February 23–27, 2013
San Antonio, Texas, USA

Association for
Computing Machinery

Advancing Computing as a Science & Profession

CSCW 2013

Proceedings of the 2013 ACM Conference on
Computer Supported Cooperative Work

Sponsored by:
ACM SIGCHI

Vol. 1 of 2

Association for
Computing Machinery

Advancing Computing as a Science & Profession

The Association for Computing Machinery
2 Penn Plaza, Suite 701
New York, New York 10121-0701

Volume 1
ISBN: 978-1-4503-1331-5 (Digital)
ISBN: 978-1-4503-2098-6 (Print)

Additional copies may be ordered prepaid from:

ACM Order Department
PO Box 30777
New York, NY 10087-0777, USA

Phone: 1-800-342-6626 (USA and Canada)
+1-212-626-0500 (Global)
Fax: +1-212-944-1318
E-mail: acmhelp@acm.org
Hours of Operation: 8:30 am – 4:30 pm ET

Printed in the USA

CSCW 2013 Chairs' Welcome

It is our great pleasure to welcome you to the *2013 ACM Computer Supported Cooperative Work – CSCW'13*. This year's conference continues its tradition of being the premier forum for research on online collaboration, social computing, and social media studies. CSCW meets a wide range of research interests, from technical communication systems building to ethnographic studies of computer-mediated collaboration in the wild. The mission of the conference is to share novel research in these domains of interest in order to advance the state of the art in CSCW.

CSCW is committed to innovation in all aspects of research. This year's conference marks the second year in which the conference used a revision cycle in the paper reviewing process. The goal of this process is to increase quality of accepted papers and grow the program to better reflect the richness of our field. 390 paper submissions were received, 139 of which were accepted for publication after going through two rigorous review cycles. This year also marks the first year in which page length limits and the Papers/Notes distinction were eliminated, resulting in an overall modest increase in the length of papers. In all, the changes to the authoring and reviewing process have generated more papers of higher quality. *CSCW '13* also has tracks for posters, demos, videos, workshops, panels, and a doctoral consortium, all of which are seeing tremendous participation. The workshops alone, for instance, have attracted almost 150 participants. For the first time, CSCW this year will have an open format "unconference" track where attendees can explore ideas in greater depth. We will also have a fitness track to start each day with some collaborative healthy activity.

In addition to the stellar technical program, *CSCW'13* hosts two exciting keynote speakers, Ron Burt and Jascha Franklin-Hodge. Ron will open the conference with a discussion of his research on volatility and advantage in networks, while Jascha will close the conference with an in-the-trenches look at modern digital democracy. Other highlights outside the papers program include a posters and videos reception and the main conference reception, both of which should provide time to connect with your fellow CSCW researchers.

Putting together *CSCW'13* was a team effort. We first thank the authors for providing the content of the program. We are grateful to the program committee, who worked hard in reviewing papers and providing feedback for authors. We heard from many authors and reviewers that the reviewing process truly helped improve the final papers. We thank the conference committee, from the papers chairs to the treasurer to the webmaster, an incredible group of people who donated countless hours of their time. We also thank Lisa Tolles at Sheridan Communications, Yvonne Lopez at RegOnline, and Ashley Cozzi and Stephanie Sabal from ACM for all of their assistance with arrangements, registration, and printing. Special thanks go out to John and Joanne Lateulere for their invaluable help with conference planning and management. Finally, we thank our sponsors ACM and SIGCHI, and generous corporate supporters, Facebook, Microsoft Research, NSF, Grand NCE, IBM Research, Yahoo! Labs, and Google.

We hope that you find this program interesting and thought provoking and that the conference provides you with a valuable opportunity to share ideas with other researchers and practitioners from institutions around the world.

Amy Bruckman
CSCW'13 General Chair
Georgia Institute of Technology, USA

Scott Counts
CSCW'13 General Chair
Microsoft Research, USA

Table of Contents

Mining Social Media Data

Monday February 25 *(14:30-16:00)*

Teams

Monday February 25 *(14:30-16:00)*

Games

Monday February 25 *(16:30-18:00)*

Collaboration and Sharing in Scientific Work

Monday February 25 *(16:30-18:00)*

Making the World a Better Place

Monday February 25 *(16:30-18:00)*

Group and Team Issues in the Health Domain

Monday February 25 *(16:30-18:00)*

Trust, Credibility, and Rumors: International Perspectives

Monday February 25 *(16:30-18:00)*

Crowdsourcing

Tuesday February 26 *(9:00-10:30)*

Local Is Where It's At

Tuesday February 26 *(9:00-10:30)*

Working Together

Tuesday February 26 *(9:00-10:30)*

Computer-Mediated Communication

Tuesday February 26 *(9:00-10:30)*

VOLUME 2

Understanding People's Practices in Social Networks

Tuesday February 26 *(9:00-10:30)*

Wikipedia Supported Cooperative Work

Tuesday February 26 *(11:00-12:30)*

Ideology, Politics, and Social Curation: Recent Work on Twitter

Tuesday February 26 *(11:00-12:30)*

Not Lost in Translation?

Tuesday February 26 *(11:00-12:30)*

Social Media Analysis and Interventions

Tuesday February 26 *(11:00-12:30)*

Collaboration in Creative Communities

Tuesday February 26 *(11:00-12:30)*

Controversy, Arguments, Rule Breakers, and Policies

Tuesday February 26 *(14:30-16:00)*

Big Issues for CSCW to Consider

Tuesday February 26 *(14:30-16:00)*

Technology to Support Family Connections

Tuesday February 26 *(14:30-16:00)*

Searching: Better Together?

Tuesday February 26 *(14:30-16:00)*

Q&A

Wednesday February 26 *(14:30-16:00)*

Crowding Out the Competition

Wednesday February 27 *(9:00-10:30)*

Computer Supported Young People

Wednesday February 27 *(9:00-10:30)*

Leveraging a Social Network
Wednesday February 27 *(9:00-10:30)*

Social Networks During a Major Transitions (Personal and Political)
Wednesday February 27 *(9:00-10:30)*

Citizen Science
Wednesday February 27 *(11:00-12:10)*

Devices Matter
Wednesday February 27 *(11:00-12:10)*

Roles

Wednesday February 27 *(11:00-12:10)*

Alternative Contexts for Collaboration

Wednesday February 27 *(11:00-12:10)*

CSCW 2013 Conference Organization

General Chairs:	Amy Bruckman *(Georgia Institute of Technology, USA)* Scott Counts *(Microsoft Research, USA)*
Program Chairs:	Cliff Lampe *(University of Michigan, USA)* Loren Terveen *(University of Minnesota, USA)*
Panels Chairs:	Darren Gergle (*Northwestern University, USA*) Sian Lindley (*Microsoft Research, USA*)
Workshops Chairs:	Jeremy Birnholtz *(Northwestern University, USA)* Andy Crabtree *(University of Nottingham, UK)*
Videos Chairs:	Sasa Junuzovic *(Microsoft Research, USA)* Carman Neustaedter *(Simon Fraser University, Canada)*
Interactive Posters Chairs:	Gary Hsieh *(Michigan State University, USA)* Chen Zhao *(Microsoft Research, USA)*
Demonstrations Chairs:	Dan Cosley *(Cornell University, USA)* Travis Kriplean *(University of Washington, USA)*
Doctoral Colloquium Chairs:	Geraldine Fitzpatrick *(Vienna University of Technology, Austria)* David McDonald *(University of Washington, USA)*
Open Space Chairs:	Eric Gilbert *(Georgia Institute of Technology, USA)* Jenn Thom-Santelli *(IBM Research, USA)*
Publications & Proceedings Chairs:	Aleksandra Sarcevic *(Drexel University, USA)* Bryan Semaan *(University of Hawaii, USA)*
Social Interaction & Publicity Chairs:	Andrea Forte *(Drexel University, USA)* Reid Priedhorsky *(Los Alamos National Lab, USA)*
Treasurer:	Nic Ducheneaut *(Ubisoft, USA)*
Student Volunteer Chairs:	Brian Keegan *(Northwestern University, USA)* Jenn Marlow *(Carnegie Mellon University, USA)*
Fitness Chairs:	Andrew Miller *(Georgia Institute of Technology, USA)* Sarita Yardi *(University of Michigan, USA)*

Program Committee:

Paul Andre *(Carnegie Mellon University, USA)*
Louise Barkhuus *(Stockholm University, Sweden)*
Jeremy Birnholtz *(Northwestern University, USA)*
Jeanette Blomberg *(IBM Research, USA)*
Geoffrey Bowker *(UC Irvine, USA)*
A.J. Brush *(Microsoft Research, USA)*
Moira Burke *(Facebook, USA)*
John Carroll *(Pennsylvania State University, USA)*
Coye Cheshire *(UC Berkeley, USA)*
Alvin Chin *(Nokia Research Center, China)*
Luigina Ciolfi *(Sheffield Hallam University, UK)*
Gregorio Convertino *(Xerox Research Center Europe, France)*
Dan Cosley *(Cornell University, USA)*
Kevin Crowston *(Syracuse University, USA)*
Edward Cutrell *(Microsoft Research, India)*
Rogerio de Paula *(IBM Research, Brazil)*
Jason Ellis *(IBM Research, USA)*
Thomas Finholt *(University of Michigan, USA)*
Geraldine Fitzpatrick *(Vienna University of Technology, Austria)*
Andrea Forte *(Drexel University, USA)*
Darren Gergle *(Northwestern University, USA)*
Eric Gilbert *(Georgia Institute of Technology, USA)*
Sean Goggins *(Drexel University, USA)*
Carl Gutwin *(University of Saskatchewan, Canada)*
Christine Halverson *(IBM Research, USA)*
Derek Hansen *(Brigham Young University, USA)*
Gary Hsieh *(Michigan State University, USA)*
Jina Huh *(University of Washington, USA)*
Tomoo Inoue *(University of Tsukuba, Japan)*
Steve Jackson *(Cornell University, USA)*
Joseph 'Jofish' Kaye *(Nokia/Yahoo! Research, USA)*
Wendy Kellogg *(IBM Research, USA)*
John King *(University of Michigan, USA)*
Hideaki Kuzuoka *(University of Tsukuba, Japan)*
Heather Lipford *(University of North Carolina at Charlotte, USA)*
Regan Mandryk *(University of Saskatchewan, Canada)*
David McDonald *(University of Washington, USA)*
Helena Mentis *(Microsoft Research, UK)*
David Millen *(IBM Research, USA)*
Meredith Morris *(Microsoft Research, USA)*
Michael Muller *(IBM Research, USA)*
Bonnie Nardi *(University of California, Irvine, USA)*
Carman Neustaedter *(Simon Fraser University, Canada)*
Oded Nov *(Polytechnic University, New York USA)*
Sergio Ochoa *(University of Chile, Chile)*

Program Committee (continued):

Gary Olson *(University of California, Irvine, USA)*
Sameer Patil *(Helsinki Institute for Information Technology/ Indiana University, Finland/USA)*
Erika Poole *(Pennsylvania State University, USA)*
Reid Priedhorsky *(Los Alamos National Laboratory/University of Minnesota, USA)*
Emilee Rader *(Michigan State University, USA)*
David Randall *(University of Siegen/Manchester Metropolitan University, Germany/UK)*
Madhu Reddy *(Pennsylvania State University, USA)*
Jennifer Rode *(Drexel University, USA)*
Mary Beth Rosson *(Pennsylvania State University, USA)*
Aleksandra Sarcevic *(Drexel University, USA)*
Frank Shipman *(Texas A&M University, USA)*
Chengzheng Sun *(Nanyang Technological University, Singapore)*
John Tang *(Microsoft Research, USA)*
Jennifer Thom *(IBM Research, USA)*
Zachary Toups *(Texas A&M University, USA)*
Hao-Chuan Wang *(Cornell University, USA)*
Rick Wash *(Michigan State University, USA)*
Naomi Yamashita *(NTT Communication Science Laboratories, Japan)*
Jun Zhang *(Pitney Bowes/University of Michigan, USA)*

CSCW 2013 Additional Reviewers

Agustina Agustina
Ban Al-Ani
Morgan Ames
Ken Anderson
Adrienne Andrew
Judd Antin
Gabriela Avram
Phoebe Ayers
Naveen Bagalkot
Brian Bailey
Kalika Bali
Nelson Baloian
Jakob Bardram
Barbara Rita Barricelli
Archer Batcheller
Scott Bateman
Eric Baumer
Natalie Bazarova
Andrew Begel
Bo Begole
Rachel Bellamy
Nicholas Berente
Michael Bernstein
Matthew Bietz
Jeffrey Bigham
Christian Bird
Torger Bjornrud
Joshua Blumenstock
Mark Blythe
Alexander Boden
Johan Bollen
Elizabeth Bonsignore
Marcela Borge
Marcos Borges
Alan Borning
Nathan Bos
Claus Bossen
Guillaume Bouchard
Mohamed Bourimi
Joel Brandt
Andy Brooks
Barry Brown
Jed Brubaker
Peter Brusilovsky
Jenna Burrell
Ayse Buyuktur
Daragh Byrne
Federico Cabitza
Kelly Caine
Stefan Carmien
Marcelo Cataldo
Melissa Cefkin
Zebin Chen
Yunan Chen
Jilin Chen
Marisa Cohn
Sunny Consolvo
Stephane Conversy
Eric Cook
Henriette Cramer
Lorrie Cranor
Jonathon Cummings
Mary Czerwinski
Laura Dabbish
Elizabeth Daly
Laurie Damianos
Catalina Danis
Munmun De Choudhury
Cleidson de Souza
David Dearman
Dominique Decouchant
Nicholas Diakopoulos
E.Ilana Diamant
Joan DiMicco
Xianghua Ding
Gavin Doherty
Jonathan Donner
Andre Doucette
Steven Dow
Jill Drury
Gaurav Dubey
Nicolas Ducheneaut
Therese Dugan
Casey Dugan
Henry Been-Lirn Duh
Shree Durga
Erik Duval
Achim Ebert
Andy Echenique
Kate Ehrlich
Nicole Ellison
Ingrid Erickson
Thomas Erickson
Jerry Fails
Robert Farrell
Rosta Farzan
Mirko Fetter
Joel Fischer
Danyel Fisher
Rowanne Fleck
Benjamim Fonseca
Jodi Forlizzi
Jacob Foster
Marcus Foth
Mike Fraser
Susan Fussell
Krista Galyen
R. Kelly Garrett
Deborah Gears
R. Stuart Geiger
Aaron Genest
Elizabeth Gerber
Werner Geyer
Fabien Girardin
Christophe Giraud-Carrier
Jennifer Golbeck
Gloria Gomez
Tijana Gonja
Victor Gonzalez
Walkyria Goode
Nicholas Graham
Raphael Grasset
Judith Gregory
Catherine Grevet
Erik Gronvall
William Griswold
Jonathan Grudin
Ning Gu
Rosanna Guadagno
David Gurzick
Francisco Gutierrez
Eben Haber

Aaron Halfaker
William Hamilton
Jeff Hancock
Benjamin Hanrahan
Thomas Hansen
David Harley
richard harper
Christopher Harris
Steve Harrison
Drew Harry
Bjorrn Hartmann
Andrea Hartzler
Kirstie Hawkey
Gillian Hayes
Brent Hecht
Libby Hemphill
Felienne Hermans
Valeria Herskovic
Morten Hertzum
Jonna Hakkila
Brian Hilligoss
Serena Hillman
Starr Roxanne Hiltz
Jon Hindmarsh
Pamela Hinds
Erik Hofer
Eve Hoggan
Nic Hollinworth
HrÌ¦nn Holmer
Henry Holtzman
James Howison
Lee Humphreys
CJ Hutto
Kori Inkpen
Keisuke Inoue
Joshua Introne
Lilly Irani
Petra Isenberg
Isa Jahnke
Lian Jian
Hao Jiang
Jinlei Jiang
Marina Jirotka
Aditya Johri
Julie Jones
Elisabeth Joyce
Tejinder Judge
Nicolas Jullien
Sanjay Kairam
Santosh Kalwar
Matthew Kam
Sep Kamvar
Bridget Kane
Victor Kaptelinin
Karrie Karahalios
Azmina Karimi
Natascha Karlova
Brian Keegan
Kerstin Keil
Patrick Kelley
Aisling Kelliher
Juho Kim
Jeffrey Kim
Taemie Kim
Jennifer King
Matthew King
Peter Kinnaird
David Kirk
Lorraine Kisselburgh
Aniket Kittur
Funda Kivran-Swaine
Styliani Kleanthous
Mark Klein
Scott Klemmer
Cory Knobel
Shin'ichi Konomi
Joseph Konstan
Vassilis Kostakos
Yong Ming Kow
Adam Kramer
Robert Kraut
Erin Krupka
Pavel Kucherbaev
Anand Kulkarni
Diana Kusunoki
Carl Lagoze
Shyong Lam
Cliff Lampe
Airi Lampinen
Walter Lasecki
Lydia Lau
Tessa Lau
Eric Laurier
Edith Law
Shaun Lawson
Christopher Le Dantec
Lucian Leahu
David Lee
Matthew Lee
Alison Lee
Charlotte Lee
Thomas Lento
Gilly Leshed
Qinying Liao
Brian Lim
Jih-Hsuan Tammy Lin
Sian Lindley
Janne Lindqvist
Greg Little
Tracy Liu
Ying Liu
Sophia Liu
Huanglingzi Liu
Kai-Uwe Loser
Tun Lu
Andres Lucero
Paul Luff
Stephan Lukosch
Alina Lungeanu
Kurt Luther
Kalle Lyytinen
Allan MacLean
Rachel Magee
Brian Magerko
Paul Maglio
Jalal Mahmud
Nasim Mahmud
Scott Mainwaring
Peter Mambrey
Lena Mamykina
Jennifer Mankoff
Osama Mansour
Gabriela Marcu
Gary Marsden
Paul Marshall
Catherine Marshall
Andrea Marshall
Christopher Mascaro
Winter Mason
Michael Massimi
Ashwin Mathew

Matthew Mayernik
Michelle Mazurek
Nora McDonald
Gregor McEwan
Claudia MÌ_ller
Andrew Miller
Zara Mirmalek
Tanushree Mitra
Pascal Molli
Wendy Moncur
Andrew Monk
Andres Monroy-Hernandez
Jonathan Morgan
Florian Mueller
Gabriel Mugar
Sean Munson
Bilge Mutlu
Brad Myers
Lennart Nacke
Dawn Nafus
Yiftach Nagar
Hideyuki Nakanishi
Kevin Nam
Tooba Nasir
Mark Newman
Duyen Nguyen
Jeffrey Nichols
Jeffrey Nickerson
Sylvie Noel
David Novick
Petteri Nurmi
Erick Oduor
Judith Olson
Elisa Oreglia
Felipe Ortega
Jahna Otterbacher
Tyler Pace
Xinru Page
Joyojeet Pal
Aditya Pal
Leysia Palen
Katherine Panciera
Carolyn Pang
Katrina Panovich
Hugo Paredes
Andrea Parker
Fabio Paterno
Sharoda Paul
Helen Petrie
Emmanuel Pietriga
Niels Pinkwart
Jose Pino
Volkmar Pipek
Anne Marie Piper
Enrico Piras
Bernd Ploderer
John Pollak
Wanda Pratt
Nathan Prestopnik
Michael Prilla
Daniele Quercia
Alexander Quinn
Andrew Raij
Rebecca Randell
Yolanda Rankin
Stuart Reeves
Tim Regan
Markus Rester
David Ribes
Romain Robbes
Lionel Robert
Michelle Rogers
John Rooksby
Carolyn Rose
Chiara Rossitto
Dana Rotman
Mark Rouncefield
Karen Ruhleder
Paul Russo
Kathy Ryall
Daisuke Sakamoto
Antti Salovaara
Nithya Sambasivan
Christian Sandvig
Cheryl Savery
Steve Sawyer
Florian Schaub
Lauren Scissors
James Scott
Stacey Scott
Melinda Sebastian
Magy Seif El-Nasr
Abigail Sellen
Bryan Semaan
Shilad Sen
Chirag Shah
N. Sadat Shami
Kalpana Shankar
Nikhil Sharma
Aaron Shaw
Cuihua Shen
Haifeng Shen
Patrick Shih
Irina Shklovski
Gavin Sim
Bart Simon
Leif Singer
Roger Slack
Madeline Smith
Jacob Solomon
Clay Spinuzzi
Tad Stach
Kate Starbird
Charles Steinfield
Gunnar Stevens
Cristiano Storni
Fred Stutzman
Ozge Subasi
Bongwon Suh
Elisabeth Sylvan
Anna-Liisa Syrjanen
Federico Tajariol
Charlotte Tang
Karen Tang
Anthony Tang
Andrea Tartaro
Yla Tausczik
Ahmed Tawfik
Nick Taylor
Jaime Teevan
Paul Tennent
Monica Tentori
Loren Terveen
William Thies
Elizabeth Thiry
Peter Tolmie
Bill Tomlinson
Mercan Topkara
Khai Truong
Manfred Tscheligi
Simon Tucker

Kathleen Tuite
Kristene Unsworth
Jan Van den Bergh
Max Van Kleek
Ravi Vatrapu
Alcides Velasquez
Theresa Velden
Kaisa Vaananen-Vainio-Mattila
Sarah Vieweg
Jesse Vig
Jessica Vitak
Juergen Vogel
Amy Voida
Mihaela Vorvoreanu
Maja Vukovic
Patrick Wagstrom
Jing Wang
Yi-Chia Wang
Hao Wang
Nadir Weibel
Suzanne Weisband
Andrew West
Ryen White
Mark Whiting
Jason Wiese
Andrea Wiggins
Heather Willever-Farr
Max Wilson
Susan Winter
Volker Wulf
Susan Wyche
Lu Xiao
Bin Xu
Yun Yang
Sarita Yardi Schoenebeck
Svetlana Yarosh
Chen Ye
Jude Yew
Zhen Yue
Mi Zhang
Qiping Zhang
Shengdong Zhao
Xiaomu Zhou
Dingyun Zhu
John Zimmerman

CSCW 2013 Sponsor & Supporters

Sponsor: SIGCHI

Supporters (Hero): NSF

Supporters (Benefactors): facebook, Microsoft Research

Supporters (Contributors): grano (Graphisme, animation et nouveaux médias / Graphics, Animation and New Media), IBM Research, Yahoo! Labs

Supporters (Friends): Google

Path Dependent Network Advantage

Ronald S. Burt
University of Chicago
Chicago, IL 60637
ron.burt@chicagobooth.edu

Jennifer L. Merluzzi
Tulane University
New Orleans, LA
jmerluzz@tulane.edu

John G. Burrows
University of Chicago
Chicago, IL 60637
jburrows@chicagobooth.edu

ABSTRACT
We analyze network volatility as something akin to the hum of a running engine. People active in a network produce vibration and wiggle where the connections and the network structure around these people changes frequently. We want to know how that vibration and wiggle affects their network advantage. We distinguish four dimensions to network volatility (churn, variation, trend, and reversals), measure them with panel data on a population of bankers, then add them to analysis predicting compensation from status and structural-hole measures of network advantage. We find that volatility does not affect performance directly. It creates a slope adjustment that enhances the returns to network advantage. We identify two stability traps that destroy advantage, but the key is not to avoid the traps so much as to avoid them in a particular way. The volatility that enhances is reversal: a pattern in which network advantage is lost then regained, producing oscillations in network metrics, as would be produced by a behavioral pattern of serial closure over time. Bankers who go through reversals enjoy significantly higher returns to their network advantage. In the absence of reversals, in fact, there are no returns to network advantage. We infer a "serial closure" hypothesis in which reversals are the result of bankers engaging and disengaging closed networks. Networks built through serial closure provide advantage well beyond the level expected from structure alone. We present evidence consistent with the hypothesis, but testing remains for future research. What we can say here is that the way a network develops has substantial implications for the advantage it provides.

Author Keywords
Social networks; Structural holes; Status; Network advantage

ACM Classification Keywords
K.6.1 Computing Mileux: Management of Computing & Information Systems, Projects & People Management: life cycle, management techniques, staffing, strategic information systems planning

INTRODUCTION
Standard practice in social capital research has been to ask what kinds of network structures provide advantage, run studies looking for higher performance from advantaged people and organizations, then talk and teach about building and securing networks that provide known advantage. The practice has worked well. The research literature provides a good sense of how advantage is associated with certain network structures, especially the status advantages of having many, well-connected contacts, and the brokerage advantages of those contacts being separated from one another by structural holes. Extensive evidence has accumulated on status and brokerage advantages associated with individual and organizational achievement. Given the empirical success of network advantage predicting achievement, models have been proposed to describe how advantage should be distributed in stable networks. The models often imply pessimistic conclusions about the theoretical feasibility of stable advantage, though people seem able to muddle through. The people who have network advantage today are often the people who had network advantage yesterday. Among the bankers to be analyzed here, for example, network status is correlated .75 from year to year across four years. Banker access to structural holes is correlated .64 from year to year. Stability in access to structural holes is becoming established with results such as Zaheer and Soda's finding that Italian TV production teams rich in access to structural holes tend to be composed of people who were rich in access several years prior. Sasovova, Mehra, Borgatti, and Schippers similarly find that continuing individual access to structural holes includes access to many of the same past structural holes along with more access to new structural holes.

These developments emerge against a backdrop of functional theory in which the imprimatur of "social structure" was reserved for stable features of networks. Networks that persist in time have meaning, serve some purpose, are real in their consequences. Much like human capital that is anchored in enduring education credentials acquired as a person moves up through a stable stratification of grade levels, social capital is studied and taught as a level of network advantage to be developed and preserved. As Laumann and Pappi expressed the sentiment during the 1970s resurgence of network images in sociology: "Despite differences in nuance associated with 'structure,' the root meaning refers to a persisting order or pattern of relations among units." And well after network images were again mainstream in sociology, Sewell broadened the observation as criticism: "structural language lends itself readily to explanations of how social life is

CSCW '13, February 23–27, 2013, San Antonio, Texas, USA.
ACM 978-1-4503-1331-5/13/02.

shaped into consistent patterns, but not to explanations of how these patterns change over time. In structural discourse, change is commonly located outside of structures."

Our purpose in this paper is to bring patterns of network change into the analysis of network advantage as a factor that can erode or enhance advantage. We know that networks change and evolve with broad potential implications for organization theory, but what are the implications for returns to network advantage?

It is possible that previous, current, and subsequent networks might only differ by random noise, whereupon we would be correct to focus on the stable levels of network advantage as we have done over the last decade. But then how do we account for the returns to a person's network advantage enhancing over time, such as the case of a rising star (previous level of advantage low, subsequently higher)? Might returns also be eroded if an employee is in a downward spiral (previous level of network advantage high followed by subsequently lower returns)? Even trendless change could be corrosive. Network status is an advantage because colleagues and clients use status as a visible signal of otherwise difficult-to-read quality. The signal is clear if a person's status is consistently low, or consistently high. The signal is unclear if status bounces up and down.

On the other hand, stability could be a stigma. In a structural holes story about brokerage, innovation, and growth, stability is a quality of the pedestrian and phlegmatic. The valuable connections that span structural holes are fragile. Their fragility can be expected for several reasons, but regardless of reason, the fact is that bridges are prone to decay. A certain amount of volatility is to be expected in the networks around successful people as some projects turn out to be productive, and others not.

We use the term network volatility to include any kind of change in a network across time. Instead of thinking about a network for its level of advantage, we think about the current network as a passing moment that came from somewhere and is on its way to somewhere. Network volatility includes the formation of new relations, and decay of the old. It includes random variation from year to year, as well as dramatic transitions and gradual trends in network structure.

While we mean volatility to include any kind of change, we are not thinking about network change in terms of a destination equilibrium or broader context. Given an image of network equilibrium, observed networks can be studied for how they should move, or evolve, toward equilibrium; for example, change toward an equilibrium defined by exchange theory, change toward an equilibrium defined by balance theory, or change contingent on context.

We study change as a characteristic property, something akin to the hum of a running engine. There is a certain amount of vibration and wiggle produced by people active in a network. We want to see how that vibration and wiggle affects network advantage.

We reach our conclusions by analyzing four annual panels of data on bankers in a large financial organization. The study population is a good place to study network volatility because the network is stable in its macro structure with a great deal of year-to-year change at the micro level.

Our analysis is in two steps. First, as a baseline, we treat network volatility as noise, which is how it has been treated in previous analyses of our study population. The "volatility as noise" treatment is legitimate since network advantage is correlated from year to year such that advantage seems to be a moving average subject to random shocks each year at the interpersonal level. However, even in a system stable in macro structure, patterns of change have implications for network advantage.

Our second pass through the data treats network volatility as signal. We distinguish four dimensions to network volatility (churn, variation, trend, and reversals), and show that much of the compensation association with network advantage depends on a banker's network being unstable in certain ways.

We infer from our analysis a hypothesis of "serial closure." Advantage is greatest in broad, open networks that have a history of shifting between open and closed. Periods of deep engagement in a closed group of colleagues are punctuated by periods of broad, open connections. In fact, bankers who maintained a consistently broad and open network show minimal average achievement. Achievement is greatest, on average, among bankers with a history of shifting between open and closed – i.e., a history of "serial closure."

Digital Democracy: How the Internet Re-elected a President

Jascha Franklin-Hodge
Blue State Digital
280 Summer St., 7th Floor,
Boston, MA 02210
jascha@bluestatedigital.com

ABSTRACT
Jascha Franklin-Hodge, CTO and co-founder of Blue State Digital -- the company whose new media team and technology powered the Obama campaign's record-breaking online fundraising and social networking program -- will share stories and lessons from winning political and advocacy campaigns. Franklin-Hodge will talk about the testing and analytics strategies used to rapidly iterate online programs, the techniques used to reduce friction in the donation experience, and how the campaign combatted supporter fatigue in a saturation media environment. You'll hear tales from the campaign trail, learn what worked in 2008 and what changed in 2012, and hear about the techniques and data behind the president's groundbreaking online campaign operation.

Author Keywords
Digital democracy; social computing.

ACM Classification Keywords
H.5.3 [Information Interfaces and Presentation]: Group and Organization Interfaces – Collaborative computing

BIOGRAPHY
Jascha Franklin-Hodge is Chief Technology Officer (CTO) and Founding Partner at Blue State Digital. Franklin-Hodge brings more than a decade's experience in software development in the corporate, nonprofit, and political spheres to his role as BSD's Chief Technology Officer. He manages the company's technology staff and operations out of BSD's technology center near downtown Boston, including our infrastructure, the maintenance and enhancement of the BSD Online Tools, and our technology client services.

For Governor Howard Dean's groundbreaking 2004 presidential campaign, Franklin-Hodge led the technology team responsible for scaling, securing, and maintaining a high-visibility, high-traffic website, which received praise from both the political and tech communities for its usability, reliability, and depth of functionality. Franklin-Hodge studied computer science at MIT, and lives in Boston.

CSCW '13, February 23–27, 2013, San Antonio, Texas, USA.
ACM 978-1-4503-1331-5/13/02.

Closure vs. Structural Holes: How Social Network Information and Culture Affect Choice of Collaborators

Ge Gao
Communication,
Cornell University
Ithaca, NY 14850
gg365@cornell.edu

Pamela Hinds
Management Science &
Engineering, Stanford University
Stanford, CA 94305
phinds@stanford.edu

Chen Zhao
Microsoft
One Microsoft Way
Redmond, WA 98052
chzha@microsoft.com

ABSTRACT
Collaboration is important to successful organizations and how coworkers are selected is crucial to the dynamics of effective collaborations. In this study we explore how people use social network information, which is increasingly accessible on enterprise systems in organizations, to choose people with whom to collaborate. We conducted a scenario-based study of 459 respondents in a global high-tech company. Our data indicate cultural differences in how social network information was valued when choosing a collaborator. The Chinese, consistent with the cultural value of Guanxi, more closely followed a *closure* model, whereas Americans favored neither a *closure* nor a *structural holes* model. These results provide new insights into how needs for social network information may vary between cultures and how social networking sites might support workers in choosing collaborators from within and across national cultures.

Author Keywords
Social network sites (SNS); closure; structural holes; guanxi; national culture; willingness to collaborate.

ACM Classification Keywords
H.5.m. Information interfaces and presentation (e.g., HCI): Miscellaneous.

INTRODUCTION
A central purpose of organizations is to coordinate among coworkers so that complex tasks can be accomplished [31]. Extensive research on coordination, dating back to at least the 1960's [8], provides insight into the formal and informal mechanisms through which coordination occurs. Little attention, however, has been paid to the formation of collaborations, despite evidence that how people choose coworkers is crucial [16, 24].

With the emergence of more distributed organizations and virtual work in recent years, teams are continually being reconfigured and, as a result, people are constantly working with new collaborators [24, 27]. Mortensen describes the emerging phenomenon of *recombinant collaboration* in which teams are highly dynamic and continually recombining resources, including project members [27]. Based on interviews with 21 employees of a large technology company, Matthews and colleagues similarly conclude that teams are increasingly dynamic with team members frequently participating on multiple teams [24]. This research on new forms of collaborative work, suggests higher levels of dynamism, but also a more central role for team members in identifying and recruiting new collaborators. Finding appropriate collaborators in modern organizations is, therefore, both more frequent and more important. Unfortunately, little is yet known about the basis on which people make these choices.

Although studies examining choice of collaborators are rare, several relevant studies are instructive. McDonald, for example, investigated how people respond to recommendation systems that used social networking information as a basis for recommending collaborators [25]. He concluded that people have mixed feelings about using social network information to find collaborators, in part because of their more nuanced understanding of their own social networks, which is hard to capture in technology. Matthews and colleagues also examined the recruiting process by which people find collaborators for dynamic projects [24]. They report that networking played a central role in finding expertise. Extensive research also examines the role of social network information in locating expertise [19, 28, 40], but with less of a focus on choosing collaborators. Another study that bears directly on our research examined the formation of student teams and concluded that people select collaborators based on reputation for competence, similarity (especially race), and familiarity [16]. Hinds and colleagues concluded that reputation is a key determinant in the selection process [16], but none of these studies directly examine how social networking information is being valued, especially how potential collaborators' connections to others affects collaboration seekers' choices.

One important way of learning about potential coworkers is by using enterprise social network sites. Here, we are interested in if and how an individual's desire to collaborate with a potential collaborator is shaped by social network information available on such sites. We also examine this question across cultures for both practical and theoretical reasons. As regards the practical aspect, although the use of social networking systems is increasingly global, little is known about how the interpretation of different social network information might vary between cultures. In terms of theory, competing theories predict different bases on which social networks are formed, thus making the predictions ambiguous for how people will use social networking information when choosing collaborators.

In this study, we investigate 1) how people's willingness to collaborate with a potential collaborator is influenced by the existence of shared contacts between the collaboration seeker and the potential collaborator, the type of network connections in the potential collaborator's network, and the size of the potential collaborator's network, and 2) if and how the value of social network information is affected by the national culture of the collaboration seeker. To answer these questions, we conducted a scenario-based study of employees of a global high-tech company in the U.S. and China.

A surprising finding in this study is that neither the U.S. nor the Chinese respondents' reaction to the social network information could be entirely predicted by structural holes theory, which has been supported by numerous studies in U.S. organizations. The Chinese data more strongly support a closure model which favors more interconnected networks, consistent with the cultural value of Guanxi. On the U.S. side, our data suggest more complexity than predicted by structural holes theory, in particular respondents sought resources through their networks, but followed neither a closure or a structural holes model entirely.

Insights gained from this study provide inspiration for designing better enterprise software to support collaborative work in modern organizations, particularly regarding which type of network information -should be included, highlighted or made visible in social profiles. In particular, we aim to inform the design of enterprise software to support diverse cultures and intercultural collaborations.

BACKGROUND AND RELATED WORK

Collaboration is crucial for the success of organizational endeavors. As a result, the factors that affect collaboration have long been examined by researchers from a variety of disciplines, including organizational behavior, communication, sociology and information science. In the CSCW and HCI communities, the impact of technology on collaboration has been emphasized [3, 14, 20, 37]. Studies in these fields have talked extensively about how the process of collaboration can be facilitated by modern technologies, but both the genesis of the collaborations and the role of culture have largely been ignored.

In fact, more broadly, few studies have examined the impact of culture on work collaboration [17]. Some research has examined the effect of cultural values on aspects of organizational behavior, such as views of autonomy and task orientation, although mostly neglects collaboration [15]. Scholars have also discussed global collaboration across cultures [32, 36], but their focus has been on the dynamics between team members rather than on the practices of each cultural group engaged in the collaboration. Some exceptions include cross-cultural research examining the effect of different media types on communication and collaboration behaviors [12, 35]. In an interview based study, Setlock and Fussell [34], for example, found that Asian users of communication media make more deliberate choices about when to use technology that conveys emotional information. Although a move in the right direction, these studies tend to emphasize communication media rather than social networking systems. To understand how design requirements for social networking systems might vary across cultures, it is critical to more deeply understand the meanings and values associated with information and interaction processes supported by technology [17, 18].

As discussed earlier, few studies in CSCW or HCI discuss the collaborator-seeking phase (for an exception, see McDonald, 2003) which is prior, but essential to the main process of collaboration. Considering the increasing spread of social networking sites in modern organizations and their presumed role in supporting the selection and recruitment of collaborators [25], it is important to consider how social network information is used during the process of choosing collaborators.

With these points in mind, our study examines how people in both China and the U.S. use social networking information as a basis for choosing collaborators. We propose and find that people from different cultures respond differently to potential collaborator's social network information when considering a potential collaboration.

Closure vs. Structural Holes

Theories that explore the development and use of social capital treat network information as an important resource. The value of social network information comes from "its representation of the social structure, of either an individual or a group, which is a kind of capital that can create, for certain individuals or groups, a competitive advantage in pursing their goal"[33]. In general, better-connected people enjoy higher returns and facilitate more coordinated actions.

The theoretical model used to explain what it means to be "better connected" has, however, been a matter for debate. Two competing models – the network closure model and the structural holes model – propose different mechanisms driving how social network information is perceived and interpreted. The strategy for choosing collaborators predicted by each model is, therefore, quite different.

The network closure model (also called the bonding model) suggests that people tend to connect with others who are located in the same collective network [1, 11]. In this model, a network with higher closure is described as a network in which more people are mutually connected. In this type of closed network, social capital is enhanced in two ways. First, information-sharing between people is more effective due to the establishment of more direct connections and communications. Second, and more importantly, a higher level of trust and cohesiveness are established within the network to facilitate the pursuit of collective goals because more redundant ties create stronger bonds and a more acute sense of obligation [6].

The structural holes model (also called the bridging model), however, implies a very different strategy. According to this model [1, 10, 11], being connected to people who are not connected to each other creates holes in the network. People can therefore construct themselves as brokers, whose relationships and connections span the holes between two disconnected groups. By becoming a broker, one's power to access and control more, otherwise inaccessible, resources increases.

Although these two competing models are not typically focused on collaboration seeking, different assumptions between the models predict two different strategies for choosing collaborators. The closure model puts more emphasis on collective achievements and interpersonal-emotional harmony. The structural holes model, however, pays more attention to the enhancement of individual achievements and task achievement realized by obtaining more unique resources and doing so more efficiently.

Although previous studies of social capital generation in the U.S. have offered support for the benefits of the structural holes model rather than the closure model, quite the opposite has been found in Asian settings [4, 7, 39]. In Xiao and Tsui's [39] study investigating how social networks influence career development in China, this contrast was explained by the cultural context in different societies. In Eastern cultures, the value of intra-group relationships and Guanxi (an enduring network of relationships characterized by reciprocity) are key to career and business success. These cultural values suggest a strong appreciation of network closure. That is, people are tightly connected in networks characterized by harmony and reciprocity. Furthermore, in Asian society, a 'broker' positioned at the boundary of two groups is generally distrusted by both groups [39], which means people might hesitate about allowing structural holes when developing collaborations. In contrast, the effect of the structural holes model is more aligned with the Western culture of open markets, free competition and an individualistic orientation [6].

The value of shared contacts

The first type of network information we examine when predicting how people will use social network information for choosing collaborators is *shared contacts*, defined as the extent to which people are connected to the same other people. If, for example, John and Joe are both connected to Jane, they have a shared contact in Jane. It is surprising that, although shared contacts have been recognized as an indispensable social profile information resource on almost all popular social network sites (e.g. Facebook, Twitter and LinkedIn), there remains little empirical knowledge about how this information facilitates further interaction and/or collaboration between people.

The network closure and structural holes models offer two theoretical approaches for analyzing the value of shared contacts in choosing collaborators. To improve the interconnections between people, the closure model would suggest that people will choose potential collaborators with whom they have shared contacts because it will strengthen closure. In contrast, the structural holes model would predict collaboration between people who do *not* have shared contacts, as the potential collaborator could enhance the seeker's social capital by getting access to resources to which others in the network do not have ready access.

Studies further suggest that workers in China and the U.S. might favor different models when choosing collaborators. As an essential value in Chinese Confucian capitalism [7, 23, 39], Guanxi represents the nature of a Chinese individual's life as living in an intricate web of personal and social interconnections [13]. In organizational settings, Guanxi is manifested in strong emotional involvement, which is often accompanied by instrumental exchange of favors between people [23]. Members highly value interpersonal harmony, cohesiveness and achieving collective goals by meeting each other's needs. It is clear that the nature of Guanxi overlaps significantly with the goal of achieving network closure, particularly the emphasis on interpersonal cohesiveness and emotional bonding. Based on this, we hypothesize that Chinese workers will follow strategies predicted by the closure model, e.g. capitalizing on shared contacts, when choosing collaborators.

The national culture manifested in organizational settings in the U.S., in contrast, is characterized by an exchange-oriented market transaction model which leads to more instrumental vs. affective ties [26]. As has been pointed out by Xiao and Tsui [39], the structural holes model better predicts how people perform in a more instrumental culture. For both a more instrumental culture and the structural holes model, focusing on self-interest and task achievement are driving considerations. Since the structural holes model enables more efficient access to unique resources, we hypothesize that U.S. workers will favor a structural holes model by creating networks devoid of shared contacts when seeking collaborators.

H1: Chinese workers will choose collaborators who share contacts with them, whereas workers in the U.S. will choose collaborators with whom they do not have shared contacts.

The value of access to expertise and interpersonal resources

The second type of network information we examined is the type of network connections of the potential collaborators. Since the process of choosing collaborators requires seeking certain informational and/or interpersonal resources [19, 25, 40], we are especially interested in whether choice to collaborate varies based on different types of resources in the candidate's network.

In both the network closure model and the structural holes model, the value of a potential collaborator is manifested in one's social network, or more specifically, in the informational and interpersonal resources contained in his/her social network [5]. Connections to important others confer resources, but also contribute to a positive reputation by validating the legitimacy of the candidate [9]. It could therefore be inferred that connection to others who have informational and interpersonal resources will increase the capital held in one's own social network and will consequentially be a basis on which to choose collaborators. In our study, we examine access to expertise, an informational resource, and access to those in important positions, an interpersonal resource.

When taking national culture into consideration, the relationship between network connections of the potential collaborator and choice to collaborate may turn out to be more complex. As we argue in previous sections, the strategy for choosing collaborators among the Chinese is likely to be based on the cultural value of Guanxi. In Confucian society, Guanxi influences how people interact with each other in the hierarchy of social relationships. In Chinese society, social hierarchy and interpersonal connections are highly valued and intertwined. It is worth noting that Guanxi links two individuals of unequal social status such that "the weaker partner can call for special favors for which they do not have to equally reciprocate" [2]. In other words, Guanxi may create more benefits for people if they can find a way to connect with those who hold important positions (e.g. managerial positions). In the U.S., however, expertise may be more tied to access to information resources necessary for the immediate and successful completion of tasks, so U.S. workers may prefer collaborating with others who have experts in their networks.

Combining this consideration with Chinese employees' assumed strategy for choosing collaborators based on the network closure model, we also hypothesize an interaction between common contacts and the type of network connections of the target candidate on the willingness of Chinese employees to collaborate with a particular candidate. In particular, we anticipate that common contacts will be more important to Chinese employees when the candidate's network includes people in important positions vs. people with expertise. We do not anticipate the same effect for U.S. employees.

H2a: Chinese workers will more strongly favor choosing collaborators who are connected to those who hold important positions whereas U.S. workers will favor collaborators who are connected to those with expertise.

H2b: For Chinese workers, connections to people in important positions will be more valuable when collaborators also have shared contacts whereas U.S. workers will not show this preference.

The value of network size

Another type of network information we examine is network size. It is surprising that, although network size has been recognized as an important piece of social information, there remains little empirical knowledge about how this information facilitates further interaction and/or collaboration between people. Many previous studies, however, have demonstrated that network size plays an important role in the process of forming an online impression. Utz's experimental study of 124 American participants, for example, found that people with more friends were perceived as more popular [38]. In another study of friends on Facebook researchers found a significant but inverted U-shape relationship between number of friends and perceived attractiveness [37]. Until the number of friends exceeded 300-500 (depending on the dependent variable), more friends were associated with more positive impressions. In an analysis of 30,773 natural Facebook profiles, Lampe and colleagues further point out that information in social profiles [20], such as user characteristics (e.g. gender and age of the account) and profile fields (e.g. high school information, birth date) can predict the person's number of friends. In sum, people with larger networks in their social profile often earn better evaluations from others.

Both the closure and the structural holes models emphasize the accumulation of social capital [5]. The value of network size is, therefore, evaluated mainly by how much it guarantees the access to resources. Holding all else equal, a higher number of connections (up to a point) should yield access to more resources, both informational and interpersonal. As a result, when choosing collaborators, workers should favor collaborators who have large rather than small social networks. We posit that this will be consistent across cultures.

H3: Workers will choose to collaborate with people who have large, rather than small, networks.

METHOD

To test our hypotheses, we conducted a scenario-based survey with a 2×2×2×2 between-subject design. In the scenario, we asked each respondent to assume the role of someone choosing a collaborator (team member) for a new project and were asked to indicate to what extent they would like to collaborate with a given candidate on a work project. Three types of social network information in the candidate's profile were presented, including the existence of shared contacts between the respondent and the potential collaboration candidate (without vs. with shared contacts), the type of connections in the potential collaboration candidate's network (e.g. whether the candidate was connected to others with expertise or others in important positions), and size of the candidate's network (large vs. small). The fourth independent variable was national culture of the respondent (Chinese vs. U.S.).

Previous research has found that a scenario-based approach is effective for studying cross-cultural differences [41]. Given technology differences across the U.S. and China, scenarios enable researchers to understand preferences independent of the technology currently available to respondents. This method has been used in HCI studies as diverse as understanding responses to breakdowns in robots [21], information demands in context-aware applications [22], and self-disclosure behavior [42]. In our study, we provided a written scenario describing a situation in which the respondent needs to choose a collaborator for a new project, followed by questions about the extent to which the respondent would like to collaborate with the candidate being evaluated. It was a between-subjects design and each respondent was presented with only one candidate and that candidate's social network information. The effectiveness of the scenario and some of the measures were pre-tested in a pilot study.

Pilot Study

Our pilot study was conducted to verify that the scenarios with social network maps were understandable and sensitive enough to detect Chinese and U.S. respondents' preferences with regard to choosing a collaborator. We also evaluated whether or not Chinese and U.S. respondents could clearly distinguish between the two different levels of social network size.

The sample consisted of 6 Chinese respondents (3 male, 3 female, M_{age} = 23 years) and 6 U.S. respondents (3 male, 3 female, M_{age} = 22 years) who were born, grew up and lived in China or the U.S., respectively. All respondents answered questions about their background so that we could discern cultural identity (e.g. *countries in which they were raised, to what extent they identified with their own culture*, etc.), read two scenarios with social network maps (see Table 1), indicated to what extent they would choose to collaborate with the given candidate in the scenario, and rated the social network information given in both textual scenarios and the social network maps. All materials were translated and back-translated by professional translators into Chinese and English.

Our pilot study results indicated that respondents in both cultures understood the scenario and were able to answer questions about the collaboration decision they would make in these scenarios. Moreover, the respondent's ratings on the social network information given in textual scenarios and social network maps showed clear distinctions between two network sizes (large network of 350 contacts, small network of 50 contacts) in both cultures.

Main Study

The main study was a survey with demographic questions, a scenario with the social network map followed by questions asking respondents to indicate the extent to which they would choose to collaborate with this candidate, and questions evaluating the effectiveness of our manipulations.

In cross-cultural experiments, one challenge is conducting controlled research with representative samples from the cultures of interest. Many cross-cultural studies rely on international students who study in U.S. universities, although limitations include a possible selection bias (e.g. students who come to the U.S. may not be representative of the average person in that culture) and concerns that the students have adapted to the U.S. culture. To avoid these issues, we conducted our study at a global company with employees in both China and the U.S.. All materials were presented in English for the U.S. respondents and Mandarin Chinese for the Chinese respondents. Materials were first developed in English by the entire multi-cultural research team and then translated into Chinese by a professional translator who was blind to the study design. Finally, consistent with practices for cross-cultural research, the materials were back-translated into English by two other professional translators to ensure that there was no change in meaning.

Participants

The survey request was sent via email to a total of 1,100 employees from a global IT company who were randomly chosen based on their work locations (China or the U.S.). The response rate was 43.64% (480). We further restricted our sample using two filter questions, including where the respondent was raised and what language(s) they spoke fluently before the age of 10, to make sure the cultural identity of each respondent in this study was strictly Chinese or American. The final sample consisted of 459 respondents (247 Chinese, 212 U.S.). There were 51 females and 156 males included in the Chinese sample and 58 females and 154 males in the U.S. sample. The mean ages of these two samples were 32.39 years (SD = 5.50) for the Chinese and 39.55 years (SD = 8.43) for the U.S.

Manipulations

We had four primary independent variables in this study, including the existence of shared contacts between the candidate and the respondent, type of network connections of the potential collaborator (expertise vs. position), size of the network, and national culture. Culture was not manipulated, but varied based on our sample of Chinese and Americans. We used the scenario and network map for our remaining manipulations by changing the content of the scenarios and presenting different network maps (as depicted in Table 1). To manipulate shared contacts, respondents were shown either a map in which they were connected to three of the same people as the candidate or

Scenario: The team you are currently working with is preparing for a new project and needs to recruit some new members from outside [The Company] over the next few months. The graph below is the social network map of a potential candidate from outside [The Company] who has been pre-screened and invited for an onsite interview. This candidate [text from manipulation 3 inserted here] for someone at this stage in their career and for this position.

The social network map show a subset of this candidate's overall network with information about all of his/her relevant contacts including the number of contacts the candidate has in common with you, information about types of the candidate's connections, and the candidate's social network size. The meaning of each shape and color in the map is listed in table.

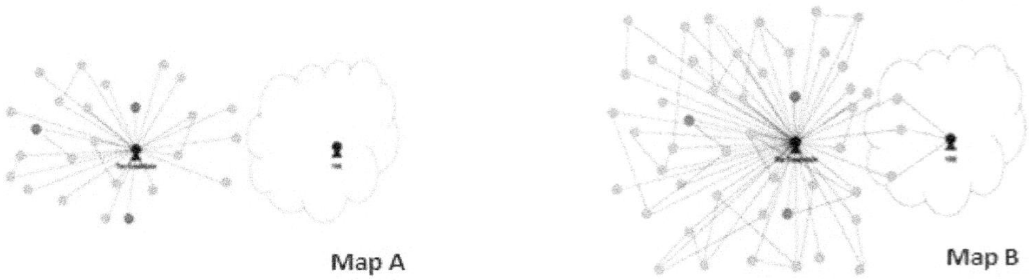

Manipulations:

Shared contacts	Manipulated in network maps (see Map A vs. B)	Social network map with contacts *(see grey dots)* connected with the candidate but not the collaboration seeker. [Map A]	Social network map with contacts *(see grey dots)* connected with both the candidate and the collaboration seeker. [Map B]
Type of network connections	Manipulated in network maps (see Map A)	Social network map with contacts *(see blue dots)* that are recognized as international leaders in a technical field relevant to the project.	Social network map with contacts *(see blue dots)* that hold high level administrative positions.
Size	Manipulated in text (above) and in network maps (see Map A vs. B)	Has about 50 contacts, which is a small number of contacts. [Map A]	Has about 350 contacts, which is a large number of contacts. [Map B]

Table 1. Scenario (top) with descriptions of the manipulations in the text and the network maps.

none of the same people as the candidate. To manipulate the type of network connections of the potential collaborator, the respondents were informed that the candidate was either connected to three people who were recognized as international leaders in a technical field relevant to the project (expertise) or to people that held high level administrative positions (position). Note that none of these connections were among the contacts shared with the respondent (see Table 1). Also, the candidate was depicted as being connected to someone who either had connections to someone with expertise or someone at a high administrative level, but was not her/himself described as having such expertise or position. Finally, network size was manipulated in the text as well as through the network map. Respondents were shown either a network map with few nodes or a network map with many nodes and told (in the text) that the candidate either had about 350 contacts (large) or 50 contacts (small). To control for density of the network, both the large and the small networks were constructed to have the same network density.

It is worth noting that we did not specify a particular social networking site in our scenarios for three reasons. First, there is no single dominant online social network site that spans China and the U.S. with all the functions and settings we were interested in for our study. Second, if we had referenced particular social software in the study (e.g. LinkedIn), we would not have been able to determine whether the differences we found in the current study were caused by culture or by specific design features of this social networking system (some of which may be culturally biased). Third, we are interested foremost in how people value social networking information, not in how they respond to a particular technology or display of the information, so having our manipulations as technology-neutral as possible enabled us to better understand peoples' underlying preferences. Consistent with this, our manipulations are not meant to replicate the way that one might see this information in a social networking system, rather to test basic assumptions about how people value social networking information when choosing collaborators and how this varies across cultures, so that design decisions can be made from a solid foundation.

To evaluate the effectiveness of our manipulations, we conducted ANOVAs which included the control variables. In evaluating our manipulation check for the existence of contacts shared by the candidate and the collaboration seeker, we found significant differences. That is, respondents in the *shared contacts* condition recognized that the candidate in the scenario shared contacts with the respondent ($F[1,430] = 815.69$, $p = .000$). In evaluating our manipulation check for connections to experts versus connections to those in important positions, respondents in the expertise vs. position conditions were significantly more likely to detect that the candidates were connected to those with expertise ($F[1,425] = 385.04$. $p = .000$) and not to those in important positions ($F[1,430] = 200.10$, $p = .000$). In evaluating our manipulation check for the size (large vs. small) of the candidate's social network, we found that those presented with the large vs. the small network recognized that the candidate in the scenario had a large (vs. small) social network ($F[1,430] = 192.46$, $p = .000$).

Although we did not manipulate culture, we validated through survey questions that 100% of our Chinese respondents were raised and lived in China and 100% of our U.S. respondents were raised and lived in the U.S.. Further, considering that both the Chinese and U.S. participants in the global high-tech company might be exposed to and influenced by each other's cultures, we measured the culture-based thinking style of all respondents based on Nisbett and Masuda [29, 30]. In our survey, we presented respondents with two photographs and asked them to choose which photo they would prefer to take of a friend. One photo was of a person sitting in a chair with office details visible in the background. The other photo was of the same person, but was only a "headshot" with a neutral background. As expected, all the U.S. respondents chose the second photo. Among the Chinese respondents, most people (91.9%) chose the photo in which the office was visible. The result show that above 90% of Chinese participants had a typical relation-based thinking style and 100% U.S. participants had a typical individual-based thinking style. In other words, participants in our study could be seen as both demographically and culturally representative Chinese and Americans regardless of their exposure to other cultures.

Dependent Variables

To test our hypotheses, we used as our dependent variable the extent to which respondents expressed a desire to collaborate with that candidate. We measured desire to collaborate using a 5-item scale ($\alpha = .91$) in which we asked about the extent to which the respondent would want to collaborate with the given candidate (on a 7-point scale anchored by 1 = *strongly disagree* and 7 = *strongly agree*).

Mediating Variables

In the logic leading up to our hypothesis, we argued that the relationships between network connections (shared contacts and type of connections) and desire to collaborate would be a result of a better reputation and access to expertise and interpersonal resources. To explore the mechanisms underlying our hypotheses, we measured general reputation by asking respondents to rate their impressions of the candidate as positive (=7) or negative (=1). We also measured three types of resources perceived as being available to each respondent through the candidates' social network, including access to *technical knowledge/advice*, *influence in the organization*, and *expanded social networks*. The three variables were measured with the items in Table 2. All items were measured on a 7-point scale where 1 = strongly disagree and 7 = strongly agree and averaged across items.

Control Variables

We measured and included as control variables respondents' demographic characteristics and experience with social networking sites. Demographics included age, gender, position in the company (individual contributor vs. management), and education (below vs. above undergraduate). For online experience, we generated a 5-item scale ($\alpha = .79$) and used the average of these items as a control variable. We also included job role as a control variable (including administrative, product manager, program manager, marketing product support, testing, design, development, research, sales, and other) in our analysis to test if different respondents may have been thinking differently in terms of what type of candidate was needed by the team. Job role was not significant so we

Technical Knowledge, $\alpha = .91$	**Influence in Organization, $\alpha = .93$**	**Expanded Social Network, $\alpha = .89$**
This candidate could offer good technical suggestions.	This candidate could use the authority of his/her position to influence others.	This candidate could introduce me to someone from whom I could get support.
This candidate could share with the team his/her considerable experience and/or training.	This candidate could influence the resources available to this team.	I could enlarge my social circle with the help of this candidate.
This candidate could provide team members with sound job-related advice.	This candidate could use his/her power to get access to special benefits for people on the team.	I could be informed about useful non-technical information by this candidate.
This candidate could influence the team by his/her professional technical knowledge.	This candidate could influence peoples' chances to get promoted.	This candidate can leverage his social network to get things done.

Table 2. Survey items used to measure types of resources.

		M	*SD*	1	2	3	4	5	6	7	8	9	10
1.	Age	35.66	7.84	-									
2.	Gender (male vs. female)	-	-	.08	-								
3.	Job position (subordinate vs. management)	-	-	.26**	-.04	-							
4.	Education (below vs. above undergraduate)	-	-	.01	-.04	-.05	-						
5.	SNS experience	3.69	1.39	-.018**	-.00	-.03	.01	.79					
6.	Shared contacts (without vs. with shared contacts)	-	-	-.01	.05	-.06	-.03	.06	-				
7.	Type of network connections (expertise vs. positional connections)	-	-	-.02	.05	.02	-.01	.07	.06	-			
8.	Size of network (small vs. large)	-	-	.06	-.12**	.02	-.02	.06	.06	.04	-		
9.	Culture (China vs. U.S.)	-	-	.46**	.08	.20**	-.20**	-.20**	-.07	.02	.07	-	
10.	Choice to collaborate	4.25	1.07	-.26**	-.03	-.17**	.06	.11*	.10*	-.14**	-.12	-.33**	.91

Table 3. Descriptive statistics and correlations between the primary variables.

removed it from our final analysis.

RESULTS

Table 3 shows the descriptive statistics and correlations between the primary variables in this study. To test our hypotheses, we used a 2×2×2×2 ANOVA analysis predicting the extent to which participants expressed a desire to collaborate with the candidate presented (Table 4).

Our first hypothesis predicted that choice to collaborate would be influenced by the existence of shared contacts and that shared contacts would be a stronger predictor for the

	F (1, 424)	*Sig.*
Age	6.13	.014
Gender	.27	.602
Education	.03	.859
Job position	2.93	.088
SNS experience	.51	.477
Shared contacts	1.71	.192
Type of connections	13.40	.000
Size	.02	.885
Culture	19.95	.000
Shared contacts × type of connections	1.07	.302
Shared contacts × size	1.08	.300
Shared contacts × culture	.04	.846
Type of connections × size	.85	.356
Type of connections × culture	.11	.736
Size × culture	1.69	.194
Shared contacts × type of connections × size	2.48	.116
Shared contacts × type of connections × culture	4.74	.030
Shared contacts × size × culture	2.91	.089
Type of connections × size × culture	.00	.957
Shared contacts × type of connections × size × culture	.40	.528

Table 4. ANOVA analysis predicting desire to collaborate with the candidate.

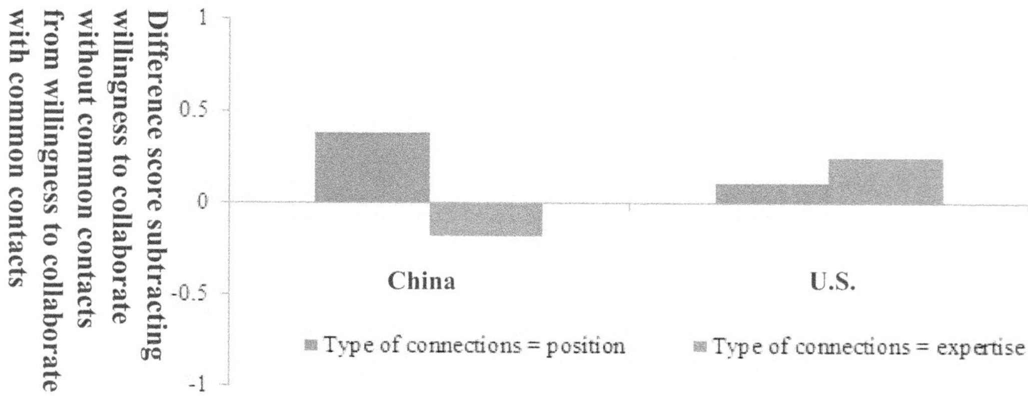

Figure 1. The 3-way interaction showing the willingness to collaborate with common contacts (vs. without common contacts) by type of connections.

Chinese as compared to U.S. participants. To test this hypothesis, we examined the two-way interaction between the existence of shared contacts (without vs. with) and national culture of the respondent (Chinese vs. U.S.). The results of the ANOVA partially support our hypothesis. Although the two-way interaction between shared contacts and culture was not significant, we found a significant three-way interaction between shared contacts, the type of network connections and the respondent's national culture ($F[1,424] = 4.74$, $p = .03$). This finding indicates that the influence of shared contacts on choice to collaborate was stronger for Chinese respondents, but only when the potential collaborator also had connections to people in important positions.

Our second set of hypotheses predicted that workers from China would choose to collaborate with candidates when the potential collaborator had access to resources by virtue of being connected to people in important positions whereas U.S. workers would choose potential candidates who were connected to those with expertise (H2a). We also hypothesized that having shared contacts with candidates who had connections to those in important positions would be important for the employees in China (H2b). A significant three-way interaction between shared contacts, type of network connections and the respondent's national culture ($F[1,424] = 4.74$, $p = .03$) was found to partially support H2a and H2b.

To explore this effect further, we tested the simple two-way interaction between the existence of shared contacts and the type of network connections in each cultural sample. For respondents from China, a significant interaction was found between shared contacts and type of network connections when predicting choice to collaborate ($F[1,231] = 6.12$, $p = .01$). To be specific, when there were connections to those in important positions included in the candidate's network, Chinese respondents preferred to collaborate with candidates who had shared contacts ($M = 4.62$, $SD = 1.14$) rather than with those who did not have shared contacts ($M = 4.25$, $SD = .91$). However, although the main effect of type of network connections is significant ($F[1, 192] = 6.91$, $p = .009$) for respondents from the U.S., the interaction was not significant ($F[1,192] = .59$, $p = .44$). The main effect of shared contacts is not significant neither ($F[1,192] = 1.20$, $p = .27$) for the U.S. respondents. That is, the Americans had a stronger desire to collaborate with candidates connected to people who were recognized as international leaders in a technical field relevant to the project (expertise, $M = 4.07$, $SD = .94$) compared to candidates connected to people who held high level administrative positions (position, $M = 3.76$, $SD = .96$) regardless of the existence of shared contacts (interaction term, $F[1,192] = .59$, $p = .44$). The mean value of desire to collaborate for the U.S. respondents when the candidate was connected to those with expertise (with shared contacts, $M = 4.20$, $SD = 1.02$, without shared contacts, $M = 3.95$, $SD = .85$) vs. important positions (with shared contacts, $M = 3.82$, $SD = 1.09$, without shared contacts, $M = 3.71$, $SD = .84$) reaffirms that U.S. respondents favored connections with experts vs. those in important positions, regardless of shared contacts.

Figure 1 illustrates these relationships by showing the difference score subtracting willingness to collaborate *without* common contacts from willingness to collaborate *with* common contacts by type of connection. As can be seen from figure 1, Chinese respondents valued common contacts when connecting to a candidate with contacts in high positions, but not when connecting to a candidate who had contacts with expertise.

To examine the mechanisms underlying our hypotheses and results, we first analyzed the effect of general reputation. We conducted a mediation analysis which included a) establishing a link between our independent variable(s) and desire to collaborate, b) establishing a link between our mediator (general reputation) and desire to collaborate, and c) if both "a" and "b" were significant, running a regression to determine if the relationship in "a" diminished when the

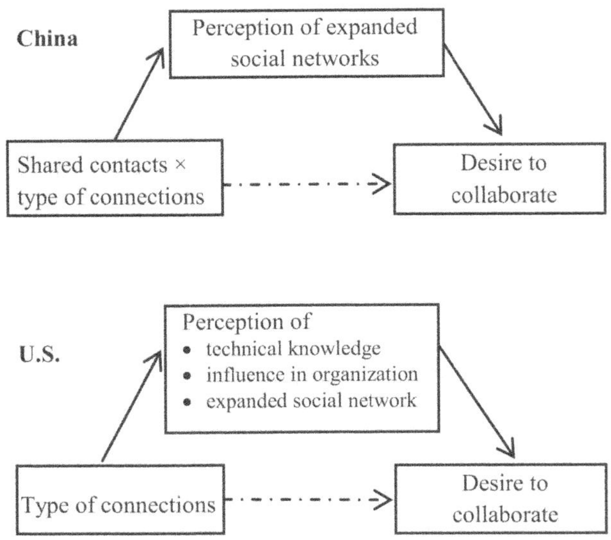

Figure 2. Mediation models for China (top) and U.S. (bottom).

mediator (general reputation) was added to the model. Our analysis indicates that although reputation was significantly related to desire to collaborate ($F[1,424] = 221.53$, $p = .000$), the effect of shared contacts on desire to collaborate was not reduced, thus ruling out mediation. This analysis establishes that reputation affects desire to collaborate, but eliminates reputation as an explanation for why shared contacts contribute to the desire to collaborate.

We also analyzed *technical knowledge*, *influence in organization*, and *expanded social networks* perceived as being available through the potential candidate as mediators. For Chinese respondents, perceiving that they would be able to enlarge their social circle through the candidate's network connections (Guanxi) served as a mediator (see figure 2). That is, the interaction between shared contacts and type of connections predicted the desired to collaborate (a), but when *expanded social network* was added to the model, it was significant ($t = 7.76$, $p = .000$) and the relationship between shared contacts/type of connections and desire to collaborate became less significant ($t = 1.80$ $p = .073$), see figure 2). In other words, Chinese respondents perceived a candidate who was connected to people in important positions and with whom the respondent had shared contacts as someone helpful to expand their own networks. This perception, in turn, lead to a desire to collaborate with that candidate. For the U.S. respondents, however, the choice to collaborate based on type of network connections was mediated by perceived access to all three types of resources. In other words, the U.S. respondents appear to perceive those who have expertise as compared to those who have positions of importance as having better access to technical knowledge, organizational influence, and expanded social networks and access to these resources affects their collaboration decisions.

To answer our research question about the relationship between network size and choice to collaborate, we examined the main effect of network size (large vs. small) within the full ANOVA. Contrary to our hypothesis, our analysis did not show any clear relationship between network size and choice to collaborate. Respondents presented with potential collaborators who had a small network reported slightly higher willingness to collaborate ($M = 4.31$, $SD = 1.01$) than those presented with candidates who had a large network ($M = 4.25$ $SD = 1.07$), but the difference was far from significant ($F[1, 424] = .02$, $p = .88$). The interaction between network size and culture was also not significant ($F[1, 424] = 1.69$, $p = .19$), although Chinese tended to prefer collaborators with smaller networks (large, $M = 4.56$, $SD = 1.15$; small, $M = 4.60$, $SD = .92$;) and Americans tended to prefer collaborators who had larger networks (large, $M = 3.90$, $SD = .90$; small, $M = 3.84$, $SD = 1.06$).

DISCUSSION

Overall, our results demonstrate the importance of national culture when using social network information to choose a collaborator. Generally, collaborator seekers from the U.S. based their decision largely on the type of connections (e.g. experts vs. people in important positions) in the candidate's social network whereas collaborators from China tended to consider the existence of shared contacts and type of connections in potential collaborators' networks together when making a decision.

Our mediation analysis further shows that how people perceive and value the resources available (access to technical information/advice, influence in the organization, or expanded social networks) determines how they attend to social network information. Although all three types of resources should contribute to the candidate's ability to get things done, Guanxi especially emphasizes one's ability to create lasting connections between people with benefits that play out over years, if not decades. Further, our measure of expanded social networks specifically included access to those who could provide support, suggesting someone who may be in a higher position hierarchically. In this sense, the mediating effect of expanding social networks for Chinese respondents is consistent with Guanxi and closure models. The U.S. respondents, in contrast, appear to value all resources equally, which is consistent with a structure holes model in which efficient, non-redundant access to a variety of resources is paramount. U.S. respondents, however, did not adhere to a structure holes model in their response to shared contacts. A structural holes model would suggest that workers prefer to collaborate with those who do *not* share common contacts, but shared contacts was not significantly related (positively or negatively) to U.S. respondents' desire to collaborate with the candidate. Finally, U.S. respondents did not significantly prefer to collaborate with a candidate who had a larger network. In sum, our results suggest that a closure model fits the preferences of the Chinese respondents relatively well, but U.S. preferences reflect neither model completely.

Given extensive support for structural holes theory in the U.S., our research calls into question its relevance for choosing collaborators and perhaps challenges its validity more generally, at least as a normative vs. prescriptive model. Of course, people likely rely on hybrid models for creating social networks, e.g. with some structural holes and some network closure. We set up two competing models – a closure model and the structural holes model – although people's preferences are rarely so black and white. Overall, our results show that U.S. as compared with Chinese use more of a structural holes model even if they do not adhere to it completely.

Still, there are other possible explanations for why a structural holes model did not entirely fit the U.S. respondents. One explanation is that peoples' behavior when using social media is different than the way that they form social networks through other means. Most research on structural holes has not examined choices made based on online social network information. Further research will need to be conducted comparing online vs. offline collaboration choices to determine the extent to which social media affects networking behavior. For example, McDonald's [25] research would suggest that some of the more nuanced social network behaviors are hard to capture in technology. Another possible explanation is that U.S. participants simply valued all types of resources and believe that expertise was the best conveyor of social capital (as suggested by the data). Perhaps when seeking collaborators in the U.S., social capital of all types is valued, regardless of the uniqueness of the resource (as argued by structural holes theory) and expertise is seen as a carrier of social capital. This is consistent with an exchange oriented market transaction model as described by Morris and colleagues [26] in which relationships are primary instrumental and carriers of resources.

We were also surprised that network size, across cultures, was not a predictor of desire to collaborate, given our expectation that more connections would be perceived as conferring more resources. One question is how people perceived network size. Evidence suggests that connecting with someone in an online community does not always mean that people have a close connection in the real world [40]. In our current study, although our manipulation check showed a significant difference between large and small networks in the respondents' evaluation of network size, we do not know how respondents perceived the strength and validity of the connections. For candidates with a large network (which included 350 contacts in our scenario), it is possible that respondents did not perceive the contacts as being resource rich, which could explain why network size did not predict to desire to collaborate with a candidate. To evaluate this, we examined the relationship between network size and the three types of resources, e.g. access to technical knowledge/advice, influence in the organization, and expanded social network. Our results suggest that, in fact, respondents saw larger networks as conferring more access to organizational influence ($F[1,428] = 9.80$, $p = .002$) and to expanded social networks ($F[1,428] = 28.38$, $p = .000$) but *not* to technical knowledge/advice ($F[1,425] = .77$, $p = .38$). There were no interactions between culture, network size, and any of these three types of resources. Given the Chinese value for expanded social networks, we were somewhat surprised that they did not value larger networks. We suspect that although a larger network is perceived to provide more access to those with organizational influence, a larger network is less consistent with a Guanxi model of tightly connected networks characterized by reciprocity and harmony.

Our findings provide new insights for the design of better enterprise software systems to enhance collaborations at work. The type of connections, as elaborated above, play a more important role for a collaboration seeker than network size. However, if we look at the current social network websites (such as Facebook and LinkedIn), the available information on the type of connections is not highlighted or made easy for users to search or sort. A better design that makes the information more visible and accessible to users might enhance workplace collaborations. There are also design implications for the design of systems when people are working globally. If, for example, Jian in China wants to collaborate with John in the U.S., how do we make sure that Jian has the information about John that Jian values? How does John develop a social network that helps him to be perceived as a valuable collaborator to potential colleagues in China? Also, how does John choose a collaborator in China who is seen as a valuable collaborator by Chinese stakeholders? The answer may lie in providing more explicit information about how the information is being valued in different cultures and allowing enough flexibility in the system to visualize information specific to the culture(s) of interest.

Of course, there are limitations to the study we report here. First, our study only included respondents from China and the U.S. Cross-cultural research often relies on broad distinctions between East and West [30] so it is possible that our results would generalize to other Eastern and Western cultures, but future studies will be required to assess the extent to which these findings generalize beyond China and the U.S. Second, we studied a multinational company in which the Chinese employees may have had extensive exposure to Western culture. On one hand, this might suggest weaker effects than a more representative sample, but it is still important to assess its impact. To assess the effect of the Chinese being exposed to Western culture, we asked several relevant survey questions. Results show that exposure to Western culture did not affect the results for Chinese employees, suggesting that the results may be robust to exposure to the West and may therefore hold for employees outside of multinational companies. Our manipulation checks for cultural also indicate that our Chinese sample was culturally Chinese and our US sample was culturally American, despite both having broad global exposure. Still, future research with a less cosmopolitan set of respondents would help to shed light on the representativeness of our results. Third, our scenario was intentionally vague about the exact work to be done by the collaborator being selected. This had the advantage of being meaningful for each individual responding to the study regardless of their situation, but it also had the possible disadvantage of being a noisy measure in that respondents may have interpreted the role of the potential collaborator and the team needs differently. To address this, future research may want to provide more specificity about the role of the candidate and/or capture more data on the mental model being held by the respondents regarding the needs of the team. Fourth, previous work indicates that reputation affects how collaborators are sought [e.g., 16]. In the current study, we examined how the relationship between general reputation of a team member candidate and desire to collaborate with this candidate would be influenced by the existence of shared contacts and other network information. To understand more specifically how reputation works in this context, future research could examine how the shared contact's impression of the team member candidate affects the attractiveness of the team member candidate. Finally, scenarios are an excellent way to get data from non-student populations and enabled us to access a fairly large sample of working professionals around the globe, but are not a substitute for capturing behavior. Future studies should validate and extend this work with laboratory experiments and observational studies. A controlled lab study would also help to validate the direction of causality between variables of interest in our study.

Despite the limitations, we believe that this work demonstrates a link between the use of social network information and national culture. Our research further suggests that selecting models that are culturally congruent (e.g. a closure for Chinese and an exchange oriented market transaction model for U.S.) may be helpful in designing culturally sensitive social networking systems.

AKNOWLEDGEMENTS

We thank the anonymous reviewers, Desney Tan, and James Landay for their insightful comments on earlier versions of this paper. We also thank Mike McGhie for his help in formulating the study.

REFERENCE

1. Adler, P.S. and Kwon, S.W. Social capital: Prospects for a new concept. *Academy of Management Review* 27, 1 (2002), 17-40.
2. Alston, J.P. Wa, Guanxi, and Inhwa: Managerial principles in Japan, China, and Korea. *Business Horizons* 32, 2 (1989), 26-31.
3. Balakrishnan, A.D., Fussell, S.R. and Kiesler, S. Do visualization improve synchronous remote collaboration? In *Proc. of CHI 2008*, ACM Press (2008), 1227-1236.
4. Bian, Y.J. Bring strong ties back in: Indirect ties, network bridges, and job searches in China. *American Sociological Research* 62, 3 (1997), 366-385.
5. Burt, R.S. Structural holes versus network closure as social capital. Pp 31-56 in Social Capital: *Theory and Research* (edited by Lin, N., Cook, K.S. and Burt, R.S.), Aldine Press, Chicago, US, 2001.
6. Burt, R. S., Hogarth, R.M. and Michaud, C. The social capital of French and American managers. *Organization Science* 11, 1 (2000), 123–147.
7. Chai, S.K. and Rhee, M. Confusion capitalism and the paradox of closure and structural holes in East Asian firms. *Management and Organization Review* 6, 1 (2009), 5-29.
8. Chandler, A.D., Jr. Strategy and Structure: Chapters in *The History of The American Industrial Enterprise*, MIT Press, Cambridge, MA, 1962/1998.
9. Cialdini, R.B., Borden, R.J., Thorne, A., and Sloan, L.R. Basking in reflected glory: Three (football) field studies. *Journal of Personality and Social Psychology*, 34, 3 (1976), 366-375.
10. Coleman, J.S. Social capital in the creation of human capital. *American Journal of Sociological Review* 64, 1 (1988), 682-686.
11. Coleman, J.S. *Foundation of Social Theory*. Harvard University Press, Cambridge, MA, 1990.
12. Diamant, E.I., Fussell, S.R., and Lo, F. Where did we turn wrong? Unpacking the effects of culture and technology on attributions of team performance. In *Proc. of CSCW 2008*, ACM Press (2008), 383-391.
13. Dunning, J.H. and Kim, C. The cultural roots of Guanxi: An exploratory study. *The Word Economy* 30, 2 (2007), 329-341.
14. Fisher, D. and Dourish, P. Social and temporal structures in everyday collaboration. In *Proc. of CHI 2004*, ACM Press (2004), 551-558.
15. Gelfand, M., Erez, M., and Aycan, Z. Cross-cultural organizational behavior. *Annual Review of Psychology*, 58 (2007), 479-514.
16. Hinds, P.J., Carley, K.M., Krackhardt, D., and Wholey, D. Choosing group members: Balancing similarity, competence and familiarity. *Organizational Behavior and Human Decision Processes*, 81, 2 (2000), 226-251.
17. Hinds, P.J., Liu, L., and Lyon, J. Putting the global in global work: An intercultural lens on the process of cross-national collaboration. *Academy of Management Annals*. 5 (2012), 1-54.
18. Irani, L., Vertesi, J., Dourish, P., Philip, K., and Grinter, R.E. Postcolonial computing: A lens on design and development. In *Proc. of CHI 2010*, ACM Press (2010),

1311-1320Kautz, H., Selman, B. and Shah, M. Combining social networks and collaborative filtering. *Communications of the ACM* 40, 3 (1997), 63-65.

19. Keegan, B., Gergle, D. and Contractor, N. Do editors or articles drive collaboration? Multilevel statistical network analysis of Wikipedia coauthorship. In Proc. of *CSCW 2012*, ACM Press (2012), 427-436

20. Lampe, C., Ellison, N. and Steinfield, C. A familiar Facebook: Profile elements as signals in an online social network. In *Proc. of CHI 2007*, ACM Press (2007), 435-444.

21. Lee, M. K., Kiesler, S., Forlizzi, J., Srinivasa, S. and Rybski, P. Gracefully Mitigating Breakdowns in Robotic Services. In *Proc. of HRI 2010*, 203-210.

22. Lim, B. Y., Dey, A. K. Assessing demand for intelligibility in context-aware applications. *In Proc. Of the 11th internal conference on Ubiquitous Computing*, ACM Press (2009), 195-204.

23. Luo, J.D. Guanxi revisited: An exploratory study of familiar ties in a Chinese workplace. *Management and Organization Review* 7, 2 (2011), 329-351.

24. Matthews, T., Whittaker, S., Moran, T., Yuen, S., and Judge, T. Productive interrelationships between collaborative groups ease the challenges of dynamic and multi-teaming. *Computer Supported Cooperative Work*, 2012, doi=10.1007/s10606-011-9154-y.

25. McDonald, D.W. Recommending collaboration with social networks: A comparative evaluation. In *Proc. of CHI 2003*, ACM Press (2003), 593-600.

26. Morris, M. W., Podolny, J. and Sullivan, B. N. Patterns of coworker relations: Interpersonal patterns in American, Chinese, German, and Spanish divisions of a global retail bank. *Organizational Science* 19, 4 (2008), 517–532.

27. Mortensen, M, From teams to recombinant collaboration: Understanding the evolution of organizational work (January 6, 2012). *INSEAD Working Paper* No. 2012/02/OB. Available at SSRN: http://ssrn.com/abstract=1980698

28. Nardi, B.A., Whittaker, S., and Schwarz, H. NetWORKers and their activity in intensional networks. *Computer Supported Cooperative Work: The Journal of Collaborative Computing*, 11, 1-2 (2002), 205-242.

29. Nisbett, R. *The Geography of Thought: How Asians and Westerners Think Differently... and Why*. New York: Free Press, 2003.

30. Nisbett, R.E., and Masuda, T. Culture and point of view. *PNAS*, 100, 19 (2003), 11163-11170.

31. Okhuysen, G. A., and Bechky, B. A. Coordination in organizations: An integrative perspective. *The Academy of Management Annals*, 3 (2009), 463 - 502.

32. Olson, G.M., and Olson, J.S. Distance matters. *Human-Computer Interaction*, 15 (2000), 139-178.

33. Ordonez de Pablos, P. Western and eastern views on social networks, *Learning Organization* 12, 5 (2005), 436– 456.

34. Setlock, L.D., and Fussell, L.R. What's it worth to you? The costs and affordances of CMC tools to Asian and American users. In *Proc. of CSCW 2010*, ACM Press (2010), 341-349.

35. Setlock, L.D., and Fussell, L.R. Culture or fluency? Unpacking interaction between culture and communication medium. In *Proc. of CHI 2011*, ACM Press (2011), 1137-1140.

36. Tang, J.C., Zhao, C., Cao, X. and Inkpen, K. Your time zone or mine? A study of globally time zone-shifted collaboration. In *Proc. of CSCW 2011*, ACM Press (2011), 235-244.

37. Tong, S.T., Heide, B.V.D., Langwell, L., and Walther, J.B. Too much of a good thing? The relationship between number of friends and interpersonal impression on Facebook. *Journal of Computer-Mediated Communication* 13, 1 (2008), 531-549.

38. Utz, S. Show me your friends and I will tell you what type of person you are: How one's profile, number of friends, and type of friends influence impression formation on social network sites. *Journal of Computer-Mediated Communication* 15, 2 (2010), 314-335.

39. Xiao, Z.X. and Tsui, A.S. When brokers may not work: The cultural contingency of social capital in Chinese high-tech firms. *Administrative Science Quarterly* 52, 1 (2007), 1-31.

40. Yuan, Y.C., Carboni, I. and Enrlich, K. The impact of awareness and accessibility on expertise retrieval: A multilevel network perspective. *Journal of the American Society for Information Science and Technology* 61, 4 (2010), 700-714.

41. Yuki, M., Maddux, W. W., Brewer, M. B., and Takemura, K. Cross-cultural differences in relationship-and group- based trust. *Personality and Social Psychology Bulletin* 31, 1 (2005), 48-62.

42. Zhao, C., Hinds, P.J., and Gao, G. How and to whom people share: the role of culture in self–disclosure in online communities. In *Proc. Of CSCW 2012*, ACM Press (2012), 67-76.

Effects of Message Content on Cognitive and Affective Processes in Cross-culture and Same-culture Instant Messaging Conversations

Duyen T. Nguyen
Department of Communication
Cornell University
tn248@cornell.edu

Susan R. Fussell
Department of Communication
Cornell University
sfussell@cornell.edu

ABSTRACT

In this paper we explore how and why communication problems such as lack of understanding, low involvement, and negative emotions emerged during the computer-mediated conversations of same-culture and cross-culture pairs. We used retrospective analysis, in which pairs of cross-culture and same-culture American and Chinese participants collaborated on a crime-solving task via Instant Messaging (IM), and later reviewed their IM conversations to report their thoughts and feelings on a minute-by-minute basis. We found differences in the types of messages people produced based on the cultural combination of the pairs. We also found that the content of their partner's messages influenced participants' involvement and negative emotions during the conversation. Our results provide insights into the conversational processes of computer-mediated intercultural teams, and have implications for the design of intercultural collaboration tools.

Author Keywords

Cross-culture communication; CMC; retrospective analysis

ACM Classification Keywords

H5.3 Group and Organization Interfaces: Computer-supported cooperative work

General Terms

Experimentation; Human Factors

INTRODUCTION

While global teams with members in different geographical locations, and from different cultures, collaborating via computer mediated communication (CMC) have been found to offer many benefits [30], previous studies have reported that challenges can arise during intercultural CMC communication [e.g. 32, 45, 7]. In order to enjoy the benefit of global collaboration, these communication problems should be prevented, or overcome. However, it is still difficult to understand the characteristics and causes of these problems. Two possible reasons may help explain this difficulty. First, while challenges often arise during the communication processes of intercultural teams [7], previous research [e.g. 27, 28] has typically assessed the presence or absence of these issues after the conversation is over, rather than associating them with aspects of the communication process. Second, prior studies of computer mediated intercultural communication show quite different patterns of results regarding the communication process of cross-culture teams, depending on the medium of communication [e.g. 39, 40], the type of task, and the cultural composition of the group [45]. Hence, the goal of the present paper is to increase our understanding of why, and how communication problems arise in intercultural CMC conversations by examining how what partners think and feel during the course of a conversation is associated with the types of messages exchanged in that conversation.

At least three interrelated types of issues can occur when communication takes place across cultural boundaries: (a) difficulty understanding a partner's message [e.g. 27, 40], (b) negative affective reactions, such as anger, anxiety, or annoyance [e.g. 32], and (c) reduced engagement or involvement in intercultural conversations [e.g. 4]. Some studies have pointed to the content of messages produced during the conversation as a source of influence on conversational outcomes such as satisfaction & recall [e.g. 29], but because participants' reactions to the conversation were measured after the conversation was over, it is impossible to pinpoint what specific aspects of the communication led to these effects.

To address the above issue, Nguyen & Fussell [32] used a *retrospective analysis* technique [14] in which cross-culture and same culture pairs of American and Chinese participants reviewed their instant messaging (IM) conversations after the fact and reported, on a moment-by-moment basis, what went wrong during the conversation. Nguyen & Fussell [32] found that the level of tension and annoyance were higher for both American and Chinese participants working with a Chinese partner than with an American partner. Qualitative analysis of participants' comments revealed that there were differences in communication styles among participants from different cultures, such as task-orientated versus relationship-orientated conversational style, which might explain the high level of annoyance and tension felt in cross-culture pairs.

Nguyen & Fussell, however, did not pinpoint how cultural differences in communication styles may lead to communication problems such as negative emotions. This is an important question to answer because it may suggest ways to improve intercultural collaboration through the prevention or remedy of communication problems. Moreover, it also contributes to the development of intercultural communication theories. It not only explores cultural differences in communication on a deeper level (specific message production practices), but also examines how such differences affect the communication process, which has not been discussed in many previous cross-culture studies. The current study extends the analysis in Nguyen & Fussell [32] to answer this question, by investigating the association between message content and participants' cognitive and affective processes, namely, the processes of developing mutual understanding, involvement, and negative emotions during an IM conversation. Pairs of participants collaborated on the crime-solving task described in Nguyen & Fussell [32]. They conversed via IM and then individually reviewed a recording of their conversation. For every two-minute period of the interaction, they reported on their cognitive and affective reactions. We also coded the messages exchanged during each two-minute interval, and examined the relationships among the cultural composition of the pair, the messages exchanged, and participants' cognitive and affective processes.

In the rest of the paper, we first review previous literature on issues in intercultural communication and present our hypotheses about the effects of message content on cognitive and affective processes in intercultural and intracultural CMC conversations. We then describe our retrospective method, explain our statistical approach, and present our findings. As we will show, the number of task-related messages produced during the conversation differed depending on the culture composition of the pair. Moreover, the type of messages produced by their partner influenced participants' self-reported levels of involvement and negative emotions during their conversations. We conclude by discussing some of the implications of our findings for theories of intercultural communication and the design of new CMC tools for intercultural communication.

BACKGROUND

In this section, we first point out several problematic cognitive and affective processes in intercultural teams. We then describe the types of message content often produced during these processes. Finally, we outline the specific hypotheses and research questions tested in our study.

Cognitive and Affective Processes in intercultural CMC

Previous studies of global virtual teams [e.g., 33, 21] suggest many issues arise during team conversations [7]. Our focus is on three interrelated types of communication problems: difficulties with cognitive processing, negative affective responses, and lower conversational involvement.

With respect to cognitive processing, participants in intercultural conversations sometimes report difficulty understanding their partners. Some of these problems arise from fluency issues or from differences in conversational styles [e.g. 27]; others arise from errors in the process of *grounding* [5], the interactive processes by which partners in a conversation establish mutual understanding. For example, Li [27, 28] found that European Canadians and Chinese participants differed in whether they would ask for clarification when needed during a conversation, and these differences affected task outcomes. The reduced affordances of CMC, such as lack of audio and visuals, may lead to even more difficulties in grounding [7, 21]. Lack of understanding, or misunderstanding may negatively affect both the team's performance and relationships among team members [21].

Participants in conversations also experience a flow of affective reactions to the ongoing interaction, which can influence team interaction and performance [22]. Intercultural teams often report more negative emotions than intra-cultural teams, including anxiety, tensions [4], frustrations and annoyance. There are a variety of possible explanations for this finding, including the fact that people enjoy being around similar others [8], or that people find the extra effort required for grounding to be annoying. Effective team communication involves attention to others' affective states, emotions and feelings. However, the lack of contextual cues in CMC may make it harder for team members to detect others' emotions [23].

Another important aspect of communication is how engaged or involved participants are in the conversation, that is, how actively they participate [3]. Involvement has been shown to facilitate affiliation, expression of intimacy, regulation of interaction [35], conversational cohesion, and better understanding [42]. However, research has found less involvement in intercultural interactions [4], possibly due to the lack of familiarity and common ground between partners. Although previous studies suggested that the inability of CMC to support non-verbal cues such as gaze and touch might lead to lack of involvement [23, 24], few studies have directly measured levels of involvement.

Cognitive processes, affective processes, and conversational involvement can be related in complex ways. For example, difficulties in understanding a partner can lead to annoyance, which in turn can lower involvement in a conversation. Previous studies of intercultural collaboration mostly pointed to the cultural differences in communication styles as the possible causes for these difficulties. Few studies, however, examined how culture affects conversations, and how the differences in conversational behaviors caused by both the cultural orientation of the participants and their partners could lead to communication issues. In this study, we examine cultural differences through the content of the messages participants said during their conversation. We also investigate how the types of messages that a person receives from his or her partner may have an impact on all three of the communication processes mentioned before. We turn to these topics in the next section.

Message Content in Task-Oriented CMC

Previous research suggests that many of the collaboration issues reported during conversations among virtual team members are associated with specific messages exchanged [7]. Thus, message content plays an important role in the emergence of collaboration challenges.

In many task-oriented conversations, participants exchange *task-related messages* that help them complete the task together (such as comments and opinions about the task content, suggestions of how to carry out the task). With respect to the crime-related conversations in our study (described in detail under Methods), two types of task-related messages can be distinguished: those that exchange facts about the case and those that express subjective feelings or opinions about the case [e.g. 34]. Since work-related conversations are composed of predominantly task-related messages, this type of messages is the main collaboration tool for any work team. Moreover, the amount of task-related communication a team member exchanged with his or her partners can shape their impressions of his or her knowledge and expertise [46].

Even when a conversation is primarily task-related, speakers use relational messages to establish and maintain their relationships with each other (such as greetings, compliments and ice-breaking small talk) [1, 40]. For example, partners who do not know each other often exchange self-introduction and greetings before starting the task, and offer compliments or congratulations to each other for doing well. While some studies found that CMC conversations were largely task-oriented and lacked relational exchanges [e.g. 23], other studies have found that CMC interaction could be used to support moderate social-emotional content [36] and develop close relationships [e.g. 44]. Studies of distributed work teams have also shown that building good team coherence and rapport is important for team success [e.g. 19].

Partners also exchange *backchannel responses* such as "uhm" or "uh huh" that are not intended to take the floor from the current speaker but rather indicate attention or understanding [37]. An addressee's back channel responses clarify whether he or she is paying attention and understanding one's messages [6, 25]. In text media, interactants produce back-channels by using transcriptions such as "uh huh", or shortcuts, and emoticons [18].

The Current Study

While previous studies have found issues in the communication processes of intercultural teams, they were not able to adequately explain these problems. Our study aims to bridge this gap by examining how culture influences the types of messages a participant produces, and how the message content, in turn, influences three types of cognitive and affective processes during CMC: (a) the grounding process of establishing mutual understanding; (b) affective responses to the ongoing interaction; and (c) participants' levels of involvement in the conversation. We focus on three types of message content: task-related messages, relational messages, and back-channel responses.

Culture differences in message production

Our first set of hypotheses pertains to the effects of cultural background on message production. In this study, we consider two cultures --American, and Chinese – which have been found to prefer different communication styles [e.g. 16, 45]. One key aspect of communication style is the emphasis placed on completing tasks vs. building rapport [41]. Some cultures, such as that of the U.S, place priority on getting work done efficiently, with minimal regard to building interpersonal relationships. Other cultures, such as that of China, tend to emphasize the need to achieve group harmony and solidarity. Consistent with these cultural differences, several studies have observed more relational communication in Chinese pairs than in American pairs, both in face-to-face communication and CMC [e.g., 27, 28, 40, 20]. Moreover, in intercultural teams, some participants may adapt to the conversational styles of their partners [e.g., 11]. For example, Wang, Fussell & Setlock [45] found that Chinese participants were more likely to reduce their use of relational communication when interacting with (more task-oriented) American partners. Based on these findings, we posed the following hypotheses:

H1A: American participants working with an American partner will produce more task-related CMC messages than Chinese participants working with a Chinese partner.

H1B: Chinese participants working with an American partner will produce more task-related CMC messages than Chinese participants working with a Chinese partner.

H2: Chinese participants will produce more relational CMC messages than American participants regardless of the culture of their interaction partners.

Less is known about the effects of culture on backchannel responses, especially in CMC. In a face-to-face setting, Li [29] found that Chinese pairs produced more backchannel responses than Canadian pairs, and that in intercultural pairs Canadians increased their use of backchannel responses although there was no effect of the cultural composition of the group on Chinese speakers. Since the implications of these findings for CMC is unclear, we asked the following question:

RQ1: In a text-based CMC environment, how does the number of back-channel responses a participant uttered during the conversation differ based on the various culture combinations of the pair?

Effects of message content on understanding
Backchannels are an important component of the grounding process, since they are used to confirm mutual knowledge during a conversation [25, [29]. Therefore, we hypothesize:

H3: A participant's level of understanding during CMC will be positively associated with the number of backchannel responses produced by his/her partner.

Little research has examined the effects of numbers of task-related and relational messages on the development of mutual understanding in CMC. Therefore, we posed the following research question:

RQ2: How is a participant's level of understanding affected by his/her partner's task-related fact-oriented messages, task-related subjective opinions, and relational messages?

Effects of message content on involvement
Involvement is the degree to which a person participates with his or her partner in the ongoing social interaction [10]. In task-oriented conversations, task-related messages from a partner can signal that the partner is actively participating and thus involved with the interaction. Since involvement is a social process whereby social actors rely on each other to maintain their own involvement [13], being confirmed about a partner's attention may in turn lead the speaker to feel more involved. Thus, we proposed that:

H4: A participant's level of involvement during CMC will be positively associated with the number of task-related messages (both fact-oriented task messages, and subjective opinions) produced by his/her partner.

Back channel responses can also signal that a listener is paying attention [29], and therefore, can also help increase the speaker's level of involvement with the conversation.

H5: A participant's level of involvement during CMC will be positively associated with the number of backchannel responses produced by his/her partner.

There have not been many studies about the effects of relational messages on involvement in CMC. Therefore, we proposed the following research question:

RQ3: How is a participant's level of involvement during CMC affected by his/her partner's relational messages?

Effects of message content on negative emotions
During a conversation, negative emotions may emerge as a result of cognitive processes, such as a lack of understanding [7], and a lack of involvement [3]. Because there been little previous work looking at how message content affects negative emotions on a moment by moment basis, we propose the following question:

RQ4: How is a participant's level of negative emotions during CMC affected by his/her partner's back-channel responses, fact-oriented task-related messages, task-related subjective opinions, and relational messages?

METHOD
In order to understand how cultural differences in communication styles affect intercultural interaction, we used a retrospective analysis technique [14]. Same-culture and cross-culture pairs first discussed and solved a crime case using a text-based IM program. Afterwards, they individually reviewed a recording of their interaction. At preset intervals, the recording was stopped and participants provided their feedback on the segment.

Participants
Participants consisted of 60 students (53% undergraduate, 65% female) studying at a large American university. Of these, 30 students were native Chinese speakers who had been born in the People's Republic of China (29) or Taiwan (1), and had spent less than 5 years in the United States or Canada. The Chinese participants spoke fluent or near-fluent English. The other 30 American participants were all born and raised in the United States or Canada and spoke English as their native language. Twenty-eight American were Caucasian and two were Asian.

Each participant was paired randomly with a partner from the same culture or from a different culture, resulting in three combinations: 10 Chinese-Chinese (CC) pairs, 10 American-American (AA) pairs, and 10 American-Chinese (AC) pairs. To control for age differences we paired graduate students with other graduate students and undergraduates with other undergraduates. Participants in a pair did not know each other prior to the experiment.

Materials
Task. The task consisted of discussing a crime story and identifying the culprit of the crime. The crime story, developed by the first author, involved a break in and a murder attempt on a victim named Alex. Alex is the leader of a rock band of four people. The other three members of the band were the three prime suspects, one of whom was the actual culprit.

Two different versions of the crime story were prepared, based on the reports of two witnesses. Each version contained 10 pieces of information important to solving the case. The two versions shared common information about the victim, crime location, and attack on the victim. They also included details complementing each other that needed to be combined to fully understand what happened, such as the time and location of each of the suspects before and after the crime. The two versions also contained three contradictory details about the crime: (a) the time of the attack, (b) the body builds of the culprit and (c) the color of the shirt the culprit was wearing as they were reported from the different perspectives of the two witnesses. These had to be resolved through discussion to identify the culprit. The details were presented on a single sheet of paper (622 words for version A; 644 words for version B). The crime-solving task was designed to reflect a common collaboration task for global virtual teams that requires not only information sharing, but also collaborative reasoning and conflict resolution.

Memory quiz. A paper and pencil *memory quiz* was created to test participants' understanding of the materials prior to discussion with their partner. The quiz consisted of 10 multiple choice questions on the key details of the crime (e.g., time, suspects).

Culprit identification form. Since every pair had to provide a common answer to the case, we created a shared Google document between the two participants in a pair, with two questions on it: one for indicating the culprit(s) of the crime, and another for the pairs' reasoning behind their identification of this culprit. Both participants in each pair were able to edit this shared document at the same time. At the end of the discussion they saved this document.

Post task survey. Participants completed an online survey asking about their reactions to the task and partner, their communication styles, and their basic demographic information.

Retrospective analysis survey. The online *retrospective analysis survey* consisted of 7 rating questions and an additional open response question that participants completed after each 2-minute video clip. The first three questions asked each participant to rate on 5-point Likert scales their level of tension (very tense-very relaxed), annoyance (very annoyed-not annoyed at all) and interest (not interested at all-very interested) in the conversation. The next two questions asked participants to rate how much their partners understood them and how much they understood their partners, respectively (1 = not understanding at all; 7 = very understanding). The remaining two questions asked the participants to rate how much their partners and they themselves felt involved with the conversation (1 = not involved at all; 7 = very involved). The final question asked whether the participant had noticed any problem with their interaction at the point of time shown in the video clip. If the answer was yes, we asked them to provide details about what went wrong and what they would have done to prevent/remedy the problem.

Equipment and Recording Processing

Participants in all pairs used identical Dell workstations running the same version of Gtalk for Window XP. We disabled the use of audio call in Gtalk. The Gtalk chat window of the two participants in each pair were recorded, synchronized and combined into a split screen video during their discussion using CamStudio 2.5 desktop capturing software and ShowMyPC 3011 remote desktop sharing software. The split screen video consisted of two frames, one for each participant's Gtalk chat window. During retrospective analysis, each participant was shown only the frame with his or her own chat window. The video clip of the participants' own chat window served to remind them as much as possible their experience during the conversation with the partner, and aspects of the dynamics of the conversation such as keystrokes and response time, which may be helpful for them to answer the retrospective analysis survey.

Two Dell workstations with Dell Ultrasharp 19 inch monitors (1140 x 900 resolution) were used to present the video clips during the retrospective analysis. The 20-minute video of the discussion was divided into 10 sequential clips of 2 minute each to be played one by one in chronological order to both participants using Quicktime Player.

Procedure

The experiment consisted of two phases: a discussion phase and a retrospective analysis phase. In the *Discussion Phase*, pairs of participants were brought into a room and assigned seats at two separated workstations with a divider in between. They signed consent forms and received task instructions. Each participant received one of the two versions of the crime story. They were given 10 minutes to read the story and learn the details of the crime, after which the hard copies were taken away and they were given the memory test. The experimenter then corrected the quiz and left the corrected quiz with the participants for the rest of the experiment. Participants were then instructed how to use the Gtalk text chat client.

Each pair then discussed the story via Gtalk for 20 minutes (Figure 1). In order to solve the crime, the pairs needed to gather all the information from both versions of the story, resolve conflicting details, and identify the culprit. All pairs were encouraged to fully utilize their 20 minutes for discussion. After 20 minutes, the facilitators stopped the discussion, no matter what the pairs were doing. At the end of their interaction, each pair submitted their conclusion about the culprit and the reasoning behind their decision in the culprit identification form. Each participant in the pair then separately filled out the post-task survey.

In the *Retrospective Analysis Phase*, the two participants were seated as in the previous phase. They were shown a series of 10 two-minute video clips of their conversation in Phase 1. After each clip, participants filled out the retrospective analysis survey. After the last clip, participants were debriefed, paid and dismissed.

Figure 1. Setting of the discussion phase.

Coding of conversational messages

The experiment was conducted on 30 pairs for a previous study [32]. In this study, the IM chat logs of the conversations of each of these 30 pairs was broken down into 10 sub transcripts corresponding to the 10 two-minute clips participants watched during the retrospective analysis phase. The first author parsed each of the 10 sub transcripts of each pair into conversational messages based on speaking turns. A conversational message was defined as a verbal structure expressing one and only one idea. Incomplete or non-meaningful structures were coded as sentence fragments and ignored in the analyses.

Two independent coders, blind to the conditions of the experiment, coded all the conversational messages in all sub transcripts of all pairs (kappa = 84.7%). The conversational messages are coded exclusively into one of the 5 categories: fact, opinion, relational messages, back channel responses, and others.

Facts are those messages (including questions) about the task of solving the crime that express an objective fact or a clue that is already given in the stories handed out to the participants in the first phase of the experiment (e.g., "According to my story, Brian is tall.", "What is Brian's height according to your story?").

Opinions are messages (including questions) about the task of solving the crime that express a subjective opinion (agreement, disagreement, or neutral) (e.g., "I think Mr. Grover was lying.", "How do you think he could do that?", "No, I don't think Carl was the one.", "Yes, I agree Brian may be the culprit.").

Relational messages are messages (including questions) not related to the task of solving the crime, but are meant to establish relationships with the conversation partners or to promote team spirit. These messages include greetings, self-introductions, cheers and motivations; messages whereby the participants self-disclosed, but which are not directly related to solving the crime case (e.g., "Hi, nice to meet you!", "What's your name?", "I think our team did great, yay!").

Backchannel responses are messages that do not have any specific meaning, and do not add more meaning to the conversation, but still serve the communicative purposes of indicating involvement in the conversation and/or understanding of the partners' utterances or complimenting the partner's utterances (e.g., "uhm", "yeah", "ok", "and?").

Others are messages not fitting any of the categories above.

Measures

The dependent variables were number of problems, levels of understanding, involvement and negative emotions, subjective outcomes and performance.

Understanding. Participant's ratings, on a 7-point scale, of how much they understood their partner (self's understanding) during each minute of their conversation were negatively skewed, so we recoded the data into three categories (1 to 5 =1, 6=2 and 7=3), roughly corresponding to problematic understanding, good understanding and excellent understanding.

Involvement. Participants' ratings, on a 7-point scale, of how much they felt involved in the conversation (self's involvement) during each minute of their interaction were negatively skewed and recoded into three groups, representing the bottom, middle and top third of the responses (1 to 5=1 "low", 6=2 "middle", and 7=3 "high").

Interest. Participants indicated, on a 5-point scale, how much interest they felt in the conversation. This measure was also negatively skewed and recoded into three groups, representing the bottom, middle and top third of the responses (1 to 3 =1 "low", 4=2 "middle", and 5=3 "high").

Negative emotions. Participants' ratings on a 5-point scale of how tense and how annoyed they felt in the conversation were negatively skewed and recoded into three groups, representing the bottom, middle and top third of the responses (1=1 "low", 2 to 3=2 "middle", and 4 to 5=3 "high").

Message counts. We counted the number of messages of each of the 4 categories (facts, opinions, relational messages, backchannels) that a participant uttered every minute of the 10-minute discussion.

RESULTS

We report the results in two parts: first, analyses of the culture differences in message content produced; and second, the effects of message content on participants' cognitive and affective responses as well as their levels of involvement in the conversation.

Cultural Differences in Message Content

Table 1 showed the distribution of each type of messages uttered per minute based on the culture of the participants.

To test H1, H2, and answer RQ1, we conducted mixed model Analyses of Variance (ANOVA) on the number of messages, with self's culture, partner's culture and the interaction of these two as the fixed effects, and pairs, individual within pairs, and time within individual as random effects. Note that in mixed models, when tests of fixed effects involve a linear combination of variances at different levels of the model (e.g., group and individual), it is standard to estimate the degree of freedoms associated with the denominators by using Satterthwaite's approximation. Therefore, non-integer degree of freedoms may occur [31]. Because our hypotheses concern the fixed effects of culture, we present only these fixed effects below.

Message Types	Number of messages per minute	
	American	Chinese
Facts	2.8 (2.54); 3	2.1 (1.73); 2
Opinions	2.0 (2.02); 3	1.6 (1.53); 1
Relational	0.5 (0.33); 0	0.2 (0.40); 0
Back channel	0.3 (0.62); 0	0.3 (0.54); 0

Table 1. Number of messages of each type uttered every two minutes by American, and Chinese participants (Mean (SD); Median)

Task related and relational messages. Hypothesis 1A proposed that Americans working with an American partner would produce more task-related messages (both facts and opinions) than Chinese participants working with a Chinese partner. Hypothesis 1B proposed that Chinese participants working with an American partner would produce more task-related messages (both facts and opinions) than Chinese working with a Chinese partner. Hypotheses 2 suggested that regardless of the culture of their partners, Chinese participants would produce more relational messages than American participants. To test these hypotheses, we conducted a mixed model ANOVA of the form outlined above, using the number of task-related facts, task-related opinions, and relational messages produced by each participant every 1 minute of the conversation as dependent variable. However, since these totals were heavily skewed, we did the analysis on the natural log transformation of these numbers instead. We did not find any significant main effects of self culture (F[1, 44.5]=1.02, n.s), partner's culture (F[1, 44.5]=1.59, n.s), nor interaction effects (F[1, 26.58]<1, n.s) on the number of relational messages, rejecting H2.

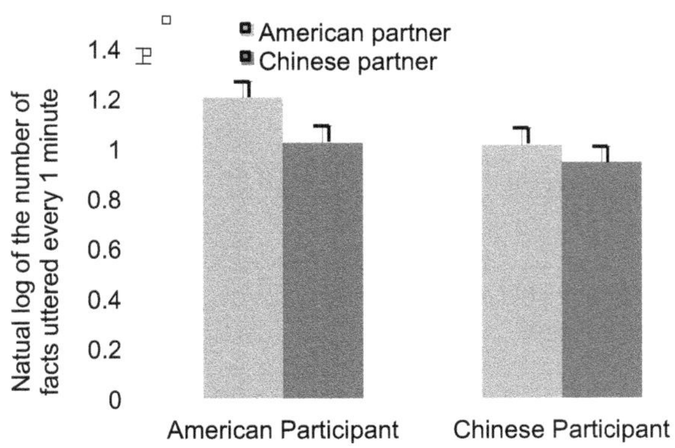

Figure 2. Culture difference in terms of the number of facts uttered every two minutes.

We found a significant main effect of self's culture (F[1, 45.49]=6.16, p=.017), and partner's culture (F[1, 45.49]=5.34, p=.025) on the number of facts, but no significant interaction effect (F[1, 27]<1, n.s). American participants said more facts (M=1.11, S.E=.048) than Chinese participants (M=.98, S.E=.048), regardless of whom they were working with. This is consistent with H1A. Participants, regardless of culture, working with an American partner produced more facts (M=1.11, S.E=.048) than working with a Chinese partner (M=.98, S.E=.048) (Figure 2). This is consistent with H1B.

We found no significant main effect of self's culture (F[1, 54.7]=2.48, n.s), or partner's culture (F[1, 54.7]<1, n.s) on the number of task-related opinions. But we found a significant interaction effect (F[1, 27]=8.99, p=.006). Same-culture American pairs said the most task-related opinions (M=.95, S.E=.06), followed by same-culture Chinese pairs (M=.87, S.E=.06), and lastly cross-culture pairs (M=.64, S.E=.07) (Figure 3). These results are consistent with H1A, but contradict H1B. Taken together, the results about the different types of task-related messages supported H1A, and partially supported H1B.

Back channel responses. RQ1 asked whether there would be any difference based on the culture combination of the pairs in terms of the number of backchannel responses produced. To answer this question, we conducted a mixed model analysis of the form outlined above, using the total of back channel responses produced by the participant every 1 minute of the conversation as dependent variable. However, since the total numbers of back channel response every minute were heavily skewed, we did the analysis on the natural log transformation of these numbers instead. We did not find any significant main effect of self's culture (F[1, 53.55]=2.17, n.s), or partner's culture (F[1, 53.55]=1.37, n.s), or any significant interaction effect (F[1, 27.20]<1, n.s) on the number of back-channel responses produced. So there was no significant difference across the culture combinations of the pairs in terms of the number of back-channel responses uttered during the conversation.

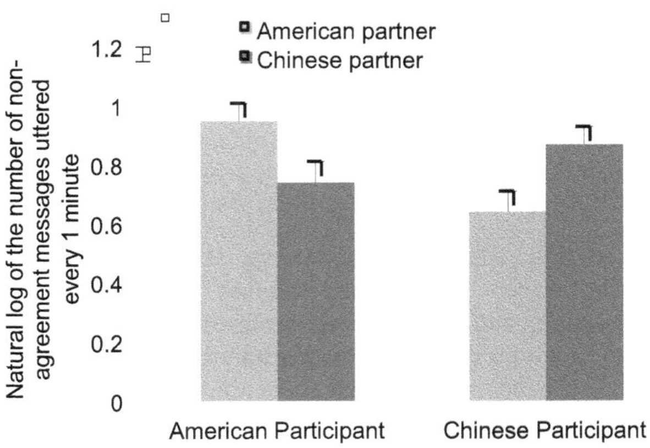

Figure 3. Culture difference in terms of the number of non-agreement messages uttered every two minutes.

Message Content and Communication Processes

To test H3, H4, H5, and answer RQ2, RQ3, RQ4 we conducted regressions using our cognitive and affective measurements as dependent variables. First, we included the effect of gender, self's culture, partner's culture, and the interaction of these two as covariates. Second, the number of messages in each of the 5 categories mentioned above was included as covariates. Since the cognitive and affective measurements (level of understanding, involvement, interest, tension, and annoyance) were taken every minute of the 10-minute long discussion for each participant in each pair, we included the lagged dependent variable (the cognitive and affective measurement taken 1 minute before the dependent variable) among the regressors, to control for the effect of the previous level of affective and cognitive responses [9]. Finally, we accounted for the non-independence of multiple observations per individual within pairs and per pair.

While there are reasons to believe that culture may also influence the effects of message content on communication processes, and thus the need to include the interactions of culture and message content as covariates, a model with these covariates added showed no significant interaction effects of culture and message content on communication processes. Removing these interaction effects from the model did not significantly change the results. Therefore, we decided not to include the interaction between culture and message content in our final model. Consequently, the independent variables consist of 4 groups: 1) random effect of 30 pairs and 60 participants nested in each pair, 2) culture variables including self's culture, partner's culture, and the interaction of these two, 3) Yt-1, or the conversational reaction being analyzed at the t-1 time, and 4) message content variables: natural log of number of facts, opinions, relational messages and back channel response each minute

We carried out this analysis in JMP statistical package. Table 2, 3, 4, 5 and 6 present the results of these regression analyses on 5 dependent variables: level of understanding, involvement, interest, annoyance and tension, respectively. As can be seen from table 2 to 6, the R^2 for the regression on all 5 dependent variables were high, implying that the models provided good explanations for communication processes. For the level of understanding, R^2= .69 (see table 2); for level of involvement R^2= .73 (see table 3); for level of interest R^2= .70 (see table 4); for tension R^2= .70 (see table 5); and for annoyance R^2= 64. (see table 6).

Effects on the level of understanding. H3 and RQ2 were about the effects of message content on the level of understanding, and tested using a regression of the form outlined above on the level of understanding reported every minute as dependent variable. Results are shown in table 2.

Dependent variable: Level of understanding				
Variables	**β**	**SE**	**DFDen**	**p**
Intercept	1.51	0.13	135.7	***
Self culture [A]	-0.05	0.08	29.7	
Partner culture [A]	0.04	0.08	29.7	
Self [A] x partner culture [A]	-0.03	0.08	19.26	
Lag_understanding	0.24	0.05	459.4	***
Fact	0.03	0.04	433.9	
Opinion	-0.03	0.04	441.1	
Back channel	0.09	0.07	424.8	
Relational	0.12	0.11	473.7	
R^2	**.69**			

Table 2. Effects of message content on understanding. ***Notes:*** **2-tailed p values: + p<=.08, * p<= .05, ** p<=.01, *** p<=.0001, A=American**

H3 predicted more back channel responses uttered by the partners would lead to higher level of understanding of the participant. The regression result showed no significant effect of the number of back channel responses uttered by the partner on the participant's level of understanding (F[1, 424.8]=1.54, n.s). H1 was not supported.

RQ2 asked what the effects of task-oriented fact, task-oriented opinions, and relational messages by the partner were on the level of understanding on a moment-by-moment basis of the participant. The result showed no significant effect of the number of factual messages (F[1, 433.9]<1, n.s), opinions (F[1, 441.1]<1, n.s), and relational messages (F[1, 473.7]=1.20, n.s) uttered by the partner on the participant's level of understanding. So in this study, we did not find any effect of task related messages and relational messages by the partner on the level of understanding of the participant.

Effects on the level of involvement and interest. H4, H5 and RQ3 were about the effects of message content on the level of involvement, and tested using a regression of the form outlined above on the level of involvement, and interest reported every minute as dependent variables. The results are shown in table 3 for the level of involvement, and table 4 for the level of interest.

Dependent variable: Level of involvement				
Variables	β	SE	DFDen	p
Intercept	1.47	0.12	163.1	***
Self culture [A]	-0.02	0.07	25.23	
Partner culture	0.06	0.07	25.35	
Self [A] x partner culture [A]	-0.06	0.06	18.08	
Lag_involvement	0.32	0.05	395.4	***
Fact	0.03	0.04	452.1	
Opinion	0.04	0.04	428	
Back channel	0.02	0.07	416.9	
Relational	-0.19	0.1	465.9	+
R^2	**.73**			

Table 3. Effects of message content on involvement. ***Notes:*** **2-tailed p values: + p<=.08, * p<= .05, ** p<=.01, *** p<=.0001, A=American**

Dependent variable: Level of interest				
Variables	**β**	**SE**	**DFDen**	**p**
Intercept	1.19	0.12	152.8	***
Self culture [A]	0.04	0.06	25.12	
Partner culture [A]	-0.01	0.06	25.14	
Self [A] x partner culture [A]	-0.04	0.06	18.52	
Lag_interest	0.35	0.05	392.5	***
Fact	0.15	0.04	458.9	***
Opinion	0.04	0.04	428.8	
Back channel	-0.09	0.07	418.8	
Relational	-0.14	0.11	472.6	
R^2	**.70**			

Table 4. Effects of message content on interest. ***Notes:*** **2-tailed p values: + p<=.08, * p<= .05, ** p<=.01, *** p<=.0001, A=American**

H3 predicted more task-related messages uttered by the partner would lead to higher level of involvement of the participant. We did not find any significant effect of the number of facts (F[1, 452.1]<1, n.s), or opinions (F[1,

428]<1, n.s) uttered by the partner on the participant's level of involvement (see table 3). H3 was not supported.

H4 predicted more back channel responses by the partners would lead to higher level of involvement of the participant. No significant effect was found for back channel responses (F[1,416.9]<1, n.s) by the partner on the participant's level of involvement (see table 3). H4 was not supported.

RQ3 asked what the effects of the frequency of relational messages of the partner on the moment-by-moment level of involvement reported by the participants are. The results in table 3 showed a near significant negative coefficient (β=-.19, F[1, 465.9]=3.67, p=.056) for the number of relational messages by the partner. So we found that higher number of relational messages by the partner lead to lower level of involvement of the participant.

Table 4 displays the results on the level of interest. It showed a significant positive effect of the number of factual messages (β=.15, F[1, 458.9]=14.02, p<.001) by the partner on the level of interest of the participant. In summary, we found that high number of task-related fact messages by the partner lead to higher level of interest in the participant. This is consistent with H3. We found no other significant effect of the number of opinions (F[1, 428.8]<1, n.s), relational messages (F[1, 472.6]=1.77, n.s), and back channel responses (F[1, 418.8]=1.43, n.s) by the partner on the participant's level of interest.

Effects on the level of negative emotions. RQ4 asked what the effects of message content said by the partner on the participant's level of negative emotions. We used a regression of the form outlined above on the level of tension, and annoyance reported every minute as dependent variables. The results are shown in table 5 for the level of tension, and table 6 for the level of annoyance.

Dependent variable: Level of tension				
Variables	**β**	**SE**	**DFDen**	**p**
Intercept	1.32	0.12	176.6	***
Self culture [A]	0.03	0.05	30.85	
Partner culture [A]	-0.06	0.05	30.94	
Self [A] x partner culture [A]	-0.08	0.06	19.44	
Lag_tension	0.33	0.05	440	***
Fact	0.10	0.04	471.7	**
Opinion	0.06	0.04	427.1	
Back channel	0.07	0.06	419.9	
Relational	-0.14	0.09	468.7	
R^2	**.70**			

Table 5. Effects of message content on tension. ***Notes:*** **2-tailed p values: + p<=.08, * p<= .05, ** p<=.01, *** p<=.0001, A=American**

First, as can be seen in table 5, there was a significant positive effect of the number of facts uttered by the partner (β=.10, F[1, 471.7]=8.16, p=.004) on the participant's level of tension. So we found that the higher the frequency of fact messages said by the partner, the more tense the participant reported. We did not find any significant effect of the number of opinions (F[1, 427.1]=2.65, n.s), relational messages (F[1, 468.7]=2.43, n.s), or back channel responses (F[1, 419.9]=1.50, n.s) by the partner.

Second, as shown in table 6, we did not find any significant effect of the number of facts (F[1, 471.7]<1, n.s), opinions (F[1, 427.1]<1, n.s), relational messages (F[1, 468.7]<1, n.s), or back channel responses (F[1, 419.9]=2.54, n.s) by the partner on the participant's level of annoyance.

Dependent variable: Level of annoyance				
Variables	**β**	**SE**	**DFDen**	**p**
Intercept	1.25	0.11	116.2	***
Self culture [A]	-0.03	0.06	38.27	
Partner culture [A]	-0.14	0.06	39.7	*
Self [A] x partner culture [A]	-0.01	0.07	21.96	
Lag_annoyance	0.23	0.05	523	***
Fact	0.03	0.04	434.1	
Non-agreement	0.03	0.04	458	
Back channel	0.1	0.06	448.2	
Relational	-0.08	0.09	480.2	
R^2	**.64**			

Table 6. Effects of message content on annoyance. ***Notes:*** **2-tailed p values: + p<=.08, * p<= .05, ** p<=.01, *** p<=.0001, A=American**

DISCUSSION

The motivation for this study is the communication problems encountered in virtual intercultural teams such as lack of understanding or negative emotions, which were often associated with the cultural differences in communication styles of team members collaborating via CMC [e.g. 33]. While Nguyen & Fussell's preliminary analysis of similar data found that American participants reported being more annoyed when they worked with a Chinese partner than with an American partner [32], this study examined the specific process and patterns of such communication problems during dyadic CMC conversations. We investigated the cultural differences in communication styles that manifested itself in message content production during the conversation in pairs of various cultural combinations. Moreover, we explored the relationships between the content of the messages exchanged and the level of understanding, involvement, and negative emotions participants reported during the interaction using retrospective analysis.

Our first set of results showed that in CMC, participants from different cultures differed in communication styles. We found that, consistent with previous studies [e.g., 15, 20], Americans participants tended to produce more task-oriented messages than Chinese participants, regardless of who they were working with. We also found that Chinese participants tended to say more task-related messages when working with an American partner than with a Chinese partner. This confirmed previous findings that Chinese would tend to adapt to the task-oriented communication style of their American partners [45]. Our results also showed that same culture pairs produced more opinions than cross-culture pairs. This may be explained by the fact that people are often more open with similar ingroups than outgroups [8]. Our results thus pointed to an issue with cross-culture teams, where team members may be less likely to share their honest opinions and restrain disagreements, while such open discussion may be beneficial for the group performance.

In summary, all the cultural differences that we found are consistent with well-known dimensions of cultural differences such as task-relationship focus, communication adaptation of high context participants, and ingroup-outgroup dynamics in communication. Our results, however, further describe how such cultural differences in values and communication strategies may manifest into specific communication behaviors during intercultural conversations. As mentioned before, the collaboration task designed for this study requires a variety of communication activities, from information sharing to collaborative sense making, which are characteristic of the collaboration task that global virtual work teams usually face [20]. Previous studies, using different experimental tasks, have found similar cultural differences in brainstorming, problem solving, or information sharing [40, 45]. Our results, therefore, may enhance our understanding of intercultural conversations in global work teams.

While we did not find any significant culture difference in terms of relational messages exchanged and back-channel responses, the insignificant results might be due to the small number of relational messages and back-channel responses spoken in a task-oriented conversation. Since the crime-solving task was rather complicated, and time was limited, most participants focused on discussing the crime case instead of exchanging pleasantries. Moreover, the reviewability and revisability of IM messages allowed participants to carefully contemplate partners' messages, as well as craft their own messages before sending. Thus, we found participants tended to send more long, thoughtful messages in their IM conversations rather than short, and less meaningful backchannel responses. Another factor that may also contribute to the small number of backchannel responses exchanged was the fact that participants in a pair might be able to hear each other despite being visually separated by a divider. Some audio cues such as typing or clicking noises may provide contextual information about one's partner, reducing the need to use backchannel responses in text.

Our second set of results helped to explain why lack of engagement and negative emotions might emerge in conversations by describing the effects of message content on these communication processes. Moreover, our retrospective analysis allowed us to separate this effect from the confounding sequential effect of the past level of involvement and negative emotions. We found a trend that more relational messages from the partner led to lower involvement in the participant. This, again, may be explained by the high focus on task completion of our pairs, as the difficulty of the task is high. Relational messages might be regarded as off-topic and distracting. In fact, Nguyen & Fussell's qualitative analysis showed that some participants thought the pair discussion should be entirely dedicated to the task, and were annoyed if their partners digressed [32]. This result appears to be consistent with our other finding that the more task messages heard from a partner; the more interested in the conversation the participant reported being. Fact messages from a partner not only helped the participants understand the task more, but also indicated cognitive effort of the partner dedicated to the task, consistent with the definition of involvement [3], and therefore, could help increase the participant's interest.

In terms of negative emotions, we found that, interestingly, more facts uttered by the partner tended to increase tension felt by the participant. As we outlined in the method section, the crime case used in our study was built on some contradicting details. It is possible that by discussing these contradicting facts from the two different versions of the crime case, the participants might feel more confused, and tense. Nguyen & Fussell's qualitative analysis also found that some participants reported being frustrated with the contradictory details [32].

Our results, taken together, could help clarify the finding in Nguyen & Fussell [32] that participants, particularly American, tended to be more annoyed working with a cross-culture partner than a same-culture partner. We found that while task-related messages from a partner could help to increase the participants' level of interest and involvement in the conversation, American participants said significantly more task-related messages than Chinese participants. We also found that more task-related opinions were exchanged in same-culture pairs than in cross-culture pairs. Nguyen & Fussell [32] found that lack of involvement was one of the main causes for frustration and annoyance. Hence, our results show that cultural differences, in terms of task focus, influence the conversational dynamics of intercultural team through the content of the messages exchanged during team interaction. The content of the messages, in turn, influence the involvement of team members in conversations. Mismatch in the level of involvement might lead to communication issues such as negative emotions. By linking culture differences in message content production and the influence of message content on communication processes, our results could provide insights into the conversational dynamics of intercultural teams, thus contributing to the development of intercultural communication theories. Moreover, they also help explain why and how intercultural teams face the various challenges in communication previous studies have reported, thus enhancing our understanding of intercultural collaboration, and providing design implications for intercultural collaboration tools which will be discussed next.

Design Implications

Our findings indirectly suggest some strategies for designing new tools to support intercultural communication. First, our results pointed out the issue of fewer subjective opinions being expressed in intercultural teams, while task-related discussion could help increase team members' involvement in team conversations. Therefore, one way tools may help improve intercultural teamwork is by encouraging more open discussion. A system might display feedback about each participant's contributions to the conversation, particularly the number of personal opinions exchanged, similar to the GroupMeter system [e.g. 26], making it obvious when one partner is providing fewer opinions than the other, to encourage more contributions from that member.

Second, our results indicate that in some situations, task-oriented discussions with a lot of task-related messages could increase pressures on team members and introduce negative emotions. Therefore, tools might incorporate strategies to minimize the negative emotions that result when team discussions become intense. We believe this is especially important given evidence that negative emotions can be contagious in CMC [17]. Significant progress has been made identifying emotions from CMC [e.g., 12], which could in turn drive interventions to increase positive mood (e.g. via pictures of positive events, color, music).

Limitations and Future Directions

There are several important limitations to the current study. First, we examined dyads, not larger groups of cross-culture members, which may be more typical of global teamwork. Our small sample size might have limited the significance of some of our results. We also focused only on two out of the many cultures of the world. Furthermore, our Chinese participants were studying or working in the U.S and do not represent the larger population of Chinese people with whom Americans might collaborate. In the future, we plan to replicate the study using a more culturally diverse sample. We also did not control for participants' experiences working in multicultural settings, which may have affected the experience of participants during the experiment.

Our next steps include exploring the influence of communication processes on the production of message content. We also want to examine how our various measures of the communication process change over time during the interaction. With the findings from these analyses, we hope we can uncover the mechanism by which the communication process could lead to communication problems in intercultural collaboration. This in turn will help us characterize these problems at a deeper level, which hopefully will provide insights into how intercultural collaboration can be improved.

CONCLUSION

In this study we explored cultural differences in message production in cross-culture and same culture teams, and examined the effects of message content on team members' cognitive and affective processes. Cross-culture and same-culture dyads of American and Chinese participants discussed a crime case together via IM, and later reviewed their conversations and reported their thoughts and feelings on a minute-by-minute. We found differences in the frequency of task-related messages produced, based on the culture combination of the pairs. Moreover, the content of a partner's messages affected participants' levels of involvement and negative emotions. Our results provide insights into the conversational processes of computer-mediated intercultural teams and implications for the design of intercultural collaboration tools.

ACKNOWLEDGMENTS

This work was funded in part by NSF grants #0803482 and #0942658. We thank Dan Cosley and Hao Chuan Wang for their thoughtful feedback on the experimental design, Stephanie Sanders, Kathryn Duerr for running participants and preparing data for analysis. We also thank Leslie Setlock and the anonymous reviewers for their feedback on past revisions of the paper. This material is based in part on work supported by the National Science Foundation, while Susan Fussell was working at the Foundation. Any opinion, findings, and conclusions or recommendations expressed in this material are those of the authors and do not necessarily reflect the views of the National Science Foundation.

REFERENCES

1. Bales, R. F. (1950). A set of categories for the analysis of small group interaction. *American Sociological Review, 15,* 257-263.
2. Black, S., Levin, J., Mehan, H. & Quinn, C. (1983). Real and Non-real Time Interaction: Unraveling Multiple Threads of Discourse". *Discourse Processes,* 6, 59-75.
3. Cegala, D. J., Savage, G. T., Brunner, C. C., & Conrad, A. (1982). An elaboration of the meaning of interaction involvement: Toward the development of a theoretical concept. *Communication Monograghs*, 49, 229-248.
4. Chen, L. (1995). Interaction involvement and patterns of topical talk: A comparison of intercultural and intracultural dyads. *International journal of Intercultural Relations*, 19, 463-482.
5. Clark, H. H., & Brennan, S. E. (1991). Grounding in communication. In L. B. Resnick, R. M. Levine & S. D. Teasley (Eds.), *Perspectives on socially shared cognition.* Washington DC: APA Press.
6. Clark, H. & Wilkes-Gibbs, D. (1986). Referring as a collaborative process. *Cognition, 22,* 1-39.
7. Cramton, C. D. (2001). The mutual knowledge problem and its consequences for dispersed collaboration. *Organization Science*, 12, 346-371.

8. Cramton, C. D. & Hinds, P. J. (2005). Subgroup dynamics in internationally distributed teams: Ethnocentrism or cross-national learning? *Research in Organizational Behavior, 26*, 231-263.
9. Cohen, J., & Cohen, P. (1983). *Applied Multiple Regression/Correlations Analysis for the Behavioral Sciences (2nd Edition)*. Hillsdale, NJ: Erlbaum.
10. Coker, D. & Burgoon, J. (1987). The nature of conversational involvement and non-verbal encoding patterns. *Human Communication Research, 13*, 463-494.
11. Gallois, C., Franklyn-Stokes, A., Giles, H., & Coupland, N. (1988). Communication accommodation in intercultural encounters. In Y. Y. Kim & W. B. Gudykunst (Eds.), *Theories in Intercultural Communication*, Newbury Park, CA: Sage.
12. Gill, A.J., French, R.M., Gergle, D., & Oberlander, J. (2008). The Language of Emotion in Short Blog Texts. *Proceedings of CSCW 2008*.
13. Goffman, E. (1967). *Interaction Rituals: Essays in Face to Face Behavior*. Chicago, IL: Aldine Publishing Company.
14. Gottman, J.M. & Levenson, R.W. (1985). A valid procedure for obtaining self-report of affect in marital interaction. *Journal of Consulting and Clinical Psychology, 53*, 151-160.
15. Gudykunst, W. B., Matsumoto, Y., Ting-Toomey, S., Nishida, T., Kim, K., & Heyman, S. (1996). The influence of cultural individualism-collectivism, self construals, and individual values on communication styles across cultures. *Human Comm. Research*, 22, 510.
16. Hall, E. T. (1976). *Beyond culture*. Garden City, N.Y: Anchor Press.
17. Hancock, J. T., Gee, K., Ciaccio, K. & Mae-Hwah Lin, J. M.-H. (2008). I'm sad you're sad: emotional contagion in CMC. *Proc. CSCW '08*.
18. Herring, S. (1999). Interactional coherence in CMC. *Journal of Computer Mediated Communication*, 4, 4.
19. Hinds, P. & Kiesler, S. (2002). *Distributed work*. Cambridge, MA: MIT Press.
20. Hung, Y. T. & Nguyen, D. (2008). The impact of cultural diversity on global virtual team collaboration – A social identity perspective. *Proc. of the 41st Hawaii International Conference on System Sciences, 10*.
21. Kayworth, T., & Leidner, D. (2000). The global virtual manager: A prescription for success. *European Management Journal, 18*, 183.
22. Kelly, J. R., & Barsade, S. (2001). Emotions in small groups and work teams. *Organizational Behavior and Human Decision Processes*, 86, 99-130.
23. Kiesler, S., Siegel, J. & McGuire, T. Social psychological aspects of computer-mediated communication. *American Psychologist*, 39, 1123-1134.
24. Kiesler, S., Zubrow, D., Moses, A., & Geller, V. (1985). Affect in computer-mediated communication: an experiment in synchronous terminal-to-terminal discussion. *Journal of Human-Computer Interaction*, 1, 77-104.
25. Kraut, R., Lewis, S., Swezey, L. W. (1982). Listener responsiveness and the coordination of conversation. *J. Personality and Social Psychology, 43*, 718-731.
26. Leshed, G., Hancock, J., Cosley, D., McLeod, P. & Gay, C. (2007). Feedback for guiding reflection on teamwork practices. *Proc. GROUP 2007*. 217-220.
27. Li, H. Z. (1999a). Grounding and information communication in intercultural and intracultural dyadic discourse. *Discourse Processes, 28*, 195.
28. Li, H. Z. (1999b). Communicating information in conversations: A cross-cultural comparison. *International Journal of Intercultural Relations, 23*, 387.
29. Li, H. Z. (2006). Backchannel responses as misleading feedback in intercultural discourse. *Journal of Intercultural Communication Research*, 35, 2, 99-116.
30. Lipnack, J. & Stamp, J. (1997). *Virtual teams: Reaching Across Space, Time and Organizations with Technology*. NY: John Wiley & Sons.
31. Littell, R., Milliken, G. A., Stroup, W. W., & Wolfinger, R. D. (1996). *SAS system for mixed models*. Cary, NC: SAS Institute.
32. Nguyen, D. & Fussell, S. (2012). How did you feel during our conversations: Retrospective analysis of intercultural and same-culture instant messaging conversations. *Proc. CSCW 2012*.
33. Olson, G. M. & Olson, J. S. (2000). Distance matters. *Human Computer Interaction, 15*, 139-178.
34. Otondo, R.F., Van Scotter, J.R., Allen, D.G., & Palvia, P. (2008). The Complexity of Richness: Media, Message, and Communication Outcomes. *Information & Management, 40*, 21-30.
35. Patterson, M. L. (1983). *Nonverbal behavior: A functional perspective*. New York: Springer-Verlag.
36. Rice, R. & Love, G. (1987). Socioemotional content in a computer-mediated communication network. *Communication Research*, 14, 1, 85-108.
37. Schegloff, E. A. (1982). Discourse as an interactional achievement: Some uses of ''uh huh'' and other things that come between sentences. In D. Tannen (Ed.), *Analyzing discourse: Text and talk* (pp. 71–93).Washington, DC: Georgetown University Press.

38. Setlock, L. D. & Fussell, S. R. (2010). What's it worth to you? The costs and affordances of CMC tools to Asian and American users. *Proc. CSCW 2010*, 341-350.

39. Setlock, L. D., Quinones, P. & Fussell, S. R. (2007). Does culture interact with media richness? The effects of audio vs. video conferencing on Chinese and American dyads. *Proc. HICSS 2007*, 13.

40. Setlock, L. D., Fussell, S. R. & Neuwirth, C. (2004). Taking it out of context: collaborating within and across cultures in face-to-face settings and via instant messaging. *Proc. CSCW 2004*, 604-613.

41. Triandis, H. C. (1995). Individualism and Collectivism. Boulder, CO: Westview.

42. Villaume, W.A. & Cegala, D. J. (1988). Interaction involvement and discourse strategies: The patterned use of cohesive devices in conversation. *Communication Monographs, 55,* 20-40.

43. Walther, J. B. (1996). Computer-mediated communication: Impersonal, interpersonal and hyperpersonal interaction. *Communication Research*, 23, 3–43.

44. Walther, J. (1995). Relational aspects of computer-mediated communication: Experimental observations over time. *Organization Science*, 6, 186-203.

45. Wang, H., Fussell, S. F. & Setlock, L. D. (2009). Cultural difference and adaptation of communication styles in computer-mediated group brainstorming. *Proc. CHI 2009*, 669-678.

46. Yuan, Y., Bazarova, N., Zhang, Z. X., & Fulk, J. (2012). Recognition of Expertise and Perceived Influence in Intercultural Group Collaboration: A Study of Mixed American and Chinese Intercultural Groups. *Paper presented at the 2012 Annual Conference of the International Communication Association, Phoenix, AZ.*

"Facebook is a Luxury": An Exploratory Study of Social Media Use in Rural Kenya

Susan P. Wyche
Michigan State University
Dept. of Telecommunication, Information Studies, and Media
East Lansing, MI 48824
spwyche@msu.edu

Sarita Yardi Schoenebeck
University of Michigan
School of Information
Ann Arbor, MI 48109
yardi@umich.edu

Andrea Forte
Drexel University
College of Information Science and Technology
Philadelphia, PA 19104
aforte@drexel.edu

ABSTRACT
Facebook use is pervasive in developed countries where computers, smartphones, high-bandwidth Internet, and electricity are ubiquitous. In this paper, we examine Facebook use in a country where social media participation is growing, but less developed technological infrastructures and uneven access to technology limit use. We conducted observations and 24 interviews at Internet cafés in rural Kenya. Our findings reveal how costs associated with using the Internet, limited access to computers and smartphones and unreliable electricity hinder online participation. We draw on these results to discuss the critical role of constraints in understanding social media use, to raise questions about broadening online participation and to highlight ethical issues researchers must consider when studying Facebook use in developing regions.

Author Keywords
Facebook; social media; social networking sites (SNS); Kenya; infrastructure; ICTD

ACM Classification Keywords
H5.m Information interfaces and presentation (e.g., HCI): Miscellaneous.

INTRODUCTION
You see, when you don't have technology it's like you are in your own world and people are in their other world... It's like traveling. When you travel you need to learn a lot, if you cannot travel it's also another way of learning a lot.

– *Kenyan Interviewee, when asked why she wants to use Facebook*

This quote captures the optimism implicit in narratives about communication technologies in the so-called developing world. The potential for Information and Communication Technologies (ICT) to support economic prosperity, education, and civic engagement in these countries has been widely discussed, however, despite their global reach and proliferation, research on social network site (SNS) use in such contexts is sparse. Consequently, we know little about how globally adopted sites such as Facebook are used in sub-Saharan Africa, where use is growing. What is the Facebook experience in contexts where the social, economic, and technical contexts affecting use differ from the American college campuses where the site was first popularized? To answer this question we conducted qualitative fieldwork in rural Kenya.

CSCW '13, February 23–27, 2013, San Antonio, Texas, USA.
Copyright 2013 ACM 978-1-4503-1331-5/13/02...$15.00.

Our findings reveal how limited bandwidth, power outages and persistent poverty shape peoples' experiences with Facebook. These factors are typically taken for granted in sites where Facebook is usually studied (the U.S. and U.K.), but were at the forefront of users' experience on the site in rural Kenya. For example, the costs of creating and maintaining a Facebook account limited use of the site among our participants. Monetary costs associated with using the Internet are rarely discussed in prior Facebook research.

We use our findings to motivate practical suggestions for improving the Facebook experience in rural Kenya, to highlight the critical role of constraints in understanding SNS use, to raise questions about broadening online participation and to offer practical insights for future researchers wanting to study Facebook in the rural Africa. Broader implications of our work include contributing to a nascent body of work aimed at understanding SNS use outside of the U.S. and Europe. Facebook is a global site with 70% of it users living outside of the U.S. and research must account for this increasing diversity [33].

BACKGROUND AND RELATED WORK

Empirical Studies of Facebook Use
Facebook research tends to be conducted in North America and Europe where technology infrastructures are highly developed [33]. These populations were the earliest adopters of the site, the first to reach market penetration levels upwards of 50% and, as such, provided rich opportunities for understanding the roles that SNS play in people's academic, social, and work lives. Notable examples of this research include Ellison, Steinfield, and

Lampe's studies of how American college students benefit from social connections on Facebook [12, 43] what kinds of connections are most useful [13], how SNS help young people transition to college, and explorations of how students use Facebook to support academic collaborations [26]. Privacy preferences and identity management have also been examined in American academic contexts, where college students negotiate multiple communities and social contexts [19, 29].

This research has contributed to the community's understanding of SNS use in valuable ways; however, these studies take place with college-educated populations living in the U.S. where Internet access is seemingly unlimited, unconstrained, and where users rarely consider the costs associated with accessing it. Growth of SNS use among these populations is plateauing and future growth for services such as Facebook, Twitter and Google+ is predicted in the developing world [22, 42]. Yet, little data exist on use of these services these regions, thus a limited set of use practices shapes scholars' understanding of an increasingly global phenomenon.

More problematic than the lack of cultural diversity in empirical accounts of Facebook use is the potential for assumptions about infrastructure, access, and market constraints to also remain unexamined. Lessig notes that social norms, laws, market forces, and architectural (both technological and physical) constraints all influence online behaviors in complex, interrelated ways [28]. Our research highlights how architecture (e.g., physical access and infrastructure) and market forces (e.g., cost and pricing structures) shape Facebook use in rural Kenya. We argue that these influences are rendered invisible if Facebook use is only studied in contexts where technological infrastructure and economies are robust.

Infrastructures and Internet Access in Kenya

An infrastructure is an underlying framework that enables a group, organization, or society to function in certain ways, such as the series of pipes, drains, and water sources that comprise a water system [27]. Our use of the term is more constrained and reflects other researchers' use of it to draw attention to taken-for-granted factors in infrastructure-rich countries (e.g., [48]).

Access to the Internet and latest ICT varies between rural and urban parts of the Kenya. In the country's capital, Nairobi, billboards advertise the latest smartphones, Apple products are available for purchase at Western style malls and Internet access is becoming increasingly ubiquitous, though slower than what many Western users are accustomed to. These and other benefits of the latest ICT are less visible in rural Kenya, where people live off electricity grids and often lack the steady income necessary to take full advantage of available technologies. In Kenya an estimated 67% of the population live outside of the country's major urban areas of Nairobi, Mombasa, and Kisumu—places where hard-wired internet first reached in 2009 [2].

Kenyans living far from theses areas tend to be older, less educated and less informed about the latest ICT compared to their urban counterparts [16]. The majority subsist on the equivalent of $1.50 to $2.00 a day and do without consistent access to water and electricity [21,39]. Despite these challenges, Facebook use is growing in Kenya and at the time of our study it was estimated that there were slightly more than 1 million Facebook users in the country. By 2012 that number was approaching 2 million (in a country of more than 40 million people) [42]. Media reports and findings from our fieldwork suggest this growth is taking place in urban, or infrastructure rich parts of Kenya and in rural, or infrastructure poor settings [22].

Social Networking Sites in the Developing World

Though examples of research examining SNS in the African continent are scarce, we are not the first to study this topic. Mäkinen and Kuira's findings demonstrate how social media acted as an alternative medium for citizen communication during the crisis following the 2007 Kenyan presidential election [30]. Their research speaks to the growing presence of Web 2.0 communication tools and services in the country. More recently, Bosch conducted qualitative studies of Facebook use among South African college students [6,7]. Her findings highlight the benefits of using Facebook in teaching and learning, particularly for the development of "educational micro-communities" at the University of Cape Town. We build on this work, but rather than focusing on crisis situations or college students, we studied Facebook use among people living in rural Kenya.

SETTING AND METHODS

This was a qualitative study and our decision to study Facebook in Internet cafés builds on both Burrell's [8] and Fair et al.'s fieldwork in urban Ghana [15]. For people who lack an Internet connection at their home or office, and are unable to afford an Internet-enabled mobile phone, cyber cafés provide an important service for getting online. This understanding, paired with popular reports in Kenyan newspapers touting the rising popularity of the site, suggested that cafés would be fruitful field sites [34].

Our findings draw from fieldwork that took place during June-August 2011. We conducted observations, read local newspapers (e.g., *Daily Nation* and *The Standard*), and interviewed 24 individuals (15 actively used Facebook and nine were not yet members). We moved between offline spaces—the most prominent being 14 cyber cafés located in rural and peri-urban sites in central and western Kenya—and online spaces. Online fieldwork included observations of participants' Facebook profiles.

When entering cafés we usually logged onto our Facebook accounts, engaged patrons in short conversations about their Internet use and conducted semi-structured interviews with customers using the computers and individuals who owned or were employed at the sites. These key informants had completed high school and were more knowledgeable about ICT compared to their customers.

Common livelihood activities among participants who did not work at cyber cafés included farming, selling homemade products, and receiving remittances from family members living in Nairobi, Mombasa, and the U.S. Personal contacts developed within the Kenyan migrant community in the U.S. led us to the following field sites: Bungoma, Eldoret, Homa Bay, Oyugis, Tala and Machakos. Eldoret was the largest site visited and had a population of 193,839, while Tala was the smallest with a population of 4,734 [1]. We complemented these formal interviews with several in situ conversations with café patrons to gain additional insights into how Facebook was used in rural Kenya.

Interviews were conducted in English, digitally recorded, and began with general questions about participants' experiences with mobile phones, computers, and the Internet. Asking about Facebook was a standard part of our protocol and these questions focused on participants' familiarity with the site, reasons for joining (or not joining) and whether or not they accessed the site on a mobile phone or at a cyber café. Our protocol was flexible enough to allow participants freedom to discuss related topics they deemed important. Finally, because gender, age, and class affect how researchers are seen in the field, we briefly describe the background of the first author, who collected the data used in our analysis [9]. The first author is a 36-year old, American-born, English-speaking, middle-class, white woman, with prior research experience in Kenya.

Data Analysis

Our fieldwork resulted in 24 transcribed interviews, 174 pages of field notes and 1,375 digital photographs. The qualitative method used to analyze data was thematic analysis, wherein patterns emerged via repeated analytic passes through the transcripts and field notes [17]. After patterns were identified, the first author catalogued them into categories that addressed the following question, "What factors affect using Facebook in rural Kenya?" After she analyzed the transcripts and drew tentative conclusions, they were discussed with the co-authors who are experts in SNS and uses of sites like Facebook. Their feedback was incorporated into the analysis. Once this was completed, the authors reread the related literature and formulated themes presented as findings in this paper.

FINDINGS: ALTERNATIVE UNDERSTANDING OF USE

Everyone interviewed was familiar with Facebook, more than half of our participants actively used the site, and those who were not yet members wanted to be. Yet the costs associated with creating and maintaining an online profile prevented them from joining the site. For low-income rural Kenyans accessing the Internet at a cyber café or on an Internet enabled mobile phone represented a significant expenditure [39].

Buying a mobile phone is an expense and so is using it to access the Internet. Most Kenyans and all of our participants use pre-paid "airtime" or "credit" plans. Credit typically comes in the form of scratch-cards that are sold in units ranging from (Kenyan Shilling) KSh 10 ($0.10) to KSh 1000, or approximately $10.00. Even those with the financial resources to use the Internet encountered challenges when using Facebook, including: frequent power outages, limited Internet access and low-bandwidth. Poverty also shaped these participants use of the site; specifically, some wanted to make online friends abroad in hopes they could use them to gain financial resources.

A Desire to use Facebook

In North America and Europe, people regularly use Facebook to reconnect with friends, update their status, and send private messages. Some rural Kenyans described similar patterns of use; for example, a young man who owned a café emphasized that Facebook was the "most popular" site in Kenya and that many patrons came to his café to "chat" with friends. He added that he accessed the site four to five times a day and valued being able to share information with his online friends.

And you can use it blog, you can also tell some...something about yourself or what you are doing, then many people access it, yeah. And the chain of friendship so the information goes to many people, because your friend is a friend to some other people.

Alex, like the other eight cyber café employees interviewed, used Facebook in ways that resembled documented practices in countries with developed technological infrastructures. Our interviews and conversations with individuals living outside of the towns where the cyber cafés were located revealed alternative practices.

Participants not using Facebook

Everyone interviewed was familiar with Facebook; however, the 10 participants living in rural communities outside of the towns where the cyber cafés were located were unclear about the purpose of the site. These areas were located off electricity grids, lacked access to water, and the roads linking them to cities were poorly maintained [4, 21]. People we talked to in Kamuu, Kakichuma, Ziwa, and Sawich villages learned about Facebook from friends living in urban Kenya, in North American and in European countries, or by watching people access the site on their mobile phones. Knowledge about Facebook also came from unexpected places, such as Kenya's transportation industry. There were references to the SNS on *matatus*, a public service mini-van used by a low and middle-income Kenyans (Figure 1). This sighting also suggests that Facebook is on par with other symbolic objects depicted on matatus such as Brazilian World Cup players and U.S. pop and rap stars. Despite an awareness of Facebook, these participants had never used the site and told us they "didn't know much about it," "did not know how to use it effectively" or lacked technological "know-how."

Hard-wired Internet reached rural parts of Kenya in 2009 [16,41], so it is unsurprising that some participants had not yet accessed Facebook and referred to it as a "new thing." Yet their familiarity with and desire to learn more about Facebook reveals how the idea of online social networks has reached those most affected by the digital divide, even if the infrastructures to support it has not kept pace. After explaining, and sometimes using our personal modem and laptop to show these individuals the Facebook site, we asked them to consider whether or not they would want to join the site. Their replies were revealing:

Yes, you could be updated and understand what is going on in the world. . .you get on Facebook, you feel advanced, you have friends, you can send them snaps and they can exchange.

Mobile phones make it cheaper and faster for people to communicate with people in regions where infrastructures to support fixed-lines phones are underdeveloped; researchers suggest this is a primary reason the device has been overwhelmingly successful in the African continent [14,44]. Facebook offers people additional ways to sustain relationships by sharing "snaps," or photos. This participants' use of the term "advanced" reveals, like others interviewed, the status that is tied to using the Internet and having a Facebook account. Indeed, this is another reason the site has become a symbol emblazoned on public transportation. Like having a mobile phone, it appeared that having a Facebook account was perceived as a status symbol and this may explain our participants' strong desire to be a part of this online community [25]. Other reasons include wanting to "understand what is going on in the world" and for this particular participant, to see photos of her nephew living in the U.S.

Facebook Costs in Rural Kenya

Participants living in the rural communities we visited consistently told us costs associated with creating and maintaining a Facebook account prevented them from joining. These remarks were surprising to a Western observer who regarded the site as free of charge, with a business model that relies on advertising rather than subscription [38]. Further questioning revealed how establishing an account could become an expense for individuals earning the equivalent of $1.50 a day. We asked café managers, who routinely created accounts for people coming to town from rural villages, about this process and learned there was a cost associated with every phase of the sign-up process.

Figure 1: Matatu with Facebook insignia.

For some people, joining Facebook required them to obtain an email address or in a few cases to "activate" an address that had expired due to lack of use. Four participants had not checked their Yahoo! accounts for two and three years and consequently they became inactive. When helping customers re-activate or create email accounts, café workers encouraged clients to use numbers they would not forget such as their mobile phone or government identification numbers as passwords. At some cafés, creating an email account was a service with a fixed price (10 KSh or $0.11), but it was more common for customers to pay for using the Internet at the café, where costs were typically (0.50 to 2 KSh/minute).

Creating, scanning, and uploading a profile picture to a new account resulted in additional costs. Digital cameras are too costly for most rural Kenyan consumers. Although mobile phones with cameras are available, our participants told us photos taken with a mobile phone were lower quality than those taken with a digital camera. Instead, they wanted a "presentable" or "smart" profile picture and understood that a picture taken with digital camera was higher quality than one taken with a mobile phone.

Rural Kenyan towns are dotted with small photo shops painted yellow and displaying the Kodak Film logo. People visit them to have photographs taken that eventually become their profile pictures. Theses paper photos have to be scanned and uploaded to Facebook, resulting in additional costs. An employee at a cyber café in Homa Bay explained this process:

It is common knowledge like if you want to be on Facebook you must have a photo, when they come, they come armed with that photo, you have to scan and upload it for them and they get excited and you see like scanning one photo is thirty shillings, thirty Kenyan shillings. Uploading is ten shillings. . .

Once an account was established there were further costs associated with maintaining it. All participant lacked domestics Internet access, so in order to use Facebook they had to travel to town from a rural village typically by paying for a ride on a bicycle, motorcycle, or matatu. Paying for each minute online at the cyber café was another expense, as was the return trip home. Prices that might seem like small amounts to Western observers represented significant expenditures for participants relative to their other daily expenses. The cost of using the Internet at a café for 30 minutes typically cost 0.50 KSh ($0.60), which is roughly the price of buying enough maize porridge to feed a family for a few days.

Those who chose to access the site told us using Facebook was a "luxury." One participant allowed himself to log-on after "finishing other expenses," and others said they would access the site if they had extra "bob," a slang term for the Kenyan schilling. Their desire to use Facebook despite coping with acute economic constraints speaks to participants' desire to be a part of what they called a "global village." Continuing to explore Facebook use in settings where costs limit use can be useful for understanding what features are most valued on the site. For our participants it was clearly the ability to "chat" with friends.

Mobile Phones and Costs

Given the widespread adoption of mobile phones throughout Kenya and sub-Saharan Africa, it was unsurprising to learn that participants accessed Facebook on these devices. We encountered six people with Internet enabled phones. They were all men, worked at the cafés we visited, and used their phones to "see what their friends were doing" or to "update their status" on Facebook. Costs impacted their experience on the mobile version of the site because like accessing Facebook at cyber cafés, participants paid to use the site on their mobile phones. Lack of electricity meant they were also paying to charge the batteries in their mobiles devices.

Small kiosks selling scratch-cards are a ubiquitous part of the landscape in rural Kenya; yet even so, lack of credit consistently affected participants' ability to access the mobile Internet. To get a sense for how much credit people generally carried, we asked them how much airtime was on their mobile devices. Amounts ranged from KSh 0 to 112 ($0 to $1.18), with the average being KSh 21 among the 24 people asked. This means at any given they could browse the Internet on their phones for approximately for 6-12 minutes (depending on the current rates of their service provider).

Underlying the practical use of mobile phone applications are assumptions about users' abilities to maintain a charged phone battery. But like most people living in rural Africa, our participants lacked access to electricity and maintaining a charged battery in their mobile handsets was difficult. A desire to "preserve the charge" on their phones limited how long respondents browsed the Internet [47]. A dead battery required taking the phone to a charging kiosk and paying 20 KSh for it to be recharged. These participants understood that accessing the Internet depleted battery life faster than using their phones to make calls and they adjusted their usage accordingly, meaning they typically spent two or three minutes looking at the mobile version of Facebook. The cost of purchasing a smartphone, or any kind of high-end device that can access the Internet, was out of reach for the majority of our participants, thus accessing the site on a desktop computer in a cyber café was more common than using it on a mobile phone.

At the time of our study the lowest cost 3G-enabled Nokia was approximately $150, while a simple handset cost the equivalent of $20. These latter phones typically have small black and white screens (unlike the larger, colored screens on popular smart phones like the iPhone or Droid), have little memory and are not Wireless Application Protocol (WAP) enabled.

USSD Version of Facebook

In response to the ubiquity of these basic phones in rural Kenya, Safaricom, Orange, and Yu—Kenya's leading mobile network operators—recently introduced an USSD version of the site called *Facebook Zero*. USSD (Unstructured Supplementary Service Data) is a protocol common to all GSM (Global System for Mobile Communications) phones. It enables services such as exchanging money via M-Pesa, the popular mobile phone based money transfer service, is accessible by dialing a number, and works on almost all mobile phones. Thus, users with older or very basic handsets without an Internet connection can access a site like Facebook. To use Facebook on these simple phones, users enter a specific code and then enter a PIN number to access the service [3,5]. The USSD version of Facebook is entirely text-based and does not support the site's most popular features, including the News Feed and photosharing [5]. We saw advertisements for this version of the site in mobile phone stores (Figure 2), but none of our participants used it. We speculate this may be because of the novelty of the service; at the time of our fieldwork it had been available for less than one year [44].

Limited Bandwidth and Power Outages

A typical Internet café was located in a small, dimly lit, and minimally decorated room containing 6-12 secondhand computers on wooden desks. The Hewlett Packard, Compaq, and Dell machines in them were bulky and showed considerable wear. Keys were missing from keyboards, dated monitors were sometimes blurry and the images on them shaky. The age of computers and limited bandwidth resulted in Facebook and other sites taking minutes rather than seconds to load. Profile pictures often remained gray before appearing and participants described waiting as "frustrating," because the delay cost money since they were paying for access by the minute.

Despite slow Internet speeds and dated equipment, we watched patrons scrolling through Facebook, engaging in chat sessions, and clicking on links at cyber cafés. Experienced Internet users developed strategies to use Facebook as efficiently as possible. For example, café employees with access to their workplaces after operating hours waited until the evening to use Facebook and other sites, including YouTube and Skype. This decision was related to their understanding that if fewer people were using the network it will be faster. They were also chatting with friends overseas in different time zones. Another strategy participants used to make the most of their time was to simultaneously browse multiple webpages, for example:

When the Internet is a bit slow, I will open two tabs and while Yahoo! loads I am on Facebook browsing, getting updates, and then checking my mails again.

Findings from Wyche et al.'s study of Internet use in urban Kenya suggests that software developers create low bandwidth versions of their sites to account for the slow Internet speeds in the country [48]. In 2009, Facebook introduced a "lite" version optimized for users with slower or intermittent Internet connections. *Facebook Lite* offered fewer services, excluded most third-party applications, and required less bandwidth [45]. We experienced and observed performance lags on the site, which indeed suggests a low-bandwidth version as a technical response; however, before implementing such a response, companies should investigate whether or not rural users *want* an alternative version of the site and, if so, what features are desired. We observed rural users developing ingenious ways to navigate slow Internet speeds and limited bandwidth, they were resourceful and figured out how to make ICT work for them in their contexts. Perhaps this explains why Facebook shut down Facebook Lite seven months after introducing it [40].

Power Outages and Interrupted Use

The quality of the Kenyan electricity grid is poor and power outages or "blackouts" are frequent. During our fieldwork, the country experienced particularly aggravating power outages attributed to natural (e.g., storms) and man-made (e.g., vandalism and overuse) events [35]. Frequent blackouts had implications for cyber cafés, the most dire being that the cafés had to close. When touring towns and entering cafés we found dark rooms and unlit monitors on more than one occasion. Café employees rarely knew when power would return. While interviewing a staff member at a café in Bungoma we experienced four blackouts during a six-hour period, each lasting between 10-45 minutes. In Tala, a café owner showed us old monitors, scanners, and desktop computers that had been "spoiled" due to power outages and corresponding surges.

Blackouts also had implications for customers using Facebook, because it meant they were unable to log off of their accounts. When logging onto our personal account, finding an open one on the shared computer was common. There were consequences of being unable to log off of Facebook. For example, Micheal, a 25-year-old, originally from a village outside of Machakos told us after experiencing a power outage, he logged onto his account three days later and found someone had updated his status to indicate he had come out as gay. A young woman, who unintentionally remained logged onto the site following a power outage, found that someone changed her status to say that she had multiple sexual partners. Unsurprisingly, she and others interviewed found these posts upsetting and worked to counter them with clarifications when they next logged onto Facebook. This required spending more time and money at the cyber café.

Power outages coupled with shared ICT affect Facebook use in Kenya. Compared to findings in prior studies, this creates an alternative depiction of people's experience with the site. Problems with power will persist in Kenya, and backup power sources are too costly for many cyber café owners. This suggests opportunities to develop versions of the site that automatically log users off after a certain amount of time or developing an "auto log off" feature. Such straightforward responses to this problem would likely limit concerns and embarrassment that result from an undesirable message being posted on one's wall.

Low-cost Communication, Poverty Reduction Strategies and Friending

In addition to preventing some participants from creating accounts and limiting the amount of time spent online, there were other ways lack of financial resources affected respondents' interactions on Facebook. Though all participants expressed concerns about power outages and costs of using the Internet, for most, the desire to connect was powerful enough to keep them coming back to the site. Here we describe two ways costs affected how our participants used Facebook to maintain and create ties with people abroad. First, because Facebook was less expensive than making overseas phone calls, participants used it to communicate with friends and family living outside of Kenya. Second, participants' wanted to expand their online networks to include people who they perceive to have more financial resources than they do.

Participants had family and friends in other countries, across Europe and North America, and in other parts of the African continent. Over the last two decades, economic difficulties, increased poverty, and political instability have resulted in large-scale migration of Africans to the U.S., including many Kenyans [24]. Thus, it was common for

Figure 2: Sign advertising USSD version of Facebook at Safaricom store in Bungoma, Kenya.

participants to have friends and family living around the world. Participants showed us the online profiles of friends who migrated to California, Michigan, New Jersey, Virginia and countries including Canada, Germany, U.K., and Malta.

Those with family abroad were accustomed to being at the receiving end of transnational communication because it was more economical for people overseas to pay for an international phone call to Kenya. However, Facebook allowed our participants to initiate contact with people overseas [48]. "Flashing" or "beeping" are commonly used to initiate phone calls with friends and family abroad. [11,46]. This process involves a person calling a mobile telephone number and then hanging up before the mobile phone's owner can pick up the call. It is a free way to alert someone that you would like him or her to call you [10]. Facebook provided participants with an alternative way to initiate conversations with friends abroad because it cost less than making an overseas phone call. *Facebook Chat* is an instant message function incorporated into the site that makes it easier to find online friends available to chat. Unlike other chat applications, such as *Skype* or *AOL Instant Messenger*, Facebook chat does not require users to download new software, making it a desirable chat option in cyber cafés where limited bandwidth complicates software downloading. A young man explained the cost and benefits of using Facebook chat when telling us about communicating with a childhood friend living California:

If I communicate with him on the phone, I spend ten shillings per minute, so if you talk for 30 minutes that is 300. But on Facebook I can chat for 30 minutes, share loads, at a lower rate.

Facebook chat alters the historically unidirectional flow of transnational communication. Those who regularly used the feature told us they preferred chatting with online friends in a real-time rather than using email. We observed café patrons exchanging short messages often using a combination of English, Swahili, and their vernacular language. Like the strategies users developed to maximize their Internet use, our participants adoption of Facebook as a low-cost way to communicate with people abroad also speaks to how they make ICT fit into their everyday lives.

The second way cost influenced participants' SNS use became evident in some of their explanations of why they would want an American friend. Facebook offers the possibility of what has come to be known as "friending." As in other social network sites, users create profiles that may contain photos and other personal information as well as a list of connections to others' profiles. Making those connections, or "Friending," on Facebook is reciprocal; a request to become a 'friend' must be accepted before the connection is recognized in the system. During our observations at cafés, patrons frequently asked to see the first author's Facebook profile and requested to add her as a friend. People add friends for a variety of reasons [18], so we probed to understand why they wanted to add her as a friend. Responses were often tied to her race and being an American. For example, a young man working at a cyber café in Homa Bay made the following comment:

I like to be connected with people in America.

A young woman in Tala told her:

I have always loved to have a white as a friend on Facebook.

Most individuals wanted foreign contacts for their own sake, but others saw a connection between having an American friend on Facebook as fulfilling other aspirations. Life in rural Kenya is unpredictable so a connection to someone perceived as a rich foreigner acted as sort of insurance policy against future hardships [15]. Our understanding of this became clear once the author returned to the U.S. and received requests for money and other forms of aid from the individuals she friended. Below is an excerpt from one of these messages:

My plea is that you kindly assist me to offset the balance I owe the university of 60,000 KSh = 637.80 USD, this will enable me have my certificates and a better chance to get employed. . .

This phenomenon is not new and anthropologists and aid workers have written about the complications that can arise when they become intertwined with peoples' income generating strategies (e.g., [37]). In the past, people sent letters asking for money, goods, and assistance with obtaining a visa to the U.S.; today, Facebook provides a more immediate way to make these connections. This example serves a reminder that, although there is much enthusiasm for the ways technology can potentially bring about social change, it can also perpetuate both perceptions and realities of long-standing inequality between developed and developing countries. Such assumptions serve an important function in ethnographically informed research and merit more attention as CSCW researchers explore ICT appropriation in developing countries.

SUMMARY AND DISCUSSION

Our findings present an alternative understanding of Facebook use with constraints that differ from those implicit in common narratives about Facebook on college campuses and other infrastructure-rich contexts. The constraints we identified include:

- **local market constraints**, which include not only the cost of obtaining hardware, an internet connection, and bandwidth, but also emergent local markets around the production and consumption of media like digital images to share on social network sites;
- **infrastructure constraints**, such as low bandwidth and slow internet connections and unpredictable electrical and communication grids; and

- **the demands of persistent poverty**, which created incentives for overcoming barriers to use, including relatively low-cost mechanisms for keeping in touch with distant loved ones and the hope of establishing social ties that may help secure economic or social stability.

In contrast to prior studies of Facebook, the marketplace and technical infrastructures are at the forefront of participants' experiences with social media, rather than removed from users' concerns.

The Critical Role of Constraints

Our findings reveal constraints that affect social network site use in rural Kenya that, to our knowledge, have not been reported elsewhere in the literature. This raises questions about the applicability of findings regarding Facebook use in more studied settings (e.g., U.S. and U.K.) to rural Africa and even in North America where uneven Internet access and limited electricity also influence peoples' online experience [31]. For example, prior research suggests that users primarily use Facebook as a way of passing time [36]. These findings are drawn from a survey of students at an American university where infrastructure and cost are largely invisible and taken for granted. In rural Kenya, Facebook use is tightly coupled with economic resources: 30 minutes at an Internet café (KSh $0.50 or $0.60) could easily consume about one third of a person's daily expenditures in rural Kenya. This raises questions about whether findings about passing time as a motivation can possibly be used to understand Facebook use in rural Kenya.

Future research on motivation and priorities in Kenya, where costs and limited access are a factor, could lead to a better understanding of what needs are met by social media and how. This work can also help designers understand what features are most valued among different populations and also where concerns should be raised. In America, Facebook and privacy is an ongoing issue for academics and society at large. In rural Kenya, where every minute on Facebook can represent real costs to a user, do questions about privacy preservation and settings become even more pressing?

We also offer preliminary insights into how friending practices intersect with economic concerns. Participants described and exhibited friending behavior predicated on desired economic and social mobility and security. What is the value of Facebook friends for these individuals? This question has been answered in the context of the American college campuses. For students who exhibit low self-esteem, Facebook use is correlated with higher levels of self esteem and social capital [14]. Can we assume these benefits of Facebook friends carry over into non-Western contexts, where friending is motivated by different needs and where online attention is a more limited commodity? The relative inability of Kenyans to access and browse Facebook for great lengths of time and the varied incentives to participate in Facebook challenge current understandings of how and why people use SNS.

The Benefits and Threats of Broadening Participation

Participants' persistent desire to use Facebook despite obstacles suggests that, although their experience does not mimic those of college students in the U.S., they do perceive social and economic benefits of using the site. If we accept this perception uncritically, that access to Facebook is desired and beneficial for users, we might anticipate that easier and cheaper access would result in more equitable benefits for rural Kenyan users. Some solutions to the question of equity are being explored; for instance, Facebook is collaborating with mobile operators to make *0.facebook.com* accessible to people without data charges [44]. Though it was a feasible option and some interviewees described using their phones to access Facebook, we concluded it was not yet a main attraction. For most the phone remains a device reserved for making short phone calls and exchanging money using M-Pesa rather than a tool to support social networking. It will take time to for users to consider and embrace different ways they can use mobile devices.

A more critical interpretation of broadening participation on Facebook highlights potential threats and vulnerabilities. The company's business model relies on users trading access to a wealth of personal information and data about their behavior for the experience of connecting with others and sharing content. If, as we have suggested, Kenyan users view the site as an economic way of contacting loved ones or as a safeguard against economic hardship, this places them in a vulnerable position. Specifically, it may be hard for them to refuse to use the service or put pressure on Facebook to amend business practices if they feel their social life and livelihood depend on it. When the cost of opting out is too great, users may compromise other areas of their life (in both Western and non-Western contexts).

Finally, this work serves as a reminder that the experience of a service being free is not possible until larger problems such as rural electrification are remedied. Businesses that rely on that experience can help engineer ways of providing access. Facebook could explore mechanisms aimed at shifting the costs of using the site away from café patrons so they can enjoy the using the site in ways taken for granted by North American and European users.

Since large-scale formal rural electrification is unlikely to extend to remote locations, like some of those we visited, other alternative power sources like wind, diesel, human-or animal-draft power, and solar photovoltaic will be needed [21]. Until then, something as simple as the cost of charging one's phone will hinder the use the mobile phone as a web-browsing platform.

A Note on Future Research

This study is our first step in studying SNS use in rural Africa. Continuing to study Facebook in infrastructure poor settings in North American and abroad is critical. As such, we offer advice and reflections for scholars who wish to conduct future research examining SNS developing countries. These recommendations are based on our experiences and also reflect lessons learned as we continue to conduct research in this space.

Participant compensation. Online surveys are commonly used in prior work examining Facebook use (e.g., [23]). For this approach to data collection to be successful in contexts like we studied, researchers should compensate participants for time spent at cyber cafés and for accessing the Internet on their mobile phones.

Increasing interview comprehension. For this study, we conducted our interviews in English. The first author has experience with both native-language interviews with an interpreter and English language interviews with ESL speakers. We believe that working closely with local interpreters and people familiar with the various tribal languages spoken in Kenya would lead to a deeper understanding of their online experiences.

Research questions. Participants' stories raised questions such as, "How is Facebook a platform for social expression among rural Kenyans?" and "How is it used to circulate rumors and gossip?" "What social and cultural norms in rural Kenya govern self-presentation online?" In part because nuance is lost in second-language interviews, and in part because we did not pursue these lines of inquiry, we have less traction to answer these questions and they remain interesting areas for future research.

Ethics and awareness. As more researchers explore social media outside of Western academic institutions, new ethical challenges will likely arise and researchers should be sensitive to these. Like others, we believe the challenge is for researchers to add value to the lives of people they are researching, to recognize them as participants and not simply sources of data [20]. Of course, these challenges have been discussed in other disciplines (e.g., Anthropology) and we see an opportunity to increase awareness of them as CSCW researchers examine SNS's in new contexts.

LIMITATIONS AND CONCLUSION

Our study was ethnographic in nature and aimed to study a small sample of users. Hence, our findings are representative of trends and patterns of behavior associated with a particular set of participants and experiences. The complexities surrounding race, gender, colonialism, and constraints including financial, technical, and infrastructural ones cannot be fully represented in an exploratory study like ours. Instead our research provides the CSCW community with a first step in understanding Facebook use in rural Kenya and highlights opportunities for future research.

We present, to our knowledge, one of the first studies of SNS use in rural and peri-urban Kenya. We conclude that by continuing to conduct research focused mainly on the U.S. we risk making global assumptions about SNS use based on local Western uses. Our study reveals that these assumptions can be impoverished and in some cases wrong. The danger here, of course, is that if we assume use in developed countries is universal, we will gloss over challenges and deeper understanding of what it means to use Facebook to connect with people in other parts of the world.

Thus it is necessary to understand SNS use in new contexts without assuming practices will necessarily mirror results from other regions of the world. As a first step in understanding how Facebook use differs between rural Kenya and more studied contexts, we showed how market forces, including cost and income, and architecture, including infrastructure, access, and electricity, affect peoples' experience on the popular social networking site. This paper underscores the need to understand technology use not only in different contexts, but with analytic approaches that help render important influences visible and point out where our data are insufficient. We see opportunities for further data collection and analysis to help us understand the social and legal aspects of Kenyan culture that may be playing a role in shaping behaviors.

ACKNOWLEDGMENTS

Thanks to Elisa Oreglia, Brooke Foucault Welles, and the anonymous reviewers for feedback on earlier drafts of this paper. A grant from the NSF/CRA "CI Fellows" program supported this research. Special thank to Nightingale Simiyu for assisting us during our fieldwork and for transcribing interviews.

REFERENCES

1. Population of Local Authorities (with towns), Government of Kenya, 1999. Available online: http://treasury.go.ke/cbs.go.ke/pdf/authority.pdf.
2. World urbanization prospects: The 2009 revision. United Nations, Department of Economic and Social Affairs, Population Division, New York, 2010.
3. Africa, IT News. "Orange enables Facebook on non-internet phones," 2012. Available Online: http://www.itnewsafrica.com/2012/02/orange-enables-facebook-on-non-internet-phones/
4. Agesa, R.U. and Kim, S., "Rural to urban migration as a household decision: Evidence from Kenya," *Review of Development Economics* 5, 1 (2001), 60-75.
5. BizTechAfrica. "Facebook for every phone on Orange," 2012. Available online: http://www.biztechafrica.com/article/facebook-every-phone-orange/2029/.
6. Bosch, T.E., "Using online social networking for teaching and learning: Facebook use at the University of Cape Town," *Communication* 35, 2 (2009), 185-200.

7. Bosch, T.E., "Young women and 'technologies of the self': Social networking and sexualities," Agenda 25, 4 (2011), 75-86.
8. Burrell, J., "User Agency in the Middle Range: Rumors and the Reinvention of the Internet in Accra, Ghana," Science, Technology, & Human Values 36, 2 (2011), 139-159.
9. Davies, C.A., *Reflexive Ethnography: A Guide to Researching Selves and Others*. Routledge, London, 2002.
10. Donner, J., "The rules of beeping: Exchanging messages using missed calls on mobile phones in sub-saharan Africa," Paper presented at the 55th Annual Conference of the International Communication Association: Questioning the Dialogue, New York. (2005).
11. Donner, J., "The rules of beeping: Exchanging messages via intentional "missed calls" on mobile phones," *Journal of Computer-Mediated Communication* 13, 1 (2008), 1-22.
12. Ellison, N., Steinfield, C. and Lampe, C., "The benefits of Facebook 'friends': Exploring the relationship between college students' use of online social networks and social capital," *Journal of Computer-Mediated Communication* 12, 3 (2007).
13. Ellison, N.B., Steinfield, C. and Lampe, C., "Connection Strategies: Social Capital Implications of Facebook-enabled Communication Practices," *New Media & Society* (2011).
14. Etzo, S. and Collender, G., "The Mobile Phone 'Revolution' in Africa: Rhetoric or Reality?," *African Affairs* 109, 437 (2010), 659-668.
15. Fair, J.E., Tully, M., Ekdale, B. and Asanta, R.K.B., "Crafting Lifestyles In Urban Africa: Young Ghanaians In the World of Online Friendship " *Africa Today* 55, 4 (2009), 29-49.
16. Freeman, H.A., Ellis, F. and Allison, A., "Livelihoods and Rural Poverty Reduction in Kenya," *Development Policy Review* 22, 2 (2004), 147-171.
17. Glaser, B.G. and Strauss, A., *The discovery of grounded theory: strategies for qualitative research*. Rutgers University Press, New Jersey, 2009, 1967.
18. Golder, S., Wilkinson, D. and Huberman, B. "Rhythms of social interaction: Messaging within a massive online network." Steinfield, C., Pentland, B., Ackerman, M. and Contractor, N. (eds.), Proceedings of Third International Conference on Communities and Technologies, Springer, 2007.
19. Hewitt, A. and Forte, A., "Crossing boundaries: Identity management and student/faculty relationships on the Facebook," Extended Abstracts of CSCW'06, ACM, 2006, poster.
20. Hugman, R., "Social Work Research and Ethics," in Shaw, K., Briar-Lawson, J., Orme, J. and Ruckdeschel. (eds.), *The Sage Handbook of Social Work Research, Sage Publications*, Los Angeles/London, 2010, 149-163.
21. Jacobson, A., "Connective Power: Solar Electrification and Social Change in Kenya," *World Development* 35, 1 (2007), 144-162.
22. Jidenman, N. "Facebook's explosive growth in Africa Next Web Africa," 2011. Available online: http://thenextweb.com/africa/2011/05/02/facebooks-explosive-growth-in-africa/.
23. Joinson, A.N. 'Looking at', 'Looking up' or 'Keeping up with' People? Motives and Uses of Facebook Proc. of CHI'08, ACM, 2008, 1027-1036.
24. Konado-Agyeman, K., Takyi, B.K. and Arthur, J.A. (eds.), *The new African diaspora in North America: trends, community building, and adaptation*. Lexington Books, Latham, MD, 2006.
25. Kwaku Kyem, P.A. and LeMarie, P.K., "Transforming Recent Gains in the Digital Divide into Digital Opportunities: Africa and the Boom in Mobile Phone Subscription," *The Electronic Journal of Information Systems in Developing Countries* 28 (2006).
26. Lampe, C., Wohn, D., Vitak, J., Ellison, N. and Wash, R., "Student use of Facebook for organizing collaborative classroom activities," *International Journal of Computer-Supported Collaborative Learning* 6, 3 (2011), 329-347.
27. Lee, C., Dourish, P. and Mark, G. "The Human Infrastructure of Cyberinfrastructure," Proc. of CSCW'06, ACM, 2006, 483-492.
28. Lessig, L., *Code 2.0*. Basic Books, New York, 2006.
29. Lewis, K., Kaufman, J. and Christakis, N., "The Taste for Privacy: An Analysis of College Student Privacy Settings in an Online Social Network," *Journal of Computer-Mediated Communication* 14 (2008), 79-100.
30. Mäkinen, M. and Kuira, M.W., "Social Media and Postelection Crisis in Kenya," *International Journal of Press/Politics* 13, 3 (2008), 328-335.
31. Melvin, R.M. and Bunt, A. "Designed for Work, But Not From Here: Rural and Remote Perspectives on Networked Technology," In Proc. of DIS 2012, ACM, 2012, 176-185.
32. Millen, D.R., "Rapid ethnography: time deepening strategies for HCI field research," Proc. of DIS '00, ACM, 2000, 280-286.
33. Miller, D., *Tales from Facebook*. Polity Press, Cambridge, U.K., 2011.
34. Mwaniki, P. "Facebook event draws crowd in Kenyan capital," *Daily Nation*, Nairobi, 2010.

35. Njoki, C. Govt blames fuel shortage on power outage, KBC News, 2011. Available online: http://www.kbc.co.ke/news.asp?nid=70049.

36. Papacharissi, Z. and Mendelson, A., "Toward a New(er) Sociability: Uses, Gratifications and Social Capital on Facebook. ," in Papathanassopoulos, S. (ed.) *Media Perspectives for the 21st Century*, Routledge, New York, 2011.

37. Pink, S., "The White 'Helpers': Anthropologists, Development Workers and Local Imaginations," *Anthropology Today* 14, 6 (1998), 9-14.

38. Postman, J. "Facebook Free? Hardly," *socialmediatoday.com*, 2011. Available online. http://socialmediatoday.com/socialized/362352/facebook-free-hardly

39. Sahn, D.E. and Stifel, D.C., "Urban–Rural Inequality in Living Standards in Africa," *Journal of African Economies* 12, 4 (2003), 564-597.

40. Scheils, M. "Facebook shut its Lite site after just seven months" BBC News, 2010. Available online: http://news.bbc.co.uk/2/hi/8623710.stm.

41. Shrum, W., Mbatia, P.N., Palackal, A., Dzorbo, D.-B.S., Duque, R.B. and Ynalvez, M.A., "Mobile phones and core network growth in Kenya: Strengthening weak ties," *Social Science Research* 40 (2011), 613-625.

42. socialbakers.com. "The rise of Asia and Africa on Facebook, statistics by continent!," 2011. Available online: http://www.kbc.co.ke/news.asp?nid=70049.

43. Steinfield, C., Ellison, N. and Lampe, C., "Social Capital, self-esteem, and use of online social network sites: A longitudinal analysis," Journal of Applied Developmental Psychology 29 (2008), 434-445.

44. Wasserman, H., "Mobile Phones, Popular Media, and Everyday African Democracy: Transmissions and Transgressions," Popular Communication 9, 146-158 (2011).

45. Williams, C. Facebook slims down for developing countries, *The Register*, 2009. Available online: http://www.theregister.co.uk/2009/08/12/facebook_lite/.

46. Wyche, S.P. and Grinter, R.E. "This is how we do it in my country": A Study of Computer-Mediated Family Communication Among Kenyan Migrants in the United States." Proc. of CSCW'12, ACM, 2012, 87-96.

47. Wyche, S.P. and Murphy, L.L. "Dead China-Make'' Phones Off the Grid: Investigating and Designing for Mobile Phone Use in Rural Africa," Proc. of DIS'12, 2012, ACM, 186-195.

48. Wyche, S.P., Smyth, T.N., Chetty, M., Aoki, P.M. and Grinter, R.E. "Deliberate interactions: characterizing technology use in Nairobi, Kenya," Proc. of CHI'10, ACM, 2010, 2593-2602.

Doodle Around the World: Online Scheduling Behavior Reflects Cultural Differences in Time Perception and Group Decision-Making

Katharina Reinecke[1], Minh Khoa Nguyen[2], Abraham Bernstein[2], Michael Näf[3], Krzysztof Z. Gajos[1]

[1]Harvard University
Cambridge, MA, USA
{reinecke,kgajos}@
seas.harvard.edu

[2]University of Zurich
Zurich, Switzerland
{nguyen,bernstein}@ifi.uzh.ch

[3]Doodle AG
Zurich, Switzerland
mn@doodle.com

ABSTRACT

Event scheduling is a group decision-making process in which social dynamics influence people's choices and the overall outcome. As a result, scheduling is not simply a matter of finding a mutually agreeable time, but a process that is shaped by social norms and values, which can highly vary between countries. To investigate the influence of national culture on people's scheduling behavior we analyzed more than 1.5 million Doodle date/time polls from 211 countries. We found strong correlations between characteristics of national culture and several behavioral phenomena, such as that poll participants from collectivist countries respond earlier, agree to fewer options but find more consensus than predominantly individualist societies. Our study provides empirical evidence of behavioral differences in group decision-making and time perception with implications for cross-cultural collaborative work.

Author Keywords

Doodle; event scheduling; cross-cultural; decision-making

ACM Classification Keywords

H.5.3 Group and Organization Interfaces:
Computer-supported cooperative work

INTRODUCTION

It might not be surprising that the origin of the popular event scheduling tool Doodle [11] lies in Switzerland—the country of accurate clocks and "Swiss efficiency". Doodle addresses the problem of deciding on a mutually agreeable time by letting users create polls with several date and time options. After participants indicate their availability, poll initiators can easily determine the best time for the event.

On the surface, such event scheduling processes may appear to be simply a matter of matching availabilities of those involved. But before it is possible to find a suitable time, poll initiators and participants have to make a range of decisions.

What, for example, if participants do not make themselves available whenever they could in order to avoid making a temporary commitment for these times? What if they indicate availability for less convenient options just because they do not want to inhibit finding a mutually agreeable time? And what if they do so because of social norms and procedures that influence their behavior?

We see event scheduling as a group decision-making process [13] in which "a set of individual preferences are transformed into a group choice by a certain social procedure" [22]. Researchers have observed that societal norms and values differ between countries and determine how groups negotiate individual choices and reach consensus [12, 3, 7]. In countries that are believed to have collectivist and more community-oriented cultures, such as China or Japan, people see themselves as part of a group, and prefer collective decision-making with distributed responsibilities [31]. In individualist countries, as for example the US, people seem to be less concerned with harmony, and are less affected by the decisions of others [31].

Such variations in social procedures between countries lead to our main research question: Does (national) culture determine how we schedule events online?

To answer this question, we analyzed more than 1.5 million anonymized Doodle date/time polls, which had been initiated in 211 countries. Our findings empirically support several assumptions of cultural differences in group decision-making and time perception. For example, we found that in comparison to predominantly individualist societies, poll participants from collectivist countries respond earlier, agree to fewer options but find more consensus. More generally, our results demonstrate that Internet users have not converged into a homogeneous subcultural group with the same behavioral norms across the world, but that their use of technology considerably differs between countries. We discuss the implications of these findings for collaborative work within and across cultures, and suggest strategies for designing scheduling tools that raise awareness of cultural differences, or encourage behavioral change.

GROUPWARE CALENDARS AND EVENT SCHEDULING

Many of today's electronic calendar systems, such as Lotus Notes or Microsoft Outlook, provide a significant advantage over their paper predecessors by allowing users to match their availabilities with others in order to schedule events. One of their downsides is that users need to ensure that all their plans are captured in their calendars. Moreover, they need to explicitly allow others to access their schedules [14] and by doing so, users automatically disclose personal availability patterns [24]. Although most systems enable users to hide any detailed information (e.g., the occasion of an event) researchers have raised concerns over people's privacy [24]. Further, these systems do not capture users' complex scheduling preferences [6], such as preferring afternoon meetings unless the meeting is with a boss or a colleague in a different time zone.

Online scheduling systems such as Doodle make a different trade-off: users disclose their availability in the context of a particular event, which allows them to keep their overall schedules private [24] and to make context-specific judgements about which times to make available for a particular activity. However, such systems impose additional work on all attendees and in some cases may create the expectation that the invitees will keep open all the times they reported as available until the results of the poll have been announced [35]. Thus, to remain in control of one's own time, people have been found to "schedule defensively" [35], or in other words, to lie about their availabilities, and to manipulate the system for their own benefit [41]. By being very selective about one's availabilities, participants could, for instance, influence the outcome of the scheduling process to suit their own preferences rather than attempting to find an option that maximizes the collective utility [41].

So far, much research has focused on inferring users' complex preferences from past scheduling decisions [6] and on mechanisms for encouraging users to report their availabilities truthfully, for example by using game-theoretic mechanisms [13], or by employing an auction system [41]. Other studies looked at the use of calendars, and at social behaviors related to sharing availabilities [2]. Palen [35, 36] conducted a study of the use of groupware calendars at Sun Microsystems, and found that users were willing to share information about their availabilities if it benefited the scheduling process within their group. Geyer et al. [14] investigated the use of a social calendar that combined calendaring and microblogging within IBM. Similarly to Palen's findings, they concluded that users were willing to share most of their availability information within the enterprise.

Our work has a different focus in that we examine the scheduling processes that emerge when people *do not* have to disclose their availabilities, as it is the case on Doodle. We extend related work by empirically investigating the social dynamics that are inherent in such group decision-making, and provide the first large-scale comparison of people's scheduling behavior between multiple countries.

SCHEDULING EVENTS WITH DOODLE

Doodle date/time polls enable an initiator to find the best time for an event, by defining a poll that lists all viable *options*.

Participants make *choices* by selecting those options that are consistent with their availability and preferences. Underneath

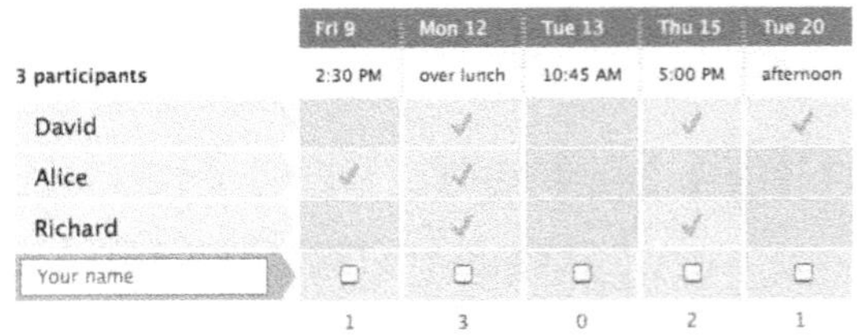

Figure 1. An example of a Doodle date/time poll, where the second option reached consensus among all three participants.

a poll, Doodle provides a summary of how many participants have selected each option, and highlights those that currently represent the majority vote. In Figure 1, for example, all three participants indicated availability over lunch on "Mon 12", so this option received *consensus* among all participants. Date/time polls also allow initiators to define optional settings, such as enabling an *if-need-be* choice (instead of just *yes* or *no*) or using a *hidden poll*, where participants cannot see each other's answers.

HYPOTHESES

Like other group decision-making processes, event scheduling follows certain "social procedures" [22]. It starts with specific choices made by an initiator ("Which times suit me best? Do I want participants to see each others' answers?") and is then passed on to individual decisions of participants ("When am I available? Should I disclose a less convenient time?"). However, instead of making our decisions independently, we usually look at the choices of others and consider how our own choice might affect the group outcome, or our standing within this group ("What have others chosen? What will they think of me if I make this choice?").

Because social procedures are formed by cultural values, we assume that both the individual decisions, as well as the social dynamics found in the overall group decision-making process will be different between countries. Indeed, previous research suggests that people's thinking, behavior, and preferences are formed by cultural influences [23] stemming from the language we speak, our religion, education, social and political norms, and values [26]. With that, culture becomes a "rich complex of meanings, beliefs, practices, symbols, norms, and values prevalent among people in a society" [37]—making it an intangible construct that does not allow easy comparison. No two people can possibly have exactly the same culture, but cultural groups often share similar thinking and behavior. Research on decision-making theory has contrasted such behavioral tendencies between countries (e.g., [1, 31]) and, thus, compared behavioral trends between *national cultures* [19].

To facilitate these comparisons, cultural anthropologists attempted to describe culture with a definite set of constructs, so-called cultural dimensions. Hall [15, 16], for example, proposed to differentiate cultures by their polychronic versus monochronic time orientation. He suggested that in countries that are predominantly polychronic (e.g., in China), human interactions are more important than time and this is often expressed by a much more relaxed attitude when needing to "get things done". On the contrary, predominantly monochronic countries (e.g., Germany) show a greater concern for time management, including advance planning and punctuality. Monochronic cultures are thought to be on clock

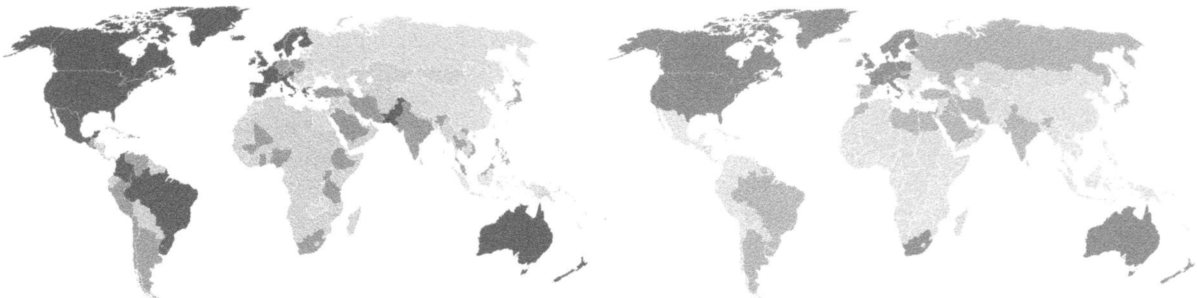

(a) Survival vs. Self-expression (b) Collectivism vs. Individualism

Figure 2. Overview of Inglehart's Survival/Self-expression values (a) and Hofstede's Individualism dimension (b). Darker colors stand for a higher Self-expression or Individualism score, respectively. Medium colors indicate scores ± 0.5 of the medium Survival/Self-expression, or ± 10 of the world average score (43) for Individualism. Gray areas mark countries that have not been included in Inglehart's or Hofstede's study.

time; in their life, an external clock dictates the start and end of events [28]. Polychronic cultures schedule their life more loosely around event time, where activities determine the course of the day, and multiple activities can take place at the same time [28]. Ending a discussion simply because another meeting is scheduled to start would be out of question for cultures on event time. Monochronic cultures can clash with this understanding, as they would expect punctuality and adherence to previously assigned schedules.

Differences in time perception have also been attributed to the extent to which people think of themselves as autonomous individuals with an interest in self-expression and a high quality of life that industrialization brought with it, in comparison to seeing themselves more as interdependent parts of a group, such as the family [38]. The phenomenon is usually described as Individualism versus Collectivism [38, 19], or Self-expression versus Survival [20].

Hofstede's Individualism/Collectivism dimension is one of five that emerged from a large-scale quantitative study at IBM in 74 countries [18]. All countries in his study received a score on each of the five dimensions, facilitating comparisons between their national cultures. Hofstede's study is older than the Self-expression/Survival scores of Inglehart [20], but the link between his Individualism scores and several behavioral phenomena has been well-explored, such as to measure variances in decision-making styles. Moreover, they have been explicitly linked to societies' concern with time, making it an interesting construct for our study to relate to.

Inglehart's Self-expression/Survival dimension emerged within the scope of the World Value Survey [40], which aims to track social and political changes with the help of country scores that have been collected in five waves of surveys, from 1981 to 2007. Thus, the scores for this dimension are arguably more up-to-date, the survey studies a broader population, and offers comparison between slightly more countries. To our knowledge, however, it has not been investigated in the context of decision-making, or directly linked to the perception of time. While the Individualism and Self-expression constructs slightly differ in their meaning, the country scores of both dimensions significantly correlate with each other [20]. In Hofstede's study, the US is the most individualist country with a score of 91, and Guatemala is "most collectivist" with a score of 6. Inglehart's Survival/Self-expression dimension ranges from -2 to around 2.5, with many Scandinavian countries being high on Self-expression and Russia, Bulgaria, or the Ukraine having one of the lowest positions on the Survival/Self-expression value axis. Figure 2 shows a world overview of countries that are believed to score higher in self-expression versus survival based on the latest scores of the world value survey [40], and which ones are more individualist or more collectivist based on Hofstede's country scores [18, 19]. We include both dimensions in our analysis to see how useful the Survival/Self-expression value is as a predictor for cultural differences in decision-making and time perception. As we will later see, both dimensions explain these cultural variations similarly well, and in combination, they help to explain some of the outliers that we see in our data.

Comparisons of national cultures always run the risk of stereotyping all people within one country [32], and thus, these kind of studies have to be seen as contrasting behavioral tendencies. This is especially interesting in our case, because Doodle users likely share a certain *subculture*, making the comparison of national cultures more meaningful [37]. Because Doodle users use the Internet, they are likely more educated and younger than the average person [34]. If we presume that Doodle users have a comparable subculture—thus, controlling for these factors—then differences in the scheduling behavior between countries are likely due to the influence of other cultural values.

Time Perception, Pace of Life, and Affluence

Doodle enhances efficiency by reducing the time required to schedule an event. We assume that Doodle users are primarily from those cultures that are highly concerned with time, which has been linked to Individualism [38]. Highly individualist societies (marked with a darker color in Figure 2(b)) are believed to emphasize individual achievements, and to feel a greater need to save time [27]. Similarly, time is used to structure days in monochronic cultures such as Germany, Switzerland, United States, and Scandinavia much more than in polychronic cultures (e.g., Egypt, Mexico, or India). We therefore hypothesize that individualist societies use Doodle more often than collectivist societies, and will compare the results with Hall's polychronic versus monochronic time orientation [15].

[H.1.1] The number of polls per internet user positively correlates with Individualism.

Researchers have also argued that some countries are more individualist than others because of their higher affluence [38]. Economic development has been attributed as a cause for cultural change, leading to a higher demand for self-expression [20]. If our first hypothesis is in fact true, then the number of polls should increase with a country's per capita gross domestic product (GDP):

[H.1.2] The number of polls per internet user positively correlates with the GDP per capita.

Additionally, we assume that people use Doodle with a higher frequency in countries with a higher tempo. Levine and Norenzayan [27] compared people's walking speed, the work speed amongst postal clerks, and the accuracy of bank clocks in 31 countries. Their study resulted in a ranking for each of these indicators, as well as in an overall pace of life index, with the fastest countries being in Western Europe and Japan, and the slowest in countries with less vital economies. We assume that the arithmetic means of each country's pace of life, as they are provided by Levine and Norenzayan, parallels how often people use Doodle:

[H.1.3] The number of polls per internet user correlates with the pace of life country ranking.

Planning Ahead, Punctuality, and Response Time

Time is often mentioned as the most striking difference between cultures that divides the world into notorious planners and those who spontaneously get together. Countries with a fast pace of life and a high Individualism are generally thought to be monochromic, and on clock time [28]. People in these countries place more importance on time management and planning [25, 38], but might be less spontaneous and plan their events more in advance:

[H.2.1] People in individualist countries initiate Doodle polls further ahead of time than do collectivist countries.

The importance of time goes in line with expectations on punctuality [4, 15, 39]. We assume that people specify the time of a meeting option more precisely in individualist societies in which people live by clock time [28]. Defining a poll option as 11:15 a.m. indicates a higher level of precision than simply clock face time, and presumably, a higher expectation of punctuality. A date with a text string, e.g.,"afternoon", or "sometime in the evening", is less precise than 11 a.m., but more precise than just a date.

[H.2.2] Countries with a higher Individualism use the time option for scheduling meetings more precisely.

Culture also influences whether we feel the need to optimize time [5]. In individualist societies, where "time is money", people feel the need to speed up negotiation processes and decisions in general [30]. We could therefore assume that participants from countries with a high score in Individualism respond to polls more quickly than collectivist participants. On the other hand, individualists, for whom time is often more important than human interactions [15], might be strategizing more by deferring a commitment to specific options as long as possible. If they respond to a poll too early, their time choices might be already outdated before the poll initiator informs of the final choice. However, if participants defer the decision, other time constraints will already be known, therefore facilitating the decision without a long-term commitment of their time. Hence, we put forward a non-directional hypothesis:

[H.2.3] The average response time per country correlates with the dimension Individualism.

Consensus and Dependency of Choices

The notion of "social proof" [9] describes the human tendency to follow other people's decisions and choices. Social proof is assumed to be more prevalent in collectivist countries (e.g., Taiwan, China, or Japan), where people have a greater desire for harmony and blending in [1]. This also parallels a higher reluctance of people in collectivist cultures to independently make decisions [31]: Study participants from Japan, Hong Kong, and Taiwan reported a higher preference for collective decisions—thus, sharing responsibility—and a higher tendency to completely hand over responsibility to an authority [31]. People in individualist countries show a different decision-making behavior, sometimes driven by the desire to be unique [1]. They report a greater confidence in their own decision-making ability, and make choices more independently of others [31].

Such autonomous decision-making has been linked to high self-expression values [20]. Society's economic success usually changes the political climate in favor of an increasing demand for democratic rights [21]. The emerging emphasis on independent choices in more democratic countries might be mirrored in people's scheduling behavior: Doodle users from highly economically viable countries and with high self-expression scores might insist on their democratic right to vote independently, and thus, pay less attention to the choices of others. In contrast, Doodle users from community-oriented, collectivist countries might try harder to match the decision of others, and to find mutual agreement.

We assume that the number of options that reach consensus within a poll is higher in collectivist countries, and the same should be true for the Survival/Self-expression dimension. We define "consensus" as reaching agreement among all participants, but not necessarily on all options.

[H.3.1] The fraction of options that reach consensus within open polls negatively correlates with Individualism.

According to the social proof theory, the decision outcome can be substantially influenced if the preferences of others are visible [9]. In particular, we hypothesize that participants have the goal to find mutual agreement, and that they will therefore adjust their availabilities to find more consensus options. The hidden polls in our data set provide us with a convenient baseline: If participants cannot see each other's choices, any influence of this sort can be ruled out. In our analysis, we will therefore also contrast the assumption of the previous hypothesis with hidden polls versus open polls:

[H.3.2] The fraction of options that reach consensus is higher in open polls than in hidden polls.

According to the findings of Mann et al. [31], we further assume that participants from collectivist countries with more group-oriented cultures tend to "pass the buck", meaning that they avoid making decisions themselves. Furthermore, collectivists have a stronger desire to comply with others [1]. This could result in a corresponding avoidance of declining an option in a poll:

[H.3.3] The fraction of options that participants agree to within open polls negatively correlates with Individualism.

Correspondingly, we assume that participants from collectivist countries prefer declining an option less decisively. We assume that participants from group-oriented collectivist countries select *if-need-be* more often than participants from individualist countries:

[H.3.4] The fraction of times that people select "if-need-be" negatively correlates with Individualism.

DATA PREPARATION AND ANALYSIS

We analyzed 1,771,430 anonymized date/time polls provided to us by Doodle. The polls were selected at random from a time period in mid-2011 and an additional time period in early 2012. Both sets of polls showed consistent results, so the following analyses report on the merged data set. As part of the data preparation, we excluded polls that did not have any participant responses. Our final data set contains 1,536,022 polls initiated by users from 211 countries[1] (m = 9.14, sd = 58.2 polls per country). On average, these polls have 5 participants (sd = 1.4) and 13.5 options (sd = 15.2).

Correlations between two variables were analyzed with Spearman's r (two-tailed) given that our data was significantly non-normal (Kolmogorov-Smirnov tests showing $p < .05$ for all variables). P-values were adjusted for multiple hypothesis testing using the Benjamini-Hochberg correction. We compared two dependent conditions (e.g., the difference between hidden and open polls) using the Wilcoxon signed-rank test, and several independent conditions (e.g., the countries) with the Kruskal-Wallis test.

The correlation analyses report on a subset of the 211 countries: First, when relating to the dimension Individualism, we employ the scores from Hofstede's study [18], which were available for 76 of the countries in our data set. Levine's study on the pace of life [27] comprised timing data for 31 countries, all of which were also included in our data set. In addition, we used the Survival/Self-expression scores of 68 of the countries included in the World Value Survey [40].

In favor of higher validity, the subset of countries was further reduced when we evaluated behavior on a poll or participant level. The advance planning and response time was analyzed for a subset of 828,560 polls and 177 countries for which we were able to retrieve the poll initiation time stamps. Our correlation analyses are based on 47 of these countries that have an Individualism score, and 50 that have a Survival/Self-Expression score. To evaluate the hypotheses related to consensus (H.3.*), we used 52 countries that had more than 100 polls and at least 5 hidden polls. Lastly, the analysis for H.3.4. compares 37 countries that have used the "if-need-be" option, received an Individualism score and had at least 50 polls.

[1] Countries were automatically derived from IP addresses with the help of the Maxmind GeoIP database. IP addresses were not revealed to the researchers at any time.

For the calculation of the advance planning time, we computed the average time difference per country between the poll initiation time stamp and the time given for the first option. For polls that only specified a date, or date and text (e.g., morning, or afternoon), we used midday as the time of the first option. The average response time per country was calculated by subtracting the average of participants' response times per poll from the poll initiation time stamp. Finally, the number of polls that reach consensus within a country was calculated by taking into account polls where participants found mutual agreement for at least one option divided by the overall number of polls per country.

To mitigate the influence of population size and internet penetration, we calculated the *number of polls per capita* and the *number of polls per internet users*. Population data and information about each country's per capita gross domestic product (GDP, available for 205 countries) was derived from [8] and supplemented with information from [33].

Variables such as consensus options were normalized based on the *number of options per poll*. For comparisons between countries, we further adjusted our data for the *number of polls per country*.

RESULTS

All hypotheses and their results are summarized in Table 1.

[H.1.1] Our results support the hypothesis that the higher a country's Individualism score, the more likely its people are to schedule events with Doodle. As Table 2 shows, it is mostly Western countries that lead the list of Doodle users. These countries are regarded as monochronic cultures that use time to structure days much more than predominantly polychronic cultures. All countries in the left column are highly individualist cultures, but the right column shows some outliers: Singapore has a score of 20, clearly marking it as a collectivist country. Lebanon and Hong Kong are regarded as collectivist societies with a score of 38 and 25, respectively. Bermuda and Cambodia were not included in Hofstede's study, but both can be assumed to predominantly show collectivist traits. There could be multiple reasons that these countries are showing a comparatively high scheduling activity: Singapore and Hong Kong are both examples of huge economic growth. Bermuda is a tax haven and it could well be that Doodle is being used by the many expats living in the country. The high scheduling activity could, however, also be the result of changing work practices in these countries.

The neighboring countries Liechtenstein and Switzerland are much more likely to schedule events with Doodle than any other country in our data set, which could be partly attributed to the fact that Doodle is a Swiss company. Doodle's uptake was highly supported by word-of-mouth communication, which suggests that its adoption rate might be higher

Time Perception, Pace of Life, and Affluence		
H.1.1	The number of polls per internet user and country positively correlates with Individualism.	$r_{s(74)} = .65, p < .001$
H.1.2	The number of polls per internet user and country positively correlates with the GDP per capita.	$r_{s(203)} = .57, p < .001$
H.1.3	The number of polls per internet user correlates with the pace of life country ranking.	$r_{s(29)} = -.67, p < .001$
Planning Ahead, Punctuality, and Response Time		
H.2.1	People in individualist countries initiate Doodle polls further ahead of time than do collectivist countries.	$r_{s(45)} = .60, p < .001$
H.2.2	Countries with a higher Individualism use the time option for scheduling meetings more precisely.	partly supported: $r_{s(56)} = .31, p < .05$
H.2.3	The average response time per country correlates with Individualism.	$r_{s(45)} = .50, p < .001$
Consensus and Dependency of Choices		
H.3.1	The fraction of options that reach consensus within open polls negatively correlates with Individualism.	$r_{s(50)} = -.32, p < .05$
H.3.2	The fraction of options that reach consensus is higher in open polls than in hidden polls.	$Z_{(58)} = -6.53, p < .001, r = -.86$
H.3.3	The fraction of options that participants agree to within open polls negatively correlates with Individualism.	Inverted: $r_{s(50)} = .62, p < .001$
H.3.4	The fraction of times that people select "if-need-be" negatively correlates with Individualism.	$r_{s(35)} = -.31, p < .1$

Table 1. Summary of the hypotheses and results. P-values were adjusted for multiple hypothesis testing using the Benjamini-Hochberg correction.

in neighboring countries and those with similar languages. However, even when excluding Switzerland from the analysis[2], the relationship between Individualism and the number of polls remains strong, $r_{s(73)} = .64, p < .001$.

Country	# of polls	per k Internet users	Country	# of polls	per k Internet users
Liechtenstein	2,540	110.430	United Kingdom	60,686	1.180
Switzerland	358,108	58.210	France	53,131	1.174
Austria	47,721	7.768	Bermuda	53	0.982
Germany	405,381	6.225	Sweden	7,963	0.948
Belgium	45,309	5.585	Malta	195	0.811
Luxembourg	1,788	4.212	Israel	3,426	0.757
Denmark	15,774	3.321	New Zealand	2,507	0.737
Canada	81,129	3.009	Singapore	2,372	0.733
USA	602,419	2.459	Netherlands	9,815	0.660
Iceland	679	2.311	Lebanon	596	0.596
Estonia	2,162	2.225	Cambodia	45	0.573
Norway	9,157	2.067	Hong Kong	2,570	0.527
Finland	8,921	2.031	Hungary	3,238	0.524
Ireland	4,161	1.367	Australia	7,321	0.463

Table 2. The 28 countries with the highest numbers of polls per thousand Internet users, and their number of polls in our data set.

[H.1.2] In line with the previous discussion on the link between scheduling activity and economic growth, we had hypothesized that the number of polls per Internet user and country correlates with the GDP per capita. Those countries with a higher affluence do indeed show more scheduling activity on Doodle, confirming H.1.2. The result also indicates that Doodle use might be a function of the amount of white-collar work in these countries with stronger economies, which usually leads to a greater need for scheduling.

[H.1.3] The number of polls per internet user and country also significantly correlates with Levine and Norenzayan's pace of life study. We found correlations with walking speed ($r_{s(29)} = -.56, p < .001$), postal speed ($r_{s(29)} = -.56, p < .001$), and clock accuracy ($r_{s(29)} = -.47, p < .01$). Thus, the faster a country's pace of life (represented by a smaller number of seconds), the higher the number of polls per Internet user. If the data is normalized instead by population size (i.e., number of polls per capita), we see the same significance. We can therefore confirm Hypotheses 1.1, 1.2, and 1.3 even when not accounting for the effect of Internet penetration. Altogether, our first set of results suggests that Internet users use Doodle with a higher frequency if they come from individualist countries with high economic viability, and a fast pace of life.

[H.2.1] In support of Hypothesis 2.1 we found that Doodle users from countries with a high Individualism plan further in advance. Figure 3 provides an overview of the advance planning times in relation to the countries' Individualism scores. There are a few outliers. Mexico, a country that is often regarded as having a laid-back, event-time culture, follows Switzerland and Germany with a high advance planning time of 28 days. In the Survival/Self-expression dimension, Mexicans have transitioned from a culture of "survival" towards a self-expression score of 1.03 over the last 10 years. In comparison, Germany has a lower self-expression score of 0.44 (West) and 0.42 (East), while Switzerland has a higher self-expression score of 1.90. Inglehart relates changes from survival to more self-expression as Mexico has experienced it to an increasing economic development and industrialization—in which time becomes more important. While the importance of time in societies with a higher self-expression has previously only been hypothesized, our data demonstrates that the dimension can be indeed a good predictor of advance scheduling time ($r_{s(48)} = -.67, p < .001$).

This also shows in another outlier: Hungary only plans ahead 13.7 days, yet with an Individualism score of 80 is regarded as a highly individualist country. Again, the low score of -1.22 in the Survival/Self-Expression dimension might be more suitable to explain the result. Lastly, American Doodle users schedule much more spontaneously (on average 17 days in advance) than their high Individualism score of 91, as well as their high Self-Expression score of 1.76 would suggest. This is very comparable to Thailand, China, Singapore, who plan between 15 and 18 days in advance, yet whose national cultures are usually thought to be strongly collectivist.

[2]Liechtenstein was not included in Hofstede's original study, and is therefore not part of our analyses involving Hofstede's scores.

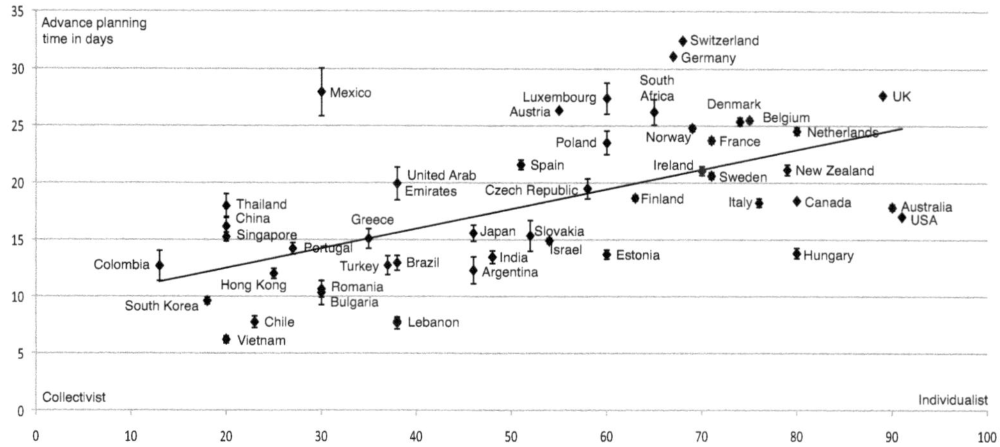

Figure 3. Average advance planning times in days in relation to Individualism scores. Error bars represent the standard error within one country.

[H.2.2] We also assumed that in countries with a higher individualism options might be specified with more detail, a hypothesis that was confirmed for polls with options defined at the 5-minute precision level (e.g., 4:35 p.m.). Individualist countries schedule their events more often with a precision of 5 minutes. The correlation was also confirmed for the Survival/Self-expression values ($r_{s(52)} = .34, p < .01$).

Interestingly, we cannot substantiate this hypothesis for polls with options at a 10 or 15 minute precision level. It is likely that the overall number of these polls in our data set is too low to fully verify a relationship between Individualism and precision level. In fact, only 2% of the polls contained options that had been defined with a 5 minute precision, 10 minute precision, or a 15 minute precision. In contrast, the plurality of polls (41%) has their option time set to the full hour.

[H.2.3] The average response time across all polls per country significantly correlates with the dimension Individualism, therefore substantiating Hypothesis 2.3. Participants in countries with a higher individualism tend to provide their choices *later* than participants of collectivist countries. A strong correlation with the Survival/Self-expression values ($r_{s(48)} = .67, p < .001$) confirms this result.

The finding can be partly attributed to the fact that countries high in individualism and self-expression plan much more in advance, as we have shown in H.2.1. Countries like Switzerland and Germany, who plan their events longest in advance, are now the ones that take longest to respond—on average 44.1 and 45.1 hours after the poll was set up. This is in contrast to Bulgaria, South Korea, Lebanon, and Vietnam with respond times ranging between 14.1 and 18.6 hours (Bulgaria being the fastest). However, even when controlling for the advance planning time, Individualism remains a strong predictor for longer response times (multiple regression, $F_{(2,73)} = 12.11, p < .001, adj.r^2 = .23$).

The cause for this is likely to be a function of individualists' least-commitment behavior. By responding late, individualists seem to defer making time commitments, perhaps because an early response requires blocking time in their calendar longer. Such least-commitment behavior in individualist countries strategically maximizes personal benefit, which collectivists tend to be opposed to [19].

A notable outlier in the correlation of response time with Individualism is China ($m = 40$, $sd = 3.6$ hours), whose participants respond similarly late as the UK and Luxembourg, yet China is thought to have a strong collectivist culture. We believe that this demonstrates where cultural dimensions alone cannot explain the variance in behavior that we are observing in our data. First of all, China has recently experienced enormous economic growth, probably resulting in a shift towards individualism. China is also classified as low on the Survival/Self-expression dimension, but Inglehart acknowledges that growing economies can be expected to result in a country's shift towards higher self-expression [21]. What we see in our data might therefore reflect "the emergence of a prosperous, educated, and self-confident middle-class" [21] that weakens the traditional values of Confucian culture. Chinese Doodle users might belong to a growing sub-cultural group that relates less to the Confucian subjectivity of time, but instead adopted a more Western time perception. This subcultural group within China could possibly become more prone to the least-commitment behavior.

Interestingly, participants respond significantly faster to open polls ($m = 35.6$, $sd = 6$ hours) than to hidden polls ($m = 45.4$, $sd = 15.8$ hours), $Z_{(17)} = -2.68$, $p < .01$, $r = .42$.[3] In hidden polls, they have the opportunity to wait before committing to block certain times in their calendars without other participants noticing. In open polls, however, people might be well aware of the fact that the first participants often strongly influence the outcome of the poll, and thus, are eager to state their availabilities earlier.

[H.3.1] The fraction of options that reach consensus negatively correlates with Individualism, supporting Hypothesis 3.1. Collectivist countries find on average more consensus than individualists. However, some countries agree on significantly more options than others, sometimes independent of what their Individualism score would predict. In India, an

[3]This analysis used only countries with more than 20 hidden polls.

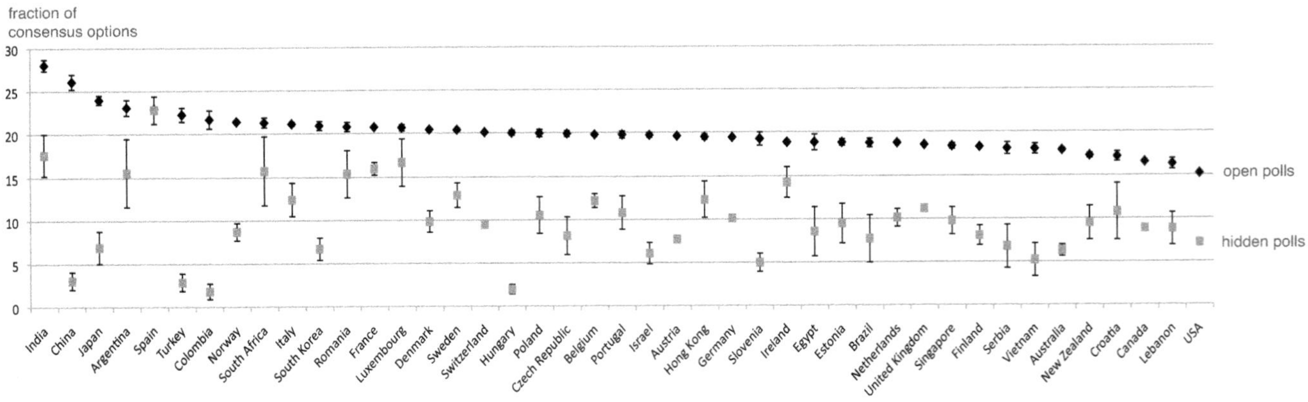

Figure 4. The average fraction of consensus options per country in open polls and hidden polls. Error bars show the standard error.

average of 28% of options find mutual agreement. As Figure 4 shows, this is the highest number in our data set and a strong contrast to the US, whose Doodle users only find consensus on an average of 15% of options. India is regarded as a collectivist country in which individual's actions are highly influenced by other's opinions. Its Individualism score of 48 seems to underestimate how much its people are willing to adjust their availabilities in order to find mutual agreement.

The countries with the second and third most consensus options are China and Japan (with 26% and 24%, respectively). Both are collectivist societies by Western standards, but China has a much stronger extended family system, which forms the basis of most collectivist societies. In contrast, Japan is usually regarded to deviate from other Asian cultures, but its collectivist values seem to remain influential: Seeking consensus can be interpreted as an active effort to keep harmony—a characteristic usually associated with collectivist cultures. In fact, Japan's high fraction of consensus options in our Doodle data verifies the findings of Mann et al. [31] who had found that Japanese participants preferred to collectively make decisions.

[H.3.2] According to the findings of our last hypothesis, people are rethinking their availabilities in an effort to find a mutually agreeable time—but they are not able to do this in hidden polls. In support of H.3.2, we found a significant difference between the fraction of options that reach consensus between hidden and open polls (see Table 1). Open polls reach almost double as many consensus options ($m = 20.3$ % options, $sd = 2.5\%$) than hidden polls ($m = 11.2\%$, $sd = 5.7$ %). This demonstrates that people are indeed highly influenced by the choices of other poll participants and are actively trying to find mutual agreement.

Figure 4 shows that the fraction of consensus options reached in hidden polls highly differs between countries. This is due to how many availabilities participants offer in general (as discussed in the results of the next hypothesis). However, the difference between the fraction of consensus options in open and hidden polls can also be regarded as the amount of effort that people put in to reach consensus in open polls, compared to the "baseline" hidden polls, in which they cannot see other's choices. This difference is largest for the collectivist countries China and Colombia, suggesting that these countries put a higher effort into finding mutual consensus.

[H.3.3] Individualism significantly correlates with the fraction of options that participants agree to. Contrary to our hypothesis, however, participants with a higher Individualism score show *more* availabilities. As might be expected, the fraction of availabilities slightly increases the further ahead of the actual event the poll was set up. However, even when controlling for the planning ahead time and the number of options (which could potentially confound the fraction of times that people are willing to commit to), the relationship remains positive and significant (multiple regression, $F_{(2,48)} = 18.72, p < .001, adj.r^2 = .41$).

Collectivists show less availabilities, yet in our analysis of Hypothesis 3.1 we found that they find more consensus options. Both findings in combination indicate that collectivists must be explicitly targeting their few availabilities at those options that are likely to reach consensus.

The correlation between the fraction of options that participants agree to and Individualism also remains true in hidden polls ($r_{s(51)} = .32, p < .05$), albeit in a weaker form. Moreover, participants agree to a significantly larger fraction of options in open polls ($m = 53.7\%$ availabilities, $sd = 3.8\%$) than in hidden polls ($m = 39.6\%$ availabilities, $sd = 10.9\%$), $Z_{(59)} = -6.38, p < .001, r = -.83$. Iceland, Lithuania, Slovakia, Philippines, Taiwan, and Serbia show the greatest change in behavior when using hidden polls by reducing their availabilities by a factor of 3.

[H.3.4] The fraction of if-need-be answers show a weak inverse relationship with Individualism, suggesting that collectivists answer with "if-need-be" slightly more often. The correlation is significant with the Survival/Self-expression dimension ($r_{s(50)} = -.52, p < .001$), indicating that these values are more predictive of a country's tendency to use if-need-be. The countries that answer if-need-be most often are Hungary, Slovenia, Latvia, Russia, Czech Republic, and China with 13% to 14.7%. With the exception of Slovenia and the Czech Republic, all of these countries rank low on the Survival/Self-expression dimension, but not all of them are regarded as collectivist cultures. Hungary and the Czech

Republic, for example, received Individualism scores of 80 and 58, respectively. In contrast, Liechtenstein, Switzerland, Luxembourg and France, countries that rank high in self-expression and Individualism, use if-need-be least often (7.6-9.1%). The relationship with Survival/Self-expression remains equally strong when regarding if-need-be answers as a resort to declining an option ($r_{s(50)} = -.57, p < .001$).

DISCUSSION

When discussing the effect of technology on culture, people often assume that the world is slowly homogenizing into a culture of Internet users, who share similar values and behavioral norms [29, 17]. Our analysis of the online scheduling behavior on Doodle argues against this hypothesis.

In fact, Doodle users around the world use the tool very differently: Our data indicates that individualists strategically respond late, perhaps in order to make fewer time commitments and maximize their own flexibility [35, 41]. Our results also demonstrate that across the world, people are steering their availabilities towards those options that have good chances to reach consensus, which shows in a significantly higher number of consensus options in open polls compared to hidden polls. But collectivists seem to make a larger effort to reach mutual agreement: Polls initiated in collectivist countries find more consensus options, while their participants indicate fewer availabilities. This is consistent with previous findings in the decision-making literature: Collectivists are more likely to conform to other people's decisions and choices [1, 31]. However, the finding also implies that collectivist participants must predominantly show availabilities for those options that have a good chance of finding consensus. Individualists show more availabilities, but seem to agree to options despite knowing that these will not reach consensus. One possible interpretation is that they want to appear flexible and willing to find consensus, while hoping to change the poll outcome to their preferred option [13, 35, 41].

Such differences in scheduling behavior can lead to misinterpretations of other's behavior and challenges in intercultural collaboration [4]. For example, if collectivists schedule more spontaneously, individualist participants might feel that showing availability close to the actual event could indicate to others that they are not as busy as they would like to appear. Conversely, if individualists set up polls a long time in advance, collectivists might expect a higher importance of the event when it may not be.

Likewise, differences in expectations towards people's response time can cause friction. Collectivists might see a late response as unsocial behavior: They are blocking time in their calendar while other participants seem to perceive their own time as more important.

Furthermore, if collectivists show less availabilities, individualists could understand this as a lower willingness to find consensus. Collectivists, on the other hand, might have a higher expectation that poll participants adjust their availabilities for the benefit of the group and that they confirm options that will likely reach consensus. Thus, a rejection of these leading options might be perceived as selfish behavior in more group-oriented cultures.

To mitigate similar misunderstandings, intercultural training usually focuses on raising awareness about cultural differences, as well as on suggesting behavioral adjustments [4]. A combination of both could also facilitate scheduling within and across cultures: One possibility to invoke a certain response behavior, for example, would be to set a deadline by which participants have to respond to polls. This has the positive side effect of removing the penalty for participants that respond quickly—those participants no longer have to keep all options they agreed to open. To increase chances of finding a mutually agreeable time, scheduling systems could also emphasize options that are likely to reach consensus, or explicitly notify a participant when s/he declines options that otherwise suited everyone. Notifications could supplement Doodle's current display of majority vote(s), but would more directly point out which choice(s) inhibit finding consensus.

Intercultural training additionally suggests to raise awareness of ethnocentric or culturally insensitive behaviors, and to provide people with the appropriate knowledge of cultural differences [4]. Scheduling systems could do so by displaying informational tool-tips and providing feedback (as suggested in [10]). This information could already support the poll setup. In some countries, for example, we have seen longer response times, or that people showed less availabilities when using hidden polls. Depending on the poll initiator's country (e.g., as indicated by her IP address), scheduling systems could inform about these likely behaviors. Moreover, the system could guide the poll setup by providing advice on optional settings, such as the pros and cons of hidden versus open polls, or when a deadline option might be appropriate. If a poll is likely to include participants from several different countries (e.g., if the initiator turns on time zone support), scheduling systems could more generally inform poll initiators about scheduling differences between cultures.

Similar information could also be useful for participants: Scheduling systems could automatically detect whether people's IP addresses suggest a multinational team, and inform about possible differences in other participants' scheduling behavior. Our findings can serve as a basis for these explanations, and help mitigate possible misunderstandings in intercultural scheduling.

LIMITATIONS, FUTURE WORK AND CONCLUSION

The results of this paper confirm our research question: Culture influences how we schedule events online. In comparison to individualist societies, such as the US, more group-oriented collectivist countries respond to polls earlier, indicate fewer availabilities, but seem to make a larger effort to reach mutual agreement. The results provide empirical evidence of these behavioral variations when people schedule online, and indicate possible reasons for misunderstandings when scheduling across cultures. We believe that increasing the awareness of these differences can help improve intercultural scheduling and support the acceptance of cultural differences as an interesting contribution to our lives.

Our analysis of Doodle date/time polls was an empirically powerful way to unobtrusively investigate such variations between countries, but it is obvious that future work needs to address several shortcomings. Specifically, we intend to follow up our findings with interviews and surveys in order to ensure that the behavioral differences observed between countries are not the result of a varying use of Doodle. For example, the current data set did not provide us with any information about the purpose for which polls were scheduled, potential hierarchies between poll participants, or whether Doodle is mostly used to schedule work or leisure time activities in a specific country. Future work also needs to clarify whether the behavioral differences are the result of varying job sectors between countries rather than the influence of national culture. Last but not least, we would be delighted to see our results compared to, and complemented with, similar event scheduling data of international organizations or of another online event scheduling service.

ONLINE APPENDIX

To enable others to validate and extend our results, our data set containing information about all 211 countries can be downloaded from http://iis.seas.harvard.edu/resources/.

ACKNOWLEDGMENTS

We thank David Gubler from Doodle for helping with the data export, and Anthony Jameson for numerous discussions on decision-making and culture. Katharina Reinecke was supported by the Swiss National Science Foundation under fellowship number PBZHP2-135922.

REFERENCES

1. Aaker, J., and Maheswaran, D. The Effect of Cultural Orientation on Persuasion. *Journal of Consumer Research 24* (1997), 315–328.
2. Birnholtz, J., Dixon, G., and Hancock, J. Distance, Ambiguity and Appropriation: Structures Affording Impression Management in a Collocated Organization. *Computers in Human Behavior 28* (2012), 1028–1035.
3. Brew, F. P., Hesketh, B., and Taylor, A. Individualist-Collectivist Differences in Adolescent Decision Making and Decision Styles with Chinese and Anglos. *International Journal of Intercultural Relations 25*, 1 (2001), 1–19.
4. Brislin, R., and Yoshida, T. *Intercultural Communication Training: An Introduction*. Thousand Oaks, CA: Sage, 1994.
5. Brislin, R. W., and Kim, E. S. Cultural Diversity in People's Understanding and Uses of Time. *Applied Psychology 52* (2003), 363–382.
6. Brzozowski, M. et al. groupTime: Preference Based Group Scheduling. In *Proc. CHI* (2006).
7. Choi, I., Choi, J. A., and Norenzayan, A. Culture and Decisions. *Blackwell Handbook on Judgment and Decision Making* (2004), 504–524.
8. CIA World Factbook. https://www.cia.gov/library/publications/the-world-factbook, last access: 08/07/2012.
9. Cialdini, R. The Science of Persuasion. *Scientific American 284* (2001), 76–81.
10. Diamant, E. I., Fussell, S. R., and Lo, F. Where Did We Turn Wrong?: Unpacking the Effect of Culture and Technology on Attributions of Team Performance. In *Proc. CSCW'08* (2008), 383–392.
11. Doodle AG. http://www.doodle.com, last access: 07/08/2012.
12. El-Shinnaway, M., and Vinze, A. S. Technology, Culture and Persuasiveness: a Study of Choice-shifts in Group Settings. *International Journal of Human-Computer Studies 47* (1997), 473–496.
13. Ephrati, E., Zlotkin, G., and Rosenschein, J. S. Meet your Destiny: A Non-Manipulable Meeting Scheduler. In *Proc. CSCW* (1994), 359–371.
14. Geyer, W., Dugan, C., and Brownholtz, B. An Open, Social Microcalender for the Enterprise: Timely? In *Proc. CHI* (2011), 247–256.
15. Hall, E. T. *The Silent Language*. Anchor, 1973.
16. Hall, E. T. *The Dance of Life: The Other Dimension of Time*. Anchor; 1st edition, 1984.
17. Hamelink, C. J. New information and communication technologies, social development and cultural change. Tech. rep., United Nations Research Institute for Social Development, Geneva, Switzerland, 1997.
18. Hofstede, G. http://www.geert-hofstede.com, last access: 12/10/2011.
19. Hofstede, G. *Cultures and Organizations: Software of the Mind*. London: McGraw-Hill, 1997.
20. Inglehart, R., and Baker, W. E. Modernization, Cultural Change, and the Persistence of Traditional Values. *American sociological review 65*, 1 (2000), 19–51.
21. Inglehart, R., and Oyserman, D. *Individualism, Autonomy and Self-Expression: The Human Development Syndrome*. Leiden, The Netherlands: Brill, 2004, 74–96.
22. Kameda, T. Procedural Influence in Consensus Formation: Evaluating Group Decision Making from a Social Choice Perspective. In *Understanding Group Behavior: Consensual Action by Small Groups*. Erlbaum, 1996, 137–161.
23. Karahanna, E., Evaristo, R., and Srite, M. Levels of Culture and Individual Behavior: An Integrative Perspective. *Journal of Global Information Management 13*, 2 (2005), 1–20.
24. Kellermann, B., and Bohme, R. Privacy-Enhanced Event Scheduling. In *Proc. Computational Science and Engineering* (2009), 52–59.
25. Kirkcaldy, B., Furnham, A., and Levine, R. Attitudinal and Personality Correlates of a Nation's Pace of Life. *Journal of Managerial Psychology 16*, 1 (2001), 20–34.
26. Leidner, D. E., and Kayworth, T. A Review of Culture in Information Systems Research: Toward a Theory of Information Technology Culture Conflict. *Management Information Systems Quarterly 30*, 2 (2006), 357–399.
27. Levine, R., and Norenzayan, A. The Pace of Life in 31 Countries. *Journal of Cross-Cultural Psychology 30*, 2 (1999), 178–205.
28. Levine, R. V. *A Geography of Time: On Tempo, Culture, And the Pace of Life*. Basic Books, 1st edition, 1998.
29. Levitt, T. The globalization of markets. *Harvard Business Review 61*, 3 (1983), 92–102.
30. Macduff, I. Your Pace or Mine? Culture, Time, and Negotiation. *Negotiation Journal 22*, 1 (2006), 31–45.
31. Mann, L. et al. Cross-cultural Differences in Self-reported Decision-making Style and Confidence. *International Journal of Psychology 33*, 5 (1998), 325–335.
32. McSweeney, B. Hofstede's Model of National Cultural Differences and Their Consequences. *Human Relations 55*, 1 (2002), 89–118.
33. Miniwatts Marketing Group. http://www.internetworldstats.com, last access: 12/10/2011.
34. Nie, N. H., and Erbring, L. Internet and Society: A Preliminary Report. *IT & Society 1*, 1 (2002), 275–283.
35. Palen, L. A. *Calendars on the New Frontier: Challenges of Groupware Technology*. PhD thesis, University of California, Irvine, 1998.
36. Palen, L. A. Social, Individual and Technological Issues for Groupware Calendar Systems. In *Proc. CHI* (1999), 17–24.
37. Schwartz, S. H. Mapping and Interpreting Cultural Differences Around the World. *Int. Studies in Sociology and Social Anthropology 93* (2004), 43–73.
38. Triandis, H. C. *Individualism and Collectivism*. Boulder, Co.: Westview, 1995.
39. White, L. T., Valk, R., and Dialmy, A. What is the meaning of "on time"? the sociocultural nature of standards of punctuality. *Journal of Cross-Cultural Psychology 42*, 3 (2011), 482–493.
40. World Values Survey Association, 2009. official aggregate v.20090901, 1981-2008.
41. Xu, C. Making Doodle Obsolete: Applying Auction Mechanisms to Meeting Scheduling. Bachelor's thesis, Harvard College, 2010.

Local–Universality: Designing EMR to Support Localized Informal Documentation Practices

Sun Young Park, Kathleen H. Pine, Yunan Chen
Donald Bren School of Information and Computer Science
University of California, Irvine
sunyp1@uci.edu, yunanc@ics.uci.edu, khpine@uci.edu

ABSTRACT
In this paper, we describe a practice that is common across multiple heterogeneous contexts but enacted differently depending on the unique constellation of resources and demands present in each local context. Using the case of informal documentation practices in two departments of a single hospital, Emergency and Labor & Delivery, we describe how clinicians in each department develop contextualized informal documentation practices after deployment of a new EMR system. We describe three underlying functions of informal documentation that are inherent to the practice of medical personnel: "memory work," abstraction work," and "future work." We then find that the newly deployed EMR technology does not support these kinds of work. We argue that hospital documentation work systems should be designed with an eye to such universal work practices, while keeping in mind that the effectiveness of informal documentation practices is rooted in its adaptive and flexible deployment in heterogeneous work settings.

Author Keywords
Documentation; Informal Documentation Practices; Locality; Universality; Electronic Medical Record (EMR)

ACM Classification Keywords
H.0; K.4.3; J.3

INTRODUCTION
A hospital is a complex organizational system comprised of dozens of medical and administrative units, each with a unique purpose and set of activities. Proper functioning of a hospital requires the alignment of the activities of multiple departments together. Researchers in CSCW have long been concerned with the development of Health Information Technologies, such as Electronic Medical Record (EMR) systems, to support hospital workflow. EMRs are designed to serve as comprehensive information infrastructures that include both the medical chart and a key component of the hospital work system [5], while simultaneously serving other multiple functions such as scheduling, entering orders, and retrieving results. This comprehensive approach promotes legibility and access to information as well as the standardization of workflows among heterogeneous departments across the hospital [22]. Overall, the centralization of patient information and standardization of work coordination enabled by a shared computer platform is expected to enhance the quality, safety, and efficiency of health care practices [1] and result in cost savings [24].

Individual departments have unique goals, tools, cultures, and workflows, making centralization and standardization difficult to achieve in practice. We borrow the term "local-universality" from Timmermans & Berg (1997) [35], who argue that standardization of artifacts such as protocols is only achieved through local adaptation of universal standards. However, we apply the term differently. In our conceptualization, local-universality applies to *a type of practice* that has stable characteristics in multiple local settings rather than a particular artifact. We employ this concept to study clinicians' informal documentation practice. Our analysis reveals that although different local departments and user groups localize informal documentation to their particular context, there are common, universal types of work in the informal documentation practice across the hospital, which are not currently supported by the EMR. Conceptualizing informal documentation as a "local-universality" allows us to analyze both the stable and flexible characteristics of this practice, which in turn will help us think about how to design computer-supported work systems that promote, rather than interfere with, informal documentation.

Although creating a "paperless" system was a goal of EMR implementation in general, researchers note that creating paperless electronic workflows through EMRs is very difficult and "paper persistence" post-implementation is pervasive in hospitals [17]. Paper persistence has been seen as a problem arising primarily from incomplete integration of health information technologies (HIT) with existing work systems. Campbell et al. [8] and Chen [9] give examples of problematic paper persistence such as using printouts from an EMR for documenting and transposing information back and forth between computer and paper forms. Unlike previous studies on incomplete integration of HITs, we focus on informal documentation practice and see the persistence of paper not as a problem in and of itself, but as evidence of the importance of informal documentation practice and a means through which we can better understand the function of informal documentation in hospital departments. We define "informal documentation" as documentation activities that take place outside the purview of the official EMR system. A key feature of informal documentation artifacts is that they are *not archived after use.* Unlike "formal documentation," informal documentation is only used as part of the practice of doing work, not as part of an official record of the work that was done. We define "formal" documentation as any documentation, paper or electronic, that is archived and thus forms part of an account of care that is retrievable and accountable for organizational, regulatory, or legal purposes.

In this paper, we present findings from an ethnographic study at a large teaching hospital to examine the informal documentation that took place in *two local departments,* in response to newly imposed formal documentation requirements presented by implementation of an EMR system deployed across the hospital. Specifically, we focused on the local practices for informal documentation in two separate departments – Emergency Department (ED) and Labor and Delivery (L&D). Although in the same hospital, these departments are radically different: ED is driven by time pressure. Multiple patients are managed by caregivers at once and the objective is to stabilize patients and discharge or transfer them to the care of another unit. In contrast, L&D specializes in a single medical domain and one-to-one patient care through the entire trajectory of labor, birth, and recovery. Our findings reveal that despite the different nature of work taking place in each department, medical workers engaged in three universal informal documentation practices, which we call *memory work*, *abstraction work*, and *future work*. These informal documentation practices arise in response to universal needs and goals in heterogeneous healthcare contexts, but take different forms depending on the local work processes, requirements, and resources. Further, we provide suggestions on how to design for such practices in future EMR system design.

RELATED WORK

The complexity of the healthcare field has been widely noted by the HCI community. Previous research has exposed a variety of issues affecting the successful design and implementation of HIT in medical workplaces, such as temporality in coordination [32] spatiality in collaboration [4], compatibility in workflows [9], and breakdowns in communications [32]. This rich stream of research indicates the magnitude of the challenges presented by designing systems for the healthcare field. Because of these unique challenges, researchers note a multitude of problems with current designs of large HIT systems. Despite expected benefits such as easy access to patients' records [23, 37] and increased quality of patient care [23], unintended consequences have also been reported, including increased documentation time [27, 31], medical errors [2], and increased mortality [19]. Others also have noted that system design has unexpected impacts on clinical work processes and practices. For example, electronic documentation changes the workflow [11,13], alters the structure of physician notes [13], and alters the physical layout of work practice [26].

Medical work is highly complex and requires coordination among multiple heterogeneous individuals and departments [34]. This creates tension when attempting to achieve meaningful use of a system designed for an entire hospital while also finding congruence with the unique constellation of practices, routines, and requirements present in each individual department [22]. Given the dynamic, contextual nature of healthcare environments, it is very challenging to design universal information systems that serve as functional work infrastructures and support the intricate and variegated nature of medical work. Because of this, recent studies assert successful EMR systems must support local variations in workflow [3] and point to the inability for local departments to customize the EMR to their own needs and existing work structures [7].

One workflow issue noted in prior studies is the persistent use of paper despite implementation of an electronic system designed to eliminate paper documentation [8,12,18]. Much research shows that clinicians deploy working records [15], nursing working documents [38], provisional information [20], transitional artifacts [9], and personal notes [25]. These paper-based informal documentation practices allow clinicians to create flexible working documents that meet the needs for records to be provisional, informal, private or hidden [16, 38] and facilitate care delivery [20] that is timely and responsive [15]. Information documented on these paper artifacts is locally evolved, maintained, and used to support delivery of care. Dykstra et al. [12] argue that the role of paper will change from an archival medium to an active medium for communication, filling gaps left by information technologies.

Much of the literature on informal documentation asserts that these practices arise from insufficient design of clinical documentation systems. It has been argued that existing computerized systems often misrepresent the use of paper-based medical records [18], lack the ability to document and use informal and provisional information [20, 38], and lack the ability to support clinicians' tailoring, presenting, and augmenting clinical information based on their roles and preferences [15]. However, these studies have not yet addressed the specific issues of informal documentation use that arise due to the local and contextual nature of work practice.

To understand the dual nature of informal documentation practice as both local and universal, our paper has two primary aims:

1. To explore how informal documentation is used and understand how informal documentation is adapted and deployed in different contexts to support distinctly different work practices.
2. To identify and describe the commonalities in informal documentation practices employed in different contexts.

RESEARCH METHODS

This study was carried out at a large teaching hospital located in the United States. Our field site is a diverse organization with dozens of departments, employing more than 3,500 personnel and serving for more than 300,000 outpatients visits and nearly 17,000 inpatients visits per year. We chose to compare the ED and L&D since these two departments present uniquely distinct work practices.

Setting

Emergency Department (ED)

The primary goal of ED care is to promptly stabilize patients' medical problems and make decisions to either discharge or admit patients; if patients are admitted, ED clinicians must choose the appropriate department and transfer the patient's care. The general ED care process consists of short patient care trajectory[1] ranging from 1-2 hours to 1-1.5 days. In addition, ED deals with a wide variety of illnesses, which range from 1-2 hours of simple care (e.g. for patients needing stitches or patients presenting with influenza) to more serious exams (e.g., patients requiring an MRI or CT scan requiring specialist diagnosis) or the treatment of life threatening injuries.

Labor and Delivery (L&D)

The primary goal of L&D is to safely care for a mother and baby throughout the entire trajectory of labor, birth, and recovery, and it is specialized in only one area of medicine (obstetrics). In addition, patients stay much longer in L&D than ED ranging from 1-2 days to up to 12 weeks or more if a patient is admitted for antepartum care[2]. The L&D department has 14 beds and approximately 55 nurses. About 1,000 deliveries per year occur in L&D. Due to legal pressures and the nature of the work, documentation requirements in L&D are much more intense than ED and a larger quantity of information must be recorded. The physical layout consists of a central nursing station with computers for documentation surrounded by several patient rooms, each of which is equipped with computer terminals for in-room documentation.

Data and Data Collection

We conducted a comparative qualitative field study using ethnographic methods. All data was collected by the first two authors, who conducted in-depth observations and interviews with clinicians in each department. The goal was to gain an in-depth contextual understanding of how ED and L&D clinicians perform their documentation work, as well as the ways different artifacts were used to support these activities. We followed key personnel and artifacts, such as patients' paper charts and admission and discharge processes, to comprehend the general workflow of ED and L&D from various perspectives. We also observed various staff meetings and trainings pertinent to documentation.

In total, 630 hours (230 in ED and 400 in L&D) of observation was conducted over a period of 2 years. Each observation session ranged between 2 and 15 hours at all times of day and night, including weekends. In the ED, we studied 19 doctors, 20 nurses and interviewed 23 clinicians. In the L&D, we shadowed 25 nurses and conducted interviews with 11 nurses and a focus group with 12 nurses. Interviews were recorded and transcribed for analysis.

After completing observations and interviews, we reviewed the data collected in the study to understand clinicians' documentation behaviors in both the ED and L&D. Data were analyzed using qualitative data analysis to identify themes. After informal documentation was chosen as the main theme, we followed a process of comparing informal documentation artifacts from each unit. We coded types of information present on different artifacts, such as "future work," then re-analyzed artifacts with these categories in mind, thus refining and defining *categories* of informal documentation and noting similarities and differences between the two departments. We also coded sections of field notes, including conversations held with participants during the course of field work, related to informal documentation for further insight in to how clinicians in each department use the informal documentation in practice. During this process, we wrote extensive memos about key themes we saw emerging from the data, which we later refined through the process of writing. During data analysis, findings were presented to participants in a series of informal conversations to contest findings and clarify pre-conceptions [25].

FINDINGS

Recently a comprehensive and large-scale EMR system was implemented at our field site. The EMR was custom-designed for our field site and has been used in all the departments across the hospital for about a year. The EMR serves as an official record system for the entire hospital and the information documented in the EMR is archived and stored digitally. Although the EMR is expected to result in a "paperless" hospital work system, nonetheless, consistent with past findings [9,15,20, 26], we observed clinicians in both ED and L&D used papers extensively after implementation, which we observed was because of the importance of informal documentation to support the performance of medical care. In this section we first describe the differences between formal and informal

---

[1] A "trajectory" is the entire course of a disease and the associated work in its different stages and phases [Strauss et al., 1986]

[2] Hospitalized bedrest due to complications with a pregnancy.

documentations, and then describe informal documentation use in ED and L&D.

Formal and Informal Documentation

In this paper, we distinguish between practices for "formal" documentation that is entered into the official medical record, and practices for "informal documentation" that are not archived in permanent records.

- Formal documentation refers to the documentation that is archived or stored (either physically or digitally) and is thus auditable by agents either within or outside the organization. E.g. all documentation that occurs in the EMR, L&D bedside flowsheet program, ED nurses' flowsheet and nursing notes.
- Informal documentation is documentation that is discarded and not stored as permanent records. E.g. single-patient worksheets, annotated daily rounds sheets, triage note print-outs, as well as notes kept on scraps of paper or jotted elsewhere.

In our field sites, informal documentation was primarily used by ED doctors and L&D nurses. Although doctors and nurses are different types of users, we chose to focus on L&D nurses and ED physicians because these were the user groups who engaged in informal documentation most intensively in each department. Our observations revealed that informal documentation practices were used universally for needs that seem to be fundamental to the emergent organization of medical work. By analyzing the informal documentation practices in each department and comparing informal documentation practices across the two departments, we identified different (*local*) needs and common (*universal*) usages for the informal documentation practices developed by ED doctors and L&D nurses.

Informal Documentation Use in ED

Two primary rationales underlie the unique informal documentation practices we observed in ED: time pressure and the need to care for multiple patients at once. Compared to other units in the hospital, ED is a time-pressured environment with short patient turnaround time and on-going care for multiple patients. Despite this short care duration, the workload in ED is very heavy. During rush hours (e.g. weekend evenings and Monday mornings), ED doctors often treat several patients in a row without having time to chart between patients. Moreover, doctors constantly perform time-sensitive coordination work to handle multiple patients care and collaborate with different patient care team members, such as bedside nurses, translators, technicians, admitting residents, and specialists.

ED doctors' informal documentation practices arose naturally from the clash between the constraints imposed by the EMR and the unique nature of ED work. Prior to EMR deployment, ED doctors used paper records for charting work at the patients' bedside, thus completing much of their documentation work during an exam. Doctors entered patient rooms with charts in hand, filled them out during the initial consultation, and carried them as they moved around the ED. However, after EMR deployment, completing charting with paper records was no longer possible. It was not possible to complete documentation efficiently with the EMR. ED doctors realized that in contrast to the paper charts, the EMR required them to document very detailed patient information. Furthermore, although ED doctors had access to wall-mounted bedside computers, they disliked typing and paying attention to a computer in front of their patients. As a result, ED doctors began using paper personal notes to bridge the gap, allowing them to complete detailed documentation in the EMR after they had left the patient's room. Now, before doctors see a new patient, they either print a triage note from the EMR system or prepare a blank paper to use for personal notes. Doctors often fold papers in half or ¼ and carry them in their pockets until patients are discharged or their shift ends. ED doctors found that the use of personal notes was particularly helpful in transferring information from the doctors' room to new patient rooms, since they could quickly preview patient information on their way to meet patients. This informal documentation practice was initiated by a few doctors and later adopted by all ED doctors (Figure 1).

Figure 1. Several personal notes (triage copies) used by ED doctor when charting at computer.

In ED, informal documentation was primarily used for supporting what we term *memory work* – the information that needs to be saved and transferred from the bedside to the EMR. ED doctors care for multiple patients at the same time and have many ongoing tasks that cannot always be instantly logged in the EMR. After the EMR rollout, ED doctors could no longer conduct the bulk of their initial documentation at the bedside and they found it impossible to rely solely on memory when charting information later. Moreover, since ED doctors often saw multiple patients in a row and were unable to chart at the bedside, a large backlog of information was created. To support memory work, ED doctors recorded brief notes on papers before or during the bedside consultation then used these paper notes as a basis for the follow up EMR-based formal documentation.

Informal documentation was also employed for *abstracting key information* from the EMR system. As they managed multiple patients at a time, ED doctors found it was essential to be aware of the "big picture" – knowing what is going on with every patient they manage. Instead of spending time checking information in the detailed EMR record, doctors narrowed down the extensive information stored in the EMR to a simplified information snapshot using informal documentation. On personal notes, doctors jotted down only basic information for each patient (e.g. age, chief complaints, medical history), and they frequently edited or updated their notes to record new procedures and medications. Some doctors drew tables to organize multiple patients' information at once. In our study, almost all ED doctors felt the need to remain aware of basic information about all the patients they managed. Informal documentation allows them to abstract key information in a personal, portable, and easy to read manner.

ED doctors also utilized informal documentation to facilitate *future planning*. In the ED, rapid decisions and coordination for next steps in patient care is important for quick turnaround and efficient patient treatment. Each of the multiple patients managed by an ED doctor at any given time has a unique care trajectory. In order to coordinate all medical tasks in a timely manner within this extremely complex environment, ED doctors must remain continuously informed of each patient's status and the possible future actions they may need to take, and they must coordinate these actions so they can manage their own time and attention to care for multiple patients at once.

In summary, the informal documentation practice was created and used to help ED doctors' memorize on-going information, abstract key information, and planning future actions. ED doctors used informal documentation to support their unique work practices that were not supported by current EMR documentation.

Informal Documentation Use in L&D

While ED work is characterized by a routine of stabilize-and-transfer, L&D is characterized by the detail-driven work of caring for a mother and baby throughout the course of labor and childbirth. The role of nurses is much different, as nursing care is one-to-one during the intense phases of labor, birth, and recovery. L&D nurses manage their patients very closely, as they monitor the health of mother and baby through labor and provide emotional support for mothers and families. They also often act as a "hub" who communicates and facilitates coordination among all of the other members of the obstetrical team. The informal documentation practices that have developed in L&D are thus uniquely suited to this context.

In contrast to ED, L&D nurses had a well-developed informal documentation practice prior to deployment of the EMR. Each evening at 7PM and each morning at 7AM, the outgoing nurses would print a worksheet from the older-generation computer order entry system. This worksheet contained patient information as well as a list of all active orders at the time of shift change. As each incoming nurse received their patient assignment from the charge nurse, he/she would report to the outgoing nurse for that patient, who would give them the newly printed worksheet before beginning a lengthy handoff conversation. During handoff between the L&D nurses, the outgoing nurse gave the incoming nurse a description of the medical history and current condition of the patient, along with many detailed narrative descriptions of the patient's labor and how it was progressing and the story of the patient's care so far. The incoming nurse would often make copious notes on the patient worksheet during handoff, and then continue to use the worksheet to make notes, organize tasks, and refer to key elements of the patient's story throughout her shift, until handing the patient off to another nurse. Many nurses would use the worksheets to create customized schedule of tasks that needed to be completed for their patients using a series of lines and checkboxes along with the times that different orders were supposed to be carried out, thus facilitating proper execution of orders and serving as a memory aid for the nurses.

However, after EMR implementation, the worksheets were no longer printed automatically, and it was not possible to print a worksheet that contained a list of active orders. The absence of a worksheet presented a disruption in the nursing work in L&D. One nurse described it simply as follows: "*I just feel blind without having the orders, and the worksheet. It's like I don't have eyes.*" With the EMR, nurses were able to log into the system to check orders, but they did not like doing so in the patient's room, and often had difficulties with the logins. Nurses disliked having to leave the room to look at orders, and the new "worklist" function on the EMR program was not as convenient or as malleable as the hand-drawn schedules for task completion that they used to draw on the worksheets. The lack of a worksheet impeded the nurses' ability to engage in *memory work* both during handoff and throughout the shift. L&D nurses experienced a disconnection between the patient and the information that they needed to take care of the patient. Nurses also realized that they had used the worksheet as much more than a reference sheet for orders. The worksheet served several other valuable functions, and they disliked having the worksheet taken away from them. L&D nurses soon compensated by creating their own worksheets using blank pieces of paper to keep track of active orders and other key pieces of information. Soon after, nurses realized that although they could not print a worksheet from the EMR, they could continue to print a worksheet from the older order entry program. The function on this program was still accessible, although they were not supposed to use it and it no longer provided a list of orders. The importance of the worksheet in L&D was evident in the commonly used nickname for it – nurses referred to the worksheet as their "brain." When nurses needed a piece of information, such as when a medication was due or what a patient's weight was, they often said, "*Where's my brain?*" or "*Let me grab my brain!*" while fishing the worksheet out of their pocket or locating it on the counter of the nurse's station.

Therefore, worksheets function as "eyes" and "brains" which allow nurses to remember orders and other key information while interacting directly with patients at the bedside.

Informal documentation was also used as a way to *abstract key information* from the highly detailed patient information that resides in multiple information systems, including the EMR. However, the granularity of the information L&D nurses collected was much finer than the information used in the ED. Instead of summarizing multiple patients' conditions on one piece of paper as ED doctors did, L&D nurses utilized one sheet per patient. An L&D worksheet contains detailed information about a patient's history and progress, even for patients' basic information, such as weight, body mass index, admission date, and other details. For example, during our observation, nurses made notes about patients' position and breathing, such as "*wheezes on left side*". This detailed but abstracted and readily accessible artifact not only allowed L&D nurses to see a clear, organized one-page overview for each patient, but also helped them to report a patient's condition to other team members. Therefore, informal documentation allows L&D nurses to control the granularity of the information they abstract and avoid checking the entire patient chart every time they need a piece of information.

Informal documentation practice also aided L&D nurses' tracking of possible future plans for the patient care trajectory. Predicting future care trajectories and their associated tasks is essential for L&D nurses because they need to carry out these orders in relation to all of the other tasks they are handling and the resources available on the unit. While ED doctors are coordinating multiple patients in relation to each other, L&D nurses must anticipate possible future tasks so they can anticipate which team members they need to contact and which materials they may need to gather. Informal documentation allows nurses to control the relationship between all the tasks to be performed in the future and to visualize the respective stage of completion, at a single glance. It also enables a safety check, so that they do not forget tasks by having them planned on papers.

To summarize, our analysis revealed intensive use of informal documentation among L&D nurses. The nature of the informal documentation that took place as well as the specific informal documentation artifacts developed by L&D nurses were quite different than those observed in the ED. L&D nurses had an increased need for specificity of information and details important to the patient's narrative, as detail-driven long-term care calls for ongoing and long-trajectory. L&D nurses also used worksheets intensively to remember and organize tasks to be carried out after the disruption caused by EMR-based formal documentation, which did not function adequately as a brain or eyes for L&D nurses. This function was not observed to the same degree among ED physicians, due both to the different nature of ED work and the occupational tasks associated with physician and nursing work. However, we observed many commonalities in both informal documentation practices, which we describe next.

Universal Informal Documentation Practice

Although the two departments are very different, informal documentation serves multiple common needs across both departments. These needs are motivated by the general characteristics of the health care practices shared by both ED and L&D. These include the high complexity of the work environment; the fact that many interdisciplinary providers and staff must work within this environment together and must coordinate their actions to care for patients; and the fact that work is highly contextual and responsive. We identified three main categories of universal needs served by informal documentation practices: *memory work*, *abstraction work*, and *future work* (Figure 2). In this section we describe how current informal documentation practices are uniquely suited to meeting these needs and bridging the gaps caused by EMR.

Memory work

The first universal use of informal documentation is to aid clinicians' memory work by managing the temporality of the patient chart. Doctors and nurses are expected to care for and attend to their patients on an ongoing basis, and also expected to "keep up" with their documentation work. In essence, clinicians must care for both the patient and the chart and choreograph these two streams of work together into one coherent flow of actions [29]. However, this is not always possible, particularly given the unpredictable and complex nature of medical work. For example, when ED doctors have to see 3-4 patients in a row at busy times and receive verbal updates from nurses in the hallways, this on-going information could easily be forgotten before it is documented. Information is captured using informal documentation before it is forgotten so that it can be documented in the formal patient record at a later time. Similarly in L&D, key pieces of information are produced on an ongoing basis, but a nurse's hands are often engaged elsewhere and he/she finds it impossible to chart in the EMR "in real time," although this is the expectation. If information is not written down, it is often quickly forgotten. A common strategy for managing both the patient and the chart is jotting down a few details on the accessible paper worksheet and completing charting details later, when there is a lull in patient work. This practice is known as "back charting" in the hospital, and it is discouraged. However, our observations reveal that using informal documentation to engage in strategic back-charting is actually a crucial practice that enables L&D nurses to stay focused on the patient during intense phases of work [29].

Lastly, informal documentation use supports memory work by retaining information that is not ready to be charted. For legal and regulatory purposes, EMR documents only factual

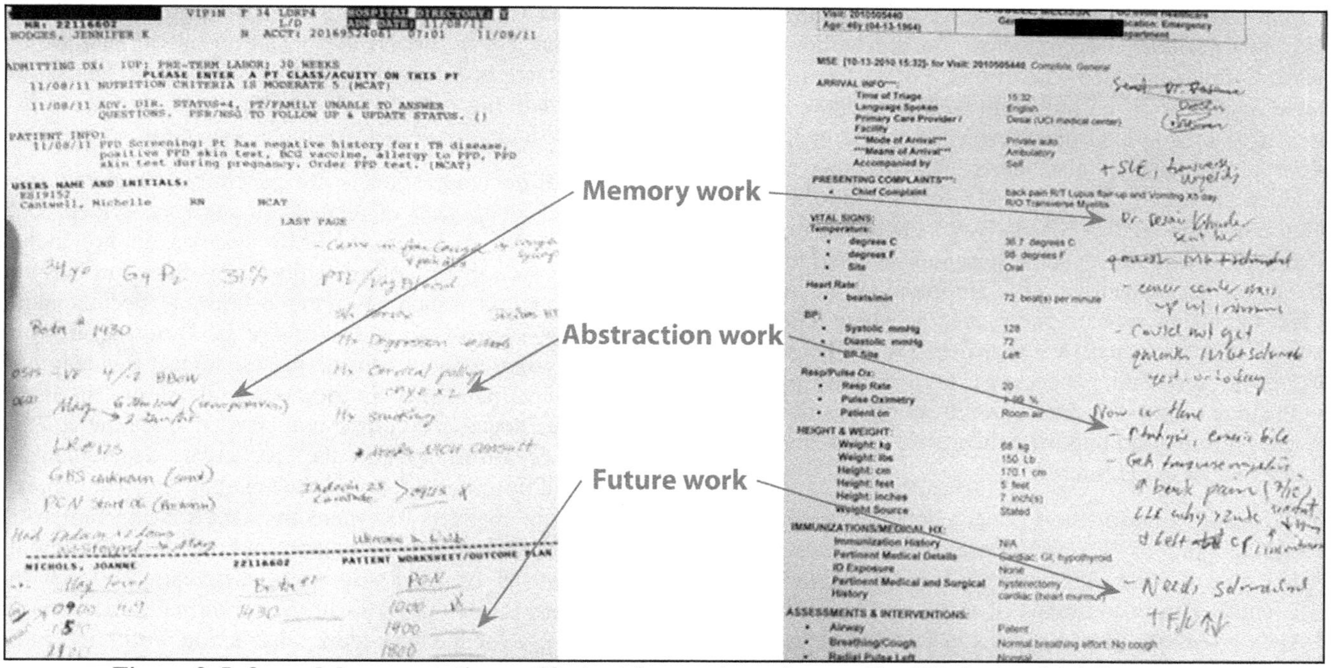

Figure 2. Informal documentation artifacts: triage note copies used by ED doctor (right) and worksheet used by L&D nurse (left)

information, not conjecture. Since doctors' diagnosis work is mostly hypothesis-driven, doctors cannot document suspected diagnoses in the EMR unless they receive lab or image results, which corroborate their suspicions. Thus, memory work serves to help doctors record items they cannot officially document.

Abstraction work

Doctors and nurses use informal documentation to create abstracted accounts from a patient's larger medical chart. An abstracted account provides a quick overview of a patient's situation. Formal EMR documentation practices collect of a huge amount of information about a patient and provide a high level of detail about the patient. However, in real medical practice, clinicians often need an information source that contains only the most important facts to allow easy and quick access. For example, an ED doctor entering a room may only want to know chief complaints or lab results. In our study, ED doctors needed highly abstracted notes that presented an overview of multiple patient situations efficiently, whereas L&D nurses required a more detailed degree of information. The degree of granularity of this abstraction in informal documentation varied depending on departments. We acknowledge that differences between the work of nurses and physicians might have influenced the degree of abstraction. We believe the more important point is that even though there is variation between the informal documentation practices of these different user groups, these practices have stable underlying functions. Creating abstractions of the lengthy formal documentation stored in the EMR also help clinicians to track key occurrences, such as major procedures or lab results, and manage their workloads.

Similar findings have been reported in separating informal notes from formal note content through tagging the important items [37]. Since documenting information in the EMR requires users to document in a precise, clear, and complete manner, key information is often buried in the lengthy and extensive patient records. To manage and coordinate multiple tasks, doctors and nurses often flag pieces of information to rank items in terms of importance. Even though the design of EMR uses red flags to draw clinicians' attention to important information, clinicians cannot control what information they want to flag. Instead, it is predefined by the system and is universally designed across the entire medical center. Thus, informal documentation provides clinicians control and flexibility by allowing them to create their own system by flagging and prioritizing key information.

Future work

Another function of informal documentation is keeping track of possible future steps – commonly known as "trajectory work." Trajectory work is essential to medical practice [34]. In contrast to abstraction work where glancing at a quick overview of current patient information, trajectory work involves anticipating actions a clinician may need to take in the future depending on how a patient's trajectory unfolds. Thus, clinicians have to note down possible future actions that may need to be taken based on the patient's current situation. This forecasting allows clinicians to prepare for upcoming tasks by prepping equipment for possible procedures, and checking available resources, hopefully preventing possible errors due to failure to anticipate an emerging situation. However, this future planning work is not appropriately supported by the current EMR design. In our study, we observed that doctors and nurses often used informal documentation to note possible future problems or events. For instance, an L&D nurse wrote "NICU consult" and drew an asterisk to remind herself to schedule a consultation for a patient later. This piece of information also alerted her to other tasks that might be required of her in the future should the baby be admitted to the NICU. Similarly, an ED doctor circled one of the lab orders for a patient to remind himself to check if the result was positive. This information would further affect the follow up care plans, such as where to admit this patient or who to call for consultations. Although nurses and physicians find it necessary to constantly plan for a wide range of possible future events, clinicians do not wish to enter information into the official record that may or may not be factual in the future.

Additionally, information documentation provides an overall picture of the patient trajectory by serving as a visual map so that clinicians can coordinate future tasks efficiently. The visual maps of tasks on paper notes were used as a reminder for clinicians of next steps, such as the task grids L&D nurses often drew on paper notes to indicate all the tasks need to be done and the stages they are currently in. Thus, mapping using informal documentation is more contextual than the task display on the EMR.

DISCUSSION

The EMR system at our field site was designed to serve as an information infrastructure supporting clinical documentation and other work activities in all departments across the entire hospital. However, our study found that the design of this EMR system does not support a key set of practices that are critical for clinical work – informal documentation practices. Informal documentation is necessary in the delivery of both medical and nursing care to sustain proper clinician documentation processes, and also serves as an artifact tailoring the formal EMR system to local work systems. In this section, we first discuss the need to re-conceptualize informal documentation as an essential practice for medical work that is often neglected by designers and administrators. Then, we consider informal documentation as a site for the development of practices that enable local users to exert control over universal infrastructures. We further discuss the need of rethinking the goal of EMR as it needs to successfully support informal documentation practice.

Redesigning for both Universality and Locality

Drawing on work from science and technology studies, processes of standardization and the creation of "unversalities" must be examined through the lens of local practice. Thus, Timmermans and Berg [35] point out that successful standards only come into being as "local universalities." They argue, "universality always rests on real-time work, and emerges from localized processes of negotiations and pre-existing institutional, infrastructural, and material relations." That is, an artifact such as a protocol, technology, or work infrastructure only becomes universal if it is successfully taken up by workers through local practices in multiple distributed work systems. We appropriate the notion of *local universality* but apply it to describe an *informal practice* rather than a *formal artifact.*

Informal documentation is not generally considered as an essential component of medical practice, as evidenced by the fact that designers of EMR systems do not include features to support informal documentation. Furthermore, administrators sometimes remove informal documentation artifacts (such as the worksheets of L&D nurses) from the work system without considering the impact this may have on medical personnel. In fact, our study shows the use of informal documentation is universal in both the ED and L&D departments, but the particular deployment of informal documentation varies depending on local contexts. The study uncovers that there are some striking similarities in informal documentation usage in both units even though the systems of work are quite different. We saw that clinicians in each department used informal documentation commonly for memory work, abstraction work, and future work. In each department, the informal documentation serves as an aid to the eyes, brain, and memory for providers to process, organize, and store the information necessary for patient care. This finding could help us understand the role of informal documentation in healthcare work systems in general, suggesting that informal documentation is fundamental to medical work.

However, discussing the use of informal documentation in general terms overlooks the multiplicity and complexity of informal documentation practices that occur in local departments. Although all departments come together in the service of the over-arching goal of providing high-quality patient care under the umbrella of a single hospital, each medical department in the hospital differs fundamentally from others since each has different medical specialties with very different functions [22]. This difference is evident in the description of work at our field site; informal documentation occurs differently in different departments. The comparison of informal documentation practices in the two separate departments shows that unique configurations of goals, contents, displays, practices, and requirements shaped the particular use of informal documentation. Therefore, the use of EMR across a healthcare organization requires designers to pay attention to not only universal use but also local use of informal documentation in order to allow the design to be flexibly adapted in several distributed localities.

Designers often focus on *artifacts* rather than *routines* - the patterns of action through which work is actually accomplished [28]. For example, when the new EMR system was deployed, although it was designed to produce clear and complete patient records as a documentation tool (*artifact*), it did not allow L&D nurses to print out worksheets which contain orders to mediate the actual work process (*routines*). So the L&D nurses developed a new routine for obtaining a suitable artifact and creating a new worksheet. Therefore, the development of local routines is a source that ensures adaptability [26] and ongoing flexibility during and after the implementation of EMR systems, to fill the gap that EMR designs inevitably leave between localized user needs and the universally designed infrastructure.

Additionally, administrators often do not consider informal documentation practice as a crucial tool for medical and nursing work. The existence of several different interests at work in hospitals affects the ways that various individuals make use of the EMR system and must be taken into account when designing and redesigning the system. While clinicians working at the bedside may have a primarily work-based interest in EMR, administrators use EMR principally as an accounting and auditing system. In contrast to clinicians, who might favor an informal system coexisting with the EMR system, administrators might resist such a system since it works against the principles of accountability and audit (and hence the way that services are priced and billed). Thus, informal documentation has often been given a negative connotation [2, 6] at the level of administration and management. However, we find that informal documentation is a crucial nexus between universal and local infrastructures. It serves critical informal functions – such as for memory, abstraction, and future work – in clinicians' documentation work, even though these functions may not be immediately pertinent to administrators and managers.

Exerting Local Control

It is well-accepted in the HCI community that design should include participation and input from the end users of a system. The design of EMR systems is no exception. The EMR at our field site was implemented only after years of system testing and extensive training of all clinicians and staff. However, as noted earlier, designers of systems intended to serve as work infrastructures are never able to anticipate all of the problems that may arise. Also, users find it impossible to anticipate all of their needs and concerns until they are actually using a system [26, 30]. Systems need to be modified by users on an ongoing basis in response to changing circumstances and the specifics of a particular situation. When the hospital work system was paper-based, it was relatively easy for clinicians and staff to make modifications on an as-needed basis. Clinicians could cross out sections of forms or write things in at their discretion. If a form became obsolete, it could be discontinued without hassle; if the need for new information arose, the department could develop a new form and have it approved by a hospital committee. Of course, the EMR can be manipulated by clinicians in an informal way such as copying, pasting, and using comment boxes to type free information. However, it is difficult for local users to make fundamental changes to their work system. Although paper-based documentation systems do not confer the same benefits as EMR for standardized workflow across departments (and, in the case of larger systems, across multiple hospitals), they are more malleable for clinicians and staff.

Additionally, EMRs introduce a level of oversight to which clinicians are unaccustomed. Through the use of warnings and restrictions, EMRs can exert pressure on users to follow certain protocols or procedures for carrying out tasks that clinicians previously were able to articulate using any number of different iterations. Finally, users often feel that EMRs are not flexible enough to allow them to control their own workflow – a flexibility that is needed to enable clinicians to accommodate the typical day-to-day variations and oddities that arise in the course of work in an organization where disruptions are constant. The design of EMRs thus exerts greater control over the actual actions that clinicians and staff engage in on a day-to-day basis, and the loss of flexibility and control over how to engage in clerical procedures can hamper medical practice [7,20, 38].

For this reason, Berg [6] argues that it is essential for EMR implementation to be top-down, yet still provide space for users to develop some control over the system. This brings up a secondary finding about informal documentation: we argue that informal documentation practices, in addition to serving several key work functions, also promote clinicians' control over local work systems. Informal documentation practices that emerged in both ED and L&D units allow clinicians to have more control over their documentation work, particularly for coordinating tasks. For example, when an ED doctor uses EMR to check lab results for a patient, she has to look at the list of all patients and go through each different lab result page. Doing so forces doctors to spend time going through several different results to locate the specific information they need. Unlike the formal EMR documentation practices, informal documentation made it possible for doctors to control how and when they would complete documentation work and to maintain their local coordination by requiring less rigid procedures or protocols.

Although retaining flexibility in documentation may be contrary to hospital procedures of governing the documentation of work, this flexibility means doctors can be actively involved and have more control over what happens in the patient care process, which is one of the main goals of patient care. Therefore, EMR systems should have the ability to be locally controlled and should respect local users' needs, activities, and work processes.

Re-thinking and Supporting Informal Documentation

Although creating a "paperless" system was a goal of EMR implementation in general, we found that clinicians in both the ED and L&D departments continued to use paper-based informal documentation practices (e.g., blank papers, printouts from the system). This finding is consistent with past research on "paper persistence" in hospital work systems. However, we assert that paper persistence is evidence of the crucial function of informal documentation, which is often performed using paper artifacts. Our findings suggest that rather than problematizing paper persistence or accepting it as inevitable, we should focus on the function of informal documentation and find artifacts that afford this practice.

At present, the EMR does not provide tools that clinicians can use to develop artifacts for informal documentation, such as the L&D nurses' worksheet. The worksheet, in turn, indicates a lack of capability for the EMR to support short-term information use (the type of information usually recorded on paper working documents), which facilitates complex patient care work [9, 20]. The EMR system's current design largely leaves it up to the individual clinician to decide if and how to record this temporal and transient yet critical information. Thus, clinicians have found that personal notes compensate for the inadequacies of EMR design. Moreover, the use of personal notes reflects clinicians' fundamental work practices and leads us to reconsider the goal of EMR systems. Should EMRs be designed to store permanent records only, or should it also be used as a site to mediate the actual work practices in each individual department?

Most policy makers accept the usefulness of EMR systems given that they serve crucial administrative functions, principle among them being the reduction of the hospital's liability for medical personnel who fail to follow best practices, evidence-based care trajectories, standardizing workflows, or other administrative requirements. However, the system's design misses some important functions of the day-to-day practice of medical care, as we have shown. For this reason, the underlying conflict resides in the contradiction between the *exclusively formal documentation* in the EMR, which is characterized by archiving information for later auditing, and *short-term informal documentation*, which supports the temporal and emergent needs of practice. Therefore, we assert that the presence of paper is not an adequate measure of the success of an EMR. Instead, EMR designs should successfully support the transitory functions of informal documentation, not simply support its material medium of paper.

DESIGN OPPORTUNITES

Through the analysis of the ED and L&D documentation practices after EMR deployment, our study demonstrates that informal documentation is not a troublesome vestige of old paper-based systems but rather an essential component of medical work. We find that the tools provided by the EMR often leave gaps that can only be filled by informal documentation practices as these practices have developed and spread into wide usage in each unit. Informal documentation practices take slightly different forms in the two units but bear surprising similarities, indicating that hospital workers use informal documentation to fill several universal needs, regardless of the department in which work is occurring. Furthermore, EMR implementation can exacerbate, rather than ameliorate, the need for informal documentation by creating new needs for memory, abstraction, and future work.

Currently, EMR systems are designed primarily with formal documentation in mind. We suggest EMR designers should consider and design for informal documentation practices through either digital or paper-based artifacts. Moreover, the design of informal documentation artifacts must afford flexible localization. For example, the EMR could give clinicians the ability to create customizable documentation artifacts to support their needs for abstraction and trajectory work in each unique unit. Each clinician could easily generate their own form of informal documentation media with whatever information they need to suit the needs of both system and management levels.

On the system-level, for example, ED doctors could create tailored, individualized forms that include only abstracted information they need, such as each patient's bed number, age, chief complaints, and key lab results. Alternatively, they could integrate tasks across multiple patients into a single timeline on the form. Just as with a doctor's personal notes, such forms could be printed and carried around. By collecting and organizing key pieces of information as needed throughout the care process, ED doctors could better oversee patients' progress and outline their future care trajectory. These artifacts would be created and used at the discretion of each individual. Thus, providing affordances for informal documentation artifacts in system design would allow local departments and individual users with different roles to customize the universal infrastructure to their own work practices.

At the management-level, managers and administrators should be aware that informal documentation is important to successful work practice and that informal documentation practices may be altered during or after EMR implementation. Managers should find ways to support informal documentation in clinicians' work. For instance, administrators should accommodate informal practices that are essential and universal to every local department. It is also necessary to acknowledge the different needs among administrators and clinicians, and to make those needs evident to each other, such as through forming workgroups. In addition, managers and administrators should recognize the need for a support local infrastructure, such as the need for medical workers to have customizable paper artifacts that are discarded and not maintained as part of the archived medical record. For example, they could examine personal note usage in ED doctors' work and make suggestions to use a better format (e.g. triage copies as personal notes) to better support their documenting process, so that doctors can use the basic information directly off triage copies without spending time writing this information onto their own notes every time.

Additionally, digital mobile artifacts could be developed to mediate various informal documentation practices.

Although the use of mobile technologies has been widely noted in facilitating health practices, these technologies need to provide affordances that are not available in existing mobile technologies. Our findings suggest that simply installing EMR systems on mobile platforms may not rule out paper usages, because what led to the use of paper notes, as we have discovered in our study, are not merely for being mobile. Instead, it is largely because the EMR design does not support informal documentation practices or afford informal documentation to the same degree that paper artifacts do, and that leads to the continuing use of paper. Digital artifacts to support informal documentation practice must provide the same affordances that paper-based artifacts do, including malleability, portability, and accessibility, and above all *delete-ability*. These characteristics promote successful informal documentation practices described above, and allow these practices to meet the demands of the specific contexts in which they are deployed. The attribute of delete-ability is echoed in prior design implications that concerned loss of hidden and psycho-social information emerged from the use of a formal system [16, 38]. It is worth mentioning that there may be political barriers to successfully implementing such artifacts. Increased oversight and precise specification of work practices are a hallmark of medical organizations at present [36]. Supporting informal documentation would require a recognition that in order for work to be effectively coordinated, some parts of the medical record may need to remain invisible to the eye of the organization. Thus, digital mobile artifacts must be designed for clinicians' working-in-use and not serve a second function as an artifact-for-accountability.

CONCLUSION

Through our analysis of informal documentation practices in ED and L&D after EMR deployment, we assert that informal documentation practices arise in response to universal needs for conducting memory, abstraction, and future work in heterogeneous healthcare contexts. Further, although informal documentation practice exhibits many stable characteristics, these practices take different forms depending on the local work processes, requirements, and resources present in each unique department. Informal documentation practices are an undervalued yet crucial part of hospital work systems and also a key site at which local users are able to take a measure of control of formal documentation work systems and adapt a hospital-wide infrastructure to local systems of work. Successful deployment of EMR across a healthcare organization requires designers to pay attention to support the crucial functions of informal documentation practices that allow clinical users to conduct memory, abstraction, and future work.

REFERENCES

1. Armijo, D., McDonnell, C., Werner, K. Electronic Health Record Usability: Evaluation and Use Case Framework. Rockville, (October 2009), *MD: Agency for Healthcare Research and Quality.*
2. Ash, J. S., Berg, M., Coiera, E. Some Unintended Consequences of Information Technology in Health care. *JAMIA,* 11(2), 104-112.
3. Balka, E., Bjorn, P. and Wagner, I. Steps toward a typology for health informatics. *Proc. CSCW 2008,* ACM Press (2008), 515-524.
4. Bardram, J. E., Bossen, C. Mobility Work: the Spatial Dimension of Collaboration at a Hospital. *Computer Supported Cooperative Work*, 14(2), 131-160.
5. Berg, M., Bowker, G. The Multiple Bodies of the Medical Record: toward a Sociology of an Artifact. *The Sociological Quarterly*, (1997). 38(3), 513-537.
6. Berg, M. Implementing Information Systems in Health Care Organizations: Myths and Challenges. *International Journal of Medical Informatics,* 64, 2-3 (2001), 143-156.
7. Boonstra, A., and Broekhuis, M. Barriers to the acceptance of electronic medical records by physicians from systematic review to taxonomy and interventions. BMC Health Services Research, 10, (2010), 231.
8. Campbell E. M., Sittig D.F., Ash J.S. Types of Unintended Consequences Related to Computerized Provider Order Entry. *J Am Med Inform Assoc.* 2006;13(5):547–556.
9. Chen, Y. Documenting Transitional Information in EMR. In *Proc. CHI 2010,* ACM Press (2010), 1787-1796.
10. Corbin, J., Strauss, A. Basics of Qualitative Research: Techniques and Procedures for Developing Grounded Theory. (2008). Los Angeles: Sage.
11. Cyert, R.M., March, J.G. A Behavioral Theory of the Firm. *Prentice-Hall*, Englewood Cliffs, NJ, USA, 1963.
12. Dykstra, R.H., Ash, J.S., Campbell, E., Sittig, D.F., Guappone, K., Carpenter, J., Richardson, J., Wright, A., McMullen, C., Persistent Paper: the Myth of Going Paperless, *in: AMIA Annual Symposium Proceedings*, 2009, pp. 158–162.
13. Embi, P.J., Yackel, T.R., Logan, J.R., Bowen, J.L., Cooney, T.G., Gorman, P.N. Impacts of Computerized Physician Documentation in a Teaching Hospital: Perceptions of Faculty and Resident Physicians, *Journal of American Medical Informatics Association* 11 (2004) 300–309.
14. Feldman, M., Pentland, B. Reconceptualizing Organizational Routines as a Source of Flexibility and Change. *Administrative Science Quarterly* (2003). 48(1), 94-118.
15. Fitzpatrick, G. Integrated Care and the Working Record. *Health Informatics Journal* 10 (2004) 291–302.
16. Hardey, M., Payne, S., and Coleman, P. (2000). 'Scraps': Hidden nursing information and its influence on the delivery of care. Journal of Advanced Nursing, 32(1), p.208-214.
17. Harrison, M.I., Koppel, R., and Bar-Lev, S. Unintended Consequences of Information Technologies in Health

Care—An Interactive Sociotechnical Analysis. *JAMIA, 14, 5* (2007), 542-549.

18. Heath, C., Luff, P. Documents and Professional Practice: 'Bad' Organizational Reasons for 'Good' Clinical Records. In *Proc. CSCW 1996*, ACM Press (1996), 354- 363.
19. Han, Y.Y., Carcillo, J.A., Venkataraman, S.T., Clark, R.S.B., Watson, S., Nguyen, T.C., Bayir, H., Orr, R.A. Unexpected Increased Mortality after Implementation of a Commercially Sold Computerized Physician Order Entry System. *Pediatrics* 116 (2005), 1506 –1512.
20. Hardstone, G., Hartswood, M., Procter, R., Slack, R., Voss, A., Rees, G. Supporting Informality: Team Working and Integrated Care Records. In *Proc. CSCW 2004*, ACM Press, 142- 151.
21. Hartswood, M., Procter, R., Rouncefield, M., Slack, R. (2003). Making a Case in Medical Work: Implications for the Electronic Medical Record. *Computer Supported Cooperative Work*, 12(3), 241-266.
22. Hayes, G., Lee, C., Dourish, P. Organizational routines, innovation, and flexibility: The application of narrative networks to dynamic workflow. *International Journal of Medical Informatics,* (2011). 80(8), 161-177.
23. Hersh, W.R. The Electronic Medical Record: Promises and Problems. *Journal of the American Society for Information Science,* 46, 10 (1999), 772-776.
24. Hillestead, R. et al. Can Electronic Medical Record Systems Transform Health Care? Potential Health Benefits, Savings, And Costs. Health Affairs, 24, (2005), 1103-1117.
25. Klein, H., Myers, M. A set of principles for conducting and evaluating interpretive field studies in information systems. *MIS Quarterly,* (1999). 23(1), 67–93.
26. Park, S.Y. and Chen, Y. Adaptation as Design: Learning from an EMR deployment Study. In *Proc. CHI 2012,* ACM Press, 2097-2106.
27. Park, S.Y., Lee, S.Y., Chen, Y. The Effects of EMR Deployment on Doctors' Work Practices: A qualitative Study in the Emergency Department of a Teaching Hospital, *International Journal of Medical Informatics*, Vol 81, Issue 3 (2012), 204-217.
28. Pentland, B., and Feldman, M. Designing routines: On the folly of designing artifacts, while hoping for patterns of action. *Information & Organization, 18* (2008), 235-250.
29. Pine, K.P. Fragmentation and Choreography: Caring for a Patient and a Chart during Childbirth. In *Proc. CSCW 2012*, ACM Press, 887- 896.
30. Pipek, V., and Wulf, V. Infrastructuring: Toward an Integrated Perspective on the Design and Use of Information Technology. *JAIS, 10, 6* (2009), 447-473.
31. Poissant, L., Pereira, J., Tamblyn, R., Kawasumi, Y. The Impact of Electronic Health Records on Time Efficiency of Physicians and Nurses: A Systematic Review. *J Am Med Inform Assoc,* 12 (2005), 505-516.
32. Reddy, M. 2002. A Finger on the pulse. Temporal Rhythms and Information Seeking in Medical Work. *In Proc. CSCW'08*, 344-353.
33. Steinbrook, R. Health Care and the American Recovery and Reinvestment Act. *New England Journal of Medicine, 360* (2009), 1057-1060.
34. Strauss, A., Fagerhaugh, S., Suczek, B., Wiener, C. The Social Organization of Medical Work. *Chicago: The University of Chicago Press.* (1997).
35. Timmermans, S., Berg, M. Standardization in Action: Achieving Local Universality through Medical Protocols. *Social Studies of Science, 27(2) (1997), 273-305.*
36. Timmermans, S., Berg, M. The Gold Standard: The Challenge of Evidence Based Medicine and Standardization in Health Care. *Philadelphia: Temple University Press (2003).*
37. Wilcox, L., Lu, J., Lai, J., Feiner, S., Jordan, D. Physician-driven Management of Patient Progress Notes in an Intensive Care Unit. In *Proc. CHI 2010,* ACM Press, 1879-1888.
38. Zhou, X., Ackerman, M.S., and Zheng, K. (2009) I just don't know why it's gone: Maintaining Informal Information Use in Inpatient Care. . In *Proc. CHI 2009,* ACM Press, 2061-2070.

Re-Coordinating Activities: An Investigation of Articulation Work In Patient Transfers

Joanna Abraham
The New York Academy of Medicine
1216 5th Avenue, New York, NY
jabraham@nyam.org

Madhu C. Reddy
The Pennsylvania State University
University Park, PA
mreddy@ist.psu.edu

ABSTRACT
The coordination of distributed activities is central to organizational work. The effective functioning of organizations hinges on their ability to manage interdependencies both within (intra-) and between (inter-) various departments. However, more than just the management of these individual interdependencies is required for smooth work system coordination. Organizations must also manage the interactions between intra- and inter-departmental activities. To investigate how these interactions manifest in organizational work, we conducted a field study examining patient transfer process. We highlight the *cross-boundary breakdowns* that occur when intra-departmental and inter-departmental activities related to patient transfers negatively affect each other. We then describe the *re-coordinating activities* performed to mitigate the effects of cross-boundary breakdowns. We discuss a framework of inter-departmental coordination work that describes the relationship between cross-boundary breakdowns and re-coordinating activities. Furthermore, we classify the re-coordinating activities as a type of articulation work performed by hospital staff. This research can help us develop empirically-driven and theoretically-based design guidelines for coordination tools to maintain overall organizational workflow by balancing the goals and requirements of the various departments.

Author Keywords
Coordination; articulation work; hospitals; patient transfers

ACM Classification Keywords
H.5.3 [Group and Organization Interfaces]: Computer Supported Cooperative Work; J.3 [Life and Medical Sciences]: Medical Information Systems

INTRODUCTION
Organizational work is characterized by interactions between individuals and teams within and across departments. Consequently, the seamless coordination of organizational work requires intra- and inter-departmental activities to be synchronized in such a way that they do not have detrimental effect on each other [1], [2]. Effective coordination can lead to more streamlined work processes, higher productivity and effective resource management [3].

Within CSCW, there has been a great deal of attention paid to either coordination activities within departments (e.g., [4]) and between different departments (e.g., [5]). However, there have been fewer studies that discuss how intra- and inter-departmental activities are coordinated in order to ensure seamless organizational workflow.

We have been studying coordination practices both within and across departments in a large academic hospital [6]. A hospital is an excellent example of an organization that has to work around and deal with various types of coordination conflicts/breakdowns on a daily basis. We specifically investigated coordination activities involved in the *patient transfer process*. Patient transfer is an "invisible" yet critical and frequent hospital process that depends on collaboration among various departments. Consequently, the success of this process depends on the effective management of interdependencies that exist between intra- and inter-departmental activities. Below is a scenario that highlights the patient transfer of a trauma patient from the emergency department (ED) to the operation room (OR).

> The ED has reached its critical capacity of seventy one patients. The ED staff is overwhelmed with the constant influx of patients. During this chaos, a trauma patient is brought to the ED. The ED attending, based on his evaluation of the patient, decides that the patient needs to undergo a surgery sometime that day. After consulting with the OR attending (on OR schedule and staff availability), the patient is directly sent to the OR from the ED although the protocol requires transfer decisions to be mediated by the admissions department staff responsible for bed placement (from IPA (inpatient access department)).
>
> Later that evening, the IPA gets a phone call from the charge nurse of the OR requesting an ICU (intensive care unit) bed for the trauma patient. Since the admissions staff member is not notified of the prior transfer sequence of this patient, she has no updates regarding the status or the physical location of this patient. Because the hospital is at critical capacity, the admissions staff member is unable to immediately locate an available ICU bed for the patient.

This case highlights the coordination challenges that occurred when decisions made to facilitate one particular activity within a department negatively impacted other activities between departments. For instance,

- The ED staff failed to notify the admissions staff about the transfer (ED to OR) due to the chaotic and time-pressured nature of the ED environment. They decided to send the patient to OR to temporarily solve the crowding crisis within ED, thereby achieving the coordination of care and flow activities within ED at the expense of inter-departmental activities between OR and IPA.
- The lack of notification about the patient transfer from ED to OR (i.e. inter-departmental activities) affected the intra-departmental activities of IPA.

The consequences of such coordination breakdowns included the use of additional resources such as the time and effort required by the IPA staff (a) to switch patients around to find an appropriate bed, (b) to contact physicians in the ED and OR requesting them to enter admit and transfer orders of the ED trauma patient, (c) to cancel a hospital transfer of a patient who was pre-assigned the last ICU bed and (d) also trying to convince the PACU (post-anesthesia care unit) charge nurse to temporarily board an OR patient.

Through this study, we have started to develop a detailed understanding of the coordination challenges that occur in the patient transfer process when intra- and inter-departmental activities negatively affect each other – "*cross-boundary breakdowns*". Failure to address these conflicts and breakdowns can potentially result in increased errors, use of additional resources, higher coordination costs, and disruption of the overall hospital workflow.

In this paper, we highlight the cross-boundary breakdowns in patient transfers and also describe a certain type of activity performed by hospital staff to mitigate the consequences of these cross-boundary breakdowns, which we label as "*re-coordinating activities.*" We argue that these activities are a type of articulation work, a well-established concept in the CSCW domain. We also present a framework on inter-departmental coordination work that highlights the relationship between cross-boundary breakdowns and re-coordinating activities.

BACKGROUND

Coordination has been a prominent research topic in a variety of domains including maritime operations, software development [7], civil work [8], and healthcare [9]. Malone and Crowston [10] defined coordination as "the act of managing the interdependencies between activities to achieve a shared goal." Within CSCW, researchers have described how the presence of interdependencies highlights the need for coordination. While intra-departmental coordination studies focus on interdependencies of teams *within* a department [9, 11], inter-departmental coordination studies examine interdependencies of teams *between* different departments [5]. Most of these studies have examined how ineffective organizational work practices can result in coordination challenges. Researchers have described how some of the challenges are caused by the specialization and decomposition of activities [12, 13], while others arise due to the need to integrate and align various interdependencies to ensure shared goals [2, 10].

Within the healthcare domain, studies have focused on coordination of patient-care activities, both within [4] and between clinical departments [5]. There has been a particular emphasis on identification of coordination challenges related to information failures [6], process bottlenecks [14], and patient handoff communication problems [15] that can result in medical errors and poor quality of care. During an investigation of the coordination activities in a surgical intensive care unit (SICU), Bardram [9] found that temporal constraints such as changes to operation schedules and schedule of surgeons, use of artifacts within a particular time frame influenced the coordination of care among the surgical team members. Similarly, Symon et al. [5] examined the use of a "radiological request form" to schedule radiology examinations between several departments and found it to be an ineffective coordination tool because of the limited information contained in the form. Furthermore, they highlighted that factors such as status influences, social and political uses of information, conflicts between goals and between motivations for coordinating activities and the role of formal and informal work practices had a detrimental impact on inter-departmental coordination.

However, only a few researchers have examined the coordination breakdowns that occur when intra- and inter-departmental activities negatively affect each other and their consequences on continuity of patient care [5], [9].

Role of Articulation Work in Ensuring Effective Coordination

The concept of articulation work [16, 17] focuses on maintaining the continuity of distributed activities and hence is an integral part of organizational work. The concept was first formulated by Strauss [17] to understand how actors cooperate to complete their work. He defined articulation work as the "specifics of putting together tasks, task sequences, task clusters – even aligning larger units such as lines of work and subprojects in the service of the work flow" [16].

Articulation work has been presented as an analytical framework to understand interdependencies between collaborating actors and to overcome coordination challenges [18]. Researchers have interpreted this particular coordination concept in different ways. For example, articulation work has been analyzed as "the coordination of lines of work" [18]. Although Strauss' definition for articulation work remains an overarching concept, different researchers have refined articulation work to explore specific aspects of work. For example, the concept has been described as the work that "gets things back on track in face of unexpected contingencies" [19] and also the "work that enables other work." Despite these different interpretations, the common thread central to articulation work is that it involves some kind of "additional work" to ensure the continuity of work.

To gain deeper insights on the role of articulation work in hospital coordination, we examined various healthcare studies related to articulation work. Articulation work has primarily been used to understand and analyze coordination activities in hospitals including critical work-arounds performed by patient care teams to maintain the continuity of clinical work [20, 21]. For instance, Bossen et al. [22] investigated the use of shared interactive displays in supporting coordination of teams in a surgical ward. They highlighted several features of the display (AwareMedia) such as on-line, updated surgery schedules, video-feeds, RFID (radio-frequency identification) tags, chat and mobile phone capabilities that improved context-awareness among the surgical team members and also reduced the amount of articulation work that is caused by the need to align different work trajectories in distributed collaboration. In another study, Faergemann et al. [21] examined the role of articulation work in supporting collaboration of activities of heterogeneous teams belonging to different units. They argued that such an articulation work exhibits a dual nature where articulation work to support cooperative work needs to be done at a local level (i.e. within local work arrangements) and at a global level (i.e. between the different local work arrangements). Although this highlights the duality in articulation work, it does not fully examine the interactions related to it. Most studies fail to highlight the nature and specific characteristics of articulation work needed to manage the consequences of the coordination challenges that arise when intra- and inter-departmental activities negatively affect each other.

To address this, we conducted a year-long qualitative research study at a major academic hospital in northeast United States. Our goals were to (1) identify *cross-boundary breakdowns* in patient transfers and evaluate their impact on hospital coordination goals, (2) examine *re-coordinating activities* in patient transfers and elucidating how and why they are a type of articulation work employed by organizational staff to alleviate the consequences of cross-boundary breakdowns.

STUDY SETTING AND METHODS

We examined the patient transfer process between two clinical departments (emergency department (ED) and neurosciences department (NSD)) and investigated the role of a non-clinical department (inpatient access department (IPA)) in managing these activities. The three departments were selected because of the large number of patient transfers that took place between the ED and NSD and the pivotal role played by IPA in facilitating these transfers (Table 1).

Roles	ED	NSD
Attending Physician	Primary physician assigned to ED patients. If she feels a patient is a potential hospital admission based on her assessment, she initiates the transfer process by contacting consulting physicians belonging to specialized services	Primary physician assigned to NSD patients
Staff Nurse	Primary nurse responsible for the care delivery of patient in the ED. Before transferring a patient to a hospital bed, the staff nurse gives patient report (summary of patient case) to the receiving department nurse accepting the patient	Primary nurse responsible for the care delivery of patient in the NSD. Before accepting a patient to the NSD, the staff nurse receives patient report (summary of patient case) from the sending department nurse
Charge Nurse	Head of the nursing staff and helps with the coordination of patient transfer activities	
Resident Physician	Physician in medical training who work under the supervision of the attending physicians	
Consulting Physician	Specialist who makes decision on whether to accept a patient to her service	

Table 1. Patient Transfer Team: Roles and Responsibilities

IPA: The IPA manages the coordination of patient admissions, discharges and transfers in the hospital. The main staff involved in patient transfer are the bed placement team which consists of non-clinical staff and an admit nurse. The non-clinical staff members ensure that beds are available for transfer patients and assign them to appropriate beds. The admit nurse helps the non-clinical staff understand the clinical needs of the patient. For example, when a non-clinical staff receives a bed request for a patient diagnosis that does not sound familiar, the nurse could explain the bed requirements of the patient based on the diagnosis. The bed placement team will be referred to as IPA in the rest of the paper.

ED: The ED is the primary gateway to the hospital. A large number of patients are admitted to the hospital via the ED, therefore it is referred to as the sending department in the patient transfer process. Patients are stabilized in the ED before they are transferred to the appropriate department where they can receive specialized care for their medical condition. The primary staff involved in patient transfer process included the charge nurse, staff nurses, attending physicians, resident physicians, and consulting physicians.

NSD: The NSD receives patients with nervous and neurological disorders from the ED and hence is referred to the receiving department. The NSD is divided into two units: the neurosciences intensive care unit (NSICU) and the neurosciences intermediate care unit (NSIMCU). The primary staff involved in patient transfer process included the charge nurse, staff nurses, the attending physician and a triage officer. The NSD staff members have similar patient transfer responsibilities as the ED staff except for one additional position in the NSD, the triage officer.

Technologies used in the Patient Transfer Process

The electronic medical record (EMR) and the bed board tracking systems were the two main technologies used in the patient transfer process.

Electronic Medical Record: The EMR is primarily used to support coordination of care activities within clinical departments. During the patient transfer process, the sending and receiving department nurses use the EMR to share patient information with each other. For example, when a patient is transferred from the ED to NSD, the ED nurse uses the EMR to provide a patient report to NSD nurse. The NSD nurse on the other hand, takes down meticulous notes from the patient's EMR onto her personal scrap paper before the patient arrives in the unit. The EMR is also used by the IPA to obtain patient admission, discharge and transfer orders entered by physicians.

Bed Board Tracking System: The bed board tracking system provides an instant snapshot of the status of beds in the hospital. It contains multiple columns, each column representing each department in the hospital. The system is primarily used by the IPA staff to assign and manage beds within the hospital. The CNs use it to identify clean and available beds in the hospital.

Data Collection and Analysis

We used multi-faceted *ethnographic methods* including general observations of departmental activities, shadowing of patient transfers, hospital staff interviews, artifact identification and collection to gain meaningful insights into the nuances and complexities of intra- and inter-departmental work practices especially with respect to patient transfers [23] (Table 2). In CSCW, these methods have been used to investigate the collaborative practices of work and the impact of technologies on work in these practices.

The first author *observed* 440 hours of work activities in the three departments over a period of twelve months. The observations provided a detailed understanding of the complex interactions of technical and organizational issues. During this time, she observed a total of 48 patient transfers. In addition to the general observations, she also *closely shadowed* 16 patient transfers between the ED and NSD. Shadowing the patient transfer process involved observing specific micro-level tasks (as they unfold in real time) of all participants involved in this process. A task template was used to record the common patterns during patient transfer activities including the current tasks performed, artifacts

Dpt.	Method	Participants		Time (hrs)
		No.	Type	
IPA	Observation	Varied among sessions	Bed placement staff and IPA manager	175
	Interviews	18	IPA staff, IPA manager and house managers	10
ED	Observation, Shadowing	Varied among sessions	Charge nurses, staff nurses, physicians, residents, consults, transport staff, emergency technicians, registration associates and patient advocates	155
	Interviews	29	Charge nurses, staff nurses, physicians, residents, consults and interim nurse manager	14.5
NSD	Observation, Shadowing	Varied among sessions	Charge nurses, staff nurses, physicians, transport staff, and unit secretaries	110
	Interviews	25	Charge nurses, staff nurses and unit secretaries	12.5

Table 2. Data Collection Activities

used, location, additional work, challenges faced during the activities including the current tasks performed, artifacts task execution, and work-arounds employed to alleviate some of these challenges. The first author also conducted 72 *formal interviews* with clinical and non-clinical staff from the various departments. Finally, *artifacts* used in the transfer process were identified and collected. The data collection and analysis was performed in an *iterative manner* where the data collection sessions were alternated with the analysis.

We followed the three steps (open, axial and selective coding) in the *grounded theory* approach [24] to code the collected data. We followed a "constant comparison" method where the codes were compared and grouped together based on their similarities and differences. We first did a line-by-line analysis of the data we collected on the patient transfer activities and labeled the various activities into general open codes. Some examples of open codes that were developed include information needs, coordination goals, role of artifacts, collaborators, various patient and information flows, examples of routine exceptions, information breakdowns, work-arounds to alleviate the coordination problems encountered. We then reanalyzed the data to examine the relationships between the open codes and developed core categories. Examples of axial codes include sequence of steps during patient transfer process, process interdependencies and their types etc. Finally, we integrated the core categories to describe the patient transfer process, the coordination challenges within and between departments and the re-coordinating activities in patient transfers. In the following section, we present the key findings identified using this analysis approach.

FINDINGS

The patient transfer process involved not only the physical movement of patients but also a transfer of their care services between the respective clinical departments. Consequently, care continuity was dependent upon the flow of right information between departments to ensure the availability of appropriate patient resources at these locations.

Description of Patient Transfer Process and Process Interdependencies

The main participants involved in the patient transfer process were the IPA department, and the sending and receiving clinical departments (i.e. ED and NSD respectively). Various patient transfer activities must be coordinated both within and between departments before the actual physical movement of the patient. These activities included finding a bed in the appropriate service, exchanging clinical information between the sending and receiving departments, arranging transport, and housekeeping services.

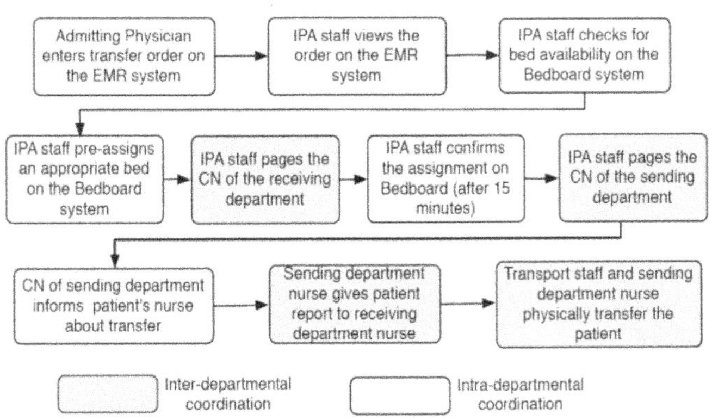

Figure 1. Patient Transfer Process

Figure 1 describes the roles of ED, NSD and IPA staff in patient transfer process. It highlights that coordination of both intra- and inter-departmental activities is crucial for a successful patient transfer. Furthermore, these coordination activities relied on effective collaboration and communication between clinical and non-clinical departments (e.g., for bed allocation), and between clinical departments (e.g., for information handoffs). Consequently, the patient transfer process comprised of a number of interdependencies that were required to be managed. Similar to interdependencies described in prior research [2, 25], we identified four prominent types of process interdependencies that need to be managed during patient transfers: information, task, role, and artifact.

Information interdependency occurred when the initiation of an activity in one department was dependent on the availability of information from another department. For example, IPA's ability to arrange a transfer from ED to NSD was dependent on receiving accurate and timely patient information from the ED and NSICU.

Task interdependency occurred when the initiation of an activity in one department depended on the completion of a particular task or set of tasks by another department. For example, the physical transfer of patient from ED to NSD required the NSD nurse to complete a set of tasks (or actions) such as taking patient report and setting up the room for receiving the patient.

Role interdependency occurred when one department's work activities depended on the specific role and responsibilities unique to a particular staff member belonging to another department. Unlike task interdependency, role interdependency required the tasks to be carried out by individuals with specific roles. For example, the transfer of a patient from the ED to a NSD bed depended on the NSD's CN's decision on whether she would accept the ED transfer or not.

Artifact interdependency was created when an activity in one department depended on an action (i.e. modification) being made on an artifact by another department. For example, the bed assignment activities of IPA department depended on physician orders documented into the EMR by the sending department. Although artifact interdependency may sound similar to information interdependency, it required the information to be recorded and archived on a *physical object* (i.e. artifact). Here, artifacts are viewed as tools that embody a whole history of social practices in their design and physical shape [26].

Although we have categorized the interdependencies into four types, they are not mutually exclusive of each other. For instance, information interdependencies occurred sometimes between individuals with defined roles (i.e. overlap with role interdependencies). However, the categorization of these interdependencies provided us with analytical insights into the inter-relationships and interactions that must be considered for ensuring a seamless patient transfer process. Such an identification of cross-departmental interdependencies is a crucial first step in understanding the patient transfer process because they can have an impact on how the departmental staff not only coordinate their intra- and inter-departmental activities but also how they work around and recover from coordination breakdowns.

Organizational Issues: Contributor to Ineffective Management of Interdependencies

We identified three organizational issues – competing goals, competing resources and competing teams that influenced the way in which these interdependencies in the patient transfer process were managed by hospital staff.

Competing Goals: Although the hospital shared a common objective of high quality patient care, the various individual departments were driven by their own functional goals and responsibilities. The smooth functioning of the organization required the proper management of the goals at local and global levels. Goals at the intra-departmental level were local goals of a specific department while goals at the inter-departmental level were global goals achieved by two or more departments coordinating with each other.

Coordination challenges in patient transfers occurred when the local intra-departmental goals of the different departments competed with the global inter-departmental goals between these departments. In other words, competing goals occur when the intra- and inter-departmental goals are achieved at the expense of each other. For example, to achieve PACU (post anesthesia care unit) patient flow goals, PACU attending physicians sometimes entered patient transfer orders for departments where beds are available even though their patients were not appropriate for the particular department. The competing goals of PACU, IPA and receiving departments had a detrimental effect on the way in which information interdependencies were managed. Consequently, this led to the lack of information sharing between the departments. Cross-boundary breakdowns occurred when the intra-departmental goals of the PACU are achieved at the expense of inter-departmental goals between the IPA and departments receiving inappropriate patient transfers. Although these cross-boundary breakdowns helped with the PACU activities, they affected the inter-departmental coordination of activities between the IPA and receiving departments.

Competing Resources: Hospital resources needed for patient care can be categorized into two main types: personnel (e.g., hospital staff) and non-personnel (e.g., hospital beds). Coordination challenges occurred when intra-departmental resources are managed by external staff members who achieved inter-departmental coordination at the expense of intra-departmental resources. These challenges were further exacerbated when the lack of critical resources such as staffed beds (i.e., beds that have staff nurses assigned to them) created competition among various clinical departments for their use. For example, the coordination challenges between ED and PACU occurred when they both tried to assign their patients to the first available private bed in the NSICU by convincing the IPA staff. The IPA staff decided to assign the ED patient to the NSICU bed because the ED had reached its surge capacity. However, cross-boundary breakdowns occurred when the intra-departmental activities of IPA affected the inter-departmental coordination activities between the IPA and PACU. The competition between ED and PACU for a NSICU bed affected the way the departments viewed and used the bed availability information on the Bedboard system.

The competing resources between the departments had a detrimental effect on the way in which artifact interdependencies were managed. Consequently, this led to the ineffective artifact use in patient transfers. This was because the departments vying for resources had complete knowledge about the available beds and allocation decisions. In the previous example, the PACU CN gets frustrated when she learns that the NSICU bed was assigned to the ED patient. This subsequently affected the coordination activities between the PACU and IPA. The PACU CN instead of waiting for the IPA staff to assign another NSICU bed when it becomes available bypassed the IPA staff and made use of the system information on bed board to transfer the PACU patient to an empty bed in the SICU. Although this transfer helped with patient flow in the PACU, it was done at the expense of SICU work activities because the PACU transfers an inappropriate post-op patient (who did not meet the care criteria) to the SICU.

Competing Teams: Coordination within and between diverse teams (e.g., clinical or non-clinical) is an important aspect of hospital work. Although it is important to ensure effective intra- and inter-departmental coordination, managing these functionally diverse teams belonging to different departments is problematic. Coordination challenges occur when intra- and inter-departmental coordination tasks of functionally diverse teams are achieved at the expense of each other. For example, to achieve rapid patient flow between the ED and OR during emergent situations, the clinical teams in these departments often fail to inform the IPA (i.e., a non-clinical team) about patient transfer to the OR. However, cross-boundary breakdowns occurred when inter-departmental coordination tasks between the ED and OR are achieved at the cost of the IPA intra-departmental tasks.

Furthermore, these clinical teams did not pay much attention to the non-clinical patient transfer activities because they did not understand the importance of non-clinical teams' work activities. Finally, the nature of professional hierarchies ingrained within clinical work practices influenced the way the diverse teams perceived and behaved towards each other. For example, some admitting physicians showed a negative attitude towards IPA staff when they questioned the appropriateness of physicians' transfer orders. This was because of the physician's perspective of their role in the patient transfer process. The house managers stated that: "There are physicians who don't like IPA staff question their orders." They also added: "The doctors need to realize that when IPA calls them, they are not questioning their intelligence, they are asking an intelligent question themselves: 'Is this what you really want for the patient?; 'Is it an appropriate place for the patient?'." The competing teams from the various departments had a detrimental effect on the way in which role and task interdependencies were managed.

Through our analysis, we identified how organizational issues led to the ineffective management of the various interdependencies, which consequently resulted in coordination challenges that led to *cross-boundary breakdowns*. These breakdowns are a unique type of coordination problem that occurred when intra- and inter-departmental activities negatively affected each other. In the following sub-section, using a single example case, we illustrate how ineffective management of task interdependencies in a particular activity such as the physician's order entry led to cross-boundary breakdowns in the overall patient transfer process.

Ineffective Management of Task Interdependencies: Contributor to Cross-boundary Breakdowns

Physician order entry refers to the physician's activity of entering instructions on the delivery of care for her patients. The EMR system allowed physicians to electronically enter orders and communicate their plan of care to other hospital staff. A typical transfer order contained the physician name, the sending and receiving locations, and service requirements that need to be considered for bed assignments. Although physician orders initiated the transfer process, the time of physician rounds influenced when the physician completed their transfer orders. Physicians often rounded, based on their individual work schedule (e.g., surgeries/scheduled procedures/clinic visits) for that particular day which contributed to bottlenecks in patient flow as illustrated by the scenario below.

> A NSIMCU patient who is ready to be discharged stays in the unit for a whole day without being discharged, waiting for physician to make his department rounds. The NSIMCU nurse commented that delays in getting the discharge orders entered into the system introduced "a time lapse there, where I could have moved this patient quicker." Another nurse noted that "Until physicians change orders, we can't do anything". Based on the pending discharge information of the patient received from the NSIMCU CN, an IPA staff already pre-assigns that particular bed for another scheduled surgery patient in the operating room (OR).

Delays caused by the time of rounds within the NSIMCU created a cross-boundary breakdown between the IPA and OR. The delayed rounds in the NSIMCU forced the IPA staff member to immediately find another appropriate bed to place the OR patient. Because of the unique requirements of the OR patient's condition, she was unable to assign the patient immediately to another bed. As a result, the patient transfer was delayed which created friction between the OR and IPA staff. The OR CN kept asking the IPA staff member to find another open bed and also informed her that the OR would not be able to hold the patient for more than an hour.

The challenge in managing interdependencies during the physician order entry task added to the complexity in the patient transfer process by contributing to cross-boundary breakdowns. In the following sub-section, we describe the consequences of such cross-boundary breakdowns in patient transfers process with respect to the delivery and continuity of patient care.

Consequences of Cross-boundary Breakdowns: Impact on Hospital Coordination Goals

The cross-boundary breakdowns had a detrimental impact on two primary coordination goals of the hospital - patient flow and patient co-localization.

Patient Flow: Patient flow refers to the movement of patients from one location to another in a health care facility. Cross-boundary breakdowns in the patient transfer process created bottlenecks in patient flow. Some of the immediate visible consequences included delays in admitting ED boarders (i.e. inpatients in the ED awaiting a hospital bed assignment) and lack of awareness of resource availability in departments. Over time, these bottlenecks in patient flow resulted in potential delays and cancellation of hospital transfers, duplication of unnecessary work, ED and PACU overcrowding, cancellation of surgeries, extended patient stay in inappropriate departments, increased costs and decreased hospital revenue and most importantly, provider and patient dissatisfaction with hospital management and services.

Patient Co-localization: Patient co-localization refers to assigning a patient to a bed within a department that can provide the appropriate service required for that patient. For instance, a patient with major heart problems should be transferred to the heart and vascular intensive care unit where the patient can receive appropriate attention from cardiology experts for his problem. Although co-localization of patients is important to achieve both patient safety and quality of care, cross-boundary breakdowns during patient transfers hampered the hospital's efforts of patient co-localization. The immediate visible consequence on patient co-localization was inappropriate bed assignments. Patients would be transferred to beds in non-suitable departments. This, in turn, led to increased risks of medical errors, duplication of similar services in different departments, and inefficient staff utilization and care provider frustrations.

The effects of cross-boundary breakdowns on these hospital coordination goals were present. Yet, despite these breakdowns, patient transfers were successfully accomplished everyday in the hospital. Very rarely did we witness a completely unsuccessful patient transfer due to these cross-boundary breakdowns. This raised the question of: *"how are staff members still able to successfully carry-out patient transfers despite the effects of cross-boundary breakdowns?"* In the next section, we describe how various departmental staff managed the cross-boundary breakdowns to maintain the continuity of patient transfer work.

Re-coordinating Activities in Patient Transfer

Hospital staff employed a set of activities to address cross-boundary breakdowns during patient transfers: (1) collaborative balancing of goals, (2) collaborative resource prioritization and (3) mediating role of integrators.

Collaborative Balancing of Goals: Goals are organizational benchmarks that have to be achieved during a particular process. For example, in the patient transfer process, the goal of sending department nurse is to give patient report to the receiving department nurse within 15 minutes from the time that the bed is assigned.

In the presence of a cross-boundary breakdown caused by competing goals, ad-hoc departmental bed meetings were held to evaluate the changes in the local departmental goals against the global goals of the hospital. For example, when inter-departmental activities between ED and IPA affected the intra-departmental activities of the NSICU, CNs from the concerned departments met with the IPA staff to discuss their respective departmental goals and their relative status on bed utilization and availability. Based on the CN's information on the status of the entire neuro-service, the staff from the different departments came to an understanding about how to manage their different goals. During this process, staff members often shared important information with each other. The collaborative balancing of goals allowed individuals representing different departments to jointly assess and evaluate their goals in order to not only identify the conflicting goals but also minimize their effect on each other's local activities and on global hospital goals of patient flow and co-localization.

Collaborative Resource Prioritization: Collaborative resource prioritization allowed individuals to jointly rank the available hospital resources in the order of increasing importance. While goal balancing focused on larger organizational needs, resource prioritization focused on specific resources needed to achieve these goals.

In the presence of a cross-boundary breakdown caused by competing resources, CNs from the particular departments whose resources were impacted by constant influx of new admissions, met with the IPA staff to evaluate their available departmental resources. During this meeting, they jointly formulated a strategy for admitting new patients and also the order of priority of boarded patients in other departments awaiting beds. In the patient transfer process, the collaborative resource prioritization discussion provided a common forum for different departments to discuss their patient care and transfer needs and resource priorities. This then allowed the various departments to jointly decide the priority (i.e. order) of patients that need to get resources. These emergent meetings were used as a venue to jointly map out and resolve issues related to personnel (e.g. nurse staffing ratios) and non-personnel resources (e.g. bed management) in the various clinical departments.

Mediating Role of Integrators: Individuals with integrator roles [27] were entrusted with the responsibility of managing coordination of hospital patient flow activities. The hospital had four individuals who were integrators in the patient flow initiative: a capacity officer, a house manager, an admit nurse and a triage officer. The capacity officer was a senior physician responsible for not only identifying but also moving patients who are assigned to inappropriate units in the hospital. The house manager was a nurse with hospital-wide duties such as planning overtime nurse-staffing ratios, convincing nurses to accept patients, and resolving conflicts between IPA staff and nurses regarding bed placement. The admit nurse in the IPA department screened patients by examining patient orders and clinical information in the EMR to ensure its appropriateness. Finally, the triage officer was a physician who screened and triaged patients belonging to a particular service/department.

Integrators took a reactive role in mitigating cross-boundary breakdowns caused by ineffective interactions of competing teams. They were contacted by the IPA staff when a cross-boundary breakdown occurred in patient transfers. Once they obtained the necessary information from the IPA staff on overall hospital bed status, and the issues of the departments involved in the cross-boundary breakdown, the integrators took immediate steps to resolve the cross-boundary breakdown. For instance, the capacity officer ensured that the various departmental CNs were making progress in their patient transfer activities by contacting them individually (either by phone or face to face) to seek more information on the status of their intra- and inter-departmental activities. This information helped them and the CNs to identify strategies to respond to the immediate patient transfer bottleneck (i.e. adding staff nurses, boarding patients in other units). Integrators particularly helped mitigate the coordination challenges related to status differences and power structures between the clinical and non-clinical departmental staff. They bridged some of the perceived perceptual and cultural gaps between staff that was caused by the differences in work orientations between the clinical (patient-oriented) and non-clinical (task-oriented) departments.

By analyzing these types of re-coordinating activities in the patient transfer process, we better understood the way staff in different departments "fix" coordination breakdowns at the boundaries.

DISCUSSION

Achieving seamless coordination and communication across a hospital is a complex activity [28]. In this section, we discuss three main aspects that can help us to re-conceptualize about inter-departmental coordination work. First, we present a framework that describes how cross-boundary breakdowns and re-coordinating activities manifest in organizational work. Second, we discuss how re-coordinating activities are a type of articulation work. Finally, implications to organizational practice are highlighted.

Inter-Departmental Coordination Work: A Descriptive Framework

A descriptive framework of inter-departmental coordination emphasizing aspects of cross-boundary breakdowns and re-coordinating activities and the relationship between them (Figure 2) was developed using a bottom-up, evidence-based approach. In addition to being descriptive, it provides a set of re-coordinating strategies and mechanisms to foster seamless inter-departmental workflow. The framework depicts the multiple levels that need to be considered in the process of inter-departmental coordination and illustrates the importance of balancing activities between local and global levels during organizational coordination.

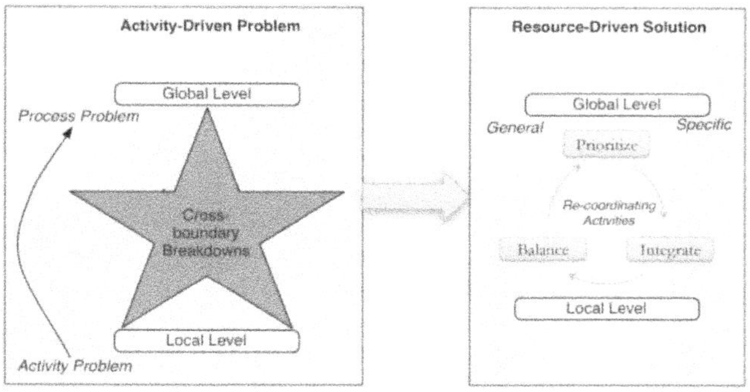

Figure 2. Inter-Departmental Coordination Framework

This framework comprises of two core aspects – cross-boundary breakdowns and re-coordinating activities (represented by blue squared boxes). Both these aspects of inter-departmental coordination process occur at the intersection of local and global levels of work.

Cross-boundary breakdowns occur when the interactions between local and global levels are not managed properly. For instance, departmental staff constantly transition between these levels to maintain effective intra- and inter-departmental workflows. The box representing the cross-boundary breakdowns highlights three main features of cross-boundary breakdowns that occur when intra- and inter-departmental coordination activities negatively affect each other.

First, the framework shows that cross-boundary breakdowns shift the focus of coordination problems from an activity problem at the intra-departmental level to a collaborative process problem at the inter-departmental level. Furthermore, cross-boundary breakdowns can be cumulative if they are not attended to in a timely manner. For instance, an intra-departmental activity of department 1 affects the inter-departmental activities between departments 2 and 3. The intra-departmental activities of department 2 can affect the inter-departmental activities between departments 4 and 5, which in turn can affect intra-departmental activities of 5, which in turn can affect the inter-departmental coordination activities between departments 5 and 6 and so forth.

Second, as we move from local to global levels of work, the degree of problem certainty increases while the functional similarity (in goals, resource needs and priorities, and teams) varies from high to low. Furthermore, these cross-boundary breakdowns occur when the degree of staff involvement with patient vary from high to low. At the local level, the degree of staff involvement in patient's treatment process is high when compared to the decreased involvement in patient's treatment process at the global level. For example, the ED staff pays more attention to the ED patient at the local departmental level. But, once she becomes an admitted inpatient (at the global level), the ED staff do not actively involve themselves in the patient's care process although the patient is still being boarded in the ED. This hampers the inter-departmental transfer and care activities such as quality of verbal patient report, the completeness of diagnostic procedures, monitoring of patients.

Finally, the cross-boundary breakdowns are caused by coordination challenges that are primarily activity-driven in nature. During patient transfer process, the inefficiencies in physician order entry process, the lack of information sharing, the ineffective interactions, and ineffectiveness of artifacts are all examples of patient transfer activity-driven problems.

Re-coordinating activities take a comprehensive approach (by evaluating all departmental activities) before resolving the conflict. The box representing the re-coordinating activities highlights two main features of re-coordinating activities.

First, re-coordinating activities occur at different levels of analysis ranging from general level (i.e. organizational) to specific (i.e. individual) level. For example, the collaborative balancing of goals takes place at a general level where the competing goals are being evaluated and balanced to ensure high-level organizational goals. The collaborative prioritization of resources takes place at a departmental level where the competing resources are being assessed and prioritized to ensure the departmental resources are optimally used. Finally, the integrators play an active role at a more specific level to ensure that individual patients' and staff concerns are being addressed in a timely manner. Since these activities are coupled with each other and therefore not mutually exclusive, there exists an overlap between them.

Second, despite these different levels of analysis, re-coordinating activities are always resource-driven. For example, the collaborative balancing of goals is driven by "how to get appropriate care for patients without overwhelming the staff?." The collaboratively prioritization of resources is driven by "how to get patients the right resources and move them to the right place at the right time?." The integrators resolve staff concerns such as identifying patient flow bottlenecks to minimize the number of ED and PACU boarders, and ascertaining the appropriateness of physician orders to ensure patient receives the appropriate care required.

Re-coordinating Patient Transfer: Articulation Work

We identified that hospital staff *re-coordinate* patient transfer activities to mitigate the coordination challenges that occur when intra- and inter-departmental activities conflict and interact with each other. This re-coordination involves additional work that is not part of formal hospital workflow but is performed in response to cross-boundary breakdowns. For example, collaborative prioritization of resources is the additional work performed by hospital staff to manage constrained resources in an optimal manner. This not only ensures that patients get the appropriate resources needed but also helps to maintain the continuity of patient services. Upon closer analysis, we identified these re-coordinating activities to be a type of articulation work that is focused on mitigating the effects of cross-boundary breakdowns in patient transfers. Below, we describe some critical characteristics that are common to different types of articulation work.

First, articulation work is invisible within formal models of work; similarly, the re-coordinating activities that address cross-boundary breakdowns are informal strategies used by departmental staff and hence are not formalized in the current hospital policies and protocols. For instance, the collaborative balancing of goals, collaborative prioritization of resources and integrator roles are informal strategies to overcome the breakdowns in coordination at the intersection of intra- and inter-departmental coordination activities.

Second, articulation work involves the coordination of tasks, goals, beliefs and standards; likewise, the re-coordination of patient transfers aim at fixing cross-boundary breakdowns that occur as a result of competing interdependencies (with respect to goals, resources and teams) at different levels of the organization.

Third, articulation work aims at a high-level end goal; similarly, the re-coordinating activities are performed to achieve a high-level goal. For example, although goals at the intra-departmental levels are different between different departments, during the collaborative balancing of goals activity, the various departmental staff work together to meet the hospital coordination goals of patient flow and co-localization. Next, we describe the fundamental types of articulation work and then show that these re-coordinating activities are a type of non-routine articulation work.

Categories of Articulation Work

Although the divisions between routine and non-routine work is often not clearly delineated, for analysis purposes, we used Hampson et al.'s [29] categorization in this paper. They mapped the basic types of articulation work into a four-cell matrix along four dimensions of routine/non-routine and invisible/visible work (Figure 3).

	Visible Work	Invisible Work
Routine Work	Cell 1 Planning, organizing, fitting, coordinating of work activities	Cell 2 Behind the scenes or work that is not part of the formal job description
Non-Routine Work	Cell 3 Explicit response mechanisms to get things back on track once unanticipated contingencies occur	Cell 4 Implicit response mechanisms to get things back on track once unanticipated contingencies occur

Figure 3. Fundamental categories of articulation work [29]

Routine work is part of the regular activities that are repeated daily. This type of work can either be visible based on the formalization of roles and services or invisible in the formalized model of work. Cell 1 consists of routine, visible work. Cell 2 consists of routine invisible work that is necessary to maintain the continuity of work. Cell 3 consists of explicit (or fully expressed) response mechanisms used to work around the non-routine contingencies that are internal to the formal workflow. Cell 4 consists of implicit (or unexpressed) response mechanisms that require actors to modify their actions and work around to accommodate unexpected contingencies that are external to the normal workflow. For example, internal contingencies are embedded in the work arrangements while external contingencies are caused by external factors such as technology, culture, and organization structure.

While cells 1 and 2 are straightforward mechanisms that focus on normal "routine activities" required to manage the continuity of work, cells 3 and 4 are informal mechanisms that focus on "response activities" to mitigate the problems resulting from unexpected contingencies in work. Re-coordinating activities fall within cell 4 of the matrix; as highlighted in the findings, they are a type of "non-routine" articulation work and are performed in response to cross-boundary breakdowns.

Non-Routine Articulation Work

We highlight the nature of this particular type of non-routine articulation work in patient transfers by examining some of its central characteristics.

First, articulation work done to re-coordinate patient transfers is performed only during instances of coordination breakdowns that are caused by unexpected problems occurring when intra- and inter-departmental activities conflict or compete with each other. Consequently, they can additionally be categorized as a type of lower-level articulation work performed to "get things back on track [19]." For instance, re-coordinating activities help to address the competition between goals, resources, and teams.

Second, articulation work done to re-coordinate patient transfers is performed for organizing and managing work activities that span multiple departments. In other words, they occur for alleviating challenges in managing interdependencies across multiple departments.

Third, articulation work in-patient transfers are dependent on identifying, assessing and ensuring that the needs and constraints of the different departments are taken into consideration during the joint decision-making process. Collaboration is a core requirement of this particular type of articulation work. In addition to the meshing of tasks and efforts, it requires that the needs and constraints of all the involved participants are taken into consideration.

Fourth, time-dependency is an important feature in re-coordination of patient transfer. Time was found to be an important factor in re-coordinating activities since these activities are always performed in response to a time-critical activity. For example, articulation work in patient transfers are focused on eliminating the delays in transferring a critical patient from the emergency department to intensive care unit that can have severe consequences on the health of the patient.

Finally, a fundamental feature underlying all these types of re-coordinating activities in organizations is that they involve an inherent management of resources. Cross-boundary breakdowns effects on inter-departmental workflows can be mitigated when the extra work performed is focused on managing resources (including personnel and non-personnel resources) in an optimal and effective manner at both local and global levels. For example in the case of patient transfers, re-coordinating activities ensure that rapid bed assignment goals can be met without compromising any individual department's resources. This is because unlike other types of articulation work, re-coordinating activities are focused on addressing the source of the breakdown in order to prevent future coordination breakdowns from happening.

Re-coordinating Activities: Implications to Practice

The investigation of the patient transfer process helps focus our attention on the significance of managing both intra- and inter-departmental workflows to understand articulation work in complex organizations (e.g., [30]). The concept of re-coordinating activities focuses on the importance of emphasizing and capturing a broader approach to articulation work in organizations. This broader approach relies on understanding the organizational setting and the relationships between humans, technologies and organizational structures such as policies [31]. It also highlights the need to support seamless collaboration between functionally diverse teams working together. The concerted effort involved in carrying out this type of articulation work helps to mitigate the challenges caused by these competing intra- and inter-departmental activities (e.g., activities with competing goals, competing resource needs and competing teams).

Many large-scale information systems have a set of assumptions about intra- and inter-departmental work practices such as work goals, teams, their rules of interaction, protocols that need to be followed and resources needed for particular activities. These systems often fail to account for the cross-boundary breakdowns discussed here. The concept of re-coordination not only orients us towards questioning design assumptions about intra- and inter-departmental work practices built into current organizational workflow systems, but also emphasizes that the effectiveness of articulation work across different organizational levels which depends on incorporating technological functionalities that can support effective intra- and inter-departmental coordination. Finally, this study highlights the importance of viewing articulation work from a socio-cognitive perspective of coordination behavior. The coordination challenges could be attributed to the social and cognitive aspects of team coordination practices. Social aspects of coordination behavior include coordination structures, policies, and protocols while cognitive aspects of coordination behavior focus on individual and team cognitive processes (such as collective expertise, team awareness, shared mental models, common ground and team cognition). Therefore, social and cognitive aspects of the various departmental teams and their effect on intra- and inter-departmental practices need to be evaluated when examining articulation work.

CONCLUSION

Organizations have to deal with a number of coordination challenges that occur on a variety of different levels ranging from a small team to the entire organization. Although CSCW researchers have focused a great deal of attention on intra- and inter-departmental activities and their respective coordination issues, there has not been significant focus on the investigation of what happens when these two different sets of activities negatively impact each other. Through our field study, we identified (a) a set of coordination challenges that occur when intra- and inter-departmental activities affect each other, which we refer to as cross-boundary breakdowns and (b) a type of non-routine articulation work that helps to mitigate cross-boundary breakdowns. The primary contribution of this research is conceptual in nature. By unpacking how people respond to cross-boundary breakdowns and their consequences, we can start to understand the complex nature of articulation work performed to re-coordinate activities necessary for ensuring smooth workflow in an organization. Building on this, researchers can also gain insights on the socio-technical issues that need to be considered when developing new or improving existing tools and technologies that can easily be integrated into the fabric of intra- and inter-departmental work practices.

ACKNOWLEDGMENTS

We want to thank the hospital staff for participating in the study. This research was supported in part by the College of IST's Tronzo Endowment for Medical Informatics.

REFERENCES

[1] Crowston, K. *A Coordination Theory Approach To Organizational Process Design*. Informs, City, 1997.

[2] Thompson, J. D. *Organizations In Action: Social Science Bases Of Administrative Theory*. Mcgraw-Hill, New York, 1967.

[3] Hee-Woong, K. *Modeling Inter- And Intra-Organizational Coordination In Electronic Commerce Deployments*. Kluwer Academic Publishers, City, 2001.

[4] Reddy, M. And Dourish, P. A Finger On The Pulse: Temporal Rhythms And Information Seeking In Medical Work. In *Proceedings Of The Proceedings Of The 2002 Acm Conference On Computer Supported Cooperative Work*

[5] Symon, G., Long, K. And Ellis, J. The Coordination Of Work Activities: Cooperation And Conflict In A Hospital Context. *Computer Supported Cooperative Work*, 11996), 1-31.

[6] Abraham, J. And Reddy, M. Moving Patients Around: A Field Study Of Coordination Between Clinical And Non-Clinical Staff In Hospitals. In *Proceedings Of The Acm 2008 Conference On Computer Supported Cooperative Work* (San Diego, Ca, Usa, 2008).

[7] Carstensen, P. H. And Nielsen, M. *Characterizing Modes Of Coordination: A Comparison Between Oral And Artifact Based Coordination*. Acm Press, 2001.

[8] Rogers, Y. Coordinating Computer-Mediated Work. *Computer Supported Cooperative Work (Cscw)*, 1, 4 1993), 295-315.

[9] Bardram, J. Temporal Coordination –On Time And Coordination Of Collaborative Activities At A Surgical Department. *Computer Supported Cooperative Work*, 9, 2 2000), 157-187.

[10] Malone, T. W. And Crowston, K. The Interdisciplinary Theory Of Coordination. *Acm Computing Surveys*, 26, 1 1994), 87-119.

[11] Mentzas, G. N. Team Coordination In Decision Support Projects. *European Journal Of Operational Research* 89 1996), 70-85.

[12] Heath, C. And Staudenmayer, N. *Coordination Neglect: How Lay Theories Of Organizing Complicate Coordination In Organizations*. Elsevier Science Inc., City, 2000.

[13] Lawrence, P. R. And Lorsch, J. W. *Organization And Environment*. Harvard Business Press, Boston, Ma, 1967.

[14] Brixey, J. J., Robinson, D. J., Tang, Z., Johnson, T. R., Turley, J. P. And Zhang, J. Interruptions In Workflow For Rns In A Level One Trauma Center. In *Proceedings Of The Amia Annual Symposium Proceeding* (2005).

[15] Dunn, M. J. G., Gwinnutt, C. L. And Gray, A. J. Critical Care In The Emergency Department: Patient Transfer. *Emerg Med J* 242007), 40-44.

[16] Strauss, A. Work And The Division Of Labor. *The Sociological Quarterly*, 26, 1 1985), 1-19.

[17] Strauss, A. The Articulation Of Project Work: An Organizational Process. *The Sociological Quarterly*, 29, 2 1988), 163-178.

[18] Strauss, A. *Continual Permutations Of Action* Aldine De Gruyter, 1993.

[19] Star, S. L. *The Sociology Of The Invisible: The Primacy Of Work In The Writings Of Anselm Strauss*. Aldine De Gruyter, City, 1991.

[20] Bossen, C. And Jensen, L. W. K. Implications Of Shared Interactive Displays For Work At A Surgery Ward: Coordination, Articulation Work And Context-Awareness. In *Proceedings Of The 2008 21st Ieee International Symposium On Computer-Based Medical Systems - Volume 00* (2008). Ieee Computer Society.

[21] Faergemann, L., Schilder-Knudsen, T. And Carstensen, P. H. The Dualistic Nature Of Articulation Work In Large Heterogeneous Settings - A Study In Healthcare. In *Proceedings Of The Proceedings Of The 9th European Conference On Computer Supported Cooperative Work* (Paris, 2005)

[22] Bossen, C. And Jensen, L. W. K. Implications Of Shared Interactive Displays For Work At A Surgery Ward: Coordination, Articulation Work And Context-Awareness. In *Proceedings Of The Proceedings Of The 2008 21st Ieee International Symposium On Computer-Based Medical Systems - Volume 00* (2008). Ieee Computer Society,

[23] Forsythe, D. *"It's Just A Matter Of Common Sense": Ethnography As Invisible Work*. City, 1999.

[24] Strauss, A. And Corbin, J. *Basics Of Qualitative Research*. Sage Publications, Thousands Oaks, Ca, 1998.

[25] Crowston, K. *A Taxonomy Of Organizational Dependencies And Coordination Mechanism*. Center For Coordination Science, Mit, 1994.

[26] Orlikowski, W. J. *Action And Artifact: The Structuring Of Technologies-In-Use*. Sloan School Of Management Working Paper, Cambridge, Ma, 1995.

[27] Brown, C. V. And Sambamurthy, V. *Linking Intra-Organizational Stakeholders ; Cio Perspectives On The Use Of Coordination Mechanisms*. Center For Information Systems Research, Sloan School Of Management, Massachusetts Institute Of Technology, City, 1998.

[28] Bardram, J. And Bossen, C. Mobility Work: The Spatial Dimension Of Collaboration At A Hospital. *Journal Of Cscw*, 142005), 131-160.

[29] Hampson, I. And Junor, A. Invisible Work, Invisible Skills: Interactive Customer Service As Articulation Work. *New Technology, Work And Employment*, 20, 2 2005), 166-181.

[30] Grinter, R. E. Supporting Articulation Work Using Software Configuration Management Systems. In *Proceedings Of The Comput. Supported Coop. Work* (1996),

[31] Zhang, J., Patel, V. L. And Johnson, T. R. Medical Error: Is The Solution Medical Or Cognitive? *Journal Of American Medical Informatics Association*, 9, 90061 (November 1, 2002 2002), S75-77.

Shared Decision Making Needs a Communication Record

Bridget Kane[*] †‡∗
NSEP, NTNU, Norway
†St. James's Hospital, Dublin
kaneb@tcd.ie

Pieter Toussaint
NSEP, NTNU∗
Trondheim, Norway
pietert@idi.ntnu.no

Saturnino Luz‡
‡Dept of Computer Science
Trinity College Dublin, Ireland
luzs@scss.tcd.ie

ABSTRACT
Increasing dependability in collaboration work among health professionals will directly improve patient outcomes, and reduce healthcare costs. Our research examines the development of a shared visual display to facilitate data entry and validation of an electronic record during multidisciplinary team meeting discussion, where specialists discuss patient symptoms, test results, and image findings. The problem of generating an electronic record for patient files that will serve as a record of collaboration, communication and a guide for later tasks is addressed through use of the shared visual display. Shortcomings in user-informed designed, structured data-entry screens became evident when in actual use. Time constraints prompt the synopsis of discussion in acronyms, free text, abbreviations, and the use of inferences. We demonstrate how common ground, team cohesiveness and the use of a shared visual display can improve dependability, but these factors can also provide a false sense of security and increase vulnerability in the patient management system.

Author Keywords
Large Shared Display; Data entry; Validation; Record-keeping; Teamwork; Collaboration

ACM Classification Keywords
H.5.3 Group and Organization Interfaces: Computer-supported cooperative work

INTRODUCTION

In this paper we describe a scenario where a multidisciplinary medical team (MDT) of clinical specialists meet to discuss their patient cases. They discuss each patient's clinical findings on examination, and review their radiological imaging and pathology results in the context of those clinical findings. The team agree a definitive diagnosis and a management plan for each patient. If information is incomplete, they will decide on further tests that may need to be performed before making their decision, or recommendation to the patient. This method of patient management, by an MDT, has become the standard of care for cancer patients in the UK, and in most European countries as well as Canada and Australia. Group decision-making in this clinical setting is considered superior to individual decision-making, because i) synchronous review of the results of independent diagnostic processes improves the diagnostic accuracy and overall reliability of the diagnostic process [31], ii) having all of the necessary specialists together is believed to improve the coordination of highly complex treatment protocols, and iii) peer review is conducted in this MDT process. The MDTM forum facilitates collaboration and knowledge is created through the interaction [17].

Communication failures are acknowledged as a leading root cause of medical error [18]. While effective teamwork is considered one of the ways to improve communication and reduce the number of errors, the majority of communication breakdowns occur in verbal communication when patients are being transferred among clinical staff [27]: a practice recognised as a frequent activity at meetings [21], a regular outcome of an MDT discussion, and an acknowledged challenge for researchers in this area [10, 27]. Moreover, inadequate medical record-keeping is known to threaten health care quality especially with respect to coordination and continuity of care, decision-making capacity and accountability [32].

In the context of an increasingly specialized healthcare system, and the development of electronic records and ICT tools, there are challenges posed in providing suitable technological support in this setting. CSCW has traditionally investigated the use of interactive tools that support collaboration, and interactive table tops and large screen displays are among those tools explored to support cooperative work. However in most of the workplace studies to date, the use of the shared display has been permanent and interactive [2, 37] rather than transient and non-interactive as in our setting. Furthermore, the function of the large displays investigated provide for *interaction* with them by the users. Frequently large displays are seen as tools to support awareness [2] and /or places where people might look for information, interaction is afforded, and people can leave notes for one another, for example. In contrast our study demonstrates the use of a transient, non-interactive, large display, the function of which is intended as an awareness mechanism that adds dependability to the worksystem. The work of building a shared meeting record is made visible, and team members have the opportunity to contribute, indirectly, to the product.

Although the essence of CSCW is described as addressing the *support requirements of cooperative work arrangements*

[*]Marie Curie (ERCIM) Fellow

[34], one of the less developed topics in supporting cooperative work is the production of records of the interactions, or of the communication and decision-making process. Records from MDT meetings serve to co-ordinate later work tasks, and provide a visible, persistent, account of shared information. Records also give testimony to collaboration among particular independent specialists, as well as providing a snapshot in time of a patient's health status.

The difference between the problems of these teams, and those issues addressed in other CSCW studies can be described as follows. i) The individual roles involved in these MDTs have a need to interact with one-another directly through talk. Technology is secondary in the setting, or a 'necessary evil', which facilitates communication (of radiological images, or videoconference, for example). ii) The team need access to a lot of information quickly. Discussion is fast-moving because of limited time. The team needs to have all of the information available on the patient that they are discussing, otherwise the patient will be adversely affected [12]. Although having the electronic patient record (EPR) provides reliability, it takes more time to query an electronic medical record than it takes to review a paper chart. iii) Information is generated in the setting that could be useful in several related processes, such as national repositories, or department of health statistics. iv) A subset of information generated at the meeting is required for the patient's 'chart' whether it is a paper or electronic record. v) Tasks are assigned within the MDT that need to be conducted once the meeting is concluded. vi) The team wants to know (eventually) that the task assigned was satisfactorily executed. In other words, we are not only concerned with the synchronous support for collaboration. We also need to take account of work tasks and processes before and after the meeting event. It is to these issues, but communication record-keeping in particular, that we address our study and our discussion.

Background

The team meetings that are the focus for this research have been observed over several years. At first, their role in medical education was quite prominent and MDTs tended to discuss a small number of 'interesting cases'. But over the past 10 years in particular, work practices have gradually changed and, like other hospitals, these meetings are now embedded in the routine work of the hospital. Since becoming a normal part of the work in managing patients, issues have arisen for which solutions have been sought. Some of the issues have been brought about by innovations and developments that have taken place independently of this MDT process. The developments that have had most impact, in our experience, are the implementation of an Electronic Patient Record (EPR) System in the hospital, the implementation of a Picture Archive and Communication System (PACS) for managing digital radiological images, and videoconferencing. Changes in recommended practice in radiation oncology, medical oncology and surgery are also impacting this work system. It is not uncommon for some cancers (depending on tumour type or anatomic location) to be treated though a complex protocol that involves these three specialities (surgery, radiation and medical oncology). Patients may receive treatments in sequence, or concurrently, or in some combination of sequences and concurrency. These complex protocols require high levels of collaboration and coordination in providing the necessary services (including diagnostic tests and monitoring) in a way that maximises the benefit of the improved treatments for the patient. When these systems that require high levels of collaboration and cooperation work well, they also deliver economic efficiencies in addition to patient benefits [15].

Examining how people work in multidisciplinary medical teams (MDTs), and how they address the problems they encounter, provides insight into collaborative work that can be applied in other non-medical work settings. The MDT forum is a valuable setting for research into problem-solving and decision-making as well as more general CSCW issues. Research themes around co-operation and co-ordination; roles and information; time, space and place; knowledge used and technology employed are all relevant to the CSCW community and can be applied to medical work and meetings [20]. Observing these work teams also gives us improved understanding of fundamental issues in modes of interpersonal communication, including speech, the use of multimedia and technology-mediated communication. Furthermore, CSCW has a unique contribution to make to medical teamwork. Indeed the grand challenge for CSCW to find ways of integrating the means to support informality into medical systems has already been posed [13]. Supporting collaboration, coordination and communication among health professionals will directly impact our health system by making it more dependable and improve peoples' lives.

METHODOLOGY

An ethomethodologically-informed ethnographic study was conducted with multidisciplinary medical teams (MDTs), and their meetings in particular, in a large tertiary-referral teaching hospital, (and designated cancer centre). The hospital ethics committee approved the study. Undertakings were given that patient privacy is respected and confidentiality is maintained in the data. Since work-processes are the object of our research, no individual patient data is gathered or used in this research. Our approach to this fieldwork conforms to the general position advocated by Randall [33] in that our aim is to achieve a deep understanding of the work, how workers communicate and share information in the course of their tasks, and how their role objectives are satisfied.

We have had the benefit of conducting a long-term ethnographic study at the teaching hospital for the past eight years. Over this period we have witnessed a number of user initiatives to address self-identified problems in their work practices, and we have also been able to observe the outcomes of those initiatives. Assessing support requirements has been one of our main objectives, and the problem of enhancing specialist collaboration within the constraints imposed by the busy hospital setting [23]. In our earlier work, record-keeping has been identified as a key concern of MDTs at this hospital [24], and it is in the context of the implementation of a record-keeping initiative that this study is undertaken.

As well as our knowledge from extensive observation of

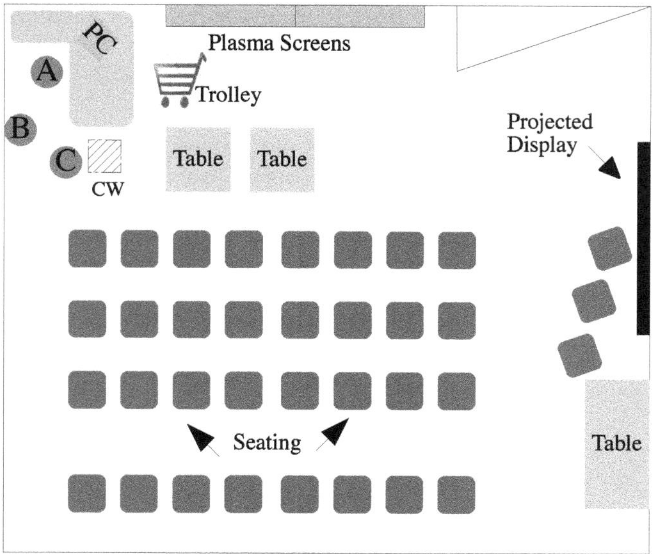

Figure 1. The layout of the meeting room. The Radiologist and Pathologist work from positions A and B. The person entering data works from station C.

MDT meetings of several MDTs, recent data for this paper were gathered through approximately 20 hours of focussed observation of the record-entry task at MDT meetings, with a single MDT. The focus is on the implementation of an initiative by the MDT to construct and validate a real-time record of the MDT discussion that is available in the patient's electronic record (EPR). Our ethnographic observations are supplemented with a survey and semi-structured recorded interviews with members from this particular MDT. By supplementing our ethnographic orientation with mixed data gathering methods (survey and interviews), we facilitate triangulation of our findings and a more robust analysis.

We confine ourselves in this paper to describing a particular initiative of one MDT, and refer to other teams' initiatives where relevant.

The MDT under particular study for this paper has approximately 30 members and comprises the following roles: surgeons, radiologists, pathologists, medical oncologists, radiation oncologists, nurses, physiotherapists, data manager, an MDT (clerical) co-ordinator and researchers. The MDT meets weekly to discuss their patients' management.

The primary objective of the survey we conducted was to help elicit user requirements for a meeting record and was distributed among all of the multidisciplinary teams in the hospital. A total of 190 responses were submitted, (of which 29 were returned from the MDT that implemented the meeting record reported here). Analysis of the 190 returns are used in compiling Tables 1 and 2. Additional analysis of the results from the MDT under study for this paper was performed separately. The results from the sample of 29 from this particular MDT followed the same general pattern and there were no significant differences to the overall result.

The semi-structured recorded interviews were conducted in follow-up to the questionnaire, with 11 members of the MDT. The 11 interviewees are made up of 4 consultant surgeons, one radiologist, two nurses, one data manager, one medical oncologist, one surgical registrar, and one radiation oncologist. Nine of the 11 interviewees from this MDT describe themselves as active vocal participants at meetings. Interviews lasted between 40 and 60 minutes, and 10 out of 11 were recorded (with participant's consent). Recordings were reviewed and annotated afterwards for salient findings.

Almost half (13, or 45%) of the MDT members in the MDT described are vocal participants at meetings. Only one-third of the MDT belong to this MDT alone. Most of the members of this MDT belong to at least two other MDTs in addition: two people are members of 5 MDTs. A single MDT is usually concerned with a single organ, biologic system, or set of diseases, for example a Breast MDT, or Lymphoma MDT. Each team will require radiologists, pathologists, medical and radiation oncologists too. These specialities tend to be highly specialised and contribute to several MDTs.

For one MDTM, one of us (BK) undertook to write (copy) simultaneously the written text being entered into the patient record and displayed on screen. The experience of this exercise is reported in the section titled 'The Data Entry Task'.

THE SETTING

The multidisciplinary team (MDT) has a co-located weekly meeting that normally lasts for approximately 1.75 hours. The room is configured in a theatre-style arrangement with two plasma screen displays in front that are used to display radiological images, and occasional pathology images. The meeting room layout is drawn in Figure 1, and the photograph in Figure 2 was taken from the front left quadrant of the room. The room was originally designed as a radiology seminar room and the workstation with PC, in the front left hand side of the room, is a radiologists workstation with high resolution displays. (See upper left hand corner of the diagram in Figure 1.) Two plasma screen displays at the front of the room are connected to this fixed workstation. An additional computer screen, from a computer-on-wheels (CW), is projected onto the right hand side-wall of the room using a ceiling-mounted projector. Figure 2 shows the radiologist seated at his workstation and the plasma screens with the relayed image (from workstation). The Specialist Registrar is entering data into the EPR using the mobile workstation. Figure 3 shows the projected image of the screen of the mobile workstation onto the side wall.

The radiologist normally sits on a stool at A in Figure 1 and the pathologist sits, or stands, nearby at location B in the Figure. The computer-on-wheels is positioned next to the radiologist's workstation, labelled CW in Figure 1, and shown in the photograph in Figure 2. Either an experienced nurse specialist, or surgical registrar occupies this position, C, and enters data in real time using the mobile workstation. The computer-on-wheels is connected to a ceiling mounted projector and the data entry screen is projected onto the right hand side wall of the room.

The MDT clerical co-ordinator transports paper charts for the patients to be discussed by the MDT in a trolley to the meet-

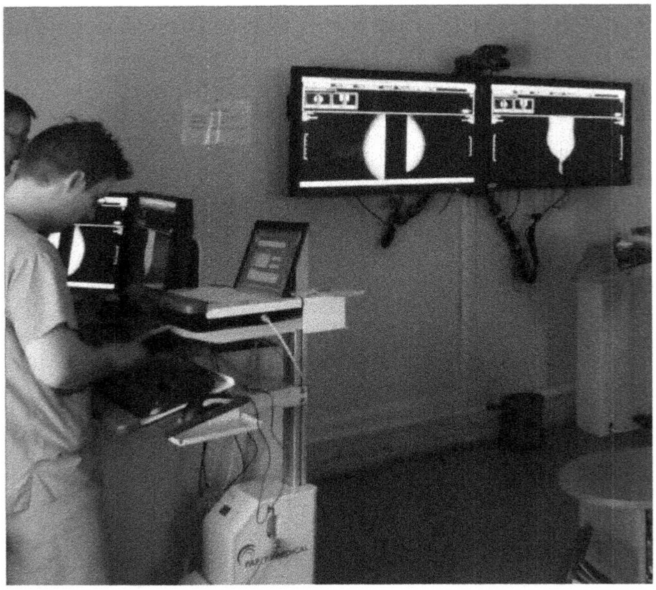

Figure 2. Radiologist talks at his workstation and the Senior Surgical Registrar enters data.

ing. The small tables in front are used to handle the charts, and facilitate consulting and probing the patient's record, during the discussion. Consultant surgeons sit nearest the tables and use the charts. The oncologists tend to sit towards the right of the group; pathologists and radiologists tend to sit to the left hand side. While the senior clinical staff tend to sit in the front row, nursing, physiotherapy and research staff sit towards the rere of the room according to a role hierarchy. The more senior nursing staff sit in the second row, and so on. The table at the back of the room is used for refreshments, and for display and dissemination of research reports, or articles of interest to the group, as well as the agenda, or list of patients, for the meeting and the sign-in attendance record sheet.

The hospital is undergoing implementation of an electronic patient record system, and currently both paper charts and electronic information are used in patient management. The electronic records contain all laboratory data, radiology images and some clinical notes. However most clinical notes are written into the patient's paper chart.

Radiological images are accessed through the picture archive and communication system (PACS). Pathology reports can be accessed though the hospital electronic patient record system (EPR) and images from pathology specimens are sometimes brought on memory stick to the meeting, loaded onto the PC at the start of the meeting, and accessed as needed during the discussion on a patient.

THE PROBLEM

Record-keeping at MDT meetings is one of the identified priorities for all of the teams surveyed, (reported in [24]), and the affordances of MDT discussion records are discussed in [23]. Here we draw attention to particular items of information, listed in Table 1, that have been requested to be part of the record of an MDT discussion, and illustrate some of the complexity of the problem of record generation.

Priorities for the Specific Information to be Included in a Record of a Patient's Case Discussion *(In order of frequency expressed importance)*
Consensus treatment or management plan agreed
Recommendation to patient
Agreed Disease staging
Summary of Patient presenting details
Choice of chemotherapy / radiation therapy clearly indicated
Lesion type, grade, stage, margin status noted
Background history summarised
The underlying basis for decision agreed
The referring consultant
Past medical history
Patient findings on Examination
Cancer molecular diagnostics
Family history
Investigation dates
Accurate smoking history

Table 1. Identified information priorities for inclusion in the record of a patient's case discussion

The problem that emerged for the MDTs is how to make a record of the discussion, and the form it should take. Prior to formal records, individuals took personal notes. However, concerns were expressed, particularly by those who reported findings to the meeting, that the notes being taken might not truly represent what was being said; that the communication may have been misunderstood, and that there was no way for the person making the utterance to be assured that they would not be misquoted in the future. For example, pathologists and radiologists issue written reports on their findings that are already in written form elsewhere. At the meeting they explain their opinion in talk and illustrate their interpretation with the patient's images. The words they may use paraphrase, summarise, or add emphasis to points made in their report to aid their colleagues' understanding. However, the written report is the official record and informal notes saying *'its benign'* have no standing when the official report might say *"this lesion is likely to be benign . . . '*. As one radiologist put it: *"...just because I think its probably benign, doesn't mean that it is benign . . . the patient needs to be followed up"*. An official record of the case discussion would clarify the meaning conveyed in the talk, and build a shared understanding of the patient's situation in the context of his / her findings that were considered. In any patient case discussion, the individual patient's test results will be reviewed (including radiology, pathology and / or endoscopy findings if any), but it is also important to remember the information, knowledge and experience that the individual experts bring to the discussion, (including recent research evidence [9]). Together with the patient information, the expert input forms the *content of information* in the discussion, a concept used by [36] in his study in the Netherlands.

Over time, MDTs developed structured or semi-structured pro forma reports to assist them in gathering information during discussion. These pro formas do not satisfy *all* of the expressed needs (in Table 1), but were a first step in develop-

Information 'Wish list' for records
Patient Information
Clinical staging
Performance status / Co-morbidity
Include Endoscopy (still & video) images
Laboratory results incorporated
Up to date staging revision
Decision-making
Basis for decision agreed
Was differential diagnosis considered?
What are Pros and Cons of the treatment options considered?
What was ruled out?
Communication Process
Print name of person who signs form
Type record and send copy to referring physician and GP
Generate a worklist of patients to be seen by a particular person
Automatic information from EPR to PATS (audit database)
Have summary distributed to team post-MDTM
Communication Interaction
Who was there?
Names of radiologist and pathologist who contributed
Names of all all specialists involved in discussion
Did X say anything about the possibility of Z option?
Other
"Microphones would help us hear"

Table 2. Expressed 'wish list' related to information to be gathered for inclusion in a case discussion record

ing a discussion record. All of the specific information items that have been deemed necessary for a record (in Table 1) are clearly made known in discussion, through talk, text and the use of images, and notes are currently taken in written records by most of the MDTs (and scanned in afterwards into the EPR system). But when reviewing notes afterwards, the information sought is not always available, a common feature of medical records and noted in several studies [38, 13, 19]. There are likely several explanations for missing information, including deliberate withholding of data [38], but noting correct information from conversation between specialists can be a difficult task, and studies have identified problems for individuals when conducting this sort of exercise [22].

The pro forma reports do not purport to address all of the information desired. The teams highlighted a 'wish list' of information they would like to be able to record somewhere on the proceedings and process, and Table 2 lists items of information that are not currently available to which team members would *like* access afterwards. At interview, some team members elaborated on items such as 'clinical staging'. It can be argued that some of the items listed in Table 2 can be provided through items in Table 1, such as 'Patient findings on examination', could infer 'clinical staging'. However, the point was made that while policy might state that certain information is collected, compliance is often less than desired. "*I wish they would fill out the form properly*", said one participant. In other words, and like others have found [30], there can be a gap between policy and practice, or gaps between the work, the patient, and the information representation which may account for adverse consequences for the patient and increased costs for the hospital [38]. This 'wish list' will be further considered in the Discussion section. Some of the items requested concern patient information, but most of the suggestions raised concern the communication and decision processes. The '*Other*' issue listed in Table 2, namely 'microphones', will be discussed separately.

As well as reducing ambiguity and avoiding potential communication misunderstandings, the most immediate and important utility of the record of the MDT discussion is to explicitly document the next steps to be taken in managing the patient, and direct staff who will be interacting with the patient on his/her next visit to their clinic.

The 'wish list' is more than about (sometimes) missing information that is normally available, and there are clear differences in the type of information listed in both Tables. The pro forma reports developed have aimed to capture *essential* information, and tend to be designed to address the information listed in Table 1. The gap between the information that people see as *essential* in Table 1, and information they would *like to have* in Table 2 points to some of the areas of concern for people in their work.

Examining the items in Table 2, we can see that there is a clear information deficit in the current system of record-keeping that is likely impacting patient care. Having an account of the treatment options that were considered, for example, is not information that was formally proposed to capture, yet it is information that many value when considering the management of their patients. While there are issues concerning the EPR system and the completeness of information gathered, there is also a clearly identified need for 'decision communication', or process record of some sort. Zhou argues that a convincing rationale should be recorded for treatment plans, but notes that critical thinking or supporting evidence is often missing from medical records [38]. For example, suppose a surgeon is reviewing records of an MDTM discussion, and sees a particular operation recommended that is not the surgical method normally advised in clinical practice guidelines for this clinical situation. In the absence of an explanation, or rationale, for the decision the surgeon cannot be certain if an error was made in the record entry that might account for this unexpected advice. If there are adverse consequences for the patient as a result of the wrong operation being carried out, the damage cannot be undone. Thus it is critically important, in the interest of patient safety and hospital efficiency, that clinicians (e.g. surgeons) are confident in the accuracy of the record.

In Table 2, we draw attention to the emerging pattern of information sought. It can be categorised as a) *patient information*, b) *decision related*, c) *process related*, or d) *interaction communication* related, as illustrated by the categories and examples in Table 2. These categories bear some relation to those identified in other MDT meetings studies, such as [36] who noted three categories of communication namely i) grounding communication, ii) making practical arrangements and iii) co-ordinating treatments.

THE SOLUTION

At interview, clinical staff were asked "What if there was a full audio-visual recording of the MDT meeting?" Without exception, team members did not like the idea of having a full audio-visual recording. They felt "*... it would be a very stifled discussion, having to be careful of every word you said ...*". Although one team member said "*I suppose that's the way things are going now, but I hope its not* [implemented] *in my lifetime*". Students when questioned felt it would be a wonderful resource for study if they could access particular types of cases, review the information used in making the diagnosis and the choice of treatment option made by the MDT in the circumstances. A Swedish oral surgery centre has reported such a system, although we note that information in this system is captured asynchronously. It is mainly used for teaching purposes, rather than routine work [6].

The reluctance of staff to consider an audio-visual record of the proceedings - a record that would be easy to make but difficult to process - highlights some of the complexity of this forum. But it is unlikely to be the difficulty in processing such a record or concerns for patient privacy, alone, that makes an audio-visual recording so unappealing. Goffman's metaphor describing 'frontstage vs. backstage' [11] is useful to help our understanding of the behaviours we witness, and describe in this paper. The informality observed in the interactions 'backstage', contrasts with the formality and transformation recorded in the formal, 'front stage' record entry. Indeed, others have also observed these dual, parallel, interaction processes in interactive, collaborative, medical work [16, 37, 5].

Having ruled-out an audio-visual record, a text-based electronic record was investigated that would be available in the patient's EPR. The particular MDT being studied designed an electronic form, with the help of the Information Services (IS) Department (and independent of our study). Information was identified, focus groups and workshops were held with the team leaders, and prototypes were tested and evaluated by members of the MDT.

The electronic form was designed to capture the key information items that the MDT agree are essential, and the design and layout of the form was negotiated with the IS department in conjunction with the EPR vendor. The form is designed over four pages and is intended to capture some items through radio-buttons, and check-boxes, and one free-text box is included for 'Other' comments. Gathering structured data electronically will facilitate audit and research later, (and potentially decision-support and analysis tools could be applied).

A user is first presented with the agenda list of patients for the meeting. Double clicking on a patient row, enters into that individual patient record and a four-tabbed form is presented facilitating structured data entry. The first three tabs provide access to separate pages for data related to clinical, radiology, pathology findings respectively. The fourth tab loads the page to record the decision made by the MDT and is depicted in Figure 4.

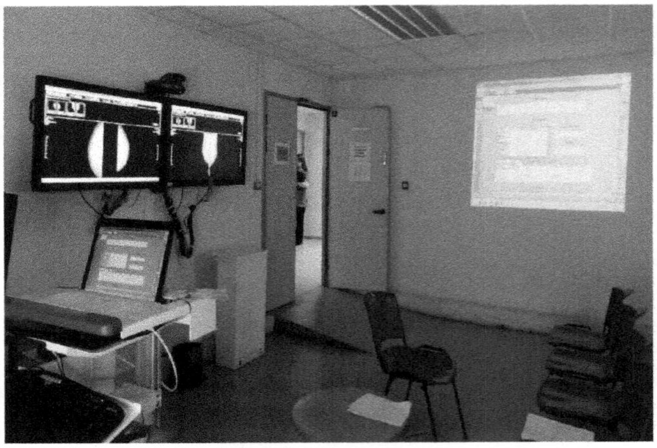

Figure 3. Meeting room showing the plasma displays in front with screen from mobile computer projected onto the side-wall of the room. Meeting participants can view the record as its being entered.

As described earlier, the data entry page to the patient's EPR is accessed on the computer-on-wheels, and projected onto the side wall of the room. Having the data entry display visible to all of the participants is similar in practice to other centres [29], although the side wall is not reported to be used elsewhere. Some team members expressed a concern that they did not want for their MDT discussion to be transformed to a "*... group form-filling exercise*". Members report their satisfaction in meeting their colleagues and sharing opinions. Concerns have been expressed that if people were to "*...focus only on the next bit of information to be entered ... it would take from* [the quality of] *the discussion*".

The side-wall facilitates a very large projected image, several times larger than a plasma screen display in front would allow (as used for radiology). The plasma screens at the front of the room and the large projected display on the side wall are illustrated in the photograph in Figure 3. Another MDT had adopted a practice of using the side-wall of their meeting room to display background information on the patient being discussed, and this had been found useful as an awareness mechanism. The choice of side-wall is likely a matter of convenience and the knowledge of its satisfactory use by another MDT. Projecting the data entry screen onto the wall means that it is available to all MDT members to view the data being entered, but is not the object of discussion. However, it allows for corrections to be made to understanding, and thus the data is validated at the MDT meeting.

Actual Use

After a short time in use, the planned utility of the tabs, linking separate sections to collect the structure, was abandoned. The time constraints on the MDT meeting have become such that it was found to take too much time to go through the form systematically. Current practice utilises the single free-text box designed for 'Other', or additional, information only.

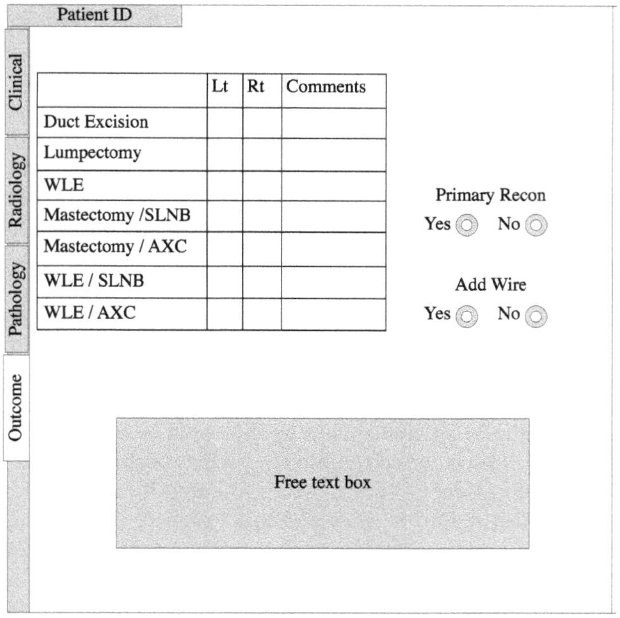

Figure 4. Representation of the data entry screen that is projected onto a side-wall of the meeting room

The check-boxes, intended to indicate the planned procedure, are not used. Neither are the radio-buttons used. At interview, staff who enter data regularly reported that it takes too much time to point the mouse and select an option. It is much faster, and easier, to type free text into the comments box. As one observed:

> "*. . . by the take your hand from the keyboard to find the mouse, point it and click or whatever, you've lost too much time . . . and the discussion has moved on*"

Entering data obtained from a fast-paced discussion requires skill and expertise. The person entering the data is either an experienced nurse or an experienced house doctor. Initially, junior doctors in training were assigned the task, but their lack of experience was found to cause them difficulty in keeping pace with the discussion.

Staff who regularly enter data report that it is a highly demanding task but that they have "*. . . got used to it, and don't mind it at all*". Prior to the data entry screen being projected, the computer-on-wheels was placed at the back of the room; the data were entered in real time and validated afterwards with the lead clinician. There is a greater demand on the person entering data to enter as much as possible, now that it is visible, compared to the pressure when the notes were being privately taken.

The physical location of the computer-on-wheels in the meeting room has had a great impact for the person entering the data. In the words of one of the staff:

> "*It makes a big difference to us, now that we are up in front beside the radiologist . . . its much easier to lean over and ask something, or check what was said. We were inclined to be forgotten about when we were at the back of the room. Now its easier . . . and they have the opportunity to point to something missing and maybe say 'don't forget to say we need to see her after she is finished with the gynae people'*[1]

The Data Entry Task

When one of us (BK) attempted to follow the data entry task by writing down the words that appeared on the large display, the challenge of the task became evident. It was extremely difficult, and not possible at times, to maintain pace with the entries being typed into the free-text box. When asked afterwards about the data entry task, the interviewee explained:

> *But its difficult for us too . . . but we're more used to it - and we still sometimes find it difficult too. Sometimes we might have to add in something afterwards from a note that someone has taken. Don't forget we are using these records afterwards and we know what we want to see. And we know this work, don't forget . . . we anticipate whats going to be said next. . . . like . . . when someone is talking - we get to know what they're going to say, and we anticipate what's coming next - so we're really thinking through . . . and anticipating . . . we know what they're saying as we're writing - we don't wait until after they've said it, if you know what I mean. But it definitely is tiring . . .*

This is certainly not a task that anyone can easily perform. The people entering the data are highly qualified and demonstrate an intimate knowledge of their work.

Lessons Learned

There are a few noteworthy behaviours that became evident and from which lessons can be learned for the CSCW community.

Speech: The talk among the MDT specialists is relaxed and informal and when describing their findings they use language that is distinct from the language used in the medical record. So, for example, a phrase "*. . . I didn't see any sign of cancer in the sample*", is recorded as "*Biopsy Lt side is negative*". Or "*It didn't come up on PET*" is recorded as "*No evidence of metastasic disease*". Or "*her mother died of cancer*" is recorded as "*Fhx ca*", meaning that she has a family history of cancer and thus may have a higher risk of developing the disease. Or if the oncologist offers "*Send her to me*", the note might say "*candidate for neoadjuvant chemo*", meaning that the patient will likely prove suitable for chemotherapy in conjunction with her surgical procedure. In this case the care for the patient will be formally transferred to that clinician, after the MDT meeting. Thus the written record is more formal and it is not a verbatim report of the relatively relaxed talk among MDT members. While it is a record of the discussion it has a more formal and objective appearance, likened by [13] as an 'act of publication' with a particular audiences or purposes in mind. It is the intended meaning, as understood in the team, i.e. the communication to be conveyed that is recorded and not the actual spoken words. Action is directed, for after the meeting.

[1] Meaning that the patient is being referred to the gynecologists for another problem that has likely a greater priority, but this MDT want to review this patient again after her gynecological issue is resolved.

Shared Understanding / Common Ground: The core team members work closely together and demonstrate a high regard for one another. They appear to be a cohesive group and have a shared understanding of their procedures and policies, so their intentions are not always articulated during discussion. When the volume of work increased to a level that eliminated time for teaching or discussion on research, they self-organised to start 30 minutes earlier and devote this time to their research interests. These once-weekly, *voluntary* meetings of the MDT[2] are held outside normal working hours at 07:15am and demonstrate the regard and dedication the MDT members have for their meetings. (Many of the members have meetings on the other mornings of the week too, because of their membership of other MDTs.)

When specialists are reporting their findings during the discussion, the information they contribute is assimilated by the team member, and transformed into an action. Examples such as "*I'm concerned that we may have missed something ... and maybe there is something nearby*" is recorded as "*repeat biopsy*". Or "*So, we are concordant then, that it is fibroadenoma - radiology and pathology agree. Is that right?*", becomes "*Reassure patient and DC*" (DC, stands for 'discharge patient'). Information is generated through interaction among the specialists - using speech gestures, and body language. This information becomes synopsised, meaning is interpreted, or inferred, and action is applied. Acronyms and shorthand are frequently used and the MDT appears to have a shared understanding of them. For example, a typical entry into the record might read (for a cancer patient):

> "*40yrs Presented large tumor Lt breast IDC. Neoadjuvant chemo good clinical response. Proceeded to wire WLE &SNBX. Path IDC G2 2.4mm DCIS. Margins all okay. Closest int @2mm. LVI present and perineural invasion. Nodes 0/3 ER + Pr - Her- MP Grade 3/5. Response ypT2N0. Plan Med Onc to see and radiation oncology*".

As one might expect, the report on a non-cancer patient is usually shorter and might read:

> "*36yrs. Core Rt breast FA 2.5cms. Path FA B2. Concordant. Reassure & DC*".

These example reports will have little meaning for most people. However they provide an important demonstration of how the MDT has developed a shared language that is a combination of the different jargons used by the several specialities in the MDT. The levels of common ground allow for statements such as "*So, its a fibroadenoma*", or "*... she has a lot of family history ...*" to trigger protocols and procedures that will be implemented by the individuals on the team whose role it is to carry out the task, such as reassuring patients or arranging genetic counselling.

Common ground and team cohesiveness likely contribute to the development of these local languages. Although it is difficult to measure behaviours in these MDTs, they have been the object of studies, as there are concerns that MDTs do not always perform effectively. There are reports that behavioural factors may account for some of the dysfunction observed [35, 7], and, drawing on the research of Clark on common ground [3, 4] our concern is how to support this grounding, and avoid breakdown. It can be anticipated that any weakening of common ground in MDT meetings will lead to breakdown in communication and ultimately affect patient safety.

Validation:

The intention in having the shared display for data entry is to afford team members the opportunity to correct entries, prompt if an omission is observed, or suggest clarification. This record of the MDT discussion has shared ownership, and it is the MDT understanding that what is written into the record will be adhered (unless the patient objects). However, there is no evidence for the MDT to know if this is the case, i.e. that this record is *valid* and that tasks are discharged. In fact there is the suggestion that the group cohesiveness may be counter productive and that individuals might not bother to pay any attention to the data being entered, or that they might be reluctant to correct the person entering the data. For the MDTMs observed utilising this method of record-entry, there were no corrections prompted, comments were rare, and any remarks made by other MDT members added emphasis such as *"be sure to write that ... "*. If MDT members fail to check the entry, or feel inhibited about correcting an incorrect entry, this could potentially lead to a false sense of validity of the discussion record. To compound matters from a hospital perspective there is currently no mechanism to ensure that an instruction in the record, such as *"repeat scan in 6/12"*, will be carried out. Indeed, some might describe this work system as "an open loop".

Missed Opportunities: The MDT meeting has a rich content of information available to the MDT, but unfortunately most of this content is unavailable afterwards and its persistence is limited by the quality of the meeting record. Other sections of the hospital, and the healthcare system could benefit from aspects of the information content if they could access it. For example, hospital management has a responsibility to be able to account for the activity of its staff, and to plan services better. Without access to quality data with regard to the types of work that is being conduced by staff, and a better understanding of the services being delivered, hospital managements are hampered in their organisation, delivery and planning of services. Indeed, Government budgets are often allocated on the basis of the 'case-mix' or other such metric, and hospitals employ staff tasked with the responsibility to gather these data, indirectly and labouriously, in patient files. The hospital also has responsibility to national repositories for public health and cancer registries and the MDT meeting is a point in the work processes where these data are available, but not captured. An ideal record from a meeting would satisfy more hospital information needs than is current practice.

Ethnographers: should be reminded that what people say, and do, and the language they may use to describe a situation can be misinterpreted by experienced researchers. Having the data entry displayed on the wall allowed for us to com-

[2]Attendance, both the research seminar and the routine MDTM, is voluntary and outside of normal work hours for most members of the MDT.

pare what was being said at the meeting from what was being written. It also gives new insights into interviews that had been conducted at earlier periods in our studies. At all times when individuals were asked about the notes they took during the discussion, the typical answer was "I take note of whatever is being said". Being able to monitor the entries and the conversation betrayed the differences.

Microphones: The use of microphones is raised repeatedly in surveys and at interview. Regular, active vocal, participants tend not to want to use them (although some say they would be willing to wear microphones if they were made available). The non-vocal participants on the other hand continually prompt (in surveys and in research interviews) that they cannot always hear what is being said. Yet, at meetings it is a very rare event for a non-vocal participant (unusually a junior, or older, member of the team) to ask a speaker to repeat what they said, or to speak louder or more clearly. From time to time senior (and vocal) members of the team have been observed to ask others to "*speak up, I can't hear you*". For junior team members the social structures are inhibiting. Older team members can also be inhibited (despite their seniority) and one explained "*I don't like to draw attention . . . that I may have an age-related hearing deficit!*".

The fact that an issue such as 'microphones' gets raised in questionnaires and interviews interested in 'record-keeping', and rarely at MDT meetings, is an indication of the complexity of the issues of information, collaboration and record-keeping in healthcare. It is not possible to entirely separate the social and technical aspects of information and its use - they are inter-twined. If utterances cannot be heard, then where, or what, is the information content?

DISCUSSION

It is our responsibility to deliver the promise to provide ICT solutions to make our health systems safer and more dependable. Evidence that our claims that ICT solutions to support collaboration between health professionals, and between patients and their carers, will transform health services and make safer and more dependable systems is still awaited. Our research identifies a shortcoming in our ability to recognise that support for collaboration, sharing and reuse of information requires new methods of capturing information and transforming it into artifacts that are accessible and 'fit for purpose', i.e. supports communication records.

We argue that we need a communication record in healthcare that will document information used in decision-making, and support several levels of user skills, knowledge and experience. The argument was made in a participant interview, for instance, that if a record says '*treat with drug Q for three times a day, for 10 days*', unless that record has the information that provided the basis for the decision to recommend that treatment, there is potential to introduce new errors into the system. While some staff roles will be satisfied with a straightforward instruction, those in more responsible positions of clinical authority need to have a full understanding of *why* that recommendation was made, i.e. the underlying rationale of the decision, and be able to validate or update the decision in the event of new evidence. One clinician said:

> "*it would all be fine if I only had a few patients to look after . . . then I could remember all the details on each one. But we are getting busier and busier, and we need systems in place that leave no room for error or ambiguity.*"

It is well recognised that as humans we can expect to make errors and that we need to design systems that make it hard for people to do the wrong thing and easy for people to do the right thing [25]. We also need to guard against precipitating new errors when we introduce electronic information systems in healthcare, and the example above where the basis of the decision is not available is one of those omissions that has already been identified as responsible for some adverse patient events [1, 26].

A record from an MDTM is something quite different from an electronic medical record for an individual patient. This research suggests that the communication record need not necessarily be structured, but it should be condensed such that it can be produced and read quickly, processed, comprehended, and provide the information required. We are not alone in pointing out the need for medical records to be as much about the collaborative work involved and services delivered as they are about repositories, or 'silos' of information strung together over a network. The need for working records that have multiple working views that are both interdependent and independent has been described [8], and [38] argues that an electronic medical record system should be designed to facilitate clinical work process representation, while simultaneously preparing information in a patient-centered representation for long-term reuse. It has been proposed that electronic patient records should afford organisational knowledge in a similar way to the way paper records allow them to be used as a means of making the activities of an organisation accountable and available in various ways [14]. Here, we add that it must be 'doable' in the time-constrained setting of an MDT meeting.

Furthermore, given the information-rich setting that the MDTM provides, it is an ideal opportunity to capture knowledge that can be used to validate other data, capture non-verbal interaction data for quantitative analysis [28], build case sets for teaching purposes, or to make the overall 'system' of work more effective. For example, by fulfilling the hospital's responsibility for notification of disease to a national repository, or for building evidence for future review and policy development. While staff regard the newly implemented electronic record system as a great improvement over the old method in many respects, they report that the current electronic record does not provide them with all the information they require and say "*we still need to be there . . . to hear, and see for ourselves . . . and take our own notes*".

We propose a communication record that is linked to the patient's EPR, but not necessarily an integrated part of it. This record is likely to be relatively unstructured and would support the backstage/ frontstage interests. It would be flexible enough to provide for individual lists of assignments ('to do' lists) according to role on the MDT, and also assure the security and privacy expected in medical work.

CONCLUSION

Electronic MDT meeting records, i.e. communication records, should be an important part of the electronic patient record (EPR) system. As well as communicating the decisions made, this communication record should provide the basis for the decisions made on a patient: by whom was the decision proposed, who contributed to the discussion, which information was provided, and what was the rationale for the decision? As well as providing a formal account of the collaborative event, the communication record is an important tool to guide later tasks.

Our study provides insight into how clinicians collaborate at MDT meetings, and argues for a record of the communication and decision-making. When discussing their opinion with one another, clinicians are explaining their motivation and providing context for their opinion (in images, text or other data). The MDT meeting is an opportunity to bridge the different clinical specialist perspectives through talk, and one of the few occasions in medical work when different specialities come together to discuss patients. We propose that the ability for an MDT to successfully negotiate this inter-disciplinary bridge and build common ground, may well account for the significant patient, and other, benefits that have been reported to result from MDT collaboration and meetings [35].

The use of large projected transient display as a dependability enhancing mechanism to reduce risk in the MDT worksystem is laudable, but its use must not undermine the benefits of co-located discussion. However, if MDT members do not consult the entries, or intervene in discussion, then there is a risk that the large display will undermine its potential benefit and give a false sense of reliability. There needs to be a balance between maintaining a fluent discussion, and having a useful record. We also need to acknowledge the importance of MDT cohesiveness in building and maintaining common ground and recognise how these teams can work very efficiently under severe time constraints. Interventions, or events, that threaten team cohesiveness will also threaten patient safety.

Developing a record that will not detract from the synchronous face-to-face collaboration between clinicians, that is easily produced, requires little (if any) processing, and provides for the multitude of potential uses is a challenge. We believe that it is a challenge worth the effort. The solution potentially has a very significant role to play in transforming our health services into more dependable, more efficient, and effective system.

ACKNOWLEDGMENTS

A sincere ‘thank you’ is extended to all of the multidisciplinary teams at St. James’s hospital, Dublin, for their ongoing co-operation in this study. Bridget Kane is a Marie Curie (ERCIM) Fellow and at the time of this study was an IRCSET Fellow, funded through the IRCSET Research Council for Science Engineering and Technology (IRCSET) Enterprise Partnership Scheme with St. James’s Hospital Board. The helpful support of Centre for Next Generation Localisation (CNGL, SFI grant 07/CE/1142) in bringing this paper to fruition is also appreciated. We thank our anonymous reviewers for their helpful comments.

REFERENCES

1. Ash, J. S., Berg, M., and Coiera, E. Some unintended consequences of information technology in health care: The nature of patient care information system-related errors. *Journal of the American Medical Informatics Association 11*, 2 (2004), 104 – 112.
2. Bardram, J. E., Hansen, T. R., and Soegaard, M. Awaremedia: a shared interactive display supporting social, temporal, and spatial awareness in surgery. In *Proceedings of the 2006 20th anniversary conference on Computer supported cooperative work*, CSCW ’06, ACM (New York, NY, USA, 2006), 109–118.
3. Clark, H. H. *Using Language*. Cambridge University Press, Cambridge, 1996.
4. Clark, H. H., and Brennan, S. E. Grounding in communication. In *Perspectives on Socially Shared Cognition*, L. B. Resnick, J. M. Levine, and S. D. Teasley, Eds. American Psychological Association, Washington, DC, 1991, 127–149.
5. Coiera, E., and Tombs, V. Communication behaviours in a hospital setting: an observational study. *BMJ 316*, 7132 (2 1998), 673–676.
6. Falkman, G., Gustafsson, M., Torgersson, O., and Jontell, M. The origin, representation, and use of collaboration patterns in a medical community of practice. In *Emerging Technologies and Information Systems for the Knowledge Society*, M. Lytras et al., Eds., vol. 5288 of *LNCS*. Springer, 2008, 403–412.
7. Firth-Cozens, J. Multidisciplinary teamwork: the good, bad, and everything in between. *Quality in Health Care 10* (2001), 65–66.
8. Fitzpatrick, G. Understanding the paper health record in practice: Implications for EHRs. In *Health Informatics Conference (HIC’2000) Integrating Information for Health Care*, Health Informatics Society of Australia (Adelaide, Australia, 2000).
9. Frykholm, O., and Groth, K. References to personal experiences and scientific evidence during medical multi-disciplinary team meetings. *Behaviour & Information Technology 30*, 4 (2011), 455–466. doi: 10.1080/0144929X.2011.553746.
10. Galliers, J., Wilson, S., Randell, R., and Woodward, P. Safe use of symbols in handover documentation for medical teams. *Behaviour & Information Technology 30*, 4 (2011), 499–506. doi: 10.1080/0144929X.2011.582147.
11. Goffman, E. *The presentation of self in everyday life*, reprint ed. Penguin, London, 1990.
12. Goolam-Hossen, T., Metcalfe, C., Cameron, A., Rocos, B., Falk, S., and Blazeby, J. M. Waiting times for cancer treatment: the impact of multi-disciplinary team meetings. *Journal of Behaviour and Information Technology 30*, 4 (2011), 467 – 471.

13. Hardstone, G., Hartswood, M., Procter, R., Slack, R., and Voss, A. Supporting informality: Team working and integrated care records. In *CSCW Chicago 2004*, ACM, ACM Press (2004).

14. Hartswood, M., Procter, R., Rouncefield, M., and Slack, R. Making a case in medical work: Implications for the electronic patient record. *Computer Supported Co-operative Work (CSCW) 12* (2003), 241 – 266.

15. Hillestad, R., Bigelow, J., Bower, A., Girosi, F., Meili, R., Scoville, R., and Taylor, R. Can electronic medical record systems transform health care? potential health benefits, savings, and costs. *Health Affairs 24*, 5 (2005), 1103–1117.

16. Ho, D., Xiao, Y., Hu, P. F., Vaidya, V. U., Straumanis, J. P., Cardarelli, M. G., Norcio, A. F., and Gurses, A. P. P. "front-stage" and "back-stage" information. In *CHI '08 extended abstracts on Human factors in computing systems*, CHI EA '08, ACM (New York, NY, USA, 2008), 3033–3038.

17. Housley, W. Category work and knowledgeability within multidisciplinary team meetings. *Text and Talk 20*, 1 (2000), 83–108.

18. Joint Commission for Accreditation of Healthcare Organizations (JCAHO). Root causes of sentinel events. Tech. rep., The Joint Commission, 2010.

19. Jordan, K., Porcheret, M., and Croft, P. Quality of morbidity coding in general practice computerized medical records: a systematic review. *Family Practice 21*, 4 (2004), 396–412.

20. Kane, B., Groth, K., and Randall, D. Medical team meetings: utilising technology to enhance communication, collaboration and decision-making. *Behaviour & Information Technology 30*, 4 (2011), 437–442. doi: 10.1080/0144929X.2011.591576.

21. Kane, B., and Luz, S. 'referring on': Passing responsibility for patient care. In *Workshop on 'Handover: Collaboration for Continuity of Work', ECSCW, 2007*, ACM (Limerick, 2007).

22. Kane, B., and Luz, S. Taking lessons from teleconference to improve same time, same place interaction. In *IEEE conference on Computer Based Medical Systems*, IEEE (Jyväskylä, Finland, 2008).

23. Kane, B., and Luz, S. On record-keeping at multidisciplinary team meetings. In *24th IEEE International Symposium on Computer-Based Medical Systems (CBMS)*, IEEE (Bristol, England, 2011).

24. Kane, B., O'Byrne, K., and Luz, S. Assessing support requirements for multidisciplinary team meetings. In *23rd IEEE International Symposium on Computer-Based Medical Systems*, IEEE (Perth, Australia, 2010), 110 – 115.

25. Kohn, L. T., Corrigan, J. M., and Donaldson, M. S. *To Err Is Human: Building a Safer Health System*. Institute of Medicine, 2000.

26. Koppel, R., Metlay, J., Cohen, A., Abaluck, B., Localio, A. R., Kimmel, S. E., and Strom, B. L. Role of computerized physician order entry systems in facilitating medication errors. *Journal of the American Medical Association 293*, 10 (2005), 1197–1203.

27. Leonard, M., Graham, S., and Bonacum, D. The human factor: the critical importance of effective teamwork and communication in providing safe care. *Qual Saf Health Care 13*, suppl 1 (2004), i85–90.

28. Luz, S. The non-verbal structure of patient case discussions in multidisciplinary medical team meetings. *ACM Transactions on Information Systems 30*, 4 (2012), article 17.

29. Napolitano, G., Ranaghan, E., Middleton, R., Fox, C., and Gavin, A. Real-time multidisciplinary team meeting management systems. a comparison with paper records for staging completeness and waiting times. *Behaviour & Information Technology 30*, 4 (2011), 473–477.

30. Northcott, D., and Llewellyn, S. Benchmarking in uk health: a gap between policy and practice? *Benchmarking 12*, 5 (2005), 419–435.

31. O'Higgins, N. Developing quality care for breast services in Ireland, 2006.

32. Pirkle, C. M., Dumont, A., and Zunzunegui, M.-V. Medical recordkeeping, essential but overlooked aspect of quality of care in resource-limited settings. *International Journal for Quality in Health Care* (2012).

33. Randall, D., Harper, R., and Rouncefield, M. *Fieldwork for Design*. Springer, 2007.

34. Schmidt, K., and Bannon, L. Taking CSCW seriously: Supporting articulation work. *Computer Supported Co-operative Work 1*, 1/2 (1992), 7–40.

35. Taylor, C., Munro, A. J., Glynne-Jones, R., Griffith, C., Trevatt, P., Richards, M., and Ramirez, A. J. Multidisciplinary team working in cancer: what is the evidence? *British Medical Journal 340* (2010), c951.

36. Verhoef, J., Toussaint, P. J., Putter, H., Zwetsloot-Schonk, J. H. M., and Vlieland, T. P. M. V. The impact of the implementation of a rehabilitation tool on the contents of the communication during multidisciplinary team conferences in rheumatology. *International Journal of Medical Informatics 76*, 1112 (2007), 856–863.

37. Wilson, S., Galliers, J., and Fone, J. Not all sharing is equal: the impact of a large display on small group collaborative work. In *Proceedings of the 2006 20th anniversary conference on Computer supported cooperative work*, CSCW '06, ACM (New York, NY, USA, 2006), 25–28.

38. Zhou, X., Ackerman, M. S., and Zheng, K. Doctors and psychosocial information: records and reuse in inpatient care. In *Proceedings of the 28th international conference on Human factors in computing systems*, CHI '10, ACM (New York, NY, USA, 2010), 1767–1776.

Caring for Caregivers: Designing for Integrality

Yunan Chen [1, 2], **Victor Ngo** [1], **Sun Young Park** [1]

[1]Department of Informatics
University of California, Irvine
Irvine, California, 92617, USA

[2] Institute for Clinical and Translational Science
University of California, Irvine
Irvine, California, 92617, USA

{yunanc, ngov1, sunpy1}@uci.edu

ABSTRACT
Health and wellness have drawn significant attention in the HCI and CSCW communities. Many prior studies have focused on designing technologies that are patient-centric, allowing caregivers to take better care of patients. Less has been done in understanding and minimizing the burden of caregiving in caregivers' own lives. We conducted a qualitative interview study to understand their experiences in caregiving. The findings reveal a great magnitude of challenges in the caregivers' day-to-day lives, ranging from the physical and social, to the personal and emotional. Caregivers have to constantly balance their personal lives with work, family, and their caregiver roles, which can be overwhelmingly stressful. We discuss how caregivers attempt maintaining this balance through two concepts: first, *giving-impact*, and second, *visibility-invisibility*. Our study's findings call for system design that focuses not only on patients but also caregivers, addressing the burdens that often impair their health and wellness.

Author Keywords
Caregiving; caregiver; health and wellness; integrality; invisibility; healthcare technology.

ACM Classification Keywords
J.3 Life and Medical Sciences, Health, Medical Information Systems; H.5.2 User Interfaces, User-centered design; H.5.3 Group and Organization Interfaces, Computer Supported Cooperative Work

INTRODUCTION
With an increasingly aging population and the spread of chronic diseases like diabetes, obesity, and dementia, managing health and wellness has become an urgent topic facing today's society. In particular, the challenges of maintaining health and wellness lie in the extremely long duration and complex nature of the issue. It is well noted that ICT systems can provide great benefits to those trying to stay well, e.g. mobile phone-based interventions for tracking and managing diabetes [19].

Maintaining health and wellness, especially for patients and older adults, is seldom a solo task; instead, there are many people involved in the caring process. Strauss et.al [30] introduced the concept of *trajectory work* to conceptualize the social organization of managing chronic care, where an illness trajectory refers *"not only to the physiological unfolding of a patient's disease but to the total organization of work done over that course [of illness], plus the impact on those involved with that work and its organization"* [30 p8]. Strauss's work [30] suggests that chronic care is collectively managed by an organization of stakeholders that can range from healthcare professionals who assist patients in clinical settings to caregivers who often provide care to patients in residential environments. Because of its collaborative nature, many previous CSCW studies have explored the caregiving process, and how technologies can be designed to offer improved physical, social, and emotional support for patients, e.g. [3]. Overall, these systems designed to support patients facilitated the coordination of necessary care endeavors and provided convenient means for caregivers to help patients.

In addition to patients, healthcare consumers also include other users, such as caregivers, who are heavily involved with day-to-day patient care activities related to chronic illness management. Caregiving-related activities may also have significant impact on caregivers' lives. Like Strauss states, trajectory work also includes *"the impact on those involved with that work and its organization* [30, p8]*."* In a sense, the work of caring for others may exert certain effects on those involved in the process. However, the "impact" Strauss deems as an essential part of the total organization of care work has seldom been studied in prior CSCW literature. In this article, we focus on the involvement of caregivers in the caregiving process. We aim to understand the impact of caring for patients on caregivers. The goal of this paper is not to examine how caregivers can better devote themselves to patient care, but rather how caregivers can manage their own health and wellness in the process of helping others.

The impact of caregiving has been widely noted in prior medical and nursing literature, with a focus on *caregiver burden* that denotes the overall impact of physical, psychological, social, and financial demands of caregiving

[9]. Studies found that there is often stress, anxiety, and even high mortality rates among caregivers, especially those for family members [26, 27]. These findings suggest that addressing caregivers' own health and wellness is an unavoidable issue. In the HCI/CSCW field, the lack of attention to caregiver burden in system design may exacerbate this already severe problem, since new chronic care management systems are often designed to facilitate caregivers to do more, and may increase the amount of burden they already have. It is clear that there is an urgent need to not only address disease management for patients, but also the overall well-being of caregivers. This insight calls for an in-depth examination of caregiver behaviors that can inform the design of future consumer health informatics systems that not only support patients' needs, but also caregivers' health and wellness.

In the rest of this paper, we present the findings of our qualitative study on caregivers. Specifically, we describe how caregivers strive to maintain their own health and wellness through four main aspects, which we term *the physical self, the emotional self, the social self,* and *the reflective self,* respectively. We further discuss these aspects using two lenses of thought: *giving-impact* and *visible-invisible*. We believe this work makes a solid contribution to the field of CSCW by advocating for the often neglected caregiver role. The insights gained in this study can inform the future design of chronic care management systems to attend to patients' needs while alleviating the burden of caregivers.

RELATED WORK

The impact of caring for caregivers is well -documented in prior medical and nursing research. Studies have suggested that caregiving often demands a variety of efforts from caregivers, ranging from physical and emotional, to financial – all of which can cause extreme stress for family caregivers [26, 27]. In particular, one study examined 392 caregivers and 427 non-caregivers who were living with their spouses and concluded that "*being a caregiver who is experiencing mental or emotional strain is an independent risk factor for mortality among elderly spousal caregivers. Caregivers who report strain associated with caregiving are more likely to die than non-caregiving controls* [26]."

The burden of caregiving is further specified into two categories, objective burdens, and subjective burdens [20]. According to Montgomery et.al. [20], objective burdens include activities associated with the caring process or practical consequences of the physical and behavioral changes in the care receiver, while subjective burdens are the emotional reactions of caregivers. It was found that the negative impact on family members mainly resulted from depression, financial strain, and disruptions in family routine and dynamics [26, 27]. One study found that nearly 80% of caregivers for terminal breast cancer patients had to miss work, an objective burden [12]. Meanwhile, their subjective burdens, such as anxiety and stress level, increased as patients' functional statuses declined [12]. In the end, it was concluded that "*strategies are needed to help reduce the psychosocial, occupational and economic burden associated with caregiving* [12]."

To that end, the use of technology as a strategy to mitigate the challenges in chronic care management has been a well-established area of study, with a majority of studies focusing on the use of technologies to assist the care of patients. For example, one study presents an innovative monitoring system that can send photos to caregivers via mobile phones. This device is designed to ensure caregivers are aware of patients' activities [7]. Similarly, other studies utilized mobile phones for remote communication among young adults with cognitive disabilities and their parental caregivers [6], in addition to GPS enabled communication tools for caregivers to track and locate Alzheimer patients [18]. As such, technologies are considered lifelines [16] that bring together the ones in need of help with those providing the help.

In addition to advanced communication capabilities, other online systems, such as Personal Health Record (PHR) systems, were also introduced with the hope of providing better information-sharing and coordination of caregiving related tasks [1, 28]. These technologies center on facilitating better care coordination among multiple caregivers. Consolvo et al. use the term *Computer Supported Cooperative Care (CSCC)* to describe the area of coordination systems that can help caregivers allocate and assign tasks [3]. Consolvo stresses that the goal of CSCC applications is to keep people healthy, and that system design has to consider issues of emotion, trust, and privacy.

It is notable that although caregiving has been studied extensively in medical and social science literature, current HCI and CSCW studies focus primarily on patients, and often neglect caregivers as potential users of patient care systems. These systems are often designed to help better execute caregiving tasks for patients. Consequently, these systems may lead to increased burden on caregivers who are the ones actually conducting the tasks. There are only a few studies primarily devoted to decreasing the burden of caregivers, *e.g.* [17]. In terms of objective burden for instance, mobile and ubiquitous computing is indicated as one promising direction for decreasing the amount of burden for caregivers, since "*everyday objects, from hearing aids and watches to alarm clocks and refrigerator doors, can serve as computing surfaces to help these individuals* [21]." Another study introduced a robotic wheelchair to support wheelchair users and reduce caregivers' workloads [15]. In terms of subjective burden, technologies are used to provide social and emotional support for caregivers. One study introduced a telecommunications system for family member caregivers of dementia patients. The system facilitated caregiver communication among family members, especially those who were far distances away. Caregivers found participation in "online discussion" groups to be very valuable also [5]. Likewise, ComputerLink was found to increase the amount of psychological support provided by nurses to a group of homebound caregivers looking after Alzheimer's patients. It also enabled caregivers to share experiences, and make new friends through a caregiver support network [8].

Despite the dominant concern on caregiver burden, recent research has turned its attention to positive aspects of caregiving, such as a sense of reward, satisfaction, and companionship [2]. Peacock et.al [25] found that caring for dementia patients was often coupled with several positive experiences, including personal growth, a sense of competence, and closer family relationships. In particular, connecting with others was found to be an effective coping strategy in managing the stress and frustration associated with caregiving [25]. These positive experiences provide opportunities for introducing early supportive interventions that can lead to better health outcomes for both patients and caregivers [2, 11, 13], in addition to influencing caregivers' experiences in their long journey [25].

Overall, the challenges and opportunities identified in prior research raise important question on how technologies can be designed to diminish the negative impacts, and meanwhile enhance the potential positive experiences associated with caregiving. Addressing this issue is critical for caregivers' own health and wellness, as well as for the patients they provide care for. We believe this is an important area for HCI/CSCW communities, since neglecting the needs of caregivers while over-emphasizing patient-centric design may lead to increased caregiver burden. To do so requires researchers to truly understand caregivers' needs, behaviors, and preferences in managing their own lives rather than focusing solely on what they do for the patient.

METHODOLOGY

To understand how caregiving tasks are managed and how technologies can help leverage the challenges of being a caregiver, we conducted a qualitative interview study centered exclusively on understanding caregivers' behaviors.[1]

Data Collection

Study participants were recruited from an outpatient clinic, where patients and their caregivers were approached and asked whether they had caregiving experience or were willing to introduce their current caregivers to us. The participants were recruited from the clinic because it was a convenient location to meet caregivers, since many caregivers accompany patients to their medical visits. It is notable that the clinic is only a location for recruitment, and the actual interviews were conducted at caregivers' homes. We studied 15 individuals, including current caregivers and those who had provided care in the past.

Semi-structured interviews were chosen as the main data collection method. Qualitative interviews provided an opportunity to gather insight into the participants' experiences and perspectives on caregiving. As previously mentioned, interviews were conducted at caregivers' homes: the locale where most caregiving activities take place. The comfort and privacy of these settings helped us to gain a better understanding of the physical caregiving environment, as well as provided access to care-related artifacts such as travel bags, notebooks, and calendars. Occasionally during the interviews, patients and other family members, e.g. spouses or children, joined the conversations and provided their insight. Talking with other family members in the household also confirmed some of the challenges perceived by the caregivers with whom we had spoken.

The study participants covered a broad range of situations: from chronic to extremely needy patient cases; and from current to past caregivers. The diversity of illnesses and types of involvements afforded us a way to understand common themes across a variety of caregiving situations, rather than focusing exclusively on a particular illness or it's associated tasks. In doing so, we uncovered common behavioral patterns across many illnesses that helped to generalize our design insights for a broader audience.

Prior to the start of the interview, participants were given a short questionnaire to gather demographic information (e.g. age, gender, ethnicity), and questions on technology-use and health-management. The interviews lasted approximately 1-2 hours in length, were audio-recorded, and later transcribed for further analysis. The approach yielded a rich set of raconteur-like retellings of the caregiver experience, with individual transcripts averaging 40 pages in length. The semi-structured interviews explored the following three sets of questions:

- *The interviewee's caregiver experience*
- *How caregiving affects the interviewee's own life behaviors*
- *Whether technologies were used in managing both the interviewee's and the patient's health, and if so, how.*

Among the 15 interviewees, 11 were female and 4 male. 9 participants were Caucasian, 3 were Asian, and 3 were Latin American. Participants were aged between 24-76 at the time of the study, with 6 over 60 years of age. 10 of our interviewees were current caregivers, while the remaining 5 were caregivers in the past. Caregivers in our study engaged in caring for individuals with of a variety of health conditions, including severe chronic back pain, glaucoma, diabetes, cancer, stroke, and dementia. With regards to the use of technologies, 13 out 15 participants were using a computer and the Internet at home, and almost everyone claimed that they used technologies on daily basis, either at home, or in work environments.

[1] Institution Review Board (IRB) approvals were obtained from both the university and the field site prior to the data collection.

Data Analysis

Data analysis for this study was guided by grounded theory [4, 10] that emphasizes the co-evolution of data and theory by conducting data collection and analysis simultaneously. Following the constant comparative method [10], immediately after the first few interviews, initial data analysis sessions were held among the three authors to identify the main issues noted down during each interview. Audio data were transcribed into text as promptly as possible. 5 interview transcripts were randomly selected for the initial round of data analysis. Sample data were analyzed using an open coding method by each researcher to identify salient concepts. The impact of caregiving activities on the caregivers' own life was identified as the main concept from this initial round of analysis. Once this core theme was identified, axial coding was then performed to extract categories of impact in the dataset. The themes produced by each researcher were compared, discussed and revised through a series of discussions until agreements were reached. Results of the sample interviews were used to guide the next stage of coding, during which one author coded the remaining data using the developed coding scheme. This second stage of the analysis generated similar concepts and themes to those identified in the initial coding stage, demonstrating the consistency of the findings. Through these activities, we were able to reveal how caregivers manage their tasks, cope with their emotions, collaborate with others, and deal with the lasting effects of caring in their own lives.

FINDINGS

Our study revealed many caregiver challenges, including a need to maintain and balance caregiving obligations with other parts of their life. For most caregivers, incorporating caregiving into their own lives is by no means an easy task, but caregiving is "*an integral part of [their] life [#06]*" that they choose to accept.

Caring for a patient, especially the elderly and those with a severe illness, can be highly demanding. Other than the obvious medically-driven tasks, such as attending a patient's doctor appointment and dispersing a patient's medication, being a caregiver also implies many non-medical tasks: from the small chores of cleaning the house, cooking meals, and picking up groceries; to providing financial assistance, emotional comfort, and even IT help. The caregivers we spoke with reported making frequent home/clinic visits, taking phone calls, dealing with various errands, and staying in constant contact with the patient in order to deal with the numerous tasks that are necessary for them. Although most of the participants we studied were healthy, working professionals, the telling of their caregiving experience revealed a sense of burden which, combined with other work and family obligations, resulted in unbearably high workloads and stresses that often were not recognized by their family and friends. Many caregivers experienced frustration and even depression; some even had to consult doctors to maintain their own wellness, thus making the health of caregivers a critical issue to address.

This high demand from all aspects of their lives forces caregivers to constantly *balance* tasks between caring for others and sustaining their own lives. This can have a major impact on the caregiver, resulting in the need for physical, emotional and social support. Meanwhile, the experience of seeing patients struggle with diseases can lead to self-reflection and new life lessons.

In what follows, we elaborate on four aspects of wellness that caregivers strive to maintain in their day-to-day lives. These four themes emerged from the iterative interview analysis process, and are considered the main findings of the study. They are the 'physical self,' the 'emotional self,' the 'social self,' and the 'reflective self'. We use participants' own quotes to illustrate the attitudes, concerns, and experiences they had in maintaining the integrality of their lives while engaging in caregiving responsibilities. To maintain patients' confidentiality, all names used in this paper are pseudonyms.

Physical Self

The first aspect of wellness is what we called the *physical self* – the needs for managing, coordinating, and handling the physical activities in one's everyday, personal, and caregiver life. We use physical to refer to the actual tangible tasks being performed by caregivers, as opposed to the emotional or social aspects of caregiving. As briefly mentioned earlier, many caregiving tasks are intrinsically medical; nevertheless, the tasks themselves can extend much further into activities that deal not only with disease management, but also with patients' quality of life. As a result of their high variability, tasks can grow in size very quickly. Since each task is important in ensuring some level of patient care, caregivers feel obligated to attend to all care tasks – even if it means sacrificing a portion of their own lives. The following example shows how patient care may conflict with a caregiver's personal obligations. Diane described how difficult it is to manage her own family while caring for her mother who suffers from dementia:

> *Diane [#09]: "...it's been challenging. It's affected my marriage. We've had a lot of talks about it, and the time away from my family. It's a balancing act. It's that sandwich generation."*

Many of the caregivers we spoke with are facing the similar dilemma in their daily lives, where they take on the major roles of caring for both older parents and younger children at the same time. Taking on the dual roles means they may be the strongest person in a family in order to coordinate, cope, and manage all forms of physical activities they are responsible for; in the multiple roles they engage in. In the case described earlier, when her mother was diagnosed with dementia, Diane was only a few years into her marriage and had a newborn baby. Caregiving certainly impacted Diane's personal life, and took away quality time with her own family. Allocating time between the patient and one's own personal commitments was a conflict we encountered consistently across all the interviewees. As Diane describes, the situation always involved a kind of *balancing act* between the caregiving life and the personal life. In her case, it is also a balance between caring for an older parent and younger child. Unfortunately, many of our participants must make two ends of responsibilities meet. This balance may not always be achieved. As a result, caregivers sometimes have to sacrifice one end in dealing with an overwhelming workload. Similarly, another interviewee told us how he had difficult times balancing the two responsibilities of his life.

> *Jeff [CG05]: At some point I definitely ignored my own family, ignored my wife and my kids because I took care of him...My dad would sometimes get upset if I was paying attention to my son, my son would get upset that I was paying more attention to my dad.*

Family was not the only personal obligation that was affected by caregiving activities. Taking time away from work also created additional strain for our caregivers, since it could affect work performance. Many interviewees also talked about the needs to coordinate work responsibilities with patient needs, such as making sure patients' medical appointments are scheduled on days they can take off from work. In such cases, communication among the patient, clinic, and employer turns into another task that caregivers must take on. This often resulted in the need to compensate missed work time by working on the weekends, further invading an already-impacted family life. Another participant, Jeremy, commented on the challenges of integrating caregiving in all aspects of his life, and wished that his sister would help with more tasks.

> *Jeremy [CG06] "So last year was me trying to get, not only worrying about my mom's health and condition and well-being, but trying to get my sister to step up... She has no children. She has no husband. She has no boyfriend. She just works... I work, too. I have a wife. I have two kids. I coach soccer. I do this. I do that..."*

Jeremy's quote not only indicates the multi-faceted roles he simultaneously engaged in, and the unbearable responsibilities weighing on his shoulders, but also reflects how other family members were unaware of how much work and time he sacrificed in taking on the main caregiver role for his mother. Indeed, the numerous tasks involved with caregiving can be as small as making phone calls to clinics and picking up medication on the way back home; however, these tasks can quickly accumulate and become overwhelming while still remaining unnoticed by others.

To address conflicts in balancing their lives, the caregivers we studied utilized various tools and technologies to coordinate their tasks, such as daily planners, 12-month calendars, and online calendars. Nevertheless, the use of these tools was not a remedy to the challenges involved with caregiving, and success varied among participants. Most interviewees emphasized that the technologies only served as tools, and were not complete remedies when handling all their tasks.

The difficulties we described in maintaining the 'physical self' clearly indicates a need to introduce new applications to help caregivers balance personal and care related tasks. However as previously noted, most current health and wellness applications are patient-centric in design, with the goal of "helping" caregivers to better serve their patient. How to incorporate the caregivers' lives in system design is a less studied topic. There is a need to design a platform to integrate the innumerous tasks caregivers manage on a daily basis. The lack of systems that support the busy and often challenging tasks of caregiving can lead to breakdowns when addressing tasks and even emotional difficulties among caregivers.

Emotional Self

Not only are caregivers physically invested in the care process, but their lives are also emotionally affected. Consistently across all the interviews, there was an indication that the caregivers felt "stress," "frustration," and "difficulty." The accumulated tasks related to care in conjunction with personal obligations can certainly take its toll on caregivers and lead to stress in handling these tasks, especially when caregivers have difficulty balancing the various facets of their life. Melissa mentioned the guilt she felt regarding her inability to take on more caregiving tasks.

> *Melissa [CG04]... always that conflict like "I can do more. I should be doing more."*

Indeed, much frustration stems from the inability to handle all the tasks involved, not to mention the helplessness a caregiver feels in watching their loved one suffer from pain or seeing their patient's health slowly decline. Many participants commented not only the challenges in managing a patient's chronic illness, but also their own emotional wellbeing – an important aspect of wellness that we term the *emotional self.* When caring for others, there are undoubtedly negative emotions involved such as stress and frustration that also affect the caregivers' own wellbeing. Not surprisingly, the inability to maintain the 'physical self' resulted in overwhelming stress for Jeremy:

> *Jeremy [CG06]: "I have a teenager now and a pre-teen here pretty quick. And he was starting to go through puberty at the same time that I had to start working with [my] mom. So actually I...*[whispering to prevent his family from hearing]*...I went to therapy for about eight months because of it and I was on some meds for a while because I wasn't handling it well. It was a lot of change. It was a lot of stress, and I didn't know what to do."*

In this case, Jeremy's 'emotional self' had to be maintained by consulting a professional therapist and taking medication. This shows the extreme emotional impact that caring for others may have on the caregiver. Notably during the interview, Jeremy whispered the fact that he had been in therapy to prevent his wife from knowing. As we quoted earlier in Diane's case, many caregivers have to take on dual roles in caring for both older adults and younger children simultaneously. Meanwhile, they are often left alone to cope with the resulting stress and negative emotions involved, since it is difficult for them to vent their emotional concerns to those who are even more vulnerable than they are. In Jeremy's case, his emotions were hidden from his wife, and there was no way that she could help care for him during these difficult times without knowing how he suffered.

Finding ways to manage the 'emotional self' is necessary among caregivers. Other than consulting healthcare professionals, caregivers in our study deployed other strategies to cope with their emotions. Darlene mentioned that the most effective way to cope was to share her feelings and experiences with her two sisters. In addition, she also wrote in her blog as a means of sorting out and dealing with her emotions.

> *Darlene [CG13]: "I did start writing a blog. And no one really knows about it. No one reads it except for me {laughs} actually. But I just started one so that I could just get down information and feelings and thoughts that I have...writing that blog I think helps me deal with all of the emotional stuff that comes along with [caregiving]."*

Darlene's experience gives interesting insight into how technology can be used to assuage the emotions that are accumulated during the caregiving process. The blog Darlene kept was not shared with others; however, writing it serves the same comforting role as talking with her siblings or consulting a therapist. In some cases, venting emotions – either with people or simply writing thoughts down – can have a calming effect. Since expressing emotional concerns with patients or family members may not always be an option for caregivers, and not everyone has the courage to consult mental health professionals, technologies can provide an alternative channel for caregivers to vent their emotions.

To deal with their feelings, the caregivers we spoke with engage in various strategies to maintain their emotional wellbeing, such as confiding in health professionals, family, and friends. Interestingly, we found that technologies like blogs were also effective. This brings new perspective into how emotions can be alleviated through technology use when other coordination strategies are not available, and what technologies can help caregivers cope with their emotions. What we found in our exploration of the caregivers' 'emotional self' suggests that compared with the obvious emotional needs patients have, the caregivers' emotional wellbeing is a more invisible and less studied area of research.

Social Self

In addition to their emotional wellbeing and their skills for everyday life management, the 'social life' of caregivers has also been impacted by the demanding role of caregiving. In many cases, the burden of caregiving both emotionally and physically diminishes opportunities to socialize with others. Maintaining social wellness can be reflected in both decreased social activities within the family and less opportunities to interact with friends. In our study, Melissa mentioned how it felt when her mother moved in her home after the stroke.

> *Melissa [CG04]: She [her mom] had that stroke in January, then she was in rehab for a while...and then she stayed with us for a while until we could figure out something else for her to do...it's very isolated here. We don't have any socialization. It's just us...everyone kind of doing their own things; the kids are in school and we all have our things to do. And so, it's not like a social – we didn't provide the same kind of social activities.*

For Melissa, staying together was not equal to "being together"; the busy caregiving-work-family schedule left almost no space for family members to catch up or to partake in social activities with each other. In such cases, being in the same household even created more of a sense of isolation since family members were busy engaging in their own activities separately.

Furthermore, the needs in accommodating to care related activities can also dramatically change the day-to-day life of caregivers. Darlene mentioned how she left her 11-year job and life in New York to become the primary caregiver for her mother in California.

> *Darlene [CG13]: Well I mean it's totally changed...I have no social life, really. I mean I have some friends, and for a long time that was never a big deal to me - being alone. But now all of a sudden it is... So, I mean, in essence my whole life has changed."*

In Darlene's case, caregiving is a "24 hour a day, 7 days a week" job (from here on referred to as 24/7). Darlene's situation is especially challenging since her life now completely revolves around care for her mother. As the interview quote indicates, not only did Darlene give up her own personal life, she also disconnected herself from her social life back in New York. Being a caregiver occupies her both physically and emotionally, and in such a situation, social connections become even more important. As Darlene said, alone was never an issue in the past, but it turned into an issue when she became a caregiver.

In both these scenarios, socializing is an important aspect of life that has been deeply disrupted by the work of caregiving. Patient care tasks may conflict with a caregiver's social life; in extreme cases, where a particularly debilitating disease is involved, 24/7 care is required that entails caregiving efforts without breaks. There can be a dramatic disruption in one's 'social self' if the caregiver does not have the resources and time to socialize, or even if the mood and time to socialize diminishes when family members are co-located in the same household. No doubt socializing is desired among caregivers, since it can eliminate their sense of isolation and offer breaks in their already stressful lives. What needs to be considered is how to connect caregivers with their social circles when they have very little time or when their other obligations overlap with social events. Also of important consideration is how to mobilize and inspire relaxing social moments to eliminate the isolation among families and individuals living in a caregiving situation, and how technologies can help facilitate this process.

Reflective Self

Even though the undesirable effects of caregiving may cause unpredicted stress and frustrations to caregivers, the care process also provides opportunities to reflect and rethink personal values. As one study participant [#01] told us "*I have a deeper appreciation for life.*" We found many participants engaged in self-reflection throughout the caregiving process. These reflections often centered on health issues, but also extended beyond to other aspects of their lives. We use the term 'reflective self' to represent the process of self-reflection and the management of new life perspectives that may change current beliefs and behaviors.

First, being a caregiver entails reliability for the patient. Caregivers need to be constantly prepared to handle unpredictable care situations and obligations. To do so, they have to be healthy themselves and attend to their own personal health issues.

> *Sean [CG 03]: I never wanted to call out sick because I knew she needed me and also because it was so hard to find somebody else that knew how she liked things because I knew that – I knew how to do what she liked and we were so compatible together.*

As this case shows, caregiving motivates Sean to stay healthy and not miss workdays. This shows a process of self-reflection that reconsiders caregiving aligned with work responsibilities so he can make himself available for the patient.

In addition, more than affecting day-to-day personal life, caregiving may have deeper impact on the way caregivers perceive and approach their lives. Caregiving is an opportunity to peer into life with a chronic disease without being the patient. Managing a patient's disease can involve learning about the illness, in turn prompting the caregiver to take preventative measures in the present to avert the onset of the disease later in their life.

> *Jeff [CG05]: but certainly one of the things that, having seen my dad being so excessively obese...is something that we're concerned...So that's what we watch our weight certainly... It's not going to change in two days or three days, but there's just that thing mentally. We watch our weight, certainly. We watch what we eat.*

As Jeff's case indicates, caregiving for his obese father and watching the difficulties he faced warns Jeff and his family to avoid obesity in their own lives. They started to proactively monitor their own weight and be cautious about food intake. Similarly, Wendy, another participant, mentioned that she recommends not eating sugary foods to her diabetic grandfather, and at the same time, avoids them herself on a day-to-day basis. Additionally, she and her husband have cut alcohol out of their lifestyle, since they recognize it as a risk factor for many diseases. The recognition of risk factors related to a patients' disease was consistent across all the interviews. Although some interviewees were not as proactive as Wendy or Jeff in changing their lifestyles, they at least acknowledged a need to change the undesirable and less healthy practices in their lives. Typical lifestyle changes included eating healthier, consuming less sugar, and exercising more frequently.

The influence of caregiving in relation to the 'reflective self' is much more profound than reading educational materials, since caring for a patient is a reminder of the everyday importance of being healthy. Thus, caregiving entails the process of reflecting on current life practices with lessons learned from the caregiving endeavor. Consequently, the caregivers' self-reflection on these life lessons may affect the way they perceive their lives.

Self-reflection touches all aspects of the caregivers' lives – some caregivers are more appreciative of what they have and what is important in life; others proactively prepare for their own future by educating their children on the procedures and costs in caring for the elderly. Here we see that caregiving has changed people's perceptions in life, creating opportunities to be more affectionate and understanding with one's own relationships and experiences, and to be even more prepared for future care of themselves and others – all positive impact on caregivers' lives. However, the benefits of these lessons serve no purpose if the caregivers do not take action. Many of the interviewees were not as proactive as Jeff or Wendy in changing their behaviors to live healthier, suggesting that there is a need to help caregivers more aggressively turn these reflective thoughts into action.

DISCUSSION

Our study on caregivers reveals a multitude of challenges they face in their daily lives. In this section, we discuss how caregivers strive to manage the integrality of their lives through two lenses of thought that both emphasize the collaborative nature of caregiving. The first is *giving and impact,* the second – *visibility and invisibility.*

Managing Integrality

The findings of this study show that caregivers have to constantly balance numerous tasks involved in caring for others, while maintaining their own physical, emotional, and social needs. The process of caregiving is by no means a small part of the caregivers' lives, but affects all aspects of their daily activities. In this sense, managing the caregiving role cannot be separated from the other parts of life. Here we use the term *integrality* to refer to the need to understand the complete spectrum of a caregiver's life, instead of separating caregiving from other life facets.

Prior studies in health management have advocated that the management of disease should be embedded in the rest of life behaviors, e.g. [14, 24]. Nevertheless, the foci of these studies are often on how patients integrate and struggle with their multi-faceted lives; the experiences of caregivers in helping patients remain a relatively underexplored area. The integrality concept can be more challenging since it involves multiple layers of impact. Here we discuss maintaining the integrality of the caregivers' lives in the following two ways. *First*, we argue that managing integrality is a multi-faceted activity that involves not only negotiating the 'physical self', but also the 'emotional', 'social', and 'reflective' self. In this sense, integrality covers multiple layers that need to be coordinated, instead of only one aspect. As we have seen in the study, the caregivers' struggles can result from the incapacity of managing physical tasks, but more profoundly, they are deeply rooted in the challenges of managing social and emotional wellbeing. While physical tasks can be reallocated easily, the emotional side of integrality is more difficult to maintain, and deserves more attention in future work. *Second*, in managing integrality, caregivers have to coordinate all aspects of their lives with individuals who are tied to other life activities, such as their spouse, children, friends, co-workers and managers. Hence, maintaining integrality is a collaborative activity that involves many people. Negotiating activities with these parties may not be easy, since the needs of a caregiver may not always be appropriately perceived, compared to the patients' cases. Design for life integrality needs to consider not only the physical involvement of the caregiver and their emotional involvement, but also the broader spectrum of people who each connect to various aspects of a caregiver's life.

Caregiving as a Collaborative Endeavor

Although the focus of the study was set on understanding what caregiving entails to caregivers' real lives, the task of caregiving is intrinsically collaborative in nature. First, caregiving is a process of devoting time, energy, and emotion to helping others better manage illness. It cannot be termed *giving* without at least two people's involvement. Second, as we mentioned in the section above, in the process of maintaining integrality, caregivers negotiate their relationships and activities with family members, co-workers, and even other caregivers. In this sense, caregiving work can be viewed as a collaborative endeavor that emanates between a patient and a caregiver, and onwards to collaboration among caregivers and others who are involved in the caregiver's multi-faceted life [Figure 1].

In the following, we elaborate on two factors we deem critical to the collaborative caregiving endeavor. Specifically, we use the idea of '*giving and impact*' to frame the impact of caring for patients on caregivers' own lives, and '*visibility and invisibility*' to explain the need for better coordination among the role of caregiver and the other roles a person undertakes simultaneously [Figure 2].

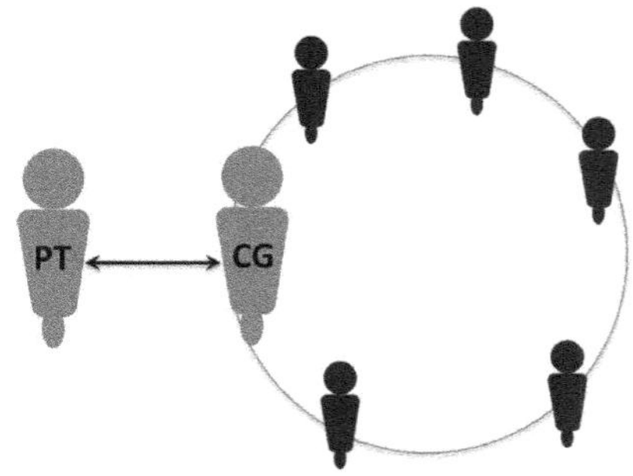

Figure 1: Collaborative Caregiving. Left side represents patient-caregiver interaction, and the right shows how a caregiver connects to others in real life.

Giving-Impact

To better understand the collaborative nature of caregiving work, we revisit the illness trajectory concept introduced at the beginning of the paper. Strauss describes an illness trajectory involving, "*not only the physiological unfolding of a patient's disease but the total organization of work done over that course [of illness], plus the impact on those involved with that work and its organization*" [30, p8]. In this definition, clearly the work involved in patient care is necessary; however, it also states that the "impact of those involved" is essential in maintaining the illness trajectory. Here we use giving and impact to categorize the process of caregiving to caregivers' own lives.

In caring for a patient, a caregiver often devotes large amounts of time, energy, financial assistance, and emotional support to the patient. While much of the previous literature is centered on understanding what patients' need from caregivers, less attention has been spent on the consequences of these activities on caregivers. We argue that the process of caregiving inevitably results in impact on caregivers, regardless if it is negative or positive. The more involved and helpful a caregiver is, the more impact s/he may experience from the act of giving. The counter-effect exerted on caregivers can be felt physically, emotionally, socially, and in other ways. This is because when a caregiver devotes more time and energy to a patient, less time and energy remains for his/her other life activities; when a caregiver is more emotionally involved in a patient's care, the more difficulty there is in maintaining emotional wellness.

The association of 'giving and impact' in this section suggests that caregiving is a balance act, where the amount of work invested in the giving effort is related to the amount of impact one may receive. As such, focusing only on the needs of patients and neglecting the potentially strong impact that caring may have on caregivers can be problematic or even dangerous. In the cases mentioned in this paper, the wellbeing of patients may be coupled with the impaired wellbeing of a caregiver. When designing technologies to facilitate better caregiving for patients, the advanced technologies may in turn increase levels of impairment exerted on caregivers unintentionally. What we have found in the study suggests that it is critical for system design to consider both the obvious beneficiaries, e.g. patients, and those who may receive the counter impact in the process of helping others.

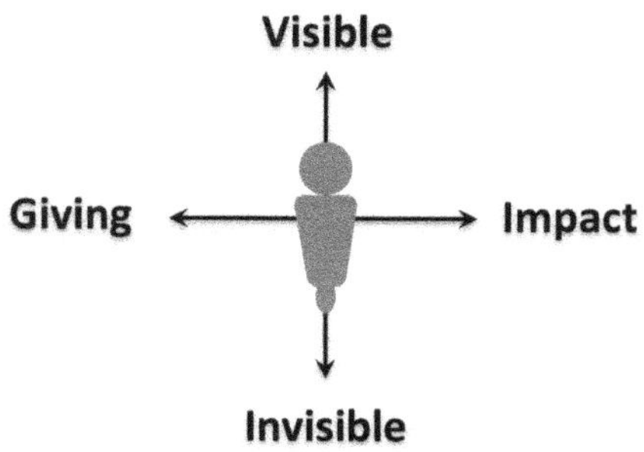

Figure 2: Factors affecting the collaborative caregiving process.

Visible-Invisible

As our study shows, the impact on caregivers largely results from the tension between the busy, multi-faceted lifestyle of caregivers, and the new tasks created by the caregiving role. Managing day-to-day wellness is actually a process of negotiating all the different social connections in a caregiver's own life – a collaboratively driven activity in nature. Nevertheless, the negotiating process may not always be successful, and sometimes may not even occur. On many occasions, even the closest of family members were not fully aware of the struggles involved in the caregiving process. For example, the accumulated task and mental stress remained only visible to Jeremy, and was invisible to those who were connected to him through only one aspect of his life. Many of our study participants took dual roles of both caring for patients and their children. The huge responsibilities imposed on them made it difficult to vent their stresses and frustrations to friends, family and co-workers. Consequently, outside individuals were unaware of the needs of these caregivers during difficult times.

The visible and invisible nature of tasks presented here is similar to what Lucy Suchman pictured in workspace collaborations [31], where certain behind-the-scenes work cannot be appreciated by collaborators and may lead to a misrepresentation of workload in system design. As we described earlier, when the amount of care and concerns stay invisible to family members and co-workers, these "collaborators" may not have a chance to offer help, especially when caregivers themselves are reluctant to reveal the challenges they have to others. In such situations, we suggest that technological design for caregivers take advantage of the *articulation work* that is deemed essential in collaborative work. By definition, articulation work is a type of "*work that gets things back 'on track' in the face of the unexpected, and modifies action to accommodate unanticipated contingencies* [29]." In caregivers' cases, articulation work can be managed at both the behavioral and system levels: caregivers can be encouraged to articulate the concerns, problems, and issues they face in maintaining their own wellbeing; systems could map out the entire workload a caregiver routinely undertakes for other people, and open opportunities for them to offer help whether physically or emotionally.

DESIGN IMPLICATIONS

This section details specific design suggestions based on the study's findings. As indicated, the design of health systems should not merely address what caregivers can do for patients, but should include how to improve the health and wellness of caregivers while attending to their patients.

Support Coordination among Care and Personal Tasks

As we have shown in the study, balancing caregiving with personal life can be challenging. Caregivers have to constantly deal with rearranging their personal tasks to accommodate caregiving obligations, and vice versa. It is not surprising that having a multitude of medical, non-medical, and personal tasks can lead to challenges in remembering and organizing tasks efficiently. Oftentimes, caregivers have to deploy various artifacts, tools, and routines to integrate and coordinate tasks from different parts of their lives. As such, it is essential that future systems help caregivers via an integrated platform that provides various mechanisms to facilitate the task coordination process. Such a design could support caregivers in balancing and navigating their caregiving responsibilities with their personal lives.

More importantly, this technology should integrate all tasks caregivers have into a single, centralized system that supports the articulation of objective burdens to the caregivers' other social connections.

We argue that such a system should be an integrated technology. This argument is based on the concept of "giving-impact" we discussed earlier, since balancing multiple parts of one's life needs to be consistently maintained in the caregiving process. A caregiver only has limited time and energy to deal with the multiple roles s/he is responsible for. Thus, it is necessary to coordinate caregivers' time and tasks in a visible way so that they can more efficiently synchronize and communicate with co-workers, friends, and family members. The enhanced awareness and improved communication afforded by this system could ease the stress and physical workload of caregivers and make their jobs easier.

For instance, the integrated care system may allow a caregiver to set up his/her comfort task zone for a day, *e.g.* 12 hours of work. It could link with calendars from work, life and caregiving activities, and automatically calculate the daily workload of a caregiver. When the calculation exceeds the threshold set by the caregiver, the system could send warning signals to remind the caregiver that there are more tasks than s/he can do on a particular day, and also send messages asking for help to the caregiver's friends, family members, and other non-primary caregivers. Although there is uncertainty in estimating one's workload, many tasks are scheduled in advance. Take Jeremy's case as an example. He knows his kids' school schedule in advance and the time needed for his job, as well as the planned medical visits for his mother. Entering these key events into the system could provide Jeremy a sense of order in properly execute different tasks, and how best to avoid task-conflicts. More importantly, this integrated tool can share the task load of a caregiver without verbal communication. Caregivers could choose to show their actual activities or just a warning signal that their workload has become too high. When co-workers, family members and other caregivers receive the warning message, they are able to intervene and offer help. The system can even automatically assign tasks to other caregivers based on their availability or expertise. In such cases, the work of a caregiver is no longer invisible; instead, it is shared with others in comfortable and non-intrusive ways.

Support Management of Social-Emotion Work

Caregiving is a long, intensive endeavor where the management of a caregiver's emotional wellbeing is as important as the patient's. In dealing with the stress and frustration of completing tasks, different caregivers utilize different strategies to cope with the subjective burden of their workloads. Many look to medical professionals for help, while others confide in siblings and friends to share their feelings and discuss stressful situations. A surprising discovery in our study revealed that blogs serve as a therapeutic tool in helping caregivers manage their emotions. This finding echoed prior work that the writing process can help individuals express "*deeply felt emotions*" [23] even without a reader. In this case, the use of technology affords new opportunities for caregivers to better manage their emotions. In the visible-invisible discussion, we mentioned that the impact to caregiving – especially those that are emotional – is invisible to the caregiver's social connections. In such cases, people who are available to help might not be aware of a caregiver's potential emotional needs. To this end, technologies can be designed to indicate the stress level of caregivers, which can later be shared with social connections.

One possible way to alleviate the caregiving burden is to offer ways to assess and support the caregiver's emotional wellbeing. For instance, in the integrated system, encouraging or rewarding messages can be sent to a caregiver automatically when the system indicates their workload is too high, or when the patient being cared for is in a difficult condition. In addition to these reminders, brief surveys can frequently be sent to caregivers to help determine their emotional states, as a previous study has suggested [17]. Depending on the levels of stress and frustration a caregiver experiences, the system could provide ways to ease their emotions through jokes, family pictures, or suggestions that the caregiver should share with family members.

In terms of making emotions visible to family members, our findings suggest that caregivers are often unwilling to explicitly reveal their emotional concerns with family members and friends, indicating more implicit and subtle emotional identifiers may be needed. For example, stress, frustration, or anxiety can be marked using different colors. A system could use red to represent different anxiety levels, and the deeper the color, the more anxiety the caregiver feels. Doing so would allow family members and friends to acknowledge a caregiver's emotional state without the caregiver revealing any details.

Technologies can also provide the social support that caregivers need, especially when it is unavailable in their physical surroundings. Just like patients can form online support groups to help and encourage each other remotely, information and communication technologies can be applied to support caregivers virtually, as the ComputerLink study offered to caregivers [8]. This type of social-emotional support is especially useful for those whose lives are deeply involved in and impacted by the caregiving process. Systems such as online groups, or broadcasted micro-blogs in a caregiver group, connect caregivers with similar experiences – especially those who care for patients at a distance. Social support is also critical for caregivers in maintaining their emotional wellbeing, since encouragement from their caregiver peers might be more effective than others' words. It's notable that many caregivers have to remain stationed around their patients and have no time to socialize with others who have similar experiences. However, it is likely that these caregivers have enough time to briefly talk with each other using the social components embedded in our proposed system, such as online chat-rooms, electronic bulletin boards, instant messaging, and text/visual micro-blogging. These social components can easily be managed during the waiting time of a patient's medical visit, or the monitoring time at home.

Encourage Reflection and Learning

Similar to the sense of competence and personal growth gained from learning and living with patients [25], we also found that constant exposure to their patients' illnesses provided caregivers the opportunity to reflect on their own lives, reminding them that they can take preventative measures to stop the onset of disease for themselves. This process, however, requires caregivers to reflect and take action in living a healthier lifestyle that can additionally influence others who are connected to the caregiver. Therefore, we suggest that the system help caregivers engage in the reflection, learning, and eventual preventative measures that can help stop the onset of disease. One way to succeed in this endeavor is to facilitate the sharing of caregiving experiences through blogs and caregiver groups, as we had proposed in the social support section previously. Expressing and summarizing insights in health and wellness through blogs was considered useful in self-reflection [23]. In addition, the insights authored by caregivers can optionally be shared with other family members, friends, or even other caregivers in a social network. The process of reflection can be encouraged through an extra 'rewarding' message, or by obtaining higher levels of status/reputation in the caregivers' communities. These features can encourage increased awareness of health risks and applicable preventative measure. Other considerations to encourage caregivers' reflection and learning include providing personalized health information for caregivers to read, and to provide them with opportunities to help each other with personal issues – health related or otherwise.

In this section, we advocate for the design of a health system that considers the critical role and potential impact of caregiving on caregivers, instead of solely focusing on patients' needs. With the tight integration of a caregiver's familial, professional, and caregiving lives, and the physical, emotional, social and reflective aspects of self-management, it is necessary to provide an integrated system that better connects the various aspects of life as a whole. The best way to know what caregivers need to do for their patients is through knowing the patients' needs. The total workload of an individual cannot be obtained if work, or family responsibilities are not included with the caregiving duties. Similarly, we view these four aspects of caregiving as overlapping and interconnected. System features that promote the wellness of one aspect will likely positively enhance the other three, such as the case of writing and sharing blogs that can pacify the negative tensions in the emotional self while also positively influencing the social and reflective selves simultaneously. Thus, an integrated platform that addresses all aspects of caregiving is likely to be a successful application.

CONCLUSION

In studying health and wellness, not only should we address the physical, social, and emotional requirements of patients, but also those of caregivers. Consideration of caregiver needs is especially important, since the burden of care may negatively impact the health and wellness of caregivers, leading to anxiety, stress or even an increased mortality rate. Nevertheless, unlike patients' needs that are clearly perceived, the counter-impact on caregivers often stay invisible, even to their closest friends and family members. In our study of caregivers' lives, we use the metaphor of giving-impact to emphasize the amount of influence caring for others may have on caregivers' lives. Surprisingly, much of the caregiving work remains invisible to other caregivers' social connections. We examined various caregiver activities, wherein we uncovered that caregivers struggle in their multi-faceted lives maintaining their physical, emotional, social and reflective selves. We argue that the future health and wellbeing systems should consider the impact of on caregivers as an integral part of the design.

REFERENCES

1. Chiu, T. and Massimi, M. A Digital Support Device Designed to Help Family Caregivers Coordinate, Communicate and Plan the Care of People with Brain Injury. *AMIA Annual Symposium*, (2006), 884.
2. Cohen, C.A., Colantonio, A., and Vernich, L. Positive aspects of caregiving: rounding out the caregiver experience. *International journal of geriatric psychiatry*. 17, 2 (2002), 184–188.
3. Consolvo, S., Roessler, P., Shelton, B.E., LaMarca, A., Schilit, B., and Bly, S. Technology for care networks of elders. *Pervasive Computing, IEEE 3*, 2 (2004), 22 –29.
4. Corbin, J.M. and Strauss, A.C. *Basics of Qualitative Research: Techniques and Procedures for Developing Grounded Theory*. Sage Publications, Inc, 1998.
5. Czaja, S.J. and Rubert, M.P. Telecommunications technology as an aid to family caregivers of persons with dementia. *Psychosomatic medicine 64*, 3 (2002), 469–476.
6. Dawe, M. Understanding mobile phone requirements for young adults with cognitive disabilities. *ACM ACCESS conference on Computers and accessibility*. (2007), 179–186.
7. Duncan, J., Camp, L.J., and Hazelwood, W.R. The portal monitor: a privacy-enhanced event-driven system for elder care. *International Conference on Persuasive Technology*. (2009), 36:1–9.
8. Gallienne, R.L., Moore, S.M., and Brennan, P.F. Alzheimer's caregivers. Psychosocial support via computer networks. *Journal of gerontological nursing. 19*, 12 (1993), 15–22.
9. George, L.K. and Gwyther, L.P. Caregiver Weil-Being: A Multidimensional Examination of Family Caregivers of Demented Adults. *The Gerontologist 26*, 3 (1986), 253–259.
10. Glaser, B.G. and Strauss, A.L. *The discovery of grounded theory: Strategies for qualitative research.* Aldine de Gruyter, Hawthorne, NY, 1967.
11. Greenwood, N., Mackenzie, A., Cloud, G.C., and Wilson, N. Informal carers of stroke survivors--factors influencing carers: a systematic review of quantitative studies. *Disability and rehabilitation 30*, 18 (2008), 1329–1349.
12. Grunfeld, E., Coyle, D., Whelan, T., et al. Family Caregiver Burden: Results of a Longitudinal Study of Breast Cancer Patients and Their Principal Caregivers. *Canadian Medical Association Journal 170*, 12 (2004), 1795–1801.
13. Hudson, P. Positive aspects and challenges associated with caring for a dying relative at home. *International journal of palliative nursing 10*, 2 (2004), 58–65.
14. Huh, J., Patel, R., and Pratt, W. Tackling dilemmas in supporting 'the whole person' in online patient communities. *CHI conference on Human factors in computing systems*. (2012), 923–926.
15. Kobayashi, Y., Kinpara, Y., Takano, E., Kuno, Y., Yamazaki, K., and Yamazaki, A. Robotic wheelchair moving with caregiver collaboratively depending on circumstances. *CHI '04 extended abstracts on Human factors in computing systems,* (2011), 2239–2244.
16. Ling, R. *The Mobile Connection: The Cell Phone's Impact on Society*. Morgan Kaufmann, 2004.
17. Liu, L.S., Hirano, S.H., Tentori, M., et al. Improving communication and social support for caregivers of

high-risk infants through mobile technologies. *Conference on Computer supported cooperative work.* (2011), 475–484.

18.Loh, J., Schietecat, T., Kwok, T.F., Lindeboom, L., and Joore, P. Technology applied to address difficulties of Alzheimer patients and their partners. *Proceedings of the conference on Dutch directions in HCI.* (2004), 18–22.

19.Mamykina, L., Mynatt, E., Davidson, P., and Greenblatt, D. MAHI: investigation of social scaffolding for reflective thinking in diabetes management. *CHI conference on Human factors in computing systems.* (2008). 477-486.

20 Montgomery, R.J.V., Gonyea, J.G., and Hooyman, N.R. Caregiving and the Experience of Subjective and Objective Burden. *Family Relations 34*, 1 (1985), 19–26.

21.Morris, M., Lundell, J., and Dishman, E. Catalyzing social interaction with ubiquitous computing: a needs assessment of elders coping with cognitive decline. *CHI extended abstracts on Human factors in computing systems*, (2004), 1151–1154.

22.Mynatt, E.D., Rowan, J., Craighill, S., and Jacobs, A. Digital family portraits: supporting peace of mind for extended family members. *CHI conference on Human factors in computing systems*, (2001), 333–340.

23. Nardi, B.A., Schiano, D.J., Gumbrecht, M., and Swartz, L. Why we blog. *Commun. ACM 47*, 12 (2004), 41–46.

24.Pratt, W., Unruh, K., Civan, A., and Skeels, M.M. Personal health information management. *Commun. ACM 49*, 1 (2006), 51–55.

25.Peacock, S., Forbes, D., Markle-Reid, M., et al. The Positive Aspects of the Caregiving Journey With Dementia: Using a Strengths-Based Perspective to Reveal Opportunities. *Journal of Applied Gerontology*, 29, 5, (2010). 640–659

26.Schulz, R. and Beach, S.R. Caregiving as a risk factor for mortality: the Caregiver Health Effects Study. *JAMA: the journal of the American Medical Association 282*, 23 (1999), 2215–2219.

27.Schulz, R., O'Brien, A.T., Bookwala, J., and Fleissner, K. Psychiatric and physical morbidity effects of dementia caregiving: prevalence, correlates, and causes. *The Gerontologist 35*, 6 (1995), 771–791.

28.Siek, K.A., Khan, D.U., Ross, S.E., Haverhals, L.M., Meyers, J., and Cali, S.R. Designing a personal health application for older adults to manage medications: a comprehensive case study. *Journal of medical systems 35*, 5 (2011), 1099–1121.

29.Star, S.L. and Strauss, A. Layers of Silence, Arenas of Voice: The Ecology of Visible and Invisible Work. *Comput. Supported Coop. Work 8*, 1-2 (1999), 9–30.

30.Strauss, A., Fagerhaugh, S., Suczek, B., and Wiener, C. *Social Organization of Medical Work.* University of Chicago, Chicago, 1985.

31.Suchman, L. Making work visible. *Commun. ACM 38*, 9 (1995), 56–64.

Mutual Assessment in the Social Programmer Ecosystem: An Empirical Investigation of Developer Profile Aggregators

Leif Singer[1], Fernando Figueira Filho[2], Brendan Cleary[3], Christoph Treude[3], Margaret-Anne Storey[3], Kurt Schneider[1]

[1]Leibniz Universität Hannover, Hannover, Germany

[2]Universidade Federal do Rio Grande do Norte, Natal, Brazil

[3]University of Victoria, Victoria, Canada

leif.singer@inf.uni-hannover.de, fernando@dimap.ufrn.br, bcleary@uvic.ca, ctreude@gmail.com, mstorey@uvic.ca, kurt.schneider@inf.uni-hannover.de

ABSTRACT

The multitude of social media channels that programmers can use to participate in software development has given rise to online developer profiles that aggregate activity across many services. Studying members of such developer profile aggregators, we found an ecosystem that revolves around the *social programmer*. Developers are assessing each other to evaluate whether other developers are interesting, worth following, or worth collaborating with. They are self-conscious about being assessed, and thus manage their public images. They value passion for software development, new technologies, and learning. Some recruiters participate in the ecosystem and use it to find candidates for hiring; other recruiters struggle with the interpretation of signals and issues of trust. This mutual assessment is changing how software engineers collaborate and how they advance their skills.

Author Keywords

Virtual Communities; Social Media; Software Development; Software Engineering; Social Code Sharing; Reputation; Motivation; Gamification

ACM Classification Keywords

H.1.2. User/Machine Systems: Human factors

General Terms

Human Factors; Management.

INTRODUCTION

The open source and free software movements have altered the way software is built by extending the development process to large numbers of volunteers, often without explicit design or plans [20]. More recently, the advance of social media has changed the way developers collaborate, how they communicate, how they learn, and how they become informed about new technologies [30]. Social media provides new ways for developers to engage in *communities of practice* [35], to articulate their interests across communities, and to follow other developers' activities online.

Collaboration-oriented websites, such as GitHub and Stack Overflow, integrate social features to expose information about developers and their activities across open source projects [7]. These social features create new ways for developers to culturally identify with their communities, and enable new social relationships between developers and organizations within an interconnected ecosystem.

Masterbranch[1] and Coderwall[2] are examples of websites specifically created for the self-display of software developers, aggregating data from other sites such as GitHub and Stack Overflow[3]. The increased exposure generated by these sites has the potential to change which communities software developers engage in, how they interact with others, and how they prioritize their tasks.

This influences how software developers manage their reputation and how other stakeholders engage with developers. Developers use social media to connect with their communities and to monitor, publicize, and grow their skill sets. Social media are connecting like-minded developers, resulting in new social ties that foster collaboration and can encourage entrepreneurship at international scale. Companies, too, are starting to take into account such public profiles when reviewing candidates.

Understanding this *social programmer ecosystem* can give us insights into how social media mechanisms play a role in software engineering skill development, hiring practices, community formation and how social media may influence the quality of software being developed in these communities. For example, social media can be used to motivate developers to engage in software engineering practices more rigorously [27]. Companies and recruiters would benefit from understanding the behaviors and attitudes of their candidates.

This paper investigates how social media, specifically tailored to software developers, can influence the varied and many

[1]`http://masterbranch.com`

[2]`http://coderwall.com`

[3]`https://masterbranch.com/html/about.html`

stakeholders in software engineering communities. By using Masterbranch and Coderwall as an entry point, we surveyed and interviewed participants and bystanders of the social programmer ecosystem. We emphasize that we consider this ecosystem to be distinct from software ecosystems as defined by Lungu et al. [18] — instead, the social programmer ecosystem is comprised of a multitude of not necessarily related developers, projects, as well as web sites and services used for development and communication. Our approach allowed us to find the different actors' motivations and strategies for participating in this ecosystem. To the best of our knowledge, this is the first study investigating the social programmer ecosystem as a whole.

In this paper, we use the following terminology. A *profile* is a webpage that contains information about a user of the associated website. Profiles play a part in managing one's *public image*, that is, the way one is perceived publicly. *Social network sites* allow their users to create a profile, to connect with each other, and to inspect each other's connections with other users of the site [5] — examples are LinkedIn, Twitter, and GitHub. Masterbranch and Coderwall are *developer profile aggregators*, as they create profiles out of several existing profiles and activities on other sites for a single user.

This paper is structured as follows. In the following section, we discuss recent trends in social software development and the social media infrastructure underpinning those trends. Then we describe a study we conducted to investigate how software developers and other actors are involved and influenced by their participation in the social programmer ecosystem. Finally, we present our findings and analysis, and draw conclusions about how our findings may impact software development practice and research.

BACKGROUND

This section gives an overview of existing research on the use of social media in software development. Following this, we introduce the two websites that we investigated as our window into the social programmer ecosystem.

Social Media in Software Development

Social media is radically changing how software developers communicate and coordinate software development activities online [2]. While the Internet as a communications platform has long been used by developers to talk about and develop software, the advance of social media has introduced new mechanisms that enable large communities of developers to share knowledge, to share code, and to collaboratively create software in a manner that is more public and traceable than previously possible.

Historically, wikis [8] and blogs [24, 23] were the first social media mechanisms used by software developers, utilized mostly in the areas of requirements engineering and documentation, and to communicate high-level concepts [17, 1, 30]. Microblogs, such as Twitter, play a role in conversation and information sharing between software developers [3]. Tags, which became popular in general social media first, now help software developers communicate their concerns in task management [33] and add semantic information to source code [29]. On a larger scale, Stack Overflow and GitHub are two examples of how this kind of social media infrastructure is having an influence on software development practices and software developers.

Stack Overflow[4] is a website that facilitates the exchange of knowledge between software developers. Users post and answer questions related to development, and may comment and rate both questions and answers. The site uses *gamification* concepts — *"the use of game design elements in non-game contexts"* [9] — to encourage and reward community participation. For example, users receive points for posting questions and providing answers, and win "badges" for specific services or contributions to the community. Since its inception in 2008, more than 3.1 million questions have been asked on Stack Overflow, nearly 6.2 million answers have been provided, and over 12 million[5] comments have been submitted — all contributing to a large repository of software development knowledge. A question asked on Stack Overflow has a median answer time of 11 minutes [19]. Member profiles on Stack Overflow contain not only the number of points and badges received for activity on the website, but also a complete record of every question asked and answer provided along with the topics or tags in which the user was most active.

GitHub[6] is a website that allows developers to host their software project repositories using the popular Git revision control system. Since its launch in April 2008, the site has become one of the most popular source code hosting services with over 2 million repositories and over 1 million users[7]. In addition to providing revision control, GitHub also acts as a social network site that enables developers to connect and collaborate with each other. Through GitHub, developers can search for software projects that they are interested in, easily "fork" those projects to make their own contributions, and follow the work of others. The site organizes software repositories by software developer, rather than by project, showing a list of each developer's repositories and their activity across GitHub in a news feed. For a developer, this effectively makes their GitHub profile an easily accessible public portfolio of their open source development activity.

Social media systems such as Stack Overflow and Github are rapidly changing how developers advertise their skills and how they manage their time learning and programming. These types of websites not only provide them with a means for exchanging information, but also enable a level of transparency never seen before in software development. The online profiles of software developers, containing code, questions, and public communication, are available to the whole world for review.

[4] `http://stackoverflow.com`
[5] `http://data.stackexchange.com`
[6] `http://github.com`
[7] `http://github.com/blog/841-those-are-some-big-numbers`

Profiles in Online Communities

The importance of public user profiles for online communities and how people choose to manage their profiles in those communities is well established. One of the most extensively studied social media communities is Wikipedia [16, 14, 25, 13]. Since its inception in 2001, the online encyclopedia has come to be a reference model for how an online community can organize, collaborate, share, and create. Online communities such as Wikipedia are by definition open collaborative spaces that allow virtually anybody to contribute. Because of this inherent openness, the quality, accountability, and trustworthiness of contributions is often suspect. Therefore, it is important that a community be able to quickly and adequately evaluate a user's contributions to that community.

Several authors have discussed the issue of trust in online communities and how trust issues can be mitigated through the application of theories of social translucence and social transparency [11, 31, 32]. In their work on social transparency, Stuart et al. identify three social dimensions of information exchange: identity transparency (visibility of the identity of an actor); content transparency (visibility of the origin and history of actions taken on information); and interaction transparency (the awareness of actors of each other's participation in an information exchange) [31].

In online communities, different levels of transparency cause different behaviors. For example, higher identity transparency increases actor accountability: members are more likely to act in an accountable manner if their profile is available for other community members to review. Also, members can better assess the quality of information based on reputational accountability of the source. This effect has been shown by Hess and Stein in a study on Wikipedia's "featured articles" (articles voted by the community to be of very high quality) [28]. They found that articles with contributions from higher reputation authors — as judged from their public profiles — were more likely to become featured articles. However, a negative consequence of higher identity transparency could be that creativity suffers due to members not wishing to contribute information that, while potentially valuable to the community, might negatively affect their reputation.

Dabbish et al. investigate how software developers manage their online profiles by studying GitHub users [7]. They found that while explicit self-promotion was frowned upon, users were actively managing their public image and that users believed visibility to be important for the success of an open source project. Watching and being watched also have benefits and requirements. Users said that having watchers was a motivation to continue making contributions. Also, they were more conscious of the quality of their contributions when a project had more watchers.

Developer Profile Management

A recent trend in social media for software development is the emergence of profile aggregation sites for developers, such as Masterbranch and Coderwall. These websites are specifically tailored to software developers and aggregate developers' activities from across several other websites, providing a combined social programmer meta-profile. Contrary to more established sites, such as ohloh[8], Masterbranch and Coderwall focus on the developer rather than on individual projects.

Both sites provide public developer profiles that are mostly generated from activities on social code sharing sites such as GitHub, BitBucket[9], or SourceForge[10]. Other sites, such as LinkedIn[11] and Stack Overflow, are also supported. The customers of both sites are companies that are looking to hire software developers, for which the sites provide them with special access to their databases of developer profiles. According to their operators, Masterbranch and Coderwall both aim to make it easier for their customers to find candidates suitable for hiring. Customers of Masterbranch so far are mainly web-focused companies of all sizes, most of them younger than 10 years, and some of them very well-known.

Masterbranch

Masterbranch was founded in 2009 by Ignacio Andreu, Juan Luis Belmonte, and Vanessa Ramos. In 2011, the creators started growing it into a community for software developers. As of February 20th 2012, more than 9,000 users had registered with the site.

Fig. 1(a) shows a screenshot of a developer profile[12]. On top, it displays the name, location, and image of the user, as well as the *DevScore* (a value calculated from the developer's activities, such as commits to projects). To the right, a button allows users to *give free beer* to the developer — a symbolic act of endorsement.

A table generated from the user's repositories displays the distribution of programming languages across these projects (see Fig. 1(b)). Next, the profile lists projects the developer has worked on. For each project, the name, duration, description, and the programming languages used are displayed (Fig. 1(c)). The blue arcs indicate the percentage of commits the user contributed to a project.

Masterbranch awards *Most Valuable Programmer* (MVP) achievement badges to their users. Each week and for each project known to the site, the most active committer of the project earns the badge.

In addition to developer and project profiles, the site randomly displays some of the most active developers on its front page. An ordered list of the 95 most active developers acts as a simple leaderboard.

Coderwall

Coderwall was founded in 2011 by Matthew Deiters. As of March 1st 2012, more than 15,000 users had registered with the site.

Similar to Masterbranch, Coderwall analyzes the repositories of developers on social code sharing sites. It awards achievement badges to developers when certain conditions are met.

---

[8] `http://ohloh.net`

[9] `http://bitbucket.org/`

[10] `http://sourceforge.net/`

[11] `http://linkedin.com`

[12] Taken from `http://masterbranch.com/lsinger`

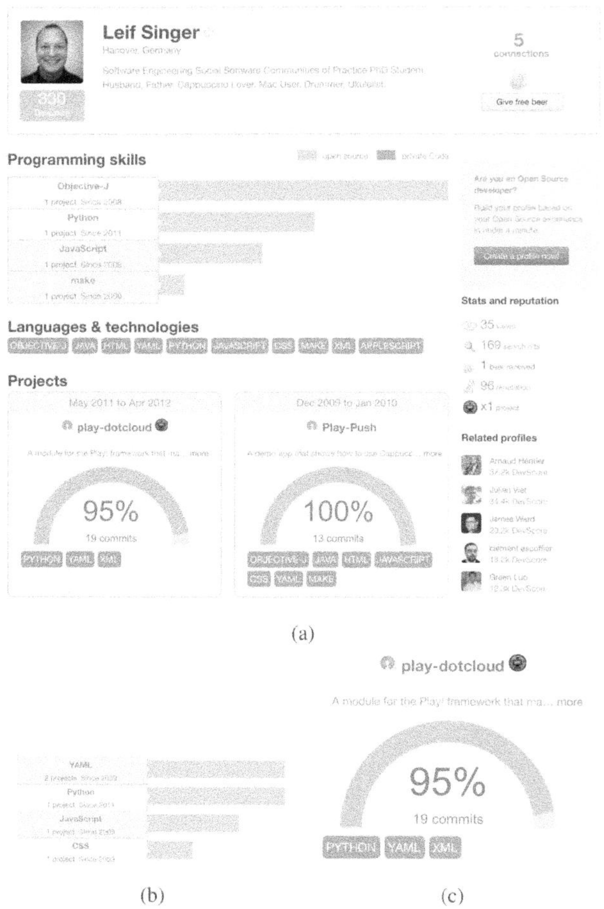

Figure 1. *Elements of a Masterbranch profile: (a) the profile itself (name/photo/URL redacted for review); (b) programming skills; (c) details for a project.*

For example, if a developer uses at least four different programming languages in the repositories she owns, Coderwall will award her the *Walrus* achievement badge (Fig. 2(a)). The *Forked* achievement is awarded if someone else forked — that is, made their own branch of — a developer's project (Fig. 2(b)).

(a) (b)

Figure 2. *Coderwall's* Walrus *(left) and* Forked *(right) achievement badges.*

Fig. 3(a) shows a screenshot of a developer profile[13]. On top, it displays the name, current company, location, and image of the user. Below this header, there is a timeline that chronologically lists events regarding that developer: when they earned which achievement, when they gave a talk, and others.

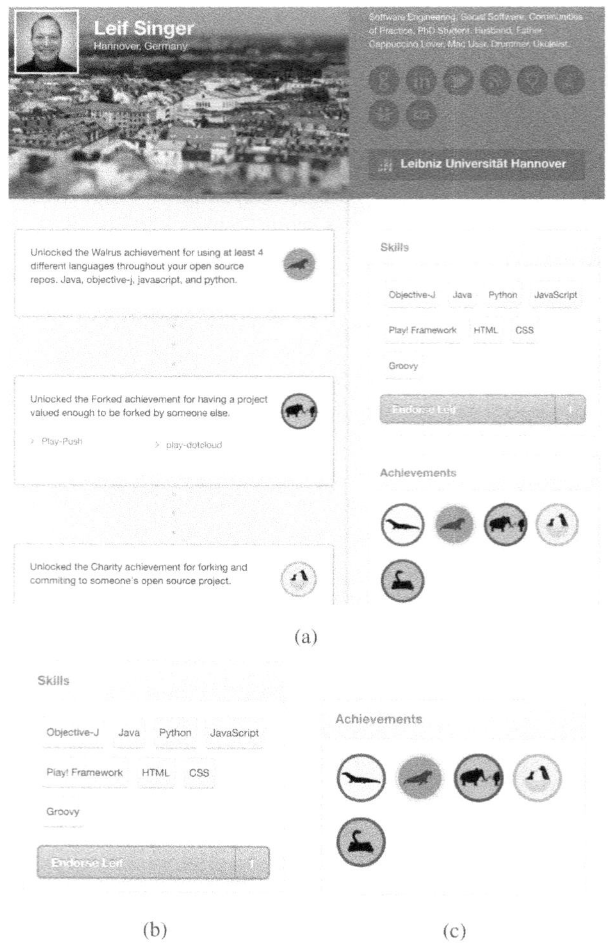

Figure 3. *Elements of a Coderwall profile: (a) the profile itself (name/photo/URL redacted for review); (b) programming skills and endorsements; (c) achievements awarded.*

The right side of the page displays the developer's skills. A button offers to *endorse* the developer — a low-effort mechanism that, similar to Facebook's *like*, might signal approval (Fig. 3(b)). Next to the button, the number of endorsements the developer has received is displayed. Finally, the profile page lists the achievements earned by the developer (Fig. 3(c)). During our study, Coderwall added a list of people the developer is connected with on Twitter (not pictured).

Developers registered with Coderwall may join a team, typically named after a company. For each team, the members' contributions are accumulated, resulting in an overall score for the team. This score determines the team's ranking on the Coderwall team leaderboard[14].

[13]Taken from `http://coderwall.com/lsinger`
[14]`http://coderwall.com/leaderboard`

STUDY DESIGN

We used a mixed methods approach to better understand how social media, specifically tailored to software developers, can influence the varied stakeholders in software engineering communities.

For the purposes of this paper, we focused on two groups of actors: software developers as well as employers and recruiters who might be using social media to assess potential job candidates and connect with them.

Research Questions

We designed a set of research questions to help us understand why software developers and other stakeholders participate in the social programmer ecosystem, how they interact, and the impact and challenges they face.

RQ1: Why are software developers and other actors participating in the social programming ecosystem?

Software developers' public display of their development activities through social media is a relatively recent phenomenon enabled by new technology platforms. Our first research question seeks to examine the motives that software developers and other actors have for participating in this emerging ecosystem.

RQ2: How do software developers and other actors interact in the social programmer ecosystem?

Users of developer profile aggregators are constantly signaling information about themselves and their work. This information might be interpreted differently by each group of actors participating in the social programmer ecosystem. We are particularly interested in how software developers might be interacting with each other using profile aggregators, but also in how recruiters and employers might be using information available on those sites to engage and interact with software developers. Research question 2 aims at examining these interactions.

RQ3: What is the impact of participating in the social programmer ecosystem?

Our third question aims to investigate the impact of participation in the ecosystem. We focus on how software developers and other actors might benefit from the environment.

RQ4: What are the risks and challenges faced by participating in the social programmer ecosystem?

Developer profiles might be interpreted differently based on differing organizational and cultural values of the participants of the social programmer ecosystem. Their interpretations may depend on community standards and conventions of practice induced by these standards [4]. Since such differences may give rise to communication problems, we investigate risks and challenges for those people using and participating in the ecosystem.

Procedures

To our knowledge, this paper is the first to report on a study of developer profile aggregators and their role in the social programmer ecosystem. As such, it is of an exploratory nature and is concerned with questions of *why* and *how*. This calls for qualitative methods, which we describe in this section.

In our study, we distributed questionnaires to Masterbranch and Coderwall users and then conducted interviews with some of them. We also interviewed employers and recruiters in order to include their perspectives.

Questionnaires

Our instrument consisted of two web-based questionnaires: one was tailored for Masterbranch users and the other for Coderwall users. The questionnaires were equal in content and order of items, except for the terminology referencing particular features of each site. We pre-tested the questionnaire by distributing it to 10 Coderwall users, of which 5 were sampled at random and 5 were taken from the site's front page. We received responses from 3 users, and 2 of those gave feedback on the survey. After minor changes in both questionnaires (wording; additional "I don't know" options), we distributed our survey to a larger sample.

We used several forms of distribution. First, the questionnaires were advertised on Twitter by some of the authors. The operators of Masterbranch and Coderwall supported us by retweeting our invitations. Masterbranch published a blog post, inviting their users to take part in the survey. In this phase, we gathered 28 responses from Codewall users and 9 responses from Masterbranch users. To increase the number of responses, we collected the profile pages and e-mail addresses of 315 random Coderwall members (Masterbranch does not provide random access to member profiles). We then e-mailed those users, inviting them to take our questionnaire. This resulted in another 46 responses.

Each form of distribution contained a URL linking to the respective questionnaire[15]. Both questionnaires were made available online using Google Forms from February 29th to April 19th 2012. Apart from an introductory cover letter, the main content sections were:

Demographics: we asked for information such as age, gender and country. We also measured respondents' professional experience in years and their current employment status, which included their primary responsibility at an organization (if employed), the organization's size and its age.

Site membership: we inquired when the respondent signed up for a profile on the respective site and asked why they did so.

Site features: for each of the features of Coderwall and Masterbranch described earlier, we asked how important they are to the respondent (on a Likert scale). We also asked some specific questions for each feature. For example, we asked respondents whether they care if people look at their profiles and what kind of profiles they are most interested in. We also asked whether they are applying explicit strategies for earning badges such as achievements on Coderwall, or the MVP on Masterbranch. Finally, we inquired about eventual strategies they might be using for earning achievements.

[15]Masterbranch: `http://bitly.com/yMo22Q`; Coderwall: `http://bitly.com/zqrCo9`

Responders were also asked to optionally submit their e-mail addresses if they agreed to be contacted for an interview with our research team. In total, we received 35 responses with e-mail addresses included, 31 of which came from Coderwall users.

Interviews

To scrutinize the answers from the survey, we invited all of the 35 survey participants who had volunteered to do interviews via e-mail. Of these 35, 14 software developers enrolled, 2 of them from the Masterbranch survey. For interviews with recruiters, we used a snowball sampling strategy, which yielded 12 recruiters volunteering. Our strategy involved sending personal messages to our acquaintances and friends working for software companies. Our sample consisted of people we already knew from our personal networks and others referred to by them. Some enrolled after reading a tweet or a blog post we created.

We then conducted semi-structured interviews with software developers and recruiters. We first asked developers about their current job situation — for example, what kind of company they work for or what the team structure is. We then used their answers from the questionnaire as a starting point for deeper inquiry, asking for the reasons and motivations for their behaviors.

In the interviews with recruiters, we asked about their strategies for evaluating candidates for software development positions in industry, especially with regard to the stages in which they would use information from the Web. We presented developer profiles available on Coderwall and Masterbranch to the recruiters, and asked them to think aloud while skimming through the page in order to get their impressions about the various features of the sites.

Interviews were conducted mostly via Skype and were recorded; for 2 of them we used a text chat. In total, we recorded 14 hours and 36 minutes of audio; the interview times ranged from 17 to 75 minutes.

Participants

Overall, we received 83 responses to our questionnaires, 74 of which came from Coderwall users. 68 of the respondents were software engineers (82%), 14 were team leaders and 1 was a non-technical co-founder of a software company. We interviewed 26 people; among them software engineers (50%), one software contractor, and recruiters (46%). Table 1 summarizes our interview participants and lists the identifiers we assigned to them.

Participants we interviewed as developers start with a *D*, while those we interviewed as recruiters start with an *R*. Note that during the interviews, we noticed that some of the developers were also involved in recruiting practices and we modified our questioning to cover these aspects as well (developers D4, D5, and D10).

Our interviewees had diverse backgrounds. To illustrate this, Table 2 provides a short introduction for some of the participants.

Software developers	
D1, D3-D5, D7, D8, D10-D13	employed in a software company
D6, D9, D14	consultant or contractor
D2	unemployed
Recruiting	
R1-R5, R7, R8, R11, R12	for their employer
R6, R9, R10	for customer companies

Table 1. *Summary of interview participants.*

Code	*Background*
D1	Developer at a Web development shop in Norway, mostly Ruby development.
D3	Developer working in an image recognition company from Spain.
D6	Developer and team coordinator in a Linux security and deployment company in the USA.
D10	Developer and team coordinator in a large software company in the USA, managing proprietary and open source efforts.
D11	Java developer for a Polish outsourcing company.
R3	CEO of a local German IT services company.
R5	CTO of a German analytics and research company.
R8	Project manager in a research subsidiary of a large German carmaker.
R9	Employee at a recruiting company based in the UK, focusing on mobile and Web developers.
R12	Hiring manager at a *Big Data* company based in Germany and the USA.

Table 2. *Backgrounds of select interview participants.*

Data Analysis

We used an approach based on grounded theory for data analysis [6]. Questionnaire data was split into two data sets and two of the authors open coded each set independently. Two authors then cooperatively engaged in axial coding our preliminary set of codes and, as a result, 15 categories emerged. We used those categories to code interview data. Then, we transcribed excerpts from the interviews that were related to our research questions. The next phase comprised of selective coding over all extracted quotes (from questionnaire responses and interview transcriptions). During this process, we iterated on our previous code system and identified both the core categories and relationships that would help us answer our research questions.

FINDINGS

This section reports the findings from the surveys and the interviews with developers and recruiters. For brevity, we provide quotes only for some of the findings. The source of each quote is noted in square brackets — *[Dx]* referring to an interview with a developer; *[Rx]* an interview with a recruiter; *[SMx]* and *[SCx]* to survey answers for Masterbranch and Coderwall, respectively.

RQ1: Reasons for Participation

To answer research question 1, we investigated *why* developers and recruiters participate in the social programmer ecosystem.

Developers

Many software developers told us that they are ***curious about technology, passionate to learn, and always trying to improve themselves as developers***. A variation of this was given in 20 of the 83 survey answers as the reason to join one of the developer profile aggregators.

Taking part in the ecosystem allows developers to discover novelty — by joining a developer profile aggregator, publishing code on GitHub, or interacting with others on Twitter. Seeing others do interesting new things with technology ***inspires*** them. A special case are ***high-profile developers*** that are vocal about their technological discoveries, respected in the community, and followed by many.

"On Twitter, I follow a few prominent software developers. For example, Kelly Sommers[16] from Canada, she's constantly trying new things. I don't think she ever sleeps. She's a great source of inspiration." [D11]

A reason that was very commonly given for participation in the ecosystem was ***enjoying the interactions*** with other developers: *"this incredible group of fascinating people that get interested in all sorts of things, makes it interesting to talk with them, and work with them" [D1]*. This was mentioned in 8 of 14 developer interviews.

Interestingly, very few participants told us that they were looking for ***competition*** with regard to the number of projects, followers, or badges one has on the different social media sites. It was mentioned by 5 developers in the interviews, and only by 3 of 83 survey respondents when asked about achievements. Related to that, there was also the theme of ***pride*** — developers said they liked showing off their achievements and comparing themselves with others. Some specifically mentioned that they were proud of being part of a great team.

The most important reason for enjoying the community was ***recognition*** of others. In the survey, 19 of 83 answers with regard to the *endorsement* features of the websites were about recognition or validation of one's work. Developers like getting respect from their peers — and from random people as well — for the work they are doing. *"I would like to have some recognition from the community [...] [my projects] are fun to me, but if they are only on my hard disk then nobody knows" [D3]*

Similarly, ***helping others*** was also very important for several developers: *"I like to be useful to others, and this is a good way to do that" [D3]* Some explicitly said that ***interacting with, and helping others, motivated them*** to contribute more and to become better developers.

Finally, a few participants mentioned that they were ***pushed into the ecosystem by their peers*** — they had been asked to join a site or a service, and to contribute code of their own. *"I started to publish because my friends told me that [a project] didn't have any [visibility]" [D3]*

A few developers mentioned that they were striving for visibility because they were ***searching for work***. Taking into account all questions of the survey, 6 of 83 respondents mentioned this. These developers said that they would like to improve their chances of being recognized by recruiters. They believe that the simplifications of experience that the developer profile aggregators provide help non-technical recruiters in assessing developers: *"I love the idea of the badges, it helps communicate to non-technical people (like recruiters) what I know" [SC14]*

As we will see in our findings for research question 4, this is not generally true. Yet, showing off diversity is important for developers, as they believe that recruiters value it as well. The insights for research question 2 will support this finding.

Recruiters

Recruiters have two main reasons for taking interest in the social programmer ecosystem. For one, they see its potential for better assessment of potential candidates. Much information on developers is now publicly available, such as public interaction and engagement. This enables recruiters to find out more about cultural fit, values, and soft skills. For example, they are looking for people who care about their work and those who are ***passionate*** about it. *"I want people who care, and I'm trying to find out whether they do care based on their activity on the Web." [D10]*

The other reason for recruiters to take part is the shortage of software developers to fill open positions. Few are available, and the really good ones are often employed and not looking for a career change. Recruiters want to use the ecosystem to ***actively engage*** with developers they might not be able to sway otherwise.

Related, recruiters are trying to ***speed up finding new candidates***. Many companies desperately need to hire developers quickly — not being able to do so hurts businesses, as it slows down their progress. *"we cannot progress as fast as we would like to. [...] the workload is enormous and that's why we try to find these guys as fast as possible." [R5]*

RQ2: Modes and Terms of Interaction

To answer research question 2, we investigated *how* developers and recruiters interact in the social programmer ecosystem.

[16] `https://twitter.com/kellabyte`

Survey Results

Table 3 shows the results regarding the subjective importance of different features of the developer profile aggregators. All 83 respondents were factored in. The questions provided a Likert-type scale ranging from *1 — very important* to *5 — not important at all*. An option reading *"I don't know that feature"* was also available.

	Mean	*Median*	*Don't know*
Achievements	2.5	2.0	1
Endorsements	2.8	3.0	27
Leaderboard	3.3	3.0	15
Featured Developers	3.3	3.0	37

Table 3. *Importance of the features of developer profile aggregators.*

The achievements feature, possibly being the most visible, was most important, followed by the endorsement feature. Strikingly, 37 of 83 respondents did not know the "featured developers" on the front pages of the developer profile aggregators. Supported by this additional data, we will now answer research question 2.

Developers

Many developers participate in the social programmer ecosystem to connect with others — peers, interesting people, or high-profile developers. To be able to do so, they need to ***assess other developers*** first.

As part of this assessment, they are investigating ***what others have created***. Thus, the open source projects of developers mediate relationships in the ecosystem. They allow developers to construct a "coder footprint" of one another. *"[When] I look at repos around this topic [data visualization], I may be interested in seeing the coder footprint of people that work in this area [...] their favorite languages, the topics they write code about, what they work on" [D6]*

Constructing such a footprint not only helps in assessing strangers on the Internet. It is also being used to ***make sense of coworkers*** who might be geographically dispersed. In a similar manner, developers are using ***common interests*** to find interesting people and connect with them. While some developers will interact with those they discover, others choose to ***passively follow*** the activity of developers.

Developers are aware that their peers are assessing them as well. This leads to developers wanting to manage their *"personal brands" [D9]*, that is, consciously constructing a public image of themselves. The social programmer ecosystem is one of ***mutual assessment***.

Developers enjoy and desire ***recognition by peers***, which was mentioned by 11 of 14 interviewed developers: *"there's the social component. So peers — developers, coders — can see that. It gives you a good feeling when others see what I've achieved" [D12]* On the other end of this interaction, developers do recognize and ***acknowledge good work***: *"I knew he worked hard in that area and felt like giving him recognition" [SC58]* This finding may be related to the relative importance of the *endorsement* feature (see Table 3).

Regarding the employment aspect, developers often view recruiters as spammers who send them irrelevant employment offers. Developers have a ***bad perception of recruiters*** and try to avoid them. Instead, they prefer utilizing their personal network and word-of-mouth for finding work. *"I don't like recruiters [...] it's largely who you know" [D5]* Amongst other insights, the following paragraphs will show how recruiters are trying to fight this perception.

Recruiters

From the perspective of recruiters, we found a diverse set of strategies for connecting with interesting software developers. Several of the recruiters we talked to used relatively traditional means: for example, ***generic professional networking sites***, such as LinkedIn or Xing.

Those who were more technical themselves, or even considered themselves or their companies as part of the *in-crowd*, often used their ***personal networks for recruiting***: *"Our lead designer, we hired through referral, basically. Our CEO is friends with [well-known entrepreneur] and [...] our lead designer was the lead designer at [entrepreneur's most successful startup]." [R11]*

Going where the developers are to connect with them — that is, on social code sharing sites or Q&A sites — was considered to be effective by most recruiters we talked to. Some recruiters actually succeeded in doing so, but many were ***struggling with technical culture***, or overcoming the ***bad reputation*** recruiters have with developers. They tried ***using social media*** to appear more authentic and become part of developers' personal networks: *"[...] we use a lot of social media [...] hearing, talking to different developers we already know is another way, recommendations are one of the best ways to find the best developers" [R10]*

When evaluating a developer, recruiters first ***filter by skills***, using skill lists provided by many web-based profiles. *"The most important point here is the tag cloud about his skills[17]" [R5]*. None of the recruiters we talked to told us that they used certifications to assess the skills of developers. When certifications were mentioned by a recruiter, it was to say that they didn't mean much to them.

When these first line filters had narrowed down the candidate pool, recruiters took a more thorough look to find out about the experiences and social skills of a developer. A common baseline check was looking at a developer's ***activity and engagement in open source***. For many recruiters, that would mean profiles on Stack Overflow, GitHub, and Twitter. However, if there was nothing to be found, recruiters said they do not outright reject the candidate — they would assume that this might be a more private person, for example.

If they find something online about developers, recruiters use a diverse set of signals to get a picture of a candidate. Regarding the technical skills and work style of the developers,

[17]Interviewee thinking aloud while looking at developer profile.

the more technical recruiters looked at whether they used ***best practices*** adequately, such as testing, version control, or commenting. *"I always look to see if they're writing tests, as a key. If they're not, I don't wanna hire them" [D10]*

Several recruiters used other people's ***endorsements of a developer's code*** as a proxy to assess their technical skills. *"[it's] very helpful if you have a project valued enough to be forked by somebody else, this is quite interesting [...] because it really shows that it has some meaning for other people[17]" [R7]*. They also use these endorsements to assess soft skills, such as communication behavior: *"In the long run, you don't get people to follow your repository by just pushing out code. It means that he's sufficiently good at other things as well, such as communication." [R4]*

Recruiters try to assess several very intangible attributes of developers using social media and open source activity. 5 of 12 interviewed recruiters mentioned that they were looking for ***diversity in developers***: for example, by looking at the number of different programming languages they are comfortable with. As we questioned this further, two underlying reasons emerged.

For one, they were looking for ***fast learners*** who are adaptable to change. Recruiters mentioned that software development is very fast-paced and technologies come and go. So employees need to be able to react to that with flexibility: *"He's relatively broad.[17] [...] we're looking for people who can get into new concepts quickly. That's what makes a good coder." [R4]*

Secondly, recruiters were often looking for ***passionate developers*** — this was mentioned by 11 of 12 interviewed recruiters. To assess passion, they mostly used social media that were not directly related to code. Many mentioned Twitter as a sign for how interested and engaged a developer was with regard to technology: *"A 9 to 5 developer is not tweeting about the latest stuff that's coming out of the W3C mailing list. A 9 to 5 developer is tweeting a picture of the hamburgers he's frying at 4:30." [D10]* The reason they were looking for passionate developers was one of drive and job satisfaction, both allegedly leading to better results.

Finally, recruiters tried to find candidates who would ***share the company's values***, for example being product-focused: *"we're looking for people who are [...] product-focused, they're gonna talk about things beyond programming. I guess you could say 'well-rounded' [...] they love coding, but it goes deeper than that" [R11]*

RQ3: The Impact of Participation

This section reports what we found with regard to research question 3, which asks about the *impact* of participation in the social programmer ecosystem.

Developers

Our interviews revealed that the ***gamification*** employed by features such as Coderwall's achievements is, in fact, at least somewhat effective: *"if I need to make a repository, I'll put it on Github, it'll exist forever, and I can get a badge for it. That's really awesome. [...] It pushed me in the right direction. It forced me to play the game for the right reasons." [D13]* In our interviews, 8 of 14 developers explicitly mentioned that they felt motivated by the developer profile aggregators. This may be related to the high importance given to the achievement feature in Table 3.

A closer look revealed that those features ***lower the barriers for participation*** in developer teams and communities. As a result, opportunities for participation are more visible and tangible: *"I have been trying to get into [the open source] scene for a while, when you see an achievement that is available for a contribution, it is the final nudge to make an actual contribution." [D2]*

Developers also reported other reasons for participation that go beyond ludic motivations and might impact their professional progress. For instance, ***learning new programming languages*** is a consequence of engaging in such an environment: *"I wouldn't think of starting a repository in a specific language just to earn an achievement, but it may push me towards choosing a new language to learn" [D6]*. Also, achievements are seen as a window for ***exploration and experimentation***. When asked about why achievements are important, one respondent said: *"they make me want to achieve something that I didn't know about before or open me up to new ideas." [SC38]*

The impact of such features is not limited to individuals. They ***motivated whole software teams to contribute more***: *"Coderwall has generally upped the game in the office amongst our engineers. It has helped to encourage all of us to publish more code online." [SC51]*

As we saw in the findings for research question 1, developers are interested in novelty. Now we find that their drive for trying new things helps them ***diffuse new ideas***. *"Generally, I sign up for every online service I think I might find interesting. [...] now our entire team is on Coderwall" [SC51]*

Recruiters

Finally, participation also has a concrete impact on recruiting practices. Features on Masterbranch and Coderwall aggregate and quantify developers' activities and artifacts. In doing so, they enable others to ***understand complex attributes*** of developers with less cognitive load. We asked a developer who also turned out to be actively involved in recruiting how fast learning can be identified in developers: *"I used to look for that manually in GitHub repositories, but Coderwall and others make it easier now" [D4]*

RQ4: Risks and Challenges of Participation

Research question 4 is concerned with potential *risks and challenges* that result from participation in the social programmer ecosystem. Backing up the necessity for this inquiry, a developer also greatly involved with recruiting told us: *"It's a new space. I think there's some value to this kind of thing [Coderwall], but I'm not sure where it is yet. Because it's a new idea." [D10]*

Developers

Many of the developers we talked to were rather isolated locally, but well-connected with weak ties on a global scale. Even though these were passionate and interested persons, they were not able to gain too much from participation in mutual assessment as implemented by developer profile aggregators: *"[Importance of leaderboard] It's not very important to me now as soon as most of my colleagues are not very interested in open source" [SC24]* They simply ***lack the social connectedness*** that seems to help in adopting such approaches. The relative obscurity of the *leaderboard* feature that can be seen in Table 3 may be related to this finding.

Even though we have found strong preferences for passionate novelty seeking, some developers mentioned that they ***struggle to keep up*** with their fast-paced environment. *"The whole 'what's new today thing' is exhausting" [D1]*

Because developer profile aggregators, social code sharing sites, and social media in general are very public by their nature, the actual audience of content cannot be determined beforehand. We found two conflicting views regarding this issue.

Several developers and recruiters are aware that ***public signals should not receive too much weight*** — they mentioned that the reasons for the existence or absence of such signals can be very different from what people might assume. *"The GitHub repository doesn't show everything though. I wouldn't discard someone with an emptyish GitHub repo. Might just show that most of his/her projects were closed-source. That's why nothing can replace a few e-mails." [D4]*

Recruiters

However, some participants involved with recruiting said they would be ***irritated by a lack of public activity*** for a developer. One recruiter told us: *"I find it kind of strange if a software developer doesn't use Twitter or GitHub[17] [...] Because git is the factual standard at the moment for version control, yeah? At least for people who try to go with the [latest] technology, the early adopters. [...] we actually want people to be passionate about technology." [R7]* For this recruiter, having adopted Git and being public about it was actually a required sign of passion for technology in a developer.

Non-technical recruiters, however, struggled with the ***interpretation of signals*** from developer profile aggregators and social code sharing sites. *"Well, I don't know all these achievements. They look fun! But they don't really help me.[17]" [R12]* As a consequence, these recruiters did not trust the sites and therefore did not use them: *"we don't use those sites [Coderwall, Masterbranch, GitHub, Stack Overflow]. We know too little about them." [R8]*

Of the 12 recruiters we interviewed, 7 had used general social media for candidate assessment before (LinkedIn, Twitter, Google+). 5 had experiences with using developer-specific social media (Stack Overflow, GitHub), and 1 had used a developer profile aggregator before (Masterbranch).

DISCUSSION

In this section, we discuss some of the most important themes that emerged from our study and their potential impact on software engineering practice.

Mutual Assessment

The core category that we found in our study was that of *mutual assessment*: developers, recruiters, and companies continually used social media to assess each other — across as well as within these groups. For this, the high degree of social transparency [31] in the social programmer ecosystem provides novel reputation signals, and known signals that are being used in novel ways. The aggregation performed by sites such as Masterbranch and Coderwall helps in quantifying the activities of the programmers in the ecosystem, and it also enables the creation of symbols for certain kinds of participation in the ecosystem.

For developers, it appears to be much more important to assess other developers, rather than recruiters or companies. Our findings indicate that developers are in the center of the ecosystem, and that securing employment is only a second priority. For the developers we studied, everything revolves around their passion for technology and learning, as well as being connected to other passionate developers. Thus, they assess each other in terms of the technologies they use and the problems they solve, using each others' *coder footprint* (see below) with the goal of finding new stimuli and collaborators.

Developers use the signals in the ecosystem to assess companies as well: *"I want to gauge the quality of developers in a certain organization, so I can determine if I'm a good fit for a position there."* The presence of a company's developers in the social programmer ecosystem is an indication of that company's philosophy with regard to using the latest technology and participating in open source. While developers do not seem to like recruiters as they are often considered spammers, we found that some recruiters are actively trying to create an authentic identity in the social programmer ecosystem for networking purposes in an attempt to fight this perception.

We suspect that this mutual assessment in the social programmer ecosystem may be supporting the dissemination and adoption of technology and software development practices. According to Rogers' *innovation-decision process* [26], to adopt an innovation, individuals first need to gain knowledge of it. The second step of that process is *persuasion*, the formation of a favorable or unfavorable attitude towards the innovation. Both processes are heavily influenced by opinion leadership. As we saw in our research, the social programmer ecosystem supports the formation of such authorities — e.g. through several reputation-relevant signals — and provides different communication channels through which to diffuse information about innovations. The mutual assessment may help creating, judging, and finding opinion leaders. For a more complete picture of adoption processes in the social programmer ecosystem, further research is needed.

Related to this, Murphy-Hill and Murphy [21] show that developers learn about new technology from chance encounters with peers. Draxler and Stevens [10] studied how Eclipse users appropriate plug-ins, distinguishing between need-driven and opportunity-driven appropriation. We see equivalents to these modes in discovery processes in social media — need-driven and opportunity-driven discovery. Nardi [22] found similar processes when studying Communities of Practice [15] of spreadsheet users. Individuals who were known for their expertise — coined *gardeners* or *tinkerers* — were approached by less proficient users about problem solutions and innovations. In our study, we saw hints that the high degree of social transparency in the social programmer ecosystem may support both serendipitous discoveries and targeted searches for solutions — however, without the requirement for physical proximity. Stack Overflow with its Q&A format seems to produce very need-driven content. On Twitter, both forms are supported: members passively follow trustable sources for opportunity-driven discovery and actively interact with others for need-driven discovery. Sites like Masterbranch and Coderwall support almost no direct interaction between users, concentrating on creating opportunities for serendipitous discoveries.

Passion

The core aim of mutual assessment, we found, was identifying *passion* in others. From the perspective of a company, the active participation of a developer in the ecosystem shows the developer's passion for technology and learning in general.

This passion appears to be the main motivation for programmers to participate in the ecosystem. The participants in our surveys and interviews love programming and creating things. The applications used in the social programmer ecosystem and their features make it easy for them to find interesting potential collaborators as well as interesting new technologies to learn. In that sense, the signals of the ecosystem are a mechanism to reduce uncertainty about technologies as well as other stakeholders.

Developer profile aggregators are a vehicle for programmers to showcase themselves and their achievements. The focus is not on job hunting, but rather on having fun, building something cool, and generally *"being awesome"* — as one of our survey respondents put it. Developers use profile aggregators to show their peers and potential collaborators how passionate they are and that they love what they do. Incidentally, it is this passion that recruiters and companies are looking for as well, in particular passion for learning, using, and mastering new technologies. This passion connects developers with each other, and — to a lesser extent — with recruiters.

As reported by Vallerand et al. [34], passion and performance are deeply connected. Therefore it makes sense for all stakeholders in the social programmer ecosystem to be looking for passionate individuals: these are more likely to perform better in companies, as recruiters, or as collaborators in open source projects. Specifically for the latter, Wu et al. [36] found that high motivation — for which passion may be a sign — may influence future engagement in open source software projects, helping others in deciding which potential employees or collaborators might be most valuable to invest in.

Coder Footprint

In several interviews with developers, the interviewees struggled to say exactly what they were looking for in other developers. Some wished to *"get a better picture"*, others wanted to *"get a feel"* for what kind of developer the other person was. They all agreed, however, that multiple factors are important: the developer's technical niche and its popularity in the community; their diversity; their passion for technology; their standing in the community. Quoting one of our interviewees, we call this their *coder footprint*. While sites such as GitHub are also suitable, developer profile aggregators in particular provide a condensed representation of the coder footprint that can be grasped quickly.

Grasping the coder footprint seems to be the primary function of the profile aggregators. Both developers and technical recruiters claimed to be trying to get a feel for what other developers were about. Non-technical recruiters seemingly lacked the technical intuition required and resorted to determining attributes that were more fact-based and easier to interpret without a technical background.

The coder footprint serves an important purpose in the social programmer ecosystem. Developers are driven by a passion for new technologies, new ideas, and learning. The coder footprint allows them to navigate a vast social space much more easily, supporting them in their search for novelty and social connectedness. While sites are still experimenting on how to get the coder footprint right, and several interviewees voiced criticism and concerns regarding the validity of the signals found on developer profile aggregators, the current iteration is an already useful glimpse at what future developers might be using to assess and explore each other.

As argued by Funder [12], any accuracy when judging the personalities of others *"stems from the relevance, availability, detection, and utilization of behavioral cues."* The social transparency [31] found on sites and services of the social programmer ecosystem provides for many such cues. For example, one interviewee explicitly mentioned that he watches how potential hires behave on public mailing lists and in issue discussions on GitHub — an application of *interaction transparency* for assessment. The coder footprint as a simplification of such behavior seems to be a useful construct helping with the aforementioned mutual assessment.

Diversity

Developers were regarded as *diverse* when they were perceived as interested in multiple technologies, ideally with different characteristics. Especially very current technologies — such as Clojure or NodeJS — and those requiring different modes of thinking — e.g. object-oriented vs. functional programming languages — were used as signals for diversity.

An essential part of the coder footprint, diversity was considered important by developers and recruiters alike. Developers tried to attain it themselves as part of their personal improvement efforts and also looked for it in other developers. Recruiters used diversity as a signal for fast learners and adaptability, which they deemed very important traits in the fast-paced software development business.

We believe this might be an indicator for a cultural change in software development. Proficiency in a certain niche is no longer enough, as developers are expected to be able to easily adapt to a changing technology landscape. Importantly, this expectation is not only one of companies or recruiters, but also one of developers — they expect it from others and also from themselves.

Several parties might be interested in leveraging this insight. Developers that are aware of it might take it as a motivation to become more diverse themselves. Others might try exploiting the potential for manipulation, for example by creating many repositories containing trivial projects in several programming languages. Recruiters that are not yet proficient in interpreting developer profiles might use it as a guideline in their assessments. Finally, developer training — for example at universities — is already somewhat diverse in that it mostly teaches concepts instead of concrete programming languages. However, these are often restricted to only one or two programming paradigms, such as object-oriented programming. Taking a cue from software development practitioners and companies, universities might want to support their students in attaining a higher level of diversity.

While most participants of our study used diversity in programming languages as a signal for actual diversity and adaptability, there might be other, more appropriate measures for this character trait. A few interviewees stressed the importance of public communication, for example on Twitter, to help in assessing this. Therefore, tag clouds and badges of programming languages might just be a first iteration of a more important idea — simplifying the assessment of diversity in developers.

As Ye and Kishida report [37], learning is an important motivation of open source developers. Diversity as a signal for being able to learn different concepts seems like a good way to gauge the motivation of a developer. Therefore, similar to passion, diversity may be an appropriate surrogate for assessing others' motivations. Again, social transparency in the social programmer ecosystem makes suitable signals publicly available.

Impact

Our findings indicate the presence of novel dynamics between the stakeholders of the social programmer ecosystem, enabled by an unprecedented social transparency in the software engineering domain. For each group of stakeholders, these dynamics may have multiple positive as well as negative impacts.

The software developers we talked to viewed participation in social media and mutual developer assessment in a largely positive light. For them, it presents opportunities to learn about new technologies and to connect with other like-minded people who they might not be able to find locally in their own organizations. Several developers also spoke of how participating in the social programmer ecosystem and knowing that other developers were following their activities propelled them to contribute more or better quality code, and to improve themselves as developers. This effect has been shown for GitHub by Dabbish et al. [7].

From a recruiting perspective, the impact is less clear. Some recruiters and companies that are already familiar with the ecosystem are able to parse the activity signals generated by developers to a degree. Others who are outside of the immediate community have more trouble interpreting developer activity in social media and weighing the value of different kinds of activities.

This study explores how a group of early adopter software developers are interacting with new social media platforms. As such, the question arises as to whether and how these trends extrapolate to the rest of the software development community. Software developers outside the early adopters group may find many of the same benefits in using social media as part of their development activities. However, motivations for participation by this group may well differ from those of the early adopters.

There is also the issue of developers feeling compelled to participate in the ecosystem to keep up with expectations of the wider software development community. Many developers are not able to participate freely in social media due to their employment circumstances; others may be dissuaded by the potential for public criticism of their work. A future developer landscape that expects a public portfolio of work available for contribution or participation in the community could have the unintended consequence of isolating these developers from the community rather than connecting them to it.

Arguably, recruiters and software companies have the most to gain from increased software developer participation in social media. Coarse-grained quality indicators such as CVs and even professional and academic qualifications have until now been the mainstay of resources for assessing developers' suitability for job opportunities. With more and more developer activity taking place in social media and archived in public portfolios, recruiters and companies will have access to much more active and historical information about candidates than previously available. As interpreting this information might be easier for recruiters with technical backgrounds, this could have an impact on the skills expected from recruiters as well.

LIMITATIONS

As with any research methodology, there are limitations with our choice of research methods.

We used a Grounded Theory approach, which involved conducting surveys and semi-structured interviews, and coding of the results from these. These methods do not allow us to infer statistical significance of our findings. However, these methods are well-suited for exploration and discovery and can suggest how and why stakeholders of the social programmer ecosystem participate in it. As this is the first study on the role of developer profile aggregators, we consider these methods and their focus on exploration to be suitable for our purposes.

With regard to developers, the responses to our questionnaires and interviews came exclusively from members of the Coderwall and Masterbranch sites, as these were the most visible when we started our research[18]. Recruiters were mostly contacted via Twitter and personal networks. Participants in both the questionnaires and the interviews were self-selected by volunteering for them. Therefore, the responses are naturally biased. We found that many developer participants exhibited traits of the *innovators* adopter category as defined by Rogers [26]: with only few local ties, they were connected globally with many weak ties and used those to bring new ideas and technologies into their own local societies — Rogers calls them *venturesome*. This character trait may have helped with the relatively good response rates for the questionnaires and interviews (e.g., 35 of 83 total respondents offered to do an interview, of which 14 were realized). Even before sending out personal invitations to members of Coderwall, most responses came from members of Coderwall instead of Masterbranch. That might be explained by the relatively high media exposure the site had recently[19].

Unfortunately, we were not able to get in contact with customer companies of Masterbranch or Coderwall that are paying for specialized access to developer profiles for hiring purposes. We believe that these companies would have added another interesting perspective to our research.

Another limitation of this study lies in the relatively low number of interviews conducted. However, we were able to increase the credibility and validity of our findings by triangulating data from interviews and survey responses. Also, the interviewees had a wide range of different backgrounds, allowing us to consider many different perspectives in this work.

The current users of developer profile aggregators are *innovators* and *early adopters*, and thus are not representative of the entire software developer population. However, they allow us to gain early insights into the role of profile aggregators in the ecosystem of social programmers, and to shed light on the potential impact of these sites for software developers, recruiters, and companies.

Coderwall and Masterbranch are among the first sites to aggregate developer data across various social media developer services. As more individuals start using these sites and other services emerge, additional studies should be conducted to gain further insights into the complex ecosystem of social programmers.

CONCLUSIONS & FUTURE WORK

In this paper, we discussed a group of software developers that are using new social media tools to communicate and share their development activity with fellow developers and other interested actors. These developers, their motivations, and the technology infrastructure they use combine to produce an ecosystem where open collaboration and public sharing of who you are and what you do is ingrained. Apart from a GitHub-specific study by Dabbish et al. [7], our work is the first to investigate the dynamics of the social programmer ecosystem.

Initially, we were motivated to understand why some developers choose to publish and promote their development activity online. In our investigation, we performed surveys and interviews with software developers and recruiters affiliated with this ecosystem. We identified their motivations for participating, how they interact with other stakeholders, what effects participation may have on their learning and job prospects, as well as risks and challenges stakeholders in this ecosystem may face.

Our findings indicate that the developers we surveyed are motivated by a strong passion for discovery and learning about new software development technologies. To satisfy this need, they explore the technology landscape through the prism of other like-minded developers' activities and coder footprints. They are aware of other developers and actively assess and are assessed by them. This process is facilitated and encouraged by the underlying technology infrastructure of the social programmer ecosystem, which places its emphasis not on software projects, but rather on software developers and their activities across multiple projects and communities. Among our study participants, the developers are at home in this ecosystem, the recruiters less so, but it is becoming an increasingly important aspect of what they do.

This study reports on relatively recent trends in social media and software development and how early adopter software developers are participating and interacting in this ecosystem. As such, our findings may have implications for the future of software engineering at large. For companies and recruiters, developer activity archived in social media is a potentially potent resource for assessing developer capability and matching developers to job opportunities. For developers, it represents opportunities for learning and discovery, staying current with trends, and benchmarking against other developers. Yet, it also poses questions about how developers who, by choice or otherwise, choose not to participate in public social media, will be viewed by the rest of the developer community. These and other populations have not yet been considered in our study.

It is also unclear which sub-communities may exist in the social programmer ecosystem, even though our study discovered some clues regarding this: for example, some developers were passionate novelty-seekers and deeply connected to the "in-crowd", others were remote and passive consumers, and we also saw some developers who were overwhelmed by having to keep on top of things. Some recruiters were using social media to their advantage successfully, others tried less successfully, and yet others were not participating at all. Several interviews hinted at an influence such communities and the high degree of social transparency may have on the learning processes of developers and the adoption of programming-specific practices and technology. We plan to investigate these issues of the social programmer ecosystem in future work, for which this study may provide a first foundation.

[18] Another recently popular site is `http://geekli.st`.

[19] `http://techcrunch.com/2012/02/27/coderwall-hacker-reputation-system/`

ACKNOWLEDGMENTS
We thank Vanessa Ramos of Masterbranch and Matthew Deiters of Coderwall for their support in conducting this research. Furthermore, we're grateful to the participants of our survey and interviews. We appreciate comments by Cassandra Petrachenko that helped improve this paper, as well as the anonymous reviewers' valuable insights.

REFERENCES
1. Ahmadi, N., Jazayeri, M., Lelli, F., and Nesic, S. A survey of social software engineering. In *Automated Software Engineering - Workshops, 2008. ASE Workshops 2008. 23rd IEEE/ACM International Conference on* (sept. 2008), 1 -12.
2. Begel, A., DeLine, R., and Zimmermann, T. Social media for software engineering. In *Proceedings of the FSE/SDP workshop on Future of software engineering research*, FoSER '10, ACM (New York, NY, USA, 2010), 33–38.
3. Bougie, G., Starke, J., Storey, M.-A., and German, D. M. Towards understanding twitter use in software engineering: preliminary findings, ongoing challenges and future questions. In *Proceedings of the 2nd International Workshop on Web 2.0 for Software Engineering*, Web2SE '11, ACM (New York, NY, USA, 2011), 31–36.
4. Bowker, G., and Star, S. *Sorting things out: classification and its consequences*. The MIT Press, Cambridge, MA, 2000.
5. boyd, d. m., and Ellison, N. B. Social network sites: Definition, history, and scholarship. *Journal of Computer-Mediated Communication 13*, 1 (2007), 210–230.
6. Corbin, J., and Strauss, A. *Basics of qualitative research: Techniques and procedures for developing grounded theory*, 3rd ed. Sage Publications, 2008.
7. Dabbish, L., Stuart, C., Tsay, J., and Herbsleb, J. Social coding in github: transparency and collaboration in an open software repository. In *Proceedings of the ACM 2012 conference on Computer Supported Cooperative Work*, ACM (2012), 1277–1286.
8. Dagenais, B., and Robillard, M. P. Creating and evolving developer documentation: understanding the decisions of open source contributors. In *Proceedings of the eighteenth ACM SIGSOFT international symposium on Foundations of software engineering*, FSE '10, ACM (New York, NY, USA, 2010), 127–136.
9. Deterding, S., Dixon, D., Khaled, R., and Nacke, L. From game design elements to gamefulness: defining "gamification". In *Proceedings of the 15th International Academic MindTrek Conference: Envisioning Future Media Environments*, MindTrek '11, ACM (New York, NY, USA, 2011), 9–15.
10. Draxler, S., and Stevens, G. Supporting the collaborative appropriation of an open software ecosystem. *Computer Supported Cooperative Work (CSCW) 20* (2011), 403–448. 10.1007/s10606-011-9148-9.
11. Erickson, T., and Kellogg, W. A. Social translucence: an approach to designing systems that support social processes. *ACM Trans. Comput.-Hum. Interact. 7*, 1 (Mar. 2000), 59–83.
12. Funder, D. On the accuracy of personality judgment: a realistic approach. *Psychological review 102*, 4 (1995), 652.
13. Gleave, E., Welser, H., Lento, T., and Smith, M. A conceptual and operational definition of 'social role' in online community. In *System Sciences, 2009. HICSS '09. 42nd Hawaii International Conference on* (jan. 2009), 1 -11.
14. Kuznetsov, S. Motivations of contributors to wikipedia. *SIGCAS Comput. Soc. 36*, 2 (June 2006).
15. Lave, J., and Wenger, E. *Situated learning: Legitimate peripheral participation*. Cambridge University Press, 1991.
16. Lih, A. Wikipedia as participatory journalism: reliable sources? metrics for evaluating collaborative media as a news resource. In *In Proceedings of the 5th International Symposium on Online Journalism* (2004), 16–17.
17. Louridas, P. Using wikis in software development. *Software, IEEE 23*, 2 (march-april 2006), 88 – 91.
18. Lungu, M., Lanza, M., Gîrba, T., and Robbes, R. The small project observatory: Visualizing software ecosystems. *Science of Computer Programming 75*, 4 (2010), 264–275.
19. Mamykina, L., Manoim, B., Mittal, M., Hripcsak, G., and Hartmann, B. Design lessons from the fastest q&a site in the west. In *Proceedings of the 2011 annual conference on Human factors in computing systems*, ACM (2011), 2857–2866.
20. Mockus, A., Fielding, R. T., and Herbsleb, J. A case study of open source software development: the apache server. In *Proceedings of the 22nd International Conference on Software Engineering*, ICSE '00, ACM (New York, NY, USA, 2000), 263–272.
21. Murphy-Hill, E., and Murphy, G. Peer interaction effectively, yet infrequently, enables programmers to discover new tools. In *Proceedings of the ACM 2011 conference on Computer supported cooperative work*, ACM (2011), 405–414.
22. Nardi, B. A. *A Small Matter of Programming*. MIT Press, 1993.
23. Pagano, D., and Maalej, W. How do developers blog?: an exploratory study. In *Proceedings of the 8th Working Conference on Mining Software Repositories*, MSR '11, ACM (New York, NY, USA, 2011), 123–132.
24. Park, S., and Maurer, F. The role of blogging in generating a software product vision. In *Proceedings of the 2009 ICSE Workshop on Cooperative and Human Aspects on Software Engineering*, CHASE '09, IEEE Computer Society (Washington, DC, USA, 2009), 74–77.
25. Priedhorsky, R., Chen, J., Lam, S. T. K., Panciera, K., Terveen, L., and Riedl, J. Creating, destroying, and restoring value in wikipedia. In *Proceedings of the 2007 international ACM conference on Supporting group work*, GROUP '07, ACM (New York, NY, USA, 2007), 259–268.
26. Rogers, E. M. *Diffusion of Innovations*, 5th ed. Free Press, 2003.
27. Singer, L., and Schneider, K. Influencing the Adoption of Software Engineering Methods using Social Software. In *Proceedings of the 34th International Conference on Software Engineering, NIER Track* (2012).
28. Stein, K., and Hess, C. Does it matter who contributes: a study on featured articles in the german wikipedia. In *Proceedings of the eighteenth conference on Hypertext and hypermedia*, HT '07, ACM (New York, NY, USA, 2007), 171–174.
29. Storey, M.-A., Ryall, J., Singer, J., Myers, D., Cheng, L.-T., and Muller, M. How software developers use tagging to support reminding and refinding. *IEEE Transactions on Software Engineering 35*, 4 (july-aug. 2009), 470 –483.
30. Storey, M.-A., Treude, C., van Deursen, A., and Cheng, L.-T. The impact of social media on software engineering practices and tools. In *Proceedings of the FSE/SDP workshop on Future of software engineering research*, FoSER '10, ACM (New York, NY, USA, 2010), 359–364.
31. Stuart, H. C., Dabbish, L., Kiesler, S., Kinnaird, P., and Kang, R. Social transparency in networked information exchange: a theoretical framework. In *Proceedings of the ACM 2012 conference on Computer Supported Cooperative Work*, CSCW '12, ACM (New York, NY, USA, 2012), 451–460.
32. Suh, B., Chi, E. H., Kittur, A., and Pendleton, B. A. Lifting the veil: improving accountability and social transparency in wikipedia with wikidashboard. In *Proceedings of the twenty-sixth annual SIGCHI conference on Human factors in computing systems*, CHI '08, ACM (New York, NY, USA, 2008), 1037–1040.
33. Treude, C., and Storey, M.-A. Work item tagging: Communicating concerns in collaborative software development. *IEEE Transactions on Software Engineering 38*, 1 (jan.-feb. 2012), 19–34.
34. Vallerand, R., Salvy, S., Mageau, G., Elliot, A., Denis, P., Grouzet, F., and Blanchard, C. On the role of passion in performance. *Journal of Personality 75*, 3 (2007), 505–534.
35. Wenger, E. *Communities of Practice - Learning, Meaning, and Identity*. Cambridge University Press, 1998.
36. Wu, C., Gerlach, J., and Young, C. An empirical analysis of open source software developers motivations and continuance intentions. *Information & Management 44*, 3 (2007), 253–262.
37. Ye, Y., and Kishida, K. Toward an understanding of the motivation of open source software developers. In *Proceedings of the 25th International Conference on Software Engineering* (2003), 419–429.

Impression Formation in Online Peer Production: Activity Traces and Personal Profiles in GitHub

Jennifer Marlow
Human-Computer Interaction Institute,
Carnegie Mellon University
5000 Forbes Ave
Pittsburgh, PA 15210
jmarlow@cs.cmu.edu

Laura Dabbish
Human-Computer Interaction Institute & Heinz College
Center for the Future of Work
Carnegie Mellon University
dabbish@cmu.edu

Jim Herbsleb
Institute for Software Research, School of Computer Science & Center for the Future of Work
Carnegie Mellon University
jdh@cs.cmu.edu

ABSTRACT
In this paper we describe a qualitative investigation of impression formation in an online distributed software development community with social media functionality. We find that users in this setting seek out additional information about each other to explore the project space, inform future interactions, and understand the potential future value of a new person. They form impressions around other users' expertise based on history of activity across projects, and successful collaborations with key high status projects in the community. These impressions influence their receptivity to strangers' work contributions.

Author Keywords
Peer production; Collaborative software development; Impression formation; Activity traces

ACM Classification Keywords
H.5.3. Group and Organization interfaces: Computer-supported cooperative work.

INTRODUCTION
Open source software development is an example of commons-based peer production where "uncertainty about the quality of others is the rule rather than the exception" [33]. In this environment, project owners often receive code contributions from previously unknown others. They must routinely form impressions about the expertise, background, and credentials of these unknown contributors. In this research we sought to understand how these impressions form and how they influence receptivity to contributions.

Surprisingly little previous research has examined impression formation in peer production environments. Research on leadership and the promotion process in Wikipedia touches on this issue, highlighting factors that influence selection for management positions [8]. However, these individuals are typically already active project contributors. Impressions of expertise and suitability for management are based on a history of interactions and quality contributions. The question remains: when and how do contributors form "first impressions" of each other? And how do these impressions influence evaluations of contributions?

At the same time, there is a rich history of research on impression formation in offline contexts. This research suggests that we quickly form judgments of strangers' expertise and trustworthiness based on limited cues (such as posture, dress, interaction style etc.). These judgments can be biased and inaccurate in a variety of ways [6], but inevitably impact how we view and interact with the person. In the work context our social judgments change the way we evaluate someone's suitability for a task or their work quality [10].

Online, a completely different set of cues are available. In online social settings like discussion forums or dating sites individuals form impressions of other participants based on cues like screen names, email addresses, or profile pictures [9, 11]. However, in an open online peer production workspace instrumented with social media, there is the potential to know about the entire collaborative world of another user. This increased amount of information may change the way we understand what someone else knows, is good at, or what they are like as a person. Activity traces have the potential to inform how we assess expertise and to shape our interactions.

Recent work by Dabbish et al. [7] suggests that open source developers make an extensive set of social inferences based on activity traces generated by social media connected to the work environment. For example, developers in their sample inferred others' commitment levels based on recency and volume of code commit activity. Their study also suggested these inferences influenced work outcomes. Participants in their sample described using inferences about individual's attributes in evaluating incoming code contributions or locating new knowledge on the site. However, their study provided only a partial picture of the types of inferences formed about individuals and their subsequent influence on receptivity to contributions.

Our goal in this work was to develop a more detailed understanding of impression formation in online peer production. We build on the distributed social cognition model [32], which posits that impression formation is an active process influenced by behavior in a network or group. This model shows that when forming impressions of others, individuals engage in an active process that involves the following steps: 1) choosing whether to obtain information about the target; 2) choosing what information is elicited, and 3) interpreting the elicited information to form a person model (an integrated interpretation of what a person is like.) The distributed social cognition model provides general guidelines about how impression formation occurs but doesn't describe what the process looks like in a specific setting. We address the following research questions to understand how distributed social cognition occurs in the online peer production setting:

RQ1: When do people seek out information about unknown others in an online peer production community?

RQ2: What information do they use to form impressions?

RQ3: How do interpersonal impressions influence evaluations of others' contributions?

In order to address these questions, we conducted an interview-based investigation of impression formation in GitHub. We find that users in this setting seek out additional information about each other to explore the project space, inform communication interactions, and understand the potential future value of a newcomer. They form impressions around other users' expertise based on project and code-related cues, which combine with interaction traces to help influence judgments about how to work with new contributors in the context of receiving and accepting pull requests (code contributions.) Our results inform the design of social technology to support online peer production communities engaged in knowledge-based work.

BACKGROUND

Open source projects rely on contributions from a global community of developers to perform various tasks ranging from bug reporting to submitting feature requests and contributing patches and code. The success of a project depends on the proactive and constructive participation of contributors to the project [30]. However, these outside contributions may vary in quality depending on the skills and expertise of the people who contributed them. Diversity in technical abilities can be helpful to a project because various types of contributions, from filing bugs to suggesting features, can be made by people with a range of expertise [30]. However, bug reports can waste time and divert developers' attention when they are misleading due to contributors' inexperience [19]. In both of these cases, the potential benefits of receiving contributions from inexperienced, unknown others may be outweighed when editing their work becomes too time-consuming to deal with, and this often results in the suboptimal outcome of contributions not being accepted to the project [28].

Although we know that individuals engaged in open source software development are continuously evaluating the contributions of others, few studies have addressed exactly when and why developers seek information about unknown others, how impressions of these people are formed, and what information is relied upon to infer an unknown developer's expertise, or other personal characteristics. In the next section, we consider previous work on impression formation and uncertainty reduction to inform our study of this process in the peer production context.

Impression formation and expertise perceptions

Forming impressions of strangers can be thought of as an uncertainty reduction process motivated by the goal of understanding their behavior and predicting how they will behave in the future [11]. When people are faced with a previously unknown person, they can use direct social interaction or information gathering to reduce uncertainty about that person [26]. During the process, the seeker fills out their mental models or mental representations of these new unknown people that help him or her to make sense of other people and their intentions, emotions and behaviors [1]. These can be models about how they will react to certain situations, but also what they know.

Research in sociology and social psychology describes interpersonal impression formation in offline settings. Goffman was among the first to describe the social inference process, by which we interpret characteristics of others based on appearance and public behavior [13]. Later work in social psychology described the cognitive processes associated with mentally placing individuals in social categories [2]. This work showed that we use these broad social categories to populate initially simplistic mental models of an individual (otherwise known as stereotyping) [24]. These initial models can be simplistic and inaccurate, and only through direct experience can we develop accurate impressions of an individual.

Limited research has examined how work-related impressions form through technology. Research in corporate settings has examined how individuals use technology to explore what other people know or are good at. For example, expertise finding is an important task in the corporate domain e.g. [29] and many internal tools have been developed to help people tag their own and others' expertise [25]. Research on impression formation in corporate settings has found that public profile information influences impressions of work-related skills [25, 29]. This previous research does not describe how the impression formation process works. It is also not clear how the presence or absence of organizational boundaries may change this process.

Open source software development is an example of a peer production community fueled by volunteer contributors interacting, via computer-mediated channels, from all over the world. Research conducted in other peer production settings, such as Wikipedia, has examined impression formation in admin promotion decisions. This work suggests editors attend to history of interaction and work on the site in order to make decisions regarding promoting people to admin status. The information that informs these decisions includes evidence of civil interactions with others, social networks and counts/types of edits made [8]. Similarly, Luther et al. [20] found that people desired information about the quality of past work (through peer ratings) as well as soft skills such as the personality of unknown collaborators when deciding who to work with in an online animation creation community.

Impression formation in software development

However, it is unclear to what extent the findings of impression formation in Wikipedia or artistic collaborations extend to evaluating non-managerial participants or to other online peer production communities, partly due to the nature of the domains. In open source development, participants have a wide range of technical abilities and skills, contribute to a project in different ways for different reasons, and may be motivated by career goals or a desire to build reputation and gain peer recognition [18]. Attribution may be less of an issue in open source development than observed in artistic communities [21, 22] in part because projects are viewed as community property and also because systems like GitHub automatically provide a record of a project's origins and contribution history.

Supporting awareness of teammates in distributed software development to improve both task and social outcomes has been an important research area. For example, Trainer et al. [36] suggest that providing visual traces of work interdependencies between team members can influence trust in distributed team members and help people understand whom to ask for assistance. Other work [37] has also pointed to the ways in which tools such as dashboards and activity feeds can help teammates get a sense of the project and plan their tasks. Begel et al. [3] point to the benefits of using social media at various stages in a software team's lifecycle, particularly with respect to coordination and communication. For example, they point to how social media can be used for effortless knowledge sharing or to help groups infer best practices by observing others' work. However, most of these studies have focused on ongoing, organized teams of developers within an organization, unlike the more volunteer-based collaborations that can occur in open source development, where contributors can vary in the length of their involvement and may not share a specific organizational affiliation. Furthermore, in contrast to teams within organizations, developers in open source settings often lack guidance from a management hierarchy, and thus need to self-coordinate and make autonomous decisions based on whatever information is available to them.

Thus, there are gaps in our knowledge about the mechanisms of impression formation in a peer production environment such as open source where participants span organizational boundaries and have extremely heterogeneous backgrounds. Open-source development has traditionally conducted much of the project-based interaction on message boards or via email lists, where it can be difficult to gain insight into who a person is or what they are good at without repeated interactions. In this type of large-scale online peer production community with hundreds or thousands of members, individuals cannot feasibly evaluate in detail every new contributor that accesses a project or submits work. Open source developers may rely heavily on stereotypes as a means of more efficiently assessing people [24].

In this paper we add depth to the previous work by focusing in greater detail on when people seek information about each other, what information they use to make judgments about others, and how they process it. We are specifically interested in the role that social information plays in the collaborative software development process, with a focus on how this information (or lack thereof) influences the openness to contributions.

Social information in the GitHub environment

In order to examine impression formation in peer production, we focused our data collection on GitHub, a software hosting website with over 2.7 million users hosting over 4.5 million repositories as of December 2012 [12]. GitHub's site design integrates social media functionality directly with code management tools. Two unique aspects of the GitHub environment set it apart from other online communities in terms of personal information available about project contributors.

The first unique aspect of GitHub is the presence of a profile for each individual site member. Figure 1 shows a typical user profile on the GitHub site. Profiles on GitHub include: a) biographical data (such as the date they joined the site and optional details about location, employer, etc.), b) a list of their projects in public repositories (including whether they own the project or forked it from another user, the coding languages used, and a histogram of project activity), as well as c) an "activity feed" that displays the most recent actions they have performed on the site (forking projects, watching other users or projects, submitting pull requests, commenting on code, discussing issues, etc.) Finally, the profile also highlights d) the number of people that follow the profile owner as well as the coders and projects that the profile owner has elected to watch.

Similar to many other social networking sites, from the profile users can interact with other users (message them), view content they posted (their code repositories), or view an "activity stream" of their recent actions and behaviors.

Profiles offering this degree of visibility of individual actions are not frequently and easily presented in other peer production environments (e.g. Wikipedia). GitHub is unique in this regard in both the software development and crowd-based work domains.

The second unique aspect of the GitHub environment is that coding is done publicly. Contributors can get involved in pre-existing projects by forking a project, making their changes, and then issuing a pull request to have their change merged back into the main branch of the project. The details of the work done by a contributor on the fork are also visible to the project owner, making it easy to see what a contributor is doing with the project.

The low effort associated with building on others' work is anecdotally associated with attracting more contributors to a project [27]. This accessibility can provide projects with many eager helpers, but project owners still have to evaluate their potential contributions before they are integrated into the master code base. At the same time, all code activity on the site is associated with a user's identity and public profile, meaning a code contribution can be vetted based on a developers entire past history of contribution on the GitHub site.

In our study we aimed to learn exactly when developers searched for more information about each other on the site, how they used this information to form impressions, and how it influenced their evaluation of code contributions.

METHOD

We conducted interviews with 18 GitHub users focusing in detail on how they formed impressions of new people they encountered on the site. Using information obtained through the GitHub API, we identified GitHub users who owned at least one open source project. Potential interviewees who had publicly-displayed e-mail addresses available on their personal profiles were contacted to see if they would like to participate in the study. We did not offer any incentives for participation.

We focused our recruitment on users with leadership positions in popular projects, who managed incoming contributions on a regular basis. These users were more likely to have recent experience handling contributions from strangers they hadn't interacted with before. We contacted GitHub users that owned at least one project with six or more authorized "editors" (people who were authorized to make changes without approval). The six editor cutoff was chosen based on a descriptive analysis of a subset of projects with activity in the 2 weeks prior to February 20, 2011. This analysis showed that projects with greater numbers of editors had more users watching them and more pull requests received per day.

Of the 18 interviewees (17 male), twelve were based in the U.S. and six were located in Europe. This sample was fairly representative of the GitHub community, where around 80% of its users come from North America and Europe [34]. Sixteen interviewees worked as professional software developers or consultants and used GitHub to host personal projects that they worked on in their spare time, while two were PhD students. Most had been members of GitHub for three to four years (based on the "joining dates" on their profiles), with the newest member having joined just under two years ago. Overall, interviewees were active site users and the largest projects they owned had a median number of 59 project watchers, 21 project forks and 451 contributions.

Interviews lasted between 30 and 60 minutes. They were conducted over Skype, with screen sharing enabled so that both interviewer and interviewee could refer to GitHub profiles and pages. The interviews followed a semi-structured format.

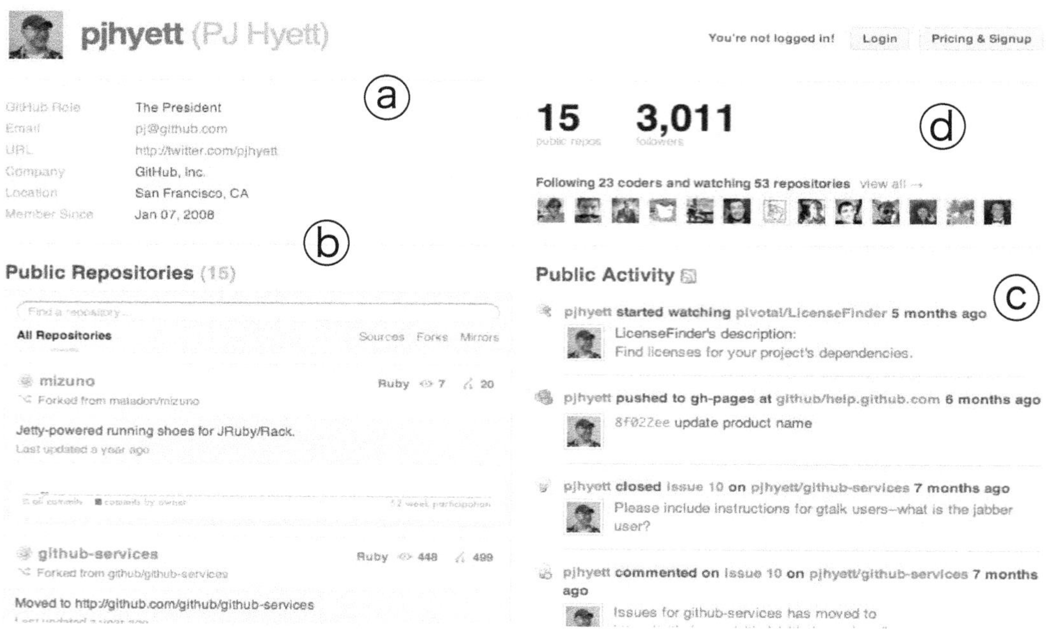

Figure 1. Sample GitHub profile (profile features labeled a-d)

To address RQ1, interviewees were first asked to identify scenarios in which they sought out more information about unknown others. Next, they were asked to go to these people's profiles and describe the information they had focused on and inferences drawn from it. To further address RQ2, each interviewee was asked to think aloud while assessing the profiles of two or three others – some of whom they knew well and others whom they did not know well. Finally, to assess the influence of profiles on work outcomes (RQ3), we also explicitly asked participants to show us examples of pull requests (i.e. code contributions they had received from others) that they had recently dealt with and either accepted or rejected. They described the process of receiving the pull request and walked through how they had handled the request, including whether or not they had consulted the profile of the requester.

Analysis

The analysis process was structured around the three stages in the distributed social cognition model and the corresponding research questions.

Our first research question focused on when people sought personal information about others. To address this question, we began by analyzing interview transcripts for instances in which participants mentioned having consulted others' profiles. Two researchers made affinity diagrams grouping instances around common themes, discussing until consensus was reached, and used these themes to develop categories for impression formation scenarios. We used qualitative analysis software (HyperResearch) to assist in coding interviews and in aggregating similar themes. We then repeated this analysis process for the other research questions.

Our second research question was about which cues individuals used in impression formation. To address this question, we identified all instances of new impressions in the transcripts. We then open coded these instances to form themes around the cues attended to and the impressions resulting from them.

Finally, to address our third research question on the impact of impressions on the working process, we focused on one of the most commonly mentioned themes in the first round of coding: receiving new pull requests from unknown others. We identified pull request interactions described by the interviewees. Next, we generated a set of categories around pull requests in terms of how the request was handled and factors leading to this decision. At some times, discussion was needed to determine the nature of some of the pull request conversations (whether there was a conflict or not) but this was resolved by matching what the interviewees said about the conversation with the correct segments of the visible discussion. Using focused coding [5], we compiled a set of pull requests that demonstrated these themes and then compared and contrasted specific pull requests to create a flow diagram of how decisions to accept pull requests were made, and how exposure to profile elements factored in to this process.

RQ1: SCENARIOS FOR INFORMATION SEEKING

We first investigated when GitHub users sought out personal information in order to learn more about another member. Our analysis identified three scenarios where users sought out more information about each other:

1) discovery, 2) informing interaction, and 3) skill assessment. Each scenario had a different triggering event, questions the user was trying to answer, and the outcome of the search for personal information is summarized in Table 1.

Scenario 1: Using profiles for discovery

Discovery was the first scenario for investigating others. This scenario involved exploring new people's profiles in the hopes of finding interesting projects they could use or learn from. This meant an outcome of discovery was staying up to date with the latest developments in open source world, whether or not these were directly related to the observer's interests and expertise.

Discovery was triggered in two different ways. The first involved encountering an unknown GitHub user with some personal relevance (e.g. the person started watching or forking the interviewee's project or were working on a friend's project). They then looked at the profile of this new person to learn about their other projects in case they were potentially useful. They would browse through the person's projects seeking out common interests, or give projects they had encountered before a second look because the owner had contributed to their project.

The second trigger for discovery was encountering a new project promoted on an external site (Twitter or HackerNews) or on GitHub's 'featured projects' page. Interviewees described becoming aware of a new project through these outlets and then exploring the profile of the project owner to see if there were any other useful projects they could use or learn from (P2, P5, P8, P10, P16). As one interviewee put it:

> *"...they may have done something really interesting, and I'll look at their other projects that they've done and see if any of those are things that I like."* (P8).

Discovery also supported learning about new coding techniques and tools. By checking out someone who had watched or forked their project and delving into what kinds of things they were working on or consulting their personal blogs, people learned about new tools and languages and knew whom they could contact in the future for questions. After viewing the blog of a user who had forked his project, one participant described how this "serendipitous" discovery helped him learn:

> *"[I learned] some very key words about natural language and would I need that at some point, I know where to look and who to contact, so somewhere in my brain, I have this guy connected."*

Scenario	Trigger	Motivating questions	Outcome
Discovery (mentioned by 10 interviewees)	T1. Receiving a new follower	M1. Curiosity: What cool things does this person do? What is their connection to me?	Find new projects, exposed to new information
Informing interaction (mentioned by 10)	T2. Receiving a pull request	M2. Are they a nice person? Are they worth helping?	Decision of how to act towards the new person based on impressions of interaction style and interests
Forming expectations about skills (mentioned by 6)	T2. Receiving a pull request from unknown person	M3. Who are they? Why are they interested in what I do?	Assessment of what they do for my project, how they can contribute based on skills

Table 1. Scenarios for interpersonal information seeking

Scenario 2: Informing interactions with new people

The second information-seeking scenario we identified focused on informing interaction. This occurred when an unknown person submitted a pull request (offering up a code contribution to the other person's project). Project owners would investigate the profile and activity of the person submitting the pull request to help them decide how to interact with the person (were they receptive to criticism? Did they argue with others?). This was most likely to happen when the project owner had the time and attentional resources to quickly look at the user's profile or when they had encountered the person on more than one occasion.

Because GitHub enables unknown people to fork a project without interacting with the owner, project owners often found themselves receiving pull requests from people they did not know. Owners in our sample were compelled to examine the profiles of these unknown others in conjunction with examining their code to understand why they were interested in the project or submitting a certain change. Learning more about a person informed how they would respond to this person and start building a working relationship: As one interviewee put it, "*I want to know you before I help you*" (P6).

Scenario 3: Forming expectations about skills

The third scenario for seeking information about other people was skill assessment. This involved investigation into a contributor's skills and abilities after they submitted a pull request to a project (P3, P6, P14, P15). Knowing what a person did helped owners to make sense of their abilities or competence as a coder, that is "*who they are and what do they do*"(P3). They looked to see if a person had contributed to other projects to understand in what capacity they might be able to help on their own project (or how much assistance or extra effort accepting their contribution would require, based on their technical abilities.)

Often times this kind of skill assessment did not occur until there had been multiple interactions with a given individual (P10, P12). As one developer explained, repeat contributions to a project made a contributor stand out, and triggered their interest in the face of extreme workload:

> *"for me there's so many different people I interact with on the Internet because my projects are pretty popular so that I just don't have the mental capacity to know each person who I interact with. But let's say if I get another bug from him and then maybe he makes other comments in the future, at some point he'll cross a threshold where I'm like okay, who is this person? What does he or she do?"* (P12).

Dabbish et al. [7] found these repeat contributors were often recruited for more central project involvement, e.g. assigned tasks to complete or bugs to fix.

RQ2: TRACES AND IMPRESSION FORMATION

Our second research question focused on how developers used visible cues in the work environment to form impressions about others. Our analysis identified three categories of impressions formed based on different activity information. Table 2 presents an overview of these categories of impressions, and the types of cues that were used to derive these impressions:

Impression category	Cues
C1. General coding ability	Amount of activity, frequency of commits, number of projects owned vs. forked, length of time on site, languages used
C2. Project-relevant skills	Types of visible activity (coding vs. discussing), specific languages used
C3. Personality and interaction style	Past discussion posts and threads

Table 2. Impression categories and associated cues

General coding ability

Interviewees often made stereotypical judgments about a user's coding ability by quickly scanning the recent activity (or lack thereof) visible on the profile. They mentally categorized other developers as one of three expertise-based personas: newcomers, novices, or competent peers.

Complete newcomers were distinguished by a lack of projects or any activity on their profiles, as well as a recent joining date that corresponded with their contribution. The lack of projects or contributions to other projects made it difficult to infer expertise or intentions. As one interviewee said:

> *"kind of hard to tell how good he is, actually. He hasn't contributed to anything else"* (P14).

Empty profiles also led to conclusions that the person wasn't a committed member of the site or only complained but never coded. One participant mentioned that seeing a person with an empty profile led him to characterize them as a certain "type of person" who signed up to report bugs but didn't actually contribute any code themselves. These people predisposed him to expect a certain type of contribution:

> *"you can usually tell when you go to a profile and they don't have any projects, and they just sign up to communicate with developers, basically. Yeah, it's a bit more frustrating because... sometimes you get bad bug reports or duplicated bug reports, and people who report them are-- I wouldn't say they're-- not negative, but they're-- yeah-- complaining, I would say."* (P13).

Novice or inexperienced users, in contrast, could potentially have started their own projects in addition to forking those of others. However, the kinds of projects that they chose to work on or the types of projects they had started themselves conveyed a lack of expertise. In the former case, one interviewee explained:

> *"Mongo DB is a database that's relatively well known for having a lot of fundamental architectural flaws and performance problems. The fact that he may choose to use this thing, again suggests to me that he's not a very experienced developer."* (P7).

Finally, *competent peers* were judged by the breadth and depth of the projects they owned, and the coding languages they used. As one interviewee described, the languages on a contributor's profile demonstrated 'geek cred':

> *"He seems like a quite talented coder. I mean, I see Pascal, I see Erlang, and yeah, he used VI, so, I mean, he validates his geek cred for all those things. So yeah, that would give me a pretty good first impression on the person, regarding the way he knows how to code"* (P4).

Project-relevant skills

Developers also formed impressions about specific areas of expertise based on a contributor's visible activity. These impressions included the types of work a person was best suited to doing or preferred to do (e.g. did they spend more time writing code or editing and managing projects?)

Activity traces led project owners to form expectations about the ways a person could assist their project. One interviewee highlighted how the portfolio of languages on a user's profile showed what they might be able to contribute to his projects (which were written in C code):

> *"if someone forks and all their other projects are web based PHP stuff, well you can sort of guess that you won't be getting any code patches from them. But if someone writes something and you see that their profile's all really hardcore C libraries, and C stuff, then you can sort of expect them to actually help out and write good C code, for example."* (P3).

Personality judgments

Interviewees also described inferring someone's personality based on how they interacted with others. They used communication activity visible in a person's recent activity feed (such as recent comments a user had made or discussions they had been involved in) to get a sense of what a person was like to work with. Arguments or 'rude' postings revealed negative personality traits such as arrogance or uncooperativeness, or led to the conclusion that someone was difficult to work with. For example, one interviewee talked about inferring willingness to help through exchanges with others:

> *"I think you can kind of look at how they respond in threads, if they're arrogant or if they're trying to be helpful, it does show through a little bit in threads"* (P15).

RQ3: IMPACT OF IMPRESSIONS ON WORK OUTCOMES

Our third research question focused on how these impressions of new contributors affected the working process. In order to address this question, we focused on the pull request evaluation process. Submitting a pull request involves proposing a code contribution to a project which can be accepted, rejected, or commented on and left open. The pull request process is important because it is the primary way open source projects attract new contributors and extend their code base. Our understanding of this process was based on the interviewee's retrospective thinkalouds of recent pull request interactions, which were publicly archived on pages linked to the pull requests.

In the open source software environment, project success is influenced by two key factors, which informed our analysis. First, code submitted to projects should be of high *quality* and not degrade the performance of the project by introducing bugs. It should also be able to be accepted with a minimum amount of effort required from the project owner, because in the open source environment project owners are limited in the amount of their own time they can devote to maintaining their projects – therefore, *efficiency* is valued. Relationship outcomes are also important to project success, because an owner needs to encourage participation from others in order to maintain the vitality of a project. Relationship outcomes suggested by Hackman [14] include *satisfaction* with the relationship, *learning* from distant colleagues, and *desire to work together in the future*. These positive outcomes are most likely to be maximized in the absence of relationship conflict, when developers interact in a polite and cordial manner. In light of these factors influencing open source software project success, we focused in our analysis on the following outcomes associated with a pull request interaction: whether the contribution was accepted, how long the exchange took, and whether conflict arose in the process.

Pull request case studies

We identified ten recent pull requests interviewees had received from contributors they had not directly interacted with before. These pull request interactions varied in terms of whether or not the project owner looked at the profile of the contributor, the nature of the code being submitted, the perceived expertise of the contributor, the amount of discussion surrounding the pull request, and two outcomes:

1) whether or not the pull request was accepted, and 2) the degree to which negative interpersonal interactions were avoided/managed. By comparing and contrasting the ten cases, we gained greater insight into factors that led to a pull request being accepted, and found instances in which impressions based on profile material influenced the attitude of the owner towards the contributor.

Accepted versus rejected pull requests

Our comparison of accepted versus rejected pull requests suggested that uncertainty was a critical factor in the code contribution review process. Owners were more certain about the value of simple changes that addressed features the owner had wanted to add, were small in scope, or fixed a known bug. Owners were less uncertain about the value of code that was suggesting a larger change, introducing a new feature, or conflicting with other existing functionality.

Code that was accepted "as is" was often either straightforward and easily verifiable, or accepted as a matter of principle (A1-A5). Few comments were involved. Declined pull requests, on the other hand, were not immediately accepted although they had the potential to be if certain fixes were made (D1-D5). These requests involved a great deal more uncertainty regarding the implications of accepting the change. These pull requests required some back-and-forth discussion between owner and contributor to explain the reasons why the code couldn't be automatically accepted or would cause problems and then to negotiate a final outcome.

When the value of submitted code was more uncertain, project owners often engaged in an assessment that involved weighing both code-based factors (e.g. perceived value of the code) and person-based factors (e.g. the perceived value of encouraging continued and sustained participation in the project by the new contributor.) For example, the cost of working with someone to fix their code so that it could be accepted (which could be high in cases where contributors were newcomers or novices) was weighed against the potential benefits of helping to mentor a new project member and potentially gain help in the future, or the risks of being annoyed by time-consuming arguments with a novice about why their contribution was not acceptable. Figure 2 summarizes the pull request acceptance decision process.

Impressions influencing mentorship : Examples

In this section we describe two of the five declined pull requests (D3, D4) where the owners reported having examined the profile of the contributor in the process of assessing the code. In both of these cases, the code being submitted was problematic in that it had stylistic issues, followed poor practices, and generally would require additional time and work by the project owner to fix to the point that it could be incorporated into the main branch of the project. However, the impressions they formed from glancing at the contributors' profiles influenced their willingness to accommodate the contributor's efforts.

When the owner of D4 consulted the contributor's profile, he discovered the contributor was a complete newcomer with no previous history. He described his subsequent reaction to this as:

> *"if I see this is their first pull request, I'm more like, 'Oh, thank you. Very nice.' And then try to be more gentle or...more friendly"* (P14).

The results of this impression were that as a result, he shaped his reaction to the code (which followed a poor practice of containing many different commits in one) to be more tolerant. In the end, the code that was submitted later proved to have some problems, so it was not accepted; however, the owner handled the issue in a way that illustrated his desire to encourage rather than sharply criticize someone whom he recognized to be a newcomer.

Similarly, in D3, the project owner received a pull request that was *"a bit problematic in the sense that it gives me a lot of work to accept a patch like this"* (P3). Since his assessment of the contributor, based on profile activity and interactions through the pull request was of *"an intelligent person who has not been coding too long, does not have too much experience in this,"* he realized that this person was *"a good person to focus but needs hand-holding."* For this reason, the owner was willing to look over his work, but rather than outright rejecting it he planned to look it over at a later time.

Impression accuracy: Examples

While we saw evidence of project owners quickly forming impressions of new contributors and using these to frame their interactions with these people, an associated question was to what extent these impressions were accurate. In the six cases where project owners elected to consult the new contributors' profiles, two users had no evidence of activity on their profiles, one was assessed as a novice user, and three were deemed to be competent peers.

In four instances, participants made judgments of others' abilities without having consulted their profiles beforehand (or consulted them after the pull request interaction had occurred.) In three of these four instances, (D1, D2, D5), the default assumption made without looking at the users' profiles was that they were new to GitHub or to coding. The owner of D2 described the contributor as: *"kind of a junior level experience guy, because anyone else would realize that these kind of changes are going to have a dramatic impact on this kind of project if they were more experienced."* (P7).

However, the sender of this pull request was one of our interviewees as well, who had been a professional programmer for over ten years and owned a popular open source project. In this case, had the project owner looked at his profile, he may have formed a different and more positive impression of the contributor's abilities.

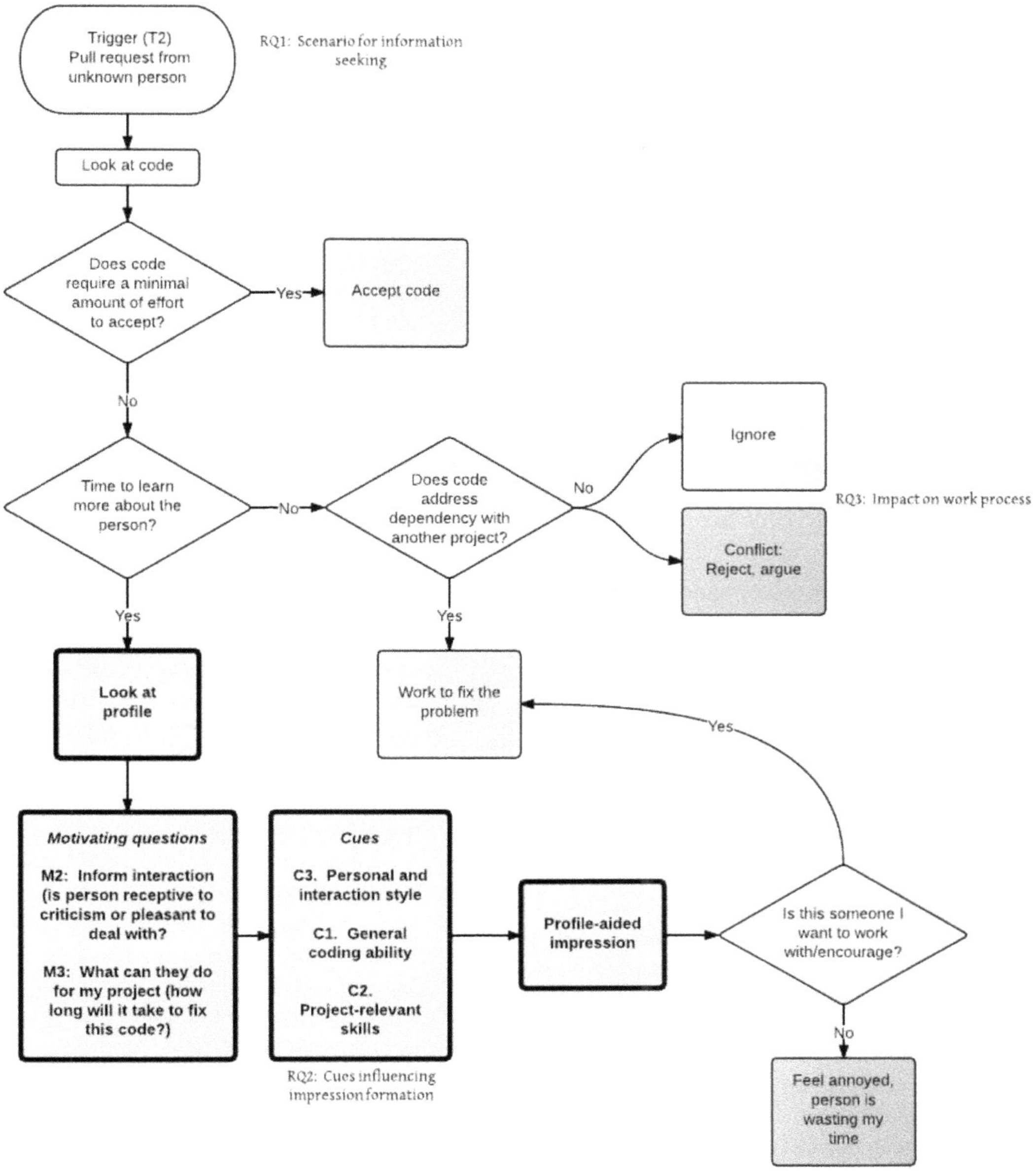

Figure 2. Flow diagram of the pull request decision-making process

DISCUSSION

Our analysis identified three key information-seeking scenarios on GitHub: discovery, informing interaction around contributions, and expertise assessment. Discovery was driven by a desire to stay up to date on new projects, and learn about new people with similar or complementary skills, and did not involve direct interaction.

Developers also sought out more information on others in response to code contributions. They sought out information about other developers' interaction style and interest to inform how they communicated with them. They also formed ability and expertise impressions based on profile information. These impressions influenced the way they handled project contributions moreso when the value of submitted contributions was uncertain, the contributor was unknown and future interactions were not expected. Owners with a stronger tendency for helping would use this information to inform mentoring style interactions to improve a contribution. Bad contributor attitudes combined with low perceived skill and ability led to annoyance, inflexibility, long arguments, and delays.

It is well known that conflict in open source software development often stems from interpersonal matters related to expertise and power. Problems arise when there is mismatched expertise and different knowledge levels [4], newcomers make arguments that are not defended with rationale [17], or people rudely advocate for features that have already been rejected [28]. These types of issues were seen in many of the example pull request negotiations we elicited. Often, the project owners tended to assume that when unknown contributors sent something for the first time, that they possessed inferior skills to the owner. This corresponds with the assertion made by Oreg & Nov [23] that contributors need to have a reasonable level of expertise and to have this expertise made public in order for them to make a creditable contribution.

The decision of what information to display about users may depend on a site's goals and the behavior it desires to promote (for example, some sites like Wikipedia minimize visible information about contributors in an attempt to create a level playing field [35].) However, when direct cues are absent, it becomes difficult to identify authors and evaluate their expertise. Our work suggests that detailed personal information can shape work outcomes in a peer production setting, particularly for complex contributions.

Design Implications

Like other peer production sites, interactions on GitHub often center around work contributions from unknown others. Our results show that the impressions formed of these users (whether based on activity traces such as profile cues or not) can influence a project owner's receptivity to contributions. In most of the cases where people reported consulting others' profiles, they perceived others as skilled when there was evidence of activity on well-known projects. Project owners may be less receptive to newcomers and developers perceived as unskilled.

Our results suggest that the design of peer production work environments can facilitate more accurate impression formation. First, sites can more accurately portray credentials of a newcomer who may in fact be quite skilled but has not yet built up a portfolio of work on the site. As Luther et al. [20] state, a contributor cannot improve their reputation without establishing an identity and ensuring that the history of contributions is linked to that identity. Finding ways of enhancing cues or links to other credentials or past work may help talented newcomers establish credibility and avoid biased impressions of their skills.

The design of contributor profiles can also help less experienced contributors gain respect from others, particularly given the importance of reputation in peer production environments [18]. A profile cue summarizing relative expertise like Halfaker et al.'s [15] NICE system in Wikipedia, could encourage awareness of and civility towards new editors. For users with some previous activity on GitHub, it could also be useful to show a visual summary of the history of their pull requests submitted to other projects along with an indication of how many of these were accepted or rejected. Such a statistic could help project owners quickly determine whether they will need to spend extra time mentoring or reviewing a person's contributions.

Contributor profiles can also provide better access to communication interaction histories. Our results suggest seeing how someone communicated with others is a useful means of assessing contributor soft skills. This interaction style information may support more effective peer production collaboration across a variety of domains [8, 20]. However, representativeness of interactions displayed is an important design consideration. Activity feeds may bias perceptions of interaction styles since only the most recent behaviors (which may or may not include comments) appear on a person's activity feed on their profile. This means it is possible that an isolated comment may be taken out of context or misconstrued.

Contributor profile design should be optimized for efficiently visualizing or summarizing the information for quick perusal. One of the most frequently mentioned reasons why project owners did *not* consult contributors' profiles was because doing so was simply too time-consuming and inefficient. Because of the site design, they had to scroll through a long list of projects and look at many different icons and cues to determine who owned which projects, what languages they worked in, and so forth. Better organizing this information or summarizing it at the top of the page (for example, a summary of languages and number of projects owned) could reduce the burden of looking at profiles of more experienced members and help more people to quickly assess their expertise and possible contributions.

These design issues around representing peer production contributors can apply to a range of communities. Succinctly summarizing expertise based on behavioral data and incorporating evidence of social interactions may support more nuanced impressions and reduce bias. In any type of peer production site where a person shares their work for others to build on, dealing with contributions from others is necessary and important. Our results show that impressions can influence receptivity to these contributions.

Limitations and future work

In this study we specifically focused on the project owners' assessments of the contributors submitting pull requests. In all cases except for one, it was not feasible to also interview the contributors involved in the pull request exchange to understand the situation from their side (often because they did not provide contact information on their profiles or were located in time zones that made it difficult to find a time for a synchronous interview.) Therefore, our findings do not apply to how contributors form impressions of project owners (however, this perspective has been to some extent covered by [28].)

We also had a limited number of pull request case studies from the interviews that met our criteria of being sent from previously unknown people (many of the other pull requests mentioned in the interviews were from people the interviewees knew and had worked with previously.) In future work, we plan to collect a larger number of instances where the pull request sender is unknown and use these to confirm or modify the model proposed here.

Finally, some of our findings may be unique to GitHub and the OSS community. These communities have their own norms, e.g. "open source" mentality emphasizes mentoring new members in a way that other communities may not share as strongly. Future work should examine the extent to which our results generalize to other open source communities and other peer production settings.

CONCLUSION

We found that open source software developers use detailed traces of an individual's project-related activities for discovery and learning. This information also informs their decisions on how to interact with new, unknown contributors to their projects. Impressions about future potential may increase receptiveness to complex contributions. Our observations suggest that interactions preceded by interpersonal information gathering had more positive outcomes (where social relations were prioritized over efficiency.)

Our results inform the design of future systems to support distributed, computer-supported work. The impression formation process may be expedited by providing more accessible cues about expertise that incorporate activity in other settings. More accurate impressions of expertise and ability may be more critical where there is a perceived gap in skill level between the owner and contributor and the technical merits of the work are unclear and up for debate.

ACKNOWLEDGMENTS

This work was supported by NSF grants IIS-1111750, SMA-1064209, OCI-0943168, a grant from the Center for the Future of Work at Heinz College, Carnegie Mellon University, and an NSF Graduate Research Fellowship.

REFERENCES

1. Antheunis, M. L., Valkenburg, P. M., & Peter, J. Getting acquainted through social network sites: Testing a model of online uncertainty reduction and social attraction. *Comp. in Human Beh.*, *26*(1), (2010), 100–109.
2. Baldwin, M.W. Relational schemas and the processing of social information. *Psychological Bulletin 112*, 3 (1992), 461-484.
3. Begel, A., DeLine, R., & Zimmermann, T. Social media for software engineering. *Proc. FSE/SDP workshop on Future of software engineering research*, (2010), 33–38.
4. Bettenburg, N., Just, S., Schröter, A., Weiss, C., Premraj, R., & Zimmermann, T. What makes a good bug report? *Proc. ACM SIGSOFT International Symposium on Foundations of software engineering*, (2008), 308-318.
5. Charmaz, K. Grounded theory as an emergent method. *Handbook of emergent methods*, (2008), 155–170.
6. Chen, S., Shechter, D., and Chaiken, S. Getting at the truth or getting along: Accuracy-versus impression-motivated heuristic and systematic processing. *Journal of Personality and Social Psychology 71*, 2 (1996), 262-275.
7. Dabbish, L., Stuart, C., Tsay, J., & Herbsleb, J. Social coding in GitHub: transparency and collaboration in an open software repository. *Proc. CSCW*, (2012), 1277–1286.
8. Derthick, K., Tsao, P., Kriplean, T., Borning, A., Zachry, M., & McDonald, D. W. Collaborative sensemaking during admin permission granting in Wikipedia. In *Online Communities and Social Computing* (Vol. 6778), (2011), 100-109).
9. Donath, J.S. Identity and deception in the virtual community. *Communities in cyberspace*, (1999), 29–59.
10. Flynn, F.J., Chatman, J.A., and Spataro, S.E. Getting to know you: The influence of personality on impressions and performance of demographically different people in organizations. *Administrative Science Quarterly 46*, 3 (2001), 414–442.
11. Gibbs, J. L., Ellison, N. B., & Lai, C. H. First comes love, then comes Google: An investigation of uncertainty reduction strategies and self-disclosure in online dating. *Communication Res.*, *38*(1), (2011), 70–100.
12. GitHub.com, https://github.com/home [Accessed December 6, 2012].
13. Goffman, E. The presentation of self in everyday life. New York: Anchor Books, 1959.
14. Hackman, J.R. *Groups That Work (and Those That Don't): Creating Conditions for Effective Teamwork*, San Francisco, CA: Jossey-Bass, 1990.
15. Halfaker, A., Song, B., Stuart, D. A., Kittur, A., & Riedl, J. NICE: Social translucence through UI intervention. *Proc. 7th International Symposium on Wikis and Open Collaboration,* (2011), 101–104.
16. Hamilton, D.L., Katz, L.B., and Leirer, V.O. Cognitive representation of personality impressions: Organizational processes in first impression formation. *Journal of Personality and Social Psychology 39*, 6 (1980), 1050-1063.
17. Ko, A. J., & Chilana, P. K. Design, discussion, and dissent in open bug reports. *Proc.iConference, (*2011), 106-113.
18. Lerner, J., & Tirole, J. Some simple economics of open source. *The Journal of Industrial Economics*, *50*(2), (2002), 197–234.
19. Lotufo, R., Passos, L., & Czarnecki, K. Towards Improving Bug Tracking Systems with Game Mechanisms. GDSLab Technical Report, University of Waterloo, 2011.

20. Luther, K., Caine, K., Ziegler, K., & Bruckman, A. Why it works (when it works): success factors in online creative collaboration. *In Proc. GROUP*, (2010), 1–10.

21. Luther, K., Diakopoulos, N., & Bruckman, A. Edits & credits: Exploring integration and attribution in online creative collaboration. *Ext. Abs. CHI,* (2010), 2823–2832.

22. Monroy-Hernández, A., Hill, B. M., Gonzalez-Rivero, J., & others. Computers can't give credit: how automatic attribution falls short in an online remixing community. *In Proc. CHI*, (2011), 3421–3430.

23. Oreg, S., & Nov, O. Exploring motivations for contributing to open source initiatives: The roles of contribution context and personal values. *Comp. in Human Beh.*, *24*(5), (2008), 2055–2073.

24. Quinn, K. A., Mason, M. F., & Macrae, C. N. Familiarity and person construal: Individuating knowledge moderates the automaticity of category activation. *European Journal of Social Psychology*, *39*(5), (2009), 852–861.

25. Raban, D. R., Danan, A., Ronen, I., & Guy, I. (2012). Impression formation in corporate people tagging. In *Proc. CHI,* (2012), 569–578.

26. Ramirez A., Walther, J. B., Burgoon, J. K., & Sunnafrank, M. Information-Seeking Strategies, Uncertainty, and Computer-Mediated Communication. *Human Communication Res.*, *28*(2), (2002), 213–228.

27. Rao, V. GitHub and the democratization of programming. http://www.forbes.com/sites/venkateshrao/2012/03/27/github-and-the-democratization-of-programming/ [Accessed 18 April 2012]

28. Rigby, P. C., & Storey, M. A. Understanding broadcast based peer review on open source software projects. *Proc. ICSE,* (2011), 541–550.

29. Shami, N. S., Ehrlich, K., Gay, G., & Hancock, J. T. Making sense of strangers' expertise from signals in digital artifacts. *Proc. CHI*, (2009), 69–78.

30. Sinha, V. S., Mani, S., & Sinha, S. Entering the circle of trust: developer initiation as committers in open-source projects. *Proc. of the 8th working conference on Mining software repositories*, (2011), 133–142.

31. Skeels, M., & Grudin, J. When social networks cross boundaries: a case study of workplace use of facebook and linkedin. *Proc. GROUP,* (2009), 95–104.

32. Smith, E. R., & Collins, E. C. Contextualizing person perception: Distributed social cognition. *Psych. Rev.*, *116*(2), (2009), 343-364.

33. Stewart, D. Social status in an open-source community. *American Sociological Review*, *70*(5), (2005), 823–842.

34. Takhteyev, Y., & Hilts, A. Investigating the geography of open source software through GitHub. http://www.takhteyev.org/papers/Takhteyev-Hilts-2010.pdf

35. Tausczik, Y.R. and Pennebaker, J.W. Predicting the perceived quality of online mathematics contributions from users' reputations. *Proc. CHI*, (2011), 1885–1888

36. Trainer, E. H., Al-Ani, B., & Redmiles, D. F. Impact of collaborative traces on trustworthiness. *Proc. of the Workshop on Cooperative and human aspects of software engineering*, (2011), 40–47.

37. Treude, C., & Storey, M. A. Awareness 2.0: staying aware of projects, developers and tasks using dashboards and feeds. *Software Engineering, 2010 ACM/IEEE 32nd International Conference,* 2010, 365–374).

Shared Prolepsis and Intersubjectivity in Open Source Development: Expansive Grounding in Distributed Work

Pål Fugelli
Research Computing Services
University of Oslo
pal.fugelli@gmail.com
+47-22852965

Leif C. Lahn
Dept. of Educational Research
University of Oslo
l.c.lahn@ped.uio.no
+47-22857076

Anders I. Mørch
InterMedia
University of Oslo
a.i.morch@intermedia.uio.no
+47-22840713

ABSTRACT
Intersubjectivity is a term used to conceptualize the psychological relationship between people during conversation, e.g. for building a shared understanding. Ragnar Rommetveit, a Norwegian social psychologist, developed a conceptual framework for intersubjectivity, treating it as a social phenomenon and a dynamic process. One technique for increasing intersubjectivity according to Rommetveit is to issue 'anticipatory cues,' i.e. referring to common knowledge and indicating future situations where the knowledge will be relevant. This framework was adapted for online communication and applied to an analysis of the mod_perl module of the Apache Web server (an open source development project). Based on observations of 215 participants' contributions to the project's mailing list over a 6-month period, we explore how processes of intersubjectivity evolve across the developer network. We conclude with a discussion of how so-called *proleptic instances* in post-and-reply messages may be significant and trigger the co-construction of shared understanding.

Author Keywords
Collaboration, empirical study, grounding, intersubjectivity, prolepsis, shared understanding, software development.

ACM Classification Keywords
H.5.2 [Information Interfaces and Presentation]: Group and Organization Interfaces – Asynchronous interaction, evaluation/methodology. K.4.3 [Computers and Society]: Organizational Impacts – Computer-supported collaborative work.

General Terms
Design; Documentation; Theory.

INTRODUCTION
The complexity of CSCW calls for the identification of sub-processes of communication and coordination that may impact overall performance. A recent effort in this regard is the study of micro coordination among a group of co-located game players playing a collaborative problem solving game [18]. Here, micro coordination refers to how participants decide who plays next and other low-level decisions that might impact overall performance. The authors argue that learning and working are intertwined at this level. In this paper, we apply a related strategy for identifying sub-processes in distributed work, studying intersubjectivity by analyzing communication patterns and message postings in an open source development (OSD) community. Intersubjectivity is a term used to conceptualize the psychological relationship between people during conversation, e.g. for learning each other's perspective and building a shared understanding. We consider this relevant for understanding aspects of communication and coordination in OSD; i.e., newcomers must learn how to get into a project and experts (core members) must learn how to sustain their understandings as the software evolves.

Intersubjectivity is perhaps most often associated with a theory of language use first proposed by the linguist Herbert Clark and referred to as the theory of common ground. Clark's theory is comparable with the theory of intersubjectivity espoused in this paper, Ragnar Rommetveit's theory of prolepsis-driven intersubjectivity. They share the assumption that individuals engaged in conversation must share knowledge in order to be understood and contribute to the conversation. Clark and Brennan said that grounding involves "mutual knowledge, mutual beliefs, and mutual assumptions" [6, p. 127], whereas Rommetveit defined intersubjectivity as a "temporarily shared social world" [25, p. 87], which is mutually accessible and partly based on so-called *proleptic instances*, a special type of utterance induced by the speaker. These proleptic instances function as anticipatory cues, expanding the space of intersubjectivity. Rommetveit's position is that the social world in the outset is not the world of the private individual but a world of intersubjectivy shared by all, to a lesser or greater extent. We depict the differences between the two perspectives in Figure 1. We argue that both perspectives have strengths and weaknesses, and we use the latter one, which we refer to as prolepsis-driven intersubjectivy or expansive grounding, to develop a conceptual framework for analysis of distributed work in OSD.

Figure 1. Two perspectives of common ground in interpersonal communication: shared cognition (left) and shared social reality (right). The picture has been simplified for illustration.

Our object of study is the community around the mod_perl module of the Apache web server. The Apache project is described as "a collaborative software development effort aimed at creating a robust, commercial-grade, featureful, and freely-available source code implementation of an HTTP (Web) server" [1]. It is a worldwide network of more or less dedicated developers and users, and the software has continually evolved since the project was launched in April 1995 as a result of new patches submitted by developers and new upgrades released by the organization.

The main aim of our research is to explore prolepsis-driven intersubjectivy as a dynamic, social phenomenon in distributed cooperative work. This has not been explored in previous work in CSCW. The second aim is to identify opportunities for learning and knowledge development. We surveyed related work to provide a rationale for our aims. For example, Lee, Tatar and Harrison [18] show in their study of micro-coordination that non-discursive behavior in decision-making needs to be accounted for in discourse analysis. Furthermore, in a case study of Second Life use, Shami, Erickson and Kellogg [29] found that implicit grounding, i.e. common ground that is established before conversation actually begins, could be supported by affordances built into in the collaboration environment. Moreover, Stahl, Koschmann and Suthers [30] studied collaborative knowledge building and suggest that the problem of intersubjectivity is of particular relevance for understanding how learning is produced through interaction, advocating for more in-depth interdisciplinary research and arguing that this issue has implications for research methods and for the design of collaboration software.

The results we report in this paper can be summarized as follows: Intersubjectivity is the 'object' of a shared understanding that evolves in the OSD project. The 'object' in this sense is neither software nor documentation, but a parallel process of building this shared understanding over some time (in our case 5 days). We have traced the roots of these processes to a certain type of utterance we refer to as proleptic instance. Proleptic instances are explicit or indirect parts of postings that can be identified as preceding or otherwise in conjunction with questions, idea proposals, etc. They are peculiar in the sense that they draw attention to themselves by triggering a series of elaborations and clarifications over several days from more experienced members of the community with the ultimate effect of expanding the group's common ground or shared understanding.

We have developed a theoretical framework to guide our efforts. We used a mixed methods approach for collecting and analyzing data. Regions of intersubjectivy were found using the social network analysis (SNA) method and included both peripheral and core members of the mod_perl development network. Our unit of qualitative analysis is conversations among developers, initiated by peripheral members and cultivated by core members who were perceived as both knowledgeable about the project (code and documentation) and good educators. We discuss the role of proleptic instances in these conversations and also how prolepses differ from 'tasks' and 'problems' in OSD.

Our work is theoretically informed but also motivated by informal examples, especially of the early stages of transitioning from natural to artificial (design) activity. We briefly describe three illustrative examples that have motivated of our own understanding of the role of proleptic instances in the early stages of cooperative work:

- *Gnu crossing*: From July through September each year herds of wildebeest gather to cross two rivers in East Africa. The transition starts by more or less random and restless attempts at finding a place to cross safely, being aware of crocodiles lurking in the water but driven by the better feeding grounds on the other side. When a few lead animals ('gunny pigs') have found a satisficing route, a vigorous activity follows as the other animals follow quickly after in more or less the same path. It shows flock behavior triggered by a sudden act of movement by a few individuals [13].
- *The Richmeister*: The role played by Roy Schneider in a series of Saturday Night Live comedy sketches in the early 1990s. The character Richard Laymer ('The Richmeister') is an office worker in a copy room who annoys people by giving them nicknames based on knowing their real names, more or less randomly issued with the goal of making friends. He is not very successful in his numerous attempts, and his behavior is characteristic of what we refer to as pre-prolepsis [31].
- *Cinema viewer capture technique*: Prolepsis is a word that has been adopted in cinema production and used as technique to capture audience attention for a long time. It means flash-forward or foreshadowing, a technique used to reveal events that will occur in a future scene, often presented in discrete ways, leading the viewer to form her own expectations about what will happen next. An example is the notorious 'kitchen knife as set decoration' in early scenes in horror films, strategically placed for later use as a murder weapon. In the opposite direction, flashbacks are often used to recount events that happened before a story's primary sequence of events or to fill in crucial backstory.

The rest of the paper is organized as follows: First, we provide a brief survey of related work in OSD. Next, we develop a conceptual framework for intersubjectivity based on a review of two theories of intersubjectivity as first proposed for face-to-face communication: Rommetveit's [24, 25] notion of prolepsis-driven intersubjectivity and Clark and Brennan's [6] extended contribution model. Two levels of analysis are employed for zooming in and out of the mod_perl developer community: macro (network structure) and micro (message content and interaction). We capture data at these two levels during a six-month logging of online communications among subscribers of the project's mailing lists. The network data provide the context (visualize regions of low and high cohesion) for the selection of messages for in-depth interaction analysis. The framework is applied to the analysis of message exchanges among the contributors in high cohesion areas to identify characteristics of prolepsis-driven intersubjectivity. At the end, we compare our findings to related work in OSD and intersubjectivity and suggest some implications for design.

OPEN SOURCE SOFTWARE DEVELOPMENT

There is little research that explicitly links OSD and intersubjectivity. We survey some of the related work below.

Bergquist and Ljungberg [3] conducted an empirical study of open source developers for a period of two years and identified a phenomenon they labeled "gift giving" culture. They found that developers communally gave and appreciated gifts, and that the open source developer community relied on gift giving as a way of "getting new ideas and prototypes out into circulation." Gifts were not physical commodities, but rather substances such as knowledge, source code and peer reviews (conceptual artifacts). They claim that examining the sharing of these resources provides a key for understanding the open source community's cultural foundations, as well as its social organization [3].

Network-level studies of open source development projects have reported that interaction patterns among participants vary depending on their roles, most notably those of core developers vs. peripheral participants [8, 9]. In one study, Long and Siau [19] applied social network analysis to three projects accessible in SourceForge.net. They reported that the interaction pattern within these projects evolved from a single hub at the beginning of a software project's life cycle into a core-periphery model as the project matured. In our study, another approach is proposed while using a similar model as a network-level contrast for analyzing message content targeting processes of intersubjectivity.

In a study by Cataldo and Herbsleb on how software engineers communicate in geographically dispersed teams, a core group of developers emerged as the liaisons (or gatekeepers) between formally defined teams [5]. Their findings revealed that "individuals in the core not only perform a critical communication role but also they are the top contributors to the actual development effort" (p. 1). Furthermore they found that the communication network of the developers evolve to adapt to the modular structure of the source code, organized into communication hubs. Moreover, the authors report that in addition to skilled developers, also less experienced developers are drawn into the communication hubs if their work assignment leads them. Our analytic attention takes inspiration from these findings and focus on how core and peripheral participants take on different roles at different times in the construction of shared understandings.

Edwards [9] studied the transition from peripheral to core participation in OSD using "community of practice" as a theoretical framework. He found that situated learning was essential for newcomers to become core members. He also found that all contributors, but especially core members, relied on a common frame of reference to coordinate their joint effort. Much of this was not the result of a conscious effort but a consequence of maintaining membership in the community. The peripheral participants contributed to user support mailing lists (e.g. how to download and install a system), whereas the core members contributed to technical discussion lists and proposed patches to improve the software. The learning curve was steep for newcomers, and the motivation of core members to sustain membership was associated with the joy of solving software-related problems [9]. Our study reveals a separation of core and peripheral participants, but little transition between them.

There are studies of global online teams other than OSD projects that use organization structures comparative to those of OSD, like management teams of large scale engineering projects [14, 17]. They reveal that distributed teams have structures that may easily dissolve because of the high demands of coordination and 'centrifugal forces' that pull the teams apart. Hemetsberger and Reinhardt [14] contrasted these findings with the persisting cohesion typical of open source collaboration. They attributed the success of coordination in OSD to a number of technological artifacts that define the process; source code is the main artifact, and serves as a coordination mechanism by providing a modular structure for organizing mailing lists. The combination of a well-defined agenda (what to do) and an organization that facilitates the recruitment of newcomers ensures stability and progress [17].

These studies show how open source development projects are collaborative, knowledge intensive, and require learning, both for newcomers and core members. Newcomers must learn how to enter a project, while core and peripheral members must learn to sustain their understandings as software evolves. The participants' interactions are organized around source code, tools for development (programming environments, programming languages, web browsers, debuggers, version control systems, and so on), releases for download, and mailing lists. These artifacts are different from the less tangible and transitory objects of knowledge that emerge during conversations in the mailing lists. These initially vague objects serve as cues and markers for evolving more durable objects of shared understanding to monitor and inform collaborative work in the OSD community.

CONCEPTUAL FRAMEWORK

We develop a conceptual framework for intersubjectivity based on a review of two theories of intersubjectivity as first proposed for face-to-face communication: Rommetveit's notion of prolepsis-driven intersubjectivity and Clark and Brennan's extended contribution model.

Intersubjectivity and Prolepsis

Nearly 40 years ago, Rommetveit proposed a phenomenological account of communication [24] that was partially inspired by the phenomenology of Husserl and social phenomenology [27] and partially by the sociology of knowledge [2]. In a nutshell, it states that the world of intersubjectivity is not the overlap of the worlds of the private individuals but a world of a shared social reality. Furthermore, it states that communicators' perspectives of this world can only be partial, never complete because the world is a generalization of experiences and it is temporarily shared (see Figure 1, rightmost situation). It is an accumulation of shared presuppositions and historical information only partly accessible. Between the 'I' and 'You' depicted in Figure 2, potential states of intersubjectivity can emerge along a three-dimensional spatial-temporal-interpersonal space. Utterances are assigned meaning through a process of joint construction that operates in this space [25].

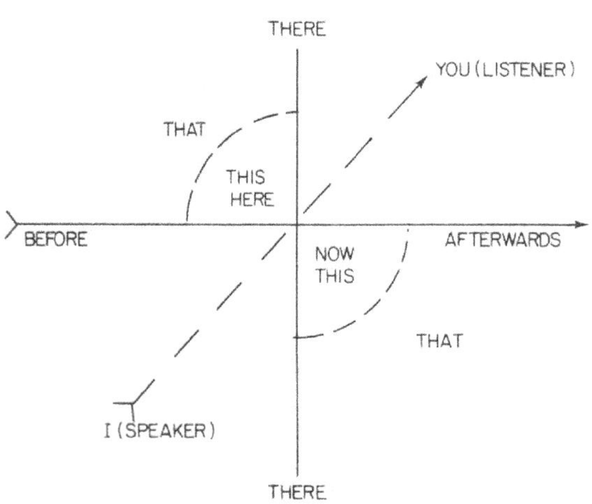

Figure 2. The spatial-temporal-interpersonal coordinates of communicative acts defining the framework of intersubjectivity for face-to-face communication [25].

Rommetveit argued that this world is "in part based upon premises tacitly induced by the speaker" [25, p. 87], by which he means that some elements are left out of a conversation and the listener is subsequently invited to step into a partially shared space of intersubjectivity and make sense of it. He called the tacitly induced elements *shared prolepses* [25], defined as a communicative act among participants in a conversation where the speaker presupposes something that has not yet been discussed, in effect creating a connection between a past situation and possible future situations. The term 'prolepsis,' meaning 'preconception' or 'anticipation' dates from ancient Greek writings. In Rommetveit's framework, prolepsis is intimately connected to intersubjectivity as a mechanism for expansion. The 'here and now' of the present situation is connected with past events (before) and future events (afterwards) as depicted by the intersection of the x-axis with the curved lines in Figure 2. At a more general level the process is dynamically changing in three dimensions (x, y, and z-axes), which is triggered by issuing proleptic instances as communicative acts.

Shared prolepsis is also a mechanism for sustaining intersubjectivity when the actors continually fine-tune their assumptions and anticipations in reaction to others' contributions and feedback [21]. Rommetveit [24] offers the following example of prolepsis in a personal letter received from a friend:

"Today, I walked with one of the psychologists here past the Mayflower cinema in Eugene, where Bergman's latest film movie is being shown. He asked me whether I had seen it. I said no, and asked if he had. He said yes, he had. I asked him how he liked it, and he said 'I liked it very much, but Mary Ann did not'; without ever explicitly having 'made known' to me that he is married and that his wife's name is Mary Ann, that they went to see the film together, and a lot of other things – and (if I am correct) without assuming that I knew all this. His utterance was proleptic in that it triggered a search on my part for a shared social reality, which in turn would provide a basis for understanding the sentence. Incidentally, it would have been barbaric and pedantic to say, 'Oh, Mary Ann is your wife'. To be precise, prolepsis here served to establish a relationship between his wife and me as persons who should at some time get together. My comment would have been a crude rejection of that implication." [24, p. 87-88]

In this story the fact that the friend has a wife and her name is Mary Ann is presupposed but not directly mentioned. This may challenge the listener and "trigger anticipatory comprehension, and what is made known will hence necessarily transcend what is said" [24, p. 88]. It may also trigger the construction of new understandings of the situation. Prolepsis can thus serve as a catalyst for making sense of not-yet-provided information; in this case, to prepare for a future meeting of three individuals. Its role in intersubjectivity is to provide prompts or cues for building a special kind of common ground: referring to shared knowledge that has not yet been introduced and pointing towards a future situation where the knowledge is relevant. As such, it is a mechanism for constructing common understanding for use in practical situations (e.g. installing a web server) inspired by phenomenology [24, 25].

The process of omitting information and, in its place, issuing more or less indirect cues of its aims, invites the listener to actively participate in the co-construction of an expanded intersubjective space [24]. The receiver of proleptic utterances ‘fills in’ the missing pieces and thus co-constructs the information needed to achieve a sufficient level of common understanding. Using proleptic instances as building blocks for conversational grounding is new in CSCW. We describe the most frequently cited work below before we present a conceptual framework for intersubjectivity in online communication, which we apply in the analysis of building common understanding in the mod_perl network.

The Extended Contribution Theory

Clark and Schaefer [7] proposed a collaborative model for human communication based on grounding, referred to as the contribution model. This model revises a more traditional sender/receiver perspective on communication, broadening the analytic frame from single utterances to contributions developed through interaction. We visualized this model informally in Figure 1 (leftmost situation). Clark and Brennan [6] extended this model and postulated that, “all collective actions are built on a common ground and its accumulation” [6]. To coordinate the content and processes of human conduct, participants must update their common ground moment by moment in what Clark and Brennan refer to as ‘grounding,’ and these grounding processes vary according to the contexts of interactions.

Clark and Brennan [6] claim that different media put different constraints on grounding processes. For example, real-time communication media like videoconferencing offer visibility and co-temporality, whereas e-mail or personal letters lack the same features, causing delays in turn taking for proper understanding. They suggest that, “people should ground with those techniques available in a medium that leads to the least collaborative effort” [6]. According to Rommetveit and his notion of prolepsis, such a shared understanding is only partially achieved and depends on access to historical information (common pre-understanding).

Early research on applying the extended contribution theory of common ground in CSCW compared face to face situations with remote collaborations, finding that grounding was reduced in distributed settings unless participants had access to media channels that simulated the contextual information of co-presence (e.g. video, shared space for communication) [22] Arguably, this is less of a problem in today’s virtual collaboration environments, which have more sophisticated means for simulating co-presence and capturing context (e.g. built-in cameras, desktop video, immersive worlds), but also because of new ways of communicating and grounding. For example in a recent study of online communication in the virtual world Second Life, Shami, Erickson and Kellogg [29] found grounding to be different (less constrained) than predicted by Clark and Brennan’s [6] theory. They found that affordances of the virtual places and situational characteristics of the environment, such as knowledge of occurring events (in their case an online conference), might facilitate grounding. They proposed an adaptation of the extended contribution theory to virtual worlds with the notion of *implicit grounding*, which refers to actions in the beginning of a conversation that refer to elements of the immediate surroundings that allows for the creation of common ground, and in Second Life this information extends the contextual information found in face-to-face conversations [27].

We propose another technique for facilitating grounding in online communication, which we apply in the empirical analysis of an OSD project, namely *shared prolepsis*, which we present next.

A Distributed Model of Shared Prolepsis

Online communication introduces new dimensions to intersubjectivity that was not present in the framework proposed by Rommetveit. In the revised framework we present here [11], intersubjectivity emerges in the intersection of distributed work and the evolution of a shared knowledge object. This is depicted by the coordinate system shown in Figure 3, where the x-axis tracks the evolution of a shared knowledge object as a temporal process from fragmented (individual) knowledge towards a shared object of attention. The y-axis represents spatial displacement, which are supported by the features of collaboration software. The z-axis represents the interpersonal communication across the network (captured by the type of messages submitted and responded to).

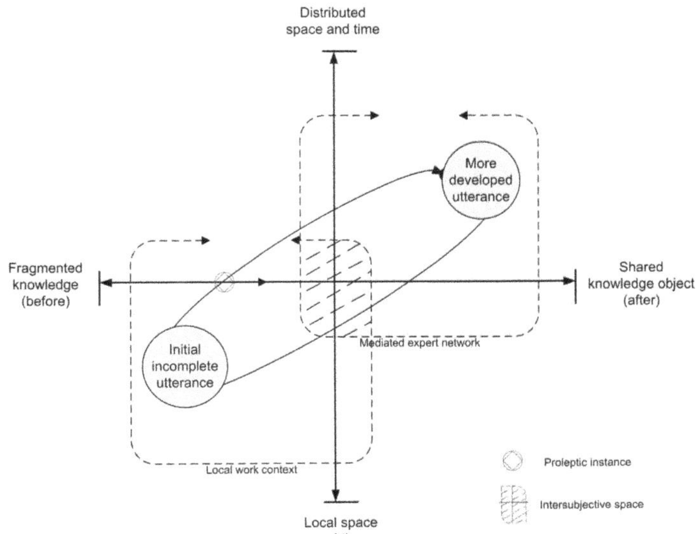

Figure 3. Framework for intersubjectivity and shared prolepsis in knowledge-intensive distributed work [11].

The complexity of this model is partly a result of viewing it as an extension of the time-place matrix of groupware [15], with a dimension of evolving shared understanding as informed by Rommetveit's theory of intersubjectivity. This is our main analytic tool for understanding intersubjectivity as a dynamic, social phenomenon in knowledge-intensive distributed work. The development of shared understanding within a group is a process represented as an emergent object of knowledge issued by an individual and moving along the x-axis, which may take a path on its own (z-axis) and involving other individuals if it is caught on, from an incomplete or vague utterance not yet fully understood, gradually leading to clarification and shared understanding based on feedback and follow up utterances from multiple individuals. This process may involve spatial, temporal, and interpersonal displacements as depicted in Figure 3.

Furthermore, two aspects of time are represented in the coordinate system: time associated with duration of work and relative geographical location, i.e. clock time (y-axis), and time associated with past, present, and future (x-axis). It entails connecting past and future with the present by expanding from the 'here and now' towards the (predicable) future (here, afterwards) and the (remembered) past (here, before), i.e. expansive time. Finally, the coordinates 'I' and 'You' in Rommetveit's original framework have been replaced by 'Initial incomplete utterance' and 'More developed utterance,' respectively (z-axis). This framework is later in the paper applied in the analysis of conversations among peripheral and core developers in the mod_perl mailing list. It is the temporal and interpersonal dimensions of the framework that we focus on. We did not collect data on the developers' geographical location, so the spatial dimension is outside the scope of our work.

Research Questions

Based on the above survey of previous work and the development of a new framework for intersubjectivy in online communication, we address the following questions regarding the intersection of OSD and intersubjectivity:

- How is intersubjectivity achieved in the mod_perl community and what role does prolepsis play?
- How can SNA and content analysis complement one another in the analysis of prolepsis-driven intersubjectivity?
- How is learning and knowledge development manifest in the OSD community?

RESEARCH METHOD

In the following section we will provide a rationale for our research design and discuss the strategies we used for collecting and analyzing our data.

Rationale for the Mixed Methods Approach

We used a mixed methods approach to address our research questions because of interdependencies between structural parameters like centrality, grouping, and density in a social network and the constitution of intersubjectivity in on-line communication We opted for a strategy to combine social network analysis and content analysis of messages between participants. The former approach computes structural parameters of interactions in terms of number of subgroups, centrality, and density of the network, whereas the latter approach follows an interpretative strategy with a focus on meaning making in the conversations between participants [16]. The structural analysis will produce network-level data and provide an empirical basis for selecting episodes of interaction among individuals, for example in high-cohesive regions of the network. In a nutshell, the process goes as follows: 1) identify regions in the network that are interesting from the point of view of intersubjectivy, 2) identify meaning making processes in the selected regions, and 3) identify the mechanisms that trigger the meaning making process.

We used UCINET [4] to carry out network-level calculations. E-mail conversations were content analyzed to highlight processes of intersubjectivity and shared prolepsis using thematic coding with Nvivo [23], a software package for qualitative data analysis.

Data Selection and Strategies for Analysis

Since Gisle Aas released the first version of mod_perl on March 25, 1996, thousands of individuals have contributed to its current state of development (http://perl.apache.org/about/history.html). All data used was obtained from the mod_perl project mailing lists related to the development of the mod_perl core, which are publically available as a text-based archive from http://mail-archives.apache.org/mod_mbox/perl-dev/. In order to strike a balance between a manageable data set and a rich data set, we decided to include all members active within a timeframe of six months. The study period lasted from 01.01.2008 to 30.05.2008 and included 215 individual contributors. The number of postings during this period was 1,154, with a mean of 6.2 postings per contributor.

The first author, then a PhD student, observed the activity in the mailing lists as it occurred, reading through previous postings and following the discussion threads without disturbing the 'naturally occurring' communication within the project. With respect to the transparency and public nature of the mod_perl project, we decided to send an informative letter introducing ourselves and explaining the study's purposes [11]. None of the authors have any affiliation with mod_perl, though the first author has some knowledge of Perl programming and has installed an Apache web server.

At the first descriptive level of analysis, formal measures associated with SNA [28, 32] were applied to render the overall communication among participants in the mod_perl project visible. The main focus at this level of analysis was to organize the message archive into sub-groups to serve as contrasts for a more detailed content analysis of individual email messages. We selected communicational ties among contributors on the mod_perl mailing list for users and developers as relation and the basic units for constructing the network. All communicational ties among the selected nodes were studied to provide a census for a full network analysis. The adjacency matrix generated from UCINET included information about each participant's communicational ties with all other participants in the population. The rationale behind this selection was to collect information about all communicational dyads in the network and to construct an inclusive overview and provide parameters to calculate centrality and density in communication, which again determine cohesion. In this way, sub-groups of core and peripheral contributors were identified for further content analysis.

We constrained the space further by selecting among four possible core-periphery dyads: 1) periphery-periphery, periphery-core, 3) core-periphery, and 4) core-core. We chose periphery-core communication as our object of study as it raised the most interesting research questions for us (heterogeneous community, boundary crossing, multiple roles, and user participation in software development). Furthermore, we made a purposeful sampling of the total data set of 215 contributors, reducing the number to five core contributors and 10 peripheral contributors. The rationale for the reduction is to carry out a qualitative analysis to address our research questions within a reasonable time frame (PhD thesis). In the next section we explain in more detail the steps we went through in order to select representative sub-groups of core and peripheral contributors and the number of contributors in each group.

The mailing lists consisted of post and reply messages. Our focus on interaction led us to ignore posts that were not responded to. The presence of interaction requires a minimum of one post and reply sequence, and this was coded as '1,' whereas non-interacting dyads were coded '0.' Consequently, messages that were not responded to were unaccounted for in our analysis. This left us with a standard asymmetric binary network for performing basic matrix operations.

DATA AND RESULTS

We organized our empirical results into two parts: 1) network-level data [28, 32] and 2) interaction data [16]. We computed density, centrality, ego networks and subgroups within the network to identify regions of high and low cohesion. We analyzed the processes of intersubjectivity within selected high cohesion sub-groups and the roles of shared prolepsis by zooming in on interactions among participants in selected sub-groups, focusing on the content of their messages and identifying proleptic instances in the message flow, and studied the impact the proleptic instances had on the conversation.

Network-Level Data

The density score of the network is 0.0127, which indicates rather low overall cohesion (a value closer to 1 would be considered high). This means that relatively few participants in the community directly and frequently communicate with each other. However, network density provides only a rough estimate of cohesion in the overall network, and centrality measures provide additional information. The *degree centrality* [10] shows the overall network activity of individuals, as the number of ties incident upon a node or "the sum of each row in the adjacency matrix representing the network" [4]. Two of the participants with the highest degree centrality score are listed in Table 1 below.

Member	OutDeg	InDeg	NrmOutDeg	NrmInDeg
dev-12	62	40	28.972	18.692
dev-29	29	19	13.551	8.879

Table 1: Freeman's degree centrality measures [10] indicate the most active participants in the mod_perl community.

The above degree centrality values indicate that dev-12 is the most central member of the mod_perl community. An Out/InDegree of 62/40 means that dev-12 has established 62 communicational ties (the number of postings) and received 40. In an asymmetric expert network such as the mod_perl community, a high InDegree may indicate prominence in the sense that other members consult the member more often. High OutDegree centralization could mean that the participant undertakes the majority of consulting in the project.

To obtain a visual impression of the prominence and influence of dev-12, the sociogram ego network of dev-12 depicts a relatively clear star structure, which indicates that this developer is one of the most active members in the community. From this diagram, one can find which other developers he interacts with frequently (e.g., dev-29 and dev-81 in the top-left region). The sociogram can also tell us what other developers dev-12 interacts with frequently, but it does not tell whether the nodes also cluster in sub-groups (cliques) around the structural center, information we need to zoom in on potential regions of intersubjectivy.

We tested multiple values for group size to identify high cohesive sub-groups that could be used for content analyses. The following four sub-groups were found for N=5. This was the smallest group size where all members had ties to each other:

1: dev-12, dev-29, dev-40, dev-81, dev-92

2: dev-12, dev-29, dev-40, dev-81, dev-144

3: dev-12, dev-20, dev-22, dev-23, dev-65

4: dev-3, dev-12, dev-38, dev-39, dev-40

These four sub-groups partially overlap, and their relationships are displayed in Figure 4.

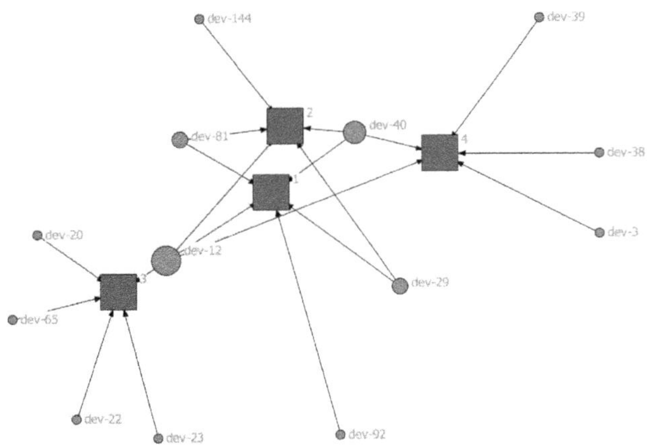

Figure 4. Sub-group sets showing central participants' co-memberships.

dev-12 and dev-40 share membership in three of the four groups, and dev-12 and dev-81 in two of the four groups. On the other hand, dev-3, dev-20, dev-22, dev-23, dev-38, dev-39, dev-65, dev-92 and dev-144 are more isolated from the rest, since they belong to only one of the sub-groups. Given that the most central nodes in the network are co-members in clearly defined sub-groups, in particular dev-12, dev-29, dev-40 and dev-81, we refer to them as the *nucleus group* in the content analysis that follows.

We adopted a similar technique (purposeful sampling) for identifying a *peripheral group* to serve as a contrast to the nucleus. However, as there were many more peripheral than core participants in the total population (202 vs. 13), we had to first reduce the data set. We opted for a practical solution and randomly extracted ten participants from the total population of peripheral participants. UCINET software was applied to categorize the participants in the two classes according to the core-periphery model [4].

The ten randomly selected participants in the peripheral group are nodes with low centrality and density measures (low cohesion). In comparison with the nucleus group, they contribute and interact infrequently to the project's mailing lists. The two contrasting (nucleus and peripheral) groups' distinguishing features are displayed in Table 2.

In the core group we obtained an intragroup (core group with its own group) with a density score of 0.436 and an intergroup (core group with other groups) score of 0.053, whereas similar scores for the peripheral regions were much lower: 0.070 and 0.005, respectively. A density value of 0.005 indicates a very low prevalence of ties among peripheral members in the network (low cohesion), whereas a density value of 0.436 indicates frequent direct communication among core members (high cohesion). Almost half of the possible ties are present. Finally, a value of 0.053 indicates relatively few ties between the periphery and core.

Group	Members	Characteristics
Nucleus N=4	dev-12, dev-29, dev-40, dev-81	High centrality and density. Densely knit around the structural center of the network. Frequent contributors to the project mailing list.
Peripheral N=10	dev-19, dev-30, dev-33, dev-95, dev-131, dev-142, dev-153, dev-169, dev-186, dev-207	Random participants with low centrality and density measures. Sparsely knit in the peripheral regions of the network. Infrequent contributors to the project mailing list.

Table 2. Contrasting features of nucleus and periphery in the mod_perl network.

Interaction Data

In the following section, we analyze the content of selected messages submitted between nucleus group participants and peripheral group participants. They were selected on the basis of involving prolepsis-driven intersubjectivity (constructing shared understandings initiated by vague or incomplete utterances that catch on). The organization of this section is as follows: first, we present a sequence of "raw" interaction data, followed by a brief explanation in "common sense" terminology before we discuss it with the conceptual framework we developed in the theory portion of this paper. The extracts show a sequence of post and reply messages spanning five days. They start with a posting by a peripheral participant (dev-186), who describes difficulties installing an Apache server, proposes a possible solution, which is followed by a question. This triggers a "sense making" discussion involving two members of the nucleus group (dev-12 and dev-81). **Extract 1** is displayed below:

[Line]	**Message from dev-186, 13 Feb 2008 14:09 GMT**
1	Hello @all,
2-4	we are just transferring our Intranet Server which used Apache 1.3 and mod_perl1 from SLES8 to SLES10 with Apache2 and mod_perl2.
5-7	The switch has to go quick and we can't redesign all of our old mp1 programs to mp2, so we try to use the compat module. But I have no luck with it.
8-11	I tested my config with SELS10, Opensuse 10.3 and Ubuntu but i hit every time the same problem. I searched the Mail Archive and the Documentation, but no luck.

12	[code]
13	I get the following output...
14	Software error:
15-16	Can't locate object method "request" via package "Apache" at /usr/lib/cgi-bin/test1.pl line 4.
17-19	For help, please send mail to the webmaster (webmaster@localhost), giving this error message and the time and date of the error.
20-22	It seems, he can't find the requested methods... How can i validate that the compat module is loaded and working?

When switching to an upgraded intranet server, dev-186 experiences difficulties with the earlier mod_perl programs (mp1, line 6). Upon searching the project's message archive and documentation (line 10), he found no adequate solution to the problem. In order to assist mod_perl peers in understanding the situation, a piece of code is posted as an attachment to the message (line 12) and the software error that appeared when he attempted to start the server is displayed in lines 15-19. He proposes a tentative solution ("It seems, he can't find the requested methods," line 20) before asking a question at the end (line 20-22).

Following Rommetveit's [25] framework for intersubjectivity, the sender of utterances is in a privileged position to control what features of the shared object will "enter the field of shared attention" [25, p. 95]. If we interpret source code as the main artifact attended to in the mailing list, the message sent by dev-186 points out a specific feature of the artifact in an effort to penetrate the shared space, namely the "compat module" (lines 7 and 21), which is used when transferring server programs written for mod_perl 1.0 to mod_perl 2.0. In the situation description, he also refers to several different server OS (SLES10, Opensuse 10.3 and Ubuntu) that are not part of the mod_perl bundle. However, a partially shared understanding of how these systems integrate with mod_perl may be important to make sense of dev-186's posting. What shared background information can be assumed or presupposed by the receivers of this message? Dev-186 explains that prior to sending the message he searched the mail archive and the project documentation (line 8-11). The previous postings stored in the mail archive and project documentation can be seen as knowledge resources that are mutually accessible to the participants.

As the initial message is addressed to all mailing list subscribers ("Hello@all," line 1), the potential 'listeners' or receivers of utterances are numerous. They are scattered around the entire developer network, ranging from peripheral to nucleus participants. It follows that 'the listener' invited into a partially shared intersubjective space is not a single individual, as in Rommetveit's framework, but rather a relatively large group of peers (developers and web server administrators). This implies that the sender somehow has to adapt the message to a potentially large number of receivers. This proleptic communication may not provide the necessary pre-understanding for establishing intersubjectivity across the network, and a selective response should be expected either from one of the core members or perhaps from another peripheral member who has been in a similar situation before. A member of the nucleus group (dev-81) replies a few hours later, on the same day. It appears that he has experienced a similar problem with his own server installations. **Extract 2** below is a reproduction of the reply:

[Line]	**Message from dev-81, 13 Feb 2008 21:49 GMT**
1	Hi.
2	About your problem below...
3-5	I am not sure that this is going to help, nor even if it is really relevant to your specific problem. Just trying to give you ideas, because it reminds me of something.
6-16	Below are two configurations, of two of our systems, which have slightly different versions of mod_perl and the rest. I went through the same kind of problems you're going through, a while ago when going from Apache 1.x to Apache 2.x, and again more recently when there were some changes in the mod_perl naming of modules between mod_perl 1.9xx and mod_perl 2.0, and then some additional things happened during a Linux Debian upgrade from Sarge to Etch, which changed the location where some of the Apache2 stuff was installed.
17-19	And there is still some differences to this day in some Perl scripts or modules between these two systems, which greatly bothers me, but it basically works.
20-23	The main difference is in the two first "use" statements in our "startup.pl" script (which I assume you are familiar with, as a way to pre-load some Perl stuff when the server starts).
24-26	I do not remember precisely which problems we had, but they were of the same "general gist" as yours, so maybe this helps. [code]

Dev-81 indicates a shared understanding of dev-186's description of a problem, but his understanding appears at first vague and suggestive ("it reminds me of something," line 5). Dev-81 continues the reply by comparing two server configurations at his site (lines 6-16), referring to a problem in the mod_perl module when the server was upgraded to a newer version (lines 8-12), and eventually pinpointing the problem by comparing the startup script in the two systems (line 20). He refers to a script called "startup.pl," (line 21) which dev-81 assumes is part of dev-186's pre-understanding (lines 21-23). However, there is no further specification of these differences and the question is left open (e.g. no response from the main recipient, dev-186). This is an example of a proleptic instance; it is well formulated but lacks detail and begs for completion (lines 20-23, "use" statements in our "startup.pl" script). It caught the attention of the nucleus group, and the sense-making discussion that followed over the next days is shown in

Extract 3. It involves two nucleus members (dev-12, dev-81) and one experienced peripheral member (dev-19):

[Line]	**Reply from dev-81, 13 Feb 2008 22:00:56 GMT**
1-5	Of course, what I forgot to mention below - and sorry if you know that already - is that whichever perl modules you pre-load in your main Apache server config via the startup.pl script, you do not need to "use" anymore in all your perl scripts or Apache/mod_perl handlers. [..]
6	**Reply from dev-19, 14 Feb 2008 14:13**
7-11	This is the first time that NOT using "use" because it was preloaded is mentioned. In fact, how would the modules compile (while testing for example)? Wasn't preloading supposed to do the exact opposite? [..]I'm at a loss here.
12	**Reply from dev-12, 14 Feb 2008 15:51:22 GMT:**
13-16	[..] I think that was just a wording mistake. When the process forks, the loaded modules are shared by the operating system's copy-on-write feature. I believe that's what he was trying to say.
17	**Reply from dev-81, 18 Feb 2008 09:40**
18-21	Well, it was not exactly what I was trying to say, but undoubtedly this reflects my incomplete personal understanding of the process anyway, and I stand ready to be educated.
22-32	What I have until now believed is that perl "code" is in fact "data" for the perl interpreter, and that as such it cannot really be "shared". What I mean is that, as soon as some bit is changed in a "page" of any perl module, that "page" is dirty and must be copied and made private to the one child process. And since there is (in my understanding) not such a clear separation as to which parts in "perl code" are data and which are code, after a while one ends up with a full duplicate in each child anyway. Probably badly explained, but not so in the general sense?
33-38	P.S. What I really meant originally, is that if the speed to make it work was of the essence, it might be easier to (find/grep) and remove the various use Apache-x() from the multiple modules or cgi scripts, and put them all in the startup script. Then later one could go back and refine things, if it makes a difference.
39	**Reply from dev-12, 18 Feb 2008 19:55:03 GMT**
40-43	Your technical understanding is correct, but in practice most pages remain shared. You can help this by using a tool like Apache::SizeLimit that kills off processes after a while.

In the above interaction sequence, the general and intended functionality of the startup.pl script's 'use' statement is the object of shared attention. With reference to the follow-up posting by dev-81 to dev-186 (""you do not need to 'use' anymore in all your Perl scripts," lines 4-5), dev-19 disagrees with dev-81's attempted explanation of how the 'use' statement works ("This is the first time that NOT using "use" because it was preloaded is mentioned," lines 7-8). It appears that the function of the 'use' statement is not sufficiently understood by the experts, and a temporary communication breakdown occurs. Another central nucleus group member (dev-12) attempts a repair sequence, suggesting that this is only a wording mistake by dev-81 (line 13), but dev-81 turns down dev-12s interpretation of his understanding. Dev-81 admits some "incomplete personal understanding" (lines 19-20) before elaborating using another example (lines 22-32), then proposing a tentative solution to the original problem raised by dev-186 (lines 33-38). At the end of the excerpt, dev-81's explanation is approved by dev-12, who is one of the most central members of the nucleus group. At this stage of knowledge development the shared understanding seems to have been brought to a new level, elaborating upon the previous incomplete information from dev-81's earlier attempts. The new understanding extends from what was partially known in advance and thus provides both an expansion of the intersubjective space and a clarification of the partly misunderstood feature [24, 25].

What we have described here is a process of constructing shared understanding for the run time configuration (installment) of a web server (Apache) using a logic that is different from programming and documentation (hierarchical organization), despite similarities for obvious reasons. It is a more dynamic and serendipitous process that involves the evolution of a shared object of attention, an 'object of knowledge' [11]. It starts with an uncompleted description of a difficult situation with a server upgrade as experienced by a peripheral contributor (involving problem formulations, knowledge sharing, and solution proposals), who describes the situation to the best of dev-186's knowledge, which is responded to by a nucleus member (dev-81), who 'fills in' uncompleted information by suggesting a more appropriate description of the problem in terms of the startup script, followed by a critical remark by dev-19, which causes a temporary breakdown regarding their understanding of how Perl modules are included in the system during compilation, later resolved by the nucleus members, thus refining the object of knowledge and expanding intersubjectivity among the group of OSD practitioners.

In summary, the main findings from this analysis are:

- *Network-level findings:* Large group of peripheral members compared with core members and relatively few interactions between periphery and core (compared with intragroup interactions in the core).
- *Interaction findings: Two types of intersubjectivity*: 1) among core members and 2) among peripheral and core members. We have assumed that core members draw heavily on a repertoire of common pre-understanding, whereas peripheral members enroll in the same common ground in a more rudimentary fashion. Previous studies have shown that peripheral members can enroll in the common ground by involvement in work tasks that draws

them to the center [5]. Based on our findings we can add another path to enrollment: being immersed in practical matters in a local setting of shared concern for a developer community, and using the community as a resource for collaborative problem solving when difficulties arise.

- *Interaction findings: Proleptic instances appear twice:* 1) An initiation phase where what is presupposed is surfaced but not necessarily picked up and acknowledged (extract 1), which may lead to partial understanding that is sufficiently clear to involve other more competent members in an 2) explication phase (extracts 2-3) that may create a new shared understanding within the group.

GENERAL DISCUSSION

In this section, we discuss our findings, organized according to our research questions, using our theoretical framework, and by comparing our findings to those reported in the literature.

How is Intersubjectivity Achieved by Shared Prolepsis

Intersubjectivity is a term we use to conceptualize the psychological relationship between people during conversation, in order to build common understanding within a group and to reach goals. The goals may diverge across sub groups (e.g. improving server software vs. installing a web server) and the individuals may not know each other well in advance. We developed a framework for the analysis of empirical data based on Rommetveit' theory of prolepsis-driven intersubjectivity, proposed for face-to-face communication [25].

Our findings indicate that many of the postings in the mod_perl mailing list are incomplete as problems, as they include problem descriptions, solution proposals, and ideas for understanding, i.e. question and answers, in the same formulation. In some situations they serve as proleptic instances, triggering prolonged discussions, and at other times they generate little or no response. This suggests a two-step process of shared prolepses: 1) initiation (sending a potentially interesting message, a pre-proleptic instance) and 2) explication (a proleptic instance vigorously followed up by joint problem solving and knowledge sharing). For explication to be possible, the pre-proleptic instances need to hit upon the 'hot spots' of shared attention in the community (at least one member in the nucleus group must find it interesting).

According to Clark and Brennan [6], two key factors shape grounding processes: purpose and medium. Purpose means that a sufficient condition for continuing the collective activity is that communicators mutually believe that the receivers "have understood what the contributor meant to a criterion sufficient for the current purpose" [6]. In the case of dev-186, reply messages provided by nucleus group members were perhaps sufficient to solve the problem of installing an upgraded Apache server. However, as the message thread continued into a discussion among more competent practitioners, the initial purpose of the communication thread seemed to change. In the second wave of replies, shown in Extract 3, the sense-making discussion moved beyond the initiation by dev-186. This is supported by the fact that dev-186 never returned to the thread with follow-up postings. We do not know whether dev-186 successfully installed the server, or if additional help was needed.

Rommetveit argues that intersubjectivity should be approached as an expansive process of creating and maintaining a temporary shared social reality among a small group of communicators. This expansive process occurs along multiple dimensions (spatial, temporal and interpersonal), which we elaborate below based on our data (we do not have data on spatial expansion as we did not ask our informants about their whereabouts).

Temporal expansion

Temporal expansion means to reach backward and forward in time (towards shared knowledge and presuppositions on one end and common goals and application of the knowledge on the other).

In Rommetveit's original work on prolepsis-driven intersubjectivy, temporal expansion seems to be the main dimension for increasing intersubjectivy and shared prolepsis being the main mechanism. It is initiated by somewhat vague (not always identifiable) anticipatory cues inserted in a conversation. These cues must refer to common preunderstanding to succeed (be picked up by more experienced participants), and should point forward to a new event of common interest: the meeting of three people in Rommetveit's example in the beginning of the paper, and successfully installing an upgraded Apache web server in our case. The common preunderstanding relates to previous postings in the mail archive and the mod_perl project documentation, general knowledge of server operating systems (SLES, Opensuse, and Ubuntu in extract 1), and the role of the 'use' statement in the 'startup.pl' script (extracts 2). This preunderstanding is not fully shared by dev-186 (the peripheral participant who triggered the conversation), and the subsequent elaboration (extract 3) indicates that information for understanding the situation was missing.

Our analysis provides tentative evidence that peripheral participants reporting difficulties will not yet be carriers of the culturally taken-for-granted knowledge that makes prolepsis effective for enrolling outsiders in the project. Our findings indicate that the former have, first of all, a pragmatic role in providing pre-proleptic instances that serve as the 'raw material' or triggers for more competent practitioners to construct instances of shared prolepsis. The nucleus group members continue with a discussion of the 'use' statement, which dev-81 assumes is part of the community's common pre-understanding ("which I assume you are familiar with," line 21-22, extract 2). 11 minutes later (line 1-5, extract 3) dev-81 becomes unsure if dev-186 has understood what was meant, and perhaps is unsure about his own understanding, and follows up with more information and excuses himself for stating the obvious ("sorry if you know that already", line 1-2, extract 2). Later on, dev-81 fine-tunes his understanding based on feedback from two experienced developers, dev-19 and dev-12 (clarifying their understanding of how the 'use' statement works and how Perl programs load). In the final reply message, dev-12 provides positive evidence that the procedure was understood sufficiently for the current purpose. The information can thus be added to the group members' common ground.

Interpersonal adaptation

Interpersonal adaptation means to adapt to the role of the person one communicates with (sender, receiver, peripheral member, core member, etc.) and to the type of their utterances (vague, incomplete, elaborated, clarified, etc.). Our network data shows there were few interactions among periphery and core members, which can partly be explained by peripheral members using the mod_perl community as a resource for problem solving when difficulties arise with a web server installation. The interaction data indicates that the peripheral participant (dev-186) did not know the audience well (e.g. "Hello @all," extract 1), whereas nucleus members and frequent contributors were more aware of whom they communicated with, and they adapted their messages differently across the conversation thread

The contributors reveal attitude towards the others based on the tone of their utterances. Dev-81 and dev-12 (two of the most active members in the mod_perl community) makes the greatest effort of adapting responses to the perspective of the person they communicate with (dev-81 → dev-186; dev-12 → dev-81). Dev-19 is a somewhat at odds with the two nucleus members when he criticizes dev-81 for having an understanding different from his own (line 7-11, extract 3). Dev-19 seems to be knowledgeable about web server configurations, but he is only a peripheral contributor in the mod_perl community. His critical attitude created a temporary breakdown and helped resolve the situation by triggering a final round of 'mutual education' ("I stand ready to be educated," dev-81 in line 20-21 in extract 3) and ("Your technical understanding is correct," dev-12, line 40, extract 3). These message sequences show a somewhat bumpy road of proposing explanations, elaboration, friction, and clarification, leading eventually to success by increasing the group's (and possible their numerous listeners') intersubjectivity.

According to Matusov [20], processes of intersubjectivity transcend specific and time-limited joint problem solving and are "not only the basis and derivative of the joint activity but also the social glue of different sociocultural activities" [20, p. 30]. Praising peers, seeking education (line 20-21 in extract 3), and validating another person's understanding of a shared object, as indicated by dev-12's last reply to dev-81 (lines 40-43 in excerpt 3), may perhaps be significant for sustaining participation in OSD projects like mod_perl.

Our study would have benefited from interviews with the above-mentioned developers (dev-186, dev-81, dev-19 and dev-12) to verify our claims. Interviews can dig deeper into the meaning of individual postings and obtain valuable feedback for supporting and/or refuting our interpretations of informants' text-based (public) conversations. This was not done in our case due to lack of time and for practical reasons (access to emails addresses). Future work ought to consider interview as a part of a mixed methods approach.

Combining SNA and Content Analysis

We approached the social phenomenon of the mod_perl community by choosing methods from the social sciences and applied mathematics (social network analysis and content analysis). These methods allowed us to identify high cohesion subgroups within the mod_perl community and study their interactions in some detail. We narrowed the scope further to zoom in on periphery-core communications, mainly for practical reasons (interest of the research team and constrained by the timeframe of a PhD thesis). Intersubjectivy was identified as an expansive process in central regions of the network in an effort to create common understanding of some topic of concern to the community of Perl developers and Apache web sever administrators. Our total data set covers a period of 6 months of mailing list discussions in the mod_perl community, whereas the data extracts chosen for content analysis had a much shorter time frame (5 ¼ days). Limitations of our work can be attributed to the short duration of the quantitative analysis and our purposeful sampling of the data set to reveal one detailed example. Further work ought to explore multiple data sets for comparison and include larger time spans for qualitative analysis (longitudinal study), to see if there are interdependencies of working, learning and knowledge development, and other characteristics of prolepsis-driven intersubjectivy that we have not yet identified.

Informal Learning and Knowledge Development

The development of shared understanding is illustrated in the extracts as an emergent object of knowledge gradually capturing shared attention. It starts by dev-186 pointing out in extract 1 a specific feature of a server configuration that does not work as a result of an upgrade, in an effort to catch the attention of more experienced members of the community who can help, and penetrate the shared space.

The original formulation issued by dev-186 is a pre-proleptic instance, which is responded to by dev-81 in extract 2 and turned into shared prolepsis by a meticulous explanation of certain parts of the system. The reformation by dev-81 turns out to be incomplete (partly "wording mistake," line 13, extract 3, dev-12; and partly "incomplete personal understanding," line 19-20, extract 3, dev-81). It generates vigorous activity by three experienced developers, and further clarification becomes necessary.

In the final stage of knowledge development the shared understanding seems to have been brought to a new level, elaborating upon the previous incomplete information from dev-81's earlier attempts. The new understanding extends from what was partially known in advance and thus provides both an expansion of the intersubjective space and a clarification of the partly misunderstood feature. However, it is not clear from our data whether or not the shared understanding created within the nucleus group also reached out to dev-186 who first raised the concern as well as the other peripheral participants who listened in on the conversation. A follow up interview with dev-186 would be able to answer this question. This was outside the scope of our work.

The literature on OSD describes paths for newcomers to become (peripheral and core) contributors to the activities taking place in the OSD communities. For example, Cataldo and Herbsleb [5] found that peripheral members' involvement in work tasks that draws them to the center provides a path for enrolling newcomers in OSD projects [5]. Edwards [9] suggests that situated learning and apprenticeship (techniques from community of practice) do apply to OSD projects. Our own study corroborates previous findings of socialization, but we did find a clear demarcation between core and peripheral members in terms of participation, which could indicate a steep learning curve for newcomers or a different motivation for involvement, but further work ought to follow this up in more detail. Presenting a problem may be one possible path to enter into the community, but a problem-proposer also faces the risk of offending others as a result of a poorly formulated question.

Prolepses vs. Problems

The notion of shared prolepsis can be compared with the notion of problem as part of a problem solving process, but they are not the same. First, prolepsis appears in two facets, pre-proleptic and shared prolepsis. Shared prolepsis is closer to a problem description than a pre-proleptic instance, as the former is tuned into a path that may lead to cooperative problem solving. Second, proleptic instances should be thought of as embryonic solutions, capturing both problem setting and skeleton solution. A proleptic instance is better described as a 'seed.' A seed contains a 'mini solution' for its own development. When it is planted in fertile soil it will grow (expand) in two directions: downward (roots) and upward (stem, leaves, etc.). In the same fashion a proleptic instance stimulates growth of knowledge in two directions: backward in time (connecting personal knowledge with shared understanding) and forward in time (applying the knowledge to solve a problem or reach a goal).

Previous organization studies in OSD report that artifacts (source code, patches, downloads, tools, documentation, mailing lists, etc.) are the main source of organizing tasks and joint work [17]. Looking ahead, we envision that a vast number of peripheral participants in the network will use social media and 'feed' the central core with pre-proleptic instances (potential problems, new ideas, etc.). As pragmatic elements in a 'collective learning system,' the swarm of actors on the outer edges monitors the evolution of the shared knowledge object and contribute 'raw material' that might trigger further development cycles in the central region.

Schön's notion of problem setting [26] is arguable the technical term that comes closest to capture the meaning of shared prolepsis. By problem setting it is meant essentially a non-technical process of deciding the boundaries to be investigated, naming the problem (if applicable), and framing the context in which it will be approached. They are not problems be solved in the outset, but problematic situations characterized by uncertainty, disorder and indeterminacy [26].

Implications for Design

We can speculate on implication for design based on our empirical work by comparing (uttered) proleptic instances to (designed) prompts, and 'sentence openers' in Web-based inquiry environments to trigger reflections, discussions, and further development. Furberg [12] reports on a qualitative study of high school students' engagement with a web-based inquiry environment system for science education aimed at prompting student reflections on processes of scientific inquiry. Her findings were that students often copied and pasted (e.g. verbatim reuses) the prompts provided by the system or by the teachers in their own work when they were told to rewrite the prompts in their own words. Her findings point to the fact that engaging in prolepsis-driven intersubjectivity is not straightforward for newcomers as it requires identifying cues, understanding their meaning and reformulating them in a language that resonates with shared knowledge within a given community.

SUMMARY AND CONCLUSIONS

We studied communication patterns and analyzed message exchanges between central and peripheral participants in the mod_perl open source software development project for a period of six months, showing how constructing a shared understanding is a subprocess of complex distributed work in this community. A framework for prolepsis-driven intersubjectivity constituted the theoretical perspective for understanding this process. We used social network analysis to identify and visualize high-cohesion sub-groups and interaction analysis to analyze conversations (contents of messages).

A key mechanism in the framework is the notion of shared prolepsis, which serves as a catalyst (a 'seed') for joint meaning making among competent practitioners. However, for pre-proleptic instances to progress into proleptic instances that will expand the project's shared understanding, the study suggests that the potential problems and solution ideas shared by peripheral participants need to be reformulated by the more competent, central developers, to serve as building blocks for a shared understanding that can be properly introduced into the intersubjective space (i.e. aligned with the community's common pre-understanding. This implies that pre-proleptic utterances are often vague and sometimes off-track, suggesting some lacking feature in the knowledge object that may invite reformulation as proleptic instances, which again may evolve into productive discussions among more competent peers.

ACKNOWLEDGMENTS

We thank the Faculty of Education, University of Oslo for funding the PhD project of the first author, and we thank our colleagues in the 'Professional Learning in a Changing Society' (ProLearn) project for providing comments and advice along the way. The authors thank the anonymous CSCW'13 reviewers for constructive, elaborated comments on two previous versions of this paper.

REFERENCES

1. Apache Software Foundation. http://apache.org/.
2. Berger, P. L. and T. Luckmann. *The Social Construction of Reality: A Treatise in the Sociology of Knowledge*. Anchor Books, Garden City, 1966.
3. Bergquist, M. and J. Ljungberg (2001). The power of gifts: organizing social relationships in open source communities. *Information Systems Journal 11*, 4 (2001), 305-320.
4. Borgatti, P., M. G. Everett, et al. *UCINET for Windows: Software for Social Network Analysis*. Analytic Technologies, Harvard, MA, 2002.
5. Cataldo, M. and J. D. Herbsleb. Communication networks in geographically distributed software development. In *Proc. CSCW 2008*. ACM Press (2008), 579-588.
6. Clark, H. and S. Brennan. Grounding in Communication, in L. B. Resnick, R. M. Levine and S. D. Teasley (eds.), *Perspectives on socially shared cognition*. American Psychological Association, Washington DC (1991), 127-149.
7. Clark, H. and E. F. Schaefer. Contributing to discourse. *Cognitive Science* 13 (1989), 259-294.
8. Crowston, K., K. Wei, et al. (2006). Core and Periphery in Free/Libre and Open Source Software Team Communications. In *Proc. 39th Annual HICSS conference, Vol. 6*, IEEE Computer Society (2006), 118-125.
9. Edwards, K. Epistemic Communities, Situated Learning and Open Source Software Development. In *Proc. Workshop on Epistemic Cultures and the Practice of Interdisciplinarity*. NTNU, Trondheim (2001), 11-12.
10. Freeman, L. C. Centrality in networks: Conceptual clarification. *Social Networks 1*, 3 (1979) 215–239.
11. Fugelli, P. (2010). Intersubjectivity and objects of knowledge: Making sense across sites in software development. PhD Thesis, Department of Educational Research, University of Oslo.
12. Furberg, A. Socio-cultural aspects of prompting student reflection in Web-based inquiry learning environments. *Journal of Computer Assisted Learning 25* (2009), 397–409.
13. Gnu crossing in East Africa, Battle at the Mara river. http://www.youtube.com/watch?NR=1&feature=endscreen&v=Mkg0E8c71IQ .
14. Hemetsberger, A. and Reinhardt, C. Collective development in open-source communities: An activity theoretical perspective on successful online collaboration. *Organization Studies 30*, 9 (2009), 987-1008.
15. Johansen, R. *Groupware: Computer support for business teams*. The Free Press, New York, 1988.
16. Jordan, B., and Henderson, A. Interaction analysis: Foundations and practice. *The Journal of the Learning Sciences 4*, 1 (1995), 39-103.
17. Lanzara, G.F. and Morner, M. Artifacts rule! How organizing happens in open source software projects, in B. Czarniawska and T. Hernes (eds.), *Actor-Network Theory and Organizing*. Liber & Copenhagen Business School Press, Copenhagen (2005), 67-90.
18. Lee, J.S., Tatar, D. and Harrison, S. Micro-coordination: because we did not already learn everything we need to know about working with others in kindergarten. In *Proc. CSCW 2012*, ACM Press (2012), 1135-1144.
19. Long, Y. and K. Siau. Social network structures in open source software development teams. *Journal of Database Management 18*, 2 (2007), 25-40.
20. Matusov, E. Intersubjectivity without agreement. *Mind, Culture, and Activity 3*, 1 (1996), 25-45.
21. Matusov, E. Intersubjectivity as a way of informing teaching design for a community of learners' classroom. *Teaching and Teacher Education 17*, 4 (2001), 383-402.
22. McCarthy, J.C, Miles, V.C, and Monk, A.F. An experimental study of common ground in text-based communication. In *Proc. CHI 1991,* ACM Press (1991), 209-215.
23. Nvivo software package, www.scienceplus.nl/Nvivo

24. Rommetveit, R. *On message structure: A framework for the study of language and communication*. Wiley, London, 1974.

25. Rommetveit, R. On the architecture of intersubjectivity, in R. Rommetveit and R. M. Blakar (eds.), *Studies of Language, Thought and Verbal Communication*. Academic Press, New York (1979), 147-161.

26. Schön, D.A. *The reflective practitioner: How professionals think in action*. Basic Books, New York, 1983.

27. Schütz, A. (1962). *Collected papers I: The problem of social reality*, with M.A. Natanson and H.L. van Breda (eds.). Martinus Nijhoff Publishers, Dordrecht, The Netherlands, 1962.

28. Scott, J. *Social network analysis: A handbook*. Sage, London, 2000.

29. Shami, N.S., Erickson, T. and Kellogg, W.A. Common Ground and Small Group Interaction in Large Virtual World Gatherings. In *Proc. ECSCW 2011*, Springer: London (2011), 393-404.

30. Stahl, G., Koschmann, T., and Suthers, D. Computer-supported collaborative learning: An historical perspective, in R. K. Sawyer (ed.), *Cambridge handbook of the learning sciences*. Cambridge University Press, Cambridge, UK (2006), 409-426.

31. The Richmeister sketch, "Copy machine." http://www.nbc.com/saturday-night-live/video/copy-machine/1353535/.

32. Wasserman, S. and Faust, K. *Social network analysis methods and applications*. Cambridge University Press, Cambridge, UK, 1994.

Activity Traces and Signals in Software Developer Recruitment and Hiring

Jennifer Marlow
Human-Computer Interaction Institute
Carnegie Mellon University
5000 Forbes Avenue, Pittsburgh PA
jmarlow@cs.cmu.edu

Laura Dabbish
Human-Computer Interaction Institute &
Center for the Future of Work, Heinz College
Carnegie Mellon University
dabbish@cmu.edu

ABSTRACT
Social networking tools now allow professionals to post and share their work in online spaces. These professionals build reputation within a community of practice, often with the goal of finding a job. But how are the visible traces of their actions and interactions in online workspaces used in the hiring process? We conducted interviews with members of the GitHub "social coding" community to understand how profiles on the site are used to assess people during recruitment and hiring for software development positions. Both employers and job seekers pointed to specific cues provided on profiles that led them to make inferences (or form impressions) about a candidate's technical skills, motivations, and values. These cues were seen as more reliable indicators of technical abilities and motivation than information provided on a resume, because of the transparency of work actions on GitHub and relative difficulty of manipulating behavior traces. The use of online workspaces like GitHub has implications for the type of information sought by employers as well as the activity traces job hunters might seek to leave.

CATEGORIES AND SUBJECT DESCRIPTORS
H.5.3 Group and Organization Interfaces – *Computer Supported Cooperative Work*

GENERAL TERMS
Design, Human Factors

KEYWORDS
Impression formation; Transparency; Hiring; Open source software development; Impression management

INTRODUCTION
Reputation and professional development have long been cited as primary motivators for contributing to online peer production communities like open-source software development projects [16]. Contributors and potential employers both view open-source software participation as a desirable way to gain relevant experience and skills [17, 23]. The pace of recruiting and career development in online production communities seems to be accelerating with the emergence of social media, evidenced by discussions among developers online sparked by blog posts such as one asserting that "GitHub is your new resume" [3].

In many online peer production environments, social networking functionality is now tied directly with the work artifacts being shared or collaboratively developed. This means contributors can get moment to moment updates about others' actions on artifacts and interactions, affording an unprecedented level of transparency around who is doing what and how work is accomplished. At the same time, there is some level of individual control over what is shared and how.

Anecdotally, the open source software community describes the traces provided by social media as affording more verifiable information about an individual's skills and abilities than a list of achievements on a resume. As John Resig, the creator of the jQuery interface library, recently tweeted: "When it comes to hiring, I'll take a Github commit log over a resume any day."

Social networking functionality, when tied with the work environment in a peer production site, provides moment-by-moment information about actions on artifacts and interactions around project decisions or activities. This means that information in these environments, compared to information on a resume, can provide much more information about how someone works. In software development, for example, sites like GitHub allow employers to view the details of the code an individual writes in each commit, or contribution, to a project, and any interactions or discussions around the code are also publicly viewable. Potential employers can effectively reconstruct exactly what someone works on, how they work, what their code looks like, how they talk about their work or negotiate changes to collaborative projects, and their speed and style of work on public projects. This level of detailed information about someone's working style is typically unavailable to a potential employer.

Research has not addressed how activity traces within online communities of practice play into the hiring process for more traditional jobs associated with the work of the community. Thus, we were interested in how employers in this environment made use of the displayed cues about developers' actions over time. Our work focused on the following research questions:

(1) How are activity traces in an online peer production community used by potential employers to find and evaluate prospective software development hires?

(2) How do job seekers attempt to manage the impressions their activity traces give off to employers?

We conducted exploratory interviews with employers and job seekers in GitHub, an online open source software hosting repository with extensive social networking functionality integrated with the development environment. This means that potential employers can view an individual's profile of projects posted on the site, and a history of their code related actions on these projects and other people's projects over time. As software developers commit changes to their software projects, these changes are broadcast to other developers watching the project. A history of commits (or contributions) to the code is recorded over time, along with conversation around changes in the form of comments. (See [5] for a detailed description of the GitHub environment.)

We interpret our interview results through the lens of signaling theory to understand how and why certain cues were viewed as reliable signals of underlying characteristics of a potential hire. Our results suggest that certain activity traces are viewed by employers as more reliable than others, in part because they serve as more trustworthy signals of underlying characteristics that are often difficult to assess in traditional interviews, such as values and motivation, but also because they are easy to verify quickly. For example, willingness to actively contribute to software and share projects openly on the site was viewed as a reliable signal of commitment to open source software ideology.

BACKGROUND

Impression formation and employment

When evaluating job candidates, either online or offline, a principal goal of the employer is to accurately evaluate applicants' job-relevant knowledge, skills, abilities, and other characteristics. These evaluations, in turn, affect selection decisions [2]. For example, related work in the online peer production realm looking at admin permission granting in Wikipedia revealed that reviewers weighed evidence of interaction style, a candidate's social network, and the amount and type of past editing work when making these decisions [6].

In addition to criteria relating to competence and expertise, employers also often place high importance on features that cannot be gleaned from a resume and need to be assessed in a job interview, such as a person's likeability and the potential person-organization fit [28]. Other work suggests that features such as whether a candidate is seen as "the right person for a job" and perceived applicant-interviewer similarity can be strong determinants of hiring decisions [14].

Increasingly, online presence on social networking sites (SNS) such as Facebook or LinkedIn are playing into the hiring process for full time jobs in the offline world. A 2008 survey [13] found that information gleaned from SNS could damage an applicant's chances of being hired if it revealed that a person had lied about their qualifications. On the other hand, SNS information could be advantageous if it helped support their qualifications or portrayed a professional image. SNS members with personal profiles are aware that employers might look at their profiles [2] and occasionally engage in management techniques to present a professional image [7].

While it is known that employers supplement resumes with online information and use this to form impressions about candidates, less is known about what specific inferences hiring managers make from this information and how useful or accurate these impressions actually are. In the software development domain, recent surveys indicate that employers examining students' OSS experience look for compatible skills (while paying less attention to the popularity of the projects,) [17] but it is unclear how exactly they go about this. This work has not considered how activity trace information would play into this process. In the next two sections we consider the impression formation and impression management process from the perspective of signaling theory.

Impression formation as signal assessment

Signaling theory provides a useful framework for understanding impression formation in the hiring process. According to this theory, we make assessments of others based on their visible characteristics and actions. These observable cues effectively act as "signals" of hidden qualities (such as experience or expertise) that are not directly observable [9]. This theory delineates two main types of signals in terms of how they are produced and interpreted: *assessment signals* are thought to be more reliable indicators of the presence of a certain quality because they are costly to produce, whereas *conventional signals* are more susceptible to being manipulated because they are more easily faked by someone not possessing the underlying quality they signal. For example, being able to lift a heavy weight is an assessment signal of someone's strength while simply wearing a Gold's Gym t-shirt would be a conventional signal of this underlying quality (something that can easily be acquired and worn even if the wearer is actually quite weak) [15].

In the online realm, signaling theory has been applied to examine how individuals in online communities attempt to convey and interpret visible cues about others as signals of their underlying characteristics (e.g. user name as a low cost or conventional signal of interest in the topic of the community) [8]. This work suggests that the degree to which a certain type of cue is viewed as reliable may depend on the context of the site: For example, the interpretation of one's number of friends or connections on a site as a signal of popularity may be more or less reliable depending on how costly it is to make a connection [9]. An additional important aspect of evaluating others' signals is the amount of effort involved, or how easy it is for the observer to verify the accuracy of these signals [18].

The impression management and formation process in online peer production communities, then, can largely be thought of as a signal production and evaluation process. Job seekers on the sites can attempt to convey or signal certain skills or abilities with the information they post on their profile or the activities they engage in. Employers must determine which visible signals of developer expertise or personality to attend to on these sites (depending partly on how hard it is to verify them), and then interpret these signals to infer the developers' underlying or actual skill or expertise.

In the hiring domain, where deception about qualifications is a concern, being able to judge signal reliability is important. When the costs of forming an incorrect impression are high, for example, in hiring for a highly-paid job, perceivers may demand a more reliable signal that is costly to fake [9]. Level of education attained is one example of a reliable signal of skills that is costly for a person to produce [22] but also potentially costly for an employer to verify. Closely related to the issue of signal evaluation is the issue of signal production, or impression management.

Impression management

Signaling theory also has important implications for impression management, because signalers may deliberately try to convey positive attributes to receivers. Given that signalers may have incentives to "cheat" [4], understanding when and how they do this (and how receivers go about verifying the signals they produce) is an important topic that we investigate in GitHub.

Initial work by Goffman [12] focused on ways in which individuals convey information about themselves to observers, which can be the "cues" they intentionally give, or their real behaviors, which may be "cues given off" through involuntary expressive behavior. Both types of information can be manipulated, either through overt deceit or through pretending. In the online realm, studies of impression formation and self-presentation in online settings have examined the cue management process in a variety of contexts and scenarios, ranging from honesty and lying about oneself in online dating profiles [10, 11] to friendship formation and other behavior on sites like Facebook [7, 15, 27] to blogging [26]. This work has primarily focused on understanding self-presentation in the context of interpersonal or non-work relationships, although Ellison et al [10] draw parallels between online dating profiles and resume submissions for jobs, as using deception in either arena can be grounds for terminating a relationship. However, work on impression management in the social realm has focused largely on how people attempt to control the impressions conveyed by their profiles or pictures on these sites, and is not centered around impressions relating to work artifacts, skills, or behaviors.

Given that site design affects the reliability of signals [9], what signals do employers attend to in a peer production environment providing a plethora of trace information about work process and collaborative activity? How do prospective employees manage these signals? In order to understand how this new set of information plays into hiring, we examined how activity traces were used as signals in an online peer production environment instrumented with social media. We wanted to understand how these traces influenced employer impressions of potential candidates and how candidates attempted to manage these impressions.

INTERVIEWS OF GITHUB USERS

Method

We conducted a series of semi-structured interviews with thirteen GitHub users to identify how activity traces are used and assessed to infer a developer's abilities and personal qualities. We began by sending a screening and recruitment questionnaire to 200 GitHub members with publicly available e-mail addresses on their profiles. As there was no way to specifically filter for our two target groups (university students and employers,) we focused on targeting people located in North American and European cities that were likely to have large populations of both technical students and companies (e.g. San Francisco Bay Area, Boston/Cambridge, Pittsburgh, Seattle, Waterloo, Toronto, London, Berlin).

The questionnaire asked people if they had ever used GitHub as part of the job application or hiring process and if they would be willing to participate in a follow-up interview on the topic. Overall, 128 people responded, 65 of whom volunteered for the follow-up interview. Participants did not receive any compensation for taking part in the study.

We contacted respondents for interviews in the order in which they replied, sampling both employees and job seekers in order to understand the hiring process from both sides. Our participants for these interviews were seven employers who reported using GitHub to identify and evaluate job candidates and six job seekers who reported using their GitHub profile to supplement their job applications. The interviews focused on how they had used GitHub during a recent hire or job application.

We asked employers to describe a recent past hire, focusing on how they used GitHub during that hiring process, what information on the site was attended to and what that information conveyed about the candidate. We asked job seekers to describe how they used GitHub, how it had played into any recent job applications or interviews, and whether and how they edited the information on their profiles or in other public places on the site.

In our analysis, we coded the interview transcripts to identify the different ways profiles were used in the hiring process, as well as the different types of inferences made about individuals being evaluated based on 'signals' in the GitHub environment. Using HyperResearch, a qualitative analysis software tool, we identified relevant sentences or broader segments in interview transcripts related to candidate evaluation, and then open-coded these segments for comments related to profile cues and inferences made from them. Next, specific instances of these themes were compared across interviewees and further refined as necessary, until a set of recurring themes about signals and the inferences drawn from them emerged. The interpretation of these from both employer and job-seeker perspectives is addressed in detail in the following sections.

EMPLOYER PERSPECTIVE

The employers (6 males, 1 female, referred to here as E1 through E7) all worked for software-related organizations based in the United States (both large and well-known internet companies and smaller startups.) These companies varied in size: three of them had less than 50 employees, two had between 200 and 500 employees, and one had more than 500 employees. On the survey, participants indicated that they had either asked job seekers to provide links to their GitHub profiles during the hiring process, or had actively searched for people on the site to recruit and/or learn more about them. The interviewees were asked to think aloud while consulting profiles of people they had hired or were thinking of hiring. We used this method to obtain detail on how information in the GitHub environment signaled developer characteristics.

Employers' use of GitHub

Our first research question focused on how employers use GitHub profiles to evaluate new hires. All interviewees expressed the belief that a GitHub account provided insight into an individual's technical abilities and/or personal qualities in a more reliable way than resumes or code samples taken out of context. The GitHub profiles provided employers with a history of the individuals' contributions over time, and further guarantee the candidate was indeed the author of any code submissions.

Table 1 summarizes the main GitHub signals and inferences mentioned by employers in the interviews. We categorize these cues based on factors that are relevant to both the profile holder and profile viewer: Signal type/reliability, and the ease with which the viewer can verify them.

In the rest of this section we describe in detail how employers used GitHub activity traces as signals of a job candidate's motivation, quality of code contributions, and soft skills or management abilities.

Signal	Inference	Signal reliability, ease of verifiability
1. Active open source involvement	Shared open source values	Reliable Easy
2. Contributions accepted to high status project	Community acceptance of work, quality of contributions	Reliable Hard
3. Project ownership	Soft skills: Initiative, project management	Reliable Easy
4. Side projects	Passion for coding	Reliable Hard
5. Number of watchers or forks of project	Project popularity	Unreliable Easy

Table 1. Summary of employer inferences from profile signals

Inferring motivation

Employers in our sample worked to assess how well job candidates would fit with their company or team culture (or person-organization fit). These factors are traditionally assessed during interpersonal interaction in face-to-face interviews through direct questioning. The employers in our sample indicated that a job seeker's profile of activity on GitHub signaled personal characteristics of the employee such as being a team player, showing commitment to their work, or demonstrating how he/she spent their free time.

Shared open source values and character

Employers care about value congruence with their employees. In the software development world, an important and hotly contested value is attitudes towards open source and whether software should be free. In fact, there is a well-documented ideology of open source software [24]. Developers who differ in their software ideology may thus be said to come from different cultures. Thus, an important character property of a developer is their attitudes and commitment to the open source ideology.

Employers in our sample used presence on GitHub and activity levels on the site as signals of the level of commitment to the open source ideology. Simple presence on GitHub (having a profile and sharing even one repository) was viewed as an indicator of a potential employee's open source values by four of seven employers. The presence of code that was developed openly and shared with others signaled even more strongly that the developer valued openness, transparency, and participation in a community. This active involvement in the open source community was a signal of the candidate's selflessness and honesty. As one employer put it:

> *"If they've devoted time to this OS project, that's a good indicator that they're in [computer science] for*

the right reasons. Software engineering is becoming a pretty lucrative career...you could liken that to a doctor working with Doctors Without Borders. They're doing something because they want to give back to their community" (E7).

Active participation in other people's projects was the most reliable signal of commitment to the open source mindset (mentioned by five out of seven employers). Cues such as recent and frequent commits in another person's project showed the candidate was indeed invested in the open source community (E2, E3, E4, E6, E7). It is rather trivial to create a profile on GitHub and fork other users' projects (meaning create a personal copy of the project in order to make changes to it). Having a copy of someone else's project did not signal investment. The effort to fork a repository was negligible, while the effort and skill required to contribute meaningfully was much higher. This was widely understood, as one respondent described:

> "*a lot of people will just fork a lot of projects kind of to collect them but not actually do anything with them. So I look for a sign that these are things he's genuinely engaged in*" (E4).

Activities within these forked projects were costlier signals of commitment, requiring much more effort to produce. This activity, publicly building on another person's work, served as an assessment signal that the candidate truly bought into the open source mindset (over and above mere presence on GitHub or simply forking projects). As one employer explained:

> "*[by looking for recent activity I was] sussing out whether they're a good sport about contributing to open source...if they're doing their job of keeping up to date and actually participating" (E2).*

Passion for programming

Organizations also differ in their working style or company culture around work life balance. Employers in our sample wanted to assess candidates' level of dedication to the work and their level of initiative. They were able to discern subtle motivational differences that suggested person-organization fit from the kinds of projects a developer worked on.

Our interviewees described going through an individual's public repositories to figure out how they spent their time outside of work. They categorized projects on a user's profile as either work-related repositories that were part of an individual's "day job" (work or schoolwork,) and non work-related side projects, which could either be contributions to open-source projects not directly related to work, or personal projects done as a hobby or for fun but not necessarily intended for a wider audience.

For many of our employers, personal projects signaled a candidate's love for programming and willingness to do it in one's leisure time as well. One interviewee (E4) saw personal projects as a signal of interest in learning and developing one's career, while two employers (E3, E5) described using this signal to assess whether the candidate shared the same enthusiasm for coding with the other members of their organization and were the type of people they liked to work with. This signal is valued because it ties into the aforementioned tendency for employers to like and seek out people who are similar to themselves and fit with their company's culture. As one employer explained:

> "*A lot of us spend our weekends working on [project name] so we want to work with people who are motivated to not just work on the code they've been assigned but to work on projects outside their job. It just shows a general excitement for the space and that's what we want to find – people that are really engaged*" (E5).

These side projects suggested a willingness to learn and revealed excitement about the software development domain. For employers this meant a potential employee who would spend their free time working, and show initiative and entrepreneurship in their work.

Inferring quality of contributions

Employers also care about a potential hire's competence and level of skill for the job. GitHub supported traditional methods of evaluating software development, allowing employers to look directly at the content of someone's code and the languages they had used. The cross-project visibility and the community on GitHub supported skill assessment beyond these traditional uses. Specifically, affiliation and accepted contributions to a popular project reliably signaled candidates' level of coding ability in the GitHub environment.

Accepted code as a seal of approval

If a candidate had contributions accepted to well-known open-source projects, it was seen as a community-level seal of approval. An accepted commit to a high-status project (a widely-used project with many contributors and watchers) signaled the candidate was someone who produced quality code. This acted as a reliable signal because it required approval of the code by others in the community, meaning it would be extremely difficult to falsify. For example, one employer described a candidate who seemed proficient because he had committed code to a high-status project:

> "*Seeing that he had commits to jQuery, was filing tickets with jQuery, and I know that's a prestigious project to work on....Just by looking at his code, if nothing else seeing that it was being merged downstream into jQuery, I recognized that has demonstrated some level of proficiency*" (E6).

Another interviewee echoed this view for candidates who had contributed to open source projects, likening it to a reference:

> "*someone else can vouch for your work because you were good enough to work on that project, be a part of that community*" (E7).

Since examining lines of a developer's code can be a time-consuming endeavor, using the reputation of previously-established projects that had accepted an individual's contribution as a proxy for quality (or lack thereof) was one way to reduce the evaluation costs of the perceiver in forming impressions about the abilities of a coder. An employer's opinion of a project's reputation in our sample was largely based on general knowledge of the wider community or past experience with its use versus visible cues at the project level such as watchers (people who have decided to "follow" the activity of a project) or forks (people who have saved a copy of the project to edit on their own.).

Popularity does not always equal quality

Employers in our sample also noted conventional signals of quality they did not trust. Primary among these were popularity signals: simple counts of watchers on a project or followers (people subscribed to a developer's activity feed). In some community settings, indicators of popularity (such as the number of votes given to an answer on a question-answering site) can serve as a proxy for the quality of the answer, while in other settings, popularity (e.g. having too many friends on a SNS) can be viewed negatively [25].

Project popularity on GitHub can be roughly assessed by the number of other people "watching" the repository along with the number of people who had forked that repository. Only one employer (E2) specifically mentioned looking at a candidate's main project to look for a large number of forks. Two employers (E4, E7) were more skeptical about the utility of the watching/forking numbers as indicators of a developer's ability. As one interviewee explained:

> "*I don't think I've hired or recruited someone specifically because they were working on a very popular project or something. There aren't enough popular projects and the popularity doesn't necessarily indicate quality for that to work.*" (E4).

Popularity was thus to some degree viewed as a signal that developers could game. Our interviewees noted that project popularity was an unreliable signal of code or developer quality because it had more to do with how much an individual promoted their work:

> "*You can see if a lot of people have watched and forked and that's a good thing, but it kind of depends on how good a marketer that person was as well on GitHub.*" (E7).

Rather than relying on numbers of forks and watchers, employers described looking at the project where the applicant had made the most commits (as presumably that was the work they were the most serious about or interested in) and then assessing the actual code that was written there to understand the individual's style and skill level.

Inferring developer "soft skills"

Finally, one employer mentioned inferring "soft skills," such as project management abilities, through a developer's activity traces. These cues were largely gleaned from their interactions in a project they had started rather than one they had forked (a distinction which is made obvious by the GitHub interface).

These projects allowed him to observe a candidate's project management skills and collaboration style. Owning a project involves tasks such as setting a design direction, managing incoming code contributions and patches, and interacting with potential collaborators. The employer described being able to infer these soft skills from projects that a person owned, stating that

> "*[Projects he owned] would give me a better sense of his long-term design skills and ability to manage a community*" (E4).

JOB SEEKER PERSPECTIVE

Our second research question was how job seekers manage their presence on GitHub. In order to address this question, we also conducted interviews with six job seekers on GitHub (referred to here as J1-J6) from four different U.S.-based universities. These participants reported using GitHub to supplement their application materials as a job seeker in our recruitment survey. Of these, two were undergraduate students in their final year, one was a PhD student, and the other three recently graduated and had been working at their current position for one year or less. They had between 4 and 28 public repositories visible on their profiles (mean= 17.3) and an average of 19 followers.

All of the interviewees had originally joined the site to host projects they were currently working on and archive past work. The projects they shared included school and class projects, projects for hackathons, samples of code written for job interviews, side projects, and open source projects, both recent and older.

They varied in the ways they shared their work on GitHub with employers. Four of them had provided a link to their GitHub accounts on their resume and stated that this had been consulted during the hiring process. One person never provided this information to the employer and instead assumed the employer had found his profile through a Google search. The final interviewee did not actively promote his GitHub account in the hiring process but stated that he would provide a link if asked for it.

In the interviews, they described the role that their GitHub account had played in recent employment searches. We asked them to describe the impressions they thought their profiles conveyed to potential employers. Finally, we talked about how they managed their profile for an actual (or imagined) audience of potential employers.

Impressions given from profile

We asked interviewees what impressions they thought their GitHub profiles conveyed about them to a potential employer. Their responses highlighted two key qualities they felt employers could see from their activity on the sight: passion for software development as an activity and field and technical expertise.

Activity signaling passion for the field

Interviewees mentioned that their visible level of activity in the site was a positive signal of passion for software development (J1, J2, J6). One person realized that it might be important from the employer's perspective to see evidence of extracurricular coding activity. Referring to some of the side projects, he mentioned,

> *"The fact that in my free time I went and coded something...I think that counts a lot"* (J2).

Our interviewees also indicated their activity in terms of following also signaled an interest in the domain. The fact that they followed a lot of projects conveyed that they were generally interested in keeping up-to-date on the latest projects and technology (J2, J3). One interviewee followed several hundred coders and projects. He thought this would show employers his interest in coding and open source even though he himself had very few projects. Another explained,

> *"The impression I would like to give off is: This guy is current with what's going on in the open source world"* (J2).

Portfolio of work signaling technical expertise

Developers were also keenly aware that the portfolio of projects on their profiles conveyed their areas of expertise to employers. One person's profile (J5) contained a lot of projects in "web-heavy" languages like Python and JavaScript. He thought revealed that his skill set focused on web development. Several interviewees noted the languages they used in their projects would signal proficiency in those languages (J4, J5, J6).

Interviewees were also aware that details of their code would influence perceived skill level. They noted that good style such as descriptive commit messages, comments, and code indentation would convey competence. Two interviewees were aware that their code was not particularly readable or well-organized, partly because the projects were originally just intended for personal use and trying new things. One person had many old projects on his site and his style had improved since. He explained,

> *"I have a lot of things in my GitHub account that I wouldn't feel comfortable putting on a resume because I didn't know how to code at the time...I'm definitely a better coder than some of the projects imply"* (J5).

Impression management

Attitudes towards profile manipulation

Although the job seekers in our sample were acutely aware their profiles gave off certain impressions about them, few reported having engaged in efforts (such as changing or editing any information visible on the profile) to control this impression. We learned in our interviews that this was partly because there were few ways of doing so and doing so was too costly and effortful. As one interviewee explained:

> *"A major component of your GitHub profile are your projects, and it's not really easy to refactor your code quickly"* (J1).

Job seekers also noted that even old or incomplete material could still be useful in conveying qualities about its creator. One interviewee intentionally left incomplete or unfinished projects on the site because they could signal thought processes such as *"how you are approaching and organizing something"* (J4).

Signal Accuracy: Cleaning up the profile

The developers we interviewed realized there might be some need to edit information on their profile, either currently or in the future, to more accurately represent their work. This profile improvement consisted of either commenting code or removing old projects. For example, one developer expressed a desire to concentrate more on "cleaning up" his profile. In lieu of having the time to improve the accuracy of the signals on the site, he provided employers with a description of the current state of projects in the repository descriptions:

> *"I try to say statuses of projects sometimes: I have a couple repositories where it says something like 'this is a super early proof of concept thing'...I make a slight effort to sort of downplay the things I'm not very proud of"* (J5).

He mentioned that in the future, he would consider stripping out everything that he was not proud of, including old and incomplete projects, in order to provide a more accurate picture of his current abilities.

Overall, we found that participants did not seem to engage in much "gaming" of the system for a variety of motives. On one hand, they often felt that they were happy with the signals given off by their profiles regarding their active involvement and participation in projects. On the other hand, they did not try to fake information because it was effortful (i.e. difficult to give a false impression about actual code they wrote.) They could influence information given off by projects by downplaying them in the repository descriptions or by adding proper comments into the code. Keeping the profile as-is, with imperfections or old information, was seen as useful, both to other developers (who might be able to learn something by viewing old projects) and to employers.

DISCUSSION

Our interviews revealed that employers used cues on GitHub as signals of underlying characteristics of potential hires. These signals varied in their reliability as a function of manipulation cost in the GitHub environment. In addition, employers' use of these signals was directly related to evaluation cost. Job seekers on the other hand, were aware that employers were using their behavior as signals of underlying properties. In addition, attempts to manipulate these signals were culturally or practically discouraged. We consider what made signals reliable and how evaluation cost influenced employer behavior.

Evaluation of signals and inferences

Reliable signals

Employers expressed a belief that some cues were not easily manipulated and thus they were reliable indicators of a potential hire's competence, values and collaboration styles. Our analysis revealed that two key properties of activity traces supported signal reliability. These were the fact that traces were: (1) archived over time - signals generated by direction of time and effort expended (commitment to open source values, passion for programming), or (2) networked - signals generated by third party affiliation.

Activity traces on GitHub are archived and persistent, meaning employers could view a history of effort on projects over time. Employers could use information about how much effort was put into different projects to draw conclusions about a person's values and motives. This signal also appeared to be an accurate indicator of motivation. For example, job seekers who committed to open source projects truly wanted to give back to the community. This kind of historical signal would be extremely costly to fake, making it a more reliable indicator of investment.

The network context of activity traces in GitHub meant that affiliation could also act as a signal. The acceptance of offerings to joint projects in the form of pull requests or code commits was archived and accessible. The fact that work had been accepted to well-known projects was not easy to fake. Connection to these high status projects increased employer perceptions of the candidate's competence or quality. These signals were deemed more trustworthy because they were generated by a third party. This is akin to the notion of warranting introduced by Walther et al. [27]. This work suggests that when forming an impression, information provided by third parties (for example, the fact that someone else had accepted the candidate's code into their work) and connection to a social network is more trustworthy than self reports. The offering and acceptance of work contributions provided a kind of third party verification of work quality.

Unreliable signals

Activity traces were deemed unreliable signals of a potential hire's characteristics if they were (1) subject to manipulation or (2) likely to be missing information because of the way they were generated. Both of these assessments required employers to have intimate familiarity with the GitHub environment and the social context surrounding project activity.

Project popularity was an example of an unreliable signal of a potential hire's ability. Although popularity was easy to assess through aggregate statistics on the number of people watching a project, it was seen as subject to manipulation and thus not closely tied to ability (the underlying characteristic employers wanted to assess). Project popularity could be artificially inflated by an applicant, and was dependent on factors distinct from coding abilities such as how well an individual marketed his or her project or what type of project it was.

Signals were also deemed unreliable if they were known to be missing information. For example, employers acknowledged that projects on an individual's profile were not always representative of their full body of work. This meant they were only partial signals of properties like technical skills and coding abilities, since private projects were not visible on GitHub. If the majority of an individual's coding activity happened behind a firewall at work (meaning they could not share it), then their GitHub account would not completely reflect their true range of abilities.

Employers were aware that certain information about a potential hire was not visible on the profile and the possible reasons it might not be visible. Despite this knowledge of the broader context or perhaps because of it, employers in our sample valued an active presence on GitHub. There was a sense from the employers we sampled that all things being equal, a candidate with a GitHub profile would still be preferred because of the added signals. One person said,

> "*I don't think you can use it as the sole way to judge someone because a lot of it's going to depend on how much time the developer is donating to maintaining their GitHub, so if this is someone who has a wife and kids and not much time to be programming out of the workplace, that doesn't necessarily mean they are not as good of a developer. But if something is up there, it's definitely a huge plus and probably one of the first things we look for – are they sharing their source code?*" (E7).

Evaluation cost

Evaluation cost seemed to influence employer's use of activity traces in GitHub. The signals summarized in Table 1 are all observable on a user's profile on the site. It is easy to quickly verify active open source involvement just by seeing that a person is a member of GitHub and has evidence of recent activity in their profile's activity feed. It is also easy to tell whether a project was original or forked, via the presence or absence of an icon.

Determining contributions to a high-status project required more effortful investigation if these commits were not in the top recent activities shown, while determining if something is a "side project," as one person mentioned, may require following up with a user to learn more about it (depending on how the repository is described in its textual summary.)

While one possible advantage of GitHub signals is the ability to view how people work with others, interviewees did not mention looking at evidence of past interactions with others to determine attitude and personality. Work on hiring has shown employers are usually interested in candidates' likeability as a team member. In other contexts such as Wikipedia, traces of civil online interactions are used as a signal of likeability and collegiality [6]. However, in GitHub, it is non-trivial to view an individual's interactions. This information requires more effort to seek out and is time consuming to review.

Site design strongly influences the cost to access information about a person. This cost may have repercussions on what information feeds into the hiring decision. The employers we interviewed favored cues that took less effort to access and verify, such as relative effort across projects or presence of forked versus owned repositories. They used these cues as a heuristic to identify people with extra passion in addition to skills, who were then set apart from general applicants or followed up with in person.

Impression management

Our second research question focused on impression management by job seekers. Participants acknowledged that they could not easily give a false impression about the actual code they wrote, but they could try to influence information given off by their projects through downplaying them in the repository descriptions or adding more proper comments into the code. Given that GitHub has relatively recently gained popularity as an employment tool, it is possible that future site members will be more conscious about managing their impressions for future employers.

Design implications

Our results have implications for the design of open transparent work environments. The effort required to access activity traces connected to a person may change what is considered during the hiring process. Our results suggest it is important to strike a balance between providing enough information to be useful while avoiding overload. This could be useful in other online peer production settings such as Wikipedia: Visualizations of an editor's work history across pages could help editors understand what kinds of tasks they would be good at performing. This kind of history could also give context to debates and arguments.

Our work also raises interesting questions about designing activity traces for multiple audiences. GitHub is a site that was not originally designed as a hiring tool. Its design also needs to support collaborative software development. Activity traces are used by developers to coordinate their work and transfer knowledge across projects. However, employers increasingly use these traces to evaluate new hires. There is a tension between using the site as a tool to carry out work and using it to manage the impression one gives to external observers.

The degree of overlap between signals that are important to manage for gaining acceptance within a given community and signals that are important to manage for external viewers such as employers or evaluators is another area that future work can tease apart and provide insight for transparent system design. As Begel et al [1] suggest, a social medium that reveals a user's knowledge, expertise, activities, or availability may be useful for finding knowledgeable others when consumed by the user's peers, but may feel like "corporate spyware" when consumed by his manager. Future systems could provide different views or privacy settings for different categories of users, while still providing the benefit of transparency of actions and reliable assessment cues.

Implications for other domains

The importance of passion for coding and active involvement in the community may be uniquely emphasized in GitHub due to the nature of the open source development community, in which people may be more motivated by self-development and reputation gaining compared to contributors to online content sites such as Wikipedia. In addition, contributing software to open-source projects also requires a certain level of expertise to pass the review process, compared to Wikipedia [19].

However, some of the issues raised here may also apply to issues pertaining to the role of publicly visible behavior in other realms outside of GitHub. For example, there are other instances in which people in technical fields may wish to promote their skill or knowledge in publicly viewable online arenas.

While there has been much concern about employers accessing individuals' personal SNS profiles, there are other areas in which employers may wish to access public work-related information, and sometimes job-seekers may wish for employers to see this information. For example, there has been discussion in the developer community about when/if one should display their StackOverflow score on their resume, including varied reactions from employers about the meaning of this score (e.g. [21]). Users of the Quora question-answering site have also mentioned that they will strategically answer questions in order to attract the attention of influential people and as a form of networking [20].

As people interact and collaborate online on sites geared towards "serious leisure," they may generate additional traces as they go about their work. It is possible to imagine a future of work in which evidence of one's abilities and what "type of person" they are is not solely gathered from their activity within a structured organization or educational program but from the aggregation of their behavior on the web. For example, are the details of a person's online Wikipedia editing activity considered to be useful by employers looking to hire journalists or writers, and do Wikipedia contributors looking for jobs actively promote the work they have done on the site? These questions suggest interesting research directions to explore.

Limitations and future work

Our sample of interviewees was limited to a small subset of people who volunteered to discuss the topic of GitHub and hiring. Another question that was not deeply addressed in the current research was ways in which impression formation occurs with other cues and information besides a GitHub profile. It would also be valuable to follow up on employers' perceptions of new hires after they have spent some time in their job role to understand how initial impressions correlate with actual performance, or how these change over time.

Future work can also include developers and employers who are not involved in the GitHub community or who participate in other sites such as BitBucket or Sourceforge to understand if they present or market themselves differently in these environments, as well as to understand why they choose not to use GitHub.

Furthermore, the role of impression formation and management in other sorts of online production communities should be examined, to uncover similarities and differences across domains outside of open source software development.

CONCLUSION

In this work we examined how activity traces on GitHub are used as signals by potential employers. Past work on impression management online has suggested people actively manipulate various observable elements of their online presence to portray an idealized self. Interestingly, we saw very little evidence of such behavior in GitHub. This may be because the effort required to manipulate activity traces that actually matter to employers (such as active participation and code style) is too great.

At the same time, employers preferred easily verifiable signals of potential hire's skills or abilities. This desire to minimize assessment effort meant they did not necessarily take advantage of the full range of transparency that GitHub can provide. They used candidates' presence and high level cues of activity on the site to infer how well the person would fit within their organization. Employers favored developers who signaled similar passion and willingness to work on coding projects both during and outside of work.

The kind of transparency pioneered by GitHub may have implications for the future of hiring. Employers may begin to expect applicants to provide a rich history of detailed work activity traces. Job seekers may in turn increasingly gravitate towards companies that will allow them to accrue a publicly-available (or shareable) portfolio of work. Businesses may find employees demand some open-source work sharing, and see policies of openness as a benefit. We are already seeing this kind of trend in fields like graphic design, as individuals often work for themselves to maintain the ability to visibly promote their work.

The implications of our results extend beyond software development as work becomes increasingly digital. Providing accessible, reliable traces of an individual's work history may support more accurate impressions of unknown contributors. These impressions will shape decisions about recruiting, hiring and promotion in tradition and new forms of organizations like Wikipedia or crowdsourcing. Such impressions are also likely to influence the collaborative dynamics of work. It is important for system designers and policy makers to consider what actions and activities can and should be recorded and made visible. Our results should help decision makers develop useful and efficient ways of providing various groups with the information they need while protecting individuals' rights.

ACKNOWLEDGMENTS

This work was supported by NSF grants IIS-1111750, SMA-1064209, OCI-0943168, grants to Dabbish from the Center for the Future of Work, Heinz College, Carnegie Mellon University, and an NSF Graduate Research Fellowship.

REFERENCES

1.Begel, A., DeLine, R., & Zimmermann, T. Social media for software engineering. *Proceedings of the FSE/SDP workshop on Future of software engineering research*, (2010), 33–38.

2.Bohnert, D., & Ross, W. H. The influence of social networking web sites on the evaluation of job candidates. *Cyberpsychology, Behavior, and Social Networking*, *13*(3), (2010), 341–347.

3.http://code.dblock.org/github-is-your-new-resume (Retrieved Aug 25, 2012).

4.Connelly, B.L., Certo, S.T., Ireland, R.D., and Reutzel, C.R. Signaling theory: A review and assessment. *Journal of Management 37*, 1 (2011), 39–67.

5.Dabbish, L., Stuart, H.C.S., Tsay, J., & Herbsleb, J. Social coding in GitHub: Transparency and collaboration in an open software repository. In *Proc. CSCW,* (2012), 1277-1286.

6.Derthick, K., Tsao, P., Kriplean, T., Borning, A.,Zachry, M., & McDonald, D. W. Collaborative sensemaking during admin permission granting in Wikipedia. In *Online Communities and Social Computing* (Vol. 6778), (2011), 100-109.

7.DiMicco, J., & Millen, D. Identity management: multiple presentations of self in facebook. *Proc. GROUP*, (2007), 383–386.

8.Donath, J. S. Identity and deception in the virtual community. *Communities in cyberspace*, (1996), 29–59.

9.Donath, J. Signals in social supernets. *Journal of Computer-Mediated Communication*, *13*(1), (2007), 231–251.

10.Ellison, N., Heino, R., & Gibbs, J. Managing Impressions Online: Self-Presentation Processes in the Online Dating Environment. *Journal of Computer-Mediated Communication*, *11*(2), (2006), 415–441.

11.Ellison, N. B., Hancock, J. T., & Toma, C. L. Profile as promise: A framework for conceptualizing veracity in online dating self-presentations. *New Media &Society*, *14*(1), (2012), 45–62.

12.Goffman, E. The presentation of self in everyday life. New York: Anchor Books, 1959.

13.Grasz, J. "One-in-Five Employers Use Social Networking Sites to Research Job Candidates, CareerBuilder.com survey finds."http://www.careerbuilder.com/share/aboutus/pressreleasesdetail.aspx?id=pr459&sd=9%2F10%2F2008&ed=12%2F31%2F2008 (Retrieved Feb 19, 2012)

14.Kristof-Brown, A., Barrick, M.R., and Franke, M. Applicant impression management: Dispositional influences and consequences for recruiter perceptions of fit and similarity. *Journal of Management 28*, 1, (2002), 27–46.

15.Lampe, C., Ellison, N., & Steinfield, C. A familiar face (book): profile elements as signals in an online social network. *Proc. CHI*, (2007), 435–444.

16.Lerner, J., Tirole, J., Some simple economics of open source. *Journal of Industrial Economics* 50 (2), (2002), 197–234.

17.Long, J. Open Source Software Development Experiences on the Students' Resumes: Do They Count? Insights from the Employers' Perspectives. *Journal of Information Technology Education*, 8, (2009), 229–242.

18.Mavlanova, T., Benbunan-Fich, R., and Koufaris, M. Signaling theory and information asymmetry in online commerce. *Information & Management*, (2012), 240-247.

19.Oreg, S. and Nov, O. Exploring motivations for contributing to open source initiatives: The roles of contribution context and personal values. *Computers in Human Behavior 24*, 5 (2008), 2055–2073.

20.Paul, S.A., Hong, L., and Chi, E.H. Who is Authoritative? Understanding Reputation Mechanisms in Quora. *Proc. Collective Intelligence,* (2012), *arXiv:1204.3724v1*.

21.http://programmers.stackexchange.com/questions/12070/would-you-put-your-stackoverflow-profile-link-on-your-cv-resume (Retrieved Aug 25, 2012).

22.Spence, M. Job market signaling. *The quarterly journal of Economics*, *87*(3), (1973), 355–374.

23.Spinellis, D. Open source and professional advancement. *Software, IEEE*, 23(5), (2006), 70–71.

24.Stewart, K.J. and Gosain, S. The Impact of Ideology on Effectiveness in Open Source Software Development Teams. *MIS Quarterly 30*(2), (2006), 291-314.

25.Tong, S.T., Van Der Heide, B., Langwell, L., and Walther, J.B. Too much of a good thing? The relationship between number of friends and interpersonal impressions on Facebook. *Journal of Computer-Mediated Communication 13*, 3 (2008), 531–549.

26.Trammell, K., & Keshelashvili, A. Examining the new influencers: A self-presentation study of A-list blogs. *Journalism and Mass Communication Quarterly*, 82(4), (2005), 968-982.

27.Walther, J.B., Van Der Heide, B., Hamel, L.M., and Shulman, H.C. Self-Generated Versus Other-Generated Statements and Impressions in Computer-Mediated Communication A Test of Warranting Theory Using Facebook. *Communication Research 36*(2), (2009), 229–253.

28.Weiss, B. and Feldman, R.S. Looking good and lying to do it: Deception as an impression management strategy in job interviews. *Journal of Applied Social Psychology 36*, 4 (2006), 1070–1086.

KinectArms: A Toolkit for Capturing and Displaying Arm Embodiments in Distributed Tabletop Groupware

Aaron Genest[1], Carl Gutwin[1], Anthony Tang[2], Michael Kalyn[1], and Zenja Ivkovic[1]
[1]Department of Computer Science
University of Saskatchewan
110 Science Place, Saskatoon, Canada
[2]Department of Computer Science
University of Calgary
2500 University Dr. NW, Calgary, Canada
[aaron.genest, carl.gutwin, michael.kalyn, zenja.ivkovic]@usask.ca, tonyt@ucalgary.ca

ABSTRACT
Gestures are a ubiquitous part of human communication over tables, but when tables are distributed, gestures become difficult to capture and represent. There are several problems: extracting arm images from video, representing the height of the gesture, and making the arm embodiment visible and understandable at the remote table. Current solutions to these problems are often expensive, complex to use, and difficult to set up. We have developed a new toolkit – KinectArms – that quickly and easily captures and displays arm embodiments. KinectArms uses a depth camera to segment the video and determine gesture height, and provides several visual effects for representing arms, showing gesture height, and enhancing visibility. KinectArms lets designers add rich arm embodiments to their systems without undue cost or development effort, greatly improving the expressiveness and usability of distributed tabletop groupware.

Author Keywords
Distributed tabletops, gestures, embodiments, toolkits

ACM Classification Keywords
H.5.3 Group and Organization Interfaces: CSCW.

INTRODUCTION
Gestural communication is a ubiquitous and important part of co-located collaboration at real-world tables. People gesture over tables in many different ways, including pointing at objects, indicating paths and areas, emphasizing elements of the conversation, and illustrating actions [2,6]. At distributed tables, gestural communication is equally important, but gestures become much more difficult to reproduce compared to face-to-face environments. There are three main problems.

First, the complexity and subtlety of many over-the-table gestures requires that systems use video-based embodiments of hands and arms (e.g., [12,18,23]). However, extracting images of people's arms from the table background can be computationally expensive, prone to error (particularly if color is used for separation), and dependent on good lighting conditions [28].

Second, information about the height of the gesture can be a critical aspect of the communication [10], but height information is usually lost in distributed settings. Gesture height is difficult to capture (traditionally requiring expensive tracking technologies), and is difficult to convey through arm embodiments that are displayed as 2D images on the remote table surface.

Third, the reduced physical presence of remote arm embodiments, coupled with low frame rates and network jitter, make remote gestures difficult to see and interpret. Prior work has suggested visual traces as a way to increase the salience of a remote gesture [9,24], but traces are difficult to gather when arms move above the table.

The result of these three problems is that gestural communication in distributed tabletop groupware is much less expressive than at co-located tables. To address these problems, we have developed a new toolkit – called KinectArms – for capturing gestures over tables and displaying arm embodiments at remote sites (Figure 1).

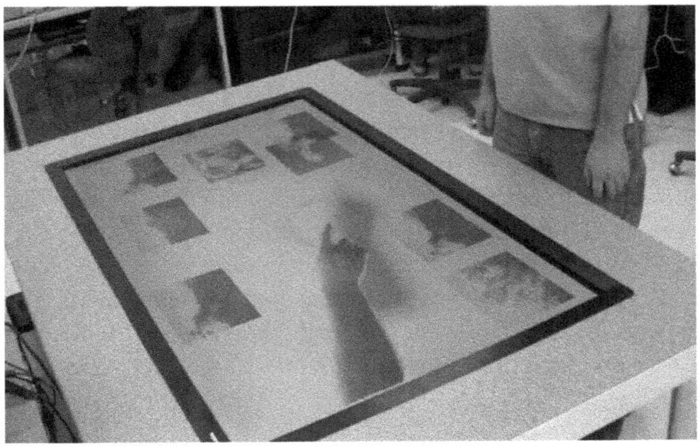

Figure 1: KinectArms used in a photo-sharing application, showing shadow and height indictor (circle).

KinectArms solves all three of the issues mentioned above. First, it uses a depth camera to quickly and efficiently extract arm images from the video stream – the system runs easily at 30 frames per second. Second, KinectArms uses the depth camera to identify fine-grained height information about the gesture, and can attach that information to extracted features of the images such as hands and fingers. Third, KinectArms provides several visualization techniques to show gesture height, to enhance the visibility of embodiments, and to highlight arm movements (e.g., abstract height indicators, color and transparency modifications, and motion lines and traces). The toolkit also provides several other capabilities, including automatic calibration to the table surface, tracking of arms in the scene, and wrappers to allow development in several programming languages.

In this paper we describe the design, implementation, and use of KinectArms. Our work makes three contributions.

- KinectArms is the first toolkit to provide a simple solution to all the aspects of remote arm embodiments, including capture and representation of gesture height. It goes well beyond standard Kinect libraries, which are not set up to recognize arms over table surfaces.
- We demonstrate that KinectArms can reproduce a wide variety of previous designs (e.g., DOVE, VideoArms, and C-Slate) and show that the platform can be used to produce new representations as well, providing an opportunity to compare different designs.
- We evaluate the toolkit in terms of performance, developer effort, expressiveness, and simplicity, and show that KinectArms provides a powerful yet easy-to-use solution to the problem of remote gestures.

With KinectArms, designers can easily add support for remote gesture to tabletops, which can dramatically improve the usability and communicative capabilities of distributed tabletop groupware.

RELATED WORK

Researchers have looked at several aspects of gestures, including representation of gestures through embodiments, techniques for enhancing remote embodiments, and capturing and representing gesture height.

Representing Gestures Through Embodiments

Gestures are an important part of collocated settings and equally valuable when people collaborate in distributed settings [2]. The design of user embodiments for showing remote gestures has long been considered in CSCW (e.g., [2,4,8]). Two approaches to embodiment design have emerged: abstract representations that visualize particular aspects of user information, and realistic representations based on video that show more details of the user.

Realistic Representations

Realistic embodiments represent collaborators with full or partial-body video, providing a rich representation of people's actions and postures. Early techniques used analog video (e.g., VideoDraw, VideoWhiteBoard, or ClearBoard, [11,25,26]); more recent designs typically use digital video, such as DOVE [18], VideoArms [23], or C-Slate [12]. Realistic embodiments provide a large amount of information about gestures, and convey considerable subtlety, but are often complex and expensive [28]. In addition, video embodiments have difficulty conveying some aspects of remote action, such as gesture height.

Abstract Representations

Abstract visualizations of particular elements of user activity can provide valuable information for collaboration. Telepointers are a well-known example that represents the pointing locations of collaborators with shapes and colors [8]; in addition, researchers have shown that abstract embodiments can be augmented with several different types of user information [22]. The abstract approach to embodiment design can convey information that is not easily available through a realistic embodiment (e.g., height can be represented directly with a specific visualization).

Combinations of Realistic and Abstract Representations

A few researchers have examined combinations of real and abstract embodiments (an approach we follow with KinectArms). Kirk *et al.* used video combined with a stylus to permit sketching [14], and Tang *et al.* added contact traces to VideoArms, an augmentation that participants described as useful [24]. A more quantitative approach to evaluating abstract components added to realistic embodiments was adopted by Yamashita *et al.* [28] who replayed entire gestures using a form of motion blur to reduce the time needed for conversational grounding.

Enhancing Gesture Visibility in Distributed Settings

In distributed collaboration, remote embodiments are much less visually obvious than people's bodies in co-located settings, and may be affected by problems such as low frame rates or network jitter; as a result, it is easy to miss actions and motions [7]. Motion traces can help to solve these problems by smoothing motion and providing a longer-lasting representation of a gesture (e.g., [8,24,29]). Most trace techniques, however, have only considered mouse movements rather than hand gestures (with Tang et al's work the notable exception [24]), and only show traces when in contact with the surface. Combining historical traces with height visualizations has been discussed [5], but only for telepointer-style embodiments.

Capturing and Representing Gesture Height

The height of deictic gestures (which indicate things in a shared environment) is valuable in communication [6]. Height, however, is not well supported in embodiment design: although some embodiments and interaction techniques incorporate differences between table touches and hover states (e.g., [24,27]), most do not, and none express a full range of height above the surface.

Part of this problem is that height is difficult to capture. There has been considerable research on using height as an input variable and capturing that height with cameras (often depth cameras). Most often, height has been used to identify touch interactions on variably distant surfaces, such as with OmniTouch [9], which used a depth camera similar to the Microsoft Kinect. Detecting touch on fixed-distance (non-touch-sensitive) surfaces has been shown to be possible using the Kinect camera (e.g., [28]). Marquardt *et al.* are one of the few to suggest that interactions should span the spaces between touch, hover, and above the surface [17]. More elaborate models of a workspace have been created with moving cameras, such as in KinectFusion [13]. For most surface-based computing, however, a fixed camera and fixed surface is a more common scenario.

Although height detection in the layer above (or in front of) a surface has been used in a variety of gesture recognition and input techniques (e.g., [1] and [12]), there are few embodiments that represent height in this space. Two exceptions are Fraser *et al.* [4], who showed that representing approaches to a surface can improve distributed interactions, and Genest and Gutwin [5], who showed that abstract representations of height can improve gesture interpretation in distributed settings. Neither solution, however, captured detailed information about the hand and arm: Fraser captured the position of the tip of a stylus and Genest used a single 3D location, tracked with a magnetic-field sensor on the user's pointing finger.

REQUIREMENTS FOR AN ARM-EMBODIMENT TOOLKIT

A new toolkit for supporting the visualization of gestures in distributed systems would be valuable for researchers and developers. With the advent of cheap depth sensors, it has become important to understand how all three dimensions of gesture can be represented in a variety of distributed settings. This cannot be easily done with the state of the art in software tools for capturing and representing gestures. A toolkit for arm embodiments has four main requirements:

1. Address the three problems described above – of easily separating arm images, capturing and displaying height information, and enhancing embodiment visibility;
2. Permit the rapid reproduction of existing embodiment techniques to allow experimentation and comparison;
3. Support easy creation of new embodiment types with both realistic and abstract representation techniques;
4. Provide simple setup and calibration.

THE KINECTARMS TOOLKIT

KinectArms is a toolkit that simplifies the capture of remote tabletop gestures and the display of those gestures through arm embodiments. KinectArms has two parts: a capture module that recognizes hands and arms above the surface, performs video separation, and identifies the height of each pixel of the separated image; and a display module that provides built-in effects to show height, to improve visibility, and to provide movement traces. Additional effects can be easily developed and added to the toolkit.

Overview and Setup

KinectTable uses an Xbox or PC Kinect sensor, fixed above the table (1.8m is optimal for the Xbox version) and pointed down. The camera need not be perfectly perpendicular to the display surface; the automatic table detection (see below) can handle small angular variation. The Kinect has a field of view of 57° horizontally and 43° vertically, so at 1.8 meters, the camera can accommodate a 1.42m by 1.95m table surface. This area can be increased for larger tables (at the cost of resolution) by raising the Kinect.

Although 2D resolution will increase as the Kinect approaches the surface, the depth image has an optimal resolution at 1.8m, with an accuracy of approximately 2mm at that distance [28]. This level of accuracy means that user touches on the table surface can be approximately determined (i.e., without requiring a touch-sensitive surface); however, our tests described below used a PQLabs touch overlay on a 60-inch LCD television.

After the Kinect is suspended above the table surface, the KinectArms software can be started (usually by a client application). On startup, KinectArms automatically detects the table surface (see details below). Table detection takes less than a second, and no further calibration is required – KinectArms is then ready to capture and process arm images, and add visual effects to these images.

The general algorithm for using KinectArms in an arbitrary tabletop application is as follows:

1. Create an instance of the KinectArms client
2. Set up initial visual effects
3. While the application is running:
   - 3.1 Get image data from the KinectArms client
   - 3.2 Apply visual effects to the current frame
   - 3.3 Draw the current frame to the table

KINECTTABLE: THE CAPTURE MODULE

The capture module of KinectArms uses a Microsoft Kinect as its primary sensor. The Kinect incorporates a full-colour camera and a depth camera (both 640x480), which can be aligned to produce a depth-mapped image. From this image, we accomplish both separation of arms and hands from the table background, and recognition of the structure of the arms in the scene. We note that this recognition is not already provided by the Kinect – although the SDK provides sophisticated body recognition, it is not designed to capture isolated arms and hands over a table surface (it needs to see the entire body for accurate recognition).

The main features provided by the KinectTable module are:

1. Fast setup and calibration, with automatic detection of the table surface.
2. An API for accessing information about arms and table:
   a. Image masks for the table and each of the arms
   b. Fingertip, palm, and arm locations in three dimensions
   c. Basic user tracking
   d. Geometric properties for each of the arms.

The KinectTable API

The C++ version of the KinectTable API provides access to image data, table information, and arm information.

Image Data

The raw color and depth images from the Kinect are available in a custom structure; the application programmer can use the raw information, or can obtain a processed image representation from the KinectViz module.

```
KinectArmsClient *client = KinectArmsGetClient();
```

```
KinectData data;
client->GetData(data);
DepthImage& depthImage = data.depthImage;
```

Table Information

KinectTable provides information about the table surface (from the automatic recognition step, as described below) including the height of the table, the table corners, and a bitmap mask where white pixels indicate the table.

```
BinaryImage& maskImage = data.tableMaskImage;
```

Arm and Finger Information

Information for each arm is stored in a C++ struct; these are provided in an array representing all arms above the table (stored in the order that they enter the space). Each struct contains the following arm information:

1. Geometric values:
   a. Mean height of the arm (using all pixels);
   b. Total number of pixels corresponding to the arm;
   c. The pixel at the geometric center of the arm;
2. An array of points defining the arm boundary;
3. A bitmap mask corresponding to the arm;
4. An array of points corresponding to fingertips;
5. An array of points for between-finger locations;
6. A point representing the center of the hand;
7. A point representing the base of the arm (i.e., the intersection of the arm with the edge of the table);
8. A unique ID, retained between frames.

The height of any point in the arm image can be obtained from the `getHeight(Point p)` function. For example, the following code retrieves the depth of an arm's first finger:

```
client->GetData(data);
Arm& arm1 = data.arms[0];
int fingerHeight = client->getHeight(arm1.fingers[0]);
```

KinectTable System Architecture

KinectTable is comprised of four components: a camera component, a table detector, an arm and hand detector, and an arm tracker (Figure 2). KinectTable makes use of the Kinect SDK or the OpenNI library (openni.org) to obtain the Kinect images, and the OpenCV library for image processing (opencv.willowgarage.com).

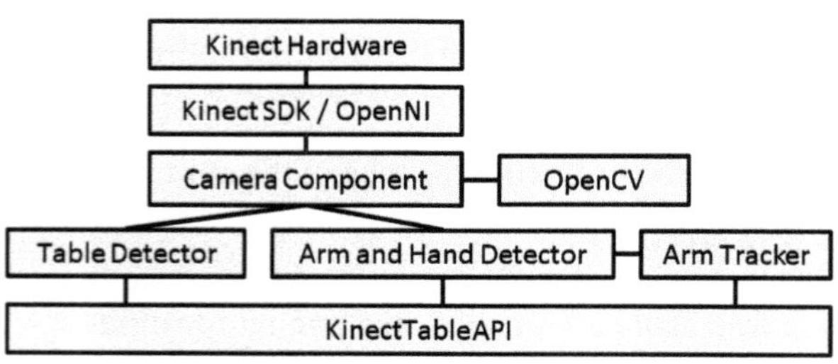

Figure 2: KinectTable system architecture.

Camera Component

The camera component fetches image data through the Kinect SDK or OpenNI sets the SDK to align the colour and depth images, and performs low-level processing to prepare the data for table, arm, and hand detection. This processing involves converting the Kinect images to our own custom C++ structure, and passing a 5x5 median filter over the image to fill in error pixels (some pixels fail to update every frame).

Table Detection

The height and extents of the table are critical for arm identification, and most systems use an interactive calibration procedure to determine these values [5,9,23]. KinectArms simplifies this step with an automatic table detector. Through the `RecalculateTableCorners()` function, KinectTable can be asked to identify the largest visible and roughly planar surface in the image as the table. After identification, any pixels in the depth map that are farther than the table, or outside its boundaries, are ignored.

Table detection is performed with the following steps:

1. A Laplacian filter and thresholding function are passed over the depth image to identify sharp changes in depth;
2. Depth edges are dilated to ensure continuity;
3. The center region enclosed by the continuous edge is filled – this region represents the table;
4. Table corners are found using k-curvature (as in [20]) on the region boundary (k-value of 30, threshold of 70°);
5. Table height is set as the lowest value of the table pixels.

Table identification is robust for slanted and curved tables, but any large non-linear changes in depth may cause incorrect table identification.

Arm and Finger Detection

Arms and fingers are identified using image processing techniques similar to those used for table detection (Fig. 3):

1. Background subtraction is performed by removing pixels in the depth image that are not above the table region. The remaining pixels are arm candidates.
2. A Canny edge detector (max threshold 200, min 150, Sobel filter order 5) finds the edges of the arms. Edges are dilated to make them continuous.
3. Contours of each arm candidate are found using OpenCV's Suzuki85 algorithm.
4. All small contours (< 40 pixels in length) are discarded as noise. The remaining contours are considered arms.
5. Geometric properties of each arm (mean depth, total pixels, center point) are calculated from the contours.
6. The base of each arm is determined by finding the intersection of the arm with the edge of the table.
7. Fingertip locations and the points between the fingers are found using k-curvature (k-value 30, threshold 85°).
8. The center of the hand is calculated using a Euclidean distance transform of the arm's boundary points.

Arm Tracking and User Identification

Arms are given unique ID numbers so that the application can track arms across multiple frames. Tracking takes advantage of the location where the arm intersects the edge of the table (a location that does not change rapidly in tabletop work). KinectTable matches arm bases in the current frame to known arm bases in the previous frame, by comparing distance and time values between the frames. If an arm in a previous frame cannot be matched, we assume it has left the table area. If an arm does not return at the same base position within five seconds, we re-use the ID for the next arm that enters the table area.

.NET Wrapper

Developers can access KinectTable through a .NET wrapper that provides .NET versions of all data structures. The wrapper's API is similar to the C++ API but also provides event mechanisms whereby methods are called automatically when new data is available.

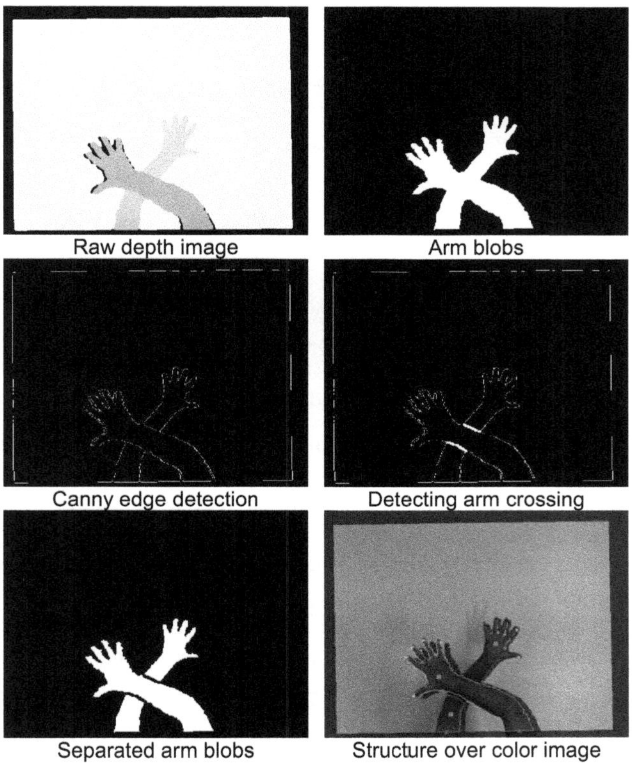

Figure 3: Steps in processing arm images.

KINECTVIZ: THE DISPLAY MODULE

KinectViz provides a set of standard effects that can be added to arm images obtained from KinectTable. The library provides effects to visualize height, increase or decrease arm visibility, improve user identification, and provide motion traces. Using these effects, it is possible to replicate many previous embodiments; KinectViz also allows programmers to design new effects. Programmers can set up effects with single API calls, and effects can be changed dynamically and can be assigned to specific height layers. Effects can be applied to all arms or to specific arms (the examples below show the global versions).

Basic Arm Representations

VideoArms. KinectViz provides full-colour background-subtracted images of hands and arms that can be drawn on top of existing tabletop objects. The basic representation (similar to VideoArms [23]) is built in a few lines of code:

```
client->GetData(data);
viz.updateData(data);
viz.applyEffects();
```

The `applyEffects()` method translates raw KinectTable data into a drawable image, and also alters the image to add any visual effects that have been chosen by the application programmer (no effects are needed for the standard arm).

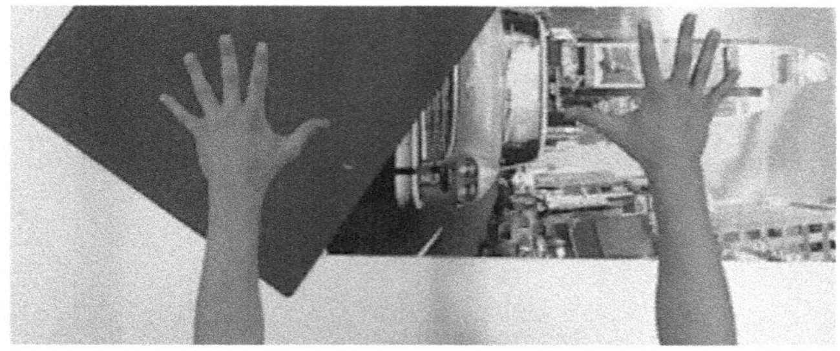

Figure 4: Standard arms drawn over table artifacts.

StructureArms. The extracted structure of the arm (base point, hand center, and finger points) can be used as the basis for an abstract representation of the arm. The main advantage over video-based embodiments is that structure information is much smaller than video, and can therefore be used even in poor network conditions. The structure points could also be used as anchors for artificial textures (e.g., cartoon arms or even images of people's real arms). The points on the structure can be accessed through KinectData (see above); as a demonstration, KinectViz includes a 'stick figure' effect in its API (Figure 5).

```
viz.getEffect(kSkeleton).enabled = true;
```

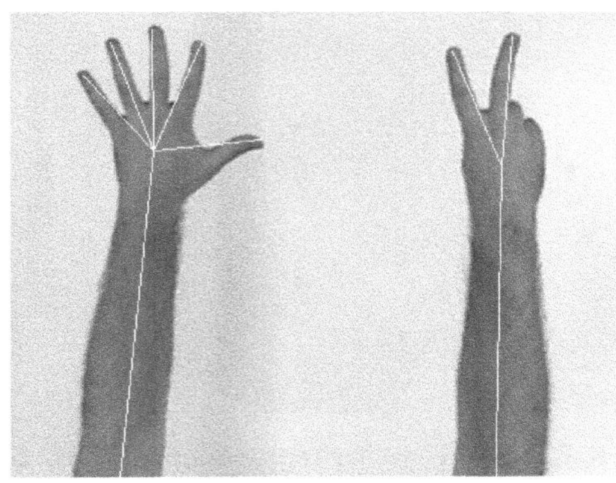

Figure 5. Stick-figure arms using structure points

Visual Effects 1: Height Indicators

Showing the height of a gesture can greatly improve people's ability to interpret the meaning of that gesture [5]. KinectViz provides three kinds of height indicator.

Circles. KinectViz can add abstract visualizations to the realistic embodiment. To show height, we add a circle that changes size and transparency based on the arm's height above the table (see Figure 6). KinectViz uses the lowest fingertip as the centre of the circle, which assumes that people are pointing downwards towards the surface.

Shadows. Arm shadows have been part of analog video representations (e.g., [24]), but are not usually captured in digital embodiments. KinectViz provides a shadow effect in which the shadow is displaced to the side as the arm moves higher above the table (Figure 7).

```
viz.getEffect(kPointerCircle).enabled = true;
```

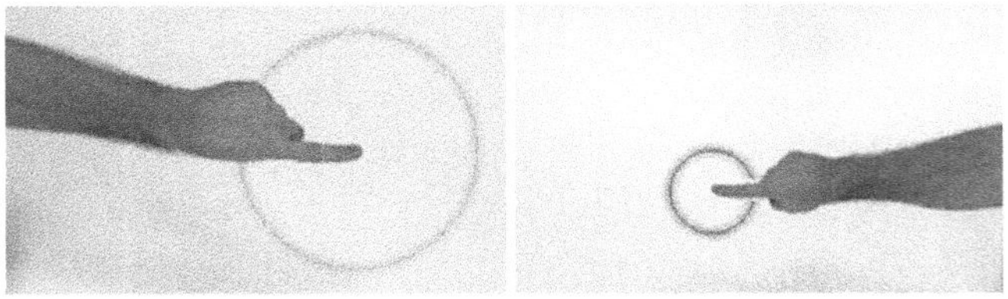

Figure 6: Circles – abstract visualization of gesture height.

```
viz.getEffect(kShadow).enabled = true;
```

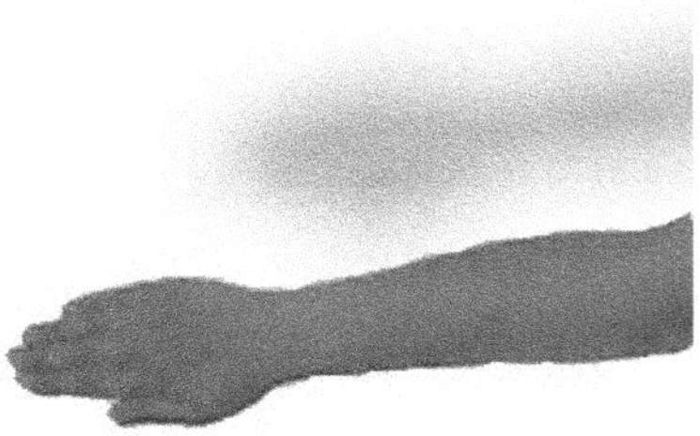

Figure 7: Shadows – simulated representation of height.

Gradients. Richer representations of arm height are also possible with KinectVis. One novel technique shows height as a false-colour gradient (see Figure 8): parts of the arm closer to the table are shown in cool colors (blues and greens); higher parts of the arm are shown in warm colors.

```
viz.getEffect(kRainbow).enabled = true;
```

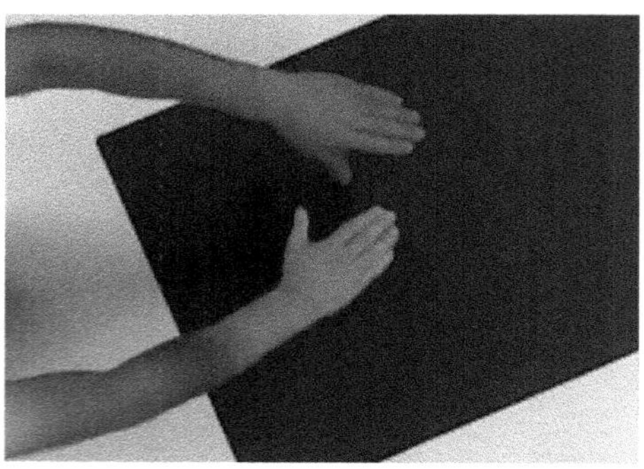

Figure 8: Gradients – richer representation of arm height.

Visual Effects 2: Visibility and Identification Enhancements

Virtual embodiments can suffer from several kinds of visibility problems: they are harder to notice and harder to see than real arms [7,19], they are often difficult to identify, and they can occlude objects on the table. To address these problems, KinectViz provides effects that manipulate the visibility of an embodiment and that assist identification.

Outlines. To increase noticeability, KinectViz includes an effect that draws a colored outline around the arm (Figure 9); the effect can be applied to one or all of the arms.

```
viz.getEffect(kOutline).enabled = true;
```

Transparency. Embodiment visibility can be varied with a transparency level defined by the application programmer, or with a level that varies according to the height from the surface (Figure 10). Transparency can be used in several ways: as a basic way to avoid occlusion, or as a dynamic effect (e.g., to reduce salience of less-active participants).

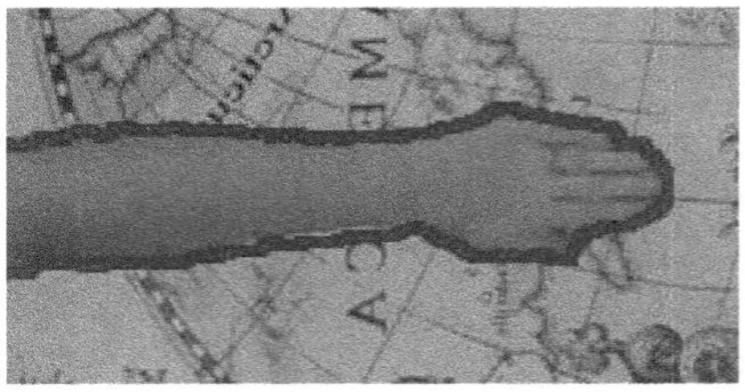

Figure 9: Outlines – visibility on complex backgrounds

```
viz.getEffect(kTransparency).enabled = true;
```

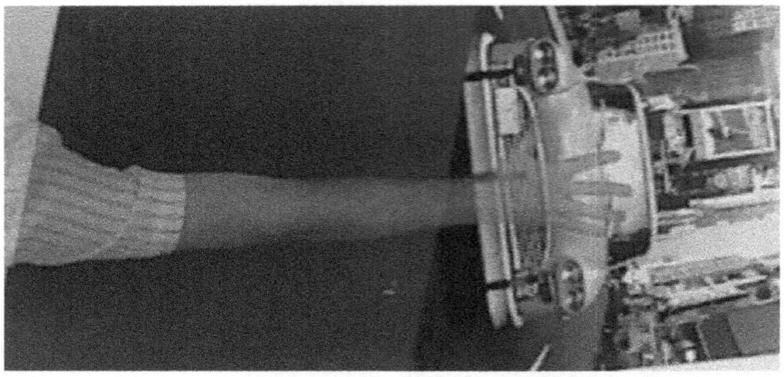

Figure 10: Transparency – reducing visibility and occlusion.

Tattoos. KinectArms can apply virtual tattoos or markings to enhance identification (Figure 11). The tattoos move with the user's arm and are maintained even if the user removes her arm from the Kinect's field of view (see description of IDs above). Tattoos can be any image or text, and are defined by providing a directory for tattoo images. Tattoos are applied in the order that arms enter the workspace, and are set up similarly to other effects:

```
viz.getEffect(kTattoo).enabled = true;
```

Figure 11: Tattoos – improving identification of embodiments.

Tinting. A second effect for helping people differentiate between several embodiments applies a semi-transparent color to the arm image. The effect is similar to the gradient effect of Figure 8, but with a single color.

```
viz.getEffect(kTint).enabled = true;
```

Visual Effects 3: Motion Traces

Gestures are easily missed in distributed settings because of the reduced salience of virtual representations, or network problems [8]. KinectViz provides two effects that help solve this problem: motion lines and motion blur.

Motion lines. Fingers can leave motion-line traces as they move above the table. This effect is created by storing the finger point, connecting the points with lines, and fading older lines to avoid cluttering the space (Figure 12). No previous embodiment technique enables these kinds of traces above the table surface.

Motion blur. A blur effect on the entire arm can help people notice and understand arm movement and gesture [29]. KinectViz produces this effect by overlaying previous frames on the current image (Figure 12), and increasing the transparency on older frames.

```
viz.getEffect(kTraces).enabled = true;
viz.getEffect(kMotionBlur).enabled = true;
```

In both effects, variable `historySize` indicates how many previous samples to use in the effect, and `maxAge` controls how quickly traces fade away.

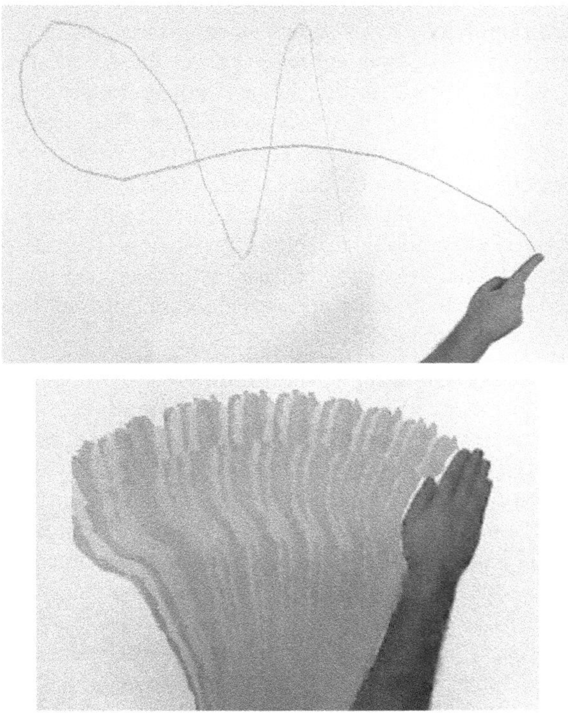

Figure 12: Motion lines (above) and motion blur (below).

Assigning Effects to Specific Height Layers and Users

People use different heights above the table surface to provide different information in a gesture [9] – for example, touching the surface, hovering, and medium and high levels above the table. Therefore, embodiments should be able to represent users differently depending on the height layer in which they are gesturing. All of the effects in KinectViz can be restricted to be visible only in certain layers above the table. For each of the API calls above, there are additional versions with two extra parameters – the lower and upper height of the layer in which the effect should be shown. This capability allows composite visualizations to be created without needing to add new code. For example:

```
viz.getEffect(kMotionBlur).minHeight = 0;
viz.getEffect(kMotionBlur).maxHeight = 1000;
```

Similar method calls allow programmers to assign effects to single users, using the user ID as determined by the library.

EVALUATION OF KINECTARMS

Our experiences with KinectArms allow an analytical evaluation of several issues: the toolkit's performance, the complexity it adds to applications, and its extensibility, generality, and expressive power.

Performance

KinectArms is fast, providing visualized arm images at about 30 frames per second, even with multiple users. KinectTable uses the depth camera and a set of fast image-processing algorithms to carry out video separation, so a major computational expense seen in other systems is avoided. The Kinect hardware produces 30 frames per second, and KinectTable easily processes at the same rate.

KinectVis carries out additional image processing and other computation to add visual effects to the arm images. Multiple or demanding effects in KinectViz, or a large number of arms that need to be processed, could reduce the frame rate depending on hardware. In our experience, with four users and simultaneous use of several of the effects described above, a standard PC (Windows 7, Core i5 processor) was able to maintain a rate of 30 frames per second. In distributed tables, networking constraints are more likely to impose the upper limit on frame rate (at remote sites) than KinectArms.

Complexity and Usability for Application Programmers

Using KinectArms with groupware applications is simple. API calls to KinectTable return arrays of hands and arms with unique identifiers that match users from frame to frame. Applications can choose how and where to display the hands and arms depending on their specific requirements. Similarly, KinectViz effects can be added with simple changes to the API, and the API allows developers to parameterize the effects (to different users and specific height layers) and change effects dynamically at runtime.

We carried out two informal tests of how easily KinectArms can be used for client application projects. First, we integrated KinectArms with a distributed photo-sharing application running on two interactive tables. With this application, users could manipulate shared images using the touch capabilities of the networked tables and see each other's gestures with KinectViz effects (e.g., Figure 1 and Figure 13). The integration of KinectArms and the photo-sharing application took less than one afternoon, suggesting that developers will be able to easily access KinectTable data and use KinectViz effects.

Second, we provided the KinectTable toolkit to another researcher in our lab (not an author) who needed a toolkit for exploring tabletop gesture recognition. Using calls to the KinectTable API, the researcher was able to begin developing gesture recognition systems within a day of starting development. The KinectTable hand structure provided enough information for the researchers to write software that recognizes hand orientations and postures (e.g., fingers up or fingers down), grasping gestures, and pointing gestures. This research is currently ongoing, and is continuing to use the KinectArms toolkit.

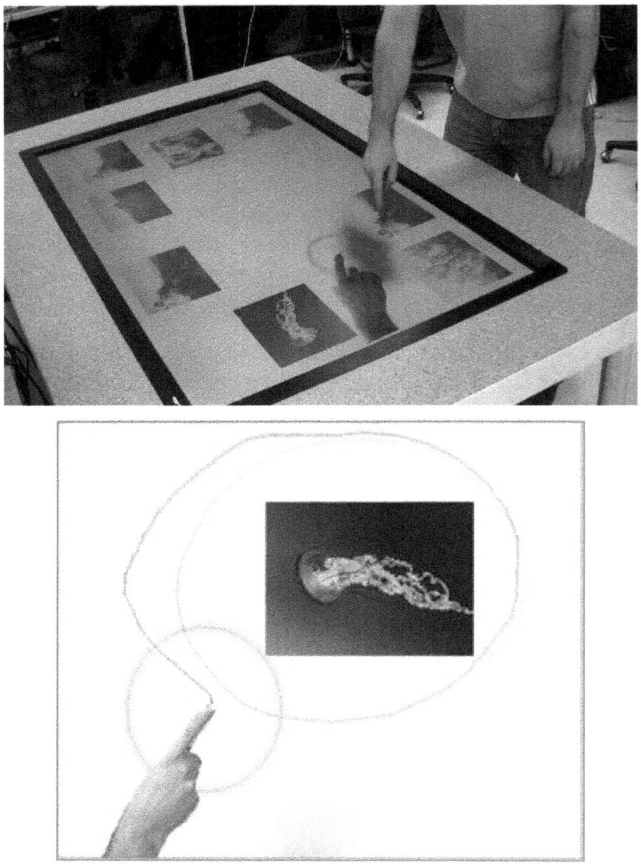

Figure 13: A remote user gesturing to indicate a shared image (below) in the photo-sharing application (above).

Expressiveness: Replicating Existing Techniques

A measure of KinectArms' breadth is its ability to duplicate other arm embodiments that have appeared in previous research. Using only the stock effects of KinectArms, we are able to reproduce embodiments from a wide range of previous work, including VideoArms [23], DOVE [18], C-Slate [12], Fraser's approach visualization [4], and Yamashita's gesture replay [29].

For example, Tang's VideoArms shows hands and arms as two-dimensional silhouettes over a workspace. A later version that used a Microsoft Surface added 'trace pearls': small, fading lines where fingers came in contact with the surface [24]. KinectViz can replicate these two techniques using its basic video arm representation, and a motion-line effect that is limited to a small layer just above the surface (0-1cm). When a pointing finger (defined as the lowest finger on a hand) enters the low layer, traces are drawn. This embodiment can be built with the following calls:

```
viz.getEffect(kTraces).enabled = true;
viz.getEffect(kTint).enabled = true;
((Tint&)(viz.getEffect(kTint))).handColors[0] =
  ColorPixel(255,100,100);
```

The monochrome image of users' hands and arms in VideoArms can also be changed to full colour at no cost (part of the basic video arm representation in KinectArms).

As a second example, both DOVE and C-Slate overlaid video embodiments on a workspace and used transparency either to reduce occlusion or to indicate that hands were further from the tablet surface. In addition, DOVE provide contact traces when the user touched the surface. These techniques can be replicated using transparency, shadows, and motion lines:

```
viz.getEffect(kTransparency).enabled = true;
viz.getEffect(kShadow).enabled = true;
viz.getEffect(kTraces).enabled = true;
```

In addition, KinectArms shows its expressive power in two other ways. First, by combining effects for different users and different height layers, KinectViz can create complex representations that go well beyond existing examples. Second, KinectViz provides several novel effects not seen elsewhere (e.g., outlines, color gradients, stick-figure arms, tints, and above-the-table motion lines); and these new effects were simple to build by using KinectArms' processed images, extracted arm structure, and detailed height information, capabilities which are not provided by any other current toolkit.

Extensibility: Defining New Effects

Although KinectViz has a wide variety of stock visualizations, developers may wish to create their own. The extensibility of the KinectArms toolkit is shown in the simplicity of the process of creating a new effect. KinectTable provides easy access to hand and arm position data and KinectViz automatically applies any enabled effect when `applyEffects` is called. Adding a new effect involves three steps:

1. Create a new class that extends class `Effect`, and implement method `applyEffect()` to manipulates the input image in the desired way.
2. Register the new effect with KinectViz, using the call `int handle = registerEffect<MyEffectClass>();`
3. The new effect can then be toggled on and off, and added to different height layers, using the handle.

Generality

KinectArms works with a wide variety of tabletop setups and table hardware. Tables with existing touch sensing can be used alongside KinectArms (and can be used to augment KinectViz effects by providing additional accuracy for touch events). Top-down projection, a problem for most video-separation techniques, works well with KinectArms, since separation is done with the depth camera, not the colour camera. KinectArms can also be used with non-interactive tables (similar to Ishii's TeamWorkStation). One-way connections can be used to show remote users the contents of a normal table, thus supporting collaboration over paper-based artifacts.

EXTENSIONS TO KINECTARMS

Although KinectArms already provides substantial support to developers of distributed tabletop groupware, there are several extensions that can further improve remote gestural communication, awareness, and system efficiency.

Texture + structure arm embodiments. Structure-based representations of hands and arms are far cheaper to transmit over networks than high quality images. KinectArms automatically extracts structure information about arms above the table, and this could allow designers to provide some of the benefits of realistic video-based embodiments without the costs of transmitting video. That is, network performance can be improved by transmitting hand and arm position data without images and adding custom images at the remote location. Images of users' arms could be taken at the beginning of a session or other kinds of representations could be used. Future research should determine the effectiveness of such cost rebalancing (GPU vs. network) and how users respond to reconstructed or artificial representations rather than live images.

Calibrating multiple distributed tables. Currently, KinectTable provides no built-in support for calibrating between two remote tables, and systems must be aligned by hand (by setting both Kinect sensors at fixed heights above the equal-sized surfaces). Based on this experience, we are currently adding an interactive calibration tool to the library, to permit the Kinect to be hung at different heights above different tables.

Storing the history of interactions. Some researchers have discussed the ability to view long term interaction traces – the historical movements of collaborators over an entire session [16]. Since KinectTable identifies hands and arms with unique IDs and stores their boundaries as well as finger and palm locations in 3D, it would be possible to archive all of the movements during a collaborative session in this way and reconstruct it at a later date. Such replays could be used to answer questions about what kinds of activity occurred during a collaborative session, or could be synchronized with audio recordings to visually identify when different spaces in the workspace were used.

Using the space around the table. KinectTable recognizes tables in its field of view and ignores everything outside of that space. However, collaboration operates in a context that includes the workspace and much research has shown that seeing what is happening outside of the workspace is valuable for both distributed and collocated activities (e.g., [4, 24]). Future versions of KinectTable could model the entire body in the same way as Microsoft's Kinect SDK, except from above. Understanding where users are situated at a table could, for example, allow identification of right and left hands, allow better identification of hands, and allow the tracking of users as they move around the table (something that currently disrupts user tracking). It can also improve awareness in distributed settings and allow systems to make assumptions about user behaviour depending on whether they are sitting or standing.

Supporting gesture recognition. KinectTable identifies several key components of hands and arms (e.g., fingertips and palms) and the current version of the toolkit is sufficient for basic, if rudimentary, gesture recognition. Future work will focus on higher levels of accuracy and added identification features, such as palm orientation, knuckle location, and wrist location. With these improvements, KinectTable can be a tool for gesture recognition as well as representation. We will use this capability to explore possible collisions of communicative gestures and command gestures in interactive systems.

Creating additional hybrid embodiments. Embodiments have previously been classified as realistic or abstract [6]. A third space, a hybrid of abstract and realistic, uses high quality images of hands and arms with abstract visual effects that accommodate for missing fidelity in the images, emphasize existing information, or add information not normally available in collocated settings. To date, few such hybrid embodiments have been built; KinectArms is the first tool to make the development of hybrid embodiments simple and fast. KinectViz allows designers to create and evaluate a wide range of hybrid embodiment designs. It will also help address some challenges with hybrid embodiment design, such as the placement of abstract elements to enhance pointing (our assumption that the pointing finger is always the lowest point of the hand and arms is correct for only some cases).

Interface gestures vs. communicative gestures. KinectArms can also help explore the tension between interface gestures meant as input, and communicative gestures between collaborators. Detailed gesture data about hands, fingers, and arms, along with information about where collaborators are positioned around a table will assist designers and researchers in determining how best to create systems that support both gestural input and gestural communication.

CONCLUSION

Representing rich and subtle gestures in distributed tabletop groupware – particularly those that use varying levels of height above the table – is often expensive, complex, and can require specialized hardware and lengthy calibration. As a solution to the problems of capturing and displaying arm embodiments for remote work, we developed KinectArms, a toolkit that helps groupware developers build arm embodiments with a minimum of effort. KinectArms handles video capture and separation, determines fine-grained height above the table, and provides visualizations that improve arm visibility, representation of gesture height, and movement. The KinectArms toolkit allows simple replication of most existing arm embodiment techniques, and enables the creation of many new types of representation.

In future work, we will carry out two kinds of further development with KinectArms. First, we will continue refinement of the current library – for example, to improve edge detection, effect speed, and camera/table alignment. Second, we will investigate the new extensions described above; these are longer-term enhancements and new functionality that will provide additional ways for people to interact around distributed tabletop systems, all made possible using cheap and easy-to-use components.

SOFTWARE AVAILABILITY

The KinectArms toolkit and the example programs used in this paper are available at www.hci.usask.ca/KinectArms.

ACKNOWLEDGMENTS

This research was supported by the Natural Sciences and Engineering Research Council of Canada, and the SurfNet Research Network.

REFERENCES

1. Ballendat, T., Marquardt, N., Greenberg, S. Proxemic interaction: designing for a proximity and orientation-aware environment, *Proc. ITS 2010*, 121-130.
2. Bekker, M., Olson, J., Olson, G. Analysis of gestures in face-to-face design teams provides guidance for how to use groupware in design, *Proc. DIS 1995*, 157-166.
3. Benford, S., Bowers, J., Fahlén, L., Greenhalgh, C., and Snowdon, D. User embodiment in collaborative virtual environments, *Proc. CHI 1995*, 242–249.
4. Fraser, M., McCarthy, M., Shaukat, M., and Smith, P. Seconds Matter: Improving Distributed Coordination by Tracking and Visualizing Display Trajectories, *Proc. CHI 2007*, 1303-1312.
5. Genest, A. and Gutwin, C. Evaluating the effectiveness of height visualizations for improving gestural communication at distributed tabletops, *Proc. CSCW 2012*, 519–528.
6. Genest, A. and Gutwin, C., Characterizing Deixis over Surfaces to Improve Remote Embodiments, *Proc. ECSCW 2011*, 519-528.
7. Gutwin, C. and Greenberg, S. A descriptive framework of workspace awareness for real-time groupware, *CSCW*, 11, 3, 2002, 411–446.
8. Gutwin, C. and Penner, R. Improving interpretation of remote gestures with telepointer traces. *Proc. CSCW 2002*, 49-57.
9. Harrison, C., Benko, H., and Wilson, A. OmniTouch: Wearable Multitouch Interaction Everywhere. *Proc. UIST 2011*, 441-450.
10. Hindmarsh, J. and Heath, C. Embodied reference: A study of deixis in workplace interaction. *Journal of Pragmatics*, 32, 12, 2000, 1855-1878.
11. Ishii, H. and Kobayashi, M. ClearBoard: a seamless medium for shared drawing and conversation with eye contact. *Proc. CHI 1992*, 525–532.
12. Izadi, S., Agarwal, A., Criminisi, A., Winn, J., Blake, A., Fitzgibbon, A. C-Slate: a multi-touch and object recognition system for remote collaboration using horizontal surfaces. *Proc. Tabletop 2007*, 3–10.
13. Izadi, S., Newcombe, R., Kim, D., Hilliges, O., Molyneaux, D., Hodges, S., Kohli, P., Shotton, J., Davison, A., and Fitzgibbon, A. KinectFusion: Real-Time Dynamic 3D Surface Reconstruction and Interaction. *Proc. SIGGRAPH 2011*, 559-568.
14. Kirk, D. and Fraser, D. Comparing remote gesture technologies for supporting collaborative physical tasks. *Proc. CHI 2006*, 1191–1200.
15. Li, J., Wessels, A., Alem, L., and Stitzlein, C. Exploring interface with representation of gesture for remote collaboration. *Proc. OZCHI 2007*, 179-182.
16. MacEachren, A., Brewer, I., Cai, G., and Chen, J. Visually enabled geocollaboration to support data exploration and decision-making. *Proc. International Cartographic Conference 2003*.
17. Marquardt, N., Jota, R., Greenberg, S., Jorge, J. The Continuous Interaction Space: Interaction Techniques Unifying Touch and Gesture on and above a Digital Surface. *Proc. Interact 2011*, 461-476.
18. Ou, J., Chen, X., Fussell, S., and Yang, J. DOVE: Drawing over video environment. *Proc. Multimedia 2003*, 100–101.
19. Pinelle, D., Guwin, C., Nacenta, M. The Effects of Co-Present Embodiments on Awareness and Collaboration in Tabletop Groupware. *Proc. GI 2008*, 1-8.
20. Segen, J. and Kumar, S. Human-computer interaction using gesture recognition and 3D hand tracking. *Proc. ICIP 1998*, 188-192.
21. Shoemaker, G., Tang, A., Booth, K. Shadow reaching: a new perspective on interaction for large displays. *Proc. UIST 2007*, 53-56.
22. Stach, T., Gutwin, C., Pinelle, D., Irani, P. Improving recognition and characterization in groupware with rich embodiments. *Proc. CHI 2007*, 11-20.
23. Tang, A., Neustaedter, C., Greenberg, S. Videoarms: embodiments for mixed presence groupware. *People and Computers 20*, 2007, 85-102.
24. Tang, A., Pahud, M., Inkpen, K., Benko, H., Tang, J., and Buxton, B. Three's company: understanding communication channels in three-way distributed collaboration. *Proc. CSCW 2010*, 271–280.
25. Tang, J. and Minneman, S. VideoWhiteboard: video shadows to support remote collaboration. *Proc. CHI 1991*, 315–322.
26. Tang, J. Minneman, S. VideoDraw: a video interface for collaborative drawing. *ToIS*, 9, 2, 1991, 170–184.
27. Wigdor, D., Williams, S., Cronin, M., et al. Ripples: utilizing per-contact visualizations to improve user interaction with touch displays. *Proc. UIST 2009*, 3-12.
28. Wilson, A. Using a depth camera as a touch sensor. *Proc. ITS 2010*. 69-72.
29. Yamashita, N., Kaji, K., Kuzuoka, H., and Hirata, K. Improving visibility of remote gestures in distributed tabletop collaboration. *Proc. CSCW 2011*, 95-104.

The Mocking Gaze: The Social Organization of Kinect Use

Richard Harper and Helena M. Mentis
Socio-Digital Systems Group
Microsoft Research Cambridge
7 JJ Thomson Av, Cambridge, CB3 0FB
[r.harper, hementis]@microsoft.com

ABSTRACT
As the Kinect sensor is being extended from gaming to other applications and contexts, we critically examine what is the nature of the experience garnered through its current use in gaming in the home setting. Through an exploratory study of family experiences with Kinect in gaming, we discuss the character of the experience as one that entails users reveling in absurdity of movement that is required by the Kinect sensor. Through this analysis, we liken the 'third-space' defined by Kinect-based gestural interaction to that of Bakhtin's mocking gaze in the contexts of carnivals. This is followed by remarks on the implications this re-specification of understanding Kinect-enabled interaction has for the term 'natural' and relatedly the emphasis on the 'user' as 'the controller' in HCI. Remarks will be made on the implications of this for the application of the Kinect sensor to distributed gaming and other non-gaming interaction spaces in the home.

Author Keywords
Kinect; Natural User Interfaces; Gesture; HCI; Home; Body-based interaction; Games; Family; Culture; Cultural Theory; Sociology.

ACM Classification Keywords
H.5.m.

PREAMBLE
The message Kinect for Xbox advertisements deliver emphasizes an absence: attention is drawn to how something is missing in the relationship between the human and the technology. The claim is made that there is no 'how' when someone interacts with Kinect; indeed, more strongly than this: if the publicity is to be believed, there is no interaction at all. This is because, as the adverts put it, with this technology, *'You are the Controller'* [11].

Obviously this is simple publicity; advertising does not pretend to be science. Nevertheless, there is much to consider in what is being emphasized in phrases such as this. Whereas once the computer mouse might have been the centre of an advertising campaign, now in a world where the technology can let you be the controller, all those sorts of technologies can go. This future holds less – less technology to get in the way. And thus, so the hype goes, we are allowed to be 'natural'. All other means of interacting with a computer are, by dint of this phrase, implied to be somehow other than natural. In this view, the keyboard was merely a technological step on a path to this 'natural' mode; the computer mouse simply a cute technological aid that, like the keyboard itself, is soon to disappear, to be found in the future only in museums and histories of innovation.

So, what is one to make of the phrase 'You are the controller' and relatedly the term 'natural'? The trouble with both is that they are pregnant with numerous meanings and interpretations – it's not that they are vague; it is that they are too evocative and besides can lead one to the wrong conclusions. Consider, the word natural is bound up with what its use implies as unnatural. Given that Kinect does away with a keyboard, one interpretation that goes with this usage could therefore be that people do not 'naturally' want to communicate by written words – the primary output of a keyboard. Doing so is an artifice of technology, one might be led to think by the Kinect publicity. Yet one only has to think of linguistics and how this argument is one of their continual bugbears. As Baron laments in her *Alphabet to Email* [5] linguists are regularly asked to explain why the written word is *not* a surrogate for some other human activity that is ordinarily preferred or more 'natural' (see also [15]). Writing is a different social act than verbal communication; it is not a replacement or a proxy. Similar errors and muddles occur when one conjures with the phrase 'You are the controller'. Is a person not a controller when they use a keyboard and mouse? Does an individual somehow relinquish some control when they use these devices? Presumably that is not what is being implied when the phrase 'you control' is coined. Perhaps it is immediacy that is being implied: with Kinect one can get the machine to do as one wishes instantly, as quickly as one can move one's hand: this brings to mind the idea of direct interaction, so beloved by some in HCI [20].

Yet both ways may be wrong - or rather beside the point. As we say, the trouble with the publicity is where it leads you. Perhaps the best way to think about Kinect is to disregard the publicity and think about what it is implying about what is meant by the verb 'to see'. For, with Kinect, the machine comes to see rather like a human: it can recognize gestures as commands, it can grasp meaning. Is this something that should give credit to the implied claim of intelligence underneath the hood of Kinect? Is there good reason therefore to, say, anthropomorphise the technology and so justify the use of the term *natural*?

Careful reflection will make it clear however that this view ignores something so startlingly obvious that it is perhaps too obvious to see when one is dazzled by the publicity: namely, the fact that both the machine (the Kinect) and the users see at the same time. Users see that the machine is looking at them, and this in turn presumably has reflexive consequences on the user's behaviour - they act so as to be seen. As Vertesi notes in her evocative article, *Seeing like a Rover* [26], what happens in situations when people try to see like a machine is not anthropomorphism but its opposite: *technomorphism*. They try and imagine themselves as machines. It is only in this way that they can accurately understand what the machine(s) in question can do for them. On this basis, they articulate their bodily actions so as to enable and support the action of the machine. Technomorphism requires, in other words, the organizing of the human body as a seen object for a machine's praxis [2012:400].

All of these possibilities highlight, then, the oddness of the phrase 'You are the controller' and, relatedly, the term 'natural'. However, though they might be odd, one ought not to think that they are therefore wrong; it is more probable that the terms need grounding in rather prosaic particularities. Vertesi was able to examine this in the distributed contexts of planetary science-work. There she saw diverse representational practices and talk but she also saw "peculiar" (p. 397) socially organised gestures and movements in the actions of the scientists trying to determine use of the Rover machine. This was 'natural' to the labs she studied. Likewise with Kinect, then: what is natural needs to be understood and evoked in reference to particular spaces where users of this technology can see and the machine can see them. One needs to look at the contexts where this mutual gaze – if gaze it is – has its 'natural' 'peculiarities', those specificities that are characteristic both of the person-machine nexus and the spaces where it is, as it were, natural for this nexus to be operationalized: in spaces where people want to game. There are numerous such places, but presumably the home is one of the more common; it is certainly salient in the Kinect publicity.

The Purpose of this Paper

The bottom line is that even though the interaction that Kinect enables in gaming might indeed be immensely appealing and may make users experience a new sense of control and wonder at how easy and 'natural' it seems to be, 'just what' the experience of Kinect is, what it affords and how it can be designed around, needs careful investigation. One should not allow publicity professionals to own it.

Curiously, and despite the evident commercial success of the technology, little research has yet to appear into this topic – though doubtless, even as this is being written, papers are appearing. There is, however, quite a great deal on gaming in general, and a substantial amount of research in particular on body-based designs, using Wii devices, for example. Though this is a quite different technology to Kinect, there are arguably numerous parallels that can be drawn between the user's experience of each.

It is this absence of empirical research on the one hand and the plethora of research on the social experience of gaming on the other, that the research reported has its motivation. More particularly, the paper will seek to offer an initial set of insights with regard to Kinect. First, it will provide a short review of some of the literature on the topic. Here we will not seek to be comprehensive – space precludes that – but wish instead to highlight what we think are the main themes that can be distilled in the literature.

We will then report on some qualitative research we undertook on the use of Kinect in home settings and in particular by families. We shall explore how the experience of using Kinect is 'produced': users have to learn to interact with it, and doing so means discovering what kinds of movements 'work' and which do not. Key to this is learning (or figuring out) how the machine 'sees' and adjusting human body movement – the user's body – so that what the machine 'sees' is what the user intends. Just as with Vertesi's planetary science researchers, so here we will see that users of the system have to develop a peculiar regime of body movements and gestures that enable the machine they are wanting to engage with to do 'its business'. We shall also see that this is a socially organised affair, with Kinect gamers having to learn how Kinect is to be used collaboratively not just for family games but even how solitary use can imply an audience (and its visible absence in some instances). It is only thus that they can come to discover what appeal it might have.

Our exploration will then turn to the consequences of the experience of using Kinect on the social group. Vertesi explores Durkheim's notion of totem and makes an analogy, as Durkheim does, between the religious role of such devices and the role of the same in the social cohesion of profane groups (i.e. non-religious ones). In Vertesi's case these groups are to be found in distributed planetary science research labs. In her view, the Rover acts as a kind of totem. But this is not a route we can go down for we shall see that the appeal of Kinect – and it has a great deal – cannot be explained in this way. The appeal is of a particular order, one that Durkheim never attended to, certainly not in the *Elementary Forms* or in the *Division of Labour* [9,10]: it has to do with play and laughter. We shall show that the various kinds of bodily movement required by the Kinect system have an effect on the audience watching these efforts. These bodily displays induce laughter, derision. Though the Kinect succeeds in 'recognising' movements, many of these movements are not simply peculiar, but are 'silly', or at least facile, pastiches of 'normal' actions – from the user's point of view. This is manifest in the talk about and accounts of action offered by users, the audience and the players alike; these accounts reflect and articulate what one might call the local 'community of practice'. We shall also note that these pastiche behaviours are sometimes difficult to do – counter to the practices of good grace and bodily elegance constitutive of social role, of what Bourdieu calls *habitus* [6]. This difficulty is something talked about and remarked upon by players. These two combined facts, that the machine's 'vision' requires a 'peculiar' set of body gesture and, secondly, the difficulty this causes for the humans technomorphising, is both the source of the competitive zeal, the constitutive of life with the technology, and the source of ridicule and mockery for those who play and watch, we shall show.

In our discussion we consider this ridicule in the social context of modern home life in reference to Bakhtin's analysis [2; 3] of the social functions of carnival in the medieval period. He argues that the particular kind of mocking laughter that carnivals allowed vented tensions in social hierarchy and this allowed stability in social relations through time. Drawing on this and Vertesi's theory of technomorphism, we will propose that the social function of Kinect is not through providing a totem of family life but through fostering laughter that binds those who participate in the production of that laughter. An important characteristic of that laughter is its mocking form, and this is related to the differences between members of family life in terms of status, identity and role – a father's efforts to act as the Kinect demands causing more giggles than the child's for example; the former's status warranting teasing, the latter more tenderness. We will add that, status notwithstanding, this laughter tends toward the affectionate rather than cruel. We will note that our findings are only preliminary however, with further studies of Kinect use required, both in scale and over time.

We shall then go on to explore why some usages of Kinect, for example for keep fit activities, are often undertaken privately by solitary users – this follows on from the nature of its appeal in collaborative use, we shall suggest. When it comes to keep fit games, users are less willing to be subject to the kinds of derision usually associated with the technology. In the context of keep fit games, it does not make fun, we note, but provokes embarrassment, even shame if the efforts of users falls short of what the game demands or in terms of everyday norms of social and body finesse. And, furthermore, the social value of laughter – the teasing of social status, the venting of restraint, does not apply in this context. Users of Kinect keep fit games prefer to use the technology alone; its value is for them, not for the group.

Our paper, then, covers quite a lot of ground even though it is a preliminary analysis of the social context of Kinect. As we say, much more research will need to be done. Our combining of Vertesi and Bakhtin might be seen to be premature, even jejune. But the issues our study points towards are, we think, quite broad and allude to substantive concerns for HCI across the board. Hence we conclude the paper with some remarks on what is understood as natural in HCI, and what in practice constitutes the actor that creates the active engagement that is computer mediated interaction in the home. From this, we discuss the implications this indicates for the application of the Kinect sensor to, for example, supporting distributed games, and thus situations when the players cannot see or watch each other *in vivo*. We will also remark on the use of the technology of interaction spaces in the home outside of gaming – for smart home type sensors and such, and whether users will be willing to technomorphise themselves in similar ways as they do with Kinect for gaming so as to make those systems usable. Though we think they could do so, we think that the appeal of this technomorphism will be weak: little laughter or fun is to be had by performing as a machine expects when switching on the lights, for example, only effort. Hassle hardly seems a way forward for domestic HCI.

LITERATURE

Given the scope of our topic, the literature that could be brought to bear is immense – space and modesty precludes a full review. But for the purposes of framing the context one might note, first of all, that Kinect would seem to point towards research on the basic principles of HCI. As noted at the outset, the publicity for Kinect highlights the various ways that users can interact with computers. Camera-based and vision reliant technologies are simply one instance of a range, each of which have various benefits and disadvantages. The theme that makes all these discussions pertinent has to do with how phrases like 'natural' and alternatives like 'intuitive' get used in publicity and more generally, in HCI for example.

Careful reflection has makes it clear that most of this debate tends to oversimplify, often disregarding the social context of use and over emphasising, for example, cognitive characteristics, and this leading to the spurious idea that, amongst other things, technologies afford something intrinsically, rather than come to have affordances through the social construction of use. As Turner notes [28], it is not that technologies never afford naturalness or intuitiveness, it is rather that how they do so nearly always needs 'coupling to the social, cultural and historic'. Evoking the cognitive or other 'essentialist' claims without this coupling is simply egregious (p. 482). Any claims about the merits of Kinect need to be based on precisely such coupling: detailed examination of the contexts in question with regard to how the affordances of the technology unfold.

This coupling is made by close examination of situated action and the role of technology in it. In the case of Vertesi, the coupling she uncovered had to do with the relationship between regimes of seeing – the machine and the human – separated by vast distances; in the case of Kinect, the unique circumstances where computer vision and 'natural interaction' occurs is in the much more prosaic setting of the home. Whether this setting has 'peculiar' social properties was an open question at the start of our research, thought as should be clear, our investigations have lead us to a view on this.

If one area of research has to do with framing the affordances of interfaces, another area of pertinent research has to do with gaming. One theme here takes a socio-cultural approach: this seems particularly rich, though it is not always addressed in CSCW especially well. CSCW research has tended to focus on ease of use, learning and efficiency of input measures and such like – important but of a different character to cultural concerns. The latter type of research is exemplified in books like Consalvo's *Cheating* [6] and Boellstorff's *Coming of Age in Second Life* [5]. The focus of these socio-cultural studies is in identity and its relationship to power, capitalism and the marketplace. At first glance this might seem somewhat distant from Kinect but closer examination will show that this is not so.

For example, Consalvo [6] looks at how cheating on on-line games fosters a culture of surveillance and counter measure, and thus deepens the way that social controls manifest themselves. Her particular concern is not only with the relationship between the individual users and the State, but also with the relationship between fellow game players: with computer games, cheating with (and even in front of) other players is almost 'normal'. Thus the technology creates a new 'social system', one where rule breaking is paradoxically the norm. The relationship between this gaming context, the local system if you like, and the larger one at a societal level, is not well articulated in Consalvo, however, probably because she is not that concerned with it, being more focused on the lived moment of cheating.

Focusing on this local level, Nicholls & Ryan [21] argue that gaming allows people to create a new domain of living, a 'thirdspace', which reorders the typical logic of everyday practice and social control. Thus, in ordinary life, the way the body moves is only part of the general regimen of interaction; in body-based gaming it takes precedence, displacing other concerns like the history of the persons involved (their education and so on) and hence things like status. As we shall see, status does play a part in the experience of Kinect, the games themselves providing opportunities to bypass and even mock status, status here meaning either social competence – the ability to perform as the camera wants, and the status that is diminished when technomorphism is at play – when fathers have to 'run' in a 'silly manner', and so forth. In these respects, cultural theory does pertain very powerfully to explanations of the experiences produced by users of Kinect.

Similarly, Swalwell [26] and also Simon [25] argue that the kinds of body movement prioritized in body-based gaming require what Simon terms 'gestural excess', a form of movement that, outside of the envelope of gaming, would cause ridicule and shame, but within not only allows the individual to be more effective at the games in question, but can also create its own kinaesthetic pleasure. The use of the body is thus peculiar, even though it might be appealing, even delightful.

This concept of gestural excess is quite well known in the HCI and gaming literature and obviously has its parallels in Vertesi's studies of planetary scientists' methods of engagement with their remote robotic camera, Rover. A difference exists, however, insofar as Simon (and Swallwell) emphasise the peculiar joy that such gestures induce for gamers while Vertesi is more interested in emphasizing its oddness, and thus the credit that ought to be given to her argument that it is through such odd behaviours that actors in her context 'engage' with a seeing machine. This difference in emphasis however should not elide the similarities, particularly as regards the relational emphasis that Swallwell, Simon and Vertesi give to the nexus between person and machine, to the idea of 'performance'. This is something that has been a persistent interest in cultural theory and gaming literature.

For example, long before body-based gaming became widespread, Darley [8] argued that a key feature of the gaming experience is that it is dialogic in ways that other screen-based activities like cinema are not. Whereas a film-goer passively consumes, the user of a computer game does not just watch but actively engages in what they see and in their reactions creates change in what is seen. In this sense, the space between the screen and the user is not inert or of no consequence; it is the domain of interaction.

This insight has implications for how we might understand the experience of Kinect. For it is suggestive that phrases like 'You are the controller' disregard the space in which that control is done, a space that can be thought of as a stage, a theatre created by two audiences: the human on one side *and* the Kinect on the other. And key to this is the possibility that these two audiences affect each other's sensibility. In the case of Kinect, just as in the case of the Rover, the user side of the interaction adopts what it thinks of as the sensibility of the other side, the machine side, so as to make their own performance more effective for the other. Vertesi suggests this is a kind of opposite to anthropomorphism: in the case of her scientists, there certainly seemed a great deal of effort in constructing the 'reasoning' and visual 'mechanics' of the remote machine, Rover, whereas with the users of Kinect, one would imagine less effort was put into this reflexive engagement. Acting on the stage of planetary science is one thing, acting to a gaming machine at home quite another.

Clearly, the space or the locale of action frames what can be done, giving it particular meaning. Studies too numerous to mention have looked at the relationship between gaming and the various spaces in which they occur, most especially the home [11; 16; 19]. Randall, for example, notes that gaming, both on-line and local, can be engaged with as a means of getting away from the social space in which the gamer finds themselves [22]. Gaming is a place one goes to, to get away. And if this is so, then something about the places that they are fleeing from is bound to the value – natural or otherwise – of the game itself: a real space makes the virtual space desirable. Thus, if gaming is popular at home, one needs to ask not just what is appealing about games, but what pushes people to games. This can be asked not just of home but of anywhere people play games: on the train to work, at work, in public spaces [5; 6].

By the same token, in certain contexts, just as an individual might use gaming to 'get away', so other persons might want to join in that gaming so as to be with the person who originally seeks absence through games. Parents try and make amends for distant relationships with their offspring by asking to join in the games their children are playing on Xbox, for example. They do so not because they particularly enjoy gaming; it is because it is an excuse for being sociable with persons that they cannot be sociable with in other spaces: their kids [14]. Of course, such requests are often resisted: after all what is the point of going to the space of a game to get away if those one wants to get away from follow [7; 5; 20]?

One can sympathize with the teenagers on this front just as we can with the parents. Relations in families are not always easy [13]. The same and related literatures also remark on the negotiation of spaces that needs to be undertaken when gaming occurs, for though the gamer might be focusing on the game at hand, their behaviour naturally affects others thereabouts. People cannot read very easily when another is using a gaming consul to play a noisy (and sometimes violent game) for example; likewise, body gaming can only be undertaken when it does not intrude on other activities or things in a room [21; 22].

INVESTIGATING KINECT USE

All of these concerns beg questions about what is appropriate and controllable; just what Kinect-based interaction might be; how the user might adopt the reasoning (so to speak) of the game technology, or more appositely here, how they might construct a sense of the vision of the machine so that they can engage with what 'it sees'. Inquiries into these concerns can help frame what it means to say that interaction 'is natural' or that a person 'is' the controller and whether the latter turns around, for example, Vertesi's technomorphism or some other form of Darley's dialogue. Inquiries can allow us to better understand the constraints imposed by the unique spatial and bodily regimen afforded by, and created through, what Kinect 'sees', in other words, and how this is dealt with by users. They can help point us towards how we need to couple the specificities of the technology to the 'social, cultural and historical' locales and ways of seeing and being seen in which that technology exists.

If there are then these resources in the literature with which to approach the problem of what happens when the experience of Kinect is 'produced', then it also happens to be the case that there are as yet few actual studies of the technology in action. As we mentioned above, although papers might be appearing soon there is, at the current time, a dearth of field studies on this technology. Given that any claims about the need to base research on the coupling of a technology to social contexts, then this means that any attempt to map this coupling – to contextualize it to put in Vertesi's terms – will be initial, and subject to the criticism that the experience of use might either settle down in something that is yet to appear or that will continue to evolve.

OUR STUDY

It was in this context that the research presented here was taken. It would make no sense to examine Kinect use in a laboratory setting; our research would not be what is often called a traditional 'user study', one that would focus on speed of learning or ease with which interaction dialogues can be selected. Rather, ours would have to be a study of how people come to adopt the technology as their own in spaces that they might also call their own through the act of gaming – where the context is central. Our research would have to look at how Kinect gets used and experienced in gaming in the home. Following on from this, our study would need to let us inquire into interaction between the use of Kinect in gaming and the management of shared spaces of home life. Finally, even though this would have to be tempered with practical constraints, it would be better if those we studied had at least some time to get used to Kinect, to meld it to at least a semblance of routine. Dropping Kinect on an Xbox in a living room and then asking people to play with it would not do; we had to come up with a way that would let them come to grips with it.

So, with this in mind, we initially recruited participants by reaching out to local schools through flyers and personal contacts for households in the spring of 2010 – about 3 months after the Kinect entered the market. By household, we mean a family unit that lives in the same home. The only requirement for participation was that there was at least one child living in the households in question and that they already owned an Xbox. At least this way we could guarantee that they would be familiar with and already adopted some of the essential properties of the kinds of computer-mediated interaction at issue: with the use of large screens, often the main screen in the house for example, and with the centrality of gaming within the domestic affairs of the house that results.

As a result of our first efforts we received interest from ten families – six of which went on to participate in this phase of the study (See Table 1). We provided each of these families with a Kinect and a representative sample of four games: Kinect Adventures, Kinect Sports, Dance Paradise, and Dr. Kawashima's Body and Brain Exercises. The games were chosen for their ability to support both individual and social use and their suitability for all family members. We also provided each family with a video camera and tripod and asked them to capture any use of their Kinects. After a month or so passed, we returned and interviewed the families on their experience with the Kinect, using video footage as part of the resource for discussion in the interviews. In the following we refer to the families as F1-F6.

ID	*No. of Adults*	*Children Ages (Gender)*	*Location of Xbox & Kinect*
F1	1	9(M)	Son's bedroom
F2	2	11(F), 15(M)	Family room
F3	1	16(M)	Living room
F4	0	11(M), 15(M)	Older son's bedroom
F5	2	5(F)	Living room
F6	1	13(F), 15(M)	Games Room

Table 1: Household Player Demographics

Our initial analysis or characterisation of the Kinect experience was of a grounded theory kind, though we don't want to make too much of what was basically a qualitative and ethnographically informed approach. Having gained some sense of what patterns of use were emerging, we then conducted further interviewing around more specific usages of Kinect. In this phase, we recruited participants by putting out a call to our own workplace for anyone who used or knew of someone who used the Kinect fitness games. As a result of this we conducted four more sets of interviews. In the following, we refer to the individuals as I1-I4.

All the interviews were transcribed and the videotapes scrutinized. An open, iterative approach was used for analysis of the qualitative data collected from the interviews; themes were garnered with what might be loosely called an ethnographic imagination. Accordingly, analysis focused on characterizing the experience as understood by the subjects. Some attempt to validate the scope of the findings were made through reference to the differing demographics of the families, but as should be clear, nothing great is being placed on the data beyond its richness. Future studies can be stringent methodologically.

The Kinect Sensor

To describe how the users experienced Kinect during gaming in the home, it is important to highlight how the technology works and the implications this has on its functioning from the user's point of view.

Kinect consists of an infrared light sensor with the quite low resolution of 640x480. This sensor generates a continual stream of depth data of all objects in a scene. From this depth information, a processor on the gaming console analyses the dynamically changing scene 30 times a second – each frame separately from the prior frames – in order to fit a notional skeleton to the human form through machine learning algorithms. This means that every three hundredth of a second the scene is analysed anew for the location and pose of the user.

The low resolution of the sensor along with the need to fit the scene to a pre-existing training set has two important implications in the system's ability to reliably ascertain a user's pose and movements.

First, Kinect requires rather gross gestures and movements. The kinds of fine-grained movement constitutive of everyday interaction between people, where small inflections of the hands, shoulders, chest or spine can convey a sense of dismay, joy, vitality or vexation are beyond the capacity of the Kinect technology to capture.

Second, the Kinect system will tend to 'lose' track of its 'target' when the position of the body makes ambiguous the existence of the skeleton. This happens most frequently when the gamer stands sideways to the Kinect sensor. When this occurs, the system may try to predict where the occluded elements of the skeleton are, and, sometimes, these predictions are wrong. This is known as 'pop-out' by the system designers (See images a & b in Figure 1).

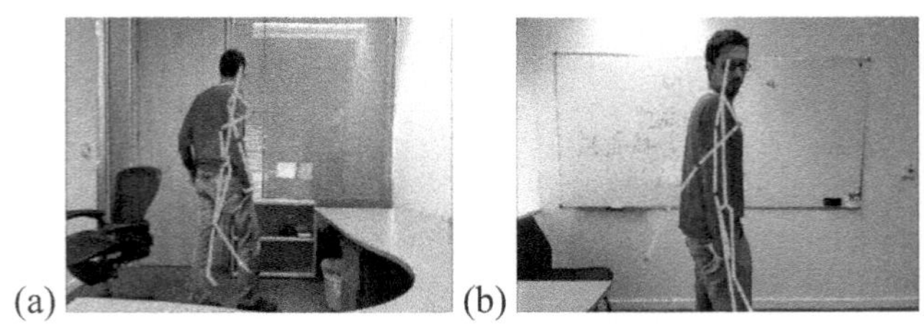

Figure 1. Incorrect interpretations of the body position by Kinect: (a) the system 'loses' the left arm and incorrectly places the left leg; (b) the system loses both arms and creates a theoretical but spurious location for one.

Third, Kinect requires a certain area of movement as, during gameplay, it is a fixed sensor and the view angle delineates a particular area of interaction. The skeletal tracking system is also dependent on a sufficient view of the floor

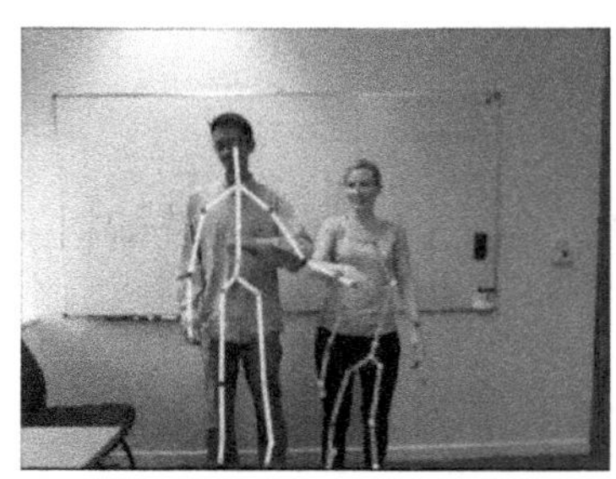

Fig 2: the system incorrectly allocates arms to players

plane on which the user is standing. Social gameplay needs to occur within this space, and can force close proximity between players. This can stress the system, both producing too much change in the viewable space and confusion of skeletons (Fig. 2).

Presented thus, these properties would suggest that the Kinect can be erratic and even difficult to use; it is neither. Rather these properties are simply something that users adapt to and 'work around' as appropriate. They also act, as we shall see, as important resources with which users come to frame and leverage their use of the technology.

The Character of Experience

If Consalvo thinks that cheating is one of the most conspicuously novel features of gaming, then it turns out that our subjects thought something similar, using the experience of cheating with prior forms of device to help approach and account for the experience they came to have with the Kinect. They also 'grokked' the system insofar as they figured out how it worked so as to better 'work to' and 'around' the system's limits. Our subjects discovered that this technology requires a particular manner of movement – gross, strident; they discovered that the kinds of particular gestures that Kinect requires are themselves very peculiar – a move of the arm had to have very particular form, for example.

The following transcript of a father and son discussing the Wii and Kinect makes both the reference to cheating and grokking clear as well as highlight how this is bound to type of device, a Wii being different to a Kinect.

F2, Son: [The Wii] is easier because you can cheat.
Father: Yeah, OK. That was the other side. You really have to, on the Kinect you really are having a go at bowling, but it was quite gross movements.
Son: Yeah, you didn't have to exaggerate your movements [with the Wii].

The exaggerated and gross movements required by the Kinect in using one's body was seen as anything but natural and this affected forms of cheating and gestural form. As a result there was a particular manner of movement, one that had to be cultivated. The way this was described and accounted for, as well as the way it was used to guide learning how to play more effectively, also evoked the idea that the machine 'sees' and that its seeing had particular properties that the gamer had to learn, to 'grok' as we say, although none of our subjects used that term. In this respect, that Kinect sees action and how this was socially understood was a common feature of the talk about and reference to Kinect in our transcripts.

F1, Father: When you do some of the games, like the raft one, you lean...when it actually wants to see you move your leg. So you lean ... 'cause you want to lean, and that's what you do in certain sports... If you're on a bike, you'd lean. But it expects you to move your leg. So that wasn't very intuitive as far as I was concerned, right.

F2, Mother: It took me a little while to get the hang of getting your knees up [when running]. That is good training – that is hard work isn't it?

These peculiarities of movement, what might be called, following the gaming literature, this particular 'regimen of gesture', are also spatially framed. A user has to learn where the area of movement needs to reside and thereafter orient to it. Part of learning to do so involves adjusting gestures to keep them within this space. Not only would this put the user out of reach of the Kinect but there was also the potential for objects to become as it were 'involved'. This sometimes had disastrous, albeit comical effects. In one instance, in F3, the son knocked down an overhead light fixture while trying to act in accord with Kinect; in another, a player was 'sacked' (i.e., caught in the game) when a hand was placed on a bookshelf which connect mistook for another player. In this respect, the ability to perform in the required way demanded what Vertesi calls the 'embodied imagination' [29: 395] of the users, one that requires them to move in a fashion that replicates what they think the machine they are dialoguing with can 'see' as recognizable, and hence game-actionable gestures.

Where actors with the Rover remote planetary mission had to imagine what spatial constraints the Rover was operating within, Kinect players had to adjust their action to the constraints of a space fixed in two dimensions: in terms of how near it is to the camera (i.e. not too near nor too far away from the camera) and in the left and right positioning. If in the planetary science lab contexts such spatialising of the remote machine was easy, some of the gestures that were required in the gaming interaction seemed almost farcically hard:

F4, Father: Sometimes you are running and you go forward and you go backward and suddenly you are on the sofa sitting. You really lose the context of where you are and you are inside the game. It is really amazing how you are pulled into the game.
Son: Yeah, [friend's name] did when he did the sprint, run straight towards the TV.
Daughter: We ended up having to go 'no [friend's name]' [mimes pulling him back]

F2, Mother: Yeah we fell over the sofa a couple of times I think. I wasn't very good at it because I didn't have much practice.

Adjusting for these constraints in order to be able to play 'freer' were some of the strategies used:

F3, Son: When my friend and I played football, we moved [the Kinect] slightly to the left so that he had room to move to the right.

Our subjects did learn to manage these precise spatial constraints – oftentimes through the sting of failure:

F3, Father: But after the first time he was all right.

Daughter: Because it tells you 'move back' and you are like 'oh right, move back'
R-Son: And he went from first to seventh
R-Daughter: Cause he stopped to look at it and then 'oh, move back'.

Some of the young children in our subject families seemed particularly affected by the need to learn embodied imagination. They struggled to control their body, to identity the right relative positioning of the body with regard to Kinect, and more generally in understanding the relationship between their movements and the functioning of the game. It may be that this difficulty had to do with their resistance to technomorphising: though their parents could suspend their everyday attitudes and 'think as the machine sees', their children found this somewhat more difficult. Besides, older persons seemed keen to avoid the demotivation of younger players and sought means to help them around these difficulties. Managing the self-esteem of the children seemed important to this. We shall come back to this point.

In any case, an additional problem small children had was that Kinect could not see them anyway; they were either too small and so slipped out of the view or, when playing, required adult assistance and this in turn made for difficulties with the system:

F4, Mother speaking of her four-year-old daughter: Sometimes when we are playing Adventures we hold hands. Because she doesn't really understand all of [the games]. With the boat one you have to go this way to get the boat to go this way and go that way...sometimes she does the opposite. So I thought OK, let's hold hands. So whenever I go I take her with me and she loves it. Now every time we play Adventures she goes 'hold my hand, hold my hand'. So she loves playing that one because we hold hands and play together.

Instances of the kinds of problems our users had when parents were with their children were often topics in our interviews:

F3, Daughter: The little one, he is three, his dad did it for him. He thought he was doing it, so he enjoyed that.

Interviewer: So he was standing behind him?
Daughter: Yeah. And it didn't confuse it either. It did pick him up but it still let him do the actions of the bowling.
Interviewer: Is it because he was so small and the sensor didn't pick him up?
Father: Well it did sometimes.
Daughter: Sometimes, but he was a bit out of range.
Son: He was a bit forward most of the time.
Father: We are all standing a foot or so from the couch there and he was standing there [points forward toward the TV] so he was a bit forward of the area, wasn't he.

Historicizing Gestural Excess

We need to say again that these vignettes and interview topics are only alluding to activities that are beginning to emerge. With the passing of time (and with more uptake of the technology), so the nature of this produced-experience might alter just as will the kinds of accounts associated with them. Nevertheless, it seems clear that even with our small amount of evidence one can begin to discern certain characteristics of the Kinect experience.

Prior studies of body-gaming make it clear that there are particular regimes of appropriate body movements. This has to do in part with the limits of the technology in question. It turns out to be easy to undertake the movements required for a Wii for example – a whole arm gesture can be converted into a simple move of the wrist. This in turn has implications for what is cheating, of course, and consequently has to do with understandings of what is and is not correct, what is cheating and what is 'playing the game straight', and so forth.

The quotes in the previous section show that Kinect likewise demands a certain form of body movement. They also show it as one that is demonstrative, where the movements in question have to be exaggerated within a constrained space akin to a stage.

In this regard, the Kinect experience is understood in part through drawing a contrast with the Wii. This is certainly attested to by the way that interaction with the Kinect was accounted for and in part predicted by referencing to using the Wii in the past (as some of the above quotes show). The Wii demands a peculiar kind of body action, an action that it turns out can be quite minimal; Kinect also demands peculiar movement because of fidelity, but in this case of the reverse kind: extreme. The performative qualities of gestures with Wii and Kinect technologies are thus different.

In both cases, it would appear that users construct a sense of how the system in question works; how Wii senses and how Kinect 'sees'. They 'grok' the technology. Certainly from our interviews it was clear that our users took on board how they thought the sensors in the Wii work. With Kinect they seemed to adopt a language that implied a greater sentience on the part of the machine than with the Wii: 'it sees' was the formula they used, and they learnt to behave such that what it sees was how they wanted it to see. Whether this sentience was merely implied in choice of words is hard to tell from our data, however. Certainly, the word 'see' has a kind of grammar to it that implies sentience in ways that use of the word 'sensor' does not. Our evidence is mute on this question however.

Be that as it may, such gestures made our users think that their behaviours were not 'like the real thing'; that they were 'different'. The contrast with the word 'natural' obviously comes to mind; we shall come back to this. So, for example, and to allude to the quotes above, running with a Kinect game did not entail running as it is normally. It could not: for one thing, furniture would get in the way. For another, a user would run out of the Kinect's view – its line of sight. Rather, running entailed running on the spot in a peculiar way, one that forced the user to, for example, "bring their knees up high". One might say, somewhat teasingly, that Kinect made people alter what they thought of the 'real' actions are so as to fool the technology into thinking they were doing the real action – running, say, or swinging a bat.

As we alluded to earlier, this might seem to make a mockery of the publicity for Kinect, but this would be to miss a much more important point. For it turns out that in requiring this kind of gestural control, the experience that Kinect thereby helped deliver was one that our subjects delighted in. They did not feel disappointed at the failure of the technology to let them move 'naturally'. We heard no complaints that Kinect demands 'unreal action'. On the contrary, the oddness of these behaviours (and the finesse or otherwise of people's attempts to enact those behaviours) would appear to become the focus – or perhaps the source – of fun produced when using the technology. The falling forward when our subjects ran too literally; the bashing of objects outside of the proper domain of action; all this made our subject's laugh. They told us about this, we saw it in our videos. This is quite different from the appeal that gestural excess delivered to those gamers that Simon and Swalwell studied: for there, the appeal was simply in the physical ability to play games, even if those abilities were kinaesthetically quite limited, like holding and manipulating a consul.

Sociality

This laughter was not solipsistic. The delight in the physical foolishness required by the Kinect was tied up in the relationship between those that are playing and those that are spectating. It was the enjoyment together that made these awkward and, sometimes, grotesque movements part of the appeal of the technology. Fig 3 shows movements that caused those watching to shout out "The maniac is alive" for example.

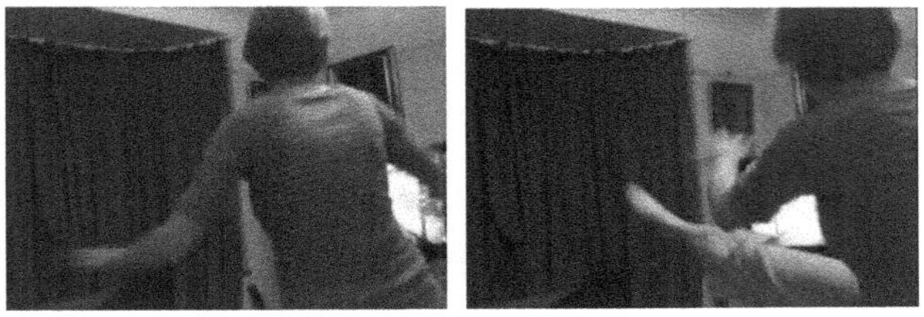

Figure 3. "The maniac is alive!"

Even when these extreme movements resulted in physical rivalry or unfortunate accidents in the home, they were still seen as part of the enjoyment of moving one's body in absurdity.

F3, Father: [Y]ou can have a bit of a laugh together. It's the social interaction isn't it? A bit of a laugh.

F4, Father: With the Kinect you really have to make the effort. So in terms of interaction it is a lot better because when we have other people you push the other you try to cheat or you do those kinds of things.

And after telling a story of an overhead light fixture being knocked down by the father's 'flailing arms' during gameplay:
Interviewer: That is quite unfortunate.
F2, Mother: Well, it was quite funny, really.

F4, Father: Yeah, it is a lot more fun to watch. Because they really have to move. And when you are in the game there is no inhibition, you have to win, so you just go for it and do whatever it takes. I'm the first person to be quite embarrassed ... but it is good fun at the end of the day.
Interviewer: So you don't feel inhibited...
Father: No, because you are playing a game. I mean sometimes you make funny faces when playing on the gamepad. Here your entire body is the controller so you just do what it takes. And if you look at [daughter's name], it is the same thing. Sometimes when we do the running she just goes all over the place [demonstrates with hands flailing around]. You completely lose it.

F3, Father: You are like mad in the air. [waves hands over head] woohoo!

The effort needed for bodily mastery or the spectacle provided through the body was considerable, then. Demonstrating one's ability to contort, constrain, and grossly over-exaggerate one's limbs so as to beat other players resulted not just in victory, though, but laughter, too: 'success' would lead to cheering and encouragement, even if this laughter was peculiar, being not with the 'victor' but at them, even as they 'run away' with a game.

The form of this laughter and the demands for peculiar movement was also related to social status, or at least this is what our subjects reported. As one father explained it:

F4, Father: Yeah it's about bringing us together you know.
Interviewer: The family?
Father: Yeah. You know it's stupid technology. It makes you run in the most ridiculous way. But when you run like that you make yourself a prat. The kids love it. Look at Dad they say. It's about making me look a fool.
Interviewer: you mean you as Dad?
Father: Yeah. It's not so funny when you laugh at the kids. Well you don't. They get upset.

This last point alludes to the difficulties of getting children to join in given that they might find it hard to adopt the skills of movement required and given also their relative lack of self-esteem and status. Laughing at Dad won't upset Dad but will please others; laughing at children is just unkind.

The Space of Kinect

This then would be the kind of 'social, cultural and historical place' that was constituted when Kinect was used in our home settings. Within this context, this situation, users came to learn that exaggerated, almost theatric type behaviours were required; ones more like mimes of everyday action than accurate proxies of normal or 'natural' movement.

Just how much our participants technomorphised themselves and their behaviour, and, at the same time, just how much they anthropomorphized the Kinect technology, cannot be judged with certainty from our evidence, however. As we noted earlier, ours is really only an initial study and besides a study at the start of familiarity and use that comes only over time. And in any case, our videos and our interview transcripts do not record the kinds of rich 'work talk' constitutive of the settings that Vertesi studied, work talk where intimations about technomorphism come to be articulated and thought about. One might make a contrast here between our data and the data Chuck Goodwin made famous in his accounts of 'professional vision' [12]. And beyond all this, one should not forget that this was gaming we are talking about, not work. Vertesi's subjects were serious about making Rover tractable to serious questions; our subjects need to be understood in reference to the creative, playful and light-hearted spirit constitutive of the kinds of games they played. As Huizinga notes [16], one of the distinguishing characteristics of games is the order of talk manifest in them: levity is allowed, even expected in those situations when the game is being played earnestly. Games are not 'serious'; only the real world is.

Nevertheless, what the evidence we gathered does show is that interacting with Kinect in the ways described, imagining how the technology sees and embodying this in one's actions, produced delight. Delight was afforded in trying to do the 'mimes' as our subjects put it; and *trying* seems to be the apposite word here. For it would appear that the difficulty people had in doing these performances, combined with the oddness of the actions themselves (what was being mimed) made the enactment of them somehow absurd, ridiculous. Our subjects laughed at themselves for failing to act as the machine would have them do; they laughed when they got it 'right'. And not only did they laugh at themselves, but they laughed at others, too. To invert Swalwell's [26] point: pleasure came not from success at the kinaesthetics, but failure at them.

Some further consequences follow on from this. It has to do with the kind of space that Kinect enabled – the version of the thirdspace mentioned by Nicholls & Ryan [21]. This has a number of features. It is not one that would only be about getting away from the presence of others, as prior research has suggested can sometimes be the case with gaming. Nor might it be about creating a new sociality with remote gamers. For Kinect seemed to be a technology that appealed because it turned around altering the relations users (or players) had with other's thereabouts, in the social and geographical space in which the games were played. The 'place' was, if you like, about the 'here and now'. Thus the relationship between Kinect and the use of games to get away from a real space is one of contrast. Kinect altered the space it was used in; other games alter a space by making it twofold: the space that the gamer is in and the space that those who are not gaming remain within. With Kinect there was no such division; it encompasses all.

Even so and though, obviously, to play a multiplayer game requires that more than one person be involved, the space that Kinect enabled entailed a shifting of the relations between the people thereabouts. This shift was not simply from normal, non-game into those that are game-like: competitive, skill-based and so forth. What it entailed was of a particular order. For this space was one were the adroitness of each player, each participant in this social system, willingly engaged in a social practice that could be and indeed would appear to most often entail, mockery. For this to be willingly engaged in, a participant needed to be prepared to risk being mocked as well as enjoy doing the mocking. Kinect was a risky technology in terms of the consequences using it had for a person:

F4, Mother: We have some friends that are kind of shy and normally wouldn't do something like that [flailing hands]...it is actually very funny to see how you totally lose that embarrassment of looking funny.

One might put it this way: playing games with the Kinect is not about showing expertise; playing games with the Kinect is about making a fool of oneself – and the willingness to do so.

F2 Mother playing with the Kinect for the first time with her daughter. She is playing Rally Ball in Kinect Adventures - waving her limbs around to try to hit the balls that are coming at her.
Mom, laughing: "There is no skill! It is just a case of waving your arms around isn't it?"
Daughter, sarcastically: "The maniac is alive. ... 55! Wow mom."
Mom, laughing: "You are very rude!"

Foolishness itself comes in degrees, of course. To win at the kind of running games that Kinect enabled, for example, was not to win because one was the best 'runner'; one would win because one was less poor than others at the kind of absurd running that Kinect required and that required one to look more foolish in the enactment of that running than others. Being willing to take this risk showed and demanded a degree of complaisance and of confidence: one must not mind being made a fool of.

Inclusive Space

Such practices would seem to be essentially to do with joint activities. But one should not imagine that this is therefore exclusively about or for multi-user games. For our research suggests that if the space that Kinect helped enable was one that was about the relations between persons in the real geographical space in which Kinect operated, then it does not necessarily require that all those persons thereabouts would actually be playing. If the thirdspace that Nicholls & Ryan [21] defined was one that was occupied by gamers and gamers alone, then the space that Kinect created would seem to affect was the actual geographical space and *whoever was in it*. Even if one was not playing with Kinect, the place that Kinect enabled was one that an individual could join in.

That this was so has a radical consequence. A person who was not playing Kinect and who was in the space could, obviously, watch the movements of those who were playing. But this watching had a *moral* overtone. For they would not just see movements, they would see odd movements; they would see the gestures for what they were: not simply as excessive, but as odd. They did not need to be playing Kinect to see that this was so: for the measure that was used here was one that involved using their knowledge of everyday gestures. Anyone could see that running on the spot is not like normal running, for example. Hence the applicability of the phrase *moral* here for the watching person judged the actions of the Kinect player and when they did so they came to laugh at it. It was risible.

Yet, and consequent on this, when people watching the gamers made such mirthful noticings, so they were doing so in a way that distinguished them from others who were playing the game. As mentioned above, to play the game entailed enjoying the fun of laughing at other's ineptitude. But this would come at the risk of being laughed at in turn. We did not have any examples of this but it was certainly implied in our interviews: that those who might laugh at others playing with Kinect but who would not play with the technology themselves would not be in a sense taking the risk that others would demand: their laughter would be of another order, a selfishness that would be almost unkind since it could never be reciprocated.

Space and the individual

This will have a reverse consequence too: one can imagine that some people want to play with Kinect and might be happy to laugh at themselves but do not want to be vulnerable to the mockery of others. Indeed, this seemed to be often the case with children, for example. In our interviews we heard that parents and siblings were often banished from the room in which children were using the Kinect. Something about the form of action entailed made the children concerned that they did it away from the hurtful eyes of a doubtlessly mirthful other.

We found something else too, that seemed to reflect the same logic. In the second phase of the study, one of our interviewees was a user of Kinect for sports and keep-fit activities. Talk with that person at first seemed to suggest a different kind of logic would apply to this kind of gaming context than the one just described for family games. She said that there were a number of reasons for using the technology – one of the appeals of the technology was that it allowed her to be lazy:

I1: The other day ( ) I did a workout with my pajamas. I thought what's the point I am going to get my pajamas in the wash so let's use them so I did it in them.

But then she went on to say that going to the gym, meanwhile, did not just require effort. Something else concerned her motivations:

[When I go to the gym] *I feel self-conscious. Well I try and not look silly for example. You know that's one of my major worries about going to the gym – it's not looking silly. If I don't know a piece of equipment I won't go near it since I don't want to look silly if I don't know how to use it, you know? If you are there, and there is a great big buff guy and you are there and without your make up and you're in your gym gear you are already on a lower foot.*

In other words, one of the concerns this person had about going to the gym was esteem: she was afraid that sometimes she would be laughed at if she could not use the machines properly or did not look as fit as 'the buff guy'.

Using Kinect seemed much less risky, she was suggesting. But then she went on to say that when she used Kinect for keeping fit by herself:

I make my husband stay out of the room. ... Cause he will laugh at me. But on those occasions when he has stayed there I have told him to leave because he just makes judgments and I don't appreciate it when I am exhausted.

Another user of Kinect for fitness we spoke to added to this insight. She reflected on her mother's need to be hidden when performing any form of physical exertion, including with the Kinect.

I2: It would be a very personal thing. She wouldn't want anyone else in the room. She would probably do it at a time when there was nobody else in the house.... Because it is <u>her</u> fitness. It is <u>her</u> body. It is not a fun thing to do where people can look and laugh and join in. ... Like she runs, but she only runs at night. She won't let anyone see her going out for a run.

What these quotes suggest then is that the need for a private performance of sorts is one consideration taken heed of when people chose whether and how to interact through gestural excess. In certain circumstances such excess is tied up in laughter and mutual understanding in play; this we saw in the bulk of our interviews and videos. Here gestural excess is fun. But if the gestural excess can lead to derision, to making a subject seem awkward or foolish in controlling their body, then such excess is relegated to the private arena when derision can be avoided. Kinect technology can be used for both, it would seem.

FROM GESTURAL EXCESS TO THE MOCKING GAZE

The contrast between these two different formulations of the experience of use, highlighting as they do opposite responses to the demands of the system, attests to the need for more investigations, particularly of a comparative kind.

Between these two opposites one might discover that several persons performing gestural excess in harmony might be at once a serious affair and a leisure pursuit, for example. Dancers might find the constraints of Kinect appealing; for example, their capacity to technomorphise might even be an additional concern that they might train for. One cannot say.

But confining ourselves to the topic of how our families used Kinect does bring to mind a comparison if its own. It brings to mind a wholly different time and place where bounded excess also enabled laughter and mutual mocking. We are thinking of Bakhtin's medieval carnivals [2]. This seems a long way from Kinect just as it seems a long way from Nicholls & Ryan's thirdspace [17]; literary theory is indeed normally well removed from HCI. But let us explain.

The carnivals that Bahktin described in his various works [2; 3] contrasted, he argued, with the tightly regimented official feasts and celebrations that were commonplace in medieval society. Whereas official celebrations were designed to help consecrate and dignify status, particularly the status of the high and mighty, carnivals, on the other hand, provided an opportunity where all could laugh at each other without fear of undermining social structure. Bakhtin's thesis is that this carnival laughter provided a vent for social tension, and, further, helped humanize people whose elevated status might otherwise make dealing with them awkward for those of low status. Through laughing in carnivals, the uneducated masses could learn that their masters were human, in other words, and thus, when the need arose, communications with them could be made. Carnivals produced a temporary world where all could transgress boundaries and challenge the usual and accepted. Bakhtin referred to this new world of carnivalistic life as "life turned inside out" or "the reverse side of the world" (monde a l'envers) [3] (p.122).

Similarly with the 'space' created in and through Kinect gameplay in the family settings we have sketched. Though the technology would seem indifferent to status, concerning itself only with the body of the gamers, this very fact helps make that status salient to the gamers. Who they are, what they have done in the past, or what rights they have viz-a-viz others in the home setting, all this is immaterial to the Kinect but not for those who play. For we have seen that the socially constructed experience of Kinect in the family affairs we have described ends up having carnival-like qualities.

In our evidence about families, Kinect was about the relationship between persons and their competence, their bodily competence and their capacity for Vertesi's embodied imagination. Kinect games created a domain in which that imagination came to be the focus or, rather, allowed people to make fun of themselves and each other through their imaginative, embodied play. With Kinect, though the laughter may have carnival-like feel – being ribald, giggling, uncontrolled – it was, importantly, also quite circumspect. It was about mocking the transformation of everyday finesse with the body, Bourdieu's bodily habitus, into the gestural excess of gaming. This might or might not have ontological footings in terms of an interplay between anthropomorphic and the technomorphic, but it is above all about the situated creation of amusement. We have suggested that has particular social organizational characteristics in our material: the higher the status of the individual making this transition, the greater the distance between the stuffiness of their normal action and the ludicrousness of their gaming behavior, the greater the fun. Dad's running in 'a stupid fashion' was funnier than kids doing it. Besides, kids didn't like being laughed at. Their self-esteem was too delicate.

It needs to be stated yet again that this fun would appear to be gentle, a kind mocking, if our subjects are anything to go by. It is the loving of families and friends who seal their relations through the teasing of each other. This is the naturalness of Kinect in gaming, not the input and output functionality of the technology; not how it sees but how it allows laughter.

That this is so has a number of consequences and design implications. First of all, it suggests that Kinect games will not find success by expanding into remote gaming scenarios if those games are intended to help foster the kind of social experiences we have described. Xbox has been remarkably successful in bringing online connections to the gaming world and so it would not seem so unlikely that efforts will be put into bringing Kinect games to this online space – indeed, this is already happening. But if our analysis is correct, then one of the key values of Kinect would be lost in this scenario: though one could see the avatar moving, the joy of Kinect comes from looking at the user trying to act as an avatar, not at the avatar itself. In other words, one needs to be with the fellow gamer, not watching the consequences of their actions on the screen. The paradox of Kinect is that it uses very advanced technology to bring renewed vitality to being together.

Of course, this claim only holds for the kinds of activities we have focused on, and excludes others we have pointed towards and imagined. Our analysis does not account for the value of Kinect in private affairs, for example, nor does it account for when gestural excess becomes a target for serious ambition, such as in dance, say.

Second, the analysis suggests that it might be quite inappropriate to use Kinect technology for many other tasks in the home. Laughter and mockery are not perhaps the most resonant forms of experience that one associates with for example, those applications one associates with the smart home [1,13,15]. Switching lights on and off, maintaining the ambient temperature at the right level, making the home secure when one leaves, all these are serious matters, albeit of various degrees of importance. Laughter doesn't come into it [19].

By the same token, while excessive movements and contortions of the body in Kinect for fitness might increase the physical benefits of the activities in question, one can hardly imagine that such effort would please the user when they seek to control the lights or lock the door. Less effort is what is desired, less excuse for awkwardness. There would be nothing very natural about using Kinect for the lights; indeed, quite the reverse.

CONCLUSION

We started our discussions by saying that the terms 'natural' and the phrase 'You are the controller' seemed too evocative, too rich to adequately capture the 'just what' of Kinect experiences. We reviewed the literature and came to see that one needs to understand this experience through linking it to the social context: to where the technology is used. Here we have focused on one domain, the home setting and the use of Kinect for one particular type of social practice within that setting, namely family gaming; we have explored this by briefly looking at Kinect and exercise.

Having done so, it should be clear that using Kinect does not entail 'natural' in the way the publicity seems to imply for the context we describe. It requires eccentric simulations of commonplace and real activities like running, golf and football, and a buckling of the apposite skills for the movements associated with these activities into a constrained regime of actions. These tend to be excessive or exaggerated, and lack the physical delicacy of the real. This will apply for other settings and usage of Kinect, so natural doubtless will be awkward and ill-fitting there too.

The does not in any way diminish the appeal of using Kinect for the setting in question however. Being natural has nothing or at least very little to do with this appeal for family gaming. Other factors do and these are related to what is constituted in the relationship between users in this context, other persons thereabouts and the Kinect-enabled computer. For gaming in home life, the use of exaggerated gestures provides an opportunity for fun and laughter, for the gentle mocking of social status as well as for satiating the threat of domestic boredom. For exercising, in contrast, excessive gestures increase the value delivered, forcing the participant never to slack but to constantly focus on the demanded movements. But such activities are sought for in private moments, away from the eye of others which is can be cruel in this context, though benign when gaming.

The phrase 'You are the controller' is not as misleading with regard to family gaming as the term 'natural' – although the way it is used in publicity is nevertheless unhelpful. For one thing, that use emphasises how unproblematic it is to control the Kinect; a misleading claim as we seen. For another, this usage is also suggestive that the relationship is a binary one, solely concerning the 'user' and the 'machine'. Our research shows that this is to misconstrue the experience of use and to misconstrue who or what the user 'is'. Just as all gaming experience creates a space into which the gamer goes, so too does Kinect, but this space is not elsewhere, other than in the here and now, in the virtual say (and here the term the thirdspace does have its applicability). Rather, what is created is a kind of theatrical performance. This performance, however, is not simply one that distinguishes the passive viewer of screen entertainment from the active gamer who alters the screen, as Darley drew attention to all those years ago. In this instance the individual user performing with the Kinect is also performing to others watching that performance. These are not so much a passive audience, but are users waiting their turn; indeed their rights to be in the audience are bound to their willingness to be a user.

And here lies the rub: for being a user comes at a price. This has to do with the difficulties of controlling *oneself*; it is not the Kinect that is difficult. These difficulties are the source of amusement both to the user(s), the individual player(s), and those watching. The carnival-like theatre that is produced by Kinect, the social space that is constructed with its use, has to do, to put it exaggeratedly, with making the failure the human the centrepiece of theatre. It is the fact that it is not easy or natural to control how one controls oneself that is at the heart of its appeal; it is that a user finds it hard to be 'natural', as the Kinect system demands, that is part of the thrill: this naturalness is not difficult in some extreme sense; it is only difficult because it forces one to focus and concentrate on being other than one normally is. And if one is successful at this, and thus good at the controlling Kinect requires, then the absurd and excessive gestures that emerge make for the laughter of others. In short, success makes a mockery of the user.

In this sense the Kinect experience appeals because its controllers are bad at their job; this makes a fool of them and this is funny. Kinect is not about the wonders of computer vision to see the intentions of the user, it is about how this technology lets users – both players and audience alike – indulge in a mocking gaze through adapting their action so as to let it be seen by a computer that 'sees' in a certain way: in a way that one that demands even as it looks, demands that say, in effect, 'act this way', 'act oddly', 'that is all I can see'. The appeal here is not in the fact that thereby all the human gamers can come to successfully interact with the machine: it is not the users' technomorphising that is at issue. It is because the gamers come to laugh at each other through mocking the demands that the machine makes of them. This is natural interaction made peculiar. This is the interaction that allows one family member to say to another, with glee and partly mocking the publicity that suffuses the media, 'You are a poor controller'.

ACKNOWLEDGMENTS

Thanks to all the participants and the encouraging reviewers of CSCW.

REFERENCES

1. Aldrich, F. (2003). Smart Homes: Past, Present, Future, In Harper, (Ed) *Inside the Smart Home,* pp17-40.
2. Bakhtin, M. (1968). *Rabelais and his world*. Cambridge, MA: MIT Press.
3. Bakhtin, M. (1984). *Problems of Dostoevsky's poetics*. Minneapolis, MN: University of Minnesota Press.
4. Baron, D. (2009). *A Better Pencil: Readers, Writers, and the Digital Revolution*. Oxford and New York: Oxford Univ. Press.
5. Boellstorff, T. (2008). *Coming of Age in Second Life*. Princeton: Princeton University Press.
6. Bourdieu, P. (1972) *Outline of a Theory of Practice*, London: C.U.P.
7. Consalvo, M. (2007). *Cheating: Gaining Advantage in Videogames*. Cambridge: MIT Press.
8. Darley, A. (2000). *Digital and Visual Culture: Surface Play and Spectacle in New Media Genres*. London: Routledge.
9. Durkheim, E. (1915[1912]) *The Elementary Forms of the Religious Life,* (Trans. J.W. Swain) London: Allen & Unwin.
10. Durkheim, E. (1947 [1892]) *The Division of Labor in Society,* (Translated by George Simpson). New York: The Free Press.
11. First Official Xbox 360 Kinect Ad – US. http://www.dailymotion.com/video/xfaytv_first-official-xbox-360-kinect-ad-u_videogames. Downloaded January 19, 2012.
12. Gaver, B. *Designing for Homo Ludens, still.* http://kmdi.utoronto.ca/documentshomepage/gaver-ludens08.pdf
13. Goodwin, C. 9(1994) Professional vision, *American Anthropologist,* 96(3):606-633.
14. Harper, R. (Ed.) (2003). *Inside the smart home: Interdisciplinary perspectives on the design and shaping of domestic computing*. Godalming & Heidleburg: Springer-Verlag.
15. Harper, R. (2010). *Texture: Human expression in the age of communications overload*. MIT Press: Cambridge, Mass.
16. Harper, R. (Ed.) (2011) *The Connected Home: the future of domestic life*. London: Springer.
17. Huizinga, J. (1950). *Homo ludens: A study of the play element in culture*. Boston: The Beacon Press.
18. Intille, S.S. (2006). The goal: Smart people, not smart homes. In C. Nugent and J.C. Augusto (Eds.), *Smart Homes and Beyond* (pp.3-6). Amsterdam: IOS Press.
19. Jameson, F. (1991). *PostModernism, or the cultural logic of late capitalism*. Durham, North Carolina: Duke University.
20. Kientz, J. A., Patel, S. N., Jones, B., Price, E., Mynatt, E.D., & Abowd, G.D. (2008). 'The Georgia Tech aware home'. In *Extended Abstracts on Human factors in computing systems*, pp. 3675-3680.
21. Nicholls, B. & Ryan, S. (2008) Gameplay as thirdspace. In Swalwell & Wilson, *Op cit*, pp167-190.
22. Randall, D. (2011). All in the game: Families, peer groups and game playing in the home. In Harper, *Op cit,* pp. 111-131.
23. Rouncefield, M., Hughes, J., O'Brien, J., & Rodden, T. (2000). Designing for the home. In R. Harper (Ed.), *Personal technologies: Special issue on home life*, Amsterdam: Kluwer, pp. 76-94.
24. Shneiderman, B. (1983). Direct manipulation: A step beyond programming languages. *IEEE Computer, 16*(8), 57-69.
25. Simon, B. (2009). Wii are out of control: Bodies, game screens and the production of gestural excess. *Loading..., 3*(4).
26. Swalwell, M. (2008). Movement and kinaesthetic responsiveness: A neglected pleasure. In Swalwell & Wilson, *Op cit*, pp72- 93.
27. Swalwell, M. & Wilson, J. (Eds.) (2008). *The pleasures of gaming: Essays on cultural history, theory and aesthetics*. Jefferson, North Carolina: MacFarland & Company.
28. Turkel, S. (1984) *The Second Self: Computers and the Human Spirit*, MIT Press: Cambridge, Mass. (See also the Preface of the second edition, 2005).
29. Turner, P. (2008). Towards an Account of Intuitiveness. *Behaviour & Information Technology*, 27(6), p.475-48.
30. Vertesi, J (2012) 'Seeing like a Rover: Visualization, embodiment, and interaction on the Mars Exploration Rover Mission, *Social Studies of Science*, 42: 393-414.

"Almost Touching": Parent–Child Remote Communication Using the ShareTable System

Svetlana Yarosh[1,3], Anthony Tang[2,3], Sanika Mokashi[3], Gregory D. Abowd[3]

[1]AT&T Research Labs
Florham Park, NJ, USA
lana@research.att.com

[2]University of Calgary
Calgary, AB, Canada
tonyt@ucalgary.ca

[3]Georgia Institute of Technology
Atlanta, GA, USA
{lana, tonyt, sanikamokashi, abowd}@gatech.edu

ABSTRACT
We deployed the ShareTable—a system that provides easy-to-initiate videochat and a shared tabletop task space—in four divorced households. Throughout the month of its use, the families employed the ShareTable to participate in shared activities, share emotional moments, and communicate closeness through metaphorical touch. The ShareTable provided a number of advantages over the phone and was easier to use than standard videoconferencing. However, it did also introduce concerns over privacy and new sources of conflict about appropriate calling practices. We relate our findings to the larger research landscape and present implications for future work.

Author Keywords
Computer-mediated communication, divorced families, children, tabletop, camera-projector system, home

ACM Classification Keywords
H.5.2. [Information Interfaces and Presentation]: User Interfaces – *User-centered design*

General Terms
Human Factors.

INTRODUCTION
The negative consequences of divorce on parents' and children's wellbeing can often be mitigated if the non-residential parent stays instrumentally involved in the child's life [2]. Kelly & Lamb advise that arrangements should provide "opportunities to interact with both parents every day or every other day in a variety of functional contexts" [22]. This is difficult to achieve for parents and children who live apart, as contact with the non-residential parent decreases dramatically after the first year apart [30].

Non-residential parents sometimes turn to technology to supplement in-person time, a practice known as virtual visitation. As of 2009, six states have passed laws allowing virtual visitation to be incorporated into custody decisions,

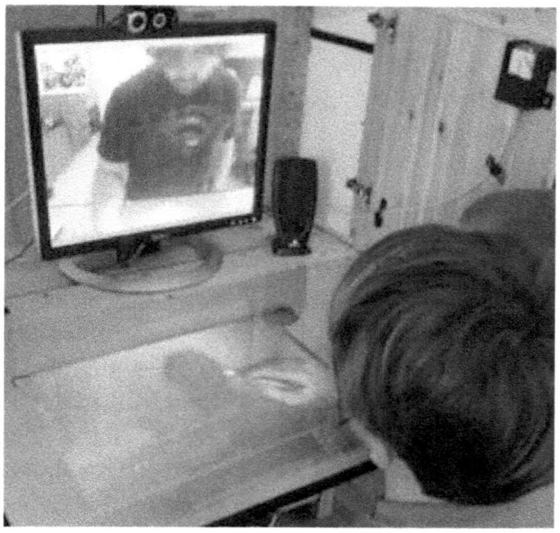

Figure 1. Parent and child using the ShareTable at home.

stating that "technology may be able to help maintain a relationship that would otherwise cease" [31]. Several recent investigations have pointed to the potential of videochat technologies to enrich remote interaction with children by providing a context for the communication and expressiveness (e.g., [3,21]). However despite these opportunities, videochat is problematic for many families because children find it difficult to initiate a videochat session and rarely do so [3] and interaction over videochat is focused on conversation rather than care and play, which are the primary ways children build closeness with their family [9].

This work contributes to the ongoing efforts to address these two challenges by presenting a field deployment of the ShareTable system, which provides easy-to-initiate videochat and a shared tabletop task space for sharing physical objects. We present the results of a month-long field deployment of the ShareTable system in four divorced households. This work has three contributions, emerging from the three research questions that drove our investigation:

- How do families use a system that combines easy-to-initiate videochat and a shared tabletop task space?
- How is such a system different from previous technologies used by these families?
- What social practices and rules emerge around the use of such a system in divorced families?

We begin a brief description of the ShareTable prototype. We proceed with an account of previous related video-mediated communication systems and investigations of remote parent–child contact. Next, we provide an overview of the study methods. Then, we present the findings of the study in the context of the three research questions above. Finally, we discuss the broader implications of our findings and provide directions for future investigations and design.

SHARETABLE SYSTEM

The ShareTable system consists of two cabinets, one in the home of the parent and one in the home of the child. To make it easy to initiate a connection and to empower the child to connect without help, we use a physical metaphor. To place a call through the system, the user simply needs to open the doors of the ShareTable cabinet. The paired table in the other household rings, as would a phone. Opening the cabinet doors answers the call; closing the cabinet doors ends it. Once a call is connected, the monitor screen of the ShareTable shows a standard face-to-face videochat view (Fig. 1). Additionally, the local table surface of the ShareTable shows a projected view of the remote table surface and vice versa. This allows the system to support the parent and child in shared activities rather than only conversation. For example, the child can draw a cat on her side and the child's parent would be able to draw a hat directly on the head of the projected cat on his table. Since the drawings are aligned and scaled on both tables, both would see the same image of the cat wearing the hat.

The face-to-face video and audio is achieved by leveraging the Skype4COM API to initiate a full-screen videochat session. The ShareTable surface is a C# component that extends the Axis Media Control API to display a processed image of the partner surface. A projector mounted above the table surface provides a 20"x16" projection on the tabletop. The tabletop surface image is captured by a 207MW Axis Camera at 1024x768 resolution and sent directly to the partner table using the Axis camera's internal server. The door sensor that triggers initiation or answering of a call is reed switch on an Arduino board mounted on the cabinet door and a magnet mounted on the table shelf. The technical challenges of this system and employed solutions are described in more detail in previous work [41].

RELATED WORK

In this section, we present relevant video-mediated communication technologies, we discuss the unique characteristics of the parent–child relationship, and we highlight the needs of parents and children in divorced families.

Video-Mediated Communication

We drew inspiration from the body of research on remote communication in the office, particularly the concept of a media space. A media space is an audio and video connection between two locations for the purpose of maintaining social and work connections. Media spaces have been used since the mid-80s to support collaborations between geographically distributed offices [6]. The audio–video connection can be supplemented with a shared workspace to support collaboration over documents, data, etc. There are a number of such media spaces which share implementation aspects with the ShareTable, including TeamWorkStation [18] and Videodraw [34].

The PlayTogether system is most similar to the ShareTable in its use of top-down projection for sharing physical objects [38]. Microsoft Research expanded this work into the domain of supporting remote communication between children [42]. Most recently, they created the Illumishare system, which significantly expands on the possibilities of camera–projector-based sharing by creating a robust echo cancellation system usable with any surface [17]. However, all these systems are early prototypes and have only been explored in the lab setting (similar to early investigations of the ShareTable [41]). The ShareTable is the first of such systems to be put in the field and tested with real families.

Remote Contact with Children

Designing for parents and young children presents unique challenges due to the (1) asymmetry in needs between the parent and child, (2) the challenges posed by the cognitive and emotional abilities of young children, and (3) a greater need for play and care than direct communication.

The parent–child relationship is characterized by asymmetry. Dalsgaard et al. found that the parent carried a greater responsibility for maintaining the relationship by creating a setting for trust and unity, providing care, and participating in play [9]. Children rarely verbally expressed affection and they self-disclosed less than their parents desired. Interviews with work-separated families highlight that parents and children have different emotional responses to separation and technology must balance the disparate needs and motivations of participants to succeed [25,39]. The second challenge is that the child's cognitive and emotional limitations may make long-distance contact difficult. Young children are still developing the communication competencies to participate meaningfully in conversations without shared context [32]. Children also have limited attention resources and motivation for remote contact, so families find it difficult to keep a remote communication session engaging enough to hold the child's attention [5]. The third challenge is that closeness in a parent–child relationship is built more through play and care together than through conversation [9]. Development literature emphasizes the importance of parental involvement in both instrumental care and play activities for secure relationships [22].

A number of systems have been targeted explicitly at supporting remote interaction in adult–child relationships. In eKiss [10] and Collage [36], children could share photos with adult family members to provide a context for later synchronous conversation. Other systems are aimed at supporting remote activities together such as playing games [11,14,25] and reading together [28]. We present a field deployment of a novel synchronous communication system quite different from other field investigations in this domain, in that it is a medium for synchronous communication that can support a number of different activities, rather than a single activity. We also approach a largely overlooked family context—divorced families.

Opportunities in Supporting Divorced Families

Two in-depth interview studies with divorced families suggest that members of divorced families balance two major goals: reducing tensions between households and maintaining closeness [27,40]. Children may try to reduce tensions by keeping the details of their involvement with the other parent as private as possible. Parents may seek to reduce conflict by maintaining only minimal contact with each other, respecting each other's autonomy, and minimizing unscheduled interruptions of the other household. However, both of these goals may conflict with the parents' desire to remain aware of the child's everyday activities to provide support and drive conversation. The parent's need to minimize interruption may also clash with the child's goal of achieving spontaneous contact, as it leads to a regimented schedule of interaction with few opportunities for spur-of-the-moment conversation. Both parents and children expressed that they would prefer to stay in touch through something richer than phone conversations, but found that asymmetric rules, technical literacy, and access to infrastructure between households often lead to the lowest common technological denominator. One of the outcomes of this work is a better understanding of these constraints.

ShareTable in the Larger CSCW Context

The ShareTable represent a long-standing CSCW tradition of taking remote communication from the office into the home space [6]. CSCW explorations of communication in the home center on the ideas of closeness (e.g., [23]) and playful contact (e.g., [33]), both central to the philosophy of the ShareTable design. Our chosen evaluation approach is in line with the typical CSCW epistemological approach of focusing on longer deployments and richer qualitative data gathered from a smaller number of families (e.g., [35]), rather than large-scale quantitative studies.

In its larger scope, this paper contributes to an ongoing CSCW discussion about designing for families [26]. Families are incredibly heterogeneous, so this investigation focuses specifically on divorced families. However, some of the findings may be extended to other forms of separation. Other investigations point out that issues of conflict, control, and motivating communication are not unique to the context of divorce (e.g., [19,39]). Studying divorced families foregrounds these issues that are present in all families but may otherwise not be discussed as primary concerns.

METHODS

The ShareTable was deployed with two Atlanta-area divorced families (four households) in an A-B design with a two-week pre-deployment and a four-weeks deployment period. The system was evaluated using a mixed-methods approach combining multiple sources data.

Participants

The two families participating in this study (all names anonymized) were selected through a professional recruitment firm, with a call for divorced families with young children interested in testing a new communication technology. We opted for the benefits of a longer deployment rather than more participants. This allowed us to see use over time and conduct a more in-depth investigation than would have been otherwise possible.

Family 1

Simon is the 7-year-old son of **Matt** and **Nadia**. Matt and Nadia have been divorced for 5 years and they currently live a 45–60 minute drive apart. Matt and Nadia both describe their current relationship as fairly low-conflict. Matt is recently remarried to **Mary** and lives with Mary and **Jeffrey**, her 3-year-old child from a previous relationship. Nadia is remarried to **Rod** and pregnant with Simon's new half-brother. Simon spends 2–3 nights per week with his father and the rest with his mom. Simon and Nadia communicate almost exclusively by phone. Matt and Simon also communicate by phone, but have recently tried videochat as well. Though Matt has purchased the necessary equipment for Nadia's home, she rarely uses videoconferencing and Matt finds it difficult to do so without her support. In Matt's home, the ShareTable was set up in the living room; in Nadia's home, it was in Simon's room.

Family 2

Taylor (11, boy) and **Kennedy** (7, girl) are the children of David and Kelly. **David** and **Kelly** have been divorced for 7 years and they currently live 60-minutes apart. Both David and Kelly describe their relationship as fairly low-conflict. Taylor lives with his father, spending alternate weekends with Kelly. Kelly lives with her partner **Jason** and Kennedy. Kennedy spends alternate weekends with David. Taylor and Kennedy spend weekends together. Additionally, David is the father of 2-year-old **Casey**. Casey lives with David's ex-girlfriend but David gets custody every other weekend. Taylor has his own mobile phone and communicates with both of his parents by calling or sending text messages. Kennedy does not have her own phone and Kelly's house does not have a land line telephone, so David usually calls Kelly's cell phone and she passes it to Kennedy to talk. Kelly and David have previously attempted videochat on special occasions, but found that it was too problematic. In Kelly's home, the ShareTable was set up in the children's room; in David's home, it was in the den.

Procedure

During the recruitment process, we made sure that both sides of the families were interested in participating. At the first meeting, specific consent procedures involved gathering informed consent from each parent, parental consent from the primary parent for each child, and the child's assent to participate. During this process, we described the potential risks and participant rights in an age-appropriate fashion, as approved by our institutional review board. To protect the privacy of each participant, interviews and questionnaires were conducted separately whenever possible.

During the pre-deployment, we interviewed each family. We spoke to any children over 6 who live in the house, both of the parents, and any cohabitating current partners. The questions focused on current strategies that each family uses to stay in touch and the specific challenges of their arrangement. We asked each parent to fill out a Network of Relationships Inventory (NRI) [15] describing their relationships to their past partner, current partner, and the children participating in the study. We asked each child to fill out a shortened NRI inventory (presenting only one question from each scale of interest) describing their relationships with their parents and any stepparents. For each communication medium that the family used regularly, we asked both the parents and the children to fill out an appropriate version of the Affective Benefits and Costs of Communication Technologies (ABCCT) questionnaire [43]. Finally, we provided each member of the family with a diary and asked them to log any remote contact between the parent and the child. The adult version of the diary asked about the length of the communication, the medium used, and the topic of the conversations. The child version of the diary asked the child to circle or draw the medium used and topic of conversation. Each family kept these preliminary diaries for at least 14 days. We conducted weekly interviews about the provided entries.

During the deployment, ShareTable was installed in each home and the system was introduced using example scenarios. We also explained that the system would log use and record any ongoing calls. However, videos were only stored locally and participants could mark any session for deletion. We asked participants to continue keeping communication diaries and we continued weekly interviews with participants for the next 28 days. Finally, each participant was asked to complete the NRI and ABCCT again.

The two deployments were conducted consecutively since only one pair of prototypes existed. At the end of each deployment, we asked each family if they had advice for the next family who would try out the system, which was a good way for us to elicit best practices. This advice from Family 1 (but no other gathered data) was passed on to Family 2 when we deployed the ShareTable. It was up to the family whether to accept this advice or not (in this case, they did not). This represents an Action Research [37] approach to an intervention. The two case study deployments should be viewed through this lens rather than as tightly controlled studies.

Analysis

There were a number of quantitative metrics gathered through the course of the study: ABCCT responses, NRI responses, and descriptive statistics of log and diary data. Because of the low number of participants in this study, we focus on general descriptive statistics in reporting this data rather than hypothesis testing. There were also numerous sources of qualitative data in this study: field notes, interviews, video logs, and diaries. These were transcribed and an initial round of open coding and memoing was conducted on all four of these sources of information. We followed the qualitative analysis process described by Seidman to create thematic connections using a data-driven approach [29]. We extracted statements of interest and grouped these together by theme. We conducted three such passes through all of the data, refining the themes with each pass until a set of distinct themes emerged. Though the process was largely data-driven, we were also influenced by the research questions posed at the outset of the study. After conducting the analysis, we grouped the themes by the research question addressed. This is the structure we use to report the results.

Limitations

One limitation of our design is that we were only able to collect self-report data for the pre-deployment communication. This was particularly problematic for the Family 2 who frequently estimated the lengths of sessions. In weekly interviews, we asked the family to specify the length of the session within a range that they thought would definitely include the actual length (e.g., "between 5 and 10"). We use the upper range in the quantitative reporting to not overestimate the effect of the ShareTable on session lengths.

Because the ShareTable is a prototype that combines a number of diverse technologies, it did not work perfectly all the time. In fact, something went wrong in 9 out of the 24 sessions with the ShareTable. These problems included choppy face-to-face video (Skype problems), projector taking more than 3 minutes to start, one of the Axis cameras failing to connect (thus one person could see the other's table, but not vice-versa), and audio being too low. In 3 of these 9 cases, the users contacted us and we were able to correct the system through remote access, but in the remaining 6 cases the families used the system as-is, thus missing out on potential benefits of the ShareTable. Most of these were minor problems and the families still continued using the system. The participants' willingness to put up with system bugs highlights the value that the system provided to their lives, even when everything did not work perfectly.

Finally, as in all such deployments [8], there is a strong potential for the observer effect and demand characteristics to bias the final findings. For example, the parents might feel the pressure to perform as a "perfect parent" for the researcher, thereby increasing the number of communication sessions and changing their content. Brown et al. recommend changes to how HCI researchers conduct field trials to help moderate these effects: diversifying methods, moving beyond success vs. failure analysis, and emphasizing the unique characteristics of each participant [8]. We act on all three of these recommendations in this work.

FINDINGS

Families used the ShareTable to provide a playful context for communication, enable instrumental support, and provide a virtual meeting place to share moments and affection. It was more effective than the previous technologies used by these families, but structuring social practices around use proved to be a challenge to both families.

ShareTable Use

The ShareTable was designed to support a number of joint activities by providing both face-to-face video and a shared workspace. We saw use of the system that fell into three categories: (1) creating a playful context for conversation, (2) providing instrumental care, and (3) using the ShareTable as a meeting place for sharing the objects and moments.

Creating a Playful Context

Parents and children used the ShareTable to create a playful context for interaction through drawing together, playing around, and show-and-tell.

Drawing together was the most common way that the families in the study used the surface. Frequently, there was a playful and collaborative nature to the drawing, as the remote participant tried to guess what the local participant was producing. Simon frequently leveraged the ability to synchronously share his drawing as it was being created, by asking his father to guess it (video logs are color coded to show remote versus local participants):

> **Simon**: *Awesome! Cool, cool. Look what I drew.*
> **Matt**: *Yeah, what is that? Is that DNA?*
> **Simon**: *No, it's like... Oh wait, it kind of does look like DNA.*
> **Matt**: *That's what I said...*
> **Simon**: *Except there's no lines... Just wait one second...*
> **Matt**: *Yep, there's the DNA.*
> **Simon**: *[Jeffrey], look at my DNA!*

After Matt provided an interesting suggestion, Simon changed his drawing to play along.

Interaction over the ShareTable was inherently playful, however unstructured playful activities were much more common than structured games. The only structured play we saw were four separate examples of playing tic-tac-toe. Other types of play were more focused on playful actions and show-and-tell. Playful actions were frequently spontaneous and child-initiated, such as dancing and playing tag with hands on the table. Parents often became the audience for playful physical show-and-tell activities:

> **Simon**: *Watch my eyes. You ready?*
> **Rod**: *Yeah [Laughs as Simon tries to roll his eyes so that only the whites of his eyes are showing]*
> **Jeffrey**: *Those are zombie eyes.*

The ShareTable became a venue for the child to show off new skills and playact new stories with toys. There were five separate examples of playful show-and-tell, including puppets and showing magic tricks. Most of these examples used the face-to-face video as a primary view, however in two of the cases the tabletop view was used as well to provide the parent with an opportunity to "touch" a particular toy that was being shared. For example:

> **Kelly**: *Where is your baby doll? Or, what's her name?*
> **Kennedy**: *Her name is Daisy ... I'll go get her...*
> **Kelly**: *Oh, there's Daisy! [strokes Daisy's hair on the tabletop] I missed you, Daisy.*

Two examples of playful activities involved mostly audio (e.g., doing funny accents to each other), five involved primarily the face-to-face video (two physical playfulness and three show-and-tell), two involved both the face-to-face video and the tabletop (show-and-tell), and four involved primarily the tabletop (all cases of tic-tac-toe).

Providing Instrumental Support

Parents provided instrumental care using the ShareTable by supporting learning and participating in co-parenting.

Parents have frequently described the frustrating interaction of trying to engage in their child's learning experience remotely (e.g., [40]). However, throughout the ShareTable deployment, we saw several examples of parents engaging with their child's learning experience. For example, Simon and his mother practiced math problems remotely:

> **Nadia**: *Good job! Let me give you one.*
> **Simon**: *Give me a math problem I'll write it.*
> **Nadia**: *OK. [Writes on the table]*
> **Simon**: *It has to be a big one.*
> **Nadia**: *It's a plus. [Waits for him to write out the answer]*
> **Nadia**: *That's right, Babbo. Good job!*

However, only two examples of supporting learning leveraged face-to-face or tabletop video. The other three involved only audio: a question-answer session, a quiz, and practicing singing a song in a foreign language.

We did not see explicit homework help activity, though this activity was compelling to the parents in this study:

> *I especially want to use it to go over homework. I feel like the other house has been slacking and [Simon] hasn't been keeping up with it. I'd love to look at the homework and get him to practice his spelling and all that.* -Matt

One aspect of the system prevented this from being a more common activity—the participants found it difficult to read small text over the surface of the table. Though we did provide 1024 X 768 resolution for the surface (best possible under bandwidth constraints), this was barely good enough for 16-point text and impractical for anything smaller. Though most of the younger children's worksheets were viewable, it was straining and much more practical for these families to defer this task until they could be together.

Parents used the ShareTable to practice co-parenting and care activities. Co-parenting is a term to describe the activity of parenting together, when both of the parents provide care and discipline to the child [12]. This is seen as a particularly rare occurrence in divorced families, where the most common approach is "parallel parenting" (dad's house, dad's rules; mom's house, mom's rules) [1]. However, we saw several examples of co-parenting in the ShareTable video logs. For example, David and Kelly collaborate to convince Kennedy to clean her room after David sees its state over the ShareTable face-to-face video:

> ***David***: *You need to clean your room, princess!*
> ***Kelly***: *Yeah, she needs to give away to feel better. She needs to go through her room today and pick some toys to give away. Otherwise, Santa won't have any room, right?*
> ***David***: *Yes, I'm going up there to inspect your room and if it isn't clean, it's not a good thing.*
> ***Kennedy***: *Okay, okay, okay...*
> ***Kelly***: *But you don't mind right, [Kennedy]? You don't mind giving away some of your toys to those in need to make room for some new ones, right?*
> ***Kennedy***: *No, I don't.*

There were four other examples of both parents parenting together from throughout the course of the logs. There were also seven additional examples where one parent remotely provided instrumental care for the child, for example:

> ***Kelly***: *Oh, hey, let me see. Are all of your teeth still there? Yeah? Okay, just making sure. Are you brushing them?*
> ***Kennedy***: *... Umm ...*
> ***Kelly***: *[Kennedy], you gotta brush those nasty teeth! ...*
> ***Kennedy***: *I'm gonna brush my teeth today.*
> ***Kelly***: *Okay, that's a great idea.*

Interestingly, children felt confident in turning to a remote adult to resolve a local situation. For example, when Jeffrey tries to take the markers from Simon's table:

> ***Simon***: *No, give back the markers! [wrestling over them] [Rod], can you make him give me? [looks at Rod on screen]*
> ***Rod***: *Play nice and share half of them, okay?*

It was encouraging to see that co-parenting and care interactions were possible and common over the ShareTable.

ShareTable as a Meeting Place

The ShareTable became a metaphorical meeting place where physical objects, special moments, and physical affection could be shared.

One aspect of being a child from a divorced family is having two homes with two mailing addresses and two distinct locations for all of your physical belongings [27], so mail became a common object to be shared using the tabletop surface. Matt shared a card from a grandparent with Simon using the ShareTable system. Thus, the card could be shared on the appropriate holiday, rather than waiting for the next in-person visit several days later:

> ***Matt***: *Grandma sent you a card, actually, a Halloween card. Do you want to wait or do you want me to open it?*
> ***Simon***: *Open it!*
> ***Matt***: *"Cooked up these happy wishes, especially for you. Because it's that time of the year, when you send a happy boo. Happy Halloween, Love Grandma & Grandpa." See? Look!*
> ***Simon***: *Cool!*
> ***Matt***: *And, you get to see this ... this is also in it.*
> ***Simon***: *Oh, a check! How much is it?*
> ***Matt***: *Grandma and Grandpa sent you a $5 check!*

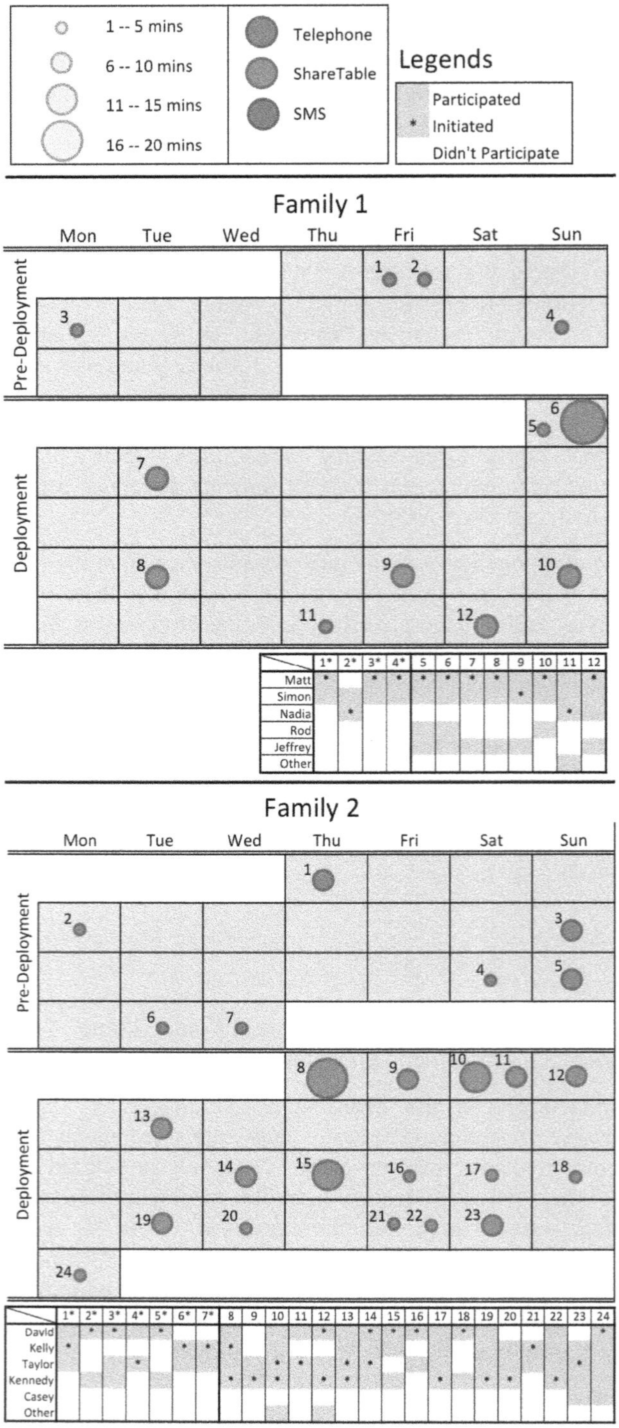

Figure 2. Specifics of each remote communication session in families 1 and 2 before and during the deployment. Medium is specified by color, length of session by size. Session labels in calendar figure correspond to columns in participation tables.

One benefit of the ShareTable over holding an item up to the face-to-face camera is that the object can remain on the table for the duration of the conversation. This particularly worked well for Family 2, where interactions typically involved three or more people at the same time, tended to get hectic, and a shared item would otherwise be overlooked:

Kennedy: Look at what daddy did to my nails? [puts her hands on table, while about 5 minutes of other conversation passes between Kelly and Taylor]
Kelly [looks down]: Oh my god! Your nails! [points to Kennedy's hand] ... Are these your nails, these long ones?
Kennedy: No, they're fake. Dad put them on.

In the logged videos, there were three cases of mail being shared, two cases of showing toys and games on the surface, and two cases of schoolwork being shown.

Family 2 frequently used the ShareTable to share special moments and everyday life. Several times, the father would call the children over the weekend before a sports game that all three of them were planning to watch. Even though the ShareTable was not used during the actual game, the father found this to be a compelling interaction:

We ended up talking around noon and before the game. So, that was almost like we were watching together! -David

The father's communication with the children in Family 2 was generally spontaneous. As such, the children frequently included him in whatever they were doing, rather than interrupting their activity to talk. In one moment, Taylor shares playtime during a friend's visit, while Kennedy narrates:

Taylor: Look, this is a game that me and [my friend] made up... [Taylor and his friend tackle each other]
Kennedy: Look. It's so funny! They tackle each other as boys.
Taylor: Then we start punching each other! [laughing]

Family 2 celebrated Christmas towards the end of the deployment period. The ShareTable became the medium for the children to share the excitement of the moment and show off their newest presents to their father. Overall, sharing the moment occurred more in the second family than in the first, because the former incorporated spontaneous messaging into their practices with the ShareTable. In the first family, Matt attempted to initiate similar sessions (e.g., calling late on Halloween hoping to see the candy that Simon received during trick-or-treating), however all spontaneous connections were usually rejected by Nadia.

The most common type of interaction with the ShareTable focused not on a specific activity or topic, but rather on building closeness and communicating love through metaphorical touch. Perhaps the best example of this type of interaction was Kelly talking to Taylor while he was sick:

Kelly: What's going on, baby?
Taylor: Well, my throat is acting up...
Kelly: Awww, well take care of yourself ... what else is wrong, sweetheart? ... You look like you're really sad, honey!
Taylor: I just don't feel good.
Kelly: All right, well listen. I love you ... Do you see my hand, holding on to your hand? [Strokes his projected hand]
Taylor: Yes, I do.
Kelly: I love you, baby.
Taylor: I love you too, mom.
Kennedy: Hey, Bubba. [Also puts her hand on the table]
Kelly: There's my hand. Keep your hand in there, we're going to do a family handshake, okay? [Kelly, Kennedy, and Taylor move their hands on the table together]

Family 1		
	Pre	Deployment
Avg. Mins/Week	5.25	17.50
Avg. Session Mins	2.63	8.75
Avg. Sessions/Week	2.00	2.00
Initiated by Child	0%	12.5%
Family 2		
	Pre	Deployment
Avg. Mins/Week	14.98	33.67
Avg. Session Mins	7.50	7.35
Avg. Sessions/Week	2.00	4.58
Initiated by Child	14.3%	64.3%

Figure 3. Aggregate session characteristics data.

The face-to-face video was key to Kelly noticing that Taylor may have been more sick than his voice sounded, but it was the ShareTable surface that allowed her to act towards him to convey emotional care through "physical" touch. All in all, there were 20 separate examples of metaphorical physical touch interaction in the video logs. Most of these were fairly brief kisses or hugs towards the end of the conversation. However, four separate cases were longer interactions as the one above and involved the table surface.

Comparing ShareTable to Previous Technologies

One goal of this investigation was to understand how the ShareTable was different from other communication technologies routinely used by the families in the study.

Participation in ShareTable Use vs. Previous Technologies

In the pre-deployment phase, we asked the parents and children to keep diaries of remote communication. Family 1 collected four diaries over the course of 14 days. All four described telephone calls. Family 2 collected seven diaries over the course of 21 days (the extra week of pre-deployment was due to a delay in getting the ShareTable installed). Six of these described phone conversations, while one described an SMS exchange. Both families continued keeping communication diaries during the deployment. Family 1 recorded eight conversations in a 28-day period, with seven of those being over the ShareTable. Family 2 recorded 17 conversations in a 26-day period, with all but one of those using the ShareTable. Figure 2 shows the specifics of each communication session before and during the ShareTable deployment. It is important to note that children initiated a greater proportion of conversations during the ShareTable deployment, ShareTable sessions generally involved a greater number of participants, and more time was spent communicating using the ShareTable than previous technologies. Figure 3 shows the overall statistics of the amount of time each family spent communicating, showing the weekly average for each family increased more than two-fold.

Effect on Relationship Quality

We asked each parent and child in the study to complete a Network of Relationships Inventory [15] before and after the deployment. The NRI uses a five-point Likert scale, asking the participant to evaluate different aspects of various relationships. Here, we highlight those aspects that changed by more than 1 point before and after the deployment, but all findings are displayed in Figure 5. The most striking changes can be seen in Taylor's inventory, which reported a more supportive relationship with his mother and a less antagonistic relationship with both his mother and father. In interviews he reflected that much of the antagonism was previously due to the fact that he did not call enough—an issue eased by the ShareTable. Kelly (Taylor's mom) reported a greater sense of intimacy with him after the deployment. The ShareTable also seemed to have the same effect on David's relationship with his daughter. Family 1 reported fewer changes on their NRI. Simon reported a higher level of satisfaction in his relationship with his father, but no other positive changes. There was a negative change that Nadia reported in her sense of reliable alliance with Matt. It seems that the table did introduce some conflict for this family that was captured by the NRI. Overall, the ShareTable may have contributed to some positive relationship outcomes for both families, though also some potentially negatives ones for Family 1. We emphasize that the quantitative findings are meant to be used to corroborate the qualitative findings, not to make broad generalizations about all families. Additionally, small changes should be treated conservatively as they can represent natural variation rather than an actual difference between pre and post measurements.

Comparison with the Telephone

The families in the study were aware of the challenges of using the phone to talk to a child even at the onset of the study. As David said, "the phone is really too short and it's so easy to get distracted and want to go do something else." This is consistent with findings from previous investigations (e.g., [5]). However, these families also faced additional challenges due to tensions introduced by divorce:

> *[Kennedy] doesn't have a phone and her mom doesn't have a landline, so I really have to call [Kelly] to talk to [Kennedy]. And that's awkward and I really can't even call every day and even when I do, it's for about 5 minutes, no more.* -David

> *[David] can be really a [problem] about it ... He wasn't picking up and [Taylor]'s phone was turned off or dead or whatever so I had no way of contacting him.* -Kelly

One contribution of this work is pointing out the specific factors that may make the phone less effective than the ShareTable. Figure 4 presents the results of the ABCCT questionnaire comparing the phone and the ShareTable. Overall, the ShareTable scored higher on each measure of benefit and lower on all but one measure of cost. Of most significant note, the ShareTable created fewer unwanted obligations to communicate, supported greater emotional expressiveness, more engagement & playfulness, and a greater sense of connectedness outside of the actual interaction (presence-in-absence) than the phone. These findings were also confirmed in the interviews:

> *Just in general, having the interaction is better. It's more fun and more like just killing time together ... It definitely makes it easier to keep it engaging for more than five minutes.* -Kelly

However, not all comparisons between the phone and ShareTable were favorable. In particular, the ShareTable introduced additional privacy concerns and did not provide the flexible mobility of a phone.

Comparison with Videochat

A previous investigation has compared the ShareTable to videochat in the lab [39]. However, in the field, the main difference between the ShareTable and videochat was that the first was used while the second was not. Though both of the families in the study reported trying out videochat, neither family used it routinely and not a single pre-deployment diary from either family described a videochat session. The father from Family 2 articulated the problem:

> *Video is nice, but getting it to work wasn't worth it ... we spent an hour and a half setting up a call, which lasted five minutes. It gets to the point when it's not worth it.* -David

It seems that without an easy way to initiate and answer a connection, videochat was simply not a usable solution for these families. In fact, these results are consistent with findings from other studies, which show that only some families who try videochat use it routinely (e.g., [39]). This was confirmed by the extremely positive feedback from families about the physical metaphor of interacting with the system. For example, Kelly stated:

> *I think the biggest thing is just being able to just open the doors and connect. We don't have to log in or anything. It's just already there.* -Kelly

Additionally, interviews revealed that participants saw the surface as a significant component of the interaction that was different from the previous technologies:

> *It really added an extra depth dimension and another layer to*

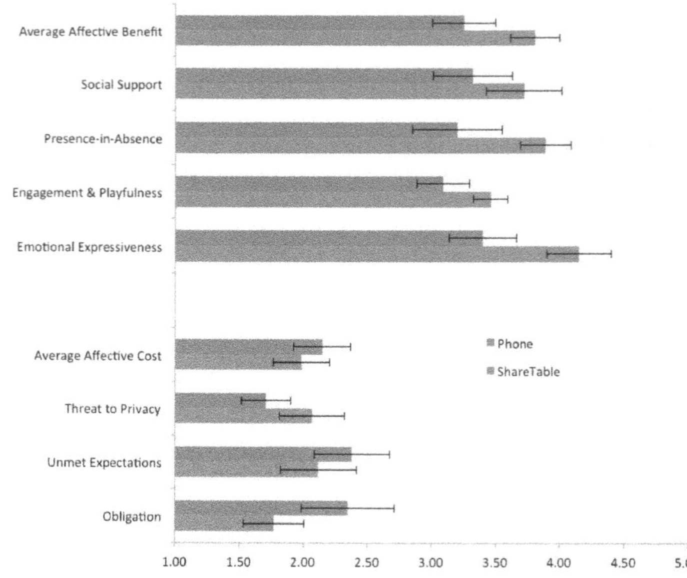

Figure 4. Results of the ABCCT questionnaire from 4 parents and 3 children in the study. Overall, ShareTable provided greater benefits but lower cost (except on the privacy scale).

the experience. I was surprised by how different it was from trying to do an online white board together. -Matt

The table itself ... there's just something about it, when you put your hand there and your daughter puts her hand on top, where you feel like you're almost touching. It's like, now I know why you called it the ShareTable. You really feel like you're sharing the moment. -David

Overall, participants recognized the ShareTable as a compelling medium and almost all parent–child communication during the deployment occurred over the ShareTable.

Social Practices around the ShareTable

During the four-week deployment, participants reflected on their experience through weekly interviews. These results provided insights into the rules and practices that emerged around use of the ShareTable system.

A big concern with the ShareTable was that remote contact might interrupt routines in the home:

If his dad calls, that just kind of means that [Simon] has to disengage from us in order to engage with his dad. -Rod

In Family 1, all contact was preceded by a telephone call to the mother to make sure that no household routines would be interrupted. Even when a ShareTable call was planned and a ShareTable connection was established, there were several times when the collocated parent decided that it wasn't a good time to talk:

***Matt**: I didn't get you guys at a bad time there?*
***Nadia**: Well, I mean. Normally, we're at the church at this time but we're really busy today, so ...*
***Matt**: Oh, all right ... Well, I'll catch you later.*

Nadia also cited concerns over interrupting the other household as the main reason she kept contact with Simon to a minimum while he was visiting his father:

I didn't use it that much and that was mostly because I feel guilty using it. We have [Simon] the majority of the time, so when he's at [Matt]'s, I want to respect that and give them time to be together. -Nadia

By contrast, in Family 2, the remote parent prioritized continued contact over the worry of interrupting the other home. While this did lead to more frequent use of the system, it also created conflict as routines were disrupted:

I did end up calling too early. You'll see mom yelling in the video because I called too early. -David

Neither arrangement was ideal for both households.

The ShareTable introduced a new source of conflict over appropriate practices around communication. One disagreement focused on the placement of the system:

I feel like right now, [Simon] would have to be in his room to hear when I call [Nadia's house]. Here, it's set up in a public space, so one of us hears it and lets him know, but there, unless he's in his room, I have to call first. -Matt

I'd say that it needs to be in a private room, especially if the divorced parents don't get along as much as we do. –Nadia

If I had known that this would be the outcome of putting it in [Taylor]'s room—that [David] feels like he can call night and day—I would have probably put it in the living room so that I could have more control over when it gets used. -Kelly

David was the only parent happy with the system's placement; all others thought that the ShareTable would be better in a different location. However, the general requirements of each parent are not contradictory. The ShareTable should be in a location where: (1) the child can hear it ring, (2) the privacy of the others is respected, and (3) parents have an appropriate amount of control over its use. However, families had trouble deciding on the appropriate amount of use.

In both families, the arrangement that was established did not work well for one of the parents. In Family 1, the dad

	Mother -> Simon	Mother -> Father	Mother -> Step-Father	Father -> Simon	Father -> Mother	Father -> Step-	Simon -> Mother	Simon -> Father	Father -> Kennedy	Father -> Mother	Kennedy -> Mother	Kennedy -> Father	Kennedy -> Step-Father	Mother -> Taylor	Mother -> Father	Mother -> Step-Father	Taylor -> Mother	Taylor -> Father
Support	-0.7	0.0	0.0	0.7	0.0	0.0	0.0	0.0	0.3	0.0	0.0	0.0	1.0	0.7	0.0	0.0	2.0	-1.0
Criticism	0.0	0.0	0.0	0.0	0.3	0.3	0.0	0.0	0.0	-0.3	0.0	0.0	0.0	0.0	0.0	0.0	-1.0	-1.0
Satisfaction	0.0	0.3	0.0	-0.7	-0.3	0.0	0.0	1.3	0.7	0.0	0.0	0.0	1.0	0.7	0.0	-0.3	0.0	0.0
Companionship	0.0	0.0	0.0	0.3	0.0	0.7	1.0	0.0	0.3	0.0	0.0	0.0	0.0	1.0	0.0	0.0	-1.0	1.0
Conflict	0.0	0.0	0.0	-0.3	-0.7	0.7	0.0	0.0	0.0	0.0	0.0	0.0	0.0	0.0	0.0	0.0	0.0	0.0
Instrumental Aid	-0.3	-0.7	1.3	-0.3	0.0	0.7	0.0	0.0	0.7	0.0	0.0	0.0	0.0	0.3	0.0	1.0	1.0	1.0
Antagonism	0.0	0.3	0.0	-0.3	0.3	0.0	0.0	0.0	0.0	0.0	0.0	0.0	0.0	0.0	0.3	0.0	-3.0	-2.0
Intimacy	-0.3	-0.7	0.0	-0.2	0.0	0.0	0.0	0.0	2.2	0.5	0.0	1.0	1.0	1.2	0.5	1.7	0.0	-1.0
Nurturance	0.0	-	-	-0.3	-	-	-	-	-0.3	-	-	-	-	1.0	-	-	-	-
Affection	0.0	0.3	0.0	-0.3	0.0	0.3	0.0	0.0	-0.7	0.0	0.0	0.0	0.0	0.0	0.0	0.0	1.0	1.0
Admiration	0.0	-0.7	0.0	-0.3	0.7	0.3	0.0	0.0	0.3	0.0	0.0	0.0	0.0	0.0	0.3	-0.3	-1.0	1.0
Relative Power	-	0.0	0.0	-	-0.3	0.0	-	-	-	-0.3	-	-	-	-	-0.3	0.0	-	-
Reliable Alliance	0.0	-2.0	0.0	-0.3	0.0	0.0	0.0	0.0	-0.3	0.0	0.0	0.0	0.0	0.0	0.0	-0.3	0.0	0.0

Figure 5. Differences in scores on each of the NRI scales, changes greater than 0.5 are highlighted (beneficial in green, detrimental in red). Children were asked to answer the NRI about each adult that they described as "part of their immediate family." The adults filled out the NRI about the non-residential/equal-custody child, their current partner, and the former partner. The "Nurturance" scale was only given to parents to describe relationship with child. The "Relative Power" scale was only given to adults to describe relationship with other adult members of the family. Small changes should be interpreted conservatively as they may show natural variation rather than an actual change in status.

had to call the mom ahead of time. This worked for Nadia, but curtailed available communication time for Matt:

> *We really try to think about it and arrange communication with the other person in mind. That's why [Matt] always messages me before calling—to make sure he's not interrupting anything.* -Nadia

> *I think that the biggest problem ... was actually the social coordination aspect of it. It seemed like it was really hard to get on. I always tried to call [Nadia] first or at least text or something to let her know what I'd be trying to ShareTable later, but that didn't always work.* -Matt

At the end of the study, we asked Nadia and Matt if they could recommend a better arrangement for the next family who would use the ShareTable. Both agreed that an ideal arrangement would be a set time every week to call.

This suggestion was passed on to Family 2 before the ShareTable was deployed. Family 2 tried to heed this, but got in the habit of calling spontaneously instead. This arrangement worked for David but not for Kelly:

> *Well, I'd say that our arrangement worked really well. We didn't really have a set time, but I could hear the ShareTable anywhere so the kids could just call any time.* -David

> *If you leave it up to a child or the dad, they really just go "Ahhh!" and use it all the time. Sometimes it felt like it was like "Enough calling! He just got to my house!"* -Kelly

After the deployment, Kelly and Taylor both agreed that an arranged time would have served the family better. However, David and Kennedy maintained that the existing way worked well. Unfortunately, the ShareTable can only work in the long run if all can agree on acceptable practices.

DISCUSSION

We provide some implications for design and consider the ShareTable deployment in the context of previous work.

Implications for Design

There are three lessons from the ShareTable that could be beneficial to other communication systems for families.

One of the big factors that contributed to the ShareTable's use was that **the connection was easy to initiate**. There was no log in screen, no user list, and no way to contact the wrong person. This allowed children initiate sessions without help. While ethnographic studies have acknowledged the difficult "work" behind videochat [3], most studies of communication technologies have not addressed this issue. In field studies of such systems, the issue has been avoided through always-on connections (e.g. [20]) or by assuming that a parent will help set up the session (e.g. [28]). Neither is a reasonable solution for divorced families. Simplifying the process of initiating a session may be beneficial to use.

Second, the ShareTable was more engaging for families than previous communication mediums because **communication focused on activities rather than just conversation**. The parents described that previous communication was characterized by the brevity of each session. Sometime after a few minutes of conversation, the parent would run out of questions and the silence would become uncomfortable. With the ShareTable, we saw these silences becoming opportunities for the children to invent activities, show-and-tell with new toys and skills, or simply hold hands and feel together. While the ShareTable allowed these activities to incorporate physical objects, digital sharing may provide similar benefits to remote parent–child interaction.

Third, one of the most valuable aspects of the ShareTable was that **presenting overlapped video of the local and remote spaces** supported emotional interactions, such as holding hands. In fact, there is something powerful about *sharing* the video space rather than a standard videochat window-in-window view. Other studies have noted the power of a shared video arrangement for creating a feeling of shared narrative [13] and for simplifying perspective taking on the part of the child [42]. In this study, we saw another benefit—this arrangement created a greater sense of closeness and a good metaphor for physical touch. Even though the ShareTable is quite different from the remote touch technologies considered in the HCI domain (e.g., [7]), it was successful at conveying an emotionally-meaningful sense of physical touch. In fact, a camera–projector system is not required to create this sense. Simply displaying the participants at the same scale on the screen, subtracting the background, and overlapping the video would let participants give virtual high-fives or even pick each other's nose.

In our future work, we will leverage tablet devices to take these lessons to a platform that can have wider penetration than a custom-built piece of furniture. All three of the lessons above can be integrated into an application. Though such an application will more likely focus on sharing digital rather than physical objects and experiences, comparing the ShareTable deployment with that of an app may help us understand the relative importance of this aspect of the system. Additionally, due to the relative ease of deployment of such an app we may be able to gather a larger number of participants and systematically vary the integration of each of the three lessons about to understand their relative importance to the family's experience (e.g., easy to initiate + built-in activities, but no overlapped video space).

ShareTable in Context of Existing Theories

Video media spaces have had a long history of exploration in the work place [6] and several CMC theories point to videochat as an appropriate medium for family communication. Media Richness Theory emphasizes that ambiguous and uncertain tasks require more immediate feedback, more cues for communication, and more emotional awareness. Remote parenting is certainly an example of such a task. Social Presence Theory suggests that video affords social awareness of the partner's state in a way that is more similar to in-person interaction than other media, and thus may be better at supporting tasks that are usually carried out in-person. However, there is significantly less theoretical grounding to consider the role of multiple streams of video on the richness of the interaction. Empirical work in the workplace highlights that videos of the collaborative task space and videos of the larger context of the remote room may often be more useful to remote participants than the face-to-face video view [16]. However, in this investigation we found that families interweaved use of the face-to-face and the tabletop video for each of the three major categories of their activity over the table. Both types of video contributed significant value to the participants.

Control and Conflict

Though the HCI community has been exploring technologies for divorced families through interview studies (e.g., [27]) and including divorced families in deployments (e.g., [10]), generally most deployments focus on more amicable types of distributed families. This study may provide insight on how communication technologies are adopted in situations where privacy and control may be of paramount importance to users and conflict is a fundamental aspect of the relationship. The idea of designing for conflict or disruption is an important thread within CSCW [24] and this work contributes to the conversation.

The ShareTable became a meeting place, essentially making the room where it is placed part of both the local house and the remote one. It may be hard for family members to develop practices around such a "cybrid misfit" [4]. For preserving privacy, the most likely place for such meeting place would be in the child's room. However, in order for it to work well in that setting the families still need to develop a reasonable agreement about appropriate times for calling.

In this study, parents struggled to control the amount of remote contact with the child. Too much remote contact interrupts household routines and takes time away from interacting with the local parent. Too little remote contact cuts the parent out of the life of the child and does not provide the remote parent with opportunities to share in the joys and burdens of childrearing. The two deployments represent two contrasting cases: one where the local parent limited the interaction considerably and another where the remote parent's spontaneous contact became a point of conflict. In both deployments, one parent ended up feeling slighted by the adopted practices. In the end, use of the ShareTable and similar technologies should be treated as a "virtual visitation" practice [31]. As such, decisions over its use need to be made explicitly and potentially with the help of a court-appointed counselor who can advise the parents in an objective manner. As it was, the ShareTable did introduce additional conflict into the lives of the families in the study. However, in the end, none of the four households rejected the technology. In fact, the ShareTable became the medium for almost all parent–child communication throughout the deployment. The benefits of this technology were seen to outweigh the costs introduced by increasing tensions over appropriate practices around its use.

CONCLUSION

We deployed the ShareTable with two divorced families for four weeks each. Remote communication more than doubled for these families while using the ShareTable and we saw an increase in the number of communication sessions initiated by the child. The ShareTable provided benefits over previous communication systems and supported activities that are impossible with other currently available technologies. One of the biggest successes of the system was in providing an overlapped video space that families appropriated to communicate metaphorical touch and a sense of closeness. However, the ShareTable also introduced a new source of conflict for the divorced parents and challenged the families as they tried to develop practices of using the system that would be acceptable to all involved. The families' experiences with the system and approach to these challenges inform future directions for investigation and design of communication systems for separated families.

ACKNOWLEDGMENTS

We thank all of our participants for volunteering their time and homes for this study. Many others helped with the logistics of running this study, especially the members of the Ubicomp Lab at Georgia Tech. This work was funded in part by a Nokia University Award.

REFERENCES

1. Amato, P.R. and Gilbreth, J.G. Nonresident Fathers and Children's Well-Being: A Meta-Analysis. *Journal of Marriage and the Family 61*, 3 (1999), 557–573.
2. Amato, P.R. The Consequences of Divorce for Adults and Children. *Journal of Marriage and the Family 62*, 4 (2000), 1269–1287.
3. Ames, M.G., Go, J., Kaye, J., and Spasojevic, M. Making Love in the Network Closet: The Benefits and Work of Family Videochat. *Proc. of CSCW*, (2010), 145–154.
4. Anders, P. Cybrids: Integrating Cognitive and Physical Space in Architecture. *Convergence: Research into New Media Technologies 4*, 1 (1998), 85–105.
5. Ballagas, R., Kaye, J. "Jofish," Ames, M., Go, J., and Raffle, H. Family communication: phone conversations with children. *Proc. of IDC*, ACM (2009), 321–324.
6. Bly, S.A., Harrison, S.R., and Irwin, S. Media spaces: bringing people together in a video, audio, and computing environment. *Commun. ACM 36*, 1 (1993), 28–46.
7. Brave, S., Ishii, H., and Dahley, A. Tangible interfaces for remote collaboration and communication. *Proc. of CSCW*, (1998), 169–178.
8. Brown, B., Reeves, S., and Sherwood, S. Into the Wild : Challenges and Opportunities for Field Trial Methods. *Proc. of CHI*, (2011), 1657–1666.
9. Dalsgaard, T., Skov, M.B., Stougaard, M., and Thomassen, B. Mediated intimacy in families: understanding the relation between children and parents. *Proc. of IDC*, (2006), 145–152.

10. Dalsgaard, T., Skov, M.B., and Thomassen, B.R. eKiss: Sharing Experiences in Families Through a Picture Blog. *Proc. of British HCI*, (2007), 67–75.
11. Davis, H., Skov, M.B., Stougaard, M., and Vetere, F. Virtual box: supporting mediated family intimacy through virtual and physical play. *Proc. of OZCHI*, ACM (2007), 151–159.
12. Doherty, W.J. and Beaton, J.M. Mothers and Fathers Parenting Together. In *Handbook of Family Communication.* Lawrence Erlbaum Associates, 2004, 269–286.
13. Follmer, S., Ballagas, R., Raffle, H., Spasojevic, M., and Ishii, H. People in Books : Using a FlashCam to Become Part of an Interactive Book for Connected Reading. *Proc. of CSCW*, (2012), 685–694.
14. Follmer, S., Raffle, H., Go, J., Ballagas, R., and Ishii, H. Video play: playful interactions in video conferencing for long-distance families with young children. *Proc. of IDC*, (2010), 49–58.
15. Furman, W. and Buhrmester, D. The Network of Relationships Inventory: Behavioral Systems Version. *International journal of behavioral development 33*, 5 (2009), 470–478.
16. Gaver, W.W., Sellen, A., Heath, C., and Paul Luff. One is not enough: multiple views in a media space. *INTERCHI*, ACM (1993), 335–341.
17. Inpen, K. and Junuzovic, S. Illumishare : Sharing Any Surface. *Proc. of CHI*, (2012), To Appear.
18. Ishii, H. and Miyake, N. Toward an open shared workspace: computer and video fusion approach of Team-WorkStation. *Commun. ACM 34*, 12 (1991), 37–50.
19. Judge, T.K., Neustaedter, C., Harrison, S., and Blose, A. Family Portals : Connecting Families Through a Multifamily Media Space. *Proc. of CHI*, (2011), 1205–1214.
20. Judge, T.K., Neustaedter, C., and Kurtz, A.F. The family window: the design and evaluation of a domestic media space. *Proc. of CHI*, ACM (2010), 2361–2370.
21. Judge, T.K. and Neustaedter, C. Sharing conversation and sharing life: video conferencing in the home. *Proc. of CHI*, ACM (2010), 655–658.
22. Kelly, J.B. and Lamb, M.E. Using Child Development Research to Make Appropriate Custody and Access Decisions for Young Children. *Family Court Review 38*, 3 (2000), 297–311.
23. Kirk, D.S., Sellen, A., and Cao, X. Home video communication: mediating 'closeness'. *Proc. of CSCW*, ACM (2010), 135–144.
24. Massimi, M., Dimond, J.P., and Dantec, C.A.L. Finding a New Normal: The Role of Technology in Life Disruptions. *Proc. of CSCW*, (2011), 719–728.
25. Modlitba, P.L. Globetoddler: Enhancing the experience of remote interaction for preschool children and their traveling parents. Masters Thesis. MIT. 2008.
26. Neustaedter, C., Brush, A., and McDonald, D.W. Designing for Families. *CSCW 2008 Workshops*, (2008).
27. Odom, W., Zimmerman, J., and Forlizzi, J. Designing for dynamic family structures: divorced families and interactive systems. *Proc. of DIS*, (2010), 151–160.
28. Raffle, H., Ballagas, R., Revelle, G., et al. Family Story Play: Reading with Young Children (and Elmo) Over a Distance. *Proc. of CHI*, ACM (2010).
29. Seidman, I. *Interviewing as Qualitative Research: A Guide for Researchers in Education And the Social Sciences*. Teachers College Press, New York, 1998.
30. Seltzer, J.A. and Bianchi, S.M. Children's Contact with Absent Parents. *Journal of Marriage and the Family 50*, 3 (1988), 663–677.
31. Shefts, K.R. Virtual Visitation: The Next Generation of Options for Parent-Child Communication. *Family Law Quarterly 36*, 2 (2002), 303–327.
32. Stafford, M. Communication Competencies and Sociocultural Priorities of Middle Childhood. In *Handbook of Family Communication*. Lawrence Erlbaum Associates, Mahwah, NJ, 2004, 311–332.
33. Strong, R. and Gaver, W.W. Feather, Scent, and Shaker: Supporting Simple Intimacy. *Proc. of CSCW*, (1996).
34. Tang, J.C. and Minneman, S.L. Videodraw: a video interface for collaborative drawing. *ACM Trans. Inf. Syst. 9*, 2 (1991), 170–184.
35. Tolmie, P. and Crabtree, A. Deploying research technology in the home. *Proc. of CSCW*, (2008), 639–648.
36. Vetere, F., Davis, H., Gibbs, M., and Howard, S. The Magic Box and Collage: Responding to the challenge of distributed intergenerational play. *Intl J of Human Computer Studies 67*, 2 (2009), 165–178.
37. Villiers, M.R. *Three approaches for interpretive information systems research: development research, action research and grounded theory.* (2005), 142 – 151.
38. Wilson, A.D. and Robbins, D.C. PlayTogether: Playing Games across Multiple Interactive Tabletops. *Workshop on Tangible Play*, (2007), 53–56.
39. Yarosh, S. and Abowd, G.D. Mediated Parent-Child Contact in Work-Separated Families. *Proc. of CHI*, (2011), 1185–1194.
40. Yarosh, S., Chew, Y.C., and Abowd, G.D. Supporting Parent-Child Communication in Divorced Families. *Intl J of Human Computer Studies 67*, 2 (2009), 192–203.
41. Yarosh, S., Cuzzort, S., Müller, H., and Abowd, G.D. Developing a media space for remote synchronous parent-child interaction. *Proc. of IDC*, (2009), 97–105.
42. Yarosh, S., Inkpen, K.M., and Brush, A. Video playdate: toward free play across distance. *Proc. of CHI*, (2010), 1251–1260.
43. Yarosh, S. and Markopoulos, P. Design of an instrument for the evaluation of communication technologies with children. *Proc. of IDC*, (2010), 266–269.

Sometimes When We Touch: How Arm Embodiments Change Reaching and Coordination on Digital Tables

Andre Doucette[1], Carl Gutwin[1], Regan Mandryk[1], Miguel Nacenta[2], Sunny Sharma[1]

[1]Department of Computer Science
University of Saskatchewan
Saskatoon, SK, Canada
{firstname.lastname}@usask.ca

[2]School of Computer Science
University of St Andrews
St Andrews, UK
mans@st-andrews.ac.uk

ABSTRACT
In tabletop work with direct input, people avoid crossing each others' arms. This natural touch avoidance has important consequences for coordination: for example, people rarely grab the same item simultaneously, and negotiate access to the workspace via turn-taking. At digital tables, however, some situations require the use of indirect input (e.g., large tables or remote participants), and in these cases, people are often represented with virtual arm embodiments. There is little information about what happens to coordination and reaching when we move from physical to digital arm embodiments. To gather this information, we carried out a controlled study of tabletop behaviour with different embodiments. We found dramatic differences in moving to a digital embodiment: people touch and cross with virtual arms far more than they do with real arms, which removes a natural coordination mechanism in tabletop work. We also show that increasing the visual realism of the embodiment does not change behaviour, but that changing the thickness has a minor effect. Our study identifies important design principles for virtual embodiments in tabletop groupware, and adds to our understanding of embodied interaction in small groups.

Author Keywords
Social norms, reaching, tabletops, embodiments.

ACM Classification Keywords
H.5.3 [**Group and Organization Interfaces**]: *CSCW*

INTRODUCTION
The way that people are embodied in tabletop groupware is determined in part by the interaction mechanism used for the system. Direct input implies that people are embodied with their real arms and hands, whereas indirect input (e.g., when using a mouse) means that a virtual embodiment must be used, such as a telepointer or a 'pantograph' line connecting their cursor to their location at the table.

CSCW '13, February 23–27, 2013, San Antonio, Texas, USA.

Direct and indirect input techniques have been studied frequently, and both have advantages and disadvantages for tabletop work. Direct input is natural and easy for novices to learn, and works well when artifacts are within arms' reach. However, direct input is problematic when tables are large and objects are farther away. Indirect input, in contrast, makes it easy for people to reach all areas of the table; studies have shown indirect input to be faster, more precise, and more efficient when targets are far away [5].

Less is known, however, about other effects of the user embodiments that arise from different input types. Direct input uses people's real arms and hands, and so provides obvious awareness cues for others around the table. Indirect input uses a virtual embodiment on the table surface, and this embodiment can take a wide variety of visual forms. Understanding how things change when systems move from real to virtual embodiments is critically important for the design of tabletop groupware, because of the strong interaction patterns that people exhibit with physical bodies. In particular, people working at a table with their real arms and hands almost never touch or cross one another's arms. This behaviour on tables may stem from the natural touch avoidance [1] that affects our spatial interactions with others, or it may be an attempt to avoid disrupting another person's activities (for example, getting in their way or occluding their view of the workspace).

People's unwillingness to touch or cross arms provides an implicit coordination mechanism for tabletop work – that is, people are careful to negotiate access to shared areas of the table, and rarely reach for the same object. In addition, people use the mechanism in other ways, such as protecting objects by laying an arm around an area of the table. What happens to this natural coordination mechanism, however, when tabletop groupware moves to indirect input and virtual embodiments? Previous research provides conflicting views: work in VR suggests that social protocols are preserved when people are represented with digital avatars, but other research suggests that people may be more likely to break social rules at digital tables. An exploratory study [19] looked at several different arm embodiments on tables, and suggested that there are differences between real and virtual arms – but did not look at these differences in a controlled fashion.

To gather stronger empirical evidence about the differences between physical and virtual embodiments on digital tables, we carried out two studies. First, we examined social protocols for arm crossing at physical tables, and found that crossing and touching are extremely rare. Second, we carried out a large controlled study to look specifically at the effects of four factors – physicality of the embodiment, visual realism of a virtual representation, embodiment transparency, and embodiment size – on crossing and touching behaviour at a digital table. In addition, we investigated whether participants' relationship (strangers, acquaintances, romantic couples) affected crossing and touching behaviour with the different embodiment types.

The study showed four main results:

- There are dramatic differences in all measures of social behaviour between physical and digital embodiments;
- Increasing visual realism had no effect – people were just as likely to cross arms with a realistic picture arm as with a simple line embodiment;
- The occlusion resulting from the embodiment type did have a small effect on crossing behaviour;
- Relationship had a strong overall effect on the number of crossings, but did not interact with the other factors.

Our study provides new evidence about the effects of embodiment type on coordination over digital tables, and provides new insights about the principles underlying these findings. In particular, our results indicate that an actual tactile sensation is much more important than the visual arm representation in the phenomena of touch avoidance and the ensuing coordination mechanism for tabletop work. In addition, our results about size and occlusion suggest that people's desire to avoid inconveniencing others also affects their behaviour on shared tables. The findings from our study provide new design implications for supporting space management issues in digital table environments, and add new empirical results to our understanding of embodied interaction in small groups.

RELATED WORK

Our work draws from previous research into physical touch, personal space in the physical and digital worlds, and tabletop embodiment and input design.

Touch and Personal Space

Touch is the most intimate interpersonal communication channel. It is "...the most carefully monitored and guarded, the most vigorously proscribed and infrequently used, and the most primitive, immediate and intense of all communicative behaviours." [28, p.24]. Touch has many social functions – for example, it can demonstrate dominance or increase compliance (see [28] for a review).

Body-accessibility research has shown that people's comfort level with being touched on different parts of their body depends on who is doing the touching, where the touch occurs, and the type of touch [13,20]. Studies have shown that people are comfortable with touches on their arms and hands, regardless of gender [18] or relationship [8]; however, other principles of social interaction – such as touch avoidance [1] or inter-personal distance norms [6] – are likely to reduce the frequency of incidental arm and hand contact in work environments. Personal space is moderated by many factors, including age, relationship, culture, and gender [7]. Although invasions of personal space are generally avoided, people can accommodate these situations when necessary (e.g., in crowded elevators) [7].

Personal Space in Digital Environments

Researchers have shown that personal space does exist in digital environments. For example, in immersive virtual environments, people stand farther away from virtual humans that engage them in mutual gaze [2] (similar to the real world). People also assign personal space to avatars. For example, research has found that people treat their avatar's personal space as they would their own [12], that they are uncomfortable with invasions of their avatar's personal space (e.g., [12,21,22]), and that they use gaze avoidance to compensate for these invasions [31]. In addition, people avoid actions that could cause others to be uncomfortable (e.g., walking though another's avatar) [21].

Previous literature looks primarily at avatars, and less is known about the physical social norms governing other embodiments. Previous researchers assumed that social protocols would be enough to guide users' behaviour (e.g., [3]); however, other researchers reported this is not always the case [11,15]. In a magnetic poetry task over a touch table, users violated each other's personal space by reaching through private workspaces to reach an item, even stealing words from other users [15]. This may be because the digital world does not have the same social norms as the physical world. For example, in a remote task, people had little issue sitting "in each others' laps" [25].

Co-located and Distributed Multi-user Collaboration

Personal space and the digital representation of users were identified early on as important issues in the design of distributed collaborative spaces. For example, ClearBoard showed a remote collaborator as if she was on the other side of the same surface [10]. Other remote collaboration systems have used varying degrees of realism in representations of people's arms [25,26,30]. Most research on distributed groupware suggests that embodiments aid collaboration by increasing awareness and reducing potential conflict.

In contrast, co-located collaboration naturally provides more information about the positions and postures of collaborators; however, digital tools may disrupt conventional coordination mechanisms that rely on the physicality of action, such as those described by Tang [27]. Prior research in this area focused on comparing direct and indirect input and the effects on performance [5], coordination and conflict [9,17,19], and spatial interference [24,29]. Some evidence suggests that indirect input changes natural collaborative behaviours such as territoriality [23], and leads to an increase in coordination problems [16].

Pinelle et al. [19] carried out a broad exploratory study that is the closest previous work to ours. Pinelle looked at ways that different arm embodiments affected behaviours in a tabletop game. Their observations suggested several hypotheses, which we use as starting points for our investigations. First, they found differences between physical and digital arms (although the low level of interaction they observed between physical arms may have been caused by the large size of the table used in the study and the resulting distance between collaborators). Second, they saw only small differences between different types of digital embodiments, but found that people preferred more realistic representations, and were less comfortable reaching with larger embodiments [19].

Overall, the results of previous research (including those of Pinelle et al.) provide conflicting messages about the effects of moving from real to virtual embodiments; we still do not clearly understand the factors that change group behaviour on digital tabletops. For example, it is unclear whether changes in people's behaviour arise from physical touch (and people's attempts to avoid it), or from an awareness of others and a desire to avoid disrupting their work. Similarly, it is unclear whether people will respect others' personal work areas on tables with different kinds of embodiments, and in what situations they will avoid interfering with each others' activities. Answering these questions is important because it is difficult to design appropriate representations of people's bodies in collaborative systems unless we know which factors are likely to influence behaviour, and how.

To address these issues in a controlled fashion, we carried out two empirical studies, focusing on reaching and coordination behaviours. In our first study, we examined these behaviours in a real-world activity at a physical table. In the second study (a controlled experiment), we investigated the effects of four specific factors – the physicality, visual realism, transparency, and size of an embodiment – on crossings, coordination, and awareness.

PHYSICAL-TABLE OBSERVATIONAL STUDY

Our first study examined how the behaviours and social protocols discussed in previous work occur in the specific setting of tabletop artifact-based work. We observed and interviewed people working with paper artifacts at a physical table, and focused on the behaviour of arm crossing to look at coordination and touch avoidance.

Participants and Tasks

Ten dyads (1 female pair, 6 male pairs, 3 mixed pairs) were recruited from a local university. Participants were instructed to build a haiku (a three-line poem) by arranging words cut from a sheet of paper and placed on the table (Figure 1, left). The two participants built their haikus at the same time, each on a different topic, and assembled the words on the table in front of where they were sitting.

Words were scattered around the table and were available to either of the participants; however, the words related to the left participant's topic were on the right side of the table, and vice versa. Participants had to reach to the other side of the table to retrieve the most appropriate words for their haiku (e.g., see Figure 1, right), which created the potential for many reaching conflicts in a short session.

Users sat side-by-side – a common way for pairs to locate themselves at real-world tables, and a necessary arrangement when working with textual artifacts. It is much easier to read text when it is oriented towards you, and previous work has shown that orientation is often used to imply ownership [14]. Our setup ensured that all words were equally available to both people.

Figure 1 - Study setup (left), and word distribution (right).

This task is interesting for CSCW because several of its attributes are common in real work tasks. First, the area is split into territories (see Figure 1), which is common for tabletop work [23]. Second, the haiku task is a mixed-focus collaborative task [4], in which users often switch between individual work and group work. The group work in the haiku task is the need to coordinate access to the shared resource (the words) in the public space of the table.

Observed Behaviours

We observed two clear behaviours in the study – touch avoidance, and territoriality – both of which led to specific kinds of space management strategies on the tabletop.

Touch Avoidance

It was very clear that people avoided touching the other person's arm or hand. Over ten sessions, with hundreds of reaching events, we observed only three crossings (i.e., where one person reached over or under the other person's arm). In informal, post-experiment interviews, people repeatedly stated that it was rude to reach over or under another person's arm, and that they avoided doing so. When we asked the three people who had been crossed how it felt, all said that they noticed the cross and felt uncomfortable.

Touch avoidance led to two mechanisms for managing table access: implicit coordination, and accommodation.

Implicit Coordination. We observed nascent reaching conflicts where both people simultaneously began reaching to the same area; however, these never became selection conflicts (where both people grabbed the same object) as groups used coordination techniques to avoid selection conflicts. The most common was the 'hallway passing' coordination technique, where both people move their arms in and out until one conceded to the other (see Figure 2). This behaviour was also observed in [9].

Figure 2 - The hallway passing technique.

Accommodation. People consistently leaned back slightly when the other person reached in front of them; this subtle behaviour was observed in all groups. People reported that they moved away not because the closeness of the other's arm made them uncomfortable, but because doing so would let the other person work without feeling uncomfortable about reaching into their personal space. This accommodation technique provides a subtle and low-effort means for giving permission to reach into personal space.

Figure 3 – Accommodation.

Territoriality

The second obvious behaviour that we observed was territoriality [23]. People immediately adopted the area in front of them as their personal territory. This organization is normal for tabletop work [23], and was also encouraged by the setup of the study; however, we also manipulated the sense of ownership in the public space of the main table, by reversing the arrangement of topic words (described above). The main way in which territoriality seemed to affect people's behaviour in the task was in protection of the personal region of the table. Over all sessions, there were no episodes where people reached into the other person's personal territory (defined by the sheet of paper where they built their haiku), even though they needed to reach in front of the other person to retrieve words for their own task.

Both touch avoidance and territoriality provided results in terms of crossing and intrusion events, and we use these concepts as the basis for the design of the digital-table study described below.

DIGITAL TABLE STUDY

We replicated the haiku-building task used in our physical-table study on a digital tabletop. We were interested in two main research questions: first, what changes occur when moving from physical to digital arm embodiments, and what happens to the touch-based coordination mechanism observed in the physical-table study; and second, how does the visual design of a digital embodiment affect behaviour.

Visual Factors of Arm Embodiment Design

Previous work in embodiment design has shown that cursors provide only low levels of awareness in group work [19], and that arm embodiments (which maintain a visual link between the cursor and the user's seated location) provide better awareness [17].

To determine which embodiments to study, we conducted small pilot studies of different digital embodiments based on Pinelle et al.'s exploratory study [19]. We tested cursors, lines, cartoon arms, transparent thick arms, and realistic-looking picture arms (a picture of the user's actual arm). In contrast to our physical table study and the observational results in [19], we observed that in many cases, people had little issue touching the digital embodiments.

Based on these results, we varied three factors of digital embodiment design: *size*, *transparency*, and *realism*. The thicker an embodiment (size), the more likely others are to notice it; however, it also occludes more of the workspace. The more transparent an embodiment, the less prominent it is, and the less it might affect a collaborator's actions. Realistic-looking embodiments may cause people to treat them more like digital extensions of a user.

Study Procedure

To investigate the role of visual embodiment design on coordination, we asked dyads to create five sets of individual haikus using the digital tabletop system. People sat side-by-side, as in the physical-table study, with their mouse to the right of their digital haiku papers.

System and Task Descriptions

Dyads used a 125cm x 88cm, top-projected tabletop system, with resolution of 1280 x 960. Participants were able to physically reach any digital word on the table, although this sometimes required them to stand to reach distant words. The size of the digital words was similar to the paper cutouts used in the physical-table study.

Participants built their haikus by moving the words on the table to the digital haiku paper in front of them – the papers measured 400x175 pixels and were positioned directly in front of each user. Each of the five haiku tasks used a different set of words belonging to a topic pair. Each participant was given one topic in the pair for their haiku. The five topic pairs were: Clothing/Book, Coffee/Cat, Car/Tree, Student/Dog, Lake/Chair. Topics were paired so that words from one topic would be less useful to the other topic (e.g., 'lumbar' is more useful for a chair haiku than a lake haiku); however, participants were told they could use any of the words on the table.

There were 36 words from each topic, plus the same 102 joiner words (e.g., 'the', 'and', 'of') as in the physical-table study, for a total of 174 words available for each haiku set. Words were split in a similar way to the physical-table study: the 'tree' words were on the opposite side of the table as the 'tree' haiku. Joiner words were distributed over the entire table. Initial locations of the words were saved, so that all groups saw the same words in the same locations.

Procedure

When dyads arrived, we took a picture of each person's right arm to be used as the base image for their virtual embodiment. Virtual arms were anchored at the right side of each haiku paper and were controlled by the mouse (the arm image stretched as users reached farther onto the table).

Participants completed five haikus, one for each topic set and embodiment (described next). During piloting, we found that groups quickly learned how to use the system and build their haikus, so no explicit training was required. Order of presentation of the embodiments was balanced using a Latin Square design. Topic pairs were presented in a single order, thus topic pairs were equally distributed across embodiment conditions over the study. We wanted to ensure we did not bias participants into thinking about personal space and awkwardness, so participants completed questionnaires only after the last haiku.

Embodiment Conditions

We tested one physical embodiment and four digital embodiments that varied in the previously identified visual factors of embodiment design. People used a mouse to control the cursor location when using digital embodiments. By using an image of the participant's arm for all digital embodiments, shape was kept constant for all conditions. The display width of the embodiment image was approximately the same as people's actual arm width.

Pens (real arms): In this condition, people moved words using direct touch on the tabletop - a cursor appeared below the tip of a pen and the embodiment was simply their physical arm. Pen location was tracked using a Polhemus Liberty tracker, and selection occurred via a button at the tip of the pen controlled by a Phidget interface board. Polhemus pens were used instead of a touch table to track hand locations at all times, not just during object selection.

Thin: the embodiment image was scaled to 5 pixels wide, and filled in with purple or green to differentiate users.

Solid: the unscaled embodiment image (approx. 200 pixels wide; everyone's arm is a different size and shape) was filled in with purple or green, and was opaque.

Transparent: the unscaled embodiment was filled with purple or green and made semi-transparent (60% opacity), so users could see the words through the embodiments.

Picture: the unchanged image of the user's arm (same size as the transparent and solid conditions).

These five embodiment conditions each varied only one visual factor of embodiment design. Solid, Transparent, and Picture embodiments all have the same size (thickness), because they use the unscaled arm image. *Physicality* was investigated by comparing Solid to Pens; *Size* by comparing Solid to Thin; *Transparency* by comparing Solid to Transparent; and *Realism* by comparing Solid to Picture.

Participants and Demographic Factors

Personal space, and people's willingness to invade or be invaded by another, is dependent on a variety of factors (e.g., culture, sex), but is highly dependent on relationship type [6,7]. To ensure that our results take the nature of relationship into account, we gathered data from three dyad types: strangers, acquainted pairs, and romantic couples.

Strangers had never met previously; acquainted pairs were dyads that interacted at least once a week and included friends and co-workers; romantic couples included dating and married couples. The median length of relationship for acquainted pairs was 1.00 years (1 month to 20 years), and 3.75 years (9 months to 10 years) for romantic couples.

Sixty people (28 female, mean age 24.1) participated – ten dyads per relationship type. Twenty-four participants had never heard of digital tables; 23 had heard of them but never used one; and 13 had used a digital table before. 42 participants reported English as their first language; 7 dyads had different first languages.

We did not control the distribution of sex in our dyads. All romantic dyads were male-female; 3 acquainted dyads were male-male, 3 were male-female, and 4 were female-female; 4 stranger dyads were male-male, 5 were male-female, and 1 was female-female.

Measures and Data Analyses

We collected a variety of objective and subjective measures that we group in three themes relevant to coordination: touch avoidance, territoriality and awareness. Subjective measures used standard 7-point Likert scales.

Touch Avoidance – We counted the number of crossing events (when embodiments crossed each other) to measure the degree of touch avoidance. We also asked participants to rate their feelings of awkwardness when crossing.

Territoriality – Previous work in territoriality (e.g., [9,23]) showed that people's reaching behaviour is mediated by the location of items on the table. To measure this, we counted the number of events (word pick up and drop) taking place on the other participant's side of the table. To measure how an embodiment's occlusion affected reaching behaviour, we collected the percent of time embodiments occluded the other person's haiku. In addition, we asked participants to rate how awkward it felt to reach to the other side of the table, and their feelings of invasions of personal space, with each embodiment type. Last, we asked them to rate their sense of ownership over various tabletop objects.

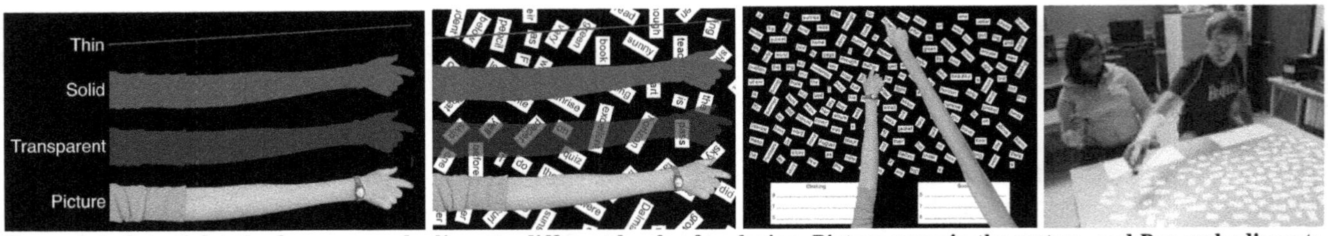

Figure 4. Left to right: the four arm embodiments, different levels of occlusion, Picture arms in the system, and Pen embodiments.

Awareness – We asked participants to rate their level of awareness of their partner's embodiment table position.

Visual inspection of the distribution of the objective counts indicate that parametric analyses were adequate; therefore we run repeated measures ANOVAs with α=0.05. When main effects were found, we performed planned post-hoc comparisons between selected techniques, motivated by four factors: Physicality (Pens to Solid), Size (Thin to Solid), Transparency (Transparent to Solid), and Realism (Picture to Solid). Post-hoc tests were adjusted for multiple comparisons by adjusting α according to the Holm-Bonferroni method.

Due to the ordinal nature of subjective measures we applied more-conservative non-parametric tests to these ratings. Post-hoc tests in subjective measures were also corrected for multiple comparisons. All results are reported for individuals, except for crossings. These are difficult to attribute to one or other participant, so we report by dyad.

RESULTS

We present analysis for the themes presented in the previous section: touch avoidance, territoriality, and awareness. Relationship effects are included in each theme. Table 1 shows the post-hoc pairwise comparison results.

Touch Avoidance

There was a main effect of embodiment on the number of crossing events ($F_{(4,116)}$=30.02, p≈0.000, η^2=0.53). The pairwise comparisons in Table 1 show that there were significant effects of physicality and size on the number of crossings, but not of transparency or realism. Figure 5 shows that physicality was the dominant factor affecting touch avoidance as measured by crossings.

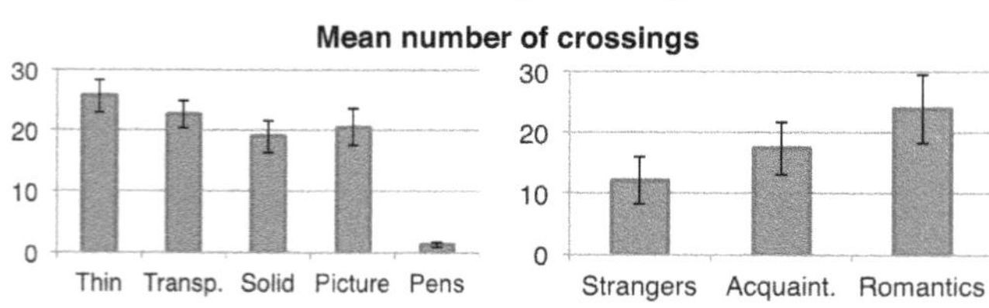

Figure 5 - Mean (±SE) number of crosses, by embodiment (left) and by relationship (right).

Although there was a main effect of relationship on the number of crosses ($F_{(2,27)}$=4.45 p=0.021, η^2=0.25), there was no interaction with embodiment ($F_{(8,108)}$=1.27, p>0.05, η^2=0.09). As Figure 5 shows, Strangers crossed fewer times than Romantics (p=0.016), and Acquaintances did not significantly differ from Strangers or Romantics (p>0.05).

We asked participants to rate their agreement with the statement: "It felt awkward to cross embodiments with this embodiment"; results are shown in Figure 6 (left). A Friedman test showed a main effect of embodiment on participants' feelings of awkwardness when crossing embodiments ($\chi^2(58)$=58.69, p≈0.000). As Table 1 shows, there were significant effects of physicality, size, and transparency, but not realism. A Kruskal-Wallis test showed no main effect of relationship on any ratings of awkwardness of crossing embodiments (all $\chi^2(2)$<3.53, p>0.17).

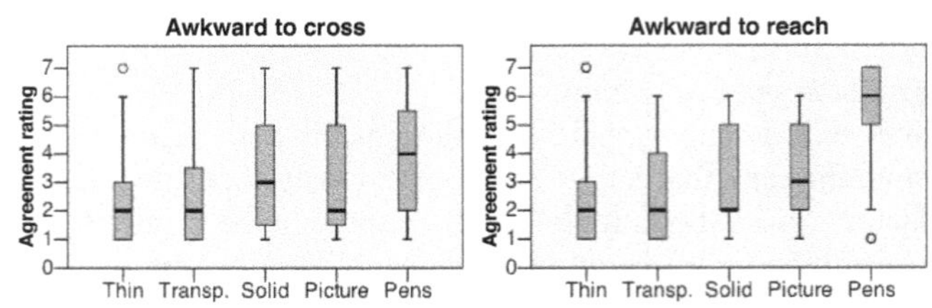

Figure 6 – Subjective feelings of awkwardness.

Territoriality

Figure 6 (right) shows agreement with the statement "It felt awkward to reach to the other side of the table with this embodiment." A Friedman test showed a main effect of embodiment on participants' feelings of awkwardness reaching to the opposite side ($\chi^2(58)$=114.16, p≈0.000). Table 1 shows that physicality and size increased awkwardness, and transparency reduced it.

There was a main effect of embodiment on the percentage of time people spent occluding the other person's haiku ($F_{(4,130.87)}$=6.254, p=0.002, η^2=0.086, Greenhouse-Geisser). Pairwise comparisons showed that Pens occluded less often than all digital embodiments, with no differences between the digital embodiments (see Figure 7).

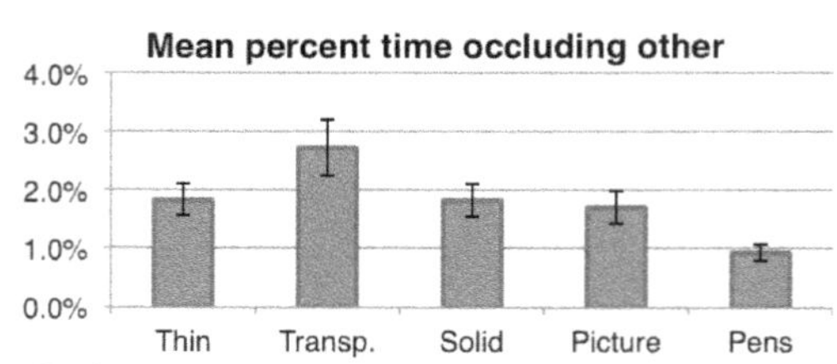

Figure 7 - Mean (±SE) percent time occluding other's haiku.

There was a main effect of embodiment on the proportion of words picked up from the other side of the table ($F_{(4,200.68)}$=5.578 p=0.001, η^2=0.086, Greenhouse-Geisser). There were no significant pairwise comparisons after adjusting for multiple comparisons.

Theme	Measure	Physicality (Pens vs. Solid)	Size (Thin vs. Solid)	Transparency (Transparent vs. Solid)	Realism (Picture vs. Solid)
Touch avoidance	Number of crosses	**Fewer crosses** ($p{\approx}0.000$)	**More crosses** (p=0.016)	No difference (p=0.082)	No difference (p=0.366)
	Feelings of awkwardness	**More awkward** (p=0.017)	**Less awkward** ($p{\approx}0.000$)	**Less awkward** ($p{\approx}0.000$)	No difference (p=0.627)
Territoriality	Proportion of events on opposite side	No difference (p=0.032)	No difference (p=0.445)	No difference (p=0.019)	No difference (p=0.541)
	Percent time embodiment occludes other's haiku	**Less time occluding** (p=0.002)	No difference (p=0.981)	No difference (p=0.061)	No difference (p=0.592)
	Feelings of awkwardness reaching to other side	**More awkward** ($p{\approx}0.000$)	**Less awkward** (p=0.001)	**Less awkward** ($p{\approx}0.000$)	No difference (p=0.268)
	Feeling of being invaded	**More invaded** (p=0.021)	**Less invaded** ($p{\approx}0.000$)	**Less invaded** ($p{\approx}0.000$)	No difference (p=0.444)
	Feeling of invading partner's space	No difference (p=0.108)	**Less invading** ($p{\approx}0.000$)	**Less invading** ($p{\approx}0.000$)	No difference (p=0.802)
Awareness	Feeling of awareness	**More aware** (p=0.018)	**Less aware** ($p{\approx}0.000$)	**Less aware** (p=0.038)	**More aware** (p=0.010)

Table 1 – Pairwise comparisons showing the effect of each factor as compared to Solid (e.g., for Physicality, Pens had fewer crosses than Solid). Bolding indicates significant difference (after correction for objective measures).

We asked participants to rate their agreement with the statements, "I felt like my partner was invading my space" and "I felt like I was invading my partner's space" (see Figure 8). Friedman tests showed a main effect of embodiment on participants' feelings of being invaded by their partner ($\chi^2(58)$=52.66, $p{\approx}0.000$) and of invading their partner's space ($\chi^2(58)$=63.69, $p{\approx}0.000$). As Table 1 shows, participants felt less awkward invading and being invaded with increased transparency and decreased size. Participants felt more awkward being invaded with a physical embodiment (Pens), but there was no effect of physicality on the feeling of invading space. Realism did not affect the awkwardness of invading or being invaded.

A Kruskal-Wallis test showed no effect of relationship on feelings of being invaded with all embodiments (all $\chi^2(2)<0.695$, $p>0.17$) except Picture ($\chi^2(2)$=8.00, p=0.018). Acquaintances were different than Strangers and Romantics (both $p<0.02$). A Kruskal-Wallis test showed no main effect of relationship on the ratings of invading partner's space (all $\chi^2(2)<2.35$, $p>0.309$).

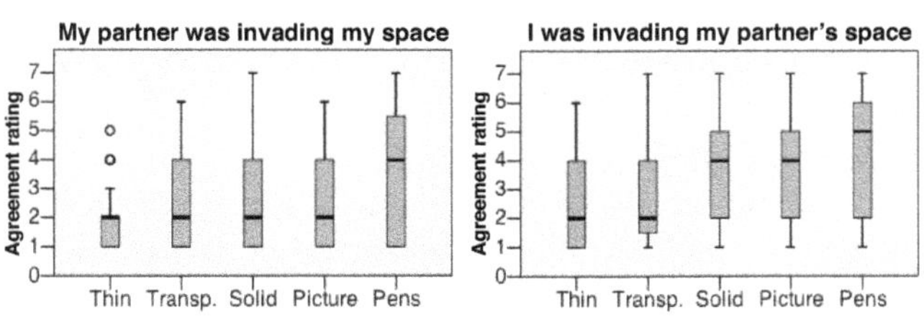

Figure 8 - Feelings of being invaded, and of invading partner.

Participants had complete freedom constructing their haikus and we did not provide instructions about whether they were allowed to reach onto another user's paper. Only 15 of the 30 groups ever accessed words on their partner's paper (3 Strangers, 6 Acquaintances, 6 Romantics), and there were large variations in the amount of this activity in the dyads. Strangers invaded their partner's paper sparingly (1-2 times), Acquaintances did so more often (1-11 times), and Romantic couples invaded most of all (3-96 times). Half of the groups did not invade their partner's paper; many stated they did not realize that they would be able to do so.

On average, invasions represented only 1% of pick and drop events. There was no main effect of embodiment on invasion ($F_{(4,236)}$=0.72, $p>0.05$, η^2= 0.01).

We also asked people to report their level of ownership over table items on a 5-point scale (1="no ownership", 5="complete ownership"). Although people felt more ownership over their paper (mean=4.07) and the words on their paper (3.75) than over their partner's paper (1.97) or words on their partner's paper (2.05), people did not differentiate ownership of words on the opposite side of the table (2.71) from words on their side of the table (2.9). There were no main effects of embodiment on these ratings.

Awareness

Figure 9 shows agreement ratings to the statement "I was aware of my partner's position on the table while using this embodiment". A Friedman test showed a main effect of embodiment on participants' feelings of awareness ($\chi^2(58)$=63.69, $p{\approx}0.000$). As Table 1 shows, increases in size, physicality, and realism increased awareness, while transparency reduced awareness.

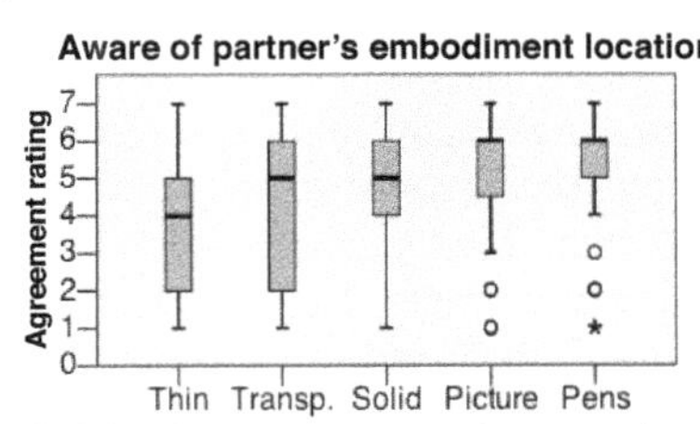

Figure 9 – Subjective awareness of partner's embodiment location.

Open-Text Questions and Observed Behaviours

In addition to finding out how participants behaved with and felt about visual embodiments, we asked two open-text questions about crossing embodiments. We grouped participant responses into categories based on the words used (one response can appear in multiple categories).

When responding to the question "briefly describe why you avoid crossing over (or under) someone's physical arm", people reported that it is rude, impolite, uncomfortable, or awkward (33 times), it is an invasion of personal space (19 times), and it causes a performance cost to the partner – occlusion, interruption, and distraction (19 times). For the question "briefly describe how crossing over (or under) someone's physical arm is different than crossing someone's digital embodiment", people reported that embodiments can't "feel" (26 times), the embodiment is not "me" or "them" (18 times), and the embodiments don't have or invade personal space (14 times).

Observations of Coordination with Physical Embodiments

In addition to clear evidence of touch avoidance (as described above), we also observed instances of implicit coordination and accommodation (e.g., see Figure 4). Another coordination policy we observed with the pens was that some people planned out the words they wanted, then quickly reached for the words, making a pile on their paper, and then organized them into sentences.

DISCUSSION

The user study shows five main results.

- All measures showed large differences between physical and digital embodiments: crossings with physical arms were rare (fewer than two per session), but were very common with all digital embodiments (twenty or more); in addition, subjective perceptions of awkwardness and invasion of space were strongly different between physical and digital embodiments.
- Increased realism of the embodiment – even photos of people's actual arms – had no effect on behaviour, but did increase subjective ratings of awareness.
- The size of the digital embodiments had the largest effect on behaviour.
- Relationship had a strong overall effect on the number of crossings, but did not interact with the other factors;
- Perception of awareness differs for physical and digital embodiments and is also affected by all visual factors.

Interpretation of Results

Differences Between Physical and Digital Embodiments

People rarely crossed physical arms, but had little issue crossing digital embodiments (even when they looked like their own physical arms). The main reasons for this dramatic difference lie in the way people felt about the arms' connection to the real bodies, and the lack of any touch sensation. First, most participants reported that they did not associate the digital embodiments with their own, or their partner's, actual body: several people said that the embodiments were "not me" and "not my partner;" others stated that the digital embodiments did not have personal space. We saw further evidence in the lack of proprioception with the digital embodiments – people often left their digital arms 'laying out on the table,' something that would likely never happen with real arms. Second, participants stated that the digital embodiments cannot "physically touch," and that they have no sense of feeling, and so the awkwardness of crossing was removed.

These statements imply that people perceive physical touch differently than a visual representation of touch, even if that visual representation is dynamic and realistic, contrary to some VR work (e.g., [12,21,22]). The touch avoidance first seen in the physical-table study appears to be dependent on a true sensation of touch rather than a visual representation. This is in part because representations of arm crossing are not subject to social norms; it is possible, however, that other representations of touch (e.g., touching while holding hands) might not be seen as being as neutral as crossing.

Nevertheless, in our tabletop systems, the lack of true touch in digital arm embodiments appears to remove most touch-avoidance behaviour. This has strong design implications, because people may perform actions in the digital world that they would strongly avoid in the physical world (e.g., crossing over an outstretched arm to steal an item).

Territoriality

People did not extend their private territories in front of them beyond their pieces of paper. This may be because we swapped the word locations, which forced people to reach into what otherwise might be the other person's territory. We also did not allow people to create their own territories in the public workspace. The system automatically moved words back to their original location when they were dropped anywhere outside of pieces of paper.

Our territoriality results also suggest there is an effect of dyad relationship on territorial behaviour (which has not been reported before). The more intimate the relationship, the more likely people are to invade personal territories. In addition, although people's public-workspace territorial behaviour was different than reported in other research (e.g., [5,23]), people's subjective ratings matched previous work (e.g., people are uncomfortable reaching to the other side of the table [9]).

Occlusion and Digital Embodiment Size

Although not nearly so strong as the effect of physicality, we also saw an effect of embodiment size on crossings and awareness. Figure 9 and Table 1 show the same trend: the thicker an embodiment is, the more aware people feel of their partner, and the less they cross. In addition, increased thickness was paired with more feelings of awkwardness reaching to the other side of the table (Figure 6, right).

These effects are likely due to both the increased visual prominence of the thicker embodiments, and the increased likelihood that the arm will occlude artifacts on the table and disrupt the partner's activities. Many of the open-text responses stated that people were concerned about disrupting their partner's work, both with physical and digital embodiments. We speculate that the cause of the differences was directly related to the level of occlusion caused by that embodiment. The lack of effect for Realism (the Picture to Solid comparison) provides additional evidence for this hypothesis, because both Picture and Solid occluded the workspace to the same degree.

Implications for Design

There are five issues from this research that designers should consider when developing tabletop systems.

Touch input (real arms) vs. indirect (digital embodiments). When designing tabletop systems, designers must choose the way that people will interact with the table. In some cases, indirect touch (and digital embodiment) are advantageous, but our study shows that this decision can greatly impact the way that people use the system. As a result, designers should think carefully about the ramifications of different choices. For example, designers might use only real-arm touch input when selection conflicts could lead to severe errors; with real touch, people will be more aware of their partner and less likely to come into conflict over the table.

Visual realism does not reproduce social protocols. The study showed that no purely visual design reproduced the degree of touch avoidance seen with physical arms. This means that designers will not be able to re-introduce social control mechanisms simply through appearance (although several participants found the picture arms 'creepy', this did not produce additional touch avoidance). As a result, systems that use digital embodiments may need to build in explicit access control to prevent uncontrolled access.

Lack of awkwardness could be useful. In some situations, such as fast-paced tasks or games, people may be able to complete their work faster when they do not have to worry about making others uncomfortable. In these cases, designers could choose digital embodiments to allow for comfortable crossings, and narrow embodiments to avoid occlusion. However, this decision also means that actions will be less obvious, decreasing awareness.

Relationships change behaviour. Reaching and territoriality behaviour is strongly dependent on the relationship of the users. This is important for public digital tabletop installations (e.g., museums), where the system may be used by anyone. Designers who know the relationship of their users may need more than simple embodiments – for example, if users are more familiar with one another, access control mechanisms might be required.

Occlusion is an important factor in embodiment design. Of the visual factors we investigated, size was the only one that had an effect on behaviour. In general, people did not want to disrupt others (this was true even for intimate couples). Transparency is easy to build into arm embodiments, and provides a reasonable combination of visual salience (for awareness) and low occlusion.

Directions for Future Research

Replacing Coordination Mechanisms on Tables

Touch avoidance provides people with a natural way of avoiding conflict, but without true touch, alternate means of managing access to the table will be needed. First, access could be controlled at the system level through roles or permissions. Previous CSCW work on explicit roles and access provides the control required and provides solutions to conflicts, but these methods are often too heavy-weight to be used in practice. We plan to explore new possibilities for light-weight access controls for tabletops (e.g., touching an object to reserve it for a short time).

Alternatively, new social protocols may appear as people become more experienced with digital embodiments. The changes that we saw may have occurred because people have so little exposure to these techniques. With more experience, groups may develop new coordination methods – for example, they may start to associate digital touching with the negative implications of physical touching, or may develop other mechanisms that do not depend on touch avoidance (e.g., more explicit turn-taking behaviours).

Mixed Input Ecologies

Our results suggest it will be important to know more about systems that allow multiple types of input and embodiment. For example, systems that combine direct and indirect input will have the two embodiments mixed together. We speculate people would have little issue crossing an arm embodiment over a physical arm, but more study is needed. Remote collaboration over distributed tables is another mixed setting: both people interact with direct touch, but are represented remotely via an arm embodiment (e.g., VideoArms [26]). It is not known whether the real-arm origin of a remote representation would change behaviour.

Other Instantiations of Social Protocols

Our work looked at the change of embodiment from a physical form to a representational form, and how this changes behaviour. We chose arm embodiments as our representation and touch avoidance as the behaviour. Although we lose touch avoidance with this representation, feelings of awkwardness and invasion are still present, so other protocols may also remain. For example, touching certain parts of another's avatar with your avatar's arm may still be considered rude, even though neither person can "feel" that touch.

CONCLUSION

In this paper, we presented two studies of tabletop reaching behaviour: a physical table study, demonstrating that people rarely cross arms, and a digital table study, demonstrating the marked difference between reaching with physical and different digital arm embodiments. We showed that the most important factor in the visual design of embodiments is the level of occlusion caused by the embodiment: the lower the occlusion, the less people are aware of each other's actions, the less awkward it is to interact in shared spaces, and the more people cross embodiments. This research is an important step in understanding the differences between physical and digital group interactions, opening up many new questions on what factors tabletop designers should manipulate to ensure that groups are able to work as naturally as they do over physical tables.

ACKNOWLEDGMENTS

This work was supported by the Natural Sciences and Engineering Research Council of Canada, the SurfNet Research Network, and the Walter C. Sumner Foundation.

REFERENCES

1. Anderson, P.A., Leibowitz, K. The Development and Nature of the Construct Touch Avoidance. *Nonverbal Behaviour.* 3(2). 1978. 89-106.
2. Bailenson, J.N., Blascovich, J., Beall, A.C., Loomis, J.M., Interpersonal Distance in Immersive Virtual Environments. *PSPB '03. 29, 7.* 819-833.
3. Greenberg, S., Marwood, D. Real Time Groupware as a Distributed System: Concurrency Control and its Effect on the Interface. *CSCW '94.* 207-217.
4. Gutwin, C. and Greenberg, S. Design for individuals, design for groups: tradeoffs between power and workspace awareness. *CSCW '98*, 207-216.
5. Ha, V., Inkpen, K.M., Mandryk, R.L., Whalen, T. Direct Intentions: The Effects of Input Devices on Collaboration around a Tabletop Display. *TABLETOP 2006.* 177-184.
6. Hall, E.T. *The Hidden Dimension.* 1966.
7. Hayduk, L.A. Personal Space: Where We Now Stand. *Psychological Bulletin.* 94(2). 1983. 293-335.
8. Heslin, R, Nguyen, T.D., Nguyen, M.L. Meaning of touch: The case of touch from a stranger or same sex person. *Nonverbal Behaviour.* 7(3). 1983. 147-157.
9. Hornecker, E., Marshall, P., Dalton, N.S., Rogers, Y. Collaboration and interference: awareness with mice or touch input. *CSCW 2008.* 167-176.
10. Ishii, H., Kobayashi, M., Grudin, J. Integration of interpersonal space and shared workspace: ClearBoard design and experiments. *T. Inf. Syst.* 11, 4, '93, 349-375.
11. Izadi, S., Brignull, H., Rodden, T., Rogers, Y., Underwood, M., Dynamo: A public interactive surface supporting the cooperative sharing and exchange of media. *UIST '03.* 159-168
12. Jeffrey, P., Mark, G. Navigating the virtual landscape: co-ordinating the shared use of space. In *Social Navigation of Information Space*, 112-131.
13. Jourard, S.M. An Exploratory Study of Body-Accessibility. *J. Soc. Clin. Psych.,* 5, 1966. 221-231.
14. Kruger, R., Carpendale, S, Scott, S.D., and Greenberg, S. How people use orientation on tables: comprehension, coordination and communication. *GROUP 2003.* 369-378.
15. Morris, M., Ryall, K., Shen, C., Forlines, C., Vernier, F. Beyond "Social Protocols": Multi-User Coordination Policies for Co-Located Groupware. *CSCW '04.* 262-265.
16. Nacenta, M.A., Pinelle, D., Gutwin, C., Mandryk, R.L. Individual and Group Support in Tabletop Interaction Techniques. *TABLETOP* 2010, 303–333.
17. Nacenta, M.A., Pinelle, D., Stuckel, D., Gutwin, C. The effects of interaction technique on coordination in tabletop groupware. *GI 2007.* 191-198.
18. Nguyen, T., Heslin, R., Nguyen, M.L. The meanings of touch: Sex differences. *Comm. '73.* 25(3). 92-103.
19. Pinelle, D., Nacenta, M., Gutwin, C., Stach, T. The effects of co-present embodiments on awareness and collaboration in tabletop groupware. *GI 2008.* 1-8.
20. Rosenfeld, L.B., Kartus, S., Ray, C. Body Accessibility Revisited. *Communication.* 26(3). 1976. 27-30.
21. Slater, M., Steed, A. Meeting People Virtually: Experiments in Shared Virtual Environments. *The Social Life of Avatars: Presence and Interaction in Shared Virtual Environments. 2002.*
22. Smith, M.A., Farnham, S.D., Drucker, S.M. The Social life of Small Graphical Chat Spaces. *CHI '00.* 462-469.
23. Scott, S.D., Carpendale, S.T., Inkpen, K.M. Territoriality in collaborative tabletop workspaces. *CSCW '04.* 294-303.
24. Tang, A., Tory, M., Po, B., Neumann, P., Carpendale, S. Collaborative Coupling over Tabletop Displays. *CHI 2006.* 1181-1190.
25. Tang, A., Pahud, M., Inkpen, K., Benko, H., Tang, J.C., Buxton, B. Three's Company: Understanding Communication Channels in Three-way Distributed Collaboration. *CSCW2010.* 271-280.
26. Tang, A., Neustaedter, C., Greenberg, S. VideoArms: Embodiments for Mixed Presence Groupware. *People and Computers, in Proc of HCI '06.* 2-18.
27. Tang, J.C. Findings from Observational Studies of Collaborative Work. *JMMS,* 34(2). 1991. 143-160.
28. Thayer, S. History and Strategies of Research on Social Touch. *Nonverbal Behaviour.* 10(1). 1986. 12-28.
29. Tse, E., Histon, J., Scott, S.D., Greenberg, S. Avoiding interference: how people use spatial separation and partitioning in SDG workspaces. *CSCW 2004.* 252-261.
30. Tuddenham, P. Robinson, P. Distributed Tabletops: Supporting Remote and Mixed-Presence Tabletop Collaboration. *TABLETOP 2007.* 19-26,
31. Yee, N., Bailenson, J., Urbanek, B., Chang, F., Merget, D. The Unbearable Likeness of Being Digital: The Persistence of Nonverbal Social Norms in Online Virtual Environments. *Cyberpsychology & Behaviour.* 10(1). 2007. 115-121.

Recalibrating the Ratio: Enacting Accountability in Intimate Relationships Using Shared Calendars

Alexander Thayer
University of Washington
423 Sieg Hall, Seattle, WA
98195
huevos@alumni.washington.edu

Behzod Sirjani
Northwestern University
633 Clark Street, Evanston, IL
60208
me@behzod.net

Charlotte P. Lee
University of Washington
423 Sieg Hall, Seattle, WA
98195
cplee@uw.edu

ABSTRACT
This study enriches the understanding of relationship work in the context of calendar sharing by examining how people negotiate and enact accountability in their intimate relationships with and around their shared calendars. We conducted 13 semi-structured interviews as part of a qualitative study of Google Calendar users. Our research discovered how participants develop understandings of how close friends and significant others structure their time using shared calendars, as well as how people negotiate and enact accounts within and beyond their intimate relationships. Our findings indicate ways in which Online Calendar Systems (OCS) can be better designed to more effectively support users' needs.

Author Keywords
Accountability; calendars; intimacy; qualitative research; relationship work.

ACM Classification Keywords
H.5.3 [**Information Interfaces and Presentation (e.g., HCI)**]: Group and Organization Interfaces.

INTRODUCTION
Over the past several years, online calendaring systems (OCS) have become an increasingly popular alternative to paper calendars [20]. Early work on OCS investigates their coordinative use in the context of corporations or large organizations [4, 10, 11, 17, 18, 19, 20, 27], while more recent studies describe calendaring practices in the context of family activity [9, 14, 15] and among young adults without children [26].

As [2, 14, 25] point out, people who share calendars continue to have face-to-face, coordinative discussions about their activities and their rationale for planning and scheduling those activities. Such coordinative activities are one aspect of *relationship work*, or the set of negotiated practices that foster, maintain, and sometimes damage friendships and feelings of intimacy. Prior work [26] determined that people in intimate relationships perform relationship work when they share calendars, resulting in different calendaring behaviors compared to familial and organizational OCS users.

The present study expands upon prior work by applying the concept of accountability as a lens for exploring the performance of relationship work with shared calendars. Feelings of intimacy are grounded in bonds of trust, which are forged when people act accountably toward one another. This study deepens our understanding of calendar sharing as relationship work by examining how our study participants negotiate accountability with and around their shared calendars, as well as attempt to act accountably from the perspective of their close friends and significant others. We explore the accounts that our participants read, interpret, and describe in their shared calendars in order to identify opportunities for the design of calendaring systems that will better support relationship work.

We therefore study OCS use by addressing the following research question in the context of the enactment of accountability: *How do OCS users perform relationship work with and through their calendars?* To answer this research question, we interviewed 13 users of Google Calendar, a popular OCS that has been freely available since 2006 and that has millions of users. The novel contributions of this paper are to describe the relationship work practices in which participants engage in the service of acting accountably, as well as discuss potential OCS interface and interaction design interventions inspired by those practices. Such interventions could help OCS users maintain their intimate relationships by more effectively supporting their performance of accountable behavior.

In the sections that follow, we first discuss the literature that is related to the topic of this study, with a focus on defining intimacy, trust, and accountability as they relate to our research. We then describe our study design and methods, followed by a detailed explanation of our findings as they relate to our research question. We conclude with a discussion of the study results and the implications for design that the results suggest.

RELATED LITERATURE

In this section, we first discuss the concept of intimacy and the different types of interpersonal relationships in which people can participate. We then describe the concept of trust, as well as how people develop intimacy and bonds of trust in their relationships. We conclude by situating intimacy and trust in the context of accountability, which we define in terms of being answerable and explainable for one's actions.

Defining Intimacy

Of the six types of interpersonal relationships [30], two can be considered intimate relationships: *reciprocal friendships* (e.g., two people who choose to be friends and who demonstrate a mutual commitment to their friendship) and *romantic relationships* (e.g., two people who are married). Hereafter, we refer to individuals in intimate relationships as close friends and significant others.

Additional relationship types include associative friendships and kin relationships. In an associative friendship, two people are friendly with one another due to a shared commitment, such as a job, and are not interested in developing intimate relationships. In a kin relationship (including relatives and direct family members), two people can decide whether they want a reciprocal friendship, or they can decide not to be friendly at all. Their genealogical connection persists regardless of how they choose to act toward one another.

At its core, intimacy can be defined as the shared knowledge that unites two people. This knowledge not only shapes current experiences but also "informs and deepens subsequent interactions between…partners" [23]. There is not necessarily a moment in every intimate relationship when both partners explicitly declare to one another that they are "close" friends. Instead, this sentiment is felt through ongoing engagement in intimate interactions.

There are three criteria for intimate interactions: "self-revealing behavior, positive involvement with the other [individual], and shared understandings" [23]. These criteria are defined as follows:

- Self-revealing behavior occurs when two people disclose aspects of themselves that are emotionally challenging to discuss or that make them psychologically vulnerable.
- Positive involvement between two people entails both individuals making it clear that they are engaged with the conversation, and is often expressed through a person's choice of words, cues drawn from body language, and so on.
- Shared understandings among partners in intimate relationships involve mutual familiarity, which develops as two partners bond through conversation and shared experiences over time.

When two partners in a relationship engage in these types of interactions, they generate *interactional intimacy* with one another. Interactional intimacy can occur in non-verbal ways [23], whether the intimate behaviors take place in person or are technologically mediated, as with a shared calendar. Interactional intimacy is also predicated on feelings of trust between two partners in an intimate relationship. In the next section we explore what it means for two people to trust one another, leading to a discussion about accountable behavior as the foundation for both intimacy and trust in an intimate relationship.

Defining Trust

The concept of trust is defined in a number of different ways depending on the theoretical perspective of the scholars who discuss it. We follow the definition that McKnight, Cummings, and Chervany [13] provide as a result of their exhaustive, interdisciplinary research into other scholars' discussions of trust.

According to [13], feelings of trust are based on beliefs and intentions. Trusting beliefs are comprised of four attributes: benevolence, competence, honesty, and predictability. [13] claim that when two people believe these attributes are sufficiently present in their relationship, they are able to establish trusting intentions whereby they decide to depend on one another. Therefore, these four trusting beliefs positively inform the decision that people make when they become willing to trust one another.

As with intimacy, feelings of trust are sustained over time as two partners continue to meet the social expectations they have established for their relationship together. In healthy intimate relationships a bond or cycle of trust develops when one partner believes the other is routinely trying to act in the best interests of the relationship. In the context of OCS use, this bond of trust is strengthened when people perform the activities they say they will perform, as indicated by the events on their shared calendars.

Feelings of trust and mistrust alike can develop as close friends or significant others decide how to balance their pursuit of individual interests with the potentially conflicting interests of their partners [24]. Specifically, mistrust can develop when one partner perceives the other to be acting in a way that is harmful to their relationship, especially if those actions appear to form a pattern over time. When trusting beliefs are negatively influenced, trusting intentions are also impacted and one partner can cease to depend on the other in given situations [13].

The definitions of intimacy and trust provided here tell part of the story about how people form and maintain their intimate relationships. As stated earlier both of these concepts are based on a more fundamental behavioral process: acting accountably toward other people. In the next section we define the concept of accountability in the context of OCS users' behavior with and around their shared calendars.

Defining Accountability and Acting Accountably with and around OCS

Prior work has explored the calendar work and life scheduling behavior of OCS users [cf. 9, 14, 15, 18, 19], as well as the relationship work of young adults in intimate relationships [26]. At a conceptual level, the performance of accountability is the foundation of coordinative behavior among partners in intimate relationships because accountability undergirds both intimacy and trust. Tracing the enactment of accountable behavior through OCS use reflects an underexplored approach to understanding the relationship work that people perform. The present study is designed to enable a richer level of analysis of the ways in which intimacy and trust play out among partners in intimate relationships by framing those phenomena in the context of enacting accountability.

Garfinkel [8] defines accountability as the organization of rational and reportable behavior enacted as an ongoing process. Similarly, Eriksén defines accountability as the ongoing process of the production and management of organized, everyday affairs [6]. Additionally, relationship work is performed in the spirit of what Troshynski, Lee, and Dourish [27] describe as socially accountable behavior.

Accountability, then, is a state of being that is continuously enacted among people in various ways. However, Garfinkel and Eriksén both acknowledge that the notion of accountability is actually comprised of two different elements. Eriksén [6] summarizes these elements using the words "answerable" and "explainable." We will use these same words to reference the two elements of accountability throughout the rest of this paper.

Being answerable is an attribute of OCS users' behavior whereby they let others know when they will be available to spend time together. The collection of events within a shared calendar provides visibility into the world of the person who owns that calendar. Close friends and significant others understand this fact, and use their calendars in a self-revealing way: They indicate when they are free and when they are busy. OCS users begin sharing calendars in order to enhance the amount of visibility they have into the lives of close friends and significant others so they can find time to hang out [26].

Whereas being answerable is about indicating whether specific times are free or busy, being explainable is about telling others what one is doing during the busy times. OCS users make themselves explainable through the titles and descriptions they write for their events, and they rely on the event descriptions of others as explanations of their behavior. Being explainable is a continuously negotiated state of being that describes how calendar owners report their activities to other people. Close friends and significant others expend a great deal of effort explaining to one another how they are spending, or are planning to spend, their time together [26].

Acting accountably, then, is comprised of being answerable and explainable for one's past, present, and future behavior. Given that OCS are collections of members' accounts [8] of how they will spend their time, as well as how they have spent their time, the act of sharing calendars makes both partners in an intimate relationship members of those calendars. As members, they agree to rely on their shared calendars as expressions of their accountable behavior.

This tacit agreement occurs even as partners struggle to understand **how** they can use shared calendars to know whether they are both acting accountably. Importantly, bonds of trust and feelings of intimacy can be damaged by inaccurate perceptions of other people's behaviors and intentions. For this reason, the practice of shared calendaring necessitates some amount of offline, coordinative discussion to clarify any discrepancies between the description and the intent of a calendar entry, or the description of an event and the resulting behavior of the calendar owner. They do not plan to have these discussions, but they become necessary when they must confirm their true intentions and clarify their behavior in the context of their calendars. In so doing, they are attempting to preserve their feelings of intimacy and bonds of trust, both of which are predicated on the perception of mutual accountability.

Summary

There are three main takeaways to draw from this section. First, trust is a prerequisite for the development and maintenance of interactional intimacy, which can be developed through non-verbal communication, as when people rely on OCS to help them arrange their social lives with others.

Second, accountability is critically important to the health of every intimate relationship. However, acting accountably requires being answerable and being explainable for one's activities. Both forms of accountability play out within and around OCS when close friends and significant others use shared calendars with one another.

Finally, given that partners' feelings of intimacy and trust are at risk when their accountability is called into question, we feel it makes sense to situate this study in the context of close friends and significant others attempting to act accountably with one another. In so doing, we enable ourselves to follow the practices on which partners in intimate relationships rely to successfully enact accountability with and through their shared calendars.

In the remainder of this paper we first outline how we designed our study to understand how OCS users enact accountability in their intimate relationships with and through their shared calendars. We then describe the subtle ways in which our participants enact accountability using their shared calendars. We conclude by discussing the combination of participants' negotiation and enactment of accountability in their intimate relationships using OCS.

STUDY DESCRIPTION

Although we know from prior research that OCS users perform relationship work with and through their calendars [26], it is unclear how OCS can be designed to more effectively support the negotiation of accountable behavior among close friends and significant others. Further, both forms of accountability (being answerable and being explainable) are often enmeshed and are challenging to separate when discussing specific cases of calendar sharing and use. The fact that these elements of accountability are so tightly woven indicates the difficulty of the design challenge at hand: effectively supporting the maintenance of intimate relationships through OCS interface and interaction design.

We developed the present study of Google Calendar use among close friends and significant others to help meet this challenge. In this section we provide an overview of our participants, describe the specific OCS application we studied, and explain the methods we used to gather and analyze our data.

OCS Application

We selected Google Calendar as the OCS for this study because it is a freely-available, widely-used OCS. Users of Google Calendar create "events," which can be titled, given a location and duration, and can include additional information ("notes").

Additionally, Google Calendar users can create and manage multiple calendars; each calendar has its own level of privacy and can be shared individually with any number of other individuals. When users view multiple calendars, they can choose from a palette of colors how to distinguish each calendar's events from all other events (refer to the screenshot in Figure 1, below). Event creators can "invite" other individuals to a specific event, making the details of that event visible, or they can "share" the contents of a calendar with another individual.

There are four possible levels of access (refer to the screenshot in Figure 2 on the next page):

- "Free/busy" is the most basic level of sharing, as it shows the date, time, and duration of calendar events but no event titles or additional information,
- "See all" lets others see the details of any event on a calendar that is shared with them,
- "Make changes to events" grants complete control to all details of any event, regardless of who created it,
- "Make changes AND manage sharing" allows for full control of the calendar and the sharing preferences.

Figure 1: A screenshot of Google Calendar, featuring two calendars that the user owns and six calendars shared with that user.

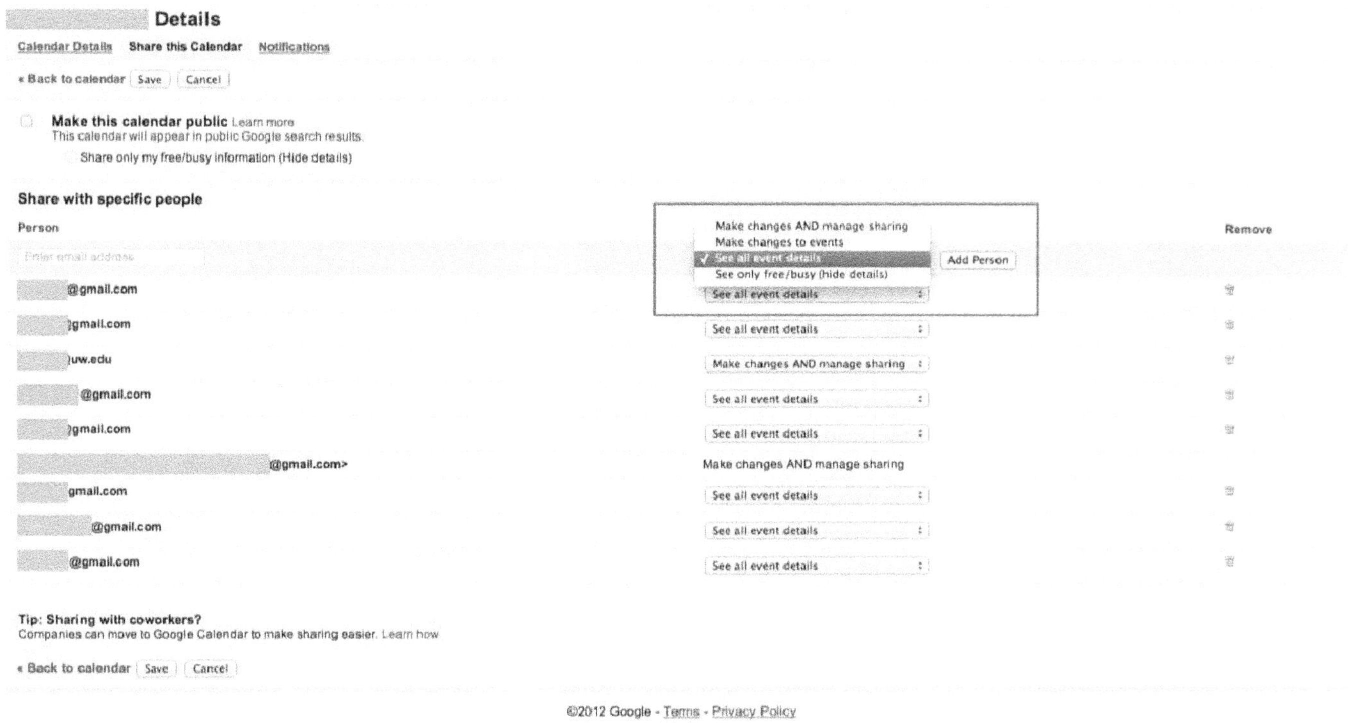

Figure 2: A screenshot of the sharing preferences for a specific calendar. The red box indicates the four sharing options that are possible for any given individual.

Participants

Our study took place from February to April 2011, during which time we conducted semi-structured interviews with 13 participants (6 women and 7 men), who had an average age of 27. Our participants included 6 students, 6 individuals with full-time jobs, and 1 individual who was unemployed.

Participants were solicited through email mailing lists associated with our university as well as through announcements of the study via personal social networks. The criteria for consideration as a participant included using Google Calendar, sharing a calendar with at least one other person, accessing at least one other shared calendar, and being older than 18 years of age. Participants were not compensated for their time.

Limitations and Differences from Prior Work

We acknowledge that Google Calendar is but one among several OCS that are available as of 2012. However, our prior work on OCS involved Google Calendar [26], and because the present study is an expansion of that prior work we chose to retain the same OCS.

Our previous work also informed our present study design as we chose to recruit a specific type of Google Calendar users for this study. We focused on interviewing individuals in their twenties and thirties who used OCS primarily with their close friends and significant others, and who did not have children around whom they would need to coordinate their lives. Additional studies of other types of participants (e.g., organizational users) could yield more types of activities and strategies to support relationship work. Further, we relied on an existing typology of interpersonal relationships as our goal was not to generate our own typology. Future research into shared calendar use could fruitfully probe the boundaries, expectations, and definitions of shared calendar users' relationships.

For the present study we wanted to dive deeper into the lives of partners in intimate relationships in order to understand more thoroughly how the enactment of accountability can be supported with and through OCS. Prior work [26] described some of the techniques that close friends and significant others use when negotiating shared activities using OCS. The present study expands upon that work by applying the concept of accountability as a lens for exploring the performance of relationship work with shared calendars.

Specifically, in this study with a new set of participants, we distinguish between being answerable and being explainable as facets of accountability. Additionally, because bonds of trust and feelings of intimacy are predicated on acting accountably with close friends and significant others, this richer definition of accountability enables us to describe and analyze accountability practices and behaviors with more precision than in our prior work..

This subtle difference is important because, as stated earlier, feelings of intimacy and trust stem from acting accountably. By situating accountability at the core of this paper, our intent is to develop an understanding of the underlying phenomena that motivate partners in intimate relationships to use OCS as they do. Acting accountably means thinking ahead about how calendar entries will be interpreted, as well as looking back to decide how specific entries were interpreted. Therefore, forward-looking and retrospective uses of OCS abound when partners in intimate relationships rely on their shared calendars to determine whether each partner is acting accountably, an observation that follows Lynch's [12] description of how people's embodied practices result in accountability (p. 33).

Finally, our study is qualitative by design, which is a particularly powerful way to obtain descriptive, empirical data that reflect real-world OCS use. In the next section we describe our qualitative methods in more detail before turning to a discussion of our findings.

Methods

Each participant was interviewed once in person using a standard semi-structured interview protocol. At the start of each interview session, the researcher filled out a survey with the participant that gathered data about the participant's relationship status (e.g., single, married, in a relationship but not living together), the identity of others with whom the participant had shared calendars (e.g., name, relationship to the participant, how long the sharing has been going on), and the identity of others whose calendars had been shared with the participant. The intent was to develop a clear view of each participant's social network as defined by his or her shared calendars.

The interview protocol included 6 questions about the relationships and calendaring practices of each person who accessed or shared a calendar with the participant (e.g., "How has sharing a calendar influenced your interactions with this person?"). The protocol also included 4 questions about general calendaring practices and relationship work (e.g., "Has your calendar use ever gotten you in trouble with someone?"). Interviewers were encouraged to ask follow-up questions and probe for greater detail and unexpected insights when possible. All interviews lasted between 21 and 51 minutes (mean: 38, median: 37, SD: 10.48); interviews were relatively brief when participants shared only one calendar and accessed only one other calendar. The interviews were recorded and transcribed, and all participant names were replaced with pseudonyms.

The research team initially coded the data using a standard codebook developed from the interview protocol. To ensure commonality of interpretation, all team members coded the same three interviews using the same codebook and discussed the results. Finally, after writing memos based on the initial codes, the team performed an open coding pass intended to identify examples of accountability, scheduling expectations and calibration activities, and accommodation of others' needs. In the following section, we describe the results of this analysis process in the context of how OCS users in intimate relationships perform accountability with, through, and around their shared calendars.

FINDINGS

We begin this section with an overview of the frequencies with which our participants share their calendars and access other people's calendars. Our 13 participants maintain and share 18 different calendars (mean: 1.36, median: 1, SD: 0.84), and access 32 different shared calendars (mean: 2.43, median: 2.0, SD: 2.31). All of the calendars have individual rather than group ownership, meaning that one person is ultimately responsible for their contents.

We observed a few particular sharing patterns across the 13 participants in this study. With regard to the calendars they owned and shared with others:

- 7 participants shared only with significant others (P1, P2, P3, P8, P9, P10, and P12)
- 4 participants shared with a mix of friends and family (P5, P7, P11, and P13)
- 2 participants shared with significant others and close friends (P4 and P6)

With regard to the calendars that participants accessed:

- 5 participants accessed only their significant others' calendars (P2, P3, P4, P8, and P12)
- 4 participants accessed a mix of significant others' and friends' calendars (P6, P7, P10, and P11)
- 3 participants accessed only their friends' calendars (P5, P9, and P13)
- 1 participant accessed a mix of significant others' and family members' calendars (P1)

As these data make clear, our participants share calendars with their close friends and significant others most frequently. Recall that the difference between a close friend and an associate is related to intimacy: Associates only disclose factual information to one another and are not interested in developing intimate relationships. Relatives and direct family members are distinct from close friends as well because of the bond of kinship that is present in these relationships. Intimate relationships are distinct from these other relationship types because close friends and significant others choose to be friends and demonstrate a mutual commitment to their relationship.

Given that our participants most frequently share and access calendars belonging to close friends and significant others, the goal of this section is to clarify the following facets of the performance of accountability among OCS users in these intimate relationships:

- **Being answerable within an intimate relationship:** How partners in intimate relationships let one another know that they are trying to act responsibly.
- **Being explainable within an intimate relationship:** How partners in intimate relationships report their activities to one another.
- **Being accountable beyond intimate relationships:** How partners in intimate relationships negotiate both elements of accountability (being answerable and explainable) when sharing calendars with one another and with a variety of other people (e.g., coworkers, casual friends).

Being Answerable within an Intimate Relationship

In this section we discuss participants' strategies for becoming answerable to close friends and significant others with and through their shared calendars. Given that OCS are socially-constructed systems that describe how people plan to spend their time, the initial challenge of sharing calendars comes from creating a schedule of events that is not just readable for the calendar owner but that is also understandable to whomever else is looking at the same calendar.

The process of becoming answerable is a mutual process whereby calendar users take steps to make themselves answerable for representations of time (e.g. a calendar event), as well as for how they act in accordance with those representations. When close friends and significant others begin sharing calendars with one another, they go through a learning process whereby they attempt to understand how their partners manage and represent time. The differences in how they perceive time are expressed in a variety of ways: how and when they decide to schedule activities, the meaning of unscheduled time during which there are no events listed, and so on.

This learning process is made more challenging for partners in intimate relationships when a particular event is not listed on a shared calendar. For example, Bernadette described the difficulty she had in trying to locate her husband Nathan based on the events in his calendar, and alludes to the discussion that resulted when she addressed this situation with him:

I was trying to get a hold of [my husband] to go home and I wanted to go home. I get cranky when I get hungry and tired. {Laughs} And I couldn't get a hold of him. And then, you know, a half hour later, an hour later, whenever his meeting was over, he called me and said, 'Well I had a meeting.' And I said, 'Well it wasn't on the calendar!'

This example demonstrates the importance that Bernadette ascribes to keeping a complete, accurate list of events on a shared calendar. When Nathan did not include an evening work event, she became upset because the missing event exposed a gap between her expectation of visibility into Nathan's life and his use of his calendar. This situation also reflects how Bernadette expects Nathan to use their shared calendars in a way that reflects his desire to be answerable to their relationship. Ultimately, Nathan began synchronizing the calendar he shared with Bernadette with his separate, private work calendar so she could see know when he would be busy due to evening work events.

The process of becoming answerable requires the development of a mutual awareness of how to use shared calendars. Our participants develop their awareness through the offline discussions that result from misunderstandings about how to gauge the exactness of calendar entries. For example, Ivan told us how the use of his calendar initially differed from that of his fiancée, Joan, with regard to their different perceptions of "free" time. From Ivan's perspective, the end times of his events are simply rough estimates of when they will end. However, Joan took these times literally and assumed that Ivan would be free immediately after his scheduled events had seemingly concluded. As Ivan described the situation:

[Joan] used to take [event times] more seriously and used to try to schedule things...right after when I said I would be done. I remember one instance in particular: We wanted to go [rock climbing] with a friend of hers. And I said I would be done by 3:30, and 3:30 turned into 4:15, and they were trying to go climb while there was still daylight. And we were really late, and they were really upset.

Whereas Ivan sees his events more as reminders of activities that lack precise endpoints, Joan regards the lack of events as equivalent to free time and so she planned other events accordingly. Therefore, Joan is holding Ivan answerable for the structure that he created with his calendar by using his events as indicators of when he is busy, and the blank spaces as free time when he is not busy. Although both partners in this intimate relationship want to be socially accountable to one another, the ways in which they use OCS to express their perceptions of time required a recalibration of those perceptions. Ivan changed how he used his calendar to make himself answerable to Joan in the way she expected based on how she perceives time. Ivan told us about this process:

It was a combination of learning to use the calendar and [becoming] more comfortable with each other and our own needs in our lives.

Being answerable includes, but entails much more than, keeping accurate records and sticking to a plan, changing actual practice and actions in response to discussions about how to use shared calendars, and demonstrating that the needs of close friends and significant others are being considered. The examples in this section reflect how, by tracing participants' interest in being answerable to their close friends and significant others, the events included within they shared calendars are meaningful to those who can view the calendars, as are the gaps between events. Additionally, although calendar events appear to have hard boundaries, not all OCS users regard their schedules in such inflexible terms. Because people bring these different ways of working with OCS to their calendar sharing practices, they must negotiate with close friends and significant others what it means to be answerable when performing calendar sharing as relationship work.

Being Explainable within an Intimate Relationship

Our participants use specific language and indicators to denote certain types of events that are more or less flexible than other events. For these events, participants write event descriptions that sometimes contain additional, highly contextual information that close friends and significant others are able to interpret and act on accordingly. This information can be more significant than the presence or absence of the events themselves because the additional context helps others know how they should act when they see such an event in a shared calendar.

Prior work [26] documents a similar phenomenon whereby OCS users rely on special event settings or codes to negotiate shared activities, keep their relationships vital, and manage different schedules. The present research explores in greater detail **how** close friends and significant others try to keep their relationships vital by tracing how they rely on shared calendars to judge whether they are acting accountably. Specifically, in this section we explore the calendaring techniques our participants use when they attempt to be explainable to others, a fundamental element of accountability and a necessity for keeping intimate relationships vital.

For example, Sarah told us that when she and her boyfriend Charles started sharing calendars, she would put events on her calendar and often not tell him, especially those that were very important to her.

when we first started sharing the calendar…I would just put down, "Oh, I'm going to the temple," and not say anything because I knew that we'd have an argument about it…so I would sneakily just put all these things on the calendar.

As their relationship developed and their time on weekends began filling up, Sarah realized that she needed a way to indicate to Charles which events she wanted to attend, but that she was flexible to his needs as well and could negotiate or sacrifice some of her events in favor of attending his. To resolve this issue, Sarah and Charles developed an event naming convention to help them differentiate between events that will definitely occur and events that require offline discussion before they are considered "real" events.

The big one that we use…is 'tentative.' And a lot of times I will put the brackets and then say 'tentative' so he knows that I am planning this but it's subject to his…I don't want to say approval, but, like, to his agreement that it's okay to do that… Like, 'These are all the days this month that I am planning on going to the temple. And is that okay?'

For Sarah, going to the temple is an important part of her week that is often non-negotiable, and so she does not describe that event as tentative. However, she also adds events to her calendar as a way to remember activities or outings that are potentially worth attending. Sarah notes those events as tentative so that Charles can look at her calendar and understand how she is planning to spend her time. This use of "*tentative*" enables Sarah to make herself explainable to Charles through their shared calendar. Sarah told us that the naming convention allowed her and Charles to have conversations about events that may be less essential, and to create space for shared time between them.

Alternatively, Ethan described how his girlfriend Nora felt that having too many events on a calendar could seem confining. Nora would often create an event that was explicitly named to suggest that no other events should be created within the same period of time. Her use of a specific phrase as well as a specific event duration became a calendaring convention that let Ethan know he should **not** schedule time with her.

She just doesn't like being locked down to commitments and so having a lot of documented appointments on the calendar is something she dislikes. So, sometimes she'll just have days where the event is not having events. This is a date where people are not allowed to schedule things...it'll just be a day event that says, 'Take it easy.'

This example reflects another way in which our participants make themselves explainable to their partners in intimate relationships. Although Nora could simply leave her calendar empty for the day, her "*take it easy*" event description makes it clear to Ethan (and others) that she does not want to be scheduled for any other events during that period of time. It is up to Ethan to decide whether his bond of trust with Nora is strong enough that he can honor her calendaring convention and see her another time.

Taken together, the examples discussed in this section demonstrate two different tactics that our participants use to make their plans and behavior explainable to others. Specifically, Sarah and Ethan add events to their shared calendars as conversation starters, whereas Nora relies on her "*take it easy*" event description as a clear statement to be left alone. In both cases, the event descriptions and the contextual information they provide are at least as important as the presence in the calendars of the events themselves. Someone who lacked the proper context could overlook the event descriptions and misinterpret the flexibility or purpose of the events, resulting in the need for clarification about what the calendar owners intended.

The next section explores how being accountable with and through OCS becomes more problematic when more than two people share the same calendar, and when calendar events are visible to people with whom the calendar owner is not intimately familiar. In particular, problems arise for our participants when they need to communicate specific information to certain individuals but not to everyone who can view the same calendar.

Being Accountable in Intimate Group Relationships

When OCS users share their calendars with people other than their significant others, they must consider how to act accountably to multiple individuals through their calendars. This broader consideration of how to behave accountably is especially challenging because, as our participants told us, it can be challenging to appear accountable to several people at the same time.

One way that our participants attempt to manage this situation is through their event descriptions. As described in the previous section, close friends and significant others sometimes use highly contextual event descriptions that other people might not understand. For example, one of our participants, Esther, shares a calendar with her husband, Frank, as well as three close friends. She labeled her wedding ceremony as "*lunch date*" and only invited Frank and a few friends as witnesses.

Instead of saying 'wedding day,' we called it a lunch date. We just really didn't want to share it with other people yet. And a lot of our friends knew, but, you know, we [secretly] put it on our calendar in advance.

Esther needed to put an event on her shared calendar so that she and her wedding guests would have time scheduled for the ceremony, but she did not want to alert anyone else about her wedding or her specific plans for the ceremony. However, Esther's close friend Christy added the event to her own shared calendar and changed the description from "*lunch date*" to something that indicated Esther's wedding plans.

Tyler, a close friend of Esther and Christy, saw this event in Christy's calendar and realized that he had not been invited to Esther's wedding ceremony. He consequently stopped sharing his calendar with both Esther and Christy. Esther was only able to repair her relationship with Tyler when she had a lengthy offline discussion with him about how small her wedding was, and why he and a number of other friends simply could not be invited. Even after a great deal of discussion about this situation, however, Tyler no longer shared his calendar with Esther or Christy.

Prior work has shown that the act of sharing a calendar is an emotionally meaningful event in an intimate relationship, an event that is not always tied to the need to coordinate time with another person [26]. However, as the situation with Esther makes clear, the decision to stop sharing a calendar can also signify an important milestone in a relationship. The decision to stop sharing is not necessarily because the need to coordinate no longer exists, but because the relationship itself is in jeopardy, as when the bond of trust between Esther and Tyler needed to be reestablished.

OCS use can help strengthen relationships as well: Sally told us how she and her group of close friends insert events into their shared calendars as a way to encourage interactional intimacy. She explained that they use an event with a specific name to indicate their desire to spend time with Leslie, one of their close friends.

Leslie recently has been in a relationship, and so she's been spending a lot of time with her boyfriend. And so, we told her that she had to maintain a one-to-one ratio between her friendships and her boyfriend. And so, you'll see on her calendar she has 'Recalibrate the ratio,' which generally means either she's having sex with her boyfriend or she is hanging out with us. So, sometimes when she's spending too much time with her boyfriend we'll put in, 'Recalibrate the ratio' as like, 'Hey, come spend some time with us.'

The use of *"recalibrate the ratio"* on Leslie's calendar demonstrates how the significance of a calendar event can come from its specific context as well as its presence. The event itself is important because it acts as a notification to Leslie that she needs to be accountable to her entire group of friends, both her boyfriend and her close friends, and the context with the event is significant because the presence of the event on Leslie's calendar forces her to ask what the current ratio of time spent amongst her friends is and which way it is out of balance. Beyond that, it forces her friends to consider both of these aspects as well. In some cases, *"recalibrate the ratio"* will appear on Leslie's calendar when her boyfriend is in town and she wants time with him, yet other times it will appear because her friends want time with her.

Our participants weave OCS into their lives as they attempt to behave in socially accountable ways with close friends and significant others. OCS are organized, continuously enacted social arrangements within which people represent their activities as calendar events, OCS users must take care to maintain awareness of the specific social expectations that apply to calendaring behavior. If they fail to do so, they run the risk of damaging the bonds of trust [25] that partners in intimate relationships construct over time as they support one another through their mutual commitment to their relationships.

DISCUSSION

The goal of this study was to address the following research question in the context of the enactment of accountability: *How do OCS users perform relationship work with and through their calendars*? We have addressed this research question by highlighting the processual struggles that partners in intimate relationships undergo when attempting to act accountably with and through their shared calendars.

In this section we consider the OCS design challenge posed by our findings: How can OCS help users through the initial learning process about shared calendaring norms and expectations? The goal is to discuss possible design interventions that could allow OCS users to more effectively supporting their negotiation and enactment of accountable behavior.

One of the biggest challenges with OCS use is the shift from "me-calendaring" to "we-calendaring," where calendar owners must realize that others will be using the information they store in their calendars. Specifically, when people first begin using OCS, they need to understand the differences in using a digital, shared calendar compared to using paper calendars and other forms of tracking one's schedule. For example, OCS users need to understand who else can see their events, as well as their titles and descriptions. While it is simple to develop this awareness when only two people share calendars with one another, it becomes tougher to trace who can see which calendar as invitations to share proliferate within groups of friends.

As calendar owners grant other people access to a shared calendar, the OCS should alert all users that changes have been made to the visibility of that calendar. Each new invitation to share is an opportune time for all calendar users to think about how their events will be interpreted by everyone else who can see and use the same calendar. This simple interface design change would allow OCS users to make decisions about how they want to be explainable to other calendar users; which events to track, how to describe those events, who they should invite, and so on.

Unlike colleagues who share Google Calendar simply to complete a specific project, close friends and significant others intend to continue scheduling their lives together forever, assuming their intimate relationships flourish and persist. One way to help partners in intimate relationships improve their ability to act accountably through their shared calendars is for OCS to offer better support for the scheduling of unscheduled time. Although this concept seems contradictory, the present work reflects the fact that people share calendars because they are quite busy and want to make time for one another.

Our prior work [26] touched on the possibility of "shades" of availability without extending that idea beyond musing about how people needed to decide on their own whether specific times could be considered available. However, our findings from the present study provide additional context that enables us to explore possible variants on the notion of "free" time. For example, OCS can include blocks of time that have differentiated levels of availability depending on who is viewing the shared calendar. Times could be shown as available for scheduling by anyone else, available only to a subset of calendar users, or entirely unavailable. The goal behind any such design changes is to enable calendar owners and users alike to generate and interpret contextual temporal information more easily than the indication of "free/busy" currently allows, or in Eriksén's words, to support the practices of being explainable.

Finally, partners in intimate relationships frequently add events to both of the calendars they share with one another, rarely sending actual invitations to events. A simple annotation system would allow OCS users to indicate how tentative their attendance might be, and whether attendance at a specific event is conditional based on other events. Selectable and customizable tags could help eliminate the need for complicated systems of textual notation within events, as well as other intricate calendaring conventions.

CONCLUSIONS

As other scholars have demonstrated [cf., 2, 19, 28], OCS support collaborative activity in part by enabling users to share their schedules of planned activities with one another. However, tools that are designed to support collaboration cannot entirely replace the variety of activities that people perform when they collaborate with one another [cf., 3]. Therefore, it is important for OCS to be designed such that the performance of accountable behavior is supported more effectively than at present, particularly considering that calendar sharing is relationship work [26] and that relationship work is predicated on acting accountably.

Given this importance of shared calendaring in people's lives, we concur with the value that [5] ascribe to designing "digital systems so that they mesh with human behavior at the individual and collective levels." Ultimately, OCS is only one channel of communication among many that are popular among partners in intimate relationships and across groups of friends. However, as technology has become increasingly interwoven into our lives, it is useful to consider how OCS can be designed to better support the accountability practices that are vitally important to the growth and ongoing health of the relationships we consider most important.

ACKNOWLEDGMENTS

This project was funded by a Google Research Award. Thanks to Katie Derthick, Betsy Rolland, and Stephanie Steinhardt for their work on this study.

REFERENCES

1. Beech, S., Geelhoed, E., Murphy, R., Parker, J., Sellen, A., and Shaw, K. The Lifestyles of Working Parents. Technical Report HPL-2003-88R1 HP Labs (2004).
2. Crabtree, A., Hemmings, T., and Rodden, T. Informing the Development of Calendar Systems for Domestic Use. in *Proc. of the Eighth European Conference on Computer-Supported Cooperative Work,* (Helsinki, Finland, 2003), Kluwer Academic Publishers, 119-138.
3. Dossick, C. F. and Neff, G. Messy talk and clean technology: communication, problem-solving and collaborating using Building Information Modelling.

Engineering Project Organization Journal, 1, 2 (2011), 83-93.

4. Ehrlich, S.F. Social and psychological factors influencing the design of office communications systems. In *Proc. CHI 1987,* ACM Press (1987), 323-329.
5. Erickson, T. and Kellogg, W. A. Social Translucence: An Approach to Designing Systems that Mesh with Social Processes. In *Transactions on Computer-Human Interaction*, ACM Press (2000), Vol. 7, No. 1, 59-83.
6. Eriksén, S. Designing for Accountability. In *NordiCHI,* ACM Press (2002), 177-186.
7. Fehr, B. *Friendship Processes*. Sage Publications (1986).
8. Garfinkel, H. *Studies in Ethnomethodology*. Prentice-Hall (1967).
9. Grimes, A. and Brush, A.J. Life scheduling to support multiple social roles. In *Proc. CHI 2008*, ACM Press (2008), 821-824.
10. Grudin, J. A case study of calendar use in an organization. *SIGOIS Bull. 17*, 3 (1996), 49-51.
11. Kincaid, C.M., Dupont, P.D. and Kaye, A.R. Electronic Calendars in the Office: An Assessment of User Needs and Current Technology. *ACM Transactions on Office Information Systems 3*, 1 (1985), 89–102.
12. Lynch, M. Against Reflexivity as an Academic Virtue and Source of Privileged Knowledge. *Theory, Culture & Society 17*, 3 (2000), 26-54.
13. McKnight, D.H., Cummings, L.L., and Chervany, N.L. Initial Trust Formation in New Organizational Relationships. *Academy of Management Review 23*, 3 (1998), 473-490.
14. Neustaedter, C., Brush, A.J., and Greenberg, S. The calendar is crucial: Coordination and awareness through the family calendar. *ACM Trans. Comput.-Hum. Interact. 16*, 1 (2009), 1-48.
15. Neustaedter, C., Brush, A.J., and Greenberg, S. A digital family calendar in the home: lessons from field trials of LINC. In *Proc. of Graphics Interface 2007*, ACM Press (2007), 199-220.
16. Orlikowski, W.J., and Yates, J.A. It's about Time: Temporal Structuring in Organizations. *Organization Science, 13, 6,* (2002) 684-700.
17. Palen, L. and Grudin, J. Discretionary adoption of group support software: lessons from calendar applications. In B.E. Munkvold (Ed.) *Implementing Collaboration Technologies in industry: Case Examples and Lessons Learned*, (2003), 159-179.
18. Palen, L. Social, individual and technological issues for groupware calendar systems. In *Proc. CHI 1999*, ACM Press (1999), 17-24.
19. Palen, L. Calendars on the New Frontier: Challenges of Groupware Technology. *Dissertation, Info. & Computer Science*, UC Irvine (1998).
20. Paul, P. A Paper Calendar? It's 2011, *The New York Times.* Retrieved April 28, 2012 from The New York Times: www.nytimes.com/2011/07/31/fashion/calendar-wars-pit-electronics-against-paper.html
21. Payne, S.J. Understanding calendar use. *Human-Computer Interaction 8*, 2 (1993), 83-100.
22. Plaisant, C., Clamage, A., Hutchinson, H.B., Bederson, B.B. and Druin, A. Shared family calendars: promoting symmetry and accessibility. *ACM Transactions on Computer-Human Interaction 13*, 3 (2006), 313-46.
23. Prager, K.J. and Roberts, L.J. Deep Intimate Connection: Self and Intimacy in Couple Relationships. In D.J. Mashek and A. Aron (Eds.) *Handbook of Closeness and Intimacy*. Lawrence Erlbaum Associates (2004), 43-60.
24. Rusbult, C. E., Kumashiro, M., Coolsen, M. K., & Kirchner, J. L. Interdependence, Closeness, and Relationships. In D.J. Mashek and A. Aron (Eds.) *Handbook of Closeness and Intimacy*. Lawrence Erlbaum Associates (2004), 137-161.
25. Sanderson, C. A., and Evans, S. M. Seeing one's partner through intimacy-colored glasses: An examination of the processes underlying the intimacy goals–relationship satisfaction link. *Personality and Social Psychology Bulletin, 27,* 4 (2001), 463-473.
26. Thayer, A., Lee, C.P., Derthick, K., and Bietz, M.J. I Love You, Let's Share Calendars: Calendar Sharing as Relationship Work. In *Proc. CSCW 2012*, ACM Press (2012), 749-758.
27. Troshynski, E., Lee, C.P., and Dourish, P. Accountabilities of Presence: Reframing Location-Based Systems. In *Proc. CHI 2008*, ACM Press (2008) 487-496.
28. Tungare, M., Pérez-Quiñones, M.A. and Sams, A. An Exploratory Study of Calendar Use. arXiv:0809.3447v1.
29. van den Hooff, B. Electronic coordination and collective action: use and effects of electronic calendar and scheduling. *Information & Management 42*, 1 (2004), 103-114.
30. Van Lear, A., Koerner, A. F., & Allen, D. Relationship Typologies. In A. Vangelisti and D. Perlmann, (Eds.) *The Cambridge Handbook of Personal Relationships*. Cambridge University Press (2006), 91-111.

Audio-Enhanced Paper Photos: Encouraging Social Interaction at Age 105

Anne Marie Piper[1,2], Nadir Weibel[2], James D. Hollan[2]

[1]Northwestern University
2240 Campus Dr., Evanston, IL 60208, USA
ampiper@northwestern.edu

[2]University of California, San Diego
9500 Gilman Dr., La Jolla, CA, USA
{weibel, hollan}@ucsd.edu

ABSTRACT

Photographs are powerful and pervasive media that facilitate communication and support reminiscence. Adding audio narrations to traditional paper photographs combines the familiarity of paper photos with the nuanced richness of voice. We enable creation of and interaction with audio-enhanced paper photographs through custom software deployed on a digital pen. This paper reports on use of a paper-digital photo album by an older adult (Ethel, age 105), her extended family, and nursing staff over a five-month field deployment. The interactive photo album was found to be easy to use and accessible, effectively engaged Ethel's and family members' interest, and provided a focal point for communication and social interaction. Family and caregivers report improvements in Ethel's social interaction. We discuss the properties of our audio-enhanced paper approach that make it a promising medium for engaging older adults and distill general design considerations for paper-digital photo albums.

Author Keywords

Communication; Digital Pen; Photos; Older Adults; Social Interaction

ACM Classification Keywords

H.5.2 User Interfaces: Input Devices and Strategies

INTRODUCTION

Aging presents challenges in many dimensions of life. One aspect of aging that is well-studied is the relationship between social interaction and late-life satisfaction. A lack of social interaction for older adults may contribute to higher rates of disability, slower recovery from illness, and even early death [25, 1]. While some work suggests that social networking technologies can prevent feelings of social isolation or loneliness [29], such outlets require technical and physical ability as well as access to a computer, presenting challenges for some older adults. Furthermore, intergenerational communication and sharing of memories is complicated by differences in technology access, ability, and interests.

CSCW'13, February 23-27, San Antonio, Texas, USA.

We present a hybrid paper-digital approach to sharing photos that is a tool for intergenerational communication, reminiscence, and social engagement. Through a case study we detail the evolution and use of an interactive audio-enhanced paper photo album. Working with a large extended family, we introduced the photo album to Ethel (age 105) and her extended family. We report on Ethel, her family, and her care staffs' use of the photo album over five months, describing how the materials engaged Ethel's interests and supported social interaction and reminiscence.

This research builds on and contributes to the growing literature on social practices of photo sharing [24, 6, 10] as well as techniques that support reminiscence for older adults [15, 22, 40, 44]. In particular, this case study documents improvement in social interaction by the older adult. Practices such as reviewing family and care staff's names and faces in the photo album seemed to help Ethel better remember these people during face-to-face interactions. The introduction of the album also provided a new focal point for interaction and stimulation, which generally enhanced quality of life. Older adults in the family, including Ethel and her children (in their 70s and 80s), had little difficulty authoring audio content or navigating the interactive photo album.

In order to situate our study we first highlight how current work in different areas informed and shaped our own work. After introducing the research methods and the deployment of the interactive photo album, we describe and analyze the authoring process, user generated content, and usage of audio-enhanced paper photos. We conclude with a discussion of the properties of audio-enhanced paper photos that make them well-suited for reminiscence and intergenerational communication and offer practical insights about deploying this technology in the field. Although derived from an extended case study of usage by one family, we anticipate that the general authoring process we developed as well as the idea of audio-enhanced paper photos for communication and reminiscence might inform a variety of applications with other populations.

RELATED WORK

This project bridges several areas of research: applications of digital pen technology, social interaction involving photographs, the notion of audio-enhanced photos, archiving of family memories, and the implications of these media for older adults. Foremost, a deeper understanding of the affordances of paper are a cornerstone of this research, drawing on studies of paper in office work [38], medicine [26], and aviation [27, 30]. Digital pens are often used to link paper and digital media [28, 43, 17]. Applications of digital pens include document editing [5], linking handwritten and audio notes [4], scientific notebooks [46], and collaborative annotations [41]. Recent work by Piper *et al* [34] suggests that digital pens are an appropriate and accessible tool for older adults. Digital pens are also affordable, costing $100 USD.[1]

Our work is not the first to use a hybrid paper-digital approach to support photo sharing and reminiscence. The Memento project introduces a hybrid paper-digital scrapbooking architecture [45]. Memento uses an Anoto pen to allow users to annotate a paper photo album and link these annotations with audio recordings and video files on a nearby computer. While the system does record and replay audio, the digital pen must be coupled with a computer, requiring the users to setup and manage bluetooth connections and ensure Internet connectivity. In contrast to this, we explore the use of a Livescribe pen with an integrated speaker and microphone to enable a standalone interactive experience. What is distinctive about our approach is the simplicity of a purely pen and paper interface.

Photographs are a powerful tool for social interaction [19] and provide anchors for discussion [39]. Our approach explores audio-enhanced photos and builds on Frohlich's extensive work on audiophotography, which indicates that ambient "sounds-of-the-moment" have potential to bring photos to life and to aid memory of events [12, 13]. Frohlich and Fennell [9] recommend audio photographs rather than video clips as a new media form, again emphasizing the importance of paper photos in contrast to a screen-based viewing experience. An interesting contrast is the idea of a "sonic souvenir" for family remembering [7]. Compared to photos, sounds were found to be more varied, familial, and creative as well as being evocative and generating reflective narrative.

Several projects involve tangible interaction as part of linking audio narrations with physical content. The Memory Box explores recording and attaching stories to memorabilia in a keepsake box [11]. Similarly, Stevens *et al* [42] examine family archiving as a way of informing the Living Memory Box project. Klemmer *et al* [20] introduce bar-code augmented paper transcripts linked to digital video interviews.

The present research focuses on supporting photo sharing and reminiscence for older adults, the so called "Kodak culture" [3]. Many digital photo sharing alternatives require a level of technical understanding, often limiting use by older generations [36], whereas paper photos have immediate affordances understandable by everyone [32]. Related work examines new approaches to bridge generational differences in the photo sharing experience (e.g., [21]).

Prior work also examines the design of tools for reminiscence later in life, specifically for individuals with memory loss. Gowans *et al* [15] introduce a multimedia tool to stimulate long-term memory and encourage conversation for adults with dementia. Kuwahara *et al* [22] enable remote photo- and video-sharing involving individuals with dementia and their therapists. As part of this literature, there is work on multimedia biographies to support communication and reminiscence between individuals with memory loss and their families [40]. Similarly, Webster [44] and colleagues designed Portrait to serve as a communication bridge between people with dementia and their caregivers.

Aging is associated with a variety of changes in cognitive abilities. After the age of 70, normally aging individuals experience a decline in short-term memory [16]. Semantic knowledge may also decline around this time [31, 37]. Changes in verbal ability generally become increasingly evident after the age of 80 [37]. Some aspects of cognitive functioning, however, remain relatively stable over the lifespan and are central to our approach. Stable aspects include autobiographical memory [14], implicit memory (accumulation of life experiences and learnings) [23], ability to process emotional information [2], and theory of mind (recognizing the viewpoints of others) [18]. Psychomotor skills can also be sustained if they receive dedicated practice [35], and our approach presents one technique for encouraging this.

METHOD

This research details the adoption and appropriation of an audio-enhanced photo album by a large extended family, primarily consisting of older adults. As part of this, we examine the system's usability by older adults as well as how the system changes the older adults' social interaction and overall wellbeing. A five-month field technology deployment with a single extended family addresses these aims.

Ethel, at age 105, is the oldest member of her family. She does not know how to use a computer nor does she regularly use a cell phone, digital camera, or tablet computer. She enjoys visiting with her family and reading novels. She has trouble remembering people's names and her relationship to them. Ethel often forgets who extended family members are, whether appearing in a photo or in person. She is also unlikely to know which day of the week it is and generally her ability to understand the passage of time has declined.

Ethel lives in a retirement community along with two of her children. In addition to onsite nursing staff, Ethel's four children (in their 70s and 80s) help care for her and visit her daily. Alice (Ethel's oldest daughter, age 78) has been Ethel's primary caregiver over the past 10 years. For this reason, much of the analysis within this paper focuses on interactions between Ethel and Alice and relies heavily on Alice's observations of her mother while using the photo album.

We selected this family as study participants for three reasons. First, initial observations of the role of paper photos in communication with Ethel was promising in terms of building on this family's existing practices. Second, Ethel's closest family member (Alice) lives in the same community with her and was available to introduce and manage the technology. Third, Ethel's 105th birthday party was approaching, an event that brings many distance-separated family members together, enabling a unique opportunity for multigenerational content generation.

[1] http://www.livescribe.com

The timing of the study allowed us to introduce the interactive photo album at Ethel's 105th birthday as a new type of guest book. A Livescribe digital pen, equipped with the TAP & PLAY software [33] was deployed with the album and allowed family members and friends to author audio messages and link them to the photos. We positioned a video camera nearby the album to capture interaction during the party. After the party we observed photo album use by a variety of family members and conducted semi-structured interviews with family members and Ethel.

The photo album remained with Ethel after the birthday party. After six weeks of heavy use, the pen's memory reached capacity for audio recordings. The family returned the photo album and digital pen to the research team. After a few days, the family requested that we return the materials so they may continue to use the materials with Ethel, as it had become an important artifact in her life. We returned the materials to the family, now with the ability to listen to existing recordings but not record new audio. After a total of five months (starting at the birthday party), we collected the photo album and digital pen to perform a final analysis.

Throughout the study we collected field notes and video data of the family using this album (both the authoring process and Ethel's usage), interviews with the family and nursing staff, email reports from the family, and log file data from the digital pen. We conducted a survey with family members and nursing staff after the initial six week deployment to understand the photo album's impact on Ethel.

Our analysis derives themes from our field observations, interviews, and the analysis of artifacts and representations over time. There are many dimensions to consider within this complex system of interaction: how family members and care staff create audio-enhanced photos, how Ethel learns to use the album, how others support her in doing this, and how the album changes social interaction and communication involving Ethel. We examine these issues below, but first we describe the role of paper photos for this family.

PAPER PHOTOS

We began research with this family by conducting an interview with Alice and observing Ethel in her room at the retirement community. Alice said of her mother:

"She was 101 when she went into the nursing home and she didn't want to interact with any of the people there, she considered them 'old.' She also didn't interact with the people taking care of her. If she had a complaint she waited until I came or my brother came and then told us. She didn't want to eat in the dining room for any of her meals."

Figure 1. Printed photos on a bulletin board in Ethel's room.

Alice is the family member who interacts with Ethel most frequently, and as such she is a key informant for this research project. She comments on the challenges of engaging her mother in conversation:

"I come in [to Ethel's room], say a few things. She doesn't really interact in the conversation, but if you start talking about who someone is in a picture, and 'do you remember that person?' It gives a focal point for communicating... It gets real easy just to go in with a book and sit with her."

While many of Ethel's interests have waned, she maintains a strong interest in her family and memories captured in photos. She has a bulletin board in her room filled with paper photos of her family (Fig. 1). Alice describes this:

"We have a bulletin board covered with pictures... in her room on the wall. She wants to engage me in a conversation, I know. She'll say, 'you know who those people are?' I say, 'oh yeah, that's so and so.' She says, 'take those pictures and move them there.' She wants to get me engaged in doing something with the pictures. It's her way of communicating."

Following a human-centered design approach, we leverage the fact that photos are already a means of fostering communication with Ethel and therefore study this family more closely as they use the interactive photo album. It is important to note that Ethel and her children are all part of the "Kodak culture" [3], generations that grew up with and still highly value photos printed on paper. Therefore, our research is most concerned with how the family creates and appropriates audio recordings coupled with the paper photos. The inherent goal is to build upon the familiar nature of paper photos, but now enhanced with audio recordings, to foster interaction between Ethel and her extended family and care staff.

INTERACTIVE PHOTO ALBUM

After observing the family's use of paper photos, we used the TAP & PLAY authoring toolkit [33] to help the family create a custom interactive photo album. TAP & PLAY runs on a Livescribe[1] digital pen. This digital pen has a built in microphone and speaker that allows users to record and replay audio. TAP & PLAY provides a pen-based interface for linking custom audio recordings to regions of paper printed with a special dot pattern recognized by the Livescribe pen.

The family sent the research team digital photos which we printed on dot pattern paper and gave back to the family as part of the photo album. Additionally, we provided the family with stickers printed with the dot pattern to attach to other paper materials (e.g., traditional photos) and integrate into the photo album. The family assembled the interactive photo album for Ethel's 105th birthday. Each year, five generations of the family gather to celebrate Ethel's birthday. Using a Livescribe pen with the TAP & PLAY software, family members recorded and saved messages for Ethel. The family placed a small control panel used for authoring on the inside cover of the album (see Fig 3). After saving audio to a page, tapping the pen on the interactive area plays the associated audio.

FIELD DEPLOYMENT & ANALYSIS

Through a five-month field deployment we observe how this family cooperatively authored interactive photos and integrated this album into Ethel's daily routine to improve communication and socialization.

Photo Album Authoring

Over the course of the study, the family added 102 photos to the album and linked 104 audio messages to these photos. Authoring began when family members placed the photo album on a table at Ethel's 105th birthday party for family and friends to add their audio messages. We videotaped interaction with the photo album during the birthday party and conducted follow-up interviews with family members. A total of 36 people (age 2-105) added audio messages to the interactive photo album. As earlier evaluations of TAP & PLAY indicate [33], there is a low learning curve for linking audio content to paper. Family members were able to quickly and easily add custom audio messages to photos within the album.

Partway through the party, the family showed the photo album to Ethel. She watched as people recorded their messages, and she even recorded her voice, with the help of her children and grandchildren (Fig. 2). Family members were particular about the messages they recorded and often revised a message before saving it. Messages could be re-recorded but not deleted from the pen. Although there were 104 audio messages linked to the album, 154 messages were saved to the pen. This indicates that roughly one-third of the audio messages were unlinked from photos and/or not wanted. The TAP & PLAY interface allows for recording, replay, and re-recording of a message. One grandchild (age 62) recorded the same message six times before he was happy with it, making only slight modifications between each version.

Alice took ownership over the album, storing it for the family and bringing it to her mother to use. Two days after the birthday party she revised the paper interface that allows people to

Figure 2. Grand daughter and daughter (Alice) introduce the interactive photo album to Ethel (age 105) at her birthday party. Authoring control panels are on the right side of the album cover. All participants consented to the use of photos for publication.

Figure 3. Alice authoring photos. Control panel for TAP & PLAY interface on photo album cover.

Figure 4. *Left:* faces as interactive regions; *Center:* interactive sticker on a birthday card; *Right:* grouping photos by family and person.

add audio to the book (Fig. 3, right). She cut up the authoring control panel and supplemented it with her own more detailed instructions. Here again we note the benefits of paper.

Most people authored content by circling a face within a photo and attaching a message directly to that area (Fig. 4, left). The pen comes with a non-marking pen tip, and several family members requested this; however, they used the marking tip during the authoring process to help Ethel identify interactive regions. Over time Alice improved upon this and learned to put a large "tap here" region lower on the page, closer to where Ethel would sit when tapping the photos:

"I have found that due to her [Ethel's] limited arm mobility it is better to have the area to be tapped at the bottom of the page so that it is easier for her to reach rather than the faces circled. Of course it is good to have faces circled if that person is actually talking to her."

Traditional paper photos (without dot pattern) and other paper objects were also integrated into the photo album. Family members added interactive dot pattern stickers that are part of the TAP & PLAY toolkit to regular photos and to greeting cards Ethel received at her party (see Fig. 4, center). Tapping on the card played an audio message associated with that object (i.e., read the birthday card aloud).

As a close caregiver of Ethel, Alice naturally became the main person in charge of the photo album. She worked to improve the album and make it a better experience for Ethel. She supplemented missing material: *"I have had to rerecord one picture because part of the sentences were missing."* She even reorganized the photos in the book: *"Using the book was a learning experience for me... as time went on, I added new pictures and began to arrange the pictures*

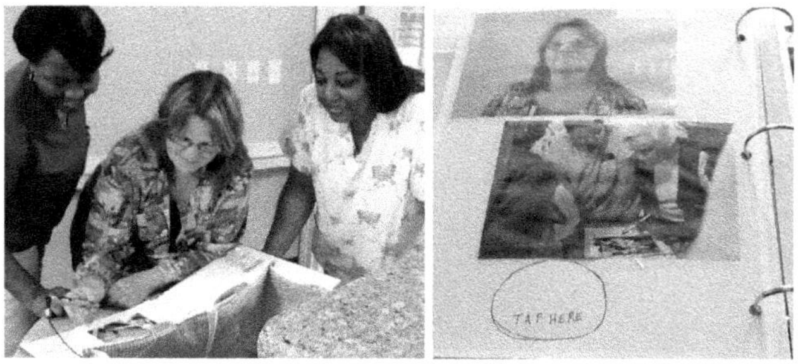

Figure 5. Nursing staff adding audio messages to the photo album. Alice took these photos, printed them, and then added them to the album.

in better order." Alice organized multiple photos of the same person into groups (e.g., stacked photos as in Fig. 4, right) and placed immediate family members near each other in the book order.

Ethel is in full-time nursing care at her retirement community and a team of nurses help care for her. Alice took photos of the nursing staff who work with her mother. She printed these out on her home printer, added them to the album, and had each person add a message for Ethel (Fig. 5).

Audio Annotations

Two researchers performed a content analysis of the photo album and coded each audio recording identifying recurring features of the audio messages. The coding scheme evolved and was updated as additional features became salient. We identified the following features of each audio recording: speaker name(s), whether multiple people are part of the audio, explicit identification of speaker, identifies others, states a relationship ("this is your husband"), identifies objects in the photo, the event captured in the photo, photo location, the purpose of the photo, a marker of time ("your 101st birthday"), asks a question, personal message ("happy birthday"), or references other photos. Figure 6 illustrates the generational relationships of family members, the total messages recorded by each member, and the average number of features in the recordings by each author.

Alice was the most prolific author, generating 46 of the 104 messages. Alice's daughter Sharon was the second most frequent author, providing 11 recordings. Although Ethel did not record any messages independently, her voice was part of seven messages. A total of 36 people added audio messages to the album, 17 of whom contributed two or more recordings.

The family understood that the photo album was intended for use by Ethel, so we analyze how people designed their messages for her. Ethel is losing her memory of individuals in her family, so it is important that people identify themselves through the audio recording. However, only 32 of the messages explicitly identified the speaker ("This is Mary"), and 15 messages assumed Ethel would know who was speaking ("This is me at the beach"). On the other hand, both Alice and Sharon almost always identified themselves when speaking even though they were the two most prolific authors. Many recordings (74 total) identified people other than just the speaker and 55 recordings discussed relationships between the people in the photo or their relationship to Ethel.

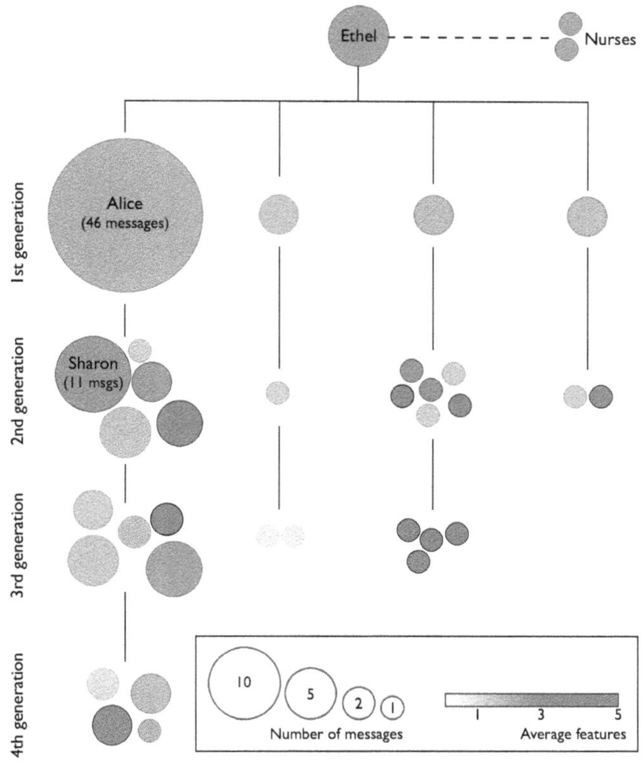

Figure 6. Audio messages visualized as part of the family tree. Every circle represents a person, its size is the number of messages recorded, and its color gradient the average number of features used in the messages.

Family members structured their messages to Ethel in a similar way, often first stating who is in the photo, then describing the context of the photo, and concluding with a personal message such as "Happy birthday Grandmom" or "We love you." Some of the recordings (15) were primarily a message such as a child singing a song or wishing Ethel "happy birthday".

People used both time and place descriptions to put the photo in context for Ethel. Twenty recordings included markers of time such as death of someone in a photo or a past birthday. For example Ethel's son David said, *"Hi Mom, this is Minnie and myself quite a few years ago before Nicole passed away, and these are your grandchildren."* Recordings also identified the event captured in the photo (24 recordings) and/or the location (21 recordings). Some recordings were more experiential in that they described details of the environment or mood during the photo. For example, Mary (Ethel's daughter) recorded rich details about a photo taken in the 1940s: *"...I can still smell the pine cones. I can remember the water. I can remember us standing and taking this picture. I don't remember a lot about my childhood, but this I do remember."*

While the system only involves a single digital pen, there were many opportunities for collaboration. The large size of the photo album enabled sharing between people. The authoring process itself generated new opportunities for interaction among co-present individuals. Eighteen audio recordings were created by multiple people at once (i.e., two or more people talking during the same recording). One recording

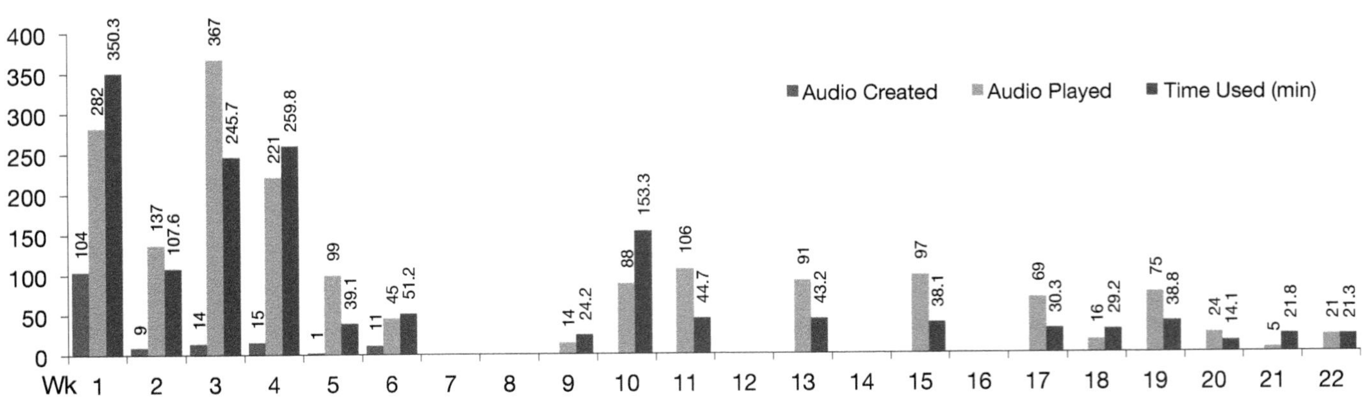

Figure 7. Amount of time digital pen was used by Ethel and her family over the field deployment. Several days had multiple sessions of use.

involved nine different speakers, including Ethel. Several of the multispeaker recordings capture instances of banter and teasing between family members (see Table 1). This dialog about the photo, called *phototalk* [6, 10], is now archived and associated with the image.

Speaker	Recorded on Pen
Alice:	*This is me, Alice, with both of my daughters. On my right is Sharon and on my left is Carol.*
Sharon:	*I'm the favorite daughter.*
Alice:	*That's Sharon. She thinks she's the favorite, and so does Carol think she's the favorite.*
Other:	*You're not the favorite, it's the one who [inaudible]*
All:	*(laughter)*

Table 1. Example of *phototalk* captured on the digital pen.

Later in the study Alice commented on the need for clear, succinct recordings: *"The people speaking need to prepare what they want to say so time is not wasted."* Alice made this comment after the pen's memory filled up, and she indicated to our research team that she would have spent less time on certain recordings, specifically narrating the birthday cards. Currently it is possible to unlink an audio recording from a region on paper, but it is not possible to permanently delete recordings through the authoring toolkit. This facility would be useful in future deployments.

Nearly all audio messages were directed towards Ethel in the second person. Audio recordings address Ethel directly (as mother, grandmother, etc) with personalized greetings. The only two audio messages that spoke of Ethel in the third person were those created by nursing staff. Fourteen recordings provided meta-information about a group of photos, while the individual photos contained more detailed specifics. Two recordings provided Ethel with additional instructions. For example, Alice recorded the following: *"This is a picture of you with all four of your children. Tap on the faces that have a circle around them to have them tell who they are."*

Photo Album Use

We observed Ethel using the photo album in her room at the retirement community several days after her birthday party. Alice demonstrated how to use the pen to tap on photos. Ethel was able to independently tap throughout the album. During this first experience, Alice helped by turning pages and pointing out interactive regions. Ethel has arthritis in her hands and is now unable to write, but she was able to hold the digital pen and tap on different parts of the page. Ethel listened to the audio played by the pen. Alice asked her mom, *"What do you think of it [the photo album]?"* Ethel replied, *"Well, it's great! Great to see all the people."* After observing her mother, Alice said, *"She did very well, especially for 105."*

An important aspect of this experience is that it is guided by a caregiver but self-paced by the older adult. It is not a passive experience; Ethel's actions are required for progression through the book. Alice continued to use the photo album with her mother and regularly sent our research team emails about usage. In an email Alice reported:

"I took it to [Ethel] today and started it up for her and she just took off. She tapped on the pictures and listened with delight, smiling a big smile. I sat with her for thirty minutes while she did it all herself and then she continued for another hour, handling it completely by herself... It was a huge success for social interaction. She was the center of attention and loved it. Earlier in the day she was dozing in her chair and not focusing on anything. This brought her to life."

After one evening session, Alice commented, *"She goes over and over it. It was time for her to get ready for bed but she didn't want to stop."* A few days later she explained that the album was even changing their daily routine: *"[Ethel] has been using it daily for the past few days... We used to watch television from six to seven when she goes to bed but now we look at pictures. She often says, 'oh, yes I remember that.'"*

Logfile Analysis

After six weeks, we collected the digital pen and photo album to examine the status of the album and the pen's log files. Ethel and her family used the digital pen for 1054 minutes (17.5 hours). Ethel's family created 154 audio messages and various messages were accessed 1151 times. Unfortunately the family filled the memory capacity of the pen after just six weeks of use. Surprisingly, the family wanted the photo album back even if it meant they could not add new audio recordings. Alice wrote to our research team: *"I missed having the book last evening. [Ethel] seemed lethargic, the book brings her truly alive. It brings back the past and it seems very happy memories."* Observing this change in her mother, Alice attempted to continue the project on her own by printing out paper photos and bringing them to her mother to discuss. Alice explained that this did not work well: *"I tried just computer pictures of the family but that didn't hold her interest. She wanted me to put them in the 'book'."* Per their request, we returned the pen and photo album to the family in a "play only" mode that would allow them to access previously saved audio but not add new recordings.

After five months of use, the family returned the album to our research team for a final analysis. The family accessed audio recordings an additional 606 times during weeks 9-22. During this extended deployment use stabilized to roughly 30 minutes per week. Figure 7 illustrates this usage data. Of the 104 linked audio recordings, 95 of them were replayed 10 or more times. Seven audio recordings were accessed 25 times or more (maximum of 33 times). Six of the seven frequently played recordings were directly related to her 105th birthday or a previous birthday. Also, six of the seven recordings were recorded by Ethel's children (the other was by her grandson).

Cognitive, Social, and Physical Impacts

We surveyed Ethel's closest family members (n=5) and her nursing staff (n=4) about their observations of Ethel after the first six weeks of the study. All nine respondents said they saw improvement in the quality of conversations they had with Ethel as well as her interest in socializing with others. Eight people reported improvement in Ethel's overall happiness, responsiveness, alertness, and willingness to interact with others. A certified nursing assistant commented, *"She seems to be more interactive in the evenings."* Five people said that they observed improvement in her range of motion of her right arm from tapping the pen on pages in the album. Alice commented, *"One physical improvement I have noticed is that she is stretching her arm out to tap the faces and is improving her arm mobility."* The physical consequences of the prototype are interesting and unexpected.

Reflection and Remembering People

The photo album provides a resource for reflecting on the past and remembering people in Ethel's life. Alice said, *"...if the pictured person spoke it made the connections stronger."* Ethel's photo album contained emotional photos of her deceased husband. The transcript and image shown in Fig. 8 are one example. Here, Ethel taps a photo of her husband. The pen plays back a conversation Ethel and Alice had about this photo several weeks prior. In the immediate situation, Ethel reflects on not only the paper image but also on the archived conversation. This example again demonstrates how phototalk is captured and revisited as part of this technology.

Alice reported a change in Ethel's behavior: *"She doesn't point to the bulletin board as she used to do, asking me if I knew all those people. I took the pictures in question off the board and put them in the book with comments telling her who they were and in some cases the circumstances of the pictures."* One certified nursing assistant (CNA) said that Ethel *"will show me family pictures on the wall and tell me who they are. She never did that before."* Ethel's daughter Mary explained, *"The good thing about the album was that it helped her to recognize those family members she does not see often."*

Pen's Playback	Real-time
Alice: Who is this man?	
Ethel: Yeah tha my husband	
	Ethel: Now I tapped him
Alice: This is Albert Trip	
Ethel: Yeah	
Alice: You were married to him for many years	
	Ethel: Yeah
Alice: And then he got sick	
Ethel: Yeah	
Alice: And then	
Ethel: He died	
Alice: He di::ed	
	Ethel: Yeahh

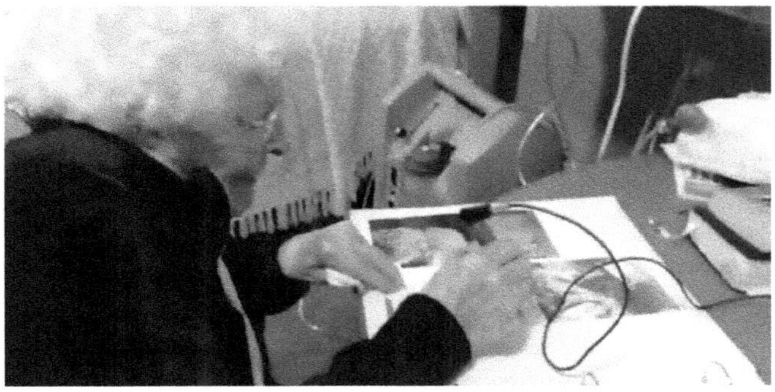

Figure 8. Ethel reflects on a photo of her husband augmented with a previous conversation between her and Alice.

At the end of the study, Alice reported via email: *"By repeating the process of looking at the pictures and hearing the recorded comments, she gradually learned who the people were... Now when she sees some of these people, she has something to attach the current people to the pictured people and remembers names much better."*

Supporting Social Interaction & Engagement

One positive effect of the photo album is that it provides a focal point for social interaction. It is evident in Alice's reports to our research team that the photo album provides an effective way for Alice to engage her mother in interaction. Several weeks into the study Alice explained, *"[The photo album] is a wonderful focal point for the hour I spend with her each evening. It serves as a bridge in fostering communication."*

The availability of the photo album also changed Ethel's interactions with other residents at the retirement community. Alice describes one such situation:

"Last evening one of the residents came to [Ethel's] door in her wheelchair and wanted to come in to visit. We had just started to use the photo album... [Ethel] was so pleased to show her the pictures and tap on them. She told her who some of them were... She actually talked to her, which is unusual because she doesn't usually interact with the other residents. The album was the focal point and stimulated interaction."

Interestingly, Alice called this event to our attention several times and said, *"it was unusual behavior for [Ethel]"*. On other occasions Ethel's care staff went through the photo album with her as part of therapy, similar to that done in [34].

Care Staff Support

While refinements are required before widespread adoption of this system is possible, the nursing staff was generally positive about the photo album and wanted one for the common area of the retirement community. Alice said of the nurses, *"Their response was overwhelming."* One nurse commented, *"This interactive photo album is an awesome tool for the elderly... It would help the elderly to work their minds and memories and give them so much pleasure."* Another nurse added, *"I think this project is so fascinating and it is such a wonderful tool for anyone to use."* It is encouraging to see nursing staff in strong support of this approach, as many older adults would rely on nursing staff to help them use such a photo album rather than immediate family as in Ethel's case. The photo album is a cooperative tool that provides opportunities for social interaction and fosters communication, and as such the success of the approach relies on shared use. The dependence on a support person to use the album, however, is also a limitation of the current design.

Limitations and Challenges of Design

Based on this field deployment, we identify aspects of the system design that need improvement. The form factor of the Livescribe pen, with its integrated microphone and speaker, worked well in the field. However, the pen's internal speaker is far from sufficient. Ethel and her children needed volume amplification through an external speaker as done in [33, 34]. Recording, listening to, and revising audio was a common pattern in authoring, and the TAP & PLAY interface enabled this with ease. A challenge is that the system does not allow users to delete audio recordings. This is intentional for research purposes but consequently contributed to the memory shortage that prevented the family from creating additional recordings. Similarly, several family members were concerned about losing the contents of the pen and wanted backup copies to be generated. Our current system does not have a way for end-users to do this, so the research team had to step in and backup the system for the family. While the play-only facilities of the pen (as in the latter part of the study) were sufficient for several months, the family still wanted to generate new content for Ethel. Content needs to be updated and improved upon regularly. This helps engage the older adult and her broader family. Enabling dynamic authoring of interactive paper photos is critical, and we are currently refining our software to allow for longer term use in the field.

DISCUSSION

In this paper we present an analysis of how one extended family authored and used an interactive paper-digital photo album to support engagement for the family matriarch. This research furthers our understanding of how people create and interact with audio-enhanced photos as well as how this media may support the unique needs of older users.

Digital tools mediate and may even interfere with the photo sharing experience for older generations [10]. Furthermore, all digital photo viewing alternatives require a certain level of technical ability, presenting potential challenges for older users [36]. Interaction through the digital pen, however, was straightforward for Ethel at age 105 and her children who are in their 70s and 80s. Building on prior work [34], we found that the digital pen integrates selection, recording, playback, and annotation in a way that is appropriate for older users.

This approach is also multigenerational, working well for young children and older adults, and allows for intergenerational expression [8]. Moreover, the interactive photo album presents an opportunity to bridge the "Kodak generation" with younger digital generations. Building on the need to include the practices of younger users as well as enable remote photo authoring, we are currently integrating our system with Facebook photo albums in a printable form.

Uniquely, our system allows phototalk to occur as it often does around traditional paper photos, but now those narratives can be recorded and replayed during subsequent viewing experiences. Lindley *et al* [24] note that captions, annotations, and digital storybooks elaborate a photo but may not afford true dynamic interaction that happens in face-to-face and in situ viewing experiences. Our approach begins to bridge this divide. Archiving this evolving narrative not only serves as an important family artifact but it may also provide anchors for improving older adults' memory as described in [15, 22].

The photo album is an interesting artifact to examine for research purposes, but at the conclusion of the study, who owns the materials? The physicality of the album and the fact that it was presented during Ethel's birthday party gives it properties of a gift item. At the beginning of the study, photos were printed on dot pattern paper with the help of the research team, but after that point the family evolved the photo album on their own. It also became an important part of Ethel's, and perhaps Alice's, life. After our final analysis, the family will maintain ownership of the materials and content.

Recommendations for Authoring

Our data indicate that the interactive paper photo album is a powerful tool for families, but particularly the primary care giver (Alice), in that they can design custom photo sharing or reminiscence activities for a loved one. As part of this, the primary care giver plays a critical role in the photo album's success. This person helps manage the album, organize it, adds and refines content, and then supports the older adult in using it. In our work we observed that Alice took on the role of curator, presenter, and primary author of the album [24]. Based on our analysis, we provide recommendations for authoring subsequent albums with the goal of engaging and stimulating an older adult.

- Photos should be large and clear. Alice suggested, *"Big and clear pictures are the best for someone who is old and may have trouble seeing."*
- Interactive regions should be indicated clearly, perhaps with additional labeling (e.g., "Tap Here"). The older

adult's arm mobility should be taken into account when determining the location of the region on the page.

- Audio narrations linked to a person's face are good if that person is talking and seem most natural when directed toward the older adult using second person language.
- The photo-audio combination is most useful when together it includes the person's name (spoken and written), the context of the photo, and a marker of time.
- Large group photos (over 5 people) can be problematic because the faces are typically smaller and there are many people for the older adult to identify within a single scene.
- Rather than a chronological ordering of the album, grouping family members and multiple photos of the same person together, may be more valuable for improving recall of names.

Curating and Further Authoring

Alice's close relationship with Ethel naturally shaped the interaction and authoring of the photo album. After the birthday party Alice became the curator and the keeper of the album. This influenced access to the album for Ethel, but also for other family members, especially in terms of further authoring. This is well visible in Fig. 6, where the family tree outlines how most of the messages have been generated in Alice's family branch. In fact, while collaborative access to the album with different family members continued throughout the study, family only present at the birthday party did not have opportunities to participate in further authoring after the party. This limited the evolving nature of the photo album.

The role of the curator is a fundamental one for enabling access to the interactive photo album for older adults, however we realized that alternative access for further authoring is desirable and would enable the album to evolve over time independent of the physical location of family members. In our current work, we are exploring ways of enabling remote access for authoring audio enabled printed photos. For example, we are designing a dedicated Facebook application to enable remote authoring, while local software installed on a computer at the retirement community would enable automatic upload to the digital pen of the audio messages recorded through Facebook. A local printer can then print the interactive photos for inclusion in the photo album. The role of the curator becomes therefore even more important.

CONCLUSION

We presented a five-month field study of the use of a paper-digital photo album designed to support late-life social interaction and engagement. We demonstrated that even for a person at age 105, digital pen technology is easy to use as an input device and supports powerful applications such as interactive audio-enhanced paper photos. Family members of all ages were able to add audio messages to the photo album. Messages identified people, described relationships, referenced past events, and had many other features. Personal photos and custom audio recordings provide meaningful stimulation and engagement. After using the interactive photo album for just six weeks, Ethel's family and caregivers reported improvements in several dimensions of social interaction. Furthermore, our research prototype became a positive part of Ethel's daily routine. While many factors may be involved in Ethel's improvements and the family's attraction to this system, the promise of technology to add personal voice recordings to normally static images is clear. Photographs have always functioned as catalysts for social interaction and anchors [39] for discussion. Making them multimodal and interactive makes it possible to explore new mechanisms for encouraging social interaction and engagement. We see great promise in exploring this approach with additional user groups who may benefit from rehearsal of peoples' names and faces as well as customized content that facilitates face-to-face social interaction.

REFERENCES

1. D. G. Blazer. Social support and mortality in an elderly community population. *Am. J. Epidemiol.*, 115, 1982.
2. L. Carstensen, H. Fung, and S. Charles. Socioemotional selectivity theory and the regulation of emotion in the second half of life. *Motivation Emotion*, 2003.
3. R. Chalfen. *Snapshot versions of life*. Bowling Green State University Popular Press, OH, 1987.
4. P. Chiu and L. Wilcox. A dynamic grouping technique for ink and audio notes. In *Proc. UIST '98*, pages 195–202, 1998.
5. K. Conroy, D. Levin, and F. Guimbretière. ProofRite: A Paper-Augmented Word Processor. Technical Report HCIL-2004-22, University of Maryland, USA, 2004.
6. A. Crabtree, T. Rodden, and J. Mariani. Collaborating around collections: informing the continued development of photoware. In *Proc. CSCW '04*, pages 396–405, 2004.
7. L. Dib, D. Petrelli, and S. Whittaker. Sonic souvenirs: exploring the paradoxes of recorded sound for family remembering. In *Proc. CSCW '10*, pages 391–400, 2010.
8. A. Durrant, A. Taylor, D. Frohlich, A. Sellen, and D. Uzzell. Photo displays and intergenerational relationships in the family home. In *BCS 2009*, 2009.
9. D. Frohlich and J. Fennell. Sound, paper and memorabilia: resources for a simpler digital photography. *Personal Ubiquitous Comput.*, 11(2):107–116, Jan. 2007.
10. D. Frohlich, A. Kuchinsky, C. Pering, A. Don, and S. Ariss. Requirements for photoware. In *Proc. CSCW '02*, pages 166–175, 2002.
11. D. Frohlich and R. Murphy. The memory box. *Personal Ubiquitous Comput.*, 4(4):238–240, Jan. 2000.
12. D. Frohlich and E. Tallyn. Audiophotography: practice and prospects. In *CHI '99 extended abstracts*, pages 296–297, 1999.
13. D. M. Frohlich. *Audiophotography: Bringing photos to life with sounds (The Computer Supported Cooperative Work Series)*. Springer-Verlag New York, Inc., Secaucus, NJ, USA, 2004.

14. P. Fromholt and *et.al.* Life-narrative and word-cued autobiographical memories in centenarians: comparisons with 80-year-old control, depressed, and dementia groups. *Memory*, 2003.

15. G. Gowans, J. Campbell, N. Alm, R. Dye, A. Astell, and M. Ellis. Designing a multimedia conversation aid for reminiscence therapy in dementia care environments. In *CHI '04 extended abstracts*, pages 825–836, 2004.

16. J. Gregorie and M. V. der Linden. Effect of age on forward and backward digit spans. *Aging Neuropsychol. Cogn.*, 4, 1997.

17. F. Guimbretière. Paper augmented digital documents. In *Proc. UIST '03*, pages 51–60, 2003.

18. F. Happe, E. Winner, and H. Brownell. The getting of wisdom: theory of mind in old age. *Dev. Psychol.*, 1998.

19. M. Hirsch. *Family Frames: Photography, Narrative and Postmemory*. Harvard Univ. Press, Cambridge, 1997.

20. S. R. Klemmer, J. Graham, G. J. Wolff, and J. A. Landay. Books with voices: paper transcripts as a physical interface to oral histories. In *Proc. CHI '03*, pages 89–96, 2003.

21. C. Kray, M. Rohs, J. Hook, and S. Kratz. Bridging the gap between the kodak and the flickr generations: A novel interaction technique for collocated photo sharing. *Int J Hum-comput St*, 67(12):1060 – 1072, 2009.

22. N. Kuwahara, S. Abe, K. Yasuda, and K. Kuwabara. Networked reminiscence therapy for individuals with dementia by using photo and video sharing. In *Proc. Assets '06*, pages 125–132, 2006.

23. D. LaVoie and L. Light. Adult age differences in repetition priming: a meta-analysis. *Psychol. Aging*, 1994.

24. S. Lindley, A. Durrant, D. Kirk, and A. S. Taylor. Collocated social practices surrounding photos. *Int J Hum-comput St*, 2009.

25. J. Lubben and M. Gironda. Centrality of social ties to the health and well-being of older adults. In B. Berkman and L. Harootyan, editors, *Social work and health care in an aging society: education, policy, practice, and research*. Springer, 2003.

26. P. Luff, C. Heath, and D. Greatbatch. Tasks-in-interaction: paper and screen based documentation in collaborative activity. In *Proc. CSCW '92*, pages 163–170, 1992.

27. W. MacKay. Is paper safer? The role of paper flight strips in air traffic control. *ACM Trans. Comput.-Hum. Interact.*, 6(4):340, 1999.

28. W. E. Mackay, G. Pothier, C. Letondal, K. Bøegh, and H. E. Sørensen. The Missing Link: Augmenting Biology Laboratory Notebooks. In *Proc. UIST '02*, pages 41–50, 2002.

29. M. Morris. Social networks as health feedback displays. *IEEE Internet Computing*, 2005.

30. S. Nomura, E. Hutchins, and B. Holder. The uses of paper in commercial airline flight operations. In *Proc. CSCW '06*, pages 249–258, 2006.

31. D. Park. Models of visuospatial and verbal memory across the adult life span. *Psychol. Aging*, 2002.

32. D. Petrelli and S. Whittaker. Personal photographs: the reassuring of the paper and the neurosis of the digital. *Collocated Social Practices Surrounding Photos, CHI 2008 Workshop*, 2008.

33. A. M. Piper, N. Weibel, and J. Hollan. TAP & PLAY: An end-user toolkit for authoring interactive pen and paper language activities. In *Proc. CHI '12.*

34. A. M. Piper, N. Weibel, and J. Hollan. Introducing multimodal paper-digital interfaces for speech-language therapy. In *Proc. ASSETS*, 2010.

35. T. Salthouse. Effects of age and skill in typing. *J. Exp. Psychol. Gen.*, 1984.

36. R. Sarvas, A. Lehmuskallio, V. Lehtinen, J. NŁsŁnen, and S. Vihavainen. Snapshot media: "kodak culture" in the 21st century. *Collocated Social Practices Surrounding Photos, CHI 2008 Workshop*, 2008.

37. K. Schaie. *Intellectual Development in Adulthood: The Seattle Longitudinal Study*. Cambridge University Press, Cambridge, 1996.

38. A. J. Sellen and R. Harper. *The Myth of the Paperless Office*. MIT Press, November 2001.

39. R. Y. Sit, J. D. Hollan, and W. G. Griswold. Digital photos as conversational anchors. In *Proc, HICSS '05*, page 109.2, 2005.

40. K. L. Smith, M. Crete-Nishihata, T. Damianakis, R. M. Baecker, and E. Marziali. Multimedia biographies: A reminiscence and social stimulus tool for persons with cognitive impairment. *Journal of Technology in Human Services*, 27, 2009.

41. J. Steimle, O. Brdiczka, and M. Mühlhäuser. CoScribe: Integrating Paper and Digital Documents for Collaborative Knowledge Work. *IEEE Transactions on Learning Technologies*, 2(3):174–188, 2009.

42. M. M. Stevens, G. D. Abowd, K. N. Truong, and F. Vollmer. Getting into the living memory box: Family archives & holistic design. *Personal Ubiquitous Comput.*, 7(3-4):210–216, July 2003.

43. L. Stifelman, B. Arons, and C. Schmandt. The Audio Notebook: Paper and Pen Interaction with Structured Speech. In *Proc. CHI '01*, pages 182–189, 2001.

44. G. Webster. Multimedia profiles as external personalities to support people with dementia and their carers. *Doctoral Dissertation, University of Dundee*, 2011.

45. D. West, A. Quigley, and J. Kay. Memento: a digital-physical scrapbook for memory sharing. *Personal Ubiquitous Comput.*, 11(4):313–328, Apr. 2007.

46. R. Yeh, C. Liao, S. Klemmer, F. Guimbretière, B. Lee, B. Kakaradov, J. Stamberger, and A. Paepcke. Butterflynet: a mobile capture and access system for field biology research. In *Proc. CHI '06*, pages 571–580, 2006.

Electric Agents: Fostering Sibling Joint Media Engagement Through Interactive Television and Augmented Reality

Rafael Ballagas
Kindoma, Inc.
Palo Alto, CA
ballagas@kindoma.com

Thérèse E. Dugan
PURE Research
Sunnyvale, CA
rezza21@gmail.com

Glenda Revelle
Human Environmental Sciences
University of Arkansas
Fayetteville, AR 72701
grevelle@uark.edu

Kochi Mori
Samsung
San Jose, CA
koichi.mori@gmail.com

Maria Sandberg
Mozilla Firefox
Mountain View, CA
mariaksandberg@gmail.com

Janet Go
Autodesk
San Francisco, CA
janet@gojanetgo.com

Emily Reardon
Sesame Workshop
New York, NY
emily.reardon@sesame.org

Mirjana Spasojevic
Kindoma, Inc.
Palo Alto, CA
mirjana@kindoma.com

ABSTRACT

Electric Agents is a multi-player game that uses augmented reality on mobile phones to facilitate in-room collaboration and promote joint media engagement around interactive educational television content in the home. Joint media engagement describes 'collaborative' consumption of media and has potential learning benefits. Our research examines whether technology can support joint media engagement, through the use of a series of prototypes that combine handheld augmented reality with web-based video. In pilot testing, sibling play patterns showed evidence of the kind of in-room collaboration and joint media engagement that previous research has shown to facilitate children in making sense of media content.

Author Keywords

Pervasive Games; Augmented Reality; Educational Games; Cross-Media; Interactive Television; Mobile Phones; Joint Media Engagement

ACM Classification Keywords

K.8; H.5

INTRODUCTION

Two major trends in television are emerging that enable new interactive and collaborative experiences. First, television is migrating to the Web. In the U.S., 172 million Internet users watched online video content in April of 2012, representing 82% of the country's online population [16]. Second, media multitasking is on the rise. Among children and young adults, 8- to 18-year-olds are media multitasking, using more than one medium concurrently, 29% of the time that they are using media [19]. Additionally, while television remains the most popular medium through which young people consume media related content [19], a recent report indicates that more and more adults, teenagers, and children are using and playing on their phones while they watch television together [16]. Furthermore, mobile devices and the Web are highly interactive by nature, whereas current interactive television experiences are just beginning to unlock the potential inherent in designing for interactivity.

There is another relevant trend in children's television viewing behaviors: they are spending more and more time watching television than any other media-related activities while at home [19]. The current average is 4.5 hours a day spent watching television content across all platforms [19]. Television is not generally perceived as a collaborative medium, but increasingly researchers have observed benefits of joint media engagement. Joint media engagement (JME) refers to people interacting together with media. Modes of JME include viewing, playing, searching, reading, contributing, and creating, with either digital or traditional media [15]. JME can support learning by providing resources in a current activity to participants for creating meaningful connections among media representations, interests, and experiences [15]. For example, children have been found to interact more with media, specifically television and video games, when peers or family members are present in the room [6, 24, 25]. Detailed examinations of JME reveal patterns of in-room interactions among co-viewers that help structure sense-making around media [6].

Our primary research question, then, is how to leverage technology to promote in-room interactions and collaborative sense-making around television content in the family. A starting point may be found in recent CSCW research that explores the sibling relationship as a context for collaborative play [10]. Through their exploration, the authors identify a number of design guidelines, such as bridging the difference in ability, allowing for different types of contributions, and avoiding common sources of conflict such as resource scarcity. We believe that the sibling relationship is also a rich context for designing opportunities for joint media engagement.

We designed and built Electric Agents as a design probe for novel collaborative experiences in the family. Electric Agents combines gameplay, mobile augmented reality, and interactive television content to create the first interactive system designed to actively promote in-room interactions around an educational television program.

RELATED WORK AND BACKGROUND

Researchers and designers have long debated how to make video games and television experiences collaborative and educational, as well as entertaining and fun. They stress that well-designed games that embody important learning principles can make remarkably good learning environments [9, 17], and that children can extend the learning and experiences they derive from video game play to other aspects of their lives [6, 24].

Scholars have suggested that siblings can learn from each other when they are engaged in cooperative activities such as games and claim that sibling collaboration engages the social aspects of learning in the sense that people learn by doing in the presence of more experienced individuals [26, 20, 9]. For example, researchers have noted that interactions with older siblings promote younger siblings' cognitive development and language skills [7]. Moreover, older siblings have also been shown to be more effective teachers compared to familiar peers when children are attempting to complete unstructured tasks [1]. Given the strongly in-room interactive nature of augmented reality games, Electric Agents is designed to encourage older siblings to help their younger siblings as they play the game together.

Mobile augmented reality systems have demonstrated potential to support collaboration that blends across physical and digital worlds. Henrysson et al. [11] demonstrated augmented reality games on mobile phones that enhance face-to-face interaction. Games such as Bragfish [27] and Art of Defense [12] explored the use of handheld augmented reality to enhance physical board games and found that players' coordination strategies leverage cues from the shared physical space. Electric Agents was designed to build on this work and use augmented reality in a mobile game to promote in-room interactions among siblings.

Electric Agents was first introduced in [3], with the main contributions being the novel technological system and examining collaboration patterns using mobile augmented reality among same-age peers. This paper's contribution focuses on how technology might promote joint media engagement within the family context.

Game Premise

Electric Agents is based on the Emmy Award winning television show, *The Electric Company*. The show features a group of children known as *The Electric Company* with literacy-related superpowers. They use their powers to counteract the mischief caused by their nemesis group, the Pranksters, and to restore order. Each episode focuses on a curriculum of domain-specific vocabulary words, phonics, and connected text.

In Electric Agents, an augmented reality game is layered on top of the episode narrative. In the supplemental meta-narrative, the Prankster Manny, invents a gadget that can steal words out of people's mouths and uses the gadget to sabotage Electric Company member Hector's rap video. In the game, siblings are 'special agents' of *The Electric Company* and must collaborate to collect and return the stolen words to the episode. The stolen words are hidden in the siblings' environment, and 'communicators' (mobile devices) are used to channel special literacy superpowers. Siblings see red word-balls and blue picture-balls floating around in their environment, which are only visible using their communicators (for a preview of this AR effect look ahead to Figure 3). Siblings must coordinate to simultaneously capture matching word-balls and picture-balls and return the words to Hector in the show.

Preliminary Game Design

The game concept was initially broken up into two main playing phases to promote in-room collaboration: (1) word collection, and (2) word return during viewing.

Word Collection:

After a brief introduction and tutorial, players must capture the five stolen words. Each sibling has a different role: Agent Red can only capture red word-balls, and Agent Blue can only capture the blue picture-balls. Players use their mobile devices to frame the correct word- or picture-ball and then capture the ball by pressing a trigger. Captured balls can be released through use of the touch screen. After both players have captured a ball, they bump the devices together to verify a match. If the balls do not match, both balls are released. If the balls match, they are combined into a single ball containing both the word and picture. If no match is made within 30 seconds of capture, the ball/s are released and must be recaptured. This 30-second timeout is a constraint designed to promote both game tension and coordination of game activity between the players.

Word return during viewing:
After the players have captured all the words, the words are randomly split between the players and the television episode begins. Each time Hector from *The Electric Company* tries to say one of the vocabulary words, the narrative is interrupted. Children must resolve the problem by selecting the appropriate word on their device and then throwing the word-ball back into the show. This action directly mimics the power of *The Electric Company* characters on the show to create and throw word-balls, pulling children who are playing into *The Electric Company* world. Returning the correct vocabulary word advances the episode, while returning the incorrect word triggers progressive hints to help the children find the correct word.

Low-Fidelity Prototyping of Mobile Augmented Reality:
We experimented with multiple low-fidelity prototypes to simulate and test different aspects of in-room interactions with our design.

In our first low-fidelity prototype, we pasted images and words around a room using post-it notes, and simulated "capture" by asking siblings to use a camera phone to take pictures of items (see Figure 1).

We used a second paper-based prototype to better approximate the viewfinder interaction of augmented reality experiences. We encoded words and pictures using a dot pattern. To the naked eye, the message was not readable (see Figure 2). Encrypted words and pictures were posted on the wall around a room. Players were given red vellum lenses about the size of a standard mobile phone screen, and the contents of the postings were only visible through the red lens.

To test our early ideas for game mechanics, we tested the low-fidelity prototype with eight pairs of siblings. Players were directed to collect matching words and pictures one at a time. A word was successfully acquired when players brought the matching word and picture pairs to the game moderator (Figure 2), who acted out the role of the system to verify matches. If a match was verified, the moderator would read a child-friendly definition as a payoff.

Observations from low-fidelity play testing both confirmed our design choices and resulted in design insights:

- Matching roles with abilities: We designed the game so that the younger sibling was assigned the role of capturing the images and the older sibling the role of capturing the words. Thus, the players' roles would be roughly matched to their abilities, while the need to coordinate encouraged them to discuss and share information. Observations during testing confirmed this to be an effective strategy for encouraging collaboration.
- Shared perspectives, but distinct roles: During testing, we observed that the shared perspective of these low-fidelity designs facilitated collaboration and mentoring in that players could help each other find matching word and picture pairs. Naturally dominant older siblings facilitated game play by reading words out loud and directing their younger siblings, but sometimes would overstep their role and take over the responsibilities of the younger sibling. In order to mitigate some of these issues of dominance, we decided that in the functional prototype players would be able to see their partner's word- or picture-balls in the air, but only be able to capture the type of ball they had been assigned to search for (either word-balls or picture-balls).
- Progressive hints: We designed the game to provide informative feedback and guidance for both players at various points in the game play. For example, a word would be read aloud for both players when either player captured a word- or picture-ball. If incorrect words were chosen, a spoken child-friendly definition

Figure 1. The first paper prototype of Electric Agents leveraged blue pictures (left) and red words (right) placed on the wall around a room. Children 'captured' the words by taking pictures of them using smartphones.

Figure 2. The second paper prototype of Electric Agents used dot patterns (top left) to encode word- and picture-balls. Vellum lenses (top right) were used to decode the balls to find a match. Children pulled the balls off the wall and bumped them together for a moderator to verify a match.

would give players increasing levels of scaffolding for unfamiliar vocabulary. Observations of the importance of these hints as delivered by the moderator during the low-fidelity prototype testing confirmed this design choice as essential to helping children succeed in the game.

- Pace of game: We witnessed lots of enjoyment during the word collection phase, but some older siblings expressed a sense of boredom during the viewing phase. One older sibling (age 10) complained that the show was 'too young' for her, illustrating a tension in finding ways to design games and media that are age appropriate for siblings with an age gap.

Overall, the testing suggested that augmented reality is a good choice to facilitate in-room interactions, and the design can be improved for engagement of older siblings.

Final Functional Prototype Design:

To address the issues around game pacing, we decided to merge the two main phases into a single play mechanic that combined word collection and word return while viewing. Every time Manny interrupted the viewing by stealing a word, children were prompted to both collect and return the correct word. The goal was to create a more balanced experience by spreading out the excitement for capturing balls across the viewing session more evenly.

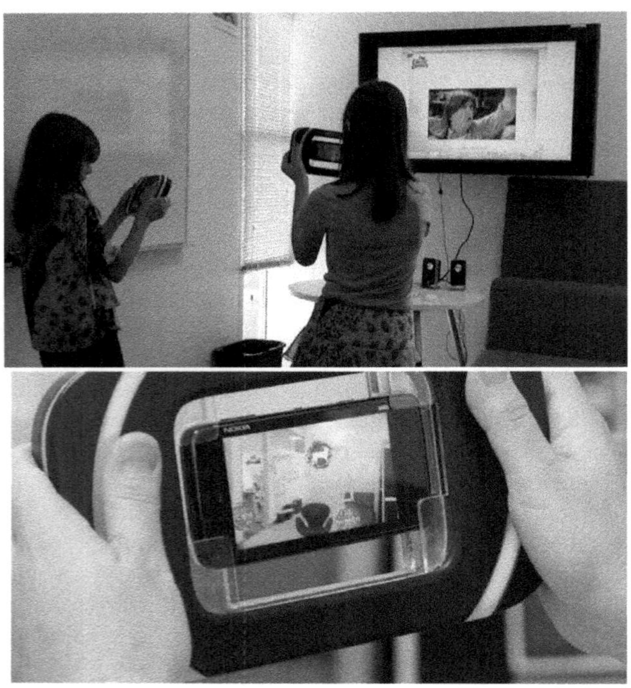

Figure 3. (Top) Siblings collaborate to find matching word- and picture-balls to resume the show. (Bottom) A close up of Agent Blue targeting the canine picture-ball.

As a result of our game pacing changes, we also chose to simplify the interaction. "Bump-to-match" interaction alongside the "throw to return" mechanism was deemed excessive. Instead, matches were automatically detected once both players had captured corresponding word- and picture-balls. In the case of unmatched captures, players could discard captured balls to find the correct matching ball. Upon a successful match, players could each throw the balls into the show to give Hector his words back. The final tested version of the prototype is depicted in Figure 3.

EVALUATION: USER STUDY WITH SIBLINGS

Each iteration of the Electric Agents prototype led to new insights on how to foster more effective collaboration, and how to balance different needs for sibling pairs with an age gap. With the final design, we hoped to gain a deeper understanding of the nature of sibling collaboration Electric Agents affords.

Data collection methods

We observed and videotaped 9 pairs of siblings ages 6 to 10 years old in our lab as they played with the augmented reality game. Siblings were recruited with the help of an external recruiter. After the gameplay children were given a semi-structured interview by a researcher. In most cases, children played the game while their parents were within view to simulate an at-home scenario.

Setting and Participants.

We designed our lab to simulate a living room in a home where siblings would typically watch TV and play videogames. There were 8 girls and 10 boys who participated (Table 1).

We strived for pairs consisting of younger siblings who were either 6 or 7 years old, and older siblings who were either 9 or 10. Similar to the approach used in previous research [10], we intentionally chose this age differentiation because we believed the corresponding differences in literacy abilities might provide the most opportunity for siblings to learn from each other. A few of the participants were familiar with *The Electric Company* television show, but participants were not screened for prior exposure.

Table 1: List of Participant Pairs

Pair	Sibling	Age (O/Y)	Agent Status
Pair 1	Sister/Brother	9/6	Blue/Red
Pair 2	Sister/Brother	9/7	Red/Blue
Pair 3	Brother/Sister	9/7	Red/Blue
Pair 4	Brother/Sister	9/6	Red/Blue
Pair 5	Brother/Brother	10/7	Red/Blue
Pair 6	Brother/Sister	9/7	Red/Blue
Pair 7	Sister/Sister	10/7	Red/Blue
Pair 8	Brother/Brother	8/7	Red/Blue
Pair 9	Brother/Sister	7/6	Red/Blue

Protocol

Before playing the game, each child was given a controller. The controller and gameplay were explained for all participants using a video-based game tutorial delivered by one of *The Electric Company* characters in the context of the game. The tutorial explained that Agent Blue's controller allowed that agent to capture pictures while Agent Red's controller allowed him or her to capture words. When picture-/word-ball pairs were found, agents were shown how to click the back of their controller to capture the ball and then physically throw it back to the screen to aid the characters in the show. As previously mentioned, our design called for the older sibling to look for words and the younger sibling to look for pictures. However, there was one pair in which this assignment was inadvertently reversed, providing us with an opportunity to observe potential issues that might arise in that case. Parents were in the room, but not given explicit instruction about whether to participate/intervene or not.

Analysis

The analysis was conducted in several iterations. First, video-taped data was reviewed to identify examples of collaborative interaction. Next, those highlighted examples from the videotaped data were transcribed using InqScribe (transcription software) and examined for instances of siblings' verbal expressions or "reflective externalizations." [18]. Price et al. [18] advocate the development of awareness of one's thinking through the externalization of one's thoughts; collaborative interaction is a potent way to encourage this externalizing process and illustrate when learning is occurring. They believe that "collaboration is essential for learning knowledge" [18].

Specifically, using Price et al.'s framework [18] as a guide, we looked for examples of:

- Clarifying information: questions clarifying what to do so that one can be less confused and information is more clearly comprehensible.
- Explaining: explaining and describing what to do.
- Reporting: an account of something that one has observed, heard, done, or investigated.
- Prompting: an action of saying something to persuade, encourage, or remind someone to do or say something.
- Structuring an activity: performing an action or demonstrating what to do.
- Asking for elaboration: asking for greater detail to understand an activity or a command.

Additionally, we were interested in how and when collaboration was occurring and who or what kind of situations were affecting this. So we located instances in sibling conversations when collaboration and cooperation were working (participants are working together to achieve a goal) [14], as well as when collaboration seemed to be contested (participants skills or history make collaboration challenging but potentially rewarding and participants must work through their interpersonal differences to complete their work together) [23], or even adversarial (participants have different goals but are still tasked with completing an action or activity together) [4]. This helped us to select examples where older siblings were helping and structuring their behavior to scaffold game play for their younger siblings and instances where sibling collaboration broke down and was not working successfully.

Finally, after this review of transcriptions was completed, clips were additionally analyzed using interaction and conversational analysis techniques [8, 22]. These techniques are derived from discourse and ethnomethodology literature and are used to help researchers trace the information that is shared through conversation.

FINDINGS

Our findings show evidence that the children in this study were able to communicate and reflect with their siblings during gameplay, and the augmented reality interactions supported in-room interactions among children in several different ways indicating the potential for learning benefits.

To explore this more, in this section we first describe different ways in which children in the study engaged in collaborative play. We then discuss, though an analysis of siblings' reflective externalizations and patterns of communication, how older children scaffolded ideas and behaviors for their younger siblings to perform. We conclude by describing some non-collaborative outcomes and exploring how they might help inform future design.

Scaffolding During Collaborative Play

Collaborative play is the cooperative, co-constructed action of two or more individuals working towards a common goal to complete an activity. Children's collaborative play includes activities such as completing a puzzle together, building a house out of toy bricks, or in this case, acting as agents and capturing word- and picture-balls together. Siblings are encouraged to share, take turns, and listen to one another in order for them to complete the game.

Throughout the study we observed older children engaging in scaffolding [20] and modifying their behavior in order to help their younger siblings better understand how to play the game. Whether the children were simply explaining what to do, coordinating with their siblings on how to complete a task, or structuring their behavior and actions so that their siblings could better follow their lead, they used a variety of strategies to help their siblings successfully learn how to play and complete the game.

We specifically discuss the following strategies:

- Using various expressive forms of communication to direct game play and achieve the goals of the game.
- Requesting clarification from older siblings to confirm actions.
- Explaining to or prompting younger children to perform certain activities.
- Exhibiting reporting behaviors while playing to guide younger children's game play.

- Demonstrating and structuring, in a positive way, what younger children should do when playing the game.

Directing play: "Look over here!"

Players used many different verbal and physical expressions to try to help their siblings find the target word- or picture-ball within the augmented reality space. While the game is designed so that the siblings must work together to find matching balls, siblings were not specifically instructed on how to do this and they had to figure out how to collaborate verbally and physically in order to achieve the game goal.

Children often used physical gestures or mentioned physical reference points when referring to digital content in the augmented reality space. Players would scout out balls for their sibling to capture by saying phrases like, "*hurry! over here! over here!*" (Pair 9) and point with their controller or with their fingers. Additionally, siblings would relate words to physical objects in the room and to other balls using the physical space of the room as a guide, "*look at the bulletin board*" (Pair 6) or the virtual space within the viewfinder "[*the picture is*] *near* [*the word*] *hypnotize*" (Pair 7).

Some sibling pairs developed techniques to physically guide each other to the balls by:

- Stacking devices to ensure a common view,
- Placing the devices side by side to ensure a common view, or
- Physically pulling a sibling's arms and relocating them to the correct position in the room to locate the digital item.

Furthermore, older siblings would sometimes guide younger siblings by describing what the picture-ball looks like, for example, "*Track! Find the picture of... um... of him... of steps.*" (Pair 9), or "*It looks something like footsteps*" (Pair 1) to find the word "track", or, "*No, it looks like a watch and with a strange dude*" (Pair 4) to find the word "hypnotize".

Similarly, the siblings used descriptions of pictures to verify they were capturing the right one.

Pair 5 brother age 10 (Agent Red), brother age 7 (Agent Blue):
Agent Blue: *The one with the doggie?*
Agent Red: *No, that's "canine", that's "track"* [pointing into viewfinder at the pictures].

Therefore, the siblings directed their collaborative play both verbally and physically in order to find the words and pictures for the show characters and ultimately solve the case. While no one directly explained to the children how to play the game beyond telling them they needed to locate and capture the word- and picture-balls within the room and throw them back into the show, the siblings co-constructed different techniques of active game play to achieve the goals of the game experience by working together and helping each other find the words and pictures within the viewing space.

Throughout the study we observed that older children often tried to help and scaffold situations for their younger siblings so that they could both play successfully. The older children usually grasped the concept of the game faster than the younger ones, and these younger players needed their older siblings' guidance in order to complete the game. In the following sections we explore these observations in greater detail using a more microanalysis of the children's external expressions while they played the game.

Attempts to clarify: "What are we supposed to do?"

When siblings attempt to clarify the task at hand, they ask questions of each other in order to understand what they are supposed to be doing, either in the context of the game or their own collaboration with one another. The purpose of providing clarifying information is to add context or guidance regarding information that may have been missed in the instructions for the game or the controls. In some cases, the act of providing clarifying information reflects the potential for collaborative learning that games such as this one can enable.

Pair 1 sister age 9 (Agent Blue), brother age 6.5 (Agent Red):
Agent Red: *Do we need to find dog?*
Agent Red: *What do we need to find?*
Agent Blue: *"Human", find "human".*
Agent Red: *I found the "human" picture.*
[Agent Red captures "human" and tries to throw it to the screen.]

In this example, the younger brother asks what needs to happen next and his older sister tells him to find a certain word that is different from the one he was looking for. Both siblings are attempting to coordinate their activities in order to collaborate successfully and complete the task presented to them. As with most instances of clarifying behavior, this coordinated activity has a strongly spatial component in that the siblings are looking around the room for the different words using the screen on the device to locate them.

With sibling Pair 1, the child who asked for clarification is also the one who found the right word and threw it at the screen in an attempt to complete the task. However, with sibling Pair 8, the older brother clarifies where the picture-ball is for his younger brother, but quickly pivots his attention to grab his word-ball before his younger brother understands what is happening.

Pair 8: brother age 8 (Agent Red), brother age 7 (Agent Blue):
Agent Red: *There's canine down low...*
Agent Blue: [inaudible] ... *I can't find it! Is it supposed to be a human?*
Agent Red: [capturing the word-ball] *Oh! I found it! Garr... Gotcha!*

Although both examples of clarifying behavior lead to physical action, one is an example of cooperative collaboration (Pair 1) while the other tends toward adversarial collaboration (Pair 8) since the brothers end up competing with one another to grab words and complete the task. Additionally, even though the purpose of providing clarifying information is to add enough context that one sibling can help the other sibling complete a task, Pair 8 reflects the fact that the siblings' behavior toward each other strongly influences the ways in which collaboration is enacted, even when the game design is carefully structured. While both boys in Pair 8 are trying to play the game and complete the mission successfully, they add their own level of sibling rivalry into the mix. But despite the added teasing, the boys successfully complete the game while working together to clarify information when needed.

Explaining and prompting: "How do we do it?"

Children used explaining and prompting phrases to help their siblings better comprehend what was being asked of them throughout the game. Explaining or prompting behavior is about providing highly directive instructions to promote understanding of the task at hand. The essential difference between clarifying and explaining behaviors is that clarifying requests are posed as questions from one sibling to another, whereas explanations are provided in response to requests for clarification or are simply provided unprompted when a sibling realizes the other sibling needs help with a task.

Pair 2: sister age 9 (Agent Red), brother age 7 (Agent Blue):
Agent Blue: *Get the "hypnotize one"*
Agent Red: *Okay.*
[Agent Red captures "hypnotize"]

Furthermore, explaining behaviors can also be physical and sometimes appear to be adversarial.

Pair 3: brother age 9 (Agent Red), sister age 7 (Agent Blue):
[Agent Red turns Agent Blue around and points at her controller intertwining his with it so that she can find the picture]
Agent Red: *Here!*
[Grabs Agent Blues controller and puts his controller in front of hers so she can find the picture.]

In this example, the older brother (Agent Red) takes control of his younger sister's (Agent Blue) controller so he can complete the task for her. In some cases, this issue of control limits the time that one sibling is able to spend playing the game; older siblings sometimes shift from explaining what to do to simply taking control of both controllers and ending the collaboration entirely. However, in this case while it first appears that the older brother is not letting his sister complete the task and the collaboration is contested, he actually was physically placing her in the vicinity of a picture-ball so that she could find it herself.

The design of the game can have a significant influence on the form that the collaboration will take. For example, when there is a time limit or some other factor in the game that requires quick and accurate task completion, the collaboration can turn from cooperative to contested to adversarial as the players try to "win" without regard for their siblings. While many of the explaining behaviors like Pair 3 (above) could appear to be somewhat contested or even adversarial in nature, we observed many of the older siblings just trying to encourage their younger siblings to finish successfully and eventually letting their younger counterparts complete the tasks on their own. That is, they led them to the answers but made sure they were gathering them together.

Reporting: "How is it going?"

Reporting behavior occurs when one sibling broadcasts his or her activities with the activity of the other sibling. Reporting is a frequent occurrence, as the siblings in this study often spoke aloud about what they were doing as they played the game. However, reporting is commonly intertwined closely with other activities, such as clarifying questions.

Pair 8: brother age 8 (Agent Red), brother age 7 (Agent Blue):
Agent Red: *There it is!*
Agent Blue: *Where?*
Agent Red: *It's right by the light!*
Agent Blue: *Oh! There it is... Oh! Garr! Gah! I almost got you... heeey!*
[Agent Red's timeout expires, the word-ball escapes]
Agent Red: *Oh, no. I've gotta find track again.*
Agent Blue: *I'll just wait for it to stumble into me.*
[Agent Red captures "track"]
Agent Blue: *I can't... Agh... I...*
[Agent Blue captures "track"]
Agent Blue: *I got it!*

All of the siblings in this study used reporting behavior to support collaborative gameplay. Reporting also offers a way for siblings to think aloud about their progress, externalizing their feelings about the work they are doing to achieve the goals that the game sets out for them, and check in with one another, as they collaborate. In some cases, these reporting statements are cues for assistance that needed to be addressed by the other sibling in the room.

Structuring: "How can I help?"

Structuring activity occurs when one sibling demonstrates what the other sibling should do in order to play the game or complete a specific task. This type of activity can take the form of one sibling physically helping the other, or it can be a verbal statement made to refocus the attention of one sibling on the task at hand (a parent may also structure an activity for both siblings).

Pair 3: brother age 9 (Agent Red), sister age 7 (Agent Blue):
[Agent Red helps Agent Blue to find "canine" by moving Agent Blue's device around]
Agent Red: *Hold it like this* [touches side of controller]
[Agent Blue: Holds up her controller next to Agent Red]
[Agent Red: Points out what to collect on Agent Blue's controller]
[Agent Blue captures "canine"]
[Agent Red captures "canine"]

In this example, the older brother physically shows his younger sister how to work with the controller, but then he quickly cedes control back to his younger sister so they can complete the task together.

Pair 6: brother age 9 (Agent Red), sister age 7 (Agent Blue):
Father: *Find it!*
Agent Red: *It was here. It's running away.*
Father: *Be systematic.*
Agent Blue: [excited inhale] *it's over there* [pointing]!
Agent Red: *Up top, please.... Oh! Yes!*
[Both devices: [Match sound]]
[Agent Red throws "hypnotize" to the screen]
[Agent Blue throws "hypnotize" to the screen]

This is an example of a father trying to guide his children by structuring the task more specifically than the interface of the game makes clear. By telling his children to systematically look for words rather than wildly waving their controllers around, the father tries to structure their collaborative activity in order to elicit a positive outcome.

Non-Collaborative Outcomes of Sibling Play

While the above sections explored how Electric Agents created an environment where siblings could collaborate creatively and even learn from and with each other as they played together, this did not always occur successfully. In some cases sibling rivalry took over and children refused to work together to play the game. In these cases, the older siblings tended to refuse to help the younger siblings play the game by taunting them or, in one case, taking over the game completely. These breakdowns in collaborative behavior are the result of the ebb and flow in everyday life of sibling relationships. However, it is helpful to review how and when these instances occurred and explore how the game design could be augmented in the future to address these situations.

Impatience and refusing to collaborate

Sometimes when the children were playing, communication and collaboration broke down. Many times these short breakdowns occurred when the older sibling would get irritated or annoyed with their younger sibling not understanding what to do. In most cases the older sibling eventually would help out the younger one. However, in some cases, like the example below, the older sibling became very impatient with helping her younger brother.

Pair 1, sister age 9 (Agent Blue), brother age 6.5 (Agent Red)
Agent Blue: *There you are.*
Agent Red: *I'm not giving you any canines. You never gave me your canines.*
[Agent blue catches "canine"]
Agent Blue: *There. Now, you have to find the one with the "c" and you only have 30 seconds to do everything.*
[Agent Blue reaches over and moves Agent Red's device around]
Agent Blue: *Go over here, go over here. There it is, there it is! No, wait, wait, wait! Get it, get it, get it!*
[Agent Red catches "canine" and throws it back]

It was intended that sibling pairs playing the game had the older child as Agent Red and the younger as Agent Blue because the younger child, being a less-experienced reader, would have an easier time locating pictures rather than words. However, in this example, it was the one case where roles were reversed, so this may have played a strong role in the tension around their collaborative behavior.

The elder Agent Blue was annoyed with the younger Agent Red for not finding words fast enough. Agent Blue begins to direct her younger brother. After the exchange above, she exasperatedly says she has tried to "help" him but he does not seem to be getting it. He first refuses to help and later she decides to tell him what to do while pulling and orienting him to the target. He finally does find the word and they continue with gameplay and yet, throughout the rest of their interactions it is clear from the older sister's behavior that she is annoyed that she has to help her younger sibling figure out how to play.

We saw similar behaviors exhibited by older siblings tasked with helping their younger sibling counterparts play the game. It seemed like a number of older siblings just wanted to play the game and not help their younger sister or brother learn *how* to play. However, even if they gave their younger sibling a hard time, they *were* demonstrating what to do or guiding them along so that they could eventually do it themselves. The sibling pairs all finished the game and successfully completed the required activities as intended, except for one pair that will be described next.

Seizing control of the game

While some older siblings gave their younger siblings a hard time while trying to learn how to play the game, in most cases the older siblings eventually scaffolded the activity so that the younger siblings could understand it enough to complete the required tasks. However, one pair did not, as is evident in the example below:

Pair 5, brother age 10 (Agent Red), brother age 7 (Agent Blue):
[Agent Red captures "human", puts his controller down and reaches over to grab Agent Blue's device]
[Agent Blue tries to defend his device from Agent Red]
Agent Red: *I need it! It's timing out.*
Agent Blue: *No.*
Agent Red: *Here, let me see that.*
Agent Red: [looking around with the blue device] No... no... no...
[Agent Blue touches the screen of the red device]
Agent Red: [Agent Blue], *quit it, you just messed it up!*
[Agent Red catches "human" on Agent Blue's device and switches back to his own device]
[Agent Red throws the red word-ball to the screen]
Agent Red: *Don't!* [directing Agent Blue to refrain from playing]
[Agent Red throws Agent Blue's picture-ball to the screen]

Instead of the older brother guiding and helping his younger brother to learn to play the game correctly, Agent Red cuts Agent Blue out of the experience by taking away his controller, telling his younger brother he is doing it wrong, and eventually playing both roles himself. Agent Blue tries several times to regain control of his controller and continue to play the game once he figures out how to do it. But even when he feels he understands what to do, his older brother still refuses to accept him as a game partner and again seizes control of his controller. By the end of the game the younger brother has given up entirely and begins to wander around the room looking sad and bored.

This breakdown in collaboration indicates that even a game designed with the best intentions with regard to collaborative play can result in unintended outcomes. If either player refuses to help the other learn and play the game, the collaborative aspect is lost. How might we design games to prevent this over dominance?

DISCUSSION

In the previous section we presented a number of examples of siblings' interaction patterns. When playing Electric Agents, the siblings' reflective externalizations and patterns of communication represent their sense-making processes with regard to achieving the goals of the game. Our findings indicate that the final prototype design supports sibling collaboration and scaffolding, with potential for achieving the same types of benefits as joint media engagement and parental scaffolding have been shown to do in the context of television viewing and video game play. In sum, given that digital games encourage players who are working together to externalize their strategies with one another, Electric Agents demonstrates the potential of augmented reality to support joint media engagement in a collaborative play environment while children are interacting with television content.

Are We Learning Yet?

It can be challenging to identify how researchers define learning when claiming that learning is evident in their work. Instead of measuring learning directly, we are demonstrating creation of a context where there is a potential for learning to occur and instances where environments can be designed to support learning experiences. Vygotsky's zone of proximal development, or ZPD, is defined as the difference between what a learner can do with the aid of a more experienced person, and what a learner can do on his or her own [26]. This would suggest that older sibling-younger sibling collaboration and subsequent behavioral scaffolding could help the younger siblings achieve game success, which they might not be capable of on their own. This theory is complementary to that of apprenticeship learning [20], whereby older, more advanced individuals scaffold younger, less experienced individuals.

Our prototype was designed to encourage cooperative problem-solving, or two children working together to solve an external problem [2]. Therefore, our conceptualization of learning and where learning is occurring stems from this set of theoretical frameworks. Instead of measuring learning directly, we observe the in-room interactions related to joint media engagement. Based on these ideas, it is clear that the observed sibling play patterns show evidence of the kind of supportive scaffolding, collaboration and joint media engagement that previous research has shown to facilitate "sense-making" – a first step toward learning.

Challenges When Children Are Tasked With Teaching

There are challenges involved in encouraging children to teach one another how to play a game, which is different from encouraging children to complete a game. As they grow up, siblings learn to share and help one another as well as how to provoke conflict [28]. However, we noticed many of our older siblings going out of their way to make sure their younger siblings were able to play the game correctly and understood how to use the controller, adapting their own behavior to help their younger siblings. Firstborn children are often seen as "surrogate...caregivers, teachers, and models...for their younger siblings," [21] and we observed many of the older siblings taking on this role.

Mitigating Negative Outcomes Through Game Design

How can we best mitigate negative outcomes through game designs that prevent seizure of control from one player? We attempted to prevent non-cooperative actions like taking over control by making a captured ball automatically release after 30 seconds, presumably requiring children to capture balls in parallel. This mechanism made it difficult (though not impossible) for the older brother from pair 5 to capture a word-ball with red controller, put it down, and capture a matching picture-ball with the blue controller before the timeout (especially when his younger brother resisted relinquishing the blue controller). The older brother had to attempt this several times before he successfully captured both. Perhaps future prototypes could be designed to prevent players from putting down their controllers, e.g. by allowing captured items to escape when put down, or controllers could sense who is handling them, preventing one player from using both. However, as previous research with siblings has suggested, there are often negative aspects of sibling dynamics [13, 10] that will most likely emerge regardless of collaboration mechanics.

Parents' perspective

We never explicitly asked parents to participate or not while their children were playing in our lab, and many of them decided to not interfere with the gameplay. However, upon further reflection during their post-game interview many parents insisted that when playing this game at home, they would be a central part of the collaborative process and help their children better understand game concepts, rules, and monitor their children's behavior.

Researcher: *If you were using this in the home would you likely have been more involved as they were playing?*
Mom [Pair 10]: *Absolutely, I was trying to bite my tongue (makes zipping gesture with hand over mouth) and not interrupt the research... but I would have said 'girls let's read the screen and discuss what word would fit'.*

Furthermore, all of the other parents interviewed felt positively about the Electric Agents experience and would be open to having their children play with something similar within their homes. Whether it was the collaborative aspects of the game pushing their children to work together or just getting their children off the couch and physically active, most parents seemed impressed. The father from Pair 8 said, "*I like how [the boys] were working together to help each other...and paying attention to the story a whole lot more... I think a little action mixed with watching is a good thing*". Moreover, the Mom from Pair 9 said "*[she] found [the game experience] to facilitate interaction a lot through team work... and it was nice to see". She was also excited about the "interactive component*" of the game that overlaid the story. She felt this helped her children pay attention and facilitated a "*strong learning component.*"

CONCLUSION

Joint media engagement is still a new concept that to date has been understudied in the CSCW community. This work serves to bring attention to the opportunities of designing new technology-supported collaborative experiences for families that amplify the power of traditional educational television.

Mobile augmented reality facilitated specific patterns of collaboration. Siblings physically coordinated to capture digital objects by gesturing in physical space, verbally referencing physical objects, and physically guiding each other's controllers. The parallel nature of the tasks also afforded verbal coordination including reporting activity status and prompting to ensure common task goals.

It should come as no surprise that designs are not always experienced as intended. Future research should explicitly address sibling dynamics (and more generally entrenched interpersonal dynamics) as a factor through iterative design. Our design iterations helped us tune the experience to be better suited for both older and younger siblings to create an environment that fostered interaction and collaboration for most sibling pairs in our study.

Joint media engagement with family members helps children process and make sense of educational content. In Electric Agents, we designed the first technology-based interactive experience that supports in-room interactions to promote joint media engagement around educational television in the family. Our study illustrates patterns of communication and collaboration that relate to effective social learning experiences. We hope this work inspires more systems that promote joint media engagement, family togetherness, and support for families in creating positive learning environments for their children.

AKNOWLEGEMENTS

This project was funded and created by the authors at Nokia Research Center in Palo Alto, CA in cooperation with Sesame Street Workshop and the Joan Ganz Cooney Center.

REFERENCES

1. Azmitia, M. and Hesser, J. Why siblings are important agents of cognitive development: A comparison of siblings and peers. *Child Development 64*, 2 (1993), 430-444.
2. Ashley, J., & Tomasello, M.. Cooperative problem solving and teaching in preschoolers. *Social Development 7*, 2 (1998), 143–163.
3. Ballagas, R., Revelle, G., Reardon, E., Cook, K., Takeuchi, L., Mori, K., Horri, H., Hayes, R., Sandberg, M., Buza, K., Tsai, Y., Go, J., Spasojevic, M. Electric Agents: Combining collaborative mobile augmented reality and web-based video to reinvent interactive television. *To appear in Computers in Entertainment*. ACM Press.
4. Cohen, A. L., Cash, D., & Muller, M. Designing to support adversarial collaboration. *Proc. of CSCW 2000*. ACM Press (2000).
5. ComScore. Video Metrix. (2012) http://www.comscore.com/Products_Services/Product_Index/Video_Metrix.
6. Dugan, T. E., Stevens, R., & Mehus, S. From show, to room, to world: A cross-context investigation of how children learn from media programming. In *K. Gomez & J. Radinsky (Eds.), Proceedings of the 9th International Conference of the Learning Sciences.* International Society of the Learning Sciences (2010), 992-999.
7. Dunn, J. Sibling relationships. In: *P. K. Smith (Ed.) Blackwell handbook of childhood social development*. Malden, Blackwell Publishing (2002), 223–237.
8. Erickson, F. *Talk and social theory: Ecologies of speaking and listening in everyday life*. Malden, MA: Polity Press (2004).
9. Gee, J. P. *What video games have to teach us about learning and literacy?* New York: Palgrave/Macmillan (2003).
10. Go, J., Ballagas, R., and Spasojevic, M. Brothers and sisters at play: Exploring sibling dynamics around game play. *Proc. CSCW '12*. ACM Press (2012).
11. Henrysson, A., Billinghurst, M., and Ollila, M. Face to face collaborative AR on mobile phones. In *Fourth IEEE and ACM International Symposium on Mixed and Augmented Reality*. IEEE, (2005) 80–89.
12. Huynh, D., Raveendran, K., Xu, Y., Spreen, K., and MacIntyre, B. Art of defense: a collaborative handheld augmented reality board game. In *Proceedings of the 2009 ACM SIGGRAPH symposium on video games*. ACM Press (2009) 135–142.
13. Kramer, L. & Conger, K. J. (Eds.). Siblings as agents of socialization. *New Directions for Child and Adolescent Development*, *126*. San Francisco: Jossey-Bass (2009).

14. Malone, T. W. & Crowston, K. Toward an interdisciplinary theory of coordination. *Computing Surveys 26*, 1 (1994), 87-119.
15. Media and Learning Group at SRI. (2010). *Joint media engagement and learning*. Menlo Park, CA: SRI International.
16. Nielsen Media Research. *Double vision – Global trends in tablet and smartphone use while watching TV* (2012). http://blog.nielsen.com/nielsenwire/online_mobile/double-vision-global-trends-in-tablet-and-smartphone-use-while-watching-tv/.
17. Prensky, M. Computer games and learning: Digital game-based learning. *Handbook of computer game studies*. Cambridge, Mass: MIT Press (2005),14 97–122.
18. Price, S., Rogers, Y., Stanton, D. and Smith, H. A new conceptual framework for CSCL: Supporting diverse forms of reflection through multiple interactions. In *Proc. CSCL 2003*. Kluwer Press (2003), 513-523.
19. Rideout, V.J., Fuhr, U.G., & Roberts, D.F. *Generation M2: media in the lives of 8- to 18-year olds*. Henry J Kaiser Family Foundation, Menlo Park, California, USA (2010).
20. Rogoff, B. *Apprenticeship in thinking: Cognitive development in social context*. New York: Oxford University Press (1990).
21. Sailor, D.H. Chapter 9: Siblings, peers, and friends. In *Supporting children in their home, school, and community*. Boston: Allyn Bacon (2004).
22. Schegloff, E. A. Reflections on studying prosody in talk in interaction. *Language and Speech 41*, (1998). 235-263.
23. Sonnenwald, D.H. Contested collaboration: A descriptive model of intergroup communication in information system design. *Information Processing and Management 31*, 6 (1995) 859-877.
24. Stevens, R., Satwicz, T., & McCarthy, L. In-game, in-room, in-world: Reconnecting video game play to the rest of kids' lives. In *K. Salen, (Ed.), The Ecology of Games: Connecting Youth, Games, and Learning. The John D. and Catherine T. MacArthur Foundation Series on Digital Media and Learning*. The MIT Press, (2007), 41-66.
25. Takeuchi, L. & Stevens, R. *The new coviewing: Designing for learning through joint media engagement*. New York, NY: The Joan Ganz Cooney Center at Sesame Workshop (2011).
26. Vygotsky, L. S. *Mind in society: The development of higher psychological processes*. Cambridge, MA: Harvard University Press (1978).
27. Xu, Y., et al. Bragfish: Exploring physical and social interaction in co-located handheld augmented reality games. In *Proc. ACE '08*. ACM Press (2008), 276–283.
28. Zahn-Waxler, C., & Smith, K. D. The development of prosocial behavior. In *V. B. Van Hasselt & M. Hersen (Eds.), Handbook of social development: A lifespan perspective*. New York: Plenum Press (1992).

"Back and Forth, Back and Forth": Channel Switching in Romantic Couple Conflict

Lauren E. Scissors, Darren Gergle
Northwestern University
2240 Campus Drive, Evanston IL 60208 USA
{l-scissors, dgergle}@northwestern.edu

ABSTRACT
This work explores the act of channel switching, or switching between forms of face-to-face (FtF) and mediated communication (e.g., text messaging, instant messaging) during romantic couple conflict. Interviews were conducted with 24 individuals currently involved in a non-cohabitating romantic dating relationship of 3 months or longer. Results revealed that many patterns of channel switching are used during conflict, including switches from mediated to FtF communication and from FtF to mediated communication. In addition, participants had a number of interpersonal motivations for initiating a channel switch, including avoiding conflict escalation, managing one's emotions, and attempting to reach a resolution. Theoretical and design implications are discussed.

Author Keywords
Channel switching; romantic relationships; conflict; computer-mediated communication (CMC)

ACM Classification Keywords
H.5.m. Information interfaces and presentation (e.g., HCI): Miscellaneous.

INTRODUCTION
Every day we make use of a variety of communication technologies to interact with others, whether the interactions are related to coordination in the workplace or management of personal relationships [2]. However, while in practice we make use of several different technologies, many research studies of technology selection focus on a single communication channel at a time rather than the variety of channels that might be used in combination or succession during an extended communication episode.

The current study aims to address this gap by examining how people make use of a collection of different communication channels during a single communication episode. We examine this activity in the context of romantic couple conflict—a domain that helps to draw out a deeper theoretical understanding of the rich and varied ways in which we use communication technologies to support our relational goals.

A particularly salient behavior that we investigate is that of "channel switching" [31], or the act of shifting between different modes of communication during a single communication episode. While this process has been examined in the context of instant messaging (IM) in the workplace, the main findings from these studies are that individuals engage in media switching either to support coordination (e.g., scheduling meetings), to multitask, or to overcome instances where a discussion becomes too "complicated" for IM [18, 13]. Our research reveals, however, that there are several more social and interpersonal reasons for channel switching.

While channel switching may occur across relational contexts, couple conflict (see [24] for a review) is a particularly useful domain for studying channel switching since interpersonal issues like face threat (threat to one's public self-image) [3], emotion regulation, and relational satisfaction are prominent and may help to explain switching motivations. For instance, while individuals may prefer to argue face-to-face (FtF) because many contextual and nonverbal social cues are present, the presence of face threat may instead make the reduced-cue environment of CMC preferable. In other words, we aim to study channel switching in a context where social motivations and the affordances of a given communication channel both contribute to understanding technology use.

The goal of this paper is to answer two major research questions: (1) What patterns of channel switching do individuals exhibit during a conflict? and (2) What interpersonal motivations drive channel switching? By identifying these patterns and motivations, we can begin to understand how individuals appropriate the different affordances of text-based and FtF communication to manage their conflicts, and uncover which patterns of channel switching may be more or less successful for relational maintenance issues such as conflict resolution. This understanding will also allow us to reevaluate existing research on channel switching and related theories of media choice in light of individuals' interpersonal motivations.

CSCW '13, February 23–27, 2013, San Antonio, Texas, USA.

RELATED WORK

Channel Switching

Though scholars have examined media or channel choice, as well as how communication technologies may be used in parallel, one topic that has received relatively little attention is the act of media or channel *switching*. In 2004, Walther called for a greater emphasis on the study of channel switching in CMC scholarship, noting "relationships are not single-channeled, despite the tendency of much of our research to control, partial, and force these limitations for the purpose of study" [31, p. 390].

Traditionally, channel switching has been examined in workplace settings. For instance, Su and Mark [27] found that individuals are strategic in their channel switching so that they can effectively manage their multitasking behaviors. Similar to findings in other studies [18, 13], these insights focus more on logistical motivations rather than interpersonal motivations. Related to channel switching is the practice of channel blending. Isaacs and colleagues recently studied how channel blending, or the act of using multiple modes of communication at the same time, allows individuals to coordinate and share experiences [14]. While Isaacs et al.'s work did not focus on channel switching per se, the current work builds on their suggestion to "think about coherent social acts that may take place over time and across channels" (p. 626) rather than focus on acts of FtF and mediated communication in isolation.

An important aspect of channel switching is choice, since the process of switching involves a choice to move from one channel to another. A recent study of media choice in the workplace by Pongolini and colleagues concluded that individuals choose certain technologies for convenience or to adapt to technical difficulties [22]. Studies of media choice often point to media richness theory, which posits that individuals will choose technologies based on the amount of cues a given communication channel can support, and suggests that more cues are preferable, particularly when clarity and connection are important [5]. This theory, however, has been widely challenged in the literature. Scholars have argued that so called "less rich" mediums such as email or IM actually contain their own set of social cues that can support interpersonal processes such as developing intimacy and trust [32]. Despite these benefits, many may find it hard to believe that one would rather engage in conflict with a relational partner via channels like text messaging when the option for FtF communication exists.

Studies of media choice and its relationship to tie strength, or degree of closeness to one's relational partner, are mixed. For instance, van den Berg and colleagues [29] found that strong tie relations are less likely to interact by email, but more likely to interact via telephone, text messaging and IM, relative to FtF communication. Alternatively, Mesch [17] found that, for adolescents, the longer one knows someone the less likely they are to communicate online, and the more likely they are to communicate FtF. Mesch suggests that "shared history may reduce the need for a more protective environment, as good friends do not feel the need to hide emotions, and, apparently feel comfortable expressing their inner concerns unmasked in this medium" [17, p. 250]. However, as we discuss in the following section, there may be certain contexts in which even the closest of ties prefer to use mediated communication.

Romantic Couples, Conflict, and CMC

Managing conflict is an inevitable part of relational maintenance, and recent work has established that couples use text-based communication technologies to argue [9, 12, 23]. Researchers know little, however, about how communication channels might impact the nature of a conflict and know even less about how individuals use multiple channels in succession to support their individual and relational goals during conflict.

During a conflict, individuals may vary in the extent to which they reveal and manage their emotions. Early work on conflicts in CMC suggested that they were more likely to escalate in mediated settings, due to the fact that the medium's relative anonymity might lead to more uninhibited behavior [25] and because CMC was not believed to be rich enough to support conflict management [5,7]. More recent theories, such as Social Information Processing (SIP) theory, have claimed that individuals can use the cues available in CMC to have intimate communication with relational partners (e.g., [30]). In a recent study about couples' use of video chat to manage their long-distance relationships, Neustaedter and Greenberg [19] highlighted a few examples of how video chat can both aid and hinder emotion management during a conflict. It is unclear, however, how these examples might apply to text-based CMC and whether they are indicative of more common patterns of communication technology use.

A critical factor that may affect how individuals manage a conflict FtF is the presence of face threat, or a threat to one's public self-image [3, 10]. Brown and Levinson [3] identified a variety of acts that might be face-threatening, including expressions of strong negative emotions, disapproval, criticism, and accusations, all of which may come up during a conflict. In fact, previous research suggests that individuals prefer to use mediated channels of communication in face-threatening contexts [20], including conflict resolution [28]. Yet, the rationale behind these choices has either not been explored [28] or been limited to identifying practical reasons such as proximity (spatial distance preventing FtF interaction), technological advances (aspects of CMC that made it superior to FtF), and convenience or ease of use [9]. It may be that there are other reasons why individuals manage a conflict in CMC rather than FtF.

While the visual anonymity or protective environment of CMC may reduce face threat and make individuals more likely to disclose information or emotions to others [15], the lack of nonverbal cues may be detrimental to conflict resolution. For example, looking one's partner in the eye is considered to be a universal rule of conversations that occur after a partner has committed a transgression [1]. This research highlights the potential benefits and drawbacks to using CMC during interactions with one's partner. With the myriad channels individuals use to manage their relationships, individuals might not limit themselves to one channel if using a combination of channels could help to support their relational goals.

This literature raises a number of questions related to the practice of channel switching from the perspective of couples during conflict. For example, do certain channels help to minimize conflict or do they exacerbate it? Are certain channels more conducive to closure than others? And, how might the desire to minimize conflict or attain closure relate to channel switching behavior? By examining channel switching in couple conflict, we can begin to identify patterns of communication across channels and eventually explore how different patterns may be more or less successful for certain couples or for conflict resolution.

This work also addresses gaps in the literature by providing insight into a broad range of interpersonal motivations for channel switching during conflict. Prior research on conflict among romantic partners suggests that many impression management and relational issues are at play. While issues like coordination, proximity, and setting up future communication may be relevant during couple conflict, the literature suggests that interpersonal processes are salient and perhaps even paramount during this type of interaction. As we show in this work, this heightened relational context can surface additional patterns of use that were previously uncovered in the workplace-based literature. Furthermore, findings that "IM is too complicated" or that CMC is preferred during conflict for "ease of use" beg to be examined on a deeper level. What interpersonal goals make CMC complicated? What relational goals impede or support the use of CMC during conflict?

METHOD

Participants

Participants (*N*=24) were undergraduate and graduate students at a mid-sized Midwestern university who were at the time involved in a heterosexual romantic relationship (self-defined). Only one individual from a couple participated. Participants' ages ranged from 18 to 30 years (*M*=21 years). Ten men (42%) and 14 women (58%) participated and 46% were Caucasian (25% Asian, 13% African-American, 8% Hispanic, 8% Mixed Race). Half of the participants considered themselves to be in a long-distance (LD) relationship, while the other half considered themselves to be in a non-long-distance (NLD) relationship. Though there is a debate over how best to conceptualize and measure LD relationships, we follow [6] by utilizing self-definition. However, we also asked participants how far apart they currently lived from their partners. Individuals in NLD relationships ranged in distance from very close (e.g., "a five minute walk away") to moderately close (e.g., "30 minutes away"). The furthest distance by miles for NLD participants was 15 miles away and the furthest distance by time was a 1-hour drive or subway ride. Participants in LD relationships also varied in how much time or distance separated them. Of participants who described distance in miles, distance ranged from 60 to 2400 miles apart. Of participants who described distance in time, distance ranged from a 5-hour drive to being separated by 12 time zones. Gender was distributed equally across relationship type. Of the participants who were in a LD relationship, all had been engaged in a NLD relationship with their current partner at some point in the past. All participants were in dating relationships; 88.5% of participants were seriously dating (self-defined) (12.5% were casually dating). Participants' relationship length ranged from 3 to 48 months (*M*=17.8 months). No participants were cohabitating with their partners, nor had they ever cohabitated with their partners.

Procedure

Participants were recruited via flyers and email listservs for a "study about communication technologies and romantic relationships." The recruitment material did not explicitly state that conflict would be the focus of the study so individuals with particular patterns of conflict in their relationships (e.g., individuals who fight a lot with their partners) were not pre-selected for the study.

Participants engaged in in-person semi-structured interviews with the researcher, which allowed for novel topics to emerge. Participants were asked to discuss all of the ways in which they communicate with their partner and how often they use each type of communication channel. Participants were then asked to discuss a recent conflict they had with their partner, and detailed questions about specific conflicts were asked. Questions focused on participants' current relational partners but participants could also discuss past relationships. All interviews occurred in a laboratory setting, were audio recorded and lasted from 30 to 65 minutes (*M*=40 minutes).

Analysis

Three research assistants transcribed the interviews to prepare them for qualitative analysis in HyperResearch. The coding process was iterative; interviews were read through several times and initial codes were evaluated to reflect a deeper knowledge of the data. We used open, axial, and selective coding [26]. Over 100 codes were generated and then sorted into concepts, and concepts were categorized into themes. Initial codes captured behaviors (e.g., "CMC then FtF"; "CMC then FtF then CMC again"; "conflict

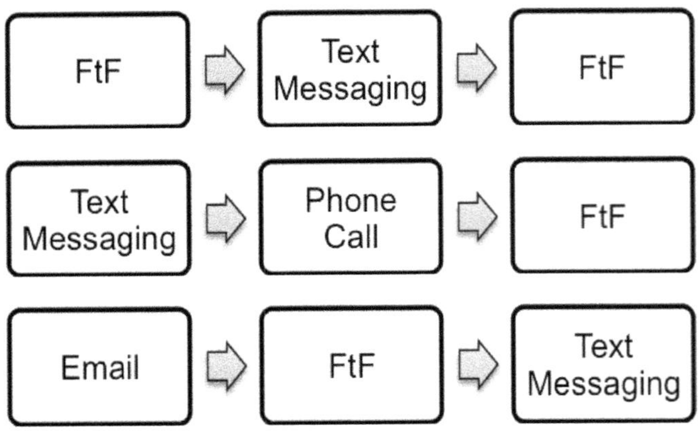

Figure 1. Examples of reported patterns of channel switching during a single communication episode.

initiated – email", "conflict initiated – FtF") while others captured the perceived pros and cons of using different mediums (e.g., "response times increase feeling upset", "CMC good for apologies"). These types of codes were later sorted into themes that reflected sets of codes. For instance, the theme of Managing Emotions included codes like "CMC get less upset", "CMC get more upset", "CMC easier to listen to partner". As themes began to emerge, the interview script was altered to reflect these discoveries. We also explicitly looked for counter examples during theme development in order to strengthen internal validity. In addition, we shared our emerging themes with participants who were interviewed later in the data collection process and asked them for feedback on our claims. This occurred after the interviews were completed. We found sufficient evidence to suggest that our themes were on the right track. This approach allowed us to use our participants to establish coding reliability as well as to test our preliminary findings. Though many themes emerged that related to the use of communication technologies during conflict in general, the current work focuses on the emergent themes related to channel switching.

Participants described a range of experiences and opinions related to using forms of technology-mediated communication during a conflict with their partners. All participants regularly used some form of mediated communication, and all reported having at least one conflict with their partner. Participants mentioned using IM, text messaging, email, and social network sites, in addition to audio calls, video chat, and FtF communication during a conflict. The frequency of reported conflicts differed; some participants rarely engaged in conflicts with their partners while other participants did so regularly. Participants engaged in conflict over a number of different topics, including issues about communication, trust, responsibilities, and scheduling.

While there are many definitions of interpersonal conflict, we utilized Hocker and Wilmot's [11] definition of conflict as "an expressed struggle between at least two independent parties who perceive incompatible goals, scare resources, and interference from the other party in achieving their goals" (p. 21). In other words, a conflict was an instance where a person's goals were incompatible or at odds with their partner's goals. During the interviews, the terms "conflict", "argument", and "disagreement" were used to reflect the varying degrees of conflict. Small tiffs or brief misunderstandings were not considered to be a conflict in our analysis. Some reported conflicts were moderate and/or resolved fairly quickly while others were more serious and/or took longer to resolve. Examples of conflicts that were reported by participants included issues about jealousy, lack of attention or responsiveness, lack of social support, and relationship status. To better understand the severity of conflict in the analysis, we examined the use of emotional language as well as descriptions of the conflict and the extent to which participants felt it had an impact on their relationships. As participants reported a variety of experiences with conflict across channels, we were able to investigate a number of patterns of communication and motivations for behavior.

PATTERNS OF CHANNEL SWITCHING

Initial results revealed that participants use a variety of channels during a conflict, including IM, text messaging, email, and FtF communication, and that the evolution of a conflict could follow a number of different patterns involving forms of mediated and FtF communication (see Figure 1 for examples). In some cases, participants reported instances of conflicts being discussed only FtF or only through one form of CMC. In other cases, a conflict was initiated FtF and then continued and resolved/terminated in some form of CMC. The opposite was also observed; participants described conflicts that were initiated in CMC but were then discussed and resolved/terminated FtF. Participants also reported cases where an argument started in one form of CMC and ended in another form of CMC. In all three of these patterns, one channel switch occurred.

Participants also reported instances of two channel switches during a conflict. In other words, the conflict was initiated in one channel, discussed in a second channel, and then resolved/terminated after a final channel switch (either back to the previous channel or to a new channel). Both FtF and mediated forms of communication served as the initial, secondary, and final communication medium. Participants explained that channel switches could be initiated by themselves, their partners, or by both partners in a couple. Participants also described conflicts with three or more channel switches, suggesting a vast number of possible communication patterns during one conflict event.

For instance, in one case, an issue was first discussed FtF between p18 and her partner, but was not resolved. As time passed and resolution was needed, the participant emailed her partner. The partner emailed back but the resolution was ultimately achieved FtF. In another case:

"It started on Gchat and then we got together face-to-face and we sorta talked it out and it was OK for a while, but some tension came back throughout the week when I realized I had a little more work than I thought I had to do, or she wasn't satisfied with how clean her apartment was yet. [This] would usually come up on Gchat. And, then, get resolved face to face. Thursday was when we were both satisfied with what we had done and the stress was off and it was kinda resolved." – p4

In this case, the conflict was initiated in Gchat (a type of IM), then discussed FtF, then discussed again via Gchat, and finally resolved FtF.

Some participants noted that the same pattern of communication and channel switching would occur with their partners across conflicts. For instance, p26 explained that when his partner became upset, he would first try to solve the issue over text message. When he was unable to come to a resolution that satisfied his partner, he would use IM with his partner. If he still could not appease his partner, then he would visit his partner FtF.

Participants noted many functional reasons for channel switching, including overcoming technical constraints (e.g., switching from texting to talking due to the cumbersome nature of typing) and dealing with logistical issues (e.g., continuing a FtF discussion over text or IM when someone has to physically leave). However, many additional reasons emerged that were more interpersonally motivated, as described below.

LONG-DISTANCE VS. NON-LONG-DISTANCE

It is important to note that there are clear and significant differences between LD and NLD couples. In the current study, the main difference reported by participants and coded for in the analysis was that individuals in LD relationships used video chat much more often than did their NLD counterparts. However, in the analysis, LD participants' language surrounding video-chat use was strikingly similar to NLD participants' language regarding FtF communication. Though we do not suggest that video chat and FtF communication are the same, the similarities between the two channels (e.g., visual communication, presence of nonverbal social cues, synchronicity) suggest that for LD couples, video chat acts a proxy for FtF communication in many ways. Therefore, since the purpose of the current study is to identify motivations for channel switching between forms of text-based CMC and FtF-style communication, we do not highlight differences between participants in LD relationships and NLD relationships in the subsequent sections. Individuals in LD relationships channel switch between video chat and other forms of text-based CMC, whereas participants in NLD relationships channel switch between FtF and forms of text-based CMC.

In fact, there were many similarities between LD and NLD participants. Participants in both types of relationships reported that they communicate with their partners throughout the day via forms of text-based CMC, had similar types of conflicts both in topic and intensity, and channel switched during conflict (either between text-based CMC and video chat or text-based CMC and FtF communication). In addition, all participants in LD relationships had spent time with their partners FtF, and so could comment on times where all types of communication were viable options. Accordingly, we asked participants in LD relationships to reflect on times where they were not distant from their partners, including times where a conflict occurred, in addition to times when they were separated from their partners. Participants in LD relationships did not have trouble recalling a recent conflict with their partners that occurred when they were geographically close.

MOTIVATIONS FOR CHANNEL SWITCHING

Avoiding Conflict Escalation

Many individuals switched channels during conflict in order to avoid conflict escalation in the distant or immediate future. For instance, some participants initiated conflict in CMC as a way to manage the nature of a future FtF discussion regarding a conflict. In one case, p9 introduced the idea to his partner that something might be wrong via IM:

"Just to let the other know that something's going on before you get into the conversation in person helps the situation itself develop later in person. ... I myself think it's a good thing that you can ease into a conversation not being in person and get to communicate a little bit rather than being exiled of each other." – p9

This tactic was seen as a way to ease one's partner into the conflict, as opposed to catching one's partner off guard by bringing it up for the first time FtF and launching into a full discussion. Here, p9 orchestrated a channel switch by starting the conversation in one mode with the explicit intention to continue the conversation in another mode. Individuals also switched channels to avoid problematic communication. For instance, p4 explained that when an issue comes up while he is texting or IMing with his partner, he tries to move the conversation to FtF ...

"... 'cause it will probably only get worse, ... what they type might get misinterpreted than what they actually meant, so it might get worse. So, that's why we usually leave something that just came up in conversation 'til later." – p4

While some participants explained how using CMC could lead to conflict escalation, others felt that CMC could actually help to minimize a conflict. For example:

"You just don't wanna start an argument or debate in person about something that probably doesn't have that much importance ... It would escalate more in person than over text. Whereas in a text [it] would be a short-lived conversation, in person it could be carried on into many

other conversations that really had nothing to do with where you started at." – p9

Here it seems that the properties of text messaging helped to streamline the conversation and helped to prevent conflicts from escalating past their initial stages.

Finally, some participants initiated a conflict in CMC so they could get it out of the way and preserve their future FtF time for happier discussions. For instance, p4 sometimes initiated the discussion of an issue via IM while he and his partner are both at work:

"While you're not face to face, staring at the computer, you might as well get all the negative things out. We're both really anxious and happy to see each other at the end of the day. Starting with a happy conversation is better." – p4

Here, p4 used CMC as way to compartmentalize his uncomfortable conversations so that the FtF relationship could be preserved. It may be that if young dating couples predict that conversations will not go smoothly, they accept this and contain their conflict-related conversations to CMC, thus avoiding a channel switch within the context of the conflict.

Managing Emotions

In addition to trying to avoid conflict escalation, many participants chose to switch channels in order to better manage their emotions. Echoing findings from previous studies (e.g., [9]), most participants felt that it was easier to express their true feelings or bring up an issue with their partners via CMC than FtF. These sentiments were often the reason for a channel switch. For instance:

"I think on Gchat ... I found that I was, maybe, more comfortable speaking what was on my mind while I wasn't face-to-face. And then, [in] face-to-face I was a little more reserved, which is probably why I didn't bring it up when it was face to face. Maybe because I was behind a computer screen I was able to show that I was a little more stressed than when I was face-to-face." – p4

In addition, p22 explained:

"It's just easier for me to be honest with a text-based communication like a text message or something that isn't personal. I'm more likely to get tied up or have trouble communicating if I'm sitting face-to-face with a person. Especially if it's negative or likely to upset them." – p22

That young adults in established romantic dating relationships may have a hard time expressing their feelings to one another may have important implications for technology adoption during conflict. If disclosure is the goal, CMC might actually be a better option through which to have an argument, at least at the beginning of the argument so both parties have equal opportunity to bring up grievances.

Not only did participants explain that it was easier to express their emotions but that it was easier to control them. For instance:

"I waited until he was out of my room to text him. Like, 'Oh, by the way you have pictures on your phone of your ex-girlfriend. Cute.' And then he actually came back and tried to talk to me in person and I locked my door and wouldn't talk to him and started doing homework ... 'cause that was a fight I couldn't handle in person 'cause I couldn't even handle looking at him. It just made me feel sick to my stomach that someone I really trusted could do that. [Then] over a text, I just told him I need my space and that I didn't want to be with him." – p25

Here, p25 switched from FtF communication to texting, a medium with fewer nonverbal cues, in order to be able to communicate without losing control of her emotions. This tactic suggests that for individuals in dating relationships, use of text-based CMC might support communication that is too *emotionally* hard to conduct FtF. Though participants generally felt more comfortable expressing themselves through mediated communication, findings were mixed on whether using CMC made participants feel more or less upset during a conflict. On the one hand, certain aspects of CMC were related to increased negative affect. For instance:

"I know when you send an angry text message, waiting for someone to respond, I'll just get angrier in that time that I'm waiting for the response and then...when I finally do get it ... by the time I get it, even if it's a nice message I'm still ready to keep fighting." – p1

Response latencies were one of the main reasons that participants reported feeling upset when arguing via text message, email, or even IM. In addition to growing angrier, some participants experienced increased anxiety while waiting for a response from their partners. For instance, p9 explained that while waiting for a text ...

..."I feel ... an emotion of, not anger, but frustration or ... waiting. Kind of just a very awkward waiting, just wanting to know what she's gonna say. Anxious, that's what I was looking for. Very anxious. A lot of times, whatever I'm doing if it's something just like studying or doing homework my mind is doing something else." – p9

Increased anxiety during an argument may be harmful, not only to a person's mental well being but also to the likelihood that a conflict will get resolved. For instance, individuals with higher levels of attachment anxiety are typically less forgiving [4], making resolution more difficult to achieve. In order to avoid these increased feelings of anger or anxiety, participants would sometimes initiate a switch to FtF communication.

On the other hand, other participants used the time between responses to reflect on the problem and come up with alternative approaches. For instance:

"I replay it, sort think about it more in depth, probably come up with a better solution, maybe it wasn't that big a problem. ... [you] lose that urge, like, if you're really upset at somebody, kinda calm down." – p5

Another participant explained that, when using CMC:

"... you stay cooler. The voices aren't raised and you don't feel the tension. You still feel angry but it's not like you say, 'No it was this way,' and he cuts you off and doesn't even listen to what you were saying before. You have time to say what you wanted to say." – p18

Not only did switching from FtF to CMC allow some participants to handle their strong emotions but it also allowed them to think independently about the situation. For example:

"My girlfriend and I, we like to talk face-to-face in person about just everything. I think we enjoy being in each other's presence more than we do texting. ... But I know maybe once or twice it's happened where we'll be talking about it in person and we'll say 'okay let's just forget about this for now, we'll talk about it later'. And we'll [end up] talking about it over text. ... Texting after you're not together gives you more time to think alone about it, so you're each independent of each other rather than codependent. ... [It's] a way to cope with situations and think about them and establish your own feelings. And then you go back to the conversation with your own thoughts." – p9

In this case, p9 was able to gain distance from his partner in order to better understand his own emotions without completely disengaging from discussing the conflict.

Adjusting to Partner Preferences

Studies of channel choice often approach this behavior as strategic but one sided. In other words, scholars assume that each individual is a rational actor in charge of a channel choice. However, what about the person on the receiving end of another's channel choice? Here, we found that preferences or behaviors of participants' partners were also a factor influencing channel switching. For instance, p5's partner preferred to email back and forth, whereas p5 preferred to chat on the phone:

"You just can't have a conflict right away, she wants to write it, read it, take time. I just automatically want a comeback. She likes a dialogue: email, email, email, email. ... She writes me a letter and I'd probably call her at that time. It's like a dialog right away. I think she likes our arguments better when she says what she needs to say and then I say it, and then she says. Back and forth, back and forth, back and forth." – p5

In another case, a participant explained how, after a fight over the phone, her partner expressed his feelings in an email, and she emailed him back. Then:

"He didn't respond. So it was up to me to call him. That's how it usually goes. Like if he's upset about something and doesn't email back I'm like, 'I'm sorry' and then I'm supposed to call." – p6

Here, a channel switch occurred because p6's partner refused to continue the conversation via the current channel that p6 was using. This example also illustrates the tendency for these couples to enact similar patterns of channel switching across conflict events. In fact, switches were sometimes initiated because participants sensed a change in their partner's behavior. For instance, p17 explained that during a conflict with his girlfriend,

"Initially we were texting back and forth and then once I could tell she was getting more upset, I ended up calling her and we talked about the rest of it on the phone. ... Because she has a tendency to... she's a really long-winded texter. Her texts very rarely get short and her texts became in succession, 'yeah', 'uh huh', 'okay'. So it's things like that. And that was a first indication to me. So I called her and asked 'what's up?' and explained the whole thing. We talked the whole thing out." – p17

In addition, some participants explained how they abandoned their own preferences for channel switching in favor of their partner's preferences. In one case, p7 preferred to bring up issues over email and then transition to FtF communication, but found that this was not working with her partner:

"We don't usually talk things through emails because he would rather talk it through the phone so we can mutually respond. ... I liked to write letters and emails to my boyfriend before. ... But I'm kind of changing the mode a bit because he feels like we should talk face-to-face instead. [Now] we have an agreement that we should talk face-to-face instead of sending him emails and not getting any feedback. So I feel like it's kind of pointless to just shoot him emails anymore because I don't get the feedback that I want." – p7

In some cases, individuals switched channels to adjust to their partner's preferences and felt mildly inconvenienced. In other cases, however, adjusting to one's partner despite competing preferences caused participants to have a more negative experience. For instance, p18 revealed:

"I feel like I don't get as frustrated when I'm talking through Gchat and I'm more willing to discuss [a conflict]. But it doesn't seem like my current partner is on that same ... he'd rather call and discuss it. But I feel like I get frustrated when we start talking face-to-face and I can't remember what I was gonna say, which is why I like using Gchat. ... He always says, 'I don't wanna talk like this' and then he calls me." – p18

Here, by deferring to her partner's preferred communication channel, the participant becomes more frustrated. Yet, her partner does not like using Gchat, a channel p18 prefers. In this case, it may be that different channel preferences and resulting channel switches can actually exacerbate a conflict, or introduce a new conflict in addition to the one already being discussed.

Conflict Resolution

The majority of participants explained that, to attain closure or resolution to a conflict, they needed to communicate FtF with their partners. For instance, after fighting with her partner via text messaging, p25 explained that a FtF apology was effective because:

"... he knows that a good way, a big way to show you're apologizing is to be ... really be repentful (sic), *to apologize and give me a hug. ... So I think he wants to meet up in person so he can show that he's truly sorry and give me a hug ... I feel like hugs resolve the conflict, that's when the conflict is truly over, when you hug someone and accept them into your life."* – p25

Many participants felt that some sort of visual or physical contact, like a smile or a hug, was required to help them truly feel better and attain closure on a conflict. Accordingly, many participants switched from texting or IM to FtF communication in order to come to a resolution. However, some participants explained that using CMC after a FtF argument was a useful way to add additional closure. Even when participants would attempt to come to a resolution in CMC, many noted that it did not seem final. Participants explained they would still have unresolved feelings and uncertainty about the issue. For instance, when asked how likely it was to resolve conflicts discussed over IM with her partner, p1 replied:

"Well definitely discussing them online just leaves some lingering bad feelings whereas face-to-face I'll be ready to move on right away. ... I mean, resolved to a certain degree? Probably only somewhat likely. Completely resolved like, end of discussion? I'd say never, almost never. ... Having text fights is not good for your relationship." – p1

p22 also explained:

"I don't remember ever getting to the end of an IM conversation and feeling better about things or like things had been resolved. There was never that sort of reconciliatory moment at the end of it. ... I do remember that we would sometimes see the solution to that as an offline communication of some sort. So, make an effort to see each other in person." – p22

Participants explained that true closure was most common at the end of FtF fights. There was some evidence, however, that CMC could provide finality to a FtF conflict. Many participants explained that, even after a resolution was achieved in a FtF argument, they or their partners would later use CMC to reiterate that they were sorry to omit any lingering doubts. For instance, p19 explained:

"Sometimes when I feel like some things are left open ended [or] I didn't express enough how I felt at the time, I send a follow-up text like, 'thanks for taking care of me last night' or 'sorry about last night', ... but it's after we've discussed it. ... It just maybe ties a knot at the situation. 'I'm sorry about what happened, I already expressed that.' I didn't communicate as clearly as I wanted so let me just summarize my feelings in a text message so we don't have any hard feelings at all." – p19

This tactic seemed to provide a final word on the matter in cases where a FtF or phone resolution did not seem final or in cases where the participant wanted to be explicitly clear about what they meant during the FtF conversation. P11 also explained that she and her partner reiterate apologies via text message after a FtF fight:

"I'll send him a text just before we go to bed saying I'm sorry that I got upset and had the argument. ... [In FtF] we resolve things but I feel like it's harder to admit in that moment, 'Oh, you know, I'm sorry that I caused that and got upset.' So we resolve it, like 'OK, I understand', but we won't give out that formal apology. ... It's easier to send that over a text then to sit there ... and admit that in that moment when we're resolving things." – p11

In this sense, CMC seems to be a useful tool for providing closure to a FtF argument, but not for providing closure during a CMC-only argument.

DISCUSSION

Implications for Theory

Overall, this work revealed that young, non-cohabitating individuals in romantic dating relationships have a number of interpersonal motivations for choosing communication channels and initiating channel switches during a conflict. These findings contribute to both the CSCW channel switching literature, which has primarily examined logistical motivations for switching and lacks distinct theories of channel switching, and to the couple conflict literature, which has given little attention to the role of communication channel during conflict. In contrast with the notion that CMC might lead to more intense arguments due to its lack of nonverbal social cues, participants explained how CMC can both lead to conflict escalation but also help to minimize conflict. Accordingly, participants switched channels from CMC to FtF and FtF to CMC in order to avoid conflict escalation and improve their situation. It is worth noting that the latter behavior is unexpected based on most social cues theories.

In addition, the notion of reduced face threat in CMC was salient for many participants, even though these were not strangers or newly acquainted partners but rather couples who had already established some level of intimacy. Interestingly, while most participants felt that it was easier to initiate a conflict and to express their honest emotions via CMC, they also felt that conflict resolution was easier to achieve FtF. In fact, one participant expressed these "competing priorities" in this way:

"I've got competing priorities there. Because on the one hand, I am far more comfortable with text-based communication than I am with in-person. I'm better able to express myself, ... and I'm better able to address a conflict productively. I'm much more able to deal with that kind of situation via text-based communication. But I sort of have this...sense or feeling that healthy conflict resolution takes place in person. I think... handling that situation correctly involves having as personal an exchange as is possible. So in terms of what my actual preference would be, ... my short term preference would be text-based, my long-term preference would be face-to-face communication." – p22

While many different patterns of channel switching occurred, including switches from the "less rich" CMC to the "richer" FtF, switches from FtF to CMC were also common. Switches in either direction seemed to occur, at least in part, to address the competing priorities of wanting to communicate through a channel with less face-threat but also wanting to communicate through a channel that supports a rich personal connection with one's partner. This observation stands in contrast to previous research that suggests individuals would prefer the richest medium possible to communicate with their partners about a conflict and that close ties do not need a channel with reduced cues to shield them from face-threatening situations with each other. Individuals do not necessarily seek the richest channels but rather seek channels with different affordances for different relational goals, and combine the use of multiple channels during one conflict episode. Furthermore, these findings extend previous knowledge of channel choice in couple conflict by not only uncovering the reasons behind preferences for mediated communication during conflict but by also suggesting that preferences are not static. In certain cases, individuals may desire or choose one channel to support their relational goals but in other instances, they may choose another channel. Thinking about channel *choice* as a more dynamic process helps us to better understand channel *switching*.

In addition, most studies of communication that consider channel choice or channel switching treat the individual as the rational actor in the situation and do not consider the role of the communication partner. For instance, it may be that an individual prefers to text during a conflict but, if one knows one's partner will not respond, one may switch to another channel in order to keep open the lines of communication. Taking into account the preferences and motivations of both partners in a couple is not only important for understanding channel switching behavior but also for highlighting potentially detrimental differences in preferences that may lead to more conflict down the line.

Finally, while understanding channel switching in relation to various issues surrounding conflict communication, one of the most important may be resolution. Conflict does not always have to be negative for a couple. In fact, resolving and moving on from a conflict can actually strengthen the bond between partners [8]. And while most participants felt that FtF communication was necessary for resolving non-trivial conflicts, some participants revealed that text-based communication technologies can be effective tools in reiterating and solidifying a FtF apology or attempt at resolution that did not seem final.

Taken together, these findings suggest that text-based communication technologies like email, IM, and text messaging can be an effective part of conflict management between romantic partners and, in some cases, can provide benefits that stem from the unique affordances that each channel provides. In this way, we see the socio-technical nature of using CMC and FtF communication during conflict, whereby individuals' social motivations are entwined with the affordances of a given medium, and that channels are chosen to optimize social outcomes. While individuals may feel that FtF is the supposed ideal channel in which to discuss a conflict, the reduction in face-threat and resulting increased perceived ability to express one's self suggest that switching "back and forth" across channels may provide unique benefits above and beyond communicating through one channel alone. Furthermore, findings from the current work suggest that by not exploring interpersonal motivations, studies of channel switching are not capturing the full picture of what drives switching behavior. By taking into account both logistical and interpersonal motivations for channel switching, we can gain a much richer understanding of which motivations are more salient across a variety of contexts.

Implications for Design

Insights from this work may help inform the design of technology for young dating couples and perhaps for others in romantic relationships. While several mobile applications for couples focus on tracking each other's whereabouts or determining whether one's partner is cheating, a new class of applications could focus instead on relationship maintenance and improvement, leveraging findings from this work and incorporating theory-driven design.

This work suggests that channel switching has multiple benefits, and that individuals switch to channels with greater or fewer affordances, depending on their motivations. In recent years many platforms have incorporated multiple communication channels, possibly to encourage or support user's transitions between channel types. For instance, Facebook supports email-like direct messages, instant messaging, and video chat in addition to the ability to post public messages. Skype supports video chatting as well as instant messaging. Google Plus aims to integrate all of users' mediated communication into one portal. Yet, there may be reason to suggest that combining channels would be detrimental to the relational strategies the participants in this study utilize. For instance, our participants suggested that switching channels could help them gain a new perspective or to manage the conflict in a particular way. Our data challenge the notion that integration of communication channels into a single platform is inherently beneficial. If all channel types were integrated into one platform, individuals might not feel as strongly that a switch has been made, and thus may not reap the potential benefits of channel switching.

It is unclear, however, whether platforms that currently integrate multiple media channels (e.g., Google Plus and Facebook) support or diminish switching behavior, since switches to FtF communication might not occur as often if there are multiple mediated channels at one's disposal. Furthermore, since tools like IM or texting seem to be helpful to one's ability to initiate a conflict, experience intense emotions while still maintaining communication with one's partner, and in some cases even calm down from a heightened emotional state, these text-based technologies may be useful in couples' therapy.

Limitations & Future Work

One limitation of this study is that we only interviewed individuals in relationships and not both members of a couple. Interviewing couples in future studies could allow us to compare each partner's experiences and preferences more directly and to explore instances where their assessments of a situation diverged. In addition, our sample indicates that our results may not be generalizable to other types of romantic couples. Our participants were in dating relationships, did not cohabitate, and were relatively young. Different patterns of channel switching or motivations for switching might emerge with a sample of cohabitating couples, married couples, or simply older couples. For instance, participants did not bring up conflicts about money or children, which are more common among older or married couples.

In addition, even though college students are quite typically used in social psychological studies of romantic relationships, caution should be exercised when generalizing to other non-student populations [21] since relationships among college students and young adults may be less serious, stable, or mature than relationships among older or married couples. For these reasons, our findings should be examined with different participant pools in order to understand how other types of arguments, living situations, and relationship statuses might impact channel switching during conflict. However, we feel that the current inquiry clearly outlines various interpersonal motivations for channel switching that can inform previous work on channel switching. In addition, we did not see any themes emerge around gender differences, though future work could explore the role of gender more explicitly.

While this study focuses on conflict, conflict is just one context in which to understand the interpersonal motivations behind channel switching. We could also look at channel switching during courtship, during acts of self-disclosure, or even during task-related events during which interpersonal issues (e.g., pride) might be salient. However, conflict is a useful testing ground on which to study the interpersonal motivations of channel switching since conflict can threaten a relationship, which in turn heightens the importance of emotions, impression management, and the ability to communicatively work toward a resolution. Similarly, we could look at channel switching among different types of relationships, including platonic friendships, family relationships, or even coworkers. For instance, how might power or signals of capability affect one's channel switching choices? Since work on channel switching stemmed from a CSCW perspective focusing on workplace communication, it would be useful to go back to a workplace context to explore whether interpersonal motivations for channel switching identified in the current work are also salient in the context of workplace communication and how these relational and instrumental motivations may be related.

Identifying patterns of and motivations for channel switching is the first step in understanding how switching influences relational outcomes. Future work can examine these patterns more systematically through surveys or diary studies in order to gain a more objective understanding of channel switching behaviors. This will help us to better understand how patterns of channel switching affect relational outcomes and make recommendations to couples on how to productively use CMC during an argument.

CONCLUSION

This work demonstrated that couples use CMC in a variety of ways during a conflict and have a number of motivations for switching between channels. While most studies of CMC focus on one type of technology at a time, this study reveals that channel switching, at least during a conflict, is common among romantic dating couples. Individuals seem to be interpersonally motivated in their channel switching, whether it be to initiate, manage, or resolve a conflict. Overall, recognizing how and why individuals move "back and forth" from one channel to another can help us to better understand and support the ways in which individuals manage their multi-modal relationships.

ACKNOWLEDGMENTS

We thank the CollabLab and the anonymous reviewers for their insightful feedback on this work. Funding was provided by National Science Foundation grant #0953943.

REFERENCES

1. Argyle, M., & Henderson, M. (1985). The rules of relationships. In S. Duck & D. Perlman (Eds.), *Understanding personal relationships: An interdisciplinary approach* (pp. 63-84). Beverly Hills, CA: Sage.
2. Baym, N.K., Zhang, Y.B., & Lin, M-C. (2004). Social interactions across media: Interpersonal communication on the internet, telephone and face-to-face. *New Media & Society, 6*(3), 299-318.

3. Brown, P., & Levinson, S. (1987). *Politeness: Some universals in language usage.* Cambridge, U.K.: Cambridge University Press.
4. Burnette, J.L., Taylor, K.W., Worthington, E.L., & Forsyth, D.R. (2006). Attachment and trait forgivingness: The mediating role of angry rumination. *Personality and Individual Differences, 42*, 1585-1596.
5. Daft, R.L., & Lengel, R.H. (1984). Information richness: A new approach to managerial behavior and organization design. In B.M. Staw & L.L. Cumming (Eds.) *Research in organizational behavior.* Greenwich, CT: JAI.
6. Dainton, M., & Aylor, B. (2002). Patterns of communication channel use in the maintenance of long-distance relationships. *Communication Research Reports, 19*(2), 118-129.
7. Daft, R.L., & Lengel, R.H. (1986). Organizational information requirements, media richness and structural design. *Management Science, 32*, 554-571.
8. Duck, S. (1988). *Relating to others.* Chicago: Dorsey.
9. Frisby, B.N. & Westerman, D. (2010). Rational actors: Channel selection and rational choices in romantic conflict episodes. *Journal of Social and Personal Relationships, 27*(7), 970-981.
10. Goffman, E. (1967). *Interaction ritual.* Garden City, NY: Doubleday.
11. Hocker, J. L., & Wilmot, W. E. (1995). *Interpersonal Conflict* (4th ed.). Dubuque, IA: William C. Brown.
12. Hovick, S.R.A., Meyers, R.A., & Timmerman, C.E. (2003). E-mail communication in workplace romantic relationships. *Communication Studies, 54*(4), 468-482.
13. Isaacs, E., Walendowski, A., Whittaker, S., Schiano, D.J., & Kamm, C. (2002). The character, functions, and styles of instant messaging in the workplace. In *Proc. CSCW 2002,* 11-20, ACM Press.
14. Isaacs, E., Szymanski, P., Yamauchi, Y., Glasnapp, J., & Iwamoto, K. (2012). Integrating local and remote worlds through channel blending. In *Proc. CSCW 2012*, 617-626, ACM Press.
15. Joinson, A.N. (2001). Self-disclosure in computer-mediated communication: The role of self-awareness and visual anonymity. *European Journal of Social Psychology, 31,* 177-192.
16. Ledbetter, A. M. (2008). Media use and relational closeness in long-term friendships: interpreting patterns of multimodality. *New Media & Society, 10*, 547-564.
17. Mesch, G. S. (2009). Social context and communication channels choice among adolescents. *Computers in Human Behavior, 25*, 244-251.
18. Nardi, B.A., Whittaker, S., & Bradner, E. (2000). Interaction and outeraction: Instant messaging in action. In *Proc. CSCW 2000,* 79-88, ACM Press.
19. Neustaedter, C., & Greenberg, S. (2012). Intimacy in long-distance relationships over video chat. In *Proc. CHI 2012*, ACM Press.
20. O'Sullivan, P.B. (2000). What you don't know won't hurt *me*: Impression management functions of communication channels in relationships. *Human Communication Research, 26*(3), 403-431.
21. Peterson, R.A. (2001). On the use of college students in social science research: Insights from a second-order meta-analysis. *Journal of Consumer Research, 28*(3), 450-461.
22. Pongolini, M., Lundin, J., & Svensson, L. (2011). Golbal online meetings in virtual teams - from media choice to interaction negotiation. In *Proc. C&T 2011*, ACM Press.
23. Ramirez, A., & Broneck, K. (2009). 'IM me': Instant messaging as relational maintenance and everyday communication. *Journal of Social and Personal Relationships, 26*(2-3), 291-314.
24. Roloff, M.E., & Soule, K.P. (2002). Interpersonal conflict: A review. In M.L. Knapp & J.A. Daly (Eds.) *Handbook of Interpersonal Communication* (3rd edition), 475-528. Thousand Oaks, CA: Sage.
25. Sproull, L. & Kiesler, S. (1991). *Connections: New ways of working in the networked organization.* Cambridge, Mass: MIT Press.
26. Strauss, A., & Cordin, J. (1998). *Basics of Qualitative Research*, 2nd Edition. Sage Publications.
27. Su, N.M., & Mark, G. (2008). Communication chains and multitasking. In *Proc. CHI 2008,* ACM Press.
28. Turner, M.M., D'Urso, S.C., Rankin, C.T., & Malone, P.C. (2003). Cognition during conflict: The impact of communication medium and perceived intentions on attributions. *Paper presented at the International Communication Association, 2003.*
29. van den Berg, P. E. W., Arentze, T. A., & Timmermans, H. J. P. (2012). New ICTs and social interaction: Modeling communication frequency and communication mode choice. *New Media & Society*, 1-17.
30. Walther, J.B. (1992). Interpersonal effects in computer-mediated interaction: A relational perspective. *Communication Research, 19*, 52-89.
31. Walther, J.B. (2004). Language and communication technology: Introduction to the special issue. *Journal of Language and Social Psychology, 23,* 384-396.
32. Walther, J., & Parks, M. (2002). Cues filtered out, cues filtered in: Computer-mediated communication and relationships. In M. L. Knapp & J. A. Daly (Eds.), *Handbook of interpersonal communication* (3rd ed., pp. 529-563). Thousand Oaks, CA: Sage.

Radiator - Context Propagation based on Delayed Aggregation

Pedro Alves
INESC-ID / Technical University of Lisbon / Opensoft
Rua Joshua Benoliel, 1, 4C, 1250 Lisboa
pedro.alves@opensoft.pt

Paulo Ferreira
INESC-ID / IST / Technical University of Lisbon
Rua Alves Redol, 9, 1000 Lisboa
paulo.ferreira@inesc-id.pt

ABSTRACT

Context-aware systems take into account the user's current context (such as location, time and activity) to enrich the user interaction with the application. However, these systems may produce huge amounts of information that must be efficiently propagated to a group of people or even large communities while still protecting the privacy of the participants.

We argue that both scalability and privacy can be ensured by delaying context propagation until certain conditions are met and then aggregating such messages both at the syntactic and semantic level. Since such conditions vary from application to application, we propose Radiator, a systematic way to model the propagation characteristics of a distributed context-aware system.

Our qualitative evaluation shows that Radiator is generic enough to model the needs of different context propagation scenarios. To assess the impact of the model on the scalability of an application, we developed twiRadiator, an adaptation of Twitter to the Radiator model which, while preserving user expectations, reduces bandwidth consumption to approx. one third.

Author Keywords

Context propagation; privacy; scalability

ACM Classification Keywords

H.4.3 Information Systems Applications: Communications Applications

General Terms

Algorithms; Human Factors; Measurement; Performance; Security

INTRODUCTION

Context-aware systems take into account the user's current context (such as location, time and activity) to enrich the user interaction with the application [12, 34]. In the last decade, this topic has seen numerous developments that demonstrate its relevance and usefulness, a trend that was further accelerated with the recent widespread availability of powerful mobile devices (such as smartphones) that include a myriad of sensors which enable applications to capture the user environment for a large number of people. Recently, some commercial applications have started to make use of this contextual information to provide real-time traffic information (Waze[1]) or universities' hotspots (Bonfyre[2]), not to mention Facebook or Twitter whose personal short messages are complemented with identity, time and location.

These applications can operate on different scales depending on their purpose: personal, group or community [25]. Whereby personal context-aware applications are designed for a single individual (e.g., personal finance), group applications are designed to propagate context among a group of people who share a common goal or concern (e.g., avoid interruptions when calling friends [32]). When attaining such goals is only possible with a large number of people, applications start operating at a community scale (e.g., traffic monitoring [20] or noise map of a city [33]).

This distinction is important because, as we move from personal to group and then to community applications, we have to face increasing problems related to scalability and privacy. In fact, it is undoubtedly much easier to propagate context to a dozen of friends than to thousands of strangers (obviously, at the individual level this is not even a concern). For example, as of 2012, there are 175 million tweets (twitter messages) being sent per day and some of these messages are distributed to over 19 million users (the number of followers of Lady Gaga).[3] Foursquare[4] has millions of users sharing their location on a regular basis, with more than 600.000 updates per day.[5] Also, we are much more sensitive in revealing personal information to such large groups than we are to our close group of friends. For example, several people have been arrested or fired because of messages they posted on Facebook.[6]

Traditionally, application designers have decided to apply completely different mechanisms to the different scales. Firstly, community applications usually anonymize all information while group applications rely on trust between group members to prevent privacy breaches. Secondly,

CSCW '13, February 23–27, 2013, San Antonio, Texas, USA.

[1] http://www.waze.com
[2] http://www.bonfyreapp.com/
[3] See http://bit.ly/zOiX8k.
[4] http://www.foursquare.com
[5] http://blog.foursquare.com/2010/05/17/607883149/
[6] http://www.huffingtonpost.com/2011/08/30/arrested-over-facebook_n_942487.html

group applications propagate context in intact form while community applications aggregate context from multiple people into single statistical measures. Thirdly, context propagation is immediate on group applications while community applications usually imply some propagation lag to prevent scalability problems. Finally, community applications usually present the information in a condensed form to avoid overwhelming the user with the sheer amount of captured information, while this is not a problem on group applications. These differences are summarized in Table 1.

Group	Community
Members trust each other	All data is anonymized
Context intact	Context aggregated
Immediate propagation	Delayed propagation
User sees all context info	User sees only aggregated info

Table 1. Differences between group and community applications

However, we believe these boundaries will tend to blur in the future, as the distinction between personal, group and community goals also start to blur. As an example, consider the case of weight loss programs assisted by a context-aware application. These applications track user's weight on a daily basis as well as her diet, what she has eaten, how many times she went to the gym, etc. The main goal is clearly individual but it's a well known fact that a group of overweight people can achieve better results if they work together.[7] On top of that, there is statistical relevant data from large communities that can help in the weight losing process, such as knowing that consuming a certain ingredient is usually related to weight losing from a statistical point of view. So, weight losing programs could benefit from the three scales but, since the mechanisms mentioned in the previous paragraph are usually applied to only one scale, application programmers usually end up choosing only one scale instead of embracing a *multi-scale* approach.

There are several other types of applications suffering from this problem. Typically, "friends location" applications are designed at group scale but if they introduce features such as "popular places" they start operating at community scale. These applications are constantly propagating context between groups of friends (i.e., their location, current activity, etc.) to improve coordination between them, promote serendipitous encounters, etc. However, since they are already receiving this contextual information, they might as well discover the most popular spots (e.g., pubs, restaurants) based on the number of people located there (regardless of being friends). In Table 2 we present more examples of this type of applications.

Even when developing applications for just one scale, application programmers spend a significant amount of time designing and programming the context propagation layer, a relatively generic component which could be reused on multiple applications. Some frameworks have been developed to provide a common layer to context-aware applications, but they are usually focused on abstracting the sensor layer (e.g., Context Toolkit [34]) or rely on a publish/subscribe model of propagation (e.g., PACE [21]) which lacks two important features for community-level applications (see Table 1): delayed propagation and anonymization.

Our goal is threefold: to propose a model that (1) is generic enough to express the context propagation and privacy needs of distributed context-aware applications[8] that are able to produce context information (according to Definition 1 outlined in the Design Section); (2) improves scalability by substantially reducing the amount of transmitted information while still fulfilling user expectations; (3) provides a privacy mechanism out-of-the-box without imposing any effort from neither the application programmer nor the user.

We address these challenges by proposing Radiator, a context propagation model that operates equally well on the different scales of context-aware systems and effectively addresses scalability and privacy. This model relies on four main principles:

- Context messages have different urgency levels for different recipients. Some recipients will tolerate (and even appreciate) some lag on the propagation of certain context messages that they do not consider very important. Therefore, some messages can be retained before being propagated.
- Messages that are being retained can be aggregated prior to their propagation. This aggregation can be a simple compression or more sophisticated semantic aggregations. In any case, the final aggregated message is normally much smaller than the sum of the original individual messages. This brings two advantages: network bandwidth reduction (therefore, improved scalability) and less information overload for the end user.
- Anonymization can be achieved through proper aggregation: by aggregating sensible data in such a way that it is not possible to match that data with the corresponding individuals while still retaining its statistical usefulness.
- Application programmers should be able to define their context propagation specific needs with a simple yet expressive model that maps seamlessly to an easily pluggable middleware component.

The remainder of this paper is organized as follows. The next section surveys relevant related work. Then we present the Radiator model, a very simple yet expressive model to define different context propagation schemes. The next section describes a middleware that implements the Radiator model and that can be easily plugged by programmers into their context-aware applications. Then, we evaluate our three goals: generality, scalability and privacy. Finally, we draw some conclusions.

RELATED WORK

In this section, we review the literature for the usage of aggregation, privacy protection and context propagation techniques on context-aware systems.

[7]Take for example the TOPS (Take Off Pounds Sensibly) organization which is based on weekly support meetings between its (more than 200.000) members.

[8]Applications where context is captured in one place and consumed in another place, therefore requiring context propagation across some network.

Aggregation

In distributed context-aware applications, aggregation may be performed at two levels: the inference/reasoning level and the distribution level.

Aggregation at the inference level provides application developers with data on a higher level of abstraction [4] and is usually materialized on some kind of semantic aggregation. For example the Activity widget provided by the Context Toolkit [34] transforms raw audio data from a microphone into "Activity Level" values (*none*, *some* or *a lot*). Many examples like this exist in the literature (e.g., [29, 38, 35]) but they usually perform the aggregation next to the sensor creating a strong coupling that prevents reuse. For example, inferring a street name from a pair of geo-coordinates is so common that it makes sense to move that logic into the middleware layer. The Solar system [8] presents a middleware where aggregation can be composed of multiple operations parametrized by each application. However, it is not able to retain messages during a certain period of time, which would increase the efficiency of the aggregation.

Aggregation at the distribution stage occurs when context was already captured and processed and is now in the process of being sent to the client application. This aggregation consists of gathering into a single large message the content of multiple smaller messages before propagating it. Even though the vast majority of the context-aware frameworks propagate context in single disaggregated messages [1], recent experiments with aggregation have achieved good results [3, 15]. In both cases, we're talking about syntactic aggregation: blindly concatenating single packets into a larger one and possibly compressing it. Although this yields good compression levels for unstructured text-based messages, we believe a higher-level semantic aggregation would be much more effective with other types of information (e.g., geo-localized messages or sensor readings). Ideally, the developer should be able to provide an aggregation function suited to his application needs that would be executed by the middleware.

Privacy

Distributed context aware applications may expose personal information such as current location or availability to a large group of people, raising privacy concerns on end-users. The increasing pervasiveness of devices that are able to communicate context information without explicit user intervention is only aggravating this problem.

In general, privacy mechanisms can be grouped into four categories [2]:

- **Privacy policies** - Applications using this technique allow the user (the context discloser) to provide rules (privacy policies) that define to whom and to what extent his context information is revealed to others. This is the most common technique on both academic and industry social applications (e.g. Facebook, Twitter) and it is tied to *control* and *accountability*, two important mechanisms for privacy protection. However, this approach has revealed multiple problems: it is cumbersome for users to specify fine-grained policies and users are not particularly good at it [11]. For example, Gross [19] found that only 1.2% of Facebook users changed the default privacy settings for profile search-ability.
- **Data perturbation** - This type of technique consists of transforming or partially omitting information before being delivered to the context consumer, in such a way that it is impossible to reconstruct the original message while still keeping (some of) its usefulness [17]. Usually, this is implemented through encryption [31], noise addition [17], blurring [24] or chunk replacement [30]. These techniques are most effective for community-scoped applications whose primary purpose is gathering statistical information.
- **Anonymization** - Using this type of technique, the information is delivered intact to context consumers, except for its author, which is removed or replaced, preventing an attacker from inferring the real author [7, 14]. The removal process must affect both directly identifiable attributes and indirectly identifiable attributes, also known as quasi-identifiers [18]. Some examples of anonymization techniques are mix routing [10], temporal-spatial cloaking [20] and hitchhiking [37]. Unlike the other types of technique, anonymization can usually be parametrized and measured using well-known metrics such as *k-Anonymity* [36], *l-Diversity* [28] and *t-Closeness* [26]. The *k-Anonymity* metric is based on the idea of generalizing a data record until it is indistinguishable from the records of at least k - 1 other individuals. For example, this idea can be applied to location information [20] by computing geographical areas large enough to contain k locations (and during a certain period of time), and propagate that area instead of the individual locations.
- **Lookup notification** - This technique consists on providing the user with information of who has consumed his context information and when [9]. This can occur in real-time (the user is alerted that someone is consuming his context information) or *a posteriori*, by keeping a log of who has seen which information. Unlike the previous three techniques, which are applied before data is delivered, this technique is applied after data delivery (that is, after a potential privacy breach) so it is usually combined with other techniques.

Despite extensive research on this subject, the community is still far from reaching a complete solution that covers the privacy needs of context-aware applications. Two major concerns are the rigid nature of most approaches and the inability to cover *multi-scale* applications (i.e., applications that work both at group scale and community scale). Consolvo [9] has shown that privacy settings can't be rigid - they must be situation-dependent. However, *privacy policies* and *data perturbation* techniques are usually applied regardless of the situation. On the other hand, *data perturbation* techniques are tied to community-scale applications (given their statistical bias) while *lookup notification* techniques are usually applied to group-scale applications (they don't scale well - the user would be overwhelmed with thousands of notifications on community-scale applications).

Anonymization techniques offer a promising solution to those concerns because they usually depend on a parameter that can be configured for each case (therefore being situation-dependent) such as, for example, the k or the l in the k-Anonymity/l-Diversity privacy metrics. Furthermore, they are easy to implement, don't depend on the user's ability to define privacy rules and actually reflect real-world social behavior (e.g., people are more comfortable with video-vigilance on crowded places than on deserted places).

Most of the context-aware frameworks don't offer any support for privacy. Some exceptions such as Context Fabric [23] and PACE [21] allow applications to manage a repository of privacy policies whose rules are enforced upon access to information. However, as already mentioned, this approach relies on users specifying their rules, which has been proven not to be very effective. Also, to the best of our knowledge, none of the public context-aware frameworks support parametrized anonymity mechanisms that can be measured using *k-Anonymity* or *l-Diversity* metrics.

Context Propagation

Several context-aware frameworks rely on traditional publish-subscribe approaches to selectively propagate context messages (e.g., PACE [21], CFN [8] and AWARE [5]). On publish-subscribe systems, users subscribe to topics (subject-based systems) or predicates (content-based systems) [16]. Then, users feed content into the system (publish) and the system distributes events matching subscribers interest with publisher content. Even though the decoupled nature of this approach makes it attractive for systems that need to address mobility and heterogeneity requirements, it assumes a relatively fixed set of matching rules. Systems where context attributes change very frequently (e.g., location, speed) require large volumes of subscribe/unsubscribe messages, leading to wasted resources and poor scalability.

DESIGN

This section describes Radiator, a generic context propagation model based on the concept of aggregation. Radiator assumes a distributed system where a group of personal sensors (sensors that capture the situation of a person) want to propagate context messages to others, regardless of their number (i.e., it works for both group-level and community-level propagation). In most cases, each person is both a producer and a consumer of context messages, but the underlying model is general enough to work on systems where producers are different than consumers. Additionally, this model assumes that context messages will always be propagated albeit some of them can be delayed and/or transformed.

Note that it is up to the application programmer to setup a model that suits the needs of her application. Even though the programmer may take into account the user's input, it is not the user's responsibility to setup Radiator.

First, we need to define context as a triplet relating people, time and the attributes that characterize the environment or situation of those people during a given time span.

Definition 1 (Context)

Let an attribute A_i to be a tuple (N, V), where N is a name representing the attribute (e.g., speed) and V is the value of that attribute (e.g., 100); P to be a finite set of people $\{P_1, P_2, .., P_n\}$; t to be a time range between two timestamps $t_i..t_j$; A to be a finite set of attributes $\{A_1, A_2, .., A_n\}$.

Context C is a triplet (P, t, A) that represents the attributes that characterize the situation of a group of people P during the time span t.

For example, suppose Alice is in New York between Jul 1st and Jul 3rd. We can define her context C as:

$C = ((\text{'}Alice\text{'}), \text{'}01/07\text{'}..\text{'}03/07\text{'}, ((\text{'}location\text{'}, \text{'}NewYork\text{'}))$.

The Radiator model also introduces the notion of context aggregation to represent a set of contexts C that share a certain attribute A, producing an aggregated context C_{Aggr}.

Definition 2 (Aggregation)

Let $\{(P_1, t_1, A_1), .., (P_n, t_n, A_n)\}$ be a set of contexts and A_c a common attribute such that $\forall A_i \in A_1...A_n : A_c \in A_i$.

$$Aggr(A_c, \{(P_1, t_1, A_1), .., (P_n, t_n, A_n)\}) = (P, t, A) \Rightarrow$$
$$\forall P_i \in P_1..P_n : P_i \in P \wedge$$
$$\forall t_i \in t_1...t_n : t_i \subseteq t \wedge$$
$$\forall A_i \in A_1...A_n : A_i \in A$$

For example, it is possible to aggregate:

$$C_{Alice} = ((\text{'}Alice\text{'}), \text{'}01/07\text{'}..\text{'}03/07\text{'}, ((\text{'}location\text{'}, \text{'}NewYork\text{'}))$$
$$C_{Bob} = ((\text{'}Bob\text{'}), \text{'}02/07\text{'}..\text{'}04/07\text{'}, ((\text{'}location\text{'}, \text{'}NewYork\text{'}))$$

into an aggregated context:

$$C_{Aggr} = ((\text{'}Alice\text{'}, \text{'}Bob\text{'}), \text{'}01/07\text{'}, \text{'}04/07\text{'}], ((\text{'}location\text{'}, \text{'}NewYork\text{'}))$$

or (if anonymity is required):

$$C_{Aggr} = ((\text{'}A\text{'}, \text{'}B\text{'}), \text{'}01/07\text{'}, \text{'}04/07\text{'}], ((\text{'}location\text{'}, \text{'}NewYork\text{'}))$$

Any function capable of aggregating contexts according to definition 2 is noted as f_{Aggr}. Aggregation can be done at the raw data level (e.g. compression) or at the semantic level, taking into account the specific properties of certain attributes. For example, if the attribute is a geographical location, a common f_{Aggr} is the minimum bounding box - the smallest rectangle where a set of coordinates are included. Other common f_{Aggr} calculates the mean for continuous attributes or the median for categorical attributes [13].

Finally, we introduce the notion of aggregability.

Definition 3 (Aggregability)

Let C_P be the current context of a given person P and C_x the context of someone else that the system wants to propagate to P. The aggregability function $G(C_P, C_x)$ represents how much aggregated C_x must be before being transmitted to P, taking into consideration his current context C_P.

Therefore, a set of contexts C_1 to C_n is only propagated to P when $\forall i \in 1..n, G(C_P, C_i) = n$, n being an integer.

Informally, the aggregability represents the number of context messages that must be retained before propagation. If we define an aggregability function (G) that always returns 4, the system will always aggregate four context messages before propagating them. In case we want immediate propagation, we can define G as a function that always returns 1. Although returning a simple number has the advantage of keeping the model very simple, we propose that G returns a tuple in the following format:

$G(C_P, C_i) \rightarrow \{type : value\}$

$type :: [volume|time|people]$

Along with the before mentioned $value$, G must tell if that value represents a quantity ($volume$), a time range ($time$) or the number of different people contained in the aggregation ($people$). If the type is $time$, context messages will be aggregated until the number of seconds between the oldest and newest retained message is equal or greater than $value$. The types $volume$ and $people$ are similar in the fact that they represent the maximum number of retained/aggregated messages, although $volume$ is the number of different messages while $people$ represents the number of different people involved on those messages. For example, if G returns $\{people : 4\}$, the system will aggregate messages until there are four different people involved, before propagating them. This distinction is important to implement privacy management mechanisms as we will describe shortly. Note that we chose these 3 metrics as the minimal set to fulfill the context propagation needs of most distributed context-aware applications (as shown in the Evaluation Section); other metrics can easily be included without changing Radiator's algorithm.

Given these definitions, we can now describe how the Radiator model works. A set of people ($P_1..P_n$) wants to propagate their current context ($C_{P_1}..C_{P_n}$) to everyone, in an efficient and privacy-manageable way. Every context C is evaluated against a set of aggregability functions G that will tell how many other "similar" C_n must be aggregated with C. If that aggregation is not possible (i.e., there are not enough aggregatable pending C_n), than C is appended to a *pending* queue. On the other hand, if there are conditions to aggregate, we can apply an aggregation function f_{Aggr} to those contexts that produces a single aggregated context C_{Aggr}. Afterwards, C_{Aggr} is propagated and the corresponding C_n removed from the pending queue.

This model is much more efficient than traditional immediate broadcast approaches because it postpones propagation until a certain level of aggregability is met. Since the aggregability function reduces a set of context messages into a single one, it effectively reduces the number of bytes transmitted over the wire. This is particularly significant when the message is propagated to a large population, as the message size reduction is multiplied by the number of recipients. Moreover, it provides a simple yet powerful mechanism for privacy management based on the concept of k-anonymity [36]. The k-anonymity principle tells that we can achieve anonymity by aggregating at least k records with a common attribute, making them indistinguishable from each other. Implementing k-anonymity using this model is straightforward - the developer only has to define an aggregability function $G \rightarrow (\{people : k\})$. Note that the model allows other anonymity metrics such as l-diversity [28] (e.g., using an aggregability function such as $G \rightarrow (\{diverse\_salary : l\})$) or t-closeness [26]. We only implemented support for k-anonymity because of its simplicity and generalized adoption.

As an example, let's say we want to propagate only context information related to at least two different people. Therefore, we define an aggregability function $G \rightarrow \{people : 2\}$.

A typical message flow would be:

t:0 Alice wants to propagate C_{Alice_1}. Since there are not enough messages to aggregate with, it's appended to the *pending* queue.

t:1 Alice wants to propagate C_{Alice_2}. There is already one message to aggregate with, but it's from the same person, so it's also appended to the *pending* queue.

t:3 Bob wants to propagate C_{Bob_1}. We can aggregate this message with the other pending messages and get an aggregated context of at least two people. So we apply $f_{Aggr}(C_{Alice_1}, C_{Alice_2}, C_{Bob_1})$ to get C_{Aggr}. C_{Aggr} is propagated to everyone.

Until now, we have considered only constant aggregability functions, that return the same value independently of the actors involved. However, consider the case where we want to have different propagation rules depending on whether people are friends or strangers. For example, a certain application may want to immediately propagate a person's context to her friends but aggregate messages up to 40 seconds when they are being propagated to strangers. We could define such function as follows:

$$G(C_P, C_{P_i}) \rightarrow \{volume : 1\} \iff is\_friend(P_i, P)$$
$$G(C_P, C_{P_i}) \rightarrow \{time : 40\} \iff is\_stranger(P_i, P)$$

We present other examples of aggregability functions as well as an evaluation of their generality in the Evaluation Section.

IMPLEMENTATION

We developed a middleware component that implements the Radiator model described in the Design Section, in order to (1) provide a reference implementation for developers who wish to use this model on their applications and (2) conduct several experiments to evaluate the model regarding ease of use and performance/scalability. The results of the latter are presented in the Evaluation Section.

The middleware component is written in Python and it can be downloaded from `https://bitbucket.org/palves/radiator`. From a client perspective (a developer who wishes to integrate her context-aware application with the Radiator middleware), there are only two classes to know about: `Context` and `RadiatorMiddleware`. The class `Context` contains all the information pertaining to a certain context message according to Definition 1: people, time and a list of attributes. The `RadiatorMiddleware` class is the primary interface from which to send and receive context messages (represented as Context objects). The constructor receives an aggregability function that complies with

#	Scenario	Description	Aggregability function
1	Traffic monitoring	Aggregate speedometer and GPS data within 300 seconds periods	$\{time : 300\}$
2	Road hazards detection	Aggregate vertical accelerometer and GPS data until 5 hazards detected	$\{volume : 5\}$
3	Popular spots Friends location	Aggregate location until 10 different people in the same spot but for friends send immediately (non-aggregated)	$\{people : 10\}$ if stranger $\{volume : 1\}$ if friend
4	Facebook likes	Aggregate likes from strangers within 300 seconds periods, likes from friends of friends until there are 5 and likes from direct friends with a maximum delay of 30 seconds	$\{time : 300\}$ if stranger $\{volume : 5\}$ if friend_of_friend $\{time : 30\}$ if friend
5	Friends location in crowded spaces (concerts, street markets)	Aggregate location based on how far you are from the recipient (further away implies more aggregation)	$\{volume : \texttt{distance}\}$
6	Stock market alerts	Aggregate stock market information during a period of time proportional to the number of shares owned by the recipient (higher number implies less aggregation)	$\{time : 1000/1 + \texttt{number\_of\_shares}\}$
7	Weight loss program	Anonymize weight information based on the recipient's weight (the closer the weight of recipient is from the sender the less anonymous it is)	$\{people : \texttt{weight\_difference}\}$
8	Anonymize twitter	Anonymize tweets with Egyptian revolution related hashtags	$\{people : 50\}$ if #sidibouzid or #Jan25

Table 2. Different context propagation scenarios and the corresponding aggregability functions

```
1  def my_aggregability(recipient, context):
2      # aggregates until 4 hazards detected or
3      # 5 minutes since the last propagation
4
5      if context.attributes['hazard_detected']:
6          return {'volume': 4}
7      else:
8          return {'time': 300}  # 300 seconds
9
10 def mean(attribute_name, attributes_list):
11     # returns the mean value of attributes named
12     # 'attribute_name' in 'attributes_list'
13     ...
14
15 # start the middleware engine
16 engine = Middleware(aggregability=my_aggregability,
17                     aggregation_functions={'hazard_detected':mean,
18                                            'speed':mean })
19
20 # register some participants
21 engine.register('p1')
22 engine.register('p2')
23
24 # propagate a context message
25 engine.propagate(Context('p2', now, { 'speed' : 100 }))
26
27 def receive(context):
28     # called whenever a context is received.
29     # the context may be aggregated.
30
31 # register the callback for receiving messages
32 engine.register_receiver(receive)
```

Listing 1. Code example of Radiator middleware usage

Definition 3 and an optional list of aggregation functions (Definition 2), as show on lines 16-18 in Listing 1. Each participant then registers itself (lines 21-22) after which it can start propagating messages as well as receiving messages propagated by others.

The rest of the process is also exemplified in Listing 1. After the `RadiatorMiddleware` initialization, the application can propagate context (line 25) or can receive context that was propagated by others (lines 27-29). Since the reception of context is asynchronous, the developer has to register a callback to do so (line 32).

Note that the actual network topology of the system is completely transparent to the developer. Even though right now this is implemented following a centralized model, it can easily accommodate other models such as the partitioned or the decentralized topologies without breaking the client application.

EVALUATION

The Radiator model is simple enough to be easily understood by application developers yet sufficiently expressive to define a wide range of needs usually found on distributed context-aware applications. In this section, we first measure its expressiveness by applying the Radiator model to eight scenarios where context propagation across the network is crucial to accomplish the application's goals. Note that, although evaluating the usability of this model (for developers) was not the goal of this paper, our experiments have given good indications on this subject.

Then, we present *twiRadiator*, a Twitter application built over the Radiator model to evaluate the impact of different propagation rules on (1) the system scalability and (2) user expectations. With over 100M users, Twitter is arguably one of the largest context-propagation applications and has faced multiple scalability problems along the time[9].

Finally, we evaluated how the Radiator model can protect the privacy of Twitter participants in sensitive situations such as the Egyptian revolution.

Is the model generic enough?

Despite the simplicity of the Radiator model, it is still powerful enough to describe a large variety of context propagation scenarios. Consider the scenarios and corresponding aggregability functions on Table 2. For example, traffic monitoring applications [20, 22] (first row of Table 2) continuously capture the speed and position of a large group of vehicles to identify places suffering from traffic congestion. This information is then broadcast to all vehicles possibly alerting

[9]See http://tcrn.ch/wi7rJ3

#	Scenario	Aggregation function
1	Traffic monitoring	`avg`(speed) by location
2	Road hazards detection	`sum`(hazards) by location
3	Popular spots	`count`(people) by location
4	Facebook likes	`sum`(likes) by object
5	Friends location in crowded spaces	`list`(people) by distance
6	Stock market alerts	`newest`(values) by share
7	Weight loss program	`list`(people) by weight
8	Anonymize twitter	`list`(people) by tweet

Table 3. Different context propagation scenarios and the corresponding aggregation functions

the drivers to take alternative routes. Since traffic congestion occurs during a relatively long period of time (at least, dozens of minutes), it can be aggregated within 5 minutes (300 seconds) periods without losing its usefulness and relevance. Using the radiator model, implementing this propagation scheme is as simple as defining an aggregability function that always returns {`time:300`}.

The aggregation itself is performed by the *aggregation function* (see Definition 2 in the Design Section). If the developer does not provide any aggregation function, Radiator applies a simple concatenation between the messages to aggregate. To achieve higher compression levels (and therefore reduce network bandwidth), the developer should provide an aggregation function that takes into account the specific needs of its application. Table 3 shows some examples of such functions. In the traffic monitoring case (first row in Table 3), we are concerned about the average speed within a geographical region. For example, if the average speed is near zero, it is reasonable to assume that there is traffic congestion within that particular region. The pseudo-code of such function is shown in Listing 2.

```
def average_speed_by_location(pending_msgs):
  return [people_within_location,
          time_range_between_oldest_and_newest,
          { 'speed': avg(speed), 'location': location}
          for location in group_by(pending_msgs, location)]
```

Listing 2. Pseudo-code of an aggregation function for traffic monitoring applications

Since the propagation scheme is continuously calculated by the aggregability function, is is possible to define more complex scenarios such as *Facebook likes*[10] (the fourth row of Table 2). Depending on the privacy settings, when a user likes a link or a photo on facebook, this action can show up on the news feed of all his friends, friends of friends and even strangers. This is important to measure the general popularity of an item when compared to the popularity within the much narrower circle of friends. Again, in the radiator model this is very simple to define. In this case, the aggregability function returns three different settings depending on whether the recipient is a friend, a friend of a friend or a stranger. In the latter, it can aggregate *likes* within 300 seconds because we only want a coarse-grained statistical value ({`time:300`}). On the other hand, we want to see *likes* from our friends with some urgency (we may want to interact with them based on their *like*), so the aggregation is much narrower (only 30 seconds - {`time:30`}). For friend of friends, we may want to set the maximum number of retained/aggregated *likes* to only five ({`volume:5`}). Here, the aggregation function can just be the sum of likes grouped by liked object (see fourth row of Table 3), so that users know the current "popularity" of a given object (e.g., 5 likes for photo X, 23 likes for article Y).

Even though the previous case is more flexible, we are still limited to a discrete set of options (friend, friend of friend, stranger). However, the radiator model allows completely continuous propagation schemes, giving rise to potentially very creative models of propagation. Rows 4, 5 and 6 of Table 2 exemplify such creative uses. For example, typical weight loss programs where users keep track of their diet on a daily basis, as well as their current weight, are very sensitive to privacy concerns [17]. On the other hand, it is a well known fact that engaging with other users on similar conditions can have a positive effect on the program, blending the user's personal goal with the community goals (e.g., Fitbit[11]). Therefore, we suggest an application that aggregates weight information proportionally to the weight difference between the sender and the recipient. Suppose Alice weights 95 Kg. If there is another user elsewhere with the exact same weight, the application shows this information to Alice unaggregated (and vice-versa). But if Bob and Carol weight 94 Kg, their weight will appear aggregated to Alice (Alice will receive $('2people', 'Today', (\{`weight' : `94'\}))$. The aggregation (and consequentially the anonymity level) increases as the weight becomes further from 95 Kg. Using the radiator model, this scenario can be defined by an aggregation function that returns a result that is itself dependent on a variable (in this case, the weight) - {*people* : `weight_difference`}.

With respect to privacy, we can turn to scenarios like the 2011 Tunisian and Egyptian revolutions that were greatly propelled by twitter, through the use of hashtags such as `#sidibouzed` (home city of Mohamed Bouazizi, following his self-immolation) or `#Jan25` (after a political demonstration in Cairo on the January 25th) [27]. The big challenge here lies in preventing the ones who start the tweets (typically, local activists) from being identified by the government in order to censor and control the dissemination of critical rebel information. Even though twitter allows the use of pseudonyms, given enough historical information one could still identify the author. Using Radiator's *k-Anonymity* style mechanism, it is possible to preserve the privacy of the actors involved by aggregating batches of messages until there are at least k people involved. This rule could be applied only to sensitive hashtags, as in the example shown on the last row of Table 2.

Delayed aggregation impact on scalability

In the Radiator model, some messages can be aggregated before being propagated. Since the compression of an aggregated message is usually much more effective than the compression of its individual parts, we evaluated this effect

[10] See http://on.fb.me/wrw9bA for information on the like feature

[11] http://www.fitbit.com

Scenario	Rel. Consumed Bandwidth	Max delay (secs)
$\{volume : 1\}$	100%	0
$\{volume : 5\}$	51%	49
$\{volume : 10\}$	43%	62
$\{volume : 20\}$	39%	66
$\{volume : 50\}$	35%	144
$\{volume : 100\}$	32%	250
$\{volume : 200\}$	29%	471

Table 4. Consumed bandwidth under different scenarios

on the consumed network bandwidth of an application built using the Radiator middleware described in the Implementation Section.

We developed twiRadiator, an adaptation of the well-known Twitter application to the Radiator model. Twitter[12] is a very popular application with over 100M users, that allows anyone to post short messages with less than 140 characters (called "tweets") with diverse content, ranging from personal thoughts to photo and link sharing. Even though Twitter may not be considered a classic context-aware application, tweets are supposed to be answers for the question *"What's happening?"*, so we are effectively talking about a huge context propagation system and therefore an excellent candidate to test the impact of the Radiator model.

```
# start the middleware engine
engine = Middleware(['p1'], # 1 participant
           aggregability=[lambda p, c: {'volume': 10}],
           aggregation_functions=
           {'tweet': aggregate_equal_tweets,
            'location': aggregate_if_all_the_same})

# iterate all the tweets in the sample
for tweet in tweet_sample:
      engine.propagate(Context(tweet))
```

Listing 3. Sample of twiRadiator showing how easy it is to setup a testing scenario with the Radiator middleware

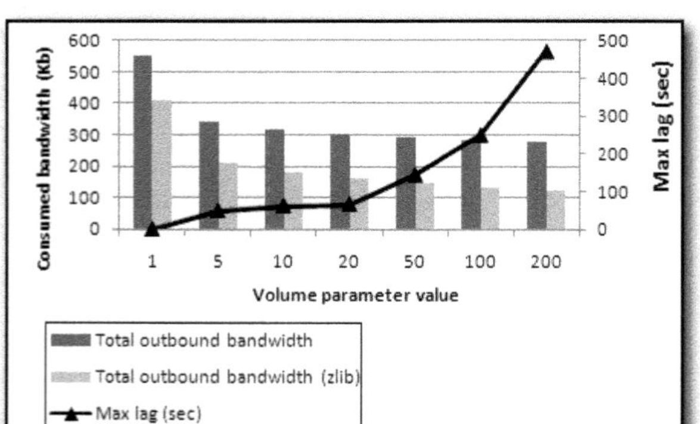

Figure 1. Bandwidth consumption under different "volume" values and its effect on the message propagation lag

We collected a sample of received tweets from a popular user (Scobleizer[13]) using Twitter's API. Scobleizer follows more than 32.000 users (i.e., receives tweets from more than 32.000 users). The sample contains all the received tweets by Scobleizer during 1 hour (on Jan 15th 2012), resulting in aprox. 2000 tweets (at least 1 tweet received every two seconds). We then fed this sample into twiRadiator, which transformed each tweet in a *context* object and used the Radiator middleware to propagate those messages. Then, we measured the total consumed bandwidth for each user, under different *volume* values. Listing 3 shows an example for these scenarios: a middleware engine is initialized with the *volume* set to 10, meaning that the engine will postpone propagation until it can aggregate 10 messages.

We have also setup two **aggreggation functions**: one to aggregate tweets with the same content into a single one (basically a count of retweets) and another to aggregate locations if they were all the same (i.e., if all the tweets contained in the aggregation share the same location, that location is only included once). Here's a simple example of how 3 different messages with the same location become aggregated.

$([\text{'}p1'], (\text{'}04:00:00', \text{'}04:00:00'),$
$(\text{'}tweet' : [\text{'}strange'], \text{'}loc' : [\text{'}NewYork']))$

$([\text{'}p2'], (\text{'}04:00:02', \text{'}04:00:02'),$
$(\text{'}tweet' : [\text{'}This\ is\ great'], \text{'}loc' : [\text{'}NewYork']))$

$([\text{'}p3'], (\text{'}04:00:05', \text{'}04:00:05'),$
$(\text{'}tweet' : [\text{'}OMG'], \text{'}loc' : [\text{'}NewYork']))$

are aggregated into:

$([\text{'}p1', \text{'}p2', \text{'}p3'], (\text{'}04:00:00', \text{'}04:00:05'),$
$(\text{'}tweet' : [\text{'}strange', \text{'}This\ is\ great', \text{'}OMG'], \text{'}loc' : [\text{'}NewYork']))$

We experimented with the following *volume* values: 1 (immediate propagation, equivalent to what Twitter does), 5, 10, 20, 50, 100 and 200 with zlib compression turned off and on. Note that, in this test, we are only propagating messages to one participant. This means that the **server**'s outbound bandwidth consumption (the focus of our experiment) equals the (single) **client**'s inbound bandwidth consumption.

From the results, shown in Figure 1, we can see that the consumed bandwidth decreases as the volume increases, even when compression is turned off. The reason is that in the aggregated messages we are not repeating the headers and other structural information that ends being repeated in every message. When we turn on the compression, the effect on the consumed bandwidth is even more clear, becoming more efficient as the number of aggregated messages increase. Comparing the compressed bandwidth used in the direct propagation scenario ($\{volume : 1\}$) with the most aggregated scenario ($\{volume : 200\}$), we can observe that the latter consumes only 29% of the former. However, we can also observe the impact on the maximum propagation delay as the volume increases. Since we are allowing the middleware to aggregate up to 200 messages before propagating, we can expect an increased delay. In the most aggregated scenario some messages would arrive with aprox. 8 minutes of delay, but if we look at the $\{volume : 50\}$ scenario, there seems to be a good tradeoff between the 2.5 minutes delay and the 35% bandwidth reduction (see Table 4). To better understand what would be a good tradeoff

[12]http://www.twitter.com
[13]http://www.twitter.com/scobleizer

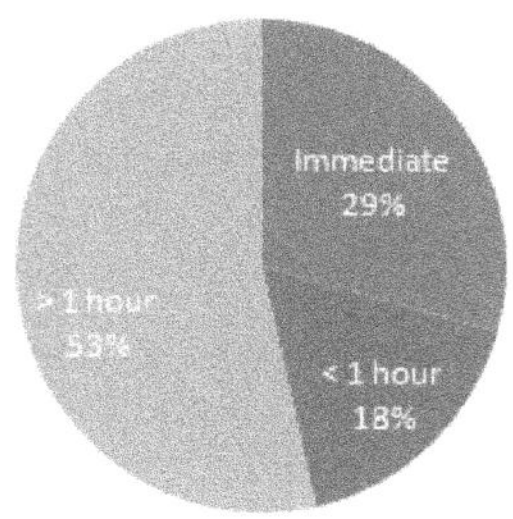

Figure 2. Answers to the question "On Twitter, what is your maximum tolerable delay for receiving a tweet?"

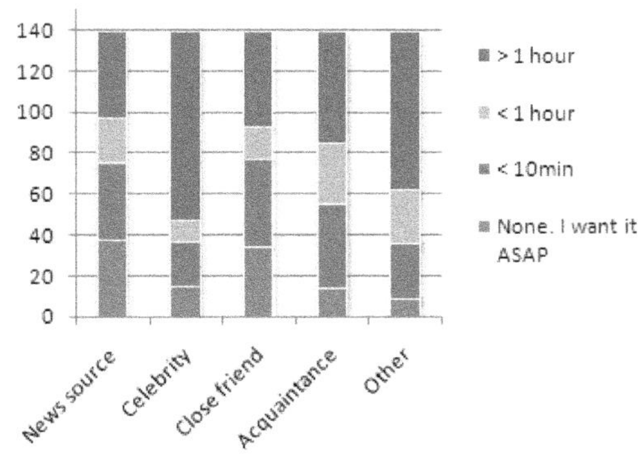

Figure 3. Tolerable delay by type of source information

from a user's perspective, we conducted a survey which we describe in the next section.

Delayed propagation impact on user expectations

To better understand the user expectations of this type of applications we designed a questionnaire that was answered by 139 (non-paid) participants that were randomly recruited through twitter. All the subjects were active twitter users and 69% of them followed more than 100 users. We asked the following question:

"On Twitter, what is your maximum tolerable delay for receiving a tweet from each type of source? That is, instead of receiving the tweet immediately, the tweet would arrive after a certain amount of time. How much time would you tolerate before becoming annoyed about it?".

Respondents had to answer this question for each of the following five types of source information: News source (e.g., CNN); Celebrity (e.g., Lady Gaga); Close friend; Acquaintance; Other. The possible answers ranged from "None. I want it as soon as possible" to "I don't care, as long as I receive it." with some time ranges in between.

Our goal was to understand (1) if users tolerate receiving tweets with a delay and (2) if that delay depends on the type of source.

The general results without taking into account the type of source, depicted in Figure 2, show that only 29% of the respondents require immediate propagation and that the majority doesn't mind receiving tweets with over an hour delay. From that, we can conclude that twitter could use a delayed propagation approach while still fulfilling the needs of most of its users.

Next, we analyze if and how user expectations depend on the type of source. The results in Figure 3 show that the source of information is indeed an important factor on the maximum tolerable delay. Tweets from close friends and media sources require the most immediacy while tweets from celebrities require no immediacy at all. Given that the tweets from some celebrities are propagated to millions of users, the bandwidth reduction of delayed propagation that we observed on the quantitative evaluation could have a tremendous impact while still fulfilling user expectations. We can also observe that the tolerance to delayed messages is much greater for acquaintances and strangers than close friends. This seems to indicate that the distance on the social network graph is correlated with the delivery urgency of the corresponding messages. We believe this correlation is a common characteristic of distributed context-aware applications and fits perfectly into the Radiator model.

Given these results, the following aggregability function would match scalability needs with user expectations, assuming a function $social\_distance$ returning the number of hops in the social network between 2 people:

$\{time : 0\}$ `if media`
$\{time : 10000\}$ `if celebrity` # a few hours
$\{time : social\_distance(p1, p2) * 3600\}$ `if !(media or celebrity)`

The specific implementation of $social\_distance$ is outside the scope of this paper but we present some hints on possible solutions. The most obvious solution, albeit cumbersome, would be to ask the user directly about how strong is his relation with each person he follows. Another solution would be to tap into other social networks (besides Twitter) that support different levels of connections such as Facebook's friends and friends of friends and Linkedin's 1st, 2nd and 3rd level connections. Finally, even on Twitter itself we can distinguish between symmetrical relationships (A follows B and B follows A) and asymmetrical relationships (A follows B but B doesn't follow A) to infer the strength of the connection.

Privacy

The Radiator model proposes a privacy mechanism based on the *k-Anonymity* principle: generalizing a data record until it is indistinguishable from the records of at least k - 1 other individuals. To evaluate how this principle applies to real-world data, we collected a sample of tweets with the hashtag `#Jan25` pertaining the Egyptian revolution (after a political demonstration in Cairo on the January 25th). Egypt and several other countries have been reported to track down activists on social networks such as twitter and facebook[14], therefore privacy is a major concern on these scenarios.

In Figure 4 we can see a sample of tweets in its original form (using the Twitter web client). The tweets are shown in a way that it is clear who is their author, making it impossible to protect his privacy. To keep the figure simple, we only show the original tweets, not the retweets from 7 other people.

Next, we setup the Radiator model with the following configuration:

[14]http://rww.to/ifg3i0

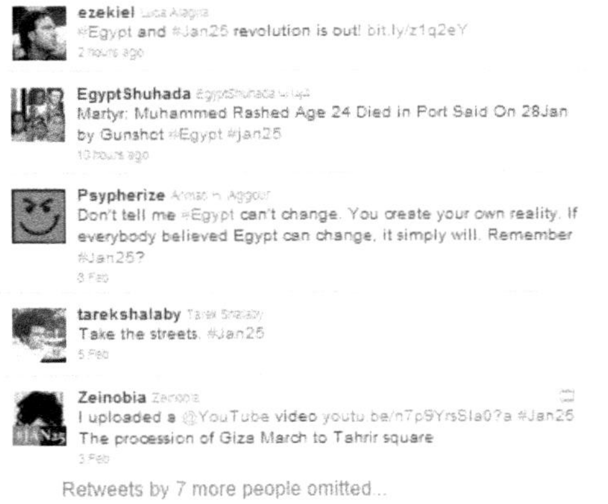

Figure 4. Sample of tweets with the hashtag #Jan25, in its original form

Figure 5. The same sample of tweets in aggregated form.

$\{people: 12\}$ if `#Jan25`

This configuration tells the Radiator to aggregate messages with the hashtag `#Jan25` until at least 12 different people are included in the aggregation. We chose the number 12 to keep the example simple: a greater number would increase privacy even more. As shown in Figure 5, applying this configuration to the same sample of tweets, we get a result that protects the privacy of the participants without losing critical information. Now, the same messages appear next to each other, with all the authors in the end, so it is no longer possible to relate tweets with their authors. Even though some local activists may be included in the authors, we are no longer sure about the specific tweet they are responsible for. They may even claim that they were just retweeting a tweet from a foreign journalist, for example (which is probably enough to get by the government control). In practice, during the peak of revolution, it would be reasonable to use much higher levels of *k-Anonymity*, with k easily going up to the thousands. Note that, in this example, we used an aggregation function that preserved the identity of the authors (although breaking the link between author and message). We could just as well used a function that replaced the identity of the authors with a count (number of authors), achieving greater privacy at the expense of some utility. The point here is that the Radiator model can be used to implement multiple levels of privacy with little effort by carefully selecting adequate aggregability and aggregation functions. For example, as suggested by Campan [6], we could take into account the social network of each participant to drive the anonymization level by using an aggregation function such as $\{people: num\_friends()\}$, where num_friends() is the number of friends of the author.

CONCLUSIONS

In this paper, we propose Radiator, a simple and generic model for propagation characteristics of distributed context-aware systems. The model revolves around the concept of delayed aggregation: it allows application developers to define which messages should be propagated immediately and which should be retained and aggregated before being propagated. This definition is formally based on the concept of $Aggregability$, representing the conditions under which messages must be retained before propagation. These conditions may depend on *volume*, *time* or *people* and can be highly dynamic as the $Aggregability$ function may return itself a function.

As our experimental results have shown, it is possible to decrease network bandwidth consumption to less than 1/3 using the delayed aggregation technique (due to higher compression efficiency) while still fulfilling user needs. Furthermore, by carefully aggregating messages coming from different people in a way that makes it impossible to distinguish individual information (borrowed from the concept of *k-Anonymity*), it is also possible to protect the privacy of the participants, a common and important issue on the design of context-aware applications.

Thus, this model is able to improve both scalability and privacy with very little effort from the developer for a wide variety of applications, from traffic monitoring and location-based services to health monitoring and social network applications.

In the future, we plan to experiment with a decentralized Radiator middleware to improve the total consumed network bandwidth as well as implementing other applications on top of this model.

ACKNOWLEDGMENTS

This work was partially supported by national funds through FCT – Fundação para a Ciência e a Tecnologia, under projects PTDC/EIA-EIA/113993/2009 and PEst-OE/EEI/LA0021/2011.

REFERENCES

1. P. Alves and P. Ferreira. Distributed Context-Aware Systems. Technical Report RT/22/2011, INESC-ID, 2011.

2. P. Alves and P. Ferreira. Privacy in Distributed Context-Aware Systems. Technical Report RT/23/2011, INESC-ID, 2011.

3. P. Alves and P. Ferreira. ReConMUC - Adaptable Consistency Requirements for Efficient Large-scale Multi-user Chat. In *Proceedings of the 2011 ACM conference on Computer supported cooperative work*, 2011.

4. M. Baldauf, S. Dustdar, and F. Rosenberg. A survey on context-aware systems. *International Journal of Ad Hoc and Ubiquitous Computing*, 2(4):263, 2007.

5. J. E. Bardram and T. R. Hansen. The AWARE Architecture: Supporting Context-Mediated Social Awareness in Mobile Cooperation. In *Proc. Conf. on Computer-Supported Collaborative Work (CSCW)*, pages 192–201, Chicago, 2004.

6. A. Campan and T. M. Truta. A Clustering Approach for Data and Structural Anonymity in Social Networks. *Privacy, Security, and Trust in KDD*, pages 0–9, 2008.
7. D. Chaum. Untraceable electronic mail, return addresses, and digital pseudonyms. *Communications of the ACM*, 24(2):84–90, 1981.
8. G. Chen, M. Li, and D. Kotz. Design and implementation of a large-scale context fusion network. In *Mobile and Ubiquitous Systems: Networking and Services, 2004. MOBIQUITOUS 2004. The First Annual International Conference on*, pages 246–255. IEEE, 2004.
9. S. Consolvo, I. Smith, T. Matthews, A. LaMarca, J. Tabert, and P. Powledge. Location disclosure to social relations: why, when, & what people want to share. In *Proceedings of the SIGCHI conference on Human factors in computing systems*, pages 81–90. ACM, 2005.
10. C. Cornelius, A. Kapadia, and D. Kotz. Anonysense: privacy-aware people-centric sensing. In *Proceedings of the 6th international conference on Mobile systems, applications, and services*, pages 211–224. ACM New York, NY, USA, 2008.
11. J. Cornwell, I. Fette, G. Hsieh, M. Prabaker, J. Rao, K. Tang, K. Vaniea, L. Bauer, L. Cranor, J. Hong, B. McLaren, M. Reiter, and N. Sadeh. User-Controllable Security and Privacy for Pervasive Computing. *Eighth IEEE Workshop on Mobile Computing Systems and Applications*, pages 14–19, Mar. 2007.
12. A. Dey and G. Abowd. Towards a better understanding of context and context-awareness. In *CHI 2000 workshop on the what, who, where, when, and how of context-awareness*, volume 4, pages 1–6, 2000.
13. J. Domingo-Ferrer and V. Torra. Ordinal, Continuous and Heterogeneous k-Anonymity Through Microaggregation. *Data Mining and Knowledge Discovery*, 11(2):195–212, Aug. 2005.
14. M. Duckham and L. Kulik. Location privacy and location-aware computing. *Dynamic & mobile GIS: Investigating change in space and time*, pages 34–51, 2006.
15. J. Dyck, C. Gutwin, T. Graham, and D. Pinelle. Beyond the LAN: Techniques from network games for improving groupware performance. In *Proceedings of the 2007 international ACM conference on Supporting group work*, pages 291–300. ACM, 2007.
16. P. Eugster, P. Felber, R. Guerraoui, and A. Kermarrec. The many faces of publish/subscribe. *ACM Computing Surveys*, 35(2):114–131, June 2003.
17. R. Ganti, N. Pham, Y. Tsai, and T. Abdelzaher. PoolView: stream privacy for grassroots participatory sensing. In *Proceedings of the 6th ACM conference on Embedded network sensor systems*, pages 281–294. ACM, 2008.
18. P. Golle and K. Partridge. On the anonymity of home/work location pairs. *Pervasive Computing*, pages 2–9, 2009.
19. R. Gross and A. Acquisti. Information Revelation and Privacy in Online Social Networks. In *Proceedings of the 2005 ACM workshop on Privacy in the electronic society*, pages 71–80. ACM, 2005.
20. M. Gruteser and D. Grunwald. Anonymous Usage of Location-Based Services Through Spatial and Temporal Cloaking. *Proceedings of the 1st international conference on Mobile systems, applications and services - MobiSys '03*, pages 31–42, 2003.
21. K. Henricksen, J. Indulska, and T. McFadden. Middleware for distributed context-aware systems. *Internet Systems 2005*, pages 846–863, 2005.
22. B. Hoh, M. Gruteser, R. Herring, J. Ban, D. Work, J.-C. Herrera, A. M. Bayen, M. Annavaram, and Q. Jacobson. Virtual trip lines for distributed privacy-preserving traffic monitoring. *Proceeding of the 6th international conference on Mobile systems, applications, and services - MobiSys '08*, page 15, 2008.
23. J. Hong and J. Landay. An architecture for privacy-sensitive ubiquitous computing. In *2nd International Conference on Mobile Systems, Applications, and Services (MobiSys)*, 2004.
24. G. Iachello, I. Smith, S. Consolvo, M. Chen, and G. Abowd. Developing privacy guidelines for social location disclosure applications and services. In *Proceedings of the 2005 symposium on Usable privacy and security*, pages 65–76. ACM, 2005.
25. N. Lane, E. Miluzzo, H. Lu, D. Peebles, T. Choudhury, and A. T. Campbell. A Survey of Mobile Phone Sensing. *IEEE Communications Magazine*, (September):140–150, 2010.
26. N. Li, T. Li, and V. Suresh. t-closeness: Privacy beyond k-anonymity and l-diversity. *IEEE 23rd International Conference on Data Engineering*, pages 106–115, 2007.
27. G. Lotan, E. Graeff, M. Ananny, D. Gaffney, I. Pearce, and D. Boyd. The Revolutions Were Tweeted: Information Flows During the 2011 Tunisian and Egyptian Revolutions. *International Journal of Communication*, 5:1375–1406, 2011.
28. A. Machanavajjhala and D. Kifer. l-diversity: Privacy beyond k-anonymity. *ACM Transactions on Knowledge Discovery from Data (TKDD)*, 1(1), Mar. 2007.
29. E. Miluzzo, N. Lane, K. Fodor, R. Peterson, and H. Lu. Sensing meets mobile social networks: the design, implementation and evaluation of the cenceme application. In *6th ACM conference on Embedded network sensor systems*, page 337, New York, New York, USA, 2008. ACM Press.
30. M. Mun, P. Boda, S. Reddy, K. Shilton, N. Yau, J. Burke, D. Estrin, M. Hansen, E. Howard, and R. West. PEIR, the personal environmental impact report, as a platform for participatory sensing systems research. *Proceedings of the 7th international conference on Mobile systems, applications, and services - Mobisys '09*, page 55, 2009.
31. K. P. N. Puttaswamy and B. Y. Zhao. Preserving privacy in location-based mobile social applications. *Proceedings of the Eleventh Workshop on Mobile Computing Systems & Applications - HotMobile '10*, page 1, 2010.
32. M. Raento, a. Oulasvirta, R. Petit, and H. Toivonen. ContextPhone: A Prototyping Platform for Context-Aware Mobile Applications. *IEEE Pervasive Computing*, 4(2):51–59, Apr. 2005.
33. R. Rana, C. Chou, S. Kanhere, N. Bulusu, and W. Hu. Ear-phone: an end-to-end participatory urban noise mapping system. In *Proceedings of the 9th ACM/IEEE International Conference on Information Processing in Sensor Networks*, pages 105–116. ACM, 2010.
34. D. Salber, A. Dey, and G. Abowd. The context toolkit: Aiding the development of context-enabled applications. In *Proceedings of the SIGCHI conference on Human factors in computing systems: the CHI is the limit*, page 441, New York, New York, USA, 1999. ACM.
35. T. Stiefmeier, C. Lombriser, D. Roggen, H. Junker, G. Ogris, and G. Tröster. Event-based activity tracking in work environments. In *Proceedings of the 3rd International Forum on Applied Wearable Computing (IFAWC)*. Citeseer, 2006.
36. L. Sweeney. k-anonymity: A model for protecting privacy. *International Journal of Uncertainty Fuzziness and Knowledge-based Systems*, 10(5):557–570, 2002.
37. K. Tang, P. Keyani, J. Fogarty, and J. Hong. Putting people in their place: An anonymous and privacy-sensitive approach to collecting sensed data in location-based applications. *Proceedings of the SIGCHI*, 2006.
38. E. Welbourne, J. Lester, A. Lamarca, and G. Borriello. Mobile Context Inference Using Low-Cost Sensors. In *Location and Context-Awareness*, pages 254–263. 2005.

An Online Experiment of Privacy Authorization Dialogues for Social Applications

Na Wang
Pennsylvania State University
University Park, USA
nzw109@ist.psu.edu

Jens Grossklags
Pennsylvania State University
University Park, USA
jensg@ist.psu.edu

Heng Xu
Pennsylvania State University
University Park, USA
hxu@ist.psu.edu

ABSTRACT

Several studies have documented the constantly evolving privacy practices of social networking sites and users' misunderstandings about them. Researchers have criticized the interfaces to "configure" privacy preferences as opaque, uninformative, and ineffective. The same problems have also plagued the constant growth of third-party applications and their troubling privacy authorization dialogues. In this paper, we report the results of an experimental study examining the limitations of current privacy authorization dialogues on Facebook as well as four new designs which we developed based on the Fair Information Practice Principles (FIPPs). Through an online experiment with 250 users, we study and document the effectiveness of installation-time configuration and awareness-enhancing interface changes.

Author Keywords

Third-party applications (apps); information privacy; privacy notice and consent; privacy awareness and control; online social networks (OSNs)

ACM Classification Keywords

D.4.6 [Security and Protection]: Access Controls; H.5.2 [Information Interfaces and Presentation]: User Interfaces – Evaluation/methodology; K.4.1 [Public Policy Issues]: Privacy

General Terms

Human Factors; Design; Security.

INTRODUCTION

With the thriving popularity of Online Social Networks (OSNs), an increasingly large number of users share personal information, activities, opinions, photos and videos on OSNs. This trend is giving rise to growing privacy concerns by consumers about the potential misuse of their information by various stakeholders including providers of OSNs, marketers, and other users [1, 16]. Privacy concerns pertain to the acquisition of personal data and the potential risks that users may experience as a result of possible privacy breaches [1]. Recently, additional complexities of studying privacy in the context of OSNs have been introduced by the increasing popularity of third-party applications ("apps"). It has been reported by the Wall Street Journal that many popular apps on Facebook have been transmitting users' personal information and their friends' information to various advertising and data tracking firms [28]. Due to the inability to monitor the data use by app providers, users need to account for the inherent uncertainty about the behaviors of many different developers rather one large OSN site (i.e., Facebook).

To address the critical privacy concerns for third-party apps, we conducted this research to investigate whether consumers can more adequately represent their preferences for sharing and releasing personal information with our newly proposed privacy authorization dialogues. Our designs draw upon the internationally recognized Fair Information Practice Principles (FIPPs) and address important interaction problems identified in our previous study [31]. Further, we conduct a series of online experiments to examine the impact of these new interfaces on users' privacy behaviors. We also compare our results with a baseline treatment, i.e., the original authorization dialogue employed by Facebook. This research is not targeted at making value judgments about desirable user practices (e.g., to decide whether an app should be installed or not). Instead, we are interested in understanding the relative observable effect of our proposed redesign elements on the practice of notice and consent on Facebook.

In implementing our online experiment, we aimed for a realistic integration of our design in the typical experience of user-to-app interactions on Facebook. To that end, we recruited real Facebook users who followed our study protocol using their own accounts. In addition, we employed an innovative experimental procedure that mimicked the Facebook's privacy authorization dialogues via Chrome browser extension. The method is similar to a Man-in-the-Middle Attack in the sense that the user expects to communicate exclusively with the OSN but in reality interacts with a modified version of the website.

Our work is significant given the wealth of data that is continuously harvested on OSNs. In addition, the practices we study are broadly alluded to recently released privacy agendas by the FTC [9], the White House Technology Office [23], and the European Union [8]. However, these developments stand in contrast to the relatively modest investments by the policy and research communities to study their effectiveness and practical implications.

RELATED WORK

Privacy Concerns Pertaining to Third-Party Desktop and Mobile Apps

In the domain of personal desktop computing, third-party apps were already widely in use and available from a variety of sources. For example, CNET's download.com hosts ten-thousands of apps for a variety of operating systems that originate from a wide range of large and small-scale software developers. Unsurprisingly, such repositories may include apps with problematic security and privacy practices. Grossklags and Good analyzed the End User License Agreements (EULAs) of the 50 most popular download.com apps (in a sample from 2006) and found that they contained highly problematic provisions regarding privacy and usage rights. In addition, they found that those statements were opaque, inaccessible and lacked readability [15].

Good et al. studied the effectiveness of providing a shortened version of the EULAs for different desktop programs with potentially harmful privacy and security aspects (which were disclosed in the text of the agreement). They found that users (when asked) appreciated the availability of a concise user notice; however, rarely stopped to study them in detail during the installation [13]. In a follow-up study which included a larger user population they recorded a statistically significant reduction of completed installations for the worst programs in their sample. Nevertheless, of the remaining users (who installed consumer-unfriendly programs) a significant share later regretted their decision [14].

Alternative solution approaches to ineffective notification that have been repeatedly suggested include the reliance on a review and reputation process as well as basic quality control. However, external certification has been criticized on the basis of adverse selection, i.e., that mostly those programs seek certification that are suffering from weak reputation and include problematic practices [7].

Recently, research has increasingly focused on privacy leakage and security concerns associated with third-party apps on smart phone systems and closed tablet computing platforms [3, 12, 17]. Those include Google Android, Symbian and Apple iOS for iPad and iPhone who all use some form of application permission and/or review process. On those markets, some apps have been classified as malware by researchers and anti-virus companies. In a recent study of 46 incidents across different mobile platforms, 28 apps were actively trying to exfiltrate user information and 4 searched for user credentials, 24 triggered premium calls or SMS messages and 8 sent unsolicited marketing messages [10].

In a closely related study, Felt et al. conducted a survey of permissions on the Android system for 100 paid and 856 free applications [11]. They found that 93% of free and 82% of paid applications included at least one potentially dangerous permission request. The authors suggested that the associated user dialogues did not allow users to meaningfully discriminate because almost all applications included potentially unwanted practices. The researchers conducted a follow-up Internet survey and usability laboratory study on Android permissions and showed that only a very small share of the study participants were attentive to the tested permissions dialogues, and could answer simple comprehension questions afterwards [12].

Anderson and his colleagues conducted case studies to examine the application markets from personal computers, mobile phones, web browsers, and online social networks. They identified security problems existing in these platforms and also proposed economic solutions [3]. Their study makes the connection to our context of investigation, i.e., authorization dialogues on online social networks, but does not directly address usability concerns.

Facebook Apps' Problematic Privacy Practices

Adding to the previously cited Wall Street Journal (WSJ) report on how apps were exfiltrating identifiable user information and data about users' sharing behavior and interests [28], Krishnamurthy and Wills report how this leaked information was in turn shared with third-party aggregators and advertising partners [21].

However, in addition to these technical findings, there is relatively little user-oriented research on third-party apps on OSNs. In a small-scale qualitative study, Besmer and Lipford examined motivations, intentions, and concerns of users when they engage with applications, as well as their perceptions of data sharing. Their results indicate that Facebook users are not truly understanding and consenting to the risks of apps maliciously harvesting profile information [4]. King and her colleagues conducted a survey study about users' misunderstandings and confusion concerning apps' functionality and information practices [20]. Survey participants self-reported their behavior with respect to the privacy authorization dialogue, but it was not studied experimentally: 44 percent responded that they had read the information, 28 percent answered that they would not read these statements, 25 percent stated that they had read a notice at some earlier time, and 3 percent could not recall whether they had read it or not.

Taking a design perspective, Hull et al. suggest visualization enhancements of the third-party apps' information accessing and publishing practices [18]. In doing so, users might have a better awareness how the app will use their information and thus users might be able to avoid some undesirable information leakage. In a small-scale design study, Tam et al. tested various user interface elements to describe privacy and security consequences (e.g., icons, paragraphs) [29]. They reported that the variation of the disclosure design had only limited impact on participants' ability to learn about the data practices. Participants further disliked designs that used verbal descriptions in the form of paragraphs (i.e., short descriptions of practices), and preferred icons and images.

THE DEVELOPMENT OF NEW DESIGNS FOR AUTHORIZATION DIALOGUES

Problems in the Current Design

In our previous work, we studied the Facebook authorization dialogue for third-party apps (Figure 1) from different perspectives and identified several significant problems in information transmission and in the options available to the user to configure important aspects of the disclosure consequences (see Wang et al. [31]).

- **Problem 1:** When an app is asking for publishing permissions and data access permissions at the same time, users are confused and may not be able to distinguish these permissions and do not know how the app will use their information.
- **Problem 2:** During the process of adding an app to users' profiles, they do not have any installation-time control to limit or configure the app's access to their information or restrict app's publishing ability. Only after users add the app, they can edit selected categories of data access or publishing options from their privacy settings.
- **Problem 3:** During the process of adding the apps to their profiles, users do not have any control to limit whether other users can see their app activities. Only after they add the app, users can change the visibility of their app activities via adjusting options that are deeply buried in their privacy settings.
- **Problem 4:** Users may easily give out particularly sensitive private information or share information with third parties from which crucial identifying data can be inferred. For example, information about an individual's place and date of birth can be exploited to predict his or her Social Security Number (SSN) [2].

These observations have helped us to identify suitable design heuristics that we outline below.

Design Heuristics

The information flow between individuals and other entities takes place in the context of ever-present and often conflicting simultaneous information needs. To better understand how to assure privacy and security, we must first understand the flow of personal information among various entities. Xu et al. [32] noted that concerns over information flow may be governed by two larger dimensions: 1) concerns over information release at the front-end where data flow in and out of users' accounts (e.g., the data exchange at the moment of installing apps in our context, i.e., installation time) within a specific platform (e.g., Facebook); and 2) concerns over unwanted access and use of personal information at the back-end where user data are transferred, stored and processed across different platforms. Based on the conceptual distinction above, the practicality and utility of the privacy enhancing interfaces and technologies will eventually depend on how a candidate solution addresses the issues related to these two dimensions.

In the past decades, the U.S. government and privacy scholars have proposed a number of principles to protect users' online privacy [22, 25, 27]. Among these principles, it has been argued that the Fair Information Practices Principles (FIPPs), which originated from a study commissioned by the U.S. Department of Health, Education and Welfare in 1973 [25], have become the de-facto global standard for ethical use of personally identifiable information by large organizations [24]. In particular, four of the total of five FIPPs (excluding enforcement/redress) are directly applicable to our problem domain and can potentially empower user control over both frond-end and back-end information flow [32]: *notice/awareness* that their personal information is being collected, *consent/choice* with regard to the authorized use of their information, *access/participation* to personal information the firm has collected, and *security/integrity* to prevent these data records from unauthorized access.

In the context of this research, we are aware of the fact that it is hard to implement all of the FIPPs without corresponding policy changes supported by Facebook or other stakeholders. However, we can investigate the impact of a limited implementation of FIPPs at the front-end where the data exchange occurs at the moment of installing apps, i.e., installation time. Consequently, we mainly focus on the following three FIPPs at the front-end: (1) notice/awareness, and (2) choice/consent, and (3) access/participation. Based on these three FIPPs, we propose the following design principles:

- **Principle 1 (Notice/Awareness):** The authorization dialogue should provide explicit information for users to learn what data would be accessed by the app and how the data would be used.
- **Principle 2 (Choice/Consent):** The authorization dialogue should provide options for users to control information access or publishing ability before adding the app to the user's Facebook profile (i.e., at installation time).
- **Principle 3 (Access/Participation):** The authorization dialogue should provide options for users to control who can see their app activities.
- **Principle 4 (Notice/Awareness):** The authorization dialogue should provide alert signals for users when the app asks for users' sensitive private information.

Permission	Number of apps requesting permission (percentage of apps requesting permission)		Total times a permission is requested by apps	Permission	Number of apps requesting permission (percentage of apps requesting permission)		Total times a permission is requested by apps
basic information	9411	100.00%	502,755,469	friends_education_history	14	0.15%	3,564,500
Email	3234	34.36%	314,855,710	friends_activities	22	0.23%	3,448,300
publish_stream	4702	49.96%	259,917,056	friends_about_me	17	0.18%	3,328,000
user_birthday	902	9.58%	138,257,300	friends_interests	13	0.14%	3,163,500
publish_actions	513	5.45%	125,686,870	user_work_history	73	0.78%	2,961,900
user_location	343	3.64%	55,077,200	friends_relationships	3	0.03%	2,912,000
offline_access	660	7.01%	42,491,210	user_photo_video_tags	98	1.04%	2,779,680
read_stream	528	5.61%	37,863,840	friends_photo_video_tags	32	0.34%	2,423,340
user_photos	491	5.22%	24,940,010	friends_likes	36	0.38%	2,385,960
user_about_me	248	2.64%	23,700,430	user_status	40	0.43%	1,827,500
friends_birthday	206	2.19%	19,237,740	user_checkins	17	0.18%	1,422,000
user_likes	214	2.27%	13,486,760	friends_checkins	6	0.06%	1,350,000
friends_photos	214	2.27%	13,051,340	user_religion_politics	19	0.20%	1,183,100
friends_online_presence	121	1.29%	10,745,500	publish_checkins	11	0.12%	980,700
user_interests	68	0.72%	9,675,600	manage_notifications	8	0.09%	976,000
user_hometown	120	1.28%	9,594,040	user_relationships	34	0.36%	969,600
user_online_presence	110	1.17%	8,298,400	friends_relationship_details	4	0.04%	741,000
friends_location	104	1.11%	8,121,000	read_friendlists	39	0.41%	603,800
xmpp_login	13	0.14%	7,744,000	user_videos	12	0.13%	560,780
user_education_history	51	0.54%	5,920,640	user_relationship_details	19	0.20%	406,200
friends_hometown	21	0.22%	5,862,500	create_event	11	0.12%	336,500
friends_work_history	86	0.91%	5,260,660	user_groups	10	0.11%	294,900
user_activities	53	0.56%	5,204,740	friends_videos	2	0.02%	230,400
manage_pages	60	0.64%	4,725,900	user_website	2	0.02%	130,000

Table 1. Most Frequently Requested Permissions by the Applications.

To further increase the relevance of our work, we also conducted a large-scale measurement study to gain a broad perspective of the data practices by the various app providers on Facebook. This study helps us to propose experimental layouts of high relevance to the Facebook user community.

Scope of Permissions

To determine the scope of permissions that should be included into our design of privacy authorization dialogues, we investigated the data practices from the 9,411 most popular third-party apps on Facebook which displayed the typical privacy authorization dialogue to users (as shown in Figure 1). We also collected data to assess the scale of data collection for the apps under consideration.

From the app developer's perspective, there were 63 types of permissions they can request from users. For each of these permissions, we first compiled a list of applications that request each type of permission. We summed up the number of monthly active users for each application on the list to get the total number of users who were affected by a certain data practice (see Table 1). Further details about the measurement methodology can be found in Wang [30].

Table 1 shows how many apps request a particular permission, and given the apps' popularity how many times users on Facebook have shared this information with app providers.

Figure 1. Example of an Authorization Dialogue Page.

As shown in Table 1, users shared their basic information more than 500 million times with apps. The next three most frequently requested permissions are: 1) "email", which allows an app to access a user's primary email address; 2) "publish_stream", which enables an app to post content, comments, and likes to a user's stream and to the streams of the user's friends; and 3) "user_birthday", which permits an app to access a user's birthday.

Based on the results shown in Table 1, we included users' basic information and an additional twelve frequently requested permissions in our design of the privacy authorization dialogue. We were able to group these permissions into three categories: 1) permissions related to users' information releasing behaviour (*email, user_photos, user_videos, user_birthday, user_hometown,* and *user_location*), 2) permissions related to users' friends' information releasing behaviour (*friends_birthday, friends_hometown, friends_location, friends_photos,* and *friends_videos*), and 3) a permission related to information reposting (*publish_stream*). By selecting these permissions, we kept our privacy authorization dialogues within a reasonable length while adequately representing the most frequently requested types of data and categories of permissions. We added the currently less utilized video permissions to account for the trend towards increased multimedia utilization.

Design Considerations about Format and Style

Kelley et al. developed a privacy "nutrition label" that presents to users the ways organizations collect, use, and share personal information [19]. Their design aims to: 1) clearly highlight the meaning of different labels so that users can easily understand different sets of information; 2) use different font highlights to separate sets of information in order to expedite the users' navigation through the list; and 3) have a bold and clear title to inform users with the purpose of the information in each section. Those ideas are derived from previous work on food safety warnings and information about nutritional content which are reviewed in Kelley et al. [19]. We also draw upon recent research by Bravo-Lillo et al. on effective warning mechanisms to protect people from privacy harms [6].

In this research, we aim to include design elements mentioned above. In particular, we present four independent and distinct interfaces covering different aspects derived from our design heuristics. By incrementally adding design elements into our interface, we can test the impact of the design heuristics in a progressive fashion which is highly beneficial given the complexity of typical interactions between users and social apps. In this way, our results are easier to replicate and to rationalize. In the following section, we describe each of our designs in detail.

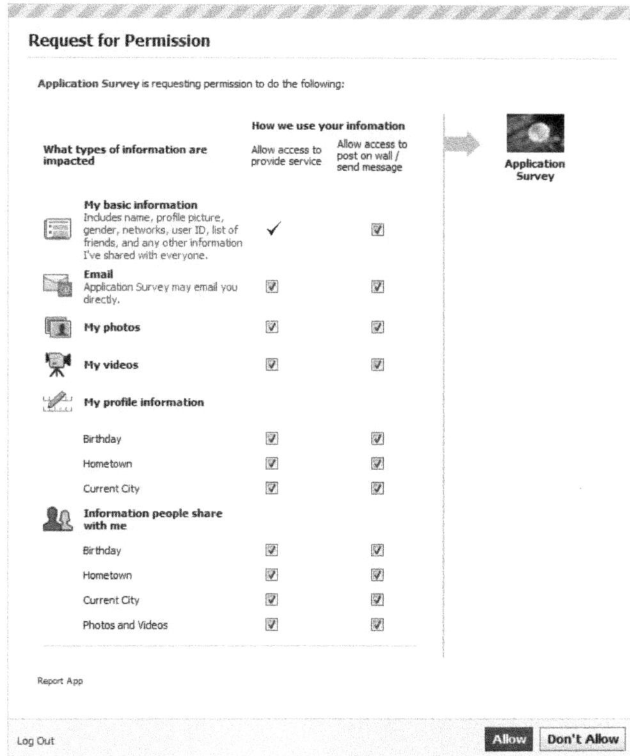

Figure 2. Proposed C Design.

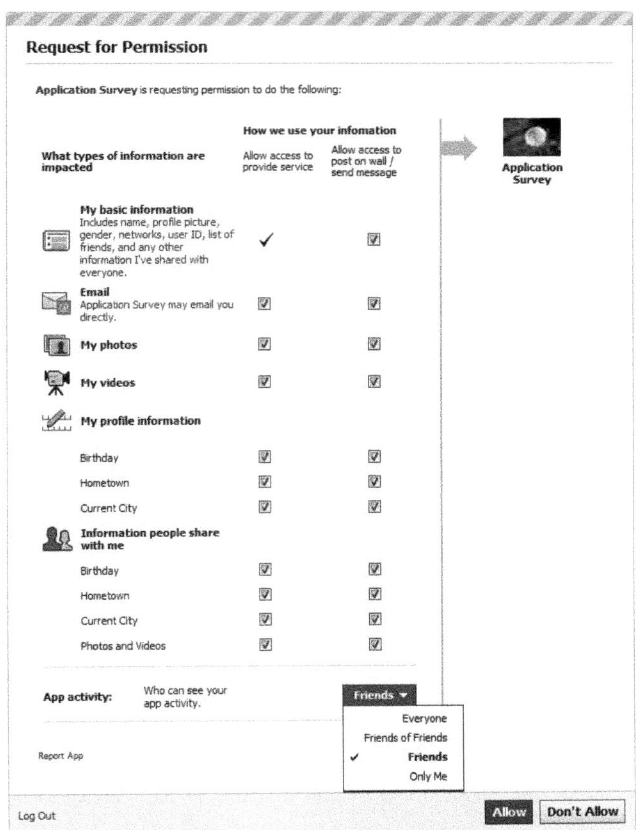

Figure 3. Proposed CAA Design

Four Designs for Authorization Dialogues

Check-box Authorization Dialogue (C): The C interface design of the authorization dialogue (see Figure 2) aims to fulfill the first two design heuristics. Below we describe our major design elements.

- **The Granular Layout of Permissions:** All types of data (basic information and data reading permissions) required by the app are listed in the first column. The top row displays the information regarding how the app will use the data (including data writing and page management permissions).
- **The Tick Marks and Checkboxes:** *Un-clickable tick marks* represent those types of information that will be accessed and used by the app and are non-negotiable. The *checked* check box means that users will allow the app to access and use certain information. When *un-checked*, users will not allow the app to access or use the corresponding information.

Taken together this design allows us to investigate the relative impact of granular installation-time configuration (opt-out) options for apps' data practices (compared to a baseline treatment of the current Facebook design applied to our scenario displayed in Figure 1).

Check-box and App Activity Authorization Dialogue (CAA): Our second design of the authorization dialogue, the CAA design, is an enhanced version of the C design, in addition to fulfilling the first two design heuristics, it also aims to address the third one (see Figure 3).

- The "App activity" Drop-down List: It allows the user to decide whether other users (i.e., Friends, or Friends of Friends, or the public) can see users' app activity on Facebook. Users can change this setting by using a drop down menu.

That is, the dialogue now offers the user control options directed towards the app developer as well as other users.

Check-box and Signal Authorization Dialogue (CS): Our third design of the authorization dialogue, the CS design, is another variation of an enhanced version of the C design; in addition to addressing the first two design heuristics, it also considers the fourth one (see Figure 4).

- **The "i" Mark and Color Scheme:** As users' basic information is always requested by the app, here we use the blue "i" signal to remind users that this information cannot be opted out. We use the red "i" signal to alert users that certain information is particularly sensitive. In our study, we highlight email, user_birthday, user_hometown, and user_location as sensitive information mainly because privacy advocates advise not to share these information with third parties [2]. Both marks have tooltip information which is accessible to users when they move their mouse pointer over the sign.

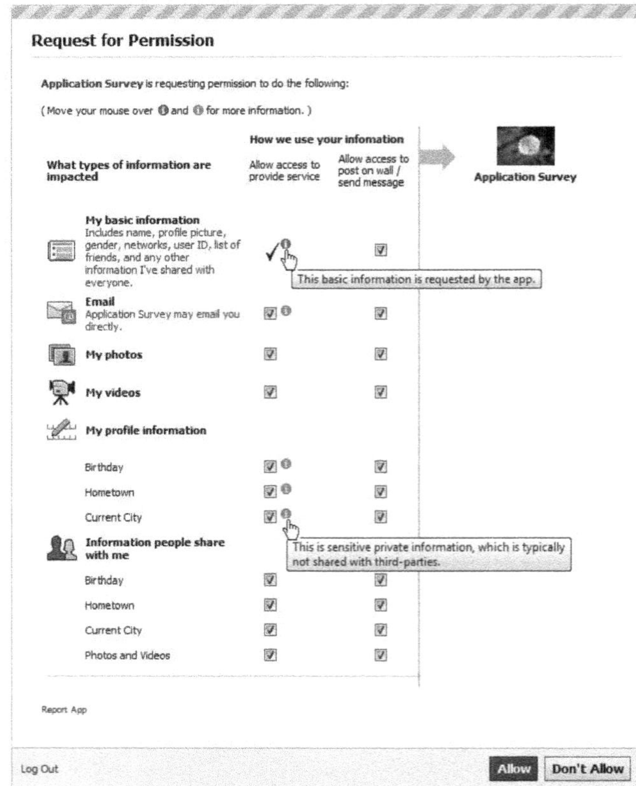

Figure 4. Proposed *CS* Design.

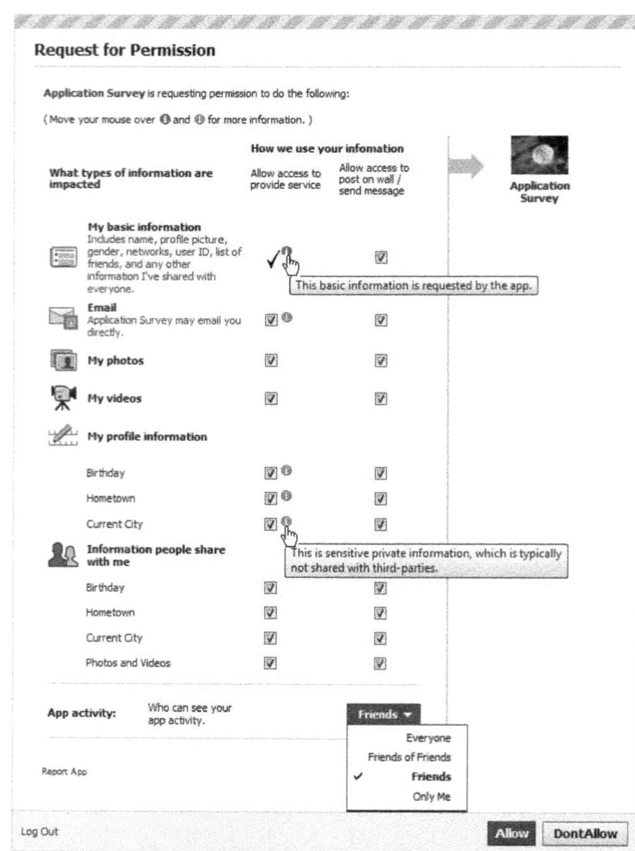

Figure 5. Proposed *CSAA* Design.

This treatment allows us to study the relative impact of awareness-enhancing interface alerts which signal when an app requests a user's sensitive private information (and allows for a comparison with the checkbox design C and the baseline treatment).

Check-box, Signal, and App Activity Authorization Dialogue (CSAA): The fourth design of the authorization dialogue, the CSAA design, addresses all four design heuristics (see Figure 5). With this interface, we want to examine whether the third and the fourth design heuristics combined together would help users better protect their privacy on Facebook.

EXPERIMENTAL DESIGN

Implementation

To implement our proposed designs, we employed a semi-functional Wizard of Oz approach to visually mimic Facebook's default third-part apps authorization dialogue. The method is similar to a *Man-in-the-Middle Attack* in the sense that the user expects to communicate exclusively with Facebook.com but in reality interacts with a modified version of the website. This approach was implemented with a Chrome browser extension that integrated into the authorization process by capturing a particular Facebook app's unique ID. Once the app's unique ID was captured, the extension replaced the original authorization dialogue with one of our four proposed designs (for treatment II-V), or left the original interface (the baseline treatment). In all cases (including the baseline treatment) we activated a redirect URL when participants clicked the "Allow" or "Don't allow" button. All these replacements were implemented by modifying the authorization page's HTML Document Object Model (DOM). The browser extension recorded users' interactions with the interface and the time they spent on that page. However, we neither recorded users' identifiable information, nor called the Facebook API to collect information from users' profiles.

Participants

We recruited participants via Amazon Mechanical Turk (MTurk: www.mturk.com). On MTurk, requesters post Human Intelligence Tasks (HITs) by uploading job descriptions onto Amazon's web portal. MTurk maintains each Turker's performance history and additional information, which requesters may use to specify who is eligible to perform a particular HIT. Eligibility may include the Turker's location (country), HIT completion rate (fraction of tasks completed among those signed up for in the past) and approval rate (fraction of tasks accepted by requesters among those completed in the past). The requester must also specify the amount of payment a Turker will receive once the task is completed and the work is accepted by the requester. Once a requester posts a HIT on MTurk, as in our application installation task, eligible Turkers can immediately view it and sign up.

We recruited 276 Turkers with a North American IP address and a previous HIT approval rate of 55% or better. Participants were also required to be Facebook users and needed to be familiar with the Google Chrome browser. To motivate Turkers to complete this study, we paid $0.80 to each participant after we did a basic evaluation of the validity of task completion. Data from 26 participants was rejected via the MTurk web interface because these participants submitted blatantly incomplete or incoherent work. We also ensured that no individual with a particular MTurk ID would participate in our study twice.

We used a between-subjects design, where the participants were randomly assigned to one of five groups, namely, the baseline group I or one of the four treatment groups II-V corresponding to our four new designs of privacy authorization dialogues (see Table 2). As expected, Chi-square tests revealed that subjects assigned to the various treatments did not differ significantly in terms of their age, education, and gender (see Table 3).

Treatment	Interface Presented
I (Baseline)	Current Authorization Interface
II (C)	Check-box Design
IV (CAA)	Check-box and App Activity Design
III (CS)	Check-box and Signal Design
V (CSAA)	Check-box, Signal, and App Activity Design

Table 2. Overview of Treatment Groups.

Among the participants, 56% were females and 44% were males; they had a wide range of education levels (from less than high school to Ph.D.) and covered a wide range of age categories (from 18 to over 50) which is consistent with the diversity of the current Facebook user base. See Table 3 for more details about participants' demographics.

	Baseline %	C %	CAA %	CS %	CSAA %	Total %
Sex						
Female	56	52	60	46	66	56
Male	44	48	40	54	34	44
Age						
18-24	52	40	44	46	36	43.6
25-29	20	34	26	24	36	28
30-34	14	8	14	10	16	12.4
35-39	10	12	12	12	8	10.8
40-49	0	4	2	6	4	3.2
50 and over	4	2	2	2	0	2
Education						
Less than	2	4	2	6	0	2.8
High school	22	26	20	16	22	21.2
Associate	8	14	14	20	4	12
Current	18	28	30	28	24	25.6
Bachelor's	38	18	24	24	30	26.8
Master's	10	6	8	6	18	9.6
Ph.D.	2	4	2	0	2	2

Table 3. Participants' Demographics.

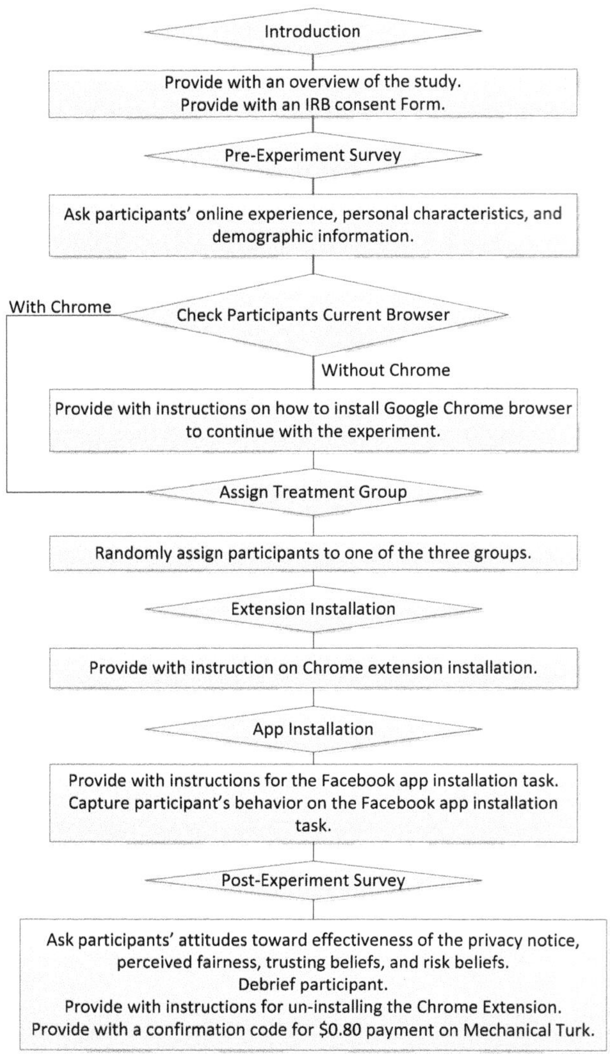

Figure 6. Experimental Protocol

Experimental Procedure and Task
Figure 6 provides an overview of the protocol in this experiment. Each participant was guided through this study protocol[1]. Upon finishing all tasks shown in Figure 6, participants were asked to complete a questionnaire that was customized to the specific treatment and asked them to evaluate usability, security, and privacy aspects related to the privacy authorization dialogues they interacted with. We also asked participants to evaluate another two alternative designs at the end of the post-experimental questionnaire. See Table 4 for details about the post-experimental survey.

Treatment	Interfaces Evaluated and Compared
I (Baseline)	Baseline, C, and CS
II (C)	C, Baselin, and CS
IV (CAA)	CAA, Baseline, and CSAA
III (CS)	CS, Baseline, and C
V (CSAA)	CSAA, Baseline, and CAA

Table 4. Post-Experimental Survey Customization Details.

RESULTS
Our analysis of the experimental results unfolds in five steps.

1. Task Completion Times:
We estimated that the study would take about 20 minutes to complete and advertised this estimate in the HIT description. The actual average across all treatment groups was 19 minutes and 36 seconds, and Tukey HSK Test revealed that subjects assigned to the five treatment groups did not differ significantly in terms of total time to complete the task.

For participants in the baseline treatment, the average time spent on the authorization dialogue was about 9 seconds, which was significantly faster than what we observed in the other treatments (28 seconds). This effect is significant with $p<.001$ for treatments II, III and V, significant with $p=.025$ for treatment IV for the comparisons with the baseline treatment. We attribute this to users' likely familiarity with the interface they interacted in the baseline condition and the complete absence of any configuration options. We observed no significant difference concerning this metric among the four new designs (i.e., treatment II to V).

2. Overall App Installation Approval Rates:
A total of 50 participants interacted with the original Facebook interface and 42 of them (84%) did "Allow" to add the app to their profiles. The alternative interfaces lowered the participants' readiness to add the apps in all cases. More precisely, 37 out of 50 (74%) for the C design, 39 out of 50 (78%) for the *CAA* design, 30 out of 50 (78%) for the *CS* design, and 30 out of 50 (60%) for the *CSAA* design, allowed the installation of the app.

For the C and CAA treatments, we are surprised to find that the availability of granular configuration options at installation-time (C and CAA) does not increase the number of installations. We would have expected that the opportunity to opt-out from unwanted practices would

1 As participants logged into their Facebook accounts, we asked them to evaluate our Facebook application. The exact instruction was as follows: We have developed a Facebook app that would help us to contact you about the study results and for potential further survey opportunities. To continue with the study, please click the following URL then log into your Facebook account to access the Facebook application's installation page. When you visit this site you can learn more about our app and decide whether you want to continue the installation or cancel the installation. Either option will allow you to continue with the study and will not impact your Mechanical Turk payment.

make the application more attractive to participants. Instead, there is a non-significant reduction of installations.

In contrast, with the presence of warning signals, we would expect lower installation rates. In fact, this effect is strongly significant for the proposed *CS* (*Chi-square*=21.429, $p<.001$) and *CSAA* (*Chi-square*=21.429, $p<.001$) designs when compared to the original Facebook interface (i.e., the baseline treatment). More importantly, in comparison to the C and CAA treatments, the effect of the signals is also significant (considering the relevant comparisons, the effect is always at least significant at $p<0.05$). Nevertheless, we are somewhat surprised by this strong finding given the recent research on attention blindness, for example, when considering security indicators for Phishing and other browser warnings [5].

3. The Effectiveness of the Layout of Permissions and Checkboxes:
The original design of the authorization dialogues (i.e., baseline treatment) provides a take-it-or-leave-it option concerning the access and publishing abilities of an app, i.e., users have to accept all of these permissions if they want to use the app. In our proposed interfaces, we separated accessing and publishing permissions into different columns and enabled users to uncheck checkboxes and thereby refuse to give certain permissions. These design components were considered as the most basic ones and were implemented in all of the four proposed designs (i.e., *C*, *CAA*, *CS*, *CSAA*). For analysis purposes, if a user clicked the "Don't Allow" button to step back from the installation of the app, we regard this as if they did not release any information to the app, which is equivalent to the decision to uncheck all the checkboxes in the authorization dialogue.

Table 5 and Table 6 show that when users are interacting with the new designs, they not only tend to release significantly less information in total, but also tend to opt out of publishing permissions to prevent the app from reposting information to their wall compared to the original Facebook interface (all comparison tests of treatments with the baseline are significant at $p<0.001$).

Treatment	%
I (Baseline)	84
II (C)	58.27
IV (CAA)	52.91
III (CS)	46.45
V (CSAA)	41.27

Table 5. Overall Information Release (in %).

Treatment	%
I (Baseline)	16
II (C)	44.55
IV (CAA)	51.45
III (CS)	56.55
V (CSAA)	61.27

Table 6. Opt-Out from Publishing Permissions (in %).

Also, in the post-installation questionnaire, participants were instructed to rate the effectiveness of the interfaces. We utilized a Likert scale (i.e., how much they agree or disagree with; 1 = strongly disagree, 7 = strongly agree), and presented the participants with the following statements:

- The proposed designs could help users better differentiate between the different purposes of data usage by the app.
- The proposed designs would allow users to better control the app's access and use of a specific type of personal information.

Participants who interacted with the four proposed interfaces rated these two questions significant higher (with $p<.01$) than participants who interacted with the original Facebook authorization dialogue. These factors indicate that the layouts of permissions in our proposed designs are likely to be more effective to attract users' attention and to utilize their options to adjust privacy parameters.

4. The Effectiveness of the App-Activity Drop-down List:
With the original design of the authorization dialogue, users cannot modify whether other users can see their App Activity before adding the app to their profile. They can only change it by going through a series of relatively complex steps after installing the app. We believe that if users could modify this setting at installation time, it will be another improvement comparing to the original authorization dialogue. To put it differently, we can investigate the users' responses when we "bring to light" deeply buried privacy configuration options.

If a participant selected "Don't Allow" to refuse to add the app to her Facebook profile, then the user's choice on this App-Activity drop-down list will have no effect in terms of controlling who can see her app activities. Thus, in this section, we only focused on those participants who did "Allow" to add the app to their profiles.

Eight participants out of 39 (20.51%) for the CAA design, and 5 out of 30 (16.67%) for the CSAA design, who added the app to their profiles, decided not to share their app activity with others, and preferred to keep this information private (Selected "Only Me"). Those individuals who tightly restricted their App-Activity also used the opt-out options for the permissions significantly more often ($p<.005$ for *CAA*, and $p<.0001$ for *CSAA*).

We also found a treatment effect in which participants who interacted with the designs of CAA and CSAA tend to release significantly less information compared to those who interacted with the design of C (see Table 7, p=.005 for *CAA* and $p=.006$ *for CSAA*). This happened because the app-activity drop-down list enhanced participants' awareness that their interaction with the app might be observed by other users on Facebook, and then triggered them to reduce the information released to the third-party app.

Treatment	%
I (Baseline)	100
II (C)	79.36
IV (CAA)	70.86
III (CS)	76.36
V (CSAA)	70.61

Table 7. Information Release by Participants' who Installed the App (in %).

5. Further Evidence on the Effectiveness of the "i" Mark Signal:

For this analysis, we continue to focus on participants who chose to add the app to their profiles. Our results indicate that the red "i" mark helped users to differentiate between information that is marked as sensitive and other information, and to recognize when a particular type of sensitive information is being collected by an app (i.e., in the designs of CS and CSAA, it affects four types of data permissions for email, birthday, hometown and current city; see Figures 4 and 5). Table 8 shows that participants who interacted with the *CS* interface released considerably less sensitive information compared with those who faced the *C* interface. Further, for subjects who interacted with the designs of CS or CSAA, ratings for the statement "*the interfaces (with "i" mark) helped them to better recognize when a particular type of sensitive information is being collected by the app*" were significantly higher than for those interacting with the CAA or CSAA dialogues *($p<.05$).*

We also conducted a separate analysis targeted at the blue "i" mark which indicates that basic information is requested by the app (see Figure 7). In particular, we were wondering whether there is a distinct effect on the publishing check box to the right of the blue mark (circled in red in Figure 7). For example, we expected that users might feel that information which is considered basic information is subject to fewer opt-outs. This presumes that participants would understand collection and usage of basic information as a bundle that should be treated equally. We find no such distinct effect (see Table 9) that applies to both relevant pairings (i.e., C/CS and CAA/CSAA).

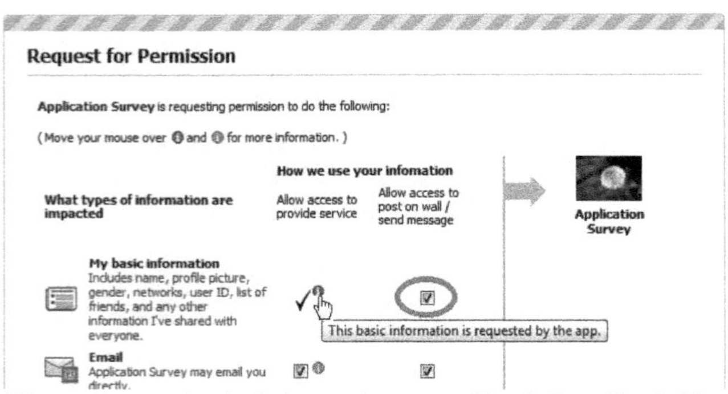

Figure 7. user_basic_information_post Check-Box Circled in Red.

In summary, the red "i" mark motivates participants to install apps less often and to release sensitive information to the experimental app less frequently. The effect of the blue "i" mark (that is attached to the permission designating access to basic information) is primarily informative. It does not appear to have a consistent behavioral impact.

So far, we have reported the overall app installation rate and the effectiveness of different design components. In the next section, we are going to discuss the findings and possible limitations of our current study and possible directions for future work.

Treatment	%
II (C)	81.08
IV (CAA)	67.31
III (CS)	70.00
V (CSAA)	60.00

Table 8. Sensitive Information Release (in %).

Treatment	%
II (C)	21.62
IV (CAA)	35.90
III (CS)	20.00
V (CSAA)	16.67

Table 9. Opt Outs for Basic Information (in %).

DISCUSSION

While in this study we mainly focus on information disclosure issues pertaining to Facebook third-party apps, similar problems also exist in other platforms, i.e., other social media platforms, smart phone platforms, and desktop platforms. The common features of these third-party app offerings are: they often provide useful services or entertainment to users; but they also typically collect users' information and then transfer it to a server outside of the purview of the platform provider and the user. Users have an extremely difficult task to understand the ramifications and consequences of these practices. Further, beyond vague policy statements there is little actual enforcement by the platform providers to assure adequate treatment of user data.

In our work, we aim to address the vulnerability of users at the front-end of this information exchange through the deployment of improved privacy notice and consent interfaces as favored by most regulatory and self-regulatory proposals. Our study provides nuanced results about the impact of such efforts.

Surprisingly, we find that offering granular configuration options at installation-time does not increase individuals' willingness to install the experimental app. Instead, there is a non-significant reduction of installations. Since more fine-grained control allows users to account for their individual privacy preferences, we would have expected that users negotiate deals that prompt them to reject the app less often. This does not seem to be the case. However, we find that users who eventually decide to install the app make use of the granular choices and opt-out from certain data collection and usage practices. In addition, users who change the default behavior of the app concerning its interaction with other OSN users opt-out even more often.

In light of research that highlights individuals' blindness to security indicators and warnings, for example, in the context of Phishing or Spyware [5], we unexpectedly find that providing additional awareness-enhancing signals in the privacy authorization dialogue significantly lowers the number of installations.

Our study also makes progress along the dimension of methodology. We implemented our new designs as working interfaces and embedded them during controlled experiments into the Facebook environment via a Chrome extension. In this way, participants can actually interact with these interfaces on their own accounts, and we are able to collect users' actual installation operations in a plausible experimental setting. Then, in the subsequent post-experimental survey, we collect additional data for the assessment of the authorization dialogue designs.

Limitations

In our study, we have logged participants' final decisions including whether they "Allow" or "Don't Allow" the app to access and use their information and specifically what kinds of their information can be accessed by the app (which check-boxes are checked). However, we did not track several other types of conceivable interaction data with the authorization dialogue (e.g., mouse movements or eye tracking). We also did not solicit a free text response about the reasons for (not) adding the app to their profiles. Such data might have enabled us to provide further intuition about the effectiveness of certain design elements, e.g., the "i" mark, and whether they attracted users' attention and enhanced participants' privacy awareness.

We mentioned in our instructions on Mechanical Turk that the app to be installed is an "application survey" (and it indeed triggered the post-experimental survey). We also mentioned to the participants that the app would enable us to contact them later about potential future survey opportunities. We selected this framing because it naturally fit our goal to include a series of survey questions in the experimental process. It would be interesting to conduct additional treatment conditions with different framings (e.g., that control for the reputation of the app developer or the type of the application).

The study use a monitoring infrastructure based on a Google Chrome extension. According to StatCounter [http://gs.statcounter.com/] Google Chrome has now achieved a market share of about 35.7% (similar to Microsoft Internet Explorer's share and significantly higher than Firefox). While we cannot categorically exclude that Chrome users are more tech-savvy or differ in some other regard, we feel that its deep market penetration will moderate such concerns.

We used Mechanical Turk as our recruitment platform and recruited our participants among those Turkers with North American IP addresses. As Smith et al. [26] noted, different countries or regions have approached privacy issues differently in their social norms and regulatory structures. Thus, in this study, we restrict eligibility to those participants with Northern American IP addresses because the technological and regulatory privacy environments in North America are relatively similar [26]. Thus a future research opportunity could be to conduct a similar study by recruiting participants from other regions (e.g., from the E.U. or Asia).

CONCLUSION

Based on qualitative and theoretical considerations and the results from a substantial measurements study on Facebook, we proposed four new designs of the authorization dialogues for third-party apps and conducted a rigorous online experiment to investigate whether users can more adequately represent their preferences for sharing and releasing personal information with these improved designs. We uncovered significant treatment effects that may contribute to improvements of the effectiveness of authorization dialogues for third-party applications and beyond.

In the future, we intend to use our experimental setup to explore a number of related questions (e.g., the relevance of opt-in versus opt-out) to provide the CSCW research community with comparable results across a spectrum of design choices. We also would like to explore opportunities for future collaboration with Facebook and application developers to conduct large-scale field experiments in the context of naturally occurring user practices.

ACKNOWLEDGMENTS

We thank the anonymous reviewers for their comments on a previous version of this paper. Heng Xu and Na Wang gratefully acknowledge the financial support of the National Science Foundation under grant CNS-0953749. Any opinions, conclusions or recommendations expressed in this material are those of the authors and do not necessarily reflect the views of the National Science Foundation. Jens Grossklags gratefully acknowledges the financial support of a Google Faculty Research Award.

REFERENCES

[1] Acquisti, A. and Gross, R. Imagined Communities: Awareness, Information Sharing, and Privacy on the Facebook. In *Proc. PETS 2006*, ACM Press (2006), 36-58.

[2] Acquisti, A. and Gross, R., Predicting Social Security numbers from public data. *Proceedings of the National Academy of Sciences* 106,27 (2009), 10975-10980.

[3] Anderson, J., Bonneau, J., and Stajano, F. Inglorious Installers: Security in the Application Marketplace. In *Proc. WEIS 2010* (2010).

[4] Besmer, A. and Lipford, H. Users' (Mis)conceptions of Social Applications. In *Proc. GI 2010*, ACM Press (2010), 63-70.

[5] Böhme, R. and Grossklags, J. The Security Cost of Cheap User Interaction. In *Proc. NSPW 2011*, ACM Press (2011), 67-82.

[6] Bravo-Lillo, C., Cranor, L., Downs, J., and Komanduri, S., Bridging the Gap in Computer Security Warnings: A Mental Model Approach. *IEEE Security & Privacy* 9,2 (2011), 18-26.

[7] Edelman, B., Adverse Selection in Online "Trust" Certifications and Search Results. *Electronic Commerce Research and Applications* 10,1 (2011), 17-25.

[8] European Commission, Proposal for a Regulation of the European Parliament and of the Council on the Protection of Individuals with Regard to the Processing of Personal Data and on the Free Movement of such Data (General Data Protection Regulation), COM (2012) 11 final, 25 January, 2012.

[9] Federal Trade Commission, Protecting Consumer Privacy in an Era of Rapid Change: Recommendations for Businesses and Policymakers. http://www.ftc.gov/os/2012/03/120326privacyreport.pdf.

[10] Felt, A., Finifter, M., Chin, E., Hanna, S., and Wagner, D. A Survey of Mobile Malware in the Wild. In *Proc. SPSM 2011*, ACM Press (2011), 3-14.

[11] Felt, A., Greenwood, K., and Wagner, D. The Effectiveness of Application Permissions. In *Proc. WebApps 2011* (2011), 75-86.

[12] Felt, A.P., Ha, E., Egelman, S., Haney, A., Chin, E., and Wagner, D. Android Permissions: User Attention, Comprehension, and Behavior. In *Proc. SOUPS*, ACM Press (2012).

[13] Good, N., Dhamija, R., Grossklags, J., Thaw, D., Aronowitz, S., Mulligan, D., and Konstan, J. Stopping Spyware at the Gate: A User Study of Privacy, Notice and Spyware. In *Proc. SOUPS 2005*, ACM Press (2005), 43-52.

[14] Good, N.S., Grossklags, J., Mulligan, D.K., and Konstan, J.A. Noticing Notice: A Large-Scale Experiment on the Timing of Software License Agreements. In *Proc. CHI 2007*, ACM Press (2007), 607-616.

[15] Grossklags, J. and Good, N. Empirical Studies on Software Notices to Inform Policy Makers and Usability Designers. In *Proc. FC 2007 and USEC 2007*, Springer Press (2007), 341-355.

[16] Hoadley, C.M., Xu, H., Lee, J.J., and Rosson, M.B., Privacy as Information Access and Illusory Control: The Case of the Facebook News Feed Privacy Outcry. *Electronic Commerce Research and Applications* 9,1 (2010), 50-60.

[17] Howell, J. and Schechter, S. What You See is What They Get: Protecting Users from Unwanted Use of Microphones, Camera, and Other Sensors. In *Proc. Web 2.0 Security and Privacy* (2010).

[18] Hull, G., Lipford, H., and Latulipe, C., Contextual gaps: Privacy issues on Facebook. *Ethics and Information Technology* 13,4 (2010), 289-302.

[19] Kelley, P., Bresee, J., Cranor, L., and Reeder, R. A Nutrition Label for Privacy. In *Proc. SOUPS 2009*, ACM Press (2009).

[20] King, J., Lampinen, A., and Smolen, A. Privacy: Is There an App for That? In *Proc. SOUPS 2011*, ACM Press (2011).

[21] Krishnamurthy, B. and Wills, C. On the Leakage of Personally Identifiable Information Via Online Social Networks. In *Proc. WOSN 2009*, ACM Press (2009), 7-12.

[22] Lederer, S., Hong, I., Dey, K., and Landay, A., Personal Privacy Through Understanding and Action: Five Pitfalls for Designers. *Personal and Ubiquitous Computing* 8,6 (2004), 440-454.

[23] Obama, B., Consumer Data Privacy in a Networked World: A Framework for Protecting Privacy and Promoting Innovation in the Global Digital Economy, 2012.

[24] Reidenberg, J.R., Setting Standards for Fair Information Practice in the US Private Sector. *Iowa L. Rev.* 80,(1994), 497.

[25] Secretary, Records, Computers and the Rights of Citizens - Report of the Secretary's Advisory Committee on Automated Personal Data Systems, 1973.

[26] Smith, H.J., Dinev, T., and Xu, H., Information Privacy Research: An Interdisciplinary Review. *MIS Quarterly* 35,4 (2011), 989-1015.

[27] Spiekermann, S. and Cranor, L.F., Engineering Privacy. *IEEE Transactions on Software Engineering* 35,1 (2009), 67-82.

[28] Steel, E. and Fowler, G., Facebook in Privacy Breach. http://online.wsj.com/article/SB10001424052702304772804575558484075236968.html.

[29] Tam, J., Reeder, R.W., and Schechter, S., I'm Allowing What? Disclosing the Authority Applications Demand of Users as a Condition of Installation, 2010.

[30] Wang, N. Third-Party Applications' Data Practices on Facebook. In *Proc. CHI 2012*, ACM Press (2012), 1399-1404.

[31] Wang, N., Xu, H., and Grossklags, J. Third-Party Apps on Facebook: Privacy and the Illusion of Control. In *Proc. CHIMIT 2011*, ACM Press (2011).

[32] Xu, H., Teo, H.H., Tan, B.C.Y., and Agarwal, R., Effects of Individual Self-Protection, Industry Self-Regulation, and Government Regulation on Privacy Concerns: A Study of Location-Based Services. *Information Systems Research* (2012), doi: 10.1287/isre.1120.0416

What a Tangled Web We Weave: Lying Backfires in Location-Sharing Social Media

Xinru Page, Bart P. Knijnenburg, Alfred Kobsa
Department of Informatics, Donald Bren School of Information and Computer Sciences
University of California, Irvine, USA
{xpage, kobsa, bart.k}@uci.edu

ABSTRACT

Prior research shows that a root cause of many privacy concerns in location-sharing social media is people's desire to preserve offline relationship boundaries in the online world. Other literature recognizes lying as an everyday phenomenon that preserves such relationship boundaries by facilitating smooth social interactions. Combining these strands of research, one might hypothesize that people with a predisposition to lie would generally have lower privacy concerns since lying is a means to preserve relationship boundaries. We tested this hypothesis using structural equation modeling on data from a survey administered nationwide (N=1532), and found that for location-sharing, people with a high propensity to lie actually have increased boundary preservation concerns as well as increased privacy concerns. We explain these findings using results from semi-structured interviews.

Author Keywords

Privacy; Lying; Boundary Preservation; Location Sharing; Social Media; Structural Equation Modeling; Survey.

ACM Classification Keywords

H.1.2 **[Models and Principles]**: User/Machine Systems – *software psychology*; H.5.m. **[Information Interfaces and Presentation]**: Miscellaneous; J.4 **[Social and Behavioral Sciences]**: *Psychology*; K.4.1. **[Computers and Society]**: Public Policy Issues – *Privacy, Ethics*.

General Terms

Human Factors; Design; Measurement; Theory.

INTRODUCTION

Location-sharing services (LSS) are rapidly inundating the technology landscape, as dedicated mobile applications (e.g. Foursquare) or in the guise of location-sharing features incorporated into other social media (e.g. Facebook Places) [67]. Although nearly half of all U.S. adults now have a smart phone, only 10% have tried location-sharing services [62]. And while 74% of smartphone owners are willing to use location-based services such as location-based search, only 18% have ever used geo-social services that share location with other people [74]. As the technology is widely available, many researchers blame various privacy concerns for the slow adoption of LSS [67]. In prior work, we identified the desire for relationship *boundary preservation* as one key driver of these location-sharing privacy concerns [52]. We demonstrated that privacy concerns increase when users are concerned about location-sharing technology changing the boundaries of their offline relationships. For example, in the qualitative portion of our study, one interviewee explained how his girlfriend didn't want him to hang out with friends who she thought were a bad influence. Since LSS would reveal his encounters with these friends, he realized that sharing his location with her could cause problems for their relationship. Once they broke up, he was fine sharing his location with her since he was no longer accountable to her in their new relationship.

In analyzing the qualitative portion of the data, we further noticed that some people admitted that they would use *lying* as a routine privacy management tactic. Lying occurred in face-to-face as well as online interactions as a way to maintain relationship boundaries. Lies were often used to hide information or to avoid going out with someone in favor of going out with others.

Some interviewees were confident that they could get away with such lies, even when sharing their location: "I probably don't have anything to hide [about my location], but even if I do, I can just cover it up...Just make up some story." On the other hand, more interviewees expressed concern about being caught in their offline lies if their location were known:

> [If] I'm calling in sick...to go somewhere like a three day trip, [I'll say I'm] sick Friday [and] sick Monday to make it more plausible [be]cause no one gets better over the weekend... I don't think I'd ever want to reveal my location to my coworkers or my boss.

Here, coworkers would question whether this interviewee is really sick if they could see that he is out of town rather than at home. A quarter of the interviewees brought up similar situations in which they had misled someone as to their whereabouts and feared being caught lying. Examples like these led us to wonder whether one's propensity to lie also plays a role in shaping one's location-sharing privacy concerns. On the one hand, people may be less privacy concerned if they feel they can count on lying to facilitate interactions. Indeed, much research characterizes lying as a common practice used to facilitate daily social interactions and to maintain relationship boundaries (e.g. [20]). Studies of deception in computer-mediated interactions show that lying also occurs as a boundary management tactic in various mediated communications [27]. On the other hand, people with a propensity to lie may be more privacy concerned for fear of being caught at some point. Moreover, the medium of communication affects one's ability to tell and detect lies (which may explain why the rates of lying vary across media [28]). In LSS, which typically give an unbiased view of one's location, these fears and concerns of seasoned liars may thus be aggravated.

Not all interviewees who lie may have admitted it during in-person interviews. Thus, to verify whether or not one's propensity to lie affects location-sharing privacy concerns, we administered a nationwide anonymous survey that probes on lying propensity alongside boundary preservation and privacy concerns (N=1532). Using structural equation modeling and a latent factor to represent Propensity to Lie, we establish that this factor has a significant effect on a large majority of privacy concerns. Interestingly, these effects are all *positive*: one's propensity to lie *increases* one's privacy concerns. Upon integrating Propensity to Lie into the boundary preservation model identified in our previous research [52], this factor continues to have a positive direct effect on privacy concerns. Additionally, we demonstrate that part of this effect is mediated by boundary preservation concerns (BPC) towards the use of location-sharing services. In other words, Propensity to Lie increases concerns about preserving one's relationship boundaries in location-sharing social media, and this in turn causes one to be more privacy-concerned. These findings indicate that the privacy management tactic of lying tends to *backfire* in location-sharing social media.

RELATED WORK

Our work falls at the intersection of research on lies and deception, and research on privacy in location-sharing services. We survey related work in these areas.

Lies and Deception

Lying can be characterized as an act that "deliberately seeks to create a false belief" in the other person [27]. Lies may be enacted for self-interests (e.g. enhancing self-image, avoiding embarrassment) or told in the interest of helping another [19]. Some reasons for lying include interactional and relational goals, relieving role strain, achieving high-value outcomes or guarding against high-risk outcomes [16]. Studies estimate that one quarter to one third of all interpersonal interactions involve some sort of deception [14, 28]. The vast majority of these lies are what researchers consider minor deceptions, such as pretending to agree with someone or making excuses to avoid interacting with someone [27]. In everyday life, many people lie about a diverse range of topics including their feelings, achievements or failures, plans, actions, and location [20]. This is often for impression management reasons (e.g. a concept popularized by Goffman [26] and further developed in subsequent empirical research by various scholars [38, 39]).

Lies can come in many forms including outright deception, equivocation, plausible deniability, and nondisclosure [47]. Studies of SMS use have identified diverse ways of creating ambiguity such as using temporal, activity-based and location-based excuses [10]. Many studies in ubiquitous computing encourage systems to support white lies for plausible deniability [31, 40]. Researchers have even addressed this in contexts where technology is always on [5].

Many scholars focus on how everyday lies are trivial and how they do not cause much distress [20]. Some even emphasize how lying is essential to maintaining close relationships [47]: partners may collaborate to maintain lies or use ambiguity rather than full disclosure [19, 22]. However, other research shows how an act of deception and subsequent concealment may instill anxiety. Deceivers may experience apprehension associated with the fear of being caught, or guilt for violating social expectations [14]. Lying to a partner can result in discomfort, less meaningful interactions, and can even cause the *liar* to trust their partner less [8]. Lying has even been connected to physiological indicators of stress, such as elevated heart rate [15], and lying tendency has been linked to survival rates for various forms of cancer [58]. These studies suggest that lying, as a coping mechanism, can have negative physiological side effects.

Rather than being pre-planned, most lies unfold as a reaction during the course of an interaction [17]. Nonetheless, psychological research shows that people differ in their tendency to resort to lying in the face of a threat [23]. In other words, although lying is triggered by a threatening situation, the *propensity* of a person to tell a lie in that situation is a disposition. Studies have also found that people's predisposition "to use their defensive maneuvers is somewhat independent of the nature of the threatening situation" [15]. This may help explain why people lie just as much offline as online [8, 17, 28], and that the importance and content of lies [28] and the motivations behind lies are similar across media [47].

However, the rates of lying vary across media, and researchers have different explanations for this. Some authors posit a Social Distance theory in which the liar chooses less rich media to put social distance between themselves and the recipient [20]. Others subscribe to Media Richness theory which views lying as equivocal work that benefits from the richest medium so that the liar can personalize and closely monitor the interaction [28]. Hancock et al. criticized these theories for ignoring three aspects: synchronicity, the ability to record the interaction, and whether the communication partners are co-present [28]. They argue that since most lies are unplanned, lying is better carried out in media that are synchronous, hence increasing the opportunities for deception to occur. Moreover, media that can record an interaction allow people to review the content, which deters lying. Lastly, being physically co-present serves as a deterrent too, since one cannot lie about the shared physical environment.

Based on media richness theory, one would predict that liars do not prefer LSS since it is a limited interaction that does not allow personalization. Furthermore, although real-time sharing in LSS might offer more opportunities to lie, it supports a limited version of physical co-presence in that both parties can observe the physical location of the person, which deters lying about it. Ability to record is also a common feature of many LSS and could deter lying. In all, it seems that for people with a high propensity to lie, LSS could be a contentious medium. It inhibits their natural coping mechanism, which impacts their ability to alleviate privacy concerns.

Although lie scales have been developed in prior literature, it is often to detect positive survey response bias, i.e. lying as a means for social conformity or impression management [23, 55, 59]. Studies often focus on the (situation-specific) *act* of lying. Those measuring the (situation-independent) *propensity* of people to lie contend that existing scales confound multiple constructs [24, 55]. When applied to new contexts, some scales have even been shown to assign high lie scores to the most honest respondents since items wrongly assume universal truths [44, 56]. We focus on people's lying *propensity* in context of *managing interactions*. Thus, we develop a new Propensity to Lie scale that treats lying as a relationship management tactic.

Location-Sharing

Location-sharing technologies come in many guises. They range from automatic, continuous, real-time location-sharing (e.g. Google Latitude) to manual check-ins (e.g. Gowalla, Foursquare), to authorized disclosures in response to requests (e.g. HeyWAY), to location tags (e.g. GPS coordinates appended to a Twitter tweet). There are a range of methods to determine the location of a mobile device including GPS, cell towers, wireless access points, and IP address. Until recently, location-sharing technologies have mainly been studied in the lab using experiments and questionnaires. Privacy has often been a primary emphasis in these studies. Researchers posit that the primary determinants of location disclosure are *who* is requesting one's location, *when,* and *why* [18, 41, 48]. Recent research has also focused on other aspects of *who* and found that one's subjective perception of closeness is enough to predict disclosure in a given set of scenarios [73]. Others focused on weighing disclosure benefits versus risks [67].

Some studies conduct field trials of location-sharing prototypes [33]. Real-time disclosures to a limited group of socially connected participants (e.g. co-workers, family, or a group of friends) can be useful for being socially connected, coordinating day-to-day activities, and making sure loved ones are okay [6, 13, 57, 70]. Researchers point out that in a household setting, location sharing creates a moral component. Family members have to account for their location and justify deviations [13]. To avoid disclosing too much location information, prototypes support nondisclosure, ambiguity, and varying level-of-detail.

Other studies concentrate on publically available location sharing services. Humphreys described how Dodgeball, a text-based application, helped people meet up at venues in the city [32]. Page and Kobsa interviewed adopters and non-adopters of Google Latitude and found that several social forces shape people's attitudes (norms, reciprocity, symbolism) regardless of whether they had adopted the technology [50]. Boesen et al. studied domestic use of Google Latitude as a way of monitoring and making sure children were where they should be [11]. They point out that despite behavioral improvements, this ability to more easily detect lies undermined the perceived trust in their relationships. Our research concentrates on privacy concerns of users and non-users of publically available LSS.

Privacy

There are diverse conceptualizations of privacy [64]. Some prominent definitions are Warren and Brandeis's "Right to be left alone" [71], Westin's "claim of individuals, groups, or institutions to determine for themselves when, how and to what extent information about them is communicated to others" [72], and Altman's "interpersonal boundary regulation" [3]. These definitions depict privacy as the ability to regulate physical, informational or social access.

Location-sharing research often focuses on informational privacy and on sharing information with, or withholding it from, the appropriate people (e.g. [73]). Some researchers have also found impression management concerns [66], worries about being disturbed or disturbing others [33], and apprehension towards potential stalkers [67].

Researchers highlight similar concerns in other social media. Social network users are concerned about who sees what, often because of the various social spheres (e.g. family, work, friends) that intersect on their Facebook page [7]. Users often limit who sees their profile to a defined audience [43, 65]. Likewise, social media users worry about self-presentation and how others' postings will reflect on them [68], sometimes getting annoyed or being overwhelmed by too much information from others [21]. Studies have also shown concerns for feeling compelled to interact with others online [41].

Nonetheless, throughout the literature there are also counterexamples to these privacy concerns. Location-sharing in families or close friend groups often engenders social connection rather than privacy concern [6]. People disclose enormous amounts of personal information in social networks despite potential embarrassment or threats to their employment, identity, or safety [1, 2, 46]. Individuals leave intimate details open to strangers online [45] without disclosing those details to their closest relationships [29]. Location-sharing services such as SinglesAroundMe.com or Skout are even used to connect with strangers nearby.

Theories of privacy as boundary regulation may shed some light on these seeming contradictions. For example, Palen and Dourish [53] extend Altman's theory [3] of offline privacy to the online world. Like in the physical world, online privacy is a regulation of various boundaries: one's desired level of privacy can be more open or more closed, and one's current level of privacy may or may not match what is desired. For example, being cut off from interaction could be a privacy violation that results in the person feeling isolated. Along similar lines, sharing more information is not necessarily a privacy problem.

We validated a model that explains a *motivation* behind online boundary regulation in location-sharing social media [52]. The desire for *boundary preservation* of offline relationships is one root cause of diverse location-sharing privacy concerns. In other words, people's privacy concerns are higher if they are concerned that location-sharing social media would redefine their offline relationships. We found a direct effect of boundary preservation concern on eight privacy concerns that ranged from informational to interactional to physical privacy (see Table 1 for the specific concerns). Furthermore, we discovered that increased social media use lowered location-sharing boundary preservation concerns and thus had an indirect effect on privacy concerns. This suggests that as people use more social media, they may become better at, and/or less concerned about, preserving their relationship boundaries. In turn, this lowers their privacy concerns. In this paper, we build upon our findings that boundary preservation is a root cause of privacy concerns.

Integrating the Different Fields

Merging the main findings from these fields, a common pattern emerges: people's privacy concerns are caused by their need to maintain offline relationship boundaries in an online environment. Lying is a commonly used strategy to maintain existing boundaries. However, some evidence suggests that upholding a lie may be much harder in location sharing systems than in other types of social media, and may therefore increase, not decrease, privacy concerns.

We tested the veracity of these claims as part of a larger study, other parts of which have been published elsewhere [50, 52]. The current paper concentrates on how one's propensity to lie, a determinant not analyzed in previous work, affects privacy and boundary preservation concerns towards location-sharing social media.

STUDY DESIGN

The data for this analysis comes from a two-phase study that comprises a larger effort to understand social media and location-sharing attitudes and adoption. In the first phase, 21 semi-structured interviews were conducted. In the second phase, a nation-wide survey (N=1532) was administered. For the first time, this paper reports on items measuring a Propensity to Lie factor, the qualitative insights that led to its construction, and new analysis that connects lying propensity to boundary preservation and privacy concerns. We thereby build upon our previous findings [52] that relate privacy to boundary preservation concerns.

Phase 1: Interview study

Previous research points out that to understand human computer interaction, it is just as important to study *non-use* of technology as it is to study *use* [9, 60]. This is particularly relevant for location-sharing technology. Despite widespread availability of smartphones and location-sharing services, adoption of these services has been low [62, 74]. Understanding concerns of non-users could shed light on what is driving people away from these services. Little is known about who is using social media and who is not [12].

We therefore interviewed *users* of a real-time location-sharing social medium, Google Latitude, as well as *non-users*. We conducted 1 to 2 hour semi-structured interviews of 7 location-sharing users, 7 who had explicitly chosen not to adopt Latitude, 4 who had abandoned the technology, and 3 who wanted to use it but could not (because the service was not yet available for their phones). This allowed us to study attitudes and privacy concerns that might impede adoption, as well as those arising from usage after adoption. Thus, our findings are applicable to the user populations as well as those who do not use LSS.

The mean age of the subjects was 28 (ages 21 to mid 40's) and there were 4 females (one of each type of users / non users). [50] reports more broadly on adoption barriers uncovered by these interviews, while the current paper focuses on propensity to lie (we described essential details here, for complete interview procedures see [50]).

We used open-coding, purposeful sampling, and constant comparison to generate grounded theory [25]. During coding phase, three types of lying emerged (see next section for items). These lies were sometimes the source of privacy concerns and other times the solution to a potential privacy breach. "Non-lying" also emerged, and was either associated with increased concerns (because these interviewees refused to lie to cover up a sticky situation), or lowered privacy concerns (because non-lying interviewees had nothing to hide). This led us to wonder whether one's propensity to lie impacts one's privacy concerns and how. Below we report (for the first time) on the development of items reflecting the three types of lying that we encountered in our interviews.

Phase 2: Nation-wide Survey

Based on qualitative insight derived from grounded theory analysis of those interviews, we developed and administered a geographically balanced survey across the U.S. Items used in the current analysis are a subset of the survey questions. In spring of 2011, we posted the survey in 13 Craigslist cities and invited participation from anyone 18 and older who had resided in the U.S. for at least 5 years (as has been done in other privacy studies to control for culture [54]). Past research shows that liars tend to be aware of their behavior and produce fairly accurate self-reports [34].

Also, anonymous online surveys have been found to elicit more honest responses for deviant behavior (such as lying) than methods where a researcher is present [30]. We did not require location-sharing or other social media use as a precondition for participation. This way, our results would be relevant for understanding both user and non-user attitudes.

The first 50 participants each received a $10 Amazon.com gift card and the first 1000 were entered into a raffle for two $100 gift cards. After removing surveys that failed two or more of seven quality checks (e.g. reverse-coded items, unrealistic completion times), we were left with 1532 valid responses. To make the sample more representative of the U.S. population, we normalized responses from each of the U.S. census-defined geographic regions by their respective metropolitan population sizes. 24.0% of the respondents had tried location-sharing services, 79.0% used social media at least weekly, 54.0% owned smart phones, 59.7% had an unlimited data plan, 66.6% were female, the education level was in line with the U.S. Internet population, and the average age was 35.5 years (range 18-73).

The valid responses were randomly split into thirds. In [52], we used the first sample for theory construction, and the second sample for its validation. For the current analysis, we pool these two samples to test our hypotheses. We refer to this as the *original* sample (N=1021). Additionally, we use the third untouched sample for the validation of our results. We refer to this as the *hold-out* sample (N=511). Throughout the paper we cross-validate our results between the original and the hold-out samples, and only report on results that are significant in both samples. This ensures the robustness of our results. The reported outcomes are based on the full sample (N=1532).

Privacy Concern Items

The survey included items that probed on privacy concerns. As reported in [52], items were developed to represent eight of the most common online privacy concerns expressed by interviewees (C1-C8). These ranged from informational (e.g. disclosing private information) to social (e.g. impression management) to physical (e.g. physical access) privacy concerns. Another item was created to represent concern for preserving relationship boundaries (BPC) when using location-sharing services. In [52], we showed that BPC causes C1-C8. Table 1 lists these items (see [52] for a detailed explanation of the construction of each item).

Participants responded to these items on 7-point scales whose values are -3 (Disagree Strongly), -2 (Disagree Moderately), -1 (Disagree Slightly), 0 (Neutral), +1 (Agree Slightly), +2 (Agree Moderately) and +3 (Agree Strongly). Location-sharing concern items (BPC, C6-C8) were worded in a way that can be answered by everyone, including non-users. Since previous research shows that people's location-sharing attitudes and concerns are intertwined with attitudes towards social media in general [51], items C1-C5 refer to attitudes towards social media that were indicative of location-sharing concerns.

To check whether privacy concerns C1-C8 could be treated as one or more privacy concern factors, we went beyond what was reported in [52], performing exploratory factor analysis (EFA) on the original sample (N=1021). The items did not constitute a well-fitting factor model since the average inter-item correlation was 0.26, whereas 0.30 is a minimal requirement for factorization [35]. Furthermore, the average variance extracted (AVE) was 0.311, below the 0.5 cut-off for factor creation [35]. These results indicate that there is a relationship between the items, but that the correlation is too low for the items to form a robust measurement scale. In fact, all inter-item correlations were low except C7,C8 (r=0.647) and C3,C5 (r=0.516)[1] and these pairs lacked face validity to be considered as a construct. Therefore, items C1-C8 are treated as separate, but correlated, indicators.[2]

BPC	I'm worried LSS will change my relationship with others
C1	I am bothered that others share so much information with me
C2	I am concerned that if I share too much information, I would bother others
C3	I worry that I might share information with more people than I intend to
C4	I worry about feeling compelled to interact with others online
C5	I worry that what my friends share will reflect badly on me
C6	I'm worried about knowing the social etiquette of using LSS (e.g. who to friend, what to share, etc.)
C7	I'm concerned about being able to control who sees my location
C8	I'm worried others would join me at an inappropriate time if I share my location

Table 1. Questionnaire items for boundary preservation and privacy concerns. LSS=location-sharing services

Propensity to Lie

The survey included items about one's propensity to lie (whether lying offline or online), which have not been previously reported. Here we describe the factor construction and validation. Because lying is a sensitive topic, we decided to represent propensity to lie as a latent factor measured by multiple indicators. For content validity, we drew on the types of lying found from the qualitative data. In analyzing the phase 1 interviews, we found that those

---

[1] Correlation of < 0.4 is considered low, 0.4 to < 0.7 is medium, and > 0.7 is high

[2] Our modeling tool, Mplus, treats single indicators as single-item latent factors.

who spoke of lying often discussed two or more of the following forms of lying: 1) I lie, 2) Everyone lies, and 3) Technology Lie (e.g., pretending to have a bad network connection as an excuse for not answering or not being visible in a location-sharing service). Table 2 shows the items developed to represent each form of lying. We describe the development of each item in detail.

Everyone Lies	Everyone lies to get out of doing something
I Lie	Sometimes I tell a lie to avoid something (e.g. I tell someone I don't have time to go out, but then go out with someone else)
Technology Lie	Sometimes I use technical difficulties as an excuse (e.g. I pretend I had bad cell phone reception)

Table 2. Questionnaire items for Propensity to Lie factor

Everyone Lies
Several interviewees thought of lying as a typical behavior used by everyone. One interviewee elaborated on how he hid his actions by removing tags that identified him in Facebook pictures: "I don't know if my friends [remove tags]. I mean, no one wants to get caught in a lie. I'm sure they must do it." Asserting that others *must* untag pictures to avoid getting caught in a lie betrays an underlying assumption: Others are lying as well. Because others are lying, they inevitably will run into similar situations. Consequently, we developed an item to reflect the belief that others also lie. This item also had a purpose beyond being an indicator for propensity to lie. We displayed this item before the other lying items in order to frame the behavior of lying as commonplace. Framing is a common technique to increase the likelihood that respondents will be comfortable admitting to what could be perceived as deviant behavior [61].

I Lie
Several interviewees mentioned lying as an offline privacy management tactic to avoid going out with someone:

> I do tell somebody [I'm] not available for something. I tell them that I'm not feeling too good – I can't come out. But I'm actually going out with another group of people that they don't necessarily get along with.

This is an example of the most common lie among our interviewees. Namely, lying to avoid going out with or being around someone. In general, people used lying as an avoidance strategy, whether it be avoiding people in the physical space or avoiding having to converse online. This is in line with other studies that have found that people lie as a way to guard against unwelcome conversations [69] or to extract themselves from an ongoing interaction [27]. This item therefore probes how much one lies as an avoidance strategy. We purposefully framed this and other items in the context of avoidance motives rather than just asking about lying in general. This was in line with motivations described by interviewees and also increased the social acceptability of our questions.

Technology Lie
As a cover up, people often accused faulty technology. An interviewee explained how he could blame technology if location-sharing ever displayed him as being at an unsavory location: "Oh, there's a library across the street. Latitude must have been a few feet off." Making excuses by blaming technology may be a more socially acceptable type of lie since it exploits a sense of ambiguity. This is consistent with past research indicating that technology is a common scapegoat to create plausible deniability [4, 5, 10, 31, 40]. Several interviewees were not comfortable lying outright, but content to allege faulty technology. To capture this form of lying, we developed an item focused on blaming technology.

Respondents rated the three lying items (Everyone Lies, I Lie, Technology Lie) on the same 7-point scale used for privacy concern items (see previous section). Using the survey results, we established the reliability and validity of the Propensity to Lie factor. Because the reliability and validity indices are consistent in both the original and the hold-out samples, we report the statistics for the full sample. The factor loadings are significant at the $p < 0.001$ level and had the following values: Everyone Lies = 0.647, I Lie = 0.883, Technology Lie = 0.700. The Cronbach's alpha of 0.74 indicates a satisfactory level of internal reliability. The Average variance extracted (AVE) of 0.565 indicates acceptable convergent validity.[3]

Controls
The survey had several control questions, including location-sharing use, social media use (a composite of how frequently participants use various social media including Facebook, Twitter, Social Media Games, Instant Messaging), smart phone ownership, and having data and/or texting plans. Demographics included age, gender, education, geographical location, marital status and parental status.

ANALYSIS
For this analysis, we created a structural model that analyzes the effect of Propensity to Lie on privacy concerns. Then we proceed to integrate Propensity to Lie into the full boundary preservation model presented in [52]. We use weighted least squares estimator (WLSMV) with ordered categorical indicators as our estimation method for both analyses.[4] This technique does not assume normality of outcome variables. We checked for outliers (+/-3 standard

---

[3] A loading > 0.7 is considered high, and a loading > 0.4 is considered medium. Accepted cutoff values for the reliability indices: Cronbach's alpha > 0.7, AVE > 0.5.

[4] Mplus uses probit regression to estimate ordered categorical outcomes.

deviations) and used bivariate scatterplots to check for homoscedasticity. All data was within normal ranges.

Initially, we modeled LSS users separately from non-users to see if their attitudes and concerns differ. We found no difference and hence combined these data for our analysis. Thus, a single model accounts for both users and non-users.

Lying Leads to Privacy Concerns

In [52], we showed that boundary preservation concern (BPC) is a root cause of eight identified privacy concerns (C1-C8). To test whether participants' propensity to lie could also be seen as a root cause of these eight concerns, we created a structural equation model in which propensity to lie (Lie) causes these concerns. We fit this model on both samples, removed effects that were not significant in either of the two samples, and ran the resulting model on the full sample. This model had a good fit (χ^2 (12) = 50.151, $p <$ .001; *CFI* = 0.991; *RMSEA* = 0.046, 90% CI: [0.033, 0.059]; *WRMSR* = 0.558)[5]. Table 3 summarizes the effects in this model.

Concern	Effect of Lie → C1-8
I am bothered that others share so much information with me (C1)	0.183***
I am concerned that if I share too much information, I would bother others (C2)	*no effect*
I worry that I might share information with more people than I intend to (C3)	0.215***
I worry about feeling compelled to interact with others online (C4)	0.235***
I worry that what my friends share will reflect badly on me (C5)	0.259***
I'm worried about knowing the social etiquette of using LSS (C6)	*no effect*
I'm concerned about being able to control who sees my location (C7)	0.116***
I'm worried others would join me at an inappropriate time if I share my location(C8)	0.161***

Table 3. The standardized effect of Propensity to Lie on the eight different concerns (C1-C8). * indicates $p < 0.001$**

[5] A significant chi-square means that the model shows some misfit. However, this statistic is known to be very sensitive in large samples such as ours. As an alternative, one may consider other fit indices, which have the following accepted cut-off values: *CFI* > 0.96, *RMSEA* < 0.05 (within [0.00, 0.10]), *WRMSR* < 0.95.

Lying Integrated with Boundary Preservation Model

We subsequently integrated Propensity to Lie into the structural model established in [52], in which social media use decreases boundary preservation concern, and in turn boundary preservation concern increases all eight of the other concerns (refer back to *Privacy* in the *Related Works* section for a more detailed description of this model). Specifically, we modeled Propensity to Lie as a cause of both boundary preservation concerns (BPC) and the eight individual privacy concerns (C1-C8).

Although it is possible to conceive a model in which boundary preservation concerns cause an increase in the *acts* of lying, research has shown that the *propensity* to lie can be considered a stable predisposition [15, 24] rather than a situation-dependent activity. This warrants our choice of the causal direction "Lie → BPC".

Would the effect of propensity to lie on boundary preservation concerns be positive or negative? First of all, the results of Lie → C1-C8 suggest that propensity to lie will increase concerns. This is in line with research results that lying can cause significant physiological and mental stress or anxiety [14, 15]; this stress could manifest itself as boundary preservation concerns and privacy concerns in social media. On the other hand, lying can facilitate maintaining relationship boundaries [47], which would mean that propensity to lie decreases boundary preservation concerns.

We tested the integrated model on both the original and the hold-out samples and confirmed that it is consistent between the two samples. We also found that age has a consistent negative effect on the propensity to lie, as well as on social media use. We ran the resulting model on the full sample. This model has an acceptable fit ($\chi^2(42)$ = 175.059, $p <$ .001; *CFI* = 0.976; *RMSEA* = 0.046, 90% CI: [0.039, 0.053]; *WRMSR* = 0.989). Moreover, all effects in the model are highly significant (see Figure 1).

The model shows that lying propensity increases not only various online privacy concerns (C1-C8), but also concerns that location sharing will affect one's ability to preserve relationship boundaries (BPC). This makes boundary preservation concern a partial mediator that amplifies the effect of lying on privacy concerns.

The resulting model also shows that there is a direct effect of age on social media use and propensity to lie. Interestingly, the indirect effects of age on boundary preservation through social media use and propensity to lie are of similar magnitude but in opposite directions and hence end up canceling each other out. The final outcome is that there is no total effect of age on boundary preservation concerns (p = 0.617). Consequently, age only affects the eight privacy concerns through Propensity to Lie.

As an aside, we did not find any effects of lying on social media use or vice versa.

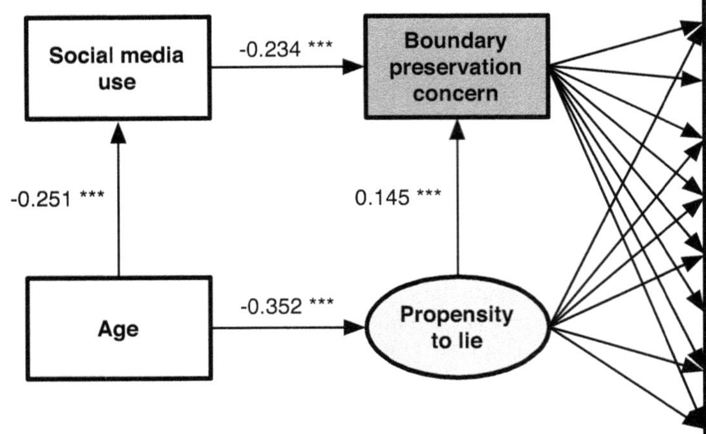

Concern	BPC	Lie
C1	0.221 ***	0.159 ***
C2	0.237 ***	*no effect*
C3	0.239 ***	0.190 ***
C4	0.294 ***	0.200 ***
C5	0.269 ***	0.215 ***
C6	0.464 ***	*no effect*
C7	0.269 ***	0.102 **
C8	0.318 ***	0.119 ***

Figure 1. Propensity to lie and boundary preservation concern (BPC) are root causes of online privacy concerns. Effects of Lie and BPC on C1-8 are tabulated, e.g. the effect of BPC on C1 is 0.221* (standardized effect sizes, *** indicates $p < 0.001$, ** $p < 0.01$)**

DISCUSSION

Lying is often depicted as a common privacy management tactic in offline relationships to mitigate concerns and to maintain relationship boundaries. Although the propensity to lie might alleviate boundary preservation concerns in other online technologies [10, 27], our model shows that in location-sharing social media, lying is likely to *backfire* and to actually increase privacy concerns. These concerns arise directly from Propensity to Lie, but also from liars' increased concerns about preserving relationship boundaries. Several interviewees recognized the risks in mixing lying with location-sharing social media:

> I don't want to tell someone, "I can't go out with you – I'm at home," and then I go out. That's dangerous. [There have] been situations where I tell someone I'm not going out tonight and then photos will be posted of me going out… One of my friends was just caught. At happy hour, she told one of her friends she wasn't going to go out. And we went out and that friend happened to show up at the same restaurant.

Location-sharing services change the premise for carrying out these lies by erasing the physical barriers and making location easily accessible.

Some location-sharing services can be used to increase the plausibility of a lie because they allow people to set an incorrect location. However, our qualitative data suggests that this can be problematic as well. Many interviewees would not consider using software to lie, and were disturbed by others who did. One interviewee forsakes using technology with friends who are not sharing their true location:

> So the point about Latitude is to know where your friends are… And so if I see a person toy with an application, I just won't pay attention to them on it. So it's like my confidence in how well they use it…. And so my confidence in the way [person's name] uses this application…was [broken]. So from now I just won't pay attention to where he is.

Another interviewee explained how he wasn't interested in Google Latitude because it allows people to set or type an incorrect location:

> People can just say they're wherever they want to say they are… It changes my perception of using Latitude as opposed to showing your accurate location all the time no matter what the users wanted…[It] becomes this unreliable source of information, becomes this messy thing.

Similarly, some interviewees even perceived the practice of blocking others from seeing location to be a deceptive act. A number of these interviewees avoided location-sharing technology and minimized participation in social media in order to keep themselves from falling into situations where lying would be a tempting solution. Several seemed to take an ethical stance against lying. These interviewees serve as a reminder that features to support lying will not appeal to everyone and could even drive users away. A value-based approach [36] would help designers understand core values such as honesty that should be supported in their design.

For those individuals motivated to avoid bad situations (rather than by ethics), several studies conclude that location-sharing technology should support plausible deniability by obscuring or hiding location [4, 5, 33]. For instance, one interviewee who would not tell blatant lies nor use technology to do so, was keeping his relationship a secret from his parents: "I would visit her but wouldn't tell my parents. I'd say I'm going to Atlanta to visit my friends. I didn't really fly to Atlanta. Well, I DID fly to Atlanta, but it was a layover on the way to another place." If he had used location-sharing at that earlier point in time, "I would have manually set it to 'break'." In other words, he wanted to maintain a partial truth by freezing his location at Atlanta or going offline and using technology as a scapegoat.

However, we question the extent to which this is possible. Obscuring location or ignoring location requests at certain moments or for certain lengths of time may violate relationship boundary expectations. For example, an employee who calls in sick for four days and whose location is unavailable the entire period might raise suspicions. Worse yet, even honest instances of being offline can then be mistaken as deception. Furthermore, as location-sharing services become more accurate and connectivity improves, and as users learn the available features, blaming technology becomes less of an option. Designers will have to better understand offline relationship dynamics in order to understand what constitutes acceptable interactions online.

Our results did not find any relationship between social media use and lying. This suggests that Propensity to Lie does not affect frequency of social media use in general, or vice versa. However, lying propensity does seem to affect concerns towards specific social media. In location-sharing we find that lying propensity increases concerns, but studies suggest that in other technologies it might decrease concerns (e.g. Hancock et al. describe the benefits of butler lies [27]). We are actively investigating whether this difference is what causes the relatively slow adoption of location sharing services.

We also did not find a consistent significant effect of lying on the concern for bothering others with too much information (C2, see Table 3). Conceptually, one can quickly see why this may be so. The Propensity to Lie factor emphasizes lying as an avoidance tactic for *self-interested* goals. Thus, it is aimed at limiting communication for the benefit of the liar. This in turn does not necessarily result in sharing too much information, nor concern for others.

Lying also did not have a significant effect on the concern for not knowing the social etiquette of LSS (C6). Upon closer inspection, we see that all of the concerns, except C6, are tangible outcomes that can result from lying. Knowing social etiquette (e.g. who to friend, what to share, etc.) has to do with defining what is considered an infraction or problem in the first place, and this may not be affected by one's lies.

In contrast to prior deception studies that focused on more homogenous samples (e.g. [10, 27]), we found that the propensity to lie significantly decreases with age. This in turn causes older participants to have lower privacy concerns. We see this play out in some of our interviews. One man explained how, as a youth, he would be especially anxious to control what his parents could see but "not so much anymore" because he is not lying to his parents about where he is. Despite common conceptions that teenagers don't care about privacy, research has shown that they actually are privacy concerned, especially in social media context [42]. Our findings shed light on one reason younger users could be more concerned: they tend to lie more.

Our model results were consistent with the hypothesis that lying propensity impacts boundary preservation concern. This direction of causality is also in line with existing theory [15]. Yet, because this is a descriptive study, it is conceivable that there is a mutual effect between lying propensity and boundary preservation concerns and thus, boundary preservation concerns could affect lying propensity over time. However, reversing the direction of causality in our model does not yield significant results. Hence, we are unable to claim a mutual effect, and leave the question to future research.

This paper uncovered lying as one privacy management tactic that affects online privacy and boundary preservation concerns. There also may be other traditional social practices that are in conflict with modern location-sharing social media. This work is a first step in exploring the interplay of location-sharing social media, our social practices, and our social relationships. Although the focus of our study was on location-sharing technology, the propensity to lie factor was framed as general practice (offline or online) and many of the privacy concern items were about social media in general, not just location-sharing social media. Thus, we suspect that lying may directly increase online privacy concerns in a range of social media that extends well beyond location sharing systems. Future research should investigate lying and boundary preservation concerns in other social media. Longitudinal studies could also shed light on how privacy-preserving social practices manifest and evolve themselves in new social media.

CONCLUSION

Our findings bring to the forefront Sir Walter Scott's admonition, "Oh! What a tangled web we weave when first we practice to deceive!" Our results indicate that lying may complicate matters even more in the online social world. This begs the question: Should technology pave the way to more transparent interactions by making it more difficult to lie? Would this force people to tell the truth, or would people avoid the technology? Or on the other extreme, should technology provide fertile grounds for facilitating lies and aim at reducing people's resulting concerns? In the middle of describing a detailed feature idea making it "convenient" to lie, one interviewee stopped himself and acknowledged this powerful, and perhaps disturbing, influence of technology:

> There are applications which force people to lie, force people to do wrong things. And I may want to take my words back. If you're writing it down, just don't write it down because I don't want to be the reason for such a bad feature.

Technology can influence social dynamics by facilitating certain practices and inhibiting others [37]. If one regards lying as undesirable, do designers have an obligation to protect people from their own propensity to lie? The answer to this may depend on one's ethical viewpoint. Our recommendation is for technology designers and researchers to think about and study the social and moral impact their technology will have once it is deployed. Technological changes can affect social practice whether we design for it or not [49]. If we understand how social practices are evolving around technology, perhaps the social and moral impacts of new technology do not have to go completely unchecked. In the realm of privacy concerns, our paper provides a first step in that direction.

ACKNOWLEDGMENTS

This work was funded by NSF grants IIS-0308277, IIS-0808783 and CNS-0831526, and by Disney Research. We thank Bonnie Nardi and the anonymous CSCW reviewers for their constructive feedback on prior drafts.

REFERENCES

[1] Acquisti, A. and Gross, R. 2006. Imagined Communities: Awareness, Information Sharing, and Privacy on the Facebook. *Privacy Enhancing Technologies*. 36–58.

[2] Acquisti, A. and Gross, R. 2009. Predicting Social Security Numbers from Public Data. *PNAS*. 106, 27 (2009), 10975–10980.

[3] Altman, I. 1975. *The Environment and Social Behavior: Privacy, Personal Space, Territory, and Crowding*. Brooks/Cole Publishing Company.

[4] Aoki, P. and Woodruff, A. 2005. Making Space for Stories. *Proc. CHI 2005* (2005), 181–190.

[5] Bagüés, S.A., Zeidler, A., Valdivielso, C.F. and Matias, I.R. 2007. Disappearing for a While - Using *White Lies* in Pervasive Computing. *Proc. WPES 2007* (2007), 80–83.

[6] Barkhuus, L., Brown, B., Bell, M., Sherwood, S., Hall, M. and Chalmers, M. 2008. From Awareness to Repartee: Sharing Location within Social Groups. *Proc. CHI 2008* (2008), 497–506.

[7] Binder, J., Howes, A. and Sutcliffe, A. 2009. The Problem of Conflicting Social Spheres: Effects of Network Structure on Experienced Tension in Social Network Sites. *Proc. CHI 2009* (2009), 965–974.

[8] Birchmeier, Z., Dietz-Uhler, B. and Stasser, G. 2011. *Strategic Uses of Social Technology: An Interactive Perspective of Social Psychology*. Cambridge University Press.

[9] Birnholtz, J. 2010. Adopt, Adapt, Abandon: Understanding Why Some Young Adults Start, and then Stop, Using Instant Messaging. *Computers in Human Behavior*. 26, 6 (2010), 1427–1433.

[10] Birnholtz, J., Guillory, J., Hancock, J. and Bazarova, N. 2010. "on my way": Deceptive Texting and Interpersonal Awareness Narratives. *Proc. CSCW 2010* (2010), 1–4.

[11] Boesen, J., Rode, J.A. and Mancini, C. 2010. The Domestic Panopticon: Location Tracking in Families. *Proc. UbiComp 2010* (2010), 65–74.

[12] Boyd, D.M. and Ellison, N.B. 2007. Social Network Sites: Definition, History, and Scholarship. *Journal of Computer-Mediated Communication*. 13, 1 (2007), 210–230.

[13] Brown, B., Taylor, A., Izadi, S., Sellen, A., Kaye, J. and Eardley, R. 2007. Locating Family Values: A Field Trial of the Whereabouts Clock. *Proc. UbiComp 2007* (2007), 354–371.

[14] Buller, D.B. and Burgoon, J.K. 1996. Interpersonal Deception Theory. *Communication Theory*. 6, 3 (1996), 203–242.

[15] Burish, T.G. and Houston, B.K. 1976. Construct Validity of the Lie scale as a Measure of Defensiveness. *Journal of Clinical Psychology*. 32, 2 (1976), 310–314.

[16] Carlson, J.R., George, J.F., Burgoon, J.K., Adkins, M. and White, C.H. 2004. Deception in Computer-Mediated Communication. *Group Decision and Negotiation*. 13, (2004), 5–28.

[17] Caspi, A. and Gorsky, P. 2006. Online Deception: Prevalence, Motivation, and Emotion. *CyberPsychology & Behavior*. 9, (2006), 54–59.

[18] Consolvo, S., Smith, I., Matthews, T., LaMarca, A., Tabert, J. and Powledge, P. 2005. Location Disclosure to Social Relations: Why, When, & What People Want to Share. *Proc. CHI 2005* (2005), 81–90.

[19] DePaulo, B.M. and Kashy, D.A. 1998. Everyday lies in close and casual relationships. *Journal of Personality and Social Psychology*. 74, 1 (1998), 63–79.

[20] DePaulo, B.M., Kashy, D.A., Kirkendol, S.E., Wyer, M.M. and Epstein, J.A. 1996. Lying in Everyday Life. *Journal of Personality and Social Psychology*. 70, 5 (1996), 979–995.

[21] Ehrlich, K. and Shami, N.S. 2010. Microblogging Inside and Outside the Workplace. *Proc. ICWSM 2010* (2010).

[22] Ekman, P. and Friesen, W.V. 1969. Nonverbal Leakage and Clues to Deception. *Psychiatry: Journal for the Study of Interpersonal Processes*. 32, 1 (1969), 88–106.

[23] Eysenck, H.J. and Eysenck, S.B.G. 1991. *Manual of the Eysenck Personality Scales (EPS adult)*. Hodder & Stoughton.

[24] Francis, L.J. 1991. The Dual Nature of the EPQ Lie Scale Among College Students in England. *Personality and Individual Differences*. 12, 12 (1991), 1255–1260.

[25] Glaser, B.G. and Strauss, A.L. 1967. *The Discovery of Grounded Theory*. Aldine.

[26] Goffman, E. 1959. *The Presentation of Self in Everday Life*. Anchor Books.

[27] Hancock, J., Birnholtz, J., Bazarova, N., Guillory, J., Perlin, J. and Amos, B. 2009. Butler Lies: Awareness, Deception and Design. *Proc. CHI 2009* (2009), 517–526.

[28] Hancock, J.T., Thom-Santelli, J. and Ritchie, T. 2004. Deception and design: the impact of communication technology on lying behavior. *Proc. CHI 2004* (2004), 129–134.

[29] Hasler, L. and Ruthven, I. 2011. Escaping Information Poverty through Internet Newsgroups. *Proc. ICWSM 2011* (2011).

[30] Hine, C. 2005. *Virtual Methods: Issues in Social Research on the Internet*. Berg Publishers.

[31] Hong, J. and Landay, J. 2004. An architecture for privacy-sensitive ubiquitous computing. *Proc. MobiSys 2004* (2004), 177 – 189.

[32] Humphreys, L. 2007. Mobile Social Networks and Social Practice: A Case Study of Dodgeball. *Journal of Computer-Mediated Communication*. 13, 1 (2007), 341–360.

[33] Iachello, G., Smith, I., Consolvo, S., Abowd, G.D., Hughes, J., Howard, J., Potter, F., Scott, J., Sohn, T., Hightower, J. and LaMarca, A. 2005. Control, Deception, and Communication: Evaluating the Deployment of a Location-Enhanced Messaging Service. *Proc. UbiComp 2005* (2005), 213–231.

[34] Kashy, D.A. and DePaulo, B.M. 1996. Who Lies? *Journal of Personality and Social Psychology*. 70, 5 (1996), 1037–1051.

[35] Kline, R.B. 2004. *Principles and Practice of Structural Equation Modeling, Second Edition*. The Guilford Press.

[36] Knobel, C. and Bowker, G.C. 2011. Values in design. *Communications of the ACM*.

[37] Latour, B. 1992. Where Are the Missing Masses? The Sociology of a Few Mundane Artifacts. *Shaping Technology/Building Society: Studies in Sociotechnical Change*. MIT Press. 225–258.

[38] Leary, M.R. and Kowalski, R.M. 1990. Impression Management: A Literature Review and Two-Component Model. *Psychological Bulletin*. 107, 1 (1990), 34–47.

[39] Leary, M.R., Tchividijian, L.R. and Kraxberger, B.E. 1994. Self-Presentation Can Be Hazardous to Your Health: Impression Management and Health Risk. *Health Psychology*. 13, 6 (1994), 461–470.

[40] Lederer, S., Hong, J.I., Dey, A.K. and Landay, J.A. 2004. Personal Privacy through Understanding and Action: Five Pitfalls for Designers. *Personal and Ubiquitous Computing*. 8, 6 (2004), 440–454.

[41] Lederer, S., Mankoff, J. and Dey, A.K. 2003. Who Wants to Know What When? Privacy Preference Determinants in Ubiquitous Computing. *Ext. Abstracts CHI 2003* (2003), 724–725.

[42] Lenhart, A. and Madden, M. 2007. *Teens, Privacy and Online Social Networks*. Pew Internet & American Life Project.

[43] Li, N. and Chen, G. 2010. Sharing location in online social networks. *IEEE Network*.

[44] McCrae, R.R. and Costa Jr., P.T. 1985. Comparison of EPI and Psychoticism Scales with Measures of the Five-Factor Model of Personality. *Personality and Individual Differences*. 6, 5 (1985), 587–597.

[45] Nardi, B.A., Schiano, D.J. and Gumbrecht, M. 2004. Blogging as Social Activity, or, Would You Let 900 Million People Read your Diary? *Proc. CSCW 2004* (2004), 222–231.

[46] Neuburger, J. 2008. Teacher Fired for Inappropriate Behavior on MySpace Page. *PBS.org*.

[47] O'Sullivan, B. 2000. What You Don't Know Won't Hurt Me: Impression Management Functions of Communication Channels in Relationships. *Human Communication Research*. 26, 3 (2000), 403–431.

[48] Olson, J.S., Grudin, J. and Horvitz, E. 2005. A study of preferences for sharing and privacy. *Ext. Abstracts CHI 2005* (2005), 1985–1988.

[49] Orlikowski, W. and Robey, D. 1991. Information Technology and the Structuring of Organizations. *Information Systems Research*. 2, 2 (1991), 143–169.

[50] Page, X. and Kobsa, A. 2010. Navigating the Social Terrain with Google Latitude. *iConference 2010* (2010).

[51] Page, X. and Kobsa, A. 2009. The Circles of Latitude: Adoption and Usage of Location Tracking in Online Social Networking. *CSE 2009* (2009), 1027–1030.

[52] Page, X., Kobsa, A. and Knijnenburg, B.P. 2012. Don't Disturb My Circles! Boundary Preservation Is at the Center of Location-Sharing Concerns. *Proc. ICWSM 2012* (2012).

[53] Palen, L. and Dourish, P. 2003. Unpacking "Privacy" for a Networked World. *Proc. CHI 2003* (2003), 129–136.

[54] Patil, S., Page, X. and Kobsa, A. 2011. With a little help from my friends: can social navigation inform interpersonal privacy preferences? *CSCW 2011* (2011), 391–394.

[55] Paulhus, D.L. 1984. Two-component Models of Socially Desirable Responding. *Journal of Personality and Social Psychology*. 46, 3 (1984), 598–609.

[56] Pearson, P.R. and Francis, L.J. 1989. The Dual Nature of the Eysenckian Lie Scales: Are Religious Adolescents More Truthful? *Personality and Individual Differences*. 10, 10 (1989), 1041–1048.

[57] Raento, M. and Oulasvirta, A. 2008. Designing for Privacy and Self-presentation in Social Awareness. *Personal and Ubiquitous Computing*. 12, 7 (2008), 527–542.

[58] Ratcliffe, M.A., Dawson, A.A. and Walker, L.G. 1995. Eysenck Personality Inventory L-scores in Patients with Hodgkin's Disease and Non-Hodgkin's Lymphoma. *Psycho-Oncology*. 4, 1 (1995), 39–45.

[59] Sackeim, H.A. and Gur, R.C. 1979. Self-deception, Other-deception, and Self-reported Psychopathology. *Journal of Consulting and Clinical Psychology*. 47, 1 (1979), 213–215.

[60] Satchell, C. and Dourish, P. 2009. Beyond the User: Use and Non-use in HCI. *Proc. OZCHI 2009* (2009), 9–16.

[61] Singleton, R. and Straits, B.C. 2005. *Approaches to Social Research*. Oxford University Press.

[62] Smith, A. 2012. *Nearly half of American adults are smartphone owners*. Pew Internet & American Life Project.

[63] Smith, H.J. and Rogers, Y. 2003. Managing One's Social Network: Does Age Make a Difference? *Proc. Interact 2003* (2003).

[64] Solove, D.J. 2008. *Understanding Privacy*. Harvard University Press.

[65] Stutzman, F. and Kramer-Duffield, J. 2010. Friends Only: Examining a Privacy-enhancing Behavior in Facebook. *Proc. CHI 2010* (2010), 1553–1562.

[66] Tang, K.P., Lin, J., Hong, J.I., Siewiorek, D.P. and Sadeh, N. 2010. Rethinking Location Sharing: Exploring the Implications of Social-driven vs. Purpose-driven Location Sharing. *Proc. UbiComp 2010* (2010), 85–94.

[67] Tsai, J.Y., Kelley, P., Cranor, L.F. and Sadeh, N. 2010. Location-Sharing Technologies: Privacy Risks and Controls. *I/S: A Journal of Law and Policy for the Information Society*. 6, 1 (2010), 119–151.

[68] Tufekci, Z. 2008. Can You See Me Now? Audience and Disclosure Regulation in Online Social Network Sites. *Bulletin of Science, Technology & Society*. 28, 1 (2008), 20 –36.

[69] Vanden Abeele, M. and Roe, K. 2008. White Cyberlies: the Use of Deceptive Instant Messaging Statuses as a Social Norm. *Proc. ICA 2008* (2008).

[70] Want, R., Hopper, A., Falcão, V. and Gibbons, J. 1992. The Active Badge Location System. *ACM Transactions on Information Systerms*. 10, 1 (1992), 91–102.

[71] Warren, S. and Brandeis, L.D. 1890. The Right to Privacy. *Harvard Law Review*. 4, 5 (1890), 193–220.

[72] Westin, A. 1967. *Privacy and Freedom*. Atheneum.

[73] Wiese, J., Kelley, P.G., Cranor, L.F., Dabbish, L., Hong, J.I. and Zimmerman, J. 2011. Are You Close with Me? Are You Nearby?: Investigating Social Groups, Closeness, and Willingness to Share. *Proc. UbiComp 2011* (2011), 197–206.

[74] Zickuhr, K. 2012. *Three-quarters of smartphone owners use location-based services*. Pew Internet & American Life Project.

Mining Smartphone Data to Classify Life-Facets of Social Relationships

Jun-Ki Min, Jason Wiese, Jason I. Hong, John Zimmerman
Human-Computer Interaction Institute, Carnegie Mellon University
loomlike@gmail.com, {jwwiese, jasonh, johnz}@cs.cmu.edu

ABSTRACT
People engage with many overlapping social networks and enact diverse social roles across different facets of their lives. Unfortunately, many online social networking services reduce most people's contacts to "friend." A richer computational model of relationships would be useful for a number of applications such as managing privacy settings and organizing communications. In this paper, we take a step towards a richer computational model by using call and text message logs from mobile phones to classifying contacts according to life facet (*family*, *work*, and *social*). We extract various features such as communication intensity, regularity, medium, and temporal tendency, and classify the relationships using machine-learning techniques. Our experimental results on 40 users showed that we could classify life facets with up to 90.5% accuracy. The most relevant features include call duration, channel selection, and time of day for the communication.

Author Keywords
Mobile social network; interpersonal relationships mining; life-facets; smartphone.

ACM Classification Keywords
H.5.m. Information interfaces and presentation (e.g., HCI): Miscellaneous.

General Terms
Algorithms; Experimentation; Human Factors.

INTRODUCTION
People enact many different social roles as they move between contexts and interact with different people. A woman might enact the role of mother, wife, daughter, sister, neighbor, supervisor, colleague, teammate, subordinate, chairperson, coach, and music patron all within a single day. Social roles provide a sort of invisible structure, guiding people in their choice of actions in various social situations. Computational systems, interestingly, often have little or no understanding of the many roles a person might play, of the behavioral expectations associated with these roles, or of the specific role a person is enacting when interacting with a system.

Even social devices and services like smartphones and social networking services (SNS) operate with a tremendously limited understanding of social role, often classifying everyone as "friend" or "friend of friend." Systems with a richer understand of role could assist people in a variety of ways. At the highest level, these systems could engage in much more situationally appropriate behavior. More pragmatically, these systems could help by organizing and prioritizing communications, by working to prevent unwanted self-disclosure or socially inappropriate behavior when sharing on SNSs, by reminding people of the role they should be enacting before taking a phone call or engaging in other mediated communication, and by mining situational enactments of different roles to help systems better understand the meaning of a place, of a situation, or of the services people might most desire.

Some computational systems provide tools for users to manually label groups and assign their contacts to these groups; however, people do not appear to use these tools. One recent study reported that only 16% of people create any contact groups on their mobile phones [20]. In addition, Facebook reported that less than 5% of users create groups within their set of friends [23]. We suspect that these features are rarely used because people do not perceive enough value in improved services to invest the time and attention necessary to categorize the hundreds of contacts they digitally maintain. The challenge is greater than simply classifying each contact once. Research shows relationships are dynamic [35,3]. Kelley *et al.* argue that groups created for privacy purposes need to be periodically updated because of changes in relationships [25].

Our goal is to develop methods for systems to infer social role at a level of granularity that allows significantly improved service offerings by mining logs of electronic communications and sensor data from smartphones and social media. Data from email and online SNSs provide rich details on the communications between groups of people. Data from smartphones provide a person's locations as well as proximity to and co-location with others. For example, previous work demonstrated how information on co-location patterns could be used to predict if two people are friends [10]. In addition, phones provide call and text message (SMS) logs, capturing the: who, when, initiator/receiver, and the duration/length of many communication events. The integration of all of this data offers the opportunity to model human behavior and social interactions at a scale and fidelity not previously possible.

This paper documents our investigation of one part of this bigger picture, namely using smartphone communication data (contact list, call logs, and SMS data) to classify the life facet of a user's contact as *family*, *work*, or *social*. Life facets are distinct domains within which people enact different roles. We chose these facets based on previous social networking research by Ozenc and Farnham [36]. While these facets are broad and coarse-grained, they provide initial evidence that concepts such as social role can be learned. Based on communication log data from 40 participants, we used machine-learning techniques to classify life facets with 90% accuracy for contacts users had communicated with.

This paper provides two contributions. First, it provides a set of extracted smartphones features that help to mine life facets. Second, it provides details of models built to classify life facets and an evaluation of these models based on a data set of 16,940 calls and 63,900 SMS messages.

BACKGROUND

Kinds of Relationships

Both social identity theory (from social psych) and identity theory (from sociology) agree that social role is a critical component in understanding human relationships [17,39,40]. People enact many different social roles and form relationships/affiliations with groups based on these roles. The degree that social role structure and granularity vary depends on individuals; however, social constructs like the life facets of *family*, *work*, and *social* are much more universal [33,36]. In exploring her work/family border theory, Clark suggested that the greater the differences across role domains, the less people engage in across-the-border communication [9]. Similarly, Farnham and Churchill found that one approach people use to manage roles and facets is to match them to specific communication mediums, such as only using the phone to communicate with your mom [17].

Relative to offline social contexts (such as face-to-face interaction), people experience new challenges in online contexts, which tend to be more broadcast oriented. This openness, particularly in online SNS, often results in unwanted self-disclosure, where information that is relevant in one life facet but inappropriate in another manages to spillover [20,26,32]. As a result, users often experience difficulty in regulating boundaries [20,26]. Ozenc and Farnham explored how users can leverage bounded, group-based sharing models with online media, in the contexts of *family*, *work*, and *social*, and emphasized the ubiquity of smartphones as an important tool for managing these relationships [36].

Together, their work suggests that the distinctions between *family*, *work*, and *social* are general enough to apply broadly to individuals, and that these distinctions are important and defining factors in people's lives. Furthermore these studies highlight the challenges of maintaining boundaries when using modern technologies. Our work is an effort to help address these concerns by providing a mechanism for systems to gain more detailed information about the specific relationship between people.

Social Network Analysis and Group Mining

Researchers have addressed social network (SN) analysis on smartphones and SNS using both supervised and unsupervised approaches [3,6,32]. Many of them have focused on tie strength, defining its properties as four dimensions: amount of time, intimacy, intensity, and reciprocal services [19]. Studies have shown that the vast majority of interaction on SNS is with small numbers of strong ties. For example, recent work by Burke suggested that the average number of friends on Facebook is around 180 [5] (though many users have many more), while most people on Facebook only interact regularly with 4 to 6 people [42]. A different study examined people who posted and tagged pictures of each other on Facebook, and found that on average people had 6.6 such "friends" [8].

Based on network information like tie strength, researchers have tried to analyze distinction of groups within a SN. Skeels and Grudin [38] found that people faced many tensions when they tried to manage the co-presence of multiple groups within their network. Lampinen *et al.* [26] showed that people address group co-presence based on behavioral strategies such as dividing the platform into separate spaces, using suitable channels of communication, and performing self-censorship. In addition, several studies have demonstrated users' desire to create groups of contacts for practical applications like multi-level access control when sharing content [12,25,38]. Olson *et al.* [34] found that people decide with whom to share information based on the type of relationship, such as family and coworker. For example, Gilbert and Karahalios suggested that privacy controls based on tie strength might help to segment a user's SN into meaningful groups, and achieved 85% accuracy on binary classification of people's strong or weak tie [18]. With their study on people's privacy concern, Jones and O'Neill found six criteria of grouping that people commonly considered: social circles and cliques, tie strength, temporal episodes, geographical locations, functional roles, and organizational boundaries [24].

Meanwhile, as smartphones have become popular and more advanced, they have become an invaluable tool for making inferences about a person's physical and social identities. Reality Mining was one of the first attempts to utilize mobile data with survey studies pertaining to human social behavior [15], showing that a user's SN could be detected by using call records, cellular-tower IDs, and Bluetooth proximity logs. Since then, numerous studies on mobile phones have inferred a broad array of attributes, including: identifying users' demographic information (ethnicity, age, and marital status) [2]; personality [7]; predicting mobile interaction [30]; predicting friendships between people based on co-location patterns [10]; predicting willingness to share different kinds of contextual information [41]; and health-related behaviors that are correlated with social interactions [27]. Relatively little work has attempted to engage the relationship mining problems using data available on mobile phones. The studies that do engage this tend to focus on one type of relationship, namely friendship (or tie-strength) [35,16], despite literature that indicates that people have overlapping groups of relationships across their personal social networks [12,26,36].

In this paper we focus on mining interpersonal relationships based on the three main life facets (*family*, *work*, and *social*) that appeared most robust and general in the aforementioned literature. We used people's mobile phone data (contact list, call logs and SMS logs) to classify relationship types, and demonstrate which features can be effective in identifying each relationship. As a first step towards testing the feasibility of this data to infer the top-level life facets, we collected historical data available on mobile phones. Our work allows us to examine the relationship between people's communication behaviors and the life facets that their social connections belong to, a topic not previously explored in the literature above.

DATA COLLECTION

Our study ran from January 2012 through April 2012. We recruited participants living in the United States by posting ads in several online bulletin boards and websites. We gathered data from their Android smartphones and asked them to self-report on their relationships with contacts to provide ground truth through our study website. To protect our participants' privacy, we anonymized contact names. While we did not collect the content of messages, we did collect descriptive information such as email domain name, first six digits of phone numbers, and postal address without street name, to use for machine learning features.

Participants and Procedure

40 participants (13 male and 27 female) were selected based on several criteria: age ($\geq$ 18), social network membership (on Facebook with at least 50 "friends"), and mobile device usage (have used the same Android phone for at least six months, to have a useful SMS and call log). 55% of our participants were graduate or undergraduate students, 35% were employed, and the rest (10%) were unemployed. The age of the participants ranged from 19 to 50 years (*mean* = 28.0 years, σ = 8.9). Participants were instructed to complete the entire study within two weeks, and were compensated $80 USD.

Participants downloaded their contact list, call log, and SMS log from their smartphones to computers by using our Android app. They also downloaded their friend list from Facebook, which we used to help select which friends they would label. Participants then uploaded these data files to our server.

Next, participants were asked to list the names of people in specific social groups, including immediate and extended family members, people they currently live with, work

Figure 1. Part of our study webpages. Each participant is asked to (a) answer questions about her relationship with a selected contact, and (b) label what groups this contact belongs to. We used this data as ground truth.

with, feel close to, and do hobbies with. We selected these labels based on past qualitative work [28,39,41]. We then created a list of 70 contacts for each participant to label with relationship information as follows: First, we included all the people each participant listed in the previous step. Next, we selected the top 15 most frequently communicated individuals via mobile phone call, SMS, and Facebook (the number of wall posts, comments, and Facebook messages from a contact), respectively. We then added randomly selected individuals from their phone's contact list and Facebook friend list. Participants resolved duplicates, including people who had different names in the different communication mediums or that had multiple listings in the contacts list. This resulted in a list of 70 distinct names for each participant (hereafter referred to as the "*70-contact list*").

We asked participants to provide basic demographic information about each contact from the *70-contact list*, such as sex and approximate age (see Figure 1a). Participants were also asked to rate their perceived closeness with each contact on a 5-point scale ranging from *very distant* to *very close* [1,5,11,37] and to indicate how many years they had known the contact. We asked participants how frequently they interact with each contact using a 7-point scale ranging from *less than yearly* to *daily*. They used this scale to describe frequency for face-to-face interaction, overall communication through mobile and online channels, mobile phone call, text messaging, and interaction via Facebook, respectively.

Finally, participants assigned each contact to at least one group (we encouraged them to indicate multiple group affiliations when relevant, see Figure 1b). For example, if a

Facet	Group-Category	# Contacts	% Participants		Example labels created by participants
Family	Immediate family	181	90	90.0	Home, Parents, Close Family, Siblings, Children
	Extended family	219		75.0	Relatives, Cousins, Uncle, Brother-in-laws, Mother's side family
	Significant other	23		35.0	Boyfriends, Husband, Ex-boyfriends, Partner, Sig other
Work	Work	305		72.5	Friends of work, Clients, Senior, Previously worked with
Social	School	1136	100	90.0	UIC, Pitt students, Indiana high school, Roommates this year
	Hobby	78		25.0	Poker, Marathon, Chess, Old dance people
	Neighborhood	139		40.0	Current neighbors, Roommate, Met while lived in Morgan park
	Religious	8		7.5	Church friends
	Family friend	100		3.3	Friends of parents, Children's friends' parents
	Know through somebody	260		55.0	People from Greensburg, Boyfriend's friends, Online friends
	Others a	452 + 22		80.0	Facebook friends, My doctor, Not sure, Mentor

a. We had an "Others" category (4% in our data set) for contacts who did not fit into one of the three facets such as "My doctor" or "Can't remember this person." Some participants used this to distinguish "best friends" from social friends. We used the self-reported closeness to assign the contacts in the Others category into the *social* facet (closeness ≥ 2, 452 contacts; or have another *social*-type label, 22 contacts), and rejected the rest 107 contacts.

Table 1. Relationship categories and examples of group labels created by our participants. Column "# Contacts" shows the number of contacts assigned into each category label (out of a total 2680 contacts from 40 participants, allowing multiple labels), and "%Participants" shows the percentage of participants that labeled at least one contact in a given category.

participant and her friend went to college together, and they both attend or attended the same church, the participant could place them in two groups. Each group was defined to be one of 11 different categories corresponding to the three life facets: *family* (immediate family, extended family, and significant other), *work*, and *social* (neighborhood, religious, family friend, knowing through somebody else, school, hobby, and others). We selected the names of these sub-categories by combining several sources [22,25,39,41], aiming to strike a balance between comprehensiveness (for richness of data) and simplicity (to prevent errors and minimize burden for participants).

RESULTS

In total we gathered the logs for 24370 phonebook contacts, 16940 calls, 63893 SMS, and 1853 multimedia messages (MMS). Note that Android automatically syncs its phonebook (contact list) with online contact lists such as Outlook/Gmail contact list and Facebook friend list. The system merges identical contacts, but there are frequently duplicates. We eliminated duplicates by matching names participants provided (the *70-contact list*) or by comparing a name and phone number. We ignored calls and messages from/to phone numbers not in a participant's phonebook.

The number of contacts in participants' phonebooks varied: 14 to 2355 contacts (Q1 = 236, Med = 519, Q3 = 962), where 12 to 772 contacts (Q1 = 125, Med = 172, Q3 = 301) had phone numbers in their profile information (the rest of these in-phonebook contacts only had "online" information like email address). Past research found that people have consistent communication with between 7 to 20 people [5,22]. This pattern bore out in our data set. For example, as shown in Figure 2c, the top 60% of calls and messages were made with just 1 to 31 contacts (Q1 = 5, Med = 6, Q3 = 8). Descriptive statistics for the *70-contact list* (40 participants × 70 contacts = 2800 contacts) are shown in Figure 2(d, e), where we rejected 120 contacts that were not in our target facets (107 contacts, see Table 1) or had no labels (13 contacts). Note that, in the *70-contact list*, we included the people who had a close relationship with the participant such as live-with, family, coworker, social friends, and most frequently communicated with. Thus, about half of the contacts in this list had a high self-reported closeness (>3 out of 5, see Figure 2e). Among the 2680 contacts in the *70-contact list*, 1847 contacts were in the phonebook list (more than 80% of them overlapped with the Facebook network as plotted in Figure 2e), and 817 contacts had communicated with our participants through mobile phone call or messaging during the logged period. In addition to the *70-contact list*, we will refer these two subsets as the "*in-phonebook list*" and "*communication list*", respectively. We will focus on these three lists for the remaining experiments and analysis.

Relationship Categories

As we described in the Introduction, we consider three classes (*family*, *work*, and *social*) rather than using all the group categories (see Table 1). In our data set, 14% of

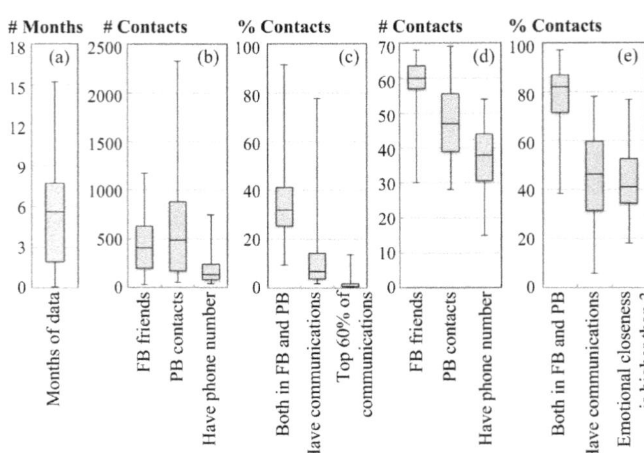

Figure 2. Outline of our data set. (a) Months of data; (b) #contacts in the Facebook (FB) and mobile phonebook (PB) from the entire data set; (c) ratio of contacts for the PB contacts in (b); (d) #contacts in the FB and PB for the *70-contact list*; and (e) ratio of contacts for the PB contacts in (d).

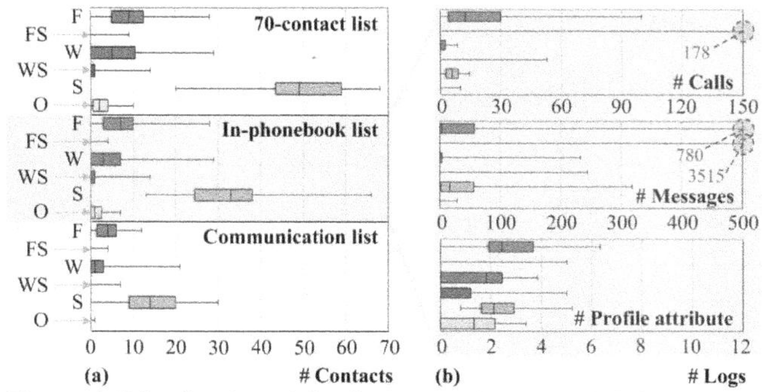

Figure 3. Distribution of *family* (F), *work* (W), *social* (S), and the others (O) contacts (FS and WS denote contacts in multiple facets; we rejected O contacts): (a) The number of contacts in each list; and (b) the log size in the *in-phonebook list*

contacts were *family* (here we included "significant other"). We had a relatively small number of *work* type contacts (11%) since more than half of our participants were students. *School* presents a difficult challenge for our analysis, where some student-participants labeled part of their relationships as *work* while others reported all of their school contacts as *social*. This demonstrates a limitation of simplifying the groups down to these three facets. We found that *social* is the most common life facet. In our data set, 70% of contacts were *social* with diverse group labels like schoolmates, poker friends, church friends, and online friends.

Note that if a contact was assigned to two or more groups crossing different faceted boundaries, he/she was labeled with multiple classes. However, most of the cross-labeled contacts were within *social* categories, such as school friends who play chess together (school and hobby) or roommates (school and neighborhood). Only 0.9% and 2.3% of contacts were in multiple facets of *family-social* and *work-social*, respectively (see Figure 3a).

APPLYING MACHINE LEARNING TO LIFE FACETS

Mobile Communication Patterns

Based on the observations of our data set and several sources of references, we defined five factors that characterize communication patterns in the context of the life facets as: intensity, regularity, temporal tendency, channel selection/avoidance, and maintenance cost.

Intensity and regularity: The number of and duration of communication actions has been used to predict tie strength in past work [22,37]. For example, as illustrated in Figure 3(b), voice calls were very common for *family* relationships. Meanwhile, office interactions and personal interactions show different regularity [13]. Figure 4 shows examples of communication patterns between a contact and a participant, where *work*-type interaction (Figure 4b) was less regular than those of *family* and *social* (Figure 4a and 4c respectively).

Temporal tendency: In their friends-acquaintances work, Eagle and Pentland observed the temporal tendency in contacting people [15]. Our participants called with their

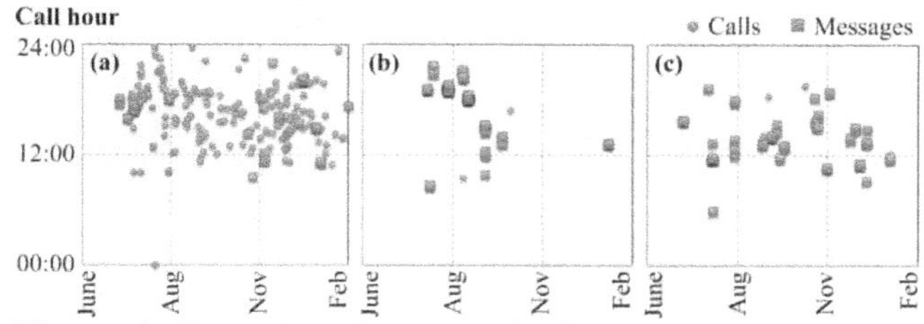

Figure 4. Examples of communication patterns between a participant and a contact: (a) *family*, (b) *work*, and (c) *social*

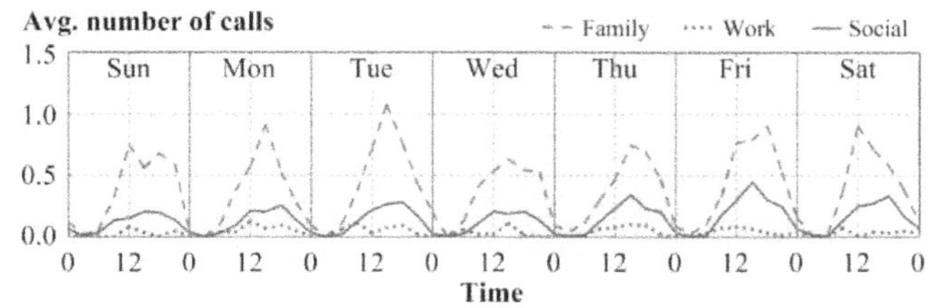

Figure 5. Averaged number of calls over the contacts in the *communication list*. Users preferred to call *social* contacts after work-hour while less with *work* facet contacts on the weekends.

family, *work*, and *social* contacts at different times of day and days of week (see Figure 5). For example, participants frequently called with their *family* members in the afternoon (12~15h) and evenings (15~18h) while they contacted with their *social* friends more on a Friday afternoon. They were less likely to call *work* contacts on the weekends.

Channel selection and avoidance: People tend to favor a certain communication medium based on the person they are communicating with [29]. According to our survey result, participants communicated via face-to-face, calls, text messages, and Facebook with different priorities based on the facets that the contacts belong to.

Maintenance cost: Roberts and Dunbar [37] suggested that people apply different amounts of effort in maintaining different kinds of relationships, where effort (cost) can be evaluated by using the time to last contact between two individuals. However, this value could be smaller than the actual cost by chance according to the data collection date. To minimize this coincidence, we measure the number of communications in the past two weeks (short-term view) and in the past three months (relatively long-term view).

In the following section, we describe how we operationalized these categories into specific machine learning features.

Feature Extraction

We defined 153 features from smartphone data: 17 from phonebook, 66 from call logs, 36 from message logs, and 34 from communication (call + message) logs (see Table 2).

Contact's profile features: We measured the similarity between our participants and their contacts based on the last name, email domain, first six digits of phone number (area code + exchange), postal-address, and company name. These features might help categorize *family* and *work* facets. For email domain, we excluded popular free-hosting

Modality		Variables	Description
Survey		Same gender; age difference; is Facebook friend; frequency seen	Available from SNS and GPS
Profile features		Similarity of {last name, email domain, company name, phone number}; has {photo, ringtone, webpage, note, affiliation, work-phone & address, home-phone & address, email}; is starred; event type; completion of profile	Contact information
Mobile-communication features	Call logs	Total {#, dur.} calls; total #lengthy-calls;	Intensity
		{AVG, STD, MIN, MAX, MED} #{outgoing, incoming} calls per week; #days called / days logged; {AVG, MAX} dur. {outgoing, incoming} calls	Regularity
		{#, dur.} outgoing calls / total calls; #{failed, missed} calls / outgoing (incoming) calls	Ch. selection & avoidance
		{#, dur.} calls at {times of a day, days of a week} / total calls; #{lengthy, failed, missed} calls at {times of a day, days of a week} / total (outgoing, incoming) calls	Temporal tendency
		{#, dur.} calls for the {past two weeks, past three months} / total calls	Maintenance cost
	MSG logs	Total {#, length} MSGs	Intensity
		{AVG, STD, MIN, MAX, MED} #{outgoing, incoming} MSGs per week; #days MSGed / days logged;	Regularity
		{#, length} outgoing MSGs / total MSGs; #replied MSGs / total MSGs	Ch. selection & avoidance
		{#, length} MSGs at {times of a day, days of a week} / total MSGs	Temporal tendency
		{#, length} MSGs for the {past two weeks, past three months} / total MSGs	Maintenance cost
	COMM (Call & MSG) logs	Total #COMMs	Intensity
		#Days had COMMs / days logged	Regularity
		#Outgoing COMMs / total COMMs; #calls / total COMMs	Ch. selection
		# COMMs at {times of a day, days of a week} / total COMMs; #calls / total COMMs at {times of a day, days of a week}; outgoing COMMs at {times of a day, days of a week, holidays} / total COMMs	Temporal tendency
		# COMMs for the {past two weeks, past three months} / total COMMs	Maintenance cost

Table 2. Extracted 153 features from mobile data. We used four time segments and four day of week segments: morning (6AM ~ noon), afternoon (noon ~ 6PM), evening (6PM ~ midnight), and night (midnight ~ 6AM); Weekdays (Mon ~ Thu), Fri, Sat, and Sun. Note that "total" communication denotes all previous (logged) communications with the contact.

domains like @gmail.com. We used the labels on each contact's phone numbers, such as *home*, *work*, *mobile*, and *other*, which are pre-defined in Android. Since only few participants had their own and contacts' postal-address in the phonebook, we simply checked if the contact's {*home*, *work*, and *other*} postal-address exists (as binary features). We had additional binary features, such as ringtones, notes, or if the contact was marked as a favorite in the Android contact list. We also calculated the completion of each profile. This serves as a weak proxy to measure the user's effort in filling in the contact information. Android phones can automatically fill contact list data by syncing with online SNS such as Google+ and Facebook. In the *70-contact list* data set, 50% of mobile contacts had photos, suggesting that about a half of participants used auto-sync. Interestingly, we still found that the majority of contacts had less than 3 profile attributes, including name, a phone number, and an email address (see Figure 3b). Thus, more contact information could still be a potentially useful signal.

Call features: We created several features to examine the *intensity* of voice communications, including total number of and duration of calls for each contact. We counted the number of lengthy calls, in which their duration is twice the average duration. To measure the *regularity* of calls, we calculated five statistical values (AVG, STD, MIN, MAX, and MED) for the number of calls per week. We also calculated AVG and MAX duration of calls to measure a simple regularity and burst-ness, respectively. We estimated users' *channel selection and avoidance* behaviors by calculating the ratio of outgoing calls, failed calls (duration < 5 seconds), and missed calls. *Temporal tendency* and *maintenance cost* were also extracted from call logs as shown in Table 2.

Message (MSG) features: We defined SMS and MMS features similar to the call features (see Table 2). Here, we counted the length of MMS as 160 characters, which is the maximum length of SMS. With their large-scale text messaging study, Battestini *et al.* applied a time metric of a 20-minute response time to group messages together as a conversation [4]. We adopted this metric to capture the ratio of replied messages.

Communication (COMM) features: Messages frequently involve other communication channels [4]. For example, people often call back in response to a text message. Therefore, we counted calls and messages equally for the COMM features. For the intensity, regularity, and channel selection features, we calculated *total #COMMs*, the *#days had COMMs / days logged*, and the ratio of calls (*#calls / total COMMs*), respectively. We also had features checking *COMMs* on four days that, in the United States, often carry some kind of meaning. These days included Thanksgiving, Christmas, New Year's Day, and Valentines' Day.

Finally, we extracted four features from the self-reported information, such as same gender, age difference, is-Facebook friend, and frequency seen, referring to them as the *survey features* (see Table 2). Current smartphones do not have these data, but we included them since they could be obtained from today's SNS and future smartphones. For example, demographic information such as gender and age can be automatically retrieved from Facebook profiles (or estimated from smartphone data [2]), and face-to-face communication could be detected by using smartphones' Bluetooth proximity [13] or GPS co-location [10].

Life Facet Classification

We evaluated how well we could classify the life facets with different sets of features across different data sets. As noted by a previous study on friends and non-friends [14], the size of different life facets are not necessarily balanced. In our data set, two-thirds of contacts were *social*, meaning that a null classifier could achieve good accuracy just by guessing "*social*." Therefore, when evaluating a given data set, we randomly sampled contacts to balance their classes (non-replacement sampling with WEKA toolkit [21]). For the classification test, we conducted three runs of 10-fold cross-validation, where we re-sampled the given set (to balance the classes) for each run. Table 3 shows the class distributions of the original datasets and resampled datasets.

Type of data set	Original data sets			Evaluation data sets		
	Family	*Work*	*Social*	*Family*	*Work*	*Social*
70-contact list	419	305	1956	501	521	537
In-phonebook list	315	227	1305	399	422	400
Communication list	168	95	554	202	198	210

Table 3. The number of contacts for the original data set and the evaluation set (sum of three runs)

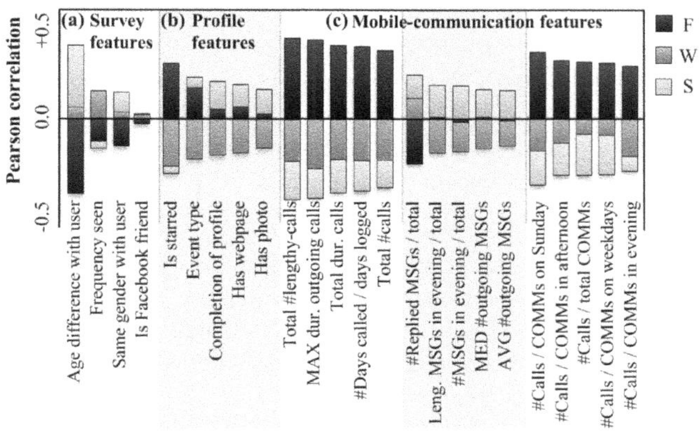

Figure 6. The most correlated (Pearson correlation) features of each modality with each life facet. Call and message features were positively correlated with *family* and *social*, respectively.

Data set	Method	Survey features	Profile features	Mobile comm. features	Profile+ mobile comm.	Using all
70-contact list	C4.5	68.0(5.1)	NA	NA	NA	74.2(4.4)
	NB	72.4(5.6)	NA	NA	NA	67.1(3.6)
	SVM	65.5(4.4)	NA	NA	NA	81.0(4.5)
In-phone book list	C4.5	69.1(6.9)	52.8(7.7)	64.7(6.0)	64.5(7.8)	76.1(7.5)
	NB	72.5(7.2)	54.3(6.6)	65.5(5.5)	65.4(5.6)	65.6(5.5)
	SVM	66.7(7.4)	51.1(7.2)	67.9(6.4)	68.5(6.0)	83.1(5.9)
Comm. list	C4.5	66.0(9.9)	53.1(8.7)	75.8(7.2)	75.9(6.7)	75.6(5.5)
	NB	69.1(10.)	55.2(9.0)	76.4(8.8)	76.4(8.8)	76.6(8.6)
	SVM	60.8(10.)	52.9(8.4)	87.1(5.0)	88.0(5.3)	90.5(4.8)

Table 4. Ave. accuracy (and Std.) of three runs of ten-fold cross-validation for predicting life facets. Note that online friends in the *70-contact list* have no mobile features (denoted by NA)

We first analyzed associations between the features to the facets based on Pearson correlations. The *communication list* data set is used to highlight people's mobile communication behaviors over different facets. As shown in Figure 6(a), *frequency seen* feature was related to *work* facet. Age difference between a user and contact was more correlated with *social* facet than the other facets, which implies that people hang out with similar age people. For the profile features, *Is-starred* (a "favorite" in the Android phonebook) and *Has-photo* were strongly associated with *family* and *social* types, respectively. Note that photos in phonebooks are mostly synced from Facebook (a socially oriented service), which explains why *Has-photo* was positively correlated with the *social* contacts. *Event type*, such as *birthday*, *anniversary*, and *other*, was also highly correlated with *family* and *social*. Among the mobile communication features, *intensity* and *regularity* were positively associated with *family* contacts, while negatively correlated with *work* contacts. Based on the correlation values from the *#Calls in evening* and *weekends*, we also confirmed that people prefer not to have calls with *work* contacts after work-hours and on weekends.

To evaluate the life facet classification, we built a model with SVMs (Polynomial kernel, $d = 2$). Since an SVM is originally a binary classifier, we built 3 pairwise SVMs (*family*-vs.-*work*, *family*-vs.-*social*, and *work*-vs.-*social*) and combined their outputs with a maximum voting method. We also compared the result with two different models using WEKA [21]: rule-based model (decision tree C4.5) and probabilistic model (naïve Bayes, NB). All the models were tested on three types of evaluation data sets shown in Table 3.

For the *70-contact list* data set, the SVMs showed 65.5% accuracy with survey features and increased to 81.0% when using all features (see Table 4). Note that half of the contacts in the *70-contact list* were Facebook friends, that is, they did not have profile and mobile-communication feature data. Nevertheless, the combination of all features achieved a 15.5% improvement in accuracy. Using profile and mobile-communication features together (without survey features), the SVMs yielded 68.5% of accuracy on the *in-phonebook list* and 88% for contacts that users actually communicated with (the *communication list* set).

When we used the profile features alone, all the classifiers showed lower accuracies since our participants did not have enough contact information in their phonebook (see Figure 3b). For example, on the *in-phonebook list*, SVMs yielded only 51.1%. Table 5a shows the confusion matrix of this result. There were 396 total *family* members evaluated; 175 were correctly classified as *family*, while 186 and 35 were misclassified as *work* and *social*, respectively. Interestingly, the profile features were effective in classifying *work*-type contacts but were not so for the other facets. This is because the profile features that strongly correlated with the *family* facet, like *last name* and *Is-starred*, were missing on many contacts or only associated with a few strongest ties. On the other hand, we could classify *family* and *social* contacts correctly by using mobile communication features while many of the *work*-type contacts were confused as *social* because of no communication logs (see Table 5b).

The combination of profile and communication features failed to classify the *work* facet, shown in Table 5(b, c). We have two possible explanations. First, the number of the profile features was much smaller than the number of the communication features (17 vs. 136), and thus might be less influential within the combined feature vector. Second, the profile features had many missing values and SVM cannot handle missing values well. To address these issues, we need a feature selection scheme or classifier combination approach with two different models built on each type of features. We defer this line of investigation to future work.

As shown in Tables 5(c, d), features from the survey reports (*same gender*, *age difference*, *face-to-face communication frequency*, and *is-Facebook friend*) resolved confusions on *work*-type contacts. Since the communication features are continuous values, SVMs performed better than the other algorithms. Meanwhile, C4.5 and NB showed higher accuracies on the survey and profile features which consist of discrete values. For the combination of the features, however, the SVMs performed much better than the others.

(a)	***Family***	***Work***	***Social***
Family	175	186	35
Work	68	247	71
Social	77	160	202

(b)	***Family***	***Work***	***Social***
Family	288	31	76
Work	49	111	198
Social	15	23	430

(c)	***Family***	***Work***	***Social***
Family	290	28	76
Work	46	114	198
Social	15	22	432

(d)	***Family***	***Work***	***Social***
Family	298	43	53
Work	27	305	44
Social	20	20	411

Table 5. Confusion matrices (row: actual, column: predicted) of SVMs for the *in-phonebook list*: the (a) profile, (b) mobile-communication, (c) both profile and communication, and (d) using all (including survey features) features. Row sum of each matrix are different because of multi-labeled samples.

	Feature name	**Info. gain (corr.)**	**Feature values and sample distribution (target : rest facets)**
F	Total dur. calls	0.547 (+)	>588 (0.90:0.11)
	Total #lengthy-calls	0.481 (+)	>2 (0.73:0.04)
	#Calls on Sun. / total COMMs	0.478 (+)	>0.02 (0.83:0.10)
	Dur. calls on Sun. / total calls	0.470 (+)	>0 (0.83:0.11)
	#Calls on Sun. / total calls	0.470 (+)	>0 (0.83:0.11)
W	Total dur. calls	0.225 (-)	>16 & ≤588 (0.65:0.17)
	Total #calls	0.217 (-)	>1 & ≤4 (0.52:0.08)
	Dur. calls on weekdays / total calls	0.144 (+)	>0.20 (0.48:0.11)
	MAX dur. incoming calls	0.140 (-)	>16 & ≤574 (0.65:0.26)
	#Calls on weekdays / total calls	0.140 (+)	>0.2 (0.40:0.08)
S	Total dur. calls	0.442 (-)	≤16 (0.72:0.09)
	#Days called / days logged	0.441 (-)	≤0.01 (0.75:0.08)
	Total #calls	0.425 (-)	≤0 (0.69:0.08)
	#Calls / total COMMs	0.421 (-)	≤0.06 (0.80:0.13)
	(#Calls / COMMs) on weekday	0.396 (-)	≤ 0.02 (0.85:0.16)

Table 6. Top five information gain (with ranker [21]) features to predict each facet (for *communication list* data; using profile and communication features together). Examples of feature values depict participants' general contact behaviors.

Table 6 shows the top five information gain features for each life facet, where the signs denote positive or negative correlations. For example, *Total duration of calls* was the strongest feature to recognize *family* facet, where the participants had longer calls (duration > 588 sec.) with their *family*-type contacts (90% of *family* contacts) and not with *work* and *social* contacts (11% of them), denoted as "0.90:0.11" in the table. *Family* was also positively associated with the lengthy-call features and Sunday-calls.

For the *work*-type relationships, call intensity features (number and duration of calls) were negatively correlated and the ratio of *weekday calls* over *total calls* was positively associated with. Participants communicated with their *social* contacts via SMS for weekdays (negative *#Calls / COMMs on weekday*). *#Days messaged* and *#Calls on Sunday* were also a negatively associated to the *work* facet (which are not shown in Table 6). After-work communications (positive *#Outgoing COMMs in evening* and negative *#Calls in morning*) and text messaging (positive *Total length of MSGs* and *#Replied MSGs*; less intensive calls) were the characteristics of *social*-type communications for our participants.

The feature values listed in Table 6 might be affected by several factors such as a logging period, user's mobile plans like unlimited SMS, and his/her personality (e.g. extrovert vs. introvert). However, the table depicts how people communicate by different facets of life, showing these patterns as concrete examples.

DISCUSSION AND FUTURE WORK

We achieved 90.5% accuracy for classifying contacts that the participant communicated with, and 83.1% for classifying all contacts in the participant's phonebook list. For each participant (by leave-one-contact-out cross validation), our model yielded 91.2% accuracy (Max = 100%, Min = 50%, and σ = 11.6), which shows its effectiveness across the different participants except for some uncommon cases. An open question is how good a system would need to be in order to effectively enhance different kinds of applications.

In our test results, errors were mainly due to the lack of information, such as minimal profile information or no call/message logs. For example, we could achieve a 14.6% improvement when we used survey features along with the profile and mobile communication features for the *in-phonebook list* data set. However, another open question here is how important it is to classify these individuals. On the one hand, no information suggests that the contact may not be important to the participant. On the other hand, the availability of alternative forms of communication—such as email, iMessage, Skype, Facebook chat, and more—means that these data are not easily available. For example, in our data set, people did not have mobile communications with over half of their phonebook contacts, including 38% of their close contacts (see Figure 2). Both of these questions are issues we plan on exploring in future work.

One limitation of our work is the maximum size of logs stored. By default, Android stores only 500 recent calls and 200 messages per contact. The logs we gathered contained roughly 100 days of communications on average. Another limitation of the results is a relatively small sample size ($n = 40$). Since our work is a preliminary study with a limited group of subjects who live in US and have been using smartphone and Facebook, we could not say that our results reflect general patterns of interaction that people have (we did not present generalizability of our results as well). There also exists a possible self-selection bias, in that potential participants concerned about privacy might not participate in our study even they aware of our privacy protection policy. Nevertheless, our results suggest that there is potential for automated tools that can help classify relationship types.

Certain aspects of a relationship such as the duration and history are difficult to measure using a data driven approach. In this paper, we explored how far we can go with relatively straightforward methods, saw where these methods fall short, and then saw what other kinds of data and features can help improve the models. For instance, incorporating location data into our models could give a better sense as to whom a person spend time with, and how much "effort" a person has put into meeting someone. As a concrete example, one idea would be to put more weight on the people contacted when a person goes to a different city. Cranshaw *et al.* showed that co-location features could be used to infer friendship between individuals [10]. Mok *et al.* found that frequency of both face and non-face communication declines with increasing distance [31]. There may be additional correlations between this behavioral pattern and the type of relationships.

Lastly, we focused on three common life facets, but as shown in Table 1, there are a variety of relationships within each facet. Misalignment between different life facets could cause many problems like inappropriate sharing, but fusing different sub-facets into one higher-order class could also be unsuitable. For example, both co-workers and clients are in the *work* facet but these two relationships are totally different in terms of their type of interaction that take place and information sharing concerns to a user. We also speculate that it may be more effective overall to have five facets, with the two new facets being school and maintenance. In our study, we saw student participants struggle with classifying people as *social* or *work*, and having a specific facet for this purpose could mitigate this problem. Adding a maintenance facet would capture contacts that do not match the other facets such as auto repair, doctor, and pizza shop. These kinds of contacts were excluded in our study, but were something that some participants commented on.

CONCLUSION

People have distinct domains within which they enact different roles, called life facets, and *family*, *work*, and *social* are people's common facets. In this paper, we defined a set of smartphone features to help classify the life facet of a contact, using profile information as well as five categories of communication behaviors, including *intensity*, *regularity*, *temporal tendency*, *channel selection & avoidance*, and *maintenance cost*.

Our models were evaluated with 40 participants. For contacts that the participant had any communication with in their smartphone logs, we could classify those contacts with 90.5% accuracy. For *family*, call intensity was positively associated. For *work*, call intensity (negatively correlated) and weekday communication behaviors were the strongest factors. For *social*, channel selection (preferring to use SMS) and communications on weekends were the most relevant features. We also found that using different modalities of features together could improve the accuracy.

ACKNOWLEDGMENTS

This work is sponsored in part by Defense Advanced Research Projects Agency (DARPA) Information Innovation Office (I2O) Program: Detection and Computational Analysis of Psychological Signals (DCAPS), ARPA Order No. 9464-00, Program Code: CHEL5, issued by SPAWAR System Center-Pacific under Contract No. N66001-12-C-4196. The views and conclusions contained in this document are those of the authors and should not be interpreted as representing the official policies, either expressly or implied, of the DARPA of the U.S. Government. The first author was also supported by the National Research Foundation of Korea (NRF-2011-357-D00210).

REFERENCES

1. Ackerman, J.M., Kenrick, D.T., and Schaller, M. Is friendship akin to kinship? *Evolution and Human Behavior*, 28 (2007), 365-374.
2. Altshuler, Y., Fire, M., Aharony, N., Elovici, Y., and Pentland, A. How many makes a crowd? On the evolution of learning as a factor of community coverage. In *Proc. Int. Conf. on Social Computing, Behavioral-Cultural Modeling, and Prediction* (2012), 43-52.
3. Backstrom, L., Huttenlocher, D., Kleinberg, J., and Lan, X. Group formation in large social networks: membership, growth, and evolution. In *Proc. KDD '06* (2006), 44-54.
4. Battestini, A., Setlur, V., and Sohn, T. A large scale study of text-messaging use. In *Proc. MobileHCI '10* (2010), 229-238.
5. Burke, M. *Reading, Writing, Relationships: The Impact of Social Network Sites on Relationships and Well-Being.* Carnegie Mellon University, Pittsburgh, Pennsylvania, 2011.

6. Chau, M. and Xu, J. Mining communities and their relationships in blogs: A study of online hate groups. *Int. J. of Human-Computer Studies*, 65 (2007), 57-70.
7. Chittaranjan, G., Blom, J., and Gatica-Perez, D. Mining large-scale smartphone data for personality studies. *Personal and Ubiquitous Computing*, (in Press).
8. Christakis, N.A. and Fowler, J.H. *Connected: The Surprising Power of Our Social Networks and How They Shape Our Lives*. Little, Brown and Company, New York, 2009.
9. Clark, S.C. Work/family border theory: A new theory of work/family balance. *Human Relations*, 53, (2000), 747-770.
10. Cranshaw, J., Toch, E., Hong, J., Kittur, A., and Sadeh, N. Bridging the gap between physical location and online social networks. In *Proc. Ubicomp '10* (2010), 119-128.
11. Cummings, J.N., Lee, J.B., and Kraut, R. *Communication technology and friendship during the transition from high school to college*. New York: Oxford University Press, City, 2006.
12. DiMicco, J.M. and Millen, D.R. Identity management: Multiple presentations of self in Facebook. In *Proc. GROUP '07* (2007), 383-386.
13. Do, T.M.T. and Gatica-Perez, D. Human interaction discovery in smartphone proximity networks. *Personal and Ubiquitous Computing*, (in Press).
14. Dong, W., Lepri, B., and Pentland, A. Modeling the co-evolution of behaviors and social relationships using mobile phone data. In *Proc. MUM '11* (2011), 134-143.
15. Eagle, N. and Pentland, A. Reality mining: Sensing complex social systems. *Personal and Ubiquitous Computing*, 10 (2006), 255-268.
16. Eagle, N., Pentland, A., and Lazer, D. Inferring social network structure using mobile phone data. *Proc. National Academy of Sciences*, 106, 36 (2009), 15274-15278.
17. Farnham, S. and Churchill, E.F. Faceted identity, faceted lives: Social and technical issues with being yourself online. In *Proc. CSCW 2011* (2011), 359-368.
18. Gilbert, E. and Karahalios, K. Predicting tie strength with social media. In *Proc. Int. Conf. on Human Factors in Computing Systems* (2009), 211-220.
19. Granovetter, M.S. The strength of weak ties. *The American Journal of Sociology*, 78, 6 (1973), 1360-1380.
20. Grob, R., Kuhn, M., Wattenhofer, R., and Wirz, M. Cluestr: mobile social networking for enhanced group communication. In. *Proc. Group '09* (2009), 81-90.
21. Hall, M., Frank, E., Holmes, G., Pfahringer, B., Reutemann, P., and Witten, I.H. The WEKA data mining software: An update. *SIGKDD Explorations*, 11, 1 (2009), 10-18.
22. Hill, R.A. and Dunbar, R.I.M. Social network size in humans. *Human Nature*, 14 (2003), 53-72.
23. Http://www.cbsnews.com/8301-501465_162-20105561-501465.html
24. Jones, S. and O'Neill, E. Feasibility of structural network clustering for group-based privacy control in social networks. In *Proc. SOUPS* (2010), 1-13.
25. Kelley, P.G., Brewer, R., Mayer, Y., Cranor, L.F., and Sadeh, N.M. An Investigation into Facebook Friend Grouping. In *Proc. INTERACT* (2011), 216-233.
26. Lampinen, A., Tamminen, S., and Oulasvirta, A. All my people right here, right now: Management of group co-presence on a social networking site. In *Proc. GROUP '09* (2009), 281- 290.
27. Madan, A., Cebrian, M., Lazer, D., and Pentland, A. Social sensing for epidemiological behavior change. In *Proc. Ubicomp '10* (2010), 291-300.
28. McCarty, C. Structure in personal networks. *J. of Social Structure*, 3 (2005).
29. Mesch, G.S. Social context and communication channels choice among adolescents. *Computers in Human Behavior*, 25 (2009), 244-251.
30. Min, J.-K. and Cho, S.-B. Mobile human network management and recommendation by probabilistic social mining. *IEEE Trans. on Systems, Man, and Cybernetics, Part B: Cybernetics*, 41, 3 (2011), 761-771.
31. Mok, D., Wellman, B., and Basu, R. Did distance matter before the Internet? Interpersonal contact and support in the 1970s. *Social Networks*, 29 (2007), 430-461.
32. Newman, M.E.J. Detecting community structure in networks. *The European Physical Journal B - Condensed Matter and Complex Systems*, 38 (2004), 321-330.
33. Nippert-Eng, C.E. *Home and Work*. The University of Chicago Press, 1995.
34. Olson, J., Grudin, J., and Horvitz, E. A study of preferences for sharing and privacy. In *Proc. CHI '05* (2005), 1985-1988.
35. Onnela, J.-P., Saramäki, J., Hyvönen, J., Szabó, G., Lazer, D., Kaski, K.,Kertész, J., and Barabási, A.-L. Structure and tie strengths in mobile communication networks. *Proc. National Academy of Sciences*, 104 (2007), 7332-7336.
36. Ozenc, F.K. and Farnham, S.D. Life "modes" in social media. In *Proc. CHI '11* (2011), 561-570.
37. Roberts, S.G.B. and Dunbar, R.I.M. Communication in social networks: Effects of kinship, network size, and emotional closeness. *Personal Relationships*, 18 (2011), 439-452.
38. Skeels, M.M. and Grudin, J. When social networks cross boundaries: A case study of workplace use of Facebook and LinkedIn. In *Proc. GROUP '09* (2009), 95-104.
39. Spencer, L. and Pahl, R.E. *Rethinking Friendship: Hidden Solidarities Today*. Princeton University Press, 2006.
40. Tajfel, H. *Differentiation Between Social Groups: Studies in the Social Psychology of Intergroup Relations*. London: Academic Press, 1978.
41. Wiese, J., Kelley, P.G., Cranor, L.F., Dabbish, L., Hong, J.I., and Zimmerman, J. Are you close with me? Are you nearby? Investigating social groups, closeness, and willingness to share. In *Proc. UbiComp '11* (2011), 197-206.
42. Wilson, C., Boe, B., Sala, A., Puttaswamy, K.P.N., and Zhao, B.Y. User interactions in social networks and their implications. In *Proc. the 4th ACM European Conference on Computer Systems* (2009), 205-218.

Mining Social Relationship Types in an Organization using Communication Patterns

Jinhyuk Choi, Seongkook Heo, Jaehyun Han, Geehyuk Lee, Junehwa Song
Computer Science Department, KAIST, Daejeon, Republic of Korea
demon@kaist.ac.kr, {leodic, jay.jaehyun, geehyuk}@gmail.com, junesong@nclab.kaist.ac.kr

ABSTRACT
Our goal is to show that it is possible to automatically infer social relationship types among people who stay together in an organization by analyzing communication patterns. We collected indoor co-location data and instant messenger data from 22 participants for one month. Based on the data, we designed and explored several indicators which are considered to be useful for mining social relationship types. We applied machine learning techniques using the indicators and found that it is possible to develop an intelligent method to infer social relationship types.

Author Keywords
Social relationship, relationship mining

ACM Classification Keywords
J.4 [Computer Applications]: Social and Behavioral Sciences – Sociology.

INTRODUCTION
People are social beings, spending most of their time interacting with others. Within any organization, while people collaborate with others in a work relationship, they also share the distractions of personal relationships. In other words, there are both social (informal) and production (formal) relations between members of an organization. According to [29], the social relation can be defined in opposition to the production relation because the social relation is not strictly related to members' work as employees. Production relations may be regarded as artificial relationships between colleagues who share the common goal of handling matters related to work; social relations are natural relationships based on interpersonal intimacy.

Many studies reveal that understanding the patterns of such relationships plays a significant role in achieving organizational goals. For example, informal, or horizontal, social relations among members seem to encourage commitment to the organization and cooperation in the workplace [7, 15, 29]. Forming a team with members who share informal relations, or enhancing the informal relations among team members, leads to improved team performance. Similarly, [1] and [12] show that the social network is as least as important as the official organizational structure for tasks ranging from immediate, local problem-solving ones (e.g., fixing a piece of equipment) to primary work functions, such as creating project teams. Therefore, finding extant social relationship types among members is important for understanding the current state of the organization.

From this point of view, we aim to create an individual intelligent agent that monitors its host user all the time and discovers social relationship types existing between its host user and other users, which can then be implemented to enhance the informal relations between its host user and other users, ultimately improving the performance of the organization that the users belongs to. For examples, based on the relationship information, the intelligent agent may recommend its host user to participate in social activities such as joint gymnastic sessions or after-work activities [2, 29] in order to make intimate relationship with a particular colleague. We may extend the agent to an organization level for some types of organizations; the agent monitors social relationship types among organization members and uses relationship information for the purpose of enhancing the communication channels for the members.

However, the formation of a social relationship can take a significant period of time and can also change dynamically and vary from individual to individual, making the identification of these relationships difficult. This means that we must first study which data to use, and how to use it, in order to identify social relationship types among organization members.

In this paper, we report the results of an initial study conducted to show the possibility of determining social relationship types among co-workers. We divided these social relationships into two types: formal and informal. We then extracted several indicators from the communication patterns that can be easily collected through cell phones and personal computers. Based on the results of our analyses, we explored a method through which social relationship types can be inferred automatically.

RELATED WORK
Social scientists have emphasized the importance of social relationships among people within an organization for achieving common goals [17, 21, 22, 23, 29]. It is well

known that human resource management determines organizational success [8], and that cooperative social relations facilitate cooperation among the members of a workplace [29]. Researchers have also studied various social relationship types. In particular, [29] divided personal relationships in an organization into two types—production and social relationships—and claimed that these two types of relationships have their own unique characteristics. Moreover, some researchers argue that one of the most important factors in distributing and sharing information and technology within an organization is the informal network of collaborators, colleagues, and friends [9, 16, 30]. In parallel with the view taken by previous studies, we concern ourselves with the challenges inherent in developing a system for mining and utilizing information on the social relationship between each member of an organization.

Despite previous theoretical research on the importance of understanding the nature of social relationship types, most studies attempting to mine social relationships focus on finding the strength of a relationship or on finding methodologies to recommend new friends to people. Most attempts in the field of social relationship mining utilize current friend relationships, personal profiles, or shared user content [10]. Many services have exploited the user profiles or communicated data stored within an online community or on-line social networking service such as Twitter or Facebook [19, 20, 28]. However, these examples have a limitation in that the profiles contain only static data such as the age, gender, hometown, and cultural background of the user, and thus they do not reflect any dynamic characteristics. In addition, online data can only be found in cyberspace, which does not reflect the characteristics of relationships among people who have direct contact with other people within the physical environments of their everyday lives.

In contrast, there have been attempts to use real world interactions to understand social relationships. Various studies utilize co-location data in this sense; some utilize wide area location information such as GPS, with others using indoor location information. Studies that used indoor information made use of Wi-Fi, RFID, Bluetooth, or Microphones to gather location information [6, 19, 26, 31, 32, 33]. Among them, [6, 19, 26, 32, 33] suggested a method of extracting new social connections by analyzing user patterns, the duration of each encounter with other people, and the number and location of encounters. Particularly, [5] attempted to identify interpersonal relationships (workplace colleagues, outside friends, people within a user's circle of friends) by exploiting periodical patterns shown by proximity, time, and location data collected from mobile phones.

Phone call logs have also been utilized for social network analysis. [24] extracted manifold features from mobile phone call logs—the number of calls, amount of time spent talking, and time that calls were either received or made—and analyzed these to understand their use in discovering which social group the user belongs to, then classifying them using a machine learning based classifier. [4] ran a mobile social network analysis, taking into account only whether or not a call has been made between users.

The most representative case using the e-mail exchange patterns in social network analysis is [14], and they used recipient list size, number of e-mails sent from the receiver to the sender, time elapsed since the last observed e-mail activity of the receiver, and e-mail size in bytes to create a "friends-of-friends" relationship graph, and then they augmented users' contact list based on those relationships.

However, most of the above studies target only large-scale social networks, or bear no relation to mining the types of social relationships themselves. To the best of our knowledge, there have been very few, if any, studies that propose methods to automatically recognize social relationship types among people in an organization, which can then be used as the basis for a system to exploit those types of relationships between each organizational member.

PROBLEM AND APPROACH

Generally, the physical location of an organization is composed of offices, meeting rooms, and lounges. People use each part of the space appropriately. People exchange information and share personal intimacy with others while conducting work-related communication in these spaces. Such instances of communication are made face-to-face or remotely via telephone calls, e-mails, and messengers. This is why we believe different types of relationships between each organization member can be mined by analyzing various sources of evidence such as co-location patterns, intended use of places, and remote communication patterns among members.

Co-location data is one of the most basic forms of data used by previous studies in an attempt to mine social relationships. Face-to-face conversations may be called the most basic method of communication, and we can generally assume that formal activities will most likely take place in meeting rooms and offices and that informal activities will occur in places such as lounges. We therefore believe that those data to be most important for inferring social relationship types. Co-location data indicates when, and how many times, a user visits a particular location at the same time as other users, and for how long. We also expected that location information (i.e., where people meet others) would be an important indicator.

Because users can communicate with others without seeing them face-to-face, instant messenger data were collected from users' personal computers to determine when and how many times a user communicates remotely with other users. We selected instant messenger data as a useful indicator for inferring different social relationship types since unlike e-mail, it is largely used for real-time communication; by

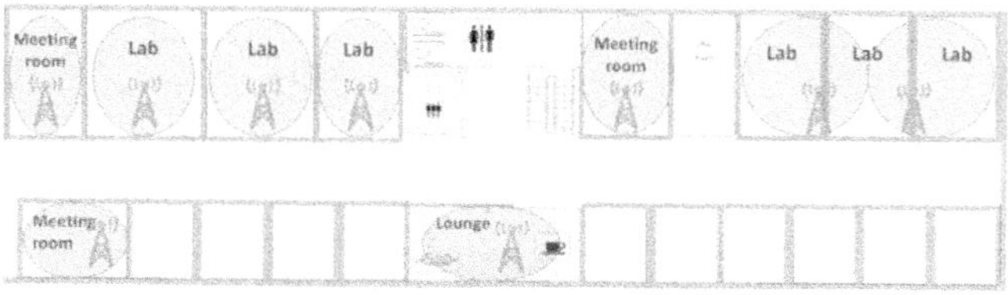

Figure 1. Map of the experimental space.

using this service, users can communicate with others without having to worry about their conversations being exposed in a shared location, unlike verbal communication through a cell phone. Such characteristics led us to believe that data patterns derived from instant messaging would properly indicate social (informal) relations. Messenger messages are also synchronous, providing easy access to various data such as the duration and number of communications. Previous studies showed that the rate of each member in a firm using instant messengers as a means of communication was very high and that using communication patterns are useful for examining mutual intimacy among members [13, 25].

Our goal is to explore a method through which social relationship types can be inferred without the user's participation, based on data that can be easily collected. As an early study, we used only indoor co-location data and instant messenger data. We understand that increased data can enhance performance. However, we extract several indicators from the data patterns, and use these to test the usefulness of each indicator, applying a machine learning based method of classification.

DATA COLLECTION

We collected two types of data potentially useful for inferring social relationship type: co-location data and instant messenger data. We also carried out surveys to determine real relationships among users. Twenty-two graduate students working on the same floor of the same building participated in our month-long experiment.

Co-location Data

To determine users' locations, we installed nine Bluetooth stations in the laboratories, meeting rooms, and lounge, as shown in Figure 1. These Bluetooth stations scanned the surrounding area at a radius of approximately 10 m, at a 20s frequency, and collected the Bluetooth IDs of devices within this area to determine their current location. During the experimental period, users kept the Bluetooth terminals of their cell phones switched on in order to allow the stations to detect their location.

Bluetooth dongles were covered with conductive bags to control the size of the scanning area. However, several cases make it possible for some noise to be included in the data. For instance, one ID can be detected from two or more stations at the same time, or the range of detection can vary according to the status of the phones. In an actual user environment, there are gray areas in between places, and the location detection system can have some type of

No	Question	Answer
1	Do you have frequent conversations with him/her about personal topics such as entertainment, sports, private affairs, and so on?	0 – never 1 – rarely 2 – occasionally 3 – frequently 4 – very frequently
2	Do you have conversations with him/her frequently about topics that are related with your works?	

Table 1. Survey Questions

internal error, and this initial study, therefore, regards them as natural noise.

Instant Messenger Data

In this study, we installed specialized logging software on users' personal computers to collect the conversation patterns of their instant messenger programs. The logging software operated in stealth mode, recording the names of participants conversed with by participants as well as the time of the conversation at one minute intervals. The contents of the conversation were considered private and, therefore, were not logged.

User Information

From our survey, we collected general information on users and their real social relationships. Among the 22 participants, 2 are female. The average age of the participants is 29.9. All participants are computer science majors, each from one of seven different concentrations, namely Computer graphics; Computer networks; Database systems; Computer architecture; Human-computer interaction; Information retrieval; and Distributed systems. Participants sharing the same concentration had their seats close to each other in a lab and regular meetings in the meeting room, with each concentration holding a meeting on a different day. There were tables, chairs, and vending machines in the lounge, providing a place to rest.

Our survey on relationships consisted of two questions, listed in Table 1. The first question was asked in order to determine each user's level of informal relationship with other participants, and the second question to determine the level of formal relationships. The participants provided their answers to these questions based on a 5-point Likert scale. Table 2 shows the number of relationships assigned a high value (>2) by users (in this study, we regarded user A's answers for user B, and user B's answers for user A, as being independent). As we can also see in Table 2, 46% of highly valued relationships are commonly found in the answers for both questions.

Highly informal relationships(HIR)	Highly formal relationships(HFR)	HIR ∩ HFR
Question 1 (>=2)	Question 2 (>=2)	Question 1 (>=2) ∩ Question 2 (>=2)
118	97	68

Table 2. Number of high level relationships

Indicators from co-location data	co-visit-duration co-visit-frequency co-visit-average-duration co-visit-hour-regularity co-visit-weekday-regularity
Indicators from instant messenger data	mess-comm-duration mess-comm number mess-comm-ave-time

Table 3. List of indicators

DATA ANALYSIS

From co-location and instant messenger data, we extracted several indicators considered useful for mining social relationship types. Table 3 shows these indicators.

Indicators from the Co-location Data

Since the time and place in which user i and j have a conversation can vary according to the social relationship types and the intimacy between the two users, we measured how long a particular user i stays with another user j at a particular location (co-visit duration, T_{ij}^k). To obtain the co-visit duration, we divided the duration in which user i and another user j remained at the same location by the total duration in which user i stayed at that location, because there may be distinctive communication patterns for each individual. The co-visit duration was calculated for the laboratories, meeting rooms, and lounge (the duration was obtained by counting the number of detections as we can see in Figure 2).

$$T_{ij}^k = \frac{t_{ij}^k}{t_i^k}$$

Here, t_{ij}^k represents the total number of instances that users i and j were detected at place k at the same time, and t_i^k represents the total number of times that user i was detected at place k.

Since the place and number of communications can differ according to social relationship type and the degree of intimacy between a particular user i and j, we measured how often a particular user i visited a location with another user j (co-visit-frequency, F_{ij}^k). In order to obtain the co-visit frequency, we divided the number of visits, f_{ij}^k, during which two users visited the same location, by the number of visits, f_i^k, during which one user visited that location. The co-visit-frequency was calculated for the laboratories, meeting rooms, and lounge (the number of visits was obtained by counting the number of groups of continuous detection as we can see in Figure 2).

$$F_{ij}^k = \frac{f_{ij}^k}{f_i^k}$$

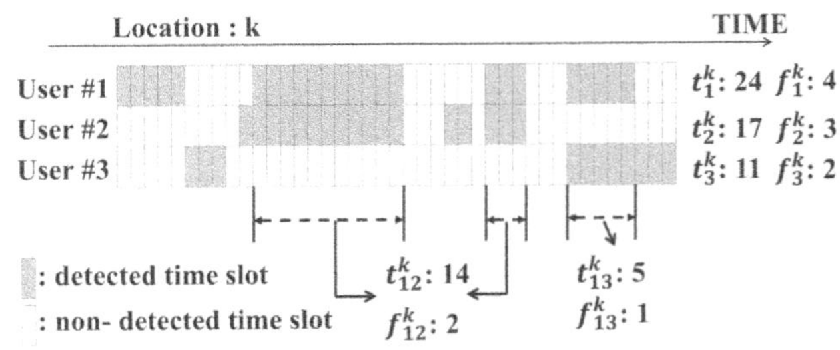

Figure 2. Concept of co-location indicators at location k.

We also measured the average duration in which a user i stayed with another user j at a particular location (co-visit-average-duration, AT_{ij}^k) as follows:

$$AT_{ij}^k = \frac{T_{ij}^k}{F_{ij}^k}.$$

In addition, we measured how regularly two users i and j met at a particular location. We found the maximum regularities at the hourly (co-visit-hour-regularity) and weekly levels (co-visit-weekday-regularity). If the two people meet at 10 every morning, the co-visit-hour-regularity goes up. If they meet up more on a particular day, the co-visit-weekday-regularity rises. We decided to find these regularities, as we expected that there would be more chances for users who have formal relationships to have regular meetings.

Indicators from Instant Messenger Data

Similar to co-location data, we measured how long and how many times a user communicated with other users using instant messenger (mess-comm-duration and mess-comm number). The average amount of time that passed while a user talked with other users (mess-comm-ave-time) was also measured. The regularity features of messenger communications were not included because we could not find any evidence of a pattern from the messenger communications.

Analyses of Indicators

We designed two classification problems. The first problem was to find the Highly Informal Relationships (HIRs) from all relationships. We divided the relationships into two classes, HIRs and non-HIRs, and explored our data to see whether the indicators existed to determine the HIRs (HIR classification). The second problem was to classify the Highly Formal Relationships (HFRs) and non-HFRs (HFR classification) in the same way as in the HIR classification.

We measured the Information Gain (IG) [27] of each indicator value. The IG of each indicator shows how much information an indicator provides for the current classification task. Table 4 shows how useful the indicators are in both HIR and HFR classification. As we can see in the figure, we found that co-visit duration in the lounge, co-visit frequency in the lounge, weekly co-visit regularity in the lounge, and the instant messenger indicators, are more

Rank	HIR classification (Location)	IG	HFR classification (Location)	IG
1	co-visit-duration (Lounge)	0.1812	co-visit-frequency (Meeting room)	0.1346
2	co-visit-frequency (Lounge)	0.1763	co-visit-average-duration (Meeting room)	0.1227
3	co-visit-weekday-regularity (Lounge)	0.1412	mess-comm number	0.1029
4	mess-comm number	0.1361	mess-comm-duration	0.1029
5	mess-comm-duration	0.1361	mess-comm-ave-time	0.0986
6	mess-comm-ave-time	0.1290	co-visit-hour-regularity (Meeting room)	0.0876
7	co-visit-hour-regularity (Lounge)	0.1178	co-visit-weekday-regularity (Meeting room)	0.0855
8	co-visit-frequency (Meeting room)	0.1026	co-visit-duration (Lounge)	0.0812
9	co-visit-hour-regularity (Lab)	0.1007	co-visit-hour-regularity (Lab)	0.0762
10	co-visit-average-duration (Lounge)	0.1	co-visit-frequency (Meeting room)	0.0702
11	co-visit-hour-regularity (Meeting room)	0.0916	co-visit-weekday-regularity (Lab)	0.0580
12	co-visit-weekday-regularity (Lab)	0.0916	co-visit-frequency (Lab)	0.0565
13	co-visit-weekday-regularity (Meeting room)	0.0887	co-visit-average-duration (Lab)	0.0559
14	co-visit-average-duration (Meeting room)	0.0864	co-visit-frequency (Lounge)	0.0533
15	co-visit-frequency (Lab)	0.0802	co-visit-weekday-regularity (Lounge)	0.0488
16	co-visit-average-duration (Lab)	0.0778	co-visit-duration (Lab)	0.0376
17	co-visit-frequency (Meeting room)	0.0729	co-visit-hour-regularity (Lounge)	0.0315
18	co-visit-duration (Lab)	0.0316	co-visit-average-duration (Lounge)	0.0278

Table 4. Rank of indicators by their information gain (IG)

useful than other indicators for HIR classification. This indicates that co-location patterns in the lounge play a more important role in determining the HIRs. On the other hand, in contrast to HIR classification, the co-location patterns in the meeting rooms are more important for determining HFRs. Interestingly, the instant messenger indicators play a role in both classification problems. This result is in contrast to our anticipation that instant messengers are useful for discovering informal relations. The co-location indicator values for the laboratories were not very useful. We believe that this low level of usefulness is due to the fact that users have spent much more time with other users in laboratories than at other locations.

MINING THE TYPES OF SOCIAL RELATIONSHIPS

We transformed each possible relationship into a multi-dimensional vector in which each element represents an indicator value. We then applied machine learning techniques using WEKA [11] to see whether HIRs and HFRs can be classified automatically. Table 5 shows the accuracy of the classification tasks (10-fold cross validation) after we applied a Decision tree and a Bayesian network. The Bayesian network was constructed using a K2 structure learning algorithm [3]. As we can see from the table, the overall classification accuracy is approximately 85% for both the HIR and HFR classifications. The Bayesian network showed a slightly better performance than the Decision tree. Notice the much greater number of non-HIR (non-HFR) relationships than HIR (HFR) relationships.

HIR classification	Decision Tree			Bayesian network		
	Precision	Recall	F-measure	Precision	Recall	F-measure
Non-HIR	0.95	0.81	0.87	0.97	0.86	0.91
HIR	0.56	0.83	0.67	0.60	0.88	0.71
Total	0.81			0.86		

(a) HIR classification

HFR classification	Decision Tree			Bayesian network		
	Precision	Recall	F-measure	Precision	Recall	F-measure
Non-HFR	0.95	0.85	0.91	0.97	0.89	0.93
HFR	0.58	0.83	0.68	0.67	0.88	0.76
Total	0.85			0.89		

(b) HFR classification

Table 5. Accuracy of classification tasks

To verify whether an individual intelligent agent can generally use this method, we built and tested the same model using "leave-one-out cross validation." We trained the Bayesian network model using all user data excluding a single user's data, and then tested the model using the excluded user data. Table 6 shows the total accuracy of the classification tasks for 12 users. Actually, we excluded 10 of the users from this test as their numbers of HIRs or HFRs were too small. Generally, the classification accuracy of the model was around 75% for both HIR and HFR classifications. This shows that we can construct a common model for both classification types useable by all individual intelligent agents. Considering the fact that we used only a limited amount of easily collectable data, these results are impressive enough to justify future research.

DISCUSSION AND CONCLUSION

We performed a study to find useful indicators for inferring social relationship types among people in contact with each other during their daily lives, using their communication patterns within an organization. We showed that there is a high possibility of inferring social relationship type with a small amount of easily obtainable data. Using the inferred social relationship types, we believe we can build an intelligent system that is able to comprehend the current status of an organization or enhance communication between each member of that organization.

User Number	1	2	3	4	5	6	7	8	9	10	11	12
HIR classification	76	82	68	70	77	75	81	79	80	73	75	72
HFR classification	77	70	75	81	69	80	77	68	83	70	82	74

Table 6. Total accuracy of the classification tasks for 12 users

This study is based on the data collected from graduate students whose activity space consists of laboratories, lounges, and meeting rooms, and only half the number of the active members within that space volunteered to participate in this experiment. For this reason, we need to conduct additional research on an organization with more diverse types of spaces and personnel. Looking at what has been accomplished so far, we believe we can achieve comparable results with an organization in which members collaborate through communication and where each place has a distinct purpose. Furthermore, in the case of an organization with greater size and number of members, there will be a need for a more efficient algorithm that specializes in dealing with bigger organizations. Based on these preliminary findings, we will conduct more extended research towards a system with which we can recognize social relationship types and adapt communication channels among members to improve organizational performance.

ACKNOWLEDGMENTS

We thank all of the subjects who participated in this study, the anonymous reviewers for their invaluable feedback on our work, and Hwon Ihm for his helpful comments that lead to significantly better presentation of our arguments. This work was supported by the IT R&D program of MKE/KEIT. [10039161, Development of core technologies for high-physicality control interfaces and personalized intelligent user interfaces based on Smart TV user experience] and the National Research Foundation of Korea grant funded by the Korea government (MEST) (No. 2012-0005733).

REFERENCES

1. Bernheim, B.D., Whinston, M.D., Multimarket contact and collusive behavior. RAND Journal of Economics 21, 1 (1990), pp. 1-26.
2. Besley, T., Coate, S., Group lending, repayment incentives and social collateral, Journal of Development Economics 46, 1 (1995), p1-18.
3. Cooper, G. and Herskovits, E. A Bayesian Method for the Induction of Probabilistic Networks from Data, Machine Learning, vol. 9, 4 (1992), p309-347.
4. Dong, Z., Song, G., Xie, K., Tang, K., and Wang, J. Statistical analysis of real large-scale mobile social network. In Proc. international conference on Fuzzy systems and knowledge discovery - Volume 2, IEEE Press (2009), p612-616.
5. Eagle, N. and Pentland, A. Reality mining: sensing complex social systems, Journal of Personal and Ubiquitous Computing, 10, 4 (2006), p255-268.
6. Eagle, N. and Pentland, A. Social serendipity: Mobilizing social software. Pervasive Computing, vol. 4, IEEE Press (2005), pp. 28-34.
7. Frey, L.R., and S. Wolf. The Symbolic & Interpretive Perspective on Group Dynamics. Small Group Research 35, 3(2004), 277–316.
8. Gerald R. Ferris, Michelle M. Arthur, Howard M. Berkson, David M. Kaplan, Gloria Harrell-Cook, Dwight D. Frink, Toward a social context theory of the human resource management-organization effectiveness relationship, Human Resource Management Review, Volume 8, Issue 3 (1998), p235-264.
9. Granovetter, M. Strength of weak ties. Amer. J. Sociology 78 (1973), p1360–1380.
10. Guy, I., Ur, S., Ronen, I., Perer, A. and Jacovi, M. Do You Want to Know? Recommending Strangers in the Enterprise. In Proc. ACM CSCW 2011, ACM Press (2011), 285-294.
11. Hall, M., Frank, E., Holmes, G., Pfahringer, B., Reutemann, P., and Witten, I. H. The WEKA data mining software: an update. ACM SIGKDD Explorations Newsletter 11, 1 (2009), 10-18.
12. Henry Kautz, Bart Selman, and Mehul Shah. Referral Web: combining social networks and collaborative filtering. Communications of ACM 40, 3 (1997), p63-65.
13. Hu, Y., Wood, J. F., Smith, V. and Westbrook, N., Friendships through IM: Examining the Relationship between Instant Messaging and Intimacy. Journal of Computer-Mediated Communication, Blackwell Publishing (2004).
14. Karagiannis, T. and Vojnovic, M. Behavioral profiles for advanced email features. In Proc. WWW '09. ACM (2009), p711-720.
15. Katz, D., and R. Kahn. The Social Psychology of Organizations. 2nd ed. New York: John Wiley & Sons (1978).
16. Kraut, R., Galegher, J. and Edigo C. Intellectual Teamwork: Social and Technological Bases for Cooperative Work. Lawrence Erlbaum (1990).
17. Kurland, N. B. and Pelled, L. H. Passing the Word: Toward a Model of Gossip and Power in the Workplace, The Academy of Management Review 25, 2 (2000), p428-438.
18. Lampe, C. Ellison, N. and Steinfield, C. A familiar face(book): profile elements as signals in an online social network. In Proc. CHI '07, ACM Press (2007), p435-444.
19. Lee, Y., Ju, Y., Min, C., Kang, S., Hwang, I., Song, J. CoMon: Cooperative Ambience Monitoring Platform with Continuity and Benefit Awareness, in Proc. MobiSys '12. ACM(2012), p43-56.
20. Li, D., Ding, Y., Sugimoto, C., He, B., Tang, J., Yan, E., Lin, N., Qin, Z., and Dong, T. Modeling Topic and Community Structure in Social Tagging: the TTR-LDA-Community Model, Journal of the American Society for Information Science and Technology, 62 ,9 (2011), p1849-1866.

21. Mehra, A., Kilduff, M. and Brass, D. j. The social Networks of High and Low self-Monitors: Implications for Workplace Performance, Journal of Administrative Science Quarterly 46, 1 (2001), p121-146.
22. Nelson, K. M. and Cooprider, J. G. The Contribution of Shared Knowledge to IS Group Performance, Journal of MIS Quarterly 20, 4, 1996, p409-432.
23. Ogata, H., Yano, Y., Furugori, N., and Jin, Q. Computer Supported Social Networking For Augmenting Cooperation, Comput. Supported Coop. Work 10, 2 (2001), p189-209.
24. Phithakkitnukoon, S. and Dantu, R. Inferring Social Groups Using Call Logs, In Proc. OTM'08 Workshops, Springer (2008), p200-210.
25. Quan-Haase, A., Cothrel, J. and Wellman, B. Instant messaging for collaboration: A case study of a high-tech firm, Journal of Computer-Mediated Communication, Blackwell Publishing (2005).
26. Quercia, D. and Capra, L., Friendsensing: recommending friends using mobile phones. in Proc. ACM RecSys, ACM Press (2009), pp. 273-276.
27. Quinlan, J.R. C4.5: programs for machine learning, Morgan Kaufmann Publishers Inc (1993).
28. Sousa, D., Sarmento, L., and Rodrigues, E. M. (2010). Characterization of the Twitter @replies Network: Are User Ties Social or Topical. In Proc. SMUC'10, ACM Press(2010), p63-70.
29. Spagnolo, G. Social relations and cooperation in organizations, Journal of Economic Behavior & Organization, 38, 1(1999), 1-25.
30. Wasserman, S. and Galaskiewicz, J., Advances in Social Network Analysis. SAGE Publications (1994).
31. Wyatt, D., Choudhury, T., and Bilmes, J. Learning hidden curved exponential family models to infer face-to-face interaction networks from situated speech data. In Proc. national conference on Artificial intelligence - Volume 2, AAAI Press (2008), 732-738.
32. Xu, B., Chin, A., Wang, H., Chang, L., Zhang, K., Yin, F., Wang, H., and Zhang, L., Physical proximity and online user behavior in an indoor mobile social networking application. In Proc. IEEE CPSCom 2011, IEEE Press (2011), p273-282.
33. Xu, B., Chin, A., Wang, H., Using physical context in a mobile social networking application for improving friend recommendations, In Proc. IEEE CPSCom 2011, IEEE Press (2011), p602-609.

Understanding Affect in the Workplace via Social Media

Munmun De Choudhury
Microsoft Research, Redmond, WA 98052

Scott Counts
Microsoft Research, Redmond, WA 98052

{munmund,counts}@microsoft.com

ABSTRACT
We investigate the landscape of affective expression of employees at a large Fortune 500 software corporation via an internal microblogging tool. We present three analyses of emotional expression among employees, based on literature in organizational behavior: its relationship to (1) exogenous/lifestyle and endogenous workplace factors, (2) geography and (3) organizational structure. We find that employees tend to make significant accommodations in affect expression when interacting with others over the organizational hierarchy. We also find that positive affect is expressed through interpersonal communications that connect disparate geographic regions. Our findings have implications for enabling emotional reflection of employees and for management in that they can help uncover emotional patterns associated with episodes of high and low productivity, allowing organizations to improve employee engagement and promote positive attitudes.

Author Keywords
affect; emotion; enterprise; microblog; social media

ACM Classification Keywords
H5.3. Group and Organization Interfaces; Asynchronous interaction; Web-based interaction.

INTRODUCTION
The 'affective climate' of an enterprise constitutes a valuable resource for its operational procedure and its organizational processes and outcomes. For instance, measures of affect of employees may help predict anxiety/ stress levels with respect to company policies, products, or organizational changes. Employment trends including more volatility and insecurity in many industries, more mobility and ability to work remotely, more expectation of or need for active employee participation in decision-making also make it increasingly important for organizations to assess employee affect and reaction to changes. The organization can thereby seek to identify the factors behind employees' joy and satisfaction, as well as their frustration towards difficulty and failure. Ideally such efforts to assess affect culminate in feedback cycles that support action plans for improved emotional counseling, workgroup dynamics, employee collaboration, and organizational structuring in the workplace environment. In short, affect analysis can help enterprises strive for positive change.

CSCW '13, February 23–27, 2013, San Antonio, Texas, USA.

Recognizing the value, organizational behavior researchers have conducted numerous ethnographic studies in a variety of workplace types and settings, validating the influence of affect on work outcomes and workplace dynamics, such as task quality, productivity, creativity, group rapport, user focus, and job satisfaction [1,6,15,29,34,39,41]. For instance, a well-established effect is that creativity in problem-solving is heightened by positive affect and is diminished when a user is in a negative emotional state [1].

Beyond self-reports from relatively small samples of workers, employee affect has been difficult to measure and leverage. Managers at organizations are supposed to monitor it in their groups and feed the information forward; human resources personnel try to monitor it and devise awards and morale events to influence it, and perhaps bring in consultants to deal with problems in a specific group. Each of these methods poses unique challenges and many are decentralized (e.g., relying on managers, who are distributed and may vary widely in the amount of attention and sophistication they give to the affect monitoring).

Annual experience surveys, in which explicit anonymous responses are sought from employees who opt-in to respond, are a common method for getting a reading on company-wide affect in a standardized manner. Although these surveys often allow the employees to enter open-ended comments and feedback on their feelings, thoughts, and attitude towards the organization, they face an inherent limitation due to the large temporal gaps in which they are conducted. The cost, staff time and effort associated with the surveys make it difficult to administer them any more frequently. Consequently, the reflections in these surveys tend to be summary in nature, even possibly imprecise, rather than a record of actual data points collected in the flow of daily work. This means that they lose the context that would tie emotional expression to specific aspects of the daily work schedule. When colleagues are separated geographically, additional complications ensue.

Some organizations today are starting to make sustained use of public, Twitter-like communication channels. Tools are being developed to monitor conversation channels and discern levels of engagement of speakers. In fact, the use of social media (e.g., Facebook, Twitter, Yammer) in enterprises has been shown to impact information sharing [7,10,12,44], collaboration, communication, and interpersonal connectivity [2,8,11, 21, 37] in the workplace. Such data sources can complement smaller sample ethnographic research while simultaneously overcoming the limitations of infrequent employee experience surveys by providing an ongoing record of employee affect.

Although creating individual profiles might alarm employees and alter their use of the channels, monitoring the collective stream of conversation, or conversations involving large groups of workers via these communication modalities, could provide a measure of how different groups interact, or how affect is being impacted by specific events or broad changes in the work processes or environment.

Analysis of employee social media posts, such as Twitter, is tempting given the volume, frequency of use, and easy availability of shared content from employees. However, many of these tools are essentially public, making it unclear how effective they are in capturing organization-specific sentiment of employees. Further given the constant eroding of work-life boundaries [2], employees are likely to use these tools for both personal and professional updates, and are unlikely to discuss company-related information in a public forum.

To this end, we take advantage of the voluntary and casual short updates posted on an *internal* Twitter-like microblogging tool within a large Fortune 500 software corporation based in the United States. Our goal is to characterize affective expression of employees at the workplace in a fine-grained, in-context, and longitudinal manner, and thereby complement traditional mechanisms, such as self-reports and annual experience surveys. The tool, called OfficeTalk was developed and launched in 2008 by a product group inside Microsoft to explore the value of microblogging in an enterprise context. It is hosted on the company's own servers, automatically restricting all content within the company, and thereby allowing sharing of internal information among users. OfficeTalk had been adopted by over 30,000 employees. This promising source of insight into the evolving affective climate in the company can thus be studied and used, while protecting individuals from exposure. The main contributions of this paper are as follows:

- A methodology to mine emotion of employees (Positive Affect or PA and Negative Affect or NA) at-scale, motivated by psycholinguistics literature.
- A series of studies, grounded by theory in organizational behavior research, that describe how affective expression in the enterprise is influenced by the following factors: (1) exogenous and endogenous workplace factors, (2) physical location/geography of organization, and (3) the organizational hierarchy.

Our analyses indicate three major findings. Employees were found to exhibit cyclic rhythms of positive and negative affect over the course of a day; with PA decreasing significantly afterhours, which could be due to employee dissatisfaction with the work-life imbalance of having to work in the evening. Next we observe that interpersonal interactions via the tool generate PA that transcends geographic and cultural homophily, connecting employees across disparate regions known to professionally collaborate. Finally, our results exhibit evidence of "affect accommodation", wherein employees with higher status in the organizational hierarchy were seen expressing increased PA and lowered NA in their conversations with their coworkers and subordinates, likely with the goal of energizing the latter with enthusiasm in order to improve task performance.

Together, our findings bear on the potential of development of systems that can enable assessment of employee affect in an anonymous and aggregated manner, including assessing performance-relevant outcomes, such as job satisfaction, judgments, attitudinal responses, creativity, helping behavior and risk-taking.

BACKGROUND: ENTERPRISE, SOCIAL MEDIA, AFFECT

As newer web-based modalities of communication have emerged, a number of studies began investigating their role in enterprises—including email [8], blogs [11,22], microblogs [12], and instant messaging [21], as well as less direct modes of interaction such as social bookmarking [26], tagging [27], and file sharing [32]. Recent studies have investigated motivations and usage of social networking/media tools in organizational settings. Broadly, these studies have either been about how publicly open tools such as Twitter and Facebook are adopted and used by employees in a workplace [2,10,33,37,43,44], or about user studies of prototypes developed inside an organization for promoting collaboration or networking (notably [7,12]). Prior work also examined and identified power users and their roles in enterprises (e.g., [37]), the traction between social and work benefits, predominantly in light of the impact of these tools on productivity (ref. [33]), as well as how content in emails can indicate the organizational hierarchy [16].

This body of work reveals the value of these social tools in enhancing information sharing among employees in large organizations, helping build common ground, and sustaining a feeling of connectedness among individuals across the organizational hierarchy [43]. Social networking tools especially were observed to help build stronger bonds via weak ties, enable employees to reach out to unknown colleagues [10] and in finding experts in the company.

However, the examination of affect expression at work, especially in light of the growing use of social tools in the enterprise [2], has received relatively less attention. In [38], a tool called Themail was developed that represented the changing nature of email correspondence between two parties over time; while in [24] an emotional prosthetic, called AffectAura combined automatic labels for valence, arousal and engagement with multimodal contextual information to construct and present affective states to employees in a software company.

THEORETICAL FOUNDATION: WORKPLACE AFFECT

Outside the domain of online social tools and platforms, organizational behavior researchers have showed considerable interest in understanding how "organizations affect their workers, and how workers affect the organizations" [6], with respect to workers' thoughts, feelings and actions. This body of work has examined affective experiences of workers from several perspectives, primarily through ethnographic studies or archived daily records of samples of employees. The purpose has been to study the impact of affect on the quality of work outcomes, productivity, creativity, and job satisfaction [1,4,15,41]. A number of factors, centered around organizational processes have thus been proposed that could lead to the production of affect among workers. In a review work by Brief and Weiss [6], the authors classified these factors broadly as: (1) exogenous factors and conditions at work, (2) physical settings, (3) leaders and organizational roles.

(1) *Exogenous and endogenous workplace factors:* Watson in [39] investigated how cycles of feelings among workers related to lifestyle, biological, and sociocultural factors. Other studies have also found that inherent personal and behavioral traits play important role in stress and job related anxiety/depression [15,20]. A number of organization and work related conditions have also been found to lead to affective expression among workers [45], such as, dealing with administration and supervision [20], time constraints [35], negative job experiences, and workplace socialization.

(2) *Physical settings/geography:* Geographic distancing and work environments [29] have been found to impact collaborative norms that are often manifested through expressions of worker affect [13]. Many enterprises today have global offices, either to access workers with appropriate skillsets, outsource parts of big projects, or for the purpose of sales and marketing. Consequently, it is useful from an organization's point of view to understand the affective expressions of its workers in and between geographic locations, in order to improve communication exchange and foster creative idea sharing and collaboration.

(3) *Leaders, organizational structure:* Emotions among workers are deeply intertwined with the process of leading and leader outcomes [34]. For example, leaders in a negative mood generate a negative group affective tone and more effort from employees, than groups with positive mood leaders. Leaders also exhibit mood convergence with respect to workers, with respect to workplace norms and task and social interdependence [36]. This pattern of convergence is referred to in the socio-linguistics literature as communication accommodation theory [17]. The theory argues that when people of different authority/status levels interact they adjust their speech, their vocal patterns and their gestures, to accommodate to others. A deeper understanding of the manner of affect expression among individuals over the organizational hierarchy can yield insights into promoting healthy collaboration and improved group performance. What is the role leaders are playing via their social media-based interactions with employees? How are employees and leaders accommodating to one another?

Research Questions. The research presented in this paper is motivated by the theory presented above in the organizational behavior literature. As mentioned, the primary method of measuring affect in these works has been through interviews, archived daily records, or other ethnographic tools. We leverage the microblogging activity of employees to investigate, at-scale, how each one of the factors that we discussed impact the affective experiences of the enterprise workers. We frame three studies:

1) *What is the role of exogenous and endogenous workplace factors on affect expression?* [RQ 1]

   We explore how exogenous factors, aggregated into diurnal cycles, impact the emotions of employees. That is, while we have no full accounting of the exogenous factors of employees, we can look for differences in emotional expression over the course of a 24 hour period to characterize broadly the effects of exogenous factors. For instance, employees may show different patterns of affective expression during lunch time or outside of normal working hours. We then examine the endogenous factors within the workplace that trigger positive or negative affect. Finally, we investigate the role of socialization within the workplace context, via microblog conversations, in the expression of affective states.

2) *What is the role of physical location / geographic disparity on affect expression?* [RQ 2]

   Our second study is geared towards understanding the impact of geographic disparity on affect expression among employees. Specifically, we are interested in understanding how employees interacting over disparate geographic regions express emotion towards one another. From an organizational standpoint this can help with understanding interaction norms, employee allocation, and ultimately establish common ground and improve group performance across geographies and cultures.

3) *What are the roles of organizational structure and the diversity of job roles on affect expression?* [RQ 3]

   In our final study, we investigate how organizational structure relates to the expression of affect. First, we will explore the affect dynamics between employees having different job roles, based on their conversations on the enterprise microblog. Next, we investigate how employees of various job levels make *accommodations* in their affective expression when communicating with colleagues.

DATA

Source: Enterprise Microblogging Tool

Our source of data is a microblogging tool, called OfficeTalk developed exclusively for internal use by the employees in Microsoft. Potential users of the microblogging tool include all employees of the corporation, who can share short posts and can consume posts from others they follow. All posts by default are public and English is the only supported language. The usernames correspond to employees' corporate email aliases and are associated with their real names. The profile associated with each username reflects the user's job title, as well as his/her position in the organizational chart. Note that the tool also allows user accounts that are non-employees, often an entity related to the company, such as the name of a product, or a team/group. The primary goal of these accounts is to disseminate product/service updates to the larger enterprise community, such as details of new upcoming features, news about future team meetings, releases or trade shows.

Although conceptually the tool is similar to Twitter, there are some key differences. The posts shared via this tool can be up to 420 characters in length. While Twitter promotes the concept of @-replies in tweets to facilitate one-to-one information exchange, this tool allows a threaded structure to the replies.

Data Characteristics

In coordination with the product group who maintained the tool, we collected all posts and their associated information shared through this tool between Dec 1, 2008 and Mar 15, 2012. There were a total of 311,054 posts from 32,813 unique users in our dataset. For the purposes of this work, we consider only the individual user accounts; which leads to 204,284 posts from the 22,968 employees. Thus the mean number of posts per user was 8.9, while the variance was 1.6e+3. Overall, we had 21% users who had more than 10 posts, while 7% who had more than 100 posts. Out of these of posts, 93,256 posts were replies to other users.

From these data we constructed a post data model and a user data model. (1) For each post, the following information defined the post data model: content of post, authoring userid, timestamp of post creation, and id of the recipient user if the post is a reply. (2) At the user level, we obtained the following information to construct the user data model: userid, user's real name, user's corporate email alias (or username), user's job title, and user's workplace location (office/building number/city/country).

Job role	Count	Job role	Count
Program Managers	1441	Sales	1335
Developers	7511	Product/IT Support	994
Testers	7041	Designer	521
Admin	625	Usability	874
Marketing	2439	Researcher	183

Table 1. Number of employees (i.e. microblog users) per job role category.

For the upcoming studies, we then categorize the users of OfficeTalk first into various generic job roles, i.e. the type of responsibilities that entail their work, and next into various levels that define their position in the organizational hierarchy at Microsoft. The job roles we considered, along with the corresponding number of users is shown in Table 1. Note that each role defines a notion of a distinct set of tasks – e.g. a *developer* is primarily entrusted with the job of programming, while a *usability* focused job role would encompass examining the clarity of a human's interaction with a computer system.

Job level	Count	Job level	Count
Executive	24	Individual contributor	13148
Manager	2092	Intern	764
Lead	6940		

Table 2. Number of employees (i.e., microblog users) per job level category.

Table 2 shows the five job levels considered in this paper along with their respective number of users. *Individual contributors* comprise employees who do not have a direct report – for instance, junior *developers* and *testers*. To illustrate the difference between *managers* and *leads*, note that typically in this company, an employee who is a *lead* is someone who supervises one or more *individual contributors*, but does not formally manage them. On the other hand, a *manager* would oversee the entire product group or a team that likely comprises *leads*, *individual contributors* and *interns*. Also note that, the *program manager* role in Table 1 is different from the *manager* in Table 2. *Program managers* are typical in tech roles within product groups, who do not manage people as a rule, they manage feature specifications and have the role of coordinating *developers*, *testers*, *designers*, and so forth, although they do not have authority over these people. Finally, while it is true that *Executives* also serve some managerial role, they are typically higher level officers heading departments and orgs, such as chairman, chief executive officer, chief operating officer, president etc. and with the general responsibility of acting as a communicator, decision maker, leader, manager and executor therein.

MEASURING AFFECT EXPRESSION

Method

We now present our methodology used to measure affect expression of users. We focus on the two broad categories of emotional expression typically used in the sentiment analysis research community [18,28] as well as the organizational behavior community (see [6] for a review) – positive affect (PA) and negative affect (NA).

In order to compute the two types of affect for the users, we utilize the textual content of the microblog posts to capture individuals' affect expressions over time. We use a prominent psycholinguistic lexicon called Linguistic Inquiry and Word Count (LIWC[1]) that identifies over 64 behavioral and psychological dimensions (e.g., "insight", "certainty", "perception") in English text, comprising a total of 4,500 words and word stems. Creators of LIWC [30] had conducted rigorous experimentation to examine how these words related to actual natural language of people – the lexicon has been found to capture around 86 percent of the words people use in written text and speech[2].

High PA post examples
@some_person1 love your shared notes. That's great!!!! Will greatly help me!!
Is ready to celebrate the (product_x) LAUNCH! Awesome times of release. Have a good weekend!
Back to work from the best vacation and happy to see the evolutions of (product_y) build!!! yeah
High NA post examples
Unknown error – seriously. And weird post caching behavior. Hate this...
I sucked at pool so bad at the launch party yesterday that I should lose against myself. Oh brother!
@some_person2 sorry I missed that! Had an emergency and couldn't come to the meeting yesterday. Damn, this sucks

Table 3. Example posts with high PA and high NA.

Turning to the social media domain, considerable work has successfully utilized LIWC to determine PA and NA, as well as a variety of emotional states including 'joy', 'anger' etc. [18,23], validating the use of LIWC for reliably measuring affect expression in short text (Twitter posts).

As in prior literature [18], we focus on the words and word stems available in the emotion categories in LIWC: for PA, we use the dimension "positive emotion", and for NA, we use "negative emotion", "sadness", "anger", "anxiety" and "inhibition". In this manner, we compile positive affect and negative affect lexicons. Based on regular expression matching of the words in each lexicon with the content of a microblog post, we determine measures of PA (or NA) respectively as the ratio of the number of positive (or negative) words in the posts to the total number of words in the post (hence PA and NA values for a given post will lie in the range {0,1}). Some example posts with high PA and high NA respectively are shown in Table 3. Note that usernames and certain terms have been replaced with dummy strings to preserve privacy.

Validation

To demonstrate the effectiveness of LIWC, we perform a validation exercise to determine if our affect measurements could truly capture the nature of affect expressed in a post[3]. For the purpose, we selected randomly a set of 50 posts, and sought feedback from three researchers (English proficient). Each researcher coded PA (and NA) separately in each post using a 1-5 Likert scale, where 1 indicated low PA (or NA) and 5 indicated high PA (or NA). We then combined mean ratings from the three researchers to obtain "ground truth" PA and NA measures (Fleiss' kappa: 0.72). In parallel, to match the Likert scale ratings, we discretized into 5 bins (bin size, 0.2), the LIWC computed affect measurements for the same 50 posts so that for each post, its PA and NA lies in one of the 5 bins. Thereafter, we compared these to the "ground truth" affect measures for all posts – the Pearson's correlation coefficient was found to be 0.83 which provides evidence that our LIWC computed affect measurements are reliable.

Note that we acknowledge a major limitation of lexicon-driven affect measurement is failure to account for negation. However, the availability of hundreds of thousands of posts in our case helps alleviate this issue, as has also been demonstrated in prior work [18]. Also, the aforementioned strong correlation with human coded posts suggests that noise in our data due to negation is minimal.

ROLE OF EXOGENOUS AND ENDOGENOUS WORKPLACE FACTORS [RQ 1]

Exogenous Factors: Rhythmic Cycles of Affect

Recall that we intend to present a summary picture of the impact of exogenous factors by examining emotional expression over the course of a day. We present in Figure 1 the mean daily trends of PA and NA over any typical 24 hour period, computed over all the users and the entire time range of analysis. We notice that NA shows a fairly stable trend throughout the day, with a minor drop in the evening. On the other hand, PA exhibits higher variability, showing a peak during morning hours between 10am and 11am, but gradual decrease through the day, with a sharp drop after 6pm. PA also is considerably greater in magnitude

[1] http://www.liwc.net/

[2] http://www.liwc.net/howliwcworks.php#index6

[3] Note that a similar human coding based validation of LIWC emotions was performed successfully for Twitter posts in [23].

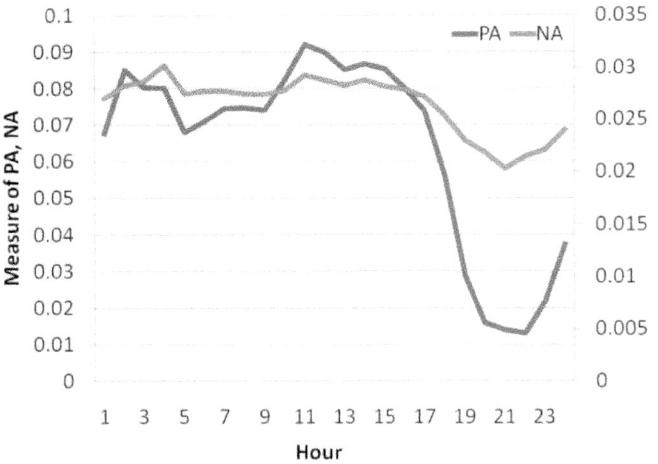

Figure 1. Diurnal trends of PA (left y-axis) and NA (right y-axis) based on enterprise-wide microblog usage. The trends show mean measures across all users and collapsed across all days in our analysis timeframe.

throughout the workday (9am-5pm), compared to NA, at least prior to the sharp drop in the evening. On average, when comparing average values per-hour of the day, employees express greater PA than NA (independent sample t-test, $p < .01$; df = 23).

These results reveal several implications about how users express their emotion in a workplace context: people generally express PA throughout the workday around various work-related issues and topics, but then exhibit a sharp drop in PA when working afterhours. It is possible that during afterhours, individuals are dissatisfied, saying fewer positive things, but because they are timid they do not express negativity. The stable expression of NA in our context may also indicate employee caution about expressing extreme NA around work-related topics.

Endogenous Factors: Work Context

We investigate the type of topical content associated with the two affect categories, PA and NA. We define topics here to be non-stopword unigrams present in the text of the posts, although more sophisticated topic models are certainly an option to explore in future work.

In Table 1, we report a list of some of the top keywords that are most frequent for each affect type. We notice distinct topic categories associated with PA and NA – out of the top 100 most frequent keywords for each of the PA and NA distributions, we find only 27.5% overlap. PA tends to co-occur with topics related to the company's products, its corporate partners, business-related updates and customers, as well as broader notions of 'positive feeling' in an enterprise context (e.g., *productivity*, *love*, and the hashtag *#bingo*, used in the sense of "you got it"). NA on the other hand, appears to be associated with work-related problems, updates and topics (e.g., *debug*, *toolbox*, *spec*, *demo*, *error*, *meeting*, *webcast*), vibes of 'negative feeling' possibly around work process or interactions (e.g., *confused*, *blocked*), some mentions of competing products and companies, as well technical issues (e.g., *security*, *servers*, *support*, *drill*, *VPN*). Broadly the observation that workplace issues/contexts increase negative affect expression thus aligns with findings in the literature that suggest that time constraints and the demands of the job responsibilities impact NA production [35].

Together, these observations reveal that the topical patterns around affect expression in the enterprise microblog are almost exclusively work-focused, with positivity shown toward company products and negativity toward IT issues.

	Frequent keywords
PA	windows, xbox, Microsoft, love, #helloworld, weekend, experience, cool, sharepoint, vision, technology, (company_corporate_partner_1), productive, ROI, potential, creative, business, kinect, customers, awesome, kudos, #bingo, media, fix, pretty, design, feedback, idea, thx, #windowsphone, favorite, openness, flawless, amazing, (company_corporate_partner_2), brilliant, money
NA	upgrade, client, discuss, meeting, question, debug, email, servers, support, data, (competing_product_1), network, suck, developers, managers, drill, VPN, security, error, urgent, webcast, interview, frustrating, notes, (competing_company), tired, late, confused, mysterious, toolbox, spec, proxy, users, demo, (competing_product_2), waiting, forbidden, blocked, (competing_product_3)

Table 4. Top keywords in the enterprise microblog posts, associated with PA and NA. Certain keywords are masked to ensure confidentiality (e.g., *competing_product_3*).

Endogenous Factors: Workplace Conversations

A key benefit of enterprise microblogs is that they promote conversations around work related topics. Ideally this fosters a sense of community and helps collaboration.

We study how a measure 'responsivity', defined as the normalized frequency of replies between pairs of users, is associated with expression of PA and NA. Figure 2 shows the measures of PA and NA over the number of replies, averaged over all pairs of conversing users. Overall, affect expression appears to have higher variance and higher extremities for lower responsivity rates (i.e., fewer replies). In fact for very high responsivities, we observe that users share very little emotional content (both PA, NA). The Pearson correlation coefficient between #replies and PA is –.28, and between #replies and NA is –.21. In other words, affect expression appears to decrease with increased frequency of responses. Additionally, it appears that, similar to the daily patterns, PA is comparatively higher than NA, given a certain reply frequency, reflecting the

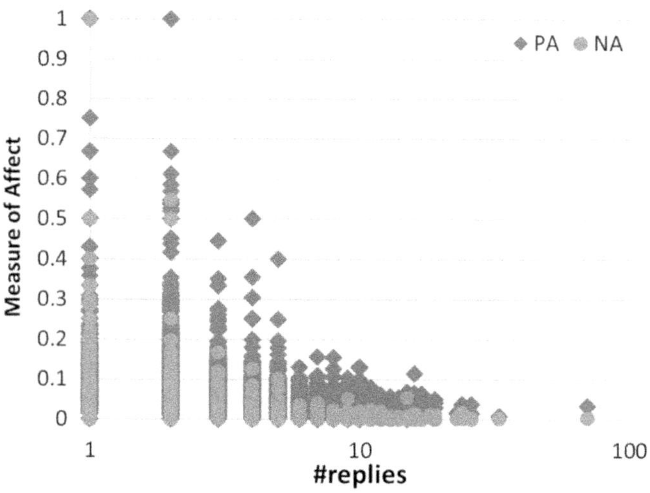

Figure 2. Responsivity (frequency of replies) between pairs of enterprise microblog users, in terms of PA and NA.

general tendency of employees to express less negativity while conversing with their colleagues.

To summarize, we observe that consistent and frequent conversations between employees tend to be focused on objective topics (e.g., discussing a common debugging issue), making conversational relationships mechanisms neutral and more for issue resolution or problem solving than for social engagement or internal networking.

ROLE OF PHYSICAL LOCATION/GEOGRAPHY [RQ 2]

In this section, we investigate the role of geographic proximity between pairs of users in the nature of affect they share through conversations. We study conversational relationships of employees, as manifested in the microblog OfficeTalk, across seven different geographical regions where Microsoft has its offices. To elaborate on our technique used here, given a particular conversing user-pair, we inferred the geographic region of the sender and the recipient, separately based on their respective office locations – we mapped the office location addresses to latitude/longitude pairs, and thereafter obtained the city, country, and region names using Bing maps API. In Table 5, we show the mean PA and NA shared and received between employees at pairs of geographic locations – for brevity, for each region, we show the region which it shares the highest PA (and the highest NA) with – measures of PA (and NA) are respectively shown in boldface font.

Across all geographic region pairs, the PA and NA distributions are significantly different from the mean levels of PA and NA (see Table 6, rows 1 and 2). That is, the distribution of values of PA (or NA) over region pairs differ significantly from the mean level of PA (or NA) expressed between region pairs. We present this to document the variability across region pairs in the expression of affect: expression of PA and NA are not the same across all regions pairs. The PA and NA distributions across region pairs are also different from one another (third row in Table 6). This means that when a region pair expresses higher PA, that pair does not also express higher NA. In fact, the Pearson correlation coefficient between PA and NA in region pairs is only .094.

Sender region	Recipient region	PA	NA
Africa	Asia	0.0211	**0.0016**
Africa	Europe	**0.09**	0.0002
Latin America	U.S./Canada	0.0266	**0.0085**
Latin America	Middle East	**0.1382**	0.0032
Australia/New Zealand	Asia	0.0301	**0.001**
Australia/New Zealand	Europe	**0.0741**	0.0007
U.S./Canada	Latin America	0.0375	**0.005**
U.S./Canada	Asia	**0.094**	0.001
Asia	Latin America	0.0185	**0.005**
Asia	U.S./Canada	**0.0415**	0.001
Europe	Australia/New Zealand	0.023	**0.007**
Europe	U.S./Canada	**0.0679**	0.0021
Middle East	Asia	0.0495	**0.003**
Middle East	Europe	**0.0743**	0.0004

Table 5. Aggregated affect expression between pairs of conversing individuals across geographical locations, based on replies in the enterprise microblog.

Further exploration shows that we do not see higher PA for geographically proximate region conversing user-pairs; neither do we notice lower NA for them (e.g., U.S./Canada → Latin America; Africa → Asia; Middle East → Asia; Table 5). In fact, strong PA is seen in Africa → Europe, U.S./Canada → Asia, and Asia → U.S./Canada relationships. While geographically coarse-grained, these results show that the (geographical/cultural) homophily of living in the same or a relatively more similar country is not a primary driver of positive emotion in workplace interactions.

	p	*t*-stat	df	std dev.
PA^	***	7.9635	46	0.0375
NA^	***	6.7727	46	0.0021
PA × NA^^	***	7.6147	46	0.0374

^ one-sample *t*-test ^^ two-tail paired *t*-test *** p<.001

Table 6. Statistical significant tests for affect expression across pairs of conversing geographical regions (there are *N*=47 region pairs). df in each test is thus based on the number of pairs of geographic regions which have conversing employees.

Rather, higher PA (and lower NA) appear more related to collaboration across regions. Precise amounts of cross-region collaboration are difficult to quantify, but it is known that employees in U.S./Canada interact extensively with those in Asia, and similarly those in Europe with Africa, on a variety of development-related and outsourced products and projects. While this warrants additional exploration, it appears that high PA (or low NA) is not a direct function of geographic or even perhaps cultural homophily, at least at a country/regional scale. An enterprise context, especially one at Microsoft which is culturally and globally diverse, may however see exchanges of PA more along collaboration ties.

ROLE OF ORGANIZATIONAL STRUCTURE [RQ 3]

Job Roles and Affect Expression

In this section, we examine the role of the organizational structure on employees' affect expression in light of their job roles. We construct network representations of affect shared among the job roles (see Table 1), in which the nodes represent the categories, and a directed weighted edge between two categories represents the mean PA (or NA) over all replies sent by the employees associated with the first job role category to those of the second.

	p	t-stat	df	std dev.
PA^	***	11.05	83	0.023
NA^	***	8.21	83	0.0045
PA × NA^^	***	12.84	83	0.0237

^ one-sample t-test ^^ two-tail paired t-test *** p<.001

Table 7. Statistical significance tests for various job roles pairs' conversational exchange. df for each test is based on the number of directed edges in the job role affect network, connecting pairs of job roles.

We observe differences in affect expression across job role categories. Like the analyses for region pairs, that the amount of expression of PA (or NA) for the job role pairs differ from the mean level of (i.e., that not all job role pairs express the same levels of PA and NA toward one another; rows 1 and 2 in Table 7) and that job role pairs differ in the expression of PA and NA toward one another (row 3 in Table 7). This establishes that job roles of the employees involved in a conversation plays an important role in the nature of affect that is expressed between them.

In Table 8, we present the mean PA (and NA) shared and received by each job role with others. Based on the network representation among the job roles, we also present in Table 8, two network metrics—betweenness centrality (that estimates how the importance of a node/job role in terms of its connectivity in the network) and clustering coefficient (that estimates how well connected a node/job role is with its neighborhood/neighboring roles).

Overall, from Table 8, it appears that shared affect (whether PA or NA) over the ties between job roles is driven strongly by the roles' professional responsibilities i.e., "who works with whom". For example, *admins* and *program managers* are more centrally connected (high betweeness centrality) to a variety of other job roles, sharing higher PA and lower NA. This likely indicates admins' role of coordinating with other employees (e.g. setup a meeting, organize a conference or trade show) and keeping up the morale of people around them. On similar lines, *program managers'* goal is ensuring successful performance of their colleagues. Hence they tend to maintain more positivity in their conversational ties. From the lower values of NA we conjecture that the *program managers*, being relatively higher up in the organizational hierarchy (compared to e.g., *developers, designers, testers* etc.) exercise caution in expression of negative emotion, instead attempting to be friendly and encouraging in their encounters on public communication channels like this enterprise microblog.

PA				
Job role	Shared	Received	Betweenness Centrality	Clust. Coeff.
Program Managers	0.0895	0.0824	231.371	0.188
Developers	0.0416	0.0052	35.071	0.386
Testers	0.0327	0.0046	24.038	0.433
Admin	0.0802	0.0782	210.254	0.232
Marketing	0.158	0.103	248.392	0.169
Sales	0.173	0.149	239.458	0.173
Product/IT Support	0.0742	0.0193	234.249	0.192
Designer	0.0374	0.0041	20.094	0.402
Usability	0.0381	0.0042	23.842	0.428
Researcher	0.0524	0.0059	31.096	0.308
NA				
Job role	Shared	Received	Betweenness Centrality	Clust. Coeff.
Program Managers	0.0025	0.0016	206.973	0.196
Developers	0.0304	0.0135	28.35	0.391
Testers	0.0273	0.0324	20.942	0.414
Admin	0.0021	0.0019	187.194	0.215
Marketing	0.0024	0.0018	228.486	0.183
Sales	0.0022	0.0013	213.288	0.195
Product/IT Support	0.0082	0.0182	213.349	0.142
Designer	0.0305	0.0245	21.354	0.395
Usability	0.0284	0.0289	20.249	0.293
Researcher	0.0125	0.0117	23.065	0.326

Table 8. Mean PA and NA shared and received by various job roles, based on conversational ties. Also shown are two types of network metrics (betweenness centrality, clustering coefficient) for PA and NA, over the different job roles.

Notable also are the *Sales* and *Marketing* individuals who generally show the highest PA shared and received, and at the same time they also share and receive low NA. They are also highly centrally connected in the network. We note here that *Marketing* and *Sales* people often are selected to be positive individuals. As a result, as a part of their role they maintain positivity, because they are interested in expanding marketing efforts, engage in professional networking and improving interactivity among groups.

On the other hand, we observe that, *designers, developers* or *researchers* are not very central in the network (low betweenness centrality) and show high local clustering of their networks in terms of affect expression, perhaps connecting extensively to other individuals of the same job role. Overall, they also show low PA in conversations with other job roles. To elaborate this observation further, with careful inspection we find that these job roles are largely *individual contributors* in the workplace (see Table 2, for job levels) – consequently they are probably less motivated to use the microblogging tool to engage in positive affect-bearing conversations with others. However with the relatively higher NA for these roles, it appears that these employees are perhaps using OfficeTalk to express their negative issues/concerns with others – for either their own problem resolution or for someone's critical task at hand. We also note here that *developers* and especially *testers* are selected to be people who look for faults, which can come across as negative.

To sum up, we note that in an enterprise context, the stratification of organizational structure appears to play an important role in explaining the nature of affect expression. Those that are central in the enterprise network tend to share and receive high positive affect. Conversely, those in individual contributor roles tend to express more negative than positive affect. This finding aligns with observations in prior work: communication patterns and affective content in organizations tend to be structured by its hierarchy [16].

Job Level and Affect Expression

As mentioned in the theoretical foundations section, job level of employees impacts their affect expression--leaders' negative affect generates negativity among their followers [34]. Here we explore this question from the perspective of the five types of job levels in the context of this company (Table 2).

We therefore define a measure called "affect accommodation", that is the degree of adaptation or adjustment a user is likely to make in her expression of affect while conversing with another user, of possibly different status, compared to her baseline level of affect that appears in her non-conversational posts. For instance, we may hypothesize that employees may be more positive than their baseline level of positivity when replying to people of high status in the organizational hierarchy. Generally, let us suppose that an individual u_i sends a reply to another individual u_j. We further suppose that u_i will make a certain degree of adjustment in her affect expression based on u_j's status (in the hierarchy).

Hence, affect accommodation is defined as the mean difference between the levels of affect (PA or NA) expressed by u_i in posts which were replies to u_j, and the level of affect expressed in posts that were not replies to anyone (non-conversational posts assumed as baseline).

More generally, for any u_i, u_j, u_k etc., we further define measures of affect accommodation separately for the sender and recipient roles in replies. We investigate (1) what degree of affect accommodation is observed for all conversations sent by u_i and received by individuals, u_j, u_k, ..., of possibly varied statuses and (2) what degree of affect accommodation is observed for all conversations sent by individuals u_i, u_k, ..., of possibly varied statuses, and received by u_j? Finally, by aggregating across the job levels associated with each pair of individuals u_i and u_j involved in conversations, we get affect accommodation measures for the sender and recipient roles respectively for pairs of job levels.

	df	*t*-stat		std dev.	
		PA	NA	PA	NA
Executive × Manager **	2,114	6.93	5.73	0.048	5.7e-3
Executive × Lead **	6,962	11.15	9.29	0.075	8.3e-3
Executive × Individual contributor ***	13,170	14.98	13.73	0.163	1.5e-2
Executive × Intern ***	786	4.02	3.14	0.014	3.6e-3
Manager × Individual contributor ***	15,238	17.66	14.85	0.224	2.1e-2
Manager × Intern ***	2,854	7.35	6.02	0.056	5.2e-3
Manager × Manager *	4,182	2.36	1.95	0.019	6.8e-3
Lead × Individual contributor ***	20,086	22.35	16.59	0.295	2.8e-2
Lead × Intern ***	7,702	12.94	10.26	0.079	7.5e-3

Table 9. Statistical significance tests to compare the degrees of PA and NA accommodation across job levels (* p<0.01; ** *p*<.001; * *p*<.0001). df for each pair is based on the number of employee-employee conversing pairs with the particular two job roles under consideration. Only pairs with significant PA and NA accommodation are shown.**

We begin by examining the differences in PA and NA accommodation shown by various job levels for the above two circumstances: (1) when (employees with) a particular job level is a sender of replies targeted to another job level, and (2) when a particular job title is a recipient of replies sent from (employees with) another job level. Overall, from Table 9, for most pairs we observe statistically significant differences in the degree of accommodation—greater accommodation is observed when the two job levels are distinct.

Further, Figure 3 shows the average measures of affect accommodation for each job level. For affect accommodation with respect to the senders, we find that

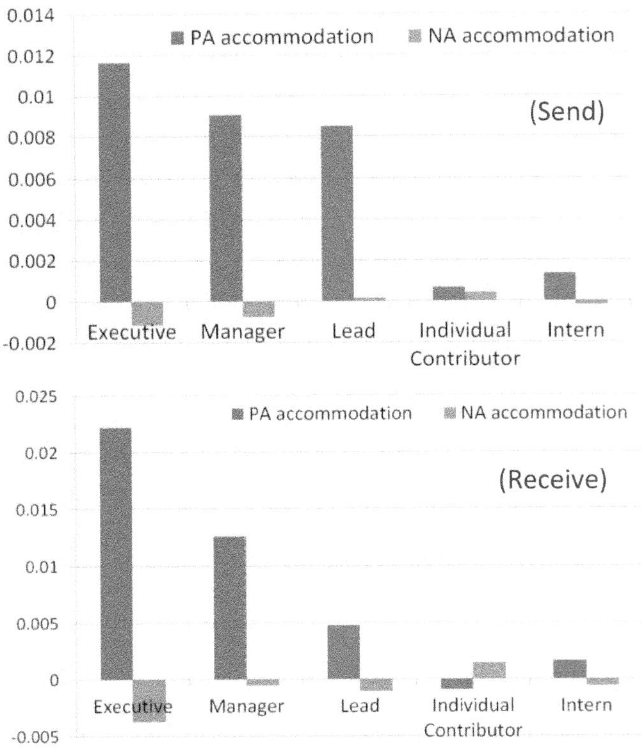

Figure 3. Affect accommodation by employees holding various job levels: (1) Accommodation while sending/sharing affective content (top), (2) Accommodation by others in receiving affective content (bottom).

most job levels tend to express positive accommodation for PA. In particular we observe that higher status job levels such as *Executives, Managers, Leads* tend to share notably high accommodation in the positive direction for PA and in the negative direction for NA; i.e., they are more positive and less negative while conversing with other employees. These results generally support the theoretical observation that transformational leaders in an organization often bear positivity to help ignite others' aspirations, eliciting enthusiasm, and conveying optimism regarding a desirable future for the workplace [14].

In contrast *Individual Contributors* and *Interns* share less PA and NA accommodation: in fact for the *Individual Contributors* NA accommodation is in the positive direction which implies that they are more negative while engaging with others, than they are on their own.

For affect accommodation with respect to recipients, there is again high PA accommodation in the positive direction for top job levels (e.g., *Executives, Managers* etc.)—employees tend to be exceedingly positive in their conversations targeted towards them. At the same time, NA accommodation towards them is negative, meaning individuals tend to be less negative than their baseline while addressing replies to them.

DISCUSSION

Theoretical Implications

The three studies presented in the previous three sections, in a broad sense, provide at-scale empirical evidence in support of the theoretical foundations behind the production of affect at workplace (refer to the three research questions in third section). They also suggest theoretical implications that can be actionable from an organization's perspective.

Exogenous factors. To begin with, the patterns of affect expressed over the course of a day exemplify findings that are actionable on the part of management. That positivity drops off dramatically in the evening is one sign that employees are less satisfied with afterhours work – an aspect that might be critical while employees are meeting deadlines, product pre-release duties, or collaborating with colleagues in distinctively different timezones. Overall, this is not surprising, but the size of the drop in positivity may be surprising or at least informative in the context of work-life balance discussions. Employees do experience *consistent* cycles of positivity throughout the day that are likely to impact their performance levels or how they accomplish targets meant for their particular job role [20]. The consistency is something management could leverage when, for instance, establishing cross-timezone collaborations. While somewhat unexpected, the similar but smaller drop in NA in the evening might indicate that afterhours work does not necessarily result in explicit negative expression. We acknowledge that this could be due to a general reticence to criticize, or simply a feeling that it is not productive to be openly critical or negative.

Endogenous factors. The analysis of topics reveals specific aspects of work that cause both anxiety and negativity, as well as feelings of positivity toward work, broadly helping the organization place employee job satisfaction in the context of workplace conditions and events (social, physical, economic) [29]. From an application standpoint, such ability to align employee emotion with specific contexts is potentially a substantial step toward an actionable, fine-grained feedback loop from employees to management.

For instance, although some of the topics we observed (e.g., the product names) are specific to the company we studied, many of the discomfort points, like the IT related issues (e.g., *upgrading, servers, support*), are found to be commonplace sources of frustration. Though this observation is not particularly a surprise, but which IT issues get discussed the most or are most associated with negative affect, can guide prioritization of managerial efforts toward amelioration; at the same time the organization can utilize this knowledge to streamline how technical issues are handled internally in order to prevent counter-productivity among the employees. Capturing these issues in the flow of daily work, versus via an annual survey, should thus provide a more accurate reflection of impediments to productivity.

Similarly, words like *urgent, meeting, confused, question* etc.'s frequent co-occurrence with NA might indicate dissatisfaction while attending to the day-to-day demands of a particular job role, which in turn might have implications in how the organization could tackle bureaucratic issues.

Finally, it is well-established that positivity within organizations can be contagious [39] and has been proposed to have diminishing effects on the dysfunctional, counterproductive emotions and behaviors barricading employees from achieving organizational goals. Frequent use of words like *awesome, kudos, #bingo, amazing, brilliant* with PA thus provides helpful evidence to the organization in this direction: that employees are sharing/ propagating their positive perceptions amongst them.

Physical Location/Geography. Our results also have implications regarding the strong role of the workplace's geographic environment [13] on the expression of affect. For instance, we saw significant differences in levels of positivity and negativity in conversational interactions depending on the geographic region of the employees. One explanation is that employees in the same geographic region share affect through other communication mechanisms (e.g. face-to-face interaction, phone conversations), minimizing the need for the use of online social tools for affect sharing. For geographically disparate colleagues, this might be reversed. Since most of their professional interactions tend to be over emails or virtual meetings, they may use the microblog for networking or engagement and thereby express higher positive affect (and lower negative affect), to compensate for not being able to share it via other physical communication means. This is furthermore supported by similar observations in the organization behavior literature – e.g., Kiesler and Sproull [46] described how people corresponding over email in an organization used capital letters to emphasize or stress important concepts, and add emotion back into a more emotionally sterile context through the use of emoticons.

Tentatively we thus conclude that regions that are geographically separated but that collaborate more tend to also share more positive emotion. The variation in affective expression across geography can inform the organization about how to distribute employees across teams who need to collaborate consistently, or how to regulate norms of the remote collaboration/communication environment, which can in turn be valuable in making outsourcing decisions with overseas clients.

Organizational Structure. There is also a considerable difference in affect expression with respect to centrality in the organizational network. Consequently we observe accommodation of affect between employees who are individual contributors versus those who lead or manage groups and teams. As an actionable item, the finding can provide helpful guidelines to managers about how to deal with administration and supervision, and how they can foster and shape the temperament of their subordinates through the use of positive affective cues in their communication, thereby improving group performance [3].

Interestingly, however, while examining the interactive effects of leader affect and group's goals within Cognitive Appraisal Theory, the authors in [14] found that leader negative affect was perceived less favorably when groups were focused on promotion goals, whereas leader negative affect was perceived more favorably in groups with prevention goals. Hence the nature of affect expression we observed across the organizational hierarchy in our studies points to a helpful guideline of how the *Managers*, *Leads* and *Executives* could utilize negative affect expression that could be deemed appropriate in the face of challenging situations.

Together, these influences highlight positive attributes of the enterprise (collaboration generating positivity), offer insight into "soft skill" requirements (*managers* and *sales* people staying positive) and suggest avenues for improvement (perhaps *developers* could be less negative when interacting with others).

Design Implications

We discuss some potential design implications of our studies. One possibility is that an organization's HR/administrative team can be assigned the role to monitor an "affect dashboard", a system that describes the prevalent mood of employees about specific topics in an anonymous manner. The team could look for affect trends over time, both daily and longitudinally, in the context of specific issues and products, and identify the affective influence exerted by different job roles. Further, they could assess emotional reactions among employees in different locations or in different departments without revealing explicit affective scores to individuals. For instance, after a change in health benefits is announced, the organization can use this dashboard to find out what type of reception the news has received among staffers. This would let the organization locate and tune into critical issues and concerns, and propagate them up to suitable authorities for requisite action or change, if necessary.

The other potential design implication could be an individual-focused "application" (e.g. a smartphone app) that the employees could use on their own for self-monitoring and self-evaluation of their stress or anxiety levels (or their coping strategies) in order to promote emotional reflection under different workplace contexts.

Privacy

Finally, we mention the issue of respecting individual privacy in reviewing employee affect via social media. We note that while our monitoring of employee microblog posts may seem a bit "big brother", our analyses as well as the design implications we discussed are aggregated over individual user behaviors where individual identities are excluded from being part of the data. That is, they would largely prevent one actually deciphering "who expressed what emotion on which topic or about whom". Our hope is that such aggregated findings maintain this minimization of privacy infringement while still providing insight into employee affect that is actionable toward positive organizational directions. However we note that it is possible that knowing this type of affect-monitoring system exists, employees might find it unsettling for themselves. The type of reaction such mining could trigger is, however, hard to gauge without qualitative feedback from them, or a pilot deployment, both being directions for future work.

Limitations

We discuss a few limitations of this work. As a critique of our affect measurement method, we again acknowledge that a lexicon driven approach via LIWC can have limitations. It is worthwhile to examine alternative lexica (e.g., POMS [25], PANAS [40]) that describe emotional states beyond PA/NA. We would also like to mention that measuring arousal or activation of affect beyond pleasure-displeasure can potentially be useful, especially given the Yerkes-Dodson law that there are optimal ranges of arousal for productivity [42]. In the future, we look forward to characterizing workplace affect through a more complex psycho-linguistic instrument such as the circumplex model [31] that can enable a more nuanced investigation of affect in terms of valence and arousal.

CONCLUSION

The emergence of social media as a data source for understanding affect of employees in organizations carries considerable potential—it can open up the "watercooler conversations" and help organizations get a real sense of what is on the mind of employees, stay abreast of their morale or assess reaction to important changes such as a corporate restructuring or a product launch.

Toward this end, we explored the landscape of emotional expression from the employees at the software corporation Microsoft, leveraging the data from an internal microblogging tool called OfficeTalk. Grounded by theoretical foundations in organizational behavior research, we examined three broad factors that have been known to influence affective expression: (1) exogenous and endogenous workplace factors, (2) geography, and (3) organizational structure. We found empirical at-scale evidence for effects of job role and level, geographic region, exogenous factors like daily life patterns, and endogenous factors like IT issues on the expression of affect. Our findings together bear the potential of development of affect assessment systems in enterprises that can reveal aggregated temporal dynamics of how employees feel. In essence, the timescale and context for affect expression in the workplace can provide a more effective tool for assessing key factors and performance-relevant outcomes, such as job satisfaction, judgments, attitudinal responses, creativity, helping behavior and risk-taking, than internal surveys or other traditional methods.

ACKNOWLEDGMENTS

The authors would like to thank Jonathan Grudin for thorough and helpful comments and feedback on early drafts of the paper. They are also thankful to the erstwhile Office Labs colleagues, Chris Slemp and Anne Archambault for help with data gathering and access.

REFERENCES

1. Amabile, T. M., Barsade, S. G., Mueller, J. S. and Staw, B. M. (2000) Affect and Creativity at Work. Administrative Science Quarterly, 50, 3 (2005), 367.
2. Archambault, A. & Grudin, J. (2012). A longitudinal study of Facebook, LinkedIn, & Twitter use. In *Proc. CHI 2012*.
3. Ashforth BE, Humphrey RH. (1995). Emotion in the workplace: a reappraisal. Hum. Relat. 48:97–125.
4. Ashkanasy, N.M., Hartel, C. E. J. and Zerbe, W. J. (2000). Emotions in the Workplace: Research, Theory, and Practice. Westport, CT: Quorum Books, 2000.
5. Bartel C.A., Saavedra R. (2000). The collective construction of work group moods. *Admin. Sci. Q.* 45(2):197–231.
6. Brief, A. P., & Weiss, H. M. (2002). Organizational behavior: affect in the workplace. Annual Review of Psychology, 53(1), 279-307.
7. Brzozowski, M. J. (2009). WaterCooler: exploring an organization through enterprise social media. In *Proc. GROUP 2009*. 219-228.
8. Dabbish, L. A., Kraut, R., Fussell, S. & Kiesler, S. (2005). Understanding email use: predicting action on a message. In *Proc. CHI 2005*. 691-700.
9. De Choudhury, M., Counts, S., & Gamon, M. (2012). Not All Moods are Created Equal! Exploring Human Emotional States in Social Media. In *Proc. ICWSM'12*.
10. DiMicco, J., Millen, D., Geyer, W., Dugan, C., Brownholtz, B. & Muller, M. (2008). Motivations for social networking at work. In *Proc. CSCW 2008*. 711-720.
11. Efimova, L. & Grudin, J. (2007). Crossing Boundaries: A Case Study of Employee Blogging. In *Proc. HICSS 2007*.
12. Ehrlich, K. & Shami, S. (2010). Microblogging inside and outside the workplace. In *Proc. ICWSM 2010*.
13. Eligio, Ulises Xolocotzin, Ainsworth, Shaaron E., Crook, Charles K. (2012). Emotion understanding and performance during computer-supported collaboration. *Computers in Human Behavior,* ISSN 0747-5632, 10.1016/j.chb.2012.06.001.
14. Gaddis, B., Connelly, S., & Mumford, M. D. (2004). Failure feedback as an affective event: Influences of

leader affect on subordinate attitudes and performance. *The Leadership Quarterly*, 15(5), 663–686.

15. George J.M., Brief A.P. (1992). Feeling good doing good: a conceptual analysis of the mood at work-organizational spontaneity relationship. *Psychol. Bull.* 112(2):310–29.
16. Gilbert, Eric. (2012). Phrases that signal workplace hierarchy. In *Proc. CSCW 2012*. 1037-1046.
17. Giles, Howard; Smith, Philip (1979). Accommodation Theory: Optimal Levels of Convergence. In Giles; St. Clair, Robert N. *Language and Social Psychology*. Baltimore: Basil Blackwell.
18. Golder, S. A., & Macy, M. W. (2011). Diurnal and Seasonal Mood Vary with Work, Sleep and Daylength Across Diverse Cultures. *Science*. 30 Sep 2011.
19. Hackman J.R. (1992). Group influences on individuals in organizations. In Handbook of I/O Psychology, ed. MD Dunnette, LM Hough, 3:199–267. Palo Alto, CA: Consult. Psychol. Press. 1095 pp.
20. Hart P.M., Wearing A.J., Headey B. (1995). Police stress and well-being: integrating personality, coping and daily work experiences. J. Occup. Organ. Psychol. 68(2):133–56.
21. Herbsleb, J., Atkins, D., Boyer, D., Handel, M. & Finholt, T. (2002). Introducing instant messaging and chat in the workplace. In *Proc. CHI 2002*. 171-178.
22. Huh, J., Jones, L., Erickson, T., Kellogg, W. A., Bellamy, R., & Thomas, J. C. (2007). BlogCentral: the role of internal blogs at work. In *Proc. CHI EA 2007*.
23. Kivran-Swaine, F., and Naaman, M. (2011). Network properties and social sharing of emotions in social awareness streams. In *Proc. CSCW 2011*.
24. McDuff, D., Karlson, A., Kapoor, A., Roseway, A. & Czerwinski, M. (2012). AffectAura: an intelligent system for emotional memory. In *Proc. CHI 2012*.
25. McNair, D.M., Lorr, M., & Droppleman, L.F. (1971). Profile of mood states. San Diego: Educational and Industrial Testing Service.
26. Millen, D., Feinberg, J., Kerr, B. (2006). Dogear: Social bookmarking in the enterprise. In *Proc. CHI 2006*.
27. Muller, M. (2007). Comparing tagging vocabularies among four enterprise tag-based services. In *Proc. GROUP 2007*.
28. Ortony, A., & Turner, T. J. (1990). What's basic about basic emotions? *Psychological Review*, 97, 315-331.
29. Parkes J. (1990). Coping, negative affectivity, and the work environment: additive and interactive predictors of mental health. *J. Appl. Psychol.* 75:399–409.
30. Pennebaker, J. W., Mehl, M. R., & Niederhoffer, K. (2003). Psychological aspects of natural language use: Our words, our selves. *Annual Review of Psychology*, 54, 547-577.
31. Russell, James A. (1980). A circumplex model of affect. *J. of Personality and Social Psychology*: 39, 1161–1178.
32. Shami, S., Muller, M., & Millen, D. (2011). Browse and discover: Social file sharing in the enterprise. In *Proc. CSCW 2011*.
33. Skeels, M., & Grudin, J. (2009). When social networks cross boundaries: a case study of workplace use of facebook and linkedin. In *Proc.* GROUP *2009*. 95-104.
34. Staw, B. M. and Barsade, S. G. (1993). Affect and managerial performance: A test of the sadder-but-wiser vs. happier-and-smarter hypothesis. *Administrative Science Quarterly*, 38: 304-331.
35. Teuchmann K., Totterdell P., Parker S.K. (1999). Rushed, unhappy, and drained: an experience sampling study of relations between time pressure, perceived control, mood, and emotional exhaustion in a group of accountants. J. Occup. Health Psychol. 4(1):37–54.
36. Totterdell P., Kellett S., Teuchmann K., Briner B.B. (1998). Evidence of mood linkage in work groups. J. Pers. Soc. Psychol. 74(6):1504–15.
37. Turner, T., Qvarfordt, P., Biehl, J. T., Golovchinsky, G. & Back, M. (2010). Exploring the workplace communication ecology. In *Proc. CHI 2010*. 841-850.
38. Viégas, F., Golder, S. and Donath J. (2006). Visualizing email content: portraying relationships from conversational histories. In *Proc. CHI '06*. 979-988.
39. Watson D. (2000). Mood and Temperament. New York: Guilford. 340 pp.
40. Watson, D., Clark, L. A., & Tellegen, A. (1988). Development and validation of brief measures of positive and negative affect: the PANAS scales. *Journal of Personality and Social Psychology*, 54(6), 1063-1070. American Psychological Association.
41. Weiss H.M., Nicholas J.P., Daus C.S. (1999). An examination of the joint effects of affective experiences and job beliefs on job satisfaction and variations in affective experiences over time. Organ. Behav. Hum. Decis. Process. 78(1):1–24.
42. Yerkes RM, Dodson JD (1908). The relation of strength of stimulus to rapidity of habit-formation. *Journal of Comparative Neurology and Psychology* 18: 459–482.
43. Zhang, J., Qu, Y., Cody, J. & Wu, Y. (2010). A case study of micro-blogging in the enterprise: use, value, and related issues. In *Proc. CHI 2010*. 123-132.
44. Zhao, D. & Rosson, M. B. (2009). How and why people Twitter: the role that micro-blogging plays in informal communication at work. In *Proc. GROUP 2009*.
45. Zohar D. (1999). When things go wrong: the effect of daily work hassles on effort, exertion and negative mood. J. Occup. Organ. Psychol. 72(3):265–83.
46. Kiesler, S., & Sproull, L. (1992). Group decision making and communication technology. Organizational Behavior and Human Decision Processes, 52, 96–123.

Statistical Affect Detection in Collaborative Chat

Michael Brooks[1], Katie Kuksenok[2], Megan K. Torkildson[1], Daniel Perry[1], John J. Robinson[1], Taylor Jackson Scott[1], Ona Anicello[1], Ariana Zukowski[1], Paul Harris[1], Cecilia R. Aragon[1]

Human Centered Design & Engineering[1], Computer Science & Engineering[2]
University of Washington, Seattle

ABSTRACT

Geographically distributed collaborative teams often rely on synchronous text-based online communication for accomplishing tasks and maintaining social contact. This technology leaves a trace that can help researchers understand affect expression and dynamics in distributed groups. Although manual labeling of affect in chat logs has shed light on complex group communication phenomena, scaling this process to larger data sets through automation is difficult. We present a pipeline of natural language processing and machine learning techniques that can be used to build automated classifiers of affect in chat logs. Interpreting affect as a dynamic, contextualized process, we explain our development and application of this method to four years of chat logs from a longitudinal study of a multi-cultural distributed scientific collaboration. With ground truth generated through manual labeling of affect over a subset of the chat logs, our approach can successfully identify many commonly occurring types of affect.

Author Keywords

Computer-mediated communication; scientific collaboration; affect; emotion; machine learning; chat; spontaneous text communication; social media.

ACM Classification Keywords

H.5.3. Group and Organization Interfaces: Computer-supported-cooperative work.

INTRODUCTION

Geographically distributed collaboration is increasingly common across many work domains, and understanding the expression of emotion in computer-mediated communications is crucial to understanding team interactions and processes.

Against prior views of emotional expression as merely inappropriate disturbances within a work setting, an increasing number of studies in the last twenty years have documented a renewed interest in understanding emotion and affect in the workplace [4,5,11]. Numerous studies have shown that affect and emotion influence performance and interactions in cooperative work environments [1,4,11,16,17]. Further, this "awakening of interest in emotion in CSCW" [16] can support the design of affect-aware information systems in the workplace.

There are many definitions of emotion, affect, sentiment, and related concepts; many definitions are overly restrictive given the wide range of emotional or affective phenomena that may be of interest in understanding cooperative work environments. In this paper we draw on Russ's broad definition of *affect* to refer to an inclusive concept spanning emotions and feelings distinct from cognition [26], and more pervasive than the neurophysiological experiences of emotions [20]. We seek to better understand how instances of this broader notion of affect manifest in collaborative text-based communication.

Text-based chat within collaborative scientific work provides a rich body of data for understanding affective processes within groups. The increasing volume of text-based communication available for study, combined with a growing awareness of the importance of affect in the workplace, have led to an upsurge in research on affect detection in text, including work in fields as diverse as sentiment analysis, affective computing, linguistics, and psychology, among others [11].

Manual coding for affect expression in chat logs can yield rich and reliable data, but this process does not scale well to larger data sets. Research on the automated detection of the overall positive or negative sentiment of long, relatively well-formatted blogs, articles, and online posts has achieved promising results with statistical classification methods based on frequencies of term occurrence, e.g. [10,14,30]. More recently these methods have been applied in more informal settings, focusing on classifying messages on social network sites, blogs, and discussion forums, which are characterized by irregular grammar and spelling practices, e.g. [26, 33].

However, more work is needed to develop classification methods robust to the varied and dynamic context of affect in collaborative and distributed online chat environments [25]. Recent work in this area has applied rule-based techniques to the detection of specific types of affect, e.g. [15,21]. Effective classification of very short, informal texts, such as chat messages, remains a challenging problem for current text classification methods.

CSCW '13, February 23–27, 2013, San Antonio, Texas, USA.

In this paper, we address the problem of detecting subjective, non-mutually-exclusive labels of affective state (*e.g.*, *joy*, *excitement*, *confusion*, *frustration*, *anger*, and *annoyance*) in workplace chat logs. We contribute (1) a novel approach to affect classification in chat logs based on an interpretation of affect as a dynamic process, (2) a novel combination of features for use in classification of affect expression in chat, and (3) *ALOE*[1] – open source software for classifying coded chat messages. Our technique was applied to a large data set of nearly 500,000 lines of chat collected over four years of an international scientific collaboration. We were able to successfully identify 13 common types of affect expression from a taxonomy developed via collaborative open coding. Automated techniques to identify affect in chat messages are a powerful addition to the analytic toolkit of researchers studying affect in distributed teams.

RELATED WORK

Previous work includes a diverse set of approaches to affect classification, differing both in the evidence (features) used as well as the classification method. The variety of ways that the problem has been studied and the many techniques that have been developed make comparison between these studies challenging.

The features used for affect classification include everything from statistics on the frequencies of word sequence occurrences (word counts, n-grams) to more linguistically informed features (e.g. part of speech). These features have been combined with countless classification methods, ranging from rule-based methods to more flexible probabilistic methods. Depending on characteristics of the data, different configurations can have different levels of success. Furthermore, different granularities of classification – whether to classify affect merely as positive or negative, or to use a finer set of categories – not only impact the success of approaches, but make results even more difficult to compare between studies.

A significant amount of research on affect or sentiment detection in text has focused on lexicon-based approaches, in which pre-determined dictionaries of words that are associated with the target affect categories are used to generate features for machine learning algorithms. The Linguistic Inquiry and Word Count tool (LIWC) uses a predefined lexicon, counting words in specific psychological categories in order to measure characteristics of a text [30]. This tool has been successfully used to study the prevalence of emotion or affect in documents [10]. Taboada et al.'s Semantic Orientation CALculator [29] used manually compiled lexicons for sentiment analysis, with consistent results across a variety of types of product reviews.

[1] http://depts.washington.edu/sccl/tools

Many sentiment analysis techniques, such as these, are most successful when applied to carefully authored, lengthier content, but often struggle when faced with informal online communication. There have been efforts to adapt some of these techniques to work with such content. Thelwall et al. detected positive, negative, and neutral emotions in MySpace blog posts, which use more informal language including nonstandard spellings and grammar. Classifying the strength of both negative and positive sentiment independently on 5 point scales, their algorithm, SentiStrength, performed well relative to other machine learning approaches because of its ability to correct misspellings and its sentiment strength lexicon, in combination with other features [31].

The Affect Analysis Model uses a database of emoticons, abbreviations, interjections, and other words that had been manually associated with nine emotions to drive a rule-based affect classification system that analyzes affect at the word, phrase, and sentence level [21]. This system was developed specifically for informal online communications, including hundreds of popular abbreviations and emoticons in its database. Over two blog post data sets, the Affect Analysis Model reached 72% and 77% accuracy, and outperformed other systems on news headlines. Although work such as this is promising, "spontaneous text communication" such as collaborative online chat presents other unique problems, with extremely short, hastily written messages and rapidly shifting topics and affective states.

There are noted challenges in applying lexicon-based approaches, such as the LIWC tool, to naturalistic or jargon-ridden language [25]. Some word associations that lexicon-based approaches rely on break down in specialized domains. In techniques developed for more formal documents, punctuation, nonstandard capitalizations, grammar, and misspellings are often discarded as noise. This makes LIWC and other existing tools inappropriate in this work. In our data set, messages often communicate affect through grammar and spelling modification, capitalization, and punctuation: e.g. "in there???" and "WHAT WHO DID THAT" (*annoyance* and *frustration*). While these issues have been studied before in the context of blog posts, very little previous work has focused on affect classification in chat messages.

In addition to lexicons, a variety of other approaches have been studied. Liu et al.'s EmpathyBuddy made use of real-world knowledge, obtained from the Open Mind Common Sense knowledgebase, to power an affective email client, which displayed Chernoff face-style feedback alongside email messages. Participants in a user study perceived the email client as more intelligent than a version which displayed random faces [15].

Other work has had some success with n-gram features, or short phrases derived from the data set itself, to inform classification. Rather than a predefined lexicon of words with known associations, the significance of the n-grams is learned from the available data. Aman and Szpakowicz experimented with lexicon-based features from the General Inquirer and WordNet-Affect [28] in addition to other features, such as emoticons, exclamation points, and question marks, for classifying blog post sentences according to a taxonomy of six basic emotions. The combination of all of these types of features was found to be the most successful configuration, compared to using any one group of features in isolation [2].

Mishne supplemented word counts with punctuation, emoticons, and length of blog post. While providing an important exploration of a feature-enhanced analysis approach, the results yielded a modest 8% improvement over the 50% baseline on average, stating that further improvement could be obtained by increasing the amount of training data [18].

Gilbert explored the relationship between the words written in emails and the rank of the email recipient in the workplace hierarchy. Recipients were ranked as higher, lower, or the same as the sender within a dataset of 2,000 messages from the Enron email corpus. A logistic regression model was used to determine the most predictive unigrams, bigrams, and trigrams from the emails. Support vector machine (SVM) classification based on these phrases achieved 70% accuracy with three-fold cross-validation [9].

Learning the terms of interest from the data set under study can provide both advantages and disadvantages. Mohammad experimented with both lexicons and n-gram features to classify affect in text. Findings showed that the efficacy of word-level lexicons (WordNet-Affect and NRC) was correlated with the size of the lexicon, with the larger lexicon (NRC) showing significant improvements over the use of n-gram features alone for sentence level affect classification. The study also found that the classification performance of n-gram features was domain specific; namely that n-gram features trained on data from one domain were unable to classify affect as well as lexicon features when transferred to a new domain [19].

Most work in this area has focused on texts written by an individual, but there has also been work on affect detection in collaborative contexts, e.g. investigating applications of modern text classification techniques for analyzing computer supported cooperative learning environments [25]. There remains a need for affect classification methods suited to chat messages from distributed collaborative work.

CLASSIFYING AFFECT IN TEXT CHAT LOGS

Our goal was to automate the process of affect labeling in a specific set of chat logs produced by an extended scientific collaboration. We begin by describing the corpus and the manual labeling process we used to generate truth data for machine learning. Then, we describe the results of experiments on different feature selection and classification configurations.

The Supernova Factory Chat Dataset

Our dataset is comprised of chat logs collected from the Nearby Supernova Factory [3], an international astrophysics collaboration of approximately 30 core members; about half of the scientists were located in the U.S. and the other half in France. The scientists were monitoring the occurrence of Type Ia supernovae, a specific type of stellar explosions that have a consistent brightness that allows them to be used to effectively measure the distances to other galaxies and trace the expansion history of the universe. The scientists, distributed across multiple time zones, operated their telescope remotely three nights per week using chat as the primary means of communication; during such operation, numerous technical and scientific decisions involving the operation of the telescope had to be made quickly and collaboratively.

There are a total of 485,045 chat messages in the corpus. The top 32 human participants contributed over 500 messages each, or 300,684 messages total, accounting for the majority of the data. Most of the rest were produced by automated programs ("bots") using chat to relay critical changes to the environment (sunrise/sunset; weather; telescope settings, etc.) [24]. Individual chat messages are very short, with the vast majority between 5 and 10 words in length. The chat logs span 1,319 days (nearly four years).

Coding for Affect

We prepared training data through a manual coding process. A subset of the data was annotated with any number of non-mutually-exclusive affect codes by between 1 and 5 undergraduate and graduate students in our research group. Below, we describe in more detail the mechanics and justification of the manual labeling process.

Because our main goal in this work was to facilitate a rich analysis of the dynamics of distributed work in a specific data set, we constructed a taxonomy of affect [27] through a combination of open, axial, and selective coding grounded in the data [6] and affective terms from Plutchik's taxonomy of emotion [22,23]. This approach was our solution to the problem of translating a large body of existing work on affect and emotion into a more appropriate and useful analytic tool for our particular data set. The resulting taxonomy allows us to examine the specific types of affective expression present in our data because it accounts for the distinct ways in which these expressions are molded by the text-based medium.

Over the course of several months we conducted iterative, open coding of the chat messages. Coders were allowed to label messages with as many affective terms as they believed applied to each message, and they were free to add new terms to the taxonomy. Messages could be coded as "no affect" to distinguish messages that had been identified as lacking affect from those which were not yet coded.

The interpretation of affect in any recorded communication is inherently subjective. In deciding which affect labels to

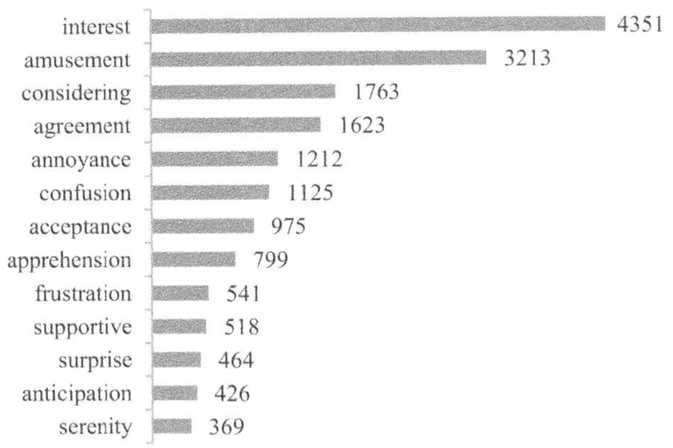

Figure 1. Number of times each of the top 13 affect codes was applied.

time	*speaker*	*message*
05:58:41	Alice	ok, so where was the f***ing SN on the image? #1: interest / anger #2: annoyance / confusion#3: interest / frustration
05:58:55	Alice	was it the bright blob? #1: interest / anger #2: considering #3: interest
05:59:03	Ben	5876 absorption is much wider than the H alpha in v space #1, #2, #3: no affect
05:59:18	Ben	Oh hmmm. #1, #2, #3: considering
05:59:28	Ben	Lemme see what [the] coordinates were... #1, #2, #3: no affect

06:13:07	Charlie	is it "well-developed"? #1: interest
06:13:18	Alice	Should be an interesting experiment. #1, #2: anticipation #3: interest
06:13:19	Dana	yes #1, #3: agreement #2: no affect
06:12:20	Dana	big!! #1: excitement / agreement #2, #3: excitement

Figure 2. Two anonymized examples of conversations from our dataset. Each segment was coded by three members of the research team; these annotations are shown below each line.

apply to a given chat message, coders were asked not to attempt to guess what emotion the speaker was feeling, nor the affect that the speaker may have intended to express. Instead, they were asked to focus on the affect that they believed was communicated by the message in the context of the conversation. Coders were encouraged to trust their own instincts as experienced human readers of chat messages from this data set.

Given the nature of this task, we did not find that any existing qualitative data analysis software was suitable. We

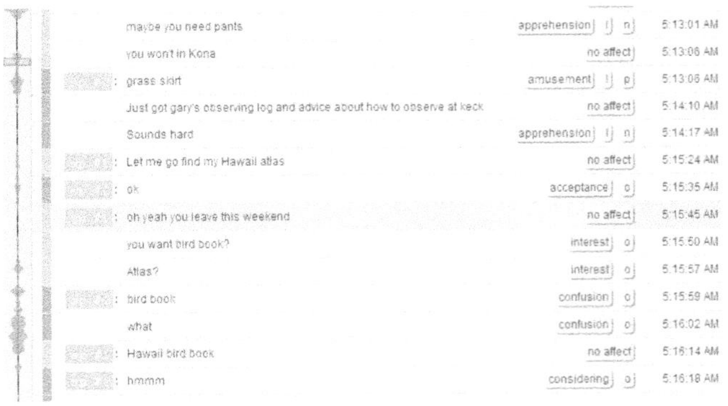

Figure 3. A screenshot of the coding tool developed by team members, as seen by an individual coder applying codes. (Codes *o, l, h, n,* and *p* refer to neutral, low, and high intensity, and negative and positive valence, respectively.)

needed to allow up to 10 human coders to efficiently work together on thousands of short, sequential lines of chat data, and this data needed to be easily accessible and transformable for machine learning procedures and statistical analysis. Thus, as part of preparing the ground truth data, we developed and used our own web-based coding tool, pictured in Figure 3, which we plan to present in greater detail in a future paper and release publicly.

As the affect taxonomy stabilized, we integrated the categories we had developed with Plutchik's taxonomy of emotion to facilitate comparison to other work and ensure that our taxonomy captured the breadth of possible expressions of emotion. We also added codes for intensity (low, neutral, and high) and valence (positive and negative) to allow for more coarse analysis and comparison to prior sentiment analysis research, which typically focuses on positive and negative sentiment. We do not address these codes in this paper. The resulting taxonomy includes 40 different categories of affect. Some of these categories – such as *interest*, *considering*, and *agreement* – are cognitive aspects of interaction that are closely linked with an affective component in the way that they are communicated or expressed by members of the group. This inclusive and flexible aspect of our taxonomy ensures that it captures the broad range of affective expressions that influence group dynamics.

With the taxonomy solidified, a team of three primary coders and five additional coders, all part of the research team, coded about 5% of the data set over a period of about 8 weeks. Of 27,344 messages coded, 15,942 (58%) were coded as 'no affect' by at least one person. About 18,000 messages were coded by exactly one rater, the rest by up to 5 raters. Most of the affect codes were used too infrequently for successful machine learning: Figure 1 shows the most commonly applied 13 affect codes, which we focus on throughout this paper.

In many cases, multiple affect codes may apply, such as *annoyance* and *frustration* applying to these three messages, sent by the same person: "Did I see a bunch of =

vs = = in there??? / WHAT / WHO DID THAT". These coincident codes sometimes overlap in meaning. At other times, multiple codes with distinct meanings may apply: *anger and confusion* were applied to a conversation about error-prone software. Example messages where this expressiveness is especially useful are included in Figure 2. Of those messages coded, 1,599 were coded with more than one affect code by at least one coder (129 were coded with more than two affect codes by at least one coder).

Reliability

Several characteristics of our data make reliability calculation challenging. There are between 1 and 5 raters per message, which can be modeled as missing data. Since the 40 codes of interest are subjective, not mutually exclusive, and may be conceptually overlapping, the criteria for agreement are atypical: non-matching codes may sometimes reflect a degree of agreement instead of disagreement. If we are to estimate the reliability of the taxonomy as a whole, rather than the reliability for each code independently, then it becomes a problem that raters could apply more than one code per message.

One of the most widely used reliability statistics, Cohen's kappa [7], is not easily applied to this data because of the variable number of coders and the large number of codes. A multitude of variations exist, such as Fleiss' kappa [8] which can work with more than two coders, but cannot handle missing data (i.e. variable number of raters). Krippendorff's alpha [13], one of the most flexible reliability statistics, handles variable numbers of raters and is nearly appropriate, but does not work with non-mutually-exclusive categories.

After studying the available techniques, we decided to modify and extend Cohen's kappa. Instead of analyzing the entire taxonomy of affect with its overlapping categories at once, we examined the reliability of each code separately. This also had the advantage of providing useful code-level information. However, we wanted to carefully control the criteria for agreement and disagreement between coders. We also wanted to use all of the data coded by multiple raters, regardless of how many raters had coded it. Although Cohen's kappa has known weaknesses [13], it is also widely understood, so we developed a way to compute a version of kappa over our coded data.

In general, kappa represents the percent agreement over data points, corrected by the probability of chance agreement. To compute it, we needed to be able to calculate two quantities: the percent of the data points where coders are observed to be in agreement, and an estimate of the probability of coders agreeing by chance. We defined agreement about a particular code on a single chat message in the following way: if more than half of raters said that the code was present, or if all of them said it was absent, then they are in agreement. Otherwise they are in disagreement.

This allows the computation of the percentage of observed agreement, in the manner of Cohen's kappa. Computing the probability of coders agreeing by chance directly is more complex because of the variable number of raters and variable number of codes.

We developed an estimate of the probability of chance agreement based on a Monte Carlo method. Similar to the calculations for Cohen's kappa, we first calculate the marginal probabilities of choosing each code for each individual coder, and the marginal probabilities of applying specific numbers of codes for each individual coder.

Code	Obs. % Agreement	Prob. Chance Agreement	Kappa
interest	0.925	0.609	0.808
amusement	0.933	0.827	0.611
agreement	0.954	0.909	0.491
considering	0.931	0.864	0.49
confusion	0.906	0.755	0.615
acceptance	0.941	0.828	0.657
annoyance	0.929	0.693	0.77
apprehension	0.876	0.737	0.529
supportive	0.961	0.906	0.583
surprise	0.968	0.93	0.543
anticipation	0.942	0.9	0.424
serenity	0.923	0.808	0.602
frustration	0.971	0.935	0.55

Table 1. Kappa statistics showing the reliability of 13 affect codes in our data set.

Next, we randomly simulate the rating of a very large number of messages. For each simulated message, we randomly generate the codes that the raters will apply, sampling from the pre-computed distributions. Counting the number of these simulated messages where agreement occurred (according to our definition) allows us to estimate the probability of random agreement. The Monte Carlo simulation continues until all probability estimates are stable to within 0.0001, generally requiring about 2 million messages to be simulated.

Finally, we calculate kappa in the usual way, given the rate of observed agreement and the probability of chance agreement. Table 1 shows the kappa values for each of the 13 affect codes that we discuss in this paper. Our kappa values ranged from 0.424 to 0.808, which is generally comparable to reliabilities obtained in previous research coding for affect or emotion [2,21].

OUR APPROACH

Our purpose in classifying affect is to automatically apply affect labels to our entire chat dataset with reasonable accuracy. With a sufficient amount of chat data coded for affect, we began developing a pipeline of data processing steps and classifier configurations, seeking the configuration with the strongest precision and recall for as many different categories of affect as possible.

Because most of the affect codes in our taxonomy still had far too few examples to use for machine learning, we focused on only the 13 affect codes that were manually applied over 300 times (Figure 1). This included a mix of positive and negative codes, as well as some closely related codes (e.g. *frustration* and *annoyance*).

We have already mentioned several significant challenges to successful classification of chat messages using current text classification algorithms. Facing these problems required numerous choices throughout the classification pipeline, including preprocessing steps, features, and classification algorithms. In order to explore this vast space to find the most successful overall pipeline, we ran a series of experiments designed to test each aspect of the pipeline in isolation. Combining these results yielded the findings we present in this paper.

We describe the options considered at each step in the pipeline, explaining how we have dealt with the challenges specific to chat messages and which choices were supported by experimental results.

Experiment Setup

In order to maximize our efficient use of the limited truth data, we used 10-fold cross validation [32] for all experiments. This helps to avoid making decisions that work well on training data but do not generalize well. Here we also describe our preparation of truth data and our software architecture.

Data preparation

For classification, we transformed the manually-labeled chat messages into training sets, one for each code, with examples labeled "present" or "absent" for each code. In order to do this, we had to decide how to use labels that raters disagreed on, and how to account for the much larger number of negative examples rather than positive for each code.

As previously mentioned, raters frequently, and often justifiably, disagree about what affect is present in a given message. For the purposes of creating truth data for classification, we assigned a given affect label in the truth data to any messages where any of the raters applied that affect code. Reliability was low for some affect codes, reflecting low internal consistency within the raters, but not low validity (i.e. low inter-rater reliability does not imply that the codes fail to capture affect). The process by which the taxonomy was developed and applied is the best assurance that the codes we used actually reflect affect expression in the data.

For all of our affect categories, there are far more messages without a given affect code (negative examples) than there are messages where that code applies (positive examples). The imbalance in the labeled data is a common problem in machine learning tasks. In such situations, it is difficult for a classification algorithm to do better than could be obtained by simply guessing the majority class. For this reason, there are many established methods for balancing data sets. We experimented with different balancing strategies including up-sampling (randomly duplicating positive examples) and down-sampling (randomly removing more-common negative examples). We found that down-sampling led to more consistent results across different affect codes.

In the experiments reported below, we applied downsampling both to the training sets and to the held-out sets in cross validation. Thus, the performance would be different on real unlabeled data where the percent of positive examples is very low. In order to evaluate classifiers with realistic unlabeled data, the relative importance of minimizing false positives vs. minimizing false negatives must be determined. These decisions depend heavily on the purpose for which labels are needed, and will vary from one project to another. We decided to downsample the held-out sets for this paper because the results generated are agnostic of the specific project context and are more easily interpreted.

Software architecture

Key to our rapid exploration of different choices for the machine learning pipeline was the use of a relational database for data storage and manipulation. Our web-based chat coding application, unlike most commercial coding systems, uses a MySQL server for storing both messages and applied codes. Our software for running machine learning experiments connects directly to this database. It is implemented in Java and relies on the popular Weka library for implementations of classification algorithms and data processing [12].

Chat Segmentation

Two significant challenges in classifying chat messages are that the messages are extremely short and highly dependent on context. We developed a segmentation procedure that reduces the number of negligibly small data points and incorporates message context.

Sparsity of feature space

Many approaches to text classification rely on "bag of words" features. The ordered list of words in the raw text is simplified by discarding all the ordering information, leaving only the number of times each word occurred in the document. This approach has been successful for many text analysis problems [32].

A corpus of text documents generally uses a large number of different words, while each individual document uses relatively few. Thus, the feature space produced by bag of words features has a high dimensionality, but is very sparse since each document has a value of 0 for most of the features. Moreover, the overlap in words between any two documents is likely to be small. Under these conditions, many machine learning algorithms are prone to overfitting. That is, they might detect and learn patterns in the data that do not generalize beyond the specific group of documents used for training.

With chat messages, this effect is even more pronounced. The average length of messages in our data is 26 characters, or about 5 words. This means that the bag of words created from each data point probably contains only a miniscule fraction of the total vocabulary in the corpus. There are likely to be many spurious patterns created by the random coincidence of these words in messages, making the patterns actually relevant to classification more difficult to detect.

Contextual dependence

Much of the information about individual messages is not present in the messages themselves, but rather in the surrounding context. Messages are often not understandable without reading many lines before (and sometimes after) in the logs, posing a challenge to message-by-message classification.

In classification problems, the data points being classified are typically assumed to be independent of one another. Yet, chat messages rarely stand on their own. Approaches which do support learning of labels in context of their surroundings, such as hidden Markov models (HMMs) or more general graphical models, are available but not commonly used for affect identification in text. We discuss our approaches to accounting for context in the following sections, leaving experiments with graphical models like HMMs for future work.

The segmentation procedure

To deal with small message lengths and to help capture message context, we split the data into segments, combining messages based on their proximity in time.

Combination of messages was determined by a simple time threshold: if two messages were separated by less than the threshold, they were grouped together. We evaluated the classification performance achieved with different segmentation configurations. Because many consecutive messages in our data set were separated by less than 25 seconds, we tested nine different time thresholds from 5 to 45 seconds at 5 second intervals.

We also developed and evaluated two different formulations of the segmentation procedure. One formulation grouped together messages by different speakers, reflecting an assumption that affective state is distributed among all of the chat participants. The second formulation did not combine messages by different speakers, presuming that affective state is bound to individuals.

Regardless of the time threshold selected, segmentation resulted in a significant reduction in data set size due to the combination of data points: a conservative threshold of 10 seconds, not separating by participant, halved the number of data points. The effect was less pronounced when we maintained separation between participants: at 10-second-segmentation, the dataset only shrank to two-thirds of its original size. In general, reducing the amount of training data makes machine learning more difficult.

However, we also observed that segmentation did have the desired effect: the number of negligibly small messages (40 characters or less, spanning only a few words) in the data set decreased, having been combined with other messages. We hypothesized that the higher word-count per data point would improve classification results. Additionally, the segmentation procedure makes contextual information available, because the messages in the immediate context of each data point are pulled in and combined.

In our experiments, the effectiveness of segmentation procedures varied from one affect code to another. For some codes, performance differences between different time threshold settings were as great as 10%. For most of the 13 affect codes we tested, the best classification performance was achieved with a time threshold of 30 seconds, keeping messages from different participants in different segments. We believe that this threshold balances the harmful effects of reducing the data set size against the benefits of increasing the size of data points.

Enriched Feature Space

Face-to-face communication relies on facial expressions and tone to communicate affect. Without these channels, chat participants use other means to communicate affect. We developed a rich set of features to help capture these aspects of chat messages, including pronoun categories, punctuation, emoticons, spelling changes, and the words in the message.

Linguistic challenges

Our data set, and chat communication generally, is rife with informal language and atypical spelling and punctuation. Unfortunately, many successful techniques for automatically analyzing text, such as LIWC [30], rely on one or more characteristics of standard written language, such as a reasonably correct vocabulary, correct grammar, and predictable punctuation.

For example, in converting a text document into a sequence of words, the text is usually split up at spaces and punctuation characters (although other techniques do exist). Indiscriminate use of this technique on chat communication risks obliterating much of the interesting content. Emoticons and other nonstandard punctuations (*e.g.* "??????!") carry a great deal of meaning in chat, but would typically be removed or distorted during this process.

As noted earlier, lexicon-based approaches to affect detection and sentiment analysis in text [10,19,28,31] are difficult to adapt to communications with frequent nonstandard spellings and abbreviations. Because of these irregularities and because of their short length, typical chat

The telescope is stuck! >:(	The exclamation point and emoticon suggest *frustration*.
The telescope is stuuuuuuuuuck...	Repetition of the letter "u" suggests *annoyance*.
The telescope is stuck??	Multiple question marks suggest *confusion*.

Figure 4. The addition of one of our features dramatically changes the meaning of the phrase.

Message Information (4 features)
duration: the length of the segment in seconds
length: the number of characters in the segment
characters per second: length / duration
rate: the average rate of messages in the segment
Pronouns (7 features)
of **1st person singular** pronouns: I, me, my, mine…
of **2nd person singular** pronouns: you, your, yours…
of **3rd person singular** pronouns: she, he, hers, his…
of **1st person plural** pronouns: we, us, ours…
of **2nd person plural** pronouns: you all, yourselves
of **3rd person plural** pronouns: they, them, theirs, their…
of **interrogative** pronouns: who, whom, whose
Punctuations (8 features)
and length of **ellipses**
and length of **question marks**
and length of **exclamation points**
and length of **?!s and !?s**
Special strings (3 features)
of **negation words**: no, not, cannot, aren't, can't…
of **swear words**
of **known people names** (list of about 18)
Low-level spelling features (8 features)
and length of **capital letters**
and length of **"hmmm"**-variants: hm, hmm…
length of **laughter** phrases: lol, hehe, heehee, haha…
and length of **repeated letter sequences** 3 or longer
Emoticons (varies, around 8-15 features)
Counts the **number of each emoticon** in the message.
Vocabulary of up to about 2200 (marshall.freeshell.org/smileys.html)
Emoticons must occur in at least 10 data points to be counted
Bag of Words (varies, around 200-300 words usually) Stemmed (Porter) and lowercased

Figure 5. A detailed list of features used.

messages may contain few if any words that are recognized by these tools. In our data, there is also a large amount of jargon and a mix of multiple languages, making the application of lexicon-based techniques especially challenging.

Features

We included duration, length, and rate of messages as features to capture this aspect of chat communication. A conversation over a short period of time, with a high rate of messages, could signal urgency or anger, such as a problem with the telescope. Whereas a conversation over a longer period of time and a lower message rate could signal one of the participants explaining a process to another, or a less stressful event.

Grammatical markers, such as personal pronouns, and punctuation, unusual spelling, and emoticons may also communicate affect. For example, the statement "*the telescope is stuck*" can have a markedly different character when expressed using various non-verbal cues embedded in the text (Figure 4).

In addition to the above features, we included more traditional bag-of-words features, based on Weka's *StringToWordVector* filter. Certain words occur more often with specific affect codes. For example, *confusion* is very often linked with phrases containing variations of "confuse," such as "confusing" and "confused." *Amusement* is often paired with phrases containing "haha," as in "You should just live there hahaha" or "Did you have enough coffee this morning? Haha."

Evaluation of feature sets

We experimented with two different configurations of the bag-of-words features: one using the Porter stemming algorithm (reducing each word to its base form), and one removing stopwords (words like "and" or "the"). Word stemming had no noticeable effect on classification performance, but the removal of stopwords consistently *decreased* performance by 2 to 3% for most affect codes we tested. Based on these results, we decided to use a stemming algorithm, but no stoplist, to generate the bag of words.

In order to determine the value of the other features outside of the bag of words, we measured the performance difference between a data set prepared with standard bag-of-words features (a large set of about 1.5k words), and similar data sets that were augmented with sets of additional features (such as punctuation, pronouns, or emoticons). Performance improvements of a few percent from each of these new types of features in isolation prompted us to continue developing and improving them, and to combine them into the extensive set of rich features summarized in Figure 5. We also applied additional reduction techniques to the bag-of-words features, such as a minimum frequency threshold and lowercasing.

Classifier Configuration

Aside from the data preparation procedure and the set of features to be used in classification, we considered a variety of options for the classification algorithm itself.

Our taxonomy of affect provides a multitude of categories into which chat messages can be classified. There are several ways that we could formulate this as a multiclass classification problem, where we would produce a single trained classifier that selected one from among the 13 affect codes for each message submitted. However, because our categories are not mutually exclusive, we decided to create a separate binary classifier for each of the affect codes tested. We plan to experiment with other configurations in future work.

Classifier	F-measure	Precision	Recall	Accuracy
Naïve Bayes	0.650	0.637	0.691	0.637
Logistic Reg.	0.730	0.731	0.731	0.730
SVM (SMO)	**0.759**	**0.766**	**0.751**	**0.761**
C4.5 (J48)	0.700	0.724	0.680	0.710

Table 2: Performance comparison of classification algorithms from preliminary experiments, averaged over 4 runs of cross validation for each of the 13 codes tested.

Our early experiments used Weka [12] to test a variety of classification algorithms including Naïve Bayes, C4.5 decision trees, support vector machines (SVM), logistic regression, voted perceptron, boosting and bagging. We tested different parameter configurations for each of these algorithms, devoting more attention in subsequent experiments to those with more promising initial results. In these initial experiments, we found that linear-kernel SVM and logistic regression were quite effective (Table 2), which is consistent with prior results [9]. Our later experimental setups focused on configurations of SVM and logistic regression classifiers, and included Naïve Bayes and decision tree approaches for comparison.

Code	F-measure	Precision	Recall	Accuracy
interest	0.925	0.925	0.926	93%
amusement	0.734	0.78	0.694	75%
agreement	0.779	0.813	0.748	79%
considering	0.761	0.774	0.749	76%
confusion	0.738	0.743	0.733	74%
acceptance	0.773	0.805	0.743	78%
annoyance	0.642	0.668	0.618	66%
apprehension	0.638	0.657	0.619	65%
supportive	0.626	0.66	0.596	64%
surprise	0.71	0.789	0.645	74%
anticipation	0.748	0.743	0.753	75%
serenity	0.663	0.74	0.601	69%
frustration	0.673	0.734	0.621	70%

Table 3: Classifier performance for each of the top 13 codes, from cross validation on data with class frequencies balanced.

RESULTS AND DISCUSSION

In this section we describe the performance of our classification pipeline on each of the 13 most commonly occurring affect codes in our taxonomy (Table 3). We also discuss which features were most useful for classifying each of the affect codes we tested (Figure 6).

Classification performance

The results of evaluating the SVM classifier with 10-fold cross validation for the top 13 affect codes are provided in Table 3. Accuracy for most affect codes fell in the 70-80% range. The SVM algorithm is designed to be robust to large feature spaces, which are typical in text classification applications [32]. Others working on affect classification in text have also found SVMs to be effective [26,33].

Predictive features

Of particular interest to researchers studying affect in collaborative text chat are the specific signals that chat participants use to communicate affect. We examined the weight vectors produced by the linear SVM training algorithm to better understand which features were most influential. Note that this analysis is limited in that it does not allow quantitative comparison from one trained classifier to another. However, it does reveal the most significant features for each affect code, as modeled by the classifier (Figure 6).

The top features span the variety of types of features; however, different codes are associated not only with specific features but specific feature types. For example, *amusement* is most clearly indicated by various emoticons. However, most of the other affect codes do not strongly rely on emoticons. Meanwhile, the *anticipation* code chiefly uses bag-of-words features, words that are often used when discussing the future. In contrast, more immediate, active affect codes, such as *frustration* and *surprise* are based mostly on punctuation, message rate, and low-level features.

Pennebaker et al. have had success using functional linguistic cues to detect emotional content [30]. In everyday speech, there are words we use that carry informational content (the semantics of what we mean to say) and those that make the utterance sensible. The latter, functional elements of text are comparatively more meaning- and context-agnostic. In contrast, EmpathyBuddy relied on real-world knowledge, extracting emotional content from semantics [15]. The evaluation of the tool did indicate that the method was able to identify some emotional content.

For some of the affect categories that we analyzed, entirely non-semantic cues like capitalization and punctuation appear to be the most important. Semantic cues, including smiley faces and content words that carry meaning, are more useful for other codes.

In prior work, it has been common for some categories of affect, e.g. negative sentiment [31], to be more easily classified than others. Our results suggest that these types of differences may stem from these researchers' different choices for features. In our experiments without emoticons, for example, the classification accuracy for *amusement* decreased significantly. This suggests that future improvements may be obtained by continuing to develop new features, focusing specifically on the worst performing affect categories.

Considering	**Annoyance**	**Frustration**
"think"	# swearing	# swearing
# question marks	"pascal"	# 1st sg. pronouns
"maybe"	"--" (dash)	msg. length
ellipsis length	"all"	ellipsis length
"or"	"damn"	capital. length
hmm length	"again"	chars/second
# hmmm	"I"	# negation words
???? length	"only"	"it"
"probably"	"me"	# repeated letters
"x"	msg. length	# interrogative prns
Surprise	**Serenity**	**Interest**
# exclamation pts.	"good"	???? length
"wow"	emoticon ":)"	# question marks
msg. length	"nice"	"je" (fr.) (-)
???? length	"cool"	"sunrise"
!!!! length	!!!! length	"bert"
"oh"	msg. length	"est" (fr.) (-)
ellipsis length	"right"	"where"
# repeated letters	"too"	"wonder"
segment duration	# 1st pl. pronouns	"sunset"
"right"	_do (-)	"interesting"
Confusion	**Apprehension**	**Amusement**
???? length	"bad"	emoticon ";)"
# question marks	"something"	emoticon ":)"
"understand"	"problem"	laughter
"confus_"	"we"	emoticon ";-)"
"why"	"seem"	"fun"
"what"	"too"	laughter length
"nothing"	msg. length	"p"
"wrong"	"not"	# people names
msg. length	# 3rd sg. Pronouns	"sleep"
"thought"	# swearing	"of"
Agreement	**Acceptance**	**Anticipation**
"yes"	"ok	"hope"
"yeah"	"okay"	"if"
"yep"	"ah"	"next"
msg. length	msg. length	"should"
segment duration	# 1st sg. pronouns	"think"
"right"	"oh"	"will"
"yup"	"yep"	"try"
"agree"	# question marks	"at"
"sure"	"put"	"like"
"okay"	segment duration	"to"
Supportive		
"good"		
???? length (-)		
msg. length		
"if"		
"about"		
"the"		
"--" (dash)		
"derek"		
"he"		
"think"		

Figure 6. Top 10 features for each of 13 classes. (-) indicates that feature negatively relates to the affect code.

Methodology

Related work by Rosé et al. in the domain of computer-supported collaborative learning research has also developed analytic tools that allow people to code data more efficiently [25], as we aim to do for analysis of affect in chat messages from distributed collaborations. One key distinction of our approach is the coding scheme itself. Although we did incorporate an existing taxonomy of emotion, we also engaged in a crucial open coding process. This method is especially important for the analysis of communication of a distributed group using an evolving digital medium that influences interactions [27]. Analyzing the role of affect in distributed collaboration by examining traces created by ever-evolving technological media requires the freedom to refine and expand coding schemes. The automation step, therefore, would best serve this type of work if it did not methodologically require a complete and stable taxonomy of manual labels.

In discussing the methodological validity of automating coding, Rosé et al. raise the issue that automated methods base their classifications on the most predictive features, which may not be relevant to the cognitive process of human coding. For this reason, it is important to use algorithms that have interpretable learned mechanisms; optimizing for quantitative performance metrics is comparatively less important than maintaining a grasp on the methodological reasonableness of the classification itself. We reported the most predictive features for the SVM classifier, but not all algorithms afford even this level of transparency. We plan to consider how to surface this kind of information, as well as allow more transparent access to the results of classification, in future work.

Gill et al. suggest that successful social engagement relies on understanding the experience and emotional cues of others, noting the challenge of doing this in a relatively impoverished computer-mediated environment [10]. Our analysis of influential features for each of the affect categories offers clues as to how different affect states might be expressed and experienced uniquely in text chat. Grammar use, punctuation, the length of responses, and other features, all form a part of this experience much the way facial cues, tone of voice, and body language might augment the emotions of face-to-face communication in different ways. These results suggest that the experience of affect in text-based chat environments may indeed be much richer and less impoverished than long imagined.

Limitations

In future work we will consider a more qualitative consideration of *which* errors classifiers make. It is possible, for example, that one classifier makes qualitatively worse mistakes than another, misclassifying more obvious examples, whereas a better classifier only missteps on nuanced cases that are difficult even for humans. This evaluation would require an additional step of human re-evaluation of code appropriateness.

Furthermore, some apparent classification errors may not actually be errors. Preliminary inspection of a selection of chat messages where the labels produced by the SVM disagreed with our own manual coding found that in many cases a strong case could be made that the classifier's label actually made sense. As classification methods become increasingly robust and accurate, reaching human accuracy in difficult problems like this one, the errors that human coders make pose a challenge. Although reliability can help to verify the internal consistency of raters, to err is human, and so perhaps classifiers ought to balance measures of confidence against models of human error to produce more verbose descriptions of labeling results than precision and recall.

CONCLUSIONS AND FUTURE WORK

The study of affect expression in distributed work can benefit considerably from traces left by digital communication media, if scalable analytic methods are available.

We contribute an application of machine learning to scale fine-grained, subjective human analysis up to a large chat log. We interpreted affect as a dynamic phenomenon by segmenting the chat data set on a temporal, per-participant basis. We further augmented a standard bag-of-words feature set with analogues of non-verbal cues, such as grammatical markers including unusual spelling and emoticons, and meta-information about the chat messages such as duration, length, and rate. These decisions led to better classification results, though other avenues of exploration may offer additional improvements.

We were able to classify text for 13 affect codes with F-measures of 70-90%. We also produced a set of predictive features for each of the 13 types of affect considered, which may be applicable in other domains. We have made our machine learning software, *ALOE*[2], open source to facilitate validation, comparison to other techniques, and further research on affect in chat messages within the CSCW community.

ACKNOWLEDGMENTS

We thank the reviewers for their feedback which greatly strengthened this paper, and we thank the scientists of the SNfactory collaboration. This work was funded in part by an NSF Graduate Research Fellowship in Computer Science.

REFERENCES

1. Amabile, T.M., Barsade, S.G., Mueller, J.S., and Staw, B.M. Affect and Creativity at Work. *Administrative Science Quarterly 50*, 3 (2005), 367–403.
2. Aman, S. and Szpakowicz, S. Identifying expressions of emotion in text. In *Text, Speech and Dialogue*. 2007, 196–205.
3. Aragon, C., Poon, S., Monroy-Hernandez, A., and Aragon, D. A Tale of Two Online Communities: Fostering Collaboration and Creativity in Scientists and Children. *Proc. C&C 2009*, ACM (2009), 9–18.
4. Ashforth, B.E. and Humphrey, R.H. Emotion in the Workplace: A Reappraisal. *Human Relations 48*, 2 (1995), 97–125.
5. Barsade, S.G. The ripple effect: Emotional contagion and its influence on group behavior. *Administrative Science Quarterly 47*, December (2002), 644–675.
6. Charmaz, K. *Constructing grounded theory: A practical guide through qualitative analysis*. SAGE, London, 2006.
7. Cohen, J. A coefficient of agreement for nominal scales. *Educational and Psychological Measurement 20*, (1960).
8. Fleiss, J.L. Measuring nominal scale agreement among many raters. *Psychological Bulletin 76*, 5 (1971), 378–382.
9. Gilbert, E. Phrases that signal workplace hierarchy. *Proc. CSCW 2012*, ACM Press (2012), 1037.
10. Gill, A.J., French, R.M., Gergle, D., and Oberlander, J. The language of emotion in short blog texts. *Proc. CSCW 2008*, (2008), 299–302.
11. Grandey, A. Emotions at Work: A Review and Research Agenda. In *Handbook of Organizational Behavior*. SAGE, London, 2008.
12. Hall, M., Frank, E., Holmes, G., Pfahringer, B., Reutemann, P., and Witten, I.H. The WEKA data mining software: an update. *ACM SIGKDD Explorations Newsletter 11*, 1 (2009), 10.
13. Hayes, A.F. and Krippendorff, K. Answering the Call for a Standard Reliability Measure for Coding Data. *Communication Methods and Measures 1*, 1 (2007), 77–89.
14. Keshtkar, F. and Inkpen, D. Using sentiment orientation features for mood classification in blogs. *Proc. NLPKE 2009*, IEEE (2009), 1–6.
15. Liu, H., Lieberman, H., and Selker, T. A model of textual affect sensing using real-world knowledge. *Proc. IUI 2003*, (2003), 125–132.
16. Mentis, H.M., Reddy, M., and Rosson, M.B. Invisible emotion. *Proc. CSCW 2010*, ACM Press (2010), 311–320.
17. Milliken, F.J., Bartel, C.A., and Kurtzberg, T.R. Diversity and creativity in work groups: A dynamic perspective on the affective and cognitive processes that link diversity and performance. In *Group creativity: Innovation through collaboration*. Oxford University Press, New York, 2003, 32–62.
18. Mishne, G. Experiments with Mood Classification in Blog Posts. *Proc. Style 2005*, (2005).
19. Mohammad, S. Portable Features for Classifying Emotional Text. *Proc. NAACL-HLT 2012*, (2012), 587–591.
20. Moore, B.S. and Isen, A.M. *Affect and Social Behavior*. Cambridge University Press, 1990.

[2] http://depts.washington.edu/sccl/tools

21. Neviarouskaya, A., Prendinger, H., and Ishizuka, M. Affect Analysis Model: novel rule-based approach to affect sensing from text. *Natural Language Engineering 17*, 01 (2010), 95–135.

22. Plutchik, R. *The Emotions*. University Press of America, Lanham, MD, 1991.

23. Plutchik, R. The Nature of Emotions. *American Scientist 89*, 4 (2001), 344–350.

24. Poon, S., Thomas, R.C., Aragon, C., and Lee, B. Context-Linked Virtual Assistants for Distributed Teams: An Astrophysics Case Study. *Proc. CSCW 2008*, ACM Press (2008).

25. Rosé, C., Wang, Y.-C., Cui, Y., et al. Analyzing collaborative learning processes automatically: Exploiting the advances of computational linguistics in computer-supported collaborative learning. *Computer-Supported Collaborative Learning 3*, 3 (2008), 237–271.

26. Russ, S.W. *Affect and Creativity: The Role of Affect and Play in the Creative Process*. Routledge, 1993.

27. Scott, T.J., Kuksenok, K., Perry, D., Brooks, M., Anicello, O., and Aragon, C.R. Adapting Grounded Theory to Construct a Taxonomy of Affect in Collaborative Online Chat. *Proc. SIGDOC 2012*, (2012).

28. Strapparava, C. and Valitutti, A. WordNet-Affect: an affective extension of WordNet. *Proc. LREC 2004*, (2004).

29. Taboada, M., Brooke, J., Tofiloski, M., Voll, K., and Stede, M. Lexicon-Based Methods for Sentiment Analysis. *Computational Linguistics 37*, 2 (2011), 267–307.

30. Tausczik, Y.R. and Pennebaker, J.W. The Psychological Meaning of Words: LIWC and Computerized Text Analysis Methods. *Journal of Language and Social Psychology 29*, 1 (2009), 24–54.

31. Thelwall, M., Buckley, K., Paltoglou, G., Cai, D., and Kappas, A. Sentiment strength detection in short informal text. *Journal of the American Society for Information Science and Technology 61*, 12 (2010), 2544–2558.

32. Witten, I.H., Frank, E., and Hall, M.A. *Data Mining: Practical machine learning tools and techniques*. Morgan Kaufmann, 2011.

Voluntary Turnover in a Distributed Work Setting: An Examination of the Role of Spatial Propinquity and Role Similarity in Project Affiliation Networks

Gopakumar Gopalakrishnan
Infosys Labs
Infosys Limited
Electronics City
Bangalore – 5600 100
Gopakumar@infosys.com

Daniel S. Halgin
LINKS Center for Social Network Analysis
University of Kentucky
Lexington, Kentucky – 40506
danhalgin@uky.edu

Stephen P. Borgatti
LINKS Center for Social Network Analysis
University of Kentucky
Lexington, Kentucky – 40506
sborgatti@uky.edu

ABSTRACT
Project affiliation networks (i.e., individuals connected through common project team memberships) create fruitful junctures to understand how individuals are connected to others in their social contexts, especially in distributed organizations. Advances in technology-mediated environments further help individuals develop connections with their colleagues who may or may not be collocated. This embeddedness creates inertial pressures on individuals and constrains them to conform to firm norms and thus stay with the firm. In this paper, we examine whether ties to those who quit the firm can trump the feeling of connection to the firm and thus motivate subsequent quit decisions. We argue that individuals with a greater number of defectors in their project affiliation networks are more likely than others to leave the firm and the influence on those focal individuals will be higher when they are collocated and occupy similar professional roles as the affiliated defectors. We analyze complete project affiliation data linking 728 geographically distributed employees at a multi-national high technology firm across five years to test these arguments. During this time 183 employees voluntarily left the firm. The findings support our arguments and suggest that project affiliation networks in such settings occasion social comparisons among employees and serve as conduits for the diffusion of their career mobility decisions. We discuss the implications of our work for managing voluntary turnover in knowledge intensive distributed organizations.

Author Keywords
Social network analysis; distributed teams; voluntary turnover.

ACM Classification Keywords
J.4 [Social AND Behavioral Sciences]: Psychology; K.4.3 [Organizational Impacts]: Computer-supported collaborative work; Employment; K.6.1 [Project and People Management]: Staffing.

INTRODUCTION
When work is organized around geographically distributed teams, effective coordination of tasks, exchange of information, and resolution of conflicts among team members become non-trivial challenges to realize optimal team outcomes [15, 18, 30]. The social network perspective has offered a fruitful lens to examine these issues in the context of distributed work. For instance, we know that dense networks among team members increase group solidarity, facilitate information exchange, and strengthen attachment to group norms [16, 45, 59, 60].

Similarly, the technology-mediated work environments help individuals accomplish interdependent work, as well as develop connections with colleagues who may or may not be collocated. Such connections further serve as conduits to the flow of signals that could influence their workplace decisions, including the one to quit the firm. However, we know very little about what happens when an individual's connected colleagues at the workplace decide to quit the firm. Does the individual view the departures as pathways to increased resources and opportunities and thus strengthen his attachment to the firm? Or, do the departures create social pressures on the focal individual to also leave? Further, what happens when a colleague who quits occupied a similar role and worked in the same geographical location as the focal individual? These questions assume significance in the contemporary free-agent labor markets [13] where career trajectories unfold in a series of short stints at multiple firms as opposed to a life-long career in a single firm [25]. Workplace connections are likely to play a different role in such scenarios and analyses of those connections stand to offer productive opportunities to advance our understanding of employee quit decisions in distributed organizations.

Recent studies report that an individual's level of attachment to an organization is influenced by connections with co-workers and the greater those connections, the slower the decay of attachment to the organization over time [11]. Ties at the workplace can provide an individual with co-worker support and a sense of belonging and are found to be negatively related to voluntary turnover [21, 44]. In essence, ties to other employees create inertial pressures on an individual and constrain him to conform to firm norms and thus stay with the firm.

While these ties bind an individual to fellow coworkers (and the firm in general), we believe that ties to others who leave the firm activate different mechanisms which can weaken these binds. Mainly, an individual who observes coworkers making career moves is likely to compare himself to those others and make behavioral changes in his own career. We propose that the observation of one or more defectors can trump a feeling of connection that the individual might feel with others who don't choose to leave the firm. Further, we suggest that the influence of those defectors will be higher when they were collocated and occupied similar professional roles as the focal individual.

In the following sections of the paper, we first provide an overview of the changing nature of careers and explain the role of social comparison mechanisms in such contexts. We highlight existing research using a relational perspective to understand voluntary turnover and subsequently introduce our hypotheses related to the role of geographical proximity and role similarity in shaping career mobility decisions.

We then proceed to present the research setting, analyses and, finally conclude with discussion of our findings and their implications. In sum, we advance theory by explaining the powerful influence of co-worker decisions on employee turnover through comparison mechanisms. In doing so, we bring together network-related ideas in organizational behavior and distributed work fields. This synthesis also has key implications for managers of distributed teams.

CAREER MOBILITY AND SOCIAL COMPARISON

Recent studies in the career field suggest that individuals manage their careers in proactive, self-directed ways driven by values and subjective success criteria [2]. Often referred to as the protean career [21, 26], it proposes that individuals must create career opportunities through networking and actions aimed at enhancing their visibility. Thus, skilled and qualified individuals frequently search for career paths and opportunities outside organizational boundaries that provide such satisfaction [29]. This differs from prior eras, where individuals had long term commitments to one firm and top performers rarely changed employers.

One aspect of the boundaryless career is that individuals are often more strongly connected to co-workers than they are to the formal firm [2]. Advances in information and communication technologies allow them access to each other's knowledge, create communities of common interest and foster collaboration across locations [58]. Classic network influence studies report that social interactions determine everything from voting behaviors to prescribing behaviors among physicians [40, 14]. We propose that increased opportunities for social interaction at the workplace can also influence behavioral changes related to career mobility. In contemporary labor markets, network ties to those who leave a firm influence career decisions through social comparison mechanisms and access to novel information.

Social comparison theory [22] suggests that individuals rely on others to make decisions and form attitudes. If comparison with a referent other reveals differences in thoughts, feelings or behaviors, the focal individual is likely to change his or her thoughts, feelings, or behaviors to become consistent with the referent other. Such comparisons are especially likely in risky and ambiguous situations. When an individual is unsure how to behave, he looks to referent others for cues. A similar mechanism is found in the heart of balance theory [28], which states that a person seeks to be congruent with those she likes. When she is not, she feels dissonance, and seeks to reduce it either by changing behaviors or changing ties.

In work settings, researchers find that working with others who are searching for a job increases the salience and perceived viability that an individual will also consider leaving for another firm [21]. We extend such work by proposing that social comparison mechanisms play an important role in shaping career mobility decisions. While new careers promote independence and subjective success, they also lack the certainty and stability of the traditional upward trajectory. As a result, individuals might look to referents to help reduce uncertainty and make sense of possibilities of a boundaryless career. Therefore, we propose that individuals are strongly influenced by the career moves of co-workers in attempts to define security, stability, and career success. When such referent others leave and cut their formal ties with the firm, the focal individual faces pressure to do the same.

Consider the example of employees A and B who work together on the same work team. If A decides to voluntarily leave the firm, employee A's departure might be viewed as an opportunity for B to obtain more resources and power within the firm. For example, in an earlier study among employees of fast-food restaurants, it was found that an individual's job satisfaction increases following the turnover of unhappy friends [38]. We believe that the boundaryless nature of professional careers makes this reaction less likely. Rather than seeing opportunities within the same firm, we believe that B is more likely to emulate A due to social comparison pressures. We propose that B's tie to A will be stronger than B's tie to the firm [25], and therefore B is more likely to seek to form new ties with new firms than to maintain his or her tie to the current firm. If B keeps her tie to the firm, she is likely to experience dissonance as well as uncertainty as to whether she is in accordance with a successful trajectory. If employee C (also a project teammate) decides to leave the firm, employee B faces additional pressure to follow suit.

In addition to social comparison mechanisms, we acknowledge that individuals with co-workers who quit are likely to gain access to new employment opportunities through these existing ties. Social ties can also serve as pipes through which resources flow [50]. Network literature has established that ties to disconnected groups in a network can be sources of novel resources and opportunities [10, 24]. In our example, when employee A joins a new firm they create bridging ties with those who remain at the organization. These bridging ties are possible sources of novel resources such as knowledge about job opportunities to those who remain. The knowledge of these opportunities would be clearly useful for them. Therefore, for the above reasons, we expect that an individual's career decisions are highly influenced by their social connections with fellow employees. Thus,

Hypothesis 1: The more connections that an individual has to co-workers who leave a firm, the more likely the individual will also leave the firm.

SPATIAL PROPINQUITY

The role of spatial dispersion has been central to several studies in the area of distributed work. Scholars have paid significant attention to understand how geographical distance influence collaboration, information exchange, trust, conflict and, shared understanding among team members and various team outcomes [36, 46, 57]. In general, it is reported that opportunities for informal, face-to-face and spontaneous communication between members who work in different geographical locations are highly constrained.

In an earlier study, Allen [1] claimed that when offices of engineers were 30 meters apart, the frequency of communication between them dropped to nearly the same level as with people working in offices that were many miles away. Further, uneven exchange of information, limited awareness of each other's social context, and ambiguities related to the interpretation of information significantly impact interactions between members working in such contexts [17, 27, 32, 35].

While significant advances have been made to design technologies to stimulate and strengthen the communication and interaction in such settings, Bradner and Mark [8] report that in computer mediated situations, people are less cooperative, less likely to be persuaded and more likely to deceive others when they work in different cities.

In the context of distributed software development in an offshoring context (this study setting), onsite members typically interact with clients to specify requirements, map change requests and, review project progress. The offshore members, who are further distributed within various offices in the host country of the focal firm, mainly focus on delivering against those requirements and meeting client expectations. This distance creates differences in workplace experiences and knowledge heterogeneity between these different groups and can trigger occasions for conflicts, increased collaboration costs and errors and ultimately delays in project delivery.

In an extensive review of proximity and distance in work groups, Kiesler and Cummings [36] report that opportunities for increased face-to-face communication that are often available for collocated members increases information exchange, interpersonal attraction, felt commitment and, greater contribution by team members. Further, repeated interactions in between members in collocated settings strengthen group identity and cohesion. Similarly, Olson and Olson [48] highlight the importance of synchronous collocated interactions such as rapid feedback and nuanced information that are essential for individuals working on software projects.

Following this line of reasoning, we propose that the information of the quit decision of an employee will more quickly spread among those in the same office location than across different locations. In a highly mobile labor market where employees actively seek cues from their colleagues to determine the acceptability of leaving a job in order to achieve career success, quit decisions of proximal employees are more likely to influence other collocated members than those in other locations.

However, not all individuals will be equally influenced by ties with proximal co-workers when making career decisions. For instance, those with established security in their careers will be more likely to be subjectively pleased with their accomplishments and perhaps less likely to seek change. In contrast, individuals with uncertainty in terms of career success will likely be more motivated to continually seek out new opportunities outside of the focal organization. We propose that individuals who feel stability in their current positions are less likely to look to others for cues regarding career movements. Job tenure is one proxy for such security. Therefore, those with greater firm tenure are less likely to be interested in external opportunities and therefore less likely to seek comparisons with those who leave. In addition, these individuals are less likely to view their careers as novel, risky, or ambiguous situations. Thus,

Hypotheses 2A: The greater percentage of those teammates who are in the same geographic office and leave, the more likely the individual will leave the firm.

Hypotheses 2B: The above relationship will be moderated by tenure such that younger employees will be more influenced by proximal others.

ROLE SIMILARITY

Extensive evidence suggests that social interactions are more likely to be triggered between similar actors in various instances ranging from marriage to investment decisions. Marriages are likely between individuals with similar level of education and religion and investors invest in same industries [41, 53]. While it is difficult to specify what dimensions of similarity will be salient in a given context, there is strong empirical support to the hypotheses that people who are similar in age, gender, ethnicity and, educational level are much more likely to interact with each other than with people who are heterogeneous in these aspects [19] .

This tendency of similar individuals to associate with one another is referred to as homophily and it suggests that similarity breeds connection. Monge and Contractor [45] highlight Byrne's [12] similarity-attraction hypothesis and self- categorization theory [54, 56] to explain homophily. Byrne postulate that people are more attracted towards those with whom they share similar attributes. Self-categorization theory proposes that people self-categorize themselves and others in terms of age, role, gender, education and so on and they use these categories to differentiate between similar and dissimilar others.

Podolny [49] offers an alternate explanation by highlighting the role of the status of people. Similarity is not required nor expected for two actors to initiate an association. If there is a generally recognizable ordering of the attributes on which actors differ, high status actors attract others. In the work setting, those who occupy higher status roles are likely to enjoy more interactions than those who are in the lower level of the hierarchy.

Although much of the studies on homophily in networks are conducted among collocated members, Yuan and Gay [60] argue that their findings are generalizable to distributed work settings as well. They argue that advances in communication technologies and their creative usage enable employees to locate and connect with similar others at work.

While much of the studies have focused on similarities in gender and race, [31, 33, 43] we focus on role homophily in our study. In highly competitive organizations, such as our study setting, people who occupy similar formal roles compete with each other another for time, attention and, resources of the shared parties and any action that one takes is likely to be emulated by the other. For instance, if employee A, who occupies role X, enrolls in an executive education program, employee B in a similar role may feel pressure to keep pace, and will thus enroll in a similar program. We believe that similar pressures influence career decisions as well.

Consider the continued example of A and B who work together on the same work team. If A and B occupy the same professional role, it is possible that they view each other as competitors and if one leaves the firm it will open up additional opportunities for the other at the firm. But we believe that the boundaryless nature of careers makes this reaction less likely. Instead, we believe that B is more likely to see A as a social referent due to shared job roles and shared work experiences and therefore emulate A. Likewise, if A decides to stay at the firm, B is likely to stay at the firm. In addition, for the reasons mentioned earlier, we propose that people with greater tenure in the organization are less likely to be influenced by the quit decisions of others who occupy similar professional roles. Thus,

Hypothesis 3A: The greater percentage of those teammates who occupy the same professional role and leave, the more likely the individual will leave the firm.

Hypothesis 3B: The above relationship will be moderated by tenure such that younger employees will be more influenced by similar others.

RESEARCH SETTING

We test our hypotheses at a global technology firm. The firm has over 130,000 employees with 2011 revenues projected to surpass 6 billion USD. Within the firm, employees are assigned to primarily work on specific client accounts. Some accounts consist of more than 1000 employees. Within the account groups, employees are further separated into project teams. Project teams are often voluntary and temporary in nature and range in size from 3 to 250 people. Most teams are formed with the goal of meeting specific client needs and typically exist for three to eighteen months. Individuals can work on more than one project team at a time. Some sets of individuals frequently work together on the same teams whereas others transition from team to team based on requirements.

During the study period the focal firm maintained a positive global reputation allowing it to be very selective in hiring highly qualified individuals. According to qualitative interviews with members of the Human Resources Department, job openings at the firm attract a large pool of candidates, allowing them to be very selective. In addition, focusing on employees from a single firm allows us to control for differences in opportunity structures of internal labor markets [4].

DATA

For our analysis, we focused on all employees associated with one client account. The client account was active from January, 2007 to August, 2011. During this time 728 individuals formed 301 project teams based on account needs. Employees assigned to this account were located at 30 offices locations throughout North America, Europe, South Asia and Asia Pacific. The largest office housed 256 of the employees in this study (the average office size was 30.2 employees, SD = 66.65). Employees occupied 64 various professional roles (the most common professional role was Test Engineer, held by 109 employees). All employees had at least a university degree and formal training in areas ranging from computer science to finance. During the study period 183 employees voluntarily left the firm.

To analyze the social influence of turnover, we used longitudinal project team data to create the project affiliation network. We first created a 3-way person-by-team-by-time stacked matrix. This allowed us to identify connections between individuals and specific project teams at each point in time. We then converted these data into person-by-person data, allowing us to identify which individuals worked on the same project teams at each point in time (between January, 2007 and July, 2011). By matching these relational data with demographic and attrition data provided by the Human Resources Department, we were able to investigate possible relational influences of voluntary turnover in the focal firm.

DEPENDENT VARIABLE

Quit. The key variable in our study is whether or not the focal individual voluntarily left the firm during the study period. Of the 728 employees, 183 quit during the study period. Part of the leaving process at this firm involves an exit interview with the Human Resource Department. During this interview the employee is asked to indicate their primary reason for leaving the firm. The most common reasons provided were leaving to join another company, and leaving for an undisclosed personal reason. Of the 183 who quit, 90 indicated that they were leaving to join a competitor or start their own firm. Forty-six of those who quit indicated that they were leaving for personal reasons.

CONTROL VARIABLE

We obtained demographic information about each individual that might have also influenced their decision to voluntarily leave the firm. Demographic data included *gender, year of birth,* and *organizational tenure*. The sample consisted of 262 women and 467 men. The average year of birth of the employees was 1982.32 (SD = 4.4). The average organizational tenure among employees was 4.56 years (SD = 2.67). We used project data to determine the number of project teams that each individual worked on and the number of project teammates who remained with the organization throughout the study period. The average *number of project teams* was 2.18 (SD = 1.88). The average *number of teammates* was 50.12 (SD = 56.12).

INDEPENDENT VARIABLES

Percentage of teammates who quit. Our key independent variable captures the presence of quitters among project team members. Using the time stamped data we determined the percentage of each individual's project team members who voluntarily left the organization. The average teammates who quit measure was 9.71 (SD = 11.58).

Collocated quitters. We used locational data to identify which sets of project teammates were located at the same office building at the same point in time. We then used this relational matrix to calculate the percentage of each individual's collocated project teammates who also quit. Among individuals with at least one coworker who quit, the average percentage of collocated teammates who quit was 18.95 percent (SD = 16.44).

Same role quitters. We used job role data to identify which sets of project teammates occupied the same professional role and used this to determine what percentage of each individual's project teammates were role similar. Among individuals with at least one coworker who quit, the average percentage of teammates with same role who quit was 16.20 percent (SD = 22.80).

ANALYSES

To test our hypotheses, we used a cross-sectional logistic regression model to test whether or not each individual quit at some point during the study period. We created all network measures in UCINET 6.365 [6] and used Stata 11.0 for regression analysis. Please see Table 1 for descriptive statistics and correlations of our study variables.

Recognizing that a cross-sectional approach does not fully capture the longitudinal nature of this process, we ran a secondary analysis using Cox proportional hazards regression model to strengthen our analysis. The Cox model is a technique typically used in survival research to explore the effect of explanatory variables upon the time that it takes for an event to occur. In this study, we created rolling six month project network windows as our time slices to analyze quit events. The model takes time into account and fits hazard ratios to the variables, which are interpreted as the effect of each variable on the risk that the focal individual will quit the firm. In other words, we used data from the projects that each individual had worked on in the past six months, to identify the influence of our independent variables on quitting behavior. The decision to use six month windows was based on our belief that ties from longer than six months ago would not have as much influence on the individual's decision (as these former teammates may no longer be viewed as referents).

		Mean	S.D.	1	2	3	4	5	6	7	8
1	Year of birth	1982.32	4.41	1							
2	Organizational tenure	4.57	2.67	-0.57	1						
3	Number of projects	2.21	1.91	-0.08	0.27	1					
4	Number of teammates	50.12	56.79	0.06	-0.03	0.15	1				
5	Teammates who quit (%)	19.02	15.49	-0.17	0.18	-0.01	0.05	1			
6	Collocated quitters (%)	18.95	16.44	-0.11	0.11	0	0.11	0.78	1		
7	Same role quitters (%)	16.20	22.80	0.08	-0.02	0.02	0.16	0.43	0.4	1	
8	Female	262 = F	NA	0.3	-0.17	0.02	-0.04	-0.08	-0.06	0.04	1
9	DV= Did employee quit	183 = yes	NA	-0.04	-0.11	-0.14	-0.08	0.18	0.13	0.11	0

Table 1: Descriptive Statistics and Correlations of Study Variables

RESULTS

Regression outputs from the logistic regression models are presented in Table 2. Model 1 provides support for Hypothesis 1 predicting that individuals with project teammates who quit are themselves more likely to quit (Model 1 $e^b = 1.03 < 0.01$). Results indicate that among individuals with at least one quitter in their project team, the greater the percentage of quitters in each individual's co-working network, the greater the likelihood that he or she also voluntarily left the firm during the study period.

	Model 1 DV Quit	Model 2 DV Quit	Model 3 DV Quit	Model 4 DV Quit	Model 5 DV Quit	Model 6 DV Quit	Model 7 DV Quit
Female	1.10 (0.21)	1.13 (0.24)	1.10 (0.23)	1.10 (0.24)	1.10 (0.24)	1.07 (0.21)	1.14 (0.24)
Number of Projects	0.84* (0.06)	0.79** (0.06)	0.79** (0.06)	0.78** (0.06)	0.79** (0.06)	0.83* (0.06)	0.80** (0.06)
Year of birth	0.94* (0.02)	0.95* (0.02)	0.95* (0.02)	0.94* (0.02)	0.94* (0.02)	0.95* (0.02)	0.95t (0.03)
Tenure at firm	0.84** (0.04)	0.85** (0.04)	0.97 (0.07)	0.84** (0.00)	0.87** (0.05)	0.93 (0.06)	0.83** (0.04)
Number of teammates	1.00** (0.00)	1.00** (0.00)	1.00** (0.00)	1.00** (0.00)	1.00** (0.00)	1.00** (0.00)	1.00** (0.00)
Percent of teammates who quit	1.03** (0.00)					1.05** (0.00)	
Collocated teammates who quit (%)		1.01* (0.01)	1.04* (0.01)				
Same role teammates who quit (%)				1.01* (0.00)	1.02* (0.01)		
Interaction of Tenure with percent of teammates who quit						0.99* (0.00)	
Interaction of Tenure with collocated quitters			0.99* (0.00)				
Interaction of tenure with same role quitters					1.00 (0.00)		
Percent who quit to join a competitor							1.03* (0.01)
Percent who quit for personal reasons							0.99 (0.02)
LL	-377.13	-318.26	-315.27	-317.63	-316.94	-374.62	-313.34
N	728	598	598	598	598	728	598

Table 2: Odds Ratios from Cross-sectional Logistic Regression Models

These results hold when controlling for number of teammates, number of projects and other demographic attributes. Model 2 provides support for hypothesis 2A, indicating that the greater the percentage of defectors who are located in the same office as the focal individual, the more likely the focal individual will also quit (Model 2 $e^b = 1.01$, $p < 0.05$). Model 3 provides support for hypothesis 2B indicating that organizational tenure moderates the influence of collocated quitters, such that individuals with greater tenure are less influenced by the career decisions of proximal teammates (Model 3 $e^b = 0.99$, $p < 0.05$).

Model 4 provides support for hypothesis 3A indicating that having teammates with the same professional role who quit increases the likelihood that the focal actor will also quit (Model 4 $e^b = 1.01$, $p < 0.05$). We fail to find support for Hypothesis 3B (Model 5 $e^b = 1.00$, $p > 0.05$). Results from our cox regression in Model 8 (see Table 3) provide additional support to our hypotheses indicating that each increase in the percentage of teammates who quit increases the risk that the focal individual will also quit the firm (Model 8 Hazard ratio = 1.02, $p < 0.05$).

	Model 8
	DV Quit at end of month
Female	0.93 (0.16)
Number of recent projects	1.21* (0.10)
Year of birth	1.09** (0.03)
Tenure at firm	1.00 (0.00)
Number of recent team members	1.00 (0.00)
Percentage of recent team members who quit	1.02* (0.01)
LL	-1522.30
Number of observations	31793

Table 3: Hazard Ratios from Cox Regression Analysis

We acknowledge two plausible alternative mechanisms that might explain our core results: (1) individuals who work on struggling project teams might all independently choose to leave due to the outcome of the projects ("struggling project"); and (2) individuals primarily base their career decisions on opportunities presented by former colleagues who now work outside of the firm ("outside ties"). To address these competing mechanisms, which might result in findings similar to our models, we created a critical experiment, in the spirit of Lave and March [39].

Table 4 presents three empirical tests (rows) to determine whether or not one theorized mechanism is superior to others. The columns correspond to competing theories and present the predicted results of each empirical test if the theorized mechanism were true. For instance, if the struggling project theory of turnover is correct, we predict the following: (1) tenure would not have a significant influence on career decisions (i.e., all members of a struggling project are likely to be equally affected regardless of tenure at the firm); (2) the reasons provided by teammates who quit would not influence each individual's career decision (in theory the decision would be based on the focal actor's experience with the struggling project); and (3) structurally equivalent actors (i.e., those with ties to the same third parties in the project affiliation network) would not make the same career choices. Note that the outside ties and social comparison theories have unique column profiles of predicted results. The actual results of multiple analytic tests are provided in the fourth column of Table 4. For instance, we find that working with those who join a competitor influences quit decisions but working with those who quit for personal reasons does not. This seemingly discounts the "poor performing project" theory. We also find that structurally equivalent actors are more likely than others to make similar career decisions seemingly discounting the "outside ties" theory. Taken together, we believe the results of these three empirical tests provide additional support for the social comparison theory and discount alternative theories as the primary mechanism.

Empirical Tests	Struggling Project Theory	Outside Ties Theory	Social Comparison Theory	Actual Findings
Are early stage employees more influenced than older employees?	No	Yes	Yes	Yes (see Models 3 & 6 in Table 2)
Are some coworker reasons for quitting more influential than others?	No	Yes	Yes	Yes (see Model 7 in Table 2)
Do structurally equivalent actors make the same career choices?	No	No	Yes	Yes (see Table 5)

Table 4: Critical Experiment with Predicted Results for Plausible Alternative Mechanisms and Actual Findings

DISCUSSION

This paper examined voluntary turnover of employees in a distributed work setting using social network perspective. We proposed that given the nature of talent mobility in contemporary labor markets, individuals' decisions to stay with or quit the firm are influenced by the extent of quitters in their project affiliation networks. Those with greater connections to defectors will quit the firm. Further, we suggested that the influence on such focal individuals will be higher when they are collocated and occupy similar professional roles as the affiliated quitters. We specified that this relationship will be moderated by firm tenure of employees. We find empirical evidence to support these hypotheses.

	Structurally similar	Same career decision
Structurally similar	1	
Same career decision	0.03*	1
*With 5000 permutations		

Table 5: Quadratic Assignment Procedure Correlation
*Table presents the relationship between the structural similarity of each pair of actors (i.e., individuals with similar patterns of ties to third parties have a corresponding value close to 1) and the career similarity of each pair of actors (e.g., $x_{ij} = 1$ if both individuals quit the firm or if both individuals stayed, and $x_{ij} = 0$ if one individual quit and the other stayed)

Existing research on networks and turnover proposes that embeddedness established through ties (or lack of ties) with other employees is a key reason why individuals choose to stay with or leave a firm [21, 44]. Our findings suggest that employee ties also serve as important reference points to provide clarity and cues of next career moves. To the extent that objective physical bases for evaluation are not available, subjectively accurate assessments of one's ability depend upon on how one compares with other person [22]. This suggests employees are purposefully alert and actively seek signals from colleagues to assess themselves as they join and leave the network. When success is defined in subjective metrics, the moves and opportunities of others become especially important.

Our findings highlight that spatial proximity assumes salience in the diffusion of quit decisions among employees in geographically distributed teams. The proximity to defectors and increased opportunities for interactions with them appears to influence the quit decisions of collocated employees more than those who work in distant offices. The findings also suggest that role similarity serve as important referent points for employees to make quit decisions. People who occupy similar professional roles are likely to share similar values, attitudes and experiences and thus, the career decisions of such similar professionals become strong signals for focal individuals to pursue outside opportunities.

We acknowledge that the networks analyzed in this study are based on project affiliation information and not direct interpersonal social relations. However, scholars [20] suggest that individuals whose activities are organized around the same focus (e.g., project teams, workplaces, family, etc.) frequently become interpersonally connected over time. This is similar to Atkin's distinction of "backcloth" and "traffic" [3] and Breiger's [9] discussion of the duality of persons and groups. Likewise, affiliations are often used as a proxy for large-scale social relationship data that might be difficult to collect [7]. The significant patterns of our findings based on such ties, which are arguably 'weaker' than direct influence ties, provide us with even greater confidence in our proposed theoretical mechanism.

IMPLICATIONS

This study updates current theoretical understanding of voluntary turnover in general and more specifically, it explains the relational dynamics and the role of spatial propinquity and role similarity in shaping quit decisions of employees in geographically distributed organizations. We extend the current research [21, 37, 44] in the employee turnover area by proposing that social comparison processes are especially pertinent in boundaryless careers and the decisions of coworkers influence an individual's career decisions.

Rather than seeking belonging and viability with others, our findings suggest that individuals are actively searching for cues among their network of colleagues for signals that provide subjective evaluations of career success. In a distributed work setting, spatial proximity allows the flow of such signals and professional role similarity serve as referent points for those cues. Collectively they influence the career mobility decisions of employees.

Our findings engage directly with the complexities of new world of work and have important implications for managers in distributed organizations. Team-based organization of work, geographically and culturally diverse team members, transient team memberships and higher levels of coordination requirements between members are salient characteristics of this new order at work. In such circumstances, employee quit decisions are likely to be influenced heavily by their workplace networks.

Unpacking those networks in a rigorous manner can provide two distinct advantages to managers in distributed organizations: (a) accurate detection of employees who are most likely to quit and (b) robust estimates of the likelihood of subsequent departures given the quit decision of an employee. Such insights will allow managers to take timely and appropriate actions to avoid the loss of valuable employees as well as manage and staff project teams in a manner that make them less vulnerable to diffusion effects of turnover.

In addition, our study methodology can be integrated with existing enterprise systems and scaled across large organizations. This implies that such insights can be derived passively and consistently in a real or near-real time fashion by intelligent computations of people and project related information that are already recorded for various purposes.

CONCLUSION

Organizations are increasingly relying on various forms of distributed work. For instance, in remote work, individuals work off-site from their employers [5] and in outsourcing and cross-organizational production or development tasks that were earlier considered as key internal activities are instead entrusted to dedicated suppliers [55]. When organizations distribute work across multiple locations, the ability of members to communicate and coordinate across the locations becomes a key source of success.

It is therefore not surprising to note that much of the research in distributed work context is focused around advancing the understanding of various social, behavioral and technological issues to improve team effectiveness in such settings. The network literature has made important contribution to this area. For instance, scholars have found that individuals tend to build ties toward information necessary for their work [42], but rely heavily on pre-existing ties for information, and often prefer to gain the needed knowledge indirectly through existing ties, rather than by establishing new ties [23].

In this paper, we took a different path and explored the role of networks in employee turnover decisions. We argued that ties to those who quit the firm can motivate subsequent quit decisions. We also postulated that when greater number of teammates in same office location quit the firm and more importantly, when they hold similar professional roles, the likelihood of an individual to follow the suit become higher. We found evidence to these arguments. Our study updates extant network research on employee turnover by specifying that in addition to ties to defectors in project affiliation networks, proximity to and role similarity with them increase the social pressure on focal individuals and trump their sense of connection with the organization.

The analysis of project affiliations used in this study can be integrated with enterprise wide workforce analytics program to create valuable and timely insights for managers while staffing people and designing interventions to ensure project success and addressing employee turnover.

The findings of this study will have special relevance for knowledge-intensive and distributed organizations that operate in highly competitive environments. Highly skilled members of such organizations are often short in supply and drawn from a highly mobile labor market. For instance, IT professionals are found to be moving across organizations, not bound to a single employer [34, 47], and moving across occupations not bound to the IT profession [51, 52]. In such contexts, networks can not only transmit work related information but also career movement signals.

ACKNOWLEDGMENTS

All authors contributed equally. We thank the associate program chair, the three anonymous reviewers, and members of the LINKS Center for social network analysis at the University of Kentucky for their insightful suggestions. We also thank managers of the study site for sharing contextual information relevant to the findings. This work was funded in part by The President APJ Abdul Kalam India Studies Research Program.

REFERENCES

1. Allen, T.J. *Managing the Flow of Technology*. Cambridge, MA: MIT Press (1977).
2. Arthur, M. B., and Rousseau, D. M. (Eds.). *The boundaryless career: A new employment principle for a new organizational era*. New York: Oxford University Press (2001).
3. Atkin, R.H. From cohomology in physics to q-connectivity in social science. *International J. of Man-Machine Studies 4* (1972)139-167.
4. Baron, J.N., Davis-Blake, A., and Bielby, W.T. The structure of opportunity: How promotion ladders vary within and across organizations. *Administrative Science Quarterly 31*, 2 (1986), 248 – 273.
5. Barsness, Z.I., Diekmann, K. A., Seidel, M.D. and L. Motivation and opportunity: The role of remove work, demographic dissimilarity, and social network centrality in impression management. *Academy of Management Journal 48*, 3 (2005), 401-419.
6. Borgatti, S.P. and Halgin, D.S. Analyzing affiliation networks. In Carrington, P. and Scott, J. (eds.) *The Sage Handbook of Social Network Analysis*. Thousand Oaks: Sage Publications, (2011).
7. Borgatti, S.P., Everett, M.G. and Freeman, L.C. UCINET for Windows: Software for Social Network Analysis. Harvard, MA: Analytic Technologies. (2002).
8. Bradner, E., and Mark, G. Why distance matters: effects on cooperation, persuasion and deception. In *Proc. ACM Conference on Computer-Supported Cooperative Work*, ACM Press (2002).

9. Breiger, R. The duality of persons and groups. *Social Forces 53*, 2 (1974), 181-190.
10. Burt, R.S. Attachment, decay, and social networks. *Journal of Organizational Behavior 22*, 6 (2001), 619 – 643.
11. Burt, R.S. Structural Holes: *The Social Structure of Competition*. Cambridge, MA: Harvard University Press (1992).
12. Byrn, D.E. *The Attraction Paradigm*. New York: Academic Press (1971).
13. Cappelli, P. *The New Deal at Work: Managing the Market-driven Workforce*. Boston: Harvard Business School Press (1999).
14. Coleman, J.S., Katz E., and Menzel, H. *Medical Innovation*. New York: Bobbs-Merrill (1966).
15. Cramton, C. D. The mutual knowledge problem and its consequences for dispersed collaboration. *Organization Science 12* (2001), 346–371.
16. Cummings, J.N. Work groups, structural diversity, and knowledge sharing in a global organization. *Management Science 50*, 3 (2004), 352–364.
17. Dougherty, D. Interpretive barriers to successful product innovation in large firms. *Organization Science 13* (1992) 77–92.
18. Espinosa, J., Cummings, J., Wilson, J., and Pearce, B. Team boundary issues across multiple global firms. *Journal of Management Information Systems 19*, 4 (2003), 157–190.
19. Feld, S. The focused organization of social ties, *American Journal of Sociology 86* (1981), 1015–1035.
20. Feld, Scott L. Structural determinants of similarity among associates. *American Sociological Review 47* (1982), 797–801.
21. Felps, W., Mitchell, T.R., Hekman, D.R., Lee, T.W., Holtom, B.C., and Harman, W.S. Turnover contagion: How coworkers' job embeddedness and job search behaviors influence quitting. *Academy of Management Journal 52*, 3 (2009), 545 - 561.
22. Festinger, L. A theory of social comparison processes. *Human Relations 7* (1954), 117 - 140.
23. Gargiulo, M., Benassi, M. Trapped in your own net? Network cohesion, structural holes, and the adaptations of social capital. *Organization Science 11*, 2 (2000), 183-196.
24. Granovetter, M. S. The strength of weak ties. *American Journal of Sociology 6* (1973), 1360-1380.
25. Hall, D. T. Careers *In and Out of Organizations*. Thousand Oaks, CA: Sage Publications (2002).
26. Hall, D. T. The protean career: A quarter-century journey. *Journal of Vocational Behavior 65*, 1 (2004), 1 – 13.
27. Hansen, M.T. The search-transfer problem: The role of weak ties in sharing knowledge across organization subunits. *Administrative Science Quarterly 44* (1999), 82-111.
28. Heider, F. *The Psychology of Interpersonal Relations*. New York: Wiley (1958).
29. Heslin, P. A. Conceptualizing and evaluating career success. *Journal of Organizational Behavior 26* (2005), 113 – 136.
30. Hinds, P., and Mortensen, M. Understanding conflict in distributed teams: An empirical investigation. *Organization Science 16* (2005), 290–307.
31. Ibarra, Herminia. Homophily and differential returns: Sex differences in network structure and access in an advertising firm. *Administrative Science Quarterly 37* (1992), 422–447.
32. Jarvenpaa, S. L., and Leidner, D. E. Communication and trust in global virtual teams. *Organization Science 10* (1999), 791–815.
33. Jehn, K. A., Northcraft, G. B., and Neale, M. A. Why differences make a difference: A field study of diversity, conflict, and performance in workgroups. *Administrative Science Quarterly 44* (1999), 741–763.
34. Josefek, R., and Kauffman, R. Nearing the threshold: An economics approach to pressure on information systems professionals to separate from their employer. *Journal of Management Information Systems 20*, 1 (2003), 87-122.
35. Kankanhalli, A.; Tan, B.; and Wei, K. Conflict and performance in global virtual teams. *Journal of Management Information System 23*, 3 (2006), 237–274.
36. Kiesler, S., and Cummings, J. N. What do we know about proximity and distance in work groups? A legacy of research. In P. Hinds, and S. Kiesler (Eds.), *Distributed work* (pp. 57–82). Cambridge, MA: MIT Press (2002).
37. Krackhardt, D., and Porter, L.W. The snowball effect: Turnover embedded in communication networks. *Journal of Applied Psychology 71*, 1 (1986), 50 - 55.
38. Krackhardt, D.M., and Porter, L.W. When friends leave: a structural analysis of the relationship between turnover and stayers' attitudes.

Administrative Science Quarterly 30, 2 (1985), 242 - 261.

39. Lave, C.A., and March, J.G. *An Introduction to Models in the Social Sciences*. (1975) New York: Harper & Row (1975).
40. Lazarsfeld, P.F., Berelson, B., and Gaudet, H. *The People's Choice*. New York: Columbia University Press (1944).
41. McPherson, J. M., and Smith-Lovin, L. Homophily in voluntary organizations: Status, distance and the composition of face to face groups. *American Sociological Review 52* (1987), 370-379.
42. Mitsuhashi H, and Greve, H. R. A Matching Theory of Alliance Formation and Organizational Success: Complementarity and Compatibility. *Academy of Management Journal 52,* 5 (2009), 975-995.
43. Mollica, K.A, Gary, B. and Trevino, L.K. Racial homophily and its persistence in newcomers' social networks. *Organization Science 14* (2003), 123–36.
44. Mossholder, K.W., Settoon, R.P., and Henagan, S.C. A relational perspective on turnover: Examining structural, attitudinal, and behavioral predictors. *Academy of Management Journal 48* (2005), 607 - 618.
45. Monge, P. and Contractor, N. *Theories of Communication Networks*. Cambridge: Oxford University Press (2003).
46. O'Leary, M.B., and Cummings, J.N. The spatial, temporal, and configurational characteristics of geographic dispersion in teams. *MIS Quarterly 31*, 1 (2007), 433 – 452.
47. O'Mahony, S., and Bechky, B. A. Stretchwork: Managing the career progression paradox in external labor markets. *Academy of Management Journal 49*, 5 (2006), 918-941.
48. Olson, G. M., and Olson, J. S. Distance matters. *Human Computer Interaction 15*, (2000). 139–178.
49. Podolny, J.M. A status-based model of market competition. *American Journal of Sociology 98*, 4, (1993), 829-872.
50. Podolny, J.M. Networks as the pipes and prisms of the market. *American Journal of Sociology 107*, 1 (2001), 22 - 60.
51. Reich, B. H., and Kaarst-Brown, M. L. Creating social and intellectual capital through IT career transitions, *Journal of Strategic Information Systems 12*, 4 (2003), 91-109.
52. Reich, B. H., and Kaarst-Brown, M. L. Seeding the Line: Understanding the transition from IT to non-IT careers, *MIS Quarterly 23*, 3 (1999), 337-364.
53. Sorenson, O, Stuart, T.E. Syndication networks and the spatial distribution of venture capital investments. *American Journal of Sociology 106*, 6 (2001), 1546–1588.
54. Tajfel, H., and Turner, J. C. (1986). The social identity theory of intergroup behavior. In S. Worchel and W. G. Austin (Eds.), *Psychology of Intergroup Relations* (2nd ed., pp. 7-24). Chicago: Nelson-Hall.
55. Takeishi, A. Bridging inter- and intra-firm boundaries: Management of supplier involvement in automobile product development. *Strategic Management Journal 22*, 5 (2001), 403-433.
56. Turner, J.C. *Re-discovering the Social Group: A Self-Categorization Theory*. Oxford: Basil, Blackwell (1987).
57. Walther, J.B. Relational aspects of computer-mediated communication: Experimental observations over time. *Organization Science 6*, 2 (1995), 186–203.
58. Wenger, E.R., McDermott, and W.M. Snyder. *Cultivating Communities of Practice.* Cambridge, MA: Harvard Business School Press (2002).
59. Wiesenfeld, B. M., Raghuram, S., and Garud, R. Communication patterns as determinants of organizational identification in a virtual organization. *Organization Science 10*, (1999), 777–790.
60. Yuan, Y. C., and Gay, G. Homophily of network ties, and bonding and bridging social capital in distributed teams. Journal of *Computer-Mediated Communication 11*, 4 (2006), 1062-1084.

Analyzing the Flow of Knowledge in Computer Mediated Teams

Joshua Introne
Center for Collective Intelligence
MIT
Cambridge, MA
jintrone@mit.edu

Marcus Drescher
School of Management
Technische Universität München
München, Germany
drescher@tum.de

ABSTRACT
In this article, we present an analysis of communication transcripts from computer-mediated teams that illustrates how different kinds of decision support impact collaborative knowledge construction. Our analysis introduces an algorithmic technique called Topic Evolution Analysis (TEvA), which tracks clusters of words in conversation, and illustrates how these clusters change and merge over time. This analysis is combined with measurements of group dynamics to distinguish between teams using different kinds of decision support.

Our analysis offers evidence that some kinds of decision support improve the apparent rationality of a team, but at the cost of collaborative knowledge construction. This result is not apparent when simply measuring team decision performance. We use this finding to motivate the utility and importance of the approach when assessing the impact of technology on collaborative knowledge processing.

Author Keywords
Collaborative knowledge construction; decision support; computer-mediated communication; online conversation; topic tracking; knowledge flow

ACM Classification Keywords
H.5.3. Group and Organization Interfaces: Computer-supported cooperative work, Evaluation/methodology, Theory and models; I.2.7 Natural Language Processing: Text analysis

INTRODUCTION
One desirable outcome of collaboration is the birth of knowledge that is somehow more than the sum of its parts. Yet collaborative knowledge construction is subject to the vagaries of interpersonal dynamics and hampered by socio-psychological biases, and can thus be an elusive end product for groups. A challenge for designers is how to build technology that can reliably improve a community's ability to exchange and fluidly recombine its available information to develop new insights.

Robust analytical techniques are necessary to determine how technology impacts collaborative knowledge construction and knowledge processing. In an ideal case, we would be able to witness the historical evolution of knowledge as it flows across a socio-technical network, and describe the impact of technology in these terms. For example, is a community better or less able to combine different pools of knowledge over time? What is the average lifespan of a new idea? How homogenous is the knowledge held by a group? Being able to observe the evolution and flow of knowledge in collaboration would allow us to better understand the broader impact of technology on the knowledge processing properties of a group.

Approaches have been developed recently to track the dynamics of topics in document corpora [2,37]. These approaches seek to label each document in a corpus with one of more topic descriptors, but topics can appear, disappear, or change over time. Using these techniques, it is possible to examine how topics can change, merge, and split, generating a rich picture of how knowledge evolves throughout the corpus [7].

This is precisely the sort of analysis we would like to perform with online communities to discover how knowledge flows across an online conversation. Unfortunately, online conversation may be too noisy and dynamic to apply document-centric topic tracking. Unlike a document, which offers a snapshot of a relatively stable distribution of topics, a conversation is an unfolding process in which the definition of a topic is continually re-negotiated. The lack of a relatively well-structured, intentionally designed document limits the utility of the machine-learning approaches that drive modern topic-tracking algorithms.

Consequently, we have sought to develop an approach that makes no assumptions about the existence of documents or their structure. Instead, we take as our unit of analysis a sequence of replies, seek to understand how clusters of words in these reply sequences change, merge, and split

CSCW '13, February 23–27, 2013, San Antonio, Texas, USA.

over time. We call this approach Topic Evolution Analysis (TEvA).

In this article, we present the algorithm, and use it to analyze a dataset collected in a prior study on decision support technology. By comparing TEvA with other indices of group dynamics we are able to identify important differences in collaborative knowledge processing of groups and better characterize the differential impact of collaborative technologies. Specifically, we show that one type of decision support appears to dampen collaborative knowledge construction, even though there is no clear impact on performance in the decision task.

The goals of our analysis are twofold. First, we demonstrate that a normative approach to collaborative decision support, intended to help collaborators engage in more rational knowledge processing, can have the unintended effect of disrupting a process that allows people to combine their individual knowledge synergistically. This bounded result contains cautions about evaluating the design of collaborative systems and the difficulty of generalizing team performance from targeted measures.

By way of this example we also hope to introduce a new approach to the assessment of online groups via the analysis of collaborative knowledge processing. By examining the movement and evolution of word co-occurrence clusters in online conversation, we can speak with more precision about the knowledge processing capabilities and characteristics of online groups. This in turn can support new ways of distinguishing between online communities and assessing the differential impacts of technology upon them, and ultimately improve our ability to design technology that supports more effective collaborative knowledge processing.

LITERATURE REVIEW

There is a growing interest in being able to observe the dynamics of information in technologically mediated communities. Approaches based on interaction analysis offer tremendous resolution on the dynamics of knowledge processing in small groups (e.g. [14,26,35]) but these techniques involve manual coding and cannot scale to the volumes of unbounded and informal collaboration now available in online settings.

To scale up to such settings, some researchers have made opportunistic use of structured content that appears in online interactions to observe information dynamics. For instance, social tagging is an affordance of some social networking platforms that users use to identify relevant information. It also provides researchers with clear markers that can be readily followed across a network. Social tagging has been used to illustrate the miscibility of different ideas and the diffusion patterns of information [6,28].

Web users have also often adopted conventional behaviors of copying and pasting snippets of text to create "memes" with enough regularity that researchers can track them across multiple networks based on their lexical similarity [20]. Unlike social tags, lexical memes have internal structure that can be analyzed, allowing researchers to observe how these memes are transformed across networks–mutating, splitting, and even merging [30].

Moving beyond markers like memes and tags, information retrieval and topic modeling techniques have been employed to trace the movement of words or groups of words across networks (e.g. [10][27]). These approaches are a more general approach to analyzing the flow of information in social networks, but as they have been applied offer only a limited view of the kinds of transformations information undergoes over time.

In the last several years, topic-modeling techniques have been applied to elucidate detailed topic dynamics in document corpora [7]. These techniques leverage statistical regularities in word frequencies that result from the structure of the documents and corpora in which they are found. A document is a designed artifact; a self-contained package of knowledge (e.g. an scientific paper, or a news story) that is intended to convey a fixed set of ideas that do not typically change over the course of the document. These topics are relatively stable across documents in a corpus at a given point in time because they describe external phenomena (e.g. news events), and may be reinforced by other communication channels (e.g. academic discourse).

Unfortunately, topic-modeling techniques are not well-suited for analyzing multi-party dialog. One difficulty is that dialog is often so dynamic that it lacks the statistical regularities that enable topic detection in document corpora. A more serious issue is that the subjective meaning of any given passage may only be clear when the hierarchical context of the overall dialog is also considered [12], so topic models based upon the local, atemporal distribution of words may not be sufficient.

Thus, we have developed an approach from the ground up that may be better suited to tracking the flow of information through online conversation. In our approach we model topics as evolving "communities" of words over sequences of replies using a well-known community identification technique developed in the social networking literature. Our approach allows us to observe both how topics evolve within threads, as well as connect across them.

INSTANCES OF KNOWLEDGE CONSTRUCTION

Our initial inspiration for TEvA was drawn from a subjective reading of transcripts of teams attempting to solve a murder mystery. In the following, we offer examples of effective and ineffective knowledge construction in different teams.

Both transcripts are taken from teams of five collaborators trying to solve a murder mystery using a threaded-chat-like tool [17]. Each post is broadcast to the team, and there is a 10–20 second lag between when a post is made and when it

Time (mm:ss)	Author	Content
02:41	P1	*[talking about Billy]* he was there, picked up thecrowbar and then ran. kinda guilty sounding
		--- posts skipped---
03:17	P2	*[talking about Billy]* the fact that it was found in the bushes makes it seem like he was framed. why would he leave the murder weapon at the scene of the crime? it looks like someone planted it there with the intention of it being found
		--- posts skipped---
16:54	P3	I think Eddie is guilty but I'm still looking for a sufficient motive, probably with his daughter.
17:44	P2	I agree
17:54	P4	I agree with this, but I want some theory on how he got billy's prints on the crowbar
19:05	P3	Good point. I think it's possible that he removed it from the scene of the crime without thinking for some reason
19:07	P1	the crowbar was leaning on the garage door so billy had to move it to the side to get the lawnmower out, seeing how billy cam every saturday to mow lawn, eddie could have planned that
19:37	P2	BINGO
19:54	P3	I didn't know that
20:30	P5	AHA

Figure 1: Collaborators (P1-P5) constructing a story to solve a murder mystery. Reported time is from the beginning of the conversation.

appears on all of the participant's screens. Conversations are roughly 30 minutes long and all teams were offered a small prize (movie tickets) if they unanimously came to the correct conclusion about the culprit. Several of the participants in each team have critical pieces of information that the others do not have. Participants were told that they might have non-identical information, but they were not aware how information is distributed or which pieces were critical.

Figure 1 is a portion of conversation extracted from a team that correctly identified the culprit, Eddie. In the first post (at 02:41) P1 reports that Billy picked up the crowbar (the murder weapon), and then ran. This evidence explains how Billy's fingerprints got on the crowbar, but none of the team members seem to notice. In a subsequent post (at 03:17) P2 observes that it was strange that the murder weapon, with Billy's fingerprints, was just lying around near the scene of the crime, and suggests that perhaps he was framed. Once again, no one else picks up on this idea.

The third post in the figure occurs roughly seventeen minutes into the conversation. By this point, several of the collaborators are suspicious of Eddie, but they have no good explanation for his motive or the presence of Billy's fingerprints on the crowbar. The conversation proceeds until the post at 19:07, when P1 repeats (but also reframes) the information she had previously presented in the first post. This time, the other team members pick up on the importance of the information—it becomes clear that Eddie framed Billy by placing the crowbar in his way, forcing him to pick it up.

Time (mm:ss)	Author	Content
11:07	P1	I think Eddie killed him heat of the moment over something with his daughter, and then tried to cover it up because he regretted it.
12:01	P2	how could he have put billy's finger prints on his crowbar?
12:36	P1	Billy might have touched the crowbar when finding the body.
12:52	P1	Or Eddie could have paid Billy off to keep quiet.
17:25	P3	That's not evidence.
18:48	P4	Yes. Billy admitted to touching the crowbar. That doesn't mean he used it to kill Blake.
19:56	P5	Did he? I didn't have that.
21:51	P2	why would he touch it?

Figure 2: A missed opportunity for knowledge construction

The bits of evidence held by different collaborators are synthesized at this point to become a complete story that explains the murder. The collaborators are aware that this has happened, as indicated by P2's enthusiastic "BINGO" and P5's "AHA." The dynamics of the conversation change in several ways at this point as well. All collaborators are present and engaged, peripheral conversations (in other active threads) die down, and posting speed increases. Conversation at this point is inclusive, focused and excited.

A second example (Figure 2) presents a section of dialog from another group that also successfully solved the same mystery. The passage begins much as the passage in Figure 1; collaborators suspect Eddie is the culprit, but lack sufficient evidence. Yet, when P4 provides the relevant piece of missing evidence (18:48), the others meet it with skepticism, and even P4 himself seems unable or unwilling to integrate it into the emerging story. Ultimately, this group chooses Eddie as the most likely suspect, but never agree upon a consistent story about how the murder occurred.

In both of the preceding examples, individuals bring different pieces of knowledge to the same passage of conversation. But in the first case, something special happens—the participants notice how the pieces of information fit together and synthesize them to create a story that makes sense. The latter example, on the other hand, can best be described as a case of missed opportunity. All of the necessary information is present, but collaborators fail to weave it together.

In the remaining sections, we describe a quantitative approach to identifying such patterns, and then apply this approach to the entire dataset. This analysis will show that the degree to which knowledge convergence correlates with posting dynamics differs significantly between groups using different kinds of decision support. With these findings in hand, we offer an explanation for the differences, and reflect upon the approach and its potential in other online contexts.

APPROACH

We seek to identify moments of a conversation where (1) collaborators bring multiple pieces of information together, and (2) the dynamics of the conversation (as observed in the posting patterns of users) change. In the following we first describe the Topic Evolution Analysis (TEvA) process, and then describe a composite measure of posting dynamics.

Topic Evolution Analysis (TEvA)

To identify topics in conversation we use patterns of co-occurrence frequencies between words in the text, and model how these frequencies change over time. There are some similarities between our approach and topic tracking in that a topic can ultimately be resolved to a set of co-occurring words found throughout the corpus, and each sample of the corpus is labeled with a set of topics. Unlike many approaches to topic-tracking, which model topics as probability distributions over words in a dictionary, and seek to identify the underlying probability distributions that generate words in documents, we use word adjacency in reply sequences as a strong hint about what a conversational topic is, and then connect these topics across different reply sequences.

Within TEvA, a topic at any point in time is represented as a network of connections between words. The approach is based upon an algorithm for modeling the dynamics of communities in social networks [23]. The procedure works by identifying communities of words—referred to here as topics—in networks extracted at a series of overlapping time intervals, and then describing how these topics change, merge, and split as the network evolves.

The overall procedure is as follows:

1. Split the conversation into overlapping windows.
2. Transform data in each window into a single network for each time slice.
3. Extract topics in each window.
4. Connect topics across windows.

Before any analysis is performed, the entire dataset is preprocessed to remove stop-words and replace alternative spellings with identical tokens (e.g. mower → lawnmower).

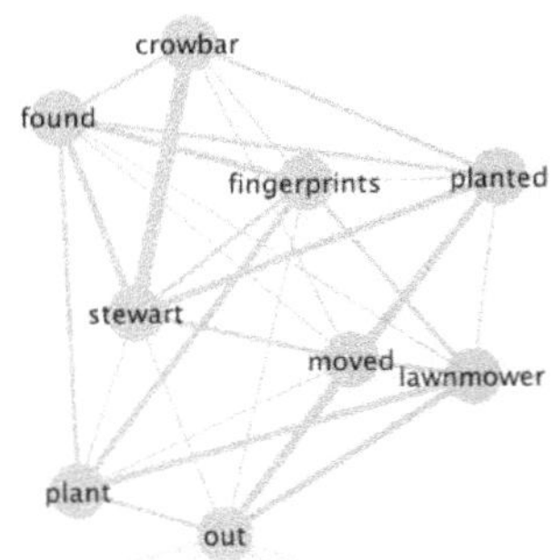

P1	His fingerprints were found on Stewart's crowbar.
P2	Stewart may have planted them somehow
P3	I don't think you can plant fingerprints
P4	Yes, but he moved it to get it out of the way of the mower.

Figure 3: Extracting the network from a transcript. Only the highlighted words (non stop-words) are processed, and stronger relationships are indicated by link width. The "Stewart-crowbar" relationship is the strongest in this frame.

Transcripts are then divided into overlapping windows. Allowing windows to overlap helps the algorithm to establish continuity between emerging topics. We expect that different datasets will require different windowing parameters depending on the amount of traffic and nature of the forum. We chose to use ten-minute windows slid over the data in one-minute increments, such that each window overlapped the previous by nine minutes. The size of the window was based on our impressions about the typical lifetime of a topic in our dataset, so that topics not mentioned for ten minutes will be "forgotten" by the topic extraction (step 3) step. The amount of time by which each window was advanced was chosen to be the approximately equal to the average time between posts in any given sequence of replies. Thus, each subsequent window on average replaces one post per thread. More general techniques for choosing a windowing method and parameters are a subject for future work.

Once the data has been split into windows, text within each is transformed into a network using a technique called Wordij [8] (see Figure 3 for an example). In Wordij, strong ties connect adjacent words, weaker ties link words that are adjacent to a common word but are not themselves adjacent, and so forth. This approach may be applied up to some maximum degree of indirection. Within a given time window, the approach is applied separately to each thread (a sequence of replies). The availability of reply sequences is important, because adjacent posts tend to be about the same topic, and adjacency relationships are what drive topic extraction. The resulting networks are merged, adding edge-weights where edges overlap, to reflect the possibility that multiple threads may be about the same topic.

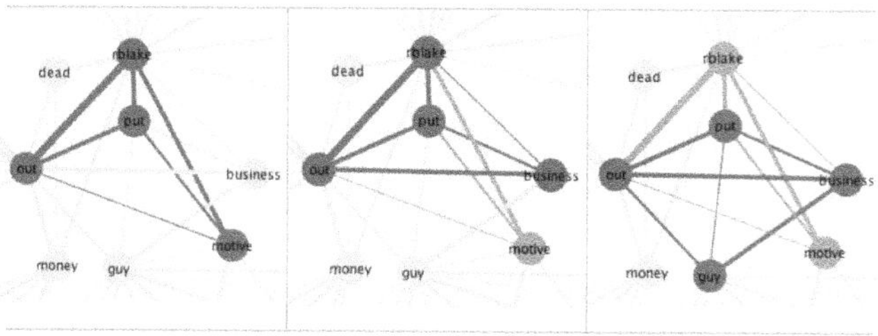

Figure 4: Rolling a *k=4* clique template across a network to identify a community. The final community consists of three cliques.

To identify topics in each network, we apply the Clique Percolation Method (CPM; [24]). CPM works by identifying a clique (a fully connected set of nodes) of some pre-determined size, and then replacing a node in this clique to obtain a new, overlapping clique of the same size. This process continues with each new clique, until no new replacement nodes can be found (see Figure 4 for an example). This is euphamistically described as "rolling" a clique template across a network. When a clique can be rolled no further, the boundary of a topic has been found. A complete set of topics can be discovered by exhaustively applying this process to the word co-occurrence network.

In the final step, we seek to connect topics across time-windows. Because some topics may disappear and than reappear, it is necessary at each point in time to consider each previously seen topic as a potential progenitor of a currently observed topic. We make a simplifying assumption that only most recent version of each historical topic is a viable candidate as progenitor of a current topic. Thus, if topic **A** existed from time *t-n-m* $(n>0;m>1)$ to time *t-n*, we would only check to see if a connection can be drawn from **A** at *t-n* to a novel topic **B** at time t. This assumption reflects our intuition that knowledge tends to accumulate for small groups that are engaged in a time bounded problem-solving task. For larger, longer-lived groups with more dynamic membership, this may not be a realistic assumption.

A simple approach to connecting topics in subsequent time steps would be to identify those pairs that have the highest relative overlap, where the relative overlap between A and B is defined as:

$$S(A,B) = \frac{|A \cap B|}{|A \cup B|}$$

However, as described by Palla et al [23], this approach will lead to spurious matches in instances where community growth is rapid and many communities overlap. Thus, following the procedure described in [23], the connections to communities at time *t* are established as follows:

1. CPM is used to extract topics from a network formed by merging networks at times *t-1* and *t* along with the most recent version of all topics that have previously been identified. We denote this set of topics as $\mathbf{C}^{merged}$.

2. We seek to connect the most recent version of topics

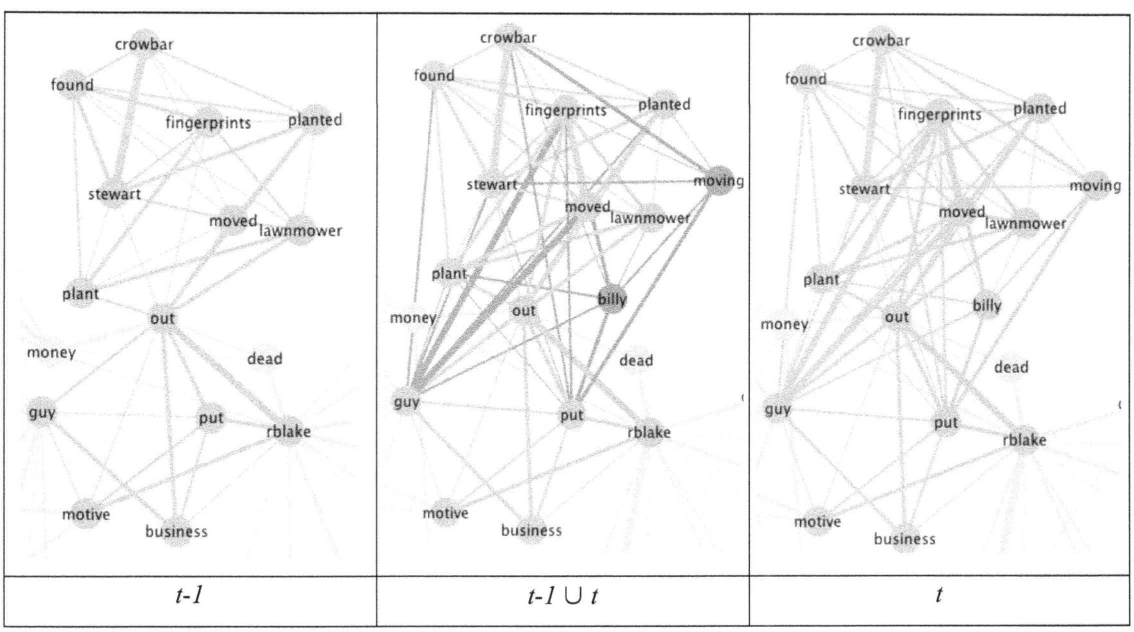

Figure 5: Establishing the connection between topics in adjacent time windows. The network at time *t* adds numerous links, causing the two topics at time *t-1* to become joined together. Note that because there is a greater overlap between topic A at *t-1* and topic identified at *t*, the new community adopts topic A's label.

that have already been identified, $\mathbf{C}^{u<t}$, to the set of topics found in the current time window, $\mathbf{C}^{t}$ as follows. For each community $c_j \in \mathbf{C}^{merged}$:

a. Identify each community $c_i \in \mathbf{C}^{u<t}$ and $c_k \in \mathbf{C}^{t}$ whose links are completely contained in c_j.

b. Compute $S(c_i, c_k)$ for all pairs (i,k).

c. Order pairs by descending score, and draw connections between the pairs of communities until all topics c_i and c_k have been accounted for.

3. Assign labels to the communities at time t according to the connections. Where a single community $c_i \in \mathbf{C}^{u<t}$ is determined to be the progenitor of $c_k \in \mathbf{C}^{t}$, c_k is simply assigned the label of the progenitor, indicating that the community has evolved. In cases where multiple communities in $\mathbf{C}^{u<t}$ are connected to a single community in $\mathbf{C}^{t}$, the destination community is labeled with the $c_i \in \mathbf{C}^{u<t}$ that accounts for the largest proportion of members.

The output of the algorithm is a set of topics that exist for some length of time during the conversation, and a set of links that indicate how different topics are connected. Topics can appear or disappear, evolve, merge, and split (Figure 6).

A final step in the analysis attempts to label the actual chat traces with the discovered topics. This is a simple matter of using the networks originally developed for each window and each thread, and finding the best match (in terms of relative overlap) with the extracted topics. At most one topic for each distinct thread in a time window is chosen.

Integrated Collaborative Intensity

As described with our knowledge construction example above (Figure 1), collaborative insights among the murder-mystery solving teams analyzed in this article often seemed to occur during portions of conversation where:

1. Posting activity among a team of collaborators is focused in one thread,
2. Posting speed increased, and
3. Most of the users were directly involved in the conversation.

Together, (1) and (3) indicate that a majority of the collaborators are contributing and attending to the conversation. A number of recent studies suggest that such

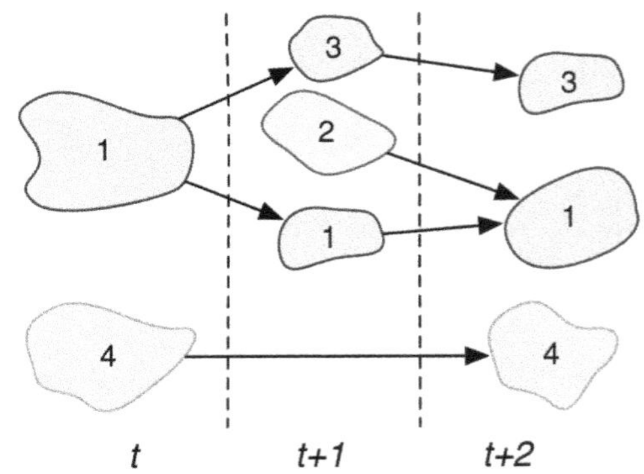

Figure 6: Illustrating the types of relationships between topics at different time steps. Topics can spawn new children (1→3), be consumed (2→1), evolve (3), or disappear and then reappear (4).

group dynamics are indeed important variables for group performance. For instance, Woolley, et al. [36] found that groups that have more balanced interaction patterns (i.e. lower variance in conversational turns among team members) are more collectively intelligent.

We developed a measurement, which we refer to as *integrated collaborative intensity* (ICI), which combines the preceding factors. The observation that activity is focused on one thread is quantified as θ_w, which is the inverse of the number of active threads (a thread is considered to be active in a time window w if there is a post in that thread in that time window) normalized by the maximum number of threads in any time window.

The speed of posting, α_{tw}, is determined by the number of posts in topic t at time window w, normalized by the maximum number of posts in any window in the conversation.

Finally, we adopt a measurement of *communication integration* (μ_{tw}) for every topic in every time window to describe how balanced and inclusive the conversation is [1]. The value is at a minimum where no team member talks to another, and at a maximum where everyone speaks directly to everyone else. In online forums where a sequence of replies may be established, communication integration is derived from the graph of who replies to whom.

More precisely, let l_{ij} be the smallest number of links between team members i and j in the reply graph for the section of conversation that is under consideration. The longest possible chain between any two members in a team of N members is N-1; if no chain exists between two members, we set the path length to N. Thus, following [1], communication integration is defined as:

$$\mu_{tw} = 1 - \frac{1}{N^2} \sum_{i \in \{1,2 \ldots N\}} \sum_{j \neq i} \frac{l_{ij}}{N-1}$$

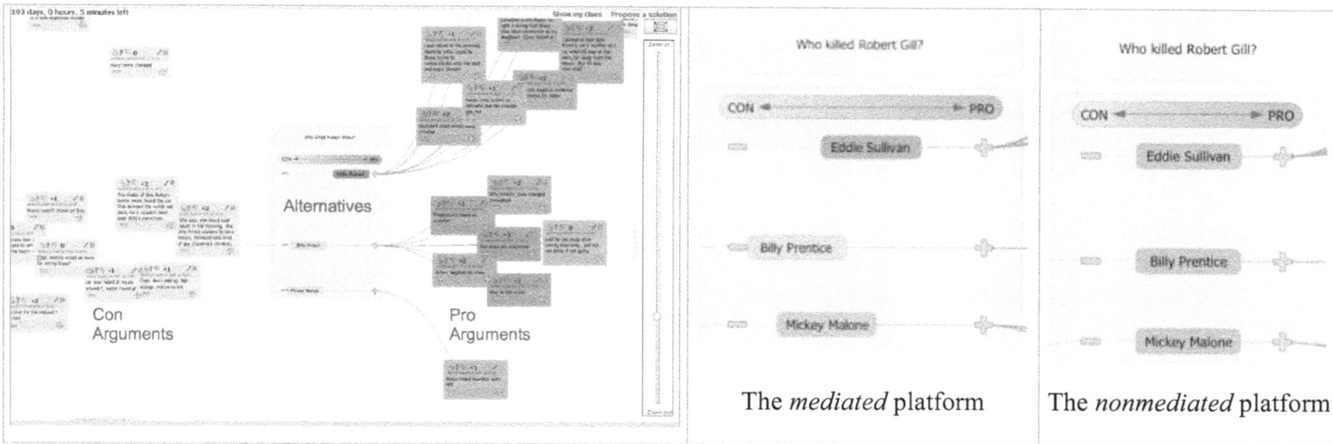

Figure 7: The platform interface. Both platforms used the same a graph-based interface. top level implicating arguments drifted to the right. In the mediated platform, cells representing the three suspects moved to the left or right depending upon the system's assessment of the suspect's guilt. In the non-mediated platform, these cells were anchored in the middle.

We adopt communication integration instead of simply counting the number of distinct users in a time window because we are interested not only in the number of unique sources of information, but also how that information might flow between people to create new collaborative insights. Our hypothesis is that such insight is most likely when online collaborators see different pieces information physically juxtaposed, but it is possible that any single individual might also carry information between two others. Thus, communication integration offers a rough approximation of the likelihood each team member will have been exposed to each other team member's information in a section of the conversation.

Each of the constituent measurements is normalized to the interval [0-1], so we express ICI for topic t in window w simply as:

$$ICI_{tw} = \theta_w \alpha_{tw} \mu_{tw}$$

DOMAIN

We used TEvA and ICI to analyze a dataset introduced at the beginning of this article. The dataset is derived from a controlled study that examined two versions of a decision platform [17]. The purpose of the study was to investigate whether a particular form of decision support could help groups avoid a pitfall of group decision making called the *common knowledge phenomenon*[31]. This phenomenon describes groups' tendencies to focus upon knowledge held by a majority of participants, and discount information held by a minority.

Both versions of the decision support platform were similar to a threaded chat forum with some specialized features (Figure 7). Each thread of discussion was anchored at a decision option (one of the suspects), and users were required to express whether a top-level post was for (implicating) or against (exonerating) the decision option it was attached to. Respondents to any existing post had to indicate whether their reply agreed or disagreed with that post. Finally, participants could vote for or against anyone else's posts.

The two platforms were identical with the following exceptions. In the *non-mediated* version the platform, teams were provided with the structure described above and a simple tool for negotiating consensus. In the *mediated* version, the system provided continuous feedback about which decision option was winning (based on analysis of the structure of the conversation and user votes). Feedback was provided via a set of sliders that moved according to the system's assessment of guilt for each suspect (Figure 7; see the detail for the two platforms). In addition, the team's final decision was constrained to match the winning option. If a team did not agree with the system, they could continue to deliberate to change the system's assessment.

The study was performed in a lab, and no contact was allowed between users outside of the system. Teams consisted of five people, and their task was to identify the correct suspect in a murder mystery. Team members were provided with a set of affidavits from characters in the mystery. The information contained in these materials was the same across all team members, but three of the team were provided with some additional information no one else had. Participants were told that some team members might have information others did not have, but no one knew which information was unshared. Teams were required to form a consensus by the end of a time-limited decision-making period, or else forfeit an opportunity to win a small prize for making the correct decision.

Twenty teams participated in the study, evenly split between the two platforms. Together, they generated roughly 1200 posts, evenly distributed across the conditions. As reported in [17], the mediated platform was found to improve the correlation of group decisions with the evidence mentioned in their conversations, and hence appeared to help participants avoid the common knowledge bias, but there was no appreciable difference in decision performance.

Subjectively however, teams in either condition appeared to solve the mystery quite differently. Teams with the non-mediated platform tended to pool their information in a single thread and attempted to create a shared story in periods of intense collaborative activity. Individuals in teams using the mediated platform appeared to operate more independently, and seemed less interested in generating a shared story to explain the evidence. We sought to use TEvA and ICI to expand upon these observations.

ANALYSIS

We applied the TEvA and ICI analyses to the collected dataset. Settings for the CPM algorithm and word co-occurrence network creation were chosen following guidance in [24] and [8], and parameters for the windowing strategy were chosen as described above. In all cases, a time windows were ten minutes long and were slid across the data in one-minute increments. Thus, a thirty-minute thread would contain at twenty windows, and each window after the first would overlap the previous window by nine minutes.

We analyzed our results in three steps. To provide initial validation of our procedure, we manually coded the dataset to extract conversational topics, and then compared the performance of TEvA and two established topic-modeling algorithms against the coded data. We then visualized TEvA's results to gain some insight into the data. Finally we performed a quantitative analysis to help make our more subjective impressions more concrete. The following sections describe each of these steps.

Validation

The validation of topic modeling approaches is somewhat complicated. Most topic modeling approaches adopt the common machine learning technique of training the probabilistic model with some subset of a corpus, and then testing the ability of the model to predict held-out documents (documents that were withheld from the training set) [33]. There have also been some efforts to determine if topic models produce psychologically meaningful topics [18]. This work has examined both the coherence of topic definitions and their fitness as labels that summarize the contents of a document. These approaches are not as useful in a discourse context where topic definitions change rapidly over time and the documents are very small. Thus, we validated the topics detected by TEvA and their assignment to posts against manually coded data. We also compared TEvA's topic assignments to two established topic-modeling approaches.

To code the data, two coders first worked together to establish a consistent methodology. Two sessions of data were randomly drawn from the corpus and used in this step. Topic assignment proceeded as follows. Within a sequence of replies (a thread), each post was considered to belong to the same evolving topic as long as local coherence was maintained and the thread did not deviate in a significant way from the inferred high-level topic for that thread. Opening and procedural posts (e.g. "Hi guys!" or "We need an answer soon!") were assigned the same topic as the temporally closest content post within a thread. If a post was encountered that for the most part replicated the contents of a thread that began earlier, it was labeled with the earlier thread's topic ID.

To establish inter-rater reliability, the coders processed two additional sessions independently. Because the number of topics and their meanings could vary, we could not apply approaches to inter-rater reliability that use a fixed classification scheme. Therefore, we approached the problem as one of assessing clustering similarity, where documents are clustered by topic ID.

We report two accepted clustering similarity metrics. The adjusted Rand index [16] compares how different clustering procedures assign pairs of items (posts, in our case) to the same or different clusters (topics). The adjusted Rand index ranges is equivalent to Cohen's Kappa [5,34], and is appealing because it is easy to interpret. However, it has the drawback of assuming a null hypothesis in which the two clusterings are drawn randomly from all possible partitions with a fixed number of clusters and fixed number of elements per cluster[22]. This is not a realistic assumption in our domain.

Because of this drawback, we also report Variation of Information (*VI*), which is a metric that addresses problems with the adjusted Rand index but is somewhat harder to interpret. *VI* is an information theoretic criterion that measures the distance between two clustering procedures based on the information gain and loss by switching from one to another method [22]. *VI* ranges from 0 to $log(n)$ with n equal the number of items to be clustered. Smaller values of *VI* indicate smaller distances between the results of two algorithms.

The two coders achieved a mean adjusted Rand index of .93 and *VI* of .05. Coders coded one session consisting of 88 posts exactly the same, and disagreed about the topic assignment for five posts in the 64 posts of the other session. This result satisfied us that the coding methodology was sufficiently robust, and the two coders split the remaining sessions to code the entire corpus.

Using the manually coded data as ground-truth, we compared the performance of TEvA and two probabilistic topic-modeling approaches: latent Dirichlet allocation (LDA) [4] and correlated topic models (CTM) [3]. We used the sliding window approach used with TEvA to prepare documents for LDA and CTM, and followed the procedure suggested by [13] to retrieve topics. Because it is necessary to specify the number of topics in advance for both LDA and CTM, we estimated models ranging from 5 to 40 topics (the maximum number of topics identified by the coders in any given session) and used the model yielding the best results for each session in our analysis.

Topics were assigned on a per window, rather than per post, basis. To compare the results of topic extraction to the manually coded data, it was therefore necessary to assign each post to a topic. To do this we labeled each post with the topic label that was assigned to the greatest number of time windows that the post appeared in. In the case of ties, we used the topic that reached its highest frequency first.

	$TEvA_{mean}$	LDA_{mean}	t	p
Adj. Rand	0.85	0.67	6.36	<.001
VI	0.10	0.26	-9.27	<.001
	$TEvA_{mean}$	CTM_{mean}	t	p
Adj. Rand	0.85	0.68	6.72	<.001
VI	0.10	0.27	-10.17	<.001

Table 1: Performance differences between TEvA and other topic extraction approaches (TEvA vs. LDA, TEvA vs. CTM) . In both cases, a two-tailed paired t-test was used. Sample size *m*=20 sessions.

Table 1 reports mean values of the adjusted Rand index and *VI* for TEvA, LDA and CTM compared against the manual coding. The results show that TEvA performs well, and is significantly more similar to the manual topic assignments than either LDA or CTM. We conclude from this initial validation step that TEvA is an effective method for extracting psychologically meaningful topics from our corpus.

Visualization

Figure 8 and Figure 9 present visualizations of TEvA's output for groups in the mediated and non-mediated conditions respectively. Time flows from left to right in the graphs, and each vertical line marks a minute of conversation. Each node is a segment of conversation (possibly containing multiple posts) about a topic detected by TEvA, and a node's size is proportional to ICI. Each color represents a different topic. The layout algorithm attempts to keep successive, connected nodes representing the same topic at the same vertical position in the graph until they merge with other topics. In some cases, topics that are active at different times appear at the same vertical position to economize on vertical space. Links indicate how topics evolve and become merged together. Because we are primarily concerned with the convergence of topics, instances where topics split are not shown and are not considered here.

Upon visualizing the data, we discovered an important difference between the mediated and non-mediated conditions. In non-mediated conditions, periods of maximum ICI tended to occur at points in the conversation where collaborators brought together the maximum number of topics. The portion of the transcript provided in Figure 8 traces the evolution of the conversation to such a point. Topic 3 occurs early on in the discussion, and concerns Billy's lying, his fingerprints on the crowbar, and the lawnmower. Topic 8 is a separate discussion about the wife not hearing Billy's loud muffler. Topic 3 merges with another topic (not shown) to become Topic 13, which is about Eddie potentially trying to frame Billy by claiming he heard his muffler. Finally, Topic 17 brings together information about the crowbar, the muffler, and Eddie's possible intent to frame Billy to arrive at the final shared story that Eddie must have framed Billy.

By the end of the session, Topic 17 has collected information from a total of five previous topics. It also reaches the maximum ICI for any point in the conversation at the second to last time window. This corresponds to the behavior observed in the subjective analysis of non-mediated teams, and is the moment where the group appears to form the story that determines the group's final decision.

In the mediated groups, periods of high ICI and topic convergence were observed, but they did not occur together as frequently. This is illustrated by Figure 9, which highlights the evolution of the conversation up to the points of highest ICI and maximum topic convergence for a mediated group. Topic 10 begins with a discussion of Billy's motive and theft of the victim's wallet, and this flows into Topic 9, which continues the discussion about the missing wallet. Topic 9 becomes quite heated as participants discuss the importance of the wallet, leading to the highest point of ICI for the conversation.

Topic 10 also flows into Topic 12, which focuses on Marble and his alibi. Topic 12 is informed by Topics 0 and 11, which cover the victim's wife's report of voices outside and Marble's motive. Topic 1 develops in parallel, and is initially concerned with Billy's tire tracks at the house on Saturday morning. Finally, Topic 16, which is about the victim's wife hearing a loud noise outside, merges along with the previously mentioned topics into Topic 1. At the point of convergence, information about Billy's car is brought in to the discussion about Marble to support the argument that Marble did not visit the victim that morning. Five topics flow into Topic 1 at this point, which is the maximum topic convergence for the conversation, but ICI remains relatively low.

Based on our observations about the difference in correlation between topic convergence and ICI across the conditions, we performed a quantitative analysis of both topic convergence and ICI across all sessions, and report the results below.

Quantitative Analysis

In the preceding analysis, we refer to *topic convergence* as the number of topics that flow into another topic at any given point in the conversation. More concretely, we can define topic convergence V as:

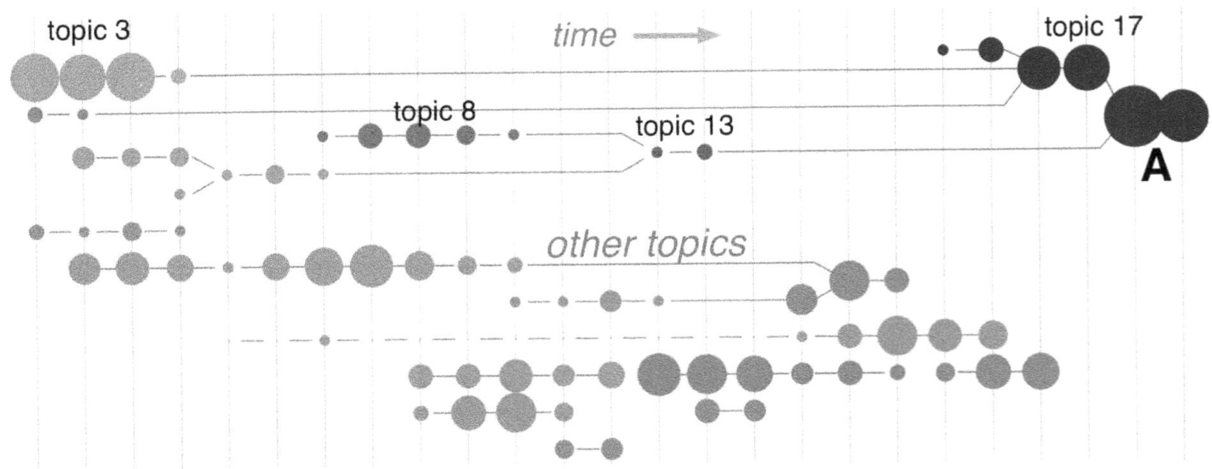

Topic 3 (Billy)	
P1	billy was VERY withholding of information
P2	Has lied to police and was caught twice.
P1	his fingerprints were on the crowboar, but he denied using it
P3	he's just a stupid scared kid
P1	and it's not his crowbar
P1	then why had he handled the supposed murder weapon?
P4	his fingerprints were on eddie's crowbar that was found in the bushes
P1	He handled it to get to the mower - claims he never used it, though.

Topic 8 (Billy)	
P5	does his car have a loud muffler?
P3	mrs blake didn't say anything about a loud muffler
P4	if his car was there also there would have been two cars, they only heard one noise

Topic 13 (Eddie)	
P1	eddie said he heard the loud muffler, and said it was billie's. was he trying to frame him?

Topic 17 (Eddie)	
P5	very much disregarded the question did he find the crowbar
P1	how would billie's fingerprints get on eddie's crowbar?
P2	Billy said he moved the crowbar to get to the mower.
P1	and would that really require throwing the murderweapo- crowbar into bushes, to be hidden?
P3	no, but eddie might of used the opportunity to frame him
P2	He never said he threw it into the bushes, just that he moved it - Eddit could move it
P2	Eddie also wants to pin this on Billy from the beginning. (muffler)
(A) Maximum Topic Convergence & Maximum ICI	
P1	what's eddie's motivation to frame billy?
P2	It's somebody that is not Eddie.

Figure 8: Non-mediated condition – Topic evolution graph with a portion of the conversation it describes. Time flows from left to right in the graph, and each vertical line represents a minute of time. Nodes represent conversation about a particular topic in a time window, and links on the graph illustrate how topics become merged together in time. Node colors distinguish between different topics, and node size reflects ICI. Passages of chat corresponding to the labeled nodes are shown beneath the graph. Point of maximum intensity and maximum convergence is indicated.

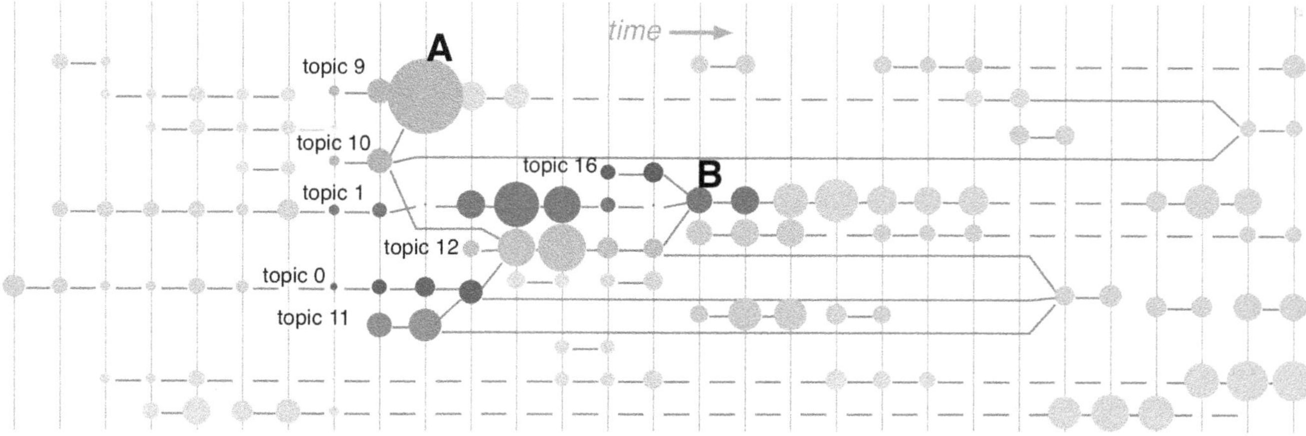

Topic 10 (Billy)	
P4	Motive?
P3	Always needed extra money. Remember Blake's wallet was stolen, and all the cash inside was taken.
P2	That's a good point, but remember he also saw the body. Maybe he just took the wallet an ran, without committing the murder.

Topic 9 (Billy)	
P5	Cash was missing. He's the only one who seems to need money
P4	They give him cash when he needs it. No need to steal.
	(A) Maximum ICI
P2	Stealing the wallet does not mean he committed the murder.
P5	Bob told his wife he was keeping an eye on billy re: money

Topic 0 (Marble)	
P4	Motive: Buisiness would be ruined by Blake
P5	Wife heard voices arguing outside
P2	Okay, but she also was alseep and is probably in shock.

Topic 12 (Marble)	
P1	called victim Saturday morning
P2	That doesn't suggest he killed the guy. He needed to talk about the golf game. They didn't want to both be there are the same time.
P4	Mrs. Blake heard a car on the driveway at 6:40, could have come and gone in that time.
P1	he left his home at 6:30-6:40 and it takes 15 minutes to get to golf, and he was there

Topic 11 (Marble)	
P1	got to his golf game on time
P4	The voices were heard at 6 am, plenty of time to get to the golf game

Topic 16 (Billy)	
P5	A very loud noise at 6:40 according to Wife; billy's car is very loud

Topic 1 (Billy + Marble)	
P5	Tire Tracks at the house on the day
P2	No, not on the day. He was there the day before. That was confirmed.
P3	The tracks were from Saturday morning. Billy admitted that he went Saturday to Blake's house and found his dead body.
	...
	(B) Maximum Topic Convergence
P3	Eddie identified the car as Billy's because he could hear its loud muffler. Billy admitted to being at Blake's Saturday morning
P3	He was at the golf course by 6:50
P4	That still fits in with the time frame of him killing Blake

Figure 9: Mediated Condition - Visualization of topic evolution with portions of the conversation it describes. Topic 1 spans multiple threads about Billy and Marble. Note that the points of maximum ICI and topic convergence occur at different points in the conversation.

$$V(t_{iw}) = \frac{|t_j \in Tree(t_{iw})|}{|\mathbf{T}|-1}$$

For topic t_i in window w, V is the number of unique topics in the tree formed by incoming edges and rooted at t_{iw}, divided by the total number of topics identified in a session minus one.

We sought to assess the relationship between the type of decision support and the two dependent variables, ICI and V. A histogram analysis revealed that both ICI and convergence were exponentially distributed, so a standard analysis of variance (which presumes normally distributed data) was inappropriate. Therefore, we used a variety of tests that are recommended for non-normally distributed data.

	Mediated (*n=989*)	Non-mediated (*n=921*)	Significance
ICI (mean)	.041	.054	$p<.01$
V (mean)	.046	.060	n.s.
Correlation (Spearman's ρ)	.27	.39	$p<.001$

Table 2. Descriptive statistics for ICI and Convergence (V); *p* values for the individual variables were determined using the Mann-Whitney's *U*. Fisher's transformation was applied to determine the significance of the difference in ρ.

Table 2 summarizes statistics for ICI and V. Both measurements were higher on average in the non-mediated condition. We used the Mann-Whitney test, which is a non-parametric alternative to Student's t and is appropriate for non-normal data [29], to evaluate the significance of this difference. The result indicates the difference in average ICI is highly significant, but that the difference in V is not.

To assess the relationship between V and ICI, we used Spearman's ρ, and compared the difference using Fisher's z transformation ([29]; p. 1071). Spearman's ρ is defined as Pearson's product-moment correlation between ranked variables, and can be interpreted similarly to r. The results indicate that correlation between ICI and V is significantly higher in groups that used the non-mediated platform.

To further elaborate these findings, we restricted our analysis to just points of maximum ICI for all groups and ranked the topic under discussion at that point according to V. Histograms reporting the percentile rank of the convergence value for the topic under discussion at points of maximum ICI are shown in Figure 10. Seven of the ten groups in the non-mediated condition experienced a maximum value of V at the same time they experienced maximum ICI. In the mediated groups, periods of maximal

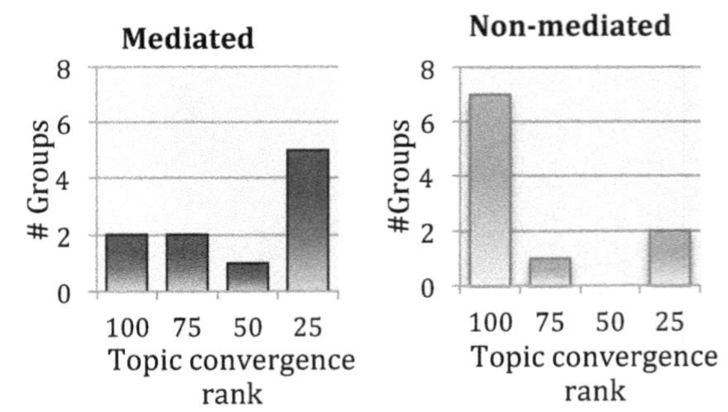

Figure 10: Topic convergence (V) at points of maximum ICI. Y-axis indicates the number of groups, x-axis the percentile rank of the topic according to V.

ICI were more highly correlated with topics that had relatively low V values.

These results confirm our initial impressions upon reading the transcripts. Groups in the non-mediated condition in experienced significantly more excited, focused collaboration as measured by ICI. Groups in either condition experienced a similar degree of convergence, but the degree of convergence correlated more strongly with the intensity of collaboration (ICI) in the non-mediated groups. It was also more likely that the most intense period of collaboration in the non-mediated groups would occur at the same time the group pooled a large amount of their information together.

In the following discussion we offer an explanation of these results, and then reflect upon our analysis methodology.

DISCUSSION

Decision Support and Knowledge Construction

Across the non-mediated groups, the passages of high topic convergence and high ICI were strongly correlated. These appeared to be passages where individuals were attempting to combine their information and develop a story that they could all agree to.

There is other evidence that individuals create narratives to solve certain kinds of problems. Pennington and Hastie demonstrated in a series of empirical studies that jurors maintain a mental model of evidence in the form of a narrative, and that these models are predictive both of their memory for evidence and ultimate verdict [25]. Based on these studies, the authors suggested that a group of jurors ultimately decide on a verdict by selecting a story that best satisfies a handful of criteria (e.g. completeness, consistency, plausibility) [15].

Our findings also suggest that story formation can be a natural part of decision making for groups if they are allowed to manage their own decision process. However, this does not appear to be a simple process of selecting the best story. Rather, individuals actively seek to construct their shared stories during highly collaborative phases of discussion.

Results from our previous work indicated that the non-mediated groups appeared to be less rational than the mediated groups because their final decision did not conform to the evidence mentioned in conversation. The analysis presented here offers an explanation; that the shared story is more important than the individual pieces of evidence. Groups may discount evidence that doesn't fit within an emerging consensual story, or infer evidence that completes it.

This is a useful perspective upon a large body of research on the common knowledge phenomenon and information pooling in general (e.g. [9,21]), which has focused on how group information pooling deviates from a rational norm. Studies in this thread of research typically rely upon domain problems in which individual pieces of information should be considered independently, and consistently report on groups' inability to make the "correct" decision under assumptions of independence. The findings have been robust enough (and troubling enough) to make their way into the popular literature [32].

The mediated platform used in this study was designed to correct the common knowledge problem. It intervened in a team's evidence aggregation procedure, and did indeed help groups to appear more rational. Yet our extended analysis shows that it also disrupted a natural collaborative process of story formation. Individuals may have still sought to create stories to explain the evidence, but the dynamics associated with teams weaving their information together to form a shared narrative were absent.

There are a variety of possible reasons for this. The presence of a referee (the mediating platform) may have reduced the scope of negotiation and hence the need for a group to form a common understanding. The system may have also had the appearance of an intransigent partner, and so participants in mediated teams would often simply accede to the opinion reflected by the system as the clock ran out. Furthermore, continuous feedback about which option was winning may have created a sense of competition that dissuaded collaboration.

More subtly, we noted during our analysis that effective narrative creation tended to occur in long, meandering threads where many pieces of information were juxtaposed in close temporal proximity. These threads did not conform well to the argumentative structure enforced by the platform. On the other hand, the combination of features in the mediated platform seemed to encourage posting behavior that did conform to this argumentative structure—threads were shorter and more focused. We might tentatively conclude that adherence to a purely argumentative formalism as a means for both communicating about and evaluating individual pieces of information makes it harder for groups to draw connections across the different pieces of information.

An approach to remedying this problem would be to provide representational support for both narrative and argument structures. This might allow collaborators to remain within the formalism yet still benefit from computational support. It has been noted elsewhere that individuals have tremendous difficulty in bringing evidence to bear upon their working theories [19], and so developing hybrid narrative-argumentative formalisms may ultimately be of great value.

Theory Driven Design and Technology Impact

In the study described here, simply assessing performance with respect to the common knowledge problem would not have uncovered the impact of the technology on collaborative knowledge construction. This reaffirms a more general lesson that is well understood by ethnographers, activity theorists and practitioners of distributed cognition: when evaluating technology that is designed to address a specific aspect of collaboration, it is important to consider how that technology affects all aspects.

How effectively any group of people can assimilate information, generate ideas, or make decisions depends upon a large number of interacting processes. By virtue of these interactions, technology designed to mediate any specific process or property can fundamentally alter the abilities of the group as a whole. We advocate the development of analytical approaches that can use digital trace data to provide a broad view of such system-wide processes, and the application of these when assessing the impact of collaborative and social technologies.

Researchers have begun to develop new methodological frameworks around systemic analyses of this kind (e.g. group informatics [11]). TEvA is a tool in this family, intended to serve as an imaging device for a socio-technical organism. It is our hope that others will begin to use TEvA and similar techniques not only for descriptive purposes, but also to critically evaluate the impact of technology on the health and intelligence of socio-technical systems.

FUTURE WORK

Our near term goal is to apply TEvA to corpora extracted from online communities that are orders of magnitude larger than the dataset analyzed here. There are challenges in doing this. One difficulty is the algorithmic complexity of the CPM algorithm, which slows exponentially if the underlying network is too densely connected. However, we can take advantage of the fact that networks of words change incrementally to reduce total computation time. If the algorithmic complexity of the CPM algorithm ultimately proves to be an insurmountable hurdle, other community detection algorithms might be used.

Another challenge in applying the algorithm to larger and more varied datasets is the variety of purposes online conversation serves. The transcripts we analyzed here contained highly focused, task-oriented discussion that was used to exchange a relatively small number of underlying ideas. In the wild, message-forums are used for a variety of additional purposes including planning, socialization, and emotional support, and they are informed by an external context that is much richer than the constrained domain of a single decision making task. We are not certain how TEvA will process such a varied substrate, but anticipate that the attempt will lead to new insights.

CONCLUSION

We have presented an analysis of computer-mediated teams using a novel approach called TEvA. This analysis allowed us to observe the historical evolution of knowledge as it flowed across a team, leading us to perceive the impact of technology in a new way. We concluded that the particular form of decision support under study disrupted a natural collaborative process, even while it improved decision making from a theoretically rational point of view.

We used the example of this study to reaffirm a more general lesson about the design of collaborative technology. The performance of a socio-technical system is governed by a complex set of interacting processes, and it is possible for a relatively small technological intervention to have much broader impacts. To understand these impacts, it is necessary to be able to observe the system as a whole.

The growing availability of digital trace data has enabled a new era of tools that allows us to analyze the global dynamics of collaborative systems in a new way. We hope that TEvA will be a useful contribution to this growing palette of techniques, and that the study presented here helps demonstrate the value and importance such analyses.

ACKNOWLEDGEMENTS

We would like to thank the reviewers for their careful review of this paper and excellent suggestions. We would especially like to thank Peter Gloor and Rob Laubacher for their many good ideas and continued encouragement throughout this project. Finally we would like to thank Thomas Malone for generously supporting this work at the MIT Center for Collective Intelligence.

REFERENCES

1. Van Alstyne, M. and Brynjolfsson, E. Global Village or Cyber-Balkans? Modeling and Measuring the Integration of Electronic Communities. *Management Science 51*, 6 (2005), 851 –868.
2. Blei, D.M. and Lafferty, J.D. Dynamic topic models. *Proceedings of the 23rd international conference on Machine learning*, ACM (2006), 113–120.
3. Blei, D.M. and Lafferty, J.D. A Correlated Topic Model of Science. *The Annals of Applied Statistics 1*, 1 (2007), 17–35.
4. Blei, D.M., Ng, A.Y., and Jordan, M.I. Latent dirichlet allocation. *J. Mach. Learn. Res. 3*, (2003), 993–1022.
5. Cohen, J. Weighted kappa: Nominal scale agreement provision for scaled disagreement or partial credit. *Psychological Bulletin 70*, 4 (1968), 213–220.
6. Conover, M.D., Ratkiewicz, J., Francisco, M., Gonc, B., Flammini, A., and Menczer, F. Political Polarization on Twitter. *Networks 133*, 26 (2011), 89–96.
7. Cui, W., Liu, S., Tan, L., et al. TextFlow: Towards Better Understanding of Evolving Topics in Text. *Visualization and Computer Graphics, IEEE Transactions on 17*, 12 (2011), 2412–2421.
8. Danowski, J. WORDij: A word-pair approach to information retrieval. *NIST special publication*, 500207 (1993), 131–136.
9. Dennis, A.R. Information Exchange and Use in Group Decision Making: You Can Lead a Group to Information, but You Can't Make It Think. *MIS Quarterly 20*, 4 (1996), 433–457.
10. Gloor, P.A., Krauss, J., Nann, S., Fischbach, K., and Schoder, D. Web Science 2.0: Identifying Trends through Semantic Social Network Analysis. *Computational Science and Engineering, IEEE International Conference on*, IEEE Computer Society (2009), 215–222.
11. Goggins, S., Mascaro, C., and Valetto, G. Group Informatices: A Methodological Approach and Ontology for Understanding Socio-Technical Groups. *Journal of the American Society for Information Science and Technology*, (2012).
12. Grosz, B.J. and Sidner, C.L. Attention, intentions, and the structure of discourse. *Comput. Linguist. 12*, 3 (1986), 175–204.
13. Grün, B. and Hornik, K. topicmodels: An R Package for Fitting Topic Models. *Journal of Statistical Software 40*, 13 (2011), 1–30.
14. Gunawardena, C.N., Lowe, C.A., and Anderson, T. Analysis of global on line debate and the development of an interaction analysis model for examining social construction of knowledge in computer conferencing. *Journal of Educational Computing Research 17*, 4 (1997), 397–431.
15. Hastie, R. and Pennington, N. Explanation-Based Decision Making. In *Judgment and Decision Making: An Interdisciplinary Reader*. Cambridge University Press, 2000, 212–228.
16. Hubert, L. and Arabie, P. Comparing partitions. *Journal of Classification 2*, 1 (1985), 193–218.
17. Introne, J.E. Supporting group decisions by mediating deliberation to improve information pooling. *Proceedings of the ACM 2009 international conference on Supporting group work*, (2009), 189–198.
18. Jonathan Chang, Jordan Boyd-graber, Sean Gerrish, Chong Wang, and Blei, D.M. *Reading Tea Leaves: How Humans Interpret Topic Models*. CiteSeerX, 2010.
19. Kuhn, D. *The skills of argument*. Cambridge Univ Pr, 1991.
20. Leskovec, J., Backstrom, L., and Kleinberg, J. Meme-tracking and the dynamics of the news cycle.

Proceedings of the 15th ACM SIGKDD international conference on Knowledge discovery and data mining, ACM (2009), 497–506.

21. Lightle, J.P., Kagel, J.H., and Arkes, H.R. Information Exchange in Group Decision Making: The Hidden Profile Problem Reconsidered. *Manage. Sci. 55*, 4 (2009), 568–581.
22. Meilă, M. Comparing clusterings—an information based distance. *Journal of Multivariate Analysis 98*, 5 (2007), 873–895.
23. Palla, G., Barabasi, A.-L., and Vicsek, T. Quantifying social group evolution. *Nature 446*, 7136 (2007), 664–667.
24. Palla, G., Derenyi, I., Farkas, I., and Vicsek, T. Uncovering the overlapping community structure of complex networks in nature and society. *Nature 435*, 7043 (2005), 814–818.
25. Pennington, N. and Hastie, R. Reasoning in explanation-based decision making. *Cognition 49*, 1–2 (1993), 123–163.
26. Poole, M.S. Decision development in small groups, III: A multiple sequence model of group decision development 1. *Communication Monographs 50*, 4 (1983), 321–341.
27. Ramage, D., Dumais, S., and Liebling, D. Characterizing microblogs with topic models. *International AAAI Conference on Weblogs and Social Media*, (2010).
28. Ratkiewicz, J., Conover, M., Meiss, M., et al. Truthy: mapping the spread of astroturf in microblog streams. *Proceedings of the 20th international conference companion on World wide web*, ACM (2011), 249–252.
29. Sheskin, D. *Handbook of Parametric and Nonparametric Statistical Procedures*. CRC Press, 2004.
30. Simmons, M.P., Adamic, L.A., and Adar, E. Memes Online: Extracted, Subtracted, Injected, and Recollected. *ICWSM 2011*, (2011).
31. Stasser, G. and Titus, W. Pooling of unshared information in group decision making: Biased information sampling during discussion. *Journal of Personality and Social Psychology 48*, 6 (1985), 1467.
32. Sunstein, C.R. *Infotopia: how many minds produce knowledge*. Oxford University Press US, 2006.
33. Wallach, H.M., Murray, I., Salakhutdinov, R., and Mimno, D. Evaluation methods for topic models. *Proceedings of the 26th Annual International Conference on Machine Learning*, ACM (2009), 1105–1112.
34. Warrens, M. On the Equivalence of Cohen's Kappa and the Hubert-Arabie Adjusted Rand Index. *Journal of Classification 25*, 2 (2008), 177–183.
35. Wise, A.F. and Chiu, M.M. Analyzing temporal patterns of knowledge construction in a role-based online discussion. *International Journal of Computer-Supported Collaborative Learning 6*, (2011), 445–470.
36. Woolley, A.W., Chabris, C.F., Pentland, A., Hashmi, N., and Malone, T.W. Evidence for a collective intelligence factor in the performance of human groups. *Science 330*, 6004 (2010), 686.
37. Zhang, J., Song, Y., Zhang, C., and Liu, S. Evolutionary hierarchical Dirichlet processes for multiple correlated time-varying corpora. *Proceedings of the 16th ACM SIGKDD international conference on Knowledge discovery and data mining*, (2010), 1079–1088.

.

Representation and Communication: Challenges in Interpreting Large Social Media Datasets

Mattias Rost
Mobile Life @ SICS
Stockholm, Sweden
rost@sics.se

Louise Barkhuus
Stockholm University
Stockholm, Sweden
barkhuus@dsv.su.se

Henriette Cramer
Yahoo! Research
Sunnyvale, CA, USA
henriette@yahoo-inc.com

Barry Brown
Mobile Life @ DSV
Stockholm, Sweden
barry@mobilelifecentre.org

ABSTRACT
Online services provide a range of opportunities for understanding human behaviour through the large aggregate data sets that their operation collects. Yet the data sets they collect do not unproblematically model or mirror the world events. In this paper we use data from Foursquare, a popular location check-in service, to argue for the importance of analysing social media as a communicative rather than representational system. Drawing on logs of all Foursquare check-ins over eight weeks we highlight four features of Foursquare's use: the relationship between attendance and check-ins, event check-ins, commercial incentives to check-in, and lastly humorous check-ins These points show how large data analysis is affected by the end user uses to which social networks are put.

Author Keywords
Social media, location-based services, empirical methods.

ACM Classification Keywords
H.3.5 [Information Interfaces and Presentation]: Online Information Services – Web-based services.

INTRODUCTION
The widespread adoption of online services has created a range of new human activities and behaviours. Since our online behaviour is invariably tracked, datasets of online activity can be used to make a range of inferences about behaviour, both in terms of the service itself and our broader lives. Large data sets in particular afford the analysis of broad social trends and activities. CSCW and HCI are no stranger to these sorts of analyses– for example, data on Facebook's relationship status has been used to infer differences in relationship formation and breakup [14], and research has even argued that happiness, as a broadly defined measure of general wellbeing, can be measured from social media status messages [19]. Location-based social media (from services such as Foursquare and Twitter) have been used to infer details about travel patterns and behaviours [11, 22] and with the increasing possibility of location sensing, large scale location data has be used to predict social events attendance [7] or to infer the nature of neighbourhoods [12] and human mobility [8].

These analyses rest upon the assumption that large-scale data sets are representative, in some quantifiable way, of real world behaviour. Extensive work has been done to understand the relationships between these databases and human behaviour, such as inferring location from humorous posts, or extracting 'real' from 'fake' online reviews. As we argue in this paper, however, this focus on the representativeness of such data inadvertently neglects the *communicative* features of social network data sets. Social media datasets are a record of communication – analysing it as only a representation of an underlying reality neglects the ways in which social media data is produced by social interactions between users. What is being analysed is a communicative system with its own contingencies, absences, and structure – genera of accounts produced and adapted for the purposes of the online system. This is particularly the case if we turn to location sharing systems. Systems such as Foursquare, Gowalla, and Facebook places (for example) are based not only on users' locations but also on an explicit declaration – and thus communication to others – of location. Using such data offers great opportunities [8, 11, 12], but taking advantage of these opportunities necessitates an awareness and discussion of the properties that these datasets have.

Through exploring one large social media dataset in particular – Foursquare check-ins – in this paper we examine how this dataset is better understood not as a representation or record of behaviour, but rather as communication amongst Foursquare users.

Foursquare check-ins
Foursquare is a mobile service allowing its users to share their location by 'checking in' to a venue. A check-in is a manual declaration of location at a semantically named venue. Users can check in to existing venues, or create venues themselves. Venues have a latitude longitude location, a name, an address, a category and users can add tips to venues. Users can keep their check-ins private, share them with their Foursquare friends, or push them to Facebook and/or Twitter. Venues are public, with the

CSCW '13, February 23–27, 2013, San Antonio, Texas, USA.

exception of those venues explicitly labelled as homes. Foursquare also employs 'gamification' elements such as 'mayorships' (the user checking in to a venue most becomes its mayor), points and badges for combinations of certain check-ins to increase usage [9, 20]. Commercial partnerships are part of Foursquare's business model with for example badges being offered for check-ins related to various brands, and merchants can also offer deals and discounts to users to reward checking in to their venue.

As with most social media systems, Foursquare collects a record of users' activity in the system. We studied data from an unedited feed of all Foursquare check-ins worldwide, for a period of eight weeks in 2010 and 2011. In studying this data, it was apparent that the use of Foursquare is not a simple indicator of location or behaviour. Rather, Foursquare is a social medium with its own properties. Broadly, we argue that the uses to which a system is put influences the kinds of data logged [3]. In particular the data that social media systems collect is broadly data about communicative action, with the richness that entails. While this data can be mined to obtain incidental representations of other activity, this is to throw away the key features of the data that make it comprehensible. Using this data we argue for how check-in data cannot be read simply as declarations of position, but should be understood as part of a broader communication system.

PREVIOUS WORK

Many aspects of online social networks have been explored, relating to particular properties of the network in terms of friendship ties and impression management [9, 13, 20], content-based user characterisation [21], as well as large-scale network structure and behaviour [16]. These online social networks, or "social-awareness streams" [21], also provide potential for modelling activity through the data sets that are available, either through scraping websites or through companies voluntarily sharing their data. More specifically, location-based networks have provided researchers with large data sets of location data that they use for creating models of prediction in terms of issues such as friend connections and human mobility [8, 11, 24], check-ins have for example been used to identify proto-neighbourhoods [11] and city 'rhythms' [8]. Cranshaw et al. [11] used public data about venues that have been checked in to (rather than check-ins) to distil canonical neighbourhoods by analysing co-occurrence patterns in place categories. Scellato et al. [24] analysed the socio-spatial characteristics of the ties between users in various location-sharing services, including Foursquare. Noulas et al. [22] presented an analysis of the geo-temporal dynamics by analysing tweets that contain check-ins and Cheng et al. [8], using tweets containing check-ins, showed that users follow reproducible patterns, that socioeconomic factors are coupled with mobility, and that content analysis of check-ins can provide interesting insights in the relationships between people and locations.

While these analyses may offer interesting insights in local differences, there are a wide variety of reasons for checking in resulting in these data points (and also for *not* checking in). Actively sharing a location is not only a practical tool for coordination and serendipitous interactions; location-sharing supports self-presentation, expression of mood, sharing of life events, and a multitude of other usage motivations [2, 9, 19]. Check-ins change location from 'a user state' into a deliberate situated act, in which considerations of audiences of other users and social norms play an important role [9]. This includes whether to share, but also on which channel(s), such as pushing check-ins to Twitter and/or Facebook as well.

More broadly, a challenge here is that check-in data, which is inherently social in nature, is approached as data indicating behaviour, i.e. that a check-in is simply an indication that a person has been at a specific place. Although most work acknowledges that data is socially based, the models and analyses rarely take into consideration the users' underlying motivations or social characteristics of the service itself in the modelling of the data. Analysis inevitably takes the form of seeing data as a view on behaviour beyond the social network, rather than as a way of studying the social network itself.

For example, Hecht et al. [18] describe the use of humorous 'fake' location descriptions in twitter users' profiles (such as 'Justin Bieber's Heart'), developing an algorithm that finds users' location to overcome this deliberate obfuscation. The paper does insightful analysis so as to obtain location data from users' tweets, broadly categorising users' location based on their similarity to users where location is already known. Thus, according to their algorithm a user who tweets about 'Crawfish' is more likely to be in Louisiana, and a user who tweets about "Clegg" (the British deputy prime minister) in the U.K. While this paper acknowledges that it only looks at one part of twitter data, to our mind this analysis neglects important aspects of the twitter data feed. Twitter data is *communicative* and not *representative*, and while as a side effect it might be possible to ascertain location data this is to ignore important aspects of this data. What is absent in this analysis is an understanding of *why* location might feature and influence what is tweeted. As a communication media that supports at a distance communication, one could image that location would disappear as a feature of tweeters' identity. Yet as this paper shows, location is so evident as a feature of actual tweets that it can be extracted with considerable accuracy from a sample of users' tweets.

This focus on representation can also be seen in more qualitative work. Brubaker and Hayes' [6] insightful discussion of relationship status in Facebook and Craigslist documents the relationship between these systems and users' lives and practices. Yet, while the paper pivots on their nature as "representational systems", it retains a focus on these systems as descriptions of reality rather than as genera of communication.

DATABASES AND REPRESENTATION

Outside CSCW and HCI the nature of databases and their proliferation have proven to be a topic of sporadic interest for social science research. Here the nature of representations has been most directly grappled with and here the database as representation has had a prominent focus. Poster, for example, writes of databases as a 'super panopticon', resonating Foucault's writings on the prison [23]. A more subtle approach is taken by Bowker [4] who writes in detail about how the authorship of particular representations is embroiled in their use. The international classification of disease, for example, is embedded in a series of medical practices in different places. This is no less the case when we look at databases of activity. This echos Garfinkel's [15] arguments concerning the nature of representations such as medical records. Since medical records are made as part of a work process the sorts of records that are made are inherently conditioned by the needs of that work. The records that are produced are not then simply objective records of the workplace, but rather records that are used as part of that work activity, produced specifically for the purposes of treating patents.

With the recent turn to 'big data', however, understanding the conditions of the production of data has been downplayed, seen as an issue of 'data cleaning', rather than an inherent feature of records of activity. As boyd and Crawford put it: "Regardless of the size of a data set, it is subject to limitation and bias. Without those biases and limitations being understood and outlined, misinterpretation is the result." [5] We can draw an analogy with public app deployments for research purposes. Large-scale app deployments, capitalizing on easy distribution via app stores and the widespread proliferation of sensor-equipped mobile devices, offer huge opportunities for researchers, but also methodological challenges including data representation, gaining informed consent from app users, and lack of context surrounding collected data points [10].

DATA

To explore this argument, let us now turn to our data, and approach. The data set was provided to us by Foursquare and we were given access to their live stream of check-in data between September 12th 2010 and March 3rd 2011. The data is acquired through a firehose API delivering anonymised check-ins as they are performed. These data points contain venue name, venue category, venue location (long/lat), user gender, timestamp and the timezone used at the location of the venue, and whether or not the user received a badge. Due to some technical problems this data had a number of missing days – we thus selected the longest continuous period of data for closer analysis - eight weeks of continuous data at the end of 2010 and beginning of 2011 (starting Nov 8). Our approach to the data was experimental in that we took focused examinations of the data to explore what venues were being checked-into, both infrequently and frequently. We then explored the data analysing how check-ins to different venues differed over time, and over different areas.

RESULTS

We start with a broad overview of the data worldwide using roughly the first four weeks of data, from Nov 8 – Dec 5, 2010. Within this set, Foursquare users checked in to 5,499,469 different venues. The data shows a long tail in terms of the number of check-ins per venue. The mean number of check-ins to each venue was 7.6, with a median of 2 and σ=46.7. The number of check-ins to the top 20% of most checked-in venues account for 74% of all check-ins. The 2% of the most popular venues account for 32% of all check-ins. Interestingly, a rather larger set of 1,963,091 venues (37%) received only 1 check-in during this period.

When we look at all check-ins and venues, we see that 2.9M (53%) of venues are in the Americas and 24M check-ins (57%), 1.8M (33%) of the venues are in Asia, with 13M (33%) check-ins, 768,953 (14%) venues are in Europe, with 4.4M(11%) check-ins and 23,267 venues in Africa (0.4%), with 108.951 check-ins (0.26%). When we look at the top 100 venues users checked into (Table 1 shows the top 10) we see that overall, venues in the US, and in particular airports, dominate (airports: 31/100, US venues: 55/100, 39/100 in Asia, Europe: 6/100 – 3 of the latter, perhaps quite characteristic for the time of year, were ski areas in Austria).

#	Check-ins	Venue
1	26,159	Siam Paragon (shopping mall), Bangkok
2	18,140	Los Angeles International Airport (LAX), US
3	17,224	MoMA Museum of modern art, NY
4	16,878	John F. Kennedy International Airport (JFK)
5	16,804	NBC Studio 1A Today Show, NY, US
6	16,564	Madison Square Garden, NY, US
7	16,404	Hartsfield Jackson Atlanta Int. Airport, US
8	15,967	San Francisco International Airport, US
9	15,239	Chicago O'Hare International Airport, US
10	12,460	New York Penn Station, NY, US

Table 1: Top checked-into venues worldwide

Why this is the case cannot be established from this data alone. This could for example indicate a difference between locales in terms of places that people visit, or the type of venues people like to share. While this data does represent human activity to a certain extent, we also see that we need to be careful for which types of purposes we use this data. The data is characterized through the motivations for sharing as identified in [9], socio-economic factors and demographics of foursquare users. As examples: the MoMa (#2) for instance receives 2.5M visitors a year according to its homepage, whereas Atlanta's airport (#3) receives over 7M passengers every year, and the order of airports does not confirm to the passenger number listings of [1], nor are all airports in the world, such as the second largest airport, Beijing, present in such data.

Snowpocalypse: Reappropriation of Location

We continue by focusing on a geographical subset of the data; we extracted data from New York City, London and Boston. These are all large urban areas and looking at these enabled us to examine more detailed local phenomena. Looking at this data showed that location-sharing services are not only used to share location; their usage data also reflect local events. When we look at #5 in the top 10, we see a TV show/studio. The venues of #13 and 19 are related to the Macy Thanksgiving Parade in NY. Events can also result in spikes in the data, Foursquare for example report the 'rally to restore sanity' in Washington, DC on 30 October with 30,525 check-ins as the most checked-into event for 2010. This number of check-ins is markedly larger than the most checked-into venue in the top 10 for our Nov-Dec period (Siam Paragon with 26,159 check-ins). We also see data likely caused by incentives, rather than actual presence at a venue, such as on #39 with 7428 check-ins, 'The Conan Blimp', a promotion in which a giant blimp promoted the Conan O'Brien show (a comedy show) across America, and a check-in to this 'venue' resulted in a badge.

One characteristic of our data is the prevalence of non-location based check-ins (not unlike previous studies of prototype systems where locations were defined as hybrids between a location and status [2]). One interesting phenomena concerned weather related check-ins. Over our sampled time period there was extreme weather with a record snowfall and low temperatures across the US and Europe. On January 25th New York snowfall broke a record held since 1925. Looking at our larger time period, in our NY data set we found 85 special venues reflecting this by searching for keywords such as "...pocalypse," "snow", "freeze" and "slush". The venues were not physical venues such as a particular restaurant, but rather they captured a shared experience of extreme weather. This is reflected through the way these venues are named; of the 85 special venues identified, 17 were based on the notion of an Apocalypse, for example Snowpocalypse, Freezepocalypse, Slushpocalypse. These are all playful ways of saying that it is snowy, cold, ice is melting etc., and that this seemed at the time extreme and very much an experience that is shared by New Yorkers.

Figure 1 shows the total for check-ins to the eight most popular expressive check-ins. The most 'checked-in' venue is Snowpocalypse 2011 peaking at 4590 check-ins on January 27th. This contrasts with other top checked in physical venues the same day – for example 378 check-ins to all Starbucks and 268 to Penn Station. There are two major spikes in the data on January 24th and 27th where Freezepocalypse accounts for 2877 check-ins on the 24th, followed by 599 the day after (but notably none the days before). Snowpocalypse on the other hand exhibits a different characteristic with 3431 check-ins on the 26th and 4590 on the 27th. In the figures we also see the snowfall during the same dates. It is clear that on days of heavy snow, large numbers of check-ins to a venue reflect an event, but the online phenomenon is also affected by the actual check-in activity itself.

We contrasted this data with similar check-ins for Boston, see figure 2 (also affected by the extreme weather). Interestingly, while Snowpocalypse-styled check-ins appear sporadically here after January 2nd, at the start of the extreme weather this was not a check-in phenomenon. The phenomenon in Boston came after NYC, despite the weather starting in Boston. Foursquare check-ins can thus be read as an indicator of a large shared experience – the severe winter of 2010/2011. The social network here has been repurposed and effortlessly reappropriated to this experience, 'redefining' location and the purpose of the service itself. The check-in data does not directly correlate with the real-world occurrences, especially Boston that did not catch on with the first big snowfall.

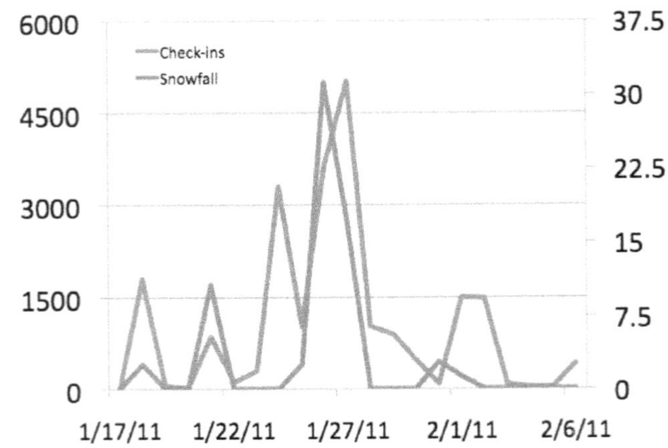

Figure 1: Snowfall and snow related check-ins for NYC

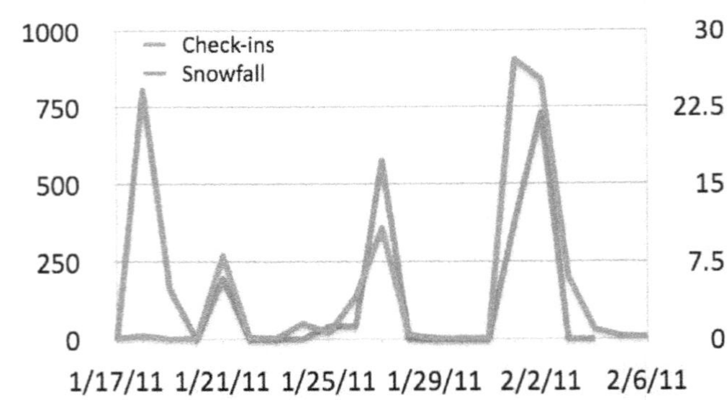

Figure 2: Snowfall and snow related check-ins for Boston

External Motivation Factors

A second feature of the check-ins we examined was the role of external motivation factors. Services such as Foursquare understandably employ various ways to increase usage, and have incentives built in to increase the number of check-ins. Game-like elements, and rewards such as discounts at retailers aim to motivate users to check in. Foursquare contains elements such as points, badges and 'mayorship' of a venue for the user who checks in the most to a venue. These game-like aspects have been highlighted in other research as well [20], and have been shown to in some cases conflict with other usage motivations to share one's location [9]. Another factor at play are third-party collaborations that are part of the Foursquare business model in which organisations can for example acquire a dedicated badge related to their brand.

The effect of these intertwined service design features can be illustrated by the introduction of a set of five new badges on November 16th 2010. In New York we found that Radioshack (an electronics chain) spiked rather quickly over a short time, going from 5 and 12 check-ins per day on 13th to 14th November, then jumping to 58, 196 and then 1323 the following days, bringing it to the top 10 venues in number of check-ins on Manhattan for three days in a row. Radioshack had introduced a special offer on November 15th where customers who checked in would receive 10% off, 15% off if the customer was a 'mayor' and 20% if the customer got a 'holiday hero badge' (obtained through checking in to a set of venues). It is perhaps not a surprise that the specific features of Foursquare, or that commercial tie-ins influence check-in data. Yet this underlines how online data can be influenced by a myriad of small features that produce anomalies and local deviations.

Humour and Communication

Past researchers have remarked upon the humorous use of location systems - where locations are used as part of banter or social repartee. In particular Barkhuus et al. [2] report on how location statuses amongst a group of friends were frequently used as a part of longstanding jokes. Hecht et al. [18] describe the use of humorous location descriptions in twitter profile location fields (such as 'Justin Bieber's Heart'), developing an algorithm that finds users' location, overcoming this deliberate obfuscation. Although it is clear that the users' intention is humour in both these papers, the nature of the humour was unexplored. In here we explored in more detail categories of humorous entries. To categorise the humorous check-ins that we had identified, we sorted the forms of humorous check-ins and agreed three categories: mis-categorisation, profanity-based invented venues, and real venue/'from-a-distance' check-ins where the user's location does not match the venue checked into.

Mis-categorisations were observed when a user specified venue name did not match its category. For example on Manhattan we found 21 venues that were clearly homes but categorized as strip clubs (verified using Google Street View). Theses were only checked into on average 2.8 times, perhaps as a short-lived joke. Examples include: "Dans apartment" [sic], "Gian's rooftop" and "Tom's bachelor pad" - all categorized as strip clubs. *Invented locations* involved imaginary location names that included profanities, often expressed as a general commentary or as an opinion of a real venue. For example, searching for the one of most common profanities we found 18 such venues just on Manhattan. They were 'places' such as 'Faux-tini: This is not f****** bartini' or 'It's My F****** Birthday!'. The snowpocalypse phenomenon was in a sense a large-scale example of such miscategorisation.

Lastly, we found several types of likely *check-ins 'from-a-distance'* due to the time or situation. For example, there were around two check-ins per day to Buckingham Palace in London between midnight and six in the morning, indicating that either people were in close enough range outside the British Royal residence or that they specifically searched for it and checked in from afar. Other check-ins from-a-distance include check-ins to venues that were closed at the time, or would be difficult to reach (such as top of the empire state building, Statue of Liberty). These check-ins highlight the *communicative* role of checking in. These are not 'fake', 'incorrect' or 'invalid' check-ins - since their intention is as a means of communication, not as a literal description of location. This means that they provide a resource for understanding particular forms of humour, and communication; they are perhaps less clearly understandable as indicating a record of location or behaviour.

DISCUSSION AND CONCLUSIONS

The core argument of this paper has been that social network data should be seen and analysed as communicative data. That is: data that is produced as a side effect of communication between users, rather than as a representation of some underling activity. What these examples above give us are cases where the check-ins make little sense as representations of a 'reality', yet make more sense as communicative events between Foursquare users.

Reviewing these behavioural characteristics in terms of check-ins, it is clear that there are broader concerns for users than simply reporting their location to the record; we here specified four topics. Looking at the data overall we observed how the number of check-ins has no clear correspondence with visitor numbers. We then described how the 'Snowpocalypse' unfolded, and had a significant affect on east coast US check-ins. Third, we described the role of promotions as a motivation for check-ins. Lastly, evidence of humour on the other hand, showed itself to be fairly sophisticated and so individually tailored that it hardly seemed to affect any large scale analysis. On the other hand this might indicate another discrepancy: that it will not be discovered as an actual feature of use. Textual search for example will not uncover all such instances; this data illustrates well how humorous use is very difficult to look for in large data sets because of its subtlety and contextual base.

While an obvious solution when approaching the data as a representation of human activity would seem to 'simply filter out such noise', this is too simplistic. Data cleaning processes are inherently subjective [5] and without taking a qualitative look at big data faulty assumptions are likely to arise, not fitting local or temporal differences in the anomalies we have described. Our contribution here does not centre on the issue of deciding what these large datasets can be used for, but rather about exploring emerging genres of communication. In conclusion we would argue more broadly for the role of check-in services like Foursquare not as location-based services, but rather as particular communication genre, with particular developing forms and style. This role may turn out to be ultimately more important than its role as a record of location. Check-in based location systems, or at least Foursquare, are distinct to continuous location updating systems. The act of 'checking in' is such that it can be used to communicate in a way quite different to the background updating of ones location. The difference between a computer and an individual reporting their location makes for a service that fits quite different purposes. Rather than asking whether this data is representative of location, we should ask what the data represents.

REFERENCES

1. Airports Council Int., Monthly Traffic ratings, Dec 2010.
2. Barkhuus, L., Brown, B., Bell, M., Sherwood, S., Hall, M., Chalmers, M. (2008) From Awareness to Repartee: Sharing Location Within Social Groups. In Proc. of CHI '08.
3. Bittner, E. and Garfinkel, H. (1967) Good organisational reasons for bad clinical records. In Studies in ethnomethodology: Prentice Hall.
4. Bowker, G.C. (2006) Memory Practices in the Sciences, MIT Press.
5. boyd, d. and Crawford, K. Six provocations for big data, A Decade in Internet Time: Symposium on the Dynamics of the Internet and Society, Sept 2011.
6. Brubaker, J. R. and Hayes, G. R. (2011) SELECT * FROM USER: Infrastructure And Socio-Technical Representation. In Proc. of CSCW '11.
7. Calabrese, F., Pereira, F.C., Lorenzo, G.D., Liu, L. and Ratti, C. (2010) The Geography of Taste: Analyzing Cell-Phone Mobility and Social Events. In Proc. of Pervasive 2010.
8. Cheng, Z., Caverlee, J., Lee, K., Sui, D. (2011) Exploring Millions of Footprints in Location Sharing Services. In Proc. ICWSM '11.
9. Cramer, H., Rost, M. and Holmquist, L. E. (2011) Performing a check-in: emerging practices, norms and 'conflicts' in location-sharing using Foursquare. In Proc. MobileHCI '11.
10. Cramer, H. Rost, M., Bentley, F: (2011) An introduction to Research in the Large, Special Issue on 'Research in the Large', International Journal of Mobile Human-Computer Interaction.
11. Cranshaw, J. and Yano, T. (2010) Seeing a home away from the home: Distilling proto-neighborhoods from incidental data with Latent Topic Modeling. Proc. NIPS'10.
12. Cranshaw, J. Schwartz, R. Hong, J. and Sadeh, N. (2012) The Livehoods Project: Utilizing Social Media to Understand the Dynamics of a City. Proc. ICWSM'12,.
13. Ellison, N. B., Steinfield, C., and Lampe, C. (2007). The benefits of Facebook "friends:" Social capital and college students' use of online social network sites. *Journal of Computer-Mediated Communication*, 12(4), article 1.
14. Facebook Data Team: The Right Time for Love: Tracking the Seasonality of Relationship Formation. Accessed at https://www.facebook.com/notes/facebook-data-team/the-right-time-for-love-tracking-the-seasonality-of-relationship-formation/10150643989093859
15. Garfinkel, H. (1967) Good organizational reasons for "bad" clinic records, Studies in Ethnomethodology. Englewood Cliffs.
16. Golder, S. A., Wilkinson, D., & Huberman, B. A. (2007, June). Rhythms of social interaction: Messaging within a massive online network. In Proc. of Communities and Technologies (pp. 41–66). London: Springer.
17. Hacking, I. (1995) Rewriting the Soul: Multiple Personality and the Sciences of Memory, Princeton University Press.
18. Hecht, B. Hong, L., Suh, B., Chi, E.H. (2011) Tweets from Justin Bieber's Heart: The Dynamics of the "Location" Field in User Profiles. In Proc. of CHI '11.
19. Kramer, A.D.I. (2010) An unobtrusive behavioural model of "gross national happiness". In Proc. CHI '10.
20. Lindqvist, J., Cranshaw, J., Wiese, J., Hong, H. and Zimmerman, J. (2011) I'm the Mayor of My House: Examining Why People Use Foursquare. In Proc. of CHI '11.
21. Naaman, M., Boase, J. Lai, C. (2010) Is it Really About Me? Message Content in Social Awareness Streams. In Proc. of CSCW '10.
22. Noulas, A Mascolo, C., Scellato, S., Pontil, M. (2011) An Empirical Study of Geographic User Activity Patterns in Foursquare. In Proc. ICWSM '11.
23. Poster, M. (1990) The mode of information: post structuralism and social context, Polity press.
24. Scellato, S., Noulas, A., Lambiotte, R., Mascolo, C. (2011) Socio-spatial Properties of Online Location-based Social Networks. In Proc. of ICWSM '11.
25. Vasalou, A., Oostveen, A. M. and Joinson, A. M. (2012) A case study of non-adoption: the values of location tracking in the family. In Proc. of CSCW '12.

A Multi-level Analysis of the Impact of Shared Leadership in Diverse Virtual Teams

Lionel P. Robert Jr.
School of Information
University of Michigan
4417 North Quad, 105 South State St., Ann Arbor, MI 48109
lprobert@umich.edu

ABSTRACT
Although, organizations are using more virtual teams to accomplish work, they are finding it difficult to use traditional forms of leadership to manage these teams. Many organizations are encouraging a shared leadership approach over the traditional individual leader. Yet, there have been only a few empirical studies directly examining the effectiveness of such an approach and none have taken into account the team diversity. To address this gap, this paper reports the results of an empirical examination of the impacts of shared leadership in virtual teams. Results confirm the proposed research model. The impacts of shared leadership are multilevel and vary by race and gender. In addition, while shared leadership promotes team satisfaction despite prior assumptions, it actually reduces rather than increases team performance.

Author Keywords
Share leadership; virtual team; team identification; multi-level analysis.

ACM Classification Keywords
H.3.5; H.4.3; K.6.0

INTRODUCTION
It is broadly recognized that teams have better informational resources than individuals, making them ideal for accomplishing knowledge-intensive work [45]. Unlike face to face teams, virtual teams allow organizations to assemble members to solve problems without the traditional requirements associated with collocation (e.g. same time and space) [16, 39, 46]. This paper defines virtual teams as teams with members who are geographically dispersed and rely primarily on some type of technology mediated communication [3, 45, 46]. The ability to manage distributed teams has become more important as organizations and their work becomes dispersed [3, 16, 46].

Prior research on leadership has typically defined it as an individual trait or individual role [12, 13]. These studies have typically focused on how one individual influences the behavior of other team members to help meet team objectives [57]. However, many problems addressed by virtual teams are often complex and require specialized knowledge to solve that no single individual possesses [45]. In these situations it is difficult to have one person in charge of the overall team. This problem is only exacerbated when these teams work at a distance [2, 3, 35]. As a result, there has been a shift away from traditional hierarchical leadership structures to a more decentralized or shared leadership [13, 40].

Virtual teams are more likely than face to face teams to be demographically diverse [30]. Race and gender diversity, like many types of diversity, have been viewed as a double edged sword [55]. Race and gender diversity provide informational benefits for decision making and creative problem-solving, yet they also pose barriers to team unity [36]. Prior research would indicate that feelings of exclusion and inequality often leave racial and gender minorities feeling socially isolated which hinders the development of team identification [33]. As a result, gender and racially diverse teams are often confronted with the challenge of determining how to mitigate the barriers to establish a unified team identity [36, 37]. This is particularly pertinent given that virtual teams are more likely to have difficulty developing internal bonds and often report lower levels of satisfaction [30].

Shared leadership is the distribution of leadership among team members and is characterized by the sharing of leadership roles [12, 13]. Shared leadership, however, offers the possibility for every team member to be included in team decisions which potentially promises more inclusion and better team experiences. This paper seeks to build on prior literature examining shared leadership in virtual teams [5, 13]. The research question this study attempts to address is: "How does shared leadership impact the identification, satisfaction and actual performance of virtual teams?" This study has three goals: 1) To examine the impacts of shared leadership on an individual's willingness to identify with their team in light of their race and gender. Team identification has been found to be an important process variable for the success of virtual teams [9, 45]. However, little research has been done to understand the conditions that facilitate team identification when these teams are racially and gender diverse. 2) Investigate the impact of shared leadership on team satisfaction. Virtual teams are often criticized for being overly sterile and too task focused [44]. As work becomes both more virtual and collaborative, understanding what factors facilitate a positive team work environment becomes increasingly important 3) Examine the impact of shared leadership on the performance of virtual teams. Prior research has only posited positive impacts between shared leadership and virtual team performance [5, 13]; however, there are reasons to believe that shared leadership could potentially decrease the performance of virtual teams.

To address these gaps in the virtual team literature this paper proposes a multi-level research model that explains the relationship between shared leadership, identification, satisfaction and team performance. A study was conducted involving 78 individuals in 22 virtual teams to empirically test the proposed model. Results generally support the research model. Overall, this paper contributes to the CSCW literature by demonstrating the important role of shared leadership in computer supported environments.

RELATED WORK

Traditional views of leadership describe it as a process whereby an individual influences the attitudes and behaviors of other individuals [12, 13, 54]. In traditional face to face settings leaders oversee the work of other team members and set standards and expectations about how the team is expected to behave [54]. The literature on face to face teams can be divided into task versus relationship based leadership or formal static versus informal emergent leadership [6, 32 56]. Task leadership behaviors are behaviors directed at performing task while relationship behaviors are focused on promoting and maintaining cohesion, motivation and communication [32, 56]. This literature tends to examine how proficient individual leaders are at directing teams during task performance and/or promoting social support [6]. Formal static leadership occur when an individual is formally recognized as the team leader before the team begins work while an informal emergent leader is someone who is not formally recognized as the team leader but emerges as the leader through a series of interactions with other team members [59]. Research examining the former focuses more on how individuals exercise influence through formal organizational mechanisms while the latter examines how emergent leaders facilitate influence over informal mechanisms.

Leadership in Virtual Teams

Although virtuality can be measured in many different ways two dimensions remain constant across all definitions: geographic dispersion and reliance on electronic communication [22, 19, 24, 46, 38]. Other definitions of virtuality have included cultural differences, time zone differences, the number of remote workers and the number of members located at each work site [22, 38]. This study examines virtuality as geographic dispersion and the inability to rely on face to face interactions as the primary mode of communication [46].

Virtual team leadership can be defined as influence mediated through information and communication technologies [4]. Geographic dispersion makes it difficult for leaders to directly oversee the work of others [21]. This lack of direct supervision and the need to influence others through information and communication technology mediation is what differentiates leadership in virtual teams from face to face teams [54]. Despite the difficulties embedded in leading virtual teams prior research has shown that leadership matters for online collaborations [27, 58]. For example, [42] found that leadership was directly and positively associated with the performance of virtual teams. Yet, leadership still remains a much understudied topic in virtual team literature [54].

Shared Leadership

Leadership can also be viewed as distributed or focused [12]. The traditional view of leadership is an example of focused leadership where one individual is the single focus point. Distributed leadership recognizes that leadership can reside in more than one individual [20]. Distributed leadership is based on the idea that leadership is a series of functions that any member can perform at any time rather than a role than one member fulfills [40]. In this view any member can be a leader at any time and members often rotate leadership positions [12].

Shared leadership is an informal emergent distributed view of leadership. It has been conceptualized as a "dynamic, unfolding, interactive influence process among individuals, where the objective is to lead one another toward the achievement of collective goals." [41]. Shared leadership can manifest through the rotation of leadership positions where one member steps forward to take charge then steps back to allow someone else to take charge [40]. Shared leadership can also take the form of a constant distribution of responsibility where each member maintains a leadership position in a particular area at all times. Prior literature has not viewed shared leadership as an example of a leaderless team but instead as a team with many leaders [41]. Self-managed teams are one example of teams that use shared leadership [13].

Shared leadership often emerges because individuals possess unique expertise [41]. In these situations no single team leader could possess the needed expertise to effectively lead a team [40]. As a result, leadership is often based on who has the expertise to address a given, specific task at the time. However, shared leadership might also emerge out of time availability. Team members might engage in taking turns based on who has the time to oversee a particular part of the team's task.

There are relatively few empirical studies that have directly examined the impact of shared leadership in virtual teams. These studies have found that shared leadership increases team cohesion and positive communication behaviors like cooperation, exchange of information, respect for others, and trust [5, 13, 26]. However, neither [5] nor [13] found a direct link between shared leadership and team performance. Carte et al. [13] did find that high performing virtual teams displayed higher levels of shared leadership than low performing virtual teams. Unfortunately, there was no statistical connection between shared leadership and team performance [25]. Lee et al. [26] did however find a positive link between shared leadership and the self-reported creativity of virtual teams. A related study by Zhu et al. [58] found that shared leadership influenced individual contributions to Wikipedia.

Team Identification in Virtual Teams

Team identification is defined as the extent to which members are psychologically identified their team [47]. When members identify with their team they will see their team's success as their success [1]. As such, when members have strong identification with their team they are more likely to engage in productive behaviors that support the team [34]. Members who are strongly identified with the team are also less likely to engage in unproductive behaviors like effort-withholding [48]. Team identification is important to the success of both face to face and virtual teams [34, 22, 45].

Although past studies in face to face teams found that race and gender can have negative impacts on team identification [52] can we expect the same problems to exist in virtual teams that are geographically separated? Fiol and O'Connor [17] thought so. They directly proposed that team diversity could reduce the salience of the team as a target for identification in both face to face and virtual teams. Recent research has indicated that differences in geographic location can act as triggers of social categorization in virtual teams [43, 38]. However, [43] found that the effects of geographic location were significantly stronger when collocated subgroups were more homogeneous in attributes like nationality. This provides evidence that demographic variables like gender and race may have an impact on constructs like identification in virtual teams over and above geographic subgroups. In addition, Cramton [15]) has shown that in teams where members are totally geographically dispersed and there are no geographic subgroups; members were still inclined to level harsher judgments against each other because they lack contextual information about dispersed others. Taken together we can expect attributes like race and gender to influence team identification in virtual teams.

RESEARCH MODEL

This paper puts forth a multilevel research model of shared leadership in virtual teams. At the individual level the paper posits that the influence of shared leadership on an individual's identification with their virtual team is moderated by that individual's gender and race. This model also proposes that shared leadership, at the team level, increases team satisfaction and decreases team performance while team identification increases both team satisfaction and team performance. Figure 1 provides a summary of these arguments, which are elaborated below

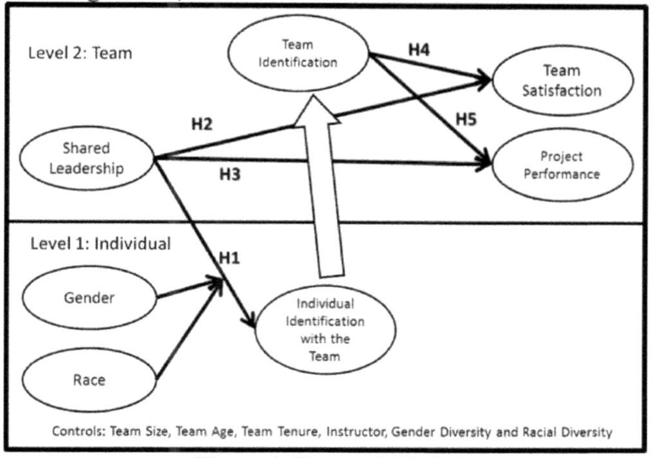

Figure 1: Research Model

Shared leadership can be described as a collective team process where individual team members share the roles and responsibilities of a traditional leader [40]. Shared leadership operates through a series of interactions and negotiations between team members that lead to the sharing of leadership responsibilities [12]. In teams with a high degree of shared leadership we would expect every member to contribute to decision making. These teams should be more inclined to consider the opinions and ideas of everyone [40]. Members of virtual teams with high levels of shared leadership will have stronger feelings of equality and greater levels of participation. Higher levels of equality and participation have been shown to be associated with increases in an individual's identification with their team [45]. As such, we would expect that shared leadership would increase an individual's identification with their virtual team.

However, we would expect this impact to be moderated by gender and race. Shared leadership necessitates the sharing of power and influence among all team members [40]. Prior research has found that feelings of inequality and a lack of influence are stronger for women and racial minorities than white males [33]. As such, we would expect that the impact of shared leadership on an individual's identification with their virtual team should be stronger and more positive for women and racial minorities than for white males. In addition, we would expect the impact of shared leadership to be stronger for racial minorities than for white females and for racial minority females than racial minority males.

H1) The effects of shared leadership on individual identification with their virtual team should vary by both race and gender.

Shared leadership results in a pattern of reciprocal exchanges among team members [12]. These patterns of interactions promote inter-team relations [41]. Virtual teams with high levels of shared leadership require all team members to engage in roles and responsibility equally. This should reduce social loafing in teams which decreases team morale [3, 49]. This, in part, explains why shared leadership has been found to promote more cohesive bonds [5]. These teams have been found to care more about each other and pull together as a team when things get tough [13]. It is likely that the strong cohesive bonds and high levels of social support should translate into a more enjoyable team experience. As such, we would expect shared leadership to increase the degree of team satisfaction.

H2) Shared leadership should increase team satisfaction in virtual teams.

Although most studies assume that the link between shared leadership and team performance is positive many empirical studies have found little or no association [13]. In fact, most of the studies that have found a strong positive relationship between shared leadership and team performance have used perceptual measures by team members as surrogates of team performance [12]. For example, Lee et al. [26] found a positive link between shared leadership and team creativity, but creativity was a self-reported outcome. There seems to be very little evidence that suggests that shared leadership increases a team level objective performance variable. Although there are many reasons to believe that shared leadership may increase team performance there are also many reasons to believe that shared leadership could reduce team performance.

Popular literature has long devalued the idea of leadership by committee [28]. When more than one person is in charge often no one is in charge. Sharing leadership functions across an entire team could lead to coordination problems like determining who is doing what and when. This, in turn, could lead to a lack of overall direction and the inefficient allocation of resources. Virtual teams with high levels of shared leadership may focus too much on trying to accommodate everyone. This could lead to virtual teams putting the maintenance of good social relations ahead of actual team performance. As such, there is some theory to suggest that shared leadership may decrease team performance.

H3) Shared Leadership should decrease the performance of virtual teams.

Team identification has been viewed as an important team process variable [9, 22, 45, and 53]. Team identification is an emotional attachment that team members have with their team [23, 50]. Identification with a team is said to occur when an individual believes that their team represents their values and beliefs [23, 50]. When members identify with their virtual team, their individual goals and personal interests recede and the goals and interest of their team dominate their actions [45]. Not surprisingly, team identification is positively associated with reduction in team conflict [16] and positively associated with satisfaction [29] and team performance [45] in face to face teams. As such, theory would suggest that team identification should be positively related to both team satisfaction and team performance in virtual teams.

H4) Team identification should positively influence team satisfaction in virtual teams.

H5) Team identification should positively influence team performance in virtual teams.

METHOD

Participants

The participants were students enrolled at a large public university. The graduate students' ages ranged from 23 to 68 with a mean of 37.83. Thirty-two percent of the students were females and 28 percent were non-white. All the participants were US citizens. A total of 78 students in 22 teams participated in the study. Team size ranged from 3 to 5. Team projects lasted from 15 to 100 days. Although the team project was a class requirement as part of their course the students received extra credit for completing the survey.

Data Collection

Data was collected from an online global campus designed to provide distance education to working professionals. Typically, individuals were randomly assigned to teams. However, the final decision was ultimately determined by each instructor. In fact, all decisions about team size, projects, scoring and so forth, were made by each instructor with no input from the paper's author(s). Instructors were not aware of the research question or hypotheses being tested and none of the classes were taught by the author(s).

Measurement

The survey was web-based. We assured team members that their responses were confidential and would not be seen by their instructors. The survey employed established multi-item scales, which we summarized below. A seven-point Likert scale was used to measure both team identification and satisfaction.

Control Variables

We used several control variables to reduce the possibility of alternative explanations. These included team age, team size and team tenure (life of the team), gender and racial diversity of the team and instructor. There were two sets of instructors/classes so a dummy variable of 0 or 1 was used. Gender and racial diversity were calculated via Blau's [7] index. Blau's index is defined as: $H=1-\sum p^{2}_{i}$. Where H is the heterogeneity score of a group, p is the proportion of team members who fall into a particular in a category, and i is the number of different categories represented in the team.

Independent Variables

Individual gender and race were obtained by asking the individual to provide a response to questions on the online survey. Race was coded as white or non-white, 0 or 1 respectively. Gender was coded as female or male, 0 or 1 respectively.

	Female	Male	White	Black
Team 1	3	1	1	2
Team 2	2	1	2	1
Team 3	2	1	2	1
Team 4	3	1	3	1
Team 5	2	2	1	3
Team 6	3	2	2	3
Team 7	3	1	4	0
Team 8	2	1	2	1
Team 9	5	0	5	0
Team 10	4	1	4	1
Team 11	3	0	2	1
Team 12	1	2	3	0
Team 13	3	0	1	2
Team 14	2	1	3	0
Team 15	3	0	3	0
Team 16	3	1	3	1
Team 17	2	2	4	0
Team 18	0	3	3	0
Team 19	1	3	2	2
Team 20	4	0	1	3
Team 21	2	1	3	0
Team 22	3	0	3	0

Table 1: Team Demographics

Shared leadership was measured via a social network approach based on density [12, 31]. Density was calculated by measuring the total amount of leadership displayed by team members as perceived by their teammates. Density was defined as: S / 7N (N-1). In this equation, S is the sum of all values that each team members would rate each other for leadership. N is the number of team members; N (N-1) is the total number of possible ties in a team. Each team member rated each of his/her teammate (1, "not at all," to 7, "to a very great extent") on the following question: "To what degree does your team rely on this individual for leadership?" Shared leadership is a team level construct, measured as the density of leadership displayed by all team members. The values ranged from 0 to 1 with the lower number indicating that only a few members displayed leadership and the high number indicating that most or all members displayed leadership.

Dependent Variables

Identification with the team was a 4 item scale, based on Brown et al. [11]. Items included, "I consider the team's success my success" and "The team is important to me as a person." Team satisfaction was measured using a two item scale that was a modified version of Briggs et al. [10]. Briggs et al. [10] focused on meeting satisfaction so the items were altered to better reflect the context of the current study. The two items were "I was satisfied with how we completed the team project" and "Looking back I was pleased with how we completed the team project."

Team performance was measured by the score the team received on their team project. The team project was an organizational needs analysis. The organizational needs analysis project included an assessment of what capabilities the organization had and what was needed in the future. The team submitted one project to their instructor. Instructors employed a slightly different grading system for the team projects. To reduce the differences among the classes a standardized score was used. The standardized score was the ratio of the number of points the team earned on the project over the maximum possible number of points that the team could have. This project performance scores ranged from 0 to 100. There were two instructors. 13 teams were graded by one instructor and 9 by the other.

RESULTS

The virtual teams in this study were composed of American graduate student teams all taking classes from different locations normally at their home. Because all subjects took courses online it was assumed that all virtual teams were fully dispersed. These teams relied heavily on the use of electronic communication. Teams were asked about their technology use. Scales range from 0 to 6, 0 indicating no use and 6 indicating extremely frequent use of electronic technology. The mean use and standard deviation of use per technology was: email 4.6 (.92), synchronous chat 2.3 (1.16), phone 2.2 (2.2) and video .10 (.4). Results indicate that most teams relied on email as the primary form of communication.

Psychometric properties were analyzed for each construct. The Cronbach alpha for team identification and team satisfaction was .78 and .97 respectively, both indicating adequate reliability [18]. Next, the intra-class correlation coefficients (ICC) were calculated for both latent constructs. The ICC is used to both justify using a multilevel analysis by providing evidence that team membership should be accounted for in the analysis and for demonstrating that the average can be used as a team level construct [46]. ICC values of above .10 have been used to provide evidence that there is a significant team effect [8]. The ICC for team identification was .25 indicating a significant team effect and providing justification for employing a multi-level analysis approach to account for team membership and the use of team identity as team level construct [8]. The ICC for team satisfaction was .40 providing justification for aggregating satisfaction to the team level of analysis [8].

Convergent and discriminant validity were accessed two ways. First a factor loading was done which is seen in Table 2. All items loaded at the .7 or above level on each of their constructs while no cross loadings were above .35. Both are clear indications of convergent and discriminant validity [18]. Second, the square root of the average variance extracted (AVE) values for each latent construct, which represent internal convergent validity, were compared with the correlations of other latent constructs. The AVEs for team identification and team satisfaction were .95 and .98. Well above the recommended .50 thus providing further evidence of convergent validity [18]. The correlation between team identification and team satisfaction was .3, found in Table 3, which was well below their respective square roots of their AVE, thus indicating discriminant validity. Table 3 presents the descriptive statistics including mean, standard deviation and the correlations for the constructs in the model.

Hypothesis 1, posited that the effect of shared leadership at the team level will be dependent on an individual race and gender. This required the use of multi-level analysis [49, 56]. To account for the nested nature of the data, SPSS 20.0 mixed model package was used to perform hierarchical linear modeling (HLM) to test the proposed model. The remaining hypotheses: 2,3,4,5 were tested using OLS regression at the team level. The results of the multi-level analysis are shown in Table 3. Model 1 shows the effects of control variables on the dependent variables. Model 2 shows the direct effects of the individual level variables. Model 3 shows the direct effects of the team level variables. Model 4 shows the impact of the two-way cross level interactions effects. Model 5 includes the three-way cross level interaction effect. We saw that there was a significant increase in the amount of variance explained between the final model and all other models.

	Team Satisfaction	Team Identification
Team Sat. 1	**.98**	.12
Team Sat. 2	**.97**	.13
Team Ident. 1	.13	**.85**
Team Ident. 2	.34	**.83**
Team Ident. 3	.19	**.70**

Table 2: Factor Loadings

Hypothesis 1, the effects of shared leadership on individual identification should vary by both race and gender, was supported. Model 1 included only the control variables. The control variables: size, tenure, team age and instructor were all non-significant in every model (see Table 3). Model 2 included the level one or individual main effect variables: gender and race. Model 3 included the level two or team level main effects. Model 4 included the two-way cross level interactions. The final model explained 17% of an individual's identification with the team ($p<.001$). The two-way cross level interactions between gender and race ($\beta= -7.16$, $p<.05$) were significant. The three-way cross level interactions between shared leadership, race and gender were also significant ($\beta= 10.5$, $p<.05$). The three-way cross level interaction is plotted in Figure 2.

Figure 2, displays four lines. Line 1 displays the slope for non-white males. Line 1 shows that as shared leadership increases within a team (or in other words as equality increases) minority males identified more with the team. Line 2 represents white males. The amount of shared leadership has relatively little or no impact on the level of identification with the team for white males. Line 3 represents minority females. Increases in shared leadership reduced the level of identification with the team. Line 4 represents white females. Line 4 clearly displays a strong positive relationship with shared leadership and identification with the team. Overall, the impact of shared leadership varied by race and gender but not necessarily in the way predicted.

Hypothesis 2-5 was tested by using OLS. The results are shown in Table 4. Model 1 shows the effects of the control variables on the dependent variables. Model 2 includes the direct effects of shared leadership and team identity and in both cases the inclusion of the direct effects significantly increased the variance explained.

Hypothesis 2, shared leadership should increase team satisfaction, was supported ($\beta= 5.01$; $p<.01$). Hypothesis 3, shared Leadership should decrease team performance, was also supported ($\beta= -28.7$; $p<.05$). Shared leadership increased team satisfaction but decreased team performance. Hypothesis 4, team identification should positively influence team satisfaction, was not supported ($\beta= .71$; $p>.05$). Hypothesis 5, team identification should positively influence team performance, was supported ($\beta= 6.21$; $p<.05$). Team identification has no effect on team satisfaction but increases team performance. The final model for team satisfaction and team performance explained 64 % and 62% percent of the variance respectively. The effect sizes for team satisfaction and team performance are 1.77 and 1.63 respectively. Both are defined by Cohen [14] as large effect sizes.

	Variable	Mean	Std. Dev.	1	2	3	4	5	6	7
1	Team Age	37.7	6.4							
2	Team Size	3.6	0.73	0.1						
3	Tenure	48.7	30.8	-0.16	0.22					
4	Shared Lead	0.71	0.12	0.28	-0.14	-0.09				
5	Gender Div.	0.27	0.21	-0.22	0.18	0.2	-0.07			
6	Racial Div.	0.27	0.29	-0.13	0.15	-0.04	-0.08	0		
7	Identification	5.56	0.54	0.13	-0.16	0.08	0.2	-0.1	-0.1	
8	Satisfaction	5.78	1	0.13	0.05	0.08	.65**	-0.2	-0.3	0

*p<.05;**p<.01,n = 22

Table 3: Correlations Matrix

Independent Variables	Model 1	Model 2	Model 3	Model 4	Model 5
Team Size	-0.12	-0.15	-0.19	-0.18	-0.12
Team Tenure	0.00	0.01	0.01	0.01	0.01
Individual Age	0.00	0.01	0.01	0.01	0.01
Instructor	0.10	0.09	0.06	0.06	0.01
Main Effects (Level 1)					
Gender		0.11	0.09	-0.22	1.87
Race		0.40	0.39	1.01	3.46
Main Effect (Level 2)					
Shared Leadership			-0.42	-0.27	1.16
Gender Diversity			0.63	0.53	0.36
Racial Diversity			0.25	0.33	0.22
Two-way Cross-Level Interactions					
Shared Leadership X Gender				0.44	-2.40
Shared Leadership X Race				-0.93	-4.20
Gender X Race				0.02	-7.16*
Three-way Cross-Level Interactions					
Shared Leadership X Gender X Race					10.50*
-2 Restricted Log Likelihood	218	216	215	215	209
Deviance Difference	3	2	1	0	6
df		2	3	3	1
R^2	0	4.9%	5.2%	4.8%	17%
Change in R^2			.3%	-4%	.12%
*: p<.05, **: p<0.01, ***:p<0.001					

Table 4. Results of Multilevel Analysis

Hypothesis	Supported	Level of Analysis and Sample Size
1	Yes	Individual, N=78
2	Yes	Team, N=22
3	Yes	Team, N=22
4	No	Team, N=22
5	Yes	Team, N=22

Table 6: Results

Independent Variables	Team Satisfaction		Performance	
	1	2	1	2
Controls				
Team Size	0.01	0.23	0.48	0.42
Team Tenure	0.00	0.00	0.02	0.01
Team Age	0.01	-0.01	0.38	0.45
Instructor	-0.40	-0.06	-9.03	-10.11
Gender Div.	-1.08	-1.33	-13.5	-13.6
Racial Div.	-1.1	-1.23	9.14	9.36
Main Effect				
Shared Leadership		5.0**		-28.7*
Team Identification		0.71		6.21*
*: p<.05, **: p<0.01, ***:p<0.001				
R^2	13%	64%	40%	62%
Change R^2		50%		22%
F	0.33	2.4	1.2	3.05
		21		21

Table 5. Results of OLS Analysis

DISCUSSION

The objective of this study was to examine how shared leadership impacts team identification, satisfaction and actual performance of virtual teams. Prior literature has assumed that the impact of shared leadership would be positive[5, 13]. However, results of this study indicate that shared leadership has both positive and negative effects on virtual teams at both the team and the individual level. At the individual level shared leadership promotes team identification and team satisfaction. However, at the individual level, shared leadership reduces team identification for non-white females and decreases team performance. Results of this study suggest that shared leadership can have both positive and negative effects (see Table 6).

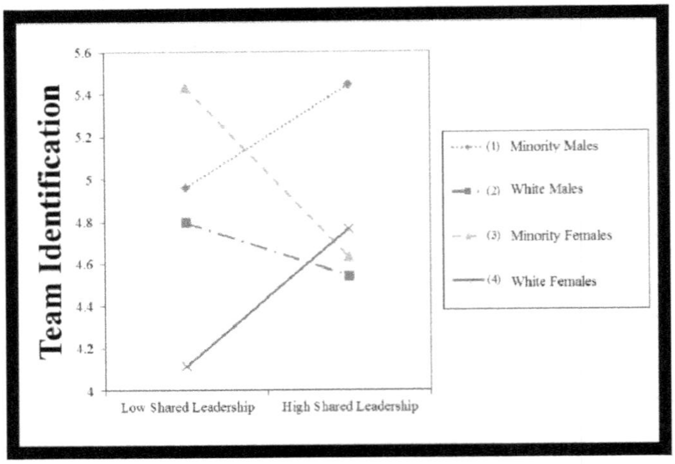

Figure 2: Multilevel Analysis of Shared Leadership

Contributions

This study makes three key contributions to the literature on virtual teams. First, this study sheds light on the impact of shared leadership in virtual teams. Although shared leadership has been shown to increase knowledge sharing, trust, constructive interactions, team cohesion and team creativity [5, 26] it has not been shown to increase objective virtual team performance [5, 13]. This study contributes to this literature by confirming that shared leadership has positive impacts on another construct measuring the quality of team interactions, satisfaction. In other words, this is another study that found that shared leadership generally improves team interactions. This study also extends the literature on virtual teams by demonstrating that shared leadership can actually decrease team performance in virtual teams. Where prior studies hoped to find positive impacts and failed to find any [5, 13], this study predicted and found negative effects in an objective measure of team performance. Whereas team relationship variables are self-reported, including Lee et al. [26] the measure of team creativity, the measure of team performance was provided by someone from outside of the team. This means that despite the fact that virtual team members generally report better interactions with more shared leadership these better interactions may come at the expense of actual virtual team performance.

Two, this study contributes to the literature on team identification and virtual teams. Prior research has found that identification in virtual teams can help reduce the negative effects of member distribution on conflict in virtual teams [22, 34]; however, few studies have directly examined and found a link between team identification and virtual team performance. This study contributes to this literature by providing evidence that team identification can have similar positive effects on the performance of virtual teams as it does in face to face teams.

Three, this study contributes to the literature on team diversity in virtual teams. Fiol and O'Connor [17] proposed that team diversity could reduce the salience of the team as a target for identification in virtual teams. Although the negative effects of team diversity on identification in virtual teams have not been empirically verified this study takes a multi-level approach to the problem. Results indicate that individuals differ in their ability to identify with the team and that those differences are based, in part, on their individual race and gender. In the case of white women and non-white males, shared leadership increases the likelihood that they would identify with the team. However, the impact on non-white females was the opposite. Nonetheless, it is clear that shared leadership plays an important role in an individual's identification with their virtual team.

Implications for Theory

This study has several implications for theory. One, most researchers have all assumed that shared leadership would increase the performance of virtual teams [13, 5, 26]. As a result, prior research has been based on the idea that shared leadership should be encouraged. However, the results of this study provided evidence that we should not always expect positive effects from shared leadership and that researchers may need to theorize about when and why shared leadership is good or bad for the performance of virtual teams.

Two, the results of this study provide evidence that the impacts of race and gender can materialize at the individual level, independent of the virtual team. The effects of gender and race in this study cannot be attributed to the composition of the team nor the interactions within the teams. In fact, the correlation between gender and racial diversity with team identification are both non-significant. In addition, table 1, indicates that women were the majority in 16 of the 22 virtual teams. This means that women were not necessarily the minority in most teams. Still, gender plays an important role in determining an individual's identification with their virtual team. Results indicate that the effects of race and gender on identification may not be the result of team interactions but individual experiences that existed before the team had any interactions.

Third, because the impact of shared leadership on non-white females had the opposite effect there is a need to rethink what mechanisms are at work. Work by Thomas-Hunt & Phillips, [51] offers additional insights on the observed effects of non-white females. Thomas-Hunt & Phillips [51] shows that female experts are less influential and less liked than male experts in mixed-gender groups because shared leadership and expertise recognition are related. It is possible that for non-white females increases in shared leadership may have been accompanied by feelings of resentment and dislike from other members. This may explain why higher levels of shared leadership lead to lower levels of identification. Nonetheless, the results demonstrate the importance of taking a multi-level approach to understanding the effects of race and gender in virtual teams.

This study has several limitations. First, like all cross-sectional research it is difficult to draw causal inferences. However, by using an objective indicator of team performance this study reduces the impact of common method bias normally associated with cross sectional research. This also uses self-reported measures of race and gender. However, other conceptualization and measures of gender and race could provide different results. This study also uses students that are enrolled in distance education course. As such, there are limits to how general the results of the study are to other contexts.

Design Implications

Despite the negative effective of shared leadership on performance in virtual teams, shared leadership has been found to increase team performance in collocated teams [12]. The difference may be due to the inability of virtual teams to coordinate their work across space and time. It may be much easier to coordinate work when teams are collocated rather than dispersed. Future collaborative systems should be designed with the intent on helping virtual teams effectively coordinate their work. Awareness systems can be designed with features that allow any member to act as a leader at any moment. These awareness systems can provide real time data and an interface which allows any user to assume control over the team operations. In summary, future collaborative systems should be designed with the intent on supporting shared leadership through the team.

Practical Implications

The paper has several practical implications. Managers may want to balance the tradeoffs between the positive and negative effects associated with shared leadership. For example, teams are often assembled with the sole purpose of building consensus. In consensus building, virtual team managers may promote shared leadership as a way of increasing better team interactions. However, when performance is important managers may appoint a single leader. Because shared leadership does not imply a leaderless team this study has implications for team leaders of virtual teams. Team leaders may want to employ some type of shared leadership when virtual team relations are bad and then centralized leadership, later to encourage performance at other times. That may translate into allowing the team as a whole to have more authority to make decisions at certain times and less authority during other times.

Conclusion

This paper also sought to extend our understanding of the role of shared leadership on race, gender and team identification in virtual teams. This paper found that the impact of shared leadership on an individual's identification with the team was moderated by their race and gender. Shared leadership increased team satisfaction but decreased team performance while team identification increased team performance but had no impact on team satisfaction. By taking a multi-level approach we were allowed to see how the impact of shared leadership on team identification was moderated by both race and gender.

REFERENCES

1. Alles, M and Datar, S. Control Implications of Worker Identification with Firm Sales Success. Management Accounting Research, 13, 2, (2002), 173-190.
2. Alnuaimi, O. Maruping, L.M. Robert, L.P. Social Loafing in Brainstorming CMC Teams: The Role of Moral Disengagement. In Proc. HICSS 2009, IEEE Press (2009), 1-9.
3. Alnuaimi, O.A., Robert, L.P., and Maruping, L.M. Team size, dispersion, and social loafing in technology-supported teams: A perspective on the theory of moral disengagement. Journal of Management Information Systems 27, 1 (2010), 203-230.
4. Avolio, B. J., Kahai, S. R., and Dodge, G. E. E-Leadership: Implications for Theory, Research, and Practices. The Leadership Quarterly. 11, 4 (2001), 615-68.
5. Balthazard, P., Waldman, D., Howell, J. and Atwater, L. Shared Leadership and Group Interaction Styles in Problem-Solving Virtual Teams. In Proc. HICSS 2004, IEEE Press (2004), 110043-110053.
6. Bass, B. M., and Stogdill, R. M. Bass & Stogdill's handbook of leadership: Theory, research, and managerial applications. (3rd Ed.). New York: The Free Press, 1990.
7. Blau, P.M. 1977. Inequality and Heterogeneity: A Primitive Theory of Social Structure. New York, NY: Free Press.
8. Bliese, P. D. 2000. Within-group agreement, non-independence, and reliability: Implications for data aggregation and analysis. In K. J. Klein and S.W.J. Kozlowski (Eds.), Multilevel theory, research, and methods in organizations: Foundations, extensions, and new directions: 349–381, San Francisco: Jossey-Bass.
9. Bos, N.D., Buyuktur, A., Olson, J.S., Olson G.M. and Voida, A. Shared identity helps partially distributed teams, but distance still matters. In Proc. Group 2010, ACM Press (2010), 89–96.
10. Briggs, R. O., Vreede, G.J . de, and Reinig, B. A. A theory and measurement of meeting satisfaction. In Proc. HICSS 2003, IEEE Press (2003).
11. Brown, R. J., Condor, F., Mathews, A., Wade, G. and Williams, J. A. Explaining intergroup differentiation in an industrial organization. Journal of Occupat. Psyc. 59, 4, (1986), 273-287.
12. Carson, J. B., Tesluk, P. E., and Marrone, J. A. Shared leadership in teams: An investigation of antecedent conditions and performance. Academy of Management Journal 50, 5 (2007), 1217-1234.
13. Carte, T. A., Chidambaram, L., and Becker, A. Emergent leadership in self-managed virtual teams: A longitudinal study of concentrated and shared leadership behaviors. Group Decision and Negotiation 15, 4, (2006), 323-343.
14. Cohen, J. Statistical Power Analysis for the Behavioral Sciences (second Ed.). Lawrence Erlbaum Associates (1988).
15. Cramton, C.D. The mutual knowledge problem and its consequences for dispersed collaboration. Organization Science. 12, 3 (2001), 346-371.
16. Dennis, A.R., Robert, L.P., Curtis, A.M., Kowalczyk, S.T., and Hasty, B.K. Trust is in the Eye of the Beholder: A Vignette Study of Postevent Behavioral Controls' Effects on Individual Trust in Virtual Teams. Information Systems Research. 23, 2, (2012), 546-558.
17. Fiol, C. M., and O'Connor, E. J. 2005. Identification in face-to-face, hybrid, and pure virtual teams: Untangling the contradictions. Organization Science, 16, 1 (2005), 19–32.
18. Fornell, C. and Larcker, D.F. Evaluating structural equations models with unobservable variables and measurement error. Journal of Marketing Research. 18, 1, (1981), 39-50.
19. Gibson, C. B., and Gibbs, J. L. Unpacking the concept of virtuality: The effects of geographic dispersion, electronic dependence, dynamic structure, and national diversity on team innovation. Administrative Science Quarterly. 51, 3, (2006), 451-495.
20. Gronn, P. Distributed leadership as a unit of analysis. Leadership Quarterly. 13, 4, (2002), 423-451.
21. Hambley, L. A., O'Neill, T. A., and Kline, T. J. B. Virtual team leadership: The effects of leadership style and communication medium on team interaction styles and outcomes. Organizational Behavior & Human Decision Processes. 103, 1, (2007), 1-20.
22. Hinds, P. J. and Mortensen, M. Understanding conflict in geographically distributed teams: The moderating effects of shared identity, shared context, and spontaneous communication. Organization Science, 16, 3 (2005), 290-307.
23. Hogg, M. A and Abrams, D. (1988). Social identifications: A social psychology of intergroup relations and group processes. London: Routledge.

24. Jarvenpaa, S. L., K. Knoll, D. E. Leidner. Is anybody out there? Antecedents of trust in global virtual teams. J. Management Inform. Systems. 14, 4, (1998), 29–64.

25. Kocolowski, M. D. Shared Leadership: Is it Time for a Change? Emerging Leadership Journeys, 3, 1, (2010), 22-32.

26. Lee, K., Lee, D., and Seo, Y. Effects of Shared Leadership on Team Creativity through Knowledge-sharing in an e-Learning Environment. In Proc. ICUIMC 2011, ACM Press (2011).

27. Luther, K. and Bruckman, A. Leadership in Online Creative Collaboration. In Proc. CSCW 2008, ACM Press (2008), 343–352.

28. Major, T. Time is running out for leadership by committee: Modern business practice is challenging German law, reports tony major: Financial Times, (2001), 29-29.

29. Marks, A. and Lockyer, C. 2005. Debugging the System: The impact of location on the identity of software team members. Intern. Journal of Human Resource Management. 16, 2 (2005), 219-237.

30. Martins, L. L, Gilson, L. L. and Maynard, M. T. Virtual teams: What do we know and where do we go from here? Jour. of Manag., 30, 6, (2004), 805-835.

31. Mayo, M. C., Meindl, J. R., and Pastor, J. C. 2003. Shared leadership in work teams: A social network approach. In C. Pierce, & J. Conger (Eds.), Shared leadership: Reframing the hows and whys of leadership: 193–214. Thous. Oaks, CA: Sage.

32. Misiolek, N., and Heckman, R. Patterns of emergent leadership in virtual teams. In Proc. 38th HICSS 2005, IEEE Press (2005).

33. Mor Barak, M. E., Cherin, D. A., and Berkman, S. Organizational and personal dimensions in diversity climate: Ethnic and gender differences in employee diversity perceptions. Journal of Applied Behavioral Sciences, 34, 1 (1998), 82-104.

34. Mortensen, M., P. J. Hinds. Conflict and shared identity in geographically distributed teams. Internat. J. Conflict Management. 12, 3, (2001), 212–238.

35. Muethel, M. and Hoegl, M. Cultural and societal influences on shared leadership in globally dispersed teams. Journal of International Management. 16, 3 (2010), 234-246.

36. Newell, J., Maruping, L.M., Riemenschneider, C. and Robert, L.P. Leveraging E-Identities: The Impact of Perceived Diversity on Team Social Integration and Performance. In Proc. ICIS 2008. http://aisel.aisnet.org/icis2008/46

37. Newell, J. Robert, L.P., Riemenschneider, C. Maruping, L.M. Influencing Individual Perceptions of Deep Level Diversity in Virtual Learning Teams (VLT), In Proc. HICSS 2009, IEEE Press (2009).

38. O'Leary, M., and Cummings, J. N. The spatial, temporal, and configurational characteristics of geographic dispersion in work teams. MIS Quarterly. 31(3), (2007), 433-452

39. Olson, G. M., and Olson, J. S. Distance Matters. Human Comp. Inter. 15, (2000), 139-179.

40. Pearce, C. L., and Conger, J. A. 2003. All Those Years Ago: The Historical Underpinnings of Shared Leadership. In C. L. Pearce & J. A. Conger (Eds.), Shared Leadership: Reframing the Hows and Whys of Leadership: 1-18. Thousand Oaks, CA: Sage Publications.

41. Pearce, C.L., Manz, C.C. and Sims, H. P. Is Shared Leadership the Key to Team Success?. Organizational Dynamics, 38, 3 (2009), 234–238.

42. Plotnick, L., Hiltz, S. R., Ocker, R.J., and Rosson, M.R. Leadership Roles and Communication Issues in Partially Distributed Emergency Response Software Development Teams: A Pilot Study, In Proc. HICSS 2008, IEEE Press (2008).

43. Polzer, J.T., B. Crisp, S.L. Jarvenpaa, J.W. Kim. Extending the Faultline Concept to Geographically Dispersed Teams: How Colocated Subgroups Can Impair Group Functioning. Academy of Management Journal. 49, 4, (2006), 679-692.

44. Powell, A., Piccoli, G., Ives, B. Virtual teams: A review of current literature and directions for future research. The DATA BASE for Advances in Information Systems, 35, 1 (2004), 6–36.

45. Robert, L.P., Dennis, A.R., and Ahuja, M.K. 2008. Social Capital and Knowledge Integration in Digitally Enabled Teams. Information Systems Research 19, 3 (2008), 1-21.

46. Robert, L. P., Dennis, A. R., and Hung, Y.-T. C. Individual Swift Trust and Knowledge-Based Trust in Face-to-Face and Virtual Team Members. Jour. of Manage. Info.Sys. 26, 2 (2009), 241-279.

47. Scott, C. R. Identification with multiple targets in a geographically dispersed organization. Management Communication Quarterly. 10, 4, (1997), 491-522.

48. Shapiro, D., Furst, S., Spreitzer, G. and Von Glinow, M. Transnational teams in the electronic age: are team identity and high performance at risk? Journal of Organizational Behaviour. 23, 4, (2002), 445-467.

49. Srinivasan, S.S., Maruping, L.M., Robert, L.P. Idea Generation in Technology-Supported Teams: A Multilevel Motivational Perspective System Science In Proc. HICSS 2012, IEEE Press (2012), 247-256.

50. Tajfel, H. and Turner, J. C. 1986. The Social Identity Theory of Inter-Group Behavior. In S. Worchel

and L. W. Austin (Eds.), Psychology of Intergroup Relations: 7-24. Chicago, IL: Nelson.

51. Thomas-Hunt, M.C. and Phillips, K. W. When what you know is not enough: The effects of gender on expert's influence within work groups. Personality and Social Psychology Bulletin. 30, 12, (2004), 1585-1598.

52. Van Dick, R., van Knippenberg, D., Hägele, S., Guillaume, Y. R. F., and Brodbeck, F. C. Group diversity and group identification: The moderating role of diversity beliefs. Human Relations. 61, 10, (2008), 1463–1492.

53. Voida, A., Bos, N., Olson, J., Olson, G. and Dunning, L. 2012. Cross-cutting faultlines of location and shared identity in the intergroup cooperation of partially distributed groups. In Proc. CHI 2012, ACM Press (2012), 3101-3110.

54. Wakefield, R., Leidner, D., & Garrison, G. A Model of Conflict, Leadership and Performance in Virtual Teams. Information Systems Research, 19, 4, and (2008), 434-455.

55. Williams, K.Y., and O'Reilly, C.A. 1998. Demography and Diversity in Organizations: A Review of 40 Years of Research. In Shaw and L.L. Cummings (Eds.), Research in Organizational Behavior 20: 77-140, Greenwich, CT: B.M. JAI.

56. Yamaguchi, R., Bos, N., and Olson, J.S., 2002. Emergent leadership in small groups using computer-mediated communications. In Proc. of CSCL'02, ACM Press (2002), 138-143.

57. Yoo, Y. and Alavi, M. Emergent Leadership in Virtual Teams: What do Emergent Leader. Do? Information and Organization, 14, 1, (2004), 27-58.

58. Zhu, H., Kraut, R.E. and Kittur, A. Effectiveness of shared leadership in online communities. In Proc. CSCW 2012, ACM Press (2012), 407-416.

59. Zigurs, I. Leadership in Virtual Teams: Oxymoron or Opportunity? Organizational Dynamics. 31, 4, (2003), 339-351.

Friends FTW! Friendship, Collaboration and Competition in Halo: Reach

Winter Mason
Stevens Institute of Technology
m@winteram.com

Aaron Clauset
University of Colorado, Boulder
Santa Fe Institute
aaron.clauset@colorado.edu

ABSTRACT
How important are friendships in determining success by individuals and teams in complex collaborative environments? By combining a novel data set containing the dynamics of millions of *ad hoc* teams from the popular multiplayer online first person shooter *Halo: Reach* with survey data on player demographics, play style, psychometrics and friendships derived from an anonymous online survey, we investigate the impact of friendship on collaborative and competitive performance. In addition to finding significant differences in player behavior across these variables, we find that friendships exert a strong influence, leading to both improved individual and team performance—even after controlling for the overall expertise of the team—and increased pro-social behaviors. Players also structure their in-game activities around social opportunities, and as a result hidden friendship ties can be accurately inferred directly from behavioral time series. Virtual environments that enable such friendship effects will thus likely see improved collaboration and competition.

ACM Classification Keywords
J.4 Computer Applications: Social and Behavioral Sciences; H.2.8 Database Applications: Database Management—*data mining*

Author Keywords
Social Mining; Group Dynamics; MMO

INTRODUCTION
Given the ubiquity of friendships in social interactions and complex social systems, the value of any particular friendship can be difficult to quantify. But some things are known: friendships are useful for finding new jobs, as in the "weak ties" or Granovetter effect [16]; they are useful for marketing because personal attributes—including fixed variables like age, ethnicity and location, as well as more fluid variables like preferences and opinions—exhibit homophily [27, 36] and thus correlate across friendship ties; and, they are useful for social filtering or search [4, 6], i.e., your friends are good at predicting what information you will like.

But, how valuable are friendships within complex collaborative environments, particularly those found online? On the one hand, teams composed of friends may perform better as a result of their extensive collaboration history, i.e., friendships may increase awareness and understanding of others' goals and motivations [33] or they may increase commitment to group objectives [22], thereby facilitating more successful collaboration. Friendships may also reduce within-group conflict [21], yielding similar results. On the other hand, friendships could detract from performance because friends spend less time focusing on group objectives and more time socializing [35].

Friendship may even be irrelevant for effective collaboration. If a competition's outcome depends mainly on team coordination, teams composed of experts may coordinate effectively regardless of within-team friendships: highly practiced individuals may simply know from experience how to work well with other experts and thus naturally anticipate or adapt to their teammates' actions (e.g., by fitting into established and effective team roles). In such a case, friendships do not matter and teams composed of skilled strangers will perform best [35]. Thus, the extent to which expertise and friendship matter to success is an open question in complex collaborative environments, particularly those found online.

Here, we focus on the topic of friendships, collaboration and competition in online game environments, and specifically in the first-person shooter (FPS) genre, in which teams of players compete against each other in non-persistent virtual worlds. We are also interested in the variety of social dynamics naturally observed in this complex environment, and the extent to which they vary with demographic and psychometric variables. There are many studies in CSCW on the design of, and human action within, multi-user dungeons [29], massively multiplayer online games (MMOGs) [5] (among others), social virtual worlds [7], and non-persistent game sites [26]. Work on friendships in online gaming has focused on how friendships and social relationships are a motivation to play games [8, 37] or how playing games builds offline relationships and social capital of the players [1, 19].

Work on guilds and parties [39] in massively multiplayer online role-playing games (MMORPGs) suggests that teams are important for individual satisfaction and performance, and anecdotal evidence suggests they are conducive to the formation of friendships. However, the impact of friendships themselves on team or individual performance has not been studied quantitatively (but see [19] for some qualitative insights). And, work on first-person shooter type games has generally focused on qualitative analysis of user actions and in-game communication [23,32,42].

Most work on the utility of friendships in teams is found in the management literature. Several such studies argue that friendships play a significant role in mitigating certain types of within-group conflicts; thus, teams of friends perform better because internal conflict handicaps performance [21,22,35]. Others have focused on designing effective teams in business or educational environments [2,3,34]. In these settings, friendships seem to improve group cohesion, satisfaction, and some measures of performance. Thus, we expect friendships to play a significant role in the collaboration effectiveness in virtual environments, including those found in the team-based competitive environments of the FPS genre.

Finally, the increasing CSCW interest in "serious games" [28] as a model for creating effective work spaces makes the study of real online games, and particularly those that allow collaboration with both friends and strangers, a valuable laboratory by which to understand the dynamics and determinants of collaboration and sociality in virtual environments.

Here, we study these questions in the context of the popular online FPS game *Halo: Reach*. We combine two large and novel data sets: one composed of rich online behavioral samples from the events within *Reach* competitions and one composed of rich demographic, play style, psychometric and friendship variables collected from players of *Reach* through an anonymous online survey. This combination of in-game behavioral data with survey data on the same participants has been used productively to study human behavior in MMORPGs [40,44] and online parlor games [26], but this study is the first time it has been applied to the FPS genre or to the question of friendship, collaboration and competition.

The survey asked participants to label their online and offline friendships with other *Reach* players, and these data allow us to test the hypothesis that friendships have a direct and significant impact on the results of these competitions. Features within the game allow us to control for the impact of expertise. An in-game "matchmaking" system draws groups of friends and individual players from the general population to create competitions; thus, players collaborate with and compete against a wide variety of teammates and competitors. Finally, we note that the sheer size of *Reach*, which is played by millions of individuals, provides a wealth of data by which to investigate these and other questions about collaboration and competition.

We find that friendships significantly improve both individual and team performance in these complex collaborative environments. Friendships are not as important to success as the raw expertise of teammates (friendship does not compensate for being a bad player), but individuals themselves perform better the more friends they play with, independent of their team's performance. Our survey shows that *Reach* players are also highly social, tending to prefer team-oriented play and experiencing a strong sense of group cohesiveness and coordination. Furthermore, older players (24 or older; 30% of players) tend to be more socially oriented and exhibit greater proclivity for pro-social behaviors. Above and beyond performance, friendships also reshape the style of play within a competition, and players structure their choices around opportunities to play repeatedly with friends. As a result, friendships can be accurately inferred directly from behavioral time seres data. These results illustrate the strong role that friendships play in complex collaborative and competitive virtual environments. They also shed light on social dynamics within FPS games and suggest algorithms designed to account for the benefits of friendship in predicting or designing competitive environments.

METHODOLOGY

Game Mechanics and Data

Halo: Reach is a multiplayer online first person shooter game played by more than ten million people worldwide. It was publicly released by Bungie Inc., a former subdivision of Microsoft Game Studios, on 14 September 2010 and *Reach* players have now generated more than 1 billion games. Players choose from among seven game types and numerous subtypes, which are played on more than 33 terrain maps with 74 weapons. Games can be played alone, with or against other players via the Xbox Live online system. Both individual game and player summaries are available through the Halo Reach Stats API. Through this interface, we collected the player details of all individuals who participated in our online survey and each of their full game histories, which yielded 2,445,617 complete games.

Among other information, each game file includes the sequence of the scoring events at the per-second resolution and a list of players by team. Scoring events are annotated with the name of the player generating the event (a unique Xbox Live gamertag), the number of points scored and the player giving up the points (if applicable).

Unlike professional sports [15], teams in *Reach* do not persist across competitions. Instead, each time a competition is created, individuals or small "parties" of players (typically friends) are grouped into teams by an in-game "matchmaking" algorithm; when the competition is complete, the players (or a subset) may choose to play together again as a party, or may reenter the matchmaking process to find new teammates or competitors. The result is that players routinely collaborate with or compete against different strangers in successive games. *Reach*'s matchmaking system uses an algorithm called TrueSkill [18] to ensure equal total "skill" for both teams, which allows us to control for this variable in our subsequent analysis.

Among the sampled games, there are three basic types: *campaign games*, a sequence of story-driven, non-competitive, player-versus-environment (PvE) maps that many players complete prior to trying other types of games; *firefight games* (also PvE), in which a team of human-controlled players battle successive waves of computer-controlled enemies; and *competitive games*, a player-versus-player (PvP) game type, in which teams of equal size (typically 2, 4, 6 or 8 players) compete to either be the first to reach some fixed number of points or have the largest score after a fixed length of time.

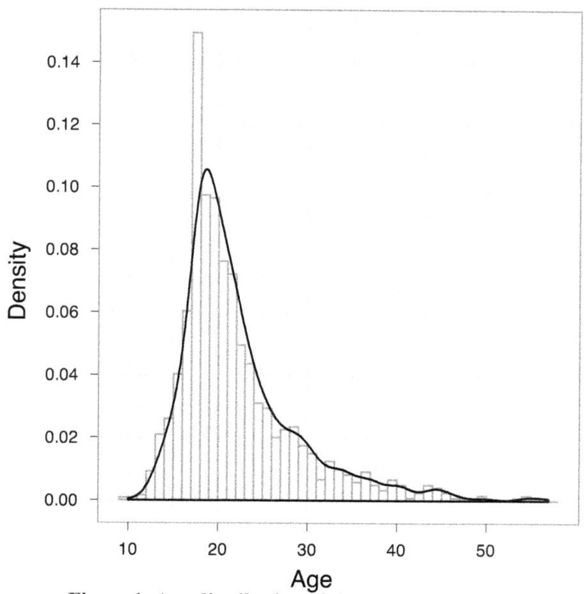

Figure 1. Age distribution of the survey respondents.

(The precise number of players per team, points required to win and length of a game depends on the game subtype.) In competitive games, players' avatars move through the game map simultaneously, in real-time, navigating complex terrain, acquiring avatar modifications and encountering opponents. Points are scored by dealing sufficient damage to eliminate an opposing avatar and for each such success, a team gains a single point. Eliminated players must then wait several seconds before their avatar is placed back into the game at one of several specified "spawn" locations.

Survey Data

In addition to the in-game behavioral data available through the API, we collected data on 1191 unique *Reach* players via an anonymous online survey.[1] The survey design incorporated extensive feedback from expert *Reach* players, including ourselves, to better frame questions in appropriate language and to focus on relevant social dynamics.

We advertised the survey through Halo-centric online forums and other community websites. While this did result in a biased sample (see below), the bias was towards participants who were active and therefore had more in-game data to draw upon. Participants supplied their Xbox Live gamertag, which we used to download their *Reach* player details and their entire *Reach* game history up to the date of survey participation. Within the survey, an initial screening was conducted based on participant age: participants who indicated their age was under 18 were routed through an additional email-based parental consent step.

The player detail files contain only summary statistics about *Reach* game play and do not contain demographic or social network information. The survey solicited these missing demographic variables (age, sex, location, highest education level, primary language), along with preferred play style (lone wolf, team leader, or team support), and psychometric responses like measures of group cohesion [38], entativity [25], and conflict [31]. In answering these questions, respondents were instructed to consider their "primary Halo group," defined as the group of friends with whom they primarily play *Reach* at the time of the survey. Finally, respondents indicated their relationship (online friend, offline friend or not a friend) with every other unique gametag that appeared in their game history. Because this list could include hundreds or even thousands of gamertags, it was sorted by the frequency of co-plays, which placed the most likely true positives at the top. The interpretation of the meaning of an online and offline friend was left to the participant, although we suggested online friends were people "you play with regularly and would say you know at least casually." This is conceptually distinct from any feature available on Halo or XBox for indicating friendships.

[1]The survey was open until November 2012, when Bungie, Inc. turned off the API. The anonymous design did not permit detailed interviews.

PLAYER ATTRIBUTES

Demographics

As is typical with many online games [41] and especially first person shooters [20], our survey respondents were mostly young men. The median age of our participants was 20, which is considerably lower than the mean age of 37 for video game players overall [14]. Of the 1191 respondents, an overwhelming majority (94.9%) reported their sex as male (compared with 80.8% male in MMO players [41] and 58% reported by the industry overall [14]). The reported age distribution of the respondents is relatively smooth, with the exception of a large spike at 18 (see Figure 1), presumably caused by individuals younger than 18 misreporting their age so as to avoid the parental consent requirement.[2]

This contrasts with the reported age distribution of MMO games, in which the plurality of players are in their 30s rather than their 20s [41]. However, the age distribution also exhibits a long right tail, with 12.8% being at least 30 years old. In agreement with the age distribution, the most frequent response indicated some college education. Although 35 countries were represented in the respondents, nearly three-quarters of respondents were from the United States, with another 14% from Canada and the United Kingdom. An overwhelming majority—94% of our respondents—indicated English was their first language.

Our respondents were very active players: they reported playing video games for an average of 23.3 hours per week. Although this number may appear high to non-gamers, it is slightly lower than the 25.9 hours per week reported by MMO players and the 27.5 hours per week reported by the industry in 2007 for video game players in general [41].

Psychometrics

[2]The initial gamertag and age screening in the survey did not hint at the subsequent parental consent requirement for under 18s; thus, misreporting of age for this group may have been an automatic response to being queried for their age. However, participants could not be prohibited from refreshing the survey, reentering their gamertag and then misreporting their age.

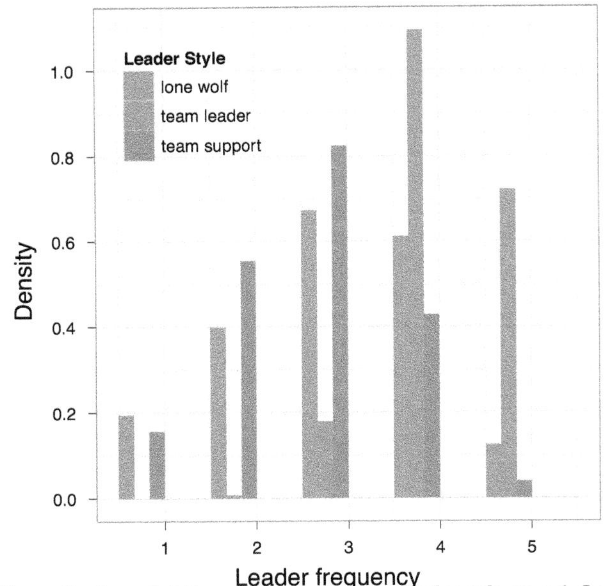

Figure 2. Reported frequency of playing a leader role on a 1–5 scale where 1 is never and 5 is always, by the preferred playing style.

We also asked participants to report their preferred playing style: team leader or team support (both collaborative styles) or "lone wolf" (a style that does not coordinate actions with the team). The survey did not provide definitions of these labels to respondents; however, feedback from our expert players indicated that their meanings should have been commonly understood within the *Reach* community. Although the popular stereotype of FPS games is non-collaborative, we find that 78.6% of players prefer playing as a team, in either the leading or supporting roles. Thus, *Reach* players are in fact strongly motivated by the collaborative aspects of the game [37,43]. When asked how often they played as a leader, participants reported typically playing their preferred role, although interestingly the lone wolves report playing a leader much more often than we would naively expect, given the anti-social nature of the lone wolf style (Fig. 2).

We find some support for the popular perception that younger players prefer the non-collaborative lone wolf role [24]. In our sample, people who preferred the team support role were indeed older (23.5 years) than those who preferred to play as lone wolves (21.6 years; $p < 0.001$). The modest size of the difference, however, suggests that while the effect is real, it is only a very weak tendency, with many younger players preferring collaborative roles and many older players preferring non-collaborative ones. Interestingly, people who preferred to play as leaders were also significantly younger (21 years) than those who played team support ($p \approx 0$).

Using our expertise as *Reach* players, we modified three classic psychometric surveys intended to assess group dynamics: entativity (how much a group is like a single entity), cohesion (how tightly-knit a group is), and conflict (how much internal conflict a group has). Past work on collaboration and team performance suggests that low-levels of conflict within a group of friends should correlate with better performance [21,22,35].

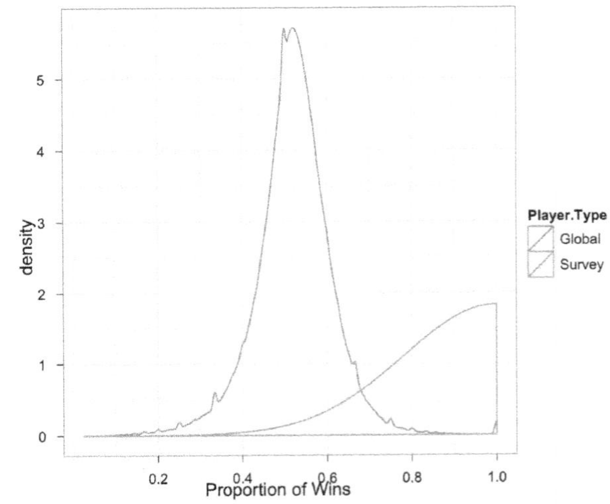

Figure 3. Proportion of games won by our respondents compared to randomly selected players

The entativity portion of the survey contained 14 questions, which had reasonable variability (SD=0.976 on a 5-point scale) and good internal consistency (Cohen's $\alpha = 0.82$). We therefore averaged the responses to create a single entativity metric. The average perceived entativity was 3.93 out of a 5-point scale, indicating respondents typically felt their teams were good at acting as one. The portion of the survey on cohesiveness contained 7 questions, which exhibited similar variability (SD=0.972) and internal reliability ($\alpha = 0.83$), so again we averaged the responses to create a single metric. In agreement with the perceived entativity, players typically felt their teams were very cohesive (4.1 out of 5). Finally, the portion of the survey on group conflict consisted of 8 questions with slightly lower variability (SD=0.92) and less internal reliability ($\alpha = 0.76$), which appears to be related to the presence of reverse-scored questions. Nonetheless, we felt the consistency was sufficient and averaged the scores. Here, perceived conflict was low (1.77), but somewhat higher than might be expected given the high entativity and cohesion ratings.

Comparison to Random Players

Advertising the anonymous survey on Halo-oriented community websites likely produced a biased sample of respondents relative to the overall population of *Reach* players. To characterize how different our respondent population was from the overall player population, we downloaded a uniformly random $1/1000$ sample of the first 400,000,000 *Reach* games from which we extracted 963,000 unique gamertags.[3] We then downloaded each of their player detail files and estimated the background distributions of various player summary statistics. Within this population, the average proportion of wins exhibited by a player is almost exactly 1/2, indicating a fairly unbiased sample of all players (Fig. 3).

Compared to the background distribution, our respondents were much better players, winning many more of their games (Fig. 3) than the typical *Reach* player. In addition to being

[3]The API does not provide a method by which to directly select a uniformly random player.

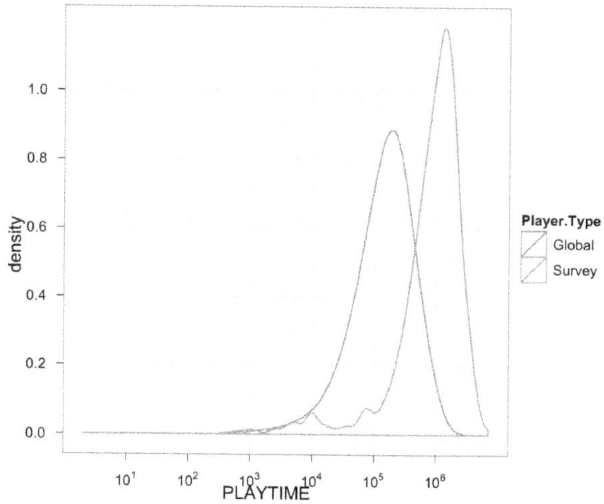

Figure 4. Time spent playing *Halo:Reach* by survey participants versus randomly selected players

more successful players, our respondents also typically invested almost 10 times more actual time playing *Reach* than the typical player (Fig. 4). That is, our respondents were serious Halo players, likely devoting a large share of their overall time spent playing video games to this particular game.

Demographics and Game Play

Although popular FPS stereotypes suggest that demographic variables like player sex may correlate with game performance, we find that males and females behave and perform similarly. For instance, males and females played roughly the same number of games (Female $= 1825.2$, Male $= 2085.0$), and the same amount of time per game (Female $= 592.3$, Male $= 620.69$; total seconds played divided by total games played). However, women died slightly more often than men (Female $= 10.69$ deaths/game, Male $= 8.86$ deaths/game, $t(1189) = 5.91$, $p < 0.007$).[4] Of course, because of the relatively small number of female players (5.1% or 61 respondents), there may be other small but real effects that we are unable to detect.

We also observed interesting differences in game play by player age. Congruent with the popular stereotypes of FPS gamers, the older a respondent was the more kills he had per game ($\beta = 0.263$, $t(1189) = 4.03$, $p \approx 0$), as shown in Figure 5. We also see older players were significantly more capable in the lone wolf role, a result that runs contrary to the suggestion that young players prefer the lone wolf role because they are more capable in the role—popularly attributed to faster reflexes—while older players must coordinate in teams in order to effectively compete [24].

One surprising age-correlated behavioral difference is in the number of betrayals (killing one's own teammate, which results in a loss of a point to the team and a longer respawn time for the offending player), as shown in Figure 5. Younger players (age ≤ 18) showed a disproportionate amount of this type of team disloyalty relative to the older players ($\beta = 0.0024$, $t(1189) = -4.71$, $p \approx 0$), with the former group exhibiting a betrayal rate about 40% higher than the latter groups. Because betrayals result in a penalty against the team's overall score, this suggests younger players exhibit significantly increased anti-social behavior while older players generally exhibit a more pro-social or cooperative orientation.

[4]For all tests, the threshold for significance (α) was corrected for the number of tests done.

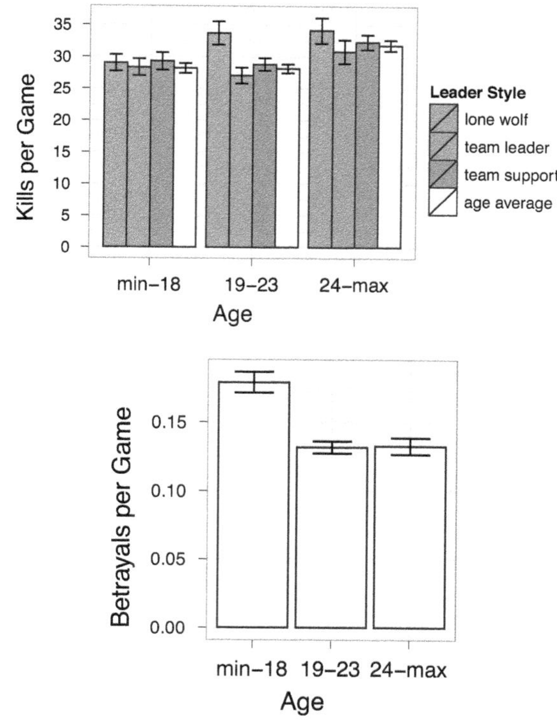

Figure 5. Kills per game (top) and betrayals per game (bottom) by age group, showing that the oldest group has significantly more kills per game than the younger groups while the youngest has more betrayals per game than the older groups.

Psychometrics and Game Play

Unlike purely survey-based studies, the access granted through the API to the detailed in-game data allows us to pair each survey response with rich independent behavioral data on the same individuals. Through this pairing, we may quantitatively verify reported variables on in-game behaviors. If the survey responses are accurate, they should predict corresponding patterns within the behavioral data, and allow us to subsequently predict survey responses from behavioral data alone. For instance, participants who report preferring the lone wolf role do indeed have significantly fewer "assists" to teammates (in which two or more team members collaborate to score a point) than participants who prefer to be team leaders ($p \approx 0$) or team support ($p < 0.005$).

We also find meaningful differences in the reported group dynamic psychometrics. For instance, the more a player sees their group as an entity, the more assists they have per game ($r = 0.13$, $p \approx 0$). Surprisingly, the opposite is true for number of kills: the more entitative groups have significantly fewer kills per game ($r = -0.16$, $p \approx 0$), perhaps because these groups travel as a pack and thus share their kills among their number. There are no significant differences in the number of deaths per game, however, suggesting perhaps that such groups are no better at warding off attacks than less entitative groups.

We observed a similar effect for perceptions of cohesiveness—more cohesive groups had significantly fewer kills per game ($r = -0.1$, $p < 0.001$), and there were no differences in the number of deaths per game. We did not, however, see the same relationship between cohesiveness and assists that we did for entativity and assists, suggesting the measures may be tapping different aspects of the players' subjective perceptions of their groups. A player going out of their way to assist a teammate, and thereby potentially giving up opportunities to score their own points, may require a greater sense of unity than mere closeness or camaraderie.

Studies of team dynamics in the management literature [21, 22, 35] suggest that groups with greater levels of internal conflict should exhibit different game play dynamics than groups with lower levels. Surprisingly, however, we found no strong or notable relationships between responses about group conflict and game play. There are several possible explanations for this pattern, but we do not explore them here.

PREDICTING FRIENDSHIPS

Before we consider the question of whether ground-truth friendship labels can be predicted purely from in-game behavioral data, we briefly discuss a few additional results from the survey data regarding friendships.

Of the 1191 respondents, 597 played at least one game with another survey respondent.[5] This overlap allows us to test whether respondents' perceptions of their online and offline friendships are reciprocal [30], i.e., when one player labels another as a friend, that friend also labels the player as a friend. For online friendships, the reciprocity is 36.9%; that is, when one of two survey respondents indicated the other was an online friend, about a third of the time did they agree they were friends. The agreement on offline friendships was higher (60.9%). While both of these values may seem low, both are in fact much higher than the rates observed in other online social networks, e.g., Twitter (22%) [17]. For a social network where friendship ties represent a significant mutual investment of time, it is not clear why we do not see rates approaching 100%, although there are a few possible reasons. For instance, we notice that there are a disproportionate number of respondents who list exactly 29 online friends, and this could indicate a number of respondents did not realize the list of teammates was scrollable. If this is the case, online and offline friends who fell "under the fold" may have been missed. Another explanation may be variability in the interpretation of the term "online friend" or actual differences in friendships of *Reach* players. This is a question for future research.

If players choose to structure their online activities in *Halo: Reach* around opportunities to play with friends, then the friendship labels respondents provided to us should be predictable from in-game behavioral data alone. Logistically, friends often synchronize their play times, at the same time of

[5]This overlap is likely attributable to the way we advertised the survey and is not representative of the background population.

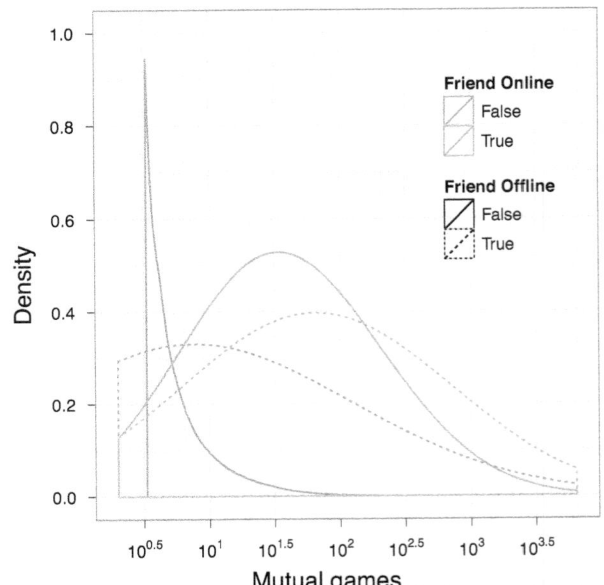

Figure 6. Number of mutual games played with players declared as online and offline friends. Dashed lines represent offline friends, and blue lines represent online friends, so the solid blue line is an online friend who is not an offline friend.

day or day of the week; this leads each player's gamertag to appear in the other player's game files in highly non-random ways. Within *Reach*, if friends are to play together, they must use the in-game "party" mechanism, in which one player "joins" another player to form a larger unit. Once they have formed this unit, the players are automatically placed together by the matchmaking algorithm into the same new competition and almost always on the same team (though splitting a party can happen, which leads to interesting in-game behavior; see below.) Thus, players who are friends will tend to appear together in a sequence of games and, within each sequence, they will typically be on the same side of a competition.[6]

We find significant differences in the frequency of playing together when a participant labeled a co-player as an online friend, offline friend, both, or neither. Pairs of players who are both online and offline friends typically played the most together, followed by online but not offline friends, then offline but not online friends and finally strangers (Fig. 6). That is, friends of both types play many more games together than do strangers.

Additionally, the party mechanism implies that when friends play together, their gamertags should appear together in a series of games, and therefore these series should be a good predictor of friendship. We define a *series* to be a sequence of consecutive games played together with no more than a one-hour gap between consecutive games. (Other gap sizes yield similar results to those reported here, indicating the robustness of this feature.) For each pair of players, we measured the number of series greater than length n and the length of

[6]By default, *Reach* will party up all players within a particular game at its conclusion, after a 10 second delay. To prevent this, a party or player must "back out" and restart the matchmaking algorithm. Most players choose to back out most of the time.

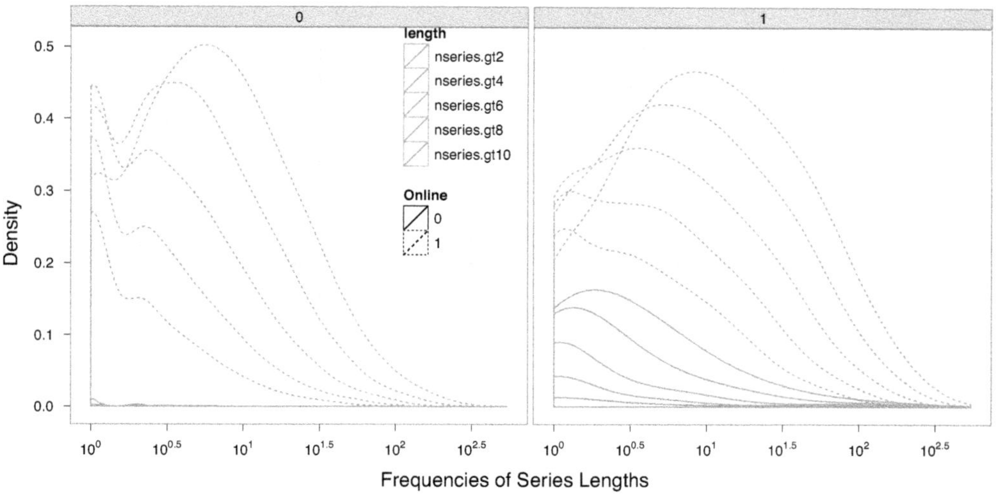

Figure 7. Number of series played for online and offline friends. Left panel shows series lengths for co-players who are not offline friends, right panel shows series lengths for offline friends. Dashed lines are online friends, solid lines are co-players who are not online friends. Colored lines show distributions for different minimum number of games played in a series.

the longest series. Figure 7 shows that online friends were significantly more likely to have played series of games together, as were offline friends. The greatest number of such series was played by pairs who were both online and offline friends. Similarly, the longest series for online and offline friend pairs is significantly longer than the longest series for non-friend pairs.

To illustrate this point, consider the average longest series. For strangers, the average was only 1.25 games in a row, indicating a strong tendency for these groups to dissolve quickly. However, for pairs of players in which either labeled the other as an online friend, the average was 10.20 and for those labeled as both online and offline friends, it was 13.15 games (corresponding to roughly two hours of clock time). That is, friends play many more games together in a sequence (on average, greater than 8 times more) than do strangers, and the structure of the party mechanism in *Reach* implies that this behavior must be actively selected for by players.

These patterns suggest that certain purely behavioral features may be highly accurate predictors of unknown friendship labels. Recovering this kind of hidden information has been done with a range of other electronic data on social interactions, including mobile phone call records [12, 13], geographic coincidences [11] and email [9], but not previously interactions within online games.

Given the number of competitions two players played and the number of those that were played together, the length of the longest series, and how many series of different length the pair played together (here: $\{2, 4, 6, 8, 10\}$, although other values could also be used), we try to predict whether either player indicated the other was an online friend (for those cases where multiple teammates responded to the survey). We fit the data to a logistic regression model, and obtain an accuracy of 98.7%, representing an AUC of 0.96. The corresponding ROC curve can be seen in Figure 8, and the ranking of the features can be seen in Table 1.

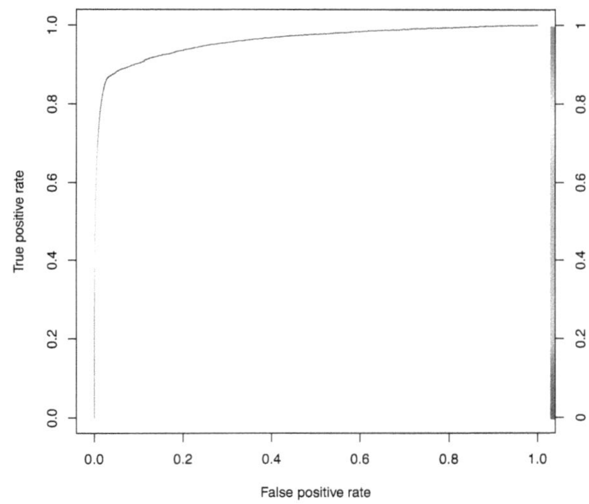

Figure 8. ROC curve for predicting whether a player is considered an online friend, given the number of mutual games together, the longest series of games, and the number of series of different lengths.

The dominant predictive feature in this model is clearly the length of the longest series the two players played together. The number of mutual games is also a strong positive feature, though it's relevance is tempered by the total number of games played. The high accuracy of the model indicates friendships in *Reach* can be reliably inferred from online behavior using simple heuristics. Given the fairly general nature of the predictive features, we expect these results will generalize to other online environments where players have the option of partying, or otherwise preferentially playing with friends. As a caveat, our labeled friendships are biased toward players with long game histories, and the most predictive features leverage this deep behavioral data. To what degree friendships can be inferred using only short behavioral histories is an important open question.

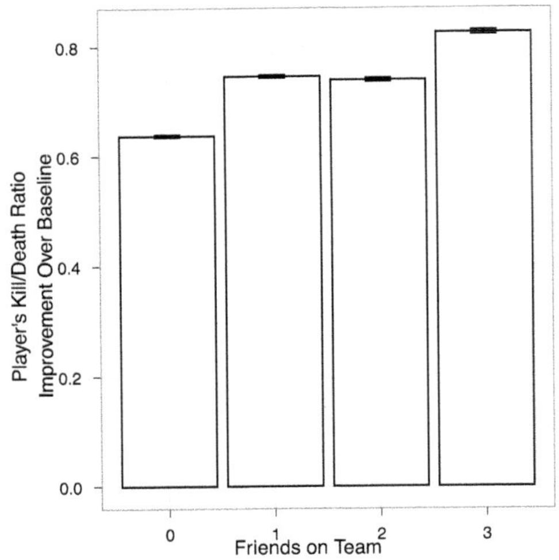

Figure 9. Average kill-death ratio, for playing with 0-3 friends. Baseline is the population average kill-death ratio (1), so even with no friends on the team participants are 65% better than average.

FRIENDSHIP AND PERFORMANCE

Because we have all competition data for each player and the participant-provided friendship labels of who they were playing with, we can investigate whether a player performs quantitatively differently when they play with or without friends. For the task of predicting winners based on the number of friends on one's (or one's opponent's) team, we take two simplifying steps. First, we focus on 4-on-4 games, which are the majority of *Reach* competitions; this controls for the number of players on each team and eliminates the need to differentiate between number of friends on a team or proportion of friends on a team. Second, we aggregate a player's online and offline friends; if a player labeled another as either an online or an offline friend, we labeled that person as a "friend".

Individual Performance

Here we ask whether the presence of friends on one's own or on one's opponent's team affects that player's performance. In other words, do people play or perform differently when they have friends on their team? If friendships impact the success of collaboration, then we expect to see performance improve as a player collaborates with more friends.

A strikingly clear result is that the amount of cooperation and defection (measured as assists and betrayals) a player exhibits depends strongly on the number of friends on their team. Specifically, the more friends on one's team, the more one assists (pro-social) and the less one betrays (anti-social) one's teammates (Fig. 10). The implication is that players actively adjust their play based on their friendships—the motivation to maintain these relationships is greater than the motivation to maintain harmony within the current team or to win the current competition.

	Estimate	Std. Error	z value	Pr(>|z|)
(Intercept)	-4.2485	0.0220	-192.81	0.0000
longest.series	0.3929	0.0030	131.80	0.0000
ngames.player	-0.0006	0.0000	-73.96	0.0000
ngames.mutual	0.0968	0.0027	35.97	0.0000
nseries.gt2	-0.1686	0.0152	-11.05	0.0000
nseries.gt4	0.0220	0.0197	1.11	0.2651
nseries.gt6	-0.2075	0.0259	-8.02	0.0000
nseries.gt8	-0.3428	0.0331	-10.36	0.0000
nseries.gt10	-1.1609	0.0350	-33.13	0.0000

Table 1. Parameters in a logistic regression predicting whether a player is labeled an online friend

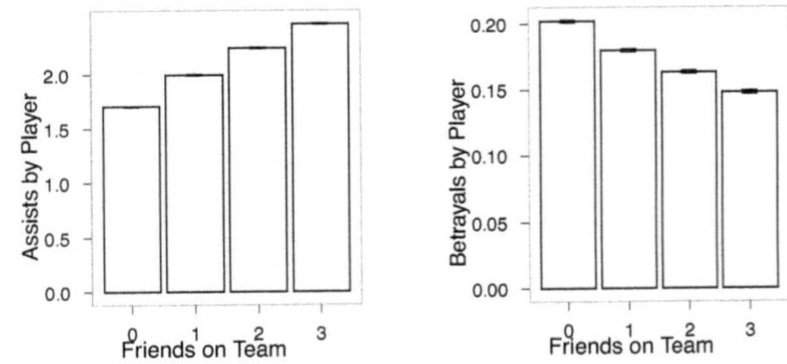

Figure 10. Assist and betrayal frequency, for playing with 0-3 friends

Playing with friends also impacts the player's success in the game, i.e., their performance. Winning and losing a competition is a team outcome (see below), but a measure of individual performance is the ratio of a given player's kill to deaths, i.e., the number of points they personally scored versus the number of points they personally provided to the opposing team. A higher individual value indicates better individual performance; by definition, the population average kill-death ratio must be 1.0, as there is one death for every kill. Figure 9 shows that even when the survey respondents are playing with no friends on their team, they do better than the average by 65%, indicating that our survey population is highly skilled. However, this already strong performance further increases with each additional friend on the team, up to an additional 20% when the entire team is a group of friends. Thus, at least for our respondents, having friends on one's team has a real and direct positive effect on one's own performance, independent of whether the team goes on to win the competition.

Team Performance

Given the effect of friends playing together on the individual's frequency of assists and betrayals, it is not too surprising that we see a similar pattern across the entire team. That is, independent of the player's own assists and betrayals, the team's assists increase, and its betrayals decrease, with the number of friends playing together.

As mentioned above, the matchmaking algorithm sometimes places members of a party on the *opposing* team, which allows us to investigate what happens when a player must

	Estimate	Std. Error	z value	Pr(>|z|)
(Intercept)	0.2027	0.0031	64.47	0.0000
own team	0.2558	0.0022	115.92	0.0000
opponent's	-0.1933	0.0069	-28.16	0.0000

Table 2. Best-fitting parameters for logistic regression model predicting whether a player won a game based only on the number of online or offline friends on their own team and on their opponent's team.

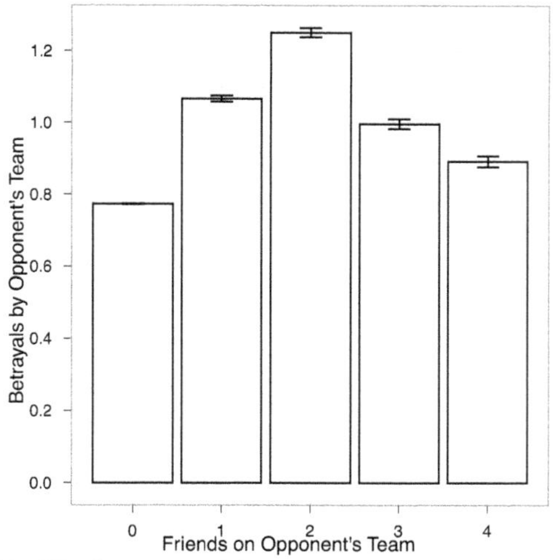

Figure 11. The frequency of betrayals on opponent's team when the team consists 0-4 of the player's friends

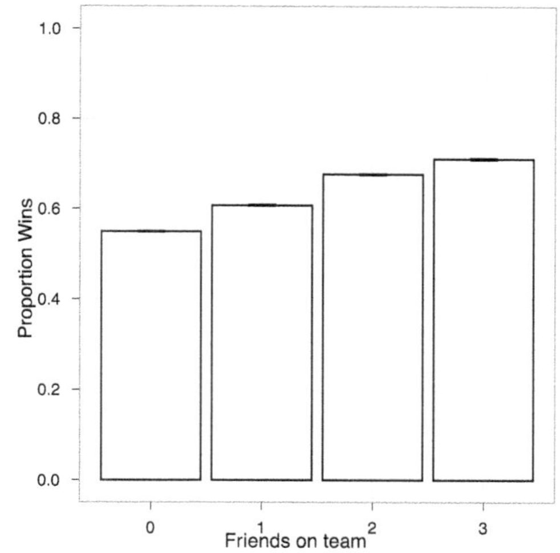

Figure 12. Proportion of wins when playing with 0-3 friends

choose between helping their teammates versus helping their friends (on the opposing team). In this case, we find an interesting pattern: as the number of friends on the opposing team increases, so too does the number of betrayals on that team. This trend continues until there is a majority of friends on the other team, at which point the number of betrayals decreases again (Fig. 11). In other words, if one or two friends find themselves playing against their friends, they are much more likely to kill their (non-friend) teammates than if they had no friends on the opposing team. The flip in the trend indicates that when a party's loyalties are divided across two teams, the smaller subset of friends is the one that defects against their teammates.

Similar to prior experimental work [2], and in agreement with our results on the kill-death ratio above, we find that players win more often when playing with friends than with strangers, and the more friends they play with the better (Fig. 12). Notably, this effect appears despite the matchmaking algorithm's effort to minimize differences in team skill [18] and thereby decrease the predictive power of non-game features like friendship. That is, the TrueSkill matchmaking algorithm used by *Reach* attempts to control for the effect of skill in improving performance, but it does not account for the performance benefits of from friendship.

We fit a logisitic regression model using only information about how many online and offline friends were on a player's own team and on the opposing team. The corresponding parameters are shown in Table 2. The model achieves an accuracy of 61.1%, with an AUC of 0.573. We note that predicting the outcome of competitions using only the number of friends on a team is a very weak signal—being friends cannot make bad players good—so it is in fact highly meaningful that there is any improvement in accuracy over random chance (AUC of 0.5).

We also tried to predict a competition's winner based on a rough metric of the players' expertise on each team. Because we do not have the entire game history of *all* players, we are unable to recreate the TrueSkill [18] estimates of the players' skill level. Moreover, despite the matchmaking algorithm's efforts to equalize skill between teams, there is still considerable variability in skill levels across competitions. Instead we use reasonable proxies for a player's skill in *Reach*, including the average number of games played by members of each team, the average progress in the single-player campaign and co-operative campaign, and the campaign difficulty level. This model performs slightly better than the friends-only model, improving the accuracy to 62.2% and the AUC to 0.614. As can be seen in Table 3, more games played on one's own team is only slightly more important than fewer games played by one's opponents.

Combining the expertise and friendship information provides a marginal improvement over expertise alone, although both the level of expertise and the number of friends on a team contribute to the model's prediction of the outcome. The three most heavily weighted parameters are the expertise on one's own team, the opposing team's expertise, and the number of online friends on one's own team (Table 4). The model has a negligible improvement in accuracy, to 62.4%, but the AUC improves slightly to 0.625.

CONCLUSION

In this paper we investigated the relationship of player demographic variables, such as age, sex and group cohesion, with player behavior, and the impact of friendships on individual and team performance in complex competitive environments. Toward this end, we used the online game *Halo:Reach*, one of the most popular games of 2010 [14] and one of the few in the FPS genre that has been studied in this way, as a model system. Our results only scratch the surface of this large and multi-faceted online system to inform our understanding of collaboration and competition in virtual environments.

Our anonymous online survey produced a number of insights into the *Reach* community, many of which likely generalize to the FPS genre as a whole. First, our respondents both invested more time in the game—but not more time than a typical video game player spends on games of all types—and were significantly more skilled than the typical *Reach* player.

	Estimate	Std. Error	z value	Pr(>|z|)
(Intercept)	0.2578	0.0051	50.10	0.0000
own.ngames	0.0001	0.0000	153.73	0.0000
oth.ngames	-0.0001	0.0000	-136.39	0.0000

Table 3. Parameters for the logisitic regression model predicting wins based on the average number of games played by one's own teammates and one's opponents.

	Estimate	Std. Error	z value	Pr(>|z|)
(Intercept)	0.1740	0.0053	33.00	0.0000
own.friends	0.1853	0.0023	78.99	0.0000
oth.friends	-0.0937	0.0071	-13.26	0.0000
own.ngames	0.0001	0.0000	125.61	0.0000
oth.ngames	-0.0001	0.0000	-132.81	0.0000

Table 4. Parameters for logistic regression predicting winners based on expertise and number of friends on one's own and one's opponent's team

Contradicting the anti-social stereotype of FPS players, our respondents were strongly motivated by social factors. More than 99.5% of our respondents indicated that they played with at least one online friend, and the typical number was 21 online friends (and 4 offline friends).[7] Nearly 80% preferred to play socially, on a team, rather than individually as a "lone wolf," and most players felt a strong sense of group cohesiveness and coordination. Thus, friendships among *Reach* players play an important role in choices of play style, game engagement and investment.

Although the typical age of our respondents was close to 20 years old, the distribution shows a long tail, with a large number of players over 30. Age correlated with several interesting aspects of game play: older players (24 or older; 30%) tend to exhibit somewhat less within-group conflict, exhibit greater pro-social tendencies (e.g., fewer betrayals), and are slightly more skilled (more kills per game). This latter point is counterintuitive given that younger players often have greater free time in which to invest in the game. We found only small differences in play statistics between male and female respondents and predictive models trained to predict sex from these values scored no better than chance. Thus, male and female players seem nearly indistinguishable from their in-game behavior.

Both team and individual performance in *Halo: Reach* are improved by friendship variables and teams composed of friends win more games on average than teams composed of strangers. However, if overall skill correlates across friendship ties, then highly skilled groups of friends could tend to win more often than groups of strangers because the skilled friends are more skilled than an average stranger. That is, skill could be homophilous. However, the TrueSkill matchmaking algorithm, which actively attempts to eliminate skill differences between teams, likely mitigates the impact of this confounding factor. TrueSkill does not control for the benefits that comes from playing with friends—benefits we observe quite clearly (Fig. 12). Admittedly, our study design does not allow us to identify the social mechanism by which friendships improve performance. A followup study that includes additional survey questions designed to distinguish among candidate mechanisms, and perhaps in depth interviews, may illuminate the answer.

That being said, our results do suggest some interesting clues. For instance, we observed more assists and fewer betrayals of teammates when there were more friends on the team, in agreement with research showing friendships decrease within-group conflict [21]. Alternatively, the large amount of time friends spend playing together may improve the division of specialized roles and improve communication within the team, leading to a better coordinated effort [22, 33].

Overall, friendships not only improve performance, but they also reshape the style of play within competitions. That is, players compete differently when they play with friends than when they play with strangers. For instance, groups of friends who are split across teams have to choose whether to compete against their friends (cooperate with their teammates) or defect against the teammates (cooperate with their friends). When this happens, friends tend to defect against their teammates, illustrated by a nearly double betrayal rate when two friends are on the opposing team. That is, friendship ties dominate teammate ties, and players sacrifice their own competitive success to help their friends. Similarly, betrayal rates (both by individuals and by teams) decrease as the number of friends on the team increase, illustrating a significant prosocial effect as compared to teams of strangers.

Although our logistic regression models found that friendship variables make marginal improvements over skill variables in our ability to predict success, this is understandable. In a context in which skill matters, a team of unskilled friends is sure to do more poorly than a team of skilled strangers. The important point is that even among skilled players, friendship ties provide a lift in both individual and team performance.

To conclude, we found a number of interesting relationships between in-game behavior within *Halo:Reach* and player demographic, group covariates and friendship ties. Most generally, we found that friendships strongly influence the social dynamics and collaboration within complex virtual environments like the FPS game *Halo: Reach*. Friendships lead to improved individual and team performance, increased prosocial behavior, and likely increased long-term appeal of and engagement in the game.

The impact of friendships is sufficiently strong, with players actively structuring their in-game activities around opportunities to play with friends, that hidden or unknown friendship ties can in fact be correctly inferred directly from behavioral time series using common sense heuristics. That is, it should be possible to automatically identify pairs of individuals who would call each other friends, if asked, merely by watching the way they interact with each other online. Collaborative systems, including online FPS games like *Reach* but also a wide variety of other systems, that can infer and account for such friendship ties could thus enable a wide range of better outcomes by providing fewer mismatches between individuals or by suggesting individuals to interact with in the future.

[7]But, the degree distribution does not follow a power law [10].

Given the increasing ubiquity of social gaming and *ad hoc* competition in general, the importance of such algorithms is likely significant.

ACKNOWLEGEMENTS

We thank Chris Schenk for help implementing the web survey, Nick Yee and Thore Graepel for helpful discussions, and the Halo community for their support and participation. This project was funded in part by a grant from the James S. McDonnell Foundation.

REFERENCES

1. Power games just want to have fun?: instrumental play in a MMOG. *Proceedings of the 1st Digra conference: Level Up*, 2003.
2. T. T. Baldwin, M. D. Bedell, and J. L. Johnson. The social fabric of a team-based M.B.A. program: Network effects on student satisfaction and performance. *Acad. of Manag. Journal*, 40:1369–1397, 1997.
3. P. Balkundi and D. A. Harrison. Ties, leaders, and time in teams: Strong inference about network structure's effects on team viability and performance. *Acad. of Manag. Journal*, 49:49–68, 2006.
4. S. Bao, G. Xue, X. Wu, Y. Yu, B. Fei, and Z. Su. Optimizing web seaerch using social annotations. In *Proc. 16th International Conference on World Wide Web*, WWW '07, pages 501–510, 2007.
5. S. Bardzell, J. Bardzell, T. Pace, and K. Reed. Blissfully productive: Grouping and cooperation in World of Warcraft instance runs. *Proc. 11th ACM Conference on Computer Supported Cooperative Work and Social Computing*, pages 357–360, 2008.
6. S. P. Borgatti and R. Cross. A relational view of information seeking and learning in social networks. *Management Science*, 49:432–445, 2003.
7. B. Brown and M. Bell. Play and sociability in *There*: Some lessons from online games for collaborative virtual environments. *Proc. 9th ACM Conference on Computer Supported Cooperative Work and Social Computing*, pages 227–245, 2006.
8. M. G. Chen. Communication, Coordination, and Camaraderie in World of Warcraft. *Games and Culture*, 4(1):47–73, Dec. 2008.
9. M. D. Choudhury, W. A. Mason, J. M. Hofman, and D. J. Watts. Inferring relevant social networks from interpersonal communication. *Proc. 19th International Conference on World Wide Web*, pages 301–310, 2010.
10. A. Clauset, C. R. Shalizi, and M. E. J. Newman. Power-law distributions in empirical data. *SIAM Review*, 51:661–703, 2009.
11. D. J. Crandall, L. Backstrom, D. Cosley, S. Suri, D. Huttenlocher, and J. Kleinberg. Inferring social ties from geographic coincidences. *Proc. National Academy of Sciences*, 107:22436–22441, 2007.
12. N. Eagle, A. Clauset, and J. Quinn. Location segmentation, inference and prediction for anticipatory computing. In *Proc. 23rd AAAI Conference on Artificial Intelligence*. AAAI, 2009.
13. N. Eagle, A. S. Pentland, and D. Lazer. Inferring friendship network structure by using mobile phone data. In *Proc. National Academy of Sciences*, pages 15274–15278, 2009.
14. Entertainment Software Association. Essential Facts about the Compute and Video Game Industry. From `http://bit.ly/kLHJ2Q`, (access date February, 2012), 2011.
15. A. Gabel and S. Redner. Random walk picture of basketball scoring. Journal of Quantitative Analysis in Sports, to appear. Preprint, `arXiv:1109.2825`, 2012.
16. M. Granovetter. The strength of weak ties. *American Journal of Sociology*, 78:1360–1380, 1973.
17. H. P. H. Kwak, C. Lee and S. Moon. What is Twitter, a social network or a news media? *Proc. 19th International Conference on World Wide Web*, pages 591–600, 2010.
18. R. Herbrich, T. Minka, and T. Graepel. TrueSkill(tm): A Bayesian skill rating system. *Adv. Neural Info. Proc. Sys.*, 20:569–576, 2007.
19. M. Jakobsson and T. Taylor. The sopranos meets everquest. In *Proc. 2003 Digital Arts and Culture DAC Conference Melbourne Australia*, pages 81–90. Citeseer, 2003.
20. J. Jansz and M. Tanis. Appeal of playing online first person shooter games. *CyberPsychology & Behavior*, 10(1):133–136, 2007.
21. K. A. Jehn and E. A. Mannix. The dynamic nature of conflict: A longitudinal study of intragroup conflict and group performance. *The Academy of Management Journal*, 44(2):238–251, 2001.
22. K. A. Jehn and P. Shah. Interpersonal relationships and task performance: An examination of mediating processes in friendship and acquaintance groups. *Journal of Personality and Social Psychology*, 72(4):775–790, 1997.
23. T. Manninen and T. Kujanpää. The hunt for collaborative war gaming - CASE: Battlefield 1942. *Game Studies*, 5(1):October, 2005.
24. G. Mastrapa. No country for old men, 2010. Wired Magazine, `http://bit.ly/dj55UW` (access date February, 2010).
25. A. R. McConnell, S. J. Sherman, and D. L. Hamilton. Target entitativity: Implications for information processing about individual and group targets. *J. Personality and Soc. Psych.*, 72:750–762, 1997.
26. G. McEwan, C. Gutwin, R. L. Mandryk, and L. Nacke. "i'm just here to play games:" social dynamics and sociability in an online game site. *Proc. 15th ACM Conference on Computer Supported Cooperative Work and Social Computing*, pages 549–558, 2012.
27. M. McPherson, L. Smith-Lovin, and J. M. Cook. Birds of a feather: Homophily in social networks. *Annu. Rev. Sociol.*, 27:415–444, 2001.
28. D. R. Michael and S. L. Chen. *Serious Games: Games That Educate, Train, and Inform*. Muska and Lipman, 2005.
29. J. Muramatsu and M. S. Ackerman. Computing, social activity, and entertainment: A field study of a game MUD. *Computer Supported Cooperative Work: The Journal of Collaborative Computing*, 7:87–122, 1998.
30. M. Newman. *Networks: An Introduction*. Oxford University Press, Oxford, 2010.
31. M. A. Rahim. A measure of styles of handling interpersonal conflict. *Acad. of Manag. Journal*, 26:368–376, 1983.
32. S. Reeves, B. Brown, and E. Laurier. Experts at play: Understanding skilled expertise. *Games and Culture*, 4(3):205–227, 2009.
33. M. Rittenbruch and G. McEwan. An historical reflection of awareness in collaboration. In P. M. et al., editor, *Awareness Systems*, pages 3–48. Springer-Verlag, 2009.
34. M. Ruef, H. E. Aldrich, and N. M. Carter. The structure of founding teams: Homophily, strong ties, and isolation among U.S. entrepreneurs. *American Sociological Review*, 68:195–222, 2003.
35. P. Shah and K. A. Jehn. Do friends perform better than acquaintances? *Group Decision and Negotiation*, 2:149–165, 1993.
36. W. Shrum, J. Neil H. Cheek, and S. M. Hunter. Friendship in school: Gender and racial homophily. *Sociology of Edu.*, 61:227–239, 1988.
37. C. A. Steinkuehler and D. Williams. Where Everybody Knows Your (Screen) Name: Online Games as "Third Places". *Journal of Computer-Mediated Communication*, 11(4):885–909, July 2006.
38. J. P. Stokes. Components of group cohesion: Intermember attraction, instrumental value, and risk taking. *Small Group Research*, 14:163–173, 1983.
39. D. Williams, N. Ducheneaut, L. Xiong, Y. Zhang, N. Yee, and E. Nickell. From tree house to barracks: The social life of guilds in World of Warcraft. *Games and Culture*, 1(4):338–361, 2006.
40. D. Williams, S. Poole, N. Contractor, and J. Srivastava. The Virtual World Exploratorium: Using Large-Scale Data and Computational Techniques for Communication Research. *Communication Methods and Measures*, 5:163–180, 2011.

41. D. Williams, N. Yee, and S. Caplan. Who plays, how much, and why? Debunking the stereotypical gamer profile. *Journal of Computer-Mediated Communication*, 13(4):993–1018, 2008.

42. T. Wright, E. Boria, and P. Breidenbach. Creative player actions in FPS online video games. *Game Studies*, 2(2):December, 2002.

43. Y. Xu, X. Cao, A. Sellen, R. Herbrich, and T. Graepel. Sociable killers: Understanding social relationships in an online first-person shooter game. In *Proc. Computer Supported Cooperative Work*, pages 197–206. ACM, 2011.

44. N. Yee, N. Ducheneaut, L. Nelson, and P. Likarish. Introverted Elves & Conscientious Gnomes: The Expression of Personality in World of Warcraft. In *Proc. 2011 Annual Conference on Human Factors in Computing Systems*, CHI '11, pages 753–762, New York, NY, USA, 2011. ACM.

Media Technologies and Learning in the StarCraft eSport Community

Yong Ming Kow
National University of Singapore
21 Lower Kent Ridge Road,
Singapore
mail@kowym.com

Timothy Young
Department of Informatics
University of California, Irvine
Irvine, CA 92697, USA
tcyoung@uci.edu

ABSTRACT
Interest-driven Internet communities often use an assemblage of media technologies to support knowledge creation and learning. In this paper, we examine the uneven functions of these media technologies in meeting the learning needs of online game players. StarCraft is an online game and electronic sport where millions around the world compete in virtual battlegrounds. To become better players, gamers actively share strategies in online forums, wiki, videos, and in person. We conducted participant observation of a StarCraft community known as Teamliquid. We performed 24 in-depth interviews with professional gamers, editors, game commentators, and community leaders. We found that the novice learners generally learned from, and participated in, public media channels, whereas the StarCraft experts congregated in small teams in which members learn from each other within private media channels and in person. We use the concepts of *informational media* and *socially-oriented media* to describe the general learning needs supported by media technologies.

Author Keywords
Communities of practice, online community, learning, online games

ACM Classification Keywords
H.5.3.

INTRODUCTION
Many Internet communities are driven by a specific interest, e.g., online gaming or modding. In these interest-driven communities, members use an assemblage of media technologies, e.g., wikis, online forums, chat rooms, video on demand on sites like YouTube, and Internet TV, to support mass collaboration. While previous studies in human-computer interaction have described interest-driven communities, these are mostly communities built on a specific media technology, e.g., Wikipedia [5,18]. Few studies have paid attention to Internet communities that utilize multiple technologies, and interrogate the different functions media technologies play in supporting the communities' activities.

The normalcy of multi-technology use in work settings has been discussed in previous studies [4]; however, few had examined such use in Internet communities. Ito [15] has suggested that Internet communities are networked publics, in which media technologies, which allow community members to interact, are also mass media. Wenger, et al. [39] suggest that community administrators and managers match media technologies to the communities' activities and their social configurations.

StarCraft (1998) is an electronic sport (eSport), organized as a set of leagues that "compete through networked games and related activities" [16]. In the StarCraft community, "metagame" is a term synonymous with strategy, but it also refers to the "planning, preparation, or maneuvering that a player does outside of actual gameplay" [23]. To master the StarCraft metagame, players attend tournaments, participate in league games, and worked with practice partners. On the Internet, players discuss the game on online forums, wiki sites, Internet telephone, and via instant messaging tools. Players often analyze StarCraft matches shown on Internet television.

From October 2011 to April 2012, we performed seven months of participant observation of a StarCraft community known as Teamliquid (Teamliquid.net). Teamliquid's website is the most popular community site for English speaking StarCraft players located in the U.S. and other European countries. We observed player interactions in Teamliquid's online forums and wiki. We participated in one local tournament and two gatherings in local bars. We performed 24 in-depth interviews with StarCraft participants including professional gamers (pro-gamers), amateur gamers, editors, game commentators (casters), and community leaders. All interviews were audio-recorded and transcribed.

In this paper, we discuss how the adoption of media technologies is uneven in the StarCraft community, e.g., some collaborative contexts may favor tools like instant messaging to online forums. We discuss social-technical formations that function alongside media technologies that support learning in Internet communities.

CSCW '13, February 23–27, 2013, San Antonio, Texas, USA.

LEARNING THEORIES

In this research, we adopt the perspective that learning is fundamentally social, and is often supported through peer-to-peer interaction [36,37,40]. Social learning is a well-established area of research, with a history that stretches as far back as the early part of the 20th century. This orientation to the social nature of learning is well established in socialcultural and "situated" theories of learning. For example, Lev Vygotsky's influential work in the 1930s suggested that learning and development happen through social interaction with a more capable person [13,35]. In this sense, our interactions with learning partners—primarily what we say to each other—shapes the way we will subsequently perceive the world [13].

Peer-to-peer and informal learning in online environments, unlike learning through classroom activities, resembles on-the-job learning [9]. Learners organize themselves to resolve new and emerging challenges, thus creating new knowledge in the process of learning [9]. Internet technologies offer immense potential as infrastructure that supports peer-based social learning [27].

Situated learning theory has had an influence in human-computer interaction research primarily through the concept of "communities of practice," which grew out of studies of work practices [20]. The concept was later applied widely to knowledge management practices, as well as various organizational contexts such as Shell and the World Bank.

A community of practice is a social group that shares a set of practices through which they gain expertise and guide new members into the group. Learners in communities of practice take the role of "legitimate peripheral participation" which is an entry point into more central participation or formal membership [37]. Social groups are important to learning because knowledge does not reside solely in individuals and in documents, but is embedded in social practices and interactions. For example, professionals often share stories that contain key lessons for other professionals. The influence of communities of practice frameworks ushered in an era when corporations began to nurture professional groups as incubators of knowledge and learning [38].

Internet communities have been found to exhibit characteristics of communities of practice [5]; however, there are key differences between Internet communities and companies. Members of Internet communities are often volunteers [1]. While companies can mandate the participation of their employees in communities of practice, Internet communities can only motivate member participation out of shared interests.

Not all Internet groups are interest-driven. Some, like eBay are market-driven, and others, like Facebook are centered on socializing rather than on specific interests. While the Wikipedia community is driven by an interest in developing an information resource [5], it has been reported as being supported by a dedicated media technology [5,18]. We have observed that most other interest-driven Internet communities adopt multiple technologies to support their activities and wikis are only some of the many technologies supporting collaborative work. In interest-driven and peer-based Internet communities, "work" often comprises the distribution, production, remixing, and consumption of digital media contents, e.g., text, graphics, videos, and software applications, in a highly-distributed collaborative setting [1].

Prior studies have examined the use of multiple technologies in industrial work settings, e.g., ship navigation [4]. Bodker and Anderson [4] interrogated use of artifacts like papers and control instruments in ships, and suggested the concept of *multi-mediation.* In multi-mediation, artifacts may mediate work all at the same time, in a chain of sequence, or in a distributed manner. In the latter, a ship's management team and engineers are using different tools to support the overarching task of navigating a ship [4].

Similarly, media technologies can connect distributed communities into a complex social-technical system, in which different social groups collaborate to solve common problems [14,39]. Research has documented how technological entrepreneurs alternate between use of social media and in-person events to foster a culture of technological knowledge sharing [6]. And more recent research on communities of practice has begun to explore the role of Internet technologies mediating distributed communities [38,39]. Wenger et al. [38] suggest that corporations pay attention to what could compromise communication among globally distributed team members, such as distance, size, culture, and the intellectual ownership of new ideas [38]. Wenger et al. [39] use the term *digital habitat* to describe a collection of Internet tools, platforms, features, and their configurations which support communities of practice.

An issue of online collaboration is that Internet media limit the transfer of knowledge between distant localities. Nonaka and Nishiguchi [26] coined the term "ba" to refer to knowledge residing within a physical context. As soon as the knowledge is re-represented into a media format, e.g., text, it loses its original depth and richness:

> Knowledge is embedded in ba, where it is then acquired through one's own experience or reflections on the experiences of others. If knowledge is separated from ba, it turns into information, which can then be communicated independently from the ba. Information resides in media and networks, while knowledge resides in ba. [26]

Knowledge written in text becomes information [33]. This view complements activity theory, which describes texts as merely the symbolic representation of what we know [36]. Learning is only effective when learners not only consume information transmitted through media technologies, but also apply the information to real-life practices.

Frameworks that have been developed in the context of communities of practice research can be productively applied and extended to online interest-driven learning environment. Other constructs, such as digital habitat and multi-mediation, are also relevant to the online context. A study of the StarCraft community—being media technology supported, peer-based, openly networked, and less institutionally bounded—can help enrich these theories by demonstrating how particular media technologies are mobilized to support learning.

STARCRAFT: THE GAME

StarCraft is an electronic sport (eSport) game with International tournaments in Asia, Europe, and North America. In 2011, these tournaments had awarded more than $2.5 million in overall prizes [30]. In the current StarCraft scene, two StarCraft versions are most popular among players, Brood War (1999) and StarCraft II (2010). By December 2010, Brood War had sold 9.5 million copies and StarCraft II had sold 4.5 million copies worldwide. StarCraft II is similar to Brood War (BW) except for improved graphics and alterations to combat units. Both BW and StarCraft II players congregate and discuss the games in the same community site, Teamliquid.net. Many of the earliest StarCraft II practices were inherited from BW. Furthermore, many StarCraft II players are also former StarCraft I players. Due to these reasons, we treated both games as residing within the same learning ecology.

A StarCraft match is played on a virtual battleground, a map containing terrains such as mineral patches, cliffs, and ramps. In a StarCraft match, a player wins when he has eliminated his opponent from the map, or when his opponent admits defeat. Each player starts at a different location, where he has a few minutes to build up his army.

A starting location includes a mineral patch containing a limited amount of resources, see Figure 1. Players collect and allocate these resources to make buildings and units. Players have to carefully deliberate the allocation of these limited resources to approximately 15 different types of buildings and 15 types of units that are available. Different unit types can do a combination of different things, e.g., collect resources, fly over terrains, or fight in combat. The units a player can make depend on buildings she had already constructed. Thus, the tasks of resource collection, building construction, and unit making, are interdependent and require careful planning on the part of the players.

StarCraft community members shared the interest of the "metagame." In general, metagame refers to "how game interfaces with life" [32]. This is a wide definition, which includes any activities that surround a game, including game prizes, strategies, and social discourses [11]. The StarCraft community adopts a narrower version of the term, which refers only to game strategies and other preparations done by the competitors in the anticipation of upcoming matches. Henceforth, the term metagame in this paper refers to this emic definition.

Within the StarCraft metagame, other concepts are constructed. For example, a "build order" is a planned sequence of actions, including collecting resources, constructing buildings, and making units. Many build orders have been developed by the StarCraft community; and each build order confers a player certain advantages and disadvantages. As a game progresses, players gradually deviate from their build orders and adjust their actions—resource gathering, building construction, and unit making—appropriately, to gain an advantage over their opponents in battles. From this point on, a match slowly exposes the full extent of StarCraft metagame, which includes how map terrains, unit types, buildings, and resource collecting rates interact in a complex way.

Figure 1 A base sitting on a plateau with a narrow ramp.

The biography of one of the best players in StarCraft history, Yohwan Lim, alias "BoxeR," provides an insight into the importance of understanding the metagame. In 2001, BoxeR was the top player in the StarCraft pro-gaming scene for 17 consecutive months, an unprecedented feat to the nascent community. He became StarCraft's first "bonjwa," or a StarCraft superstar who had dominated professional tournaments for an extended period of time [22].

BoxeR's strategy featured an unpopular unit known as a "dropship," a slow-flying transport that carries a small number of combat units. A dropship is slow moving, and thus most players had found it unwieldy during actual matches. But BoxeR would revolutionize its uses, as he describes in his biography:

> [T]he covert dropship exposes itself in the enemy base, after having taken the unrevealed route at an unexpected moment. *Even if the opponent had predicted it, he cannot stop me.* That is my strategy. Using the enemy buildings as shields, I destroy the units and buildings one by one, but quickly, even before his reinforcements arrive. I still have a second force left even if my tired units are eliminated by the

> reinforcements. I have to defend my base as perfectly as I execute the attack. [21] (Emphasis added)

BoxerR's strategy included not just plans to attack, but also how he would have defended himself against a myriad of possible counter attacks (counters). BoxeR's speed at handling the keyboard and mouse allowed him to proficiently manage his attacks, buildings and units production, and defenses all at once, perfecting his scheme. BoxeR's strategy was well thought-out and difficult to defeat, even if the opponent had seen it coming. Such strategies emerged out of the player's hundreds of hours of analyzing and playing matches. Becoming one of the best StarCraft players is difficult, and the community developed a saying that these players need 'the finesse of a pianist, and the intelligence of a chess master.'

METHOD

Teamliquid (Teamliquid.net), founded in 2002, is the main StarCraft community site visited by players. A majority of StarCraft participants, e.g., game casters, professional gamers, amateur league participants, and event organizers, had considered themselves to be members of the Teamliquid site. Teamliquid is also a hub containing a large repository of StarCraft information, e.g., articles, online forum discussion, and weblinks.

Between October 2011 and April 2012, we performed participant observation at Teamliquid—at major and minor tournaments, bar events, and on its websites. Teamlquid.net contained StarCraft online forums and a StarCraft wiki. The online forum included edited articles of bonjwas and their landmark matches, and weblinks to videos of common player matches. We analyzed the contents of relevant wiki articles, forum posts, and edited articles. Between December 2 and December 4, 2011, we conducted field observations at an international StarCraft tournament, the North American Star League Grand Finals in Ontario, California. We attended two bar events in California.

In all, we conducted 24 interviews with pro-gamers, casters, amateur league players, Teamliquid editors, tournament organizers, and community leaders. Our interviewees ranged between 15 and 30 years old, with an average age of 21.8. There were 22 males and 2 females. There were 4 professional gamers, among whom 3 were retired but still actively involved in other community roles. There were 11 working adults, 1 graduate student, 4 college students, and 7 high school students. One interviewee did not disclose his work or school status. Other data, specifically those of BoxeR and the player "re dir," were obtained from articles and online forums in the public domain.

Skype is an Internet telephone with an instant messaging function. The interviews were conducted in person, over Skype, and on the phone. Our interviews centered on two key questions: What role do you play in the community? How do you learn to become a better player? All interviews were audio-recorded and transcribed.

We performed our analysis only on technologies mentioned by our interviewees. Some media technologies popular among StarCraft gamers, e.g., reddit and stream chats, did not emerge in our interviews. One possible reason for this could be that these technologies do not play central roles in supporting the learning of the metagame. For example, reddit as a social news site may not contain enough content on strategies.

THE FINDINGS

In this section, we will discuss how players learn the metagame. We first discuss learning through mass media like Internet TV and tournaments. Then, we discuss the practice of learning from match partners and practice partners. Next, we discuss how textual and video-based media facilitate learning. Finally, we report on how members of different StarCraft interest groups are similarly configured.

Learning using Mass Media: Internet TV and Tournaments

To master StarCraft, community members have to maintain a high level of engagement with its evolving media contents, which are centered on tournaments and competitions [7]. Michael Santos, male 29 and owner of a wine business, was a semi-professional player of another online strategy game WarCraft III. After his success in WarCraft III tournaments, he tried to compete in the StarCraft II pro-gaming scene, but he was unable to keep up with the shifting metagame:

> The game is just so fast and complex. There are counters [to a strategy] and anti-counters and counters to those counters. It's just insane how quickly the pro-game strategies change. So you get stuck watching GSL [Global StarCraft II League—the most competitive professional StarCraft II league in the world]. [You may] try strategies that GSL use versus other players doing stuff that's older. Yet, [someone else would] beat you because you don't realize the reason it worked in the GSL is that it was a counter to another strategy that was countering the original strategy.

In StarCraft, learners fall behind when they are out of touch with the community's contents and media.

Professional gamers like BoxeR are able to motivate StarCraft gamers to learn the StarCraft metagame through their performance at gaming tournaments. Mona Zhang was a college student at Princeton University. Zhang is also the founder of the Collegiate Starleague, a StarCraft II league consisting of 316 U.S. and European universities. She discussed her fascination with watching StarCraft professional matches:

> When I watched [an upcoming bonjwa] vs. Boxer, and realized that there was a Korean pro scene. It was that summer where I started

> watching pro league, and I fell in love with all the Korean players and all the eSports that was going on in Korea. You have these pro-gamers who are just constantly trying to get better, constantly toppling BoxeR. In the game that I was watching, [BoxeR's opponent] was the new legend. He ended up losing to Boxer in that set, but I think it was a premonition of what was to come, and that's the type of stuff that gives people nerd chills. And that's why I love StarCraft.

Pro-gamers like BoxeR often come out with new and effective strategies, which draw players to watch StarCraft professional matches. Many players learn by copying what pro-gamers do, as suggested by Elly, male 21, who is also a writer at Teamliquid:

> A very common advice to newbies [new players] is just to copy a pro-gamer's build. Just copy what they do, don't even think about it, just copy what they do and do it over and over and over again until you see what happens, until you see why something is useful. Mainly, I think most learning comes from kind of watching and then playing and copying.

Much of the rationale behind a good strategy come from the anticipation of what an opponent may be doing, analysis of the map terrains, and resource availability. These hidden rationales may surface as a player repeatedly uses the same strategy in a series of matches.

StarCraft learners are often preoccupied with identifying holes and gaps in their own understanding of the metagame. Thus, players who spectated StarCraft matches are often absorbed in the pro-gamers minute actions, looking for instances where pro-gamers deviated from how the players would had played the game. Novel strategies that win games are templates on which these spectators rethink their very own. Following these templates are important to good gamers who want to catch up with understanding the StarCraft metagame.

Between 2005 and 2011, Internet TV sites like BlipTV and TwitchTV were launched. Internet TV allows pro-gamers or ordinary players to "stream" their matches, or to showcase these matches live over the Internet for free and for anyone to see. Streamers with high viewership receive part of the Internet TV's advertisement profit [2,34]. Primadog, who is 22 year old, is a co-founder of BarCraft, an organized StarCraft II event where local players gather in one bar or restaurant to spectate a professional StarCraft II tournament over Internet TV. He estimated as many as 120,000 online spectators may be watching any professional StarCraft match online, at home or at a BarCraft. A player who has missed these live events can also watch the replays on video on demand sites such as YouTube.

Internet TV and video on demand have brought a deeper analysis of StarCraft matches closer to the amateur player. Using these technologies, many retired pro-gamers and expert players have streamed video commentaries (screencasts) of notable matches. Day9TV (day9.tv), that carried the slogan "Be A Better Gamer," is a website that streams screencasts of "Day[9]" or Sean Plott, male 26, who was a StarCraft Pan American Champion in 2007. Day[9] founded the After Hours Gaming League, a StarCraft II league comprised of employees from Silicon Valley companies, including AMD, Intel, Facebook, Google, and Microsoft. Day[9] shared with us the beginning of Day9TV:

> [With Internet TV] Live streaming suddenly became inexpensive and reliable, finally. Pretty much for any live event before then, bandwidth was the number one cost by far. For a big event the bandwidth you need is .5 million dollars today. Other events back then 80% of our budget was just getting our stream out. It's really weird. And then all of sudden it was free and easy. I said, "Huh, download this program and hit go and see what happens." That's almost the entire story behind the whole TV thing. This is cool, "I can do video, oh, it's free and easy."

Day[9] streamed and commented on a variety of professional matches that took place in Korea, the U.S., or in Europe. Day[9] also streams amateur matches to discuss basic practice methods and strategies. Since Day9TV was launched in 2009, Day[9] has streamed 423 videos. Most Teamliquid members suggested that each Day[9] stream had the potential to attract between 10 to 20 thousand live viewers.

Pro-gamers like BoxeR represent the community's mastery of StarCraft metagame. Internet TV and video on demand bring these practices to the players. In the next section, we examine how novice players turn this information into shared practices with their practice partners.

Practicing Together: Battle.net, LAN and Practice Partners

Good StarCraft II players practice a lot, both online and with co-located partners. Since the first StarCraft version, Blizzard has provided players with a Battle.net platform where players manually find opponents online, see Figure 2.

In StarCraft II, Blizzard automated this matchmaking process and helped players find others who are similarly skilled. The players' skill levels are calculated using the results of their recent matches. Based on each player's skill level, Battle.net assigns players into one of six leagues: Grand Master, Master, Diamond, Platinum, Gold, Silver, and Bronze. The Grand Master league is made up of the top 200 players of a particular region, e.g., the U.S. The Master league is made up of the top 2% of all players in the same region. The rest of the players are similarly ranked and divided somewhat equally into Diamond, Platinum, Gold, Silver, and Bronze leagues. Battle.net may promote the top performers of a league to the next higher league, or likewise demote the worst performers into the next lower league. Due to this ranking system, StarCraft II players have referred to Battle.net as the "ladder."

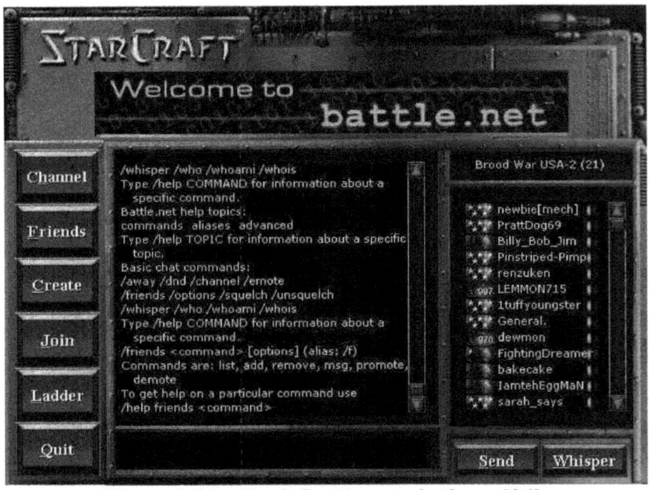

Figure 2 StarCraft Battle.net platform [24].

Brendan Ko, male 28, was a doctoral candidate at Stanford University. He represented the university in the Collegiate Starleague. He practiced online with random partners identified by the Battle.net:

> These days the StarCraft II ladder system is very good so I can meet a lot of players that are the same level with me, so I could play with them as like a practice partner, and that's all my StarCraft II playing. I sometimes play a game with my teammates [at Stanford University], but it's not actually very interesting because we already know each other very well—I can predict what my friend will do and the game will be really not interesting. That's the reason I usually play the ladder.

At a Master level, Ko was able to execute a plan correctly, anticipate and adapt to what his opponent was doing, and, at the same time, hide his own plans. Yet, that was the limit of his learning on Battle.net. Ko tried to advance in the ladder towards the Grand Master level, but the results of his matches with Grand Master level players were disappointing. Unable to comprehend the work needed to become a Grand Master player, he gave up becoming one.

Players with the ambition to learn deep practices often identify long-term learning partners, also known as "practice partners." Practice partners meet regularly on live-streams or in person to help each other improve. We interviewed Sen, a 25 year old male from Taiwan, who won third place at the international StarCraft II tournament North American Star League (NASL) in 2011. He told us the benefits of working with practice partners:

> If you practice with good players, you will improve very quickly. There are many little things in StarCraft that are easy to fix, but you do need a keen observer to tell you. They may say it using only a few words. But if you are working on your own, you may never be able to figure them out.

Practice partners spend much more time with each other than with random partners on Battle.net. Practice partners are committed to each other. They do not just play games with each other but also spend time analyzing each other's matches.

Small group learning may also take place at a LAN event. A LAN event refers to an on-site activity where video game players come together to play multiplayer games. A LAN event is supported by technologies including LAN, Wireless LAN, and the Internet. Duran Parsi, who is a 24-year-old male and co-founder of the NASL, began hosting LAN events in 2005 in California. He was then a pro-gamer. In the same year, Day[9] came to attend Harvey Mudd College located in the same state. Parsi met Day[9] at one of his LAN events, and they became friends. Thus, Parsi spent a great deal of time going over strategies with Day[9]. A LAN event allows players to exchange strategies within a preselected group of participants. Participants can exchange quick pointers. LAN events are also platforms on which participants can identify their practice partners. Parsi recounted how lucky he was to find practice partners who were pro-gamers:

> The real challenge for any player [who wants to compete at the highest level] is getting noticed, and getting good practice partners. I think there's definitely a sort of elitism among the top tier of players and they're hesitant to open up to new players and players that they don't know.

Players like the pro-gamers are entrenched in close-knit teams to sharpen their practices. Pro-gamers tend to prefer practice with other top players in Battle.net, or those whom had won tournaments.

Unfortunately, professional players congregating within tight-knit teams may accumulate knowledge that is hidden from the public media. Players like BoxeR had surprised spectators with novel strategies they had practiced in secret. In the next section, we examine how these strategies, as soon as they come to light at major tournaments, get analyzed and taken apart by the StarCraft community.

Theorycrafting: Video, Casters, and Writers

In video games, *theorycrafting* describes the process in which players reveal the game's mechanics [25]. The StarCraft community has performed much theorycrafting based on analysis of professional matches. These contents are presented in formats allowable by media technologies including Internet TVs, video on demand, online forums, and wikis. For a majority of players outside the boundaries of pro-gaming partnerships, these media can be powerful resources for learning the game. Consider how this SC player, "re dir," describes on an online forum his mind-blowing experience watching a match casted by Day[9]:

> My entire view of StarCraft, has just been flipped on its head, talk about a major paradigm shift. Beyond the unit composition, nothing seemed really out of place. Then I went on to watch [the same game casted by] Day[9]. To be frank it blew my mind. I completely overlooked [the professional player's] game plan. The things he did that seemed so unusual, now made perfect sense. I would watch a battle, and suddenly remember that I had already seen it, but it was strange, I was looking at it from such a different perspective. [8]

In StarCraft, the casters' analyses help reveal a strategy's hidden rationales. Day[9] is a popular caster because he had revealed much metagame unknown to common players.

Theorycrafting helps advance the overall knowledge level of the StarCraft community. An example comes from how StarCraft players have interacted with their keyboards. Players who can think fast, but who are unable to issue these commands on time, are unable to win matches. As such, a player's interaction with his keyboard became an important aspect of the StarCraft metagame.

In StarCraft, the keyboard keys "1" to "10" are shortcuts that can be used to quickly select units and buildings. In Day9TV's video titled "Mental Checklist: Exercises!," Day[9] suggests that players use keys "2" to "6" for the most commonly selected units and buildings [28]. These keys are most easily accessed by our left hand fingers, see Figure 3.

In the earliest days of Brood War, StarCraft players had commonly used only the mice to control every action in the game—a slow and inefficient process; however, keyboard practices are now widely known, thanks to theorycrafting by members like Day[9].

Theorycrafting produces a range of media, such as videos, forum posts, and wiki articles. Interestingly, the utility of these media for learning did not weigh evenly among StarCraft players. For example, Elly, a Platinum league player, did not read online forums and wikis for strategies:

> Sometimes I read wikis, but never the forums. I don't feel—I don't gain anything from them. Well, sometimes I'll read the original posts because they'll have an interesting build order, or they say, "Oh, I watched this game and it had a really cool build order, let me list it out for you so you can copy it." But the replies and stuff, I don't feel they're useful.

Elly found online forums and wikis useful only for researching build orders, which is similar to a procedural list of things-to-do. Build orders worked only in the first few minutes of a StarCraft match, where the opponents had not met in battles, and when game events were relatively predictable; however, as a match goes on, written procedures become less useful as game events become contingent on both players' actions and reactions.

Figure 3 Keyboard numeric keys that align well with our left hand middle fingers [3]

There are exceptions to how texts may describe complex strategies. An article, titled "The Marginal Advantage" and written by Day[9], discusses the general idea that each practice, e.g., keyboard management and build order, only confer a very small advantage to a player [29]. While each practice alone may seem inconsequential to the outcome of a StarCraft match, these practices, when orchestrated together, differentiate the winner from the loser.

Experienced players like Elly had generally relied on screencasts, rather than textual discourses of StarCraft strategies:

> The best part is you see the game. A screencast is like you actually have a teacher almost. With Day[9], he can pause a replay, he can point out things on a replay, or in a tournament he can just on the fly tell you what's behind the strategy in his experience. In many ways, people really like casters who can help them learn.

Screencasts contain videos, which are able to showcase how strategies are contingent upon match conditions, rather than procedural and stepwise. While players are watching how pro-gamers are reacting to these contingencies, casters are able to verbalize strategies that are not obvious to viewers. As a result, video-based technologies become extensions to text-based technologies when it comes to support learning among experienced players.

Other Interest Groups in StarCraft

Teamliquid contains other interest groups on the periphery of its competitive scene. These groups include the editing and melee mapmaking teams. These are highly-specialized interest groups embedded within a community, in which discourse is accented by professional competitions.

Teamliquid has an editing team that produces long articles. These articles discuss pro-gamers, tournaments, notable matches, StarCraft history, and game strategies. For example, Day[9]'s article, "The Marginal Advantage," was a product of this team. Its chief editor, known by his alias Waxangel, handpicked most of his team members among online forum posters, in particular those who were well-liked and actively contributing:

> We have people who are very, very detail oriented and want things to be very specific. We have people who are very laid back and very big picture. Honestly, it's just like, having a passion for StarCraft, being able to work hard on important things and just getting along, really, with the rest of the people who are already on staff. I can't really measure what a good personality is, but if you get along with a lot of other people on our staff, then you're probably someone everyone is going to like.

Like practice partners, the editing team is not opened to just anyone who had signed up. Players who want to become editors or writers have to first contribute actively and voluntarily in the online forums. They also had to show the ability to interact cordially with other Teamliquid members. Teamliquid editors and writers interact away from public media, in a private online forum.

Melee maps are StarCraft maps that are designed specifically for competitions. These maps differ from other type of StarCraft maps, which are essentially StarCraft mods containing games that have nothing to do with the eSports scene. The melee mapmaking community was active in Teamliquid, and contributed to the StarCraft metagame. For example, BoxeR's success with dropships was relying on his knowledge of maps, particularly the covert flight routes. The melee mapmakers designed these maps to balance the way maps would favor such well-known strategies.

Anyone who has an interest in melee mapmaking can discuss issues in the Teamliquid online forum, but the best melee mapmakers also joined one of the two teams, namely ESV and TPW. Skype provides a feature for users to invite other users into private chat channels known as Skype Conversations. A Conversation channel remains online, with its chats archived, even when channel members have logged off Skype. Members of ESV and TPW interact mostly in private Skype Conversations. An award-winning mapmaker from team ESV, known by his alias Superouman, told us, "99% of our discussions are on Skype [Conversation]."

Superouman discussed how ESV had tended to recruit only the most skilled and committed mapmakers as members:

> I can't remember even one person in a team who didn't post some maps on Teamliquid. I'd prefer determined people who would like to continue to make map for a long time. I'd also like people who take suggestions into consideration. I remember some people [in the online forums] who always ignored people's advices and even sometimes claimed they were better than the more experienced people. Everyone dislikes them.

Like practice partnerships and the editing team, melee mapmaking teams have selected members who are equally knowledgeable, equally committed, and likely to work well with others.

DISCUSSION

In this paper, we identified social-technical formations that support learning within the StarCraft community. Despite the availability of media technologies like online forums supporting mass communication and interaction, experts of the StarCraft metagame have socialized deep within private groups, such as practice partnerships, editing teams, and melee mapmaking teams. Yet, the mass media are not without learning functions. They facilitate knowledge dissemination to amateur players, so that the community as a whole becomes more knowledgeable along with the experts.

Our findings expose two functions of media technologies supporting this necessary structure of learning, comprising general learners socializing in public media on the one hand, and the highly-committed expert learners socializing in private media on the other. These functions include: (1) to convert knowledge into symbolic representations accessible by general learners, and (2) to support social practices among private groups of experts.

From Knowledge to Information: Informational media

Expert gamers, mapmakers, or editors were practicing within private social groups. At the periphery of these expert groups, *informational media* are primary sources of information useful to general learners. One unexpected, but nonetheless important, function of informational media is to entertain and encapsulate a large pool of novices to participate in common discourses within a media platform. StarCraft players like Zhang were encapsulated within the discourses of professional game play shown on Internet TV, thus eager to learn StarCraft and its metagame.

Textual media like online forums and wikis are unable to represent the full spectrum of information needed by experts like Sen; however, they are still useful in stating factual and procedural information useful to budding players. Players like Elly had occasionally used online forums to keep up to date with emerging build orders.

General learners had used public media like Internet TV and video on demand for learning StarCraft strategies. In video replays of StarCraft matches, players analyzed how professional gamers had responded to a myriad of contingency situations otherwise difficult to textualize. Digital videos are mutable artifacts. Screen casters can overlay commentaries over video streams, or pause, replay, rewind, and slow down video segments, which had helped players like "re dir" analyze a match from different perspectives. Elly suggested that Day[9] was almost like a teacher in his screencasts.

Public media, like online forums, are mostly unregulated mass-communication platforms [15]. In StarCraft, players from the levels of Bronze to Grand Masters can respond to forum discussions. Forum posts by unskilled players may not be helpful to other forum users. The experts of the StarCraft community kept their deep discourses away from these crowds, and within private groups.

From Information to Knowledge: Socially-oriented media

In-depth learning is a highly social process because knowledge resides within contexts containing our physical practices, mental practices, and technological artifacts [36,26]. The social presence of experts is important to learners, as experts can provide instantaneous guidance and feedback, which help learners solve incrementally harder problems—a necessary process of learning [40]. In this respect, a class of *socially-oriented media* facilitates social learning among experts in the StarCraft learning ecology.

Socially-oriented media are technologies which are designed to support online social interactions among a selected group of users. The purpose of socially-oriented media is to sustain small group interactions among learners, so that each learner may receive ample support and guidance from other learners. In close proximity, whether through on-site or online presence, experts benefitted from learning from other experts.

Socially-oriented media are not strictly social media. For example, many social media, like online forums and wikis, are public media open to anyone. Also, the Battle.net was designed to facilitate online competition, but was actually socially-oriented and supported the most pervasive type of social learning in StarCraft. Players like Ko had used its automatic matchmaking feature to find practice partners. In other words, whether a technology is actually a socially-oriented medium or not depends on the function it serves, rather than on its form.

For advanced players like Duran and Day[9], actual practices had happened during LAN events. LAN events as invitational events have informal membership boundaries, but nonetheless are targeted at the experts or their affiliates. For expert mapmakers and editors, private chat channels provide enclosures where they can engage in deep discussions with other experts. Mapmakers like Superouman had used private Skype Conversation extensively when working on his maps. Private channels are social tools because crowds' opinions, whether they are uninformative or unruly, are filtered away from these interactive spaces. Within private teams, professional gamers develop new practices, such as keyboard interaction methods. Socially-oriented media construct enclosures in which learning and knowledge deepen within silos of experts.

Mobilizing Media Technologies for Mediated Communities of Practice

Unlike the novices who learned from mass media, many StarCraft experts learn in private media and from other experts. Some of our informants are members of gaming teams in other games, e.g., Warcraft III. And competitive gamers commonly migrate between popular eSport games. Thus, we believe that the learning structure we have identified is prevalent at least among interest-driven communities of competitive games.

This social-technical formation—of experts learning in small groups within online communities—is of interest to human-computer interaction. Technically speaking, media technologies have enabled any Internet user to collaborate with any other users they like, i.e., "everyone is connected." Yet, our findings have shown that small group practices have remained important to experts, even with the availability of mass media like online forums and wiki [12].

Learners who become experts do not just rely on their technical skills. Embodied within their interactions with others are social values embraced by other experts. In practice, teams commonly admit only members who are able to socialize with others, and are open to criticism. Good learners who also display these virtues are welcome by teams, and subsequently gain cumulative advantages by leveraging the opportunity of peer-based learning within these teams. This learning activity operates outside the purview of informational media.

The social formation—of experts socializing with other experts in spaces inaccessible to novices—is not wholly different from what is described in "legitimate peripheral participation." Wenger et al. [37] provide examples where novice learners were kept out of workspaces of the experts. These experts will share stories of what happened in these workspaces after the fact. When experts socialize using socially-oriented media, such social formations are recreated in a networked environment.

Another finding of interest is that the relative advantages of those who are privileged enough to learn in private teams suggest a new inequality in learning opportunities even on the Internet. We cannot blame the experts for developing knowledge behind closed doors. We may think that money corrupts, that professional gamers need the secrecy to maintain their competitive edge, but we have observed the same formations even among volunteers in the editing and mapmaking teams. This shows that other factors, such as small group learning being the effective and preferred way to learn for motivated learners, are influencing these social-technical formations.

A solution to this knowledge divide is to query the possibility of motivating experts to contribute information to mass media. Reputation is one major motivator of online participation [14]. And we may design systems that reward experts with compelling forms of reputation. In this respect, reputation research studies in HCI have often been framed from an information receiver's perspective: How does a user know that a piece of information given by a stranger on the Internet is reliable (see [17,31])? In this question, the information contributor takes the form of a member of the nameless "crowd," whose opinion is to be suspected. But, for the purpose of motivating experts to contribute to mass media, the research question ought to be framed from the information contributor's perspective: How can we design reputation systems that attract experts' contributions? For example, some experts may be more motivated if that reputation carries with it monetary rewards, or its equivalents, that may transform voluntary contributions into a career [19].

Corporations nurturing virtual communities should consider providing both socially-oriented and informational media to support collaboration and learning. Large-scale collaboration is not just everyone talking in the same room, but also involves experts of different interests reflecting on different facets of a community's predicaments [10]. For example, while HCI experts in a company may deepen their practices by receiving peer-to-peer support from other HCI professionals, they can also contribute information to more open forums that help management, design, and marketing professionals acquire basic HCI knowledge.

Although experts are key actors producing new knowledge, the common periphery, a public social space populated by mostly novices, is equally important to sustain learning. The periphery is where information, which experts divulge intentionally or unintentionally, diffuses into public media. The periphery is where novices may become experts, earn memberships to teams, and improve further. Expert teams are not self-sustainable, but require an influx of new experts into their memberships. From this perspective, public media are catchment media that nurture, identify, and attract potential participants into the specialized teams. The public is a relative term. To a pro-gamer, a melee mapmaker who is not a qualified practice partner is a member of the public. Thus, the periphery, the public, is also cross-pollinating knowledge between specialized groups—nurturing the learning ecology.

CONCLUSION

In this research, we anchored our interviews and observations to an interest-driven activity, and examined varying media technologies as community support tools. We found that experts do not generally pay attention to every novice participating in Internet communities. Public media, which are mass media in essence, provide for the needs of general learners. In contrast, experts had quite unequivocally opted to learn in small groups.

Based on these findings, we identified two classes of media technologies. The first is informational media, which are powerful public media that draw novices to participate in learning practices. Informational media can also re-represent complex information into formats that are accessible by novices. The second is socially-oriented media, which support the development of private channels where experts can engage in intense interaction and learning. These private channels allow for intimate social learning where knowledge deepens and is stored within the silos of experts.

ACKNOWLEDGMENTS

We thank all StarCraft community participants who have provided valuable support in the process of our study. We are very grateful to the anonymous reviewers for their encouraging remarks, which motivate us to deepen the content of this paper. And many thanks to Tri Choontanom, Ruy Cervantes, Sharon Ding, Adam Ingram-Goble, Mimi Ito, Bonnie Nardi, and Bryan Semann for their valuable critiques on early versions of this paper. This research is supported by the Singapore National Research Foundation under its International Research Centre @ Singapore Funding Initiative and administered by the IDM Program Office. We also acknowledge the grant (#1097-572-000-USP) from the John D and Catherine T. MacArthur Foundation that supported this research.

REFERENCES

1 Benkler, Y. *The Wealth of Networks: How Social Production Transforms Markets and Freedom.* Yale University Press, London, 2006.

2 BLIP NETWORKS. *Discover the best in original web series.* http://blip.tv/about, 2012.

3 BobYoMeowMeow. *Korean Gamers: APM Demonstration.* http://www.youtube.com/watch?v=YbpCLqryN-Q&feature=related, 2010.

4 Bodker, S and Andersen, P. Complex Mediation. *Human-Computer Interaction*, 20 (2005).

5 Bryant, S., Forte, A., and Bruckman, A. Becoming Wikipedian: Transformation of Participation in a Collaborative Online Encyclopedia. In *GROUP'05* (2005), ACM Press.

6 Cervantes, R and Nardi, B. Building a Mexican startup culture over the weekends. In *ICIC* (2012), ACM Press.

7 Cheung, G and Huang, J. Starcraft from the Stands: Understanding the Game Spectator. In *CHI'11* (Vancouver, Canada 2011), ACM Press.

8 dir, r. *Paradigm Shift.* http://sc2armory.com/forums/topic/21321, 2011.

9 Engeström, Y. Expansive Learning at Work: Toward an activity theoretical reconceptualization. *Journal of Education and Work, 14:1* (2001).

10 Fischer, G. From Reflective Practitioners to Reflective Communities. In *HCI International 2005* (Las Vegas 2005), Lawrence Erlbaum Associates.

11 Garfield, R. Metagames. In *Horsemen of the Apocalyse: Essays on Roleplaying*. Jolly Roger Games, 2000.

12 Goggins, S, Laffey, J, and Gallagher, M. Completely Online Group Formation And Development: Small Groups As Socio-Technical Systems. *Information Technology & People*, 24, 2 (2011).

13 Hung, D. Theories of Learning and Computer-Mediated Instructional Technologies. *Educational Media International* (2001).

14 Ito, M. Amateur Media Production in Networked Ecology. In *Computer Supported Cooperative Work, Planetary Keynote* (Savannah, Georgia 2010), ACM Press.

15 Ito, M. Networked Publics. Introduction. In *Networked Publics*. MIT Press, Massachusetts, 2008.

16 Jin, D. *Korea's Online Gaming Empire*. MIT Press, Massachusetts, 2010.

17 Jøsang, A, Ismail, R, and Boyd, C. A Survey of Trust and Reputation Systems for Online Service Provision. *Decision Support Systems, 43(2)* (2007).

18 Kittur, A and Kraut, R. Beyond Wikipedia: Coordination and Conflict in Online Production Group. In *CSCW'10* (Savannah, Georgia 2010), ACM Press.

19 Kow, Y and Nardi, B. Mediating Contradictions of Digital Media. *UC Irvine Law Review, 2 (2)* (2012).

20 Lave, J and Wenger, E. *Situated Learning: Legitimate Peripheral Participation*. Cambridge University Press, Cambridge, 1991.

21 Lim, Y. *Crazy As Me. Translated by Marencielo.* http://www.teamliquid.net/forum/viewmessage.php?topic_id=288614, 2004.

22 LIQUIPEDIA. *Bonjwa.* http://wiki.teamliquid.net/starcraft/Bonjwa, 2012.

23 LIQUIPEDIA. *Metagame.* http://wiki.teamliquid.net/starcraft/Metagame, 2012.

24 Meco. *Battle.net.* http://starcraft.wikia.com/wiki/Battle.net, 2012.

25 Nardi, B and Choontanom, T. Theorycrafting: The Art and Science of Using Numbers to Interpret the World. In *Games, Learning, and Society: Learning and Meaning in the Digital Age*. Cambridge University Press, Cambridge, 2012.

26 Nonaka, I and Nishiguchi, T. *Knowledge Emergence: Social, Technical, and Evolutionary Dimensions of Knowledge Creation*. Oxford University Press, Oxford, 2001.

27 Paavola, S, Lipponen, L, and Hakkarainen, K. Epistemological Foundations for CSCL: A Comparison of Three Models of Innovative Knowledge Communities. In *CSCL'02* (2002), International Society of the Learning Sciences.

28 Plott, S. *Day[9] Daily #360 P1 - Mental Checklist: Exercises!* http://blip.tv/day9tv/day-9-daily-360-p1-mental-checklist-exercises-5635566, 2011.

29 Plott, S. *The Marginal Advantage.* http://www.teamliquid.net/forum/viewmessage.php?topic_id=64514, 2007.

30 ProGamingTours.net. *2011 Best Paying eSports.* http://www.progamingtours.net/index.php?/StarCraft-2/best-esports-2011.html, 2012.

31 Resnick, P, Zeckhauser, R, Friedman, E, and Kuwabara, K. Reputation Systems. *Communications of the ACM, 43 (12)* (2000).

32 Salen, K and Zimmerman, E. *Rules of Play: Game Design Fundamentals*. MIT Press, Massachussetts, 2004.

33 Tuomi, I. *Networks of Innovation*. Oxford University Press, Oxford, 2006.

34 TWITCHTV. *TwitchTV Partner Program.* http://www.twitch.tv/partner/signup, 2012.

35 Vygotsky, L. *Mind in Society: The Development of Higher Psychological Processes*. Harvard University Press, Cambridge, MA, 1978.

36 Vygotsky, L. *Thought and Language*. The MIT Press, Cambridge, 1986.

37 Wenger, E. *Communities of practice: Learning, meaning, and identity*. Cambridge University Press, Cambridge, 1998.

38 Wenger, E, McDermott, R, and Synder, W. *Cultivating Communities of Practice*. Harvard Business School Press, Boston, 2002.

39 Wenger, E, White, N, and Smith, J. *Digital Habitats: Stewarding Technology for Communities*. CPsquare, Portland, 2009.

40 Zinchenko, V. Developing Activity Theory: The Zone of Proximal Development and Beyond. In *Context and Consciousness*. The MIT Press, Cambridge, 1996.

Functional or Social? Exploring Teams in Online Games

Yun Huang, Wenyue Ye, Nicholas Bennett
Northwestern University
2240 Campus Drive, 1-459
Evanston, IL 60208, U.S.A
{yun,wenyueye2012,nick}@northwestern.edu

Noshir S. Contractor
Northwestern University
2145 Sheridan RD, TECH D241
Evanston, IL 60208, U.S.A
nosh@northwestern.edu

ABSTRACT
Team collaboration in multi-player online games provides opportunities for players to interact with each other. Facilitating teams has become one of the main design principles to increase social activities. However, there is no research evidence that collaborating on tasks in game teams can produce the desired relational outcome. This paper examines more than half a million solo and team activities during a week in *Dragon Nest*, an MMO game. We measure the degree of team engagement using the percentage of time played in teams and the percentage of play with repeated teammates, and we then identify different types of players using this. The results show that solo players and team players are two distinct populations and they are highly predictable based on players' in-game status. Moreover, we find that spending more time in teams does not always lead to more social interactions. The interviews with players are conducted to validate the findings.

Author Keywords
Online games; MMORPG; team engagement; team collaboration; network sociality; solo player.

ACM Classification Keywords
H.5.m. Information interfaces and presentation (e.g., HCI): Miscellaneous.

INTRODUCTION
Massively multiplayer online role playing games (MMORPGs) create an immersive virtual environment for players to experience intellectual challenges and make it possible for players to socially interact. Compared to traditional video games, team collaboration or confrontation in combat activities is an important game mechanism to create social dynamics among players and increase the user stickiness and loyalty of the game.

In online games, players are self-organized into teams (also called knots [4]) to accomplish challenging tasks and fulfill common goals in a short period of time. According to Activity Focus Theory [5], the team tasks and goals act as the common foci and catalyze relation building. As a consequence of team activities, individuals involved are more likely to develop interpersonal relations since they are more exposed to each other. Therefore, promoting team activities has become one of the primary design goals in many online games.

On the other hand, different from social groups, Wittel [19] suggested that short-term teams and visual communities are a type of network sociality, in which "social relations are not 'narrational' but informational." Short-term projects, flexible tasks, and increasing turnover make it difficult to develop a common narrative. A good team player should have the ability to establish relations on a task-by-task basis and help achieve a higher performance. Tasks are both the goal of, and the reason for, the existence of task teams. For example, players may form groups with randomly selected teammates for one-time quests. Once the task is accomplished, teams will disband and individuals are free to join other teams. These pickup groups (PUGs) may not induce enduring bonding relationships.

In order to understand the true nature of teamwork and social environments in game, we need to characterize the patterns of team activities in game. By exploring different types of players and their team activities, we try to answer a fundamental question: Why does a player choose to join a team vs. play solo?

This paper examines more than half a million solo and team activities extracted from one week of server logs in Dragon Nest, an MMO game. By characterizing solo and team players, we connect players' in-game status with their teamwork behavior. Based on two measures of team engagement, the percentage of time played in teams and the percentage of play with repeated teammates, we explore functional-oriented and social-oriented players and evaluate the outcomes of in-game incentives for team collaboration.

RELATED WORK

Communities vs. Network Sociality
German sociologist Ferdinand Tonnies described two ideal types of human society, community and association (*Gemeinschaft und Gesellschaft* in German), in 1887 [15]. *Gemeinschaft* is a social group based on personal relations and a common basis of traditional social mores. In contrast, *gesellschaft* characterizes associations that consist of rational and self-interested individual. Relationships in

CSCW '13, February 23–27, 2013, San Antonio, Texas, USA.

these associations are usually impersonal and indirect compared to persistent social bonds such as family and friendship based face-to-face interactions.

In the physical world, communities and associations usually overlap: people in one community can form many associations and individuals in a business association can develop social relations based on face-to-face interactions. However, advanced information and communication technologies (ICTs) have facilitated a new form of virtual associations such as online communities, short-term task-oriented teams, and new media. In these groups, relations are primarily informational and based on ephemeral exchange of data. Wittel [8] considered short-term teams and visual communities as network sociality, in which "social relations are not 'narrational' but informational." The functional features of network sociality such as short-term projects, flexible tasks, and increasing turnover make it difficult to develop long-lasting social ties.

Task and Project Teams

ICT-enabled task or project teams enable collaborations with others worldwide [8, 13]. Individuals are self-organized into groups based on common interests or activities [1, 5, 10] such as scientific research [7] and open source software (OSS) [6]. They have the freedom to choose what they work on and with whom they work according to their interests and expertise. After finishing team activities or tasks, teams are dissolved and individuals do not have to maintain relations with previous teammates.

Although virtual teams are short-term and task-oriented, many studies find that social relations and interactions do exist in such teams. For example, Crowston et. al. [2] find that people in OSS teams meet in-person and speed up certain kinds of tasks. Readers of Ms. Nielson's blog developed strong bonds with her and helped fund-raising after a plane crash [18].

Teams and Social Interactions in Games

Players frequently group together forming a type of task teams to finish challenging tasks in game. Only a few studies examine players' social interactions and validate whether the interactions in game teams have relational meaning for the participants.

Ducheneaut et al [3] is the first quantitative study using in-game data to explore social interactions in MMORPGs and found that online games are less social than people expected. They posit that this is because players are exposed to a social environment but not engaged in social dynamics. Using records collected by data scripting, they found that many World of Warcraft (WoW) players do not join groups before they reach level 55 and they only team up for difficult endgame dungeons. However, because data scripting techniques do not capture the team composition and actual player relations, their study focuses more on the impact of guilds, i.e. in-game player organizations, and provides limited information about task teams in game.

Nardi and Harris [11] enumerate different types of collaborative play in WoW such as parties, raids, friends, and guilds in an immersive ethnographic study. They find that raw time is a problematic metric for capturing sociability while informal collaborations such as chatting and PvP (Player versus Player) play are key aspects of socializing in WoW. This reveals that function-oriented measures such as play time contribute much less to players' social interactions than narrational activities do.

Some research studies player collaboration in different types of games. Xu et al. [20] explore the meaning of social relationships in Halo 3, a First-Person Shooter games. Qualitative interviews and game match records suggest that people tend to connect to a small set of offline friends and family members. On the other hand, participants played with 93% of playmates only once. McEwan et al. [9] study social dynamics and sociality in PlayOK, an online casual game site. Their analysis of game records show that although the site seems very social with many activities and subgroups, the population is highly transient without any social history or interaction: most people stay for only a few days, engage in very little verbal communication, and consistently play with new and unknown partners only once.

However, Halo 3 and PlayOK do not provide an immersive game world and corresponding team structures as there are in MMORPGs. Players have different motivations and they are more likely to compete against each other as opponents than to collaborate on specific tasks.

Motivations of Game Play

Yee [21] categorizes the player motivations into three overarching components: achievement, social, and immersion. The natures of team collaboration in MMORPGs illustrate two sides of task teams: functional and social. Playing in teams allows players to progress more rapidly and optimize their performance, and thereby fulfill the advancement and mechanics factors in the achievement component [21]. On the other hand, teams act as a special mechanism to bring players together to support the social component by: having an interest in helping others (i.e. socializing), deriving satisfaction from being part of a group effort (i.e. teamwork), and the desire to form long-term meaningful relationships (i.e. relationship).It is not clear, however, how the two sides are connected in task teams.

TEAMS IN DRAGON NEST

Dragon Nest is an action-oriented MMORPG developed by Eyedentity, a South Korean game developer. As a free-to-play game, Dragon Nest has been released in eight countries including South Korea, Japan, China, the United States, and other countries in South East Asia since 2010. Operated by Shanda Games Limited, the Chinese version of Dragon Nest hosts over 400,000 concurrent users with ten million dollars of in-game purchases per month according to THISISGAME, a Korean game news site.

In Dragon Nest, players create characters, explore the virtual land of Lagendia, fight evil dragons, and find power stones that enable them to communicate with the sleeping goddess and save the world. As in many multiple player online games, characters have four distinct classes: warrior, archer, sorceress, and cleric. The classes are designed to have unique skills and equipment and to play different roles in team: as tanks, warriors have strong physical attack ability and specialize in defense; as damage dealers, archers make long-range attacks and move while attacking; as debuffers, sorceresses have medium-range spells and inflict a variety of harmful spells; as healers, clerics heal and protect others in their team. Characters can play alone or in a small team in instanced (the team interacts privately with the environment) dungeons to fight dangerous monsters, earn experience points, and advance their levels.

Incentives of Teamwork

Unlike other MMORPGs, Dragon Nest encourages teamwork for players at any - not just high - level and has implemented two unique design mechanisms to promote team collaborations: multiple task difficulties and fatigue points for game play.

In Dragon Nest, task difficulty is an option to make dungeons progressively harder. Players can select the difficulty of each dungeon before entering it. Five types of difficulties are available for most tasks in the game, in order of difficulty: easy, normal, hard, master, and abyss. Difficult tasks have more monsters and result in better outcomes, and therefore may need more players. Easy and normal tasks are for solo players; a team of 2 is recommended for hard tasks and a team of 4 for master and abyss. The difficulty mechanism provides open choices for team settings. Any character, even at entry levels, can choose to play alone at easy/normal task difficulty, or choose to form a team for higher difficulty types and consequently better outcomes. They also have the option to play solo for abyss difficulty and team up for easy difficulty.

Moreover, Dragon Nest uses a fatigue point system to introduce costs for engaging in dungeon tasks. Every character is assigned 700 fatigue points per day and spends a certain amount of points to engage in each dungeon activity. Higher level and more difficult dungeon activities require more fatigue points. Players cannot enter dungeon activities after running out of points. In order to use the points more efficiently and play more activities, players can join a team and pay fewer points for the same activity compared to what they would pay if they engaged in it as a solo activity. For example, a dungeon requiring 40 points for a solo player only costs 17 point per person for a team of four. Since players spend fewer points in larger teams, the fatigue point system encourages players to form teams to reduce the cost of play.

Dragon Nest uses a few routine game interfaces to facilitate forming teams, choices of task difficulties, and consumptions of fatigue points, and therefore reinforces the two mechanisms designed to facilitate team formation. For example, as shown in Figure 1, players need to decide whether to join a team (called a party in game) each time they enter a dungeon.

Figure 1: Pop-up window with "Find Party" each time entering fields.

Data Set

Because all teams are freely formed and have similar sizes (i.e. from 2 to 4), Dragon Nest provides a simplified environment to explore the nature of team activities in online games and evaluate the effectiveness of designing mechanisms to facilitate team activities. We acquired from Shanda three months of server logs of the Chinese version of the game. To avoid local holiday and school schedules, we chose the 4th week of February in 2011 as the sampling period, i.e. February 22nd to 28th, 2011. We identified all 35,057 player characters in the population who registered before February 21st, 2011 and played during the sampling week. For each player, we measured their levels, classes, guild status, and numbers of friends on February 21st, 2011.

ID	Level	Class	In guild	Gender
P1	50 [a]	Sorceress	Y	Female
P2	31	Warrior	N	Male
P3	35	Archer	N	Male
P4	60 [a]	Warrior	Y	Male
P5	50 [a]	Cleric	Y	Male
P6	40	Archer	Y	Female
P7	36	Warrior	N	Male
P8	60 [a]	Cleric	Y	Male
P9	16	Sorceress	N	Female

[a]. Top-level has been increased to 60 since our data snapshot.

Table 1: Information of nine interviewees.

To characterize the nature of team play and reveal potential player motivations, we apply mixed research methods. First, employing the "social accounting" techniques used in previous studies, e.g. [3, 9], we identified all solo and team combat activities in the sample population within the sampling week from player vs. environment (PvE) logs. In each combat activity, one player or a team of up to four players enter a dungeon instance and kill monsters in a finite amount of time. Since the id number of each dungeon instance (or activity) is unique, we can separate solo and team activities and recover the team membership. Second, we interview 9 players in the game with open ended and rating questions and use their opinions to validate our findings. The basic information of the interviewees is included in Table 1.

TEAM COMPOSITION AND TEAM ENGAGEMENT IN DRAGON NEST

Among 568,763 combat activities identified, 82% involve only one player, 4.6% are completed by teams of two, 2.0% are teams of three, and 11.3% are teams of four.

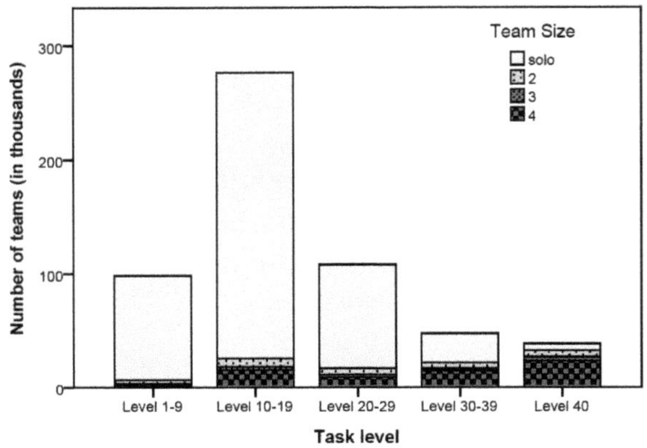

Figure 2: Numbers of teams by task level and team size.

Usually in each combat activity, a player or a team tries to finish a task at a level that matches with the player's level. Figure 2 shows the detailed distribution of solo and team activities by levels of tasks involved and team sizes. In general, there are more team activities for higher level tasks. For example, there are only 6,338 teams for tasks at Level 1-9 but 32,368 teams worked on level 40 tasks. Alongside this disparity in team activity, the decrease in the number of solo player activities in high level tasks is very dramatic. There are only 6,059 solo activities for Level 40 tasks compared to 251,289 for Level 10-19 tasks.

At all levels, setting aside solo players, the team of size 4 is the dominant team type. Because more fatigue points are needed for high level tasks, especially at level 40, playing in a big team is a more efficient way to maximize the return of investment (in terms of outcomes) on individual fatigue points.

As mentioned earlier, to promote team activities, each task offers five types of difficulties for different team sizes. Figure 3 shows the detailed distribution of solo and team activities according to task difficulties.

Although the recommended team sizes for normal, hard, master, and abyss tasks are 1, 2, 4, and 4, respectively, Figure 3 shows that the vast majority of teams are formed for abyss tasks and there are only a few team activities for other difficulties. It is clear that most teams are outcome driven and only focus on highest payoffs at abyss difficulty. Still, solo players account for more than a quarter of the abyss activities. Comparing to the distribution of solo activities by task levels shown in Figure 2, we find that many high level players solo for abyss versions of low level tasks to get some easy points and attractive items.

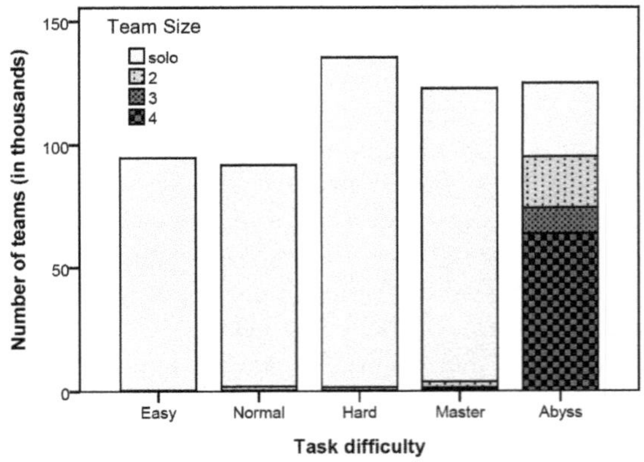

Figure 3: Numbers of teams by task difficulty and team size.

Team Engagement

Of the 35,057 player characters active during the sampling period only some were involved in team collaboration. In order to estimate their levels of team engagement in the game, we develop two measures: the percentage of time spent playing in teams and the percentage of play with repeated teammates.

Percentage of time in teams

The percentage of time in teams is defined as time played in teams of 2, 3, or 4 divided by all play time spent on Player versus Environment (PvE) activities. This time-based measure of team engagement has been used in many studies such as [3].

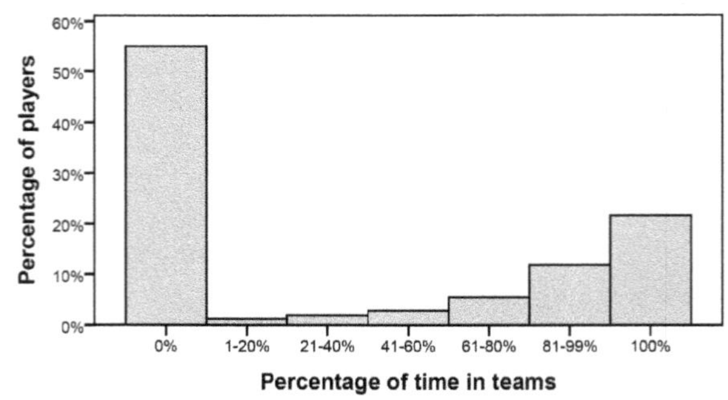

Figure 4: Numbers of players by the percentage of time played in teams (N=35,057).

In Figure 4, the histogram of the percentage of time in teams reveals a polarized player population: 55% of players spent 0% time in teams and 21.6% of players spent 100% time in teams. Only 23.4% players play both solo and in teams. The lack of intermediate population, especially the players who spent 1-60% time in teams, indicates that the solo and team players are two distinct populations and solo players do not evolve into playing with others gradually. Instead, it seems that there is a phase shift in team engagement: many users are mostly solo players and only some switch over to become active team players at some point. One possible explanation is that teams are designed for difficult tasks: after finishing the easy, soloable tasks players need to spend a lot of time teaming for difficult ones. We will validate this hypothesis by looking at player levels in the next section.

Percentage of repeated teammates

While the time measure of engagement captures amount of time in teams, it does not capture if there is a strong relational quality that might develop in teams [11]. Hence we also investigated players' team engagement from a relational perspective. There are 15,773 characters who played in at least one team, i.e. spent more than 0% time in teams, and some of them played with the same teammates many times. The percentage of repeated teammates over all distinct teammates reveals whether players tend to play in teams with prior teammates (stronger relational quality) or with strangers: 100% of repeated teammates indicates that a person plays with each of his or her teammates together in at least two team activities and 0% of repeated teammates indicates that a person never plays with others more than once.

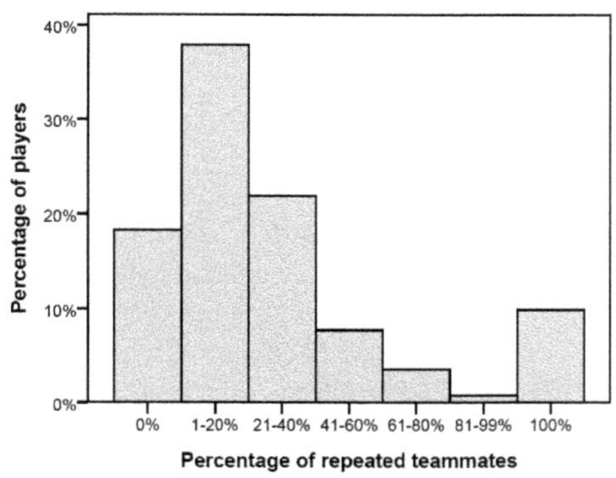

Figure 5: Player distribution by the ratio of repeated teammates (N=15,773).

Similar to the distribution pattern of the time based measure of team engagement, there are two extreme types of team players: 9.9% of players who always play with prior teammates (i.e. 100% repeated teammates) and 18.3% of players who play with strangers all the time (i.e. 0% repeated teammates).

All our interviewees joined pick up groups (PUG, teams formed by game mechanism) in game and P1 and P3 even spent 80% time in PUGs. They all agreed that "must finish a specific dungeon/quest" is the main reason for joining a PUG. When they have some specific tasks, it is easy and fast to use in-game tools to find players with the same interests and work together. PUGs become the most efficient way if you cannot finish a task alone. Interviewee P1 said,

"Even in the same guild, people have different online time. If somebody in my guild needs to do the same quest, we can play together. However, usually we cannot find the same time. Moreover, people need different things. So most of time I played in pick-up teams ... Teaming with guild members is more fun since we can talk while doing quests. Pick-up groups are just to finish tasks." (P1)

Clearly not all teams produce repeated interactions. Because of PUGs and one-time matching, even though 45% of the population played in teams at least once, the players with repeated relations are not as high as expected. This confirms the relational finding suggested in [11]: spending more time in teams does not necessarily mean having more frequent social interactions with others.

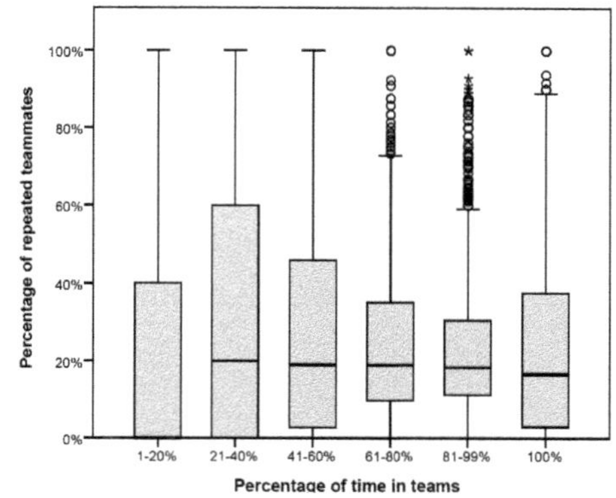

Figure 6: Percentage of repeated teammates by percentage of time in teams (N=15,773).

It is interesting that the relational measure of team engagement is not correlated to the time based measure of team engagement. Figure 6 shows that five player groups who spend from 20% to 100% of their game time in teams (indicated by the 2nd to 6th box plots) have the similar medians of the percentage of repeated teammates around 20%. These results suggest that spending more time in teams does not increase the likelihood of playing with others repeatedly, which show that team time and repeated teammates are two distinct perspectives in measuring players' interactions in teams. As a very clear example, the 1st box plot, i.e. players who spend less than 20% of their play time in teams, has a median at 0% because half of them only play once in teams resulting in zero repeated teammates by definition.

Although characters tend to have a low ratio of repeated teammates, there is a small group of more social players. The outlier in the upper right corner of Figure 6 indicates 932 players out of 15,773 who spent 100% of their time in teams with repeated teammates only.

WHO ARE MORE ENGAGED IN TEAMS?

Player level, class, in-game guilds, and friend lists are the common elements of game design in many MMORPGs. In this section, we examine the detailed impacts of these four factors on team engagement in game.

Player Levels

Player level is the most important measure of a player's experience in the game. In the sample population, character levels range from 2 to 40 with an average of 26. Similar to the strong increase in grouping starting after level 55 discovered by Ducheneaut et al [3] in WoW, we find a point of inflection at level 33 in Dragon Nest. The average percentage of time in teams is almost constant at 20% for the players below level 33. The average increases to 70%

for players between levels 33 and 40. Although the change is much bigger than what was found in [3], it supports the previous hypothesis that high level players spend more time in teams.

Because the player population has a bimodal distribution based on their time in teams, the average numbers do not reveal the true connection between players' levels and their time spent in teams. Considering players with 0% team time as solo players and the rest as team players, Figure 7 shows the two distinct populations at different character life stages.

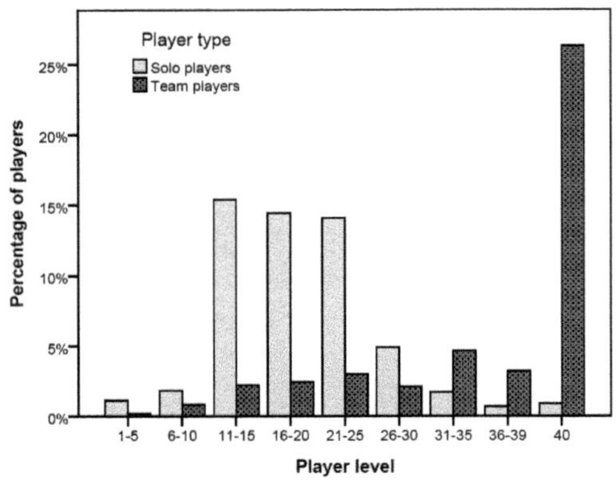

Figure 7: Solo and team players by player levels.

At low levels, characters mainly play solo. Players may prefer efficiency at the early stage of the game. High-level players, especially end game players at level 40, are facing tasks with high difficulty and more costs in fatigue points. Therefore, players need to join teams to help each other and achieve high performance.

In the interviews, all players acknowledged that they were aware that low and high levels have different requirements for fatigue points, experience points, and play time to advance. 6 of 9 felt strongly that dungeons suddenly became very difficult for solo play at a certain level. As a result, all of them spent much more time in teams at high levels, even for 4 of them who never joined a team at low levels. A top-level Cleric said,

"At low levels, while the dungeons are easy, playing in teams will get less experience points (for each person). Therefore solo will be faster. At high levels, although teammates still need to share experience points, solo play is much more difficult. Solo may take half an hour while it is just 10 minutes for a team. So I play more in teams." (P8)

The paradox is that although high-level players are more likely to team play, they tend to have a lower ratio of repeated teammates. Figure 8 shows that when player levels increase from 11 to 40, the median percentage of repeated teammates decrease from 40% to less than 20%. In the interviews, when asking for the scenarios of their first team experience, 5 of 9 reported they started at low levels with someone they know offline such as sisters, friends, and classmates and the rest 4 played with strangers for difficult tasks at high levels. The small amounts of team players at low levels usually have pre-existing social connects in game and therefore they tend to play with them repeatedly for relational proposes. On the other hand, the teams at high levels are more functional and task-driven. Players are less likely to play again together after finishing a task.

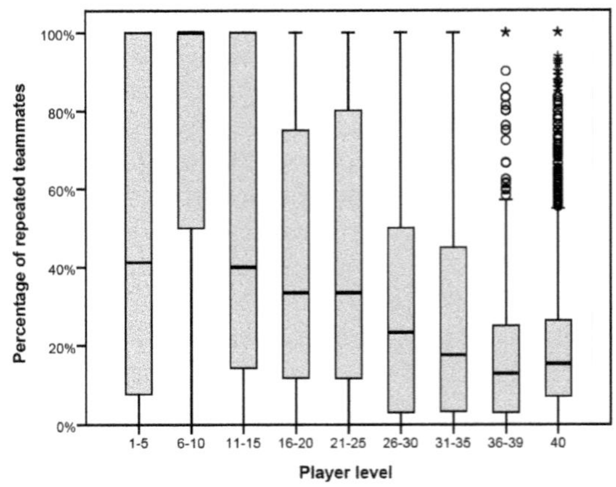

Figure 8: Ratio of repeated players by player levels.

From both time and relational perspectives, instead of the generic claim that high level players are more social, a more accurate description is that all players are performance driven and choose different play styles according to the tasks at their levels. Low-level players only need a relatively small amount of experience points to advance. Therefore, most of them finish the tasks by themselves and achieve a higher efficiency. After reaching a certain level, they have to work together for team tasks. Finding strangers and collaborating in one-off pick-up teams becomes the key to improving efficiency at higher levels.

In fact, the functional nature of teams at high levels may hurt the development of social relations. The following example show the different play styles in teams for high-level and low-level tasks:

"I usually prefer mentoring new guild members to finish mandatory tasks but not the teams for challenging abyss tasks. ... Challenging tasks have very high requirements. Sometimes a single mistake from one person fails the entire task. With this pressure, one time is fine. If play it very often, I feel very tired mentally. In contrast, mentoring others in team is easy. I can have some small talk with teammates while finishing the task. It is impossible in teams for abyss tasks since you need to run around following the leaders and make precise actions according to your class." (P8)

Player Classes and Team Roles

Dragon Nest has a traditional class design to implement various team roles. Based on the skill set specified in game, Warrior and Cleric are more independent classes, while Archer and Sorceress are supporting classes. From the game design perspective, an independent class is more balanced between attack and defense. They have better survivability than supporting classes when engaged in independent combat in dungeons. To engage in combat in dungeons with greater efficiency, supporting classes have a greater need to play in teams. The team play dynamics of the 4 classes are basically motivated by their needs and potential contribution to teams: because Clerics have the ability to heal, they are the most popular class as a teammate, while they also have no trouble to play solo; Warrior can play solo but their abilities – high self-defense – is not necessarily needed by teams; Archers and Sorceresses cannot play solo with high efficiency due to their low survivability, so they need to play with other Archers or Sorceresses to enhance attacking power, reduce the damage dealt by monsters, or play with Clerics for their healing ability. The interviewees' responses are consistent: they ranked Archers or Sorceresses as the most team-oriented classes followed by Clerics; Warrior is considered a more solo-oriented class.

In our sample, 41.9% of characters are warriors, 22.3% are archers and sorceresses, and 35.8% are clerics.

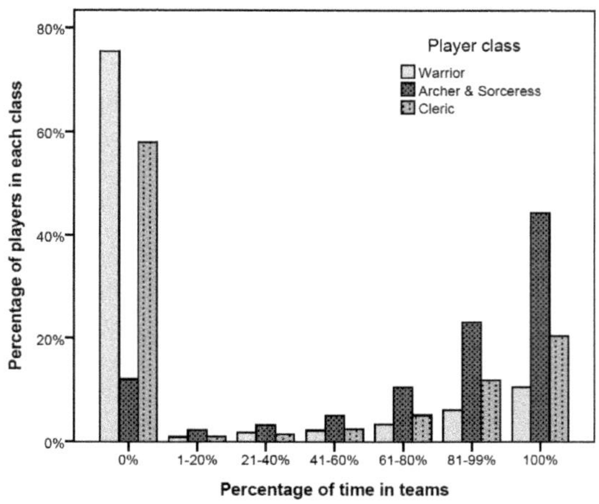

Figure 9: Time in teams by player classes.

Figure 9 shows that different classes have different team preferences: 75.5% of Warriors and 57.9% of Clerics play solo; Archers and Sorceresses are the dominant team players and 44.3% of them spend 100% of their time in teams. The differences among the three class groups are significant, $F(2,35054) = 5212.28$, $p < .001$.

Although Warriors are more capable of fighting solo and Archers and Sorceresses are more team-oriented, the two groups have no difference in percentage of play with repeated teammates, $t(6896.44) = 1.632$, $p = .103$. This suggests that Archers and Sorceresses play more in teams not because they are more social. In fact, the class design makes teamwork the only efficient play method for them. On the other hand, Clerics have about 4% more repeated teammates than other classes, $t(9506.76)=-7.629$, $p<.001$.

Interviews confirm the strong associations between classes and the level of team engagement. All interviewees except one agree or strongly agree with the two statements: "you choose character classes to meet your preference of playing solo or in teams" and "your character class influences your time of playing solo or in teams." This shows that team behavior has been stereotyped in characters' functional design and has less relational meanings.

Guild Ranks

66.9% of team players are in a guild. In Dragon Nest, guilds themselves have multiple ranks: higher level guilds have more members and more money.

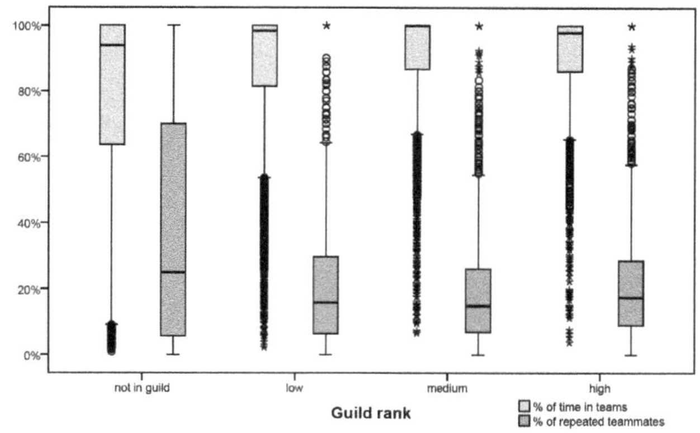

Figure 10: Team engagement by guild rank.

On average, players in a guild spend 88.8% of their time in teams and those not in a guild spend 78.9% of their time in teams. The difference is significant, $t(7534.79)=23.283$, $p<.001$. However, players in a guild play much less with previous teammates: guild players have 22.2% of repeated teammates but non-guild players have 38.7%, $t(7259.64)=-28.942$, $p<.001$. Among differently ranked guilds, players in low rank guilds spend a slightly smaller amount of time in team engagement while players in medium ranked guilds have the smallest average ratio of repeated teammates.

This suggests that guilds provide an organizational mechanism to facilitate the formation of task-oriented teams and make their members spend more time in teams. However, guild members tend to have a low percentage of repeated teammates probably due to the variety of tasks or more selective processes of choosing teammates. On the other hand, non-guild players tend to organize teams based on their relations. Although they spend less time in teams, they are most likely to play with the same players repeatedly.

Friends in Game

In-game friendship, as formalized by the friend list game mechanic, has a similar impact on team engagement. One is not required to play only with friends in this game. In general, team players with more players on their friends lists tend to spend more of their time in teams: players with no friends on average spend 72% of their time engaged in teams; players with 1 to 20 friends have 84%; and players with more than 20 friends have 91%. However, team players with at least one friend only have 24% repeated teammates compared to an average of 55% for players with no friends, $t(1886.74)=-30.727$, $p<.001$. Having more friends does appear to help finding teammates and encourage team collaboration, but more friends do not necessarily lead to more persistent team relations.

On average, interviewees reported that their friend lists have less than 10% static friends. Players use friend lists mostly for tracking new players and to play together occasionally when they are online. They have no intention to further develop their relations. One example is:

"I have no more than 10 contacts in my friend list. 3 or 4 are people I know offline. Others are I met online but I have almost no connections to them. I just take game as an entertainment but not a way to get friends." (P7)

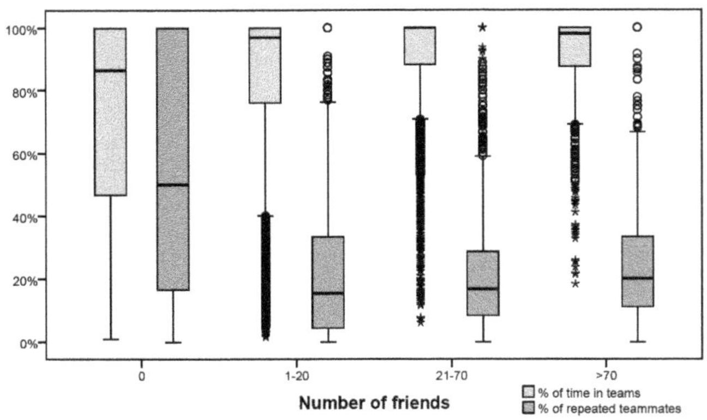

Figure 11: Team engagement by number of friends.

PREDICTING TEAM PLAYERS

Since the players in game measures are related, e.g. high-level players are more likely to join guilds and usually have more friends, we use three binary decision models to illustrate their joint impacts on social interaction levels using logistic regressions. Model 1 uses in-game status to predict solo players (i.e. 0% of time in teams) versus team players based on their levels, warrior class dummy variable, guild ranks, and the number of friends we discussed in the previous sections. Model 2 uses dichotomized versions of the level, guild, and friend variables for the same prediction: level higher than 32, in-guild (i.e. rank is low, median, or high), and has-friends (i.e. the number of friends bigger than 0). Since players who spend more time in teams are not necessarily more social, we use the percentage of repeated teammates to examine the relational side of team engagement among players in teams in Model 3. Since the medium number of the percentage of repeated teammates is around 20% for most user groups (shown in Figure 6), we assume the players with more than 20% of repeated teammates are more social than others who tend to play with different team members. Samples are thus divided into two populations, PUG team players and social team players, with similar sizes.

	Model 1	Model 2	Model 3
Prediction target	Team player	Team player	Social team player
Player level	0.07*	[a]1.59*	-0.71*
Warrior class	-1.31*	-1.04*	-0.15*
Guild rank	1.20*	[a]1.13*	-0.003
# Friends	0.20*	[a]3.32*	0.01*
Constant	-2.43*	-2.00*	2.00*
N	35,057	35,057	15,773
[b]Psudo-R^2	0.71	0.78	0.10
[c]Accuracy	89%	92%	64%

[a]. Variables are dichotomized: Level >32, Guild rank >0, # Friends >0; [b]. Nagelkerke R Square; [c]. correctly classified at the cut value .5; * indicates p<0.001

Table 2: Predicting team players and social team players.

Model 1 shows some factors that successfully facilitate team collaborations: advanced players with higher levels, non-Warrior classes, high ranked guilds, and more friends are more likely to be team players. Considering the distinct solo and team player populations, Model 2 has the same findings and binary measures offer slightly better explanatory power, which demonstrates that the impacts of in-game statistics are not linear. Whether a player is above or below Level 33, is of the warrior class or not, has at least one friend, and is in a guild or not, can predict solo and team players with 92% accuracy.

Overall our results suggest that players' decisions to join a team are mostly functional and highly predictable by their status in game. The game has two different stages: tasks that can be handled solo at the early stage and challenging end-game tasks that require teams. At both stages, players just adapt to the game mechanisms and follow the most efficient play styles to advance their levels.

Model 3 suggests that reasons for playing repeatedly with others are different from joining teams. High-level players are less likely to play with others repeatedly and guild status has no effect on the social perspective of team engagement. The low prediction accuracy shows that the game design and in-game status are less important considerations when players choose repeated teammates.

DISCUSSION

Phase Shift from Solo to Team Players

In Dragon Nest, solo players and team players are two distinct populations and are closely associated with the game design. Most of the characters play solo at the early stage of the game. Team players are characterized by a set of four status characteristics in the game: above level 33, non-warriors, in guild, and having friends on their friend list.

The increase of team players after the point of inflection at level 33 is much steeper than it is in WoW [3]. There is almost no transitional population, i.e. players do not gradually increase their involvement in teams. Playing in teams is based more on being at an advanced stage of the game rather than players' choices. When solo players reach certain levels in game, solo tasks can no longer provide enough experience points and items to advance their levels in the game quickly. All interviewees agreed that "spending less time and get experience points more efficiently" and "getting help from others" are the two main reasons to join teams at high levels. In this case, team collaboration is still functional and outcome-oriented instead of a social motivation.

Dragon Nest introduces more difficult versions of beginner tasks and tries to promote teamwork as early as possible. However, our analysis shows that, instead of facilitating teams of low-level players, this mechanism actually attracts many high-level characters to play solo in abyss versions of low-level tasks. Low-level players prefer to solo even for tasks at a master level of difficulty, which is designed for teams of four.

Team tasks at the early stage do not break the bimodal pattern. Since higher difficulty versions of beginner level tasks are not mandatory team tasks, low-level players stick to their solo behavior as long as they have a choice.

Contributing to Teams is Better than Relying on Teams

Most MMORPGs design a unique team role for each of the classes by granting them different skills. This is intended to stimulate collaboration among players across classes. Ideally each class should have its own irreplaceable contributions and therefore equally motivated to join teams. Dragon Nest illustrates different modes of class differentiation as well as their consequences in team engagement.

As a baseline, warriors have a balanced skill set with high defense abilities. Even though joining teams can reduce their expense of fatigue points, they still highly prefer to play solo. Archers and Sorceresses are incentivized for teamwork by having diminished defense skills, which make it difficult for them to survive alone. Because their attacking capability is not unique, their roles are replaceable and less attractive to teams. As a result, although the two classes spend most of their time in teams, they have the same percentage of repeated teammates as Warriors do. On the other hand, Clerics have a unique healing power, which can protect themselves as well as others in teams. Although capable of playing alone, they are very popular in teams and have a higher percentage of repeated teammates than all other classes.

These findings show that incentives of team collaboration work better than disincentives of solo play: contributing to teams with unique skills leads to social-oriented interactions while relying on teams for help leads to functional outcomes. From the design perspective, introducing the demand for long-ranged attacks and tank roles in tasks could generate more balanced team engagement across classes.

Task Teams Erode Relationships

In many MMORPGs, players at higher levels, in guild, and with many friends spend more time in teams. High level players have enough experience and good equipment and in turn more control over their own activities. Guilds and friend lists provide easy organizing tools to find tasks and teammates. Teamwork becomes temporal, i.e. coming together for a specific task and then disbanding, which in turn promotes performance-driven collaboration.

Many of the phenomena observed here are related to Sennett's conceptualizations of *decentralisation and control*, *flexibility*, and *teamwork*, which lead to the erosion of enduring relationships [14]. "Teamwork is the group practice of demeaning superficiality," Sennett writes. A good team player should have the ability to establish relations on a task-by-task basis and achieve a quick and higher return. Therefore short-term teams might not be able to bring people together.

Consistent with Sennett's arguments we find that players with high "*social*" status and more time spent in teams actually have a lower ratio of repeated teammates than those at low levels, not in a guild, and having no friends.

Implications for Design

Although some studies suggest that online gaming may result in strong social ties [16], this paper shows that teams still play a functional role in MMORPGs. Teaming is a necessary component of difficult tasks and to some extent is required by specific game mechanisms such as end game tasks and class design. The main motivation of players to join teams is to finish tasks more efficiently. Even though they spend a lot of time playing with others, it does not help in building long-lasting relations.

The design of many games tries to facilitate emerging social relations online through spontaneous self-organized groups [17]. More difficult tasks, better in-game teammate searching, and team incentive (or solo disincentive such as fatigue points) do increase the team activities. However instead of building potential relations, they become more professional in exploiting the methods, i.e. "analyzing the underlying rules and system in order to optimize character performance" [21]. This suggests that team mechanisms cannot force people to be more social. Although this finding is based on Asian players, the same scenario can be observed in many other games. This online blog [12] provides an example of similar discussions among western WoW players:

"While I think MMOs should absolutely support group play, and offer group options for all solo content, there should also be enough solo content that is fun and challenging to keep a solo player's attention. Trying to push them into groups just make those players unwilling or unable to group leave the game. WoW, unfortunately, features no solo content that is actually a challenge." (DarkWalker)

Instead of focusing too much on the functional side, providing a relaxed environment in teams may be more effective in bringing players together. Many players in our interviews mentioned that they enjoyed chitchats in teams and had more fun than tasks themselves. Consistent with previous studies, informal collaborations in teams are key aspects of socializing [11]. Similarly for virtual teams, due to their concentration on functional and informational features, informal activities are especially important to provide a persistent narrative in building long-lasting ties.

CONCLUSION

This paper explores the detailed patterns of solo and team activities in Dragon Nest and provides a comprehensive picture of players' in-game status and team engagement. We find that solo and team players are two distinct populations, which can be explained largely by game design mechanisms. We find that collaborating on tasks in teams is more functionally-driven and is not motivated by a desire for relational outcomes.

Of course informal collaboration as suggested by Nardi and Harris [11] could be more effective in facilitating the process of relation building rather than the formal PvE task teams we investigated. Future research should explore other types of player interactions and their impact of sociality in game.

ACKNOWLEDGMENTS

This study was supported by the National Natural Science Foundation (Grant No. CNS-1010904, OCI-0904356, & IIS-0841583) and Army Research Lab (W911NF-09-02-0053). We thank Yifan Li and Tianyang Lou, who conducted the interviews, and CSCW reviewers, who provided helpful comments.

REFERENCES

1. Corman, S. R., Scott, C. R., Perceived Networks, Activity Foci, and Observable Communication in Social Collectives, *Communication Theory* 4 (3) (1994) 171-190.
2. Crowston, K., Howison, J., Masango, C., Eseryel, U. Y., The Role of Face-to-Face Meetings in Technology-Supported Self-Organizing Distributed Teams, *IEEE Trans. Prof. Commun.* 50 (3) (2007) 185-203.
3. Ducheneaut, N., Yee, N., Nickell, E., Moore, R. J., "Alone together?": exploring the social dynamics of massively multiplayer online games, In *Proc. CHI 2006*.
4. Engeström, Y., Engeström, R., Vähäaho, T., When the center doesn't hold: The importance of knotworking, in: S. Chaiklin, M. Hedegaard, U. Jensen, (Eds.), *Activity Theory and Social Practice*, AarhusPress, Denmark, 1999.
5. Feld, S. L., The Focused Organization of Social Ties, *The American Journal of Sociology* 86 (5) (1981) 1015-1035.
6. Hahn, J., Moon, J. Y., Zhang, C., Emergence of New Project Teams from Open Source Software Developer Networks: Impact of Prior Collaboration Ties, *Information Systems Research* 19 (3) (2008) 369-391.
7. Jones, B. F., Wuchty, S., Uzzi, B., Multi-University Research Teams: Shifting Impact, Geography, and Stratification in Science, *Science* 322 (2008) 1259-1262.
8. Maznevski, M. L., Chudoba, K. M., Bridging space over time: Global virtual team dynamics and effectiveness, *Org. Sci.* 11 (2000) 473-492.
9. McEwan, G., Gutwin, C., Mandryk, R. L., Nacke, L., "I'm just here to play games": social dynamics and sociality in an online game site, In *Proc. CSCW 2012*.
10. McPhee, R. D., Corman, S. R., An activity-based theory of communication networks in organizations, *Commun. Monogr.* 62 (2) (1995) 132-151.
11. Nardi, B., Harris, J., Strangers and friends: collaborative play in world of warcraft, In *Proc. CSCW 2006*.
12. Root, N. (2011, Augest 27). Breakfast Topic: Are you a solo player? Available: http://wow.joystiq.com/2011/07/31/breakfast-topic-are-you-a-solo-player/
13. Schiller, S. Z., Mandviwalla, M., Virtual Team Research: An Analysis of Theory Use and a Framework for Theory Appropriation, *Small Group Research* 38 (1) (2007) 12-59.
14. Sennett, R., The Corrosion of Character: The Personal Consequences of Work in the New Capitalism W. W. Norton & Company, New York/London, 1998.
15. Tönnies, F., Gemeinschaft und Gesellschaft: Studien zu Gemeinschaft und Gesellschaft, *VS Verlag für Sozialwissenschaften*, 2012, pp. 213-219.
16. Trepte, S., Reinecke, L., Juechems, K., The social side of gaming: How playing online computer games creates online and offline social support, *Computers in Human Behavior* 28 (2012) 832–839.
17. Vogiazou, Y., Eisenstadt, M., Designing multiplayer games to facilitate emergent social behaviours online, *Interactive Technology and Smart Education* 2 (2) (2005) 117 - 130.
18. Williams, A., After Blogger's Plane Crash, Virtual Becomes Personal, in The New York Times, ed, 2008.
19. Wittel, A., Toward a Network Sociality, Theory, *Culture & Society* 18 (6) (2001) 51-76.
20. Xu, Y., Cao, X., Sellen, A., Herbrich, R., Graepel, T., Sociable killers: understanding social relationships in an online first-person shooter game, In *Proc. CSCW 2011*, ACM Press.
21. Yee, N., Motivations for play in online games, *Cyberpsychology and Behavior* 9 (6) (2006) 772-5.

ExerSync: Facilitating Interpersonal Synchrony in Social Exergames

Taiwoo Park, Uichin Lee[†], Bupjae Lee, Haechan Lee, Sanghun Son, Seokyoung Song, Junehwa Song

Department of Computer Science, KAIST and [†]Department of Knowledge Service Engineering, KAIST
Daejeon, 305-701, Republic of Korea

{twpark, bupjae, haechan, shson, sysong, junesong}@nclab.kaist.ac.kr, [†]uclee@kaist.edu

ABSTRACT
Social exergames provide immersive experiences of social interaction via online multiplayer games, ranging from simple group exercises (e.g., virtual cycling/rowing) to more structured multiplayer games (e.g., cooperative boat racing). In exergame design, interpersonal synchrony plays an important role as it enhances social rapport and pro-social behavior. In this paper, we build ExerSync platform that supports various assistive mechanisms for facilitating interpersonal synchrony even with heterogeneous exercise modalities. We consider a rhythm of body movements in repetitive aerobic exercises and explore the design space of incorporating rhythm into exergames. We build a prototype system and comparatively evaluate the effectiveness of various assistive mechanisms. The experiment results show that rhythm significantly lowers the perceived workloads and provides better competence and engagement, but the accuracy of interpersonal synchrony is not dependent on the use of rhythm.

Author Keywords
Synchrony; synchronization; exergame; rhythm.

ACM Classification Keywords
C.3 [**Special-purpose and Application-based Systems**]: Real-time and embedded systems; H.5.2 [**Information Interfaces and Presentation**]: User Interfaces—*evaluation/methodology, input devices and strategies, prototyping*

General Terms
Design, Human Factors, Experimentation

INTRODUCTION
Aerobic exercises (e.g., treadmill running, elliptical training) have many well-known health benefits such as lowering the risk of diseases (e.g., high blood pressure, cancer), maintaining body shape, and improving psychological well-being [47]. The monotonous nature of aerobic exercises, however, is regarded as one of the key demotivating factors to exercise adherence [19, 13]. In recent years, there is a growing awareness among researchers and fitness professionals that working out in groups (e.g., exercising with friends or talking group cycling/rowing classes) can effectively mitigate this problem, as social interaction in group exercise settings promotes encouragement and motivation (known as social support) [12].

Social exergames are designed not only to reap the benefits of group exercises but also to provide immersive experiences of social interaction via online multiplayer games where physical activities are used as game input [30, 55, 1, 32, 29]. The spectrum of social exergames ranges from simple online group exercises (e.g., Jogging over a Distance [30]) to more structured multiplayer interactive games (e.g., Table Tennis for Three [26], Swan Boats [1], Push'N'Pull [27], Heart Burn [43], Balloon Burst [44]). The main departure from traditional group exercises is that social exergames relax the physical constraints of co-located exercises and provide rich socio-physical interaction during workout. Further, computer-mediated interaction in social exergames can address heterogeneity of individual exercise preferences, capabilities, and goals; e.g., maintaining balanced exertion experiences based on an exerciser's fitness level [43, 29], collaboratively steering a boat using treadmill and bike [29].

One of the important components in social exergames is to facilitate interpersonal synchrony that has positive social effects of improving rapport and entitativity (or social unit) and also making exercises more enjoyable [17, 20, 18, 6, 49, 46]. Due to online nature of social interactions, we loosely define interpersonal synchrony as the state in which physical movement rhythms of game players or physiological states are in unison on the basis of given game metrics such as speed, heart rates, and a mixture of both. For instance, in a boat racing game like Swan Boat, to steer a boat on a straight line a pair of players on the treadmill should run at the same speed; in Jogging over a Distance, distant joggers could experience interpersonal synchrony by balancing their running speed based on partner's heart rates.

We consider a range of social exergames that use exercise intensity as game input and support heterogeneous exercise devices. In existing social exergames, a rhythm of body movements is captured by using a simple intensity metric

CSCW '13, February 23–27, 2013, San Antonio, Texas, USA.

like angular speed/frequency (e.g., RPM of stationary cycles). Game players use this speed information to adjust rhythmic body movements for interpersonal synchrony. In practice, however, the use of speed information is less natural, because humans feel more comfortable when coordinating rhythmic movements by tuning one's movement cycles directly to the perceived movement cycles (or the beats in music) [52, 42, 34]. For instance, to walk at the same speed, two people use the auditory or/and visual perceptions of each other's gait cycles (swing-stance pairs) to adjust their step frequencies; as a result, they will walk in step (and at the same speed). Further, interpersonal synchrony would become even more elusive, particularly when heterogeneous exercise modalities are involved (e.g., treadmill and bike).

In this paper, we build the ExerSync platform that supports various assistive mechanisms of facilitating interpersonal synchrony. Unlike existing work, we consider a rhythm of body movements to design a new assistive mechanism and comparatively evaluate various mechanisms via user studies. To be more precise, ExerSync extracts both frequency (or intensity) and phase of the current movement cycles; e.g., how fast a person is walking (step frequency), and what the current phase is (e.g., hill strike event has just happened). Given that self-stabilizing, distributed synchronization requires considerable time and effort as group size increases [34], ExerSync uses simple leader-directed group synchronization for fast convergence where a leader is elected in a game play (like a coxswain in team rowing), and the rest of users follow the leader's rhythm. Inter-person and -device heterogeneity is dealt with balancing methods proposed in the literature [43, 29, 32]; e.g., given that each user has a preferred range for exercise devices, balancing can be achieved by mapping one range to the other proportionally [32]. In this way, the leader's rhythm is translated to an individual's view (based on a preferred range and device type), and each individual uses this balanced rhythm for synchronization.

To validate the feasibility and effectiveness of rhythmic cues for synchronization in social exergames, we consider four types of equipment-based exercises, namely walking/running, cycling, hula-hooping, and jump-roping and then design novel mechanisms for extracting major phases within the movement cycles. We report the detailed design processes and the lessons learned while developing our prototype systems; i.e., (1) smart shoes that can detect hill/toe strikes to capture the stance phase of walking/running and the load/landing phases of jump-roping, (2) a wearable vest that can detect the impulse generation phase of hula-hooping, and (3) a modified bike that can monitor power-recovery phases of cycling. We perform a user study to characterize the effectiveness of rhythm cues for synchronization, to analyze synchronization performance under inter-device heterogeneity, and to understand the user experiences (e.g., intrinsic motivation, engagement).

The main contributions of this paper are two-fold. First, we analyze four kinds of repetitive aerobic exercises and explore the ways of extracting movement rhythm. Second, we build prototype systems and evaluate the effectiveness of assistive mechanisms under various configurations of exercise devices. The user study results show that when compared with the speed gauge cues, rhythm cues significantly lower the perceived workloads and provide better competence and engagement. Interestingly, even though participants reported significant improvement on perceived performance, our quantitative analysis of user study traces disproves such claims; we fail to provide statistically significant evidence that rhythm cues perform better than speed gauge cues. The rest of this paper is organized as follows. We illustrate background and related work and then detail ExerSync system by explaining its main components, namely Exercise Rhythm Extractor, Rhythm Translator, and Audio-visual Rhythm. We report our user study that examines effectiveness of synchronization, inter-device heterogeneity, and user experience studies. We discuss the implications and limitations of our main findings and conclude the paper.

BACKGROUND AND RELATED WORK

It is well known that interpersonal synchrony within group activities provides many social-psychological advantages. To name a few, it enhances cooperation between group members and binds them together [15, 23, 53]. Also, it increases social rapport, pro-social behavior and performance of joint-activity [7, 25, 48, 54]. Examples of interpersonal synchrony include dance, drill, and group exercises (e.g., aerobic dances, cycling/rowing classes); people in a group move together in time and feel strong engagement from their synchronized activities [23, 12]. Therefore, it is very important to explore interpersonal synchrony to enhance the quality of group experience in social exergames.

Before we illustrate the details, we examine interpersonal synchronization that is a process of coordinating body movement rhythms between interacting individuals [42, 34]. In the theory of synchronization [34], a rhythm of body movements (e.g., repeated stance-swing patterns of walking/running) is characterized using the angular speed/frequency (i.e., the number of movement cycles per time unit), and the phase (i.e., the quantity that increases within one cycle, proportional to the fraction of the cycle period). Interpersonal synchrony is said to occur when two people performing the same rhythmic body movements reach a common angular frequency (e.g., walking at the same speed). Note that this state does not imply that the entrained cycles coincide. In other words, there could be an arbitrary *phase shift* between movement cycles; e.g., stance-swing phases of synchronized individuals are not necessarily in unison. In particular, when there is no phase shift, this state is called in-phase synchronization (e.g., identical stance-swing phases); and when the phase shift is 180 degrees, this state is called anti-phase synchronization

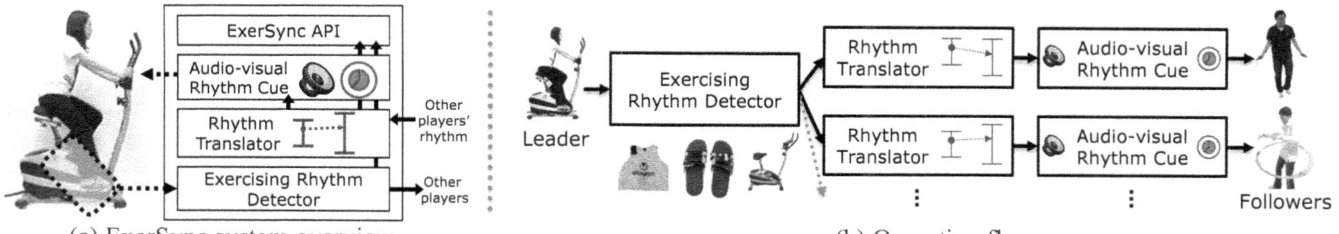

(a) ExerSync system overview (b) Operation flow

Figure 1. Conceptual overview of the proposed system.

(e.g., reversed stance-swing phases, meaning that a person's left foot coincides with the other person's right foot). Interestingly, researchers found that when visual movement information of partners (visual perception) is solely given, humans can only stably maintain without practice in-phase and anti-phase synchronization [41, 40]. In the following, we review how existing exergame attempt to facilitate interpersonal synchrony by offering audio/visual cues.

As mentioned earlier, due to online nature of interactions in social exergames, we extend the concept of interpersonal synchrony such that game players' physical movement rhythms or physiological states are in unison on the basis of given game metrics such as speed, heart rates, and a mixture of both. Having said that, interpersonal synchrony in existing social exergames can be summarized as follows. Mueller et al. developed 'Jogging over a Distance' [28] that provides joggers in different locations with a sense of presence of others. It also helps them to balance their exercising intensity by synchronizing each other's heart rate. A rhythm action game 'Dance Dance Revolution' provides Unison Mode which promotes synchronized movements of two collocated players; following shared step arrows, the players should step together in time. Another interesting example is 'Magical Truck Adventure,' an arcade pump car racing game. To move forward a pump car, two players should push their pumping bars alternately, and thereby, they have sense of synchrony and fun.

In several exergames, synchronous behavior occurs within some game contexts. Park et al. proposed 'Swan Boat,' a cooperative paddle-boat racing game [1, 33, 32] which actively utilizes exercising speeds with the exercise equipment (e.g., treadmills, stationary cycles); to steer a boat on a straight line, a pair of players should exercise at the same speed. In 'Push 'N' Pull' [26], a pair of players use resistance training devices and manipulate virtual objects. Synchrony occurs when they push and pull the devices in the same direction. In 'Truck Pull' [44], two players engage in a virtual tug-of-war by pedaling on their respective stationary bikes; synchrony can happen when they pedal at their maximal speed. Note that competitive social exergames that do not use cooperation usually lack interpersonal synchrony. For instance, in a racing game called `Heart Burn,' each player individually controls a car using bike (speed) and game pad (direction) [43].

Besides exergames, there are also other computer-supported collaborative applications that facilitate interpersonal synchrony. Carroll et al. proposed ChoNo, a video-based annotation tool that uses an audio-visual cue to help a dance team to practice together [9]. There are several works in the domain of networked music performance [3, 4], which supports on-line synchronous and collaborative music practice. Similarly, Reidsma et al. introduced a notion of virtual conductors interacting with human musicians [37]. However, these applications mainly use a predefined or programmed rhythm, whereas our system dynamically extracts players' exercise rhythm and shares it with other players for inter-player synchrony.

EXERSYNC SYSTEM DESIGN

System Overview

As shown in Figure 1, ExerSync consists of three key components: *Exercise Rhythm Extractor*, *Rhythm Translator* and *Audio-visual Rhythm Cue*. They are designed to effectively deal with the challenges in providing synchrony while playing pervasive social exergames. *Exercise Rhythm Extractor* detects repetition frequency of exercising players. It includes a variety of wearable sensors and sensor-enabled exercising devices. Each repetitive aerobic exercise has a series of movement phases constituting a repetition unit, which required exercise type-specific considerations to accurately detect the repetition frequency. *Rhythm Translator* converts a repetition frequency value of one player to its relative value in other players' predefined frequency ranges. For this, players define their own preferred frequency ranges in advance. Through the rhythm translation, players avoid receiving excessively high or low frequency of others that they cannot synchronize with. *Audio-visual Rhythm Cue* is designed to effectively convey the converted frequency information between players. It actively utilizes audio-visual rhythmic representation and additional visual hints to help players recognize and anticipate rhythm information, respectively. To facilitate rhythm-based group exergames, the system also supports application-program interface (API) which provides rhythm information of exercisers for game applications.

Exercise Rhythm Extractor

To extract exercise rhythm, we developed several types of hardware devices including wearable sensors and sensor-enabled exercise devices. We carefully designed these devices by multiple iterations of observing exercise movements, while creating and evaluating prototype devices.

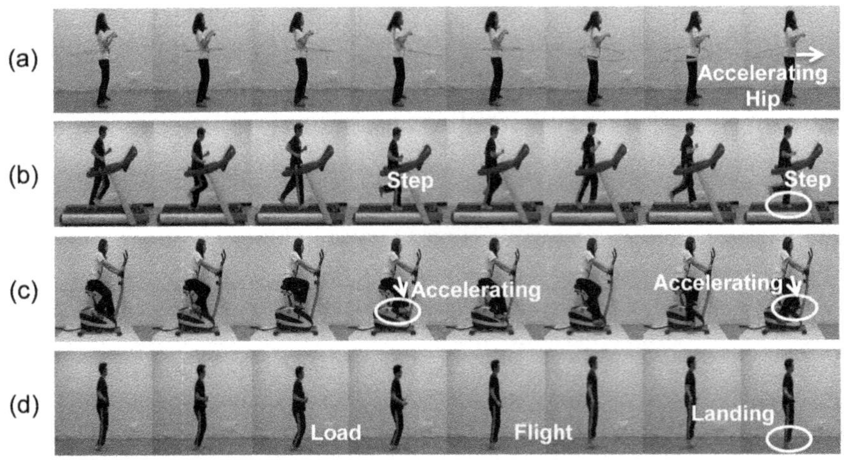

Figure 2. Repetition of exercises. (a) hula hooping, (b) treadmill running, (c) stationary cycling, (d) rope jumping.

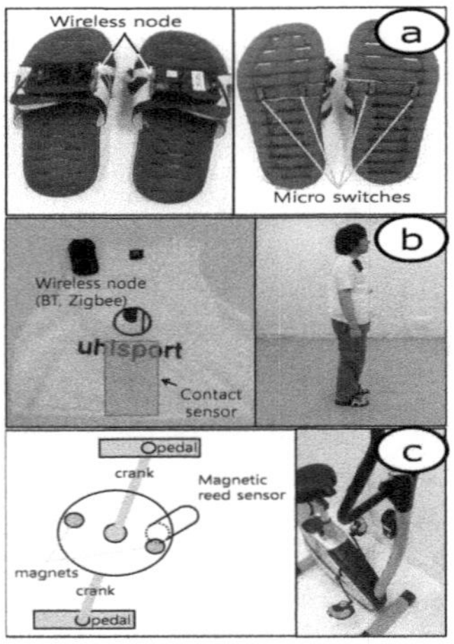

Figure 3. Prototype devices for exercise rhythm detection.

Empirical study on exercise movement and rhythm

We define exercise rhythm in terms of repetition frequency and phase of a given exercise; here, a repetition unit is a series of well-defined movement phases. For instance, Zehr et al. [56] analyzed the movement phases of walking and cycling and showed that leg flexion and extension results in feet acceleration toward and away from the pelvis, respectively. Jump roping has load, flight, and landing phases [21], and hula hooping has joint acceleration of hip/ankle and maintenance phases [11].

While these phases are defined based on the mechanics of body movements, we need to confirm how people actually identify the beginning point of repetition in each exercise. We conducted a user study of observing the moments that the participants define as the beginning of repetition. 16 paid participants were recruited. Their ages range from 18 to 28. We asked participants to perform four kinds of exercises, but we allowed them to exclude the ones that they cannot do well with. We also asked the participants to count their repetitions like as 'one, two, one, two, …' After videotaping, we analyzed the counting behavior of the participants as well as exercising movements.

We found that there are two classes of exercises depending on whether there is an explicit phase transition. First of all, running and rope jumping have 'steps,' the moments when exercisers' feet strike the floor. Participants counted repetitions along with the steps. In the case of running, one exceptional case happened; a male participant counted with his left steps only. He said that it is more natural to do so because it is very similar to the physical training that he had during his military service. For the other exercises, namely cycling and hula hooping, it is elusive to exactly pinpoint the beginning of a cycle. After careful examination, we were able to find that most of participants wanted to count rhythm when they start accelerating the pedal on the foot or the hula hoop along with the waist (see Figure 2).

Note that there exists movement symmetry in running, cycling and hula-hooping. We found that people have different preferences in terms of selecting the beginning point (i.e., 0°); yet, most of the participants prefer to select their left leg as the beginning.

Creation and Evaluation of Prototype Devices

Accelerometer-based rhythm extractor prototypes. For the first prototype, we tried to utilize 3-dimensional accelerometers which are commonly equipped on off-the-shelf smartphones. Since they are widely used to detect specific movements including walking steps, we implemented a peak-detection-based step detector [57] on top of Google Nexus One. We placed the smartphone at the right flank of participants as suggested. Similarly, we adapted the step detection algorithm for detecting exercising rhythm of hula hooping and cycling, because the waist and leg movement of these two exercises also generate near-sinusoidal waves of which the frequency is almost the same as the repetition frequency of the movement.

During preliminary tests, however, we found that this approach had a significant drawback of incurring a large detection delay. Since it continuously monitors the acceleration pattern whether it increased, reached a peak, and decreased, the algorithm inherently produces detection latencies, and even these are not consistent, ranging from 80ms to 200ms in our experiment. In the case of treadmill running, the repetition frequency at 8Kph is about 3Hz (300~350ms in a repetition period), and thus, the latencies significantly degraded the detection accuracy.

Contact-sensing-based rhythm extractor prototypes. To minimize a detection latency, we decided to focus on detecting contact events that indicates the beginning of repetitions. As shown in Figure 2, all exercises have these contact points between exercisers' body and exercise device (hula hooping, treadmill running), exercisers' body and the floor (rope jumping), and subparts of exercise device (stationary cycling). In the case of treadmill running and rope jumping, we can easily detect the step by monitoring contacts between soles of shoes and the floor. We implemented a contact sensor-enabled smart shoes which

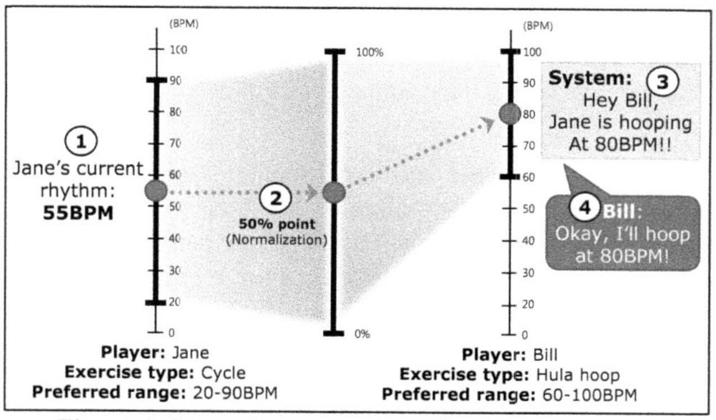

Figure 4. Conceptual example of rhythm translation.

detect the floor contacts (see Figure 3). For a stationary cycle, we attached a magnetic switch on the pedal shaft and made it detect the timing when the cranks are passing through the front vertically centered position. For a hula hoop, we utilized the fact that a hoop naturally touches around the navel when the participants start to move their waist forward. We developed a smart vest which detects pressure on the front side of belly. All of these smart devices send the contact information immediately using wireless communication channels such as Bluetooth or ZigBee. To evaluate the second prototypes, we ran a pilot test. We programmed that the participants hear a beep sound when the devices detects the beginning of the repetitions. In this experiment, all the participants strongly agreed that the devices detected their exercising rhythm accurately and immediately.

Rhythm Translator

Rhythm Translator is designed to provide a sense of synchrony between exergame players with different physical competences or heterogeneous exercise modalities. The translator converts the repetition frequency of a leader to its relative value of each following player. In brief, it maps the repetition frequency of a leader based on the preferred range of each player, as if the leader had the same physical ability and performed the same exercise with the player. Our translation mechanism is similar to the previous works [28, 32] which provide balanced and fair game play under the similar situation as this work. In the training phase, each player P_i performs the exercise at the minimum and maximum frequencies and sets her preferred range of exercise frequency as (f_{min_i}, f_{max_i}). The user's current frequency f_i is then converted to a target frequency f_{i_t} in such a way that the ratio of the target frequency f_{i_t} in the target range (f_{min_t}, f_{max_t}) is kept the same as that of the original frequency f_i in the original range (f_{min_i}, f_{max_i}).

Figure 4 shows a simple example. Jane, a stationary cyclist, with her preferred frequency range of (20, 90 BPM) runs with Bill, a hula-hooper with a range of (60, 100 BPM). Her current running pace is 55 BPM as measured by the rhythm extractor. The rhythm translator then converts it and notifies to Bill that her current frequency is 80BPM as if she performs the same exercise, i.e., hula-hooping, within the same preferred frequency range with him.

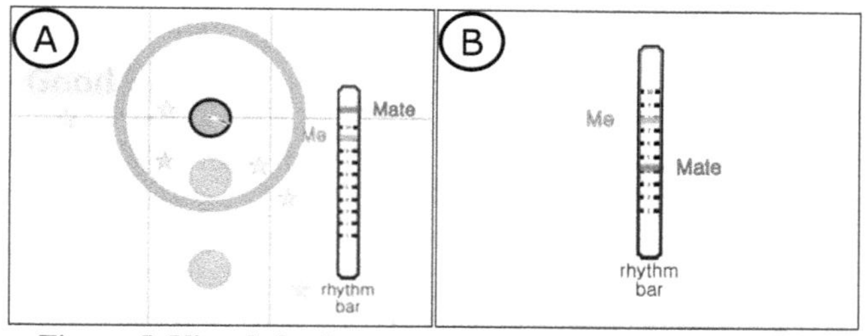

Figure 5. Visual rhythm cues. (a) proposed visual cue with rhythm rate gauge (b) rhythm rate gauge only.

Audio-visual Rhythm Cue

Each player uses audio-visual cues to coordinate her movements based on the balanced rhythm of the leader (supplied via the Rhythm Translator). The cue periodically gives auditory and visual stimuli to players; auditory cues correspond to the beginning of a cycle, and visual hints help players to intuitively estimate the remaining time till the next beat. For the auditory stimulation, we utilized a machine-generated tone with sound frequency of 4,000Hz whose duration is 50ms. This is very similar to the rhythmic sensory stimulation used for gait assistance of Parkinson's disease patients [5, 10].

We carefully designed visual stimulation considering that the frequency changes over time as the leader changes his repetition frequency. So, we designed assistive visual hints as well as traditional visual stimulation (turning on a light signal for a period of 50ms). To our knowledge, assistive visual cues have not been extensively studied in the past. However, we could find a visual metronome with assistive visual information [14]. It simply displays a moving LED light from one side to another repetitively. Also, we investigated the commercial rhythm beat games which provide assistive visual cues. Our extensive survey results show that there are two rhythm beat games featuring assistive visual hints, namely Elite Beat Agents and Hatsune Miku: Project DIVA. The former game utilizes one fixed (smaller) circle and one shrinking (bigger) circle. To help players estimate the next beat, the bigger circle getting smaller at a constant rate, and the two circles meet exactly at the beat. The latter game provides a clock hand, which rotates at a constant angular velocity and hits the direction of 12 o'clock exactly at the beat. As these two hint types do not conflict with each other in visualization, we combined the two types of visual hints without hurting or confusing them, as shown in Figure 5(a). In addition, we presented the frequency rate differences between the player and her partner using the color of the circles, similar to the colored cue suggested by Wilson et al. [52]

USER STUDY

In this user study, we seek to improve our understanding of interpersonal synchrony between exercisers, including effectiveness of the synchronization mechanisms and inter-personal and -device heterogeneity. Specifically, we examined the following research questions:

1. **Synchronization effectiveness**: Do these two mechanisms, i.e., visual gauge only vs. rhythmic cue

with visual gauge show differences on synchronization performance (e.g., perceived workloads and measured accuracy of synchronization)? Is there a significant difference on synchronization performance between exercise types?

2. **Synchronization between heterogeneous devices**: Do exercise types of a leader or followers have significant impact on synchronization performance? Will a pair with homogeneous exercise show better performance than that with heterogeneous exercises?
3. **User experience**: What kind of affordance does our system provide to users through interpersonal synchrony? Are there any differences on user experiences, e.g., intrinsic motivation, engagement, entitativity and attentional focus, between two synchronization mechanisms?

We answer these research questions by conducting three different experiments specifically focusing these questions. In the rest of this section, we first share the design of the three experiments and then report the results and findings.

Experimental Design 1

The first experiment is performed mainly to see the effectiveness of the proposed system in synchronization. We select two rhythm presentation methods, i.e., audio-visual rhythmic cue with a frequency rate gauge and the case only with a frequency rate gauge, and measure the workloads as seen by the exercisers and the accuracy of synchronization.

Participants and Apparatus

For this study, 40 participants (19 females and 21 males) were recruited on campus from the age group of 18 to 28. All of them had (corrected-to-) normal vision and hearing. During the recruitment, we announced that the participants should specify one exercise type in which they are skillful enough, among the four exercise types we stated earlier. As a result, we set four exercise-specific groups and each group consists of ten participants. The participants went through a training session for about 5 to 20 minutes in order to familiarize themselves with the way to naturally change their exercising speed. During the training session, we measured the preferred range of repetition frequency (f_{min_i}, f_{max_i}) for each participant.

To detect the exercise rhythm of two players in a pair, we used the smart shoes and vests, and the sensor-enabled stationary cycles that we described earlier. We chose off-the-shelf hula hoops and jump ropes. The dimension of a hula-hoop is about 95cm in diameter, and 500g in weight. The jump rope is about 100g in weight (including handles and a rope) and the maximum length of this rope is 270cm. We used FITEX-670U stationary cycles in which we attached the rhythm detectors. Lastly we used Frevola-T7A interactive treadmills which adjust the speed automatically on the basis of the players' current running paces [1]. To provide audio-visual information, we used 23-inch LCD screens (resolution of 1920x1080) and Samsung HS3000 stereo Bluetooth headsets. The headsets are utilized to provide auditory stimulation as well as a shared voice channel between two participants in a pair.

Tasks

We made two types of experimental tasks which are different in rhythm presentation methods: (1) an audio-visual rhythmic cue with a frequency rate gauge (Figure 5a) and (2) the case only with a frequency rate gauge (Figure 5b). Participants experienced each type of tasks for five times subsequently, and the sequence of the task types is counter-balanced.

For each task, a participant receives a workout program including five representative frequencies, namely 10%, 30%, 50%, 70%, and 90% point in the preferred repetition frequency range (f_{min_i}, f_{max_i}). The workout program is designed to have 2 minutes of total duration, consisting of 8 sections, each with 15 seconds. Each section has one of the representative frequencies, and the participant is informed of the frequency information through the rhythmic cue and/or the frequency rate gauge. We carefully randomized the frequency rates over the sections, while letting the participants experience all frequency rates. Also, we had the participants to experience all possible frequency transitions (i.e., ±20%, ±40%, ±60% and ±80%) at least once in a workout program. (As this experiment investigates the effectiveness of rhythmic cues in synchronization, it was originally designed to be performed for pairs of exercisers, namely a leader and a follower. However, with the initial design, it was difficult to sort out the effectiveness clearly since the results were affected by the leaders' stability as well as the followers' synchronization efforts. This current design is a revised version to sort out and focus on the synchronization efforts, in which each follower attempts to synchronize to the system providing the leader's frequencies.)

After performing each task, participants were asked to answer a questionnaire for subjective workload assessments. We used the NASA-TLX (Task Load Index) [16]. It consists of six items: Mental Demands, Physical Demands, Temporal Demands, Own Performance, Effort Level and Frustration Level. Because the task explicitly defines the duration, we omitted Temporal Demands and used other five items. Each item has a five-point Likert scale, ranging from Very Low (1) to Very High (5). We also logged the exercise data and calculated *degree of asynchrony* [10] (DoA), defined as the sum of the differences between each participant's current frequency rate and the target frequency rate over a time period.

Experimental Design 2

This experiment is performed to see the effectiveness of the rhythmic cue over different exercise types.

Participants and Apparatus

Similar to the first experiment, 20 participants (8 female and 12 male) were recruited on campus from the age group of 18 to 29. To closely examine differences on user experiences between different exercise types, we chose two exercise types, stationary cycle and hula hoop, which have different characteristics in terms of the controllability to follow a given frequency rate, and shows the best and worst performance, respectively. (See the result of the first experiment.) We set two exercise-specific groups and each group consists of ten participants. We also let the participants go through a training session and measured the preferred frequency ranges. We used the same devices in this experiment as we used in the first experiment.

Tasks

In this experiment, we focus on followers' experiences and accuracies when using different exercise types. Therefore, we made two types of tasks which are different in a leader's exercise type, i.e., stationary cycle and hula hoop. All participants experienced each type of the leader's exercise for five times subsequently, and the sequence of the leader's exercise types is counter-balanced.

To control the variability on the leader's skillfulness, condition and stamina effect, we used pre-recorded workout programs obtained from the first experiment. During the first experiment, we precisely recorded all of the frequency changes of participants with timestamps during tasks. We carefully examined the recorded files and chose five representative ones for hula hoop and stationary cycle. These representative log files, namely pre-recorded workout programs, have the most similar characteristics with the exercise types, in terms of degree of asynchrony (DoA) values. In this experiment, we implemented a recorded log-file playback application and let participants to follow the pre-recorded workout programs. Duration of a program is two minutes, as they are recorded from the first experiment. After performing each task, participants were asked to answer the same questionnaires (5 items from NASA-TLX), and we logged the exercise data and calculated DoA values.

Experimental Design 3

The goal of this experiment is to understand the user experiences with two different assistive mechanisms by using various psychology metrics.

Participants and Apparatus

For this study, 7 pairs of students, 14 students in total (6 female and 8 male), were recruited on campus from the age group of 19 to 28 (average: 23.3, SD: 2.97). To mimic realistic social exergame scenarios, we encouraged the participants to join the study with people whom they were familiar with. We let the participants go through a training session and measured the preferred frequency range as we did in the two previous experiments. We also used the same devices as in the previous experiments. After the training session, each participant went into different exercise rooms that are about 50 meters apart.

Tasks

We let participants experience two roles (i.e., leader and follower) with two different rhythm presentation methods: (1) audio-visual rhythm cue, and (2) the gauge only. The sequence of the task types is counter-balanced. We went through a pilot test with two pairs of participants to validate the experiment configuration. Reflecting a feedback to enhance the social presence of the leader, we decided to use low frequency sounds of drum beats.

Each task session lasts 5 minutes and is composed of sub-sessions (each with 150 seconds). In the beginning of a task, a random participant takes the role of a leader and the other does the role of a follower. At the end of the first sub-session, our software automatically switches the roles and announces that their roles have just been changed. We did not provide any workout program to the participants to create realistic exergame environments; e.g., naturally discussing their workout plans and freely synchronizing their pace.

Since the goal of this experiment is to understand the user experiences, we decided to consider a scenario where two exercisers are working out on stationary cycles. We used the same devices in this experiment as we used in the first experiment. In addition, we used stereo headsets to provide a shared voice channel between two participants in a pair.

After performing each task, the participants were asked to answer a set of questionnaires including intrinsic motivation, focused attention, engagement, entitativity and perceived exertion rate. The details of the questionnaires will be presented in the following sub-section. After the questionnaire, we conducted a semi-structured interview to collect participants' experiences, including leader/follower roles, and rhythm representation.

Survey Metrics

The Intrinsic Motivation Inventory (IMI) [39] was used to assess participants' subjective experience related to a target activity. IMI has been widely used in user studies related to intrinsic motivation and self-regulation. Using this instrument, we mainly examined the following factors, namely interest/enjoyment (7 items), perceived competence (6 items), and felt pressure/tension (5 items).

Engagement Survey Instrument (ESI) was used to measure engagement or a quality of user experience [31]. Only the factors/items relevant to our study are used for evaluation: namely, focused attention (7 items), usability (7 items), endurability (4 items), and involvement (3 items).

The Attention Focus Questionnaire (AFQ) consists of 30-items of various attention behaviors that are rated on a seven-point scale after each session. The AFQ has three factors: (1) association that are task-related mental strategies (11 items; e.g. "monitoring specific body sensations", "focusing on staying loose and relaxed"), dissociation that are task-unrelated mental strategies (12 items; e.g. "singing a song in your head", "focusing on the outside environment"), and distress (7 items; e.g. "wishing the task would end", "thinking about how much you want to quit").

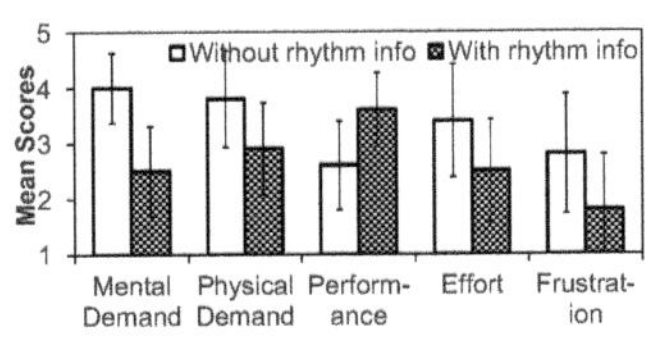

(a) Jump rope

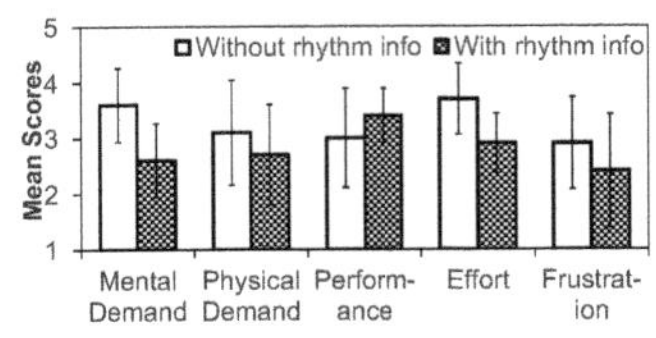

(b) Cycle

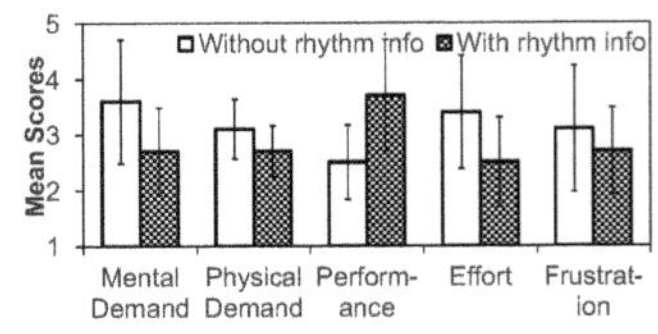

(c) Treadmill

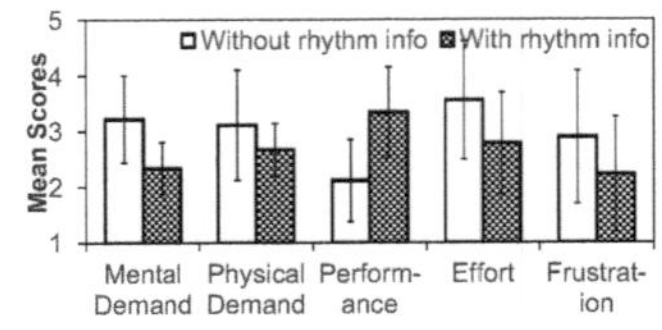

(d) Hula hoop

Figure 6. NASA-TLX questionnaire scores for each exercise type

	Mental demand	Physical demand	Performance	Effort	Frustration
(a) Exercise type - main effect, F(3,72)	F=1.174, p=0.326	F=1.419, p=0.244	F=1.191, p=0.319	F=0.75, p=0.526	F=1.11, p=0.350
(b) Cue type - main effect, F(1,72)	**F=37.878, p<0.001 ***	**F=9.037, p=0.004 **	**F=29.064, p<0.001 ***	**F=17.11, p<0.001 ***	**F=7.605, p=0.007 **
(c) Interaction effect, F(3,72)	F=0.574, p=0.634	F=0.423, p=0.737	F=1.242, p=0.301	F=0.02, p=0.996	F=0.315, p=0.814

Table 1. Two-way ANOVA result (exercise type and cue type) on NASA-TLX questionnaire scores

The Borg Scale, a simple method of rating perceived exertion (RPE) has been widely used to gauge an individual's level of intensity in sports training. We use a RPE version with a 15-point scale that ranges from 6 to 20 where 7 is "very, very light" and 19 is "very, very hard." Researchers showed that there is a strong correlation between RPE and physiological variables (e.g., 0.8-0.9 on heart rates) [8].

We measure entitativity (perception as a social unit) and rapport (an affective state of mutual attention and positivity) using Entitativity questionnaire (4 items) by Postmes et al. [35], and Rapport questionnaire (5 items) adapted from Puccinelli et al. [36]. Examples of entitativity items include feeling as a unit and acting in unison, and those of rapport items include feeling coordinated with each other and being aware of each other.

Experiment Results 1

The main effect of different cue types was found in all NASA-TLX subscales (See Table 1). The results show that when compared with the gauge, the rhythmic cue helped reduce the perceived task workloads of the participants. It is interesting to see that the rhythmic cue also decreases the perceived physical demand. Several users state why they gave high ratings on physical demand after performing the gauge task; the participants overly used their muscle to maintain constant speed when following the gauge. (It is important to note that the results are based on the subjective measures reported by users. The study at the current stage does not aim at providing rather objective measurement of the exercise intensities.) As for the Performance, users commented that they synchronized their body movements with the rhythm sound, and this gave the feeling they could perform better with the rhythmic cue. We also see the effect of the exercise type, but the result was not statistically significant.

We also tried to measure the accuracy of synchronization via degree of asynchrony (DoA) between the target speed (leader) and the following speed (follower). The result shows that the two cue types did not show significant differences over DoA. (See Table 2b) We further tested DoA over different exercise types. (See Table 2a), and main effect was found. The cycle shows the lowest value of DoA, and the hula hoop, the highest. For deeper analysis, we divided the synchronization times into two phases, i.e., the adaptation and the retainment phase. We divided the duration of 15 seconds into two halves, considering the first half as the adaptation phase, and the second half the retainment phase. From this analysis as well, the cycle showed the best performance in both adaptation and retainment phases. For the adaptation phase, the other three exercises, jump roping, running, and hula hooping, showed similar DoA. For the retainment phase, cycling showed the best performance, jump roping and treadmill running being in the middle, and hula hooping the worst.

Players generally liked the case with the rhythm cue. Most of them felt easier and more comfortable in the case. They expressed many different reasons for their preference with the rhythm. Players mentioned that the rhythm helps concentration, gives the feeling of being together, gives more fun, is more intuitive, and is easier to check their own speed and to adapt, etc.

> "*I can easily prepare my breath by matching it with the rhythm, however, without it, it is easy to lose the breath*". [P3]

> "*With the gauge, I should have paid constant attention to maintain my tempo, and hence constant mental strain. I was not sure if I was doing well. With the rhythm, my objective became simpler; I needed to simply match my rope hitting the floor with the rhythm. In the beginning, I paid attention to both audio and visual rhythm. However, once I became in sync with the rhythm, I concentrate only on the sound*". [P11]

> "*I often lose my concentration. Without rhythm I become constantly blank. The rhythm helps concentration*". [P4]

However, several participants also indicated negative points of the rhythm.

> "*I needed to pay more attention with the rhythm since there is more information to process*". [P6]

> "*With the rhythm I felt much more comfortable. However, it still leaves slight obsession*" [P10]

> "*The rhythm sound was sharp. While more comfortable, the sound gave stress when out of sync*". [P2]

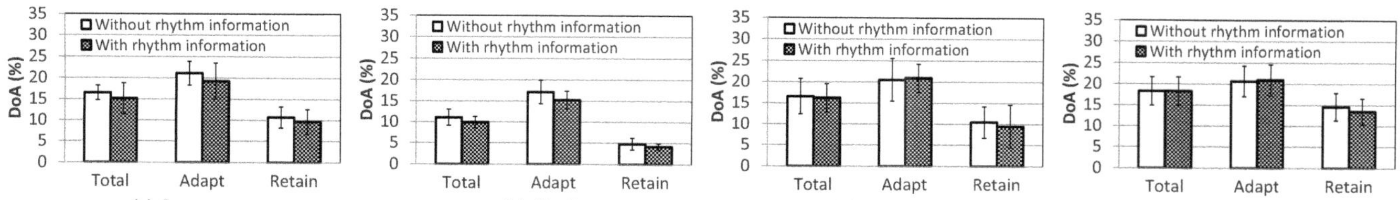

(a) Jump rope (b) Cycle (c) Treadmill (d) Hula hoop

Figure 7. Degree of Asynchrony (DoA) values for each exercise type

	DoA (Total)	DoA (Adapt)	DoA (Retain)
(a) Exercise type - main effect, F(3,72)	**F=24.177, p<0.001 *****	**F=7.704, p<0.001 *****	**F=31.577, p<0.001 *****
(b) Cue type - main effect, F(1,72)	F=1.209, p=0.275	F=0.957, p=0.331	F=1.877, p=0.175
(c) Interaction effect, F(3,72)	F=0.210, p=0.889	F=0.667, p=0.575	F=0.022, p=0.996

Table 2. Two-way ANOVA result (exercise type and cue type) on DoA values

Experiment Results 2

Table 3 shows the results for TLX questions and the DoA. We tested the answers with 2-way ANOVA. For the Mental Demand, the main effects were found neither from followers' nor leaders' exercise types. As for the Physical Demand, the main effect was found for the follower's type; following with hula hoop shows lower values than when following with cycles ($F(1,36)=9.081$, $p<.01$). For the Performance, on the contrary, the main effect was found for leader types. The perceived performance of cyclists was highly affected by leaders' exercise type, whereas that of hula hoopers was not: the leaders' effect: $F(1,36)=22.253$, $p<.001$, the followers' effect: $F(1,36)=4.846$, $p<.05$. Hula hoopers also expressed difficulties as followers. It is interesting that a user (cyclist 3) commented the following:

> *"I could follow well, but it was difficult because the leader changed his speed (frequency) too often"*. [P8]

However, in this case, the interaction effect is significant: $F(1,36)=8.011$, $p<.01$. In the case of cyclists, Figure 7 (left) clearly shows this effect: homogeneous configuration (cycle-cycle) performs much better than heterogeneous configuration (hula hoop-cycle).

As for Effort, the main effect was not found, but the average Effort value is quite higher than that in Experiment 1. Several people commented that it was quite 'stressful' and requires more effort since the target value was continuously changing. This in part explains why Mental Load does not show statistically significant differences.

As for Frustration, following hula hoop's rhythm is more difficult than following cycle's rhythm ($F(1,36)=5.769$, $p<0.05$).

As for DoA, the main effect was found with the followers' exercise type ($F(1,36)=89.641$, $p<.001$). It was also affected by leaders' exercise type ($F(1,36)= 5.786$, $p<.05$). The cycle followers can quickly adapt to the changes regardless of leader's exercise type (Figure 7(right)). In contrast, the hula hoop followers are less responsive (lower controllability as predicted in Experiment 1, see Figure 7), meaning that their DoA is much greater than that of cyclists.

From the experiment, we conclude that a leader's exercise type (e.g., cycle vs. hula hoop) is a critical factor on the perceived workload. This is also supported by the results of exit interviews; most of the participants answered that they prefer synchronizing with a leader with less speed fluctuation. The results of average error rates in Experiment 1 show that the highest and lowest speed fluctuation is given as hula hoops and cycles, respectively. The controllability of an exercise device (i.e., lower fluctuation or error) does not always guarantee lower perceived workload; when the followers use highly controllable devices, a leader's fluctuation level determines the followers' perceived physical workload. For followers with highly controllable devices, homogeneous exercise configuration always results in better perceived workloads (e.g., C-C > H-C); in contrast, for the followers with less controllable devices, homogeneous exercise configuration does not always result in better perceived workloads (e.g., H-H < C-H) due to the aforementioned reasons.

Experiment Results 3

We conducted reliability analysis on IMI, ESI, AFQ, Entitativity, and Rapport questionnaires. The Cronbach's alpha was 0.729, 0.954, 0.806, 0.925, and 0.932, respectively. It is widely accepted that when the Cronbach's alpha value is greater than 0.7, the results are assumed to be very reliable.

In IMI, the subscale of interest/enjoyment and competence were statistically significant ($t(13)=2.76$, $p<0.01$, $t(13)=2.66$, $p<0.01$, respectively). Note that some of the Interest/enjoyment items include "*enjoyed doing this activity*", "*was fun to do*"; some of the Competence items include "*pretty good at this activity*", "*satisfied with my performance*", etc. The subscale of pressure/tension (e.g., feel nervous, anxious, pressured, etc.) was not statistically significant, but its average value is slightly lower. This subscale is quite related to NASA-TLX's mental workload that was not statistically significant either.

In ESI, the subscales of focused attention, endurability and involvement were statistically significant ($t(13)=2.14$, $p<0.05$, $t(13)=2.35$, $p<0.05$, $t(13)=2.25$, $p<0.05$ respectively). Focused attention measures how much a participant focused on the activity; endurability measures whether the participants are likely to recommend this activity to others; involvements measures the participants' perceived feeling drawn to the activity. The perceived usability was not statistically significant ($t(13)=1.73$, $p=0.054$), but the average value of the rhythm cue was

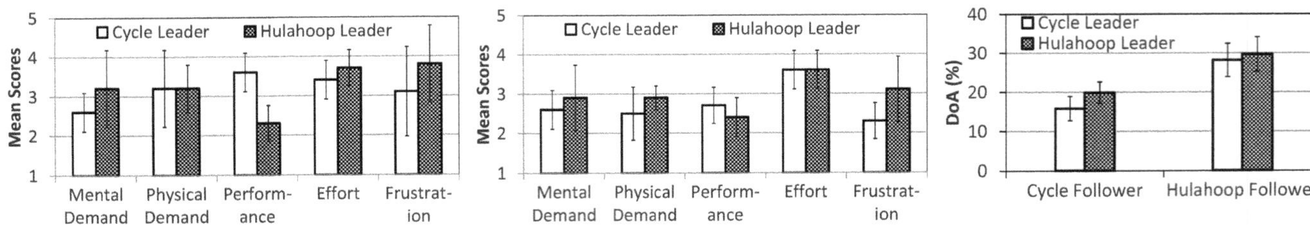

Figure 8: NASA-TLX questionnaire scores of cyclist followers (left) and hula hooper followers (center), and DoA values (right)

	DoA	Mental demand	Physical demand	Performance	Effort	Frustration
(a) Leader type - main effect, F(1,36)	**F=5.786, p=0.021 ***	F=3.329, p=0.076	F=0.363, p=0.551	**F=22.253, p<0.001 *****	F=0.095, p=0.760	**F=5.769, p=0.022 ***
(b) Follower type - main effect, F(1,36)	**F=89.641, p<0.001 *****	F=0.041, p=0.851	**F=9.081, p=0.005 ****	**F=4.846, p=0.034 ***	F=0.095, p=0.760	F=2.077, p=0.158
(c) Interaction effect, F(1,36)	F=1.139, p=0.293	F=0.041, p=0.851	F=1.009, p=0.322	**F=8.011, p=0.008 ****	F=0.853, p=0.362	F=0.026, p=0.874

Table 3 Two-way ANOVA result (exercise type and cue type) on DoA values and NASA-TLX questionnaire scores

slightly greater than that of the gauge cue. In general, the participants believe that the rhythm cue helps better engage in the paced exergames.

In AFQ, only distress subscale was statistically significant ($t(13)=-2.38$, $p<0.05$). This result is in line with NASA-TLX values, meaning that interpersonal synchrony with a rhythm cue is less demanding. The association subscale was not statistically significant; participants were able to equally concentrate on the task related items in both cases. The dissociation (or distraction) subscale was not statistically significant either, but it appears that the rhythm cue were able to slightly lower potential distraction.

RPE measures the perceived exertion, and the result shows that a rhythm cue's RPE is lower than a gauge cue's RPE ($t=-1.99$, $p<0.05$). Due to lower distress factor (AFQ, distress subscale) and task workloads (NASA-TLX), participants may feel that perceived exertion would be lower with a rhythm cue.

Finally, the results of social aspects, namely entitativity and rapport were not statistically significant ($t(13)=0.54$, $p=0.299$, $t(13)=-0.036$, $p=0.486$). Nonetheless, the rhythm cue has a slightly higher entitativity value on average partly due to coordinated movements. Interestingly, when we ask the participants to compare the results with the case where only real-time videos are available (without any of these assistive mechanisms), we find that the levels of entitativity and rapport were much lower than assistive mechanisms for interpersonal synchrony. In other words, tightly coupled collaboration in the virtual game can potentially provide enough rapport/entitativity, regardless whether participants are in complete synchronization (in-phase).

Post-experiment Interview Results

We conducted post-experiment interviews to (1) study the different user experiences depending on the roles, i.e., the leader and the follower, and to (2) understand the effects from the use of the gauge alone, and plus the rhythm.

Overall, we could observe quite even votes on both roles in terms of user preference; 7 participants preferred playing as a leader, 6 as a follower, and 1 equally liked both. Most of the preferences on being a leader came from its relative simplicity, mental freedom, and feeling of comfort. The participants' comments elaborate those such as

> "*I like playing as a leader because I feel free and independent*". [P10] and

> "*I understand that I was supposed to give guidance to the followers, but I soon found myself doing exercise at my own pace*". [P5]

We received minor opinions stating the difficulties of being a leader as well, such as

> "*Every single moment, I kept focusing on giving my follower proper exercise speeds and fun. That's why I frequently changed my pace, but it made me soon exhausted*". [P11] and

> "*I feel pressure in the leader's responsibility to guide the follower*". [P14]

On the other hand, notable comments on being a follower were regarding the feeling of achievement and the effectiveness of workouts, such as

> "*I think being a follower gives me more fun, because I feel I'm fulfilling some goals especially with the rhythmical cues*". [P7] and

> "*I feel I'm doing more exercises when I play as a follower*". [P6]

Interestingly, two participants preferred being a follower mainly because they felt more comfortable when simply following the leader's guidance, while many responded that being a follower was more difficult as it required extra attention to meet the guidance.

In either role, the participants mostly agreed that the conversation was quite beneficial. Notably, we could hear from two participants respectively that,

> "*Talking to each other makes me forget the pain of exercise. Even I got the sympathy that I am not the only one feeling hard, which encouraged me a lot*". [P7] and

> "*At first it was weird for me to play separately from each other. But as I keep talking to him and pacing with him, I was no longer aware of such a feeling*". [P8]

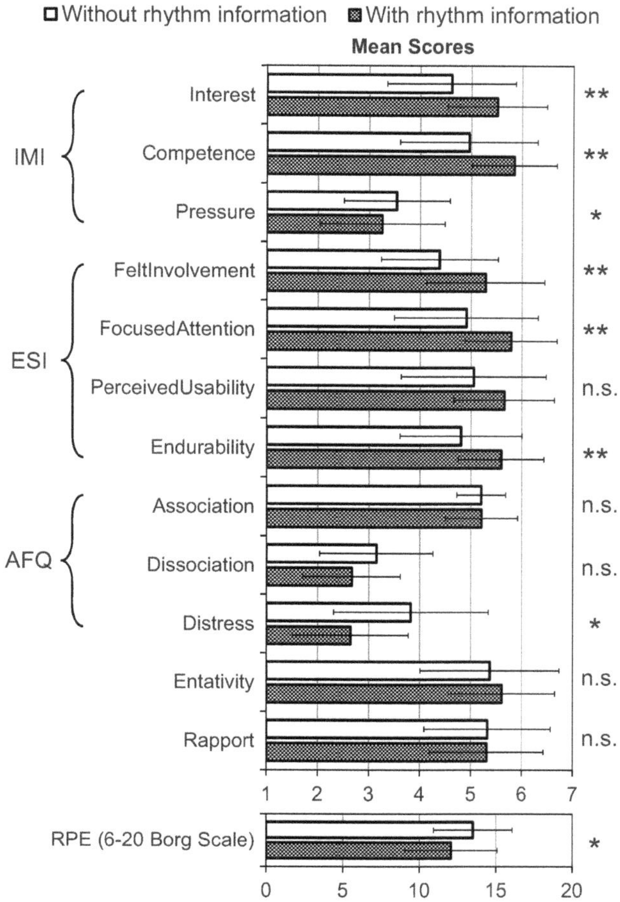

Figure 9. Mean scores of questionnaires for two cue types

From the comparative interviews regarding the gauge and the rhythm, we could understand that using the rhythm effectively facilitated easier plays, while notably, solely using the gauge stimulated unique fun originating from the higher challenges. Many leaders agreed that, with rhythms, they felt that their followers did better in keeping the paces closely. Similarly, many followers stated that the rhythms made it very simple to follow the leader's guidance. A brief comparison was that,

> "*The gauge is like something I watch and then follow, but the rhythm is just what I feel!*" [P14]

A participant elaborated,

> "*With listening to the rhythms, I found myself already got synchronized. (...) With the gauge alone, I had to concentrate on it and think more*". [P1]

However, we also received a few noteworthy opinions regarding the fun in using the gauge alone, such as

> "*Without the rhythms, my follower asked me more questions. Well, eventually it was very interesting that we could talk a lot to each other*". [P7] and

> "*I think keeping eyes on the gauge was more intuitive for me to find out the leader's intent*". [P11]

It was interesting to observe the opposing effects of using the rhythms. A participant commented,

> "*It was a great fun to me when I get the exact sync with the rhythmical sounds. But it was so annoying when I was out of beats!*" [P3]

A pair of participants gave very different comments; one said,

> "*I felt more comfortable to have signs to which I can conform*" [P12]

But the other said,

> "*I felt more comfortable to have only the gauge, because the rhythms are more like extra information for me to keep aware of*". [P10]

DISCUSSION

The user study results show that when compared with speed gauge cues, the rhythm cues lower the perceived workloads (NASA-TLX) with less distress (AFQ) and have positive impacts on perceived competence (IMI), performance (NASA-TLX), and involvement (EQ). We think that the mental and physical workloads will be an important factor on game performance and user experience, and should be thoughtfully considered in exergame design. Exergame players frequently perform multiple tasks simultaneously. A game is often designed with multiple different gaming devices (e.g., various game items, map structure, game rules) on top of a core game mechanic (e.g., exercising speed and interpersonal synchrony), which interact with each other, creating and enriching additional fun factors and new gaming experiences. For example, a player may concurrently perform one task of controlling exercise interfaces (e.g., maintaining synchrony), and another task of keeping track of game plays (e.g., making decisions on what items to take in a game) under a highly competitive situation. These tasks make players experience divided attention and impose continuous demands on the attention, potentially resulting in *dual-task interference;* performance gains on one task will come at the cost of performance deterioration on the other [51]. This relationship implies that lowering the mental and physical workloads of synchrony may have a positive effect on game performance and user experience, and allows more freedom to explore in game design. It is part of our future work to thoroughly investigate the impact of dual-task interference in exergame design; one way is to design a set of experiments in which participants perform elementary cognitive tasks relevant to exergame design (e.g., recall, pattern recognition, spatial awareness, perception/reaction) while continuously maneuvering exertion interfaces (e.g., adaptation, retainment tasks).

ExerSync provides a useful tool for gamifying existing group exercises/sports where leader-follower roles are rather clear, and interpersonal synchrony is important. Several game design scenarios include enabling online group exercises such as virtual rowing/spinning classes, and designing collaborative/competitive games out of group exercises with diverse exercising modalities. For example, in the design of a boat racing game, a virtual coxswain (leader) guides the rest of rowers (followers), and there could be multiple teams competing with one another.

As briefly mentioned earlier, a rhythm of body movements has two key factors, namely speed and phase. So far existing exergames use only exercise speed as game input from exercise devices. While we have not tested its feasibility, we discuss how phase information can be used as an additional game input. Interestingly, there are few convincing game design scenarios where the phase information can be used. For instance, in rowing, it is obvious that in order to achieve maximum speed, the crew must perfectly synchronize their rowing strokes (i.e., in-phase synchronization). In this case, the physics of rowing should be incorporated in the exergame design such that detailed rowing strokes dynamically determine boat movements.

For efficient rhythm coordination, the leader should be aware of the rhythm of followers. In the current design, the leader can only monitor the follower's status from the speed gauge. Yet, this activity would be cognitively demanding as the size of a group increases—there will be too many speed bars in a gauge. It is part of our future work to design intuitive and scalable mechanisms for delivering group status information. In a boat racing game, a good alternative would be animating each crew's rowing strokes such that the leader can instantly tell whether the crew members are performing well.

When knowing that both players are exercising with difference devices, some of our participants felt that interpersonal synchrony with heterogeneous exercises provides less social support than that with homogeneous exercises. One way of improving social affordance is to introduce a virtual avatar that animates translated rhythm; e.g., the rhythmic movements of a cyclist can be translated into a virtual avatar running on a treadmill at the cyclist's speed. An alternative method would be designing a game scenario that provides immersive social experience; in a boat racing game, we allow the crew members to directly maneuver the rowing strokes of virtual avatars.

In ExerSync, the software architecture of synchronization is based on a client-server model as in network time synchronization (NTP) [24], where exercise gamers (clients) exchange messages through the game server. Each cycle of a leader's rhythm (or gait phase) has a sequence number, and this rhythm information is broadcast to the followers with arbitrary network latency. The game server coordinates the rhythm responses from the followers on the basis of sequence numbers such that the leader can have a consistent view. In ExerSync, the worst case end-to-end round trip time (RTT) along the path of leader-server-follower is critical for group synchronization; e.g., a follower with one way latency of 150ms (comparable to 3G network latency) will always see a leader's rhythm generated 150ms ago. Fortunately, in ExerSync the time scale of interpersonal synchronization is usually much greater than that of network latency, and thus, players would be less sensitive to the network latency. In most exercises, changing a rhythm takes at least few seconds; e.g., cycles take around 2-3 seconds, and hula hoops take around 4-5 seconds. We believe that the network configuration of our user studies was no significant impact on user experiences since we used campus wireless LAN whose worst case RTT was smaller than 10ms. It is part of our future work to systematically investigate user experience under different network delay/jitter conditions in a controlled environment using Dummynet [22].

LIMITATION

The participants of user studies were mostly drawn from the university population (average age: 21.7, SD: 3.06). We recruit the study participants through campus bulletin boards and participants' referrals, indicating that the experiments involve equipment-based exercises, and the participants should be comfortable with maneuvering a chosen exercise device. This homogeneous selection of participants (who are likely young and fit) can provide an internal validity of experiments, but this would restrict the generalizability of findings. Whether our main findings are transferrable to other populations remains to be determined.

Given that only short-term experiments were carried out, we cannot determine whether ExerSync usage influences the long-term motivation. Yet, our user study results show the positive effects such as lowering the mental/physical load and distress, improving interest/enjoyment and competence, which may lead to improved long-term motivation. As reasonable as this interpretation may seem, direct confirmation requires a longitudinal study.

As it is currently, our primary interest lies in investigating the effectiveness of a rhythm cue in synchronization under group exercise environments. Our study currently does not investigate the exercise benefits of interpersonal synchrony (e.g., improved endurance, burnt calories). To this reason, the user studies are mostly composed of a series of short exercise sessions where each session takes about two minutes to complete. In the user study with five minute sessions, we asked the participants to report rating of perceived exertion (RPE) to roughly see whether the exercise amount differs between rhythm cue and speed gauge conditions–RPE is a good metric as it is highly correlated with heart rates [8]. The results show that RPE values were statistically significant, and there may be some difference between these conditions. A thorough investigation must be followed to validate whether there are the exercise benefits of interpersonal synchrony (e.g., running exhaustive tasks).

CONCLUSION

We proposed the ExerSync platform that supports various assistive mechanisms of facilitating interpersonal synchrony and handles inter-person and -device heterogeneity. In this paper, we detailed the core components of ExerSync, namely Exercise Rhythm Extractor, Rhythm Translator, and Audio-visual Rhythm. For rhythm extraction, we analyzed four kinds of repetitive aerobic exercises, namely rope jumping, hula hooping, stationary cycling and treadmill running and designed novel mechanisms for extracting major phases within the movement cycles. Rhythm translation mechanisms are based on a leader-directed model of group synchronization for fast convergence and efficiently handle inter-person and -device heterogeneity. The extracted rhythm of the leader is broadcast to the followers using thoughtfully designed audio/visual rhythm cues such that they can effectively coordinate their movement cycles. We built the prototype platform and validated the feasibility and effectiveness of synchronizing rhythm via extensive user studies.

ACKNOWLEDGEMENTS

We thank all of the subjects who participated in this study. Special thanks to Inseok Hwang, Yuhwan Kim and Changhoon Lee for their assistance. This work was supported by the National Research Foundation of Korea grant (No. 2012-0006422) funded by the Korean Government (MEST), and the SW Computing R&D Program of KEIT (2012-10041313, UX-oriented Mobile SW Platform) funded by the Ministry of Knowledge Economy of Korea.

REFERENCES

1. Ahn, M., Kwon, S., Park, B., Cho, K., Choe, S., Hwang, I., Jang, H., Park, J., Rhee, Y., and Song, J. Running or gaming. *In Proceedings of the International Conference on Advances in Computer Enterntainment Technology*, ACM (2009), 345-348.
2. Ainsworth, B., et al. Compendium of physical activities: an update of activity codes and met intensities. Medicine & Science in Sports & Exercise 32, 9 (2000), S498.
3. Akoumianakis, D., Vellis, G., Milolidakis, I., Kotsalis, D., and Alexandraki, C. Distributed collective practices in collaborative music performance. *In Proceedings of the 3rd international conference on Digital Interactive Media in Entertainment and Arts*, ACM (2008), 368-375.
4. Alexandraki, C., and Akoumianakis, D. Exploring new perspectives in network music performance: The diamouses framework. Computer Music Journal 34, 2 (2010), 66-83.
5. Arias, P., and Cudeiro, J. Effects of rhythmic sensory stimulation (auditory, visual) on gait in parkinson?s disease patients. Experimental Brain Research 186, 4 (2008), 589-601.
6. Ashton-James, C., Van~Baaren, R., Chartrand, T., Decety, J., and Karremans, J. Mimicry and me: The impact of mimicry on self-construal. Social Cognition 25, 4 (2007), 518-535.
7. Bernieri, F. Coordinated movement and rapport in teacher-student interactions. Journal of Nonverbal behavior 12, 2 (1988), 120-138.
8. Borg, G.A. and others. Psychophysical bases of perceived exertion. Med sci sport exerc. 14. 5 (1982), 377-381.
9. Carroll, E., Lottridge, D., Latulipe, C., Singh, V., and Word, M. Bodies in critique: a technological intervention in the dance production process. In Proceedings of the CSCW 2012.
10. Chen, Y., Repp, B., and Patel, A. Spectral decomposition of variability in synchronization and continuation tapping: Comparisons between auditory and visual pacing and feedback conditions. *Human Movement Science 21,* 4 (2002), 515-532.
11. Cluff, T., Robertson, D., and Balasubramaniam, R. Kinetics of hula hooping: An inverse dynamics analysis. Human movement science 27, 4 (2008), 622-635.
12. Fraser, S.N. and Spink, K.S. Examining the role of social support and group cohesion in exercise compliance. Journal of behavioral medicine.25.3, (2002), 233-249.
13. Gavin, J., McBrearty, M., and Seguin D. The psychology of exercise, IDEA Health & Fitness Source. 3. 2 (2006).
14. George, B. Visual metronome, 1987. US Patent 4,649,794.
15. Haidt, J., Seder, J., and Kesebir, S. Hive psychology, happiness, and public policy. *The Journal of Legal Studies 37, S2* (2008), S133-S156.
16. Hart, S., and Staveland, L. Development of nasa-tlx (task load index): Results of empirical and theoretical research. *Human mental workload 1* (1988), 139-183.
17. Hove, M., and Risen, J. It's all in the timing: Interpersonal synchrony increases affiliation. *Social Cognition 27*, 6 (2009), 949-960.
18. Karageorghis, et al. Psychophysical and ergogenic effects of synchronous music during treadmill walking. Journal of sport & exercise psychology.31, (2009), 18-36.
19. Karvitz, L. Exercise Motivation: What Starts and Keeps People Exerciseing? http://www.unm.edu/~lkravitz/Article%20folder /ExerciseMot.pdf, (2011).
20. Lakens, D. If they move in sync, they must feel in sync: Movement synchrony leads to attributions of rapport and entitativity. *Social Cognition. 29.* 1, (2011), 1-14.
21. Lee, B. Jump Rope Training-2nd Edition. 2010. http://www.humank inetics.com/excerpts/excerpts/learn-three-phases-of-rope-jumping.
22. Luigi Rizzo. The Dummynet project. http://info.iet.unipi.it/~luigi/dummynet/ (2009).
23. McNeill, W. Keeping together in time: Dance and drill in human history. Harvard Univ Pr, 1997.
24. Mills, D.L. Internet time synchronization: The network time protocol. Communications, IEEE Transactions on.39.10(1991) 1482-1493.
25. Miles, L., Nind, L., and Macrae, C. The rhythm of rapport: Interpersonal synchrony and social perception. *Journal of experimental social psychology 45*, 3 (2009), 585-589.

26. Mueller, F., Stevens, G., Thorogood, A., O'Brien, S., and Wulf, V. Sports over a distance. Personal and Ubiquitous Computing 11, 8 (2007), 633-645.
27. Mueller, F. Vetere, F. and Gibbs, M. The Design of Networked Exertion Games. J. of Virtual Reality and Broadcasting.5.13, (2008).
28. Mueller, F., Vetere, F., Gibbs, M., Edge, D., Agamanolis, S., and Sheridan, J. Jogging over a distance between europe and australia. In Proceedings of the 23nd annual ACM symposium on User interface software and technology, ACM (2010), 189-198.
29. Mueller, F., Vetere, F., Gibbs, M., Edge, D., Agamanolis, S., Sheridan, J., and Heer, J. Balancing exertion experiences. In Proceedings of the 2012 ACM CHI, ACM (2012), 1853-1862.
30. O'Brien, S., and Mueller, F. Jogging the distance. In Proceedings of the SIGCHI conference on Human factors in computing systems, ACM (2007), 523-526.
31. O'Brien, H.L., Toms, E.G., Kelloway, E.K. and Kelly, E. Developing and evaluating a reliable measure of user engagement. Proc. of the American Society for Information Science and Technology, 2008
32. Park, T., Hwang, I., Lee, U., Lee, S., Yoo, C., Lee, Y., Jang, H., Choe, S., Park, S., and Song, J. Exerlink: enabling pervasive social exergames with heterogeneous exercise devices. In Proceedings of the ACM MobiSys, ACM (2012), 15-28.
33. Park, T., Yoo, C., Choe, S., Park, B., and Song, J. Transforming solitary exercises into social exergames. In Proceedings of the ACM CSCW 2012, ACM (2012), 863-866.
34. Pikovsky, A., Rosenblum, M., and Kurths, J. Synchronization: A universal concept in nonlinear sciences,. Cambridge Univ Pr, 2003.
35. Postmes, Social Identity Formation and Team Performance. University of Groningen (2008).
36. Puccinelli, N.M., and Tickle-Degnen, L. Knowing too much about others: Moderators of the relationship between eavesdropping and rapport in social interaction. Journal of Nonverbal Behavior. 28. 4 (2004), 223-243.
37. Reidsma, D., Nijholt, A., and Bos, P. Temporal interaction between an artificial orchestra conductor and human musicians. Computers in Entertainment (CIE) 6, 4 (2008), 53.
38. Repp, B., and Penel, A. Rhythmic movement is attracted more strongly to auditory than to visual rhythms. *Psychological Research 68*, 4 (2004), 252-270.
39. Ryan, R.M. Control and information in the intrapersonal sphere: An extension of cognitive evaluation theory. *Journal of personality and social psychology. 43*. 3 (1982), 450.
40. Schmidt, R.C., Bienvenu, M. Fitzpatrick, P.A and Amazeen, P.G. A comparison of intra-and interpersonal interlimb coordination: coordination breakdowns and coupling strength. J. of Experimental Psychology : Human perception and Performance.24.3, (1998), 884.
41. Schmidt, R.C. and Turvey, M.T Phase-entrainment dynamics of visually coupled rhythmic movements. Biological cybernetics.70.4, (1994), 369-376.
42. Schmidt, R., and Richardson, M. Dynamics of interpersonal coordination. Coordination: Neural, behavioral and social dynamics (2008), 281-308.
43. Stach, T. Graham, T.C. Yim, J. and Rhodes, R.E. Heart rate control of exercise video games. Proceedings of Graphics interface 2009, Canadian Information Processing Society, (2009), 125-132.
44. Stach, T. and Graham, T. Exploring haptic feedback in exergames. Human-Computer Interaction—INTERACT 2011. (2011), 18-35.
45. Stein, N. Jumping rope vs. kettlebells, 2011.http://www.livestr ong.com/article/552088-jumping-rope-vs-kettlebells/.
46. Stel, M. Effects of mimicking: acting prosocially by being emotionally moved, 2007. http://onlinelibrary.wiley.com/doi/10.1002/ejsp.472/abstract.
47. U.S. Department of Health and Services, Physical activity and health: a report of the Surgeon General. (1996).
48. Valdesolo, P., and DeSteno, D. Synchrony and the social tuning of compassion. *Emotion 11*, 2 (2011), 262.
49. van Baaren. Mimicry and pro-social behavior, 2004. http://pss.sagepub.com/content/15/1/71.short.
50. Weir, J. How to calculate calories burned with a hula hoop, 2011. http://www.livestrong.com/article/89945-calculate-calories-burned-hula-hoop/.
51. Wickens, C.D. The structure of attentional resources. Attention and performance.8 (1980).
52. Wilson, A., Snapp-Childs, W., Coats, R., and Bingham, G. Learning a coordinated rhythmic movement with task-appropriate coordination feedback. Experimental brain research 205, 4 (2010), 513-520.
53. Wilson, D., et al. Multilevel selection theory and major evolutionary transitions implications for psychological science. Current Directions in Psychological Science 17, 1 (2008), 6-9.
54. Wiltermuth, S., and Heath, C. Synchrony and cooperation. Psychological Science 20, 1 (2009), 1
55. Yim, J. and Graham, TC. Proceedings of The 2007 conference on Future Play. ACM, (2007), 166-173.
56. Zehr, E., Balter, J., Ferris, D., Hundza, S., Loadman, P., and Stoloff, R. Neural regulation of rhythmic arm and leg movement is conserved across human locomotor tasks. The Journal of Physiology 582, 1(2007), 209-227.
57. Zhao, N. Full-featured pedometer design realized with 3-axis digital accelerometer, 2010. http://www.analog.com/static/imported-files/tech_articles/pedometer.pdf.

Meanings and Boundaries of Scientific Software Sharing

Xing Huang[1], Xianghua Ding[1], Charlotte P. Lee[2], Tun Lu[1], Ning Gu[1]

[1]School of Computer Science
Fudan University
Shanghai 201203, China
{xinghuang, dingx, lutun, ninggu}
@fudan.edu.cn

[2]Human Centered Design & Engineering
University of Washington
423 Sieg Hall, Seattle
WA 98195, USA
cplee@uw.edu

ABSTRACT

In theory, software, like other digital artifacts, can be freely copied and distributed. In practice, however, its effective flow is conditioned on various technical and social factors. In this paper, drawing on ethnographic work primarily with a bio-informatics research team in China, we report on meanings of scientific software sharing as embedded in social practices of learning, apprenticeship, membership, publication, and reputation. We illustrate that while free flow is important, boundary management is equally important for the effective travel of software to its appropriate destinations. Our study highlights a number of issues that are important to consider for effectively supporting sharing and collaboration in science.

Author Keywords

Software sharing; scientific collaboration.

ACM Classification Keywords

H.5.m [Information Interfaces and Presentation]: Miscellaneous; H.5.3 [Information Interfaces and Presentation]: Group and Organization Interfaces - Computer-supported cooperative work.

General Terms

Design; Human Factors.

INTRODUCTION

Sharing is central to contemporary science. In the *open science* system famously characterized by Merton [31], scientists openly publish their scientific findings and knowledge, and are rewarded with academic credit. This is in great contrast to previous eras when knowledge of nature was considered to be sacred secrets (e.g. ancient alchemy) [15]. Although contemporary research groups still self-consciously conceal research results to compete for recognition of discovery priority [19, 28], sharing is generally positively perceived and actively encouraged [16, 50].

In CSCW in particular, fostered by the development of IT, new research programs exploring the use of IT to provide new sites for scientific sharing and collaboration are on a rapid rise, under terms of "collaboratories", "cyberinfrastructure", "eScience", or others [20, 27, 34]. With its great potential to enable communication and the move of information rapidly and relatively inexpensively across time and space, there is a high expectation that IT can substantially speed up and widen the access of resources among scientists [27]. Three interrelated aspects of sharing are typically explored: instrument sharing focusing on the sharing and access of key or expensive physical instruments remotely [26, 27, 32], data sharing concerning making scientific data openly available for verification and other investigations [6, 8, 48], and knowledge sharing focusing more on the exchange of talents, expertise and effort [10]. Studies of these projects show that, for scientific sharing, while IT provides great potential to overcome distance barriers, there are still many other socio-cultural barriers, such as cross-institutional barriers [10], disciplinary and institutional cultures [11, 44], credit systems [7], and so on. These studies point to the importance of understanding relevant social and cultural practices to effectively support scientific sharing with IT.

While in these programs software as part of the *infrastructure for sharing* has been extensively explored, software as *an object for sharing* itself is largely overlooked. However, understanding software sharing is of great importance for scientific collaboration and innovation, mainly for two reasons. First, software plays an increasingly critical role in scientific research, including but not limited to data storage, integration, analysis, processing, representation, and others. Not only does it make work easier, faster or more efficient, but also it changes the very nature of doing research, such as in emerging new interdisciplinary fields including bio-informatics. Second, software is distinct from other aspects of sharing in fundamental ways, and warrants separate study. As with other digital artifacts and unlike the more physical instruments, "*software can be copied and distributed at essentially no cost*", which provides unlimited potential for sharing [22]. At the same time, software is defined as a set of programs directing what to do and how to execute certain tasks on a computer, which is essentially different from data or knowledge. So it may play very different social roles in science, which can greatly influence how it is shared and how we can support it.

In this paper, we report on an ethnographic study at a bio-informatics research center in China, with an aim to deepen the understanding of software sharing practices in science, and inform the design of computing systems to better support them. We define scientific software broadly as *all kinds of software that are used to support scientific research*. With *scientific software sharing*, then, we concern ourselves with social practices related to the creation, navigation, use, selection, and distribution of all these sorts of software, and seek ways to better support them. By focusing on this new emerging discipline, bio-informatics, in which software plays a central not a secondary role, as well as China as the particular context, we hope to be able to highlight some of the issues that might be obscured in more traditional or familiar sites, shed light on scientific sharing, and derive design implications.

RELATED WORK

For software sharing in general, probably the most studied topic is open source software. Extensive research attention is paid to the contribution and motivation mechanisms behind the development of open source software, including how the social context and social networks influence the project licensor's decision [45], how the choice of license influences people's passion for contribution [12, 35, 38, 39], and how meeting one's own needs motivates people's participation [9]. Studies also show that factors such as the readability of code and manual documents are important for user acceptance [18]. Others describe work practices, development processes, and community networking of open source software communities [13, 40]. While open source software plays a large part in scientific research, however, how it is used or shared in science still has not been closely examined.

For scientific software in particular, sharing has also been of concern for a while, especially in software research. Many found that scientific software is hard to maintain and is limited for long-term use [1, 23, 36]. Some point out that scientific software documentation is problematic, including comments in the code, user guides, manuals, and so on [33, 37, 42]. Others attribute scientific software problems to developers' lack of software engineering training [24]. This line of work suggests that although software can be copied and distributed at essentially no cost, software quality issues can prevent software from being widely applied.

More recent research focuses on developing middleware, adapters, and protocols to support "collaboration transparency", through which a single-user application can be shared between more than two people [5, 47]. By combining these sharing approaches with the development of grid computing [17], web services [4] and cloud computing [3], software can then be delivered by means of services, in hopes of further fostering software sharing across time and space.

Overall, scientific software sharing has mainly been examined from a technical perspective and few have focused on its social practices. The recent exception is Howison and Herbsleb's work on how incentives impact software production [21, 22]. Similarly from a social perspective, however, our work is distinct by looking into details and meanings of software sharing with respect to broader collective social practices, beyond software production and the issues of incentives.

RESEARCH SITE, BACKGROUND AND METHOD

Our study is primarily based on a center for bio-informatics technology in China. Bio-informatics is defined as the application of computational techniques to understand and organize the information associated with biological macromolecules. Bio-informatics emerged in recent years as the surge in biological data demanded computation to handle it [30]. The center was established in 2002, and as a non-profit organization, the mission of the center is to promote the advancement of Life Sciences, Biotechnology and the Biopharmaceutical industry by engaging in life science database construction and bioinformatics software development. The center is organized with a number of research teams focusing on various topics including functional genomics, system biology, translational medicine, pathogen genomics and so on.

As with most research teams in China, the research center is organized and managed in the form of Tidui (echelon, "梯队"). A Tidui is usually composed of one senior faculty, several junior faculty, and many graduate students. As the team is often large (20 or more), its management also tends to be hierarchical, in that new junior students are directly mentored by senior students as their ShiXiong/ShiJie (师兄/师姐, senior brother/sister apprentice) for everyday help, all students are managed by junior faculty as their team leaders, and all students/junior faculty are advised and directed by the senior faculty. As a research center with no graduate program, our site, though, is different from other research teams in universities, in that there are no graduate students officially affiliated with the center. However, as the head of the center is also a professor affiliated with a number of institutions and universities, his students from these institutions and universities are also involved in various projects at the center. So the center is a spatially distributed group as most junior students still need to spend time on their own campuses for coursework, and can only be at the center occasionally.

For this study, we have mainly engaged with the team led by Liu, a PI in the center. The team's research area is translational medicine, involving proteomics related bioinformatics, transcriptional regulation and oncology related bioinformatics. Their main focus and contribution is on developing software for analysis, and is mainly based on open data (which is important for the independence of the discipline), except for collaborative projects with other teams (e.g. a team from a hospital) who provide data and they apply algorithms to analyze the data. We have been collaborating with the team to develop an open platform to support collaborative protein analysis by integrating related software and communication tools, which partially motivated our investigation on software sharing in science in the first place.

In building the platform over the past two years, we attended monthly meetings with the team, were often invited to attend their seminars, occasionally engaged in discussion meetings with other related teams, and often worked together with the team to fix technical problems. These were the main forms of our participant observation at the center, and, in total, we spent 150 hours in the field and collected 23 meeting memos. Through this process, we noted many factors that have shaped how scientific software circulates within and without the team.

Partially motivated by our observations, we conducted more in-depth interviews to directly inquire how software is shared in practice. We completed semi-structured interviews with 15 informants in total. Interview times ranged from 25 to 120 minutes, with 50 minutes the average. In our interviews, we asked about the participants recent research projects, and details of how scientific software was produced, selected, used, and distributed with regard to these projects. When possible, concrete cases and examples were sought. Of the 15 informants, 13 were from Liu's team, and 2 were from their collaborator – the Tidui led by Ceng from another research institute. Ceng's team focuses on wet lab experiments, original data production, and some preliminary data analysis. Most of our informants only write scripts such as R, Python and Perl to integrate software for analysis, and only one informant (from Ceng's team) could be categorized as a *professional* end user developer who writes programs in Java or C++, and his main responsibility was to develop software for the rest of the team to do research. Our informants' positions were: 4 master students, 2 junior Ph.D. students, 4 senior Ph.D. students, 1 graduated Ph.D. student (now a post-doc abroad), 3 regular full time researchers, and 1 PI (Liu). All interviews were conducted in Mandarin Chinese, and the participants and interviewers were all native Chinese speakers. Quotes used in this paper were later translated to English.

We then applied a grounded theoretical approach for the analysis of the data [46]. We started analysis while the data was being collected. Through open and axial coding of the data, themes started to emerge (while our participatory observation greatly influenced our interview questions and analysis, coding and analysis was primarily based on our interview data). In this paper, we will use representative individual quotes to illustrate our points. All of the names used are pseudonyms.

TYPES OF SOFTWARE IN BIO-INFORMATICS

In bio-informatics, the development of software for the management and processing of biological data forms the main contribution of their research work. So unlike other disciplines [22], software production plays a central, rather than a secondary, role in their research. Specifically, from our study, we identify four types of software involved in their daily research work: *published academic software, open source software, homemade scripts, and commercial software products*. *Published academic software* refers to software that is published in the form of a paper that contains relevant rationales, methods, algorithms, and information about the software. Paper publication indicates novelty and significance of the software to the community, and corresponding software is usually made publicly available once published. *Open source software,* freely available in the form of source code, can be used, distributed and modified by anyone under an open-source license, and is found to be heavily used in their research. *Homemade scripts*, written to do particular data processing, or to stream different steps of software work together, are also commonly used but usually only written for personal purposes, not intended for sharing. *Commercial software products* are relatively the least used, since they are too expensive for individuals to afford, and many times, there are free alternatives available in terms of *open source software* or *published academic software* (often as good and are well recognized by the community). Of course, these categories are not entirely exclusive, and occasionally, one type can be transitioned into another. For example, some homemade software, originally written for personal or internal use, may later be published or contributed to an open source software community. Overall, we found while researchers heavily rely on open source and published academic software, always write and use scripts in their research, and occasionally use commercial software products, their main contribution or output is the published academic software. Next, we will elaborate in more details of how and why software is circulated, and how a range of boundaries are leveraged or contrived to regulate its flow.

MEANINGS OF SCIENTIFIC SOFTWARE SHARING

In our study, we believe two social entities are central to characterize the meanings and mechanisms of scientific software sharing: the local team, and the research community. The local team (or Tidui) in China is the "internal us", in which resources are centrally managed and coordinated. It is largely a people-oriented unit, where members may not necessarily share the same space or the same institution, but they all share the same leadership and management. In our case study, for example, most of our student informants were from different universities and institutions, but were all advised by the same professor and managed by the same team leader. Moreover, it is also a basic unit where junior members learn and grow into qualified and independent researchers, through "peripheral participation" or apprenticeship [29]. The research community, on the other hand, is more a topic-oriented social configuration, where members are connected by common interests, mutual engagement and a shared repertoire [49]. In this section, we will explicate why and how scientific software is shared with respect to these two social entities: internally with the local team and externally with the research community.

Apprentice and Membership: Sharing Internally with the Local Team

Within the local team, characterized as a close-knit and highly inter-dependent social entity where members mutually help each other and are generally aware of what each other is up to through regular group meetings and project participation, software and related information are generally well shared. Especially, homemade scripts and work-in-progress academic software are mainly shared within this unit and rarely travel beyond it. Particularly, the meanings and mechanisms of software sharing are highly related to apprenticeship and membership of this group.

Experience Sharing through Apprenticeship

As mentioned, one important component of a research team is learning/training, mainly through apprenticeship. In our case study, we found that it was common for new junior members to be assigned with more senior members (usually above the third year in their graduate program), or Shixiong/Shijie in their words, for everyday help, advice, and guidance. New junior members, by engaging in marginal work and with the help of Shixiong/Shijie and advisors, learn the tricks of the trade of doing research, and obtain relevant research skills including program writing. So learning, training and passing down experiences through apprenticeships are inherent themes that define the identity and culture of this group, which in turn, have greatly shaped how ideas, information, resources and software circulate within it.

First of all, by sharing their experiences, Shixiong/Shijies work as important gatekeepers to help them navigate through and choose from all the publicly available software out there (e.g. open source software and published academic software). In the field of bio-informatics, there is a consensus that published or academic software should be made publicly available for free. Throwing software out there, however, does not directly lead to effective use of it. As a matter of fact, with all of the *published academic software* as well as other *open source software* made available, it becomes a big challenge in terms of how to choose and navigate through it, especially for new members. Almost all informants reported that Shixiong/Shijies were of critical help in this regard. Li described a typical case, "*oh, Shijie said... the Shijie who helps me... she said that was a common method. So I tried it.*" So by simply following what Shixiong/Shijies use or what they recommend, new members learn what is commonly used and practiced in the community.

Further, Shixiong/Shijie's experiences are also important for them to build up programming skills. They help by engaging in discussions, checking software codes, and providing relevant resources. Hu commented that discussion with his Shijie was helpful, "*mainly in terms of thoughts. She will tell you how to think about it, but for details, in terms of how to write, you should do it yourself.*" Wu reported that his Shixiong's hints such as a package's name were useful for him to locate relevant resources. Others provided relevant documents and examples for new members to learn, as Wu said, "*he directly gave it to me... all the documents corresponding to each package, and there were examples and others, and I studied them myself.*" Of course, sometimes, it involved direct software sharing, "*I checked with my Shixiong, what functions or what packages shall be used for drawing it this way, and he said, 'I would give you this script and it could solve the problem', so I just took it and used it.*" As we can see here, how software is shared in this context is clearly associated with experience sharing between apprenticeship relationships. And, with more and more open source and academic software becoming publicly available, experience sharing for software navigation might be more important than the sharing and distribution of copies of software themselves.

Interestingly, the motivation to learn also shapes their decisions regarding whether to reuse others' software or to rewrite it on their own, especially for simple scripts. Script writing is an integral component of learning and training for junior members to grow into qualified bio-informatics researchers. Consequently, sometimes, even if there were scripts available to meet their requirements, the junior members would still opt to write one themselves, as Lian described, "*The problem was too simple to use others' scripts, and it was also a way for me to practice my script writing skills, so I wrote it all by myself.*" It reminds us that in a culture where learning/training is an inherent component, directly sharing a copy of software itself might not always be desirable, but rather, sharing relevant resources for learning and software making might be more helpful.

Moreover, we note that sharing through apprenticeship is mainly through the "request-and-give" social protocol. That is, junior members request and their Shixiong/Shijies respond with relevant information, as part of their mentoring responsibilities. It is also important to note that such a "request-and-give" social protocol is critical for experience and software sharing in this context. Considering an important component of knowing is embedded in what we do, tacit, subconsciously held [41], and not readily available for transferring to others, the request-and-give protocol, then, provides an important mechanism to turn the tacit knowing into explicit and transferrable information.

Software Sharing as Part of Membership

While sharing through apprenticeship can be accounted as part of responsibility, sharing among peers works more as markers of membership. Dourish and Anderson, drawing on social studies of secrecy, note, "*the practices of keeping and sharing secrets are ways in which affiliation and membership are managed and demonstrated*" [14]. By analogy, in our study, we similarly found that the practices of keeping and sharing software are ways in which affiliation and membership are managed and demonstrated.

Sharing as part of membership is most clearly seen from the sharing of *homemade scripts* within the team. Bai, when asked whether he would give a piece of software to his teammate, answered that being part of the same lab justified this sharing, "*I will give for sure. We are all from the same lab after all. If someone emails me, I will give it to him for sure.*" Interestingly, he further stressed "*There was nothing so secret, and you don't have any copyright*". It suggests to us that, for simple homemade scripts, since they are not as valuable (in terms of innovation and labor taken) as some academic or commercial software, there is little obstacle to constrain their flow. Yet, at the same time, it is exactly the low value that confines its capability to travel too far. As a result, sharing of homemade software is mainly contained within the local team.

In our case study, we did not find any central place to store and manage the homemade software, and sharing was also mainly through the request-and-give social protocol within the team. Yin mentioned a case, "*later, another teammate also came to me and asked for it. As he was doing similar things, so he asked and I gave it to him.*" When asked whether software sharing was always very open in her lab, she responded by explicitly pointing out that homemade software was mainly shared through private requests, email or verbal, "*not like that, but if someone asks in private, I will give. It is not like we have a public platform for it, not like that.*" Our data further suggests that many factors may contribute to the non-use of an open and centralized place for storing and sharing for this kind of software. First, most of the software is written for personal use to address a problem at hand, and it is unexpected that one day others may also find it useful. Second, as it is mainly written for personal purposes, it may not be so readable or understandable for others to use the software [24]. So sense of belonging is important for the sharing of homemade software within a team, which is similar to open source software [2]. However, unlike the production of open source software, which is communal with centralized management and coordination [38], the production of scientific software is mainly base on distributed individual effort.

For the request-and-give social protocol to work among peers, awareness of what each other is doing is a key component. As expected, regular group meeting is an important means for them to learn what each other is doing. Zan described, "*We will present (our work) in our group meetings. There are so many people in the lab, and generally we know what each other is doing.*" Qiangrui revealed a typical situation for software sharing in his group, "*you will talk about your work and your progress in your group meetings. And there will be people who may encounter the same problem for sure. If you have solved the problem, they will ask you how you solved it. And you will say, oh, I wrote something. Then he would say 'could you share the code with me', and I would give the code.*" It suggests that, for the effective circulation of homemade software, using computing to enhance awareness of what each other is doing can be valuable here, especially when members are quite distributed, as in our case study.

Publications and Natural Software Selection: Sharing Externally with the Research Community

For software with certain innovation and scientific significance, it may appeal to wider audience, go beyond the local environment, and become academic software open to the external research community through publication. In this section, we are mainly concerned with the circulation of *published academic software* within the community. Unlike the local team, the research community is largely a practice-oriented social configuration. While members may share common research interests and engage in similar research activities, there is no official social affiliation involved, and "*practice is the source of coherence of a community*" [49]. As an academic community, it is also dominated by a "reputation economy based on substantial publications" [22]. Howison and Herbsleb, in their study of the production of software, point out that "*Software is a secondary player in the world of scientific work*" [21]. Fortunately, in bio-informatics, scientific software plays a central, not a secondary, role, and substantial part of scientific software is produced and shared exactly through the reputation economy and the publication system. Authors gain academic credit directly from publishing the software, and software publications are well recognized as their primary contributions. Once the software is published, papers, citation mechanisms, reputation systems, as well as the culture and norms of the research community start to take their way to shape the evolution and circulation of software. As such, it is impossible to talk about the circulation of academic software without talking about the mechanisms and functions of publications.

Sharing through Publications

The circulation of academic software aligns well with the circulation of publication. In the bio-informatics community, of our study especially, there is a consensus that once the paper is published, relevant software should be made publicly available in one way or the other. Now it is not the issues of availability, but the issues of visibility, documentation, awareness, navigation, evaluation, selection, reputation and others that have become critical in shaping the circulation of academic software, and all of these are dependent on the publication mechanism.

Firstly, the paper reviewing and publication process helps to normalize software and relevant documentation, and sets a bar for the selection of software quality for the community in the first place. All academic software is associated with at least one paper, which contains relevant rationales, methods, algorithms, and more, as part of the norms for publication. Bai put it, "*the essence of documentation about a piece of software is in its published paper*". In a sense, publications serve as a persistent shared repertoire [49] of knowledge, information, references, authorship, and others, and they can reach out to a wider audience far beyond the space and time constraints. While the lack of documentation is commonly complained as one of the main factors constraining the widespread use of scientific software [37, 42], the correlation between software contribution and paper publication together with the reviewing process seem to provide a way to relieve this issue.

Further, visibility and awareness obtained through publication is important for the wide distribution of software. Our informants were fully aware of how important publication was for their software circulation. Huang described, "*it (widespread use) is mainly dependent on paper publication. If it cannot be published, others will not use it.*" It is especially helpful if it is published in high quality journals, as Liu mentioned, "*I never make specific efforts to recommend it, except I attend conferences, and we have lectures. But if we have good papers, that is if we publish our software tools in the internationally well known journals, it is a good recommendation in itself.*" On the other hand, almost all of our informants reported that they were highly reliant on publications to learn about methods, software, and relevant knowledge. When talking about software selection, Ji said, "*Usually, when the paper is published, they will compare their own tools with other previous tools. Usually, that will be part of the paper. So you can take a look, and choose one that might be used more often.*" Some will particularly go for overview papers for this purpose, as revealed by Hu, "*if you want to do phosphorylation, there will be overview papers about phosphorylation for sure, and usually they will mention (relevant software tools). You will know what are out there after you read a few.*" As people turn to the publication mechanism for software awareness and selection, publication and software circulation are clearly correlated.

Moreover, publications can also serve as communication channels through which demands and supplies are connected, and it may further drive the evolution of software. Bao's is a case in point. He published a paper on a piece of software, and then received several requests for more features, which motivated him to upgrade the software in the end. He said, "*others read your paper, and emailed to us, asking whether we can do some predictions for them, something they are working on. I got a few of these emails, so I developed (a piece of software) for all. It is publicly open to everyone.*" This piece of work also resulted in a publication. So publications are not merely a shared repertoire, but also communication channels through which people of similar concerns are connected.

Natural Software Selection

With more and more academic software made available, how to select high quality software becomes an issue. After all, not all published software is of equal quality. Actually, we often heard our informants complaining how some people only care about publishing the paper and never care about maintaining the software once it is published, which greatly limits the long term applicability of the software. Further, as mentioned, although in the bio-informatics community, most published software is theoretically publicly available, however, whether it is practically applicable or not is conditioned by many technical factors. For example, the extensibility of software could be an issue. Since it was mainly developed to address a specific question, and only tested with limited data, it may not be applicable or extensible to other situations [33, 43]. Besides, user interactivity also plays a role. Often a GUI is provided to make the software more user friendly, however, we found its demand for user interactivity often meant less usable for more skilled programing users. Bai reported he preferred command interface over GUI, "because the one with *GUI can't run on the server...because, the matter of computation...it is only part of the whole work procedure. If you write a whole work procedure in the script, you don't need to watch for it, otherwise, for example, if there is GUI, it will stop and you need to click for it to continue, which is too much trouble.*" Other issues such as compatibility, performance, and the lack of maintenance could also influence its widespread use. So publication itself does not ensure good maintenance, technical compatibility or wide applicability, which are critical for the circulation of software.

In this regard, citations together with paper publications provide a natural software selection process through which high quality and more sharable software can stand out. Qiangrui described how citation worked as a natural selection mechanism, "*if you want to solve a problem, you will check the literature. When you look at the literature, you may see 5 or 6 software tools that can do the same thing. You can try, and you will find which tool is good or not good to use, in terms of usability, interface, analysis capability, and so on. You can feel it. After you feel it, you choose the good one to use, and you will cite corresponding paper of that software in your paper. The tool... the more people use, it will gain more reputation naturally. For others that are not so good, it will be eliminated naturally.*" A high citation count is perceived to be highly correlated with good quality software, as Liu put it, "*usually we use the best software in the field, the most used software, which is the most cited in the literature.*" When asked how he knew which software was the most used, Bao answered, "*for example, like, how many times the (software) paper is cited, things like that.*" In a word, more citations mean it is well tested by more people and is more stable, and our informants reported that they almost always chose those well cited and well recognized software to use, so that the quality of the software can be ensured.

Besides, big names in the community also have great impact on the selection process. Zan described, "*We use what Danius (*magnates*) use or what good papers use. In the field of biology, those very big projects, like the thousand people gene program…what sequence software they use…and we will keep consistence with them. If the paper is written this way, there will be less chance for them to argue, otherwise, it may be troublesome, if you do it your own way.*" It is interesting to note in this case, that the function of reputation is not only to find the high quality software, but also to reduce unnecessary trouble or argument. Lian mentioned that the reputation of other elements, such as corresponding databases or journals or developers, were also important here, "*For this online software, there is a very good database connected to it, quite authoritative. If you do things with it, it will be more authoritative.*" As such, academic software is also part of the reputation economy of academia. Indeed, the circulation of software is very much like the circulation of papers, and only the best will stand out and have wide impact.

BOUNDARIES AND SCIENTIFIC SOFTWARE SHARING

In the last section, we discuss how software and related information are freely shared within the local team and the research community, and how meanings and mechanisms of sharing are embedded in respective social practices. However, software sharing is not always and everywhere free, but rather, many times there are obstacles involved to prevent it from widespread circulation, especially for work-in-progress and commercial software. Issues of boundaries are related to scientific software sharing mainly in two senses. First, software sharing involves tensions between sharing and control, to protect Intellectual Property but also to prevent immature software from wide distribution, and boundary management is a means to resolve it. It is the boundary at which determinations are made about whether to give the software (or the right to use the software) or not and how. Second, there are existent boundaries that regulate the free flow of software, including social boundaries (e.g. between different teams) and technical boundaries (e.g. between different networks). Now we will turn to issues of boundary as an aspect of software sharing, and explicate how tensions arise and how boundaries are managed through contrived means or along existent social or technical ones.

Tension and Boundary Management

Our data shows, tensions between sharing and the simultaneous need to control often arise in the sharing of scientific software, and strategic boundary management is key for its resolution.

Firstly, tension arises when software is still in its production. On one hand, as we know, to make software truly useful, it is important to involve users in the software making processes, the classic participatory design approach [25]. On the other hand, since it is still in production, its wide circulation should be limited. In our case study, we found several successful software tools were directly resulted from involving end users in the production process. For example, one of Huang's published software tools, BuildSummary, was clearly driven by the research needs from his own lab. According to his teammate Qiangrui, this software tool took 10 years to evolve. Over this period, new requirements were continuously fed into its production before it was ready for publication. PFind, a protein identification software tool that was developed by a computing institute in China, was also resulted from its close user involvement from the very beginning. Each year, they sent developers or even had them work at the users' site (including Liu's and Ceng's teams) for one or two months to collect requirements and address issues encountered. After being developed over 10 years, PFind has finally become powerful enough for commercialization right before this writing.

However, while reaching out and involving users are important for software evolution, its distribution should be limited since it is still a work in progress. We found a range of means was employed to balance this tension and manage the boundary. For example, Huang chose different media to share based on whether the software was mature or not, "*If it is not mature enough, or if it is only for mutual (idea) exchange, I will send it over email. And if it is sufficiently mature, they can download it online.*" The limited end-to-end email exchange, rather than the online web, was then chosen as a more appropriate means to share at its early stage. Similarly, for PFind in production, the boundary was strategically managed by socio-technical means. Liu reported a case. She once brought 20 hard copies of PFind to an international conference for academic exchange. The form of hard copy became a way to limit its distribution while at the same time encouraged some to try it, as Liu put it, "*yeah, for example, I took 20 copies with me… That is a limitation. It is not like you can download it for free.*" Moreover, the copy recipients were also asked to contact the authors for license if they wanted to try it, "*At that point, it was mainly to encourage people to try it, and we told them, they should contact us and they can only use it after we assign a license code.*" Segal mentioned, scientific software development is iterative [42], and user participation is important over the process. But for scientific research, little mistake may cause great impact on results, and boundary management is critical here when software is still in production.

Secondly, there is an inherent tension for the circulation of commercial software. For commercial software to be financially successful, broad visibility is important. And yet, to protect its economic interests, its availability shall be well controlled. As a matter of fact, as software can be freely copied and distributed, it makes the management of this boundary trickier. As mentioned, for academic software, publication was an important means to increase visibility. For commercial software, visibility is mainly achieved through active software promotion. Liu observed that software promotion was fairly common at conferences or other venues. For example, she reported, in good international conferences, such as the 3rd Asian Forum on Proteomics, a lot of people would introduce their software in detail so that more people would know the software and use it, even for software that was well known already and where people had already been using it. She also revealed that it was common for salespeople to come to their center and provide free courses and training sessions on their software, in a hope that they would buy it. Other promotion strategies include distributing copies at conferences with limited functions or with several months of probation, or sending copies to famous researchers, etc.

At the same time, for commercial purposes, the availability of software also needs to be carefully controlled. One common strategy reported by our informants is that software is provided for free first as an incentive to try, and then they will charge for upgrading it later. Liu described, "*We've been using it, and after we've used it for a while, all of sudden, they start to charge for fees. If you would continue to use it, you may buy it.*" For PFind, the boundary is managed by binding the software to a hardware based license code. Qiangrui said, "*They gave a license to us, and it was a machine code. That is, if you want to use it on your computer, they will send you a copy of software, and it will read your machine's code, which will then be returned to them to form a serial code, something like that. After you get that code, you can start to use it on your computer.*" Interestingly, it is exactly because software can be freely copied that extra effort is contrived to manage its distribution. It sounds like a contradiction, but considering the extra work and cost commercial software takes to offer high-quality services (e.g. performance, stability, usability, etc.), the contrived boundary starts to make sense.

Thirdly, there may be tension concerning the control of unwanted use of software. Software, unlike hardware and others, is more readily open for secondary development, so ownership of a copy often means a range of things they can do on top of it, especially for skilled programming users. Some of these might not be intended or desirable by the original developers. Social agreement is one means to address this tension. Liu reported a case where she got a piece of software from one of her collaborators abroad, and they signed a contract to keep it from unintended use, "*(the contract terms include), for example, it can only be used for academic purposes, and we don't have the right to transfer the copy to others. That is, we can only use it ourselves. Because, it is like a mirror site, if you want to use it yourself, you can use it on his website, but you will have limited functions. That is you can only search, something like that. But if I install the database locally, I can make improvement on it, or, you can even localize it into Chinese.*" It is similar to license use in open source software to define the users' rights to modify and redistribute the software's source code. With the use of social agreement, it is hoped that the original intention, e.g. for academic use only, can go unchanged over software distribution.

Existent Socio-Technical Boundaries

As illustrated, since software can be copied for free, many times, extra effort is needed to limit its wide spread use and balance the tension between sharing and controlling. Yet, other times, when there is a range of existent social and technical boundaries already there to regulate its movement and use, it is crossing these boundaries that demands extra work. In this respect, existent social or technical boundaries are conditioning, and manifested through software sharing.

Social boundaries between different teams play certain roles here. We've mentioned how homemade software was openly shared within the close-knit and interdependent research team. However, if it is across teams, things become a lot different. For instance, Huang's awareness of how his software was used and his responsibility for its use was largely confined to his team, "*we've been using it internally, and I don't quite know about other teams.*" We also noted that extra resources (e.g. social capital, social negotiation, and financial charge, academic credit) were needed for software to travel across teams, especially for homemade and unpublished software. Bai, for instance, when asked whether they were allowed to use Huang's software (they were from the different teams) suggested social capital was important, "*we are (allowed), because he is a former student of our director.*" Other times, social negotiation were required, as Liu described explicitly, "*yeah, in theory, it is fine, but he belongs to another lab after all, so if we want to use his software tool, we need to go ask for his permission, and he might need to get permission from his lab director.*" She further suggested that the negotiation process was important as a way to express respect to the boundary, "*usually, if you go ask him, he is nice and is willing to give, but a negotiation process is needed after all.*" It suggests that, what matters here is the negotiation itself and the attitude of respect to the boundary expressed through asking.

The purchase and shared use of commercial software are further shaped by and manifest the existence of social boundaries. In our study, the purchase decision of commercial software was always made at the team level, never individual. On one hand, the cost of commercial software was too high for individuals to afford. On the other hand, as one informant pointed out, even if they paid for commercial software, it could not guarantee to solve the problem, as research was essentially explorative after all. So it was rare for individuals to purchase software, and all reported that they would try the best to find free software when possible. Once the commercial software was purchased, its use was usually freely shared within the team, as Bai put it, "*usually if it is lab owned software, all members of the lab can use.*" Others outside the team but in the same institution could use it, but they were of secondary priority in terms of its use and were usually not allowed to control it. Liu described main and marginal roles of different teams, "*After it was purchased, it was mainly our team who used it. Other teams could if they wanted...but it was mainly our team who used it, and that would be fine.*" Essentially, the difference between ownership and use of software marks the boundary between inside and outside the team.

Interestingly, when the software is super-expensive, or requires certain expertise to use, the boundary becomes more visible. Qiangrui described, "*If it is within our own institute, just let them use. Unless the software is very very expensive, and then we might charge (for fees to use it).*" We did encounter cases that the software was expensive, and it took special expertise to use it. In that case, others could only use the software through services provided by the team, as described by Qiangrui, "*we help them identify protein with our techniques, and we go through the whole procedure by ourselves, without their involvement, so they are not able to access the software directly.*" They also charged certain fees based on how much time it took to use the software to do analysis, "*yeah, yeah, if it takes longer to output the data, the fee will be higher, and in contrast, if it is some simple identification work, it will be lower.*" Other times, it took academic collaborations or academic credit to use software across the boundary, "*usually it is because when there are many samples to work on. Considering the funding constraints, then they will (choose this approach). It is a kind of compromise. That is, I don't need to pay that much by letting them co-author our paper.*" It also suggests that the effect of social boundaries on software sharing depends on expertise required and effort needed to use the software.

Besides social boundaries, software sharing may also be regulated and managed along technical boundaries. For example, the intranet provides a natural boundary for managing and controlling the use of commercial software. The use of EndNote is a case in point, as described by Qiangrui, "*Because almost everyone will use it, our institute purchased it, and you could download it for free within the whole institute's IP addresses. That is, our institute has paid for the copyright. It is restricted by the IP address, and you can't use it beyond it.*" Interestingly, sometimes, the scope of an intranet itself can be leveraged to manage the sharing tension for work-in-progress software, as shown in Bao's case, "*It is only used in the intranet for testing, and it becomes public when it is published.*" Therefore, these boundaries are not there simply to negatively constrain the spread of software, but to positively resolve various tensions involved in software sharing.

DISCUSSION

In this paper, we have shown how scientific software sharing is conditioned by a range of technical and social factors, similar to the sharing of other scientific resources. Particularly, we illustrate how different types of software are shared within different social arrangements, according to different circulation mechanisms, associated with different social meanings, and subject to different boundary regulations. Specifically, homemade scripts and work-in-progress software are mainly circulated within one's own or related teams, shared based on membership, through personal requests or exchanges, and regulated largely along the internal and external boundary. Published academic software is made publicly available and is circulated mainly within the research community, relying on paper publication and citation mechanisms for its awareness and selection, and calling for peripheral participation practices for new members to acquire effective access to it. Commercial software products are developed, released and purchased mainly at the level of institution or team, where social-technical boundaries are leveraged and contrived to regulate its flow. Open source software comprises a great portion of scientific software, and its circulation is subject to the norms of open source software licenses. Its use in science also relies on peripheral participation practices for new members to navigate through it effectively. As such, the sharing of software is conditioned upon the interaction between the characteristics of software and its corresponding social configurations.

Software can be conceptualized as being in between digital data and physical instruments. As with digital data, it can be easily copied and distributed through IT infrastructures, and as with physical instruments, its key lies in the execution of certain tasks. To a certain extent, software, as a set of computer programs, essentially is an instrumental tool in the digital form. Of course, data, instruments and software are not separate, but many times are interrelated. Data is usually collected by instruments, and stored and managed with software. As a matter of fact, when our informants talked about software, often they meant database. The database may not be the direct subject of their scientific analysis, but forms an important means for the analysis of other data. Also, software can be part of the physical instrument, and subject to physical constraints for being moved.

However, it is the different situations and the different roles software plays in science that fundamentally transforms what is critical for the effective flow of software. Previous studies of scientific sharing revealed that scientists carefully maintain good control of their resources and are reluctant to share so that they can exchange for some other benefits, such as authorship, funding and others [8]. However, the issues of concealment and reluctance did not appear very salient for software sharing in our study. Arguably, two factors contribute to this difference. One, since a wide range of open source software and published academic software is already widely available, it is hardly a case that people gain greater priority than others by simply possessing a piece of software. Two, while critical, software might not be as central or as uniquely valuable as the data for scientific discovery, especially when the tools are not directly producing data. Consequently, the critical issue of software sharing transitions from issues of simply making the resource available to issues of awareness, selection and navigation. Just as when more and more information is available online, what becomes problematic is not the availability of information itself, but how to locate, navigate through, and select relevant and high quality information. In our study, we found awareness gained internally through group interactions as well as externally through publications, paper reviewing, citation, and experience sharing have all become important means for software location, selection and navigation. While awareness, selection or navigation issues are also relevant to the sharing of other digital resources such as data, they appear to be more pronounced in software sharing, mainly because the bar for software production is much lower than that of data production. While only scientists or related staff in the domain can produce data or operate the instrument, far more people can use their computers to produce software, which makes issues of quality control, software selection, awareness, or navigation more salient.

Nonetheless, not all software in science can move freely without resistance. Issues of resistance and strategies for boundary management are still quite relevant, especially for work-in-progress software or commercial software. In our study, we uncover various tensions between sharing and controlling, and people even intentionally contrive socio-technical means to set boundaries and resistance to its flow. We believe it is the inherent value associated with software that makes the resistance and boundaries necessary. Although it can be freely copied, essentially, software is not value free, as its production involves labor, profession and innovation. The value may be realized through reputation economy or financial economy, and boundaries are essential for these systems to work. Here, what makes software different from data is probably that it takes longer to be produced and mature. As shown in our study, many times, the software is continuously being improved over time, and users' involvement and feedback is crucial in this process, which makes the tension between sharing and controlling even more salient. Yet for digital resources, such as software and data that are less bound with physical instruments, managing boundaries becomes more difficult and complex. In our study, we show that not only are existing technical and social boundaries leveraged to resist the free flow of commercial software products or work-in-progress academic software, but also people strategically contrive socio-technical mechanisms to manage its flow such as binding the use of software to physical machines by generating machine related code, choosing different media for sharing (physical copy, email or web), and so on.

CONCLUSIONS AND IMPLICATIONS

By focusing on software as an object of sharing, not as part of the infrastructure or site for sharing, we do not limit ourselves to sharing issues of crossing distances, disciplines, and organizations as did most studies of collaboratories [11, 44]. But rather we were able to take a close look at social practices of scientific software sharing both locally and remotely. In particular, with an bio-informatics team in China, we uncover different meanings and mechanisms of sharing within different social contexts – learning, apprenticeship and membership at the local, and papers, citations, and reputation at the communal, as well as a set of boundaries, existent or contrived, regulating the travel of software.

In particular, we draw a number of conclusions and implications based on the study, and hope to incorporate them into our future work in designing computing platforms to support relevant practices.

First, not only software itself but also the special situation of software, including the existence of open source software, the role it plays in the field (e.g. a central role in bio-informatics), as well as the local culture (e.g. Tidui in China), plays important roles in shaping how software is used and circulated and what is critical for its use and circulation.

Second, we uncover how mechanisms and meanings of scientific software sharing are embedded within different collective social practices, such as learning, apprenticeship and so on, which shall be carefully considered when designing relevant computing support for scientific practice. For example, considering learning is an important theme within a team, sharing source code directly might not always be desirable, and enhancing interactive learning experiences might be more important.

Third, as with more and more software made publicly available, and especially considering the more universal production and ubiquitous nature of software, we argue that what is important is not simply making more software available, but addressing issues of navigation, selection and awareness. For example, enhancing awareness of what each researcher or research group has done at the local scale could be highly valuable here.

Four, in a related vein, we argue that experience sharing is important for addressing issues of software selection and navigation, and that the request-and-give social protocol is an appropriate means to turn tacit experience into sharable information. It suggests that computing enhancement to the sharing of experiences through the request-and-give protocol, rather than the sharing of software itself, might make a better fit for the corresponding social practices.

Finally, instead of forcing the sharing or the moving of software, respecting corresponding boundaries and seeking ways to support related social negotiation processes are also important, especially for work-in-progress software or commercial software products. After all, although software can be copied and distributed for free, it is essentially not "value free". Its value can be realized through either a reputation economy or financial economy, and boundaries are essential for these systems to work.

ACKNOWLEDGMENTS

We would like to thank our informants for their support, and Drew Paine for his editorial assistance. The work is supported by the National Natural Science Foundation of China (NSFC) under Grants No. 61272533 & No. 61233016, and the Shanghai Science & Technology Committee Key Fundamental Research Project under Grant No. 11JC1400800.

REFERENCE

1. Akhlaq, U. Impact of Software Comprehension in Software Maintenance and Evolution, *Blekinge Institute of Technology*, 2010.
2. Androutsellis-Theotokis, S. Open Source Software: A Survey from 10,000 Feet. *Foundations and Trends in Technology, Information and Operations Management*, 4, 3-4 (2010), 187-347.
3. Armbrust, M., Fox, A., Griffith, R., Joseph, A.D., Katz, R., Konwinski, A., Lee, G., Patterson, D., Rabkin, A. and Stoica, I. A view of cloud computing. *Communications of the ACM*, 53, 4 (2010), 50-58.
4. Atkinson, M., DeRoure, D., Dunlop, A., Fox, G., Henderson, P., Hey, T., Paton, N., Newhouse, S., Parastatidis, S. and Trefethen, A. Web Service Grids: an evolutionary approach. *Concurrency and Computation: Practice and Experience*, 17, 2 - 4 (2005), 377-389.
5. Begole, J., Rosson, M.B. and Shaffer, C.A. Flexible collaboration transparency: supporting worker independence in replicated application-sharing systems. *TOCHI*, 6, 2 (1999), 95-132.
6. Bietz, M.J. and Lee, C.P. Collaboration in metagenomics: Sequence databases and the organization of scientific work. *ECSCW 2009*, (2009), 243-262.
7. Birnholtz, J.P. What does it mean to be an author? The intersection of credit, contribution, and collaboration in science. *Journal of the American Society for Information Science and Technology*, 57, 13 (2006), 1758-1770.
8. Birnholtz, J.P. and Bietz, M.J. Data at work: supporting sharing in science and engineering. *In Proc. GROUP'03*, ACM (2003), 339-348.
9. Bonaccorsi, A. and Rossi, C. Comparing motivations of individual programmers and firms to take part in the open source movement: From community to business. *Knowledge, Technology & Policy*, 18, 4 (2006), 40-64.
10. Bos, N., Zimmerman, A., Olson, J., Yew, J., Yerkie, J., Dahl, E. and Olson, G. From shared databases to communities of practice: A taxonomy of collaboratories. *Journal of Computer - Mediated Communication*, 12, 2 (2007), 652-672.
11. Carlson, S. and Anderson, B. What Are Data? The Many Kinds of Data and Their Implications for Data Re - Use. *Journal of Computer - Mediated Communication*, 12, 2 (2007), 635-651.
12. Colazo, J. and Fang, Y. Impact of license choice on open source software development activity. *Journal of the American Society for Information Science and Technology*, 60, 5 (2009), 997-1011.
13. Crowston, K., Wei, K., Howison, J. and Wiggins, A. Free/Libre open-source software development: What we know and what we do not know. *ACM Computing Surveys (CSUR)*, 44, 2 (2012), 7.
14. Dourish, P. and Anderson, K. Collective information practice: Exploring privacy and security as social and cultural phenomena. *Human-Computer Interaction*, 21, 3 (2006), 319-342.
15. Evans, J.A. Industry collaboration, scientific sharing, and the dissemination of knowledge. *Social Studies of Science*, 40, 5 (2010), 757-791.
16. Fischer, B.A. and Zigmond, M.J. The essential nature of sharing in science. *Science and Engineering Ethics*, 16, 4 (2010), 783-799.
17. Foster, I. The grid: A new infrastructure for 21st century science. *Physics Today*, 55, 2 (2002), 51-63.
18. Gentleman, R.C., Carey, V.J., Bates, D.M., Bolstad, B., Dettling, M., Dudoit, S., Ellis, B., Gautier, L., Ge, Y. and Gentry, J. Bioconductor: open software development for computational biology and bioinformatics. *Genome Biology*, 5, 10 (2004), R80.
19. Hackett, E.J. Essential tensions. *Social Studies of Science*, 35, 5 (2005), 787-826.
20. Hey, T. and Trefethen, A.E. Cyberinfrastructure for e-Science. *Science*, 308, 5723 (2005), 817-821.
21. Howison, J. and Herbsleb, J. Socio-technical logics of correctness in the scientific software development ecosystem. *In Proc. CSCW'10 Workshop*, ACM (2010).
22. Howison, J. and Herbsleb, J.D. Scientific software production: incentives and collaboration. *In Proc. CSCW'11*, ACM (2011), 513-522.
23. Kelly, D. and Sanders, R. Assessing the quality of scientific software. *In Proc. Workshop on Software Engineering for Computational Science and Engineering* (2008).
24. Kelly, D.F. A software chasm: Software engineering and scientific computing. *Software, IEEE*, 24, 6 (2007), 119-120.

25. Kensing, F. and Blomberg, J. Participatory design: Issues and concerns. *Computer Supported Cooperative Work (CSCW)*, 7, 3 (1998), 167-185.
26. Kibrick, R., Conrad, A. and Perala, A. Through the far looking glass: Collaborative remote observing with the WM Keck Observatory. *Interactions*, 5, 3 (1998), 32-39.
27. Kling, R., McKim, G., Fortuna, J. and King, A. Scientific collaboratories as socio-technical interaction networks: a theoretical approach. *In Proc. Americas Conference on Information Systems (Long Beach, CA).* (2000).
28. Knorr-Cetina, K. *Epistemic cultures: How the sciences make knowledge*. Harvard Univ Pr, 1999.
29. Lave, J. and Wenger, E. *Situated learning: Legitimate peripheral participation*. Cambridge Univ Pr, 1991.
30. Luscombe, N.M., Greenbaum, D. and Gerstein, M. What is bioinformatics? An introduction and overview. *Yearbook of Medical Informatics*, 1 (2001), 83-99.
31. Merton, R.K. *The sociology of science: Theoretical and empirical investigations*. University of Chicago Press, 1979.
32. MYERS, J.D. Tools for Collaboration. *Collaboratories: Improving Research Capabilities in Chemical and Biomedical Sciences: Proceedings of a Multi-Site Electronic Workshop*, National Academies Press (1999.
33. Nguyen-Hoan, L., Flint, S. and Sankaranarayana, R. A survey of scientific software development. *In Proc. ESEM'10*, ACM (2010), 12.
34. Olson, G.M., Atkins, D.E., Clauer, R., Finholt, T.A., Jahanian, F., Killeen, T.L., Prakash, A. and Weymouth, T. The upper atmospheric research collaboratory (uarc). *ACM Interactions*, 5, 3 (1998), 48-55.
35. Rosen, L. *Open source licensing: Software freedom and intellectual property law*. Prentice Hall PTR, 2004.
36. Rother, K., Potrzebowski, W., Puton, T., Rother, M., Wywial, E. and Bujnicki, J.M. A toolbox for developing bioinformatics software. *Briefings in bioinformatics*, (2011).
37. Sanders, R. and Kelly, D. Dealing with risk in scientific software development. *Software, IEEE*, 25, 4 (2008), 21-28.
38. Santos Jr, C.D. and Kon, F. ATTRACTIVENESS OF FREE AND OPEN SOURCE PROJECTS. *European Conference on Information Systems*, (2010).
39. Santos Jr, C.D., Cavalca, M.B., Kon, F., Singer, J., Ritter, V., Regina, D. and Tsujimoto, T. Intellectual property policy and attractiveness: a longitudinal study of free and open source software projects. *In Proc.CSCW'11*, ACM (2011), 705-708.
40. Scacchi, W. Free/open source software development: Recent research results and methods. *Advances In Computers*, 69 (2007), 243-295.
41. Schön, D.A. *The reflective practitioner: How professionals think in action*. Basic books, 1983.
42. Segal, J. Some problems of professional end user developers. *In Proc. VLHCC'07*, IEEE (2007), 111-118.
43. Segal, J. Models of scientific software development. *In Proc. Workshop on SECSE'08* (2008).
44. Shrum, W., Genuth, J. and Chompalov, I. *Structures of scientific collaboration*. Cambridge: MIT Press, 2007.
45. Singh, P.V. and Phelps, C. Determinants of open source software license choice: A social influence perspective. *Available at SSRN:http://ssrn.com/abstract=1436153.* (2009).
46. Strauss, A.L. and Corbin, J. *Basics of qualitative research*. Sage Newbury Park, CA, 1990.
47. Sun, C., Xia, S., Sun, D., Chen, D., Shen, H. and Cai, W. Transparent adaptation of single-user applications for multi-user real-time collaboration. *TOCHI*, 13, 4 (2006), 531-582.
48. Vertesi, J. and Dourish, P. The value of data: considering the context of production in data economies. *In Proc. CSCW'11*, ACM (2011), 533-542.
49. Wenger, E. *Communities of practice: Learning, meaning, and identity*. Cambridge Univ Pr, 1998.
50. Willinsky, J. The access principle: The case for open access to research and scholarship. Cambridge, MA: MIT Press, (2006).

Beyond Trust and Reliability: Reusing Data in Collaborative Cancer Epidemiology Research

Betsy Rolland[1,2] and Charlotte P. Lee[2]
[1]Public Health Sciences Division, Fred Hutchinson Cancer Research Center, 1100 Fairview Avenue North, M4-B402, Seattle, WA 98109, USA
[2]Human Centered Design & Engineering, University of Washington, 423 Sieg Hall, Seattle, WA 98195, USA
brolland@fhcrc.org, cplee@uw.edu

ABSTRACT
While previous CSCW research on data sharing and reuse has focused on how researchers assess the trust and reliability of the data of others, we know little about scientists' data use practices after that decision has been taken. This qualitative study of post-doctoral researchers' use of preexisting datasets investigates the practices of cancer-epidemiology post-docs working to understand their "Small Data" datasets. We report the ongoing and iterative nature of information seeking inherent in using unfamiliar data and the time-consuming and highly-collaborative process post-docs used to understand aspects of the dataset important to their scientific questions. Understanding data use practices can help inform the design of both Small Data projects and large cyberinfrastructure projects where multi-source data are collected and combined.

Author Keywords
Data sharing; data reuse; collaboration; data; information seeking; qualitative research.

ACM Classification Keywords
H.5.3 [Information Interfaces and Presentation]: Computer-supported cooperative work

General Terms
Human Factors; Design.

INTRODUCTION
Cyberinfrastructure and eScience studies have been of increasing interest to the field of CSCW as an exemplar of the challenges inherent in collaborative work [1,2,11,12]. Such studies have identified data sharing as a key problem within collaborative research. Recent work has discussed the importance of support for data sharing in collaborative science, focusing primarily on the issues of trust and reliability that must be addressed before researchers can comfortably use data collected by others [4,5,7,8,20]. Other work has focused on why researchers share [6] and the effects of sharing on future citations [17,18].

However, there has been little study of how researchers actually use data collected by others once trust and reliability have been established. Without such knowledge, it is challenging to develop systems and practices that support better curation and reuse of existing data. Until we understand both how to prepare data for reuse and to reuse data more efficiently, the challenges of data sharing will continue to slow down collaborative research and data repositories will remain underutilized [16]. A first step toward the goal of understanding the full data reuse lifecycle is to investigate how researchers determine how to use variables from an existing dataset appropriately for their own analyses. In this paper, we report on research that investigated the data reuse practices of scientists, specifically cancer-epidemiology post-doctoral researchers (PhD-level trainees brought in for specific projects) at the Fred Hutchinson Cancer Research Center (FHCRC) in Seattle, Washington, USA, as they worked to understand the datasets recommended for their use by their mentors. In all cases, the mentors had first-hand knowledge of the quality and reliability of the data, either through participation in the original data collection or through their own previous use of the data. This prior vetting by the mentors permits us to move beyond issues of trust and reliability as factors affecting the decision to use the data, allowing us to concentrate on the actual reuse practices of the post-docs.

BACKGROUND
From *The New York Times* to *Nature*, Big Data is a hot topic, while Small Data rarely gets mentioned. In many biomedical research fields, such as cancer epidemiology, small datasets collected for individual studies, when combined or used for new analyses, represent a potential for new discoveries similar to that attributed to Big Data [3,8,9,16]. However, reuse of these small data sets is fraught with challenges. Small datasets can be difficult to find, as they are rarely deposited in repositories, but, rather, live on investigators' local hard drives or lab servers. Documentation is often informal, spotty or nonexistent

except for minimal details documented in the methods section of published papers. Original study staff may have moved on or forgotten how the study was conducted or how variables were interpreted, creating enormous potential for misinterpretation and misuse of the data. Data curation, the active preservation of data with its accompanying documentation, is rarely a formal process in these small studies.

Such small datasets stand in marked contrast to large, publicly available datasets such as GenBank or government databases with deposit guidelines or standardized data requirements, where documentation is available and vetted (formally or informally) by a community of users, and the infrastructure is maintained by a funded organization of some sort. It is also different than, though related to, data sharing and reuse within cyberinfrastructures (CIs) or large databases constructed in consortia. Such groups spend significant time designing and developing databases to accommodate the different data structures that will be included and generally employ data managers and/or programmers to assist with this process. In order to bring together data from multiple studies into one standardized database, conversations must take place between original study staff and the system developers to ensure everyone involved is clear on the meaning of the variable, the context in which it was collected and assumptions made when coding the variable into its current form. It is these types of conversations that we detail in this paper, albeit in the context of Small Data.

Calls for sharing and reusing data are increasingly loud and urgent, as exemplified by a recent editorial in *The Lancet* by the leaders of prominent funding agencies in the US and UK [19]. The editorial asserts that not sharing research data is harming public health and proposes several steps that the field of biomedical research can take to improve data sharing, encouraging foundations to require data sharing and deposit by all grantees. The US National Science Foundation (NSF) and National Institutes of Health (NIH) have also recently tightened their requirements for data sharing as a condition of funding. Yet calls for deposit and sharing of data rarely address how the eventual recipients of those datasets actually use the data [6]. In fact, we know very little about the practices of researchers who use data collected by others.

Data Reuse: A Definition

The terms "data reuse" and "data sharing" are often used interchangeably. Borgman (2011) notes that calls for "data sharing" are rarely explicit about what they mean by this term, but suggests this possible definition: "… the release of research data for use by others. Release may take many forms, from private exchange upon request to deposit in a public data collection. Posting datasets on a public website or providing them to a journal as supplementary materials also qualifies as sharing" [6]. Data reuse, then, is the work done by the recipient of those shared data. It involves identification of a dataset of interest, receipt of the dataset and appropriate use of the data for analysis.

Advantages and Disadvantages of Data Sharing

There is general agreement that data sharing and reuse can have tremendous benefits for society, if done well. These benefits include the ability to ask larger questions than any individual study might be able to ask on its own, due to a larger and more complex data set; the ability to take advantage of existing datasets rather than spending time collecting new data; and potentially large cost savings because there is no need to assemble new projects. Benefits to individuals include more publications and potentially higher-impact publications, at that, due to the bigger questions being asked.

Such data sharing and reuse are increasingly common in scientific research, in large part due to the development of technological support for doing so. Increased bandwidth and ubiquity of communication technologies allow researchers to share virtually anything with anyone. Furthermore, scientists are culturally accustomed to sharing within their trusted social networks. This stands in contrast to the for-profit world, where data are considered proprietary and rarely sent outside of the walls of the corporation without strict legal agreements.

However, the field of CSCW has documented significant challenges inherent in data sharing. These include difficulties in the interpretation of data and appropriately conveying contextual details of how the data were collected [5]; issues of trust in the quality of data [8,20]; and a reluctance to give away intellectual property [5]. The process of assessing data for reuse can be tricky and time-consuming for both the sharer and the user. However, the cost of an inaccurate assessment of the quality or an incorrect understanding of the data is much higher in terms of both money and reputation. This applies to both the original study collectors sharing their data and the investigator seeking to use it; a retraction of results due to inappropriately used data or the use of bad data is an embarrassment for everyone involved.

Cancer Epidemiology

Epidemiology is the study of disease risk at the population level. Some examples of populations studied by epidemiologists may include post-menopausal women, prostate-cancer survivors, or children. Studies focus on exposures such as tobacco use, family medical history, diet, or exposure to workplace toxins. Cancer-epidemiology datasets possess a number of characteristics that make their use particularly interesting to study. First, epidemiologic data are generally collected by questionnaire. As such, questions must be straightforward enough for a non-scientist to administer and a participant to answer. Although epidemiology questions are often not standardized (although this, too, is an area of change (see, for example, http://www.p3g.org/)), there are some generally accepted practices that make it easier for researchers to understand one another's data sets. For example, anyone collecting lifestyle data will want to collect smoking data with both frequency and duration in order to produce the derived variable "pack-years," a measure of the amount of cigarettes smoked over time. Additionally, epidemiologists are asking similar questions over different populations. Studying the association between smoking and breast cancer in post-menopausal women is not that different, at a high level, from studying the association of smoking and prostate cancer in Hispanic men. All of these characteristics make for datasets that are easier, if not easy, to combine.

Most importantly, cancer epidemiologists have a history of sharing data within their trusted social networks. This is partially attributable to the similarity of data collected but also speaks to a core belief within the cancer-epidemiology community that a dataset can be explored in multiple ways for a variety of associations. One of the defining characteristics of epidemiologic data is that they are not reproducible, given that they are collected in a specific time and place on a specific group of individuals. Even if another similar group is assembled, the data from the studies can never be identical. This makes epidemiologic data extremely valuable and useful for sharing. The sharing researcher gets fuller use of the data while the user gains access to a gold mine of data without the time and money required to produce them. In times of scarce funding, data sharing and reuse allows science to continue to move forward with fewer funds. By pooling shared data, epidemiology researchers can attack new questions without spending a lot of money.

SITE DESCRIPTION AND METHODS

This research took place at the Fred Hutchinson Cancer Research Center, a National Cancer Institute (NCI)-designated cancer center in Seattle, Washington, USA. This class of research institute is categorized by a high level of scientific excellence and patient-centered research. FHCRC has approximately 3,000 employees and is organized into five divisions. One of these divisions is the Public Health Sciences (PHS) Division, home to most of the organization's cancer epidemiologists. In 2011, FHCRC ranked 19th in total NIH funding, receiving in excess of $270 million, ahead of much larger institutions [15], and 3rd in funding from the NCI. One of the authors of this paper is an employee of FHCRC and works primarily on cancer epidemiology projects, including previous work on one of those described in these interviews. However, the author had little or no prior interactions with any of the participants in this study, meeting most of them for the first time when conducting the interviews.

The National Postdoctoral Association defines a postdoc as "an individual holding a doctoral degree who is engaged in a temporary period of mentored research and/or scholarly training for the purpose of acquiring the professional skills needed to pursue a career path of his or her choosing" [14].

Post-docs at FHCRC are generally brought in to do new analyses on data that have already been collected, either as an extension of the original aims or to undertake a completely different project. They work with a specific mentor, most often the Principal Investigator (PI), the researcher in charge of the project, who originally collected the data under analysis. In some cases, post-doc positions were written into grants and appropriate hires made; in other cases, they were funded under training grants. All post-docs at FHCRC are subject to ethics education requirements and their research projects must receive appropriate Institutional Review Board (IRB) approvals.

We chose to interview post-docs for several reasons. First and foremost, post-docs represent a user group just one step removed from the original data collectors. They must use data someone else collected, with all of the difficulties that entails, yet they still have direct access to those who collected the data, which means access to answers to their questions. Because they were given access to the dataset either by their mentors or via their mentors' professional relationships, they are able to bypass the thorny issues of trust and reliability so well documented by previous CSCW research. Thus, we are able to concentrate on the actual reuse practices of the post-docs. Finally, as junior researchers, post-docs are expected to be learning and developing professional practices while also doing a great deal of work independently; as such, their situation is conducive to reflection.

Over the course of six weeks, we conducted semi-structured interviews with a diverse group of post-doctoral researchers in cancer epidemiology at FHCRC, including four men and seven women. Participating post-docs hailed from several different institutions and fields, including medicine and public health (MD/MPHs), behavioral epidemiology, and molecular epidemiology. They worked with different mentors and had been working in their post-doctoral fellowships anywhere from 3 months to 2 years. Each post-doc was interviewed once, in a conference room at FHCRC, and interviews lasted between 30 minutes and one hour. Participants were asked about all the projects on which they had used preexisting datasets as part of their post-doc, then asked to pick one upon which to focus for the remainder of the interview. The interviews were recorded and transcribed, and all participants were given pseudonyms. While not a full grounded theory study, we did utilize a grounded theory approach to analyze our transcripts. Data were first coded for specific interview questions, then reanalyzed for emerging themes.

FINDINGS

In order to better understand data reuse, we investigated how post-docs determine appropriate use of preexisting data for their own analyses. We asked participants about the process they went through when starting to work with a new dataset and paid particular attention to the information sources they used, as well as their personal strategies for engaging with the data. In this section, we detail the data analysis process followed by our participants and describe a typology of information needs experienced by post-docs as they went through this process. We then discuss in detail one of these information needs; namely, how the dataset's variables were constructed. Understanding the construction history not only gave post-docs grounding in the conduct of the study but gave them critical information required for their own analyses.

Data Analysis Process

In general, the process post-docs undertook was remarkably similar across participants, despite the fact that they came from a variety of disciplines and universities, worked with different mentors and were working on quite different projects. They described a project proposal phase, during which they worked with their mentors to locate an appropriate dataset and mapped out the project. These project proposals required approval from either their mentor or a full study committee intimately familiar with the data before they could proceed, ensuring a trustworthy, reliable and appropriate dataset for the post-doc's work. Only one of our participants worked directly on the main study database; the rest all received copies of the main database, generally a subset containing only the variables they had requested. The data had been cleaned to varying extents; meaning, the data manager had removed obviously incorrect records or corrected mistaken entries in the database. All post-docs noted they were not allowed to share their dataset with anyone else.

Some post-docs received many derived (i.e., calculated) variables, while others derived their own. For example, the post-doc might receive a variable for "total Vitamin D intake" in addition to data on Vitamin D intake for all the individual food sources asked about on the questionnaire. Deriving variables requires that decisions be made about precisely how to calculate them. Some such calculations are standard, such as Body Mass Index, which is calculated as the weight in kilograms divided by the square of the height in meters. Others may be calculated in a variety of ways according to the scientific thinking of the PI or data manager. In our Vitamin D example, the Vitamin D content of each individual food the participant reported consuming (e.g., carrots, milk, broccoli) will be calculated based on average Vitamin D content of that food according to a government database. Another example might be a derived variable "socio-economic status" which takes answers to questions about education level and family income to create categories of high, medium and low economic status. The study team would make decisions about how much weight to give to each input variable (education and income) and where the upper and lower limits of the categories might be. This scenario could be further complicated by regional differences if done within a multi-site study. High economic status in Manhattan and Ames, Iowa, require very different cutoff points. As we will see later, understanding such decisions is crucial for appropriate use of the data.

Upon receipt of the dataset, post-docs began to get a feel for the data by talking with the study's data manager, running summary statistics (e.g., mean, median, missing, distribution) and checking those against previously published manuscripts. As they performed their analyses, post-docs presented interim results to their mentor and study groups, often getting feedback about their work and their use of the data.

Finally, they wrote up their results into a manuscript for submission to a relevant journal, relying heavily on the comments in their own analysis code to remember the details of the decisions they made along the way. This manuscript was distributed to coauthors for feedback. Throughout this collaborative process, post-docs encountered numerous situations where they needed more information in order to use the data appropriately.

Typology of Information Needs

Post-docs needed answers to a series of questions as they progressed through their project, beginning from the proposal stage through submission of the manuscript for publication. These questions are shown in Table 1. Just as the process of science is not linear, neither is the process of scientific analysis. While the questions generally came in this order temporally, they could arise at any time, and post-docs often looped iteratively and unpredictably through the questions. A colleague's suggestion to utilize an additional variable from the dataset in the analysis could drive the post-doc to return to seeking information about previous analyses which used that variable. It is important to note that questions arose primarily about those aspects of the study that were of greatest importance to the post-doc's current analyses. They were not seeking information for the sake of a vague understanding of "context" of the study; rather, they sought specific details about the study that directly or indirectly affected the work they were doing. The most difficult, time-consuming and interactive questions centered around how and why the data had been constructed the way they appeared in the dataset given to the post-doc. For purposes of this paper, only question 6 about the construction of data will be discussed at length. Other questions will be addressed in more detail in future work.

Question Type	Examples
1. What datasets are available to use in my research?	What datasets does my advisor have access to around my research area?
2. Will this dataset help me answer my research question?	Does this dataset have the population, study design and outcome data I need?

3. What else has been done with this dataset?	What manuscripts have been previously published from this study?
4. Where do I find the information I need to understand this study?	Where can I find copies of the questionnaire and codebook? Which copy of the dataset should I use?
5. How was this dataset constructed?	On what basis did the original study include or exclude participants? Why was this question included on the questionnaire?
6. How were these data constructed?	**How did the original study staff code my variables of interest? Why are so many participants missing data on the variable "alcohol use"?**
7. What do my variables of interest mean?	How did the original study define the variables "heavy smoker" and "frequent aspirin user"?
8. Am I using the data and the dataset correctly?	Does my interpretation of the meaning of this variable match that of previous data users? Did I select the correct data file?
9. What have I done with this dataset?	How did I define my categorical variables in my analysis and how should I represent that in my manuscript?

Table 1: Types of questions asked by post-docs during their project.

Information Seeking Strategies

To obtain the information they needed for their analyses, post-docs in our study employed a number of strategies, taking full advantage of the resources available to them. They started their projects with conversations with their mentors, using the mentor's vast knowledge of existing datasets to identify interesting and available datasets, then narrowing their research interest to a plausible research question for this dataset. Again, questions of trust and reliability were never raised as post-docs assumed their mentors would only point them to good data. Once this data selection had been completed, post-docs began using available written sources of information such as project websites, codebooks and study questionnaires to bolster the information gleaned from previous discussions. Inevitably, questions arose that were not answerable via available documentation, leading post-docs to have further conversations with their mentors and study staff to find appropriate answers. These conversations could lead either to a pointer to new documentation or to new knowledge that didn't exist in any written form, only in someone's memory.

Conversations were occasionally a straightforward recounting of a fact such as what year the study stopped enrolling participants; more frequently, they consisted of unraveling a trail of decisions and interpretations to answer a question such as: Why are so many participants missing tumor stage and how has that been handled in previous analyses? In the case of the missing tumor stage, Stewart received his dataset and found that a large percentage of participants were missing this key variable. After checking the study documentation, he began asking study staff about this issue. Several conversations later, he learned that one data collection site of this multi-site study was unable to share tumor stage from patient medical records due to legal restrictions. Without this knowledge, Stewart may have been forced to delete these participants from his analyses under the assumption that their records were incomplete and unusable. When asked about documenting this discovery for other, he laughed and replied, *"No, it's more like an oral tradition" (Stewart, 352)*. Uncovering answers to such complicated questions could involve interactions with any number of people, ranging from just the local PI to collaborating study staff and PIs at other institutions. Post-docs described hours, even days, spent with data managers uncovering how variables were coded, as well as weeks emailing with the PIs at non-FHCRC study sites attempting to ascertain their study procedures and the resulting data. These efforts represent significant delays in scientific progress.

An Iterative and Ongoing Process

Sometimes understanding one aspect of the study simply opened the door to more questions by revealing the need for more information about other aspects. This happened in one of two ways. First, post-docs sometimes found they had used the data incorrectly or had used the wrong data altogether due to missing or incomplete information. Several participants noted that they had discovered problems with or gaps in their analyses while talking with their mentors and colleagues about their results. Kristina described presenting her analysis of the effects of dietary intake to her study group, only to find that she had used the wrong dataset. Because the datasets were not clearly labeled and several contained similarly-named variables, she had simply chosen the wrong one. Because no one in the study group could tell her the precise name of the correct dataset, she was forced to return to the study documentation and the files on the shared drive to try to identify the correct one by opening each one and comparing the variables inside to the ones she needed. This came after weeks of work on the incorrect dataset, significantly delaying her progress.

Ginger talked about how frustrating it was to go through this iterative process and how unproductive it made her feel, especially when compared to her previous work at another institution. She noted that having to constantly redo analyses based on the replacement of bad information with new information not only was a waste of time but made her look incompetent to her mentor. She stressed that better access to information could have prevented many of the issues she had experienced.

> *What happens is, I start off seeking the information, and I'm thinking about the study, so I have an idea of what information I wish I had, and then I have to do the analysis. And then I get a little bit of information, and so I say, 'I'm sorry; that analysis that I sent you was invalid,' and so then you look bad, which is just bad. And then you redo the analysis, and you're like, 'Oh no, in light of this new information it's apparently not appropriate to think of this way, and it would be better if this exclusion was made given the nature of the study sampling.'(Ginger, 177).*

The second possible cause for iterative information seeking was that the post-doc learned something scientifically interesting, either through their analyses or through conversations with colleagues, that required additional data be incorporated or explored. For example, learning that aspirin had a certain effect on the cancer of interest might compel the post-doc to look at the effect of other pain relievers or aspirin's effect on another cancer. As epidemiologists search for associations between variables and incidences of particular types of cancer, these additional factors (confounders and correlates) that are intertwined with, but not necessarily the cause of, the phenomenon under study must be addressed. What these factors are, precisely, can be different for different cancers or different populations and is based on deep understanding of both the dataset and current scientific knowledge. For example, smoking may have an effect on one type of cancer, but not another. Additionally, smoking can be a confounding variable for weight, because smokers tend to be of lower weight, making it difficult to know if the smoking or the weight is responsible for the association present in the data analysis. Irene talked about having her initial proposal and resulting manuscript reviewed by the study committee, who then recommended she consider incorporating other variables from the dataset into her analyses by addressing additional confounding variables, as well as exploring correlation between variables in the dataset.

> *So the first step is more of the content, or here's some other things you might want to look at. And also, if they have [done] that analysis on the same data set, they will tell you these are the useful variables, these variables might be confounding, so check for [those]. So those [are the] kinds of information I get and kind of, this variable is highly correlated with each other, don't use this one or [that] kind of information. But after the analysis I get lots of analysis comments as well, [about] the data and variables (Irene, 319).*

The first scenario was a frustrating setback and generally a waste of time, while the second was the result of interesting scientific work and moved the post-doc forward toward his or her goal. This second type of iteration is a normal result of a healthy scientific project, and we saw post-docs moving among the different question types noted in Table 1 throughout the entire data analysis lifecycle. In all cases, the post-docs once again returned to their information sources, both human and written, and sought the answers they needed to move forward with their analyses.

Understanding the Construction of Variables

As has been shown by previous CSCW literature, data are highly social, reflecting the values and practices of those who engage with the research and the data [5]. Data are also constructed as a result of the plethora of small, often seemingly insignificant, decisions and actions taken during a research project. However, knowledge of such decisions or actions often lives exclusively in the heads of those who took them, not through negligence but through pragmatism. Much like software engineers responsible for documenting changes in code specifications [13], it is simply impossible for researchers to document each decision formally while still moving their work forward. These decisions and actions may or may not be apparent in the data as irregularities or missing data. In either case, they can have a profound impact on the outcome of the data analyses if not understood, as they reflect the myriad of assumptions and interpretations, some explicit and some tacit, made by researchers and study staff along the way. In this section, we describe questions post-docs asked about the construction of variables as they worked to understand their data. These questions focused not just on the meaning of the variables, but on the decisions and actions that led to the current state of the dataset as presented to the post-doc.

How were these data constructed?

In order to use the data appropriately, post-docs needed to understand not just what a variable (e.g., "smoking status") meant, but how it had been constructed. In fact, the majority of difficult and time-consuming questions post-docs reported fell into this category. These were questions that focused on how specific variables were coded, how to match the questions on the original study questionnaires with the variables in the database and why the original study did what they did to the study data, including why they coded and analyzed variables the way they did. Such questions were often difficult to answer, as they involved digging deeply into analysis code, study documentation or people's memories, often across institutional borders. This process was rarely independent, but involved significant collaboration between the post-doc and the study staff.

Ginger struggled mightily with understanding how treatment variables in her dataset had been coded. She was interested in how a specific class of medications affected the risk of cancer in her population. According to the labels in the database, her variable described the duration of the medication use in months for a given individual. After completing her analyses, she worried that something wasn't quite right. Lengthy discussions with the data manager, which involved excavating five-year-old code and painstakingly reviewing each line in the coding of this variable, revealed inconsistencies between the label and the way the variable had been coded. This inconsistency had not been an issue in the original study because the variable was not a part of those analyses, as it was outside the study's specific aims.

> *I had received a variable for exposure to [medication] use that was months of [medication] use, and I assumed from the labeling of the variable in the dataset ... that an individual was coded as a 1 if they had used at least one month of [medication], and so I said that our study excluded women who didn't have less than a month of [medication]. But apparently, women with one day of [medication] were counted as a one because it was really a zero to one month. And that took forever to figure out ... because then [the data manager] had to go back to the original code in which she had created the variable and reinterpret the code to break down exactly what had happened, and it was like all this looping. So things like that were frustrating. We had a lot of setbacks where you're like, "So what does this variable really mean?" and every time you ask, "What does this variable really mean?" it's never straightforward (Ginger, 55).*

Had she simply accepted the label and not questioned it, Ginger's analyses would have been incorrect, and she would have made inaccurate claims in her paper. For any scientist, this is a terrifying prospect.

Some variables were difficult to understand because of the way the original question was asked. Stewart mentioned a variable whose question was vague, leading him to wonder how the variable had been interpreted in the coding scheme. In the excerpt below, Stewart wants to know if a given individual had a screening colonoscopy, as opposed to one that was diagnostic, a question that is difficult to answer based on the way the original question was asked. Yet understanding this distinction was crucial for his analysis. So he finds himself interpreting what the original study "thought they were asking."

> *It's also just sometimes there's nuances you want to understand. You know, someone's colonoscopy history, there's some questions about that, and you want to understand it, trying to rule out the colonoscopy that was used to diagnose the colorectal cancer. So you want to know if they were screened ever. And actually, that's kind of hard in this dataset because of the way the questions were asked, which is unfortunate. But so you're using like a time between diagnosis and when they say they had a colonoscopy to infer maybe what that was about. ... And you have to go back to the data dictionary, for sure, but I find myself going back to the questionnaire to see what I think the question really was asking, you know. Because the data dictionary... it's just descriptive, it's kind of what they thought they were asking... it's like oh, the value can be one or two. One is yes and two is no. And, you know, it'll say had a colonoscopy [Laughter]. But when you look at the question, it's have you ever had a colonoscopy, you know, more than two years ago or something? So there's a difference. So there can be differences (Stewart, 162).*

Here, Stewart is questioning not just the actual meaning of the variable in the database, but how the question used to collect the data from research subjects was interpreted by researchers as the variable was constructed during the original study. In fact, some of the most difficult questions to answer in this category centered around the interpretation and decision-making history of a given variable. Post-docs noted that it wasn't simply a case of how the variable had been coded but why it had been coded a certain way. There is scientific knowledge encoded in these decisions, and post-docs were wary of proceeding with analyses that may have contradicted that previous knowledge or decision.

Stewart also mentioned that he wished more of the standard variables for his study, like pack-years of smoking, were derived by the study's central coordinating center, as opposed to being derived by each individual user with whom the dataset has been shared. He noted that variables were derived for previous papers in a certain way, and it was important to keep that consistent, yet those variables were each derived by individual investigators instead of by the central authority, leaving open the possibility for future mistakes by others. He felt it would reflect badly on the study and raise doubts about his analyses if he came up with a different result for, say, the average number of pack-years of smoking in the study than that which had been reported by earlier studies.

Reconstructing the history of a variable, then, is a complex, time-consuming and highly collaborative process. For their variables of interest, post-docs required a greater understanding of not only how the variable arrived at its current state, but also why. Various information sources were deployed to answer these questions; codebooks, questionnaires and the databases themselves were often used in tandem to ascertain an answer. Previous manuscripts were consulted to see how the data had been written about in the past, and to try to pin down how a derived variable may have been constructed. Data managers, original study staff and PIs were, however, the most frequently used information sources for finding answers to these questions. There was simply no substitute for the institutional memory of those most intimately involved in the collection, coding and analysis of the data. Answering questions about the construction of the data often required substantial time and effort on the part of our participants and others. Amy discussed tracking down former study members in their new jobs, years later, in order to get answers to her questions. Without such information, post-docs did not feel comfortable moving forward with their analyses.

DISCUSSION & IMPLICATIONS FOR DESIGN

Our investigation of post-docs' use of preexisting data reveals new considerations for the support of collaboration around data reuse. While previous research has examined the difficulties of sharing data, focusing on assessing trust and reliability of the data, here we have focused on the issues post-docs faced while actually using data collected by others. They utilized a variety of strategies in their practice of science to gather enough information about the data that they felt comfortable using the data they had been given. Once we have moved past the issues of trust and reliability to focus on the actual use of preexisting data, questions of appropriate use become first and foremost.

It is clear that, even between trusted colleagues, sharing and reuse of data is still complex and fraught with pitfalls. That said, there was a logic in how post-docs went about answering the questions that kept them from completing their analyses. We have described here the different actions in which researchers engage to ensure proper usage of data, including nine questions to which post-docs needed answers as they moved their projects forward. One way to support better reuse of data is to provide better support for finding answers to this set of questions through better information management. Given that the majority of questions, and the most difficult and time-consuming questions, focused on the construction of specific variables, it would seem that documenting decision histories and variable coding procedures would be a good place to start. However, it is not practical to expect researchers to document a dataset sufficiently for all potential future uses. What we can do, though, is lend support to the collaborative process of information seeking by both helping studies organize their information better and aiding the conversations between the original study staff and the new data users.

The process of understanding data is not simply a matter of access to documentation of facts about or context of a study. Post-docs were not concerned only with details such as number of participants or what the variable "smoking status" meant, but with intricate decision histories of specific variables. As discussed above, however, completed studies and datasets are composed of a multitude of such decisions, some large and some small, some explicit and some tacit, all of them affecting the structure and scientific meaning of the data. For all practical purposes, it is simply not possible to document them all or to anticipate accurately which ones will be required by new investigators later. Without a mandate or cultural expectation to do so, it is also not realistic to expect that study personnel will spend significant amounts of time and money documenting a study not for their own purposes but for as-yet-unknown others. Our participants had direct access to all of the documentation available for a given study, as well as the original study personnel, and yet they still struggled with understanding certain aspects of their dataset. Furthermore, even if study personnel could somehow sufficiently document all of these decisions made about the data, we do not currently have a way to store such information that makes it easily accessible to data users.

In addition, post-docs were not concerned with an overall documentation of the context of a study, but with the documentation of the specific aspects of interest to their own, new analyses. The post-doc's areas of interest could be quite different than those of the original study staff. Much like a scientific database is designed to support specific research question [4], the information resources about a study are designed to support a specific project. When someone comes in to do new analyses on the data, especially if those new analyses are in a different discipline, they will require information not required by the original study.

For the post-docs in our study, the work of understanding a dataset and its variables is an ongoing and potentially unending process. Participants were working on complex, multi-institutional studies of hundreds or thousands of patients over long periods of time; there is always more to understand if one goes digging. Precisely which aspects of the study post-docs required understanding of depended entirely on their research question; they were concerned exclusively with those aspects that impacted their own projects. Information seeking stopped when they felt they had sufficient information to use the data correctly.

CONCLUSION

In this paper, we have explored the data reuse practices of post-doctoral researchers in cancer epidemiology as they worked to understand preexisting data for their own, independent analyses. We found that our participants had unmet information needs throughout the lifecycle of the research project, needs they addressed through a variety of strategies, including the use of both written and human information sources. This work of understanding the data was collaborative, iterative and ongoing, as new knowledge about one aspect of the data often sent post-docs back to their information sources to gain a deeper understanding of other aspects. Of special interest to our participants was the decision history that led to the construction of their specific variables of interest. They wanted to know not just how a variable was constructed, but why it was constructed the way it was.

As researchers are required to deposit their data into shared repositories, as funding agencies and open science advocates are demanding, they must do so with the assurance that others will be able to use the data in a way that is scientifically appropriate. Otherwise, the time spent documenting data for future use will simply be wasted effort.

This study has shown that even those investigators with direct access to all available study documentation and original study staff still struggled to make sense of the data they had been given. While enhanced documentation is a worthy goal, it is an elusive one when we consider the myriad of ways a dataset can be used by future investigators, ways which we cannot even imagine now. Supporting data reuse requires much more than just better documentation and creation of repositories. Rather, it requires the development of practices and processes that simultaneously support data sharing and reuse for the future while still supporting the current study. In other words, investigators need ways to engage in data curation in support of tomorrow's research without delaying today's. Finally, data reuse also would benefit greatly from funding agency incentives to data collectors to engage in data curation throughout the entire scientific process, as well as support for answering questions from users in the future.

The field of CSCW can play an important role in developing practices and systems that support the complex scientific collaborations that are now working to solve some of society's most pressing problem in energy, the environment, and health—including helping to treat and prevent cancer, as with our study participants. As scientific research continues to increase in both size and scope, data reuse, data sharing, and collaboration become increasingly important to the conduct of scientific research. Current practices in data sharing and reuse carry significant costs in time and effort, delaying science and diverting those resources from new discoveries. Systems and tools that could help staff document their data in such a way that users can find the right dataset the first time, or that could uncover the coding scheme behind variables without requiring weeks reading comments in analysis code, would go a long way toward creating greater efficiency and productivity in data reuse. Researchers need guidance on how to organize their information and to track those aspects of a study most likely to be questioned in the future; identifying those best practices will require more study on our part.

As more focus is turned to data reuse, we must continue to investigate ways to support more efficient data practices throughout the lifecycle of scientific projects. This includes a deeper understanding of how much information is enough to make a data user feel comfortable with their dataset, as well as what types of information best serve that need. Further, is it possible to develop training guidelines for both study personnel and new data users that highlight best practices in data reuse? Perhaps frustration levels can be minimized simply through better organization of information or the presentation of information at different stages of the project lifecycle. These are all questions for future research. Building on our knowledge of issues of trust and reliability, we have much to gain by developing an understanding of how scientists can use data collected by others in order to answer difficult scientific questions, allowing us to alleviate some of these difficulties and better support scientific innovation.

ACKNOWLEDGMENTS

This research was supported in part by the Fred Hutchinson Cancer Research Center and by NIH award R03CA150036. We would like to thank our participants for their generosity with their time and our anonymous reviewers for their thoughtful feedback. We also thank Dr. John D. Potter for sharing his expertise on epidemiology and Dr. Polly Newcomb for early discussions on post-docs and data sharing that sparked this research question.

REFERENCES

1. Baker, K.S., & Yarmey, L. (2009). Data stewardship: Environmental data curation and a web-of-repositories. International Journal of Digital Curation, 4(2), 1-12.
2. Bietz, M.J., Baumer, E.P.S., & Lee, C.P. (2010). Synergizing in Cyberinfrastructure Development. Computer Supported Cooperative Work, 19(3-4), 3-4.
3. Bietz, M.J., Ferro, T., & Lee, C.P. (2012). Sustaining the development of cyberinfrastructure: an organization adapting to change. In *Proc. CSCW 2012*, ACM Press (2012), 901-910.
4. Bietz, M.J., & Lee, C.P. (2009). Collaboration in Metagenomics: Sequence Databases and the Organization of Scientific Work. In *Proc. ECSCW 2009*, Springer-Verlag (2009), 243-262.
5. Birnholtz, J.P., & Bietz, M.J. (2003). Data at work: supporting sharing in science and engineering. In *Proc. ACM SIGGROUP*, ACM Press (2003), 339-348.
6. Borgman, C.L. (2011). The conundrum of sharing research data. *Journal of the American Society for Information Science and Technology*, 63(6), 1059-1078.
7. Edwards, P.N., Batcheller, A.L., Mayernik, M.S., Borgman, C.L., & Bowker, G.C. (2011). Science friction: Data, metadata, and collaboration. *Social Studies of Science*, 41(5), 667-690.
8. Faniel, I.M., & Jacobsen, T.E. (2010). Reusing Scientific Data: How Earthquake Engineering Researchers Assess the Reusability of Colleagues' Data. Computer Supported Cooperative Work, 19(3-4), 355-375.
9. Fortier, I., Burton, P.R., Little, J., et al. (2010). Quality, quantity and harmony: The DataSHaPER approach to

integrating data across bioclinical studies. *International Journal of Epidemiology*, 39(5), 1383-1393.

10. Fortier, I., Doiron, D., Little, J., et al. (2011). Is rigorous retrospective harmonization possible? Application of the DataSHaPER approach across 53 large studies. *International Journal of Epidemiology*, 40(5), 1314-1328.

11. Karasti, H., Baker, K., & Halkola, E. (2006). Enriching the Notion of Data Curation in E-Science: Data Managing and Information Infrastructuring in the Long Term Ecological Research (LTER) Network. *Computer Supported Cooperative Work*, 15(4), 321-358.

12. Lee, C.P., Dourish, P., & Mark, G. (2006). The Human Infrastructure of Cyberinfrastructure. In *Proc. CSCW 2006*, ACM Press (2006), 483 - 492.

13. Lethbridge, T.C., Singer, J., & Forward, A. (2003). How Software Engineers Use Documentation: The State of the Practice. *IEEE Software*, 20(6).

14. National Postdoctoral Association. 2009. Accessed May 29, 2012. <http://www.nationalpostdoc.org/policy/what-is-a-postdoc>

15. National Institutes of Health Research Portfolio Online Reporting Tools (RePORT). 2012. Accessed May 29, 2012. <http://report.nih.gov/award/index.cfm?ot=&fy=2011&state=&ic=&fm=&orgid=#tab2>

16. Nelson, B. (2009). Data sharing: Empty archives. *Nature*, 461(7261).

17. Piwowar, H.A. (2011). Who Shares? Who Doesn't? Factors Associated with Openly Archiving Raw Research Data. *PloS one*, 6(7), e18657.

18. Piwowar, H.A., Day, R. S., & Fridsma, D. B. (2007). Sharing detailed research data is associated with increased citation rate. *PloS one*, 2(3).

19. Walport, M., & Brest, P. (2011). Sharing research data to improve public health. *The Lancet*, 6736(10), 9-11.

20. Zimmerman, A. (2007). Not by metadata alone: the use of diverse forms of knowledge to locate data for reuse. *International Journal on Digital Libraries*, 7(1-2), 5-16.

Explaining Field Differences in Openness and Sharing in Scientific Communities

Theresa Velden
Department of Information Science, Cornell University
301 College Avenue, Ithaca, NY 14850, USA
tav6@cornell.edu

ABSTRACT

This paper explores field differences in openness and sharing of scientific knowledge based on a comparative ethnographic field study of research groups in two research specialties. Tensions between cooperation and openness on the one hand and competition for priority and secrecy on the other hand are common in science. However, fields differ in how these tensions play out, influencing what information is exchanged when and how among research groups in a field. This paper develops an explanatory framework that identifies assumptions made in the generic model of the collective production process in the sciences and specifies epistemic and material field characteristics that affect to what extent those assumptions hold for a specific field, explaining field differences in openness and secrecy behaviors. I suggest that these field-inherent sources for differences in openness and sharing behaviors need to be accounted for in research policies and in the design of information and communication systems that aim to support and advance the collective production of knowledge in science.

Author Keywords

ethnography, scientific communication, scientific collaboration, field differences, openness, sharing, secrecy.

ACM Classification Keywords

H.5.3. Group and Organization Interfaces: [Computer-supported cooperative work]

INTRODUCTION

The emergence of the World Wide Web provides opportunities to increase the extent to which scientific knowledge is publicly shared within a scientific community, overcoming existing technical and social barriers [13, 6, 12, 17]. However, disciplines and fields differ in the extent to which they use these new opportunities. This is demonstrated e.g. by the contrast of the popularity of preprint servers[1] in some areas in physics, and the failure of preprint servers in the life sciences and chemistry [27, 26]. Social and cultural arrangements of research fields play a major role in the shaping and use of new information and communication technologies [19, 8, 32, 5, 25, 39]. This suggests that the design of new technologies to support scientific communication and collaboration needs to take account of the specific arrangements and needs in a field[2].

How to best support scientific collaboration and the sharing of scientific information and data within and across scientific fields has been an area of recent interest within CSCW and its related literature, motivated by the opportunities provided by the world wide web to better support knowledge sharing and remote collaborations, and by recent investments made into the development of cyberinfrastructures. Empirical and theoretical works on scientific collaboration have revealed challenges such as the costs of research team integration [2], the difficulty of alignment of temporal rhythms in scientific collaboration [24], and of incentive structures in scientific software production that discourage collaboration [22]. An important focus of attention have been data sharing practices in science. It is acknowledged that improvements e.g. of collaborative data generation and reuse require "a deeper understanding of the social and technical circumstances" [33]. Ethnographic observations and interviews provide evidence that data-sharing practices not only vary across fields [3], but that they need to be understood as part of a "data economy": data derive their value not just from their context of use or exchange, but also from the specific context of their production, integral to the research process [38].

The present paper focuses on openness and sharing behaviors[3] versus behaviors of withholding and secrecy within scientific communities. It investigates how work and communication practices in the basic sciences are affected by com-

[1] A web server where scientific authors can publish research manuscripts without first undergoing peer-review.

[2] An insight highlighted already in the early 1970's when the spread of the academic Internet triggered visions of the potential for computer based enhancements to scientific communication ([9] cited in: [8]).

[3] By 'openness' I understand in this context an act of disclosure that is undirected with regard to who exactly will partake of a certain piece of information or knowledge, whereas 'sharing' assumes a conscious interaction between two or more parties, possibly involving expectations of some form of reward or reciprocating behavior.

petition dynamics and aims to inform initiatives that set out to develop cyberinfrastructures and open science policies to enable new forms of collaborative science. To support a systematic understanding of field differences it builds on a sociological model of the collective production of scientific knowledge and proposes a theoretical framework that describes the inherent tension between openness and secrecy in scientific communities. Based on an ethnographic study it identifies generic assumptions made in the framework that are susceptible to field specific variation and identifies three important field characteristics that affect to what extent those assumptions hold for a specific field. The analytic framework resulting from this study can provide a valuable theoretical tool to the CSCW community engaged in the development of cyberinfrastructures to support the assessment and understanding of the social dynamics of knowledge sharing in scientific fields that are targeted.

THEORETICAL BACKGROUND

The analysis presented in this study builds on a sociological model of the collective production of scientific knowledge introduced by Gläser [13]. This model explains and puts into context a number of observations that have been reported in the social studies of science literature since the 1960's about the uneasy balance of cooperation and openness versus competition and secrecy in fields of basic research.

For basic science, secrecy cannot be attributed to outside factors such as the commercial value of the information created for commercial applications. Instead, secrecy arises from competition for priority of research discoveries [21, 10]. However, as scientific knowledge creation is a collective process that requires communication, a balance needs to be struck between competitive and cooperative behaviors. Figure 1 I propose a theoretical framework that explains the contradiction between openness and secrecy in science as a systemic tension inherent to the collective production of scientific knowledge and points to sources for field specific variations. This framework, and its underlying sociological model, is described in more detail below.

The Collective Production of Scientific Knowledge

Gläser's sociological model of the collective production of scientific knowledge seeks to explain how reliable scientific knowledge can be produced under the condition of producers that are "autonomous, and incompletely informed about one another" and that face the challenge that the definition of research tasks and how to approach them are imbued with great insecurity[4] [13] (p. 362).

The model assumes that members of the scientific community in a research specialty decide autonomously[5] about the definition of research tasks and how to approach them. However, these decisions are guided by the researchers' local interpretation of the shared knowledge base of a scientific community. Researchers orient their actions towards creating knowledge that they can offer as novel contributions to the shared knowledge base. Hence the shared knowledge base ensures coordination of a collective of autonomous producers. This coordination is decentralized, and not enforced by institutions or direct coordinating actions. The social order[6] of a scientific production community is an emergent property (ibid, p. 261). Sociologically, the coordination of collective production in a community is distinct from other well-known production systems, namely organizations, networks and markets [14].

The knowledge base of a scientific community consists of various types and forms of scientific knowledge. There is the published archive of scientific knowledge whose public accessibility is a crucial precondition for the coordinating role of the shared knowledge base [13](p. 163). Knowledge also exists in unpublished formats such as preprints, technical reports, procedures, or materials that are typically exchanged between researchers on request. Further, there is knowledge that is orally communicated, and then there is local, tacit knowledge [4] or implicit knowledge that can be acquired only through actual visits, through presence and learning by imitation in the local work environments [13](p. 114).

The orientation of research activities towards the shared knowledge base of a scientific community serves to increase the chances of eventual integration of locally produced results into the shared knowledge base [13]. This integration proceeds in several stages during which various forms of scientific communication are important. Initially, as research tasks are being derived and defined locally the knowledge base is referred to to establish open questions and new approaches, to support decisions on methods to use, and to assess the competitive situation, chances of success, potential collaboration partners, and results that others have produced (ibid, p. 83/84).

During the execution of research tasks researchers make use of the knowledge base of a scientific community to solve unanticipated problems as they arise. Further, the moving research front is monitored and task definitions and approaches may have to be adapted to retain chances for later integration of the locally produced knowledge into the shared knowledge base (ibid, p. 115).

As locally produced results get ready to be published, the next step of coordination with the common knowledge base of the scientific community begins. Through authoring and peer-review the local contribution is adapted to the community mainstream to increase its utility, e.g. by incorporating a peer reviewer's interpretation of the common knowledge base into the presentation and interpretation of research results[7](ibid, p. 130).

Eventually, research results offered in the form of publications may get integrated into the shared knowledge base of a scientific community. Integration happens through the uptake of results, repeated re-use and eventual convergence over time

[4] in contrast to e.g. the routinized work tasks in manufacturing.

[5] although influenced by power relations and access to resources (ibid, p. 81), such as research funding.

[6] Defined by Gläser as "coordinating the individual actions of actors to achieve a stable, beneficial state for the collective" (ibid, p. 52)

[7] In this integrative process Gläser sees the main function of peer-review, not in quality control, as peer-review had been proven insufficient for quality control.

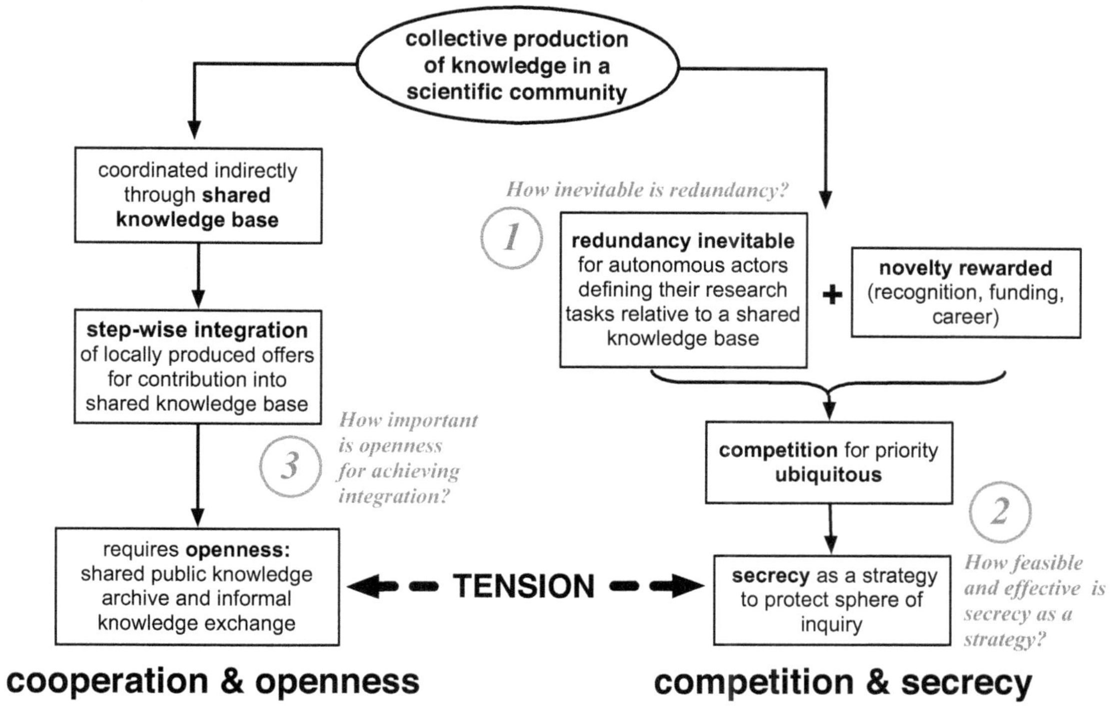

Figure 1. Theoretical framework that explains the contradiction between openness and secrecy in scientific fields as a systemic tension inherent to the collective production of scientific knowledge. Questions (1) - (3) point to sources of field specific variation.

of how users interpret those results (ibid, p. 139). The robustness of a knowledge base is achieved by re-use and testing in various local contexts providing variation in perception of results through the diversity of individual researchers' research biographies and local work contexts (ibid, p. 148/49).

What makes Gläser's model fruitful for an investigation of field differences in openness and sharing behaviors is that it does not set apart scientific communication as a detached domain of activity. Instead it emphasizes how various forms of scientific communication and exchange are an integral and necessary part of the research process. It is crucial for the decentralized coordination of research activities within a scientific community and for the integration of research results into the shared knowledge base as part of a collective production process [12].

Systemic Tension Between Openness and Secrecy

Based on Gläser's model of the collective production of scientific knowledge and observations in the science studies literature he builds on, I suggest the theoretical framework depicted in figure 1 for the analysis of openness and sharing behaviors in scientific communities. Gläser emphasizes how cooperation and communication between researchers or research groups are required at various stages of the research process. Given that researchers and research groups autonomously define their research tasks while orienting their activities toward contributing to a shared knowledge base, overlap of research tasks and redundancy of results is to be expected [13, 16]. Since the goal of scientific activity is to advance knowledge by contributing new knowledge, novelty is an important criterion for the attribution of recognition and reward. Success in publishing prominently and recognition for the originality of work are essential preconditions for success in mobilizing research funding and building a scientific career. Consequently, competition around who can claim priority of a research finding is ubiquitous [13, 16]. The results is an enduring, systemic tension between cooperativeness and competitiveness in science [15, 1, 23, 11, 16].

Different strategies might be used to cope with competition for priority. Given sufficient connectivity, i.e. a small size of the field and open communication channels, researchers can cooperate to divide up the field and pro-actively avoid that their spheres of inquiry collide [13, 7, 11]. Or they may embrace competition both as a motivating force and for its epistemic value, as redundancy and replication allow them to calibrate, cross-validate and hence to fortify results. At other times, researchers employ secrecy to protect their sphere of inquiry[8] from intruders to avoid getting anticipated,

[8]A sphere of inquiry is a set of research problems that a scientist or group of scientists can pursue based on the specific ensemble of research technologies that they can mobilize [15, 21]. An ensemble of research technologies is defined by Hackett as an "arrangement of materials, techniques, instruments, ideas, and enabling theories". Ensembles of research technologies both enable and constraint the research questions that can be pursued by an individual researcher or a research group [15, 34]. Hence 'sphere of inquiry' refers to the range of research questions a researcher or a collective of researchers (knowingly or unknowingly) has the capability to address in order to produce novel contributions to a shared knowledge base.

or 'scooped' [16]. The balance between competition and secrecy versus cooperation and openness can be rather dynamic, requiring a careful management of information exchanged [18, 1].

Sources of Field Specific Variation

Differences in research culture among research fields are likely to influence competition dynamics and the balance struck between openness and secrecy. Kohler suggests fields develop 'moral conventions' to achieve a field-specific balance between cooperation and competition, referring to this balance as the 'moral economy' of a scientific community [29](p.12).

This paper aims to help develop a systematic understanding of the origins of field specific variations in openness and secrecy behaviors. Certain elements in the theoretical framework in figure 1 are susceptible to field-specific variations as they make idealized assumptions that do not hold to the same degree in every field. The questions to ask when trying to assess a field's sources for openness or secrecy in interactions between research groups, are (1) "How inevitable is redundancy?" - to what extent is redundancy of research efforts in a field indeed inevitable or are there mechanisms in place that reduce redundancy e.g. by limiting the autonomy of actors; (2) "How feasible and effective is secrecy as a strategy?" to protect a sphere of inquiry and to avoid getting anticipated or scooped; and (3) "How important is openness to achieve integration of knowledge the field?" - to what extent are cooperation and openness between research groups needed to produce relevant research findings? I will argue below that answers to these questions can be found by examining three characteristics of the epistemic and material culture of a research field.

METHODS

Field Study Design

This study of communication behaviors compares two research specialties in the chemical and physical sciences[9]The first one is a research specialty within synthetic chemistry (**field 1**) and was intended to represent a mainstream chemistry field[10], to see whether it would shed light on a disciplinary context that seems reluctant to embrace new, web-based communication models that increase openness and sharing of scientific knowledge [37]. The second research specialty (**field 2**) is situated between chemistry and physics and was selected to include a perspective from a setting with an additional disciplinary influence, namely physics, where new web-based communication models had been successfully introduced already in the 1990's.

Between 2007 and 2009, I visited five research groups, each for a minimum of four to six weeks. Two groups were active in field 1 and three active in field 2. The ethnographic analysis reported in this paper focuses on two of the research groups, one in each field to investigate and compare in an exemplary way how communication behavior and research culture are intertwined. Those two groups were chosen from a very similar organizational environment (the same University) to reduce conflating external factors (such as academic institution, national research system). Occasionally, I will also include statements from researchers in the other groups when they contain insights about the field or community as a whole.

Observational Approach

During the field visit with a group, I would typically have a desk either in a visitor office by myself, or share an office with other group members, tag along for coffee breaks and lunches, and attend group meetings, seminars or other academic events. During the period of my field visit various opportunities would arise to observe research activities and experiments, and to attend meetings where new data were discussed, experiments planned and logistic or technical problems tackled, or publications in an advanced stage of preparation discussed. This would allow me to get an insight into various stages in the life cycle of research projects, and to develop a basic understanding of the research conducted by the group, and the social organization of the group.

All three groups that I studied in field 2 are involved in experiments conducted at shared radiation facilities, such as synchrotrons. They take advantage of what once was seen merely as a side-product of high energy experiments, namely the highly energetic radiation emitted by accelerated charged particles such as electrons and protons. Today, synchrotrons, and the most recent innovation, x-ray free electron lasers (XFELs), are run to serve a diverse user community with research groups from a large variety of scientific fields such as physics, chemistry, structural biology, and archaeology. To familiarize myself with these experimental research practices, I came along to one such experimental run, a so called 'beamtime', that makes use of the high radiation beam provided at a radiation facility to investigate the structure and dynamics of small matter particles or clusters of molecules. To familiarize myself with research practices in field 1, I used shadowing

---

Unknowingly, because not all exact research questions within that sphere have necessarily been clearly articulated (yet). Unknowingly also refers to surprise findings - situations where one stumbles in ones research across an answer to a question that one was not asking. Capability refers to being in possession of and skilled in the use of research technologies such as instruments, methodologies, material, data, and theories. Obviously, a sphere of inquiry is dynamic and its evolution may progress through gradual as well as abrupt extensions of those capabilities.

[9]In the following I will use the labels 'field1' and 'field 2' for these research specialties. Groups within these specialties come from different (sub)disciplinary backgrounds, hence I will identify the groups in this study by those (sub)disciplinary affiliations such as 'organic chemistry' or 'experimental physics'. This does not imply that the observed behaviors are representative for the entire disciplinary culture of those (sub)disciplines. Therefore I will take care in the discussion section to refer to the research specialties (field1, field2) that provide the immediate context of my observations rather than suggesting a generalization to entire (sub)disciplines.

[10]Two thirds of the 900,000 chemical papers published in 2001 reported on the chemical synthesis (the creation of new chemical substances through chemical reactions) and the analysis of new chemical substances (to determine their molecular structure and chemical properties) [36].

(following a group member around for an entire work day) to get a sense of the daily research routine in a synthetic chemistry laboratory. In addition to observing the groups in their immediate research environments, I participated in a workshop in field 2 and attended national society meetings in both fields.

Interview Analysis

I also conducted semi-structured interviews with most of the research group members at each site. I followed an informal outline of topics, such as: research practices and goals of research; research biography; everyday research activities; communication and collaboration with colleagues in and outside group; role of scientific community; scientific communication and the opportunities opened up by the World Wide Web. Interviews took between half an hour and up to two hours. In total I audio recorded more than 60 hrs of interviews with members of all five research groups.

The interviews were transcribed and analyzed using a set of tags developed and refined over the course of this study. The initial tag set reflected the major topics covered in the interviews and was refined and extended bottom-up during analysis of the interviews to capture themes emerging from the interviews as certain topics got repeatedly mentioned or offered themselves for comparison between interviewees and groups. The TAMS software[11] was used for tagging and extraction of combinations of subsets of tagged passages.

RESULTS

Based on ethnographic field observations and interviews, this section compares the social organization of the two research groups, their research practices and the experiences of group members with regard to openness and secrecy when communicating with other researchers in their research specialty.

Research Technologies and Epistemic Culture

In both groups the research efforts of the group members are united by the overarching research program of the professor who is leading the group (called in the following PI for principal investigator). The person and research interests of the PI lend continuity to the research group over decades, and his or her accumulation of knowledge and research experiences serves to guide the research group's activities. In both groups the majority of group members are PhD students. They form the backbone of the group for the execution of research tasks - whether conducting the day to day activities needed to create chemical substances and develop syntheses routes or to build instruments and capture data of physics experiments that the group sets up at shared radiation facilities. The informal knowledge and the tacit knowledge required for accomplishing these tasks is generally recognized as a critical resource and maintained by the group as long as there is no interruption of personnel continuity and training.

Beyond these commonalities, however, the social organization of the two research groups is quite distinct, emphasizing different values. What emerges from my observations is that the synthetic chemistry group represents a research culture that is invested in individual skill and personal reputation. By contrast, in the experimental physics group joint leadership, team effort and a valuation of collective achievements prevail.

My ethnographic observations further suggest differences in research culture between the two groups that have implications for the way critical knowledge is learned and how the groups organize to achieve their research goals[12]. These observations put into context the differences in valuation of individual achievement versus team spirit[13]. In the synthetic chemistry group the day-to-day practice of research foregrounds personal skill in doing syntheses and the value of knowledge that an individual accumulates and internalizes over his or her lifetime as a researcher. In the experimental physics group on the other hand, the material culture foregrounds communal efforts. The knowledge generating power of the group is externalized in the experimental apparatus that it builds and that can be applied to generate data from beamtime experiments on a range of different research objects.

Research practice in the synthetic chemistry group is characterized by the continuous, day-to-day effort of conducting chemical syntheses at the lab bench. Known or new chemical substances are produced, isolated and characterized, new syntheses routes developed, and catalysts tested. The focus in synthetic chemistry is on the creation of substances [20]. The majority of those newly created substances are of interest not for their direct technical or practical use in industrial applications, but for the advances they bring to synthetic chemistry itself by improving its synthetic capability [36, 35]. Individuals identify strongly with the 'chemistry' they are experienced in and that they have expertise in doing. A common phrase is to talk about 'my' chemistry, or 'his' or 'her' chemistry - referring to chemical reactions that one is most familiar with, as exemplified by this quote:

> *I mean, in the fluid phase you are so well rehearsed, that you know what you have to do. There are sometimes days, where I feel like a laboratory technician, because I don't have to think at all, I just do my chemistry. I do a column, I produce a spectrum, and so on and so forth.*
>
> [field 1: PhD Student, organic chemistry]

[11] by Matthew Weinstein, released under the GPL v2 license at `http://tamsys.sourceforge.net/`

[12] For a much more comprehensive account and comparison of epistemic cultures, in high energy physics and molecular biology, see [28]

[13] Balancing tensions is one of the core requirements for conducting research and leading research teams [15]. Hence, the contrasts emphasized here rarely represent exclusive alternatives, but rather a relative emphasis when negotiating between one set of values or behaviors and another. For example, the habilitants in the experimental physics group are required to prove themselves as team players. At the same time, to position themselves for an academic career they also need to acquire individual distinction. One strategy involves the significance given within a community to the order of authors on a paper. As one of the habilitants in the group explained to me, he would see to it that the first publication opening up a new stream of research would list him as a first author, the students' names in the middle, and the PI of the group in last position. After that, having signaled his ownership of the topic by first authorship, he would then give up the lead position on subsequent publications to whichever of the students did the analysis and interpretation of data that the respective publication is based on.

Doing one's chemistry successfully is not only a matter of manual skill and practical intuition. Also important is the chemical knowledge a chemist accumulates and internalizes over his or her career. It serves as a personal toolbox for developing synthesis ideas and intuitions, as described in the following quote:

I like organic chemistry, because it is like solving riddles. Also when you do a retrosynthesis, and then you have such a problem in front of you, then you have to puzzle. The more knowledge you have, the more easy it becomes. And it also... the feeling I have is that, everything I learn I can apply. [...] So in the end, I always say, we are learning a toolbox with which you can build houses. Therefore it is worth learning each and every reaction. A human being collects more and more knowledge such that it can do ever more, solve problems. And that's so fascinating to me, I don't see this in any other chemical area... that's organic chemistry for me, this knowing more and more, and solving riddles, and so on, that has always excited me.

[field 1: PhD Student, organic chemistry]

Although typically several students work alongside in a lab space, direct collaboration between group members, beyond occasional consultations and discussions on how to solve a synthetic problem, is limited. One occasional scenario is that a student is charged with (re)producing a certain substance that he and others need for their syntheses. Aside from meeting a practical need, the person fulfilling such a task benefits by learning and getting familiar with a certain 'chemistry' - hence typically a new member of the group is charged with it or someone who moves into a new topical area.

The majority of research projects in the experimental physics group is organized around beamtimes at shared national or international radiation facilities. The group has to apply for beamtime and beamtime is typically granted for a one to two week period at a time, several times a year. Beamtime experiments are complex apparatuses consisting of different parts such as vacuum chambers, particle sources and detectors, and are planned and built locally in the group's lab at the University. They undergo several years' of construction and evolve through optimization, extensions or adaptations to new tasks. The different components are transported to the synchrotron facility and assembled there for the beamtime. From these experimental runs the team brings along measurements (data) that are analyzed and interpreted back at the groups's home base at the University.

A typical range of research activities of a PhD student in this group includes desk work, ordering of parts, the computer aided design of custom made instruments and testing of those instruments in the lab. It culminates in assembling the instrument at a radiation facility and using the high energy beam provided during the beamtime to run the experiment the instrument was designed for. All students need to collaborate closely when building and running the experiment, as explained by one of the subgroup leaders:

We use this apparatus for all our experiments. It is so complex that it cannot be run by a single person. That means in the working group are eight to ten people. Everyone has their own topic but we all work with the same apparatus. That is required for the measurement runs or beamtimes, since we have 24 hours operation, and we work in shifts of two people. You cannot get this done any other way. In principle everyone works together on each project, but for the interpretation and analysis of the data, this is divided up again.

[field 2: subgroup leader, experimental physics]

The pressure of making optimal use of the beamtime allotted, the stress of setting up the experiment in limited time, dealing with occasional failures, enduring the continuous noise of the vacuum pumps, and working night shifts, make these periods exceptionally intense and exhausting. But they also provide for gratifying experiences of team success.

This whole project that I work on has virtually been a 'Napoleon-conquers-Russia-thing'. Really. Virtually from the beginning it was too big for us, and we did it in spite of that, and I believe we did really extremely well. The experiment that we have now standing there is a totally fine experiment. But it always was - this is also where the mountain of data comes from - the experiment has always been larger than we are and always precision landing after precision landing after precision landing.

[field 2: PhD student, experimental physics]

The data generated at beamtimes is assigned to individual group members for analysis and interpretation. Students in the group own tasks that contribute to the building of the common experimental capability of the group, and they are rewarded by subsets of data to analyze and to write their thesis about. Hence the projects in the experimental physics group are highly interdependent. Only the completion of a complex experimental set-up that all group members contribute to enables them to take measurements and to collect data to answer the scientific questions they are asking.

Information Resources

Chemical databases that specify the molecular structures of chemical substances, that document known chemical reactions and provide links into the chemical literature play a central role for doing synthetic work in organic chemistry. This is reflected by the following statement of one of the PhD student who describes the use of this databases when planning the chemical synthesis of a new substance that may need to make use of already know steps or might be achieved by varying already know steps:

Whenever you want to do something, somehow you envision a reaction, then most of the time you go to the computer, enter the type of reaction it should search for, or your molecule, and then it eventually retrieves reactions that have been done before, perhaps with similar molecules, or just generally and then you can select things that fit best to what you have in mind, and then you try it out. If these things have been done before, you do not have to think for yourself and sit in front of it for three years to find out something someone else has already done. So this is the main source to explore publications.

[field 1: PhD Student, organic chemistry]

To help define a research task, to double-check the novelty of a chemical reaction or substance, to develop a synthesis plan or to solve synthesis problems, the students and postdocs frequently turn to chemical databases[14], as well as the synthesis protocols published in the method sections of journal articles or included in the PhD theses of former group members.

The value of group members as a resource to discuss and help solve problems is highlighted by comments the students make on the utility of online fora or blogs. Whereas one member of the group reports a positive experience of using an online forum to solve a practical problem to purify a substance, most group members reject the idea of discussing synthesis details 'in public'. They argue that their co-workers are the most valuable resource for discussing and getting advise on problems since they provide the right mix of expertise: some of them are not too close so that they can provide a new perspective on a problem while other co-workers are highly specialized in the particular chemistry that one is working on.

To stay up to date with the research front in their field the chemists in the synthetic chemistry group fall back on the officially published literature. Many of them regularly and systematically scan between a handful of core journals up to lists of 15-20 journals relevant to their research. They forward to one another articles they deem relevant and tell their colleagues about them at the weekly group seminar. As will be discussed in the next section, getting scooped is a relatively common experience, and typically the only way of learning about it is through the published literature.

By contrast to the chemists for whom the chemical databases play a central role when planning their syntheses, members of the experimental physics group primarily mention discussions with co-workers and subgroup leaders in the early phases of planning an experiment and instrument design, as exemplified by the following quote:

During experiments and during the planning of the set up and so, I actually fall back constantly on what (the sub group leader) knows, simply his experience and the many experiments that he has already seen, and build, such that he just knows, "it is obvious to me, at this point there is this problem" and he knows how to solve it. That's simply the conversation with him. And by now also with other people, for example - I love chatting with (a fellow PhD student) if I am confused about something specific.

[field 2: PhD student, experimental physics]

The students of the group further emphasize the value of knowledge that they gain in informal discussions from researchers outside the group, e.g. at community workshops, during beamtimes or user meetings at radiation facilities. They seem to have significantly more access to informal and tacit knowledge about approaches other groups are taking than students in the synthetic chemistry group:

It is different than when you read a publication, where everything is nicely trimmed and all the problems are not listed that are actually decisive when you carry through such an experiment. Naturally you are interested in the results, but when you want to reproduce such a set up or do something similar, then you are interested in the problems, you want to know why did it almost fail. And there you can simply see it. You squat down with the groups... for example there was a group that also did pump probe experiments, also using infrared lasers, and that is new for our group. I asked them, whether I could join and observe them for a day, that timing, how they do it, and I just set down with them and asked stupid questions and wrote everything down. That what I wanted, these problems, I could directly see them.

[field 2: PhD student, experimental physics]

Students in the experimental physics group refer more often than students in the synthetic chemistry group to alternative information resources on the internet, beyond online journals and databases, that help to solve problems. Websites of other groups with photographs of their experimental set up may provide useful details, as well as theses offered for download.

The physicists in the experimental physics group would expect to hear early about a relevant experiment that may duplicate their own results. New developments in the field are tracked through several channels: before publication one may already learn about an unpublished result at a conference, receive a preprint from a colleague, or learn via the beamtime application process about a planned experiment.

The main conclusion that emerges from these observations on how information needs get addressed is that in the synthetic chemistry group the published body of chemical knowledge, reported in journal articles and made accessible through chemical databases is the most crucial knowledge resource. By contrast, in the experimental physics group more informal and unpublished knowledge is available through various channels for group members, in addition to the published journal literature that remains important.

Observations on Openness and Sharing

In the interviews I find a number of striking differences between the synthetic chemistry group and the experimental physics group with regard to the risk of getting scooped and the latitude with which group members communicate information about their work and findings to researchers outside of the group.

In the synthetic chemistry group people repeatedly talk about experiences of scooping. Getting scooped, and sometimes scooping another group is a relatively common experience.

The [Miller] research group in [US American city] works with, you know, different ligands but they are not far from ours. So it is well possible that they are already working on the same ligands, and are developing the same catalysts, you cannot prevent that from happening, that's usually the case, and it happens over an over again, that other working groups are faster, or that we are faster than others, that's not uncommon.

[field 1: PhD student, organic chemistry]

Some group members also talk about suspicions about people who steal ideas from other groups. One incident concerns a professor who met the PI of the group at a conference, and allegedly got information that she used to her advantage, thereby scooping the group.

[14]The databases used by the group are SciFinder(CAS) and Beilstein.

[...] what I think has happened, is that she saw at a conference how (our group does) a natural product with [a specific type of reaction the group is expert in] and she has combined the two methods, and produced a very similar natural product, of the same family. And I believe she very often does that.

[field 1: PhD student, organic chemistry]

The PI confirms that by talking about details of the work of his group to outsiders before the work was published, he has enabled others to scoop his group. He says he has learned from this experience to be cautious:

I simply had to make the experience... in early years I was more relaxed with those things, and it has happened that I reported in talks but did not follow up by publications fast enough, that I waited too long. That then meant that quite unexpectedly works appeared that clearly were derived from information I had given. Obviously, this implies that in future you will exercise restraint.

[field 1: PI, organic chemistry]

The PI has instructed the group members not to talk about details of their work with outsiders, and the group members respect and accept this precaution. Secrecy is not only used in informal communications. The PI sees information withholding also as a legitimate strategy when publishing results that have promise to open up a new sphere of inquiry or expand the existing sphere of inquiry of the group. One strategy is to delay publication and inhibit the dissemination of PhD theses that can be mined and expanded on in future work:

There are always aspects that are leading further. Because things build on one another and if this is a promising story where I want to avoid that others join in too early, then I try to prevent that by controlling the information. [...] An obvious example are PhD theses. A PhD has to be published, made publicly available. [...] You can, and that is the most simple method for co-workers the cheapest simplest method, to put the work online. This implies though that the whole world has immediate access to it. There is also the option to say, ok, let's not put that online right away, only after a year's time... A third option is, not to put it online, but that there will be printed copies of this work that get disseminate to libraries, and again, there is the option to not publish the printed copy immediately, but only a year later... if a thesis is particularly rich in content, and you cannot work on and follow up all aspects that are included, and you want to avoid that that provides too much inspiration for others, then there will only be a printed copy. Then the likelihood that many people will make us of it is much, much smaller.

[field 1: PI, organic chemistry]

Adding to this picture of strategic information withholding is the notion that synthesis protocols published in the literature in organic chemistry are not reliable. My interview partners suggest that authors deliberately leave out some decisive detail to hold competition at bay, leading to frustrations and disillusionment among students as they try to make use of published synthesis procedures in their work. To cite just one example:

That's really done quite often, when they publish a procedure, they leave away something small, a detail, so no one can reproduce it. Because this is an art in itself: 'we can do it, we can do it with so many systems, but no one else can.' So we can look forward to a lot of nice publications, and every one else is left behind.

[field 1: PhD student, organic chemistry]

In contrast to the synthetic chemistry group, members of the experimental physics group report only very rare incidents of scooping. This is in spite of the fact that beamline experiments happen in the public space of a shared radiation facility makes it much more difficult to maintain secrecy than it would be for an experiment conducted in a group's private lab. However, the atmosphere is described as very collegial and open:

[...] you do an experiment in such a huge hall, where concurrently other experiments are running, and where you see all the other people that do similar things, and meet and make arrangements, where it is already public, your experiment is public. That is very special, since that is really rather unusual within physics. This way you are forced to cooperate, other people come by an ask 'what are you doing?' It happens spontaneously that you get to know everybody. I was along for only one beamtime, a few weeks in March, April, and I already know almost everybody we are cooperating with, just because within a month everybody has come by and we have been eating out or had coffee or we have been at the experiment.

[field 2: PhD student, experimental physics]

Since building an instrument takes several student years and its optimization generations of students, the experimental capability to reproduce someone else's results is not instantly available. Hence, as group members explain to me, chances that another group develops the same experimental capabilities without them hearing about it are low.

The following quotes acknowledge the existence of competition in the field, but also describe how in spite of it information flow is relatively open and the attitude between groups is cooperative:

There is competition at times, but people still talk, I would say, a lot with one another, especially (in a sub area of field 2), that is an area, that is comparably strongly contested, since many groups do that. [...] there are quite a number of people, and still people talk with one another and exchange information on where they are, talk about interpretations and so on. I would say... that this is not an idealized picture, I would say that is truly so.

[field 2: subgroup leader, experimental physics]

The things you are currently working on are being communicated very freely, sometimes without boundaries that it seems strange, but you still do it. For example there is this [some PI name], a Japanese scientist, who is the lead at this [name of a free electron laser project], with whom we cooperate, but where you know, this Japanese FEL this still is a direct competition. And nevertheless he was standing at my experiment, and I explained everything to him and (my group leader) signaled to me through eye contact, yes, tell him, and I was always like, 'shall I really, yes shall I really?' and I showed him as well where I adjust the skimmer slit, that's an adjustable slit that determines how many clusters are in the interaction zone, where did I buy it, what do you have to look out for, and what is the idea here with the protection against scattering light, this is information for which we needed two beamtimes to figure that out, that this is the decisive problem, and that without that we do not get a signal on which to adjust. That's not what generates data that you publish, but this is what needs to happen first, what takes a lot of time, and still, this is being communicated.

[field 2: PhD student, experimental physics]

The view of of group members on competition in their field is shaped by recent experimental successes they have had, the recognition of having excellent access to synchrotron facilities (one being in the same city) and beamtimes, and a perception that one is, at least temporarily, leading the field.

I would say in (our research specialty) this all is, at least it was like that so far, very friendly. That's partly due to, the things we do here no one else can do, so we can be generous. There are groups that want to catch up, but you know those groups [...] how far advanced everyone is, and at meetings, regularly, you provide tips to those people.

Interviewer: One does not deliberately withhold information?

No, because that does not make any sense. One shares the desire to generate knowledge, and also.... I am rather at the forefront of a field and have a tail of people behind with the same experiment, because then everyone acknowledges that one is in front. But if I am at the top and would stamp everyone else to the ground then a) that's no fun, and b) it does not help one. I find that what we are doing momentarily is an area where it would be good if it did grow, we can't do it all by ourselves anyway, and then it is good for us, purely egoistically, that our predominance is recognized, does not do harm if you would like to have a job later sometime.

[field 2: subgroup leader, experimental physics]

Hence a successful competitive strategy for this group is to focus efforts to gain leadership in the field. Since for more complex research tasks collaborators from the same or other fields are required, a cooperative attitude prevails. In comparison to the synthetic chemistry group, members of the experimental physics group do not see their own position compromised by providing practical help to other groups within the field, and convey a stronger interest in seeing the entire community advance.

In conclusion, the picture that emerges is multifaceted. Competition with groups working in the same field is experienced by the synthetic chemistry group as well as by the experimental physics group. However, there are distinct policy differences between the two groups that reflect the fact that the synthetic chemists rely on a competition strategy that maintains secrecy around practical and conceptual details of syntheses, whereas the experimental physicists pursues a cooperative competition strategy that invests into the advancement and strength of the community as a whole.

DISCUSSION

The ethnographic observations made above suggest that differences in openness and sharing behavior are linked to the different research cultures of the two fields. I suggest that these differences can be understood at a theoretical level by considering three epistemic and material characteristics of the two scientific fields, namely the ordering power of their respective knowledge bases, the autonomy of research groups to control the research technologies they are using, and the vulnerability of spheres of inquiry. These field characteristics affect to what extent the generic assumptions in the functional model in figure 1 hold, and act as sources of field-specific variation of the balance between openness and secrecy among research groups within a scientific community.

A. The Ordering Power of Knowledge Bases

Gläser suggests the concept of "ordering power of a scientific knowledge base" to capture an important aspect of how scientific knowledge bases differ between fields, and he hypothesizes that the strength of ordering power of a scientific knowledge base influences the social order with a scientific community. He defines ordering power as the specificity of the criteria to assess the chances for a locally produced knowledge contribution to get eventually integrated into the shared knowledge base of a scientific community. Such decision criteria support in particular the identification of relevant research tasks and of legitimate methods for producing contributions [13](p. 248, 259). A scientific knowledge base with a high ordering power imposes tighter constraints on what counts as legitimate and valuable results. However, if the ordering power of a knowledge base is low, it requires greater cooperative and communicative efforts among researchers in the field to co-construct results in a way that they have a high chance for getting integrated into the shared knowledge base.

From my field study observations I conclude that the ordering power of the knowledge base in field 1 is stronger than in field 2. This difference is alluded to in the following quote of a senior researcher whom I interviewed in field 2, who had been working most of his career in a research group in physical chemistry:

"In chemistry you must put something on the table at the end, a substance or so. This means you have to somehow produce gold. And in physics you can talk well about gold, and then this is enough."

[field 2: senior researcher, physical chemistry]

The suggestion that physicists can get away with talk may seem counterintuitive at first, given that in common rankings of scientific rigor physics is placed above chemistry. However, the notion that chemists have to produce ('create') rather than talk ('understand') emphasizes the material craft aspect of synthetic chemistry. Knowledge contributions in synthetic chemistry are new molecules or synthesis routes, and it has been suggested that the growth of knowledge in synthetic chemistry can be measured by the growth in the number of known chemical substances [35]. All known chemical substances and many of the known reactions are captured in chemical databases, and can be effectively searched, facilitating the assessment of the novelty of a knowledge contribution. The centrality of these databases in the research practice of synthetic chemists indicates a high level of order and standardization of chemical knowledge.

Further evidence for a strong ordering power of the knowledge base in organic chemistry is that group members repeatedly refer to specific performance properties of their results that can be measured and translate into an assessment of the quality of the results; for example the efficiency of a natural product synthesis that can be measured by the number of synthesis steps, the overall yield and the selectivity of the product, or the assessment of the longevity of a catalysts by turnover numbers. Finally, the use of off-the-shelf instruments to support specific synthesis steps and to measure properties of chemical substances produced, indicates a high standardization of methods and measurements, which reduces the need to explain and justify the methods used to obtain a result.

This contrasts with the focus on 'understanding' as a research result in field 2. A new knowledge contribution is not as easily accessed in its meaning and relevance nor straightforwardly localized in a standardized whole. No physics database comparable to the respective chemistry databases that comprehensively capture what is known in the field of synthetic chemistry exist[15]. The instruments used to generate data are custom made, locally designed and built, and not standardized, off-the-shelf products. This means that in field 2 more translation work is needed to explain the workings of an instrument and of an experimental set up to a community member, and to argue the validity of results obtained. In this context a positive attitude toward the reproduction of a result by other groups can be found. Instead of inducing feelings of threat for fear of competition, such duplication of efforts is oftentimes valued to help solidify a result and develop a joint interpretation, as expressed by the following remark:

Here, if someone does something similar, this is rather good, because then you can calibrate and see, is that correct what one has obtained, or is there another interpretation. That's why this is an area I quite like working in. Tough use of elbows, that's something I am not interested in.

[field 2: junior researcher, experimental physics]

Researchers in this field compensate for the lack of ordering power of their knowledge base through increased engagement with colleagues and potential referees in discussions and mutual education about the methods used to obtain data and their interpretation. Informal interactions within a community of experts is valued and enjoyed as part of the research process, as exemplified by the following quote about the experience at the initial workshop of what has become a regular bi-annual workshop series:

And then all people could meet one another face to face ... and then discussions started, and they are still going on, so that's very, very important, right? [...] in the coffee breaks, they are deliberately long - right? And then you go 'You said something earlier, that I do not believe that you can even measure that' - and then 'what, really???' and then it get's going, then you can talk about such things, and the learning is unbelievably effective.... This is according to my.... perspective the most productive, productive working atmosphere at all, the small specialized meeting of a circle of adepts who do similar things, and who sit together p...] that you show the other colleagues 'this is what we will try to publish soon'. The referees are there as well.... They referee each other, without knowing who it is in each and every case - who, who else should be it? I mean, when I send a paper to a European physics journal on [field 2], then one of those people who are sitting there... is the referee. With certainty. Or.... With very great probability, you know?

[field 2: junior researcher, physical chemistry]

These differences in the ordering power of knowledge bases affect how new contributions get integrated into it. This process requires a tighter network of communication in field 2 than in field 1 and 'openness' e.g. by communicating results early, pre-publication, and discussing methodological approaches in detail, have greater value in field 2 than in field 1. Hence the ordering power of the knowledge base in a field affects the degree to which assumption (3) in the theoretical model in figure 1 holds, namely that openness and cooperation are important to integrate knowledge and advance the field.

B. Control Over Research Tools

The two fields contrast with regard to the control research groups have over the research tools for producing research results. The synthetic chemistry group routinely uses tools (lab bench, chemical glassware, measurement instruments, chemicals etc.) that are commonly available at moderate costs. They are owned by the group or used as part of the shared infrastructure of the university. The large majority of experiments conducted in the experimental physics group however require access to several weeks of beamtime at radiation facilities every year. The control over access to beamtime at a facility is in the hands of a 'beamtime allocation commitee', a group of researchers from a wide range of disciplines who have been appointed to review the experiments proposed in beamtime applications.

Also, the research groups work with different affordances of laboratory spaces. The 'privacy' of lab-based research in synthetic chemistry facilitates a strategy of secrecy about the technical details of the research work, whereas the 'publicness' of the facility where the beamtime experiments take place would make such secrecy much more difficult to attain:

... Well, inevitably you are open, because there are more than enough people running around, peeking over your shoulder... you cannot really prevent that from happening, that someone peeks over your shoulder. I mean, if someone asked, hey can I copy your data, then we presumably would not do that [laughs], ahm, but when someone asks may I see that spectrum, or what is it what you are doing right now, then that is somehow... Yes, and most of all, I believe, it is very evident in this community who has done what, just because there is only this one laser, and anything that has been measured has been measured there, and there are perhaps ten working groups or so, hence that means, nobody can come and say 'oh, by the way, yesterday in my cellar I did' - I think that is more problematic (in other fields) where practically anybody can do the same at home, where everybody knows how it works - in our case it is quite, I mean no one will come forward and say 'we will do the exact same thing you are doing' that likely would not work, if only because you would get no beamtime.

[15] The factual databases that exist would not be considered representing the core knowledge produced in the field, but represent only very specific, limited data sets.

[field 2: PhD student, experimental physics]

As indicated by the quote above the control of the beamtime allocation committee has two relevant effects: the review of proposals by beamtime committees is seeking to reduce duplication of efforts in order to increase the diversity and novelty of science enabled by a certain facility. This means there oftentimes is an explicit policy to reduce redundancy and avoid granting beamtime to directly competing proposals thereby reducing competitive pressure and reducing the danger of unwarranted duplication. Second, the beamtime application process introduces a degree of publicness of a proposal that makes secretive moves impossible:

[...] since you know the others dont really have a chance to overtake you in secret, we play with very open cards. Very early on ideas are put on the table, it is communicated and presented what one plans to do and so on. Which, in case every body had their own laboratory experiment at home, people would likely not do in this way.

[field 2: subgroup leader, experimental physics]

Hence, the control over research tools and the affordances of lab spaces in a field of research affect the degree to which assumptions (1) and (2) in the functional model depicted in figure 1 hold for that field: the degree to which actors are autonomous in selecting and defining research tasks and redundancy is indeed 'inevitable', and the degree to which secrecy is a feasible and effective strategy to avoid competition and protect one's sphere of inquiry.

C. Vulnerability of Sphere of Inquiry

The specific research technologies of a group define a group's sphere of inquiry. How openly groups in a field communicate with each other is influenced by how easily this sphere is intruded on by other groups, and the risk of a scooping event ensuing from such an intrusion.

The synthetic chemistry group in field 1 protects its sphere of inquiry against intrusion of other groups by being secretive about research ideas as well as technical details and know how. Given the ubiquitous availability of the necessary tools, the relatively standardized methods and the short amount of time it takes to reproduce a result (days, weeks or months rather than years), sharing a small piece of information can enable one group to jump ahead of another group. Competition is direct, and due to the rather secretive behavior few communication channels are open that would provide specific information about the chances of getting anticipated. Usually a direct competition is only recognized after the fact, when the scooped results have been published. Since the group's sphere of inquiry is relatively vulnerable, the PI considers legitimate to withhold PhD thesis from circulation when they contain results that allow the extension of a group's sphere of inquiry. Not acknowledged but pointed out in other's behavior is e.g. the stealing of ideas, in explicit the deliberate intrusion into another group's sphere of inquiry through information gleaned e.g. at a conference; or the seemingly deliberate omission of details from synthesis protocol - another tactical move to retain the exclusivity of one's research technologies and hence protect the sphere of inquiry of the group.

By contrast, in field 2 the controlled allocation of beamtime and the necessity of getting beamtime granted, as discussed in the previous section, work as a buffer against intrusion by another group into a research group's sphere of inquiry. In addition to those factors that relate to the control over research tools, the vulnerability of the group's sphere of inquiry is further determined by other material and epistemic properties of the research in this field. The complex, custom-made instruments developed in the lab to conduct the beamtime experiments require several student or postdoc years of development, and sometimes collaboration with another group or expert from another group to optimize a specific component. The time and resources needed to realize an experimental strategy means that any advance that another group might make when learning a specific piece of information is unlikely to propel them ahead in a way that would allow them to anticipate results the original group was aiming for. Therefore groups can afford openness with regard to technical details and know-how, as well as the interpretation of results.

However, the group's sphere of inquiry is vulnerable to leaked information at other points in the research process. When it comes to ideas for beamtime proposals, or to the actual data measured, the experimental physics group in field 2 becomes much more protective and reluctant to share. In spite of the professed openness regarding the discussion of 'early ideas' within the community, those ideas that support actual research or beamtime proposals in the pipeline are kept close to the chest.

What is not shared are the ideas for upcoming experiments. What is written in a proposal, is, we for example have a folder that contains all proposals of the last few years, so that we get an insight what experiments are planned, money for what has been applied for. Jenny [a PhD student in the group] had this folder along [during a beamtime at a radiation facility] because she was reading up on it [...] but she always kept it under lock, because there are people running around, who could write the same kind of proposal, and these are ideas that we want to keep for ourselves.

[field 2: PhD student, experimental physics]

So the fact that redundancy is controlled for by the beamtime committee, leads to increased competition for getting a unique beamtime proposal in. In a way, the competition for priority in this field is moved from the later stage of submitting an article for publication to the much earlier stage of submitting an original beamtime proposal.

Further, the exclusivity of a group's sphere of inquiry would also be compromised when the measured data was publicly shared before the group has had a chance to analyze it and publish their results. I observed the PI joking to his group how this curious and potentially damaging idea, of making the data measured during a beamtime publicly available, had been brought up at a recent workshop that he attended. He reported that someone suggested to require groups to publicly release their measurement data from beamtimes within a certain number of months. The reactions of the group members to his account showed that it was understood that such a policy would be damaging to their group since they had been tremendously successful in the last few years in acquiring beamtime and was currently struggling with a large backlog of analysis of these data. The large investments the group had made in terms of person months and PhD years into assembling their specific and productive ensemble of research technologies granted the group relative exclusivity of their sphere of inquiry. This would be undermined by sharing that data.

Hence the field-specific vulnerability of the sphere of inquiry affects to what extent assumption (2) of the functional model depicted in figure 1 holds, namely whether secrecy is a feasible and effective strategy to protect a sphere of inquiry. From this discussion we take along in particular, that secrecy and openness are not a monolithic concepts, but that the specific acts of sharing specific types of knowledge at specific points in the research process are affected differently by the epistemic and material characteristics of a field, and that neither a group nor a field are all-open or all-secretive. Whether a groups is open to sharing certain information depends on whether sharing this type of information at that point in the research process presents a threat to the exclusivity of a group's sphere of inquiry.

CONCLUSION

The flows of scientific knowledge in a scientific community reflect how research groups balance cooperation and competition for priority of discoveries. The trade-offs between secretive behavior to further a group's competitive position and openness and sharing to strengthen and accelerate the collective process of knowledge production are field specific, arising from the epistemic culture in a field and the ensemble of research technologies used.

Based on empirical observations from a comparative ethnographic field study of two research specialties, this study develops a theoretical framework for analyzing field differences and how they affect openness and sharing behaviors in scientific communities. It highlights the assumptions made in the generic model of the collective production of scientific knowledge that are susceptible to field-specific variation and discusses three field specific epistemic characteristics that account for field differences. I argue that the ordering power of a knowledge base affects the importance of openness to produce valid results and advance the field, that the control the research technologies affects the assumption of redundancy being inevitable by compromising the autonomy of actors and the assumption of secrecy being a feasible and effective strategy to protect a group's sphere of inquiry, and that the vulnerability of the sphere of inquiry also affects the assumption of secrecy being a feasible and effective strategy.

Notably, the field study observations suggest a relatively more individualistic research culture in synthetic chemistry versus a team-oriented research culture in experimental physics that would seem to extrapolate in a straightforward way to secretive versus open communication cultures. However, as shown in the discussions above, openness and secrecy behaviors of research groups are not monolithic but nuanced and context dependent, and careful consideration of the specific factors influencing competition dynamics in basic research and the value of either secrecy or openness as a strategy is warranted.

Implications for Design

Even though it has been argued that greater openness and sharing will facilitate and speed-up problem solving [31] this study suggests that a one-size-fits-all approach to policy and technology design with regard to openness and sharing of research information is problematic. The analysis refines our understanding of how some scientific fields' inertia to embrace data and knowledge sharing initiatives is rooted in their specific collaborative and competitive dynamics. It underlines that the design of infrastructures that support the broad sharing of scientific data and knowledge represent a significant socio-technical challenge [30] and that field specific dynamics around information sharing need to be considered in policy development and system design. This result complements the observation of the importance of the context of production to understand scientific data sharing [38]. The data also suggest that neither of these communities is all open or all secretive. Therefore opportunities exist that could be identified and expanded on given a more systematic understanding of the differences in the social dynamics at play in different scientific settings.

The analytic framework developed in this paper that links the generic model of collective production in the sciences and its inherent tension between cooperation and competition to specific field characteristics can be used to guide future evaluations of these dynamics in specific fields that designers turn their attention to. It protects the analyst from drawing simplistic intuitive conclusions (obviously they need to share as they need to collaborate, or obviously they are secretive because they work independently) and cautions against binary attributions of openness or secrecy to actors or entire fields. Instead it supports the comprehensive evaluation of field characteristics to explain the more subtle dynamics at play. To refine our theoretical understanding of these issues for the design of systems that support 'open science', further research is needed that breaks down and analyses in greater detail how the sharing or withholding of specific types of information at specific points within the research process can be explained by field characteristics.

ACKNOWLEDGMENTS

I gratefully acknowledge the participants in my field studies. Without their support and their consent to participate in the study this work could not have been accomplished. This material is based upon work supported by the National Science Foundation through a Doctoral Thesis Improvement Grant No. 0924445 and under Grant No OCI-1025679.

REFERENCES

1. Atkinson, P., Batchelor, C., and Parsons, E. Trajectories of collaboration and competition in a medical discovery. *Science, Technology & Human Values 23*, 3 (1998), 259–284.

2. Balakrishnan, A., Kiesler, S., Cummings, J., and Zadeh, R. Research team integration: What it is and why it matters. In *Proceedings of the ACM 2011 conference on Computer supported cooperative work*, ACM (2011), 523–532.

3. Birnholtz, J. P., and Bietz, M. J. Data at work: supporting sharing in science and engineering. In *GROUP '03: Proceedings of the 2003 international ACM SIGGROUP conference on Supporting group work*, ACM Press (New York, NY, USA, 2003), 339–348.

4. Collins, H. The TEA Set: Tacit Knowledge and Scientific Networks. *Science Studies 4*, 2 (1974), 165–185.
5. Cronin, B. Scholarly communication and epistemic cultures. In *Scholarly Tribes and Tribulations: How Tradition and Technology Are Driving Disciplinary Change. ARL, Washington, DC, October 17, 2003* (2003).
6. de Sompel, H. V., Payette, S., Erickson, J., Lagoze, C., and Warner, S. Rethinking scholarly communication — building the system that scholars deserve. *D-Lib Magazine 10*, 9 (2004).
7. Edge, D. Competition in modern science. In *Solomons House Revisited. Science History Publications. Canton MA*. 1990, 208–232.
8. Fry, J., and Talja, S. The intellectual and social organization of academic fields and the shaping of digital resources. *Journal of Information Science 33*, 2 (2007), 115.
9. Garvey, W. D. *Communication: the Essence of Science*. Pergamon Press, 1979.
10. Gaston, J. Secretiveness and competition for priority of discovery in physics. *Minerva 9* (1971), 472–492. 10.1007/BF01558020.
11. Gilbert, G. Competition, differentiation and careers in science. *Social Science Information 16*, 1 (1977), 103–123.
12. Gläser, J. What Internet use does and does not change in scientific communities. *Science studies 16*, 1 (2003), 38–51.
13. Gläser, J. *Wissenschaftliche Produktionsgemeinschaften - die soziale Ordnung der Forschung*, vol. 906 of *Campus Forschung*. Campus Verlag, Frankfurt / New York, 2006.
14. Gläser, J., and Laudel, G. The social construction of bibliometric evaluations. In *The Changing Governance of the Sciences*, R. Whitley and J. Gläser, Eds. Springer, 2007, 101–123.
15. Hackett, E. Essential tensions. *Social Studies of Science 35*, 5 (2005), 787–826.
16. Hagstrom, W. Competition in Science. *American Sociological Review 39*, 1 (1974), 1–18.
17. Hilgartner, S. Biomolecular databases: New communication regimes for biology? *Science Communication 17*, 2 (Dec. 1995), 240–263.
18. Hilgartner, S. Selective flows of knowledge in technoscientific interaction: information control in genome research. *The British Journal for the History of Science FirstView* (2012), 1–14.
19. Hine, C. *Systematics as Cyberscience: Computers, Change, and Continuity in Science*. MIT, 2008.
20. Hoffmann, R. What might philosophy of science look like if chemists built it? *Synthese 155*, 3 (2007), 321–336.
21. Hong, W., and Walsh, J. For money or glory? commercialization, competition, and secrecy in the entrepreneurial university. *Sociological Quarterly 50*, 1 (2009), 145–171.
22. Howison, J., and Herbsleb, J. Scientific software production: incentives and collaboration. In *Proceedings of the ACM 2011 conference on Computer supported cooperative work*, ACM (2011), 513–522.
23. Hull, D. A mechanism and its metaphysics: An evolutionary account of the social and conceptual development of science. *Biology and Philosophy 3*, 2 (1988), 123–155.
24. Jackson, S., Ribes, D., Buyuktur, A., and Bowker, G. Collaborative rhythm: temporal dissonance and alignment in collaborative scientific work. In *Proceedings of the ACM 2011 conference on Computer supported cooperative work*, ACM (2011), 245–254.
25. Kling, R., and McKim, G. Not just a matter of time: Field differences and the shaping of electronic media in supporting scientific communication. *Journal of the American Society for Information Science 51*, 14 (2000), 1306–1320.
26. Kling, R., McKim, G., and King, A. A bit more of it: Scholarly communication forums as socio-technical interaction networks. *Journal of the American Society of Information Science and Technology 54* (2003), 47–67.
27. Kling, R., Spector, L. B., and Fortuna, J. The real stakes of virtual publishing: The transformation of E-Biomed into PubMed central. *Journal of the American Society for Information Science and Technology 55*, 2 (2004), 127–148.
28. Knorr Cetina, K. *Epistemic Cultures - How the Sciences Make Knowledge*. Havard University Press, 1999.
29. Kohler, R. *Lords of the fly: Drosophila genetics and the experimental life*. University of Chicago Press, 1994.
30. Lagoze, C., and Patzke, K. A Research Agenda for Data Curation Cyberinfrastructure. In *Proceeding JCDL '11* (2011), 373–382.
31. Lakhani, K. R., Jeppesen, L. B., Lohse, P. A., and Panetta, J. A. "the value of openness in scientific problem solving.". Working Paper No. 07-050, 2007, Harvard Business School, 2007.
32. Nentwich, M. Cyberscience: modelling ICT-induced changes of the scholarly communication system. *Information, Communication & Society 8*, 4 (2005), 542–560.
33. Oleksik, G., Milic-Frayling, N., and Jones, R. Beyond data sharing: artifact ecology of a collaborative nanophotonics research centre. In *Proceedings of the ACM 2012 conference on Computer Supported Cooperative Work*, ACM (2012), 1165–1174.
34. Rheinberger, H. Experimental complexity in biology: Some epistemological and historical remarks. *Philosophy of Science* (1997), 245–254.
35. Schummer, J. Scientometric studies on chemistry II: Aims and methods of producing new chemical substances. *Scientometrics 39*, 1 (1997), 125–140.
36. Schummer, J. Why do chemists perform experiments? In *Chemistry in the Philosophical Meldting Pot, Frankfurt am Main, Peter Lang*. 2004, 395–410.
37. Velden, T., and Lagoze, C. Communicating chemistry. *Nature Chemistry 1*, 9 (2009), 673–678.
38. Vertesi, J., and Dourish, P. The value of data: considering the context of production in data economies. In *Proceedings of the ACM 2011 conference on Computer supported cooperative work*, ACM (2011), 533–542.
39. Walsh, J. P., and Bayma, T. Computer networks and scientific work. *Social Studies of Science 26*, 3 (1996), 661–703.

Incentives and Integration In Scientific Software Production

James Howison
University of Texas at Austin
Austin, TX
jhowison@ischool.utexas.edu

James D. Herbsleb
Carnegie Mellon University
Pittsburgh, PA
jdh@cs.cmu.edu

ABSTRACT
Science policy makers are looking for approaches to increase the extent of collaboration in the production of scientific software, looking to open collaborations in open source software for inspiration. We examine the software ecosystem surrounding BLAST, a key bioinformatics tool, identifying outside improvements and interviewing their authors. We find that academic credit is a powerful motivator for the production and revealing of improvements. Yet surprisingly, we also find that improvements motivated by academic credit are less likely to be integrated than those with other motivations, including financial gain. We argue that this is because integration makes it harder to see who has contributed what and thereby undermines the ability of reputation to function as a reward for collaboration. We consider how open source avoids these issues and conclude with policy approaches to promoting wider collaboration by addressing incentives for integration.

Author Keywords
Collaboration; software development; incentive systems; science policy

ACM Classification Keywords
H.5.3 Group and Organization Interfaces: Computer-supported cooperative work

INTRODUCTION
Software is ubiquitous in science. In current practice, scientific software originates in a diverse set of production systems that differ markedly in their incentive structures for creating, using, sharing, and enhancing software [7,18,24]. A sea change is in progress, however, as science shifts toward cyberinfrastructure, offering to reduce duplicated effort and enhance large scale collaboration [3,9,33,43] both in science and in the production of scientific software. Science policy makers are seeking understanding of how best to shape the practice of science to enable this vision. An open collaboration approach has been successful in the production of open knowledge in Wikipedia and open source software [4,27,30]. Given the communitarian principles of science it is not surprising that open collaboration is a promising candidate [19,40,41].

This paper examines openness as a road to more effective collaboration and co-creation of scientific software. We report on results of an empirical study of the socio-technical structure of innovation around a central piece of infrastructural software, the Basic Local Alignment Search Tool (BLAST). BLAST is arguably one of the most important pieces of scientific software ever written, to a large extent enabling the bioinformatics revolution. By 2003 the original paper describing the BLAST algorithm had become the third most cited paper of all time [38].

Understanding the shifting and sometimes conflicting incentives for sharing and collaboration in scientific software will deepen our understanding of coordinating collaborative work more broadly. This is because "the republic of science" [29] contrasts with environments where open collaboration has previously been examined. The contrast is especially clear in terms of overall incentive structure. Free revealing through publication, thereby building long-term academic reputation in science, contrasts both with the financial incentives common in for-profit environments, as well as the combination of use-value, learning and localized reputation motivating open-source participation [e.g., 37]. By examining the effect of different kinds of incentives, this paper advances work on incentives in large-scale collaboration, a key theme of research in CSCW [e.g., 21].

BACKGROUND

Studies of software work in science/infrastructure
Research in CSCW has recognized the importance of "the human infrastructure of cyberinfrastructure" [25], including the environment in which those producing cyber-infrastructure work. Researchers have, for example, identified a tension between the academic research goals of computer scientists and the implementation oriented needs of domain scientists [14,23] and the need to "synergize" efforts in production of cyberinfrastructure tools, especially in shifting, dynamic funding environments [7]. In the related area of data, research has shown how differential valuations of data in different scientific fields result in varying incentives, which are key to understanding data-

sharing practices in different scientific fields [43]. Recognizing academic publication as a primary motivation is key to understanding the challenges of collaborative production of scientific software [18]. Perhaps glossing over these distinctive academic incentives, many have pointed to the success of open source software development and argued that it provides a model for sustainability of software development in science [1,15,20,41].

Incentives in Peer Production

Incentives for participating in open source software projects have long been a subject of study. Expending effort for no pecuniary return was initially seen as a puzzle, explained in early literature in fairly idealistic terms, as supporting a form of freedom of expression [39], in terms of use value or "scratching one's itch" [36], or as symptomatic of a "gift economy" [36]. As academic attention turned to the question of incentives, focus began to center on the desire for reputation, for example, as a labor market signal [26] that might lead to a better salary. Surveys identified a complicated mix of incentives, including the desire to build a skill, share technical knowledge, and participate in a new form of cooperation [16,22]. Studies looking at the larger incentive picture have shown a complicated mix of intrinsic, extrinsic, and use value motivations, with various effects on developers' output [37]. Increasingly, open source developers often participate as paid employees of commercial firms, who invest in open source for commercial reasons [45]. Recent work has argued that there can be separate and different incentives for different elements of open source work such as production of code, revealing code and integrating code back into the shared source tree [5]. In a similar vein, other recent work has shown varying incentives for joining, contributing to, and becoming committed to online communities more generally [21].

As the novelty of open source software development has worn off, and as the commercial and open source worlds continue to intermingle, reputation seems to have reemerged as a primary motivation, as new environments make it increasingly easy to observe and evaluate others' work and popularity. For example, the number of "followers" a developer has is viewed as a signal of status in GitHub [13]. Indeed, online reputation accounting systems have emerged (e.g., Masterbranch.com and Coderwall.com) making reputation even more visible and explicit.

Recent work in scientific software has also shown a complicated mix of incentives in which reputation features prominently [18]. Yet in the scientific world there is the added twist that scientists, who write most of their software themselves, tend to be motivated by scientific reputation, not reputation in the software world. A physicist writing software gets little or no reputational credit unless the software enables physics work that enhances one's reputation as a physicist. This shift—working in one domain (software) while experiencing reputation incentives in another (science)—can produce mismatches [18], and may lead to patterns of activity that do not accord with those observed in non-scientific contexts. Moreover, these mismatches may lead to situations that do not serve the software needs of scientific communities well and provide difficulties for the vision of shared and communally-developed software infrastructure driven by open peer production.

A study of the BLAST innovation system

To explore these issues we studied the development and improvement of BLAST [2]. BLAST is an important piece of scientific infrastructure, realized in software code, which performs the lookup of primary biological sequences, including DNA and higher-level sequences including amino acids that make up proteins. These sequences are matched against annotated databases, especially GenBank, returning similar sequences based on appropriate statistics. These lookups facilitate scientific results including the identification of organisms, assessing their functions and, in combination with other tools, analyzing their likely evolutionary origins.

Our specific research questions are the following:

1. Who created, maintains and improves BLAST?
2. What code was integrated with BLAST?
3. What motivates the creation, release and integration of improvements to BLAST?

Data and Analysis method

The results discussed below are based on an analysis of semi-structured interviews and inspection of published literature. We identified those involved with BLAST through a combination of searching in the published scientific literature, internet searches for versions of BLAST, and through asking each interviewee to identify participants and provide feedback on our searching strategy. Conscious of the possibility of selection bias due to examining the published literature we specifically asked each interviewee if they were aware of unpublished BLAST versions (discussed below).

We conducted interviews with informants who were well-placed to provide insight into the origins of improvements to BLAST and to explain their motivations in undertaking their work. The informants, and their relationship to the improvements we studied are shown in Table 1. The interviews were semi-structured using a protocol with three sections, the background of the interviewee and the relevant project, the source and nature of the BLAST innovation and motivations for the interviewee's software work, including how they make their case for impact. We sought permission to record the interviews for research purposes and all but one participant agreed. One interview (with two participants) was conducted face to face; the remaining interviews were conducted over the phone. Overall we conducted seven interviews with eight informants, representing seven cases of BLAST improvements. We identified four other improvements of BLAST through literature and web-searches but our requests for interviews went unanswered. In these cases we have examined published papers and respective websites (where these exist).

#	Improvement	Informant role and perspective
1 2	NCBI BLAST	• Original author/Founder of NCBI • 10+ year maintainer of NCBI BLAST
3	WU-BLAST	• Original software author and 10+ year maintainer
4	Digital/Compaq	• Tech. Marketing lead who worked between clients and the developers
5	Mac OS X Port	• Software developer who undertook the port
6	Apple/ Genetech Blast	• Software developer at Apple who built optimizations and integrated them into NCBI BLAST
2	NCBI BLAST+	• 10+ year maintainer of NCBI BLAST; author on BLAST+ paper
7	GPU-BLAST	• Software author and first author on GPU-BLAST paper • Software author and second author on GPU-BLAST paper

Table 1: Informants and their roles/perspectives

For all interviews we made contemporaneous notes and developed summary memos immediately afterwards. We then developed near transcripts of the interviews and expanded our memos. Simultaneously we were returning to the research literature and we met periodically to discuss the interviews in light of this literature. In this way we developed systematic analysis artifacts focusing on organizing the cases according to their incentives for different activities. These are summarized following each case and together in the discussion. As our results developed we actively sought alternative explanations, challenging our emerging understanding. These alternative explanations, together with the rich case narratives, provide transparency into our analysis, allowing readers to see and judge the logic by which we arrive at our conclusions.

In the remainder of the paper we first report qualitative narratives of cases of BLAST improvement, focusing on answering our research questions for each. In the discussion that follows we consider alternative explanations of these findings (generality of solutions, integration costs, intentions and incentives) in their best possible light. We argue that one explanation, based on incentives, is most consistent. We then consider the theoretical and practical implications of that explanation.

RESULTS

NCBI BLAST

BLAST was conceived as an algorithm and piece of software by a small group of academics at the National Center for Bioinformatics (NCBI) together with a tenure-track biologist at Penn State and a tenure-track computer scientist at the University of Arizona. The NCBI was funded by the National Library of Medicine, an Institute of the National Institutes of Health and managed the GenBank DNA database. The software continues to be developed and maintained primarily by employees of NCBI most of whom have a background as PhD trained biologists who shifted career tracks to software work in the service of science, but for whom participation in science is an important element of their professional identity (as opposed to an identity as software developers who incidentally work in a science domain).

Our interviews revealed that the creation of BLAST was motivated by a combination of use value (for the working biologists in the group) and academic credit (all authors sought to publish to build academic reputation). Ongoing maintenance is motivated as a service project for science. The developers of BLAST express interest in following the improvements of BLAST created outside of NCBI, and have integrated some outside contributions (see below) but have not sought explicitly to encourage the development of BLAST as a community project.

Project	Motivation for …		
	Development	Revealing	Integration
NCBI BLAST	- Academic Credit - Use Value	Academic Credit	N/A (Original)

WU-BLAST

BLAST, as originally released, lacked the ability to conduct searches with gaps in the sequence. WU-BLAST was the first package to provide a "gapped BLAST." Its author had originally been employed at NCBI to work on NCBI BLAST after having been recruited out of a technician position at UC Berkeley. Seeking a more academic track, he left NCBI for a tenure-track biology position at the Washington University in St. Louis where he intended to make gapped BLAST "my research project by which I would be judged on my own merits for tenure," as well as using it for the sequencing of a key study organism. NCBI began working on their own implementation of gapped BLAST and the author of WU-BLAST did not release his source code for fear that his "improvements would be consumed". WU-BLAST did not apply for grant funding (due to an expectation that funders believed that there "shouldn't be two BLASTs"), but it was maintained as a separate project achieving some success, additional features and speed, and a loyal user base. The author did not get tenure and left academia, obtained the copyrights from his university and renamed the project AB-BLAST, planning to sell commercial licenses.

The primary incentives for the development and maintenance of WU-BLAST were therefore academic credit and use value; all financial benefits were applied to further his science. The author of WU-BLAST did not want his code integrated with mainline BLAST.

Project	Motivation for … Development	Revealing	Integration
WU-BLAST	- Academic Credit - Use Value	Academic Credit	Counter-motivated (Academic Credit)

Digital/Compaq BLAST

The original BLAST code would not run on the DEC Alpha computing platform. As was common with hardware companies at the time, DEC maintained a vertical technical marketing group whose focus was to ensure that software relevant to their market segment ran smoothly on their specific hardware. In 1999, Compaq acquired DEC but the Alpha business continued to run as it had under DEC. Our informant was a member of the Pharma technical marketing group. In the course of his work, he increasingly encountered potential and current clients engaging in sequence analysis. To serve this group the technical marketing group collaborated with an engineering group within the old DEC structure that had created an Alpha port of the NCBI BLAST code. The technical marketing group used that port to generate benchmarks showing the improved performance of the Alpha platform in running BLAST. These benchmarks, and the software improvements, were used to "sell hardware." There was no interest in publishing academic papers describing these improvements. The incentives for development and maintenance were financial: DEC/Compaq gained access to a market segment and sought to increase their income.

It was common practice at the time for DEC to provide ports to the originators of the software. Our informant indicated that this was important for two reasons: first it ensured that DEC was no longer responsible for maintaining a forked codebase as the software's original authors improved their code. Second, customers were "more confident" obtaining and using code provided by original authors. In the case of BLAST that meant customers preferred to use NCBI BLAST. In keeping with this practice DEC/Compaq reached out to NCBI and worked with them to integrate the Alpha port into the mainline NCBI tree; NCBI acknowledges this contribution in the paper that describes BLAST+ [12]. In this way the incentives for integration were also financial, ensuring continued sales while reducing maintenance costs.

Project	Motivation for … Development	Revealing	Integration
Digital/ Compaq BLAST	- Revenue from sales of complementary goods	- Revenue from sales of complementary goods	- Revenue from sales of complementary goods - Reduced maintenance costs

Mac OS X port

In the late 1990s and early 2000s Apple transitioned to a unix based operating system, known as Mac OS X. BLAST was ported to Mac OS X primarily by our informant. Our informant held a PhD in biology and on graduation had asked "what does a person do that enjoys biology and computers at the same time?" He found himself at the Whitestone Institute as part of the Human Genome Project. The majority of sequencing work there was done on DEC Alpha workstations that remained in the office and doubled as developer machines. Our informant, however, preferred to work on his Apple laptop. Yet the majority of the emerging bioinformatics tools at the time did not compile for Mac OS X out of the box, leading our informant to use time during his 1 hour daily train commute to port these applications. He thus became active in a community of like-minded enthusiasts who ported relevant applications. He enjoyed this activity and was thus driven by a combination of personal use-value and fun ("there was no credit that I was competing for"). He saw releasing the port for others to be an ethical responsibility, based on reciprocating the open work of others.

Apple provided "a great deal of support" to the porting community, including trips to Apple HQ in Cupertino and Apple computers. Although our informant was not privy to this at the time, documents show that Apple was planning to release their Xserve rack-mounted server and increasingly saw life sciences as an important market, both in academia and in industry.[1] In this sense Apple's support of our informant was financially motivated.

Our informant maintained the Mac OS X port for a year or two, providing "courtesy binaries" via FTP. Apple also distributed these binaries on DVD images at life sciences computing conferences to ensure that their customers had access to the code that worked on their hardware. Our informant expected and hoped that the projects he ported would intergrate his changes in, because he wanted to have impact and to reduce the support workload of making them available and updating them. Most projects integrated his changes rapidly, yet "BLAST was by far the slowest." He found himself "doctoring" each new release of BLAST from NCBI, sending his changes to an NCBI contact that he was introduced to by Apple, who also wanted the port integrated. Eventually he stopped being asked for the code and found his port had been incorporated in mainline NCBI BLAST, as part of the interaction between Apple and NCBI described below. The incentives for integration, then, were reducing maintenance costs on behalf of our informant and increasing sales of complementary goods on behalf of Apple.

Project	Motivation for … Development	Revealing	Integration
Mac OS X Port	Use Value Enjoyment	Ethics	- Reduced maintenance costs (informant) - Revenue from sales of complementary goods (Apple)

A/G BLAST

A/G BLAST was developed by Apple Computer in conjunction with Genetech, a life sciences company, as a

[1] Stewart (2001) "Bioinformatics meets OS X" O'Reilly Media. http://oreilly.com/pub/a/mac/2001/12/14/macbio.html

lead user and collaborator. A/G BLAST primarily took advantage of the "Velocity Engine" that was part of the G4 PowerPC chip, but also included other optimizations not specific to the PowerPC. The "Velocity Engine" enabled parallel throughput of some kinds of calculations and therefore provided significant speed increases that were key to Apple's marketing efforts.

Development of this BLAST improvement was thus motivated by complementary goods sales, i.e., making the software available in order to facilitate chip sales. They hoped to ensure that the G4 chip with its Velocity Engine was used to its potential for this application. In the words of a contemporaneous press release introducing A/G BLAST Apple extolls the virtues of their hardware for science in a section entitled, "Velocity Engine and Mac OS X: The Ultimate Science Platform."[2] A/G BLAST was touted as superior, able to deliver "five times the performance of the nearest competing desktop system running standard NCBI BLAST."[2]

The source code for A/G BLAST was freely revealed and made available through Apple's websites as well as distributed at life science conferences. In a manner similar to the Digital/Compaq Alpha port, because the code only ran on Apple's hardware there was no effort to restrict the availability of this code. Moreover at the time Apple had a strategic push towards open source software and the open source community. The Advanced Computing Group, to which our informant belonged, did publish academic papers from time to time, but did not publish a paper describing A/G Blast, nor otherwise attempt to earn academic credit for the improvements in A/G Blast. Rather Apple made the code available on an Apple-branded website and publicizing through press releases and presentations at industry venues, such as sites and conferences organized by O'Reilly Media.[3] In the words of our informant the code was distributed not by its authors but "via PR." Thus the incentives for development were financial through sales of complementary goods.

Apple sought to have its improvements moved back to the "industry standard" NCBI BLAST, which was more trusted and, for Apple's customers, easier to justify using in academic papers ("this is *real* BLAST"). Moreover the A/G optimizations could be better kept in sync with the ongoing development of NCBI BLAST, reducing effort for Apple's programmers and ensuring that new features from NCBI were available to purchasers of the G4 Apple Hardware. The NCBI BLAST team initially became aware of A/G BLAST through publicity associated with the O'Reilly Bioinformatics conference and was eventually invited to Cupertino where engineers described the Velocity Engine and other optimizations. NCBI ported these to their main source tree soon afterwards. As with Compaq's contributions NCBI acknowledges Apple's contributions in their BLAST+ publication [12]. The incentives for integration were thus financial primarily through increased sales of Apple hardware (since the port would be more trusted as part of the mainline distribution) and through reduced maintenance costs.

Project	Motivation for … Development	Revealing	Integration
A/G Blast	- Revenue from sales of complementary goods	- Revenue from sales of complementary goods	- Revenue from sales of complementary goods - Reduced maintenance costs

BLAST+

BLAST+ is a complete rewrite of BLAST by the core BLAST team at NCBI. It was released in 2009 and described in a contemporaneous academic publication [10]. The paper argues that the inclusion of new features over time had undermined the BLAST source code: "the continual addition of unforeseen modifications made the BLAST code fragile and difficult to maintain." [10] The primary goal of the rewrite was that, "the code structure should be modular enough to allow easy modification." In addition the re-write process enabled the NCBI authors to add features, including some that had been demonstrated by external improvements and provided by forked code versions hosted outside NCBI for some time (FSA-BLAST and MegaBLAST). The BLAST+ codebase provides substantial improvements to most, but not all, BLAST operations and is now the primary non-historical version of BLAST available from NCBI.

The authors of BLAST+ were motivated by use-value, although it was a different use-value than the use-value indicated by working biologists. The use-value here was to make the NCBI's overall task of service provision to the bio-informatics community more efficient and effective. The production of an academic publication to describe the code was primarily justified as the appropriate way to announce and document the new code, but since the NCBI operates in a quasi-academic environment there was a secondary motivation of academic credit associated with the article publication. Since BLAST+ replaced BLAST integration was part and parcel of development and so we did not code this separately.

Project	Motivation for … Development	Revealing	Integration
BLAST+	- Service Provision - Academic Credit	- Service Provision - Academic Credit	N/A (replacement)

GPU-BLAST

GPU-BLAST is an effort to exploit the parallelism available in modern GPU platforms, specifically the

[2] http://www.apple.com/pr/library/2002/feb/07blast.html

[3] Originally hosted at http://developer.apple.com/hardware/ve/acgresearch.html and as of May 2011 still available at http://developer.apple.com/opensource/tools/blast.html, although optimizations were eventually integrated into NCBI BLAST. See http://www.apple.com/pr/library/2002/feb/07blast.html and http://www.xml.com/pub/r/1327

NVIDIA GPU [44]. It was developed by two academics whose focus is primarily on computational optimization, and neither considers themselves biologists or bio-informaticians. Whereas previous attempts to implement BLAST on GPU hardware have provided significant speed-ups they have not provided identical results; GPU-BLAST ensures an exact results match with mainline BLAST.

GPU-BLAST, unlike other BLAST improvements considered in this paper, was built on the re-modularized BLAST+ codebase. The GPU-BLAST authors indicated that the BLAST+ code was very well written and was relatively easy to modify. They indicated that they only needed the code itself and did not rely on documentation nor seek help from NCBI. Nonetheless they did not see that as a reason to base their work on the BLAST+ codebase, arguing that the original BLAST code was also well-written and easy for their modifications. They chose to base their work on BLAST+ "only to be up to date," rather than seeking to exploit the more modular and easier to integrate structure of the codebase.

The authors of GPU-BLAST were clearly motivated by academic credit: they focus on optimization in general not only in bioinformatics, and they moved quickly to publish a description of GPU-BLAST in the academic literature. As part of that publication they made their source code available, hosting GPU-BLAST on their own website. That website is very specific about their expectation that users would provide academic credit through citations to their publication: "Please cite the authors in any work or product based on this material."

The software is also promoted by the NVIDIA's GPU platform developer's program as part of a bioinformatics distribution. NVIDIA found the GPU-BLAST software as they prepared a bid to sell hardware to a large hospital and added it to this collection. Following this NVIDIA donated "a few cards" to the GPU-BLAST authors, much as DEC and Apple had before them. Other than this post-hoc donation GPU-BLAST authors receive no royalties or financial benefits from their code and did not consider this donation an incentive for their work.

In our interview we asked whether the authors would like to integrate their GPU-BLAST with the NCBI-BLAST codebase. It is clear that they understand that NCBI-BLAST is the gold standard and that their potential users prefer to work with the NCBI-BLAST codebase as closely as possible. The question of which papers would be cited was key to their thinking about integration. Currently they expect that their users should cite both the original BLAST paper and their GPU-BLAST paper. They indicated that they would be very pleased to integrate, but with a clear reservation: "the ideal for us would be that NCBI comes to us and says let's write another paper and have them cite this from now on. Let's work together to make sure we design it the best possible way ... [A joint paper?] ... right, that would be the ideal ... for us". The final "for us" was inflected in such a way that indicated that they understood that such an undertaking might not be ideal for NCBI.

Project	Motivation for … Development	Revealing	Integration
GPU-BLAST	Academic Credit	Academic Credit	Conditional on joint publication, otherwise counter-motivated

Other Improvements

We identified four additional improvements for which we were unable to obtain interviews: commercial internal improvements, and three improvements described in academic publications (CUDA-BLAST, FSA-BLAST and CS-BLAST). Our informants indicated that they believed that commercial users of BLAST had internal improvements which they did not release publicly, while our informants did not have specific inside knowledge they indicated their belief that these were motivated by financial incentives in that they provided competitive advantage to the firms.

Improvements in the second group were found through literature searching but we were not able to interview the authors. In each case the code was released simultaneously with publication through the author's own websites. Although not as reliable as reasoning based on interview data, we infer a desire to obtain academic credit from the authors undertaking publication of these articles. In the two older cases the code is no longer available at the links provided. However, as with the "gapped" improvement in WU-BLAST the core NCBI team has incorporated the ideas, but not the source code, of those publications.

RESULTS SUMMARY

As our cases proceeded we created systematic analysis artifacts that summarized our answers to our second and third questions: Was the code integrated? And, what motivated development, release and integration (if it occurred)? These artifacts bring our results together in a systematic manner and we present them in this section.

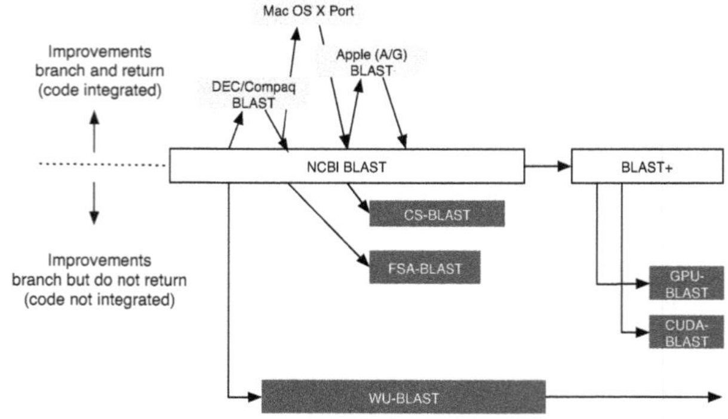

Figure 1: Forking and integration in the BLAST software ecosystem

Figure 1 summarizes the branching structure of the BLAST improvements we studied. At the core is NCBI-BLAST, transitioning to BLAST+. We found all improvements to be based on this line of code. Thus we found all our improvers sought to base their improvements on the core NCBI distribution, and to do so on whichever version was most up to date, transitioning from BLAST to BLAST+ when the NCBI did.

The path of these improvements can be divided into two basic structures: those that branch and return, being integrated with the NCBI code (shown above NCBI BLAST in light gray) and those that branch but whose code is not integrated (shown below NCBI BLAST in dark gray). Those that were not integrated were maintained separately for some time by their authors, typically having them available on personal websites. Our informants indicated that they intended to make their versions available and update them to be in sync with new versions from NCBI, but they were not sure how long they would do so; we found that forks tended to be maintained for relatively short periods of time and their authors, rather than announcing an end to the project appear to simply stop updating their websites.

What can explain the differences in whether the improvements had their source code integrated? Through our analysis we developed four competing explanations: generalizability, integration costs, intentions and motivational conflicts.

Generalizability. *The providers of a popular distribution may not want to increase the size and complexity of the distribution unless some large fraction of users will benefit.*

Integration requires willingness on both sides. Our NCBI informants indicated that they felt that outside contributions were often quite specific to the needs and interests of their authors, whereas NCBI has general responsibilities. Including every specific improvement would complicate the codebase too much for too little gain. This provides a content-based explanation for our observed pattern: improvements that were generally useful would be integrated, while more specific improvements would not. Certainly the commercially motivated computing platform based improvements, which were all integrated, fit with this explanation: all uses, if not all users, of BLAST could benefit from porting to DEC Alpha and Mac OS X and exploiting the parallelism in Apple's "Velocity Engine." However there are quite general improvements in the cases where the code was not integrated, including gapped BLAST from WU-BLAST, the improvements in CS and FSA BLAST and the code from GPU-BLAST. Thus a content-based generality does not provide a consistent explanation for the observed patterns, nor was it emphasized by our informants.

Integration costs. *It takes technical effort—sometimes a great deal of technical effort—to integrate new functionality into a large, complex piece of software, and to maintain it over time.*

A plausible explanation for why some outside improvements came to be integrated while others did not is that some simply required more effort to integrate and were thus either not considered worthwhile or the improvement was incorporated by writing code from scratch. Our NCBI informants indicated that they often found outside code to be impenetrable and that it was difficult to isolate the useful improvements. One key cause of high integration costs is related to the modularity of the codebase. The more modular a codebase is the lower integration costs should be [4]. Our informants indicated that the original BLAST codebase was fairly monolithic and that the BLAST+ codebase was clearly more modular (as intended by its authors). This explanation would thus predict that code based on BLAST would be less likely to be integrated than code based on BLAST+. Admittedly we have only one case of code based on BLAST+, but we have more cases based on BLAST. In neither condition, however, does this explanation appear to explain the observed patterns, in fact the opposite holds. All the cases of integrated code were originally based on BLAST, while the case based on BLAST+ was not integrated. If the integration costs explanation held this pattern should have been reversed. Given the small number of cases here, in our opinion it is more telling that our informants did not emphasize this explanation, focusing far more on maintenance costs than on integration costs. Either way integration costs does not seem a sufficient explanation.

Intentions. *Improvements were integrated unless their creator did not intend to have them integrated.*

The simplest explanation would be that the authors, as copyright holders, did not want their code integrated. However, in all cases other than WU-BLAST, the outside contributor clearly expressed a desire to re-integrate their contributions with NCBI-BLAST, acknowledging both the on-going maintenance costs of branches and that potential users strongly preferred to use "real BLAST" whenever possible. Yet for those that were not integrated this desire to integrate was clearly conditional on how integration would occur, turning on the question of whether and how future users would acknowledge the outside contributions. Thus the authors intentions explanation appears consistent but merely asks a deeper question: why did different authors hold these different intentions? To answer that we turn to our data on incentives.

Project	Motivation for ...		
	Development	Revealing	Integration
DEC/Compaq	Revenue (sales)	Revenue (sales)	Reduce maintenance costs Revenue (sales)
A/G BLAST	Revenue (sales)	Revenue (sales)	Reduce maintenance costs Revenue (sales)
Mac OS X Port	Fun	Ethics	Reduce maintenance effort Revenue (sales)
NCBI BLAST	Academic Credit Use Value	Academic Service Provision	N/A
NCBI BLAST+	Academic Service Provision	Academic Service Provision	N/A
WU-BLAST	Academic Credit	Academic Credit	Counter-motivated (Academic Credit)
GPU-BLAST	Academic Credit	Academic Credit	Highly conditional (Academic Credit)
CS/FSA/CUDA BLAST	Academic Credit	Academic Credit	Unknown

Table 2: Integration status and motivations for development, revealing and integration (shading refers to Figure 1).

Motivational conflicts*. The form of motivational rewards that participants seek may mean that conditions under which integration would be mutually beneficial are difficult to achieve. Specifically, the requirements to access academic credit undermine the incentive to integrate, resulting in the maintenance of separate codebases.*

Table 2 combines of our findings regarding integration and incentives: the cases are shaded according to their code integration status (as in Figure 1), light gray showing those that were integrated and dark gray those that were not. The cells indicate our findings regarding incentives for the three different elements of participation in open collaboration [5].

There is a clear association between integration and incentives: those improvements that were not integrated were motivated in development and revealing by academic credit; those that were integrated were motivated in development and revealing by a mix of motivations, but in integration by a combination of reducing effort and earning revenue through sales of complementary goods.

In essence we found that BLAST innovations from those motivated to improve BLAST by academic reputation are motivated to develop and to reveal, but not to integrate their contributions. Either integration is actively avoided (WU-BLAST) to maintain a separate academic reputation or it is highly conditioned on whether or not publications on which they are authors will receive visibility and citation.

Conversely, other motivations (including use-value, fun, ethics, as well as complementary goods) do not seem to conflict with integration. In fact these motivational rewards seem to be consistent with or actively favor integration, either as a means to reduce on-going maintenance costs or, in the case of complementary goods, to ensure the highest level of comfort using the BLAST improvement that helps sell particular hardware.

We find this explanation to be the strongest: academic reputation as a motivational reward creates conditions that are difficult to satisfy in a mutually beneficial manner, while other motivations do not. This explanation is consistent with all our cases and it was key to the explanations that informants themselves provided.

DISCUSSION

Our result is surprising because reputation has been seen as a key and unproblematic incentive for participation in open software development, as discussed above [e.g., 5,26,37]. Similarly a reputation economy is key to science, with some authors going as far as to describe a separate "republic of science" where reputation and building on each other's work replaces the dominance of competition for money in other domains [30]. This raises two questions: First, why does reputation appear to be problematic in the production of scientific software, while use-value, fun, learning and even money appear to encourage open collaboration? Second, why does reputation appear problematic for integration in scientific work but not in open source?

We explore possible answers to these questions by examining how different incentives, in content and form, relate to collaboration by using a division of claims approach [5]. The division of claims approach posits that a fundamental issue in collaboration is answering the question of how the overall value resulting from collaboration is distributed amongst those who have contributed. To the extent that that division results in adequate rewards for participants then collaboration will be possible; if that division is not satisfactory collaboration will be threatened.

Fun and learning. A number of the incentives discussed above have rewards that are independent of the overall performance of the system because they are delivered immediately. The fun and learning involved in porting BLAST to OS X was experienced in the activity itself and existed whether the code was integrated and the overall project improved or not. Thus the rewards of these type of motivations don't have to be divided or transferred to other participants and such motivations are particularly well-suited for open collaboration.

Use-value. The desire of the authors to use their own improvements is an important motivation. This is well known from studies of open source software where developers indicate that they participate to improve the software for their own use [12,37]. In science, use-value derives from one's ability to accomplish (non-software or domain) scientific work that will eventually be published in an academic paper. This type of software has been called "incidental software production" [18] and is clearly powerful for motivating development. It may not, however, be necessary to reveal developments because not doing so may preserve a competitive advantage. In this sense revealing may cause a reduction in the relative value of the use-value to the original author. In science, however, revealing may be a complement to the use-value of development work to the extent that norms of openness and reproducibility (or explicit journal/conference policies) require the full revealing of code in order to publish results based on it (and thus unlock the scientific use value of the software work). Integration, however, appears unlikely to be a complement to use-value (since journals require only revealing and not integration) and so the decision about integration is likely to be based on a separate assessment of on-going costs of maintaining a separate codetree.

Money. Money is a quintessential motivational reward in part because it facilitates a division of claims easily. This is clear in the simple case of for-profit collaboration. If two partners work together to create a valuable system and earn money by selling it they can divide that money in a way that provides sufficient reward to each of them.[4] Revenue from complementary goods sales, as observed above, is more complex but is still a division of claims facilitated by money. In this case the overall value from the improved system is sufficient to generate demand for computers to use the software with. If the software was also sold for money it would be clear that the customer's money was being divided between hardware and software contributors. Money is ideal for valuing and rewarding contributions since it can be divided and distributed easily.

Reputation. Reputation, by contrast, is potentially problematic when viewed through a division of claims framework. Reputation is something that is enacted by others through their future actions, especially the extent to which they reveal their regard to others. In the context of BLAST reputation is an anticipated reward for the development and revealing of software improvements. The improvers anticipate that others will come to value the improvements and therefore regard the improver as a contributor to science. Such regard is useful for career advancement, especially in terms of tenure and respect that leads to jobs, grants and other rewards.

As a motivational reward reputation is not delivered immediately like fun or learning, nor independently like use-value. Rather the value of reputation comes over time and at distance. The fact that reputation is enacted by others means that it is hard to control, just as it is hard to control any actions of others. This is a very strong contrast to financial rewards because once money is received it can be stored, re-directed and divided. In contrast a partner whose rewards come as reputation must work hard to cause the valuable reputation to be redirected or divided, perhaps even to the extent of correcting others each and every time they do not adequately divide their regard appropriately amongst contributors.

The division of reputation is easier to the extent that each individual's contribution is clearly marked in the final product, making a user (or an evaluator) perceive the multiple contributors. When that is the case integration does not diminish reputational reward, and in fact may enhance it by virtue of its inclusion in a more highly-functional product (as with the expected reputation benefit of having one's code included in "real BLAST"). Yet where individual contributions are not visible in the final product, there exists a risk that contributions may be undervalued. Concern over this issue has been seen in sciences with ever-increasing large author lists [8].

More concretely, integrating a piece of code into an existing project risks losing the identity and visibility of that contribution. If the existing project is already firmly associated with its originators, then there is considerable, difficult work to be done to alter the behavior of future users in order to have them recognize the contributions of those whose contributions been incorporated.

Reputation in open source and science

In open source the issues with reputation and collaboration discussed above seem less problematic than in the academic reputation economy. We see two reasons for this.

The first is that open source projects, and the systems they use, provide insight into the specific, sub-project, contributions of contributors. This can be seen in the use of THANKS files, listing the names of contributors, but even

[4] Of course any division is likely a result of power and other strategies but the simple divisibility of money facilitates these strategies.

more clearly in the source code management systems where contributions are identified by name, allowing a view of contribution that is disaggregated from the project level. In this way systems like Coderwall can "reach into" integrated products and provide an accounting of contribution in a way that accomplishes a division of claims. Scientific software projects rarely have open repositories that indicate authorship, in BLAST any integrations were performed by core staff under their usernames, not by the author whose code or idea was integrated.

The second is that reputation is more direct in open source than in the academic reputation system. In short reputation in academia is about scientific contribution, whereas reputation in open source is about software work. Scientific contribution, for better or worse, is most often measured through publications, not through other artifacts [17]. This has two implications.

The first implication of indirectness is that contributions have to be substantial enough to warrant a publication that describes them. Since the bar to publication is relatively high, especially in higher quality venues, this seems likely to exert pressure to produce larger contributions, resulting in many lines of code changes. This is a clear contrast to open source where the unit of contribution is the patch and contributions are relatively small [31:324]. Indeed open source norms encourage contributions to be as small as possible.[5] Since smaller contributions are easier to understand they are easier to integrate and so reduce integration costs.

The second implication of indirectness is that contributions must be visible in publications and in citations to those publications. Our informants were clear about this (even as they indicated they were not necessarily pleased about it): they must make their cases through publications and citations. Thus even if a source code repository were to record their integrated contributions if that contribution didn't result in a publication on which they were an author, or if it resulted in shifting citations from one on which they were an author to one on which they were not, then integration would be counter-motivated. Claims from system improvement would not be appropriately divided.

In seems, then, that for collaboration in scientific software work to solve the division of claims problem and motivate integration, contributions must remain visible not only at the software level but at the publication and citation level. This is made even more difficult because papers, unlike source code repositories, are static objects; their author lists do not change over time and thus integrated contributions from those who were not authors would need to occasion a new, joint publication and commitment from the original authors to direct all citations to that new paper.

POLICY IMPLICATIONS AND FUTURE RESEARCH

Science policy makers are looking for tools and approaches to improve the efficiency and effectiveness of cyber-enabled science, including software development. The success of open collaborations in open source software development and knowledge environments like Wikipedia provide interesting templates, and existing policy suggestions draw heavily on these analogies [19,32,41]. However our work suggests reasons to believe that the specifics of the scientific reputation environment may not adequately motivate academics to integrate their contributions, thus failing to meet the hopes held for open collaboration. Accordingly we argue that policy should address this situation in four ways.

The first approach is to improve returns for integration work. One way is to fund integration directly. For example, funding agencies could provide funding exclusively for integration, bringing together leaders of different projects and requiring the creation of joint papers that not only describe the integration work but provide an appropriate citation target. A related strategy would be to provide funding to groups less as direct sources of software and more as ecosystem "stewards" who are motivated to incorporate and integrate outside contributions [6]. Appropriate models for these include foundations such as Apache or Debian that attend to questions of the software ecosystem but do not directly develop software, aiming to side-step conflicts between core insiders and outsiders. Finally, given such stewards aiming for integration, scientific publishers could exploit the importance of publication and require contributors to go beyond revealing their source code and require them to have integrated their code into common packages before accepting papers for publication (if the claimed contribution is software that others can use). A downside of this approach is that scientists working in this area might see this funding as reducing the money available for their science.

A second approach would be to promote new integration models through architecture. This would imply an explicit preference for an ecosystem with minimal cores and most functionality delivered through separate components, each with their authors clearly identified. Such architectures have been recommended for separate reasons [11,34] but our work suggests that these architectures may be particularly important for collective innovation on scientific software, given the difficulties of direct integration.

A third broad approach would be to attempt to alter the academic reputation economy to reduce the disincentives for integration. One common suggestion is to reward academics for contributions other than journal articles, including data sets [35] and, more rarely, software [17]. Our work suggests that the specific form of non-journal

[5] These norms are summarized, with multiple references, in answer to a question about "code bombs" on StackOverflow: http://programmers.stackexchange.com/questions/152733/what-is-the-term-for-a-really-big-source-code-commit

contributions that would be acknowledged would be important in encouraging collaboration. Rather than replacing a static journal article with a record for a static software contribution, encouraging dynamic repositories that facilitate and record small units of contribution may be appropriate. The GitHub model of rapid and open forking may be more appropriate than a centralized model where improvers seek permission to have their improvements added.

A fourth approach, perhaps requiring less alteration to existing practice, would be to provide additional resources for software-contributing scientists to make their case for contribution and to provide disaggregation of contributions. Science policy makers can work with journals, conferences and professional societies to improve the citation of software in publications, specifically encouraging the citation of multiple papers or projects whose code or approaches have been integrated into the packages actually used. This creates a direct visibility for integrated code without needing to alter currents practices too widely. The software itself could provide the appropriate set of citations, keeping track of which code, including integrated code, actually ran and providing a set of citations ready for use in papers.[6] Another resource would be to help software-contributing scientists gather data on the use of their scientific software, through counts of downloads or through instrumentation of the code or distributions [28,42]. Ideally such data would link to publications and expose integrated contributions and thereby allow those making software contributions to demonstrate their scientific impact even when their code has been integrated, much as services like Coderwall and Ohloh re-aggregate contributions in open source.

Finally, the work in this paper also has implications beyond science. As CSCW systems continue to facilitate the growth of novel collaborations at scale, designers will increasingly wrestle with the challenges of working with alternative motivational rewards and their varying socio-material characteristics. We contribute to this effort by showing that different elements of open collaboration—development, revealing and integration—should have their motivations analyzed separately. In particular our results should encourage researchers and designers to consider how their reputation systems realize recognition of contribution at a sub-project level and thus support an appropriate sharing of the spoils of open collaboration.

---

[6] The R statistics community provides part of this solution. Each package is encouraged to provide an implementation of the `citation()` command. This returns a citation appropriate for a citation manager and use in papers. Currently, however, this command does not return citations for dependencies of that package; such an extension is possible. Similarly it ought to be possible to analyze a set of analysis scripts and return appropriate citations.

ACKNOWLEDGMENTS

This material is based upon work supported by the National Science Foundation under Grant Nos. IIS-1111750, SMA-1064209, and OCI-0943168.

REFERENCES

1. Alexander, J. *Software Sustainability through Investment*. 2009.
2. Altschul, S.F., Gish, W., Miller, W., Myers, E.W., and Lipman, D.J. Basic local alignment search tool. *J Mol Biol 215*, 3 (1990), -410.
3. Atkins, D. Report of the National Science Foundation Blue-Ribbon Advisory Panel on Cyberinfrastructure. 2003. http://www.nsf.gov/od/oci/reports/toc.jsp.
4. Baldwin, C.Y. and Clark, K.B. *Design Rules: The Power of Modularity*. Harvard Business School Press, 2001.
5. Baldwin, C.Y. and Clark, K.B. The Architecture of Participation: Does Code Architecture Mitigate Free Riding in the Open Source Development Model? *Management Science 52*, 7 (2006), 1116–1127.
6. Berente, N., Howison, J., and King, J.L. *Report on Workshop on "Managing Cyberinfrastructure Centers"*. University of Georgia.
7. Bietz, M.J., Ferro, T., and Lee, C.P. Sustaining the development of cyberinfrastructure: an organization adapting to change. *Proceedings of the ACM 2012 conference on Computer Supported Cooperative Work*, ACM (2012), 901–910.
8. Birnholtz, J. When Authorship Isn't Enough: Lessons from CERN on the Implications of Formal and Informal Credit Attribution Mechanisms in Collaborative Research. *Journal of Electronic Publishing 11*, 1 (2008).
9. Bower, G.C., Edwards, P.N., Jackson, S.J., and Knobel, C.P. The Long Now of Cyberinfrastructure. In *World Wide Research: Reshaping the Sciences and Humanities*. MIT Press, Cambridge, MA, 2010.
10. Camacho, C., Coulouris, G., Avagyan, V., et al. BLAST+: architecture and applications. *BMC bioinformatics 10*, 1 (2009).
11. Cataldo, M., Herbsleb, J.D., and Carley, K.M. Socio-technical congruence: a framework for assessing the impact of technical and work dependencies on software development productivity. *Proceedings of the Second ACM-IEEE international symposium on Empirical software engineering and measurement (ESEM '08)*, (2008).
12. Crowston, K., Wei, K., Howison, J., and Wiggins, A. Free (Libre) Open Source Software Development: What We Know and What We Do Not Know. *ACM Computing Surveys 44*, 2 (2012), open–source–software–development–what–we–know–and–what–we–do–not–know.
13. Dabbish, L., Stewart, C., Tsay, J., and Herbsleb, J.D. Social Coding in GitHub: Transparency and

Collaboration in an Open Software Repository. *CSCW*, (2011).

14. Faniel, I. *Unrealized Potential: The Socio-Technical Challenges of a Large Scale Cyberinfrastructure Initiative*. 2009.
15. Gambardella, A. and Hall, B.H. Proprietary versus public domain licensing of software and research products. *Research Policy 35*, 6 (2006), -892.
16. Ghosh, R.A., Robles, G., and Glott, R. *Free/Libre and Open Source Software: Survey and Study FLOSS*. 2002.
17. Hafer, L. and Kirkpatrick, A.E. Assessing open source software as a scholarly contribution. *Commun. ACM 52*, 12 (2009), 126–129.
18. Howison, J. and Herbsleb, J.D. Scientific software production and collaboration. *Computer Supported Collaborative Work (CSCW 2011)*, (2011).
19. Ince, D.C., Hatton, L., and Graham-Cumming, J. The case for open computer programs. *Nature 482*, 7386 (2012), 485–488.
20. Knepper, R. and Repasky, D. *Open Source Writ Large: Advantages of a Foundation Community Model for Cyberinfrastructure*. 2009.
21. Kraut, R.E. and Resnick, P. *Building Successful Online Communities: Evidence-Based Social Design*. The MIT Press, 2012.
22. Lakhani, K. and Wolf, R.G. *Why hackers do what they do: Understanding motivation efforts in Free/F/OSS projects*. 2003.
23. Lawrence, K.A. Walking the Tightrope: The Balancing Acts of a Large e-Research Project. *Computer Supported Cooperative Work 15*, 4 (2006), 411.
24. Lee, C.P., Bietz, M.J., Derthick, K., and Paine, D. A Sociotechnical Exploration of Infrastructural Middleware Development. (2012).
25. Lee, C.P., Dourish, P., and Mark, G. The human infrastructure of cyberinfrastructure. *Proceedings of the 2006 20th anniversary conference on Computer supported cooperative work*, ACM (2006), 483–492.
26. Lerner, J. and Tirole, J. Some simple economics of Open Source. *Journal of Industrial Economics 52*, 2 (2002), -234.
27. MacCormack, A., Rusnak, J., and Baldwin, C.Y. Exploring the Structure of Complex Software Designs: An Empirical Study of Open Source and Proprietary Code. *Management Science 52*, 7 (2006), 1030.
28. McConahy, A., Eisenbraun, B., Howison, J., Herbsleb, J.D., and Sliz, P. Techniques for Monitoring Runtime Architectures of Socio-technical Ecosystems. *Workshop on Data-Intensive Collaboration in Science and Engineering (CSCW 2012)*, (2012).
29. Merton, R.K. and Sztompka, P. *On Social Structure and Science*. University of Chicago Press, 1996.
30. Merton, R.K. The Matthew effect in science, II: Cumulative advantage and the symbolism of intellectual property. *Isis 79*, 4 (1988), 623.
31. Mockus, A., Fielding, R.T., and Herbsleb, J.D. Two Case Studies Of Open Source Software Development: Apache And Mozilla. *ACM Transactions on Software Engineering and Methodology 11*, 3 (2002), -346.
32. Morin, A., Urban, J., Adams, P.D., et al. Shining Light into Black Boxes. *Science 336*, 6078 (2012), 159–160.
33. Olson, G.M., Zimmerman, A., Bos, N., and Wulf, W. *Scientific Collaboration on the Internet*. 2008.
34. Parnas, D.L., Clements, P.C., and Weiss, D.M. The modular structure of complex systems. *IEEE Transactions on Software Engineering 11*, 3 (1981), 266.
35. Piwowar, H.A., Vision, T.J., and Whitlock, M.C. Data archiving is a good investment. *Nature 473*, 7347 (2011), 285–285.
36. Raymond, E.S. The Cathedral and the Bazaar. *First Monday 3*, 3 (1998).
37. Roberts, J.A., Hann, I.-H., and Slaughter, S.A. Understanding the Motivations, Participation, and Performance of Open Source Software Developers: A Longitudinal Study of the Apache Projects. *Management Science 52*, 7 (2006), 999.
38. Science Watch. Twenty Years of Citation Superstars. *Science Watch 14*, 5 (2003).
39. Stallman, R. and others. The GNU manifesto. *Dr. Dobb's Journal of Software Tools 10*, 3 (1985), 30–35.
40. Stewart, C.A., Almes, G.T., and Wheeler, B.C., eds. NSF Cyberinfrastructure Software Sustainability and Reusability Workshop Report. 2010. http://hdl.handle.net/2022/6701.
41. Stodden, V., Donoho,, D., Fomel, S., et al. Reproducible Research. *Computing in Science and Engineering 12*, 2010, 8–13.
42. Thain, D., Tannenbaum, T., and Livny, M. How to measure a large open-source distributed system. *Concurrency and Computation: Practice and Experience 18*, 15 (2006), John Wiley and Sons Ltd.–2019.
43. Vertesi, J. and Dourish, P. The Value of Data: Considering the Context of Production in Data Economies. *CSCW 2011*, (2011).
44. Vouzis, P.D. and Sahinidis, N.V. GPU-BLAST: Using graphics processors to accelerate protein sequence alignment. *Bioinformatics*, (2010).
45. Wagstrom, P., Herbsleb, J.D., Kraut, R.E., and Mockus, A. The Impact of Commercial Organizations on Volunteer Participation in an Online Community. *Presentation at the OCIS Division, Academy of Management Conference*, (2010).

Designing for Reflection and Collaboration to Support a Transition from Welfare to Work

Nathalie Colineau, Cécile Paris and Surya Nepal
CSIRO ICT Centre
PO Box 76, Epping, 1710
NSW, Australia
FirstName.LastName@csiro.au

ABSTRACT
Online support groups have proven to be very effective, in the health domain in particular, to provide their members with social, emotional and moral support. Drawing from this success, we are exploring the use of an online community to build a support group for parents currently in receipt of income support but needing to transition to find a job. Complementing the financial and informational support offered through existing welfare transition programs, our work aims to help people improve their prospect of finding a job to become financially self-sufficient and develop a support network to help them in their transition back to work. In this paper, we present the design of a journey of reflection and collaboration to encourage reflective thinking and foster relationships between community members.

Author Keywords
Reflective thinking; Collaborative work; Online communities; Welfare.

ACM Classification Keywords
H.5.3. Information interfaces and presentation: Group and Organization Interfaces.

General Terms
Design; Human Factors.

INTRODUCTION
Over the years, the Internet has become a social place where people come to exchange ideas, share experiences and support each other. Capitalising on this success, we are exploring the use of an online community to support parents currently in receipt of welfare payments and who are now required to find a job, as their youngest child is reaching school age. The transition back to work can be difficult for some people, in particular for single parents and people who have been out of the work force for several years. Our work aims to help this specific target group be better equipped to find a job and develop a support network to assist them during this transition period.

Through focus groups followed by a survey, we first sought to gain an understanding of what would be useful for families during this transition process, the difficulties and/or obstacles they faced, and whether online support and an online community of the type we were envisaging might be useful [2]. We found that people were not entirely sure how to look for a job, that they currently felt they had no support around them, that they sometimes resented the government for forcing them to return to work and did not want to do so. We also found that they were open to the idea of the community, in particular to the opportunity to share and work with other people in similar situations. We designed an online community to help with these issues. It was launched in March 2012, by invitation only, in partnership with the Australian Government's Department of Human Services. As in other online communities, members have an individual profile page; they can post on discussion forums, access a variety of resources, get advice and share experiences. In contrast to other online social networking sites, this community aims to help parents prepare their return to the work force through a journey of reflection and collaboration. This journey is intended to support the different levels of reflection identified by Fleck and Fitzpatrick [3] and follow the process of online group development, as specified by Waltonen-Moore *et al.* in [14].

In this paper, we first briefly review previous research on reflective practices, and how the design of technology can support reflection. We then introduce the journey of reflection we developed. Finally, we present the design and implementation of the activities that allow community members to work individually or in small groups.

RELATED WORK
Over the years, the benefits of reflective thinking have been recognised in various disciplines and used to help people understand their environment, learn new things, uncover obstacles and barriers, accept changes and develop new beliefs or practices. In education, for example, work has focused on how reflective thinking can improve teaching practices or help students develop professional knowledge (e.g., [6] and [12]). In the domain of health, a large body of work in psychology has demonstrated the beneficial health effects of writing exercises (e.g., [7] and [9]) and their ability to reshape thoughts (e.g., [4]).

Personal reflection has also been shown to benefit from peer-interactions, helping deepen thoughts and developing awareness of oneself (e.g., [10], [12] and [14]). Waltonen-Moore *et al.* showed how the use of online discussion boards could encourage interactions between participants and contribute to the building of an online learning community [14]. This work suggests that providing an environment that allows people to write, reflect and interact with others can promote critical thinking and contribute to the development of an online group.

In parallel, researchers in Human-Computer Interaction (HCI) have looked at designing for reflection (e.g., [3] and the CHI 2009 Workshop on Designing for Reflection on Experience [13]). A number of design and technologies have emerged recently, in particular in the health domain, to encourage people to reflect on their health, without necessarily asking them to modify their behaviour (e.g., [1], [5], and [11]). Fleck and Fitzpatrick provide a framework in which to place the various techniques and technologies designed to support reflection [3]. They identify different levels of reflection: "R1 Level", *reflective description*, "R2 Level", *dialogic reflection* and "R3 Level", *transformative reflection*. These progressive forms of reflection lead an individual (or a group of individuals) to look at their behaviour or beliefs, provide justifications for them, question or revisit points of view to challenge one's beliefs and adopt new perspectives on things.

In our work, we are investigating whether reflective writing can be employed to get people to overcome the barriers to work they may perceive, and whether reflection can help them review their skills, experiences and beliefs to change their attitude towards finding a job and returning to work. We would like to provide a space for community members to reflect, individually and collectively though their interactions with other members, on their feelings about getting back to work and on what might prevent them to do so.

A JOURNEY OF REFLECTION

As our online community is meant to support people going through a transition, we developed a *journey of reflection*. This journey is meant to guide parents through a series of steps to help them face obstacles, regain confidence and plan their return to work.

Reflection as a Way to Move forward

Following Fleck and Fitzpatrick's review on techniques and technology designed to support reflection [3], we articulate the purpose for the reflection, the conditions in which it will take place and the various levels of reflection we would like to support. In our online community, the aim of the reflection is to enable a critical self-review (with respect to attitudes, beliefs, skills and aspirations), self-development and empowerment. Recognising that reflection takes time and encouragement, we designed a *series* of reflective exercises (a series of activities), releasing them to community members one at a time, in a structured format. Our design aims to support the three levels of reflection identified by Fleck and Fitzpatrick.

A Path to Transition

The activities were designed with the help of social workers from our government collaborators. There are two types of activities:

- Activities to help people be better equipped to look for a job. Here, we addressed a number of issues, such as explicitly identifying one's skills and exploring the type of jobs one desires, overcoming perceived barriers to work, as well as writing a CV, preparing for an interview, creating a budget or organising child care.
- Activities that encourage people to form connections (i.e., build relationships with others in similar situations) and build a sense of community, thus helping them develop a support network. While we have specific activities for this purpose, this is also supported through other ways, in particular through collaborative activities and discussions in the forum.

Some activities are to be done individually. They are meant to encourage either personal reflection (R1 level) or connections with others in the community, a step towards collaboration. Others are designed to foster relationships between community members and encourage reflection through the exchange of views and perspectives (R2 level). They need to be accomplished collaboratively. It is also hoped that, through the collaborative activities, participants will not only share different perspectives but might also challenge each other's assumptions and beliefs (R3 level).

Activities are organised as a progression, or a journey, taking care to mix the different concerns and ensure variety. This is illustrated in Figure 1. Activities labelled with a "C" explicitly support making connections with others. All other activities address some aspects of helping someone to be better equipped to return to work. A dark background and a thick outline indicate that the activity is collaborative. Each week, one or more activities are proposed to community members. People are free to do as much (or as little) as they want or need. The activity journey is not tailored to the needs of specific individuals, and we expect people to pick and choose activities appropriate for them. For example, some people may stay in the community for a couple of weeks, others for several months; some may do all activities, others may selectively choose a subset.

Each activity is accompanied by resources, which provide information to support people in the activity. Experts are also available through a series of "Live Chat sessions" to discuss issues raised by members. In addition, each activity is complemented by specific topics of discussion in the forums, to which participants are encouraged to contribute. This again supports the three levels of reflection: by providing a comment on a topic, one might be describing a personal experience and reflecting on it (reflective description). By entering into a discussion with others in the

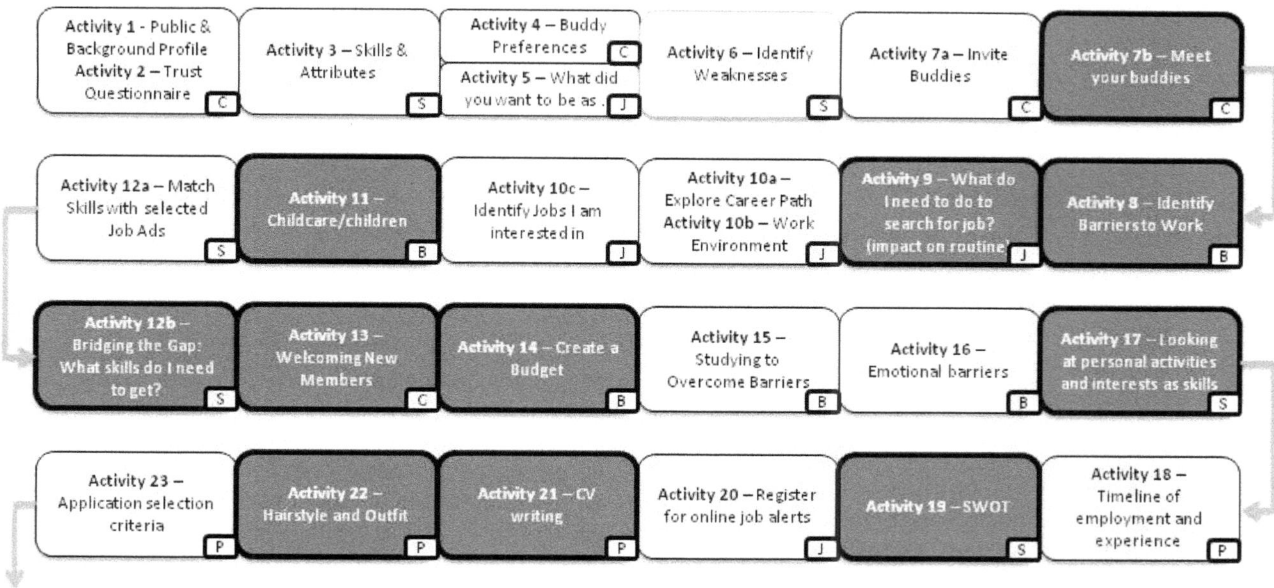

Figure 1. Activity path – the labelling of the activities reads as follows. The "C" label (i.e., 1, 2, 7a&b and 13) represents activities to introduce members to each other and build a sense of community. The "S" labelled activities (i.e., 3, 6 12a&b, 17 and 19) are to help people uncover and develop their skills. The "J" label (i.e., 5, 9, 10a, b&c and 20) indicates activities to assist people to explore career path and look for job. The "B" label (i.e., 8, 11, 14 to 16) represents the activities to support people overcome their barriers to work. Finally, the "P" label (i.e., 18 and 21 to 23) indicates activities to help people present themselves to potential employers.

forum, we may obtain a dialogic reflection. Finally, a discussion can lead to people challenging each other's perceptions, beliefs or assumptions, thus entering the realm of transformative reflection.

The aim of the journey is several-fold. It is to bring people to think explicitly of specific issues they need to address in order to be able to return to work (e.g., know how to apply for a job; think of how to organise their family life differently). It is also to get people into the practice of reflection, by encouraging them to reflect on a specific topic every week, asking them to potentially explore new ideas. It is hoped that, in this way, participants can reach another level of reflection (transformative reflection), where they confront their personal assumptions and aspects of their belief system, and they can start to challenge the barriers they perceive to their return to work. This particular type of reflection aims at a change in understanding, possibly in attitude and, in some cases, at a course of actions.

JOURNEY AND ACTIVITY DESIGN

In the "*Activity Journey*" part of the online community, participants can see the list of activities that is current for them at any point in time. The journey is presented visually in two complementary ways:

- At the top, a banner visualises a list of six activities, with their titles. An arrow on either side of the horizontal "*timeline*" enables community members to go forward or backward in the journey.
- The activities are also displayed in a vertical list, with the most recently released activity at the top. This list indicates the time by which the activity is meant to be completed and the status of the activity.

The status of an activity is specific to individual community members. When an activity is released, it is displayed with a "*pending*" status (colour coded as red), showing that this activity has not been initiated. Once the person starts working on the activity, it is displayed as "*in progress*" (colour coded as yellow) until it is completed and submitted. Once submitted, the activity is shown as "*completed*" (colour coded as green). Activities to come are also listed to inform community members of activity topics scheduled in the following weeks. These are displayed as "*coming soon*" (colour coded as grey).

Participants can access any of the activities that have already been released. They can access completed activities, if they want to examine what they wrote. This can be a reflective experience, and, according to Fleck and Fitzpatrick [3], an R2 level reflection, as people may now see something done in the past from a different perspective. They can access pending activities, if they want to start on them now. They can also access activities currently in progress, if they want to continue working on them and complete them. Only the activities that are "*coming soon*" are unavailable for inspection, beyond their indicative title.

Generally, activities are scheduled on a weekly basis, but depending on the amount of work involved, they can also run over two weeks. We decided to provide a timeframe for the activities for several reasons. First, because the activities are organised in a progression (for example, reflecting on one's skills and experience and the type of jobs one could do must come before applying for a job), it would be good for activities to be completed in the right order. Second, we wanted to provide structure and encouragement to participants to accomplish the activities. Third, we know from goal-setting theory [8] that people are more likely to achieve a goal if it is specific, with respect to both what is to be accomplished and when it needs to be done.

An activity is technically closed when it has been explicitly submitted. This is an indication that the person considers the activity as completed. When an activity is closed, people still have access to what they submitted, but they can no longer change it. Reflection is an iterative process that requires time, and it may be beneficial to revisit certain activities as people learn new things, are becoming more confident, etc. We take this into account through a three-step process. First, a set of activities initiates the reflection process around people's strengths, weaknesses, the barriers they perceive, and the opportunities they see. Then, follow-up activities build upon these initial reflections. Finally, the initial activities are revisited, asking people to reconsider their thoughts and see if there is anything they would like to change (e.g., they may have a more positive appraisal of their skills, consider a wider range of career paths, etc.). In addition, the display of the journey in itself can promote reflection, as it allows participants to see where they have come from, where they are at, and what is coming up, i.e., where the journey has taken them so far and where it is heading. We now examine specific activities in more detail.

Individual Activities

Individual activities are meant to support the first level of reflection (reflective description) as described by [3] or to help make connections with others within the community, as the first step towards collaboration.

The activities designed for reflection are to assist parents in their search for a job. For example, one activity first invites people to remember what they wanted to do as a child and as a teenager, and then asks them if that is still what they would like to do now. Another activity looks at identifying the types of work environments that are best suited to one's personality. For the activities designed to help build relationships between community members, we took inspiration from the work by Waltonen-Moore *et al.* [14] about the evolution of online group development. In their work, Waltonen-Moore and colleagues describe the process of online group development as a five-step process: (1) a phase of introduction, where participants present themselves to others; (2) a phase of identification, where participants start to identify with individuals and relate to the group; (3) a phase of interaction, where participants exchange ideas, comment and respond to one another; (4) a phase of involvement, where cooperative behaviour starts to emerge; (5) finally a phase of inquiry, where participants start to practice what was learnt and seek opinions from others. Following this process, we created a series of activities as follows:

- At the beginning, an activity encourages people to setup their profile page and introduce themselves to the community so others get to know them. This is the first step in the socialisation process.
- Later in the journey, an activity asks people to set up their buddy preferences by thinking of what particular characteristics they are seeking in their buddy. This can help people to start thinking about the person to whom they relate.
- Later again, an activity encourages people to form relationships by asking them to invite others to be their buddy (and accept invitations from others).

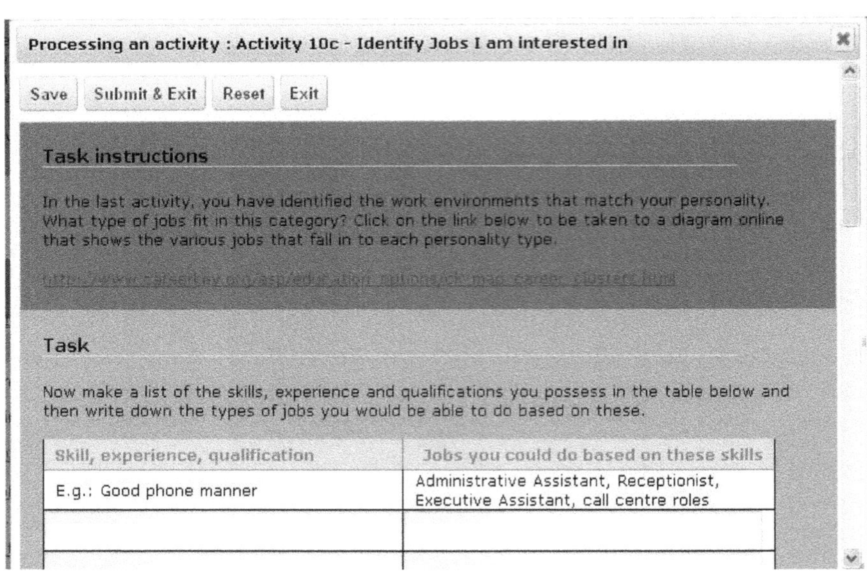

Figure 2. Example of individual activity

These activities are the building blocks which help form the initial ties between community members and upon which the following stages (i.e., the interaction and involvement stages as described in [14]) can be built.

Figure 2 illustrates how individual activities are typically presented to participants. This specific activity explores one's skills, the jobs matching these skills and potential gaps. At the top of the form, the instructions for the activity are presented, often including a statement about how the activity fits into the journey so far (e.g., "*last week, you have identified…*"). These are followed by the task itself, usually a set of questions with space for answers in a variety of format, depending on the questions. This is where the reflection process occurs. In the example task shown in the figure, members are asked to reflect on their skills, experience and qualifications. Participants also have to think about what jobs these skills and/or qualifications support. This is followed by more questions that promote descriptive reflection, in this case: *is there a gap between your skills and the job you want? How would you fill this gap? Are there specific difficulties?* Not shown in the figure but provided to participants is the activity duration period: its start and end times.

As mentioned earlier, to help them with the task, participants are provided with a set of resources. These are listed as part of the instructions. In this case, the resource is a link to a website that provides information about Career Clusters and a map linking interests to career paths. To complement the reflection process initiated through the activity, one or more discussion topics directly related to the activity are initiated in the forum when the activity is released. For the activity shown in Figure 2, for example, one of the discussion topics initiated for this activity is: *Do you find that there is a large gap between the jobs you can perform and the job you ultimately want? Do you know why this gap exists?* Discussion topics attempt to draw members into a discussion with each other, hopefully leading them to dialogic and may be transformative reflections.

Participants can save the product of their reflection at any time and exit to continue later. Once they decide that they have completed their activity, they must click on the "*submit*" button. At that stage, the activity is considered completed, and its status will be updated accordingly.

Collaborative Activities

Whereas individual activities encourage members to reflect on their own, collaborative activities are meant to be done by engaging with others. Participants are asked to invite one or more of their buddies to work on the activity as a group. This is meant to help individuals build a support network. It is also to build a sense of cohesion amongst community members, as described in [14].

While similar to the individual activities, in that they also ask questions and require someone to think and provide an answer, collaborative activities are done as a group. Each participant in the group has access to a collaborative space in which they see the questions to be answered, their own answers and the answers provided by other people in their group. This is illustrated in Figure 3 with the activity "*Identify Barriers to Work*", where Lillian and Frank have formed a group. This design supports the second level of reflection described by [3], the dialogic reflection, by providing different perspectives and points of views.

The collaborative space for these activities includes a discussion board for the specific group only, where group members can have discussions amongst themselves, hopefully asking each other challenging questions, potentially questioning assumptions, all the time supporting each other. These activities aim to support both reflection and collaboration.

As with the individual activities, collaborative activities have start and end times, instructions, resources and topics in the discussion forum. Like individual activities, they also require an explicit action on the part of participants to be completed (i.e., all participants must submit their part of the activity by clicking on the "*submit*" button).

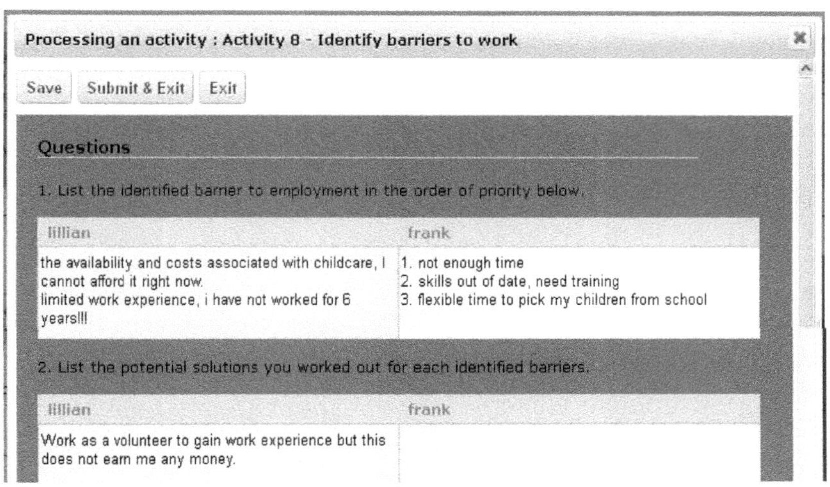

Figure 3. Portion of a collaborative activity page – in this case, we have a group of 2 people (Lillian and Frank). Each of them has an individual space in which to write, and they can see what their partner has contributed.

CONCLUSION

In this paper, we presented the design and implementation of a journey of reflection and collaboration meant to guide an online community of parents currently in receipt of income support through their transition back to work. This journey aims to promote reflective thinking and support personal reflection. It is also intended to facilitate the exchange of perspectives through collaborative activities and foster relationships amongst community members. Borrowing from various techniques and technologies designed to support reflection, we designed an environment to enable individuals to review their attitudes to work, their beliefs, skills and aspirations through self-reflective activities. This environment also enables groups of individuals to interact, engage, support and may be challenged each other through collaborative activities.

The community has been launched in March 2012 and is meant to run for one year, with several rounds of invitations. As of September 2012, the community has about 90 members, and activity in the community is slowly ramping up. Although we have observed that some members do their weekly activity regularly and that groups started to form, we have not yet looked at the content participants submitted. As part of the evaluation of the activity journey, we are interested to investigate who did their activities and assess whether our design has indeed fostered reflection and change. To do this, we are planning to analyse the content of the activities submitted. We did a survey in October 2012 to gather feedback from participants as to whether the activities proposed were appropriate with respect to progression, frequency, topic variety and relevance, and whether the activity journey helped them in their transition, provided them with a personal space to reflect, and with the opportunities to share and discuss issues with others. We are currently analysing the results.

ACKNOWLEDGEMENTS

This research has been funded under the Human Services Delivery Research Alliance (HSDRA) between the CSIRO and the Australian Department of Human Services. We would like to thank Payam Aghaei Pour, Sanat Bista, Hon Hwang, Brian Jin, Alex Sun and Bo Yan at CSIRO for their contribution to the implementation of this work, and Gina Beschorner and her team at the Australian Government's Department of Human Services for feedback on the design.

REFERENCES

1. Colineau, N. and Paris, C. Motivating Reflection about Health within the Family: The Use of Goal Setting and Tailored Feedback. *User Modeling and User-Adapted Interaction*, 21(4), Special Issue on Personalisation in e-Health, (2001), 341-376.
2. Colineau, N. Paris, C. and Dennett, A. Capitalising on the Potential of Online Communities to Help Welfare Recipients. In *Proc. of the International Reports on Socio-Informatics* (IRSI) 8, 2 (2011b), 58-65.
3. Fleck, R. and Fitzpatrick, G. Reflecting on reflection: framing a design landscape. In *Proc. of OZCHI 2010*, ACM Press (2010), 216-223.
4. Francis, M. E. and Pennebaker, J. W. Putting stress into words: The impact of writing on physiological, absentee, and self-reported emotional well-being measures. *American Journal of Health Promotion*, 6(4) (1992), 280-287.
5. Grimes, A., Bednar, M., Bolter, J.D. and Grinter, R.E. EatWell: Sharing Nutrition-Related Memories in a Low-Income community. In *Proc. of CSCW 2008*, ACM Press (2008), 87-96.
6. Lee, H.-J. Understanding and assessing preservice teachers' reflective thinking. *Teaching and Teacher Education*, 21(6), (2005), 699-715.
7. Lepore, S. J. and Smyth, J. M. (Eds.). *The writing cure: How expressive writing promotes health and emotional well-being*. American Psychology Association, Washington, DC, 2002.
8. Locke, E. A. and Latham, G. P. Building a Practically Useful Theory of Goal Setting and Task Motivation. *American Psychology* 57(9), (2002), 705–717.
9. Lowe, G. Health-related effects of creative and expressive writing. *Health Education* 106(1), (2006), 60-70.
10. Lucey, T.A., O'Malley, G.S. and Jansem, A. Using online reflection and conversation to build community. *Journal of Interactive Online Learning*, 8(3), (2009), 199-217.
11. Mamykina, L., Mynatt, E.D., Davidson, P.R., and Greenblatt, D. MAHI: Investigation of Social Scaffolding for Reflective Thinking in Diabetes Management. In *Proc. of CHI 2008*, ACM Press (2008), 477-486.
12. Manouchehri, A. Developing teaching knowledge through peer discourse. *Teaching and Teacher Education*, 18 (2002), 715-737.
13. Sas, C. and Dix, A. Designing for reflection on experience. Designing for reflection on experience. In *CHI '09 Extended Abstracts on Human Factors in Computing Systems*. ACM Press (2009), 4741-4744.
14. Waltonen-Moore, S., Stuart, D. Newton, E., Oswald, R. and Varonis, E. From virtual strangers to a cohesive online learning community: the evolution of online group development in a professional development course. *Journal of Technology and Teacher Education*, 14(2), (2006), 287-311.

Hollaback!: The Role of Collective Storytelling Online in a Social Movement Organization

Jill P. Dimond, Michaelanne Dye, Daphne LaRose, Amy S. Bruckman
School of Interactive Computing, GVU, Georgia Institute of Technology
{jpdimond, mdye, dlarose3, asb}@cc.gatech.edu

ABSTRACT
CSCW systems are playing an increasing role in activism. How can new communications technologies support social movements? The possibilities are intriguing, but as yet not fully understood. One key technique traditionally leveraged by social movements is storytelling. In this paper, we examine the use of collective storytelling online in the context of a social movement organization called Hollaback, an organization working to stop street harassment. Can sharing a story of experienced harassment really make a difference to an individual or a community? Using Emancipatory Action Research and qualitative methods, we interviewed people who contributed stories of harassment online. We found that sharing stories shifted participants' cognitive and emotional orientation towards their experience. The theory of "framing" from social movement research explains the surprising power of this experience for Hollaback participants. We contribute a way of looking at activism online using social movement theory. Our work illustrates that technology can help crowd-sourced framing processes that have traditionally been done by social movement organizations.

Author Keywords
Social Movements; Emancipatory Action Research; Feminist HCI; Social justice; Activism; Storytelling

ACM Classification Keywords
H.5.m. Information interfaces and presentation (*e.g.*, HCI): Miscellaneous.

"Posting it did a weird thing to me though... I used to be able to brush off a lot of the stuff I get on the street and at work... but now I think it means something more to me..." --P7

INTRODUCTION
The CSCW and HCI communities are beginning to examine the role of technology in social justice issues. Researchers in CSCW have moved beyond the workplace and have started to engage with social issues such as the experiences of marginal users [60], health [26,43], the environment [17,44], and international development (ICTD) [12,33]. Movements such as the Arab Spring and Occupy Wall Street, that have taken advantage of social media, have piqued interest within the HCI research community [54]. But there is little work within HCI that examines activists who contend with issues of social justice and are using collaborative information communication technologies (ICTs) to do so. Furthermore, there is little work that positions activism within the context of social movements. By social movements, we refer to Tarrow's definition that distinguishes social movements from political parties and advocacy groups. He states social movements are contentious and "better defined as collective challenges, based on common purposes and social solidarities, in sustained interaction with elites, opponents, and authorities" [57]. Examples of social movements include the civil rights, anti-globalization, and feminist movements.

Storytelling and narrative have long played a part in social change and social movements [4,13]. According to scholars of social movements, storytelling is how people learn and exercise agency, shape identity, and motivate action [19]. In this paper, we examine the role of collective storytelling online in the context of a social movement organization, Hollaback. Hollaback uses collective storytelling online to draw awareness to a newly named, but old phenomena, called street harassment. This term refers to harassment in public spaces directed towards traditionally marginalized groups such as women, non-whites, and LGBTQ (Lesbian, Gay, Bi, Transgender, and Queer) people. Specifically, this paper examines the role of storytelling using technology in a social movement organization. We investigate how the social movement concept of framing can help to explain participants' experiences of sharing stories on Hollaback. We explore how sharing stories of harassment online has impacted those who have shared them and examine if these stories have influenced what the organization focuses on in terms of activism.

More broadly for the CSCW community, this work contributes, first, a model for a CSCW system that embodies the values of feminist HCI [3]. Second, it is a model for the use of CSCW technology by activists, where the software architecture supports a transnational decentralized federation of activists who coordinate globally and do actions locally. Third, this work is an example of the power of storytelling in a social movement organization supported by collaborative software. For more detail on all of these focuses, see [15]. For this paper, we focus on the connections between social movement theory and storytelling online, and the ways in which CSCW technology makes a new kind of meaning making possible for social movements. First we examine street harassment in more detail and further describe the organization we have been working with called Hollaback.

HOLLABACK

Hollaback (http://ihollaback.org) is a social movement organization whose mission is to end street harassment. Street harassment is a new term to describe gendered harassment in public. Yet, there is not a unified definition amongst scholars and activists because it is so newly named. According to Hollaback, street harassment can be anything from verbal harassment to groping, stalking, leering, flashing, and sexual assault. Although this term is fairly new, early studies indicate that street harassment is very common and harmful globally, yet rarely legislated against. Research shows that 80% of women in Canada experienced harassment in public, which had a detrimental impact on their perceived safety in public spaces [36]. In Egypt, 83% of women reported experiencing harassment and half said they experience it daily [32]. In Delhi, India, 80% of 3,816 women surveyed said that they experienced harassment and their mobility was restricted as a result [30]. In the US, there are no population-level studies. However, in Indianapolis, 100% of their 293 sample had experienced harassment [20] (for more information on other community and city level studies see [32].) Yet, each of these studies independently defines what street harassment constitutes. Defining the boundaries and extent of street harassment is part of the work that Hollaback is trying to accomplish.

Hollaback started as a blog in New York City in 2005 as a way to share stories of street harassment, calling attention to this phenomenon as well as providing a way to understand its boundaries and pervasiveness. Hollaback is about storytelling and generating awareness of street harassment. Since then, Hollaback has developed iPhone and Android apps to collect stories, and has developed a web platform to support local Hollaback organizations, which at the time of writing represents 50 cities, 18 countries, and 9 languages around the world (shown in table 1 and figure 1.) Hollaback has collected over 3,000 stories of harassment worldwide and is an organization that is part of the anti-street harassment movement. Since the term street harassment is new and the behavior is not necessarily problematized or even recognized as a phenomenon, it is not surprising that Hollaback has not collected more stories. Diagnosing street harassment as a problem is part of the work that Hollaback is trying to accomplish. For this paper, we focus on the experiences of women in the United States and the United Kingdom.

Hollaback Cities/Locale	
Argentina: Buenos Aires	**Honduras:** Tegucigalpa
Belgium: Brussels	**India:** Chandigarh, Delhi, Mumbai, Chennai
Canada: Ottawa, Alberta, Winnipeg, Halifax, Montreal	**Israel**
Chile: Santiago	**Mexico:** Mexico City, Queretaro
Colombia: Bogota	**New Zealand:** Wellington
Croatia	**South Africa**
Czech Republic	**Turkey:** Istanbul
France	**United Kingdom:** Birmingham, Bristol, London, West Yorkshire, Gwynedd, Portsmouth
Germany: Dresden, Berlin, Duesseldorf	**United States:** Atlanta, Berkeley, Baltimore, Boston, Chicago, Columbia MO, Des Moines, El Paso, Houston, New York, Philadelphia, Portland, Puerto Rico, Richmond, SoCal, San Jose, Twin Cities

Table 1. List of Local Hollabacks Organizations as of June 2012

Figure 1. iHollaback.org and Hollaback Buenos Aires

RELATED WORK

We position our work within research in CSCW and HCI that examines storytelling and social movement theory.

Storytelling and Technology

In CSCW research, there have been many systems designed to support collaborative storytelling for different contexts and end-goals. In the area of education, collaborative storytelling systems help children [7] learn programming [41], develop creative projects [8], and preserve their cultural heritage [35]. Other collaborative storytelling systems support families and organizations in building and sharing collective histories [48] and archival digital artifacts [11]. There is also research that examines how collaborative storytelling systems can promote healthy eating habits [25]. In non-western contexts, storytelling systems have been designed to support different technologies such as radio [55] and mobile phones [18]. These systems have also been used to support post-conflict reconciliation [51].

Storytelling is also used as a method to inform and position design [16]. This technique has been used in different contexts such as in international development [6]. Some of these applications have been inspired from "digital storytelling," a particular technique and kind of storytelling that uses video [34]. However, there is little work concerning storytelling in the context of activism, and in particular that use the theory of social movements. We position our work in this gap.

Technology and Social Movements

Although there is an increasing amount of work in collective action and activism more broadly, there is less work within social movements. Social movements are a specific kind of collective action that happens mostly outside of existing political structures and are contentious [57]. Thus, they are different from civic participation, voter mobilization, or other actions that seek to reform rather than fundamentally change existing political, economic, or societal structures. Some have expressed skepticism about the possibility of a true social movement mediated by the Internet [24]. Online participation with low time commitment has been labeled "slacktivism" [9,42,47]. The study of social movements, such as feminism and the civil rights movement, is an area of research in sociology that examines "organized collective contentious activity that usually happens outside of political structures" [52]. As part of the social movement literature, there are three concepts that are prevalent within this field, across many theories: mobilizing structures, opportunity structures, and framing processes [38]. These ideas help to explain the strategies of Hollaback, and build on previous research. We will define each of these concepts as it relates to work in CSCW.

Mobilizing Structures

According to Garrett, information communication technologies (ICTs) present a new way to mobilize people by creating a collective identity [21]. One example of how ICTs can be used in this space is Voz Mob, a text message blogging platform that gives immigrant communities a voice, who may not have regular access to smart phones or computers [1]. Another example is Turkopticon, a way for Mechanical Turk workers to hold employers accountable, and as a way to organize around worker's issues within crowd sourcing digital work [50]. In 1994, the Zapatista movement in Mexico used the Internet to build a transnational solidarity network [22]. More recently, the Arab Spring and Occupy movements have also used social media, such as blogging and social network sites, to mobilize and provide a collective voice [27,54,58]. While ICTs present a new ways of organizing traditional contentious activities such as protests, they also provide a new method for conducting contentious activities, such as specific technical acts or "hacktivism" [31]. Examples of this include hacking and denial of service attacks on websites, easily distributing leaked information as in the case of Wikileaks, and the Occupy Movement [10].

Opportunity Structures

Opportunity structures are resources and climates that social movements can take advantage of [38]. Technology can help gauge particular moods and climates. There is much work in this space outside of social movements, particularly regarding natural disasters and the stock market [23]. For example, the use of mobile text messaging donation campaigns after a natural disaster takes advantage of the technology and immediate emotions of the event, as in the case of the Haiti earthquake and wildfires [49,53]. Resources, such as ICTs, can also be examined to look at the diffusion of information within the context of social movements. Meier examined whether the diffusion of ICTs as a resource predicted anti-government protests. His results suggest that ICTs do empower resistance movements, but possibly at the expense of regimes with high levels of access to technology [39]. Within social media such as Twitter, there are many large scale studies that examine how information propagates through out these networks, but fewer (such as [14,46]) apply their analysis to a specific context where the results could suggest certain effective tactics useful for social movement activists in particular.

Framing Processes

We use the concept of frames, commonly used to study social movements, to analyze the impact of storytelling on Hollaback. The concept of a frame is derived from Goffman, who defined a frame as a "schema of interpretation" that enables people to "to locate, perceive, identify, and label" their individual experiences within the experiences of society [38]. Frames help individuals to interpret individual experiences, and then to guide action. Within social movement theory and related to social movement organizations, collective action frames are "action-oriented set of beliefs and meaning that inspire and legitimate the activities and campaigns" [5]. Rather than a fixed set of beliefs, collective action frames are the outcome of a negotiated shared meaning. Frame alignment processes are the ways in which individuals and social movement organizations link or align their frames.

Benford and Snow identify frame alignment processes as the process through which individual frames become linked with collective understandings [5]. In our work we focus on two of these: frame transformation and frame extension. *Frame transformation* is a process that produces a change in the individual level specifically "in cognitive orientation and emotional sensitivities." People shift from one way of seeing and understanding an issue and oneself to a different way. For example, there is research that looks at how Black feminists worked to transform the frame of sexual violence within Black communities [59]. They were seeking to transform the common understanding that sexual violence was a result of racism; they wanted to shift that understanding to also incorporate sexism and classism. As a result of this frame transformation, women in the Black community were able to stand up and speak out against sexualized violence in their communities.

Frame extension occurs when social movement organizations expand the boundaries of what is considered part of the frame. Using the same example as above, the Black feminist collective extended their frame to include the criminalization of Black men; specifically, they expanded their efforts to also focus on rehabilitative justice within and outside of the prison system [59]. The collective's reason to extend their frame to include criminalization was to incorporate concerns within the community about addressing sexual violence with out sending more men to prison. By doing so, the collective was able to frame sexual violence as part of a larger issue within their community.

Bedford and Snow identify the specific actions or core framing tasks that social movement organizations use to try to invoke these different framing processes. Core framing tasks include diagnosing a problem, proposing a solution, and eliciting a call to action or providing a rational for action [59].

METHODS

In working with Hollaback, we employ methods both from emancipatory action research and feminist methodologies as described by Bardzell and Bardzell [2]. In order to position and describe our participation with Hollaback, we will provide researcher self-disclosure and reflexivity. Subsequently, we describe our data collection processes and analysis.

Emancipatory Action Research

Action research or participatory action research is an "orientation of inquiry that seeks to create participative communities of inquiry" [45]. Rather than separate the researcher and subjects of study, action research is a practice of participation that starts from working *with* others towards change, rather than changing others. Within the many definitions of what exactly constitutes action research, four major themes exist: empowerment of participants, acquisition of knowledge, collaboration through participation, and social change [45]. Furthermore, action research projects typically engage in systemic cycles from action phases, where members can try out new methods and techniques, to reflection phases, where members can then try to make sense of data to inform new action phases. Although the explicit use of action research is new to HCI, Hayes argues that there are many methods and issues within action research that are familiar to HCI researchers, such as fieldwork and iterative design [37], but there are also some key differences. For example, in action research, the researcher is often positioned as a "friendly outsider." Research questions and interventions are also co-constructed with members of a community or group that the researcher is working with. That is, the position of the researcher with respect to the people they are working with is changed.

However, there are different strands and types of researcher participation that can disrupt the role of the researcher as a "friendly outsider" such as emancipatory action research. Although we do not delve into all of the different strands of action research and researcher participation here, our research constitutes this specific kind of action research along with methods from Feminist HCI. Emancipatory or liberation action research has its roots in radical social movements of Marxism, anarchism, feminism, anti-racism, environmentalism, and liberationist movements in Latin America (e.g. Paulo Freire [28].) In addition to co-constructed research and action, this approach also works towards ending intersecting layers of oppression such as racism, sexism, and classism, and seeks to unravel dominant epistemologies and structures. That is, emancipatory action researchers take a political stance and become aligned with those whom they are conducting research with---they are not necessarily outsiders [29,37]. The purpose of doing action research with Hollaback is to work towards ending street harassment and continue to grow and support the organization. This research study was co-constructed with the Hollaback "mothership" (the leaders in New York City) because we wanted to understand how storytelling impacts those who share.

Researcher Self Disclosure and Reflexivity

A method used in feminist social sciences and action research is researcher/practitioner self-disclosure and reflexivity [29,37]. For researcher self-disclosure, in action research and feminist methodologies, the researcher must disclose his/her position in the world, goals, and intellectual and political beliefs [2]. Accordingly, we describe our involvement and position within Hollaback. The first author started working with Hollaback as a volunteer. Previously, the author was doing research in domestic violence and ICTs, and was interested in working with an organization that was using technology to address violence, rather than studying how technology was implicated in violence. The author initially learned about the organization through Twitter, and contacted them in the spring of 2010 to see if there was any technological help needed, and to get involved. At that time, Hollaback was a group of people who had been administrating a blog since 2005 to share stories of harassment in New York. One of the people from the group, Emily May, decided to run the organization full-time and to expand it beyond New York. At the time the first author contacted her, they were planning on making an iPhone app to collect stories of street harassment. The author had experience in Android and offered to make an Android app as well to help launch the iPhone app. The first author then subsequently developed, with other technical volunteers and the third author, the Hollaback web platform, which included a network of Wordpress sites, geocoding, story submission forms, and localization. The design was in collaboration with the founding Hollaback group in New York and other Hollaback volunteers. The first author also participates in a local Hollaback organization and helps with events and blogging.

The first author and the Hollaback team share similar political values and experiences that are pertinent to the project. For example, both consider themselves feminist and have been subject to street harassment. The second and fourth authors do not consider themselves members of the Hollaback community, while the third author has worked with a local Hollaback organization. Due to the first author's close involvement with the organization, the authors who were not involved with Hollaback helped to minimize bias in data collection and analysis as suggested in [29].

According to feminist social science, reflexivity is a method that helps researchers to question whether their work improves human quality of life and addresses issues of social oppression [2]. In our work we seek to understand how collective storytelling online impacts those who experience street harassment; by examining this, we believe our research helps to understand how storytelling frames this phenomenon and how it has impacted contributors. However, this work represents the experiences of Western women who have experienced gender-based harassment and is not representative of all kinds of harassment in all locales. More work is needed to examine how collective storytelling online affects those who experience harassment at the intersections of race, gender, class, sexual orientation, and other signifiers.

Data Collection and Analysis

We interviewed 13 people who submitted a story through the website. We selected participants by sampling from a variety of different Hollaback sites within the United States and the UK as well as selecting for a variety of different street harassment experiences such as verbal, stalking, and assault. We emailed this sample and asked if they would like to participate in a research interview about Hollaback. In the email, the first author disclosed both her role as the technical developer for Hollaback and her position as a graduate student doing research. The first author conducted six of the interviews and the second author (who is not involved with Hollaback) conducted seven. Because of the first author's involvement with Hollaback, this approach helped to minimize bias.

Because of the potentially emotional nature of the topic, we offered to conduct the interview through either phone or instant message. Four of the thirteen participants opted for instant message because they felt more comfortable over that medium. One participant stated that it was a very emotional topic for her and she felt more comfortable talking about it using text. We recruited participants until we felt that the data we were getting was saturated. The list of participants who we interviewed is in Table 2. All participants were women.

Participant	City	Age	Occupation
P1	New York City	29	Graduate Student
P2	Baltimore	19	Student
P3	Richmond, Virginia	22	Student
P4	Baltimore	27	Graduate Student
P5	Atlanta	33	Public Health
P6	Richmond, Virginia	20	Student
P7	Los Angeles	23	Server/Improv Actress
P8	Los Angeles	25	Student
P9	Houston	20	Student
P10	Boston	25	Non-Profit
P11	New York City	29	Graduate Student
P12	London, UK	30	Human Resources
P13	London, UK	36	Non-Profit

Table 2. Participant Demographics

We used a semi-structured interview because we wanted to understand why people contributed stories and how it affected them, but we also wanted to allow freedom for the conversation to go off-topic [29]. Each interview lasted 30-90 minutes. We first asked participants to recount the story they decided to share on the Hollaback site, their motivations for doing so, and how they felt after sharing. Based on our interviews with Hollaback site leaders (activists who run the local sites), we also asked the women if they thought they were "doing activism" by posting the story. We also asked them demographic information including their age and occupation. We did not ask participants their ethnicity, sexual orientation, or gender presentation. In further research, we will look at how these intersections affect sharing stories on Hollaback.

Type of Harassment	# of Ppts
Assault	1
Groping	3
Attempted Abduction	1
Stalking	2
Verbal	6

Table 3. Participant Harassment Experiences

We then transcribed the phone interviews approaching the data analysis qualitatively using inductive and deductive approaches informed by grounded theory and other qualitative analysis methods [40,56]. The first two authors separately open coded the interview data and then used axial coding to identify themes. That is, we used a Straussian approach to deductively and inductively identify themes based on social movement theory and emergent themes grounded in the data [56]. We also selected themes based on interest to the CSCW and HCI research communities. Some themes are of interest primarily from a practical standpoint (for example, that the mobile apps were not working in some cases), and those are omitted here.

FINDINGS

Participants had a range of experiences of harassment, but the most prominent was verbal harassment (shown in Table 3.) We did not interview anyone with harassment due to sexual orientation, race, or gender non-conformance.

Prior Structural Impediments

Participants stated that they felt that there was a lack of ways to process and cope with their experience with street harassment. There are several structural factors that impeded participants from emotionally dealing with or taking action in response to their experience. There were several reasons why they did not feel comfortable talking about their experience with other people.

Participants said they were hesitant to talk about their experience with friends or family because they had often been called "too sensitive" or told they were overreacting when they had tried to discuss it in the past. P3 stated,

"I think that awareness is the best way to call attention to a problem, especially one like street harassment that`s so easy to overlook (I'm often called "sensitive" for getting upset about it) and I decided that I also wanted to share mine."

Others felt that their friends or family might criticize them for the way they handled the harassment even if they felt proud of the way that they dealt with the situation.

"...the reactions I got from just telling people about it just face to face or on the phone. The reaction I got every single time was just "what if you had been hurt, what if they had come after you." And then I felt like I had to say, if it had been dark and I was the only person there I wouldn't have done that. Then they say oh ok. I feel like that shouldn't be the initial reaction and on the Hollaback site it really is not."

In sharing their experience with others, two participants were fearful that mentioning it to their family might have limited their independence and freedom.

"Oh I've shared it with a lot of over people besides my family because I know that they already don't want me here by myself in Baltimore. And because I'm short and I look young for my age they're very overprotective. I have a very overprotective family; lots of older brothers. If they knew it wouldn't go over well. I'm not sure how they would react. Especially now since I want to eventually move off of campus it might not be wise to tell them." -- P2

Three participants tried to elicit the help of the police and were unsuccessful and experienced further blame in doing so.

"...when you get told by the cop that "you shouldn't have done this, you asked for it, and you shouldn't have called" it's hard not to question yourself. Like...maybe I am over-reacting?" --P10

One participant sensed that posting her story limited her ability to contact the police. In her case, she had verbally attacked her harasser in return and she posted this on the Hollaback website. Although she only posted her first name, she felt that the police might find that evidence and hold it against her. She was frustrated and angry that in the eyes of the law she could not defend herself.

Participants also stated that they have been taught a script from an early age that the best thing to do is to ignore street harassment and walk away. However, this made them feel like they had lost some power and, as a result, were not able to deal with the harassment as it kept happening, sometimes on a daily basis.

"I've always been taught that if a guy yells at you, you should just ignore it and walk quickly away. But sharing my story reminded me of all the times I've been made to feel uncomfortable by some asshole who somehow expects me to react to what he's saying to me." --P3

Diagnosing a Problem and Frame Extension

By visiting the Hollaback website, participants were able to problematize their experience with street harassment whereas before, they considered it as a part of life that they had to accept. This is an example of a core-framing task used by social movement organizations to elicit a frame shift. For example, the following two participants were able to diagnose harassment as a problem whereas before they thought harassment was just a part of life.

"I was reading everyone else's [stories] and came to the realization that this was actually a really big problem." -- P3

"Before reading those stories, and posting, I accepted it as the norm to get harassed all the time. "--P7

As a result of problematizing their experience, two participants were able to extend the frame of street harassment to something greater. That is, the Hollaback platform gave them a way to position their experiences of street harassment within a greater frame: the position of women in society and their right to be in a public space without the fear of harassment. As we saw in the epigraph:

"Posting it did a weird thing to me though...I used to be able to brush off a lot of the stuff I get on the street and at work, because I've been getting it consistently since I was in high school, but now I think it means something more to me to be able to just walk down the street and be left alone." --P7

"But it's not something that I really thought about as a serious problem. But now, I think it definitely portrays how people think about women. I think it's disgusting." --P9

Traditionally, social movement organizations undertake this framing work. But on the Hollaback platform, story contributors are helping to extend the frame of street harassment to the greater frame of participation in public space. Design features such as the map of harassment incidents helps reinforce frame extension by illustrating the extent that harassment happens on a wide-scale.

Frame Transformation

Posting and reading stories on Hollaback changed the way that participants thought and felt about their experience, both cognitively and emotionally. That is, they experienced a frame transformation in their beliefs and feelings about the experience of being harassed.

Change of Emotions

By reading other people's stories of harassment on the site, participants felt that their own experience was validated and that they were a part of a larger epidemic that warrants change.

"It felt reassuring to realize that so many other people are also fed up with getting harassed going about their daily business."--P3

"Yeah, I mean before I personally had felt that it was not OK but it was very validating to know that there was a whole group of people out there that felt the same way I did and that could articulate, better than I could, why it was not OK. " --P10

One participant mentioned that by posting her experience, she could, in return, be a marker on the map of harassment for someone else:

"Just like for me, it makes me feel better to know that there are other women going through the same thing and trying to put a thought to it. I know I can be a little star on the map for someone else so they know they are not alone either and part of the collective activism."--P8

The women interviewed also felt that by posting their story, they were able to reclaim some power that was lost when they were harassed.

"Contributing to Hollaback was productive. That was a scary situation for me as a teenager and it was a way to make something positive out of it. "--P9

"I felt empowered posting my story on the website whether or not anyone read it. Obviously, someone did. It made me feel a lot better knowing it was out there." --P6

"I felt better. I didn't do much but I felt I had done something. Made me feel that I was taking back some of the power."--P13

Furthermore, reading other stories helped them feel like it was not their fault, and helped shift the blame and burden of the experience.

"I became more sure in my conviction that I was right to consider what happened was really, really wrong. Not to just accept it as part of life. " --P5

However, for one participant posting the story made her feel that she was not regaining any power back and that she was still acting like a victim.

"Well, because it didn't feel like it was from a position of power. It was good putting it out there, but it also felt like complaining and just leaving it there, instead of it leading to action." --P12

When this participant experienced the harassment, she was angry and wanted to do something about it. She posted to Facebook about starting a site similar to the "Microaggressions" site, a place where people submit seemingly benign experiences of racism or other oppression. On her Facebook wall, one of her friends pointed out Hollaback and encouraged her to post. In this case, the participant wanted to do more than only posting a story. She had already connected the experience of being harassed with a lack of power in society.

But for four participants, the experience of writing or sharing artwork about their experience was therapeutic and cathartic.

"I think well after experiencing it, I don't know how to put it into words, I felt like I had to articulate better the actual experience of what had happened." -- P6

Shifting to the Collective

After sharing their story and reading the stories of others, participants shifted from believing the experience was limited to "just them," to viewing it as part of a broader, collective phenomenon and as part of a community. They also wanted to understand how their individual experience related to a collective one and what they should do about it. In this way, participants experienced a frame transformation in the way that they connected their individual experience under the umbrella of street harassment.

"Sharing is like standing with the group of people who will understand what it feels like to be threatened and scared but who have not accepted what society tells us about it being "okay" and that we shouldn't complain " --P5

"It made me feel like I was a part of something. There was an excitement that came across in the other women's postings with what they were sharing. It was a camaraderie out of something that's pretty negative. But they're trying to change things and I felt that from reading the other stories."--P2

"I think it was to see if other women had this shared experience. Like what the temperature was; how other people were dealing with it or feeling about it. Because it's just a constant, and I think I may have said this in my post, but it feels like constantly that I'm getting comments or whistles and it's even happened to me again since my post. I actually got groped again in a very public place. I was actually at a bar with my boyfriend you know so like it's just so ridiculous and I wanted to see how other people are reconciling this in their daily lives."--P1

Hollaback as a Networked Public

Stories serve as a networked public and are visible to anyone on the Internet [56]. By networked public, we specifically refer to boyd's definition of "spaces and audiences that are bound together through technological networks" that include the properties of persistence, searchability, replicability, and invisible audiences [34]. As a result, these factors impact individuals who share their stories online Participants talked about how it felt good that their story was "out there" in a fixed medium.

"I felt like I got the complete story in a fixed medium and that maybe other people would see it and it was kind like alright, like checking a box. It was a good feeling"--P1

Others used the public nature of the site to thank those who helped them---something they were not able to do during the time that the harassment occurred.

"On the off chance he had told the story to someone or found the website, that he would know that I was really grateful. I feel really bad for never getting the chance to thank him because he was so nice."--P6

Two participants submitted art pieces that expressed their feelings of their experience because they thought the website would have an audience that would appreciate and understand their art.

"I felt cool for posting my painting because I have never shown at a gallery or anything. It felt good to have an audience to appreciate what it was about. "--P8

Some participants viewed the Hollaback website as a safer space than Facebook. They felt that Facebook was not a safe space for them to share their story.

"If I had posted that story on Facebook, people could take what they wanted out of it. Like thinking I wanted attention. But by posting it on the Hollaback website, you know the context of the website is like these are people submitting their harassment stories. So I felt really good about it."--P6

"I did share it on Facebook and people who read it came up to me and said, "you need to be careful." I just think that's ridiculous. It's kind of close to victim blaming. I just think that women that we always have to be afraid of men and there's no other way to exist."--P10

However, one participant used Facebook to garner support, and then posted to Hollaback later as a way of giving back or doing activism.

"Facebook narrows down the people who are reading your posts. People who know you know and support you on a personal level, people who may or may not think about things the same as you. So I had friends and for the most part people who think along the same lines as I do, supporting that but more than just discussing it among my own friends and my own social network, Hollaback is more open to the public." --P11

Due to the public nature of Hollaback, one participant wanted to make sure she posted a story that would not call into question that she did anything wrong.

"I've been harassed countless times as I'm sure tons of people have, but I chose that particular story because it was so blatantly wrong. It was broad daylight and I was in a public place. I thought people should realize that street harassment happens everywhere, not just in dark alleys."--P3

Responding Back and Dealing

For some participants, posting a story also changed the way that they reacted to harassment later. According to framing processes, a new way of framing an experience can help to guide future actions. One participant started talking back and learning how to stand up for herself:

"But I've also started getting what you might call "sassy" at work to guys who try to hit on me. You have to read the table and be careful, because if you get too bitchy you might get a complaint to the manager about you being rude, but lately I've just been as bitchy as can be to people who think they can talk down to me. Or people who call me "sweetie" or ask me to sit at the table and eat with them. I have to keep an air of "it's all in good fun," but I'm definitely talking back more. It makes me feel like I can actually let them know I'm a human being. Plus after I sass them, they'll usually laugh, but they'll stop hitting on me. Back when I was just nice, it would continue until the check came." --P7

After sharing her story on Hollaback, another participant said she started talking to more people about her experience, such as her Dad.

"But I found myself forcing myself to bring it up and to tell people about it and to, even like, people I wouldn't normally tell this to, like my Dad. It's something weird to

talk about but I wanted people to know this happened to me, it's not cool, and you should support me. Hollaback cultured my feeling that this should be shared." --P1

One participant read other stories to help her be better prepared to respond to street harassment in the future.

"It almost prepares you if you're ever in a bad situation. You've already thought about it. It gives you a head start. " --P9

One participant experimented with calling out someone who was harassing another person. She didn't feel as though she did it in the best way and is trying to negotiate how to respond to a harasser.

Unpacking Activism

For participants, activism and feminism were loaded terms---they felt uncomfortable with the potential baggage the labels carried. We asked if they felt that sharing their story on Hollaback was "doing activism." Some were hesitant about the label.

"Sort of. I'm not really much of an activist, but I do theatre, so I feel like story-sharing is a big part of helping the human condition." --P7

"I don't consider myself an activist in this area but I knew when I saw the site that it's an activist site and that posting to it would be contributing to that cause not just to document a story but to agitate for change but I can see sharing stories in a non-activist's way still being important."--P5

"When I was thinking about this whole thing last year and stuff and writing down my stuff I was wondering if someone would call me a feminist and stuff because some people have negative connotations if I like start making art like this. "--P2

For some, storytelling online was a good way to frame doing activism because it did not carry the same baggage as "being an activist." However, others thought that sharing their story was definitely a part of doing activism.

"I think so. I think the first step towards change is acknowledging there's a problem and raising awareness. I feel very strongly about sharing my stories with people so that they know they're not alone. This is why I also share that I was sexually assaulted two years ago. I think some of the best activist work comes from letting others know they're not alone and that what is happening to them is not ok." --P3

"Yeah I do. That is part of the reason I like Hollaback, part of the activism for this issue at this point in time is making people aware of it. I think that is how it starts, once people realize it's a problem then you can do something about it. Until people realize it's a problem it's hard to make anything happen." --P4

DISCUSSION

Due to structural impediments that prevented participants to interpret and respond to the harassment, Hollaback provided an alternative online space for participants to share their experiences in a way that they could not do offline. The act of writing their story changed how participants felt and thought about the experience. That is, sharing their story fundamentally changed their experience with street harassment. The concept of framing helps to explain these shifts and technology plays a new role into how framing is traditionally done.

Crowd-Sourced Framing Online

As a result of reading and writing stories on Hollaback, participants went through a frame shift [5]. Participants experienced frame transformation---the act of writing their experience and reading other stories changed their cognitive orientation toward how they viewed the occurrence, problematizing the experience as street harassment and connecting it to a greater phenomenon. In addition, design features such as the map of locations where the harassment occurred and the archive of stories worked to illustrate a collective phenomenon. Writing and reading also changed participants' emotional sensitivities. Participants shifted from blaming themselves to transferring that blame to the problem of street harassment and getting angry about it. Some participants also experienced a frame extension, where they connected the experience of street harassment with a greater frame of not being able to participate in public space and the position of women in society in general. We also have evidence that framing the incident as street harassment also changed how participants responded to it later.

Telling and sharing stories online provided a different way of performing traditional core framing tasks (e.g. diagnosing a problem, proposing a solution, eliciting a call to action) that elicit frame shifts. Because the stories are crowd-sourced or told by people around the world, participants themselves are also doing the core framing tasks rather than just the social movement organization. That is, storytellers help to define what the problem is and how to respond. As a result, contributors also experience frame shifts such as frame transformation and frame extension. Traditionally, social movement organizations have had more access to the media and positions of power, and have played an active role in defining the problem, proposing solutions, and calling to action. On Hollaback, people read other's stories of how they define harassment and ways that they cope and respond back. Beyond raising "awareness," crowd-sourced storytelling helps to fundamentally change the way that people think and respond to a phenomenon.

Concealed and Resistance Stories

Historically, storytelling has been used in many social movements, and, in particular, anti-racist movements. According to the theoretical framework for a critical examination of racism through storytelling, there are different types of stories that accomplish different things [4]. Stock stories are stories that are told through dominant groups that rationalize the status quo, and help to reveal and uncover biases. Concealed stories are stories told from non-dominant groups that counter stock stories, and uncover different ways of experiencing the world. Resistance stories are stories about how people have resisted and challenged stock stories and experiences. Emerging/transforming stories are constructed to "challenge the stock stories, build on and amplify concealed and resistance stories, and offer ways to interrupt the status quo to work for change" [4]. For the participants we talked to, we can categorize their stories as concealed and resistance stories. That is, they told stories that they felt they were unable to tell other people due to structural impediments (concealed) as well as stories about how they tried to fight back (resistance). Participants also told stories about how they were sick of "victim-blaming" and how ignoring street harassment (which is how society dictated them to act) was not working.

Sharing these concealed stories helped to frame street harassment as problematic. Furthermore, sharing concealed stories has helped site leaders to diagnose the problem and decide what to actions to take. For example, in Buenos Aires, there were a lot of stories being posted by teenage girls. The site leader decided to hold workshops in schools and to target youth. In France, there were many stories of sexual assault which led the site leader to gather and post resources on help lines and to learn more about how to respond to these intense cases. In New York City, there were a lot of stories of how bystanders failed to help out. In response, the "mothership" started a Bystander Campaign, where people who witness street harassment are also called on to share their story, and given ways and ideas to intervene. In this way, Hollaback is trying to amplify the frame of street harassment to include everyone. Some site leaders have started telling transformation stories through their own personal experiences. For example, one site leader in Winnipeg, Canada, told a story about how a man asked if he could compliment her. She gave him consent, and he told her that he really liked her hair. She experienced that public exchange as the way in which she felt comfortable about it because she gave consent.

This type of storytelling is different than the method of "digital storytelling." Digital storytelling is a particular technique and kind of storytelling that uses video to share stories [34]. However, there are some disadvantages to this approach. For one, it is impossible to be anonymous and many people do not have access to video editing software or technical skill. Also, there is not always a public forum to publish or participate in the telling of these stories. As we have seen in the responses from the Hollaback site leaders, there also may not be a social movement organization to respond to this data. Thus, the medium (the availability of text or images to remain anonymous) and a community are important in order to publish this information, as discussed in the next section.

Safe Space vs. Networked Public

Hollaback works as both a networked public and, to a degree, as a safe space, but there is tension between these roles. The stories on Hollaback are open to anyone to read and to potentially comment on (the site leaders moderate comments.) Additionally, some stories of harassment from Hollaback have been replicated through traditional media. As mentioned in previous sections, the public property is important in order for a collective framing of street harassment to happen. But for some participants, Hollaback was the only place that they could talk about their harassment experience---for them, there was no one else they could talk to, online or offline. However, Hollaback is an imperfect safe space. Participants were afraid of those invisible audiences, that they would be criticized by the way they reacted the situation. One participant was worried that it would impede their ability to contact the police or they were worried about their safety by posting the story. This fact is also variable depending on laws in different countries.

Yet, for participants, posting these stories was an act of reclaiming power and doing activism, although sometimes they did not see it through the lens of activism. Thus, there is a need for a safe space online where people who do experience harassment and do not feel that they have any other way of dealing with it, can work through their emotions and understandings of it with out fearing criticism. Yet the networked public property of Hollaback is important for reclaiming power and doing an act of resistance in response to harassment. For some participants, it was also training to talk about it offline, in public, to their friends and family.

Methodological Considerations

In the course of this study, there were additional findings related to method. At first with our recruitment email, we offered to conduct interviews over the phone. However, early on, one participant asked if she could do the interview over instant message because she felt more comfortable with the medium for such an emotionally laden topic. After that, we decided to offer the option of either phone or instant message interview. Out of 13 interviews, four chose to do them over instant message. Thus, for more emotionally laden topics, it is important to offer different types of medium choices for conducting interviews.

Similar to our experience in interviewing intimate partner violence survivors (citation omitted for blind review), we often found that we had to support and validate the participants in their experience. That is, even though they often went off topic and spent more time talking about the experience of their harassment, it was important for us to not push the conversation onto how their experience related to technology. Because of the emotionally heavy topic, it was important to act as someone who will just listen and validate their experience. This is different than research interview methods that recommend researchers to be neutral and to not show any emotions about what participants are saying. In this case, both the first and second authors were also supporting the participants and helped them deal with traumatic experiences. Participants also commented on how part of the reason they were doing the interview was another way for them to give back, and to fight against street harassment. That through participating in the research, they were doing another form of activism or giving back. This fits within the action research paradigm on how research is connected with action.

CONCLUSION

Telling the story of a traumatic experience is a typical way for an individual to make sense of that experience. CSCW technology makes it possible to tell stories to a different and larger audience. We began our study of this online story telling with a somewhat skeptical outlook. How much difference, after all, could a blog posting make? However, our empirical investigation of women who have shared stories on Hollaback has shown that it makes a great deal of difference, both to individuals struggling to understand their own experiences and to the collection of those individuals together. Whether this makes a substantial difference to others outside that group of direct participants is more difficult to discern, and is an intriguing topic for further work. We need to expand our toolkit of methods of empirically understanding the use of CSCW technology in the service of social movements.

In this research, we have, first, contributed a case study of the successful use of CSCW technology by a social movement. Second, on a more theoretical level, we have contributed a way of thinking about activism using the theories of social movements and framing. We have shown how the concept of framing helps demonstrate the effect of collective storytelling online. Specifically, sharing stories online with the Hollaback community helped to shift the way that people thought about and responded to street harassment. Telling and sharing stories on a networked public provides a different way of performing traditional core framing tasks typically done by social movement organizations and those in positions of power. Because the stories are crowd-sourced, people who experience harassment in public are helping to define what street harassment is and what to do about it. We have also provided a case of Emancipatory Action Research as an approach to doing research in the context of social justice issues.

Hollaback is an example of a social movement organization mediated by online communication. As the field of social movements and technology develops, we expect that a number of different kinds or genres will emerge. This example is grounded in storytelling as its fundamental mode of interaction. In future work, we hope to continue investigating the potential of collaborative technologies for social change.

ACKNOWLEDGMENTS

We thank Emily May, Veronica Pinto, Alex Alston, Amalia Sirica, and all of the site leaders of Hollaback. We also thank our participants for doing these interviews and sharing their story with us again.

REFERENCES

1. Bar, F., Brough, M., Costanza-Chock, S., Gonzalez, C., Wallis, C., and Garces, A. Mobile Voices: A Mobile, Open Source, Popular Communication Platform for First-Generation Immigrants in Los Angeles. *Unpublished paper presented at the Preconference workshop at the International Communication Association*, (2009).
2. Bardzell, S. and Bardzell, J. Towards a Feminist HCI Methodology: social science, feminism, and HCI. *CHI (2011)*
3. Bardzell, S. Feminist HCI: Taking Stock and Outlining an Agenda for Design. *CHI* (2010).
4. Bell, L.A. *Storytelling for social justice: Connecting narrative and the arts in antiracist teaching*. Taylor & Francis, 2010.
5. Benford, R. and Snow, D. Framing Processes and Social Movements: An Overview and Assessment. *Annual Review of Sociology 26*, (2000), 611–639.
6. Bidwell, N.J., Reitmaier, T., Marsden, G., and Hansen, S. Designing with Mobile Digital Storytelling in rural Africa. *CHI (2010)*
7. Di Blas, N., Paolini, P., and Sabiescu, A. Collective Digital Storytelling at School as a Whole-Class Interaction. *IDC* (2010)
8. Cao, X., Lindley, S.E., Helmes, J., and Sellen, A. Telling the Whole Story: anticipation, inspiration and reputation in a field deployment of TellTable. *CSCW (2010)*
9. Christensen, H.S. Political activities on the Internet: Slacktivism or political participation by other means? *First Monday 16*, 2-7 (2011).
10. Coleman, G. Anonymous: From the Lulz to Collective Action. *The New Everyday: A Media Commons Project 6*, (2011).
11. Crabtree, A., Rodden, T., and Mariani, J. Collaborating around collections: informing the continued development of photoware. *CSCW (2004)*
12. Cutrell, E. Technology for emerging markets at MSR India. *CSCW (2011)*
13. Davis, J.E. *Stories of change: Narrative and social movements*. State Univ of New York Pr, 2002.
14. Diakopoulos, N.A. and Shamma, D.A. Characterizing debate performance via aggregated twitter sentiment. *CHI* (2010)
15. Dimond, J. Feminist HCI For Real: Designing Technology in Support of a Social Movement. Dissertation. Georgia Institute of Technology 2012.
16. Erickson, T. Design as storytelling. *Interactions 3*, 4 (1996), 30–35.
17. Foth, M., Choi, J.H., and Satchell, C. Urban informatics. *CSCW (2011)*
18. Frohlich, D.M., Rachovides, D., Riga, K., et al. StoryBank: mobile digital storytelling in a development context. *CHI (2009)*

19. Ganz, M. The power of story in social movements. *unpublished paper for the Annual Meeting of the American Sociological Association, Anahem, California, August*, (2001).
20. Gardner, C.B. *Passing by: Gender and public harassment*. Univ of California Pr on Demand, 1995.
21. Garrett, R.K. Protest in an information society: A review of literature on social movements and new ICTs. *Information, Communication & Society 9*, 2 (2006), 202–224.
22. Gelsomino, M. The Zapatista Effect: Information Communication Technology Activism and Marginalized Communities. *Faculty of Information Quarterly 2*, 2 (2010).
23. Gilbert, E. and Karahalios, K. Widespread worry and the stock market. *ICWSM (2010)*
24. Gladwell, M. Twitter, Facebook, and social activism. *The New Yorker*, 2010.
25. Grimes, A., Bednar, M., Bolter, J.D., and Grinter, R.E. EatWell: sharing nutrition-related memories in a low-income community. *CSCW (2008)*
26. Grimes, A., Tan, D., and Morris, D. Toward technologies that support family reflections on health. *GROUP*, ACM (2009)
27. Hardt, M. and Negri, A. The Fight for'Real Democracy'at the Heart of Occupy Wall Street. *Foreign Affairs [Online] 11*, (2011).
28. Hayes, G. The Relationship of Action Research to HCI. *Transactions on Computer-Human Interaction 18*, 3 (2011).
29. Herr, K. and Anderson, G.L. *The action research dissertation: A guide for students and faculty*. Sage Publications, Inc, 2005.
30. Jagori and UNIFEM. Safe City Free of Violence against Women and Girls Initiative. (2010).
31. Jordan, T. and Taylor, P.A. *Hacktivism and cyberwars: rebels with a cause?* Psychology Press, 2004.
32. Kearl, H. *Stop street harassment: Making public places safe and welcoming for women*. Praeger Publishers, 2010.
33. Kolko, B.E., Hope, A., Brunette, W., et al. Adapting collaborative radiological practice to low-resource environments. *CSCW (2012)*
34. Lambert, J. Digital storytelling: capturing lives creating community. (2006).
35. Lu, F., Tian, F., Jiang, Y., et al. ShadowStory: creative and collaborative digital storytelling inspired by cultural heritage. *CHI (2011)*
36. Macmillan, R., Nierobisz, A., and Welsh, S. Experiencing the streets: Harassment and perceptions of safety among women. *Journal of Research in Crime and Delinquency 37*, 3 (2000), 306–322.
37. Masters, J. The History of Action Research. *Action Research Electronic Reader*, (1995).
38. McAdam, D., Zald, M.N., and McCarthy, J.D. *Comparative perspectives on social movements*. Cambridge University Press Cambridge, 2004.
39. Meier, P.P. The Impact of the Information Revolution on Protest Frequency in Repressive Contexts. *International Studies Association annual meeting, New York, NY, March*, (2009), 1994–2003.
40. Miles, M.B. and Huberman, A.M. *Qualitative data analysis: An expanded sourcebook*. SAGE publications, Inc, 1994.
41. Monroy-Hernáandez, A. and Yun, F. A monkey and a stick figure: stories of remixing and social creativity. *CSCW (2012)*
42. Morozov, E. The brave new world of slacktivism. *Foreign Policy 19*, (2009).
43. Newman, M.W., Lauterbach, D., Munson, S.A., Resnick, P., and Morris, M.E. It's not that I don't have problems, I'm just not putting them on Facebook: challenges and opportunities in using online social networks for health. *CSCW (2011)*
44. Pousman, Z., Rouzati, H., and Stasko, J. Imprint, a community visualization of printer data: designing for open-ended engagement on sustainability. *CSCW (2008)*
45. Reason, P. and Bradbury, H. *The SAGE handbook of action research: participative inquiry: participative inquiry and practice*. Sage, 2007.
46. Romero, D.M., Meeder, B., and Kleinberg, J. Differences in the mechanics of information diffusion across topics: Idioms, political hashtags, and complex contagion on Twitter. *Proceedings of the 20th international conference on World wide web*, (2011), 695–704.
47. Rotman, D., Vieweg, S., Yardi, S., et al. From slacktivism to activism: participatory culture in the age of social media. *Extended Abstract CHI (2011)*.
48. Shen, C., Lesh, N.B., Vernier, F., Forlines, C., and Frost, J. Sharing and building digital group histories. *CSCW (2002)*
49. Shklovski, I., Palen, L., and Sutton, J. Finding community through information and communication technology in disaster response. *CSCW (2008)*
50. Silberman, M.S., Ross, J., Irani, L., and Tomlinson, B. Sellers' problems in human computation markets. *Proceedings of the ACM SIGKDD Workshop on Human Computation*, (2010), 18–21.
51. Smyth, T.N., Etherton, J., and Best, M.L. MOSES: exploring new ground in media and post-conflict reconciliation. *Proceedings of the 28th international conference on Human factors in computing systems*, ACM (2010), 1059–1068.
52. Snow, D.A. and Soule, S.A. *A primer on social movements*. WW Norton, 2010.
53. Starbird, K. and Palen, L. "Voluntweeters": self-organizing by digital volunteers in times of crisis. *CHI (2011)*

54. Starbird, K. and Palen, L. (How) will the revolution be retweeted?: information diffusion and the 2011 Egyptian uprising. *CSCW (2012)*
55. Sterling, S.R., O'Brien, J., and Bennett, J.K. Advancement through interactive radio. *Information Systems Frontiers 11*, 2 (2009), 145–154.
56. Strauss, A. and Corbin, J. *Basics of Qualitative Research: Techniques and Procedures for Developing Grounded Theory*. Sage Publications, 1998.
57. Tarrow, S. *Power in movement: Social movements and contentious politics*. Cambridge University Press, 2011.
58. Tufekci, Z. and Wilson, C. Social Media and the Decision to Participate in Political Protest: Observations From Tahrir Square. *Journal of Communication 62*, 2 (2012), 363–379.
59. White, A.M. Talking Feminist, Talking Black: Micromobilization Processes in a Collective Protest against Rape. *Gender & Society 13*, 1 (1999), 77–100.
60. Wyche, S.P., Oreglia, E., Ames, M.G., et al. Learning from marginalized users: reciprocity in HCI4D. *CSCW (2012)*

Working & Sustaining the Virtual "Disaster Desk"

Kate Starbird
ATLAS Institute
University of Colorado, Boulder
Boulder, CO 80309-0430
kstarbi@uw.edu

Leysia Palen
Department of Computer Science
University of Colorado, Boulder
Boulder, CO 80309-0430
palen@colorado.edu

ABSTRACT
Humanity Road is a volunteer organization working within the domain of disaster response. The organization is entirely virtual, relying on ICT to both organize and execute its work of helping to inform the public on how to survive after disaster events. This paper follows the trajectory of Humanity Road from an emergent group to a formal non-profit, considering how its articulation, conduct and products of work together express its identity and purpose, which include aspirations of relating to and changing the larger ecosystem of emergency response. Through excerpts of its communications, we consider how the organization makes changes in order to sustain itself in rapid-response work supported in large part by episodic influxes of volunteers. This case enlightens discussion about technology-supported civic participation, and the means by which dedicated long-term commitment to the civic sphere is mobilized.

Author Keywords
Civic participation; crisis informatics; CSCW; digital volunteers; knowledge commons; virtual organizations

ACM Classification Keywords
H.5.3 Groups & Organization Interfaces—collaborative computing, computer-supported cooperative work; K.4.2 Social Issues

INTRODUCTION
In the aftermath of the 2010 Haiti earthquake, a group of geographically dispersed people came together after discovering each other through social media as they individually tried to aid the response efforts [26]. For a small number of these digital volunteers, their emergent work progressed to a point of formalization that included division of labor and coordinated activity [15], shifting soon after into an incorporated non-profit organization called Humanity Road. Their intention was to continue to support Haiti relief after international attention faded, and then prepare to support other crises and humanitarian events internationally. Early in its life, group members began organizing themselves around information tasks that could be performed entirely online; these included verification of information, routing of information to those who could act on it, and matching of publicized needs to offers.

Today Humanity Road remains an entirely virtual organization with a global membership of volunteers in support of humanitarian relief. Virtual organizations are "geographically distributed [organizations] whose members are bound by a ... common interest or goal, and who communicate and coordinate their work through information technology" [1]. Describing the from-scratch conditions of virtual organizing, Finholt et al. write that the "absence of prior structure means group members must develop new structures for sharing information, for example, norms or rules for reporting progress and division of labor" [8 p. 292]. As a virtual organization, Humanity Road has grown from improvised ways of operating in the chaotic information space of disasters to an increasingly established organization with a steadier social structure, identity, production functions, rules and procedures.

This paper accounts for the progression of Humanity Road from the point after its emergence as a set of loosely connected individuals as first described in [26] to a virtual organization of both long-term and episodic volunteers. Through analysis of the group's communications, we consider how its members manipulate the social media-based information that is produced during and after disaster events in an effort to create information resources for victims and responders—and to demonstrate to emergency management that such resources are valuable and such volunteer work is possible.

Social Computing in a Virtual Volunteer Organization
Exploring relationships between traditional volunteer (non-profit) organizations and social computing, Voida et al. [27] report that these organizations, contrary to the perceptions of many, do not need help recruiting new volunteers—a perceived application of social media tools. Volunteer coordinators feel that the "episodic" volunteering encouraged by public, "all call" social media broadcasts is not useful to them. Instead, they see potential for social computing to help them meet other priorities, including fostering community among current volunteers and supporting a deep engagement with these volunteers. Voida et al. [27] describe this potential of social computing as yet unrealized in traditional non-profit organizations.

But what of the purely virtual, volunteer organization? Humanity Road (HR), an early member of the emerging ecosystem of virtual volunteer humanitarian response groups, provides an opportunity for examining this relationship between volunteerism and social computing in a virtual, non-profit organization. Virtual organizations rely entirely upon social media and other ICT for their organizing, and for HR, these tools are tightly woven into the social structure of the organization—shaping who they are, what they do and how they do it.

HR represents an opportunity for exploring virtual volunteerism within a domain for which it may be particularly well suited. Response and relief work is characterized by *convergence* of people, information and resources. It is also characterized by *improvisation*, with volunteers and formal responders alike innovatively adapting to unique and changing conditions, using resources in new ways, taking on new tasks and assembling into new organizational forms [7,9,15]. During disasters, many physically located on-lookers shift into roles of helping [7,9,14] and we see the same in the online arena [12]. HR emerged from digital, spontaneous volunteerism [26], which remains a constitutive element of the organization. Their continued incorporation of spontaneous volunteers intentionally differs from how traditional volunteer organizations, specifically the American Red Cross, function.

Additional features of the disaster domain are that action is often fast-paced and social structures are emergent [15]. We see the same in online social convergence, and because of the traces of the digital communication they leave behind, examination of the small but rapidly graduating steps from social convergence to social organization are detectable.

This paper follows the trajectory of HR from an emergent group as first described in [26], to a formal non-profit, now considering how its work, its articulation of work, and the ICT it adopts in order to operate in and on the virtual sphere are interrelated, and how they together express the virtual organization it has become. Throughout, we maintain a particular focus on how the organization sustains itself over time in a domain that is comprised of a set of long-term volunteers as well as a regularly changing corps of episodic volunteers who "spontaneously" converge in response to individual disasters [9]. The case of HR enlightens the discussion around what is possible—or not possible—with technology-supported civic participation over an extended period of time, and the means in which dedicated long-term commitment to the civic sphere is mobilized.

RESEARCH: METHOD & ANALYTICAL FRAME

Participant Observation

This study is based primarily upon participant observation by the first author, who spent more than 16 months as a participant observer within HR, taking part in several efforts to respond to disaster events in 2011 and 2012. In this capacity, she acts both as a digital volunteer within and as a researcher of the organization. When interacting within the group's Skype windows, she makes this dual role explicit in her handle, which appears to all conversation participants as *Kate Starbird – student/researcher*.

In addition to field notes, the primary data are the digital traces of communication that HR members leave behind via their online interactions. The environments they use include Skype, Google Docs, Twitter, and their own webpage. Most of these tools maintain archives of interactions, which are our data sources. To capture Twitter data related to HR, this research used custom Twitter search software [2] to collect the full tweet streams of each HR volunteer during the length of the study, and to execute keyword searches during specific disaster events to which the group responded.

Usernames and Twitter accounts are pseudonymous here. However, with their permission, HR leaders Graham and Thompson are explicitly recognized.

Interpretive Frame

We employ the analytical lens of structuration to help explain the evolution of HR from a loose band of helpers to a coordinated, sustained organization of volunteers, as evidenced in illustrative excerpts.

Giddens' theory of structuration explains how social structures, defined as rules and resources or transformational relations, are both the products and the pathways of human action [10]. Employing the concept of *duality of structure*, Giddens contends that social action both shapes and is shaped by these structures. Orlikowski [20] provides a *duality of technology* framework for applying structuration theory to research on the role of information technology (IT) within organizational change, where IT is both the product of human action and a medium of human action, functioning to enable and constrain it. The *communication constitutes organization* perspective again extends structuration to communicative processes, claiming that communication and the organization co-produce and co-adapt [23], and provides a helpful approach for examining organizing within the virtual organization though the digital traces of its communication [4].

OBSERVATIONS

Origins of Humanity Road: From Social Convergence in Response to Disasters

Though HR incorporated in April 2010, its origins can be traced to 2005, when Catherine Graham and Christine Thompson, recognizing deficiencies in efforts to meet informational needs of affected people, deployed "Internet Cafés" for disaster victims of Hurricane Katrina [13]. Then, in the summer of 2009, Thompson was among a small group of volunteers who converged on-line to help provide first-aid information to people involved in the Iran Election protests. Less than a year later, the January 12, 2010 Haiti earthquake catalyzed a core group of online volunteers including Graham and Thompson. A subset of this cadre who found each other through Twitter, and soon identified as *voluntweeters* or *crisis tweeters*, went on to become the founding members of HR, formally incorporating four months after the Haiti earthquake struck [26].

Early activities to support the earthquake response began on January 14 when volunteers created a "Help Haiti Heal" website (helphaitiheal.wordpress.com). Not long after the earthquake struck, the group published a list of "Twitter Commandments," giving other crisis tweeters guidance about sorting accurate from inaccurate rumor, and for "tweeting responsibly" during disasters (Thompson, personal communication).

Twitter Commandments

1. **Do No Harm** – It is safer to share no news than to share inaccurate news. Rumors put lives at risk.
2. **Do Not Panic** – You do not need to know it all.
3. **Take a Deep Breath** – Do not be distracted by noise & confusion.
4. **Verify Source**. If you do not know for sure the source is reliable – do not RT the information. Use 2 reliable independent sources for major news.
5. **Verify Facts**. Get facts, locations, address, specific need, # of people impacted, population at risk, dig deep into details, the more the better.
6. **Listen to the official & experts**. Use caution & reason & follow those who appear to have a "handle" on how to respond in these situations.
7. **Use Tweak the Tweet** – We recommend formatting your tweet using Tweak the Tweet.
8. **Not sure where to start?** Pick one topic and stick with it. Become an expert on fielding, research facts and providing help on specific topic.
9. **Repeat the first 3** Twitter Commandments as needed.

Figure 1. Humanity Road's Twitter Commandments

This list represented a formalization of lessons learned from the volunteers' ad hoc but growing experience as crisis tweeters. Thompson claims that the structure of the Commandments offered in complement to the group's online presence helped recruit new members.

Developing Identity as a Virtual Volunteer Organization

Upon incorporation, HR declared their mission:

> We are a global citizen's action team of experienced and focused individuals dedicated to educating the public by providing accurate, critical recovery information, before, after and during a catastrophic disaster. We are a non-governmental not for profit organization aligned with the United Nations global disaster response clusters as well as US state federal and local disaster response groups. We pledge to act responsibly and quickly in identifying, facilitating, collecting and disseminating required information and solutions to the public affected by the event.

This statement strongly echoes the activities they were engaged with at the time: response in an immersive information context of rapid social media posting. The language of "before, after and during" also reflects an underlying awareness of the disaster cycle that includes, along with response and recovery, phases of preparedness and mitigation [6]. Their understanding of the needs of the domain stems from extensive previous volunteer experience by HR leaders Graham and Thompson.

Later, the mission statement was "reduced … and [made] easier for folks and volunteers to remember" (Graham, personal communication):

> *Driven by Need, Led By Experience, Powered by Volunteers.* Humanity Road's mission is to educate the public before, during and after disasters on how to survive, sustain and reunite with loved ones. Humanity Road volunteers are trained and equipped to use Internet and mobile communications technology to collect, verify and route information online during sudden onset disaster. Using the Internet, they provide public safety information as well as directing the public to governmental and aid agencies that are providing assistance for the disaster.

Though many features from the initial mission statement have been carried over, the new statement more clearly positions HR as a virtual organization that relies on ICT to organize and execute its work. Volunteer activities described here align more closely with earlier efforts by digital volunteers to assist the humanitarian response during the 2010 Haiti earthquake [26] and the 2009 protests in Iran, and are less focused on the concerns of traditional emergency response. Indeed, the organization in its early life is best understood as a sum of the practices of the individuals who identified with the organization. Though they had together forged the new identity and practices of digital volunteerism [26], the distillation of why and what they do together as an organized group emerges through the ongoing work of responding to disaster after disaster around the world. In the data presentation to come, we show this distillation of purpose as it is "discovered" in the conduct of the work, and discuss the effects this has had on making episodic volunteerism viable, on making constant response viable, and on making the event-driven products of work both viable—and, critically, *visible*.

Membership

HR relies on a small but steady group of six now-seasoned volunteers who devote considerable time and resources to HR activities both during and between disaster events.[1] The composition of the team's leadership and core volunteers has shifted since its 2010 incorporation. An aim of the organization is to be "24 always on, ready to go." In contrast to strategies employed by the non-profits described in Voida et al. [27], HR also regularly leverages a larger temporary workforce of episodic and spontaneous volunteers who activate during disaster events to help the organization meet increased needs during response efforts. Later HR will ask the new volunteers to formally register as members. Of these, some members persist across events and participate in monthly planning events, and others activate only episodically. The number has gradually risen to about 20 active members. The workforce is global with people reporting in from the U.S. and Canada as well as countries in Africa, Asia, the Caribbean, Europe, the Middle East, and South America—a feature that supports its "24-7" capacity.

---

[1] During 2011, in addition to full-time activity by HR's two leaders, four volunteers responders to more than 30 events each, and three of those reported over 1000 hours of service.

Nature of Work

HR members conduct nearly all their work online: the subject of their work is the online communication that pertains to disaster response and preparation, *and* the organization works in a virtual, distributed fashion. In this section, we discuss what comprises their work—In-Between Event work and Response—as well as *how* that work is conducted ("the work to make response work work" to borrow from Bowers [3]).

During a Spring 2012 "All hands conference call"—a monthly meeting that takes place on Skype through a combination of multi-person voice and textual chats—HR members identified their "core business functions" as Disaster Preparedness and Education, Disaster Response, and Process Improvement. This declaration reinforces their mission statement, and then, with the addition of "Process Improvement," makes a move toward overt formalization of their current processes, a topic to which we will return.

In-Between Event Work

Disaster Preparedness and Education is a long-standing role for the organization that was declared early on in its mission statement. HR devotes considerable resources to preparedness and education, using its website, its @HumanityRoad Twitter account, and the Twitter accounts of several volunteers to distribute "crisis communications" to the public. For example:

> **@AlexanderB** (Mar 15, 2012): #Tornado: Watch for flying debris. Flying debris causes most injuries/fatalities. http://1.usa.gov/9kqUn3 #hmrd #miwx #ohwx

The tweet content aligns to the operational strategy of the group at the time, i.e. whether the group is actively responding to an event or not. Tweets sent during event impact and response periods, called "just in time" messages, are designed for two purposes: to give information about what to do in the moment to those immediately affected and to educate others about how to respond to a certain type of event at a time when HR believes they are most receptive to learning—that is, when an event of a type likely to affect them is happening to someone else.

This next tweet was sent during a time when volunteers were not actively responding to disasters:

> **@HumanityRoad** (Mar 27, 2012): Today's #Sustain tip > Fresh clean water is critical to surviving in disaster. Add or rotate a fresh gallon in your supply kit today. #hmrd

HR conceptualizes this between-disaster period (for them) as a *before* period for those who are affected by seasonal hazards, which would be some small portion of their global audience. For HR, between periods are times to change focus from the high-action, real-time, information processing activities of event responses, to education messaging concentrating on prevention and preparation advice, an illustration of their structuring of their work vis-à-vis the external temporalities of disaster events and hazards seasons [18].

Over time, HR has developed a way to standardize preparedness and educational messaging through what they call *tweetables*, pre-fabricated messages that offer information about how to prepare or respond to specific kinds of disasters. A large percentage of HR's outgoing Twitter communications, including those in the above example, are tweetables. Tweetables serve to structure the social group by constraining, directing and—critically—*sustaining*, a volunteer's activities with clear things to do during and between events. Inexperienced volunteers can engage in work by retweeting tweetables as they are broadcast by the @HumanityRoad account (an account managed by veteran volunteers), and then moving on to issuing tweetables themselves from the pre-approved list. Issuance of tweetables persistently broadcasts HR's presence and purpose. As tweets are added to the list of tweetables, members continue to define what the group's message is and how it appears to the outside world.

HR's most frequently broadcast tweetable is:

> **@HumanityRoad:** Verify twice. Tweet once. Rumors put lives at risk. #hmrd

Early crisis tweeters saw verifying as an important aspect of their work [26]. Humanity Road has incorporated these foundational lessons and assumed the role of educator to others about the "right" way to do crisis tweeting.

Response Work

A central function of HR is *Disaster Response*. Members process information and collectively create publicly available resources for victims during disaster events. HR's mission statement states that they "collect, verify, and route information," but they also filter, synthesize, and reformat it into standardized data formats.

In the initial period after a disaster event has been identified as a candidate for an HR response, collection efforts initially focus on improving situational awareness of volunteers so they can make decisions about how they should respond—how much effort should they expend; how much should they shift resources from other HR activities; whether they should activate offline volunteers; how many disaster-based information resources should they create and of what kind; when they should stand down, etc.

As volunteers work to process information for their own situational awareness, and as questions about whether and how to respond are answered through sensemaking activities, information-collating efforts simultaneously begin to serve the second goal of creating resources for the affected public and responding agencies. These resources are published and regularly updated on HR's website, linked to in members' outgoing tweets, and routed to other response groups—including those on the ground as well as other remote-response organizations—through tweets, email, conference calls, and in text-based Skype chats.

Hurricane Jova

Catherine Graham - Monday, October 10, 2011

Hurricane Jova is targeting the Pacific Coast of Mexico with anticipated broad impacts to several Mexican states. Stay informed with weather updates from your local weather service such as The Weather Channel - Hurricane Central and to see current wave heights with Hurricane Jova, visit ocean weather. Be sure to follow local official guidance regarding preparations and evacuations. Below are helpful links for some local official sources.

Local Officials
Red Cross Mexico @Sedenacional
Mexico Meteorological Service @huracanconagua
Mexico Meteorologist Alberto Unzon @chaac_tlaloc
State of Colima, Mexico Civil Protection @PC_Colima
State of Colima, Mexico Governor @gobernador_mam
Mexico Seismological @sismologicoMX

Public Instructions:
(Colima) Los fenómenos más comunes que provocan desastres en nuestro país son incendios, huracanes, sismos e inundaciones. Este plan es una medida preventiva que requiere la participación de todos los miembros de la familia; incluso los niños y los ancianos. Se trata que todos los integrantes de la familia sepan qué hacer antes, durante y después de un desastre. Plan familiar de Protección Civillan

(Manzanillo) Manzanillo, Colima.- Ante la cercanía del **huracán "Jova"** a las costas de Manzanillo, el Sistema Municipal de Protección Civil pide a la población en general observar una serie de medidas precautorias. ¿Qué hacer antes, durante y después de un huracán?

Media
@MetMex
@Ntelevisa_Com
Manzanillo TV Online
The Weather Channel - Jova
@climamexico

Major Hashtags: #Jova, #huracn #hurricane
Micro hashtags: #Colima #Vallarta #Michoacan #Jalisco #Nayarit

Figure 2. Event Diary for Hurricane Jova, Original Format

During high-impact events that the group determines to warrant a response effort, an HR member will create an entry within the *Event Diary* like the one in **Figure 2**. While many volunteers contribute by reporting information they gather to a shared Skype chat window, a single person, usually one of HR's leaders, creates and edits the Event Diary page. The Event Diaries are by design publicly visible products of the group's efforts to process information during the event, containing a range of information including a high-level account of the event, lists of relevant websites and Twitter accounts, warnings broadcast by official sources, locations and capacities of nearby hospital and shelters, hashtags to follow, etc.

Members turn to Twitter to send information about unfolding events, routing information to both specific people and organizations who are involved in the response as well as broadcasting information to a broad audience.

Widely broadcast information might be intercepted by victims looking for information, or by those trying to help them, or by potential volunteers who might support HR efforts. The outbound tweets closely connect to the information processing activities of the group happening at the time. Selected tweets from HR volunteers during a series of tornados that struck the southeast US in March 2012 illustrate some of this information processing work and resulting Twitter activity:

```
@AlexanderB (Mar 2, 2012): RT @foxnewsradio:
#Tornado warning sirens are sounding in
#Harrisburg, IL
```

```
@SallyB (Mar 2, 2012) #alwx RT @JimCantoreAL -
descending funnel cloud reported just NW of Jeff
and Nick Davis Rd .. valid now
```

These tweets show HR volunteers retweeting accounts of official sources, amplifying the messages of those accounts. By monitoring their friend/follower networks and executing multiple hashtag searches, volunteers filter the public stream of Twitter messages, identify trusted sources, (including but not only on-the-ground Twitterers), and identify the relevant hashtags to monitor.

Volunteers also respond directly to people in the impact zone of disasters, using @mentions and private direct messages (DMs) to provide preparedness information and relay information about current conditions:

```
@SallyB (Jan 26, 2011): @madmain You'd best get
yourself south of the river--roads are not
getting any better!
```

One of HR's goals is to help people who are "sheltering in place," and they use Twitter to connect and communicate with these "clients" of the organization.

An Extended Examination: Responding to a Large Earthquake, Peru, October 2011

This section focuses around an extended excerpt of HR activities during a response to a large earthquake in Peru on October 28, 2011. The 6.9 magnitude earthquake struck Peru in the early afternoon, at 1:56pm[2], near the town of Ica. Though later assessment showed the impact of this event to be relatively low, the initial report of earthquake location and magnitude led HR volunteers to activate for the event. The response included eight volunteers, including the first author (hence the reference to "we" in this section), and took place over approximately three hours, beginning informally just minutes after the earthquake, at 2:06pm, and ending officially when Thompson announced that we were "standing down" at 5:11pm.

This extended excerpt demonstrates the fluidity of HR's social system—how organizational change, sometimes significant change, occurs while responding to events. In some cases, that change later becomes a fixture around which the group organizes itself, designs its work practice, and even hones parts of its identity.

Using Skype Chats as Virtual Workrooms

Much of HR's activity occurs on Skype through text-based, synchronous chats. Volunteers participate in several Skype chats at once, with different windows hosting different kinds of conversations: an *Urgent Events* window hosts real-time response activities; the *Useful Links* window is a place to post links to websites and tools for use in current or future efforts; volunteers are encouraged to go to the *Work*

[2] Timestamps for the digital communications presented here are adjusted to be consistent across all volunteer accounts and are normalized around PET, the time zone of the affected area in Peru.

Diary window to report their recent activities; and the *HR Café* is a casual space for off-topic conversation. Occasionally, group leaders or veteran volunteers create a new window for a specific event, or special windows where they invite volunteers from outside HR to collaborate.

Within these virtual workrooms, volunteers come and go throughout the day. Greetings signal to others that a volunteer is available to help if a disaster event occurs. The following excerpt from the *HR Café*, which occurred in the moments leading up to the October 2011 Peru earthquake, shows volunteers essentially hanging out, mixing disaster talk and availability updates with casual conversation:

Peru Excerpt, Part 1: Skype Chat – *HR Café* – 10/28/11

HR Sam (1:47:46 pm): Good evening, Hope everyone is well
HR Chris (1:48:15 pm): doing well thanks, hope you are too
marc123 (1:48:35 pm): evening?! where art thou?
HR Sam (1:49:04 pm): Thou art on *** Island, UK
HR Chris (1:49:18 pm): the 5.4 kermadec didnt produce any effects, the Bangkok flooding is still bad - but with language barriers - we have not had much success in that area of the world
marc123 (1:49:27 pm): aha. i skipped your kingdom this summer
HR Sam (1:50:21 pm): Shame!! My kingdom of *** Island is wonderful!
kaitlin_rice (1:52:59 pm): Thanks for the update, Chris! Hi to Sam and Marc!
marc123 (1:53:21 pm): hi!
HR Sam (1:54:31 pm): Hi Kaitlin
kaitlin_rice (1:57:17 pm): Hi Sam. Nice to C U virtually! Sorry I can't chat much now - am working - just made a quick stop at the Cafe - I hope you have a nice weekend!

In addition to coordinating and enacting their response work, HR volunteers also use their virtual chat environment to build community. These backchannel conversations in the *HR Café* help to strengthen relationships between volunteers, relationships that may be important to sustaining their participation over time.

Activating the "Disaster Desk"

Just minutes after this casual exchange, HRSally shares two posts in the *HR Urgent Events* window:

Peru Excerpt Part 2: Skype Chat – *HR Urgent Events* 10/28/11[3]

1 **HR Sally** (2:06:30 pm): http://earthquake.usgs.gov/earthquakes/recenteqsww/Quakes/ at00ltshuy.html
2 **HR Sally** (2:06:51 pm):
3 2011 October 28 18:54:32 UTC
4 Details/Maps/Tsunami/Earthquake Details
5 Magnitude
6 6.9 (Preliminary magnitude — update expected w/in 15 mins)
7 Date: Friday, October 28, 2011 at 01:54:32 PM at epicenter
8 Location: 14.500°S, 75.800°W
9 Depth: 15 km (9.3 miles) set by location program
10 Region: NEAR THE COAST OF CENTRAL PERU
11 Distances
12 52 km (32 miles) S (180°) from Ica, Peru
13 ...

[3] This is the beginning of a long excerpt revealed in sections throughout this paper. Line numbers indicate progression of this conversation within the *HR Urgent Events* window.

Sally had been online, tweeting, when she reported about the earthquake. Her first post in the *Urgent Events* window (line 1), about 12 minutes after the earthquake, was a link to the United States Geological Survey (USGS) website page generated for this event, and the second post (lines 2-13) was an earthquake report copied and pasted from it. This post became the starting point for HR's work around the quake. The conversation continued:

Peru Excerpt Part 3: Skype Chat – *HR Urgent Events* – 10/28/11

14 **HR Catherine** (2:07:28 pm): ooh
15 **HR Sally** (2:08:00 pm): http://wcatwc.arh.noaa.gov/
16 **HR Sally** (2:08:33 pm): No tsunami warning, watch or advisory so far
17 **HR Chris** (2:08:43 pm]: wow
18 **HR Sally** (2:09:03 pm): https://twitter.com/#!/search/peru
19 **HR Catherine** (2:10:12 PM): no dart buoys near it - none triggered http://www.ndbc.noaa.gov/?lat=20.0&lon=-120.0

HRCatherine, one of the two HR leaders, was the first to respond to HRSally's post. Her short comment (line 14), "ooh," signaled that she had seen HRSally's post, and that perhaps this could be a significant event requiring humanitarian response. HRChris's "wow" remark (line 17) imparted the same effect. These are often the conditions for activation of HR's *Disaster Desk*.

The *Disaster Desk*, operated from HR's Skype chatrooms by one or multiple members, is the active state of the volunteers during disaster response efforts, but has also come to imply the monitoring of possible events as well. At a minimum, its most commonly understood description is a set of pre-articulated tasks that volunteers complete during events, such as monitoring social media for information, verifying and analyzing information, and communicating situational awareness and response information.

The four other posts in Part 3, which all occurred soon after HRSally's first post, show the activation of HR's *Disaster Desk*. HRSally and HRCatherine moved quickly to self-selected tasks, executing Twitter searches (line 18) and checking for tsunami reports (lines 15-16; 19).

Division of Labor and ICT Tool Use

In the next section of the excerpt, volunteers began to coordinate their activity, explicitly articulating their intentions to take on specific tasks using specific tools.

Peru Excerpt Part 4: Skype Chat – *HR Urgent Events* – 10/28/11

20 **HR Catherine** (2:10:28 PM): I'm in Tweet tracker so i'll take a look there
21 **HR Chris** (2:10:41 PM): I am @HR and will begin tweeting
22 **kaitlin_rice** (2:13:38 PM): I can RT from kaitstweets for a few

In this excerpt, three experienced HR members explicitly announced their intentions for what they planned to work on next. These declarations are important for creating a shared awareness of distributed coordination.

Part 4 also indicates a relationship between ICT and the division of labor. HR volunteers use several applications during their response efforts. Here we see volunteers turning to Twitter in different ways to gather and disseminate information. For the former task, different tools allow different forms of mining—e.g. the TweetTracker tool [16] referenced here is a tweet analysis tool for disaster relief that collects and maps tweets with geolocation metadata. There is no single tool that HR uses to do all of their Twitter monitoring—no tool that allows them to filter by multiple terms and hashtags, filter by geographic range, translate, and geolocate tweets all in the same place. For this reason, volunteers select different third party Twitter applications, often ones with which they are uniquely proficient. The division of labor is therefore shaped by tool as well as by task.

Through the selection of these tools and tasks, human capacity, tool capacity, and the functions of the organization become mutually structuring. The affordances of available tools enable the organization to take on certain types of tasks. Over time, by selecting or being assigned to certain types of tasks that require certain tools, members develop expertise in different areas, and this collective expertise comes to shape the overall work practices and work products of the organization.

Identifying On-the-Ground and Official Sources

Some of the first tasks that volunteers take on during disasters are identifying on-the-ground and official sources. Gathering information from these sources fits the larger goal of increasing situational awareness—for themselves, victims, and responders—and will later become the raw material for the resources that members generate. The following passage from the excerpt shows members moving to identify these sources, verify them, and pull information from them into their shared workspace.

Peru Excerpt Part 5: Skype Chat – *HR Urgent Events* – 10/28/11

23 **HR Catherine** (2:14:19 pm): This Author appears to be in the area of the quake
24 Author: dsanchez
25 Location:Lima
26 Date-Time:2011-10-28 12:04:35
27 Tweet:Joder, magnitud 7 en Ica #Terremoto #Temblor
28 Latitude:-12.0459739, Longitude:-77.0306154
29 ...
30 **HR Sally** (2:16:13 pm): Ica (32 mi), Chincha Alta (76 mi) , Puquio (114 mi) and Lima *186 mi) are nearest towns/cities--seeing tweets that buildings in Lima shook.
31 **HR Catherine** (2:17:42 pm): Sorry dsanchez is in LIma - the tweet was located in Peru my mistake
32 **HR Chris** (2:17:45 pm): anybody got an official source?
33 **HR Chris** (2:17:59 pm): s'ok - I am seeing reports that the quake was felt in Lima

HRCatherine's first post (lines 23-29) in this section contained information she found using TweetTracker in her quest to locate on-the-ground sources. On line 30, HRSally was also searching for information from the ground, using an Advanced Twitter Search that lets her set geographical boundaries for the search and therefore pick up tweets likely to have originated in the affected area. Both Tweet Tracker and the Advanced Twitter search, because they rely on tweet metadata and user-reported information to determine location, provide incomplete and sometimes inaccurate results. However, volunteers work to verify sources both individually and collectively (e.g. lines 30-33).

The "Checklist": Dynamic Inscription of Process

At this stage of the event response, about 30 minutes after the earthquake, there were three volunteers working the *Disaster Desk*, collecting information and sharing it with each other in the *Urgent Events* window.

At 2:30pm HRChris suggested to HRCatherine, her co-leader, that they initiate an *Event Diary* (see **Figure 2**). At about this time, several people checked in to offer help:

Peru Excerpt Part 7: Skype Chat – *HR Urgent Events*– 10/28

34 **HR Chris** (2:30:27 pm): Cat - event diary page?
35 **HR Catherine** (2:32:45 pm): Yes Chris, I think this should be an Event Diary
36 ...
37 **HR Sam** (2:35:04 pm): what would u like me to do?
38 **HR Sam** (2:35:21 pm): monitor?
39 **Deepak** (2:36:22 pm): Can I help in any way ?
40 **Kate Starbird - student/researcher** (2:36:56 pm): Let me know if I can help as well.

In the initial part of the response (Excerpts Parts 1-6), the effort was largely decentralized with volunteers following established patterns. However, as more people, some of them inexperienced, joined the chat and offered to help, a need arose for a more explicit and directed division of labor. HRChris began proposing tasks to the group at large to populate the Event Diary (lines 41-46), but then moved on to assigning them to specific volunteers (lines 48-51):

Peru Excerpt Part 8: Skype Chat – *HR Urgent Events*– 10/28/11

41 **HR Chris** (2:37:30 pm): we need the official weblinks for national and regional - the FEMA like links for Peru
42 **HR Chris** (2:38:13 pm): we are creating an event page
43 **HR Chris** (2:39:17 pm): Use this page as a template of the types of links to collect - http://www.humanityroad.org/EarthquakeTurkey
44 **HR Chris** (2:39:37 pm): Also the useful links window contains our official checklist of what we do on an emerging event
45 **HR Chris** (2:40:31 pm): We also need someone to monitor for urgent needs
46 **HR Chris** (2:40:40 pm): so just tell us which piece you are working on
47 ...
48 **HR Chris** (2:42:43 pm): Deepak - can you monitor Tweet tracker for urgent needs? Kate - can you Google search for information on impacted hospitals, buildings, people
49 ...
50 **kaitlin_rice** (2:43:21 pm): Please repeat nearest cities to epicenter
51 **HR Chris** (2:43:21 pm): Sam - can you collect the best twitter ids to monitor - some are already in this window

This represented a significant shift in activity coordination. In the early stages of the response, a few experienced volunteers appeared to be self-organizing by self-selecting tasks, differentiating them from others, and then articulating these to the group. That small group's efforts were largely guided by pre-established routines that these experienced volunteers intersubjectively shared. Some of the volunteers joining the efforts later did not share this knowledge, which required a shift from a mostly leaderless, self-organizing style to a more hierarchical, centralized one.

Attempting to both direct and educate, HRChris then pointed to two digital documents that contain information about how the organization "works" during disasters: the *Event Diary* page (like the one in **Figure 2**) that had been created for a previous event, and the official *Checklist* which she posted in the HR Useful Links window:

Peru Excerpt – Checklist – *HR Useful Links*– 10/28/11

> **HR Chris** (2:16:40 pm): Checklist
> **HR Chris** (2:16:48 pm): What happened, did it really happen, where, when, details
> If yes – share information on texting
> If no – share information on verifying before tweeting
> Who is the Event Official Source
> Examples: Hurricane, Tornado, Flood, Earthquake, Wildfire, Health
> What is the potential impact to the population
> Examples: collapsed buildings, approaching fire, tornado, storm
> ...

The routine prescribed in the *Checklist* encapsulates a cluster of organizational know-how, including pre-existing domain knowledge and lessons learned from experience by HR's members. The *Checklist* is a dynamic document, built through members' media monitoring experiences as digital volunteers, and continuously evolving as members incorporate lessons learned and leaders seek to clarify and streamline the inscribed work process. Existing as a digital document that can be copied and pasted into current activity windows or electronically distributed as a PDF file, the *Checklist* is a resource that leaders and experienced volunteers use referentially in their own work practice and prescriptively when training others. In both capacities, the *Checklist*, as well as the *Event Diary* from an earlier event, are elements that structure the organization and its work. Digital documentation of action facilitates the structuration: that is, *what we just did* becomes *what we do*. Action and routine have a recursive, co-adaptive relationship [10].

An Innovative Return to the "Self-Directed Team Approach"

At this point in the excerpt, a problem with the current work practice became clear to several volunteers: the multiple, simultaneous use of the *HR Urgent Events* window as a place for activity coordination, information sharing and resource building, as well as the staggered arrival of new volunteers onto the virtual scene of the response efforts, resulted in a confusing work environment. While some tasks were being repeated, others were forgotten, and even though volunteers made an effort to articulate their intentions and their actions, it was hard for members to keep track of what was being done. Addressing this problem, one of HR's leaders introduced a new tool, which readily changed not only the activity in the moment, but also how the organization would respond to subsequent disasters when multiple volunteers are active.

Following a request by kaitlin_rice for information about nearest cities (Part 8, line 50), Sally dropped her current task and went to retrieve that information. As she was posting the distances to the window for the second time (lines 53 & 55), another episodic volunteer, Jiro, joined the conversation:

Peru Excerpt Part 9: Skype Chat – *HR Urgent Events*– 10/28/11

> 52 **Jiro** (2:43:34 pm): whats up guys!
> 53 **HR Sally** (1:43:54 pm): [3:16:09 PM] HR Sally: Ica (32 mi), Chincha Alta (76 mi) , Puquio (114 mi) and Lima *186 mi) are nearest towns/cities--seeing tweets that buildings in Lima shook.
> 54 **kaitlin_rice** (2:44:02 pm): TY
> 55 **HR Sally** (2:44:30 pm): [3:06:42 PM] HR Sally: Distances
> 56 52 km (32 miles) S (180°) from Ica, Peru
> 57 122 km (76 miles) SSE (163°) from Chincha Alta, Peru
> 58 ...
> 59 **HR Chris** (2:44:38 pm): hello Jiro
> 60 **Kate Starbird - student/researcher** (2:45:07 pm): no damage immediately reported ... http://www.bloomberg.com/news/2011-10-28/peru-hit-by-magnitude-7-quake-tsunami-center.html
> 61 **Jiro** (2:45:13 pm): hello Chris, i have been offline for a while because of low current here in my area
> 62 **HR Chris** (2:46:10 pm): (thumbs up)

The interaction grew confusing. Coordination and communication problems began to take a toll on efficiency. Work became redundant, and responses began to arrive out of order. Though these activity coordination efforts already reflect some adaptation to the affordances of Skype—for example, how volunteers explicitly articulate availability and current tasks—this response effort brought to light some of its constraints. A few minutes later, HRChris acknowledged the issue, exclaiming:

> 63 **HR Chris Thompson** (2:51:13 pm): < insert process improvement on data collection here >

Under the stress of the situation, with too many people doing too many things at once, the socio-technical infrastructure that underlies their work practice was breaking down. Star and Ruhleder [25] explain that infrastructure becomes visible only at these points of breakdown. Volunteers directed their attention to their social configuration as the critical infrastructure here (the technical infrastructure remains taken-for-granted). At 2:57pm, not quite an hour after HR began its response to the Peru earthquake and about six minutes after HRChris's remark about the need for "process improvement," HRCatherine posted a link in the *HR Urgent Events* window introducing a Google Docs spreadsheet to help coordinate their information collation activities.

> 64 **HR Catherine Graham** (2:57:56 pm): https://docs.google.com/document/d/5555555
> 65 **HR Catherine Graham** (2:58:54 pm): I have created a document to collect the items we need for publishing i.e. put hospitals links in the links column. I'll start collecting whats already here in the urgent window for it

To create the *Event Monitoring Google Doc* (Figure 3), HRCatherine pulled the categories in the left column directly from an *Event Diary* entry created for a previous event (**Figure 2**).

Humanity Road Event Monitoring
6.9 Peru Earthquake
Volunteers reporting in: Alexander, Kate, Sally, Chris, Cat, Kaitlin, Sam

National and Regional Links	@AlertaNews24 @info_emergencia http://www.peru.gob.pe/
Emergency Numbers	Ambulance: 131 Fire: 132 Police: 133. 137 maritime emergencies, Conaf 130, PDI 134.
Nearest Airports (Kate looking)	Pisco Airport (PIO) GPS: 13° 44' 41" S, 76° 13' 13" W
News and Social Media links (Sam Getting)	@Info_emergencia @SubTVChile @terratvperu @news_in_peru @AlertaNews24 @perutweet
Hashtags (Sam Getting)	#pisco #peru #sismo #Earthquake #Temblor #Lima
...	...

Figure 3. Replica of Google Doc for Event Monitoring.
The black text represents the original state of the document. Black plus blue (or gray) text is an intermediate state at 3:08am PET

The *Event Monitoring Google Doc* is a manifestation of existing HR work practices; however, the shift from single editor control to all-member control that the Google Doc afforded had radical consequences on the way the group conducted its work. Within ten minutes, seven volunteers were working there, and the chat rooms suddenly quieted. Both long-term and episodic volunteers used the format to guide collection efforts. Working together, they quickly moved the previously collected information to this document, and continued to fill in other areas.

Further adaption of this document occurred to support coordination when we realized we needed to know who was working on what parts. We soon developed a technique of writing our names in the left column of the row we were working on. Newly arrived volunteers no longer needed to be told what to do, and people did not have to additionally monitor the work of others through the chat windows. Instead, members looked for holes in the document and began working to fill them. Speech acts in the chat window were no longer as frequently required because the work activity itself was now visible and members were mutually aware [5]. In other words, the articulation work [24], which had to be made explicit previously, became in part implicit by being embedded in the document and in the actions taken upon the document.

Not long after this socio-technical reorganization, the group completed the document, and HRCatherine copied the Google Document directly into the *Event Diary* blog entry on the HR website (Figure 4).

The Google Doc approach for organizing and generating the *Event Diary* thereafter became standard for organizing response efforts when multiple volunteers were reporting. It also replaced the overt, verbal top-down organizing that had become necessary by the linear nature of the Skype chat environment, shifting back to a "self-directed work team approach," the intended operational strategy of the organization (Graham, personal communication).

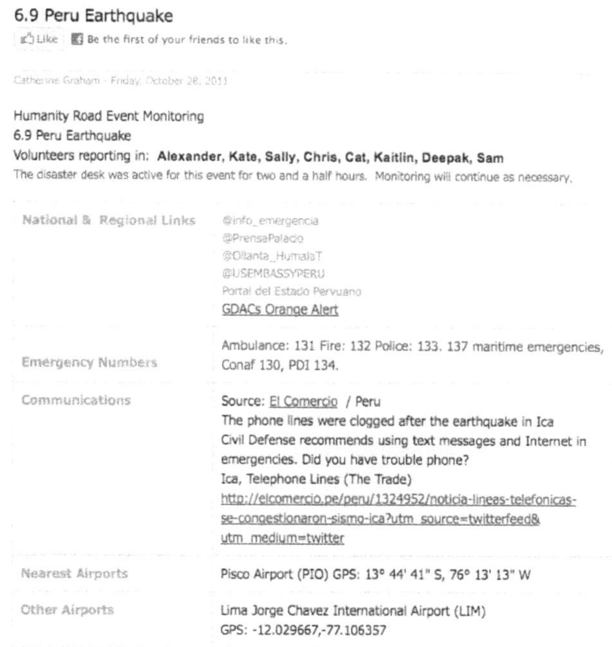
6.9 Peru Earthquake

Like Be the first of your friends to like this.

Catherine Graham - Friday, October 28, 2011

Humanity Road Event Monitoring
6.9 Peru Earthquake
Volunteers reporting in: **Alexander, Kate, Sally, Chris, Cat, Kaitlin, Deepak, Sam**
The disaster desk was active for this event for two and a half hours. Monitoring will continue as necessary.

National & Regional Links	@info_emergencia @PrensaPalacio @Ollanta_HumalaT @USEMBASSYPERU Portal del Estado Peruano GDACs Orange Alert
Emergency Numbers	Ambulance: 131 Fire: 132 Police: 133. 137 maritime emergencies, Conaf 130, PDI 134.
Communications	Source: El Comercio / Peru The phone lines were clogged after the earthquake in Ica Civil Defense recommends using text messages and Internet in emergencies. Did you have trouble phone? Ica, Telephone Lines (The Trade) http://elcomercio.pe/peru/1324952/noticia-lineas-telefonicas-se-congestionaron-sismo-ica?utm_source=twitterfeed&utm_medium=twitter
Nearest Airports	Pisco Airport (PIO) GPS: 13° 44' 41" S, 76° 13' 13" W
Other Airports	Lima Jorge Chavez International Airport (LIM) GPS: -12.029667,-77.106357

Figure 4. Event Diary Reflecting Google Document Structure

With this adaptation, the overall direction of the work had become more teleological than before—that is, more designed toward a clear, shared end goal—eliminating the tax of overt verbal orchestration, which re-enabled independent work. The Google document, then, became a replacement form of top-down organization, but also created new degrees of freedom for the organization and its individual members.

As the group moves forward to subsequent events, we discover that this innovation enables episodic volunteers to more freely enter and exit. This allows the organization to take advantage of the around-the-clock, around-the-world coverage that the inclusion of episodic volunteers makes possible. In turn, the reduction in moment-by-moment oversight allows long-term volunteers to diversify their attention to other organizational goals.

DISCUSSION

We now expand the discussion to consider the larger environmental and institutional context in which this organization exists. Externalities structure internal operations, and shape decisions about who the personnel are and what they do. The desire to be a legitimate change agent within the larger ecosystem of emergency response refines how they express and organize around what we believe to be their ultimate objective—to be stewards of the virtual "knowledge commons" [11].

Positioning vis-à-vis External Temporalities

A dominant feature of disaster events is their temporal ordering, or perhaps their temporal *dis*ordering. Human life in part organizes around the temporality of the world around it: biological temporality, environmental temporality, and—to a degree that often overrides these seemingly incontrovertible natural temporal orders—the socio-temporality of social institutions like the schedule, the week and the work shift [28,29]. Disasters might be one of the few natural events that override the socio-temporal order; indeed, damage to the routines of social life is a defining characteristic that separates disasters from local emergencies and other disruptions.

What, then, of organizations that exist to respond to such unexpected calamities? Older, physical-space emergency response organizations have established what it means to continue to work even between disaster events. The American Red Cross, which is federally mandated to respond to domestic disasters, maintains a relatively small group of employees at the national level. They respond by expanding [7] with certified volunteers who activate to support the site-based headquarters and shelters.

The ambitions of HR to respond to events globally puts demands on the pace of work. Their early mission therefore places them in a struggle between the external temporalities [18] of the subject of their work and the limits of their internal resources to do that work. Over time, these conflicts give rise to questions about how to temper the relentless surprise of world-wide disasters, and the answers come in part through its workforce composition.

Sustaining through Episodic Volunteerism

Humanity Road emerged from on-line spontaneous volunteerism [12]. Unlike other non-profits in the disaster domain as well as elsewhere who understandably see this workforce as too taxing to the organization [27], HR continues to accept spontaneous volunteers into its activities. As they have implicitly conceptualized it, episodic volunteerism supports the basic requirements of a disaster organization: to be alerted as fast as possible from any reliable source and to respond around-the-clock until the effects of a disaster reaches some stable point.

However, as we have seen in the excerpt presented in this paper, incorporating episodic volunteers takes work by the organization; HR is essentially "baking in" mechanisms into their work that make this operational strategy possible. They are even defining their work around the capacities and limitations of this workforce, co-adapting their membership and work practices with what their particular brand of worker can do. They rely on experienced volunteers to quickly train new recruits, who give them well-scoped tasks initially. Later, when response efforts stabilize, HR attempts to recruit them into official membership, asking them to register on HR's website and to participate in volunteer training. The organization has formalized several simple tasks to assign to inexperienced volunteers, including media monitoring of specific feeds looking for specific kinds of information (e.g. Part 8) and outgoing messaging using pre-crafted tweetables. As time goes on, volunteers are given increased amounts of responsibility, an indication of their centrality to the organization [17].

However, organizational social "processes" were not enough, as demonstrated earlier, to sustain HR's work from event to unexpected event. The composition of HR's members created the conditions for an innovation that only slightly adapted an existing work practice, but significantly transformed the coordination abilities of the organization.

Negotiating a Place in the Ecosystem of Disaster Response

In the two years since incorporation, HR's rapid evolution has brought it to the point of wrestling anew with the limits of its responsibilities in a new craft that it is in large part responsible for creating.

A Matter of Ethics

How do they decide to whom they respond? What resources limit them? What happens when little information is coming from a disaster site, and they have no local volunteers? During fatal flooding and mudslides near Rio de Janeiro in Brazil in January 2011, HR recruited three Brazilian volunteers who helped the group understand the geographical and cultural aspects of the disaster and translated incoming and outgoing communications. HR was then able to support the event for several weeks. A comment indicates that HR had less success supporting similar flooding events in other parts of the world:

> **HR Chris**: ... the Bangkok flooding is still bad - but with language barriers - we have not had much success in that area of the world

Recently, in late summer of 2012, an HR principal wrote to her cadre of volunteers responding to multiple simultaneous events around the world:

> Thought for the day: with 195 countries (one can debate that number) in the world - it is ok to focus on those we can truly help - and explain why we are not as effective in or on behalf of those we can not provide as much help.

This ongoing process of reflection indicates that the organization is working toward a degree of sustainability where choices regarding limits especially as they relate to the ethics of disaster response must be explicitly made.

A Matter of Relevance

What are the ways in which a virtual volunteer organization can leave its mark on the field of practice they are trying to create? Asking this question indicates another longer-term view toward sustainability. Above, we note how HR uses outgoing tweets to instruct members of the public on how to best use social media during disaster. HR has also developed formal relationships with emergency managers to educate them on how to leverage social media as well as digital volunteers during emergency response.

As another clear indication of their desire to align with the institution of emergency response, on July 27, 2012, the HR principals renamed *Event Diaries* to *Situation Reports,* or "sitreps" as they are colloquially referenced in the emergency management world. When queried about this shift, they say:

[We] made the change…to more closely align with common verbiage used by emergency response organizations and improve search engine results for finding information about recent events supported by Humanity Road. "Event Diary" is somewhat casual and seems to portray past tense but "Situation Report" provides a more current description of information contained within the site….this more accurately reflect(s) the information we are providing to the public and to aid agencies…

Working toward Inclusion in the Ecosystem of Emergency Response as a Change-Agent

This research highlights an ultimate challenge for the organization and for other groups of digital volunteers: How might they have influence? And in this particular case, how might they connect their efforts with the processes of formal emergency and humanitarian responders?

For HR, their consistent production of Event Diaries (now Situation Reports) is one way they attempt to address this challenge. By continually working to collect and synthesize information during events, and by making this work visible, HR is demonstrating some of the new capacities of digital volunteerism. They are not alone in these efforts; *Standby Task Force* has similar aims to establish a similar role for themselves in the ecosystem of emergency response.

In the context of disaster, social media and other ICT are enabling the manifestation of a "knowledge commons" [11], a shared information space for victims, onlookers, and the convergent digital volunteers. We interpret HR to be acting as a "steward of the commons" [11] through its consistent activity to organize the data there into visible, consumable information. In doing so, its members simultaneously model this behavior for others who might want to constructively participate online, an activity that complements its explicit work to educate others. Ostrom claims that "governing the commons" is best done by community members and not external authorities [21], and we see this happening naturally here early in the life of such a burgeoning commons. However, since HR members (alongside other digital volunteers) are helping to create the commons by making it more visible and navigable for the purpose of broader participation, we see HR's objective as striving towards a future where emergency managers not only recognize the existence of the commons, but then also move into the role of participants of the commons.

To meet the dual objectives of maintaining a usable knowledge commons and connecting those efforts to formal response, HR believes that it must educate the emergency response community through persistent demonstration of rigorous practice and production. In effect, the work of collectively organized digital volunteers is out ahead of the institution of emergency response. Volunteers organize virtually to process information, but many affected people and responders do not yet know to tap these new collated information resources and the workforce behind them. In probably most cases, formal responders and victims do not even know that such trustworthy efforts exist.

What we are seeing is that HR—as part of a growing movement of responsible advocators of social media in emergency response—is trying to show not that social media alone is the answer to disaster's problems, but rather that the collective system of people and data that underlie it can be shaped into new forms of rapid, highly localized assistance. Through persistent work in disaster after disaster, HR has steadily uncovered and crystallized their organizational mission and the practices that make episodic voluntary participation viable. In its display of the work, HR is trying to demonstrate worth, be visible, and ultimately be a change agent to the very traditional system of emergency management.

Conclusion

We examine a case of a purely virtual organization based on volunteerism in disaster response—Humanity Road. Its origins arose largely from the spontaneous convergence of people who reacted to news of disaster events by coming into the social media space, listening and looking for information. Those who persisted saw an opportunity to create an organization that could formalize a set of information processing activities, including collating and verifying the stream of information produced in disaster situations. The group negotiates tasks, division of labor, membership and objectives with respect to its internal resources and its ambitious aims of serving an external purpose that places high demands on the temporal ordering of work—that of helping others by changing and finding a new place in the ecosystem of emergency response.

The challenges of sustaining a public service group based entirely on volunteerism are in part mitigated by designing the very heart of the work to leverage such a workforce. In addition, with a commitment to global response, and sensitivity to limitations of their cultural knowledge, HR essentially makes it a self-requirement to access episodic volunteers from the locality they want to support. Humanity Road's inclusion of episodic volunteers also goes to an ideology of "the commons," which we propose shapes their ultimate objective: to participate in emergency management as a change agent by introducing new forms of work and work production to benefit the institution.

ACKNOWLEDGMENTS

We thank Humanity Road for granting us access to the inner workings of their organization and for being so generous with their time—helping us to understand their history, mission, and day-to-day organizing. We thank both the anonymous reviewers for their insightful critique, and Edwin Hutchins for comments on early work. We are also grateful to the US National Science Foundation, which funded this research through a Graduate Research Fellowship and grant IIS-0910586.

REFERENCES

1. Ahuju, M.K., & Carley, K. Network structure in virtual organizations, *Journal of Computer-Mediated Communication, 3*, 4 (1998).
2. Anderson, K. & Schram, A. Design and Implementation of a Data Analytics Infrastructure In Support of Crisis

Informatics Research. In the *33rd Intl Conference on Software Engineering*, (2011) 21-28.

3. Bowers, J. The Work to Make the Network Work: Studying CSCW in Action. *Proc. CSCW 1994*, ACM, (1994) 287-298.
4. DeSanctis, G., P. Monge. Communication processes for virtual organizations. *Organization Science, 10*, 6 (1999), 693–703.
5. Dourish, P. & Bellotti, V. Awareness and Coordination in Shared Workplaces. *Proc. CSCW 1992*, ACM (1992) 107-114.
6. Drabek, T. E. *Human Responses to Disaster: An Inventory of Sociological Findings*. New York: Springer-Verlag, 1986.
7. Dynes, RR. *Organized Behavior in Disaster*. Heath, 1970.
8. Finholt, T., Sproull, L., & Kiesler, S. Communication and performance in ad hoc groups. In J.Galegher, R.Kraut and C.Egido, (Eds.), *Intellectual teamwork* (pp. 291–325). NJ: Lawrence Erlbaum Associates, 1990.
9. Fritz, C. E. & Mathewson, J. H. *Convergence Behavior in Disasters: A Problem in Social Control, Committee on Disaster Studies*, National Academy of Sciences, National Research Council, Washington DC, 1957.
10. Giddens, A. *The Constitution of Society: Outline of the Theory of Structuration*. University of California Press, 1986.
11. Hess, C. and Ostrom, E. (Eds) *Understanding Knowledge as a Commons: From Theory to Practice*. Cambridge, MA: MIT Press, 2006.
12. Hughes, A., L. Palen, J. Sutton, S. Liu, & S. Vieweg. "Site-Seeing" in Disaster: An Examination of On-Line Social Convergence. *Proc. of Information Systems for Crisis Response and Management Conference (ISCRAM) 2008*.
13. Humanity Road. 2010 Annual Report. *Humanity Road, Inc.* (2011) Boydton, VA. Available at: www.humanityroad.org
14. Kendra, J.M. & Wachtendorf, T. Reconsidering Convergence and Converger: Legitimacy in Response to the World Trade Center Disaster. *Terrorism and Disaster: New Threats, New Ideas: Research in Social Problems and Public Policy* 11, (2003), 97-122.
15. Kreps, G. A. & Bosworth, S.L. *Organizing, Role Enactment, and Disaster: A Structural Theory*. Cranbury, NJ: Associated University Presses, 1994.
16. Kumar, S., Barbier, G., Abbasi, M.A., & Liu, H. TweetTracker: An Analysis Tool for Humanitarian and Disaster Relief. In *Proc. of ICWSM* (2011), 661-662.
17. Lave, J., & Wenger, E. *Situated learning: Legitimate peripheral participation*. Cambridge University Press, Cambridge, UK, 1991.
18. Lervik, J.E., Fahy, K.M., & Easterby-Smith, M. Temporal dynamics of situated learning in organizations, *Management Learning, 41*, (July 2010), 285-301.
19. Malone, T. W., Laubacher, R. & Dellarocas, C. N., Harnessing Crowds: Mapping the Genome of Collective Intelligence (February 3, 2009). MIT Sloan Research Paper No. 4732-09.
20. Orlikowoski, W. J. The duality of technology: rethinking the concept of technology in organizations. *Organization Science*, *3*, 3 (1992), 398-472.
21. Ostrom, E. *Governing the Commons: The Evolution of Institutions for Collective Action*. Cambridge, UK: Cambridge University Press, 1990.
22. Preece, J., & Shneiderman, B. The Reader-to-Leader Framework: Motivating Technology-Mediated Social Participation, *AIS Transactions on Human-Computer Interaction*, 1(1) (2009), 13-32.
23. Putnam, L.L., Nicotera, A.M., & McPhee, R.D. Introduction: Communication Constitutes Organization. In *Building Theories of Organization: The Constitutive Role of Communication*, Putnam, L.L. & Nicotera, A.M. eds., Routledge, New York, 2009.
24. Schmidt, K. & L. Bannon. Taking CSCW Seriously: Supporting articulation work. *Computer Supported Cooperative Work Journal, 1,* 1 (1992) 7-40.
25. Star, S.L. & Ruhleder. K. Steps towards an ecology of infrastructure: complex problems in design and access for large-scale collaborative systems. *Proc. of CSCW 1994,* ACM, (1994) 253-264.
26. Starbird, K. & Palen, L. "Voluntweeters:" Self-Organizing by Digital Volunteers in Times of Crisis. *Proc. of CHI 2011*, ACM, (2011) 1071–1080.
27. Voida, A. Harmon, E. & Al-Ani, B. Bridging between organizations and the public: volunteer coordinators' uneasy relationship with social computing. In *Proc. of CHI 2012*. ACM, (2012) 1967-1976.
28. Zerubavel, E. *Patterns of Time in Hospital Life: A Sociological Perspective,* University of Chicago Press, 1979.
29. Zerubavel, E. *The Seven-Day Circle: The History and* Meaning of the Week, Free Press, 1985.

Contextualized Spoken Web Browser for Low Literate Users

Mahelaqua[1] Sara Basson[2] Nitendra Rajput[3] Kundan Shrivastava[3] Saurabh Srivastava[3] John C. Thomas[2]

Samsung Design Delhi[1]
Logix Park, Noida
m.mahelaqua@samsung.com

IBM T.J Watson Research Centre[2]
Yorktown Heights, New York
Sbasson, jct@us.ibm.com

IBM Research - India[3]
Vasant Kunj, New Delhi
rnitendra, kushriva, saurabhsrivastava@in.ibm.com

ABSTRACT
Heavy penetration of mobile devices in rural areas enables access to information services to low-literate users. While connectivity solves a major issue, concepts such as browsing and searching are not intuitive to such users. This paper presents the design of a multimodal (speech+icons) voice browser for low-literate users in rural India. We conducted a field study to determine their current communication styles and preferences. Based on this, we designed three browsers, each influenced by a specific way of communicating – persona based roles, storytelling and direct interaction. The prototypes were evaluated in a task-based study with 62 low-literate users and were compared with a baseline Interactive Voice Response (IVR) browser. Our results suggest that there is clear acceptance and understanding of the necessary concepts if the browser is designed using the design constructs of persona based roles and storytelling.

Author Keywords
Spoken web; mobile; low-literate; browser; ethnography; multimodal; icons.

ACM Classification Keywords
H.5.m

INTRODUCTION
A browser is perhaps the most widely used application on a computer. However, 91% of the world population lives in less-developed geographies [1] where computer penetration is 18% and internet penetration is 15% [2]. Phone penetration, however, has reached nearly 80% in these geographies [2]. The phone is therefore expected to be the most ubiquitous device for information access in less developed countries for the near future. An additional barrier to information access is the literacy rate in these countries. In 2001, census literacy rates in India were 71 percent for males and 46 percent for females [1]. Providing oral information over mobile devices has the potential to reach the 3 billion users for whom the current internet based model is still not ubiquitous [3].

This paper focuses on enabling information access to rural populations in such less-developed regions. Access to information in this study is provided through Spoken Web, which is predicated on "VoiceSites" that are analogous to web sites [16]. These VoiceSites have audio content and can be accessed by dialing a phone number. Spoken Web works successfully on low end telephones and requires no text usage, making this a compelling medium for information access in poor, low literacy environments. In order to effectively navigate content using Spoken Web, however, browsing concepts such as *search* and *history* become important. While users are able to understand the content because it is in their own languages and is presented auditorily, explaining browsing concepts to such users is a challenge. The goal of this paper is to build a browser that can explain the browsing concepts through constructs that low-literate users can relate to.

From a technology perspective, most research in the area of designing interfaces on mobile devices focuses on how to effectively utilize the small screen size to provide good content organization and navigation [4,5]. With features such as touch screens and accelerometers, novel interaction paradigms such as gesture search [6] and haptic interaction [7] are now emerging on mobile devices. Most of these research initiatives presume that the users already know the concepts of search and browsing; they focus on novel ways of enabling these features on mobile devices. Our research is focused on users who are unfamiliar with search and browsing concepts. Therefore the browser design needs to illustrate these concepts in ways that the users can relate to.

There has been substantial work on low-literate users in terms of understanding their information needs [8,9] and also in terms of studying their adoption of existing technologies [10,11]. We wish to explore the space where an existing technology has been contextualized to facilitate its acceptance by low-literate users. Since the browser is the most used application on computers, we wish to design the browser for Spoken Web such that it is easily understandable by the target users.

Our field study provided the insight that users in rural areas have specific people who are entrusted with specific responsibilities; one person is considered worldly-wise; one records the history of the village; one is always ready to help, and so on. The first browser design is motivated by this finding and uses multiple personas for personification of search, history and help features. The second prototype is based on the finding that folk stories are popularly used to provide information to villagers; it uses a mechanism of story telling to illustrate the same concepts. The third prototype uses a single persona while the fourth prototype is a standard voice browser, to enable comparative evaluation. The main contributions of this paper are summarized below:

- We conducted a one-month field study in a rural village. The study focused on understanding the consumption and dispensation of information on a daily basis;
- We designed three specific prototypes of the Spoken Web browser that were motivated by the findings from the field study;
- We developed relevant content and asked users in different rural villages around Sohna region (Haryana, India) to use one of the browsers to navigate to that content. This study determines the effectiveness of each browser design and establishes the usefulness of designing a browser based on local constructs.
- While this study was conducted in the context of a particular rural village in India, we feel that this browser interface may prove broadly useful. More broadly, the method of discovering existing communication patterns and using those to drive design may prove useful for other low literacy populations who are unfamiliar with new communication technology.

The challenge in designing a browser for these users is that they do not have an idea about what *search* or *history* or *bookmark* means. To teach these concepts in the framework of a service, browsers were designed that illustrate these features through concepts from their daily (non-technology-aware) life. The browser design concepts are derived from a field study in one village in India – but we found no reason to believe it an atypical village in India and hence the findings can be generalized to a certain extent. The evaluation study presented at the end of the paper clearly establishes the need for such a contextual design for this specific population.

RELATED WORK

The work presented in this paper builds upon the concepts of Spoken Web, which is explained first. It uses research in the domain of multimodal mobile interfaces, explained next. This work also relates to other speech based systems that have been developed on mobile devices.

Spoken Web

VoiceSites are voice-driven applications that are hosted in the telecom network [12]. They can be accessed from any phone, mobile or landline, through an ordinary phone call to that number. The phone does not require any extra features or software to be installed on the device. VoiceSites are therefore analogous to websites in the WWW but information can be heard rather than being read or seen. Creation of content on a VoiceSite is made easy by the VoiGen system [12]. Any user (irrespective of literacy level) can create a VoiceSite without reading or typing. Such a system enables easy local audio-content creation.

A VoiceSite can link to other VoiceSites through Hyper-speech Transfer Protocol (HSTP) [13]. Such interconnected VoiceSites result in a network that we refer as the Spoken Web or World Wide Telecom Web (WWTW) [14]. System-level technology research on WWTW has been presented in [12] where the authors present technologies for VoiceSite creation. The Hyper speech Transfer Protocol has been presented in [13] and it enables linking of one VoiceSite with another in the Telecom Web. A solution based on these technologies [15] can organize heretofore unorganized urban micro-businesses. A preliminary Spoken Web browser and its features are presented in [16]. As mentioned earlier, the focus of work presented in this paper is to design a browser that can help in explaining concepts such as *bookmarks, history* and *search* to low-literate users.

Multimodal Mobile Interfaces

Recent research has shown that interfaces that use multiple modalities (such as speech, images, icons) are easier to use in many scenarios [17]. Multimodal systems are especially useful in route navigation [18,19], where the user needs speech interaction because their hands are occupied for driving and the driver also needs to see maps at the same time. In such cases, the directions are provided in speech and maps are shown as images. Multimodal systems are also used in situations where the content is too rich for a single modality to render it, as in the case of museums [20]. Even with low-literate users, multimodal applications on mobile devices have been more effective compared to their single modality counterparts [21]. However, most multimodal systems aim to use the different modalities to enrich content rendering, the work presented in this paper aims to use multimodality to make the features more contextual so that users can understand and use them.

Speech on Mobile

Rich interaction with a mobile device is generally limited by the form factor of the display. Speech has therefore been used as an additional channel for device input/output. The SearchVox system [22] presents a multimodal search interface where the user can perform mobile voice search. When the speech modality fails to recognize user commands, it presents touch and text as alternate modalities. The Dial and See system [23] provides a mechanism to interact with the Interactive Voice Response (IVR) system (dial) and in parallel, provides a visual snapshot of the IVR (see) to aid interaction with the IVR. Live search for mobile [24] enables people to search for local businesses on mobiles, using a speech interface. The PhoneBrowser [25] proposes browsing the WWW using a phone instrument where the user hears a verbal description of each visited Web page using a synthesized voice. The concept of non-visual browsers has also been studied in the context of visually impaired users [26]. CSurf [27] is a non-visual browser for blind users that extracts relevant information from a web page and renders it using a screen reader. In a study with a similar population, Sherwani et. al. [28] recommend making conversational voice user interfaces using interface metaphors and lengthier responses for better efficiency of voice based systems. Indrani et al. [29] recommend the introduction of dramatized full context video in UI to assist users in seeking information in a PC. The work presented in this paper differs from the above approaches as it presents the cultural insights that determined the design points for the Spoken Web browser.

FIELD STUDY

The study was conducted in Kadharpur village, which is 50 miles from the national capital of New Delhi in India. Like many Indian villages, this has an agriculture based infrastructure, ranging from very small to medium farmers. Villagers who are not farmers are employed as property dealers, local shop owners, vendors and so on. Land here is fertile and supports a variety of harvests, ranging from wheat and sunflower which are the primary cash crops to peanuts and chickpeas. Farming is done year round, with no seasonal gaps in between. It has a mostly illiterate population with social bias of caste and power. Little importance is given to education, particularly for girls. Those who are reasonably educated move to big cities nearby for better career opportunities. There is nonetheless very high penetration of mobile phones. With the expansion of the city Gurgaon and overlooking a horizon marked with silhouettes of modern construction all around, the village location highlights the stark differences between rural and urban India.

During this study, there were periodic visits to the villages in the region. We conducted an initial study for a period of one month and it involved 75 users. The goal of the study was to understand the consumption and dissemination of information in the village on a daily basis. Research during this phase was conducted through a series of visits to the village. Initial visits were observational, with an aim to grasp the essence, cultural context and societal behavior of the village and its people. Later, interviews were carried out with local politicians, government servants and village panchayat (organizing society) heads to gain an understanding of the statistical, demographic, and infrastructure standing of the village. In order to truly gauge the perceptions, needs, and behavior of the residents, interviews, surveys and discussions were carried out with the residents. These included men, women and children from different professions, age groups, and financial backgrounds. The study consisted of contextual enquiries and semi-structured interviews. The observations and interactions were focused towards gaining information on the following factors:

- Understanding the type of information that is consumed and disseminated;
- Understanding how information is consumed and disseminated;
- Analyzing characteristics and navigational patterns of popular media of communication;
- Understanding metaphors that are used in the social settings.

The data collected positioned the villagers in demographic and techno-graphic detail. Technographic segmentation in this case was developed to measure and categorize consumers based on their ownership, usage patterns, and attitudes toward information, communication and entertainment technologies. This study revealed individual as well as public opinions of the residents regarding their motivations and goals. We also captured opinions about how they expect technology to influence their lives to make positive changes. A number of inputs were taken from the participants which were related to the kind of information they searched, the methods of exchanging information, and preferable media of information exchange in day to day life.

While general observations were continuously made, focused sessions were conducted with 20 participant users. All the participants were small-to-medium farmers, practicing farming around Kadharpur. Out of 20 participants, 17 were male and 3 were female. No participant had more than a primary level of education (less than five years of formal education), except for one male, who pursued a bachelor's degree. We had one on one interviews with each participant which lasted for about an hour. In this part of the study, we focused on finding out how information becomes the basic unit of consumption – how information gets dispensed, molded, understood and finally used. What were the types of information consumed or dispensed and what were the related media?

We collected past experiences and stories that participants shared. We also discussed their preferences of using various

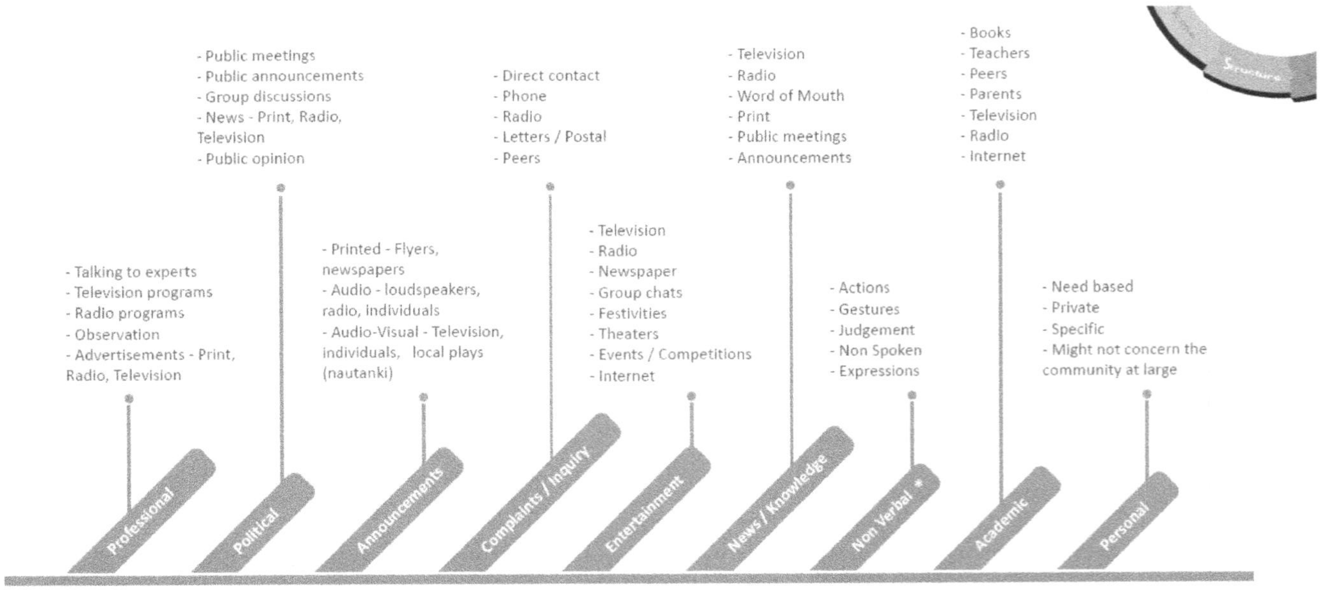

Figure 1. Different types of information exchange happening in the villages.

media such as TV, radio, newspapers, books etc. From all these insights collected during the field study, analysis and affinity mapping was done. We discuss our findings in the next section.

Literacy

The literacy rate is approximately 67% in Haryana; Kadharpur appears to be no exception.

Phone Usage

Nearly 80% of users had a mobile phone which was being used as a personal or a shared resource. The pattern of features used by farmers was highly dependent on the age of the users. Farmers who used multiple features in their mobile phones, besides making and taking calls, were all below the age of 40. In this user segment, camera and radio/mp3 emerged as the most used features. All these users had managed to learn the use of such features on their own, with minor help from friends and younger children. However, the use of SMS was very low. This was attributed to the fact that the users were not very literate and so their inability to read, understand or write the 'English' language was a barrier for SMS use. Low usage of SMS was consistent across the all age groups. However, most users were familiar with the use and functioning of IVR systems; a majority of them used services such as caller tunes and balance inquiry. Despite using IVRs, some users expressed a lack in confidence in using them, for the fear of making mistakes and thereby losing money.

Information consumed and disseminated

To determine the flow of information exchange in a rural setting, we analyzed the interviews and did the mapping to reach to the categories as shown in Figure 1. The flow of information among residents is extensive. Exchange takes place between all individuals at one level or another. Apart from information being exchanged between users through speech, information consumed and dispensed could be categorized into Professional Talks, Political Announcements, Complaints/Inquiries, Entertainment, News/Knowledge, Non Verbal, Academic and Personal conversations.

The media to exchange this information were Television, Radio, Non Verbal media, Phone, Print, Internet and Electronic gadgets (Figure 2). The representation in Figure 2 is central to this paper. It shows the different media of exchanging information among the residents of the village. Each medium has characteristic features that have the ability to catch and prolong the users' attention towards the information being supplied.

The nature of **television** and its ability to hold the users attention by presenting varied information through a **storytelling** model, was one of the most sought after features of the medium among the villagers. As pointed out by a villager himself, *"I can relate to the characters on television; it's like they are a reflection of our lifestyle and us"*. Such insights helped establish the importance of a good story telling model and **personification** of information disseminating mediums among villagers.

Even in the case of serious information exchange, such as news and public announcements, the users showed better reception to the information when it was more personal and colloquial rather than being standardized. An example of the same came from the widespread appeal of a local news program, wherein the crime reporter takes up the character of a police officer; he dresses like one and speaks in an authoritative tone, while reporting incidents of crime around the city. Such personification managed to hold the attention and interest of the audience in the village more than other crime reporters.

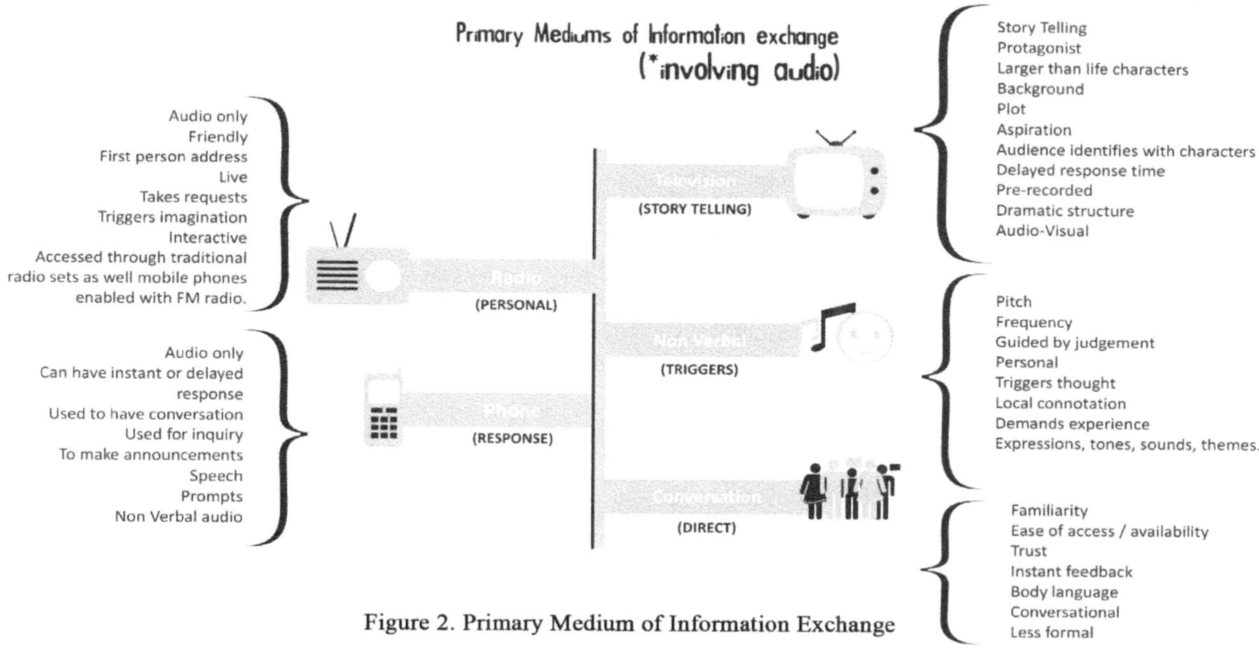

Figure 2. Primary Medium of Information Exchange

Story telling and **personification** thus emerged as possible characteristics of media of information exchange.

The second medium is the **radio**; the characteristic feature here was the personal touch of the medium. The reach of radio among the residents of the village is far more than that of television because of mobility, cost, and the fact that a user may listen to radio while doing other tasks such as farming. This reach is further amplified with the presence of radios on mobile phones (including low end mobile phones). Users pointed out that the person (radio jockey) on the other side was friendly, easy to talk to, and pleasant. Users mentioned that even though the radio jockey was probably addressing a huge audience at a given point of time, they felt that he was only talking to them. This feature of the medium, where the **radio jockey addresses the audience in first person,** elicited widespread appreciation. The listeners felt more important and hence listened with more attention.

The first-person presentation emerged as the preferred style for designing a browser interaction.

The third medium was **Non Verbal Audio**. This included all audio based mediums that did not involve the use of speech, i.e. common tunes, beats, human expressions such as making a grunting noise to show anger or disapproval and so on. As pointed out by the users, the most characteristic feature of Non Verbal Audio was the **emotional trigger** they created; for example, villagers claimed that they could easily distinguish a happy sound from a sad one by the emotion it generated.

The fourth medium was the **telephone**. With the widespread availability and penetration of mobile phones in villages of India, the usage of this medium has increased dramatically. The most characteristic feature of the phone was its ability to bring an **instant response** to the user. When compared to other media of communication such as letters and post cards, residents at the village pointed out the ability of the phone to create instant response, which not only helped save time but also ensured prompt communication during emergency situations.

Direct contact was the fifth medium. The most characteristic or liked feature was the **personal** nature of the conversations. . In face-to-face contact, both parties were felt to have the ability to analyze each other, build trust or act on judgment. Such conversations were viewed as more candid, warm and flexible.

Multimodal Spoken Web Browser Design

After extensive user research, which was primarily focused at understanding the information consumption habits of the target users and defining the key criteria and elements that would guide the design of the spoken web browser, we explored four prototypes. The design of the prototypes and the rationale behind the design will now be presented in this section. We used a display phone for each prototype to more fully illustrate the concepts chosen.

Standard Browser

First we will present a standard Spoken Web browser to illustrate the features that we wish to develop in the contextual browser. This standard browser also acts as a baseline for comparing the effectiveness of the other browser designs.

This browser greets the user and then provides two options: if the user knows the phone number (equivalent of a URL in the Spoken Web world) of the VoiceSite, she can press 1; If she does not know the phone number, she presses 2. The visual screen for this browser is a standard keypad as shown in Figure 3. If the user presses 2, then she is presented with three options: press 1 for *search*; press 2 for history and bookmarks; press 3 for *help*. On pressing 1, a search interface is presented to the user where she can submit her query. On pressing 2, all the previously visited VoiceSites and their numbers are presented to the user in a sequence. The help consists of a detailed prompt that explains these features and can then take the user back to the first prompt.

(a) (b)

Figure 3 (a) The initial screen is the same for all browser prototypes; (b) the visual interface of a standard browser is a simple keypad.

The audio prompts for this browser are very straightforward. For brevity, we will not present the English transcript of all the audio prompts, but only for the one main prompt that takes the user to the search/bookmarks/history/help option. For the standard browser, the prompt is the following:

"To search for content, press 1. To retrieve your bookmarks and history, press 2. If you need help, press 3."

If a user does not understand the terms *search/bookmarks/history* in the context of browsing, she will not be able to effectively browse the Spoken Web. A user will have to be trained to learn such concepts.

Single Persona Browser

The Single Persona browser prototype derives inspiration from the insight that users tend to associate services and functions with personas or characters that are relatable and emulate the character of the service itself. When users engaged in conversation over the phone, even when they knew that they were conversing with a machine (such as using a caller tune service), they made many inferences about the kind of person they were speaking to. Most of these inferences were formed by elements such as the voice quality, accent, grammar, level of formality. These insights led to the development of a browser prototype that extends its character to the user by designing the speech system and the visual screens based on the lines of a persona.

The main prompt for the Single Persona browser is the following:

"If you wish to ask a question, press 1; if you wish to access numbers that you had previously dialed, press 2; or if you want any kind of help from me, please press 3."

The visual screen for this browser changes with the state of interaction with the user. Typically it has the photo of Pooja along with the possible options that a user can press at a given time.

Figure 4. Persona of Pooja in the browser.

Personification of Functions Browser

The primary functions of the browser are *search, history, bookmarks* and *help*. Keeping in mind the same concept of the association of personas with the character of the service, this prototype explores the possibility of further personifying each one these functions with personas that the users in the village would imagine to be associated with these tasks. This has been done to create more engaging and familiar experiences for the user as well as extending the brand image of the service to emphasize that it understands and is aware of the practices and people of Indian villages, to whom this browser is primarily targeted.

Persona A: SEARCH

For the purpose of personifying the function of search, the persona of a middle aged school teacher has been used. From our study we found that image and respect for school teachers in these villages were extremely high. Not only were they considered as one of the most knowledgeable people in the village, but they were also associated with awareness, patience, general knowledge and righteousness. Such a personality best suits the search function of the browser, since 'search' also refers to a service where people can ask any question relevant to the topic and expect appropriate answers; just as they do with the school teacher or in colloquial terms 'Master ji'. The name of the persona is 'Mohan Master ji'.

Persona B: HISTORY AND BOOKMARKS

In Indian villages, book keeping is one job that is widely associated with that of a village 'Patwari' – a village book keeper who meticulously manages and keeps the financial and other records of the villagers at government offices such as the post office. The functions of 'History and bookmarking' are very similar. In simple language they refer to the task of record keeping for the user's activity on the Spoken Web platform. The persona of 'Pankaj Patwari' (the book-keeper) was hence used to personify this function.

(a) (b)

Figure 5. (a) The three personas on the left, and the introductory persona on the right; (b) as seen on the phone.

Persona C: HELP

In situations where the villagers are in need of advice and guidance, they turn to their elders in their village, hoping to gain from the wisdom, hands on experience and knowledge of these elderly people. One of the most common names for elders (male) in the villages of Haryana is that of 'Tau' which literally translates to 'big brother'. Tau is an old man who has seen the ups and downs of life and is equipped with experience and wisdom to help younger people with such problems. The 'HELP' menu thus derives the persona from that of 'Surender Tau'.

Non Verbal Audio: The role of Non Verbal Audio in this prototype was very crucial. Since the functions have been personified, the presence of apt non verbal audio helped ensure that the user could relate to the personas. For example, when the user accesses the functions related to the book keeper, Pankaj Patwari, the audio-icons as well as the background music help create the feel of an office, filled with records and books. Similarly, when the book keeper accesses the records to check for the user's desired book marks or history list, sounds such as the flipping of pages help create a realistic feel, one that can help the user form a suitable mental picture of the function in use, based on his/her conditioning, past knowledge and upbringing.

The visual screen for this prototype keeps changing based on the specific feature that the user is accessing. Figure 6 shows the snapshot of a screen at the time the user is asked to make a choice of the features. The figure also shows how the screen looks on the real phone on which the system was evaluated. The main prompt for this browser is very elaborate as it introduces each persona at this point:

"For the purpose of helping you, we have an in-house panel of experts who can help to answer your queries.

Our first expert is Professor Mohan. A highly learned man, he keeps track of all that's happening around the world. He can find answers to all your queries. To talk to Prof. Mohan press 1.

Our second expert is Book keeper 'Pankaj'. His ability to keep and maintain records is unmatched. All the information regarding your previous history of voicesites visited as well as your favourite bookmarks are kept safe with him. To talk to Pankaj press 2.

And our third expert is our very own uncle 'Surender'. Known for his wisdom, experience and knowledge, uncle Surender can help you understand 'how to use the service'. To talk to him, please dial 3."

Storytelling Prototype

The final prototype builds on the insight that storytelling is a strong medium that manages to hold the attention of users. This is based on the insights derived from the television viewing patterns of the users in Kadharpur village. The field study also revealed that the level of association and recall from stories is extremely high. For the purpose of creating a voice browsing experience that is based on storytelling, the first step was to find a common story, one that is widely known to a large user base. After interviewing a set of users from different age groups and identifying the popular stories in the village from the elderly to the young, the following was used.

The Folklore

Akbar-Birbal stories are an integral part of rich Indian heritage. These are one of the most popular stories among all age groups that inculcate moral values and virtues. This collection of stories is based on the relationship shared between Akbar, an illiterate king and Birbal, a learned man who was appointed by Akbar in his court as a minister. Through their stories and dialogues the duo exchanges wisdom and sentiments with each other while solving problems of the people in their kingdom. By becoming a part of the story itself, the choices made by the user during the course of using spoken web become challenges for Birbal to solve; Akbar keeps the experience interactive.

Setting

The story is set in the court of the famous emperor Akbar. Akbar is in conversation with his beloved and wise minister 'Birbal', when suddenly the user taps on the palace's door. The user is heartily welcomed by the emperor himself and offered help and service. What follows is a series of dialogues, in which the user's journey across the spoken web platform is woven. User can chose from options of direct dialing, search, history and bookmarking as well as help. Being an audio modality, the setting also makes use of a sense of navigating within a physical space; giving the user experience more depth. The corresponding visual shows the palace and changes based on where the user is navigating in the palace. This is shown in Figure 6. The translated script for the main prompt is shown below:

"Now listen carefully, I have three doors in front of me, behind each door lies an option that can help you proceed further. By opening door number 1, you can ask me any question, and I will find you voicesites that can answer it.

Door number 2 keeps safe all your previous records, be it the voicesites you visited earlier as well as the voicesites you've put in your 'star list'

The door number 3 opens your opportunity to access help, on how you can use the Spoken Web to your advantage."

(a) **(b)**

Figure 6. Storytelling prototype (a) Akbar-Birbal greeting the user; (b) Birbal explaining the three choices, i.e. doors.

Evaluation

All four prototypes were implemented in flash. The final evaluation study was performed on a Nokia N97 since it provided a large screen and an option for users to use the touch screen. However, the same browsers can be implemented on other equivalent platforms using HTML5 type languages. The design itself does not impose any restriction on the implementation. Using a standard phone across all users and all prototypes ensured that the study was resistant to any such phone biases. While this phone is perhaps a higher-end device than what the farmers typically use, none of the additional features were exposed to the user and so would not impact the results of the experiments.

A controlled study was performed to enable us to evaluate and compare the designs of the browser prototype against the different communication styles.

Demographics

The experiment was conducted with 62 participant users over a period of 8 days. All participants were small-to-medium farmers, practicing farming around Sohna town, in Haryana, India. The experiments were conducted in villages other than Kadharpur so that we could verify whether the constructs that were identified in the ethnography study are generic enough to be applicable in other areas. Ten participants were college literate; the others were either illiterate or had two years of primary education. Out of 60 users, 2 users failed to participate in the experiment due to numerical illiteracy. All participants were male, and were aged between 24-55 years. Women in this rural Indian setting were not heavily involved in agricultural work and hence their knowledge about the crop and techniques is limited. Therefore none of the women met the user criteria needed for this pilot.

Tasks and Study Method

All four prototypes had exactly the same content. The content was related to information on seeds, pesticides and the price of different crops. The content in different sections was prerecorded and had static data; for example, in the history and bookmark sections, we played voice site numbers of agriculture-related voice sites. While we introduced the study protocol to the users, we asked them to assume that they had connected to these voice sites in their previous attempts. The tasks asked users to find the relevant content using one of the browser prototypes. This ensured that we could isolate the differences due to the different browser prototypes. Each participant was met individually, and was introduced to the study and a particular prototype. Then they were provided instructions on operating the touch screen. Participants were assigned the following four tasks.

1. Find information on new seeds for wheat (*search task*).

2. Find information about the market rate (*search task*)

3. Find the information on pesticides used in wheat farming (*search task*).

4. Find the phone number of nearest seed centre, which has already been dialed earlier (*history task*).

A single user was supposed to do all the tasks using a single prototype only. No other prototype was introduced to him. While participants completed this task, the researcher observed their behaviors and methods used in navigating the browser and finding information.

Figure 7. Participants performing the task in different settings in the villages.

After completing this task, participants completed the questionnaire which was a modified version of NASA TLX, to rate their usage of the system. This was primarily done as a trigger to start the qualitative verbal feedback (and not, as is typical, as a standardized test). We believe TLX helped us to open up the conversation with the participants. The meaning of each category of the questionnaire (Mental Demand, Physical Demand etc.) was explained and elaborated verbally by giving users examples. Finally, participants were asked for their opinion on the verbal feedback based on their usage of system.

Four users were shown all the prototypes to determine relative ranking and their qualitative feedbacks. Quantitative results were not considered for these participants as they could have introduced learning bias. The quantitative analysis is therefore performed over 14 participant users for each prototype.

Quantitative Results

Figure 8 shows the number of attempts required to complete a task were very high for the Standard prototype. Rather than marking a task as incomplete, users were asked try a task multiple times, to keep their interest alive and to not be rude. To complete 56 tasks (4 tasks per user and for 14 users), participants took 100 attempts in Standard browser, 72 attempts in Single Persona, 59 attempts in Personification of Function and 64 attempts in Storytelling.

Since the length of voice prompts was different in the prototypes, we calculated the ratio of time taken for task completion with length of the voice prompts for that prototype. We call this as the normalized-time. As an example, a normalized-time of 1 implies that the participant listened to the full prompts and navigated correctly; normalized time greater than 1 implies that the user took more time than he should ideally have.

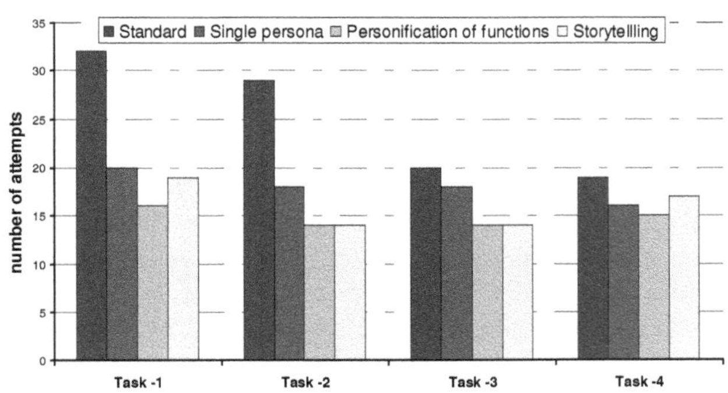

Figure 8. Total number of attempts (across all users) required to complete each task (14 users for each prototype).

Normalized-time taken for task completion by subjects in Standard Browser was more than twice the time taken in Single Persona (Figure 9). T-test shows a statistical significance ($t = 15.33 > t_{crit} = 2.779$, $p < 0.005$). Time taken for task completion was better in Storytelling than in Single Persona prototype. ($t = 1.198 < t_{crit}$). T-test shows a significant difference ($t = 3.75 > t_{crit} = 2.799$, $p < 0.005$) between the time taken for task completion between Personification of Function and Storytelling prototypes. The tasks were completed more efficiently in Personification of Function prototype

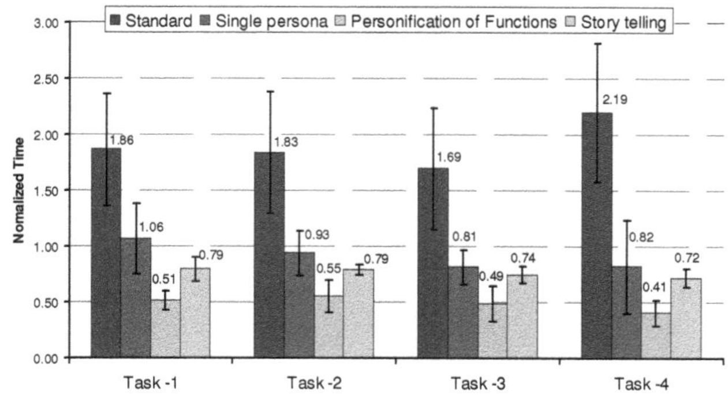

Figure 9. Average time taken to complete a task for the different prototypes.

Qualitative results

After the experiment, a questionnaire based on NASA-TLX ratings was presented to the participants. Although done primarily as a conversation starter, we also examined the quantitative results. No significant differences were found when considering any of the subjective ratings. Since this test was conceived of and normalized for very different populations and circumstances, this is not surprising.

Verbal feedback and observations

Most users liked the concept of getting agricultural information on the phone. Enthusiastically, they presented their ideas about how we can make this service better. We will now discuss the verbal comments for each prototype, focusing on suggestions for improvement. For the Standard browser, most people complained about the terminology such as history, bookmarks and help. They asked to replace the prompts with ones in their local language.

Eight of fourteen users believed that the prototype should be in a male voice. One participant said – *"In our area, males handle the farming decisions. We do not want a female telling us how to farm."* A few told us to put images of Panchayat (the local court) or sounds and photographs of the tractors so that application feels related to farming. The social setting of the villages where the study was done was based on the caste system. Most of the villages had residents from a particular caste. A user said – *"I would like to hear the voice of a person from the same caste. The name of the person should be mentioned. I would believe him more if the person would be from my caste"*.

For Single Persona, 7/14 participants wanted to use the persona of Jamindaar (Land lord) rather than the lady. The other half preferred a female voice in the system. A user complained and asked to put an attractive image in persona. An enthusiast participant asked us to put tractor sounds in the beginning of application. He even handed us the ringtone he had recorded from his new tractor. An elderly participant suggested –"*it is better to put images of crops rather than a female. We can see the photo of diseases and then apply the relevant pesticides.*" As described earlier this prototype was based on a persona, who guides you if you need help. Six of fourteen of the users tried to get help during navigation. We observed that they preferred the help command in the main menu but not using the persona. One participant accidently pressed the persona character and hence he went to the help section. Another participant said- "*You should try to incorporate a video, rather than a static picture. Video is more interesting to watch.*" One of the participants commented – "*this software wouldn't be used by farmers. They are illiterate and this would not help* "

For Personification of Functions, most of the participants mentioned that images are good for farmers. They found the voice very clear. A participant questioned – "*this is about agriculture, you should have used the Persona of Agro-Doctor instead of Masterji.*" We observed that most of users who were able to complete all the tasks successfully relate the characters in persona in context with the content. A participant said – "*we can get all information related to deposits in our bank account from Patwari.*" This character was intended to give information about history and bookmarks. Another participant said – "*Maybe Patwari can help us to get a good sale for our land.*" An important thing to note was that both these participants associated it with the real-world interactions that they had with Patwari.

For the Storytelling prototype, most participants carefully listened to the narrative. A participant said – "*I do like the Akbar-Birbal narrative, but I believe it would have been better if you had taken characters from Krishi Darshan, Lado behan, Rampal Bhai.*" Krishi darshan was a farming related talk show hosted on national television, which had these characters. Another said – "*You can use a farmer explaining concepts of farming to his wife.*" Others complained – "*Akbar-Birbal are not related to farming and hence it's not a good idea to use these characters.*"

An interesting observation was that most users did not look at the screen constantly, except for users of the Standard prototype; though the visuals of Standard prototype only had numbers. We believe that this might have been due to difficulty in navigation with the audio prompts of the Standard prototype.

Of the four participants that were asked to do a comparative evaluation, all preferred the Personification of Functions prototype to be the best, followed by the Storytelling and then the Single Persona prototype. Even from the other verbal comments, this order of preference can be derived for all the users in the study. The quantitative and qualitative results seem to report this order as well. The consistency in results therefore justifies the design of a browser based on the local constructs in the villages.

CONCLUSION

This paper presents the design of a contextual Spoken Web browser. The goal was to design a browser that helps low-literate users understand concepts such as *search* and *history*. The design was based on inputs from a one-month field study that derived important information regarding the type and media of information used by the villagers. Results clearly indicate that contextualization of these features to local constructs provide a statistically significant improvement in normalized task completion times. On the other hand, a few of the user comments indicated that they may over generalize the types of information available based on their real world interactions with characters. While the majority of comments were positive, there were also many suggestions for further improvements as illustrated above.

Encouraged by this result, we will now determine whether these constructs, especially the personification of features, are applicable to other areas of rural India which have similar folklore and similar existing communication practices. Future work might also help determine the pros and cons of this general method of basing interfaces for new communication services on existing communication patterns and attitudes. Experimenter bias is always a potential confound but this may particularly so in HCI4D because the context generally requires face to face interaction and some flexibility in protocol. In addition, users may want to please an experimenter perceived of as high status. Testing these concepts in a variety of situations will help ameliorate but not completely solve this problem.

The application of the results of the lengthy field study about existing communication patterns and attitudes were used to provide an interface for framing new forms of communication. It is quite possible that the resulting prototypes may be limited in their usefulness to application domains (like web browsing) which are also essentially communicative in nature. They may be less appropriate for other kinds of materials (e.g., learning mathematical skills). That would have to be examined empirically.

In the current context of low literacy Indian farmers, being able to complete a task at all (in order to retrieve potentially vital information) is far more critical than the total time taken to do the task. However, it is also worth exploring whether the rather lengthy prompts used in the single persona, personification and storytelling interfaces can serve successfully as scaffolding to a more concise interface for longer term use. We also want to determine the effectiveness of this approach with audio only phones.

ACKNOWLEDGMENTS

We sincerely thank Prof. Mamta Rao from National Institute of Design, Bangalore for her valuable inputs during this project. We also thank all the moderators and the users for participating in this project and sharing their insights.

REFERENCES

1. Population Reference Bureau, 2010 World Population Data Sheet. http://www.prb.org/pdf10/10wpds_eng.pdf. *Last accessed on March 23, 2012.*
2. Internet Usage World Wide by Country. http://www.infoplease.com/ipa/A0933606.html. Last accessed on January 24, 2011.
3. UNESCO Institute for Statistics. Global Education Digest 2010: Comparing Education Statistics Across the World. 2010.
4. De Bruijn , O., Spence, R., and Chong, M.Y. RSVP Browser: Web Browsing on Small Screen Devices, *Personal and Ubiquitous Computing*. Vol. 6, Issue 4, 2002.
5. Rist, T., and Brandmeier, P.,Customizing Graphics for Tiny Displays of Mobile Devices, *Personal and Ubiquitous Computing*. Vol. 6, Issue 4, 2002.
6. Li, Y. Gesture search: a tool for fast mobile data access, In *Proc. UIST*, 2010.
7. Arnab, S., Petridis, P., Dunwell, I.and , and de Freitas, S. Enhancing Learning in Distributed Virtual Worlds through Touch: A Browser-based Architecture for Haptic Interaction, Serious Games and Edutainment Applications, Part 3, 2011. 149-157.
8. Heeks, R. Information Systems and Developing Countries: Failure, Success, and Local Improvisations, *The Information Society*, Vol. 18, 2002.
9. Seshagiri, S., Sagar, A., and Joshi, D., Connecting the bottom of the pyramid: An exploratory case study of India's rural communication environment, in P*roc. WWW,* China, 2007.
10. Kolko, B., Rose, E., and Johnson, E.,Communication as information-seeking: The case for mobile social software for developing regions, in *Proc. WWW,* Canada, 2007.
11. Matthee, K., Mweemba, G., Pais, A., Stam, G.V., and Rijken, M., Bringing internet connectivity to rural zambia using a collaborative approach, in *Proc. ICTD*, India, 2007.
12. Kumar, A., Rajput, N., Chakraborty, D., Agarwal, S. and Nanavati, and A.A. Voiserv: Creation and delivery of converged services through voice for emerging economies. In Proc. *WoWMoM'07,* Finland, 2007.
13. Agarwal, S., Chakraborty, D., Kumar, A., Nanavati, A.A., and Rajput, N.. HSTP: Hyperspeech Transfer Protocol. In *ACM Hypertext 2007*, UK, 2007.
14. Kumar, A. *et.al.* WWTW: A World Wide Telecom Web for Developing Regions. In *ACM SIGCOMM Workshop on Networked Systems For Developing Regions*, 2007.
15. Kumar, A., *et. al.*. Organizing the unorganized – employing it to empower the under-privileged. In *Proceedings of the World Wide Web*, 2008.
16. Agarwal, S.K.,Kumar, A.,Nanavati,A., and Rajput, N., The world wide telecom web browser. In *Proc. WWW*, 2008.
17. Yin, M., and Zhai, S.,The benefits of augmenting telephone voice menu navigation with visual browsing and search. In *Proc. SIGCHI*, Canada. 2006.
18. Hurtig, T., A mobile multimodal dialogue system for public transportation navigation evaluated. In *Proc. Mobile HCI 07*. 2006.
19. Klante, P., Krösche, J. and Boll, S. AccesSights -- A Multimodal Location-Aware Mobile Tourist Information System. In *Proceedings of ICCHP*. 2004.
20. Santoro C., Paternò, F., Ricci, G., and Leporini, B., A multimodal mobile museum guide for all. In *Proc. Mobile HCI*. 2007.
21. Medhi, I., Gautama S. N., and Toyama, K., A Comparison of Mobile Money-Transfer UIs for Non-Literate and Semi-Literate Users. In *Proc. SIGCHI*, 2009.
22. Bongshin, Y.C., Paek, L.T., and Thiesson, B. Search Vox: Leveraging Multimodal Refinement and Partial Knowledge for Mobile Voice Search. In *Proc. UIST*, USA, 2008.
23. Yin, M. and Zhai, S. Dial and see: tackling the voice menu navigation problem with cross-device user experience integration. In *Proc.UIST*, USA, 2005.
24. Acero, A., Bernstein, N., Chambers,R., Ju, Y.C.,Li, X., Odell, J., Nguyen, P., Scholz, O. and Zweig, G. Live search for mobile: Web services by voice on the cellphone. In *Proc. ICASSP*, 2008.
25. Brown, M. K., et al. PhoneBrowser: A Web-Content-Programmable Speech Processing Platform, in *The W3C Workshop on Voice Browsers*. Cambridge, MA 1998.
26. Takagi, H. Asakawa, C., Fukuda, K., and Maeda, J.. Site-wide annotation: reconstructing existing pages to be accessible. In *ACM SIGACCESS Conf. on Assistive Tech. (ASSETS)*, Scotland, 2002.
27. Mahmud, J.U.,Borodin, Y., and Ramakrishnan, I.V.. Csurf: a context-driven non-visual web-browser. In *Proc. WWW*, Canada, 2007.
28. Sherwani, J., Ali, N.,Tongia, R., Rosenfeld, R., Memon, Y., Karim, M., and Pappas, G. HealthLine: Towards Speech-based Access to Health Information by Semi-literate Users. In *Proc. Speech in Mobile and Pervasive Environments,*Singapore, 2007.
29. Medhi, I. and Toyama, K.- Full-Context Videos for First-Time, Non-Literate PC Users. In IEEE/ACM International Conference on Information and Communication Technologies and Development 2007

ACES: A Cross-Discipline Platform and Method for Communication and Language Research

Joshua Hailpern*, **Marina Danilevsky**†, **Andrew Harris**†,
Sunah Suh†, **Reed LaBotz**†, **Karrie Karahalios**†
*HP Labs, Palo Alto, CA †University of Illinois, Urbana, IL
*joshua.hailpern@hp.com †(danilev1,harris78,sunahsuh,labotz1,kkarahal)@illinois.edu

ABSTRACT
While conducting research focused on individuals with impairments is vitally important, such experiments often have high costs (time and money), and researchers may be limited in the instructions they can give, or participant feedback they can gather (due to the impairment). We present how an impairment emulation system (ACES) can be used by researchers in the behavioral sciences. By repurposing this new technology within the context of a "traditional" psychology experiment, we were able to analyze impaired linguistic and communication in a manner that was not possible without a system such as ACES. Our experiment on 96 participants provided strong support for a theory in the aphasia psychology community, and uncovered new understandings of how people communicate when one interlocutor's speech is distorted with aphasia. These findings illustrate a new direction of HCI research that directly helps researchers in Psychology, Communication, and Speech and Hearing Science.

Author Keywords
Aphasia; Assistive Technology; Disabilities; Empathy; Emulation Software; Language; Speech; Messaging

ACM Classification Keywords
K.4.2 Social Issues: Assistive technologies for persons with disabilities

INTRODUCTION
Working with individuals that have impairments can be challenging for researchers from Computer Science to Psychology to Speech and Hearing Science. Researchers need expertise in the specific impairment, experimental costs are often higher to accommodate the physical/cognitive/language challenges, and the studies themselves can take longer and cost more to run [21]. In addition, if there is a language, cognitive or perceptual impairment, instructions given or gather able participant feedback may be limited.

Given these challenges, consider the large and lasting impact of a tool that can allow researchers (in technology or behavioral sciences) to more easily conduct experiments to aid/study individuals with impairments by running "simulated" studies with "typical" individuals. Such a tool/technique could reduce the impairment specific burden on researchers, while allowing them to test theories, run studies with more complex instructions, gather more detailed participant feedback, and quickly explore solutions before running a large N study with the target population. For those researchers with Institutional Review Boards, such a tool would expedite the approval process because participants would not be from a "vulnerable" population. Note that we are not advocating the abandonment of studies that directly work with individuals that have an impairment; rather we are advocating a solution to improve such studies, making them more time- and cost-effective by emulating a disorder through software.

In 2011, the **A**phasia **C**haracteristics **E**mulation **S**oftware, or **ACES**, was first published. ACES allows its users (e.g., caregivers, therapists and family) to experience, firsthand, the communication-distorting effects of aphasia [16]. The original goal was to allow users to build empathy and understanding by "walking in the shoes" of someone who has aphasia. Later that year, the authors validated the realism of their aphasia emulation by running (and passing) two Turing Tests [17]. We hypothesize that ACES' applications and implications are far broader than the original authors had intended and have implications for technologists and non-technologists alike.

This paper illustrates how emulation systems, like ACES, can be used by researchers in traditional Psychological, Communication or Speech and Hearing Science research. Unlike working directly with many individuals that have cognitive or communication impairments, ACES' users are neurologically typical, can provide full oral and written responses to questions, and can understand and cary out complex instructions. Through an experiment with 96 participants, we show that ACES-like systems can provide a cheap, fast and effective tool to conduct research on "simulated" individuals with impairments. We demonstrate how this approach can uncover new understandings about interpersonal communication, and provide new evidence to support theories of aphasia communication that *could not have been found without a system like ACES*. Thus, the foremost contribution of this paper is the demonstration that ACES-like CMC systems have many benefits to test and validate theories, and run "traditional" Psychology experiments targeting individuals with impairments.

RELATED WORK

As this work leverages an aphasia emulator, we describe aphasia and other tools that have emulated non-language disorders. We then highlight the relevance of ACES-like solutions for researchers by briefly discussing how language and communication is examined the existing technical and non-technical literature.

Aphasia

Aphasia is a term that describes an acquired language disorder that impairs an individual's ability to produce and understand language [5] in both written and spoken forms[6]. Aphasia is associated with individuals that have brain damage (e.g. stroke), though the manifestation (symptoms and severity) can vary based on the location and type of damage to the brain. Based on the variety of aphasia "flavors," classification systems were created to help researchers, clinicians, and individuals [15, 42]. HCI research on aphasia has largely focused the remedying communication challenges via image based communication in mobile phones [3], and day-to-day interaction [9, 1]. Also of note is the technology based research to aid individuals with aphasia in speech therapy [34] and scheduling their daily activities [31].

Disorder Emulation

In 1967, Weizenbaum et. al. introduced Eliza [47], a computer AI that attempted to emulate a Rogerian psychotherapist. Four years later, Colby et. al. published PARRY [11], and interactive computer model of paranoia. While both Eliza and PARRY were emulation systems, they did not allow a "typical" individual to experience what it was like to communicate *as* a psycho-therapist or have paranoia. These stand in sharp contrast to ACES, which allows the user to experience what it is like to have aphasia. While not a language-based emulation, Takagi's built an emulator [43] that allows a web developer to see (through obfuscation) the readability of web content to a blind screen-reader user.

The Study of Communication

Through a detailed examination of the subtle but important language patterns within conversations, researchers can uncover and quantify these changes in interpersonal communication. The examination of these patterns is not an invention of this research, nor of the computer age. Many researchers in fields such as Communication, Linguistics, and Psychology have explored how and why people communicate [14, 7, 10, 4, 48]. It is in this large corpus of existing work that we see future applications and uses of ACES, and we draw on these works in defining measures to study ACES' impact.

The examination of language and textual communication has permeated the field of human computer interaction, most notably in the field of **C**omputer-**M**ediated **C**communication (CMC). Issues of trust in computer, textual and other forms of CMC have been widespread [8, 49, 45, 32]. While some of these works has focused on examining language, others

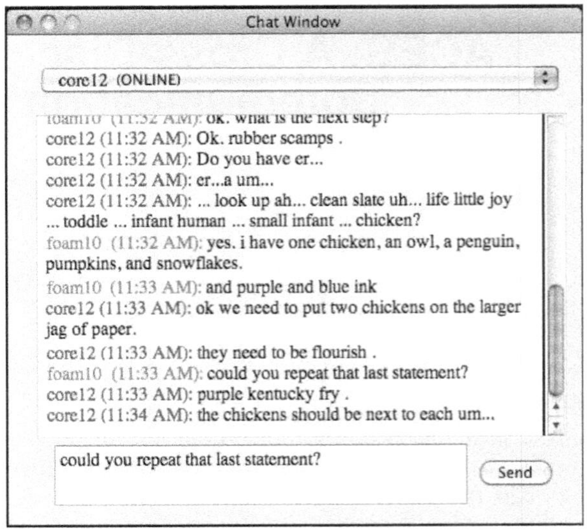

Figure 1. ACES Instant Message Window
Screenshot is of a conversation from the study in this paper. The current (red) user's partner (blue) has their text distorted.

explore the outcome of the interactions. Scissors [39, 40] examined the alignment of text and mimicry. Specifically in the domain of **I**nstant **M**essage (**IM**), Wang et. al. [46] studied, via hand-coding, the content of messages (e.g. as ideation, strategy, responses). Their focus was on the examination of conversational distance (using the divergence metrics for distribution of categories). Leshed's PhD. dissertation [28] examined language features to explore interpersonal behaviors on which people interact over IM. These works closely parallel the type of CMC questions posed in this paper (pertaining to linguistic impact and conversation outcomes). We draw on these works, and others in the CMC literature to ground many of the linguistic measures we employ.

A BRIEF OVERVIEW OF ACES

Given the prominence of ACES in this work (though the system itself is not a contribution of this paper), we briefly highlight its functioning here. For a complete description of its system and validation, please see [16, 17]. ACES is a configurable probabilistic model of the linguistic distortions associated with aphasia situated in an IM client. ACES' design is highly robust, and can emulate many types and severities of aphasia. When a user sits at a computer, they type their message into a IM window (Figure 1). This message is then distorted (based on the current settings in ACES' probabilistic model), and sent over the AOL IM network. The distorted message is then received by a conversation partner[1]. Nowhere in this process do either conversation participant role-play[2] or guess "how" the messages should be distorted [16]. Rather, the distortions provided by ACES are highly realistic, in that they passed two Turing Tests on speech disorder experts [17]. Further, ACES creates full logs of all conversations including the message *intended* to be sent, as well as the distorted message that *was* sent. In contrast to this prior work on ACES

[1] ACES allows the user to see or not see the distorted message. This parallels how some individuals with aphasia know they are making errors, while others do not.

[2] As currently done in many Speech Therapy classrooms.

which focused on the fidelity of the system and peoples emotional response, this paper examines the impact of distortions on the conversation itself (linguistics and quality).

MOTIVATION, SCOPE & RESEARCH QUESTIONS

We consider ACES-like systems to have many benefits to Researchers in Psychology and Communication beyond that of empathy building (as shown in [16]):

- **Controls:** ACES can consistently emulate a type of aphasia (unlike real individuals, who can have huge variation in their aphasia manifestations), allowing for a highly controlled experimental setup.
- **Customizable:** ACES' distortions can be easily manipulated to allow for conversations to simulate mild to severe aphasia across multiple sub-types, allowing researchers to test any specific community they wish to target.
- **Low Cost:** Unlike working with individuals that have an impairment [21], using ACES is lower in cost, time, and recruitment effort. In addition, there are few individuals with a given impairment within a population, whereas ACES' users can be nearly anyone from the population.
- **Feedback:** Many individuals with aphasia (or other impairments) have substantial challenges understanding instructions and/or responding to questions. All ACES participants can easily answer questions about their experience because they do not have aphasia themselves.
- **Intent:** With language disorders that alter grammar and syntax, it is very difficult (if not impossible) to truly understand what an individual intends to say. ACES provides researchers with transcripts of both what was said, and what individuals *intended* to say.

Research Questions

However, these broader potential applications of ACES have never been validated. Our goal is to demonstrate how systems like ACES can be used in traditional research settings in Psychology, Communication or Speech and Hearing Science and uncover new understandings of how people communicate when one interlocutor's speech is distorted with aphasia. To this end, we seek to answer the following research questions:

Question 1 Can ACES be used in a known experimental paradigm from Psychology, Communication or Speech and Hearing Science? *Showing that ACES can be integrated in traditional research setting.*

Question 2 Can ACES' distortions impact conversation style in a known way? *Showing that ACES interactions produce known changes in conversation style.*

Question 3 Can transcripts of *intended* conversation style be useful? *Showing that one of the main features of ACES transcripts over "real" transcripts has utility to researchers.*

Question 4 Can ACES be used to uncover new understandings of interpersonal interaction? *Showing that ACES is a rich platform for uncovering new phenomena.*

	Description
Step #1	Demographic Questions
Step #2	Conversation with Partner, Structure #1
Step #3	Questions About 1st Conversation
Step #4	Conversation with Partner, Structure #2
	Participant Roles & Task are Switched
Step #5	Questions About 2nd Conversation
Step #6	Final Set of Questions

Table 1. Study Session Order

It should be noted, that while we are seeking to design, and execute a traditional-style experiment that may be found in Psychology, Communication or Speech and Hearing Science, **it is not our goal to conduct every possible analysis that a research in said field would run.** Rather, we wish to demonstrate that this class of technology has new, broader applications beyond empathy building.

We use these questions to guide and shape our experimental design, measures and analysis.

STUDY DESIGN

To directly address our Research Questions we followed a known experimental design[3] from Psychology and Communication called Novice-Novice Design [7, 10, 4, 48]. In these studies, two participants are asked to perform a specific activity together (in which neither have prior experience or expertise with[4]). One such example is the "map task," developed by Anderson & Bard in the UK [4]. In the "map task," each participant has a map with landmarks on it. One participant's map has a path drawn/highlighted on it, and that participant must give the path (via conversation) to their partner, so as to recreate the path. This experimental paradigm is used to explore language, communication, approach to problem solving, shared perspective, and many more other psychological and communication questions.

The specific style of Novice-Novice design we followed will be referred to as "**W**rite **I**t - **D**o **I**t" design (**WIDI**), following the work of [7, 10]. In this experimental context, two participants are separated and assigned a ***Task***. One of the participants (***Writer Task***) is told to instruct the other participant (***Doer Task***) in building a replica of a pre-built ***Structure*** which is only visible to the *Writer*. Both participants are allowed to communicate, though only the *Writer* is allowed to view and manipulate (though not take apart) the pre-built *Structure*, while only the *Doer* is allowed to view and manipulate the raw pieces.

Ninety-six individuals (grouped in subject-pairs) engaged in WIDI IM conversations using ACES. To test our above research questions, we utilized a between-subject 2x3 factorial design. The first factor in our factorial design compared the *Writer Task* to the *Doer Task*. The second factor in our factorial design compared a ***Control Group*** (where subjects did not experience aphasic distortions) to two ***Treatment Groups***: an ***Aphasia Writer Group*** (where the participant in the *Writer*

[3]Directly addressing Research Question 1.

[4]Compared to Expert-Novice where one participant has expertise in the activity.

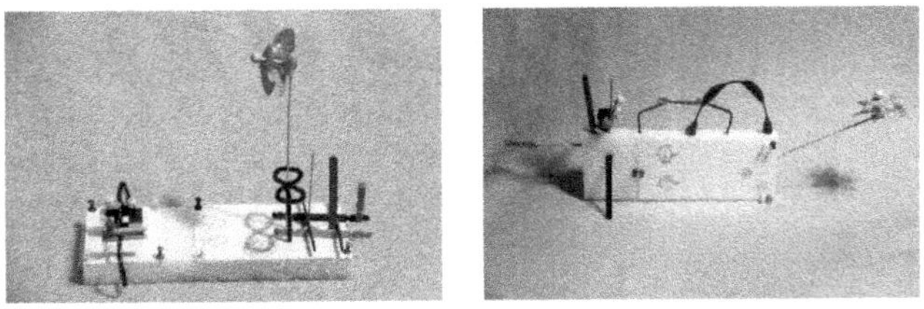

Horizontal Structure *Vertical Structure*

Figure 2. Pictures of Structures Used in Experiments

Task experienced distortions of their text first-hand) and an ***Aphasia Doer Group*** (where the participant in the *Doer Task* experienced distortions of their text first-hand)[5]. We refer to the participants who have their text distorted as having the ***Aphasia Role***[6], and to the participants receiving distorted text as having the ***Typical Role***.

All participants received the same experimental protocol, same activity, and same *Structures* to build. Subjects did not know about any other *Groups*, and were blind with respect to which *Group* they were assigned.

Experimental Protocol

Each study **Session** consisted of 6 steps lasting a total 90 minutes (Table 1). A session involved two 30-minute IM conversations between a pair of participants (a subject-pair) who did not know each other. Each participant played both *Roles*: the *Aphasia Role* in one conversation and the *Typical Role* in the other. Each participant also performed both *Tasks*: the *Writer Task* in one conversation and the *Doer Task* in the other. Participants switched *Role* and *Task* between conversations (see Table 2). Subject-pairs remained physically separated. Each member of a pair was placed in separate identical rooms with identically set-up 21" iMac computers. All questionnaires were administered digitally.

All participants completed a brief demographic survey to assess their background and prior knowledge of aphasia (if any). This allowed us to ensure equal background and pre-knowledge across *Groups*. Upon completion of these pre-study questionnaires, all participants were given an identical explanation of the study protocol. All participants (regardless of *Group*, *Role* or *Task*) were told that they would have two thirty-minute IM conversations with each other [7].

During these conversations one member of the subject-pair would take on the *Writer Task*, while the other member of the subject-pair would take on the *Doer Task*. The *Writer* would be given a completed *Structure* (assembled and glued), while the *Doer* would be given a bag with all the pieces needed to recreate said *Structure* (plus some extras). Participants were told that after the first conversation, they would switch *Tasks* (ensuring that each participant would play both *Tasks*). Only

[5]Given that the two *Tasks* require different goals, we were unsure if the language and communication would be differently effected by ACES distortions. We therefore employed three *Groups* rather than just two (Control vs. Treatment) by linking *Task* and *Role*, attempting to account for any inherent bias from the *Task*.

[6]In this experiment, participants in the *Aphasia Role* could not see the distorted message. This parallels how some individuals with aphasia do not know their errors.

[7]Participants were logged into IM accounts created for this study, not requiring subjects to disclose their own user names or passwords.

Conversation #1		Conversation #2	
User A	User B	User A	User B
APH Writer	TYP Doer	TYP Doer	APH Writer
Structure #1	*Structure #1*	*Structure #2*	*Structure #2*
APH Writer	TYP Doer	TYP Doer	APH Writer
Structure #2	*Structure #2*	*Structure #1*	*Structure #1*
APH Doer	TYP Writer	TYP Writer	APH Doer
Structure #1	*Structure #1*	*Structure #2*	*Structure #2*
APH Doer	TYP Writer	TYP Writer	APH Doer
Structure #2	*Structure #2*	*Structure #1*	*Structure #1*
TYP Doer	TYP Writer	TYP Writer	TYP Doer
Structure #1	*Structure #1*	*Structure #2*	*Structure #2*
TYP Doer	TYP Writer	TYP Writer	TYP Doer
Structure #2	*Structure #2*	*Structure #1*	*Structure #1*

Table 2. Counter Balance Permutations of *Role*, *Task*, and *Structure*
APH = Aphasia Role — *TYP* = Typical Role

participants in the *Aphasia Writer & Aphasia Doer Groups* were informed about aphasia and the aphasia distortions; both participants were told that the distortions would occur, and which participant would be having their text distorted.

Two different *Structures* (see Figure 2) were used (one for each conversation). All participants used the same *Structures* (though the order of *Structures* were fully counterbalanced). *Structures* were built from assorted craft items and toy bricks (following [7]). While some pieces did overlap between the two *Structures*, each *Structure* contained components not found in the other *Structure*. Further, for any piece in a *Structure* "alternative extras" were available (different color, size, type, etc.) for the builder to choose from. This helped ensure a lively dialogue during the conversations.

At the end of both IM conversations, participants were administered a questionnaire to gauge their perspective on conversation quality. This questionnaire consisted of short answer questions, and a series of Likert Scale questions (see Dependent Measures below). Participants were remunerated $25 for their participation in the experiment. A $30 bonus was awarded to the winning team in each *Group*, as determined by the team whose assembled *Structure* was the most complete (see *Objective Quality* in Dependent Measures bellow).

Confound Counterbalancing

Given the number of other factors inherently present in this type of experimental setup, there were at least three potential confounding effects (*Structure* order, *Task* order, and *Role* order). To help control for these potential confounding effects, we used counterbalancing, a method commonly employed to help avoid confounding from order of task and presentation. When counterbalancing, all permutations of the confounders are included in an attempt to minimize any bias due to these confounders that are not central to the experimental question.

We fully counterbalance *Structure*, *Task*, and *Role* in Table 2, requiring each pair to switch both *Role* and *Task* between conversation #1and #2. This requires a minimum of 8 subject pairs to fully counterbalance the experimental design. Our cohort of ninety-six individuals therefore consisted of three *Groups*. Thirty-two subjects were in the *Aphasia Writer Group*. thirty-two in the *Aphasia Doer Group* and thirty-two in the *Control Group*. Thus we had 16 subject-pairs in each *Group* (doubling the minimum number of subject pairs to fully counterbalance the design). Because the final data set has an equal number of logs from conversation #1 and #2, we have also counterbalanced for learning effects.

Types of Aphasia

Based on the Boston classification system[15, 42], there are numerous types of aphasia each of which can manifest in varying severities. Subsequently, there are many permutations of distortions that could be applied in this study. To ground this experiment, we leveraged one of the models created and validated during the Turing Test study of ACES[17]. This model was based on an Anomic subject named Wolf from the unpublished data files used in [29, 30] provided to the researchers by Lise Menn, University of Colorado. Individuals with Anomic aphasia have difficulty with selecting and producing correct content words, though their grammar is generally correct. For example, words may be replaced by other words that are semantically related ('birthday' with 'anniversary' or 'cake'), that have no semantic relationship (cat with airplane), that have similar phonetic sounds ('population' with 'pollution'), or non-words ('castle' with 'kaksel').

Dependent Measures

Conversation Quality can be measured in two important and different ways [23, 12]. First is ***Objective Conversation Quality***, or a measure of the effectiveness of the conversation, that can be measured consistently regardless of the persons measuring. *Objective Quality* does not take opinion or subjective judgment into account. The second measure is ***Perceived Conversation Quality***, or how each conversation partner felt about their experience or conversation. This technique dispenses with the objectively measurable features in favor of more intangible issues of assessing performance.

To produce an *Objective Quality* score, each *Structure* built during a conversation will be scored on completeness and accuracy. For both *Structures* a list of all the connections was created. A *connection* is where one piece touches another, or how one piece is deformed/shaped/placed. A connection can be graded (as applicable) on both placement and orientation (1 point each). For every piece put on a *Structure* which does not belong, one point was deducted. Both *Structures* are of the same relative complexity[8]. To ensure cross *Structure* comparisons we can use percentage completion rather than raw score.

To assess each participant's *Perceived Conversation Quality*, a post conversation questionnaire was utilized. The questionnaire consisted short answer questions, the **I**owa **C**ommunication **R**ecord (**ICR**) [13] and the **I**nterpersonal **C**ommunication **S**atisfaction **I**nventory (**ICSI**) [20]. The ICR[9] and ICSI[10] are a series of Likert Scale questions, whose mean is an indication of *Perceived Quality*.

In addition to the two measures of *Conversation Quality*, ACES logged all IM messages sent. For the *Aphasia Writer & Aphasia Doer Groups*, both intended *and* distorted versions of each message was logged. Thus, the language used during the activity can also be analyzed (see next subsection).

[8] The horizontal and vertical *Structures* have 57 and 58 connections respectively.

[9] Ten 9 point likert scale questions, the lower the ICR score, the better the conversation.

[10] Nineteen 7 point likert scale questions, the higher the ICSI score, the better the conversation. Because the measure is intended to assess spontaneous conversations, some questions did not relate to the experimental design. We therefore asked a subset of 10 question (#1,2,3,5,8,9,11,12,14,16,18).

	Control Group	Aphasia Writer Group	Aphasia Doer Group
Size (N)	32	32	32
Group Age	30.75 (10.76)	29.75 (9.41)	27.00 (11.69)
Sex (% male)	46.88	43.75	50.00
Educational Attainment †	2.00 (1.30)	1.94 (1.22)	1.44(1.37)
% Know what Aphasia is	43.75	46.88	31.25
% Taken Class on Aphasia	21.88	25.00	12.50
% Worked with Aphasia	3.12	6.25	0.00
% Family/Friend with Aphasia	3.12	3.12	0.00

Table 3. Write-it Do-it Participants
Continuous variables presented as mean (sd), p-values calculated by GEE
† Education attainment scores were 0=High School, 1=AA, 2=BS/BA, 3=MS/MA, 4=PhD

Language, Linguistics and Parts of Speech

To address the research questions directly targeted in this paper (specifically Q2 and Q3), we must examine the language uses by participants (as recorded by ACES logs). Raw number of lines (how many messages sent) and words (how many words were sent over all their messages) are coarse linguistic metrics that can be extracted from ACES logs. Parts of Speech (POS) is an important set of linguistic metrics for researchers in psychology, communication, NLP [22] as well as CMC [33, 39]. Measures such as POS, and number of lines/messages, are accepted measures for analyzing conversations, that have been used in the past to examine aphasic speech [37]

At a high level, POS can be divided into Function Words (e.g. articles, pronouns, interjections etc) and Content Words (e.g. nouns, verbs, adjectives). Function Words provide the grammatical structure to a sentence, while Content Words provide the the meaning to a sentence. To this end, we extracted Function Words and Content Words, and further subdivided Content Words into Adjectives, Verbs, Nouns, and Adverbs. There is, however, a problem with using raw occurrence of each POS, since, as users talk more (increasing the number of words generated), the occurrence of each POS will increase as well. To normalize across users, we therefore examine the ratio of each POS metric to the total words produced, rather than raw counts (allowing for comparison between the 3 *Groups*).

Analysis

To address our above Research Questions, we propose the following analytical process. By conducting a WIDI experiment, and demonstrating that participants can perform the assigned activity we demonstrate that ACES can be used within a known experimental paradigm (Question 1).

There exists a well established theory in the Psychology literature, Aphasia Adaptation Theory, that states that while aphasic distortions are imposed upon and individual by their impairment, they can learn behaviors that change their speech patterns in constructive ways [27, 19, 24]. These changes may be "preventative adaptation" or "corrective adaptation" [36, 35]. Regardless, [26] suggest that many of the "symptoms" or characteristic output of individuals with aphasia may

Language	Control Group	Aphasia Writer Group	Aphasia Doer Group
Writers' Lines	84.53 (40.63)	99.06 (54.81)	81.63 (40.90)
Writers' Words	797.60 (173.78)	602.19 (243.53)	771.88 (249.80)
Doers' Lines	57.72 (27.29)	68.47 (41.97)	56.25 (22.78)
Doers' Words	282.88 (103.72)	376.81 (192.56)	228.16 (124.67)

Table 4. Raw Count (#) of Users' Language
Values represent Mean (sd)

not be the disorder itself, but the adaptation of the individual to the impairment. However, it would be very difficult to test this theory with individuals that have aphasia, because we cannot know what those individuals *intend* to say, or examine their manipulations of their language. Given that ACES logs the intended messages sent by participants in the *Aphasia Writer & Aphasia Doer Groups*, we can compare their syntactic changes to those individuals in the *Control Group*. The existing literature attributes many specific syntactic changes made by individuals with aphasia to Adaptation Theory. Based on the theory, because patients know that it's hard to talk they concentrate on producing shorter sentences [25] with high-information words, such as nouns [38], and dropping low information words, like function words, verbs, adverbs, etc [44, 27]. If Aphasia Adaptation Theory holds, we would expect to see such changes in our logs (in the intended messages, before distortion is applied), and would we could confirm Research Questions 2 and 3

Lastly, to address Question 4 we can examine the relationship between *Perceived Quality*, *Objective Quality* and linguistic features of the conversations (see following section on Language, Linguistics and Parts of Speech).

Statistical Tests

The scalar nature of our quantitative measures would suggest using a Two-Sample Wilcoxon Rank-Sum (Mann-Whitney) test, a more conservative metric than a T-Test as it makes no assumptions about the data distribution (normal or otherwise). However, a Rank-Sum does not account for the correlated nature of the data: each pair of participants had two conversations, and their interactions will clearly be correlated. Generalized Estimating Equations (GEE) [18] with a linear regression[11] were used to account for these correlations.

To test for correlations, we likewise used GEEs to account for the correlation in data. In this correlation analysis, we produce a coefficient that indicates the slope of the regression (and the direction of correlation). However, this coefficient is not the same as an R^2 or correlation coefficient, and cannot be treated as such. Therefore, the GEE tests' coefficients are not as easy to interpret as a Pearson's Coefficient. We therefore *also* ran a pairwise correlation coefficient using the Pearson's Correlation test. Sadly, Pearson's Correlation test does not account for the correlated nature of the data, so we cannot report the p-value, and the calculated correlation coefficient value should only be treated as an indication of the correlation magnitude (and not a hard-and-fast 'true' value). Pearson's Correlation coefficient values range from -1.0 (negatively correlated) to 1.0 (positively correlated).

[11]Linear regressions were used to test associations with scalar responses as outcomes.

Writer's Language	Control Group	Aphasia Writer Group	Relative Change
% Function Words	0.43 (0.02)	0.40 (0.06)	▽
% Content Words	0.57 (0.02)	0.60 (0.06)	△
% Adjectives	0.12 (0.03)	0.13 (0.03)	–
% Verbs	0.13 (0.02)	0.11 (0.02)	▼
% Nouns	0.28 (0.03)	0.32 (0.05)	▲
% Adverbs	0.05 (0.01)	0.04 (0.01)	▼

A. Control & Aphasia Writer Groups' Comparative Statistics
Arrows Indicate direction of change from Control to Aphasia Writer Group

Writer's Language	Aphasia Doer Group	Aphasia Writer Group	Relative Change
% Function Words	0.43 (0.03)	0.40 (0.06)	▽
% Content Words	0.57 (0.03)	0.60 (0.06)	△
% Adjectives	0.11 (0.02)	0.13 (0.03)	△
% Verbs	0.13 (0.02)	0.11 (0.02)	▼
% Nouns	0.27 (0.03)	0.32 (0.05)	▲
% Adverbs	0.05 (0.01)	0.04 (0.01)	▼

B. Aphasia Doer & Aphasia Writer Groups' Comparative Statistics
Arrows Indicate change direction from Aphasia Doer to Aphasia Writer Group

Table 5. Comparative Statistics for Adaptation Theory
Values represent Mean (sd) Part of Speech usage
▽△ is significance $p \leq 0.05$, ▲▼ is significance $p \leq 0.01$ with GEE

By having a fully counterbalanced study design, we minimize the impact of learning/order effects. For a robust analysis, we examine the impact of order/learning through GEE, comparing both conversation quality, and linguistic measures.

SUBJECTS

All 96 participants did not know each other, and were assigned randomly to a *Group*, *Task* and *Role*. Participants were recruited from a large state school, and the surrounding town. No particular prior knowledge about aphasia was required for inclusion. At the beginning of each session, we asked participants a series of demographic questions. Table 3 contains the mean and standard deviation for participants in each cohort. In addition, we tested to see if our cohorts' makeup was statistically different (Table 3). There were no statistical differences in age, gender, educational attainment, or prior knowledge of aphasia between any of the *Groups*.

RESULTS

All participants in our study were able to understand and perform the WIDI activity. No subject-pair was able to complete the activity (given that the thirty minute time provided was too short). Across all three *Groups*, the *Writers* communicated more (produced statistical more Lines and Words) as compared to the *Doers* (*p≤0.01*), see Table 4.

Overall, there was a variation in structure completeness (*Objective Quality*) within and between the *Control Group* (μ=31.52%, sd=13.98, histogram:), *Aphasia Writer Group* (μ=17.23%, sd=6.12, histogram:) and *Aphasia Doer Group* (μ=30.71%, sd=18.19, histogram:). In statistical analysis, the difference between the *Aphasia Writer Group* and both the *Control Group* and *Aphasia Doer Group* was statistically significant (*p<0.01*). However, there was no statistical difference between the *Control Group* and the *Aphasia Doer Group* (*p=0.84*).

Quality Measure	Control Group	Aphasia Writer Group	Aphasia Doer Group
Objective (%)	31.52 (13.98)	17.23 (6.12)	30.71 (18.19)
Doer's ICSI	5.48 (1.25)	4.64 (1.31)	4.91 (1.25)
Writer's ICSI	5.15 (1.41)	4.53 (1.22)	4.99 (1.07)
Doer's ICR	3.74 (1.17)	4.79 (1.15)	4.13 (1.14)
Writer's ICR	3.79 (1.11)	4.87 (1.20)	4.26 (0.96)

A. Summary Statistics for **Conversation Quality**

Values represents Mean (sd) of each measure of Conversation Quality

Quality Measure	CG to AWG	CG to ADG	ADG to AWG
Objective	▼	–	▼
Doer's ICSI	▽	–	–
Writer's ICSI	▽	–	–
Doer's ICR	▲	–	△
Writer's ICR	▲	–	△

B. Comparative Statistics for **Conversation Quality**

Arrows Indicate change in direction

▽△ *is significance $p \leq 0.05$,* ▲▼ *is significance $p \leq 0.01$ with GEE*

Table 6. Comparative and Summary Statistics for *Conversation Quality*
ICR (lower is better), ICSI (higher is better)
Control Group (CG), *Aphasia Writer Group* (AWG), *Aphasia Doer Group* (ADG

Aphasia Adaptation Theory

To examine the presence (or absence) of aphasia adaptation theory, we compared the intended language and POS usage for participants playing the *Aphasia Role* with participants in the *Control Group* (performing the same *Task*). When comparing the *Writer* in the *Control Group* (no distortion) to the *Writer* in the *Aphasia Writer Group* (with distortions) we see a large shift in language (Table 5A). While the number of messages (Table 4) statistically remained the same ($p > 0.05$), the number of words fell ($p \leq 0.01$). When examining what types of words were reduced or sacrificed, we observed that participants sacrificed function words, verbs, and adverbs, while increasing noun production.

When comparing the *Doer* in the *Control Group* to the *Doer* in the *Aphasia Doer Group* (with distortions) we see no statistically significant shift in language. Number of lines, words and POS distributions remained unchanged ($p > 0.05$). Subsequently, when we compared the *Writer* in the *Aphasia Writer Group* (with distortions) to the *Writer* in the *Aphasia Doer Group* (without distortions) we observed the same relative change as seen between the *Control Group* and the *Aphasia Writer Group* (Table 5B).

Conversation Quality

When we compare the conversation quality between the three *Groups* (Table 6B), we see that across all 5 measures of *Conversation Quality*, there is a statistical difference between the conversation quality in the *Control Group* and the *Aphasia Writer Group*. We also see several significant differences between the *Aphasia Writer Group* and *Aphasia Doer Group* (though not in the ICSI measures). There was no statistical difference between the conversation quality of the *Control Group* and the *Aphasia Doer Group*. Though not shown, there was no statistical difference in *Perceived Quality* between the *Writer* and *Doer* within each of the three cohorts[12].

[12]Lack of statistical significance does not equate to statistical similarity. Further analysis would be needed to prove the distributions are the same.

	Objective	Writer ICSI	Writer ICR	Doer ICSI	Doer ICR
Objective	–	–	–	–	–
Writer ICSI	0.09	–	–	–	–
Writer ICR	-0.22	-0.60 ‡	–	–	–
Doer ICSI	0.14	0.22	-0.10	–	–
Doer ICR	-0.08	-0.25	0.11	-0.84 ‡	–

A. **Control Group**

	Objective	Writer ICSI	Writer ICR	Doer ICSI	Doer ICR
Objective	–	–	–	–	–
Writer ICSI	0.17	–	–	–	–
Writer ICR	-0.36 †	-0.74‡	–	–	–
Doer ICSI	-0.02	0.10	-0.09	–	–
Doer ICR	-0.05	-0.13	0.15	-0.75 ‡	–

B. **Aphasia Writer Group**

	Objective	Writer ICSI	Writer ICR	Doer ICSI	Doer ICR
Objective	–	–	–	–	–
Writer ICSI	-0.03	–	–	–	–
Writer ICR	0.30	-0.39 †	–	–	–
Doer ICSI	0.44†	-0.27	0.34 †	–	–
Doer ICR	-0.11	0.41†	-0.12	-0.72‡	–

C. **Aphasia Doer Group**

Table 7. Correlations between *Conversation Quality*
Pearson's Correlation Coefficients for Indication of Magnitude
† is $p \leq 0.05$, ‡ is $p \leq 0.01$ with GEE
ICR (lower is better), ICSI (higher is better)

In theory, the 5 measures of *Conversation Quality* should all reflect the same thing: the quality of the conversation. To examine the inter-relationship between these five measures, we calculated correlations between each measure of *Conversation Quality* using a GEE. For those measure of *Conversation Quality* that were statistically correlated, we present Pearson's Correlations coefficients in a correlation matrix (Table 7).

Across all three *Groups*, the only two consistently significant correlations were between the measures of *Perceived Quality* (ICSI and ICR). Further, the correlation between *Writers*' ICSI and *Writers*' ICR, and between the *Doers*' ICSI and *Doers*' ICR are both negative with a high effect size. Having a negative correlation is expected, because while the higher the ICSI outcome is the better the conversation, the ICR uses lower scores to signify better conversations.There was *no* significant correlation found between *Objective Quality* and any of the *Perceived Conversation Quality* measures.

DISCUSSION

We now discuss the results within the context of our four Research Questions.

Question 1

Can ACES be used in a known experimental paradigm from Psychology, Communication or Speech and Hearing Science?

This experiment demonstrates that ACES can be integrated within a typical experimental design from the Psychology and Communication literature. Participants were able to understand the activity and their assigned *Tasks*. Participants also had varied objective performance, which was to be expected given the existing literature on this class of study design [7, 10, 4, 48]. Further, with the introduction of a distorted or impaired communication channel (*Aphasia Writer Group*), performance decreased[13] (also, as would be expected). We can therefore see that ACES can be integrated in traditional research setting.

Question 2

Can ACES' distortions impact conversation style in a known way?

Our analysis did find striking similarities between the intended messages sent by our participants with distortions, and behavior described in Aphasia Adaptation Theory. When *Writers* had their text distorted, they increased the percentage of words that were nouns while sacrificing verbs, adverbs, and function words. This suggest that *Writers* adopted a more curt method of communication, focusing on the object rather than the action. In other words, participants were adapting their language in a way that is evocative of how real non-fluent aphasics behave[14]. These findings show that ACES interactions produce known changes in conversation style. Perhaps more importantly, the parallels between our subjects adaptations and individuals with aphasia lends strong supporting evidence that the ACES emulator is suitable for further psychological testing.

Question 3

Can transcripts of intended *conversation style be useful?*

One of the challenges with Aphasia Adaptation Theory is that it concerns what an individual does (consciously or subconsciously) to adapt to their impairment *before* communicating and having their language be distorted. Using traditional transcripts containing only what an individual "said" would not be able to differentiate what participants changed in their language, versus which changes were generated due to distortions. Therefore our findings and their support for Aphasia Adaptation Theory could only have been conducted and uncovered with transcripts of *intended* messages. ACES, coupled with these findings, opens the door to other questions about user adaptation and changes to linguistic distortions (from aphasia or other language disorders).

Question 4

Can ACES be used to uncover new understandings of interpersonal interaction?

Our analysis of *Conversation Quality* uncovered that there is no relationship between *Objective Quality* and *Perceived Quality* (Table 7), however our two measures of *Perceived Quality* were highly correlated. Further, for both *Objective Quality* and *Perceived Quality*, Aphasic Distortions made *Conversation Quality* worse[15] (see Table 6).

[13] Interestingly, we did not see a difference between the *Control Group* and the *Aphasia Doer Group*. This observation opens up a new question; is the Shannon Information [41] sent from the *Doer* to the *Writer* not as important as the information conveyed from the *Writer* to the *Doer* (so therefore any distortion does not matter or has minimal impact)? This may be supported by the statistically lower number of Lines and Words being sent from the *Doer* to the *Writer*. Another explanation is that the "amount" of information that needs to get across from the *Doer* to the *Writer* smaller/easier to understand (e.g. short pragmatics or continuers like "ok", or "got it"). It is outside of the scope of this paper to explicitly measure Shannon Information in each message, so we therefore cannot assess if the Writer has more (in quantity) information, or more complex information to convey. However we see this as a promising future research question.

[14] While this one study isn't definitive "proof" of Adaptation Theory, it does strengthen the arguments for the theory of Aphasic adaptation.

[15] While we do not see statistically significant differences in ICSI scores between the Aphasic Writer and Aphasic Doer Cohorts, this may be due to statistical power.

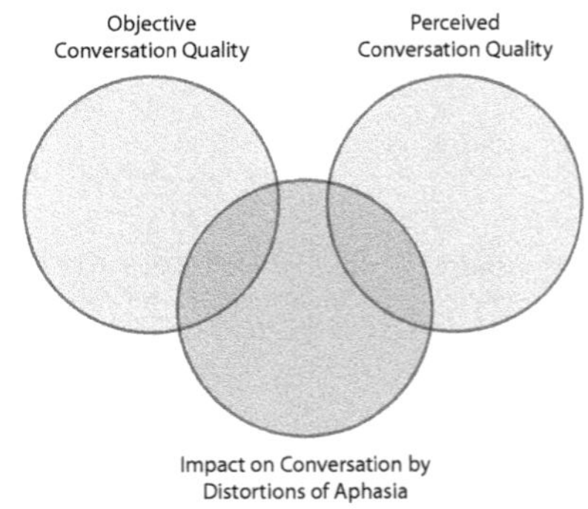

Figure 3. Venn Diagram of Conversation Quality and Distortion Impact

Thus, when considering these two findings in concert, we conclude that distortions of aphasia (by ACES) impact *Conversation Quality* in two distinct, and independent ways, as illustrated by Figure 3, by affecting both the product (or goal) of the conversation (*Objective Quality*), as well as the interpersonal interaction(*Perceived Quality*). These new understandings about interpersonal communication are clearly grounded in the quality of the measures used. While the Objective Conversation Quality is, by definition, objectively observable, perceived quality is not. However, by having two measures that have a high effect size correlation (*correlation coefficient* > 0.6) and are highly significant ($p < 0.05$), we can infer that they are valid and verifiable measures. This supports the conclusion that aphasia (or, to be precise, ACES' distortions which simulate aphasia) impacts both how we feel about the interaction as well as the conversation output quality/goal. It is important to note that gathering this type of user feedback (perceived conversation quality metrics via questionnaires) would be extremely difficult with individuals who have aphasia. These findings, and the unique ability to gather them from "typical" individuals using ACES highlights how ACES is a rich platform for uncovering new phenomena.

LIMITATIONS

Whenever there is interaction that is not face-to-face, many backchannels (e.g. gestures or intonation) are lost. This is a limitation (or control) of many study designs and many forms of CMC (e.g. IM or Email). While this limitation is important to note, Novice-Novice Designs are well accepted study designs to investigate interpersonal communication. Further, individuals with aphasia actively use many CMC applications [2], and their linguistic deficits in writing are generally consistent with those of the person's spoken language [6].

IMPLICATIONS & FUTURE WORK

Beyond explicitly answering our four research questions, we see multiple implications of the findings from our study for both technologists and non-technologists.

CMC Emulation Systems

While prior studies on ACES have shown the realism of its distortions[17] and its impact on improving user empathy[16], this is the first study to show that CMC emulation systems can impact *how* users communicate and the quality of their conversations. Moreover, these changes appear to be similar to those observed in individuals with aphasia. To our knowledge, this is the first such system demonstration of its kind (for any disorder).

These findings (coupled with the prior work on ACES) suggest the need to create system that emulate other language[16] or perception disorders. Beyond explicit disorders, technologists could investigate systems that build empathy and study communication in other contexts (e.g. English as a second language, or exposure to cultural differences). ACES research shows that CMC systems can do more than just facilitate communication. They can build empathy[16] and explicitly study communication when one interlocutor's speech is impaired.

Aphasia & Communication

We believe a rich area of future exploration is using ACES-like systems to test theories of communication, and exploring some of the current gaps in understanding how people with disorders communicate. Given the strong initial results and rich data set collected during this experiment, there are many more exciting questions that may be asked of this data. What linguistic changes (be they semantic, syntactic or structural) impact *Conversation Quality*? What types of questions asked by participants provoke the most useful responses? As alluded to above, what is the difference in Shannon Information between the two *Tasks*? owever these and other questions fall well outside the scope of this paper and this publication venue, given its technical grounding. Ideally, these questions would be addressed by Psychologists and published in Psychology research journals. Given how many provocative questions have emerged from this study, we are highly optimistic that our work here has demonstrated that this new technology has a wide variety of future applications.

Based on the new findings related to the relationship between types of *Conversation Quality*, we hypothesize that there are two aspects of conversation that can be targeted for "improvement." First, we can attempt to mediate the information conveyed to generate a more productive output (*Objective Quality*). We can also attempt to change how people feel and react to challenging interactions (*Perceived Quality*). While both goals are important, it is the task of improving perceived conversation that **must** be targeted, since improving only the objective output itself may not improve the perceived quality (since the interaction will still be challenging). Given previous work on ACES improving empathy[16], understanding and patience for conversation partners, we hypothesize that by providing users (and potential conversation partners, clinicians, and/or doctors) with the experience of communicating with aphasia (through ACES), we can effectively improve perceived conversation quality (this would need to be verified in a future experiment.)

These future directions of ACES beg the questions " how far can this system be pushed?" and "where does the line between emulation and broad implications for treatment lie?" Given the parallels between adaptation theory shown in this paper, and the turing test validation shown in [17], we are optimistic. However, exploring this relationship for aphasia, or other disorder emulation, is an important direction for future exploration.

[16]ACES-like systems could be tailored to their users by analyzing their linguistic patterns and word usage (e.g. by analyzing emails), thus personalizing the distortions.

Research with Individuals with Impairments

Finally, it should be noted that to conduct this study we recruited 96 participants, none of whom had aphasia. Subsequently, this study required no special accommodations or extra time to accommodate a language impairment. All instructions *and* questions were given once, and participants' responses to questions were easily understood. This is a striking contrast to the additional complexity of running a study with participants that have an impairment [21]. As a result, more participants were able to be included (increasing N), over a shorter time-frame (3 months), with less financial cost. Further, we were able to control the exact manifestation of aphasia, which would not be possible in a traditional setting. These are benefits for technologists and non-technologists alike. For example, imagine that a communication researcher theorizes that, if an individual with aphasia alters their language in some particular way or uses an new UI, they will have an improved experience with their conversation partner. ACES could be used to test this theory, examining such an intervention's impact on the language and conversation quality. Then, based on these initial findings, the researcher could then run a better designed large-N study with individuals who have aphasia (or re-run the design to adjust for the findings).

CONCLUSION

This paper illustrates how a CMC impairment emulation system (ACES) can be integrated within a traditional Psychology and Communication research experiment. Not only did our participants understand and complete the activity, but we appear to provide new evidence towards validating an existing theory in the Psychology literature on aphasia. Moreover, this supporting evidence would be nearly impossible to construe without a system like ACES. Further, our ACES study was able to uncover new understandings about interpersonal communication and its impact on *Conversation Quality*. By situating ACES within this "traditional" experimental context, we show that this new technology can provide many unique and important benefits to researchers (control, customization, low cost, user feedback, and pre-impairment intent) that are not present when working directly with individuals that have an impairment. We believe that our novel and important findings for researchers in Psychology, Speech and Hearing, and Communication research. Further, the findings highlight the need for and potential applications of ACES-like CMC systems as a new direction for HCI research with direct and tangible real-world impact.

ACKNOWLEDGMENTS

We would like to thank our participants. We would also like to thank Gary Dell and Sarah Brown-Schmidt whose advice throughout this experimental design, execution and analysis proved invaluable.

REFERENCES

1. Al Mahmud, A., Gerits, R., and Martens, J. Xtag: designing an experience capturing and sharing tool for persons with aphasia. In *Proceedings of the 6th Nordic Conference on Human-Computer Interaction: Extending Boundaries*, ACM (2010), 325–334.
2. Al Mahmud, A., and Martens, J. Understanding email communication of persons with aphasia. In *Extended abstracts on Human factors in computing systems*, ACM (2011), 1195–1200.
3. Allen, M., McGrenere, J., and Purves, B. The design and field evaluation of phototalk: a digital image communication application for people. In *Proceedings of the 9th international ACM SIGACCESS conference on Computers and accessibility*, ACM (2007), 187–194.
4. Bard, E., Anderson, A., Chen, Y., Nicholson, H., Havard, C., and Dalzel-Job, S. Let's you do that: Sharing the cognitive burdens of dialogue. *Journal of Memory and Language 57*, 4 (2007), 616–641.
5. Benson, D. *Aphasia, Alexia and Agraphia: Clinical Neurology and Neurosurgery Monographs*. Churchill Livingstone, New York, 1979.
6. Benson, D. *The neurology of thinking*. Oxford University Press, USA, 1994.
7. Beun, R., and Cremers, A. Object reference in a shared domain of conversation. *Pragmatics &# 38; Cognition, 6 1*, 2 (1998), 121–152.
8. Bos, N., Olson, J., Gergle, D., Olson, G., and Wright, Z. Effects of four computer-mediated communications channels on trust development. In *Proceedings of the SIGCHI conference on Human factors in computing systems: Changing our world, changing ourselves*, ACM (2002), 135–140.
9. Boyd-Graber, J., Nikolova, S., Moffatt, K., Kin, K., Lee, J., Mackey, L., Tremaine, M., and Klawe, M. Participatory design with proxies: developing a desktop-pda system to support people with aphasia. In *Proceedings of the SIGCHI conference on Human Factors in computing systems*, ACM (2006), 151–160.
10. Brown-Schmidt, S., and Tanenhaus, M. Real-time investigation of referential domains in unscripted conversation: A targeted language game approach. *Cognitive science 32*, 4 (2008), 643–684.
11. Colby, K., Weber, S., and Hilf, F. Artificial paranoia. *Artificial Intelligence 2*, 1 (1971), 1–25.
12. Cushman, W., and Rosenberg, D. Human factors in product design. *Advances in human factors/ergonomics 14* (1991).
13. Duck, S., Rutt, D., HOY, M., and STREJC, H. Some evident truths about conversations in everyday relationships all communications are not created equal. *Human communication research 18*, 2 (1991), 228–267.
14. Giles, H. *A study of speech patterns in social interaction: Accent evaluation and accent change*. PhD thesis, University of Bristol, Bristol, UK, 1971.
15. Goodglass, H., Goodglass, and Kaplan. *Boston Diagnostic Aphasia Examination: Stimulus Cards–Short Form*. Lippincott Williams & Wilkins, 2001.
16. Hailpern, J., Danilevsky, M., Harris, A., Karahalios, K., Dell, G., and Hengst, J. Aces: Promoting empathy towards aphasia through language distortion emulation software. In *Proceedings of the ACM's SIG CHI Conference 2011 Conference.*, CHI 2011, ACM (Vancouver, BC Canada, 2011).
17. Hailpern, J., Danilevsky, M., and Karahalios, K. Aces: Aphasia emulation, realism, and the turing test. In *Proceedings of the ACM SIGACCESS- ASSETS 2011 Conference.*, ASSETS 2011, ACM (Dundee, Scotland, 2011).
18. Hardin, J., and Hilbe, J. *Generalized estimating equations*. Chapman and Hall/CRC, New York, 2003.
19. Hartsuiker, R., and Kolk, H. Syntactic facilitation in agrammatic sentence production. *Brain and Language 62*, 2 (1998), 221–254.
20. Hecht, M. The conceptualization and measurement of interpersonal communication satisfaction. *Human Communication Research 4*, 3 (1978), 253–264.
21. Henry, S. *Just ask: integrating accessibility throughout design*. Lulu. com, 2007.
22. Jurafsky, D., Martin, J., Kehler, A., Vander Linden, K., and Ward, N. *Speech and language processing: An introduction to natural language processing, computational linguistics, and speech recognition*, vol. 163. MIT Press, 2000.
23. Kirvesoja, H. *Experimental ergonomic evaluation with user trials: EEE product development procedures*. Oulun yliopisto, 2001.
24. Kolk, H. A time-based approach to agrammatic production. *Brain and Language 50*, 3 (1995), 282–303.
25. Kolk, H., and Heeschen, C. Adaptation symptoms and impairment symptoms in broca's aphasia. *Aphasiology 4*, 3 (1990), 221–231.
26. Kolk, H., and Heeschen, G. The malleability of agrammatic symptoms: A reply to hesketh and bishop. *Aphasiology 10*, 1 (1996), 81–96.
27. Kolk, H., and Van Grunsven, M. Agrammatism as a variable phenomenon. *Cognitive Neuropsychology* (1985).
28. Leshed, G. *Automated language-based feedback for teamwork behaviors*. PhD thesis, Cornell University, 2009.
29. Menn, L., Kamio, A., Hayashi, M., Fujita, I., Sasanuma, S., and Boles, L. The role of empathy in sentence production: A functional analysis of aphasic and normal elicited narratives in Japanese and English. *Function and Structure* (1998), 317–356.

30. Menn, L., Reilly, K., Hayashi, M., Kamio, A., Fujita, I., and Sasanuma, S. The interaction of preserved pragmatics and impaired syntax in Japanese and English aphasic speech. *Brain and language 61*, 2 (1998), 183–225.

31. Moffatt, K., McGrenere, J., Purves, B., and Klawe, M. The participatory design of a sound and image enhanced daily planner for people with aphasia. In *Proceedings of the SIGCHI conference on Human factors in computing systems*, ACM (2004), 407–414.

32. Nguyen, D., and Rosé, C. Language use as a reflection of socialization in online communities. *ACL HLT 2011* (2011), 76.

33. Niederhoffer, K. G., and Pennebaker, J. W. Linguistic style matching in social interaction. *Journal of Language and Social Psychology 21*, 4 (2002), 337–360.

34. Piper, A., Weibel, N., and Hollan, J. Introducing multimodal paper-digital interfaces for speech-language therapy. In *Proceedings of the 12th international ACM SIGACCESS conference on Computers and accessibility*, ACM (2010), 203–210.

35. Ruiter, M., Kolk, H., and Rietveld, T. Speaking in ellipses: The effect of a compensatory style of speech on functional communication in chronic agrammatism. *Neuropsychological rehabilitation 20*, 3 (2010), 423–458.

36. Ruiter, M. B. *Speaking in ellipses: The effect of a compensatory style of speech on functional communication in chronic agrammatism*. PhD thesis, Radboud University Nijmegen, Nijmegen, Netherlands, 2008.

37. Saffran, E., Berndt, R., and Schwartz, M. The quantitative analysis of agrammatic production: Procedure and data. *Brain and Language 37*, 3 (1989), 440–479.

38. Salis, C., and Edwards, S. Treatment of written verb and written sentence production in an individual with aphasia: A clinical study. *Aphasiology 24*, 9 (2010), 1051–1063.

39. Scissors, L., Gill, A., Geraghty, K., and Gergle, D. In cmc we trust: the role of similarity. In *Proceedings of the 27th international conference on Human factors in computing systems*, ACM (2009), 527–536.

40. Scissors, L., Gill, A., and Gergle, D. Linguistic mimicry and trust in text-based cmc. In *Proceedings of the 2008 ACM conference on Computer supported cooperative work*, ACM (2008), 277–280.

41. Shannon, C., and Weaver, W. *The mathematical theory of communication*, vol. 19. University of Illinois Press Urbana, 1962.

42. Shewan, C., and Kertesz, A. Reliability and validity characteristics of the western aphasia battery (wab). *Journal of Speech and Hearing Disorders 45*, 3 (1980), 308.

43. Takagi, H., Asakawa, C., Fukuda, K., and Maeda, J. Accessibility designer: visualizing usability for the blind. In *ACM SIGACCESS Accessibility and Computing*, no. 77-78, ACM (2004), 177–184.

44. Thompson, C., Ballard, K., Tait, M., Weintraub, S., and Mesulam, M. Patterns of language decline in non-fluent primary progressive aphasia. *Aphasiology 11*, 4-5 (1997), 297–321.

45. Toma, C. Perceptions of trustworthiness online: The role of visual and textual information. In *Proceedings of the 2010 ACM conference on Computer supported cooperative work*, ACM (2010), 13–22.

46. Wang, H., and Fussell, S. Groups in groups: Conversational similarity in online multicultural multiparty brainstorming. In *Proceedings of the 2010 ACM conference on Computer supported cooperative work*, ACM (2010), 351–360.

47. Weizenbaum, J. Contextual understanding by computers. *Communications of the ACM 10*, 8 (1967), 480.

48. Wilkes-Gibbs, D., and Clark, H. Coordinating beliefs in conversation. *Journal of Memory and Language 31*, 2 (1992), 183–194.

49. Wilson, J., Straus, S., and McEvily, B. All in due time: The development of trust in computer-mediated and face-to-face teams. *Organizational Behavior and Human Decision Processes 99*, 1 (2006), 16–33.

Understanding Visual Attention of Teams in Dynamic Medical Settings through Vital Signs Monitor Use

Diana S. Kusunoki[1], Aleksandra Sarcevic[1], Zhan Zhang[1], Randall S. Burd[2]

College of Information Science and Technology[1]
Drexel University
Philadelphia, PA 19104
{diana.s.kusunoki, aleksarc, zz87}@drexel.edu

Emergency Trauma and Burn Services[2]
Children's National Medical Center
Washington, DC 20010
rburd@childrensnational.org

ABSTRACT
The purpose of this study was to understand how vital signs monitors support teamwork during trauma resuscitation—the fast-paced and information-rich process of stabilizing critically injured patients. We analyzed 12 videos of simulated resuscitations to characterize trauma team monitor use. To structure our observations, we adopted the feedback loop concept. Our results showed that the monitor was used frequently, especially by team leaders and anesthesiologists. We identified three patterns of monitor use: (i) periods with a low frequency of short looks (glances) to maintain overall process awareness; (ii) periods with a medium frequency of long looks (scrutiny) to monitor trends in patient status; and (iii) peaks with a high frequency of glances to maintain attention on both the patient and monitor during critical tasks. Approximately 75% of looks were 3 seconds or shorter, but many looks (25%) ranged between 3 and 26 seconds. Our results have implications for improving displays by presenting the status of the patient's physiological systems and team activities.

Author Keywords
Visual attention; information behavior; video analysis; health informatics; trauma resuscitation; feedback loop.

ACM Classification Keywords
H.5.3 [Groups & Organization Interfaces]: Collaborative Computing, Computer-Supported Cooperative Work, Organizational Design; K.4.3 [Organizational Impacts]: Computer-Supported Collaborative Work

General Terms
Design; Human Factors

INTRODUCTION
Trauma resuscitation is a complex, dynamic, and safety-critical process in which multidisciplinary medical teams treat critically-ill patients early after injury. Although seeing and examining the patient already provides important information, monitoring patient status using the vital signs monitor is essential for determining indications for and responses to life-saving treatments. The vital signs monitor, however, provides limited contextual information about patient status, team activities, treatments and outcomes. To obtain and interpret contextual information about the patient, past and current activities, administered treatments and outcomes, as well as pending tasks, team members mainly rely on verbal and non-verbal communication. Although communication is essential for team situation awareness and ensuring safe patient care, information reported verbally is often inaccurately transmitted or inaudible [4]. Poor information sharing has been observed even among experienced trauma teams, resulting in procedural errors, inefficiency, and delays [27]. In an environment where providers' attention is limited, it is important to assess the feasibility of supplementing existing displays with information that supports teamwork and decision making. In this paper, we examine the use of the vital signs monitor to derive design requirements for additional information displays.

In the visual attention literature, there are many studies of gaze patterns across a range of tasks, including car driving [21], laparoscopic surgery [17], and information search [12]. By using eye-tracking equipment, these studies examined search patterns and dwell times of individual participants engaged in visual problem-solving tasks while looking at a single display. A recent study of the distribution of visual attention in anesthesia providers has shown that 30% of visual attention was directed to the vital signs monitor, particularly during crisis situations [23]. Few studies, however, have explored the distribution of visual attention that interdisciplinary medical teams use to gather the information for maintaining situation awareness in dynamic domains such as trauma resuscitation. We believe that knowledge obtained through this type of study will offer valuable insight into the design of information technology that supports complex and dynamic teamwork processes. In this work, we analyzed vital signs monitor use during resuscitation to understand how trauma teams might use other types of information displays in this setting.

Information Displays in Safety-Critical Teamwork
A common approach to supporting information sharing and situation awareness among medical teams is the use of status whiteboards and large wall displays. Information

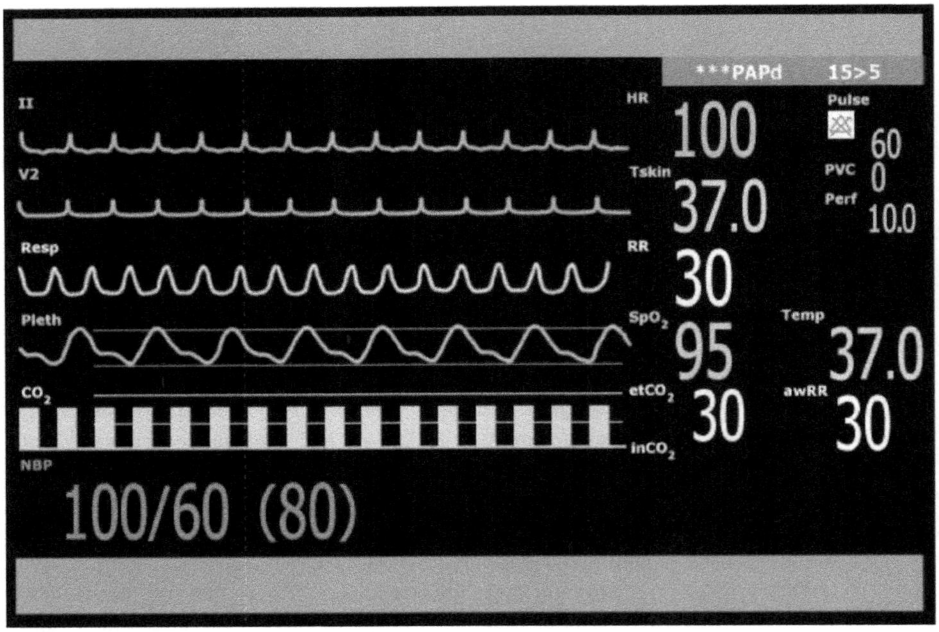

Waveforms		
II	EKG lead selection	C
V2	EKG lead placement site	C
Resp	Respiration	B
Pleth	Plethysmography (lung volume/capacity)	B
CO_2	Carbon Dioxide levels	A, B
Numerical Values		
HR	Heart Rate	C
Pulse	Pulse	C
Tskin	Skin Temperature	S
PVC	Premature Ventricular Contractions (arrhythmia)	C
Perf	Perfusion (blood flow)	C
NBP	Noninvasive Blood Pressure	C
RR	Respiratory Rate	B
SpO_2	O_2 Saturation Percentage	A, B
Temp	Temperature	S
$etCO_2$	End-Tidal (exhaled) CO_2	A, B
$inCO_2$	Inspired (inhaled) CO_2	A, B
awRR	Airway Respiratory Rate	A, B

Figure 1: Vital signs monitor displaying waveforms and numerical values of vital signs. The table on the right defines the displayed information. The last column indicates the ATLS protocol steps in which this information is used.

displays have been proposed for augmenting team situation awareness in a variety of medical settings, including emergency departments [25,26], operating rooms [3,5,20], critical care units [29], anesthesia [7], and even patient rooms. These displays and status boards have been shown to support both collocated and distributed work by facilitating task coordination, resource planning, communication, and problem solving. Effective integration and display of large amounts of data has also been used for improving awareness in other safety-critical settings, including traffic control rooms [13,14,15] and nuclear power plant control rooms [19]. As a safety-critical, socio-technical system, trauma resuscitation remains one of the few medical settings without information technologies that support teamwork. Introducing large displays that include vital signs data augmented with contextual information about patient status and team tasks could provide additional support for maintaining situation awareness.

BACKGROUND & CONCEPTUAL FRAMEWORK

Trauma Resuscitation Process Overview

Trauma resuscitation is a specialized medical domain in which critically injured patients are treated in a dedicated room in the emergency department (*trauma bay*). During resuscitation, an interdisciplinary team of medical specialists (*trauma team*) must identify and treat potentially life-threatening injuries, with the need for a critical decision about once a minute [8]. The resuscitation process is one of the most demanding in healthcare, requiring the team to focus on a common task for a short time period (on average, 20 minutes) while adapting to complex and changing circumstances driven by patient injury. Unlike other clinical settings, patient management during resuscitation relies mostly on emerging rather than existing information.

To improve efficiency, reduce errors, and guide the initial evaluation of patient injuries, the Advanced Trauma Life Support (ATLS) protocol has been developed and adopted by medical professionals worldwide [1]. The protocol includes the basics of early trauma care and focuses on identifying life-threatening conditions by adhering to the following sequence of steps ("ABCDE"): (1) **A**irway assessment and maintenance [A]; (2) **B**reathing assessment and ventilation [B]; (3) **C**irculation assessment [C]; (4) **D**isability or neurological status assessment [D]; and (5) **E**xposure and environmental control [E]. These initial assessment and management procedures are done sequentially, in the order of importance, with periodic reevaluation of each system to identify any deterioration in the patient status [1]. Steps following the initial evaluation include a head-to-toe evaluation for other injuries (Secondary survey [S]) and the initiation of definitive care [1]. Although patient evaluation is complex and sometimes requires deviation from the protocol, this structure provided a framework for analyzing the tasks performed by the team.

Vital Signs Monitor

Because adequate resuscitation is best assessed by improvement in physiological parameters (e.g., heart rate, blood pressure, pulse), the vital signs monitor is central to patient care and team performance. The monitor is currently the only electronic display in the trauma bay at most hospitals. The information displayed on vital signs monitors, however, is based solely on data read from sensors attached to the patient's body. This sensor-based data is displayed in the form of waveforms or numerical values (or both), and includes heart rate (HR), blood pressure, pulse, oxygen saturation levels (SpO_2), carbon dioxide levels (CO_2) inhaled and exhaled from the lungs, respiratory rate (Resp and RR), and temperature (Temp and

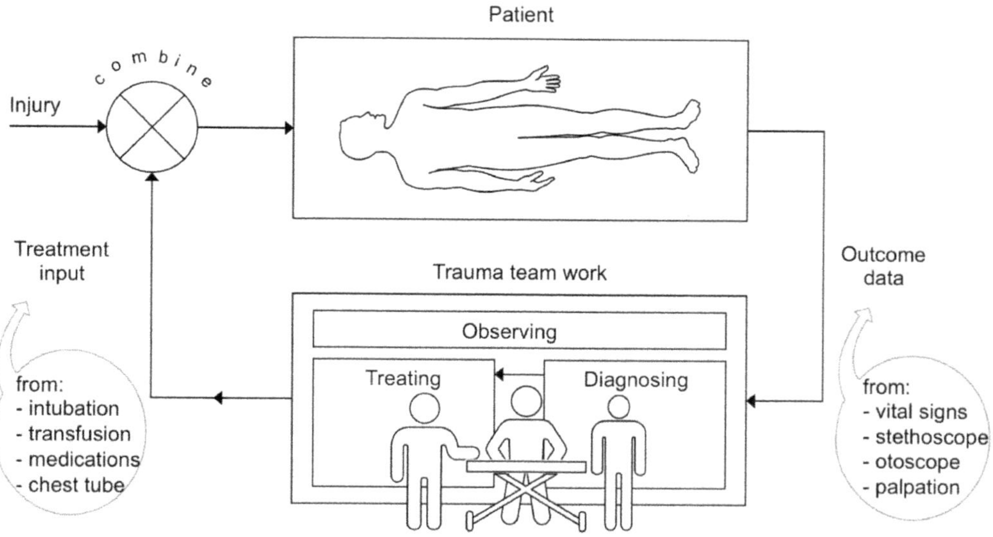

Figure 2: Feedback loop representation of the resuscitation process.

Tskin) (Figure 1). The waveforms represent the most recent trends of selected vital signs, but only span a short amount of time (less than a minute).

Trauma teams use the vital signs information to make critical decisions when treating severely injured patients. The vital signs display, however, mainly supports teams with information about the patient's airway [A], breathing [B] and circulation [C] (table in Figure 1). For example, information about oxygen saturation in the blood is used to determine if adequate levels of oxygen are being maintained or if an intervention for improving oxygenation (e.g., intubation) needs to be performed. To identify hypotension or hypertension (circulation issues), teams rely on heart rate, pulse, and blood pressure measurements. The vital signs monitor does not include information obtained through direct patient examination, such as airway obstructions [A], breath sounds [B], heart sounds [C], cognitive impairment [D], and types or extent of physical injuries [S]. It also lacks contextual information about team activities, treatments, and outcomes. Although the vital signs monitor provides a summary of the patient' condition, which in turn depends on the status of major physiological systems, the problems in each system are diagnosed and treated independently of each other.

Conceptual Framework: Feedback Loops in Trauma Resuscitation

Feedback loops are viewed as powerful mechanisms for augmenting human performance [28]. An example of a simple and successful feedback loop application is a speed limit sign coupled with a radar sensor attached to a large digital readout announcing "Your Speed," also known as driver feedback signs [11]. More recently, research in HCI and UbiComp has leveraged this concept by featuring technologies and applications that allow fast and easy collection of energy usage data and personal health data to trigger behavior change [9,10].

In the context of medical work, feedback allows clinicians to identify and correct poor decisions before they lead to undesirable outcomes [28]. Drews and colleagues studied how anesthesiologists used visual display feedback for maintaining the level of anesthesia administered during surgery [6,7]. They found that feedback helped anesthesiologists formulate drug-dosing strategies, particularly during critical moments. In contrast, our work views the entire trauma team involved in multiple feedback loops, with each feedback loop addressing a major physiological system (Airway, Breathing, Circulation, and Disability), as outlined by the ATLS evaluation protocol. We can view the resuscitation process as consisting of several independent feedback loops for two reasons. First, although connected, physiological systems are sufficiently independent from one another to allow clinicians to treat each system independently during resuscitation. For example, airway patency depends on whether there are obstructions in the patient's airway; breathing depends on the status of the chest; and circulation depends on the status of circulatory system. In fact, the ATLS protocol recommends that the evaluation of these systems be performed sequentially and independently of each other. During the primary survey, the team diagnoses and treats complications in each physiological system by collecting evidence about its status, determining and administering treatments, and interpreting patient responses to those treatments (Figure 2). Each feedback loop originates with an event (e.g., injury or treatment) and continues with the team's observations of the effects of this event (e.g., injury symptoms or response to treatment). Based on the feedback obtained, the team then decides whether to perform a treatment, pause and temporarily switch to another physiological system (different feedback loop), or conclude the current feedback loop (Figure 2). Second, all major interventions (e.g., intubation or chest tube insertion) are closely coordinated and supervised by a single person (team leader), making it difficult to perform two interventions simultaneously. In addition, each intervention is followed by a waiting period to evaluate the effects of the treatment (feedback). The timeliness of this feedback depends on how fast the team can perform treatments and how fast the patient reacts to those treatments. The team may start working on a different system while waiting for feedback, but often cannot perform major work on more than one physiological system at the same time.

Viewing the resuscitation process using a feedback loop perspective allowed us to situate monitoring activities within the context of work. This perspective yielded new insights into team dynamics and the role of vital signs monitor in supporting trauma teamwork. In short, understanding the dynamics of different feedback loops, as well as team activities associated with those feedback loops, will help inform what information to display, when in the process, and for how long.

RESEARCH GOALS, QUESTIONS & CONTRIBUTIONS

The goal of this paper is twofold. First, we examine when in the resuscitation process references to the vital signs monitor happen. Second, within this feedback loop-driven process of evaluation and treatment, we characterize the role that the vital signs monitor plays in supporting teamwork. We structure our observations by adopting the feedback loop concept to understand how teams use the vital signs monitor to reach diagnoses, decide on treatments, and monitor patient outcomes. We ask: Who are the most frequent users of the vital signs monitor? How often is the monitor used? When is the monitor used? How much time is allocated to the monitor?

The key contributions of this paper are:

- Characterization of the role of a visual display in time-critical medical teamwork.
- Identification of three types of information behaviors in time-critical medical teamwork relative to a visual display.
- Empirical quantification of the length of a safe amount of look-away time from the patient in emergency situations.

METHODS

Dataset: Simulated Resuscitations

We analyzed 12 high-fidelity simulated resuscitations from a pediatric Level 1 trauma center in the US mid-Atlantic region. There were 12 unique trauma teams in total, each composed of a team leader (senior surgical resident or emergency medicine physician), physician doer (junior surgical resident), anesthesiologist, primary nurse, scribe nurse, technician, respiratory therapist, and medication nurse. These team members were recruited from individuals usually serving in these roles.

The simulations were performed in an actual trauma bay with high-fidelity patient mannequins and the usual medical equipment and materials available. Team members positioned themselves around the patient according to their prescribed roles and positions: anesthesiologist and respiratory therapist stood at the head of the stretcher for easy airway access; scribe nurse and team leader stood at the foot of the bed for better overview of the patient and team; physician doer was positioned to the right and primary nurse to the left of the stretcher for performing interventions; technician was positioned to the right for easy access to the monitor and sensors; and medication nurse stood near the medication bench off to the left (Figure 3). The mechanism of injury and other pre-hospital information was relayed to the team when the patient mannequin was brought into the trauma bay. Real-time patient vital signs (e.g., heart rate, oxygen saturation, and respiratory rate) were displayed on the monitor after the technician connected the sensors to the mannequin. Vital signs and symptoms were manipulated electronically based on a preset script, and depended on the interventions performed by the trauma team. Information about the patient's conditions that could not be discerned from the mannequin (e.g., pulses or Glasgow Coma Scale (GCS) score to determine neurological disabilities) was verbally provided when prompted by team member actions.

We analyzed two scenarios performed by trauma teams. The first scenario (*Scenario A*) involved a 5-year-old female who was in a high-speed car accident. Teams needed to respond with interventions including intubation (a procedure in which a tube is inserted into the trachea to assist the patient's breathing) and fluid administration to stabilize blood pressure. The second scenario (*Scenario B*) involved a 3-year-old male who was hit by a car and dragged. Trauma teams were expected to perform chest decompression using a needle to release increased air pressure in the space between the lung and chest wall (tension pneumothorax), and fluid administration to stabilize blood pressure. The mannequins had features that allowed the teams to perform the resuscitation procedures required for each scenario (e.g., listen to breath sounds, insert tubes, and feel for injuries). The mannequins were also marked by artificial injuries for scenario realism.

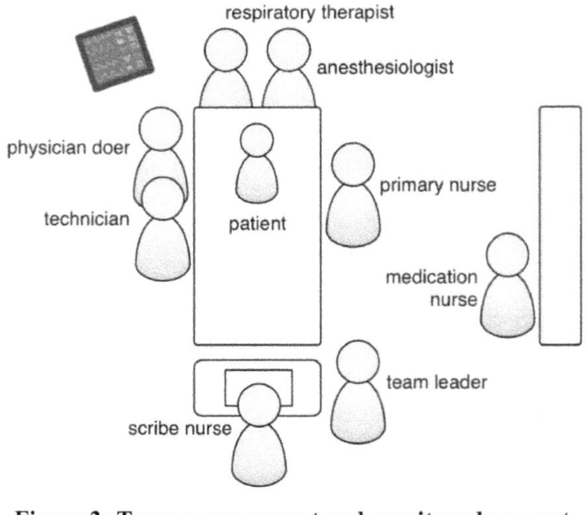

Figure 3: Team arrangement and monitor placement.

Two video cameras captured the simulations, providing different views of the trauma team and the trauma bay. One camera provided a rear, overhead view of the trauma room and the other provided a closer side view of the team and the vital signs monitor. The average length of the simulations was 9 minutes, ranging from 5 to 13 minutes.

Benefits and Limitations of Using Simulated Resuscitations

While the simulations were of high fidelity, it was not possible to replicate all aspects of the patient injuries and responses to interventions. There were, however, several benefits to implementing simulations versus observing live resuscitations. By performing simulations, we were able to videotape the resuscitations and perform detailed analyses not possible through direct observation. With simulations, the scenarios and patient conditions were presented to the teams in a consistent manner to control for variability in injuries, treatment, and outcomes, allowing us to focus on the larger themes of teamwork, workflow, and vital signs monitor use. The resuscitation scenarios we analyzed allowed us to explore several kinds of interventions. They did, however, limit the diversity of information that was exchanged and tasks that we observed.

Data Analysis

We used a three-step process for data analysis. We started with a detailed transcription of simulation videos and coding of team tasks and communication to enable subsequent analyses of tasks and monitor use behaviors within feedback loops. We then analyzed monitor looks, their distributions and frequency. Finally, we analyzed team tasks associated with different feedback loops to understand the context in which the monitor was being used.

Transcription and Coding of Simulated Resuscitations

One researcher transcribed the simulations into a spreadsheet by recording the tasks in the order that they were performed. The tasks included patient assessments, diagnoses, medication preparation, interventions, and references to information sources for both gathering data and obtaining feedback. We also transcribed team dialog, including the speaker, listener, and statement to understand the context of the tasks. A data dictionary was created to standardize the transcription and coding process; it included the tasks performed according to ATLS with a corresponding code (ABCDES). Two researchers coded the transcripts independently and applied multiple codes where necessary. Coding disagreements were minimal and were mainly concerned with tasks that were not initially categorized based on the protocol. All disagreements were resolved through discussion and codes in the transcripts were updated to reflect the decisions.

While the videos afforded rich and unobtrusive analysis, there were several difficulties encountered during the transcription process. Due to the fast-paced, noisy environment and diverse teams, it was sometimes difficult to hear what people were saying or to identify the speaker. The transcriber was able to slow speech and actions and record them in the greatest possible detail. Having two simultaneous videos from different angles also alleviated transcribing difficulties. To assess the representativeness of the transcripts, we performed checks with trauma experts and the individuals that facilitated the simulations.

Analysis of Vital Signs Monitor Looks

Using the transcripts and videos, another researcher recorded the instances in which team members looked at the vital signs monitor, including how many times each individual looked and the amount of time they spent looking at the monitor. We used the time-stamping function in Transana, an open source video transcription software, to record the start and end times of monitor looks by each team member. To manage multiple, overlapping looks at the monitor, the data was placed into a separate spreadsheet and sorted by start time and then by team member. Start times were then matched with end times, and lengths of looks were calculated, which also allowed us to check for accuracy and missing data points.

Using this data, we created histograms showing the frequency of durations of looks across all simulations (see Figure 7), as well as the look durations for each team member (see Figure 8). Based on the observed drop in the frequency of monitor looks over 3 seconds, we chose 3 seconds as a reasonable threshold to distinguish between short and long looks (see Figure 7). Monitor looks ≤3 seconds were considered *glances* and looks that were >3 seconds were considered *scrutiny* [24].

In addition, for each simulation, we graphed the distribution of monitor looks by showing (a) the total number of monitor looks per 30-second interval, and (b) the total duration of monitor looks per 30-second interval (see bottom two charts in Figure 4 and Figure 5). If a look extended into another 30-second interval, it was counted in the frequency of the first 30-second interval that it appeared in to facilitate our data analysis. We further differentiated the distributions of monitor looks for leaders and anesthesiologists because they viewed the monitor longer or more frequently than other team members.

Analysis of Feedback Loops

To situate monitor use behaviors in the context of work, we also visualized tasks that teams performed for each feedback loop (or ATLS component) on a timeline, for each simulation (e.g., top chart in Figure 4). To create these visualizations, we first used the transcripts to identify tasks within each feedback loop and then used videos to place the tasks on a timeline. Visualizations of feedback loops and graphed distributions of monitor looks were then aligned, resulting in a three-part visualization for each simulation (e.g., Figure 4). We used these charts to identify and explain monitor use behaviors in the context of the tasks.

RESULTS

We report our results in three parts. First, we describe the trauma team workflow from a feedback loop perspective to

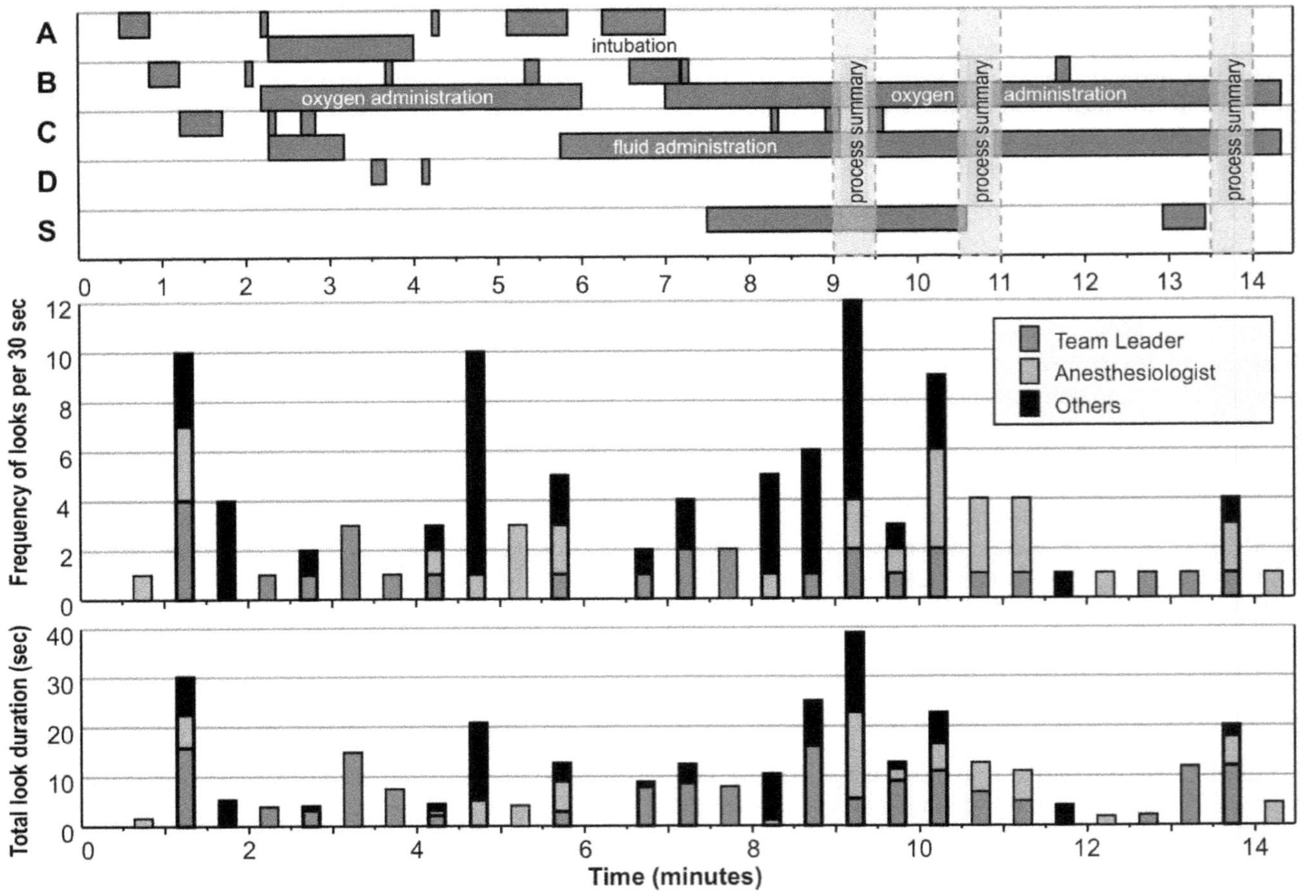

Figure 4: Top chart: Visualization of resuscitation tasks corresponding to feedback loops or ATLS steps for Scenario A, Team 1 (A stands for the Airway step or feedback loop, B for Breathing, C for Circulation, D for Disability, and S for Secondary survey). Bottom two charts: Distribution of frequency and total duration of monitor looks per 30-second interval.

help situate our analysis of monitor looks. We then characterize the use of the vital signs monitor within the context of trauma teamwork. Finally, we discuss team roles and how their work was distributed across feedback loops to gain further insight into team workflow and how best to support it with supplemental information displays.

Situating Vital Signs Monitor Use in Feedback Loops

Although we created three-part visualizations of tasks and monitor looks for all 12 teams, due to space constraints we show visualizations for only two teams, each from a different scenario (Figure 4 and Figure 5).

Our observations showed that teams initially followed the resuscitation protocol (from A through C), starting with a quick survey of the Airway [A] (by stabilizing the neck and assessing the airway patency), Breathing [B] (by listening for breath sounds and providing supplemental oxygen), and Circulation [C] (by palpating for pulses), as shown in top charts in Figure 4 and Figure 5. After completing these initial evaluation steps, the teams focused on the feedback loop involving the most critical intervention: intubation of the trachea [A] in Scenario A, and chest decompression or chest tube placement [B] in Scenario B. Critical tasks included monitoring oxygen saturation and blood pressure, as well as examining breath sounds and pulses.

We found that the frequency and duration of monitor looks varied over the course of resuscitation and depended on the tasks and team activities. The middle charts in Figure 4 and Figure 5 show the frequency of monitor looks over time for all team members. The bottom charts show the total duration of monitor looks. A possible explanation for this variability may be that the types of information sought during periods of frequent scrutiny differed from those sought during periods of frequent glances. Alternatively, it may be that teams limited the duration of their looks because they needed to focus on the patient. We next discuss these observations in greater detail.

Iterations of Feedback Loops

Teams continuously monitored the status of different physiological systems through corresponding feedback loops. Most of the time, teams were able to address the problems they diagnosed within a single iteration of a loop. For example, Team 1 in Scenario A decided that the patient needed additional oxygen and intubation based on decreased oxygen saturation and the lack of patient responsiveness at 2′15″ (Figure 4, top). They successfully

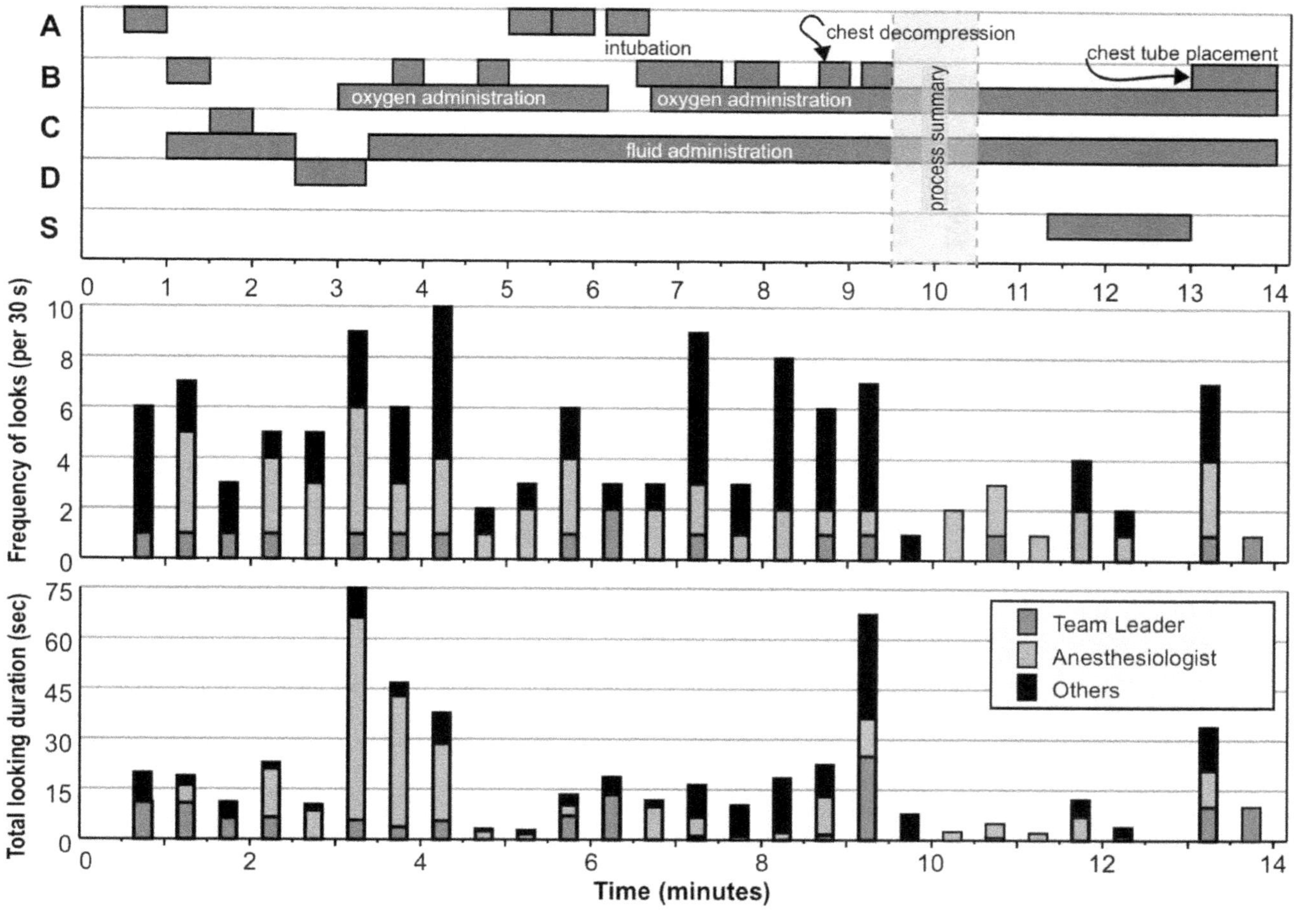

Figure 5: Top chart: Visualization of resuscitation tasks corresponding to feedback loops or ATLS steps for Scenario B, Team 5 (A stands for the Airway step or feedback loop, B for Breathing, C for Circulation, D for Disability, and S for Secondary survey). Bottom two charts: Distribution of frequency and total duration of monitor looks per 30-second interval.

completed intubation at minute 7 and then continued monitoring the airway status through brief assessments and summaries of vital signs ("process summary" in Figure 4).

Teams sometimes reiterated one or two feedback loops several times until multiple interventions finally led to patient improvement. For example, Team 5 in Scenario B iterated the Breathing feedback loop three times before successfully addressing the tension pneumothorax (Figure 5, top). At minute 1, they first diagnosed diminished breath sounds [B] and ordered oxygen administration, which started at minute 3. They then assessed breath sounds several times to observe the effects of oxygen administration (at times 3′40″ and 4′40″). After seeing no improvement, the team decided to intubate the patient, believing that this intervention would help (note their switch to the Airway loop). Breath sounds, however, remained diminished, leading the team to finally diagnose the patient with a tension pneumothorax and perform chest decompression at 8′40″. Even this second iteration did not fully address the underlying problem, triggering the third iteration and chest tube placement at minute 13.

Summaries of vital signs and patient status served as a mechanism for maintaining team situation awareness and ensuring that all critical tasks were completed. Team leaders often provided a process summary (and in some cases multiple summaries) at the beginning, middle, or end of the resuscitation. As an example, the team leader on Team 5, Scenario B summarized the process at 9′30″, including the mechanism of injury, interventions, and tasks in progress (Figure 5, top):

"*While he's putting the tube in, let's summarize. 2 year old, MVC [motor vehicle crash] hit and drag. Came in with an airway. We intubated secondary to hypoxia, needle decompressed, followed along with chest tube and fluids. Otherwise, external marks include tire tracks on the left chest and abrasions on left lower extremity as well as the left head. Anything else?*"

Switching between Feedback Loops

Trauma teams often switched between tasks from different feedback loops. For example, all teams in Scenario A began by assessing the Airway and ordering intubation, but temporarily switched tasks to the Circulation loop and prepared intravenous (IV) access for administering intubation medications. Another example occurred in Scenario B, when Team 5 switched from assessing breath sounds in the Breathing loop to intubating the patient in the

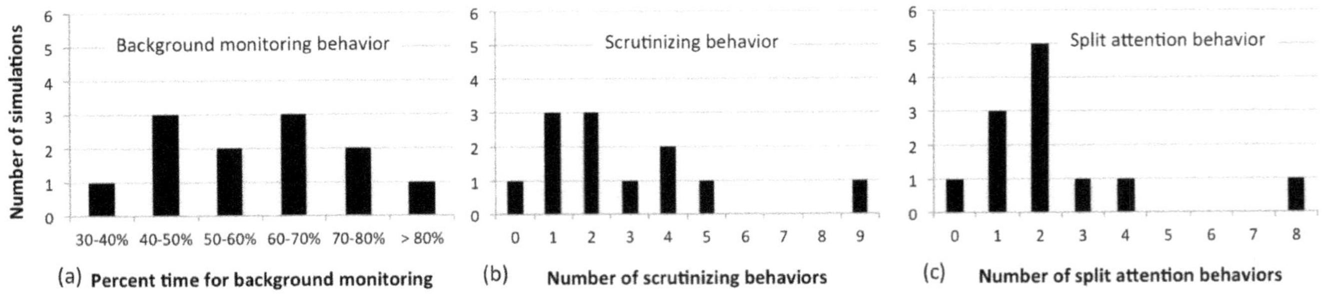

Figure 6: Vital signs monitor use behaviors across all 12 simulations. (a) Distribution of background monitoring behavior. (b) Distribution of scrutinizing behavior. (c) Distribution of split attention behavior.

Airway loop, and then back to Breathing where they decompressed the chest, as described above.

Some tasks had sequential order requirements as well. Intravenous access [C] needed to be established to administer fluids [C] or medications necessary for intubation [A]. It was also important to assess for brain injury before medicating the patient by examining the pupils and assigning a GCS score, an indicator of the patient's neurological status [D].

Switching between feedback loops seemed to occur for three reasons: (1) the requirement to attend to overlapping tasks from different feedback loops; (2) the need to suspend major tasks in the current loop while preparatory work for that loop was being completed; and (3) the sequential task dependencies across different loops, when one feedback loop could not proceed without completing tasks from another feedback loop.

Monitor Use Behaviors & Intensity of Looks over Time

Overall, the frequency and duration of monitor looks were relatively low during resuscitations, representing *background monitoring* of the patient's vital signs while focusing on patient care. These quick looks correspond to low bars in both frequency and duration—the bars with up to five looks in frequency and up to 10 seconds in total duration (see bottom two charts in Figure 4 and Figure 5). We chose 10 seconds for total duration as a reasonable threshold because each of the five looks is then about 2 seconds long, representing a glance. The background monitoring behavior was prevalent across all resuscitations, accounting for more than 50% of monitor looks in 8 out of 12 events (Figure 6(a)).

We also observed peaks (high bars) in both the frequency and duration of looks, representing *scrutinizing behavior*. These peaks occurred while teams were diagnosing patient conditions, followed by major interventions ("diagnosing" in Figure 2), and during "process summaries." For example, Team 1 in Scenario A had two high frequency peaks in the intervals 1′–1′30″ and 4′30″–5′ (Figure 4). The first peak occurred during initial evaluation of the airway, breathing, and circulation when the team diagnosed the need for oxygen administration [B] and intubation [A]. The second peak occurred while the team was waiting for the start of IV fluid administration, which then enabled them to start treating the airway by administering intubation medications. The remaining peaks coincide with process summaries, during which teams continued monitoring and diagnosing. We observed that all team members looked at the monitor during summarization, especially when the leader noted any changes in vital signs, as shown in this example: "*Open to suggestions guys. We're well ventilated and well oxygenated. Our heart rate has come down dramatically. Our blood pressure is up with the IV fluid.*"

Similarly, during the 1′–5′ interval, Team 5 in Scenario B had several high peaks in frequency and duration corresponding to the observation and diagnosing phases within the Breathing feedback loop (Figure 5). Another peak occurred during the interval 7′–8′30″, when they diagnosed the patient with a tension pneumothorax after assessing the patient's breath sounds. Peaks were also observed after chest decompression from 9′–9′30 and as the team performed chest tube placement between 13′–13′30″. During these interventions, the team needed to monitor the patient's oxygen saturation and carbon dioxide levels after intubation. They also needed to ensure that the chest tube was placed properly and the patient's breath sounds were improving. On average, we found 2.8 scrutinizing behaviors per resuscitation (Figure 6(b)). This low number of scrutinizing behaviors overall can be explained by the fact that most teams succeeded in diagnosing the complications in one to two loop iterations. The outlier team with nine scrutinizing behaviors (Team 4 in Scenario B) had a less experienced physician doer, but a proactive team leader who made diagnoses quickly and called out interventions promptly. Most of the monitor looks in this event came from the anesthesiologist, who monitored the vital signs for everyone and reported them aloud. The team leader noticed this behavior and used the anesthesiologist as a proxy so he could focus on the patient.

Finally, we observed that some high peaks in frequency did not have corresponding peaks in duration. We defined this behavior as *split attention*, which occurred during complex procedures when the team needed to maintain attention on the patient while also monitoring the displayed vital signs.

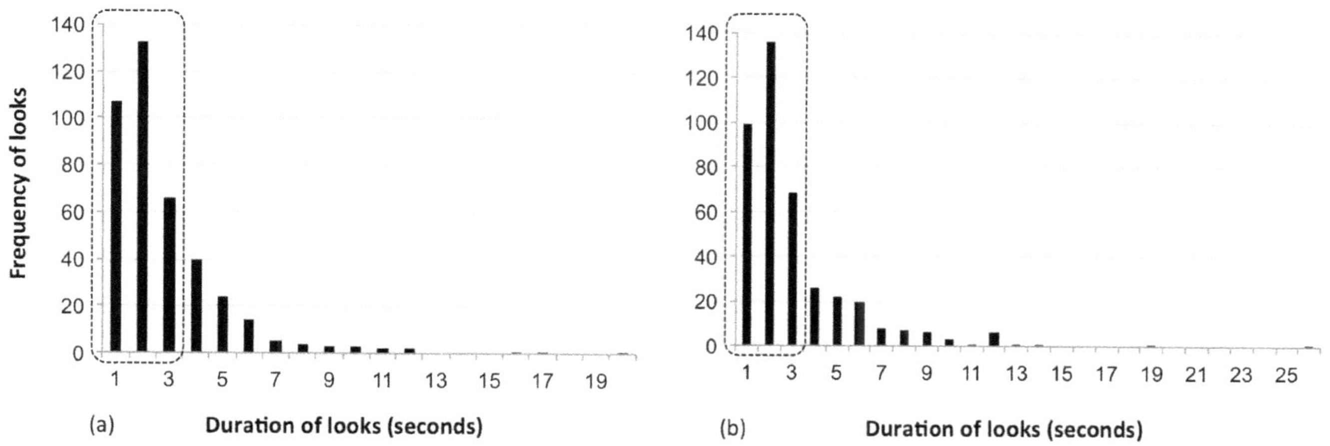

Figure 7: Durations of the vital signs monitor looks across 6 simulations for Scenario A (a) and 6 simulations for Scenario B (b).

For example, peaks in frequency during intervals 4′–4′30″, 5′30″–6′, and 7′–9′ for Team 5 in Scenario B (Figure 5, middle) do not have corresponding peaks in duration (Figure 5, bottom). During the first interval (4′–4′30″), the team was addressing a Breathing problem by frequently looking at both the patient's chest and the vital signs monitor. Similarly, during the 5′30″–6′ interval, the team was addressing the patient's deteriorating airway. The team was preparing for intubation and had to maintain attention on both the patient and the monitor. Shortly after intubation, the scribe nurse pointed out that the oxygen saturation was falling to dangerously low values. As a result, the team continued splitting attention between the patient and the monitor during the 7′–9′ interval, especially as they performed chest decompression. On average, we found 2.3 split attention behaviors per resuscitation (Figure 6(c)). This low number of split attention behaviors overall can be explained by the fact that the patients required only a few complex procedures. Team 5 in Scenario B was an outlier, exhibiting a total of eight split attention behaviors. As described above, it took this team several loop iterations before diagnosing the problem, which required more time for both patient and vitals monitoring. The leader was also less proactive, mainly asking for information, reminding the team of protocol steps, and summarizing the process.

Although all team members looked at the monitor, the team leader and the anesthesiologist had more frequent and longer looks than others. This finding is not surprising given their roles—the team leader is supervising the process and anesthesiologist is responsible for airway management, which involved one of the critical conditions that needed to be addressed. As seen in Figure 4 and Figure 5, the leader had a relatively low frequency of looks, but was dominant in terms of the duration of looks.

Monitor Looks	Scen. A	Scen. B	Total
Glances (≤3 s)	305 (75%)	303 (75%)	608 (75%)
Scrutiny (>3 s)	100 (25%)	103 (25%)	203 (25%)
Total	**405**	**406**	**811**

Table 1: Distribution of glances and scrutiny across teams and scenarios, relative to the 3-second threshold.

Distribution of Looks across Teams and Scenarios

Our analysis of vital signs monitor looks in the context of feedback loops showed that trauma teams used the monitor to identify conditions that could not be found through physical examination of the patient. The monitor was an integral part of the resuscitation process and provided an information source that team members used to establish common ground and maintain situation awareness. We further examined how teams used the vital signs monitor with a particular focus on (a) how much time was allocated to the monitor and how often team members looked, and (b) the frequent users of the monitor.

Time Allocation and Frequency of Monitor Looks

Our data showed that most monitor looks were quick glances—3 seconds or shorter (75%) (Figure 7). This large percentage of glances is directly related to the prevalence of background monitoring behavior. The data also revealed many looks that were between a little over 3 seconds and 26 seconds (25%) (Table 1). Scrutiny was not as prevalent as glances, but we can infer that teams do have opportunities to look away from the patient and view the monitor in relative detail. The monitor look ratio of glances to scrutiny is approximately 3:1. Although we examined 12 unique teams in two scenarios (6 teams per scenario), it appears that the total numbers of glances and scrutiny were highly consistent between Scenarios A and B.

Five outlying monitor looks were longer than 15 seconds, all of which were made by team leaders or anesthesiologists (Figure 7). These unusually long looks at the monitor appeared to help team leaders and anesthesiologists track the changes in the patient's vital signs to determine the overall outcome of the treatments. These looks occurred during diagnosis or following major treatments. For example, after intubation, the team leader on Team 5 in Scenario A looked at the monitor and reported, "*Okay. She's improving with the [fluid] boluses. [...] We've secured our airway.*" Similarly, the anesthesiologist and team leader on Team 1 in Scenario A both looked at the

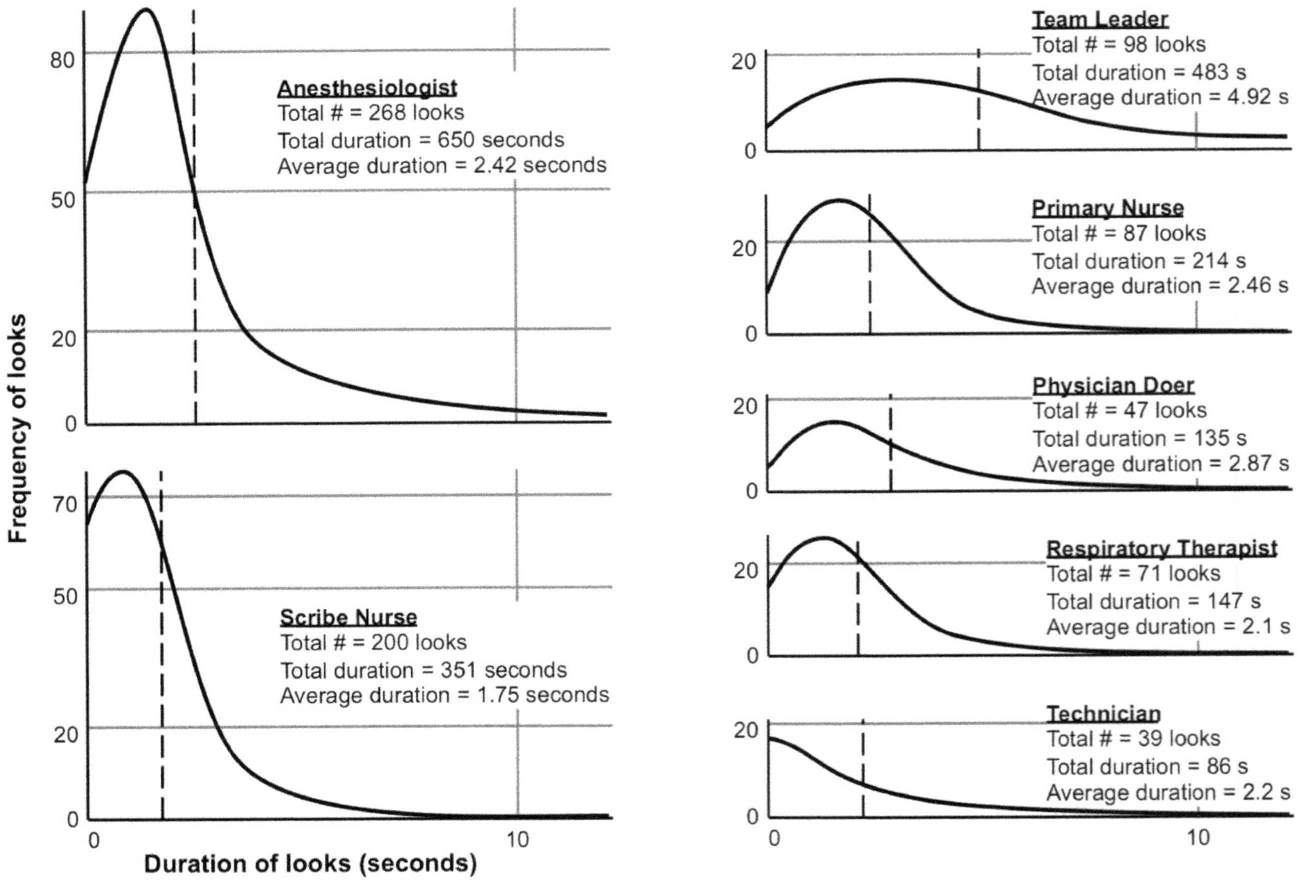

Figure 8: Curve-fitted approximation of the frequency of durations of the vital signs monitor looks for individual team members across all 12 simulations. Dashed lines mark the averages of durations.

monitor after the patient was intubated. The team leader reported, "*End-tidal [CO_2 exhalation level] is 33 guys, so from a respiratory point of view we're looking alright. Heart rate still coming down. Blood pressure is going up just a little bit so that's good.*" The longest look (25.4 s) came from the leader on Team 5 in Scenario B. Scenario B was more complex than Scenario A, and team members had difficulty diagnosing problems with the patient's breathing.

Monitor Attention across Team Members

We were also interested in understanding the different ways team members and teams as a whole used the monitor throughout the resuscitation process to identify design requirements for future displays. As our data showed, monitor use varied by team member role (Figure 8). Team leaders and anesthesiologists on all teams appeared to depend on the vital signs monitor the most, but exhibited distinctly different patterns of use. Team leaders were not among those who looked most often, but spent significantly longer amounts of time looking at the monitor than others (Figure 8). Based on our data, we concluded that most leaders relied on the monitor to maintain a high-level awareness of the patient's status and outcomes of the interventions performed. They appeared to analyze the monitor more deeply to determine the patient's conditions and the appropriate interventions. Team leaders also used the monitor to analyze trends in vital signs, which is demonstrated by the frequency of their scrutiny (Figure 8).

Anesthesiologists looked significantly more often, but on average spent about the same amount of time as everyone else except the team leader (Figure 8). Anesthesiologists used the monitor to ensure that the patient's vital signs were within a safe range, and to detect any adverse reactions to medications or interventions, especially those involving the airway and breathing. For example, the anesthesiologist in Team 4 of Scenario B looked at the monitor often and reported the feedback gathered back to the team.

Physician doers and technicians looked at the monitor less frequently than the rest of the team (Figure 8). They looked at the monitor mostly when silencing monitor alerts or when everyone else was looking. Physician doers typically focused their attention on the patient rather than on the monitor. They spent most of their time examining the patient, relying on other team members to report vital signs.

Technicians checked the monitor when connecting sensors to the patient. Their time was largely spent preparing IV access and retrieving materials for the team. Moreover, the team and room configuration positioned the physician doer and technician facing away from the monitor (Figure 3). They had to turn around to view the monitor and did so mostly when their eyes and hands were not busy.

Primary nurses, similar to physician doers and technicians, were busy with patient care—removing the patient's clothing, administering fluids and medications, and retrieving materials for the team. Respiratory therapists sometimes checked the oxygen saturation on the monitor when administering additional oxygen to the patient, but usually looked when other team members were also looking. Scribe nurses looked at the monitor frequently, but only for a few seconds at a time to gather information for documentation.

In short, decision making roles (team leader) looked significantly longer than others. They analyzed the display data for diagnostic purposes. Team members directly involved in patient care looked least frequently and for the shortest times. It also appeared that a fraction of monitor looks were the result of other people looking at the monitor or reporting information currently displayed, representing more of a confirmatory behavior for updating awareness of the changes in vital signs.

Roles and Work Distribution across Feedback Loops

Understanding roles and work distribution across feedback loops will help us further determine how to support the work of trauma teams with supplemental information displays. We need to know who is responsible for which tasks, what kinds of information they need for task completion, and how their work overlaps with the work of others. Established principles and guidelines for optimal trauma care published in [2] imply that there is a general division of labor defining specific tasks that each team member performs based on their role. We observed, however, that certain team members assumed the roles of others despite being "in charge" of particular tasks. This role switching behavior depended on differences in level of experience, position around the patient, or availability to perform a task. For example, the physician doer was normally responsible for examining the patient across different feedback loops, such as assessing the airway [A], listening for breath sounds [B], palpating for pulses [C], and assessing the patient's pupils [D]. Our observations showed that anesthesiologists often took over these tasks due to their convenient positioning at the head of the bed. Anesthesiologists also helped independently confirm the physician doers' findings.

Our research site is a teaching hospital where care providers frequently engage in on-the-job learning, and where teams are dynamically composed of team members with varying levels of experience and expertise. Several physician doers did not have experience with performing chest decompressions or chest tube placement, and followed directions from leaders and anesthesiologists. One anesthesiologist performed chest decompressions because the physician doer was uncomfortable with performing the procedure. Although the anesthesiologist's role is mainly to manage the patient's airway and oxygen administration, they are also skilled in performing other respiratory-related procedures. As confirmed by medical experts on our research team, these types of unpredictable circumstances also arise during actual resuscitations.

Primary nurses and technicians also frequently covered each other's tasks, filling in where the other left off on multi-stage tasks. For example, to complete the Circulation loop, technicians would place an IV access and primary nurses would prepare the fluids, connect the IV line to the infuser, and then hand the line to the technician to connect it to the access.

These observations imply that team members are distributed across multiple feedback loops. Team leaders acted as overseers of the process, and thus multiple feedback loops. They accounted for completed and incomplete tasks, pushed for information to conclude feedback loops, and determined what feedback loops needed to be reiterated. Managing multiple feedback loops required the leaders to maintain a high-level awareness of all the tasks completed, in progress, and pending. Because team members switch roles and engage in multiple feedback loops, it is important that they maintain awareness of information important to all roles, especially when temporarily assuming a different role.

DISCUSSION

During trauma resuscitation, teams collect evidence, diagnose, treat, and interpret patient responses, creating separate feedback loops for each component of the ATLS protocol. Our findings offer insights into how this feedback loop-driven process of trauma teamwork can be improved. Physical examination, verbal communication, and use of the vital signs monitor all serve as channels for receiving feedback to maintain situation awareness and support workflow. The vital signs monitor provides an overall summary of the patient's condition based on up-to-date sensor data (Figure 1), but does not provide the rich, contextual information needed to support situation awareness during the resuscitation process. We believe that trauma teams may benefit from additional displays to supplement the vital signs monitor with contextual information, provided that displayed information can be absorbed within a safe amount of look-away time from the patient. We have examined the frequency and duration of the vital signs monitor looks, and demonstrated how these variables are influenced by role and the stage of the resuscitation. Our study offers empirical evidence about the length of this look-away period, showing that medical teams have the time and cognitive resources to look at monitors in emergency situations.

Supporting Monitor Use Behaviors

We identified three distinct types of information behaviors relative to the vital signs monitor: (i) periods with a low frequency of glances, to maintain overall awareness of the process and patient status; (ii) peaks with a high frequency of glances, to split attention between the patient and the monitor; and (iii) periods with a medium frequency of scrutiny, to monitor trends in patient status over time.

Periods with a low frequency of glances (background monitoring behavior): Intervals with low numbers of glances occurred often and were distributed over the entire resuscitation (low bars in both frequency and duration charts in Figure 4 and Figure 5). During these intervals, the team was focused on their work and monitor viewing was a background activity for maintaining overall awareness. To support this monitor use behavior, the display should be peripheral, simple, and contain only essential information. Current vital signs monitors, which are mainly meant to provide a quick reference to current patient status, appear to meet the information needs during background monitoring.

Peaks with a high frequency of glances (split attention behavior): Intervals with high numbers of glances (high bars in frequency and low bars in duration charts in Figure 4 and Figure 5) occurred during critical moments in the resuscitation (diagnosis and intervention), when the team had to maintain attention on the patient while also checking for important information on the monitor. To support this monitor use behavior, displays should be peripheral and simple, but highlight information specific to the task at hand. Ideally, displays should be placed as near to the patient as possible to minimize the time spent switching between looking at the patient and the monitor. Also, display distance should be chosen in a way that does not require frequent changes in eye accommodation. A key issue, however, is that a computer system needs to distinguish split attention behavior from background monitoring for it to adjust the displayed information. Once the correct behavior is detected, task-specific information can be highlighted to make it easier to absorb within a short amount of time.

Periods with a medium frequency of scrutiny (scrutinizing behavior): Intervals with medium numbers of scrutiny (high bars in both frequency and duration charts in Figure 4 and Figure 5) occurred during diagnostic stages, when teams were collecting information and making diagnoses, and after major treatments. Because the monitor looks were relatively long (on the order of tens of seconds), the display could cease to be peripheral and provide richer information, and perhaps even include simple interaction. Designing displays to support this information behavior poses several challenges. First, there is still an issue of detecting scrutinizing behavior and distinguishing it from other monitor use behaviors. Second, once the scrutinizing behavior is detected, the question is whether the rich, contextual information should replace the basic vital signs monitor information, or whether to show this detailed information on a separate display. Replacing the vital signs monitor with a more detailed display may not be practical. Vital signs are critical to patient care and must always be presented to the team. Third, even if detailed information is shown separately, one may ask why it is not shown at all times, rather than only when scrutinizing behavior is detected. Although answering this question requires further investigation, we believe that having detailed information presented at all times may be unnecessary and distracting. Finally, the challenge is also in identifying what information to display given the large amount of information types relevant to the resuscitation process.

Providing Rich Contextual Information

Our data showed that a significant amount of time was spent on viewing the vital signs monitor. In particular, the leaders (decision making roles) appeared to scrutinize the displayed information for relatively long time periods and may benefit from richer contextual information, including (1) mechanism of injury; (2) highlights of changes in vital signs; (3) diagnoses, interventions, and outcomes; and (4) process-oriented information about the status of tasks for each feedback loop. This additional information may help the leaders manage the activities of multiple feedback loops from a high-level perspective by keeping track of the observations, treatments, and outcomes that occurred in each feedback loop during the resuscitation. Their summarizing behaviors also suggest that a display providing a reminder of the "story" with contextualized details of the resuscitation may be beneficial. These reminders would support team leaders when they review critical information to ensure that all injuries were assessed properly and to help prevent or remedy inconsistencies in team situation awareness. The challenge here is enabling seamless switching from basic to more complex information, or from peripheral to focal modes of viewing.

Time and space constraints, as well as proximity to monitors [18], prevent most team members from engaging in direct interaction with information displays in the trauma bay. Previous research has looked at using the nurse scribe as a proxy for capturing and displaying information for trauma teams in real time [22]. This solution would allow the nurse scribe to function as a human filter for the information relevant to teamwork without the need for team members to interact with an interface. Some interaction, however, such as panning and zooming in on vital signs with highlighted changes and events, would allow hands-off roles to conduct deeper analyses of the resuscitation process. Natural interaction modalities such as gestures could be used here as a way of addressing sterility and proximity issues [18].

Supporting Role Distribution across Feedback Loops

Despite being in charge of certain tasks, team members needed to be flexible to manage changing circumstances. Team members often performed tasks across different feedback loops, coordinated and shared work, covered other team members' tasks, and learned and taught new procedures. The nature of dynamic and tightly coordinated teamwork may necessitate a general information display for non-leadership roles to avoid tunnel vision for any particular role. Such a display could provide the status of tasks in each feedback loop to promote a shared awareness among the team. There may also be opportunities to assist trauma team members in training with quick visual guides for recalling how to do procedures such as locating chest tube insertion points. Multiple monitors displaying the same information in different positions around the stretcher would allow roles such as the physician doer and technician to view patient information more easily and may also reduce the reliance on others to call out information.

Finally, monitor usage data can be used for explaining or even predicting tasks and behaviors in the stressful trauma bay environment. For example, increased split attention behavior may be correlated with increased stress levels and workload because clinicians may be having difficulty making diagnoses or needing to make a lot of interventions to resuscitate the patient. Displaying this type of information through ubiquitous, context-aware technologies may help clinicians outside the trauma room discern the severity or difficulty of the case, and whether to offer assistance. Further research is required to determine why teams engage in different monitor use behaviors.

FUTURE WORK

In future work, we plan to implement other techniques to enhance the data collected about monitor usage. Mounting additional cameras on the monitors themselves may help us better identify when and how long team members are looking at the monitor. Although eye-tracking technology is commonly used in studies of visual scanning and monitoring [12,17,21,23], we found this technology inadequate for the trauma bay environment for several reasons. First, current eye-tracking technology does not support gaze tracking of multiple people at a time. Second, the distances at which eye-tracking can currently be used is less than 10 feet, which is insufficeint for the trauma bay coverage. We also plan to conduct interviews with team members to learn more about their monitor use and, in the case of team leaders, how they analyze trends in vital signs. Additional analyses of simulated resuscitations performed under different injury scenarios will allow us to better identify patterns in team workflow and use of the vital signs monitor. Finally, we hope to extend our work into the field where we can analyze actual trauma resuscitations.

ACKNOWLEDGMENTS

This material is based upon work supported by the National Science Foundation under Grant No. 0915871. We thank the medical staff at the research site for participating in this study. Thanks also to the anonymous reviewers for their helpful feedback.

REFERENCES

1. American College of Surgeons, *Advanced Trauma Life Support® (ATLS®)*, 8th Edition, Chicago, IL, 2008. Online at: http://www.facs.org/trauma/atls/.
2. American College of Surgeons, Committee on Trauma, *Resources for Optimal Care of the Injured Patient*, Chicago, IL, 2006.
3. Bardram, J.E., Hansen, T.R., and Soegaard, M. AwareMedia: A shared interactive display supporting social, temporal, and spatial awareness in surgery. *Proc. CSCW 2006*, ACM Press (2006), 109-118.
4. Bergs, E.A, Rutten, F.L, Tadros, T., Krijnen, P., and Schipper, I.B. Communication during trauma resuscitation: Do we know what is happening? *Injury 36*, 8 (2005), 905-911.
5. Bitterman, N. Technologies and solutions for data display in the operating room. *Journal of Clinical Monitoring and Computing 20*, 3 (2006), 165-173.
6. Drews, F.A., Syroid, N., Agutter, J., Strayer, D.L., and Westenskow, D.R. Drug delivery as control task: Improving performance in a common anesthetic task. *Human Factors 48*, 1 (2006), 85-94.
7. Drews, F.A. and Westenskow, D.R. The right picture is worth a thousand numbers: Data displays in anesthesia. *Human Factors 48*, 1 (2006), 59-71.
8. Fitzgerald, M.C. et al. Trauma resuscitation errors and computer-assisted decision support. *Archives of Surgery 146*, 2 (2011), 218-225.
9. Froehlich, J., Findlater, L., and Landay, J. The design of eco-feedback technology. *Proc. CHI 2010*, ACM Press (2010), 1999-2008.
10. Froehlich, J., Larson, E., Saba, E., Campbell, T., Atlas, L., Fogarty, J., and Patel, S. N. A longitudinal study of pressure sensing to infer real-world water usage events in the home. *Proc. Pervasive 2011*, 50-69.
11. Goetz, T. The feedback loop. *Wired Magazine*, July 2011 issue, p. 126.
12. Granka, L., Joachims, T., and Gay, G. Eye-tracking analysis of user behavior in WWW search. *Proc. ACM SIGIR 2004*, ACM Press (2004), 478-479.
13. Heath C. and Luff, P. Collaboration and control: Crisis management and multimedia technology in London underground line control rooms. *Computer Supported Cooperative Work 11*, 1-2 (1992), 69-95.
14. Hourizi, R. and Johnson, R. Unmasking mode errors: A new application of task knowledge principles to the knowledge gaps in cockpit design. *Proc. INTERACT 2001*, 255-262.
15. Hutchins, E. How a cockpit remembers its speeds. *Cognitive Science 19*, 3 (1995), 265-288.
16. Landry, S.J. Human centered design in the air traffic control system. *Journal of Intelligent Manufacturing 22*, 1, (2011), 65-72.
17. Law, B., Atkins, M. S., Kirkpatrick, A. E., and Lomax, A. J. Eye gaze patterns differentiate novice and experts in a virtual laparoscopic surgery training environment. *Proc. Symposium on Eye Tracking Research & Applications*, ACM Press (2004), 41-48.

18. Mentis, H.M., O'Hara, K., Sellen, A., and Trivedi, R. Interaction proxemics and image use in neurosurgery. *Proc. CHI 2012*, ACM Press (2012), 927-936.

19. Mumaw, R.J., Roth, E.M., Vicente, K.J., and Burns, C.M. There is more to monitoring a nuclear power plant than meets the eye. *Human Factors 42*, 1 (2000), 36-55.

20. Parush, A., Kramer, C., Foster-Hunt, T., Momtahan, K., Hunter, A., and Sohmer, B. Communication and team situation awareness in the OR: Implications for augmentative information display. *Journal of Biomedical Informatics 44*, 3 (2011), 477-485.

21. Rogers, S. D., Kadar, E. E., and Costal, A. Gaze patterns in the visual control of straight-road driving and braking as a function of speed and expertise. *Ecological Psychology 17*, 1 (2005), 19-38.

22. Sarcevic, A., Weibel, N., Hollan, J., and Burd, R.S. TraumaPen: A paper-digital interface for information capture and display in time-critical medical work. *Proc. PervasiveHealth 2012*, 17-24.

23. Schulz, C.M. et al. Visual attention of anaesthetists during simulated critical incidents. *British Journal of Anaesthesia 106*, 6 (2011), 807-813.

24. Sekuler, R. and Blake, R. *Perception*. McGraw-Hill Publishing Company, 1990.

25. Wears, R.L. and Perry, S.J. Status boards in accident and emergency departments: Support for shared cognition. *Theoretical Issues in Ergonomics Science 8*, 5 (2007), 371-380.

26. Wears, R.L., Perry, S.J., Wilson, S., Galliers, J., and Fone, J. Emergency department status boards: user-evolved artefacts for inter- and intra-group coordination. *Cognition, Technology and Work 9*, 3 (2007), 163-170.

27. Westli, H.K., Johnsen, B.H., Eid, J., Rasten, I., and Brattebø, G. Teamwork skills, shared mental models, and performance in simulated trauma teams: An independent group design. *Scandinavian J. Trauma, Resuscitation & Emergency Medicine 18*, 1 (2010), 47.

28. Wickens, C. D., Lee, J. D., Liu, Y., and Gordon Becker, S. E. *An Introduction to Human Factors Engineering*. Upper Saddle River, NJ: Pearson Education, Inc., 2004.

29. Wilson, S., Galliers, J., and Fone, J. Not all sharing is equal: The impact of a large display on small group collaborative work. *Proc. CSCW 2006*, ACM Press (2006), 25-28.

30. Xiao, Y., Lasome, C., Moss, J., Mackenzie, C.F., and Faraj, S. Cognitive properties of a whiteboard: A case study in a trauma centre. *Proc. ECSCW 2001*, 259-278.

31. Xiao, Y., Schenkel, S., Faraj, S., Mackenzie, C.F. and Moss, J. What whiteboards in a trauma center operating suite can teach us about emergency department communication. *Annals of Emergency Medicine 50*, 4 (2007), 387-395.

Privacy Management in Dynamic Groups: Understanding Information Privacy in Medical Practices

Yunan Chen
University of California, Irvine
5066 Bren Hall, Irvine, CA, 92697
yunanc@ics.uci.edu

Heng Xu
The Pennsylvania State University
316H IST Building, University Park, PA 16802
hxu@ist.psu.edu

ABSTRACT
Recent wide adoption of Electronic Medical Record (EMR) systems provides health practitioners with easy access to patient private information. However, there is a dilemma between the easy access to patient information and the potential privacy infringement brought by such easy access. This paper elaborates three types of group dynamics that identify challenges of privacy management in medical practices: team members, temporal involvement, and different levels of information sensitivity. Drawing on the theory of *contextual integrity,* this work identifies the appropriate actors, information access, and information transmission principles for understanding the norms of information flows. The findings of the study shed lights on the design insights that privacy enhancing features should be appropriately aligned with the dynamic group behaviors of medical practices.

Keywords
Electronic Medical Record (EMR); access control; information privacy; privacy-by-redesign; patient care teams; group dynamics.

ACM Classification Keywords
K.4.1 [Public Policy Issues]: Privacy, H.0 [information systems], K.4.3 [organizational impacts], J3.Life and Medical Sciences: Health, Medical Information Systems.

INTRODUCTION
As medical practices speed into the digital age, privacy has become an ever-present challenge. One particular challenge is how to prevent inappropriate access, use, and diffusion of private patient information in Electronic Medical Record (EMR) systems. EMR is an organization-wide IT infrastructure that contains patients' entire medical records assembled from various sources. It is projected that the adoption of EMR systems will exceed 70% in U.S. healthcare organizations by 2019 [38]. EMR offers a magnitude of benefits to future medical practices, *e.g.* accurate diagnosis, error prevention, easy communication, and patient care -- all relying on the improved accessibility of patient information. However, EMR's anticipated value is potentially discounted because of concerns involving highly personal and sensitive nature of healthcare data and associated privacy.

To protect patients' privacy rights, prior research advocated implementing privacy safeguards to reduce privacy concerns and protect sensitive health information [1]. Nevertheless, these privacy safeguards do not seem effective [36] and privacy breaches frequently occur. Since 2005, the Privacy Rights Clearinghouse has reported over 22 million healthcare-related privacy breaches [34]. Situations where personal health information is stolen or disclosed without authorization have been widely discussed in the media and have raised broad awareness about the digitization and use of personal health information in medical practice. For example, it was reported in 2011 that employees at a University Medical Center in Tucson inappropriately accessed the U.S. Rep. Gabrielle Giffords' medical records through the hospital-wide EMR system, following the shooting rampage at a local supermarket five days earlier [41]. The three clinical support staff members and a contracted nurse were soon fired due to the violation of patient privacy, since none of them were involved in the treatment or care of Giffords.

According to the privacy rules of Health Insurance Portability and Accountability Act (HIPAA) in the United States, individuals need to have a legitimate reason to legally access a patient's medical records, such as participating in a patient's treatment, care, or billing. Those who work in the same health organization, but are not involved in a patient's case, have no right to access. In the Giffords' case of privacy breach, the hospital officially stated that, "UMC uses sophisticated technology to help prevent and detect inappropriate access to patient information [41]." Technologies, such as access controls implemented in EMR systems facilitate the detection of inappropriate access to patient information. However, these cases indicate that many current EMR systems may not prevent inappropriate access before it occurs. With the wide adoption of EMR systems, insider abuse of personal health information is by no means a rare case. What is left to be solved is -- *how can EMR systems help prevent such privacy breach from happening?*

CSCW '13, February 23–27, 2013, San Antonio, Texas, USA.

Even though privacy management[1] has been well studied, prior studies often focused on *organization-wide* privacy practices, i.e., establishing preventative measures such as organizational policies, privacy enhancing technologies, and administrative processes [31], to alleviate concerns for the privacy of the organizations' customers. Nevertheless, these organizational-level privacy practices may not align with employees' actual information behaviors [5, 21], especially in a dynamic and collaborative environment such as healthcare, where teamwork is crucial to the execution of patient care tasks. From this perspective, largely missing from current understandings of privacy management are studies examining *group* level privacy concerns, i.e., the collective concerns that group members have regarding the privacy of information to which the group possesses and has access in an organization [6].

This void in extant privacy literature has also been identified by Murphy et al. [25], who highlights the need for studying group-level privacy practices in the healthcare setting. As noted by Murphy et al. [25], sensitive health data are often co-managed by different groups of medical employees who collectively share, use, and communicate patients' medical records in their medical practices. Therefore, the accuracy and confidentiality of a patient's medical records is the joint responsibilities of multiple medical teams who provide care to that patient.

Drawing insights from three recent ethnographic studies in the use of EMR systems at various medical settings, this paper identifies three forms of group dynamics that are particularly challenging in designing privacy safeguards. We believe that this work contributes to the privacy research in several important ways. First, this research provides new theoretical insights into understanding privacy management by studying group dynamics in complex medical practices. Second, Smith et al. [37] call for more qualitative research to study privacy management, and the challenge is that studies in organizational settings "*are necessarily more complex and less conducive to 'quick' data collection techniques such as written and online surveys*" (p. 1006). In response to this challenge, this research aims to understand privacy management in health organizations through ethnographic field studies. Third, Fitzpatrick [17] has noted it is critical to emphasize policy driven innovations. In particular, she mentioned, "*CSCW research will not have significant impact unless it engages in such advocacy alongside undertaking studies* [17]." In line with this thought, the insights obtained through our field studies are likely to contribute to both the technical development, as well as the privacy policy design in similar collaborative and dynamic working environments.

[1] In this research, we focus on privacy management problems resulting from information practices in terms of collection, use, security, and distribution of personal information [13]. Consistent with Culnan and Williams [13], we define security as one aspect of privacy and argue that privacy includes more than security. According to Culnan and Williams ([13], p.675), "privacy is broader and encompasses permission and use of personal information. Privacy is difficult to achieve without security. However, organizations can successfully secure the personal information in their databases but still make bad decisions about subsequent use and distribution of personal information, resulting in a privacy problem."

RELATED WORK

Collaborative Work and Privacy Management

The collaborative nature of medical work has been studied extensively in the CSCW literature, with a focus on understanding work behaviors and system use in real health contexts [17]. This is because the success of patient care often relies upon effective team collaboration, and collaborative work behaviors cannot be obtained without studying work behaviors *in situ*. Compared with other static collaborative settings, collaboration in the medical field is characterized as dynamic and information-rich [7, 24, 35]. As such, many studies have been conducted to examine complex medical practices *in situ*, in the hopes of gaining insight to inform the design of systems deployed in these settings. Various and important aspects of group-level work practice have been discussed in prior literature, including temporal coordination [35], spatiality and mobility [3], and formality of artifacts [10]. In particular, one study shows that groups are dynamically formed and evolve rapidly *in situ* [23]. Collectively, this body of literature indicates the needs of grounding design in the group dynamics of medical practices, since the lack of consideration of collaborative work often leads to system failures in organizations [19].

As opposed to group-based work practices studied in the CSCW field, prior privacy studies mainly consider privacy management at the organizational level, and fail to recognize the need for privacy protection at the group level. This void in extant privacy research has been identified by a recent interdisciplinary literature review [37] that highlights the need for more privacy management research at the team or small group level, as well as by online privacy research in the HCI field, *e.g.* [29]. To provide a richer conceptual description of privacy management, this study is targeted to this under-researched level of analysis.

Effectiveness of Privacy Safeguards in Healthcare

There is a growing body of privacy research examining organizational responses to privacy threats in the context of healthcare [15, 30]. Parks et al. [31] suggest that health organizations respond to privacy threats through a combination of technical and behavioral means. Technical safeguards such as access control [33], anonymization [28] and encryption [22] have been studied in prior literature. Nevertheless, implementing these technical safeguards in medical practices may impede the operational activities of medical employees [2]. In term of behavioral means of privacy safeguards, prior research has investigated the impact of training, promoting, and educating medical professionals about privacy and security awareness [32]. In the pursuit of privacy compliance, organizations implement these privacy safeguards that may change medical workers' operational workflow [12]. As a result, users may not always react positively to implemented changes, especially when privacy safeguards disrupt their work routines [8]. Therefore, establishing safeguards in harmony with the "actual day-to-day procedures" remains one of the major challenges of healthcare organizations [11].

THEORETICAL FOUNDATION

To better understand privacy expectations and the norms of the transmission of personal information in a given context, the theory of *contextual integrity* [26, 27] because it theorizes the **context-relative informational norms** which "*regulate the flow of information of certain types about an information subject from one actor (acting in a particular capacity, or role) to another or others (acting in a particular capacity, or role) according to particular transmission principles*" (p.141). Specifically, context-relative information norms are characterized by four key parameters: *contexts, actors, attributes, and transmission principles* [27]. Among these parameters, *contexts* are the circumstances in which the information flows are situated in; *actors* including information recipient (who receives information), information subject (whom the information is about), and information sender (who transmits the information); *attributes* are defined as the types of information in the information flow; *transmission principles* are the constraints to the information flow from one party to another in a given context.

Applying Nissenbaum's framework to understand the informational norms in medical practices, we consider the *context* as the circumstances in which an act of information handling is prescribed by medical employees. In this research, the *actors* we concern about are medical employees who write, share, and communicate patient's information (information senders and recipients); while patients (information subjects) are not examined in this study. In a healthcare context, there are different *attributes* or types of information being used and distributed in EMR systems, such as patients' diagnose information, contact information, medical histories and etc. In U.S., the *transmission principles* that govern the flow of information is the HIPAA regulation, which requires that accessing protected health information follow the minimum necessary rule. Under the general minimum necessary rule, medical employees have to have a legitimate reason, such as participating in a patient's treatment, care, or payment process, to access a patient's medical records.

In addition, the norm of **appropriateness** is a distinctive notion from the theory of contextual integrity [26]. Appropriateness dictates what personal information is appropriate to handle or reveal in a given context wherein data practices and actions are performed [26]. In medical practices, we interpret the norms of appropriateness as a set of norms as to whether the information accessed by a medical employee is considered appropriate to the role s/he serves, and the specific context at the moment of access. To that end, although the healthcare industry has established legislative efforts in HIPAA, aligning norms in harmony with actual dynamic work practices remains one major challenge. In particular, the normative guidance provided by HIPAA regulation does not define the appropriate levels of privacy protection corresponding to the types of personal information and the specific situation under which the information is accessed and revealed.

Therefore, understanding the informational norms in medical practices are no easy tasks, since norms are not static. Instead, they are dynamically changing when the parameters of informational norms change. New norms are emerged and have to be considered when information distribution is passed to a new recipient, encountered under a new situation, or with new constraints. In this work, we aim to: (a) understand the informational norms in medical practices, and (b) investigate the extent to which privacy safeguards designed in current EMR systems may align or misalign with the contextual informational norms in medical practices.

In this paper, we base our argument on the theory of contextual integrity [26] because it ties privacy protection to *"norms of specific contexts, demanding that information gathering and dissemination be appropriate to that context and obey the governing norms of distribution within it*" (p.101). In other words, the informational norms should be engrained into medical teams' daily data practices to determine *who* can access or distribute *what kinds of information under what situations and constraints*. Consequently, privacy protection mechanisms should be designed and enforced at an appropriate level in order to facilitate appropriate information flow and to establish norms of appropriate information use in a specific situation.

METHODOLOGY

As Barkhuus [4] points out, in the privacy literature, "*it is rare to see studies that implemented real systems with real data sharing or which [are] used in-situ data.*" To respond to such a compelling call for "*contextually-grounded research that explores privacy issues in the wild* [4]," we obtained data from qualitative field observations to study the group-level privacy practices mediated through the EMR systems-in-use and to understand the norms of information flows that challenge the privacy management in actual clinical work practices. The research context is the patient care conducted in health organizations. Users who have the right to access the patient data held in EMR systems are doctors, nurses, case managers, billing personnel, and lab technicians -- those who actually engage in patient cases in the medical setting. Other users, such as researchers who access patient records for chart review studies, or health consumers, such as patients and their family members, will not be discussed in this study.

The data reported in this paper were drawn from three recent qualitative studies (see Table 1) examining the use of EMR systems in different health settings. Although these studies were originally designed and carried out for studying the use of EMR systems in diverse clinical settings, the data obtained from these field observations give us an opportunity to study the norms of information flow and the EMR systems-in-use at our field sites. It should be noted that this study does not intend to reveal privacy infringements, nor to criticize the design of privacy enhancing features in the EMR systems we studied. Instead, our intention is to understand the nature of group dynamics in medical practices in order to examine the extent to which the design of EMR systems effectively supports information flow in medical teams' work practices.

Site	Organizational Context	EMR
ED	Regional healthcare center	System A
Clinic 1	Technology pilot site for a nationwide health system	System A
Clinic 2	Free Clinic serving for the poor	System B

Table 1: Summary of the ethnographic studies

Studies

Ethnographic study methods, including field observations, in-depth interviews, and informal probes, were used in all three studies[2]. Specifically, the field observations allowed us to uncover nuanced information behaviors in the real working environments. Formal and informal interviews were used to gather medical employees' perceptions, attitudes and preferences about technology-in-use.

Emergency Department (ED): Work Efficiency & EMR Use

The first study was conducted in an ED affiliated with a large regional hospital. ED work practices and workflows are extremely complex because of its diverse patient situations and their urgent care needs. At the time of this study, a full-functioning EMR system had already been implemented in the ED. However, the use of the newly introduced EMR system was coupled with decreased work efficiency and complicated workflow. The ED study was set forth to examine ED workflow and efficiency with EMR use accordingly.

A total of 120 hours of field observations were conducted during a period of three months. Each observation session lasted for 4-5 hours, during which brief notes were jotted down using pen and paper, and detailed notes were transcribed after the observation sessions finished. Brief informal interviews were probed with ED staff members during and after each observation session. During the study, we observed the general activities in the ED, shadowed ED employees, asked questions, tracked critical incidents and followed various patient cases. Our observations were able to cover most of the ED employees during work, either briefly in the public area or through close shadowing. The observations started with the overall activities on the ED floor. We followed 6 entire patients' treatment processes, shadowed 5 ED doctors, 4 triage nurses, 5 room nurses, and 2 case managers. In addition, we observed other employees, such as receptionists, billing personnel, technicians, social workers, and specialists.

Clinic 1: EMR Usages in an Outpatient Clinic

The second study aims to examine the use of the EMR system in an outpatient clinic affiliated with a large healthcare organization. Unlike the ED setting, medical conditions being treated in an outpatient clinic are usually not urgent, but are oriented towards disease management and prevention. The main purpose of the Clinic 1 study was to understand the impact of the EMR system on patient-provider interactions during routine medical visits. The EMR system at the field site had been in use since 2008 and was integrated as part of routine work practices. We shadowed 5 out of the 9 primary care physicians in the clinic, with a total of 140 patient visits during the study. Observation data on doctors were primarily collected in the exam-rooms and physicians' offices. In addition, we also observed other medical and administrative staff members, including medical assistants, front desk personnel, team leads, and schedulers to obtain a broader understanding of work practices. In total, we collected 180 hours of field observations over 6 months. In the exam-room, when patients were present, we passively stayed behind-the-scenes, writing down notes related to technology-use and clinicians' behaviors. Observations in the offices were conducted through a think-aloud manner, where we sat at the back of the office observing physicians' behaviors while the doctors explained their activities and the reasons behind the tasks they were doing. Data from the informal interviews and observations were noted using pen and paper on-site, and then transcribed in more detail later.

Clinic 2: EMR Rollout in a Free Clinic

The third study was an examination of the rollout of an EMR system at a free outpatient clinic primarily serving for low-income and homeless population. Patients in this clinic normally do not have health insurance, and many even require further social services. Most of the employees at this free clinic are those who also hold jobs at other health organizations and are volunteering at the clinic temporarily. The unique practices of this clinic are useful in studying how the EMR system is used in a volunteer dominant working environment. Approximately 40 hours of field observation, both before and after the EMR rollout, were conducted. Field observation data were collected in the same way as we described in the previous two studies. In addition, we also conducted in-depth interviews with 14 clinic staff members after the EMR rollout to gather their opinions regarding the new system. Interviewees included medical directors, nurses, medical assistants, medical record coordinators, as well as volunteers in the free clinic.

[2] The human subject research approvals were obtained in all the field sites prior to the studies.

Interviews lasted between 30-45 minutes, and were audio-recorded. One medical director was also interviewed before the EMR rollout in order to understand the process of the system's deployment. Together, a total of 15 interviews were collected, which include most paid employees and selected volunteers in this free clinic.

Data Analysis

Although these ethnographic studies were not designed to specifically study privacy managements, the deep understandings of how work practices are performed during real patient care inspire one central question in privacy management – *who uses what types of information according to what transmission principles?* Answering this question is crucial to the understanding of how privacy features should be designed to align with actual work processes. With this goal in mind, we first reviewed observation notes and interview transcripts, and extracted data that were relevant to the use of patient information in medical practices, with specifically attention paid to the users (actors), the types of information (attributes) as well as the ways how information is shared within teams (transmission principles). The extracted notes were then analyzed using grounded theory approach [18] to uncover behaviors of information practices across all three field sites. We focused on the differences between how information is accessed and used in actual patient care, and how such information is stored and protected in the systems. The initial information usage patterns were coded, with an open coding approach to identify new concepts from the data. This process was followed by an iterative process of collapsing our first round of codes into conceptually distinct themes. Through this coding process, we identified team members, temporality, and information sensitivity as the three main norms for patient information flow in medical practices.

FINDINGS

In this section, we describe the information accessibility afforded by EMR systems, and the privacy control mechanisms designed in EMR systems from our field sites. We then discuss three forms of group dynamics identified through field observations to highlight the unique challenges of privacy management in medical practices. We argue that these group dynamics are embedded in the norms of appropriateness and information flow, as they reveal the ways in which privacy safeguards designed in current EMR systems may or may not align with the norms of appropriateness and information flow.

Better Accessibility Afforded by EMR Systems

Accessing patient information online anywhere and anytime is a major benefit that EMR systems intend to bring to medical practices. With these centralized systems, there is no longer one physical copy of a medical chart that can be used by only one user at a single location; instead, multiple clinicians can simultaneously read, review and document in the same electronic record from their work settings or other offsite locations (see Figure 1). This enhanced accessibility was illustrated through the ubiquitously placed EMR systems at all three field sites. At the ED site, desktop terminals to access the EMRs were available almost everywhere, at patients' bedsides, in hallways, and at doctors' desks. Similarly, in the outpatient clinics, EMR systems were available in exam-rooms, doctors' private offices, front desks, and in the medical assistants' desks located in the hallways. In addition, most doctors can access the EMRs from outside clinical environments (e.g., when they work from home).

Figure 1: ED doctors checking (left) and documenting (right) in the shared EMR system.

The improved accessibility of the systems enables the EMRs to mediate various collaborative practices among different medical team members synchronously. For instance, in the ED setting, when a nurse updates a patient's progress in the EMR system at a patient's bedside, the doctor, who is in charge of the patient, can view the updated note immediately from his end. After orders are prescribed in the EMR system, nurses and technicians can be notified when they logon to the system. Likewise, primary care physicians can oversee patients' situations by reading the medical notes authored by other specialists. These observations demonstrate that EMR systems are not only record-keeping tools, but also universal infrastructures that mediate various forms of collaboration and communication that are often distributed across time and location in medical settings.

Privacy Enhancing Features in EMR Systems

Consistent with prior research that identifies both technical and behavioral means to assure health privacy [30], we also observed both behavioral and technical safeguards in our field sites. In terms of behavioral safeguards, medical employees are expected to follow the privacy guidelines set by health organizations. As we witnessed at our field sites, summaries of HIPAA privacy rules are posted on flyers or are even set as the background on computer screens to remind employees that, without a legitimate reason, they should not access patient medical records. In terms of technical safeguards, the EMR systems we studied are designed with privacy protective features that allow only authorized users to access the patient information stored in the system. Medical employees working in a given healthcare organization are provided with user names and passwords in order to access the organization-wide EMR. This password protection mechanism is designed to prevent outsiders from accessing patient records.

Within each health organization we studied, the EMR system was initially designed by a vendor company and was then customized based on the organization's work routine, operational procedures, local considerations, as well as patient care needs. Consequently, the privacy enhancing features in these systems were also customized by each organization. Nevertheless, we observed a universal access control mechanism through an *all-or-nothing* approach, i.e., employees were either allowed or denied access to patient information in the system. Such a static approach often fails to recognize the specific roles employees from different departments serve in different medical practices.

At our field sites, there was also a lack of differentiated access for different types of medical groups. Consequently, privacy features were rarely enacted at the *group* level in the system to prevent and detect illegitimate access among multiple medical teams. The need for access control at the group level arises due to the inability to monitor all team members and their privacy practices. On one hand, medical teams collaborate on various medical tasks and make decisions based on their gathering, accessing, analyzing, and sharing of patients' medical records. On the other hand, the effectiveness of these collaborative medical practices impact whether or not the privacy and confidentiality of the records will be maintained.

In what follows we describe three types of group dynamics that are unique to medical practice and discuss why group-level privacy protection is a particularly challenging issue to tackle.

Group Dynamics in Medical practices

As illustrated in the *illness trajectory* concept, the health management of a patient contains the entire course of a disease and the associated work in its different stages and phases [39]. For instance, a diabetic patient's trajectory work includes the treatments s/he receives from all emergency, routine, and medical specialists, *e.g.* podiatrist visits in different stages and times of the overall diabetic care. Health practitioners involved in patient cases are all reliant on the use of the private information documented in the medical records to make informed decisions and to continue with follow-up treatments. In this sense, being users of shared, yet private, patient information is the basis for team collaboration in healthcare, and such collaboration is often across temporal and departmental boundaries. Nevertheless, the highly dynamic nature of medical teams makes it difficult to define the boundaries of groups in medical practice, and consequently, makes group-level privacy management more difficult to implement.

In this section, we outline three types of group dynamics found in medical practice, and use cases drawn from our ethnographic studies to illustrate the question of *who uses what types of information according to what transmission principles*. The three types of group dynamics are:

- The constantly changing group members,
- The dynamic life spans of team formation, and,
- The different levels of information sensitivity.

1. Dynamic Team Members

Different from other collaborative teams which are more static (e.g. those in regular office settings), patient care teams are dynamically formed *in situ* with distinctly different team members. Because of this, it is not easy to predefine who will be in which patient team before a patient's arrival. In many cases, even the roles required for a patient's care cannot be determined beforehand and are decided *in situ*, when the patient has been presented. This unpredictability in determining patient care team members adds to the challenges of defining and designing group-based privacy control features. In this section, we describe the patient treatment processes at our sites to demonstrate the dynamic nature of medical teams.

Group dynamics are a salient issue in ED settings since patients in the ED present a wide range of medical situations with varied urgencies. Teams can only be formed when a patient has arrived on site, and the teams continue evolving when new progress, new orders and new situations occur. To illustrate the dynamics of team members, here is a typical patient treatment drawn from field observations conducted in the ED.

When a patient walks into the ED, s/he first checks in at the front desk, where a nurse and a receptionist ask for the chief compliant and measure the patient's vital signs. Then the patient is called into the triage for a more detailed assessment. Triage assessment determines the severity of the patient case, and assigns the patient to a specific room according to the severity of the situation and doctor's expertise, e.g. adult or pediatric care; the main ED or the urgent care unit. Once the patient is assigned to a room, the nurse, who is in charge, starts monitoring his/her situation. The room nurse then conducts a more detailed assessment and marks the case as ready in the EMR system. On the other end of the ED, doctors constantly browse through newly admitted patients in the EMR, and pick patients based on their expertise and availability. The doctor sees patients in their rooms, and return to his/her desk to prescribe medications, or lab orders. After receiving the orders, the room nurse and technicians work on them respectively. Lastly, after the patient's situation is stabilized in the ED, a case manager will start preparing the transfer or discharge paperwork for the patient.

In the scenario described above, an ED patient care team usually consists of a receptionist, a triage nurse, a room nurse, an ED doctor and a case manager, as well as technicians and other professionals, during the few hours of the patient's stay. Among these different roles, the doctor and the room nurse act as the *core team members* since these roles are required for the patient's entire stay, and the others serve as *peripheral members* since they only join the team as needed. Other more complicated patient cases often have to deal with situations like discussions with doctors in other departments or hospitals; treating urgent, traumatic cases; and managing patients with other social and financial needs. These complicated situations, as we have seen in the study, involve various specialists, primary care physicians, admission doctors and social workers, who often do not work in the ED.

The challenge of dynamic team members also exists in outpatient care, especially in clinics that have multiple physicians. As seen in the Clinic 1 study, doctors and medical assistants work in pairs to treat patients, yet doctors do not always collaborate with the same assistant. In fact, our observations with the two schedulers at Clinic 1 show that the full schedule of each day was usually planned every morning at 7 am – only one hour before the operation of the clinic began. In addition, there were different medical assistants who covered lunch breaks and took over during shift changes. For instance, we frequently saw medical assistants handoff their job in the middle of a patient case at 5pm when one assistant had to leave and the other arrived at work, while doctor had to stay longer to finish all the scheduled appointments. Further, the different shift changes and availabilities among random radiology technicians, nurses, and team leads also complicated what was otherwise relatively routine outpatient care. In these cases, although the doctor of each patient was scheduled in advance, the rest of the patient care team was formed dynamically *in situ*.

In addition to the group dynamics of a patient care team, each medical employee often participates in multiple care teams that all have distinctly unique configurations simultaneously. As our observation shows, an ED nurse takes care of 4-5 patients, and an ED doctor is usually in charge of 8-10 patients at a time. We also observed that nurses in the ED are assigned to patients based on rooms, while doctors are assigned to patients based on their expertise and availabilities. Thus, teams generally do not have the same doctor or nurse. Similarly, a family doctor may work with many different medical assistants, nurses, specialists and technicians for the patients in his/her panel. Together, such cross-team involvement forms an intricate care network where the boundaries of the teams are difficult to define (Figure 2).

In summary, the challenge of defining the scope of a patient care team in medical work is tri-folded. First, the roles of a patient care team are defined as the treatment evolves *in situ*; second, the specific person who works in these roles are dependent on the situation at the moment; and third, medical employees are always involved in multiple patient care teams, and each team has its own team members. The dynamic nature of scoping exact team members presents great challenges for defining which individuals constitute a patient care team, and who should be granted access to a patient's records in the EMR system.

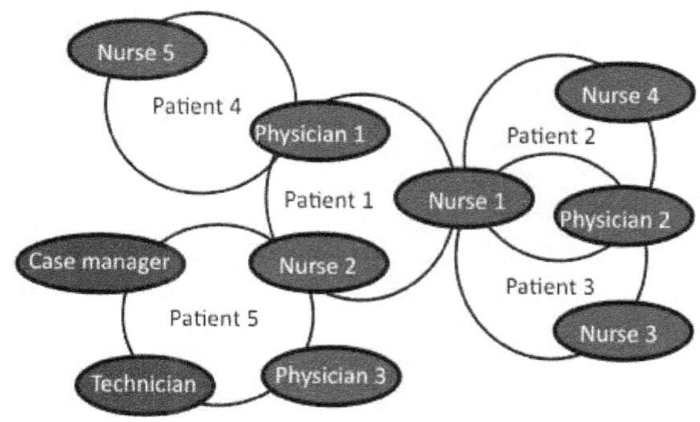

Figure 2: Team Dynamics in Medical Practices. Each patient care team constitutes both core team members (in black) and peripheral members (in blue). Meanwhile, cross-team involvement is a common practice in health settings.

2. Diverse Life Span of Teams

In addition to dynamic team members, the duration of teams also vary dramatically depending on each patient situation. As we described earlier, when a patient arrives at a health setting, the patient care team is formed dynamically on site. Similarly, when the patient care work is completed, the patient care team disassembles, and members of the team take on other patient cases to continue their work. Since a patient care team is only temporarily formed, access to private patient information should be granted accordingly in a time-sensitive manner. Thus, the temporal dimension becomes another concern that adds to group dynamics in medical practice. Temporality is a rather complicated factor to measure in healthcare group dynamics. In this section, we illustrate two aspects of temporality: 1) the dynamic life span of teams in medical practice; and 2) the volatile time span for core and peripheral team members.

The two types of medical teams we studied at our field sites introduced us to diverse forms of team durations. The nature of ED care determines that patients do not visit the department on a routine basis. The actual time span of each ED visit is dependent on the severity of the patient case, the psychological responses to treatment, and other logistical factors. Our observations showed that an ED visit could be as short as 2-3 hours or as long as 1-2 days. In contrast, patients often visit their family doctors routinely over a long period of time, *e.g.* on many occasions we shadowed patients who had been with a doctor for over multiple years. Visits to outpatient clinics usually have a prescheduled and fixed duration: patients schedule an appointment for 20-30 minutes in advance; the core team member, usually the primary care doctor, stays in the patient team longitudinally, regardless of changing medical assistants, specialists, nurses and technicians. In this sense, the patient care team in outpatient care can be viewed as a long-term oriented team with a fixed core and ever-changing peripheral members. Long and short term team durations often co-exist in a patient overall health trajectory, making it a challenging task to define the duration of team access, and consequently, difficult to define the temporal dimension of group-level access to patient information.

Another group dynamic lies in the volatile time involvement of the patient care team members, especially for core and peripheral members. As stated by Strauss [39], a doctor and nurse are required to cover therapeutic and monitoring levels of patient care throughout an entire hospital stay, but other team members just treat the patient briefly. Cases such as this were observed in the ED, where a doctor and a room nurse, who represent the core team members, stay in the team from a patient's arrival till discharge. Other peripheral members only join the team for a short period of time. In our study, we found that a technician only participates in patient care during the time of taking an EKG, a case manager only joins the team after the decision for hospital admission has been made, and a receptionist deals with appointment scheduling and registration. Although a family doctor sees a patient for years, constantly there are different medical assistants, nurses and specialists who join and leave the patient care team. Granting core and peripheral members access to private patient information for the same duration can be problematic since those people should not access the records after they leave the care team.

In addition, the access and use of medical records may occur both before and after the formation of medical teams. Although it is expected that doctors will review patient information, conduct medical consultations, and document relevant information in the EMR at the of a visit, their heavy workload and working styles often prevent them from doing so. For instance, some doctors we studied in Clinic 1 prefer to review patients' charts one or two days prior to their visits, and most doctors only have time to complete their documentations hours after the patients' visits have been completed. On many occasions, we observed outpatient doctors chart in patient records during lunch breaks, evenings or early morning the next day. Many of the ED doctors we shadowed also hold patient information till the end of 12-hour shifts and document them in the system all at once, since only then do they have the uninterrupted time to write long progress notes. This prolonged working time, which exceeds the actual patient care time, also complicates the duration of the chart using time, and consequently challenges access-control from the perspective of temporality.

The prolonged charting time often makes doctors open patient charts longer than the actual medical visit period. One outpatient doctor we studied even complained that she got warning messages from the IT department since she kept the charts open for too long. This observation suggests that privacy policies and features have to be compatible with the temporal dynamics of patient care teams, instead of implementing a one-size-fits-all policy for the use of medical charts.

In summary, the dynamic life span of medical teams also affects group-level privacy practices. What we have seen at field sites suggests that both the durations of patient care teams, and the length of the team members' involvement, vary on a case-by-case basis. Designing a group-based access control that aligns with the dynamic and volatile temporal aspect of team formation is a critical, yet challenging, issue to consider in protecting patient privacy at the group level.

3. Different Levels of Information Sensitivity

Last, the extent to which a team member should be granted access to patient information also varies greatly. Patient records in an EMR system contain a broad range of information from a person's name, address, date of birth and phone numbers to diagnoses, medications, radiology images and medical and social histories. These records may also cover information regarding a wide range of patient diseases, from the common cold to more sensitive mental and psychological disorders. The lengthy personal and medical data accumulated over time are all packed into one medical record in the centralized system. With the diverse and ever-changing users of the records, granting everyone the same amount of access without differentiating sensitivity levels can be problematic. In this section, we use cases collected from the two outpatient clinic studies to exemplify the need for having layered access control for different types of information with different levels of sensitivity in a single medical chart. These cases point to the need for granting different levels of privacy control for team members who serve different roles, indicating that patient information has different levels of sensitivity.

In Clinic 1, we studied the use of the EMR system among primary care physicians. The major role of primary care physicians is to oversee a patient's whole spectrum of health and to serve as a gatekeeper for other emerging and specialized illnesses. Because of this, physicians always read and review medical notes authored by other healthcare providers, as they are obligated to know why their patients went to an ED prior to their current medical visit or what the progress has been with other specialists and therapists in between a patient's two routine visits. Having easy access to a patient's entire medical record has greatly benefited primary care physicians. However, at Clinic 1, there was a privacy control feature being implemented to limit primary care physicians from accessing patients' mental health records. Frequently during observations we saw primary care physicians become frustrated about not being able to view the notes made in the system by psychiatrists and psychologists. Physicians can see the medications a psychiatrist prescribed, but cannot access the medical documentation associated with the orders. There was one case observed in the study, when a physician found out that her patient had depression, and had been consulting with a psychiatrist in the same healthcare organization for more than a year. The doctor was shocked and frustrated that she had not known, since she would have otherwise prescribed medications differently. In this case, when a mental illness was concealed from a primary care physician, diagnoses and prescriptions may be based on incomplete and inaccurate health information. During the study, to show how important it is to access this highly sensitive information, a doctor even told the researcher to follow her to a neighboring doctor's office. When asking about the mental health records, the other doctor replied, *"YES, I want to see that all the time, and I need to know what's going on with my patients!"* In this example, protecting highly sensitive information, on one hand, eliminated bias and improper access, but on the other hand, hindered effective information use among team members. It is worth noting that only at Clinic 1 did we observe the protection of highly sensitive information based on department codes. The other study sites treat all patient information equally.

At Clinic 2, we studied the rollout of an EMR system. As a free outpatient clinic serving the poor, this clinic relies heavily on volunteers to facilitate its daily operations. One main task that was taken on by volunteers prior to EMR adoption was reaching out to patients, either for medical appointments, medication refills, or social services. Prior to the EMR adoption, the clinic had 400 student volunteers who worked on these tasks. Volunteers pulled medical charts from shelves, printed letters, filled in envelopes and called patients using the patient information in their paper records. However, after the system deployment, volunteers lost access to the medical information kept in the EMR and were no longer able to work at the clinic. One reason that accounts for this change is that the EMR treats patient contact information the same as other medical information, and it is no longer accessible to volunteers, since accessing the whole package of the patient's information requires the clinic to purchase user licenses for the constantly changing student volunteers who normally only work in the clinic for a few months. In addition, it is not appropriate for students, who do not have medical expertise, to access private information stored in the records. In the Clinic 2 study, it was clear that treating contact information and other private health information with the same level of sensitivity hindered the information flow in the normal work practices.

The two cases described above indicate that a strict cut-off access for both mental health information and contact information are both inappropriate and blocked the flows of information. These cases raise the question of whether all the private information stored in a patient's medical record should be regarded with the same level of sensitivity, and if there are different levels of sensitivity, that is, whether patient care team members should all be granted the same level of access, regardless of the information needs of their specific role. The earlier descriptions of both dynamic team members and the temporal involvement of team members suggest that core team members who stay with patients and provide long-term medical assistance are in need of accessing the entire spectrum of information. Other peripheral members, such as specialists, technicians, and even volunteers, may only require a small subset of low sensitivity information that is relevant to the completion of their tasks. The cases also suggest that restricting access to a patient's records simply based on the roles a health employee has taken on, instead of whether this person is involved in the patient care process, is not appropriate.

DISCUSSION AND DESIGN IMPLICATIONS

Using cases drawn from our ethnographic studies, we have identified three forms of group dynamics that are unique to health practices, including (a) the constantly changing team members, (b) the dynamic life spans of teams, and (c) the varied sensitivity levels of patient information. These findings fall into four core components outlined in the theory of contextual integrity, as we identified actors (team members), attributes (types of sensitivity), and changes in principles of transmission (time span of the teams). In this section, we discuss how to maintain the right level of appropriateness in medical employees' information practices.

The Appropriate Actors in Context

Nissenbaum's theory [26] suggests that the norms of information flow should be engrained into the daily data practices of medical teams. However, the cases extracted from our field observations show that the boundaries of medical teams are difficult to define in advance, as they are always formed dynamically *in situ* and that the team members of groups are constantly evolving when patient situations change. Because of this, it is not easy to predict the full scope of actors, as it is almost impossible to determine who will be in which patient team before a patient's arrival. For instance, whether a trauma patient in the ED needs an X-ray or MRI exam is dependent on the locations and the type of the injuries a patient has; and whether Dr. Smith or Dr. Taylor will join a patient team may be dependent on their availabilities at that moment.

To address the challenge of dynamic actors, we borrow the token-based access control mechanism proposed in prior study [14] to apply in healthcare context. For example, an ED doctor can grant a token to an EKG technician for a patient's records when s/he orders an EKG test in the EMR system. Or a primary care physician can grant an access token to a physical therapist when a patient is in need of physical therapy treatment. When a link is created to add a team member through an access token, only that member with the access token can view the patient's chart. Under such a mechanism, medical employees who work in the same hospital, but who lack an access token to a patient case, cannot view that patient's chart without first obtaining tokens either through orders or request by an existing team member; the team can dynamically reconfigure as the patient situation changes in context. In doing so, the example of the clinical support members who illegally accessed Giffords' medical records could be prevented before the privacy breach occurred. Meanwhile, if an employee has a valid reason to view highly sensitive information, s/he can explain the reason for access and obtain a token accordingly.

The Appropriate Information Access

According to Nissenbaum [26], the norms of appropriateness circumscribe how different types of information should be handled or revealed in a given context wherein data practices and actions are performed. Privacy control in medical practices should consider the norms of appropriateness in terms of different types of information, different levels of information sensitivity, and different responsibilities and duties medical employees hold. This suggestion is consistent with the findings of this work that indicate even within a single patient's medical record, there are different levels of information sensitivity. In such cases, adopting an *all-or-nothing* control mechanism can be problematic because such static access-control mechanism does not consider the dynamic norms of information flows in actual medical practices. For instance, in our case of restricting access to mental disease records, the static privacy control mechanism does not incorporate the situations of the legitimate use of these records by family doctors. Likewise, the free clinic study also indicates when the privacy control mismatches with norms of information flows in work practices, it may hinder the work practices supported by patient information. The problems of these one-size-fits-all privacy safeguards reflect the misalignment of privacy management with group-level work practices. That is to say, the norms in actual medical practices were not mapped with the privacy control mechanisms employed by the organizations, where access to patients' records were cut off by departments' codes, or roles' of employees. In other words, access at the right level of appropriateness should be granted to those who need to work on a patient case, regardless of the roles or organizational boundaries of the department.

To address this issue, we suggest role-based access control mechanisms that have been proposed in prior studies [40]. The role-based access control mechanism determines users' access privileges through assigning them with the appropriate roles in the system. Applying this approach to our findings, although group members are dynamic and unpredictable, the cases we described earlier suggest that a patient care team contains both core and peripheral roles, where the core members stay throughout the patient's entire treatment, and the peripheral members only join the team briefly as needed. Since certain roles, such as doctors, are indispensable in a patient care team, information access at the team level can be granted for core members, or the one who first opens a patient chart, and the peripheral members can be added based on their roles. However, this strict access restriction cannot compromise care in an emergency situation. To achieve the balance between information availability and restricted access, a strategy often proposed in this context is "break-the-glass" access [16], in which restrictions can be selectively over-ridden – as if breaking the glass plate that covers a fire alarm – to provide proper access, with the assumption that the threat of a subsequent audit will provide an adequate disincentive for abuse.

The Appropriate Information Transmission

The theory of contextual integrity [27] suggests that, in a given context, transmission principles may change with the changes of other parameters (actors and attributes) and consequently, changes in principles of transmission should be established in context. This notion of establishing changes in transmission principles is extremely important in medical context, since group members are consistently reconfiguring and reforming in context. In temporarily formed medical groups with a high variety of team members, it is obvious that accessing patient information at the time of use should not equal permanent access. On one hand, the information that resides in one's medical records continues to grow and will reach far beyond the amount of information that was granted to a medical employee at the time of access. On the other hand, a one-time access and use of health information does not mean that an employee can always access and use the private information. This temporal dimension is extremely important in dynamic medical teams, since group members are consistently reconfiguring and reforming in context.

The dynamic life span of teams and the volatile time span of different team members make it challenging to define and control the temporal aspect of privacy practices. One strategy that can be proposed to address these challenges is a behavior-based access control mechanism, in which access controls will be built upon an initial set of rules and modified over time based on users' behavioral patterns [20]. Under such an access control mechanism, behavioral logs of the access and use of patients' medical charts and other personal information are analyzed and mined for consistent patterns. For example, mining real behavioral patterns would suggest ED doctors continue accessing a patient's record hours after the patient's discharge for the purpose of documenting progress notes. In such cases, access to patient information can be extended for ED doctors based on the analysis of their behavioral patterns. An effective behavior-based access control mechanism should be able to detect patterns of deviation and provide administrators with feedback and an opportunity to either accept common workarounds; initiate training sessions or interventions to change behavior; or redesign the access control mechanism. More importantly, an effective behavior-based access control mechanism will learn from patterns of behavior, leading to iterative improvements in access management, thereby tightening access options in EMR systems to the minimum necessary rule.

Design Implications

Although our findings highlight the importance of group level privacy practices in the healthcare context, the question of *how* this understanding of group dynamics can be turned into concrete system-level and policy-level recommendations is still a challenge. Clearly illustrated in our study is that a one-size-fits-all privacy policy cannot accommodate the group dynamics in medical practices. We suggest that it is crucial to align the privacy technologies and policies with users' dynamic needs for data access in context. Towards this end, future research should consider the approach of *Privacy by ReDesign* [9]. This approach indicates that it is not always possible to design appropriate privacy safeguards from the outset; instead, privacy-enhanced solutions should be based on an understanding of the actual system-in-use in real work practices. This notion of redesign is in line with well-recognized design principles in which design of socio-technical solutions is grounded in understanding user behaviors in *context*. Our discussions on group dynamics, in regards to the three layers of contextual integrity, suggest that privacy solutions should consider: (a) establishing appropriate actors in context (defining contextual boundary of dynamic groups), (b) establishing appropriate information access (defining levels of information sensitivity in matching with employees' roles and responsibilities), and (c) establishing changes in principles of transmission (defining pertinent time spans).

In addition, we argue that, because the healthcare information environment is dynamic and event-driven, there are continuous cycles in which procedures need to be updated and re-aligned with new privacy issues or problems that may emerge from work practices. Privacy by redesign should be a continuous and iterative process where constant efforts are expected in ensuring the contextual integrity of privacy in real work practices.

LIMITATIONS AND CONCLUSION

There are several limitations of the study. First, the purpose of this study was not to achieve statistical validation or generalizability but rather to discover patterns for the purpose of better understanding of the main issues in its context. Thus it is reasonable to assume that the findings may not apply to other settings which are distinctly different than what we have studied. Second, the findings are based on the health organizations in U.S., and privacy researchers demonstrated that different countries have approached privacy issues differently in their social norms and regulatory structures [37]. Therefore, a future research opportunity could be to conduct a comparative study in another country.

Though prior research has examined individual-level privacy practices in terms of *how* users react and *what* their privacy practices (via behavioral and technological means) could be, few studies have explored *why* users have reacted the way they do. In this work, we took an approach of studying "*contextually-grounded research that explores privacy issues in the wild* [9]" and addressed the issues of workspace privacy in dynamic medical practices. In particular, we identified group-level dynamics that can be mapped to the contextual integrity theory [26] and argued that group-level privacy is deeply grounded in actual medical practice. Design for group-level privacy compliance is complicated by the fact that team collaborations in health practices are dialectic and dynamic, varying significantly based on the diverse team members, the information appropriateness, and the volatile life span of teams. The insights obtained from our studies on EMR systems point to a new design direction that calls for research focusing on group-level privacy practices. Future designs of privacy control mechanisms should enhance the group-level privacy control features that allow only appropriate team members to access patients' private information while balancing convenient data access with the monitoring and detection of illegitimate access in a real-time fashion.

REFERENCES

1. Agrawal, R. and Johnson, C. Securing Electronic Health Records without Impeding the Flow of Information. *International Journal of Medical Informatics* 76, 5-6 (2007), 471–479.
2. Aronsky, D., Jones, I., Lanaghan, K., and Slovis, C.M. Supporting Patient Care in the Emergency Department with a Computerized Whiteboard System. *Journal of the American Medical Informatics Association* 15, 2 (2007), 184–194.
3. Bardram, J.E. and Bossen, C. Mobility Work: The Spatial Dimension of Collaboration at a Hospital. *Computer Supported Cooperative Work (CSCW)* 14, 2 (2005), 131–160.
4. Barkhuus, L. The mismeasurement of privacy: using contextual integrity to reconsider privacy in HCI. *Proceedings of the CHI 2012*, 367–376.
5. Bauer, L., Cranor, L.F., Reeder, R.W., Reiter, M.K., and Vaniea, K. Real life challenges in access-control management. *Proceedings of CHI 2009*, 899–908.
6. Bélanger, F. and Crossler, R.E. Privacy in the digital age: a review of information privacy research in information systems. *MIS Quarterly*. 35, 4 (2011), 1017–1042.
7. Berg, M. Accumulating and Coordinating: Occasions for Information Technologies in Medical Work. *Computer Supported Cooperative Work (CSCW)* 8, 4 (1999), 373–401.
8. Bulgurcu, B., Cavusoglu, H., and Benbasat, I. Information Security Policy Compliance: An Empirical Study of Rationality-Based Beliefs and Information Security Awareness. *MIS Quarterly* 34, 3 (2010), 523–548.
9. Cavoukian, A. and Prosch, M. Privacy by ReDesign: Building a Better Legacy. 2011. http://www.ipc.on.ca/english/Resources/Discussion-Papers/Discussion-Papers-Summary/?id=1070.
10. Chen, Y. Documenting transitional information in EMR. *Proceedings of CHI 2010*, 1787–1796.
11. Choi, Y.B., Capitan, K.E., Krause, J.S., and Streeper, M.M. Challenges Associated with Privacy in Health care Industry: Implementation of HIPAA and the Security Rules. *Journal of Medical Systems* 30, 1 (2006), 57–64.

12. Coiera, E. and Clarke, R. E-Consent: The Design and Implementation of Consumer Consent Mechanisms in an Electronic Environment. *Journal of the American Medical Informatics Association* 11, 2 (2004), 129–140.
13. Culnan, M.J. and Williams, C.C. How ethics can enhance organizational privacy: lessons from the choicepoint and TJX data breaches. *MIS Quarterly*. 33, 4 (2009), 673–687.
14. Dmitrienko, A., Sadeghi, A.-R., Tamrakar, S., and Wachsmann, C. SmartTokens: Delegable Access Control with NFC-enabled Smartphones. *Proceedings of the 5th International Conference on Trust & Trustworthy Computing (TRUST)*, Springer, 325–339.
15. Earp, J.B. and Payton, F.C. Information privacy in the service sector: An exploratory study of health care and banking professionals. *J. Organ. Comp. Electron. Commer.* 16, 2 (2006), 105–122.
16. Ferreira, A., Cruz-Correia, R., Antunes, L., et al. How to break access control in a controlled manner. *Proceedings of the IEEE International Symposium on Computer-Based Medical Systems*, (2006), 847–854.
17. Fitzpatrick, G. and Ellingsen, G. A Review of 25 Years of CSCW Research in Healthcare: Contributions, Challenges and Future Agendas. *Computer Supported Cooperative Work*. (2012). 1-57.
18. Glaser, B.G. and Strauss, A.L. *The discovery of grounded theory*: Strategies for qualitative research. Aldine de Gruyter, Hawthorne, NY, 1967.
19. Grudin, J. Why CSCW applications fail: problems in the design and evaluationof organizational interfaces. *Proceedings of CSCW 1988*, 85–93.
20. Gunter, C.A., Liebovitz, D.M., and Malin, B. Experience-Based Access Management: A Life-Cycle Framework for Identity and Access Management Systems. *IEEE Security and Privacy* 9, 5 (2011), 48–55.
21. Heckle, R., Lutters, W.G., and Gurzick, D. Network authentication using single sign-on: the challenge of aligning mental models. *Proceedings of the Symposium on Computer Human Interaction for Management of Information Technology* (2008), 6:1–10.
22. Kluge, E.H.W. Secure e-Health: Managing Risks to Patient Health Data. *International Journal of Medical Informatics* 76, 5-6 (2007), 402–406.
23. Lee, S., Tang, C., Park, S.Y., and Chen, Y. Loosely formed patient care teams: communication challenges and technology design. *Proceedings of CSCW 2012*, 867–876.
24. Luff, P. and Heath, C. Mobility in collaboration. *Proceedings of CSCW 1998*, 305–314.
25. Murphy, A., Xu, H., Reddy, M., and Ringel, B. Exploring Collaborative Privacy Practices. *CHI 2011 Workshop on Privacy for a Networked World: Bridging Theory and Design.*
26. Nissenbaum, H. Privacy as Contextual Integrity. *Washington Law Review* 79, 1 (2004). 101-139.
27. Nissenbaum, H. *Privacy in Context: Technology, Policy, and the Integrity of Social Life*. Stanford Law Books, 2009.
28. Ohno-Machado, L., Silveira, P.S.P., and Vinterbo, S. Protecting Patient Privacy by Quantifiable Control of Disclosures in Disseminated Databases. *International Journal of Medical Informatics* 73, 7-8 (2004), 599–606.
29. Palen, L. and Dourish, P. Unpacking "privacy" for a networked world. *Proceedings of CHI 2003*, 129–136.
30. Parks, R., Chu, C.-H., Xu, H., and Adams, L. Understanding the Drivers and Outcomes of Healthcare Organizational Privacy Responses. *Proceedings of 32nd Annual International Conference on Information Systems (ICIS)*, (2011).
31. Parks, R., Chu, C.-H., and Xu, H. Healthcare Information Privacy Research: Issues, Gaps and What Next. *Proceedings of the 17th Americas Conference on Information Systems (AMCIS)*, (2011).
32. Patel, V.L., Arocha, J.F., and Shortliffe, E.H. Cognitive Models in Training Health Professionals to Protect Patients' Confidential Information. *International Journal of Medical Informatics* 60, 2 (2000), 143–150.
33. Peleg, M., Beimel, D., Dori, D., and Denekamp, Y. Situation-Based Access Control: Privacy Management via Modeling of Patient Data Access Scenarios. *Journal of Biomedical Informatics* 41, 6 (2008), 1028–1040.
34. PRC. http://www.privacyrights.org/data-breach. 2012.
35. Reddy, M. and Dourish, P. A finger on the pulse: temporal rhythms and information seeking in medical work. *Proceedings of CSCW 2002.* 344-353.
36. Siponen, M. and Vance, A. Neutralization: New insights into the problem of employee information systems security policy violations. *MIS Quarterly* 34, 3 (2010), 487–502.
37. Smith, H.J., Dinev, T., and Xu, H. Information Privacy Research: An Interdisciplinary Review. *MIS Quarterly* 35, 4 (2011), 989–1015.
38. Steinbrook, R. Health Care and the American Recovery and Reinvestment Act. *New England Journal of Medicine* 360, 11 (2009), 1057–1060.
39. Strauss, A., Fagerhaugh, S., Suczek, B., and Wiener, C. *Social Organization of Medical Work*. University of Chicago, Chicago, 1985.
40. Zhang, W., Gunter, C., Liebovitz, D., Tian, J., and Malin, B. Role Prediction using Electronic Medical Record System Audits. *Proceedings of the 2011 American Medical Informatics Association Annual Symposium* (2011), 858–867.
41. Hospital personnel fired for accessing records of Tucson victims. CNN. http://articles.cnn.com/2011-01-12/us/arizona.hospital.records_1_patient-hospital-personnel-medical-records?_s=PM:US.

Non-Static Nature of Patient Consent: Shifting Privacy Perspectives in Health Information Sharing

Aisling Ann O'Kane
UCL Interaction Centre
University College London
London, United Kingdom
a.okane@cs.ucl.ac.uk

Helena M. Mentis
Socio-Digital Systems
Microsoft Research
Cambridge, United Kingdom
hementis@microsoft.com

Eno Thereska
Systems and Networking
Microsoft Research
Cambridge, United Kingdom
etheres@microsoft.com

ABSTRACT
The purpose of the study is to explore how chronically ill patients and their specialized care network have viewed their personal medical information privacy and how it has impacted their perspectives of sharing their records with their network of healthcare providers and secondary use organizations. Diabetes patients and specialized diabetes medical care providers in Eastern England were interviewed about their sharing of medical information and their privacy concerns to inform a descriptive qualitative and exploratory thematic analysis. From the interview data, we see that diabetes patients shift their perceived privacy concerns and needs throughout their lifetime due to persistence of health data, changes in health, technology advances, and experience with technology that affect one's consent decisions. From these findings, we begin to take a translational research approach in critically examining current privacy enhancing technologies for secondary use consent management and motivate the further exploration of both temporally-sensitive privacy perspectives and new options in consent management that support shifting privacy concerns over one's lifetime.

Author Keywords
Privacy; temporality; medical records; chronic illness; illness trajectory.

ACM Classification Keywords
H.5.2 [Information Interfaces and Presentation]: User Interfaces - Interaction styles.

General Terms
Human Factors; Design; Measurement.

INTRODUCTION
The National Health System (NHS) in England offers lifetime medical services with an eye towards capturing detailed health records on a national scale for medical and public health research needs. This is motivated firstly by the purported benefits of sharing a patient's medical records between the healthcare providers that treat and care for that patient. However, the digitized and comprehensive nature of such medical records is also particularly supportive of the patient data needs of organizations (e.g. a hospital trust tracking mortality rates), national (e.g. disease tracking), and research agendas (e.g. treatment efficacy studies). In late 2011, approval was granted in the UK for health information to be made available to both industry and academic researchers [7, 23] through the Secondary Uses Service (SUS), a single, comprehensive repository for UK healthcare data [29]. In order to use collected data, though, patients must provide consent to secondary medical data use. Secondary use refers to the use of data for purposes other than it was initially collected for. In healthcare, this may include the transfer of a general practitioner's patient records into a national center's database for use in public health disease tracking or research on medication efficacy. Current guidelines in the UK provided by the General Medical Council [11] stipulate how to gain consent for particular data usage for research and the necessary security measures put into place (both in terms of policy as well as system design). This is in order to ensure the continued maintenance of patient privacy of their medical information that is transferred to the SUS for secondary medical data use [11].

However, medicine is temporal in nature [34] and perspectives on data sharing and privacy can change [19]. This raises questions as to how current perspectives on gaining consent and maintaining anonymity are temporally restrictive and could provide a hindrance in future medical and public health research, possibly breaching a patient's sense of privacy. Issues relating to the non-static nature of patient consent are particularly relevant for conditions that can last a lifetime, such as with chronic illnesses. This includes a particularly large swath of the population, as chronic illness conditions affect approximately half of all American and British adults – 133 million Americans and 17.5 million Britons [6, 48] – and these numbers are expected to continue to rise [43]. Chronic illnesses generally progress slowly with long durations [47] and thus some require a lifetime of on-going care and communication between the patient and their specialized healthcare providers, along with a lifetime of medical documentation [44].

An understanding of how patients regard the privacy of medical information they generate, share, and use to collaborate care is necessary to select mechanisms to securely and properly share health data in order to benefit medical research pursuits as well as ensure patient privacy and control over their data. Patient privacy, which includes the ability to exclude others from knowledge about one's health [19] is not an absolute right, as it has to be balanced with societal and other's rights in the healthcare domain [3]. However, confidentiality, including the respectful handling of disclosed personal knowledge in a trustful relationship [19], has traditionally been an essential part of healthcare worldwide [3]. Therefore, any understanding of patient privacy concerns and needs should be balanced with information and compliance needs of the patients' network of healthcare providers and the needs of those reliant on the SUS.

In the following exploration of perspectives on medical information privacy and sharing, we have focused on one particularly prevalent chronic health condition: diabetes. Through interviews with diabetic patients and diabetes health specialists on prior experiences with sharing health information, we have uncovered a clear trend that attitudes towards sharing sensitive health information had shifted due to factors such as changing concerns over the persistence of health data, health and lifestyle changes, technology advances, and technology experiences. Shifts can be towards the patient wanting to allow more or less of their health information to be shared with other parties than they had previously allowed. However, the occurrence of changes in one's privacy needs without the complimentary mechanisms of allowing a patient to change their prior consent exposes a gap in current consent management techniques.

Our interest in this question is in order to benefit a translational research agenda in design solutions for effective consent management systems and procedures and encourage further exploration of time sensitive privacy perspectives and technology solutions. After we present our findings on the non-static nature of patient privacy perspectives in sharing their health information, we turn our attention to a critical review of two current popular Privacy Enhancing Technologies (PETs). As an example of how it could be addressed, we then introduce a substantially different alternative that would require a shift in the collection and sharing of private health information (particularly for secondary uses) and a mechanism for achieving this system. Thus, our aim with this paper was to (1) bring the occurrence of shifting perceptions to light in order to stimulate a discussion within the CSCW health informatics community as well as (2) discuss the failure of current design mechanisms in addressing some of issues uncovered and how they could be addressed.

BACKGROUND

Studies exploring people's attitudes towards sharing medical information to inform research have hinted towards shifting perspectives and concerns over future data use being a factor in a patient's health data privacy preferences and perceptions. For instance, in one study of 1,230 Canadian adults in 2005, 56% reported an increased concern over their privacy in the previous five years [46]. A larger study of 4,659 US adults in 2007-2008 found that 37% worried that their DNA, medical information, and lifestyle information being collected and used in genetic research could be used against them in the future [16]. And a survey in 2008-2009 of 1,159 older (>64) US genomic research patients showed that 14% indicated that they would choose not to consent to sharing their information with a secondary database such as the National Genotypes and Phenotypes database due to concerns about future uses of the data [21]. Of course, privacy attitudes do not exist in a vacuum as they are "part of a larger social, cultural, political, and economic world" [35, p. 42]. In the UK in particular, attitudes towards privacy of health information have changed significantly as "unfettered access to personal health information is a thing of the past" [3, p. 725].

Although there are many factors that influence health information sharing concerns, changing perceptions of privacy are importance when considering the growing concern in many western countries over the management and tracking of chronic illnesses [6]. A chronic illness is one that can be controlled but not cured and therefore requires a lifetime of on-going, continually shifting care [33]. As a chronic illness can change and morph over time [20], the constant tracking of this information is of importance for a patient's own health records and trajectory as well as for public health monitoring [6]. This is in line with Strauss and Fagerhaugh's illness trajectory [40], which refers to the physiological unfolding of a patient's disease and the practices of care surrounding it over time, along with the claims of those in the CSCW community such as Reddy, Dourish and Pratt who argue that clinical information seeking and sharing is temporally coordinated [34] and Palen and Aaløkke who showed that a patient's home-based care is attuned to temporal rhythms [32].

A particular chronic illness of growing importance is that of diabetes. It affects the production of insulin, which is needed to process digested sugars, with Type I patients having no insulin production and Type II patients with deteriorated insulin production. The nature of diabetes means that onset could occur from childhood and last until late in life, making it a valuable context for studying the temporal nature of privacy attitudes. Type I is commonly associated with childhood onset and Type II with late adulthood, but this is not necessarily the case [17] and this is represented within our sample of patients. Diabetes is growing more prevalent every year, with estimates by the World Diabetes Association that one in ten will have the condition by 2030 worldwide [15]. Low glucose levels can lead to ill health effects immediately, but long-term excess levels of sugar can eventually lead to serious complications including eye, foot, kidney and heart disease. Both the maintenance of Type I and Type II diabetes require a range of treatments including diet, exercise, and medication, all of which need to be balanced by the patient to self-control their levels of ingested glucose [15]. There is no one-size-fits-all treatment plan for either diabetic condition; whether they are Type 1 or Type II, the patient must coordinate with their health providers to determine a sustainable health plan. To add to the complexity of care, the lifelong nature of these chronic conditions means that patients' health and lifestyles will change [30] along with the technology and treatments involved in their care [18].

As chronically ill patients have more experience with the transformation and use of temporally situated health data than the general patient population, the focus of this study was on how diabetes patients and caregivers have perceived their data sensitivity and privacy needs throughout their lifetime of care. Our findings show that the nature of a patient's illness trajectory and other temporally-situated outside influences can impact how patients perceive security and privacy concerns, ultimately impacting efforts in using shared health information for secondary uses.

METHODS

Research Setting

In this study, our focus was on the chronic condition of diabetes. The original intent was to study a group of patients affected by one chronic illness and although many patient groups were initially considered, a strategic decision was made early on in the study to focus on diabetes patients. Despite concerns over limits to the generalizability of eventual results, this proved to be a fruitful choice because of ease of access for the research team to this particular patient population.

This research was carried out in Eastern England, with support from local hospitals' diabetes service groups. The study centered on interviews of two important groups in a diabetic patient's care and information management: diabetic patients and diabetic specialists. Diabetic patients are people who have been diagnosed with Type I or Type II diabetes and are in charge of their own self-care (i.e. they are not a child, invalid, etc.). Diabetic specialists are those trained medical and health practitioners who specialize in diabetic care.

Sampling Procedure

The study used a theoretical, non-probabilistic sampling procedure [22]. Interviews with diabetes patients were first conducted in person with patients known personally to the researchers. We then conducted further patient interviews by telephone with diabetes patients recruited from the UK Internet board Gumtree, a weekly student union news email to a local university's undergraduate population, local diabetes support groups, physical advertisements in grocery stores around Eastern England, and directly emailing three popular diabetes patient bloggers. In addition, we conducted a group interview with a diabetes support group in the Greater London area. This ensured a wide range of interviewees with varied experiences and backgrounds, including those with Type I diabetes since childhood, two men with Type I diabetes onset in their early thirties and forties, elderly Type II patients, and a late twenties male with Type II diabetes. Each of these interviewees was rewarded with a £10 or $15 Amazon gift certificate. Demographics are in Table 1.

Gender	
Male	15
Female	12
Age (year range 18-73)	
<30	5
30-50	8
>50	14
Years Since Diagnosis (year range 2-32)	
1-5	5
6-10	4
11-15	7
>15	11
Diabetes Type	
TI	12
TII	15
Comfort With Technology	
Very	11
Somewhat	13
Not	3
Interview Source	
Group Interview	12
Support Group Follow-up Contact	2
UK Internet Board Gumtree Advertisement	1
University Newsletter Advertisement	2
Grocery Store Advertisement	5
Personally Known to the Researchers	2
Contacted by Email (Bloggers)	3

Table 1. Diabetes Patient Participant Demographics (N=27)

In interviewing diabetes specialists, convenience sampling was used. We interviewed six UK based diabetes health specialists: two senior diabetes consultants, a diabetes midwife, a diabetes nurse, a diabetes podiatrist, and a diabetes dietician. They were recruited from diabetes services groups in two hospitals in Eastern England through the head of one of the services groups. The interviews were conducted by phone except for the diabetes nurse and first consultant, who were interviewed at their hospital in person. Each interview concluded when the interviewer felt a clear picture of the participant's perspectives on medical information sharing and privacy experiences were covered. Each interview was at least 30 minutes.

Data Collection Procedure

The interviews, including the group interview, were conducted by the first author and audio recorded for all sessions. These recordings were transcribed verbatim and the qualitative research software Atlas Ti was used to manage the dataset. All interviews were conducted in a semi-structured format with interview questions probing people's experiences with their medical information exchange networks as well as their attitudes towards it.

Topic	Questions
Experience with the condition	Could you describe how it affects a diabetes patient's day? Is there anything about diabetes that makes it unique from other conditions?
Online information use	Have you used any online diabetes health resources? Have you ever used Twitter or Facebook for diabetes information? Do you read blogs and forums for diabetes information?
Medical information use	What kinds of documents are used for diabetes care? Have you used electronic medical records before? What kinds of documents are shared?
Accessing medical information	Who should have full access to medical records? Who should have partial access to medical records? Who should decide who has access?
Expectations for medical information	When do you expect a new caregiver to first have access to a medical record? For how long do you expect a caregiver to have access to your medical record?
Changing medical information	Who do you think should have the right to modify portions of a health record? Over time, should some information be withheld or retired from access?
Sharing medical information	Have you ever encountered any issues with privacy and health records? What are your views on privacy and online health documents? Do you have any concerns with the shift from paper to electronic records?

Table 2. Interview and Group Interview Questions

Similar questions were asked of the two user groups with changes to the language based on the participant, as seen in Table 2. During these interviews, patients reflected on their current privacy concerns, prior experienced privacy breaches, and concerns about future privacy issues.

Data Analysis

A descriptive, exploratory research approach such as thematic analysis is well suited to uncover the nature of privacy concerns for chronically ill patients. Thematic analysis was chosen to systematically analyze the data whilst also allowing us to tap into latent themes that manifested in the data collected [1], going beyond observations to more tacit themes [24]. Subsequent integration of these latent themes with the researchers' interpretation of the literature uncovered the need for further studies to explore the realities of the changing perceptions of and attitudes towards one's health information privacy. The emergent themes formed the basis for the introduction of a mechanism that supports the temporally sensitive perspectives on privacy [9].

Thematic analysis was conducted using an open, iterative coding scheme on the qualitative data collected from the interviews conducted [1]. A three-step approach was used for coding the data. Coding was organized first around the broad theme of 'shifts'. The evidence that attitudes towards privacy are not consistent led to further classifying the qualitative data by changes in technology, changes in health, and changes in lifestyle. Finally, this coding allowed deeper analysis into the changing perspectives of the patients and specialists around the sharing and use of sensitive medical information. The study's findings were assessed through an evaluation of validity and reliability by ensuring that we included patients with variation in diabetes experiences, triangulation of data collection and analysis methods (interviews and group interview), and through the relationship to prior literature [12].

RESULTS

Solutions for instituting protection for patient health information privacy tend to address one's privacy attitudes as a static state: that a successful model of privacy need only be concerned with the proper anonymisation after consent has been gained from a patient [32, 41, 42]. However, because this study's focus is specifically on how and why a patient's perceptions of privacy can shift and change, four related but different themes emerge from the data that encompass the shifting nature of privacy perceptions: concerns over the persistence of health data, health changes, technology advances, and technology experiences.

Persistence of Health Data and Its Changing Relevance

Despite the political and technological push towards the collection of a lifetime of digitized health records, we found that a predominant concern of diabetes patients who have a lifetime of health records in relation to their chronic illness is the perseverance of health information. Their concern in keeping much of the information that was previously recorded private, is primarily due to patients' interest in maintaining their dignity and privacy, which can outweigh their interest in their health [4]. For instance, one's indiscretions when young can be deemed private information to a recently diagnosed, middle aged, Type II diabetic. Although a patient may provide consent for data to be accessible to others at one time, this does not mean that in ten years patients might not want to hide such data. Likewise, if the collection of current data also requires the collection of previous data, the relevancy of this need may not be immediately obvious to a patient [39]. This is because, oftentimes, previous health and behavior is a contributing factor to current health issues and behavior. Thus, many things could be relevant or could lead researchers to ascertain a relationship between seemingly disparate data.

> The things that happened in the past often are still affecting the patient in the future. Let's say they've been anorexic or something. It may get deleted from the record and you don't know. You wonder why they're not eating properly and not wanting to see a dietician and not taking care of themselves. – *Podiatrist*

However, patients do not realize this information is what specialists and researchers need to know. When asked to share such personal, sensitive, and seemingly irrelevant information, the first reaction of many patients is of distrust. Moreover, if another party was privy to that information, then anger can ensue.

> They had gotten information that had nothing to do with anything really and I felt that that was inappropriate and too personal. Yeah, you know the podiatrist again, just qualified, knows nothing about me, doesn't know anything but I've got corns, why should they know [...] that my diabetes was out of control when I was 18? [...] It's got to be relevant, surely. – *Patient 3*

Patients do not always understand the complex interrelated workings of their health [2]. Thus many of our patient interviewees wished to have a greater discussion over what is and what is not relevant in their records. However, in situations such as these, it was not clear as to who should decide relevancy while also being cognizant of patient trepidation of the persistence and distribution of prior data.

> I suppose there are always going to be plenty of things which have ceased to be relevant but somebody somewhere has got to make a decision about these and I would feel that the making of the decision of which records to expunge is probably taking up time which any professional will have in short supply and might be – might want to use in a more effective way. – *Patient 11*

This is an important question as even healthcare practitioners are not omniscient in knowing what data will and will not be relevant. For example, it was not that long ago that the link between a diet high in refined carbohydrates was linked to a greater risk of Type II diabetes [14]. Some participants understand that when more information is made available, the better it is for their own healthcare as well as for research. But the requirement for privacy is even greater as increasingly sensitive information is being shared with unknown third parties.

> If health professionals are looking at your health records, they want to see the whole picture. ... And if they suddenly discover that there is a certain trend or suspect or do research on the fact that there is a certain trend in diabetes or whatever condition you have actually got... Say for example the fact that you smoked when you were 20, if you want to take that piece of information out of your records they are not going to be able to find it, so I don't think it actually helps treatments longer term, so I would say no, I think your records should stay even if there is stuff there that you would like to be taken off. – *Patient 8*

> I think there's a lot of people who care that 'what if I don't want them to know this about me?' It doesn't matter. They need to know everything that's going on in your health. If you had an STD or if you're on a certain kind of medication, a certain doctor still needs to know about that. – *Patient 15*

As one's behavior changes, one's perception of the sensitivity of previously recorded and shared data may change as well. However, retroactively removing previously recorded data that at the time was considered acceptable, but now the patient perceives it as sensitive, is not a possibility.

Health Changes Influence Privacy Attitudes

As a chronic condition such as diabetes changes over time, the nature of a person's condition can also change their views on their health information privacy. Although some people might be open to sharing information on their diabetes, if the associated effects of the illness changed or if a person was afflicted with something else in addition to diabetes, they become more or less private about their health information, such as with sharing information about a stigmatized illness [45]. In our interviews, the majority of patients acknowledged the way they share information, whether it be with family members or online, may change based on his or her condition.

> I'm out there blogging and sharing my life with diabetes with my real name and my picture and stuff like that, so I consider my diabetes world kind of an open book. But there are other people who I definitely think would be very concerned about the privacy of their health records. Now if it were to cross over into health issues that maybe were not diabetes related, I think I would feel a little differently about that. – *Patient 13*

The open sharing behavior and privacy attitudes of the diabetes patients we interviewed differs from the behavior and attitudes of other chronically ill patients, perhaps with stigmatized illnesses such as mood disorders and HIV [45].

These health changes would be beneficial to capture in a medical record that could inform large-scale medical data aggregation, but this might not always be preferable to patients as new health scenarios could bring about different attitudes.

> Well privacy is an interesting thing, right. A scenario could change very quickly, and I could easily see myself being more concerned with the privacy aspect of it than the control. – *Patient 13*

Beyond changes in the nature of a patient's medical health, it cannot be assumed that the way he or she values privacy will be consistent while dealing with a chronic condition that could last their lifetime. New responsibilities, such as having children who manifest a chronic illness, cause people to alter their perceptions of the privacy of their own health data and the importance of medical research purposes, while on the other hand, responsibilities may diminish as complications arise in older diabetics. Patient 9 developed cancer and required an arm amputation causing a lifestyle change that required him to rely on his wife to handle his health documentation. Subsequently, he expressed a reduction in anxiety when asked about his views on the privacy of his medical records.

> I am not really bothered. I am happy I should be told what I want to know and they should do what they need to do… Because I do get help so it doesn't bother me. My wife does most of the computer work…I don't do much since I lost my arm. – *Patient 9*

Thus, a change in health itself can change one's perspective of privacy. On the one hand, the onset of new illnesses, such as a mental illness, may cause a once open patient to want to be more private about their information whereas other health onsets cause one to loosen their perspective on privacy as we see with the patient who lost his arm and had already given up autonomy to his wife.

Technology Advances Lead to Greater Perceived Privacy Risks

As time passes, new types of medical care options are available for diabetes patients through innovations in medical research and technologies [8]. These advances can lead to changes in the way patients want to share their health information and their attitudes towards privacy. With the move to networked electronic medical records, patients that may be currently very comfortable with technology believe there is potential for additional security issues and worry more about privacy, as per the Canadian study mentioned in the Background [46].

> I mean banks can get hacked, I care about my money, but I do care about my health more. So I would rather... it's just the security of that information. I mean if they're online, people having access to things that they shouldn't have access to, I don't know. It makes me nervous though I understand the necessity of it, but it does make me a little nervous. – *Patient 14*

These increased privacy concerns are not necessarily justified based on the technology change, but are linked with other factors such as patients' previous exposure to technology in general [31]. Issues with privacy are perceived to be more important as they are more noticeable or more easily captured with new technology compared to previous solutions, such as the security concerns surrounding paper receiving far less attention than its digital equivalent [5]. Evidence of this is highlighted in stories of security breaches that have occurred with both electronic and paper health records.

> Well we have had some instances in the [hospital] that we've had to take action when people have accessed records inappropriately. The interesting thing about that is, had there been paper records, we would have never been able to prove it or sort it out. – *Consultant 2*

When patients are not familiar with these new systems or have little experience with newer technologies, they can be wary of them [31]. This is seen through technology advances such as new glucometers or insulin pumps bringing up brand new privacy concerns for diabetes patients.

> Actually I had one patient the other day email me about, her husband worked for IT, and had found this article about how insulin pumps can be interfered with and overdose you with your insulin, and certain companies can kind of…I'm not sure where it really came from, but obviously I directed her to that company to bring it up with them. – *Diabetic Nurse*

Technology innovations that patients and care providers have already experienced have been shown to affect their views towards the privacy of their medical records. Technical innovations as well as the shift towards EMRs show that patients are wary of what this means for the security of their information. As new information and news stories emerge, they can lead to a patient changing his or her mind regarding privacy needs. One may want to revoke their consent in having their information listed in a repository, such as the SUS. Although all stakeholders recognize there is great potential in the collection of this information for medical research, the patients will have concerns that may or may not be well founded based on their knowledge of new technologies.

Technology Experience Leads to Fewer Privacy Concerns

Newfound worries changed patients' perception of the risks to their privacy yet there is no mechanism to revoke the agreements they made in the past. However, although the access to new technologies brings up new privacy concerns for patients, they are increasingly sharing sensitive health information through another technology: the Internet and specifically social media. Patients are going online to aid in their own care, often facilitated by sharing with a large online community [13]. This acts as social and emotional support, which can be very important in caring for a chronic condition that can be "unrelenting". Diabetes patients use social media as "social support".

> [Its popularity] comes from openly sharing our vulnerabilities and some of our fears and sharing our hard times as well as our good times - *Patient 13*

> Just that it is extremely supportive and there's a huge value to people, to being surrounded by people who understand and who are like you. This community has grown at such a rate I think because there was a net organic need for it, and intrinsic need for it. – *Patient 14*

This is a massive shift in patients' care that is growing as this type of social support treatment is becoming easier to access [10]. The use of social media seems to be a fine balance between openly sharing sensitive medical information whilst also remaining in control of what is considered private.

> If you want to talk about the worst thing that you've done to your diabetes, or you are really ignoring it, or you're in a dark place, you can share that information without sharing your name, without alerting your employer to your potential issue or alerting your family even. You can keep those feeling private but share them publicly in a way gets the support without putting you out there like you're waving a flag saying 'I'm diabetic and I want everyone to look at me!' right? – *Patient 14*

Apart from health information, people are increasingly sharing sensitive information through social media [25]. The growing popularity of social media for medical knowledge and social support is changing people's perspectives as to what is private and what is not private, based on how vulnerable they feel. In these cases, people may choose to view previously held privacy beliefs as overly cautious and want to reveal more about their previous medical history, but they still have their own individual levels of comfort. Although Patient 13 would write his diabetes blog under his own name and picture as mentioned above, one group interview participant did not feel comfortable with this level of privacy.

> I think it would be alright to share information about how your, maybe how your blood sugars go…[…] but I don't think it is necessary to say your name and your address or anything like that. You can have a blog where everyone has a user name or something. And then I think it's really helpful. I don't think you really need to identify yourself. – *Group Interview Participant*

The benefit of easy to obtain information and social support over the Internet has increased the amount of sensitive medical information patients share, albeit not for the purposes of, say, aggregating large-scale medical data but rather for engaging with the 'Diabetes Online Community' [13]. Because they personally benefit from shared information and are able to directly see others benefit from their own medical information, patients seem to be happy to share sensitive healthcare details and employ their own tactics to keep their personal data anonymous. They have the control to reveal or hide information, revoke access to old posts, or open access up to all new content.

DISCUSSION

Due to the persistence of health data, changes in health, technology vulnerability, and technology experience, a patient's privacy attitudes can change over their lifetime. This lends evidence to the ever-changing notion of privacy and the consideration of mechanisms to allow for changes in privacy preferences to be accommodated. In the aim to start the discussion around addressing temporally-sensitive patient privacy in secondary medical data use in England, we turn our attention to two common, but surprisingly ineffective Privacy Enhancing Technologies (PETs). Then we describe a new mechanism that relies on zero-knowledge cryptographic proofs.

A Critical View of Current PET Mechanisms

Two popular mechanisms for PET support some of the issues we have outlined from our study: sealed envelope and pseudonymisation. Both of these have been considered in the design of the NHS health database [28, 26]; however, our discussion of these two mechanisms highlights how they are inadequate in addressing the privacy needs of patients over their lifetime as various circumstances shift their perspectives.

A 'sealed envelope' is a concept that provides security around parts of a shared electronic record to which a patient wishes to restrict access [28]. A wish may be expressed, for example, that sensitive information can be accessed by a patient's mental health practitioner, but not shared with a national health registry. If another health practitioner or public health researcher believes the sealed information to be important for their uses, they may request access to the information from the patient to 'un-seal the envelope'. Although sealed envelopes support the loosening of privacy perspectives due to either a change in circumstances or growing need to contribute to research, sealed envelopes do not support one's tightening of privacy perspectives due to concerns over new technologies or previously disclosed health data. In other words, although a retrospectively sealed envelope prevents future access, it does not remove data from SUS.

There has also been a strong movement towards protecting the identity of a patient through anonymisation; i.e., removing all identifying data of a patient. The problem with anonymisation is that it is a permanent process and once anonymised, it is not possible to link the data back to a particular individual. This may not always be acceptable, as a researcher may need to know that the patient who engaged in heavy drinking as a youth is the same patient who was diagnosed with diabetes at a later date. The mechanism of pseudonymisation, sometimes described as "reversible anonymisation" provides a solution [26, 27]. In effect substituting true patient identifiers with pseudonyms where the true identities are retained in a secure part of the information system allowing the relationship between old and new data to manifest. However, again, this mechanism does not support one's tightening of privacy perspectives as once consent is given, data is copied as a permanent part of the SUS and pseudonymised which again conflicts with our findings regarding concerns over new technologies or previously disclosed health data.

Thus, just as these two popular mechanisms show, the focus of PETs has been on the secure provision of medical information to secondary sources and, once provided, the assurance of anonymity [26-28]. However, this focus is missing the need to remove medical information from secondary repositories such as SUS and support the retroactive tightening of privacy settings for health care information.

A Fresh Take on Privacy Enhancing Technologies

Another option is potentially more supportive of temporally sensitive privacy. It was developed in the context of privacy-preserving smart metering [36] where a household's privacy may be threatened by allowing the electricity provider to access fine-grained electricity consumption data, from which privacy-sensitive user behavior in a household could be deduced. The intuition behind the solution is that metering and data aggregation does not have to happen at the electricity provider, but can happen at the households. The electricity provider would provide each household with a function to run over the user's electricity data, which guarantees privacy since the provider does not gather the household's data.

So, how would this model apply to the NHS and SUS? In England, the NHS has moved to a networked system model [38]. Although the initial plan was a centralized repository, this failed in its implementation; thus, now a distributed model is being used where all patient data is to be stored at the patient's general practitioner (GP). This same model can be used for secondary uses. First, the medical data always resides with the GP and is not stored elsewhere. Second, in many cases the researcher could create hypotheses to be run on the GP networked systems without having to look at the fine-grained user data.

This allows the medical information to stay at the place of origin – the GP – thus allowing for changes requested by patients, perhaps based on changing privacy attitudes, to be fulfilled at their local GP's office. This would support the loosening and tightening of privacy expectations by patients as they can make these changes at the local GP's office, alleviating some of the concerns found in this study.

There are several technical challenges with this approach. First, there is a bootstrapping process that requires all devices onto which data is held to provide a proof that the original data has not been tampered with by the user. This bootstrapping phase will require GP systems capable of some basic cryptographic capabilities. There is evidence that these capabilities are minimal and current system architectures support them [36]. In addition, the medical community might not readily accept the proposed design as it ultimately calls for the data to be stored with the GP and not with the SUS. This decentralized architecture will have to allow privacy-preserving statistical aggregation of data to be transmitted to the researchers to support medical studies.

Limitations of the Current Study

Because the ultimate goal of mechanisms for privacy of medical data in secondary use is to uncover relationships and trends that can positively affect public health, having rich narrative data explicating the patient's perspective of privacy is both crucial and necessary. Nevertheless, the research agenda must go further to validate the concepts we have generated through further studies of other patients with diabetes, as well as other groups of chronically ill patients, and even people unaffected by a chronic illness. In addition, a longitudinal study of patients' actual changes in health information sensitivities would be helpful to compare to their recalled previous experience and envisaged future changes in privacy perceptions. It is hoped that the emergent concept of temporally situated patient privacy perspectives can then be applied in a more structured manner to guide the formative evaluation of secondary data use systems to empower patients toward greater participation in health reporting.

CONCLUSION

A chronic condition can affect a person from their childhood to late in life, and when one ponders the massive changes that can occur over lifetime, it is naïve to assume that the privacy concerns and the willingness to share health information will be anything close to consistent or static. Change in one's experience with technology and the nature of one's lifestyle or condition will influence one's willingness not only to share information that will be collected in a medical record but also how likely one will be to share information for the purpose of large scale medical data aggregation. A one-time consent management system would not respect the patients' wishes in the long-term so future systems should be able to adapt to changing attitudes that include both tightening and loosening of privacy sensitivities. Designers of these medical information systems supportive of large-scale medical data aggregation should be mindful of these implications and what this might mean for the quality of the data in these systems.

REFERENCES

1. Braun, V. and Clarke, V. Using thematic analysis in psychology. *Qualitative Research in Psychology 3*, 2 (2006), 77-101.
2. Bridson, J., Hammond, C., Leach, A. and Chester, M.R. Making consent patient centred. *British Medical Jour. 327*, 7424 (2003), 1159-1161.
3. Chalmers, J. and Muir, R.. Patient privacy and confidentiality. *British Medical Jour 326*, (2003), 725-726.
4. Chochinov, H.M. Dignity and the essence of medicine: The A, B, C, and D of dignity conserving care. *British Medical Jour 335* (2007), 184.
5. Cleeff, A., Dimkov, T., Pieters, W. and Wieringa, R. Realizing Security Requirements with Physical Properties: A Case Study on Paper Voting. In *Proc. IT Convergence and Security 2011*. Springer Netherlands (2012), 51-67.
6. Department of Health. Improving Chronic Disease Management. http://www.dh.gov.uk/en/Publicationsandstatistics/Publications/PublicationsPolicyAndGuidance/DH_4075214.
7. Department of Health. Newly available Health Data will support Medical Research and Patient Empowerment. http://mediacentre.dh.gov.uk/2011/11/29/newly-available-health-data-will-support-medical-research-and-patient-empowerment/.
8. Diabetes UK. Current Research. http://www.diabetes.org.uk/Research/Current-research/.
9. Forsythe, D.E. Using ethnography to build a working system: rethinking basic design assumptions. In *Proc. Computer Applications in Medical Care 1992*. McGraw-Hill (1992), 510–514.
10. Fox, S., and Jones, S. The social life of health information. *Pew Internet*. www.pewinternet.org/Reports/2009/8-The-Social-Life-of-Health-Information.aspx.
11. General Medical Council Standards. Confidentiality guidance: Research and other secondary uses. http://www.gmc-uk.org/guidance/ethical_guidance/confidentiality_40_50_research_and_secondary_issues.asp.
12. Golafshani, N. Understanding reliability and validity in qualitative research. *The Qualitative Report 8*, 4 (2003), 597-607.
13. Greene, J.A., Choudhry, N.K., Kilabuk, E. and Shrank, W.H. Online social networking by patients with diabetes: a qualitative evaluation of communication with Facebook. *Jour. General Internal Medicine 26*, 3 (2011), 287-292.
14. Gross, L.S., Li, L., Ford, E.S. and Liu, S. Increased consumption of refined carbohydrates and the epidemic of type 2 diabetes in the United States: an ecologic assessment. *American Jour. of Clinical Nutrition 79*, 5 (2004), 774-779.
15. International Diabetes Federation. One Adult in Ten Will Have Diabetes by 2030. http://www.dh.gov.uk/prod_consum_dh/groups/dh_digitalassets/@dh/@en/documents/digitalasset/dh_4075213.pdf.
16. Kaufman, D.J., Murphy-Bollinger, J., Scott, J. and Hudson, K.L. Public opinion about the importance of privacy in biobank research. *American Jour. of Human Genetics 85*, 5 20(2009), 643-54.
17. Kaufman, F.R. Type 2 diabetes mellitus in children and youth: a new epidemic. *Jour. of Pediatric Endocrinology and Metabolism*, *15*, Supplement (2011), 737-744.
18. Koro, C.E., Bowlin, S.J., Bourgeois, N. and Fedder, D.O. Glycemic control from 1988 to 2000 among US adults diagnosed with type 2 diabetes. *Diabetes Care 27*, 1 (2004),17-20.
19. Lowrance, W.W. Learning from experience. *Privacy and the seconda3ry use of data in health research.* Nuffield Trust (2002).
20. Lubkin, I.M. NS Larsen, P.D. *Chronic illness: Impact and interventions*. Jones & Bartlett Learning (2006).
21. Ludman, E.J., Fullerton, S.M., Spangler, L., Trinidad, S.B., Fujii, M.M., Jarvik, G.P., Larson, E.B. and Burke, W. Glad you asked: participants' opinions of re-consent for dbGap data submission. *Jour. Empirical Research on Human Research Ethics 5*, 3 (2010), 9-16.
22. Mays, N. and Pope, C. Qualitative research: rigour and qualitative research. *British Medical Jour 311*, 6997 (1995), 109.
23. Medical Research Council. e-Health Informatics Research – Securing the UK as a world leader. http://www.mrc.ac.uk/Ourresearch/ResearchInitiatives/E-HealthInformaticsResearch/index.htm.
24. Merton, R.K. Thematic Analysis in Science: Notes on Holton. *Science 188*, 4186 (1975), 335-338.
25. Narayanan, A. and Shmatikov, V. De-anonymizing social networks. In *Proc. Security and Privacy 2009*. IEEE (2009),173-187.
26. National Health Service. Pseudonymisation Implementation Project.

http://www.connectingforhealth.nhs.uk/systemsandservices/pseudo.

27. National Health Service. Pseudonymisation Implementation Project (PIP): Implementation Guidance on Local NHS Data Usage and Governance for Secondary Uses. http://www.connectingforhealth.nhs.uk/systemsandservices/pseudo/impguide.pdf.

28. National Health Service. "Sealed Envelopes" Briefing Paper: "Selective Alerting" Approach. http://www.connectingforhealth.nhs.uk/systemsandservices/infogov/confidentiality/sealedpaper.pdf.

29. National Health Service. Secondary Uses Service (SUS). http://www.ic.nhs.uk/services/secondary-uses-service-sus.

30. Nied, R.J. and Franklin, B. Promoting and prescribing exercise for the elderly. *American Family Physician 65*, 3 (2002), 419-430.

31. Or, C.K.L. and Karsh, B.T. A systematic review of patient acceptance of consumer health information technology. *Jour. of the American Medical Informatics Association 16*, 4 (2009), 550-560.

32. Palen, L. and Aaløkke. Of pill boxes and piano benches: Home-made methods for managing medication. In *Proc. of CSCW 2006*, ACM Press (2006), pp. 79-88.

33. Paterson, B.L. The shifting perspectives model of chronic illness. *Jour. of Nursing Scholarship 33*, 1 (2001), 21-26.

34. Reddy, M.C., Dourish, P. and Pratt, W. Temporality in medical work: Time also matters. *Computer Supported Cooperative Work 15*, 1 (2006) 29-53.

35. Regan, P.M. *Legislating privacy: Technology, social values, and public policy*, University of North Carolina Press (1995).

36. Rial, A. and Danezis, G. Privacy-preserving smart metering. In *Proc. Workshop on Privacy in the Electronic Society 2011*, ACM (2011), 49-60.

37. Rind, D.M., Kohane, I.S., Szolovits, P., Safran, C., Chueh, H.C. and Barnett, G.O. Maintaining the confidentiality of medical records shared over the Internet and World Wide Web. *Annals Internal Medicine 127*, 2 (1997), 138–141.

38. Robertson, A., Cresswell, K., Takian, A., Petrakaki, D., Crowe, S., Cornford, T., Barber, N., Avery, A., Fernando, B., Jacklin, A., Prescott, R., Klecun, E., Paton, J. Lichtner, V., Quinn, C., Ali, M., Morrison, Z., Jani, Y., Waring, J., Marsden, K. and Sheikh, A. Implementation and adoption of nationwide electronic health records in secondary care in England: qualitative analysis of interim results from a prospective national evaluation. *British Medical Jour 341*, (2010).

39. Roter, D.L. and Hall, J.A. Physicians' interviewing styles and medical information obtained from patients. *Jour. General Internal Medicine 2*, 5 (1987), 325-329.

40. Strauss, A.L. and Fagerhaugh, S. *Social organization of medical work.* Transaction Publishers (1997).

41. Sweeney, L. Guaranteeing anonymity when sharing medical data: the Datafly system. In *Proc. AMIA Annual Fall Symposium 1997*, PubMed Central (1997), 51–55.

42. Sweeney, L. Replacing personally-identifying information in medical records: the SCRUB system. In *Proc. AMIA Annual Fall Symposium 1996*, PubMed Central (1997), 333–7.

43. Tunstall-Pedoe, H. Preventing Chronic Diseases. A Vital Investment: WHO Global Report. *Jour. Epidemiology 35*, 4 (2006), 1107.

44. Wagner, E.H., Austin, B.T., Davis, C., Hindmarsh, M., Schaefer, J. and Bonomi, A. Improving Chronic Illness Care: Translating Evidence Into Action. *Health Affairs 20,* 6 (2001), 64-78.

45. Wicks, P., Massagli, M., Frost, J., Brownstein, C., Okun, S., Vaughan, T., Bradley, R. and Heywood, J. Sharing health data for better outcomes on PatientsLikeMe. *Jour. Medical Internet Research 12*, 2 (2010).

46. Willison, D.J., Schwartz, L., Abelson, J., Charles, C., Swinton, M., Northrup, D. and Thabane, L. Alternatives to Project-specific Consent for Access to Personal Information for Health Research: What Is the Opinion of the Canadian Public? *Jour. American Medical Informatics Association 14*, 6 (2007), 706-712.

47. World Health Organization. Chronic diseases. http://www.who.int/topics/chronic_diseases/en/.

48. Wu, S. and Green, A. Projection of chronic illness prevalence and cost inflation. RAND Health (2000).

Globally Distributed System Developers: Their Trust Expectations and Processes

Ban Al-Ani[1] Matthew J. Bietz[1] Yi Wang[1] Erik Trainer[1] Benjamin Koehne[1] Sabrina Marczak[2] David Redmiles[1] Rafael Prikladnicki[2]

[1]Department of Informatics
University of California, Irvine
Irvine, CA 92697-3425, USA
{balani|mbietz|yiw|etrainer|bkoehne|redmiles}@ics.uci.edu

[2]Faculdade de Informática
Pontifícia Universidade Católica do Rio Grande do Sul
Porto Alegre, RS, Brazil
{sabrina.marczak|rafael.prikladnicki}@pucrs.br

ABSTRACT
Trust remains a challenge in globally distributed development teams. In order to investigate how trust plays out in this context, we conducted a qualitative study of 5 multi-national IT organizations. We interviewed 58 individuals across 10 countries and made two principal findings. First, study participants described trust in terms of their expectations of their colleagues. These expectations fell into one of three dimensions: that socially correct behavior will persist, that team members possess technical competency, and that individuals will demonstrate concern for others. Second, our study participants described trust as a dynamic process, with phases including formation, dissolution, adjustment and restoration. We provide new insights into these dimensions and phases of trust within distributed teams which extend existing literature. Our study also provides guidelines on effective practices within distributed teams in addition to providing implications for the extension of software engineering and collaboration tools.

Author Keywords
Trust; Trust expectations; Trust processes; Systems development; Globally distributed teams; Multi-national organizations; Empirical study.

ACM Classification Keywords
H5.3 Group and Organization Interface: Computer-supported cooperative work; K.4.3 Computers and Society: Organizational Impacts: Computer-supported collaborative work.

INTRODUCTION
Globally distributed system development (DSD) faces a number of sociotechnical challenges [11]; trust is just one challenge that must be overcome for effective and efficient collaboration in this area [1]. One of the most prevalent definitions sees trust as a belief that the trustee (individual, team and/or organization) will meet the positive expectations of the trustor (individual, team and/or organization) [1]. While we take this understanding of trust in terms of expectations as a starting point, we seek to gain a deeper understanding of what these expectations are and the processes that influence trust in DSD teams. Specifically, our guiding research question is: *How does trust play out among globally distributed development team members?* By contributing to a better understanding of trust *in this specific context*, we hope to inform the organization and management of these teams as well as the design of communication and collaboration tools to support this work.

To achieve our goal, we interviewed individuals working in DSD teams within 5 multi-national organizations. We specifically sought to investigate three aspects based on our understanding of trust as a dynamic process which involves expectations. First, we sought to understand what individuals within DSD teams expect from others during their collaboration. Second, we are interested in gaining insights into how individuals experience trust during their collaboration. Finally we wanted to identify the factors that influence the trust development process. This deeper understanding of trust can guide the development of future collaborative tools and extend existing tools to better support DSD teams.

We found our participants' expectations of others fell within one of three dimensions: *moral social order*, *concern for others,* and *technical competency*. We also found that the study participants described various phases of trust *processes*. We discuss these findings in the context of DSD, thus we extend existing literature. These findings are discussed in subsequent sections following our review of relevant literature to present an understanding of trust. The paper concludes with a discussion of our findings and directions for future work.

AN UNDERSTANDING OF TRUST

Trust has long been considered an important aspect of all social relationships [4]. It is a fundamental part of effective collaborations, as collaborators are more likely to collaborate, share knowledge and accept others' contributions when trusted [1].

We derive our understanding of trust from our previous work and from the literature. Furst et al. [9], for example, conclude that an individual's trust in their team refers to the likelihood that team members will live up to expectations, whereas Sabherwal [19] considers trust a "state involving confident positive expectations about another's motives with respect to oneself in situations entailing risk." In other words, trust can be considered one individual's expectations of another, and the former's willingness to be vulnerable based on those expectations [2]. These definitions of trust suggest that expectations, and consequently a sense of trust, can form and possibly change over time as an individual interacts with others. Trust formation and change over time in turn suggests that trust is a *dynamic process*.

We found two expectations frameworks particularly useful in analyzing our data: Barber's categories of expectations [4] and Fulmer et al.'s process model [8]. Barber [4] posits that all social interactions are acting upon expectations, which are part cognition, part emotional and part moral. He found that people's expectations develop into various *structures* and *processes*. Structures are often used to refer to people's expectations like referring to a person in their team as a manager, programmer, or tester. Although our discussions of trust are generally presented as positive expectations; we also consider changes in expectations from positive to negative, e.g. the expectation that an individual will fail to meet a deadline. This expectation of failure may lead to negative trust [1]. We therefore do not consider trust a static relationship but rather a complex dynamic *process* influenced by many factors that evolve and adapt in harmony with individuals' perceptions and changing expectations. Fulmer et al [8], consider this dynamic process as a series of three phases: trust formation, dissolution and restoration which denote met expectations, failure to meet expectations and instances in which individuals' trust is restored, respectively.

Barber [4] goes on to outline three different categories of expectations, namely: expectations of persistence of the natural and moral social orders, technical competency, and finally the expectation that the trustee will meet fiduciary obligations and responsibility in certain situations. Based on our review of his work, we understand these expectations to be as follows:

1. Social order: The expectations of the persistence of the natural and moral social orders refer to the internalized expectations that life will continue as usual. Such expectations within the context of systems development can be used to refer to the predictability of behavior e.g. people will behave as expected in a given situation.

2. Technical competency: The expectations of technically competent role performance within a given role may be dependent on knowledge, skill or other factors that enable an individual to perform the tasks within their roles. In this context, expectations are typically based on perceptions of what a certain role entails and the anticipated level of knowledge and technical facility.

3. Concern for others: What Barber refers to as "fiduciary" expectations include the expectations of obligations and responsibility that go beyond technical competence, such that an individual demonstrates concern for others' interest above their own. This includes team members fulfilling their role within the team regardless of their own agenda.

A breach of one or more of any of these expectations can have a negative impact on trust. Barber uses these dimensions of trust to frame his discussions of individuals' trust within the context of family, foundations, politics, and modern institutions (business and professions). We will use his dimensions to frame our research findings as we sought to understand what globally DSD team members expect from others, how they experience trust and the factors that influence this dynamic process.

METHOD

We conducted an empirical study across five Fortune 500 organizations that share the common characteristics of being multi-national and a leader in the development of computer-based systems worldwide. We recruited 58 subjects through a combination of email sent through a cross section of the organizations' mailing list and word of mouth (snowball sampling).

We interviewed 17 female and 41 male employees who were assigned to a wide range of projects within their organizations. The one-on-one semi-structured interviews lasted for an average of one hour and consisted of two main sections. The first section focused on the participant's demographics, role in the organization, and current project. For example, we asked the participant to choose a current or recent project (completed in the last year) in which one or more of the team members were geographically distributed. Each participant was a member of a team that was globally distributed across temporal and spatial locations. Participants described the project and discussed their trust in their team members.

The second section of the interview was designed to elicit deeper discussions about trust in the context of the participants' work. We began this section with a discussion of the meaning of trust; the interviewer asked the participant "*what do you mean when you say you trust John or Jane?*" A discussion ensued and typically concluded with a shared understanding that trust is about *expectations*, *reliance* and *risk*. Subsequent discussions typically included these key concepts associated with trust. We then presented participants with hypothetical scenarios, for example, "If you were forming a team to work on the next version of your current project, who would you choose for that team and why?" We then followed such questions with a discussion of their response. We also asked participants to tell us stories of instances when trust became an issue in their current project and others they have been involved in.

One of two researchers conducted each interview either face-to-face (F2F), over the telephone or through VOIP. Participants were drawn from 10 different countries of the world: the United States (33), Brazil (16), Mexico (2), Costa Rica (1), Ireland (1), Israel (1), Poland (1), China (1), Taiwan (1), and Malaysia (1). It was common for a participant to be working on the same project with team members located at different sites. Participants had an average of 11 years' experience working in distributed teams and 12 years' experience in the organization. Overall, participants had an average of 21 years of work experience. The participants' roles in the distributed team fell into one of three broad categories: managers - 20 (e.g. project manager), developers - 33 (e.g. systems architect), and support staff - 5 (e.g. lawyer). We refer to them collectively as developers as they are all members of a DSD team working toward developing an IT-related product.

Data Analysis

All interviews were transcribed, and transcriptions were prepared for analysis in the ATLAS.ti qualitative data analysis software [3]. Qualitative coding proceeded in stages. A team of five researchers were involved in the analysis and coding process. Due to issues of timing and site access, it was not possible to conduct simultaneous or iterative data collection and analysis. Instead, we treated the interviews as a fixed dataset, and analyzed them using techniques adapted, in part, from grounded theory approaches [6, 7].

Analysis began by dividing the interviews equally among the researchers. Each researcher conducted open-coding on a subset of transcripts, with the instructions to identify any statement in which the participant provided a definition of trust, an explanation of why they trust someone, or a rationale that drives a behavior or decision. The researchers then discussed the code lists each had generated, collapsing and unifying codes where there was commonality, and identifying unique codes that only one or two researchers had identified for further investigation. Each researcher then returned to her subset of the documents in order to unify the coding, look for instances of codes that had been identified by the other researchers, and generate new codes as needed. In the next phase of analysis, all of the documents were combined in a single ATLAS project file, and the researchers each took responsibility for a subset of the codes, writing descriptive memos about the emergent categories. Analysis continued in parallel, as the researchers wrote, shared and discussed memos, added to and refined the coding scheme, and analyzed the primary documents.

As the coding scheme was refined, we used a technique of comparison against findings and frameworks in the literature to identify the extent to which our developing insights fit existing theoretical explanations. Trust research is a theoretically flooded area (e.g. [4, 12, 14]). Rather than add to the general confusion of trust models, our goal is to specifically identify how existing frameworks apply (or do not) to the specific site of DSD. As such, rather than adopt Glaser's call to avoid the research literature [10] we engage with it directly. We used existing theoretical frameworks in the literature as a way to interrogate and challenge our developing category scheme. We paid special attention to which of our categories matched easily, which were struggles to fit, and those categories that did not fit a given framework. For example, when comparing our categories to a decision-theory framework [15], we found that the language of constraints could be useful for thinking about issues of organizational and geographical distance, but that the distinction between internal and external mental processes was less salient in our data. This process, repeated against several different trust frameworks from our literature review, then generated and informed further coding, memoing, and group discussion.

In the sections that follow, we discuss our findings, using two theoretical frameworks that we found to be most consistent with our data: Barber's model of expectations [4] and Fulmer's model of trust stages [8], both of which are outlined in the previous section.

FINDINGS

The context for this study is globally distributed systems development (DSD), and it is important to understand the ways that certain characteristics of the organizational and task context shape our findings. First, all of our participants are employed by large, multi-national firms engaged in systems engineering. These organizations typically have central headquarters and many satellite offices around the world (operating as separate divisions, wholly-owned subsidiaries, or sub-contractors). Second, almost all of our participants work in matrix organizations where they are members of a specific functional unit and are assigned to one or more product/project teams. For example, someone may be a test engineer (unit) working on a piece of accounting software (product). These large organizations work to promote strong corporate cultures through various organizational procedures, policies, and training events. Employees often have relatively long tenures within these organizations: the average among our participants is 12 years, with several of our participants reporting more than 30 years with the same firm. Global collaboration is becoming the dominant mode of work in these organizations, and it is typically supported through information technology infrastructure with specific tools for collaboration support including project management and communication tools.

Finally, risk plays an important role in many definitions of trust [1], and the organizational structure in which most of our participants live plays a significant role in shaping the risk preference. Systems development in other contexts, even if it is globally distributed, is likely to look very different in terms of how trust plays out. Arenas like community-based open-source development or small start-up firms are likely to be higher-risk ventures, or at least will not have the same set of organizational resources available to manage the risks. This clearly places limits on the generalizability of our study.

Trust as Expectations

We found that most participants discussed trust in terms of their expectations of others and whether or not these expectations were met. For example, one female developer located in the US justified her trust towards others in her team stating: "*I can always rely on them to meet my expectations.*" (P7)

Expectations have been identified frequently as an important aspect of trust e.g. [2, 4, 16]. In this section, we adapt the framework proposed by Barber to structure our discussion, and to highlight the specific ways that expectations play out in global systems engineering context.

Barber's model, outlined in our discussion of trust, suggests that trust relies on meeting three kinds of expectations: *social order*, *concern for others,* and *technical competency*. In the rest of this section, we discuss how each of these plays out in our data.

Maintaining the Social Order

In Barber's framework [4], trust relies on expectations that others will act in a way that is consistent with the social order. In other words, we expect that others will act in a way that is consistent with cultural, organizational, and other social norms. We found that our study participants typically discussed aspects of professionalism, and our analysis led us to conclude that maintaining a certain level of professionalism is essential to the persistence of social order. The primary concerns discussed include: honesty, politeness, and meeting commitments.

Honesty is a common form of moral social order. Many of our participants have an expectation that others tell the truth and think that honesty is "*one factor*" that is important to establishing trust. It is especially prized in difficult situations, for example, when giving critical feedback. Many participants emphasized the importance of not withholding *negative* feedback especially, and providing such feedback in a timely and appropriate manner. As one female manager located in the US, explained: "*They were absolutely honest with me. So, if things were not going right, instead of - they would let me know, but they'd let me know in an appropriate manner.*" (P6)

Here, we find that the participant describes an implied social order where she expects others to be honest. Many other participants emphasized that it is expected that others would freely (but appropriately) share information, outcomes, and opinions. P6's statement exemplifies others who valued negative feedback.

Appropriate professional conduct was also frequently cited as contributing to trust. One male manager, located in the US, explained an incident which led to the dissolution of trust: "*This man started swearing at people. And immediately that broke quite a good bit of trust with certain individuals who personally found that offensive.*" (P18).

Our participants also frequently cited a particular aspect of expectation of professionalism that was very important: whether or not others met their commitments. It is not surprising that meeting commitments plays such a large role in distributed development. The work tends to be deadline driven, and cooperative work is often managed through a divide-and-conquer strategy, in which distributed individuals and subgroups are assigned portions of the task that will be their responsibility. However, if someone does not complete their portion of the work on time and to specification, it can cause delays and other problems across the whole project. Monitoring others' activities from a distance is difficult. A clear sign of lack of trust is how much monitoring and follow-up is required. One male manager located in the US explained that his trust in someone depended on "*how many times I have to go back and keep asking them, or even worse, call them on the phone and walk through it.*" (P40)

Response to emails is also considered by many participants as a basis of trust and a characteristic of professionalism. One participant, a male developer located in Brazil, explained his expectations of others to respond to his queries as follows: "*if these people takes more than three or five hours to answer you back, it's hard to trust in other things.*"(P33). Another stated that "*trust is really shook up*" if a response is not received "*within a week" (P36)*. Others recalled instances in which a non-response led them to assume that their remote team members may have a public holiday and created negative trust when the team member claimed the email was not received (e.g. *P33*). Some participants stated that they would appreciate some form of acknowledgement, even if only it is an email to inform them it would take a few days to provide an answer (e.g. P35).

Expectations about meeting one's commitments are an important aspect of trust and a complicated one. In global development, the teams typically include people from a number of different cultural backgrounds. What it means to make a commitment, and the behaviors associated with making that commitment, tend to vary across cultures. As one male manager, located in the US, explains his experiences with others of different cultures: "*Certainly different cultures have different ways of saying yes and no or they'll say it and they don't mean or it's difficult... People are very willing to say yes when they're not committed, especially in other cultures. They just don't want to disappoint you, but they're not really committed and I was surprised by that a few times.*" (P3)

In international and cross-cultural interactions, expectations about maintaining the social order become particularly fraught. The meanings of a "yes," appropriate modes of expressing conflict, expectations about working in the evenings or on weekends, and many other aspects of organizational life, are all part of culturally-specific social orders. If the social order varies depending on the location of the team member, trust can suffer, not because of a personal failing, but as a result of differences in understandings of the social order [2].

Demonstrating Concern for Others

Barber [4] refers to "expectations of fiduciary obligations," or expectations that others will demonstrate concern and interests that extend beyond their own personal needs and gains. We take a broad view of this category that includes a consideration of others' needs and also one's dedication to the team and organization, sometimes including an "*element of self-sacrifice*" (P17).

We found that our participants typically discussed their sense of commonality as being important to their sense of trust towards others. This could involve shared goals, meanings, styles of working, or morality. This commonality led our participants to feel that they could predict others' performance. We found instances where participants stated that they could predict others' behavior because they shared emotion (e.g. passion for the project), ideals (e.g. conviction), culture or shared goals and agendas.

One way this category emerged in the data is that participants are more likely to trust others who share their emotions about the project or product. One male software engineer located in Costa Rica described how he picked collaborators: "*The idea is if you can include people that have an excitement about it either as part of the idea or can be excited about executing it, then we try to assign those folks.*" (P3)

Similarly, a female lawyer located in the US, said: "*I think it would be dependent upon whether or not they were passionate about the idea as well. So I think it would be more knowledge and passion.*" (P7)

Being passionate about the project also demonstrates a commitment to something outside of ones' own self-interest, and our respondents both tended to trust and want to work with enthusiastic and passionate people more.

Participants' trust also relied on their sense that others shared their ideals and work ethic, implying that this commonality engenders trust. One participant, a male manager located in the US, stated: "*I felt that we were all working towards common goals, I felt that they demonstrated technical credibility and that they had the respect of their peers and I have several personal experiences with them in difficult situations that showed that they could deliver.*" (P10)

In this statement, we find that the participant uses his experience of others on his team to predict future behavior. First, we find that he has determined that others shared his goals and those of the team, therefore they will collaborate and commit as he does. Second, he was able to determine a certain level of technical competence and assumes this will continue. Finally, he uses the insights gained from his peer network and his sense that those peers respect team members to conclude that others have found them reliable and predictable. Ideals such as confidentiality and loyalty are also important traits that participants listed amongst their expectations of others' moral correctness. We observed that loyalty to the team is a core expectation whereas loyalty to the individual is often considered an additional bonus.

Other participants demonstrated an awareness of the role that culture, *shared culture* in particular, plays in determining others' understanding of moral obligations. They acknowledge that people from different cultural backgrounds may vary on moral obligation. One developer located in Brazil, for example, typically sought others born in Brazil as their contact in remote locations i.e. (P33).

These findings suggest that there is a degree of overlap between expectations of *social order* and *demonstrating concern for others*. We observe that some participants expect team members to collaborate within the norms of their ideals and we therefore treated these expectations as part of the *natural social order*, whereas other participants regard others sharing such ideals to be beyond the norm and we therefore considered them showing *a concern for others* which extends beyond their own personal needs and gains.

Demonstrating Technical Competency

In general, system development requires a high degree of technical skill. We made four overarching observations regarding our data. First, we observed that study participants generally expected that all team members would possess the requisite technical competence to do their job. Participants believe that specific organizational structures, processes and practices make it possible to simply assume a certain level of skill from their team members. In other words, our participants expect that team members will have the required technical abilities because their organization's stringent performance reviews and intensive internal training maintain a universally high level of expertise among all employees. For example, when asked about technical competence, a male developer located in the US stated: "*... there's also something to be said for the fact that they are [org_name] employees and one of the criteria for getting in the group is that you've been with [org_name] for a while. And so, absolutely, I'm not saying that just having an [org_name] badge makes you a trustworthy person, but it certainly is one factor.*" (P49)

Second, we found that participants were generally confident in their understandings of the roles that each team member and remote site played within the context of their project. For example, a male developer located in China felt it was important to understand the role of each location during the collaboration: *"... and [we know] what kind of role the Shanghai team will be playing, what kind of role in Malaysia team will be playing, what kind of role the U.S. team will be playing.*" (P46)

This understanding of roles allowed participants to appreciate when their team members went beyond the confinement of their role to support others working on the project. The following statement, made by a male support staff member located in Malaysia, illustrates that he has often encountered team members that fulfill their role and go beyond his expectations thereby giving him a sense of team cohesion: "*...today I look at that team as one that has a very teamwork and lots of positive surprises where people would go the second and third mile to accommodate some of the needs that I'm facing over here in Penang.*" (P5)

Finally, we found that participants valued other competencies that impacted *how* they carried out the tasks associated with their role. One key form of competency was an organizational or process competency, e.g. people who could successfully navigate corporate bureaucracy or evaluate ideas for their organizational as well as technical acceptability. Study participants often implied that they trusted others who could provide insight into the dynamics of their team interactions. It was important that decisions be clearly communicated, but also that the rationales (especially if non-technical) should be clear. When rationales weren't explained, trust could be hurt e.g. (P35).

Interestingly we found instances where participants stated that they valued moral correctness more highly than technical knowledge. In such instances, participants acknowledged the importance of being able to rely on fellow team members and not need to second-guess their actions or tasks once these had been discussed.

In sum, Barber's framework of trust is a lens through which we can categorize our results into 3 categories of expectation: *social order*, *concern for others,* and *technical competency*. We found that professionalism, honesty, politeness, and meeting commitments are values that form expectations about social order.

In addition, we found that participants were more likely to trust others who share their emotions about the project or product. Demonstrating this passion to others and being aware of shared culture allowed participants to predict each other's behavior which in turn resulted in more trust. Additionally, participants trusted those who demonstrated competency in technical and organizational areas, as well as team interactions. Thus, our results indicate that these expectations form the foundation upon which trust rests.

Trust as a Process

While our findings about the types of expectations are consistent with Barber's model, we also found that, for our study participants, trust is a *dynamic process* that cannot be fully explained by Barber's model. To understand this aspect of trust, we engage the work of Fulmer et al [8], which describes trust as evolving through three stages: trust *formation*, *dissolution*, and *restoration*. *Trust formation* is the phase in which individuals develop trust over time, whereas *trust dissolution* occurs when trust erodes as a result of others failing to meet an individual's expectations. *Trust restoration* can occur when trust stops declining after violation and eventually reaches some relatively stable state. We observed these stages in our study, and also observed an additional phase - that of *trust adjustment*. Trust *adjustment* occurs when individuals adjust their expectations so that they can be met by others and it therefore enables *trust restoration*. While we identify these phases with distinct names, we recognize that they do not necessarily occur in distinct phases. We found that these phases intertwine and overlap; moreover, the sequence of these phases can also change.

In the next sections, we describe each of these stages in more detail in relation to our participants' experiences.

Trust Formation

Our participants typically discussed *trust formation* as occurring over an extended period of time as a result of interpersonal interactions. They discussed the formation of trust as being contagious, an emotional process which involves developing empathy with others in the distributed team and an awareness of different cultures (work styles, language, etc.). Their statements also suggest that while many felt that they had a baseline level of trust that exists because of their trust in the organization's hiring process, they also recognized that different forms of trust developed based on the roles of the trustor and the trustee within the team (e.g. peer-peer vs. team member-manager). Finally, we found that many relied on others' previous performance to initiate the trust formation phase; conversely, we also found instances where participants stated they preferred providing their team mates with an opportunity for a *"fresh start"* (P54).

Our study supports findings that trust is built over time [1]. We found many instances in which our study participants referred to trust developing either through a planned strategy to test others' trustworthiness or through the opportunities afforded to demonstrate their own trustworthiness. For example, the following general quote from a male developer located in Brazil illustrates the need to form trust gradually over time: "... *trust is something that you need to build, it's not something that you're gonna get on your first meeting. You don't know that person, you don't know the skills that uh she or he has, and things like that.*" (P13)

Similarly, another participant located in the US considers trust formation as process that is forged from shared experiences and *"common battles together"*. These statements exemplify many participants' perception that their trust in others has developed over an extended period of time through a series of interactions. This perception of participant's trust towards others is extended by an awareness that others trust' towards them must be gained by meeting others' expectations to "*build up that bank account with them*", as one male manager located in the US explained (P18).

Our participants had mixed thoughts about whether trust could successfully be built without face-to-face (F2F) interaction. For some, F2F meetings were crucial to gain insights into others' concerns and understand where they were coming from. Others felt that they acclimatized to non-F2F interactions and focused more on the nature of their interactions rather than the medium. There is, however, a general agreement that *frequent* contact is important, and that, if given the choice, F2F is preferable to non-F2F, and that richer mediating technologies (e.g. video- and audio-conferencing) are better for trust development than leaner (e.g. e-mail).

Personal networks are also very important in trust formation. Participants are more likely to trust others who have been introduced or referred by someone they trust. Our analysis of such statements suggests that people who have long-term experience in the organization could play an important role in supporting the development of trust. For example, a US-located manager was confident that he could form trust with most people he needed to collaborate with: "*... I've been at [org_name] for 18 years. I know a lot of people inside [org_name]. And never do I go to a meeting where there isn't somebody there that I know who can introduce me to somebody else.*" (P21)

Participants reported that frequent interactions promoted an understanding of other cultures in terms of diverse working styles, humor, use of language, and shared knowledge. Frequent interactions also helped participants read the "tone" of someone's communications. Tone is often implicitly implied in written communications or explicitly heard in spoken communications. Such cues are often the only clues team members have when interacting with others in remote locations. For example, one manager located in Brazil described why he liked to meet with his French colleagues: "*I think talk is really important... when I come and go to talk about that with people they take it easier. Okay, he's like that. He's not angry at me; he's just like that.*" (P17)

His statement suggests that he feels that the French team members are better calibrated to his way of expressing emotion and tone because he spent time with them and they met F2F.

The formation phase of the trust process is considered by some as an emotional process in which the role within the team determines the level of involvement and the degree of empathy which can be felt by the participant. For example, a manager located in the US (*P3*) explained how his sense of trust is formed within the boundaries of team members' roles and determines the nature of the collaboration. Another participant, a developer located in Brazil (*P34*), describes the emotional aspect of trust formation as developing an *empathy* towards trusted others.

Trust Dissolution

Trust formation and growth do not always continue unchecked, but rather can undergo *dissolution*. Others have found that trust breaks down in electronic contexts [18], but our findings suggest that there are a variety of reasons for trust dissolution. Participants often reported instances in which their trust towards others declined as a result of others failure to meet their expectations. Participant's trust in others also declined if they sensed that others did not trust them (e.g. questioned the truthfulness of participant's statements). *Trust dissolution* is also often precipitated by fear of job loss, negative reputation or differences in culture coming to the fore.

Previous work has led us to conclude that the dissolution of trust in distributed development teams can lead to individuals working in isolation or re-doing others' work, which leads to the erosion of team cohesiveness [2]. In previous sections, where we discussed trust expectations, we discussed instances in which others failed to meet study participants' expectations and the participants' attempts to cope with such failure. The following statement, given by a male manager located in Malaysia, exemplifies the general sentiment that some basic level of baseline trust can exist and grow, unless the participant finds that such trust is unfounded: "*I'm a person that I would trust you until - unless you give me reason not to.*" (P5)

We conclude from statements similar to these that failure to meet expectations, regardless of which category these expectations fall under, can lead to the decline of trust.

Our analysis of coded data led us to observe that the dissolution of trust typically occurs when a change of context arises. Changes in context occur as a result of the participant working with others on a new project, or when others employment status changes from an employee of the organization to a consultant or contractor. In such instances, while participant's expectations remain the same the new context may mean that team member fails to meet those expectations. The following statement, for example, made by a male developer located in Brazil illustrates the influence of roles within the team (i.e. business team): "*People who are the [business unit] are having difficulty to get the trust from the business partners because.... those guys, they are not always open to share.*" (P13)

Other instances of trust dissolution were a result of fear of job loss or failure to meet the participant's expectations regarding communication, in terms of timeliness, truthfulness, or honesty. The dissolution of trust because of the fear of job loss is closely associated with poor communications and a perceived lack of transparency. For example, one manager located in the US explains others' experience of fear of job loss as leading to dissolution of trust: "*Every time you tell them, no, look at how this is structured. They don't believe you because everybody is so d--n (expletive) scared about getting shut down.*" (P21)

Participants also discussed less positive encounters with agendas of some of the remote locations that competed for project ownership. Such statements often include the participants' description of their coping strategies e.g. the need for extra control by attending meetings, checking up on others to make sure they followed through or enforcing a reporting hierarchy.

Others experienced the dissolution of trust as a result of communication breakdown caused by the relatively large team size. The benchmark for the optimum team size varied greatly. This may imply that it is not so much the size of the team in some instances, but rather the mismatched expectations of the team members.

Other mismatches could be caused by cultural traits of the distributed team members. The awareness of differences in culture often leads to participants anticipating differences during interactions and arousal of suspicion between diverse collaborators. Participants described how they had to bridge between two or more mismatched cultures that caused trust dissolution within the team as a whole, e.g. (P6).

Trust Adjustment

While Fulmer [8] claims that trust restoration occurs when "trust stops declining after violation and starts to rebound, eventually being relatively stable", we found that this transition from dissolution to restoration requires an adjustment of expectations. Participants generally discussed their need to make adjustment to other cultures which they determined was the cause of the dissolution. The period of adjustment phase allowed many of our study participants to transition into the next phase of the trust process - trust restoration.

A failure to meet expectations often leads to a decline in trust or trust dissolution. Our analysis of the phases as experienced by study participants and within the trust process proposed by Fulmer [8], led us to identify a phase that has not been widely reported. Practitioners assigned to a project cannot typically leave the project if negative trust has developed towards one or more of their team members. We found that participants typically attempted to *adjust* their expectation when they were not met - such that they can be met by others.

We found many instances in which participants chose to continue working with others who had not met their expectations when presented with a hypothetical scenario where they could choose team members to work with. They acknowledged the existence of negative trust towards some of the current team members but rationalized their choice by stating that they now knew what to expect and had learned to cope. As such, *trust adjustment* refers to the phase in which individuals reflect on their expectations of others, why these expectations were not met, and how they need to revise their expectations during interactions to *restore* some level of trust.

One participant, an experienced lead developer located in Brazil, described the adjustment of her expectations regarding her PM. This adjustment took some time because they both expected different work styles, as she explains: "*And about the PM. Uh, now because we are working for some time I would say we can, we have a high trust. But at the, at the beginning you don't have, we didn't have because she has a totally different way of working. I've never worked with a PM like her before.*" (P52)

We found that participants typically reflected on their experiences with others to identify the cause of the discord and guide them through the adjustment phase of the trust process. One software engineer located in Brazil described what led him to adjust his expectations as follows: "*...by my interaction with them. By experience. By situation where I was trusting them, there was a certain action item. I figured out that wasn't exactly the product; it wasn't exactly what happened. So it's based on experience.*" (P17)

One senior US manager discussed the dissolution of trust in his team, and acknowledged that his failure to nurture the team affected the level of trust. His statement suggests that he did not expect team members to need guidance and his reflections imply he has revised his expectations to more closely reflect the team members' ability to perform and work together: "*And that's the part that I think I could have made a difference in the overall trust of the team had I been able to spend the time working with that team in a more one on one guidance, leadership type basis; take the politics out of the discussions.*" (P21)

Participants predominantly reported that they needed to adjust to others because the cause of the dissolution was cultural; some reporting that their exposure to other cultures and travel has enabled them to gain a better understanding of others and revise their expectations. Such cultural adjustments are not limited to interaction among team members from different countries; they also include adjustment to different regions within the same country as highlighted by a manager in Mexico (P32).

Trust Restoration

Trust restoration typically occurs when individuals attempt to rebuild their sense of trust towards others. We found that many participants discussed instances in which trust *restoration* can occur as a result of the *adjustment* of expectations. Once individuals have reflected on and revised their expectations, they can then begin to rebuild trust using expectations that more closely reflect the reality of their collaborations with others. While restoration is possible, it is not an easy phase or necessarily one that can be taken for granted. A portfolio manager in Brazil made the following comment: "*I mean, if you break that [trust], the work required to regain trust is very high.*" (P12). Other participants explicitly stated that they were never able to restore trust towards their team members and this typically led to a breakdown in their collaboration.

Participants also recalled working in teams and having to restore trust amongst disparate cultures of two geographically isolated sites. An experienced female manager in US found that previous negative experiences among team members or units led to ineffective collaboration: "*There was a lot of historical bad feeling, as I said earlier. So, part of my job was to bring this into a cohesive team to deliver the capability in the most efficient manner for [org_name]. My recommendation towards the end of the program was actually an org change. That we [re]org these people so that they could work better together.*" (P6)

She further illustrated her points with an example of differences in working styles between the participant located in the US and team members located in Israel: "*It absolutely, it was my learning that I needed, for these people-we're talking engineers, we're talking technical people-is that it will - in fact it has helped me with the Israel folks. I deal with them now, and I know how to do it so much better than I did before. And it's different than I do in the US. It's very different...Although it was painful, it was really - it was good.*"

As in the formation phase of trust development, we found that participants reported trust restoration can be more readily restored when they have an opportunity to meet F2F. A female project manager (P10) in the US described how F2F interaction helped the restoration phase and went on to explain how she continues to rely on and trust the team members she met in her first visit.

In sum, our results corroborate previous research that indicates that trust is a dynamic process that occurs in multiple stages: trust formation, trust dissolution, and trust restoration. However, while we found support for this model, our data indicates that there is an additional phase in the process: *trust adjustment.* Trust *adjustment* occurs when individuals adjust their expectations so that other individuals can meet them. The adjustment phase enables *trust restoration.*

DISCUSSION

Trust is an important element of most interactions and allows individuals to work together effectively and share information openly. It must be developed over an extended period of time. We have also extended other work in reporting that trust is experienced through a series of phases, trust *formation*, *dissolution* and *restoration*. We identify a phase discussed by many of our study participants that of *adjustment*. In reporting the activities within each of these phases we have extended our understanding of the trust process and provided new insights into how individuals in DSD teams refer to trust in such contexts. Our analysis of participants' adjustments implies that trust is a dynamic process which evolves over time in response to elements in the environment and is similar to other conceptual constructs that have been defined by researchers.

Researchers, for example [17], discuss people's continuous management and negotiation of expectations and behaviors within the context of privacy, and we find this is echoed in our data. Their description of a dynamic process in which individuals continuously respond to circumstance is similar to the process of adjusting and recalibrating the expectations which form the basis of trust. People act in a variety of capacities simultaneously: as individuals (e.g., team members, project managers, developers) and as representatives of work units or of a specific team. Trust judgments are not isolated to single events, but rather evolve based on the outcome of a sequence of previous collaborations and adjustments. Based on their past experiences, some participants sought to "understand" one another and adjust.

We adapted Barber's [4] constructs to structure the understanding of developers' expectations, reported in this paper. It allows us to provide information that can be used to more accurately reflect what individuals expect of others in their globally DSD team. For example, our findings suggest that not only is communication clarity important but also the timeliness and appropriateness of communications are additional factors that can influence trust. Such an understanding of expectations, which many of our study participants discussed during our interviews, can be used to further extend existing tools adopted by development teams. Indeed, existing qualitative studies of e-mail responsiveness suggest that a reply within the same work day or within 24 hours of receiving a message is a reasonable expectation [21]. The authors cite contextual cues such as e-mail, shared calendars, and job role that can be integrated into existing applications such as e-mail clients where they can help developers form expectations about their colleagues' response times.

For instance, a new feature to an existing email application can include deriving the average response time for individuals on the team. Consider a scenario where a developer "John" sends an e-mail to another team member "Jenna". Our results suggest that extending John's e-mail application such that it informs him that Jenna typically needs 3 working days to respond to any e-mail can help him know when to expect a reply. Providing such information (with respect for appropriate privacy considerations) can help developers set their expectations at a level in line with a team member's typical response time.

Truly globally distributed software developers can especially benefit from contextual cues they might otherwise miss. Yet responsiveness is but one indicator of trustworthiness, and other relevant cues will likely depend on the task at hand. For example, when assembling new teams for especially *innovative* software projects, managers may value expertise over responsiveness, despite the fact that that expertise may be distributed throughout many time zones. Cues such as personnel profiles and org. chart information will be more appropriate than emails and calendars. On the other hand, new developers who are being "onboarded" to such a project will likely need to quickly learn the inner-workings of the system as well as who to go to for help. This requires knowing about their colleagues' expertise. As such, cues like source-code and work items may be more meaningful because these are the artifacts that demonstrate said expertise.

The findings reported in this paper have informed the construction of a "design space" for DSD tools that gives guidance on what contextual cues can be used in the design of tools to maximize factors that influence trust among globally distributed software developers. Using the example of responsiveness as a trust factor, the design space suggests that cues such as one's e-mail reply time, time zone overlap, the number and priority of work items assigned to them, and their working hours overlap can help set expectations [20]. Our findings provide guidance for designers about what kinds of expectations are important and the role they play in the process of building and maintaining trust.

We found our study participants' expectations remarkably consistent across sites and organizations. We also found, however, that many of our participants had encountered many instances in which others had failed to meet these expectations. This suggests that while these expectations are widespread there is a certain level of ignorance of how to effectively collaborate with others in DSD teams. We conclude that the expectations we report in this paper can be used to develop a more substantial set of expectations which can serve as guidelines for effective practices in DSD teams and can be used for training purposes.

Finally, it is worth pointing out a kind of "meta-finding" that arose from our analysis process. We worked to compare our emergent categories to frameworks proposed in the literature, but we found no single framework that could explain the richness of our data. Here we draw on the two frameworks that fit our data the best, but both were incomplete. Barber discusses expectations, but does not shed light on how they come to be or change over time. Fulmer allows us to see dynamic processes, but does not help us to understand which expectations are important. Like these two frameworks, models of trust tend to be either static models that emphasize particular determinant factors or dynamic models with a process focus. We found this dichotomy to be inconsistent with our data. For our participants, trust in someone is always a matter of both who that person is and what kinds of experiences they had shared together.

STUDY LIMITATIONS

We had a rare opportunity to conduct an empirical study *in situ*, to discuss trust with individuals working in globally distributed systems development (DSD) teams. We strove to off-set the limits that may have been introduced in the recruitment process (self-selection and snowball sampling) by increasing the sample size, and diversity of sites included in our participant pool to increase our confidence regarding our insights into trust within DSD teams. Our study is one of a few which gains insights from practitioners through an open discussion of current projects rather than laboratory studies involving students (e.g. [5,14]) or a survey targeting off-shore developers (e.g. [19]). Furthermore, the interviewees are not limited to software engineers, but range from very technical jobs (e.g., developers) to support staff (e.g., lawyers). This inclusion is also not typical of studies of trust in distributed teams. The researchers have no conflicts of interests with the interviewees.

As with any interview study, certain aspects of trust may have been invisible to our method. For example, while in-group/out-group effects are likely to affect trust in global collaborations, social stigma and the human tendency for post-hoc rationalization make it difficult to uncover issues like cultural prejudice through interview data.

Given the aims of this study, we believe the method was appropriate. As we have discussed, our goal was to explore the applicability of existing trust frameworks in this particular context. However, we caution against simplistic generalizations to other contexts that do not share similar organizational structures, forms of expertise, and task constraints.

CONCLUDING REMARKS

In conclusion, we report several key contributions in this paper. These include:

- A description of what people expect from others when collaborating: We demonstrate that these expectations cut across gender, roles and geography and consequently cultures. We adopted Barber's [4] construct to frame our findings and provide structure to expectations discussed by our study participants. These expectations give insights on *what* engenders trust.

- An extension of existing theory based on practitioners' accounts of their experiences of the trust process: We extended the phases identified by Fulmer [8], based on our analysis of these accounts, to include an *adjustment* phase. The *adjustment* phase explains how individual transition from trust *dissolution* to *restoration*, which will allows them to continue to collaborate with others more effectively.

- Integration of existing frameworks for understanding trust: We found that to adequately explain our findings, we needed to draw on two kinds of theories: one that described categories of expectations, and another that dealt with trust as a dynamic process.

- Suggestions on how to extend existing collaboration tools: Our findings provide new insight into both the factors that engender trust and the phases that are part of the trust process. These can be utilized to both extend existing tools and to help develop effective collaboration practices that are key to improving future collaborations among DSD team members.

We have three specific goals for our future work on this project. First, we continue to explore our data in different ways, including investigating the existence of any correlations between the findings reported in this paper and other characteristics of the individuals (e.g. demographics) or collaborative projects (e.g. team structure, cultural distribution, etc.). We also have introduced here an extension of the grounded theory method that, rather than focusing on generating new theory, takes as its goal the assessment of theoretical validity and fit within a particular context. We are working to refine and extend this method as we use it to explore this and other data. Finally, as mentioned above, we have already begun to utilize our current findings to extend existing tools such that they can support the development of trust in distributed teams by helping the team members build proper expectations, and we expect to pursue this work further.

AKNOWLEDGEMENTS

This work was supported by NSF awards #0943262, #0808783, and #1111446. We thank the participants of our study for collaborating with us.

REFERENCES

1. Al-Ani, B., and Redmiles, D. In strangers we trust? Findings of an empirical study of distributed Development. In *Proc. ICGSE 2009*. IEEE Press (2009), 121-130.
2. Al-Ani, B., Trainer, E., Redmiles, D., and Simmons, E. Trust and surprise in distributed teams: Towards an understanding of expectations and adaptations. In *Proc. ICIC 2012*, ACM press (2012), 97-106.
3. Atlas.ti v. 6 [computer program]. ATLAS.ti Scientific Software Development GmbH (2011).
4. Barber, B. *The Logic and Limits of Trust*. Rutgers University Press (1983).
5. Bos, N., Olson, J., Gergle, D., Olson, G., and Wright, Z. Effects of four computer-mediated communications channels on trust development. In *Proc. CHI 2002*. ACM Press (2002), 135-140.
6. Charmaz, K. *Constructing grounded theory: A practical guide through qualitative analysis*. Sage (2006).
7. Corbin, J. M. and Strauss, A. L. *Basics of qualitative research: Techniques and procedures for developing grounded theory, 3rd edition*. Sage (2008).
8. Fulmer, C. Ashley and Gelfand, Michele Joy, Dynamic Trust Processes: Trust Dissolution and Restoration. In *Proc. IACM 23rd Annual Conference,* (2010).
9. Furst, S., Blackburn, R., and Rosen, B. Virtual team effectiveness: A proposed research agenda. *Information Systems Journal 9 (1999)*, 249-269.
10. Glaser, B. G. *Basics of grounded theory analysis*. Sociology Press (1992).
11. Herbsleb, J. D., Mockus, A., Finholt, T. A., & Grinter, R. E. (2000). Distance, dependencies, and delay in a global collaboration. In *Proceedings of the ACM 2000 Conference on Computer Supported Cooperative Work*, p. 319-328. New York: ACM Press.
12. Hosmer, L.T. Trust: The connecting link between organizational theory and philosophical ethics. *Academy* of Management Review 20, 2 (1995), 379-403.
13. Jarvenpaa, S. L., Knoll, K., and Leidner, D. E. Is anybody out there? Antecedents of trust in global virtual teams. *J. Manage. Inf. Syst.* 14, 4 (1998), 29-64.
14. Jarvenpaa, S. L., Shaw, T. R., and Staples, D. S. Toward contextualized theories of trust: The role of trust in global virtual teams. In *Information Systems Research 15, 3 (2004)*, 250-267.
15. March J. G., and Heath C. *A primer on decision making: How decisions happen*. Free Press (1994).
16. Olson, G. M., and Olson. J. S. Distance matters. *Hum.-Computer Interaction 15, 2 (2000)*, 139-178.
17. Palen, L., and Dourish, P. 2003. Unpacking "privacy" for a networked world. In *Proc. Conference on Human factors in computing systems, (CHI). ACM, NY, NY,* 129-136.
18. Rocco, E. (1998). Trust breaks down in electronic contexts but can be repaired by some initial face-to-face contact CHI '98 Conference Proceedings ACM, NY, NY, (pp. 496-502). New York: ACM.
19. Sabherwal, R. The role of trust in outsourced IS development projects. *Communications of the ACM* 42, 2 (1999), 80-86.
20. Trainer, E. and Redmiles, D.F. "Foundations for the Design of Visualizations that Support Trust in Distributed Teams," In *Proceedings of the 2012 ACM International Conference on Advanced Visual Interfaces (AVI 2012, Capri Island, Italy)*, 34-41.
21. Tyler, J. R. and Tang, J. C. 2003. When Can I Expect an Email Response? A Study of Rhythms in Email Usage. Proceedings from *ECSCW '03: European Conference on Computer-Supported Cooperative Work*, 239- 258.

Microblog Credibility Perceptions: Comparing the United States and China

Jiang Yang[1]
[1]University of Michigan, IBM
[1]105 S. State St., Ann Arbor, MI 48109, U.S.
yangjiang78@gmail.com

Scott Counts, Meredith Ringel Morris, Aaron Hoff[2]
[2]Microsoft Research
[2]One Microsoft Way, Redmond, WA 98052, U.S.
{counts, merrie, aaronho}@microsoft.com

ABSTRACT

Microblogs have become an increasingly important source of information, both in the U.S. (Twitter) and in China (Weibo). However, the brevity of microblog updates, combined with increasing access of microblog content through search rather than through direct network connections, makes it challenging to assess the credibility of news relayed in this manner [34]. This paper reports on experimental and survey data that compare the impact of several features of microblog updates (author's gender, name style, profile image, location, and degree of network overlap with the reader) on credibility perceptions among U.S. and Chinese audiences. We reveal the complex mechanism of credibility perceptions, identify several key differences in how users from each country critically consume microblog content, and discuss how to incorporate these findings into the design of improved user interfaces for accessing microblogs in different cultural settings.

Author Keywords

Twitter; Microblogs; Credibility; Cultural differences.

ACM Classification Keywords

H.5.m [Information interfaces and presentation (e.g., HCI)]: Miscellaneous;

INTRODUCTION

Social media are becoming an important and general information source beyond status post sharing within social networks [27]. Every day, more than 1.6 billion queries are issued on Twitter's search portal [49], and major search engines like Google [12] and Bing [46] have integrated status updates in order to provide timely and socially-relevant information. The rise in prominence of social media as an information source has led to an increase in the scrutiny of the credibility of these sources from mainstream media and researchers alike. This scrutiny is not unfounded, as end users are particularly wary of content posted to social media. Schmierbach and Oeldorf-Hirsch [45] showed that even when describing the same stories, people viewed the information on a website as more credible than the information on a Twitter feed. Thus, to best leverage the potential of social media as an information source, we need to design user experiences that maximize both the credibility and the perception of credibility of social media-based content.

Researchers have started to understand the mechanisms of microblog credibility perception. A recent study conducted by Morris et al. [34] revealed that people rely on a variety of non-text clues when assessing tweet credibility, identifying message topic, user name, and profile image as features that affect users' perceptions. They also found that altering the profile image made a greater difference in the context of entertainment topics than for science or political topics. This suggests that the factors influencing tweet credibility perception can be diverse, making the mechanism underlying perceptions of credibility complex and hard to predict.

Culture also influences people's preferences and use styles in sociotechnical systems [62, 63]. In particular, there are significant differences between the West (e.g., North America and Europe) and East Asia, corresponding to the contrasts between the analytic and holistic cognitive patterns and between the individualism and collectivism social orientations [30, 36]. These cognitive patterns and social orientations co-evolve with a number of cultural factors, including the development of a country's political systems [14], economic ideology [42], industrialization [26], intellectual traditions (Aristotelian vs. Confucian) [29, 40], languages [56], and religions [8]. Within the technology domain, these cultural characteristics may, affect how information is created and used, causing significant challenges in designing for information sharing in social media across cultures. In this study, we contrast the United States and China to identify and understand differences in how information and users are perceived in social media in each country. This is particularly timely and important given the exploding use of microblogging in China, where the two most popular microblogging services have 324 million and 425 million users respectively [22].

To our knowledge this is the first systematic study investigating cultural differences in how people perceive the credibility of social media content. Our results describe how several profile factors (gender, name style, profile image, location, and network overlap) and the topical domain of the content itself interact with one another and

CSCW '13, February 23–27, 2013, San Antonio, Texas, USA.

with culture to affect credibility assessments. We first show a number of main effects and interactions of these features on credibility perceptions. Next, consistent with their high-context cultural characteristic, we show that Chinese respondents demonstrated stronger effects and more complex interactions among these social media features. We then discuss how to incorporate our understanding of these credibility perception mechanisms into user experiences for consuming microblog content.

RELATED WORK

Microblogs and Credibility

Due to the efficiency, volume, and timeliness of information, microblogging services (e.g., twitter.com and weibo.com) have become prominent information sources [27]. According to the Twitter blog, there were on average 340 million tweets generated per day as of March 2012 [54]. In addition to receiving information from people that they "follow," people have been increasingly searching for topically-relevant tweets (e.g., the over 1.6 billion queries of Twitter's search portal per day). In particular, learning about breaking news is often an important motivation for people to read tweets [51], for example, in order to keep updated on local emergencies [58].

To serve this huge information demand, major third-party search engines such as Google [12] and Bing [46] have incorporated microblog updates into their search results. Encountering microblog posts through search, rather than through network relationships, increases credibility concerns [34]. To start to tackle this and related issues, researchers have been working on filtering and recommendation algorithms that can help identify topically-relevant tweets or high-authority information (e.g., [4, 38]), and some interactive tools have also been developed to aid information finding and exploration of Twitter content such as [2, 43].

Nonetheless, the speed and volume of the spreading of various kinds of undesirable information, such as spam [35, 44, 50], surreptitious advertising [15], imposter accounts [37, 53], and false rumors [6, 24, 32, 41] have surfaced serious concerns about the veracity of microblog posts. Thus it is crucial to understand how and how well people make assessments of credibility of microblog content. This understanding can guide the design of tools that help people to make informed, high quality judgments about content and source credibility of microblog information.

Due to the decentralized nature of the Internet, the credibility of online information has long interested researchers and practitioners. Information scientists have identified important dimensions (e.g., authority, accuracy) and models (e.g., cognitive authority) in credibility assessment (see [33] for a complete review). The factors that may affect Web page credibility perceptions, for example, can be very diverse, including visual features [28], user factors (e.g., prior experience [9]), technical properties (e.g., web functionality [11]), and the context of encountering the content (e.g., search engine ranking [19]). Integrating these findings, some techniques have been designed to support credibility assessment in search results [47] [60].

In contrast, research on microblog credibility is relatively nascent and faces new challenges and opportunities. Different from Web pages, the compact content (usually a limit of 140 characters) and brief author profile in microblog environments provides relatively sparse information for consumers to leverage when making credibility judgments. This paucity of contextual information is exacerbated when microblog content is presented in mainstream search results, as the content is even further removed from information about the author. Finally, while some work has shown promise in using structural and time-series features (e.g., [41, 44]), there is no standard algorithmic solution for automatically identifying credible tweets analogous to using PageRank to identify high quality web pages.

Given the strong social component of microblogs as an information source, algorithmic solutions to content selection would do well to incorporate an understanding of human cognition. Identifying the factors that influence credibility judgments in the minds of users not only can enhance the feature set for machine learning approaches to content selection, but also can suggest proper information presentation for tweets in varying contexts. To identify such influential factors, Pal and Counts [39] examined how the user name can affect whether people consider a tweet "interesting" or the author "authoritative." They found that more popular authors (with more followers), names representing organizations, and topically-related names contributed to higher ratings of the content and the author. In their survey study, Morris et al. [34] revealed that various tweet features might impact credibility assessments, such as "contains URL," "bio suggests topic expertise," and "account has verification seal." Morris et al.'s experiments also indicated that the tweet features might interact with different topical contexts. For example, the difference of default image versus other image types appeared to be the strongest for tweets on the topic of entertainment. This implies that users' credibility perception might be context-dependent.

Microblogging in China and Cultural Differences

Since the first notable microblog service Fanfou (饭否) was launched with its beta version in 2007, China has experienced an astonishing growth of microblog services, or Weibo (in Chinese *Pinyin*). There now are several popularly used Weibo services, including Sohu Weibo, NetEase Weibo, and Tencent Weibo. As mentioned, the largest among them, Sina Weibo and Tencent Weibo reach 324 million and 425 million users respectively [22] (Twitter, in contrast, had 100 million active users as of September 2011 [55]). Note that the Chinese government actively censors many forms of media, including the Internet; consequently Twitter, the iconic example of microblogging in the West, is banned in China.[1]

Significant cultural differences exist between the West and East Asia, notably the contrasts between the analytic and holistic cognitive patterns, and between the individualism and collectivism social orientations [30, 36]. Related to these two cultural dimensions, high- and low- context is one index related to information processing and communication. High-context (corresponding to East Asian cultures) is characterized by implicit and nonverbal expression, high uncertainty, and situational and context-based knowledge in communication. This corresponds to East Asians' strong and long-term social relationships and high value on the interdependence and connectedness in their social structure. In contrast, people of low-context cultures use explicit and transferable knowledge, and maintain a greater number of weaker and independent social relationships [17, 52]. As mentioned, these cultural characteristics may co-evolve with a number of cultural factors (e.g., the development of a country's political systems [14], economic ideology [42], and intellectual traditions [29, 40]). With respect to the technology domain, these interactions among the various cultural factors may affect how information is produced and disseminated, and shape the technology status and system designs in a country. In particular in China, perceptions of media credibility may also be influenced by the culture of government censorship and the on-going dramatic social and technical transformation. In this paper, we use the term "culture" to broadly encompass these many intertwined factors.

In the field of CSCW, Asian users have been found to prefer features supporting high-context communication, such as multi-party chat, audio-video chat, and emoticons in Instant Messaging (IM) [25], and to be less satisfied with asynchronous communication [31]. Yang et al. [63] revealed that Asian users prefer IM over a scheduling tool, express less sentiment in electronic conversations, and vary their sentiment levels more depending on contexts. [48] and [1] also found that Asian users tend to integrate more contextual and social concerns when choosing an appropriate medium for communication and motivating social queries.

Cultural differences have been found in profile presentation in online social media. For example, U.S. students disclosed more than Chinese students on a variety of topics [5], and Chinese users prefer to customize their profile images more than Americans [64]. However, to our knowledge, there is no literature about cultural differences in *perceiving* the information credibility in social media. Given the tremendous volume of information generated and huge popularity of microblogs in China, it is important to know whether people share similar patterns in credibility perception and whether credibility-relevant algorithms and designs can be transferred into another culture (e.g., from the research on U.S. users in [34] to users in China). In fact, Yang et al.'s [62] cross-cultural study on community based Q&A sites suggests that even using very similar designs, people might behave very differently across sites because of a complex interaction between cultural characteristics and social-technical status.

As such, we examine culture as an influence on perceptions of content credibility in microblogs. To do so, we compare the effects of various pieces of tweet metadata on credibility perceptions among U.S. and Chinese participants. In terms of the metadata, as described in detail below, we start with factors that [34] examined in a U.S. context (gender, user name, profile image), and then add the additional factors of location and degree of network overlap that we hypothesize will be valued differently by Western and East Asian cultures. Our hypotheses below detail our predicted effects of each type of metadata on U.S. versus Chinese participants, along with a cultural differences-based rationale in each case.

RESEARCH QUESTIONS AND STUDY DESIGN

In order to test for differences in microblog credibility perceptions between the U.S. and China, we ran an online study in which participants rated the credibility of stimuli tweets, with each of the factors of interest manipulated. In this section we describe the profile factors introduced above and associated hypotheses, followed by our study design and content creation process.

Study Factors and Hypotheses

Gender. Gender differences have been shown to impact perceptions of credibility of information and people in other media (e.g., [7, 10]), though Morris et al. [34] found no impact of gender on credibility perceptions of tweets by U.S.-based users. We manipulated gender by varying whether the author's image was male or female (user names were selected to be gender-neutral).

H1: Overall, people will find tweets from men more credible than those from women.

> **H1a**: This gender effect will be more pronounced in China than in the U.S., because China is higher than the U.S. in its masculinity index, which implies that the values of genders differ more in China [21], and furthermore Chinese females are traditionally less preferred and of lower socio-economic status (e.g., in [3, 16]).
>
> **H1b**: This gender effect will be more pronounced for political tweets because the credibility of men and women will be more equitable for health than for political content, since prior studies show that generally men are more interested and informed in politics [57].

[1] For brevity we use the term "tweet" generically throughout this paper to refer either to microblog posts on Twitter or to those on the Chinese Weibo services.

User name. The user name presents a unique piece of information about the author, and has been shown to systematically bias perceptions of authors and of those authors' content [34, 39]. For user name style, we extracted the two most polarized conditions found among U.S. users in [34]: *topical-style* (e.g., "Political_news" and "健康资讯") and *Internet-style* (e.g., "Akalala99" and "Sleep 休止符"). We verified that these names were gender-neutral, and were not actual registered account names on the relevant microblog services.

H2: People will find tweets from users with topical user names more credible than those with Internet-style user name. This replicates the finding in [34].

Given the stronger influence of social context, Chinese respondents might be more influenced by differences in user name style (who the tweet is from is particularly important). However, the direction of this influence may be driven by different factors. For example, a topical user name may indicate profession and dedication in a particular topical area, but also may be related to certain intentions to spread spurious information or spam. With respect to the censorship in China, some authors who provide quality but politically sensitive content may want a non-topical user name to avoid censorship. Thus we make no specific prediction about how username style interacts with culture and topical domain, but we explore this issue in depth.

Profile image. The profile image can provide rich identifying and self-disclosure information about the author. [34] found that authors using the default Twitter icon received lower credibility assessments by U.S.-based users. Chinese users might have different perceptions on the variety of profile images, for example, [64] found that customizing one's profile image is more prevalent than using untreated photos in Chinese SNS sites.

For the profile image, we used either a photo of the author (*Photo*), or a generic icon depicting a gendered silhouette (*Anonymous*) (Figure 1). Coloring (pink for women and blue for men) was used to further distinguish between genders in the *Anonymous* condition (this color-gender association is common in both the U.S. and China). Images in the *photo* condition were selected from profile images of real social media users who were young adults with simple headshots (a method also used in [34]). All photos used for the U.S. version of the experiment depicted people of Caucasian heritage, while those used in the Chinese version depicted people of Asian descent.

H3: People will find tweets using photos as profile images more credible than those using anonymized images. This also replicates the finding in [34].

> **H3a:** This effect will be less pronounced for Chinese respondents, because they might be more accepting of using anonymous photos as a way to avoid censorship.

Location. The location of the author might imply some latent properties of the author, such as political views and educational or socio-economic status [13]. Prior studies have shown that authors on Twitter often obscure or generalize their true location for a variety of reasons [14], though the presence of accurate location information on microblogs may be important since U.S.-based users reported in a survey that Twitter authors whose location is near to their own location are viewed as more credible [34].

For the author's location, we manipulated whether the location was stereotyped as being *liberal* or *conservative*. To select locations for the U.S. experiment, we used a 2010 Gallup Poll [23] listing the most liberal and conservative states. We chose eight states from each list, and then selected two cities from each state (for a total of 32 city/state pairs). Cities were chosen by viewing the Wikipedia entry for the given state, which features lists of large and small cities. For the liberal states, two of the large cities were selected, and for the conservative states, two small cities were chosen (since larger cities tend to be associated with liberalism [59]). Examples of locations constructed in this manner include "Portland, Oregon" and "Cambridge, Massachusetts" (liberal) and "Biloxi, Mississippi" and "Provo, Utah" (conservative). In China, the differentiation between liberal and conservative corresponds mainly to a few large cities on the East Coast versus the small and under-developed interior areas. Thus, we randomly selected from the counties in the 4 metropolises like Beijing and Guangzhou for liberal locations, and non-capital cities in interior provinces like Gansu and Jiangxi for conservative locations.

H4: Participants will find tweets from people in more liberal locations to be more credible than tweets from people in more conservative locations. This is because for both countries, people from more liberal regions are more likely to have better access to information and new technologies, and in general they also tend to be associated with higher educational background and better economic status than people from more conservative regions [13].

> **H4a:** This effect will be less pronounced in the U.S. because its level of modernization is more uniform than China.
>
> **H4b:** This effect will be more pronounced for political tweets because we anticipate that the location difference will matter more in access to, evaluation of, and stereotypes regarding political information [13] than health information, which would be more neutral and of more universal interest.

Network overlap. There are many ways to measure the social network status of the author and social relationship with the reader. For example, [39] found that higher in-degree (popularity) authors received higher interestingness evaluations. We chose a measure of closeness between the stimuli authors and the study participants (the number of your friends who are following the author) to capture the social influence from one's direct social network in a credibility judgment. This measure was manipulated with two conditions: *Overlap*, in which the study participant was told a random number between two and five of her friends were following the content author (the random variation was used to make the deception more plausible), and *no overlap*, in which case no connection between the author and participant was indicated (see Figure 1).

H5: People will find tweets from authors who their friends also follow more credible. Survey participants in [34] reported having greater trust in tweets from people they followed, leading us to surmise that tweets from second-degree network connections may be perceived as more credible than those from unconnected users.

> **H5a**: This effect will be more pronounced in China than in the U.S. because participants' perceptions might be more affected by other people, given the collectivist culture where people are highly connected and social relationships are stronger and more influential [17, 18].

H6: Overall, Chinese users will find microblog updates more credible than U.S. users, since government censorship of traditional media in China and a collectivist culture that places high value on social relationships may improve users' valuation of peer-produced content. [61] reported that Chinese users rely more on SNS in information seeking than the U.S. users.

Study Design

In order to test the above hypotheses we designed a within subjects experiment [gender × user name × profile image × location × network overlap]. To limit the experiment to a reasonable length, we simplified each factor to two conditions, as described above [$2 \times 2 \times 2 \times 2 \times 2 = 32$ combinations].

We made culture a between-subjects factor, such that participants were in either a China or U.S. condition, seeing stimuli tailored to their culture (described below). Finally, participants were randomly assigned to either a politics or health topical condition, such that they only saw content on one of those topics. The topic condition was included for generalizability and because we felt political topics may show distinct effects in China (see above hypotheses) but kept between subjects in order to maintain a reasonable time frame for each experimental session.

Tweet content

In order to have tweet content for participants to rate, we authored sets of 32 original tweets for the four (topic × culture) between-subjects conditions (128 total tweets). The 64 tweets in the Chinese culture condition were written in Chinese characters by a native Chinese speaker, while those in the U.S. condition were written by a native English speaker. Similar to [34], these tweets used standard grammar and spelling to remove the influence of message style on credibility perceptions. Since Chinese tweets can contain significantly more information with the same character limit, we controlled the length of Chinese tweets based on a similar amount of information that can be conveyed in a 140-character English tweet. Each tweet described a topically-relevant current event, followed by a shortened URL (using the different shortening conventions common in the U.S. and China).

We wanted the tweets to be as relevant to participants as possible. Therefore, all tweets in the politics topic condition were only about local events within each country. However, Chinese tweets in health were translated from English tweets, as they all describe generally relevant health topics.

Importantly, the stimuli messages were false, designed to describe events that had never taken place, but which were plausible. To ensure all messages had a similar level of plausibility, we pilot-tested them on a group of native speakers in our organization and iteratively revised and verified that the messages all fell into a small range of a plausibility assessment scale. Prior work [34] found that users were unable to accurately distinguish true tweets from false ones designed in this manner. The falsehood of the stimuli messages, randomly combined with different profile conditions, allowed us to best isolate the effect of the factors of interest (location of the author, network overlap with the participant, etc.) on credibility assessments in each culture.

The messages, in combination with the aforementioned profile features, were rendered using a .css style similar to that of Twitter.com (and also the Chinese Sina-Weibo). One important modification was the addition of the location

Figure 1. Four sample tweets from our experiment with different condition combinations:

(A) female×topical_ID×anonymous_image×liberal_location×no_overlap×health×U.S.

(B) female×internet_ID×photo image× conservative_location ×overlap×politics×U.S.

(C) male×internet_ID×anonymous_image×liberal_location×no_overlap×health×China

(D) male×topical_ID×photo_image× conservative_location× overlap×politics×China

feature and (in the *overlap* condition) the network overlap feature, which were rendered underneath the message using the position and styling that Twitter typically uses for timestamps (which were not included in our rendering). All 32 conditions for the profile features were combined for each of the four between-subjects conditions, and generated into images that were rated by the participants in our experiment (Figure 1). A sufficiently-sized set of photos, user names, locations, and tweets was generated such that no component was repeated.

EXPERIMENT AND SURVEY

We built an online experiment site to implement this study. Participants from the two countries were directed to the corresponding version of the website (in either English or Chinese), and randomly assigned into either of the two topical conditions (health or politics). Users were prompted to provide their Twitter or Weibo user name, so that they would assume that our experimental software had crawled their network in order to compute the network overlap features (although this feature was in fact randomly generated). After the experiment and survey was complete, participants read a debriefing message explaining that the message content and network overlap information had been falsified for the purposes of the study.

The set of 32 tweets for the appropriate culture×topic condition were displayed one at a time, in a random order. Participants were asked to rate how much they agreed that the microblog update contained credible information, using a 7-point Likert scale. For each rating task, the participants were instructed to not leave the page or perform additional Web searches (the updates themselves were rendered as images rather than as HTML, so that the URLs contained were not clickable). After completing the 32 rating tasks, participants were asked to take a survey that collected their demographic data and data on their use of microblog services.

Since our main goal was to extract cultural differences in the mechanism of perceiving microblog credibility, we confined our study in the two countries to comparable user samples: participants were recruited from a global software company with offices in both the U.S. and China. Although these participants do not necessarily reflect a representative sample of a country's general population, they do represent user groups with similar job type, educational background, socioeconomic status, and technology access between the two countries. This helps us attribute our findings more confidently to cultural, rather than educational or socio-economic, differences. But we also should note that for some microblog-usage results, technologically savvy people tend to be early adopters and their behavior may be leading the trend of the following few years.

We invited participants via email (randomly selecting from the company email lists in the two countries). The invitation email indicated that a precondition to be eligible for the study was to be a microblog user and read microblog

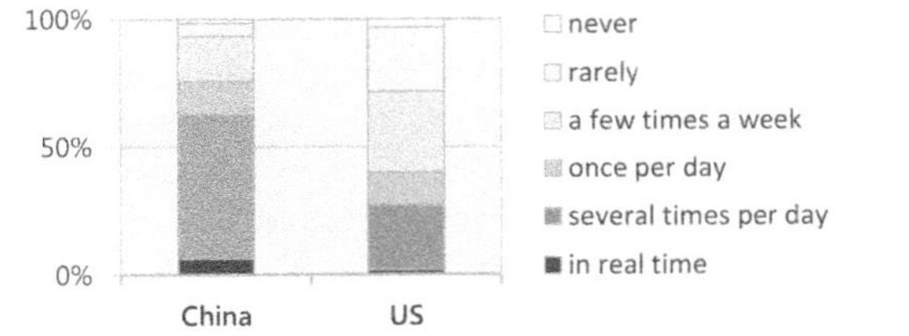

Figure 2. Frequency of reading microblogs in each culture.

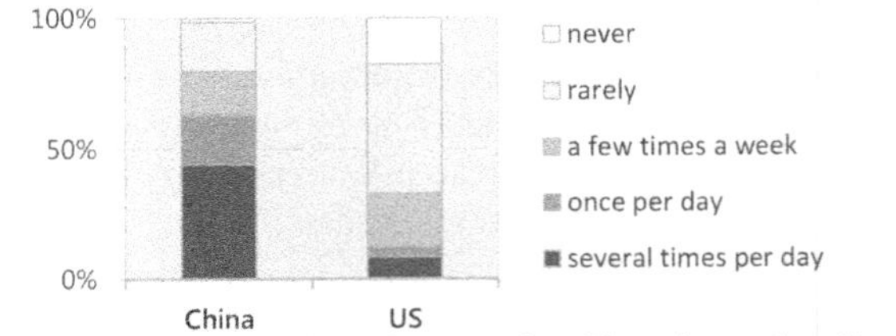

Figure 3. Frequency of posting to microblogs in each culture.

updates occasionally (microblog usage was re-verified with survey questions). As an incentive to participate, participants were entered into a drawing for an online gift-certificate from a shopping site in their country.

Participants

The online study was conducted during March 2012. In total, 3000 invitation emails were sent and 256 Chinese and 153 U.S. respondents completed the study. Due to the technical nature of this company, there were more males (320) than females (89) overall, though the gender ratios were similar (CN: 75%, U.S.: 83%) between the two cultural groups. In terms of age distribution, the two groups had similar ratios for the 18-24 range (CN: 5.1%~U.S.: 5.9%) and 35-44 (CN: 33.3%~U.S.: 37.9%). However, the Chinese group had more people in the 25-34 range (60.4%, compared to U.S. 35.9%); while the U.S. group had more in the 45-54 range (18.3%, compared to CN 1.2%). We incorporated these major demographic variables into our analysis as controls (see Table 1).

SURVEY RESULTS

The survey revealed that cultural differences significantly impact microblog usage and credibility perceptions. First, consistent with findings in [61], Chinese users appeared to be more engaged in microblogs in terms of both sharing and consuming information (Figure 2-3: Chinese respondents reported higher frequencies of reading and posting tweets). This stronger preference for microblogs might be a combined result from two factors: 1) with a collectivist cultural orientation, Chinese people may prefer more social types of media to serve their informational and social needs; and 2) the information control and centralization due to government censorship can significantly limit people's exposure to rapidly updated, diverse, and sensitive information, prompting use of peer-produced media.

In fact, Chinese respondents rated microblogs with much higher importance scores as an information source, measured by the percentage of everyday information obtained from microblogs on different topics (from 1: never

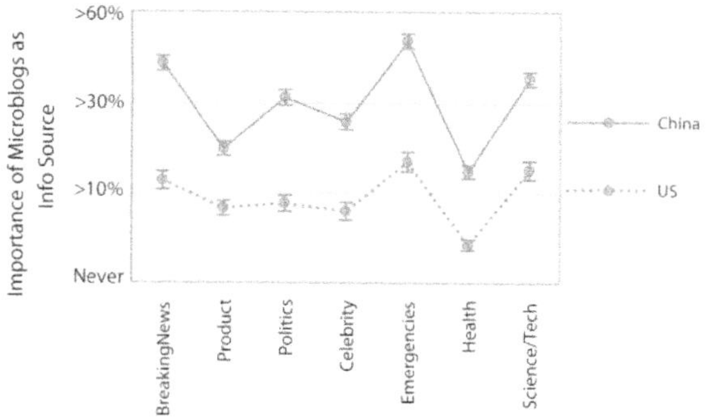

Figure 4. Mean reported importance of microblogs as an information source for several news topics.

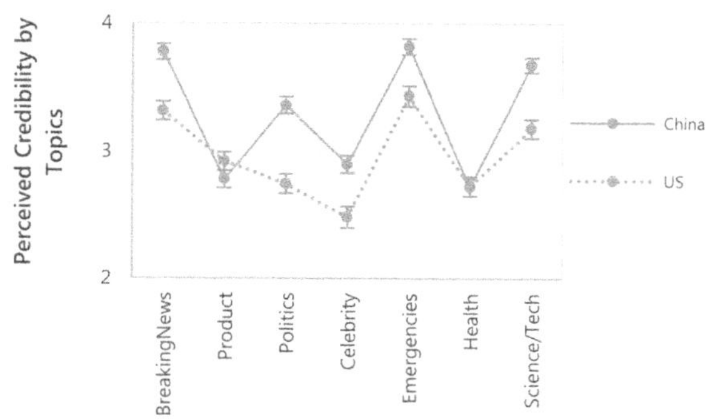

Figure 5. Mean reported perceptions of microblog information credibility on several topics (five-point scale).

to 5: >90%). As shown in Figure 4, mean values for Chinese respondents ranged around 3 across topics, which suggests that on average they use microblogs as a source of almost 50% of their information. Comparatively, U.S. respondents reported that they obtained less than 25% of their information from microblogs (*p* in t-test on each topic <.001).

The Chinese users' preference for microblogs is also reflected in their consideration of credibility (measured by a 5-level Likert scale from 1-point: "not credible at all" to 5-point: "tweets are all of very high credibility"). As Figure 5 indicates, except for *Products* and *Health* that were similar across countries, Chinese respondents consider information from microblogs to be more credible than U.S. respondents ($p<.001$). It is not clear whether this difference is due to inherent differences in the credibility quality of microblog information in the two cultural contexts, or to the different ways people perceive the credibility of microblog information and/or other information sources. However, this does reveal the substantial difference in the attitude toward and use of microblogs across these two cultures.

EXPERIMENTAL RESULTS

In total, 409 respondents completed our online experiment and each of them rated 32 tweets in one of the four topic×cultural contexts. This generated 13,954 tweet ratings. As described in the "Hypotheses" section, we tested each of the hypothesized factors (including interactions) in predicting the final rating for a tweet's credibility.

Predictor factors	F value	df	Pr(>F)
Culture	385.845	1	.000
Topic	82.397	1	.000
Gender	14.542	1	.000
User name	27.856	1	.000
Profile image	22.916	1	.000
Location	32.107	1	.000
Network overlap	50.122	1	.000
Culture * Topic	200.780	1	.000
Culture * Gender	.506	1	.477
Culture * User name	60.786	1	.000
Culture * Profile image	4.926	1	.027
Culture * Location	8.279	1	.004
Culture * Overlap	2.888	1	.089
Topic * Gender	4.664	1	.031
Topic * Profile image	.153	1	.695
Topic * User name	15.223	1	.000
Topic * Location	22.503	1	.000
Topic * Overlap	28.690	1	.000
Culture *Topic * Gender	8.439	1	.004
Culture *Topic * User name	21.052	1	.000
Culture *Topic * Profile image	1.883	1	.170
Culture *Topic * Location	6.116	1	.013
Culture *Topic * Overlap	5.644	1	.018
Controlled variable: Reader's Age	13.797	4	.000
Controlled variable: Reader's Gender	4.142	1	.042
Controlled variable: Reader's job role	22.637	9	.000

Table 1. Impact of microblog factors on credibility

We applied mixed-design ANOVA to test the effect of all the predictor factors (segregating within- and between-subjects factors) and their interactions on credibility ratings. Table 1 lists the test results with all hypothesized factors and controlled demographic variables of age, gender, and job role (note: more complicated interaction terms might be significant but adding those into the model did not significantly alter the results in the current table). In the remainder of this section, we present the test results for each hypothesized factor and we report the significance from the ANOVA model (additionally, we check the directions of the differences to verify the hypotheses). Note that for main effects we report means in the text, while for interaction effects for readability we report p-values only and refer the reader to the figures to see means.

Gender

H1: (Supported) People find tweets from men (M_{male} = 3.87) more credible than those from women (M_{female}= 3.75, $p < .001$).

H1a: (Not supported) The interaction between gender and cultural context is not significant ($p = 0.477$).

H1b: (Supported) The gender difference is more salient in political tweets, with tweets from male authors rated as more credible ($p < .05$, Figure 6).

The non-significance of the interaction term (H1a) between gender difference and culture inspired us to explore this issue further, looking at the three-way interaction of these two factors with topical context. The result indicates that

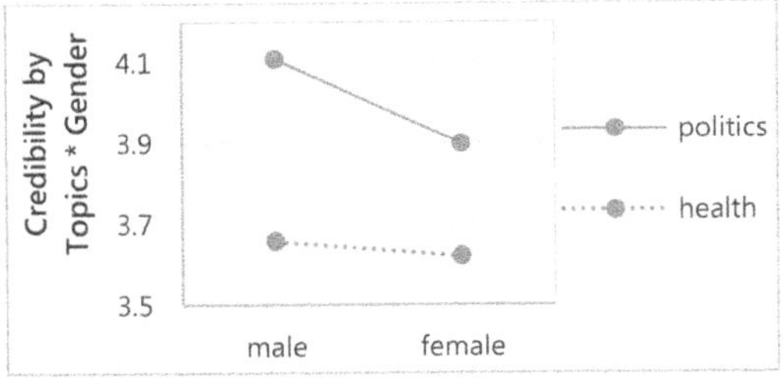

Figure 6. Interaction of gender*topic

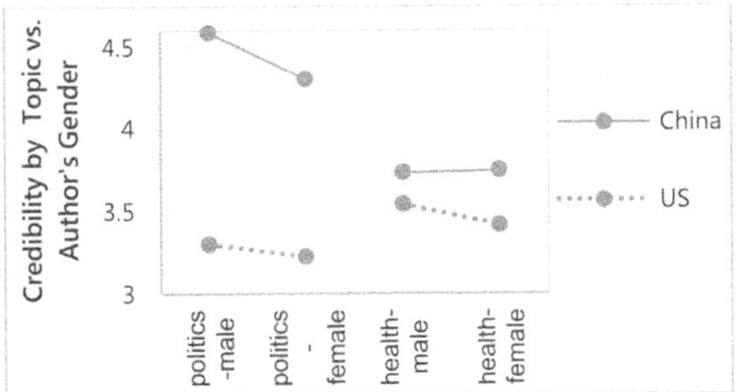

Figure 7. Interaction of gender*topic*culture

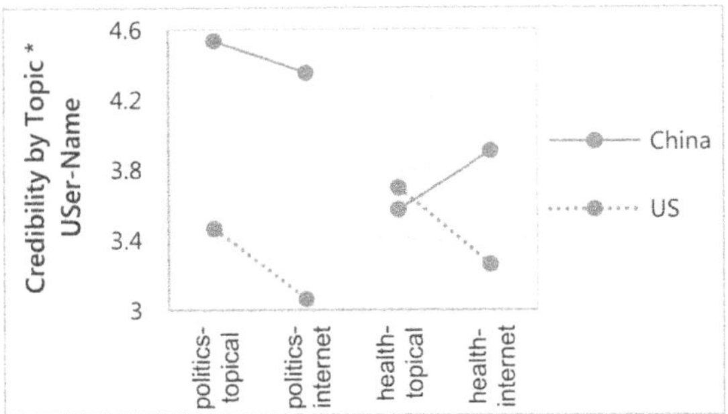

Figure 8. Interaction of user name*topic*culture

gender matters differently in the two cultures, depending on the topical domain ($p<0.005$). As shown in Figure 7, Chinese respondents present stronger gender difference on the politics topic, while for the U.S. respondents the differences appear to be consistent across topics.

This favor to males' tweets is also consistent between the respondents' genders. However, we found that in the U.S. condition, female respondents tend to systematically rate all tweets as less credible than males ($p < 0.001$).

User Name

H2: (Supported) People find tweets from users with topical user names ($M_{topic} = 3.86$) more credible than those with Internet-style user names ($M_{internet} = 3.76$, $p < .001$).

However, the interaction between user name and culture is complex, due to an additional interaction with topic ($p <$ .001, Figure 8). The differences in credibility based on user name styles are fairly consistent for the U.S. respondents, with internet style names viewed as less credible (replicating Morris et al.'s finding [34]). Interestingly, Chinese respondents present opposite patterns across topics: consistently they find tweets with topical-style user names more credible than those with Internet-style user names for the political topic, while they find tweets with topical-style user names less credible for the health topic.

A possible explanation may be that Chinese respondents believe that health tweets with internet-style user names have been authored by everyday individuals, who themselves believed the news to be credible. In contrast, users with topical user names are possibly sources of spurious health tweets, for promoting products, spamming, or other purposes. For political tweets, topical user names may imply that the author is closer to political information sources, which often are inaccessible to normal individuals in China.

Profile Image

H3: (Supported) Consistent with [34], people find tweets using photos for the profile image ($M_{photo} = 3.88$) more credible than those using generic images ($M_{anon} = 3.74$, $p <$ .001).

H3a: (Supported) There is significant interaction between profile image and culture ($p < .05$) as predicted, Chinese respondents are less sensitive to using anonymized images (Figure 9).

Location

H4: (Supported) People find tweets from people in more liberal locations ($M_{liberal} = 3.92$) to be more credible than tweets from people in more conservative locations ($M_{conservative} = 3.71$, $p < .001$).

Since our sample tends be biased to people from liberal regions (>89%) and they might believe information from those who are more similar to them, we coded the U.S. respondents based on the liberal-conservative schema. These two types of respondents similarly rated tweets from liberal locations as more credible. Overall, respondents from conservative regions tend to rate all tweets as more credible than participants from liberal regions (t-test: p <.001). We could not perform this analysis for Chinese respondents because they were all from liberal regions.

H4a: (Supported) The interaction between location difference and cultural context is significant ($p < .005$). As predicted, the location effect is more salient in China, where tweets from people in more liberal locations tend to be perceived as even more credible (Figure 10).

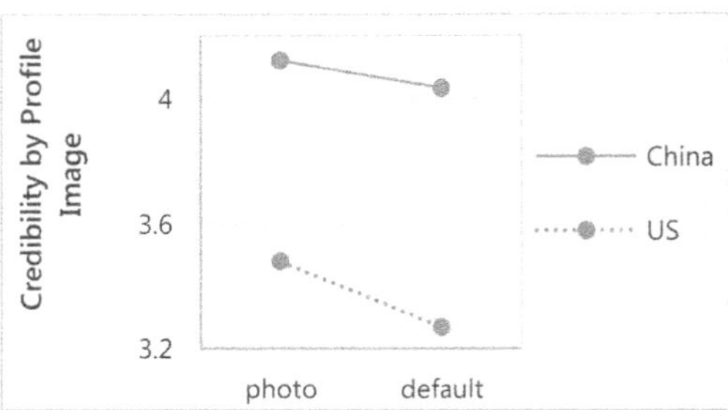

Figure 9. Interaction of profile image*culture

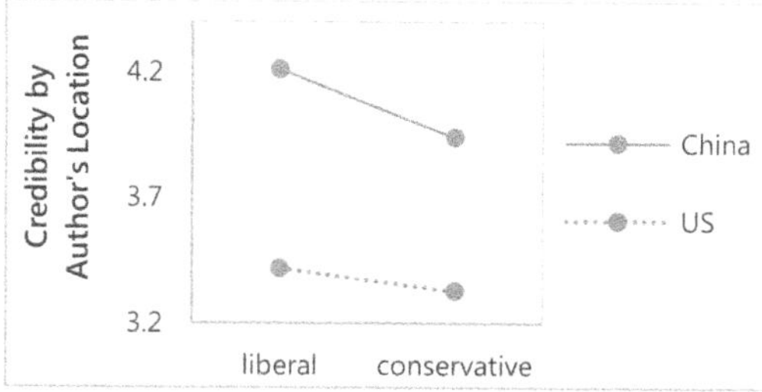

Figure 10. Interaction of location*culture

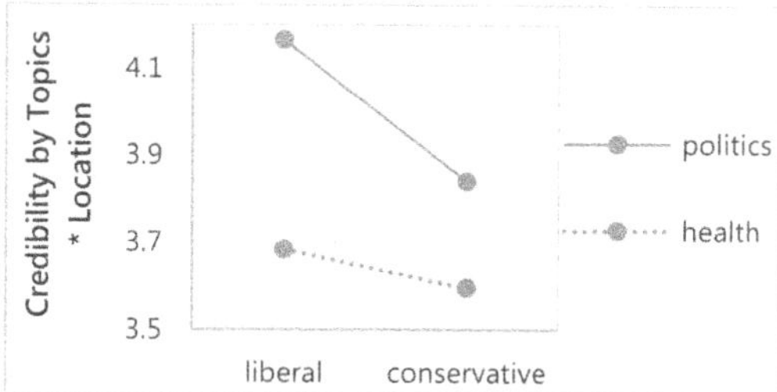

Figure 11. Interaction of location*topic

H4b: (Supported) The interaction between location difference and topical context appears to be even more significant ($p < .001$). As predicted, the tweet credibility difference between liberal and conservative locations is more prominent for political tweets (Figure 11).

Network Overlap

H5: (Supported) People find tweets from authors who their friends also follow ($M_{overlap} = 3.92$) more credible, and tweets from authors who have no social connections with them ($M_{none} = 3.71$, $p < .001$) less credible.

H5a: (Not supported) The interaction between network overlap and cultural context is not significant ($p = .089$).

However, our exploratory test on the three-way interaction between network overlap with the two topical domain factors indicates insightful results ($p < .05$, Figure 12): U.S. respondents present fairly consistent difference patterns between the two overlap conditions, while for Chinese respondents, they believe political tweets from outside their closer social network as more credible. This again reminds us of the special credibility and accessibility status of political information in China. Note also that political tweets were rated as highly credibly by Chinese users regardless of network overlap. Taken together, these findings suggest that Chinese users are likely to view social media as a reliable information source for politics, potentially in contrast to state-controlled media and other more easily censored information sources, but that they also know that their own social network is unlikely to have access to authentic and reliable political information.

General Cultural Attitudes

H6: (Supported) Chinese users overall view microblogs as a more credible source of information than U.S. users. Our survey findings (reported in the previous section), indicated that Chinese users viewed microblogs as equally or

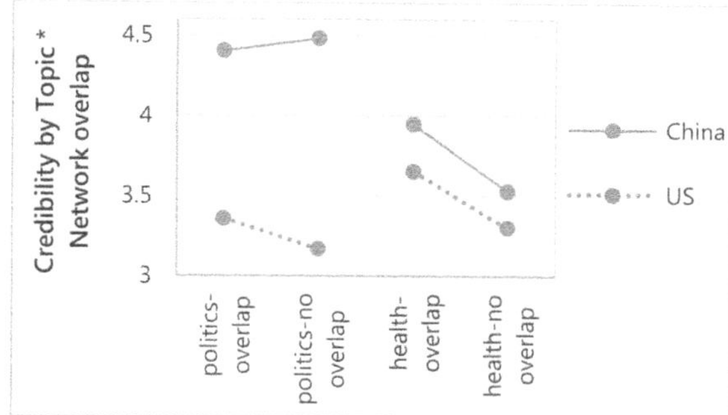

Figure 12. Interaction of overlap*topic*culture

significantly more credible than U.S. users for a large selection of topics. In our experiment, Chinese users rated tweets as significantly more credible overall (comparing health tweets because the contents were matched across languages: $mean_{china} = 3.75$, $mean_{US} = 3.48$, $p < 10^{-9}$).

One limitation in the credibility ratings is that some of the difference may be caused by systematic differences in using the scale between U.S. and China-based participants. However, we see support for H6 from multiple sources: the consistency between survey answers and experimental ratings, and the correlation between the Chinese respondents' higher credibility evaluations and their more frequent usage of microblogs and heavier reliance on microblogs as an information resource. In addition, this result is consistent with the finding in [61] that Chinese users rely more on SNS in information seeking than the U.S. users.

Synthesizing the Tests

The ANOVA test results in Table 1 present an overview of all single and interaction predictors, from which we can extract the relative significance among different factors. First, the *Culture* and *Topic* factors yield the largest differences in terms of affecting credibility judgment. In particular, consistent with the finding in [61] in which culture accounts for the most variance in predicting people's social querying behavior, here culture appears to be a dominant influence on social media credibility perceptions. The five profile features are also very important predictors. In particular, variations on the location and overlap factors are associated with highly significant changes in credibility assessments.

A prominent pattern in our test is that the interactions among these profile and cultural factors pervasively and significantly exist in multiple levels. Particularly, Chinese respondents' behavior tends to be more complex and unpredictable: they often vary their credibility assessments according to different combinations of conditions, and even present opposite patterns due to changes in the factors tested. For instance, the effect of network overlap was dependent on the topic for the Chinese respondents.

DISCUSSION

Our experiment showed how culture interacts with microblog profile features (gender, user name, profile image, location, and network overlap) and topical context to affect content credibility assessments. These interactions reveal a complex and context-dependent mechanism for microblog credibility perceptions, particularly among Chinese users, suggesting caution in interpreting and designing based on effects of single factors. Credibility ranking algorithms should incorporate interactions among factors. When representing microblog information, such as in search results, the relative importance among different features might vary by context. For example, the location information about the tweet author should be more important and salient for a search in political news, while other features may need to be moved down or off due to limited space.

Our experiment found that two factors, location and network overlap, although often neglected in tweet representation (for example, these are not shown in the default view of updates on Twitter.com), actually account for more influence in credibility assessments than the other profile factors studied. Even if a user might not reveal her/his actual location information, it is relatively easy to approximate through minimal tweet content analysis [20], and could be displayed or used to filter or rank microblog search results. Location information together with various social structural features, such as network overlap and social distance, can be generated at relatively low cost, but may yield great utility in discovering credible information.

We have for the first time examinined cultural differences in the credibility perceptions of social media information. These cultural differences that are embedded in how people process information and conduct social interactions, interacting with other cultrual factors such as the social and technology status of the country, generated significant differences in credibility perceptions in the social information networks studied. In fact, culture appears more influential than the properties of the tweet itself. Chinese respondents were more sensitive to context, changing their judgements based on small variations of the conditions. For instance, while U.S. respondents showed the same effect for username type across topics, Chinese users showed opposite effects depending on whether the content was political or health related (Figure 8). This implies a new form of software "localization", as direct transfer of content ranking algorithms for social media across cultures is suboptimal. In this case, Chinese people's more context-dependent perceptions may require that algorithms incorporate additional content and social dimensions. For the user experience, Chinese users are likely to utilize (with or without explicit conscious awareness) additional metadata when evaluating microblog content. Thus, for search or other alternative microblog interfaces, simply extracting part of the user profile along with the tweet may fail to support user confidence in the credibility of the message content sufficiently. For highly context-sensitive cultures like China, providing additional metadata will better align with how such users evaluate social media-authored information.

The importance of tailoring metadata presentation to specific cultures is reflected in the survey and experiment results that showed that Chinese users believe microblogs to be more credible and that they rely on this information source more than U.S. users. Note that our study does not investigate whether this trust is warranted (although the fact that Chinese users gave high credibility ratings to the tweets, even though they were all false, indicates that this group may be placing too much confidence in the authenticity of social media). This preference may be related to their social-oriented information consumption behavior, the information deficiency from other sources due to censorship, or current design (culturally localized) and status of microblog services in China.

Current Chinese microblog services do provide some of this additional metadata (e.g., on Sina Weibo, a rough sense of the network overlap with the author is presented to the reader) though most have yet to be included. Similarly, some of the interface features on Chinese microblog sites, such as retweet chains linking back to the original source, representing a whole sequence of social filtering actions, might aid U.S. (and other) microblog consumers is making accurate assessments of credibility. Closer examination of leveraging these interface cues in non-Chinese microblog environments is an exciting opportunity for future work.

Finally, although with relatively smaller effect, credibility perceptions can vary by demographic factors such as age and gender. Our explorations also found people from liberal regions tend to systematically view tweets as less credible. Thus it is important to investigate different user groups in addition to cultural factors, and design user experiences with user-group-oriented customizations. We are interested in exploring this in our future work.

CONCLUSION

As microblogs become an increasingly important news source in both the U.S. and China, understanding how to help users discern the quality of microblog information takes on increased importance. In this paper, we presented the first investigation of cultural differences in the perception of microblog credibility between the U.S. and China. We provided survey and experimental results illustrating the impact that an author's gender, profile image, user name, location, network overlap with the end user, and message topic have on credibility perceptions, and find key differences between the two countries. Chinese users show relatively high trust in and dependence on microblogs as an information source, greater acceptance of anonymously and pseudonymously authored content, and they tend to more depend on and integrate multiple metadata when evaluating microblog credibility. We hope that our reflections on the implications of these findings assist designers of search engines and other tools for aggregating microblog content in better conveying credibility to end-users within and across cultures.

ACKNOWLEDGMENTS

We would like to thank Brent Hecht, Xiang Cao, and Darren Edge for their help. This work was partly funded by NSF IIS-0948639.

REFERENCES

1. Barabás, A.L., Jeonga, H., Néda, Z., Ravasz, E., Schubert, A., and Vicsek, T., Evolution of the socialnetwork of scientific collaborations. *Physica A: Statistical Mechanics and its Applications* 311, 3-4 (2002), 590-614.
2. Bernstein, M., Suh, B., Hong, L., Chen, J., Kairam, S., and Chi, E.H. *Eddi: Interactive topic-based browsing of social status streams*. in *Proc. 23rd ACM Symposium on User Interface Software and Technology (UIST)*, ACM (2010), 303-312.
3. Bishop, J.A., Luo, F., and Wang, F., Economic transition, gender bias, and the distribution of earnings in China. *Economics of Transition* 13, 2 (2005), 211–420.
4. Castillo, C., Mendoza, M., and Poblete, B. *Information credibility on twitter*. in *Proc. WWW*, ACM (2011), 675-684.
5. Chen, G.M., Differences in Self-disclosure Patterns among Americans versus Chinese: A Comparative Study. *Journal of Cross-Cultural Psychology* 26, 1 (1995), 84-91.
6. Corcoran, M., *Death by Cliff Plunge, With a Push From Twitter*, in *The New York Times*. 2009.
7. Darley, W.K. and Smith, R.E., Gender Differences in Information Processing Strategies: An Empirical Test of the Selectivity Model in Advertising Response. *Journal of Advertising* 24, 1 (1995), 41-56.
8. Dollinger, M.J., Confucian ethics and Japanese management practices. *Journal of Business Ethics* 7, (1988), 575–584.
9. Flanagin, A.J. and Metzger, M.J., Perceptions of Internet information credibility. *Journalism & Mass Communication Quarterly* 77, 3 (2000), 515–540.
10. Flanagin, A.J. and Metzger, M.J., The perceived credibility of personal Web page information as influenced by the sex of the source. *Computers in Human Behavior* 19, 6 (2003), 683–701.
11. Fogg, B.J., Soohoo, C., Danielson, D.R., Marable, L., Stanford, J., and Trauber, E.R. *How do users evaluate the credibility of Web sites? A study with over 2,500 participants*. in *Proc. the Conference on Designing for User Experiences*, (2003).
12. Google. *Official Google Blog. An Update to Google Social Search. February 17, 2011.*
13. Gould, P. and White, R., *Mental Maps*. 1986: Psychology Press.
14. Greenfield, P.M., Maynard, A.E., and Childs, C.P., Historical change, cultural learning, and cognitive representation in Zinacantec Maya children. *Cognitive Development* 18, (2003), 455–487.
15. Grover, R., Ad.ly: The Art of Advertising on Twitter. *Businessweek* January 6 (2011).
16. Gupta, M.D. and Shuzhuo, L., Gender Bias in China, South Korea and India 1920–1990: Effects of War, Famine and Fertility Decline. *Development and Change* 30, 3 (1999), 619–652.
17. Hall, E.T., *Beyond Culture*. 1976: Anchor Books.
18. Hall, E.T., *Understanding Cultural Differences, Germans, French and Americans*. 1990, Yarmouth: Intercultural Press.
19. Hargittai, E., Fullerton, L., Menchen-Trevino, E., and Thomas, K.Y., Trust Online: Young Adults' Evaluation of Web Content. *Int'l. Journal of Communication* 4, (2010).
20. Hecht, B., Hong, L., Suh, B., and Chi, E.H. *Tweets from Justin Bieber's heart: the dynamics of the location field in user profiles*. in *Proc. CHI*, ACM (2011), 237-246.
21. Hofstede, G. *http://www.clearlycultural.com*.
22. http://companies.caixin.com/2012-05-18/100391626.html.
23. Jones, J.M., Mississippi Rates as the Most Conservative U.S. State. *Gallup Politics* (2011).
24. Kanalley, C., Facebook Shutting Down Rumor Goes Viral: Site Said to be Ending March 15, 2011. *The Huffington Post* January 9 (2011).
25. Kayan, S., Fussell, S.R., and Setlock, L.D., *Cultural differences in the use of instant messaging in Asia and North America*, in *Proc.*CSCW, 2006, ACM: Banff, Alberta, Canada. p. 525-528.
26. Kitayama, S., Park, H., Sevincer, A.T., Karasawa, M., and Uskul, A.K., A cultural task analysis of implicit independence: Comparing North America, Western Europe, and East Asia. *Journal of Personality and Social Psychology* (2009).
27. Kwak, H., Lee, C., Park, H., and Moon, S. *What is Twitter, a social network or a news media?* in *Proc. WWW*, ACM (2010), 591-600.
28. Lazar, J., Meiselwitz, G., and Feng, J., Understanding Web Credibility: A Synthesis of the Research Literature. *Foundations and Trends in Human-Computer Interaction* 1, 2 (2007), 139-202.
29. Lloyd, G.E.R., *Science in antiquity: The Greek and Chinese cases and their relevance to the problems of culture and cognition*, in *Modes of thought: Explorations in culture and cognition*, D.R. Olson and N. Torrance, Editors. 1996, Cambridge University Press: Cambridge, UK.
30. Markus, H.R. and Kitayama, S., Culture and the self: Implications for cognition, emotion, and motivation. *Psychological Review* 98, (1991), 224–253.
31. Massey, A.P., Hung, Y.-T.C., Montoya-Weiss, M., and Ramesh, V., *When culture and style aren't about clothes: perceptions of task-technology "fit" in global virtual teams*, in *Proc.GROUP*. 2001, ACM: Boulder, Colorado, USA. p. 207-213.

32. Mendoza, M., Poblete, B., and Castillo, C. *Twitter under crisis: can we trust what we RT?* in *Proc. Workshop on Social Media Analytics*, ACM (2010), 71-79.
33. Metzger, M.J., Making sense of credibility on the Web: Models for evaluating online information and recommendations for future research. *American Society for Information Science and Technology* 58, 13 (2007), 2078 - 2091
34. Morris, M.R., Counts, S., Roseway, A., Hoff, A., and Schwarz, J. *Tweeting is Believing? Understanding Microblog Credibility Perceptions*. in *Proc. CSCW*, ACM (2012).
35. Mustafaraj, E. and Metaxas, P., From Obscurity to Prominence in Minutes: Political Speech and Real-Time Search. *Web Science* (2010).
36. Nisbett, R.E., Peng, K., Choi, I., and Norenzayan, A., Culture and systems of thought: Holistic vs. analytic cognition. *Psychological Review* 108, (2001), 291–310.
37. Owens, S., How Celebrity Imposters Hurt Twitter's Credibility. *Mediashift* February 20 (2009).
38. Pal, A. and Counts, S. *Identifying Topical Authorities in Microblogs*. in *Proc. WSDM*, (2011).
39. Pal, A. and Counts, S. *What's in a @name? How Name Value Biases Judgment of Microblog Authors*. in *Proc. ICWSM*, AAAI (2011).
40. Pye, L.W., *Asian power and politics: The cultural dimensions of authority*. 1985, Cambridge, MA: The Belknap Press of Harvard University.
41. Qazvinian, V., Rosengren, E., Radev, D.R., and Mei, Q. *Rumor has it: identifying misinformation in microblogs*. in *Proc. the Conference on Empirical Methods in Natural Language Processing* (2011), 1589-1599.
42. Ralston, D.A., Holt, D.H., Terpstra, R.H., and Kai-Cheng, Y., The impact of national culture and economic ideology on managerial work values: A study of the United States, Russia, Japan, and China. *Journal of International Business Studies* (2007), 1-19.
43. Ramage, D., Dumais, S., and Liebling, D. *Characterizing Microblogs with Topic Models*. in *Proc. ICWSM*, (2010).
44. Ratkiewicz, J., Conover, M., Meiss, M., Goncalves, B., Patil, S., Flammini, A., and Menczer, F. *Truthy: Mapping the Spread of Astroturf in Microblog Streams*. in *Proc. WWW*, ACM (2011), 249-252.
45. Schmierbach, M. and Oeldorf-Hirsch, A., A little bird told me, so I didn't believe it: Twitter, credibility, and issue perceptions. *Association for Education in Journalism and Mass Communication* August 4, (2010).
46. Schwartz, B., Bing Adds Twitter Smart Answers. *Search Engine Land* (2009).
47. Schwarz, J. and Morris, M.R. *Augmenting Web Pages and Search Results to Support Credibility Assessment*. in *Proc. CHI*, (2011).
48. Setlock, L.D. and Fussell, S.R. *What's it worth to you?: the costs and affordances of CMC tools to asian and american users.* . in *Proc. CHI*, ACM (2010).
49. Siegler, M.G., *At 1.6 Billion Queries Per Day, Twitter Finally Aims To Make Search Personally Relevant*, in *TechCrunch*. 2011.
50. Sullivan, D., Twitter's Real Time Spam Problem. *Search Engine Land* June 6 (2009).
51. Teevan, J., Ramage, D., and Morris, M.R. *#TwitterSearch: a comparison of microblog search and web search*. in *Proc. ACM international conference on Web search and data mining* (2011), 35-44
52. Triandis, H.C., The self and social behavior in differing cultural contexts. *Psychological Review* 3, (1989), 506-520.
53. Tumbridge, J., Twitter: who's really there? *Journal of Intellectual Property Law & Practice* 5, 2 (2010), 116-118.
54. Twitter. http://blog.twitter.com/2012/03/twitter-turns-six.html *March 21, 2012*. March 14, 2011.
55. Twitter. *One Hundred Million Voices.* http://blog.twitter.com/2011/09/one-hundred-million-voices.html *September 8, 2011*.
56. Varnum, M.E.W., Grossmann, I., Kitayama, S., and Nisbett, R.E., The Origin of Cultural Differences in Cognition: The Social Orientation Hypothesis. *Current Directions in Psychological Science* 10, 1 (2010), 9-13.
57. Verbaa, S., Burnsa, N., and Schlozmana, K.L., Knowing and Caring about Politics: Gender and Political Engagement. *The Journal of Politics* 59 (1997), 1051-1072
58. Vieweg, S., Hughes, A.L., Starbird, K., and Palen, L. *Microblogging during two natural hazards events: what twitter may contribute to situational awareness*. in *Proc. CHI*, ACM (2010), 1079-1088
59. Williamson, T., Sprawl, Spatial Location, and Politics: How Ideological Identification Tracks the Built Environment. *American Politics Research* 36, 903-933.
60. Yamamoto, Y. and Tanaka, K. *Enhancing Credibility Judgment of Web Search Results*. in *Proc. CHI* ACM (2011).
61. Yang, J., Morris, M.R., Teevan, J., Adamic, L.A., and Ackerman, M.S. *Culture Matters: A Survey Study of Social Question and Answer Behavior*. in *Proc. ICWSM*, IAAA (2011).
62. Yang, J., Wei, X., Adamic, L., and Ackerman, M. *Activity Lifespan: An Analysis of User Survival Patterns in Online Knowledge Sharing Communities*. in *Proc. ICWSM*, IAAA (2010).
63. Yang, J., Wen, Z., Adamic, L., and Ackerman, M. *Collaborating Globally: Culture and Organizational Computer-Mediated Communication*. in *Proc. International Conference on Information Systems (ICIS)*, (2011).
64. Zhao, C. and Jiang, G. *Cultural Differences on Visual Self-Presentation through Social Networking Site Profile Images*. in *Proc. CHI*, ACM (2011), 1129-1132.

She Gets a Sports Car from Our Donation: Rumor Transmission in a Chinese Microblogging Community

Qinying Liao
IBM Research - China
Bldg. 19 Zhongguancun Software Park
Beijing, 100193
liaoqy@cn.ibm.com

Lei Shi*
State Key Laboratory of Computer Science
Institute of Software, Chinese Academy of Sciences
Beijing, 100190
shil@ios.ac.cn

ABSTRACT
In this paper we report on a case study of rumor transmission during a nationwide scandal via China's most popular microblogging service, weibo.com. Specifically, we explore dynamics of the rumor discourse by characterizing different statement types and their evolution over time. We examine the roles that different user groups play in the rumor discussions. Through qualitative and statistical analyses, our results identify seven reaction patterns to rumors and their different development trends. We reveal a three-stage pattern of the change of leadership during the rumor discussions. By connecting social theories on rumor transmission to the large scale social platform, this paper offers insight into understanding rumor development in social media, as well as utilizing microblogging data for effectively detecting, analyzing and controlling public rumors.

Author Keywords
Microblogging; social media; rumor transmission; China

ACM Classification Keywords
H.5.m. Information interfaces and presentation (e.g., HCI): Miscellaneous.

General Terms
Human Factors.

INTRODUCTION
Rumors are unconfirmed messages, but prevalent in everyday communications. With the flourishing of social networking services (SNS, e.g. Facebook, Twitter), one has good reasons to believe that rumors could travel much faster and wider today than ever before. Researchers have been interested in examining the credibility of information on SNS (e.g., [11][20]) and developing technologies to identify rumors (e.g., [20][28]), under a common view that rumors are "misinformation" and "disinformation".

In many ways, however, rumors are not merely destructive. Social scientists have believed rumors to be an attempt to relieve anxieties [25]. Recently others suggest that rumors are a communication strategy [33]. CSCW research has however overlooked this perspective of understanding rumoring behavior, which is common on SNS. Furthermore, little is known so far about how a rumor is transmitted or discussed on SNS. Practically, we believe understanding various rumor discussions could help to design and develop technologies for identifying, tracking and responding to rumors that could have a massive impact in the society.

In this paper, we report findings from a case study on rumor transmission in China's largest microblogging system, Sina Weibo. In 2011, rumors around a young lady's wealth and her possible connections with a government-owned charity caused a nationwide credibility crisis. We are interested in understanding how people participated in the rumor discussions and how the rumor developed over time. Specifically, we examine two aspects of the rumor transmission: evolution of content patterns and different user roles in the rumor-related discussions. We categorize different rumor statement types and analyze their development trends. Key leaders are identified that drive major discussions during the course. By bringing together social theories and empirical studies on microblogging, we propose a model of rumor discourse evolution for understanding large-scale rumor transmission processes, and examine the potential of using microblogging data to respond to rumors that are of public concern.

The rest of this paper is structured as follows. We first briefly review the existing research on rumor transmission and microblogging. We then describe the background of our case, as well as our methods of data collection and analyses. After that we report and discuss our results.

RELATED WORK
We review literatures on two main topics related to our study: First, we summarize known characteristics of rumor transmission from researches in psychology and sociology. Second, we examine recent work on the role of microblogs in generating and disseminating breaking news. We then introduce our research questions.

CSCW '13, February 23–27, 2013, San Antonio, Texas, USA.

* Corresponding author

Rumor Theory

Rumor discourse has been regarded as a form of collective behavior in social sciences (e.g., [7][8][12][25]). While the authenticity of the unconfirmed message could be a matter of debate, whether a rumor is truthful or not is unimportant in studying its transmission [10]. It is the building-up of collectively sanctioned explanations of ambiguity that drives social scientists' research interest. Despite the existence of different definitions of rumor, they share common ideas of two essential features: *importance* and *uncertainty*. Rumors tend to arise in situations that bear topical relevance to people involved but are cognitively unclear and largely outside of their own control [4][5][10][23][24]. Such conditions are associated with people's stress of "collective ambiguity and anxiety" [25]. When people fail to obtain necessary and assured information from credible sources, they circulate unofficial news in the community to relieve the tensions of such uncertainty and anxiety [25]. Rumor transmission, as a social process for people to collect, evaluate and interpret information [15], provides meanings to the ambiguity and offers its participants a sense of control over the situations [23][25].

Despite the development of the theoretic frameworks, previous rumor research has been suffered from the lack of empirical evidence due to the difficulties in conducting natural observations. Allport and Postman [4] have explored the social factors in rumor transmission using the serial reproduction paradigm in experimental situations. In their theory, rumors would lose most details (*leveled*) during the discourse, while only certain details are selected and emphasized (*sharpened*). Moreover, according to them, rumors are often distorted in the telling to fit one's unconscious affection and intellectual motivations (*assimilation*). This framework, however, has been criticized for not resembling rumor transmission in real life which tends to be an exchange [10][23] and involves feedback from listeners actively.

More recent work on rumor spread utilizes small scale data collected in computer-mediated communication (CMC) settings (e.g., [6][7][8][9]) and indicates rumor interactions to be a rich conversational process. In these studies, different transmission patterns (*aka.* the Rumor Interaction Analysis System) are identified [7], including apprehensive, interrogatory, authenticating, sensemaking, belief and disbelief, etc. Four stages of interactions are suggested. In the first stage, the rumor is tentatively introduced; in the second and third stage, sensemaking increases and then dominates; in the fourth stage, the rumor fades out and other topics take over [7]. Besides, temporal analysis on group dynamics reveals that rumor discussions via CMC largely follow the face-to-face group development patterns [8]. These findings are consistent with the sociological view of rumoring as group problem-solving.

Researchers have also been interested in understanding individuals' role in rumor discourse. Shibutani discussed the communication styles of *messenger* and *interpreter* [25] although without any empirical evidence. Bordia and Rosnow [9] analyzed eight clusters of communication profiles on rumor messages in CMC groups, for example, skeptical disbelievers, investigators, curious responses, etc. More recently, Bordia and DiFonzo [7] created a topology of what they called *communicative postures* with eleven clusters, such as evaluating, verifying, information-reporting, accepting, etc.

In retrospect, the rumor phenomenon is an old problem that seemed intractable due to the difficulty of study in naturalistic settings until the use of data in CMC groups. However, existing CMC studies only examined rumors in small (e.g. 30 participants [8][9]) and relatively closed groups (e.g. discussion groups [7]), and the rumors discussed were very light (e.g. number of most postings <60 [7][9]). With the latest development of SNS (e.g. Facebook, Twitter), substantial content especially breaking news nowadays is distributed widely in a speed that one can never imagine before. This not only offers an opportunity for observing the new patterns of rumor transmission, but also poses novel challenges of analyzing large scale social data of rumoring, which have not been addressed in literature. Next we review the work on news spread and crisis response with micrblogging, mainly on Twitter.

Microblogging

Since its release in 2006, Twitter has been the mainstream microblogging service worldwide. People share their everyday activities, report news, and seek for information on Twitter [14]. Research has suggested that Twitter is more an information spreading medium than a social networking tool. The study by Kwak *et al.* [16] with a large-scale data collection showed a much lower reciprocity in the follower-followee links on Twitter than Facebook-like SNS. Recently more research has been conducted to understand and model the information flows on Twitter. Wu *et al.* [31] discovered that 50% URLs received on Twitter were created by the top 20,000 elite users and the information flows on Twitter possessed high homophily in that one category of people (e.g. celebrities) tended to follow people of the same kind.

One typical social impact of Twitter is to break grand news [13][16]. For example, the work by Hu *et al.* reveals that Twitter has convinced the mass audience of bin Laden's death even earlier than the traditional media [13]. In order to identify such emerging news, several methods have been developed to track the short-term topic trends on Twitter [17][32].

More recent work has paid intensive attention to the role that Twitter and other microblogging systems play during large public events, such as disasters and crises. In [27][29], the Twitter usages after the Red River flood and Oklahoma Grassfires are studied. Researchers have found and discussed an information production life-cycle of generation, derivation, synthesis and innovation on Twitter

[27]. Information vital to situational awareness, such as vulnerable geographical area, is shown to be traceable on Twitter for a better emergency management [29]. As a whole, microblogging has been considered as a wide-scale interaction platform [21] for hosting situation updates, communicating emotions [22], distributed problem-solving [21], as well as self-organizing rescuing activities [26] during large public events.

More relevant to our work, Mendoza *et al.* investigated the dissemination of false rumors and valid news on Twitter [19] under the similar context of disasters. By manually tagging user interactions over a few typical rumors and news, they obtained preliminary results that the Twitter users tend to question the baseless rumors while few ever deny the confirmed news. Another piece of work by Morris *et al.* has systematically studied the credibility issue of microblogging [20]. Through carefully designed surveys and online experiments, they verified a list of critical features (e.g. message topic, user name and user image) that could heavily impact the credibility of Twitter's messages. These findings suggested feasible methods for Twitter users and social search engines to enhance their credibility.

To the best of our knowledge, none of the existing work has studied the crowd's various reactions to rumors and how rumor discussions develop over time via microblogging. Taking the social perspective of rumor transmission, we are interested in exploring the following research questions:

Q1: How are public rumors generated and how do they develop in the microblogging community? What kinds of statements do people post on microblogs and how do they change over time during rumor discussions?

Q2: Do people play different roles in transmitting rumors with microblogging? Who leads the discussions? Do their roles change in the different phases of the rumor discourse?

STUDY OVERVIEW

In this section we first introduce the background of Sina Weibo and the Guo Meimei Incident, and then describe our method of data collection and analyses.

Sina Weibo (Sina Microblogging)

Launched in 2009, just about three years after Twitter, Sina Weibo [1] is by far the most popular microblogging platform in China. Till March 2012, Sina Weibo has more than 300 million registered users with over 100 million messages (i.e., "tweets" or "*weibo*s") sent every day [2].

Sina Weibo is similar to Twitter, but different in many senses. One of the most striking differences is the volume of information communicated via each microblog in Chinese versus English. Both Sina Weibo and Twitter restrain the word count to 140 characters, but 140 characters in Chinese could convey much more information than that in English [30]. Such a language efficiency turns microblogging in China into a blog-like platform. Moreover, besides re-posting ("re-tweeting" or "*zhuanfa*") a message, Sina Weibo allows users to comment on others' posts or add a comment when re-posting a message (with an extra 140 words). These features could promote more communications on Weibo by invoking new discussions and spreading messages.

Similar to [22], in this paper we use the word "post" for the publishing of a message, and "re-post" for the forwarding of an existing message. A "message" (*weibo*) could be a post or a re-post.

Guo Meimei and the Red Cross Incident

Guo Meimei (@ 郭美美 Baby), a 20-year-old woman, stirred China's Internet in summer 2011. In a number of messages on her microblog, she posted pictures of her piles of luxury handbags and sports cars (e.g. Figure 1). At the same time, she appeared in her verified Weibo profile to hold the position of "commercial general manager" at China's Red Cross Society, a government-backed charity.

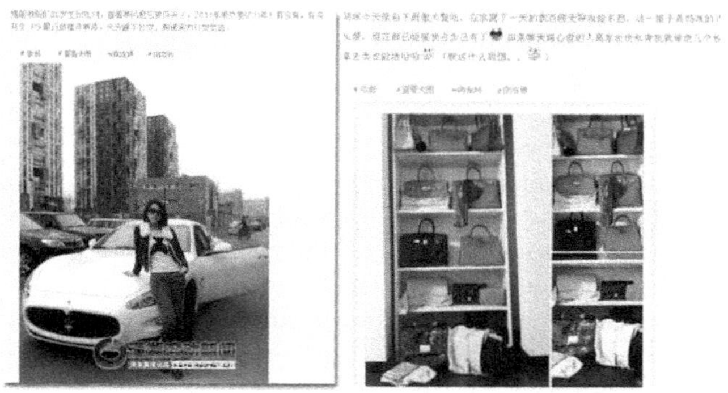

Figure 1. Two sample posts of Guo Meimei about her luxurious lifestyle on Sina Weibo. Left: "*Just got my 20-year-old birthday gift. The Year of 2011 is a lucky year, right?*" Right: "*These were my mommy's loving bags and now they are mine!!! If one day I left home with my lover and took away some of them, we can live off them, hahah*"

On the night of June 21st when some anonymous micro-bloggers began to notice and pointed out Guo Meimei's scandalous posts, the young lady ignited a firestorm. On June 20th, Guo Meimei had only 2,126 people following her. In just three days, her followers increased to 190,000. By June 27th, the number had grown to 700,000.

Suspecting that Guo might have financed her lifestyle out of the money from charity, furious people started a *human flesh search*[1] hoping to find out who Guo Meimei was and how she became connected with the Red Cross. Rumors flushed out all over the Internet, with more and more stories told and details added. Guo afterwards denied her having any ties with the Society and posted apologetic messages declaring that her title was fabricated for fun out of her

[1] *Human flesh search* is a Chinese Internet phenomenon of collectively identifying and exposing individual's profile to the public using social media, e.g., forums and microblogs.

ignorance. The Red Cross also held numerous press conferences to deny the rumor. But the suspicions were not relieved. The public did not even buy in the police's investigation which said Guo and the Society had no direct ties with each other. For months, disclosures of inside stories and disputes continued to flood. Ms. Guo and the Red Cross had been the most talked-about subject among China's five hundred million netizens through the year. The Guo Meimei Incident, as it is called, ranked as the largest public affair generated from Sina Weibo in 2011.

It is not our intent to examine the credibility of information or the trust issue associated with this incident on Sina Weibo. As prior research [10] pointed out, the authenticity of a rumor is not important for studying its transmission. In our paper, we focus on understanding different discourse behaviors and user roles in the rumor spreading. Next, we describe our method of data collection and analyses.

Data Collection

A keyword search of posts with "Guo Meimei" (郭美美) on Sina Weibo now returns 9.7 million messages. Due to the huge volume of data, we decided to employ a sampling method for data collection. We only collected the relevant data from the website for 41 days, starting from June 21 when Guo Meimei's posts first came into the public notice, until July 31. According to Baidu Index[2] [3], the number of online posts about Guo Meimei dramatically went down in late July. Although there were discussions related to Guo Meimei in August as well, most posts during this period were around Guo Meimei's appearance on several TV shows instead of her rumored connection with the Red Cross. We thus decided to exclude the messages posted after July and focus on the major rumor discourse.

For practical reasons, we constrained our sample to the original posts that contain "Guo Meimei" (郭美美) in their messages. We are aware that we miss a portion of messages which do not contain "Guo Meimei". But that would require intensive technical work to identify text meanings and we believe the number of such posts is small.

During these 41 days, a total of 474,000 original posts had been published on Sina Weibo according to the search result. However, only a list of 50 pages with 20 posts per page (1,000 posts in total) was available for each search on Sina Weibo. We then made advanced search queries on a per-hour and per-province basis. The peak hour for original posts from Beijing was around 10AM on June 23 and the number of posts was 878, which is smaller than 1,000. Theoretically we have made a full coverage of the relevant data by making such advanced searches. Based on the search results, we periodically collected posts for 10 consecutive seconds in every minute, and sampled roughly 16% of all the posts (76,128) during those 41 days.

To exclude the spamming messages (e.g., advertisement) that also contain "Guo Meimei" but are irrelevant to the rumor discussions, two researchers examined 17,000 posts in the sample and identified about a hundred spam-patterns. These patterns were then applied to all the collected posts with the help of SQL queries to remove the spams. The final cleaned sample contains 49,725 posts, which we call the *large sample* throughout this paper.

For each post in the large sample, we collected data on author's name, time of publication, message content, number of comments, number of reposts, and full lists of associated comments, reposts and their authors, all through Sina Weibo API. For each user appearing in these 49,725 posts, we collected their profiles including geographical location, background, total number of posts, followers, followings and the status of certification on Sina Weibo. As a result, we collected profiles for 38,221 unique users in total.

Data Analysis

Statement Coding

Our first goal of the study was to understand different content of rumor discussions and the evolution over time. To identify the types of statements people posted during the Guo Meimei Incident, a smaller sample with 1,000 messages was created for manual coding and the in-depth qualitative analysis. A uniform sampling method similar to the large sample is adopted so that the temporal development trend of the *small sample* strictly follows that of the large sample.

We mixed a top-down and a bottom-up strategy to develop our coding framework. First, we built an initial coding scheme based on the Rumor Interaction Analysis System (RIAS) [7]. Two researchers applied the scheme to a random collection of 150 messages independently. Then they discussed their results and revised the coding scheme together. After three rounds of iteration, the RIAS scheme was revised and a final list of seven categories of statement was determined (see Table 2). Specifically, we combined three RIAS categories (*prudent*, *authenticating*, *personal involvement*) into *providing information*, replaced *apprehensive* with *emotional statements* to cover both the positive and negative, and added a new category of *opinions* which included the former *belief*, *disbelief* and *sarcastic statements*. The reason for such revisions was that some of the original categories in RIAS appeared too rare in our sample. The basic unit of our coding scheme was a 'statement' instead of a message as a message could contain several complete thoughts and belong to multiple categories.

[2] *Baidu index* is a keyword research and trend analysis tool developed by Baidu, China's largest search company.

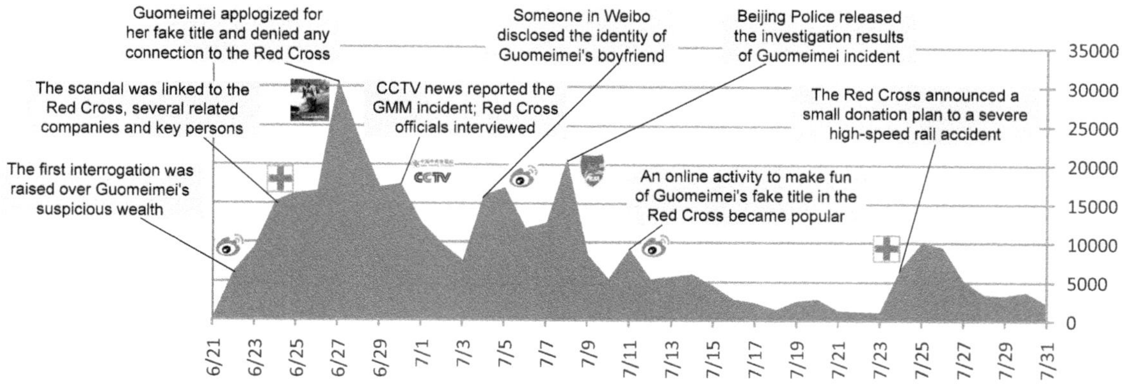

Figure 2. The trend of the original messages related to the rumor (49,725 posts).

The two researchers then applied the final coding scheme independently to all the 1,000 messages in the small sample. After that, they discussed together and found about 15% classifications different. They examined each of the disagreements until reaching consensus. As a result, a total of 1,186 statements were coded from the 1,000 messages.

Category	Verified Type	# Follower	Example
Celebrity	Personal	>= 10000	Entertainment/Sports Star, President of large corporations
Certified	Personal	< 10000	Manager of small companies
Mass Media	Media	—	Xinhua news, Times
Organization	Enterprise/ Academic/ Non-profit	—	Shopping mall, car company
Website	Website	—	Guangzhou portal
Internet Star	N/A	>= 10000	Bloggers, personalized content providers, online opinion leaders
Ordinary	N/A	< 10000	Other Microblog users

Table 1. Sina Weibo user categorization.

User Categorization

Our second research goal was to understand the different roles microblogging users play in the rumor discourse. We first determined a method to categorize Sina Weibo users according to their profiles and online behaviors. Then we applied this method to our large sample of 49,725 messages from 38,221 unique users.

Sina Weibo provides publicly visible "VIP-titles" to verified users. There are multiple types of certifications, including individuals, media agencies, organizations (enterprise, academic and non-profit) and websites. To build our user categories, we incorporated users' microblogging behavior with their certifications provided by Sina Weibo. We applied a cut-value of 10,000 in the number of followers to identify the top 1.96% users, who attracted 79.9% followers in the entire user base. The final user categories are shown in Table 1.

RESULTS

What Did People Talk About?

In this section, we first present the overall trend of rumor discussions on the Guo Meimei Incident. Then we examine different types of statements people posted during the rumor discussions and their evolvements over time.

Overall Trends

We analyzed the overall trends of the 49,725 posts collected during the 41 days (June 21~July 31). 28.5% of these posts have at least one comment, 27.5% are reposted at least once. In total, these posts have 133,318 comments and 343,596 reposts by a total of 245,847 unique users.

We then examined the development curve of these posts upon some key dates and the associated events during the rumor discussions, as illustrated in Figure 2. The rumor was generated on the late night of June 21 and immediately exploded. People gathered rapidly and engaged heavily in the discussion. Multiple peaks appeared during the 41 days. The first peak emerged around June 27 after Guo Meimei posted her apologetic messages. Around June 30, a second peak was achieved, following the mass media's interview with the Secretary General of the Red Cross Society. The post number dropped a bit in the coming few days, and then surged again on July 4 when another rumor was leaked out indicating Guo's boyfriend to be a high-level official at the Red Cross. Intensive discussions continued and then reached another peak with the police investigation results released on July 8. Later on July 11, a small peak was caused by a popular online competition activity which made fun of Guo's fabricated title at the Red Cross (messages were automatically posted to the microblogs of people who joined this activity, e.g., "*Now I am seriously showing off my wealth: I am pleased to accept the offer of the position of the Commercial General Manager at the Red Cross Society. I have beaten 1087 people!*"). After that, discussions about Guo Meimei became quieter until the Society announced a small donation plan for a severe high-speed rail accident which touched upon the public's sensitive nerve again on July 24.

Statement Types and Trends

Table 2 shows the overall distribution of the 1,186 statements we manually coded. Most statements fell into three major categories: providing information (410, 34%), expressing emotions (226, 19%) and opinions (315, 27%). Notably, about 10% (122) of the statements were those attempting to analyze and interpret the situation, which was not seen in people's responses to other extreme events discussed on Sina Weibo (e.g., a major disaster [22]). Another 3% asked for information explicitly for clarifying the rumors.

Categories	Description	%
Providing information	**Definition**: Statements adding material to the rumor, e.g. 'factual' details, evidences, situation updates, inside stories, personal involvements, etc. **Example**: *"Insiders leaked the identity of Guo Meimei's boyfriend [URL]"*	34
Opinion related statements	**Definition**: Statements indicating people's attitude towards the rumor, e.g. belief/disbelief, criticizing/agreement, etc. **Example**: *"You suspect when they don't deny. But when they deny, they are actually telling you the rumors are true."*	27
Emotional statements	**Definition**: Rumor-related emotions, both positive and negative, including fear, anxiety, apprehension, surprise, stress, anger, wish, excitement, etc. **Example**: *"Guo Meimei P.K. Red Cross! I am totally astonished!!!"*	19
Sense-making statements	**Definition**: Statements attempting to analyze and interpret the situation, e.g. disputing, justifying one's views, etc. **Example**: *"During the whole course, the biggest problem lies in Sina Weibo's verification system."*	10
Interrogatory statements	**Definition**: Question seeking information **Example**: *"#Guo Meimei incident# How did all this happen? Can anybody tell me?"*	3
Directive statements	**Definition**: Statements suggesting action. **Example**: *"Why don't we put Guo Meimei into a human flesh search?"*	3
Digressive statements	**Definition**: Off the topic. Statements irrelevant to the rumor. **Example**: *"Will this girl become the next Guo Meimei?"*	4

Table 2. Statement types and distribution (1,186 statements from 1,000 messages).

We studied how posts of different statement types were reposted and found that the messages providing information (6.31 reposts in average) and disseminating opinions (8.82) were the most disseminated. All the other types, such as conveying emotions (0.98) and sensemakings (0.73) were rarely reposted in average. Overall, 80% reposts were made within the first 12 hours after the original messages were posted.

Our analysis of the statement trends revealed interesting patterns in the distribution of different conversation types over time. Figure 3 shows the combined trend, while Figure 4 gives a clearer view to the evolution of each statement type separately.

The rises and falls of messages *providing information* are quite similar to the overall waves of discussions. A closer look at the content of these posts also showed high relevance of the messages with the key phases illustrated in Figure 2. For example, one group of typical posts in this category is those to contrast and question Guo's wealth against her title in the early phase: *"A 20-year-old young woman. Maserati, Lamborghini. Pure descent racehorse from Germany. Tens of Hermes handbags. First class airplane tickets. And…Commercial General Manager, Red Cross China." (@公益高剑)*

" 'The role of Red Cross is to help the people in need.' Said Guo Meimei, the Commercial GM. This 20-year-old girl lives in a palatial villa, drives a Maserati." (@乐活山西)

Meanwhile, new materials were synthesized from various sources about Guo's hometown, family background, educations and personal life. Later on, another group of posts kept updating the Red Cross' reactions and news from other media. For example, "*The Society says: Guo Meimei has no connection with the Red Cross [URL]*", "*The National Television calls Red Cross to prove itself innocent [URL]*" and "*Beijing Police: Guo Meimei has nothing to do with the Red Cross. [URL]*".

Generally, the emotional curve reached its peaks a bit later than the informational curve in each stage, although not much. This is probably because people tend to express their emotions as intuitive reactions to unfamiliar situations. The surge of emotional statements could be roughly divided into three phases. The first phase was from the beginning of the rumor to the first two peaks of discussions around June 27 and June 30. The second phase followed the rumors about Guo's boyfriend and the police investigation during July 3 to 11. The last phase was generated around the Red Cross' donation to the railway accident victims in late July. Our preliminary qualitative analysis indicated people's different emotions in the different phases of rumor discussions. In the first phase, people expressed a lot of anxiety and worry. For example, "*Guo Meimei has set a fire on the Internet!*" "*OMG! Guo Meimei! Explosive news! I can't go to work anymore!*" "*I can't bear this if this issue is not solved.*" Later, disappointment rose. "*It has already been a week. I*

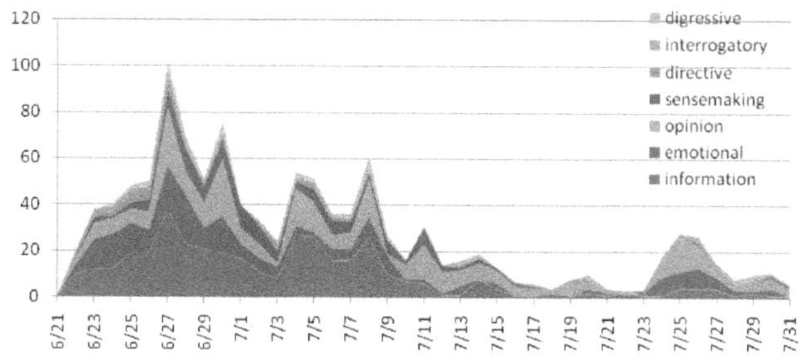

Figure 3. Statement trend accumulated (1000 messages).

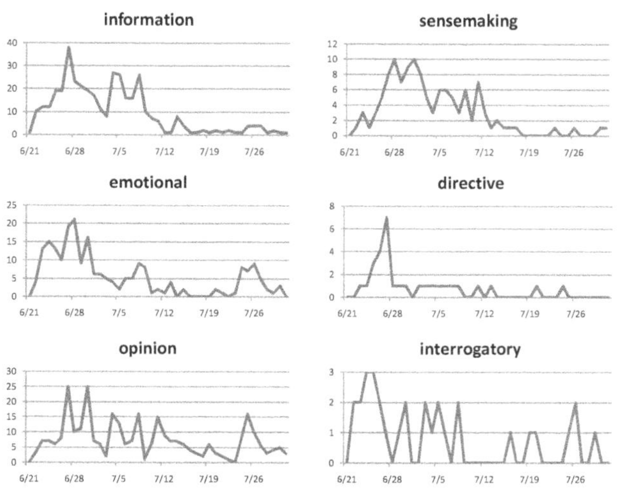

Figure 4. Statement trends separated (1000 messages)

am disappointed at the government." "*I am totally depressed.*" In the second phase, we observed more anger and sarcasm. For example, *"I feel like eating a worm in the apple.*" "*We all have to thank Guo Meimei. She is a hero!*" During the last peak, some became indifferent and sneered down the Society's small donation to the "7-23" railway accident victims: "*Oh Red Cross! Save your donation for Guo Meimei's handbags!*"

Interestingly, it is observed that people's emotional statements around the Guo Meimei scandal sometimes follow certain patterns of expression. For example, on the second day, a narrative format became very popular on Sina Weibo, which contains the pattern of "I am not in the mood": *"Guo Meimei's identity remains unclear, I am not in the mood to sleep." "Guo Meimei's identity uninvestigated, I am not in the mood to write my paper".* This pattern appeared 20 times in the first phase of the emotional surge.

The opinion curve progressed differently. Both the informational and the emotional curves faded out gradually after the police investigation results came out on July 8th. Overall the opinion curve covered the whole span of the rumor discourse quite actively. Our preliminary observation suggested that the crowd tended to believe the rumor was true and question the credibility of the government. Even after the police released their investigation results which denied the rumor, the typical opinions on Weibo were disbelief and criticism. For example: "*The Guo Meimei Incident challenges transparency of the charity: the society has lost its credibility*" (@G友 138159553), "*The police is humiliating themselves! Yes Guo Meimei has no connection with the Red Cross Society but she has connections with the Red Cross officials!*" (@冬去春来 9). Others challenged the government system: "*We saw the fall of the whole society. Our philanthropy has become another source of corruption. Should we think more about the down side of our own system?*" (@中国茶神)

Sensemaking statements, interestingly, peaked a little time later than informational, emotional and opinion-related statements. For example, the latter three reached their first peak on the same day of June 27, while sensemaking did that on June 28. Posts in this group increased quite slowly before its first peak. Similarly, while the other three had a second peak on June 30, sensemaking still peaked one day later. After that, it decreased, with several small peaks. One explanation for this latency could be that analyzing and interpreting the uncertain situation would depend on the understanding of information collected; so the sensemaking curve surged later than the informational curve. Compared to emotional expressions, which are more spontaneous, sensemaking utilizes one's rational decision rules and could involve more efforts. Opinions, at the least, could be formed from one's prior experience and thus surge before statements of sensemaking.

Lastly, directive and interrogatory statements showed novel trends. The directive messages emerged mainly with the first peak of the information curve and the first phase of the emotional surge. Posts in this category mainly asked for actions to put Guo Meimei into the *human flesh search* engine and to boycott the Red Cross. It is not surprising that the messages seeking information appeared immediately when the rumor was introduced. It is however notable that the interrogatory curve peaked a bit earlier than all other curves but disappeared after the information curve reached its peaks. This result could be explained by people's needs to collect information before they try to understand the situation.

So far we have examined different statement types of the rumor discussions and their evolution along with the rumoring trend. Next we explore different user roles in the rumor transmission.

Who Led the Discussions?

To understand the different user roles in the rumor discussions around Guo Meimei, we classified the 38,221 users in our dataset into seven categories as shown in Table 1. We then analyzed the *contributions* and *influences* of each user group. Here contribution was measured by the number of participating users and messages *posted.* Influence was measured by the number of comments and reposts *received.* Table 3 summarizes our results.

Categories	Contribution		Influence	
	% users	% posts	% commented	% reposted
Celebrity	2.27	2.54	22.38	29.40
Certified	5.46	5.20	4.42	2.05
Mass Media	0.45	0.72	25.90	22.78
Organization	0.77	0.84	1.04	1.22
Website	0.71	0.88	1.20	1.55
Internet Star	2.74	4.21	18.23	28.74
Ordinary	87.62	85.61	26.85	14.25

Table 3. User categories and distribution in terms of contribution and influence.

As expected, the ordinary users were the most engaged. They occupied more than 85% share in both the number of participating users and messages posted during the rumor discussions. Their posts, however, were not often reposted or commented by others. In together, the ordinary users only received about 14% of the total reposts and 27% of the total comments. In contrast, three smaller groups invoked most discussions and occupied most reposts. They were, namely, celebrities, mass media and Internet Stars (iStar). The mass media, notably, while being the smallest group, received the second most comments. The Celebrities and iStars only posted a small number of messages related to the rumor (less than 7%); but their messages were the most broadcasted (received about 60% of all the reposts).

We then examined how users in different categories drove discussions along with the rumor's development. We analyzed the temporal trends of different user groups' influence in generating discussions and reposts with their original messages. As shown in Figure 5, in the early stage after the rumor broke out (June 21~25) and before the first peak (June 27), messages posted by *iStars* were the most widely disseminated (55%~83%). After that, around the first peak on June 27 when Guo Meimei made her online apologies (June 26~July 2), the *celebrity* took the flag and their posts were heavily forwarded (41%~65%). During the next two peaks around the Beijing police's investigation (July 4~July 10), the *mass media* made a strong presence, with their reports and investigations most circulated (39%~85%). Later, rumor discussions cooled down after more and more media reports came out trying to clarify the truth and people began to lose interests. It was not until July 24, the next day after the "7-23" high-speed train accident, that the Guo Meimei incident was recalled. In this stage, discussions were again led by celebrities and iStars.

Figure 6 shows different user groups' strength in attracting comments along with the rumor evolution. The overall trend revealed a similar pattern to the influence on reposts (Figure 5): *iStars* first took the leadership followed by *celebrities* and the *mass media* respectively. Notable differences were that the ordinary people were more capable of generating discussions (receiving more comments) than producing wide-spread messages (receiving reposts), while iStars were the opposite.

In summary, our analysis of different user groups' influence over time reveals a 3-stage pattern of the changes of leading role in the rumor discussions on Weibo. In this pattern, the iStars first took the lead and generated the buzz. Then the celebrities broadcast the rumor to a larger audience. After that, the mass media take the leadership with their strong capabilities in providing substantial information.

DISCUSSION

In our case study, we categorized seven types of statements around rumor discussions and identified four major categories: providing information, expressing emotions, opinions, as well as analyzing and interpreting the situations. We also identified three leading user groups in the rumor discussions. While we do not generalize our findings to other microblogging communities (e.g., Twitter) or other extreme events, it's worth comparing our work with other case studies on the microblogging behavior in public crises (e.g., [19][22][27][29]) to understand the unique characteristics of rumor transmission.

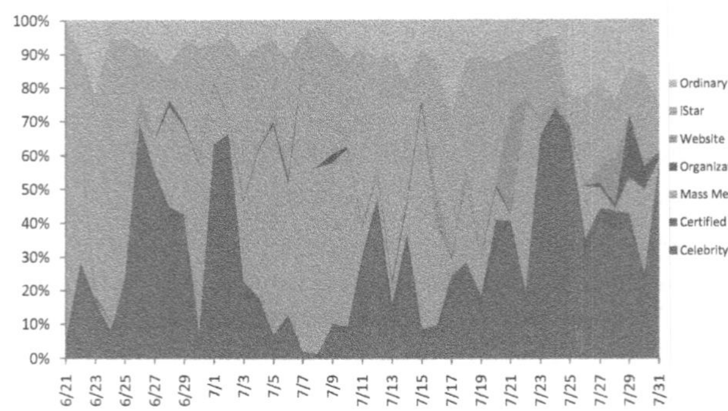

Figure 5. The trend of user categories in receiving reposts.

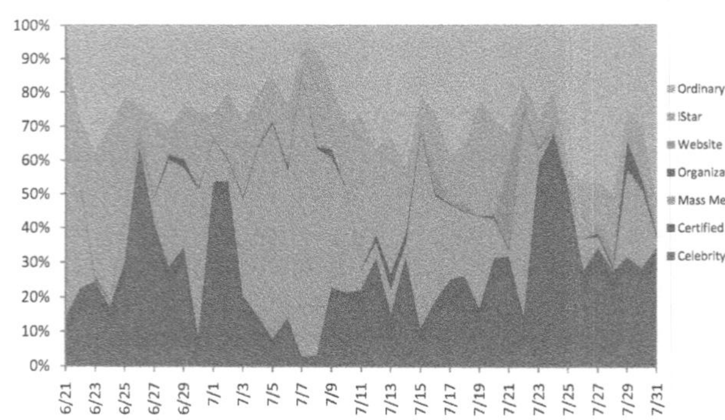

Figure 6. The trend of user categories in receiving comments.

Rumor discussions are more dynamic in terms of its various statement patterns. First, the primary job after a natural disaster or public event is to take immediate responses for rescues. Messages on situational awareness and actions are the essential. Under a public rumor, the major goal is to reduce the uncertainty, where providing new evidence, expressing opinions and making interpretations could be the driving force. Second, in all the previous studies on information spreading during extreme events, the posting trends largely follow the model proposed in [17][18]: the curve is shaped by a spike of breaking news and a power-law decay. Rumor discussions, however, are structured by various types of discussions that try to construct the truth or achieve a shared explanation. Next we discuss the contribution of our case study.

Conceptual Contribution to Rumor Theory

In this paper we take the social perspective that rumor transmission is a group explanation process for reducing collective anxiety in uncertain situations [7] [25]. Our study provided preliminary large-scale empirical evidence for the rumor theories that had been hindered by the difficulties in acquiring data under a natural observation and limited to small scale studies before the flourishing of SNS. As the next step, we plan to conduct deeper analysis on the interplay among the different types of statements. Conceptually we are interested in examining the relationship among uncertainty, anxiety and sensemaking activities. In our case, difficulties in finding credible evidences and the high public concern added to the complex of the rumors. Our case suggested that availability of reliable information sources, consistence in the information collected, variety of the materials as well as the scale of participants could be candidate indicators for measuring the uncertainty associated with rumors.

Furthermore, from our analysis we form a preliminary argument of the large-scale rumor transmission processes. We propose that at the early stage of rumor discourse, people post most messages for information seeking and emotion relieving, to address their intensive stress caused by the situation of great ambiguity. They form and share their opinions based on the situation and their past experience to give their initial explanations. Questions are asked for collective information gathering. When rumors continue to develop, with more details added to the situation, uncertainty increases. People put more effort in finding references, analyzing and making sense of the story. After that, emotional expressions decrease and interpretations increase. When people gradually build a collectively acceptable version of understanding, authenticating and emotional statements fade out.

While the contribution of our work is the rumor discourse analysis over a large scale of data, not much in-depth analysis has been included in this paper. Future work should be done to pin down and examine our above models proposed with more thorough analysis. It is also worth the effort to dig the roles and impact of different user groups while examining the model.

Microblogging during Massive Rumor Discourses

Our findings could inform the design and development of tools based on microblogs to respond to public rumors that may create collective stress in the society.

First, our results suggest that examining the combination of people's different statements may serve as an indicator for analyzing and predicting rumor development automatically, as well as measuring its impacts. For example, classifiers can be trained based on our analysis to classify the real-time large data on SNS that are related to rumor discussions. Our observation on different statement types has suggested many features that could be applied in machine learning technologies, e.g., statements in the "providing information" group often contain a URL link that points to other news websites, blog articles, or video sharing sites, and possess several patterns, e.g. "[entity] published an article". Emotional statements, as another example, often contain several exclamatory marks or mood-related keywords. Future work should be done to investigate the best features and measure their effectiveness for automatically identifying statement types accurately. Based on reliable large-scale statement classifications, portions and evolution trends of each statement types could be computed to build an index for understanding different rumor stages. Furthermore, the patterns of user behaviors for situation clarification and emotion relieving could be used to evaluate the levels of the importance and relevance of the topic, as well as the public anxiety induced by the uncertainty.

Second, technologies could be developed to analyze different user roles and identify key influencers that drive the direction of rumor discussions. In doing this, one should consider multiple dimensions for gauging different users' role in the microblogging community. Our analysis revealed different results on user roles between their contribution and influence. Interesting variances were also observed in different types of influences, e.g. capabilities for attracting comments versus reposts. While we did not include content analysis in measuring the user contribution and influence, future work could consider mining the text of users' discussions. For example, in our case, the mass media and celebrities have made the strongest presence in generating popular posts. However, it remains unclear *how* their posts are perceived and *how* their opinions influence the crowd. More in-depth research on the detailed interactions among different users should be done for identifying users that could help reduce uncertainty. With this understanding, future technology could be developed to detect opinion leaders, together with the analysis on the discourse patterns, to identify best strategies and channels for intervening and controlling the development of public rumors.

Social Media Transforming China's Civil Society

Lastly, our work also shed light on how social media is used in China under its social transitions. Recent years have witnessed the fast development of social media including microblogging in China since 2008, e.g. Kaixin001.com, Renren.com, weibo.com, etc. One of the reasons, we believe, lies in social media's great potential in driving public interests towards numerous controversial subjects that have been emerging under China's social reforms. Bringing together the advantages of both blogging and social networking, Sina Weibo provides a great channel for the grassroots to voice their opinions towards public affairs, to collectively examine topics of shared concerns, and to form the power of the crowd in impacting government decisions of public interests. Our case study provides an example of how powerful an anonymous microblogger can be in the social transition that China has been going through. Rumor discussions on Guo Meimei and her rumored connection with the Red Cross urged the government-owned charity to be more transparent to the public. As a response to the furious crowd, the Red Cross has built a system to publicize how each donation is used and open itself to public supervisions. Future research could be conducted to obtain a deeper understanding of how social technologies change people's civic life in China.

CONCLUSION

In this paper, we have reported a case study on rumor transmissions in a Chinese microblogging community. Our content analysis on 1,000 messages identified seven different statement types and revealed their evolution dynamics as rumors developed over time. Another analysis of 38,221 unique users from 49,725 messages suggested different patterns of people taking the leading role in consecutive rumoring phases. Overall, our work provided preliminary evidence to social scientists' perspectives of viewing rumor transmission as a collective problem solving process. Our findings offered implications to unleashing the potential of using microblogging data to understand and control the public rumor development. Lastly, our study documented a case that added to the understanding of how social media is used in China for civil engagement.

ACKNOWLEDGMENTS

We would like to thank our colleagues John C. Thomas and Weijia Shen for their proofreading the paper and their valuable comments. Thank our anonymous reviewers for their insightful feedback, which helped us revise and improve the paper.

Lei Shi is supported in part by the National Basic Research Program of China (973 Program) under Grant No. 2010CB328105, National Science Foundation of China (NSFC) under Grant No. 60932003 and 60973144.

REFERENCES

1. Sina Weibo. http://weibo.com
2. Sina Weibo Wikipedia Entry. http://en.wikipedia.org/wiki/Sina_Weibo
3. Guo Meimei in Baidu Index. http://index.baidu.com/main/word.php?word=%B9%F9%C3%C0%C3%C0
4. Allport, G. W. and Postman, L. J. (1947).*The psychology of rumor*. New York: Holt, Rinehart and Winston.
5. Anthony, S. (1973). Anxiety and Rumor. *The Journal of Social Psychology* (89), pp. 91- 98.
6. Bordia, P. Studying verbal interaction on the Internet: The case of rumor transmission research, *Behavior Research Methods*, Vol. 28, No. 2 (1996), 149-151.
7. Bordia, P., and DiFonzo, N. Problem Solving in Social Interactions on the Internet: Rumor as Social Cognition. *Social Psychology Quarterly* 67(1), 2004: 33-49.
8. Bordia, P., DiFonze, N., and Chang, A. Rumor as Group Problem Solving: Development Patterns in Informal Computer-Mediated Groups. *Small Research Group* 30(8), 1999, pp.8-28.
9. Bordia, P., and Rosnow, R.L. Rumor Rest Stops on the Information Highway: Transmission Patterns in a Computer-Mediated Rumor Chain. *Human Communication Research* 25(2), 1998, 163-179.
10. Buckner, H. T. A Theory of Rumor Transmission, *Public Opinion Quarterly*,, Vol. 29, No. 1, Spring 1965, pp. 54-70.
11. Castillo, C., Mendoza, M., Poblete, B. Information Credibility on Twitter. In *Proc. WWW*, (2011).
12. DiFonzo, N., Bordia, P. and Rosnow, R. L. (1994). Reining in rumors. *Organizational Dynamics* 23, 47–62.
13. Hu, M., Liu, S., Wei, F., Wu, Y., Stasko, J., Ma, K., Breaking News on Twitter, In *Proc. CHI'12.*
14. Java, A., Song, X., Finin, T., and Tseng, B. Why we twitter: understanding microblogging usage and communities. In *Proc. WebKDD/SNA-KDD '07*, ACM (2007), 56–65.
15. Krull, D. S. and Craig A. A. (1997). The Process of Explanation. *Current Directions in Psychological Science 6*(1):1-5.
16. Kwak, H., Lee, C., Park, H., and Moon, S. What is twitter, a social network or a news media? In *Proc. WWW '10*, ACM (2010), 591–600.
17. Leskovec, J., Backstrom, L., and Kleinberg, J. Meme-tracking and the dynamics of the news cycle. In *Proc. KDD '09*, ACM (2009), 497–506.
18. Matsubara, Y., Sakurai, Y., Prakash, B. A., Li, L. and Faloutsos, C. Rise and Fall Patterns of Information Diffusion: Models and Implications. In *Proc. KDD '12*, ACM (2012), 6–14.
19. Mendoza, M., Poblete, B. and Castillo, C. Twitter Under Crisis: Can We Trust What We RT? KDD 2010 Social Media Analytics Workshop.
20. Morris M. R., Counts, S., Roseway, A., Hoff, A., Schwarz, J. Tweeting is Believing? Understanding Microblog Credibility Perceptions, In *Proc. CSCW 2012.*
21. Palen, L. and Vieweg, S. (2008). The Emergence of Online Widescale Interaction: Assistance, Alliance and Retreat. In *Proc. CSCW'08.*
22. Qu, Y., Huang, C., Zhang, P., Zhang, J. Microblogging after a Major Disaster in China: A Case Study of the 2010 Yushu Earthquake, In *Proc. CSCW 2011.*

23. Rosnow, R. L. (1980). Psychology of rumor reconsidered. *Psychological Bulletin*, 87, 578–591.

24. Rosnow, R. L. and Kimmel. A.J. (2000). Rumor. *Encyclopedia of Psychology*, Vol. 7, edited by Kazdin., A.E. New York: Oxford University Press. pp. 122-123.

25. Shibutani, T. *Improvised News: A Sociological Study of Rumor*. Indianapolis: Bobbs-Merrill, 1966.

26. Starbird, K., Palen, L. "Voluntweeters": Self-Organizing by Digital Volunteers in Times of Crisis. In *Proc. CHI* 2011.

27. Starbird, K., Palen, L., Hughes, A. L. and Vieweg, S., Chatter on The Red: What Hazards Threat Reveals about the Social Life of Microblogged Information. In *Proc. CSCW* (2010).

28. Qazvinian, V., Rosengren, E., Radev, D. R., and Mei. Q. Rumor has it: identifying misinformation in microblogs. In *Proc. EMNLP '11*, (2011), 1589–1599.

29. Vieweg, S., Hughes, A. L., Starbird, K. and Palen, L., Microblogging during two natural hazards events: what twitter may contribute to situational awareness. In *Proc. CHI*, (2010), 1079-1088.

30. Wu, D. K. Aligning a parallel English-Chinese corpus statistically with lexical criteria. In *Prof. ACL'94*, 80-87.

31. Wu, S., Hofman, J. M., Mason, W. A., and Watts, D. J. Who says what to whom on twitter. In *Proc. WWW '11*, ACM (2011), 705–714.

32. Yang, J. and Leskovec, J. Patterns of temporal variation in online media. In *Proc. WSDM '11*, ACM (2011).

33. Bernardi, D., Cheong, P. H., Lundry, C. and Ruston, S. W. *Narrative Landscapes: Rumors, Islamist Extremism, and the Struggle for Strategic Influence*. Rutgers University Press, 2012.

Trust in Online News: Comparing Social Media and Official Media Use by Chinese Citizens

Yiran Wang and Gloria Mark
Department of Informatics
Donald Bren School of Information and Computer Sciences
University of California, Irvine
{yiranw2, gmark@uci.edu}

ABSTRACT
Since 2006 social media use has grown dramatically in China. Social media has become a stage for citizens to report and disseminate news and to vocalize viewpoints, at times competing with reports from highly curated official media sources. These competing news channels, oftentimes presenting contradictory information, raise questions about citizens' trust in these different media. This study explores the level of trust Chinese Internet users place on news from social media versus official media. We conducted a large-scale anonymous survey in China that revealed that official and citizen news attract different audience groups and each group uses different features to assess news trustworthiness. We present a model for predicting preference for news from citizen media. The results reveal features of social media that explain why some citizens trust it as a channel for news. The results also suggest that in highly regulated news environments, citizen media has the potential to become an alternative news channel where citizens can trust each other for information.

Author Keywords
Social media; citizen journalism; trust; news; authoritarian government.

ACM Classification Keywords
H.4 [Information Systems Applications]: Miscellaneous; H.5.3 [Group and Organization Interfaces]: Computer-Supported Cooperative Work.

INTRODUCTION
In April, 2012, Chen Guangcheng, a human rights activist from Shandong Province, China, daringly escaped from house arrest and arrived at the U.S. embassy in Beijing. Chen, who is a lawyer and who is blind, had been a vocal advocate for womens' rights and the welfare of the poor in rural China. Due to his exposure of alleged violence in the enforcement of family-planning policy, as well as his organization of local protests, he experienced four years of jail, house arrest, and apparent physical abuse from local police forces. At the U.S. embassy, Chen negotiated his case with both U.S. and Chinese top authorities.

Chen's case immediately attracted national and international media attention given its political sensitivity. Within 24 hours of his entry to the U.S. Embassy, Chen's name, his initials "CGC" and the phrase "the blind man" had all been blocked by Chinese censorship on user-generated content websites [1]. Official Chinese media outlets, on the other hand, offered a series of brief reports.

The official Chinese media reports communicated a very different story than what was expressed in social media. As reported in Chinese official newspaper reports and editorials, Chen, a "political pawn," was taken into the U.S. Embassy by Hillary Clinton via abnormal means and left of his own volition after a six-day stay [7]. The official Chinese media accused Chen of cleverly playing a role of a dissident to seek benefits from a Western power [27]. Later, the Chinese official media conveyed a negative impression of the U.S. by Chen's change of heart when he expressed his disappointment about the U.S. government [26].

However, despite government censorship, content about Chen's case still secretly circulated in Chinese social media sites. During a week of online observation, the first author observed dozens of posts from China's most popular microblogging site: Sina Weibo. In the posts, Chen was depicted as a "normal citizen" unaware that he had gained international attention and who reflects the authentic life of Chinese citizens living under the authoritarian system. Citizens reported that he should be well respected given his contribution and the injustice he endured. In short, users of social media sites showed empathy, understanding and positive interest toward Chen.

The plight of Chen Guangcheng illustrates the complexity of the role of social media in a society where an authoritarian government regulates news. What information should a citizen believe when social media citizen accounts contradict media reports from "official" sources? In any society, there are different channels through which news can be reported and disseminated: from the informal permeable word-of-mouth, to conventional television, newspapers and magazines which follow a strict production

CSCW '13, February 23–27, 2013, San Antonio, Texas, USA.

cycle, to the Internet, which is regarded as the ideal medium where varied forms of information can converge [19].

The purpose of this study is to examine, in an authoritarian society where the media is under strict government control, why some citizens trust news more from such official media, and why others trust news more from user-generated social media. This is an extremely important question not only in China, but also in other authoritarian-ruled countries where citizens face similar choices about trusting news from official and citizen-generated channels.

In this paper, we define trustworthiness as perceived believability of information [5]. Instead of focusing on the innate credibility of news, we seek to investigate trust from the audience perspective [8]. The reasons are two-fold: first, personal interpretations of news (such as news commentary), which often comprises reported news, cannot necessarily be assessed by "truthfulness"; second, how much a news consumer trusts the news has a direct impact on how the news is interpreted and further disseminated.

The News Media Environment in China

By *official media*, we refer to enterprises that are run or influenced by the state, generally involving professional journalists and editorial procedures. In China, examples of official media outlets run by the state are Xinhua, CCTV, and People's Daily. Independent commercial news portals or news sites such as Sina or Tencent that need a license from the government are only allowed to reproduce news from official (i.e. government) accounts. Thus, they do not have the autonomy to produce original news content [11, 31]. We refer to both state-run and commercial media companies under governmental control as official media.

By *citizen media*, we refer to news that is posted and disseminated by citizens using various forms of social media. According to the 29th statistical report on Internet development in China [9], the number of micro-blog (**MB**) users tripled within 2011, making up 48.7% of the total 500 million Internet user population in China, while users of social-network sites (**SNS**s) comprise 47.6% of the Internet population. With the wide adoption of these two platforms, in this paper we concentrate on citizen-generated news that is only shared through SNSs and MBs. These two media channels have become a stage for users to vocalize their viewpoints and report original eyewitness reports, which often compete with, if not contradict, those from highly curated official media sources.

However citizen media is not completely free of government influence. "Opinion guidance", as translated from Chinese, is a unique phenomenon in Chinese user-generated sites. Here, Internet commentators hired by the government (yet appearing to be citizens) are speculated to post comments favorable to the Party in order to subtly guide public opinion. Opinion guidance introduces "the hand of the state" secretively into citizen media by guiding dialogue on social and politically sensitive topics, oftentimes, news. For example, in the most popular online forum Tianya (tianya.cn/bbs), a comment about an online information filter application sponsored by the Chinese government was widely regarded as "opinion guidance." It said: "I think 80% of all Internet users are supporting this software…we finally have access to a free copy to this software, thank you government!" Irrespective of the personal sentiments in this comment, it distorted the fact that the software is not well accepted by the public. We believe it is important to investigate the potential influence of opinion guidance because it hinders citizen media from becoming a true public sphere. A public sphere, as Habermas [15] explains, is where rational debate is not manipulated (e.g. by an authoritative power), and is open to inspection by citizens. When the state exerts control over the discourse through opinion guidance, then this challenges the role of citizen media channels as public spheres with free and open dialogue.

Contrasting "Official" and "Citizen" Media

There are some fundamental differences between news generated and disseminated through professional, "official" channels and by citizens [11, 30, 34]. In traditional news production, news is written by professional journalists, whose practices and values adhere to institutional authority and economic resources [30]. Because official news is subject to diligent fact-checking, editorial oversight and governmental curation (in China), a certain level of accountability and objectivity is therefore expected. However, official news generally sets agendas [23] by choosing what news goes on the front page and what news should be hidden from the public. This design of news essentially directs news consumers what to read, which for some might cause suspicion or even aversion towards official media. Also, news consumers may lower their trust in official reports due to biases and the promotion of particular viewpoints, which direct them "how to think". In addition, in a society ruled by an authoritarian government, there may be censorship of significant events (as in the case of Chen Guangcheng).

In citizen-generated news media, production rules are more relaxed. News can be written, filtered, interpreted, mutated and redistributed in the complex chain of dissemination, out of citizens' simple desire to report news, express commentary or pass on hearsay. Although average citizens do not have as many resources compared to professional journalists, those who happen to be present at a newsworthy event can provide eyewitness accounts in what Lasica [21] calls a "random act of journalism," which is "report what you observe, analyze events in a meaningful way but, most of all, just be fair and tell the truth as you and your sources see it." Even if only a small proportion of social media users each report a tiny slice of news information, given the large number of reports, they might potentially provide enough news with sufficient impact, as the long tail theory suggests [2]. In contrast to official news reports, which strive to be "objective", citizen reports can also convey emotion, commentary, sentiment and reflection on events. Such shared emotions can stimulate a sense of community and a sense of transparency among news consumers, which can further enhance trust.

The consumer-turned–into-producer opportunity, however, has its own drawbacks. Considering that user-generated news often only contributes "soft news", Thurman [33] raised the concern that citizens who do not have power or access to professional resources can hardly adequately report hard news such as stories at the national level. Another disadvantage is that the increasing interactive options can possibly make it harder for users to effectively digest or follow news [3]. Besides, people are found more likely to interact with those who share the same views for conformity [32]. Since citizen media can easily link like-minded people together, the consequent opinion polarization [32, 36] can potentially limit people's ability to engage in meaningful discussion. Thus, citizen media as a news channel is two-sided: it can increase trust because of the citizen-centric values it embodies but it can also decrease trust due to poor quality of information.

Comparing Trust in Official and Citizen Media in China

Considering the frequent discrepancies in news from these two media as we discussed, news trustworthiness has become a pressing issue. A number of recent studies (e.g. [5, 10]) have examined the credibility of news information in social media in Western countries. While a considerable amount of attention has been paid to the impact of social media in China, e.g. [29, 30, 35], research is lacking that explicitly examines the trustworthiness of news generated from social media in China. We feel that it is very important to examine the trust that Internet users place on news from official and citizen media, because the Internet has the power to shape opinion about events [4]. Further, it is important to learn what features of social media potentially can enhance trust in news as this can benefit the future design of social media tools.

Trust in News: Research Questions

Our main research question addresses what leads citizen to trust or distrust news from official or citizen media. Based on the research literature, we focused on eight aspects detailed below that we expect to influence trust in online news: types of readers, participation, commentary sources, alignment with government views, strength of ties, anonymity, content, and collective behavior.

Who Trusts What News Channels: Types of Readers

Official media can promote trust due to fact-checking, editorial oversight and governmental curation. However, features of Chinese official media such as agenda-setting, censorship, biases and propaganda of particular viewpoints can also lower people's trust in it. With citizen media, trust can be leveraged by personal relationships, the collective contribution and assessment by the crowd, and multiple viewpoints. On the other hand, concerns about news information quality and informality could also hinder trust.

The current media environment in China has been experiencing change amidst the overall rapid changes in the country. As the old meets the new (e.g. culturally and economically), we expect the emergence of different citizen groups who might have different preferences and trust in these different media. We will investigate first what kinds of news channels citizens trust more, and then, based on our data, whether we can identify different types of news consumers with different preferences and trust in news from official and citizen-generated channels. We will also consequently identify other ways that these news reader types might differ. Understanding how news reader types differ can provide insight into why some citizens trust or distrust certain news channels in an authoritarian government society. We thus ask RQ1: *Do Chinese news readers place more trust in official media or citizen media? Can we identify news reader types based on their different trust levels of media?*

Participation in News Activities

To understand trust in media channels, it is important to gain an overview of to what extent news consumers are passive spectators or active participants. According to a Pew research center report [28], in 2010, 37% of U.S. Internet users have contributed to the reporting of news, commented about it, or disseminated it using social media. It is possible that the more people participate in news activities the more they may trust news from citizen media channels. We thus ask RQ2: *How much do Chinese news readers participate in creating and commenting on news?*

Authors of News Commentary and Trust

News commentary helps consumers to make sense of news, which influences further dissemination of the news. News commentary from professional editorialists are more formal and more likely to reflect the public agenda whereas citizen news commentators are more likely to express a broad range of personal interpretations and opinions. Thus, these two types of commentary differ, e.g. in quality, style, and background research. Trust in commentary refers to trust in an author's rationality in constructing arguments or opinions. Citizens may have higher trust in commentary from professionals, associated with official media, who may be better educated and informed on an issue. On the other hand, citizens may trust commentary more from fellow citizens due to the democratic nature of expressing a range of opinions which may be agenda-free, i.e. interests of citizens rather than of the government. We thus ask RQ3: *What is the level of trust in news commentary from different types of news authors (professionals vs. citizens)?*

Perspective of News and Trust

Chinese citizens generally perceive official media as the mouthpiece of the government [35]. Even Chinese professional journalists share the same view that information generated by the Chinese official media is of low credibility [31]. Together with the potential effect of opinion guidance in citizen media as we discussed earlier, Chinese Internet users may have different trust in news that affirms government views than those that criticize them, regardless of the news source. We thus ask RQ4: *What is the level of trust in news information with different views (affirmative, critical and neutral) on the government?*

Strength of Ties and Trust

SNSs (and to a large degree MBs) use both strong and weak ties. One fundamental difference why people might retrieve news from SNSs or MBs compared to a government-sanctioned institution is that people often (perhaps unconsciously) trust information from individuals who they trust. Readers may trust news that is generated by their friends [13] or by those who are "like them" based on the strength of strong ties [20] and homophily [24]. The stronger the tie (family, close friends), the more similar two actors are in terms of information, experience, and values [20]. Because of this, people may place high trust on news information written or re-posted from strong ties in SNSs or MBs. Weak ties (acquaintances, friends' friends), on the other hand, help disseminate novel information and bridge local networks into a larger community [14]. With SNSs and MBs, news consumers tend to access new information or different viewpoints from weak ties [14]. There may be a positive relationship between placing high trust in social media and in newsworthy information from weak ties. For news written or re-posted from strangers, there is no social tie to introduce either pre-existing trust or accountability associated with social capital [22]. People may therefore have different levels of trust in news from strangers, compared to strong and weak ties. We ask RQ5: *What is the relationship between trust in news (posted or re-posted) and strength of ties in the source delivering the news?*

Anonymity and Trust

Citizen reporting can be anonymous (i.e. with a non-identifiable user name or user image) or identifiable (i.e. with a perceived real name or profile image). User profile characteristics such as a profile image have been found to influence perceived trustworthiness [25]. Identifiable accounts may therefore affect news readers' trust in citizen media news [25]. We ask RQ6: *How does anonymity of the source affect trust in citizen media news?*

Content Features and Trust

Content-related features could also potentially have an effect on news trustworthiness. Posting a URL to an original news source was reported to boost trust as it provides more evidence [25]. However, those URLs most likely linked to news from official sources. Since Chinese news readers may be skeptical of official sources, we might expect different findings. We ask RQ7: *How do content features, such as a URL, affect trust in news?*

Collective Participation and Trust

Since social media involves large-scale participation, posts can easily be re-posted, commented or "liked". Such a collective "crowd effect" from social media users can enhance trust since an aggregation of group opinions could imply credibility; on the other hand, it could also hinder trust due to an artificial inflation of re-posts that could be manipulated by a commercial agenda [37]. We ask RQ8: *how does reflection of the crowd (e.g. comments or affirmations) affect trust in citizen news?*

METHOD

We conducted a large-scale anonymous online survey within China. The survey was in the Chinese language, deployed through snowball sampling using multiple links to the authors' contacts of family, friends, and professional colleagues. The survey link was spread via emails to contacts throughout China. It was also posted in Chinese social network sites, microblogging sites, online forums, and university bulletin board systems. In addition, we asked for recommendations of other contacts from all survey respondents, which we used to further disseminate our survey. After a one-month deployment in April, 2012, we received 578 responses. The survey provides us with both quantitative and qualitative data concerning trust in official and social media. The full questionnaire can be accessed here (http://www.ics.uci.edu/~yiranw2/China_News_Consumption_Survey.pdf). Survey questions that address our research questions are in Appendix A.

We asked two open-ended questions: (Q1) If you have experienced opinion guidance, to what extent has it influenced your understanding or opinion toward current news events? and (Q2) Do you have any open comments on trustworthiness of news in social media in China?

Two coders conducted content analysis on these last two questions. The first coder used a bottom-up approach to develop categories for coding and both coders applied these on the data. Cohen's Kappa was 90.5% for Q1 and 89.4% for Q2, indicating satisfactory inter-coder reliability.

RESULTS

Overview of Results

We first present demographic information about our sample in Table 1. The gender distribution of our sample population is very similar to the Chinese Internet population [9]. The age distribution is in line with the social media user population [17]. Our sample is most representative of the Chinese population who has higher education.

Gender	Female: **45.5%**		Male: **54.5%**		
Age	18-25: **47.6%**	26-30: **30.6%**	31-40: **9.1%**	41-50: **10.2%**	50+: **2.5%**
Education	Middle/High school: **3.8%**		College: **47%**	Graduate school: **49.2%**	
Location	Urban: **87.9%**		Suburban: **7.3%**	Rural: **4.7%**	

Table 1. Demographic information of sample population

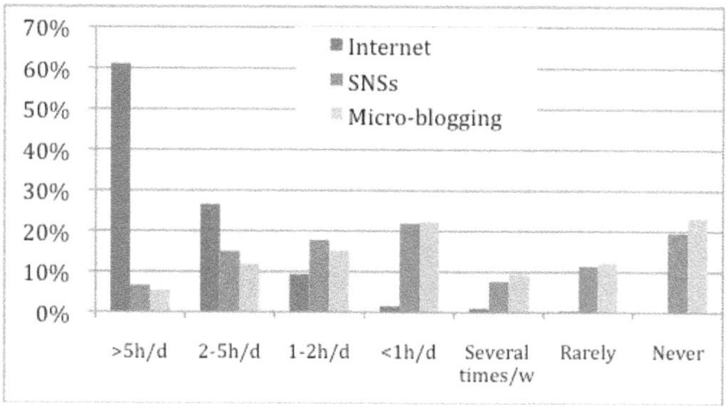

Figure 1: Internet, SNSs and MBs usage

Figure 1 shows the reported amount of overall Internet, SNS, and MB usage. Social media users tend to use it 1-2 hours a day or less. About one fifth of our respondents do not use SNSs or MBs and we exclude these in our analyses that specifically relate to trust in citizen media news.

Respondents do read news actively (i.e. deliberately reaching out for news, such as buying newspapers, going to online news sites, or checking RSS feeds). We found that 36.8% of our respondents read news several times a day and 27.2% read news once a day. Only 2.8% of the sample do not read news. For our analyses related to news consumption in our survey, we excluded those respondents who reported that they do not read news.

However, specifically when they visit SNSs or MBs, most respondents reported they tend to find news by chance. On a 7-item scale (1=completely by chance, 7=deliberately search), the mean is 2.84 (sd=1.89) and 3.01 (sd=1.82) for SNSs and MBs respectively. On a typical day 65.6% and 54.3% of respondents read at least one news item daily from SNSs and MBs respectively; 22.7% and 36.6% of respondents read over 10 news items daily from SNSs and MBs respectively.

These numbers illustrate that social media users do get a fair amount of news exposure through SNSs and MBs but they tend to find it by chance. For example, a person might log into her SNS account and happen to read a news post shared by her friend.

Results of Research Questions

We report the findings for each research question in the following sections. All questions regarding trust used a 7-point scale, where 1=strongly distrust, 7=strongly trust. For RQ2–RQ8, we report the findings on the entire sample, followed by comparisons between news reader types. A repeated measures ANOVA was used for analyses comparing survey responses. For analyses on news reader types, the survey question response is the within-subjects variable and news reader type is the between-subjects variable. RQ5-RQ8 concern trust specifically in citizen media.

	Cynical	Gullible	**Traditional**	**NG**
Male	64%	48.3%	**40.7%**	**61.7%**
Female	36%	51.5%	**59.3%**	**38.3%**
Total no.	75	60	**54**	**47**

Table 2. Percent responses to four newsreader types

RQ1: Who Trusts What

The results show that Chinese news consumers place moderate trust in both official (mean=4.07, sd=1.63) and citizen (mean=3.92, sd=1.22) media with no significant difference t(391)=1.66, p<.10, even though the two media have a different set of advantages and disadvantages.

However, if we investigate our sample more closely, we might identify types of news readers: different subsets of respondents with different types of trust preferences for media. We combined ratings of 5, 6, 7 into 'high trust' and ratings of 1, 2, 3 into 'low trust' and created four categories of respondents: 'Traditional' (**T**) (high trust in official, low trust in citizen), 'New Generation' (**NG**) (low trust in official, high trust in citizen), 'Cynical' (low trust in official, low trust in citizen) and 'Gullible' (high trust in official, high trust in citizen) as shown in Table 2. Trust rating 4 in official and/or citizen media is not counted; thus not every respondent is associated with a "reader type".

Our goal in this study is to understand why citizens prefer to trust one media channel over another. Therefore, to best understand reasons for trust and distrust among citizens we focus our further analyses on the reader types with the most contrasting (or discerning) opinions: the Traditionals, mean (official media)=5.68, sd=0.67; mean(citizen media)=2.53, sd=0.58) and the New Generation (mean(official media)=2.30, sd=0.70; mean(citizen media)=5.39, sd=0.49). Because the Cynicals and the Gullibles report trusting both media types similarly (low and high trust, respectively), our reasoning to not focus on them is that they may not distinguish the channels as much as the other reader types.

How can we characterize the differences between these groups other than their trust in media? Ts have a higher proportion of women than the NGs (chi-sq(1) = 4.41, p<.04), but surprisingly do not differ significantly in age or other demographics. NGs adopted SNSs earlier than Ts (chi-sq(3)=8,07, p<.05), but there is no significant difference with MB adoption (chi-sq(3)=2.08, p<0.56).

RQ2: Participatory News Activities

Table 3 shows results of our respondents' participation in online news production and dissemination, such as contributing original news content, commenting, posting or sharing URLs to news articles on social media, as well as feeling a sense of community with such participation.

The respondents are relatively active in writing and modifying news. Of all the respondents, 81.6% have participated in at least one type of news activity. Commenting and sharing URLs to news articles in social media are the most prevalent forms of participation.

Type of online participation	T	NG	Entire sample
Tag or Categorize online news	32.1%	39.1%	28.9%
Contribute orig'l news content*	**39.6%**	**63.0%**	44.5%
Comment	69.8%	83.6%	69.6%
Organize/participate online news events	37.7%	43.5%	36.7%
Post URL on SNSs**	**41.5%**	**67.4%**	48.2%
Share URL on SNSs	58.5%	71.7%	60.4%
Post URL on MBs	49.1%	63.0%	48.6%
Share URL on MBs	64.2%	69.6%	60.7%
Feeling a sense of community *	**15.2%**	**33.3%**	18.1%
Overall participation (participated in at least one type of activity)	83.0%	89.1%	81.6%

Table 3. Percentage of respondents who participate in online news activities. (*p< .05; **p< .01)

When asked why they participate in generating or disseminating news, 63.5% agree (responding 1, 2, or 3 on a 7-point scale) that they want to inform others by participation, 62.2% reported doing so in order to socialize with others, yet only 18.1% felt a sense of community while participating.

We also observe that a larger proportion of NGs have participated in different types of news activities than Ts. Using a Z-test on proportions, we find that significantly more NGs contribute original news content (z=2.39, p<.02) and post URLs on SNSs (z=2.68 , p<.01) compared to the Ts. Trends show that NGs participate in more commenting, sharing URLs on SNSs and posting URLs on MB sites but these did not reach significance. We also find significantly more NGs have experienced a sense of community (z=2.12, p<.04) in their participation. In sum, our sample shows a relatively high participation in online citizen news activities, with a trend that more NGs participate than Ts.

RQ3: Authors of News Commentary and Trust

How much do people trust commentary from professionals versus other citizens? Figure 2 shows the results of trust in news commentary. For the entire sample, we found that Chinese news consumers have moderate trust in news commentary from both professional writers (e.g. editorialists in official media) and non-professional citizen commentators with a trend for higher trust in professional commentary (F(1,393) =3.61, p<.06).

However, Ts and NGs have quite different views on these two news commentary sources. A significant Commentary x Type interaction (F(1,97)=56.68, p<.001) shows that Ts have higher trust in commentary by professionals whereas NGs have higher trust in citizen commentary. News Commentary does not show significant differences but there is a slight trend of difference in reader type (F(1,97)=3.028, p<.09).

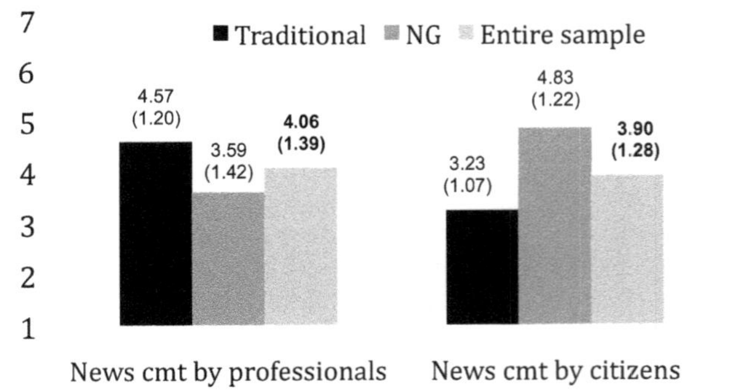

Figure 2. Trust in news commentary sources for Ts, NGs and the entire sample. Means and sd's shown.

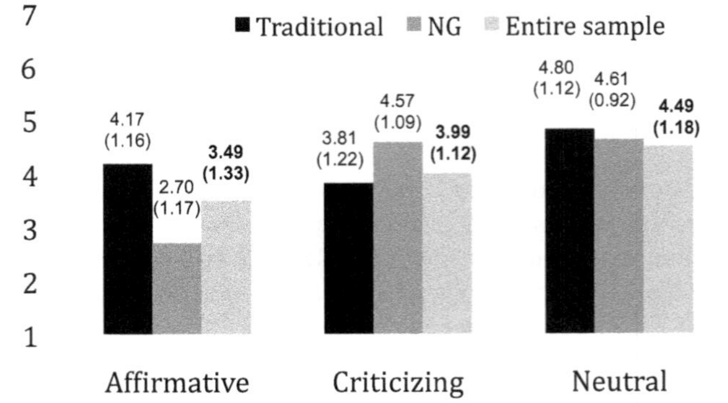

Figure 3. Perspective of government views and trust for Ts, NGs and the entire sample. Means and sd's shown.

RQ4: Perspective of News and Trust

How much do people trust news that supports the government? Figure 3 shows the results for RQ4. Chinese news consumers in general have the lowest trust in news that affirms the government perspective, moderate trust in news that criticizes the government perspective, and highest trust in neutral portrayals of the government. Though a small effect, these three trust levels are significantly different (F(2,778)=93.52, p<.001). A Bonferroni post hoc test shows all means to be significantly different (p<.001).

Focusing on Ts and NGs, the three trust levels are significantly different (F(2,192)=27.02, p<.001; A Bonferroni post hoc test shows all means to be significantly different (p<.001)), while Type is not significant. However, there is a significant Perspective x Type interaction (F(2,192)=23.68, p<.001): Ts have higher trust in news that affirms the government perspective; NGs have higher trust in news that criticizes the government perspective.

RQ5: Strength of Ties and Trust

What is the relation of strength of ties in the news source and trust in the news? Figure 4 shows the results for RQ5. For the entire sample we found a significant difference between strength of ties and level of trust (F(2,696)=176.08; p<.001). A Bonferroni post hoc test shows a significant difference among all levels: strong ties

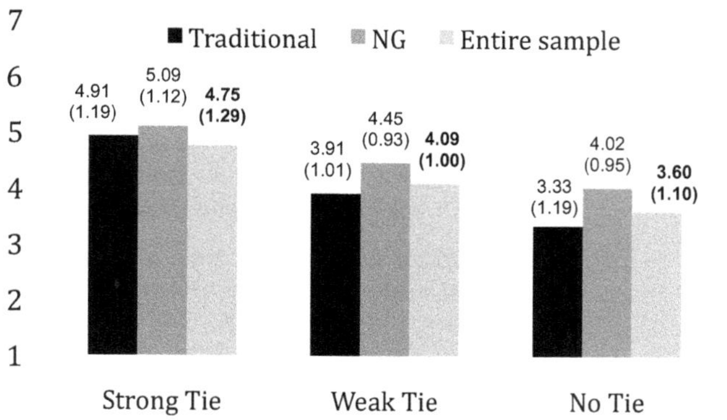

Figure 4. Tie strength and trust for Ts, NGs and the entire sample. Means and sd's shown.

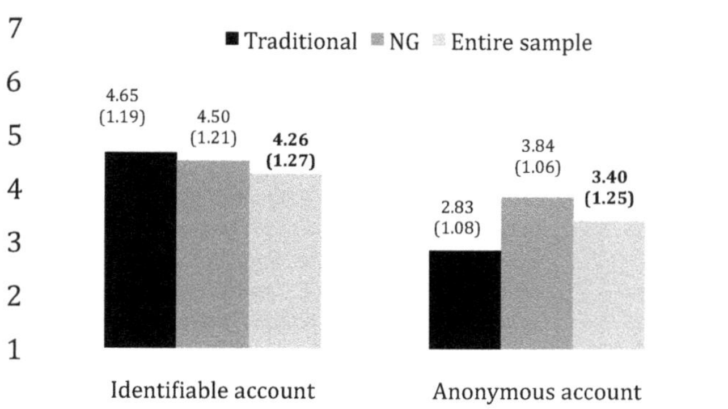

Figure 5. Anonymity and Trust for Ts, NGs and the entire sample. Means and sd's shown.

produce the highest trust, followed by weak ties, and then posts from strangers (p<.001).

Similarly, for Ts and NGs there is a significant difference among Tie Strength (F(2,172)=63.69, p<.001). A Bonferroni post hoc test shows that there is significant difference among all levels (p<.001). There is also a significant main effect of Type (F(2,172)=7.16, p<.009). There is a trend for an interaction of Tie Strength x Type (F(2,172)=2.50, p<.09): as the tie strength grows weaker, the level of trust declines less for NGs than for Ts.

RQ6: Anonymity and Trust

What is the effect of news coming from an anonymous vs. an identifiable source in citizen media? Figure 5 shows the results for RQ6. The entire sample reports significantly higher trust for identifiable accounts than anonymous accounts (F(1,351)=113.00, p<.001).

While Ts and NGs show little difference in trust in identifiable accounts, a significant Anonymity x Type interaction (F(1,88)=11.79, p<.001) shows that Ts have much lower trust in news from anonymous accounts than NGs. Main effects of Anonymity (F(1,88)=53.49, p<.001) and Type (F(1,88)=5.94, p<.02) are both significant.

RQ7: Content Features and Trust

Does including URLs as part of news content increase trust in news? Figure 6 shows the results for RQ7. For the entire

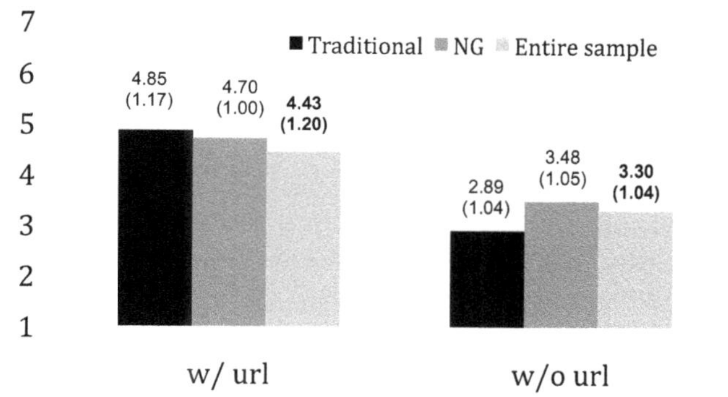

Figure 6. Content features and trust for Ts, NGs and the entire sample. Means and sd's shown.

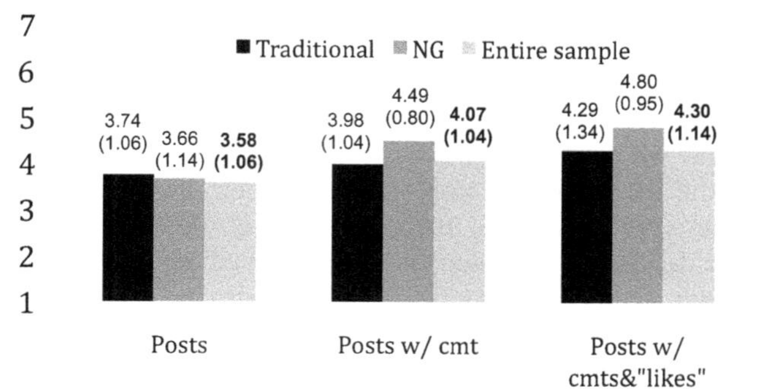

Figure 7. Comments & "Likes" and Trust for Ts, NGs and the entire sample. Means and sd's shown.

sample, respondents reported significantly higher trust in posts with URLs than those without URLs (F(1,351)= 258.95, p<.001).

Comparing Ts and NGs, the main effect of URL is significant (F(1,88)=102.54, p<.001); whereas Type is not significant. However, there is a significant URL x Type interaction, indicating that the absence of a URL affects trust for Ts more than NGs (F(1,88)=5.38, p<.03).

RQ8: Collective Participation and Trust

Compared to the content posted in citizen media, comments show how others reflect on the news. How does the "crowd effect", i.e. comments or "likes" from other citizens, affect a consumer's trust in news? Figure 7 shows the results for RQ8. For the entire sample, we found a significant increase in trust among "plain" posts, posts with comments, and posts with both comments and "likes" (F(2,688)=95.28, p<.001; A Bonferroni post hoc test shows all three groups to be significantly different (p<.001)).

Specifically, NGs have higher trust than Ts in posts with comments and in posts with both comments and "likes". The interaction of Crowd Effect x Type is significant (F(2,172)=5.64, p<.005). Crowd Effect is significant (F(2,172)=25.84, p<.001) but not the main effect of Type. These results suggest that as comments and "likes" from the crowd enhance people's trust in news in general, NGs value collective interpretation and affirmation more than Ts.

Dependent Variable	Independent Variables	β	t	p
Preference for citizen media	(Intercept)	0.441	.187	.852
	Trust in news commentary from citizens	0.466	8.885	<.001
	Frequency of Commenting	0.159	3.111	.002
	Trust in news that affirms gov't accounts	-0.331	-5.330	<.001
	Trust in news commentary from news professional	-0.306	-4.811	<.001

Table 4. Regression coefficients for model of preference for citizen media

A Model Predicting Preference of News Channels

If we were to randomly select an Internet user in China, could we predict their preference for trusting one type of media for news? To answer that question, we used a step-wise regression model using responses of the entire sample. Our dependent variable is preference of citizen over official media, as measured by trust ratings of citizen media minus trust ratings of official media. This measure ranges from +6 to -6. People who highly trust both citizen and traditional media channels would score a 0, as would those who highly distrust both channels. Our interest is focused on *trust preference*. We include all factors that might be relevant to trust in media as input for the independent variables: demographic information, media use habits, news participatory activities, and trust ratings that apply to both media. As shown in Table 4, we found that respondents' favorability of citizen media over official media is most positively associated with the trust in news commentary by citizens and the frequency of posting comments in social media, while it is negatively associated with trust in news that affirms government accounts and news commentary from professionals (adjusted R^2=0.455, $F(4,208) = 44.86$, $p<.001$).

Qualitative Analysis of Open-ended Questions

Opinion Guidance Impact

When asked if they have experienced opinion guidance online, 63.4% responded that they have. .Among the 63.4%, 204 respondents commented on its impact. Of these, more than one third self-reported being susceptible to the manipulation of citizen media by governmental postings. However, the reliability of self-reported vulnerability to persuasion is suspect for two reasons: first, there does not exist clear criteria that people can use to determine whether a comment is opinion guidance. Second, even if such criteria existed, it can be difficult for people to assess how they might be affected by opinion guidance. Because of this methodological concern, this is a topic for future research.

Code (%)	Sample Comments (translated from Chinese)
Negative (45.97%)	*"There's no way to tell truth from lies."* *"There is lots of false or unverified information, they get popular because they arouse panic of the public. This kind of information blind people's eyes. Also, audience are lacking rational judgment..."* *"most official media tend to candy-coat stuff, while unofficial media environment tends to be misguided by different situations such that untruthful, or unverified information gets spread around."*
Hope /Suggestion (12.1%)	*"There shouldn't be censorship in social media."* *"Information on social media is very easy to disseminate, there should be more regulation."* *"If every social media user is prudent when they speak, higher quality of shared information can be achieved."*
Neutral (10.48%)	*"It's not a matter of trust or no trust to me, I'm just killing time there."*
Strategy (8.87%)	*"For the information circulated in SNS, I won't judge its trustworthiness just by its source. I will judge by information comparison. I'll see if it makes sense. If some information is in line with existing information, and the logic is self-sustaining, then it's easy to trust it, even if it turns out to be false."*
Negative and Positive (6.45%)	*"The good side is that it provides sources for information that is not available on official sites. The bad side is that, because Chinese citizens are gullible, with poor critical judgment, social media can cause unnecessary panic."* *"Information is easy to disseminate, and easy to be misleading."*
Positive (5.64%)	*"It's more comprehensive, and truthful, comparatively."* *"Very convenient, lots of grassroots information."* *"The freedom in China depends solely on it (social media)."*
Other (9.67%)	"These are sharp questions, we should get some explanations from a formal institution."

Table 5. Open comments on trustworthiness of social media.

Open Comments on Trustworthiness in Social Media

Comments were included in 124 of the surveys. Based on our content analysis on open comments about news trustworthiness in social media, to our surprise, negative views (45.97%) dominate. Table 5 summarizes sample quotes that are representative of the coded categories.

The reoccurring negative concerns cover mainly three themes. First, there is much false rumor and misinformation, and it is difficult to verify the authenticity of news information. Especially when there are too many re-posts, the artificially inflated popularity can make it even more difficult to objectively assess the information quality. Second, because of censorship, site moderators can easily delete posts that involve sensitive but oftentimes valuable news information. Thus citizen media users do not feel encouraged to report. However, there is nothing to prevent users from blindly spreading unverified news information, extremely biased views or "junk". Third, news is often too subjective, personal, and emotional in citizen media.

Among all respondents who gave negative views, 20.05% are from Ts, and 12.28% are from NGs. Yet reasons for Ts and NGs negative views differ. Ts primarily emphasize the problem of false rumors in citizen media. They express that it is difficult or impossible for them to assess the trustworthiness of citizen-reported news, and they tend to believe it as false. NGs, however, suggest that objectivity and rationality is lacking when people report or discuss news in citizen media, and describe the lack of freedom of speech. Although those comments are all negative, the attitudes from Ts appear more pessimistic towards citizen media, while the comments of NGs are more evaluative and analytic, discussing potential causes of the drawbacks.

DISCUSSION

In this study, we investigated how people trust news in a society where official news is subject to authoritarian government control and new citizen media is continuing to gain popularity. In this changing media environment in China, our survey responses show that Chinese citizens do receive a fair amount of news from citizen media but mostly by chance. Citizens are adopting citizen media as a news form: nearly half contribute news content and over two-thirds comment on news. At this point in time, Chinese news consumers show no significant difference in trust in official and citizen news channels, professional journalists or citizen commentators, yet they show particularly low trust in news that affirms governmental accounts.

These results all highlight the complex conditions of the Chinese news information environment. In 2003, the deliberate information blockade and distortion about the SARS incident evoked a national dispute around information control from the government. We infer that the low level of trust in official media is largely due to the reoccurrence of incidents of this kind (e.g. a recent case is the dispute surrounding the 2011 Yongwen train crash). In addition to recent media scandals, Chinese news media has historically been reported to cause people to distrust the government [6]. So how does the advent of citizen media--SNSs and MBs in our study, come into play in such an authoritarian society?

We argue that citizen media provides an alternative news channel to government-controlled channels, one which leverages the advantage of personal relations and crowd confirmations in news information. Instead of relying on centralized institutions run by the state for news, citizen media now provides a platform for citizens to rely on and trust each other for information. Our results support this by showing that features of citizen media related to strong ties and the collective interpretation and affirmation from the crowd enhance people's trust in news significantly.

We found that embedding a URL to an original news source (which are mostly official media sources), boosted trust. We infer that people tend to perceive the official news to be more trustworthy when it is passed on by their friends or other peer citizens, even if they are strangers. This is in line with Katz and Lazarsfeld's [18] model of "personal influence": information often flows from traditional forms of mass communication (e.g. radio or print) to the influential readers and then on to a less active audience (the influenced readers) who regard news from their fellow citizen as guidance or social confirmation. The notion of interpersonal relationship as a mediating factor in news dissemination suggests that in an authoritarian society, citizen media can change how people perceive official media reports, perhaps even leading to more positive views.

As citizen media grows in popularity, it may not necessarily be a rivalry to official channels. By taking advantage of the action and wisdom of the crowd, it can provide unique news, complementary information to original news content and opinions, and can help news consumers to process and filter official news. Yet despite potential advantages, our survey results show that the value of citizen media may not yet be recognized; most citizens only moderately trust it.

To understand differences in trust for official and citizen media, we identified and focused on two types of news readers, contrasting trust in official and citizen media: NGs have high trust in citizen media and low trust in official media; Ts have the reverse pattern. What is interesting is that NGs trust features of citizen media more than Ts; they trust news commentary more by citizens, news from weak ties and strangers, from anonymous accounts, and the collective interpretations and affirmations of news.

One reason why Ts and NGs have very different trust levels on affirmative and criticizing news about the government could be due to their different political views. Our findings are in line with that of Choi et al. [8] who found that Americans with anti-governmental views on the Iraq War perceived the Internet as the most credible news source, in spite of it lacking editorializing and gatekeeping, compared to other traditional media sources such as newspaper or TV. It may be more likely for people who disagree with government views to turn to citizen media for news as it may be easier there to find news critical of the government.

Compared to NGs, Ts have less trust in news posted by anonymous sources and trust declines more as social ties weaken. Although other studies (e.g. [12]) have found that women have less risk-taking attitudes in online social networks, we did not find an effect of gender to explain the difference between Ts and NGs. Another explanation could be due to a "familiarity effect" [16] since NGs adopt citizen media earlier and are more active in online news participation than Ts. We found that NGs are more likely than Ts to trust comments and "likes" from the crowd. We cannot say however that higher involvement caused NG's high trust in citizen media because it is possible that NGs generally trust users of citizen media which leads to their high trust in the features of citizen media. It could also be the reverse: NGs participate in citizen media more and as a result of usage, they gain higher trust in citizen media.

Many of the open comments revealed reasons why citizen media is only partially accepted by Chinese news consumers. The existence of false rumors and misinformation is reported to be a major issue. This may be due to the lack of a mechanism for preventing the reporting and re-posting of false information. There is also governmental intervention (censorship on citizen media) for valuable newsworthy information. As NGs point out, citizen media channels can lack objectivity and rationality. In the current environment in China, it may rest on the crowd to design ways to be more diligent in writing, to be more rational in reading, and to be more responsible in disseminating news.

Based on our study, we propose that within an authoritarian state, citizen media is becoming an alternative news channel that provides a platform for citizens to trust each other for information. Because of this, citizen media could become a force for citizen empowerment. Yet there are still many challenges. High trust in citizen media in China does not currently exist and will take time. We identified a group of Chinese news consumers who embrace and take advantage of citizen media, while others are still struggling to trust it as a channel for news. Taken together, our study begins to explain how news generated in citizen media could impact China-- news trustworthiness is a critical element.

Generalizability and Limitations

We believe that our findings can generalize to other societies where the official media environment is strictly controlled by the central government while the popularity of citizen-generated media is currently fast growing. Syria is a timely case.

Since we used multiple seeds in our snowball sampling through different media channels, we believe that we reduced selection bias in our sample. Seeds were sent through various social networks using a variety of contacts in different areas across China. However, one limitation of our study is that our sample is most representative of the Chinese population who have higher education and who are from urban areas. We can thus only generalize our findings to this type of population. In addition, because opinion guidance exists in China, we cannot rule out the possibility that some respondents may have been hired by the government. Another limitation is that we asked people to self-report their general perception of trust. We feel this approach is valid because the credibility of news is not simply an innate quality of news content or sources, but is rather a subjective perception by its audience through sensemaking [8]. However, examining subjective perceptions can possibly reveal people's actual behavior when encountering news information. In future work, we will use alternative methodologies to triangulate our findings.

CONCLUSION

Citizen media is changing the way that people worldwide are receiving news. This is especially important in societies such as China where the official media is subject to strict government control. We are optimistic in the power of citizens to generate, disseminate and to assess news. Such signals from the collective, such as 'likes' or comments, can serve to empower citizens in continuing to generate and judge news. Our study was a first step in assessing the nature of trust in competing forms of news generation in authoritarian societies. We hope this will spark further research in this topic.

ACKNOWLEDGEMENT

We thank Judy Olsen and Gary Olsen for their insightful feedback. This project was supported by NSF grant #0910640.

REFERENCES

1. BBC News, Activists debate China lawyer Chen Guangcheng's escape, 4.27. 2012. http://www.bbc.co.uk/news/world-asia-china-17865439
2. Anderson, C. *The Long Tail: Why the Future of Business is Selling Less of More*. New York: Hyperion (2006).
3. Bucy, E. The Interactivity Paradox: closer to the news but confused', in: E. P. Bucy and J. E. Newhagen (Eds), *Media Access: Social and Psychological Dimensions of New Technology*, Mahwah, NJ: Lawrence Erlbaum (2004), 47-72.
4. Castells, M. Communication, power and counter-power in the network society. *int'l J Comm* (2007).
5. Castillo, C., Mendoza, M., and Poblete, B. Information credibility on twitter. In *Proc. WWW'11*, 675–684.
6. Chen, X., and Shi, T. Media effects on political confidence and trust in the People's Republic of China in the post-Tiananmen period. *East Asia*, 19, 3 (2001), 84–118.
7. China demands U.S. apology on Chen Guangcheng's entering U.S. embassy, Xinhua News, 5.2.2012. http://news.xinhuanet.com/english/china/2012-05/02/c_131564125.htm
8. Choi, J. H., Watt, J. H., and Lynch, M. Perceptions of news credibility about the war in Iraq: Why war opponents perceived the Internet as the most credible medium. *J of Computer-Mediated Comm*, 12 (1), (2006). Retrieved April 13, 2007 from http://jcmc.indiana.edu/vol12/issue1.choi.html
9. CNNIC, 29th Statistics Report on Internet development in China, 2012, available online: http://research.cnnic.cn/img/h000/h12/attach201102211453210.pdf
10. Diakopoulos, N., Choudhury, M. D., and Naaman, M. Finding and assessing social media information sources

in the context of journalism. In *Proc CHI'12,* ACM Press (2012), 2451–2460.
11. Esarey, A., and Xiao, Q. Digital communication and political change in China. *International Journal of Communication,* 5 (2011), 289–319.
12. Fogel, J., and Nehmad, E. Internet social network communities: Risk taking, trust, and privacy concerns. *Comp in Hum Beh*, 25, 1 (2009), 153–160.
13. Ganley, D. and Lampe, C. The ties that bind: social network principles in online communities. *Decision Support Systems,* 47, 3 (2009), 266–274.
14. Granovetter, M. S. The strength of weak ties. *American J of Sociology,* 78, 6 (1973), 1360–1380.
15. Habermas, J. *The structural transformation of the public sphere*. Cambridge: MIT Press (1989).
16. Hawkins, S. A. and Hoch, S. J. Low-involvement learning: memory without evaluation, *J of Consumer Research*, 19, 2 (1992), 212-225.
17. iResearch report, 2011, available online: http://www.iresearch.com.cn/Report/View.aspx?Newsid=146991
18. Katz, E., and Lazarsfeld, P. F., *Personal Influence: the part played by people in the flow of mass communications*, Glencoe, IL: Free Press, (1955).
19. Klinenberg, E. Convergence: news production in a digital age, *The ANNALS of the American Acad of Political and Soc Sci,* 597, 1 (2005), 48-64
20. Krackhardt, D. The strength of strong ties: The importance of philos in organizations. In N. Nohria and R. Eccles (Eds.). *Networks and Organizations: Structure, Form, and Action* (1992), 216-239.
21. Lasica, J.D., Blogs and journalism need each other. *Nieman Reports,* 57, 3 (2003), 70–74.
22. Li, P. Social tie, social capital, and social behavior: Toward an integrative model of informal exchange. *Asia Pacific J of Mgt,* 24, 2 (2007), 227–246.
23. McCombs, M.E., and Shaw, D.L. The agenda-setting function of mass media. *Public Opinion Quarterly,* 36, 2 (1972), 176–187.
24. McPherson, M., Smith-Lovin, L. and Cook, J. M., Birds of a feather: Homophily in social networks, *Annu. Rev. Socil.*, 27 (2001), 415-44
25. Morris, M. R., Counts, S., Roseway,A., Hoff, A., and Schwarz, J. Tweeting is believing?: Understanding microblog credibility perceptions. In *Proc. CSCW 2011.*
26. Nation's human rights progress has no shortcut, Global Times, 5.4.2012. http://www.globaltimes.cn /NEWS/tabid/99/ID/707744/Natons-human-rights-progress-has-no-shortcut.aspx
27. One leaf is not the whole forest, China Daily, 5.4.2012, http://www.chinadaily.com.cn /opinion/2012-05/04/content_15204886.htm
28. Purcell, K., Rainie, L., Mitchell, A., Rosenstiel, T. & Olmstead, K. Understanding the participatory news consumer. Pew Internet and Amer Life Proj (2010).
29. Qu, Y., Huang, C., Zhang, P. and Zhang, J., Microblogging after a major disaster in China: a case study of the 2010 Yushu earthquake. In *Proc. CSCW'11*
30. Reese, S. D, and Dai, J. Citizen journalism in the global news arena: China's new media critics'. In Allan & Thorsen (Eds.) *Citizen Journalism: Global Perspectives*, NY: Peter Lang (2009): 221–231.
31. Stockmann, D. What kind of information does the public demand? Getting the news during the 2005 Anti-Japanese protests. In: S. Shirk, (Ed.), *Changing Media, Changing China*, Oxford: Oxford U Press (2010).
32. Sunstein, C., The law of group polarization, In Fishkin J. S. & Laslett P. (Eds.), *Debating deliberative democracy* (2008), 80-101.
33. Thurman, N. Forums for citizen journalists? Adoption of user generated content initiatives by online news media. *New Media & Society,* 10, 1 (2008), 139–157.
34. Wall, M. 'Blogs of War' Weblogs as news, *Journalism*, 6, 2 (2005), 153-172.
35. Xiao, Q. The rise of online public opinion and its political impact. In: Shirk, S. (Ed.), *Changing Media, Changing China*, Oxford: Oxford Univ Press (2010).
36. Yardi, S., and boyd, D., Dynamic debates: An analysis of group polarization over time on Twitter, *Bulletin of Science Technology Society*, 30, 5 (2010), 316-327.
37. Yu, L., Asur, S., Huberman B.A. Artificial Inflation: The True Story of Trends in Sina Weibo (2012) (Submitted) available at: http://arxiv.org/abs/1202.0327v1

APPENDIX A. SURVEY QUESTIONS THAT ADDRESS THE RESEARCH QUESTIONS.

Research Questions	Survey Questions (All questions used a scale of 1-7, originally in Chinese.)
RQ1: Trust and news channels (official vs. citizen)	In general, how much do you trust news items (news or news comment) from: 1) Official channels (e.g. China Daily, Xinhua); 2) Unofficial channels (e.g. Renren, Sina Weibo)
RQ2: Online news participatory activities	1) Please rate how much you engage in each of the following eight news consumption activities. 2) My main goal of commenting, sharing, or contributing my own newsworthy information online is to INFORM / SOCIALIZE with other people. 3) When you participate in online news dissemination and production, how much do you feel you are part of an online community of news readers/writers?
RQ3: Trust and types of news	In general, how much do you trust the following: 1) News reporting (e.g. newspaper article); 2) News commentary from professional journalists (e.g. editorials); 3) News commentary from citizens (e.g. blog posts, microblogs, SNS posts)
RQ4: Trust and news perspectives toward government	In general, how much do you trust news commentary articles or posts with the following different types of perspectives? 1) Perspectives that AFFIRM official account; 2) Perspectives that CRITICIZE official account; 3) Perspectives that are NEUTRAL
RQ5: Trust and strength of ties in citizen media	In general, on social network sites or microblogging sites, how much do you trust news items written by: 1) Close friend; 2) Acquaintance; 3) Person you don't know; 4) Government source; 5) Media outlet; 6) Public figure
RQ6: Trust and anonymity in citizen media	In general, on social network sites or microblogging sites, how much do you trust news items written by: 1) An identifiable account; 2) An anonymous account
RQ7: Trust and news content feature in citizen media	In general, how much do you trust news items on social network sites or microblogging sites as follows: 1) Posts with links to an original source; 2) Posts without links to an original source; 3) Posts with image; 4) Posts without image
RQ8: Trust and crowd effects in citizen media	In general, how much do you trust news items on social network sites or microblogging sites as follows: 1) Post only; 2) Post with comments; 3) Post with "likes"; 4) Post with both comments and "likes"

Putting Ubiquitous Crowd-sourcing into Context

Afra Mashhadi
Bell Labs
Alcatel Lucent
Dublin, Ireland
afra.mashhadi@alcatel-lucent.com

Giovanni Quattrone
Dept. of Computer Science
University College London
Gower Street
London WC1E 6BT, UK
g.quattrone@cs.ucl.ac.uk

Licia Capra
Dept. of Computer Science
University College London
Gower Street
London WC1E 6BT, UK
l.capra@cs.ucl.ac.uk

ABSTRACT
Ubiquitous crowd-sourcing has become a popular mechanism to harvest knowledge from the masses. OpenStreetMap (OSM) is a successful example of ubiquitous crowd-sourcing, where citizens volunteer geographic information in order to build and maintain an accurate map of the changing world. Research has shown that OSM information is *accurate*, by comparing it with centrally maintained spatial information such as Ordnance Survey. However, we find that coverage is low and non uniformly distributed, thus challenging the suitability of ubiquitous crowd-sourcing as a mechanism to map the whole world. In this paper, we investigate what contextual factors correlate with *coverage* of OSM information in urban settings. We find that, although there is a direct correlation between population density and information coverage, other socio-economic factors also play an important role. We discuss the implications of these findings with respect to the design of urban crowd-sourcing applications.

Author Keywords
Crowd-sourcing; Volunteered Geographic Information; Socio-Economic Factors

ACM Classification Keywords
H.2.8 Database Management: Database Applications—*Spatial Databases and GIS*

INTRODUCTION
Cities are highly dynamic entities, with urban elements such as businesses, cultural and social Points-of-Interests (POIs), housing, and the like, continuously changing. Maintaining accurate spatial information in these settings has become an onerous task, rendering some centrally-maintained public datasets obsolete [14]. A solution made possible by the rise of social media is crowd-sourcing, where user-generated content can be cultivated into meaningful and informative collections, as exemplified by sites like Wikipedia [24]. This form of crowd-sourcing is no longer confined to the Web: equipped with powerful mobile devices, citizens have become surveyors, with council-monitoring applications like FixMyStreet;[1] reporters, with micro-blogging sites such as Twitter;[2] and cartographers, with geo-wikis like Cyclopath[3] and OpenStreetMap.[4]

OpenStreetMap (OSM) is perhaps one of the most successful examples of ubiquitous crowd-sourcing, with currently over 547,270 users, collectively building a free, openly accessible, editable map of the world. OSM exhibits *ubiquitous* features, because of the spatio-temporal nature of the knowledge it gathers (map elements of the changing world). Furthermore, Hecht et al. [9] have shown that the "localness" of participation in repositories of user-generated content with geospatial component is high if the available editing tools make use of GPS, as is the case with OSM (accessible and editable via mobile phone applications). It can thus be assumed that editing urban elements in OSM is predominantly done by citizens who have actually visited that location.

The geographic information stored in OSM has been demonstrated to be of high quality, where quality has been mainly measured in terms of positional accuracy. Indeed, OSM's accuracy has shown to sometimes supersede the most reputable geographic datasets, performing especially well in urban areas [6, 13]. However, relying entirely on user-generated content for urban mapping raises concerns, not only in terms of accuracy of the collected information (which, for OSM, is presently high), but crucially in terms of *coverage*. In other words, *what part* of the physical world is being digitally mapped? Studies that looked at who the main contributors of crowd-sourcing systems (i.e., Wikipedia) are have shown these to be a group of predominantly young and educated male [3]; they also reported a large gender gap among editors (87% male vs. 13% female). As the crowd-sourcing user base is not representative of the world population, can we expect the geographic content they contribute to be representative of the whole physical world? To answer this question, we performed a study in the area of Greater London, UK, where OSM was originally created and launched, and where the community of contributors is particularly active. As we shall demonstrate in the paper, OSM map features are

[1] http://www.fixmystreet.com/
[2] https://twitter.com/
[3] http://cyclopath.org/
[4] http://www.openstreetmap.org/

not uniformly distributed across the city. This raises a fundamental question: what contextual factors contribute to coverage of volunteered geographic information in urban settings? Answering this question is necessary, so to understand *where* crowd-sourced map information can be relied upon (and crucially where not), with direct implications on the design of applications that rely on having complete and unbiased map knowledge.

In this work, we investigate to what extent various socio-economic factors of urban areas correlate with coverage of crowd-sourced geo-spatial data. Although this research question has been studied extensively in the social sciences [22, 7], it has received limited attention from the ubiquitous computing community. Thus, in this paper, we report on a study that aims at discovering the contextual factors that impact coverage of information in OSM for the city of London, UK. As one can expect, we find that coverage is directly correlated with population density; however, we also find that other socio-economic factors are highly significant.

The rest of this paper is structured as follows: after a brief overview of the state-of-the-art in ubiquitous crowd-sourcing research, we describe the dataset at hand, the metrics we computed, and the methodology we adopted. We then illustrate the results of our analysis, before moving on to the discussion section, where we state the implications of these findings for the design of ubiquitous crowd-sourcing applications. We finally conclude the paper and elaborate on future directions of research.

BACKGROUND AND RELATED WORK

Ubiquitous crowd-sourcing is a form of collective gathering of user-generated content that has seen an uptake in recent years, thanks to the combined and wide adoption of mobile technology and social media. A popular example of user-generated content is volunteered geographic information (VGI), such as that maintained by OSM. In order for businesses (e.g., Foursquare) to rely on VGI as opposed to proprietary datasets (e.g., Google Maps), quality of the contributed information must be high. For years, the research community has studied the quality of such information [4], compared to traditional geographical datasets maintained by national mapping agencies, as well as proprietary datasets maintained by commercial companies such as Navteq.[5] The findings show very high accuracy: for example, Haklay et al. [5, 6] measured the positional accuracy of OSM road networks in the UK and found it to be very high (i.e., on average within 6 meters of the position recorded by Ordnance Survey). The authors have also investigated the impact of the number of contributors on positional accuracy, and estimated that high accuracy is achieved when there are at least 15 contributors per square kilometre. Works such as [2, 12] have confirmed these observations for countries like France, Germany and Switzerland. Moving from accuracy to coverage of OSM data, a recent study by Zielstra et al. [25] shows that coverage in Germany sharply decreases as we move away from city centres; Girres et al. [2] also discovered a correlation between the number of OSM objects in an area and number of contributors in that area (i.e., areas with up to three contributors per square kilometre had ten times more contributions than areas with only one contributor, and areas with more than three contributors had up to hundred times more contributions).

A limitation to the studies conducted by the VGI community on OSM is the focus on road networks only. However, the contribution process associated with editing roads and that associated with editing Points-of-Interests, such as restaurants and cafes, differ greatly: indeed, the former is typically done by a selected number of users who have high expertise in both the geography of an area and the editing tools required to digitally represent it; the latter can be performed by any city dweller owning a GPS-enabled smart-phone instead. It is the latter that is most representative of citizen engagement. In this work, we thus focus on eliciting the factors that relate to *coverage* of crowd-sourced POIs in urban areas.

OSM is not the only example of crowd-sourced urban information. For example, Cyclopath is being successfully used to digitally map route information for bicyclists in Minneapolis. The system has been widely studied by the academic community, both in terms of its design and rationale [18], its effectiveness [20] and in terms of user's participation and behavioural analysis [19, 15, 16]. In [19], for example, the authors investigated the techniques and motivations that lead to an increased amount of volunteered geographic information in Cyclopath. They found that visually highlighting contribution opportunities and asking users to work on an area that they are mostly familiar with, lead to better coverage. Similarly, [18, 20] discovered that cyclists were interested in sharing their expertise with each other, to cover gaps in terms of missing routes in the geo-wiki, thus increasing coverage of the crowd-sourced information.

These studies offered valuable insights into the *motives* behind user's participation and the impact they have on urban crowd-sourcing. Another important aspect is understanding the *contextual* factors that may affect crowd-sourcing coverage. This line of research has been explored extensively in Wikipedia, where contextual factors of contributors have been analysed in relation to coverage. For example, [10] studied gender imbalance in Wikipedia, and reported on how topics of particular interest to females were substantially less covered than topics of specific interest to males. In [8], the indegree summation (i.e., number of inlinks per article in the Wikipedia Article Graph) on 15 different language editions of Wikipedia was analysed; their findings suggest that population is not the most important factor to be considered, and other factors such as *fluency* in languages are more strongly correlated with indegree instead. They conclude that, when developing technologies to rely upon community maintained repositories, contextual factors of the contributors, such as language and culture, must be carefully examined. This has been done in other user-generate content datasets too; for example, [17] proposes a machine learning technique for estimating location and gender of Flicker users based on the tags they associate to the content they produce.

The work we present in this paper falls into the stream

[5]http://www.navteq.com/

of research that aims to understand the relation between contextual factors and coverage of user-generated content. More precisely, we focus our attention on OSM, an example of ubiquitous crowd-sourcing, where content has a distinct spatio-temporal nature. In this domain, we aim to understand the impact that *urban factors*, such as population density, distance to the city center, poverty, and the like, have on OSM coverage. We delve into this study next.

RESEARCH METHODOLOGY

Dataset Description

We begin our study with a detailed description of the crowd-sourcing dataset at hand, that is, OpenStreetMap. The dataset is freely available to download and contains the history of all edits (since 2006) on all spatial objects performed by all users. In OSM jargon, spatial objects can be one of three types: *nodes*, *ways*, and *relations*. Nodes are single geospatial points, defined using latitude/longitude coordinates, and they typically represent POIs; ways consist of ordered sequences of nodes, and mostly represent roads (as well as streams, railway lines, and the like); finally, relations are used for grouping other objects together, based on logical (and usually local) relationships (e.g., administrative boundaries, bus routes).

For the purpose of this study, we restricted our attention to nodes only. In particular, as our choice of sampling strategy, we focused on those that represent urban elements commonly interpreted as *leisure* POIs, such as cafes, restaurants, pubs and bars. These are the categories that are most common to mobile applications such as MyCityWay,[6] Google HotPot[7] and Foursquare,[8] which are used by city dwellers to navigate the urban landscape. To ensure we are considering genuine crowd-sourcing contributions, and not those made by bots (i.e., mass imports), we have eliminated from the dataset those users who performed an excessive number of edits in a very short time (i.e., those who edited more than 40 POIs in a single *changeset* session in OSM, with the threshold of 40 chosen after manual inspection of the per-user edit distribution). Finally, we focused on the area of Greater London, UK, which is an example of urban city with many administrative districts with different socio-economic factors (as we shall present later). The resulting crowd-sourcing dataset consists of 818 users, editing 9,573 POIs by means of 19,139 edits overall.

In order to compute coverage of OSM, we required *(i)* a benchmark against which to compare OSM POIs and *(ii)* a matching algorithm to map OSM POIs to those in the benchmark dataset.

Benchmark. We required a ground-truth dataset, containing all POIs physically present in each chosen area. For this purpose, we selected Navteq, the leading global provider of maps and location data, covering not only roads but also millions of POIs of varying nature, from restaurants to hospitals and gas stations. Being a commercial service, Navteq's primary objective is to ensure the highest level of accuracy of its data (the information contained there is factually correct and up-to-date).

[6]http://www.mycityway.com
[7]http://www.google.com/hotpot
[8]https://foursquare.com

Amenity	*Perc. in OSM*
Post box	18%
Nightlife	15%
Place of Worship	6%
Restaurant	6%
Bicycle Parking	6%
School	5%
Cafe	4%
Other	40%

Amenity	*Perc. in Navteq*
Restaurant	12%
Vehicle Repair	8%
School	8%
Clothing Store	6%
Nightlife	6%
Cafe	5%
Grocery Store	3%
Other	52%

Table 1. Amenity Distribution in OSM and Navteq

Table 1 reports on the most popular amenity categories in OSM and Navteq separately. It is worth noting that, while OSM also deals with objects that are of interest to the community, such as post boxes (18%) and bicycle parking (6%), Navteq is primarily concerned with commercial entities instead, such as restaurants (12%) and clothing stores (6%). In this work, we restrict our attention to what we call *leisure* POIs, to indicate those categories which have a presence in both OSM and Navteq.

POI Matching Algorithm. To be able to measure coverage, we first need to relate POIs in OSM with the same POIs in the ground-truth dataset in an automatic way. In both OSM and Navteq, a POI is defined as a tuple: $poi = \langle name, (lat, lon)\rangle$, where $name$ is the POI's name, and (lat, lon) are the coordinates determining its geographical position. We then define and quantify, for each POI in OSM, two measures: *geographic error* and *lexicographic error*. More precisely, let poi_{x} be a single POI, and POI_{x} the set of all POIs, with x being either the OSM dataset or the ground-truth dataset (to which we will refer, for convenience, simply as *gt*). We thus state that poi_{osm} is *equivalent* to poi_{gt} if *both* their geographic distance *and* lexicographic differences are below some specific thresholds. The geographic distance $geo_{Err}(\cdot,\cdot)$ is computed as the Euclidean distance between the two points, while the lexicographic difference $lexical_{Err}(\cdot,\cdot)$ is computed as the Levenshtein[9] distance between the POI names normalized between [0,1] by the length of the POI names.

To determine suitable thresholds to use in our POI matching algorithm, we proceeded as follow: we first considered a subset of 100 POIs from OSM, computed geographic and lexicographic distance to all ground-truth POIs, and determined the 'closest match' for each of these. We then manually inspected which of these were indeed matches, and which were not. Based on this inspection, we empirically derived a threshold of 100 meters for the geographic distance, and a threshold of 0.33 for the lexicographic difference. To further validate these choices, we ran the matching algorithm using these thresholds; upon completion, we selected a small (different) subset of 30 POIs, and manually inspected the correctness of the matches. We found that 97% of these had been correctly matched, while only 3% were not. For illustrative purposes, Table 2 presents some examples of POIs that

[9]It is worth to remind that Levenshtein distance is a string metric defined as the number of single-character edits required to change one string into the other

OSM name	*ground-truth name*	geo_{Err}	$lexical_{Err}$	*Equiv.*
Rondhouse	Rondhouse	0 m	0	Yes
The Green Gate	Green Gate	33 m	0.28	Yes
Smollenskys Bar	Smollensky's	48 m	0.33	Yes
Eardley Arms	Eardley Garage	145 m	0.29	No
Whittington Stone	Whittington NHS	180 m	0.29	No

Table 2. Some example of POIs in OSM and ground-truth dataset with different values of geographic distance and lexicographic difference

our matching algorithm correctly relates (first three), despite some lexicographic and geographic error; it also illustrates two examples of correct mismatches (the POIs in OSM are pubs, while those in Navteq are a garage and a hospital respectively).

Metric. Based on the above mapping, we have evaluated coverage of OSM POIs for Greater London as:

$$coverage = \frac{\#(\{\text{POIs in OSM}\} \cap \{\text{POIs in Navteq}\})}{\#\{\text{POIs in Navteq}\}}$$

with $coverage \in [0, 1]$. The higher the coverage, the higher the extent to which the ground-truth POIs are also present in OSM.

Contextual Factors of OSM

Our hypothesis is that there is a strong relationship between socio-economic characteristics of an urban area and the level of coverage that can be expected of this area by means of volunteered contributions. To validate this hypothesis, we focus on OSM coverage for London at a finer level of granularity than the city level, that is, the level of wards. We have chosen this level of granularity as wards are the smallest regions defined by local authorities in London.[10]

London presently comprises 600 wards. Figure 1 illustrates the frequency distribution of ground-truth POIs at ward level. As it can be seen from the head of the distribution, there are many wards with less than 5 POIs, and a long tail of a few wards with many POIs. To avoid biased analysis due to sparsity of this data, we have considered only wards that have 5 or more POIs. In so doing, we disregarded 120 wards, analysing 480 of the original 600. For each ward, we have collected the following contextual factors:

Population. Using UK Census 2011 data published by the National Statistics Office,[11] we have information about population at ward level. Previous studies of OSM coverage for road networks have revealed a correlation between the number of contributors in an area and the number of OSM objects digitally mapped in that area [2]. We have thus selected population as an attribute for investigation in this study, as it can give us an expectation of contributions per area. Although higher population density does not directly translate into higher number of contributors, we may expect more contributors per unit area to exist in denser areas. The hypotheses we thus want to test are: *(i)* the higher the *population density* of an area (that is, population divided by ward size), the higher the coverage; and *(ii)* the higher the population per POIs in an area (that is, population divided by number of POIs), the higher the coverage.

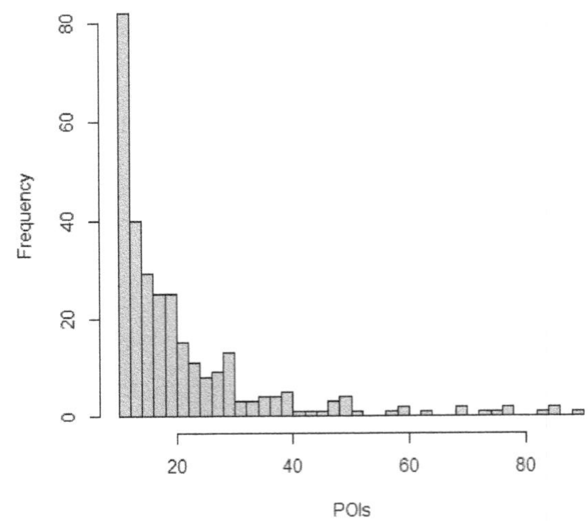

Figure 1. Frequency Distribution of POIs at Ward Level

Poverty. Analysing the relationship between poverty of an area and coverage is important, as it may reveal the impact that (lack of) technology adoption (e.g., use of smartphones and Internet), as well as (lack of) available leisure time, has on it. In this regard, UK Census data contains information about the Indices of Multiple Deprivation (IMD). IMD are a set of indicators, published by the UK Office for National Statistics, measuring deprivation of small geographic areas known as Lower-layer Super Output Areas (LSOA) in England. IMD consist of seven domain indicators. The one we are interested in this study is the Income Deprivation Index, that measures the number of people claiming income support, child tax credits, or asylum; we refer to this factor as *poverty* henceforth. The hypothesis under test is that poverty of an area is negatively correlated with digital mapping of its POIs. This is another important aspect to look into, if we are to rely on volunteered mapping information alone, as it may reveal where gaps arise, thus enabling intervention via contingency plans.

Dynamic Population. While the previous two factors capture 'static' characteristics of the residents of an area, they do not reveal much about the actual pulse of the city, that is, where city dwellers (i.e., the potential contributors of ubiquitous crowd-sourced information, be them residents or tourists) spend time. We thus add a dynamic attribute based on Foursquare check-ins, which we refer to as *dynamic population.*

We acknowledge that Foursquare and OSM share commonalities: neither represents fully the urban population, with a bias towards young, educated and wealthy people; furthermore, the type of content they gather has a common spatio-temporal nature. However, despite these commonalities, we do not expect the behaviour of the crowds

[10] http://data.london.gov.uk/datastore/package/ward-profiles-2011

[11] http://www.ons.gov.uk/ons/guide-method/census/2011/census-data/2011-census-prospectus/index.html

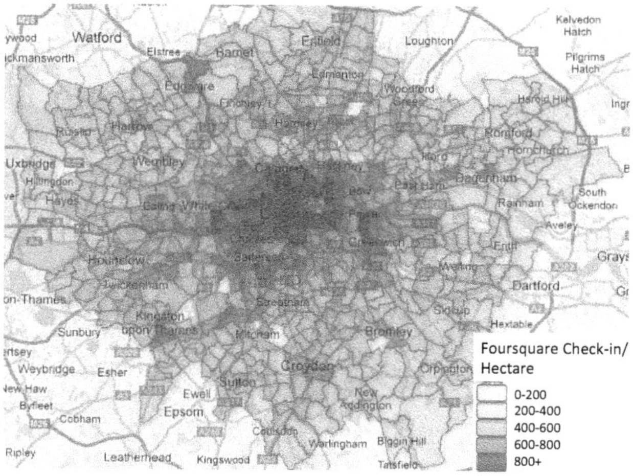

Figure 2. Choropleth map of Foursquare check-ins - Darker wards have higher check-in density

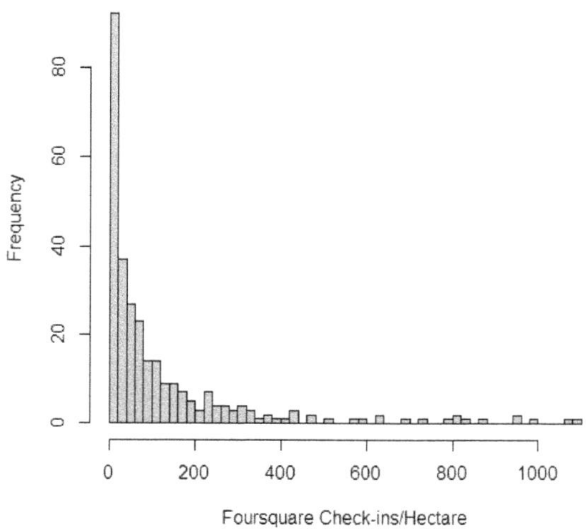

Figure 3. Frequency Distribution of Foursquare Check-in Density

that contribute to these systems to be the same: this is because, in Foursquare, users contribute data (check-ins) to show/share their location and social life with their friends, reflecting an *egocentric* behaviour, whereas OSM editors contribute in order to improve the existing map, thus exhibiting a *community* behaviour. We are thus interested in studying what dynamic population can reveal with respect to coverage. We measure dynamic population based on the last four years of Foursquare activity in London, computing the density of check-ins per ward (i.e., the total number of check-ins in a ward divided by its size); Figure 2 shows a choropleth map of such density distribution across all wards in London: the darker the ward, the higher the density of check-ins. Similarly Figure 3 illustrates the histogram approximating the frequency distribution of density of Foursquare check-ins at ward level: as shown, there are many wards with very low check-ins density, and a long tail of wards with higher check-ins density.

Distance to the Closest Poly-centre. The last factor we consider is the distance from where the social and economic activities happen. Previous studies on OSM have shown that road coverage decreases when moving away from the city centre [25]. Similarly, we are interested to examine the effect of distance from the city centre on coverage. However, in metropolitan areas there is not just one centre but multiple urban hubs [1]. Specifically, a recent study [21] has found that London has 10 different polis. In this work, we thus computed the Euclidean distance from the geographic centre point of each ward to the geographic centre point of each of the 10 polis. We then used the shortest distance as our 'distance from the centre' factor, and tested the hypothesis that the closer to the centre, the higher the coverage.

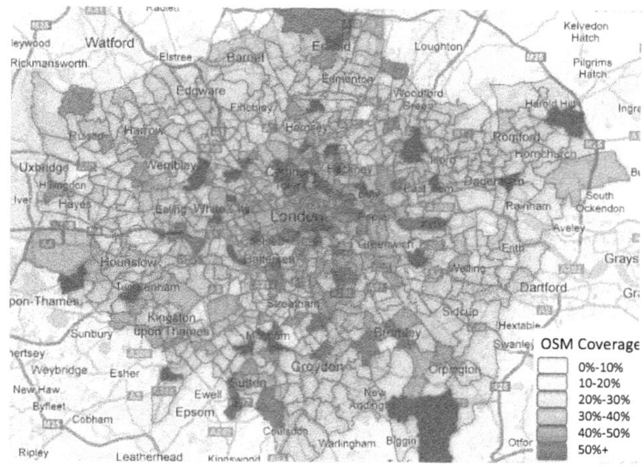

Figure 4. Choropleth map of OSM coverage for Greater London- Darker wards have higher coverage

RESEARCH RESULTS

This section reports on the results of our analysis. We first considered the area of Greater London as a whole, for which we found coverage to be 0.35. However, this single aggregate value does not reveal much in terms of what areas of London are being digitally mapped. Figure 4 illustrates the choropleth map of London's coverage, where each tile represents a ward. As shown, coverage is non-uniformly distributed across the city. Previous studies on coverage of OSM for road networks have revealed that distance from the city centre is inversely related to coverage [25]; although at a first approximation a similar pattern seems to emerge for POIs too (i.e., the further away we move from the city centre, the worse the coverage), we can also identify various suburban areas with high coverage instead. We thus hypothesise that distance from the city centre cannot fully explain coverage.

Figure 5 further shows the histogram approximating coverage distribution at ward level. As shown, there are many wards where coverage is very low (≈ 0), and a few wards where coverage is quite high (≈ 0.6) instead. We now proceed to analyse what contextual factors contribute to this distribution. The factors we are interested in are those listed in the previous section, that is: population density, population per POI, poverty, dynamic population, and distance from the closest poly-centre. To quantify the extent to which coverage is related to such parameters, we proceeded in two steps: first,

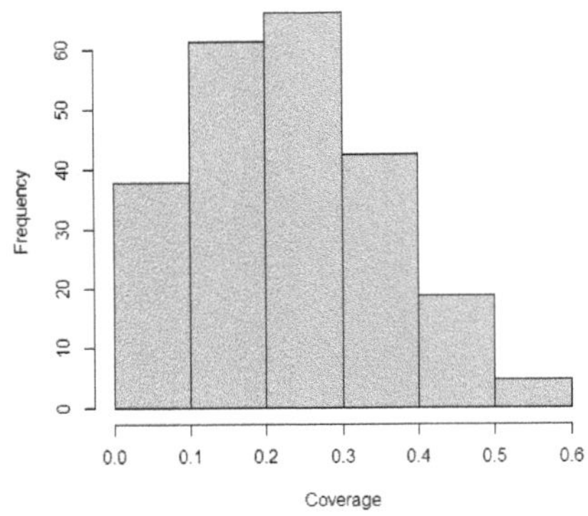

Figure 5. Frequency Distribution of Coverage

Factor	β	R^2	*p-value*
Population Density	0.075	0.10	***
Population per POI	0.005	0.00	
Poverty	-0.021	0.01	*
Dynamic Population	0.090	0.15	***
Distance from the Nearest Poly-centre	-0.085	0.13	***

Table 3. β Coefficient, Multiple R^2 and p-value of Single Linear Regression Models of Coverage on Socio-Economic Factors at Wards Level (p-value significance. codes: 0.0001 '*', 0.001 '**', 0.01 '*', 0.05 ' ')**

we used single linear regression, considering one parameter at a time as independent variable, and analysed how coverage varies with it. Second, we applied a multiple regression model, so to control for the various parameters at play simultaneously. In all models, all our parameters followed normal distribution, with the exception of dynamic population for which we computed the natural logarithm. Finally, in order to easily interpret the β coefficients of the regression models, we computed the z-scores of each parameter; in so doing, β coefficients indicate the increment in coverage for one unit of standard deviation increment of the corresponding parameter.

We begin analysing the results of the five single linear regression models independently. For each such model, Table 3 reports *(i)* the *β coefficient*, representing the independent contribution of each factor to coverage, *(ii)* R^2, indicating how well each regression model fits the data, and *(iii)* p-value, indicating the significance level of each presented result.

Population Density

We first focus our attention on population density, i.e., the number of people over the number of hectares of each ward. Our intuition is that citizens care a lot about the area where they live, thus being actively involved in digitally mapping their space. As a consequence, we expect that suburban areas are less well-covered than urban areas. Table 3 indeed confirms that population density is positively correlated with coverage ($\beta = 0.075$, $R^2 = 0.10$, p-value < 0.001). In particular, the β coefficient of 0.075 indicates that an increment in population density of 50 people per hectare (i.e., of one unit of standard deviation) would improve coverage of that ward by 0.075. If we consider the distribution of coverage of Greater London (as shown in Figure 5), this increment corresponds to 25% increase in coverage for the average case. The R^2 value is however fairly low, suggesting that a regression model purely based on population density does not fully explain the residual between actual and expected coverage.

To further understand the relation between coverage and population density, the box plot of Figure 6 shows how coverage varies with the change in population density. In particular, the plot for each range of population density presents: a bin graphically depicting the smallest observation, the lower quartile, the median, the upper quartile, and the largest observation for that range of population density. The circles in the figure are the observations that are considered to be outliers. From Figure 6, we can thus see the effect that population density has on coverage (as one grows, so does the other). It is worth noting that there exist very few outliers, thus confirming the validity of our results (i.e., positive correlation between population density and coverage).

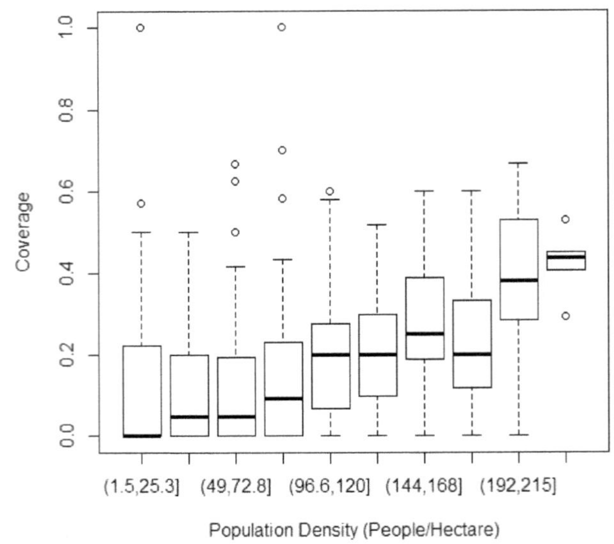

Figure 6. Coverage vs. Population Density

Population per POI

We now move our attention to population per POI, that is, the number of people over the number of (ground-truth) POIs for each ward. The hypothesis we examine here is whether having more people per POI in an area means better coverage of the information in that area. If so, we could then aim to identify a minimum number of people per POI that is required to expect the POI to be mapped, as done in [6] for roads. Interestingly, our analysis (Table 3) reveals otherwise ($\beta = 0.005$, $R^2 = 0.00$, p-value > 0.05). The box plot of Figure 7 depicts variation of coverage with regards to population per POI; as shown population per POI bears no correlation with coverage. In other words, having a higher number of residents per POI does not translate into those POIs being mapped.

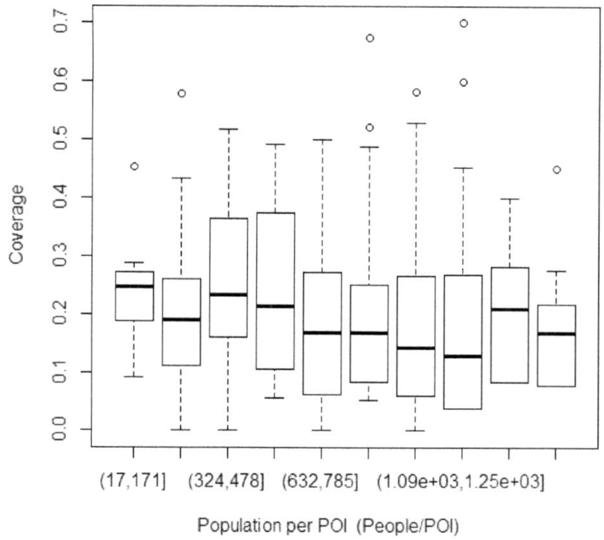

Figure 7. Coverage vs. Population per POI

Poverty

We next examine how poverty of an area plays a part in that area being mapped. Studies such as [10] have revealed the contributors of crowd-sourcing to be predominantly a group of young, educated and wealthy males. We thus hypothesise that poverty of an area (measured as deprivation of its residents) is negatively correlated to coverage of that area. Table 3 confirms that poverty of an area has a (weak) negative correlation (β=-0.021) with coverage; that is, a decrement of one unit standard deviation of poverty in a ward would improve coverage of that ward by 0.021 (this increment corresponds to 7% increase in coverage for the average case). Note that $R^2 = 0.01$ is significantly lower than that found for other factors such as population, suggesting that, although significant, poverty itself is only a secondary factor in explaining coverage residual, as computed via linear regression. This is confirmed also by Figure 8 which displays how coverage changes with variations in poverty level. We will return to this point when considering all factors together in a multiple regression model.

Dynamic Population

We now turn our attention to dynamic population. Our hypothesis is that the higher the number of check-ins/visits in an area is, the better mapped such area will be. One may wonder whether poverty of an area and dynamic population of an area (measured as density of Foursquare check-ins) are surrogate of each other, the idea being that poorer areas attract fewer people, while richer areas are expected to attract more businesses and thus more visitors too. However, by performing a correlation analysis between poverty and dynamic population, we discovered the two to be non correlated; in other words, there are areas in London whose residents are income-deprived (e.g., Camden and Hackney) and yet attract large crowds.

Table 3 confirms that dynamic population is highly and significantly correlated with coverage ($\beta = 0.090$, $R^2 = 0.15$, and p-value < 0.001), with β and R^2 values higher than those computed for previous factors. The box plot of Figure 9 also confirms that dynamic population of an area has a positive correlation with coverage.

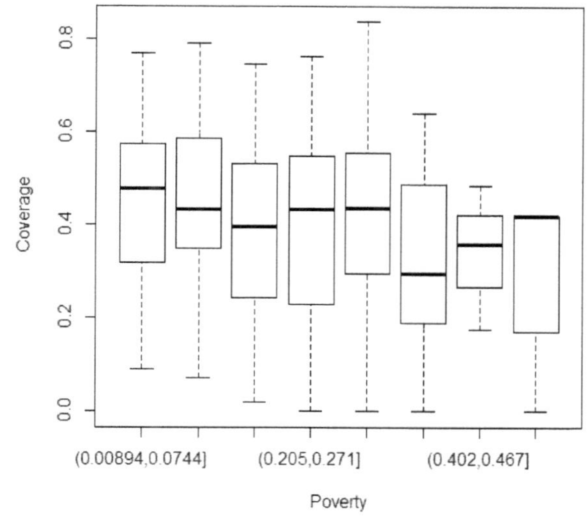

Figure 8. Coverage vs. Poverty

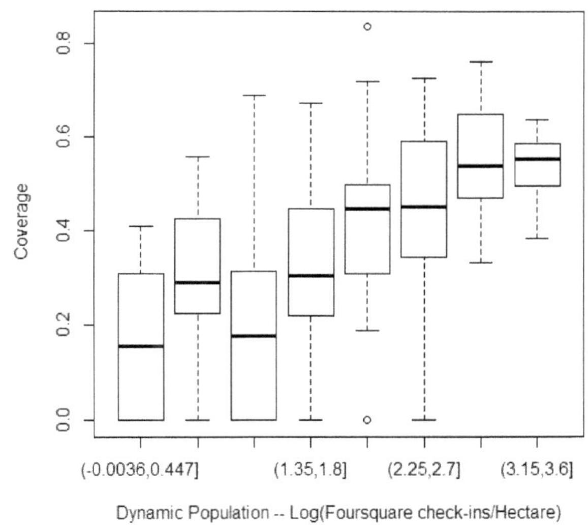

Figure 9. Coverage vs. Dynamic Population

Distance from the Closest Poly-centre

We now turn our attention to the last factor under examination, that is distance to the closest poly-centre. Our hypothesis is that the closer a ward is to the nearest poly-centre of London, the better its coverage. This intuition is confirmed by Table 3, which shows that distance from the closest poly-centre is inversely correlated with coverage ($\beta = -0.085$,

$R^2 = 0.13$, p-value < 0.001). In particular, the β coefficient of -0.085 indicates that a decrement of 5km in distance from the closest poly-centre (i.e., of one unit of standard deviation) would improve coverage of that ward by 0.085 (this increment corresponds to 28% increase in coverage for the average case). Similarly to what we noted before for population density, the R^2 value of a single linear regression model based on distance is relatively low, suggesting that distance from the closest poly-centre does not fully explain the residual between actual and expected coverage.

The box plot of Figure 10 shows how coverage varies as one moves further away from the closest poly-centre: note that, for short distances from the nearest poly-centre, correlation with coverage is indeed rather high; however, as distance increases, this correlation weakens considerably. We will return to this observation in the next section.

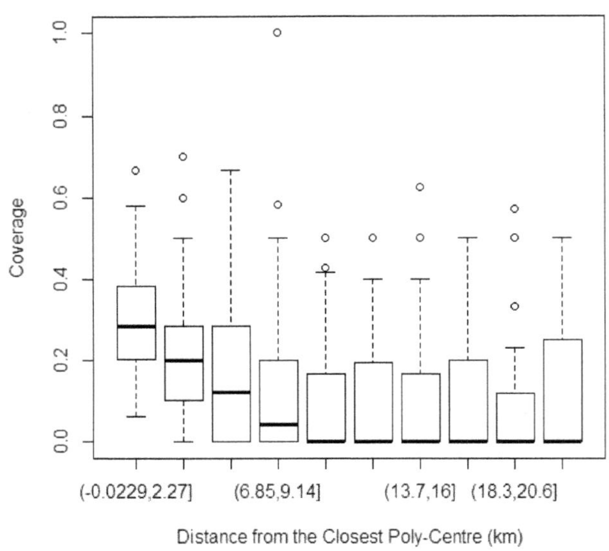

Figure 10. Coverage vs. Distance to the Nearest Poly-centre

Understanding Mediating Influence

Although the previous single predictor models afford us valuable insights into the relations at play between each such variable independently and coverage, in practice we expect coverage to depend on these factors as a whole. We thus need to analyse these parameters together, and understand the relative importance of each of them while controlling for others. We do so by means of a multiple linear regression model.

Table 4 presents the results of such model, reporting β coefficients for each factor and their level of significance, along with adjusted R^2. As shown, dynamic population, distance from the nearest poly-centre and population density are the dominant factors, with higher contribution weight and lower p-values. This analysis confirms that population per POI does not contribute to coverage of an area. Finally, the low β coefficient and the high p-value associated with poverty confirms that the correlation between poverty and coverage (as presented in Table 3) is of secondary importance when we consider the mediating influence of all other factors.

Factor	β	*p-value*
Population Density	0.027	*
Population per POI	0.010	
Poverty	-0.007	
Dynamic Population	0.054	***
Distance from the Nearest Poly-centre	-0.031	*
Adjusted R^2	0.17	***

Table 4. β Coefficient, Multiple R^2 and p-value of Multiple Linear Regression Models of Coverage on Socio-Economic Factors at Wards Level (p-value significance codes: 0.0001 '*', 0.001 '**', 0.01 '*', 0.05 ' ')**

If we now compare the adjusted R^2 value for the adjusted regression model (Table 4, $R^2 = 0.17$) with the R^2 value for the best fitting single regression model (Table 3, $R^2 = 0.15$ for dynamic population), we observe only a marginal improvement in terms of model fit. There may be two reasons for this: on one hand, the factors we examined in this work only partly capture the facets of urban context that relate to coverage; future work is required to examine other aspects not included so far. On the other hand, there might be interactions between the factors under study that a simple multiple linear regression model does not capture. In order to evaluate the extent of the impact of these interactions we also considered a multiple regression model with bilinear interactions across all pairs of predictors. We found that the adjusted R^2 value of the model with interactions is 0.24 with p-value < 0.001; this means that the model with interactions fits 41% better than the model without, revealing that the effect of interactions between our socio-economic parameters is not negligible. We do not delve further into modelling interactions in this paper; however, we note that, as one moves from understanding the relevance of contextual factors on coverage (i.e., the goal of this work) into building predictor models of coverage growth, such interactions should be explored further (for examples, by means of non-linear models such as SVM).

So far we have attempted to build a model that explains coverage in terms of socio-economic factors, while looking at the area of Greater London as a whole. However, London is a large and complex metropolitan city, and one may wonder whether different regression models should be built and analysed for different sub-areas instead, with the expectation that the same predictors would play a rather different role in such sub-areas. We did so by dividing Greater London in two: Inner London and Outer London, as depicted in Figure 11.[12] The distinction comes from the London Government Act 1963[13] where Inner London is defined as the richest area in Europe, albeit widespread poverty towards the East and South.

We built two multiple regression models for Inner and Outer London separately; we used the model without interactions so to afford direct interpretation of the β parameters with those derived for Greater London as a whole (Table 4). Results for Inner London are reported in Table 5; results for Outer London are aligned with those for the whole of Greater London and thus not repeated in the interest of space. Note that, while

[12]This image has been taken from http://wikitravel.org

[13]http://www.legislation.gov.uk/ukpga/1963/33

Figure 11. Inner and Outer London

Factor	β	*p-value*
Population Density	0.013	
Population per POI	0.024	
Poverty	-0.028	*
Dynamic Population	0.008	
Distance from the Nearest Poly-centre	-0.380	***
Adjusted R^2	0.16	***

Table 5. β Coefficient, Multiple R^2 and p-value of Multiple Linear Regression Models of Coverage on Socio-Economic Factors for Inner London (p-value significance codes: 0.0001 '*', 0.001 '**', 0.01 '*', 0.05 ' ')**

dynamic population and population density were primary factors in relation to coverage when looking at the whole of Greater London, they become secondary factors when we focus on Inner London instead (their β values are lower, and their p-values higher compared to those in Table 4). For Inner London, it is poverty that now shows correlation with coverage (higher β value and lower p-value compared to those reported in Table 4). As an example, we considered two wards in Inner London, one in Chelsea (just north of the river) and one in Battersea (just south of the river, opposite Chelsea). We found that the former has low poverty and high coverage, while the latter has high income deprivation and much lower coverage. Note also that, when focusing on Inner London, distance from the nearest poly-centre is much more strongly related to coverage ($\beta = -0.380$) than when looking at Greater London as a whole ($\beta = -0.031$) . This insight is in accordance with Figure 10, which highlights how distance matters on short and medium length, but less so as one moves away from the center.

DISCUSSION

Limitations

In the previous section we have shown results of an investigation into the relationship between socio-economic factors of an area and the coverage of its POIs in OpenStreetMap. A number of limitations have to be highlighted in relation to the findings previously reported. First, our findings are valid for London, but cannot be directly translated to other cities. We chose to study London because it is an example of a large and complex metropolitan setting, and also because of the rich set of information about this city that is freely available for investigation: being the birth city of OSM, it has a large community of active contributors; furthermore, details of the socio-economic status of its administrative regions is available at a very fine level of granularity. While we cannot expect the findings reported in the previous section to hold true for other cities, the general approach we have presented can be followed to understand what contextual features correlated with coverage in ubiquitous crowd-sourcing domains. For example, one may analyse the extent to which factors such education are correlated with coverage in cities in the developing countries, where there exists a much bigger gap between different groups of the society than in London.

A second limitation relates to the choice of POIs that we have examined (leisure POIs, such as cafes, restaurants, pubs and bars). Our findings cannot be generalised to the mapping of other spatio-temporal information, as it may take place during disaster recovery efforts [26].

Finally, we used census data released in 2011 by the UK Government as measure of population and wealth. This data is valuable, but limited in that it only offers aggregate values per ward. Should we have been in possession of further information, such as wealth distribution and standard deviation within a ward, we could have delved into a more fine-grained assessment of the relationship between these variables and coverage.

Implications

How does the study reported in this paper affect the development of urban crowd-sourcing applications? As our results have highlighted, coverage of VGI in OpenStreetMap varies depending on a variety of contextual factors, in particular distance from the center, dynamic population and population density. Furthermore, in a large metropolitan city like London, the relative importance of each such factor may vary when looking at different geographic clusters; for example, in Inner London coverage is strongly related to poverty but not to dynamic population. Understanding the contextual factors that relate to coverage is important for developers of ubiquitous crowd-sourcing applications, so they can better engineer one. For example, a variety of incentive schemes, spanning from financial rewards to gamification (e.g., in the form of competitions or mapping parties) to location-based social network features [23, 11] can be planned, so to nudge the crowds toward mapping areas that would otherwise be naturally neglected (e.g., because far from the city center, or because they are poor areas within the center).

Understanding the contextual factors of the areas being mapped is only one aspect that developers need to consider in building successful ubiquitous crowd-sourcing applications. Two further aspects require investigation: on one hand, understanding the characteristics of the crowd that the application attracts (for example, locals vs. visitors), and on the other hand the characteristics of the urban objects that such crowds actually map (for example, services as opposed to leisure POIs). Both directions deserve future investigation.

CONCLUSION AND FUTURE WORK

The study presented in this paper has shown that coverage in OSM, a ubiquitous crowd-sourcing dataset, is non-uniformly distributed across the city. Different contextual factors, including population density, dynamic population, distance from the center and poverty are correlated with information coverage. Raising awareness of the factors that correlate with (lack of) coverage is a first step towards planning interventions, such as developing incentives to nudge the community to take part in a more guided crowd-sourcing act (e.g., to geo-map areas that would otherwise be neglected). Being aware of the contextual factors that affect coverage of crowd-sourced urban information is important for end-users too, so to understand where they can rely on the crowd-sourced information (the risk, in fact, is to make decisions based on partial and biased information).

We are continuing the work started in this paper along two main directions. On one hand, having analysed what contextual factors correlate with coverage in OSM, the next step is to study the crowd-sourcing process as it happens over time. The aim is to build dynamic models that leverage the previously elicited parameters to accurately *predict* what areas will be covered and, crucially, what areas will not, so to direct resources towards targeted interventions.

On the other hand, we are looking at the crowd-sourcing process from a contributors perspectives, rather than from a spatial one. A study focused on OSM contributors will enable us to understand what human factors (both static, such as age and gender, and dynamic, such as mapping patterns) contribute to coverage, and of what type of information. In so doing, we aim to offer a better understanding of the sustainability of crowd-sourcing as a means to gather information about our changing world.

ACKNOWLEDGMENTS

The research leading to these results has received funding from the European Community's Seventh Framework Programme (FP7/2007-2013) under the Grant Agreement n. 234239.

REFERENCES

1. S. Brunn, J. Williams, and D. Zeigler. *Cities Of The World: World Regional Urban Development*. Rowman & Littlefield Publishers, 2003.
2. J. Girres and G. Touya. Quality Assessment of the French OpenStreetMap Dataset. *Transactions in GIS*, 14(4):435–459, 2010.
3. R. Glott, P. Schmidt, and R. Ghosh. Wikipedia Survey–overview of results. *United Nations University: Collaborative Creativity Group*, 2010.
4. M. Goodchild. Citizens as sensors: the world of volunteered geography. *GeoJournal*, 69(4):211–221, 2007.
5. M. Haklay. How good is volunteered geographical information? A comparative study of OpenStreetMap and Ordnance Survey datasets. *Environment and Planning B: Planning and Design*, 37(4):682–703, 2010.
6. M. Haklay, S. Basiouka, V. Antoniou, and A. Ather. How Many Volunteers Does it Take to Map an Area Well? The Validity of Linus Law to Volunteered Geographic Information. *Cartographic Journal, The*, 47(4):315–322, 2010.
7. E. Hargittai and E. Litt. The tweet smell of celebrity success: Explaining variation in twitter adoption among a diverse group of young adults. *New Media & Society*, 13(5):824–842, 2011.
8. B. Hecht and D. Gergle. Measuring self-focus bias in community-maintained knowledge repositories. In *Proceedings of the 4th International Conference on Communities and Technologies*, pages 11–20. ACM, 2009.
9. B. Hecht and D. Gergle. On the localness of user-generated content. In *Proceedings of the 13th International Conference on Computer supported cooperative work*, pages 229–232. ACM, 2010.
10. S. T. K. Lam, A. Uduwage, Z. Dong, S. Sen, D. R. Musicant, L. Terveen, and J. Riedl. WP:Clubhouse? An Exploration of Wikipedia's Gender Imbalance. In *Proceedings of the 7th International Symposium on Wikis and Open Collaboration*, pages 1–10. ACM, 2011.
11. D. Laniado, R. Tasso, Y. Volkovich, and A. Kaltenbrunner. When the Wikipedians Talk: Network and Tree Structure of Wikipedia Discussion Pages. In *Proceedings of the 5th International AAAI Conference on Weblogs and Social Media*. 2011.
12. I. Ludwig, A. Voss, and M. Krause-Traudes. A Comparison of the Street Networks of Navteq and OSM in Germany. *Advancing Geoinformation Science for a Changing World*, 1(2):65–84, 2011.
13. A. Mashhadi, G. Quattrone, L. Capra, and P. Mooney. On the Sustainability of Urban Crowd-sourcing for Maintaining Large-scale Geospatial Databases. In *Proceedings of the 8th International Symposium on Wikis and Open Collaboration*. ACM, 2012.
14. I. Masser. *Governments and Geographic Information*. Taylor and Francis, London, 1998.
15. K. Panciera, R. Priedhorsky, T. Erickson, and L. Terveen. Lurking? Cyclopaths? A Quantitative Lifecycle Analysis of User Behavior in a Geowiki. In *Proceedings of the 28th International Conference on Human factors in computing systems*, pages 1917–1926. ACM, 2010.
16. K. A. Panciera, M. Masli, and L. G. Terveen. "How should i go from _ to _ without getting killed?": Motivation and Benefits in Open Collaboration. In *Proceedings of the 7th International Symposium on Wikis and Open Collaboration*, pages 183–192, 2011.
17. A. Popescu and G. Grefenstette. Mining user home location and gender from Flickr tags. In *Proceedings of the 4th International AAAI Conference on Weblogs and Social Media*. 2010.

18. R. Priedhorsky, B. Jordan, and L. Terveen. How a Personalized Geowiki Can Help Bicyclists Share Information More Effectively. In *Proceedings of the 3rd International Symposium on Wikis and Open Collaboration*, pages 93–98, 2007.
19. R. Priedhorsky, M. Masli, and L. Terveen. Eliciting and Focusing Geographic Volunteer Work. In *Proceedings of the 13th International Conference on Computer Supported Cooperative Work*, pages 61–70. ACM, 2010.
20. R. Priedhorsky and L. Terveen. The Computational Geowiki: What, Why, and How. In *Proceedings of the 11th International Conference on Computer Supported Cooperative Work*, pages 267–276. ACM, 2008.
21. C. Roth, S. M. Kang, M. Batty, and M. Barthlemy. Structure of Urban Movements: Polycentric Activity and Entangled Hierarchical fFows. *PLoS ONE*, 6(1), 01 2011.
22. J. Schradie. The Digital Production Gap: The Digital Divide and Web 2.0 Collide. *Poetics*, 39(2):145–168, 2011.
23. Y. Volkovich, S. Scellato, D. Laniado, C. Mascolo, and A. Kaltenbrunner. The Length of Bridge Ties: Structural and Geographic Properties of Online Social Interactions. In *Proceedings of the 6th International AAAI Conference on Weblogs and Social Media*. 2012.
24. J. Voss. Measuring Wikipedia. In *Proceedings of the 10th International Conference of the International Society for Scientometrics and Informetrics*, pages 24–28, 2005.
25. D. Zielstra and A. Zipf. A Comparative Study of Proprietary Geodata and Volunteered Geographic Information for Germany. In *Proceedings of the 13th International Conference on Geographic Information Science*, 2010.
26. M. Zook, M. Graham, T. Shelton, and S. Gorman. Volunteered Geographic Information and Crowdsourcing Disaster Relief: A Case Study of the Haitian Earthquake. *World Medical and Health Policy*, 2(2), 2010.

Pay by the Bit: An Information-Theoretic Metric for Collective Human Judgment

Tamsyn P. Waterhouse
Google, Inc.
345 Spear Street, 4th Floor
San Francisco, CA 94105-1689
tpw@google.com

ABSTRACT

We consider the problem of evaluating the performance of human contributors for tasks involving answering a series of questions, each of which has a single correct answer. The answers may not be known *a priori*.

We assert that the measure of a contributor's judgments is the amount by which having these judgments decreases the entropy of our discovering the answer. This quantity is the pointwise mutual information between the judgments and the answer.

The expected value of this metric is the mutual information between the contributor and the answer prior, which can be computed using only the prior and the conditional probabilities of the contributor's judgments given a correct answer, without knowing the answers themselves.

We also propose using multivariable information measures, such as conditional mutual information, to measure the interactions between contributors' judgments.

These metrics have a variety of applications. They can be used as a basis for contributor performance evaluation and incentives. They can be used to measure the efficiency of the judgment collection process. If the collection process allows assignment of contributors to questions, they can also be used to optimize this scheduling.

Author Keywords

human computation; information theory; crowdsourcing

ACM Classification Keywords

H.5.3. Information Interfaces and Presentation (e.g. HCI): Group and Organization Interfaces

INTRODUCTION

Background

Human computation, as defined by Quinn and Bederson [21] (*quo vide* for more discussion of it and related terms), is the performance of computational tasks by humans under the direction of a computer system. The term is sometimes confused with crowdsourcing, which encompasses a broader definition of tasks, performed by workers sourced openly online.

In this paper we restrict ourselves to a specific human computation paradigm we call *collective human judgment*: tasks phrased in the form of a question with discrete possible answers, such as the Freebase curation tasks described by Kochhar, Mazzocchi, and Paritosh [16]. Each question is presented independently to a number of contributors, and their judgments are synthesized to form an estimate of the correct answer.

Some examples will clarify this concept. A subjective or creative task such as writing ad copy [8], summarizing a written article, or rating others' work, sourced out to workers via a service such as Amazon Mechanical Turk, CrowdFlower, or oDesk, is crowdsourcing but is not collective human judgment. An objective computational task given to an established team of contributors, as in the case of Freebase data curation [16], is collective human judgment but is not crowdsourcing. Classification of a large data set using volunteers sourced online, such as the Galaxy Zoo project [19], is both crowdsourcing and collective human judgment. The present work is not applicable to the first example but is applicable to the other two.

Collective human judgment presents an interesting quality-control problem: How do we measure and manage the performance of human computers?

Salaried human computers are often under pressure to perform well, which usually means some combination of "faster" and "better". Definitions of these terms, and how they are weighted in evaluating workers' performance, can often be vague or capricious.

Crowdsourced workers, on the other hand, work online for low pay with minimal supervision. There is a financial incentive to perform the most work with the least effort, which can lead to laziness, cheating, or even adversarial behavior. Such behavior can be modeled and accommodated without difficulty in the processing of collective human judgments, but it still comes with a cost: Employers must pay workers, even for worthless work. Most solutions to this problem involve terminating (or blocking) low-quality workers and offering extra financial incentives to high-quality workers.

Thus, there is a growing need for objective measurements of worker performance in human computation tasks, especially in cases where the workers are crowdsourced.

Aside from the need to be able to evaluate workers' contributions, the benefits of proactive management of human computers have been studied by Dow et al. [8]. Shaw, Horton, and Chen [24] explore the effect of several different incentive mechanisms on Mechanical Turk workers performing a website content analysis task. But without an objective metric for contributor performance, we have no way of knowing that we're incentivizing behavior that is actually beneficial.

Once answers are estimated, we could simply score workers by percent of answers correct. But this has serious shortcomings. In many cases, a good worker can produce judgments that are highly informative without ever being correct. For example, for classification problems over an ordinal scale, a well-meaning but biased worker can produce valuable output. If the distribution of classes is not uniform, a strategic spammer can often be correct simply by giving the most common answer every time. Problems over interval scales, for example the image-cropping task described by Welinder and Perona [30], can be resolved by modeling contributor estimates of the correct answer as discrete Gaussian distributions, with even a very good (accurate and unbiased) contributor having a very low probability of getting the answer exactly correct.

Many collective judgment resolution algorithms implicitly or explicitly include parameters representing contributors' skill. But such parameters are specific to their models and may not even be scalars, making it impossible to use them directly to score workers.

Ipeirotis, Provost, and Wang [15] introduce a data-based metric for contributor performance that calculates the hypothetical cost incurred by the employer of using that contributor's judgments exclusively. It depends on confusion matrices (and thus is restricted to classification problems) and takes a cost-of-errors matrix as input.

Paritosh [20] champions experimental reproducibility, specifically using Krippendorff's alpha [17] to measure the reliability of data from human contributors. Alpha is a descriptive statistic that measures aggregate agreement between contributors in a task. It's useful as a general measure of the statistical health of a task, but it doesn't say anything about the performance of individual contributors.

We propose a metric which we feel provides an objective and widely-applicable measurement of workers' contributions, in naturally-motivated units of information. Unlike Ipeirotis, Provost, and Wang's cost function, our metric is explicitly intended to be agnostic to the purpose for which the results are used: Workers are measured strictly by the information content of their judgments.[1]

The proposed metric also allows us to measure the redundancy of information obtained from multiple contributors during the judgment collection process. We can therefore measure the information efficiency of the process, and even tune the assignment of questions to contributors in order to increase the amount of information we obtain from a given number of judgments.

[1]However, we will see that we have the latitude to adjust incentives by attaching weights to different outcomes in the calculation of the metric.

Information Theory

The field of information theory [22, 23] deals with the mathematical aspects of the storage and communication of data.

The central concept of information theory is entropy, a measure of the expected (or asymptotic) minimal number of basic symbols (for example, bits) required to encode each of a sequence of outcomes of a random variable.

If X is a discrete random variable, the *self-information* of the outcome $X = x$ is defined to be

$$I(X = x) \equiv -\log P(X = x),$$

where the base of the logarithm determines the units in which the information is to be expressed. The most common choices are bits (base 2) or nats (base e), though familiar units from computing (decimal digits, bytes, etc.) can be used just as easily.

The *entropy* of X is defined to be the expected value of $I(X = x)$ over all x in the associated sample space, and is written as

$$H(X) \equiv E_X[I(X)] = \sum_x P(X = x)\left(-\log P(X = x)\right).$$

The definition of entropy is characterized, up to the choice of base, by four properties:

Continuity with respect to each probability $P(X = x)$.

Symmetry under exchange of outcomes $x \leftrightarrow x'$.

Maximization when all outcomes are equiprobable, with $P(X = x) = P(X = x') \forall x, x'$.

Additivity with respect to combining systems. The entropy of two independent variables X and Y is equal to $H(X) + H(Y)$.

Introductions to information theory are widely available, but Shannon's 1948 paper [22] remains both accessible and relevant today.

Information theory has been previously applied to topics in human-computer cooperation. For example, Card, Moran, and Newell [2] were among the first to describe human perception, cognition, and performance in computational terms, paraphrasing Hick's Law [14] as "to a first order of approximation, the response time of people is proportional to the information-theoretic entropy of the decision." Yang-Peláez and Flowers [34] discuss the information content of visual presentations of relational data. Chi and Mytkowicz [5] apply measures of information to search-and-retrieval tasks over the documents in a social tagging system. In the field of prediction markets, Hanson's logarithmic market scoring rules [11] yield payoffs proportional to the relative entropy of the probability distributions before and after a trader changes the market probability [4]. In evolutionary programming, Card and Mohan [3] propose using mutual information in the evaluation of genetic algorithms.

Collective Human Judgment

We work under the regime of Bayesian inference, in which the posterior probability of a given correct answer, given a set of judgments, is proportional to its prior times the probability of obtaining those judgments given that answer.

Hence, in order to perform this inference, we need a model that provides the probability of obtaining a particular set of judgments for a given question. Assuming that the contributors' judgments are conditionally independent of each other, conditioned on the correct answer, then the model need only prescribe the probability distribution of each contributor's judgments given a correct answer. These models are typically parametrized by a vector of parameters for each contributor, but question-dependent parameters are also possible.

The choice of model depends strongly on the nature of the problem. Classification tasks have a common set of classes for all questions, and so a model that incorporates a contributor's possible confusion of one class with another is appropriate: This is the family of *confusion matrix* models. For tasks whose answers are numbers, an entirely different model based on continuous probability distributions may be appropriate. We'll discuss these issues in more detail later.

Although a model can provide all of the probabilities needed to compute a posterior answer distribution, we still need the values of the model's parameters. Simple approaches to inference typically make point estimates of these parameters, for example maximum-likelihood estimates obtained using the expectation-maximization algorithm, and use these point estimates to compute posteriors. A more rigorous approach is to perform marginal integration over the space of possible parameter values, but this requires more sophisticated numerical or analytical techniques and is more computationally intensive.

A common property of all of these techniques is that they are attempting to solve a hidden-data problem. If we knew all the answers, then we could easily determine the parameter likelihoods. Likewise, with known parameter likelihoods, we could determine answer posteriors. With no answers known, a bootstrapping process is necessary. Expectation-maximization addresses the problem by alternating between estimating answers from parameters and estimating parameters from the estimated answers, eventually converging to maximum-likelihood parameter values for the full hidden-data problem. Marginalization treats both answers and parameters as unknowns and integrates the answer posteriors over all possible parameter values, weighted by their likelihoods. In both regimes it's possible to inject "golden" data, in other words a subset of answers that are known *a priori*, to increase the accuracy of the inference.

Model and inference algorithm selection present many subtle issues that lie beyond the scope of the present work, and there is a great deal of relevant literature. Models for various task types are proposed by Whitehill et al. [31] (a logistic model linking a contributor skill parameter to a question difficulty parameter), Welinder and Perona [30] (simple models for several tasks including numeric ones), and Welinder et al. [29] (a probit model using vectors to represent problem domains and contributor skill domains). The expectation-maximization algorithm was introduced by Hartley [12], named by Dempster, Laird, and Rubin [7], and popularized by Dawid and Skene [6]. Numerical marginalization for high-dimensional inference problems generally follows the Markov chain Monte Carlo paradigm [13] (generating a sequence of samples from the domain of integration in which each sample is conditioned on the one before it) and may involve Gibbs sampling [10] (iteratively sampling each variable conditioned on all the others) or substitution sampling [27] (iterating between sampling the parameters and sampling the hidden data, in a stochastic analogue to expectation-maximization); see Gelfand and Smith [9] for an accessible introduction to these methods. Analytic approximations through variational Bayesian methods are also possible [1, 26] but are more mathematically challenging.

For our purposes, we will prefer simple models and use expectation-maximization to perform inference. We'll mention the limitations of this approach as we encounter them. The critical limitation is this: The metrics presented in this article are only as good as the model parameters that they're based on. With too little data, a poor choice of model, or an inaccurate resolution algorithm, our metrics will be inaccurate.

Notation

We use the term *task* to refer to a set of questions and the judgments collected for those questions.

Let $\mathcal{Q}$ be the set of questions. Let $\mathcal{H}$ be the set of contributors. Let $\mathcal{A}$ be the set of possible answers. Let $\mathcal{J}$ be the set of possible judgments. In many applications we have $\mathcal{J} = \mathcal{A}$, but this isn't strictly necessary. When $\mathcal{J} = \mathcal{A}$, we'll refer to the set simply as the answer space.

Let A be a random variable producing correct answers $a \in \mathcal{A}$. Let J and J' be random variables producing judgments $j, j' \in \mathcal{J}$ from two contributors $h, h' \in \mathcal{H}$. J and J' are assumed to depend on A and to be conditionally independent of one another given this dependence. Since each h corresponds to one random variable J, we will often represent contributors by J instead of h when there is no risk of confusion.

For brevity and to keep notation unambiguous, we'll reserve the subscript a to refer to answer variables A, and the subscripts j and j' to refer to judgment variables J (from contributor h) and J' (from contributor h') respectively.

Thus, let $p_a = P(A = a)$ be the prior probability that the correct answer of any question is a. Let $p_{a|j} = P(A = a | J = j)$ be the posterior probability that the correct answer to a question is a, given that the contributor represented by J gave judgment j. Other probabilities for variables A, J, and J' are defined analogously.

THE VALUE OF A JUDGMENT

Information Content of an Answer

Suppose first that we have no judgments for a given question. The probability distribution of its correct answer is simply p_a, the answer prior. The information content of a particular answer $A = a$ is

$$I(A = a) = -\log p_a.$$

The choice of base of the logarithm here simply determines the units (bits, nats, digits, etc.) in which the information is expressed. We'll use bits everywhere below.

$I(A = a)$ is often introduced in the literature as a measure of surprise: It measures how surprised we should be at finding the outcome a. For example, if the correct answer turns out to be a, we'd be more surprised by it with a prior $p_a = 0.1$ than we would with a prior $p_a = 0.5$.

We could also write the information as $I(A)$, a random variable that depends on A. Its expected value is the *entropy* of A:

$$H(A) \equiv E_A[I(A)] = -\sum_a p_a \log p_a$$

Information Content of a Judgment

Suppose that we have a single judgment $J = j$ (from contributor h). Now the information content of the outcome $A = a$, conditioned on this information, is

$$I(A = a|J = j) = -\log p_{a|j},$$

and the expected value of $I(A|J)$ over all combinations of x and y is the *conditional entropy* of A given J,

$$H(A|J) \equiv E_{A,J}[I(A|J)] = -\sum_{a,j} p_{a,j} \log p_{a|j}.$$

Given a question $q \in \mathcal{Q}$, a judgment $j \in \mathcal{J}$, and the correct answer $a \in \mathcal{A}$, the information given to us by J is the amount by which the information content of the outcome $A = a$ is decreased by our knowledge of J: in other words, how much less surprising the outcome is when we have $J = j$. This quantity is

$$\Delta I_{a,j} \equiv I(A = a) - I(A = a|J = j) = \log \frac{p_{a|j}}{p_a}, \quad (1)$$

the *pointwise mutual information* of the outcomes $A = a$ and $J = j$.

We propose $\Delta I_{a,j}$ as a measure of the value of a single judgment from a contributor. If the judgment makes us more likely to believe that the answer is a, then the value of the judgment is positive; if it makes us less likely to believe that the answer is a, then its value is negative.

To compute $\Delta I_{a,j}$ for a single question, we must know the answer a to that question. In practice, we find a using a judgment resolution algorithm applied to a set of contributor judgments. Although knowing a is the goal of judgment resolution, we can still compute a contributor's aggregate value per question without it, simply taking the expected value of $\Delta I_{a,j}$ over all values of A and J. This is

$$E_{A,J}[\Delta I_{a,j}] = H(A) - H(A|J) \equiv I(A; J),$$

the *mutual information* of A and J, a measure of the amount of information the two random variables share. We can expand this as

$$I(A; J) = \sum_{a,j} p_{a,j} \log \frac{p_{a|j}}{p_a}. \quad (2)$$

Although ΔI can be negative, $I(A; J)$ is always non-negative: No contributor can have a negative expected value, because any behavior (even adversarial) that statistically discriminates between answers is informative to us, and behavior that fails to discriminate is of zero value.

a	j	$p_{a,j}$	$p_{a\|j}$	$I(A = a\|J = j)$	$\Delta I_{a,j}$
a_1	a_1	0.5	$\frac{2}{3}$	0.58 bits	0.42 bits
a_2	a_1	0.25	$\frac{1}{3}$	1.58 bits	-0.58 bits
a_2	a_2	0.25	1	0	1 bit

Table 1. Outcomes for the classification example.

Example

Say we have a task involving classifying objects q into two classes, a_1 and a_2, with uniform priors $p_{a_1} = p_{a_2} = 0.5$, so that $I(A = a_1) = I(A = a_2) = 1$ bit, and $\mathcal{J} = \mathcal{A}$.

Consider a contributor, represented by a random variable J, who always identifies a_1 objects correctly but misidentifies a_2 as a_1 half the time.

The possible outcomes for the random variables are listed in table 1.

This contributor is capable of giving a judgment that reduces our knowledge of the correct answer, with $\Delta I_{a_2,a_1} < 0$. However, the expected value per judgment from the contributor is positive: $I(A; J) = E_{A,J}[\Delta I_{a,j}] \approx 0.31$ bits.

Worker Incentives

If contributor rewards are linked to mutual information $I(A; J)$, then we are rewarding contributors for the degree to which they help us arrive at answers to our questions. If the computation task results in valid estimates of the answers, then we can say a few things about using $I(A; J)$ in a worker incentive mechanism.

It's important to note that $I(A; J)$ doesn't reward *honest* behavior so much as it rewards *consistent* behavior. A biased, or even adversarial, contributor who consistently swaps classes A and B in a classification problem, or one who consistently underestimates answers by 10 units in a numeric problem, is still providing us with useful information. In the former case we can reverse the swap, and in the latter case we can simply add 10 to the contributor's judgment, in order to get a good estimate of the correct answer.

There is one important caveat, however: We must have good estimates of the contributor parameters in order to have a good estimate of $I(A; J)$. This is a particular hazard if the number of judgments is small and the resolution algorithm uses point estimates of parameters rather than marginal integration. This is analogous to the problem of guessing the ratio of colors of balls in an urn from a small sample: If I draw one red ball, the maximum-likelihood estimate is that all the balls are red.

It's also critical that contributors work independently of one another, because any resolution algorithm, even one incorporating golden data, can be misled by workers colluding to agree on answers to questions.

The point is that our ability to estimate worker performance is only as good as our ability to estimate answers. As we discussed in the Introduction, the resolution of answers in collective human judgment problems is a fertile area of research, beyond the scope of this article, and involves choosing both an appropriate statistical model for contributor behavior and an appropriate means of performing statistical inference over the model.

COMBINING JUDGMENTS

We typically have several judgments per question, from different contributors. The goal of judgment resolution can be expressed as minimizing $H(A|J, J')$, or in the general case, minimizing $H(A|J, \ldots)$. To do so efficiently, we would like to choose contributors so as to minimize the redundant information among the set of contributors assigned to each question.

Suppose we start with one judgment, $J = j$. If we then get a second judgment $J' = j'$, and finally discover the correct answer to be $A = a$, the difference in information content of the correct answer made by having the second judgment (compared to having just the first judgment) is the *pointwise conditional mutual information*

$$\begin{aligned} \Delta I_{a,j'|j} &\equiv I(A = a|J = j) - I(A = a|J = j, J' = j') \\ &= \log \frac{p_{a|j,j'}}{p_{a|j}}. \end{aligned} \tag{3}$$

Below, we'll consider two situations: assigning a second contributor represented by random variable J' to a question after receiving a judgment from a first contributor represented by J (the sequential case), and assigning both contributors to the same question before either gives a judgment (the simultaneous case).

This section tacitly assumes that we have a good way to estimate probabilities as we go. This requires us to work from some existing data, so we can't use these methods for scheduling questions until we have sufficient data to make initial estimates of model parameters. What constitutes "sufficient data" depends entirely on the data and on the resolution algorithm, and these estimates can be refined by the resolution algorithm as more data is collected.

For example, one could break the judgment collection process into N batches of judgments. Contributors are assigned to questions at random for the first batch, after which the resolution algorithm estimates answers and contributor metrics and then assigns questions to contributors optimally for the next batch, and so on. After all N batches have been collected, the resolution algorithm computes final estimates of answers and metrics.

Sequentially

The expected information gained from the second judgment, conditioned on the known first judgment $J = j$, is

$$E_{A,J'|J=j}[\Delta I_{a,j'|j}] = \sum_{a,j'} p_{a,j'|j} \log \frac{p_{a|j,j'}}{p_{a|j}}, \tag{4}$$

which is similar in form to equation (2).

This expression allows us to compute the expected value of $\Delta I_{a,j'|j}$ for each choice of second contributor J' and to make optimal assignments of contributors to questions, if our judgment collection system allows us to make such scheduling decisions.

Simultaneously

If we must choose contributors for a question before getting judgments, we take the expectation of equation (3) over all three random variables rather than just A and J'. The result is the *conditional mutual information*

$$I(A; J'|J) = E_{A,J,J'}[\Delta I_{a,j'|j}] = \sum_{a,j,j'} p_{a,j,j'} \log \frac{p_{a|j,j'}}{p_{a|j}}, \tag{5}$$

which is the expected change in information due to receiving one judgment from J' when we already have one judgment from J.

Two contributors are on average at least as good as one: The total information we gain from the two judgments is

$$I(A; J, J') = I(A; J) + I(A; J'|J) \geq I(A; J),$$

since $I(A; J'|J) \geq 0$. In fact, we can write

$$\begin{aligned} I(A; J, J') &= I(A; J) + I(A; J'|J) \\ &= I(A; J) + I(A; J') - I(A; J; J'), \end{aligned}$$

where $I(A; J; J')$ is the *multivariate mutual information* of A, J, and J'.[2] Here it quantifies the difference between the information given by two contributors and the sum of their individual contributions, since we have

$$I(A; J; J') = I(A; J) + I(A; J') - I(A; J, J').$$

$I(A; J; J')$ is a measure of the redundant information between the two contributors. Because contributors are responsible only for their own judgments, it might not be fair to reward a contributor's judgments based on their statistical interaction with another contributor's judgments. However, we can use this as a measure of inefficiency in our system. We receive an amount of information equal to $I(A; J) + I(A; J')$,

[2]Unfortunately, the same notation is used for the interaction information, which differs from multivariate mutual information by a factor of $(-1)^n$, where n is the number of variables involved.

but some is redundant and only the amount $I(A; J, J')$ is useful to us. The overlap $I(A; J; J')$ is the amount wasted.[3]

More than Two Judgments

Generalizing to higher-order, the relevant quantities are the combined mutual information

$$I(A; J_1, \ldots, J_k),$$

which gives the total information we get from k judgments, the mutual information conditioned on a set of known judgments $\{J_1 = j_1, \ldots, J_{k-1} = j_{k-1}\}$,

$$E_{A,J_k|J_1=j_1,\ldots,J_{k-1}=j_{k-1}}[\Delta I_{a,j_k|j_1,\ldots,j_{k-1}}] = \sum_{a,j_k} p_{a,j_k|j_1,\ldots,j_{k-1}} \log \frac{p_{a|j_1,\ldots,j_k}}{p_{a|j_1,\ldots,j_{k-1}}}, \quad (6)$$

which gives the expected increase in information from the kth judgment with the previous $k-1$ judgments already known, and the conditional mutual information

$$I(A; J_k | J_1, \ldots, J_{k-1}),$$

which gives the increase in information we get from the kth judgment with the previous $k-1$ judgments unknown. Higher-order expressions of multivariate mutual information are possible but not germane to our work: We are instead interested in quantities like

$$\left[\sum_{i=1}^{k} I(A; J_i)\right] - I(A; J_1, \ldots, J_k)$$

for measuring information overlap.

PRACTICAL CALCULATION

The equations we derived in the previous section are rather abstract, phrased as sums involving quantities like $p_{a|j}$. In this section we'll discuss how to compute these quantities in the context of real-world human judgment tasks.

Regardless of the type of task, we generally have a statistical model for questions and contributor behavior which defines probabilities p_a (answer priors) and $p_{j|a}$ and $p_{j'|a}$ (probability of a judgment given an answer). Other probabilities, such as $p_{a|j}$ (probability of an answer given a judgment), must be computed from these.

Pointwise mutual information, equation (1), is

$$\Delta I_{a,j} = \log \frac{p_{a|j}}{p_a} = \log \frac{p_{j|a}}{\sum_{a'} p_{a'} p_{j|a'}}. \quad (7)$$

Mutual information, equation (2), is

$$I(A; J) = \sum_{a,j} p_{a,j} \Delta I_{a,j} = \sum_{a,j} p_a p_{j|a} \log \frac{p_{j|a}}{\sum_{a'} p_{a'} p_{j|a'}}. \quad (8)$$

[3] $I(A; J; J')$ can in theory be positive or negative, but in most cases it's positive, representing redundant information. Cases in which it's negative represent information present in the combination of two judgments in excess of the sum of their individual contributions. Such cases can be contrived but have not been observed in our experiments.

To compute probabilities involving more than one judgment, we must assume conditional independence of judgments given the correct answer. This means, for example, that $p_{j'|a,j} = p_{j'|a}$.

Pointwise conditional mutual information, equation (3), is

$$\Delta I_{a,j'|j} = \log \frac{p_{a|j,j'}}{p_{a|j}} = \log \left(p_{j'|a} \frac{\sum_{a'} p_{a'} p_{j|a'}}{\sum_{a'} p_{a'} p_{j|a'} p_{j'|a'}} \right). \quad (9)$$

Mutual information conditioned on one point $J = j$, equation (4), is

$$E_{A,J'|J=j}[\Delta I_{a,j'|j}] = \sum_{a,j'} p_{a,j'|j} \Delta I_{a,j'|j} = \sum_{a,j'} \frac{p_a p_{j|a} p_{j'|a}}{\sum_{a'} p_{a'} p_{j|a'}} \log \left(p_{j'|a} \frac{\sum_{a'} p_{a'} p_{j|a'}}{\sum_{a'} p_{a'} p_{j|a'} p_{j'|a'}} \right). \quad (10)$$

Conditional mutual information, equation (5), is

$$I(A; J'|J) = \sum_{a,j,j'} p_{a,j,j'} \Delta I_{a,j'|j} = \sum_{a,j,j'} p_a p_{j|a} p_{j'|a} \log \left(p_{j'|a} \frac{\sum_{a'} p_{a'} p_{j|a'}}{\sum_{a'} p_{a'} p_{j|a'} p_{j'|a'}} \right). \quad (11)$$

Although these expressions may seem intimidating, the arguments of the logarithms are Bayes' Rule calculations that must be performed by the resolution algorithm, so that little additional work is required to compute these information-theoretic quantities.

Combined mutual information is then

$$I(A; J, J') = I(A; J) + I(A; J'|J),$$

and multivariate mutual information is

$$I(A; J; J') = I(A; J') - I(A; J'|J).$$

The exact nature of the statistical model depends in part on the type of problem we're trying to solve. Below we'll examine three different types of tasks, which we'll refer to as *classification*, *search*, and *numeric*.

Classification Tasks

Classification tasks are the bread and butter of the human computation literature. Such tasks ask contributors to bin objects into a predetermined set of classes or to determine for each object whether a given proposition is true. A good example of a classification task is Galaxy Zoo [19], which uses volunteers to classify galaxy morphology from photographs.

Although other models are possible, contributor behavior for classification problems can usually be modeled well with confusion matrices, $p_{j|a} \equiv \pi_{a,j}$, and the small size of the answer space relative to the number of questions allows us to make good estimates of the class priors p_a. In other words, we have a model that contains a confusion matrix $\pi_{a,j}$ for each contributor and a prior p_a for each class.

As long as our model provides $p_{j|a}$ and p_a, we can evaluate equations (7) to (11) directly using these quantities.

However, due to the multiple sums over the answer and judgment spaces that appear in the above equations, a few words on computational complexity are appropriate here.

Calculating contributor performance goes hand-in-hand with the main problem of turning human judgments into estimates of correct answers to questions. Our metrics can be computed at the same time as these estimates.

In the following section's examples, we'll assume for simplicity a judgment resolution algorithm which makes pointwise estimates of model parameters. Although this is a common simplification in the literature and in practice, full statistical inference involves marginal integration over the space of possible parameter values, for example using Markov chain Monte Carlo methods (see Walsh's notes [28] for an introduction). Instead of computing, say, $I(A; J'|J)$ using point estimates of parameters like p_a and $p_{j|a}$, we marginalize by integrating $I(A; J'|J) = \int_{\boldsymbol{\alpha}} I(A_{\boldsymbol{\alpha}}; J'_{\boldsymbol{\alpha}}|J_{\boldsymbol{\alpha}})d\boldsymbol{\alpha}$, where $\boldsymbol{\alpha}$ represents the full set of parameters governing the model.

Because these numerical methods are computationally intensive, we should consider how much additional burden our metrics would impose in such cases.

Let $m = |\mathcal{H}|$ be the number of contributors, $s = |\mathcal{A}|$ be the number of possible answers, and $t = |\mathcal{J}|$ be the number of possible judgments. Computing first-order quantities $I(A; J)$ for all contributors using equation (8) has run time $O(m \cdot s \cdot t)$, and computing a second-order quantity such as $I(A; J, J')$ for all contributor pairs using equation (11) has run time $O(m^2 \cdot s \cdot t^2)$. Higher-order quantities become challenging, though: In general, computing $I(A; J_1, \ldots, J_k)$ for all contributor k-sets has run time $O(m^k \cdot s \cdot t^k)$.

By comparison, estimating answers to all questions in a task from a single set of model parameter values can be accomplished in run time proportional to the total number of judgments received, which is typically of order 10 times the number of questions.

Search Tasks

Classification problems are characterized by a small answer space shared by all questions and sufficient data to estimate priors p_a and confusion matrix elements $\pi_{a,j}$.

We'll refer to problems that don't satisfy these conditions as "search problems", because unlike classification problems, we have little prior knowledge of what the answer could be: Our contributors are searching for it.

Search problems can have very large answer spaces. For example, the answer space for the question "Find the URI for company X's investor relations page" is the set of all valid URIs.

Problems with large answer spaces have large entropies, naturally incorporating the increased difficulty of searching over these spaces. The set of all Freebase MIDs (canonical topic identifiers), for example, presently numbers in excess of 20 million entities, so $H(A) \sim 24$ bits for problems over this space.

Large answer spaces aren't strictly necessary for a problem to fall into the search category, though: A typical multiple-choice exam also has the property that answer A on question 1 is unrelated to answer A on question 2, so confusion matrix models are inappropriate.

As we noted above, our metrics require a run time which is polynomial in the size of the answer spaces. For large answer spaces this becomes unviable. Fortunately, the same challenge is faced by the judgment resolution algorithm, and its solution can be ours too.

Without enough information to model contributor behavior using confusion matrices (or with answer spaces too large for confusion matrices to be computable), we usually use models with agnostic answer priors and a single value π that gives the probability of a contributor answering a question correctly. π may depend on the contributor, the question, or both; see Whitehill et al. [31] for an example of the latter case.

That is, we generally have $\mathcal{J} = \mathcal{A}$ and uniform answer priors $p_a = \frac{1}{s}$ (although this can change if we have information beyond just the contributors' judgments), where as above we let $s = |\mathcal{A}|$. Our conditional probabilities are

$$p_{j|a} = \pi\delta_{a,j} + \frac{1-\pi}{s-1}(1-\delta_{a,j}),$$

where $\delta_{a,j}$ is the Kronecker delta. This means that with probability π, the contributor answers the question correctly, and with probability $1-\pi$, the contributor gives a judgment chosen randomly and uniformly from among the incorrect answers.

All of the equations above now simplify (in terms of computational, if not typographical, complexity). The normalization term in equation (7) is

$$\sum_a p_a p_{j|a} = \sum_a \frac{1}{s}\left[\pi\delta_{a,j} + \frac{1-\pi}{s-1}(1-\delta_{a,j})\right] = \frac{1}{s}.$$

Conditional probability is

$$p_{a|j} = \frac{p_a p_{j|a}}{\sum_{a'} p_{a'} p_{j|a'}} = p_{j|a}.$$

Mutual information is therefore

$$I(A; J) = \pi\log(s\pi) + (1-\pi)\log\left(s\frac{1-\pi}{s-1}\right).$$

Note that $I(A; J) \sim \pi\log s = \pi \cdot H(A)$ as $s \to \infty$. In figure 1, we plot $\frac{I(A;J)}{H(A)}$ for various values of s.

We can also compute higher-order quantities. For example, letting π be the probability-correct parameter for J and π' be

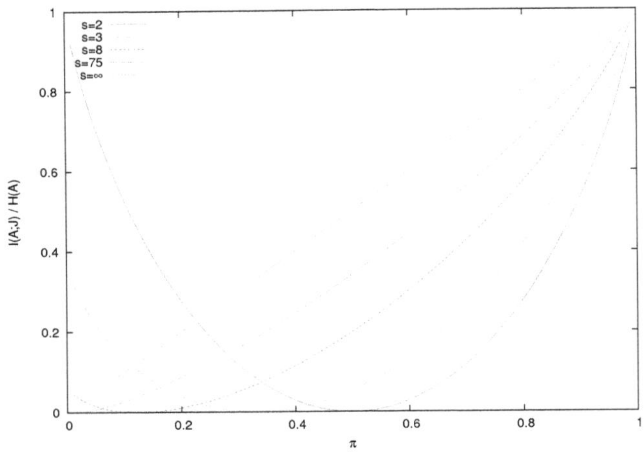

Figure 1. $\frac{I(A;J)}{H(A)}$ **as a function of the probability-correct parameter** π**, for various sizes** s **of the answer space.**

the probability-correct parameter for J', we have

$$\sum_a p_a p_{j|a} p_{j'|a} = \begin{cases} \frac{1}{s}\left[\pi\pi' + \frac{(1-\pi)(1-\pi')}{s-1}\right] & \text{if } j = j' \\ \frac{1}{s}\left[\frac{\pi+\pi'-2\pi\pi'}{s-1} + \frac{(1-\pi)(1-\pi')(s-2)}{(s-1)^2}\right] & \text{if } j \neq j' \end{cases}.$$

For large s, we can approximate this as

$$\sum_a p_a p_{j|a} p_{j'|a} \approx \begin{cases} \frac{\pi\pi'}{s} & \text{if } j = j' \\ \frac{1-\pi\pi'}{s(s-1)} & \text{if } j \neq j' \end{cases}.$$

This simplification happens because for a large answer space, $j = j' \neq a$ occurs very rarely, so the $j = j'$ case is dominated by $j = j' = a$. This is another example of the assumption of contributor independence: Two contributors' wrong answers are assumed to be uncorrelated.

However, higher-order quantities are less useful for search problems than for classification problems, because with lower-dimension model parameters for each contributor, there is less to differentiate contributors from each other and thus less to be gained from attempting to optimize scheduling. In the case of just one parameter π per contributor, contributor skill is literally one-dimensional.

In any event, what matters is that for search problems, we can eliminate the sums in equations (7) to (11) to produce computationally simple quantities.

Numeric Tasks

A third class of human judgment problem is that of estimating a numerical value. Such tasks differ from search tasks in that the answer space is interval rather than categorical: A judgment close to the correct answer can still be informative. Welinder and Perona [30], for example, consider the problem of determining a bounding rectangle around a desired object in an image. Human contributors were shown a series of images, each of which contained a bird, and asked to draw a "snug" bounding box around the bird in each image. The judgments and answers to these questions are integer 4-tuples representing the x and y coordinates of each edge of the bounding box.

Evaluating equation (8) for numeric tasks is the same calculation as in the classification task case, albeit at high dimension. There is no shortcut to performing this calculation in general. Nevertheless, in the example to follow, we were able to calculate a contributor's $I(A;J)$ with an answer space of size $s = 400$ in a few seconds using a quick-and-dirty Python script.

Additionally, some special cases allow simplification.

In the case of a uniform answer prior, $p_a = \frac{1}{s}$, equation (8) reduces to

$$\begin{aligned} I(A;J) &= \frac{1}{s}\sum_{a,j} p_{j|a}\log(s\cdot p_{j|a}) \\ &= \log s + \frac{1}{s}\sum_{a,j} p_{j|a}\log p_{j|a}. \end{aligned}$$

This form follows the definition $I(A;J) = H(A) - H(A|J)$, with $H(A) = \log s$ and $H(A|J) = -\frac{1}{s}\sum_{a,j} p_{j|a}\log p_{j|a}$.

If we further assume that we can extend the answer space indefinitely in the positive and negative directions and that $p_{j|a}$ depends only on the difference $\delta \equiv j - a$, writing $p_\delta \equiv p_{j|a}$, we then have

$$H(A|J) = -\sum_\delta p_\delta \log p_\delta.$$

Now that we've reduced the sum to one dimension, if we interpolate p_δ by a continuous probability distribution $f(x)$, we can consider $H(A|J)$ as a Riemann approximation of the *differential entropy* $h[f] \equiv -\int_{\mathbf{R}} dx f(x)\log f(x)$. That is,

$$I(A;J) \approx \log s - h[f].$$

From this it's clear where we might expect the approximation to break down: for values of $h[f]$ close to 0 and close to $\log s$. However, the integral $h[f]$ has a known closed form for many commonly-used continuous probability distributions [18], making the approximation quite versatile.

The case in which $p_{j|a}$ is a Gaussian function of $\delta = j - a$ is of special importance, since a product of Gaussians is also a Gaussian, as is a convolution of Gaussians. This yields closed-form approximations to higher-order quantities like $I(A;J;J')$, as we'll see later.

EXAMPLES

In this section we will present the results of applying our metrics to human judgment tasks from several domains. In addition, we will show how online estimation of contributor

Contributor	$I(A;J)$
1	0.94 bits
2	1.06 bits
3	1.03 bits
4	1.15 bits
5	1.05 bits

Table 2. Mutual information for the contributors in Wilson's experiment.

Patient	Resolution	#2		#3		#4	
2	4	4	3.91	3	2.58	3	1.10
11	4	4	3.91	4	2.32	4	3.32
20	2	1	-2.75	3	-0.08	2	1.16
22	2	2	0.93	2	1.06	2	1.16
32	3	3	2.03	2	0.10	3	2.36
39	3	3	2.03	4	2.58	3	2.36

Table 3. Pointwise mutual information for several patients in Wilson's experiment, for contributors 2, 3, and 4.

$I(A;J'\|J)$	#1	#2	#3	#4	#5
First #1	0.31	0.40	0.37	0.43	0.38
First #2	0.27	0.30	0.33	0.42	0.32
First #3	0.28	0.37	0.33	0.37	0.36
First #4	0.22	0.33	0.25	0.27	0.28
First #5	0.26	0.34	0.33	0.38	0.35

Table 4. Conditional mutual information for second judgments, given the first contributor.

parameters and real-time scheduling of contributors to questions can improve the efficiency and accuracy of some human judgment tasks.

Wilson's Patients

We'll start by applying our metrics to Wilson's data in Dawid and Skene [6], the paper which popularized the use of the expectation-maximization algorithm for hidden-data problems. The data is taken from real pre-operative assessments by 5 contributors of 45 patients' fitness for anesthesia. The judgment and answer spaces are a set of four categories numbered 1, 2, 3, 4.

Each contributor $h \in \{1,2,3,4,5\}$ gives a single judgment $j \in \{1,2,3,4\}$ to each patient $q \in \{1,\dots,45\}$, except for contributor #1, who gives three (presumed independent) judgments for each patient.

Dawid and Skene proceed as follows. The contributors are modeled using confusion matrices: Each observer is assigned a 4×4 matrix whose j, j' entry is the probability of that observer giving judgment j' when a patient's actual condition is j. Each of the four conditions has a model parameter representing its prior probability for any given patient. Using the expectation-maximization algorithm [7, 12], the 315 judgments collected from the contributors are used to make maximum-likelihood estimates of the model parameters and priors, and these parameter estimates are used to estimate the actual condition of each patient.

We duplicated Dawid and Skene's results, up to what we believe to be an error in their final estimates for patient 7, where we get probabilities of ≈ 0.981 and ≈ 0.019 for categories 1 and 2 respectively, instead of Dawid and Skene's 0.986 and 0.014. We used the maximum-likelihood parameter estimates to form point estimates of the information-theoretic quantities of interest to us.

$I(A;J,J')$	#1	#2	#3	#4	#5
#1	1.25	1.33	1.31	1.36	1.32
#2		1.37	1.40	1.48	1.39
#3			1.36	1.40	1.39
#4				1.42	1.43
#5					1.40

Table 5. Mutual information for two combined contributors.

$I(A;J;J')$	#1	#2	#3	#4	#5
#1	0.63	0.67	0.66	0.72	0.68
#2		0.76	0.70	0.73	0.73
#3			0.69	0.78	0.70
#4				0.87	0.77
#5					0.70

Table 6. Multivariate mutual information for two contributors.

Using the priors and confusion matrices thus obtained (corresponding to Dawid and Skene's Table 2), we measured $I(A;J)$ for each contributor J. The results are shown in table 2.

From the prior $p_a = [0.40, 0.42, 0.11, 0.07]$, the entropy of the answer priors is $H(A) \approx 1.67$ bits.

We also computed pointwise judgment values using the estimated answers (Dawid and Skene's Table 4). In cases where the estimated answer was a probability distribution, we computed the expected judgment value over this distribution.

In table 3, we list the contributors' judgments and the corresponding values of ΔI, in bits, for a selection of patients for each of contributors 2, 3, and 4.

Note that in many cases, a contributor giving the wrong answer still gives us a positive amount of information, because the correct answer is more likely given that judgment. This is to be expected with an answer space of cardinality larger than two: An answer that a contributor is known to confuse with the correct answer narrows down the possibilities for us.

We also computed combined, conditional, and mutual information for pairs of contributors.

Table 4 contains the conditional mutual information between correct answers and a second contributor, conditioned on a first contributor.

Table 5 shows the mutual information between correct answers and two combined contributors.

Table 6 shows multivariate mutual information between correct answers and two contributors.

These data make it clear that although contributor #4 gives us the most information in a single judgment ($I(A;J_4) \approx$ 1.15 bits), a second judgment from the same contributor has low expected additional value ($I(A;J_4|J_4) \approx 0.27$ bits). Pairing #4 with #2 gives the most total information ($I(A; J_2, J_4) \approx 1.48$ bits), with relatively little overlap ($I(A; J_2; J_4) \approx 0.73$ bits, which is less than any other pairing except $I(A; J_1; J_4) \approx 0.72$ bits).

Welinder and Perona's Bounding Boxes

Next, we considered one of Welinder and Perona's bounding box experiments, introduced previously. In this experiment, 343 contributors gave judgments on 24,642 images, with no image receiving more than 4 contributors' judgments. For simplicity, we restricted our attention to the x-coordinate of the left edge of each bounding box, and we assumed a uniform prior over the columns of each image. Thus the problem is one of estimating an integer value from 0 to $s - 1$, where s is the number of columns in the image. s can be different for each image, ranging from a minimum of 88 to a maximum (and mode) of 500.

We chose a simple model for contributor performance, in which each contributor's judgments follow a Gaussian distribution with parameters for bias and variance: $J \sim N(a - \eta, \sigma^2)$, where the *bias* η and *variance* σ^2 are contributor-dependent parameters. The probability of a contributor giving judgment j when the correct answer is a is thus

$$p_{j|a} \propto e^{-\frac{1}{2}\left(\frac{j-a+\eta}{\sigma}\right)^2}.$$

We also assumed an agnostic prior $p_a = \frac{1}{s}$, so that the probabilities of answers given judgments are simply $p_{a|j} \propto p_{j|a}$.

The normalizing constant for the continuous Gaussian distribution is $(\sigma\sqrt{2\pi})^{-1}$, but since we are still assuming a discrete space of possible answers (integer pixel values from 0 to $s - 1$), we must calculate the correct factor by brute force, summing

$$\sum_{j=0}^{s-1} e^{-\frac{1}{2}\left(\frac{a-j-\eta}{\sigma}\right)^2}.$$

In particular, the tails of the distribution are cut off by the lateral boundaries of the image.

The continuous approximation to the mutual information $I(A|J)$ is

$$I(A; J) \approx \log s - \log(\sigma\sqrt{2\pi e}) = \log \frac{s}{\sqrt{2\pi e \sigma^2}}. \quad (12)$$

The continuous approximation breaks down, as expected, for values of σ close to 0 and close to $s/\sqrt{2\pi e}$. We can improve it somewhat simply by truncating it at these values. In figure 2 we plot this corrected approximation along with the actual values of $I(A; J)$ for various values of η and σ^2, with $s = 100$.

The continuous approximation also breaks down when the bias η approaches s in absolute value. This is more a property of our simplistic model than a failure of the approximation, because the model asserts that contributors with large η must be giving uninformative judgments close to one or the other edge of the answer space. The continuous approximation to $I(A; J)$, on the other hand, has no η dependence, because it

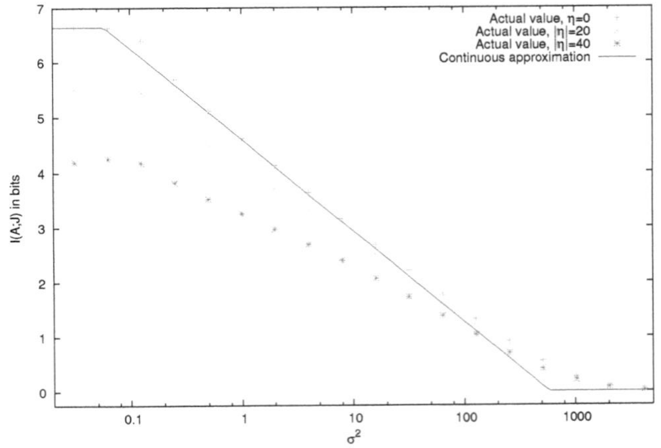

Figure 2. $I(A; J)$ **in the bias-and-variance model as a function of the variance** σ^2**, for three values of the bias** η**, with an answer space of size** $s = 100$**. The solid line is the truncated continuous approximation.**

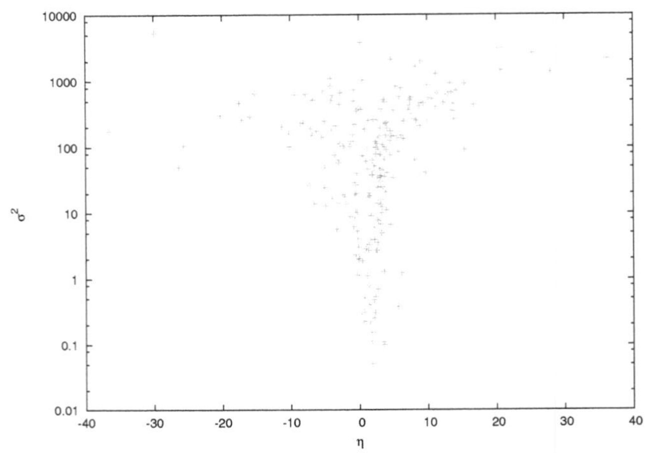

Figure 3. Scatter plot of maximum-likelihood bias and variance for 229 contributors in one of Welinder and Perona's experiments.

extends the answer space to the entire real line, on which a contributor with large bias but small variance is as valuable to us as one with small bias and the same variance.

The fact that the product of two Gaussian functions is also a Gaussian makes it very easy to estimate correct answers given judgments and model parameters. We implemented the expectation-maximization algorithm over this model and ran it on data from one of Welinder and Perona's experiments.

We note again the important limitation of point parameter estimation approaches such as expectation-maximization, that maximum-likelihood estimators of model parameters are unreliable when there is little data. In particular, the maximum-likelihood estimate $\hat{\sigma}^2$ of the parameter σ^2 for any contributor with only one judgment is zero. (The unbiased estimator $\frac{n}{n-1}\hat{\sigma}^2$ isn't helpful either, as it's undefined for $n = 0$.) A more statistically rigorous approach would be to use marginal integration rather than point parameter estimation, but we chose our approach for the sake of clarity and will simply omit the 114 such contributors in what follows.

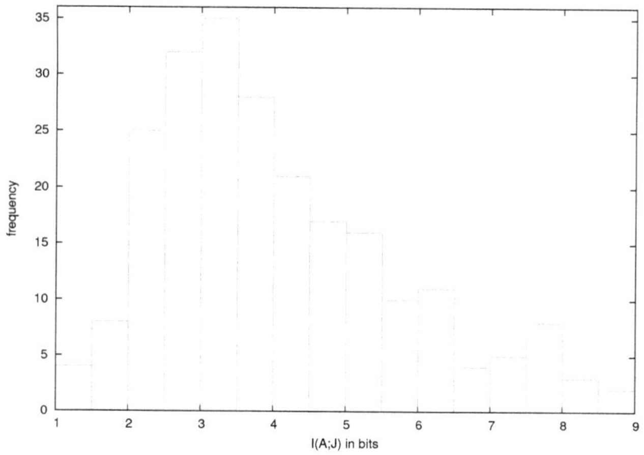

Figure 4. Histogram of mutual information $I(A;J)$ for the contributors in one of Welinder and Perona's experiments, with $s = 500$.

A scatter plot of the maximum-likelihood estimates of contributor parameters η and σ^2 for the remaining 229 contributors is presented in figure 3.

Using these parameter estimates, we calculated the mutual information $I(A;J)$ for each contributor for a hypothetical image of width $s = 500$ (the most common value in the experiment). figure 4 shows a histogram of the results. The upper bound on $I(A;J)$ is $H(A) = \log 500 \approx 9$ bits.

Using the continuous approximation, it's easy to work out higher-order information measures. The posterior probability of answer a given judgments j and j' is

$$p_{a|j,j'} = p_a \cdot p_{j,j'|a} = p_a \cdot p_{j|a} \cdot p_{j'|a}$$

under the assumption of contributor independence. As long as these three factors are all Gaussian, their product is also Gaussian.

For example, if p_a is a constant, $p_{j|a}$ is a Gaussian with variance σ^2, and $p_{j'|a}$ is a Gaussian with variance σ'^2, then $p_{a|j,j'}$ is a Gaussian with variance $\frac{\sigma^2\sigma'^2}{\sigma^2+\sigma'^2}$. That is,

$$H(A|J,J') \approx \log\left(\sigma\sigma'\sqrt{\frac{2\pi e}{\sigma^2+\sigma'^2}}\right).$$

Using the formula $I(A;J,J') = H(A) - H(A|J,J')$ for the combined mutual information, we can compute the information overlap between two contributors with respective variances σ^2 and σ'^2 as

$$\begin{aligned} I(A;J;J') &= I(A;J) + I(A;J') - I(A;J,J') \\ &= H(A) - H(A|J) - H(A|J') + H(A|J,J') \\ &\approx \log\frac{s}{\sqrt{2\pi e(\sigma^2+\sigma'^2)}}. \end{aligned}$$

Comparing this to equation (12), we see that there is little to be gained by pairing a contributor having high variance with one having low variance: The information given to us by the latter is mostly redundant. It's more efficient to trust low-variance contributors and to pair high-variance contributors with each other.

APPLICATION TO SCHEDULING

Scheduling of human resources is an active area of research. Yan et al. [33] discuss optimal assignment of contributors to questions for a binary classification task with a logistic contributor model. Welinder and Perona [30] present an algorithm that adaptively categorizes contributors as "experts" or "bots" and requires fewer judgments per question as it identifies more and more contributors. Additionally, Sheng, Provost, and Ipeirotis [25] discuss several strategies in the context of cost-effectively collecting binary classification labels to be used as training data for an ML classifier.

We'll demonstrate question-contributor scheduling using mutual information conditioned on one or more points, equations (4) and (6). We conducted the following three experiments, one using simulated data and two using real data.

Wilson's Patients

First, we simulated a continuation of Wilson's experiment, with a pool of 50 new patients drawn from the estimated prior distribution and contributors' judgments drawn from their estimated confusion matrices.

We implemented a simple queuing system in which a patient with condition A is drawn at random and assigned to an available contributor, where "available" means "has given the fewest number of judgments so far".

The first contributor J for each patient is chosen randomly from the set of available contributors. Once every patient has been judged by one contributor ($J = j$), we repeat the process to get a second judgment. In control runs, we choose the second contributor randomly again from the pool of available contributors. In test runs, we instead choose for each patient the available contributor J' that maximizes $E_{A,J'|J=j}[\Delta I_{a,j'|j}]$. Using the same contributor both times for one patient is permitted in both cases.

Once two judgments have been collected for each patient, we look at the patient's actual condition a and use the estimated posterior probability of that condition $p_{a|j,j'}$ from the two judgments $J = j$ and $J' = j'$ as a score for our resolution. (This does away with the question of thresholding answer probabilities, which isn't relevant to the experiment.) So a perfect resolution gets a score of 1.0, and a completely incorrect resolution gets a score of 0.0.

We repeated the experiment ten thousand times for each of the control and test runs and computed mean scores of 0.876 for the control group and 0.937 for the test group. That is, using the most likely answer for each patient, if we assign two contributors randomly, we can expect to get the patient's condition correct 87.6 percent of the time, and if we assign the second contributor to maximize expected information gain, we get the patient's condition correct 93.7 percent of the time.

Freebase Reconciliation

For the second experiment, we wished to demonstrate the benefit of a scheduling algorithm even while bootstrapping our estimates of contributor parameters.

Freebase (`http://www.freebase.com`) is a structured knowledge base with an underlying graph model: Topics (graph vertices) are connected to each other by subject-predicate relations (edges).

We considered a Freebase curation task [16]. Sixteen human contributors, engaged in an ongoing basis for this and other tasks, were presented with pairs of Freebase entities representing politicians and political parties and, for each pair, were asked if the politician "is/was a member of" the party. The allowed judgments were "yes", "no", and "skip" (to indicate a problem with a question). Five to seven judgments were collected for each pair, so not every contributor saw every question. There were 10,750 questions and 54,201 judgments in total.

We used a three-by-three confusion matrix model for contributor behavior. We recreated the collection process as follows: First we collected all available judgments for each of 250 questions. We ran the expectation-maximization algorithm over these judgments to obtain initial estimates of the answer priors and contributor confusion matrices.

For the remaining 10,500 questions, we recreated the data collection process using a scheduling algorithm that chose contributors for each question and yielded their real answers from the original data set. This allowed us great flexibility and control in repeating the same experiment under different conditions, without having to collect new data.

In the control groups, the scheduling algorithm chose n contributors for each question, randomly and uniformly without replacement, from the set of contributors from whom a judgment was available for that question. In the test group, the algorithm again chose n contributors, selecting at each step the available contributor with the highest expected information contribution, just as in the above experiment on Wilson's data. The algorithm was free to drop contributors whose judgments were found to be less informative. After every 1,500 questions, we reran the expectation-maximization algorithm over the current set of accumulated judgments, to refine our estimates of the model parameters.

Lacking *a priori* known correct answers to every question, we scored this experiment as follows. For a given set of posteriors from an experimental run, we computed the element-wise dot product of this set with the set of posteriors estimated by running expectation-maximization over the entire data set. We then computed a normalized score by dividing this dot product by the product of the total-data posterior with itself. (We dropped 6 questions whose answer was determined to be "skip".)

For the control groups, we obtained a score of 0.86 with $n = 2$, a score of 0.90 with $n = 3$), a score of 0.90 with $n = 4$, and a score of 0.91 with $n = 5$. For the test groups, we obtained a score of 0.89 with $n = 2$ and a score of 0.91 with $n = 3$.

In other words, by choosing contributors with a high expected information contribution, we were able to achieve results with only two or three contributors per question comparable to those obtained from four or five contributors per question chosen arbitrarily.

Galaxy Zoo 2

The Galaxy Zoo project [19] is an ongoing crowdsourcing effort to classify galaxies from deep-field surveys. The component known as Galaxy Zoo 2 [32] (`http://zoo2.galaxyzoo.org`) asked its users to answer a sequence of questions in order to identify each object. For example, if a user identified an object as an elliptical galaxy, the next question asked the galaxy's shape; on the other hand, if the user identified the object as a spiral galaxy, subsequent questions would ask for the number and packing density of the spirals.

To simplify the data set, we first collapsed each set of judgments for a given object and contributor into a single classification judgment. We dropped several questions in order to reduce the dimension of the answer space to the following nine classes: three classes of elliptical galaxies (round, cigar-shaped, and intermediate), one class for disk galaxies seen edge-on, four classes for disk galaxies with or without bars and with or without spirals, and one class for non-galaxies. This simplification made judgment resolution easily tractable using a nine-by-nine confusion matrix for each contributor.

As in the Freebase experiment above, we ran the experiment by selectively replaying contributors' actual judgments. In order to have sufficient flexibility in scheduling, we needed a data set comprising contributors with lots of judgments. From the 13,880,502 recorded judgments of 355,990 objects by 83,906 contributors, we iteratively subtracted objects with fewer than 15 judgments each and contributors with fewer than 800 judgments each, repeating the process until the set stabilized at 6,159,423 judgments of 272,270 objects by 2,956 contributors.

We generated reference classifications for each object by running expectation-maximization over all the judgments in this data set using the confusion matrix model and taking the most likely classification in each case. We computed the per-question entropy to be 2.72 bits. Contributor mutual information ranged from 0 bits (for a contributor who gave 997 judgments, all "non-galaxy") to 1.68 bits per question.

We scored our algorithm and two control-group algorithms at various points by running expectation-maximization over all the data they had collected so far and computing the proportion of the resulting classifications that matched the reference classifications.

Each algorithm was given ten rounds in which to assign objects to contributors. Each round consisted of collecting 92 judgments from each contributor.[4]

[4]This batch size was chosen as a computational convenience, with the mean number of judgments collected per round approximately equal to the total number of objects, although the judgments were not evenly distributed between the objects. Also, some contributors ran out of judgments before the end of the experiment.

Our algorithm, in order to play fair, started with no knowledge of the contributors' confusion matrices. In the first round, we had it assign to each contributor the set of 92 available objects (where "available" means "classified by this contributor in the real experiment but not yet in this simulation") with the most judgments already collected, thus collecting judgments for only a small number of objects. Although this approach is inefficient at determining actual classifications, it has the benefit of giving the algorithm a good initial estimate of the contributors' confusion matrices.[5] In each subsequent round, the algorithm formed new maximum-likelihood estimates of the confusion matrices by running expectation-maximization over all judgments collected so far, and then assigned to each contributor the subset of 92 available objects with the highest values of mutual information conditioned on the judgments already collected for that object, as defined by equation (6).

We compared our algorithm to a "least-answered" algorithm, which assigned to each contributor at each round the subset of 92 available objects with the fewest judgments collected so far, thus attempting to equalize the number of judgments collected across all objects.

We also included a "random-assignment" algorithm, which assigned to each contributor at each round a randomly chosen subset of 92 available objects.

We scored each of the three algorithms after each round of judgment collection. The results are presented in figure 5. Our algorithm showed poor results after the first round in which it accepted redundant judgments in order to bootstrap its estimates of the confusion matrices, but then quickly caught up and consistently outperformed the two control algorithms. In later rounds the gap closed because there were fewer available judgments to choose from, a limitation of the "replay" nature of this experiment, so the three algorithms' judgment sets and classifications began to converge to the full data set and its reference classifications.

We expect that we have only scratched the surface of the scheduling problem. Although the models we discussed above for search and numeric tasks are too one-dimensional to benefit from online contributor scheduling, one can imagine more sophisticated statistical models that incorporate a notion of domain expertise, for which a scheduling algorithm like those above would progressively identify the domain of a question and assign contributors skilled in that domain.

CONCLUSIONS

We developed the pointwise mutual information metric $\Delta I_{a,j}$, a measure of the amount of information in a contributor's judgment that we use to estimate the correct answer to the question, together with its expected value, the mutual information metric $I(A;J)$, which measures the average information obtained per question from a contributor.

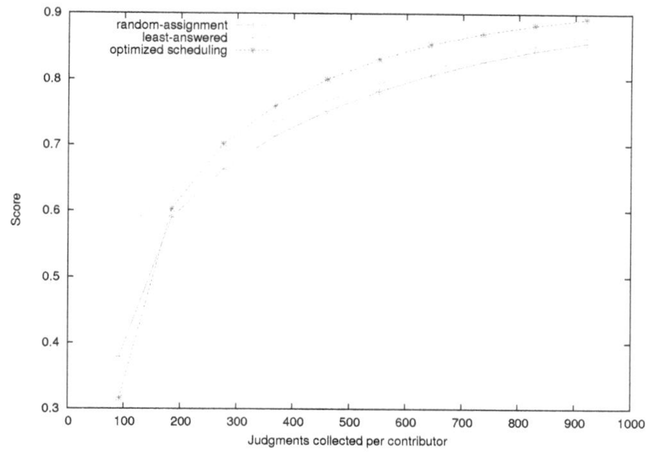

Figure 5. Scoring of three judgment collection algorithms for the Galaxy Zoo 2 experiment at each round of data collection. Our algorithm performs poorly at first because it focuses on getting good initial estimates of confusion matrices, then quickly overtakes the two control group algorithms.

We then explored the use of conditional and multivariate mutual information to capture the interaction between judgments from different contributors (or between multiple judgments from the same contributor).

We showed how to compute these quantities in an experimental environment, and how they can be adapted to different statistical models of contributor behavior, specifically discussing the differences between confusion matrix models and probability-correct models. We provided a simplification that makes our metrics easy to compute even over a very large answer space.

We then described how to use them to optimize question-contributor scheduling, demonstrating the utility of this technique in three experiments.

We believe there is much potential in the information-theoretic approach to contributor evaluation. We will conclude by briefly introducing several possible extensions to the work presented in this paper.

Evaluating Resolution Algorithms

It's important to emphasize that mutual information does not measure correctness of the judgments given. Judgments are collected in order to help us find the correct answers to questions, but we acknowledge that the end result of the collection process must inevitably be *estimates* of the correct answers, not the correct answers themselves. We are only measuring the amount by which contributors help us to arrive at these estimates.

Therefore, our metrics depend very strongly on the estimation techniques used. For example, if the answer to each question is estimated using majority voting among the judgments collected for that question, than we are rewarding conformity and nothing else. If we use a probability-correct model where a confusion matrix model would be more appropriate, then we are ignoring (and punishing) the judgments of biased workers. If we use a probability-correct model for questions

[5] When we tried the experiment without this seeding approach, the results were no better than the control groups, we believe because of the sparsity of the incidence matrix between contributors and objects in such a large-scale crowdsourcing project.

over interval scales, then we reward the single contributor the model decides is most likely correct and punish the others even if their answers are very close to the estimated correct answer.

In summary, the value of contributors' judgments is linked to our use of those judgments. If we make good estimates of the answers to our questions, then we value good judgments highly, and if we make poor estimates, then we place little value on good judgments.

Turning this problem around, we arrive at another application for our metrics: as a test of the health of a resolution algorithm. If an algorithm yields low values of $I(A;J)$ for many contributors, then by definition, that algorithm is making very little use of those contributors' judgments. Another algorithm that yields higher values of $I(A;J)$ is making more use of the same judgments and is likely to be producing better-informed estimates of the correct answers.

Interaction with Reproducibility

The use of Krippendorff's alpha as a measure of the overall statistical health of the collection process can be coupled with the information-theoretic approach.

Since alpha is computed using only the judgments and does not depend on the resolution algorithm, it can be used as an early warning system for ill-defined tasks or poorly-briefed contributors.

We expect that, in addition to Paritosh's argument [20] that reproducibility is a prerequisite for accurate resolutions, reproducibility is also a prerequisite for obtaining high value from judgments.

The reason for this is that a task with low alpha is one in which judgments for the same question are not well-correlated with each other, and therefore cannot be well correlated with the correct answers. Hence, a set of judgments with low alpha must necessarily have low information, under any resolution mechanism.

Establishing a mathematical or empirical relationship between alpha and mutual information is a potential topic for future work.

Normalized Information

$I(A;J)$ measures contributor performance in extensive physical units. In some applications, we may instead be more interested in a normalized (intensive) score for contributor performance, on a fixed scale.[6]

We can exploit the inequality

$$0 \le I(A;J) \le H(A),$$

which expresses the limits that a worst-case contributor yields no information to the resolution process and that a perfect contributor gives us exactly as much information as is present in the question itself.

[6]For the non-physicists: *extensive* quantities are those which depend on the amount of stuff being measured and are additive, like mass; and *intensive* quantities are those which are invariant under the quantity of stuff being measured, like density.

Thus, we normalize $I(A;J)$ by dividing by the theoretical optimal performance $H(A)$, defining a normalized score

$$C(A;J) \equiv \frac{I(A;J)}{H(A)}$$

for a given contributor, with $0 \le C(A;J) \le 1$.

Weighted Entropy

If we place a higher value on certain outcomes and we wish to incentivize contributors accordingly, we can attach weights $\boldsymbol{w}$ to the outcomes in equation (1), subscripted either by a or by a and j together, yielding weighted information $w_a \cdot \Delta I_{a,j}$ or $w_{a,j} \cdot \Delta I_{a,j}$. Then equation (2) becomes

$$I_{\boldsymbol{w}}(A;J) = \sum_a w_a \sum_j p_{a,j} \log \frac{p_{a|j}}{p_a}$$

or

$$I_{\boldsymbol{w}}(A;J) = \sum_{a,j} w_{a,j} p_{a,j} \log \frac{p_{a|j}}{p_a},$$

respectively.

For instance, if we consider it especially important to identify objects of class a_2 correctly in the example above, we can use weights $w_1 = 2$ and $w_2 = 1$, so that our contributor's work on objects the resolution algorithm determines to be in class a_2 is given twice as much weight as that contributor's work on objects of class a_1.

On the other hand, if we wish specifically to discourage mistaking objects of class a_2 for class a_1 (as our contributor is known to do), we can set $w_{2,1} = 2$ and $w_{a,j} = 1$ otherwise, thus punishing our contributor for making that mistake. This works as long as $\Delta I_{2,1} < 0$; if $\Delta I_{2,1} > 0$, then the mistake actually helps rather than hinders the resolution process, so the added weight incentivizes the mistake.

ACKNOWLEDGMENTS

Many thanks to colleagues Praveen Paritosh, Ronen Vaisenberg, Reilly Rose Hayes, Jamie Taylor, Stefano Mazzocchi, Ellen Spertus, Colin Evans, Viral Shah, Micah Saul, Robert Klapper, and Dario Amodei, for valuable comments, conversations, and suggestions during this work.

We are especially grateful to Chris Lintott and Arfon Smith for providing us with data from Galaxy Zoo 2, to Peter Welinder for sharing with us the raw data from an early bounding-box experiment, and to Michael Shwe for providing us with the data from the Freebase political parties task.

REFERENCES

1. Beal, M. J. *Variational algorithms for approximate Bayesian inference*. PhD thesis, Gatsby Computational Neuroscience Unit, University College London, 2003.
2. Card, S. K., Moran, T. P., and Newell, A. The model human processor: An engineering model of human performance. In *Handbook of Perception and Human Performance*, K. R. Boff, L. Kaufman, and J. P. Thomas, Eds., vol. 2: Cognitive Processes and Performance. Wiley-Interscience, 1986, ch. 45, 1–35.

3. Card, S. W., and Mohan, C. K. Ensemble selection for evolutionary learning using information theory and price's theorem. In *Proc. GECCO 2006*, ACM Press (2006), 1587–1588.
4. Chen, Y., Dimitrov, S., Sami, R., Reeves, D. M., Pennock, D. M., Hanson, R. D., Fortnow, L., and Gonen, R. Gaming prediction markets: Equilibrium strategies with a market maker. *Algorithmica 58*, 4 (2010), 930–969.
5. Chi, E. H., and Mytkowicz, T. Understanding the efficiency of social tagging systems using information theory. In *Proc. HT 2008*, ACM Press (2008), 81–88.
6. Dawid, A. P., and Skene, A. M. Maximum likelihood estimation of observer error-rates using the EM algorithm. *Applied Statistics* (1979), 20–28.
7. Dempster, A. P., Laird, N. M., and Rubin, D. B. Maximum likelihood from incomplete data via the EM algorithm. *Journal of the Royal Statistical Society. Series B (Methodological) 39*, 1 (1977), 1–38.
8. Dow, S., Kulkarni, A., Bunge, B., Nguyen, T., Klemmer, S., and Hartmann, B. Shepherding the crowd: managing and providing feedback to crowd workers. In *Ext. Abstracts CHI 2011*, ACM Press (2011), 1669–1674.
9. Gelfand, A. E., and Smith, A. F. M. Sampling-based approaches to calculating marginal densities. *Journal of the American Statistical Association 85*, 410 (June 1990), 398–409.
10. Geman, S., and Geman, D. Stochastic relaxation, Gibbs distributions, and the Bayesian restoration of images. *IEEE Transactions on Pattern Analysis and Machine Intelligence*, 6 (1984), 721–741.
11. Hanson, R. Logarithmic market scoring rules for modular combinatorial information aggregation. *The Journal of Prediction Markets 1*, 1 (2007), 3–15.
12. Hartley, H. O. Maximum likelihood estimation from incomplete data. *Biometrics 14*, 2 (June 1958), 174–194.
13. Hastings, W. K. Monte carlo sampling methods using markov chains and their applications. *Biometrika 57*, 1 (1970), 97–109.
14. Hick, W. E. On the rate of gain of information. *Quarterly Journal of Experimental Psychology 4* (1952), 11–26.
15. Ipeirotis, P. G., Provost, F., and Wang, J. Quality management on Amazon Mechanical Turk. In *Proc. HCOMP 2010*, ACM Press (2010), 64–67.
16. Kochhar, S., Mazzocchi, S., and Paritosh, P. The anatomy of a large-scale human computation engine. In *Proc. HCOMP 2010*, ACM Press (2010), 10–17.
17. Krippendorff, K. Estimating the reliability, systematic error and random error of interval data. *Educational and Psychological Measurement 30*, 1 (1970), 61–70.
18. Lazo, A. V., and Rathie, P. On the entropy of continuous probability distributions. *IEEE Transactions on Information Theory 24*, 1 (1978), 120–122.
19. Lintott, C. J., Schawinski, K., Slosar, A., Land, K., Bamford, S., Thomas, D., Raddick, M. J., Nichol, R. C., Szalay, A., Andreescu, D., Murray, P., and van den Berg, J. Galaxy Zoo: Morphologies derived from visual inspection of galaxies from the Sloan Digital Sky Survey. *Monthly Notices of the Royal Astronomical Society 389*, 3 (2008), 1179–1189.
20. Paritosh, P. Human computation must be reproducible. In *Proc. First International Workshop on Crowdsourcing Web Search* (2012), 20–25.
21. Quinn, A. J., and Bederson, B. B. Human computation: a survey and taxonomy of a growing field. In *Proc. CHI 2011*, ACM Press (2011), 1403–1412.
22. Shannon, C. E. A mathematical theory of communication. *The Bell System Technical Journal 27*, 3 (1948), 379–423. Part 1 of 2.
23. Shannon, C. E., and Weaver, W. *The Mathematical Theory of Communication*. University of Illinois Press, 1949.
24. Shaw, A. D., Horton, J. J., and Chen, D. L. Designing incentives for inexpert human raters. In *Proc. CSCW 2011*, ACM Press (2011), 275–284.
25. Sheng, V. S., Provost, F., and Ipeirotis, P. G. Get another label? Improving data quality and data mining using multiple, noisy labelers. In *Proc. KDD 2008*, ACM Press (2008), 614–622.
26. Simpson, E., Roberts, S., Psorakis, I., and Smith, A. Dynamic Bayesian combination of multiple imperfect classifiers. *ArXiv e-prints* (June 2012).
27. Tanner, M. A., and Wong, W. H. The calculation of posterior distributions by data augmentation. *Journal of the American Statistical Association 82*, 398 (June 1987), 528–540.
28. Walsh, B. Markov chain Monte Carlo and Gibbs sampling, 2004. Lecture Notes for EEB 581.
29. Welinder, P., Branson, S., Belongie, S., and Perona, P. The multidimensional wisdom of crowds. In *Advances in Neural Information Processing Systems*, vol. 23, NIPS (2010), 2424–2432.
30. Welinder, P., and Perona, P. Online crowdsourcing: rating annotators and obtaining cost-effective labels. In *Proc. CVPR 2010*, IEEE (2010), 25–32.
31. Whitehill, J., Ruvolo, P., Wu, T., Bergsma, J., and Movellan, J. Whose vote should count more: Optimal integration of labels from labelers of unknown expertise. *Advances in Neural Information Processing Systems 22* (2009), 2035–2043.
32. Willett, K. W., Lintott, C. J., et al. In preparation.
33. Yan, Y., Rosales, R., Fung, G., and Dy, J. Active learning from crowds. In *Proc. ICML 2011*, IMLS (2011), 1161–1168.
34. Yang-Peláez, J., and Flowers, W. C. Information content measures of visual displays. In *Proc. InfoVis 2000*, IEEE (2000), 99–103.

Enhancing Reliability Using Peer Consistency Evaluation in Human Computation

Shih-Wen Huang and Wai-Tat Fu
University of Illinois at Urbana-Champaign
Department of Computer Science
201 N Goodwin Avenue
Urbana, IL 61801
{shuang51, wfu}@illinois.edu

ABSTRACT
Peer consistency evaluation is often used in games with a purpose (GWAP) to evaluate workers using outputs of other workers without using gold standard answers. Despite its popularity, the reliability of peer consistency evaluation has never been systematically tested to show how it can be used as a general evaluation method in human computation systems. We present experimental results that show that human computation systems using peer consistency evaluation can lead to outcomes that are even better than those that evaluate workers using gold standard answers. We also show that even without evaluation, simply telling the workers that their answers will be used as future evaluation standards can significantly enhance the workers' performance. Results have important implication for methods that improve the reliability of human computation systems.

Author Keywords
Crowdsourcing; Human Computation; User Behavior; Mechanical Turk; Evaluation

ACM Classification Keywords
K.6.0 [Management of Computing & Information Systems]: General.

INTRODUCTION
Human computation [15] is a technique that utilizes human activities to replace traditional digital computers to perform certain computational tasks. The benefit of human computation is that some problems that are often difficult for machines can be accomplished relatively easily for humans (e.g., vision, natural language processing). The ESP game [29], for example, encourages players to generate image labels while enjoying the game. Human computation is also used for security [1], speech-to-text translation [17], and generation of labeled data for natural language processing [27]. These examples have merely begun to demonstrate the potential of human computation as a social computing technique that can be applied in a wide range of situations.

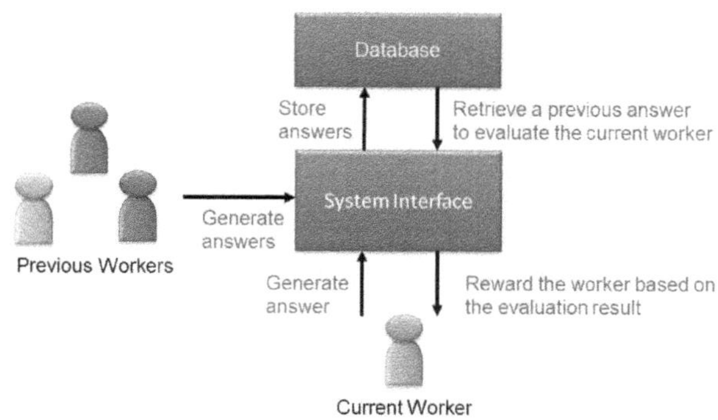

Figure 1. A graphical representation of peer consistency evaluation. Every worker in the system is evaluated by the answers provided by the previous workers, which means it is a very scalable mechanism.

One of the biggest challenges for developing effective human computation systems is the reliability of the outcomes [11]. Unlike traditional computational systems, workers in a human computation system may fail to reliably generate correct outputs for many reasons. One notable reason is that workers may not have the incentives to put forth enough effort to finish the task assigned to them [24]. Another reason is that the instructions given to the workers may not be clear enough for them to follow [23]. These factors have made it difficult to build a reliable human computation system. The potential unreliability may in general decrease the utility of human computation systems. Systematic testing of methods that can potentially enhance the reliability of human computation systems is therefore critical for their success.

Peer consistency evaluation in output agreement games
Games with a purpose(GWAP) [30] harness the power of human computation by making their players work while enjoying the games. An output agreement game is one of the earliest and most popular forms of GWAP. A typical output agreement game has the following procedure: the game first randomly matches multiple players and provides them the same set of inputs, which can be images [29], words [26], or any

data that the game designer wants to label. Then, the players start to generate outputs that are related to the inputs. The players will be rewarded if the outputs generated by different players reach a certain level of agreement. When the game ends, some versions of the agreed outputs will be collected as the labels that describe the data.

Output agreement games use the *consistency between the players to ensure the quality of the collected data.* Although previous research questioned whether peer consistency evaluation used in an output agreement game can persuade workers to generate high-quality outputs [25], recent research [9] has shown that the gaming environment not only could encourage the players to generate answers that matched other players' responses, but could also encourage players to generate high-quality answers.

These results allow us to hypothesize that human computation systems with peer consistency evaluation could outperform those without any evaluation because peer consistency evaluation provide evaluation standards that can approximate correct answers. This is our first hypothesis.

H1: *Peer consistency evaluation can serve as a valid evaluation method to motivate workers to generate outcomes with high-quality. Therefore, workers with peer consistency evaluation have better performance than those without evaluation.*

Peer consistency as a better evaluation mechanism

Existing human computation systems often use gold standard answers to evaluate their workers [6, 16, 22, 24]. A gold standard answer is an objectively determined correct answer. For example, gold standard answers for a part-of-speech (POS) tagging task can be the correct POS of each word in the sentences or articles of the tasks determined by human experts (e.g., linguists). Therefore, gold standard evaluation is considered one of the most objective mechanisms that can accurately measure the performance of workers.

However, gold standard answers of a task can be very costly [22]. Thus, people often compromise by mixing a few tasks that have the gold standard answers with the majority of tasks without them, and evaluation is often only based on those that have the gold standard answers. This may decrease the effectiveness of the evaluation because repeated workers can find out and only work hard on the evaluation questions [22]. On the other hand, peer consistency evaluation directly utilizes outputs of previous workers to evaluate outcomes of future workers, such that the system can generate abundant questions to evaluate workers. Therefore, an important focus of the current article is to investigate the extent to which peer consistency evaluation can be as effective as gold standard evaluation to encourage high quality outcomes from workers, because *peer consistency evaluation is much more scalable and cost-effective.*

Compared with gold standard evaluation, a potential advantage of peer consistency evaluation is that it may also increase the perception that workers are connected to other workers in the system, as workers are informed that their answers will be evaluated by the answers of others and their answers will also be used to evaluate future workers' answers. *The implicit social interactions among workers* could serve as a form of social motivation for workers to work harder. For example, workers may be motivated to match the performance of others - a competitive motive; or to provide good answers to evaluate future workers - an altruistic motive [9]. Peer evaluation *also makes the rewards of the workers dependent on each others' answers.* This is because if one worker does not generate the correct answer, the other workers would be incorrectly penalized due to this erroneous evaluation standard. This can be another incentive for them to put more effort into the tasks because it is possible that workers may have the altruistic tendency to adjust their effort level to avoid unfair evaluation to future workers [2]. As a result, workers may realize that their performance not only affect their personal reward, but also the reward of their "colleagues".

Therefore, the altruism of workers can provide another motive for them to generate high-quality outcomes, which is our second hypothesis:

H2: *Peer consistency evaluation can further motivate workers utilizing the altruism of them. As a result, the workers with peer consistency evaluation can perform better than those with gold standard evaluation.*

On the other hand, this may also increase the perception of unfairness in the evaluation because it sometimes incorrectly penalizes the workers – i.e., if previous workers provided bad answers, the new workers might be penalized even if they generate good answers. The perception of unfair evaluation may decrease the incentives for the workers to provide good answers. This leads us to the third hypothesis:

H3: *The unfairness of peer consistency evaluation can discourage workers to put effort in generating good work, which harms the reliability of the system.*

The experiments

In the current study, we aim at examining the three hypotheses mentioned above by experiments that teased out different effects.

Our first experiment tested whether systems with peer consistency evaluation can generate reliable outcomes compared with systems with gold standard evaluation and with no evaluation (**H1**). Because it is possible that financial incentives may interact with the evaluation method, we also created three bonus levels in each evaluation condition to investigate their effects. Moreover, our second experiment separated the effects of evaluation and altruism of peer consistency evaluation to see if altruism itself was effective in enhancing worker performance (**H2**). Finally, we analyzed how the unfairness (incorrect penalty) affected the performance of workers in peer consistency evaluation (**H3**).

RELATED WORK

Human computation and crowdsourcing are two highly overlapped fields. However, the focus of the fields are slightly different – human computation tends to focus more on replacing digital computers with humans while crowdsouring focus more on replacing traditional human workers with online workers [24]. Therefore, the research in crowdsourcing often focuses more on managing the workflow to solve complex work [12, 13, 14]. On the other hand, research in human computation focuses more on generating reliable answers to questions that are difficult for digital computers to solve [24]. Given our goal is to understand tasks that are often difficult to handle by digital computers (e.g., natural language processing), we choose to use the term human computation throughout. We, however, believe that research in crowdsourcing is highly relevant to our research.

Many approaches have been proposed to enhance the reliability of human computation. Some researchers used statistical methods to eliminate errors and biases of the outcomes generated by the workers [3, 7, 11, 18, 27]. Other researchers proposed different task designs to induce workers to produce high-quality outputs. Huang *et al.* [8] proposed a prediction model that helped the requester achieve an optimized task design by varying the variables in the design (e.g. price, number of tasks). Dow *et al.* [4] showed that instant self-assessment and external-assessment could enhance the quality of the work. Sun *et al.* [28] found that it is easier for workers to pick the better answer than generate the good answer. Therefore, they designed a tournament selection method that asks the workers to pick the better answers at each round. Mason and Watts [21] studied the relation between the financial incentives and the performance of the workers. They found that the amount of financial incentives did not affect the performance of the workers, but some compensation schemes did yield better outcomes. Lin *et al.* [19] designed AGENTHUNT, a system that can dynamically switch between alternative workflows to achieve better worker performance. Little *et al.* created Turkit [20], a framework that allowed the workers to iteratively improve the previous workers' work. Liem *et al.* [17] further incorporated a dual pathway structure to the system. The dual pathway structure evaluated the workers in one path using the works of the workers in the other path, and rewarded the workers based on the similarity between their works. They showed that the system with their proposed structure could achieve 96.6% accuracy on a speech-to-text transcription task. Although they did show that a system with peer consistency evaluation could have good performance, they focused on a particular application and did not analyze how and why peer consistency evaluation could enhance the reliability of the systems. Therefore, the main contribution of their study and ours differ.

Gold standard evaluation

Gold standard evaluation is another mechanism that often adopted by human computation researchers [6, 16, 22] and industry (e.g., CrowdFlower[1]) to ensure the quality of human computation outcomes. Le *et al.* [16] studied how to spread the gold standard evaluation questions to enhance the reliability of collected outcomes. Harris [6] also showed that providing positive incentives for workers to match gold standard answers yield better works. Oleson *et al.* [22] noticed that gold standard data is difficult and costly to get, but the size of gold standard data is important to quality assurance. They solved this problem by using previous matched answers with high confidence as "programmatic gold" to expand the size of gold standard data. Though both programmatic gold and peer consistency evaluation use answers of previous workers to evaluate newer workers, the former mechanism aims to create more gold standard answers in a cost-effective way, while the latter directly tell the workers that their answers will be evaluated by an answer of a previous worker. Therefore, programmatic gold cannot benefit from the possible social interactions between the workers of peer consistency evaluation.

To the best of our knowledge, our study is the first one that makes a systematic comparison between peer consistency evaluation and traditional gold standard evaluation and proves that peer consistency evaluation is a valid mechanism to enhance the reliability of human computation.

EXPERIMENTAL DESIGN

The goal of our experiment is to see whether peer consistency evaluation can improve the reliability of human computation systems. We recruited 270 subjects from Amazon Mechanical Turk (AMT)[2], a platform that recruits online workers to solve human intelligence tasks (HITs) [10]. We asked the workers to perform tasks on systems with no evaluation (N), gold standard evaluation (GS), and peer consistency evaluation (PC). We also varied the level of bonus the workers could receive when passing the evaluation to study if there were interactions between the financial incentives and evaluation methods.

Noun counting task

The workers in our experiment were asked to count the words with a particular part-of-speech (noun) in a list of 30 words. Each word in the word list had equal probabilities to be a noun or not a noun. We created 1,000 tasks, and the answers to the tasks ranged from 7 to 23. Since we recruited 270 workers in our experiment and each worker completed five tasks, 1,350 tasks were randomly picked from the task pool. There were two advantages of this task that made it a very good test-bed for us to examine the ability of the evaluation mechanisms to enhance reliability. First, it had a ground truth (objectively correct answer) to serve as the gold standard, so the quality of an answer could be measured by the difference between the answer and the gold standard. Moreover, the workers needed to put in a certain level of effort to solve the task[3]. This task is also representative of the tasks used in previous human computation systems (e.g., [27, 29]). An example interface of the task is shown in Figure 2.

Evaluation mechanisms in the systems

In our experiment, we compared the systems with three evaluation mechanisms:

- **No evaluation (N)**: The system with no evaluation was used to imitate a basic human computation system. The workers who worked in the system received a bonus regardless of the quality of the answers that they generated.

[1] https://crowdflower.com/

[2] https://www.mturk.com/mturk/welcome

[3] The difference between an average answer and the gold standard was 3.78, which supports our argument.

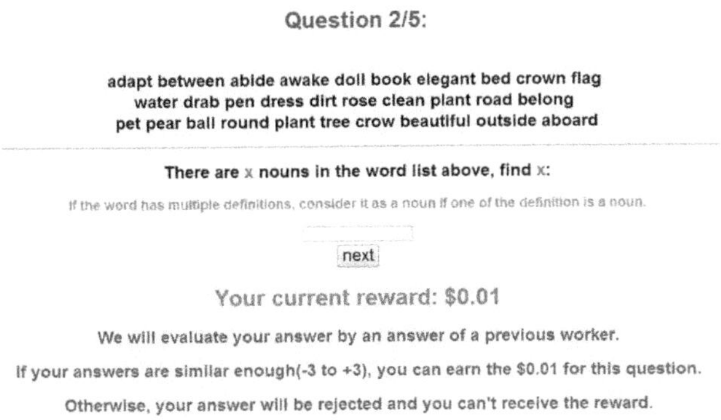

Figure 2. An example interface of the noun counting task

- **Gold standard evaluation (GS)**: In the system with gold standard evaluation, the answers generated by the workers were evaluated by the correct answers. The workers earned a bonus if their answer was accurate enough. We allowed the workers to make some minor mistakes by accepting the answers with difference to the gold standards less than or equal to three[4].

- **Peer consistency evaluation (PC)**: Peer consistency evaluation was similar to gold standard evaluation, but the standards used to evaluate the workers were different. When a worker was working with a system utilizing peer consistency evaluation, the system first randomly picked a previous worker and used the answer generated by that previous worker as the standard of evaluation. Then, the worker who was performing the task could earn a bonus if the difference between the answer of the current worker and the evaluation standard was less than or equal to three (the same difference as in gold standard evaluation).

Bonus levels

The workers who worked in the experiment could earn a low bonus ($0.01), a medium bonus ($0.05), or a high bonus ($0.10) if they passed the evaluation of the task. We chose these three bonus levels based on an empirical study [10] that shows that more than 90% of the HITs on AMT have a price tag less than $0.10, and 70% of them have a price tag less than $0.05. These are also the three financial incentive levels used in [21]. Of course, the reasonable price of a task should be determined by many factors (e.g., difficulty of task, interestingness of work). However, the purpose of this manipulation is to understand the extent to which the effects of different evaluation methods might interact with those induced by different levels of financial incentives.

Subject recruitment on Amazon Mechanical Turk

We published our HITs on AMT from 5/13/2012 to 5/22/2012. The title and the description of these HITs were both "Count the nouns in a word list". We did not require our workers to pass any qualification tests, but we did require them to have more than 100 approved HITs and a HIT approval rate higher than 95%. This is a quality assurance mechanism usually used by requesters in AMT, and it prevented the results of our experiment from being affected by too many spammers. The price tags for the HITs were $0.05, which were the rewards the workers could earn regardless of their performance. On the HIT page, we provided a link to route the workers to our experiment website and a text area for the workers to enter a unique eight-digit completion code. When the workers completed their jobs, our website showed them the total bonus they could earn for their performance and the completion code that they could enter in the original HIT page on AMT. We then paid the workers both of their rewards (performance independent) and bonuses (performance codependent) based on the completion codes they entered.

Experimental interface

After the workers visited the experiment website, they were randomly assigned to one of the 9 conditions[5]. On the introduction page, the system told the workers that they had to answer 5 questions about counting the nouns in a word list. It also showed how much bonus they could earn for each question. After starting the task, the workers could see the interface for performing the noun counting task (Figure 2). In the upper part of the interface, the system showed a word list and an input box for them to provide their answers. The system specifically told the workers to count a word as a noun if one of its definition is a noun because it is possible for a word to have multiple definitions and only some of them are nouns. This made the gold standard answer of the question clearer to the workers. The system also told the workers how it would evaluate them in the lower part of the interface. The exact words used in this part by different systems are summarized below:

- **No evaluation (N)**: You can earn bonus[6] for providing the answer.

- **Gold standard evaluation (GS)**: We will evaluate your answer by the correct answer. If your answer is similar enough (-3 to +3) to the correct answer, you can earn bonus for this question. Otherwise, your answer will be rejected and you can't receive the reward.

- **Peer Consistency Evaluation (PC)**: We will evaluate your answer by an answer of a previous worker. If your answers are similar enough (-3 to +3), you can earn the bonus for this question. Otherwise, your answer will be rejected and you can't receive the reward.

When the workers finished each question, the system informed the workers whether they passed the evaluation or not. If they passed the evaluation, the system added the bonus of the question to the total bonus earned by the workers and show it in the middle part of the interface. After finishing 5 questions, the workers would be redirected to a completion page which showed them the amount of bonus they could earn and the completion code.

[4]We tried only accepting the answers that were exactly correct, but this greatly hurt the performance of the workers as providing the exact number of nouns in a long word list can sometimes be very difficult.

[5]3 evaluation mechanisms X 3 bonus levels.

[6]It showed the amount of bonus: $0.01, $0.05, or $0.10

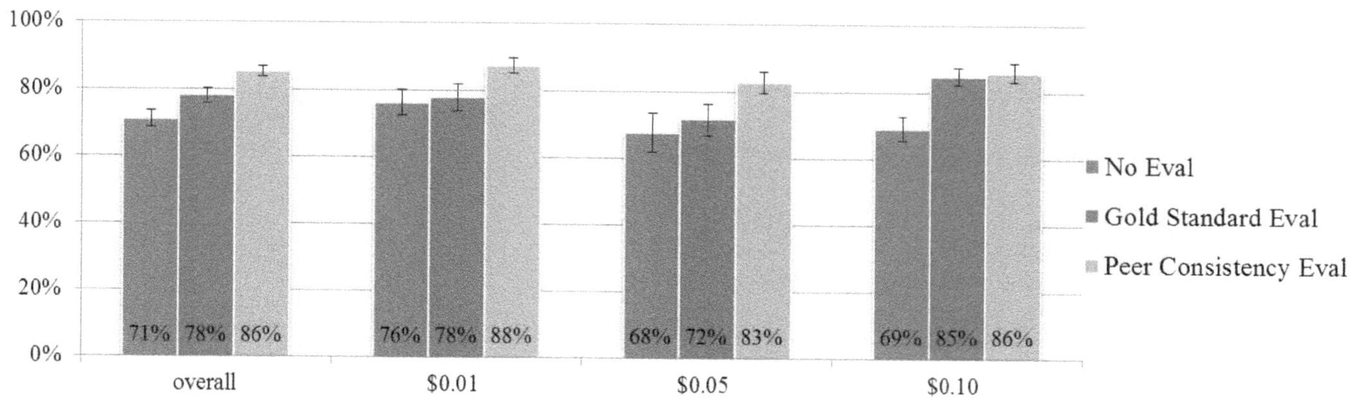

Figure 3. The mean of the average label accuracies of the workers under different evaluation mechanisms and bonus levels (with standard error). In general, the workers under peer consistency evaluation outperformed the ones under gold standard evaluation and without evaluation.

	N vs. GS	N vs. PC	GS vs. PC
overall	71%(24.7%) vs. 78%(21.3%)* (t(174) = 2.04, p < 0.05)	71%(24.7%) vs. 86%(14.6%)* (t(144) = 4.75, p < 0.001)	78%(21.3%) vs. 86%(14.6%)* (t(158) = 2.62, p < 0.005)
0.01	76%(21.5%) vs. 78%(21.7%) (t(58) = 0.26, p = 0.79)	76%(21.5%) vs. 88%(11.8%)* (t(45) = 2.47, p < 0.01)	78%(21.7%) vs. 88%(11.8%)* (t(45) = 2.13, p < 0.05)
0.05	68%(31.6%) vs. 72%(25.5%) (t(56) = 0.53, p = 0.60)	68%(31.6%) vs. 83%(16.8%)* (t(44) = 2.32, p < 0.05)	72%(25.5%) vs. 83%(16.8%)* (t(50) = 2.01, p < 0.05)
0.10	69%(19.6%) vs. 85%(13.5%)* (t(52) = 3.64, p < 0.001)	69%(19.6%) vs. 86%(15.1%)* (t(55) = 3.77, p < 0.001)	85%(13.5%) vs. 86%(15.1%) (t(57) = 0.33, p = 0.74)

Table 1. The comparison between the mean (standard deviation) of the average label accuracy of different evaluation mechanism at various bonus levels and their t-test statistics. The significant results (p-value < 0.05) are marked with *.

RESULTS

270 subjects (30 subjects per treatment) were recruited from AMT, each of them completed 5 noun counting task and generated 5 labels, so 1,350 labels (150 labels per treatment) were collected for our result analysis.

To evaluate the results of our experiment, we first computed the label accuracy of each collected label. The label accuracy shows how close the label is to the gold standard answer. Therefore, the formula for label accuracy is:

$$Label\ Accuracy = 1 - \frac{|N_{GS} - N_{worker}|}{Max(30 - N_{GS}, N_{GS})}$$

Where N_{GS} is the correct number of nouns in the list, N_{worker} is the number of nouns in the list reported by the worker. Therefore, the numerator of the second term in the formula is the distance between the label generated by the worker and the gold standard answer, and the denominator of it is the distance between the worst possible answer and the gold standard answer. (If $N_{GS} > 15$, the worst possible answer is 0. Otherwise, it is 30.) Therefore, the label accuracy is a number between 1 and 0, where 1 represents that the label is exactly the same as the gold standard, and 0 means that the answer is the worst possible answer. Then the average label accuracy of each worker was computed by averaging the label accuracy of the five labels generated by the worker. We used the average label accuracy of the workers to measure their quality of works.

We conducted a 3X3 ANOVA to see if there were significant effects of the evaluation mechanisms, bonus levels, and their interactions. The results showed that the evaluation mechanisms did significantly affect the average label accuracy of the workers ($F(2, 261) = 11.08$, $p < 0.001$). Moreover, the effect of bonus levels was marginally significant ($F(2, 261) = 2.72$, $p = 0.067$). However, the effect of the interactions of the two factors were not significant ($F(4, 261) = 1.15$, $p = 0.34$). Because the analysis shows that the effects of bonus levels is only marginal to significant and the interaction between evaluation method and bonus levels was not significant, in the current result analysis, we focus on the effects of the evaluation mechanisms.

The effects of the evaluation mechanisms

The mean of the average label accuracies for the workers with different evaluation mechanisms and bonus levels are summarized in Figure 3 and the comparisons between different conditions are summarized in Table 1. The results show that the average label accuracy of the workers in the systems with peer consistency evaluation was significantly higher than the systems with no evaluation. In addition, there was also a significant difference between the performance of the workers in the systems with gold standard evaluation and the systems with no evaluation. Interestingly, *the workers in the systems with peer consistency evaluation also outperformed the workers in the systems with gold standard evaluation.*

When we further analyzed the results of the systems with different bonus levels, we observed that with low or medium bonuses ($0.01 or $0.05), the workers under peer consistency evaluation performed significantly better than the workers under no evaluation and the workers under gold standard evaluation. In addition, there was no significant difference between the workers assessed via no evaluation and gold standard evaluation.

However, when we increased the bonus to the highest level ($0.10), there was nearly no difference between the workers under peer consistency evaluation and the ones under gold standard evaluation, and the difference between the workers under gold standard evaluation and the ones under no evaluation became significant.

These differences, of course, need to be interpreted cautiously, as the overall interaction effect between bonus and evaluation method was not significant. Nevertheless, we can see that the difference between the ability to enhance reliability between the two evaluation methods is larger when the workers received low or medium bonuses. While the main effects of evaluation methods and bonus levels are strong, future studies can further test their possible interaction effect by introducing more levels of bonus in different evaluation methods.

Peer consistency as valid evaluation mechanism

Previous research [9] on peer consistency evaluation in output agreement games provided a game theoretic analysis for why it could generate higher quality works in a gaming environment. The analysis showed that because both players in the game would like to earn points, the player chooses the answer that is most likely to be the same as the answer generated by the other player. Thus, the best strategies for both players are putting more effort to select the correct answer for the task (or the answers that are close to it). The reason is that since the players cannot communicate with each other during the game, high-accuracy answers can serve as a protocol for the two players. By choosing the answers that are close to the gold standard answer, it increases the probability for them to generate similar answers and earn points.

Similar analysis also applies to our current study; in our human computation systems with peer consistency evaluation, workers did not know which previous worker would be chosen in the evaluation. As a result, there was no way for them to communicate with each other or agree on some particular answers in advance. Therefore, putting more effort to provide answers with high accuracy would be generally a desirable strategy for workers, which could be a factor that enhanced the overall reliability of the system. This analysis explains why the system with peer consistency evaluation had a higher reliability compared to the systems without evaluation in our experiment. This supports **H1** that *peer consistency evaluation can serve as a valid evaluation mechanism to motivate workers to generate high-quality work.*

Reciprocal altruism facilitating worker performance

A notable difference between peer consistency evaluation and gold standard evaluation is that because the system with peer consistency evaluation used the answers of previous workers as evaluation standards, the performance of the workers not only affected their own bonus, but also the bonus of the future workers of the system. If workers did not put enough effort into selecting a high-quality answer, not only would they lose the chance to earn the bonus, future workers evaluated by this erroneous answer might also not get the bonus. Therefore, workers might have an altruistic motive to put more effort into the task in order to maximize the bonus-earning potential of their "colleagues". (**H2**)

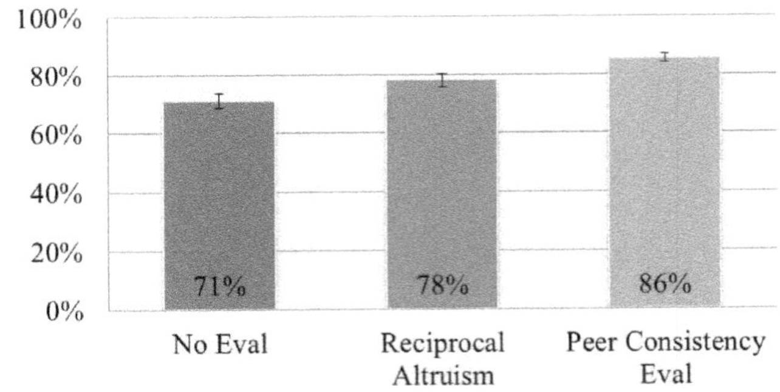

Figure 4. The mean of the average label accuracy of the system with reciprocal altruism compares to the system with no evaluation and peer consistency evaluation.

To test if this hypothesis is true, we created another human computation system with a condition we called *reciprocal altruism (RA)* and recruited 90 workers[7] to conduct the same noun counting task on this system. The workers of the system in the RA condition were not evaluated, but they were told that their answers would be used as evaluation standards to evaluate future workers. In other words, the condition was similar to the peer consistency evaluation condition, *except* that workers were told that their answers would not be evaluated. The exact words we put on the interface were as follows:

- **Reciprocal altruism (RA)**: You can earn bonus for providing the answer. We will use your answer as an evaluation standard for future workers. They can only earn bonus if their answers are similar to yours.

The mean of the average label accuracy of the system with reciprocal altruism is shown in Figure 4. The results showed that even without any evaluation, the workers with reciprocal altruism ($\mu = 78\%$, $SD = 20.8\%$) performed significantly better than those without reciprocal altruism ($\mu = 71\%$, $SD = 24.8\%$) ($t(173) = 2.02$, $p < 0.05$). This provides support to **H2** that the *altruistic motive did make the workers provide more reliable answers*. The other thing we found was that workers under peer consistency evaluation still performed significantly better than those in the RA condition ($t(160) = 2.80$, $p < 0.001$). One reasonable explanation is that both reciprocal altruism (that their answers were used to evaluate future workers) and evaluation feedback (that their answers were evaluated using previous workers answers) are factors that provide additive effects that made workers perform better. Peer consistency evaluation allows its system to benefit from the additional motivating effects of both factors.

[7]30 workers each bonus level

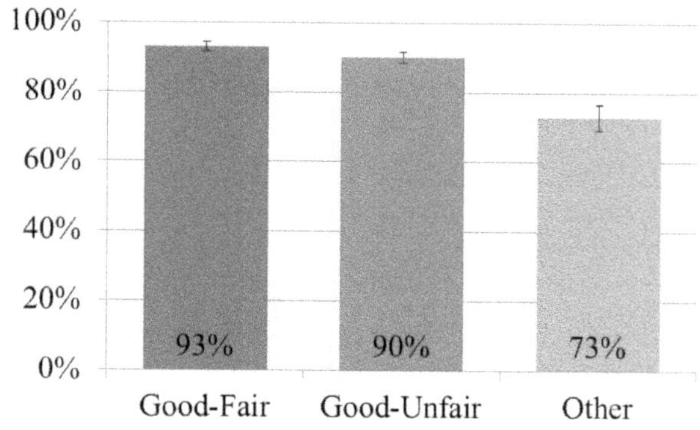

Figure 5. The comparison between the performance of the good workers were treated fairly, unfairly, and other workers under peer consistency evaluation.

Unfairness as insignificant factor in worker performance

It is reasonable to assume that the workers under gold standard evaluation had higher incentives to work harder because peer consistency evaluation sometimes penalized workers even if they put more effort to generate correct answers. (**H3**) Our results, however, clearly showed the opposite effect: workers in peer consistency evaluation conditions outperformed those in gold standard evaluation conditions.

To understand this seemingly counter-intuitive result, we analyzed whether the unfairness of peer consistency evaluation hurt the performance of workers. We divided the 5 questions answered by each worker into two groups, and used the first half (first two questions) to identify those that were *good workers* in peer evaluation condition. Specifically, workers were considered good workers if they generated answers that were similar to the gold standard answers (distance less than 3) in the first 2 questions. These *good workers* should have earned the bonuses if the system evaluated their answers using gold standard answers. 62 out of 90 workers in the systems with peer consistency evaluation were considered good workers by this definition. These good workers were further divided into two groups: the first group was treated fairly, in the sense that they actually earned the bonus because the answers used to evaluate them were also close to the gold standard answers. In contrast, the second group of them were treated unfairly, in the sense that they failed to pass peer consistency evaluation for at least one of the first two questions because they were evaluated by answers that were different from the gold standard answers. 33 good workers were treated fairly, and the other 29 good workers were treated unfairly by the system with peer consistency evaluation in the first two questions. By comparing how these two groups of good workers performed in the next three questions, we could test the extent to which the fairness of evaluation could impact performance.

The mean of the average label accuracies on the next 3 questions (the second half of the 5 questions) of these two groups and other workers that did not do well in the first 2 questions are shown in Figure 5. Although the good workers who were treated fairly ($\mu = 93\%$, $SD = 1.2\%$) performed slightly better than those who got penalized incorrectly ($\mu = 90\%$, $SD = 1.5\%$), the difference of the performance between these two groups was not significant ($t(55) = 1.45$, $p = 0.15$). Moreover, the workers who were treated unfairly still performed significantly better than the other workers that did not perform well in the first two questions ($\mu = 73\%$, $SD = 20.5\%$) ($t(39) = 4.22$, $p < 0.001$). This is in accordance with the previous research that there is a very low correlation between the performance of the workers and the quality of evaluation standard [9]. Therefore, at least in our samples of workers, *we did not find that unfairness of evaluation in peer consistency evaluation could discourage good performance*, which contradicts **H3**.

Implicit social interaction as possible factor in enhancing human computation reliability

Research has shown that social interaction can attract workers to voluntarily conduct tasks for human computation systems [9]. In our experiment, when the workers could earn high levels of bonus, both peer consistency evaluation and gold standard evaluation could enhance the reliability of the systems. However, when the workers only could earn low or medium bonuses, peer consistency evaluation seemed more effective. It is possible that peer consistency evaluation produced a feeling among the workers that they were not doing the task alone because they knew that their answers were to be evaluated by other workers in the systems, and that their answers also would be used to evaluate other workers. This implicit social interaction created a social motivation to encourage them to put extra effort into solving the task. This could explain why the systems with peer consistency evaluation outperformed the systems with gold standard evaluation, especially when workers only receive a minimum level of bonus. In future studies, it will be useful to conduct a series of carefully controlled experiments that focus on how the implicit social interactions created by peer consistency evaluation affect workers' performance.

Possible effects of financial incentive levels

Although the ANOVA results show that the effect of bonus level was only marginally significant, we found weak evidence of a possible trend in our results that might provide useful insights for future studies. Specifically, we found that the means of the average label accuracies of the workers dropped from 81% to 74% when we increased the bonus from \$0.01 to \$0.05, and this number climbed back to 80% when we further raised the bonus to \$0.10. This is in accordance with the findings from previous research [5] that financial incentives not only bring the utility of monetary reward to the workers, they also reduce the intrinsic values (e.g., enjoyment, altruism) for the workers to perform the tasks voluntarily. We believe that this potentially interesting interaction between financial incentives and social motivation will be an important topic for human computation research.

CONCLUSIONS AND FUTURE WORK

In this paper, we show that peer consistency evaluation is effective in enhancing the reliability of human computation systems. Even though the system does not evaluate its workers by gold standard answers, the mechanism is effective in motivating workers to put in their effort to generate answers that are close to the gold standard answers. In fact, we found that although peer consistency evaluation sometimes incorrectly penalizes the workers, the potential unfairness in evaluation does not seem to have a large effect that significantly harms the performance of good workers. Moreover, we show that reciprocal altruism (i.e., preventing future workers from being penalized incorrectly) may even make peer consistency evaluation a better mechanism than traditional gold standard evaluation. Since gold standard answers are costly to generate, this result provides researchers and practitioners in human computation (including crowdsourcing) a much more cost-effective option to ensure system reliability.

In addition, we found that the implicit social interaction of peer consistency evaluation might be another factor that helps to improve reliability. In our experiment, the workers under peer consistency evaluation performed well even when the bonus they could earn was low. This showed that implicit social interaction might provide some form of a social motivation to workers, even when the financial incentive was low. This points to the need to conduct more systematic studies on how social interactions of the workers in a human computation system affect different forms (social, finanicial, or others) of incentives and performance. One possible way is, for example, to test if the workers under peer consistency evaluation are willing to do more tasks than those without it. This could show whether the implicit social interaction really motivates the workers to do the tasks voluntarily. Another possibility is to strengthen the social interactions (e.g., reducing anonymity, message boards) to test how it affects the reliability of the system.

We believe that more studies are needed to test the limitation of peer consistency evaluation by applying it to different kinds of tasks. It is possible that certain tasks may have a wider range of variability of performance, or certain systematic biases may be observed in workers' responses. In these situations, peer consistency evaluation may either lead to worse performance because of the general perception that answers from a previous worker are more likely to be wrong than correct; or that certain biases may be magnified as workers start to perceive that previous workers may likely generate wrong answers (i.e., future workers adapt to bad answers rather than being encouraged to provide good ones). While these are some of the many possible directions that are worthy of pursuing, we believe that results from the current study provides a small but significant step towards better understanding of the complexity involved in a human computation system that are useful for the CSCW community.

ACKNOWLEDGEMENTS

Many thanks to the anonymous reviewers for their valuable comments for us to improve the earlier draft of this work. This paper is also benefited from the discussion with Pei-Fen Tu, Jessie Chin, and Vera Liao.

REFERENCES

1. Ahn, L. V., Blum, M., Hopper, N. J., and Langford, J. Captcha: using hard ai problems for security. In *Proceedings of the 22nd international conference on Theory and applications of cryptographic techniques*, EUROCRYPT'03, Springer-Verlag (Berlin, Heidelberg, 2003), 294–311.
2. Bandiera, O., Barankay, I., and Rasul, I. Social preferences and the response to incentives: Evidence from personnel data. *The Quarterly Journal of Economics 120*, 3 (2005), 917–962.
3. Dawid, A. P., and Skene, A. M. Maximum likelihood estimation of observer error-rates using the em algorithm. *Journal of the Royal Statistical Society. Series C (Applied Statistics) 28*, 1 (1979), pp. 20–28.
4. Dow, S., Kulkarni, A., Klemmer, S., and Hartmann, B. Shepherding the crowd yields better work. In *Proceedings of the ACM 2012 conference on Computer Supported Cooperative Work*, CSCW '12, ACM (New York, NY, USA, 2012), 1013–1022.
5. Gneezy, U., and Rustichini, A. Pay enough or don't pay at all. *The Quarterly Journal of Economics 115*, 3 (2000), 791–810.
6. Harris, C. G. You're hired! an examination of crowdsourcing incentive models in human resourse tasks. In *Proceedings of WSDM 2011 Workshop on Crowdsourcing for Search and Data Mining* (2011).
7. Hirth, M., Hossfeld, T., and Tran-Gia, P. Cost-optimal validation mechanisms and cheat-detection for crowdsourcing platforms. In *Innovative Mobile and Internet Services in Ubiquitous Computing (IMIS), 2011 Fifth International Conference on* (30 2011-july 2 2011), 316 –321.
8. Huang, E., Zhang, H., Parkes, D. C., Gajos, K. Z., and Chen, Y. Toward automatic task design: a progress report. In *Proceedings of the ACM SIGKDD Workshop on Human Computation*, HCOMP '10, ACM (New York, NY, USA, 2010), 77–85.
9. Huang, S.-W., and Fu, W.-T. Systematic analysis of output agreement games: Effects of gaming environment, social interaction, and feedback. In *Proceedings of HCOMP12: The 4th Workshop on Human Computation* (2012).
10. Ipeirotis, P. G. Analyzing the amazon mechanical turk marketplace. *XRDS 17*, 2 (Dec. 2010), 16–21.
11. Ipeirotis, P. G., Provost, F., and Wang, J. Quality management on amazon mechanical turk. In *Proceedings of the ACM SIGKDD Workshop on Human Computation*, HCOMP '10, ACM (New York, NY, USA, 2010), 64–67.
12. Kittur, A., Khamkar, S., André, P., and Kraut, R. Crowdweaver: visually managing complex crowd work. In *Proceedings of the ACM 2012 conference on Computer Supported Cooperative Work*, CSCW '12, ACM (New York, NY, USA, 2012), 1033–1036.

13. Kittur, A., Smus, B., Khamkar, S., and Kraut, R. E. Crowdforge: crowdsourcing complex work. In *Proceedings of the 24th annual ACM symposium on User interface software and technology*, UIST '11, ACM (New York, NY, USA, 2011), 43–52.

14. Kulkarni, A., Can, M., and Hartmann, B. Collaboratively crowdsourcing workflows with turkomatic. In *Proceedings of the ACM 2012 conference on Computer Supported Cooperative Work*, CSCW '12, ACM (New York, NY, USA, 2012), 1003–1012.

15. Law, E., and Von Ahn, L. *Human Computation*. Synthesis Lectures on Artificial Intelligence and Machine Learning. Morgan & Claypool Publishers, 2011.

16. Le, J., Edmonds, A., Hester, V., and Biewald, L. Ensuring quality in crowdsourced search relevance evaluation: The effects of training qustion distribution. In *Proceedings of the SIGIR 2010 Workshop on Crowdsourcing for Search Evaluation* (2010).

17. Liem, B., Zhang, H., and Chen, Y. An Iterative Dual Pathway Structure for Speech-to-Text Transcription. In *Proceedings of the AAAI Workshop on Human Computation (HCOMP)* (2011).

18. Lin, C., Mausam, M., and Weld, D. Crowdsourcing control: Moving beyond multiple choice. In *Proceedings of HCOMP12: The 4th Workshop on Human Computation* (2012).

19. Lin, C. H., Mausam, and Weld, D. S. Dynamically switching between synergistic workflows for crowdsourcing. In *AAAI* (2012).

20. Little, G., Chilton, L. B., Goldman, M., and Miller, R. C. Turkit: tools for iterative tasks on mechanical turk. In *Proceedings of the ACM SIGKDD Workshop on Human Computation*, HCOMP '09, ACM (New York, NY, USA, 2009), 29–30.

21. Mason, W., and Watts, D. J. Financial incentives and the "performance of crowds". *SIGKDD Explor. Newsl. 11*, 2 (May 2010), 100–108.

22. Oleson, D., Sorokin, A., Laughlin, G., Hester, V., Le, J., and Biewald, L. Programmatic gold: Targeted and scalable quality assurance in crowdsourcing. In *Proceedings of HCOMP11: The 3rd Workshop on Human Computation* (2011).

23. Paritosh, P. Human computation must be reproducible. In *Proceedings of CrowdSearch: Crowdsourcing Web search 2012* (2012).

24. Quinn, A. J., and Bederson, B. B. Human computation: a survey and taxonomy of a growing field. In *Proceedings of the 2011 annual conference on Human factors in computing systems*, CHI '11, ACM (New York, NY, USA, 2011), 1403–1412.

25. Robertson, S., Vojnovic, M., and Weber, I. Rethinking the esp game. In *Proceedings of the 27th international conference extended abstracts on Human factors in computing systems*, CHI EA '09, ACM (New York, NY, USA, 2009), 3937–3942.

26. Seemakurty, N., Chu, J., von Ahn, L., and Tomasic, A. Word sense disambiguation via human computation. In *Proceedings of the ACM SIGKDD Workshop on Human Computation*, HCOMP '10, ACM (New York, NY, USA, 2010), 60–63.

27. Snow, R., O'Connor, B., Jurafsky, D., and Ng, A. Y. Cheap and fast—but is it good?: evaluating non-expert annotations for natural language tasks. In *Proceedings of the Conference on Empirical Methods in Natural Language Processing*, EMNLP '08, Association for Computational Linguistics (Stroudsburg, PA, USA, 2008), 254–263.

28. Sun, Y.-A., Roy, S., and Little, G. D. Beyond independent agreement: A tournament selection approach for quality assurance of human computation tasks. In *Proceedings of HCOMP11: The 3rd Workshop on Human Computation* (2011).

29. von Ahn, L., and Dabbish, L. Labeling images with a computer game. In *Proceedings of the SIGCHI conference on Human factors in computing systems*, CHI '04, ACM (New York, NY, USA, 2004), 319–326.

30. von Ahn, L., and Dabbish, L. Designing games with a purpose. *Commun. ACM 51* (Aug. 2008), 58–67.

Quality Control Mechanisms for Crowdsourcing: Peer Review, Arbitration, & Expertise at FamilySearch Indexing

Derek L. Hansen
Brigham Young University
Provo, UT
dlhansen@byu.edu

Patrick Schone
FamilySearch
Salt Lake City, UT
BoiseBound@aol.com

Douglas Corey
Brigham Young University
Provo, UT
corey@mathed.byu.edu

Matthew Reid
Brigham Young University
Provo, UT
matthewreid007@gmail.com

Jake Gehring
FamilySearch
Salt Lake City, UT
GehringJG@familysearch.org

ABSTRACT

The FamilySearch Indexing project has enabled hundreds of thousands of volunteers to transcribe billions of records, making it one of the largest crowdsourcing initiatives in the world. Assuring high quality transcriptions (i.e., indexes) with a reasonable amount of volunteer effort is essential to keep pace with the mounds of newly digitized documents. Using historical data, we show the relationship between prior experience and native language on transcriber agreement. We then present a field experiment comparing the effectiveness (accuracy) and efficiency (time) of two quality control mechanisms: (1) Arbitration – the existing mechanism wherein two volunteers independently transcribe records and disagreements go to an arbitrator, and (2) Peer Review – a mechanism wherein one volunteer's work is reviewed by another volunteer. Peer Review is significantly more efficient, though not as effective for certain fields as Arbitration. Design suggestions for FamilySearch Indexing and related crowdsourcing initiatives are provided.

Author Keywords

Crowdsourcing, transcription, historical documents, quality control, peer review, FamilySearch Indexing, genealogy.

ACM Classification Keywords

H.5.m. Information interfaces and presentation (e.g., HCI): Miscellaneous.

INTRODUCTION

Crowdsourcing projects such as Wikipedia, IMDB, Project Gutenberg, and FamilySearch Indexing (FSI) are responsible for the creation of millions of information artifacts. Their output is used daily by the masses and increasingly integrated into other systems. Despite our increasing reliance on peer-produced content, our understanding of how to assure its quality is still in its infancy. The work presented here sheds light on this topic by examining FSI, the world's largest historical document transcription service.

Specifically, we examine the role of expertise and different quality control mechanisms on accuracy and efficiency.

FSI volunteers have been responsible for transcribing (i.e., indexing) billions of historical records making them freely available on the Internet in machine-readable format for genealogists and historians around the globe to search. Documents include census records, vital records (e.g., birth, death, marriage, burial), church records (e.g., christening), military records, legal records, cemetery records, and migration records from countries around the globe. These documents are often hand-written, making their transcription challenging, particularly when the document authors used cursive letters that differ from those used today. These challenges make the role of experience and learning vital.

The volunteer workforce has included nearly 400,000 contributors with over 500 new volunteers signing up each day. Volunteers use special client software that shows an image alongside data entry fields (Figure 1). The software and funding for the project are provided by the Church of Jesus Christ of Latter-day Saints. Despite their tremendous effort, users cannot keep pace with the mass of newly digitized documents prompting the need for more efficient, yet equally effective transcription processes.

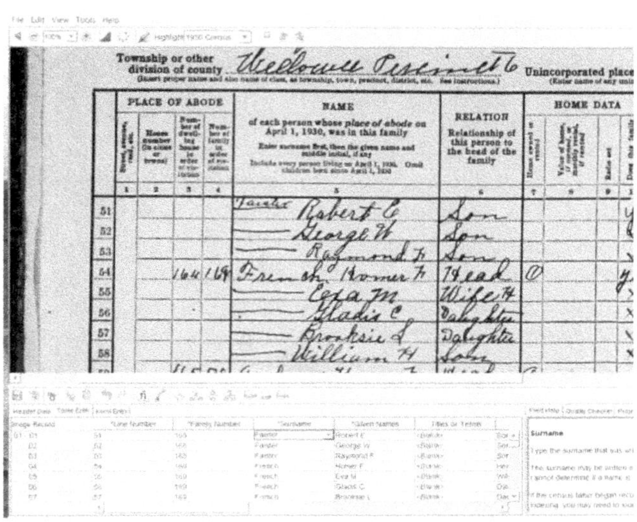

Figure 1. FamilySearch Indexing client software. Original image on top and structured data entry fields and notes on bottom.

Since its inception, FSI has sought to create high-quality transcriptions. To increase accuracy, FSI has used an *arbitration-based* quality assurance process, whereby two individuals (A and B) independently transcribe an image and any discrepancies between their outputs are passed to an experienced arbitrator (ARB) who makes the final decision. We refer to this model as A-B-ARB. While this process presumably provides a high standard of quality, it comes at a high cost, since each image must be fully transcribed by two people plus pass through the arbitration stage.

An as-yet untried, alternate method is to use a *peer review* quality assurance process. This entails the transcription of a record by one person (A) which is passed along to a reviewer (R) who identifies and fixes any errors she can find. We refer to this model as A-R. Optionally, changes made by the reviewer can be arbitrated by a third party contributor (RARB). We refer to this model as A-R-RARB.

If reviewing a document takes significantly less time than transcribing it from scratch, the peer review method will more efficiently allocate volunteer efforts. More documents can be transcribed in the same amount of time. However, peer review's impact on quality is not clear. On the one hand, reviewers may be too prone to agree with the original transcriber, which would lead to mistakes that would have been caught had the reviewer independently transcribed the work. Alternatively, reviewers may spend more time on difficult cases leading to a more careful review.

This paper explores quality control within FSI using two complementary approaches. First, we analyze historical data created using the arbitration mechanism to better understand the relationship of prior experience and native language on transcriber agreement and time spent. Then, using a subset of data from the 1930 US Census, we present a field experiment comparing the effectiveness (accuracy) and efficiency (time spent) of A-B-ARB, A-R, and A-R-RARB. We finish by discussing design implications, many of which can be applied to other crowdsourcing projects.

BACKGROUND

Crowdsourcing, a term coined by Jeff Howe in 2006, broadly describes "the act of taking a job traditionally performed by a designated agent (usually an employee) and outsourcing it to an undefined, generally large group of people in the form of an open call" [13]. Though exact definitions of crowdsourcing vary, they typically involve the completion of discrete tasks by voluntary contributors who have varying levels of expertise [10]. Many crowdsourcing initiatives, such as Wikipedia, IMDB, Project Gutenberg, and FSI create open access information resources freely available to the public. Crowdsourcing systems must recruit users, orchestrate their activity (e.g., break tasks into modular components), aggregate their contributions, and discourage deviant behavior [8]. FSI is a prototypical example of crowdsourcing, as it takes a task formerly performed by professional transcribers, breaks it up into discrete tasks completed by volunteers, and aggregates their contributions into a final product.

FamilySearch Indexing work is also a good example of human computation, because the transcription work (1) might someday be solvable by computers (i.e., it is a "computational" task), and (2) is completed by humans who are directed by a computational system or process [21]. Other human computation systems include Games With A Purpose (GWAP) such as the ESP game [25], services such as Mechanical Turk, and a range of others focused on topics as diverse as translation, annotation [14], document editing, transcription, and image recognition [21]. As is typical of many human computation systems (as well as "lightweight peer production" systems [12]), FSI is currently organized in such a way that largely anonymous contributors independently complete discrete, repetitive tasks provided by authorities. Though members of local religious congregations and genealogical societies help train and motivate one another to participate in FSI, the FSI system does not yet support "heavy-weight peer production" wherein contributors develop strong-tie relationships and internally-negotiated community norms and policies [12].

Despite the success of many crowdsourcing and human computation initiatives, the processes that lead to high quality output are not fully understood. Quinn and Bederson describe nine types of quality control mechanisms for human computation (e.g., redundancy, multi-level review) [21], though most systems rely on a single mechanism. Paul Duguid shows that existing "laws of quality" invoked by peer production systems (e.g., given enough eyeballs all bugs are shallow) do not always hold up under scrutiny at Project Gutenberg, Wikipedia, and other peer production systems [9]. Work on optical character recognition, a task similar to transcription, illustrated how simple techniques like independent agreement don't work well for difficult tasks or ones with many possible answers [18].

The strategies used to assure high quality depend largely on the tasks and outputs of crowdsourcing projects. For complex unstructured tasks, such as contributing to a Wikipedia article, quality is largely affected by the number and diversity of contributors, coordination practices, and policies [15,22]. For concrete, structured tasks, such as those at FSI, automated methods can be used to aggregate user contributions in a way that promotes high quality [8]. For example, some systems use the reputations of contributors as weights in determining which of multiple contributions is most likely accurate (e.g., [19]). Others use peer or expert oversight to increase quality and quantity of contributions [5]. Some new techniques, like the Find-Fix-Verify pattern [3] or the tournament selection approach [23], work well in some conditions, but come at a cost of more total effort needed and people involved. Despite the recognized importance of producing high quality output from crowd-sourcing initiatives, few studies have compared alternate quality control processes in a large-scale project.

METHODS

Study Design

We use a two-pronged approach to better understand the effect of experience and quality control mechanisms at FSI. First, we perform an analysis of historical agreement data between independent transcribers (A and B) to understand the impact of experience on quality (i.e., agreement) and effort (i.e., time). Second, we perform a field experiment of a proposed peer review quality control process and compare it to the current arbitration model.

Data Sources

Data for the historical analysis and the field experiment was drawn from the database containing data associated with the FSI transcription software. The database includes the transcription text entered for each field (e.g., surname, given name, birthyear), name of the transcriber, her role (e.g., A transcriber, B transcriber, arbitrator), her native language, time spent transcribing, time spent idle (i.e., more than 30 seconds without any activity), number of keystrokes entered, and meta-data associated with the image being transcribed (e.g., language, collection).

The historical dataset includes all transcribed records from various FSI data collections (e.g., U.S. Census records, Canadian Census records) completed by February 2011. The field experiment dataset is based on a random sample of 2,000 images pulled from 25 of the 48 states that participated in the 1930 Federal U.S. Census for which data were available. Each census page includes up to 50 records, each of which describes an individual person and their information (e.g., surname, given name, birthplace). Images with less than half of the 50 rows completed were excluded to assure sufficient data.

A truth set transcription of the 2,000 images was created to calculate the accuracy of the two quality control mechanisms tested in the field experiment. A professional transcription company was hired to create a truth set with at least 99% accuracy. Two FamilySearch internal auditors reviewed the truth set. They tagged one row from 380 of the images (which included 18 fields each) and identified errors in the truth set. They found a total of 17 errors (e.g., Allan vs Allon; Evins vs Enins), which results in an estimated 99.75% accuracy. Errors in the field experiment were identified when a transcribed field did not match the truth set.

Historical Data Analysis

The goal of the historical data analysis was to understand the impact of a transcriber's experience and native language on quality and efficiency. Efficiency was measured as the total amount of non-idle time spent indexing a particular image. Native language is self-reported by users.

Users' experience was measured by totaling the number of images a volunteer had transcribed up until a given point in time. In February 2012, the top five transcribers of all time had each transcribed between 206,000 and 269,000 full images. In comparison, 26,459 of the nearly 400,000 transcribers only annotated a single image. To account for the skewed distribution, we used a log transformation of number of pages transcribed. For clarity, users are grouped into nine experience levels based on the following formula:

$$EL(U) = \text{round}(\log_5(N(U)))$$

Where U represents the transcriber, N(U) is the number of images that U has transcribed, and EL(U) is the experience level of U. A volunteer who has transcribed only 1 page has an experience level of 0, while the top transcriber has an experience level of 8. The median number of images transcribed is 50, which equates to a skill level of 2.

Since no truth set exists for the large historical data corpus, accuracy is estimated by examining *agreement* between A and B transcribers. In contrast, the field experiment (described below) compares each transcription with the truth set to determine *accuracy*. An analysis of the 2,000 image sample showed that A and B agreement was strongly correlated with accuracy as compared with the truth set (when A and B agreed, the transcription matched the truth set 98% of the time on average for all fields in the dataset). This suggests that patterns observed in the historical data using agreement between A and B likely mirror patterns that would be observed based on actual accuracy.

Experimental Design

The goal of the field experiment was to evaluate three different quality control mechanisms as outlined below:

- A-B-ARB Condition: A and B transcribe a page independent of one another and any discrepancies are passed to a third arbitrator (ARB) who makes the final decisions. This is the currently used model at FSI. The FSI user interface has been optimized for this process. For example, when transcribers type in a location not on a pre-approved list it is highlighted to indicate it may be an error. Likewise, arbitrators have a special view that highlights fields that are different in the A and B transcriptions and allows them to quickly choose one or the other, or (as rarely happens) enter something else.
- A-R Condition: A transcribes a page and R reviews the transcription by identifying and correcting any errors he finds. The same FSI software was used to perform the review, with the original A transcription being flagged as "incomplete" so that R could have access to it. No specialized tools were developed to support peer review (e.g., no highlighting of suspected errors). Instructions were provided to volunteers on how to perform peer review, since this process was new to FSI volunteers. The newness of the peer review process to volunteers and the lack of optimized tools to support peer review likely underestimate the potential of this process. In other words, our findings provide a lower bound on the quality of peer review compared to arbitration.

- A-R-RARB Condition: A transcribes a page, R reviews the page, and any discrepancies are reviewed by a third arbitrator (RARB). Data from the A-R Condition above was passed to an arbitrator using the same arbitration software as is typically used. The arbitrator was presented with both A and R fields, without knowing which was which, since the standard arbitration tool does not give precedence to one transcription over another.

Recruitment and Limitations

Historical data from 2011 was used for the A-B-ARB condition. The original A transcription was used in the A-R and A-R-RARB conditions as well. However, FSI volunteers were recruited from five active U.S.-based user groups in January and February of 2012 to play the role of R and RARB. Each group had a known leader who helped notify their volunteers, point them to the instructions for the new peer review process, and answer any questions they had. Volunteers were asked to only complete a handful of pages each, to solicit a wide range of experience levels among volunteers and more independent assessments.

Despite our efforts to recruit a representative sample for the R and RARB roles, analysis of the experience distribution of our volunteers showed that R and RARB were on average less experienced than A, B, and ARB transcribers (see Figure 2). Even with the narrower spectrum of experience for R and RARB, there is evidence that R's experience is positively associated with higher accuracy. As a result, our A-R and A-R-RARB accuracy numbers may be lower than expected from a set of volunteers who directly matched the experience distribution of A-B-ARB volunteers. However, the distribution of R was spread out enough to see the expected positive relationship of higher experience and accuracy, though this was not true for RARB (see Field Experiment Results). For this reason, we control for experience of the original transcribers, arbitrators, and reviewers in our statistical models (see next section).

Some of the data fields in the B transcription data were not created via the typical transcription method, requiring us to make a special adjustment. Some fields, including surname and given name, were transcribed initially by a company, after which FSI volunteers transcribed the remaining fields.

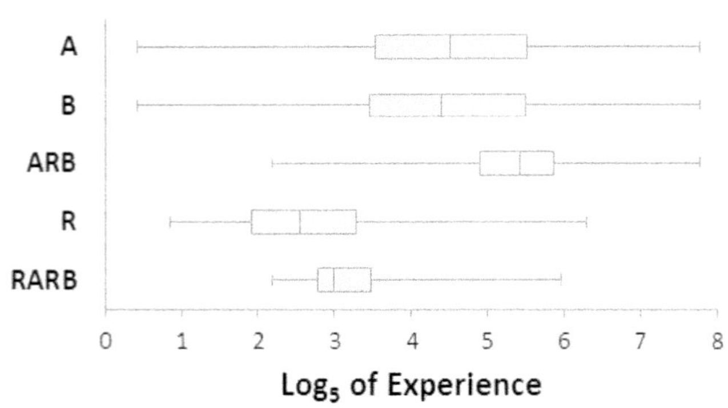

Figure 2. Box plots of experience distributions of A (n=1,550), B (n=1,588), ARB (n=1,010), R (n=344), and RARB (n=47)

The result was that for most fields, the B transcription was slightly, but consistently higher quality (compared to the truth set) than the A transcription which was created completely by FSI transcribers. We report the raw A-B-ARB results, as well as adjusted A-B-ARB results which estimate the amount of error that would have occurred had the B transcription been the same quality as the A transcription.

To estimate the adjusted A-B-ARB transcription quality, the following method was used. First, calculate how often there is a discrepancy between A and B and only one of them is correct. For example, for surname, A is correct 5.3% of the time when B is wrong, and B is correct 7.1% of the time when A is wrong, totaling 12.4%. Next, calculate how often ARB chooses the correct answer among the 2 options (e.g., 81% of the time for surname). Then, adjust B down to the same level as A (i.e., 5.3%) and multiply 10.6 (5.3% + 5.3%) by the percent of the time ARB is correct for this field (81%). This gives us an estimate of the adjusted value-added of ARB (8.7%) assuming that B is the same quality as A. Subtracting this from the actual value-added of ARB (10.1%) gives the adjustment amount (i.e., accuracy goes down by 1.4%). This approach is reasonable because ARB only reviews records where A and B disagree, ignoring records where A and B agree (whether or not their agreed value was correct).

Statistical Analysis

The historical data analysis is descriptive, while our analysis of the field experiment uses a statistical model to identify significant differences between experimental conditions. The dependent variable in each of our models is the volunteer's accuracy, a binary variable that indicates whether the volunteer's transcription matched the truth set or not. We measure a match in 3 different ways as described in the following section. Our independent variables include the experimental condition (described below) and the experience of the volunteer. The experience variable was used to control for possible differences among volunteers in different conditions. This is particularly important given the difference in expertise levels between the conditions as discussed earlier and in Figure 2.

The data has a complicated structure that violates key assumptions of standard t-test or OLS regression. Volunteers transcribed an entire census page (i.e., image) of records at a time, each of which included up to 50 records in what is called a batch. Batches of records were transcribed by several individuals playing the role of A, B, ARB, R, and RARB. Thus, the independence assumption needed for simpler analyses was unreasonable because records on the same census page have more highly correlated accuracy rates than records on different pages (due to the common handwriting of the census taker, repeated surnames and placenames, etc.). Also, records transcribed by the same person have more highly correlated accuracy rates than those transcribed by different people. To account for these unique properties, we used a mixed model [6] with random effects that included records nested in batches and cross-nested between two transcribers (or a transcriber and a peer reviewer) and an arbitrator.

Each model was used to estimate or compare accuracy rates of different quality control processes (A vs A-R; A vs A-B-ARB; A-R vs A-B-ARB; and A-R vs A-R-RARB) controlling for the expertise of the volunteers as well as the random effects for batch, transcribers (or reviewer), and arbitrator. Expertise was measured, as mentioned before, by a log transformation of the number of batches that had been transcribed by an individual up to the time of their transcription of the experimental records. For A, B, and ARB this was February, 2011. For R and RARB this was February, 2012 since their data was collected a year later. Each model was run separately for each field (surname, birthplace, etc). We used a logistic regression model because we were testing accuracy rates with an outcome of each model as a 1 (correctly transcribed) or 0 (incorrectly transcribed).

Accuracy Measures

Agreement between two transcriptions (e.g., A and the truth set) was calculated in 3 ways for the field experiment:

- Exact Match: A standard string comparison, where each string (including punctuation and spaces) had to exactly match the other one ("Washington D.C." did not match "Washington DC")
- Known Variants: Matches were counted in cases where the transcriptions were exact matches or effectively equivalent as determined by a 1930 Census expert working for FamilySearch. These included obvious abbreviations (e.g., W in the Race column matched with White; "Wash DC" in a location column for "Washington DC" and other variants with periods), extra spaces in names (e.g., "Mc Arthur" matched "McArthur"), and unnecessary details added by the census taker (e.g., "Montgomery County" matched "Montgomery"). The equivalency matches were developed by looking at the most common errors.
- Authorities Variants: Matches were counted in cases where the transcriptions were known variants or where a surname, given name, or placename was identified as equivalent in the authorities tables used by FamilySearch's search engine. These tables have been iteratively developed over 40 years by FamilySearch, primarily from observed variations where there were multiple records which seemed to refer to the same person but with name/place differences. For example, Katia and Katherine match. The authorities variants are not statistically motivated, so there can be names that occur with relatively high frequency but which are lumped together because of some limited number of variants (e.g., Mike, Michael, and Chiel, which are translations of each other).

Transcribed Field	Agreement
Gender	98.8%
Given Name	82.5%
Surname	74.7%
Birthplace	96.1%
Relationship to Head of House	95.0%
Age	91.6%
Birth Date	97.8%
Father's Birthplace	96.7%
Mother's Birthplace	96.7%
Immigration Year	90.0%

Table 1. A-B Agreement percent by Field for all US Census records in our corpus.

HISTORICAL ANALYSIS RESULTS

A-B Agreement Analysis

Agreement between A and B varied dramatically depending upon the field of data that was transcribed. Table 1 shows the percent agreement for each field in the U.S. Censuses from 1850 to 1920. Other collections included similar differences between fields. As expected, fields with few possible values had extremely high agreement (e.g., gender = 99%), while fields with many possible values had much lower agreement (surname = 75%).

Differences in accuracy were also observed based on the language of the census taker. The Canadian 1871 Census data used the exact same census forms to record data in both English and French, allowing for a comparison. Agreement was much higher for English-language transcriptions than for French-language transcriptions. Comparing just the given name and surname fields, the French Canadian census records on average have only a mere 62.7% and 48.8% accuracy compared to 79.8% and 66.4% for the English Canadian records. This may be due to the fact that nearly all transcribers are native English speakers.

Finally, results from our analysis of agreement and prior experience of the transcribers is presented. The heatmap presented in Figure 3 shows agreement levels between all possible experience matchups. The lowest agreement values (shown in blue) occur when inexperienced transcribers are matched up with other inexperienced transcribers (in the bottom-left-region of the graph), while the highest agreement occurs between experienced transcribers (in the upper-right region of the graph). Though the general trend is not surprising, the continued improvement even at the very high levels is worth noting. It is consistent with lab experiments conducted by cognitive psychologists who show continued improvement at tasks even at extremely high levels of practice, though with diminishing returns [1].

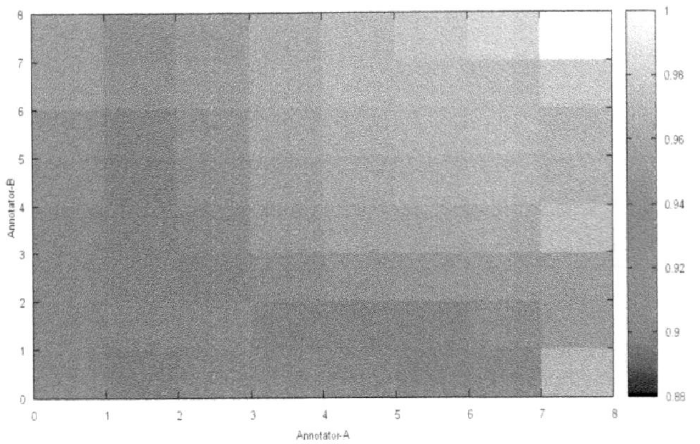

Figure 3. Heatmap of A-B agreement by Experience Level for Birthplace in all US Censuses in our corpus.

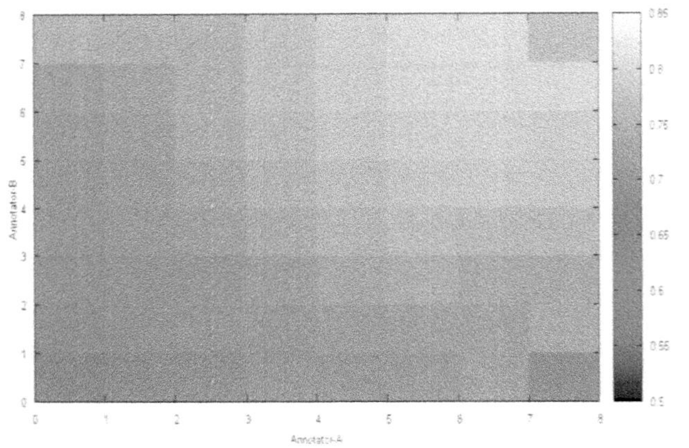

Figure 4. Heatmap of A-B agreement by Experience Level for Surname in all US Censuses in our corpus.

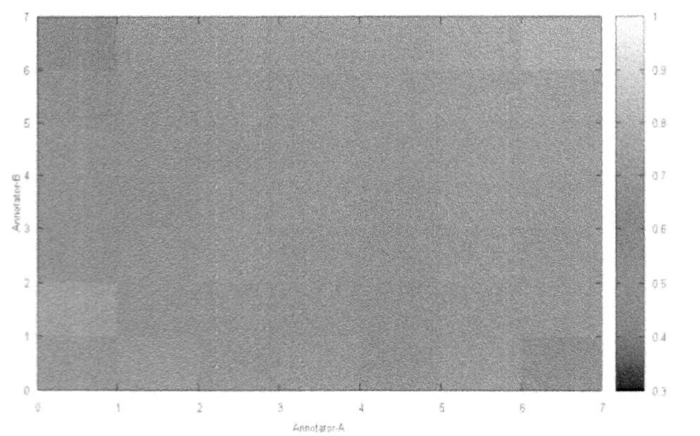

Figure 5. Heatmap of A-B agreement by Experience Level for Birthplace in the English-speaking Canadian Census.

This pattern of continuous improvement was found in other fields such as surname (Figure 4) and given name. Improvements in agreement for gender were noticeable but very small since agreement was so much higher for all experience levels. Agreement for birthplace did not improve for certain other datasets including the English-speaking Canadian Censuses (Figure 5). For this field, unlike with gender, the agreement remained relatively low. It is likely that the predominantly U.S. transcribers were unfamiliar with Canadian places, contributing to this effect. This suggests that transcription expertise is partially tied to domain knowledge, and that expertise in one domain (e.g., U.S. locations) does not necessarily translate into expertise in another domain (e.g., Canadian locations).

Transcription Time Analysis

Data on non-idle time and keystrokes was not available for specific fields, since the time was based on completion of an entire image. There are cases where some transcribers may be completing other tasks on their computer concurrently or take frequent breaks while working on projects, which would skew time results. For this reason outlier times that were in excess of two hours or less than 20 seconds were discarded.

The number of keystrokes and the time spent decreased for those with more experience (Table 2). The estimated average of keystrokes per line for the US records in our dataset had a small but consistent downward trend, except for those transcribing their very first record (Experience Level 0 people who were given easy batches to get them acquainted with the system). Since the same amount of data needed to be transcribed on each line irrespective of experience level, it is likely that experienced transcribers revised their entries less often (e.g., re-type in a surname after realizing they got it wrong the first time).

Changes in time per line (measured in seconds) are far more dramatic. Experienced volunteers can be up to 4 times faster than novices. The weighted average of the times for the first three experience levels (0-2), which includes the skill level of the median contributor to FSI, is double the weighted average of the three highest experience levels (6-8). This lowers the average Time per Keystroke.

Experience Level	Avg Keystrokes per Line	Avg Time per Line	Avg Time per Keystroke
0	18.74	65.79	4.31
1	19.25	63.10	3.96
2	19.42	55.54	3.47
3	18.53	48.21	3.22
4	18.03	41.53	2.92
5	17.67	34.71	2.57
6	17.50	28.87	2.22
7	17.44	23.16	1.82
8	17.65	14.95	1.18

Table 2. Time and Keystroke data by Experience Level for all US Censuses in our corpora

Experience Level of Transcriber	Avg Keystrokes of ARB	Avg Time of ARB	Avg Time per Keystroke
0	35.1	466.6	13.3
1	35.0	492.1	14.1
2	35.4	482.1	13.6
3	33.8	467.9	13.8
4	31.6	445.0	14.1
5	28.9	421.7	14.6
6	27.4	399.7	14.6
7	26.7	386.7	14.5
8	24.1	370.8	15.4

Table 3. Time and Keystroke data by Experience Level for the 1910 US Census

Differences in time and keystrokes based on language were also observed. The English-speaking 1871 Canadian Census was 2.68 seconds faster per line than the French version, despite the fact that it required more keystrokes. Though this sounds small, when aggregated over the 3 million+ French-language census lines, it amounts to over 2,000 hours of additional time, or about a year's work by one full-time employee. This difference was likely due to a lack of native French-speaking volunteers.

As expected, arbitrators spent more time reviewing content transcribed by novices. Table 3 shows this using data from the 1910 US Census. All US Censuses were not combined in this analysis because each Census had a different number of columns and rows. Because there were fewer errors to correct in records transcribed by experienced users, fewer keystrokes and less time were required. The average time per keystroke was not dramatically different, though there was a slight upward trend as experience levels increased. This was likely because cases where experienced volunteers differed (particularly amongst themselves) were often the hardest cases that required more time to evaluate.

FIELD EXPERIMENT RESULTS

Accuracy Analysis

Consistent with findings from the historical analysis of A and B agreement, there were dramatic differences between accuracy across fields, with the lowest accuracy in surname and given name fields (Table 4). This pattern is consistent for all 3 quality metrics (exact match, known variants, and authorities variants) and experimental conditions.

Surprisingly, the impact of the additional arbitration (RARB) of the peer reviewed content (R) failed to improve the quality. No statistically significant results were found at the .05 level. Furthermore, arbitration of peer reviewed content actually lowered the accuracy for all fields, though only slightly. In other words, when presented with A and R discrepancies RARB chose the wrong one more times than they chose the right one. Since the majority of R's changes improved accuracy (54-86% depending on field), it appears that RARB chose A instead of R too often. As mentioned earlier, the RARB volunteers were not as experienced as expected, though they were more experienced than R (see Figure 2). Even so, the fact that R's edits were mostly improvements suggests that the need for RARB does not seem justified by the extra effort required. For this reason we now focus on A-B-ARB and A-R quality control models.

Results for the Known Variants quality metric are shown in Figure 6. They show lower error rates than those based on Exact Match (Table 4), since field values such as "Washington D.C." match with known variants such as "Washington DC". Both quality control mechanisms (A-B-ARB and A-R) resulted in statistically significant reductions to A's original error rates ($p < .001$ for all fields). For most fields, A-B-ARB (even with the adjustment) outperforms A-R, though only 3 of the fields found the improvement to be statistically significant at the .001 level (see Figure 6).

Another key observation relates to the two main types of error: missed error and introduced error. Missed error refers to errors that were made in the original dataset (A) that the quality control mechanism did not catch. These make up the vast majority of errors. Introduced errors refer to the errors that the quality control mechanism introduced. In other words, A had it right, but the quality control mechanism changed the correct answer into an incorrect answer. In nearly all cases the A-R process introduces fewer errors than the A-B-ARB process, though R also missed more errors than B-ARB. As mentioned earlier, no customized tools were provided to R in order to help identify potential errors, so the R results should be interpreted as a minimum threshold of quality.

	A	ARB	R	RARB	N
Surname	82.2%	87.0%*	84.2%	83.9%	97,600
Given Name	84.0%	89.1%*	86.5%	86.1%	98,496
Age	96.9%	98.2%*	98.3%	97.7%	98,402
Relationship	97.9%	99.3%*	98.6%	98.2%	98,188
Race	99.8%	99.9%*	99.9%	99.8%	98,516
Birthplace	97.8%	98.6%*	98.4%	98.0%	98,512
F_Birthplace	96.5%	97.3%	97.0%	96.6%	98,499
M_Birthplace	96.5%	97.3%	97.0%	96.7%	98,497
Gender	99.2%	99.7%	99.5%	99.2%	98,517
Marital	99.2%	99.7%	99.5%	99.1%	98,316

Table 4. Unadjusted Exact Match accuracy by field for A, ARB, R, and RARB. The B transcription was transcribed by a company and B for those fields with *s.

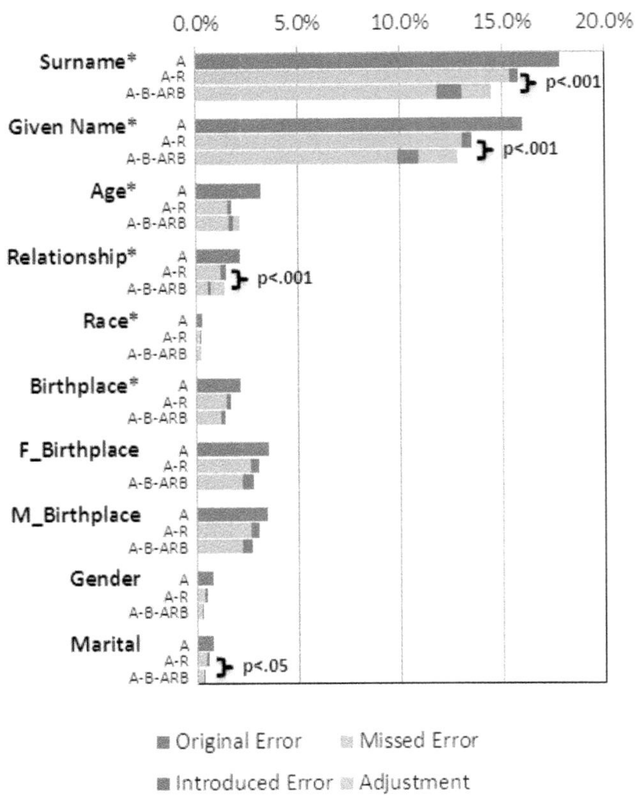

Figure 6. Errors based on Known Variant matching by field and quality control mechanism. Fields with a * require an adjustment (shown in gray) because B was transcribed by a company and B rather than just B volunteers.

Adding Known Variant matches to Exact Matches made the biggest difference in location-based fields (e.g., birthplace fields), where the error rate was reduced by just over a third. Adding Search Variant matches reduced surname error rates by11% for ARB and R, and given name error rates by 21% for ARB and R. Changes to location-based fields were negligible.

The statistical models allowed us to parse the variation in accuracy rates between image, transcriber(s), reviewer (if present), and arbitrator. Using this data, it was possible to identify which factors contributed the most to the variability in accuracy. Table 5 displays the upper and lower bounds based on the estimated random effects of the model for the surname field. These bounds were found by taking two standard deviations above and below the log-odds mean and translating those values into percentages (since it was not a linear transformation the interval was not centered around the mean). The values represent reasonable upper and lower bounds in a category assuming other categories contributed their average effect.

For example, for a typical transcriber (A), reviewer, and arbitrator, a particular image could end up with 50.8% accuracy at the low end or 98.7% accuracy at the high end.

	Lower Bound	Upper Bound
Image	50.8%	98.7%
A	81.5%	94.9%
Reviewer	88.8%	91.2%
Arbitrator	87.7%	92.0%

Table 5. Lower and Upper bounds for different sources of variation in accuracy of the surname field. These bounds assume an average result for the other sources of variation.

This a dramatic effect, likely driven by factors such as differences in handwriting of the census taker and the complexity of surnames and placenames that show up together in the same image. In contrast, with an average difficulty image, the best transcribers would get 94.9% accuracy while the worst would get 81.5% accuracy. Overall, the image is by far the most important driver of accuracy variance followed by the transcriber. The effect of reviewer and arbitrator are much smaller.

The effect of experience on the review process is consistent with findings from the historical analysis. For instance, the experience of the initial transcribers and the reviewers is significantly related to the accuracy of most fields, but the effects, although significant, are relatively small. Because most of the fields are transcribed with high accuracy, comparing experienced transcribers to novice transcribers gives a difference in accuracy of less than 1% – even when the effect is significant.

The effect of experience on more difficult fields (surname and given name) is more dramatic. For example, the effect (in log odds) on the surname field is .018 per unit increase in the log of experience. A volunteer who has completed 22,000 batches has about a 1.9% increase in accuracy over a person who only transcribed 9 batches. The effect of experience on accuracy is about 4% for the same comparison when looking at the given name field. The experience of a reviewer has about the same effect on accuracy as the experience of the initial transcriber. We did not find evidence that the experience of arbitrators matters, perhaps because all arbitrators must meet a minimum level of experience and expertise to be accepted in that role.

Time Analysis

As expected, A-R (and A-R-RARB) required significantly less time to complete than the A-B-ARB process. Overall, peer reviewing a document takes about half as long as transcribing a document from scratch. The end result is that the A-R process takes about 70% as long as the A-B-ARB process (Figure 7), which is significantly different at the .001 level. Data based on medians instead of averages was similar, though faster (e.g., Median for A-B-ARB process is 61 min; Median for A-R-ARB process is 46 min).

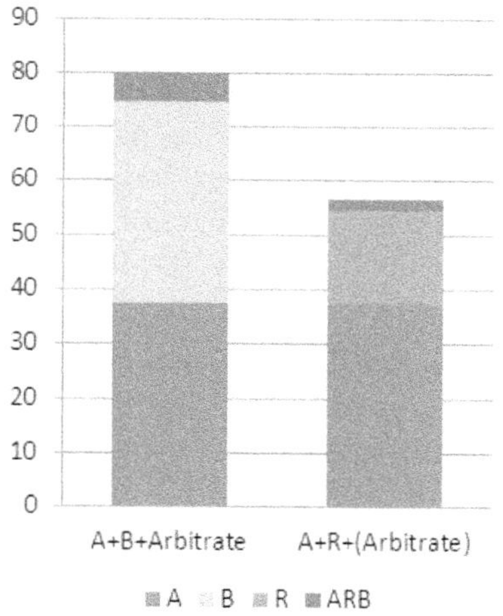

Figure 7. Average minutes per page for different quality control mechanisms.

DISCUSSION & DESIGN IMPLICATIONS

Below is a discussion of our findings and their design implications. Though we focus on improving transcription work, many of our suggestions have natural applications to other crowdsourcing endeavors such as image labeling [20], truth set creation [7], and database entry (e.g., IMDB) [5].

The role of Expertise on Quality & Efficiency

Both our historical and experimental data showed significant differences between experienced and novice volunteer efforts. Not only did quality increase for more experienced transcribers, but the time to complete the work was much less. As is typical of crowdsourcing projects [27], the distribution of expertise and the amount of work contributed is highly skewed with the majority of contributions made by a minority of highly experienced contributors. The findings suggest the importance of retaining experienced members and helping motivate less experienced members to contribute more (see [16,17] for a discussion of design strategies to promote contributions).

However, the historical analysis also gives us reason to be cautious about how prior transcription experience does and does not impact current tasks. Overall experience was not strongly related to fields such as Canadian placenames, which are likely unfamiliar to the largely U.S. based volunteers. This may indicate the importance of the transcribers having some contextual knowledge (e.g., knowledge of Canadian placenames) that may indirectly benefit them when performing transcription work. This knowledge may be completely independent of their transcription experience (e.g., ability to read cursive handwriting and use the FSI system). Tools that leveraged people's contextual knowledge by, for example, intelligently recommending images to transcribe based on a volunteer profile, may improve quality. Additionally, tools that helped volunteers gain contextual knowledge (e.g., by providing county maps and sending sets of images from the same county) could improve quality. Though not tested in this paper, it is likely that those who work extensively with Canadian Census records would come to know the Canadian placenames and improve over time. Likewise, those working with certain languages will likely improve over time, though recruiting native speakers to transcribe within their own language seems essential given our findings on language accuracy.

Systems, such as the new FSI mobile application or reCAPTCHA [26], which allow users to transcribe single records (as opposed to entire images) should take this into consideration. If they serve a user randomly selected images, the user's prior experience is less likely to benefit their future performance. Conversely, if they serve a user similar fields (e.g., placenames) from the same collection (e.g., Canadian census), that user's experience will help him with future transcriptions. More generally, a system that breaks down large heterogeneous tasks into their constituent subtasks (i.e., a census image broken into specific field entries) can promote the development of specialist experts who are served up similar subtasks. This will likely improve quality as well as reduce time to complete, though its effect on user satisfaction is unclear. Future work should examine learning effects in crowdsourcing environments more directly. Interventions designed to more rapidly improve expertise could be developed, such as sending novices common errors identified through arbitration or peer review.

Improving Peer Review

One of the most surprising results was the lack of a need for arbitration of peer reviewed content (i.e., the lack of benefit provided by RARB). Peer reviewers seemed to make changes only when they were certain that their change would fix a mistake, as shown by the low number of introduced errors by reviewers. Adding a verification step (as proposed in the Find-Fix-Verify pattern [3]) was unnecessary in the FSI context, since it increased the amount of time without improving quality.

Our findings related to strict peer review (A-R) are mixed. On the one hand, it took considerably less time to complete than the A-B-ARB method. On the other hand, the resulting quality was, in some cases statistically inferior to the A-B-ARB method. As discussed earlier, the peer review data from our study likely understates the quality of the mechanism because (a) the tools are not customized for reviewing, while they are customized for A-B-ARB, (b) the peer review process was new to the volunteers, while the A-B-ARB process was not, and (c) the average experience levels of the reviewers was low due to a selection bias. Given these factors, our findings suggest that peer review should be carefully considered as a viable alternative to the current A-B-ARB model, particularly if steps are taken to improve the tools and experience of reviewers.

Several techniques could be used to improve the quality of peer review, all of which could be empirically tested in future work. First, reviewers could be provided with an estimated number of errors per page (or field) in order to set their expectations within a reasonable range. The high variability in quality among pages and initial transcribers suggests that such estimates should be customized based on the page and expertise of the original transcriber.

Second, tools could highlight entries that have a high probability of error. The current system does this for transcribers by literally highlighting entries that do not match other entries in existing databases (e.g., county names or surnames that are not in an authorities table). This is a good start, but more sophisticated techniques may prove useful. For example, prior A-R data could be used as a training set to help identify potentially erroneous entries (see discussion in [7] of various techniques). Alternatively, the original transcriber could flag items that they have low confidence in. This allows for the decoupling of the identification of potential problems with the provision of the solution, which was found to be a useful strategy in the Find-Fix-Verify pattern [3] (though without the heavy overhead of including as many people in the process). It may be that novices can accurately identify difficult records, even if novices can't accurately transcribe them. While these approaches may slow down the review process, they have the potential to pay off in increased quality.

Third, entries that are likely to contain errors (based on the earlier techniques mentioned) could be routed to more experienced reviewers, while entries estimated to be accurate could be routed to novice reviewers. Caution would need to be applied in this approach, since it may be in conflict with the goals of training newcomers to become more expert (see prior section).

Alternate Quality Control Mechanisms

Though A-B-ARB and A-R both provide significantly better results than using a single transcription, there is significant room for improvement for difficult fields such as surname and given name. Our data provides some hints at alternate mechanisms that could be used to improve quality without dramatically increasing the amount of effort.

One alternative quality control method would be double review where an original transcriber is reviewed by one person and the updated file is passed on to another reviewer for a final pass. Our data shows that reviewing a completed transcript takes about half as long as transcribing one from scratch. Thus, an A-R_1-R_2 process would take about the same amount of time as the current A-B-ARB process. Yet, a single review pass is almost as good as the A-B-ARB process, so it may prove that a second round of review would continue to improve the accuracy. This seems likely, since, for some fields (e.g., surname, given name), there are many missed errors left for the second reviewer to catch. It may make sense to assure that the second reviewer is an expert.

The A-R_1-R_2 method could be combined with other recommendations mentioned earlier. For example, the first reviewer could flag fields that they want the second reviewer to review. Furthermore, some fields with a low probability of error (e.g., gender) could skip the second stage of review to improve efficiency. Indeed, even the first round of review could be skipped for some fields if there is a high enough probability that the original transcriber was accurate (based on her expertise and/or machine learning-based predictions like those used in other contexts [7]).

Another promising approach, which could provide increased efficiency, is to blend human transcription with algorithmic transcriptions (e.g., [24]). A growing body of literature uses image processing techniques to automatically transcribe historical texts [2]. Though accuracy of interpreting cursive writing in documents such as U.S. Censuses is not nearly as good as human transcription, for some fields with a limited set of entries (e.g., gender, relationship) it is becoming viable [24]. Automatic transcription could be used in several ways. It could perform the initial transcription that is reviewed by a human. It could act as the reviewer. Or, it could help intelligently determine if human peer review is needed on a given entry.

One exciting possibility would be the creation of a large-scale machine learning training dataset, which could be developed as part of the standard workflow. For example, if automatic transcription algorithms served as the original transcriber (A), they could be reviewed by humans as part of the A-B-ARB, A-R, or A-R_1-R_2 quality control process. Data on the correct and incorrect transcriptions could be fed back into learning algorithms, helping to improve future (or even prior) classifications. Such a process could create a training set of millions and possibly billions of records, orders of magnitude larger than existing sets. While this approach would not be based on a truth set, for many of the simpler fields, it would create a training set that is above 95% accurate. If successful, such approaches could increase the rate of transcription by orders of magnitude.

Another approach that could augment existing quality control mechanisms would be to allow users of the transcriptions to make corrections. Like a wiki, the existing transcription would become a living document that is constantly updated. While this introduces more opportunities for vandalism, it also provides people with the most content knowledge (e.g., the grandson of a person in a census record) the ability to fix it, an approach that helps sites like Wikipedia [22]. One difficulty associated with this approach would be dealing with the many definitions of accuracy. In this paper we focused on accurately transcribing what was written on the historical page. However, those writing the historical documents were not perfect, particularly in time periods when spelling norms were not established. Allowing users to fix, or annotate, direct transcriptions would help genealogists and historians in their efforts to identify individuals whose names may be written in several different forms.

Finally, models that made transcription more social and intrinsically rewarding may motivate more people to participate. Currently, transcription work is an isolating experience, where tools outside of the existing software must be used to get help. This is contrary to the highly collaborative work that genealogists enjoy. Allowing users to request help on a difficult record from an expert, or even their Facebook friends may add enjoyment, speed up the learning process, and attract new volunteers. Making the transcription task part of an intrinsically rewarding game may also attract a different audience. There is precedence in games that help identify optical character recognition errors (i.e., scannos) [4] and image recognition errors [11]. Additionally, adding a more explicit community component may also allow volunteers to take a more active role in improving the process as a whole, which is currently dictated almost entirely by FSI. This could move the project into a "heavy-weight peer production" environment, which raises new challenges and opportunities [12].

CONCLUSION

This paper has provided an in-depth look at quality control mechanisms within FamilySearch Indexing, one of the world's largest crowdsourcing projects. Analysis of historical agreement data showed that experienced transcribers are more likely to agree than novices, as are those working on English language transcriptions compared to other languages. Furthermore, experts take less time, suggesting the need to retain experts and train novices as opposed to treating all users as interchangeable.

A field experiment comparing the existing arbitration-based process (A-B-ARB) and two proposed peer review processes (A-R and A-R-RARB) showed that peer review took dramatically less time, though it did not achieve quite as high accuracy. This may be in part due to the lack of customized tools to support peer review and other limitations in our experimental data. Interestingly, arbitration (i.e., validation) of the peer reviewer's edits did not increase quality, suggesting that a simple A-R process is preferable in this context. Tools customized to better support peer review (e.g., help reviewers identify potential errors or set their expectations) could likely lead to more efficient quality control that achieves comparable or better quality over existing methods. Alternate models such as double peer review (A-R_1-R_2), integration of human and machine transcription, and intelligent routing of difficult records may improve quality and efficiency above existing golden standard approaches.

ACKNOWLEDGMENTS

We would like to express our appreciation to Rose Pierson, Zane Jacobson, Katie Gale, Stephen Pew, Paul Starkey, and LDS missionaries for their tremendous assistance in helping to create and implement the field experiment.

REFERENCES

1. Anderson, J. *Cognitive psychology and its implications*, 7th edition. Worth Publishers, 2009.
2. Barret, B., Brown, M.S., Manmatha, R., and Gehring, J. *Proceedings of the 2011 Workshop on Historical Document Imaging and Processing*, ACM Press (2011).
3. Bernstein, M. S., Little, G., Miller, R. C., Hartmann, B., Ackerman, M. S., Karger, D. R., Crowell, D., and Panovich, K. Soylent: a word processor with crowd inside. Proc. UIST '10, ACM Press (2010), 313-322.
4. Chrons, O. and Sundell, S. Digitalkoot: Making old archives accessible using crowdsourcing. *Human Computation: Papers from the 2011 AAAI Workshop*, (2011).
5. Cosley, D., Frankowski, D. Kiesler, S., Terveen, L., and Riedl, J. 2005. How oversight improves member-maintained communities. In *Proc. CHI 2005*, ACM Press (2005), 11-20.
6. Demidenko, E. *Mixed Models: Theory and Applications*. Wiley-Interscience, 2004.
7. Dligach, D., and Palmer, M. 2011. Reducing the need for double annotation. In *Proc. of the 5th Linguistic Annotation Workshop* (LAW V '11), (2011), 65-73.
8. Doan, A., Ramakrishnan, R., and Halevy, A. Y. Crowdsourcing systems on the World-Wide Web. *Commun. ACM* 54, 4 (April 2011), 86-96.
9. Duguid, P. 2006. Limits of self-organization: Peer production and "laws of quality". *First Monday*, 11 (10).
10. Estellés-Arolas, E., and González-Ladrón-de-Guevara, F. Towards an integrated crowdsourcing definition. *J. of Information Science*, 20, 10 (2012), 1-14.
11. Hansen, D., Jacobs, D., Lewis, D., Biswas, A., Preece, J., Rotman, D., and Stevens, E. Odd Leaf Out: Improving visual recognition with games. In *Proc. SocialCom '11*, IEEE (2011), 87-94.
12. Haythornthwaite, C. Crowds and Communities: Light and Heavyweight Models of Peer Production. In *Proc. HICSS '09*, (2009), 1-10.
13. Howe, J. Crowdsourcing: Why the Power of the Crowd is Driving the Future of Business http://www.crowdsourcing.com/
14. Hsueh, P., Melville, P., and Sindhwani, V. Data quality from crowdsourcing: a study of annotation selection criteria. In *Proc. NAACL HLT 2009 Workshop on Active Learning for Natural Language Processing (HLT '09)*, (2009), 27-35.
15. Kittur, A., and Kraut, R. E. 2008. Harnessing the wisdom of crowds in wikipedia: quality through coordination. In *Proc. CSCW '08*, ACM Press (2008), 37-46.
16. Kraut, R.E. and Resnick, P. Building Successful Online Communities: Evidence-Based Social Design. The MIT Press, 2012.
17. Ling, K., Beenen, G., Ludford, P., Wang, X., Chang, K., Li, X., Cosley, D., Frakowski, D., Terveen, L., Rashid, A.M., Resnick, P., and Kraut, R. Using social psycholo-

gy to motivate contributions to online communities. *JCMC*, 10, 4 (2005).

18. Little, G. and Sun, Y. Human OCR: insights from a complex human computation process. *Workshop on Crowdsourcing and Human Computation, Services, Studies and Platforms, ACM CHI*, (2011).

19. McCann, R., Doan, A, Varadajan, V., and Kramnik, A. Building Data Integration Systems via Mass Collaboration. In *International Workshop on the Web and Database*, (2003).

20. Nowak, S., and Rüger, S. How reliable are annotations via crowdsourcing: a study about inter-annotator agreement for multi-label image annotation. In *Proc. MIR '10*. ACM Press (2010), 557-566.

21. Quinn, A. J. and Bederson, B. B. Human computation: a survey and taxonomy of a growing field. In *Proc. CHI 2011*, ACM Press (2011), 1403-1412.

22. Stvilia, B., Twidale, M., Smith, L. C., Gasser, L. Information quality work organization in Wikipedia. *JASIST*, 59(6), (2008), 983–1001.

23. Sun, Y., Roy, S., and Little, G. D. Beyond independent agreement: a tournament selection approach for quality assurance of human computation tasks. *Papers from the 2011 AAAI Workshop on Human Computation*, (2011).

24. Toselli, A.H., Romero, V., and Vidal, E. Rodriguez, L. Computer Assisted Transcription of Handwritten Text Images. *Proc. ICDAR '07*. IEEE (2007), 944-948.

25. von Ahn, L. Games with a purpose. *Computer, 39*(6), (2006), 92-94.

26. von Ahn, L., Maurer, B., McMillen, C., Abraham, D., and Blum, M. reCAPTCHA: Human-based character recognition via web security measures. *Science* (2008),1465-1468.

27. Wilkinson, D.M. Strong regularities in online peer production. In *Proc. EC '08*. ACM Press (2008), 302-309.

Indebtedness and Reciprocity in Local Online Exchange

Airi Lampinen[1,4], Vilma Lehtinen[1,4], Coye Cheshire[2], Emmi Suhonen[3]

[1]Helsinki Institute for Information Technology HIIT/ Aalto University P.O. Box 15600, 00076 Aalto, Finland firstname.lastname@hiit.fi

[2]School of Information University of California, Berkeley 102 South Hall, Berkeley CA 94720-4600, USA coye@ischool.berkeley.edu

[3]Aalto University P.O.Box 17800, 00076 Aalto, Finland

[4]University of Helsinki Department of Social Research, P.O. Box 54, 00014 University of Helsinki, Finland

ABSTRACT
Many existing and emerging online systems allow people to share content and coordinate the exchange of goods and favors in local geographic settings. We present a qualitative case study of user experiences concerning exchange and reciprocity in local online exchange. Findings from eleven in-depth interviews (containing forty-nine separate exchange experiences) reveal an aversion to indebtedness and several user behaviors that lessen these negative feelings: (1) offering small tokens of appreciation to exchange partners, (2) understanding and accepting the indirect nature of generalized exchange, (3) managing expectations by framing offers and requests carefully, (4) minimizing efforts needed in exchange processes, and (5) bartering and exchanging for a third party. The paper contributes to our understanding of emergent behaviors and norms in local online exchange systems. We discuss design implications from these empirical insights that can help alleviate the discomfort of indebtedness and better encourage and sustain participation in systems of indirect reciprocity.

Author Keywords
Computer-mediated communication; online community; social exchange; gift economies; reciprocity; debt of gratitude

ACM Classification Keywords
K.4.3 Computer-Supported Collaborative Work, H5.m. Information interfaces and presentation (e.g., HCI): Miscellaneous.

General Terms
Human Factors

INTRODUCTION
Social exchange is a fundamental human activity that helps to explain social behavior through the process of exchanging valued goods and services [3]. Beyond the material value of exchange, participation in systems of social exchange can produce social value for participants and for communities as a whole, including commitment, emotional attachment, and solidarity [5]. While social psychologists have long noted the value of participating in various forms of social exchange at the interpersonal and societal levels [35, 3, 19], the problem of learning about norms of exchange in a given community remains a challenge for theory and practice.

We present a qualitative case study focusing on *indirect exchange experiences* (where giving is not contingent on receiving gifts or favors). We focus on users of Kassi, a local online exchange system where individuals can engage in indirect exchange, as well as other forms of direct exchange. Kassi is a service in which users can lend, rent, give away and sell items, give and get help, or share rides with people nearby. By scoping our analysis on indirect exchange, we only examine non-monetary exchanges such as giving and getting help, giving away goods, and lending goods and services.

This paper seeks to advance our understanding of how individuals *interpret* and *respond* to norms of indirect social exchange within a socio-technical system. Our focal problem raises several theoretical and practical sub-questions that we address through our empirical study: How do individuals make sense of indirect reciprocity and understand how to make use of a novel system of online exchange? And, what can we do as designers, researchers, and practitioners to alleviate and address feelings of discomfort while facilitating ongoing indirect exchange?

This work contributes to our understanding of emergent behaviors and norms in local online exchange systems - an important area for CSCW research, especially among designers and practitioners who build and maintain online systems that facilitate social exchange. We discuss how the design of the Kassi system supports social exchange and indirect reciprocity, which in turn creates an opportunity for feelings of indebtedness to emerge among users. Following our empirical study, we conclude with a discussion of three broader design implications: (1) the importance of matching *similarity and status characteristics* for combating feelings of indebtedness, (2) publicly sharing experiences as *recipients* of gift exchange, and (3) the critical role of exchange *process* rather than just outcomes in online social exchange.

EXCHANGE, RECIPROCITY AND INDEBTEDNESS

Social exchange is vital to social interaction. Social exchanges are a core part of romantic relationships, friendships, barters, negotiations, favors and gifts. Most empirical research identifies three major types of social exchange [4]: negotiated exchange, reciprocal exchange, and generalized exchange. *Negotiated exchange* tends to include economic exchanges such as bargaining and prior agreements on trades or purchases. *Reciprocal exchange* includes direct reciprocity such as gifts or favors that are sometimes repaid, but lacking any terms or agreements such as those in negotiated exchange.

Generalized exchange describes acts of indirect reciprocity in the form of either collective goods (where individuals contribute to an outcome that benefits many) or networks of indirect gifts and favors where the providers rarely receive benefits from the same recipients (e.g., stranded motorists helping one another on the highway) [8, 38]. Anthropologists first observed and described systems of sustained generalized exchange in the Kula Ring: a stable exchange of decorative items with no real monetary value, but substantial symbolic value among the Trobriand Islanders of Papua New Guinea [23, 21]. Mauss [23] described this and other similar systems as *gift economies* to contrast them with systems of bartering and negotiation.

A central aspect of all types of social exchange is the norm of reciprocity: the empirical observation that individuals tend to feel a sense of responsibility after someone provides a gift or another act of kindness. Gouldner [15] found that while the application of reciprocity varies widely by culture, the norm is largely ubiquitous across societies. Furthermore, the expressive value of reciprocity can increase solidarity between exchange partners through either symbolic or communicative value, "*over and above the instrumental value of the benefits provided*" [25]. In Emerson's formulation of social exchange theory in the 1970's, he viewed reciprocity as the foundation of exchange, where norms of obligation emerge to *reinforce* reciprocity [9, 10].

In addition to the positive benefits of solidarity from acts of reciprocity, there are also some psychological challenges for individuals. People tend to reciprocate the kind acts of others, and non-reciprocated actions can leave one with an uncomfortable sense of *indebtedness*—even if the original action or gift was unsolicited. An essential part of Gouldner's description of the norm of reciprocity is that, "*people should help those who have helped them, and people should not injure those who have helped them*" [15]. Greenberg [16, 17] extended Gouldner's argument by describing the basic psychological state of indebtedness as, "*a state of tension having motivational properties such that the greater its magnitude, the greater will be the efforts to reduce it*".

The problem of indebtedness can be a significant concern for any system designed to facilitate and encourage social exchange. An aversion to indebtedness may lead potential exchange partners to be unwilling to accept gifts or help, especially if one does not expect to be capable of reciprocation in the future. Prior research indicates that individuals tend to feel an obligation to return the benefits they receive from others, but they are also psychologically and emotionally averse to over-benefitting from social interactions [36]. As we detail below, the challenge of dealing with indebtedness is a core theme in our empirical research.

SOCIAL EXCHANGE IN ONLINE COMMUNITIES

To date, the largest body of work on online exchange processes has primarily dealt with direct negotiated exchange in online systems such as EBay[1] and other economic exchange markets. In this domain, a central challenge is to reduce uncertainty among people who come together in an online market to negotiate compensation for goods and services. The main focus of research on these online economic exchange markets includes outcomes such as compensation, reputation, and trust [7, 6, 31, 20].

Of course, not all online exchange systems exclusively deal with direct economic exchange. Vast online information pools and other forms of content creation and sharing online create *group-generalized exchange*: where individuals receive rewards from a collective good without contributing to it (e.g., free-riding in collective action) [38, 8]. There are many examples of online systems where group-generalized exchange is prevalent, including Wikipedia [1], corporate knowledge sharing systems [11], peer-to-peer file sharing networks [12], and geographically local online communities such as Cyclopath [29, 22]. In each case, individuals make contributions that collectively create a public resource that benefits everyone—including those who never contribute.

An emerging body of research focuses on *network-generalized exchange*, where individuals engage in indirect reciprocity within a defined community [38]. Studies of online exchange communities comparing direct exchange on Craigslist[2] and generalized exchange on Freecycle[3] [37] support the finding from prior laboratory research that network generalized exchange creates stronger feelings of solidarity than direct exchange for both givers and receivers [25]. In addition, repeated receipt of unilateral gifts can lead to group identification, or positive feelings that are then attributed to the group as a whole [13].

Finally, some of the aforementioned online exchange systems combine online and offline participation with the

[1] http://www.ebay.com/

[2] http://www.craigslist.org/

[3] http://www.freecycle.org/

same users over time. For example, Freecycle and NeighborGoods[4] support the indirect exchange of goods and services in geographically local contexts: Individuals connect online, but exchanges take place face-to-face. Encouraging and sustaining participation is a central challenge for these different systems, regardless of whether they function online, offline, or in online-offline hybrid forms (e.g. [11, 27, 28, 29]).

KASSI – A LOCAL GIFT EXCHANGE SYSTEM

Kassi is an online gift exchange system designed to support the exchange of goods and services in geographically local communities. The purpose of the service is to help people in the course of their everyday lives by enabling them to help each other in any way they see fit – by sharing information or goods, using their special skills, or by participating in time-consuming tasks. Kassi is an example of a system that spans the online-offline dichotomy, similar to online bulletin board and classified advertisement systems (e.g, Craigslist.org). Physical location and face-to-face interaction are often crucial in Kassi, since few exchanges can be completed solely online.

Kassi users have stable user names that persist in the system as they interact over time. Many users choose to use their real names while others use pseudonyms. By using stable online identities in a geographically local context (e.g., university or other existing location), Kassi encourages a sense of community and trust that is difficult to create in large-scale anonymous social exchanges [7].

The main content on Kassi's front page is user offers and requests (see Figure 1). These listings can be searched and browsed by other users. When a user finds something of interest, she can contact the person who posted the listing either by sending them a private message or by commenting the listing publicly. Once individuals agree to make the exchange, they can then discuss logistics with Kassi messages or via e-mail, text messages, or telephone. An exchange takes place when an item or favor is successfully transferred between any two users. Kassi's interface directs users to post and/or browse offers and requests.

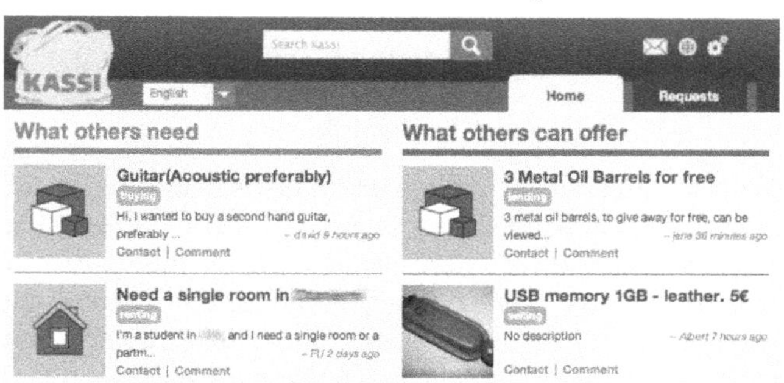

Figure 1. Examples of exchange proposals on the front page of the local gift exchange system Kassi.

[4] http://neighborgoods.net/

Users are free to offer and/or request as many favors, services and items as they like. The service is designed to support direct communication to allow all forms of exchange without implying any particular type of interaction such as negotiation or gifting (e.g., participants are completely free to decide how they want to offer or request goods and services). Typical activities in the community include selling textbooks, searching housing, and offering favors to others.

RESEARCH MATERIAL AND METHOD

This paper focuses on the use of Kassi within a university community (including both students, staff and faculty) in the capital region of Finland. In the end of April 2012, the community had 4464 members. In a pattern typical of many online communities, more than half of the members never posted a listing on Kassi, while a group of less than a thousand members produced most of the content on the site. Between May 2011 and April 2012, there were on average 2243 weekly visits to the site. During this year, altogether 2833 listings were posted, 2176 of them offers and 657 requests. Users gave feedback after a completed exchange 679 times. Of the 2833 listings, eight percent were free offers and gifts, while another eight percent dealt with lending and borrowing. The combined 16 percent of non-monetary exchanges (gifts, lending, and borrowing) constitute the focus of our empirical analysis of indirect exchange experiences below.

We chose a qualitative approach for this research in order to build a rich understanding about (1) how norms of exchange and reciprocity are interpreted and applied in the context of local online exchange, and (2) ways to lessen uneasy feelings of indebtedness in indirect exchange processes. Our primary research material consists of eleven semi-structured individual interviews from which we identified 49 distinct accounts of exchange processes using the Kassi service.

Participants

In this research, we study *active, experienced participants*: individuals who have given and/or received goods and/or services with other Kassi users at least once. The number of exchange experiences for each participant in our sample ranged from one to eight. Among these active users, the average number of offers or requests was between one and two.

We recruited individuals who engaged in one or more exchanges by screening Kassi usage logs for active participation during the previous academic year. We focus explicitly on active, experienced participants because only those participants who have engaged in at least one gift/favor exchange can relate their experiences, responses and behaviors from prior interactions. By confining our scope to only active, experienced participants, we lose the opportunity to get an inclusive picture of *all* Kassi users (e.g., lurkers and new users with no experience). However, our purposive sampling is justified precisely because our theoretical focus (feelings of indebtedness and reciprocity created after an exchange) requires that participants have had an opportunity to develop opinions from experience rather than conjecture.

We contacted twenty-four users by email and asked them to participate in an interview. We also recruited potential interviewees through an interview request posted to Kassi. We sought as many interviews as possible, and we stopped taking additional interviews when our primary thematic categories related to perceptions of exchange norms and indebtedness began to repeat substantially.

This led us to a combined total of eleven participants. We interviewed six male and five female participants. Four participants created their accounts soon after Kassi's open beta release in 2009. Another three used the service for 7 to 20 months. The final four used the service for less than 6 months. Most of the participants (N=7) were technology students in the age range from 21 to 27 who were introduced to Kassi through study-related activities. The exceptions were two students from other campuses, and a relatively older employee of the university. Finally, we interviewed one student from another university who originally found Kassi through a search engine.

Interview Procedure

Two of the authors split the interviewing tasks, using the same semi-structured interview outline. The senior interviewer trained the second interviewer on the format and style of interviews to ensure internal consistency. All interviews were conducted in spring and summer 2011 by one of the two interviewers. The interviews lasted from 30 to 90 minutes. The interviews were arranged in locations convenient for the interviewees, such as the campus library, a café, or the participant's home.

Our interview questions focused on participants' views and feelings concerning exchange processes in Kassi. In each interview, the discussion centered on specific exchange experiences. The interviewer and the participant talked through participants' experiences of exchange processes in a detailed manner. We focused on participants' perceptions of their exchange interactions, as well as any apparent 'significant moments' in the exchange experience. We prompted discussion on reciprocity with questions, such as "did anything surprising happen?", or "what would have made the experience worse?" about participants' initial expectations towards local online exchange, and later, their reflections of exchange processes. The questions covered topics including worries and hopes concerning reciprocity, indebtedness, and fairness. We did not ask direct questions about reciprocity (as a specific word), though we did ask follow-up questions once participants raised an issue about reciprocity, exchange, or related concepts.

Interview Focus: Exchange Processes

Most exchanges (30 out of 49) described by our participants were completed successfully. However, the interviews revealed a variety of ways in which an exchange process might not be fully successful. For instance, a person who offered to help with sewing had to turn down a request for help when she deemed that the task was too difficult. In other cases, the item to be exchanged had already been given away to someone else or it did not meet the needs of the person who requested it. All attempts at exchange are important for our analysis since the outcome is only a small part of the exchange process (requesting, offering, reciprocating, coordinating practical arrangements, etc).

The exchange processes in our data concerned a wide variety of goods and services, ranging from giving away an unneeded table, providing avalanche gear, sharing a ride to another city, getting advice on how to take care of plants, to receiving help in moving from an apartment to another. This study set out to understand non-negotiated social exchanges, though there were some mentions of negotiated exchanges (e.g. selling or renting items/housing) in our interviews (N=11). For this research, our primary analysis is centered on the thirty-eight exchanges in our material concerning lending or giving away goods (N=26), and providing favors (N=12).

Method of Analysis

We frame our analysis from the perspective of social exchange theory, which emphasizes the role of interpersonal relationships in the trade of socially and/or economically valuable resources. We chose to apply qualitative, interpretive methods [33] because they allow a grounded exploration of participants' conceptions of reciprocity, indebtedness, and fairness in the context of local online exchange. In brief, our analytical approach was grounded in, and driven by the research material.

We began the analysis by identifying the instances that we considered illustrate (1) experiences and perceptions of reciprocity and indebtedness and (2) ways to lessen uneasy feelings of indebtedness in exchange processes. After picking up these instances from the transcripts, we compared them to one another to identify themes that would describe the phenomena. Following the principles of constant comparison [14], we again reflected the themes we had constructed to the material, and modified them, until all the instances would fit under the themes. The themes are presented as subchapters in the following sections.

With the exception of two international students whom we interviewed in English, all interviews were conducted in Finnish. Thus, most interview excerpts in this paper are translations from original Finnish transcripts. To protect the anonymity of the participants and their friends and exchange partners, the names mentioned in the following excerpts are pseudonyms. Participants (PX) are identified by numbers (in place of "X") in the interview excerpts.

SOCIAL EXCHANGE EXPERIENCES WITH KASSI

We discuss participants' exchange experiences along two primary themes: (1) the aversion to indebtedness and perceptions of fairness, and (2) eagerness to provide something of value to others in the local community.

Aversion to Indebtedness and Perceptions of Fairness

An aversion to feeling indebted at the completion of an exchange was widely present in our interview material. Four participants explicitly stressed that they did not want to ask for something without giving something in return. Participants noted that indebtedness feels unpleasant and worrisome. An appreciation for the norm of reciprocity was present also in the other seven interviews, albeit in a less explicit form, in participants' expectations that neither of the exchange partners remains indebted.

One participant expressed an extreme view of how one should live without being dependent on others: "*The way I see it people should survive on their own. I don't want to bother others in that way. I somehow avoid the sense of being indebted.*" (P4) Other participants did not share such a strict perspective against asking for help from anyone as far as possible, but the good will of others was considered so precious that one should resort to it only when in a serious need. The worry of burdening others was well illustrated by one participant's comparison: "*If you don't really need it, then it feels a little like being a parasite, that you bother others without a reason.*" (P1)

In the initial process of making requests and responding to offers, participants expressed concern about being a burden or a nuisance by asking for excessive efforts from others. One participant illustrated this sentiment as he recalled the delighted surprise of noticing that the person lending him an electronic drill was so happy to help him use it: "*Well, I assumed that I would be more of a nuisance to that fellow. But on the contrary, he seemed really happy [in the situation]--*" (P1)

Another participant remembered a good experience of receiving a favor via Kassi. However, as she did not have an opportunity to return a favor to anyone in the community yet, she felt stuck with a sense of indebtedness: "*I don't think it could have gone any better. But I have not gotten a chance to return the favor to anyone, so I still owe that favor.*" (P2)

Next to expressing an aversion to feeling indebted to others, participants also indicated that they don't want to be cheated by a bad or unfair deal. It was considered best to aim for what the participants considered 'fair reciprocity'. For instance, one participant who offered proofreading of English texts on the site explained the boundaries of her willingness to help without compensation: "*I think if it's a small thing, I could just do it for them but if they wanted me to proofread like a thesis, or really, something really big, then that should be more like some kind of trade or service.*" (P 10) She was also wondering whether the reason she had not yet been contacted was that others did not know what to offer in return: "*--maybe people expect that you have to trade the service-- so they have to think 'what can I offer?', like a fair exchange, maybe people are thinking about what to offer.*" (P10)

When it comes to non-negotiated exchanges, our interviewees seemed to be more preoccupied with being fair-minded and avoiding indebtedness than worried about being taken advantage of or treated unfairly by others. Put differently, the norm of reciprocity is consistently more salient in our interviews than profit-driven self-interest. Among our participants, it was considered better to give too much or to withdraw from participating altogether rather than to feel indebted to others. The interviewees expected compliance to this norm from their exchange partners as well.

Eagerness to Contribute

Another characteristic that describes our participants' experience of exchanges is the eagerness to contribute to the community by offering something to others. Participants expressed the most reward from actions that clearly contributed something of value to others in the community. The possibility to do something concrete that was also in line with their personal values, such as altruistic sharing, recycling and sustainability, was another aspect that rendered participation meaningful. As the following excerpt illustrates, experiences of being able to help out and contribute were rewarding: "*It makes me feel good, when I lend things. -- And then it makes me feel good, too, to be able to help someone else own fewer things. By lending what I have.*" (P11) Participants expressed getting a lot out of 'helping others' (by responding to a request or offering something to others), especially when they felt that their efforts were valued and appreciated: "*I noticed that people are grateful that someone comes and helps them, that makes me feel good for sure*" (P5).

Participants appreciated opportunities to 'give (back)' whenever they received something from someone else. Recipients often tried to reciprocate either directly with another individual or by making an effort to provide something of their own to the community. Participants indicated that they would sometimes post an offer on the site after they received something from others, especially if their offer for direct reciprocation had been rejected. We identified five exchange processes were an offer a participant had posted had not been taken up by others. These participants were hoping that someone would contact them so that they would get a chance to contribute: "*--I have a somewhat anticipating feeling, like 'come on, someone request something now'. Or a little like that, it's not so dramatic. A slight anticipation. I'd like to get to try it out, that would be fun, I wish I would get the chance to lend something, even if it would be only something like lending a hammer, like 'here you go'" (P1)*

It seems that in our participants' minds, providing an item, a favor, or some other kind of 'help' to others are all aspects of community engagement. Even though participants enjoyed making such contributions, they did not necessarily expect others to feel the same way. On the contrary, they expressed concern about burdening or bothering others with their needs. This general sentiment is well illustrated in the aforementioned comparison of accepting help without becoming a 'parasite' to the contributor. In sum, participants held somewhat contradictory framings of their own participation in social exchange versus the participation of others. The disconnect between one's own needs and those of the 'generalized other community member' may lead to a failure to appreciate the value that one provides in their role as a beneficiary of others' contributions.

EMPIRICAL INSIGHTS: REDUCING INDEBTEDNESS IN SOCIAL EXCHANGE PROCESSES

Having identified our participants' reluctance to risk feeling indebted to others, we analyzed the research material for *intentional or unintentional* behaviors that lessen uneasy feelings of indebtedness. While our interviews are specific to a particular, dense student community embedded in the generally trusting and cooperation-oriented Finnish society, our insights from user responses and behaviors can apply to local online exchange in other societies. In the following sections we present five key ways that participant behaviors alleviated feelings of indebtedness in exchange processes or created a situation where personal obligation was significantly lessened: (1) offering small tokens of appreciation to one's exchange partners, (2) understanding and accepting the indirect nature of generalized exchange, (3) managing expectations by framing offers and requests carefully, (4) minimizing the efforts needed in the exchange process, and (5) bartering and exchanging for a third party.

Offering Small Tokens of Appreciation

Based on participants' experiences, potential compensation for efforts related to exchanges were often negotiated face-to-face at the end of the exchange process. However, when it comes to providing favors, donating goods, or lending items, direct compensation is not appropriate or sometimes even possible. We identified five accounts of exchange processes where participants navigated their way out of indebtedness by offering little tokens of appreciation for their exchange partners.

Small, unsolicited gifts can be understood as a symbolic gesture that eases feelings of obligation by converting a unilateral giving situation into one that approximates direct reciprocity. For instance, one participant *insisted* on giving a small token of appreciation for the person who helped him. Finding a way to pay back the favor was especially important to him: "*Well first I felt a little unsure and anxious of how this will go and whether it really is ok that I borrow the power drill. -- But then afterwards I had a really positive feeling of how easy it was and then of course I gave him a little cash for coffee so that also made me feel good that I at least somehow paid the favor back to him. So then; I did not feel at all that I would have been a burden for him.*" (P1)

Another participant explained how he offers to reciprocate, without a serious expectation that his offer would necessarily be accepted. Whenever he receives a book from someone, he invites them to take in return one from his collection: *I have received books from there (via Kassi), and in that sense it has been reciprocal, that books have been exchanged, or I have had some extra ones, so 'if you happen to be interested, feel free to take one'. Returning the favor, in a way.* (P4)

Furthermore, giving public feedback can be considered as a small token of appreciation—especially in a system that does not require feedback or use reputation metrics to the same extent as some other systems such as Ebay or Couchsurfing. In Kassi, the point of giving public feedback is to acknowledge the value the exchange partner has provided and to thank her/him. A participant who was not willing to accept cash as a reward for an exchange valued feedback, and subsequently expressed disappointment when she did not receive it after a successful exchange: "*Another time, I gave away mugs to a young student, and she offered to give me a little cash for coffee, so I was like, I don't want any money, just take them (the mugs) and put them in use -- But then it was a little curious that she didn't for instance give me feedback in Kassi*" (P7)

Importantly, these small tokens of appreciation were not supposed to be a direct compensation (e.g., exchanges that approximate equivalent value) for the efforts and value provided by one's exchange partner. When the exchange was not clearly a monetary transaction like buying or selling goods, paying for an item or a favor was not expected. However, it was deemed important to find a way to express gratitude – and, on the flipside, to feel acknowledged and appreciated for participation. As one participant explains, an unexpected, small acknowledgement can give a positive afterglow: "*I think that he was really grateful for that, you could see from how he left that box of chocolates for me. It made me feel really good, since he really didn't have to do that, as I had been the one to offer lending that item.*" (P11)

Offering small tokens of appreciation, gratuitously accepting them, or rejecting gifts as "kind but unnecessary" is important for acknowledging one's exchange partner and managing feelings of indebtedness. The interpersonal discussions stemming from the small gestures of appreciation liberated participants from a sense of indebtedness and feelings of unfairness or disappointment due to an ungrateful exchange partner. Alleviating such feelings was important for the participants and sometimes encouraged further participation.

Understanding and Accepting the Indirect Nature of Generalized Exchange Over Time

Our research material included instances of indirect reciprocity where individuals paid their debts of gratitude not directly to their exchange partner but to someone else in the community, that is, they engaged in network-generalized exchange [38]. Being able to give back to someone in the community made it easier for the participants to accept the lack of direct reciprocity. One participant explained the idea of reciprocating with the community instead of with one's direct exchange partner in the following way: "*It feels like 'okay, I can borrow this'. And then if someone needs, for instance, a hammer from me, I'll lend it. That way we'll be okay with the community.*" (P1)

The idea of evening out any debts of gratitude with the community, not directly with one's exchange partner, has been a part of the philosophy underlying Kassi since the service was first created. However, this idea is not communicated to users in any explicit way (e.g., the Kassi platform and user interface does not explain or otherwise elaborate on expectations of exchange aside from the idea of sharing with the community). While three participants expressed explicitly that the "pay it forward to the community" aspect of Kassi appealed to them and was a motivation to participate, engaging in indirect, network-generalized exchange was not instinctive or self-evident. One participant told how her feelings of being indebted were lessened when an exchange partner (in this case, one of the developers of the service) had explained to her that direct reciprocation is not necessary: "*Well I guess I did remain indebted but then he explained that to me, that I can offer a favor to someone else, something I can do, so then we'll be square.*" (P2)

Amongst our participants, those who had had more exchange experiences were more prone to advocate indirect reciprocity within the community – a finding that indicates that network-generalized exchange was understood and accepted as an idea only after some initial period of learning and familiarization. In the following excerpt, a participant explains how his thinking changed after a first, positive exchange experience: "*Well at least after that first exchange event, I was feeling open to it and I listed also the rest of my tools there (on Kassi), so then, if nothing else, if I can't pay back my debt of gratitude to that person, then at least I can lend things to others if they need something so in that way the common good is sustained.*" (P1)

Managing Expectations of Reciprocity by Framing Offers and Requests Carefully

As Kassi does not spell out how exactly users should manage and coordinate exchanges, people may hold different expectations for how the exchanges should take place. As we have seen in the previous sections, some participants were happy to reciprocate indirectly, while others (sometimes the same people in different exchange processes) were more comfortable when they could offer a little token of appreciation directly to their exchange partner. Three participants brought up the helpfulness of spelling out expectations of reciprocity when making an offer or a request. In other words, these individuals emphasized the importance of framing the initial requests and offers as a way to reduce uncertainty about the exchange.

A good example of the importance of framing came from a participant who used Kassi to join a carpool. While the compensation of the driver's efforts and investments were eventually (and successfully) negotiated face-to-face, the participant explained that the process would have felt even easier if the expectation of sharing fuel costs would have been expressed explicitly from the beginning: "*Well, I don't know whether that might have frightened people, but maybe it could have been even smoother if in the offer there would have been a mention of sharing the costs of gas, like 'let's split gas' or something like that. I mean, it is a Finnish assumption of politeness that of course we'll share but (it would have been easier if it was spelled out)*" (P3)

Another participant made an offer to help people who were moving in or out of an apartment. He stated that he did not expect compensation but that he would not reject it either. Such a wording, perhaps unsurprisingly, had led others to reward him in a variety of ways. The participant felt comfortable about the situation since although no explicit agreement had been made, there was also no need for negotiating the 'right' level of compensation or reward: "*In this latter case, it went in line with my offer where I had written something like 'I don't expect a compensation but if you want to give something in return, feel free.' So in this case, either, it had not really been agreed upon. But the person wanted to (give a reward). And I, on the other hand, didn't reject that.*" (P5)

Finally, one participant noted that the offer he responded to stated that the item offered was free, so there was no need to reciprocate directly or offer anything tangible to express his gratitude: "*There was nothing like that. She had said it's for free. So then I didn't suggest a packet of coffee or anything like that in exchange.*" (P4)

In all of these cases, initial online postings on Kassi facilitated subsequent face-to-face interactions. When some form of expectations management concerning reciprocity was clearly explained from an initial posting, participants felt less awkward about entering an exchange. Framing an exchange offer or request carefully in terms of what to expect and how to reciprocate is helpful in managing expectations, reducing uncertainty, and building a shared understanding of the aims of the exchange process.

Minimizing the Efforts Needed in Exchange Processes

The desire to simplify exchange processes is another way to lessen indebtedness in exchange. Participants attempted to keep exchange processes as effortless as possible to reduce the burden to others as well as for their own convenience. Switching to a more convenient communication channel is one common way to simplify an exchange. The following excerpt depicts a typical flow of communications during an exchange – the switching from one medium to another as the exchange process proceeds: "*I think, we did talk through Kassi first but maybe he preferred e-mail, so we went for e-mail and then I called him, to see when he had the time for me to come over but after that (we switched over to) sending text messages 'cause I don't want to call all the time and disturb him.*" (P10)

Participants were troubled when coordinating an exchange turned out to require more effort on their part than they had originally intended. This was especially evident if the person receiving an item or a favor was not actively working to complete the exchange. For example, one participant's experience taught her to be stricter about clarifying what she is or is not willing to do for others. While the particular exchange ended successfully with positive feedback, the participant disapproved of being left to make the practical efforts the exchange necessitated – especially since she was giving away an item for free: "*There was this coffee table that he couldn't pick up, really. I guess I could have pressured him a little more -- but then I said 'ok, I'll bring it on the bus to you' -- so that was a little [burdensome]. -- But then he did thank me in the feedback so that made me feel good about it*" (P7)

Another participant expressed similar concerns regarding the need to retrieve items that were loaned rather than given away. In this case, the participant lent a backpack to a fellow student: "*Sophie returned it by bringing it back to our place. -- That, in my opinion, was a nice gesture since when I have lent something to someone it is nice if the borrower brings it back to me so that I don't need to bother (to pick up the item)*" (P11). What is inherent in the participant's perspective is that kind deeds done for others imply that the recipient should be the one who makes further efforts to follow up and return loaned items. This was reiterated in her account of another exchange event: "*Yeah, there was then a little bit of a hassle, I had a lot of work and he was always busy in the evenings. But then, I took the attitude that he has to come and pick it up from me from here if he wants to borrow it (a backpack)*" (P11)

When expectations of responsibility and accountability were not met, participants felt burdened and expressed an overall sense of imbalance in the exchange. Participants worried not only about potential conflicts resulting from material damage, but also about the flow of the exchange process before lending their possessions to others: "*Well, of course if the items get broken. Or then the exchange of the items, like if it turns into a huge hassle, like they can't pick it up from the student village (where the interviewee lives) or they can't return it here, if they are like 'come and pick it up'. Things like that, that would cause me trouble, would disappoint me.*" (P6)

In sum, indebtedness stems from both exchange outcomes and efforts made during exchange processes. Participants' experiences with issues of practice and procedure were critical to their overall perceptions of successful exchange and their desire to continue participating in the future.

Bartering and Exchanging for a Third Party

Finally, we identified an unexpected usage pattern that illustrates how local online exchange not only embodies a "pay it forward" philosophy, but also sometimes creates a "search it forward" mentality in which individuals find goods and services for others in their existing social groups. We identified four instances where a Kassi user turned to the service in order to solve someone else's problem. For instance, one participant promised a friend to keep an eye out for skates. When she stumbled upon the right size of skates, she set up a meeting for the friend and the seller: "*And then, in the end, that friend of mine went to get the skates himself, as they were not even for me, I just said that I can keep an eye out for skates of his size and then there happened to be a pair [on offer].*" (P7)

In another case, a participant's partner had a broken computer screen, so she decided to make a request, to which another Kassi user replied: "*Well, he had an old CRT display, an incredibly huge one. A screen he just wanted to get rid of. He said that 'come take it away and don't bring it back'. -- So that's how I got it for Luca, we carried it over to his place, with a car.*" (P11) Luca, an exchange student at the time, donated the screen to a neighbor when he returned to his home country. While this last transfer was not organized through Kassi, the participant expressed that successfully recycling the screen constituted a further victory for local exchanges of gifts and favors.

In the third instance, a Kassi user borrowed a mattress from a community member in order to accommodate his brother who was coming for a visit. In the final case, a single individual managed an exchange on behalf of a larger group. A group of housemates used Kassi when they needed rugs for their common room. One of the participants posted a request for the group, with the promise that they could all compensate any donated rugs by baking something in return. Although the entire household needed the rugs, the participant was the one to bring up the issue in Kassi: "*Well, it was posted under my name and, in principle, it was my idea, too, but in a way that 'we are looking for this to our shared household'.*" (P3)

Later on, the abovementioned participant explained how she considered Kassi especially useful for collective causes, such as furnishing and decorating shared spaces, where no one is willing to invest a lot of money or effort but everyone in the group benefits if something matching the need can be found. She stated that if she needed something for her own room, she would most likely purchase it from a store but that she would turn to Kassi for collective purposes: "*But if I wanted a shelf to our common room, I would ask for it in Kassi. The way we decorate our common room together, everything is pretty much how it happens to be, almost everything is second hand and I still think it's cozy.*" (P3)

Kassi members sometimes screen and post listings with the intention of finding something that a friend, a significant other, or a housemate needs. Though almost certainly not intentional, this is another effective way to distance oneself from obligations of reciprocity: When one barters for others, he or she may cognitively restructure the situation in a way that lessens his or her personal connection to the exchange. Such cognitive shifts in framing are an effective way to reduce the magnitude of indebtedness that one might otherwise perceive [18]. Similarly, the third parties who receive benefits may experience less of a personal connection (and therefore less indebtedness), too, since they did not initiate the exchange.

DESIGN IMPLICATIONS

The norm of reciprocity is a core social norm that persists in all forms of exchange, including local online exchange. Given the strong aversion to indebtedness and the various ways that participants handle uneasy feelings of obligation, what can we do as designers and practitioners of online systems to help address it in a real-world context? In light of the outcomes of our analysis of user experiences, attitudes and behaviors discussed above, we identify three broader implications for designers who want to design effective online exchange systems.

Matching Similarity and Status Characteristics

Among Kassi users, we found that an aversion to indebtedness was often accompanied by a strong willingness to contribute by providing some kind of help to others. Indeed, we found that the possibility to help a community member can sometimes be even more rewarding than benefiting from the help or resources of others. Yet, it is not always clear *who* one could contribute to, or *what* one could contribute that would lessen feelings of indebtedness. Combined with principles of group similarity and status from social psychology, our empirical findings illuminate a few ways to encourage positive responses to feelings of indebtedness.

Prior sociological and social psychological research shows that individuals tend to seek favors or assistance from those who are most similar to them (e.g., individuals in similar situations within a given community), even if the assistance is not as valuable as that which could be obtained from someone else [17]. The theoretical and empirical explanation for this effect is that individuals tend to accept support from those "*of a kind they could themselves return on occasion.*" [18]. This generates a straightforward, but significant implication for the design and structure of online exchange systems: designs that facilitate linking or matching individuals based on similarity on a variety of metrics (e.g., socio-economic, needs-based, social affiliation, etc) create an opportunity for individuals to give and receive from those with comparable social status and likeness. Designing systems that make individuals aware of who is in a similar situation to one's own (with regard to various similarity characteristics) can provide a simple, yet empowering way to guide individuals towards pro-active behaviors when feelings of indebtedness are salient.

Highlighting the Value of being a Recipient

Our participants were quick to note the value that they personally receive from giving goods and favors to others, yet these same individuals often failed to perceive their value in their most frequent and generally common role: a *recipient* of others' goods and favors. In general, recipients do not recognize that they provide others with rewarding experiences by allowing contributors to be helpful, needed community members. To date, the role of recipient is largely ignored in almost all online exchange systems, perhaps because the incentive to receive benefits is taken for granted. However, our research on users' experiences clearly shows that in gift and favor exchange, exchange recipients play a critical role for providers of gifts and favors.

There are many design solutions that can address this problem by providing necessary feedback to users about their role as both a contributor *and a recipient*. We invite designers to explore the potential of feedback beyond basic, user-to-user rank/rate reputation systems. Prior work clearly shows that individuals contribute more when they know the unique value of their contribution [2, 30]. Extending this logic further, designers could highlight one's role as a *recipient* of others' efforts as a logical next step. By clearly explaining how and why a recipient is important to individual providers (and the community as a whole), such feedback can reduce the sense of imbalance and inequity that leads to strong, negative feelings of indebtedness. For example, one's user page in a given online exchange system could actively highlight the extended benefits to the community that are created by participation of all types—including the role of exchange recipient.

One of the simplest design choices that can effectively highlight the role and value of recipients more broadly is to actively promote user experiences as a core part of the user interface and home page experience in a given system. Many aforementioned online systems such as Freecycle and Neighborgoods provide examples of user experiences, yet this information is often relegated to areas of the site other than the primary interface (e.g., instructional videos, frequently asked questions, and 'about' pages).

Highlighting Exchange Processes and Outcomes

Finally, another important design issue stems from the finding that user experiences of social exchange are often more about process than just outcomes. The flow of communication between providers and recipients, as well as the smoothness of coordination are crucial elements of the entire exchange process.

One clear design consideration comes from our observation of informal tokens of appreciation after an exchange. Formalizing the exchange of tokens of appreciation and/or linking such behavior to one's online reputation or profile would be antithetical to the spirit of indirect exchange. However, designers could provide a way for recipients of these small gifts to share their experiences in an anonymous, public fashion through the site. Highlighting this aspect of the exchange process is a way to spread awareness of this type of emergent behavior and to help reduce some of the trepidation that was so common among users.

More broadly, designers should leverage user feedback as a way to accumulate best practices for handling exchanges and for dealing with issues of reciprocity and indebtedness. Passing along (and frequently refreshing) suggestions about best practices through the user interface as users prepare an offer or request is a deceptively simple, yet important way to address these issues. A subtle but critical point is that the emphasis of such feedback should be on the exchange *process* as a whole instead of the specific community member (e.g., reputation metrics). For instance, solicitations for user feedback in local online exchange systems could be framed in terms of 'sharing one's exchange experience with the community' instead of 'rating one's exchange partner'.

Whether feedback about the exchange process is positive or negative, it can create a shared benefit by (a) reducing uncertainty and concern among newer community members, and (b) informing all community members about less helpful or even harmful behaviors that hinder successful exchange. Of course, it is sometimes hard to infer norms and codes via the lean channels of computer-mediated systems [34]. Nevertheless, the experiences we documented in our research lead us to believe that showcasing successful *and* less successful examples of exchange processes can help diffuse community norms in an organic way.

CONCLUSION: EMBRACING INDEBTEDNESS IN ONLINE SOCIAL EXCHANGE

Our research documents months (and in some cases slightly less than two years) of user experiences, opinions, and behaviors with the Kassi system. Indebtedness is clearly a negative feeling that was a prominent part of our participants' experiences during this time, but it would be a mistake to try to 'design away' indebtedness. After all, the norm of reciprocity and indebtedness are part of the same social process [9, 10, 16]. Feelings of indebtedness motivate individuals to give something back to the community. The key for designers is to redirect feelings of indebtedness towards positive, participatory outcomes rather than frustration, hesitation, and non-participation.

The overall design goal should not be an eradication of the discomforts of indebtedness in social exchange. Instead, local online exchange systems have an opportunity to channel such feelings into pro-active behaviors of sharing and ongoing community participation. By lessening burdens and highlighting benefits, participants can 'get over the hump' of understanding and accepting the indirect nature of reciprocity in generalized exchange. If successful, local communities can potentially use online systems to reap the benefits of stronger group identities [13] as well as positive affect, trust, and solidarity [34].

ACKNOWLEDGMENTS

This work has been supported by the OtaSizzle research project, funded by Aalto University (formerly Helsinki University of Technology TKK) "Technology for Life" campaign donations as well as the TEKES funded research project Possi. We thank Antti Oulasvirta, Suvi Silfverberg, Eeva Raita and our other colleagues at Helsinki Institute for Information Technology HIIT, as well as the anonymous reviewers for their many valuable comments. Furthermore, we are grateful to Juho Makkonen and Antti Virolainen for fruitful discussions and help in accessing the Kassi usage logs.

REFERENCES

1. Antin, J. and Cheshire, C. Readers are not free-riders: reading as a form of participation on wikipedia. In *Proc. CSCW 2010*, ACM Press (2010), 127-130.
2. Beenen, G., Ling, K., Wang, X., Chang, K., Frankowski, D., Resnick, P. and Kraut, R. E. Using social psychology to motivate contributions to online communities. In *Proc. CSCW 2004*. ACM Press (2004), 212-221.
3. Blau, P.M. *Exchange and Power in Social Life*. J. Wiley, New York (1964).
4. Cheshire, C., Gerbasi, A. and Cook, K.S. Trust and Transitions in Modes of Social Exchange. *Social Psychology Quarterly 73*, 2 (2010), 176-195.
5. Cook, K. and Emerson, R. Power, Equity and Commitment in Exchange Networks. *American Sociological Review 43*, 5 (1978), 721-739.
6. Cook, K. S., Cheshire, C. and Gerbasi, A. Power, Dependence and Social Exchange. In Burke, P. (ed.), *Research Programs in Social Psychology*. Stanford University Press (2006).
7. Cook, K. S., Cheshire, C., Gerbasi, A. and Aven, B. Assessing Trustworthiness in Providers of Online Goods and Services. In K.S. Cook, C. Snijders, V. Buskins and C. Cheshire (eds.), *eTrust: Forming Relationships in the Online World*. Russell Sage Foundation (2009), 189-214.
8. Ekeh, P.P. *Social exchange theory: the two traditions*. Heinemann Educational, London (1974).
9. Emerson, R.M. Exchange Theory, Part I: A Psychological Basis for Social Exchange and Exchange Relations in Network Structures. In *Sociological Theories in Progress*. Houghton Mifflin, Boston, MA (1972), 38-87.
10. Emerson, R.M. Exchange Theory, Part II: A Psychological Basis for Social Exchange and Exchange Relations in Network Structures. In *Sociological*

Theories in Progress. Houghton Mifflin, Boston, MA (1972), 38-87.

11. Farzan, R., DiMicco, J. M., Millen, D. R., Brownholtz, B., Geyer, W., & Dugan, C. Results from Deploying a Participation Incentive Mechanism within the Enterprise. In *Proc. CHI 2008*, ACM Press (2008), 563-572.
12. Feldman, M., Lai, K., Stoica, I., & Chuang, J. Robust Incentive Techniques for Peer-to-Peer Networks. In *Proc. EC 2004*, ACM Press (2004), 102-111.
13. Flynn, F. Give and Take: Psychological Mindsets in Conflict. In De Cremer, D., Van Dick, R., & Murnighan, J. K. (eds.) *Social Psychology and Organizations*. Routledge (2011), 231-250.
14. Glaser, B. & Strauss, A. *The Discovery of Grounded Theory*. Aldine, Chicago (1967).
15. Gouldner, A. The Norm of Reciprocity: A Preliminary Statement. *American Sociological Review 25*, 2 (1960), 161-178.
16. Greenberg, A. W. A preliminary statement on a theory of indebtedness. In M. S. Greenberg (Chm.), *Justice in Social Exchange*. Symposium at the Western Psychological Association, San Diego (1968).
17. Greenberg, M. S. and Shapiro, S. P. Indebtedness: An Adverse Aspect of Asking for and Receiving Help. *Sociometry 34*, 2 (1971), 290-301.
18. Homans, G. Social behavior as exchange. *American journal of sociology 62* (1958), 597-606.
19. Homans, G. C. *Social Behavior: Its Elementary Forms*. New York: Harcourt, Brace and World (1961).
20. Kollock, P. The Production of Trust in Online Markets. *Advances in Group Processes 16* (1999), 99-123.
21. Malinowski, B. *Argonauts of the Western Pacific*. New York: E.P. Dutton (1992).
22. Masli, M., Priedhorsky, R., & Terveen, L. Task Specialization in Social Production Communities: The Case of Geographic Volunteer Work. In *Proc. Weblogs and Social Media'11*, AAAI (2011), 217-224.
23. Mauss, M. *The Gift: The Form and Reason for Exchange in Archaic Societies*. New York: W.W. Norton (1923 [1990]).
24. Molm, L. D. Power, Trust and Fairness: Comparisons of Negotiated and Reciprocal Exchange. In Thy, S. R. and Skvoretz, J. (eds.) *Advances in Group Processes: Power and Status 20* (2003), 31-65.
25. Molm, L. D., Collett, J. & Schaefer, D. Building Solidarity through Generalized Exchange: A Theory of Reciprocity. *American Journal of Sociology 113*, 1 (2007), 205-242.
26. Molm, L. D., Schaefer, D. R. and Collett, J. L. The Value of Reciprocity. *Social Psychology Quarterly 70*, 2 (2007), 199-217.
27. Muller, M., Shami, N.S., Millen, D. & Feinberg, J. We are all lurkers: consuming behaviors among authors and readers in an enterprise file-sharing service. In *Proc. GROUP 2010*, ACM Press (2010), 201-210.
28. Muller, M. Lurking as Personal Trait or Situational Disposition? Lurking and Contributing in Enterprise Social Media. In Proc. CSCW 2012, ACM Press (2012), 253-256.
29. Panciera, K., Priedhorsky, R., Erickson, T. and Terveen, L. Lurking? Cyclopaths? A Quantitative Lifecyle Analysis of User Behavior in a Geowiki. In *Proc. CHI 2010*, ACM Press (2010), 1917-1926.
30. Rashid, A. M., Ling, K., Tassone, R. D., Resnick, P., Kraut, R. and Riedl, J. Motivating participation by displaying the value of contribution. In *Proc. CHI 2006*. ACM Press (2006), 955-958.
31. Resnick, P., Zeckhauser, R., Swanson, J. and Lockwood, K. The value of reputation on eBay: A controlled experiment. *Experimental Economics, 9*, 2 (2006), 79-101.
32. Rice, Eric. R. *The Effect of Social Uncertainty in Networks of Social Exchange*. Ph.D. Dissertation. Stanford University (2002).
33. Strauss, A. & Corbin, J. *Basics of Qualitative Research*. Sage, Newbury Park, CA (1990).
34. Suhonen, E., Lampinen, A., Cheshire, C. and Antin, J. Everyday Favors: A Case Study of a Local Online Gift Exchange System. In *Proc. GROUP 2010*, ACM Press (2010), 11-20.
35. Thibaut, J. & Kelley, H. *The Social Psychology of Groups*. Wiley, New York (1959).
36. Uehara, E. S. Reciprocity Reconsidered: Gouldner's 'Moral Norma of Reciprocity' and Social Support. *Journal of Social and Personal Relationships 12*, 4 (1995), 483-502.
37. Willer, R, Flynn, F. J. and Zak, S. Structure, Identity, and Solidarity: A Comparative Field Study of Direct and Generalized Exchange. *Administrative Science Quarterly*, forthcoming.
38. Yamagishi, T. & Cook, K.S. Generalized Exchange and Social Dilemmas. *Social Psychology Quarterly 56*, 4 (1993), 235-248.

Consequences of Content Diversity for Online Public Spaces for Local Communities

Claudia López
University of Pittsburgh
135 North Bellefield Ave, Pittsburgh, PA 15260
cal95 @ pitt.edu

Brian Butler
University of Maryland
2117B Hornbake Bldg, College Park, MD 20742
bsbutler @ umd.edu

ABSTRACT
While there is significant potential for social technologies to strengthen local communities, creating viable online spaces for them remains difficult. Maintaining a reliable content stream is challenging for local communities with their bounded emphases and limited population of potential contributors. Some systems focus on specific information types (e.g. restaurant, events). Others allow many different information types. This paper reports our findings about the consequences of content diversity from a study of neighborhood-oriented Facebook groups. The findings raise questions about the viability of designs for local online communities that focus narrowly on single topics, goals, and audiences.

Author Keywords
Local online groups, design decisions, sustainability

ACM Classification Keywords
H.5.3. Group and Organization Interfaces: Web-based Interaction

INTRODUCTION
Communicative ecology refers to the mix of media that people use to connect to others [31]. Residents of local communities rely on many systems to communicate and propagate information [14]. Traditional media, internet-enabled systems and word of mouth comprise the communicative ecology of a neighborhood. A recent study has shown that local newspapers, radio, and TV continue to be important sources for many kinds of local information [28]. Word of mouth is also identified as a frequent source of community news [28].

Internet-based systems that rely on user-generated content also play a role as local information sources. Specialty websites provide information about restaurants and other local businesses [25]. Search engines enable users to discover locally-constructed information sources [25]. However, mobile applications and online social platforms such as Facebook and Twitter, while widely used in US, are only slowly developing as channels for local information [28]. Listservs are rarely mentioned as source of local information [28]. In spite of the potential for peer-based online systems to propagate local information, development and deployment of these systems is still in the early stages.

One of the main challenges of online social systems is maintaining a sufficient level of content contribution. Even with a potentially global reach, online discussion communities often fail to maintain a critical mass of activity [13, 24]. Given the much smaller population of potential participants, building sustainable online spaces for local communities is even more challenging.

Systems that provide user-generated information about local communities vary significantly with respect to the diversity of content allowed. Some sites focus on providing information of a single type. Urbanspoon[1] enables users to share reviews about restaurants. Metromix[2] is a network of local entertainment websites that allows users to comment on the advertised establishments. Eventful[3] uses the same mechanisms to advertise events. Each of these sites organizes content and activity in hierarchically-structured sections corresponding to particular regions and communities. Then within each community area, the type of information allowed is focused on a particular type of content.

At the other extreme are sites that allow individuals to post information on a broad range of topics. Websites for traditional media often collect information from individuals on a range of topics (traffic, school closings, sports and entertainment, politics, etc.). Craigslist[4] allows users to post information ranging from discussion contributions to classified advertisements for all kind of services. e-democracy[5] supports moderated online forums within a local community. i-neighbors[6], Neighborland[7], EveryBlock[8] and NextDoor[9] aim to provide a centralized website for each neighborhood where users can meet online, discuss and stay informed about any aspect of their neighborhood. While these information sources also have subsections focused on particular locations, their content

CSCW '13, February 23–27, 2013, San Antonio, Texas, USA.

[1] http://www.urbanspoon.com
[2] http://www.metromix.com/
[3] http://eventful.com/
[4] http://www.craigslist.org/about/sites
[5] http://forums.e-democracy.org/
[6] http://i-neighbors.org/
[7] https://neighborland.com/
[8] http://www.everyblock.com/
[9] https://nextdoor.com/

diversity is much greater than seen in the specialized sources described above.

Our larger research agenda focuses on determining how design decisions and community characteristics affect the viability and impact of locally-focused online social systems. To achieve this goal, we are developing and testing a data collection protocol for both online and offline information systems and information sources that are part of a neighborhood's communicative ecology. As part of this developing stream of research, we have collected data about neighborhood-oriented Facebook groups, websites that advertise local events, local media sites and offline bulletin boards in a sample of urban neighborhoods in Pittsburgh.

The study reported in this paper examines how a single system characteristic (content diversity) affects one aspect of local online system viability (level of activity) in a single type of online spaces for local communities (local Facebook groups). Community networks [30] –information systems that aim to support communication within a neighborhood– have usually tended to increase the diversity of their content over time, as reported in [7]. Therefore, we hypothesize that the diversity of the purposes and content affects future content volume and frequency of information exchanges within a system. In the context of a local community, we expect that the more diverse the communicative purposes and content, the more subsequent posts there will be within the system. However, we expect that this positive relationship will be subject to diminishing effects as higher levels of content diversity leading to problems such as information overload.

RELATED WORK

This work is focused on analyzing the diversity of content and its correlation to the level of activity of online groups for local communities. Our research question is based on three research areas: community networks, public displays and the impact of diversity on online communities. This section reviews the relevant work in these areas.

Community Networks

It has been observed that technology can reshape many aspects of people's lives [26]. Among them, researchers have studied how internet access changes the communication patterns with local social ties [16, 20], and how internet-based systems designed for neighborhoods can affect community involvement and social capital [17, 19]. Although it has been argued that the Internet can diminish the importance of neighborly proximity by enabling people to maintain friendship ties with others regardless of their location [34, 26], place and neighborhoods remain an important focus for many sociotechnical research efforts [1, 2, 7, 15, 18].

Community networks are "computer-based networks created by and for a local community" [7]. They are intended to support communities' efforts to achieve social goals such as greater community awareness and involvement [30].

Community Memory of Berkeley, California [11] is recognized as the first exemplar of community networks. It was known as an "electronic bulletin board" and it was used for a wide range of topics such as housing, finding people with similar interests (e.g. musicians), organizing groups (e.g. car pooling), buying and selling things, and reviewing restaurants. Additionally, it developed some unexpected uses as users added poems, shared graphics, and started dialogues with others in the system [11]. The Cleveland Free-Net [5] was initially conceived as an online question & answer bulletin board for health issues, but was later extended to incorporate other topics such as law, arts, and government issues.

The PEN project in Santa Monica [27] offered access to public information such as event and bus schedules, city council agendas, public safety tips, and the library catalog. It also included a discussion forum where the neighbors could participate in or initiate discussions about local issues. Two-thirds of the overall activity in the community network took place in these open discussion forums. Generally, community networks tended to offer a broad range of topics with the range of content expanding over time.

Web-based versions of community networks also allowed for high levels of content diversity. The Blacksburg Electronic Village (BEV) [8] offered a wide variety of information and services ranging from health and education information to museums and library services. Particularly, it was also noticed that the BEV-news listserv – that was originally intended to host discussion about BEV policies – was used for a much broader range of discussion topics including event announcements, restaurant reviews, and even personal topics.

Netville [16] offered chat rooms and email lists where neighbors could initiate any kind of conversation. e-Neighborhood [17] offered different forums for reviews of local business and services, classifieds and events. The Carlisle Community Center designers reported that some discussion topics such as politics and local issues related to danger and novelty were more appealing to the neighbors as they generated more participation in the discussion forums [21]. Based on this observation, they suggested that purposefully seeding these sorts of topics might be an effective approach to increasing participation in community networks. e-Democracy [3], a discussion forum seeking to encourage civic engagement within neighborhoods, has specifically hired staff to seed new content in the discussion forums as a mechanism to encourage more activity in the discussion forums. Its studies of content diversity have revealed different proportions of each type of content (announcements, opportunities, requests, news and issues) in different neighborhoods [3].

Although it is often asserted that content diversity is positively related to participation rates, none of these projects have actually tested this hypothesis. Our work is particularly focused on studying the relationship between these two variables in local online groups.

Public Displays

Physical public displays are another prominent form of social information system where neighbors can find local information. Bulletin boards, store windows, light poles, and other features of the physical environment are often used to share local information. These physical objects provide a low cost mechanism for disseminating information about events, activities, and organizations within a neighborhood [10, 32]. There have also been efforts to develop electronic announcement boards and other forms of publicly accessible, computerized information public displays [10, 22, 29] in order to increase community awareness and involvement.

The content posted in public displays has been previously studied. Based on observation of bulletin boards in three local areas in California and interviews with residents, Churchill et al. [10] concluded that bulletin boards serve as a communication media to seek and advertise (1) viewpoints, (2) activities, (3) events and (4) services. In another observational study, Alt et al. [4] determined that there is an interplay among a bulletin board's location, its stakeholders (the manager, the content providers and the viewers) and its content. Content that has no relation to the location is rarely posted. Besides, each bulletin board develops an "identity" as its managers remove posters related to undesired topics. Munson et al. [22] stated the goals and norms of use of a public display are negotiated among the participants over time. Our work aims to further investigate content in public online displays. We want to analyze how the decisions about the (allowed) diversity of content relate to subsequent content contribution rates.

Diversity in Online Communities

Diversity has been generally associated with participation measures in online communities. Diversity of tenure among editors of Wikipedia groups had a curvilinear association to the group's members withdrawal [9]. While very low and very high levels of tenure diversity were related to high turnover, moderate levels of diversity of experience in Wikipedia were associated with lower rates of withdrawal.

User population diversity in chat channels at their inception stage was a significant predictor of the likelihood of channels' long term sustainability [24]. Channels with more diverse populations were more likely to survive than those with more homogeneous populations. However, the diversity measure used in this study assessed how stable the user population was at an interval of time and did not assess diversity of any characteristic of individual posters.

Regarding content diversity, a study of e-mail-based online groups found that topic diversity was a significant mediator of the relationship between group size and group membership variation. Size was positively related to content diversity, and both measures had a negative association with the subsequent measure of group size [6]. Larger groups had greater content diversity in their communication and these two factors were associated with losing larger proportions of membership. Another study analyzed the consequences of content diversity in Twitter. It was observed that lower content diversity was associated with a larger and more connected group of followers (i.e. readers) [33]. In contrast, our study focuses on understanding the consequences of content diversity on the creation of content in neighborhood-oriented online groups.

HYPOTHESIS

As reviewed in the previous section, prior work on community networks has usually reported a broad range of topics being offered or discussed [7]. A diverse spectrum of content can potentially be relevant to more people within the neighborhood, which in turn can lead to more people being motivated to create content in the online group. Given that the potential audience of a local online group is limited (compared to global online groups), we believe that the negative effects of content diversity in larger online groups [33, 6] will not be as detrimental in local online groups.

We hypothesize that the diversity of communicative purposes and content affects subsequent content volume and frequency of information exchanges within a system. In the context of a local community, we expect that the more diverse the purposes and contents, the more posts there will be within the system at later periods of time. However, we expect that this positive relationship will be subject to diminishing effects as high levels of content diversity lead to problems such as information overload and identity confusion.

DATA COLLECTION

Previous work on public displays and community networks has measured and qualitatively analyzed the diversity of content published in these social information systems [3, 4, 10, 21, 22]. This work aims to supplement the prior work by quantitatively examining the relationship between content diversity and subsequent content contributions in online groups related to neighborhoods. To examine the consequences of content diversity, we collected data from Facebook groups related to five urban neighborhoods in Pittsburgh.

Facebook Groups

Examining the consequences of design and contextual factors for local online systems requires a sample of sites that vary with respect to community characteristics, technology capabilities, and system features. This study of Facebook groups is an initial step in an ongoing effort to gather data from a diverse sample of local systems that make up a neighborhood's communicative ecology. Our sample includes local-oriented Facebook groups, websites, e-mail discussion lists, and offline bulletin boards from different communities.

Although Facebook is itself a large-scale, global, online social system, Facebook groups can be used to create online spaces for local communities. We chose this platform for this study because content diversity is not predefined by the technology itself, but rather it is developed and negotiated by the group's members. Facebook groups that are used to discuss local community issues have the potential to vary significantly with respect to content diversity in ways that are not directly determined by design decisions or technology affordances (as every group uses the same technology). Furthermore, as Facebook groups were not designed to be community networks, the groups are more likely to have naturally evolved, without the biases generated by planned interventions, participatory design or purposefully seeded content. Additionally, Facebook is already a very popular site, so many people have the technical skills needed to use it as a medium to share local information. Thus, low levels of participation in groups can be more reliably associated with the content that was shared in the group than with other factors such as usability or general awareness of the platform.

Neighborhoods

We aim to understand what contextual factors can affect the sustainability of local online groups, therefore we sampled neighborhoods that differ with respect to attributes that might be relevant to the activity in online groups. The sampled neighborhoods vary with respect to population size, age demographics, and median income (Table 1).

Table 1. Neighborhoods' Descriptive Data [10]

Neighborhood[10]	Population	% Over 60	Median Income
Bloomfield	9,089	21.60%	15K - 25K
East Liberty	6,871	18%	15K - 25K
Highland Park	6,749	16.90%	35K - 50K
Oakland Central	5,281	7.80%	10K - 15K
Squirrel Hill North	10,408	14%	50K - 75K

Central Oakland has the smallest population (5,281 residents), the lowest proportion of older residents (7.80%) and the lowest median income (10K - 15K) among the sampled neighborhoods. It is also distinctive because two universities (University of Pittsburgh and Carnegie Mellon University) are located there. Squirrel Hill North has the highest median income (50K - 75K) and the largest population. Bloomfield has the highest proportion of older residents (21.6%) and the second lowest median income. Highland Park has an average population size, average proportion of older residents and above average mean income. This small, but heterogeneous sample of urban neighborhoods is a starting point for understanding the design and contextual factors that affect the viability of local online social systems.

The data collection procedure

The following procedure was used to identify Facebook pages and groups associated with each neighborhood:

- A Facebook search was conducted using the neighborhood's name, "Pittsburgh" and "Facebook group" as the search keywords. The top ten search results were recorded.
- A Google search was conducted using the same search keywords and the additional constraint that results be from Facebook.com (site:facebook.com). The first twenty search results were recorded.

Duplicate sites and non-Facebook sites were removed based on manual inspection of the recorded search results. The resulting sample included 16 Facebook pages or groups (2-4 per neighborhood). We collected data about "likers" and posts for each of them using the Facebook developers API. We pulled the page that contained the most recent posts for each site in late October, 2011 (Time 2). We also retrieved their prior (older) page of posts (Time 1). The number of posts per page varied depending on post frequency and length. In total, 794 posts were collected. This raw data is the basis for the analysis sample that contains measures of each site's communication activity and participants.

[10]Neighborhoods are based on City of Pittsburgh maps. While assessing their accuracy is beyond the scope of this study, these designations are generally consistent with those used by residents, local media, and other organizations.

[10]Source: Census 2000 data - `http://www.city.pittsburgh.pa.us/cp/assets/census/2000_census_pgh_jan06.pdf`

Table 2. Content Coding Scheme

Goal's verb: What is the message's intention?	
Request	Solicit something from the reader, e.g. vote for a campaign
Provide	Provide something to the reader, e.g. inform about an accident.
Goal's noun: What is being requested/provided?	
Information	Objective information
Action	A physical action
Opinion	A subjective opinion
Audience' scale: How many people are needed?	
Peer	Only one reader (e.g. greeting someone for her birthday, selling a car)
Few people	Few (less than 100) readers (e.g. inviting to a meeting in a coffee shop)
Many people	As many readers as possible (e.g. signing an online petition)
Audience' involvement: What should they do?	
Passive	A passive action (e.g. read an online news)
Audience	Go to a place and be part of a passive audience (e.g. listening a concert)
Active	A physical activity needed to participate in the event (e.g. run a marathon)
Topic: What is the message about?	
Event	A happening that includes date and location and has been organized in advance (e.g. invitations to political meetings)
Activity	Organized actions that perform a function and require a higher commitment than attending an event once (e.g. join a band)
Cause	A perspective or request related to a community project (non-profit) or any community issue (e.g. donate food to a shelter)
Service	An occupation that is being advertised or a product that can be traded (e.g. babysitter wanted, carpool partners sought)
Fact	A happening that includes date and location that has not been organized in advance by the community (e.g. news)

CODING LOCAL FACEBOOK POSTS

Facebook posts were automatically parsed to identify the date, type (i.e. status, link, photo, video), author, and number of likes and comments. To measure content diversity we applied a coding scheme to characterize the posts in terms of their communication goal, the scope of the intended audience, and their topic. This categorization scheme, summarized in Table 2, is a modified version of the classification schemes used in [4, 10].

A message's communication goal is indicated by a goal's verb and noun. The goal's verb refers to the intention of the mes-

Table 3. Categorization of Sample Messages

Example 1: *"Councilman Patrick Dowd hosts Council to Go in Bloomfield! Councilman Dowd will be at Crazy Mocha in Bloomfield on February 8th to hear your ideas, concerns, and complaints. Please stop by! Monday, February 8, 2010 5:30pm - 7:00pm Crazy Mocha Coffee Company - 4525 Liberty Avenue. We hope to see you there!"*	
Goal's verb:	Solicit
Goal's noun:	Action
Audience's scale:	Few people
Audience's involvement:	Active
Topic:	Event
Example 2: *The Allegheny River sometimes seems distant from Highland Park even though we're really close. What do you think about having riverfront access, perhaps via bike or pedestrian connections (which have been discussed for years)?*	
Goal's verb:	Solicit
Goal's noun:	Opinion
Audience's scale:	Many people
Audience's involvement:	Passive
Topic:	Cause
Example 3: *Geotechnical drilling along Penn Avenue between Evaline and Mathilda will occur on 9/19 and 9/20 in the evening hours. This drilling takes samples to determine pavement depth at different locations, in preparation for the Phase 1 reconstruction project due to begin in 2013. It may look like Marcellus shale drilling, but it's not!*	
Goal's verb:	Provide
Goal's noun:	Information
Audience's scale:	Many people
Audience's involvement:	Passive
Topic:	Fact

sage (request or provide). The goal's noun indicates what is being communicated or requested (information, action, or opinion). By default every message aims to provide information. The other categories were designed to further capture the more specific goal of a given message. For example, the first message in Table 3 is providing information about a meeting with a city council member, but it is also *soliciting* neighbors to take an *action* by attending and participating in the meeting. In the second example in Table 3, the message poses a question about what others think about an infrastructure project/idea in the neighborhood. In this case, the message was categorized as *soliciting* neighbors' *opinion*. The last example shows a message that informs about drilling at a particular location in the neighborhood. However, readers are not asked to do anything else. This message was categorized as *providing information*.

The intended audience assesses the scale of the target audience being engaged through the message (only one peer, few people, or many people) and the type of action required for involvement (passive, audience, or active). Table 3 also shows the intended audience codes associated with each example message. Example 1 mentions a meeting that is to be held in a coffee shop; therefore, the number of people that can attend is limited. This contrasts with other messages that invite larger numbers of people. For example, the following message *"Little Italy Days this weekend! September 23, 24 and 25! Free entertainment (including Live On Liberty bands) free parking and food, lots and lots of delicious food!"* also encourages readers to attend an event, but this event is held in the streets of the neighborhood, so it clearly intends to engage several hundred people. This case was coded as *many-people* in the audience's scope category. We defined a threshold equal to a hundred people to distinguish between few-people and many-people categories. In general, events that were located in coffee-shops and meeting rooms were coded as *few-people*. Events that were located in theatres or streets and actions that could be performed online (read an article or vote online) were classified as *many-people*. An example of message that was coded as *peer* for the audience's scope is: *"Anyone eat at Cioppino restaurant in the strip? I have a $50 gift certificate that will expire next week. I am selling it for $40.00 or best offer. Hurry up it will expire July 14"*. Although many people can read the message, only a single reader can participate in the purchase of the gift certificate.

Additionally, the kind of audience involvement describes the level of activity being requested of the audience. Example 1 in Table 3 encourages readers to go to a specific meeting place and express their ideas and concerns at that event. To respond to this message, the audience needs to be *active*. The message's goal would not be achieved if individuals do not attend and actively participate in the discussion. On the other hand, examples 2 and 3 only require readers to perform an action online (write their opinion or read the information), which is coded as a *passive* action. An intermediate category was defined as *audience*. This category refers to messages that invite people to attend an event in a specific place, but participation in that event is passive. The following message: *"The Reservoir of Jazz concert series will launch on Sunday, August 7, at 5 p.m. with a performance by the BOILERMAKER JAZZ BAND"* was classified as *audience* because readers are encouraged solely to go as spectators at an event that would be performed in the same way whether they attend or not.

Finally, message topic refers to the main subject of the message: event, activity, cause, fact, or service. Events are gatherings that are planned and scheduled in advance that have a location and date. Example 1 in Table 3 refers to an *event*. An activity requires more commitment. It implies that the intended audience commits to perform a certain action in a more sustained fashion. For example, *"ELPC's performing arts outreach program is looking for some great teens who might be interested in becoming part of HAT Co (Hope Academy Theater Company). If you are one, please apply. If you know one, please forward this on."* was categorized as an *activity* because it is trying to engage teens in a ongoing theatre program. An sample of *cause* is shown in Example 2. The message sender is sharing their concern about an issue and asking others to share their thoughts about it. Example 3 is a sample of a *fact*. Although it is a happening that has location and date, it does not request people to attend or participate. Other examples of *facts* are accident reports, crime alerts and any kind of news. Finally, *services* are occupations or products that are being advertised. An example of a service is: "*Come by our lemonade stand today to support the library! We'll be serving lemonade until 1PM.*"

Each post was coded by two judges trained with the coding scheme. Intercoder agreement for each feature was assessed with Cohen's Kappa coefficients. The Kappa coefficients were: 0.61 (topic), 0.61 (audience's scale), 0.63 (goal's noun), 0.67 (audience's involvement), 0.74 (goal's verb). These minimally adequate Kappa values suggest that the coding scheme may not be fully refined. In particular, posts containing multiple goals, topics and audiences contributed to lower than expected levels of coder agreement. To evaluate the feasibility of increasing the reliability of the coding, the posts in Time 2 were re-coded with instructions to focus on primary aspects of the message. After this iteration, the coefficients for the messages were: 0.65 (goal's noun), 0.75 (audience's involvement), 0.78 (topic), 0.84 (goal's verb), and 0.89 (audience's scale). Based on this improvement in the coefficients, the coded sample was determined to be adequate for preliminary analysis. Any remaining disagreements between coders were resolved based on discussion.

DESCRIPTIVE ANALYSIS OF FACEBOOK GROUPS

Table 4 summarizes the number of posts, the time interval, and posting frequency for each of the 16 Facebook sites at Time 1 and Time 2. During Time 2, there were 430 posts in 16 groups with an average of 26.88 posts per group. The average interval of time in which they were posted was 172.16 days (range: 24.55 – 893.32 days). The average post frequency was 0.41 posts per day (range: 0.01 – 1.59 messages per day).

Table 4. Summary of Posts and Audience

	Time 1			Time 2			
site	n	days	freq	n	days	freq	likers
B-1	41	57.5	0.71	39	24.6	1.59	461
B-2	31	98.1	0.32	28	65.8	0.43	219
B-3				12	893.3	0.01	
E-1	6	6.9	0.87	26	99.2	0.26	58
E-2	29	37.9	0.76	25	50.6	0.49	100
E-3	43	115.8	0.37	36	116.3	0.31	126
E-4	30	204	0.15	27	326.6	0.08	124
H-1	26	75.7	0.34	26	118.2	0.22	225
H-2				27	237.5	0.11	93
O-1				11	312.2	0.04	
O-2	7	6.1	1.15	31	102.0	0.30	106
O-3	27	23.9	1.13	29	48.0	0.60	535
O-4	31	49.1	0.63	32	37.0	0.87	329
S-1	31	76.0	0.41	29	41.9	0.69	717
S-2	34	125.1	0.27	27	223.1	0.12	160
S-3	28	35.6	0.79	25	58.2	0.43	287
All	364			430			
Mean	28	70.1	0.61	26.9	172.2	0.41	252.9
Min.	6	6.1	0.15	11	24.6	0.01	58
Max.	43	204	1.15	39	893.3	1.59	717

The Time 1 sample consists of the second most recent batch of posts for each group. There were 364 posts in 13 groups. Three of the sampled groups (B-3, H-2 and O-1) did not have enough history and activity to populate a prior page of posts in Facebook. Their frequency of posts per day is .01, .11 and .04, which are very low compared to the average frequency of the other groups in Time 1 (.61). As these three groups have existed over a long time (B-3: 893.3 days; H-2: 237.5 days; and O-1:312.2 days), we concluded that these online spaces had not managed to remain viable over time. Among the 13 groups that had sufficient activity, the mean number of posts in Time 1was 28 and the mean time interval was 70.13 days.

The number of people who "liked" each Facebook site was collected at Time 2 as a measure of the potential audience for each site (Table 4). Two groups (B-3 and O-1) did not report this measure. For the other 15 groups, the average was 252.86 people (range: 58 – 717 people).

Ten groups were associated with nonprofits. Three groups (E-1, 0-1, S-3) belong to a public library and two other groups (E-3, E-4) were related to churches. A single group (B-3) was created by an individual.

Posts' Authors

Groups also varied with respect to the number of posters and the concentration of posts written by the most active authors (Table 5). The average number of people posting in each group is 5.77 at Time 1 and 6.44 at Time 2. Overall the number of posters ranged from 1 to 16.

Table 5. Summary of Audience and Posters

	Time 1		Time 2	
	posters	top 80%	posters	top 80%
Mean	5.77	0.21	6.44	0.45
Min.	1.00	0.00	2.00	0.20
Max.	16.00	0.50	13.00	1.00

Poster concentration was measured by calculating the proportion of authors who accounted for 80% of the posts. This measure ranges from 0 to 1. The lower its value, the higher the level of concentration (i.e. a smaller percentage of the posters account for the majority of the posts). The average poster concentration was 0.21 (Time 1) and 0.45 (Time 2). In Time 1, the sites were more concentrated, in part because of two groups in which only one user posted all the messages. However, in Time 2 there was a shift to lower levels of concentration with a mean of 45% of the posters accounting for 80% of the posts. This change holds true if we removed the most inactive groups (B-3. H-2, O-1). In that case, 37% of the posts' creators accounted for 80% of the posts on average (range: 30% - 56%).

In general, the Facebook groups' owners were the most active posters. In Time 1, the owners' contribution ranged from 32% to 100% of the posts with a mean of 76%. In Time 2, the proportion of posts accounted for by group owners dropped to an average of 64% (range: 4% - 93%). This result was affected by the characteristics of the least active groups in our sample (B-3. H-2, O-1). Their owners contributed very little to their groups (8%, 45%, 4%). After removing them from the sample in Time 2, the owners' share of posted message in Time 2 (mean: 74%, range: 38% - 93%) is similar to Time 1.

Analyzing the persistence of authors over time, we found that in most groups approximately half of the contributors in Time 1 contributed to the group again in Time 2 (average: 48%, range: 35% - 100%). Changes in group size also varied (with median change percentage: 0%). Five of the groups had fewer members in Time 2 than in Time 1 with member loss ranging from 25% to 50%. Three groups had exactly the same size in both periods. Another five groups increased their size ranging by between 1.23 and 4 times.

Content Diversity

Among the collected posts, 45% were related to events, 24% were about services, 20% are associated with facts, 9% discussed causes and 2% advertised activities (Figure 1a). None of the topic types were present in all of the groups. None of the groups had only one topic type accounting for 80% of posts. On the other hand, seven groups had high topic diversity with three quarters of their topic types accounting for 80% of their posts.

The majority of posts (64%) solicited action. 20% solely provided information, and 11% provided an opinion about an issue. Posts soliciting information (3%) or support (2%) were far less common (Figure 1b). The sampled groups were generally moderate with respect to post goal diversity, with only two groups exhibiting a high concentration (low diversity) and one having low goal concentration (high diversity).

39% of messages sought to engage large audiences in passive activities such as reading specific online news, voting online, or viewing published photos. Another segment of posts (34%) invited small groups of people to get involved in more active happenings such as community meetings. Only 12% of the posts sought to encourage large numbers of people to actively participate in events such as marathons or cleaning campaigns (See Figure 1c). Intended audience diversity among the posts in each group was also moderate.

During the data collection period, there were two street festivals in Bloomfield, which were mentioned in 19% of the posts in the Bloomfield groups (B-1,B-2,B-3). More than 40% of the posts in East Liberty and Squirrel Hill groups announced events or services provided by the Facebook group's owners. Squirrel Hill also had the highest rate of posts offering volunteering opportunities and fundraising campaigns. 23% of the posts were advertising local businesses. Two group owners whose organization aimed to promote local business development and artists largely defined that pattern.

DIVERSITY AND SUSTAINABILITY

To test our hypotheses regarding content diversity and content contribution levels, we used regression analysis to predict the frequency of posts at Time 2 with independent variables from Time 1. Groups that had no activity in Time 1 (B-3, H-2, O-1) were excluded. The number of distinct goals, audiences and topics present in each group in Time 1 were used as measures of different forms of content diversity.

The number of goals (# goals) counts how many different types of message goals were found in a given group in Time 1. A goal type was formed by combining a goal verb and a goal noun. The possible values for goals were: "solicit action", "solicit information", "solicit opinion", "provide information" and "provide option". If a group has messages that were all coded as "solicit action", then the number of goals would be 1. If a group has some messages that were categorized as "solicit action" and others that were coded as "provide opinion", the number of goals would be assessed as 2. Figure 2 shows a scatter plot between the number of distinct types of goals observed in Time 1 and the frequency of posts in Time 2, illustrating the relationship between one type of content diversity and subsequent post frequency,

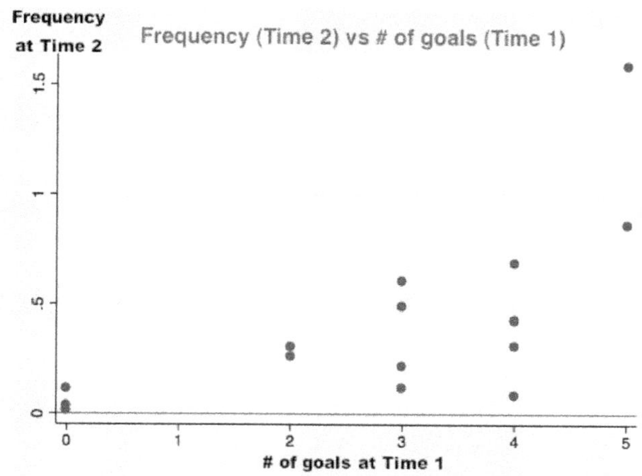

Figure 2. Frequency vs. Number of Goals

The number of audiences (# audience) measured the diversity of message target audiences. Distinct audiences were identified by combining audience scale and audience involvement level codes. Thus, potential audience values included: "peer-active", "peer-audience", "peer-passive", "fewPeople-active", "fewPeople-audience", "fewPeople-passive", "manyPeople-active", "manyPeople-audience" and "manyPeople-passive". The variable # audience was created by calculating the total number of different audience values that were found in each group.

The number of topics (# topics) assessed topic diversity. It was calculated by counting the number of different topic types (i.e. events, facts, causes, services and activities) present in the messages posted in each group.

In the regression models of post frequency, we also controlled for the number of authors and frequency of posts in Time 1. Dummy variables were included to assess neighborhood differences. However, none of the dummy variable were statistically significant in any of the analyses and hence have been excluded from the final results.

Table 6 reports a reduced model with the most significant predictors and the full model containing all the diversity variables. The reduced model was significant (p = 0.001) and it explains 81% of the variability in the frequency in Time 2. Diversity of goals was positively associated with high subsequent posting frequency after controlling for the number of authors and the frequency in Time 1. These two control variables were also significant factors to predict frequency of

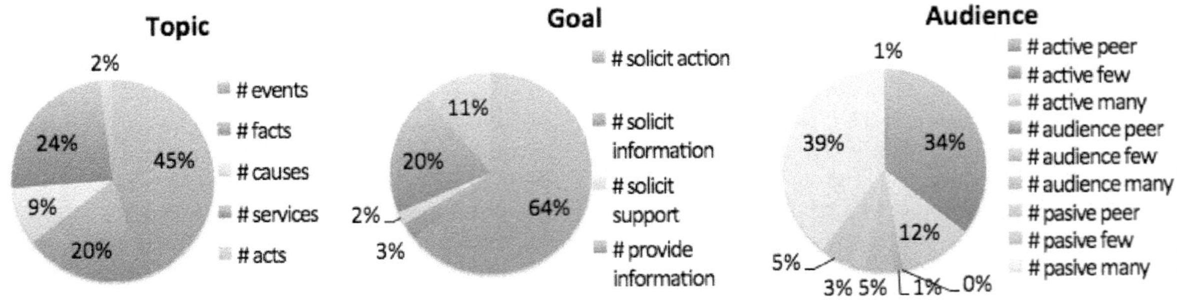

Figure 1. Topic, Goal and Intended Audience

posts in the next period. The number of authors and the frequency in Time 1 are positively associated with the frequency of posts in the next interval of time. A full model that includes all of our content diversity variables was also tested. The full model was significant (p = 0.015), however neither topic diversity (# topics) nor intended-audience diversity (# audience) were significant contributors to the full model.

Table 6. Predicting Frequency

	Reduced Model		Full Model	
Predictor	B	SE	B	SE
frequency (T1)	.740***	.196	.743**	.219
# authors (T1)	.042*	.019	.053	.033
# goals (T1)	.243***	.084	.262**	.096
# audience (T1)			-.057	.102
# topics (T1)			.049	.071
_cons			-1.102	.421
Reduced Model:	R^2=.81, $R^2_{adjusted}$=.74, p = .0014			
Full Model:	R^2=.82, $R^2_{adjusted}$=.69, p = .0150			

*: p¡.1 ; **: p¡.05 ; ***: p¡.01

Jackknife residuals, leverage and Cook' s distance analyses were conducted to assess the robustness of the results. A potential outlier was identified in most of the analyses. The group B-1 had an extremely high frequency of posts compared to the rest of the groups. Both regression models were estimated again after removing this data point and the results were qualitatively the same regarding the diversity of goals. After removing this potential outlier, the p-value of some of the control variables were above the significance level 0.5. However, diversity of goals remained a significant predictor of frequency of posts in the next period of observation. This suggests that the models are robust to outliers.

Multicollinearity tests were conducted using the Collin Stata package. The results show a moderate level of multicollinearity among the independent variables in the reduced model (VIF = 1.61, CN = 14.64) and a higher level of collinearity in the full model (VIF = 3.01, CN = 21.04). The Pearson correlation score between number of authors and number of goals is .64. The number of authors was highly correlated to the number of audiences (r = .86), which is the highest correlation among the independent variables. This may explain the insignificance of the number of authors in the full model.

We also evaluated the possibility that concentration measures of each category, retention rates of authors and concentration of contributors might be associated with the frequency of posts in the subsequent period. However, none of these variables was a significant predictor in the regression analyses.

DISCUSSION

Our results confirm the hypothesis that content diversity, in terms of goals, is a significant factor in the development and maintenance of content streams in online spaces for local communities. Greater variety of message goals is associated with higher levels of activity in subsequent time periods. This result differs from other analyses of the consequences of content diversity in larger-scale systems, which have found that higher content diversity is associated with negative outcomes [6, 33]. This may mean that that focused streams of information are more desirable in larger-scale social systems, while in smaller, bounded contexts content diversity is more beneficial because it leads to a sufficiently active content stream, which in turn helps the group remain viable over time.

Our results also raise questions about the consequences of the design decisions made when implementing online communities for cities. Single-focus communities such as Eventful and Urbanspoon can engage a considerable number of users globally (their global ranking in Alexa is 5410 and 1699, respectively). However, these goal/topic-limited designs can lead to a segregated distribution of local information online. While this strategy may work in environments where the number of restaurants and events is sufficient to maintain the content stream, our results suggest that a broader content approach may be necessary in many local communities. This may be a factor behind the currently limited role of the online social systems that rely on user-generated content as a source for local information. Even when specialty sites (e.g. restaurant or entertainment event sites) are relevant sources of local information [25], people still rely on traditional media and word-of-mouth to acquire other relevant local information about events and services [28]. Interestingly, local events and services were the more popular topics in our sample of local Facebook groups. Future work should further examine the consequences of content type segregation on use of online local information sources and the role of less constrained platforms, such as Facebook, in propagating information about the local events and services.

We also observed that the majority of the Facebook groups

had highly participative owners. Owners accounted for more than 70% of the posts in the groups with high frequency of posts. Inequality of contribution in online groups is a phenomenon that has been observed in most successful large-scale online communities [23]. Therefore, it is not surprising to also find this behavior in these smaller groups. Although the content in an online community is meant to be provided by many of its members, it seems to be necessary to have a core of very active users that contribute enough content to regularly attract new members and retain existing ones. This can be especially difficult when a local online group is not created by the neighbors, but offered as an external service. However, a community network that aims to serve a neighborhood would need to find and motivate a group of residents to become the core contributor group.

Although the rate of members' retention was not found to be a significant predictor of post frequency, the continuous involvement of 48% of authors (on average) shows that repeated contributions to a local online group is not uncommon. Future work should consider its antecedents and consequences. Who are repeat contributors to local community online groups? What types of content do they post? Is there a relationship between the users' participation in an online local group and their role in their neighborhoods or affiliations with certain organizations? Does the presence of repeat contributor encourage or discourage new participants? As with any group, core participants have the potential to be both critical resources and stifling influences, suggesting that further understanding of these individuals' motivations and behaviors is important when creating local online groups.

Despite the fact that we expected to find an effect of the neighborhoods' characteristics on the online groups, our analysis did not reveal any significant effect. Although some neighborhoods had more groups than others, neighborhoods did not systematically differ with respect to the frequency of posts in their associated Facebook groups. This was especially surprising because one of the neighborhoods (Central Oakland) has a major proportion of transient residents as students who attend nearby universities largely compose its population. Several hypotheses regarding the lack of significant results can be raised. It is possible that our study design has obscured the location effects. For example, we decided to use the official maps to delineate the boundaries of each neighborhood and therefore its characteristics. These boundaries can differ from the boundaries that residents perceive among different sectors in the city, as it is discussed in [12]. If this were the case, we could have been relating local groups to incorrectly defined local communities. It is also possible that there are indeed no neighborhoods' factors that affect the sustainability of online groups. It is feasible that these groups are mainly run for people who are highly committed to the local community (e.g. long-term residents) which are present in any neighborhood, and that more transient (less committed) residents do not significantly impact the viability of these groups as they do not actively participate in them. Further replication of our study in a larger and more heterogeneous sample of online groups needs to be undertaken to fully understand the implications of this result.

As with any study, this research has limitations that must be taken into account when considering its implications. First, our dataset only contains public Facebook groups. Third parties cannot access private Facebook groups; therefore our results only apply to public online spaces. Private groups may function differently because of their association with more cohesive groups. Furthermore, Facebook groups were not particularly designed to support interaction among neighbors. A follow up study should consider the effects of content diversity in neighborhood-oriented network sites such as EveryBlock or NextDoor, in which the design decisions about structure may directly affect the types and consequences of content diversity. Moreover, we looked at the Facebook groups in isolation from other local media. Future work will focus on studying content diversity in a more diverse sample of the local communicative ecology.

Our results depend upon the nature of the coding strategy. Messages that combined different goals, topics, and audiences introduced noise into the measures that may have obscured the relationship between posting frequency and other types of content diversity. Development of coding schemes and models that take into account within-message diversity may provide a clearer characterization of these relationships. Despite these limitations, our findings shed light on aspects of use of online groups for local communities and the consequences of diversity in these groups.

CONCLUSION

This paper reports initial findings regarding the dynamics of local online systems. We collected, coded and analyzed more than 750 posts from 16 Facebook groups associated with five neighborhoods in an US city. The hypothesis that content diversity in local online groups would promote future posting activity was partially supported. Diversity of communication goals was significantly associated with higher frequency of posts in a subsequent time period. More generally, these local Facebook groups all contained a variety of posts with 45% of posts about events and 24% about services; 64% requesting some action and 20% providing information; and, 39% aiming to engage a large audience in passive actions and 34% inviting smaller audiences to join active happenings.

While not conclusive, these results raise questions about the viability of designs for local online systems that focus narrowly on single content and message types. A narrow scope risks the viability of the online group in a local setting, by neglecting one way that a sufficiently active content stream may be maintained. Future work should consider this and other design choices for information systems for local communities with data from a greater variety of communities, technologies, and system designs.

ACKNOWLEDGMENTS

Claudia López's PhD studies are funded by CONICYT, Chile (The National Commission for Science Research and Technology) and a Fulbright Scholarship.

REFERENCES

1. Special issue: Supporting community and building social capital. *Commun. ACM 45*, 4 (2002).

2. Special issue: Urban computing. *IEEE Computer 39*, 9 (2006).

3. Inclusive social media project: Participatory evaluation. Tech. rep., e-democracy.org, 2010.

4. Alt, F., Memarovic, N., Elhart, I., Bial, D., Schmidt, A., Langheinrich, M., Harboe, G., Huang, E., and Scipioni, M. Designing shared public display networks: Implications from today's paper-based notice areas. In *Pervasive Computing* (2011), 258–275.

5. Beamish, A. Communities on-line: Community-based computer networks. Master's thesis, Department of Urban Studies and Planning. Massachusetts Institute of Technology, 1995.

6. Butler, B. S. Membership size, communication activity, and sustainability: A resource-based model of online social structures. *Info. Sys. Research 12*, 4 (2001), 346–362.

7. Carroll, J. M. *The Neighborhood in the Internet.* Routledge, 2012, ch. What are community networks?, 23–47.

8. Carroll, J. M., and Rosson, M. B. Developing the Blacksburg electronic village. *Commun. ACM 39*, 12 (1996), 69–74.

9. Chen, J., Ren, Y., and Riedl, J. The effects of diversity on group productivity and member withdrawal in online volunteer groups. In *Proceedings of the 28th international conference on Human factors in computing systems* (2010), 821–830.

10. Churchill, E. F., Nelson, L., and Denoue, L. *Communities and technologies.* Kluwer, B.V., 2003, ch. Multimedia fliers: information sharing with digital community bulletin boards, 97–117.

11. Colstad, K., and Lipkin, E. Community memory: a public information network. *SIGCAS Comput. Soc. 6*, 4 (1975), 6–7.

12. Cranshaw, J., Schwartz, R., Hong, J., and Sadeh, N. The livehoods project: Utilizing social media to understand the dynamics of a city. In *ICSCW* (2012).

13. Cummings, J. N., Butler, B., and Kraut, R. The quality of online social relationships. *Commun. ACM 45* (2002), 103–108.

14. Foth, M., and Hearn, G. N. Networked individualism of urban residents: discovering the communicative ecology in inner-city apartment buildings. *Information, Communication & Society 10*, 5 (2007), 749–772.

15. Gordon, E., and de Souza e Silva, A. *Net Locality: Why Location Matters in a Networked World.* Wiley-Blackwell, 2011.

16. Hampton, K., and Wellman, B. Neighboring in Netville: How the internet supports community and social capital in a wired suburb. *City & Community 2*, 4 (2003), 277–311.

17. Hampton, K. N. Neighborhoods in the Network Society the e-Neighbors study. *Information, Communication & Society 10*, 5 (2007), 714–748.

18. Haythornthwaite, C., and Kendall, L. Internet and community. *American Behavioral Scientist 53*, 8 (2010), 1083–1094.

19. Kavanaugh, A. L., and Patterson, S. The impact of community computer networks on social capital and community involvement. *American Behavioral Scientist 45*, 3 (2001), 496–509.

20. Kraut, R., Kiesler, S., Boneva, B., Cummings, J., Helgeson, V., and Crawford, A. Internet paradox revisited. *Journal of Social Issues 58*, 1 (2002), 49–74.

21. Millen, D. R., and Patterson, J. F. Stimulating social engagement in a community network. In *CSCW* (2002), 306–313.

22. Munson, S. A., Rosengren, E., and Resnick, P. Thanks and tweets: comparing two public displays. In *CSCW* (2011), 331–340.

23. Ortega, F., Gonzalez-Barahona, J., and Robles, G. On the inequality of contributions to wikipedia. In *HICCS* (2008), 304–308.

24. Raban, D. R., Moldovan, M., and Jones, Q. An empirical study of critical mass and online community survival. In *CSCW* (2010), 71–80.

25. Rainie, L., Purcell, K., Mitchell, A., and Rosenstiel, T. Where people get information about restaurants and other local businesses. Tech. rep., Pew Research Center, 2011.

26. Rainie, L., and Wellman, B. *Networked: The New Social Operating System.* The MIT Press, 2012.

27. Rogers, E. M., Collins-Jarvis, L., and Schmitz, J. The pen project in santa monica: Interactive communication, equality, and political action. *Journal of the American Society for Information Science 45*, 6 (1994), 401–410.

28. Rosenstiel, T., Mitchell, A., Purcell, K., , and Rainie, L. How people learn about their local community. Tech. rep., Pew Research Center, 2011.

29. Schroeter, R. Engaging new digital locals with interactive urban screens to collaboratively improve the city. In *CSCW* (2012), 227–236.

30. Schuler, D. Community networks: building a new participatory medium. *Commun. ACM 37*, 1 (Jan. 1994), 38–51.

31. Tacchi, J. A., Slater, D., and Hearn, G. N. *Ethnographic Action Research: A User's Handbook.* UNESCO, India, 2003.

32. Taylor, N., Cheverst, K., and Mller, J. Affordances and signifiers of community noticeboards. In *Workshop on Pervasive Advertising* (2009), 1–4.

33. Wang, Y.-C., and Kraut, R. Twitter and the development of an audience: those who stay on topic thrive! In *CHI* (2012), 1515–1518.

34. Wellman, B. Physical place and cyberplace: The rise of personalized networking. *International Journal of Urban and Regional Research 25*, 2 (2001), 227–252.

Finger On The Pulse: Identifying Deprivation Using Transit Flow Analysis

Chris Smith
University College London
London, UK
chris.smith@ucl.ac.uk

Daniele Quercia*
Yahoo! Research
Barcelona, Spain
dquercia@yahoo-inc.com

Licia Capra
University College London
London, UK
l.capra@ucl.ac.uk

ABSTRACT
A common metaphor to describe the movement of people within a city is that of blood flowing through the veins of a living organism. We often speak of the 'pulse of the city' when referring to flow patterns we observe. Here we extend this metaphor by hypothesising that by monitoring the flow of people through a city we can assess the city's health, as a nurse takes a patient's heart-rate and blood pressure during a routine health check. Using an automated fare collection dataset of journeys made on the London rail system, we build a classification model that identifies areas of high deprivation as measured by the *Indices of Multiple Deprivation*, and achieve a precision, sensitivity and specificity of 0.805, 0.733 and 0.810, respectively. We conclude with a discussion of the potential benefits this work provides to city planning, policy-making, and citizen engagement initiatives.

Author Keywords
public transport; urban computing; well being; data mining

ACM Classification Keywords
H.1.2 User/Machine Systems: Human information processing; H.5.m Information Interfaces and Presentation: Miscellaneous

INTRODUCTION
Large contemporary cities exhibit complex spatial and temporal dynamics, such that quality of life and the environment can vary significantly between adjacent areas and change over relatively short time periods. It is well known that the planet is undergoing a rapid population shift towards urban environments, with an estimated growth of 5 million new city dwellers each month in developing countries. With rapid growth comes an ever increasing need for effective planning and management of urban infrastructure. Indeed, a 2008 United Nations report into the state of the world's cities showed that inequality in urban environments is on the rise, as some areas and communities benefit more than others from economic growth and investment in public services [20]. The report states that urban inequality has a detrimental effect on citizens' health, education and participation in society and the economy, which in turn leads to social unrest and the diversion of resources from productive public investment toward security services, thus exacerbating the problem further. Therefore the importance of averting and rebalancing such inequality cannot be overstated.

To efficiently allocate limited resources, policymakers and agencies first need to identify which areas are in most need of intervention in order to alleviate deprivation. Assessment of city neighbourhoods' relative prosperity or deprivation may take place only once every few years, and the larger the assessment window, the more likely that problem areas will deteriorate. Thus, developing new methods of identifying urban inequality swiftly and at low cost would offer significant social and economic benefits. In this paper we ask whether we can identify deprived areas of the city by analysing the flow of people on public transport systems. Cities worldwide are adopting the use of RFID smart-card and sensor based automated fare collection systems to provide access to public transport systems, such as London's Oyster card which accounts for more than 84% of all journeys.[1] With such high coverage, these systems offer a detailed real-time picture of peoples' movement between different parts of the city. To test the hypothesis that automated fare collection systems can be used as rapid, low cost deprivation detectors, we define a number of features derived from transit data and use them to build and test classification models.

BACKGROUND AND RELATED WORK
Since 2000 the UK Office for National Statistics has published, every three or four years, the The Indices of Multiple Deprivation (IMD), a set of indicators which measure deprivation of small census areas in England known as Lower-layer Super Output Areas [13]. These census areas were designed to have a roughly uniform population distribution so that a fine grained comparison of the relative deprivation of different parts of England is possible. The formulation of the IMD follows the principles set out by Townsend [19], in which the author argues that deprivation ought to be defined in such a way that it captures the effects of several different factors. In particular, the IMD consists of the following seven components, here listed with examples (not exhaustive) of factors they measure: Income Deprivation - number of people

*This work was undertaken while at the Computer Laboratory of the University of Cambridge

[1] http://www.whatdotheyknow.com/request/oyster_card_usage - Retrieved 9/03/12

CSCW '13, February 23–27, 2013, San Antonio, Texas, USA.

claiming Income Support, Child Tax Credits or Asylum; Employment Deprivation - number of claimants of Jobseeker's Allowance or Incapacity Benefit; Health Deprivation and Disability - including a standard measure of premature death, rate of adults suffering mood and anxiety disorders; Education, Skills and Training Deprivation - education level attainment, proportion of working adults with no qualifications; Barriers to Housing and Services - homelessness, overcrowding, distance to essential services; Crime - rates of different kinds of criminal act; Living Environment Deprivation - housing condition, air quality, rate of road traffic accidents; and finally a composite measure which is a weighted mean of the seven domains. Note also that the IMD provide relative, rather than absolute measures of deprivation. This is less than ideal, since inequality could be reduced by lowering standards of living in less deprived areas, as well as the more desirable reverse, and with a relative measure we would be unable to determine which has occurred.

The indices have been used by central government as criteria for allocating resources to regeneration programmes and grants to community groups; by local authorities to identify areas in need of support or intervention; and also by residents to hold authorities to account [13]. However, not disregarding the clear utility of this kind of information, one shortcoming is the time frame associated with collating and publishing the data. For example, the latest version of the English IMD, which we use in this study, was published in 2010 yet pertains to data mostly from 2008 and even partly from as early as 2001. To overcome this limitation, researchers have recently proposed several techniques for data collection from ubiquitous sources, such as social media, phone call records and smart card sensors, in order to provide low cost, real-time proxy measures for community well being. For example, Kramer [10] found that the difference between the number of positive and negative words used in Facebook status updates covaries with self-reported "satisfaction with life" in the US. Similarly, Quercia *et al.* found that sentiment expressed in tweets [16] and the topic of tweets [17] in London, aggregated by the area associated with the tweet or Twitter profile, correlates with the composite IMD score of that area. A limitation noted in these works, however, is the large demographic bias of Twitter users. The majority of Twitter users are male, under 35 and with a relatively high income. Mislove *et al.* [14] also suggest that the ethnicity of twitter users in the US is not representative of the general population. Similarly, although Facebook has a more even gender distribution, in the UK around 60% of users are less than 35 years of age.[2]

Research that does not suffer such a population bias involving the IMD includes Eagle *et al.* [5], in which the authors derive a measure of communication diversity from phone call records in England, and find that higher diversity (i.e., the more evenly dispersed a person's communications between people and places) tallies with the composite IMD score aggregated to telephone exchange areas. We adapt this diversity measure to the urban mobility case, but we do not aggregate IMD census areas, since the scores of adjacent areas can differ significantly, thus we offer a finer grained analysis. Furthermore, we do not limit our analysis to the composite IMD score, but additionally investigate each of the seven domains separately.

Other work that analyses the relationship between urban public transport use and composite IMD score is Lathia *et al.* [12], in which the authors find that more deprived areas tend to receive passenger flow from a higher number of other areas compared to less deprived areas, and they also uncover some evidence of social segregation. However, the focus of [12] is the investigation of social mixing and homophily based on trip data. Thus far, no work has been done which explicitly attempts to mine automated fare collection data in order to measure and predict urban social deprivation. In the following sections we introduce the data analysis and classification methods we adopt to do just this.

MINING TRANSIT DATA

In this section we first introduce the dataset and its context, before describing how we extract features of passenger flows and the hypotheses guiding the process.

London and Oyster Card Data

The public transport system in London consists of several interconnected subsystems, incorporating multiple modes of transport. These include the London Underground (known colloquially as the Tube), the Overground rail system, an extensive bus network, water-borne transport and parts of the UK National Rail network, of which many services terminate in London. In 2003, the operators of this system, Transport for London, introduced an RFID-based technology, known as Oyster card, which serves to replace traditional paper-based magnetic stripe tickets. Oyster cards offer access to the entire multimodal system and thus have the potential to provide a complete picture of public transport in London. We are presently limited to data pertaining to the rail subnetworks, which include a total of 588 stations. Our initial dataset consists of a record of every journey taken on the London rail network using an Oyster card in the 31 days of March 2010. A record in the dataset is a tuple of the form: $\langle u, (o, d), t_o, t_d \rangle$, recording that a user with anonymised id u travelled from station o at time t_o, to station d at time t_d. In total the dataset contains 76.6 million journeys made by 5.2 million users.

Formulating the Hypotheses

Our goal is to successfully identify areas in London with high deprivation, so we first need to find characteristics of passenger flow patterns, aggregated at the station level, which relate to the IMD scores at the station location. Specifically, we derive parameters related to the following hypotheses based on the literature.

1. *Passenger flow is affected by deprivation.* Like an fMRI scanner detecting poor brain function when blood-oxygen

[2] `http://www.insidefacebook.com/2010/06/08/whos-using-facebook-around-the-world-the-demographics-of-facebooks-top-15-country-markets/` - retrieved 29/05/2012

flows are not as expected, we propose to capture poor mobility 'function' by measuring the residual between observed flow sizes and those estimated by a simple yet widely used interaction model. This kind of model often incorporates additional parameters to account for the influence of socio-economic factors (e.g., [4, 7]), which leads us to surmise that deprivation will likely impose restrictions on human mobility that we can measure.

2. *Modality choice is affected by deprivation.* The London Travel Demand Survey [1] reports that income is strongly related to public transport use. Compared to rail and tube journeys the rate of bus use tends to increase as household income decreases, and conversely, the rate of car use tends to increase with higher household income. Additionally, the survey finds that mode choice is related to age and disability. Thus, we expect there to be a population bias in rail users related to the level of deprivation in their home areas.

3. *Diversity increases well being.* We expect diversity in the places people visit to reflect the diversity of their social ties, since the more diverse one's contacts are, the less likely they are to be concentrated in a small number of places. Eagle *et al.* [5], using phone calls as a proxy for social connections, have shown that individual level social and economic benefits of social network diversity scale to the population level. Here we use individual travel patterns as a proxy for a social network, and we expect to see a relationship between diversity of travel behaviour and IMD scores.

Processing the Data

We begin by constructing an $N \times N$ matrix F such that N is the number stations in the dataset and $F_{i,j}$ is equal to the average daily number of unique users who have made a trip between stations i and j. We do not take into account direction of travel, so $F_{i,j} = F_{j,i}$. We also find M_i, the set of users who reside near to station i. Since users in the dataset are anonymous we do not know where they live, so instead we infer their home stations using a ranking method that exploits the regularity of human travel patterns [6]. For each user u, we rank station o based on the frequency with which user u has departed from o. To distinguish genuine London residents from occasional visitors, we prune trips not departing within the morning peak period, 6:30am to 9:30am, on the assumption that the vast majority of journeys in this period will be commutes from u's home to a place of work. In so doing, we also avoid counting departures from u's other frequented stations, such as work place in the evening. The downside is that we may exclude residents whose main use of the rail network is not for commuting. For every user, we then compute a ranking vector $R_u = [r_1, \ldots, r_N]$, where r_k is the number of times u has departed from station o_k (with o_1 being the most frequently visited origin station). We then assign users a home station according to the following set of rules applied in sequence: (a) if $r_1 \leq 2$ (the user's most visited origin station has been visited no more than twice in a whole month), the user is not assigned a home station; (b) if $r_1/r_2 > 0.5$, assign o_1 as home station; (c) if $r_1/r_2 \leq 0.5$ and $r_2/r_3 > 0.5$, assign both o_1 and o_2 as home stations; (d) otherwise, the user is not assigned a home station. Note that up to two stations can be designated a home station for a user, since in some parts of London there may be more than one station within equal distance from a user's residence, and the choice of which one to depart from may depend on factors which vary day to day. Finally, $m_i = |M_i|$ is the number of users who have i as a home station. The above steps discard 76% of users whose travel records do not reveal any preferential origin station (case (d)), but what is left still amounts to more than 1.2 million users.

Feature Extraction

Metrics for hypothesis 1. Next we derive the first set of features which involves using a gravity model to estimate the number of travellers moving between each pair of stations. First introduced by Zipf in 1946 [22], gravity models rest on the hypothesis that the size of flow between two areas is proportional to the mass (i.e., population) of those areas, but decays as the distance between them grows. Despite some criticisms (see for example [18]), the model has been successfully used to describe 'macro scale' interactions (e.g., between cities, and across states), using both road and airline networks [3, 8] and its use has extended to other domains, such as the spreading of infectious diseases [2, 21], cargo ship movements [9], and to model intercity phone calls [11].

Here we posit that a gravity model can be used to estimate passenger flow at the *intra*-city level. The model takes the form:

$$F_{i,j}^{est} = g \frac{m_i m_j}{d_{i,j}^2} \tag{1}$$

where $F_{i,j}^{est}$ is the estimated flow, or number of users moving between stations i and j, g is a scaling constant fitted to the data, and $d_{i,j}$ is the distance between them, for which we use the mean travel time between i and j computed from the transit data. Flows between areas with large mass (large number of home users) and at short distances are predicted to be large, whereas flows at longer distances or between areas with low mass are predicted to be small. Overall, the correlation between the observed traffic flows and gravity model estimates, measured with the Pearson Correlation Coefficient, is as high as .72, which suggests that overall the gravity model provides a good description of the movement of passengers between stations, but also that there is still a significant amount of variation not accounted for by the model.

We posit that this unexplained portion is due to prevailing socioeconomic factors. Thus, we are interested in where the model *fails* to fit well, that is, the cases where the residual (prediction error) between the observed and estimated edge weight is high. For example, the residual between observed and estimated flow between London Bridge and Canada Water, two areas with similar IMD scores, is just 7.9. Conversely, for Liverpool Street and Bethnal Green, which are a similar distance apart but with very different IMD scores, the residual is -1074.742. Figure 1(a) shows the cumulative distribution of the mean residual at each station. We see that not only is there an acute tendency for the gravity model to overestimate, but also a significant number of stations exhibit

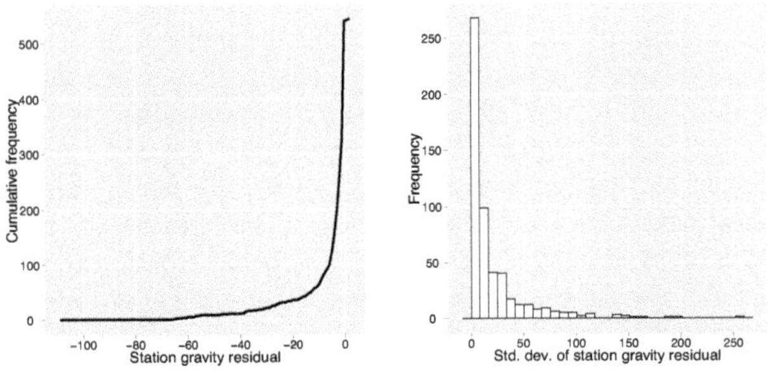

(a) Station Gravity Residual (b) Station Gravity Residual Std. Dev.

Figure 1. (a) Cumulative distribution of the mean of gravity residuals at each station. Note that less than 1% of stations have a positive gravity residual, meaning that the gravity model tends to overestimate flows (this is not a plot of G^{μ} which is the mean *absolute* residual); (b) frequency distribution of standard deviations of station gravity residual G^{σ}.

a large negative mean residual. As parameters in our classification model, for station i we compute the mean (Equation 2) and standard deviation (Equation 3) of the absolute residual on the edges connected to i:

$$G_i^{\mu} = \frac{1}{k_i} \sum_{j \in S_i} |F_{i,j}^{est} - F_{i,j}| \quad (2)$$

$$G_i^{\sigma} = \sqrt{\sum_{j \in S_i} (F_{i,j}^{est} - F_{i,j})^2} \quad (3)$$

where S_i is the set of stations such that $F_{i,j} > 0, \forall j$, and k_i = $|S_i|$. For example, Drayton Green has below average IMD scores and $G^{\mu} = 0.282$ and $G^{\sigma} = 0.809$. In contrast Canary Wharf, which has above average levels of deprivation despite being a busy financial business centre, has $G^{\mu} = 38.295$ and $G^{\sigma} = 117.032$.

Metric for hypothesis 2. The next feature we derive aims to exploit the previously mentioned discrepancy in bus usage between those in high and low income brackets. All else being equal, we would expect m_i to be proportional to the size of the population around i. Thus, we define the population bias as the residual between the observed number of home users, m_i, and that estimated from the population. First we define the population P_i around station i as the sum of a fraction of the population of each census area whose population-weighted centroid is within $1km$ of i. We choose a $1km$ radius based on London Travel Demand Survey finding that the percentage of journeys made by walking is 90% for journeys less than $0.5km$, 60% for 0.5-$1km$ and dropping to below 25% for longer journeys [1]. The size of each fraction is determined with a probability proportional to the distance between the centroid and the station. This method allows the population of each census area to be distributed between several nearby stations which reflects the fact that a person's closest station may not always be on the shortest path to a given destination. Finally, the formula for population bias at i is:

$$Q_i = \log(m_i) - (\alpha + \beta \log(P_i)) \quad (4)$$

where coefficients α and β are fitted by linear regression. Large negative values of Q_i are associated with a bias towards other forms of transport. Large positive values on the other hand are associated with a bias toward using the rail system. Figure 2(a) shows the distribution of population bias, which is roughly normal. We also include the mass, m_i, of the census area in order to control for population size.

Metric for hypothesis 3. Finally, we define two measures of diversity of travel behaviour. For those users for whom we have assigned a home station we follow [5] and measure the diversity of user u's connections as:

$$diversity(u) = \frac{-\sum_{i \in S_u} v_{u,i} \log(v_{u,i})}{\log(|S_u|)} \quad (5)$$

where S_u is the set of stations visited by u, and $v_{u,i}$ is the proportion of all u's visits to station i. The numerator in this equation is the Shannon entropy associated with u's travel behaviour, which is normalised by the log of the number of stations u has visited. Users who visit many places with equal propensity have high diversity, whereas users who tend to concentrate their visits to a few places are considered to have low diversity. The user diversity at station i, denoted H_i, is then the mean of the diversity of all users assigned to i.

$$H_i = \frac{1}{m_i} \sum_{u \in M_i} diversity(u) \quad (6)$$

As a second measure of the diversity of a station, we also include the degree of station i, or the number of other stations to which it is connected, k_i. We include this as we expect the number of connections an area has to increase opportunities for social and economic development, thus lessening the likelihood of deprivation. We include the distribution of station diversity and degree in Figures 2(b) and 2(c) respectively.

TESTING THE HYPOTHESES

To determine whether our hypotheses are valid, we use linear regression analysis. At each station the 8 IMD scores (7 domains and composite) are defined as those of the census area whose population weighted centroid is closest. Figure 4(a) shows the geographical layout of census areas in London. Areas that contain a railway station are coloured according to composite IMD score, where 1 is most deprived. For these areas, each of the 8 IMD scores then becomes the outcome variable for regression, with the features described above in Section (and summarised in Table 1) as the predictor variables. Where necessary, predictor variables undergo a logarithmic transformation, and in addition, we take the z-score of each variable, with allows us to judge the relative influence of each factor in terms of their unit standard deviation. For brevity, in Table 2 we present only the results of the composite IMD score, Living Environment, which has the highest R^2 out of the composite plus 7 domains, and Crime, which we include to demonstrate the variation in the influence of each feature. In all three examples, G^{μ} and G^{σ}, which correspond to hypothesis 1, as well as Q, which corresponds to hypothesis 2, are significant. The sign of the coefficient of G^{μ} is negative, which indicates that deprivation is expected to increase as this factor decreases. Recall that G^{μ} is the mean

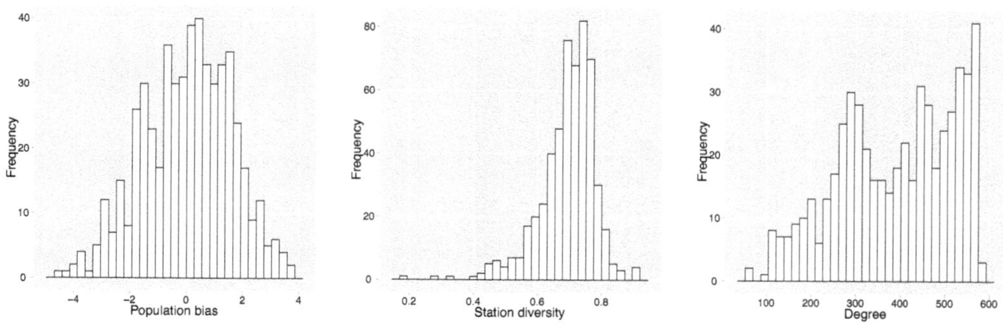

(a) Population Bias (b) Station Diversity (c) Degree Distribution

Figure 2. Frequency distributions of (a) population bias Q; (b) station diversity H; and (c) station degree k.

F_i	H1	Total flow of station i.
G_i^{μ}	H1	Mean absolute gravity residual at i.
G_i^{σ}	H1	Standard deviation of gravity residual at i.
Q_i	H2	Population bias at i.
m_i	H2	Mass of i, or number of home users.
H_i	H3	Mean user diversity at i.
k_i	H3	Degree of station i.

Table 1. List of parameters for the classification models - column 2 gives the corresponding hypothesis.

of the absolute value of residuals, and from Figure 1(a) we see that the vast majority of residuals are negative, so larger values of G^{μ} correspond to overestimates. This means that the more the gravity model overestimates the flows in and out of a station, the more likely that station is in a deprived area. Therefore, this supports our hypothesis that deprivation may represent a restriction to travel, although we cannot infer a causal link. The variance in gravity model error, G^{σ}, has a positive sign, meaning that deprivation tends to increase as this factor increases. In other words, in cases where the gravity predicts flows between areas to be similar, but in fact they differ, we also see a rise in deprivation - a result which is arguably also in support of hypothesis 1.

The coefficient of transit mode bias, Q, has a negative sign; however, unlike G^{μ}, this factor has a mean of approximately zero, even before the z-score is taken. So in this case, when more people use the tube than expected (when Q is positive) the regression model expects deprivation to be lower. On the other hand, when less people use the tube than expected (when Q is negative) the model expects deprivation to be higher - this supports hypothesis 2. The support for hypothesis 3, however, is less clear at this stage. Diversity, H, is significant and positive for Composite and Living Environment, which tells us to expect deprivation to increase as diversity increases - the opposite of our hypothesis - although the coefficient of H for living environment is very small. A possible explanation is that diversity of travel behaviour is not a reliable proxy for social network diversity (recall that this was part of the motivation behind hypothesis 3), but instead it may reflect the need of residents to travel to several different places due to lack of provision in their local area. In contrast, we find that the coefficient of the degree of a station, k, is negative, which is in line with our hypothesis that degree may reflect a higher level of economic opportunity (although k is not significant for Living Environment or Crime). In any case, with the exception of Living Environment, the values of R^2 indicate that only around $9-13\%$ of the variance in deprivation can be explained by the flow attributes. For this reason, we also tested for interactions between the attributes by including all pairwise products in a linear model, the results of which are shown in Table 3.

	Composite	Liv. Env.	Crime
Intercept	.361 ***	.487 ***	.583 ***
F	.252 *	.070	-.086
G^{μ}	-.180 ***	-.111 ***	-.060 *
G^{σ}	.104 *	.231 ***	.109 **
Q	-.141 **	-.229 ***	-.089 **
m	.074	.074	.162 ***
H	.022 *	.001 ***	.009
k	-.116 ***	.031	-.045
R^2	.092 ***	.344 ***	.085 ***
Adjusted R^2	.080 ***	.336 ***	.073 ***

Table 2. Estimated coefficients of Composite, Living Environment and Crime domains (Significance codes: * $p < 0.05$, ** $p < 0.01$, *** $p < 0.001$).

For reasons of space, we do not attempt a detailed interpretation of each of the coefficients, and again we show only three example domains. Note, however, that each of the features derived from passenger flow has a significant effect at some point, either alone or in combination. Furthermore, the R^2 values have increased, suggesting that the features explain up to 20% of the variance in deprivation - given the complexity of the problem, we believe this is a good result. An interesting result is that none of the interaction terms are significant for Living Environment, suggesting that either the linear relationships found above exhaust the effect of the features on deprivation in this domain, or, on the contrary, the dependency between each feature is more complex.

Finally, we repeat the above analysis but this time we prune the data points that fall in second and third quartiles of each domain score, thus, we concentrate on the extreme examples and effectively treat the intermediate cases as noise. Note that different stations will appear in the pruned sample for differ-

	Composite	Liv. Env.	Crime
Intercept	.369 ***	.467 ***	.583 ***
F	.449 ***	.232 *	-.153
G^{μ}	-.248 ***	-.226 ***	-.020
G^{σ}	.110	.221 ***	.106 *
Q	-.044	-.199 ***	-.085 *
m	-.202 *	-.017	.142 *
H	.035 **	-.003	.018
$F : G^{\mu}$	.216	.102	.303 *
$F : G^{\sigma}$	-.466	-.171	-.624 *
$F : Q$	.705	.205	.776 **
$F : H$	.221 *	.105	.266 **
$G^{\mu} : H$	-.084	-.029	-.104 *
$G^{\mu} : k$	-.343 *	-.071	.012
$G^{\sigma} : m$	.312	.003	.568 *
$Q : m$	-.152 **	-.069	-.124 **
$m : k$	.169	.145	.288 *
$H : k$	-.073 *	-.041	-.112 *
R^2	.199 ***	.392 ***	.195 ***
Adjusted R^2	.154 ***	.358 ***	.151 ***

Table 3. Estimated coefficients of Composite, Living Environment and Crime domains, including pairwise interactions. Predictor variables which no significance in any of the three examples have been omitted. (Significance codes: * $p < 0.05$, ** $p < 0.01$, *** $p < 0.001$).

ent IMD domains. At this point there are two things worth pointing out: the values of R^2 have risen, which shows that by treating the middle quartiles as noise we are able to discern a stronger dependency between the flow features and deprivation in each of the three examples, and the significance of some features has changed. In particular, H is no longer a significant factor by itself in any of the examples, and for the Living Environment domain we now find that some interaction terms are significant. In general, the change in significance of various attributes suggests that as circumstances change in an area, different factors come in to play, and serves to highlight the complexity of the situation.

In conclusion, the nature of the relationship between the flow features we derived from transit data has thus far evaded a precise description. Nevertheless, we have seen strong support for hypotheses 1 and 2, with a clear dependency between the corresponding features and deprivation in various domains. It is less clear at this stage whether or not hypothesis 3 has any validity.

We next describe how we use the features of passenger flow to build classification models which can identify areas of high deprivation.

IDENTIFYING DEPRIVED AREAS

We formulate the problem as one of binary classification, in which the goal is to identify areas which fall into the top quartile of each of the 8 IMD scores (higher scores corresponded to higher deprivation). We define the response variable as $y_i = 0$ if station i is in the 1st quartile and $y_i = 1$ otherwise. As before, we prune the middle quartiles, since we are interested in classifying the extreme examples. In so doing, we also ensure a roughly $1:1$ ratio of positive to negative examples in each class, as opposed to a $1:3$ ratio had we

	Composite	Liv. Env.	Crime
Intercept	.382 ***	.504 ***	.586 ***
F	.434 *	.103	-.088
G^{μ}	-.351 ***	-.194	-.119 *
G^{σ}	.223 *	.387 ***	.162 *
Q	-.238 **	-.346 ***	-.134 *
m	.122	.057	.252 **
H	.037	.010	.005
k	-.199 ***	.082	-.079 ***
R^2	.160 ***	.508 ***	.146 ***
Adjusted R^2	.138 ***	.494 ***	.123 ***

Table 4. Estimated coefficients of Composite, Living Environment and Crime domains after pruning the second and third quartiles (Significance codes: * $p < 0.05$, ** $p < 0.01$, *** $p < 0.001$).

	Composite	Liv. Env.	Crime
Intercept	.422 ***	.468 ***	.595 ***
F	.728 **	.587 **	-.192
G^{μ}	-.454 ***	-.558 ***	-.054
G^{σ}	.371 **	.399 ***	.186 *
Q	-.053	-.235 ***	-.161 *
m	-.451 **	-.210	.228
k	.116	.113 *	-.029
$F : G^{\sigma}$	-.927	-.662	-1.103 *
$F : m$	-.417	-1.609 *	-.175
$F : k$	-.316	.537 *	-.304
$G^{\mu} : k$	-.457	-.658 **	.027
$G^{\sigma} : m$	.078	.404	.499
$Q : m$	-.373 ***	-.028	-.211 **
$H : k$	-.033	-.023	-.115 *
R^2	.345 ***	.587 ***	.283 ***
Adjusted R^2	.269 ***	.539 ***	.200 ***

Table 5. Estimated coefficients of Composite, Living Environment and Crime domains, including pairwise interactions after pruning the second and third quartiles. Predictor variables which no significance in any of the three examples have been omitted. (Significance codes: * $p < 0.05$, ** $p < 0.01$, *** $p < 0.001$).

retained the 2nd and 3rd quartiles. We compare the results of two linear regression models, the first with each feature as a predictor variable (LR1), and a second model with each pairwise interaction included (LR2). Since the response variable is $y = \{0, 1\}$ we transform the output of the regression models, y', in the following way:

$$y = \begin{cases} 0, & y' \leq 0.5 \\ 1, & y' > 0.5 \end{cases} \tag{7}$$

Since our previous analysis points toward a complex relationship between the flow features and deprivation, we also try a support vector machine (SVM) with a radial basis function for the kernel function. The SVM has the advantage that by projecting the input variables onto a higher dimensional space, it is better able to split the input data. The downside to this, however, is that we cannot interpret the role played by each of the predictors, unlike linear regression, for which we can determine the significance of each. For each model, we randomly split the data into a 90% training set and 10% test set, and cross validate by repeating this 10 times.

	Precision	Sensitivity	Specificity	R^2
Composite	.597	.634	.666	.109
Income	.609	.527	.692	.127
Employment	.571	.429	.699	.084
Health	.642	.506	.687	.099
Housing	.714	.605	.747	.184
Crime	.771	.782	.764	.162
Liv. Env.	.819	.771	.826	.521
Education	.702	.753	.649	.141

Table 6. Classification scores for LR1

	Precision	Sensitivity	Specificity	R^2
Composite	.803	.666	.848	.353
Income	.731	.740	.734	.358
Employment	.725	.673	.758	.301
Health	.760	.704	.772	.354
Housing	.742	.712	.799	.428
Crime	.777	.784	.779	.372
Liv. Env.	.852	.832	.834	.621
Education	.687	.787	.643	.312

Table 7. Classification scores for LR2

	Precision	Sensitivity	Specificity
Composite	.805	.733	.810
Income	.705	.729	.733
Employment	.694	.701	.718
Health	.779	.736	.648
Housing	.779	.662	.818
Crime	.761	.756	.769
Liv. Env.	.902	.793	.928
Education	.644	.723	.615

Table 8. Classification scores for SVM

Performance measures. The performance of each model is assessed using three measures:

$$precision = \frac{TP}{TP + FP}$$

$$sensitivity = \frac{TP}{|P|}$$

$$specificity = \frac{TN}{|N|}$$

where TP is the number of true positives, or correctly identified high deprivation stations; FP is the number of false positives, or stations incorrectly identified as having high deprivation; and $|P|$ and $|N|$ are the total number of positive and negative cases respectively. In the present context, precision measures the proportion of areas classified as highly deprived which are in fact highly deprived. If we assume that a verification cost would be incurred for each area classified as highly deprived, precision would represent the confidence that this cost would not be wasted. It is therefore important that this score is high. Sensitivity (or recall rate) is the proportion of positive examples (stations with high deprivation) in the test set that are correctly identified (i.e., a sensitivity of 1 means all high deprivation areas have been identified). This is perhaps the most important performance measure in the present context, since the idea is to quickly identify areas in need of intervention. Low sensitivity would mean several areas go unreported, thus negating the utility of this kind of classifier. On its own, however, sensitivity is unreliable, since a classifier which labels all examples as positive will have a sensitivity of 1. Specificity is the proportion of negative examples correctly identified as such. High specificity means that for an area identified as deprived, there is a high probability that it is deprived. For the linear regression models we also give the mean value of R^2 for the training data, which represents the proportion of variance in the response variable explained by the predictor variables. This gives an idea of how well the model fits the training data.

Results. We report the mean of the 10 iterations for LR1, LR2 and SVM in Tables 6, 7 and 8 respectively, and for easier visual comparison we have plotted precision, sensitivity and specificity for each model in Figures 3(a), 3(b) and 3(c). The performance of each model can be interpreted relative to a baseline random classifier, which after a sufficient number of iterations averages out with a precision, sensitivity and specificity of 0.5. As expected, the most easily predictable form of deprivation is the Living Environment component. This is the only domain in which LR1 performs well, with high precision, sensitivity and specificity. Note that R^2 differs from that reported in Table 2 since it is computed against the response variable $y = \{0, 1\}$, as opposed to $y = (0, 1)$.

Overall, the best results come from LR2 and SVM. For the composite IMD score, SVM correctly identifies high deprivation 80.5% of the time, and correctly identifies low deprivation 81% of the time. Figures 4(b) and 4(c) provide a geographic illustration of the performance an example SVM model for the composite IMD domain. Each census area is coloured according to class (i.e., bottom quartile or top quartile). Note that only census areas containing stations, and which fall in the 1st or 4th quartile are coloured, hence the map is very sparse. Interestingly, LR2 achieves higher specificity in the composite score, as well as higher sensitivity than SVM in Living Environment, Housing, Crime and Education, suggesting that it may be pertinent to test a mixed classification model in order to achieve the best possible results. A pleasing result is that scores are fairly high across all domains, which demonstrates the potential for identifying specific kinds of problems, rather than just an overall indication of community well being.

To assess the level of support for our three hypotheses we also trained an SVM model to classify areas in terms of composite IMD, using only features corresponding to each hypothesis separately. Again, we report the average of 10 runs, and the results are presented in Table 9. Each of the performance scores in Table 9 is higher than that expected from a random classifier, with the exception of sensitivity for Hypothesis 2. This tells us that the features related to this hypothesis, population bias Q_i, and mass m_i, struggle to pick out deprived areas and instead tend to classify the majority of areas as undeprived. We can, however, still conclude that Q_i and m_i have predictive power, since an SVM model trained without these features (last row in Table 9) performs less well than one

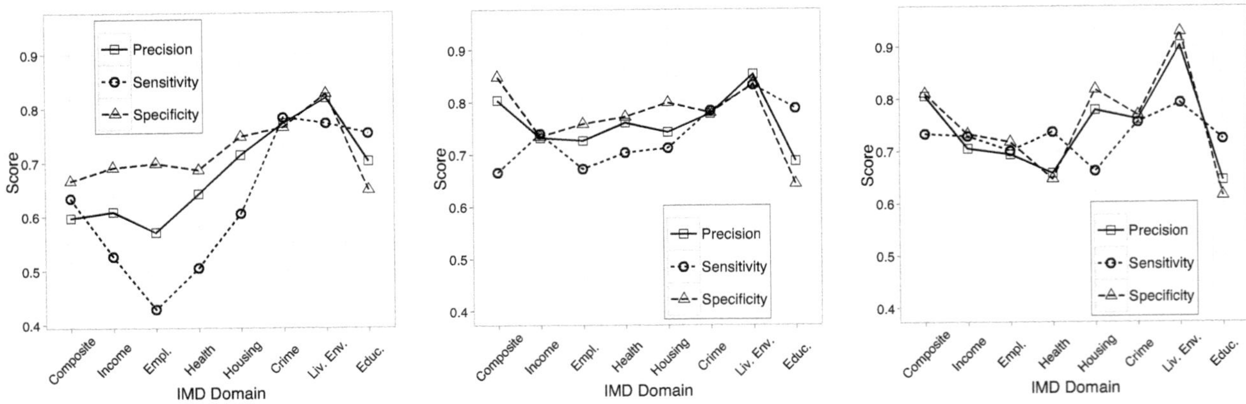

(a) LR1 Scores (b) LR2 Scores (c) SVM Scores

Figure 3. Graphical representation of classification scores.

	Precision	Sensitivity	Specificity
Hypo. 1	.640	.539	.702
Hypo. 2	.716	.413	.816
Hypo. 3	.679	.662	.643
Hypo. 1 + 3	.774	.548	.856

Table 9. Performance of SVM classification using features from each hypothesis.

with these features. In general the results suggest that each group of features offers some predictive value, that is, each of the hypotheses has some support, although more work is needed to determine the precise relationship between each of the features and the level of deprivation in a census area.

DISCUSSION

In this section we begin by discussing the main contributions and implications of our work, before examining its limitations and detailing proposals to extend the research.

Implications

This work adds to the growing literature exploring the ways in which ubiquitous technologies can be used to unobtrusively track the well being of communities [5, 10, 12, 16, 17]. We demonstrated a significant link between census area measurements of deprivation in multiple domains, and patterns of passenger flow in public transport systems. Moreover we have shown that the relationship between passenger flow and urban deprivation is strong enough to build a classification model that uses features extracted from flow data to identify areas of high deprivation. In the spirit of 'smart-cities', predictions derived from transit data could form an element of a 'city dashboard' style application[3], providing real-time information to city planners, policymakers and community members. By providing an early warning, such a tool would dramatically reduce the time frame within which local authorities identify areas of high deprivation, thereby increasing the efficiency with which limited resources are allocated to regeneration and renewal initiatives.

[3]e.g., `http://citydashboard.org/london/`

The ability to identify well being and inequality could also benefit communities by enabling residents to asses the effects of regeneration projects and hold local authorities to account. Presently, this is only possible after a number of years, when census based data has been collated and published. Additionally, a city health monitor could help facilitate community-directed campaigns and projects, such as participatory mapping initiatives like `mappingforchange.org.uk`, where residents are asked to vote for what they need the most, and then plan how to spend money accordingly, and `digitaldemocracy.org`, a platform which allows anyone to initiate and garner support for local campaigns. This kind of tool could provide a source of evidence for these types of projects and enable a comparison between areas by assessing the benefits of implementing different policies.

Limitations and Extensions

As previously mentioned, we acknowledge that as we pruned intermediate data points from the training and testing process, there is further work needed to be done in order to verify the results. This would involve classifying all data points in the first three quartiles as not deprived, or introducing a third class to represent moderately deprived areas. Possible ways to improve the models to overcome this limitation include exploiting other variables available in the Oyster data, such as ticket price and card type (e.g., standard, student, elderly and disabled). We have also begun to develop methods to capture implicit semantic information such as trip purpose, and derive new features such as a gravity residual for each trip type, which we believe are important factors to consider. For example, the rate of commuting may be related to the Employment domain, the number of leisure trips may be related to Income or Crime domains. A further modification would be to measure flows bidirectionally, rather than unidirectionally. This would give us information regarding stations acting as both origin and destination, and allow us to define an asymmetrical gravity model.

A further limitation is that our dataset includes only rail trips and as such we do not have a complete picture of passenger

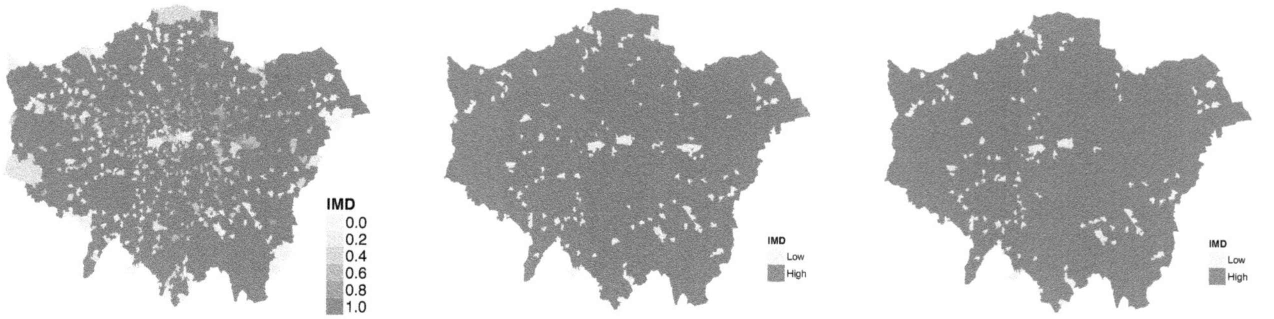

(a) Real composite IMD score (b) True class (c) Predicted Class

Figure 4. a) Census areas containing stations coloured according to real composite IMD score; b) stations which fall in the 1st or 4th quartile for composite IMD, classified as high or low; and c) predicted classifications for the same areas.

flow patterns in London. Relatedly, the number of areas for which we can make predictions is limited by the geographical coverage of the rail system. Out of a total of 4766 census areas in London, 588 (that is, 11.2%) contain tube or rail stations.

With a similar analysis of passenger flow between bus stops we would be able to extend the coverage to the whole of London. Unfortunately we are unable to perform the same analysis on bus trips, since there is no requirement to scan an Oyster card at the end of a bus journey, thus only the origin is recorded. We have, however, developed a proxy for bus usage bias (Q_i) which could potentially be extended beyond the rail/tube network.

We have thus far only tested the models laterally, that is, training and testing on different stations from the same period in time. To establish the genuine worth of building such predictive models, we plan to perform a longitudinal study in which models are tested on newly available data pertaining to trips made several months after the data on which they were trained. Furthermore, a second important verification step is to test our method on data pertaining to different cities, although at present we do not have transit data from other cities at our disposal. Finally, we plan to investigate the utility of supplementing transit data with sources such as Foursquare (and other similar location oriented applications) check-in data, which has been used previously to study global and city scale human mobility patterns [15]. By combining different datasets we can build a multiplex network (i.e. network with multiple types of edge), which may offer additional insights into the relationship between mobility, social structure and well being.

Acknowledgements. The research leading to these results has received funding from the European Community under Grant Agreement n. 234239.

REFERENCES

1. London travel demand survey. Technical Report 1, Transport for London, Greater London Authority, 2009.
2. D. Balcan, V. Colizza, B. Gonalves, H. Hu, J. J. Ramasco, and A. Vespignani. Multiscale mobility networks and the spatial spreading of infectious diseases. *PNAS*, 106(51):21484–21489, 2009.
3. A. Barrat, M. Barthélemy, R. Pastor-Satorras, and A. Vespignani. The architecture of complex weighted networks. *PNAS*, 101(11):3747–52, Mar. 2004.
4. P. Congdon. Modelling Migration Flows between Areas: An Analysis for London Using the Census and OPCS Longitudinal Study. *Regional Studies*, 23(2):87–103, 1989.
5. N. Eagle and M. Macy. Network Diversity and Economic Development. *Science*, 1029, 2010.
6. M. C. González, C. a. Hidalgo, and A.-L. Barabási. Understanding individual human mobility patterns. *Nature*, 453(7196):779–82, June 2008.
7. T. Grosche, F. Rothlauf, and A. Heinzl. Gravity models for airline passenger volume estimation. *Journal of Air Transport Management*, 13(4):175–183, July 2007.
8. W. Jung and F. Wang. Gravity model in the Korean highway. *EPL (Europhysics Letters)*, 81, 2008.
9. P. Kaluza, A. Kölzsch, M. T. Gastner, and B. Blasius. The complex network of global cargo ship movements. *Journal of the Royal Society, Interface / the Royal Society*, 7(48):1093–103, July 2010.
10. A. D. I. Kramer. An Unobtrusive Behavioral Model of Gross National Happiness. In *Proceedings of the 28th ACM CHI*, 287–290, 2010.
11. G. Krings, F. Calabrese, C. Ratti, and V. D. Blondel. Urban gravity: a model for inter-city telecommunication flows. *Journal of Statistical Mechanics: Theory and Experiment*, 2009(07):L07003, May 2009.
12. N. Lathia, D. Quercia, and J. Crowcroft. The Hidden Image of the City : Sensing Community Well-Being from Urban Mobility. In *Proc. of Pervasive*, 1–8, 2012.
13. D. Mclennan, H. Barnes, M. Noble, J. Davies, and E. Garratt. The English Indices of Deprivation 2010. Technical report, 2011.

14. A. Mislove, S. Lehmann, Y. Ahn, and J. Onnela. Understanding the Demographics of Twitter Users. *Fifth International AAAI*, 554–557, 2011.

15. A. Noulas, S. Scellato, and C. Mascolo. An empirical study of geographic user activity patterns in foursquare. *ICWSM'11*, 70–573, 2011.

16. D. Quercia, J. Ellis, L. Capra, and J. Crowcroft. Tracking Gross Community Happiness from Tweets. In *Proceedings of ACM CSCW 2012*, 2012.

17. D. Quercia, D. O. Seaghdha, and J. Crowcroft. Talk of the City : Our Tweets , Our Community Happiness. In *Proc.of AAAI ICWSM*, 2012.

18. F. Simini, M. C. González, A. Maritan, and A.-L. Barabási. A universal model for mobility and migration patterns. *Nature*, 8–12, Feb. 2012.

19. P. Townsend. Deprivation. *Journal of Social Policy*, 16:125–146, 1987.

20. United Nations Human Settlement Program. *State of the World'd Cities 2008/2009*. EarthScan, 2008.

21. C. Viboud, O. N. Bjø rnstad, D. L. Smith, L. Simonsen, M. A. Miller, and B. T. Grenfell. Synchrony, waves, and spatial hierarchies in the spread of influenza. *Science (New York, N.Y.)*, 312(5772):447–51, Apr. 2006.

22. G. Zipf. The P 1 P 2/D hypothesis: On the intercity movement of persons. *American sociological review*, 11(6):677–686, 1946.

Digital Neighborhood Watch: Investigating the Sharing of Camera Data Amongst Neighbors

A. J. Bernheim Brush, Jaeyeon Jung, Ratul Mahajan, Frank Martinez
Microsoft Research
One Microsoft Way, Redmond, WA 98052
{ajbrush, jjung, ratul, fmartin}@microsoft.com

ABSTRACT
In a neighborhood watch group, neighbors cooperate to prevent crime by sharing information and alerting police of suspicious activities. We propose a digital neighborhood watch (DNW) in which security cameras of individual homes work together to monitor the neighborhood. DNW could augment neighborhood watch by providing digital evidence of crime, increasing visibility of neighborhood activity, and automatically sending alerts when suspicious events occur. We investigate the appeal of sharing camera data with neighbors through semi-structured interviews with 11 households. Our participants validated the potential of sharing data with neighbors, particularly to provide evidence after an incident. But they also had security and privacy concerns about divulging their cameras' field of view and giving ongoing access to neighbors. For some participants, these concerns can be alleviated by enabling sharing of processed cameras views that include only the foreground activity or only public property (e.g., sidewalks).

Author Keywords
Sensing technology; neighborhood; privacy; security camera.

ACM Classification Keywords
H.5.1 Multimedia Information Systems.

INTRODUCTION
Neighborhood watches are groups of neighbors that cooperate to prevent crime (e.g., burglaries, vandalism) by watching neighborhood activity and alerting authorities when criminal activities are suspected. The U.S. National Sheriffs Association created a National Neighborhood Watch program in 1972 and many countries have similar programs. Rising crime in our own neighborhoods motivated us to investigate whether sharing data from sensors such as cameras and microphones across households could enhance neighborhood watch. At community meetings that we attended, law enforcement officers emphasized the need for residents to be the "eyes and ears" of the neighborhood and the power of sharing information among neighbors.

We envision a Digital Neighborhood Watch (DNW) system that is composed of sensors such as security cameras of individual households.[1] We investigate if such a system can augment neighborhood watch by: (1) providing digital evidence of incidents, (2) increasing visibility of neighborhood activity, and (3) automatically detecting and alerting for suspicious events (e.g., unfamiliar car drove by several times). DNW is in contrast to local authorities or governments installing and monitoring networks of cameras (e.g., CCTV cameras in England). Given the reluctance of many communities and authorities (including our own) towards such "big brother" technologies, we wanted to explore the feasibility of neighbors voluntarily sharing their own camera data with each other. Such sharing can enable inferences that data from individual homes cannot enable (e.g., a car cruising the neighborhood, without stopping at any home).

While the feasibility of DNW depends on several social, technical, and legal factors, in this paper, we focus on an important social factor—the value versus the privacy and security risks that households perceive with sharing camera data. Through semi-structured interviews we gather households' perspectives on sharing data for DNW with their neighbors, law enforcement, and security companies.

We find that DNW is a promising concept, but it entails challenges. Our participants were willing to share camera data with neighbors after an incident, which meets the goal of providing digital evidence. But the other two goals, increasing visibility and automatically detecting suspicious activities, are harder to meet because participants had concerns about divulging the location and field of view of cam-

[1] Currently a wide range of home security systems from professionally installed and monitored systems to less expensive do-it-yourself systems are available. ABI Research estimates that in 2006, roughly twenty-six million systems were deployed in the U.S (~21% of households) and twenty-three million in Europe (~8% of households). It also predicts increased adoption as hardware becomes inexpensive. Of particular interest to us are the decreasing prices of cameras, making camera-based systems more affordable.

eras and giving ongoing access to neighbors. These concerns led us to propose and evaluate two processed camera views that only include the foreground activity and public property. We find that these views alleviate the concerns and encourage some participants to allow greater access for neighbors and police.

Our main contribution is uncovering what camera data people will share with neighbors for neighborhood safety and highlighting concerns that must be addressed to build a successful DNW system. Although our work focuses on sharing home security camera data, our findings about situations when neighbors would share and about data abstractions that remove sensitive parts of information can be applicable for other neighborhood-based sharing applications (e.g., water usage, coordinating electricity usage).

RELATED WORK

As usage of information and communication technologies (ICT) became more common, researchers studied the impact on local communities. Studying the wired suburb of "Netville" from 1997-1999, Hampton and Wellman found the community mailing list facilitated neighborhood-based interactions, led to knowing and chatting with more people in the neighborhood, and lowered barriers to collective action including organizing against the housing developer [9]. Kavanaugh et al.'s longitudinal survey of 100 households in the Blacksburg Electronic Village in 2001 and 2002 also showed that Internet use can strengthen community engagement and social contact [12].

Focusing on people working together to address crime in their neighborhoods, Lewis and Lewis analyzed a Chicago community crime forum [15]. Their study suggested crime prevention technologies should facilitate communication and discussions among residents. Our study of the potential for households to share data from their own security systems with neighbors meshes well with how the community crime forum was used. For example, forum members discussed sharing information and collecting evidence (e.g., writing down license plates numbers, wanting to observe property damage to cars overnight without staying up all night) both of which could potentially be supported by a digital neighborhood watch system.

Privacy concerns around video capture and recording, primarily in public spaces, have been studied by many researchers. For example, using the principles of Value Sensitive Design, Friedman et al. interviewed both people watching video from a university plaza (direct stakeholders) and those being watched (indirect stakeholders) [8]. They found participant's privacy judgments often included consideration based on physical harm, psychological wellbeing, and informed consent, and that more women expressed concern regardless of whether they were watching the video or being watched in the plaza.

Nguyen et al. [17] studied perceptions of pervasive video recording among indirect stakeholders for video recording encountered during their own lives (e.g., in restaurants and public places). Building on the Concern for Information Privacy (CFIP) model they asked participants about collection of data, improper access, unauthorized secondary use, and errors. Study results suggested ways to extend CFIP and indicated participants frequently assumed collection of video data when outside their home or private spaces in the U.S.A. These and other similar studies (e.g., of CCTV) provide valuable information about video-related privacy concerns, particularly among indirect stakeholders, for video captured in public or semi-public spaces. In contrast, our study focuses on household members, primarily as direct stakeholders, and their willingness to share video captured from personal security systems located at their homes to address neighborhood crime.

Related to our interest in cameras for security, Tullio et al. interviewed law enforcement personal including CCTV managers and police officers that use video from seven sites across the U.S. and U.K. [20]. Their findings included the value of human monitoring of CCTV to detect incidents and challenges around managing digital evidence (e.g., finding important parts of recordings). Our focus on individual households' complements Tullio et al.'s focus on law enforcement as well as other studies of CCTV.

One study that considered cameras in households was Beckman et al.'s study of 15 homeowners installing mock-sensors inside their homes for a home energy tutor application [1]. They recommended not using highly directional sensors such as cameras and microphones due to privacy concerns and installation errors where the mock sensors were not aimed to capture items of interest. Rather than studying cameras inside homes, we focus on external cameras for capturing spaces outside the home, having participants indicate to us which parts of their property they wanted to be captured by security cameras.

Finally, our study design, especially for privacy related questions, was inspired by previous work that presents principles and guidelines for designing privacy-sensitive systems [10, 13]—most notably the first stage of Iachello and Abowd's Proportionality Design Method assessing the legitimacy or appeal of an application [10]. We also share the general goal of understanding people's reactions to recording technologies in daily life with several projects (e.g., [8], [10], [16], and [17]), but our study is grounded in the context of DNW giving a unique focus on privacy and security concerns related to data sharing with neighbors.

STUDY METHOD

We conducted 11 semi-structured in-home interviews with 24 participants (13F, 11M) living in the northwest USA between Dec. 2011 and Feb. 2012. All but one home had at least 2 members over 14 years old. Households were compensated with a choice of software gratuity for each participant, up to four per household.

Given our interest in whether electronic sensor data could augment neighborhood watch activities we recruited only households that belonged to a block watch group or neighborhood association. Beyond this requirement, we recruited households for diversity in terms of socioeconomic status, neighborhood crime rate, and experience with security systems. Our participants had a range of occupations including electrician, accountant, wine store owner, and retired. None were associated with our organization.

Five households (H7-H11) are in a neighborhood with a high crime rate relative to the region. For example, this neighborhood had 16 burglaries, 8 thefts, 5 arrests and 4 assaults from Jan. to Mar. 2012. The median household income in this neighborhood is $47,461, which is close to the national median ($49,445 in 2010). When asked about security concerns in the neighborhood, residents described frequent break-ins, hearing gunshots, and problems with drugs. These households were recruited through a neighborhood mailing list and personal requests by one of the authors who lives in this neighborhood. The author did not participate in interviews in his neighborhood so that the participants felt comfortable sharing their opinions about other neighbors. For consistency, he excluded himself from all interviews.

We recruited the other six households (H1-H6, interviewed first due to scheduling constraints) using a recruiting service. We worked with the service to locate eligible households by reaching out to police liaisons, block captains, and neighborhood associations. These six households were selected to be in different neighborhoods so we could interview people in different locations. We explicitly asked about neighborhood crime, and while we heard about occasional problems (e.g., mailbox theft, stolen cars left on the street), the level of incidents and the general concern was much lower than in the high-crime neighborhood.

Our goal in recruiting households with different levels of neighborhood crime was to explore how perspectives on sharing data might change with the level of recent crime. For instance, households in the high-crime neighborhood represent a population that might perceive considerable value in sharing sensed data with neighbors to prevent future crimes. If even these households have insurmountable security and privacy concerns, it seems unlikely that systems like DNW would be adopted in practice.

With regards to experience with security systems, six households (three in the high-crime neighborhood) have existing security systems, primarily door and window sensors, from different companies (e.g., ADT, Monitronics). Two of these six, both in the high-crime neighborhood, had experience with camera-based systems, either currently (H11) or recently (H9). This mix of participants allowed us to interview both people with the experience of living with security systems and people who could describe their ideal system without being biased by prior experience.

Interviews

We interviewed household members together. We began by asking about existing security precautions. Participants then

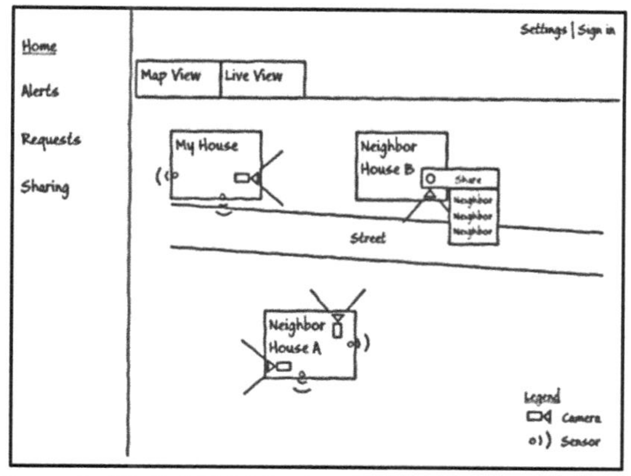

Figure 1. Digital Neighborhood Watch Paper Mockup

indicated on aerial maps of their house and neighborhood where, if desired, they would place cameras. We asked about what features they would want in a security system, how they would want to access it, and whether they would tell their neighbors if they had the cameras.

Next, we asked about their involvement in their neighborhood group and how frequently they interacted with their neighbors. We then asked about their willingness to share data from the cameras they had specified in the first part of the interview with neighbors. To ground this discussion we showed participants low-fidelity, paper mockups of a possible web interface for sharing (Fig. 1). These mockups were intended as probes to give participants some context and visuals to react to. In the interviews, we emphasized that we had not built a system and encouraged them to share their candid feedback and ideas. This effort was successful as the results will demonstrate that participants almost universally rejected the idea of sharing cameras feeds directly with neighbors that was illustrated in the mockups.

Lastly, we filled out a sharing chart through discussion with participants. The chart had rows describing groups they might share with: proximate neighbors (e.g., in view of cameras), other neighbors, law enforcement, and a security company that provided a service for detecting suspicious activity by analyzing information across multiple cameras. The chart had columns showing different types of data that could be shared (Fig. 2). Motivated by a desire to understand how data fidelity might affect sharing, we originally asked participants about sharing high fidelity data (2a), low resolution data (2b) and data that had been processed into textual descriptions of events (2e). Feedback described in the next section led us to add processed camera views showing only foreground activity (2c) or public property (2d) starting in the fifth interview.

For each row-column combination we asked participants if they would "Always", "Sometimes" (by request or under specific circumstances) or "Never" share. We used the sharing chart to stimulate discussion, allowed participants to rename groups as they desired, and prompted them to explain their choices.

(a) High fidelity (b) Low resolution (c) Foreground only (d) Public property only (e) Events

Figure 2. Raw and processed camera data similar to those we asked participants about sharing with different groups of people. Starting with H5 Options (c) and (d) were added and Option (b) was discontinued, based on feedback from first 4 interviews.

Each interview lasted about two hours and was semi-structured as we discussed different relationships with neighbors, neighborhood groups, and law enforcement. We audio recorded and transcribed each interview. We then extracted over 700 items from interviews and field notes and analyzed the data using the affinity diagramming technique [2] based on a grounded theory approach. The authors collaborated on an iterative bottom-up affinity analysis of the items to derive key themes and findings.

A limitation of our study is that some of the participants' reactions could be speculative, given the difficulty of studying people's perceptions toward a new technology. We used interface mockups and image data from an existing surveillance camera to reduce this effect. Another limitation is that our study is based on a relatively small number of participants drawn from a few neighborhoods in the USA. Our findings, however, can form the basis for a broader survey.

RESULTS

A DNW system requires individual households to install camera systems. Perhaps not surprisingly given participants agreed to participate in an interview study about the use of cameras and sensing for home security, all our participant households except H8 were interested in having cameras that recorded videos outside their home. H8 felt their home was occupied most of the time and located such that criminals would be highly visible to others; however, they were open to cameras in the neighborhood to enable DNW.

More interesting to us, eighteen participants (at least one in each household) indicated they would be willing to participate in DNW by sharing some camera data. We discuss below the household sensing system features that appealed to households and challenges that affect the design of DNW.

Household Sensing Systems Desired

Participants wanted a median of 4 outdoor cameras per home. Typical placements included views of front yard, back door, and side yards. When asked about how long they would want to store the camera data, half wanted it retained less than a month (4 of those one week only). A computer at home and a T.V. were ranked as the most important places to view data from security cameras, but access on a mobile phone from outside the home was also highly ranked.

Participants described perceived security benefits including awareness, deterring crime, and for evidence. H11_M (M denotes speaker gender), currently using cameras, also highlighted non-security benefits such as watching themselves complete a major yard project ("it was cool because we built a really nice cedar fence and it [the camera] had documented that whole process") and watching animals ("I hung a bird feeder right in front of the camera one time just for kicks"). H3 also mentioned neighbors had shared video of a bear captured by their camera system. Not surprisingly, cost was a concern, but all ten households with interest in cameras indicated a willingness to pay.

We also asked participants if cameras should capture audio data. Somewhat surprising to us, 14 participants across 9 households wanted audio captured. Participants desiring audio described using it to detect specific sounds such as gunshots or glass breaking rather than to record voices (e.g., "The only reason I would consider audio would be for like a glass break sound" H9_M).

Two female participants, who did not want audio captured, explicitly mentioned not wanting to record conversations and one also felt audio would not offer much value saying "a crooked person would not be talking probably (H4_F)." We found it interesting that in four of the five households where participants disagreed on whether audio should be recorded, female participants did not want it recorded. This could be a similar effect for audio privacy that Friedman et al. [8] found for video with a much larger sample; women expressed more concern about video privacy regardless if they were watching the video or being watched.

Trust Not Proximity for Sharing Existence of Cameras

We asked households if they would inform their neighbors about installed cameras, a pre-requisite for sharing any sensed data. We initially thought participants might treat neighbors in the view of installed cameras (e.g., next door) differently. However, it quickly became clear that participants divided neighbors into groups based on trust, not proximity. Five households renamed the "proximate neighbors" group to "trusted neighbors" in the sharing chart.

While nine households said they would tell trusted neighbors they had installed cameras, they described several reasons for not telling other neighbors in the block watch, including those in view of the camera. For example, four households thought neighbors would think they were spying on them even if that was not intended.[2] Households in the high crime neighborhood told us they had been warned about certain houses by law enforcement. H10 specified that street-facing cameras must be disguised so untrusted neighbors would not realize that they were being observed.

When asked what they would expect from neighbors with cameras (when household members would be the indirect stakeholders being captured by neighbors), most households were consistent, not expecting neighbors to share presence or location of cameras with them. Four households preferred that other households tell them if they installed cameras, but had no expectations. H10_F said, "I wouldn't have any expectation that they would have an obligation to inform us anymore than we would have an obligation to inform them." Two households explicitly mentioned they had no expectation of privacy in public spaces.

Reluctance to Divulge Camera's Field of View

Participants described a reluctance to divulge a camera's field of view (FoV) even to people they would tell about the existence of cameras (e.g., "not your coverage, because you're opening yourself up" H3_M). The concern was security related—divulging the FoV leaks information about "blind spots" of the home security system. No household would consider sharing the camera's FoV with members of their neighborhood group and four would not share even if sharing is limited to trusted neighbors. Not being able to trust "friends of friends" and "kids of friends" was frequently mentioned as a reason to limit disclosure.

The parents in H2 went further and wanted to limit kids' knowledge of the FOV of some of the cameras ("H2_F "I would not want them [kids] to know exactly where they were") to deter sneaking out of the house. More generally, we asked the four households with children in them (H1, H2, H3, H6) about who in the household should have access to camera data. In all cases, the adults felt they would be the only ones with access to any recorded video, but kids should be able to see some of it live (e.g., in H2, they wanted images from a camera mounted at the front door visible on the TV so kids could check it).

Based on FOV concerns expressed in the first four interviews, starting with H5 we additionally asked participants about a foreground-only data sharing option (Fig. 2c), that shares the camera data without divulging the FoV. Three households, all in the high crime neighborhood, indicated they would share this processed data with more groups including other neighbors and police than high-fidelity data (Fig. 2a). (H11_F "we want to tell that we have a camera, we just don't want to tell them where it is. And this way we could show them the guy in the yellow shirt, but they wouldn't know [the FoV]").

Will Share Evidence with Good Reason

One potential benefit of DNW is providing digital evidence of incidents. All ten households with interest in installing cameras indicated that they would sometimes be willing to provide data from their cameras as evidence. However, some participants stressed the need for a good reason for the request ("it really depends on the context on what they're asking for" H9_M) and that the severity of the incident would influence willingness to share ("if it was a murder, whether I didn't like you or not, I'd probably still share that information" H10_M).

While people had concerns about neighbors, five of the six households that we asked explicitly were willing to share existence and cameras' FoV with law enforcement, and all except H5 were willing to share high-fidelity video on request. In fact, H4_M said he would provide evidentiary data directly to law enforcement, rather than to neighbors ("I feel more comfortable sharing the images with the police department because they're the ones who need to take the action.") Again, certain participants stressed the need for a valid reason before they would share data.

We initially asked about sharing low-resolution data (Fig. 2b) as blurred video could reduce privacy risks while not compromising situational awareness [3]. However, starting with H5, we stopped asking about it; all earlier households felt that if they were going to share they would share high-fidelity data ("why would anybody have low resolution, what's the point?" H4_M).

Limited Willingness to Share Direct Access to Cameras

A DNW system could provide greater visibility into neighborhood activity by sharing ongoing access to cameras. For instance, a person could access a neighbor's camera to view parts of the neighborhood that are not visible in her own cameras. However, households were universally reluctant to provide direct, ongoing access to their cameras to neighbors, even trusted ones (e.g., "if an incident happened we'd be willing to share, but I don't think I would want anybody to have free access" H2_M). In a few special cases, participants would share access. Three households were willing to provide access to their cameras while they were on vacation, one when teenage children were home alone, and two would trade access with neighbors that also have cameras.

Given the reluctance to grant access, starting with H5, we asked about sharing processed data that only contained public property (Fig. 2d) such as sidewalks and parks. Three households were willing to "Always" share this data (from certain cameras) with trusted neighbors and law enforcement. H10 and H11 were also willing to provide this data to other neighbors in their neighborhood group.

When asked, four households were positive about adding cameras to public spaces, suggesting problem spots like parks. However, in general, participants were more con-

[2] While laws in the USA vary by city and state, to the best of our knowledge it is generally legal to point cameras and record videos of streets and outside parts (e.g., yards) of others' homes. In such places, there is no reasonable expectation of privacy [11]. Recording videos of inside parts or recording audio is not legal without consent. EU directive 95/46 appear more restrictive than laws in the USA, but its implementation by member states varies [4].

cerned about these cameras than household systems, wanting to avoid "turning into what England has" (H5_M), and questioning who should be able to access them (e.g., all neighbors). The primary concern was privacy—participants felt that being digitally watched by anyone in the neighborhood (without their knowledge) was worse than someone visible watching from the street.

Cautious Interest in Suspicious Activity Detection

Several of the suspicious activities that police detectives recommend watching for (e.g., an unknown car driving by several times) would be easier to detect by comparing data from multiple households. So, we asked participants about what fidelity of data, if any, they would contribute to a service that could potentially detect some of these activities using computer vision techniques [e.g., 19].

Some participants had a positive response to the idea of using data from multiple households. H9_F described how data from several neighbors' cameras had been combined to catch someone following a UPS truck and stealing packages saying "they got a face of her off of one house and they got her license plate because she parked her car next door from the house." H10_F compared suspicious activity detection to the community policing program, saying "a little bit like what Eyes on the Street [is] doing right now."

Five households, four in the high crime neighborhood, indicated they would share events (Fig. 2e) with a detection service on an ongoing basis; the other five with interest in a household sensing system were willing to do so only sometimes. Seven households were willing to share high-fidelity data upon specific requests with a suspicious activity detection service (e.g., if police were looking for a specific car).

However, participants also raised concerns about suspicious activity detection including who would run the service, data retention policies, and bandwidth requirements. Three households strongly preferred that a detection service run on their own computers and exchange data peer-to-peer rather than sending to a third-party service. Another major concern was incorrect or overwhelming notifications. Seven households, including all six with existing security systems, expressed concerns about false alerts from an automatic system. Two had modified their existing systems due to frequent occurrences of falsely detected motion.

DISCUSSION

Neighborhood Types vs. Acceptability of DNW

When planning the study we hypothesized that level of crime in a neighborhood could impact how much benefit households perceived in sharing their security data with neighbors and their willingness to do so at all. We were surprised by the broad similarity in attitudes we found in high and low crime neighborhoods. Households were equally willing to share data for evidence, and interest in sensing audio was present in both types of households.

As described earlier, we did observe two differences, however. First, households in the high crime neighborhood indicated a greater willingness to share events with a detection service on an ongoing basis (4 of the 5 households from the high crime neighborhood were interested). Second, due to untrusted or even known-to-be dangerous neighbors, participants in high crime neighborhoods emphasized the importance of hidden cameras to limit possible reprisals against them from collecting and sharing camera data. However, households in the low crime neighborhoods also had concerns about who they would share with and about leaking the camera's FOV (and thus blind spots).

Although we did not investigate them in this study, other attributes of a neighborhood may impact the acceptability of DNW, including household structure (e.g., apartment buildings vs. single family houses), cultural norms, and residents' lifestyle (e.g., urban vs. rural). We leave the study of these attributes as avenues to explore next.

Complex Neighborhood Trust

We began our study with a belief that participants might treat proximate neighbors differently and might treat all other neighbors in the block watch equally (e.g., choosing to share or not). As we described, participants quickly made clear to us that their trust and relationship with the neighbors was more important than proximity and had reasons they might not share the presence of cameras with members of the block watch. This suggests to us that, when designing a DNW system, allowing neighbors to construct their own ad-hoc sharing groups might be a more viable approach than having a "block watch" group. However, the challenge of facilitating broader sharing still remains as DNW likely becomes more effective as the number of participating households increases.

The increasing mobility of people can further complicate neighborhood trust relationships. In our study, participants showed heightened concerns over sharing camera data with renters in the neighborhood. One interesting issue to examine is to understand existing practices people use to develop trust with their neighbors and to find ways to help them grow their trust network with technical assistance. For instance, when a new neighbor moves in, there should be ways for newcomers to easily discover existing DNW groups and to introduce themselves to interesting groups. Neighborhood social networking sites such as Nextdoor.com may be a useful way to bootstrap a trusted community for DNW.

Sharing Security Camera Data vs. Other Data Types

Participant's concerns about divulging their cameras' FOV highlights a key difference compared from findings of studies of sharing other types of context, particularly mobile context such as location [e.g., 5, 14]. The placement and FOV of household cameras are highly sensitive and even a single disclosure could leak information about blind spots of a home security system. In contrast, sharing your current location might be considered less sensitive and its sensitivity potentially reduces with time, allowing participants to make different decisions about sharing with the same person at different times without long term consequences.

The importance our participants placed on knowing "why" people would be requesting their camera data was also found to be an important decision factor for sharing location in Consolvo et al. [5]. However, in contrast to this study and the findings of Lederer et al. [14], which showed that "who" was requesting the information was the most important factor, for our participants, "why" data was needed seemed to be at least equally important and sometimes more important than "who" was asking. One reason for this may be that the stakes are higher if camera data is misused (e.g., accidental leakage of personal moments, repurposed as video evidence in court). Another reason could be that we asked about sharing with very different groups (e.g., neighbors, law enforcement) than those typically studied in context sharing (e.g., family, friends, co-workers).

Implications for Other Neighborhood Sharing Systems

We focused on whether and how participants might share camera data with neighbors for security reasons; other examples of sensing applications that require data sharing amongst neighbors include coordinating electricity usage to reduce peak load on local transformers, comparing neighbors water usage (e.g., [7]), or sharing commute patterns to identify carpooling opportunities. Our findings suggest interesting ways to reconsider sharing of other types of data with neighbors.

First, systems for sharing sensed data (e.g., water usage, electricity) often collect data from large numbers of households and then share back anonymized data. However, our participants were generally more receptive to sharing data based on specific events (e.g., police looking for a specific car) than sharing ongoing information. Considering ways that neighbors can be alerted to situations and asked to respond to specific actions rather than sharing ongoing data may be fruitful. For example, for reducing peak load on transformers, alerting households to high loads and incenting them to reduce usage at that moment might be a viable alternative to collecting data for neighbors and trying to coordinate usage. Similarly, we can look for spikes in water usage at the neighborhood level and alert households to those events.

For DNW, we also found that abstractions of the data that preserved appropriate levels of privacy (e.g., foreground only or public-property views) tended to increase the willingness of some participants to share. Exploring whether similar abstractions exist for other types of data, particularly for situations when fully anonymous data is either not possible or less useful, is an interesting research opportunity. For example, neighborhood water saving competitions might be more successful if neighbors know who they are competing against, but households may be more willing to participate if they can share data at a level of abstraction that prevents neighbors from seeing specifics (e.g., showing a comparison outcome of which neighbor had higher usage instead of total daily usage which could leak when people are on vacation).

While these may or may not be good ideas in a given context, we believe our findings suggest alternatives for other researchers working on neighborhood data sharing systems to consider as they pursue their specific scenarios.

CONCLUDING REMARKS

Our findings make us cautiously optimistic about the feasibility of DNW. All but one of our households, including those outside the high crime neighborhood, saw advantages in deploying a camera-based security system. All households were willing to participate in DNW to provide digital evidence. Interest in sharing data to support awareness and detect suspicious activity was limited, however, due to security and privacy concerns. But we were encouraged by the interest in activity detection from households in the high crime neighborhood and comparisons to community policing. Further, the options of sharing processed camera data, with only foreground and public-property, helped address concerns for some households.

Informed by our study, we are building on top of HomeOS [6] an easily-installable, low-cost home camera system that incorporates features to support the types of sharing towards which our households indicated they were open. For example, we are making it easy to archive and share sections of recorded video to allow households to provide evidence when needed as well as share foreground-only and public-property camera views to support sharing without fully divulging the location and field of view of their cameras. Incorporating mechanisms that allow people to share more or less data will be necessary to allow ongoing negotiation through a DNW system as situations change [18]. We are also investigating advances in computer vision, including techniques to track objects over obfuscated videos [21], which may enable an effective DNW system that respects people's privacy and security concerns.

During our research, our own neighborhoods have continued to experience crimes including daytime burglaries and gun incidents. These events continually renew our motivation to explore ways in which technology can help reduce crime while being sensitive to the privacy and security concerns of household members. We are aware that a DNW system, like CCTV, can be abused (e.g., to spy on neighbors). While our participants felt that neighbors' cameras did not alter their expectation of privacy, we plan to revisit this issue as we deploy prototypes.

REFERENCES

1. Beckmann, C., Consolvo, S., LaMarca, A. Some Assembly Required: Supporting End-User Sensor Installation in Domestic Ubiquitous Computing Environments. UbiComp 2004, 107-124.
2. Beyer, H., Holtzblatt, K. Contextual Design: Defining Customer-Centered Systems. Morgan Kaufmann, 1998.
3. Boyle, M., Edwards, C., and Greenberg, S. 2000. The effects of filtered video on awareness and privacy. CSCW 2000, 1-10.

4. British Institute of Internal and Comparative Law, The implementation of Directive 95/46/EC to the Processing of Sound and Image Data, 2003.
5. Consolvo, S., Smith, T., LaMarca, A. Tabert, J., Powledge, P., Location Disclosure to Social Relations: Why, When & What People Want to Share. CHI 2005, 81-90.
6. Dixon, C., Mahajan, R., Agarwal, S., Brush, A., Lee, B., Saroiu, S., Bahl, P., An Operating System for the Home. NSDI'12, 337–352.
7. Erickson, T., Podlaseck, M., Sahu, S., Dai, J., Chao, T., Naphade, M., The Dubuque Water Portal: Evaluation of the Uptake, Use and Impact of Residential Water Consumption Feedback. CHI 2012, 675-684.
8. Friedman, B., Kahn, P, Hagman, J., Severson, R., The Watcher and the Watched: Social Judgments About Privacy in a Public Place. Human-Computer Interaction, vol. 21, 2006, 235-272.
9. Hampton, K., & Wellman, B., Neighboring in Netville: How the Internet Supports Community and Social Capital in a Wired Suburb. City & Community vol. 2, no. 3 2003, 277-311.
10. Iachello, G., & Abowd, G.D. Privacy and proportionality: adapting legal evaluation techniques to inform design in ubiquitous computing. CHI 2005, 91–100.
11. Katz v. United States. 389 U.S. 347;88 S. Ct. 507 (1967)
12. Kavanaugh, A., Carroll, J., Rosson, M., Zin, T., Reese, D., Community Networks: Where Offline Communities Meet Online. Journal of Computer-Mediated Communication, 10(4), article 3.
13. Langheinrich, M. Privacy by design-Principles of privacy-aware ubiquitous systems. UbiComp 2001, 273–291.
14. Lederer, S., Mankoff J., Dey, A.K., "Who Wants to Know What When? Privacy Preference Determinants in Ubiquitous Computing". CHI Extended Abstracts 2003, 724-5.
15. Lewis S., and Lewis, D., Examining Technology that Supports Community Policing. CHI 2012, 1371-1380.
16. Massimi, M. et al. (2010). Understanding recording technologies in everyday life. IEEE Pervasive Computing, 9(3), 64–71.
17. Nguyen, D., Bedford, A., Bretana, A., Hayes, G., Situating the Concern for Information Privacy through an Empirical Study of Responses to Video Recording. CHI 2011, 3207-3216.
18. Palen, L., & Dourish, P. Unpacking "Privacy" for a Networked World. CHI 2003, 129–136.
19. Song B., Ding C., Kamal A. T., Farrel J. A., Roy-Chowdhury A. K., Distributed Camera Networks. IEEE Signal Processing, vol. 28, issue. 3 May 2011, 20-31.
20. Tullio, J., Huang, E., Wheatley, D., Zhang, H., Guerrero, C. Tamdoo, A., Experience, Adjustment, and Engagement: The Role of Video in Law Enforcement. CHI 2010, 1505 – 1514.
21. Upmanyu M., Namboodiri A. M., Srinathan K., Jawahar C. V., Efficient Privacy Preserving Video Surveillance. ICCV 2009, 1639-1646.

Complementarity of Input Devices to Achieve Knowledge Sharing in Meetings

Himanshu Verma, Flaviu Roman, Silvia Magrelli, Patrick Jermann, Pierre Dillenbourg
CRAFT, École Polytechnique Fédérale de Lausanne (EPFL)
Switzerland
{himanshu.verma, flaviu.roman, silvia.magrelli, patrick.jermann, pierre.dillenbourg}@epfl.ch

ABSTRACT
In co-located meetings, participants create and share content to establish a common understanding. In this paper, we present a collaborative environment that enables group members to create and share content simultaneously by providing them with different kinds of individual input devices and a shared workspace. We also report on an exploratory study to investigate the influence of the input device used on the shared knowledge produced by the group. The results suggest that driven by the affordances, various input devices complement each other. We thus recommend groups to be equipped with multitude of them to support diverse meeting task demands. Additionally, we observed that groupware usage differs across various phases of the problem-solving activity. This provides implications for the design of collaborative environments to assist each of the respective phases of the task, in order to extend their usefulness for the group.

Author Keywords
Single display groupware; co-located collaboration; shared workspaces; multiple input devices; CSCW

ACM Classification Keywords
H.5.3 Information Interfaces and Presentation: Group and Organizational Interfaces—*Computer-supported cooperative work*.

General Terms
Human Factors; Experimentation.

INTRODUCTION
Meetings are a widespread way of decision making and problem solving in a collaborative way. In order to support the construction of shared understanding, participants create artifacts such as written notes, drawings, annotations and so forth. However, content creation is often a distributed activity as attendees have their own copy of notes, and they are not aware of their peers' actions. In order to support an idea or to express their opinion, participants share these artifacts among each other. Sharing requires either the transfer of artifacts to others or explicit acquisition of control over the shared resources such as a flip-chart or a whiteboard. Transfer of artifacts is sometimes inconvenient and the shared information is only visible to a subset of group members who are in proximity to the artifact. This may lead to reduced visibility of the artifact within the group. In addition, acquisition of shared resources by a participant could lead to floor monopolization. Also, whiteboards are often used in meetings to facilitate sharing of content, but the shared content over white-boards is not permanent, cannot be replicated and is hard to modify [26].

As our research is oriented towards co-located brainstorming and meetings, we hypothesize that a Single Display Groupware (SDG) as defined by Stewart et al. [27] can mitigate these issues relating to sharing and creation of content in meetings. Kaplan et al. [14] identified that technologies allowing for collective manipulation and group awareness (which are supplied by a SDG) support co-located collaboration. A SDG embodies the benefits of a shared workspace coupled with simultaneous interaction ability that is enabled by multiple input devices - one for each user. Presence of a shared workspace assists group members to collaborate over a common task at the same time. In addition, supplying each group member with an input device of her own makes sharing more probable and helps in avoiding situations where a user claims ownership over the shared resources, thus moderating floor monopolization. Further, the affordances of the input device also influence the kind of activity best supported by the device. For example, a keyboard is a convenient way of inputting text to a computer, while a pen is more effective for drawing schemas and figures on paper or white-board. Therefore, it is crucial to leverage these factors into the design of a collaborative meeting environment which can facilitate the auxiliary activity of content creation and sharing.

In this paper, we present a collaborative environment to support content creation and sharing in meetings for small groups. The system incorporates a shared wall-mounted workspace where users can interact using either mouse and keyboard or pen and paper. We also present an exploratory user study comparing the two input configurations, to understand the role of input devices on the way users share content within the group and how this can influence the task outcome.

RELATED WORK

Many researchers have studied SDGs in diverse scenarios ranging from education of school children [18] to organizational meetings [12, 13]. Dillenbourg et al. [4] identified that shared workspaces as comprised in SDG, offer potential benefits such as increased awareness, facilitate the process of grounding, and could act as group memory due to the persistence of information shared over it. Further, large wall-mounted displays such as whiteboards facilitate the fluid transitions between individual and group work [28], as well as enable shared visualization and give an overview of the shared content [9]. Considering the simultaneous interaction ability (as enabled by SDG), Rogers et al. [19] observed more balanced participation within a group in terms of verbal utterances, when each group member was supplied with her own input entry point. Besides, SDG was observed to positively affect the collaboration among children due to the increased awareness about the shared artifacts and fellow group members. In a study conducted by Scott et al. [21], an increase in children's participation, engagement level and enjoyment of the activity was observed, while using a SDG to solve a collaborative puzzle task.

However, existing SDG systems are restricted in the way users can interact with the system. For example, the interaction with the shared display is limited to individual claimed spaces in Dynamo [12] and users have to compete for the screen space in order to share. In PointRight [13] the interaction itself is restricted due to technological constraints and the system allows only one mouse pointer per display, thus reducing chances of collaboration. Also, some SDG systems require multi-touch tables to interact with the system as in WeSpace [33]. This can be cumbersome to use, as shared content on the table has reduced visibility among the group mainly due to orientation of the users around the table [23] and occlusion [22]. Moreover, the space over the multi-touch tables is meant for interaction and cannot be used to lay physical objects [10]. Furthermore, their prolonged usage results into fatigue [32].

In addition, these systems require users to learn the functionality of the system and perform extra effort every time to keep it operable, such as connecting individual laptops or PDAs to share content [12, 26, 33]. This additional effort required in proportion to a small collective benefit, motivates users to revert back to conventional means of collaboration using paper and flip-charts, and thus causes the groupware to fail in its purpose as emphasized by Grudin [5].

Despite the presence of varied systems supporting meetings, pen and paper are still preferred as they are a quicker way of expressing an idea or making a point. Perennial research has been done to leverage the pen based interaction into interfaces supporting collaboration. For example, NoteLook [2], NotePals [3] and We-Met [34] use stylus over PDA and tablets to enable note taking during meetings, while in NiCE Discussion Room [6] group members can use pen and paper to create and share content. NotePals [3] is a system to share meeting notes among the group using a shared note repository, however the interaction is restricted due to the small size of the PDA screen. NoteLook [2] facilitates users to generate meeting minutes by annotating directly over the meeting images (extracted from the video cameras in meeting room and signifying meeting activity and important events), but is not suitable for brainstorming where group members frequently generate ideas in the form of drawings or schemas. The pen and paper interface in NiCE Discussion Room [6] does not allow multiple users to work simultaneously on a single problem. Wolf et al. [34] observed that pen based interfaces are unobtrusive and do not interfere with interpersonal communications during collaboration. This suggests that an obtrusive input device increases the extraneous cognitive load of the user resulting in attentional shift from the collaborative task to the device usage.

Figure 1: Collaborative environment with the meeting table in the Mouse and Keyboard setup.

Researchers have also studied the impact of various aspects of groupware on the collaborative processes in face-to-face meetings. Inkpen et al. [11] conducted an ergonomic field study to investigate the influence of seating arrangement, orientation of group members, size and number of displays on co-located collaboration. In addition, Mandryk et al. [16] studied the effects of privacy and user's proximity to the display on the collaborative processes. The results suggest that varied display types have different affordances: horizontal displays are perceived to be more natural and comfortable for co-located collaboration, whereas vertical displays offer a better perspective on the shared information. Seating arrangement around the table was found to influence the distribution of roles within the group in face-to-face setting [24]. Likewise, orientation around the table was observed to affect the coordination, communication and comprehension among the group members [15]. Furthermore, Ryall et al. [20] have examined the effects of table size and group size on group interactions around a single, shared-display groupware. The results suggest that group size affects the way digital shared content was organized and used by the group members.

Figure 2: Meeting table in the Pen and Paper setup.

TECHNICAL SETUP

Our proposed system design incorporates a front projected display of 2m×2m size, as well as a meeting table placed in front of the public display (see Figure 1). The meeting table has a specific shape (wave-like shape as shown in Figure 2) designed to ergonomically facilitate face-to-face interaction between participants as well as interaction with the public display. The system consists of two setups - in the first setup each user is equipped with a wireless mouse and keyboard (MK, Figure 1), while in the other each user is supplied with a digital pen[1] and paper (PP, Figure 2). Each input device is color coded, which helps users identify their respective cursors on the public display in both the setups. The public display as well as the input devices are connected to a single computer.

Design Rationale

Wallace et al. [32] have established that single-display groupware (SDG) is beneficial for coordinating over the shared resources whereas multi-display groupware (MDG) is advantageous for individual task duties. This was our initial design decision to select SDG over MDG. Tang et al. [29] have demonstrated that collaborative coupling (both loose and tight coupling) between participants during meetings is influenced by the physical arrangement of the meeting place. This led us to the wave-like design of the meeting table (see Figure 2), which can ergonomically facilitate smooth transitions between different coupling styles as well as transitions between individual and group activities.

Next, we chose mouse and keyboard as the preferable input devices instead of multi-touch tables. Mice offer a higher degree of pointing accuracy and keyboards are a faster, convenient and robust means of entering text as compared to touch-based or on-screen keyboards [8]. Furthermore, a comparison between multi-mouse SDG and multi-touch tables suggests that users are more efficient with the multi-mouse SDG, but prefer the multi-touch setup [7]. During the iterative development of our system, we tested it in several meetings and brainstormings in our lab. We experienced that mouse was a very efficient device to move, edit and delete objects (text and images). However, the mouse was not very efficient when users quickly wanted to express an idea by drawing a schema or a diagram, as the users had to change between different tools frequently (for example from lines to circle). Even though we chose to provide users with the minimal number of tools required to create and share content, the mouse was not found to be easily compatible with the real time dynamics of a meeting. Furthermore, using a mouse for the purpose of drawing increased the extraneous cognitive load of the users and thus made it hard for them to focus on the ongoing collaboration simultaneously while using the mouse.

This led us to use pen and paper in our collaborative system as creation of content such as drawings and schemas is considerably quicker and more efficient using a pen instead of a mouse [34]. Further, availability of multiple pens during meetings (one for each user), will reduce the chances of a user acquiring explicit control over the shared resources, thus moderating floor monopolization. Terrenghi et al. [30] point out that tangibility of an artifact and the surrounding space allows for easy manipulation of the artifact. As pen and paper are tangible as compared to digital objects over multi-touch table, we decided to use the former for our collaborative meeting environment.

Shared Workspace over Public Display

Similar to the conventional paper-based flip charts, we use a page metaphor for our shared workspace. Our shared workspace allows multiple users to simultaneously add and manipulate artifacts such as graphics, text and images. In case of space shortage on the current page, users can create a new blank page while concurrently saving the previous work. In the mouse and keyboard setup, the group is provided with a *Page Manager* widget designed to enable the group to browse through previously created pages (see the top part of Figure 3a).

In the pen setup, users are provided with normal A4 sheets upon which is marked the area mapped to the entire public display. Anything written within this area is concurrently reflected on the public display in the color of the device color code (see Figure 3b). Changing of page on the public display is accomplished by tapping the pen over one of the two squares printed on the top left corner of the paper indicating the direction of the page change.

Tool Collection

We wanted to provide users only with the minimal functionality necessary to support the task at hand, as abundance of tools consume a lot of screen space and involves higher anticipated learning efforts and time. This might result in an increase in extraneous cognitive load and would leave less cognitive capacity for the execution of the task; i.e. bringing the content creation and sharing (which is a supporting activity going on in the background) to the forefront and push the

[1] IRISNotes Pen : www.irisnotes.de

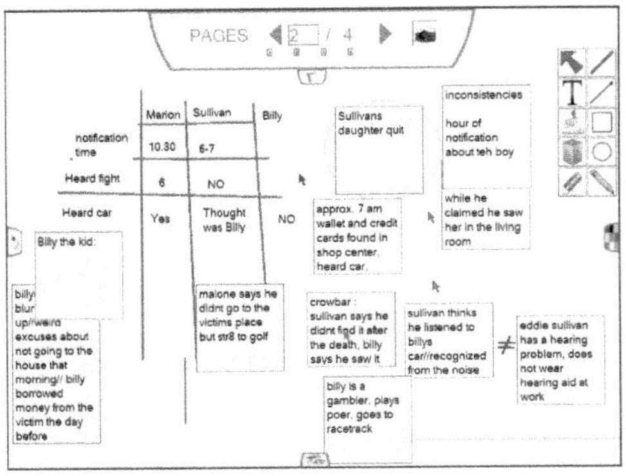

(a) Mouse and Keyboard Condition

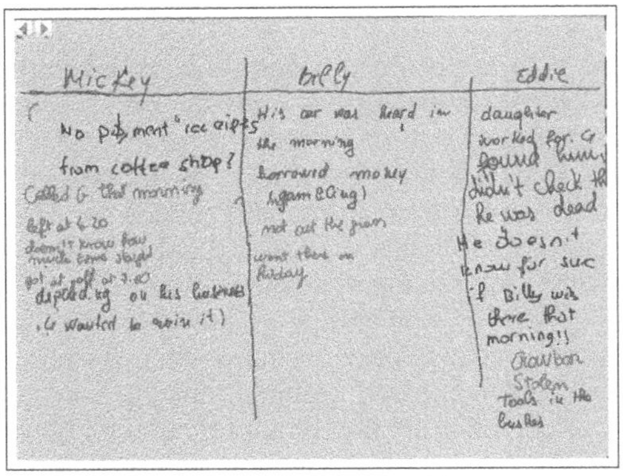

(b) Pen and Paper Contition

Figure 3: Snapshot of the shared workspace in MK condition (top) and PP condition (bottom).

collaborative task in the background. In the mouse and keyboard setup the basic toolset includes lines, arrows, ellipse, rectangle, free-hand drawing and post-its. The users are provided with two identical toolsets containing the above mentioned functionalities; one of the toolbars is displayed next to each mouse pointer, the other one is public for everyone to use (see the top right corner of Figure 3a). In this setup, users can arrange the digital content (post-its and images) over the shared workspace by simply dragging the object from one place to another, as well as stack artifacts on top of others. Furthermore, any user can annotate and manipulate the digital artifacts created by other group members; thus enabling group members to simultaneously work on the same problem without requiring to divide it into sub-problems.

In the pen system no additional tools are provided to the user, like an ability to create predefined shapes from strokes on the paper or moving artifacts over the public display. The pen is intended to be used in the natural way.

USER STUDY

We hypothesized that affordances of an input device may render it appropriate for a specific type of interaction. Thus, users might perceive one input device as an efficient (and faster) way of creating one type of shared representation than another. For example, a keyboard might more often be used to create textual elements and pen for drawing elements, while a mouse is more efficient to move and organize artifacts. In order to investigate the differences between the input devices, and how this difference influences the kind of shared representations created by groups, we conducted an exploratory user study.

Participants

Sixty-six participants (23 females and 43 males) aged 17–35 years (average age of 23) were recruited for the study, from the Swiss Federal Institute of Technology, Lausanne. The participants were all university students studying various engineering domains. Groups of 4 participants passed the experiment task, except for two cases where the experiment was performed with a group of 3 participants (both groups in the pen and paper condition). The participants were randomly assigned to the groups across the two conditions. There were 11 mixed-gender groups, 2 groups were all female groups and 4 were all male groups. Regarding the familiarity among the subjects, there were 7 (out of 17) groups where at least 2 participants were acquainted with each other. However, to increase familiarity between all participants, we asked each group member to introduce themselves before each experiment. In addition, 2 subjects (out of 66) reported themselves to be colorblind, one for red and green pair and the other for blue colors. Participants were paid 25 Swiss Francs each for their participation in the study.

Experimental Task

During the experiment, each group was asked to complete the murder mystery task designed by Stasser et al. [25], where group members were required to use the collaborative environment to generate and share content. It is a hidden profile task where some crucial information about the suspects is unshared among the group members. The correct identification of the murderer requires the group members to combine the information by sharing and discussing as much as possible, as incomplete information may lead to inferior solutions and premature solution convergence [17]. Furthermore, as identified by Mennecke [17], group members share more information in situations where they are explicitly made aware about the unshared information. We informed each group about the hidden pieces of information (but not the location) in the experiment booklets (containing various interviews with the characters of the story) at the start of the experiment.

This task was chosen because it resembles a collaborative problem solving strategy common to meetings where the group has some shared knowledge about the task as well as some unshared information which could prove to be important towards the end result. In addition, the choice of the input device to create and share information using a groupware might influence the sharing behavior of participants. Groups using different collaborative tools (mouse and keyboard (MK) versus pen and paper (PP)) might have different shared representations of the murder mystery. For example, group members in the MK condition might share facts and link them, while groups in the PP condition might come up with the timeline of the murder.

Procedure

Firstly, the group members were welcomed and asked to choose their preferred seat around the table. Once seated, the group members were asked to complete a pre-experiment questionnaire recording basic demographic data and were requested not to change their seating position, as this information was also recorded in the questionnaire. Next, the group was introduced to the collaborative system which they were about to use (either mouse and keyboard or pen and paper), and they were given some time to try out the system and familiarize themselves with the tools. After this, the experiment booklets were provided to the group members, and the group was asked to complete the task by determining the most likely suspect to have committed the crime. The group members were then asked to complete a post-experiment questionnaire recording their perception about the groupware usage and collaboration. Finally, after disclosing the true identity of the murderer and the motives involved in the study, all the subjects were given the compensation and were thanked for their participation.

Design

We used a two input configurations (mouse and keyboard (MK) versus pen and paper (PP)), between-subjects design for our user study. Groups of 4 participants completed the experimental task in one of the two conditions. The task was not time bound, but an upper limit of 2 hours was set and the groups were asked to suggest the name of the suspect most likely to have committed the crime. However, the average time required to complete the task by all the groups was 90 minutes. In total, there were 17 groups during the study (15 groups with 4 participants, 2 groups with 3 participants). Nine groups completed the experiment in MK condition and eight groups in PP condition.

Data Collection

Each participant was asked to complete two questionnaires; one before and one after the study. The pre-experiment questionnaire collected basic information about participants including working preferences (if the subject prefers to work alone or in groups), weekly time spent in meetings and type of meetings attended. We also asked if the subject suffered from colorblindness and of what kind, because the content created over the shared workspace by different group members is represented in different colors corresponding to the input device color code.

The post-experiment questionnaire recorded participant's perception of the task, the emerging social structure, the usage of the collaborative tool and the purpose for which the tool was used. This questionnaire contained statements that the participant had to rate on a 5-point Likert scale, with 1 as strong disagreement and 5 as strong agreement. The information related to the task concerned the perception of a participant about the group's consensus on the solution, time sufficiency and difference in opinion among the group members. The statements about the emerging social structure relate to the presence of a group leader, individual's perception about participation and acceptance of her contributions by the group. Further, the usage information in the questionnaire records effort required to create artifacts (text, drawings and linking information) and effort required to coordinate. Finally, the questionnaire recorded the perceived purpose of the collaborative tool: whether the group used the tool to collect facts, make hypotheses about the suspects or recreate the story line. Space was also provided for the users to add some open ended comments.

In addition, two observers manually recorded the number of deictic gestures and utterances for each participant in the group. The utterances were classified either to be relating to the task or to the organization of group activities. Similarly, deictic gestures were divided so as to refer to the task material (booklets given to the participants) or to the content shared on the public display. Further, all the interactions with the collaborative environment were recorded in system log files.

Research Hypotheses

We hypothesize that affordances of an input device render it appropriate for a specific kind of task activity. As a pen is more efficient and quick to draw figures or schemas and a keyboard is a faster way of entering text, we expect that there will be more drawing elements in the PP condition (**H1a**), and more textual elements in the MK condition (**H1b**). Furthermore, as more users simultaneously share content in the PP setup, and due to the absence of visual feedback from other users on the paper, there will be more chances of content overlapping (or coordination breakdowns). However, in the MK setup as users directly look at the shared workspace while interacting, there will be less overlap of content (due to location coordination) and coordination may be easier (**H2**).

In addition, the difference in the input mechanism can also lead to different shared representations of the problem solving task being produced by the group members. For example, as entering text is faster using a keyboard and users are accustomed to moving objects (files, folders etc.) on their desktop using a mouse, the MK setup can be used to collect facts about the suspects. On the contrary, as drawing is quicker with a pen on paper, we assume that the group members will produce a more conceptual representation of the murder mystery such as a timeline of the murder.

RESULTS AND ANALYSES

Input Devices

An analysis of variance with task time as the dependent and experiment condition as the independent variable reveals that groups in the PP condition completed the task in significantly less time as compared to the MK condition ($F(1,15)=11.70$, $p<.01$). One possible explanation for this could be that group members are more efficient with pen and paper. But this observation does not inform us about the amount of content created. Next, we look at the type of content created by the group members; i.e. the amount of textual elements and drawing elements generated. The number of textual elements corresponds to the number of words generated by each participant in each group during the experiment. Similarly, a count was made for the drawing elements, where each drawing stroke (line, ellipse, etc.) was counted as a single drawing element. A significant difference was found in the amount of text generated using the groupware across the two conditions, with more text generated in the MK condition ($F(1,64)=4.08$, $p=.04$). Thus, our hypothesis H1b is statistically validated. On the contrary, more drawing elements were created in the PP condition, but this difference was not found to be statistically significant and therefore there is not enough statistical evidence to validate hypothesis H1a. Also, no significant difference was found in the number of pages created across the two conditions.

Regarding the questionnaire data about the subject's perception of the effort required to create artifacts, we observed that it required significantly more effort to create text in the PP condition ($F(1,63)=4.30$, $p=.04$). On the other hand, creating drawing elements was perceived as significantly easier in the PP condition ($F(1,62)=5.71$, $p=.02$). This goes in line with the aforementioned observation that larger number of textual elements were created in the MK condition. In addition, this effort might also suggest that users perceive keyboard as an efficient way of inputting text, and pen as a quicker way of creating drawing elements. Thus, indicating that the affordances of an input device in usage might influence a specific task activity.

Next, considering the effort required to avoid overlapping of content over the shared workspace (i.e. avoiding coordination breakdowns), the participants responded that it was easier to coordinate in the PP setup. However, this difference is not statistically significant. This observation is contrary to our hypothesis H2, and a possible explanation for this could be the lack of transparency of the post-its and text objects in the MK setup. Also, these text objects automatically adjust their size depending on the quantity of text contained, as more text is added the post-its grow in size possibly occluding the artifact under it as indicated by Zanella and Greenberg in [35].

Task Outcome

Considering the success (or failure) of a group across the two conditions (i.e. identifying the correct suspect as the murderer), we observed that there was no significant difference ($\chi^2=0.04$, $p>.05$, Kruskal-Wallis Test). However, success in hidden profile tasks is influenced by other factors as well, such as the information the group is aware of, effective sharing of information, motivation of the group members and the importance of information perceived by them [25]. Different input techniques can only assist to facilitate the process of effective sharing. In addition, as indicated by Mennecke [17], enabling groups to share information simultaneously reduces the chances of production blocking (i.e. lack of opportunity for group members to share ideas they have created). But, this parallelism in sharing might also impede groups from discovering the true hidden profile as the individuals fail to consume the information shared by the group (see Figure 4b), i.e. *consumption blocking*. In other words, as shown in Figure 4b if group members create and share information using the groupware for the most part of the meeting without pausing to discuss and assimilate this information, it might result in a bad decision quality or failure in the task. This suggests that groups should follow phases of sharing and phases of assimilation (with very few actions on the shared workspace) of

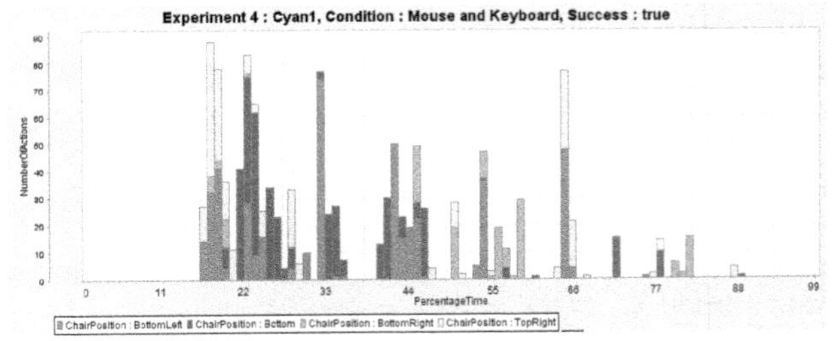

(a) Success in Task

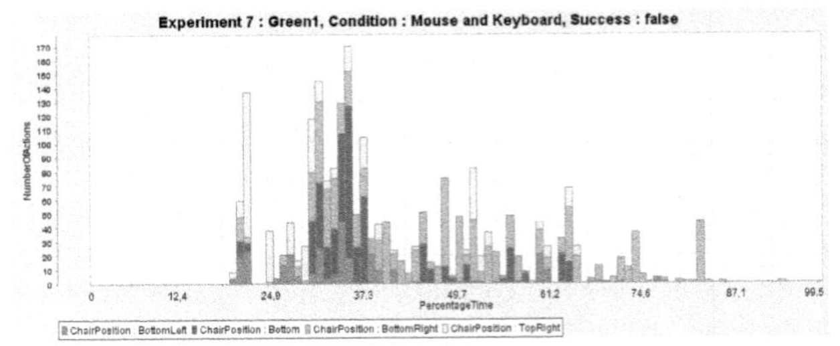

(b) Failure in Task

Figure 4: Activity map for each subject (in different color) in a group during the experiment. The X-axis represents the elapsed time in percentage, and the Y-axis represents the number of actions.

the information in order to achieve success (Figure 4a). However, we did not observe such a pattern while looking at the activity maps of all the successful groups.

Furthermore, we observed that successful groups produced more utterances but this difference was not statistically significant. On the contrary, significantly less gestures were made towards the public display ($\chi^2 = 12.86$, $p<.001$, Kruskal-Wallis Test) as well as towards the experiment material ($F(1,64)=4.32$, $p=.04$) by the successful groups. Also, significantly higher number of pages were created by the successful groups ($\chi^2=8.51$, $p<.01$, Kruskal-Wallis Test), which confirms that effective sharing is essential for success in hidden profile tasks. Taking into consideration the Likert scale value denoting the difference in opinions among group members regarding the murderer, we observed that members of successful groups were significantly more differing in their opinions ($F(1,64)=27.29$, $p<.001$). This corroborates the fact that difference in opinion results into dialogue among the group members, and thus making the true discovery of hidden profile highly probable. This dialogue might also provide the appropriate platform to reconsider the problem from a completely different viewpoint.

Shared Knowledge Representations

The experiment booklets distributed among the group members contained interviews between detectives, suspects and other characters. Few excerpts from these interviews were left unshared in a way that only one group member had this information, while the others didn't. In order to correctly identify the murderer, the group members should unify the initially shared (common to all the group members) as well as the initially unshared (specific to each user) information. Ac-

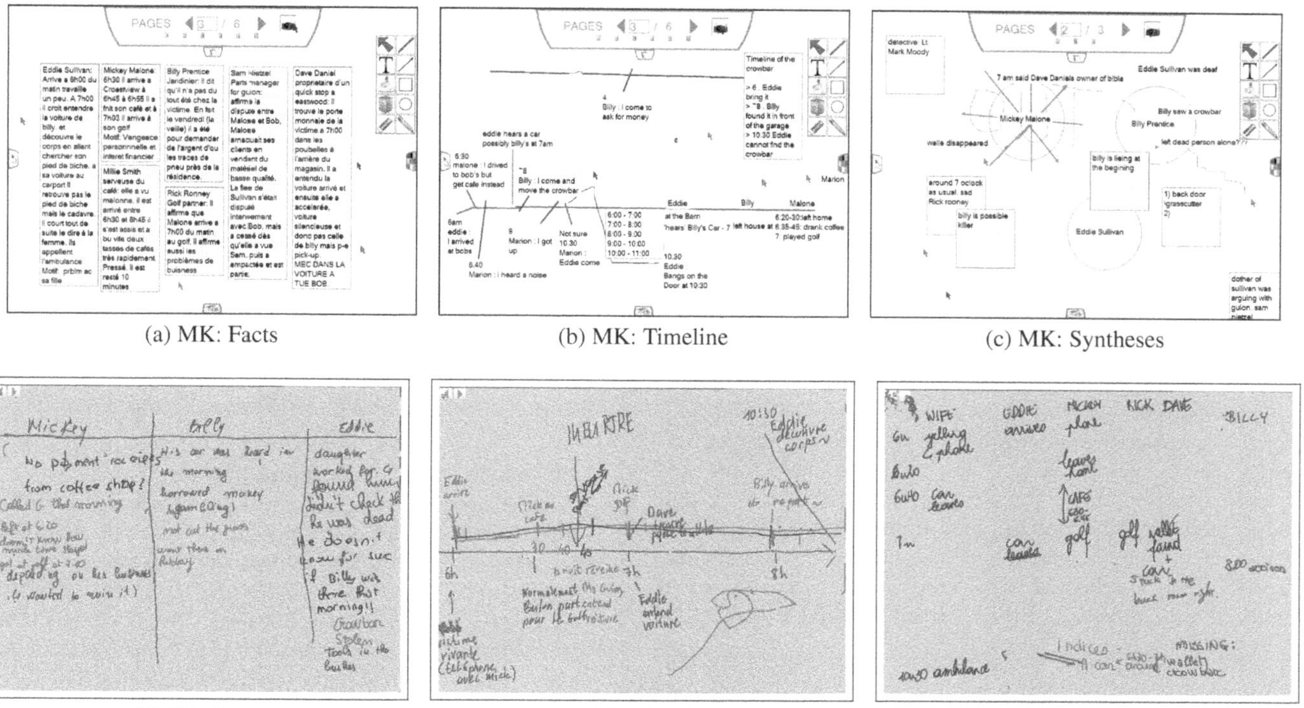

(a) MK: Facts (b) MK: Timeline (c) MK: Syntheses

(d) PP: Facts (e) PP: Timeline (f) PP: Syntheses

Figure 5: Classification of the shared content over the public display.

complishing this requires that group members simultaneously collect facts about the suspects, connect and associate the shared facts to create the narrative. During the experiments, we observed that groups created similar kinds of knowledge representations over the shared display in both the conditions. We can briefly classify the shared knowledge representations into three categories - *facts* (Figures 5a & 5d), *timelines* (Figures 5b & 5e) and *syntheses* (Figures 5c & 5f).

Facts were collected mostly during the starting phase of the experiment while reading the experiment booklets. The group members tended to partition the available space over the shared workspace; in each partition facts about one of the suspects or characters was collected as shown in Figures 5a and 5d. In the MK setup, different post-its denoted the separation of one character from another (Figure 5a), and with time the facts were added to the appropriate post-it by the group members. On the other hand, in PP setup one group member took the initiative to partition the space manually after discussing on the number of partitions (Figure 5d). In some cases, the group members skipped (the fact collection phase) directly to a more schematic representation such as a timeline or a grid. In order to do so, the group members showed each other their experiment booklets to find the differences in the text, thus reducing their effort to share a lot of information and sharing only the crucial episodes of the story.

The **timelines** were usually made towards the end of the reading phase, and mark the phase where group members start assimilating the facts. The timelines in both the conditions, looked more or less the same as shown in Figures 5b and 5e. In the MK condition, a timeline was made by situating the post-its at appropriate positions (Figure 5b) followed by linking these post-its to the horizontal timeline. Whereas in the PP condition, group members wrote directly at the exact spot (see Figure 5e). However, we observed that only one group (out of 9 groups) created a timeline in the MK condition. On the contrary, many such representations were made in the PP condition. A possible explanation for this could be that drawing in the MK condition consumed a lot of time, as users frequently have to change modes while writing text, drawing lines and even to drag post-its from one position to another. However, drawing was much faster in the PP condition, as the users simply have to write on the paper while looking at the public display to coordinate.

Syntheses representations were usually created during the convergent phase of the discussion, where users were considering the key episodes of the story and debating about the most likely suspect. In this representation the shared workspace served as a temporary storage of relevant facts which could assist the group in reaching a decision. In the MK condition, the syntheses resembled a screen with randomly distributed textual facts which were later assigned to different clusters or concepts as the discussion progressed (Figure 5c). The clusters were represented by explicitly drawing circles to contain related facts, or by placing post-its over one another with slight overlap. Similarly, in the PP condition, participants browsed for the relevant facts from the previous pages and created a hybrid representation of crucial episodes and links (see Figure 5f).

Considering the typology of produced content by the groups, we see a transition between individual sharing activity and collaborative information processing as observed by Tang et al. in [28] in case of whiteboards. The group members start with collecting information as facts and figures, and towards the end of the discussion build a more global knowledge about the story. This important group dynamics is probably driven by the transitions between these shared representations created by the group.

Task Efficiency and Input Devices

Analysis of experiment data reveals that groups created more text in the MK condition and more drawings in PP condition. In addition, mouse in MK condition allows moving, deleting and editing objects which is not possible in PP condition. These observations can possibly be attributed to the participant's efficiency with an input device. Also, the affordances of an input device favor the usage of the device for one kind of task activity than another. Pen might prove to be a faster way of expressing ideas as a schema as compared to a mouse. Similarly, keyboard could be a faster (and convenient) way of inputting large quantity of text as compared to pen.

In order to confirm that an input device is good for a specific task activity, we conducted a micro study with 10 colleagues from our lab. Each subject was asked to create text and drawing elements in both the conditions. For the text creation activity two short stories of exactly the same length (100 words each) were chosen, and the participants were asked to use the keyboard (in MK condition) and pen[2] (in PP condition) to write these stories. The time taken by the participant was recorded while using the keyboard and the pen. Similarly for the drawing activity, each participant was asked to play tic-tac-toe with oneself under a constraint that the match should end in a draw. This constraint ensures that the participants do not randomly fill in the cells but use cognition to carefully place the move so that no one wins. This is to ensure that the task is of the same difficulty for the subject across the two conditions in within-subject design. The time taken by the participant was again recorded while performing the task using a pen (PP condition) and a mouse (MK condition).

We used a two input configurations, within-subject design for this micro study. The conditions as well as the activities were counterbalanced. A Paired t-test was performed over the task completion time of subjects in the text and drawing activity, across the two conditions. The results of the analysis reveal that subjects were significantly quicker and more efficient in creating text using a keyboard as compared to pen ($t(9)=2.87$, $p=.01$). On the other hand, subjects took significantly less time to create drawings using a pen as compared to mouse ($t(9)=5.15$, $p<.001$). The analysis indicates that keyboard is an effective way of creating text as compared to pen, whereas pen is much quicker in a drawing task than a mouse. In addition, mouse is suitable for activities requiring higher pointing accuracy, such as dragging, selecting objects and changing modes. Also, the observations from this micro study confirm with the previous observations regarding different type of content produced across the two conditions.

[2]IRISNotes Digital Pen

This study suggests that the affordances of the input device in usage can influence the kind of content created and shared while using a single display groupware. Further, as group members choose to create a specific type of shared content, they would preferably go for the input device which is efficient, fast and highly convenient for such a representation, and this decision seems to be made implicitly by the user and does not involve cognitive load. This might explain why only one group (out of 9) created the timeline in MK condition, whereas more timelines were created in the PP condition. For such a representation, mouse was a very slow alternative for drawing lines and consumed a lot of time, therefore the groups preferred not to make timelines. However, in the PP condition as participants can draw lines and link facts quickly, this representation was more frequent in this condition.

Differences in Group Composition

Considering the familiarity among subjects and its influence on the group processes across the two conditions (MK and PP), we performed a Chi-Square test to study if previously-acquainted subjects were distributed differently across the conditions. The results demonstrate that there is no significant difference in distribution ($\chi^2(1,N=66)=1.25$, $p=.26$). Next, results of Chi-Square test demonstrates that there are significantly fewer than expected females assigned to the MK condition than to the PP condition ($\chi^2(1,N=66)=4.40$, $p=.03$). This might appear as a bias in our user study, consequently we investigated if the amount of shared content produced (number of textual elements and drawing elements) and participation (utterances and gestures) varied with gender. Results of a mixed-effect ANOVA show that no significant difference was found in the amount of text generated ($F(1,64)=0.92$, $p=.34$) and the amount of drawing elements generated ($F(1,64)=0.04$, $p=.84$) across gender. This signifies that the amount of shared content produced is not influenced by gender or familiarity among subjects. Furthermore, we found no significant gender differences in the number of gestures towards the shared workspace ($F(1,63)=0.08$, $p=.78$) as well as towards the experiment booklets ($F(1,64)=0.46$, $p=.5$). Likewise, the number of utterances made by the group members were not statistically different across gender ($F(1,64)=0.28$, $p=.59$). Consequently, we can conclude that gender did not play a significant role in group processes.

Groupware Usage Transition and Leadership

Our observations of the various shared representations produced by the group on the shared workspace at different points in the task (as previously discussed), show a transition from primarily factual content towards a conceptual shared representation. An examination of the concurrent usage (number of participants simultaneously interacting with the system) of the collaborative environment, exhibits similar transition. We observed that all the groups used the collaborative environment concurrently (more than one participants interacting simultaneously) during the divergent or information collection phase of the group work. However, the collaborative environment was used in a single-user mode during the discussion or convergent phase of task activity, where one group member took the responsibility of interacting with the system while others chose to be part of the ongoing discussion. Ryall et al. [20] observed a similar transition from an individual (or parallel) activity mode to a collective mode of operation during task for groups with 4 participants. Our observation either implies that roles emerged within the group, or indicates the problems related to the ergonomics of the collaborative environment.

Regarding the emergence of roles during the task, we consider only one role of a *group leader*. After each experiment the two observers were asked to rate (on a 5-point Likert scale) each group member on having the qualities of a group leader. The participant in each group with the highest average rating from both the observers was identified as a group leader. However there might be a limitation in this method of specifying a group leader, as the observers might have different perception about leadership. Moreover, the results of regression analysis demonstrate that group leaders interacted 12.67% more with the shared workspace (number of actions including creating text and drawing as well as moving artifacts) than other group members ($t(48)=2.63$, $p=.01$). In addition, group leaders had significantly higher number of utterances (19.28 utterances) than other subjects ($t(47)=3.15$, $p<.01$). Further, higher number of gestures towards shared workspace (3 gestures, $t(47)=2.73$, $p<.01$) as well as gestures towards experiment booklets (7.49 gestures, $t(48)=4.06$, $p<.001$) were observed for group leaders. These results indicate that group leaders were speaking and gesturing more, as well as took the responsibility of interacting with the system during the convergent phase of task (which is also demonstrated by the analysis of system logs).

Further, in order to investigate if problems with the ergonomics of the system resulted in one subject taking control of the system, we analyzed if the seating position around the table (or orientation with the shared workspace) influenced the emergence of leadership. The result of the Chi-Square test exhibits that there is no significant difference in leadership across the different seating positions around the table ($\chi^2(4,N=66)=5.14$, $p=.27$).

These observations emphasize on a very important group dynamics of task validation and coordination. The convergent phase of the task (information assimilation and decision making) requires relatively higher coordination among the group members as well as multiple perspectives to the shared knowledge. As a result, one of the group members acquires the control of the groupware and interacts with it while simultaneously validating (with other group members) each interaction with the shared content (such as annotating or organizing crucial facts about the suspects). These phases in group activity are consistent with the ones indicated by McGrath et al. [1] and Tschan [31]. In addition, we see a transition from a multi-user mode to a single-user mode as shown in Figure 6, where each group transits into the single-user mode by sliding down what we call a *Cliff of Convergence*. The cliff of convergence denotes the transition from the divergent phase (center of Figure 6) to the convergent phase (right side of Figure 6), whereas the region on the left side of Figure 6 denotes the phase where group members familiarize themselves with

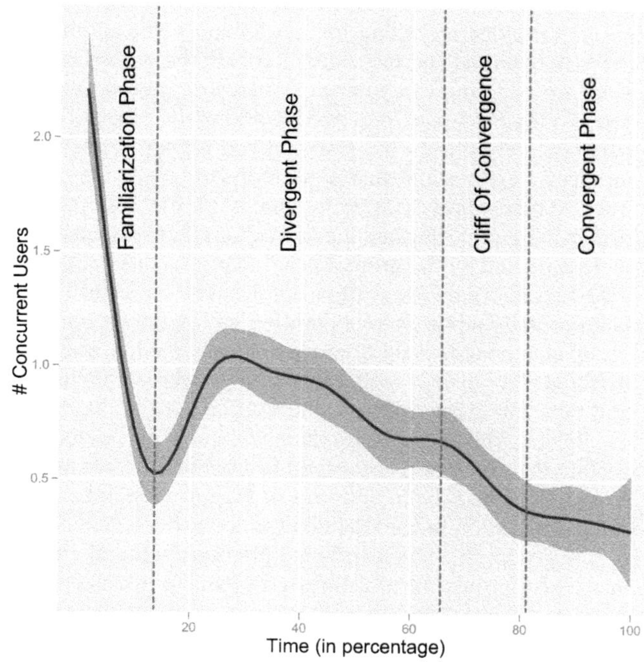

Figure 6: Moving average plot with confidence interval. X-axis represents the normalized time for all the groups and the Y-axis represents the number of users concurrently using the system.

the system before the task starts. Most existing SDGs assist only in the divergent phase of group activity by facilitating content creation and sharing. However, the existence of this phenomenon suggests that groups would benefit from SDGs that also support the convergent phase of activity.

Factor Analysis

In order to check if few experiment variables correlate well with each other, so that they can be aggregated and meaningful analysis can be made with them, we performed a factor analysis. We separated the experiment variables into two sets before performing the factor analysis. The first set regards the collaboration (or teamwork) among the group members, while the second set considers the groupware usage (or task work) during the task. This division was made based on the classification suggested by Wallace et al. [32]. The experiment variables in the first set concern the perceived participation of the individual in the group activity, opinion about the task outcome and the observed participation of the subject (utterances, gestures etc.). The second set of variables include participant's perception about effort required to create content and coordinate, content shared by the user and the perceived purpose of the system.

The first factor analysis shows the emergence of two main dimensions, namely *active participation* and *group acceptance*. Experiment variables concerning the utterances, gestures and the groupware usage are significantly correlated with the active participation dimension, whereas participants preferring to work alone are strongly anti-correlated. Furthermore, variables recording the participant's perception about the task outcome and individual's role in the group are correlated to the group acceptance dimension. We observe that group members who preferred working in groups, participated actively during the task and had higher number of utterances, gestures and shared more information. On the contrary, subjects preferring individual work had less participation in the group. Further, the individuals whose contributions were accepted by the group tended to participate actively and vice versa. This observation emphasizes on a very important group dynamic of trust building within the group. As the group acknowledges the contributions of an individual, the individual recognizes a higher level of involvement in the group and thus continues making contributions. Also a higher level of engagement of the group members could be related to the feeling that the group converged to a common consensus. Finally, the difference in opinions of the group members about the murderer might lead to higher acceptance of contributions by the group. Also as mentioned previously, the members of successful groups were differing in their opinions about the murderer. These results could provide a convincing evidence for the characteristic of successful groups. During the task the group members had different opinions about the outcome, resulting in dialogues and negotiations which finally led to a better quality decision.

The second factor analysis provides some interesting aspects about groupware usage. Experiment variables relating to the coordination aspects of the groupware usage are found to be strongly correlated to one dimension, referring to the effort required by individuals to coordinate the task activity. We observe that, if it is hard to coordinate using a groupware (more coordination breakdowns due to the overlapping of shared information on the public display or group members simultaneously using the same part of the display), the groupware is not used for a conceptual representation of the murder mystery, such as a timeline of important events. Rather the groupware is used more as a group memory to collect and store factual information about the suspects. From our previous observation we see that as it is easier to coordinate in the PP condition as compared to MK condition, more timelines were created in the PP condition than in the MK condition. In addition, significantly more amount of text was created in the MK condition. These results point out that the PP setup was used by the groups to create conceptual representation of the murder story, whereas the MK setup was used more often to collect facts. This is again coherent with the analysis of different shared representations from the previous section. The perceived affordances of an input device influence the user's choice of one input device over another for the collaborative task, which in turn affects the type of shared representations produced.

DISCUSSION

The collaborative meeting environment presented in this article was designed to assist the content creation and sharing activity in co-located meetings of small groups. Prior research has suggested that SDGs positively influence the collaboration [21, 32]. We conducted a user study to investigate the effects of different input techniques on the way participants share knowledge about the task. Our experiment findings provide some important implications towards the design of single display groupware. In problem solving meetings, creation and sharing of content is not a main activity but a supporting activity for the task at hand. During the task, group members can choose to create diverse representations of their shared knowledge depending on the task demands. For example, a group discussing about a murder mystery (as in our user study) might choose to make a timeline, whereas a group designing a database might go for a relational schema. Therefore, considering that different tasks demand varied representations, it is impractical to restrict the interaction with the groupware by choosing only one input mechanism. In other words, if group members are supplied with just one type of input device to interact, it limits the number of shared representations which could possibly be produced by the group.

The experiment results clearly indicate that there exists a mapping between the input device affordances and the knowledge representation which the task demands. Presence of multiple kinds of input devices for each user provide the user with an opportunity to select the input mechanism most appropriate to adequately support the task at hand; i.e. an ecology of input tools capable of supporting various kinds of content representations. In other words, instead of supplying users with just one input mechanism (such as mouse and keyboard *OR* pen *OR* just multi-touch table), the group members might wish to be equipped with more than one kind of interaction techniques. So, when there is a demand for a specific shared knowledge representation, the group members make the mapping between the perceived affordance of the suitable input device and the task demand. We call this phenomenon *opportunistic sharing*, as the mapping between the input device and shared representation is made opportunistically by the user herself.

An analysis of the artifacts shared by the groups lead us to classify them into three kinds based on the time when they were created, visual differences and the immediate purpose the content served. We observed that during the whole task, groups created many representations. The classification exhibits some important characteristic of the shared workspace (wall mounted public display); the role of the shared workspace and the transitions in the collaborative coupling of the group members. During the task the shared workspace is used by the group members to offload their cognitive load (group memory) by sharing information. At the later stage this information is processed, conceptualized and comprehended by the group and acts more as the group knowledge which leads to decision making. Regarding the collaborative coupling, we see a transition from loosely coupled group (individual task of sharing and surfacing facts) to a more tightly coupled group where the group members build a shared understanding. These observations are in line with the research done by Tang et al. in [28, 29]. Additionally, we observed that such a transition happened only once during the task, whereas one can expect such transitions to occur several times during the problem solving activity. However, these transitions might depend on the type of activity and certain activities might have transitions during each iteration (or phase) of the group activity.

Further analyses of the groupware usage shows that the group members used the collaborative environment concurrently during the *information collection phase*, whereas during the *decision making phase* only a single group member used the groupware. This transition from a divergent phase of the group activity to the convergent phase happens over a *Cliff of Convergence*, after which the interactions with the shared workspace are done only by the group leader while others prefer to be part of the ongoing discussion. This observation implies that SDGs will better assist groups (or group leaders) during the convergent phase of the task if they provide tools or agents which facilitate the organization of shared content in formats that enable discussion about it. This is an important design implication as existing SDGs are situated in the divergent phase of group activity requiring creation and sharing of content.

Concerning the coordination of the task activity while using the groupware, the factor analysis provides interesting results. The effort required by the users to coordinate defines the purpose of the collaborative environment. If it requires a lot of effort to coordinate, the groupware is used as a group memory to store information which could be referred later during the task. In such a situation, the collaborative environment is regarded disconnected with the task by the group and becomes invisible to the group as the task progresses. On the other hand, the easier it is to coordinate, the more tightly coupled is the group activity with the collaborative environment and the shared workspace is at the center of discussion. Further, the factor analysis emphasizes some crucial aspects of collaboration and group dynamics, and is explained by the emergence of two factors namely active participation and group acceptance.

In our user study we did not extensively test for the differences in the types of users and their behaviors across the two input configurations. In addition, participant's preferences for input devices were not accounted for in the analyses, as a keyboard (and mouse) and a digital pen do not have the same prevalence in our sample population. This is because most of the subjects were not familiar to the digital pen, and consequently preference would not be informed by experience but rather by novelty.

CONCLUSION

We have presented a collaborative meeting environment to support content creation and sharing in co-located meetings, which enables group members to concurrently interact with the shared workspace while mitigating issues such as floor monopolization. The collaborative environment is composed of a shared wall-mounted workspace and two different input configurations - mouse and keyboard AND pen and paper along with a meeting table by which the setup is supported. We have also conducted an exploratory user study to investigate the effect of difference in input configurations on the way group members create and share content. We observe that different input devices complement each other with regard to the shared representations that can be produced using these input devices, where one kind of content can be conveniently produced with one input configuration. We conclude that, group members should be equipped with varied input devices so that they can opportunistically map the adequate input device to the representation demanded by the task. We call this phenomenon *opportunistic sharing*. Finally, we observed that the usage of the groupware varies with the phase of the problem solving activity and this provides important implications for the design of collaborative environments to assist each of the respective phases of the task.

ACKNOWLEDGMENTS

First of all, we would like to thank the anonymous reviewers for their comments and suggestions, which greatly helped us to improve the paper. Next, we would like to thank Cristián Alcoholado Moenne and Olivier Guédat for their contribution to the development of this system. Thanks to all the students who volunteered to observe the meeting sessions, also special thanks to all the students who participated in the study. Finally, we would like to thank the Swiss Post for supporting our research.

REFERENCES

1. Arrow, H., McGrath, J. E., and Berdahl, J. L. *Small Groups as Complex Systems: Formation, Coordination, Development, and Adaptation*. Sage Publications, Inc., 2000.

2. Chiu, P., Kapuskar, A., Reitmeier, S., and Wilcox, L. NoteLook: Taking notes in meetings with digital video and ink. In *Proceedings of the seventh ACM international conference on Multimedia (Part 1)*, MULTIMEDIA '99, ACM (1999), 149–158.

3. Davis, R. C., Landay, J. A., Chen, V., Huang, J., Lee, R. B., Li, F. C., Lin, J., Morrey, III, C. B., Schleimer, B., Price, M. N., and Schilit, B. N. NotePals: Lightweight note sharing by the group, for the group. In *Proceedings of the SIGCHI conference on Human factors in computing systems: the CHI is the limit*, CHI '99, ACM (1999), 338–345.

4. Dillenbourg, P., and Traum, D. Does a shared screen make a shared solution? In *Proceedings of the 1999 conference on Computer support for collaborative learning*, CSCL '99, International Society of the Learning Sciences (1999).

5. Grudin, J. Why CSCW applications fail: Problems in the design and evaluation of organizational interfaces. In *Proceedings of the 1988 ACM conference on Computer-supported cooperative work*, CSCW '88, ACM (1988), 85–93.

6. Haller, M., Leitner, J., Seifried, T., Wallace, J. R., Scott, S. D., Richter, C., Brandl, P., Gokcezade, A., and Hunter, S. The NiCE Discussion Room: Integrating paper and digital media to support co-located group meetings. In *Proceedings of the 28th international conference on Human factors in computing systems*, CHI '10, ACM (2010), 609–618.

7. Hansen, T. E., and Hourcade, J. P. Comparing multi-touch tabletops and multi-mouse single-display groupware setups. In *Proceedings of the 3rd Mexican Workshop on Human Computer Interaction*, MexIHC '10, Universidad Politécnica de San Luis Potosí (2010), 36–43.
8. Hartmann, B., Morris, M. R., Benko, H., and Wilson, A. D. Augmenting interactive tables with mice & keyboards. In *Proceedings of the 22nd annual ACM symposium on User interface software and technology*, UIST '09, ACM (2009), 149–152.
9. Hilliges, O., Terrenghi, L., Boring, S., Kim, D., Richter, H., and Butz, A. Designing for collaborative creative problem solving. In *Proceedings of the 6th ACM SIGCHI conference on Creativity & cognition*, C&C '07, ACM (New York, NY, USA, 2007), 137–146.
10. Hinrichs, U., Hancock, M., Collins, C., and Carpendale, S. Examination of text-entry methods for tabletop displays. In *Horizontal Interactive Human-Computer Systems, 2007. TABLETOP '07. Second Annual IEEE International Workshop on* (Oct. 2007), 105 –112.
11. Inkpen, K., Hawkey, K., Kellar, M., Mandryk, R. L., Parker, R., Reilly, D., Scott, S., and Whalen, T. Exploring display factors that influence co-located collaboration: Angle, Size, Number and User Arrangement. In *Proceedings of HCI International*, Lawrence Erlbaum Associates (2005), 22–27.
12. Izadi, S., Brignull, H., Rodden, T., Rogers, Y., and Underwood, M. Dynamo: A public interactive surface supporting the cooperative sharing and exchange of media. In *Proceedings of the 16th annual ACM symposium on User interface software and technology*, UIST '03, ACM (2003), 159–168.
13. Johanson, B., Hutchins, G., Winograd, T., and Stone, M. PointRight: Experience with flexible input redirection in interactive workspaces. In *Proceedings of the 15th annual ACM symposium on User interface software and technology*, UIST '02, ACM (2002), 227–234.
14. Kaplan, F., DoLenh, S., Bachour, K., Kao, G. Y.-i., Gault, C., and Dillenbourg, P. Interpersonal computers for higher education. In *Interactive Artifacts and Furniture Supporting Collaborative Work and Learning*, P. Dillenbourg, J. Huang, and M. Cherubini, Eds., vol. 10 of *Computer-Supported Collaborative Learning Series*. Springer US, 2009, 1–17.
15. Kruger, R., Carpendale, S., Scott, S. D., and Greenberg, S. How people use orientation on tables: comprehension, coordination and communication. In *Proceedings of the 2003 international ACM SIGGROUP conference on Supporting group work*, GROUP '03, ACM (New York, NY, USA, 2003), 369–378.
16. Mandryk, R. L., Scott, S. D., and Inkpen, K. Display factors influncing co-located collaboration. In *In Conference Supplement to ACM CSCW'02 Computer Supported Cooperative Work* (2002), 137–138.
17. Mennecke, B. E. Using Group Support Systems to discover hidden profiles: An examination of the influence of group size and meeting structures on information sharing and decision quality. *International Journal of Human-Computer Studies 47*, 3 (1997), 387 – 405.
18. Moraveji, N., Inkpen, K., Cutrell, E., and Balakrishnan, R. A Mischief of Mice: Examining children's performance in Single Display Groupware systems with 1 to 32 mice. In *Proceedings of the 27th international conference on Human factors in computing systems*, CHI '09, ACM (2009), 2157–2166.
19. Rogers, Y., Lim, Y.-k., Hazlewood, W. R., and Marshall, P. Equal Opportunities: Do shareable interfaces promote more group participation than single user displays? *Human–Computer Interaction 24*, 1-2 (2009), 79–116.
20. Ryall, K., Forlines, C., Shen, C., and Morris, M. R. Exploring the effects of group size and table size on interactions with tabletop shared-display groupware. In *Proceedings of the 2004 ACM conference on Computer supported cooperative work*, CSCW '04, ACM (New York, NY, USA, 2004), 284–293.
21. Scott, S., Mandryk, R., and Inkpen, K. Understanding children's collaborative interactions in shared environments. *Journal of Computer Assisted Learning 19*, 2 (2003), 220–228.
22. Shen, C., Ryall, K., Forlines, C., Esenther, A., Vernier, F. D., Everitt, K., Wu, M., Wigdor, D., Morris, M. R., HancocK, M., and Tse, E. Collaborative tabletop research and evaluation. In *Interactive Artifacts and Furniture Supporting Collaborative Work and Learning*, P. Dillenbourg, J. Huang, and M. Cherubini, Eds., vol. 10 of *Computer-Supported Collaborative Learning Series*. Springer US, 2009, 1–17.
23. Shen, C., Vernier, F. D., Forlines, C., and Ringel, M. DiamondSpin: An extensible toolkit for around-the-table interaction. In *Proceedings of the SIGCHI conference on Human factors in computing systems*, CHI '04, ACM (2004), 167–174.
24. Sommer, R. Small group ecology. *Psychological Bulletin 67*, 2 (Feb 1967), 145–152.
25. Stasser, G., and Stewart, D. Discovery of hidden profiles by Decision-Making groups: Solving a problem versus making a judgment. *Journal of Personality and Social Psychology 63*, 3 (1992), 426–434.
26. Stefik, M., Foster, G., Bobrow, D. G., Kahn, K., Lanning, S., and Suchman, L. Beyond the Chalkboard: Computer support for collaboration and problem solving in meetngs. *Commun. ACM 30* (January 1987), 32–47.
27. Stewart, J., Bederson, B. B., and Druin, A. Single Display Groupware: A model for co-present collaboration. In *Proceedings of the SIGCHI conference on Human factors in computing systems: the CHI is the limit*, CHI '99, ACM (1999), 286–293.

28. Tang, A., Lanir, J., Greenberg, S., and Fels, S. Supporting transitions in work: Informing large display application design by understanding whiteboard use. In *Proceedings of the ACM 2009 international conference on Supporting group work*, GROUP '09, ACM (2009), 149–158.

29. Tang, A., Tory, M., Po, B., Neumann, P., and Carpendale, S. Collaborative coupling over tabletop displays. In *Proceedings of the SIGCHI conference on Human Factors in computing systems*, CHI '06, ACM (2006), 1181–1190.

30. Terrenghi, L., Kirk, D., Sellen, A., and Izadi, S. Affordances for manipulation of physical versus digital media on interactive surfaces. In *Proceedings of the SIGCHI conference on Human factors in computing systems*, CHI '07, ACM (2007), 1157–1166.

31. Tschan, F. Ideal cycles of communication (or cognition) in Triads, Dyads, and Individuals. *Small Group Research 33*, 6 (Dec 2002), 615–643.

32. Wallace, J., Scott, S., Stutz, T., Enns, T., and Inkpen, K. Investigating teamwork and taskwork in single- and multi-display groupware systems. *Personal and Ubiquitous Computing 13* (2009), 569–581.

33. Wigdor, D., Jiang, H., Forlines, C., Borkin, M., and Shen, C. WeSpace: the design development and deployment of a walk-up and share multi-surface visual collaboration system. In *Proceedings of the 27th international conference on Human factors in computing systems*, CHI '09, ACM (2009), 1237–1246.

34. Wolf, C. G., Rhyne, J. R., and Briggs, L. K. Communication and information retrieval with a pen-based meeting support tool. In *Proceedings of the 1992 ACM conference on Computer-supported cooperative work*, CSCW '92, ACM (1992), 322–329.

35. Zanella, A., and Greenberg, S. Reducing interference in single display groupware through transparency. In *ECSCW 2001*, W. Prinz, M. Jarke, Y. Rogers, K. Schmidt, and V. Wulf, Eds. Springer Netherlands, 2002, 339–358.

Dependency-conflict Detection in Real-time Collaborative 3D Design Systems

Agustina
BeingThere Centre, Institute for Media Innovation
Nanyang Technological University, Singapore
agustina@ntu.edu.sg

Chengzheng Sun
School of Computer Engineering
Nanyang Technological University, Singapore
czsun@ntu.edu.sg

ABSTRACT
One core issue in real-time collaborative 3D design systems is *dependency-conflict* caused by concurrent access to object replicas in *Dependency Graph* (DG) states – the common underlying structure of 3D design systems. Prior work has provided an *Operational Transformation* (OT) solution to dependency-conflict resolution, assuming dependency-conflict can be detected. But dependency-conflict detection is a complex and challenging issue because dependency relations among targets of concurrent operations – a necessary condition for dependency-conflict – is dynamic in nature and the detection must refer to prior DG states that are often unavailable during dependency-conflict detection. Conflict detection was never a difficult issue in prior OT work based on well-defined linear data models because conflict relations are readily derivable from operation position parameters without having to refer to prior document states. This work is the first to recognize and solve the dependency-conflict detection problem, which complements prior work in dependency-conflict resolution to provide a complete solution to dependency-conflict problem in real-time collaborative DG-based systems. Both theoretical verification and real implementation have been applied to validate the proposed dependency-conflict detection solution.

Author Keywords
Consistency maintenance; dependency-conflict detection and resolution; operational transformation.

ACM Classification Keywords
H.5.3 [**Information Interfaces and Presentation**]: Group and Organization Interfaces – *Collaborative Computing*, *Synchronous Interaction*, *Theory and model*.

INTRODUCTION

Real-Time Collaborative 3D Design Systems and Dependency-Conflict Issues
Real-time collaborative 3D design systems allow multiple users to edit shared documents of 3D data objects at the same time over the Internet [1, 2]. The free and concurrent editing capability is important for collaborative 3D design systems to support ad hoc, spontaneous and fine-grained interaction and collaboration which often arise during complex and unstructured processes of 3D content creation. To support free and concurrent editing, a *replicated* system architecture, which duplicates shared documents and applications at all collaborating sites, is commonly adopted [4, 22]. In such systems, user interactions with the application are applied immediately to the local copy before being propagated to remote collaborating sites. Concurrent user interactions may conflict and result in inconsistent replicated documents [2, 20, 24, 26]. One technique to resolve conflict in real-time collaborative editing systems is *Operational Transformation* (OT) [4]. Due to its lock-free and unconstrained collaboration properties, OT has emerged as the choice of conflict resolution technique for a wide range of Internet-based collaborative systems, and has been increasingly adopted in industrial real-time collaborative systems, including Google Docs[1], Novell Vibe[2], Codoxware[3], and IBM OpenCoWeb[4]. The work reported in this paper focuses on novel OT techniques to resolve special conflicts in real-time collaborative 3D design systems [2].

To support sophisticated 3D graphic functionalities (e.g. modeling, rigging, animation, deformation, etc.), 3D objects are commonly represented internally as data objects in a *Dependency Graph* (DG) structure [8, 14, 16]. In a DG, nodes represent graphic objects, and arrows represent *attribute-dependency relations* (or *dependency relations* for short) among connected objects: when the attribute of one object is changed, the changed attribute value will propagate from this object to all dependent objects in the DG. The dependency relations among nodes are also useful for representing constraints among 3D objects. For example, the 3D model in Figure 1a has, among others, three nodes: node A represents the radius of the candle, node B represents the size of the candle holder, and node C represents the width and depth of the box. The dependency relations of these nodes, and hence the constraint relations among the candle, holder, and box, are shown in Figure 1b.

[1] https://docs.google.com
[2] http://www.novell.com/products/vibe
[3] http://www.codoxware.com
[4] http://opencoweb.org

CSCW '13, February 23–27, 2013, San Antonio, Texas, USA.

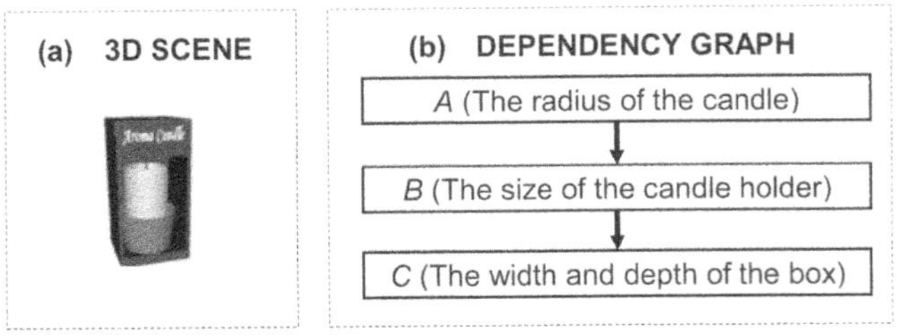

Figure 1. Dependency relations of an aroma candle (Adopted from [2]).

These dependency relations mean that the change of the radius of the candle will also change the size of the holder and subsequently, the width and depth of the box.

Real-time collaborative editing of DG-based documents may cause a special kind of *dependency-conflict*: inconsistency may occur when concurrent operations are targeting objects with dependency relations [2]. To illustrate, consider a scenario of two users concurrently modifying the candle model in Figure 1: the first user intends to make the candle fatter while the second user intends to remove the dependency relations of the three nodes so that s/he can change the box design for containing multiple candles. This scenario is illustrated in Figure 2. The two sites share a common initial DG state, denoted as $A(1)\rightarrow B(1)\rightarrow C(1)$, where $N(x)$ represents a node N with an attribute value x and the arrow "$\rightarrow$" denotes a dependency relation between two nodes in the DG. To achieve their purposes, the first user (at *site-1*) generates $O_1 = UP(A, 2)$ to update node A with attribute value "2" so that the candle will be twice fatter; the second user (at *site-2*) generates $O_2 = DC(B, C)$ to remove the dependency relation between node B and C and $O_3 = DC(A, B)$ to remove the dependency relation between node A and B. In this scenario, O_1 is concurrent with both O_2 and O_3 because O_1 is generated before the execution of O_2 and O_3 at *site-1* [4], and O_1 has dependency-conflict relations with both O_2 and O_3 because their executions in different orders will result in inconsistent DG states [2]:

1. At *site*-1 (Figure 2b-d), O_1 is executed *before* O_2 and O_3, and the resulting DG state is $A(2)$ $B(2)$ C(2), with the candle and its holder still fit into the box.
2. At *site*-2 (Figure 2f-h), O_1 is executed *after* O_2 and O_3, and the resulting DG state is $A(2)$ $B(1)$ C(1), with the candle is fatter than, and thus no longer fits into, its holder and box.

Clearly, the two 3D models and their final DG states are different as the attribute values of nodes B and C are different; i.e. $B(2)\neq B(1)$ and $C(2)\neq C(1)$. The main reason for this inconsistency is that A (the target of O_1) has dependency relations with both B and C (targets of O_2 and O_3) in the initial DG state (Figure 2a and 2e); the effect of O_1 (i.e. updating the attribute value of A to "2") is propagated to B and C when O_1 is executed before O_2 and O_3 at *site-1*, but not propagated when O_1 is executed after O_2 and O_3 at *site-2*.

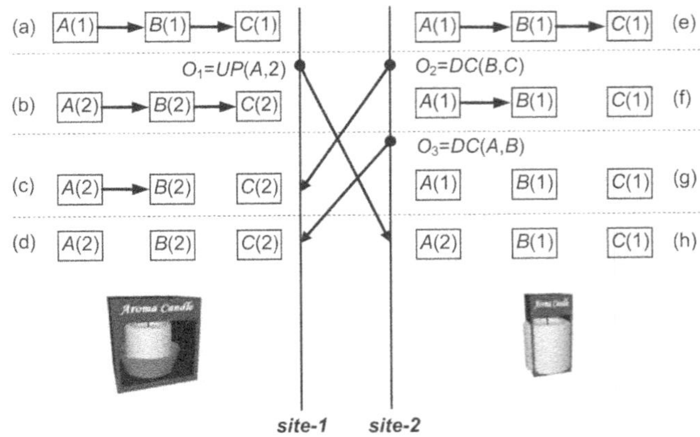

Figure 2. A dependency-conflict scenario.

Dependency-Conflict Detection Issue

The problem of dependency-conflict in real-time collaborative 3D design systems was first identified and studied in [2]. A complete solution to this problem must contain two key components: one is *conflict detection*; the other is *conflict resolution*. In [2], an OT-based solution has been proposed to resolve dependency-conflict under the *assumption* that the dependency-conflict relations among concurrent operations can be detected. For the example in Figure 2, if it can be detected that O_1 has a dependency-conflict relation with O_2 and O_3, then the OT solution in [2] will transform O_1 into a new form (a sequence of mini-operations) that will apply attribute updates on A, B, and C, respectively. In this way, the final DG states at both sites will be $A(2)$ $B(2)$ C(2), which are not only consistent, but also preserve the effects of all operations: the candle, holder, and box are twice fatter and no longer dependency related [2]. In this paper, we focus on dependency-conflict detection – the other key component of a complete dependency-conflict solution.

Correct and efficient detection of dependency-conflicts in real-time collaborative 3D design systems is complex and challenging because dependency relations among targets of concurrent operations are dynamic in nature and require the knowledge of prior DG states from which those concurrent operations were generated/defined, but such prior DG states are often unavailable at the time of conflict detection. To illustrate, consider again the scenario in Figure 2. If the initial DG state (Figure 2a and 2e), from which O_1 and O_2 were generated, is used to determine the dependency-conflict between O_1 and O_2, then their dependency-conflict relation can be correctly detected by the fact that A (the target of O_1) is connected to B (the target of O_2) in the initial DG state. However, when O_1 arrives at *site-2*, the initial DG state is no longer available as it has been changed (by O_2 and O_3) into $A(1)$ $B(1)$ $C(1)$ (Figure 2g), in which A and B are no longer connected (their connection has been removed by O_3). If the current DG state (Figure 2g) were used to determine the dependency relation of A and B, O_1 and O_2 would be falsely declared as being compatible as their target objects A and B are not connected in the current DG state! Without correct dependency-conflict detection, applying the dependency-conflict resolution in [2] would not achieve document consistency: at *site-1*, the candle, holder, and box are all twice fatter and the candle still fits into the holder and box, but at *site-2*, only the candle is twice fatter thus no longer fits into the holder and box (Figure 2). The final result at *site-2* also violates the original constraint defined by the users to always have the candle fits into the holder and box.

The scenario in Figure 2 is rather simplistic for the purpose of illustrating the basic issues involved in dependency-conflict detection, but real DG states and dependency-conflict relations among operations can be arbitrarily complex in real-time collaborative 3D design systems. In general, DG states from which operations are generated, called *original DG states,* are different from the DG states on which those operations are to be executed, called *execution DG states*, due to the execution of concurrent operations in different orders. However, dependency-conflict relations among operations are defined on their original DG states, rather than the current execution DG states. Therefore, it is necessary to know the original DG states of operations to correctly determine the dependency-conflict relations among those operations.

No prior OT work has ever encountered, let alone addressed, conflict detection that requires prior document state. Most prior OT algorithms were designed for document states that can be modeled as a sequence of objects (e.g. a string of characters) [4, 21, 22, 26] or a hierarchy of object sequences [9, 17, 25]. With those special data models, parameters of the operations being transformed are adequate to assess their relative positions in the document state and to detect their *overlapping*-conflict [24] or *positional-shifting*-conflict [22], without having to refer to the actual document. In string-based data and operation model, for example, the positional-shifting-conflict can be determined by simply comparing operation types (*Insert*, *Delete*, or *Update*) and position parameters, thanks to the well-defined positional shifting effects of those basic operations in the well-defined string-based operation model. In DG-based data and operation models, however, it is no longer possible to derive the dependency-conflict relation between two operations by using their parameters alone. For example in Figure 2, it is impossible to determine whether there is a dependency-conflict between O_1 and O_2 by examining solely their parameters because their target objects *A*, *B*, and *C* are all different!

The goal of this work is to devise novel techniques that can correctly derive an unknown prior DG state from the current DG state and detect dependency-conflict relations among concurrent operations by means of the derived DG states. The rest of this paper is organized as follows. First, we introduce the causal and context theories of OT, the DG data and operation model, and the dependency-conflict problem. Then, we discuss the requirement for correct dependency-conflict detection and describe the basic idea of our innovative solution of dependency relation detection using a *DG difference*. Afterwards, we discuss the issues and solutions for creating a DG difference of two DG states without knowing one of them, and the issue and OT-based solution of recursive dependency-conflict in creating the DG difference. Next, we present the solution to detecting dependency relations in the prior-matching DG state derived from the created DG difference and the current DG state. Finally, we discuss the implementation of this work in the *CoMaya* real-time collaborative 3D design system, conclude the paper and discuss directions for future work.

BACKGROUND

Causality and Context Theories of OT

One underlying theory of all OT algorithms is the causality theory [4, 21]. Following Lamport [12], the causal and concurrent relations among operations are defined in term of their generation and execution orders as follow [21]:

Definition 1. Causal Relation "→". *Given two operations O_a and O_b, generated at site i and j, respectively, O_a is* causally before *O_b, denoted by $O_a \rightarrow O_b$, if and only if:* (1) *$i = j$ and the generation of O_a* happened before *the generation of O_b*; (2) *$i \neq j$ and the execution of O_a at site j* happened before *the generation of O_b*; *or* (3) *there exists an operation O_x such that $O_a \rightarrow O_x$ and $O_x \rightarrow O_b$.*

Definition 2. Concurrent Relation "||". *Given two operations O_a and O_b, O_a and O_b are* concurrent, *denoted by $O_a \parallel O_b$, if and only if neither $O_a \rightarrow O_b$ nor $O_b \rightarrow O_a$.*

For example in Figure 2, we have $O_1 \parallel O_2$, $O_1 \parallel O_3$, and $O_2 \rightarrow O_3$. Based on the causality theory, OT systems enforce causally related operations to be executed in their causal order, but concurrent operations may be generated and executed in different orders at different collaborating sites [4,21].

Another core theory of OT is the theory of operation context. In OT systems, every operation O is associated with a *context*, denoted as $C(O)$, which represents the document state on which O is defined [23]. The context of O can be represented as a *set* of original operations that have been executed to create the document state on which O is defined [23].

Definition 3. Document State. *A* document state, *denoted as DS, is represented as follows*: (1) *the initial document state is represented as $DS = \{\ \}$*; (2) *after the execution of an operation O on DS, the new document state is represented as $DS' = DS \cup \{org(O)\}$, where $org(O)$ denotes the* original *form of O.*

For example in Figure 2, the *DS* for the initial DG can be represented as $DS_0 = \{\ \}$ since no operation has been executed yet. After executing O_2, O_3, and O_1 in sequence at *site-2*, the corresponding *DS* at each step are: $DS_1 = \{O_2\}$, $DS_2 = \{O_2, O_3\}$, and $DS_3 = \{O_2, O_3, O_1\}$.

Definition 4. Operation Context. *The context of an operation O, denoted as C(O), is represented as follows:*

1. *For an* original *operation O (generated by the user), C(O) = DS, where DS is the document state from which O is generated;*
2. *For a* transformed *operation O' (obtained by transformation),* $C(O') = C(O) \cup \{org(O_x)\}$, *where* $O' = T(O, O_x)$ *and T is a function that transforms O into O' by adjusting O's parameters according to the execution impact of* O_x.

When an operation is generated, it is associated with an *original context*, which is the document state from which the operation is generated (Case 1 in Definition 4). For example in Figure 2, O_1 and O_2 were generated from the same initial DG with an empty DS_0, so their original contexts are: $C(O_1) = C(O_2) = DS_0 = \{\ \}$. O_3 was generated from the DG with $DS_1 = \{O_2\}$ (after executing O_2), so the original context of O_3 is: $C(O_3) = DS_1 = \{O_2\}$. After its generation, the context of an operation may be changed by transformation (Case 2 in Definition 4). For example, when O_1 arrives at *site*-2, O_1 will be transformed against O_2 and O_3 in sequence (for conflict resolution) [2] into: $O_1' = T(O_1, O_2)$, $O_1'' = T(O_1', O_3)$; and the contexts of the transformed O_1 will be: $C(O_1') = \{O_2\}$, $C(O_1'') = \{O_2, O_3\}$, respectively.

The significance of operation context is that it provides a basis for interpreting the effect of an operation and reasoning about the relations among operations, which are essential for ensuring correct operation execution and transformation. Among others, two essential context-based conditions are:

1. *Context-equivalence condition for execution*: an operation O can be correctly executed only if its *definition context* $C(O)$ (the document state on which O is defined) equals to its *execution context DS* (the document state on which O is to be executed), i.e. $C(O) = DS$.
2. *Context-equivalence condition for transformation*: two operations O_1 and O_2 can be correctly transformed by invoking $T(O_1, O_2)$ only if they have the same definition context, i.e. $C(O_1) = C(O_2)$.

DG Data and Operation Models

In design documents, data objects are organized into a DG, which is composed of a collection of *nodes* and *arrows*, where a node represents a graphic object with an attribute and an arrow represents *an attribute-dependency relation* between two objects, as defined below [2].

Definition 5. Dependency Graph. *A* dependency graph *DG is represented as* $DG = (\mathcal{N}, \mathcal{A})$, where:

1. $\mathcal{N} = \{n_1, n_2, \ldots, n_r\}$ *is a set of nodes, and each node* n_i, $1 \le i \le r$, *represents a graphic object with an attribute value represented by* $n_i.v$;
2. $\mathcal{A} = \{(s_1, d_1), (s_2, d_2), \ldots, (s_k, d_k)\}$ *is a set of arrows, and each arrow* (s_i, d_i) *represents a dependency relation from the source node* s_i *to the destination node* d_i, *where* $s_i, d_i \in \mathcal{N}$ *and* $d_i \neq d_j$ *for* $i \neq j$ *and* $1 \le i, j \le k$.

For examples, the DG states in Figure 2b-d are represented as $DG_b = (\{A, B, C\}, \{(A, B), (B, C)\})$, $DG_c = (\{A, B, C\}, \{(A, B)\})$, and $DG_d = (\{A, B, C\}, \{\ \})$, respectively.

Definition 6. Dependency Relation. *Given two nodes,* n_1 *and* n_2, *in a* $DG = (\mathcal{N}, \mathcal{A})$, *i.e.* $n_1, n_2 \in \mathcal{N}$, n_1 *and* n_2 *have a* dependency relation, *denoted as* $DR(n_1, n_2)$, *if and only if*: (1) $n_1 = n_2$; (2) *there is an arrow from* n_1 *to* n_2, *i.e.* $(n_1, n_2) \in \mathcal{A}$; *or* (3) *there is a node* $n_i \in \mathcal{N}$, *such that* $DR(n_1, n_i)$ *and* $DR(n_i, n_2)$.

The notation $DR(n_1, n_2)^d$, where $d \ge 0$, is used to indicate the distance d (i.e. the number of arrows) between two dependent nodes n_1 and n_2. If $d = 0$, n_1 and n_2 are regarded as self-dependent; such a relation is also known as an *overlapping relation* [20]. Among others, three dependency relations among objects in Figure 2a are $DR(A, A)^0$, $DR(A, B)^1$, and $DR(A, C)^2$.

For simplicity and clarity, we have assumed: (1) each node has only one attribute; hence a node may have only one input arrow, i.e. $d_i \neq d_j$ in Definition 5, but may have multiple output arrows; and (2) a node always stores the input attribute value as-is, without making any change to it; hence all dependency related nodes in a DG share the same value, i.e. $\forall\, n_1, n_2 \in \mathcal{N}\ (DR(n_1, n_2)^d \rightarrow n_2.v = n_1.v)$. In real systems, each node may have multiple attributes (and thus multiple input arrows), and may apply an internal function to transform the input value (received from an upstream node) into a new value (to be stored by the node and to be propagated to downstream nodes). Adaptations, such as [25], are necessary to apply the solutions presented in this paper for detecting dependency-conflict in real systems with multiple attributes per node and functional transformation at each node: the multiple attributes can be adapted into multiple nodes in our DG model [1], thus multiple input connections can be supported; and the input value transformation can be seen as the generalization of the *identity* transformation function used in our DG model.

In DG-based systems, there are five basic operations:

1. ***X* := *CR*(*g*):** *Create* a new object g and return the identifier X.
2. ***DL*(*X*):** *Delete* an existing object X.
3. ***UP*(*X*, *v*):** *Update* the attribute of object X with value v and propagate the change to downstream dependent objects.
4. ***CN*(*S*, *D*):** *Connect* a source object S to a destination object D and propagate the attribute value of S to D and downstream dependent objects.

5. **DC(S, D):** *Disconnect* a source object S from a destination object D.

In addition to those basic DG operations, DG-based systems may have a wide-range of rich and complex operations such as a *revolve* operation to revolve 2D curves into 3D objects, a *deform* operation to deform the shapes of 3D objects, etc. To use the solution presented in this paper on such systems, each of those complex operations can be mapped into a compound of the above five basic DG operations [1]. For example, a *revolve* operation can be mapped into two *Create* operations for creating a *revolve* object and a *surface* object, and two *Connect* operations to establish the dependency relation between the input *curve* object and the *revolve* object and the dependency relation between the *revolve* object and the *surface* object.

For a DG operation to be successfully generated and executed, certain *preconditions* must be satisfied [2]: (1) all operations, except *CR*, must not target objects/connections that do not exist; (2) a *DL* must not target an object that has an existing input or output connection; (3) an *UP* must not target an object that has an existing input connection; and (4) a *CN* must not target a destination object that has an existing input connection.

Dependency-Conflict

Operations in real-time collaborative editing systems may have conflict/compatible relations, as defined below.

Definition 7. Conflict Relation "⊗". *Given two operations, O_1 and O_2, they have a* conflict relation, *denoted as $O_1 \otimes O_2$, iff:* (1) *O_1 and O_2 are concurrent; and* (2) *different execution orders of O_1 and O_2 result in different document states.*

Definition 8. Compatible Relation "⊙". *Given two operations, O_1 and O_2, they have a* compatible relation, *denoted as $O_1 \odot O_2$, iff they do not have a conflict relation, i.e. $\neg(O_1 \otimes O_2)$.*

Conflicts may take different forms and may require different conditions to occur in real-time collaborative editing systems with different data and operation models. Under the data model in which data objects are independent (e.g. in most word processors), concurrent operations are conflicting only if they are targeting the same object [20, 24]. But, in complex graphic editing systems where data objects are organized into a DG, concurrent operations are conflicting if their targets have a dependency relation, as stated in Theorem 1.

Theorem 1. *Given two concurrent DG operations, O_1 with a target X_1 and O_2 with a target X_2, defined on the same state DG, O_1* and *O_2 are dependency-conflicting only if X_1 and X_2 have a dependency relation, i.e. $O_1 \otimes O_2 \rightarrow DR(X_1,X_2)^d \vee DR(X_2,X_1)^d$ where $d \geq 0$.*

Proof: We show that if X_1 and X_2 have no dependency relation, then O_1 and O_2 must be compatible. From Definition 5 (on DG) and the semantics definitions of all DG operations, the effect of any DG operation must be confined to its direct target objects and downstream objects (if any). From the assumption that X_1 and X_2 have no dependency relation, we can derive that there must exist two disjoint sub-graphs DG_1 and DG_2 in DG, i.e. $(DG_1 \subset DG) \wedge (DG_2 \subset DG) \wedge (DG_1 \cap DG_2 = \emptyset)$, with X_1 and X_2 as their roots, respectively (by Definition 5 and Definition 6). From the fact that DG_1 and DG_2 are disjoint, the execution effect of O_1 will be confined in DG_1; and the execution effect of O_2 will be confined in DG_2. Therefore, the execution of O_1 and O_2 in different orders will result in the same DG state, which means O_1 and O_2 are compatible (by Definition 7 and Definition 8). Conversely, for O_1 and O_2 to be dependency-conflicting, X_1 and X_2 must have a dependency relation and the theorem follows. □

Since a dependency relation is a necessary condition for two concurrent operations to conflict in collaborative DG-based systems, such a conflict relation is called *dependency-conflict* [2]. The precise dependency relation conditions for assessing whether two concurrent operations have a dependency-conflict relation can be found in [2].

THE CONTEXT-MATCHING DG STATES REQUIREMENT

Under the OT-based dependency-conflict resolution in [2], when a new operation O arrives at a remote site, O is checked for dependency-conflict with any concurrent operations previously executed at this site. If no conflict is detected, O will be executed as-is; otherwise O will be transformed into a proper new form O' so that the execution of O' after those conflicting operations will achieve consistent and desirable results. In this conflict detection and resolution (i.e. operation transformation) process, a suitable OT control algorithm (e.g. COT [23]) must be used to ensure the context-equivalency of the two concurrent operations for transformation. However, ensuring the context-equivalence condition for transformation is only part of the requirements for OT correctness; another essential correctness requirement is the *context-matching* DG state condition for conflict detection, i.e. the DG state used to detect the dependency-conflict relation between two context-equivalent operations must match the common context of these two operations. As illustrated in Figure 2, if an incorrect DG state (e.g. the current execution DG state) is used in detecting dependency relations between target objects of operations (e.g. O_1 and O_2) in concern, the system will falsely declare conflicting operations as being compatible (or compatible operations as being conflicting) and fail to achieve consistency.

The identification of *context-matching* DG states as a requirement for dependency-conflict detection is an important step towards a correct solution for dependency-conflict detection, and a contribution to the OT technology. In prior OT work [4, 20, 22, 24, 26], conflict relations of context-equivalent operations can be derived from the parameters of the operations without having to refer to the actual document. But, in DG-based data and operation models, it is no longer possible to derive the dependency-conflict relation between two context-equivalent operations by using their parameters alone; it is necessary to know the corresponding context-matching DG state, which is not encoded in or derivable from the parameters of DG operations. What makes dependency-conflict detection more challenging is the unavailability of the context-matching DG state at the time of detecting and resolving dependency-conflict as OT systems keep only the current DG state at each collaborating site. In the rest of this paper, we will discuss our novel approach in overcoming this challenge in dependency-conflict detection.

THE DG DIFFERENCE APPROACH

The challenge in correctly detecting the dependency relations among concurrent operations is how to efficiently obtain an unknown prior context-matching DG state from the current known DG state. One possible, but inefficient and undesirable, way is to undo all operations that have been executed to bring the prior context-matching DG state to the current DG state. Those operations to be undone are available in the *history buffer* of an OT system, which keeps all executed operations for future transformations [22,23]. After the undo, the DG state is restored to the prior DG state (readers are referred to [19] for discussion on how to achieve correct *undo-effect* in the face of concurrent operations) that matches the context of the operations in concern, and can then be directly used in checking dependency relations among target objects. After the dependency relation detection, those undone operations must be redone to bring the prior DG state back to the current DG state. This undo-redo-based approach works correctly, but it is inefficient and may cause undesirable user interface effects (the undo and redo effects may be visible on the user interface and cause confusion to users). The redo of undone operations can be avoided by making a separate copy of the current DG state and applying the undo on the copied DG state instead. However, this approach is still costly as the size of the DG state for a real 3D document is often large, but usually only a small subset of the DG is relevant for dependency relation detections.

Instead of using the above naïve approach of undoing operations on the actual or copy of the current DG state to recover a context-matching DG state, we propose a novel approach to *derive* the context-matching DG state by means of the *DG difference*: the collection of different nodes and arrows between the context-matching DG state and the current DG state. This *DG difference* approach is based on two key insights: (1) the *DG difference* between a prior DG state and the current DG state can be reliably derived without knowing the prior DG state (to be discussed in detail in the next section); and (2) an unknown context-matching DG state can be correctly derived from the known current DG state and the *DG difference* (discussed in the rest of this section). This DG difference approach avoids the overhead of undoing and redoing operations and the associated user interface disturbance, and has limited space and time overhead constrained by the number of concurrent operations, which is small in real-time collaborative editing systems [23].

Simplified DG Data and Operation Models

In search of an effective and efficient way of representing DG differences, we observed that for the purpose of detecting the dependency relation between two graphic objects, only the structure of a DG (i.e. the nodes and arrows) is relevant because attribute values in the DG play no role in determining whether two objects are connected or dependent (by Definition 6). This observation has led us to the notion of *Simplified Dependency Graph* (SDG), defined below.

Definition 9. Simplified Dependency Graph. *Given a DG, a* Simplified Dependency Graph, *denoted as SDG, has the same structure and represented with the tuple* $(\mathcal{N},\mathcal{A})$ *as the DG, but the nodes in the SDG have no value.*

In a SDG-based system, an *UP* operation is no longer relevant as an *UP* does not change the structure of a DG, so there are only four basic operations: *CR*, *DL*, *CN*, and *DC*. Furthermore, the semantics of a *CN* operation in a SDG has also been simplified: it only creates a connection between two objects, without the effect of propagating the attribute value from the source object to the destination object and its downstream objects because there is no attribute value in a SDG.

In detecting dependency relations among objects, the SDG, instead of DG, data and operation model will be used.

SDG Difference

In this section, we introduce the concept of SDG difference between two SDGs and discuss the relationship of the SDG difference and the two SDGs.

Definition 10. Partial SDG Difference. *Given two SDG states,* $SDG_1=(\mathcal{N}_1, \mathcal{A}_1)$ *and* $SDG_2=(\mathcal{N}_2, \mathcal{A}_2)$, *a* Partial SDG Difference *from* SDG_1 *to* SDG_2 *is represented as* $SDG_1 \backslash SDG_2=(\mathcal{N}_{1\backslash 2},\mathcal{A}_{1\backslash 2})$, *where*:

1. $\mathcal{N}_{1\backslash 2} = \{n \mid (n \in \mathcal{N}_1) \wedge (n \notin \mathcal{N}_2)\}$ *represents a set of nodes that are in* $\mathcal{N}_1$ *but not in* $\mathcal{N}_2$, i.e. $\mathcal{N}_{1\backslash 2} = \mathcal{N}_1 \backslash \mathcal{N}_2$.
2. $\mathcal{A}_{1\backslash 2} = \{(n_1, n_2) \mid ((n_1, n_2) \in \mathcal{A}_1) \wedge ((n_1, n_2) \notin \mathcal{A}_2)\}$ *represents a set of arrows that are in* $\mathcal{A}_1$ *but not in* $\mathcal{A}_2$, i.e. $\mathcal{A}_{1\backslash 2}=\mathcal{A}_1 \backslash \mathcal{A}_2$.

Definition 11. SDG Difference. *Given two SDG states,* $SDG_1 = (\mathcal{N}_1, \mathcal{A}_1)$ *and* $SDG_2 = (\mathcal{N}_2, \mathcal{A}_2)$, *the* SDG difference *between* SDG_1 and SDG_2, denoted as $SDG_1 \Delta SDG_2$, *is represented as a pair of partial SDG differences*: $SDG_1 \Delta SDG_2=(SDG_1 \backslash SDG_2, SDG_2 \backslash SDG_1)$.

For example, given a SDG state corresponding to Figure 2f: $SDG_1 = (\{A, B, C\}, \{(A, B)\})$, and another SDG state corresponding to Figure 2a: $SDG_2 = (\{A, B, C\}, \{(A, B),$

$(B, C)\})$, their SDG difference is $SDG_1 \Delta SDG_2 = ((\{\ \}, \{\ \}), (\{\ \}, \{(B, C)\})$.

It is worth highlighting that the two SDG partial differences $SDG_1 \setminus SDG_2$ and $SDG_2 \setminus SDG_1$ are mutually exclusive, i.e. the node sets $\mathcal{N}_{1\setminus 2}$ and $\mathcal{N}_{2\setminus 1}$ are disjoint: $\mathcal{N}_{1\setminus 2} \cap \mathcal{N}_{2\setminus 1} = \emptyset$, and the arrow sets $\mathcal{A}_{1\setminus 2}$ and $\mathcal{A}_{2\setminus 1}$ are disjoint, i.e. $\mathcal{A}_{1\setminus 2} \cap \mathcal{A}_{2\setminus 1} = \emptyset$. This is because $\mathcal{N}_{1\setminus 2}$ and $\mathcal{A}_{1\setminus 2}$ cover those objects and arrows that are in SDG_1 but not in SDG_2, representing the reduction from SDG_1 to SDG_2; but $\mathcal{N}_{2\setminus 1}$ and $\mathcal{A}_{2\setminus 1}$ contain those objects and arrows that are in SDG_2 but not in SDG_1, representing the expansion from SDG_1 to SDG_2.

If we know both SDG_1 and SDG_2, we can derive $SDG_1 \Delta SDG_2$ according to Definition 10 and Definition 11. Conversely, if we know only SDG_2 (or SDG_1), but also know $SDG_1 \Delta SDG_2$, then we should be able to derive the unknown SDG_1 (or SDG_2) from the known $SDG_1 \Delta SDG_2$ and SDG_2 (or SDG_1). This reverse relationship among $SDG_1 \Delta SDG_2$, SDG_2, and SDG_1 is formally established in Theorem 2. To help the proof of this theorem, we first introduce the following five equalities from the algebra set theory [18]: (1) $A \setminus A = \emptyset$; (2) $A \setminus \emptyset = A$; (3) $A \cup \emptyset = A$; (4) $A \cup B = B \cup A$; and (5) $A \cup (B \setminus C) = (B \cup A) \setminus (C \setminus A)$, where A, B, and C are sets.

Theorem 2. *Given $SDG_1 \Delta SDG_2 = (SDG_1 \setminus SDG_2, SDG_2 \setminus SDG_1)$, and $SDG_2 = (\mathcal{N}_2, \mathcal{A}_2)$, we have $SDG_1 = (\mathcal{N}_1, \mathcal{A}_1)$, where $\mathcal{N}_1 = (\mathcal{N}_2 \cup \mathcal{N}_{1\setminus 2}) \setminus \mathcal{N}_{2\setminus 1}$, and $\mathcal{A}_1 = (\mathcal{A}_2 \cup \mathcal{A}_{1\setminus 2}) \setminus \mathcal{A}_{2\setminus 1}$.*

Proof: First, we show $\mathcal{N}_1 = (\mathcal{N}_2 \cup \mathcal{N}_{1\setminus 2}) \setminus \mathcal{N}_{2\setminus 1}$:

$$
\begin{aligned}
&(\mathcal{N}_2 \cup \mathcal{N}_{1\setminus 2}) \setminus \mathcal{N}_{2\setminus 1} \\
&= (\mathcal{N}_2 \cup (\mathcal{N}_1 \setminus \mathcal{N}_2)) \setminus (\mathcal{N}_2 \setminus \mathcal{N}_1) && \text{-- by Definition 10} \\
&= (\mathcal{N}_1 \cup \mathcal{N}_2) \setminus (\mathcal{N}_2 \setminus \mathcal{N}_2) \setminus (\mathcal{N}_2 \setminus \mathcal{N}_1) && \text{-- by (5)} \\
&= (\mathcal{N}_2 \cup \mathcal{N}_1) \setminus (\mathcal{N}_2 \setminus \mathcal{N}_1) && \text{-- by (1),(2),(4)} \\
&= \mathcal{N}_1 \cup (\mathcal{N}_2 \setminus \mathcal{N}_2) && \text{-- by (5)} \\
&= \mathcal{N}_1 && \text{-- by (1) \& (3)}
\end{aligned}
$$

Second, following the same reasoning, we can prove that $\mathcal{A}_1 = (\mathcal{A}_2 \cup \mathcal{A}_{1\setminus 2}) \setminus \mathcal{A}_{2\setminus 1}$. Therefore, the theorem holds. □

The reverse relationship captured in Theorem 2 may look trivial, but it is fundamental for solving an important problem in dependency-conflict detection: how to obtain a (unknown) prior context-matching SDG state (represented as SDG_1) from the (known) current SDG state (represented as SDG_2). The basic idea of our solution is the following: if we are able to create $SDG_1 \Delta SDG_2$, without knowing SDG_1, then we will be able to derive SDG_1 from the created $SDG_1 \Delta SDG_2$ and the known SDG_2 by the reverse relationship captured in Theorem 2. The challenge is of course how to create the $SDG_1 \Delta SDG_2$ without knowing SDG_1, which is discussed next.

CREATING SDG DIFFERENCE FROM CONTEXT DIFFERENCE

Bridging Context Difference and SDG Difference

From prior OT work [23], we know that when a new remote operation O arrives at a collaborating site, it will be checked to see whether the following *context-inclusion* condition is satisfied: $C(O) \subseteq DS$, where $C(O)$ denotes the *Context* of O, consisting of the set of operations performed on the DG state from which O was originally generated (Definition 4), and DS stands for *Document State* and is represented by the set of operations already performed on the current DG state (Definition 3). O will be held until this condition is met. Then, O will be examined and transformed against a set of operations in the following *Context-Difference* (CD): $CD = DS \setminus C(O)$, which contains all operations that have been executed in the current DG state (corresponding to DS) but not in the DG state from which O was generated (corresponding to $C(O)$).

From the correspondences between DS and the current DG state, and between $C(O)$ and the prior context-matching DG state, we can infer the correspondence between CD and the SDG difference of the two DGs. It is those operations in the CD that provide the key to solving the problem of creating the SDG difference without knowing the prior context-matching DG state. For example in Figure 2, when O_1, with $C(O_1) = \{\ \}$, arrives at *site*-2, the current DG state (Figure 2g) corresponds to $DS = \{O_2, O_3\}$ due to execution of O_2 and O_3. Since the context-inclusion condition $C(O_1) \subseteq DS$ is satisfied, O_1 will be transformed against operations in $CD = DS \setminus C(O_1) = \{O_2, O_3\}$. By examining operations O_2 and O_3 in CD, we can see that they are responsible for creating the SDG difference between the initial SDG state (matching the context of O_1) and the current SDG state: O_2 removes the connection between B and C, and O_3 removes the connection between A and B. In general, it can be shown that all structure changes between a prior SDG state and the current SDG state must be created by operations in the CD; and all structural changes created by operations in the CD must be captured by the corresponding SDG difference (Definition 11). In the following section, we present a novel OT technique invented to create the SDG difference by means of the operations in the CD.

Creating SDG Difference

Given a context difference CD corresponding to the SDG difference between SDG_1 and SDG_2, we can derive the SDG difference $SDG_1 \Delta SDG_2$ by analyzing the effect of each operation in CD. CR and CN operations expand the structure from SDG_1 to SDG_2 by adding nodes and arrows into SDG_1; thus, their targets should be included in $SDG_2 \setminus SDG_1$. DL and DC operations reduce the structure from SDG_1 to SDG_2 by removing nodes and arrows from SDG_1; thus, their targets should be included in $SDG_1 \setminus SDG_2$. However, DL, CN, and DC may not change SDG_1 but instead cancel the effects of other CR, DC, and CN that are also in CD, thus, the effects of those operations will compensate each other and their targets should be neither in $SDG_1 \setminus SDG_2$ nor in $SDG_2 \setminus SDG_1$. Since CD is derived from a document state and an operation context which all correspond to full DGs, it may include UP operations that are irrelevant for creating the SDG difference; also, CN operations in CD have the additional functionality of propagating the attribute value of the source object to the destination and its dependent downstream objects, which is also irrelevant for creating the SDG difference. Therefore, in converting operations in *CD* into the SDG difference, we should ignore all *UP* operations and the value propagation capability of *CN* operations in *CD*.

In the following, we first present the *ConvertO2GD* algorithm to convert a single operation O_x in *CD* into *GD* – a SDG Difference, then we will discuss the issues and present the algorithm to convert a whole *CD* into *GD*. The algorithm *ConvertO2GD* takes two input parameters: the operation O_x and the reference to $GD = SDG_1 \Delta SDG_2$; and updates the input *GD* to include the effect of O_x. The precondition for the algorithm is that $C(O_x)$ corresponds to the combination of the SDG state derivable from SDG_1 and the input *GD*. The routine $Type(O_x)$ returns the type of O_x (i.e. *CR*, *DL*, *UP*, *CN*, or *DC*). The dot notation is used to refer to a parameter of a SDG operation, e.g. $O_x.X$ refers to the target X of operation O_x. The variables $\mathcal{N}_{1\backslash 2}$, $\mathcal{A}_{1\backslash 2}$, $\mathcal{N}_{2\backslash 1}$, and $\mathcal{A}_{2\backslash 1}$ refer to those sets in *GD*.

Algorithm 1. *ConvertO2GD(Ox,GD)*

```
// N_{1\2}, A_{1\2}, N_{2\1}, and A_{2\1} refer to those sets in GD
switch(Type(O_x)){
   case CR: N_{2\1} := N_{2\1} ∪ {O_x.X};
   case DL:
      if O_x.X ∈ N_{2\1} then N_{2\1} := N_{2\1} \ {O_x.X};
      else N_{1\2} := N_{1\2} ∪ {O_x.X};
   case CN:
      if (O_x.S, O_x.D) ∈ A_{1\2} then
         A_{1\2} := A_{1\2} \ {(O_x.S, O_x.D)};
      else A_{2\1} := A_{2\1} ∪ {(O_x.S, O_x.D)};
   case DC:
      if (O_x.S, O_x.D) ∈ A_{2\1} then
         A_{2\1} := A_{2\1} \ {(O_x.S, O_x.D)};
      else A_{1\2} := A_{1\2} ∪ {(O_x.S, O_x.D)};
   default: return; } // includes the UP case
```

ConvertO2GD works as follows. In case that O_x is a *CR* operation, the target object X is added into $\mathcal{N}_{2\backslash 1}$. In case that O_x is a *DL* operation: if the target X is already in $\mathcal{N}_{2\backslash 1}$ due to a prior *CR* operation, then X is removed from $\mathcal{N}_{2\backslash 1}$; otherwise X is added into $\mathcal{N}_{1\backslash 2}$. In case that O_x is a *CN* operation: if the arrow $(O_x.S, O_x.D)$ is already in $\mathcal{A}_{1\backslash 2}$ due to a prior *DC* operation, then $(O_x.S, O_x.D)$ is removed from $\mathcal{A}_{1\backslash 2}$; otherwise $(O_x.S, O_x.D)$ is added into $\mathcal{A}_{2\backslash 1}$ (note: in converting a *CN*, its value propagation effect is ignored). In case that O is a *DC* operation: if the arrow $(O_x.S, O_x.D)$ is already in $\mathcal{A}_{2\backslash 1}$ due to a prior *CN* operation, then $(O_x.S, O_x.D)$ is removed from $\mathcal{A}_{2\backslash 1}$; otherwise $(O_x.S, O_x.D)$ is added into $\mathcal{A}_{1\backslash 2}$. In default case, including that O is an *UP*, O is ignored.

To convert the set of operations in a *CD* into a *GD*, we need to deal with the issue of the ordering of operations in *CD* are selected for conversion. This order must be the same as the order used for selecting those operations for execution by a context-based OT system [15, 23]. This is because *GD* is incrementally created by converting operations in the *CD* one by one; the original execution order ensures that operations can be correctly converted by examining the effects of prior converted operations accumulated in *GD*. Based on the context theory of OT [23], an operation O_x in *CD* will be selected for execution/conversion if the context-inclusion condition is met: $C(O_x) \subseteq C(O)$, where O is the new remote operation in concern. After the effect of an O_x is recorded in *GD* by invoking *ConvertO2GD*, $C(O)$ should be updated to include O_x, i.e. $C(O) = C(O) \cup \{O_x\}$, to reflect the effect of O_x has been included in *GD* and to ensure the correct ordering in selecting the next operation from *CD*. For example in Figure 2, $CD = \{O_2, O_3\}$ is for creating the *GD* between $C(O_1) = \{\ \}$ and the $DS = \{O_2, O_3\}$ corresponding to the current SDG when O_1 arrives at *site*-2. As $C(O_2) = C(O_1)$, O_2 is selected first and $C(O_1)$ is updated to $C(O_1)' = \{O_2\}$. Afterwards, as $C(O_3) = C(O_1)'$, O_3 is selected next.

In the following, we present an algorithm to sequentially convert each operation in a *CD* into *GD*. The *ConvertCD2GD* algorithm takes two input parameters: the operation O in concern and *CD*; and returns *GD* – the SDG difference converted from *CD*. This algorithm first generates the context of O and assigns it to a local variable: $CO = C(O)$, and initialize *GD* to an empty SDG difference. Then it repeats the following steps until *CD* becomes empty: (1) select and remove an operation O_x from *CD* where $C(O_x) \subseteq CO$; (2) invoke the $CovertO2GD(O_x, GD)$ to convert the effect of O_x; and (3) update *CO* to include O_x, i.e. $CO := CO \cup \{org(O_x)\}$.

Algorithm 2. *ConvertCD2GD(O, CD)*

```
CO := C(O);
GD := (({ },{ }),({ },{ }));
repeat until CD={ }:
   Select and remove O_x from CD, where C(O_x) ⊆ CO;
   ConvertO2GD(O_x, GD);
   CO := CO ∪ {org(O_x)};
return GD;
```

RECURSIVE DEPENDENCY-CONFLICT RESOLUTION

We have so far deliberately postponed one tacit but important issue in converting operations in *CD* into SDG difference: operations in *CD* may have dependency-conflict relations! Without considering and dealing with those conflicts, the created SDG difference may be incorrect. For example, consider a more complex concurrency scenario with three collaborating sites in Figure 3. The three sites share a common initial DG state: $A(1)$ $B(2)$→$C(2)$ (Figure 3a, g, and m). Five operations O_1, O_2, O_3, O_4, and O_5 are concurrently generated with the causal relation $O_1 \parallel O_5 \parallel (O_2 \rightarrow O_3 \rightarrow O_4)$, where $O_1 = UP(A, 3)$ generated at *site*-1; $O_2 = CN(A, B)$, $O_3 = DC(B, C)$ and $O_4 = DC(A, B)$ generated at *site*-2; and $O_5 = CN(A, B)$ generated at *site*-3. When O_1, with $C(O_1) = \{\ \}$, arrives at *site*-2, the current DG state is $A(1)$ $B(1)$ $C(1)$ (Figure 3k) and $DS = \{O_2, O_3, O_4, O_5\}$ (after the execution of O_2, O_3, O_4, O_5; O_5 has been transformed by the dependency-conflict resolution in [2] into a null operation

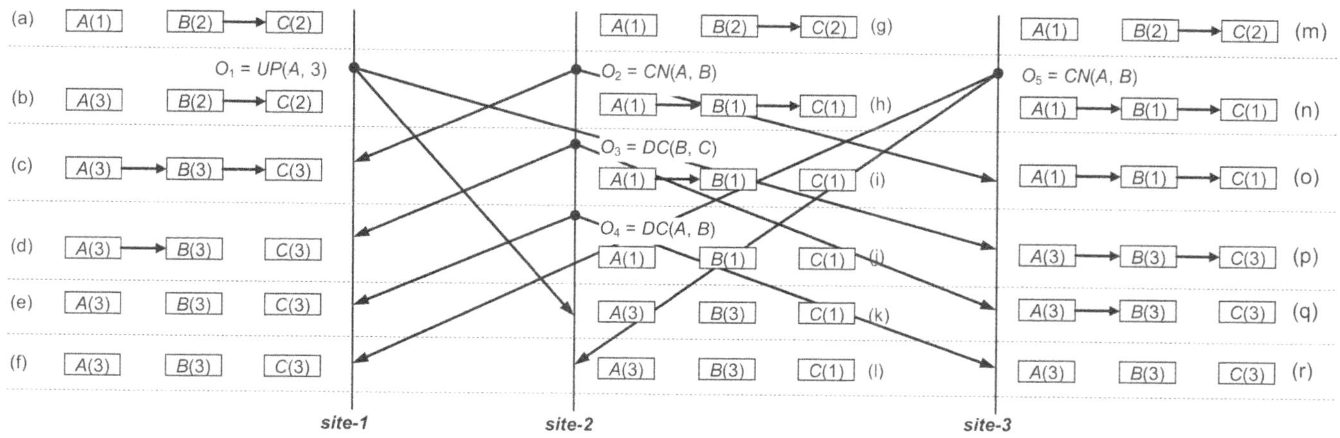

Figure 3. An example of a recursive dependency-conflict in a dependency relation detection.

as O_5 is assumed to have a lower priority than the conflicting O_2; the execution of the transformed O_5 does not change the DG state). As the context-inclusion condition $C(O_1) \subseteq DS$ is met, O_1 will be transformed against operations in $CD = DS \setminus C(O_1) = \{O_2, O_3, O_4, O_5\}$ before being executed.

In this example, we focus on the dependency-conflict detection in the transformation of O_1, which has original context $C(O_1) = \{\ \}$, against O_3, which has original context $C(O_3) = \{O_2\}$. O_1 will be first transformed against O_2 and then O_3 according to the context-theory. The transformation of O_1 against O_2 does not change O_1, i.e. $O_1' = O_1$, as an *UP* and *CN* are always compatible [2] but the context of O_1 is upgraded to $C(O_1') = \{O_2\}$, which meets the context-equivalency condition for O_1' to be transformed against O_3, i.e. $C(O_1') = C(O_3)$. For detecting the dependency-conflict of O_1' and O_3, the context matching SDG state SDG_1 corresponds to $C(O_3)$ is the simplified graph of the DG in Figure 3h, the current SDG state SDG_2 is the simplified graph of the DG in Figure 3k, and $CD = DS \setminus C(O_3) = \{O_3, O_4, O_5\}$ is for creating the SDG difference. *ConvertCD2GD* algorithm will convert *CD* into $GD = SDG_1 \Delta SDG_2 = ((\mathcal{N}_{1\setminus 2}, \mathcal{A}_{1\setminus 2}), (\mathcal{N}_{2\setminus 1}, \mathcal{A}_{2\setminus 1}))$, where $\mathcal{N}_{1\setminus 2} = \{\ \}$, $\mathcal{A}_{1\setminus 2} = \{(B, C)\}$ from the conversion of O_3, $\mathcal{N}_{2\setminus 1} = \{\ \}$, and $\mathcal{A}_{2\setminus 1} = \{\ \}$ from the conversion of O_4 and O_5. This *GD* is incorrect as $\mathcal{A}_1 = (\mathcal{A}_2 \cup \mathcal{A}_{1\setminus 2}) \setminus \mathcal{A}_{2\setminus 1} = \{(B, C)\}$ (by Theorem 2) does not reflect the arrow sets in SDG_1; the arrow (A, B) should also be in SDG_1 (see Figure 3h)! Due to this incorrect *GD*, O_1' and O_3, which are dependency-conflicting, will be detected as compatible because *A* (the target of O_1') and *B* (the target of O_3) will be detected as not dependency related!

Dependency-Conflict among SDG Operations

At first glance, we seem to be in a *conflict-detection-cycle*: to detect dependency-conflicts among concurrent operations, we devised a solution which requires a dependency-conflict detection (and resolution) solution of its own! Fortunately, our investigation found that concurrent SDG operations may have dependency-conflict relations only if their direct target objects are overlapping, thanks to the fact that nodes in a SDG do not have values. The following theorem formally establishes this necessary condition for SGD operations to conflict.

Theorem 3. *Given two context-equivalent SDG operations, O_1 with a target X_1 and O_2 with a target X_2, O_1 and O_2 are conflicting only if X_1 and X_2 are overlapping,* i.e. $O_1 \otimes O_2 \rightarrow X_1 = X_2$.

Proof: We show that if X_1 and X_2 are not overlapping, then O_1 and O_2 must be compatible. From Definition 9 (on SDG) and the semantics definitions of all four SDG operations, the effect of any SDG operation must be confined to its direct target objects only. From the assumption that X_1 and X_2 are not overlapping, executions of O_1 and O_2 in different orders must result in the same overall SDG state, which means O_1 and O_2 are compatible (by Definition 8). Conversely, for O_1 and O_2 to be conflicting, X_1 and X_2 must be overlapping and the theorem follows. □

Detecting overlapping objects can be achieved by simply comparing the object identifiers, without having to refer to any SDG state: if the object identifiers are equal, then the target objects are overlapping. Thus, the conflict-detection-cycle is broken! However, we must know under what exact conditions SDG operations are compatible or conflict, and resolve those dependency-conflicts once they are detected. We have conducted comprehensive analysis of dependency-conflict relations for every pair of the four SDG operations, and summarized the results in Table 1. Unlike in DG data model on which five pairs of DG operation conflicts, only two pairs of SDG operations: *DL-CN* and *CN-CN,* may be conflicting if and only if their

Table 1. SDG Conflict relations and detection conditions

	$CR(g_2)$	$DL(X_2)$	$CN(S_2, D_2)$	$DC(S_2, D_2)$
$CR(g_1)$	⊙	⊙	⊙	⊙
$DL(X_1)$		⊙	$\otimes \leftrightarrow (X_1 = S_2) \vee (X_1 = D_2)$	⊙
$CN(S_1, D_1)$			$\otimes \leftrightarrow D_1 = D_2$	⊙
$DC(S_1, D_1)$				⊙

targets overlap as their executions in different orders result in different SDG states. Other pairs are always compatible (*CR-CR*, *CR-DL*, *CR-CN*, *CR-DC*, *DL-DL*, *DL-DC*, *CN-DC*, and *DC-DC*) as their executions in any order would always result in the same SDG state.

We have also conducted theoretical verification on the conflict/compatible relations and conditions for every pair of SDG operations. In Theorem 4, we provide one theoretical verification of *CN-CN* conflict to show basic ideas of our verification method.

Theorem 4. *A* $CN(S_1, D_1)$ *conflicts with another* $CN(S_2, D_2)$ *defined on the same state* $SDG = (\mathcal{N}, \mathcal{A})$ *iff* D_1 *and* D_2 *are overlapping, i.e.* $CN(S_1, D_1) \otimes CN(S_2, D_2) \leftrightarrow D_1 = D_2$.

Proof: To prove the theorem holds for $CN(S_1, D_1) \otimes CN(S_2, D_2) \rightarrow D_1 = D_2$, we show that if the targets' overlapping relation is not $D_1 = D_2$, then $CN(S_1, D_1) \odot CN(S_2, D_2)$. For those cases in which the targets of the two *CN* operations have no overlapping relation, they must be compatible by Theorem 3 and Definition 8. From the assumption that the overlapping relation is not $D_1 = D_2$, the possible overlapping relation is one of the following two: $S_1 = S_2$ or $D_1 = S_2$ (symmetrically, $D_2 = S_1$). Under the relation $S_1 = S_2$ or $D_1 = S_2$, executing the two *CN*s in different orders would always result in the same SDG state. In case $CN(S_1, D_1)$ is executed before $CN(S_2, D_2)$: (1) $CN(S_1, D_1)$ will add an arrow (S_1, D_1) to $\mathcal{A}$, resulting in $SDG_1 = (\mathcal{N}, \mathcal{A}_1)$, where $\mathcal{A}_1 = \mathcal{A} \cup \{(S_1, D_1)\}$; (2) the precondition of $CN(S_2, D_2)$ must be met because $CN(S_1, D_1)$ adds an incoming arrow to D_1 but not D_2 as $D_1 \neq D_2$, so $CN(S_2, D_2)$ will add an arrow (S_2, D_2) to $\mathcal{A}_1$, and result in $SDG_1' = (\mathcal{N}, \mathcal{A}_1')$ where $\mathcal{A}_1' = \mathcal{A} \cup \{(S_1, D_1), (S_2, D_2)\}$. In case $CN(S_2, D_2)$ is executed before $CN(S_1, D_1)$: following the same reasoning, the resulting SDG state will be $SDG_2' = (\mathcal{N}, \mathcal{A}_2')$ where $\mathcal{A}_2' = \mathcal{A} \cup \{(S_1, D_1), (S_2, D_2)\}$. From $SDG_1' = SDG_2'$, we conclude $CN(S_1, D_1)$ and $CN(S_2, D_2)$ are compatible under the condition $S_1 = S_2$ or $D_1 = S_2$ by Definition 8. Hence, we derive $CN(S_1, D_1)$ and $CN(S_2, D_2)$ are compatible if the targets' overlapping relation is not $D_1 = D_2$. Conversely, $CN(S_1, D_1)$ and $CN(S_2, D_2)$ are conflicting if $D_1 = D_2$.

Then, we show the theorem holds for $D_1 = D_2 \rightarrow CN(S_1, D_1) \otimes CN(S_2, D_2)$. In case $CN(S_1, D_1)$ is executed before $CN(S_2, D_2)$: (1) $CN(S_1, D_1)$ will add an arrow (S_1, D_1) into $\mathcal{A}$, and result in $SDG_3 = (\mathcal{N}, \mathcal{A}_3)$, where $\mathcal{A}_3 = \mathcal{A} \cup \{(S_1, D_1)\}$; and (2) $CN(S_2, D_2)$ will fail and have no impact on SDG_3 due to the its precondition-violation: D_2 will have an input connection due to the prior execution of $CN(S_1, D_1)$ and $D_1 = D_2$. In case $CN(S_2, D_2)$ is executed before $CN(S_1, D_1)$: following similar reasoning, the resulting SDG state will be $SDG_4 = (\mathcal{N}, \mathcal{A}_4)$, where $\mathcal{A}_4 = \mathcal{A} \cup \{(S_2, D_2)\}$. By comparing SDG_3 and SDG_4, we have $SDG_3 \neq SDG_4$ and conclude $CN(S_1, D_1)$ and $CN(S_2, D_2)$ conflicts under the condition $D_1 = D_2$ by Definition 7. Hence, the theorem holds under all circumstances. □

OT-Based SDG Conflict Resolution

To create a correct SDG difference, each operation O_x in *CD* must be transformed against operations in the context-difference $CD_x = C(O) \setminus C(O_x)$, where O is the new remote operation in concern, so that the potential dependency-conflict of O_x can be detected and resolved. This OT-based conflict resolution can be encapsulated in a routine $Transform(O_x, CD_x)$, which is adopted from the COT algorithm in [23] and specified in Algorithm 3 below for easy of reference.

Algorithm 3. $\boldsymbol{Transform(O_x, CD_x)}$

```
repeat until CD_x = { }:
    Select and remove O_y from CD_x, where C(O_y) ⊆ C(O_x);
    Transform(O_y, C(O_x) \ C(O_y));
    O_x := T(O_x, O_y); C(O_x) := C(O_x) ∪ {org(O_y)};
```

The *Transform* routine should be incorporated into an extended *ConvertCD2GD* algorithm, named as *COT_ConvertCD2GD*, at the place before invoking *ConvertO2GD*, as shown below:

Algorithm 4. ***COT_ConvertCD2GD(O, CD)***

```
CO := C(O); GD := (({ },{ }),({ },{ }));
repeat until CD = { }:
    Select and remove O_x from CD, where C(O_x) ⊆ CO;
    Transform(O_x, CO \ C(O_x));
    ConvertO2GD(O_x, GD);
    CO := CO ∪ {org(O_x)};
return GD;
```

Inside the recursive $Transform(O_x, CD_x)$ routine, the function $T(O_x, O_y)$ performs the real transformation of O_x against O_y from CD_x to resolve their SDG conflict. One important correctness requirement is the combined effects among concurrent SDG operations must be the same as the combined *structural* effects achieved by the OT-based dependency-conflict resolution in [2]. This requirement ensures the SDG difference created from SDG operations in a *CD* correctly reflects the same structural changes made by DG operations, even in the face of dependency-conflicts. As the conflict/compatible relations, conflict conditions, and combined effects are different in SDG operation model than in DG operation model, the OT-based dependency-conflict resolution in [2] cannot be used for resolving the conflict among SDG operations, thus new OT-based conflict resolution technique must be devised.

The basic transformation strategy of $T(O_x, O_y)$ is as follows: assume O_y has been executed, assess the impact of O_y on the SDG state and derive what should be executed to achieve their combined effect. The following example illustrates this idea. Consider the conflict between $CN(S_1, D_1)$ and $CN(S_2, D_2)$. Their combined effect should be only one of the connection is established, depending on the priority of the two *CN*s [2]. Let us assume $CN(S_2, D_2)$ has a higher priority than $CN(S_1, D_1)$, so only the connection (S_2, D_2) should be established after the execution of both *CN*s.

If $CN(S_1, D_1)$ is executed before $CN(S_2, D_2)$, the execution of $CN(S_2, D_2)$ will fail because of the precondition violation due to the prior execution of $CN(S_1, D_1)$. To successfully execute $CN(S_2, D_2)$ and achieve the combined effect of preserving the connection (S_2, D_2), an additional $DC(S_1, D_1)$ should be performed first to disconnect the connection (S_1, D_1) established by the execution of $CN(S_1, D_1)$. From the OT point of view, $CN(S_2, D_2)$ should be transformed (against $CN(S_1, D_1)$) into a list of two operations: one is the new $DC(S_1, D_1)$ operation and the other is the original $CN(S_2, D_2)$. The execution of the transformed $CN(S_2, D_2)$ will achieve the combined effect for a pair of *CN*s. On the other hand, if $CN(S_2, D_2)$ is executed before $CN(S_1, D_1)$, the combined effect has been achieved by the execution of $CN(S_2, D_2)$, so $CN(S_1, D_1)$ should be transformed (against $CN(S_2, D_2)$) into a null operation. The execution of the transformed $CN(S_1, D_1)$ will not change the document state and the combined effect will be achieved as well.

As shown in the example above, the SDG conflict resolution may transform an operation into a *list of operations* (*LO*). To facilitate transformations at *LO* level, an interface function like the *LOT* algorithm in [2] is needed to bridge *Transform* and *COT_ConvertCD2GD* algorithms to deal with *LO*s; e.g. *Transform* algorithm should invoke *LOT*, instead of *T* algorithm; *COT_ConvertCD2GD* algorithm should invoke *ConvertO2GD* for each operation in the transformed *LO*, etc. Details of *LOT* algorithm can be found in [2].

The $T(O_x, O_y)$ below transforms O_x against O_y in such a way that the conflict between the two SDG operations is resolved and a consistent combined effect is achieved.

Algorithm 5. $T(O_x, O_y)$

if $Type(O_x)=DL$ **and** $Type(O_y)=CN$ **then**
    return $Tsdlcn(O_x, O_y)$;
else if $Type(O_x)=CN$ **and** $Type(O_y)=DL$ **then**
    return $Tscndl(O_x, O_y)$;
else if $Type(O_y)=UP$ **then return** $TsOI(O_x, O_y)$;
else if $Type(O_x)=UP$ **then return** $TsIO(O_x, O_y)$;
else if … // other cases are omitted for conciseness

Based on the types of O_x and O_y, the *T* function invokes a type specific transformation function $Tspq(O_x, O_y)$, where *p* and *q* are the operation types of O_x and O_y, respectively. For the conflicting pairs, three transformation functions are defined: two for handling the two different orders of execution of *DL-CN* pair and one for handling the *CN*s pair. For the compatible pairs, there are two cases that involve precondition violations (i.e. *DL-DL* and *DC-DC* pairs) that require the operations to be nullified for not affecting subsequent transformations. In addition, we define two transformation functions for handling the two different execution orders of an operation *O* in any type and an *Identity* operation *I* (i.e. an operation that is not in the SDG operation model). The transformation functions for the *Identity* operation are necessary for handling the transformation involving an *UP* operation (regarded as an *Identity* operation), which may be included in the SDG operation context that corresponds to a full DG. These transformation functions are sketched in Algorithm 6 below. These transformation functions have been theoretical verified for their convergence property.

Algorithm 6. SDG Transformation functions

$Tsdlcn(DL(X), CN(S,D))$:
if $DL(X) \otimes DC(S,D)$ **then return** $[DC(S,D), DL(X)]$;
else return $[DL(X)]$; //for $DL(X) \odot DC(S,D)$

$Tscndl(CN(S,D), DL(X))$:
if $CN(S,D) \otimes DL(X)$ **then return** [ ];
else return $[CN(S,D)]$; //for $CN(S,D) \odot DL(X)$

$Tscncn(CN(S_1,D_1), CN(S_2,D_2))$:
if $CN(S_1,D_1) \otimes CN(S_2,D_2)$ **then** {
    if $HigherPriority(CN(S_1,D_1), CN(S_2,D_2))$ **then**
        return $[DC(S_2,D_2), CN(S_1,D_1)]$;
    else return [ ];
else return $[CN(S_1,D_1)]$; //for $CN(S_1,D_1) \odot CN(S_2,D_2)$

$Tsdldl(DL(X_1), DL(X_2))$:
if $X_1=X_2$ **then return** [ ];
else return $[DL(X_1)]$;

$Tsdcdc(DC(S_1,D_1), DC(S_2,D_2))$:
if$(S_1=S_2$ **and** $D_1=D_2)$ **then return** [ ];
else return $[DC(S_1,D_1)]$;

$TsOI(O,I)$:
    return $[O]$;

$TsIO(I,O)$:
    return [ ];

//Details for transformation functions *Tscrcr*, *Tscrdl*,
//*Tsdlcr*, *Tscrcn*, *Tscncr*, *Tscrdc*, *Tsdccr*, *Tsdldc*, and
//*Tsdcdl* are omitted for conciseness because they always
//return the original operation.

In the following, we describe the transformation function for a pair of *CN*s (description of other transformation functions follows similarly, so details are omitted). The combined effect for a pair of concurrent $CN(S_1, D_1)$ and $CN(S_2, D_2)$ in both execution orders should be only the higher priority connection is established as explained above. Only one *Tscncn* is needed for transforming $CN(S_1, D_1)$ against $CN(S_2, D_2)$. In case of conflict, if $CN(S_1, D_1)$ has a higher priority than $CN(S_2, D_2)$, it returns a list of two operations: $DC(S_2, D_2)$ to remove the connection from S_2 to D_2 for satisfying the precondition of $CN(S_1, D_1)$, followed by $CN(S_1, D_1)$; else it returns [ ]. In case of compatible, it returns $[CN(S_1, D_1)]$.

In the example in Figure 3, $CD=\{O_3, O_4, O_5\}$ is for creating the SDG difference $GD = ((\mathcal{N}_{1\setminus 2}, \mathcal{A}_{1\setminus 2}), (\mathcal{N}_{2\setminus 1}, \mathcal{A}_{2\setminus 1}))$ between $CO=C(O_1')=\{O_2\}$ and $DS=\{O_2, O_3, O_4, O_5\}$. The conversion for each operation in *CD* by *COT_ConvertCD2GD* algorithm is as follows. As $C(O_3)= CO$, O_3 will be selected first: O_3 is transformed but unchanged because $CD_3 = CO \setminus C(O_3) = \{\ \}$, the conversion of O_3 into *GD* will add (B, C) into $\mathcal{A}_{1\setminus 2}$ and *CO* is updated to $CO' = \{O_2, O_3\}$. Afterwards, as $C(O_4) = CO'$, O_4 will be selected next: O_4 is transformed but unchanged because $CD_4 = CO' \setminus C(O_4) = \{\ \}$, the conversion of O_4 into GD will add (A, B) into $\mathcal{A}_{1\setminus 2}$ and CO' is updated to $CO'' = \{O_2, O_3, O_4\}$. Finally, as $C(O_5) = CO''$, O_5 will be selected: O_5 is transformed against $CD_5 = CO'' \setminus C(O_5) = \{O_2, O_3, O_4\}$ which results in $O_5' = [\ ]$ by *Tscncn* as O_5 conflicts with and has a lower priority than O_2, the conversion of O_5' will not change GD, and CO'' is updated to $CO''' = \{O_2, O_3, O_4, O_5\}$. The final SDG difference is $GD = ((\{\ \}, \{(A, B), (B, C)\}), (\{\ \}, \{\ \}))$, which correctly reflects the changes from the context-matching SDG state in Figure 3h and the current SDG state in Figure 3k.

DEPENDENCY DETECTION USING SDG DIFFERENCES

Given two operations, O_1 with a target X_1 and O_2 with a target X_2, we can detect whether O_1 and O_2 are dependency-conflicting by detecting the necessary and sufficient dependency relation condition of X_1 and X_2. In this paper so far, we have discussed a technique (*COT_ConvertCD2GD*) to correctly derive the SDG difference $SDG_1 \Delta SDG_2$ between the context-matching SDG state SDG_1 (corresponding to $C(O_1) = C(O_2)$) and the current SDG state SDG_2 (corresponding to the current document state *DS*). $SDG_1 \Delta SDG_2$ can then be used to derive SDG_1 on which the dependency relation between X_1 and X_2 can be correctly detected. In this section, we present the high level algorithm for dependency relation detection and the technique to search for the dependency relation of X_1 and X_2 in SDG_1 based on SDG_2 and the information in $SDG_1 \Delta SDG_2$, without actually creating SDG_1.

The *DR_Detection*(X_1, X_2, O, DS, DG) algorithm below detects whether the dependency relation condition: $DR(X_1, X_2)^d$, is met in SDG_1 (to be derived from input parameters *O* and *DS*). It takes five input parameters: the upstream object X_1, the downstream object X_2, the operation *O* in concern, the current document state in the set representation *DS*, and the reference to the current DG state *DG* (its simplified graph is SDG_2). First, it invokes *COT_ConvertCD2GD*(O, CD) to create $GD = SDG_1 \Delta SDG_2$ from *CD*, where $CD = DS \setminus C(O)$. Afterwards, it invokes *Search*(X_1, X_2, GD, DG) to detect the dependency relation $DR(X_1, X_2)^d$ in SDG_1. This *DR_Detection* algorithm can be integrated with any dependency-conflict detection and resolution system such as [2].

Algorithm 7. *DR_Detection*(X_1, X_2, O, DS, DG)

```
GD:=COT_ConvertCD2GD(O,DS\C(O));
return Search(X1,X2,GD,DG);
```

To search whether X_1 has a downstream path to X_2 (i.e. whether $DR(X_1, X_2)^d$) in SDG_1, a brute-force graph traversal algorithm, such as Depth-first Search (DFS) or Breadth-first Search (BFS) algorithm, starting from X_1, can be used. But such algorithms are inefficient because of the large searching space in a realistic 3D document, yet many of the searches are unnecessary; e.g. in case of DFS, many incorrect branches may have to be searched first before the correct branch can be searched. From our observation, each node in our SDG model has only one upstream path but multiple downstream paths. Hence, searching backward from X_2, as adopted in this paper, is more efficient than the typical forward traversal from X_1. This is because there is only one path to traverse in each dependency relation detection: if X_1 is visited in the traversal, X_1 and X_2 are concluded as dependency related (i.e. $DR(X_1, X_2)^d$ where $d \geq 0$); otherwise X_1 and X_2 are concluded as not dependency related (i.e. $\neg DR(X_1, X_2)^d$).

Before we can present our backward search algorithm, there is one issue to address: given SDG_2 and $SDG_1 \Delta SDG_2 = ((\mathcal{N}_{1\setminus 2}, \mathcal{A}_{1\setminus 2}), (\mathcal{N}_{2\setminus 1}, \mathcal{A}_{2\setminus 1}))$, how to efficiently obtain SDG_1, which is necessary for the SDG search? Based on Theorem 2, SDG_1 can be obtained by first making a copy of SDG_2, then adding the nodes in $\mathcal{N}_{1\setminus 2}$ and arrows in $\mathcal{A}_{1\setminus 2}$ into the copied SDG_2, and removing the nodes in $\mathcal{N}_{2\setminus 1}$ and arrows in $\mathcal{A}_{2\setminus 1}$ from the copied SDG_2. However, deriving a real SDG_1 is space and time inefficient as SDG_1 may be large (due to a large SDG_2). Moreover, we found a real SDG_1 is not necessary for checking the dependency relation of two objects. Instead, we can deduce whether an arrow (Y_1, Y_2) is in SDG_1 from $SDG_1 \Delta SDG_2$ and SDG_2 on the fly: an arrow is in SDG_1 if it is in $\mathcal{A}_{1\setminus 2}$ or in SDG_2 but not in $\mathcal{A}_{2\setminus 1}$ by Theorem 2.

Based on this idea, *isConnectedBy_InCM* algorithm to query which object Y_1 is connected to object Y_2 in the context-matching SDG state is sketched in Algorithm 8. The algorithm takes three input parameters: the downstream object Y_2, the SDG difference *GD*, and the current DG state *DG* (its simplified graph is SDG_2); and one output parameter: Y_1. When an object is found to be connected to Y_2 (i.e. the connection is in $\mathcal{A}_{1\setminus 2}$ or in *DG* but not in $\mathcal{A}_{2\setminus 1}$), the algorithm returns *true* and sets Y_1 to the found object; otherwise, it returns *false*. One reminder: *DG* is a real graph while *GD* is the set representation of the SDG difference. The querying whether an object is connected to Y_2 in a real DG can be done by invoking the *isConnectedBy*(Y_2, Y_1) routine that is commonly available in DG-based 3D design systems: if Y_2 is connected by another object, the routine sets Y_1 to the identifier of this object and returns *true*; otherwise, the routine returns *false*.

Algorithm 8. *isConnectedBy_InCM*(Y_2, GD, DG, Y_1)

```
//A1\2 and A2\1 are the sets in GD
if DG.isConnectedBy(Y2, Y1) and (Y1, Y2)∉A2\1 then
    return true;
else if (Y1, Y2)∈A1\2 then
    return true;
else return false;
```

The *Search* algorithm in Algorithm 9 performs the backward search. It takes four input parameters: the upstream object X_1, the downstream object X_2, the SDG difference *GD*, and the reference to current DG state *DG*.

The algorithm starts with checking whether X_1 and X_2 are overlapping, i.e. $X_1 = X_2$: if they are overlapping then they are also dependency related (by Definition 6), so the algorithm returns *true*. Otherwise, the algorithm traverses the context-matching SDG state deduced from the inputs *GD* and *DG*. First, the algorithm sets the variable Y_2 to X_2. Then, the following repeats for each arrow (Y_1, Y_2) in SDG_1, which is in the upstream of X_2, by invoking *isConnectedBy_InCM*(Y_2, *GD*, *DG*, Y_1): if the upstream object X_1 is visited (i.e. $X_1 = Y_1$), the algorithm returns *true* and terminates as X_1 has been found in the upstream of X_2; otherwise, Y_2 is set to Y_1 so that the next iteration will continue to check the object connected to the new Y_2. Lastly, if there is no more arrow (Y_1, Y_2) on the upstream of X_2 in SDG_1, the algorithm returns *false* as X_1 is not in the upstream of X_2.

Algorithm 9. *Search*(X_1,X_2,*GD*,*DG*)

```
if X1 = X2 then return true; //X1 and X2 overlaps
else {
  Y2:=X2;
  while (isConnectedBy_InCM (Y2,GD,DG,Y1)){
     if X1=Y1 then
        return true; // X1 is in the upstream of X2
     Y2:=Y1; }
  return false;} //X1 is not in the upstream of X2
```

The complexity of the *Search* algorithm, in term of the number of object traversed, is *min*(*u*, *d*), where: (1) *u* is the number of upstream objects of X_2, i.e. $u=|\mathcal{U}|$, where $\mathcal{U}=\{Y| (Y\in\mathcal{N})\wedge DR(Y, X_2)\}$; (2) *d* is the distance between X_1 and X_2 if they are connected, else ∞; and (3) *min*(*u*, *d*) is the minimum of two values *u* and *d*.

IMPLEMENTATION IN COMAYA

Issues in dependency conflict detection and resolution are identified and solved during our exploratory construction of a real-time collaborative 3D design system, named *CoMaya*. CoMaya is *transparently adapted* (TA) from a commercial single-user 3D design system, Autodesk Maya, without changing the source code of the original system [1, 25]. CoMaya has been used as a research vehicle for studying a range of technical and user interface issues in 3D collaborative systems, including these issues addressed in this paper.

The CoMaya system is composed of three layers [1]. On the top layer is the single-user Maya, which provides multi-level user interfaces for manipulating 3D objects and their internal DG-based graphic objects. The bottom layer is the OT-based *Generic Collaboration Engine* (GCE) layer, which provides generic collaboration mechanisms for consistency maintenance, undo, workspace awareness support, etc. The middle layer is the Maya-specific *Collaboration Adaptor* (Maya-CA), which bridges the gap between Maya API and GCE.

As GCE was originally developed for supporting collaborative applications with a (hierarchical) linear data model and an operation model with three basic operations *Insert*, *Delete*, and *Update* [25], it is unable to provide full support for detecting and resolving dependency-conflict in collaborative DG-based 3D systems. To keep GCE generic, we have chosen to implement the main solutions of dependency-conflict detection (reported in this paper) and resolution (reported in [2]) in the middle-layer Maya-CA. As these solutions are generally applicable to DG-based real-time collaborative systems, they can be separated from Maya-CA and implemented as a sub-layer between Maya-CA and GCE, and this sub-layer can be shared by a range of DG-based collaborative systems for supporting dependency-conflict detection and resolution.

CONCLUSION AND FUTURE WORK

We have contributed a novel dependency-conflict detection solution, which is significant for dependency-conflict resolution in real-time collaborative 3D design systems. Dependency-conflict detection is a complex and challenging problem due to the dynamic nature of dependency relations among targets of concurrent operations and the need of the context-matching SDG (Simplified Dependency Graph) state that are often unavailable at the time of dependency-conflict detection. This work is the first to identify and solve the dependency-conflict detection problem in real-time collaborative 3D design environments. No such conflict detection issue has ever been encountered and addressed in prior Operational Transformation (OT) work. All algorithms and techniques presented in this paper have been implemented in the CoMaya real-time collaborative 3D design system.

Main elements of contributions include: (1) identification of the context-matching SDG state as one requirement for correct dependency relation detection; (2) identification and specification of SDG data and operation model for dependency relation detection; (3) a novel SDG difference technique to derive an unknown context-matching SDG state from the current SDG state, without undoing and redoing executed operations; (4) a novel OT-based solution to the problem of creating the SDG difference from context-difference operations; (5) identification of overlapping relations, instead of dependency relations, as the necessary condition for conflict among SDG operations, thus breaking the conflict-detection-cycle involved in creating the SDG difference; (6) an OT-based solution to SDG conflict; and (7) a novel SDG traversal algorithm based on the SDG difference and the current DG state, without deriving a real context-matching SDG state.

One main future work is to support group undo in the face of dependency-conflicts in real-time collaborative 3D design systems. Undo is essential to support the explorative nature of 3D design; hence, must be supported in real-time collaborative 3D design systems. Supporting group undo in real-time collaborative 3D design systems is expected to be as challenging as supporting the concurrent do due to the dependency-conflict problem.

ACKNOWLEDGEMENT
This research is partially supported by an Academic Research Fund Tier 1 Grant from Ministry of Education Singapore, and by Singapore National Research Foundation under its International Research Centre @ Singapore Funding Initiative and administered by the Interactive Digital Media Programme Office. The authors wish to thank anonymous reviewers for their insightful and constructive comments and suggestions.

REFERENCES

1. Agustina, F. Liu, S. Xia, H.F. Shen, and C. Sun. CoMaya: incorporating advance collaboration capabilities into 3D digital media design tools. In *Proc. ACM CSCW 2008*, 5-8.
2. Agustina, C. Sun, and D. Xu. Operational transformation for dependency conflict resolution in real-time collaborative 3D design systems. In *Proc. ACM CSCW 2012*, 1401-1410.
3. P. Dourish. Consistency guarantees: exploiting application semantics for consistency management in a collaboration toolkit. In *Proc. ACM CSCW 1996*, 268-277.
4. C.A. Ellis and S.J. Gibbs. Concurrency control in groupware systems. In *ACM SIGMOD 1989*, 399-407.
5. R. Galli and Y. Luo. Mu3D: a causal consistency protocol for a collaborative VRML editor. In *Proc. ACM Web3D-VRML 2000*, 53-62.
6. S. Greenberg. Sharing views and interactions with single-user applications. In *ACM SIGOIS and IEEE CS TC-OA 1990*, 227–237.
7. S. Greenberg and D. Marwood. Real time groupware as a distributed system: concurrency control and its effect on the interface. In *Proc. ACM CSCW 1994*, 207-217.
8. G. Hesina, D. Schmalstieg, A. Fuhrmann, and W. Purgathofer. Distributed Open Inventor: a practical approach to distributed 3D graphics. In *Proc. ACM VRST 1999*, 74-81.
9. C. Ignat and M. Norrie. Tree-based model algorithm for maintaining consistency in real-time collaborative editing systems. *Fourth International Workshop on Collaborative Editing, CSCW 2002, IEEE Distributed Systems online*, 2002.
10. C. Ignat and M. Norrie. Draw-Together: graphical editor for collaborative drawing. In *Proc. ACM CSCW 2006*, 269-278.
11. R. Kanawati. Licra: a replicated-data management algorithm for distributed synchronous groupware application. *Parallel Computing*, 22, 1997, 1733-1746.
12. L. Lamport. Time, clocks, and the ordering of events in a distributed systems. *Communication of ACM*, 21(7), 1978, 558-565.
13. J. Munson and P. Dewan. A concurrency control framework for collaborative systems. In *Proc. ACM CSCW 1996*, 278-287.
14. M. Naef, E. Lamboray, O. Staadt, and M. Gross. The blue-c distributed scene graph. *ACM IPT/EGCE Workshop 2003*, 125-133.
15. D.A. Nicholas, P. Curtis, M. Dixon, and J. Lamping. High-latency, low-bandwidth windowing in the Jupiter collaboration system. In *Proc. ACM UIST 1995*, 111-120.
16. K.P. Picott, B. McPherson, W.D. Angus, and I.V. Nagendra. System and method for using dependency graphs for the control of a graphics creation process. *U.S. Patent No. 5,808,625*, 1998.
17. H. Shen and C. Sun. Achieving data consistency by contextualization in web-based collaborative applications. *ACM TOIT*, 10(4), 2011.
18. R. Stoll. Set Theory and Logic. *New York: Dover Publications*, 1979.
19. C. Sun. Undo as concurrent inverse in group editors. *ACM TOCHI*, 9(4), 2002, 309-361.
20. C. Sun, D. Chen. A multi-version approach to conflict resolution in distributed groupware systems. In *Proc. IEEE ICDCS 2000*, 316-325.
21. C. Sun and C.A. Ellis. Operational tranformation in real-time group editors: issues, algorithms, and achievements. In *Proc. ACM CSCW 1998*, 59-68.
22. C. Sun, X. Jia, Y. Zhang, Y. Yang, and D. Chen. Achieving convergence, causality preservation, and intention preservations in real-time cooperative editing systems. *ACM TOCHI*, 5(1), 1998, 63-108.
23. D. Sun and C. Sun. Context-based operational transformation in distributed collaborative editing systems. *IEEE TPDS*, 20(10), 2009, 1454-1470.
24. D. Sun, S. Xia, C. Sun, and D. Chen. Operational transformation for collaborative word processing. In *Proc. ACM CSCW 2004*, 437-446.
25. C. Sun, S. Xia, D. Sun, D. Chen, H.F. Shen, and W. Cai. Transparent adaptation of single-user applications for multi-user real-time collaboration. *ACM TOCHI*, 13(4), 2006, 531-582.
26. C. Sun, H. Wen and H. Fan. Operational transformation for orthogonal conflict resolution in real-time collaborative 2D editing systems. In *Proc. ACM CSCW 2012*, 1391-1400.
27. H. Tramberend. Avocado: a distributed virtual reality framework. In *Proc. IEEE VR 1999*, 14-21.

XPointer: An X-ray Telepointer for Relaxed-space-time WYSIWIS and Unconstrained Collaborative 3D Design Systems

Agustina
BeingThere Centre, Institute for Media Innovation
Nanyang Technological University, Singapore
agustina@ntu.edu.sg

Chengzheng Sun
School of Computer Engineering
Nanyang Technological University, Singapore
czsun@ntu.edu.sg

ABSTRACT
Telepointers are a real-time collaborative feature to indicate pointing at shared objects. Existing telepointing techniques are, however, restricted to pointing at the foremost object underneath a mouse cursor in *relaxed-space* but *strict-time* WYSIWIS environments. In real-time collaborative 3D design systems with animation creation capabilities, multiple 3D objects can be simultaneously visible underneath mouse cursors for users to freely and concurrently work on and point at (*unconstrained* collaboration), and multiple users can view 3D workspaces and point from different viewing perspectives (*relaxed-space* WYSIWIS) and animation time frames (*relaxed-time* WYSIWIS). This paper contributes a novel *XPointer* technique with the capability of pointing through objects correctly and consistently from different viewing perspectives and time frames, even in the presence of concurrent editing work. This work is the first to identify and address these advanced 3D telepointing needs and capabilities, and to extend the concept of relaxed WYSIWIS to include the time aspect. The XPointer has been implemented in the *CoMaya* real-time collaborative 3D design system (demonstration video: http://cooffice.ntu.edu.sg/comaya/videoXPointer.php).

Author Keywords
X-ray telepointers; workspace awareness; real-time collaborative 3D design systems; unconstrained collaboration; relaxed WYSIWIS; consistent telepointing.

ACM Classification Keywords
D.2.2 [**Software Engineering**]: Design Tools and Techniques – User Interfaces; H.5.3 [**Information Interfaces and Presentation**]: Group and Organization Interfaces – Computer-Supported Cooperative Work.

INTRODUCTION
Telepointers are representations of remote users' mouse cursor positions on shared workspaces in real-time collaborative systems. Telepointers can be used to refer to shared objects of common interest [2, 9, 17, 24] and make gestures in overlapped workspaces [11], and hence help simplify verbal communication and achieve fluid and natural collaboration. Prior research has shown that telepointers are also important in improving the usability of real-time collaborative systems [10].

Many real-time collaborative systems have benefited from using telepointers. In this paper, we are particularly interested in telepointing techniques for real-time collaborative 3D design systems with *relaxed WYSIWIS* and *unconstrained collaborative* environments, i.e. systems that allow multiple geographically dispersed users to freely and concurrently view and edit any 3D object in the shared 3D workspace from different viewing perspectives and animation time frames [1]. Such techniques are required to support ad hoc, spontaneous and fine-grained interaction and collaboration that often arises during complex and unstructured processes of 3D content creation. In the interaction and collaboration process, designers often need to refer to shared 3D objects of common interest, e.g. for clear and precise discussion on design problems and solutions of specific shared 3D objects. Telepointers are not only a useful but also a necessary tool for real-time collaborative 3D design systems.

A telepointer in desktop-based real-time collaborative 3D design systems is typically controlled using a mouse [3]. To point at an object, the user moves the mouse cursor to overlap with the pointing target and telepointers at remote collaborating sites are relocated accordingly to reflect this pointing. The target of the pointing is the object that is directly underneath the mouse cursor [3]. The target of the pointing is clear if there is only one object underneath the cursor. However, if there are multiple such objects (e.g. the transparent cup, apple, and tree are all underneath the mouse cursor in Figure 1), which of these objects should be the target? Any of these objects could be a valid target!

In professional single-user 3D design systems, such as Autodesk Maya[1] and 3ds Max[2], objects may be displayed semi transparently to allow users to see through and

[1] http://usa.autodesk.com/3ds-max/
[2] http://usa.autodesk.com/maya/

CSCW '13, February 23–27, 2013, San Antonio, Texas, USA.

Figure 1. The mouse cursor is on top of multiple objects: the (transparent) cup, apple, and tree (time frame 24).

efficiently work on objects behind/within other objects. For example in Figure 1, the cup is made transparent to allow users to view and edit the apple, cherry, and peanuts within the cup, and the tree behind the cup. Such useful features should be retained in real-time collaborative 3D design systems. With the ability of seeing through objects, collaborating users will naturally expect a similar capability of telepointing at any object they can see. However, existing telepointer techniques (both 2D [9, 17, 24] and 3D [3, 8, 14]) have never considered such scenarios and restrict the telepointing at the foremost object only, even though there are multiple objects visible underneath the cursor. For the cursor position in Figure 1, only the transparent cup can be pointed using existing telepointer techniques.

If existing telepointer techniques are used to point at blocked objects (e.g. the apple in Figure 1), users have to resort to an ad hoc solution: to change their viewing perspectives or move/hide blocking objects so that the pointing target is no longer blocked and becomes the foremost object. Those ad hoc solutions work in some circumstances, but they are inconvenient, inefficient, and even impossible under some other circumstances. First, in complex 3D scenes, objects of interest may be blocked by various objects in different viewing perspectives, thus multiple actions are needed to find/create a suitable viewing perspective for the pointing. Second, objects of interest may be blocked from all viewing perspectives (e.g. the apple in Figure 1 is blocked by the cup from all directions), thus changing the viewing perspective will never unveil the blocked object for pointing. Last and most important, moving/hiding blocking objects will interfere with the work on these objects by other collaborating users, particularly those users who are not involved in the discussion related to the pointing. Concurrent viewing, pointing, and editing are characteristics of unconstrained collaboration to be supported by advanced real-time collaborative 3D design systems. Under those circumstances, pointing through blocking objects is the only solution. This is the motivation behind our work of a novel x-ray telepointing technique, named as *XPointer*. As we will show later, it is challenging to support XPointers in advanced real-time collaborative 3D design systems with unconstrained collaboration and relaxed-space-time WYSIWIS supports.

For users to obtain meaningful reference information, it is important that XPointers are *correct* and *consistent* at all collaborating sites [3, 24], i.e. all XPointers of the same user must point precisely at the same point on the target

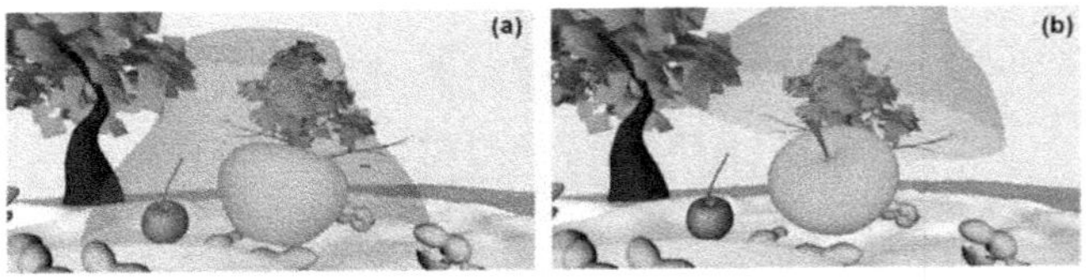

Figure 2. Remote workspaces in different time frames: (a) time frame 24, and (b) time frame 6.

object and penetrating through the same set of objects as defined by the user. In unconstrained collaborative environments, an XPointing operation may be generated concurrently with multiple editing operations that change the objects underneath the mouse cursor and hence the penetrated and/or target objects of the XPointing. Without a special concurrency control measure, XPointers may inconsistently penetrate through and point at different objects at different collaborating sites. A few telepointer consistency maintenance techniques have been proposed [3, 24]. But, none of those techniques can be directly used for maintaining the consistency of XPointers because those techniques are invented for telepointers with the capability of pointing at the foremost objects only, but XPointers are capable of pointing beyond the foremost objects.

XPointers must also correctly and precisely point at the same point on the target even when they are viewed from different viewing perspectives and animation time frames (*relaxed WYSIWIS* (What You See Is What I See) [9, 17, 18]). Relaxed WYSIWIS is one requirement of unconstrained collaboration, which complements the group need for *strict WYSIWIS*, in which all collaborating users see the same information [18]. In different viewing perspectives (*relaxed-space WYSIWIS*), different objects are within the viewing scope and the same object can be rendered onto different locations of a 2D viewport. In different time frames (*relaxed-time WYSIWIS*), the same object can be in different positions, orientations, shapes, etc. in the 3D space according to their animation, thus objects can also be in different locations of the viewport even though the viewing perspective is the same (see Figure 2). Prior research has recognized the need for supporting telepointers in relaxed-space WYSIWIS environments [9, 17]. Nevertheless, none of existing telepointing techniques has dealt with the relaxed-time WYSIWIS requirement. As a result, telepointers may point at different targets or different points on the target as objects may be in different positions, orientations, sizes, physical appearances, etc., in different animation time frames. The XPointer will be designed to support telepointing in both relaxed-space and relaxed-time WYSIWIS. Such telepointing capabilities will be useful and favorable in discussing animation-independent aspects of shared objects since the pointing effort can be reduced by eliminating the need to synchronize the users' viewing time frames before the pointing. For example, a texture artist in time frame 24 (Figure 1) can directly use the XPointer to point at a cup model for a quick discussion on the cup's texture with an animator in time frame 6 (Figure

2-(b)) who views the cup on a different 3D position and orientation. Such pointing is meaningful because the texture of the cup is not animated and it does not matter from which time frame it is viewed, pointed and discussed.

This work is the first to identify the needs for and issues in supporting telepointing through objects in relaxed-space-time WYSIWIS and unconstrained collaborative 3D environments. The XPointer has the following capabilities: (1) XPointing at any point of any object, whether it is the foremost or blocked object, in the shared 3D workspace; (2) consistent XPointing in dynamic content changes by concurrent editing operations in unconstrained collaborative environments; and (3) correct XPointing in relaxed-space-time WYSIWIS environments. Our aim is to make telepointing effortless so that more instant and informal interaction can be encouraged and consequently, the quality of real-time collaborative 3D design work can be increased.

The rest of the paper is organized as follows. First, we discuss some related work in the field of 3D user interface for virtual reality, and introduce the pointer-target association concept. Afterwards, we present the design of XPointers and their user interfaces for supporting effective XPointing, and we discuss the issues raised by concurrent work and relaxed-space-time WYSIWIS environments and present their solutions. Then, we discuss the extension of XPointers for supporting XPointing at the 3D space. Next, we discuss various combinations of relaxed/strict space/time WYSIWIS that can be supported by XPointers. Finally, we outline the usability questions and tasks for future evaluation study and summarize the main contributions of this work.

RELATED WORK IN 3D USER INTERFACE

The XPointer work is related to the work in the field of 3D user interfaces, particularly the distant object interaction, occlusion management, and collaborative object manipulation in virtual reality. Existing techniques for pointing/selecting objects at distance are hand extension techniques (e.g. *go-go* [16]), in which the avatar's hand is extended to the target; and ray-casting techniques (e.g. *put-that-there* [6]), in which a ray is casted from the user's (or avatar's) hand to intersect with the target. Those techniques are generally limited to pointing/selecting only the closest object and do not deal with occluded targets.

In contrast, the *WIM* [19] allows users to view the miniature of the 3D space from different perspectives, thus supporting interaction with blocked objects from different perspectives. The *Flexible Pointer* [13] allows users to bend the ray cursor to point at *partially* occluded objects. However, none of these techniques allows users to point at *fully* occluded objects from the same view. The *3D Bubble Cursor* and *Augmented Depth-Ray* [22] are two techniques that allow selection of, instead of pointing at, fully occluded objects, thus cannot be used to point at different surface points on a target object. There are other techniques

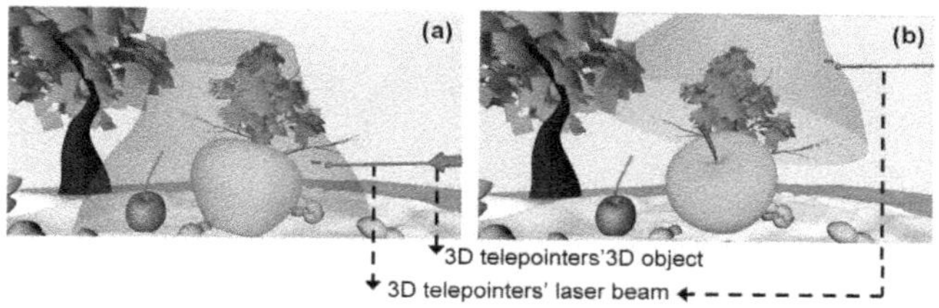

Figure 3. Remote pointer-target associations at the cup in different time frames: (a) time frame 24; and (b) time frame 6.

for overcoming occlusion [7], but they are designed for visualization, not for pointing either. Moreover, none of those techniques was designed for and capable of working in real-time unconstrained collaborative 3D design environments, where the blocked targets or blocking objects may be freely and concurrently changed by multiple users.

There exist some 3D interaction techniques for supporting collaboration in immersive virtual environments, such as the work by Pinho et al. [15] that allows concurrent manipulations on the same object by combining those manipulations. But these techniques are for manipulating the foremost object, not for pointing at the foremost or blocked objects; thus, they cannot be used to pointing at different points on the same object. In addition, these techniques do not address consistency issues involving multiple objects, e.g. in the scenarios of concurrent pointing and object manipulation addressed in this work.

BACKGROUND ON 3D TELEPOINTERS AND POINTER-TARGET ASSOCIATION

A pointing action establishes a *pointer-target association* relationship between the pointing device and the pointed target [3]. In both desktop-based single-user and multi-user 3D design systems, the mouse is the commonly used input device and the user moves the mouse cursor to point at an object. The pointer-target association is established by the fact that the mouse cursor is on top of the target object in the 2D screen display. The same association is reflected at remote sites by relocating the telepointers.

Pointer-target associations in distributed collaborative 3D design systems are subtle. In those systems, a telepointer is represented as a 3D object (e.g. a 3D arrow) embedded inside the shared 3D workspace [3, 8, 14]. A telepointer's 3D object is placed in the 3D workspace at the viewing position of the mouse user and oriented towards the target. To establish the pointer-target association, remote users must be able to identify the object that is in the pointing direction. This association is non-trivial and could easily go wrong because users are often viewing from different perspectives and there is a space gap between the telepointer's 3D object and the target [3,23].

To help the establishment of pointer-target associations at remote sites, prior research has proposed various explicit visual effects (e.g. laser beam [3, 14], stretchable arm [8], etc.) between the telepointer's 3D object and the target. Thus, the pointer-target association is established by the

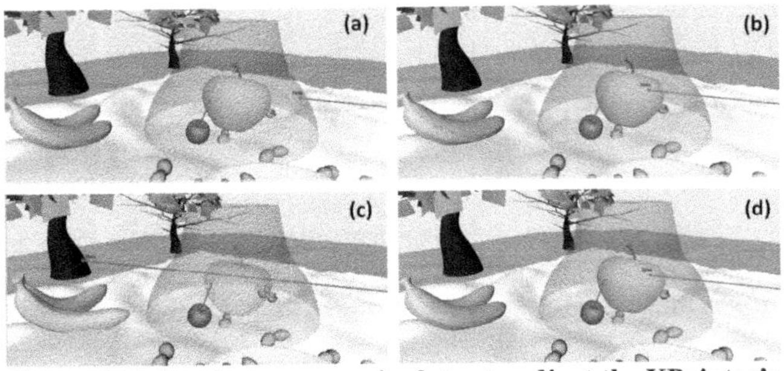

Figure 4. Using the x-ray manipulator to adjust the XPointer's penetration border-object to: (a) near plane (initial and default); (b) the cup (first increment); (c) the apple (second increment); and (d) the cup again (a decrement). After each penetration adjustment, the XPointer is pointing at: (a) the cup; (b) the apple; (c) the tree; and (d) the apple again.

fact that the explicit visual effect from the telepointer's 3D object ends at the target. Figure 3-(a) shows an example of a pointer-target association establishment of a 3D telepointer and the transparent cup at a remote site, based on the cursor position in Figure 1.

MAIN COMPONENTS OF XPOINTERS

XPointers retain the normal user experience of using a mouse and the capability of a conventional 3D telepointer to point at the foremost object. To point beyond the foremost object, the XPointer's penetration can be adjusted using the *x-ray manipulator*. The target of the XPointer is always the object in the pointing direction immediately after the last object penetrated by the XPointer (called the *penetration border-object* or *border-object* for short). To help the mouse user in establishing the pointer-target association, the XPointer is augmented with the *oblique-view* – an additional view from a different perspective.

The X-ray Manipulator

The *x-ray manipulator*, one of the fundamental components of the XPointer, is an interface technique for adjusting the XPointer's penetration. By default, the border-object of an XPointer is the *view frustum*'s *near plane* [3] and the XPointing target is the closest object to the XPointer in the pointing direction as in a conventional 3D telepointer. The mouse user can use the x-ray manipulator to increase or decrease the XPointer's penetration, thus changing the XPointing target to a further or closer object in the pointing direction. As a new pointer-target association is established, the new XPointing target will be highlighted, objects that are penetrated by the XPointer will be displayed semi-transparently (the degree of transparency is adjustable by the user), and objects that were previously penetrated but are now not penetrated by the XPointer will be displayed in solid. It is worth pointing out that originally semi-transparent objects are not implicitly assumed as objects that must be penetrated by the XPointer because the user may still want to point at these objects. This x-ray manipulator interface can be attached to input devices in various ways, e.g. a keyboard shortcut can be assigned to activate and attach the x-ray manipulator to the mouse

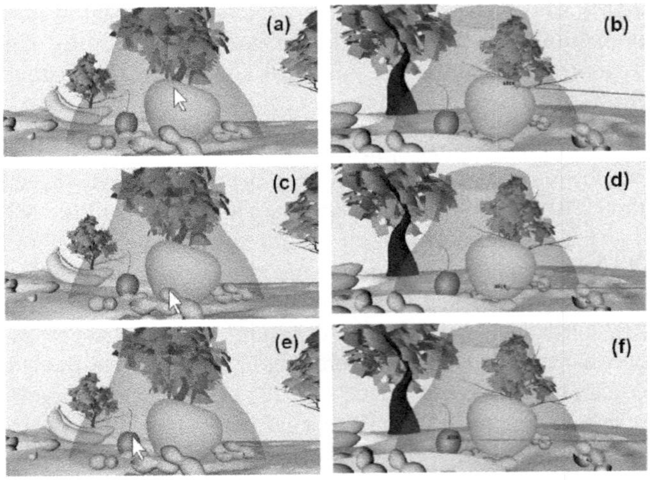

Figure 5. For different mouse cursor positions in (a), (c), and (e), the XPointer at a remote site, which is in a different viewing perspective, intelligently maintains the cup as the penetration border-object and points at the apple in (b) and (d), and the cherry in (f).

wheel so that scrolling up or down the mouse wheel will increment or decrement the XPointer's penetration.

Consider the mouse cursor position in Figure 1. Initially the XPointer is pointing at the cup, which is the foremost object underneath the mouse cursor (Figure 4-(a)). After the first penetration increment, the XPointer is penetrating through the cup and pointing at the apple (Figure 4-(b)), and after the second increment, the XPointer is penetrating through both the cup and the apple and pointing at the tree (Figure 4-(c)). Notice that the second penetration increment does not result in pointing at the back surface of the cup because the penetration is applied to the entire object, rather than a specific surface. After a follow-up penetration decrement, the XPointer is pointing at the apple again (Figure 4-(d)).

Once the mouse user has determined the XPointer's penetration border-object, s/he can freely move the mouse cursor while the system intelligently maintains the penetration border-object by: (a) automatically penetrating (and displaying in semi-transparent) those objects that were not penetrated in the prior pointing direction but are now closer than the border-object in the current pointing direction; and (b) not penetrating (and displaying in solid) those objects that were penetrated in the prior pointing direction but are now further than the border-object or no longer in the current pointing direction. If the border-object is no longer in the new pointing direction, the XPointer will automatically set its new border-object to an object in the current pointing direction that was the furthest before the original border-object in the prior pointing direction.

These XPointer's behaviors are useful when collaborating users are discussing about objects beyond certain blocking objects because the mouse user can conveniently XPoint at any object beyond the border-object without having to repeatedly adjust the XPointer's penetration whenever the

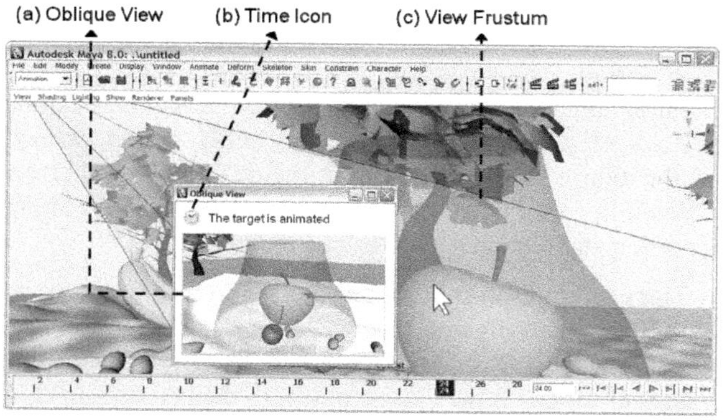

Figure 6. The visual components of XPointers: (a) an oblique-view; (b) a time icon indicates that the target is animated; and (c) a view frustum (the yellow truncated pyramid) reflects the remote user's viewing scope and time frame (dimmer if the time frame is different).

objects along the pointing direction changes as the mouse moves. Figure 5 illustrates these XPointer's behaviors to maintain the cup as the border-object. Figure 5-(a), (c), and (e) show the workspace of the mouse user, and Figure 5-(b), (d), and (f) show the workspace of a remote site that is in a different viewing perspective than the mouse user. Originally, the mouse cursor is hovering the apple (Figure 5-(a)) and the XPointer's border-object is the cup and the target is the apple (Figure 5-(b)). When the user moves the mouse cursor to be on top of the bottom of the apple (Figure 5-(c)), the XPointer maintains the apple as the target and the cup as the border-object by penetrating through the peanut (which is closer to the XPointer than the border-object), in addition to the cup. And when the user moves the mouse cursor to be on top of the cherry (Figure 5-(e)), the border-object at the cup is unchanged either, but the peanut that is no longer in the pointing direction is no longer penetrated and the XPointer is now pointing at the cherry (Figure 5-(f)).

The x-ray manipulator is similar to the *depth marker* control of the Depth Ray tool [22]. However, the depth marker is not able to intelligently maintain the border-object. Besides, its behavior in unconstrained collaborative environments is not discussed. As pointed out earlier and will be discussed in details in the next section, there are special and challenging telepointing consistency issues in unconstrained collaborative 3D design environments.

The Oblique View

In a conventional 3D telepointer, the pointer-target association is simple and intuitive to the local mouse user since the target is always the foremost object underneath the mouse cursor. In XPointers, however, the target can be any 3D object underneath the mouse cursor, how can the mouse user know whether his/her XPointer has penetrated beyond the right object to point at the right target, and whether further penetration adjustments should be done?

To address this issue, we augment the XPointer with the *oblique-view*, which provides a 90 degree difference view of the 3D workspace from the main view as shown in Figure 6-(a). In this view, a *virtual local* XPointer appearing from the right of the view is used to assist the local pointer-target association: the target is the 3D object at which the XPointer's light beam ends. To better assist the mouse user in establishing the local pointer-target association, this view has a focused scope covering the border-object and ending point of the light beam. An oblique-view is available throughout the XPointing process and its content is updated instantly upon a mouse move, a view change, or an XPointer's penetration adjustment.

Other Visual Components for Effective XPointing and its Interpretation in Relaxed WYSIWIS

For an effective XPointing in relaxed-space-time WYSIWIS, the local mouse user must be provided with necessary information to judge whether a remote user will be able to see the pointing. The pieces of information to make this judgment include: (1) the remote user's viewing scope; (2) the remote user's working time frame; and (3) whether the target is animated. To reflect the viewing scope of a remote user, the XPointer is augmented with the *view frustum* awareness widget (Figure 7-(c)) [3, 8]. To indicate that the remote user is in a different time frame, the view frustum is displayed dimmer. To indicate to the mouse user that the target is animated, a time icon is shown on the top of the oblique-view window (Figure 6-(b)) and a sound effect is played upon the pointer-target association.

In interpreting an XPointing, remote users may need to know whether the XPointing is initiated from the same or a different time frame. An XPointer records the information about the *pointing time frame* (i.e. the time frame of the mouse user when the XPointing operation is issued) and the XPointer is displayed in a dimmer color if the pointing time frame is different from the *viewing time frame* (i.e. the time frame of a remote user when the XPointer is viewed). Though it is not required, it can be beneficial to view an XPointing from the same time frame in some situations (e.g. when the target is invisible in the viewing time frame). In such cases, the pointing time frame information recorded in the XPointer can be used to allow remote users to quickly jump to the pointing time frame for viewing the XPointing.

SUPPORTING XPOINTERS IN UNCONSTRAINED COLLABORATIVE ENVIRONMENTS

XPointer Correctness and Consistency

An XPointer should reflect the mouse's current cursor position on the viewing plane, pointing direction, and the x-ray penetration. The mouse user can change the XPointer by: (1) moving the mouse cursor, which changes the position of the XPointer's 3D object on the viewing plane; (2) changing the view perspective, which changes the location of the viewing plane, and thus the position of XPointer's 3D object, in the 3D workspace; and (3) incrementing/decrementing the XPointer's penetration using the x-ray manipulator, which changes the penetration border-object. Mouse cursor movements and view changes may also change the objects penetrated by the XPointer,

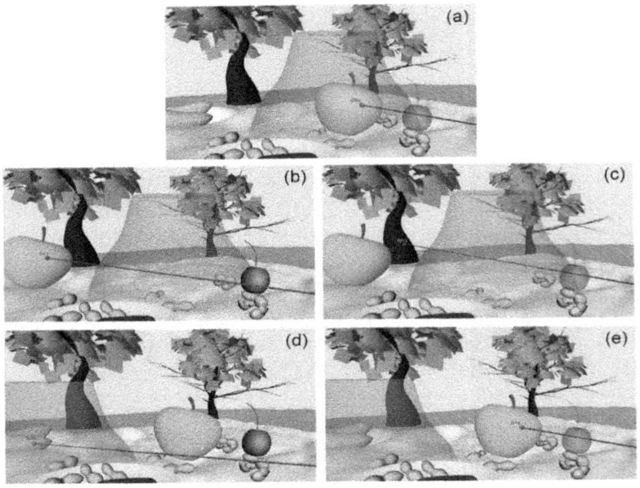

Figure 7. XPointer consistency. (a) the XPointer user intends to penetrate both the cherry and cup and point at the apple. (b) incorrect XPointing at the apple in a different remote workspace state, which was changed as the apple was moved out of the pointing direction; (c) correct XPointing at the tree, preserving the cup border-object in the same remote workspace state as in (b); (d) incorrect XPointing at the banana in a different remote workspace state, which was changed as the cup was moved out of the pointing direction; and (e) correct XPointing at the apple with the cherry as the border-object in the same remote workspace state as in (d).

and all these activities may change the pointer-target association as well. We need to detect these changes and propagated them as *XPointer update* operations to remote sites to adjust XPointers' positions, penetrations, and/or pointer-target associations.

One naïve way of adjusting the XPointers at remote sites could be: (1) record the viewing position and the identifier of the new target and the mouse in the XPointer update operation; and (2) at each destination site: (a) use the recorded mouse identifier and viewing position to find the XPointer and reposition the XPointer's 3D object; and (b) use the recorded target identifier to find the target, reorient the XPointer's 3D object towards the target, and establish the new pointer-target association: a virtual light-beam is extended from the XPointer's 3D object to the target penetrating all objects in-between by displaying them in semi-transparent. This scheme works only if the destination workspace state is the same as the local workspace state from which the XPointer update operation was generated, but fails in the face of concurrent editing and XPointer update operations.

Before the XPointer update operation arrives at a remote site, the remote workspace state may have been changed concurrently by other users; e.g. the original target object (the apple in Figure 7-(a)) may have been moved to a different place in the 3D workspace such that it may no longer in the original pointing direction (see the apple in Figure 7-(b)). If the pointer-target association establishment were based on the target identifier captured in the XPointer update operation (as in Figure 7-(b)), then this XPointing may be *incorrect* for two reasons. First, the XPointing direction may no longer reflect the original mouse user's pointing direction. Second, the associated target may not be the closest object to the penetration border-object defined by the mouse user (i.e. the cup in Figure 7-(a)). The correct XPointing should be preserving the original pointing direction and border-object (as in Figure 7-(c)).

A naïve solution to this incorrect XPointing problem is to record the identifier of the border-object, instead of the target, in the XPointer update operation; and use this identifier to search the closest object to the border-object to be the new associated target. This solution will solve the problem in remote workspace states that are changed due to the original target object has been moved away (as in Figure 7-(c)). But, it will fail on other workspace changes, e.g. instead of the target, the original border-object (the cup in Figure 7-(d)) is the one that has been moved out of the pointing direction. If the original border-object were used in establishing the pointer-target association (as in Figure 7-(d)), the XPointer may still be incorrect as the XPointing direction may still no longer reflect the original mouse user's pointing direction. The question is what should be the new border-object in the pointing direction used in determining the pointer-target association?

As an XPointer is a device for pointing beyond objects, the x-ray penetration defined by the mouse user should be preserved as far as possible. If the original border-object is no longer in the pointing direction, the object immediately before the original border-object should be the new border-object. If this object is no longer in the pointing direction either, then the object immediately before it should be the new border-object, and so on. This behavior is a favorable behavior to the mouse user, because his/her XPointer will remain pointing at the same target as long as it is still in the pointing direction, even though the border-object has changed; and will remain penetrating the objects s/he intends to point beyond, even though objects in between the original border-object and XPointer object have changed. In the previous example, the new border-object should be the cherry, and the XPointer should be pointing at the apple as shown in Figure 7-(e).

To summarize, an XPointing is *correct* only if:

1. the XPointing's position and direction reflect the mouse user's pointing position and direction;
2. the border-object is the furthest object that the mouse user intends to penetrate and is still in the pointing direction; and
3. the target of the XPointing is the closest object to the current border-object in the pointing direction.

One can argue that an XPointing should preserve the pointing target, not the penetration, defined by the mouse user. This argument is valid and indeed a desired XPointer behavior if the mouse user has settled with the XPointing and is in the middle of the discussion about the target object. But, if the mouse user is still making the XPointing, e.g. s/he is in the process of adjusting the penetration using the x-ray manipulator or moving the mouse to be overlapping with the target s/he intends to point, then the *penetration-preservation* XPointer will be more desirable. This is because if the penetration of the XPointer is preserved, the mouse user needs not readjust the XPointer penetration even though the penetrated objects and/or border-object have been changed by other users concurrently. Therefore, the target-preserving XPointer and the penetration-preserving XPointer are complementary to each other: the penetration-preserving XPointer should be used when the user is in the process of making the XPointing, and the target-preserving XPointer should be used when the user has fixed the pointing target. In our current implementation, we set the XPointer to be penetration-preserving by default, but the mouse user can switch the XPointer to be target-preserving through a keyboard shortcut. In the future, we plan to increase the usability of the XPointer by enhancing the XPointer with an automated adaptive penetration capability, i.e. the penetration behavior of the XPointer can be automatically adjusted according to the mouse user's XPointing activities.

In unconstrained collaborative environments, an XPointing update operation can be generated concurrently with not only one, but multiple editing operations that change the workspace states and affect the XPointing. XPointers are *consistent* if after executing the same set of XPointing update and editing operations, they are identical across all collaborating sites. In the remaining of this section, we will discuss how to maintain correct and consistent XPointers in unconstrained collaborative 3D design environments.

Maintaining Consistent XPointing

An XPointing update operation may be generated concurrently with editing operations that change the objects in the pointing direction, thus affect the border-object and target of the XPointer. In establishing a correct pointer-target association at a remote site, the target of the XPointer should be decided based on the current border-object, and the border-object should be decided based on the original penetrated objects. Therefore, the information about which objects and the order they are being penetrated by the XPointer when the XPointing update operation is generated is crucial for the remote XPointer's pointer-target association establishment, and thus, should be recorded in the XPointing update operation together with the mouse user's identifier, viewing position, and pointing direction.

The *Dynamic XPointing Effects Determination* (DXED) algorithm sketched in Algorithm 1 dynamically determines the correct and consistent target and border-object based on the execution context. *DXED* takes three inputs parameters, the list of identifiers of penetrated objects (called *Penetration List* (*PL*)), the pointing position *pos* and the pointing direction *dir*, which are recorded in the XPointing update operation. Objects in *PL* are sorted according to their distances to the XPointer object, from the furthest to the closest; hence, the first object in *PL* is the border-object set by the XPointer user.

Algorithm 1: *DXED*(*PL*, *pos*, *dir*)

PDL[ ] := objects in pointing direction *dir* from position *pos*;
BO_index := *BOD*(*PL*, *pos*, *dir*, *PDL*);
if *BO_index* < *PDL.length*() **then return** *PDL*[*BO_index* + 1];
else return *far_end*; //pointing at the far-end

Routine 1: *BOD*(*PL*, *pos*, *dir*, *PDL*)

for each *PL*[*i*] **where** $1 \le i \le PL.length()$ **do**
  for each *PDL*[*j*] **where** $1 \le j \le PDL.length()$ **do**
    if *PL*[*i*] = *PDL*[*j*] **then return** *j*;
return 0; //the boder-object is the near plane

The *DXED* algorithm first obtains the list of objects along the pointing direction *dir* starting from the pointing position *pos*, and stores them in a sorted list (called *Pointing Direction List* (*PDL*)) based on their distances to the XPointer object (from the closest (left-most) to the furthest (right-most)). Then DXED invokes the *Border-Object Determination* (*BOD*) routine to determine the valid border-object; i.e. the furthest object in *PL* that is still in the pointing direction.

The *BOD* routine works as follows. The border-object in *PL* is checked to see whether it is still in the pointing direction (i.e. whether it is in *PDL*). If yes, the index of the border-object in *PDL* is returned. But if the border-object in *PL* is no longer in *PDL*, the object next to the border-object in *PL* is taken as the new border-object and the same check is performed to see whether it is in *PDL*; this process repeats until all objects in *PL* are examined but none of them is found in *PDL*. In that case, the routine returns 0 to indicate that the border-object is the near plane of the XPointer user's viewing frustum.

After *BOD* routine returns, *DXED* determines and returns the closest object to the border-object as the target. If the border-object is not the right-most object in *PDL*, it returns the identifier of the object after the recorded index in *PDL* as the target; otherwise, it returns the far-end information. After the target is determined, the XPointer's representation is updated accordingly to reflect this new XPointing effect.

Correcting the XPointer after Editing Operations

In-between two XPointing update operations, the XPointing effect may be changed by subsequent editing operations that change the objects along the pointing direction, such as the original target is moved/deleted, the border-object is moved, and other objects are moved out of/into the pointing direction. The XPointing effects must be corrected at all collaborating sites (including at the mouse user site) upon the generation and execution of such editing operations by invoking the *DXED* algorithm with the current penetration list, pointing position, and pointing direction of the XPointer as the input parameters.

Editing operations that affect XPointing effects may be generated sequentially or concurrently. There is one special

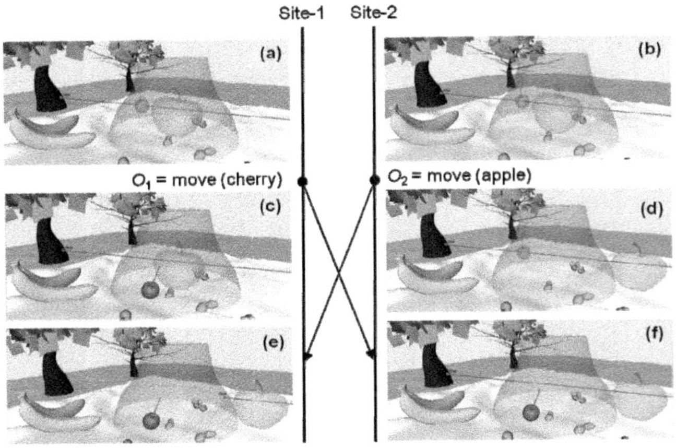

Figure 8. Inconsistencies due to concurrent editing operations after XPointing: (a) and (b) initially pointing at the same tree with the cherry as the border-object; (c) pointing at the tree after the cherry is moved and the border-object is updated to the apple; (d) still pointing at the tree after the apple is moved as the cherry remains as the border-object; (e) pointing at the cup with the apple as the border-object after all operations are executed; and (f) pointing at the tree with the cup as the border-object after all operations are executed.

consistency issue if multiple editing operations concurrently change the objects along the pointing direction, as illustrated in Figure 8. Initially the XPointer is pointing at the tree penetrating through the cherry (the border-object), apple, and cup (Figure 8-(a) and (b)). Two editing operations are concurrently generated: O_1 to move the cherry out of the pointing direction at *site-1*, and O_2 to move the apple before the cup but still in the pointing direction at *site-2*. At *site-1*, after the generation of O_1 (Figure 8-(c)), as the cherry is no longer in the pointing direction, the apple, which was the object immediately before the cherry (Figure 8-(a)), becomes the new border-object, but the XPointer remains pointing at the tree, which is still the closest object to the new border-object. And after the execution of the remote operation O_2 (Figure 8-(e)), the XPointer is updated to point at the cup, which is now the closest object to the same border-object, the apple. At *site-2*, after the generation of O_2 (Figure 8-(d)), the XPointer remains pointing at the tree, which is still the closest object to the same border-object, the cherry. And after the execution of O_1 (Figure 8-(f)), as the cherry is no longer in the pointing direction, the cup, which was the object immediately before the cherry (Figure 8-(d)), becomes the new border-object, but the target is still the tree, which is the closest object to the cup. After the execution of both editing operations and corrections of XPointers in different orders, the XPointers at the two sites are inconsistent: the XPointer at *site*-1 is pointing at the cup (Figure 8-(e)) but the XPointer at *site*-2 is pointing at the tree (Figure 8-(f)).

This inconsistency issue is caused by concurrent and independent updates of the XPointer's border-object at different sites based on a different current XPointer's penetration list changed by the concurrent editing operations. To solve this problem, the original penetration list determined by the XPointer user (propagated in the XPointing update operation and to be recorded by the XPointer afterwards) should always be the one used as the input to the *DXED* algorithm, i.e. instead of the current penetration list of the XPointer. Consistency can be guaranteed because there is only one user that can change the border-object, i.e. the XPointer user.

For the scenario in Figure 8, objects in the original penetration list are the cherry, apple, and cup. After the execution of both operations, *site*-1 and *site*-2 will invoke the *DXED* algorithm based on this original penetration list. As the workspace states and input penetration lists are identical at the two sites (which is guaranteed by the document consistency maintenance technique such as in [2, 20]), the *DXED* at both sites will determine the same object, i.e. the cup, as the XPointer target. This is because at both site, the border-object is updated to the apple based on the original penetration list as the previous border-object (i.e. cherry) is no longer in the pointing direction.

SUPPORTING XPOINTERS IN RELAXED-TIME WYSIWIS ENVIRONMENTS

In different time frames of relaxed-time WYSIWIS environments, the target of the XPointer can be in different positions, orientations, shapes, etc. in the shared 3D workspace. Regardless which time frame remote users are working in, XPointers must point at not only the same 3D object but also the same point on the 3D object. For example in Figure 4, the XPointer must point at the same point of the cup in both time frames 24 and 6.

However, the basic *DXED* algorithm presented in Algorithm 1 can achieve consistent XPointing effects only if the viewing time frame is the same as the pointing time frame. This is because objects in *PDL*, which play an important role in the *DXED* algorithm, are different in different time frames. Consider the XPointing at the cup in time frame 24 in Figure 1 (since the cup is the closest object, *PL* is an empty list). Upon receiving this XPointing operation at a remote site that is in viewing time frame 6 (Figure 2-(b)), the basic *DXED* algorithm is invoked based on this viewing time frame; the *DXED* algorithm determines that the target is the apple, which is the closest object in the pointing direction in this time frame. This XPointing is incorrect and inconsistent with the XPointing at the cup initiated by the mouse user.

To achieve correct and consistent XPointing effects in relaxed-time WYSIWIS, the *DXED* algorithm must be coupled with a *time-translation* scheme: firstly, the basic *DXED* algorithm is invoked to determine the target in the original pointing time frame; then the UV coordinate (i.e. a 2D coordinate on a 3D object typically used in texture mapping [4]) where the XPointer's light beam and the target intersects in the original pointing time frame is determined; afterwards, the 3D coordinate of this UV coordinate in the viewing time frame is calculated, which is then used to calculate the new pointing direction in the viewing time frame; and finally, the XPointer is reoriented

Figure 9. The mouse cursor is on top of multiple surfaces of an object: the handle, front surface, and back surface of the cup.

and its virtual light beam is adjusted accordingly to reflect this consistent XPointing. If the target is invisible in the viewing time frame (e.g. because the visibility or color transparency property of the target is animated), the end point of the XPointer's laser beam will be hanging on the point in the 3D space where the target should have been if it were visible and users are informed about this invisible target through a notification message. Users may use the recorded information in the XPointer to quickly jump to the pointing time frame for viewing the target.

This *time-translation DXED* should be used at remote sites which are in different viewing time frames than the pointing time frame whenever XPointers need to be updated due to an XPointing update by the mouse user, the execution of an editing operation, and the change of the viewing time frame. The XPointing update due to a time-frame change needs not be propagated to other collaborating sites unless the time frame change is global (i.e. in the strict-time WYSIWIS to be discussed later).

EXTENDING XPOINTERS WITH THE CAPABILITY OF XPOINTING AT 3D POINTS IN 3D SPACES

The Need for XPointing in 3D Spaces

Collaborating users need to XPoint at not only 3D object but also a point in the 3D space. For example, consider the scenario of a director guiding the revision on the animation of the cup from a remote collaborating site. In discussing the revised location of the cup at time frame 6 (Figure 2-(b)), there are two references for the communication: the first one is the cup object and the second is a point in the 3D space where the cup should have been.

However, the XPointer discussed so far is limited to pointing at a 3D object at any depth in the pointing direction, and incapable of pointing at a point in the 3D space. This limitation is because the x-ray manipulator increments/decrements the x-ray penetration by a 3D object and the target of an XPointing is always the closest object to the border-object. In the previous example, the first reference (the cup) can be pointed using the XPointer as it is a 3D object, but the second reference, which is a 3D point and not a 3D object, cannot be pointed using the XPointer. So, after the first reference for the communication is established using the XPointer, the director must resort to an ad hoc method in guiding the revision: to repeatedly use various verbal communications, such as "move it more to the left!" The need for constructing additional verbal communication in discussing a point in 3D spaces reduces the communication efficiency.

The XPointer is also limited to pointing at the closest surface of the target 3D object along the pointing direction. However, 3D objects typically have multiple surfaces in the XPointing direction as illustrated in Figure 9: not only the front and back surfaces of the cup are in the pointing direction but also the cup handle. Users may need to point at any of these surfaces, but the XPointer can only point at the cup handle (i.e. the closest surface to the XPointer object) and unable to point at the front/back surface of the cup. Thus, users must again resort to an ad hoc method of constructing verbal descriptions of the target surface.

To improve the efficiency of communication that references to points in 3D spaces and other surfaces of 3D objects, XPointers must be extended with a new capability of pointing at points in 3D spaces. This new capability also allows pointing at other surfaces of a 3D object by pointing at the 3D point where the target surface is. With this new capability, the XPointer becomes an *anywhere* x-ray telepointer that can point through any object and target any surface of any 3D object and any point in the 3D space.

The Fine-grained X-ray Manipulator

The x-ray manipulator discussed before is only suitable for pointing at a 3D object because it adjusts the XPointer's penetration at a *coarse-grained* level by one 3D object. To point at a point in the 3D space, a *fine-grained x-ray manipulator* is required. The fine-grained x-ray manipulator increases or decreases the XPointer's penetration by a unit distance. The target of the XPointer is a 3D object or 3D point depending on where the XPointer's light beam ends. The following details how the border-object and target of an XPointer changes as its penetration is adjusted using the fine-grained x-ray manipulator:

1. If the XPointer's fine-grained penetration is decreased such that it touches the front surface of the border-object: (a) that 3D object is no longer the border-object; (b) the new border-object is the last penetrated 3D object before the previous border-object; and (c) the new target is no longer a 3D point but the previous border-object.
2. If the XPointer's fine-grained penetration is increased from the front surface of a target 3D object: (a) that target 3D object becomes the new border-object; and (b) the target is no longer a 3D object, but a 3D point where the XPointer's light beam ends.
3. If the XPointer's fine-grained penetration is increased such that it touches the front surface of the 3D object next to the border-object in the pointing direction, the target is no longer a 3D point, but that 3D object.

To reach the target 3D point faster, the adjustment speed of the fine-grained x-ray manipulator can be accelerated overtime when the adjustment is done continuously.

With this new XPointing capability, the XPointer must intelligently maintain not only the border-object, but also

Figure 10. The XPointer intelligently maintains the relative penetration distance from the border-object (i.e. the apple) to the next closest 3D object (i.e. the cup) in the pointing direction.

the *relative* penetration distant from the border-object to the next closest object in the pointing direction. This behavior is illustrated in Figure 10. This behavior is not only useful but also necessary as it allows the mouse user to freely move the mouse around without having to readjust the XPointer's penetration, regardless how the surface curvature of the border-object and next 3D object in the pointing direction changes.

The coarse-grained x-ray manipulator and the fine-grained x-ray manipulator are complementary to each other. The coarse-grained x-ray manipulator should be used to quickly adjust the border-object to the closest one to the target point in the 3D space. Then, the fine-grained x-ray manipulator should be used to adjust the fine-grained pointing from the border-object towards the target 3D point.

Supporting XPointing at 3D Objects and 3D Points in Unconstrained Collaborative Environments

To support XPointing at a 3D point in unconstrained collaborative environments, the *DXED* algorithm to dynamically determine the correct and consistent target and border-object based on the execution context must be extended to handle a target that is a 3D point. The extended *DXED* (*XDXED*) algorithm is sketched in Algorithm 2 below. In addition to the three input parameters as in *DXED*, the algorithm also takes in as an input the *relative* penetration distance *rdist* from the border-object to the next closest object in the pointing direction.

Algorithm 2: *XDXED(PL, pos, dir, rdist)*

```
PDL[ ] := objects in pointing direction dir from position pos;
BO_index := BOD(PL, pos, dir, PDL);
posBO := PDL[BO_index].pos;
If BO_index < PDL.length() then
   posNO := PDL[BO_index + 1].pos;
else posNO := far_end.pos;
return (postBO + (rdist × (posNO – posBO)));
```

XDXED first obtains the current penetration list *PDL* as in *DXED* (algorithm 1) and then invokes the *BOD* routine to determine the valid border-object. Afterwards, instead of returning the identifier of the target 3D object after the border-object or the far-end as in *DXED*, the target 3D point is calculated as the 3D point that is *rdist* distance away from the border-object to the next 3D object in the pointing direction. The notation *PDL*[i].*pos* denotes the 3D coordinate where the XPointer's light beam intersect with the object in *PDL*[*i*]. The *XDXED* algorithm is also applicable for determining the target that is a 3D object; in this case, *rdist* is equal to one.

Supporting XPointing at 3D Space in Relaxed-Time WYSIWIS Environments

In relaxed-time WYSIWIS environments, the XPointer must point at a 3D point that preserves the same relative penetration distance. To achieve this, the *XDXED* is coupled with a similar time-translation scheme discussed earlier. After the border-object and next closest object in the pointing direction are determined, the UV coordinates of these two objects where the XPointer's light beam intersects in the pointing time frame are calculated. Next, the 3D coordinates of these UV coordinates in the viewing time frame are determined, which are then used to calculate the target 3D point that is *rdist* away from the border-object in the viewing time frame.

XPOINTERS IN VARYING DEGREES OF STRICT- AND RELAXED-SPACE-TIME WYSIWIS ENVIRONMENTS

A proof-of-concept prototype implementation of XPointers is conducted on the *CoMaya* real-time collaborative 3D design system. CoMaya is transparently adapted from Autodesk Maya offering a real-time unconstrained collaboration capability [1, 21]. To meet different collaboration needs, we extend CoMaya to allow users to customize the WYSIWIS mode; the space and time aspects of WYSIWIS can be separately controlled in relaxed or strict degrees.

A relaxed-WYSIWIS aspect allows each user to individually control the aspect of his/her workspace without affecting the workspaces of others [18]. Hence, different users may have different views of shared 3D workspaces. Relaxed-WYSIWIS aspects are naturally supported by CoMaya and other collaborative applications with a replicated architecture [1,5,21].

A strict-WYSIWIS aspect enforces all users to have the same setting for that aspect. One or more users may concurrently change the strict aspect and the change will be reflected in workspaces of all other users. If only one user is allowed to change the aspect at a time, a distributed synchronized protocol is used to block all but one setting change and a floor control system is used to decide who can change the setting [21]. If multiple users are allowed to concurrently change an aspect, a consistent synchronized aspect must be maintained using a conflict resolution strategy [3,20].

Since the two WYSIWIS aspects – space and time – can be controlled separately, there are four combinations of WYSIWIS modes as follows (Figure 11 shows the control panel for choosing a WYSIWIS mode in CoMaya):

1. *Relaxed-Space and Relaxed-Time* (*RSRT*) mode allows multiple users to view the shared 3D workspace from any perspective and time frame. This is the most relaxed mode of all and corresponds to the unconstrained collaborative environment [20].

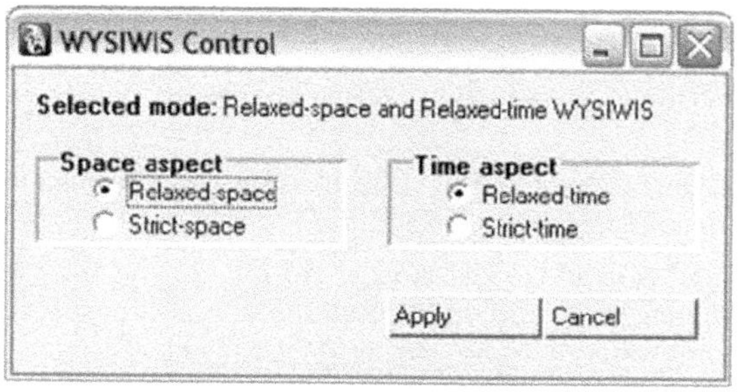

Figure 11. WYSIWIS control panel in CoMaya.

2. *Relaxed-Space and Strict-Time* (*RSST*) mode allows multiple users to view the shared 3D workspace from different perspectives but enforces the same time frame. This mode is equivalent to the relaxed WYSIWIS mode in collaborative 3D applications without animation creation supports (i.e. no time frame concept).
3. *Strict-Space and Relaxed-Time* (*SSRT*) mode allows multiple users to view the shared 3D workspace from different time frames, but enforces all users to view from the same perspective. This mode is equivalent to the relaxed WYSIWIS mode in collaborative 2D systems with an animation creation support and time frame concept.
4. *Strict-Space and Strict-Time* (*SSST*) mode enforces all users to view the shared 3D workspace from the same perspective and time frame. This is the most restricted mode of all and effectively is the strict WYSIWIS in early collaborative editing systems. This mode is useful for tightly-coupled collaboration.

XPointers can support all four WYSIWIS modes even though they are originally motivated by the need for supporting the RSRT mode. The representation of XPointers as 3D objects embedded inside the shared 3D workspace allows users to view XPointers from any perspective, including the same perspective as the XPointer user. This means XPointers can be viewed meaningfully in both the strict- and relaxed-space WYSIWIS. XPointers can also be viewed in the strict-time WYSIWIS; in this case, the basic DXED algorithm is adequate for determining the XPointing effects. Figure 12 shows XPointers are pointing at the stem of the apple in the four WYSIWIS modes.

FUTURE WORK

Although the XPointer technique has been motivated by general needs in supporting unconstrained 3D design collaboration, designed with technical arguments and justification, and implemented for proof-of-concept and feasibility validation in CoMaya, no empirical evaluation of its real usefulness and benefits to end-users has been conducted yet. One main future work is to conduct usability study to evaluate the effectiveness, efficiency, and user experiences of using the XPointer, in comparison to using non-x-ray 3D telepointers, for supporting real-time collaborative 3D design activities. We will seek to answer the following usability questions in our evaluation study:

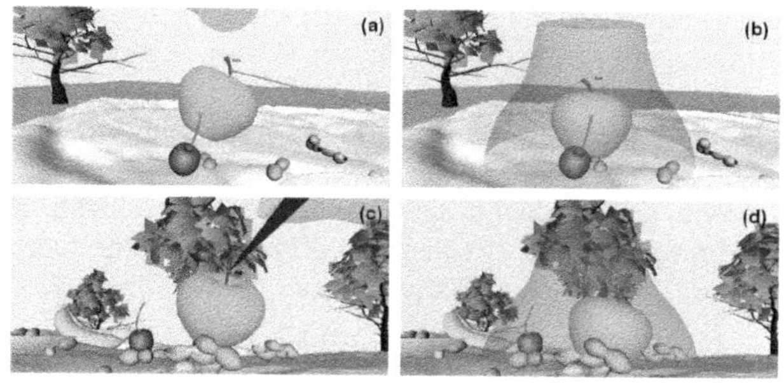

Figure 12. XPointers are pointing at the stem of the apple in different WYSIWIS modes: (a) relaxed-space and relaxed-time; (b) relaxed-space and strict-time; (c) strict-space and relaxed-time; and (d) strict-space and strict-time.

Q1. Whether the XPointer enables users to point at a blocked target, regardless whether the target is invisible or visible due to semi-transparent blocking objects, faster and more convenient than using a non-x-ray telepointer.

Q2. Whether the XPointer provides adequate information for the mouse user to make correct and accurate pointing.

Q3. Whether the XPointer provides adequate information for remote users to interpret the pointing target and understand the mouse user's pointing context.

Q4. Whether the mouse user can determine, with a low error rate, the new target of the XPointer when it is affected by remote concurrent editing operations.

Q5. Whether the XPointer's capability to perform x-ray telepointing and telepointing from different time frames can facilitate effortless communication and promote instant and ad hoc interaction among collaborative designers.

We will design suitable testing scenarios, in which participants will be asked to perform XPointing to blocked targets selected by the testing system (related to Q1 and Q2), to identify the target of XPointers (related to Q3), to identify the new target of the XPointer after the execution of remote editing operations (related to Q4), and to be engaged in realistic 3D design tasks (related to Q5). The feedback from evaluation study will be used to refine and improve the XPointer design and implementation.

CONCLUSIONS

In this paper, we have contributed a novel XPointer technique for consistent x-ray telepointing in relaxed-space-time WYSIWIS collaborative 3D design systems and an extension of the relaxed WYSIWIS concept to include the animation time frame aspect. The XPointer is motivated by the need for pointing at objects and 3D points at arbitrarily depths in relaxed-space-time WYSIWIS collaborative environments, which are not supported by prior 3D telepointing techniques. Maintaining a correct and consistent XPointing in unconstrained collaborative environments, that allow concurrent editing and pointing, is challenging because the penetration and target of XPointing can be affected by multiple concurrent operations.

The XPointer has the following distinctive features: (1) free and fine-grained telepointing at any 3D object and 3D point in the shared 3D workspace; (2) integrated with an oblique view and other awareness widgets for efficient XPointing; (3) flexible and fine-grained XPointing in varying degrees of strict- and relaxed-space-time WYSIWIS collaborative environments; and (4) consistent XPointing in the face of dynamic content changes due to concurrent editing work.

The XPointer work has also enriched our understanding of the notion of relaxed WYSIWIS: a combined space and time relaxation in WYSIWIS is needed for supporting new advanced collaborative applications. To meet different collaboration needs, users should be able to customize the WYSIWIS mode by varying the degree of relaxed- and strict-WYSIWIS, and telepointing techniques should be able to flexibly support these modes. This work is the first to address these advanced telepointing needs and extend the concept of relaxed WYSIWIS to include the time aspect. The demonstration video of the XPointer is available at http://cooffice.ntu.edu.sg/comaya/videoXPointer.php.

ACKNOWLEDGEMENT
This research is partially supported by an Academic Research Fund Tier 1 Grant from Ministry of Education Singapore, and by the Singapore National Research Foundation under its International Research Centre @ Singapore Funding Initiative and administered by the Interactive Digital Media Programme Office. The authors wish to thank anonymous reviewers for their insightful and constructive comments and suggestions.

REFERENCES
1. Agustina, F. Liu, S. Xia, H.F. Shen, and C. Sun. CoMaya: incorporating advance collaboration capabilities into 3D digital media design tools. In *Proc. ACM CSCW 2008*, 5-8.
2. Agustina, C. Sun, and D. Xu. Operational transformation for dependency conflict resolution in real-time collaborative 3D design systems. In *Proc. ACM* CSCW *2012*, 1401-1410.
3. Agustina and C. Sun. Televiewpointer: an integrated workspace awareness widget for real-time collaborative 3D design systems. In *Proc. ACM Group 2010*, 21-30.
4. Autodesk. Introduction to UV mapping. http://download.autodesk.com/us/maya/2010help/index.html?url=UV_mapping_overview_Introduction_to_UV_mapping.htm,topicNumber=d0e251306, last retrieved Dec 2012.
5. J. Begole, M. Rosson, and C. Shaffer. Flexible collaboration transparency: supporting worker independence in replicated application-sharing systems. *ACM TOCHI*, 6(2), 1999, 95-132.
6. R.A. Bolt. "Put-that-there": Voice and gesture at the graphics interface. *SIGGRAPH Computer Graphics*, 14(3), 1980, 262-270.
7. N. Elmqvist and P. Tsigas. A taxonomy of 3D occlusion management for visualization. *TVCG*, 14(5), 2008, 1095-1109.
8. M. Fraser, S. Benford, J. Hindmarsh, and C. Heath. Supporting awareness and interaction through collaborative virtual interfaces. In *Proc. ACM UIST 1999*, 27-36.
9. S. Greenberg, C. Gutwin, and M. Roseman. Semantic telepointers for groupware. In *Proc. OzCHI 1996*, 54-61.
10. C. Gutwin and S. Greenberg. The effects of workspace awareness support on the usability of real-time distributed groupware. *ACM TOCHI*, 6(3), 1993, 243-281.
11. C. Gutwin and R. Penner. Improving interpretation of remote gestures with telepointer traces. In *Proc. ACM CSCW 2002*, 49-57.
12. S. Kita. Pointing and Placing. *Pointing: Where language, culture, and cognition meet*, 2003, 243-268.
13. A. Owal and S. Fiener. The Flexible Pointer: an interaction technique for selection in augmented and virtual reality. In *Proc. ACM UIST 2003*, 81-82.
14. A. Pang and C. Wittenbrink. Collaborative 3D visualization with CSpray. In *Proc. IEEE CG&A 1997*, 32-41.
15. M.S. Pinho, D. Bowman, and C. Freitas. Cooperative object manipulation in immersive virtual environments: framework and techniques. In *Proc. ACM VRST 2002*, 171-178.
16. I. Poupyrev, M. Billinghurst, S. Weghorst, and T. Ichikawa. The go-go interaction technique: non-linear mapping for direct manipulation in VR. In *Proc. ACM UIST 1996*, 79-80.
17. K.J. Rodham and D.R. Olsen. Smart telepointers: maintaining telepointer consistency in the presence of user interface customization. *ACM TOG*, 13(3), 1994, 66-106.
18. M. Stefik, D.G. Bobrow, G. Foster, S. Lanning, and D. Tatar. WYSIWIS revised: early experiences with multiuser interfaces. *ACM TOIS*, 5(2), 1987, 147-167.
19. R. Stoakley, M.J. Conway, and R. Pausch. Virtual reality on a WIM: interactive worlds in miniature. In *Proc. ACM CHI 1995*, 265-272.
20. C. Sun, X. Jia, Y. Zhang, Y. Yang, and D. Chen. Achieving convergence, causality-preservation, and intention-preservation in real-time cooperative editing systems. *ACM TOCHI*, 5(1), 1998, 63-108.
21. C. Sun, S. Xia, D. Sun, D. Chen, H.F. Shen, and W. Cai. Transparent adaptation of single-user applications for multi-user real-time collaboration. *ACM TOCHI*, 13(4), 2006, 531-582.
22. L. Vanacken, T. Grossman, and K. Coninx. Exploring the effects of environment density and target visibility on object selection in 3D virtual environments. *IEEE 3DUI 2007*, 117-124.
23. N. Wong and C. Gutwin. Where are you pointing? The accuracy of deictic pointing in CVEs. In *Proc. ACM CHI 2010*, 1029-1038.
24. S. Xia, D. Sun, C. Sun, and D. Chen. Object-associated telepointer for real-time collaborative document editing systems. *IEEE CollaborateCom 2005*.

Drawing Practices in Image-Enabled Collaboration

Jaime Snyder
Syracuse University
School of Information Studies
245 Hinds Hall, Syracuse NY 13244
jasnyd01@syr.edu

ABSTRACT
Advances in image-making tools have greatly increased our opportunities to use images to collaborate. Much current research in the area of visualization focuses on building systems to generate visual representations of large data sets. A small but growing subset of this research focuses on collaborative aspects of information and data visualization. In order to expand the scope of collaborative visualization research, a qualitative study examined the role that spontaneous drawing practices play in face-to-face conversations. Empirical examples describe the creation and use of drawing as a form of social interaction. This study provides a methodological and theoretical basis for viewing the process of generating a visual artifact in a collaborative context from an interactional sociolinguistic perspective. Findings identify affordances of drawing related to both material object (artifact) and communicative performance (activity). Implications for design are discussed in terms of both refined heuristics and enhanced features for image-enabled collaborative tools.

Author Keywords
Collaborative visualization; drawing; image-enabled discourse.

ACM Classification Keywords
H.5.1. Information interfaces and presentation (e.g., HCI): Multimedia Information Systems: Evaluation/methodology.

General Terms
Human Factors; Design; Theory.

INTRODUCTION
From information graphics to complex data visualizations, images play an increasingly important role in communication and collaboration, especially in cross-disciplinary contexts [9, 21]. Our cultural relationship with images, combined with advances in image-making tools, has greatly increased our opportunities to use visual information artifacts to collaborate in both personal and professional domains.

Motivation for the creation of information-driven images is often social in nature. Mathison [21] posits that widespread use of images in a range of contexts reflects assumptions we have about images and their ability to transcend communication barriers. We use images to communicate because we believe (or intuit) that information presented in a visual format enables communication gaps to be bridged and provides access to broader audiences.

Current approaches to collaborative visualization [17], tend to focus on either the image generated (the chart, the map, diagram) or the technology used to create the image (the algorithm, the interface, the digital paint brush). In contrast, this paper draws attention to the *act* of image making as a collaborative, communicative activity.

Even when image-making tools are no more sophisticated than pen and paper, creating images within the context of an ongoing conversation is a technology-mediated event. Since before the advent of digital technologies, the ability to spontaneously create and share images in order to clarify, explain, or enhance a conversation has been part of our communication toolbox. Although the ease with which we can make and share images on the fly has greatly increased due to technological advances, these tools are enhancing behaviors that in many ways were already embedded in our communication practices. For this study, spontaneous drawing practices used in face-to-face conversations were examined as naturally occurring, minimally technology-mediated instances of collaborative visualization.

Image-enabled discourse [31] refers to the broader phenomenon of using images for specific communicative, information-driven purposes, particularly in collaborative or conversational situations. This study focuses on a particular type of image-enabled discourse where drawing occurs spontaneously during a face-to-face interaction without consideration for any possible wider application (i.e., visual representations drawn on napkins or whiteboards during the course of an ongoing conversation). These types of images have been called "sketches" [36] as well as "spontaneous visualizations" or "freeform representations" [39]. In this paper, "drawing" will be used to refer to both the practice of leaving a visible, tangible mark on a surface and the artifact produced by that process. The choice of this term intentionally draws attention to associations borrowed from the domain of art, discussed next.

MOTIVATION

In the field of painting and drawing, the term "mark making" is used to isolate and highlight the practice of using an instrument to leave a trace on a surface or canvas. Sometimes employed by art historians and critics when discussing the gestural qualities of a painted or drawn image, artists frequently use this term to refer to the way that a mark (or series of marks) indicates the presence of the maker. During training, art students develop a range of mark-making skills. From this perspective, marks left on a surface convey particularly potent information about the moment of expression and act of creation. A hand gesture is not a drawing, but a series of scratches in the dirt is a drawing. Drawings can contain alphanumeric characters but do not have a strict directional orientation in order to be meaningful [7]. For example, a phone number written on a napkin is not a drawing because it needs to be "read" from left to right to make sense; a diagram showing numbered measurements for constructing a box is a drawing.

Two examples of artifacts created as a result of spontaneous drawing activities are shown below (Figure 1). These so-called "napkin drawings" are notoriously cryptic for those not present during their creation. As will be seen later in the discussion of findings, however, the creation of such images can be deeply implicated in moments of collective coordination or insights.

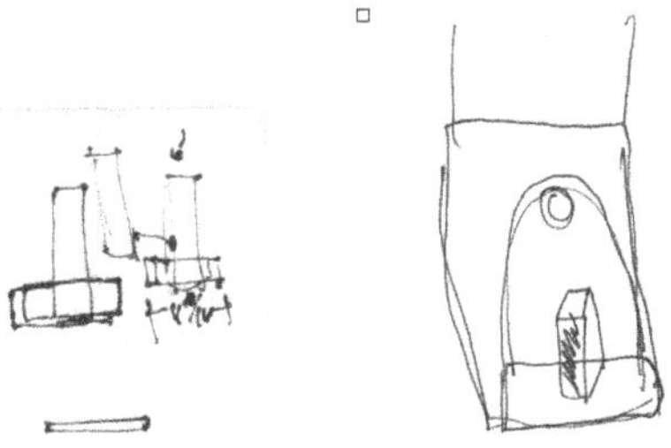

Figure 1. Examples of spontaneous drawing

In removing information regarding the context in which drawings like the ones shown in Figure 1 were created, we can only find meaning in especially representational figures or symbols. Without taking into account the social interaction in which the activity of creation is embedded, we remain blind to the dynamic role that the act of image making can play as a communicative maneuver. This study addresses this gap by providing empirical support for a theory of image-enabled discourse.

The research presented here takes a sociolinguistic perspective on the process of spontaneous drawing during face-to-face conversations in order to focus on the intuitive, complex, and sophisticated methods we use for deploying visual information (even the most rudimentary instantiations) in face-to-face conversations. The study from which this paper was derived sought to 1) identify the communicative activities that take place when people draw during face-to-face conversations, 2) learn about the roles these activities play in managing conversational involvement and coordination, and 3) shed light on affordances of drawing for image-enabled discourse strategies. This paper discusses findings related to the final point, presenting affordances of drawing as both artifact and activity in relation to notions of materiality and performativity.

This work contributes to the CSCW community by providing a basis for enhancing heuristics used to evaluate increasingly sophisticated tools that seek to replicate the fluidity and intuitiveness of face-to-face interactions. Additionally, understanding the specific ways that image-enabled communication practices influence coordination will help system builders to pinpoint communicative behaviors that would benefit most from technology interventions.

The next section provides a brief summary of related research. It is followed by a description of the research design, including data collection and analysis techniques. Findings are then presented followed by a discussion that expands the activity/artifact dichotomy introduced in prior work [30] to encompass the notions of material object and communicative performance. The paper concludes with implications for design relevant to the CSCW community.

RELATED RESEARCH

Studies focused on the creation or use of drawing during the collaborative process generally come from CSCW, human computer interaction (HCI) and information visualization (InfoVis) communities. This investigation of spontaneous drawing practices complements and extends previous work by building a bridge between research focused on production of a visual artifact and research focused on the use of that artifact within a specific context. Review of related work will focus on three themes: 1) perceived benefits of drawing for supporting collaborative outcomes; 2) drawing within a situated collaborative process; and 3) systems for creating digital drawings.

Benefits of collaborative drawing

Studies that examine the influence of drawing practices on role-based group dynamics (such as between engineers) and on specific collaborative outcomes (such as design ideation) typically focus on the social or collaborative benefits of drawing.

Sketching is a term often used in the design literature to refer to the process of creating a visual representation in a rough or quick way. As discussed by Tversky et al. [36], design sketches are frequently associated with the ideation process and, in fact, most designers are trained to some degree or another in sketching as a form of concept development according to a specific set of aesthetic or technical requirements. Taking a cognitive approach, Tversky and colleagues found that senior designers are more adept at taking advantage of creative opportunities presented through sketching.

Van der Lugt et al. conducted an experimental study to investigate the benefits of sketching for idea generation during design meetings [37]. They concluded that sketching supports the re-interpretation process while improving access to earlier ideas that might have been lost during an iterative work cycle, basing this claim on the persistence of the drawn object as a reminder or stimulus for further thought. Bastéa-Forte and Yen [2] created a collaborative sketching system using tablet PCs with styluses and a shared digital canvas to be used during brainstorming sessions. While their system resulted in less time spent sketching during interactions, it helped equalize contributions from meeting participants (compared to traditional face-to-face methods). Researchers concluded that the sketching system increased awareness of the quality and number of ideas contributed.

"Microsketching" is a method for producing rapid prototypes developed by Forlizzi and DiSalvo [8] for use in collaborative design contexts. Drawings that focus on a single feature or detail combined with ethnographic probes can successfully mediate feedback between designers and users. Tohidi et al. [35] used a similar approach, conducting usability testing via user sketching protocols in order to elicit feedback from participants.

Henderson's study of engineering drawings as boundary objects highlights the role that visual literacy plays in the social practices embedded in the design process [16]. Roth and McGinn [28] looked at the rhetorical role that inscriptions (i.e., graphical representations as opposed to mental images) play in the classroom, focusing on the public nature of these images enabling the drawn object to be a boundary object in classroom interactions.

In these studies sketching is generally described as a skill associated with certain professions, carrying implications of intent and performance. Mark-making is implied in the sketching activities described, however is generally underspecified. In focusing predominately on task performance, questions remain regarding how exactly the activity of drawing, particularly the making of a visible mark, supports communicative activities. This contextual information is important for developing and enhancing specific features for collaborative visualization tools.

Drawing within a situated context

Studies focused on collaborative visualization practices in situated contexts have allowed researchers to gather requirements, learn about workflow, and establish baselines for system evaluation. These studies show that systems that enable drawing (and other spontaneous visualization techniques) can enhance collaborative work. For example, Prante, Magerkurth and Streitz [26] asked participants to work on creative problems using mapping and whiteboard tools in order to learn more about the shared idea space created by collaborators. Their findings were ultimately turned into a list of requirements for a suite of collaborative software, including a drawing application for a networked handheld device. Bly [3] compared interactions between designers that were mediated by audio only compared to audio/video. Findings showed that similar drawing activities occurred in each communication environment, highlighting the importance of supporting the activity of drawing during the design process not just the sharing of a completed image. Through these studies, researchers uncovered instances where the creation of a drawing was implicated in higher-level work processes. These studies sought to support that process but did not unpack the "sub-process" of drawing itself.

Systems for creating digital drawings

Systems for electronic drawing, such as digital whiteboards, have been in development for at least twenty years. For example, in the early 1990s, a collaborative drawing interface called *VideoDraw* was created by Tang and Minneman [32]. This tool enabled users to share a "virtual sketchbook" and was based on observations of the ways in which individuals used graphic representations as collaborative tools in face-to-face exchanges. Ishii and Kobayashi's work on the ClearBoard system [18] is also an example of relatively early HCI research that evolved from observations of whiteboard use in collaborative situations. Around the same time, Tivoli was developed by researchers at Xerox PARC [25]. This system also attempted to replicate the simplicity, ease of use, and basic functionality of conventional whiteboards.

More recently, attention has been given to physical cues and movements associated with drawing in collaborative settings. Ju, Lee and Klemmer [20] designed an interactive whiteboard to support distributed ad hoc meetings. Their system included position sensors to identify speakers/authors; automatically make room on the writing surface; and enable clustering or grouping of ink strokes. Rekimoto's system [27] provided users with individual handheld tablets networked to a shared whiteboard canvas, inspired by the sort of palette used by artists. This provided contributors with increased access to the communal canvas, allowing them each to add visual objects or text to the shared interface.

Other digital tools have also been inspired by physical mark making implements. The I/O brush [29] looks like a regular physical paintbrush but contains a camera and sensors that "pick up" colors and textures from the environment, and allows a user to "paint" on a digital drawing canvas. Weibel et al [41] created PaperSketch, an interactive paper-digital pen application for sketching, including a GUI for communication and collaboration.

In these cases, attention to the material aspects of drawing focused on replicating with digital tools the tangible experience of drawing or writing, such as the weight, stroke and resistance of pen on paper or marker on whiteboard. Other material aspects of mark making will be discussed below, such as temporal features related to watching an image evolve and change over the course of a conversation.

Summary

This brief review shows a shared interest across CSCW and related communities in the use of drawing as a form of information exchange in collaborative contexts. However, research to date has not yet developed a rich understanding of the mechanics of image-enabled social interaction. In the next section a methodology will be described to more closely examine not just if, but *how* drawing practices contribute to social interaction, coordination, and conversational involvement.

RESEARCH DESIGN

Interactional sociolinguistic methodology

An interactional sociolinguistic approach guided analysis of face-to-face conversations involving spontaneous drawing with communicative intent (i.e., *not* doodling). Interactional sociolinguistics addresses the ways in which meaning is generated through the interactive use of language [12]. Gumperz showed that specific strategies related to choices about not only *what* we say, but *how* we say it provide important contextualization cues that are used to interpret meaning.

For example, code-switching is a discourse strategy that has specific parallels with spontaneous drawing practices. Code-switching refers to instances where multilingual conversants switch from a dominant to an alternate language (or to a sublanguage such as slang) in the midst of a conversation, based on a variety of cultural or communicative motivations [12]. Drawing during a conversation can be viewed as a form of code or "mode" switch, similar to this type of linguistic shift, which has the potential to signal contextual cues related to the social landscape and intended meaning.

Based on this line of reasoning, an initial theoretical parallel was drawn between linguistically-based discourse strategies, like code-switching, and the modal switch that marks a transition to drawing activities. An analytic framework connected verbal and non-verbal indicators of social interaction with discursive strategies such as framing [33], footing [10] and stance-taking [19]. Drawing and mark making were operationalized as a distinct type of non-verbal marker (similar to gestural forms of expression) that indicates the use of specific communicative strategies [11].

This framework provided a basis for multimodal discourse analysis of conversations involving spontaneous drawing. The analysis of both verbal and non-verbal markers revealed the interconnectedness of modes of communication such as spoken words, gestures, and drawing practices.

Data collection

Adopting a framework derived from interactional sociolinguistics required that data be conducive to very close analysis of communicative practices. The protocol for the study allowed for systematic recording of spontaneous drawing practices in a naturalistic, observable environment. The protocol was administered to 8 pairs of participants (16 volunteers from undergraduate and graduate student populations at a large university in the northeastern region of the US), with 3 pairs in a pilot, and 5 pairs taking part in the main study.

Participants were not told that drawing was the focus of the study. Instead, during recruitment and briefing, they were told that the study was about informal information sharing among peers. They were told that they would be asked to engage in conversation with another person about a set of open-ended topics. The rationale for this approach was provided by anecdotal evidence and pilot testing that supported the assumption that drawing during face-to-face conversation is not a rare event. If enough conversations are recorded, at least some will involve spontaneous drawing practices, providing a dataset for analysis.

Participants engaged in conversation with a peer in an informal, meeting room setting, with an array of typical office supplies available. A series of conversation prompts were provided to each pair of participants in order to spark discussion and seed social interactions. Details regarding prompts are discussed below.

Instigating conversation

A set of standardized conversation prompts in the form of questions to be answered by the participants was used to initiate and focus interactions between volunteers.

Burgoon et al. [4] employed a similar approach in their work looking at deception detection using a protocol that presented participants with opportunities to engage in deceitful communication with a partner. Hancock et al. [13] built on this protocol to develop a corpus for automatic linguistic analysis for deception detection.

The intent of using conversation prompts was not to create a controlled experiment, but instead to devise a situation for making consistent and unobtrusive observations while creating an authentic experience for participants. In this case, participants were college students. The situation was similar to the first meeting of a pair of students randomly assigned to work together on a group project, a familiar experience for students that enabled them to engage in a natural way. Analogous instances of establishing frames of reference for communication around an unfamiliar or assigned problem can also be found in professional settings.

Conversation prompts

The primary and exclusive role of the conversation prompt in this protocol was to enable direct observations of communication behaviors by instigating a naturalistic conversation. Conversation prompts were designed to provide opportunities for the creation of drawings, while not being overly prescriptive.

During a preliminary study, approximately 50 respondents provided narratives describing conversations they had participated in during which drawing had taken place.

These stories informed the design of questions to be used as prompts. Candidate questions were variable with respect to level of abstraction, conceptual familiarity, and degree to which ideas needed to be transformed or changed over the course of conversation (i.e., convincing someone of something versus recounting details). Further evaluation of candidate questions determined if prompts 1) were answerable within a 10-20 minute conversation, 2) did not require specialized knowledge, and 3) were not overly deterministic about requiring the use of drawing to respond.

Participants were explicitly informed that a correct response was not necessary, but that they should do their best to come up with an answer with which both participants were comfortable. Pilot testing confirmed the ability of participants to respond to the questions while still engaging in naturalistic interactions with a peer participant.

Examples of questions used in the study include:

- What is the most stable way to build a set of shelves?
- What determines weather patterns around the globe?
- How far is it from the earth to the sun in relation to the whole solar system

Because pairs responded to some of the same questions, this protocol enabled comparisons to be made between conversations about similar topics, in similar situations, where one involved drawing and another did not. The method for making such comparisons is described next.

Analysis

Video recordings of prompted conversations provided empirical data for analysis. Initial review of recordings for quality and richness confirmed that the data corpus size was adequate for the qualitative, inductive approach to analysis typical of discourse-oriented studies.

Each of the 5 pairs in the main study responded to 3 prompts. Video data was logged based on conversation prompt, yielding 15 conversation clips (3 per pair), each approximately 5-15 minutes in length. Drawing spontaneously occurred in 7 of those 15 conversations. For each of the five pairs, at least one participant drew at some point during their interactions.

Transcription

Detailed transcription of video data included all 15 conversations, enabling comparisons of interactions involving drawing with those that did not. The video transcription process (Table 1) was informed by Charmaz's approach to grounded theory [5], which advocates a two-phased inductive procedure to qualitatively identify emergent themes within a dataset (*initial coding*), and then apply structured codes derived from these themes (*focused coding*) to create rich, systematic descriptions. Heath et al., who describe a very similar approach to the analysis of video data, include a third phase, *analytic search* [15], which involves gathering candidate instances of particular phenomenon, actions or processes of interest.

Initial coding	Verbatim transcripts Narrative transcripts Collection of emergent themes
Focused coding	Transcripts annotated for: • Drawing behaviors • Framing behaviors (Topic, Agreement, Boundaries, Stance, and Vector)
Analytic search	Sets of contrasting affordances

Table 1. Analytic process.

In this case, initial coding resulted in two transcripts for each conversation: *verbatim*, which recorded verbal utterances and included annotation of nonverbal behaviors (Table 2); and *narrative*, which included prose descriptions of multimodal communication events such as passages where speech, body orientation, and drawing practices were tightly coupled, as well as "non-events" such as long periods of silence.

Behavior	Dimensions
Gestures	Hand, shoulders, head Degree of articulation (high to low) Frequency/repetition (habitual to rare) Mirroring, echoing Touching Tilt, nod/shake
Overlap	Overlapping speech Simultaneous speech and gesture/movement
Gaze	Position and orientation of head/face Direction
Drawing behaviors	Picking up implement Picking up or orienting paper Drawing Hovering implement over surface of paper Putting down implement Using implement to direction attention
Body position	Distance Orientation Trunk, arms/hands, head/face Mirroring and echoing

Table 2. Non-verbal communication behaviors.

Focused coding involved more detailed analysis of drawing episodes. *Episodes* are passages of discourse that are coherent and reflect thematic unity based on the purpose of the speaker [22, 38]. Episodes can be nested or overlapping, but have a coherent self-referential structure. In each of the 7 conversations where drawing took place, there were 2-6 distinct instances of drawing, yielding 26 discrete drawing episodes. At this point, common discourse structures related to establishing and maintaining a frame of reference [34] were identified across all 15 conversations, supporting comparisons across interactions with and without drawing.

Analytic search was used to collect information about the ways in which affordances of drawing were evident in the communicative behaviors of participants. A list of affordances was created and categorized according to whether each attribute was more closely associated with the activity of drawing or with the drawn artifact. More details of this categorization are provided in the Findings section.

Limitations

This research took a deeply qualitative approach, involving social interaction analysis of video data guided by principles of grounded theory. While providing both a structure for detailed analysis of image-enabled discourse in a situated context and the ability to compare across communicative practices both within and across pairs of participants, this approach also carried certain limitations. The close analysis of conversations is labor intensive and by definition focused on many micro-level interactions, limiting the number of conversations examined. The use of prompts may also limit the generalizability of findings. Future work can help to mitigate these limitations by applying research outcomes as heuristics for existing or planned systems to strengthen ecological validity, as well extending the investigation of collaborative drawing practices to broader contexts and more diverse populations.

FINDINGS

Visual representation is an embodied process wherein ideas, thoughts and expressions are given physical form [1]. The action of mark making instantly leaves a visible, tangible record of a communicative expression, unlike verbal utterances or gestures. This means that as drawing is deployed during a conversation, it can simultaneously function as a stable, persistent waypoint (characteristics of the physical artifact), and also serve as a mutable, dynamic discourse strategy (characteristics of the social activity of communicating). Drawing is deeply *embedded* within conversation structures, and at the same time the drawn object exists *outside* the communicative structure of a conversation.

Artifact and activity

The process of image making produces both situated activity and discrete artifact, each having distinct and sometimes contradictory attributes or affordances. Existing in a state of entanglement, these different aspects of drawing can be exploited within a single conversation or interaction, sometimes virtually at the same time.

Image making during face-to-face interactions produces both a *visual artifact* that is discrete and able to exist independently from an overall discourse structure, and a *communicative activity* that is embedded in that structure. The image artifact and image-making activity are not separated in practice. However, when viewed in terms of enabling characteristics, these two aspects of image-enabled communication are analytically distinct. Table 3 shows contrasting characteristics of drawing associated with creating and establishing conversational involvement and coordination. For example, both *persistence* (continuous presence) and *mutability* (ability to be changed) were important features of drawing in the conversations.

Artifact	Activity
Persistent	Intermittent
Stable	Mutable
Discrete	Embedded
Static	Performative
Unordered	Sequential

Table 3: Attributes of image-enabled communication practices

The focus of this paper is to expand the initial dichotomy represented by this table. The concepts of materiality and performativity are used to focus attention on the ways that the social and the material are entangled in spontaneous drawing practices, reflecting a sociomaterial relationship [24].

DISCUSSION

In discussing these findings, the dichotomy of artifact and activity reflect specific notions of *material objects* and *communicative performance*. The interactional sociolinguistic perspective that guided analysis provides a basis for conceptualizing drawing as embodied social interaction [11] and stance-taking performance [19]. The affordances of the drawn *artifact* are presented in a discussion of the material nature of visual representations: the physical and tangible. The attributes of the *activity* of drawing are seen through the lens of communicative performance, or the dynamic, improvised nature of conversational exchanges. This is done for two reasons.

First, this reinforces the importance of the drawn image as a physical, tangible, persistent object in the world. The term "artifact" is being used in the same way that one refers to a physical object in a museum. And like an artifact in a museum, the physical characteristics of that item are important clues to its social role.

Second, highlighting the notion of performance clarifies the use of the term "activity." An interactional sociolinguistic perspective provides a methodology for close analysis of communication activities [14] within a situated context, expanding scope and providing a vocabulary to describe communicative behaviors in terms of overarching discourse strategies.

In practice, this analytic division between artifact and activity is artificial. However, positioning findings in this way highlights the distinct but deeply co-constituted nature of these two aspects of visual representation in situated contexts. It also encourages an inclusive approach to imagining future collaborative visualization tools and environments, one that embraces the importance of both the image artifact and the image-making activity for collaborative social interactions.

Affordances of drawing will now be discussed in terms of materiality and performativity, showing the ways the artifact/activity relationship can be extended to discuss the role of visuality in communication and coordination.

Material objects

Persistent and stable

Persistence refers to the ability of marks made on a surface (or images displayed on a screen or printed on a paper) to endure over time. In the data, persistence was evident when participants used the drawing to manage body position, gaze, orientation, and attention, in addition to using it as a physical record of progress in the conversation. The drawn artifact was also deployed in ways that exploited its relatively *stable* qualities, meaning it has the ability to not only endure, but to exist in a consistent, constant state. Persistence is associated with a mark enduring over time, not fading like speech. Stability adds that the artifact not only does not fade, but remains in a steady state. Stability does not mean that the artifact will not ever change, but that if it does become altered or morph, it will do so in a controlled and controllable way.

For example, Gavin and Walter[1] drew a diagram of the solar system in order to respond to the question: "How far is it from the earth to the sun, in relation to the whole solar system?" Gavin and Walter had only a vague idea of where to begin to answer the question. For them, the drawing provided a kind of stable playing field or sandbox, allowing Gavin to spill out what he knew about the topic in a non-linear fashion and providing Walter with the opportunity to fill in the gaps with his own knowledge.

Stability also allowed the drawing to be used to document the progress of the conversation as physical manifestation of the current state of their interaction. In his discussions of common ground, Clark [6] refers to this as *external representation of public events so far*, used for creating coordination and cohesion in a conversation. In another conversation about the question "What is the most stable way to build a set of shelves?", Denise used the stable quality of the drawn object to firmly establish and maintain a frame of reference, keeping her partner Mike focused on the material object and therefore the topic at hand. Even when Mike did momentarily veer off-topic, she was able to use the drawing to bring him back to the frame of reference they had previously established, preventing his diversion from derailing the conversation.

[1] All names have been changed to protect privacy of participants. All participants have consented to use of images in reporting and publication.

Discrete and static

The drawings that were created during the conversations in this study are undeniably *discrete* objects independent of the conversation itself. While the conversation (including the activity of mark making) can be seen as an ephemeral event tied to a specific point in time, the drawing exists beyond and separate from this event.

For example, when Gavin and Walter decided to tackle the question, "If you could live in any kind of house, what would it be like?" they both immediately reached for paper and pencil and began to sketch their dream house (Figure 2). They maintained conversational involvement with each other by narrating their drawing activities and by periodically glancing at each other's drawing. When it came time for them to confirm that they each fully understood the other's requirements and wishes for an ideal home, they physically swapped drawings. They could do this because the drawings existed as discrete objects.

Figure 2. Gavin and Walter draw in parallel

The *static* quality of the drawn artifact is very closely aligned with its persistence, stability, and existence as a discrete object. Something that is static can be associated with a certain degree of authority because we assume it will not change over time. The static nature of a drawing came into play when it was used as a point of reference in the midst of uncertainty. At the end of Gavin's conversation with Walter about the distance from the earth to the sun in relation to the whole solar system, Gavin announced their response by saying, "How far is the distance… So it's about half way in between, out of this whole thing," as he drew a long line along the left side of the paper, spanning the distance where he had drawn the circles. It was the static quality of the drawn artifact that enabled Gavin to use it in tandem with an indexical statement (i.e., "this"). The authority of the drawn line allowed them to conclude their conversation with this drawing-indexical response, satisfied that they had visually represented the relevant relationship and answered the question.

Unordered

Another characteristic of the drawn artifact that serves as a resource for maintaining conversational involvement is the *unordered* quality of images. This refers to the ability of images to represent information "all at once," not relying on a specific linear starting point or sequential unfolding, as most verbal expression do. The image creator's choices may guide the eye in a specific direction, but the interpretation of the picture does not always depend on being "read" in a specific direction. The non-linear format of the drawn image came into play when a participant referred to a previous part of the conversation by calling attention to an element in the drawn image. The drawing supported and in some cases inspired a lack of continuity, while also supporting conversational involvement and coordination. Because a drawing has the ability to facilitate non-linear segues, participants used them to quickly re-direct conversation and re-establish frames of reference.

Towards a materiality of drawing

The persistent record of the drawn artifact allowed participants to maintain conversational involvement by providing a physical record. As Arnheim notes [1], these durable qualities allow the drawing to represent thoughts and expressions with more detail and higher resolution than a fleeting gesture is able to do. As Norris points out, the flow of attention and awareness during an exchange is a dynamic process [23]. The durable and stable quality of the drawing supported multiple levels of attention and awareness across different modes of expression throughout the course of an exchange. The drawing remains available even when it is not the primary focus of the conversation. At times, it sits stable and unchanged, providing a persistent point of orientation throughout a dynamic conversation. These observations provide a basis for enhancing interfaces to permit more flexible manipulation of attention and awareness in digital environments through features that allow users to establish stable visual waypoints through behaviors such as panning, zooming, magnification, or segmentation.

Communicative performance

Shifting now to a discussion of the characteristics of drawing as an activity, one of the most salient attributes of drawing as observed in the data was the *performative* nature of this communicative practice.

Performative

Interactions that take place between actor and audience during a performance on a stage are distinctly different from typical conversations. Engagement looks different. Performers do not traditionally speak directly to members of the audience. However, they often speak of the connection they feel with the audience, the sense of attentiveness and involvement that is generated collectively through very different means than those typically deployed in face-to-face interactions. In this sense, a performative attention was observed in conversations when drawing was involved. The person watching the drawing unfold behaved similarly to an audience in a theatre.

When Henry and Mary began their conversation about the solar system, Henry immediately turned to face the large whiteboard mounted on the wall behind where they were sitting, saying, "I really like whiteboards. I am a huge whiteboard person." Mary gestured to the whiteboard, inviting him to go ahead. Henry stood and walked to the board as he and Mary began to discuss the definition of an astronomical unit (AU) (Figure 3).

With his back turned to Mary, Hank began by writing the definition of an AU on the board, continuing with, "And then we can probably draw a diagram..." He drew a series of circles on the whiteboard, verbally identifying each planet as he drew it, then drew and labeled a bracket indicating one AU. As Figure 3 shows, their positions in relation to each other reflects someone performing on a stage. Similar interactions were also observed in less dramatic instances. Body positioning and orientation during drawing episodes reflected the same sort of spectator/performer relationship. Although these highly performative passages were marked by ambiguous verbal indexicals and cues, long pauses, and a distinct lack of eye contact, participants were able to use other means (such as drawing) to establish and maintain conversational involvement.

Figure 3. Henry and Mary discuss the solar system

For example, when Denise and Mike were discussing the most stable way to build a set of shelves, they found themselves on a tangent. Mike suggested the idea of a pyramid-shaped bookshelf as a particularly strong and stable form. He gazed out the window as he speculated at length about the triangular-shaped books that would go on such a shelf. He was clearly drifting off topic. As he spoke, Denise's gaze was turned down to the paper on the table in front of her. She began to draw. Mike trailed off as Denise's drawing took shape. His attention migrated to the image she was making (Figure 4). If Denise had spoken over Mike instead of drawing, her behavior could have been considered rude. By drawing, she successfully redirected the conversation and brought Mike's attention back to the question at hand.

Lack of eye contact and Denise's unilateral redirection of the conversation could be seen as signs of decreasing coordination, involvement, and attention. For Mike and Denise, this passage actually marked a recommitment to coordination and involvement. Throughout the data, the cumulative effects of establishing and maintaining a frame of reference through drawing activities worked with (not against) overall discourse structures, rarely corresponding with decreased coordination.

Figure 4. Denise redirects Mike's attention.

The act of picking up a drawing instrument is related to the idea of performativity. Making a mark can be seen as an embodied form of stance-taking, indicating that a person is committing to being involved or having a certain type of relevant knowledge. When we take a stance, we are self-identifying as being part of a community or an interaction, or as having a particular type of knowledge (known as epistemic stance). Jaffe states that "speaker stances are...performances through which speakers may align or disalign themselves" [19] in terms of one or more social identities. Goodwin also discusses the close relationship between body position and stance-taking in face-to-face conversations [11]. This can be seen in the example above when Henry declared his love of whiteboards, stood, picked up a marker and began to engage with the topic of the question.

Jaffe makes further connections between performance theory and stance saying that "the notion of sociolinguistic stance is a fundamentally performative one in the sense that a stance-based perspective views social identities as discursively constructed rather than fixed" [19]. For example, several people who drew made disclaimers about the poor quality of their drawing as they got started, even those who were trained in art and design. The performative nature of embodied stance-taking can be seen in the following comments from drawers indicating self-awareness, and in many cases self-consciousness, about their task performance.

For example, at one point Denise said, "This is the worst drawing..." And Mark's statement, "...let's see if I can draw it," reflected an awareness that the person doing the drawing is performing a feat. Even comments such as Gavin's admonishment to Walter, "Don't steal my ideas," as they set off to draw their dream houses, reflects a self-awareness of the performative aspects of drawing.

Given the connection between performance and conversational involvement seen in these conversations, it would be interesting to investigate more closely specific communicative benefits of developing interfaces that explicitly encourage stance-taking and performative interactions during collaborative exchanges.

Embedded, sequential, intermittent, and mutable

When drawing is used to establish stance, it shows that visualization practices are *embedded* in higher-level discourse structures, contextually deployed in response to other communicative events and improvisations. While examples like the conversation between Gavin and Walter when they swapped drawings show the ways in which images can function as discrete objects within the communication landscape, many of the drawing episodes analyzed were nested, layered and embedded in broader, overarching discourse structures. Sharp distinctions were not made between passages of drawing and other modes of expression. Participants were often fluid and seamless in their mode-switching.

They also exploited the time-based characteristics of the performed activity. The activity of drawing sometimes emulated a sequenced building of ideas or instructions. The *sequential* construction of the image was witnessed and watched by the conversation partner. This was most apparent when participants described how to build or make something, adding elements to the drawing in the same order that they would follow if they were physically constructing the thing. For example, when addressing the question, "What is the most stable way to build a set of shelves?" many used drawing with verbal narration to explain how they would go about constructing a set of shelves, with the order of drawn elements reflecting their hypothetical shelf-building process. Observations regarding sequentiality suggest that features such as annotated playback for drawing interfaces would enable users to more finely control a shared locus of attention over time. This is one way that technology-mediation can augment communication behaviors, taking us beyond pen and paper while still retaining the intuitive benefits of spontaneous drawing practices.

Interestingly, this unfolding of the timeline can happen in fits and starts. This reflects the *intermittent* quality of drawing. The conversations in this study included many examples of people drawing periodically over the course of discussion, starting and stopping, returning to a drawing or creating a new one. This type of discontinuous expression can be challenging to maintain in verbal modes, but a drawing can gradually evolve through a syncopated process while still retaining its power as a communication tool because it has the ability to become so embedded in our communicative practices.

While establishing frames of reference relies on a degree of stability, the evolution of interactions also requires flexibility. For example, while Denise exploited the unchanging character of the artifact in order to maintain Mike's attention, she was also able to change and alter the image in response to the evolution of their conversation, reflecting the *mutable* character of drawing. One moment the drawn artifact was used to confirm boundaries or maintain a frame of reference (requiring a degree of constancy), and the next moment the plastic, malleable nature of the drawing activity was exploited in order to add to a picture, erase parts of it or reconfigure it.

Drawing as performance

Drawing performed in the context of a conversation is a means to engage and interact. The accumulation of marks on a page reflects a dynamic process of exchange and coordination. Early in this paper, examples of spontaneous drawing were provided with no explanation of their content or meaning. It was clear that information about these images was missing. While we might be tempted to assume that simply knowing the subject or author of the drawings would clarify these images, this discussion of the performative aspects of image making highlights the many other things that contribute to the situated meaning of those pictures in the context in which they were created.

IMPLICATIONS FOR DESIGN

Visualizations, ad hoc or computational, reflect our intentions, priorities, and values just as other types of communication do. This is especially true in collaborative contexts were visualizations have the ability to transcend disparate vocabularies and synchronize frames of reference. Aspects of collaborative visualization are increasingly important in the CSCW field as our tools and expectations shift to more image-enabled communicative environments.

Even if you do not consider yourself a "visual" person, you can probably think of an instance where you were involved in a conversation when someone pulled out a pen and started drawing. And, even if you do not consider yourself a person who draws, you knew what to do. You picked up on the various signals and cues that occurred during the course of the conversation. You did not become offended when your conversation partner averted their eyes. You followed along, in spite of the muttering and incomplete sentences that might have been offered by the person working to visualize their thoughts. Mark making is both embedded in our overall communication structures and exists as a distinct communication resource. This study revealed aspects of visual representation as a form of social interaction that can inform the design and evaluation of collaborative visualization tools. Although the technology involved in the interactions described here is minimal, comprised simply of paper and pen, these conversations reflect the potential that visualization practices can play in creating and maintaining coordination and involvement in both face-to-face and virtual collaborative environments.

At one point in time, visualization was seen as a cognitive activity, a process. More recently the word has come to mean a computer-based object representing the digitized and graphical presentation of data. As Ware points out, visualizations have gone "from being an internal construct of the mind" to being "an external artifact supporting decision making" [40]. Viewing drawing as a performance is a call for a return to practice-based view of visualization. This is an initial step towards developing a practical understanding of visual materiality, which has implications for the ways that visual information is represented in digital environments.

Specific design implications for CSCW systems include the needs for 1) more flexible means of controlling attention and awareness with the image artifact, and 2) encouraging performativity to enhance coordination and involvement. This study raises heuristic questions that can be adapted for practical application. Does the system allow me to exploit the stable, persistent aspects of my image to establish a shared focal point for my discussion? Does it also allow me to access the sequential nature of the drawing process when I need to maintain attention over time in a dynamic setting? The notion of performativity was highlighted to better understand the dynamics of drawing as a means to establish and maintain coordination. Do current collaborative visualization systems support this process as well as they could? This study focused on the humble napkin drawing as a form of collaborative visualization, analogous to speech and gesture, and just as important to communication practices, modeling a methodology for studying collaborative visualization not just in terms of system-building but as a form of social interaction.

REFERENCES

1. Arnheim, R. *Visual Thinking*. University of California Press, Berkeley, CA, 1969.
2. Bastéa-Forte, M. and Yen, C. Encouraging Contribution to Shared Sketches in Brainstorming Meetings. Working note in *Proc. CHI 2007*. ACM Press (2007), 2267-2272.
3. Bly, S.A., A use of drawing surfaces in different collaborative settings. *Proc. CSCW '88*, ACM Press (1988), 250-256.
4. Burgoon, J., Buller, D. and Floyd, K. Does Participation Affect Deception Success? *Human Communication Research*, *27* (4). 503-534.
5. Charmaz, K. The grounded theory method: An explication and interpretation. In Emerson, R.M. ed. *Contemporary Field Research*, Univ. California, Waveland Press, Prospect Heights, IL, 1983, 109-126.
6. Clark, H.H. *Using Language*. Cambridge Univ. Press, NY, NY, 1996.
7. Elkins, J. *The Domain of Images*. Cornell Univ. Press, Ithaca, NY, 1999.
8. Forlizzi, J. and DiSalvo, C. Microsketching: Creating Components of Complex Interactive Products and Systems. *Proc. C&C '09*, 87-95.
9. Fox, P. and Hendler, J. Changing the Equation on Scientific Data Visualization. *Science*, *331*. 705-708.
10. Goffman, E. Footing. *Semiotica*, *25* (1/2). 1-29.
11. Goodwin, C. Participation, stance and affect in the organization of activities. *Discourse & Society*, *18* (1). 53-73.
12. Gumperz, J.J. *Discourse Strategies*. Cambridge Univ. Press, Cambridge, UK, 1982.

13. Hancock, J., Curry, L., Goorha, S. and Woodworth, M. Lies in conversation: An examination of deception using automated linguistic analysis. *Proc. Cognitive Science Society* (2004), 26. 534-540.
14. Hanks, W.F. *Language & Communicative Practices*. Westview Press, Boulder, CO, 1996.
15. Heath, C., Hindmarsh, J. and Luff, P. *Video in Qualitative Rsearch: Analysing Social Interaction in Everyday Life*. Sage Pub., Thousand Oaks, CA, 2010.
16. Henderson, K. Flexible Sketches and Inflexible Data Bases: Visual Communication, Conscription Devices, and Boundary Objects in Design Engineering. *Science, Technology & Human Values*, *16* (4). 448-473.
17. Isenberg, P., Elmqvist, N., Scholtz, K., Cernea, D., Ma, K.-L. and Hagen, H. Collaborative Visualization: Definition, Challenges, and Research Agenda. *Information Visualization*, *10* (4). 310-329.
18. Ishii, H. and Kobayashi, M. ClearBoard: A Seamless Medium for Shared Drawing and Conversation with Eye Contact. *Proc. CHI 1992*, ACM Press (1992). 525-706.
19. Jaffe, A. *Stance: sociolinguistic perspectives*. Oxford University Press, Oxford, UK, 2009.
20. Ju, W., Lee, B. and Klemmer, S. Range: Exploring Proxemics in Collaborative Whiteboard Interaction *Proc. CHI 2007*. ACM Press (2007), 2483-2487.
21. Mathison, S. Seeing is Believing: The Credibility of Image-Based Research and Evaluation. in Donaldon, S.I., Christie, C.A. and Mark, M.M. eds. *What Counts as Credible Evidence in Applied Research and Evaluation Practice?*, Sage Pub., London, 2009, 181-196.
22. Nakatani, C., Grosz, B., Ahn, D. and Hirschberg, J. Instructions for annotating discourses, Center for Research in Computing Technology, Harvard Univ., Technical Report Number TR-21-95. Cambridge, MA, 1995.
23. Norris, S. *Analyzing multimodal interaction: A methodological framework*. Routledge, NY and London, 2004.
24. Orlikowski, W. Sociomaterial Practices: Exploring Technology at Work. *Organization Studies*, *28* (09). 1435-1448.
25. Pedersen, E.R., McCall, K., Moran, T.R. and Halasz, F.G. Tivoli: An Electronic Whiteboard for Informal Worksgoup Meetings. *Proc. InterCHI 1993*. 391-398.
26. Prante, T., Magerkurth, C. and Streitz, N. Developing CSCW Tools for Idea Finding– Empirical Results and Implications for Design. Proc. *CSCW'02*. ACM Press (2002), 106-115.
27. Rekimoto, J. A Multiple Device Approach for Supporting Whiteboard-based Interactions. *Proc. CHI 1998*. ACM Press (1998), 344-351.
28. Roth, W.-M. and McGinn, M.K. Inscriptions: Toward a Theory of Representing as Social Practice. *Review of Ed. Research*, *68* (1). 35-59.
29. Ryokai, K., Marti, S. and Ishii, H. I/O Brush: Drawing with Everyday Objects as Ink. *Proc. CHI 2004*. ACM Press (2004), 1-8.
30. Snyder, J. Activities & artifacts: the dual nature of image-making in communicative practice. *Proc. iConference*. ACM (2012), p.10-17.
31. Snyder, J. Image-Enabled Discourse: A Conceptual Framework. Paper presented at *Intl. Visual Soc. Association (IVSA) Conference*, (2011).
32. Tang, J.C. and Minneman, S.L. VideoDraw: A Video Interface for Collaborative Drawing. *ACM Trans. on Info. Systems*, *9* (2). 170-184.
33. Tannen, D. *Framing in Discourse*. Oxford University Press, NY, NY, 1993.
34. Tannen, D. What's in a Frame? Surface Evidence for Underlying Expectations. In Tannen, D. ed. *Framing in Discourse*, Oxford Univ. Press, NY, NY, 1993, 14-56.
35. Tohidi, M., Buxton, W., Baecker, R. and Sellen, A. User Sketches: A Quick, Inexpensive, and Effective Way to Elicit More Reflective User Feedback. *Proc. NordCHI*, (2006). 105-114.
36. Tversky, B., Suwa, M., Agrawala, M., Heiser, J., Stolte, C., Hanrahan, P., Phan, D., Klingner, J., Daniel, M.P. and Lee, P. Sketches for design and design of sketches. In Lindemann, U. ed. *Human Behavior in Design*, Springer, Berlin, 2003, 79-86.
37. van der Lugt, R. Functions of Sketching in Design Idea Generation Meetings. *Proc. C&C '02*, 72-79.
38. van Dijk, T.A. Episodes as units of discourse analysis. In Tannen, D. ed. *Analyzing Discourse: Text and Talk*, Georgetown Univ. Press, Georgetown, DC, 1981, 177-195.
39. Walny, J., Carpendale, S., Riche, N.H., Venolia, G. and Fawcett, P. Visual Thinking in Action: Visualizations as Used on Whiteboards. *IEEE Transactions on Vis. and Comp. Graphics*, *17* (12). 2508-2517.
40. Ware, C. *Information Visualization: Perception for Design*. Morgan Kauffman, SF, CA, 2000.
41. Weibel, N., Hofstetter, H., Signer, B., Jetter, H.-C., Norrie, M.C. and Reiterer, H. PaperSketch: A Paper-Digital Collaborative Remote Sketching Tool. *Proc. IUI '11*. (2011), 155-164.

Understanding How the Projection of Availability State Impacts the Reception of Incoming Communication

Jaime Teevan
Microsoft Research
Redmond, WA USA
teevan@microsoft.com

Alexander Hehmeyer
Microsoft Corporation
Redmond, WA USA
alexheh@microsoft.com

ABSTRACT

Many communication systems infer and project information about a user's availability, making it possible for others to decide whether and how to contact that user. Presumably when the system infers people are busy, they are less open to interruption. But analysis of 103,962 phone calls made using a popular enterprise communications tool reveals that people are actually significantly more likely to answer the phone when the system projects that they are busy than at other times. A follow-up survey of 569 users of the system suggests that this seemingly counter-intuitive fact may arise because people care a lot about the recipient's availability when initiating phone communications and are unlikely to attempt to call someone who appears to be busy unless the communication is important. Recipients thus perceive incoming calls as more important when they are busy than at other times, making them more likely to answer.

Author Keywords

Interruptions; communication; calls; presence; availability.

ACM Classification Keywords

H.5.3 [**Group and Organization Interfaces**]: Collaborative Computing—*synchronous interactions, CSCW.*

INTRODUCTION

Imagine that you are busy. Now imagine that the phone rings. It seems reasonable to assume that you would be less likely to answer the call at that point than if you were available. Phone calls, like any type of communication, are established via a negotiation between the initiator of the communication and the recipient. The person placing the call chooses when to place it, and the person receiving the call chooses whether to answer it. One way a busy person can partake in the negotiation is to ignore incoming calls.

Surprisingly, however, when analyzing over a hundred thousand enterprise phone calls we observed that people were more likely to answer the phone when busy than at other times. Via a survey of hundreds of system users we demonstrate that this counterintuitive finding appears to arise from the fact that, in the population we studied, the initiator of each phone call had access to information about the recipient's availability and could use that information to appropriately tailor their communication timing and mode. As a result, busy people perceived incoming phone calls as particularly important because they knew the caller chose to call regardless of their being unavailable. Call importance is a primary reason people answer the phone, so this shared knowledge that the recipient was busy is likely to explain why people answered the phone more when busy.

CSCW '13, February 23–27, 2013, San Antonio, Texas, USA.
Copyright 2013 ACM 978-1-4503-1331-5/13/02...$15.00.

This paper presents evidence that the interruption decisions of a caller can impact the acceptance decisions of the recipient. Previous research has shown that establishing communication involves a negotiation between the parties involved [10, 13, 15], and that initiators use information about the recipient's availability in this negotiation [1, 5, 14]. But we are unaware of research that shows recipients' communication decisions are impacted by the fact that they know that information about their availability is visible to others. Additionally, previous studies have only looked at data collected from a handful of users on prototype systems; all papers cited here, for example, used fewer than 80 participants. In contrast, we study large-scale log data collected by a working enterprise communication system. The system was used by thousands of users within hundreds of different companies as they made real world, natural communication decisions. Because log data show what people do but not why, we supplement these data with a survey of hundreds of system users.

After a discussion of related work, we describe the details of the communication system we studied, highlighting how it indicates a person's availability. We then present the results of a large-scale analysis of the system's logs, which reveals that users were significantly more likely to answer the phone when the system thought they were busy than at other times. To explain why this was the case, we present the results of a survey of 569 users of the system that shows that phone call recipients use of the fact that the initiator of a call knows whether or not they are available to influence how they interpret the importance of the incoming call.

RELATED WORK

Requests for communication can be disruptive to a person's current task or social situation. A phone call from a colleague may lead to valuable new insight, but can also be distracting if one is working on a different project. Such disruptions have real costs. Czerwinski et al. [4] found that receiving communications during a desktop computing task can result in slower task completion times.

There are many methods people employ to mitigate the cost of interruption. For example, people control the phone calls they receive by turning off their phone's ringer [15] and by screening calls [1]. Grandhi et al. [10] explored several factors that lead people to answer or reject mobile phone calls. Bogunovich and Salvucci [3] found, via a controlled study of 20 users, that people are much more likely to respond to a phone ring during periods of lower workloads. Surprisingly, the large-scale analysis we present of real-world data reveals that users of our system did the opposite. We present the results of a survey that suggests this unexpected observation arises because call recipients believed the caller was thoughtful about when to call.

A well-timed interruption can reduce the impact of the interruption [12], and people initiating communication sometimes chose when to interrupt someone so as to minimize the disruption. De Guzman et al. [6] conducted a diary study with 13 users to understand the cues call initiators want to know about the recipient's context, and what recipients wish others would consider before calling. They found that information related to the recipient's current activity is particularly important. Avrahami et al. [1] studied the effectiveness of contextual information when establishing calls by asking 78 people to imagine the situations in which they might place or receive call and measuring the agreement between the recipients' desires and callers' decisions. Contextual information about the recipient appears to help people make more accurate decisions about placing a phone call.

Many of the cues found to be valuable in these studies of interruption have been used to create digital representations of one's availability. Researchers have explored inferring availability using device activity [2, 8, 14], calendar status [9], speech [8, 9], and physical presence [2, 8, 14]. This information can be presented to potential interrupters directly. However, Dabbish and Kraut [5] found abstract displays of availability allow people to make comparable interruption decisions as information-rich displays, while requiring much less effort on the part of the interrupter. The system described here employs this approach.

In summary, the work presented in this paper builds on previous research to explore how availability information relates to people's communication decisions. While earlier work focused on how availability information impacts the people initiating communication, we focus on its impact on the decisions of the recipient. Further, we are able to study this behavior at a much larger scale than previously possible by looking at the users of a popular enterprise communication system that infers its users' availability.

DESCRIPTION OF THE COMMUNICATION SYSTEM

To study how availability information impacts incoming communication decisions, we studied Lync, a popular commercial enterprise communication system by Microsoft. Lync provides an integrated communication experience, enabling users to connect via instant messaging, screen sharing, email, voice, and video conferencing. The system is widely used throughout the world in large enterprises.

Each Lync user projects an *availability state* to other users within the same company. Availability state is intended to communicate context to facilitate interruption decisions. It is inferred using activity and calendar information, and can be manually set by the user. Below is a list of the possible availability states and how they are inferred. Users are considered *active* if they have interacted (e.g., by typing on a keyboard or moving a cursor) with one or more of the devices tracked by the system (e.g., desktop computer, laptop computer, phone, mobile phone) within a configurable time window, set by default to 20 minutes.

Available A person is active, and the system has no additional information to suggest they are busy.

Busy A person is active, and is on the phone or has an appointment scheduled on their calendar.

Do not disturb (DND) A person has manually set the state. When set, the person can only receive communication from a manually configured list of team members.

Away A person is not active on any device.

Offline A person is not logged into any device.

Table 1 shows how the different availability states are represented graphically. These representations are displayed in email messages next to the recipient's email address, in instant message windows next to all participants' names, and in a list of contacts provided by the system. Additional text related to a person's availability (such as "in a call" or "in a meeting" when *busy*, or the amount of time the person has been away when *away*) can be accessed in a variety of manners, such as by mousing over the representation.

LOG ANALYSIS OF SYSTEM USE

By analyzing the logs of Lync's use across thousands of users and multiple organizations, we are able to build a picture of how a person's availability state relates to that person's willingness to accept incoming phone calls.

Log Analysis Methodology

The data we analyze were logged in the aggregate from anonymous opt-in users of the system. Although Lync is used primarily for internal communication within a single company, many different companies use it and the logs were drawn from a cross-section of these. The logging is a part of the system itself and information is aggregated internally so as to not record or reveal any identifying information about the enterprises or individual users.

Due to these privacy preserving measures and the fact that the system is a production system deployed worldwide with many external constraints, there are limitations to depth and richness of the log data collected. Although large-scale log analyses of communication systems have not been reported

Table 1. How often a phone call was answered or missed, by the projected availability state of the recipient. The most common action for each state is highlighted in bold.

	Answered		Not Answered		Other	
	#	%	#	%	#	%
Avail.	22916	44%	**27183**	**53%**	1602	3%
Busy	**22926**	**67%**	10561	31%	737	2%
DND	**190**	**54%**	147	42%	14	4%
Away	2662	41%	**3585**	**55%**	238	4%
Offline	4487	40%	**6137**	**55%**	577	5%

previously, the limitations we encounter in our analysis are similar to the well-understood limitations that exist in areas that commonly use log analysis like web search [11]. For example, there is additional information that could have been logged that was not. We apply standard log analysis techniques to process and clean the data [7].

Our analysis focuses on a subset of the logs that represent *internal phone calls*, or calls directed from one person in an organization to another person in the same organization. Limiting our analysis to these calls ensures that both the phone call initiator and the recipient had access to the communication system and to the availability state of the other member of the call. To minimize expected or pre-scheduled calls, we excluded conference calls. However, because escalation events were not logged, the log data do include calls that were initiated as person-to-person calls but later escalated to multi-party calls.

In our analysis we look at the logs of 103,962 phone sessions for which the recipients' status was one of the five states presented in Table 1. We then look at the portion of sessions in which the recipient either chose to *answer* or *not answer* the call. Calls that are not answered continue to ring until the call goes to voicemail or the caller disconnects. Other less common actions the recipient can take include actively rejecting the call or sending it straight to voicemail.

Log Analysis Results

Table 1 shows the actions phone call recipients took, broken down by their availability state. For most states, calls were more likely to go unanswered than be answered. When people were *available*, 53% of calls were not answered, and when they were *away*, 55% were not answered. Likewise, when people were *offline*, 55% of calls went unanswered while only 40% were answered. The fact that people sometimes answered the phone while *offline* or *away* results from the fact that the user may be present to answer the call even if not actively using a device monitored by the communication system. For example, a person reading a printed document in their office may appear *away* but choose to answer the phone when it rings. The states can also be set manually by active users.

In contrast to recipients' behavior while *available*, *away*, or *offline*, recipients in the *do not disturb* state or in the *busy* state were much more likely to accept a call than to miss it. Only 31% of incoming calls were missed when a person was *busy*, and only 42% of the calls to people who had actively set their status to *do not disturb* were missed. It is surprising that when recipients had actively asked other people not to interrupt them (i.e., set the *do not disturb* state), they were more likely to answer the phone than when they were available. And they were even more likely to answer the phone when their status indicated that they were *busy*, either because they had a calendar appointment, on the phone, or had explicitly stated that they were busy.

If the logs contained information about the amount of time an individual spent in each availability state, we might also be able to show that people who projected a *busy* state received phone calls at a different (presumably lower) rate. Nonetheless, the data that was logged reveals very strong trends in answering behavior, with the reported differences being much larger than what is typically seen in large-scale log analysis in other domains, and these trends are further confirmed by the follow-up survey.

SURVEY OF INTERRUPTION DECISIONS

Although the log data reveals a strong and surprising trend, it provides no insight into people's motivations for answering the phone when busy. To build a richer picture of why this behavior might occur, we surveyed hundreds of system users about how they use availability information to manage phone interruptions.

Survey Methodology

In addition to collecting basic demographic information, the survey consisted of three sections:

- The first contained four questions about availability state use, including the respondent's awareness of one's own and other's availability states, how often the user set their state manually and to what,
- The second contained six questions about the placing of internal phone calls, including how often the respondent placed calls and the factors they considered when calling (including the recipient's availability state), and
- The third contained six questions about receiving internal phone calls, including how often the respondent received internal calls, factors the respondent considered when answering, and how their state impacted their response to incoming calls.

The survey questions were developed based on semi-structured interviews with 34 system users (26 male), each from a different company. Interview subjects were chosen to represent a variety of job roles, including executives, IT professionals, information workers, and management.

The resulting survey was completed by 569 Microsoft employees. Consistent with the demographics of the company, 429 (75%) were male and 412 (72%) held a technical position. To ensure familiarity with the software, all participants were required to have used it for at least 2 months, and most (75%) reported using it for at least a year.

Table 2. Recipient states, ranked by which callers see as most acceptable to call.

	Ok to Call in State (5 = most acceptable)
Avail.	4.69
Away	3.19
Offline	3.05
Busy	2.65
DND	1.42

Table 3. Perceived importance of a call by the recipient, based on the recipient's state.

	Importance of Call (5 = most important)
Busy	3.30
DND	3.30
Avail.	3.07
Away	2.69
Offline	2.64

For most of the questions in the survey, participants were asked to rate a set of availability states or factors on a five-point scale. We used these ratings to rank them within-subject, and then compared the rankings between-subjects. All differences are significant ($p < .0001$) according to nonparametric Friedman tests. Post-hoc pairwise Wilcoxon tests using Holm's sequential Bonferroni procedure reveal significant ($p < .01$) differences between all pairwise subjective responses except as indicated in the text. Table cells with values that are not significantly different are separated by dashed lines rather than solid lines.

Survey Results

Analysis of the survey responses reveals that participants use availability state to make communications decisions, and consider it unacceptable to call someone who is *busy* or has set *do not disturb* unless the call is important. As a result, participants reported perceiving incoming calls to be particularly important when in these states. Because people said they were more likely to answer important calls, this may explain the log data. We now dive into how availability state is used to establish a call, and how assumptions about call importance are incorporated while doing so.

Availability State Used to Establish Calls

Participants appeared to care a lot about the availability state they project to others. They tended to know what state they were in, with 80.5% of respondents reporting they "always" or "often" knew it, and only 1.8% reporting similar measures of surprise at their state. This awareness appeared to exist even in the absence of active monitoring, with 66.7% of all participants saying they "always" or "often" knew their state without looking. Participants also put effort into controlling the state they projected, with 82.2% saying they had manually set it at some point; 29.3% of those people said they did so at least daily. The most popular states to set were *busy*, *do not disturb*, and *away*.

Knowledge of other's availability state also appeared important. Over a third (34.3%) of participants reported checking on the state of other users more than 10 times a day, and all but 9.0% said they checked someone else's state at least daily.

Other's state information was used to decide when and how to contact them. Participants were asked to judge, on a 5-point scale, how acceptable they found it to call someone in each availability state. These responses were used to create a partial ordering of the states for each individual. The mean rank of these orderings can be found in Table 2. Participants consistently found it most acceptable to call *available* recipients, and least acceptable to call *busy* or *do not disturb* recipients.

Table 4. The rank of the different factors that participants reported considering when deciding whether to place or answer a phone call.

	Placing (5 = most important)	Receiving (5 = most important)
Recipient's availability	3.32	3.46
Importance to respondent	3.29	2.78
Importance to other	2.62	2.18
Closeness of relationship	2.36	2.32
Recipient's location	1.99	2.26
Relative status	1.42	2.00

Participants reported varying the mode of communication they used based on the availability state of the person being contacted. For example, they were more likely to try to IM someone who was *available* than *busy*, and more likely to email a *busy* person. The decision to call was particularly likely to be influenced by the recipient's availability state, with 425 (75%) participants selecting the phone as a potential way to contact someone who was *available*, compared to only 80 (14%) who said they would use the phone to contact a *busy* person. Given callers make interruption decisions based on the recipient's state, it is likely that people who are *busy* receive fewer calls from a different set of people than they do in other states, and this probably impacts how the incoming calls are received.

Most (69.2%) participants believed their availability state was taken into account when an internal colleague called them. Nonetheless, not all incoming calls were wanted. Consistent with previous work [15], participants used various strategies to avoid such calls. Almost half (44.3%) reported switching their availability state when receiving an unwanted phone call, in effect enabling others to make better interruption decisions in the future.

To understand the relative importance of the recipient's availability state when establishing voice communication, participants rated the importance of a number of potentially influential factors and these ratings were used to create a partial ordering. The mean rank of a subset of the factors considered is shown in Table 4. The recipient's availability emerged as the most important factor for both the person placing and receiving the call.

Factoring in the Importance of the Call

Another central factor that participants reported considering when establishing voice communication was the importance of the message. As can be seen in Table 4, when placing a call participants were as likely to consider the importance of the message to themselves as they were to consider the recipient's availability state. This is consistent with the fact that 87.2% of participants agreed they might interrupt someone with a call in a state they normally would not if the message were important. Likewise, when receiving a call the perceived importance of the message to the recipient was second only the recipient's actual availability.

Interestingly, participants perceived an incoming phone call to be differentially important as a function of their availability state. Each state was rated by how important an incoming call was thought to be given the participant was in that state. The responses were used to create a partial ordering, and the mean rank is shown in the third column of Table 3. Incoming calls were thought to be significantly more important if received while *busy* or in *do not disturb* compared to calls received while *away* or *offline*.

It appears that not only does someone who places a call consider the recipient's state and the message importance to make an informed interruption decision, but that the recipient assumes the person placing the call has considered these factors. As stated by one participant, "I hope that others honor my [state] in the same way I do theirs, but I also understand and respect that the importance of the call to either them or me may cause them to ignore my [state]."

This mutual understanding of availability state, coupled with knowledge of one's own projected state, seems to be incorporated into how incoming calls are understood by recipients. Given message importance is a significant factor when deciding whether to answer a call, this may explain why a person in a *busy* or *do not disturb* state is particularly likely to answer the phone, as observed in the logs.

CONCLUSION

We have explored how the interruption decisions of people placing phone calls impact the acceptance decisions of the call recipients. Large-scale log data analysis of a popular communication system revealed the surprising fact that people were more likely to answer phone calls when they projected a *busy* or *do not disturb* availability state. Via a survey of 569 system users, we found evidence that this could be because the people who place phone calls to someone in one of these states choose to do so only if they think the call is important. As a result, phone call recipients perceive incoming calls from other system users to be more or less important as a function of the state they are projecting. The recipient and the initiator use availability information to jointly negotiate the best time and mode for communication based on message importance.

This paper is the first that we are aware of to show that a recipient's communication decisions are impacted by the fact that they know that their availability state is visible to others. Our findings could be used to build systems that help recipients make better acceptance decisions by providing them with additional information about what the initiator knows when starting a communication.

ACKNOWLEDGMENTS

This work benefited greatly from the advice and input of Amy Karlson, Shamsi Iqbal, A.J. Brush, Kori Inkpen, and the OCG User Research Team.

REFERENCES

1. Avrahami, D., D. Gergle, S.E. Hudson and S.B. Kiesler. Improving the match between callers and receivers: A study on the effect of contextual information on cell phone interruptions. *Journal of Behaviour & Information Technology*, 2007:26(3), 247-259.
2. Begole, J., N.E. Matsakis and J.C. Tang. Lilsys: Sensing unavailability. In *Proceedings of CSCW 2004*, 511-514.
3. Bogunovich, P. and D. Salvucci. The effects of time constraints on user behavior for deferrable interruptions. In *Proceedings of CHI 2011*, 3123-3126.
4. Czerwinski, M., E. Cutrell and E. Horvitz. Instant messaging and interruption: Influence of task type on performance. In *Proceedings of OZCHI 2000*, 356-361.
5. Dabbish, L. and R.E. Kraut. Controlling interruptions: Awareness displays and social motivation for coordination. In *Proceedings of CSCW 2004*, 511-514.
6. De Guzman, E.S., M. Sharmin and B.P. Bailey. Should I call now? Understanding what context is considered when deciding whether to initiate remote communication via mobile devices. In *Proceedings of GI 2007*, 143-150.
7. Dumais, S.T., R. Jeffries, D.M. Russell, D. Tang and J. Teevan. Designing and analyzing large scale logs studies. Course at *CHI 2011*.
8. Fogarty, J., S.E. Hudson, C.G. Atkeson, D. Avrahami, J. Forlizzi, S.B. Kiesler, J. Lee and J. Yang. Predicting human interruptibility with sensors. *TOCHI*, 2005:12(1), 119-146.
9. Fogarty, J., J. Lai and J. Christensen. Presence versus availability: The design & evaluation of a context-aware communication client. *IJHCS*, 2004:61(3), 299-317.
10. Grandhi, S. A., R.P. Schuler and Q. Jones. Telling Calls: Facilitating phone conversation grounding and management. In *Proceedings of CHI 2011*, 2153-2162.
11. Grimes, C., D. Tang and D.M. Russell. Query logs alone are not enough. *WWW 2007* workshop on Query Log Analysis: Social and Technological Challenges.
12. Iqbal, S.T. and B.P. Bailey. Effects of intelligent notification management on users and their tasks. In *Proceedings of CHI 2008*, 93-102.
13. Nardi, B.A., S. Whittaker and E. Bradner. Interaction and outeraction: Instant messaging in action. In *Proceedings of CSCW 2002*, 78-88.
14. Oulasvista, A., R. Petit, M. Raento and S. Titta. Interpreting and acting on mobile awareness cutes. *HCI*, 2007:22(1), 97-135.
15. Wiberg M. and S. Whittaker. Managing availability: Supporting lightweight negotiations to handle interruptions. *TOCHI*, 2005:12(4), 356-387.

How and Why Teenagers Use Video Chat

Tatiana Buhler, Carman Neustaedter, and Serena Hillman
School of Interactive Arts and Technology, Simon Fraser University
250 – 13450 102nd Avenue
Surrey, BC, Canada, V3T 0A3
[tda6, carman_neustaedter, shillman]@sfu.ca

ABSTRACT
Teenagers are increasingly using video chat systems to communicate with others, however, little research has been conducted to explore how and why they use the technology. To better understand this design space, we present the results of a study of twenty teenagers and their use of video chat systems such as Skype, FaceTime, and Google Hangouts. Our results show that video chat plays an important role in helping teenagers socialize with their friends after school and on weekends where it allows them to see emotional reactions and participate in activities like shared homework sessions, show and tell, and performances over distance. Yet video chat is also used to engage in more private activities such as gossiping, flirting, and even the viewing of sexual acts. This presents an interesting design challenge of supporting teen use of video chat while mitigating privacy and parental concerns.

Author Keywords
Teenagers; video chat; video conferencing; social media

ACM Classification Keywords
H.5.3 [Information interfaces and presentation]: Group and Organization Interfaces - *Computer Supported Cooperative Work;*

INTRODUCTION
For many adolescents, connection with friends for socialization, relationship-building, and 'hanging out' now takes place online [4,22]. The social expectations and pressures that are created by constant connectivity are also evident amongst teens [19]. Given this, a large amount of research has focused on how teenagers make use of a variety of communication technologies. This includes text messaging [8], instant messaging [9,10], and social networking sites such as Facebook [1,4,22].

Over the last several years, we have seen the use of video chat for communication amongst family and friends rapidly proliferate with the availability of free video conferencing systems like Skype, Apple FaceTime, and Google Hangouts. This has resulted in studies exploring the ways in which video chat is used by families with children [2,13,16], grandparents and grandchildren [25], long distance partners [24], etc. In 2012, a study showed that 37% of teenagers aged 12 to 17 used video chat [17]; however, we have yet to see any studies that specifically document *how* and *why* teenagers use such systems. Without this, we do not know how video chat supports (or does not) the needs of this unique demographic and how such systems could be better designed.

For this reason, we have conducted a study with twenty teenagers—between thirteen and eighteen years of age—who use video chat to communicate with their friends or family at varying frequencies. Our results outline the ways in which video chat is used by teenagers, when and why teenagers choose to use video chat over other technologies, and what challenges they face in using the technology. To foreshadow, like prior studies of adult use of video chat [2,6,13,16,24], teenagers valued being able to *see* their friends, they engaged in open connections in order to share activities longer term, and some teenagers even engaged in sexually explicit activities over video chat. Like pre-teens' usage of asynchronous video [12], teenagers also engaged in 'Show and Tell' sessions and 'Performing Acts'.

Beyond this, teens also showed new and different patterns of usage. Video calls were most often spontaneous, multi-person calls were more frequent, and, most fundamental, teenagers had a more localized sense of distance than adults. That is, video chat was about 'hanging out' with neighborhood friends, rather than trying to feel closer to people across long distances (as found for adults [2,6,16]). Overall, our results point to interesting challenges focused on designing video chat systems to better support the needs of teenagers while also mitigating parental concerns

First, we outline the related work on video chat and teenagers' use of technology for communication. Second, we describe our interview study methodology. Third, we outline our results. We conclude by discussing our results and what they mean for the design of future video communication systems for teenagers.

RELATED WORK
To ground our study, we outline the related literature on studies of teenagers' use of technology. Some of these studies are several years old and, given the rapidly changing use of technology, practices may have changed since then. Following this, we describe studies of video chat systems.

CSCW '13, February 23–27, 2013, San Antonio, Texas, USA.

Text Messaging

As of 2008, 71% of American youth aged 12-17 had a mobile phone where 85% used their mobile phones to send text messages or 'text' [19]. Texting is very popular among teenagers because it is fast and efficient, convenient, and private [10]. That is, teenagers feel they can communicate with friends without the eyes and ears of parents, siblings, or classmates knowing about their activities [8,22], though there is care to ensure texts do not always remain on one's phone for surreptitious browsing [20]. Texting most commonly occurs between people who know each other, while messages from advertising companies and strangers were seen as intrusive and unwelcome [10]. Studies of teenagers' texting habits revealed that they used texting to coordinate activities with others, initiate communication, and simply to chat [8,10,20]; however, within this, they experienced challenges in understanding the intent behind messages as well as an evolving 'texting language' [8,10]. Texting was also highly valued because teenagers could perform multiple tasks while communicating with friends [1,8]. In addition to this, we also now see reports of teenagers 'sexting' where they text sexually explicit messages or revealing photos of themselves to others [27].

Instant Messaging

Instant messaging (IM) is another popular communication medium amongst teenagers. Studies have shown that, as of 2007, 82% of the teenagers who used the Internet also used an IM client to communicate with friends [19]. Teenagers' typically used IM with their school friends (as opposed to people they might meet online) and it allowed them communicate at nearly all hours of the day [9,11]. IM was used for socializing, event planning, and joint schoolwork from home [9]. Within these activities, teenagers would multi-task what they were doing, and also multi-task their conversation [9]. While using IM, teenagers were concerned about others looking over their shoulder because they often used computers in public home locations [20]. They also expressed privacy concerns about messages being saved on the computer and read by others and would carefully use IM status indicators and messages to enforce their autonomy and provide awareness of presence [9].

Social Media and Social Networking Sites

Teenagers also make heavy use of social networking sites such as Facebook. Again, they are primarily used by teens to connect with friends whom they already know as opposed to strangers [1,4,22]. Social networking sites were found to be used by teens to build stronger connections, express one's self, participate in work, care for others, gain knowledge on social contacts, and maintain their existing relationships [1,4,10,18]. For many teenagers, the benefits of social networking sites were deemed to be so strong that they often outweighed privacy concerns [4]. Benefits include building reputation, popularity, social status, and connection [4]. According to studies by boyd in 2007, teenagers who do not participate in social networking sites can be divided into two categories: disenfranchised teens and conscientious objectors [4]. Marwick and boyd discuss how teenagers use social media to engage in discussions of "drama," interpersonal conflicts similar in nature to bullying, gossip, and relational aggression but with their own distinct connotation [21]. In a study of parents in 2011, Yardi and Bruckman found that parents try to create rules about computer and social media usage but it can be hard to enforce them [27]. Parents worry their children are going to say something or get involved in a conversation that can have devastating consequences, especially because of the permanency of some communications [27]. Parents typically want visibility in the technology their children use: some parents want their children to know their online behavior is being watched and other parents want to watch surreptitiously, waiting for children to make a mistake and expose a "teachable moment" [27].

Video Chat

Several studies have investigated how adults and children (non-teenagers) use video chat to connect with family and friends. These have shown that it is often challenging to maintain calls long term because of infrastructure issues and software crashes [2] but many people "put up" with these because of the benefits of video chat. There are also challenges in knowing when people are available and willing to use video chat as opposed to other technologies like the phone [2,13,16]. Despite these issues, people find great value in video chat systems because they allow them to feel more 'present' with their remote family or friends [6,24] and they are able to see body language and other visual cues depicting emotion [6,16,24]. Because of the unique benefits of video chat, people are more likely to accommodate distance in their personal relationships [6]. Many people are concerned about their appearance over a video link [7], yet this diminishes with usage [6].

There also exists a phenomenon where people will leave video connections open for longer periods of time and focus on sharing activities over distance rather than just conversation [6,13,16,24]. This may occur in a single location, but many people prefer to move around their home [6,24]. Grandparents watch their grandchildren play for long periods of time [13], parents and their adult children perform activities together such as cooking [6], adults may watch television together [6,24], and some long distance partners engage in sexual acts over the video link [24]. Given the trend of people using open video connections, several systems have been designed to better support these needs and the sharing of activities rather than just conversation. These have included always-on video links between one or more households [14,15] and even mobile devices [23]. We have also seen the design of systems targeted for specific activity or life situations such as reading between grandparents/children [25,26] or shared activities between divorced parents and their children [28].

Thus, while there has clearly been a large amount of research in the space of video chat, there are no studies specifically targeting teen use. The notable exception comes from Kirk et al.'s study, which contained two teenage participants (of 17 in total) [16]. Here they state that they sensed teenage usage of video chat was very different from adult users, but with the small sample were unable to expand deeply on this. This provides further motivation for our current study. Closely related to our work is a study by Inkpen et al. that describes how pre-teen girls (aged 9 and 10) used an *asynchronous* video messaging system [12]. Uses included conversing, show and tell, sharing activities, and play-acting / performing. Our study illustrates how these and more occur during *synchronous* video exchanges by teenagers.

STUDY METHODOLOGY

We conducted an interview study with teenagers who used video chat to understand their usage of the technology.

Participants

We recruited twenty teenage participants (10 male and 10 female) through snowball sampling, word-of-mouth, and by posting ads on sites such as Facebook and Craigslist. Four teenagers were between the ages of 13 and 15, and sixteen were between the ages of 16 and 18. Participants varied in terms of how frequently they used video chat. Fifteen were frequent users and would use video chat weekly, while five were infrequent users who used video chat every 2-3 months. The frequent users helped us understand the motivating factors behind video chat usage and the ways in which video chat tools were used. The infrequent users gave us insight into why teenagers may *not* use video chat frequently and what technologies were used instead of video chat. Twelve participants had used video chat for over a year and the other participants had all used video chat for several months to a year. All participants lived in a major metropolitan city in North America and were from middle class families of a variety of ethnicities.

Interview Method

We conducted semi-structured interviews with each participant individually in Spring 2012. Interviews lasted between 60 and 90 minutes. Prior to the interview, each participant was given an outline of what types of questions to expect and were told that data would remain confidential and anonymous. It is our university's ethical policy to breach confidence in situations involving potential suicide, child abuse or violence; no such situations arose. Parental consent was obtained for all interviews; however, parents were not present during the interviews and they did not see their teenager's data. We hoped this would allow the participants to openly discuss their technology usage.

Five interviews were conducted in person at local coffee shops, six interviews were conducted in person at the participants' high schools, and the remaining were conducted at the participants' homes. Each participant was paid $20 for the interview. Interview questions asked the participants about their communication practices using video chat, the motivation behind these practices, and their preferences on systems and devices for video chat usage. For example, questions included "Which video conferencing tools do you use?" and "When do you use video chat?" We also asked participants to tell us stories about memorable video calls and their more typical calls.

The interviewer was a trained, undergraduate student researcher in her early 20s. In retrospect, we feel this helped considerably in gathering information from participants. The participants repeatedly engaged with the interviewer in conversations outside the topic of the interviews (e.g., pop culture, activities at school), which suggests that they saw her more as a peer than a parental figure. This latter situation could have easily arisen if the interviewer was an older, more senior researcher. For future studies with teenagers, we certainly advocate our approach.

We also had the first seven participants (4 females, 3 males) (3 under 16 years of age) complete a private online diary about their communication routines over a 3-week period where they received $1 per daily diary entry. We had hoped this would provide more 'in-the-moment' data, yet we only received 65 entries across the 7 participants (average 8 per person) and the content did little to inform our findings. We suspect that our monetary incentive was not high enough and, perhaps more importantly, the teenagers were less interested in doing a repeated activity over a longer time period. Because of this, we do not report on data from the diaries; we mention it here as a consideration for future studies though.

Data Collection and Analysis

We kept handwritten notes for all interviews along with audio recordings. We transcribed audio recordings and then performed a thematic analysis on the transcribed data (diaries and interviews). Our analysis revealed several themes that form the focal points of our results and the subsequent sections. In our results, we list representative quotes along with the gender and age group of the participant. 'Older' refers to teens 16 years of age and older and 'Younger' refers to teens under 16 years of age. We have chosen to not include exact ages next to quotes to further anonymize our results, given the sometimes sensitive nature of participants' comments.

Our results first discuss the general practices that teens had for video chat, including who they talked with, how video chat compared to their uses of other technologies, and how they initiated video calls. Following this we look at the variety of activities that occurred over video chat including both 'focused' and 'open' activities. Next we outline privacy and trust issues that arose for the teens.

GENERAL PRACTICES FOR VIDEO CHAT

Our participants used a variety of video chat systems and devices. Four of our participants used laptops consistently while eight participants used laptops along with other devices such as iPhones, iPods, and desktop computers. Three participants consistently used desktop computers and two of these also used iPods. Two participants reported constantly using their iPhones to participate in video chats and the remaining participant reported to use an iPad and iPhone. Fourteen participants used multiple video chat systems where the most common was Skype (18/20) followed by FaceTime (10/20), Tinychat (3/20), MSN Messenger (3/20), and Google Hangouts (1/20). All participants favored being able to use a portable or mobile device for video chatting such as a laptop, tablet, or phone. However, one participant did explain that he had to hold his iPhone at awkward angles during video calls.

Desktop computers used for video chatting were often located in a central area of the home where other family members also had access to it. Areas like the office, living room, and kitchen were the most common areas to keep a desktop computer. Teenagers using laptops would also stay located in one location for the majority of a video call. Most participants who had access to a laptop would keep it in their bedroom and calls were often initiated from this location. Some participants reported moving laptops around the home based on their location.

Who Was Called and When

For those who used video chat frequently, it was primarily used as a tool to connect with a close group of friends, regardless of how close they lived. While they would regularly have a large number of contacts in their video chat contact lists (e.g., 50-100), they would really only video chat with a select few with whom they were comfortable calling. This included close friends, boyfriends, or girlfriends. Participants also typically had very few family members on their video chat contact list, e.g., less than five.

Those participants who were infrequent video chat users would only use the technology with family members who lived far away. In contrast to frequent users, they preferred to talk with friends who lived nearby in person and made comments such as, “*"why would I chat with my friend over Skype, when I can just see her in person."* This may also be explained by the mobility of our infrequent video chat users: all had a driver’s license and could drive as needed to visit friends. Not all of our frequent users had this luxury.

"Before, when I had [Skype], I didn't have a car or anything and it was just like, after school, just like talk to a person. I think it's more fun if you can see the person's face, like you know, you can see what they're doing" -P14, Older Female

Most participants did not trust people who were anything less than an acquaintance when it came to video chat. Yet, in the extreme, we did have one participant who reported regularly conversing over video with people she had met online and did not know in person. She explained to us that these online friends acted like a support group to whom she could ‘vent’. With her online friends, she did not worry about gossip spreading or judgment because they did not have mutual friends in common, she did not see them in person, and they did not go to her school.

Video calls typically lasted between thirty minutes and one hour, though some reported calls of several hours where connections were left open. We discuss this in detail later.

Initiating Video Calls

Only one participant had scheduled video chat sessions. This was with an extended family member where the participant’s mother would schedule a time over email for her daughter to video chat with her aunt. For all others, video chat was a spontaneous activity that occurred at varying points in the evening or on the weekend. This is likely because video chat usage amongst teenagers was tied more to local friends than extended family.

"I don't really need to like schedule a time to like talk to my friends, like I see them every day at school so it's like if they want to talk more I guess it's like, there should be like a reason, it's not like 'Okay, six tonight and every Monday'. It's just cuz like, yeah, I guess if like they want to talk or something, then you just sporadically be like 'Hey I want to talk' and then yeah. That's why I guess it's not as scheduled" - P15, Younger Female

Participants reported logging into their video chat system and seeing who was online before making a video call. Skype and MSN Messenger, for example, reveal the status of the user whether they are online, away, or offline. This online presence indicator was enough to prompt a video call for half of our participants. The other half said that their online status did not indicate their availability and at times, it did not indicate the availability of others. It is worth noting that each participant *was* actively trying to discern whether or not the online status indicated availability though. If a contact was not online, participants said that they would send them a text message, quick phone call, or Facebook message to tell the other person to go online.

“People usually use Facebook over Skype so they’ll message me and say what’s up” – P4, Older Female

Video Chat Compared to Other Technologies

As a comparison, we asked participants about their use of communication technologies other than video chat and found fairly specific uses. Participants commonly used Facebook when they were bored or wanted to ‘catch up’ with people quickly by reading status messages, looking at photos, or posting wall comments. Thus, it mostly served to fulfill a ‘browsing’ need, rather than direct communication. As mentioned, Facebook was also used to find people to video chat with. Text messaging was primarily used for exchanging short and quick messages with friends. It was often the technology our participants turned to if they did not want to feel obligated to have a long conversation with someone.

"Text can be short and quiet but um, Skype really requires you to sit down and give it a lot of attention. Calls can go on from anywhere from like thirty minutes to a couple of hours... If it's something, like, really important than I'd

rather say it to them in person and if, in that case, Skype is accessible then I would use that." -P16, Older Male

Similar to other studies [24], video chat played a communication role that was different and beyond other technologies. It was most often *not* the most frequent communication technology they used, however, our participants unanimously explained that video chat was the closest thing to face-to-face communication. It allowed them to see what the remote person was actually doing and to 'hangout' with them. Participants also felt they could more easily empathize with the recipient of the call because their facial expressions were visible and it was less likely that a conversation was taken the wrong way. This was useful when discussing sensitive topics (e.g., during arguments). Participants also valued seeing facial expressions when telling jokes or showing something funny. What was striking was that video chat was not first and foremost seen as a way to feel closer to the remote person (like was found for adults [6,16,24]) since the teenagers would see each other at school typically daily.

"I enjoy that one, you can catch up and chat with them. It's not just like a phone where you hear them, like you hear a bang and are like "What Is that?" but if you video chat you can see them and like see what they're doing... Just for the fact that you can see their facial expressions and if you tell a joke you can see if they actually did laugh or if it's a fake laugh ... if you don't want to cross boundaries with someone, like say you're discussing a topic with someone that is kind of iffy. You can tell by their face if they're like 'Oh, what's this person saying?'... Like conversations that could be taken in a good way or go completely downhill." – P6, Older Male

Although the participants preferred video for conversing, users expressed irritation with problems such as a lack of Internet connection (e.g., FaceTime over Wi-Fi), software glitches, poor audio quality, or picture distortion. Several teenagers said that if video transmission started to lag or interfere with audio, they would end the video connection in preference for a clear audio-only conversation.

ACTIVITIES DURING VIDEO CHAT

All of our participants divided their attention between multiple activities at the same time while on a video call. Many of them reported to simultaneously browse the Internet, chat on social networking sites, or watch television while video chatting. For most of the participants, multitasking was a habitual behavior. The activities and types of conversations carried out by the participants over video chat fell into one of two categories: *focused conversations* or *open connections*. This reflects Kirk et al.'s categorization [16]. Within each category, we learned about several nuanced activities that occurred.

Focused Activities

Focused conversations and activities were reported by all of the participants. For some of them, it was a sporadic call where there was a sudden desire to share news or to show something. For others, these focused activities would occur during an existing video call.

Show and Tell. Show and Tell activities occurred most often amongst our participants. Whether it was clothing or personal accomplishments, teenagers enjoyed sharing these things with one another and compared it to having friends in the room. One teenager expressed excitement and happiness as she told us a story about showing her friend some new clothes that she bought.

"I'll be in my room and I'll just sit on my bed with a Skype call on and I'll show them some stuff like if I got new clothes or something... we always like look at our outfits and stuff... It's like [having] a new best friend in my room." - P1, Older Female

The framing of the camera sometimes made it difficult for the teenagers to show the recipient exactly what they intended. In this case, they would spend time lining up the camera accordingly. 'Show and Tell' calls could occur in virtually any room of the house, where some locations may be less conducive to laptop or phone placement, e.g., a bedroom. One participant described how his friend called him on FaceTime from the kitchen after cooking:

"The last time my friend wanted to show me something he was trying to cook and it went completely awful and he was telling me how he spilled and it was all over the floor and he was going to clean it up, he was going to get the dog to eat it. Then the dog started eating it and he was showing me over FaceTime, kind of funny." – P6, Older Male

Sometimes the location of the call itself was the point of the 'Show and Tell' call. The same participant talked about a call he received from someone in the washroom:

"Uh one of the times I just couldn't stop laughing at this...he FaceTimes me and I didn't really pay attention to what was in the background and he had it so I could just see his face and then he paused it on the face and flushed [the toilet], and played it as he flushed it. It's potty humor, I know but it was just so random. – P6, Older Male

Gossip. Another common 'focused' activity done by teenagers over video chat was gossiping. Here teenagers actively conversed with their friends where they would talk about other friends from school, boyfriends or girlfriends, parents, siblings and more. This type of conversation was beyond simply talking about one's day and focused more on interpersonal relationships. Marwick and boyd refer to this type of talk as part of teenager "drama" [21]. Three participants talked about gossiping that turned into rumors being spread about them.

"I used [Skype] the last time to vent to [my friend] about the problems I was having with my boyfriend. I just kind of needed to get it off my chest and didn't really want him to see that I used that and I felt a lot better." – P4, Older Female

"I think girls gossip a lot [over video], but guys gossip maybe ten times more. I don't know if it's just our generation, but we talk a lot. We'll like pick somebody and we'll all like have a couple of things to say about that person and then okay that guys done, how about this person... In a sense, I guess you can think of it as bullying but it's kind of like we're venting out whatever we have to say." - P13, Older Male

Participants expressed keen interest in topics that revolved around peers or 'theatrical' occurrences in their daily lives. What made video the best tool for this activity was the instant gratification of venting to friends without having to travel distances. The video systems allowed our participants to see their friends' expressions so they could laugh with them when they mocked others. This would be difficult to detect over text and even a phone call.

Flirting, Nudity, and Sexual Acts. Some participants also talked about flirting with others over video chat. In these cases, participants said they would be talking directly with another person and as the conversation continued, both genders would begin to 'show skin', and in some cases, even masturbate with one another over video chat. This typically occurred late at night in the participants' bedrooms. We note that only older teens (4 male, 1 female) brought this up. Participants explained that sex talk and activities over video were better than on the phone because you could actually see the person doing the activity.

"Yeah, well my friends try to get girls to show [their breasts]... like take their shirt off." – P11, Older Male

"A lot of guys brag about how they get all of these bitches and what not, like 'oh yo, you should see what we did' ... [there's] the casual strip teases and what not. Just like showing each others' junk, I guess you can call it ... [Sex talk is] easier, isn't it? with video, cuz you can see each other. It's like, some parents are really strict and they don't want you to see each other then why not just do it on the video. You got your room locked, you have your privacy." – P13, Older Male

A female participant told us a similar story about being asked to strip and dance for a boy over video chat.

"I remember like on MSN, a guy would ask me to go on and stuff, but then he'd be like 'Ooh, do something else', but like I was kind of uncomfortable because I was only 13 or 14 so I was like 'Nooo'... He was my age and just pervy, more or less. So he just wanted me to, I don't know, like dance around." -P14, Older Female

Two participants shared stories with us about their friends who would make video calls while naked or with the intention to get naked:

"I've had some friends who intentionally go naked [on Skype] just to liven up the conversation, I guess" – P12, Older Male

"A friend of mine, her and her friend, in front of a web cam played strip poker with like two other guys on the opposite web cam. And they just, boobs and all, just straight on the web cam." -P14, Older Female

Open Connections & Activities

Like families with children and long distance couples [6,13,16,24], the teenagers in our study also kept their video chat calls open for longer periods of time where they would engage in a variety of activities visible on the video channel. In these cases, they wouldn't necessarily be engaged in focused conversations or acts with others like were the case for the previously described activities. Instead, they would simply be 'hanging out' together over video chat, much like friends would be together in person. This type of open connection would typically last longer than more focused calls.

"[I] just set [Video Chat] up and I could be doing my homework, eating food, watching TV [while] talking to someone on Face Time." – P6, Older Male

Our analysis showed several interesting situations revolving around these 'open connections.' We outline each next.

Multi-Person Calls. Three participants described their practices of video chatting with multiple friends at the same time. In this case, each would connect from his or her own home using Group Skype calling. While one might expect this to be a 'focused activity,' participants described it as an open activity where they would fluidly move in and out of conversation with people in the group. Here they did not feel an obligation to stay in front of the video chat software. Instead, they felt freer to watch television in the background or get up to move around the house without making an announcement. Teenagers were more inclined to watch others communicate until it was their turn to talk.

For example, one participant described being in a multi-person call where some of his friends started to flirt with others in the call. He expressed feeling 'left out' in this situation. This exclusion from the conversation gave him opportunities to go to and from the computer as he pleased. As he described, he would often go into the kitchen to grab snacks as the video call continued. Another participant also reported similar feelings of neglect during a multi-person conversation. He explained the difficulty of talking over the other participants in the call and the frustration that could arise. Instead of staying on camera, he would wait his turn to talk and in the mean time did not feel tied to the computer as his friends carried on the conversation. In this way, teens were able to 'hangout' in a multi-person call.

"I've talked to 5 people at once.... It's not exactly fun because everybody talks over each other." – P10, Younger Male

Teenagers were more likely to participate in group calls later in the evening or on weekends because others were more likely available at these times. For example, one participant reported having a multi-person conversation with a friend at a slumber party. Teenagers were also more likely to participate in multi-person conversations when using software such as Google Hangouts and Tinychat. One participant used Skype to connect with multiple people via video, but unlike the other software, multi-person calls in Skype are not free. As such, this participant described how she took advantage of Skype's free trials:

"You have to pay for conference calling [over Skype] but you can get a seven day trial... So I'll just create a new e-mail and a new Skype... I probably have about 52 Skypes already but only one main one that I use."- P1, Older Female

Homework. Six participants (3 Younger, 3 Older) used open calls while working on school coursework. They would leave the video chat running while completing their assignments on the computer. During this time, they would multitask and look up multiple websites in different web browser tabs. Occasionally, these participants would return to the video call and ask their friend a question or check up on progress. Overall, convenience was the main reason teenagers chose to do their homework over Skype rather than in person. For example, one teenager told us a story about doing homework in the evening when his parents were not able to drive him to a friend's house:

"[With Skype] You have the visual aid, you can show them what you've done rather than just try to explain it... It's the convenience factor, being able to do it from home. Let's say I'm at home, it's like after dinner, usually parents are just like 'Okay we're really not going to be leaving the house at like seven or eight o'clock' but you do have like this difficult [homework assignment]. It's just again the convenience factor you don't have to leave the house you can just be like 'Okay let's go on Skype, we'll figure this out' rather than you have to drive fifteen to thirty minutes, like wherever you may live in town to come help me with this problem" -P16, Older Male

Performing. At times, participants felt the need to share activities with others over for video chat. Four participants shared stories with us about 'performing' over video chat. For example, one participant told us a story about how he, along with his friends, would skateboard in front of the camera and get feedback or encouragement on their tricks. In this case, video chat took place on the participant's iPhone over FaceTime. The friends enjoyed this activity and video chat allowed them to be together for it remotely.

"[My friend and] I skate board so like sometimes he'll go in his garage and he'll show me a new trick he learned, like he'll set his camera up and he'll try it a bunch until he learns it." – P6, Older Male

Despite the benefits, setting the camera up for these situations and properly framing the video was a challenge. The participant ran through his trick a few times, positioning the phone at different angles before lining the camera up in the correct view to get feedback from his friends. The convenience in showing something instantaneously was the main reason why teenagers preferred to perform over video chat rather than in person. Other participants shared stories about dancing in front of the camera or watching their friends play instruments over video chat.

"Sometimes I dance [over video] but that's just cuz it's hilarious... It's more convenient, so it's just like, if the person lives a while away you're just like 'Okay go on [Skype] and I'll show you'." - P14, Older Female

"My friends...practice [guitar] over Skype...It's the ease of use; you don't have to bring the guitar to their house. You can just be like 'I just want to brush this by you and see what you think' and you can quickly show them... It's the convenience factor. It's just way easier to just do it over video than to have to leave the house." - P16, Older Male

Gameplay. Two participants talked about using video chat while playing games either on an external device or on the same computer used for video chatting. Although their interactions were minimal, when needed, they shared tips with one another on how to complete levels and shared the excitement of completing a challenge.

"A lot of people when they play video games like to have a mic to chat with their friends and then if you don't want to go out and purchase a mic it could be easier to just have your laptop set up next to your equipment and be able to talk to them ... it's just like having them in the room with you." - P16, Older Male

PRIVACY AND TRUST

Although we initially thought that video chat would raise serious privacy concerns amongst teens, participants generally felt comfortable and at ease with the technology. This was largely because they typically only conversed with those people who they knew well. However, participants did describe challenges with appearance, the chance of parental invasion, and background viewers.

Room and Personal Appearances

Eleven of our participants said that they were concerned about the appearance of the location being captured over video chat and what this might do to their 'image.' Yet rather than cleaning up an area, participants explained that they could simply tilt the camera away from a mess.

"You don't want to be called a slob." – P5, Older Male

"If you don't want people seeing a certain area, you just kind of tilt the camera one way and just leave it there." - P6, Older Male

Some participants used desktop computers that were situated away from a wall, and did not have the luxury of tilting the camera. In this case, it was even more important for them to clean an area prior to initiating a video call.

"[When we're on Skype] I feel like he's at my house and obviously if I bring someone over I'm not just gunna have, you know, my underwear lying around. I like to clean it up." - P14, Older Female

Eleven of our participants said that were concerned about their own appearances on camera; this is similar to findings with adults [7]. Participants were more likely to 'beautify themselves' before having a conversation with the opposite sex. Several people said that looking nice on camera made them feel better about themselves and gave them more confidence. One participant described how her appearance depended on which friend she was connecting with:

"Sometimes I do my makeup a little bit because [not wearing any] makes me feel washed out [and] like crap. But it depends who I'm on [Skype] with because if it's like [friend's name] then I don't care. I'll be like 'Oh I'm not wearing any make up' [and] she won't be wearing any makeup [either] but she looks gorgeous all the time so yeah. I just sit over here and just like hide." – P1, Older Female

Another participant also talked about the challenges of her video chat system 'controlling' her appearance, rather than being in control of it herself:

"The worst is when [Skype] crashes or the picture is frozen, and you can just hear the person... The problem is that it freezes on like the ugliest face ever." – P9, Older Female

Parental Invasion

Parental invasion was an issue with our participants for any communication technology. Teenagers who used social networking sites were okay with using a computer in a populated area and would conceal their information by changing their privacy settings or blocking out family members from seeing their photos or posts on their social networking accounts. Yet video chat presented a different challenge: Our participants had to worry about parents overhearing or overseeing video calls and told us they would often carefully think about how to hide certain chats from their parents. In particular, this included gossiping, flirting, and sexual activities. Naturally, teenagers preferred to perform these activities in private areas because they were afraid of being caught and punished. Participants who did not have access to a computer in a private area showed frustrations and wanted a computer in their bedroom.

"I usually won't turn my camera on if I'm with my family. I really like having the privacy, myself, when I have the camera on... If you're having a private conversation with your friends, like a lot of that stuff you just wouldn't talk around your family or you wouldn't talk around other friends and it's the same thing, like it doesn't matter which platform you're saying it on, you still want that privacy." - P16, Older Male

Only two parents explicitly regulated the computer usage of participants in our study and tried to carefully watch what their teenage children did online. These were the parents of two thirteen-year-old males. Both sets of parents had the passwords for their teenager's social networking sites and would implement curfews or set times when their teenagers could use the computer. One participant told us a story about how his parents grounded him when they found a conversation that he had with a friend over Facebook. Conversely, nobody reported being disciplined because of conversations they had over video chat.

Background Viewing and Listening

Teenagers showed concern about talking to others over video chat and not always knowing who was in the vicinity during a call. Due to camera restrictions, only a limited view of the area was visible. Our participants explained the ease of controlling the angle of the camera to focus on less distracting areas like a wall. Some apprehension was noticeable here, as constricted views of the room raised privacy concerns for the teens and held them back from openly talking about deep subjects. They also gossiped less when they thought others might be able to hear them.

"Like as I was saying you can't be as open [over Skype] because you never know if someone else could be um, in the room with them like listening... Because you can't see the whole room."- P8, Older Female

Interestingly, none of our participants brought up video framing and background viewing as a concern while participating in sexual activities over video chat. We suspect that this was because sexual activities always occurred in the evening after parents were asleep and they were done only by participants who had the ability to video chat from their bedroom. Six participants openly talked about their concern of hackers connecting to their camera and watching them as the changed clothes or slept. All of these participants took preventative measures such as not adding strangers to their video chat accounts or by putting tape over their video camera when it was not in use.

DISCUSSION AND CONCLUSIONS

We now compare our findings to previous studies of teenagers' technology usage and video chat studies of adults/kids. Following this, we discuss design implications.

Comparison to Teen Messaging

Like IM and texting [8,9,10], teenagers use video chat primarily with their friends and highly value the ability to multi-task while doing so. Multi-tasking even takes the form of multi-person video calls, which is also found in IM [9] but not possible over text messaging. Video chat also allows teenagers to converse and 'hangout' with their friends outside of typical 'in-person' socializing hours, as found with IM and text [8,9,10]. Participants described the initiation of video calls in a similar manner to how past studies described the initiation of IM chats where availability status indicators and messages were carefully used and watched [9]. In this way, teenagers regulated their autonomy with video chat, much like IM [9].

Like IM and text [8,9,10], video chat can be done outside of the radar of parents. This was especially the case for teenagers who had their own laptop or phone that supported video chat because they could use them in their bedroom. Teenagers who could only video chat from public home locations were concerned about parents looking over their shoulders during a call; this is the same as studies of IM [20]. With IM, teenagers were also concerned about others reading saved copies of chat messages *after* the conversation [9]. With video chat, privacy concerns were typically 'in-the-moment' because video chat systems do not save content (unless third party software is used).

Comparison to Adult and Child Video Chat

Like prior reports of adult use of video [13,16,24], teens shared the benefits of seeing body language and facial expressions during a video call. Teenagers also participated in open video link connections over extended periods of time, similar to adults and children [13,16,24]. Yet the difference with teenagers is that calls were nearly always spontaneous. This contrasts with typical behaviors by adults where video calls were most often scheduled [13,24].

Pre-teen children were found in prior studies to engage in 'Show and Tell', 'Activity Sharing', and 'Performing Acts' over *asynchronous* video [12]. We saw these same practices occur for teenagers over *synchronous* video. Yet teenagers also performed different activities: Similar to long-distance couples that use video chat [24], some teenagers performed sexual acts over video links.

Our results also showed that teenagers have different notions of 'distance' as compared to adults. Adults typically use video chat with family members who live in different cities, across country, or across the world [13,16]. Teenagers have a much more localized sense of distance. That is, teenagers would most frequently participate in video chats with other teens in their own neighbourhood. This is mainly because many teenagers do not have the luxury of driving to meet with others in town. They also often face parental restrictions about what time of day they can leave home. In some cases, it can also be cumbersome to travel with objects in order to show them or use them as part of activities (e.g., new clothes, musical instruments, skateboard ramps). In these situations, video chat provides a convenient alternative for hanging out with friends. It also means that video is not used first and foremost to feel 'close' to someone since teenagers see each other in person typically the next day at school. This contrasts adults where the focal point of video calls *is* to feel close to the remote people given the long distances [6,16,24].

Existing studies show that multi-person calls are not typical amongst adults [2,6,13,16]. Our results showed that teenagers engage in them more frequently. We suspect this is the case because of teenagers' needs to hangout rather than use video chat to feel close. The need for feelings of closeness amongst adults creates a preference for more intimate, one-on-one calls [6].

Teenagers showed little patience for bad connections. When the Internet connection was slow, teenagers would drop the video feature and continue an audible conversation only, or they would drop the call all together. Conversely, adults often endure slow connections in order to get a glimpse of their loved ones [6]. This suggests again that teenagers' desire to see the remote person is not necessarily about feeling close to them; instead, it is about hanging out and, if video fails, they will quickly switch to another technology.

Design Implications

While we feel it is beyond the scope of this paper to provide full design ideas as to how one might design 'better' video chat systems for teens, we do discuss several challenges that we think are pertinent for this design area.

First, there are clearly issues that teenagers face with video chat technology. Teenagers move between locations (both inside and outside the house) and need to capture a variety of activities on camera. Here camera framing is an issue as is laptop or phone placement and movement. In multi-party calls, it can be hard to hear over people despite the desire to have such calls. Teens are also concerned about knowing what is captured on camera and who might not be captured but still able to see or hear the video call. For the most part, these all suggest better cameras with wider fields of view, multiple cameras, better placement options for cameras, etc.

Yet looking at the teenagers' perspective of wanting to maintain a large degree of privacy, a small laptop screen and single camera lend themselves more naturally to not being seen or overheard by others. Clearly this is a challenging paradox that any future design needs to address. Unlike social networking sites, teenagers cannot easily block parents' access to video chat calls by adjusting privacy settings and such. Parents can simply stand within earshot or a visible distance of the screen. Instead, physical obstacles and architecture (e.g., a bedroom) play a clear role in regulating privacy when it comes to teen video chat.

Second, from the parents' perspective, there are other issues relating to teenager use of video chat. While we did not study parents or their rules for video chat usage, past studies show that parents are concerned about what their children do online and fear they will do something with lasting consequences [27]. For example, video chat makes it easy for teenagers to perform sexually explicit activities that are viewable by others. This clearly puts them at risk. Yet it is a different type of risk than is commonly taught at schools around sexual education and the promotion of abstinence or safe sex. Parents may need to worry less about 'real world' sex, but instead be fearful of cybersex and public viewing or recording of such acts. Thus, yet again, we see a paradox: Teenagers want technologies that support 'private' activities with their friends, while parents likely do not want their children engaging in such activities.

However, video chat is also used by teenagers for more positive activities such as doing homework together, visiting with friends when one is not able to travel, etc. Teenagers can stay 'under the roof' of their parents yet still engage in activities with their friends. This could easily help alleviate likely parental concerns associated with 'going out,' such as drunk drivers, pre-marital sex, physical violence, etc. This suggests that the best way to manage the use of video chat systems is through social exchanges and education. For example, parents should be aware of the benefits and risks associated with video chat and attempt to openly discuss them with their teenage children. Alternatively, designs focused on providing parents with means to monitor teenage video chat activities would likely not work. Teenagers would simply find workarounds.

This leaves interesting design and social challenges for the topic area. Our own future work will continue to explore the design of video chat systems for teenagers as part of our broader focus on video systems for families.

ACKNOWLEDGEMENTS

We thank the Natural Sciences and Engineering Research Council of Canada and the GRAND Networks of Centres of Excellence for funding this research. We also thank the reviewers for their very helpful revision suggestions.

REFERENCES

1. Agosto, D., & Abbas, J., High School Seniors' Social Network and Other ICT Use Preferences and Concerns, *Proc. ASIST*, (2010).
2. Ames, M., Go, J., Kaye, J., Spasojevic, M., Making Love in the Network Closet: The Benefits and Work of Family Videochat, *Proc. CSCW,* ACM Press (2010).
3. Agosto, D., & Abbas, J. Teens and Social Networking: How Libraries are Responding to the Latest Online Trend, *Public Libraries*, 48(3), (2009), 32-37.
4. boyd, d., Why Youth (Heart) Social Network Sites: The Role of Networked Publics, *In Buckingham, D. (Ed), MacArthur Foundation Series on Digital Learning,* MIT Press (2007).
5. Brown, J. Growing Up Digital, *Change*, 32(2), (2000), 10-20.
6. Brubaker, J., Venolia, G., and Tang, J. Focusing on Shared Experiences: Moving beyond the camera in video communication, *Proc. DIS*, ACM Press (2012).
7. Filho, J., Inkpen, K., and Czerwinski, M. Image, Appearance and Vanity in the Use of Media Spaces in Videoconferencing, *Proc. GROUP,* ACM Press (2009).
8. Grinter, R.E. and Elridge, M. y do tngrs luv 2 txt msg?, *Proc. ECSCW,* Springer (2001), 219-238.
9. Grinter, R.E. and Palen, L., Instant messaging in teen life, *Proc. CSCW,* ACM Press (2002), 21–30.
10. Grinter, R.E., Palen, L., and Eldridge, M., Chatting with Teenagers: Considering the Place of Chat Technologies in Teen Life, *Transactions on CHI,* ACM Press (2006).
11. Gross, E. Adolescent Internet Use: What we expect, what teens report, *Applied Developmental Psychology*, 25, Elsevier (2004), 633-649.
12. Inkpen, K., Du, H., Roseway, A., Hoff, A., and Johns, P. Video Kids: Augmenting Close Friendships with Asynchronous Video Conversations in VideoPal, *Proc. CHI,* ACM Press (2012).
13. Judge, T.K., & Neustaedter, C., Sharing Conversations and Sharing Life: Video Conferencing in the Home, *Proc. of CHI,* ACM Press (2010).
14. Judge, T.K., Neustaedter, C. and Kurtz, A., The Family Window: The Design and Evaluation of a Domestic Media Space. *Proc. CHI*, ACM Press (2010).
15. Judge, T. Neustaedter, C., Harrison, S., and Blose, A., The Family Portals: Connecting Families Through a Multifamily Media Space. *Proc. ACM CHI*, (2011).
16. Kirk, D., 2010. Home Video Communication: Mediating 'Closeness', *Proc. CSCW,* ACM Press (2010).
17. Lenhart, A. Teens and Online Video: shooting, sharing, streaming, and chatting, Washington, DC: Pew Internet & American Life Project (2012).
18. Lenhart, A. Teens, Kindness and Cruelty on Social Network Sites, Washington, DC: Pew Internet & American Life Project (2011).
19. Lenhart, A., Madden, M., Macgill, A., and Smith, A. Teens and social media, Washington, DC: Pew Internet & American Life Project (2007).
20. March, W. and Fleuriot, C. Girls, Technology and Privacy: "Is my mother listening?", *Proc. CHI,* ACM Press (2006).
21. Marwick, A. and boyd, d. The Drama! Teen Conflict, Gossip, and Bullying in Networked Publics, *Symposium on the Dynamics of the Internet and Society*, (2011).
22. Marwick, A.E., Murgia-Diaz, D., and Palfrey, J., Youth, Privacy, and Reputation, *Berkman Center Research Publication, No. 2010-5,* (2010), 4-65.
23. Neustaedter, C. and Judge, T. Peek-A-Boo: The Design of a Mobile Family Media Space, Video, *Proc. Ubicomp*, Springer (2010).
24. Neustaedter, C., and Greenberg, S., Intimacy in Long-Distance Relationships over Video Chat, *Proc. CHI,* ACM Press (2012).
25. Raffle, H., Ballagas, R., Revelle, G., Horii, H., Follmer, S., Go, J., Reardon, E., Mori, K., Kaye, J., and Spasojevic, M. (2010) Family story play: reading with children, *Proc. CHI,* ACM Press (2010).
26. Raffle, H., Revelle, G., Mori, K., Ballagas, R., Buza, K., Horii, H., Kaye, J., Cook, K., Freed, N., Go, J., Spasojevic, M. Hello, Is Grandma There? StoryVisit: Family Video Chat and Connected E-Books, *Proc. CHI,* ACM Press (2011).
27. Yardi, S. and Bruckman, A. Social and Technical Challenges in Parenting Teens' Social Media Use, *Proc. CHI,* ACM Press (2011).
28. Yarosh, S., Cuzzort, S., Mueller, H., and Abowd, G.D., Developing a Media Space for Remote Synchronous Parent-Child Interaction, *Proc IDC*, ACM Press (2009).

Butler Lies from Both Sides: Actions and Perceptions of Unavailability Management in Texting

Lindsay Reynolds[1], Madeline E. Smith[3], Jeremy Birnholtz[3], Jeff Hancock[1,2]

[1]Department of Communication
[2]Department of Information Science
Cornell University
Ithaca, NY 14853
llr448@cornell.edu, jth34@cornell.edu

[3]Department of Communication Studies
Northwestern University
Evanston, IL 60208
jeremyb@northwestern.edu,
madsesmith@u.northwestern.edu

ABSTRACT
In an always-connected world, managing one's unavailability for interaction with others can be as important and difficult as coordinating mutual availability. Prior studies have identified the butler lie, a linguistic strategy commonly used to manage unavailability, and examined message-level data to examine how message senders' use of butler lies varies across media and situations. This study is the first to examine how butler lies are perceived by those who receive them. Pairs of student participants provided messages sent to each other in real conversations and indicated whether these messages were deceptive or not. These messages were then passed to the partner, who indicated perceived deception and provided an explanation. Results suggest that participants expect butler lies regularly although not as often as they are actually produced, and participants are not very accurate in identifying butler lies. Moreover, detailed analysis of messages and explanations suggests that butler lies play a relational role that is expected by both parties in a dialog.

AUTHOR KEYWORDS
Availability management; butler lies; SMS; texting

ACM Classification Keywords
H.5.3. Group and Organization Interfaces

INTRODUCTION
A significant success of today's communication environment is that social connectivity – the ability to communicate with others – is virtually constant [1,6,21]. Even as the always-on world facilitates easy interaction and novel modes of coordination, however, people increasingly report being overwhelmed or distracted by interaction opportunities [29]. In a recent Pew study, for example, 29% of participants said they had recently turned off their mobile device simply to get a break from using it [26]. Moreover, Leonardi et al. [15] observed telecommuters strategically using communication technology to avoid rather than enable interaction, thus increasing perceived distance between them and their co-workers.

These problems reflect a fundamental shift in availability management, a phrase we use to refer to activities and social processes related to initiating, concluding or coordinating social interactions. Historically, people were not co-present (either physically or in a mediated environment) most of the time, so availability management was largely a function of coordinating co-presence (either face-to-face or in a particular medium): establishing a time and place for interaction and/or initiating an interaction once co-presence was established [28].

In an always-on world where constant connectivity and virtual co-presence are assumed, however, coordinating co-presence is no longer the key challenge in availability management. Rather, people today frequently seek to avoid communication when it is technically possible, but conversation would be socially awkward, inappropriate or disruptive [21,33]. In these cases, co-presence does not suffice to indicate availability, and additional effort is needed to explain why – despite mediated co-presence and seeming availability – interaction cannot take place now or did not take place in the past [1,30].

Prior work has identified the butler lie, a common linguistic strategy for availability management [12]. Butler lies draw on ambiguity inherent both in communication media (e.g., about one's location or current activity) and in the social conventions for their use (e.g., appropriate response times, locations for conversation). These studies, however, have primarily analyzed messages from the sender's perspective. This leaves open questions about how often these messages occur relative to other types of lies, how they are perceived by others, and their emotional and relational impact.

In the paper that follows, we present an examination of butler lies in SMS text messaging in a student population at a US university. The same messages are analyzed from the perspective of both senders and receivers. We examine the rate of butler lies relative to other types of lies, assess how accurately receivers detect deception in butler lies, and examine the relational function and impact of messages.

BACKGROUND

Deception in Availability Management

While not previously labeled as availability management, this concept has been preliminarily explored in recent literature. Aoki and Woodruff [1] argue that technologies should provide space for users to make stories about when and why they want to interact. If, for example, a person does not want to be available for a call, they could tell their interlocutor that they are in a poor phone reception area.

A key insight from Aoki and Woodruff's paper was that people sometimes use deception as a strategy for dealing with the always-on nature of modern communication (see also [4]). Salovaara et al. [24] further found that mobile device users felt a need to explain unavailability, but did not feel these explanations had to be truthful. Specifically, deception has been defined as the intentional misleading of another person [16]. To be clear, we use "lying" to refer to a subcategory of deception that involves deceptive statements by one person, that intentionally create a false belief in another person.

Following Aoki and Woodruff's approach for examining how lying can be used with technology to facilitate coordination, several studies have investigated a particular linguistic strategy for availability management, called the butler lie, which people use to avoid social interaction or to account for a failure to communicate. Butler lies were first documented in a study that asked participants to identify the lies they told in instant messaging (IM). Many butler lies involved coordinating the entry and exit of conversations, with an eye toward managing interpersonal impressions when face-threatening actions occurred, such as ending a conversation prematurely or avoiding interaction [12].

Since that initial study, several other papers have reported on how butler lies are used to manage social interactions in other text-based media, including instant messaging, SMS and BBM text messaging [12,3,23]. The resulting body of work has contributed observations about how and why butler lies are produced. First, butler lies are relatively common. Over the course of three studies, people reported lying in about ten percent of their messages overall. Of these lies, about one fifth of them are butler lies intended to manage availability, suggesting that butler lies are an important strategy for dealing with the pressures and constraints of always-on communication.

Second, butler lies draw on ambiguities that emerge from online communication, such as where someone is, what they're doing, or when they received a message. These ambiguities can be exploited in accounting for past behavior (e.g., "sorry, just got your message") or explain current or future behavior (e.g., "going to bed") in ways that are often not possible in co-present interactions where much more contextual information is shared.

Third, patterns of butler lies are affected by the norms associated with different media. IM butler lies, for example, are mostly about exiting a conversation (e.g., "Sorry, I have to go eat lunch"), while butler lies in SMS texting are most often concerned with avoiding other social interactions (e.g., "Can't meet up later, busy"), presumably because an important use of SMS among young people and students is managing their social life and interactions [11, 14]. Lastly, an important function of butler lies appears to be the management of interpersonal relationships and impressions. Explanations that people provide for their butler lies frequently involve concerns about avoiding hurting their communication partner's feelings or trying to make themselves look better. The relational importance of butler lies is also highlighted be the observation that when using a closed texting network, such as BBM, participants told more butler lies to those they coordinated with most, suggesting that butler lies are important for managing social interactions in key relationships [23].

Multiple Perspectives on Butler Lies

Several critical questions remain, however, about butler lies and their role in availability management. Perhaps the most important gap in our understanding is how receivers of butler lies perceive them. Are butler lies viewed as deceptive, and if so, are they frequently detected? Do people have expectations around butler lies, such as how often they take place? To date, behavioral research on butler lies has focused exclusively on the liar and their perceptions of their own messages.

This state of affairs, in which we know one person's perspective of their own lying behavior, parallels that of the general deception literature, in which research has focused either on how lies are produced (e.g., [8,13]) or detected (see [31] for a review). We are aware of no research that has examined how both the liar and their interaction partner perceive the same message.

A second question around butler lies that remains understudied is the relationship between butler lies and other types of lies. We know the rate as which butler lies occur from previous research. We do not, however, know whether butler lies occur more or less frequently than other types of lies. Relatedly, we do not know if receivers judge butler messages to be more or less deceptive than other lies.

THE PRESENT STUDY

The present study aims to address these questions by considering multiple perspectives on butler and other types of lies. We accomplish this and build on the prior results described above by examining message-level data from both the senders' and receivers' perspectives, drawing on both quantitative and qualitative analyses.

Terminology

Before presenting our research questions, we must define key terms that will be used throughout the paper. We refer to the producer of a text message as the *sender*, and to the person that received the text message as the *receiver*. We use these terms for their straightforwardness and because they align with the structure of the technology (in which each message has a clear sender and receiver). At the same time, we acknowledge two drawbacks to these terms. First, and most importantly, language use is a dynamic and collaborative process, and autonomous models of language that assume a sender transmitting a message to a receiver have been shown to be overly simplistic [7]. Second, communication partners are both senders and receivers of messages. Despite these drawbacks, we use these terms to be clear about participant roles for any given text message.

Next, we consider two types of deceptive messages. Following previous research, we separate messages into two broad categories: 1) *butler messages*, are those that pertain to the entry, exit or arranging of social interactions [12], 2) *other messages*, which refer to messages that served different purposes. Thus, deceptive butler messages are *butler lies*, and other deceptive messages are *other lies*. In using these terms, we recognize that the other lies category will involve many kinds of lies, many of which have been more extensively studied by others (e.g., [8]).

Research Questions

Our first question concerns the rates at which lying occurs and is expected to occur. That is, how often do senders report lying in butler messages relative to other messages? Given the pressures we note above on managing availability, we wondered whether butler messages would be deceptive more often than other messages. We also wondered how often receivers expect senders to lie to them. In particular, do receivers expect butler messages to be deceptive more or less frequently than other messages?

RQ1: What are the actual (sender perspective) and perceived (receiver perspective) rates of lying in text messaging?

RQ1 examines independently the rates at which senders tell and receivers expect deception in their SMS conversations. By combining these two measures we can assess the accuracy with which receivers detect lies, another area that previous studies have not explored.

Previous work more generally on the detection of deception has shown that people are not particularly accurate at detecting deceptive messages. A recent meta-analysis of laboratory studies, in which participants were presented with equal numbers of deceptive and truthful messages, showed an average accuracy rate of 54%, only slightly above chance [5]. Even under circumstances that would seem most favorable to those assessing lies, such as when participants receive detection training prior to making their assessments, accuracy rates still do not exceed 75% [9].

This 54% accuracy rate may be an artifact of study designs, however. Accuracy rates are impacted by the *truth bias* [19], which is the reliable tendency for people to assess messages as truthful. As such, when a set of messages contains more lies, the truth bias should lead people to make more errors be less accurate. Levine et al. [16] demonstrated this by varying the proportion of deceptive messages presented to participants, and found that this proportion had a linear relationship with detection accuracy rates. When half of the messages were deceptive, participants' accuracy rates were about 50%, or similar to the chance rates noted above. On the other hand, when no messages were deceptive accuracy improved to 65% [17].

This effect of truth bias on accuracy has important implications for everyday conversation. While deception is considered to be a common element of communication, previous research suggests that only a small fraction of all messages sent involve deception [8,13,3], but this can vary considerably between individuals [25].

Given this background, we wondered if there would be any differences in how accurately receivers perceive butler and other messages as deceptive. If, for example, RQ1 reveals a difference in the proportion of deceptive messages produced by senders between butler and other content, this may affect receiver's accuracy [16]. Additionally, there may be truth bias differences between butler lies and other lies. If RQ1 reveals that receivers are more or less suspicious of butler messages relative to other messages, this may also impact accuracy. We asked:

RQ2: How accurate are receivers when predicting which messages are deceptive?

The previous two research questions focused on the act of producing and perceiving deceptive messages. We are further interested in the emotional impact of these deceptive acts. Past psychological research has identified that people experience discomfort when telling lies in everyday life [32]. Additionally, some have argued that deception can undermine personal relationships [20] while research on butler lies suggests that they can actually be face-saving and supportive of relationships [12].

Our final research question focuses on the potential emotional impact of telling and perceiving butler lies, another area not previously investigated. Past studies on butler lies have yielded data about the senders' emotions when sending a butler lie, but have not investigated the receivers' side. The design of the present study allows us to collect multiple perspectives on the same messages for the first time. Thus we can compare the emotional impact of these types of messages on both senders and receivers.

RQ3: What is the emotional impact of telling and being told butler lies?

Method

We use a combination of qualitative and quantitative methods. Quantitative analyses are used to address the three research questions, and qualitative analyses provide more depth in understanding participant's perspectives.

Participants

Participants included 82 dyads (164 individuals), all students at a large U.S. university. We have demographic information from 126 participants. Their ages ranged from 18-34 (M=20.85), and 72% were female. This is in contrast to the overall undergraduate population (50% female), which indicates possible selection bias. On average, participants had used some form of text-based messaging for 5.86 years. Due to a database failure, demographic information for the other 38 participants was not recorded.

Students were recruited via an on-campus web-based recruitment system, and signed up for the study in pairs, with instructions that their partner should be somebody with whom they exchange texts with on a regular basis and have a friendly – but specifically non-romantic – relationship. Virtually all participants (93.3%) brought friends as partners, so there was little variance in relationship type. All received either course credit or $10.

Procedure

Participants arrived in pairs and the procedure was explained to them, clearly indicating that they would be entering messages in an online survey and that their partner would then see these messages. Partners were then separated and seated at individual computers for the duration of the study. After completing an online consent form, they read a short tutorial, which provided definitions and examples for deceptive content and butler content. The deception tutorial provided a clear definition of deception (based on the definition cited above) along with several examples and counter-examples. The butler tutorial was developed for this study, but used a similar approach and was tested with members of our laboratory.

Next, participants completed a short questionnaire including demographic questions and questions about their text messaging behavior (e.g., how long they have used text messaging, people with whom they most often exchange text messages). They then completed Phases 1 and 2.

Phase 1: Using a web-based questionnaire, each participant entered the last 15 text messages that she had sent to her study partner (or fewer if she had not sent 15). The number of messages entered per participant ranged from 3 to 15 (Mode = 15), with only 16 participants providing fewer than 15 messages. For each message participants indicated whether the message was deceptive (measured using a 6-point scale, anchored by 0, "not deceptive," and 5, "extremely deceptive"). If a message was marked as deceptive, participants explained why the message was deceptive, and indicated how bad they would feel if the receiver found out the message was deceptive (measured using a 5-point scale, anchored by 1, "would not feel bad at all," and 5, "would feel extremely bad").

Each participant also answered questions about their relationship with their study partner, both in terms of their categorical relationship (e.g., "family member," "acquaintance," "close friend") as well as the closeness of their relationship (5-point scale, anchored by 1, "not close at all," and 5, "very close").

Phase 2: In this phase, participants rated the messages just submitted by their partners. For each message read, participants indicated whether they believed the message was deceptive (using the same scale noted above). If they believed a message was deceptive, they were asked to explain why they thought so and to indicate how bad they would feel if they found out the message actually was deceptive (using the same scale described above).

Message Coding

Of the 2,341 messages we collected, 239 were marked deceptive by senders and 215 were judged deceptive by receivers. We coded these messages for jocularity to exclude messages that were clearly not intended to create a false belief in the recipient (e.g., the message "lol" was not technically true because the participant was not actually laughing out loud, but was not likely intended to mislead the recipient; see [12]). All messages marked as deceptive by senders or receivers were coded for jocularity by two independent coders. The coders together rated a subsample of messages until they reached 80% agreement, and then independently rated the remaining messages. Percent agreement between coders was 92.5% for sender ratings and 89.0% for receiver ratings. Twenty messages initially rated as deceptive by senders and 25 by receivers were coded as jocular and treated as non-deceptive.

Senders indicated that 450 of the messages contained butler content. To verify that butler lies had been correctly identified, we then coded the 219 deceptive messages for butler content, as defined above. For example, "I like your dress." was other content while "I'm on my way." was considered butler content. The coders first rated a sample of these messages and after they reached 80% agreement they continued independently. Final percent agreement between coders was 77.3%. We then tested the rate of agreement between coders and participant ratings for the butler lies and the percent agreement was 71.7%. As this was an adequate rate of agreement, participants' butler content ratings were therefore used for the non-deceptive messages. In total, 474 messages were coded as butler content and as 1,867 other content.

RESULTS

We divide our presentation of results according to the research questions presented above, followed by a qualitative discussion of messages and their explanations.

RQ1: What are the actual and perceived rates of lying in text messaging?

Rate of lying

Our first research question focused on the actual (sender perspective) and perceived (receiver perspective) rates of lying in text messaging. First we looked at the percentage of deceptive and non-deceptive messages containing butler and other content. In our corpus of 2,341 messages, 219 (9.4%) were coded as deceptive based on the senders' ratings and explanations. One hundred sixteen (6.2%) of the

1,867 other messages and 103 (21.7%) of the 474 butler messages were deceptive.

To examine rates of deception, we used a linear mixed model with rate of lying as the dependent variable. In this model, messages were nested within participants, participants were a random variable nested within pairs, and pairs were also set as a random variable. Relationship closeness and content type (butler vs. other) were included as fixed variables. The results of this model suggest that, when controlling for relationship closeness, senders produced a significantly higher proportion of lies in butler content (M=27.1%, SE=1.5%) than in other content (M= 6.4%, SE=2.0%), $F[1,168.08]=47.06$, $p<0.001$[1]. Thus the rate of lying in messages about social interactions (entering, exiting, or arranging), or butler messages, was higher than the rate of lying in other messages. However, the difference in the severity of deception between butler and other messages was not significant.

Perceived rate of lying
Next we looked at the percentage of messages perceived to be deceptive by receivers. Again, we looked at the difference between messages containing butler content and other content. Of all messages, receivers perceived 192 (8.2%) as deceptive, including 23 (9.1%) of the 474 butler messages and 149 (8.0%) of the other messages.

We used the same linear mixed model described above to examine the perceived rate of deception as a function of content type (butler vs. other) while controlling for relationship closeness. The difference between the perceived rate of lying for messages containing butler and other content was marginally significant, $F[1,230.41]=2.75$, $p<0.1$. On average, receivers perceived more butler messages (M=10.4%, SE=1.5%) to be deceptive than other types of messages (M= 8.0%, SE=1.4%). These data suggest that receivers perceive butler messages as marginally more likely to be deceptive than other messages.

Figure 1 shows the average rates of sent and perceived lying for butler and other messages. Several important patterns, supported by the statistical analysis above, are visible. First, the receivers' estimate for the rate of lying in other messages was remarkably similar to what the senders reported actually producing (8.0% vs. 6.4%). In contrast, the receivers substantially under-estimated the rate of lying for butler messages, estimating less than half the actual rate that the sender reported producing (10.4% vs. 27.1%), suggesting that senders were lying in their butler messages more than was anticipated by receivers.

[1] Note that the denominator degrees of freedom in linear mixed models are estimated using a Satterthwaite's approximation, which can yield non-integer degrees of freedom [27].

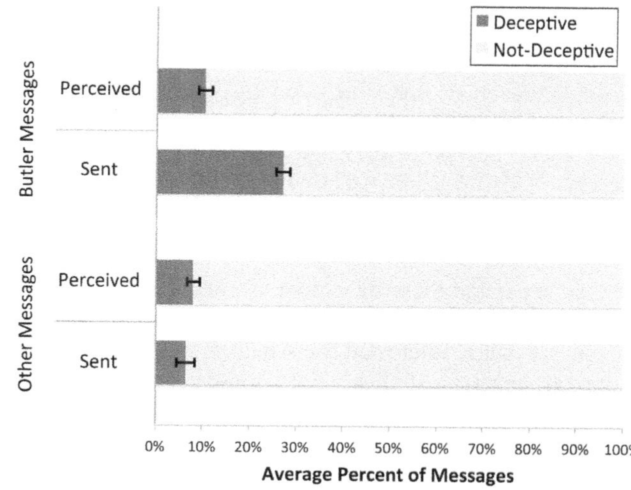

Figure 1: Comparison of actual and perceived rates of lying

While these data tell us about the rates of actual and perceived lies in the partner's text messages to one another, they do not tell us about how *accurately* the receiver detected lies. This is addressed in the next section.

RQ2: How accurately do receivers predict deception?
Our second research question focused on the accuracy of receivers when perceiving deceptiveness in text messages. We examined the sender and receiver indicators of actual and perceived deceptiveness for each message.

Overall, receivers correctly judged 2024 of the messages for an overall accuracy rate of 86.5%, including 373 (78.9%) of the 474 butler messages and 1,650 (88.4%) of the 1,867 other messages.

We used the same linear mixed model as above to test for accuracy as a function of content type while controlling for relationship closeness. The difference in accuracy rates between other (M=87.1%, SE=1.6%) and butler messages (M=71.1%, SE=1.8%) was statistically significant, $F[1,222.47]=18.82$, $p<0.001$, suggesting that receivers were less accurate in detecting butler lies than other lies.

When these data are considered along with the results from RQ1, we see that receivers substantially underestimated the rate at which butler lies are produced, and consequently that they are significantly less accurate at detecting them.

RQ3: What is the emotional impact of lies?
Our third research question focused on senders' emotions when sending deceptive messages and receivers' emotions when they believed they were lied to. We asked senders how bad they would feel if their partner found out they were lying, and receivers how bad they would feel if they found out their partner was lying. We refer to this here as the emotional impact rating.

We again used a linear mixed model with average emotional impact rating as the dependent variable. In this model, messages were nested within participants,

participants were a random variable nested within pairs, and pairs were also set as a random variable. Relationship closeness, content type (butler vs. other content), and role (sender or receiver) were included as fixed variables. The results of this model indicate that senders feel significantly worse about deceptive messages (M=1.75, SE=.08) than receivers (M=1.53, SE=.07), F[1,303.09]=8.3, p<.005. There was no effect of content type and no interaction between content type and role.

We then separated these deceptive messages into those that were detected as deceptive by receivers, and those that were not, as we were interested in whether that affected the emotional impact of lies. For non-detected deceptive messages, there were no significant differences between content type and role, and no significant interaction.

For detected deceptive messages, however, on average senders felt significantly worse about deceptive messages (M=2.09, SE=.16) than receivers (M=1.40, SE=.16), F[1, 34.82]=12.18, p<.001 (see Figure 2). There was no significant effect of content type and no significant interaction between content type and role.

Overall, this pattern of results indicates that senders feel worse about lying than receivers feel about being lied to, but only when the lie is detected. In general, these data are consistent with previous research indicating that people experience negative emotions when lying [32]. The present data indicate that, in fact, people also feel worse when they are the target of the lie. Although senders felt worse than receivers when telling detected lies, their emotional responses were indeed correlated for both butler (r=.25, p<.05) and other lies (r=.27, p<.05), suggesting that the emotional impact of telling lies in text messaging was felt similarly for both senders and receivers.

Given these important emotional effects associated with butler lies, we next sought to examine the relational effects and functions of butler lies by examining the explanations that our participants provided about their lies and their perceptions of their partner's lies.

Analysis of Messages and Explanations

To better understand how people perceived messages as butler lies, we examined their explanations for why they perceived messages to be deceptive. We found that, generally, there were two themes in their explanations.

Relational Coordination

Many messages were rated deceptive based on a combination of the receiver's understanding of their partner and expectations around the situation.

In some cases, butler lies were used simply to expedite the coordination of interaction, such as ensuring co-presence for a later conversation. One participant, for example, texted "*I'm walking in the upstairs door right now.*" Their partner correctly identified this message as deceptive, noting "I don't think he was actually walking in the door. I

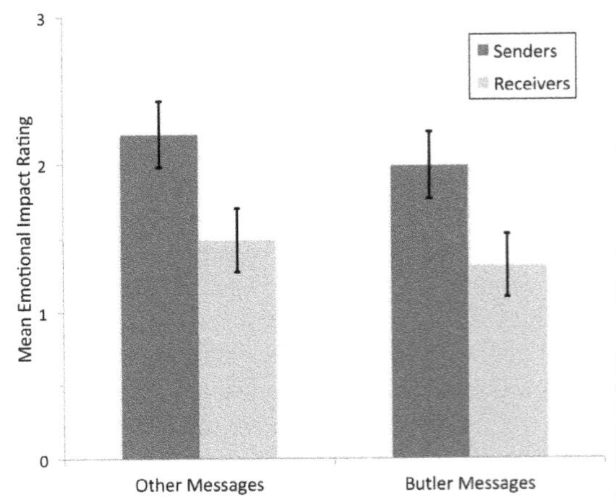

Figure 2: Emotional impact ratings for detected lies

think he was a little further away." This exactly reflects the sender's explanation, "I was not yet near the door. i could see it... but I was still about 50 yards from being there. Written to assure the message receiver that I would be there shortly plus by the time she saw it, I might actually be at that place." Neither of them indicated they would feel bad if this was known to be deceptive, as both rated the emotional impact as '1,' the low point on the scale, reflecting the implicit purpose of expediting co-presence at the door and the low stakes of the deception.

As participants tended to come to the lab with people they knew relatively well, their explanations often referenced prior experience with the partner. This experience also affected how butler lies were used and interpreted. In one case, for example, the sender texted "*I'm going to bed.*" The receiver rated the message as deceptive, explaining, "knowing this person i highly doubt this is a true statement." In fact, the message was deceptive, with the sender explaining "...it was already near midnight and he hadn't shown up. i was pissed and wanted him to think i didn't care if he was coming or not." Here the explicit message was to convey unavailability for interaction, but the implicit message – which draws on a shared understanding of expected bedtimes – was to convey frustration and possible trouble in the relationship. The sender's explanation makes clear that they were acting strategically and in anticipation of a particular response from the receiver, and the sender's emotional impact rating ('1') reflects this intent to convey frustration. The receiver did not provide an emotional impact rating.

There were also cases where implicit relational messages were more positive or routine. One participant, for example, texted "One last game sweety (sic)," with emotional impact rating of '3' His partner rated this as deceptive, noting that "usually he says one last video game and ends up playing two or three more games," but rated the emotional impact as '1'. The sender did indicate that the message was deceptive, explaining that "I texted saying that I would be playing one more game to express the fact that I would be leaving soon. In reality I don't believe I was going to come back soon. Most likely it would still take some time for me to come back." Both sender and receiver explanations here reflect an understanding that this message is not literally true, and some shared sense that the actual purpose of the message was to convey that the sender would continue playing games, but be available later. That the sender feels worse about the deception than the receiver, moreover, is consistent with the above analysis, and suggests that the recipient is willing to accept the deceptive message.

As noted above, many true messages were also perceived as deceptive. This was often true when the message involved a common butler lie. One participant, for example, texted "*Hii sorry I didn't have ym hpone* (sic)," which was not marked as deceptive. The receiver, however, marked it as deceptive, rating emotional impact '1,' and explained, "I bet she had her phone just mentally texted back (read it and forgot to respond)." This combination of the plausible explanation and ambivalence about the deception (i.e., the receiver would not feel bad) suggest a willingness to accept the message whether it is true or not.

Receivers were not always willing to accept deceptive messages, however, and their explanations sometimes revealed frustration or the desire to confront their partners. One participant, for example, texted "*ok sry 4 my horrible txting abilities i am done that awful wrk sht!* (sic)" This seemed to frustrate her partner, who rated the emotional impact '2' and said that "The fact that she didn't text me back for a long period of time because she was busy with 'wrk sht' was deceptive, because she had time to eat two different leisurely lunches with friends as she later told me but not 10 seconds to text me back?". The deception here was subtle, moreover. The sender marked the message as deceptive with an emotional impact of '2' though she was, in fact, working on a worksheet, but also admitted to having time for replying to texts from others (but does not mention lunch): "I wasnt able to respond to several of her texts that morning because I had a worksheet to do. However, i did send a few texts which needed to be immediately received from some other people, while I was doing my work."

This is interesting in that there is a mutual recognition that the message sender is conveying the message that she is too busy to interact with the recipient, but not too busy to interact with others. The recipient is thus unhappy not that the sender could not talk to the recipient, but that the sender had time to talk to others and not the recipient. This highlights an important tension in the management of social inattention: that people juggle many different priorities, and thus different levels of availability for different others. Successful balance of these tensions seems to require either that the process of managing these interactions be shielded from view (e.g., via ambiguity about what is actually taking place), or reflect a mutual agreement about priorities. Otherwise the result is the type of frustration revealed here.

Factually False Messages

In some cases, participants knew messages to be factually false, so could classify them as deceptive outright. Often this was because they had other sources of information available when they received the message. One participant, for example, texted "Yo, come up to 205. [Fred] just got here, he just started drinking. [Bob]'s here too." His partner rated this as deceptive, noting that "I knew for a fact that our friend [Fred] had been drinking for awhile." In fact, the sender's explanation confirms this, saying that "I said that [Fred] had just started drinking, but he had actually started drinking 3 hours earlier and was hammered…."

In another case, the recipient had additional information at the time of the study that they did not have when they received the message. One participant deceptively said "i am walking about want me to meet u sumwhere and take u" (explanation: "I was walking about previously, but was actually currently in my room.") Her partner correctly rated this message as deceptive, explaining "A few minutes later she said she was in [her dorm] so she probably wasn't 'walking about.'" This is, of course, somewhat problematic in that the rating of deceptiveness is retrospective, rather than "in-the-moment." Thus, this is more an artifact of our study design than a reflection of participants' immediate perceptions upon receiving the messages. This occurred only a small number of times in our data set, however, so should not affect the results above.

DISCUSSION

We have presented evidence from quantitative and qualitative analyses of butler lies used in a population of American university students, from both the senders' and receivers' perspectives. The data suggest that, proportionally, butler lies occur more frequently in everyday text messaging than other types of lies, and that receivers have less accurate perceptions about the expected rate of deception – as measured via the proportion of messages that they identified as deceptive – for butler lies than other types of lies. Receivers also tended to be less accurate at detecting which butler messages were deceptive than other types of lies. On average, senders reported feeling worse about their deceptive messages than the receivers. We saw from the explanations participants provided that messages were perceived to be deceptive when considered along with additional information about the situation or the individual, or when they contained verifiably false facts.

Our first major finding is that a significantly higher proportion of butler messages were deceptive when compared with other messages. The implication is that deception is a common practice in availability management via text messaging, and appears to occur more frequently than other types of everyday deception [8]. This suggests evolving social norms around availability management practices, a reaction consistent with recent work suggesting that people feel pressure to be connected constantly and commonly seek to avoid communication [1,33].

We next looked at people's expectations around deception. Receivers expected marginally more butler lies than other types of lies, suggesting that they were more suspicious, or less truth biased, for butler messages than other messages. Despite this reduced truth bias, receivers significantly underestimated the actual frequency of butler lies, with the expected rate of deception less than half that of the actual rate. Moreover, receivers detected butler lies less accurately than other lies. The implication of these results, particularly when combined with analysis of the explanations participants provided, is that people expect to be lied to about availability management, even if they do not always know when. This points toward the possibility of a more nuanced approach to understanding deception in availability management, in which people's expectations and overall relational goals are considered alongside the literal message text and deceptive practices.

Considering the detection result in more detail, why did receivers perform so poorly at detecting butler lies relative to other lies? There are several possible explanations for this. One is that butler lies are simply lower stakes than other lies and thus harder to detect, similar to "little white lies." Previous research has pointed out that lies not involving high stakes (e.g., punishment or significant reward) are difficult to detect [10]. This explanation, however, seems unlikely given that the emotional impact between butler lies and other lies was virtually identical, suggesting that the stakes of butler lies are not necessarily lower than other kinds of lies.

Our findings point to a second, more plausible explanation, that accuracy rates are directly related to the increased proportion of deceptive butler messages produced by the sender and the receiver's failure to fully anticipate this higher rate of deception. As Levine et al. [16] suggested, the truth bias plays a major role here in that people expect most statements to be true. Our receivers expected about 92% of butler messages to be truthful, when in fact senders reported telling truthful butler messages only about 73% of the time. This mismatch generated by the truth bias, we argue, underlies our participants low accuracy in detecting butler lies relative to other lies. In terms of the bigger picture, this pattern of results suggests that people have not yet adjusted their expectations around the frequency with which butler lies are used in managing availability.

All of this is especially interesting in light of our finding that senders were more emotionally impacted by lies than receivers. On the one hand, this is consistent with previous research that has shown people to experience negative emotions when lying [32]. What is novel here, however, is that our data provided multiple perspectives on the same messages, which allowed us to discover that 1) liars not only feel bad, they actually feel worse than the target of the lie, and 2) the emotional impact of the lie on the sender and receiver are correlated, suggesting that both parties are aligned in their perceptions of how emotionally negative the deceptive message may be.

Again, this points toward the possible utility of a more nuanced approach to deception in availability management. Indeed, prior work has shown that deception is an everyday behavior [8] and our findings suggest that people expect to be lied to, although they have trouble identifying the specific deceptive messages. If a receiver expects to be lied to, particularly in situations where they know the liar and understand possible implicit relational messages, it is reasonable that they would not be upset when it happens. The sender cannot be sure that the receiver is expecting deception, however, so it is reasonable for them to be more adversely emotionally impacted. Further research is needed to fully understand the emotional effects of butler lies.

Implications for Design

It is clear from our findings and prior work [12,3,23] that butler lies are a commonly used linguistic strategy for availability management that draw on ambiguities resulting from features of communication technologies and the social norms surrounding their use. Our analyses here strongly suggest that senders and receivers of messages recognize the social value of these messages, even when receivers believe them to be false. Moreover, receivers are not very accurate in detecting butler lies.

A naïve response to these results would be a push to design systems that make it easier for people to detect when they are being deceived, thus improving accuracy and reducing deception (but ignoring social value issues discussed throughout this paper). Interestingly, this is exactly what designers of recent commercial systems have done. Despite the potential value in the types of ambiguity commonly drawn on in butler lies, these appear to be under threat. BBM and Apple's iMessage both provide notification when a text message has been read, for example; and Lotus Notes provides a similar feature ("return receipt") in its email system. Automatic location sharing is also becoming more common, and already accompanies status updates and other posts made via GPS-enabled mobile devices on Facebook. Location-aware messaging is also available on some systems, and location sharing is facilitated by systems like foursquare, Facebook, Latitude, Glympse and Twist.

Our results suggest that designers should not – and users likely will not – take this additional information at face value. Reynolds et al. [23] observed BBM users, for example, who intentionally delayed opening messages to avoid generating "read" notifications; and Birnholtz et al. [2] observed an office in which it was not normatively acceptable to use the return receipt feature in Notes. This builds directly on Aoki and Woodruff's [1] notion of making space for stories, and our results build further on these ideas by showing people expect to be deceived some of the time, and are careful consumers of these messages. They also value the social niceties conveyed and enabled by these practices, however. In other words, they value having "space for stories."

Our primary design suggestion, therefore, is to allow for more discretion and latitude in the use of these features. At a minimum, this would mean allowing users to turn features on or off selectively. Allowing for some manipulation or obfuscation of automated information could be useful as well. One could set "read" notifications, for example, to appear only after a certain amount of time has passed; and also set "read" messages to appear as "unread." In this way, one could look briefly at a message within the pre-specified time window, and the sender would still believe it to be unread and not be upset by a delayed reply. In effect, such features would create new types of ambiguity around who uses particular features, when they are or are not enabled, and whether or not they are being used to share accurately.

Another finding here from the analysis of receiver explanations is that people use many sources of information in assessing the content of messages. With today's systems, however, it may be difficult for message senders to know what the receiver is aware of (e.g., "Did she see my Facebook post tagged with my Chicago location?"). This can make it more difficult to construct plausible and coherent explanations, as discussed by [22]. We therefore urge designers to consider ways of making message senders in various media aware of information known to be available to a message recipient. In a simple form, this could include a set of checkboxes (i.e., "Receiver may know: __ my location; __ when I read my messages; __ my calendar), with links to the potential source of the information. This will allow senders to craft plausible rationales, even as sources of ambiguity (i.e., who has access to what and what features are enabled) themselves may be ambiguous. To be clear, we are not advocating helping people deceive and possibly hurt others, but we do want to help them manage their availability and avoid communication overload. This means being sensitive not just to the need for ambiguity and crafting plausible explanations, but also sensitivity to factors that influence perceptions and usage of butler lies.

Limitations and Future Work

There are several limitations that should be considered when interpreting these findings, and that motivate important future work. First, we studied students at a university in the United States and these results may not generalize to other populations. However, college-aged young adults are the most active users of text messaging [26], so this sample is useful for understanding everyday text messaging behavior. At the same time, we urge future study of butler lie usage and perception in cultures that may have very different views of deception [18], among other demographic groups that may use SMS differently [26], and in non-social contexts such as work, where behavior may differ as well [2, 15].

Second, our design and recruitment strategy meant that most participants came to the lab with relatively close friends. There was little variance on the dimensions of relationship type and closeness. We can therefore draw few inferences about the role of these factors in availability management. We urge future research that explicitly examines participant interactions with partners from multiple relationship categories (e.g., romantic partners, close family members, distant family, acquaintance, etc.) to more closely examine these phenomena, which we believe likely impact behavior.

Third, our participants were disproportionately female. We ran all analyses controlling for gender and found no gender effects. However, we are missing demographic information due to a database failure for a significant number of participants. We do not know what effects missing data could have on our findings, but we have no reason to expect that data would be significantly different than the demographic data we do have.

Last, our survey method relies on self-reports of lying, and requires participants to be honest about their deceptive behaviors. The method used here, however, in which participants rated and explained actual messages and deceptions, improves upon other self-report deception methods, such as diary studies, that rely on the participants memory for prior conversations. Future studies may improve on this method further by directly collecting messages from participants' phones rather than having them enter them into a survey. Additionally, while the explanations participants provided in this study gave us insight to multiple perspectives on the same messages, future qualitative work is required to more thoroughly explore this rich area through interviews with people who regularly use text messaging.

ACKNOWLEDGEMENTS

This work is supported in part by the National Science Foundation (Award #IIS 0915081). We acknowledge valuable research assistance from Jon Culver, Mark Thomas, and Jin Zhao.

REFERENCES

1. Aoki, P., & Woodruff, A. (2005). Making space for stories: ambiguity in the design of personal communication systems. *Proc. ACM CHI*, 181-190.
2. Birnholtz, J., Dixon, G., & Hancock, J. (2012). Distance, ambiguity and appropriation: Structures affording impression management in a collocated organization. *Computers in Human Behavior*, 28, 1028-1035.
3. Birnholtz, J., Guillory, J., Hancock, J. T., & Bazarova, N. (2010). "on my way": Deceptive Texting and Interpersonal Awareness Narratives. *Proc. ACM CSCW*, 1-4.
4. Boehner, K., & Hancock, J.T. (2006). Advancing ambiguity. *Proc. ACM CHI*, 103-107.

5. Bond, C. F. and DePaulo, B., M. (2006). Accuracy of Deception Judgments. *Journal of Personality and Social Psychology*, 10 (3), 214-234.
6. Chen, B. X. (2011). *Always on: how the iPhone unlocked the anything - anytime - anywhere future--and locked us in*. Cambridge, MA: Da Capo Press.
7. Clark, H. H. (1996). *Using language*. New York: Cambridge University Press.
8. DePaulo, B.M., Kashy, D.A., Kirkendol, S.E., Wyer, M.M., and Epstein, J.A., (1996). Lying in Everyday Life. *Journal of Personality and Social Psychology*, 70(5), 979-995.
9. Fielder, K. and Walka, I. (1993). Training Lie Detectors to Use Nonverbal Cues Instead of Global Heuristics. *Human Communication Research*, 20(2), 199-223.
10. Frank, M.G. & Ekman, P. (1997). The ability to detect deceit generalizes across different types of high stake lies. *Journal of Personality and Social Psychology, 72*, 1429-1439.
11. Grinter, R., & Eldridge, M. (2003). Wan2tlk?: Everyday Text Messaging. *Proc. ACM CHI*, 441- 448.
12. Hancock, J. T., Birnholtz, J., Bazarova, N., Guillory, J., Perlin, J., & Amos, B. (2009). Butler lies: awareness, deception and design. *Proc. ACM CHI*, 517-526.
13. Hancock, J., Thom-Santelli, J., and Ritchie, T. (2004). Deception and design: the impact of communication technology on lying behavior. *Proc. ACM CHI*, 129-134.
14. Häkkilä, J., and Chatfield, C. (2005). 'It's like if you opened someone else's letter' – User Perceived Privacy and Social Practices with SMS Communication, *Proc. ACM MobileHCI*, 219-222
15. Leonardi, P. M., Treem, J. W., & Jackson, M. H. (2010). The Connectivity Paradox: Using Technology to Both Decrease and Increase Perceptions of Distance in Distributed Work Arrangements. *Journal of Applied Communication Research*, 38(1), 85-105.
16. Levine, T. R., Park, H. S., & McCornack, S. A. (1999). Accuracy in detecting truths and lies: Documenting the "veracity effect." *Communication Monographs*, 66, 125-144.
17. Levine, T. R., Kim, R. K., Park, H.S., & Hughes, M. (2006). Deception detection accuracy is a predictable linear function of message veracity base-rate: A formal test of Park and Levine's probability model. *Communication Monographs*, 73, 243-260.
18. Ma, F., Xu, F., Heyman, G. D., & Lee, K. (2011). Chinese children's evaluations of white lies: Weighing the consequences for recipients. *Journal of Experimental Child Psychology*, 108, 308-321
19. McCornack, S. A., & Parks, M. R. (1986). Deception detection and relationship development: The other side of trust. In M. L. McLaughlin (Ed.), *Communication yearbook 9* (pp. 377-389). Beverly Hills, CA: Sage.
20. Miller, G. R., Mongeau, P.A., & Sleight, C. (1986). Fudging with Friends and Lying to Lovers: Deceptive Communication in Personal Relationships. *Journal of Social and Personal Relationships*, 3, 495-512.
21. Perry, M., O'Hara, K., Sellen, A., Brown, B., & Harper, R. (2001). Dealing with mobility: understanding access anytime, anywhere. *ACM TOCHI*, 8, 323-347.
22. Read, S. (1992). Constructing accounts: the role of explanatory coherence. *Explaining the self to others*. M. L. McLaughlin, M. J. Cody and S. Read. Hillsdale, NJ, Lawrence Erlbaum Associates: 3-19.
23. Reynolds, L., Gillette, S., Marder, J., Miles, Z., Vodenski, P., Weintraub, A., et al. (2011). Contact stratification and deception. *Proc. ACM CSCW*, 221-224.
24. Salovaara, A., Lindqvist, A., Hasu, T., Häkkilä, J. (2011). The Phone Rings but the User Doesn't Answer: Unavailability in Mobile Communication. *Proc. ACM MobileHCI*, 503-512.
25. Serota, K.B., Levine, T.R., and Boster, F.J. (2010). The Prevalence of Lying in America: Three Studies of Self-Reported Lies. *Human Communication Research*, 36(1), 2-25.
26. Smith, A. (2011). *Americans and Text Messaging*. Washington, DC: Pew Research Center's Internet & American Life Project.
27. SPSS Technical Report. *Linear Mixed Modeling*. http://www.spss.ch/upload/1107355943_LinearMixedEffectsModelling.pdf.
28. Tang, J. C. (2007). Approaching and leave-taking: Negotiating contact in computer-mediated communication. *ACM TOCHI*. 14 (1), Article 5.
29. Turkle, S. (2011). *Alone Together: Why We Expect More from Technology and Less from Each Other*. New York: Basic Books.
30. Vanden Abeele, M., & Roe, K. (2008). White cyberlies: The use of deceptive instant messaging statuses as a social norm. *Presented at Conference of the International Communication Association*.
31. Vrij, A. (2008). *Detecting lies and deceit: pitfalls and opportunities*. Chichester: Wiley.
32. Waidd, W. M., Orne , M. T. (1981). Cognitive, Social, and Personality Processes in the Physiological Detection of Deception, In: Leonard Berkowitz (Ed.), *Advances in Experimental Social Psychology*, Academic Press, 14, 61-106.
33. Weilenmann, A. (2003). "I can't talk now, I'm in a fitting room": formulating availability and location in mobile-phone conversations. *Environment and Planning A*, 35, 1589-1605

Virtually Dining Together in Time-Shifted Environment: KIZUNA Design

Mamoun Nawahdah
Graduate School of Library, Information and Media Studies
University of Tsukuba
nawahdah@slis.tsukuba.ac.jp

Tomoo Inoue
Faculty of Library, Information and Media Science
University of Tsukuba
inoue@slis.tsukuba.ac.jp

ABSTRACT
Dining with a remote person requires that both participants are available at the same time to eat together. Because of time-zone differences and other such contingent factors, this condition can often be hard to fulfill. One solution may lie in time-shifted communication. A person can enjoy a meal while watching an earlier recorded video of a remote person's dining. However, in a time-shifted environment, achieving dining synchronization is a challenge. In this research, we propose a time-shifted tele-dining system (KIZUNA) enabling people to enjoy a meal together in a virtual environment. The system adapts the displayed video's playback speed to the difference in dining progress between the local and remote person. This is likely to enhance communication and increase enjoyment while dining. A validation experiment revealed that the proposed KIZUNA adaptation method enhanced diners' communication behavior, and significantly enhanced the perceived presence of the remote person, in comparison with conventional time-shifted tele-dining. This result suggests a promising future for the KIZUNA system.

Author Keywords
Tele-dining; time-shifted communication; videoconferencing; adaptation; social networking.

ACM Classification Keywords
H.5.3 Group and Organization Interfaces: Asynchronous interaction

INTRODUCTION
During meals, families have a chance to catch up on what has happened in their lives, and to strengthen the bonds that hold the family together. The busy lifestyles of our time, however, often make such family dining very difficult; especially with older people living independently, younger people living alone, and working people traveling more and/or working from afar [21]. In these cases, family members must often eat alone, which is a possible source of loneliness and unhappiness [5][16], in contrast to the pleasure and longer duration typical of social dining [6].

A variety of inexpensive videoconferencing technologies offer a decent solution for distant family members to maintain a sense of social connectedness, which is defined as "positive emotional appraisal, characterized by a feeling of staying in touch within ongoing social relationships" [20]. But when family members are located far away from each other, this often means they are also living in different time-zones, and this difference is likely to present further difficulties for communication between distant family members. The main difficulty lies in the misalignment of daily schedules between the two parties [1], and this is clearly apparent at mealtimes.

In this paper, we propose the "KIZUNA" system to overcome the problem of eating alone. The system is principally based on time-shifted communication involving the transmission of recorded video messages (Fig. 1). To achieve fine synchronization between local dining and the displayed recorded video, KIZUNA adapts the displayed video's playback speed to the difference in dining progress (DDP) between the local and remote user. KIZUNA system usage will vary with circumstances; it can be used occasionally or frequently, by family members or friends. The system is currently under development, with numerous modules having already been completed and tested. The KIZUNA's adaptation algorithm was validated by an actual dining experiment using the Wizard of Oz (WoZ) system simulation technique. Utilizing WoZ, we replicated an envisaged future scenario for the KIZUNA system, and the experimental results revealed that the proposed KIZUNA adaptation method enhanced diners' communication behavior and significantly enhanced the perceived presence of the remote person, in comparison with conventional time-shifted tele-dining.

RELATED WORKS
Numerous studies have investigated ways to utilize information and communication technology in minimizing the gap between people living apart. In this section, we briefly review research related to people dining together despite being located in remote places and/or different time-zones.

Synchronous Dining
Family members and close friends tend to have meals together, but lack of time or proximity often makes this hard to

Figure 1. User dines while watching a recorded video message.

achieve. To overcome this situation, the international consulting firm Accenture introduced a tele-dining prototype called the Virtual Family Dinner that would allow families to dine together in a virtual environment[1]. This prototype was essentially a videoconferencing system targeting people with limited knowledge of technology, such as the elderly. Thus, Accenture made it highly automated and easy to operate. The system monitors the site and when it detects a meal dish on the table, it goes through a list of contacts, trying to reach one who is available for a dinnertime chat.

The advertising agency Wieden+Kennedy's Amsterdam office produced a website called Virtual Holiday Dinner[2], enabling scattered friends and family to have a dinner party of up to five people via Skype[TM]. Guests can call into the dinner, and their faces are shown on the displays as the heads of models physically sitting around a dining table. The models are equipped with video cameras fitted with facial tracking software, so each guest can look around the dining table, 'from' the respective model, by moving his/her head.

The sense of coexistence among family members is likely to be affected when living apart. To maintain a heightened sense of coexistence among family members, a system called CoDine was introduced [25]. This system consists of a dining table embedded with interactive subsystems that augment and transmit the experience of communal family dining. CoDine connects people in different locations through shared dining activities, such as gesture-based screen interaction, mutual food serving, ambient pictures on an animated tablecloth, and the transmission of edible messages.

Dining together is also an enjoyable experience. In some cultures, meals are typically consumed in groups, usually made up of family members or close friends. Examples of popular group meals are the Chinese Hot-Pot, the Japanese Nabe, and the Arabic Mansaf. In this regard, remote group-meal communication was investigated to render such meals more enjoyable [2]. In the study (of the Chinese Hot-Pot meal), three factors essential to the group-meal experience were identified: interacting with food as a group, a central shared hot-pot, and a feeling that others are nearby.

All such previous research primarily focused on synchronous dining among a group of people living apart, assuming that all participants are available at the same time. Our research, in contrast, focuses on the cases where only one participant is currently available for dining.

Asynchronous Dining

When all participants are available at the same time, dining together can be achieved by a variety of videoconferencing systems. However when only one participant is available, things become more difficult. In this situation, asynchronous (time-shifting) collaboration techniques offer a general solution. Because users can receive the information they want when it is most convenient for them, such techniques have been widely employed in work settings, but they may lack a sense of immediacy. For example, in the distant-learning domain, Ocker et al. revealed that asynchronous collaboration is as effective as face-to-face collaboration in terms of learning, quality of solution, solution content, and satisfaction with the solution quality [18]. However, students were less satisfied with the asynchronous learning experience in terms of both the group interaction process and the quality of group discussion. This suggests that asynchronous interaction is satisfactory for some requirements, but not for others, such as affective satisfaction or social connectedness. Asynchronous video messages have also been employed to support interpersonal relationships in separated families [26]. Here, the recipient views the video messages asynchronously, creating a non-stressful, continuous line of communication. This is believed to enhance the connectedness and intimacy between separated family members. Inkpen et al. showed that despite enjoying face-to-face interaction, close friends used asynchronous video communication tools extensively to augment their existing relationships [9]. Time-shifting has also been considered for meetings in the workplace. Tang et al. introduced a system enabling a distant person to contribute to a meeting by pre-recording comments to be played during the meeting when needed [23]. The conducted field experiment showed that most of the recorded messages were played in the meetings; however, a lesser percentage of the messages generated in the meeting were reviewed by the distant person.

In the dining domain, Tsujita et al. proposed the system "CU-Later", to be used in time-shifted dining [24]. This system plays a recorded video of remote dining after a specific time-shift, when the local user is in front of a display placed on a dining table, enabling the local user to watch the video automatically when he/she is eating. As the video is played, the system records the local user's session as well, so that the remote user can watch the local user's session later on-rather like a video mail exchange with automatic playback and recording.

Social dining communication means more than just information exchange; it typically also involves affective satisfaction and social connectedness, and may thus be seen as a form of 'consummatory communication' (which involves the

[1] http://gizmodo.com/accenture-virtual-family-dinner/
[2] http://www.virtualholidaydinner.com/

sharing of experiences, emotions, knowledge, and/or opinions [3]). To support this type of communication, a sense of co-presence is often crucial. Thus, our proposed system addresses these more complex needs, and further explores the potential of video exchange, but is more focused on the social connectedness between remote users, based on the assumption that synchronizing the dining activities of remote participants may significantly enhance the users' dining experience.

KIZUNA SYSTEM

Figure 2 shows a conceptual illustration of the KIZUNA ('bond' in Japanese) system scenario. In this scenario two persons, local user A and remote user B, are dining together in a virtual environment, although they are physically dining in different spaces and/or at different times. First (Fig. 2 Session 1), a recorded video message from the remote user B is created while dining.

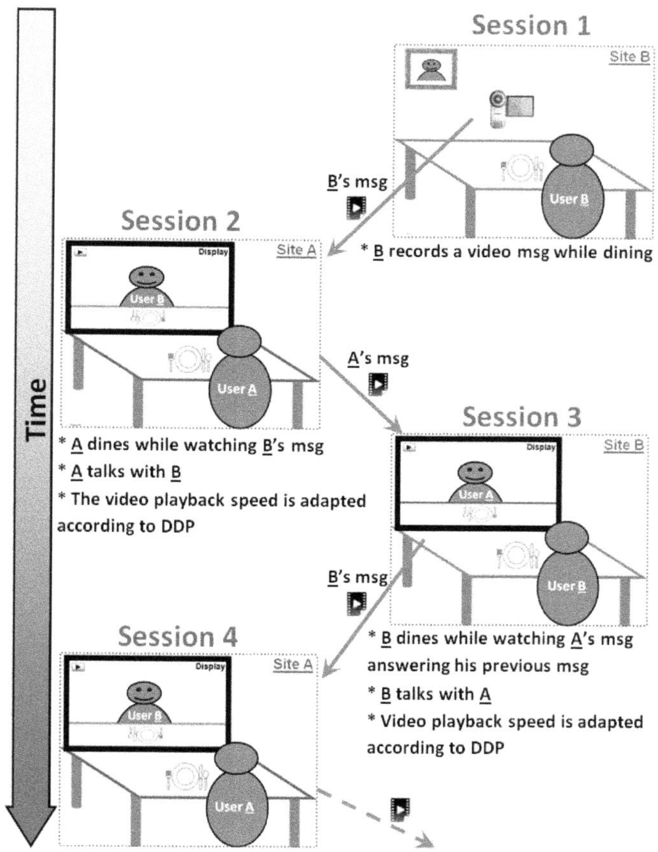

Figure 2. KIZUNA system scenario.

The system automatically starts working at site A when the local person A gets seated and some dishes are placed on the dining table (Fig. 2 Session 2). This increases the system-usage portability, especially for people with limited knowledge of the technology. The system starts playing the video of remote user B (recorder earlier) on a large display in front of the local dining table, at life-size scale. It also starts recording the local user A's dining and his/her reaction to user B's video message. Similarly, the system automatically starts working at site B when the local person B gets seated and some dishes are placed on the dining table (Fig. 2 Session 3). The system then starts playing the video of user A, and the same process is repeated. This automatic playback and recording of videos provides the illusion of co-dining for the users, though they may be dining at different times and/or in different places. We assume that merely watching the other user's video may not, by itself, arouse a sense of co-dining; but that the synchronization of both dining activities (not only the start and end time but also the entire process) may be significant. Specifically, this synchronization can be achieved by controlling the video playback speed according to the DDP between the local and remote user. In this way, the local user can enjoy the company of the remote user throughout his/her meal. Also in this way, we ensure that the local user can see the entire remote dining session while he/she is eating. These factors appear likely to enhance the dining experience.

System Design

Based on the system proposal, we defined the following set of design requirements to implement the KIZUNA system: **Dining detections**: dining status and progress are necessary information to control the system. This includes the following:

- User detection: the system must be highly automated and easy to operate. User presence at the dining table should activate the system and display the remote participant's recorded dining video. This will ensure high system usability and portability, especially for people with limited knowledge of the technology.
- Food detection: detecting a user at the dining table is not sufficient to ensure that a dining session is about to begin; the system must also detect whether food has been placed on the dining table or not.
- Amount of food detection: based on the above information, the system can assess the user's dining behavior, particularly the user's dining progress.

Video manipulation: in the proposed KIZUNA system, users can communicate through the exchange of recorded video messages. Therefore, the following video manipulations are required:

- Video recording: to record the local dining session.
- Video streaming and controlling: to control the displayed video's playback speed according to the DDP.

System Implementation

An experimental time-shifted tele-dining system is under construction based on the KIZUNA system proposal and relevant design requirements. The experimental site is equipped with the following: dining table, chair, large flat-panel display, two USB cameras, speakers, microphone, motion detection sensor, two spotlights, and computer. Figure 3 shows the preliminary system's physical workspace.

Figure 4 shows the system procedure flowchart, comprised of the following major modules:

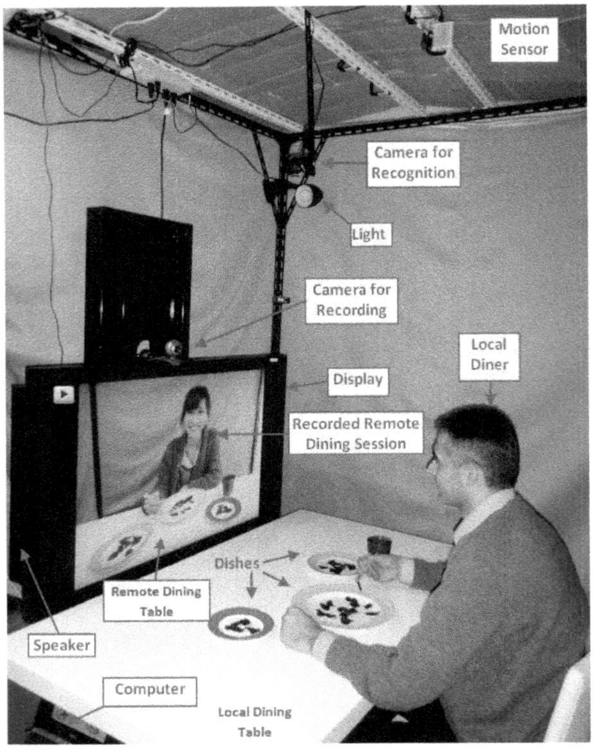

Figure 3. System's physical workspace.

User detection: The system utilizes a generic motion sensor to detect any human motions within a specified interest volume. The human motion sensor "AT Watch NET IR_mini" is used for this purpose. This sensor is fixed above the dining table at a height of 230 cm. This way, the sensor is able to detect any motion within a ground radius of 230 cm.

Food detection: This module detects any food placed on the dining table, in two steps; first step: detecting dishes on the dining table; second step: detecting the total amount of food in the detected dishes. In this study, we assumed that all the food would be served 'upfront', with the food placed directly onto the plates and brought to the table at once [7].

- Dish detection: this is performed using shape and color recognition. A previously devised method [11] is used to detect the dishes. A USB camera is fixed above the dining table at a height of 200 cm, to exclusively capture the dining table from above. At this stage of construction, we considered white circular dishes only. In addition, we used dishes with solid colored rims to easily distinguish the dishes. The free OpenCV library is utilized to perform this task, and to determine the dishes' position on the dining table.

- Amount of food detection: this is achieved using image processing techniques. A previously devised method [11] is used to estimate the remaining food from a 2D image of the dishes. At the beginning of the dining session, all the detected amount of food in all the dishes is summed together to produce a total initial amount of food. Periodically, this detection is repeated to determine the amount of consumed food compared to the total initial amount. The process ends when the user is no longer present at the dining table and/or the remaining amount of food becomes zero.

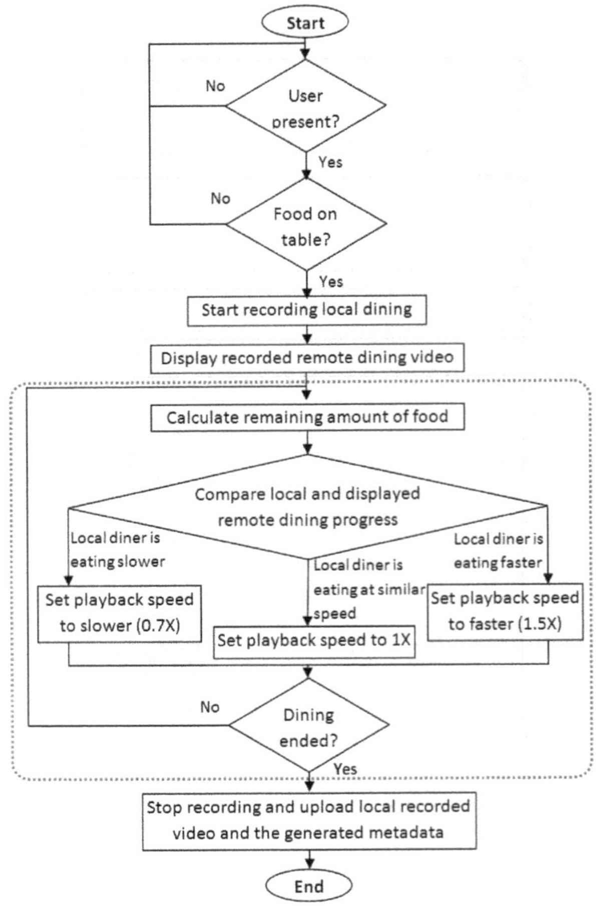

Figure 4. System's procedure flowchart.

Video recording: Recording of a dining session starts when actual dining activity is detected. This includes a person sitting at the dining table (User detection), and food placed on that table (Food detection). Accordingly, the beginning of a dining session is indicated by the diner moving his/her hand over one of the dishes. This is achieved using hand detection by the background subtraction method. A previously devised method [11] is used to detect the user's hands on the dining table.

As soon as a dining session starts, a USB camera placed over the large display in front of the person starts capturing images, and a pin microphone starts capturing sounds. The Microsoft DirectShow application programming interface (API) is used to create a media file (.avi) from the captured images and sounds. During the dining session, periodic dining progress information is collected and saved to a designated metadata file. This information includes a time stamp, a meal progress percentage, and whether or not user motion was detected at that time.

At the end of each dining session, the recorded video and the metadata file are uploaded to cloud storage in a designated user's folder. Figure 5 shows the internal folder structure of the cloud storage. In this structure, each user has a folder containing all the recorded dining sessions. Each dining session consists of a single video file and a designated metadata file. Dining sessions seen by other users are automatically archived in the user's old dining sessions folder.

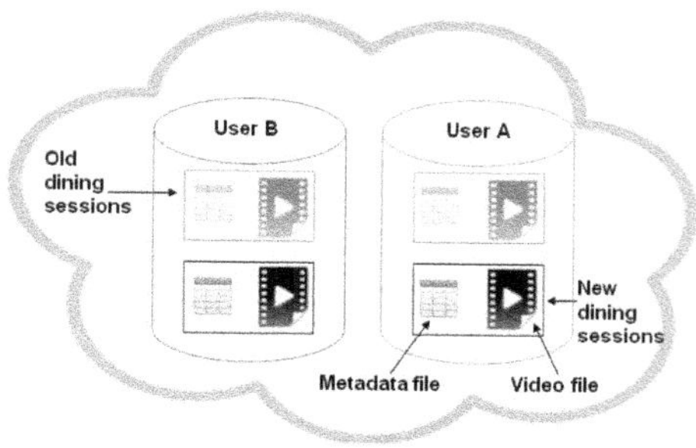

Figure 5. Internal folder structure of the cloud storage.

Video streaming and controlling: As soon as an actual dining session starts, the most recent recorded remote dining video is streamed and displayed on a large display in front of the local diner. The libVLC API[3] is used to play and control the streamed video. In order to ensure that the displayed recorded remote dining progress status matches the local dining progress status, the displayed video playback speed is controlled. The system accesses information from the metadata file and compares it to the current detected local dining progress. Based on this comparison (remote percentage eating progress minus local percentage eating progress), the system sets the displayed video playback speed. Through experimentation, we found that diners can watch a video with adjusted playback speed in a range from 0.7X to 1.5X without losing any information or sensing any distortion. Thus, the playback speed adaptation method is based on this range. If the percentage DDP is less than a specific amount, the playback-speed is set to slow-speed mode (0.7X). If the percentage DDP is greater than a specific amount, the playback speed is set to fast-speed mode (1.5X). Otherwise, the playback speed is set to normal-speed mode (1X).

THE VALIDATION OF THE ADAPTATION METHOD

In this section, the experimental validation of the KIZUNA's adaptation method is discussed. The main objective of the experiment was to determine whether using KIZUNA's adaptation method would enhance a given diner's communication and sense of presence of the remote diner, in comparison with conventional time-shifted tele-dining. Synchronizing the recorded remote dining activity with the local dining progress is expected to enhance these factors. The participants' feelings and feedback were assessed by means of a questionnaire filled out after each tele-dining experimental session.

Recording Remote Dining Video Messages

In real-life social dining, a person usually enjoys the company of familiar people, such as family members, friends or co-workers. This way, the person feels more relaxed, communicating easily and without constraint [6]. In the validation experiment, we achieved this by inviting potential participants to dine while watching a recording of another familiar person (or 'actor'). This limited the pool of participants. To extend the pool of participants, we recorded three dining sessions, each with a different actor, in a different language (Japanese, Chinese and Arabic). To achieve consistent eating progress among actors, we recruited three adult male graduate students ($A1$: Japanese, $A2$: Chinese, and $A3$: Arab). The actors were instructed to dine at a normal, relaxed speed, and provided with a list of general questions and comments to be delivered in their native languages, at specified times, while eating. Table 1 shows the list of these general questions and comments, and the time at which they are to be delivered. The questions and comments were collected and extracted from a typical basic dialog between two persons conversing at a distance. The time between each question and comment was determined based on the expected average length of reply.

Begin	Q) Hello, how are you today?
00:45 (mm:ss)	The weather here is so nice today, I like the summer season.
01:30	Q) Do you like your meal?
02:15	Delicious, I like curry rice.
03:00	Q) By the way, What's your favorite food?
03:45	Personally, I like the (Italian) food a lot.
04:30	Q) Where do you live?
05:15	I like (Tsukuba) city. It's safe, clean and the people are so friendly.
06:00	Q) Do you have any plan for the summer vacation?
06:45	I like the sea a lot, so most probably I will go to a beach and have some relaxed time.
07:30	Q) Which country would you like to visit?
08:15	Nice, I like to visit (Italy). I want to go there to eat (Italian) food.
End	Thank you. I am looking forward to meeting you again in the next video.

Table 1. List of general questions and comments.

In the recording sessions, we used 400 g of curried rice and a glass of juice as the meal. This amount is considered sufficient for an adult person. We chose curried rice as a widely enjoyed meal. Moreover, this kind of food is often eaten with a spoon, while other kinds of food might involve the use of different utensils, such as forks or chopsticks, and this, we found through experimentation, might affect the dining progress. Analysis of the actor's recorded video showed that this amount of food (400 g) was consumed in nine minutes on average.

Dining Conditions

In the experiment, we considered the following two time-shifted tele-dining conditions:

- **Normal condition**: participant dines while watching a recorded video of a familiar person eating sometime earlier.
- **KIZUNA condition**: same as normal condition, but with the video playback speed adjusted according to the DDP.

[3]http://www.videolan.org/

Using the same amount of food in the experiment as in the recording sessions caused small variations in terms of the DDP. Furthermore, 400 g may represent either a large or small amount of food to different participants, which may cause them to feel uncomfortable while dining. Accordingly, after surveying meals sold in the market, as well as participant preferences, we decided to use the following meal amounts in the experiment, according to each participant's preference:

- Small meal: 300 g of curried rice (25% less than the amount used in the recording sessions)
- Large meal: 500 g of curried rice (25% more than the amount used in the recording sessions)

We performed a preliminarily dining experiment, and ran a simulation, to investigate the playback-speed adaptation method, and to determine the adaptation values. Figure 6 shows one participant's eating progress (large meal) compared to that of the displayed remote diner. The overall DDP was around 3 minutes, with an average of 14% DDP over the length of the meal.

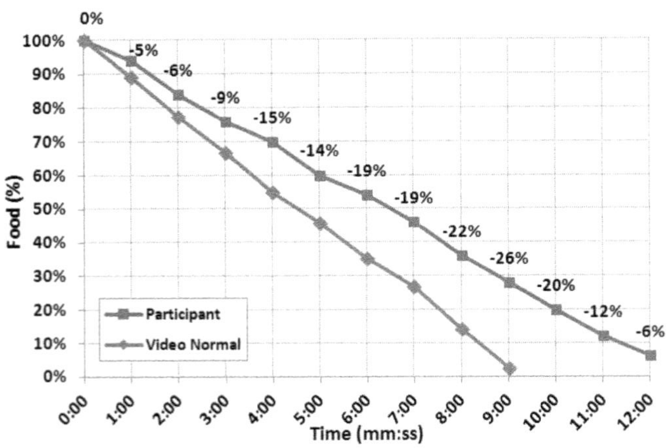

Figure 6. A participant's eating progress compared to that of the recorded remote diner. (The numbers above the chart data point indicate the percentage difference in DDP between the sessions.)

To achieve fine synchronization using the specified meal amounts, the following adaptation values were determined:

- More than -5% DDP: the local diner is considered to be eating slower than the displayed video, and the video playback speed should be changed to slow-speed mode (0.7X).
- More than 5% DDP: the local diner is considered to be eating faster than the displayed video, and the video playback speed should be changed to fast-speed mode (1.5X).
- Between -5% and 5% DDP: the local diner is considered to be eating at a normal speed compared to the remote diner, and the video playback speed should be set at normal speed (1X).

Figure 7 shows a participant's eating progress compared to the displayed remote diner progress under the KIZUNA condition. After 2 minutes of dining, the DDP exceeded the limit (-5%), so the playback speed was changed to slow-speed mode (0.7X). At the 6th minute, the DDP decreased to -2%, so the playback speed was changed to normal-speed mode (1X). At the 7th minute, the DDP increased to -5%, so the playback speed was again changed to slow-speed mode (0.7X). Under this condition, the overall DDP was reduced to only 30 seconds, with an average of -4% DDP over the length of the meal, because of the playback-speed adaptation.

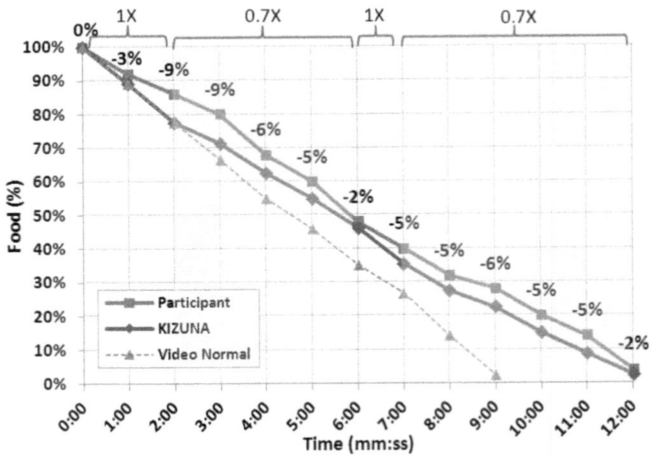

Figure 7. A participant's eating progress compared to that of the recorded remote diner, under the KIZUNA condition.

Setup

The validation experiment for the proposed adaptation dining method took place in a custom-built time-shifted tele-dining booth. The booth was enclosed by a curtain to isolate it from the lab environment. Figure 8 shows the booth's internal setup. In the tele-dining site, we used a USB camera, placed over the display, to record the participant's facial expressions and hand gestures. A small flat cooking scale was placed under the plate to accurately measure the food amount. A second USB camera was used to capture and record the cooking scale reading.

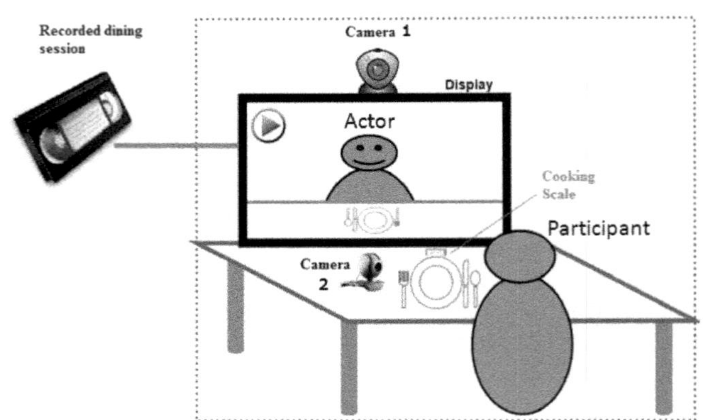

Figure 8. Tele-dining site setup.

For KIZUNA validation, the assessment of the participant's eating progress was performed by employing the WoZ system simulation technique. The second USB camera was connected to a display placed outside the tele-dining site. The researcher monitored the DDP and periodically altered the displayed video playback speed.

Group 1					Group 2				
Particpant	Sex	Video #	Bond	Meal (g)	Particpant	Sex	Video #	Bond	Meal (g)
d1	M	V2	Roommate	300	d12	F	V3	Friend	500
d2	M	V1	Friend	500	d13	F	V3	Spouse	300
d3	F	V2	Friend	300	d14	M	V1	Friend	500
d4	M	V1	Friend	500	d15	F	V1	Friend	300
d5	M	V1	Friend	300	d16	F	V2	Friend	300
d6	F	V1	Friend	300	d17	F	V2	G-Friend	500
d7	F	V3	Friend	500	d18	M	V2	Friend	500
d8	F	V3	Friend	300	d19	M	V1	Friend	300
d9	F	V1	G-Friend	500	d20	F	V1	Friend	500
d10	M	V1	Friend	500	d21	M	V1	Roommate	500
d11	M	V1	Friend	500	d22	F	V2	Friend	300

Table 2. Experimental session arrangements.

Participants

A total of 22 healthy participants took part in the experiment (12 females and 10 males). The participants' ages ranged from 21 to 32 years old (average = 24.1 years, s.d. = 2.7); most were undergraduate or graduate students; and 13 participants had had previous experience of videoconferencing systems. Most had used videoconferencing mainly to talk to remote family members and/or friends. The participants were divided into two groups: Group 1 participants ($d1 - d11$) performed under the Normal condition, while Group 2 participants ($d12 - d22$) performed under the KIZUNA condition. All the participants experienced each condition for the first time.

Participants were given their choice of the amount of food (small or large meal) they would consume in the experiment, and 10 participants chose the small meal, while the other 12 chose the large meal. Participants were also given the choice of dining at lunch or dinner time, and 17 participants chose lunch, while the other 5 chose dinner. Table 2 shows the participant-video arrangements, the diners' relationship, and the chosen meals, for the two groups; Where $V1$, $V2$, and $V3$ are recording of $A1$, $A2$, and $A3$ dining sessions respectively.

Procedure

Each tele-dining experiment began with the researcher asking the participant to sign the experiment consent form, and to complete a basic demographic survey form. Following this step, the researcher guided the participant to the tele-dining site and introduced the system environment. We asked the participant to imagine him-/herself dining and talking with a family member or friend who lives in a different time-zone. At this point, we displayed the familiar partner's static image on a display in front of the dining table. We explained to the participant that he/she would be dining while watching a previously recorded video of his/her partner. The participant was told that the partner would talk to him/her while dining and then later review the current recorded session. The participant was instructed to dine as he/she normally does. The participant was not apprised of the respective experimental dining condition (normal or KIZUNA). The researcher then left the dining booth and activated the recorded video as an indication of the beginning of the dining session. After each dining session, the participant was instructed to complete a questionnaire about the session he/she had just experienced. The dining sessions were recorded on tape. Afterward, the sessions were reviewed, and the DDP calculated for each condition.

Under the KIZUNA condition, the researcher played the role of WoZ, by monitoring the participant's dining progress and controlling the displayed video playback speed accordingly. The alterations were performed each minute, according to the adaptation values noted above, to achieve fine synchronization.

The experimental design was between-subject, and the analysis was performed on the results of the participants' first-ever experience of tele-dining (whether in Group 1 or Group 2).

Questionnaire

In the questionnaire, we asked the participants to evaluate a series of statements according to the feelings they experienced during the time-shifted dining session. The principal aim of the study was to assess participants' communication with their partner, and to determine whether synchronizing the dining sessions would affect communication or not, using a selection of straightforward questions from related questionnaires from [12][22]. The following statements were used for this purpose:

- C1) "*I wanted to talk to the partner.*"
- C2) "*I enjoyed talking with the partner while eating.*"
- C3) "*The partner's talking distracted me from my meal.*"
- C4) "*The content of the conversation was natural.*"
- C5) "*The timing of the partner's delivery was natural.*"
- C6) "*I could communicate with the partner naturally.*"

The sense of the partner's presence while tele-dining is another important aspect to consider in assessing the proposed system; and synchronizing the dining sessions is believed to affect this sense of the partner's presence. In this study, we sought to determine whether our proposed system would enhance this sense or not, using common questions from related questionnaires from [14][17][8]. To investigate the participants' sense of presence under each condition, the following statements were used:

- P1) "*I felt as if the partner and I were eating together in the same room.*"
- P2) "*I felt distant from the partner.*"
- P3) "*The partner's facial expressions were easy to recognize.*"
- P4) "*The partner's gaze direction was easy to recognize.*"
- P5) "*I was able to make eye-contact with the partner.*"
- P6) "*The partner's gestures were easy to recognize.*"

All of the above statements were rated on a 9-point Likert scale, where 1 = strongly disagree, 3 = disagree, 5 = neutral, 7 = agree, and 9 = strongly agree.

Statistical Results

Figure 9 shows the average results of participants' communication-related feedback on their dining experience, under the two conditions. Comparison was done using a between-groups t-test, to examine whether the means under the two conditions differed significantly from one another. We found significant differences in participants' feelings of distraction caused by the partner talking (C3: $t(20) = 2.62$, $p < 0.05$) and in the timing of the partner's delivery (C5: $t(20) = 3.66$, $p < 0.01$); while no significant differences were found in participants' willingness to talk with the partner (C1: $t(20) = -0.68$), enjoyment of talking with the partner while eating (C2: $t(20) = -1.6$), content of the conversation (C4: $t(20) = -1.4$), or ability to communicate with the partner naturally (C6: $t(20) = -0.81$).

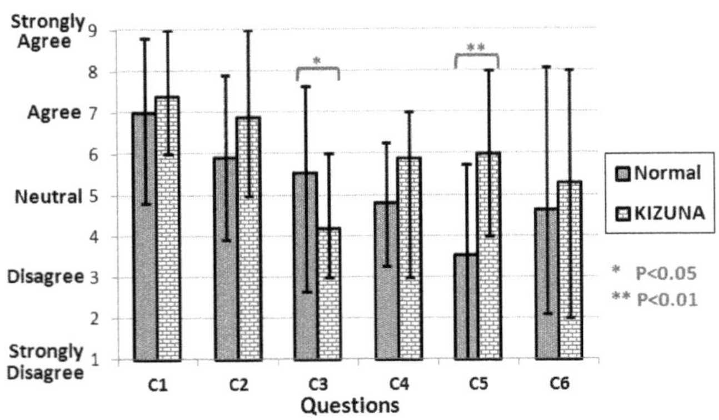

Figure 9. Participants' average communication-behavior results.

Figure 10 shows the average results of participants' felt sense of the partner's presence while dining, under the two conditions. We found significant differences in participants' sense of the partner's presence as if in the same room (P1: $t(20) = -3.48$, $p < 0.01$), and participants' felt distance from the partner (P2: $t(20) = 2.07$, $p < 0.1$); while no significant differences were found in recognizing the partner's facial expression (P3: $t(20) = -0.11$), the partner's gaze direction (P4: $t(20) = -0.61$), or the partner's gestures (P6: $t(20) = -0.51$), or in the ability to make eye-contact with the partner (P5: $t(20) = 0.28$).

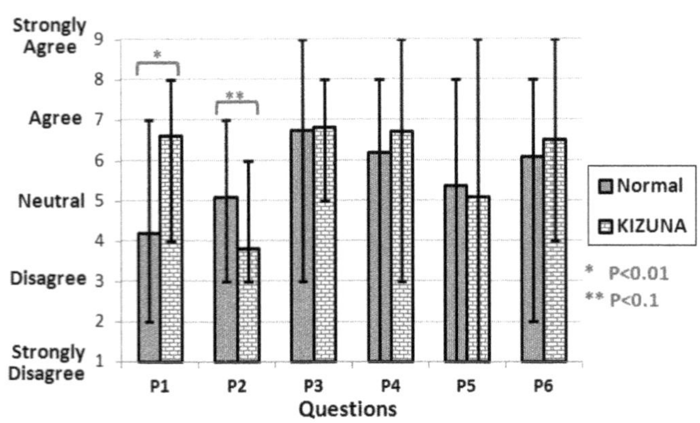

Figure 10. Participants' average sense of presence results.

The exact deployment of the $V1$ to $V3$ videos was not identical in both conditions, although all the actors were instructed to behave in the same manner, according to the scenario in Table 1: the $V1$ video was used 7 times, the $V2$ video 2 times and the $V3$ video 2 times under the Normal condition; while the $V1$ video was used 5 times, the $V2$ video 4 times and the $V3$ video 2 times under the KIZUNA condition. To determine whether the videos had any effect on the ratings, correlations between the videos and the ratings were examined for $P1$, $P2$, $C3$, and $C5$, which indicated the differences between the conditions. We found a weak correlation in Normal $P2$ ($\rho = 0.41$) and no correlation for the others. However, this Normal $P2$ used more $V1$ videos than under the KIZUNA condition, and the $V1$ video actually had relatively lower ratings on average. This suggests that the marginal significant difference in $P2$ is not caused by the video effect.

The proposed adaptation algorithm meant to synchronize the participant's and partner's dining progress by keeping the DDP within a specific range ($\pm 5\%$). This in turn reduced the overall DDP. For the Normal sessions, the average DDP was 117 seconds (s.d. = 48.8), while for the KIZUNA sessions, the average DDP was only 19 seconds (s.d. = 15.9), and this suggests a significant difference in the DDP ($t(20) = 6.07$, $p < 0.001$).

DISCUSSION

The questionnaire results revealed that the proposed time-shifted tele-dining method improved participants' communication while dining, in comparison with the Normal mode. This result supports our assumption that synchronizing the dining sessions (local and remote recorded dining sessions) would increase the realism of virtual social dining. In particular, participants found that the partner's talk in KIZUNA dining was less distracting than in Normal dining (Fig. 9 - C3). This may be a result of the close alignment of the dining progress. Moreover, participants found the partner's conversational delivery timing more natural under KIZUNA dining conditions than under Normal dining conditions (Fig. 9 - C5).

Since a sense of the remote participant's presence affects the local diner's communication, we tried to enhance this sense of presence by depicting the latter's life-sized image on a large display [10][13][19], and by matching the furniture [4] of the local and remote dining environments. The large display was placed in front of the local dining table, at the same level; hence the remote dining table appeared as if it was an extension of the local dining table (Fig. 1). We also assumed that synchronizing both dining sessions would further enhance the sense of presence. The questionnaire results support our assumption, confirming that participants felt as if the partner and they were eating together in the same room during KIZUNA dining (Fig. 10 - P1), and that participants felt less distance from the partner during the KIZUNA dining sessions (Fig. 10 - P2).

Though participants were aware that they were watching a recorded video, we noticed that some communicated more naturally with their partners during KIZUNA dining sessions, and many asked more questions in responding to the recorded video (with an average of 1.02 questions asked, compared to 0 in the Normal dining sessions). Many participants noted that it felt strange not to receive a direct response to their questions. This reaction is very similar to the "uncanny valley" telepresence reaction caused by humanoid robots that are highly similar to humans [15]. In the experiment, the remote person's life-sized representation, combined with the matching furniture and dining utensils, misled local viewers into trying to interact with the remote person in real time.

The proposed system achieved better communication and sense of presence by merely controlling the playback speed of the large displayed video. Our proposed algorithm had three playback-speed modes (normal, fast and slow). The fast and slow modes were carefully chosen so that viewers would not sense any distortion in the picture or sound. In this regard, we asked participants to judge their partner's dining speed. Despite the varying playback-speed mode, most participants said that the partner's dining speed was normal in general. However, a few participants noted that they felt the partner's motion was slightly slower in some sections, and attributed this to a problem with the video player. No comments were made, however, regarding the fast mode, which may indicate that this mode was acceptable.

It is natural for a person to look at their dinner partner while dining, and to observe their dining progress. In this regard, some participants noted that they adopted the strategy of watching their partner's plate, which gave them an indication of their partner's dining progress, by which they estimated how much time remained for the dining session. We also noticed a common behavior among participants, to echo their partner's actions, most noticeably the action of drinking. Whenever the partner performed a drinking action, the local participant performed a similar action, either synchronously or once he/she had finished their current action. We found no difference between the two conditions in this regard.

The controlled dialog during the experimental dining sessions was meant to be general and uniform for all participants. The dialog consisted of a series of questions and comments, delivered at specified times based on the dining progress. The preliminary conversational analysis showed that almost all the partner's questions were answered by participants, though only half of the partner's comments were responded to, usually in the form of a new question or agreement (or disagreement) with the respective comment. And again, no differences were found between the two conditions. When we reviewed the recorded experimental dining sessions, we found that the dialog was typically natural, especially when the partner's follow-up question or comment was a natural reply to the participant's utterance. This tended to engage participants more in the dialog, as noted by one participant: *"I was surprised when the partner answered my question immediately, as if we were talking face-to-face."* However, some participants found the pre-set question/answer dialog style abnormal, preferring a dialogue style based on a story or the latest news.

As with any study, there are limitations on our ability to generalize from the achieved results. For example, the validation experiment was performed in a lab environment and the number of participants was quite small (3 actors and 22 participants). Additionally, the experimental setup assumed that all the food would be placed on the dining table beforehand and served on one plate only. In addition, our current system is designed for two diners; in the future, we will study how KIZUNA usage would scale if more than two diners wished to dine together. Moreover, there were other ecological shortcomings, such as participants' age, location, bond, nationality, and culture. Our study was limited to young student participants and actors (from 21 to 32 years old), and the participants and actors were located in the same city, which meant that they see each other frequently. The relationship between the participants and actors was mainly one of friendship (Table 2). We would also like to validate and extend the current findings with qualitative studies, such as longitudinal observations and investigations of dining behavior.

All these concerns will be taken into consideration when performing the actual system evaluation, once the system is fully implemented. The completed system will be deployed in participants' homes and the participant sample will consist of actual family members living apart. In addition, the system will be deployed for a considerable length of time, to investigate the ongoing communication/dining exchanges between local and remote participants.

CONCLUSION

In this paper, the design and validation of a proposed time-shifted tele-dining system is presented. This KIZUNA system is meant to enhance communication and the sense of connectedness between family members and friends who live apart in different time-zones. The system involves recording the remote person's dining sessions and then displaying these sessions for the local person when he/she starts eating, and vice versa. Based on the difference in dining progress, the system adapts the playback speed of the displayed remote recorded dining session.

A validation experiment was conducted to thoroughly investigate the proposed adaptation method, and the results revealed that the KIZUNA system effectively enhanced communication and the sense of the other person's presence, by synchronizing the dining sessions.

In future, we plan to integrate and extend the system to support time-shifted group tele-dining as well, which would benefit large families where more than one person is living apart. At this stage, we implemented a simple means of adapting the video playback speed by comparing the local and recorded dining progress. This can be further enhanced by analyzing the video content and locating 'rich' sections in the recorded dining sessions; for example, those that include an abundance of conversation and/or dining actions. Finally, the method assumed discrete levels of video playback speeds (slow, normal and fast), and this may affect the diner's viewing experience.

ACKNOWLEDGMENTS

This research was partially supported by the JSPS Grant-in-Aid for scientific research 22500104, 23500158, the Telecommunications Advancement Foundation, and the Research Projects of Graduate School of Library, Information and Media Studies, University of Tsukuba.

REFERENCES

1. Cao, X., Sellen, A., Brush, A. B., Kirk, D., Edge, D., and Ding, X. Understanding family communication across time zones. In *Proceedings of the 2010 ACM conference on Computer supported cooperative work*, CSCW '10 (2010), 155–158.
2. Foley-Fisher, Z., Tsao, V., Wang, J., and Fels, S. Netpot: easy meal enjoyment for distant diners. In *Proceedings of the 9th international conference on Entertainment computing*, ICEC' 10 (2010), 446–448.
3. Fukuda, S., Ed. *Emotional Engineering: Service Development*, 1 ed. Springer, 2010.
4. Gibbs, S. J., Arapis, C., and Breiteneder, C. J. Teleport towards immersive copresence. *Multimedia Systems 7* (May 1999), 214–221.
5. Heather, K. Identifying nutrition problems in senior patients. *Geriatrics and Aging 7* (2004), 62–65.
6. Hetherington, M., Anderson, A., Norton, G., and Newson, L. Situational effects on meal intake: A comparison of eating alone and eating with others. *Physiology and Behavior 88* (2006), 498–505.
7. Hupfeld, A., and Rodden, T. Laying the table for hci: uncovering ecologies of domestic food consumption. In *Proceedings of the 2012 conference on Human Factors in Computing Systems*, CHI' 12 (2012), 119–128.
8. Ichikawa, Y., Okada, K., Jeong, G., Tanaka, S., and Matsushita, Y. Majic videoconferencing system: experiments, evaluation and improvement. In *Proceedings of the 4th conference on European Conference on Computer-Supported Cooperative Work*, ECSCW'95 (1995), 279–292.
9. Inkpen, K., Du, H., Roseway, A., Hoff, A., and Johns, P. Video kids: augmenting close friendships with asynchronous video conversations in videopal. In *Proceedings of the 2012 conference on Human Factors in Computing Systems*, CHI' 12 (2012), 2387–2396.
10. Inoue, T. Mixed reality meeting system enabling user to keep and share interpersonal distance in the real world. *Journal of Information Processing Society of Japan 50*, 1 (2009), 246–253.
11. Inoue, T. Adaptive tabletop dish recommendation by the real-time recognition of dining status. In *Proceedings of the fifth International Workshop on Informatics (IWIN'11)* (2011), 174–180.
12. Inoue, T., Okada, K., and Matsushita, Y. Integration of face-to-face and video-mediated meetings: Hermes. In *Proceedings of the international ACM SIGGROUP conference on Supporting group work: the integration challenge*, GROUP '97 (1997), 405–414.
13. Ishida, T., Sakuraba, A., and Shibata, Y. Proposal of high realistic sensation system using the large scale tiled display environment. In *Proceedings of Network-Based Information Systems (NBiS)* (2011), 444–449.
14. Kies, J. K., Williges, R. C., and Rosson, M. B. Evaluating desktop video conferencing for distance learning. *Computers and Education 28*, 2 (1997), 79–91.
15. Mori, M. Bukimi no tani the uncanny valley. *Energy 7* (1970), 3335.
16. Nakagawa, M., Nagatsuka, M., Nishiyama, M., and Yoshida, Y. The function and the possibility of kyoshoku (eating together). *HortResearch*, 64 (2010), 55–65.
17. Nakanishi, H., Kato, K., and Ishiguro, H. Zoom cameras and movable displays enhance social telepresence. In *Proceedings of the 2011 annual conference on Human factors in computing systems*, CHI '11 (2011), 63–72.
18. Ocker, R., and Yaverbaum, G. Asynchronous computer-mediated communication versus face-to-face collaboration: Results on student learning, quality and satisfaction. *Group Decision and Negotiation 8*, 5 (1999), 427–440.
19. Okada, K.-I., Maeda, F., Ichikawa, Y., and Matsushita, Y. Multiparty videoconferencing at virtual social distance: Majic design. In *Proceedings of the 1994 ACM conference on Computer supported cooperative work*, CSCW '94 (1994), 385–393.
20. Romero, N., Markopoulos, P., Baren, J., Ruyter, B., Ijsselsteijn, W., and Farshchian, B. Connecting the family with awareness systems. *Personal Ubiquitous Comput. 11*, 4 (2007), 299–312.
21. Sellaeg, K., and Chapman, G. E. Masculinity and food ideals of men who live alone. *Appetite 51*, 1 (2008), 120–128.
22. Sellen, A. J. Speech patterns in video-mediated conversations. In *Proceedings of the SIGCHI conference on Human factors in computing systems*, CHI '92 (1992), 49–59.
23. Tang, J., Marlow, J., Hoff, A., Roseway, A., Inkpen, K., Zhao, C., and Cao, X. Time travel proxy: using lightweight video recordings to create asynchronous, interactive meetings. In *Proceedings of the 2012 ACM annual conference on Human Factors in Computing Systems*, CHI' 12 (2012), 3111–3120.
24. Tsujita, H., Yarosh, S., and Abowd, G. D. Cu-later: a communication system considering time difference. In *Proceedings of the 12th ACM international conference adjunct papers on Ubiquitous computing*, Ubicomp '10 (2010), 435–436.
25. Wei, J., Wang, X., Peiris, R. L., Choi, Y., Martinez, X. R., Tache, R., Koh, J. T. K. V., Halupka, V., and Cheok, A. D. Codine: an interactive multi-sensory system for remote dining. In *Proceedings of the 13th international conference on Ubiquitous computing*, UbiComp '11 (2011), 21–30.
26. Zuckerman, O., and Maes, P. Awareness system for children in distributed families. In *Proceedings of the Conference on Interaction Design and Children (IDC)*, ACM Press (2005).

Author Index